BROOKL
WEYBRID

Me

D0589638

John Noble, Sandra Bao, Susan Forsyth, Beth Greenfield, Michael Grosberg,
Morgan Konn, Andrew Dean Nystrom, Suzanne Plank, Michael Read,
Daniel C Schechter, Iain Stewart, Wendy Yanagihara

Contents

Northwest Mexico p297

Baja California p252

Central North Mexico p337

Northeast Mexico p365

Northern Central Highlands p571

Central Pacific Coast p409

Western Central Highlands p502

Around Mexico City p176

Mexico City p94

Oaxaca State p696

Central Gulf Coast p642

Tabasco & Chiapas p772

Yucatán Peninsula p841

Destination Mexico

To explore Mexico is to walk through rain forests and along tropical beaches, to traverse vast deserts and gaze at snow-capped volcanoes, and to walk the streets of teeming cities, sleepy indigenous villages, chic resorts and the ruined cities of the great Aztec, Maya and other civilizations that flourished here centuries ago.

Mexico offers a multitude of cultures, cuisines, landscapes, activities, music, environments, languages, handicrafts, art and history. Its Spanish conqueror, Hernán Cortés, when asked to describe Mexico, simply crumpled a piece of paper and set it on a table. The rugged mountainous topography he was indicating has yielded a boundless colorful variety of distinct places, people and traditions – which today are more accessible than ever before. Thanks to steadily improving communications and innovative tourism initiatives, it has never been easier to hike Mexico's remote canyons, watch whales or flamingoes, climb volcanoes, dive waters teeming with tropical fish or bike ride to remote indigenous villages.

If you're slightly less activity-minded, delight your senses with Mexico's endless palm-fringed beaches, world-class museums and galleries, unbeatable handicrafts shopping, hectic markets, distinctive tasty food, hospitable hotels and beautiful colonial cities.

At the end of the day, sit back with a margarita or a cold Mexican beer and take it all in at a beach bar or in a plaza with splashing fountains. After dark, indulge in the bars, music and stylish nightclubs of Mexico's cities and hip travel destinations. Or lose yourself in the color, music, fun, fireworks and spectacle of one of the country's noisy fiestas: there's one happening almost every day, not far from you!

JOHN ELK III

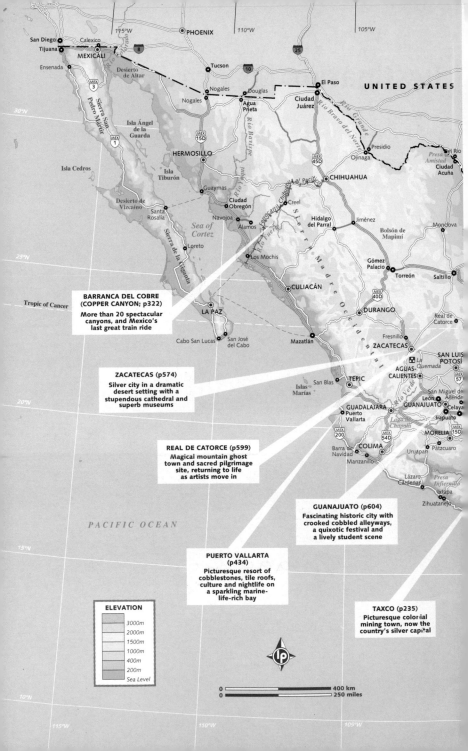

BARRANCA DEL COBRE
(COPPER CANYON; p322)

More than 20 spectacular
canyons, and Mexico's
last great train ride

ZACATECAS (p574)

Silver city in a dramatic
desert setting with a
stupendous cathedral and
superb museums

REAL DE CATORCE (p599)

Magical mountain ghost
town and sacred pilgrimage
site, returning to life
as artists move in

GUANAJUATO (p604)

Fascinating historic city with
crooked cobbled alleyways,
a quixotic festival and
a lively student scene

PUERTO VALLARTA
(p434)

Picturesque resort of
cobblestones, tile roofs,
culture and nightlife on
a sparkling marine-
life-rich bay

TAXCO (p235)

Picturesque colonial
mining town, now the
country's silver capital

ELEVATION

3000m
2000m
1500m
1000m
400m
200m
Sea Level

0 ——— 400 km
0 ——— 250 miles

UNITED STATES

PACIFIC OCEAN

Tropic of Cancer

Sea of Cortez

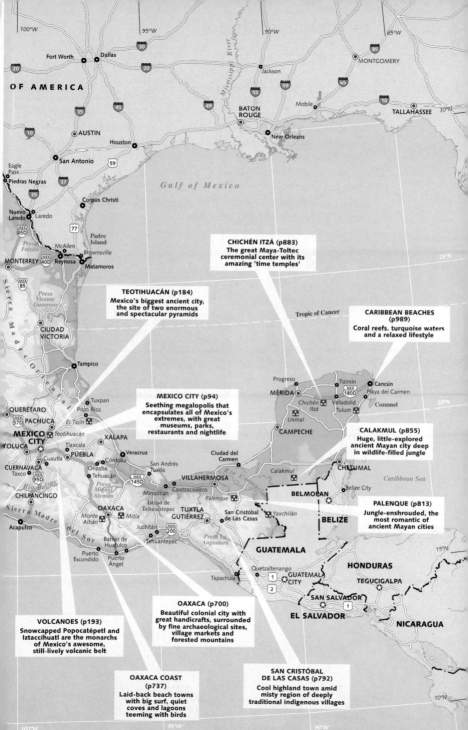

CHICHÉN ITZÁ (p883)
The great Maya-Toltec ceremonial center with its amazing 'time temples'

TEOTIHUACÁN (p184)
Mexico's biggest ancient city, the site of two enormous and spectacular pyramids

CARIBBEAN BEACHES (p989)
Coral reefs, turquoise waters and a relaxed lifestyle

MEXICO CITY (p94)
Seething megalopolis that encapsulates all of Mexico's extremes, with great museums, parks, restaurants and nightlife

CALAKMUL (p855)
Huge, little-explored ancient Mayan city deep in wildlife-filled jungle

PALENQUE (p813)
Jungle-enshrouded, the most romantic of ancient Mayan cities

VOLCANOES (p193)
Snowcapped Popocatépetl and Iztaccíhuatl are the monarchs of Mexico's awesome, still-lively volcanic belt

OAXACA (p700)
Beautiful colonial city with great handicrafts, surrounded by fine archaeological sites, village markets and forested mountains

OAXACA COAST (p737)
Laid-back beach towns with big surf, quiet coves and lagoons teeming with birds

SAN CRISTÓBAL DE LAS CASAS (p792)
Cool highland town amid misty region of deeply traditional indigenous villages

Mexico's ever-changing landscapes always amaze with their drama. Ascend **Pico de Orizaba** (p686), Mexico's highest mountain. Drive Baja California's **Transpeninsular highway** (p253) through wild desert landscapes. Explore on the breathtaking **Barranca del Cobre** (Copper Canyon, p322) in the great Sierra Madre Occidental mountains. Cool off in the lush, verdant cloud forests of Oaxaca's **Sierra Norte** (p730). Relax and soak up the sun on the superb beaches in and around the charming resort of **Puerto Vallarta** (p434). Take advantage of bird-watching opportunities at **San Blas** (p450), with its abundant wildlife. Catch some waves in the superb surf at **Puerto Escondido** (p737) on the Oaxaca Coast. Explore underwater vistas in the crystalline waters of **Cozumel** (p913).

JON DAVISON

Venture into the Caribbean in Quintana Roo (p894)

Admire the domes of the Iglesia de San Diego, Guanajuato (p604)

JAMES LYON

Walk the magical deserts around the ghost town of Real De Catorce (p599)

PETER PTSCHELINZE

LEE FOSTER

Explore El Arco, a natural arch eroded out of the rocky cliffs at Land's End (p293)

Embrace the colors of El Mirador (p265), Ensenada
DAVID PEEVERS

WOODS WHEATCROFT

Pay respect to the huge cacti of Baja California Sur (p273)

The magnificent handicrafts turned out by Mexico's talented artisans don't just make for exciting shopping, they add color and art to everyday life throughout the country. View the dramatic human and animal figures carved from ironwood by the indigenous **Seri people** (p308) of northwest Mexico. Appreciate the striking earthenware based produced by the potters of **Mata Ortiz** (p348). For marvelous handmade silver jewelry, visit the silversmiths of **Taxco** (p235). Get lost in the mythical, mystical world of the **Huichol people** (p600), depicted in wonderfully colorful yarn and bead 'paintings.' Appreciate the textile skills of southeast Mexico's Maya people, most evident in and around **San Cristóbal de Las Casas** (p792).

RICHARD I'ANSON

Be fooled by papier mâché fruit and vegetables

Try a new kind of ceramics: Mexico's festival crafts (p75)

JEFF GREENBE

RICHARD CUMMINS

Serenade your fellow travellers – ukuleles

WITOLD SKRYPCZAK

Get arty with some local textiles, Todos Santos (p295)

NEIL SETCHFIELD

Give thanks: Patron saint of Mexico for sale, Basílica (p139)

Keep your small stuff safe: painted wooden boxes from a Saturday bazaar (p165), Mexico City

RICHARD I'ANSON

Look beyond the silver and spook yourself with traditional wooden carvings and masks, Taxco (p242)

RICHARD NEBESKY

Mexicans love the color, noise, music and spectacle of a fiesta: one may break out any time, wherever you are. Experience Pátzcuaro's **Día de Muertos** (Day of the Dead; p556); Mexico's most characteristic festival is celebrated vividly here. Join the millions of people who converge on Mexico City's Basílica de Guadalupe for the **Día de Nuestra Señora de Guadalupe** (Day of Our Lady of Guadalupe; p143). Visit festive Veracruz in spring to see it lit up by **Carnaval** (p675). Watch Mexico's colorful folk dances, which are showcased at the Guelaguetza in **Oaxaca** (p711). Enjoy a cultural extravaganza at the Festival Internacional Cervantino in **Guanajuato** (p611) in October. See a reconstructed battle from medieval Spain in **Zacatecas** (p579) at the August La Morisma.

JOHN NEUBAUER

Fall in love with a folk dancer in
Tlaxcala (p195)

Marvel at the headdresses of Quetzal
dancers (p73)

JEFFREY N BECOM

Praise the plumage: a Native Mexican dancer outside the Santuario de la Virgen de
Guadalupe (p286), La Paz

RICK GERHAR

Justly famous for the heritage of its mighty pre-Hispanic civilizations, Mexico presents a magnificent array of temples, cities and pyramids. Don't miss the huge pyramids of **Teotihuacán** (p184) near Mexico City. Be sure to visit the **Templo Mayor** (p122) in Mexico City itself – the center of the ancient Aztec universe. Journey east to the unique niched pyramids of **El Tajín** (p660). Visit the ancient Zapotec capital **Monte Albán** (p723), a superb site overlooking Oaxaca city. Journey deep into the rainforest to little-explored **Calakmul** (p855), seat of an ancient Maya superpower.

Be awed by the Mayan deity Chac-Mool at Uxmal (p871)

KIM GRANT

JON DAVISON

Investigate the beautiful Mayan architecture of Palenque (p813) in its emerald-green jungle setting

Wonder at the mysteries of the Mayan calendar at El Castillo, Chichén Itzá (p885)

KIM GRANT

In addition to national favorites such as grilled meats, seafood cocktails and the ubiquitous *antojitos* (snacks) such as tacos, guacamole and enchiladas, Mexican food has wonderful regional variety. Visit Puebla to sample the spicy chocolate sauce **mole poblano** (p208). Head to Oaxaca, which offers seven different **moles** (p715). All of coastal Mexico serves up magnificent seafood, such as Veracruz's fish *a la veracruzana*, smothered in tomatoes and olives. Taste the delectable fish tacos of **Sayulita** (p434). Northerners are especially fond of their meat: a Monterrey favorite is grilled *cabrito* (baby goat). People on the Yucatán Peninsula adore their *sopa de lima* (lime soup) and *pollo pibil* (baked banana-leaf-wrapped chicken).

Brave the Mexican chili

RALPH LEE HOPKINS

Grab a snack at a fruit stall while you explore the sights of San Ángel (p133)

RICK GERHARTER

KRAIC

Try some olives, Baja California Sur (p273)

Getting Started

Mexico requires as little planning as you like. You can just get on the plane or bus or into your car and go! You'll rarely have trouble finding suitable accommodation on any budget, travel by road or plane within Mexico is easy and you'll discover so much to do and see that any plans you have may change in any case. Equally, if you have limited time and specific goals, you can work out a detailed itinerary and reserve accommodations in advance. If this is your first trip to Mexico, especially if it's your first trip outside the developed world, be ready for more crowds, noise, bustle and poverty than you're accustomed to. But don't worry – most Mexicans will be only too happy to help you feel at home in their country. Invest a little time before your trip in learning even just a few phrases of Spanish – every word you know will make your trip that little bit easier and more enjoyable.

See the Language chapter (p993) for some basic Spanish words and phrases.

WHEN TO GO

Any time is a good time to visit Mexico, though the coastal and low-lying regions, particularly in the southern half of the country, are fairly hot and humid from May to September (these are the months of highest rainfall and highest temperatures almost everywhere). The interior of the country has a more temperate climate than the coasts. In fact, it's sometimes decidedly chilly in the north and the central highlands from November to February.

See Climate Charts (p948), Festivals & Events (p953) and Holidays (p954) for information to help you decide when to go.

July and August are peak holiday months for both Mexicans and foreigners. Other big holiday seasons are mid-December to early January (for both foreigners and Mexicans), and a week either side of Easter (for Mexicans). At these times the coastal resorts attract big tourist crowds, room prices go up in popular places, and rooms and public transportation can be heavily booked, so advance reservations are advisable.

DON'T LEAVE HOME WITHOUT...

- checking your foreign ministry's Mexico travel information (p950)
- all the necessary paperwork if you're driving (p970)
- clothes to cope with Mexico's climatic variations and air-conditioned and non-air-conditioned rooms (and buses)
- any necessary immunizations or medications (p984) and any special toiletries you require, including contact lens solution and contraceptives
- a flashlight (torch) for some of those not-so-well-lit Mexican streets and stairways – and for power outages
- an inconspicuous container for money and valuables, such as a small, slim wallet or an under-the-clothes pouch or money belt (p950)
- your favorite sunglasses
- a small padlock
- a small Spanish dictionary and/or phrasebook
- adequate insurance (p955)

COSTS & MONEY

All the travel necessities remain fairly inexpensive in Mexico. Mid-range travelers can live well in most parts of the country for US$50 to US$80 per person per day. Two people can usually find a clean, comfortable room with private bathroom and fan or air-conditioning for US$30 to US$55, and have the rest to pay for food (a full lunch or dinner in a typical good restaurant costs around US$12 to US$15), admission fees, transport and incidentals. Budget travelers should allot US$20 to US$30 a day for accommodation and two meals a day in restaurants. Add in other costs and you'll spend more like US$30 to US$45.

The main exceptions to this are the Caribbean coast and parts of Baja California, where rooms can easily cost 50% more than elsewhere.

Extra expenses such as internal airfares, car rentals and handicrafts shopping will push your expenses up, but if there are two or more of you, costs per person drop considerably. Double rooms often cost only a few dollars more than singles, and triple or family rooms only a few dollars more than doubles. A rented car costs no more for four people than for one. Children under 13 pay reduced prices on many buses and flights, and at some sights and attractions.

At the top of the scale are a few hotels and resorts that charge upwards of US$200 for a room, and restaurants where you can pay US$50 per person. But you can also stay at classy smaller hotels for US$60 to US$90 a double and eat extremely well for US$25 to US$40 per person per day.

TRAVEL LITERATURE

British writer Isabella Tree takes peyote with the Huicholes and meets the matriarchs of Juchitán in *Sliced Iguana: Travels in Unknown Mexico* (2001), a warm, perceptive account of Mexico and its indigenous cultures.

On Mexican Time by Tony Cohan (2000) is a gringo's affectionate, quirky account of making a new life in San Miguel de Allende, among a cast of assorted Mexicans and other expats.

Ronald Wright offers an insightful understanding of the cultures of southeast Mexico, Belize and Guatemala in *Time Among the Maya* (1989), an investigation of the Mayas' concept of time and their tragic modern history.

In the 1930s, a time of conflict between Catholics and an atheistic state, Graham Greene wandered down eastern Mexico to Chiapas. *The Lawless Roads* (1939) traces his journey and yields perceptive insights into what makes Mexicans tick.

The People's Guide to Mexico (12th edition, 2002) by Carl Franz is less a guidebook, more a witty, affectionate portrait of a country and an introduction to the nitty-gritty of Mexican travel. It's still a classic after a quarter of a century.

Elijah Wald's *Narcocorrido* (2001) is both travel narrative and investigation of a popular Mexican song genre built around the travails of ordinary folk involved in the dangerous business of drug-running on Mexico's northern border.

For further understanding of the unique border scene, dive into John Phillip Santos' *Places Left Unfinished at the Time of Creation* (1999), a fascinating multi-generational tale of the author's north Mexican–south Texan family.

In *Sacred Monkey River* (2000), Christopher Shaw explores by canoe the basin of the remote, jungle-bound Río Usumacinta which divides Mexico from Guatemala – a great read.

TOP 10s

ADVENTURES

Adventure tourism is a burgeoning industry, with countless options for outdoor enthusiasts. See the regional chapters for detail on these adrenalin rushes.

- surfing the big Pacific waves at Puerto Escondido (p737)
- volcano hiking on Pico de Orizaba (p686)
- diving and snorkeling the crystal clear Caribbean reef waters (p915)
- canyon hiking in the Barranca del Cobre (p322)
- watching whales at Laguna Ojo de Liebre (p274)
- cloud forest hiking in Oaxaca's Sierra Norte (p730)
- snorkeling with sea lions at Isla Espíritu Santo (p286)
- hanging from a ledge in the rock-climbing mecca Potrero Chico (p398)
- taking the rough road to the pristine jungle lake, Laguna Miramar (p811)
- sport-fishing at Mazatlán (p417)

FIESTAS

You'll really catch the Mexican mood at these events (see p953 for further information).

- Carnaval (Carnival), week leading up to Ash Wednesday, late February or early March, celebrated most vividly in Veracruz (p675), Mazatlán (p418) and La Paz (p286)
- Semana Santa (Holy Week), Palm Sunday to Easter Sunday, particularly colorful in San Miguel de Allende (p626), Taxco (p239) and Pátzcuaro (p556)
- Feria de San Marcos, mid-April to mid-May, Aguascalientes (p588)
- Guelaguetza, last two Mondays of July, Oaxaca (p711)
- La Morisma, last weekend of August, Zacatecas (p579)
- Grito de la Independencia (Cry for Independence), September 15, Mexico City (p143)
- Festival Internacional Cervantino, second half of October, Guanajuato (p611)
- Día de Todos los Santos (All Saints' Day), November 1, and Día de Muertos (Day of the Dead), November 2, celebrated nationwide
- Día del Jumil (celebrating the *jumil* beetle), first Monday after Día de Muertos, Taxco (p239)
- Día de Nuestra Señora de Guadalupe (Day of Our Lady of Guadalupe), December 12, Mexico City (p143)

MOVIES

Mexico has inspired Mexicans and non-Mexicans alike to make great films set here.

- *Frida* – the atmospheric 2002 Hollywood Kahlo biopic, starring Salma Hayek
- *Traffic* – Steven Soderbergh's four-Oscar cross-border drug movie with Michael Douglas, Catherine Zeta-Jones and Benicio del Toro (2000); don't watch this the night before you leave for Mexico
- *Amores Perros* (Love's a Bitch) – Alejandro González Iñárritu's raw, ground-breaking movie of modern Mexico City life (2000)
- *Y Tu Mamá También* (And Your Mother Too) – Alfonso Cuarón's 2002 road movie, the most successful Mexican film ever
- *Puerto Escondido* – wry, funny 1992 travel-and-crime movie directed by Italy's Gabriele Salvatores
- *Viva Zapata!* – Marlon Brando and Anthony Quinn star in Elia Kazan's romanticized 1952 version of the revolutionary's life
- *Los Olvidados* (The Forgotten Ones) – Luis Buñuel's 1950 condemnation of Mexico City poverty portrays a gang of nasty teenage thugs, with haunting dream sequences adding a surreal touch
- *The Treasure of the Sierra Madre* – Bogart gets gold fever in Huston's 1948 greed-stoked adventure
- *El Crimen del Padre Amaro* (The Crime of Father Amaro) – Carrera's 2002 tale of the corrupt church
- *El Mariachi* – legendary low-budget 1992 action film, shot by Robert Rodriguez in two weeks for US$7000, about a wandering musician (Carlos Gallardo) who gets mixed up in mob violence

INTERNET RESOURCES

Lanic (http://lanic.utexas.edu/la/mexico) Best broad collection of Mexico links, from the University of Texas.

Lonely Planet (www.lonelyplanet.com) Succinct summaries on travel in Mexico ; the popular Thorn Tree bulletin board; travel news; and the subwwway section with links to travel resources elsewhere on the Web.

Mexican Wave (www.mexicanwave.com) 'Europe's gateway to Mexico,' a fund of travel, culture and food-related material.

Mexico (www.visitmexico.com) Colorful and informative site of Mexico's tourism ministry – a useful place to start.

Mexico Online (www.mexonline.com) News, bulletin boards and a huge variety of other content and links.

Planeta.com (www.planeta.com) Great articles and listings for anyone interested in Mexican travel or the Mexican environment.

Itineraries

CLASSIC ROUTES

CENTRAL OVERLAND ROUTE   Two Weeks

Don't rush the top half of Mexico. The journey from the US border to the nation's capital acquaints you with the contrast and fascination of the real Mexico: the northern deserts and the colonial silver cities. Start by crossing the Rio Grande from El Paso, Texas, to **Ciudad Juárez** (p340). Head south to lively **Chihuahua** (p349) and peaceful **Hidalgo del Parral** (p357), old stamping grounds of revolutionary Pancho Villa. Continue via friendly **Durango** (p361) to beautiful **Zacatecas** (p574), northernmost of the fabled silver cities, a cultured town amid the arid deserts. Continue to the fertile Bajío region and gorgeous **Guanajuato** (p604) where cultural attractions are piled on top of each other amid impossible topography. Eastward, gringo-friendly **San Miguel de Allende** (p621) has more galleries than you can shake a *churro* at.

Explore the charms of **Querétaro** (p633), where history and tradition hold sway in its tranquil plazas. Then give way to the magnetic pull of **Mexico City** (p94), the crucible of everything Mexican – a must-see, or unavoidable. Plan to stay long enough to hook into its culture, history and entertainment scene; or hope for a smog-free stint and try not to get stuck in traffic.

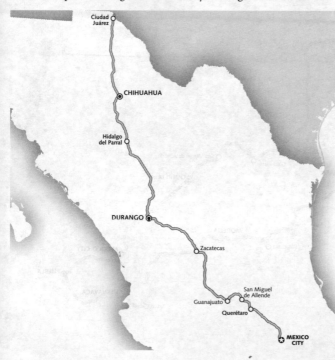

This 1740km trip from the US border to the Mexican capital crosses the northern deserts and passes through the fertile Bajío region with its colonial cities. With adequate time to enjoy the best stops along the way, it takes around two weeks.

COLONIAL HEARTLAND
Three Weeks

The nation's capital is ringed by a necklace of colonial cities blessed with carved-stone buildings, broad plazas, splashing fountains and lively modern cultural scenes – Mexico's historic, architectural and artistic gems.

After checking out the colonial center of **Mexico City** itself (p94), head east for **Puebla** (p200) which has the country's greatest concentration of restored colonial architecture. South of the capital, **Cuernavaca** (p225) has been a retreat from Mexico City ever since Cortés built his fortress-palace there in the 1520s. Further south, head to charming hillside **Taxco** (p235) which harbors many surprises in its lovely cobblestone alleyways.

Go west to Michoacán's capital **Morelia** (p542), home to an imposing cathedral and many well-preserved buildings. **Pátzcuaro** (p552) is a handsome highland town where indigenous Purépecha sell their wares around one of Mexico's loveliest central plazas. Further west, *muy mexicano* **Guadalajara** (p505) isn't as quaint as its neighbors but retains several pleasant plazas and plenty of fine architecture in its historic central district.

To the north, trip up to prosperous **Zacatecas** (p574), a stylish silver city with a stupendous cathedral set amid arid semidesert. Back toward Mexico City, in the Bajío region, lively **Guanajuato** (p604) awaits in a ravine awash with quixotic *callejones* (alleys) and vibrant student life. The lack of stoplights is only part of the charm in the festive expat capital of **San Miguel de Allende** (p621). En route back to Mexico City, stop off in **Querétaro** (p633), with several fine museums and a very walkable historic center.

> The entire loop around all the finest colonial cities, starting and finishing in Mexico City, is 2130km and would take around three weeks, allowing a few days at each stop en route. Many travelers are selective and cover only their chosen parts of the route.

DEEP SOUTH

One Month

This magnificent journey starts in Mexico's colonial heartland and ends on its glorious Caribbean beaches. Start by exploring fascinating **Mexico City** (p94), including a visit to the awesome pyramids of **Teotihuacán** (p184). Then head east to colonial **Puebla** (p200) before crossing the mountains southward to **Oaxaca** (p700), a lively and lovely colonial city with Mexico's finest handicrafts, and at the heart of a beautiful region with many indigenous people.

If you have time, divert south to one of the sun-baked beach spots south of Oaxaca, such as **Puerto Escondido** (p737), **Zipolite** (p753) or **Bahías de Huatulco** (p759). Then move east to **San Cristóbal de Las Casas** (p792), a lovely highland town surrounded by intriguing indigenous villages; and **Palenque** (p813), perhaps the most stunning of all ancient Mayan cities, set against a backdrop of emerald-green jungle.

Head northeast to the Yucatán Peninsula, with a stop at historic **Campeche** (p845) before you reach colonial, cultural **Mérida** (p857), the base for visiting **Uxmal** (p871) and other fine Mayan ruins nearby. Next stop is **Chichén Itzá** (p883), the Yucatán's most awesome ancient Mayan site. From here, head direct to **Tulum** (p926) on the Caribbean coast, a Mayan site with a glorious beachside setting, and then make your way northward along the 'Riviera Maya' toward Mexico's glitziest resort, **Cancún** (p894). On the way, halt at lively **Playa del Carmen** (p920) and/or take a side trip to **Cozumel** (p913) for a spot of world-class snorkeling or diving.

This 2800km, one-month adventure takes you from Mexico's geographic and cultural center through the states of Oaxaca and Chiapas – with their colorful indigenous populations, pre-Hispanic ruins and dramatic scenery – to the ancient Mayan cities and beaches of the Yucatán Peninsula.

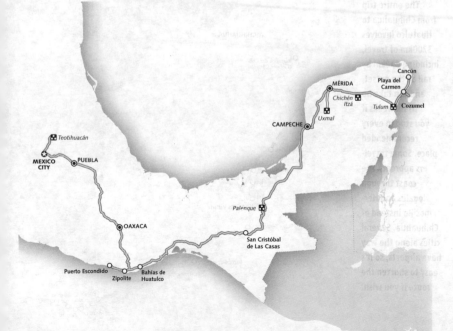

BARRANCA DEL COBRE & PACIFIC COAST   Four to Six Weeks

Mexico's Pacific coast is a glittering sequence of large, famous resorts, pristine, empty, jungle-lined beaches and every grade of coastal dream in between. A great approach to the coast is from **Chihuahua** (p349) via the awesome **Barranca del Cobre** (Copper Canyon; p322) with its dramatic railroad and spectacular hiking.

Spend an evening sipping margaritas on the lively plaza in **Mazatlán** (p412) before continuing to the ancient island of **Mexcaltitán** (p425) and the wildlife-rich lagoons of laid-back **San Blas** (p425). Hang ten in **Sayulita** (p433), then it's on to discos, gourmet food, whale-watching and shopping in **Puerto Vallarta** (p434).

Isolated beaches abound on the Costalegre, home to some of the world's most luxurious resorts. Spend a day snorkeling here at **Playa Tenacatita** (p450) and don't miss the street tacos in **Melaque** (p451). Rent a beach-bum bungalow on internationally renowned surf beach **Barra de Nexpa** (p464); novice surfers should head to **Caleta de Campos** (p465). Surf, snorkel and take romantic sunset walks in **Troncones** (p468) before hiring a fishing boat in **Zihuatanejo** (p473).

Pick up the pace to hit the discos, go bungee jumping and learn a little Mexican history in **Acapulco** (p486). **Puerto Escondido** (p737) has grade-A surf and a lively little after-dark scene. To end your trip, lie back in a hammock at the low-budget paradise beaches of **Mazunte** (p756) or **Zipolite** (p753), or relax at Mexico's newest resort, **Bahías de Huatulco** (p759), set along a string of beautiful, sheltered bays.

The entire trip from Chihuahua to Huatulco involves 3200km of travel, including 670km by rail at the outset, and can take up to six weeks if you stop in every recommended place. Some travelers approach the coast through Nogales and Hermosillo instead of Chihuahua. Several cities along the way have airports, so it's easy to shorten the route if you wish.

ROADS LESS TRAVELED

MICHOACÁN
Two Weeks

This relatively little known western state offers an amazing variety of attractions. Coming from Mexico City, the logical first stop is the **Santuario Mariposa Monarca** (p550), the spectacular winter home for millions of glorious monarch butterflies. Pretty **Morelia** (p542), Michoacán's capital, offers colonial ambience, stimulating nightlife and university culture. Continue to **Pátzcuaro** (p552), a beautiful town of cobbled streets and tile roofs, with island-filled **Lago de Pátzcuaro** (p559) nearby. The Pátzcuaro area is famous for its vibrant Day of the Dead celebrations.

A little further west is typically Mexican **Uruapan** (p563), with the wonderful little **Parque Nacional Eduardo Ruiz** (p565) within its city limits. An hour beyond is still-steaming **Volcán Paricutín** (p568), easily climbed in a day – don't miss the buried church at its foot. Take the highway down to the port of **Lázaro Cárdenas** (p466), starting point for a coastline of incredible Pacific surf beaches.

Playa Azul (p465) is a great introduction to this laid-back coast of dramatic cliffs and palm-lined coves on the way to **Caleta de Campos** (p465). International surfers lounge in cabañas, between sets at **Barra de Nexpa** (p464). Isolated **Playa Maruata** (p464) is paradise for turtles and campers, while **La Ticla** (p464) and **San Juan de Alima** (p464) have gorgeous rolling breaks. From here, continue up Mexico's Pacific coast or inland to Colima and Guadalajara.

This 940km route (measured from the Santuario Mariposa Monarca to San Juan de Alima) combines the relatively cool Michoacán highlands with a spell on the steamy Pacific coast in a neat trip of around two weeks.

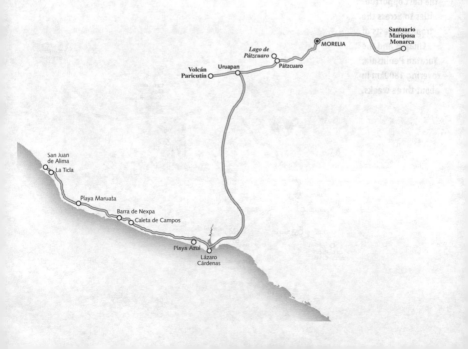

SOUTHEASTERN JUNGLES   Three Weeks

This trip from highland Chiapas to the Caribbean coast provides close encounters with exotic wildlife and visits some of Mexico's most exciting archaeological sites. Starting at graceful **San Cristóbal de Las Casas** (p792), head north to **Ocosingo** (p809), close to the jungle-backed Mayan ruins of **Toniná** (p810), and then on to remote **Laguna Miramar** (p811), an exquisite rainforest lake where howler monkeys greet the dawn.

Return to Ocosingo and head north to the thundering **Agua Azul** (p812) waterfalls and jungle-clad **Palenque** (p813), arguably the most beautifully proportioned of all Mayan cities. A fascinating side-trip leads southeast to **Bonampak** (p822) and **Yaxchilán** (p822), two fine Mayan sites situated in dense forest where you stand a good chance of spotting toucans, monkeys and other wildlife.

Return to Palenque and make your way east across the base of the Yucatán Peninsula to the huge **Calakmul Biosphere Reserve** (p855) which protects hundreds of species of rainforest wildlife and shelters important archaeological sites including the awesome metropolis of **Calakmul** itself (p855). A visit here provides a good chance to spot a variety of exotic birds and animals. To the northeast, on the Caribbean coast, the jungle, marshes and islands of the **Sian Ka'an Biosphere Reserve** (p933) are home to a huge variety of land, air and water life, best visited with an expert local guide.

This route offers the best opportunities to access the tropical forests of Chiapas and the Yucatán Peninsula, covering 1800km in about three weeks.

NORTHERN DESERTS, CANYONS & FORESTS   One Month

Awesome natural configurations and bizarre discoveries await adventurous travelers in the remoter reaches of Mexico's north. Make **Paquimé** (p346), with its pre-Hispanic desert trading settlement, your first goal. From here visit the renowned potters' village **Mata Ortiz** (p348). Then head south along winding roads to the pre-Hispanic cliff dwellings at **Cuarenta Casas** (p348) and the town of **Madera** (p348), set among forested mountains.

Move southeast to **Cuauhtémoc** (p356) where you can board the **Ferrocarril Chihuahua al Pacífico** (p322) for explorations of the spectacular **Barranca del Cobre** (Copper Canyon; p322). Next, investigate a colorful episode of Mexican history at sites where revolutionary Pancho Villa lived and died in **Chihuahua** (p349), **Hidalgo del Parral** (p357), **Canutillo** (p359) and **Torreón** (p359).

En route to Torreón, visit **Mapimí** (p360) and the ghost town of **Ojuela** (p360), at the heart of a once booming mining area. Head east for a snorkel and swim in the bizarre desert pools of **Cuatro Ciénegas** (p400), then go south to taste a drop of desert wine at **Parras** (p407). Move on to laid-back **Saltillo** (p402) with its first-class desert museum. Then turn south to the magical ex-ghost town of **Real de Catorce** (p599), a former silver-mining center coming back to life with annual floods of Catholic pilgrims, indigenous Huichol people (and others) seeking the hallucinogenic cactus peyote, and artists, filmmakers and other pioneering creative types. For one more natural marvel, head east over to the cloud forests of **El Cielo Biosphere Reserve** (p383).

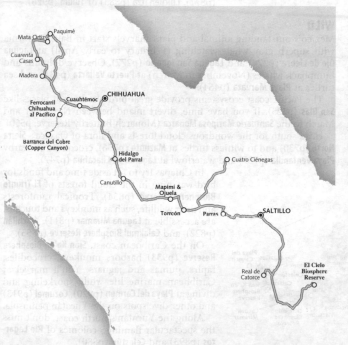

Running in a roughly northwest-to-southeast direction across some remote areas of northern Mexico, this trip needs a month if you are to enjoy every major attraction along the 3200km route from Paquimé to El Cielo.

TAILORED TRIPS

RUINED

The mysterious and awe-inspiring cities and temple complexes left behind by Mexico's pre-Hispanic cultures are unforgettable. Excellent museums at or near many sites help to interpret what you see. Begin at the center of the Aztecs' universe, the **Templo Mayor** (p122) of their capital Tenochtitlán, today in downtown **Mexico City**, followed by the capital's comprehensive **Museo Nacional de Antropología** (p129).

Then visit some of the fine sites within day-trip distance of the capital: awesome **Teotihuacán** (p184), with its gigantic pyramids; **Tula** (p181), the Toltec capital; and hilltop **Xochicalco** (p234).

Journey east to **El Tajín** (p660), the highest achievement of the Classic Veracruz civilization, and to see the best artifacts of the mysterious Olmec civilization of the Gulf coast in **Xalapa's Museo de Antropología** (p665) and **Villahermosa's Parque La Venta** (p779). **Monte Albán** (p723), the ancient Zapotec capital, is superbly situated on a hilltop overlooking the city of Oaxaca.

Southeast Mexico was the land of the ancient Maya, whose legacy is of unmatched beauty. Don't miss the marvels of **Palenque** (p813), **Uxmal** (p871), **Chichén Itzá** (p883) or **Tulum** (p926).

WILD

Mexico's outstanding animal and plant marvels start in Baja California with superb gray whale-watching (February to early April) at **Laguna Ojo de Liebre** (p274) and **Laguna San Ignacio** (p277). Observe dolphins and humpback whales (November to March) at **Puerto Vallarta** (p434) and sea turtles at **Playa Maruata** (p464).

The Pacific coast ecosystems provide great bird-watching at places like **San Blas** (p425). If you have time, divert inland between November and March to the **Santuario Mariposa Monarca** (Monarch Butterfly Reserve; p550).

Head south for the wondrous cloud forests and flora of Oaxaca's **Sierra Norte** (p730) and to witness turtles at **Mazunte** (p756), crocodiles at nearby **Playa Ventanilla** (p757) and waterfowl at **Lagunas de Chacahua** (p747).

In Chiapas try to set aside time and funds for bird-watching in the cloud forests of **El Triunfo Biosphere Reserve** (p834). Tropical rainforests and their wildlife, such as monkeys and toucans, are accessible at **Laguna Miramar** (p811), **Yaxchilán** (p822), and **Calakmul Biosphere Reserve** (p855).

On the Caribbean coast, **Sian Ka'an Biosphere Reserve** (p933) harbors monkeys, crocodiles, tapirs, pumas and jaguars. You'll marvel at Caribbean marine life while snorkeling and diving at **Playa del Carmen** (p920), **Cozumel** (p913) and other dive spots on the Yucatán peninsula.

Along the Yucatán's north coast, don't miss the spectacular flamingo colonies of **Río Lagartos** (p893) and **Celestún** (p880).

BEACHED

For an end-to-end trip encompassing Mexico's most peerless *playas*, start off in Baja California by picking your own pristine beach south of **Mulegé** (p280), then head to **Loreto** (p280), Baja's water-sports paradise, for more action.

Over on the mainland, make a beeline for the lagoon-backed beaches of **San Blas** (p425) and the popular surf village **Sayulita** (p433) before you hit **Puerto Vallarta** (p434) with its beach parties and marine wildlife. Slow down on the nearly empty beaches of the **Costalegre** (p450) before soaking in the rolling waves of **Melaque** (p451).

Zip down to **Barra de Nexpa** (p464) where international surfers rule, and don't miss the crashing waves of **Troncones** (p468). Revive on the sooth-ing bay at **Zihuatanejo** (p473) before taking on high-energy **Acapulco** (p486).

On the Oaxaca coast, the 'Mexican Pipeline' is even a challenge to experienced surfers at lively **Puerto Escondido** (p737), or you can sim-ply lie back in a hammock at the backpackers' haven **Zipolite** (p753).

Move over to the Caribbean for party time at **Cancún** (p894) followed by a spot of snor-keling and relaxation at nearby **Isla Mujeres** (p904). **Tulum** (p926), with beachside Mayan ruins and palm-fringed white sand, is a highly popular place to end a trip, but to the south the pretty beaches of the **Xcalak** (p935) area are less developed.

The Authors

JOHN NOBLE
Coordinating Author, The Culture, Environment, Inland Oaxaca State, Directory, Transport

John has felt the pull of Mexico ever since reading about Cortés and the Aztecs as a teenager in his native England. Since a backpacking trip over 20 years ago he's been returning for extended visits, including as an author of seven editions of this guide (five as coordinating author), exploring almost every part of the country. He loves Mexico's art, archaeology, history, music, ethnic diversity, languages, food, drinks, beaches, wildlife and stunningly varied landscapes – and the fact that life here always has that uniquely Mexican edge to it. John now lives in Spain, which provides yet another angle on what makes Mexico tick.

My Favorite Trip

I always return to beautiful, mysterious Chiapas. My trip starts with some beach relaxation at ultra-laid-back Puerto Arista (p835). Then I head up into the misty mountains to cool off at San Cristóbal de Las Casas (p792), a romantic town at the heart of Mexico's most deep-rooted indigenous region. I descend northward to Ocosingo (p809) then take the long, rough road to Laguna Miramar (p811), a pristine jungle lake. Next stop, the magical Mayan ruins of Palenque (p813), then I'm off to Frontera Corozal (p824) for a boat along the jungle-lined Río Usumacinta to Yaxchilán (p826), another marvelous Mayan site, where I climb Edificio 41 and look across the top of the rainforest to the hills of Guatemala as the roars of howler monkeys echo through the trees around me.

SANDRA BAO
Western Central Highlands

Born and raised in Buenos Aires, Argentina, to Chinese parents, Sandra reluctantly came to the US when she was nine. Despite her introduction to the country being a winter in Toledo, Ohio, she became a naturalized citizen and eventually wound up with a BA in Psychology from UC Santa Cruz. Sandra has traveled extensively, including to many parts of Mexico, both before and after joining up with Lonely Planet. She now despairs at having to give up a healthy vegetable garden and promising rock climbing career for her peripatetic lifestyle. Sandra lives in Portland, Oregon, with husband, fellow Lonely Planet writer Ben Greensfelder. The two hope to someday acquire a Siamese cat.

SUSAN FORSYTH
Oaxaca State

Susan Forsyth, mother, English teacher and travel writer, has been traveling in Mexico and around for well over a decade, sometimes *en familia*, sometimes alone. Her first trip was with her one-year-old daughter when both could speak barely a word of Spanish. They hung out in Oaxaca, chasing balloons in the *zócalo*, while husband and fellow author John Noble rushed around researching an earlier incarnation of this guide. Now, with better Spanish and a better understanding of the Hispanic world (aided by home being southern Spain for 10 years) Susan still loves to travel to Mexico, especially the lush Oaxaca coast, which she thinks is one of the most beautiful places on the planet.

BETH GREENFIELD   Central North Mexico
Beth, a New Jersey native now living in New York City, jumped at the chance to return to Mexico, where she first fell in love with the food, the people and the landscapes during her first trip there several years ago. Covering the central north region for this guide was wonderful for many reasons, most of all the tacos of Juárez, *huitlacoche quesadillas* of Chihuahua and the fruit-stand treats of Durango. (Food obsessed, yes – but in a good way!) The endless bus rides and car trips were made beautiful by the magical deserts on the other side of the windows. And the warmth of the folks she met along the way never ceased to amaze her.

MICHAEL GROSBERG   Northeast Mexico
Raised in the Washington, DC area, Michael studied philosophy in Michigan and Israel, then worked in business on a small island in the Northern Marianas. After a long trip through Asia and across the US, including several stops in border towns in Mexico, he was a journalist and worked with non-governmental organizations in South Africa. Michael's interest in Mexico began in earnest while pursuing graduate work in literature in New York City. Trips to Ecuador and Panama improved Spanish language skills and provided the confidence to try to get to know the neighbor to the south. He has since taken many random jobs and currently teaches at university in between trips abroad.

MORGAN KONN   Central Pacific Coast
Morgan's first fireworks and first travel writing assignment were in Mexico. Now after roaming several continents, including Antarctica, she prefers to watch fireworks from a distance and favors Mexico to just about everywhere else. She mostly resides in Berkeley, California, where she fancies herself a visual artist and enjoys long walks, hot baths and cooking. Recently she has contributed to Lonely Planet's *South America on a Shoestring* and *Bolivia* guidebooks.

ANDREW DEAN NYSTROM   Around Mexico City, Northern Central Highlands
Andrew learned Espanglish while playing soccer in the streets of Southern California. After several trips south of the border for youth *fútbol* tournaments, he was hooked on seeking out Mexico's less touristed bits. He drove 7000 miles – without hitting anything – for this edition. When not out rambling, he hangs his *hamaca* in a garden cottage straddling the San Andres Fault in Alta California. He has also written about Mexico's Pacific coast for Lonely Planet and Chiapas and Oaxaca for Fodor's.

SUZANNE PLANK   Yucatán Peninsula

Growing up, Suzanne lived primarily in Berkeley but also in Boston, Bethesda and Bahía, Brazil. (She eventually moved farther down the alphabet.) She first traveled to Mexico when she was five. Drawn by the depth of the culture and warmth of the people, she has returned repeatedly over the years to travel, to live and to work. Suzanne studied International Relations and has an MA in Latin American Studies with emphases on political economy and literature. She first visited the Yucatán Peninsula in 1990, when MTV had yet to invade Cancún and Playa del Carmen was still a quiet fishing town.

MICHAEL READ   Baja California, Northwest Mexico

Michael Read has not worked as a steamboat captain, a fry cook, a llama wrangler, or a precious gems speculator (that unpleasant episode in Bangkok notwithstanding). He has, however, spent countless hours packing and unpacking his backpack on the train platforms and river taxi docks of the world. When not chasing the horizon, Michael can be found in Oakland, California, where he has worked with the Lonely Planet web team and as an independent author, graphic designer, exhibitions curator and photographer.

DANIEL C SCHECHTER   Mexico City

After almost a decade in Mexico City, Daniel now checks the pollution levels before going out and picking up tamales with the morning paper. He arrived in 1994 to teach English at the Tec de Monterrey university, then joined the staff of the *News,* Mexico City's English-language daily. There, until its demise in 2002, he began writing on *cochinita pibil, pozole, alambre* and other mysterious Mexican foods. He continued this obsession at *Business Mexico,* the American Chamber magazine, where he also contributed pieces on Mexican travel, music and environmental matters. For this, his second edition of this guide, Daniel covered his adopted megalopolis.

IAIN STEWART   Tabasco & Chiapas

Iain Stewart is based in Brighton, UK, but daydreams of swapping the city's pebble beach for a palm-fringed version. He first visited Tabasco and Chiapas in the early 1990s, and has returned to the region regularly since then. Iain has written and cowritten several guidebooks about Central America and the Maya region for other publishers. An offer from Lonely Planet to revisit subtropical Mexico for another bout of temple trampling and mosquito slapping was far too tempting to turn down.

WENDY YANAGIHARA   Central Gulf Coast

Wendy's ties with Mexico trace back to her grandfather, a Japanese immigrant who stowed away on a ship, winding up in Mexico before crossing the border to settle in the US. Nowadays, her father spices most of his food with fresh *salsa bandera* and peppers his conversation with expressions like *'íjole!*, and Wendy listens to Maná as she wonders about the life she might have had as a Japanese Mexican. Since first visiting the Yucatán at age 10, she's learned enough Spanish to debate the distinction between a *chelada* and a *michelada*, and has traveled from Frontera BC to Nayarit to Quintana Roo. She spent a steamy six weeks on the central Gulf coast updating that chapter for this book.

CONTRIBUTING AUTHORS

Dr David Goldberg wrote the Health chapter. David completed his training in internal medicine and infectious diseases at Columbia-Presbyterian Medical Center in New York City, where he has also served as voluntary faculty. At present, he is an infectious diseases specialist in Scarsdale, New York state, and the editor-in-chief of the website MDTravelHealth.com.

Kenneth Pearce co-wrote the History chapter. Ken is the author of three books dealing with Mexican history and culture: *A Traveler's History of Mexico*; *The View from the Top of the Temple: Ancient Maya Civilization and Modern Maya Culture*; and *Aztec: The Death of a Nation*.

James W Peyton wrote the Food & Drink chapter. James has written three books on Mexican cooking as well as articles for magazines such as *Fine Cooking, Texas Highways* and *Food & Wine*. He appears on television, conducts cooking classes and lectures on Mexican cuisine. In addition Jim maintains a website, Jim Peyton's Lo Mexicano at www.lomexicano.com, providing information about Mexico and Mexican cooking. Jim also consults on recipe development and menu design for the Mexican food industry. Jim's recipes were selected to appear in the 2000 and 2001 issues of Houghton Mifflin's *The Best American Recipes*. His latest book is *Jim Peyton's New Cooking from Old Mexico*.

Snapshot

In the final straight of his six-year presidency (it ends in late 2006), Vicente Fox is already considered a caretaker. Having defeated the once all-powerful PRI (Institutional Revolutionary Party) for the first time in 70 years in 2000, Fox, of the right-of-center PAN (National Action Party), soon found himself in a political and economic quagmire. Lacking a majority in Mexico's national Congress, Fox has been unable to raise taxes or introduce private investment into the energy sector, reforms that he believes are necessary to stir Mexico's slumbering economy. The government lacks the money it needs to improve education, social welfare and roads, which would help to stem the flow of Mexicans heading north to the USA.

Though he remains personally popular, the 6ft 4in rancher is now perceived as a man who cannot get much done. Mexicans' overall standard of living is much the same as it was when he took power.

When talk turns to Fox's successor, the name you'll most often hear is Andrés Manuel López Obrador. This dynamic, populist mayor of Mexico City represents the left-of-center PRD (Party of the Democratic Revolution), but has built his success to some degree on a partnership with big business – especially Mexico's richest man, entrepreneur Carlos Slim.

Mexicans have been enjoying a certain social liberation since the PRI's grip was prized loose. Government is more transparent, honest and accountable, and Mexicans, aware that their rulers are now subject to more or less fair elections, are more confident about expressing their opinions and asserting their rights. Fine new Mexican music, films and art (see Arts p59) are reflecting the dreams and frustrations of the young and the socially aware. Urban Mexicans (and foreign visitors) have an ever-improving social scene to enjoy, including clubs, restaurants, theater and music.

Fox has failed to achieve a deal with the indigenous Zapatista rebels in the southern state of Chiapas, but his government did manage to pass a law on indigenous language rights. Fox also hoped to improve the status and conditions of Mexican workers in the USA – a hope that appeared forlorn after the September 11, 2001, attacks on the US but which was revived in 2004 when US President George W Bush, angling for Latino votes in an election year, announced plans to allow the millions of illegal immigrants in the US (most of them Mexican) to apply for three-year, renewable work permits.

Crime, a major preoccupation of late-1990s Mexico, may be a little less rampant. Mexico City has the feel of a safer city today than a few years ago. In a push against Mexico's mighty drug cartels, 14,000 people were arrested in the first two years of the Fox administration, although the news took on a more familiar complexion in 2003 when the army was called in to dismantle Mexico's deeply corrupt anti-drug police.

FAST FACTS

Population: 101 million

Foreign tourists entering Mexico per year: 20 million (2002)

Life expectancy: 73 (US: 77)

Area: 1.9 million sq km

Length of Mexico-US border: 3326km

GDP per person: US$6260

US share of Mexican exports: 77%

Adult literacy: 91% (US: 99%)

Tortillas eaten daily: 1200 million

Annual carbon dioxide emissions per person (tons): 3.9 (US: 19.9)

History   John Noble & Kenneth Pearce

Mexico's story is always extraordinary, at times barely credible. How could a 2700-year tradition of ancient civilization – the Olmecs, the Maya, the Aztecs…intellectually sophisticated, aesthetically gifted, yet at times astoundingly bloodthirsty – crumble in two short years at the hands of a few hundred adventurers from Spain? How could Mexico's 11-year war for independence from Spain lead to three decades of dictatorship by Porfirio Díaz? How could the people's revolution that ended that dictatorship yield 70 years of one-party rule? How was one-party rule finally ended in 2000?

Travel in Mexico is a fascinating encounter with this unique story and its modern consequences. From the awesome ancient cities to the gorgeous colonial palaces, the superb museums and the deep-rooted traditions and beliefs of the Mexicans themselves – be they the mixed-ancestry *mestizos* or the millions of indigenous direct descendants of the ancient civilizations – Mexico's ever-present past will never fail to enrich your journey.

John Noble has been fascinated since his teens by Mexico's history, and in more than 20 years of travel writing on the country, he has developed a detailed on-the-ground knowledge of what happened where and when in Mexico.

Kenneth Pearce has written three books on Mexican history and culture, including *A Traveler's History of Mexico*.

BEGINNINGS

It's accepted that, barring a few Vikings in the north and some possible direct transpacific contact with Southeast Asia, the pre-Hispanic inhabitants of the Americas arrived from Siberia. They came in several migrations between perhaps 60,000 and 8000 BC; during the last ice age, crossing land now submerged beneath the Bering Strait. The earliest human traces found in Mexico date from about 20,000 BC. These first Mexicans hunted big animal herds in the grasslands of the highland valleys. When temperatures rose at the end of the Ice Age, the valleys became drier, ceasing to support such animal life and forcing the people to derive more food from plants.

Archaeologists have traced the slow beginnings of agriculture to the Tehuacán valley in Puebla state where, soon after 6500 BC, people were planting seeds of chili and a kind of squash. Between 5000 and 3500 BC they started to plant mutant forms of a tiny wild maize and to grind the maize into meal. After 3500 BC a much better variety of maize, and also beans, enabled the Tehuacán valley people to live semipermanently in villages and spend less time in seasonal hunting camps. Pottery appeared by 2300 BC.

OLMECS

Mexico's ancestral civilization arose near the Gulf Coast in the humid lowlands of southern Veracruz and neighboring Tabasco. These were the Olmecs, a name coined in the 1920s meaning 'People from the Region of Rubber.' Their civilization is famed for the awesome 'Olmec heads', stone sculptures up to 3m high with grim, pug-nosed faces and wearing curious helmets. You can view Olmec heads and other artifacts at Mexico City's Museo Nacional de Antropología (p129), Xalapa's Museo de Antropología (p665) and Villahermosa's Parque-Museo La Venta (p779).

The first known great Olmec center, San Lorenzo in Veracruz state, flourished from about 1200 to 900 BC. The basalt material for eight Olmec heads and many other stone monuments known to have been

Cenotes, the deep wells that reach a vast network of underground rivers and streams in the Yucatán, may have been formed by a comet that wiped out the dinosaurs 65 million years ago.

20,000 BC or earlier	6500 BC
First humans in Mexico	Beginning of agriculture – chili seeds are planted

carved here was probably dragged, rolled or rafted from 60km to 80km away. Finds at San Lorenzo of such faraway objects as obsidian (volcanic glass) from Guatemala and the Mexican highlands suggest that San Lorenzo controlled trade over a large region.

The second great Olmec center was La Venta, Tabasco, which flourished for a few centuries up to about 600 BC. Several tombs were found here with jade (a favorite pre-Hispanic ornamental material) making an early appearance in one of them. La Venta produced at least five Olmec heads.

Olmec sites found in central and western Mexico, far from the Gulf Coast, may well have been trading posts/garrisons to ensure the supply of jade, obsidian and other luxuries for the Olmec elite. Both San Lorenzo and La Venta were destroyed violently, but Olmec art and religion, and quite possibly Olmec social organization, strongly influenced later Mexican civilizations. Apart from the were-jaguar, Olmec gods included fire and maize deities and the feathered serpent, all of which persisted throughout the pre-Hispanic era.

> For a concise but relatively complete account of the ancient cultures of Mexico and Guatemala, read *Mexico: From the Olmecs to the Aztecs* and *The Maya*, both by Michael D Coe.

TEOTIHUACÁN

The first great civilization in central Mexico emerged in a valley about 50km northeast of the center of modern Mexico City. Teotihuacán grew into a city of an estimated 125,000 people during its apogee between AD 250 and 600, and it controlled what was probably the biggest pre-Hispanic Mexican empire. Teotihuacán had writing and books, the bar-and-dot number system and the 260-day sacred year.

The building of a magnificent planned city began about the time of Christ. The greatest of its buildings, the Pirámide del Sol (Pyramid of the Sun; p186), was constructed by AD 150. Most of the rest of the city, including the almost-as-big Pirámide de la Luna (Pyramid of the Moon; p186), was built between AD 250 and 600.

Teotihuacán probably became an imperialistic state some time after 400. It may have controlled the southern two-thirds of Mexico, all of Guatemala and Belize, and bits of Honduras and El Salvador. But it was an empire probably geared toward tribute-gathering rather than full-scale occupation.

Within Teotihuacán's cultural sphere was Cholula (p211), near Puebla, with a pyramid even bigger than the Pirámide del Sol. Teotihuacán may also have had hegemony over the Zapotecs of Oaxaca during the zenith of their capital, Monte Albán (p723), which grew into a city of perhaps 25,000 in the years between 300 and 600. In about 400 Teotihuacán invaders reached what is now Guatemala.

In the 8th century, Teotihuacán was burned, plundered and abandoned. It is likely that the state had already been weakened by the rise of rival powers in central Mexico or by environmental desiccation caused by the deforestation of the surrounding hillsides.

But Teotihuacán's influence on Mexico's later cultures was huge. Many of its gods, such as the feathered serpent Quetzalcóatl (an all-important symbol of fertility and life, itself inherited from the Olmecs) and Tláloc (the rain and water deity) were still being worshipped by the Aztecs a millennium later.

3500 BC	2300 BC
People move from seasonal hunting camps to semi-permanent villages	Pottery appears

CLASSIC MAYA

By the close of the Preclassic period in 250, the Maya people of the Yucatán Peninsula and the Petén forest of Guatemala were already building stepped temple pyramids. During the Classic period (about 250 to 900), these regions produced pre-Hispanic America's most brilliant civilization.

The Classic Maya region comprised three areas. The northern is the Yucatán Peninsula; the central area is the Petén forest of northern Guatemala and adjacent lowlands in Mexico (to the west) and Belize (to the east); and the southern consists of the highlands of Guatemala and a small section of Honduras. It was in the northern and central areas that Mayan civilization flowered most brilliantly. Many of the major Mayan sites are outside Mexico, with Tikal in Guatemala supreme in splendor.

Scholars used to think the Classic Maya were organized into about 20 independent, often warring city-states. But advances in the understanding of Mayan writing have yielded a new theory that in the first part of the Classic period, most of the city-states were grouped into two loose military alliances centered on Tikal and Calakmul, in Mexico's Campeche state. Tikal is believed to have conquered Calakmul in 695, but to have been unable to exert unified control over Calakmul's former subject states.

In the second half of the 8th century, trade between Mayan states started to shrink and conflict began to grow. By the early 10th century, the central Mayan area was virtually abandoned; most of its people probably migrated to the northern area or the highlands of Chiapas. Population pressure and ecological damage have been considered probable reasons for this collapse. Recent research also points to a series of devastating droughts and Tikal's inability to control the conquered Calakmul territory after 695 as causes.

A Traveller's History of Mexico by Kenneth Pearce expands on the topics introduced in this chapter.

Cities

A typical Mayan city functioned as the religious, political and market hub for the surrounding farming hamlets. Its ceremonial center focused on plazas surrounded by tall temple pyramids (usually the tombs of deified rulers) and lower buildings, so-called palaces, with warrens of small rooms. Stelae and altars were carved with dates, histories and elaborate human and divine figures. Stone causeways called *sacbeob*, probably built for ceremonial use, led out from the plazas. Classic Maya centers in Mexico fall into four main zones: one zone in Chiapas in the central Mayan area and the other three in the Yucatán Peninsula.

The chief Chiapas sites are Yaxchilán (p822), its tributary Bonampak (p822), Toniná (p810) and Palenque (p813), which to many people is the most beautiful of all Mayan sites. Palenque rose to prominence under the 7th-century ruler Pakal, whose treasure-loaded tomb deep inside the fine Templo de las Inscripciones was discovered in 1952.

Noted for their lavishly carved buildings, the Río Bec and Chenes zones are in a wild, little-investigated area of the southern Yucatán. The archaeological sites here, which include Calakmul (p855), draw few visitors.

The Puuc zone was another focus of northern Classic Maya culture. Its most important city was Uxmal (p871), south of Mérida. Puuc ornamentation, which reached its peak on the Governor's Palace at Uxmal, featured intricate stone mosaics, part geometric but also incorporating

1200 BC–600 BC	AD 250–900
Olmec civilization	Classic Maya civilization flourishes

Maya: The Blood of Kings (from Time Life's Lost Civilizations video series) tries to re-create the story of this civilization that flourished during Europe's Dark Ages. Includes interviews, spectacular photography and exceptionally good narrative.

faces of the hook-nosed sky-serpent/rain-god, Chac. The amazing Codz Pop (Palace of Masks) at Kabah (p874), south of Uxmal, is covered with nearly 300 Chac faces. Chichén Itzá (p883), east of Mérida, is another Puuc site, though it also owes much to the later Toltec era (see p35).

Calendar

The Maya developed a complex, partly pictorial, partly phonetic writing system with 300 to 500 symbols, whose decipherment in the 1980s greatly advanced modern understanding of the culture. They also refined a calendar used by other pre-Hispanic peoples into a tool for the exact recording of earthly and heavenly events. They could predict eclipses of the sun and the movements of the moon and Venus. The ancient Dresden Codex, a copy of which can be seen at the Villahermosa Parque-Museo La Venta (p779), contains a table predicting possible solar eclipses.

Religion

Religion permeated every facet of Mayan life. The Maya believed in predestination and had a complex astrology. To win the gods' favors they carried out elaborate rituals involving the consumption of the alcoholic drink *balche*; bloodletting from ears, tongues or penises; and dances, feasts and sacrifices. The Classic Maya seem to have practiced human sacrifice on a small scale, the Postclassic on a larger scale. Beheading was probably the most common method. At Chichén Itzá, victims were thrown into a deep cenote (well) to bring rain.

The Maya inhabited a universe with a center and four directions (each with a color: east was red; north, white; west, black; south, yellow; the center, green), 13 layers of heavens, and nine layers of underworld to which the dead descended. The earth was the back of a giant reptile floating on a pond. (It's not *too* hard to imagine yourself as a flea on this creature's back as you look across a lowland Mayan landscape!) The current world was just one of a succession of worlds destined to end in cataclysm and be succeeded by another. This cyclical nature of things enabled the future to be predicted by looking at the past. The current world is scheduled to come to an end in December 2012 – so stay alert!

Mayan gods included Itzamná, the fire deity and creator; Chac, the rain god; Yum Kaax, the maize and vegetation god; and Ah Puch, the death god. The feathered serpent, known to the Maya as Kukulcán, was introduced from central Mexico in the Postclassic period. Also worshiped were dead ancestors, particularly rulers, who were believed to be descended from the gods.

CLASSIC VERACRUZ CIVILIZATION

Along the Gulf Coast, in what are now central and northern Veracruz, the Classic period saw the rise of a number of statelets with a shared culture, together known as the Classic Veracruz civilization. Their hallmark is a style of abstract carving featuring pairs of curved and interwoven parallel lines. Classic Veracruz appears to have been particularly obsessed with the ball game (see p56); its most important center, El Tajín (p660) near Papantla, which was at its height from about 600 to 900, contains at least 11 ball courts.

Around 1325	1517
Tenochtitlán, site of present-day Mexico City, founded by the Aztecs	Spanish Francisco de Córdoba 'discovers' Mexico

TOLTECS

In central Mexico one chief power center after the decline of Teotihuacán was Xochicalco (p234), a hilltop site in Morelos state, with Mayan influences and impressive evidence of a feathered serpent cult. Cholula may have been another. Tula (p181), 65km north of Mexico City, is thought to have been the capital of a great empire referred to by later Aztec 'histories' as that of the Toltecs (Artificers).

Tula

It is hard to disentangle myth and history in the Tula/Toltec story. A widely accepted version is that the Toltecs were one of a number of semicivilized tribes from the north who moved into central Mexico after the fall of Teotihuacán. Tula became their capital, probably in the 10th century, growing into a city of 30,000 to 40,000. The Tula ceremonial center is dedicated to the feathered serpent god Quetzalcóatl, but annals relate that Quetzalcóatl was displaced by Tezcatlipoca (Smoking Mirror), a newcomer god of warriors and sorcery who demanded a regular diet of the hearts of sacrificed warriors. A king identified with Quetzalcóatl, Topiltzin, fled to the Gulf Coast and set sail eastward on a raft of snakes, promising one day to return.

Tula seems to have become the capital of a militaristic kingdom that dominated central Mexico, with warriors organized in orders dedicated to different animal-gods: the coyote, jaguar and eagle knights. Mass human sacrifice may have started at Tula.

Tula's influence was great. It is seen at Paquimé (p346) in Chihuahua, at Gulf Coast sites such as Castillo de Teayo (p657), and in western Mexico. Pottery from as far south as Costa Rica has been found at Tula, and there's even probable Tula influence in temple mounds and artifacts found in the US states of Tennessee and Illinois.

Tula was abandoned about the start of the 13th century, seemingly destroyed by Chichimecs, as the periodic hordes of barbarian raiders from the north came to be known. Many later Mexican peoples revered the Toltec era as a golden age.

UNAM, the national university in Mexico City, has the world's largest mosaic mural. Created by Juan O'Gorman, the 4000 sq meters of mural depict scenes of Mexican history.

Chichén Itzá

Mayan scripts relate that toward the end of the 10th century much of the northern Yucatán Peninsula was conquered by Kukulcán, who bears many similarities to Quetzalcóatl. The Mayan site of Chichén Itzá (p883), in northern Yucatán, contains many Tula-like features, from flat beam-and-masonry roofs (contrasting with the Mayan corbeled roof) to gruesome *chac-mools*, reclining human figures holding dishes for sacrificial human hearts. Tiers of grinning skulls engraved on a massive stone platform suggest sacrifice on a massive scale. There's a resemblance that can hardly be coincidental between Tula's Pirámide B (Pyramid B) and Chichén Itzá's Temple of the Warriors. Many writers therefore believe Toltec exiles invaded the Yucatán and created a new, even grander version of Tula at Chichén Itzá.

AZTECS

Aztec legend relates that they were the chosen people of their tribal god Huizilopochtli. Originally nomads from the north or west of Mexico who were led to the Valle de México (site of present-day Mexico City)

1519–21	1810
Hernán Cortés lands near Veracruz, later captures Aztec god-king Moctezuma II and takes over Tenochtitlán	Miguel Hidalgo y Costilla begins War of Independence

by their priests, the Aztecs settled on islands in the lakes that then filled much of the valley.

The Aztec capital, Tenochtitlán, was founded on one of those islands in the first half of the 14th century. Around 1427 the Aztecs rebelled against Azcapotzalco, then the strongest statelet in the valley, and themselves became the most powerful.

In the mid-15th century the Aztecs formed the Triple Alliance with two other valley states, Texcoco and Tlacopan, to wage war against Tlaxcala and Huejotzingo, east of the valley. The prisoners they took would form the diet of sacrificed warriors that their god Huizilopochtli demanded to keep the sun rising every day. For the dedication of Tenochtitlán's Templo Mayor (Great Temple, see p122) in 1487, the Aztec king Ahuizotl had 20,000 captives sacrificed.

The Triple Alliance brought most of central Mexico – from the Gulf Coast to the Pacific, though not Tlaxcala – under its control. The total population of the empire's 38 provinces may have been about five million. The empire's purpose was to exact tribute of resources absent from the heartland. Jade, turquoise, cotton, paper, tobacco, rubber, cacao and precious feathers were needed for the glorification of the Aztec elite and to support the many nonproductive servants of its war-oriented state.

Ahuizotl's successor was Moctezuma II Xocoyotzin, a reflective character who believed, perhaps fatally, that the Spaniard Hernán Cortés, who arrived on the Gulf Coast in 1519, might be Quetzalcóatl returned from the east to reclaim his throne.

For a wealth of information about the Aztecs, including a Nahuatl dictionary and lessons in the language, see www.mexica.net. Beyond the Aztecs, the site contains miscellaneous information about Mexico's indigenous peoples and history.

Economy & Society

By 1519 Tenochtitlán and the adjoining Aztec city of Tlatelolco (p138) probably had more than 200,000 inhabitants, and the Valle de México, as a whole, over a million. They were supported by a variety of intensive farming methods using only stone and wooden tools, including irrigation, terracing and swamp reclamation.

The basic unit of Aztec society was the *calpulli*, consisting of a few dozen to a few hundred extended families, owning land communally. The king held absolute power but delegated important roles such as priest or tax collector to members of the *pilli* (nobility). Military leaders were usually *tecuhtli*, elite professional soldiers. Another special group was the *pochteca*, militarized merchants, who helped extend the empire, brought goods to the capital and organized large markets which were held daily in big towns. At the bottom of society were pawns (paupers who could sell themselves for a specified period), serfs and slaves.

Culture & Religion

Tenochtitlán-Tlatelolco had hundreds of temple complexes. The greatest, located on and around modern Mexico City's Zócalo, marked the center of the universe. Its main temple pyramid was dedicated to Huizilopochtli and the rain god, Tláloc.

Much of Aztec culture was drawn from earlier Mexican civilizations. They had writing, bark-paper books and the Calendar Round (the dating system used by the Maya, Olmecs and Zapotecs). They observed the heavens for astrological purposes. Celibate priests performed cycles of

1821	1822
Mexico gains independence from Spain	Augustín de Iturbide becomes Emperor of Mexico

great ceremonies, typically including sacrifices and masked dances or processions enacting myths.

The Aztecs believed they lived in the 'fifth world,' whose four predecessors had each been destroyed by the death of the sun and of humanity. Aztec human sacrifices were designed to keep the sun alive. Like the Maya, the Aztecs saw the world as having four directions, 13 heavens and nine hells. Those who died by drowning, leprosy, lightning, gout, dropsy or lung disease went to the paradisiacal gardens of Tláloc, the god who had killed them. Warriors who were sacrificed or died in battle, merchants killed while traveling far away, and women who died giving birth to their first child all went to heaven as companions of the sun. Everyone else traveled for four years under the northern deserts in the abode of the death god Mictlantecuhtli before reaching the ninth hell, where they vanished altogether.

OTHER POSTCLASSIC CIVILIZATIONS

On the eve of the Spanish conquest most Mexican civilizations shared deep similarities. Each was politically centralized and divided into classes, with many people occupied in specialist tasks, including professional priests. Agriculture was productive despite the lack of draft animals, metal tools and the wheel. Maize tortillas and *pozol* (maize gruel) were staple foods. Beans provided important protein, and a great variety of other crops were grown in different regions: squash, tomatoes, chilies, avocados, peanuts, papayas and pineapples. Luxury foods for the elite included turkey, domesticated hairless dog, game and chocolate drinks. War was widespread and often connected with the need to take prisoners for sacrifice to a variety of gods.

The 'Toltec' phase at Chichén Itzá lasted until about 1200. After that, the city of Mayapán (p870) dominated most of the Yucatán Peninsula until the 15th century, when rebellions broke out and the peninsula became a quarreling-ground of numerous city-states, with a culture much decayed from Classic Mayan glories.

After 1200 the remaining Zapotec settlements in Oaxaca, such as Mitla (p728) and Yagul (p728), were increasingly dominated by the Mixtecs, who were famed metalsmiths and potters from the uplands around the Oaxaca-Puebla border. Mixtec and Zapotec cultures became entangled before much of their territory fell to the Aztecs in the 15th and 16th centuries.

The Totonacs, a people who may have occupied El Tajín in its later years, established themselves in much of Veracruz state. To their north, the Huastecs, who inhabited another web of probably independent statelets, flourished from 800 to 1200. In the 15th century the Aztecs subdued most of these areas.

One group who avoided conquest by the Aztecs were the Tarascos, who ruled modern Michoacán from their capital, Tzintzuntzan (p561), about 200km west of Mexico City. They were skilled artisans and jewelers.

SPANISH CONQUEST

Ancient Mexican civilization, nearly 3000 years old, was shattered in the two years from 1519 to 1521 by a tiny group of invaders who destroyed the Aztec empire, brought a new religion to Mexico and reduced the native people to second-class citizens and slaves. So alien to each other were the newcomers and indigenous people that each doubted whether the other was human (the Pope gave the Mexicans the benefit of the doubt in 1537).

'Luxury foods for the elite included turkey, domesticated hairless dog, game and chocolate drinks'

1824	1836
The Constitution of 1824 establishes 19 states and four territories	President Santa Anna attacks the Alamo in February, and suffers defeat at San Jacinto in April

From this traumatic encounter arose modern Mexico. Most Mexicans are *mestizo*, of mixed indigenous and European blood, and thus descendants of both cultures. But while Cuauhtémoc, the last Aztec emperor, is now an official hero, Cortés, the leader of the Spanish conquerors, is seen as a villain and his indigenous allies as traitors.

Early Expeditions

The Spaniards had been in the Caribbean since Columbus arrived in 1492, with their main bases on the islands of Hispaniola and Cuba. Realizing that they had not reached the East Indies, they began looking for a passage through the land mass to their west, but were distracted by tales of gold, silver and a rich empire there.

Early expeditions from Cuba, led by Francisco Hernández de Córdoba in 1517 and Juan de Grijalva in 1518, were driven back from Mexico's Gulf Coast by hostile locals. In 1518 the governor of Cuba, Diego Velázquez, asked Hernán Cortés, a Spanish colonist on the island, to lead a new expedition westward. As Cortés gathered ships and men, Velázquez became uneasy about the costs and Cortés' loyalty. He tried to cancel the expedition, but Cortés ignored him and set sail on February 15, 1519, with 11 ships, 550 men and 16 horses.

The confrontation between the Machiavellian Cortés and the Aztecs, no shabby players of military politics themselves, would be one of the most bizarre in history.

'The subversion of a great empire by a handful of adventurers...has the air of a romance rather than of sober history, and it is not easy to treat such a theme according to the severe rules prescribed by historical criticism' (William H Prescott, in his classic work, *History of the Conquest of Mexico*).

Cortés & the Aztecs

The Spaniards landed first at Cozumel, off the Yucatán, then sailed around the coast to Tabasco, where they defeated local resisters and Cortés delivered the first of many lectures to Mexicans on the importance of Christianity and the greatness of King Carlos I of Spain. The locals gave him 20 maidens, among them Doña Marina (La Malinche), who became his interpreter, aide and lover.

The expedition next put in near the present city of Veracruz. In the Aztec capital of Tenochtitlán, tales of 'towers floating on water' bearing fair-skinned beings reached Moctezuma II, the Aztec god-king. Lightning struck a temple, a comet sailed through the night skies and a bird 'with a mirror in its head' was brought to Moctezuma, who saw warriors in it. According to the Aztec calendar, 1519 would see the legendary god-king Quetzalcóatl return from the east. Unsure if Cortés really was the god returning, Moctezuma sent messengers to attempt to discourage Cortés from traveling to Tenochtitlán.

The Spaniards were well received at the Gulf Coast communities of Zempoala (p663) and Quiahuiztlán (p663), which resented Aztec dominion. Cortés thus gained his first indigenous allies. He set up a coastal settlement called Villa Rica de la Vera Cruz (p663) and then apparently scuttled his ships to stop his men from retreating. Leaving about 150 men at Villa Rica, Cortés set off for Tenochtitlán. On the way he won over the Tlaxcalan people who became valuable allies.

After considerable vacillation, Moctezuma finally invited Cortés to meet him, denying responsibility for an ambush at Cholula that had resulted in the Spanish massacring many of that town's inhabitants.

1846–48	Late 1840s
After the Mexican-American War, a treaty gives California, Texas, Utah, Colorado and most of New Mexico and Arizona to the US	Mexico almost loses the Yucatán to the indigenous Maya in the War of the Castes

The Spaniards and 6000 indigenous allies thus approached the Aztecs' lake-island capital, a city bigger than any in Spain. Entering Tenochtitlán on November 8, 1519, along one of the causeways that linked it to the lakeshore, Cortés was met by Moctezuma who was carried by nobles in a litter with a canopy of feathers and gold. The Spaniards were lodged, as befitted gods, in the palace of Moctezuma's father, Axayácatl.

Though entertained in luxury, the Spaniards were trapped. But Moctezuma continued to behave hesitantly, and the Spaniards took him hostage. Believing Cortés a god, Moctezuma told his people he went willingly but hostility rose in the city, aggravated by the Spaniards' destruction of Aztec idols.

> **DID YOU KNOW?**
> At 17 years of age, Moctezuma's only surviving heir, Tecuichpo, bore Cortés' illegitimate daughter, Doña Leonor Cortés y Moctezuma.

Fall of Tenochtitlán

When the Spaniards had been in Tenochtitlán about six months, Moctezuma informed Cortés that another fleet had arrived on the Veracruz coast. It was led by Pánfilo de Narváez, sent by Diego Velázquez to arrest Cortés. Cortés left 140 Spaniards under Pedro de Alvarado in Tenochtitlán and sped to the coast with the others. They routed Narváez' much bigger force, and most of the defeated men joined Cortés.

Meanwhile, things boiled over in Tenochtitlán. Apparently fearing an attack, the Spaniards struck first and killed about 200 Aztec nobles trapped in a square during a festival. Cortés and his enlarged force returned to the Aztec capital and were allowed to rejoin their comrades – only then to come under fierce attack. Trapped in Axayácatl's palace, Cortés persuaded Moctezuma to try to pacify his people. According to

---

THE EYEWITNESS

Moctezuma led us into a large chamber with an ornately carved wooden ceiling. Inside the shrine were two altars, and upon each sat a massive figure. Both were monstrous with grotesquely fat bodies. The idol on the right was Huichilobos, the god of war. The face was broad and the eyes fiendish. The body was inlaid with jewels, gold, and seed pearls. Huge serpents coiled about its waist, and jewels in the coils reflected the dim light of the chamber. About its neck hung necklaces of blue stone, gold faces, and silver hearts. In one hand the idol held a bow, and in the other an arrow.

The blackened hearts of three Indians sacrificed that day lay smoldering before the altar. The floor was bathed in blood and encrusted layers of blood blackened the walls of the shrine. The stench was overwhelming.

The idol on the opposite side of the shrine was Tezcatepuca, the god of the infernal regions. This idol had the face of a bear, and its mirrored eyes seemed to glow with a light from some inner, evil, source. The waist was girdled with figures that resembled tiny devils with tails like serpents. That day they had offered the idol the hearts of five Indians, and the stench that rose from the floor, still slippery with fresh blood, was more sickening than that of any slaughterhouse in Castile. I cursed them for the dried blood that covered everything in sight, and I could not wait to leave the stink of this slaughterhouse and the abominable sight before us.

Leaving the shrine, we examined a large drum mounted on a platform near the edge of the cue. The drumhead was made of snakeskin, and when they beat this instrument of hell, its hollow throbbing could be heard for a distance of more than two leagues.

Bernal Díaz del Castillo, a Spanish soldier, upon arrival at Tenochtitlán

---

1857	1861
The Constitution of 1857 restricts military and clerical privileges and property rights, abolishes slavery and more	Benito Juárez becomes the first indigenous Mexican president

one version of events, the king went up to the roof to address the crowds but was wounded by missiles and died soon afterward; other versions of the story have it that the Spaniards killed him.

The Spaniards fled on the night of June 30, 1520, but several hundred of them, and thousands of their indigenous allies, were killed on this Noche Triste (Sad Night). The survivors retreated to Tlaxcala, where they prepared for another campaign by building boats in sections, which could be carried across the mountains for a waterborne assault on Tenochtitlán. When the 900 Spaniards reentered the Valle de México they were accompanied by some 100,000 native allies. For the first time, the odds were in their favor.

Moctezuma had been succeeded by his nephew, Cuitláhuac, who then died of smallpox which was brought to Mexico by one of Narváez's soldiers. He was succeeded by another nephew, the 18-year-old Cuauhtémoc. The Spanish attack started in May 1521. Cortés had to resort to razing Tenochtitlán building by building. By August 13, 1521, the resistance had ended. The captured Cuauhtémoc asked Cortés to kill him, but was kept alive until 1525 as a hostage, undergoing occasional foot-burning as the Spanish tried to make him reveal the whereabouts of Aztec treasure.

You can still see the ruins of Tenochtitlán's main temple and a large-scale model of Tenochtitlán can be seen at the Museo Nacional de Antropología (p129).

COLONIAL ERA

The Spaniards renamed Tenochtitlán 'México' and rebuilt it as the capital of Nueva España (New Spain) as they named their new colony. Cortés granted his soldiers *encomiendas*, which were rights to the labor or tribute of groups of indigenous people.

By 1524 virtually all the Aztec empire, plus other Mexican regions such as Colima, the Huasteca area and the Isthmus of Tehuantepec, had been brought under at least loose control of the colony. In 1527 Spain set up Nueva España's first *audiencia*, a high court with government functions.

Central America had been conquered in the 1520s by Spanish forces from Mexico and Panama, and in the 1540s the subjection of the Yucatán Peninsula was accomplished. In the north, Nueva España's territory ended roughly at a line between modern Tampico and Guadalajara, beyond which dwelt fierce seminomads. In 1540 Spain sent Francisco Vásquez de Coronado north in search of gold and treasures rumored to be hidden in the fabled Seven Cities of Cibola. He never found Cibola, but he did 'find' a territory as large as France and Germany and claimed it for Spain.

Big finds of silver in Zacatecas in the mid-1540s, followed by further finds at Guanajuato, San Luis Potosí and Pachuca, spurred Spanish attempts to subdue the north. They did not succeed until the 1590s. The northern borders were slowly extended by missionaries and a few settlers, and by the early 19th century Nueva España included most of the modern US states of Texas, New Mexico, Arizona, California, Utah and Colorado, though control there was tenuous.

The populations of the conquered peoples declined disastrously, mainly from epidemics of new diseases brought by the Spaniards. The population of Nueva España fell from an estimated 25 million at the conquest to little over a million by 1605.

Learn about the rise of Moctezuma's empire and the conquest through firsthand Spanish and Aztec accounts in *Aztec: The Death of a Nation* by Kenneth Pearce.

1862	1863
Mexican army defeats the French at Pueblo	French defeat Mexican army at Puebla and take over Mexico City

The indigenous peoples' only real allies were some of the monks who started arriving in Nueva España in 1523 to convert them. Many of these missionaries were compassionate, brave men who distinguished themselves by protecting local people from the colonists' worst excesses. The monks' missionary work helped extend Spanish control over Mexico. By 1560 they had carried out millions of conversions and built more than 100 monasteries (some fortified), including one in Acolman (p183). Indigenous slavery was abolished in the 1550s and partly replaced by black slavery.

A person's place in Mexican colonial society was determined by skin color, parentage and birthplace. Spanish-born colonists *(peninsulares)* were a minuscule part of the population but were at the top of the tree and considered nobility in Nueva España, however humble their origins in Spain.

Next on the ladder were criollos, people born of Spanish parents in Nueva España. By the 18th century some criollos had acquired fortunes in mining, commerce, ranching or agriculture. Haciendas (large estates) had begun to spring up as early as the 16th century. Not surprisingly, criollos sought political power commensurate with their wealth.

Below the criollos were the mestizos (people of mixed ancestry), and at the bottom of the pile were the indigenous people and African slaves. Though the poor were paid for their labor by the 18th century, they were paid very little. Many were *peones*, bonded laborers tied by debt to their employers. Indigenous people still had to pay tribute to the crown.

Criollo discontent began to simmer in the late 18th century, and the catalyst for rebellion came in 1808 when France's Napoleon Bonaparte occupied most of Spain and put his brother Joseph on the Spanish throne. Direct Spanish control over Nueva España evaporated. Rivalry between *peninsulares* and criollos in the colony intensified.

INDEPENDENCE

In 1810 a criollo coterie based in Querétaro began planning a rebellion. News of the plans leaked to the colonial authorities, so the group acted immediately. On September 16 one of its members, Miguel Hidalgo y Costilla, priest of the town of Dolores (p618), summoned his parishioners and issued his now-famous call to rebellion, the Grito de Dolores (basically 'Death to the Spaniards!').

A mob formed and marched on San Miguel, Celaya and Guanajuato, massacring *peninsulares* in Guanajuato. Over the next month and a half the rebels captured Zacatecas, San Luis Potosí and Morelia. On October 30 their army, numbering about 80,000, defeated loyalist forces at Las Cruces outside Mexico City, but Hidalgo hesitated to attack the capital. The rebels occupied Guadalajara but then were pushed northward by their opponents. Their numbers shrank and in 1811 their leaders, including Hidalgo, were captured and executed. As a warning to other rebels, his head was displayed for 10 years at Alhóndiga in Guanajuato; see p607.

José María Morelos y Pavón, a former student of Hidalgo and also a parish priest, assumed the rebel leadership, blockading Mexico City for several months. He convened a congress at Chilpancingo which adopted guiding principles for the independence movement including universal male suffrage, popular sovereignty and abolition of slavery. Morelos was captured and executed in 1815, and his forces split into several guerrilla

'On September 16, 1810, Miguel Hidalgo y Costilla issued his now-famous call to rebellion, the Grito de Dolores'

1864	1867
Emperor Maximilian and Carlota enter Mexico	Napoleon III withdraws French forces from Mexico, and Maximilian is executed

bands, the most successful of which was led by Vicente Guerrero in the state of Oaxaca.

In 1821 the royalist general Agustín de Iturbide defected during an offensive against Guerrero and conspired with the rebels to declare independence from Spain. Iturbide and Guerrero worked out the Plan de Iguala, which established three guarantees – religious dominance by the Catholic Church, a constitutional monarchy and equal rights for criollos and *peninsulares*. The plan won over all influential sections of society, and the incoming Spanish viceroy in 1821 agreed to Mexican independence. Iturbide, who had command of the army, soon arranged his own nomination to the throne, which he ascended as Emperor Agustín I in 1822.

MEXICAN REPUBLIC

Iturbide was deposed in 1823 by a rebel army led by another opportunistic soldier, Antonio López de Santa Anna. A new constitution in 1824 established a federal Mexican republic of 19 states and four territories. Guadalupe Victoria, a former independence fighter, became its first president. Mexico's southern boundary was the same as it is today (Central America had set up a separate federation in 1823). In the north, Mexico included much of what is now the southwestern USA.

Vicente Guerrero stood as a liberal candidate in the 1828 presidential elections and was defeated, but was eventually awarded the presidency after another Santa Anna–led revolt. Guerrero abolished slavery but was deposed and executed by his conservative vice president, Anastasio Bustamante. The struggle between liberals, who favored social reform, and conservatives, who opposed it, would be a constant theme in 19th-century Mexican politics.

Texas & War

Intervention in politics by ambitious military men was also becoming a habit. Santa Anna, a national hero after defeating a small Spanish invasion force at Tampico in 1829, overthrew Bustamante and was elected president in 1833. Thus began 22 years of chronic instability in which the presidency changed hands 36 times (11 of those terms went to Santa Anna). Economic decline and corruption became entrenched, and Santa Anna quickly turned into a conservative.

Santa Anna is remembered for helping to lose large chunks of Mexican territory to the USA. North American settlers in Texas, initially welcomed by the Mexican authorities, grew restless and declared Texas independent in 1836. Santa Anna led an army north and wiped out the defenders of an old mission called the Alamo in San Antonio, but he was routed on the San Jacinto River a few weeks later.

In 1845 the US Congress voted to annex Texas, and US president James Polk demanded further Mexican territory. In 1846 that led to the Mexican-American War, in which US troops captured Mexico City. At the end of the war, by the Treaty of Guadalupe Hidalgo (1848), Mexico ceded Texas, California, Utah, Colorado, and most of New Mexico and Arizona to the USA. The Santa Anna government sold the remainder of New Mexico and Arizona to the USA in 1853 for US$10 million in the

'At the end of the war, Mexico ceded Texas, California, Utah, Colorado, and most of New Mexico and Arizona to the USA'

1877–1911	1910
Porfirio Díaz serves as president, brushing aside 'no reelection' laws	Francisco Madero runs for presidency, is jailed by Díaz, and after his release calls for revolution

Gadsden Purchase. This loss precipitated the liberal-led Revolution of Ayutla which ousted Santa Anna for good in 1855.

Mexico almost lost the Yucatán Peninsula, too, in the so-called War of the Castes in the late 1840s, when the Maya people rose up against their criollo overlords and narrowly failed to drive them off the peninsula.

Benito Juárez, the French & Porfirio Díaz

The new liberal government ushered in the era known as the Reform, in which it set about dismantling the conservative state that had developed in Mexico. The key figure was Benito Juárez (see p706), a Zapotec from Oaxaca and a leading lawyer and politician. Laws requiring the church to sell much of its property helped precipitate the internal War of the Reform (1858–61) between the liberals, with their 'capital' at Veracruz, and conservatives, based in Mexico City. The liberals eventually won and Juárez became president in 1861. But Mexico was in disarray and heavily in debt to Britain, France and Spain. These three countries sent a joint force to collect their debts, but France's Napoleon III decided to go further and take over Mexico, leading to yet another war.

The French were defeated at Puebla in 1862, but then took Puebla and Mexico City a year later. Napoleon sent Maximilian of Hapsburg over to rule as emperor in 1864, but he didn't last long. In 1867 he was executed by Juárez loyalists.

Juárez immediately set an agenda of economic and educational reform. For the first time, schooling was made mandatory. A railway was built between Mexico City and Veracruz. A rural police force, the *rurales*, was organized to secure the transport of cargo through Mexico.

Juárez died in 1872. His office is still maintained at the Spanish Palacio Nacional (p121). Sebastián Lerdo de Tejada took over and ruled until 1876. The following president, Porfirio Díaz, ruled for the next 33 years, a period known as the Porfiriato. Díaz brought Mexico into the industrial age, launching public works projects throughout the country, particularly in Mexico City. Telephone and telegraph lines were strung and the railway network spread.

Díaz kept Mexico free of the civil wars that had plagued it for over 60 years, but at a cost. Political opposition, free elections and a free press were banned. Many of Mexico's resources went into foreign ownership, peasants were cheated out of their land by new laws, workers suffered

> For an outstanding history of postcolonial Mexico and profiles of prominent personalities such as Emiliano Zapata, Pancho Villa and Porfirio Díaz, see *Mexico: Biography of Power*, by Enrique Krauze.

JUANA CATA

It was in Tehuantepec that Porfirio Díaz met Juana Catalina Romero, known familiarly as Juana Cata, who would be his lifelong friend and mistress. During the day she rolled cigarettes, and in the evening played billiards with Díaz and other leading citizens. He built a chalet for Juana, and changed the route of the transisthmian railroad to pass within six feet of the chalet's entry. Now each morning he could step into the train from her front door.

Juana could neither read nor write until she was 30, but in her time she became a leading political figure in Tehuantepec. She owned factories and sugar mills, founded a Marist college, and traveled through Europe and the Holy Land. When she grew old, she often dined with Díaz and his wife Catalina. It is rumored that when he was dying, Díaz often cried out for Juana Cata.

1910–20	1917
Almost two million people die and the economy is shattered in the Mexican Revolution	The Constitution of 1917 guarantees civil rights, introduces election reforms and protects Mexico from foreign exploitation

The best movie of the Mexican Revolution is the 1952 film *Viva Zapata!* starring Marlon Brando. John Steinbeck's script is historically sound for the first phase of the revolution, up to the meeting between Pancho Villa and Emiliano Zapata in Mexico City. Beyond that point it flounders until Zapata is assassinated.

appalling conditions, and the country was kept quiet by a ruthless army and the now-feared *rurales*. Land and wealth became concentrated in the hands of a small minority. In late 1910 all this led to the Mexican Revolution.

MEXICAN REVOLUTION

The revolution was a 10-year period of shifting allegiances between a spectrum of leaders in which successive attempts to create stable governments were wrecked by new outbreaks of devastating fighting.

Francisco Madero, a wealthy liberal from Coahuila, campaigned for the presidency in 1910 and would probably have won if Díaz hadn't jailed him. On his release on November 20, Madero called for the nation to rise in revolution. The revolution spread quickly across the country. When revolutionaries under the leadership of Francisco 'Pancho' Villa (see p352) took Ciudad Juárez in May 1911, Díaz resigned. Madero was elected president in November 1911.

But Madero was unable to contain the factions fighting for power throughout the country. The basic divide was between liberal reformers like Madero and more radical leaders such as Emiliano Zapata (see p224) from the state of Morelos, who was fighting for the transfer of hacienda land to the peasants with the cry *'¡Tierra y Libertad!'* (Land and Freedom!). Madero sent federal troops to disband Zapata's forces, and the Zapatista movement was born.

Conservatives brought down Madero's government in 1913 and Madero was executed. President Victoriano Huerta only fomented greater strife. In March 1913 three revolutionary leaders in the north united against him under the Plan de Guadalupe: Venustiano Carranza, a Madero supporter, in Coahuila; Pancho Villa in Chihuahua; and Álvaro Obregón in Sonora. Zapata was also fighting against Huerta. Terror reigned in the countryside as Huerta's troops fought, pillaged and plundered. Finally he was defeated and forced to resign in July 1914.

In 1913 Ambrose Bierce's daughter received a letter from her father in Chihuahua. That was the last anyone heard from him. The movie *Old Gringo* is based upon a novel by Carlos Fuentes, in which Bierce becomes an unwanted but willing participant in the Mexican Revolution. While the story itself is fictional, it captures both the spirit of the revolution and its unbending discipline for rank and file.

Carranza called the victorious factions to a conference in Aguascalientes but failed to unify them, and war broke out again. Carranza eventually emerged the victor and formed a government that was recognized by the USA. A new reformist constitution, still largely in force today, was enacted in 1917.

In Morelos the Zapatistas continued to demand reforms. Carranza had Zapata assassinated in 1919, but the following year Obregón turned against Carranza, chased him out of office and had him assassinated. Pancho Villa was killed in 1923. His hacienda (complete with a bullet-ridden Dodge) is now the Museum of the Mexican Revolution (p351) and is open to visitors.

The 10 years of violent civil war cost an estimated 1.5 to two million lives (roughly one in eight Mexicans) and shattered the economy.

FROM REVOLUTION TO WWII

As president from 1920 to 1924, Obregón turned to national reconstruction. More than a thousand rural schools were built and some land was redistributed from big landowners to the peasants. Top artists, such as Diego Rivera, were commissioned to decorate important public buildings with large, vivid murals on social and historical themes.

1920–24	1929
President Alvaro Obregón presides over a reconstruction period, with rural schools built and land redistributed to peasants	The Partido Nacional Revolucionario (PNR) is founded

Plutarco Elías Calles, president from 1924 to 1928, built more schools and distributed more land. He also closed monasteries, convents and church schools, and prohibited religious processions. These measures precipitated the bloody Cristero Rebellion by Catholics, which lasted until 1929.

At the end of Calles' term in 1928, Obregón was elected president again but was assassinated by a Cristero. Calles reorganized his supporters to found the Partido Nacional Revolucionario (PNR, National Revolutionary Party), a precursor of today's Partido Revolucionario Institucional (PRI) and initiator of a long tradition of official acronyms.

Lázaro Cárdenas won the presidency in 1934 with the PNR's support and stepped up the reform program. Cárdenas redistributed almost 200,000 sq km of land – nearly double the amount distributed before him – mostly through the establishment of *ejidos* (peasant landholding cooperatives). Thus, most of Mexico's arable land was redistributed, and nearly one-third of the population received land. Cárdenas also set up the million-member labor union Confederación de Trabajadores Mexicanos (CTM, Confederation of Mexican Workers) and boldly expropriated foreign oil-company operations in Mexico in 1938, forming Petróleos Mexicanos (Pemex, the Mexican Petroleum Company). After the oil expropriation, foreign investors avoided Mexico, slowing the economy.

Cárdenas reorganized the PNR into the Partido de la Revolución Mexicana (PRM, Party of the Mexican Revolution), a coalition of representatives from agriculture, the military, the labor force and the people at large.

After Cárdenas, the presidency of Manuel Ávila Camacho (1940–46) marked a transition toward more conservative government at the end of the first two postrevolutionary decades. Camacho sent Mexican troops to help the WWII Allies in the Pacific and supplied raw materials and labor to the USA. The war's curtailment of manufactured imports boosted Mexican industry and exports.

MODERN MEXICO

As the Mexican economy expanded, new economic and political groups demanded influence in the ruling PRM. To recognize their inclusion, the party was renamed the Partido Revolucionario Institucional ('El Pree'). President Miguel Alemán (1946–52) continued development by extending the road system and building hydroelectric stations, irrigation projects and UNAM, the National Autonomous University of Mexico (p134). Pemex grew dramatically and, with the rise of other industries, spawned some of Mexico's worst corruption.

Alemán's successor, Adolfo Ruiz Cortines (1952–58), began to confront a new problem: explosive population growth. In two decades Mexico's population had doubled, and many people began migrating to urban areas to search for work. Adolfo López Mateos (1958–64), one of Mexico's most popular post-WWII presidents, redistributed 120,000 sq km of land to small farmers, nationalized foreign utility concessions, implemented social welfare and rural education programs, and launched health campaigns. These programs were helped by strong economic growth, particularly in tourism and exports.

DID YOU KNOW?

A contingent of 250,000 Mexican and Mexican-American men fought in WWII. One thousand were killed in action, 1500 received purple hearts and 17 received the Congressional Medal of Honor.

1946	1968
The Partido de la Revolución Mexicana, formerly the PNR, is renamed Partido Revolucionario Institucional (PRI)	Government troops kill hundreds of protesters during the Tlatelolco massacre one week before the Olympic Games in Mexico City

Unrest, Boom & Bust

President Gustavo Díaz Ordaz (1964–70) was a conservative with an agenda that emphasized business. Though he fostered education and tourism, and the economy grew by 6% a year during his term, he is better remembered for his repression of civil liberties. He sacked the president of the PRI, Carlos Madrazo, who had tried to democratize the party. University students in Mexico City were the first to express their outrage with the Díaz Ordaz administration. Discontent came to a head in the months preceding the 1968 Olympic Games in Mexico City, the first ever held in a developing nation. Single-party rule and restricted freedom of speech were among the objects of protest. More than half a million people rallied in Mexico City's Zócalo on August 27. On October 2, with the Olympics only a few days away, a rally was organized in Tlatelolco, Mexico City. The government sent in heavily armed troops and police. Several hundred people died in the ensuing massacre.

José López Portillo (1976–82) presided during the jump in world oil prices caused by the OPEC (Organization of the Petroleum Exporting Countries) embargo of the early 1970s. He announced that Mexico's main problem now was how to manage its enormous prosperity: on the strength of the country's vast oil reserves, international institutions began lending Mexico billions of dollars. Then, just as suddenly, a world oil glut sent prices plunging. Mexico's worst recession for decades began.

Miguel de la Madrid (1982–88) was largely unsuccessful in coping with the problems he inherited. The population continued to grow at Malthusian rates; the economy made only weak progress, crushed by the huge debt from the oil boom years; and the social pot continued to simmer. Things were not helped by the 1985 Mexico City earthquake, which killed at least 10,000 people, destroyed hundreds of buildings and caused more than US$4 billion in damage.

In a climate of economic helplessness and rampant corruption, dissent grew, even inside the PRI. There were sometimes violent protests over the PRI's now routine electoral fraud and strong-arm tactics.

Salinas & Zedillo

Harvard-educated Carlos Salinas de Gortari (1988–94) transformed Mexico's state-dominated economy into one of private enterprise and free trade. The apex of this program was North American Free Trade Agreement (Nafta), which came into effect on January 1, 1994. Salinas' term did not end in a blaze of glory, however – far from it. Firstly, January 1, 1994 also saw the start of the Zapatista uprising in Mexico's southernmost state, Chiapas (see p793). Then in March 1994 Luis Donaldo Colosio, Salinas' chosen successor as PRI presidential candidate, was assassinated in Tijuana. Conspiracy theories abound (by the time of the murder relations between Salinas and Colosio had deteriorated markedly).

During Salinas' term, drug trafficking grew into a huge business in Mexico and many Mexicans believe his stance on the issue was too soft. Vilified also for the economic crisis into which Mexico plunged after he left office, Salinas ended up as the ex-president that Mexicans most love to hate.

Ernesto Zedillo (1994–2000) of the PRI was a quiet, uncharismatic economist president, but he brought the Mexican economy back from

In addition to general information, www.mexonline.com has some good history links.

1985	1994
Magnitude 8.0 earthquake strikes Mexico City, killing more than 10,000 people	The North American Free Trade Agreement (Nafta) comes into effect

a nasty slump engendered by his predecessor. He also made real history by reforming the country's politics so that power was peacefully transferred to a non-PRI successor – the first ever peaceful change of regime in Mexican history. While Zedillo was perceived as more honest than his predecessors, he was unable to make many inroads into the burgeoning power of Mexico's drug mobs.

Within days of President Zedillo taking office in late 1994, Mexico's currency, the peso, suddenly collapsed, bringing on a rapid and deep economic recession that hit everyone, especially the poor, hard. It led to, among other things, a big increase in crime, intensified discontent with the PRI, and triggered large-scale Mexican emigration to the USA. It was estimated that by 1997 more than 2.5 million Mexicans a year were entering the USA illegally. Zedillo's policies pulled Mexico gradually out of recession and by the end of his term in 2000, Mexicans' purchasing power was again approaching what it had been in 1994.

By 2000, thanks to Zedillo's efforts to set up a new, independent electoral system, 11 of Mexico's 31 states had elected non-PRI governors and half the population (including Mexico City) had non-PRI mayors. The PRI remained at its most repressive and antediluvian in southern states such as Guerrero and Chiapas, both scenes of armed left-wing insurgencies. When Guerrero's famed Pacific resort, Acapulco, elected a mayor from the left-wing Partido de la Revolución Democrática (PRD, Party of the Democratic Revolution) in 1999, several prominent PRD figures and members of their families suddenly found themselves arrested, kidnapped, tortured and in one case killed.

The Drug Trade

Mexico has long been a marijuana and heroin producer, but a huge impetus to its drug gangs was given by a mid-1980s US crackdown on drug shipments from Colombia through the Caribbean to Florida. As a result, drugs being transported from South America to the USA went through Mexico instead. Three main Mexican cartels emerged: the Pacific or Tijuana cartel, the (Ciudad) Juárez cartel and the Matamoros-based Gulf cartel. These cartels bought up politicians, top antidrug officials and whole police forces. Many Mexicans believe organized crime in the early 1990s was actually controlled by the PRI, with President Carlos Salinas and his brother Raúl deeply involved.

By 1997 most illegal drugs entering the USA were going through Mexico. President Zedillo brought the armed forces into the fight against the drug mobs, but in 1997 his trusted top drug fighter was arrested on charges of being in the pay of the Juárez mob. Tijuana was the scene of literally hundreds of drug-related murders, including those of judges, witnesses, honest police and journalists, in the late 1990s. President Vicente Fox (2000–) has won praise for the arrest of several major drug-cartel leaders, but in 2004, he was still facing an uphill battle. The mobs are just too powerful with too many highly placed friends to be easily defeated.

'By 1997 most illegal drugs entering the USA were going through Mexico'

The Fox Presidency

Rancher, former chief of Coca-Cola's Mexican operation and former state governor of Guanajuato, Vicente Fox stands at almost 2m (6ft 4in) tall

1998	2000
Population reaches 97 million	Vincente Fox is elected president, with PRI losing 70-year grip on presidency

THE LESS THE MERRIER?

Overpopulation still looms as perhaps Mexico's greatest problem. The population in 1944 was 22 million, and by 1998 it had reached 97 million. The situation seemed hopeless in 1968 when the Vatican banned all methods of contraception. In 1970, more than 600,000 Mexican women underwent illegal operations, and 32,000 died.

Government-sponsored clinics were established to offer birth control literature, and by 1992 more than 6000 family planning centers were established. The goal of government and privately funded programs is to reach a balance between births and deaths by 2005.

Mexifam is the largest nongovernment family planning service, concentrating on the poorest areas of the country. By April 2000 it became evident that Mexifam and the government programs were working. Population growth had been reduced from 3.4% in 1970 to 1.7% in 2000 – from seven children per woman to 2.28. (Mexifam does not advocate abortion but does provide information on 'morning after' pills to prevent pregnancy.)

and has a penchant for wearing jeans and cowboy boots. He is Mexico's first non-PRI president since the PRI (or, strictly speaking, its predecessor the PNR) was invented in 1929. Although Fox represents the right-of-center (PAN, National Action Party) he is more of a centrist social democrat himself. He entered office with the goodwill of a wide range of Mexicans who hoped a change of ruling party would bring real change in the country. Fox picked a broad-based ministerial team ranging from ex-PRI officials to left-wing academics, and did not, as incoming Mexican administrations traditionally do, replace the entire governing apparatus with his own friends and hangers-on. He made an early, though unsuccessful, attempt to resolve the Zapatista conflict in Chiapas (see p793). Another early Fox initiative was to try to resolve some of the problems of the Mexico/US border and Mexican emigration to the USA (see p53).

Despite the high hopes that accompanied him into office, Fox's presidency is likely to go down as a disappointment for most Mexicans. Though personally popular, he has come to be seen as a man who can't get much done. He was bequeathed a booming economy by President Zedillo, only to have things seriously complicated by the recession of 2001. By 2004 Fox had still not succeeded in passing key tax legislation to pay for better education and social welfare programs. He was not helped by tensions with the orthodox establishment of his own party nor by the PAN's lack of overall majority in Congress, which made it harder for him to push through reforms. The economy idled and Fox's pledge to lead an environmental government is yet to be fulfilled.

Fox did achieve some success against the drug barons, and in 2002 he appointed a special prosecutor to investigate human rights abuses, leading to the high-profile arrest in February 2004 of former federal security chief Miguel Nazar Haro (in connection to the kidnapping of a leftist activist in 1975). In 2003 relations between the US and Mexico grew cold when Fox refused to give Mexico's support for the resolution to invade Iraq. At the time of writing, relations had begun to thaw.

2003	2004
Relations with the US are jeopardized when Mexico refuses to support the US-led war in Iraq	Relations with US begin to thaw

The Culture

THE NATIONAL PSYCHE

Mexicans will not easily be pinned down. They love fun, music and a fiesta, yet in many ways are deeply serious. They work hard but relax to the max in their time off. They're hospitable and warm to guests, yet are most truly themselves only within their family group. They will laugh at death, but have a profound vein of spirituality. You may read about anti-gringo sentiment in the media, but Mexicans will treat you, as a visitor to their country, as an individual and with refreshing warmth and courtesy. Ask for help or information and people will go out of their way to give it. (The word 'gringo', incidentally, isn't exactly a compliment, but nor is it necessarily an insult: the term can simply be, and often is, a neutral synonym for 'American' or 'citizen of the USA.')

Mexico is, of course, the home of machismo, that exaggeration of masculinity whose manifestations may range from a certain way of trimming a moustache to aggressive driving, heavy drinking or the carrying of weapons. The other side of the machismo coin is the exaggeratedly feminine female. But gender equalization has come a long way in a few decades: you'll find most Mexican women and men, especially among the increasingly educated and worldly younger generations, ready to relate simply as one person to another – even if the cliché Mexican family dynamic (son adores mother and must protect virtue of sisters and daughters but other women are fair game) does still contain a dose of truth.

Mexico's 'patron saint' – not actually a saint but a manifestation of the Virgin Mary – is the dark-skinned Virgin of Guadalupe, who made her appearance before an indigenous Mexican in 1531 on a hill near Mexico City. Universally revered, she's both the archetypal mother and the preeminent focus of Mexicans' inborn spirituality, which has its roots both in Spanish Catholicism and in the complex belief systems of Mexico's pre-Hispanic civilizations. Elements of these ancient nature-based beliefs survive alongside Catholicism among the country's many indigenous people. Many Mexicans, when sick, prefer to visit a traditional *curandero* – a kind of cross between a naturopath and a witch-doctor – rather than resort to a modern *médico*. Nor have Mexicans left behind that awareness of death and afterlife that was so central to the pre-Hispanic cultures. The famous Día de Muertos festival (Day of the Dead, November 2), when the departed are believed to revisit the living, is perhaps a way of building a bridge between this life and whatever follows it.

On a more mundane level, you'll find most Mexicans are chiefly concerned with earning a crust for themselves and their strongly knit families – and also with enjoying the leisure side of life to the full, whether it be raging at clubs, parties, bars or fiestas or relaxing over a long, extended-family Sunday lunch at a beachside restaurant. Nobel Prize–winning Mexican writer Octavio Paz argued in *The Labyrinth of Solitude* that Mexicans' love of noise, music and crowds is no more than a temporary escape from a deeper personal isolation and gloom – but make your own judgment!

On a political level, the country is, slowly, democratizing, but most Mexicans still despair of it ever being governed well. Mexicans mock themselves for their country's failings. At the same time they are proud – proud of their families, their villages and towns, proud of Mexico. They don't like perceived slurs or any hint of foreign interference. So close to the USA, where millions of Mexicans have spent years of their lives, they take on

A Nahua *curandera's* secrets of physical and spiritual health are revealed in *Woman who Glows in the Dark* by Elena Ávila with Joy Parker (1999).

board a certain amount of US technology, fashion and products, but they also strongly value the positives they see in Mexican life – a more human pace, a stronger sense of community and family, their own very distinctive cuisine, their unique heritage and their thriving national culture.

LIFESTYLE

Around three-quarters of Mexicans now live in cities and towns, and this percentage continues to increase as rural folk are sucked in by the hope of raising their standard of living. Most urban dwellers inhabit crowded, multi-generational, family homes on tightly packed streets in crowded neighborhoods with few parks or open spaces. Fly into Mexico City and you'll get a bird's eye view of just how little space is not occupied by housing or roads. Around the edges of the city, new streets climb the steep slopes of extinct volcanoes, while the city's poorest new arrivals inhabit shacks on the fringes made of whatever they can lay hands on – a few concrete blocks, wooden boards, sheets of corrugated tin. Many of these people barely scrape a living in the 'informal economy,' as street hawkers, buskers or home workers, rarely earning much more than US$5 a day.

More affluent neighborhoods in inner cities often have blocks of relatively spacious, well-provided apartments. In the wealthiest quarters, imposing detached houses with well-tended gardens and satellite dishes sit behind high walls with strong security gates. Domestic staff can be seen walking dogs or babies while tradespeople and delivery drivers talk through intercoms to gain admittance to the fortresses of the privileged. Many of these homes' owners will have other properties too – a ranch in the country or a coastal holiday home.

Out in the villages, people often inhabit a more spacious environment, working on the land and with homes comprising a yard surrounded by a few separate small buildings for members of an extended family – buildings of adobe, wood or concrete, often with earth floors, and with roofs sometimes of tile but more likely of cheaper tin. Inside these homes are few possessions – beds, a cooking area, a table with a few chairs and a few aging photos of departed relatives. These villages may or may not be reached by paved roads, but will nearly always be accessed by decrepit buses, pickups or some other public transport, because few of their inhabitants own cars.

The contrasts between poor and rich couldn't be greater: while kids from rich families go out nightclubbing in flashy cars and attend private universities (or go to school in the USA), poor villagers may dance only at village fiestas and be lucky to complete primary education.

Family and hometown ties remain strong among all Mexicans despite influences that might be expected to drive generations apart, such as youth culture, computers, study and work away from home, and emigration to the USA. Even if they are not actually living together, large family groups take holidays or Sunday lunches together, while Mexicans in the USA send money back to their families or to fund projects, like schools and clinics, in their hometowns. Gender roles are relaxing among the middle class: education and jobs are more accessible for young women, and women now hold 23% of seats in Mexico's Congress and 41% of the country's professional and technical jobs. A Mexican woman today will have 2.8 children on average; in the early 1970s the average was 6.5. Among the poor, women still tend to play out traditional domestic and mothering roles, though they may also have part-time jobs or sell produce at market.

Mexico is more broad-minded about sexuality than you might expect. Gays and lesbians tend to keep a low profile but rarely attract open dis-

Journalist Sam Quinones gets right under Mexico's skin in a superb collection of essays and reports, *True Tales from Another Mexico* (2001).

crimination or violence. Relatively open gay scenes exist in a few of the bigger cities and major coastal resorts.

Tradition remains powerful. The calendar is filled with saints' days and festivals such as Semana Santa (Holy Week), Día de Muertos (Day of the Dead, November 2), the Día de la Virgen de Guadalupe (December 12) and Christmas. These events bring people together for the same processions and rituals year after year. A belief in some form of the supernatural – often a strange mixture of Christian faith and remnants of pre-Hispanic cults – is abiding, even among the most urbane. So is the faith that so many Mexicans have in their traditional forms of medicine – a mixture of charms, chants, herbs, candles and incense.

POPULATION

In 2000 Mexico's population was estimated at 97.5 million. By 2003 it had increased to around 101.5 million (compared with 20 million in 1940 and 81 million in 1990).

About 75% of Mexicans live in towns or cities, and one-third are aged under 15. The biggest cities are Mexico City (with around 18 million people), Guadalajara (with a conurbation estimated at four to five million) and Monterrey (conurbation estimated at 3.5 million). Tijuana, Puebla, Ciudad Juárez, and the León and Torreón conurbations all have populations above one million. The most populous state is the state of México, which includes the rapidly growing outer areas of Mexico City and has more than 14 million people.

The population is growing at 1.5% a year, which is down from rates of more than 3% between 1950 and 1980 but still means an extra 1.5 million mouths to feed every year. Of equal concern is the growth of the cities, which attract thousands of newcomers from the poorer countryside every day.

MANNERS FOR MEXICO

In most places travelers visit in Mexico, the locals are accustomed to foreign visitors and tolerant of their strange ways. But it's still recommended that women dress conservatively in small towns and in places that are off-the-beaten-track (avoid shorts, skimpy tops etc). Everyone should lean toward the respectful end of the dress spectrum when visiting churches. It's also appreciated if you start off any conversation with a few words of Spanish. If it turns out that the person you're talking with speaks better English than your Spanish, then you can slip into English.

Mexicans like to hear that you're enjoying their country. As a rule they are slow to criticize or argue, avoiding direct confrontation in discussion and expressing disagreement more by nuance than blunt assertion. An invitation to a Mexican home is an honor for an outsider; as a guest you will be treated hospitably and will enter a part of the real Mexico to which few outsiders are admitted. If you have time to prepare for the visit, take a small gift.

Away from tourist destinations, your presence may evoke any reaction from curiosity to shyness or, very occasionally, brusqueness. But any negative response will usually evaporate as soon as you show that you're harmless and friendly. Just a few words of Spanish will often bring smiles and warmth, probably followed by questions. Then someone who speaks a few words of English will dare to try them out.

Some indigenous people adopt a cool attitude toward visitors: they have come to mistrust outsiders after five centuries of rough treatment. They don't like being gawked at by tourists and can be very sensitive about cameras. If in any doubt at all about whether it's OK to take a photo, always ask first.

Ways you can help poor communities are to patronize community organizations – ecotourism initiatives, crafts cooperatives and the like – and to buy crafts and commodities direct from villages or from the artisans themselves, rather than through urban entrepreneurs.

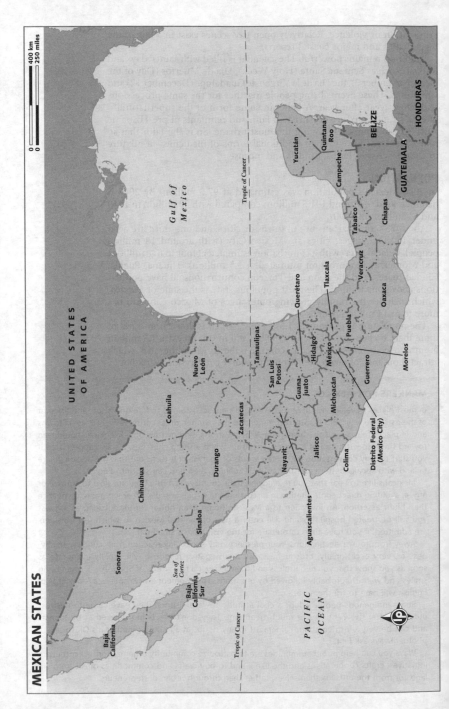

MEXICAN STATES

UNITED STATES OF AMERICA

Baja California

Baja California Sur

Sonora

Chihuahua

Sinaloa

Durango

Coahuila

Nuevo León

Tamaulipas

Zacatecas

Nayarit

Aguascalientes

Jalisco

Colima

San Luis Potosí

Guanajuato

Querétaro

Michoacán

Hidalgo

México

Distrito Federal (Mexico City)

Tlaxcala

Morelos

Guerrero

Puebla

Veracruz

Oaxaca

Tabasco

Chiapas

Campeche

Yucatán

Quintana Roo

BELIZE

GUATEMALA

HONDURAS

Gulf of Mexico

PACIFIC OCEAN

Sea of Cortez

Tropic of Cancer

400 km

250 miles

Mexico's Many Peoples

Mexicans are not a uniform people – far from it! In ethnic terms the major distinction is between mestizos and *indígenas*. Mestizos are people of mixed ancestry – usually a compound of Spanish and indigenous, although African slaves and other Europeans were also significant elements. *Indígenas* (indigenous people, less respectfully called *índios*, Indians) are descendants of Mexico's pre-Hispanic inhabitants who have retained a distinct ethnic identity. Mestizos make up the great majority of the population, and together with the few people of supposedly pure Spanish ancestry they hold most positions of power and influence in Mexican society.

Researchers have listed at least 139 vanished indigenous languages. The 60 or so remaining indigenous cultures – though some now with only a few hundred people – have survived largely because of their rural isolation. Each group has its own language and traditions and, often, its own unique costumes. Indigenous people generally remain second-class citizens, often restricted to the worst land or forced to migrate to city slums or the USA in search of work. Their main wealth is traditional and spiritual, and their way of life is imbued with communal customs, beliefs and rituals bound up with nature.

In the most recent national census (in 2000), some 7% of Mexicans listed themselves as speakers of indigenous languages, but people of predominantly indigenous ancestry may total as many as 15% – around 15 million people. The biggest indigenous group is the Nahua, descendants of the ancient Aztecs. Over two million Nahua are spread around central Mexico, chiefly in the states of Puebla, Veracruz, Hidalgo, Guerrero and San Luis Potosí. Southeastern Mexico has a particularly high indigenous population. The approximately 1.5 million Yucatec Maya speakers on the Yucatán Peninsula are direct descendants of the ancient Maya, and the Tzotzils and Tzeltals of Chiapas (around 500,000 of each) are probably descendants of the Maya who migrated there at the time of the Classic Maya downfall.

Also directly descended from well-known pre-Hispanic peoples are the estimated 780,000 Zapotecs, mainly in Oaxaca; the 760,000 Mixtecs, mainly in Oaxaca, Guerrero and Puebla; the 400,000 Totonacs, in Veracruz and Puebla; and the 150,000 Purépecha in Michoacán (descendants of the pre-Hispanic Tarascos).

Since 1994 the Zapatista rebels in Chiapas have spearheaded a campaign for indigenous rights. The San Andrés Accords of 1996, agreed between Zapatista and government negotiators, promised a degree of autonomy to Mexico's indigenous peoples, but the government of the day, under President Ernesto Zedillo, refused to turn the accords into law. In 2001 President Vicente Fox presented Mexico's Congress with a

Anthropologist Guillermo Bonfil Batalla argues in *México Profundo: Reclaiming a Civilization* (1996) that Mexico's urban and rural poor, mestizo and indigenous, constitute a uniquely Mesoamerican civilization quite distinct from Mexico's European and American-influenced middle class.

NORTH OF THE BORDER

An estimated 10 million Mexicans live in the USA, where average wages are six times higher than in Mexico. Mexicans in the US each send back, on average, US$1000 a year to their families in Mexico. Some 400,000 more Mexicans move north each year, many of them paying an average US$1200 to be smuggled across the border by 'coyotes.' Around two million more are apprehended annually in the attempt, and 200 or so die each year from drowning or thirst (in the deserts straddling the border) or from being hit by vehicles on US highways. In 2004 it was estimated that five million Mexicans were in the USA illegally. Hopes for improved status and conditions for them were raised that year when President George W Bush announced plans to allow illegal immigrants to apply for fixed-period work permits, which would give them full legal rights and entitlement to minimum wages.

bill closely based on the San Andrés Accords, but Congress passed only a watered-down version, which the Zapatistas rejected as a basis for peace talks, and which most Mexican states with large indigenous populations refused to accept in any case.

At least the cause of indigenous languages took a step forward with the passing of a Law of Linguistic Rights in 2002. This recognizes indigenous tongues as 'national' languages and aims to promote, through teaching, Mexico's linguistic plurality. A new National Institute of Indigenous Languages (Inali) has been set up to promote the use of indigenous languages in the media, on signs and in government propaganda, and to offer language options for official purposes.

SPORTS
Soccer (Football)

No sport ignites Mexicans' passions as much as *fútbol*. Games in the 20-team national Primera División (First Division) are watched by large crowds and followed by millions on television. The country has some impressive stadiums and Mexico City's Estadio Azteca (Aztec Stadium) hosted the 1970 and 1986 World Cup finals. Attending a game is fun; rivalry between opposing fans is generally good-humored. Tickets are sold at the entrance for anything from a couple of dollars to US$20, depending on the quality of the seat.

The two most popular teams in the country are América, of Mexico City, known as the Águilas (Eagles), and Guadalajara (Chivas, the Goats). They have large followings wherever they play and matches between the two, known as 'Los Clásicos,' are the biggest games of the year. Flag-waving crowds of 100,000 fill the Estadio Azteca when the two meet in Mexico City. Other leading clubs are: Cruz Azul (known as La Máquina,

---

HUGOL

Mexican soccer teams have many players from Central and South American countries, but few Mexicans make a name for themselves outside their home country. The great exception was Hugo Sánchez. No Mexican has ever known how to score goals like 'HuGol.' When Sánchez and the ball were near each other close to goal, goalkeepers could do little but hope. Agile and with lightning reactions, HuGol knocked them in with his right foot, his left foot and his head, always celebrating with a famous somersault learned from his sister, an Olympic gymnast. He was also an expert at scoring from free kicks, knocking the ball over the defensive wall and beyond the goalkeeper's reach.

At the age of 18, Sánchez helped Mexico City's Pumas to their first-ever Mexican championship in the 1976–77 season. The following season he was the leading scorer in Mexico with 26 club goals. After another Pumas championship in 1980–81, Sánchez moved to Europe to join Atlético Madrid and became Spain's leading scorer in 1984–85 (19 goals). He was then prized away from Atlético by their city rivals, the world-famous Real Madrid. Such was the Atlético fans' humiliation at losing their hero to their arch-enemy that the Atlético bosses had to stitch together a face-saving deal whereby they sold Hugo back to Pumas, who in turn sold him to Real.

HuGol's seven-year spell with Real Madrid earned him soccer immortality. Real won the Spanish championship in every one of his first five seasons, and in four of them he was the leading scorer in Spain. His 1989–90 tally of 38 goals, at the age of 31, is still the highest ever in one season in Spain's First Division. HuGol left Real in 1992, having scored 234 goals in 347 games in Spain. He played with clubs in three other countries before retiring in 1997. During his career he also knocked in 46 goals in 75 games for the Mexican national team, participating in three World Cups. At the time of writing he was back where he started in Mexico City, as coach of the Pumas.

The Machine), UNAM (Universidad Autónoma de Mexico, known as Pumas) and Atlante, all from Mexico City; Universidad Autónoma de Guadalajara (Los Tecos) and Atlas, both from Guadalajara; Monterrey and Universidad Autónoma de Nuevo León (Los Tigres), both from Monterrey; Toluca, Pachuca, Necaxa of Aguascalientes and Santos of Torreón. It was at Pachuca that the game was introduced to Mexico by miners from Cornwall, England, in the 19th century.

Crowds at Primera División games normally range between a few thousand and 70,000. Games are spaced over the weekend from Friday to Sunday; details are printed in the newspapers. The Primera División's season is divided into the Torneo de Apertura (Opening Tournament, August to December) and the Torneo de Clausura (Closing Tournament, January to June), each ending in eight-team playoffs (La Liguilla) and eventually a two-leg final to decide the champion. There's a uniquely complicated system of promotion and relegation with the Primera División A, which you'd need the astrological capabilities of an ancient Aztec priest to understand.

Mexico's national team, known as El Tri (short for Tricolor, the name for the national flag), reached the last 16 of the World Cup in 1994, 1998 and 2002 – though it will take Mexicans a long time to get over the disappointment of the 0-2 defeat by the USA in Korea in 2002! In international club competition, Cruz Azul lost only on a penalty shoot-out to Boca Juniors of Argentina in the final of the 2001 Copa Libertadores, the Latin American clubs' championship.

Bullfighting

Bullfighting is another Mexican passion, though less widespread than soccer. Fights take place chiefly in the larger cities, often during local festivals.

To many gringo eyes the *corrida de toros* (bullfight) hardly seems to be sport. To Mexicans it's as much a ritualistic dance as a fight, and it's said that Mexicans arrive on time for only two events – funerals and bullfights.

The *corrida de toros* (literally, running of the bulls) or *fiesta brava* (wild festival) begins promptly at an appointed time in the afternoon, usually on a Sunday. To the sound of a Spanish *paso doble,* the matador (literally, killer), in his *traje de luces* (suit of lights), and the *toreros* (his assistants) give the traditional *paseillo* (salute) to the fight authorities and the crowd. Then the first of the day's bulls (there are usually six in an afternoon) is released from its pen.

Each bull is fought in three *suertes* (acts) or *tercios* (thirds). First, the cape-waving *toreros* tire the bull by luring him around the ring. After a few minutes two *picadores*, on heavily padded horses, enter and jab long lances *(picas)* into the bull's shoulders to weaken him. Somehow this is often the most gruesome part of the whole process.

After the *picadores* leave the ring the *suerte de banderillas* begins, as the toreros attempt to stab three pairs of elongated darts into the bull's shoulders without getting impaled on his horns. Finally comes the *suerte de muleta*, the climax in which the matador has exactly 16 minutes to kill the bull. Starting with fancy cape work to tire the animal, the matador then exchanges his large cape for the smaller *muleta* and takes sword in hand, baiting the bull to charge before delivering the fatal *estocada* (lunge) with his sword. This must be done into the neck from a position directly in front of the animal.

If the matador succeeds, and he usually does, the bull collapses and an assistant dashes into the ring to slice its jugular. If the applause from the crowd

Soccer Age (www .soccerage.com) is a good English-language website for Mexican scores, standings, upcoming games and other things fans need to know. The Spanish-language Mundo Soccer (www.mundosoccer .com), FutMex (www .futmex.com), Es Mas (www.esmas.com) and the Mexican Football Federation's site (www .femexfut.org.mx) have even more detail; FutMex has links to clubs' websites.

For details of upcoming fights, biographies of matadors and much more on bullfighting, visit Portal Taurino (www .portaltaurino.com /mexico/mexico.htm), in Spanish and (sort of) English.

warrants, he will also cut off an ear or two and sometimes the tail for the matador. The dead bull is dragged from the ring to be butchered for sale.

A 'good' bullfight depends not only on the skill and courage of the matador but also the spirit of the bulls. Animals lacking heart for the fight bring shame on the ranch that bred them. Very occasionally, a bull that has fought outstandingly is *indultado* (spared) – an occasion for great celebration – and will then retire to stud.

In northern Mexico the bullfighting season generally runs from March or April to August or September. In Mexico City's Monumental Plaza México, one of the world's biggest bullrings, and other rings in central and southern Mexico, the main season is from October or November to March. The veteran Eloy Cavasos, from Monterrey, is often acclaimed as Mexico's top matador. Eulalio 'Zotoluco' López and Miguel 'Armillita' Espinosa are other big names. Rafael Ortega, Ignacio Garibay, Fernando Ochoa, José María Luévano and Fermín Spínola are younger stars in their 20s or early 30s. Bullfights featuring star matadors from Spain, such as Enrique Ponce, El Juli or José Tomás, have added spice.

DID YOU KNOW?

One variant of the Purépecha ball game, the *juego de la pelota encendida*, is played with a ball in flames, symbolizing the sun. Players need sufficient dexterity to avoid being burned!

Baseball

Professional *béisbol* has a good following. The winner of the October-to-January Liga Mexicana del Pacífico (www.ligadelpacifico.com.mx), which incorporates teams from northwest Mexico, represents Mexico in the February Serie del Caribe (the biggest event in Latin American baseball) against the champions of Venezuela, Puerto Rico and the Dominican Republic. The two strongest clubs are the Tomateros of Culiacán (who won the Caribbean title in 1996 and 2002) and the Naranjeros of Hermosillo. Younger American players on the way up often play in the Pacific league. The Liga Mexicana de Beisbol (www.lmb.com.mx), with 16 teams spread down the center and east of the country from Monclova to Cancún, plays from March to September. The sports newspaper *Afición* has good baseball coverage.

THE BALL GAME, THEN & NOW

Probably all pre-Hispanic Mexican cultures played some version of the Mesoamerican ball game, the world's first-ever team sport. The game may have varied from place to place and era to era, but had certain lasting features. Over 500 ball courts have survived at archaeological sites around Mexico and Central America. The game seems to have been played between two teams, and its essence was to keep a rubber ball off the ground by flicking it with hips, thighs, knees or elbows. The vertical or sloping walls alongside the courts were likely part of the playing area. The game had (at least sometimes) deep religious significance, serving as an oracle, with the result indicating which of two courses of action should be taken. Games could be followed by the sacrifice of one or more of the players – whether winners or losers, no one is sure.

The ancient ball game survives, somewhat modified (and without human sacrifice!), in two main forms in Mexico today. Both are team sports of around five a side, played on whatever open ground is available. The Pelota Mixteca (Mixtec Ball Game) is played regularly in numerous towns and villages in Oaxaca state, including Ejutla, Nochixtlán and Bajos de Chila near Puerto Escondido. Participants hit the ball with a thick heavy glove. A competition is held in Oaxaca city at the time of the Guelaguetza festival in late July. Oaxacan migrants have exported the game to other parts of Mexico and even to Santa Barbara and Fresno, California.

The Juego de Pelota Purépecha (Purépecha Ball Game) is played in the state of Michoacán, chiefly around the Lago de Pátzcuaro and at Angahuan, Zacán and Aranza. Participants use a stick to hit the ball.

The Mesoamerican Ballgame (www.ballgame.org) is an interesting educational website about the indigenous ball game, with film of a contest in action.

Other Sports

Charreadas (rodeos) are held particularly in the northern half of Mexico during fiestas and at regular venues often called *lienzos charros*. Horse racing takes place from February to November at Mexico City's Hipódromo de las Américas.

Mexico has produced many world champions in boxing, among them Julio César Chávez, who achieved an amazing 90 consecutive wins after turning pro in 1980, and won five world titles at three different weights. Chávez was a classic Mexican boxer – tactically astute but also able to take punishment and hand out even more. The highly popular *lucha libre* (wrestling) is more showbiz than sport. Participants in this pantomime-like activity give themselves names like Shocker, Karate Boy, Virus and Heavy Metal, then clown around in fancy dress. See *Lucha Libre* (p163) for more on this social phenomenon.

DID YOU KNOW?

The largest crowd in boxing history, 130,000, filled Mexico City's Estadio Azteca to see Julio Cesar Chávez beat Greg Haugen in five rounds in 1993.

RELIGION
Roman Catholicism

Nearly 90% of Mexicans profess Catholicism. Though its grip is under challenge today, Catholicism's dominance is remarkable considering the rocky history that the Catholic Church has had in Mexico.

The church was present in Mexico from the very first days of the Spanish conquest. Until Mexico's independence it remained the second most important institution after the crown's representatives and was really the only unifying force in Mexican society. Almost everyone belonged to the church because, spirituality aside, it was the principal provider of social services and education. The Jesuits were among the foremost providers and administrators, establishing missions and settlements throughout Mexico. Their expulsion from Mexico in 1767 marked the beginning of stormy church-state relations. From that time until 1940, Mexico passed numerous measures restricting the church's power and influence. The bottom line was money and property, both of which the church amassed more successfully than the generals and political bosses. The 1917 Mexican constitution prevented the church from owning property or running schools or newspapers, and banned clergy from voting, wearing clerical garb and speaking out on government policy. Church-state relations bottomed in the 1920s, when the Cristeros (Catholic rebels) burned government schools, murdered teachers and assassinated a president, while government troops killed priests and looted churches. But most of the anti-church provisions in the constitution ceased to be enforced during the second half of the 20th century, and in the 1990s President Salinas had them removed from the constitution. In 1992 Mexico established diplomatic relations with the Vatican.

The Mexican Catholic Church is one of Latin America's more conservative. Only in the south of the country have its leaders become involved in political issues such as human rights and poverty. The most notable figure in this regard is Samuel Ruiz, long-time bishop of San Cristóbal de Las Casas, who retired in 1999.

The Mexican church's most binding symbol is Nuestra Señora de Guadalupe (www.interlupe.com.mx), the dark-skinned manifestation of the Virgin Mary who appeared to an Aztec potter, Juan Diego, on a hill near Mexico City in 1531. The Virgin of Guadalupe became a crucial link between Catholic and indigenous spirituality, and as Mexico grew into a mestizo society she became the most potent symbol of Mexican Catholicism. Today the Virgin of Guadalupe is the country's patron, her blue-cloaked image is ubiquitous, and her name is invoked in religious ceremonies, political speeches and literature.

Other Christian Faiths

Around 7% of Mexicans practice other varieties of Christianity. Some are members of the Methodist, Baptist, Presbyterian or Anglican churches set up by US missionaries in the 19th century. Others have been converted since the 1970s by a wave of American Pentecostal, evangelical, Mormon, Seventh-Day Adventist and Jehovah's Witness missionaries. These churches have gained millions of converts, particularly among the rural and indigenous peoples of southeast Mexico, sometimes leading to serious strife with Catholics, notably in and around San Juan Chamula in Chiapas.

Indigenous Religions

The missionaries of the 16th and 17th centuries won the indigenous people over to Catholicism by grafting it onto pre-Hispanic religions. Often old gods were simply renamed as Christian saints, and the old festivals continued to be celebrated much as they had been in pre-Hispanic times, but on the nearest saint's day. Acceptance of the new religion was greatly helped by the appearance of the Virgin of Guadalupe in 1531.

Today, despite modern inroads into indigenous life, indigenous Christianity is still fused with more ancient beliefs. In some remote regions Christianity is only a veneer at most. The Huichol people of Jalisco have two Christs, but neither is a major deity. Much more important is Nakawé, the fertility goddess. The hallucinogenic drug peyote is a crucial

WHEN THE DEAD RETURN

Mexico's most characteristic and perhaps oddest fiesta, Día de Muertos (Day of the Dead), has its origins in the belief of the pre-Hispanic Tarasco people of Michoacán that the dead could return to their homes on one day each year.

The underlying philosophy is that death does not represent the end of a life, but the continuation of the same life in a parallel world. This day when the dead could return was a month after the autumn equinox. The occasion required preparations to help the spirits find their way home and make them welcome. An arch made of bright yellow marigold flowers was put up in each home, as a symbolic doorway from the underworld. Tamales, fruits, corn and salt were placed in front of the arch on an altar, along with containers of water because spirits always arrived thirsty after their journey. Traditionally, the spirits of departed children visited on the first night and the spirits of dead adults came on the following night, when they joined their living relatives to eat, drink, talk and sing.

Come the Spanish conquest, the Catholic celebrations of All Saints' Day (November 1) and All Souls' Day (November 2) were easily superimposed on the old 'day of the dead' traditions, which shared much of the same symbolism – flowers for the dead, offerings of food and drink, and the burning of candles. All Souls' Day is the Catholic day of prayers for those in purgatory; All Saints' Day was understood as a visit by the spirits of children who immediately became angelitos (little angels) when they died. The growing mestizo community, of mixed European and indigenous ancestry, evolved a new tradition of visiting graveyards and decorating graves of family members.

Though the idea that the dead could return on a specific day of the year seems to have been unique to the Tarascos, archaeological evidence suggests that all the cultures of ancient Mexico believed in places where people went after death, and in deities who ruled over the worlds of the dead. Thus the Aztec death god Mictlantecutli, who was often depicted with a skull-like face in pre-Hispanic artifacts, reappeared symbolically as a skull on Day of the Dead, alongside Christian images like the cross.

Día de Muertos persisted in the guise of Catholic celebration throughout the colonial period, when the idea of death as a great leveler and release from earthly suffering must have provided source of wisdom in the Huichol world. Elsewhere, among peoples such as the Tarahumara and many Tzotzil people in highland Chiapas, intoxication is an almost sacred element at festival times.

Even among the more orthodox Christian indigenous peoples, it's not uncommon for spring saints' festivals, or the pre-Lent carnival, to be accompanied by remnants of fertility rites. The famous flying Totonac *voladores* (see p662) enact one such ritual. The Guelaguetza dance festival, which draws thousands of visitors to Oaxaca every summer, has roots in pre-Hispanic maize-god rituals.

In the traditional indigenous world almost everything has a spiritual dimension – trees, rivers, plants, wind, rain, sun, animals and hills have their own gods or spirits. Witchcraft, magic and traditional medicine survive. Illness may be seen as a 'loss of soul' resulting from the sufferer's wrongdoing or from the malign influence of someone with magical powers. A soul can be 'regained' if the appropriate ritual is performed by a *brujo* (witch doctor) or *curandero* (curer).

ARTS
Painting & Sculpture

Mexicans have had an exciting talent for painting since pre-Hispanic times. The many murals decorating Mexican walls and the wealth of modern and historic art in Mexico's many galleries are highlights of the country.

comfort for the overwhelmingly poor populace. After independence it remained a popular event in the Mexican year, and poets used the occasion to publish verses ridiculing members of the social elite by portraying them as dead, with all their wealth and pretensions rendered futile. The great Mexican engraver José Guadalupe Posada (1852–1913) expressed similar sentiments in his famous *calaveras* – skeletal figures of death cheerfully engaging in everyday life, working, dancing, courting, drinking and riding horses into battle. One of his most enduring characters is La Calavera Catrina, a female skeleton in an elaborate low-cut dress and flamboyant flower-covered hat, suggestively revealing a bony leg and an ample bust that is all ribs and no cleavage.

In predominantly indigenous communities, most notably the Purépecha of Michoacán (descendants of the ancient Tarascos), Día de Muertos is still very much a religious and spiritual event. For them, the observance is more appropriately called Noche de Muertos (Night of the Dead) because families will actually spend whole nights at the graveyard – the night of October 31/November 1 with the sprits of dead children, the following night with the spirits of dead adults.

For Mexico's mestizo majority, Día de Muertos is more of a popular folk festival and family occasion. The mestizos may visit a graveyard to clean and decorate family graves, but they do not usually maintain an all-night vigil. And though they may pray for the souls of the departed and build special altars in their homes to welcome them back, the Catholic belief is that those souls are in heaven or in purgatory, not actually back on earth on a visit from the underworld. Sugar skulls, chocolate coffins and toy skeletons are sold in markets everywhere as gifts for children as well as graveyard decorations; they derive as much from Posada's work as from the icons of the ancient death cults.

Many Mexicans today are concerned about the impact on Día de Muertos of the American Halloween tradition, widely seen in pumpkin heads, friendly ghosts and kid's costume parties, and inadvertently promoted by tourists who give candy to children for 'trick or treat.' But Día de Muertos expresses a uniquely Mexican attitude to life and death that is deeply rooted, profoundly fatalistic yet eternally optimistic. It will probably absorb the pagan festival of Halloween just as it adapted to Catholicism over 400 years ago.

PRE-HISPANIC

Mexico's first civilization, the Olmecs of the Gulf Coast, produced remarkable stone sculptures, depicting deities, animals and wonderfully lifelike human forms. Most awesome are the huge Olmec heads, which combine the features of human babies and jaguars. The earliest outstanding Mexican murals are found at Teotihuacán, where the colorful *Paradise of Tláloc* depicts the delights awaiting those who died at the hands of the water god, Tláloc. The Teotihuacán mural style spread to other places in Mexico, such as Monte Albán in Oaxaca.

The Classic Maya of southeast Mexico, at their cultural height from about AD 250 to 800, were perhaps ancient Mexico's most artistically gifted people. They left countless beautiful stone sculptures, complicated in design but possessing an easily appreciable delicacy of touch. Subjects are typically rulers, deities and ceremonies. The art of the Aztecs reflects their harsh world-view, with many carvings of skulls and complicated symbolic representations of gods.

Other pre-Hispanic peoples with major artistic legacies include the Toltecs of central Mexico (10th to 13th centuries), who had a fearsome, militaristic style of carving; the Mixtecs of Oaxaca and Puebla (13th to 16th centuries), who were excellent goldsmiths and jewelers; and the Classic Veracruz civilization (about AD 400–900), which left a wealth of pottery and stone sculpture.

COLONIAL PERIOD

Mexican art during Spanish rule was heavily Spanish-influenced and chiefly religious in subject, though later on portraits grew in popularity under wealthy patrons. The influence of indigenous artisans is seen in the elaborate altarpieces and sculpted walls and ceilings, overflowing with tiny detail, in churches and monasteries, as well as in fine frescoes such as those at Actopan monastery in Hidalgo state. Miguel Cabrera (1695–1768), from Oaxaca, was probably the most talented painter of the era; his scenes and figures have a sureness of touch lacking in others' more labored efforts. They can be seen in churches and museums all over Mexico.

INDEPENDENT MEXICO

The landscapes of José María Velasco (1840–1912) capture the magical qualities of the country around Mexico City and areas farther afield, such as Oaxaca.

The years before the 1910 revolution saw a break from European traditions and the beginnings of socially conscious art. Slums, brothels and indigenous poverty began to appear on canvases. The cartoons and engravings of José Guadalupe Posada (1852–1913), with their characteristic *calavera* (skull) motif, satirized the injustices of the Porfiriato period and were aimed at a wider audience than most previous Mexican art. Gerardo Murillo (1875–1964), who took the name Doctor Atl (from a Náhuatl word meaning 'water'), displayed some scandalously orgiastic paintings at a 1910 show marking the centenary of the independence movement.

The best books on Mexican artists include Diego Rivera's autobiography *My Art, My Life*; Patrick Marnham's biography of Rivera, *Dreaming with his Eyes Open*; Hayden Herrera's *Frida: A Biography of Frida Kahlo*; *Frida Kahlo* by Malka Drucker; and *Mexican Muralists* by Desmond Rochfort.

THE MURALISTS

In the 1920s, immediately following the Mexican Revolution, education minister José Vasconcelos commissioned leading young artists to paint a series of murals on public buildings to spread a sense of Mexican history and culture and of the need for social and technological change. The trio of great muralists were Diego Rivera (1885–1957), José Clemente Orozco (1883–1949) and David Alfaro Siqueiros (1896–1974).

Rivera's work carried a clear left-wing message, emphasizing past oppression of indigenous people and peasants. His art pulled the country's indigenous and Spanish roots together in colorful, crowded tableaus depicting historical people and events or symbolic scenes of Mexican life, with a simple moral message. To appreciate them it helps to have a little knowledge of Mexican history and, preferably, an explanation of the details. Many of Rivera's greatest works are in and around Mexico City (see Frida & Diego, p136).

Siqueiros, who fought on the Constitutionalist side in the revolution (while Rivera was in Europe), remained a political activist afterward, spending time in jail as a result, and leading an attempt to kill Leon Trotsky in Mexico City in 1940. His murals lack Rivera's realism but convey a more clearly Marxist message through dramatic, symbolic depictions of the oppressed, and grotesque caricatures of the oppressors. Some of his best works are at the Palacio de Bellas Artes, Castillo de Chapultepec and Ciudad Universitaria, all in Mexico City.

Orozco, from Jalisco, focused more on the universal human condition than on historical specifics. He conveyed emotion, character and atmosphere. By the 1930s Orozco grew disillusioned with the revolution. His work reached its peak in Guadalajara between 1936 and 1939, particularly in the 50-odd frescoes in the Instituto Cultural Cabañas.

Rivera, Siqueiros and Orozco were also great artists on a smaller scale. Some of their portraits, drawings and other works can be seen in places like the Museo de Arte Moderno and Museo de Arte Carrillo Gil in Mexico City and in the Casa de Diego Rivera in Guanajuato.

Among their successors, Rufino Tamayo (1899–1991) from Oaxaca (also represented in Mexico City's Palacio de Bellas Artes) was absorbed by abstract and mythological scenes and effects of color. Many of his works are easily identified by his trademark watermelon motif, doubtless the result of being the son of a fruit seller. Juan O'Gorman (1905–81), a Mexican of Irish ancestry, was even more realistic and detailed than Rivera. His multicolored mosaic interpretation of Mexican culture on the Biblioteca Central at Mexico City's Ciudad Universitaria is probably his best-known work.

OTHER 20TH-CENTURY ARTISTS

Frida Kahlo (1907–54), physically crippled by a road accident and mentally tormented in her tempestuous marriage to Diego Rivera, painted anguished, penetrating self-portraits and grotesque, surreal images that expressed her left-wing views and externalized her inner tumult. Kahlo's work suddenly seemed to strike an international chord in the 1980s, almost overnight becoming hugely popular and as renowned as Rivera's. Thanks to the 2002 Hollywood biopic *Frida*, she's now better known worldwide than any other Mexican artist.

After WWII, the young Mexican artists of La Ruptura (The Rupture) reacted against the muralist movement, which they saw as too didactic and too obsessed with *mexicanidad* (Mexicanness). They opened Mexico up to world trends such as abstract expressionism and pop art. One leader of La Ruptura was José Luis Cuevas (b 1934), some of whose work you can see at the Mexico City art museum founded by and named for him. Other interesting artists to look for include Zacatecan Francisco Goitia (1882–1960), who conveyed the hardships of indigenous life; brothers Pedro (1923–85) and Rafael (b 1931) Coronel, also from Zacatecas; and Oaxacans Francisco Toledo (b 1940) and Rodolfo Morales (1925–2001).

Despite faint critical praise, *Frida*, Julie Taymor's 2002 factually informative movie biography, shouldn't be missed for its strong Mexican period atmosphere and fine performances by Mexican Salma Hayek as Ms Kahlo and Englishman Alfred Molina as Diego Rivera.

CONTEMPORARY ART

The unease and irony of postmodernism found fertile ground among Mexico's ever-questioning intelligentsia from the late 1980s onward. The many privately owned galleries that have sprung up display an enormous diversity of attempts to interpret the uncertainties of the early 21st century. Frida Kahlo, with her unsettling, disturbing images from a pre-mid-century (pre-'modern') era from which many postmodernists drew inspiration, stands as a kind of mother figure amid the maelstrom. Contemporary Mexican artists are mostly ironic individualists who can't be categorized into movements or groups. A few artists who incorporate Mexican themes, such as Dulce María Núñez, Nahum B Zenil and Rocío Maldonado, are labeled 'Neo-Mexicanists'. The colorful canvases of Núñez juxtapose popular icons such as saints, sports figures and cacti to show their impact on the everyday lives and psyches of Mexicans. Zenil, perhaps emulating Kahlo, is best known for his self-portraits, which confront contemporary social issues including homosexuality and AIDS. Maldonado, from Tepic, features diffusely drawn classical male nudes in designs that resemble toys or puzzles, using the bright colors of Mexican folk art. Sergio Hernández incorporates the indigenous iconography, craft motifs and popular culture of his native Oaxaca state into his abstract, colorful canvases and sculptures.

The abstract painting of the Castro Leñero brothers – Francisco, Miguel, Alberto and José – is considered a direct extension of La Ruptura. Francisco, one of Mexico's greatest modern painters, is a minimalist who employs collage and geometric forms and uses color sparingly; his works have been likened to musical compositions. In general, however, the pendulum has swung away from abstraction to hyper-representation and photo-realism. Artists are rediscovering the lost pleasures of grace, harmony and fantasy: in the work of Maldonado, Rafael Cauduro and Roberto Cortázar you'll see classically depicted figures against amorphous, bleak backgrounds. Cauduro paints photo-realistic landscapes of eroded urban surfaces, often populated by prostitutes and other street characters, the cast-off remains of civilization. Cortázar places his figures in stark, often monochrome surroundings and gives them disturbingly uncertain and imprisoned gazes.

Mexicans also play a role on the international performance art scene. Hector Falcón (www.hectorfalcon.com) uses his own body as a medium to explore norms of physical beauty. In one recent feat, he used steroids, aerobic exercise and a high-protein diet to attain the classic notion of an ideal body, recording the process through videos, photos and a log. Not just artists but an entire creative collective is Bacaanda (www.bacaanda.org.mx), an amalgam of pioneering creative folk who stage a broad range of arts and multimedia performance events in and around Mexico City.

The best way to catch up on what's happening is simply to visit some of the better contemporary galleries. See the individual sections in this guide for recommendations. The current epicenters of contemporary Mexican art are Mexico City and Oaxaca. Monterrey, with its Museo de Arte Contemporáneo (Marco) is another focus. La Jornada newspaper has a great cultural section with daily listings of exhibitions and culture of all kinds.

Hook into the contemporary Mexico City art scene through Arte Mexico (www.arte-mexico.com), with a calendar of exhibitions, data on artists and galleries, maps and more, or Artes Visuales (www.artesvisuales.com.mx).

Architecture

Mexico has a beautiful and awe-inspiring architectural heritage from the pre-Hispanic and colonial eras that ranks among its biggest attractions.

PRE-HISPANIC

The ancient civilizations of Mexico produced some of the most spectacular, eye-pleasing architecture ever built. At sites such as Teotihuacán,

Monte Albán, Chichén Itzá and Uxmal you can still see fairly intact pre-Hispanic cities. Their spectacular ceremonial centers were designed to impress, with great stone pyramids, palaces and ball courts. Pyramids usually functioned as the bases for small shrines on their summits. Mexico's three biggest pyramids are the Pirámide del Sol and Pirámide de la Luna, both at Teotihuacán, and the Pirámide Tepanapa at Cholula, near Puebla.

The Art of Mesoamerica by Mary Ellen Miller is a good survey of pre-Hispanic art and architecture. On colonial architecture, the most important book is George Kubler's *Mexican Architecture of the Sixteenth Century* (1948).

There were many differences in style between the pre-Hispanic civilizations: while Teotihuacán, Monte Albán and Aztec buildings were relatively simple in design, intended to awe by their grand scale, Mayan architecture paid more attention to aesthetics, with intricately patterned façades, delicate 'combs' on temple roofs, and sinuous carvings. Buildings at Mayan sites such as Uxmal, Chichén Itzá and Palenque are among the most beautiful human creations in the Americas. Most Mayan roof combs, formed by gridlike arrangements of stone with multiple gaps, were originally taller than what remains of them today. Mayan buildings are also characterized by the corbeled vault, their version of the arch: two stone walls leaning toward one another, nearly meeting at the top and surmounted by a capstone.

COLONIAL

Many of the fine mansions, churches, monasteries and plazas that today contribute so much to Mexico's beauty were created during the 300 years of Spanish rule. Most were in basic Spanish styles, but with unique local variations.

Gothic and renaissance styles dominated colonial building in Mexico in the 16th and early 17th centuries. Gothic is typified by soaring buttresses, pointed arches, clusters of round columns and ribbed ceiling vaults. The renaissance saw a return to the disciplined ancient Greek and Roman ideals of harmony and proportion, with shapes such as the square and the circle predominating. In Mexico, it usually took the form of plateresque (from *platero*, silversmith, because its decoration resembled elaborately ornamented silverwork). Plateresque commonly appears on the façades of buildings, particularly church doorways, which had round arches bordered by classical columns and stone sculpture. A later, more austere renaissance style was called Herreresque, after the Spanish architect Juan de Herrera. Two of Mexico's outstanding renaissance buildings are Mérida's cathedral and Casa de Montejo. The cathedrals of Mexico City and Puebla mingle renaissance and baroque styles.

Gothic and renaissance influences were combined in many of the fortified monasteries that were built as Spanish monks carried their missionary work to all corners of the country. Monasteries usually had a large church, a cloister and often a *capilla abierta* (open chapel), from which priests could address large crowds of indigenous people. Notable monasteries include Actopan and Acolman in central Mexico, and Yanhuitlán, Coixtlahuaca and Teposcolula, in Oaxaca.

The influence of the Muslims who had ruled much of Spain until the late 15th century also reached Mexico. The Muslim-influenced Spanish style known as Mudejar can be seen in some beautifully carved wooden ceilings and in the decorative feature known as the *alfiz,* a rectangle framing a round arch. The 49 domes of the Capilla Real in Cholula almost resemble a mosque.

Baroque style, which reached Mexico from Spain in the early 17th century, combined renaissance influences with other elements aimed at a dramatic effect. Curves, color, contrasts of light and dark, and increasingly elaborate decoration were among its hallmarks. Painting and sculpture were integrated with architecture, most notably in ornate, often enormous altarpieces *(retablos)*. Fine baroque buildings in Mexico include the marvelous façade of Zacatecas' cathedral and the churches of Santiago Tlatelolco in Mexico City, San Felipe Neri and La Soledad in Oaxaca, and San Francisco in San Luis Potosí. Mexican baroque reached its final form, churrigueresque, between 1730 and 1780. This was characterized by riotous surface ornamentation – witness the Sagrario Metropolitano in Mexico City, the Ocotlán sanctuary at Tlaxcala and the churches of San Francisco Javier in Tepotzotlán, Santa Prisca in Taxco, and San Francisco, La Compañía and La Valenciana in Guanajuato.

Indigenous artisans added profuse sculpture in stone and colored stucco to many baroque buildings, such as the Capilla del Rosario in the Temple of Santo Domingo of Puebla, and the nearby village church of Tonantzintla. Arabic influence continued with the popularity of *azulejos* (colored tiles) on the outside of buildings, particularly in and around Puebla.

Neoclassical style, predominant in Mexico from about 1780 to 1830, was another return to sober Greek and Roman ideals. Outstanding examples include the Palacio de Minería in Mexico City and the Alhóndiga de Granaditas in Guanajuato. Eduardo Tresguerras and Spanish-born Manuel Tolsá were Mexico's most prominent neoclassical architects.

19TH TO 21ST CENTURIES

Independent Mexico in the 19th century saw revivals of Gothic and colonial styles. In the late 19th and early 20th centuries many buildings copied recent French or Italian styles. The Palacio de Bellas Artes in Mexico City is one of the finest buildings from this era.

After the revolution of 1910–21, art deco appeared in some buildings but more important was an attempt to return to pre-Hispanic roots in the search for a national identity. This trend was known as Toltecism, and many public buildings exhibit the heaviness of Aztec or Toltec monuments. Toltecism culminated in the 1950s with the UNAM campus in Mexico City, where many buildings are covered with colorful murals.

More modern architects have provided some cities with a few eye-catching and adventurous buildings as well as a large quota of dull concrete blocks. Best known is Luis Barragán. Strongly influenced by the functionalists Le Corbusier and Alvar Aalto, Barragán's work also exhibits a strong Mexican strain in its use of vivid colors, textures, scale, space, light and vegetation, with small interior gardens. Barragán's oeuvre includes a set of wacky colored skyscraper sculptures at the gateway to Ciudad Satélite, a Mexico City suburb; the Faro del Comercio, a tall orange concrete slab in the main plaza of Monterrey; and on a more domestic scale, the Casa Museo Luis Barragán in Tacubaya, Mexico City, Barragán's home which he designed in 1947.

Pedro Ramírez Vásquez is a modernist who designed two vast public buildings – the 1960s Museo Nacional de Antropología and the 1970s Basílica de Guadalupe – in Mexico City. His work makes few references to Mexican traditions. It's a similar case with Alberto Kalach, who in 2003 won an international competition to design the new national library in Mexico City, the major architectural project of the Fox presidency. Kalach is an iconoclast who favors high-tech elements, full of metallic and industrial details. His controversial library – hidden from the outside world by curtains of jungle-like foliage – was described by one of the competition judges as 'a monotonous succession of identical and inflex-

'Modern architects have provided some cities with a few eye-catching and adventurous buildings as well as a large quota of dull concrete blocks'

ible halls…an interminable warehouse from whose roof hang, with little structural verisimilitude, clustered towers of bookshelves.'

Music

In Mexico live music may start up at any time on streets, plazas or even buses. These musicians are playing for a living and range from marimba (wooden xylophone) teams and mariachi bands (trumpeters, violinists, guitarists and a singer, all dressed in smart wild-west-like costumes) to ragged lone buskers with out-of-tune guitars and sandpaper voices. Mariachi music (perhaps the most 'typical' Mexican music of all) originated in the Guadalajara area but is played nationwide (see Mariachis, p523). Marimbas are particularly popular in the southeast and on the Gulf coast.

On a more organized level, Mexico has a thriving popular music business. Its outpourings can be heard live at fiestas, nightspots and concerts, or bought from music shops. Finding out who's playing where and when is mainly a matter of keeping an eye on posters and the entertainments pages of the press. Ticketmaster Mexico (www.ticketmaster.com.mx) has a certain amount of information in its Buscar Eventos search section.

ROCK, RAP & HIP-HOP

So close to the big US Spanish-speaking market, Mexico can claim to be the most important hub of Spanish-language rock. Talented Mexico City bands such as Café Tacuba and Maldita Vecindad took *rock en español* to new heights and new audiences (well beyond Mexico) in the '90s, mixing a huge range of influences – from rock, hip-hop and ska to traditional Mexican *son*, bolero or mariachi. Café Tacuba's exciting handling of so many styles, yet with their own very strong musical identity, keeps them at the forefront of Mexican rock today. The albums *Re* (1994), *Avalancha de Éxitos* (1996), *Tiempo Transcurrido* (2001) and *Cuatro Caminos* (2003) are all full of great songs, while the 1999 double album *Revés/YoSoy* is an excursion into more electronic realms.

Maná from Guadalajara are an unashamedly commercial band with British and Caribbean influences, strongly reminiscent of the Police. They have been around since the '80s and get ever stronger. They're the best-known Mexican band outside Mexico, having worked hard to build an international following. Collaboration with Carlos Santana on the song *Corazón Espinado* on Santana's hit *Supernatural* album (1999) and on their own *Revolución de Amor* (2002) helped their cause.

The city of Monterrey has produced most of the major more-recent arrivals, including hip-hop twosome Plastilina Mosh, a kind of Mexican Beastie Boys, whose 1998 debut album *Aquamosh* was a huge success. Rap-metal-hip-hop band Molotov attract controversy with their slang- and expletive-laced lyrics in a mix of Spanish and English – and are respected by many as the band that never sold out. They're angry about everything. Their major albums are *¿Dónde Jugarán la Niñas?* (1997), *Apocalypshit* (1999) and *Dance and Dense Denso* (2003). The much-aired track *Frijolero* from their last album is an aggressive attack on US attitudes to Mexicans, with its Spanish-language lines sung in a gringo accent.

Other big bands from Monterrey are Zurdok, with a Britpop-like sound (*Hombre Sintetizador*, 2002), ska merchants Inspector (*Alma en Fuego*, 2001), and hip-hop-rap trio Control Machete. Still one of the country's most popular bands is Jaguares, mystical Def Leppard–type rockers who spearheaded the coming of age of Mexican rock in the 1980s under the earlier name Caifanes. (Foreign rock acts were not allowed to play in Mexico until the late '80s, which somewhat hindered the development

'Foreign rock acts were not allowed to play in Mexico until the late '80s' of the genre.) Jaguares' 1999 double album *Bajo el Azul de tu Misterio* was a big success in both Mexico and the USA.

Not to be forgotten are El Tri, the grandfathers of Mexican rock, who after more than 30 years are still pumping out energetic rock and roll. Further interesting performers you may come across are virtuoso jazz-rock guitar hero Julio Revueltas and the self-consciously weird jazz-rockers Santa Sabina featuring the eerie vocals of Rita Guerrero.

POP
If you've been anywhere near a TV music channel in recent years you'll have seen the skinny form of Paulina Rubio, Mexico's answer to Shakira and Britney Spears. Rubio has also starred in several Mexican films and TV series. Balladeer Luis Miguel (born in Veracruz in 1970), meanwhile, is Mexico's Julio Iglesias. If you don't know his voice you've probably heard about his love life.

Natalia la Fourcade, a young singer with a strong voice able to tackle varied styles, made her name with the title track on the 2002 film *Amar te Duele,* a romanticized Romeo and Juliet story set in contemporary Mexico City. Sometimes compared with Canada's Nelly Furtado, la Fourcade released her debut album *Natalia la Fourcade* in 2003.

One name that Mexicans will never forget is Gloria Trevi, dubbed the 'Mexican Madonna' until she vanished in 1998 after Chihuahua authorities ordered the arrest of her and her manager Sergio Andrade for alleged sexual abuse and kidnapping of minors. The story went that the school for young female talent run by the couple was actually a harem for Andrade. The pair were on the run for over a year before being arrested in Rio de Janeiro in 2000. Both were eventually extradited to Mexico to face the courts.

ELECTRONIC MUSIC
Mexico has a big *punchis-punchis* (as they accurately call it) scene: almost every weekend there's an event somewhere in the country (usually in or around one of the big cities), where you can check out the country's top DJs and also international guests from countries such as Germany or Israel. Top names include DJ Klang (house and trance) and DJ Vazik (psychedelic). Kinetik.tv (www.kinetik.tv) has details of upcoming raves and parties.

The Tijuana-based Nortec Collective is a group of northern DJs, centered on DJ Bostich and chemical engineer Pepe Mogt, that has melded traditional Mexican music with electronica into a unique genre known as Nortec. Look out for *The Nortec Sampler* (2000) or *Tijuana Sessions Vol 1* (2001).

Kinky, a band from Monterrey, successfully fuse Latin rock with electronics and are great live performers. Their albums are *Kinky* (2002) and *Atlas* (2003). If you like techno-pop listen out for Moenia, a trio who have released several albums including *Moenia* (1997) and *Televisor* (2003).

REGIONAL & FOLK MUSIC
The deepest-rooted Mexican folk music is *son* (literally, 'sound'), a broad term covering a range of country styles that grew out of the fusion of indigenous, Spanish and African musical cultures. *Son* is essentially guitars plus harp or violin, often played for a foot-stamping dance audience, with witty, frequently improvised lyrics. The independent Mexican label Discos Corasón has done much to promote these most traditional of Mexican musical forms.

'The deepest-rooted Mexican folk music is *son*, a fusion of indigenous, Spanish and African musical cultures'

Particularly celebrated brands of Mexican *son* come from four areas:
The Huasteca, inland from Tampico *Son huasteco* trios feature a solo violinist and two guitarists singing falsetto between soaring violin passages. Keep an eye open for *son* festivals or performances by the top *son huasteco* group Camperos de Valles.
Jalisco *Sones jaliscenses* originally formed the repertoire of many mariachi bands.
Río Balsas basin, southwest of Mexico City With the elaborate violin passages of its *sones calentanos*, this hot region produced perhaps the greatest *son* musician of recent decades, violinist Juan Reynoso.
Veracruz The local *son jarocho*, performed preeminently by harpist La Negra Graciana, is particularly African-influenced. Grupo Mono Blanco lead a revival of the genre with contemporary lyrics (look out for their album *El Mundo se va a Acabar*, 1998).

An exciting talent is Oaxaca-born Lila Downs, who has an American father and Mixtec indigenous mother. At one stage a Deadhead (Grateful Dead camp follower), and also influenced by her relationship with US jazz pianist Paul Cohen, Lila has emerged as a passionate reinterpreter of traditional Mexican folk songs. Her major albums are *La Sandunga* (1997), *Tree of Life* (2000) and *Border* (2001). She sang several songs on the soundtrack of the 2002 movie *Frida*.

Modern regional music is rooted in a strong rhythm from several guitars, with voice, accordion, violin or brass providing the melody. *Ranchera* is Mexico's urban 'country music.' It's mostly melodramatic stuff with a nostalgia for rural roots – vocalist-and-combo music, maybe with a mariachi backing. The hugely popular Vicente Fernández, Ana Bárbara, Juan Gabriel and Alejandro Fernández (Vicente's son) are among the leading *ranchera* artists now that past generations of beloved stars like Lola Beltrán, Lucha Reyes, Chavela Vargas, Pedro Infante and Jorge Negrete have passed away or retired. The popular and powerful performers Eugenia León and Astrid Haddad include some *ranchera* in their versatile repertoires but range widely over Mexican song forms.

Norteño is country ballad and dance music, originating in northern Mexico but nationwide in popularity. Its roots are in *corridos*, heroic narrative ballads with the rhythms of European dances such as the polka or waltz, which were brought to southern Texas by 19th-century German and Czech immigrants. Originally the songs were tales of Latino-Anglo strife in the borderlands or themes from the Mexican Revolution. Today's ballads, especially the gritty variety known as *narco-corridos*, tend to deal with drug-runners, coyotes and other small-time crooks trying to survive amid big-time corruption and crime, and with the injustices and problems faced by Mexican immigrants in the USA. The superstars of the genre Los Tigres del Norte, originally from Sinaloa but long based in California, play to huge audiences on both sides of the frontier. *Norteño* groups *(conjuntos)* go for 10-gallon hats, with backing centered on the accordion and the *bajo sexto* (a 12-string guitar), along with bass and drums. Los Tigres del Norte added saxophone and absorbed popular *cumbia* rhythms from Colombia. Other leading *norteño* exponents include Los Tucanes de Tijuana, Los Huracanes del Norte, vocalist Marco Antonio Solis and accordionist Flaco Jiménez.

Banda is a 1990s development of *norteño*, substituting large brass sections for guitars and accordion, playing a combination of Latin and more traditional Mexican rhythms. Banda del Recodo from Mazatlán are the biggest name in *banda*.

MÚSICA TROPICAL
Though its origins lie in the Caribbean and South America, several brands of *música tropical* or *música afroantillana* have become integral

'Today's ballads tend to deal with drug-runners, coyotes and other small-time crooks trying to survive amid big-time corruption and crime'

parts of the Mexican musical scene. Two types of dance music – *danzón,* originally from Cuba, and *cumbia,* from Colombia – both took deeper root in Mexico than in their original homelands (see Dance, p72). Some *banda* and *norteño* groups play a lot of *cumbia.* The leading Mexican exponents were probably Los Bukis (who split in 1995).

TROVA

This genre of troubadour-type folk music has roots in 1960s and '70s songs. Typically performed by singer-songwriters *(cantautores)* with a solitary guitar, it's not a field where much new is happening, but is still popular with an older generation. Nicho Hinojosa, Fernando Delgadillo and Alberto Escobar are leading artists. Many *trova* singers are strongly inspired by Cuban political singer-songwriter Silvio Rodríguez and include his songs in their repertoires.

Cinema

A clutch of fine, gritty movies by young directors has thrust Mexican cinema into the international limelight, garnering commercial success as well as critical acclaim after decades in the doldrums. These films confront the ugly and the absurd in Mexican life as well as the beautiful and sad. Alfonso Arau's *Como Agua para Chocolate* (Like Water for Chocolate; 1992) and Guillermo del Toro's 1993 horror movie *Cronos* set the ball rolling, then in 1999 Mexicans flocked to see Antonio Serrano's *Sexo, Pudor y Lágrimas* (Sex, Shame and Tears), a comic but sad tale of young couples' relationships, and Luis Estrada's black comedy of political corruption *La Ley de Herodes,* a damning indictment of the Partido Revolucionario Institucional (PRI).

But the first new Mexican movie to really catch the world's eye, in 2000, was *Amores Perros* (Love's a Bitch), directed by Alejandro González Iñárritu and starring Gael García Bernal. Set in contemporary Mexico City, with three plots connected by one traffic accident, it's a raw, honest movie with its quota of graphic blood, violence and sex.

Y Tu Mamá También (And Your Mother Too), Alfonso Cuarón's 2002 'growing up' tale of two teenagers from privileged Mexico City circles, became the biggest grossing Mexican film ever, netting US$11 million in Mexico and US$13.6 million in the US. The teenagers (Gael García Bernal and Diego Luna) venture out of the city with an older woman in search of a paradisiacal beach called Boca del Cielo (Heaven's Mouth). On the way they discover lots of things about themselves and their country, raising themes such as class, sexuality and loyalty. The filming location was Bahías de Huatulco.

In Carlos Reygadas' 2002 movie *Japón* (Japan) a middle-aged Mexico City man goes to a village in Hidalgo state to commit suicide – and finds that the change of scene and personnel upsets all his certainties. It's a slow, meditative, no-easy-explanations film that some people love and others find frustrating (not least because it has nothing to do with Japan).

The 2002 success *El Crimen del Padre Amaro* (The Crime of Father Amaro), directed by Carlos Carrera and again starring Gael García Bernal, paints an ugly picture of corruption in the Catholic church in a small Mexican town.

Will Mexico's new cinematic talents continue to film in, and about, Mexico? After *Amores Perros,* Alejandro González Iñárritu moved to Hollywood to direct *21 Grams* with Sean Penn, Benicio del Toro and Naomi Watts (highly acclaimed on its 2003 release). Alfonso Cuarón

DID YOU KNOW?

Arguably the most famous of all Mexican film actors was Zorba the Greek – Anthony Quinn (1915–2001), born Antonio Quiñones in Chihuahua. His family moved to the US when he was four months old.

stepped from *Y Tu Mamá También* to directing the third Harry Potter movie, while Gael García Bernal and Diego Luna also went to the US to make, respectively, *The Motorcycle Diaries* (2004), in which García Bernal played Che Guevara, and *Dirty Dancing: Havana Nights* (2004).

The golden age of Mexican movie-making was WWII, when in the absence of much output from Hollywood, Mexico helped fill the gap in the Latin American market with over 50 films a year, typically epic, melodramatic productions. Hollywood reasserted itself after the war and Mexican film makers have been struggling for funds ever since. In 2002 just 13 films were made in Mexico. But there is cause for hope: Mexico has the world's seventh-biggest cinema audience figures and numbers are growing. In 2002 box-office takings reached US$450 million, an increase of 20% from 2001, with locally-made films attracting 10% of this audience. Mexico still has a high-class movie-making infrastructure, with plenty of technical expertise and up-to-the-minute equipment. In October 2003 the city of Morelia held its first international film festival (www.moreliafilmfest.com), an event intended to further promote Mexican cinema in international circles. Government funding for the large Churubusco studios and government film school in Mexico City has been under review, but meanwhile Mexico's first privately financed studio complex, The Film Colony, is being built at a cost of US$48 million in San Miguel de Allende. It will feature six sound stages and a film school for up to 350 students.

Literature

Mexicans such as Carlos Fuentes, Juan Rulfo and Octavio Paz have produced some of the great modern Spanish-language writing, although – with the exception of a wave of new writing from northern Mexico – cinema and popular music have taken a more head-on approach to the harsh realities of contemporary life.

Mexico's best-known writer internationally is the prolific novelist and commentator Carlos Fuentes (b 1928). Fuentes' first novel, *Where the Air Is Clear* (1958), is one of his most highly regarded. It traces the lives of various Mexico City dwellers through the post–Mexican Revolution decades in a critique of the revolution's failure. *The Death of Artemio Cruz* (1962) takes another critical look at the post-revolutionary era through the eyes of a dying, corrupted ex-revolutionary turned press baron and landowner. Fuentes' *Aura* (1962) is a magical book with one of the most stunning endings of any novel. *La Silla del Águila* (The Eagle Throne, 2003) again treats of political corruption and cynicism. It's set in 2020 at a time when an all-powerful USA has cut off Mexico's access to telecommunications and computers, Condoleezza Rice is US president, Fidel Castro is still in power, and a vicious struggle is being played out for the lifetime presidency of Mexico.

In Mexico, Juan Rulfo (1918–86) is widely regarded as the supreme novelist. His *Pedro Páramo* (1955), a work of scary, desolate magical realism with a plot about a young man's search for his lost father among ghostlike villages in western Mexico, has been described as 'Wuthering Heights set in Mexico and written by Kafka.' Some acclaim it as the ultimate expression of Latin American existence – and Rulfo certainly never felt the need to write anything else afterward. His only other book, *The Burning Plain* (1953), is a collection of short stories of Jalisco peasant life.

Octavio Paz (1914–98), poet, essayist and winner of the 1990 Nobel Prize in Literature, wrote a probing, intellectually acrobatic analysis of

DID YOU KNOW?

Recent Hollywood movies shot in Mexico have included *Titanic, Pearl Harbor, Troy* and the Leonardo di Caprio version of *Romeo and Juliet.*

Mexico's myths and the Mexican character in *The Labyrinth of Solitude* (1950). Decide for yourself whether you agree with his pessimistic assessments of his fellow Mexicans. Paz's *Sor Juana* (1982) reconstructed the life of Mexico's earliest literary giant, Sor Juana Inés de la Cruz, a 17th-century courtesan-turned-nun (and proto-feminist) whose love poems, plays, romances and essays were aeons ahead of their time.

Elena Garro (b 1920) is a relatively little-known but highly influential writer who probes the limits of language with stylish, poetic prose. Her *Recollections of Things to Come* (1963), set in post-revolutionary rural Mexico, is thought to have had a big influence on Gabriel García Márquez. In 1998 Garro published *First Love & Look for My Obituary: Two Novellas*, a pair of love stories whose characters struggle for freedom and identity against the weight of stereotypes and convention.

There is no doubt that northern Mexican writers, mostly born in the 1960s and focusing on themes such as violence, corruption, drug trafficking, the border and conflicts of identity, are producing some of the most immediate and gritty Mexican writing today. Juan José Rodríguez (*Mi Nombre es Casablanca*, 2003), Raúl Manríquez (*La Vida a Tientas*, 2003) and Élmer Mendoza (*Un Asesino Solitario*, 1999) all tell of explosive violence provoked by drug conflicts. Some writers' work, like Luis Humberto Crosthwaite's *Instrucciones para Cruzar la Frontera* (2002) and Rafa Saavedra's *Lejos del Noise* (2003), are enriched by the linguistic influence of *spanglish*. Other writers, such as Felipe Montes (*El Enrabiado*, 2003) and Daniel Sada, consciously reject Anglo influence.

> 'Northern Mexican writers, mostly born in the 1960s, are producing some of the most immediate and gritty Mexican writing today'

The Mexican Revolution yielded a whole school of novels: the classic is *The Underdogs*, the story of a poor peasant who becomes a revolutionary general, by Mariano Azuela (1873–1952). Contemporary writers are still inspired by the revolution and its aftermath: Ángeles Mastretta (b 1949) views the era through a woman's eyes in the amusing *Tear This Heart Out* (1985), written as the memoirs of the wife of a ruthless political boss. Laura Esquivel (b 1950) made her name with *Like Water for Chocolate* (1989), a passionate love story interwoven with both fantasy and cooking recipes set in rural Mexico during the revolution. Another fine contemporary writer is Cristina Rivera Garza whose *No One Will See Me Cry* (1999) tells of the tragic relationship between a photographer and an ex-prostitute he recognizes while photographing in a mental hospital in the 1920s.

Rosario Castellanos (1925–74), from Chiapas, who was an early champion of women's and indigenous rights, wrote of the injustices that provoked the 1994 Zapatista rebellion, decades before it happened. *The Book of Lamentations* (1962) draws on earlier real historical events for its story of an indigenous uprising in the 1930s.

Elena Poniatowska (b 1941) is a prolific intellectual talent who combines fiction, history, journalism and social commentary. Her fiction draws closely on the lives of real people, as in *Here's to You, Jesusa* (1969), which spans half a century of Mexican history through the colorful, sad tale of a poor but independent woman from Oaxaca; and *Tinisima* (1996), which reimagines the life of Tina Modotti, Hollywood actress, Soviet agent, friend of Diego Rivera, and model and lover of photographer Edward Weston.

In poetry, the great figures of the 20th century were Octavio Paz (see earlier) and Jaime Sabines (1925–99), a reclusive figure from Chiapas who treated themes of love and death with stark, vivid imagery. The contemporary poetry scene focuses on Mexico City and Guadalajara and is headed up by such poets as David Huerta, Francisco Hernández and Elsa

Cross (all born in 1946) and, at the forefront of a younger 1960s-born generation of much variety and vitality, the likes of Ernesto Lumbreras, Jorge Fernández Granados and Luis Vicente de Aguinaga.

NON-MEXICAN AUTHORS

Of course Mexico has inspired much fine writing from non-Mexicans. Graham Greene's *The Power and the Glory* dramatizes the state-church conflict that followed the Mexican Revolution. *Under the Volcano* (1938) by British dipsomaniac Malcolm Lowry follows a British diplomat in Mexico who drinks himself to death on Day of the Dead. DH Lawrence's *Mornings in Mexico* is a collection of short stories set in both Mexico and New Mexico.

B Traven is best known as the author of the 1935 adventure story of gold and greed in northwest Mexico, *The Treasure of the Sierra Madre*. However, he wrote many other novels set in Mexico, chiefly the six of the Jungle series – among them *The Rebellion of the Hanged, General from the Jungle* and *Trozas* – focusing on pre-revolutionary oppression in Chiapas. The identity of Traven himself is one of literature's big mysteries.

The beat generation spent plenty of time in Mexico: William Burroughs' early novel *Queer* chronicles the guilt, lust and drug excesses of an American in Mexico City in the 1940s. The city was also the scene of parts of Burroughs' *Junky* and Jack Kerouac's *On the Road* and *Tristessa*, and was where Kerouac wrote his long poem *Mexico City Blues* and two other novels.

The 1990s brought some fine new English-language novels set in Mexico. Cormac McCarthy's marvelous *All the Pretty Horses* is the laconic, tense, poetic tale of three young latter-day cowboys riding south of the border. *The Crossing* and *Cities of the Plain* completed McCarthy's Border Trilogy. James Maw's *Year of the Jaguar* catches the feel of Mexican travel superbly, taking its youthful English protagonist from the US border to Chiapas in an exciting search for a father he has never met. Harriet Doerr's *Consider This, Señora* tells of a handful of Americans who settle in a well-evoked rural Mexico. Her *Stones for Ibarra* (1978) had trodden similar ground with its story of a US couple in their forties who come to reopen a copper mine once owned by the man's grandfather.

For travel writing set in Mexico, see p14.

> 'The city was where Kerouac wrote his long poem *Mexico City Blues* and two other novels'

Dance

INDIGENOUS DANCE

Colorful traditional indigenous dances are an important part of Mexican fiestas. There are hundreds of them, some popular in several parts of the country, others danced only in a single town or village. Many bear traces of pre-Hispanic ritual, having evolved from old fertility rites and other ancient practices. Other dances tell stories of Spanish or colonial origin – the Danza de las Plumas (Feather Dance) from Oaxaca state represents the Spanish conquest of Mexico, while the fairly widespread Moros y Cristianos reenacts the victory of Christians over Muslims in 15th-century Spain.

Nearly all traditional dances require special colorful costumes, sometimes including masks. The Danza de las Plumas and the Danza de los Quetzales (Quetzal Dance), from Puebla state, both feature enormous feathered headdresses or shields.

Today some of these dances are often performed outside their sacred context as simple spectacles. The Ballet Folclórico in Mexico City brings together traditional dances from all over the country in a spectacular stage show. Other folkloric dance performances can be seen in several cities and at festivals such as the Guelaguetza, in Oaxaca on the last two Mondays of July.

LATIN DANCE

Caribbean and South American dances are highly popular in Mexico. This is tropical ballroom dancing, to percussion-heavy, infectiously rhythmic music that often includes electric guitars or brass. Mexico City has a dozen or more clubs and large dance halls devoted to this scene: aficionados can go to a different hall each night of the week (see p159), often with big-name bands from the Caribbean and South America. One of the more formal, old-fashioned varieties of Latin dance is *danzón,* originally from Cuba and associated particularly with the port city of Veracruz. *Cumbia,* originally from Colombia but now with its adopted home in Mexico City, is livelier, more flirtatious and less structured. It rests on thumping bass lines with brass, guitars, mandolins and sometimes marimbas.

Salsa developed in New York in the 1950s when jazz met *son,* cha-cha and rumba from Cuba and Puerto Rico. Musically it boils down to brass (with trumpet solos), piano, percussion, singer and chorus – the dance is a hot one with a lot of exciting turns. Merengue, mainly from the Dominican Republic, is a *cumbia*/salsa blend with a hopping step; the rhythm catches the shoulders, the arms go up and down. The music is strong on maracas, and its musicians go for puffed-up sleeves.

Folk Art

Mexicans' skill with their hands and love of color, beauty, fun and tradition are expressed most ubiquitously in their myriad appealing *artesanías* (handicrafts). The highly decorative crafts that catch the eye in shops and markets today are counterparts to the splendid costumes, beautiful ceramics and elaborate jewelry used by the nobility of Aztec, Mayan and other pre-Hispanic cultures. Many modern craft techniques, designs and materials are easily traced to pre-Hispanic origins. It's no surprise that the areas producing the most exciting *artesanías* are often those with prominent indigenous populations, in states such as Chiapas, Guerrero, México, Michoacán, Nayarit, Oaxaca, Puebla and Sonora. Selling folk art to tourists and collectors has been a growing business for Mexican artisans since before WWII.

TEXTILES

If you get out to some of Mexico's indigenous villages you'll be intrigued by the variety of intensely colorful, intricately decorated everyday attire, differing from area to area and often village to village. Traditional costume – more widely worn by women than men – serves as a mark of the community to which a person belongs. Much laborious, skillful work goes into creating such clothing.

Four main types of women's garments have been in use since long before the Spanish conquest:

Enredo A wraparound skirt, almost invisible if worn beneath a long *huipil.*

Faja A waist sash that holds the *enredo* in place.

Huipil A sleeveless tunic, often reaching as low as the thighs or ankles, though some are shorter and may be tucked into a skirt. The *huipil* is found mainly in the southern half of the country.

Quechquémitl A shoulder cape with an opening for the head, now worn mainly in the center and north of the country.

DID YOU KNOW?

Diamond shapes on some *huipiles* from San Andrés Larrainzar, in Chiapas, represent the universe of the villagers' Mayan ancestors, who believed that the earth was a cube and the sky had four corners.

Blouses, introduced by Spanish missionaries, are now often embroidered with just as much care and detail as the more traditional garments.

The *rebozo,* which probably appeared in the Spanish era, is a long shawl that may cover the shoulders or head or be used for carrying. The male equivalent of the *rebozo,* also dating from the Spanish era, is the *sarape,* a blanket with an opening for the head.

Some garments are woven or embroidered with a web of stylized animal, human, plant and mythical shapes that can take months to complete.

The basic materials of indigenous weaving are cotton and wool, though synthetic fibers are now common too. Dye, too, is often synthetic today, but some natural dyes are still in use or are being revived – deep blues from the indigo plant; reds and browns from various woods; reds, pinks and purples from the cochineal insect (chiefly used in Oaxaca state).

The basic indigenous weaver's tool – used only by women – is the backstrap loom *(telar de cintura),* on which the warp (long) threads are stretched between two horizontal bars, one of which is fixed to a post or tree, while the other is attached to a strap that goes around the weaver's lower back; the weft (cross) threads are then woven in. A variety of sophisticated techniques is used to weave amazing patterns into the cloth. The *huipiles* of indigenous women in the southern states of Oaxaca and Chiapas are among Mexico's most intricate and eye-catching garments.

Indigenous costume and its patterning may have a magical or religious role, usually of pre-Hispanic origin. Among the Huichol people, who live in a remote region on the borders of Nayarit, Jalisco and Durango states, waist sashes are identified with snakes, which are themselves symbols of rain and fertility, so the wearing of a waist sash can be a symbolic prayer for rain.

One textile art that's practiced by men is weaving on a treadle loom, a machine introduced to Mexico by the Spanish, which is operated by foot pedals. The treadle loom can weave wider cloth than the backstrap loom and tends to be used for blankets, rugs, wall hangings, *rebozos, sarapes* and skirt material. It allows for great intricacy in design. Mexico's most famous rug-weaving village is Teotitlán del Valle, Oaxaca.

The 'yarn paintings' of the Huichol people – created by pressing strands of wool or acrylic yarn onto a wax-covered board – make for colorful and unique decorations. The scenes resemble visions experienced under the influence of the drug peyote, which is central to Huichol culture.

Chloe Sayer's fascinating *Arts and Crafts of Mexico,* 1990, traces the evolution of crafts from pre-Hispanic times to the present, with many fine photos.

CERAMICS

Because of its durability, pottery has told us much of what we know about Mexico's ancient cultures. Today the country still has many small-scale potters' workshops, turning out everything from the plain cooking pots to elaborate decorative pieces that are true works of art.

One highly attractive variety of Mexican pottery is Talavera, made chiefly in Puebla and Dolores Hidalgo and characterized by bright colors (blue and yellow are often prominent) and floral designs. Another very distinctive Mexican ceramic form is the *árbol de la vida* (tree of life). These elaborate candelabra-like objects, often a meter or more high, are molded by hand and decorated with numerous tiny figures of people, animals, plants and so on. The Garden of Eden is a common subject, but trees of life may be devoted to any theme. Some of the best are made in Acatlán de Osorio and Izúcar de Matamoros, Puebla, and Metepec, in the state of México. Metepec is also the source of colorful clay suns.

The Guadalajara suburbs of Tonalá and Tlaquepaque are also renowned pottery centers, producing a wide variety of ceramics.

MASKS

Two mouthwateringly illustrated books on crafts are *Mask Arts of Mexico*, 1995, by Ruth D Lechuga and Chloe Sayer, two experts in the field, and the recent *Mexican Textiles* by Masako Takahashi (2003).

Like so many other Mexican crafts, mask-making dates back to pre-Hispanic times. Masks were and are worn for magical purposes in dances, ceremonies and shamanistic rites: the wearer temporarily becomes the creature, person or deity whose mask he wears. Today, these dances often have a curious mixture of pre-Hispanic and Christian or Spanish themes. A huge range of masks is employed and you can admire their artistry at museums in cities such as San Luis Potosí, Zacatecas, Morelia and Colima, and at shops and markets around the country. The southern state of Guerrero has probably the broadest range of fine masks.

Wood is the basic material of most masks, but papier-mâché, clay, wax and leather are also used. Mask makers often paint or embellish their masks with real teeth, hair, feathers or other adornments. 'Tigers' – often looking more like leopards or jaguars – are fairly common, as are other animals and birds, actual and mythical, and masks depicting Christ, devils, and Europeans with comically pale, wide-eyed, mustachioed features.

Today, masks are also made for hanging on walls.

LACQUERWARE & WOODWORK

Gourds, the hard shells of certain squash-type fruits, have been used in Mexico since antiquity as bowls, cups and small storage vessels. Today they serve many other uses, including children's rattles, maracas and even hats. The most eye-catching gourd decoration technique is the lacquer process, in which the outside of the gourd is coated with layers of paste or paint, each left to harden before the next is applied. The final layer is painted with the artisan's chosen design, then coated with oil varnish to seal the lacquer. All this makes the gourd nonporous and, to some extent, heat resistant.

Wood, too, can be lacquered, and most lacquerware you'll see in Mexico today is pine or a sweetly scented wood from the remote town of Olinalá, Guerrero. Olinalá boxes, trays, chests and furniture are lacquered by the *rayado* method, in which designs are created by scraping off part of the top coat of paint to expose a different-colored layer below.

Among the finest wooden crafts made in Mexico are the polished *palo fierro* (ironwood) carvings of the Seri people of Sonora. The Seri work the hard wood into dramatic human, animal and sea-creature shapes. Also attractive are the brightly painted copal dragons and other imaginary beasts produced by villagers around Oaxaca city.

Paracho, Michoacán, turns out Mexico's finest guitars, as well as violins, cellos and other musical instruments.

BARK PAINTINGS

Colorful paintings on *amate*, paper made from tree bark, are sold in countless souvenir shops. Many are humdrum productions for an undiscriminating tourist market, but others qualify as genuine art, showing village life in skillful detail. Bark paper has been made in Mexico since pre-Hispanic times, when some codices – pictorial manuscripts – were painted on it. The skill survives only among women in one small, remote area of central Mexico, where the states of Hidalgo, Puebla and Veracruz converge. One chief source of the paper is the village of San Pablito. Most of the product is bought by Nahua villagers from the state of Guerrero, who have been creating bark paintings since the 1960s.

JEWELRY & METALWORK

Some ancient Mexicans were expert metalsmiths and jewelers, but the Spanish banned indigenous people from working gold and silver for a time during the colonial period. Indigenous artisanship was revived in the 20th century – most famously in Taxco, by the American William Spratling, who initiated a silver-craft industry that now supplies more than 300 shops in the town. Silver is much more widely available than gold in Mexico, and is fashioned in all manner of styles and designs, with artistry ranging from the dully imitative to the superb.

Precious stones are less common than precious metals. True jade, beloved of ancient Mexicans, is a rarity; most 'jade' jewelry is actually jadeite, serpentine or calcite.

Oaxaca city is the center of a thriving craft of tinplate, stamped into low relief and painted in hundreds of attractive, colorful, small designs.

RETABLOS

An engaging Mexican custom is to adorn the sanctuaries of saints or holy images with *retablos* (also called *exvotos*), small paintings giving thanks to a saint for answered prayers. Typically done on small sheets of tin, but sometimes on glass, wood or cardboard, these *retablos* depict these miracles in touchingly literal images painted by their beneficiaries. They may show a cyclist's hair's-breadth escape from a hurtling bus or an invalid rising from a sickbed, beside a representation of the saint and a brief message along the lines of 'Thanks to San Milagro for curing my rheumatism – María Suárez, June 6, 1999.' The Basílica de Guadalupe in Mexico City, the Santuario de Plateros near Fresnillo in Zacatecas and the church at Real de Catorce in San Luis Potosí state all have fascinating collections of *retablos*.

FESTIVAL CRAFTS

Some folk art is produced for specific occasions. Mexicans' obsession with skull and skeleton motifs, by which they continually remind themselves of their own mortality, reaches a crescendo in the days before Día de Muertos (Day of the Dead, November 2). Families build altars in their homes, and stores and markets fill with miniature coffins, skulls and skeletons made of chocolate, candy, paper, cardboard or clay, many of them engaged in highly un-skeletonlike activities such as riding bicycles, playing music or getting married!

Most Mexican children's birthdays would be incomplete without a piñata, a large, brightly decorated star, animal, fruit or other figure, constructed around a clay pot or papier-mâché mold. At party time, the piñata is stuffed with small toys, sweets or fruit and suspended on a rope. Blindfolded children take turns bashing it with a stick until it breaks open and showers everyone with the gifts inside. Piñatas also are broken after the traditional pre-Christmas processions called *posadas*, held in some towns. Another Christmas craft is the creation of *nacimientos* (nativity scenes) in homes or town plazas. Clay or wood figures of the personages in these scenes may be reused year after year. Some larger-scale *nacimientos* even feature live sheep and goats.

> 'Mexicans' obsession with skull and skeleton motifs reaches a crescendo in the days before Día de Muertos (Day of the Dead)'

Environment

Mexico is one of the most geographically and biologically diverse countries on earth, home to more than 1000 bird species, 400 mammals, 700 reptiles (more than any other country), and about 26,000 plants – in each case, about 10% of the total number of species on the planet, on just 1.4% of the earth's land. Unfortunately, more than 1200 species are threatened or in danger of extinction.

Ron Mader's *Mexico – Adventures in Nature* has practical information on visiting some 60 sites of natural interest all around Mexico.

THE LAND

Covering almost two million sq km, Mexico is big: it's nearly 3500km as the crow flies (4600km by road) from Tijuana in the northwest to Cancún in the southeast. Its spectacularly rugged topography not only determines the possible routes of travel but has yielded a diversity of regional cultures and ecosystems that is one of the most fascinating aspects of travel here.

The northern half of Mexico is dominated by a southern extension of the mountains and uplands of the western half of the USA. In Mexico this elevated zone takes the form of a group of broad central plateaus, known collectively as the Altiplano Central, fringed by mountain chains – the Sierra Madre Occidental on the west and the Sierra Madre Oriental on the east. The Altiplano Central rises in altitude from about 1000m in the north to more than 2000m in central Mexico. Its northern part, most of which is a sparsely vegetated desert, the Desierto Chihuahuense (Chihuahuan Desert), extends northward into Texas and New Mexico; the southern part of the Altiplano is mostly a series of rolling hills and broad valleys and includes some of the best farm and ranch land in Mexico, north of Mexico City.

Routes through the mountain chains fringing the Altiplano Central are tortuous and rare. Only two traverse the wide and rugged Sierra Madre Occidental: the Ferrocarril Chihuahua-Pacífico (Chihuahua-Pacific Railway), which runs through the awesome canyon country of the Barranca del Cobre (Copper Canyon); and the dramatic Hwy 40 from Durango to Mazatlán.

Narrow coastal plains lie between the *sierras madre* and the sea. The Gulf Coast plain, an extension of a similar plain in Texas, is crossed by many rivers flowing down from the Sierra Madre Oriental. On the west side of Mexico, a relatively dry coastal plain stretches south from the US border almost to Tepic, in Nayarit state. Its northern end is part of a second great desert straddling the Mexico-US border – the Desierto Sonorense (Sonoran Desert). This desert also extends down onto the 1300km peninsula Baja California, which is divided from 'mainland' Mexico by the Sea of Cortez (Golfo de California). Baja California's mountainous spine is a southward extension of the coastal ranges of California, USA.

DID YOU KNOW?

Mexico's youngest volcano, Paricutín (2800m), in Michoacán, only arose in 1943.

The two *sierras madre* meet where they run into the Cordillera Neovolcánica. This spectacular volcanic chain strung east-to-west across the middle of Mexico includes the active volcanoes Popocatépetl (5452m) and Volcán de Fuego de Colima (3820m), as well as the nation's other highest peaks – Pico de Orizaba (5611m) and Iztaccíhuatl (5286m). Mexico City lies in the heart of the volcanic country, in a broad valley surrounded by extinct and active volcanoes including Popocatépetl.

South of Cabo Corrientes (west of Guadalajara), the Pacific plain narrows to a thin strip as the coast turns more east than south. Between here and the central volcanic belt there's another mountain chain, the Sierra

Madre del Sur, which stretches west-to-east across the states of Guerrero and Oaxaca, ending at the Isthmus of Tehuantepec, the narrowest part of Mexico at just 220km wide. The north side of the isthmus is a wide, marshy plain, strewn with meandering rivers.

East of the isthmus, Mexico's southernmost state, Chiapas, rises sharply from a fertile Pacific plain called El Soconusco to highlands almost 3000m high, then falls away to lowland jungles that stretch into northern Guatemala. The jungle melts into a region of tropical savanna on the Yucatán Peninsula, a flat, low limestone platform separating the Gulf of Mexico from the Caribbean Sea. The tip of the peninsula is arid, almost desert-like.

WILDLIFE

From the whales and giant cacti of Baja California to the howler monkeys and toucans of the southeastern jungles, Mexico has an exotic and fascinating fauna and flora. You need to make an effort to see the best of it; sometimes you have to head for some pretty remote areas. Fortunately the possibilities for doing just this are greater than ever before, with a growing number of ecotourism and active tourism firms ready to take you out to the most exciting natural sites Mexico has to offer. You'll find details on all these places, and how to reach them, in this book's destination chapters.

Planeta.com (www .planeta.com) brims with information and links for those wanting to delve deeper into Mexico's flora, fauna and environment.

Animals

In the north, domesticated grazing animals have pushed the larger wild beasts, such as the puma (mountain lion), bobcat, wolf, deer and coyote, into isolated, often mountainous, pockets. Raccoons, armadillos and skunks are still fairly common, however. The Cuatro Ciénegas valley (p400), a strange oasis in the northern deserts, is renowned for its endemic species including several kinds of turtle and fish.

Baja California is famous for whale-watching in the early months of the year – gray whales swim 10,000km from the Arctic to breed in its coastal waters – but it's also a breeding ground for other big sea creatures such as sea lions and elephant seals. More than one-third of all the world's marine mammal species have been found in the Sea of Cortez. For more information on whale-watching hotspots, see California Gray Whales (p274).

Mexico's coasts, from Baja California to Chiapas and from the northeast to the Yucatán Peninsula, are among the world's chief breeding grounds for sea turtles. All eight species are in danger of extinction, and seven of them inhabit Mexican waters, some female turtles swimming huge distances (right across the Pacific Ocean in the case of some loggerhead turtles) to lay eggs on the beaches where they were born. The beaches of the smallest, most endangered sea turtle, the Kemp's ridley, are nearly all in the northeastern Mexican state of Tamaulipas (p380). By contrast, Playa Escobilla, near the Oaxaca town of Puerto Escondido, is one of the world's main nesting grounds for the least endangered turtle, the olive ridley. Some 700,000 turtles come ashore here in about a dozen *arribadas* (landfalls) between May and January.

DID YOU KNOW?

Killing sea turtles is illegal in Mexico, which has 122 protected nesting beaches. Even so, an estimated 400,000 eggs are taken illegally each year.

Dolphins play along much of the Pacific coast, while some coastal wetlands, mainly in the south of the country, are home to crocodiles or caimans. Underwater life is richest of all on the coral reefs off the Yucatán Peninsula's Caribbean coast, where there's superb diving and snorkeling.

Back on land, the surviving tropical forests of the southeast still harbor spider and two types of howler monkey (all endangered), jaguars, ocelots, tapirs, anteaters, peccaries (a type of wild pig), deer and some mean tropical reptiles, including boa constrictors. The big cats (all endangered species) are reduced to isolated pockets mainly in eastern Chiapas, though they also exist around Celestún in Yucatán. You may well see howler monkeys, or hear their eerie growls, near the Mayan ruins at Palenque (p816) and Yaxchilán (p826).

In all warm parts of Mexico you'll meet two harmless, though occasionally alarming, reptiles: the iguana, a lizard that can grow a meter or so long and comes in many different colors; and the gecko, a tiny, usually green lizard that may shoot out from behind a curtain or cupboard when disturbed. Geckos might make you jump, but they're good news because they eat mosquitoes.

Coastal Mexico is a huge bird habitat, especially on the estuaries, lagoons and islands of the northeast, the Yucatán Peninsula and the Pacific coast. Inland Mexico abounds with eagles, hawks and buzzards, and innumerable ducks and geese winter in the northern Sierra Madre Occidental.

Tropical species such as trogons, hummingbirds, parrots, parakeets and tanagers start to appear south of Tampico in the east of the country and from around Mazatlán in the west. The jungles and cloud forests of the southeast are still home to colorful macaws, toucans, parrots, guans and even a few quetzals. Yucatán has spectacular flamingo colonies at Celestún and Río Lagartos. Twenty of Mexico's 22 parrot and macaw species are classified at some level of risk.

Another unforgettable marvel is the Santuario Mariposa Monarca (p550) in Michoacán, where the trees and earth turn orange when millions of monarch butterflies arrive every winter.

Plants

Northern Mexico's deserts are sparsely vegetated with cacti, agaves, yucca, scrub and short grasses. Between the deserts and the mountains a lot of land has been turned over to irrigation or grazing, or has become wasteland, but there are still natural grasslands dotted with mesquite, a hardy bush of the bean family. Baja California, because of its isolation, has a rather specialized and diverse flora, from the 20m-high cardón, the world's tallest cactus, to the bizarre boojum tree (see Baja Biodiversity p255).

The Sierra Madre Occidental and Oriental, the mountains of central Mexico and the Sierra Madre del Sur still have big stretches of pine forest and (at lower elevations) oak forest. In the southern half of the country, high-altitude pine forests are often covered in clouds, turning them into cloud forests, an unusual environment with lush, damp vegetation, an enormous variety of colorful wildflowers, and epiphytes growing on tree branches. The Sierra Norte (p730) of Oaxaca and El Triunfo Biosphere Reserve (p834) in Chiapas preserve outstanding cloud forests.

The natural vegetation of much of the low-lying areas of southeast Mexico is evergreen tropical forest (rain forest in parts). This forest is dense and diverse, with ferns, epiphytes, palms, tropical hardwoods such as mahogany, and fruit trees such as the mamey and the *chicozapote* (sapodilla), which yields *chicle* (natural chewing gum). Despite ongoing destruction, the Selva Lacandona (Lacandón Jungle) in eastern Chiapas is the largest remaining tropical forest area in the country, contributing a large number of Chiapas state's 10,000 plant species. The Yucatán Peninsula changes from rain forest in the south to dry thorny forest in the north, with its thorny bushes and small trees (including many acacias) resembling the predominant vegetation of the dry Pacific coastal plain.

PARKS & RESERVES

Mexico has some spectacular national parks and other protected areas – about 8% (144,000 sq km) of its territory is under some category or other

---

Dedicated birders who can read Spanish should seek out *Aves de México* by Roger Tory Peterson and Edward L Chalif. English-language alternatives are Ernest Preston Edwards' *Birds of Mexico & Adjacent Areas*, and *Birds of Mexico & Northern Central America* by Steve NG Howell and Sophie Webb.

DID YOU KNOW?

More than 900 of the world's 1500 or so cactus species are found in Mexico; 118 of them are threatened or endangered.

In *Oaxaca Journal*, scientist Oliver Sacks travels to Oaxaca, home to 700 fern varieties, and makes quirky, amusing observations, not only of a scientific nature but also on the fern fanatics he traveled with.

YOU CAN HELP

You can do your bit for Mexico's environment by not buying turtle, iguana, crocodile or black coral products, by not disturbing coral or nesting turtles, and by not collecting wild cacti, their seeds or wild orchids. You can also patronize projects that promote sustainable development. If the human inhabitants of forests and wetlands can earn a living from hosting low-impact ecotourism, then they may not cut down their forests or fish their lagoons dry. Many ecologically conscious enterprises in Mexico are community-run, which ensures that any profit made from your visit goes to the people you have visited (who are usually poor), and not to entrepreneurs from elsewhere.

of federal, state or municipal protection. Sadly, governments have never had the money to properly police protected areas against unlawful hunting, logging, farming, grazing or species collection.

National Parks

Mexico's 64 national parks *(parques nacionales)* total around 14,000 sq km. Many are tiny (smaller than 10 sq km) and most were created between 1934 and 1940, often for their archaeological, historical or recreational value rather than for ecological reasons. Some have no visitor infrastructure and draw few people; others are alive with weekend picnickers. Despite illegal logging, hunting and grazing, national parks have succeeded in protecting some big tracts of forest, especially the high coniferous forests of central Mexico.

Biosphere Reserves

Biosphere reserves *(reservas de la biósfera)* came into being as a result of a 1970s initiative by Unesco, which recognized that it was impractical for developing countries to take many ecologically important areas out of economic use. Biosphere reserves encourage sustainable local economic activities within the reserves, except in strictly protected core areas *(zonas núcleo)*. Today Mexico has 23 biosphere reserves, covering 87,610 sq km. Twelve of these are included in the Unesco biosphere reserves network; the others are recognized only at a national level. They range from deserts through dry and temperate forests to tropical forests and coastal areas. All focus on whole ecosystems with genuine biodiversity. Controlled tourism is seen as an important source of income in several of them, though they tend to be harder to access than national parks.

Mexican biosphere reserves have had varied success. Sian Ka'an on the Caribbean coast is one of the most successful, with some villagers turning from slash-and-burn farming and cattle grazing to drip irrigation and multiple crops, thus conserving the forest and increasing food yields. In addition, lobster fishers accepted a two-month off-season for egg-laying and began returning pregnant females to the sea. Sian Ka'an is one of two Mexican natural sites with Unesco World Heritage listing: the other is the whale sanctuaries within El Vizcaíno biosphere reserve in Baja California.

ENVIRONMENTAL ISSUES

From early in the 20th century, Mexican governments saw urban industrial growth, intensive chemical-based agriculture, and the destruction of forests for logging, grazing and development as the paths toward prosperity. A growth in environmental awareness since the 1970s has achieved only limited changes. Even when they have the will, governments rarely have the funds to implement major pro-environment programs. The Fox

Joel Simon's *Endangered Mexico* examines Mexico's varied environmental crises, from dumping on the northern border to the destruction of the Lacandón Jungle, with the benefit of excellent first-hand journalistic research – a compelling and frightening read.

Park/Reserve	Features	Activities	Best time to visit	Page
Parque Nacional Sierra San Pedro Mártir	canyons, granite peaks & pine forests, with desert bighorn sheep, bobcats, coyotes	hiking, camping	May-Oct	p268
Parque Nacional Pico de Orizaba	Mexico's highest peak (5611m)	volcano hiking & climbing	Oct-Mar	p686
Parque Nacional Iztaccíhuatl-Popocatépetl	live & extinct volcanic giants on rim of Valle de México	hiking, climbing	Oct-Feb	p193
Parque Nacional Volcán Nevado de Colima	live & extinct volcanoes; pumas, coyotes, pine forests	volcano hiking	Sep-Feb	p541
Parque Nacional Lagunas de Chacahua	coastal lagoons, beaches, waterbirds	bird-watching, boat trips	year-round	p747
Parque Nacional Cañón del Sumidero	800m-deep flooded canyon	boat trips, adventure sports	year-round	p792
Parque Marino Nacional Arrecifes de Cozumel	coral reefs, clear waters, awesome variety of marine life, beaches	diving, snorkeling	year-round	p915
Parque Marino Nacional Bahía de Loreto	islands, shores & waters of Sea of Cortez	kayaking, diving, snorkeling	year-round	p280
Reserva de la Biósfera Sian Ka'an	Caribbean coastal jungle, wetlands & islands with incredibly diverse wildlife	bird-watching, snorkeling & nature tours, mostly by boat	year-round	p933
Reserva de la Biósfera El Vizcaíno	deserts & coastal lagoons where gray whales calve	whale-watching, treks to pre-Hispanic rock art	Feb–early Apr	p273
Reserva de la Biósfera El Cielo	mountainous transition zone between tropical & temperate ecosystems; birds, bats, 40 orchid species	hiking, fishing, rafting, 4WD trips	year-round	p383
Reserva de la Biósfera Montes Azules	tropical jungle, lakes, rivers; jungle wildlife	hikes, kayaking, wildlife-watching	year-round	p811
Reserva de la Biósfera La Encrucijada	coastal wetlands & sand bars: monkeys, jaguars, waterfowl	boat trips, wildlife-watching, turtle-breeding center	year-round	p836
Reserva de la Biósfera El Triunfo	cloud forests; many rare birds including resplendent quetzals	guided hiking & bird-watching	Nov-Apr	p834
Reserva de la Biósfera Calakmul	rain forest with major Mayan ruins	visiting ruins, wildlife observation	year-round	p855
Reserva de la Biósfera Río Lagartos	estuary with large flamingo colony & other water birds	bird-watching	year-round	p893
Parque Nacional Barranca del Cobre	canyons up to 1879m deep, subtropical to alpine vegetation	hiking, mountain biking, horseback riding, bird-watching, vehicle tours	Sep-Oct, Feb-Jun	p322
Santuario Mariposa Monarca	forests festooned with millions of monarch butterflies	butterfly observation	Dec-Feb	p550

government's proposal to dam the Río Usumacinta, a great jungle water-way of southeastern Mexico, is redolent of grandiose 'man-over-nature' schemes from bygone eras.

Mexico's most infamous environmental problem is Mexico City itself, a huge and ever-growing high-altitude metropolis that is now even spreading over the mountainous rim of the Valle de México and threatening to fuse with the separate cities of Puebla and Toluca. The ring of mountains traps polluted air in the city, causing health problems for residents. In an effort to contain pollution levels, many vehicles are banned from the roads one day a week. Mexico City also consumes two-thirds of Mexico's electricity and, despite extracting its own groundwater at a rate that causes the earth to sink all over the city, it still has to pump up about a quarter of its water needs at great expense from outside the Valle de México. One of the rivers from which the capital draws water is the Lerma, which then receives sewage and industrial effluent from many other towns on its way into poor Lago de Chapala, Mexico's biggest natural lake, near Guadalajara. Lago de Chapala itself is shrinking because Guadalajara takes more water out of it than its feeder rivers now bring in.

Waste water leaves the city by a system of pumps and tunnels. Liquids from one 50km tunnel eventually feed into the Río Pánuco, which enters the Gulf of Mexico at Tampico carrying some 2000 tons of sewage a day. The Pánuco is far from alone among Mexican rivers in being polluted by sewage or industrial or agricultural wastes. Along the US border, about 45 million liters of sewage enter the Río Tijuana daily and flow into the Pacific Ocean off San Diego. The Rio Grande receives more than 370 million liters of sewage, pesticides and heavy metals a day, yet so much water is extracted from it that it dries up before reaching the sea.

Urban growth is not only problematic in the capital. In some expanding towns near the US border, little more than half the population has running water or sewerage.

In rural areas, a crucial issue is forest depletion. Before the Spanish conquest, about two-thirds of Mexico was forested, from cool pine-clad highlands to tropical jungle. Today only around 15% of this (300,000 sq km) remains, and this is being reduced at a rate of about 10,000 sq km a year for grazing, logging and farming. The southern states of Chiapas and Tabasco have probably lost more than half their tropical jungles since 1980, with concomitant habitat loss for many of Mexico's most exotic species of wildlife. Deforestation followed by cattle grazing or intensive agriculture on unsuitable terrain often leads to erosion, another problem for the Mexican countryside. Around 13% of Mexican land is considered severely eroded, and some 2000 sq km of fertile land are estimated to be lost annually.

Some large-scale tourism developments threaten to wreck fragile ecosystems. Developments along the 'Maya Riviera', south of Cancún, may kill off large sections of coral reef, mangrove swamp, turtle-nesting beaches and everything in between. In a few places, such as the Pueblos Mancomunados of Oaxaca, genuine ecotourism projects are trying to preserve environments by providing alternative, sustainable income for local people.

Environmental campaigning today is carried out mainly by small organizations working on local issues, though some successful campaigns in recent years have rested on broader-based support, even from outside Mexico. One was the defeat in 2000 of the plan for a giant saltworks at Laguna San Ignacio in Baja California, a gray whale breeding ground. Another was the annulment in 2001 of a large hotel project at the Caribbean beach of Xcacel, an important turtle nesting ground.

Bioplanet@ (www.bio planeta.com) is the site of an impressively wide grouping of community projects, companies, organizations and institutions committed to environmentally sustainable development in Mexico; it has an online purchasing facility for ecological products.

To see what a couple of big international conservation groups are up to in Mexico, see Conservation International (www .conservation.org) and Greenpeace (www .greenpeace.org.mx in Spanish).

Food & Drink Jim Peyton

James W Peyton has written three books related to Mexican cooking, including *El Norte: The Cuisine of Northern Mexico* and *Jim Peyton's New Cooking from Old Mexico*. In addition, he has written articles for *Fine Cooking*, *Texas Highways* and *Food & Wine*, appears on TV, conducts cooking classes and lectures on Mexican cuisine.

Regardless of your principal reason for visiting Mexico, if you delight in finding new and delicious foods, your culinary discoveries will be etched in your memory beside a bright, gold star. You can dine in an elegant restaurant in Mexico City where the meal's presentation was designed by an artist. You can sample local specialties in colorful, out-of-the-way villages, or time travel with chefs who are rediscovering the cuisines of pre-Hispanic Mexico. So vast and regional is Mexican cooking that your only challenge will be to get beyond the highlights.

For those whose culinary tastes run to the tried and true, and for whom a sprinkling of black pepper is enough heat, hotel dining rooms and restaurants catering to tourists offer delicious renditions of familiar salads, steaks, seafood and pasta, with the heat confined to little bowls on the side. Whatever your tastes, you will quickly learn that Mexicans are extremely knowledgeable about their cuisine, and ever conscious of its cultural importance. More importantly, you will discover that they are anxious to share it with you.

When the Spanish arrived in Mexico, they found a diet based on corn, beans, squash, chilies, wild game and fish. While Spanish soldiers brought meats, nuts, fruits, cheese and spices, they forgot to bring cooks! So, in the time-honored tradition of invading armies, they enlisted local women who promptly mixed the new ingredients with their own, then either misunderstood or ignored the instructions. The result was that the Spanish ingredients, instead of being made into Spanish foods, were used to create new versions of native dishes.

During the next, nearly 500 years, the two food cultures – with contributions from France, Africa and Spain's outposts in the East – continued to fuse, creating the cuisine with countless regional variations that you will enjoy during your stay. People from all cultures will find the vast majority of Mexican food appealing, partly because it has been influenced by so many of their own traditions.

AUTHORS' TOP 10 RESTAURANTS

The *Mexico* authors put together a list of their favorite restaurants throughout Mexico, based on food quality, ambience, location, popularity with locals and general greatness. Here are some of their top picks.

- **Cien Años** (p260) Tijuana
- **Café de Tacuba** (p150) Mexico City
- **Jardines de Xochimilco** (p306) Hermosillo
- **Fonda de Santa Clara** (p209) Puebla
- **La Pigua** (p850) Campeche
- **La Capilla** (p630) San Miguel de Allende
- **Mayambé** (p802) San Cristóbal de las Casas
- **Restaurante Los Danzantes** (p716) Oaxaca
- **El Sacromonte** (p520) Guadalajara
- **Cenaduria Antelia** (p480) Zihuatanejo

Today, Mexican cooking includes many aspects. The best known outside the country are the universally beloved *antojitos mexicanos,* literally 'little Mexican whims,' including tacos, enchiladas and quesadillas. In addition to *antojitos,* you will encounter Mexico's traditional dishes, including soups, *moles* and *pipianes* – special stews, often with more than 30 ingredients. Along Mexico's Gulf and Pacific coasts you will discover an amazing variety of creative seafood dishes. For those who enjoy sophisticated, upscale dining, Mexico's contemporary cooking style, *nueva cocina mexicana* (new Mexican cooking) will be a gift from the food gods.

STAPLES & SPECIALTIES

Mexicans traditionally eat three meals each day, but not always at the time some visitors are accustomed to. *Desayuno* (breakfast) conforms to the normal schedule, and is eaten any time between about 7am and 10am. It consists of anything from coffee and *pan dulce* (delicious 'sweet breads') to the ever-present *huevos rancheros* (a corn tortilla with fried eggs and a sauce of tomato, chili and onion) and a large selection of omelettes, filled with everything from squash blossoms to *chorizo* (a Mexican-style sausage). You will also find *chilaquiles,* made by heating meat or chicken in a red or green chili sauce with crispy tortilla chips, and topping it with cheese and often with a fried egg or dollop of cream. Tropical fruits, yogurt and granola are also popular all over Mexico, and the latter two have a delightfully rich, homemade quality. Coffee, tea, milk, and fresh-squeezed juices are commonly served with breakfast, as is *pan tostado* (toast).

The *comida* (lunch) is the main meal of the day, and is usually taken between about 1:30pm and 4pm. Nevertheless, restaurants catering to tourists often open by 11:30am or noon. (A terrific way to beat the crowds is to arrive between 1pm and 1:30pm.) This meal usually consists of an appetizer, soup or salad, a main course of meat, poultry or seafood, usually served with rice and/or beans and steaming hot tortillas. Dessert can be anything from pastry to flan, other confections and fresh fruit. While Mexicans prefer to spend a relaxing two or more hours over this meal, they have not escaped the stress of modern life, and there are ample coffee shops and fast food outlets available for quick meals at nearly any time.

The *cena* (supper) in Mexico usually consists of a light meal, perhaps some soup or a few tacos around 8pm or 9pm. However, most restaurants are happy to serve the larger dinner that so many visitors desire, throughout the normal evening hours.

Besides being great entertainment, *Like Water for Chocolate* conveys the importance of food in Mexico, and the magic-realism used in the book/film showcases the way so many Mexicans view life.

Regional Specialties

If you are at all adventurous in culinary matters, what you eat in Mexico will depend to a large extent on where you are. The country has nearly every imaginable climate. Each produces different foods and has developed a distinctive regional cuisine. Here are some of the most famous and interesting (for Oaxaca cuisine, see p715).

IN & AROUND MEXICO CITY

Tlacoyos are turnover-shaped *antojitos* made with smooth, fragrant corn dough – sometimes from blue or green corn – filled with everything from squash blossoms to *huitlacoche* (see 'Mexican Truffles', p84) and cooked to a crispy, golden perfection on ungreased griddles.

Sábana means 'sheet,' and that perfectly describes these fork-tender, tenderloin steaks that are pounded to a diameter of up to one foot and less than ⅛-inch thick.

MEXICAN TRUFFLES

Huitlacoche, sometimes spelled 'cuitlacoche', is a delicacy that is virtually unknown outside Mexico. It's actually an inky-black fungus that grows on corn kernels and is used as a filling for everything from crepes to quesadillas. Its promoters often refer to it as 'Mexican truffles,' or 'corn mushrooms.' *Huitlacoche* imparts both its enchanting flavor and striking color to everything it touches, and is found most often around Mexico City and Puebla.

Crepas de flor de calabaza are similar to French dinner crepes but made into exotic temptations with their fillings of squash blossoms and inky *huitlacoche*.

Barbacoa (Mexican-style barbecue) is often still smoked in earthen pits. Around Mexico City, it is usually made by smoking seasoned lamb wrapped in leaves of the maguey plant (the agave from which both tequila and mezcal are made).

Mexico City is full of *torterías* where Mexico's unique sandwiches (called *tortas*) are served.

PUEBLA

Mole poblano is Mexico's most famous dish, and one that represents the mixing of Spanish and indigenous Mexican cultures. Mexico's second most famous dish (and the most expensive), *chiles en nogada*, is also from Puebla.

Tacos árabes are tacos made with thin, tortilla-like Arab bread, filled with pork grilled with herbs on huge vertical skewers, and served with *jocoque* (ho-co-kay), a type of yogurt, honey, and sometimes herb-infused olive oil.

Cemitas are *tortas* made with hollowed-out brioche-type rolls.

See p208 for more on these specialties.

THE YUCATÁN

The Yucatán's cuisine has its roots with the Maya, rather than the Aztecs and other tribes, and is quite distinct.

Cochinita pibil literally means 'pork, pit-style.' Pork is marinated in a *recado* (regional spice rub) wrapped in banana leaves, and smoked or baked. *Pollo pibil* is a version of *cochinita pibil* made with chicken.

Sopa de lima is lime soup made with a flavorful broth, shredded chicken, special limes found only in the Yucatán, and sizzling hot, fried corn tortilla strips.

Huevos motuleños is fried eggs sandwiched between quickly seared corn tortillas and topped with ham, green peas, tomato salsa and grated cheese.

Papadzules is a light and tasty cross between enchiladas and soft tacos – corn tortillas are dipped in a pumpkin seed sauce and rolled around chopped hard-boiled egg and garnished with a mild tomato sauce and pumpkin seed oil.

Diana Kennedy is the acknowledged doyenne of Mexican food. Her latest book, *From My Mexican Kitchen: Techniques and Ingredients*, captures the essence of Mexico's complex food, and manages to make it available to cooks outside the country.

MICHOACÁN

Enchiladas de plaza, a specialty of the city of Morelia, consists of cheese enchiladas served with poached and fried chicken, garnished with potatoes, carrots, onion and chilies.

Pescado blanco (literally 'white fish') is found in the city of Pátzcuaro. A mild freshwater fish is sautéed in a filmy coating of egg and often served *al mojo de ajo* (with minced garlic sautéed in olive oil). *Charales* are tiny, dried fish used in appetizers, tacos and soup.

Carnitas are chunks of pork simmered in lard until crisp and tender, then served with corn tortillas and guacamole. They are lighter than they sound, but don't tell your cardiologist!

Sopa tarasca, named for the local Tarascan people, is perhaps the original and best version of tortilla soup. *Uchepos* are the region's delicious tamales, made with fresh rather than dried corn.

VERACRUZ

Veracruz, where the Spanish first arrived, maintains strong Spanish food traditions, mixed with those of the Caribbean's African-based food traditions, and those of the original inhabitants. *Huauchinango veracruzana* (red snapper Veracruz-style) is a dish where the fish is broiled or sautéed and served with a sauce of tomatoes, olives, capers and vinegar.

GUADALAJARA

Guadalajara is often said to be the most Mexican of cities in that it embodies the mestizo (combination of Spaniard and indigenous Mexican), and it certainly does so with its food.

Pozole is made by simmering hominy with meat (see p479). *Birria* is a regional *barbacoa* where lamb seasoned with chili is smoked, then steamed and served with a very special broth.

NORTHERN MEXICO

Although it encompasses a vast, diverse area from the Pacific Ocean to the Gulf, it has many similar foods, many of which are prepared *al carbón* (char-broiled over mesquite coals) and served with flour tortillas as often as corn.

Tacos al carbón consists of tortillas filled with char-broiled meats and poultry. In Tijuana you will find them made from New York cut steak, and in other areas from different cuts of meat and chicken.

Chimichangas (deep fried burritos) are made with huge, paper-thin *tortillas de agua* (water tortillas) and filled with minced, sun-dried beef called either *carne seca* or *machacado.*

Black bass is referred to by its English name. The very fresh fish come from Chihuahua's reservoirs and rival the popularity of beef.

Cabrito al pastor (shepherd-style kid) is a specialty of Monterrey. The whole animal is cooked on a spit over glowing coals.

In *Zarela's Veracruz,* restaurateur and chef Zarela Martinez has provided the perfect guide to the regional cooking of Veracruz. Part travelogue, it is filled with anecdotes and recipes from places you can visit, and is a terrific resource for anyone planning a trip to the area.

WE DARE YOU

A current culinary renaissance in Mexico features pre-Hispanic foods that are often accompanied by copious amounts of tequila's fiery cousin, mezcal. One of the most popular foods is *chapulines* ('grasshoppers' - purged of digestive matter and dried, you will be happy to hear). They come in large and small sizes, with the latter often smoked, and are served in many ways: from a taco filling to sautéed in butter and flamed in brandy. The small, smoked variety are actually quite tasty, and are less likely to leave bits of carapace and feelers protruding from your teeth!

Jumiles are beetles, actually a type of stink bug, esteemed in central Mexico during their season in late fall and early winter. They are usually either ground with chilies, tomatoes and *tomatillos* to make a sauce, or are used as a taco filling, either toasted or live. In discussing the latter, Diana Kennedy says in *My Mexico,* 'The more fleet-footed ones have to be swept back into the mouth and firmly crunched to prevent them from escaping.' The flavor is unforgettable by nature and forgettable by choice.

Other favorites include stewed iguana, which tastes like a cross between chicken and pork, as do armadillos whose copious, small bones are their most irritating quality.

Parrillada is a platter heaped with a selection of char-broiled beef and poultry in the state of Coahuila – the ultimate mixed grill.

DRINKS
Alcoholic

Before the Spanish arrived, two of Mexico's most important drinks were tapped from maguey (agave) plants. *Aguamiel* is the nonalcoholic, sweet juice as it comes straight from the plant. After fermentation it becomes pulque, a delicious beverage with the alcohol content of beer that was consumed by indigenous Mexicans for more than 5000 years. Now it's often flavored with coconut and other fruits. It is not bottled, and is found almost exclusively in special (often seedy) bars called pulquerías (see p188).

After their arrival in Mexico, Spaniards quickly discovered that by roasting the hearts of agaves, then extracting, fermenting, and distilling the liquids they could produce fiery alcoholic beverages called tequila (see p528) and mezcal (see p719).

Contrary to popular belief, the margarita is not the most popular way to drink tequila in Mexico. That ubiquitous cocktail, whose origin is the subject of several legends, is largely an American invention whose popularity has recently spread south of the border. Outside establishments accustomed to tourists, finding a properly made margarita can still be problematic, and a tequila sour is often a safer bet. Tequila is customarily imbibed straight, followed either by a lick of salt and a bite of lime wedge, or by a chaser of *sangrita*, a mixture of orange juice, grenadine, a dash of chili, and sometimes a dollop of tomato juice. Mezcal, whose finest examples are produced in Oaxaca, is traditionally taken neat.

> 'Contrary to popular belief, the margarita is not the most popular way to drink tequila in Mexico'

During the 19th century beer, made by immigrants with roots in Germany and Switzerland, became popular in Mexico. To this day, the country produces some of the world's best examples, with Bohemia, Corona, Dos Equis, Pacífica, Tecate and Modelo being favorite brands.

Brandy is popular all over Mexico. Although not of the quality of the better French cognacs, Presidente, Madero and Viejo Vergel produce decent renditions at very reasonable prices.

Spain, in an effort to reduce competition to its home industry, carefully controlled the production and use of wine in Mexico, much of which was restricted to use for Catholic communion. Nevertheless, the family of President Madero (also of brandy fame) operated a winery for many years, originally begun in 1597 near Parras. Although its production has either dwindled or ceased, there has been a renaissance of wine-making in Mexico, particularly in Baja near Ensenada (see p263) and near Fresnillo in Zacatecas. Often run by international corporations, the quality of Mexican wines is making great leaps. Ask your waiter for recommendations, and conduct your own taste test! But be aware that wine drinking in Mexico is still pretty much restricted to upper-class establishments, and that in other spots the word *vino* is often used to include distilled alcoholic drinks in general.

Mexico is full of lesser-known alcoholic beverages, many of them generically called *aguardiente* and a bit on the crude side, but others that are quite interesting. There is *rompope*, a type of eggnog originally developed in monasteries and convents that is bottled throughout the country. In Baja, a sweet liqueur called Damiana is made from an herb with purported aphrodisiac qualities, that makes a terrific addition to margaritas.

Nonalcoholic

Mexico has a long tradition of good nonalcoholic drinks. Many of them are teas made from herbs and other items steeped in boiling water and mixed with sugar. The most popular include *tamarindo,* made with tamarind pods, and *jamaica,* made with dried hibiscus leaves.

Aguas frescas, literally 'fresh waters,' are a mix of pulped fruits, corn meal or rice blended with water. *Horchata* is one made with melon fruit and seeds and/or rice, and limeade is ubiquitous. These delicious, fruity drinks are sold from large, keg-shaped, glass containers, often garnished with mint leaves. Note that although these are prepared with boiled water, sometimes the ice is untreated.

Mexicans also enjoy a variety of smoothies and milk shakes called *licuados,* made with milk, fruits, yogurt and honey. Orange juice, nearly always freshly squeezed, is available everywhere, as are juices of other fruits and vegetables. Many of these drinks are found in street *puestos* (stalls) and larger, bar-like establishments.

Some of the best coffee is the world is grown in Mexico, especially in Veracruz. Mexicans have a unique, traditional way of making it, called *café de olla* (coffee from the pot), where it is brewed in a special clay vessel with a raw sugar called *piloncillo. Café con leche* (coffee with milk) is very popular. Waiters will often pour both items at the table according to your instructions. For ordinary coffee, with cream on the side, simply ask for *café con crema* (ka-*fe* kon *kre*-ma).

Chocolate originated in Mexico, and Moctezuma, the last Aztec king, finished nearly every meal with a hot cup of it. Mexican chocolate often includes cinnamon and some crushed almonds, and has a unique flavor and texture. As a drink, it is mixed with milk or water and sugar, and whipped to a cappuccino-like froth with a decorative wooden implement called a *molinillo.* Sometimes a little ground cornmeal is added to create a delicious pre-Hispanic drink called *champurrado.*

DID YOU KNOW?

English sailors coined the term 'cocktail' upon discovering that their drinks in the Yucatán port of Campeche were stirred with the thin, dried roots of a plant called *cola de gallo,* which means 'cock's tail'.

CELEBRATIONS

The importance of food in Mexican celebrations cannot be overemphasized. When the Spanish arrived they were surprised to find many similarities between their own religious fasts and food traditions and those of the Aztecs. They were horrified to find ceremonies where blood mixed with ground amaranth was eaten in a manner resembling their own communions. One result was that amaranth, which was of great importance as the earliest ripening crop, was banned. To this day it is seldom used except in the famous *alegría* candies where amaranth seeds are mixed with honey.

Food is a vital aspect of virtually every celebration in Mexico. Perhaps the most important is Día de Muertos (see p58). In the week leading up to it, people bake and buy a special sweet bread called *pan de muertos* (bread of the dead) and make tamales, which are part of nearly every other celebration, as they were in pre-Hispanic times.

During Lent special meatless menus appear in restaurants. Favorites include *romeritos, revoltijo* and *tortas de camarón,* all of which are made with the special green vegetable *romeritos,* and dried shrimp. These same dishes are also popular during Holy Week and at Christmas. Another Easter favorite is *capirotada,* an elaborate pudding made with bread, cream, fruit, cinnamon, cheese, and brandy or rum. *Bacalao,* Spanish-style, dried codfish, is traditionally served at Christmas, as are the ubiquitous celebratory tamales, and turkey is a New Year's favorite.

WHERE TO EAT & DRINK

You will have a nearly dizzying array of places to eat in Mexico, from simple street vendor stalls called *puestos* to fine restaurants rivaling the world's best in both food and decor.

Hotel restaurants and cafés are a good bet for breakfast, with the former often offering opulent buffets. In the afternoon, you can choose anything from a *taquería* (a place specializing in tacos, sometimes with 20 or more different varieties) to upscale restaurants. In between are small, middle-class restaurants offering reasonably priced *comidas corridas* (prix-fixe menus). There are also *torterías*, specializing in sandwiches; *loncherías*, offering light meals like sandwiches and tacos; and cafés, resembling American coffee shops.

Within the central *mercados* (markets) you will find numerous small eating places called either *fondas* or *comedores* that serve everything from sandwiches to *comidas corridas*, and sweets, including ice cream. Most cities in Mexico also have branches of US fast-food outlets. You will find *panaderías* (bakeries) with traditional items all over Mexican towns; for a terrific light breakfast, dessert or snack, stop and pick up a selection. The system requires you to grab an aluminum tray and a pair of tongs, place your treats on the tray, and bring it to the cashier. You will be amazed at how much you get for so little cost.

'Adventurous food tastes will be attracted to the countless *puestos* or street stalls'

If you have adventurous food tastes you will be attracted to the countless *puestos* or street stalls. They offer tacos and other *antojitos* in every imaginable form – steamed or char-broiled corn, rotisserie-broiled chicken, creative hot dogs, seafood cocktails, ice cream, and just about anything else you can imagine. Many are very popular and well patronized, but hygiene can be a risk. Deciding whether to use them is a matter of judgment; those with a lot of customers are likely to be the best and safest.

It is a good idea to avoid food that spoils easily like mayonnaise, salads that may not have been properly washed, and fruit that has not been recently washed and peeled. Nevertheless, with a commonsense approach you should have no problems, other than what might be expected when you introduce new foods into your system.

Most 1st-class hotels have restaurants that serve a combination of typical Mexican meals and international favorites. Even restaurants catering mostly to tourists will usually serve authentic Mexican food, albeit a bit blander than the usual. Most restaurants that offer a full complement of meals throughout the day are open from 7am or 8am until 10pm to midnight. However, be aware that some of them may not begin serving lunch until 1pm or 1:30pm.

Both cantinas and bars serve alcoholic beverages, and are quite different. Cantinas are the traditional gathering place for men (women were actually barred from them by law until recently), and each one has its own culture: think the US TV show *Cheers*, with an edge (also see 'Welcome to the Cantina,' p157.) They are famous for their *botanas* (appetizers), which include things like pickled pigs' feet and dried shrimp soup. While women may now be allowed in cantinas, it is not recommended unless you are with a regular. Bars in Mexico fit the traditional definition of drinking places and range from upscale establishments appointed with leather, brass and stained glass, to the just plain sleazy. Instead of the more elaborate food items found in cantinas, bars usually serve only salty snacks.

TIPPING & TAXES

While a 15% IVA (value-added tax) is, by law, added to restaurant checks in Mexico, gratuities are not. Expected tips are about the same as those in the US, with 15% about the average.

VEGETARIANS & VEGANS

There is good and bad news for vegetarians traveling in Mexico, but ultimately it is mostly good. Before the Spanish arrived the people had a very low-fat, nearly totally vegetarian diet. However, following the conquest they became committed carnivores. These days, even medium-sized towns will usually have at least one vegetarian establishment and most restaurants have a fine selection of salads and vegetable side dishes, including beans and rice, that can be combined for a terrific meal.

More good news is that Mexico has many interesting vegetables such as the broccoli-like *huauzontles* and chewy greens called *romeritos*. *Nopalitos* (cactus paddles) are prepared many ways and are both delicious and a folk treatment for diabetes. Other common vegetables are *verdolagas* (purslane), Swiss chard and a variety of both domestic and wild mushrooms. *Chiles rellenos* stuffed with cheese can be a good bet if they have not been cooked in animal fat. There's also a plethora of both familiar and exotic fruits.

Mexican waiters are generally knowledgeable about what they serve and are anxious to please. However, they are often not aware of the specific requirements of vegetarians, and especially vegans, and may find the concept difficult to understand. Most Mexicans do without meat only because they can't afford it, and many Mexican vegetarians eat vegetables because they're healthy, not for ethical or philosophical reasons. So you must make your requirements very plain. One problem is that your server may believe he is bringing you a vegetarian meal when the items have been flavored with beef or chicken broth, or cooked in lard. The more upscale the restaurant, the better your chances of being understood and accommodated.

One website that does a comprehensive job of covering both Mexico and its foods is www.mexconnect.com.

WHINING & DINING

Mexicans adore children, and the country is a child-friendly place. Most waiters will cheerfully do anything special within reason to please your child, and virtually all restaurants have high chairs; just ask for a *silla para niños*. Mexican supermarkets carry a full range of American and international brands of baby food. For more on children, see the Directory chapter (p947).

HABITS & CUSTOMS

With a couple of exceptions, you will find that Mexican eating customs are similar to those in other Western countries. The *comida* is traditionally taken between 1:30pm and 4pm. It is meant to be a leisurely family or business affair and usually lasts at least two hours and up to three or four. However, the necessities of modern life mean that not everyone can do this, and many families are only able to follow this tradition on Sundays, and commonly do so. Try the Mexican schedule, and after a few days you may love it!

To obtain the full experience, plan on arriving about 2pm, and staying until at least 4pm. But no one will look askance if you order nothing but a small entree or appetizer, or grab a few tacos at a nearby *taquería*, and save your main meal for the evening. Nearly every meal is accompanied by a basket of hot tortillas; diners take one, usually the second from the top, and request a refill when the basket is nearly empty.

Mexico's attitude toward liquor is usually quite liberal. However, be aware that in many communities liquor cannot be sold on election days or when the president is visiting. Also, while alcoholic beverages are usually considered a normal part of life, some towns frown on drinking on the streets, and drinking while driving is a serious no-no!

DID YOU KNOW?

In addition to many other items, such as corn and turkey, two of the world's most beloved edibles, chocolate and vanilla, originally came from Mexico.

> **THE CHECK PLEASE!**
>
> Do not expect your meal check to be brought until you ask for it. That would be considered impolite, and the staff will often remain long after normal hours to accommodate guests taking time over coffee and brandy. Simply say *La cuenta por favor* or make the universal scribbling sign.

If you are invited to someone's home it is considered polite to bring a gift; a box of chocolates or a bottle of wine is perfect. Most people are aware that Mexicans are not always prompt, and being a half hour late or even more rarely causes notice, especially in Mexico City where traffic can be a serious problem. More promptness, however, is expected at restaurant meetings.

During Lent you will find restaurants offering special menus, many with interesting and delicious items that will appeal to vegetarians. During Holy Week, Mexicans often visit family or take vacations, and you may find smaller restaurants closed for the week.

Note that, unless given great provocation, it is de rigueur to treat waiters with respect.

COOKING COURSES

Two cooking schools, which offer quite different experiences, are heartily recommended. Seasons of My Heart is operated by well-known cookbook author Susana Trilling at her ranch just outside the city of Oaxaca. See p710 for more information.

Owned and operated by transplanted New Yorker Magda Bogin, Cocinar Mexicano (www.cocinarmexicano.com) is located in the enchanting village of Tepoztlán, near Mexico City. The program offers week-long classes that include transportation from Mexico City, luxury accommodations, nearly all meals, a market tour, attendance at a local fiesta, cooking lectures and demonstrations, workshops by guest chefs and hands-on cooking for US$2300 per week. Spanish language instruction is also available.

Jim Peyton's website, www.lomexicano.com, is updated quarterly and offers regional Mexican recipes, food-related travel articles and a large glossary of Mexican food terms.

EAT YOUR WORDS

In any foreign country, visitors who attempt to speak the language, even inexpertly, tend to endear themselves, and often enhance their experiences. It is the same in Mexico. For non-Spanish speakers, travel and dining in Mexico is usually no problem. However, a few words in Spanish indicate a respect for the locals and their culture, not to mention a willingness to risk embarrassment, and that can make a huge difference.

For pronunciation help, see p993.

Useful Phrases

Are you open?   *¿Está abierto?*
e·*sta* a·*byer*·to

When are you open?   *¿Cuando está abierto?*
kwan·do e·*sta* a·*byer*·to

Are you now serving breakfast/lunch/   *¿Ahora, está sirviendo desayuno/la comida/*
dinner?   *la cena?*
a·o·ra e·*sta* ser·vyen·do de·sa·yoo·no/la ko·mee·da/la se·na

I'd like to see a menu.   *Quisiera ver la carta/el menú.*
kee·*sye*·ra ver la *kar*·ta/el me·*noo*

Do you have a menu in English?   *¿Tienen un menú en inglés?*
tye·nen oon me·*noo* en een·*gles*

Can you recommend something?   *¿Puede recomendar algo?*
   pwe·de re·ko·men·*dar* al·*go*

I'm a vegetarian.   *Soy vegetariano/a.* (m/f)
   soy ve·khe·te·*rya*·no/a

I can't eat anything with meat or poultry   *No puedo comer algo de carne o aves,*
products, including broth.   *incluyendo caldo.*
   no *pwe*·do ko·*mer* al·go de *kar*·ne o a·ves een·kloo·*yen*·do kal·do

I'd like mineral water/natural bottled water.   *Quiero agua mineral/agua purificada.*
   kee·*ye*·ro a·gwa mee·ne·*ral/a*·gwa poo·ree·fee·*ka*·da

Is it (chili) hot?   *¿Es picoso?*
   es pee·*ko*·so

The check, please.   *La cuenta, por favor.*
   la *kwen*·ta por fa·*vor*

Menu Decoder

antojitos – 'little Mexican whims,' corn- and tortilla-based snacks like tacos and gorditas

arroz mexicana – pilaf-style rice with a tomato base

buñuelos – tortilla-size fritters with a sweet, anise sauce

carnitas – pieces of pork simmered in lard until golden brown and very tender

chilaquiles – fried tortilla strips cooked with a red or green chili sauce, and sometimes meat and eggs

chile relleno – chili stuffed with meat or cheese, usually fried with egg batter

chiles en nogada – mild green chilies stuffed with meat and fruit, fried in batter and served with a sauce of cream, ground walnuts and cheese

cochinita pibil – pork, marinated in chilies, wrapped in banana leaves, and pit-cooked or baked

coctel de frutas – fruit cocktail

costillas de res – beef ribs

crepas – crepes (thin pancakes)

enchiladas – corn tortillas dipped in chili sauce,wrapped around meat or poultry, and garnished with cheese

ensalada – salad

filete – filet

filete al la tampiqueña – steak, Tampico style, a thin tenderloin, grilled and served with chili strips and onion, a quesadilla and enchilada.

gorditas – small circles of tortilla dough, fried and topped with meat and/or cheese

guacamole – mashed avocado, often with lime juice, onion, tomato and chili

huachinango veracruzana – Veracruz-style red snapper with a sauce of tomatoes, olives, vinegar and capers

huevos motuleños – fried eggs sandwiched between corn tortillas, and topped with peas, tomato, ham and cheese.

huevos rancheros – fried eggs served on a corn tortilla, topped with a sauce of tomato, chilies and onions

milanesa – thin slices of beef or pork, breaded and fried

mixiote – chili-seasoned lamb steamed in agave membranes or parchment

mole negro – chicken or pork in a very dark sauce of chilies, fruits, nuts, spices and chocolate

mole poblano – chicken or turkey in a sauce of chilies, fruits, nuts, spices and chocolate

nopalitos – sautéed or grilled, sliced cactus paddles

pechuga de pollo – breast of chicken

pipián verde – stew of chicken, with ground squash seeds, chilies and tomatillos

pozole – soup or thin stew of hominy, meat, vegetables and chilies

pulpos – octopus

puntas de filete al albañil – beef tips stewed with smoky chipotle chilies

quesadillas – cheese folded between tortillas and fried or grilled

queso fundido – cheese melted, often with chorizo or mushrooms, and served as an appetizer with tortillas

sábana – filet mignons pounded paper thin and seared
sopa de ajo – garlic soup
sopa de cebolla – onion soup
sopa de pollo – chicken soup
sopes – a type of gordita
tacos – filling of meat, poultry or vegetables wrapped in a tortilla
tinga poblana – a stew of pork, vegetables and chilies

Food Glossary

a la parilla	grilled
a la plancha	pan-broiled
adobada	marinated with adobo (chili sauce)
agua	water
agua mineral	mineral water or club soda
agua purificado	bottled, uncarbonated water
al albañil	'bricklayer style' - served with a hot chili sauce
al carbón	char-broiled
al mojo de ajo	with garlic sauce
alambre	shish kebab
albóndigas	meatballs
arroz	rice
aves	poultry
azucar	sugar
biftec	steak
brocheta	shish kebab
cajeta	goat's milk and sugar boiled to a paste
calabacita	squash
calamar	squid
caldo	broth or soup
camarones	shrimp
cangrejo	crab
carne	meat
carne de puerco	pork
carne de res	beef
carnero	mutton
cebolla	onion
cecina	thin cut, partially dried meat, flavored with chili and sautéed or grilled
cerdo	pork
chalupas	open-faced, canoe-shaped cooked corn dough, topped with meat and chilies
chorizo	Mexican-style bulk sausage made with chili and vinegar
chuleta de puerco	pork chop
coco	coconut
cordero	lamb
crepas	crepes or thin pancakes
empanada	pastry turnover filled with meat, cheese, or fruits
empanizado	sautéed
flor de calabaza	squash blossom
fresa	strawberry
frito	fried
helado	ice cream
hígado	liver
huevos fritos	fried eggs
huevos revueltos	scrambled eggs

huitlacoche	corn mushrooms, a much esteemed fungus that grows on corn
jaiba	crab
jamón	ham
jugo de manzana	apple juice
jugo de naranja	orange juice
jugo de piña	pineapple juice
langosta	lobster
leche	milk
lengua	tongue
lomo	loin
lomo de cerdo	pork loin
mantequilla	butter
mariscos	seafood
menudo	stew of tripe
nieve	sorbet
ostras	oysters
pan	bread
papas	potatoes
papas fritas	french fries
pastel	cake
pato	duck
pechuga	breast
picadillo	a ground beef filling that often includes fruit and nuts
plña	pineapple
plátano	banana or plantain
platillo regional	regional specialty
pollo	chicken
postre	dessert
pulpos	octopus
queso	cheese
sopa	soup, either 'wet' or 'dry' as in rice and pasta
sope	a type of gordita
té de manzanillo	chamomile tea
té negro	black tea
tocino	bacon
toronja	grapefruit
tuna	cactus fruit
verduras	vegetables

MEXICO CITY

Mexico City

CONTENTS

Mexico City is a place to love and loathe. Spread across more than 2000 sq km of a valley high in Mexico's central uplands, it encapsulates the best and worst of Mexico. The result is a seething, cosmopolitan megalopolis that is by turns exhilarating and overpowering. One moment Mexico City is music, glamour and excitement; the next it's drabness, poverty, overcrowding and foul smells. This is a city of colonial palaces and sprawling slums; of ear-splitting traffic and peaceful plazas; of huge wealth and miserable poverty; of green parks and brown air.

Its setting is a most unlikely one for a megalopolis. Because of its perch at 2200m, millions of liters of water must be pumped up from lower elevations at enormous expense. Severe pollution from traffic and industry is intensified by the mountains that ring the Valle de México, preventing air from dispersing.

Yet despite its problems, Mexico City is a magnet for Mexicans and visitors alike, because with nearly a fifth of Mexico's population, it outstrips anywhere else in the country in economic, cultural and political importance. One resident summarized it's dominance in this way: 'Lo que ocurre en México, ocurre en el DF' ('What happens in Mexico, happens in Mexico City').

With its great museums, bohemian neighborhoods and spring-like climate, the capital surprises visitors who often stick around longer than they'd planned. The historic core of the city alone is worthy of extended exploration.

The city is known to Mexicans simply as México (Meh-hee-ko). If they want to distinguish it from Mexico the country, they call it either la ciudad de México or el DF (el de eff-eh). The DF is the Distrito Federal (Federal District), where in fact only half the city lies. The outlying parts of Mexico City lie in the state of México, which surrounds the Distrito Federal on three sides; the state of Morelos is on the fourth.

HIGHLIGHTS

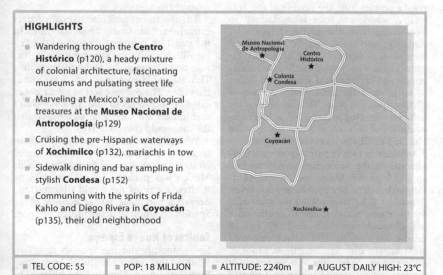

- Wandering through the **Centro Histórico** (p120), a heady mixture of colonial architecture, fascinating museums and pulsating street life

- Marveling at Mexico's archaeological treasures at the **Museo Nacional de Antropología** (p129)

- Cruising the pre-Hispanic waterways of **Xochimilco** (p132), mariachis in tow

- Sidewalk dining and bar sampling in stylish **Condesa** (p152)

- Communing with the spirits of Frida Kahlo and Diego Rivera in **Coyoacán** (p135), their old neighborhood

(map labels) Museo Nacional de Antropología · Centro Histórico · Colonia Condesa · Coyoacán · Xochimilco

| ■ TEL CODE: 55 | ■ POP: 18 MILLION | ■ ALTITUDE: 2240m | ■ AUGUST DAILY HIGH: 23°C |

HISTORY

As early as 10,000 BC, humans were attracted to the Lago de Texcoco, the lake that then covered much of the floor of the Valle de México. After 7500 BC the lake began to shrink, hunting became more difficult, and the inhabitants turned to agriculture. A loose federation of farming villages had evolved around Lago de Texcoco by 200 BC. The biggest, Cuicuilco, was destroyed by a volcanic eruption about AD 100.

Breakthroughs in irrigation techniques and the development of an economy based on the cultivation of maize contributed to the rise of a civilization at Teotihuacán, 40km northeast of the lake. For centuries Teotihuacán was the capital of an empire whose influence was felt as far away as Guatemala. However, unable to sustain its burgeoning population, it fell in the 8th century. The Toltecs, possibly descended from the nomadic tribes who invaded Teotihuacán, arose as the next great civilization, building their capital at Tula, 65km north of modern-day Mexico City. By the 12th century the Tula empire had collapsed as well, leaving a number of small statelets to compete for control of the Valle de México. It was the Aztecs who emerged supreme.

Aztec Mexico City

The Aztecs, or Mexica (meh-*shee*-kah), arrived a century after the decline of the Toltecs. A wandering tribe who claimed to have come from the mythical region of Aztlán in northwest Mexico, they offered their skills as fighters to the dominant Tepaneca tribe who resided on the lake's western shore. The Tepanecas allowed the Aztecs to settle upon the inhospitable terrain of Chapultepec, but other Valle de México inhabitants objected to Aztec habits like wife-stealing and human sacrifice (to appease Huizilopochtli, the hummingbird god).

In the early 14th century warriors of Culhuacán, on the southern shore, launched an attack on the Tepanecas, their chief rivals, taking the Aztec mercenaries as slaves. Eventually the Aztecs played the same role for their new masters, and Cocoxtli, ruler of Culhuacán, sent them into battle against nearby Xochimilco. The Aztecs delivered 8000 human ears to Cocoxtli as proof of their victory. When the Aztecs sought a marriage alliance with Culhuacán, Cocoxtli rashly offered his daughter's hand to their chieftain. But when he arrived at the wedding banquet, his pride turned to horror: a dancer was garbed in the flayed skin of his daughter, who had been sacrificed to Huizilopochtli. Fleeing from the vengeful wrath of Culhuacán, the Aztecs wandered around the swampy fringes of the lake, finally reaching an island near the western shore around 1325. There, according to legend, they witnessed an eagle standing on a cactus and eating a snake, which they interpreted as a sign to stop and build a city, Tenochtitlán. (The eagle depicted on the Mexican flag is a reference to that event.)

Tenochtitlán rapidly became a sophisticated city-state whose empire would, by the early 16th century, span most of modern-day central Mexico from the Pacific to the gulf and down into far southern Mexico. The Aztecs built their city on a grid plan, with canals as thoroughfares and causeways to the lakeshore. At the city's heart stood the main *teocalli* (sacred precinct), with its temple dedicated to Huizilopochtli and the water god, Tláloc. In the marshier parts of the island, they created raised gardens by piling up vegetation and mud and planting willows. These *chinampas* gave three or four harvests a year but were still not enough to feed the growing population. Versions of these can still be seen at Xochimilco (p132) in southern Mexico City.

To supplement their resources, the Aztecs extracted tribute from conquered tribes. In the mid-15th century they formed the Triple Alliance with the lakeshore states Texcoco and Tlacopan to conduct wars against Tlaxcala and Huejotzingo, which lay east of the valley. The purpose was to gain a steady supply of prisoners to sate Huizilopochtli's vast hunger for sacrificial victims, so that the sun would rise each day.

When the Spanish arrived in 1519, Tenochtitlán's population was an estimated 200,000 to 300,000, and the whole Valle de México was perhaps 1.5 million, making it already one of the world's biggest and densest urban areas. For an account of the Spanish conquest of Tenochtitlán, see p38.

Capital of Nueva España

So assiduously did the Spanish raze Tenochtitlán that only a handful of Aztec structures remain in Mexico City today. The

Templo Mayor (p122) is the most interesting of these, followed by the small pyramids of Tlatelolco (p138), north of the center. Having wrecked the Aztec capital, the Spanish chose to rebuild it as their own. The conquistador Hernán Cortés hoped to preserve the arrangement whereby Tenochtitlán siphoned off the bounty of its vassal states.

Ravaged by disease the population of the Valle de México shrank drastically – from 1.5 million to fewer than 100,000 within a century of the conquest, by some estimates. But the city emerged by 1550 as the prosperous and elegant capital of Nueva España. Broad, straight streets were laid out, and buildings constructed to Spanish designs with local materials such as *tezontle,* a red volcanic rock that the Aztecs had used for their temples. Hospitals, schools, churches, palaces and a university were built. But the city suffered floods caused by the partial destruction in the 1520s of the Aztecs' canals. Lago de Texcoco often overflowed, damaging buildings, bringing disease and forcing the relocation of thousands of people.

Independence
On October 30, 1810, some 80,000 independence rebels, fresh from victory at Guanajuato, overpowered Spanish loyalist forces just west of the capital. But they were ill equipped to capitalize on this triumph, and their leader Miguel Hidalgo chose not to advance on the city – a decision that cost Mexico 11 more years of fighting before independence was achieved. By 1821 the city's population had swelled to 160,000, making it the biggest in the Americas.

Mexico City entered the modern age under the despotic Porfirio Díaz, who ruled Mexico for most of the period from 1877 to 1911 and attracted much foreign investment. Díaz ushered in a construction boom, building Parisian-style mansions and theaters to house and entertain the city's elite. Some 150km of electric tramways threaded the streets, industry grew, and by 1910 the city had 471,000 inhabitants. A drainage canal and tunnel finally succeeded in drying up much of Lago de Texcoco, allowing further expansion.

Modern Megalopolis
After Porfirio Díaz fell in 1911, the revolution brought war, hunger and disease to the streets of Mexico City. Following the Great Depression, a drive to industrialize attracted more money and people to the city. By 1940 the population had reached 1.7 million. In the 1940s and '50s, factories and skyscrapers rose almost as quickly. The supply of housing, jobs and services could not keep pace with the influx of people; shantytowns appeared on the city's fringes, and Mexico City began growing uncontrollably.

Despite the continued economic growth into the 1960s, political and social reform lagged behind. Discontent came to a head as Mexico City prepared for the 1968 Olympic Games. On October 2, 10 days before the games started, some 5000 to 10,000 student marchers gathered in Tlatelolco, north of the center, to demonstrate against alleged repression, including police brutality, torture and 'disappearances' of left-wing activists. Troops and police encircled the demonstrators; to this day, no one knows how many perished in the ensuing massacre. The official count was just 24 dead, but other estimates have been put at several hundred. (In 2002 President Vicente Fox opened an investigation into the Tlatelolco atrocities, which included an interrogation of former President Luis Echeverría, who was Interior Minister at the time of the massacre. But human rights groups claim the probe hasn't gone far enough.)

In the 1970s Mexico City continued to grow at a frightening rate, spreading beyond the DF into the state of Mexico and developing some of the world's worst traffic and pollution, only partly alleviated by the metro system (opened in 1969) and by attempts in the 1990s to limit traffic. On September 19, 1985, an earthquake measuring over eight on the Richter scale hit Mexico City, killing at least 10,000, displacing thousands more and causing more than US$4 billion in damage. But people continued to pour in.

Since 1940 Mexico City has multiplied in area over 10 times, yet it's still one of the world's most crowded metropolitan areas. Today the population is estimated at 18 million. Though growth has slowed in the last decade, there are still some 600 newcomers daily and the population is expected to top 20 million by 2010. It is the industrial, retail, financial, communications and cultural center of the country; its industries generate more than one-third of Mexico's wealth, and its people consume two-thirds of Mexico's energy. Its cost of living is the highest in the nation.

Heavy subsidies are needed to keep the place from seizing up, and more than half the country's spending on social welfare is used here. Water extraction from the subsoil makes the city sink steadily – parts of the city center sank 10m in the 20th century. Even so, one-third of the city's water must be pumped in at great cost from outside the Valle de México, and because there is no natural drainage, waste water must be pumped back out. The poverty and over-crowding that always existed were exacerbated by the recession of the mid-1990s. One effect of the crisis was a big rise in crime. During the economic boom of the late 1990s the situation improved somewhat, but street crime remains such a serious concern that in 2002 the DF government hired Rudolph Giuliani to size up the situation, paying the former New York mayor US$4.3 million for the assessment. The city's police chief has promised to follow Giuliani's recommendations, which included raising salaries for police, better tracking of crime statistics and empowering police to investigate crimes, though he wasn't sure when the funds would become available to implement them.

From 1928 to 1997 the DF was ruled directly by the federal government, with federally appointed 'regents' heading notoriously corrupt administrations. Since 1997 the DF has had political autonomy and the chance to elect its own mayor. In 2000 Andrés Manuel López Obrador, a member of the left-leaning PRD, was elected. *Capitalinos* have generally approved of the populist mayor's initiatives, which include an ambitious makeover of the Centro Histórico. The PRD's overwhelming victory in the capital in 2003's mid-term elections boosted López Obrador's potential as a candidate for the national presidency in 2006.

ORIENTATION

Mexico City's 350 *colonias* (neighborhoods) sprawl across the ancient bed of Lago de Texcoco and beyond. Though this vast urban expanse is daunting at first, the main areas of interest to visitors are fairly well defined and easy to traverse.

Note that some major streets, such as Av Insurgentes, keep the same name for many kilometers, but the names (and numbering) of many lesser streets switch every few blocks.

Full addresses normally include the name of a *colonia*. Often the easiest way to find an address is by asking where it is in relation to the nearest metro station.

Centro Histórico & Alameda Central

The historic heart of the city is the wide plaza known as the Zócalo, surrounded by the presidential palace, the metropolitan cathedral and the excavated site of the Templo Mayor, the main temple of Aztec Tenochtitlán. The Zócalo and its surrounding neighborhoods are known as the Centro Histórico (Historic Center) and are full of notable old buildings and interesting museums. North, west and south of the Zócalo are many good, economical hotels and restaurants.

Av Madero and Av 5 de Mayo (or Cinco de Mayo) link the Zócalo with the Alameda Central park, eight blocks to the west. On the east side of the Alameda stands the magnificent Palacio de Bellas Artes. The landmark Torre Latinoamericana (Latin American Tower) pierces the sky a block south of Bellas Artes, beside one of the city's main north–south arterial roads, the Eje Central Lázaro Cárdenas.

Plaza de la República

Some 750m west of the Alameda, across Paseo de la Reforma, is the Plaza de la República, marked by the somber, domed art deco-style Monumento a la Revolución. This is a fairly quiet, mostly residential area with many budget and mid-range hotels. The districts called San Rafael and Juárez are respectively west and south of here.

Paseo de la Reforma

Mexico City's grandest boulevard, flanked by major hotels, embassies and banks, runs through the city's heart, connecting the Alameda to the Zona Rosa and the Bosque de Chapultepec.

Zona Rosa

The Zona Rosa (Pink Zone) is a glitzy shopping, eating, hotel and nightlife district bound by Paseo de la Reforma to the north, Av Insurgentes to the east, and Av Chapultepec to the south.

Bosque de Chapultepec

The woods of Chapultepec, known to gringos as Chapultepec Park, are to the west of the aforementioned districts. This large expanse of greenery and lakes is Mexico City's 'lungs,' and holds many major museums, including the renowned Museo Nacional de Antropología. North of the park is the swanky Polanco district, filled with embassies and upscale shopping and dining establishments.

North of the Centro

Five kilometers north of the center is the Terminal Norte, the largest of the four bus terminals. Six kilometers north is the Basílica de Guadalupe, Mexico's most revered shrine.

South of the Centro

Av Insurgentes Sur connects Paseo de la Reforma to most points of interest in the south. Just south of the Zona Rosa is Colonia Roma, a quaint area of Porfiriato-era architecture, art galleries and plazas. West of Roma, 1km to 2km south of the Zona Rosa, is Colonia Condesa, a trendy neighborhood with pleasant parks, quiet streets, and plentiful restaurants and cafés. Five to 10km further south are the atmospheric former villages of San Ángel and Coyoacán and the vast campus of the national university. In the southeast are the canals and gardens of Xochimilco.

The Eje System

Besides their regular names, many major streets are termed Eje (axis). The Eje system superimposes a grid of priority roads on the maze of smaller streets, supposedly speeding up transport. The key north–south Eje Central Lázaro Cárdenas, running all the way from Coyoacán in the south to Tenayuca in the north, passes just east of the Alameda Central. Major north–south roads west of the Eje Central are termed Eje 1 Poniente (also called Guerrero, Rosales and Bucareli through the central area), Eje 2 Poniente etc, while roads to the east of Eje Central are labeled Eje 1 Oriente, Eje 2 Oriente and so on. The same goes for major east–west roads to the north and south of the Alameda Central and Zócalo – Rayón is Eje 1 Norte, Fray Servando Teresa de Mier is Eje 1 Sur.

Maps

Mexico City tourist modules hand out useful color maps with enlargements of the Centro Histórico, Coyoacán and San Ángel,

---

MEXICO CITY IN...

Two Days

Watch the city awaken over breakfast at **Las Sirenas**, near the Zócalo. Stroll through the **Catedral Metropolitana** and admire the murals at the **Palacio Nacional**. Hop on the **Turibús** for an overview of the city. Break up the tour at **Polanco** or the **Zona Rosa** for lunch and shopping. In the evening, enjoy a relaxing dinner near your hotel, or if you're up for it, share the evening with the mariachis at Plaza Garibaldi. The next day, delve into Mexico's past at the **Museo Nacional de Antropología** and **Castillo de Chapultepec**.

Four Days

With a couple more days, head out to the pyramids at **Teotihuacán**. Spend a day around the **Alameda Central** to see the exhibits at the **Palacio de Bellas Artes** and the **Museo Franz Mayer**. Have lunch at **Los Girasoles**, overlooking **Plaza Tolsá**, then do some *artesanías* shopping at **La Ciudadela**. Spend an evening amid the lively **Condesa** scene.

One Week

With a week available, catch the **Ballet Folclórico** at the Palacio de Bellas Artes. Spend a day visiting the **Museo Frida Kahlo** and the **Museo de Culturas Populares** in Coyoacán. Another day, head south to visit the **Anahuacalli** or the **Museo Dolores Olmedo Patiño**, then float along the canals of **Xochimilco**. On Saturday wander around Plaza San Jacinto and **Bazar Sábado** in San Ángel.

as well as a confusing map of the transportation system. Those needing more details should pick up a Guía Roji fold-out map of Mexico City (US$7), or for even more detail a Guía Roji Ciudad de México street atlas (US$14), updated annually, with a comprehensive index. Find them at Sanborns stores, Librería Sama (see p101) and at larger newsstands.

Inegi, Mexico's national geographical institute, publishes informative tour booklets of certain districts with color map inserts, as well as topographical maps covering the whole country (subject to availability). In the Centro Histórico, there are several **Inegi outlets** Juárez (Map pp108-10; ☎ 5512-8331; Balderas 71 near metro Juárez; ☼ 9am-4:30pm Mon-Fri); airport (☎ 5786-0212; Sala A2; ☼ 8am-8pm); headquarters (Map pp104-5; ☎ 5278-1000, ext 1207; Av Patriotismo 711, Colonia Mixcoác near metro Mixcoác; ☼ 9am-9pm Mon-Fri).

INFORMATION
Bookstores

Books in English and other languages can be found in top-end hotels and major museums, as well as most of the following bookstores.

CENTRO HISTÓRICO   Map pp108–10
American Bookstore (☎ 5512-0306; Bolívar 23; ☼ 10am-7pm Mon-Sat) Novels and books on Mexico in English, Lonely Planet guides.
Gandhi (☎ 5510-4231; Av Juárez 4; ☼ 10am-9pm Mon-Sat, 11am-8pm Sun) Good source of books about Mexico and Mexico City, and novels in English, plus a worthwhile music section.
Librería Madero (☎ 5510-2068; Madero 12) Great selection of Mexican history, art and architecture, including many used books.
Palacio de Bellas Artes (☎ 5521-9760; Av Juárez 1; ☼ 10am-9pm Tue-Sun, 11am-7pm Mon) Excellent arts bookstore with some English-language titles.

OTHER AREAS
Rare-book aficionados can dig up some gems in the used bookstores along Av Álvaro Obregón in Colonia Roma.
Cenca (Map pp116-17; ☎ 5280-1666; Temístocles 73B, Polanco; ☼ 8am-10pm Mon-Fri, 9am-9pm Sat & Sun) Huge variety of magazines in Spanish and English, plus bestsellers in English.
Gandhi (Map p111; ☎ 5661-0911; Av Quevedo 121-134; ☼ 10am-9pm Mon-Sat, 11am-8pm Sun) This large San Ángel branch, with outlets on both sides of Quevedo, features a popular upstairs café. Also see branch in Centro Histórico, above.

La Bouquinerie Zona Rosa (Map pp112-13; ☎ 5514-0838; Casa de Francia, Havre 15; ☼ 10am-6pm Mon-Sat); San Ángel (Map p111; ☎ 5616-6066; Camino al Desierto de los Leones 40; ☼ 10am-8pm Mon-Sat, noon-6pm Sun) French bookstore with *Le Figaro* and *Libération* among other publications.
Librería Italiana (Map pp114-15; ☎ 5511-6180; Plaza Río de Janeiro 53, Colonia Roma; ☼ 10am-7pm Mon-Fri, 10am-2pm Sat)
Librería Pegaso (Map pp114-15; ☎ 5208-0174; Álvaro Obregón 99, Colonia Roma; ☼ 8am-midnight Mon-Sat, 9am-8pm Sun) Inside the Centro Cultural Casa Lamm; carries mostly Spanish-language titles with small sections devoted to French and English literature. Good selection of Lonely Planet guides.

Emergency
Sectur (☎ 5250-0123, 800-903-92-00) is available by phone 24 hours a day to help tourists with problems and emergencies. See p103 for more details.

Mobile units of the PGJDF (Federal District Attorney General's Office) can assist crime victims; call ☎ 061 for help on the spot from these units. You can report crimes and get legal assistance at the **PGJDF office** (Map pp112-13; ☎ 5346-8731; Av Florencia 20) in the Zona Rosa. It's always open and has English-speaking staff available.

Other useful numbers:
Fire, Ambulance (☎ 080)
Cruz Roja (Red Cross; ☎ 5395-1111)

Internet Access
Public Internet services are particularly abundant in the Zona Rosa. Rates range from US$1.50 to US$2.50 per hour, unless otherwise noted.

ZONA ROSA   Map pp112–13
Biblioteca Benjamín Franklin (☎ 5080-2733; Liverpool 31; ☼ 11am-7pm Mon-Fri) Free access for 30 minutes; sign up for a computer at the circulation desk.
Conecte Café (Génova 71, cnr Londres; ☼ 10am-midnight Mon-Sat, 10am-9pm Sun)
Mac Coffee (☎ 5525-4385; 1st fl, Londres 152; US$1 per hr; ☼ 10:30am-9pm Mon-Fri, 11:30am-9pm Sat) Haven for Macintosh users.

CENTRO HISTÓRICO   Map pp108–10
Esperanto (☎ 5512-4123; Independencia 66; ☼ 8am-8pm Mon-Sat, noon-6pm Sun)
Telmex (☎ 5130-0400; Venustiano Carranza 51; ☼ 9am-6pm Mon-Sat) Users insert Ladatel phone cards at a rate of $0.70 per 15 minutes.

OTHER AREAS

C@lling Home (☎ 5207-2586; Calle Jalapa 51, Colonia Roma; per hr US$1; 🕑 9am–9pm Mon–Fri, 10am–4pm Sat, 10am–2pm Sun)

Museo Tecnológico de la CFE (Map pp116–17; ☎ 5516-0964; in the Bosque de Chapultepec, 2a Sección; free access 9am–4:30pm)

Papelería Prado (Map p119; ☎ 5659-5547; Allende 45, cnr Cuauhtémoc, Coyoacán; 🕑 9am–8pm Mon–Sat, 10am–7pm Sun)

Tecnoinformática Integral (Map pp114–15; ☎ 5211-6784; Tamaulipas 75, Condesa; 🕑 9am–8pm Mon–Sat, noon–8pm Sun)

Internet Resources

The following sites compile oodles of information on the capital. Some offer the option of viewing pages in English, but the English pages are often not as thorough or barely comprehensible.

Arte Mexico (www.arte-mexico.com in Spanish) Calendar of art-related events and how to find them.

Artes Visuales (www.artesvisuales.com.mx in Spanish) Well-organized site covering DF galleries and museums.

Centro Histórico Ciudad de México (www.centro historico.com.mx/rescate.html in Spanish) Excellent overview of Centro Histórico places and events including real-time webcam views.

Consejo Nacional Para la Cultura y las Artes (www.cnca.gob.mx in Spanish) Up-to-date guide to what's happening at DF museums, theaters and other cultural institutions.

Secretaría de Turismo del Distrito Federal (www.mexicocity.gob.mx) Tourism department's exhaustive listings with plenty of practical information.

Secretaría de Cultura del Distrito Federal (www.cultura.df.gob.mx in Spanish) Covers DF festivals and museum events.

Sistema de Transporte Colectivo (www.metro.df .gob.mx in Spanish) Everything you need to know about the Mexico City metro.

Laundry

Self-service Laundromats have yet to catch on here. The following *lavanderías* charge US$4 to US$6 to wash and dry a 3kg load for you, only slightly less if you do it yourself.

Édison (Map pp108–10; Édison 91, near Plaza de la República; 🕑 10am–7pm Mon–Sat)

Esmafga (Map pp108–10; ☎ 5709-6473; Mesones 42, Centro Histórico; 🕑 10am–6pm Mon–Fri, 10am–4pm Sat)

Lavajet (Map pp112–13; ☎ 5207-3032; Río Danubio 119B, btwn Lerma & Pánuco; 🕑 8:15am–5:30pm Mon–Fri, 8:15am–4pm Sat)

Lavandería Roma (Map pp114–15; ☎ 5514-7348; Orizaba 42, Roma; 🕑 8:30am–7pm Mon–Fri, 9am–5pm Sat, 9am–3pm Sun)

Libraries & Cultural Centers

Of the following foreign-run libraries, the French, British and German ones are part of their respective national cultural centers, each of which presents films, exhibitions, concerts and other events from their home countries.

Biblioteca Benjamín Franklin (Map pp112–13; ☎ 5080-2733; Liverpool 31; 🕑 11am–7pm Mon–Fri; metro Cuauhtémoc) Housed in the US Trade Center, the library subscribes to a wide range of periodicals, from *Foreign Affairs* to *Mad*. Free Internet is available (see p100). Leave your passport at the gate.

British Council (Map pp116–17; ☎ 5263-1900; www .britishcouncil.org.mx; Lope de Vega 316; 🕑 8am–3pm Mon–Fri; metro Polanco)

Canadian Embassy Library (Map pp116–17; ☎ 5724-7960; Schiller 529, Polanco; 🕑 9am–12:30pm Mon–Fri; metro Auditorio)

Casa de Francia (Map pp112–13; ☎ 5511-3151; www .francia.org.mx in French; Havre 15, Zona Rosa; 🕑 10am–8pm Mon–Sat; metro Insurgentes) The library here includes a video screening room and Internet (US$2 per hour).

Instituto Goethe (Map pp114–15; ☎ 5207-0487; www .goethe.de/hn/mex in German; Tonalá 43, Roma; 🕑 9am–1:30pm & 4-7:30pm Tue–Thu, 10am–1:45pm Sat; metro Insurgentes) Subscribes to *Die Zeit* and other German periodicals.

Media

Mexico City's equivalent to an English-language daily newspaper is *The Herald,* a Mexico edition of *The Miami Herald,* with two pages of Mexico news coverage and a Sunday what's-on section. It's available at Sanborns and top hotels. *Tiempo Libre,* the city's Spanish-language what's-on weekly, comes out on Thursday and is sold at newsstands everywhere.

Recommended Spanish-language daily newspapers include *La Jornada,* with excellent cultural coverage, and *Reforma.* The latter is not sold at newsstands but at convenience stores and in some metro stations.

North American and European newspapers and magazines can be found at **Librería Sama** (Map pp112–13; ☎ 5525-0647; Florencia 57; 🕑 8am–8pm Mon–Fri, 9am–5pm Sat & Sun) and **La Torre de Papel** (Map pp108–10; ☎ 5512-9703; Mata 6A; 🕑 8am–8pm Mon–Fri, 8:30am–3pm Sat). The latter also stocks newspapers from around Mexico.

Medical Services

For recommendation of a doctor, dentist or hospital, call your embassy or the 24-hour help line of **Sectur** (☎ 5250-0123), the tourism ministry. You can find an extended list of Mexico City hospitals and English-speaking physicians (with their training and credentials) on the US embassy website at www.usembassy-mexico.gov/medical_lists.html. A private doctor's consultation generally costs between US$25 and US$70.

Dalinde Centro Médico (Map pp114-15; ☎ 5265-2800, emergency ☎ 5265-2805; Tuxpan 25, Roma Sur) Less expensive and often with a doctor on-call who speaks English; short walk from metro Chilpancingo.

Hospital ABC (American British Cowdray Hospital; Map pp104-5; ☎ 5230-8000, emergency ☎ 5230-8161; Sur 136, cnr Av Observatorio, Colonia Las Américas) One of the best hospitals in Mexico. There's an outpatient section and English-speaking staff, but fees can be steep. Metro Observatorio is about 1km southeast.

Hospital Ángeles del Pedregal (☎ 5652-2011; emergency ☎ 5449-5500; Camino a Santa Teresa 1055, Colonia Héroes de Padierna) First-rate hospital.

The pharmacies that are found inside Sanborns stores are among the most reliable, as are the following.

Farmacia París (Map pp108-10; ☎ 5709-5349; Rep de El Salvador 81, 85 & 97, Centro; ☼ 8am-11pm Mon-Sat, 10am-9pm Sun)

Médicor Zona Rosa (Map pp112-13; ☎ 5533-4642; Insurgentes Sur 82); Alameda Central (Map pp108-10; ☎ 5512-0431; Independencia 66; ☼ 10am-6pm Mon-Sat) Specializing in homeopathic medicines.

Money

Exchange rates vary a bit among the numerous money-changing outlets, so check two or three beforehand. Most banks and *casas de cambio* (exchange offices) will change both cash and traveler's checks – but some will change only Euros and US or Canadian dollars.

The greatest concentration of ATMs, banks and *casas de cambio* is on Paseo de la Reforma between the Monumento a Cristóbal Colón and the Monumento a la Independencia, but there are others all over town, including 24-hour branches at the airport.

BANKS & ATMS

Mexico City is chock-full of banks, most with ATMs. The most beautiful bank in town is the Banamex at the corner of Isabel la Católica and Venustiano Carranza, inside the old Casa de los Condes de San Mateo de Valparaíso.

CASAS DE CAMBIO

Centro Cambiario Indice (Map pp112-13; ☎ 5080-0080; Paseo de la Reforma 422; ☼ 9am-5:30pm Mon-Fri, 9am-2:30pm Sat)

Casa de Cambio Puebla (Map pp112-13; ☎ 5207-9485; Paseo de la Reforma 308A; ☼ 9am-5pm Mon-Fri, 10am-2pm Sat)

Casa de Cambio Tíber (Map pp112-13; ☎ 5208-5289; Río Tíber 112 at Río Lerma; ☼ 8:30am-5pm Mon-Fri)

Mexcambios (Map pp108-10; ☎ 5512-9536; Madero 13, downtown, near Latin American Tower)

AMERICAN EXPRESS

American Express (Map pp112-13; ☎ 5207-7282; Paseo de la Reforma 350; ☼ 9am-6pm Mon-Fri, 9am-1pm Sat) Change Amex traveler's checks here at good rates.

WIRE TRANSFERS

Western Union's 'Dinero en Minutos' wiring service is available at several locations.

Elektra (☼ 9am-9pm) Alameda Central (Map pp108-10; ☎ 5510-2185; Balderas 62) Colonia Roma (Map pp114-15; ☎ 5514-0716; Tonalá 15 at Insurgentes) Zócalo (Map pp108-10; ☎ 5522-7227; República de El Salvador 125 at Pino Suárez)

Telecomm (Map pp114-15; ☎ 5629-1100, ext 3035; Oaxaca 1; ☼ 8am-7:30pm Mon-Fri, 9am-4:30pm Sat, 9am-12:30pm Sun)

Using the US Postal Service's 'Dinero Seguro' service (in the US ☎ 888-368-4669; www.usps.com), you can send cash within 15 minutes to any branch of **Bancomer** Alameda Central (Map pp108-10; ☎ 5512-1669; Balderas 92); Zona Rosa (Map pp112-13; ☎ 5208-4302; Liverpool 109); Centro Histórico (Map pp108-10; ☎ 5226-8495; Bolívar 38).

Post

Palacio Postal (Map pp108-10; ☎ 5512-0091; Tacuba 1), across from the Palacio de Bellas Artes, is Mexico City's central post office. This is a lovely early-20th-century building in Italian Renaissance style. (Note in particular the marble stairway with bronze banisters.) The stamp windows, marked *'estampillas,'* stay open beyond normal post office hours (until 8pm Monday to Friday, and on Sunday). The *lista de correos* window (similar to poste restante) is on the right side.

Other post office branches are scattered around town. Here are a few:

Plaza de la República (Map pp108-10, ☎ 5592-1783; Arriaga 11)

Plaza Colón (Map pp108-10; ☎ 5535-7436; Reforma 77)

Zócalo (Map pp108-10; ☎ 5512-3661; Plaza de la Constitución 7, on the west side of the Zócalo)

Zona Rosa (Map pp108-10; ☎ 5514-3029; Londres 208)

Telephone & Fax

There are thousands of Telmex card phones scattered around town. Pick up phone cards at any shop or newsstand bearing the blue-and-yellow 'De Venta Aquí Ladatel' sign.

Some Internet cafés, especially in the Zona Rosa (see p100), let you make reduced-rate international calls via an Internet server line. Typical rates are US$0.20 per minute to the USA and US$0.30 a minute to Canada or Europe.

Some stationery stores, copy shops and Internet cafés offer a fax service; look for 'fax' or *'fax público'* signs. Esperanto (see p100), near the Alameda Central, is a perfectly good option. Sending one page to the USA or Canada costs about US$2; receiving a fax costs US$0.50.

Tourist Information

The Mexico City Ministry of Tourism has 11 tourist information modules in key areas and at the four bus stations. These provide information on Mexico City only, including a decent map and a practical 'Guía General.' At least one staff member usually speaks English.

The following offices are all open from 8am or 9am to 6pm or 7pm daily, unless otherwise indicated.

Antropología (Map pp116-17; ☎ 5286-3850; Paseo de la Reforma & Calz Gandhi, at entry to Museo Nacional de Antropología)

Basílica de Guadalupe (Map pp108-10; ☎ 5748-2085; Átrio de América)

Bellas Artes (Map pp108-10; ☎ 5518-2799; cnr Av Juárez & Peralta, btwn Bellas Artes & Alameda)

Catedral (Map pp108-10; ☎ 5518-1003; Monte de Piedad, west of the Catedral Metropolitana)

Coyoacán (Map p119; ☎ 5659-6009; Jardín Hidalgo 1, in the Casa de Cortés)

Del Ángel Tourism Module (Map pp112-13; ☎ 5208-1030; Paseo de la Reforma & Florencia, Zona Rosa side of Monumento a la Independencia)

San Ángel (Map p111; Plaza San Jacinto 11, at Bazar del Sábado market; ☉ 10am-6pm Sat)

Templo Mayor (Map pp108-10; Seminario, east side of Catedral Metropolitana)

Xochimilco (Map p118; ☎ 5653-5209; Calle del Mercado, at the Nuevo Nativitas boat landing)

Zona Rosa (Map pp112-13; ☎ 5525-9380; Amberes 54 at Londres)

Xochimilco also boasts its own **tourist information office** (Map p118; ☎ 5676-0810; Calle Pino 36; ☉ 8am-8pm), just off the central Jardín Juárez.

In addition, the office of **Corazón de México** (Map pp108-10; ☎ 5518-1869; Gante 15, btwn Carranza & 16 de Septiembre; ☉ 10am-6pm) provides information on five central Mexican states: Hidalgo, Morelos, Michoacán, Guerrero and Estado de México.

The national tourism ministry, **Sectur** (Map pp116-17; ☎ 5250-0123, 800-903-92-00; Av Presidente Masaryk 172, near metro Polanco; ☉ 9am-6pm Mon-Fri, 9am-3pm Sat) has staff who willingly answer queries and hand out stacks of brochures on Mexico City and the rest of the country.

Tourist Card Extensions

Instituto Nacional de Migración (Map pp116-17; ☎ 5281-2418; Ejército Nacional 862, Polanco; ☉ 9am-1:30pm Mon-Fri) It's advisable to phone the office first to ask what documents are needed.

Travel Agencies

A number of mid-range and top-end hotels have an *agencia de viajes* (travel agent) on-site or can recommend one nearby.

La Casa del Viaje (Map pp112-13; ☎ 5242-9400; www.lacasadelviaje.com in Spanish; Hamburgo 36, Zona Rosa; ☉ 8:30am-7:30pm Mon-Fri, 9am-2pm Sat)

Mundo Joven (www.mundojoven.com in Spanish; ☉ 9am-8pm Mon-Fri, 10am-5pm Sat) airport (☎ 2599-0155; Sala E3, international arrivals; ☉ 8am-10pm Mon-Fri, 9am-8pm Sat, 10am-7pm Sun); Polanco (Map pp116-17; ☎ 5250-7191; Eugenio Sue 342, cnr Homero); Zócalo (Map pp108-10; ☎ 5518-1755; Guatemala 4) Specializes in cheap travel for students and teachers, with worthwhile fares on domestic and international flights from Mexico City. Mundo Joven can issue ISIC, ITIC and IYTC and HI cards.

Turismo Zócalo (Map pp108-10; ☎ 5518-3606; turizmozocalo@hotmail.com; Venustiano Carranza 67, Local 3, Centro; ☉ 10am-7pm Mon-Fri) Inside the Centro Comercial Venustiano Carranza.

Viajes Educativos (Map pp104-5; ☎ 5661-4235; Insurgentes Sur 1690, near Barranca del Muerto; ☉ 9am-8pm Mon-Fri, 10am-5pm Sat) Also issues ISIC etc.

(Continued on page 120)

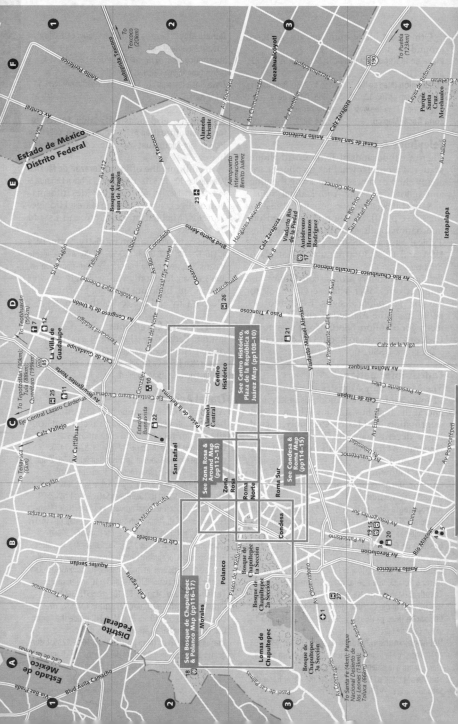

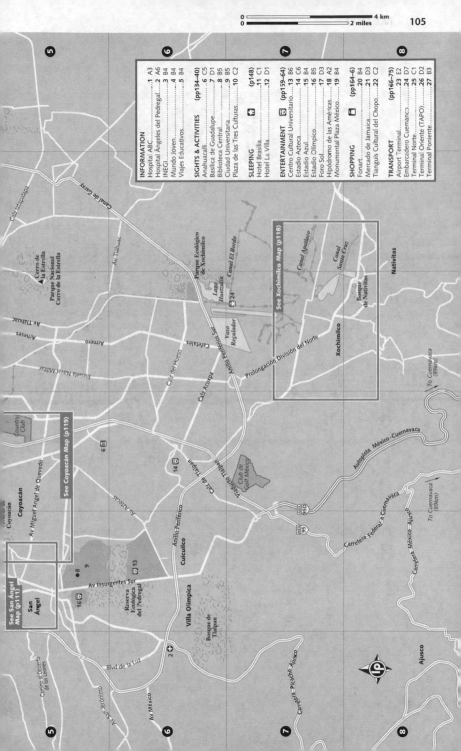

INFORMATION
Hospital ABC...............................1 A3
Hospital Ángeles del Pedregal.......2 A6
INEGI..3 B4
Mundo Joven...............................4 B4
Viajes Educativos.........................5 B4

SIGHTS & ACTIVITIES (pp134-40)
Anahuacalli.................................6 C5
Basílica de Guadalupe..................7 D1
Biblioteca Central........................8 B5
Ciudad Universitaria.....................9 B5
Plaza de las Tres Culturas............10 C2

SLEEPING ⛺ (p148)
Hotel Brasilia.............................11 C1
Hotel La Villa............................12 D1

ENTERTAINMENT 🎭 (pp159-64)
Centro Cultural Universitario.......13 B6
Estadio Azteca..........................14 C6
Estadio Azul.............................15 B4
Estadio Olímpico.......................16 B5
Foro Sol...................................17 D3
Hipódromo de las Américas........18 A2
Monumental Plaza México..........19 B4

SHOPPING 🛍 (pp164-6)
Fonart......................................20 B4
Mercado de Jamaica..................21 D3
Tianguis Cultural del Chopo........22 C2

TRANSPORT (pp166-75)
Airport Terminal........................23 E2
Embarcadero Cuemanco.............24 D7
Terminal Norte..........................25 C1
Terminal Oriente (TAPO).............26 D2
Terminal Poniente.....................27 B3

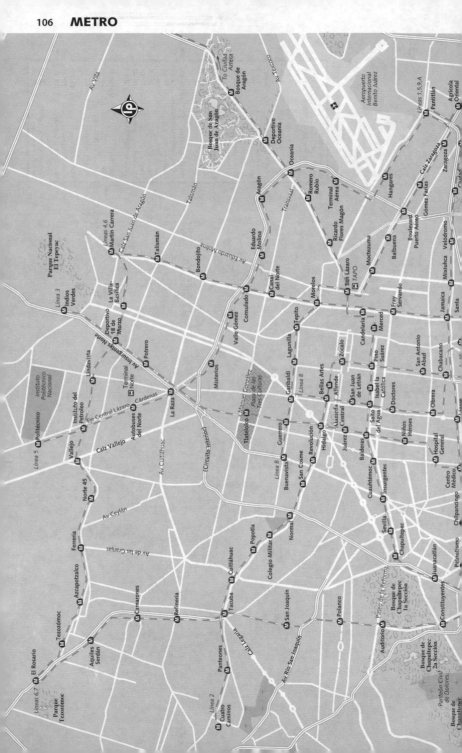

Ⓐ Ⓑ Ⓒ Ⓓ

❶ ❷ ❸ ❹ ❺ ❻

Buenavista Ⓜ
Línea B
Tianguis Cultural del Chopo
Mosqueta
Guerrero Ⓜ Guerrero
Guerrero

Moctezuma

Magnolia

Pedro Moreno

Línea 2
San Cosme Ⓜ
Dr AH
González Martínez
140 52
Ribera de San Cosme
Mina
Violeta
Héroes
Zarco
Guerrero (Eje 1 Poniente)

Altamirano
Rosas Moreno
Miguel Schultz
Serapio Rendón
del Castillo
Sadí Carnot
Av Insurgentes Centro
Edison
Montes
Edison
Iglesias
Revolución Ⓜ ●167
Buenavista
Ramos Arizpe
Orozco y Berra
Mina
Panteón de San Fernando

SAN RAFAEL

Puente de Alvarado
Plaza de San Fernando

Gómez Farías
Mariscal
21 ⊗
59
7
Atenógenes
Frontón de México
Alcázar
Baranda
Empalán
Terán
Lotería
Plaza Buenavista
51
85
77
84
58
Hidalgo Ⓜ 71
Vadillo
142 169
Rosales
Paseo de la Reforma

Serapio Rendón
Antonio Caso
64
79 128
Av de la República
Plaza de la República
39
49
96
68
81
Ignacio Vallarta
Ramírez
Lafragua
Lotería Nacional
33
Colón
119 154
Av Juárez
164
141
Iturbide
Humboldt
166
120 92
82
47 99
Jardín de la Solidaridad
Revillagigedo

70
90
Sadí Carnot
Madrid
París
20 ⊗
91
37
163
75
Av Morelos
Guerra
165
Bucareli
Balderas
Juárez Ⓜ 9
149
17
14 ●
72

Jardín del Arte
38
Plaza Villalongín
Sullivan
Jardín Luis Pasteur
Monumento a Cuauhtémoc
Paseo de la Reforma
Atenas
Ayuntamiento
$ 2
Victoria
102

Río Neva
Río Marne
Río Tíber
Roma
General Prim
Lucerna
Viena
Milán
Lisboa
Versalles
86
Plaza de Danzón
150
Donda Plaza José María Morelos
Márquez Sterling
Pugibet

Hamburgo
JUÁREZ
Londres
Berlín
Liverpool
Bucareli (Eje 1 Poniente)
Abraham González
La Ciudadela
Enrico Martínez
Luis Moya
Revillagigedo
103

Havre
Nápoles
Dinamarca
Marsella
Bruselas
Turín
Tolsá
Tolsá
Balderas Ⓜ
Arcos de B

Niza
Av Insurgentes Centro
Cuauhtémoc Ⓜ
Bucareli (Eje 1 Poniente)
Av Chapultepec
Dr Río de la Loza
Niños Héroes

Línea 1
Av Chapultepec
Flora
Frontera
Morelia
Cuajimalpa
Av Cuauhtémoc
Dr Carmona y Valle
Dr Lucio
137
Dr Lavista
Línea 3
Dr Jiménez
Dr Vertiz

Orizaba
Córdoba
Mérida
Frontera
Morelia
Real de Romita
Puebla
Durango
ROMA
Jardín Dr Chávez
Dr Liceaga
Dr Bernard

0   500 m
0   0.3 miles

INFORMATION
ATM (Banorte)..................1 C3
Gandhi..............................2 F2
Gandhi..............................3 F2
La Bouquinerie...................4 D1
Post Office.........................5 C3
San Ángel Tourist Module....6 C2

SIGHTS & ACTIVITIES (pp133–4)
Centro Cultural San Ángel....7 D2
Iglesia de San Jacinto.........8 C3
Monumento a Álvaro
    Obregón.........................9 D2
Museo Casa del Risco.........10 C2
Museo Casa Estudio Diego
    Rivera y Frida Kahlo.......11 B1
Museo Soumaya.................12 C4
Templo y Museo de El
    Carmen.........................13 D2

EATING (pp154–5)
Cluny...............................14 D2
Fonda San Ángel...............15 C2

Saks................................16 C2
San Ángel Inn...................17 B1

DRINKING (pp155–9)
La Martinera.....................18 B4
Sibarita............................19 B4

ENTERTAINMENT (pp159–64)
Blu...............................(see 14)
La Planta de Luz................20 C4
Mama Rumba.....................21 C2
Ticketmaster (Mixup)..........22 C4

SHOPPING (pp164–6)
Bazar Sábado.................(see 6)
Casa del Obispo................23 C2
La Carreta........................24 D2

TRANSPORT (pp166–75)
San Ángel Pesero Terminal...25 D3

OTHER
Flower Market...................26 D2

A

INFORMATION
American Express..........................1 E3
Bancomer.....................................2 F4
Biblioteca Benjamín Franklin........3 G3
Casa de Cambio Puebla................4 D4
Casa de Cambio Tiber...................5 D3
Casa de Francia.............................6 F3
Centro Cambiario Indice................7 C4
Conecte Café................................8 E4
Del Ángel Tourism Module.............9 D4
La Bouquinerie.........................(see 6)
La Casa del Viaje........................10 F3
Lavajet..11 D3
Librería Sama..............................12 D5
Líneas Azteca Office....................13 E4
Mac Coffee..................................14 E4
Médicor.......................................15 F3
PGJDF Office................................16 D4
Post Office...................................17 D5
Post Office...................................18 H2
UK Embassy.................................19 D3
US Embassy..................................20 D3
Zona Rosa Tourism Module..........21 E4

SIGHTS & ACTIVITIES (pp120–40)
Centro Bursátil (Bolsa)................22 E3
La Diana Cazadora......................23 C4
Monumento a la Independencia
    (El Ángel)................................24 D4
Museo de Cera (Wax Museum)...25 G3
Museo Ripley's.......................(see 25)
Torre Mayor................................26 B5

SLEEPING (pp143–8)
Casa González............................27 D3
Four Seasons Hotel.....................28 B5
Hostel Mansión Havre.................29 F4
Hotel Bristol...............................30 D2
Hotel del Ángel...........................31 D3
Hotel del Principado....................32 F3
Hotel María Cristina....................33 E2
Las Dos Fridas Hostel..................34 B5
María Isabel-Sheraton Hotel........35 D3
Suites Hotel Reforma...................36 C4

EATING (pp148–55)
Beatricita....................................37 D5
Buenos Aires Grill.......................38 E4
Delicity.......................................39 D5
El Campirano...............................40 D5
El Perro de Enfrente....................41 E4

B

Fonda el Refugio.........................42 E5
Konditori.....................................43 E4
La Góndola..................................44 E4
Les Moustaches...........................45 E3
Restaurante Vegetariano Yug......46 D4
Sanborns.....................................47 E4
U Rae Ok....................................48 C5
VIPS..49 D4

DRINKING (pp155–9)
Auseba..50 D4
Bar Milán....................................51 G2
BGay BProud Café México..........52 D4
Cantina Las Bohemias.................53 E4
Sanborns Café............................54 E4
Starbucks....................................55 D3
Yuppie's Sports Café...................56 E4

ENTERTAINMENT (pp159–64)
Cabaré-Tito Fusión......................57 E4
Cabaré-Tito Neón...................(see 67)
Cabrería El Péndulo.....................58 E4
Cine Diana..................................59 C4
El Almacén..................................60 D4
El Taller..................................(see 60)
Lumiere Reforma.........................61 C4
Mixup (Ticketmaster)..................62 E4
Papa Beto...................................63 C1

SHOPPING (pp164–6)
Fonart...64 G2
Jardín del Arte............................65 F2
Mercado Insurgentes...................66 E5
Plaza del Ángel Shopping Arcade.67 D4
Plaza La Rosa Shopping Arcade...68 E4

TRANSPORT (pp166–75)
Aero California............................69 D4
Aeroméxico.................................70 B4
Alitalia..71 C3
American Airlines.........................72 D4
Avianca.......................................73 F3
Avis..(see 4)
Copa Airlines.........................(see 77)
Delta Airlines..............................74 C4
Japan Air Lines...........................75 D3
Mexicana....................................76 D4
Thrifty Car Rental....................(see 4)
Ticketbus Reforma......................77 C4
Turibús Stop............................(see 9)
United Airlines............................78 D4

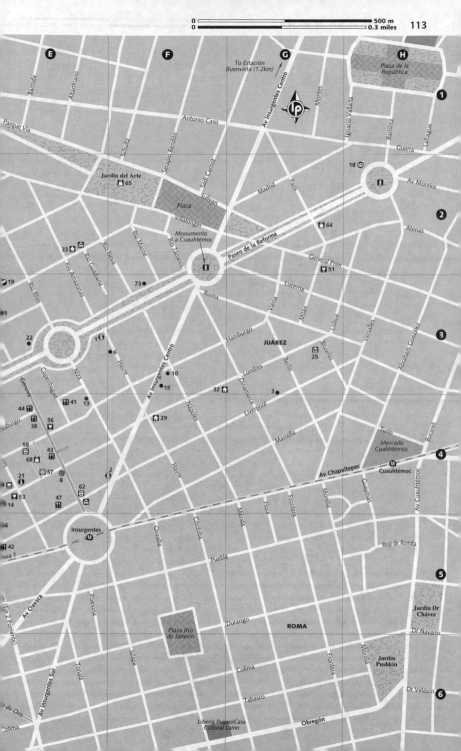

0 — 500 m
0 — 0.3 miles

E **F** **G** **H**

Plaza de la República

To Estación
Buenvista (1.2km)

Barreda
Altamirano
Parque Vía
Antonio Caso
Av Insurgentes Centro
Montes
Ignacio Villalta
Ramírez
Lafragua
Guerra

Schultz
Serapio Rendón
Sadi Carnot
Sullivan
Madrid
París
Av Morelos

Jardín del Arte
65

Plaza
Villalongín

18

Atenas

33
Río Neva
Río Guadiana
Río Amazonas
Río Marne
Río Támesis

Monumento
a Cuauhtémoc
Paseo de la Reforma
64
General Prim
51

19
Río Rhin
73
Roma
Lucerna
Viena
Milán
Lisboa
Versalles
Abraham González

22
Niza
1
6
Havre
Hamburgo
JUÁREZ
Berlín
Bruselas
25

Copenhague
Génova
10
15
Londres
Dinamarca
Liverpool
3

44
41
13
32
Nápoles
29
Marsella

38
56
58
43
68
57
8
21
53
14
2

Mercado
Cuauhtémoc
Turín
Bucareli
Av Chapultepec
Cuauhtémoc

Havre
Flora
Frontera
Morelia
Guaymas
Cuauhtémoc
Av Cuauhtémoc

62
47

Insurgentes

42
nea 1

Orizaba
Córdoba
Mérida
Puebla
Real de Romita

Av Oaxaca
Av Insurgentes Sur
Pomona
Durango

Plaza Río
de Janeiro

Jardín Dr
Chávez
Dr Navarro

ROMA

Jalapa
Colima
Frontera
Morelia

Jardín
Pushkin

Dr Velasco

Toríala
Tabasco
Obregón

-de-Oro
-olima

Librería PegasoCasa
Cultural Lamm

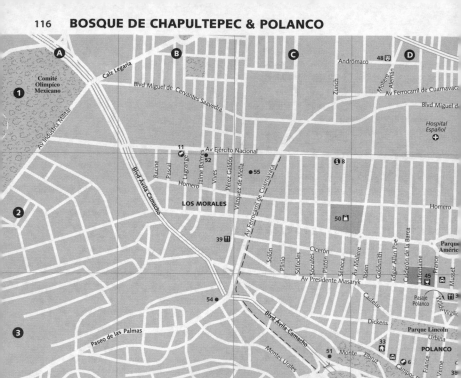

INFORMATION
Antropología Tourism Module	1 F4
Australian Embassy	2 G3
British Council	3 F2
Canadian Embassy & Library	4 F3
Cenca	5 E3
French Embassy	6 D3
German Embassy	7 E3
Instituto Nacional de Migración	8 C2
Liverpool Polanco (Ticketmaster)	9 G3
Mundo Joven	10 E2
New Zealand Embassy	11 B2
Sectur	12 F3
Spanish Embassy	13 E2

SIGHTS & ACTIVITIES (pp120–40)
Castillo de Chapultepec	(see 24)
Fuente de Tlaloc	14 D6
Fuente de Xochipilli	15 D5
Hall of Mirrors	16 G4
La Feria	17 D5
Los Pinos Presidential Residence	18 E6
Monumento a los Niños Héroes	19 G4
Museo de Arte Moderno	20 G4
Museo de Historia Natural	21 D6
Museo del Caracol	22 F5
Museo Nacional de Antropología	23 F4
Museo Nacional de Historia	24 G5
Museo Rufino Tamayo	25 F4
Museo Tecnológico	26 E6
Papalote Museo del Niño	27 E6
Zoológico de Chapultepec	28 F4

SLEEPING (pp143–8)
Camino Real México	29 G3
Casa Vieja	30 D3
Habita Hotel	31 E3
Hotel Park Villa	32 F5
Hotel Polanco	33 D3
W Mexico City Hotel	34 E3

EATING (p154)
Chez Wok	35 E3
El Lago	36 D5
Klein's	37 D3
La Estrella de Galicia	38 D3
La Hacienda de los Morales	39 B2
La Parrilla Suiza	40 E3
Restaurante del Bosque	41 D6
Rincón Argentino	42 F3
Villa María	43 E2

DRINKING (p158)
Área	(see 31)
Bar Fly de París	(see 45)
Dubliner	44 G2
La Martinera	45 D3

ENTERTAINMENT (pp159–64)
Auditorio Nacional	46 E4
Centro Cultural del Bosque	47 E4
Cinemex Casa de Arte	(see 45)
Salón 21	48 D1
Teatro de la Danza	49 E4

SHOPPING (pp164–6)
Plaza Moliere	50 C2

TRANSPORT (pp166–75)
Air Canada	51 C3
Air France	(see 52)
British Airways	52 B2
Continental Airlines	53 E3
KLM	(see 53)
Lufthansa	54 B3
Mexicana	55 C2
Ticketbus Polanco	56 F3

0 .... 1 km
0 .... 0.5 miles

INFORMATION
Banamex...........................1 D2
Xochimilco Tourism Module......2 E3
Xochimilco Tourist Office.........3 D2

SIGHTS & ACTIVITIES (pp131–2)
Museo Dolores Olmedo Patiño...4 A2
Parroquia de San Bernardino de
Siena..............................5 D2

TRANSPORT (pp166–75)
Embarcadero Caltongo...........6 E2
Embarcadero Fernando Celada....7 C2
Embarcadero Nativitas...........8 E3
Embarcadero Saltire.............9 D2
Embarcadero San Cristóbal......10 D2

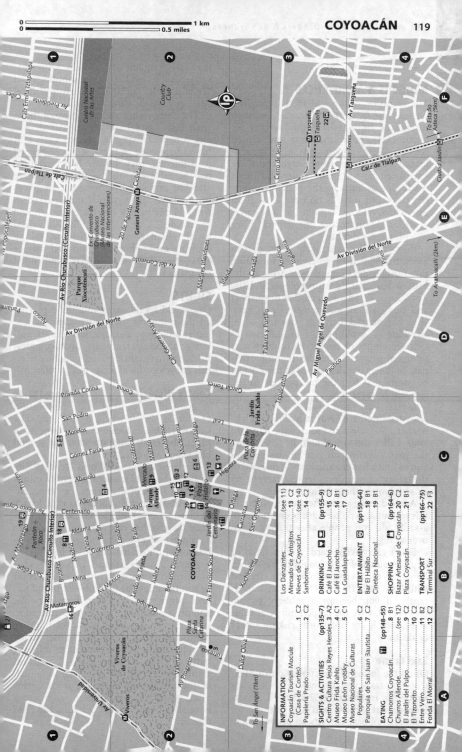

INFORMATION
Coyoacán Tourism Mocule
(Casa de Cortés)..................................1 C2
Papelería Prado.....................................2 C2

SIGHTS & ACTIVITIES (pp135–7)
Centro Cultura Jesús Reyes Heroles....3 A2
Museo Frida Kahlo................................4 C1
Museo León Trotsky..............................5 C1
Museo Nacional de Culturas
Populares..6 C2
Parroquia de San Juan Bautista...........7 C2

EATING (pp148–55)
Chamorros Coyoacán.............................8 B1
Churros Allende.............................(see 12)
El Jardín del Pulpo..............................9 C2
El Tizoncito..10 C2
Entre Vero...11 B2
Fonda El Morral..................................12 C2

Los Danzantes...............................(see 11)
Mercado ce Antojitos..........................13 C2
Nieves de Coyoacán.......................(see 14)
Sanborns..14 C2

DRINKING (pp155–9)
Café El Jarocho....................................15 C2
Café El Jarocho....................................16 B1
La Guadalupana...................................17 C2

ENTERTAINMENT (pp159–64)
Bar El Hábito.......................................18 B1
Cineteca Nacional...............................19 B1

SHOPPING (pp164–6)
Bazar Artesanal de Coyoacán 20 C2
Plaza Coyacán.....................................21 B1

TRANSPORT (pp166–75)
Terminal Sur..22 F3

(Continued from page 103)

DANGERS & ANNOYANCES

The recession of the mid-1990s brought a big increase in crime in Mexico City, with foreigners among the prime targets for pickpockets, purse-snatchers and armed robbers. Despite increased police surveillance, crime levels remain high and there have been far too many violent incidents (including assaults *by* the police) to deny the risks. But there is no need to walk in fear whenever you step outside; a few precautions greatly reduce any dangers. (See p950 for general hints.)

Robberies are most likely to happen in areas frequented by foreigners, including the Bosque de Chapultepec, around the Museo Nacional de Antropología and the Zona Rosa. Be on your guard at the airport and bus stations, and remember to keep your bag or pack between your feet when checking in. Avoid pedestrian underpasses that are empty or nearly so; robbers may intercept you in the middle. If you participate in rallies or celebrations in the Zócalo, be aware that half the pickpockets in the city will be there too.

Metro cars and buses, particularly crowded ones, are favorite haunts of pickpockets. Stay alert and keep your hand on your wallet and you should be fine. Using the metro during off-peak hours enables you to find a less crowded car (at one end of the train), where thieves are less likely to get close to you without being noticed.

Avoid driving alone after hours. Not only thieves but also police have been known to assault and rob people after pulling them over at night.

Don't carry ATM cards, credit cards or large amounts of cash; assailants have been known to force victims to tour the city and withdraw cash from ATMs. Most importantly, if you become a robbery victim, don't resist. Give the perpetrator your valuables, which are not worth risking injury or death.

Taxi Crime

Of all the forms of transportation in Mexico City, taxis are the most notorious for robberies. In December 2003 the US State Department website had this warning for visitors: 'Robbery assaults on passengers in taxis are frequent and violent, with passengers subjected to beating, shootings and sexual assault.' For updates see http://travel .state.gov/travel_warnings.html.

The importance of taking precautions with taxis can't be overemphasized. Ask any foreigner living in Mexico City: if it hasn't happened to them, it has happened to someone they know. Many victims had hailed a cab on the street and were attacked or robbed by armed accomplices of the driver. In particular taxis parked in front of nightclubs or restaurants should be avoided, unless specifically authorized by the management. Instead of taking cruising cabs, phone a radio taxi service *(sitio)*. See p175 for a list of recommended companies.

SIGHTS

One could spend many months exploring all the museums, monuments, plazas, colonial buildings, monasteries, murals, galleries, historical remnants, archaeological finds, statuary, shrines and religious relics this encyclopedia of a city has to offer.

Centro Histórico   Map pp108–10

A good place to start your exploration of Mexico City is where it all began. The Centro Histórico focuses on the large main plaza, the **Zócalo**, and stretches for several blocks in each direction.

Declared a Unesco World Heritage Site in 1987, the 34-block area presents a mind-boggling array of sites from the Aztec, colonial and prerevolutionary eras, a legacy of the incomparable wealth and importance the city has enjoyed, and is home to a number of absorbing museums. It also bustles with modern-day street life.

Mayor Andrés Manuel López Obrador has made it a priority to spruce up the center to suit the image as the hub of a proud nation. More than US$50 million in public and private funding has been earmarked to repave streets, refurbish buildings, improve lighting and traffic flow, and bolster security. The mayor has also fought an ongoing battle to clear the many sidewalk stalls off Centro Histórico streets. Because much of the investment has come from Carlos Slim, Mexico's richest man, *capitalinos* have slyly begun to call the zone the Slim Center.

ZÓCALO

The heart of Mexico City is the Plaza de la Constitución, though city residents began calling it the Zócalo, meaning base, when a statue of the Spanish monarch Carlos IV was removed after independence, leaving only the pedestal. (The statue now stands on the Plaza Tolsá in front of the Museo Nacional de Arte.) The name has been adopted informally by many other Mexican cities for their main plazas.

The ceremonial center of Aztec Tenochtitlán, known as the Teocalli, lay immediately northeast of the Zócalo. Today *conchero* dancers remind everyone of this heritage with daily gatherings in the Zócalo for a sort of pre-Hispanic aerobics, in feathered headdresses and *concha* (shell) anklets and bracelets, to the rhythm of booming drums.

In the 1520s Cortés paved the plaza with stones from the ruins of the Teocalli and other Aztec buildings. Until the early 20th century, the Zócalo was more a maze of market stalls than an open plaza. With each side measuring more than 200m, it's one of the world's largest city squares.

The Zócalo is the home of the powers-that-be in Mexico City. On its east side is the Palacio Nacional (the presidential palace), on the north the Catedral Metropolitana, and on the south the offices of the Distrito Federal government. The plaza is also a place for political protesters to make their points, and it's often occupied by makeshift camps of strikers. The PRD city government has made it a venue for free concerts and other popular entertainment with a temporary stage usually installed to one side.

Each afternoon at 6pm the huge Mexican flag flying in the middle of the Zócalo is ceremonially lowered by the army and carried into the Palacio Nacional.

PALACIO NACIONAL

Home to the offices of the president of Mexico, the Federal Treasury and dramatic murals by Diego Rivera, the **National Palace** (☎ 9158-1245; Plaza de la Constitución; admission free; ⏰ 10am-6pm) fills the entire east side of the Zócalo.

The first palace on this spot was built of tezontle by Aztec emperor Moctezuma II in the early 16th century. Cortés destroyed the palace in 1521 and rebuilt it with a large courtyard so he could entertain visitors with Nueva España's first recorded bullfights. In 1562 the crown bought the palace from Cortés' family to house the viceroys of Nueva España. Destroyed during riots in 1692, it was rebuilt and remained the vice-regal residence until Mexican independence.

As you face the palace you will see three portals. On the right (south) is the guarded entrance for the president and other officials. High above the center door hangs the **Campana de Dolores**, the bell rung in the town of Dolores Hidalgo by Padre Miguel Hidalgo in 1810 at the start of the Mexican War of Independence. From the balcony underneath it, the president delivers the *grito* (shout) *Viva México!* on September 15 to commemorate independence.

Enter the palace through the center door. The **Diego Rivera murals** around the courtyard, painted between 1929 and 1935, present Rivera's view of Mexican civilization from the arrival of Quetzalcóatl (the Aztec plumed serpent god) to the 1910 revolution. To the rear of the main patio is a tranquil botanical garden containing plants from all over Mexico.

CATEDRAL METROPOLITANA

Construction of the **Metropolitan Cathedral** (☎ 5510-0440, ext 123; Plaza de la Constitución; admission free; ⏰ 8am-8pm), on the north side of the Zócalo, began in 1573 and took two and a half centuries to complete. Because of its placement atop the ruins of the Aztec temple complex, the massive building has been sinking unevenly since its construction, resulting in fissures and cracks in the structure.

While visitors may wander freely, they are asked not to do so during mass. Free guided tours conducted in Spanish are on offer from 11am to 3pm Monday to Friday and 10:30am to 1:30pm Saturday; sign up at the information booth just inside the church entrance. Visitors can also climb the **bell tower** (admission US$1.20; ⏰ 11am-2pm & 4-7pm Mon-Sat). A US$1 donation is requested to enter the **sacristy** or **choir**, where docents provide ongoing commentary.

Another way to explore the cathedral is the evening **Maravillas de Catedral tour** (tour US$5; ⏰ 8pm Mon), a sound and light show with a guided tour (in Spanish) around the installations. For tickets, contact Ticketmaster (see p159) or visit the **church ticket booth** (⏰ 9am-2:30pm & 3:30-7pm).

With a three-nave basilica design of vaults on semicircular arches, the cathedral was built to resemble those of Toledo and Granada. The grand portals facing the Zócalo, built in the 17th century in baroque style, have two levels of columns and marble panels with bas-reliefs. The central panel shows the Assumption of the Virgin Mary, to whom the cathedral is dedicated. The tall north portals facing Rep de Guatemala date from 1615 and are in pure Renaissance style.

The upper levels of the towers, with unique bell-shaped tops, were added in the late 18th century. The exterior was completed in 1813, when architect Manuel Tolsá added the clock tower – topped by statues of Faith, Hope and Charity – and a great central dome.

Inside, the cathedral's chief artistic treasure is the gilded 18th-century Altar de los Reyes (Altar of the Kings), behind the main altar. It's a masterly exercise in controlled elaboration and a high point of Churrigueresque style. The two side naves are lined by 14 richly decorated chapels. At the southwest corner, the Capilla de los Santos Ángeles y Arcángeles (Chapel of the Holy Angels and Archangels) is another exquisite example of baroque sculpture and painting, with a huge main altarpiece and two smaller ones decorated by the 18th-century painter Juan Correa. Unfortunately, this masterpiece is poorly lit, making it difficult to appreciate.

Also worthy of admiration are the intricately carved late-17th-century wooden choir stalls by Juan de Rojas and the huge, gilded Altar de Perdón (Altar of Pardon), all in the central nave. The sacristy, the first component of the cathedral to be built, should be seen for the enormous painted panels that grace its walls. Two of New Spain's masters created them; *La Asunción de la Virgen*, by Correa, depicts the ascension of Mary, while *La Mujer del Apocalípsis*, by Cristóbal de Villalpando, dramatically portrays the apocalyptic vision of the Apostle St John.

Adjoining the east side of the cathedral is the 18th-century **Sagrario Metropolitano** (☎ 5521-2447; ⏰ 7am-7pm). Originally built to house the archives and vestments of the archbishop, it is now the city's main parish church. Its front entrance and mirror-image eastern portal are superb examples of the ultra-decorative Churrigueresque style.

TEMPLO MAYOR

The Teocalli of Tenochtitlán, demolished by the Spaniards in the 1520s, stood on the site of the cathedral and the blocks to its north and east. It wasn't until 1978, after electricity workers happened on an 8-ton stone-disc carving of the Aztec goddess Coyolxauhqui, that the decision was taken to demolish colonial buildings and excavate the **Templo Mayor** (☎ 5542-0606; Seminario 8; admission US$3.50; ⏰ 9am-5pm Tue-Sun). The temple is thought to be on the exact spot where the Aztecs saw their symbolic eagle, with a snake in its beak, perching on a cactus – the symbol of Mexico today. In Aztec belief this was, literally, the center of the universe.

The entrance to the temple site and museum is east of the cathedral, across the hectic Plaza Templo Mayor, with a model of Tenochtitlán. A set of three brochures, in Spanish, describing the archaeological zone, ceremonial precinct and museum contents, is available at the entrance for US$1.

A walkway reveals the temple's multiple layers of construction. (Explanatory material is all in Spanish.) Like other sacred buildings in Tenochtitlán, the temple, first begun in 1375, was enlarged several times, with each rebuilding accompanied by the sacrifice of captured warriors. In 1487 these rituals were performed at a frenzied pace to rededicate the temple after one major reconstruction. By some estimates, as many as 20,000 sacrificial victims went under the blade in this single ghastly ceremony, which went on for four days.

What we see today are sections of the temple's different phases. Unfortunately, hardly anything is left of the seventh and last version, built about 1502, which was seen by the Spanish conquistadors. At the center is a platform dating from about 1400; on its southern half, a sacrificial stone stands in front of a shrine to Huizilopochtli, the Aztec tribal god. On the northern half is a *chac-mool* (a Mayan reclining figure that served as a messenger to the gods) before a shrine to the water god, Tláloc. By the time the Spanish arrived, a 40m-high double pyramid towered above this spot, with steep twin stairways climbing to shrines of the same two gods.

Other features of the site include a late-15th-century stone replica of a tzompantli, carved with 240 stone skulls, and the mid-15th-century **Recinto de los Guerreros Águila** (Sanctuary of the Eagle Warriors, an elite band of Aztec fighters), decorated with colored bas-reliefs of military processions.

As you approach the museum, notice the large-scale quotes chiseled on its west walls. These are awe-struck descriptions of Tenochtitlán from three of its earliest European visitors – Hernán Cortés, Bernál Díaz del Castillo and Motolinía.

The **Museo del Templo Mayor** houses artifacts from the site and gives a good overview of Aztec civilization, including chinampa agriculture, their systems of government and trade, and their beliefs, wars and sacrifices. Audio guides, in English, are available at the museum entrance (US$3). Pride of place is given to the great wheel-like stone of Coyolxauhqui (She of Bells on her Cheek), best viewed from the top floor vantage point. She is shown decapitated – the result of her murder by Huizilopochtli, her brother, who also killed her 400 brothers en route to becoming top god. Other outstanding exhibits include full-size terra-cotta eagle warriors.

CALLE MONEDA

Heading back toward the Zócalo from the Templo Mayor, Moneda is the first street on your left, a pedestrian thoroughfare lined with tezontle buildings and often clogged with *ambulantes* (mobile street vendors). The **Museo de la Secretaría de Hacienda y Crédito Público** (Museum of the Secretariat of Finance; ☎ 9158-1245; Moneda 4; admission US$0.80, free Sun; ⏲ 10am-5:30pm Tue-Sun) exhibits works from its vast collection of Mexican art, with an emphasis on 20th-century painters. The former colonial archbishop's palace also hosts a full program of cultural events (many free), from puppet shows to chamber music recitals.

Constructed in 1567 as the colonial mint, the **Museo Nacional de las Culturas** (National Museum of Cultures; ☎ 5512-7452; Moneda 13; admission free; ⏲ 9:30am-6pm Tue-Sun) exhibits art, dress and handicrafts of the world's cultures. An uncharacteristically realistic Rufino Tamayo mural in the entry hall presents a scene of revolutionary brutality. A block further east, then a few steps north, is a former convent housing the **Museo José Luis Cuevas** (☎ 5542-8959; Academia 13; admission US$1, free Sun;

⏲ 10am-5:30pm Tue-Sun). A haven for Mexico's fringe art scene, the museum showcases the works of Cuevas, a leading modern Mexican artist, and of his contemporaries. Cuevas' *La Giganta*, a 9m-high bronze figure with male and female features, dominates the central patio, while the Sala de Arte Erótico is an intriguing gallery of the artist's sexual themes.

PLAZA SANTO DOMINGO

Two blocks north of the Zócalo is this smaller, less formal plaza. Modern-day scribes, with typewriters and antique printing machines, work beneath the **Portal de Evangelistas**, along its west side. The maroon stone **Iglesia de Santo Domingo**, dating from 1736, is a beautiful baroque church, decorated on its east side with carved figures of Santo Domingo and San Francisco. Below the figures, the saints' arms are symbolically entwined as if to convey a unity of purpose. The church's front (southern) façade is equally beautiful, with 12 columns around the main entrance. Between the columns are statues of San Francisco and San Agustín (St Augustine) and at the top is a bas-relief of the Assumption of the Virgin Mary.

Opposite the big church is the 18th-century Palacio de la Escuela de Medicina, headquarters of the Holy Inquisition in Mexico until it was abolished in 1820. It now houses the **Museo de la Medicina Mexicana** (Museum of Mexican Medicine; ☎ 5529-7542; República de Brasil 33; admission free; ⏲ 9am-6pm), with displays ranging from a model of a *temazcal* (an indigenous sauna, used for spiritual purification) to a reconstruction of a 19th-century pharmacy.

MURALS

In the 1920s the post-revolution minister of education, José Vasconcelos, commissioned talented young artists – among them Diego Rivera, David Alfaro Siqueiros and José Clemente Orozco – to decorate numerous public buildings with dramatic, large-scale murals conveying a new sense of Mexico's past and future. One of those buildings was the former convent that housed the newly established **Secretaría de Educación Pública** (Secretariat of Education; ☎ 5328-1067; República de Brasil 31; admission free; ⏲ 8am-8pm Mon-Fri). The entrance is opposite the Plaza Santo Domingo; you may need to leave ID as you enter.

The two front courtyards (on the opposite side of the building from the entrance) are lined with 120 fresco panels painted by Diego Rivera in the 1920s. Together they form a great tableau of 'the very life of the people,' in the artist's words. Each courtyard is thematically distinct: the one nearest the República de Argentina entrance deals with labor, industry and agriculture, and the top floor holds portraits of Mexican heroes. The second courtyard depicts traditions and festivals. On its top level is a series on capitalist decadence and proletarian and agrarian revolution, underneath a continuous red banner emblazoned with a Mexican *corrida*. The likeness of Frida Kahlo appears in the first of these, as an arsenal worker.

A block back toward the Zócalo, then east, is the **Antiguo Colegio de San Ildefonso** (☎ 5789-6845; www.sanildefonso.org.mx in Spanish; Justo Sierra 16; admission US$3.25, free Tue; ☉ 10am-5:30pm Tue-Sun). Built in the 16th century as the Jesuit college of San Ildefonso, it later became a prestigious teacher training college. In the 1920s, Rivera, Orozco, Siqueiros and others were brought in to adorn it with murals. Most of the work on the main patio and staircase is by Orozco, whose caustic interpretation of prerevolutionary Mexican history suggests a grotesque pageant of exploitation and brutality. The amphitheater, off the lobby, holds Rivera's first mural, *La Creación*, commissioned by Vasconcelos upon Rivera's return from Europe in 1923. Mural tours in Spanish are given at 1pm and 6pm Tuesday and Sunday. Nowadays, the San Ildefonso hosts outstanding temporary exhibitions, as well as the Filmoteca of the national university.

PLAZA TOLSÁ

Several blocks west of the Zócalo is this handsome plaza, named after the illustrious late-18th-century sculptor and architect who completed the Catedral Metropolitana. He also created the bronze equestrian statue of the Spanish king Carlos IV (who reigned from 1788 to 1808) that is the plaza's centerpiece. It originally stood in the Zócalo, then on Paseo de la Reforma, before being moved here in 1979 ('as a work of art,' a chiseled plaque emphasizes). King Carlos rides in front of the **Museo Nacional de Arte** (National Art Museum; ☎ 5130-3411; www.munal.com.mx in Spanish; Tacuba 8; admission US$3, free Sun; ☉ 10:30am-

5:30pm Tue-Sun). Built around 1900 in the style of an Italian Renaissance palace, it holds collections representing every school of Mexican art up to the early 20th century. A highlight is the work of José María Velasco, depicting the Valley of Mexico in the late 19th century – with Guadalupe and Chapultepec far outside the city.

Opposite the art museum is the **Palacio de Minería** (Palace of Mining; ☎ 5623-2982; Tacuba 5; admission US$2.50; tours ☉ 11am & 1pm Sat & Sun), where mining engineers were trained in the 19th century. Today it houses a branch of the national university's engineering department. Considered a neoclassical masterpiece, the palace was designed by Manuel Tolsá and built between 1797 and 1813. The palace contains a small **museum** (admission US$1; ☉ 10am-7pm Tue-Sun) on Tolsá's life and work.

AVENIDA MADERO

A landmark for disoriented visitors since 1952, the **Torre Latinoamericana** (Latin American Tower; ☎ 5518-7423; Eje Central Lázaro Cárdenas 2; admission US$4; ☉ 9am-10:30pm) was Latin America's tallest building at the time of its construction. (Today it's Mexico City's fifth tallest.) Views from the 44th floor observation deck are spectacular, smog permitting.

A block east toward the Zócalo stands one of the city's gems, the **Casa de Azulejos** (House of Tiles; ☎ 5518-6676; Av Madero 4; ☉ 7-1am). Dating from 1596, it was built for the Condes (Counts) del Valle de Orizaba. Although the superb tile work that has adorned the outside walls since the 18th century is Spanish and Moorish in style, most of the tiles were actually produced in China and shipped to Mexico on the Manila *naos* (Spanish galleons used up to the early 19th century). The building now houses a Sanborns restaurant in a covered courtyard around a Moorish fountain. The staircase to the upper floor has a 1925 mural by Orozco.

Continuing eastward you'll encounter the beautiful baroque façade of the late 18th-century **Palacio de Iturbide** (☎ 1226-0247; Av Madero 17; admission free; ☉ 10am-7pm). Built for colonial nobility, in 1821 it became the residence of General Agustín Iturbide, a hero of the Mexican struggle for independence. To the cheers of a rent-a-crowd, Iturbide was proclaimed Emperor Agustín I in 1822. But he abdicated less than a year later, after

General Santa Anna announced the birth of a republic. Acquired and restored by Banamex bank in 1965, the palace now houses the Fomento Cultural Banamex (the cultural promotion section of Banamex). In the courtyard exhibits feature art and historical objects from the vice-regal period to the late 19th century, as well as handicrafts by contemporary Mexican masters.

UNIVERSIDAD DEL CLAUSTRO DE SOR JUANA

Considered the greatest Spanish-language poet of the 17th century, Sister Juana Inés de la Cruz composed many of her sonnets in the former convent of San Jerónimo, today the **University of the Cloister of Sor Juana** (☎ 5130-3300; Izazaga 92, near metro Isabel la Católica; admission free; ⊗ 9am-6pm). Its magnificent two-level cloister, dating from 1585, now buzzes with students of gastronomy, literature and philosophy. To the east is the painstakingly restored Iglesia de San Jerónimo containing Sor Juana's tomb and a 1750 portrait of the poetess. The series of tiled niches on its south wall is what remains of the confessionals. Adjacent is the **Museo de Indumentaría Mexicana** (⊗ 10am-5pm Mon-Fri) displaying regional outfits from around Mexico.

MUSEO DE CHARRERÍA

If you've ever had the urge to don spurs and leather chaps, you'll want to see the **Charrería Museum** (☎ 5709-4793; Isabel la Católica 108, cnr Izazaga; admission free; ⊗ 11am-5pm Mon-Fri; metro Isabel la Católica), a rich compendium of cowboy dress, history and culture. Roughly equivalent to the American rodeo, *charrería* originated as an attempt to preserve the skills and traditions of the big cattle haciendas as they faded from the Mexican landscape. Boots, spurs, saddles, and men and women's *charro* outfits are displayed in the 16th-century Capilla de Montserrat, also the headquarters of the National Charrería Federation.

Alameda Central & Around   Map pp108–10

The only sizable downtown park, the Alameda Central is surrounded by some of the city's most interesting buildings and museums. A little less than 1km from the Zócalo, it is bordered by two metro stations, Bellas Artes on its east side, and Hidalgo on its northwest corner.

ALAMEDA CENTRAL

Created in the late 1500s by mandate of then-Viceroy Luis de Velasco, the Alameda took its name from the *álamos* (poplars) planted over its rectangular expanse. By the late 19th century, the park was graced with European-style statuary and a bandstand and lit by gas lamps. It became the place to be seen for the city's elite. Today the Alameda is a popular refuge from the city streets, particularly on Sunday when families stroll its broad pathways and gather for an open-air concert.

PALACIO DE BELLAS ARTES

Dominating the east end of the Alameda is the splendid white-marble **Palace of Fine Arts** (☎ 5521-9251; Av Juárez 1; admission US$3, free Sun; ⊗ 10am-6pm Tue-Sun), a concert hall and arts center commissioned by President Porfirio Díaz. Construction began in 1904 under Italian architect Adamo Boari, who favored neoclassical and art nouveau styles. But the heavy marble shell sank into the spongy subsoil, and work was halted. Architect Federico Mariscal eventually finished the interior in the 1930s, utilizing the more modern art deco style.

Immense murals dominate the upper floors; free tours are given at 12:30pm on Saturday and Sunday. On the 2nd floor are two striking, early-1950s works by Rufino Tamayo: *México de Hoy* (Mexico Today) and *Nacimiento de la Nacionalidad* (Birth of Nationality), a symbolic depiction of the creation of the *mestizo* identity.

At the west end of the 3rd floor is Diego Rivera's famous *El Hombre, Controlador del Universo* (Man, Controller of the Universe), originally commissioned for New York's Rockefeller Center. The Rockefellers had the original destroyed because of its anti-capitalist themes, but Rivera re-created it here in 1934. Capitalism, accompanied by war, is shown on the left; socialism, with health and peace, on the right.

On the north side of the 3rd floor are David Alfaro Siqueiros' three-part *La Nueva Democracía* (New Democracy) and Rivera's four-part *Carnaval de la Vida Mexicana* (Carnival of Mexican Life); at the east end is José Clemente Orozco's eye-catching *La Katharsis* (Catharsis), depicting the conflict between humankind's 'social' and 'natural' aspects.

The 4th-floor **Museo Nacional de Arquitectura** (☎ 5512-1410, ext 203) features changing exhibits on contemporary architecture.

The Bellas Artes theater (only available for viewing at performances) is itself an architectural gem, with a stained-glass curtain depicting the Valle de México. Based on a design by Mexican painter Gerardo Murillo (aka Dr Atl), it was assembled by New York jeweler Tiffany & Co from almost a million pieces of colored glass.

In addition, the palace stages outstanding temporary art exhibitions and the Ballet Folclórico de México (see p160). A worthwhile bookstore and elegant café are on the premises too.

MUSEO FRANZ MAYER

An oasis of calm and beauty north of the Alameda, the **Franz Mayer Museum** (☎ 5518-2266; Av Hidalgo 45; admission US$2, free Tue; ◔ 10am-5pm Tue-Sun) is the fruit of the efforts of Franz Mayer, born in Mannheim, Germany, in 1884. Earning the moniker Don Pancho in his adopted Mexico, Mayer amassed the collection of Mexican silver, textiles, ceramics and furniture masterpieces that is now on display at the museum.

Taking up the west side of the compact Plaza de Santa Veracruz, the museum is housed in the old hospice of the San Juan de Dios order. The main part is to the right of the entrance. To the left is a superb colonial patio; along its west side is a suite of rooms decorated in antique furnishings, with a particularly lovely chapel. The Cafetería del Claustro is on the patio's north side.

MUSEO MURAL DIEGO RIVERA

Among Diego Rivera's most famous works is *Sueño de una Tarde Dominical en la Alameda* (Dream of a Sunday Afternoon in the Alameda), painted in 1947. In the 15m long by 4m high mural, the artist imagined many of the figures who walked in the city from colonial times onward, among them Cortés, Juárez, Emperor Maximilian, Porfirio Díaz, and Francisco Madero and his nemesis, General Victoriano Huerta. All are grouped around a *Catarina* (skeleton in prerevolutionary women's garb). Rivera himself, as a pug-faced child, and his wife, Frida Kahlo, stand beside the skeleton. Charts identify all the characters.

Just west of the Alameda, the **Diego Rivera Mural Museum** (☎ 5510-2329; cnr Balderas & Colón; admission US$1, free Sun; ◔ 10am-6pm Tue-Sun) was built in 1986 to house the mural, which had been in the nearby Hotel del Prado until that building was wrecked by the 1985 earthquake.

Plaza de la República & Around
Map pp108–10

This plaza, to the west of the Alameda Central, is dominated by the imposing, domed Monumento a la Revolución. The grand art deco building northeast of the plaza is the Frontón de México, a now-defunct jai alai arena. Metro Revolución is nearby.

MONUMENTO A LA REVOLUCIÓN

Begun in the 1900s under Porfirio Díaz, the Monumento a la Revolución was originally meant to be a meeting chamber for senators and deputies. But construction (not to mention Díaz' presidency) was interrupted by the revolution. The structure was modified and given a new role in the 1930s: the tombs of the revolutionary and post-revolutionary heroes Pancho Villa, Francisco Madero, Venustiano Carranza, Plutarco Elías Calles and Lázaro Cárdenas are inside its wide pillars (not open to the public).

Underlying the monument, the **Museo Nacional de la Revolución** (National Museum of the Revolution; ☎ 5546-2115; Plaza de la República; admission US$1.30, free Sun; ◔ 9am-5pm Tue-Fri, 9am-6pm Sat & Sun) covers an 80-year period, from the implementation of the constitution guaranteeing human rights in 1857 to the nationalization of Mexico's oil reserves by President Lázaro Cardenas in 1938. Enter from the northeast quarter of the plaza.

MUSEO NACIONAL DE SAN CARLOS

The **Museum of San Carlos** (☎ 5566-8085; Puente de Alvarado 50; admission US$2.50, free Mon; ◔ 10am-6pm Wed-Mon) exhibits a formidable collection of European art from the 16th to the early 20th century, including works by Rubens, Van Dyck and Goya. Occupying the former mansion of the Conde de Buenavista, the unusual rotunda structure was designed by Manuel Tolsá in the late 18th century. It later became home to Alamo victor Santa Anna and subsequently served as a cigar factory, lottery headquarters and school before being reborn as an art museum in 1968.

Paseo de la Reforma

Paseo de la Reforma, Mexico City's main boulevard, runs southwest across the city past the Alameda Central and through the Bosque de Chapultepec. Emperor Maximilian of Hapsburg laid out the boulevard to connect his castle on Chapultepec Hill with the old city center. The López Obrador administration has undertaken a thorough restoration of Paseo de la Reforma, paving the broad pedestrian medians with mosaic cobblestones and planting attractive gardens along its length. You'll almost certainly pass along Reforma at some point, or call at one of the nearby banks, shops, hotels, restaurants or embassies.

Paseo de la Reforma links a series of monumental *glorietas* (traffic circles) and is studded with impressive architecture. A couple of blocks west of the Alameda Central is a major landmark, **El Caballito** (Map pp108–10). A bright yellow representation of a horse's head by the sculptor Sebastián, it commemorates another equestrian sculpture that stood here for 127 years and today fronts the Museo Nacional de Arte (p124). A few blocks southwest on Reforma is a traffic circle at the center of which stands the **Monumento Cristóbal Colón** (Map pp108–10), an 1877 statue of Columbus by French sculptor Charles Cordier.

Reforma's busy intersection with Av Insurgentes is marked by the **Monumento a Cuauhtémoc** (Map pp108–10), memorializing the last Aztec emperor. Two blocks northwest is the **Jardín del Arte**, site of a Sunday art market (p165).

The **Centro Bursátil** (Map pp112–13), a glass arrow housing the nation's stock exchange (Bolsa), marks the northeast end of the Zona Rosa. Continuing west past the US Embassy, you reach the symbol of Mexico City, the **Monumento a la Independencia** (Map pp112-13; admission free; 9am-5pm). Known as 'El Ángel' (the Angel), this gilded statue of Victory on a 45m pedestal was sculpted by Antonio Rivas Mercado for the independence centennial of 1910. The female figures around the base portray Law, Justice, War and Peace; the male ones are Mexican independence heroes. Inside the monument are the skulls of Miguel Hidalgo, Ignacio Allende, Juan Aldama and Mariano Jiménez (retrieved from an 1811–21 stint hanging outside the Alhóndiga de Granaditas in Guanajuato).

At Reforma's intersection with Sevilla is **La Diana Cazadora** (Diana the Huntress; Map pp112-13), a 1942 bronze statue of the Amazonian archer, a tribute to the strength of Mexican women. Southwest from here, marking the eastern entrance to Bosque de Chapultepec, stands the newest addition to the Mexico City skyline, the **Torre Mayor** (Map pp112–13). Designed by Canadian architect Heberhard Zeidler, the sleek green-glass tower rises 225m above the capital, making it Latin America's tallest building. Inaugurated in 2003, the 55-story structure contains 43 floors of offices, 13 parking levels and a shopping mall.

Reforma continues through the Bosque de Chapultepec and then becomes the main road to Toluca.

GETTING THERE & AWAY

Metro Hidalgo is on Reforma at the Alameda Central; Insurgentes station is at the southern edge of the Zona Rosa, 500m south of Reforma. Any 'M(etro) Auditorio' bus heading southwest on Reforma will continue on through the Bosque de Chapultepec, while those marked 'M(etro) Chapultepec' terminate at Chapultepec station, just south of Reforma at the east end of the Bosque de Chapultepec. In the opposite direction, 'M(etro) Hidalgo,' and 'La Villa' buses head northeast up Reforma to the Alameda Central and beyond.

Zona Rosa   Map pp112–13

Both glossy and sleazy, the Pink Zone is an integral piece of the Mexico City jigsaw. People-watching from its sidewalk cafés reveals a higher degree of diversity than elsewhere: it's the city's principal gay and lesbian district and an expat haven, with a significant Korean population.

Museo de Cera de la Ciudad de México (Wax Museum; 5546-3784; Londres 6; adult/child US$4/2.50; 11am-7pm) has famous figures from Mexican history, politics, film and myth enshrined in wax, along with a number of personages from around the globe. A combined ticket (adult/child US$6.50/4) includes entry to the adjacent **Museo Ripley's** (Ripley's Believe It or Not Museum; 5546-7670; Londres 4; 11am-7pm).

Condesa & Roma   Map p114–15

Colonia Condesa's architecture, palm-lined medians and idyllic parks echo its early

20th-century origins as a haven for a newly emerging elite. La Condesa is now known as a trendy neighborhood of informal restaurants and sidewalk cafés. Amsterdam, Tamaulipas and Mazatlán, with central pedestrian paths, are worth strolling around to admire the art deco and California Colonial–style buildings. A focus is the peaceful **Parque México**, whose oval shape reflects its earlier use as a horse-racing track. It makes for a delightful ramble, especially in spring when lavender jacaranda blossoms carpet the paths. Two blocks northwest is **Parque España** with a children's fun fair.

Parque México is a 500m walk north from metro Chilpancingo. Alternatively, take an Av Insurgentes bus to the intersection with Av Michoacán (there's a Woolworth store on the corner) and walk two blocks west. The main cluster of bistro-type eateries in Condesa (see p152) is about 500m west of Parque México, near the intersection of Michoacán and Tamaulipas. Patriotismo and Juanacatlán metro stations are also within walking distance.

Colonia Roma, home to numerous artists and writers, was established in the late 19th century on the hacienda lands surrounding the center. Northeast of Condesa, its Parisian-style buildings (many damaged in the 1985 earthquake) are a reminder of the Porfiriato era's admiration for all things French. Two lovely plazas – Río de Janeiro, with a giant statue of David, and Luis Cabrera with dancing fountains – reinforce the old world character. When in Roma, browse in the used bookstores, linger in the cafés and check out a few art galleries (see Galleries, this page). On weekends browse the antique market along Av Álvaro Obregón, the main thoroughfare. The neighborhood holds literary notoriety as the site of William S Burroughs' William Tell incident, in which the beat novelist fatally shot his wife Joan while aiming for a martini glass on her head. Their home at Orizaba 210 has been razed and replaced by an apartment block.

GALLERIES
The Roma neighborhood is dotted with art galleries – see www.arte-mexico.com (in Spanish) for a map.

Centro Cultural Casa Lamm (☎ 5511-0899; www .casalamm.com.mx in Spanish; Álvaro Obregón 99; admission free; ✺ 10am-6pm Tue-Sun) houses a contemporary art gallery, plus the Manuel Álvarez Bravo photo collection, with more than 2000 original images by masters like Henri Cartier-Bresson, Edward Weston and Tina Modotti.

Other galleries of note:
MUCA Roma (☎ 5511-0925; Tabasco 73; ✺ 10am-6pm) Roma branch of university museum.
OMR (☎ 5511-1179; www.galeriaomr.com; Plaza Río de Janeiro 54; ✺ 10am-7pm Mon-Fri, 10am-2pm Sat)
Salón de la Plastica Mexicana (☎ 5511-6720; Colima 196; ✺ 10am-6pm Tue-Sun)

Bosque de Chapultepec   Map pp116–17
Chapultepec – 'Hill of Grasshoppers' in Náhuatl, the Aztec language – served as a refuge for the wandering Aztecs before eventually becoming a summer residence for their noble class. It was the nearest fresh water supply for Tenochtitlán and an aqueduct was built to channel its waters over Lago de Texcoco to the pre-Hispanic capital. In the 15th century, Nezahualcóyotl, ruler of nearby Texcoco, designated the area as a forest reserve.

The Bosque de Chapultepec remains Mexico City's largest park. It now covers more than 4 sq km and has lakes, a zoo and several excellent museums. It also remains an abode of Mexico's high and mighty, containing the current presidential residence, Los Pinos, and a former imperial and presidential palace, the Castillo de Chapultepec.

The park is busiest on Sunday, when vendors line its main paths and throngs of families come to picnic and crowd into the museums. It is divided into two main sections by two major north–south roads, Calz Chivatito and the Anillo Periférico. Most of the major attractions are in or near the eastern **1a Sección** (First Section; ✺ 5am-4pm Tue-Sun), while a large amusement park and children's museum dominate the **2a Sección**.

MONUMENTO A LOS NIÑOS HÉROES
The six asparagus-shaped columns marking the eastern entrance to the park, near Chapultepec metro, commemorate the 'boy heroes,' six brave cadets who perished in battle at the national military academy. On September 13, 1847, more than 8000 American troops stormed Chapultepec Castle, which then housed the academy. Mexican General Santa Anna retreated before the onslaught, excusing the cadets from fight-

ing, but the youths, aged 13 to 20, chose to defend the castle at the cost of their lives. Legend has it that one of them, Juan Escutia, wrapped himself in a Mexican flag and leapt to his death rather than surrender.

CASTILLO DE CHAPULTEPEC

The castle on Chapultepec Hill was built in 1785 as a residence for the viceroys of Nueva España. After independence it became the national military academy. When Emperor Maximilian and Empress Carlota arrived in 1864, they refurbished it as their residence. Later the castle became home to Mexico's presidents until 1939 when President Lázaro Cárdenas converted it into the **Museo Nacional de Historia** (National History Museum; ☎ 5241-3114; admission US$3.50; ☺ 9am-4:15pm Tue-Sun).

Recently renovated, the museum includes two sections. Historical exhibits chronicling the period from the rise of colonial Nueva España to the Mexican Revolution occupy the former military academy. The east end of the castle preserves the palace occupied by Maximilian and Carlota, flanked by a patio with expansive views. On the upper floor are Porfirio Díaz' sumptuous rooms, opening onto a central patio where a tower marks the top of Chapultepec Hill, 45m above. The lower southwest room covers the battle of Chapultepec, with portraits of the six heroic boys (see opposite).

Interpretations of Mexican history by leading muralists grace the walls of the academy, including Juan O'Gorman's *Retablo de la Independencia* (Panel of Independence) in room 5, and David Alfaro Siqueiros' *Del Porfiriato a la Revolución* (From Porfirism to the Revolution) in room 13.

To reach the castle, walk up the road that curves up the hill behind the Monumento a los Niños Héroes. Alternatively, a little road-train (US$1 round-trip) runs up every 10 minutes while the castle is open.

At the base of the castle is one of the park's perennial attractions, a **Hall of Mirrors** (admission US$0.30), housing 16 fun-house mirrors imported from Spain in 1932.

MUSEO DEL CARACOL

From the Castillo de Chapultepec, the **Museo del Caracol** (☎ 5553-6285; admission US$3; ☺ 9am-4:15pm Tue-Sun) is a short distance back down the road. Shaped somewhat like a *caracol* (snail shell), this 'gallery of history' traces the origins of Mexico's present-day institutions, identity and values through a series of audio-enhanced dioramas reenacting key moments in the country's struggle for liberty. The 12 exhibit halls spiral downward. Along the way they depict the cry for independence at Dolores Hidalgo, the May 5 battle of Puebla, the execution of Maximillian, and the triumphant entrance of Madero into Mexico City. The tour ends at a circular hall that contains only one item – a replica of the 1917 Constitution of Mexico.

MUSEO DE ARTE MODERNO

The **Museum of Modern Art** (☎ 5553-2243; cnr Paseo de la Reforma & Gandhi; admission US$1.50, free Sun; ☺ 10am-5pm Tue-Sun) exhibits work by Mexico's most noteworthy 20th-century artists. The main building consists of four skylit rotundas, housing canvasses by Dr Atl, Rivera, Siqueiros, Orozco, Kahlo, Tamayo and O'Gorman, among others. *Las Dos Fridas*, possibly Frida Kahlo's most well-known painting, is in the Sala Xavier Villarrutia. Temporary exhibitions feature prominent Mexican and foreign artists. Just northwest of the Monumento a los Niños Héroes (access is via Paseo de la Reforma), the museum has a pleasant café beside a sculpture garden.

ZOOLÓGICO DE CHAPULTEPEC

The **Chapultepec Zoo** (☎ 5556-4104; Calle Chivatito; admission free; ☺ 9am-4:30pm Tue-Sun) houses a wide range of the world's creatures in large open-air enclosures. The only place outside China where pandas have been born in captivity, the zoo has three of these rare bears, descendants of the original pair donated by the People's Republic in 1975. Endangered Mexican species include the Mexican grey wolf and the hairless Xoloitzcuintle, the only surviving dog species from pre-Hispanic times.

Part of Chapultepec forest was given over to a bird sanctuary as far back as Moctezuma's reign; today, parrots, macaws, toucans, flamingos and other Mexican bird species swoop around the Aviario Moctezuma (only 20 visitors allowed in at a time).

There are various fast food franchises on the premises.

MUSEO NACIONAL DE ANTROPOLOGÍA

The **National Museum of Anthropology** (☎ 5553-6381; www.mna.inah.gob.mx in Spanish; cnr Paseo de la Reforma & Gandhi; admission US$3.50; ☺ 9am-7pm Tue-Sun), among the finest of its kind, stands in an extension of the Bosque de Chapultepec.

The vast museum offers more than most people can absorb in a single visit. Concentrate on the regions you plan to visit or have visited, with a quick look at some of the other eye-catching exhibits. Everything is superbly displayed, with much explanatory text translated into English. 'Audio guide' devices, in English, are available at the entrance (US$6).

In a clearing about 100m in front of the museum's entrance, indigenous Totonac people perform their spectacular voladores rite – 'flying' from a 20m-high pole (see p662) – several times a day.

The spacious complex, constructed in the 1960s, is the work of Mexican architect Pedro Ramírez Vázquez. Its long, rectangular courtyard is surrounded on three sides by two-story display halls. An immense umbrella-like stone fountain rises up from the center of the courtyard.

The 12 ground-floor *salas* (halls) are dedicated to pre-Hispanic Mexico. The upper level shows how Mexico's indigenous descendants of those pre-Hispanic civilizations live today. With a few exceptions, each upstairs section covers the same territory as the archaeological exhibit below it. Here's a brief guide to the ground-floor halls, proceeding counterclockwise around the courtyard:

Sala Culturas Indígenas de México presents an overview of the belief systems shared by Mesoamerican cultures, displaying objects associated with the myths, rituals and ceremonies of Mexico's indigenous peoples.

Sala Introducción a la Antropología introduces visitors to the field of anthropology and traces the emergence of homo sapiens from their hominid ancestors.

Sala Poblamiento de América demonstrates how the hemisphere's earliest settlers got here and survived in their new environment.

Sala Preclásica Altiplano Central focuses on the Preclassic period, approximately 2300 BC to AD 100. These exhibits highlight the transition from a nomadic hunting life to a more settled farming life in Mexico's Central Highlands.

Sala Teotihuacán displays models and objects from Teotihuacán – the Americas' first great and powerful state. The exhibit includes a full-size replica of part of the Templo de Quetzalcóatl.

Sala Los Toltecas y Su Época covers cultures of central Mexico between about AD 650 and AD 1250 and is named for one of the most important of these, the Toltecs. On display is one of the four basalt warrior columns from Tula's Temple of Tlahuizcalpantecuhtli.

Sala Mexica is devoted to the Mexicas, aka Aztecs. Come here to see the famous sun stone, unearthed in a fractured state beneath the Zócalo in 1790. Though often erroneously identified as a representation of the Aztec calendar, it is probably a sacrificial altar. It depicts the face of the fire god, Xiuhtechtli, at the center of a web of symbols representing the Mexica vision of the cosmos. Other exhibits include a model of the Tlatelolco market, an 'aerial view' painting of Tenochtitlán, and other graphic evidence.

Sala Oaxaca is devoted to Oaxaca state's cultural heights, scaled by the Zapotec and Mixtec peoples. A tomb from the hilltop site of Monte Albán is reproduced full-size below the main exhibit hall.

Sala Golfo de México spotlights the important civilizations along the Gulf of Mexico including the Olmec, Classic Veracruz, Totonac and Huastec. Stone carvings here include two magnificent Olmec heads.

Sala Maya has exhibits from southeast Mexico, Guatemala, Belize and Honduras. A full-scale replica of the tomb of King Pakal, discovered deep in the Templo de las Inscripciones at Palenque, is breathtaking. On the outside patio are reproductions of the famous wall paintings of Bonampak and of Edificio II at Hochob, in Campeche, constructed as a giant mask of the rain god, Chac.

Sala Culturas de Occidente profiles cultures of western Mexico from Nayarit, Jalisco, Michoacán, Colima and Guerrero states.

Sala Culturas del Norte covers the Casas Grandes (Paquimé) site and other cultures from arid northern Mexico and traces their links with indigenous groups of the US Southwest.

MUSEO RUFINO TAMAYO

A multilevel concrete and glass structure east of the Museo Nacional de Antropología, the **Tamayo Museum** (☎ 5286-6519; www.museotamayo.org in Spanish; cnr Paseo de la Reforma & Calz Gandhi; admission US$1, free Sun; ��� 10am-6pm Tue-Sun) was built to house the collection of international modern art donated by Oaxaca-born Rufino Tamayo and his wife, Olga, to the people of Mexico. Ten naturally lit halls display the works of major 20th-century artists, including Picasso, Miró and Tamayo himself, as well as innovative temporary exhibitions.

SEGUNDA (2ª) SECCIÓN

The second section of the Bosque de Chapultepec lies west of the Periférico. In addition to family attractions, there are two lake-view restaurants (see p154).

Kids will enjoy **La Feria** (☎ 5230-2112; passes from US$1; ��� 10am-6pm Mon-Fri, 10am-9pm Sat & Sun), an old-fashioned amusement park with some hair-raising rides. A 'Super Ecolín' passport (US$5.50) is good for all the rides except the roller-coaster and a few others; a 'pase mágico' (US$1) includes several dozen children's rides and five big kids' rides. There's separate admission for the white whales show.

Your kids won't want to leave **Papalote Museo del Niño** (☎ 5237-1777; www.papalote.org.mx in Spanish; adult/child 2-11/senior US$6/5/5 per 4hr session, with Imax admission US$8/9/8; ✆ 9am-1pm & 2-6pm Mon-Fri, 7-11pm Thu, 10am-2pm & 3-7pm Sat & Sun). At this innovative, hands-on museum, kids can put together a radio program, lie on a bed of nails, join an archaeological dig and try out all manner of technical/scientific gadget-games. Everything is attended by child-friendly supervisors. The museum also features a 3-D Imax movie theater.

Just north of Papalote, the **Museo Tecnológico** (☎ 5516-0964; admission free; ✆ 9am-5pm), managed by the Federal Electricity Commission, showcases Mexico's technological development, with interactive exhibits on electricity and transportation as well as a planetarium. Railcars, oil-drilling machines and other industrial equipment have been put out to pasture around the building. The **Museo de Historia Natural** (Natural History Museum; ☎ 5515-2222; admission US$1.75, free Tue; ✆ 10am-5pm Tue-Sun), a 10-minute walk west of Papalote, presents the evolution of life on earth under a series of colored domes.

Circling around the Lago Menor, you'll find the **Fuente de Tlaloc** by Diego Rivera, a huge mosaic-skinned sculpture of the rain god lying in an oval pool. The pavilion behind it houses the **Cárcamo Tlaloc** (admission free; ✆ 10am-4:30pm Tue-Sun), the Chapultepec water works, built in the 1940s to channel the waters of the Río Lerma, 62km west, into giant cisterns to supply the city. Rivera painted a series of murals entitled *Water, Origin of Life,* to decorate the walls of the basin the water flowed through. This gripping tableau has recently been restored for public viewing. To the north is the beautiful **Fuente de Xochipilli**, dedicated to the Aztec 'flower prince,' with terraced fountains around a *talud-tablero*-style pyramid.

GETTING THERE & AWAY
Chapultepec metro station is at the east end of the Bosque de Chapultepec, near the Monumento a los Niños Héroes and Castillo de Chapultepec. Metro Auditorio station is on the north side of the park, 500m west of the Museo Nacional de Antropología.

From anywhere on Paseo de la Reforma west of the Alameda Central, buses saying 'M(etro) Chapultepec' or 'M(etro) Auditorio' will reach Chapultepec metro station, and the latter pass right outside the Museo Nacional de Antropología. Returning downtown, any 'M(etro) Hidalgo/La Villa,' 'Alameda,' or 'Garibaldi' bus, from either metro Chapultepec or heading east on Reforma will go along Reforma at least as far as metro Hidalgo.

To get to the 2a Sección and La Feria, from metro Chapultepec take the 'Paradero' exit and catch a 'Feria' bus at the top of the stairs. These depart continuously and travel nonstop to the 2a Sección, dropping off riders at the Papalote Museo del Niño, Museo Tecnológico and La Feria.

Polanco   Map pp116–17
This affluent residential quarter north of Bosque de Chapultepec, where the streets are named after writers and scientists, contains lots of restaurants, art galleries and embassies, some luxury hotels and the Sectur tourist office (p103). Much of the architecture is in the California Colonial style of the 1930s and '40s, with carved stone doorways and window surrounds. A tour of Polanco could be combined with a visit to the nearby Museo Nacional de Antropología (p129).

Xochimilco & Around
About 20km south of downtown Mexico City, the urban sprawl is strung with a network of canals lined by gardens. These are the so-called 'floating gardens' of Xochimilco ('so-chi-*meel*-co'), remnants of the chinampas where the Aztecs grew their food. Gliding along the canals in a *trajinera* (gondola) is an alternately tranquil and festive experience. Nearby attractions include an ecological theme park and one of the city's best art museums.

MUSEO DOLORES OLMEDO
PATIÑO   Map p118
Set in a peaceful 17th-century hacienda, the **Olmedo Patiño museum** (☎ 5555-1016; Av México 5843; admission US$1; ✆ 10am-6pm Tue-Sun),

2km west of Xochimilco, has perhaps the biggest and most important Diego Rivera collection of all. You'll see Xoloitzcuintles, a pre-Hispanic hairless canine breed, roaming the estate's extensive gardens.

Dolores Olmedo Patiño, who resided here until her death in 2002, was a socialite and a patron of Rivera, amassing a large collection of his art. The museum's 137 Rivera works – including oils, watercolors and lithographs from various periods – are displayed alongside pre-Hispanic figurines and folk art. Another room is reserved for Frida Kahlo's paintings.

To get there take the Tren Ligero (light rail) from metro Tasqueña and get off at La Noria. Leaving the station, turn left at the top of the steps, walk down to the street and continue to an intersection with a footbridge. Here turn a sharp left, almost doubling back on your path, onto Antiguo Camino Xochimilco. The museum is 300m down this street.

XOCHIMILCO Map p118

Xochimilco, Náhuatl for 'Place where Flowers Grow,' was an early target of Aztec hegemony, probably due to its inhabitants' farming skills. The Xochimilcas piled up vegetation and mud in the shallow waters of Lake Xochimilco, a southern offshoot of Lago de Texcoco, to make fertile gardens called chinampas, which later became an economic base of the Aztec empire. As the chinampas proliferated, much of the lake was transformed into a series of canals. Approximately 180km of these waterways remain today and provide a favorite weekend destination for Chilangos (citizens of Mexico City). On weekends a fiesta atmosphere takes over as the town and waterways become jammed with people arranging boats and cruising the canals. For a more relaxed atmosphere, come on a weekday.

East of Jardín Juárez stands the 16th-century **Parroquia de San Bernardino de Siena**, with elaborate, gold-painted *retablos* (altarpieces) and a large tree-studded atrium. To the south is the bustling **Mercado de Xochimilco**.

Hundreds of colorful *trajineras* wait to cruise the canals at village's nine *embarcaderos* (boat landings). Nearest to the center are Salitre and San Cristóbal embarcaderos, both 400m east of the plaza; and Fernando Celada, 400m west on Guadalupe Ramírez. Official cruise prices are posted at the embarcaderos. A 10- to 12-person boat (blue roof) is US$14 an hour; and a 20-person boat (green), US$16. On Saturday, Sunday and holidays, 60-person *lanchas colectivos* run between the Salitre, Caltongo, and Nativitas embarcaderos charging US$1 per passenger.

Fixed prices for food, drink and even mariachis on the boats are also posted at the embarcaderos. You can get a taste of Xochimilco in one hour, but it's worth going for longer; you'll see more and get a proper chance to relax. You can arrange for your *trajinera* to stop at Nativitas embarcadero for some shopping at its large *artesanías* market.

To reach Xochimilco, take the metro to Tasqueña station, then continue on the Tren Ligero (US$0.20) to its last stop, Xochimilco. Upon exiting, turn left (north) and follow Av Morelos to the market, plaza and church. If you don't feel like walking, bicycle taxis will ride you to the embarcaderos (US$3). The last Tren Ligero back to Tasqueña leaves Xochimilco station at about 11pm. Another option, instead of returning to central Xochimilco, is to catch a 'Metro Tasqueña' pesero from outside Nativitas landing.

PARQUE ECOLÓGICO DE XOCHIMILCO Map pp104–5

A landscape comprising lakes, a botanical garden and a surprising variety of water birds lures stressed urbanites to this 2-sq-km **park** (☎ 5673-8061, Periférico Oriente 1; adult/senior/child US$1.50/0.50/0.20; ☺ 9am-6pm), about 3km northeast of downtown Xochimilco. Stroll the pleasant (though shadeless) pathways or hire a bicycle, pedal boat or, better yet, a *trajinera*. A visitors center has displays on plants and birds.

To see the genuine chinampas of northern Xochimilco, hire a *trajinera* at Embarcadero Cuemanco, just 2km west of the park entrance.

To reach Parque Ecológico de Xochimilco, take a 'Tlahuac' pesero northbound on Calz de Tlalpan outside metro General Anaya (Línea 2). From the center of Xochimilco, take a 'Villa Coapa' pesero to the 'Vaqueritos' traffic circle. Walk up to the intersection with the Periférico and go right, where you can board a 'Cuemanco' pesero to the park entrance, beside a blue footbridge with spiral towers at either end.

San Ángel   Map p111

Just a little over 60 years ago, San Ángel was a village separated from Mexico City by open fields. Today it's one of the city's most charming suburbs, with many quiet cobblestoned streets lined by both old colonial houses and expensive modern ones, and a variety of things to see and do.

Av Insurgentes Sur and Av Revolución run north to south through eastern San Ángel.

PLAZA SAN JACINTO & BAZAR SÁBADO

Every Saturday the **Bazar Sábado** (p166) brings a festive atmosphere, masses of color and crowds of people to San Ángel's pretty little Plaza San Jacinto.

Enter the 16th-century **Iglesia de San Jacinto** and its peaceful gardens by walking 50m west up Benito Juárez from the northwest corner of the plaza. The **Museo Casa del Risco** (☎ 5550-9286; Plaza San Jacinto 15; admission free; ♥ 10am-5pm Tue-Sun) occupies an 18th-century mansion which has a fascinating mosaic fountain in a pretty courtyard. Inside you'll find a permanent exhibition of 14th- to 19th-century European art and 17th- to 19th-century Mexican art, as well as temporary exhibitions.

MUSEO CASA ESTUDIO DIEGO RIVERA Y FRIDA KAHLO

One kilometer northwest of Plaza San Jacinto is the **Diego Rivera & Frida Kahlo Studio Museum** (☎ 5550-1518; Rivera 2 at Altavista; admission US$1, free Sun; ♥ 10am-6pm Tue-Sun). The famous artist couple (see p136) lived in this 1930s avant-garde abode – with a separate house for each of them – from 1934 to 1940, when they divorced. Though they remarried soon after, Kahlo moved to a house in Coyoacán, while Rivera stayed on until his death in 1957.

The museum has only a few examples of Rivera's art and none of Kahlo's, but it holds a lot of memorabilia. Rivera's house (the pink one) has an upstairs studio. Across the street is the **San Ángel Inn** (p155), in the 17th-century Ex-Hacienda de Goicoechea, once the home of the marquises of La Selva Nevada and the count of Pinillas. The former pulque hacienda is where

Pancho Villa and Emiliano Zapata agreed to divide control of the country.

TEMPLO Y MUSEO DE EL CARMEN

The peaceful Templo de El Carmen, a 17th-century tile-domed church, houses a **museum** (☎ 5616-2816; www.museodeelcarmen.org in Spanish; Av Revolución 4; admission US$3, free Sun; ♥ 10am-5pm Tue-Sun) in the former monastic quarters. The museum is devoted to colonial-era furniture and religious art, but its big draw is the mummified bodies in the crypt, which are thought to be 18th-century monks, nuns and gentry. You can also walk out into the garden, which was once a source of cuttings and seeds for much of colonial Mexico.

JARDÍN DE LA BOMBILLA

This pleasant park lies just east of Av Insurgentes. The **Monumento a Álvaro Obregón** marks the spot where the Mexican president was assassinated during a banquet in 1928. Obregón's killer, José de León Toral, was involved in the Cristero rebellion against the government's anti-Church policies.

PLAZA LORETO

Plaza Loreto, 600m south of Plaza San Jacinto, is an attractive shopping mall converted from an old paper factory. Several patios and courtyards are set between the brick buildings. The plaza features a mini-amphitheater for performances, several boutique shops, a variety of eateries and the **Museo Soumaya** (☎ 5616-3731; admission US$1; ♥ 10:30am-6:30pm Thu-Mon, 10:30am-8:30pm Wed), housing one of the world's three major collections (70 pieces) of the sculptures of Auguste Rodin (1840–1917), plus work by Degas, Matisse and other masters.

GETTING THERE & AWAY

'San Ángel' peseros and buses run south on Insurgentes. Most terminate on Dr Gálvez between Av Insurgentes and Av Revolución. Peseros also depart from metro Chapultepec, running south on Revolución to Río Magdalena and Plaza Loreto. For the Bazar Sábado, get off at the yellow Centro Cultural San Ángel, south of the flower market.

Alternatively, take the metro to Barranca del Muerto, then a 'San Ángel' pesero outside the 'Revolución Poniente' exit.

Returning north to the city center, 'M(etro) Indios Verdes' and 'M(etro) La Raza' buses

MEXICO CITY

run up Av Insurgentes to the north of town; 'M(etro) Insurgentes' vehicles go to the Zona Rosa. Going up Av Revolución, 'M(etro) Chapultepec' peseros stop at metro Barranca del Muerto, continuing up Av Patriotismo past the Condesa neighborhood.

To Coyoacán, a 'M(etro) Tasqueña' bus along Av MA de Quevedo will take you to the corner of Carrillo Puerto, five blocks south of the Jardín del Centenario.

Ciudad Universitaria   Map pp104–5

The University City, 2km south of San Ángel, is the main campus of Latin America's largest university, the Universidad Nacional Autónoma de México (UNAM), and a modern architectural showpiece. To see a map go to www.mapa.unam.mx (in Spanish).

The university was founded in the 1550s but was suppressed from 1833 to 1910. Most of it was built between 1949 and 1952 by a team of 150 young architects and technicians. It's a monument both to national pride and to an idealistic education system in which almost anyone is entitled to university tuition. However, in recent years, UNAM has struggled to compete academically with increasingly prestigious private universities.

UNAM has some 260,000 students and 31,000 teachers. It has often been a center of political dissent, most notably prior to the 1968 Mexico City Olympics. In 1999/2000 the university was closed for nine and a half months by a student strike. Initially protesting a proposed rise in tuition (from a token US$0.02 a semester to US$65), the strikers developed wider demands such as a far-reaching reorganization of the university. Eventually police retook the occupied campus. It was a testament to the scars left on Mexico's psyche by the 1968 Tlatelolco massacre that they carried no firearms and no one was injured.

Most of the faculty buildings are scattered over an area about 1km square at the north end. As you enter from Av Insurgentes, it's easy to spot the **Biblioteca Central** (Central Library), 10 stories high, almost windowless, and covered with mosaics by Juan O'Gorman. The south wall, with two prominent zodiac wheels, covers colonial times, while the north wall deals with Aztec culture. The east wall shows the creation of modern Mexico; and the more abstract west

wall may be dedicated to Latin American culture as a whole.

La Rectoría, the administration building, at the west end of the wide, grassy Jardín Central, has a vivid Siqueiros mosaic on its south wall, showing students urged on by the people.

South of the Rectoría stands the **Museo Universitario de Ciencias y Arte** (MUCA; ☎ 5622-0273; admission by donation; ⏰ 10am-7pm Mon-Fri, 10am-6pm Sat & Sun), with eclectic exhibits from the university collection and contemporary art.

The **Auditorio Alfonso Caso**, at the east end of the Jardín Central, bears a mural by José Chávez Morado showing the conquest of energy, with humanity progressing from the shadow of a primitive jaguar god into an ethereal future. Further east, illustrating the **Facultad de Medicina**, is an intriguing mosaic by Francisco Eppens in which Spanish and indigenous profiles combine to form a mestizo face.

Rebuilt for the 1968 Olympics, the **Estadio Olímpico**, to the west of Av Insurgentes, holds 80,000. A Rivera mosaic designed to resemble a volcanic cone graces the main entrance.

A second section of the campus, about 2km south, contains the **Centro Cultural Universitario** (CUC), hosting the performing arts in its theaters and concert halls (see p160); and the **Museo Universitario de Ciencias** (Universum; ☎ 5622-7287; www.universum.unam.mx in Spanish; admission US$3; ⏰ 9am-6pm Mon-Fri, 10am-6pm Sat & Sun), the university's science museum. Other attractions here include UNAM's botanical gardens; the Unidad Bibliográfica, housing part of Mexico's National Library; and the Espacio Escultórico (Sculptural Space), focused on a striking work by Mathias Goeritz consisting of triangular concrete blocks around a lava bed.

Student cafés, open to everyone during academic sessions, are in both the architecture and philosophy buildings at the Jardín Central's west end, and in the Centro Cultural Universitario.

GETTING THERE & AWAY

Orange RTP (municipal) buses marked 'Villa Olímpica' travel down Av Insurgentes from the center of town to the west side of the campus. Alternatively take a pesero down Av Insurgentes to San Ángel, where you can catch a 'Perisur' pesero to the university.

For the northern part of the campus, get off at the first yellow footbridge crossing Av Insurgentes, just before the Estadio Olímpico. For the southern section, get off at the second yellow footbridge after the Estadio Olímpico.

Otherwise, take the metro to Universidad station, on the east side of the campus. The university runs three bus routes (free) from the metro station between 6:30am and 10:30pm Monday to Friday. Ruta 1 goes west to the main part of the campus; Ruta 3 heads southwest to the Centro Cultural Universitario.

Coyoacán

About 10km south of downtown, Coyoacán ('Place of Coyotes' in Náhuatl language) was Cortés' base after the fall of Tenochtitlán. It remained a small outlying town until urban sprawl reached it 50 years ago. Close to the university and once home to Leon Trotsky and Frida Kahlo (whose houses are now fascinating museums), Coyoacán still has its own identity, with narrow colonial-era streets, plazas, cafés and a lively atmosphere. Especially on weekends, assorted musicians, mimes and crafts markets (see p164) draw large but relaxed crowds from all walks of life to Coyoacán's central plazas.

VIVEROS DE COYOACÁN   Map p119
A pleasant approach is via the **Viveros de Coyoacán** (Coyoacán Nurseries; ☎ 5554-1851; admission free; ☉ 6am-6pm), a swath of greenery 1km west of central Coyoacán. It's popular with joggers and perfect for a stroll, but watch out for belligerent squirrels! From metro Viveros, walk south along Av Universidad, then take the first street on the left, Av Progreso; or enter on Av México near Madrid.

A block south of Viveros is the pretty **Plaza Santa Catarina**. The adjacent **Centro Cultural Jesús Reyes Heroles** (☎ 5659-3937; Francisco Sosa 202) is a lovely colonial estate hosting art exhibits, concerts and culinary demonstrations in a Talavera-tiled kitchen. The 700m walk east along **Av Francisco Sosa** to Plaza Hidalgo takes you past some beautiful 16th- and 17th-century houses.

PLAZA HIDALGO &
JARDÍN DEL CENTENARIO   Map p119
The focus of Coyoacán life, and scene of most of the weekend fun, is its central

plaza – actually two adjacent plazas: the eastern **Plaza Hidalgo**, with a statue of Miguel Hidalgo; and the western **Jardín del Centenario**, with a coyote fountain.

A tourist office is inside the Casa de Cortés, the former Coyoacán town hall, on the north side of Plaza Hidalgo (see p103). This is where conquistador Cortés established Mexico's first municipal seat during the siege of Tenochtitlán and later had the defeated emperor Cuauhtémoc tortured to make him divulge the location of Aztec treasure. Cortés resided here until 1523 when the Spanish government moved to Mexico City.

The 16th-century **Parroquia de San Juan Bautista** and its adjacent ex-monastery dominate the south side of Plaza Hidalgo. Half a block east, the **Museo Nacional de Culturas Populares** (☎ 5554-8968; Av Hidalgo 289; admission free; ☉ 10am-6pm Tue-Thu, 10am-8pm Fri-Sun) hosts innovative exhibitions on popular culture, covering such topics as *lucha libre* (wrestling) and the role of maize in society. Outside, an amazing tree of life from Metepec marks the 500th anniversary of the meeting of old and new worlds.

MUSEO FRIDA KAHLO   Map p119
The **'Blue House'** (☎ 5554-5999; Londres 247; adult/child 6-12 US$3/2; ☉ 10am-6pm Tue-Sun), six blocks north of Plaza Hidalgo, was the longtime home of artist Frida Kahlo (see p136).

Kahlo and her husband, Diego Rivera, were part of a glamorous but far from harmonious leftist intellectual circle (which included, in the 1930s, Leon Trotsky), and the house is littered with mementos. In addition to their own and other artists' work, it contains pre-Hispanic objects and Mexican crafts collected by the couple.

The Kahlo art expresses the anguish of her existence; one painting, *El Marxismo Dará la Salud* (Marxism Will Give Health), shows her casting away her crutches. In the upstairs studio an unfinished portrait of Stalin stands before a poignantly positioned wheelchair. The folk art collection includes Mexican regional costumes worn by Kahlo, and Rivera's collection of *retablo* paintings, plus a number of intriguing *exvotos* (small paintings done by the devout to give thanks for miracles).

MUSEO LÉON TROTSKY   Map p119
Having come second to Stalin in the power struggle in the Soviet Union, Trotsky was

FRIDA & DIEGO

Diego Rivera, born in Guanajuato in 1886, first met Frida Kahlo, 21 years his junior, when he was painting at the prestigious Escuela Nacional Preparatoria, where she was a student in the early 1920s. Rivera was already at the forefront of Mexican art and a socialist; his commission at the school was the first of many semi-propagandistic murals on public buildings that he was to execute over three decades. He had already fathered children by two Russian women in Europe and in 1922 married Lupe Marín in Mexico. She bore him two more children before their marriage broke up in 1928.

Kahlo, born in Coyoacán in 1907, contracted polio at age six, leaving her right leg permanently thinner than her left. In 1925 she was horribly injured in a trolley accident that broke her back, right leg, collarbone, pelvis and ribs. She made a miraculous recovery but suffered much pain thereafter and underwent many operations to try to alleviate it. It was during convalescence that she began painting. Pain – physical and emotional – was to be a dominating theme of her art.

Kahlo and Rivera both moved in left-wing artistic circles and met again in 1928; they married the following year. The liaison, described as 'a union between an elephant and a dove,' was always a passionate love-hate affair. Rivera wrote: 'If I ever loved a woman, the more I loved her, the more I wanted to hurt her. Frida was only the most obvious victim of this disgusting trait.' Both had many extramarital affairs.

Kahlo's beauty, bisexuality and unconventional behavior – she drank tequila, told dirty jokes and held wild parties – fascinated many people. In 1934, after a spell in the USA, the pair moved into a new home in San Ángel, with separate houses for each of them, linked by an aerial walkway. Rivera and Kahlo divorced in 1940 but remarried soon after. She moved into the Blue House and he stayed at San Ángel – a state of affairs that endured for the rest of their lives, though their relationship endured too. Kahlo remained Rivera's most trusted critic, and Rivera was Kahlo's biggest fan.

Kahlo had only one exhibition in Mexico in her lifetime, in 1953. She arrived at the opening on a stretcher. Rivera said of the exhibition, 'Anyone who attended it could not but marvel at her great talent.' She died, at the Blue House, the following year. Rivera called the day of her death 'the most tragic day of my life... Too late I realized that the most wonderful part of my life had been my love for Frida.'

expelled in 1929 and condemned to death in absentia. In 1937 Trotsky found refuge in Mexico. At first Trotsky and his wife, Natalia, lived in Frida Kahlo's Blue House, but after falling out with Kahlo and Rivera they moved a few streets away, to Viena 45.

The **Trotsky home** (☎ 5658-8732; entrance at Av Río Churubusco 410; admission US$3; ☻ 10am-5pm Tue-Sun) remains much as it was on the day in 1940 when a Stalin agent finally caught up with the revolutionary and killed him here. High walls and watchtowers (which were once occupied by armed guards) surround the house and garden. These defenses were built after a first attempt on Trotsky's life, on May 24, 1940, when attackers led by the Mexican artist (and Stalinist) David Siqueiros pumped bullets into the house. Trotsky and Natalia survived by hiding under their bedroom furniture. The bullet holes remain.

The fatal attack took place in Trotsky's study. Assassin Ramón Mercader, a Catalan, had become the lover of Trotsky's secretary and gained the confidence of the household. On August 20, 1940, Mercader approached Trotsky at his desk and asked him to look at a document. He then pulled an ice axe from under his coat and smashed the pick end into Trotsky's skull. Mercader was arrested and spent 20 years in prison.

Memorabilia and biographical notes are displayed in outbuildings, and videos on the life of the revolutionary are continuously screened in a room off the patio, where a tomb engraved with a hammer and sickle contains the Trotskys' ashes.

EX-CONVENTO DE CHURUBUSCO   Map p119
The 17th-century former Monastery of Churubusco, scene of one of Mexico's heroic military defeats, stands east of Av División del Norte.

Though Kahlo's work was little appreciated during her lifetime, it has become the most highly valued of any Mexican painter – or of any female artist – fetching more at international auctions than Rivera's. (Kahlo's *Self-Portrait with Curly Hair* sold for US$1.3 million at a Christie's auction in 2003.)

Frida, the 2002 hit biopic, brought the painter even wider recognition. Though the film did very well in Mexico, it got mixed reviews from intellectuals who complained that none of the actors (except Salma Hayek, who played Kahlo) were Mexican – and even worse, that they spoke English, a betrayal of the vocally anti-American Frida.

Kahlo & Rivera Sites in Mexico City

There's much more of his work than hers on view – partly because he was a more prolific, public and versatile artist, partly because some of her best work is in private collections or other countries.

- **Anahuacalli** (below) – fortress-like museum designed by Rivera to house his pre-Hispanic art collection
- **Antiguo Colegio de San Ildefonso** (p124) – the former Escuela Nacional Preparatoria
- **Museo Casa Estudio Diego Rivera y Frida Kahlo** (p133) – their double house
- **Museo de Arte Moderno** (p129) – includes works by Kahlo and Rivera
- **Museo Dolores Olmedo Patiño** (p131) – 137 Rivera works and a room of Kahlos in the excellent collection of a Rivera patron
- **Museo Frida Kahlo** (p135) – the 'Blue House'
- **Museo Mural Diego Rivera** (p126) – holds Rivera's mural *Sueño de una Tarde Dominical en la Alameda*
- **Palacio de Bellas Artes** (p125) – 1930s Rivera murals
- **Palacio Nacional** (p121) – Rivera's mural history of Mexican civilization
- **Secretaría de Educación Pública** (p123) – 120 fresco panels painted by Rivera and helpers in the 1920s

On August 20, 1847, Mexican troops defended the monastery against US forces advancing from Veracruz in a dispute over the US annexation of Texas. The Mexicans fought until they ran out of ammunition and were beaten only after hand-to-hand fighting. General Pedro Anaya, when asked by US general David Twiggs to surrender his ammunition, is said to have answered, 'If there was any, you wouldn't be here.' Cannons and memorials outside recall these events.

Most of the monastery now houses the interesting **Museo Nacional de las Intervenciones** (National Interventions Museum; ☎ 5604-0699; cnr 20 de Agosto & General Anaya; admission US$3, free Sun; 9am-6pm Tue-Sun). Displays include an American map showing operations in 1847, and material on the French occupation of the 1860s and the plot by US ambassador Henry Lane Wilson to bring down the Madero government in 1913. Parts of the monastery gardens are also open.

To reach Churubusco, catch an eastbound 'M(etro) Gral Anaya' pesero or bus on Xicoténcatl at Allende, a few blocks north of Coyoacán's Plaza Hidalgo. Alternatively, it's a 500m walk from the General Anaya metro station.

ANAHUACALLI   Map pp104–5

This dramatic **museum** (☎ 5617-4310; Calle del Museo 150; admission US$3; 10am-6pm Tue-Sun), 3.5km south of Coyoacán, was designed by Diego Rivera to house his collection of pre-Hispanic art. It also contains one of his studios and some of his work.

The fortress-like building is made of dark volcanic stone and incorporates pre-Hispanic stylistic features. Its name means 'House of Anáhuac' (Anáhuac was the Aztec name for the Valle de México). If the air is clear, there's a great view from the roof. In November elaborate Day of the Dead offerings pay homage to the painter.

The archaeological exhibits are mostly of pottery and stone figures, chosen for their artistic qualities. Among Rivera's own art are studies for major murals such as *El Hombre, Controlador del Universo*, now displayed in the Palacio de Bellas Artes.

To get to Anahuacalli, take the Tren Ligero (from metro Tasqueña) to the Xotepingo station. Exit on the west side and walk 200m west to División del Norte; cross and continue 600m along Calle del Museo, curving to the left at first, then going slightly uphill.

GETTING THERE & AWAY

The nearest metro stations (1.5km to 2km) to the center of Coyoacán are Viveros, Coyoacán and General Anaya. If you don't fancy a walk, get off at Viveros station, walk south to Progreso and catch an eastbound 'M(etro) Gral Anaya' pesero to Allende; alternatively from Coyoacán station, go south on Av Universidad to Av México (follow signs to Museo Leon Trotsky) and catch a 'Coyoacán' pesero.

Returning to these metro stations, 'M(etro) Viveros' peseros go west on Malitzin, and 'M(etro) Coyoacán' and 'M(etro) Gral Anaya' peseros depart from the west side of Plaza Hidalgo.

San Ángel-bound peseros and buses head west on Av MA de Quevedo, five blocks south of Plaza Hidalgo. To Ciudad Universitaria, take a 'CU' pesero west on Belisario Domínguez, from the corner of Centenario.

Parque Nacional Desierto de los Leones

Cool, fragrant pine and oak forests dominate this 20-sq-km **national park** (6am-5pm) in the hills surrounding the Valle de México. Some 23km southwest of Mexico City and 800m higher, it makes a fine escape from the carbon monoxide and concrete.

The name derives from the **Ex-Convento del Santo Desierto de Nuestra Señora del Carmen** (admission US$1; 10am-5pm Tue-Sun), the 17th-century former Carmelite monastery within the park. The Carmelites called their isolated monasteries 'deserts' to commemorate Elijah, who lived as a recluse in the desert near Mt Carmel. 'Leones' may stem from the presence of wild cats in the area, but more likely refers to José and Manuel de León, who once administered the monastery's finances.

Built from 1606 to 1611, the monastery was abandoned two centuries later when the monks chose to escape the too wet, too cool climate and their too frequent visitors, relocating to a new compound outside Tenancingo.

The restored Ex-Convento has exhibition halls and a restaurant. (Better value meals are available in the nearby comedores.) Tours in Spanish (weekends only) are run by guides garbed in cassock and sandals who explore the patios within and expansive gardens around the buildings. Visitors are also led through underground passageways and to a 'Chapel of Secrets,' where the friars, under an oath of silence, could communicate their innermost thoughts, thanks to the structure's ingenious acoustics.

The rest of the park has extensive walking trails. (Robberies have been reported, so stick to the main paths.) One good walk is from the spot known as Cruz Blanca up to the chapel-crowned **Cerro San Miguel** at about 3800m. The route (two hours each way) follows the perimeter wall of the old monastery's property. To reach Cruz Blanca, turn right up a side road, immediately before a vehicle toll barrier (US$1) halfway from Hwy 15 to the Ex-Convento. It's about 4km up to Cruz Blanca, where you should find a forest warden who can direct you to Cerro San Miguel.

GETTING THERE & AWAY

Take one of Flecha Roja's frequent 'Toluca Intermedio' buses from the Terminal Poniente bus station to La Venta, on Hwy 15 (US$1, 30 minutes). Tell the driver your destination and you should be dropped at a yellow footbridge just short of a *caseta de cobro* (toll booth). Cross the footbridge and you'll see the Desierto de los Leones signpost on a side road to the south. On weekends taxis may wait here to take people up the 4km paved road to the Ex-Convento. Other days you'll probably have to walk, but traffic will be light and it's a pleasant, gently rising ascent.

Tlatelolco & Guadalupe   Map pp104–5
PLAZA DE LAS TRES CULTURAS

So named because it symbolizes the fusion of pre-Hispanic and Spanish roots into the Mexican mestizo identity, the **Plaza of the Three Cultures** (5583-0295; Eje Central Lázaro Cárdenas, cnr Flores Magón; admission free; (Y) 8am-6pm) displays the architectural legacy of those three cultural facets. the Aztec pyramids of **Tlatelolco**, the 17th-century Spanish **Templo de Santiago** and the modern **Secretaría de Relaciones Exteriores** (Foreign Ministry) building, on the plaza's south side. A calm oasis north of the city center, the plaza is nonetheless haunted by echoes of its somber history.

Tlatelolco was founded by an Aztec faction in the 14th century on a separate island in Lago de Texcoco and later conquered by the Aztecs of Tenochtitlán, who built a causeway to connect the two ceremonial centers. In pre-Hispanic times it was the scene of the largest market in the Valle de México. Cortés defeated Tlatelolco's Aztec defenders, led by Cuauhtémoc, here in 1521. An inscription about that battle in the plaza translates: 'This was neither victory nor defeat. It was the sad birth of the mestizo people that is Mexico today.'

Tlatelolco is also a symbol of more modern troubles. On October 2, 1968, 300 to 400 student protesters were massacred by government troops on the eve of the Mexico City Olympic Games. The area subsequently suffered some of the worst damage of the 1985 earthquake when apartment blocks collapsed, killing hundreds of people.

You can view the remains of Tlatelolco's main pyramid-temple and other Aztec buildings from a walkway around them. Of particular interest is **Temple M**, south of the main temple, with bands of 13 calendrical glyphs on its three outer walls. Recognizing the religious significance of the place, the Spanish built a monastery here before erecting the Templo de Santiago in 1609. Just inside the main (west) doors of this church is the baptismal font of Juan Diego (this page). Outside the north wall of the church, a monument erected in 1993 honors the victims of the 1968 massacre. The full truth has yet to be revealed despite a recent investigation ordered by President Fox to bring the perpetrators to justice, in which the former president Luis Echeverría, minister of the interior at the time of the killings, was summoned for questioning. (For more information, see p97).

Northbound 'Central Autobuses del Norte' peseros and trolleybuses pass right by the Plaza de las Tres Culturas. Catch them on Eje Central, north of Bellas Artes.

Alternatively, from metro Tlatelolco, exit on to the plaza of the Tlatelolco housing complex. At the far end of the plaza, turn left past a playground and follow the path to Lerdo. Cross Lerdo and continue through a park and another housing project to Eje Central. Go south and cross over a footbridge to the Plaza de Tres Culturas.

BASÍLICA DE GUADALUPE
In December 1531, as the story goes, an indigenous Christian convert named Juan Diego, stood on Cerro del Tepeyac (Tepeyac hill), site of an old Aztec shrine, and beheld a beautiful lady dressed in a blue mantle trimmed with gold. She sent him to tell the bishop, Juan de Zumárraga, that he had seen the Virgin Mary, and that she wanted a shrine built in her honor. But the bishop didn't believe him. Returning to the hill, Juan Diego had the vision several more times. When the lady's image was miraculously emblazoned on his cloak, the church accepted his story, and a cult grew up around the place.

Over the centuries Nuestra Señora de Guadalupe (named after a Spanish manifestation of the Virgin whose cult was particularly popular in early colonial times) came to receive credit for all manner of miracles, hugely aiding the acceptance of Catholicism by Mexicans. In 1737, after she had extinguished an outbreak of plague in Mexico City, she was officially declared the patron of Mexico. Two centuries later she was named celestial patron of Latin America and empress of the Americas. Today her image is seen throughout the country, and her shrines around the Cerro del Tepeyac are the most revered in Mexico, attracting thousands of pilgrims daily and hundreds of thousands on the days leading up to her feast day, December 12 (see p143). Some pilgrims travel the last meters to the shrine on their knees.

By the 1970s the old yellow-domed basilica, built around 1700, was swamped by worshipers and was sinking slowly into the soft subsoil. So the new **Basílica de Nuestra Señora de Guadalupe** was built next door. Designed by Pedro Ramírez Vázquez, architect of the Museo Nacional de Antropología, it's a vast, round, open-plan structure with a capacity for thousands. The image of the Virgin hangs above and behind the main altar, with moving walkways to bring visitors as close as possible. By walking around the outer edge of the sanctuary, you can view the image anytime the church is open.

The rear of the Antigua Basílica is now the **Museo de la Basílica de Guadalupe** (☎ 5577-6022; admission US$0.50; ⏱ 10am-6pm Tue-Sun), with a fine collection of *exvotos* and colonial religious art.

Stairs behind the Antigua Basílica climb about 100m to the hilltop **Capilla del Cerrito** (Hill Chapel), where Juan Diego had his vision, then lead down the east side of the hill to the **Jardín del Tepeyac** (Tepeyac Garden). From there a path heads back to the main plaza, reentering it beside the 17th-century

Capilla de Indios (Chapel of Indians), near the spot where Juan Diego is said to have lived until his death in 1548. In 2002 Pope John Paul II canonized Juan Diego.

An easy way to reach the Basílica de Guadalupe is to take the metro to La Villa-Basílica station, then walk two blocks north along Calz de Guadalupe. You can reach the same point on any 'M(etro) Hidalgo-La Villa' pesero or bus heading northeast on Paseo de la Reforma. To return downtown, walk to Calz de los Misterios, a block west of Calz de Guadalupe, and catch a southbound 'M(etro) Hidalgo' or 'M(etro) Chapultepec' pesero.

WALKING TOUR

The historical hub of the whole country, the Centro Histórico is the most densely packed and fascinating part of the city and worthy of extended exploration. The obvious point of departure is the Zócalo. Take it all in from one of the **lookout restaurants** (**1**; p150) on the west side of the plaza, then investigate the sites around it: the **Catedral Metropolitana** (**2**; p121), **Palacio Nacional** (**3**; p121) and **Templo Mayor** (**4**; p122).

At this point, you could detour east along Moneda for a look at the Americas' first university, now housing the country's

Distance: 2.2km to 3.8km
Duration: 3½ to 5 hours

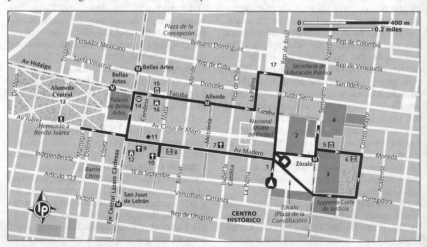

oldest cantina, **El Nivel** (5; p157); and New Spain's first mint, now the **Museo Nacional de las Culturas** (6; p123).

Circle around the Palacio Nacional, returning via Corregidora to the Zócalo, then continue west along Av Madero. A number of extraordinary colonial buildings stand alongside the jewelry shops and opticians on this stately avenue, notably the baroque **Iglesia de la Profesa** (7; ☎ 5521-8362; Isabel la Católica 21), the **Palacio de Iturbide** (8; p124) and the **Iglesia de San Francisco** (9; ☎ 5521-7731; Av Madero 7), a remnant of the vast Franciscan convent that was built over the site of Moctezuma's private zoo in the 16th century and divvied up under the reform laws of the 1850s. To see the convent's magnificent cloister, retrace your steps down Madero, turn right at Gante and enter the Methodist **Iglesia de la Santísima Trinidad** (10; ☎ 5512-5304; Gante 5).

Near the north end of Madero, stop for refreshments at Sanborns inside the beautiful **Casa de Azulejos** (11; p124), then continue a block west to the **Torre Latinoamericana** (12; p124), where you could zoom up to the observation deck. Conclude by taking a bench in the **Alameda Central** (13; p125), or continue your explorations heading up the Eje Central to Tacuba for a glimpse of the ornate **Palacio Postal** (14; p102). Turn right at Tacuba to find the Plaza Tolsá with its monuments to art and industry, the **Museo Nacional de Arte** (15; p124) and **Palacio de Minería** (16; p124).

Continue east along Tacuba, with a possible detour north on La Palma to observe the activity at the **Plaza Santo Domingo** (17; p123), before returning to the Zócalo.

COURSES

A number of language institutes can help get your Spanish up to speed.

Alliant International University (Map pp114-15; ☎ 5264-2187; www.usiumexico.edu; Álvaro Obregón 110, Roma) Small private US university offering short, intensive 'survival' Spanish courses for travelers (US$120-150) and degree programs with classes taught in English; also hosts guided cultural tours and open lectures and seminars.

Centro de Enseñanza Para Extranjeros (Foreigners Teaching Center; ☎ 5622-2470; www.cepe.unam.mx; Av Universidad 3002, Ciudad Universitaria) Six-week intensive classes meeting three hours daily (US$350). Despite the large group size (up to 20 students), courses have received good reports.

Tepeticpac Tlahtolcalli (Map pp108-10; ☎ 5518-2020; tepeticpac@hotmail.com; Dr Mora 5, Alameda Central) Indigenous cultural center offering courses in Náhuatl and Zapotec languages (US$6-10), as well as folk dance, codice reading and corn husk art (US$10-40); classes meet once or twice a week.

MEXICO CITY FOR CHILDREN

As elsewhere in Mexico, kids take center stage in the capital. Many theaters stage weekend children's plays and puppet shows, including the **Centro Cultural del Bosque** and the **Centro Nacional de las Artes** (p160). Cartoons are a staple at cinemas around town, including weekend matinees at the **Cineteca Nacional** (p159), but keep in mind that children's films are often dubbed in Spanish (unlike other films which are subtitled). Consult the Niños sections of *Tiempo Libre* and *DF* magazines for current programs.

Museums often organize hands-on activities for kids, and the **Museo Nacional de Arte** (p124) offers children's art workshops from 11:30am to 4pm Saturday and Sunday. A sure hit is the **Wax Museum** (p127) with a basement full of gruesome torture devices and mythical bogeymen; there's more grossness next door at **Ripley's Believe It or Not Museum**.

Mexico City's numerous parks and plazas are usually buzzing with kids' voices. Bosque de Chapultepec is the obvious destination, with the **Papalote Museo del Niño** (p131), **La Feria** (p130) and **zoo** (p129), not to mention several lakes with rowboat rentals. But also consider Condesa's **Parque México** (p128), where Sunday is family activities day. There are craft activities and face painting and you can rent bicycles for a spin around the lush grounds. **Plaza Hidalgo** (p135) in Coyoacán is another fun-filled spot with balloons, street mimes and cotton candy.

Be sure as well to take the kids through a market for an eye-opening tour of local fruits, piñatas and pig's heads.

QUIRKY MEXICO CITY

Anyone who's spent time in Mexico will understand why French poet André Bretón once called it 'the surrealist country par excellence.' Though it's hard to put your finger on it, something strange lurks beneath the surface of everyday life, popping up in the oddest places.

El Cuadrilátero (Map pp108-10; ☎ 5518-1821; Luis Moya 73; ⏱ 7am-8pm Mon-Sat), owned by *luchador* (wrestler) Super Astro, is 4½ blocks south of the Alameda Central, and features a wall of wrestlers' masks, many donated by Super Astro's ring pals and enemies. The place is just as renowned for its very large tortas, versions of which are displayed at the entrance. If you manage to put away a 1.3kg cholesterol-packed Torta Gladiador in 15 minutes, it's free.

Part cantina, part bullfighting museum, **La Faena** (Map pp108-10; ☎ 5510-4417; Carranza 49; ☼ noon-11pm Sun-Thu, until 2am Fri & Sat) has seen better days but retains a tumbledown grandeur. On a good night, the cavernous former hotel dining hall, three blocks west of the Zócalo, echoes with musical trios, and the colorful bar fuels a certain degree of revelry. Between drinks, admire the dusty statues of renowned matadors encased in glass and pastoral tableaus of brave bulls.

Museo del Calzado (Map pp108-10; ☎ 5512-1311, ext 35; Bolívar 27; admission free; ☼ 10am-2pm & 3:30-6pm Mon-Fri, 10am-2pm Sat) is a place Imelda Marcos could love: it contains what must be the world's largest footwear collection. On display are President Fox' cowboy boots, Louis XIV's high heels, clown shoes, shoes from around the world, and upstairs, cases and cases of miniature shoes.

Tianguis de Niños de Dios (Map pp108-10; Plaza Alonzo García Bravo) The New Year is nigh and it's time to get your baby Jesus dressed up. In January, Chilango families flock to the Tianguis de Niños de Dios and surrounding shops in the Candelaria district to clothe and accessorize their rosy-cheeked *niño* dolls with capes, crowns, *huaraches* and other essentials for his trip to church on February 2, Día de la Candelaria.

Virgen del Metro (Map pp108-10; cnr Paseo de la Reforma & Zarco) is evidence of a recent miracle, housed in a small tiled shrine. Metro riders in June 1997 noticed that a water leak in Hidalgo station had formed a stain on the floor that was a likeness of the Virgin of Guadalupe. After the discovery was made, thousands of faithful flocked to witness the miraculous vision. The stone section was removed and placed in a glass case at the Zarco entrance to Hidalgo metro.

Mercado de Sonora (cnr Fray Servando & Rosales) has all the ingredients for Mexican witchcraft. The aisles are crammed with stalls hawking things like Lucky Hunchback potion, amulets, voodoo dolls and other esoterica.

Located a few blocks south of Mercado de la Merced, this is also the place to get a *limpia* (spiritual cleansing), a ritual in which you're clouded with incense and brushed with herbs.

TOURS

Many travel agencies can book you on bus tours within and outside the city, with English-language guides. A half-day whirl around the Zócalo area and the Museo Nacional de Antropología costs around US$30; full-day tours to Teotihuacán are US$35.

Turibús Circuito Turístico (www.turibus.com.mx in Spanish; adult/child 5-12 & senior over 65 US$10/5, 2-day pass US$14/7, 3-day pass US$18/9; ☼ 9am-9pm) provides a good overview of some of the key areas. The total *recorrido* lasts about three hours, but you can get off and back on at any of the designated stops along the way. Tickets are sold on board for the red double-decker bus. Red banners mark stops along Reforma, at the southwest corner of the Zócalo, by the anthropology museum and Auditorio Nacional. Buses pass every 30 minutes or so. The fare includes headphones for recorded explanations in English, French, Italian, German, Japanese and Spanish.

Tranvía (☎ 5512-1012, ext 202; adult/child US$3.50/2; ☼ 10am-5pm) runs a motorized version of an early 20th-century streetcar around a 45-minute circuit of the Centro Histórico, with guides relating fascinating bits of lore (in Spanish) along the way. On Thursday night there's a special **cantina tour** (US$10, including margarita). Tours depart from Av Juárez by Bellas Artes. Similar **tours around Coyoacán** (☎ 5662-8972; adult/child US$3.50/2; ☼ 10am-5pm Mon-Fri, 10am-6pm Sat & Sun) depart from Av Hidalgo outside the Museo Nacional de Culturas Populares.

Paseos Culturales del INAH (☎ 5616-5228; www .inah.gob.mx; Frontera 53, Tizapán San Ángel; tours US$20; ☼ 9am-3pm Sat or Sun), the national anthropology institute, has tours almost every weekend, conducted in Spanish. Most go out of town, but some provide an in-depth view of Mexico City's sites and backstreets. Reservations can also be made at the Museo Nacional de Antropología (p129).

Recorridos Dominicales (☎ 5662-7690, ext 528; culturaldf@hotmail.com; admission free; ☼ 10:45am-1pm Sun) offers Sunday walking tours in Spanish. The route varies each week with participants divided among 10 guides. The meeting point changes with the tour route, so call ahead.

FESTIVALS & EVENTS

Mexico City celebrates some unique local events in addition to all the major nationwide festivals (see p953), which often take on a special flavor in the capital.

Festival de México en el Centro Histórico (www .fchmexico.com; late March) The Historic Center's plazas, temples and theaters become venues for a slew of international artists and performers.

Semana Santa (late March or early April) The most evocative events of Holy Week are in the Iztapalapa district, 9km southeast of the Zócalo, where more than 150 locals act out a realistic Passion Play. Palm Sunday sees Christ's triumphal entry into Jerusalem. On Holy Thursday the betrayal by Judas and the Last Supper are played out in Iztapalapa's plaza, and Christ's address in Gethsemane is enacted on La Estrella hill. The most emotive scenes begin at noon on Good Friday, when Christ is sentenced, beaten, and crowned with real thorns. He then carries his 90kg cross 4km up Cerro de la Estrella, where he is tied to the cross and 'crucified.'

Grito de la Independencia (September 15) Thousands gather in the Zócalo on the eve of the Independence Day national holiday to hear the Mexican president's version of the Grito de Dolores (Cry of Dolores), Hidalgo's famous call to rebellion against the Spanish in 1810, from the central balcony of the National Palace at 11pm. Afterwards, there's a spectacular fireworks display over the cathedral.

Día de Muertos (November 2) In the lead-up to Day of the Dead, elaborate ofrendas (offerings) show up everywhere from public markets to metro stations. Some of the best ones are at Anahuacalli (p137) and the Museo Dolores Olmedo Patiño (p131), while a city-wide contest for the most creative ofrenda is held on the Zócalo. Major vigils take place in the Panteón Civil de Dolores cemetery, west of Bosque de Chapultepec; and at San Andres Mixquic, in the extreme southeast of the Distrito Federal.

Fiesta de Santa Cecilia (November 22) The patron saint of musicians is honored with special fervor at Plaza Garibaldi.

Día de Nuestra Señora de Guadalupe (December 12) At the Basílica de Guadalupe, the Day of Our Lady of Guadalupe caps 10 days of festivities honoring Mexico's religious patron. On December 11 and 12, groups of indigenous dancers and musicians from across Mexico perform on the basilica's broad plaza in uninterrupted succession for two days. The numbers of pilgrims reach the millions by December 12, when religious services go on in the basilica almost round the clock.

SLEEPING

Mexico City offers a range of places to stay, from basic guesthouses to top-flight hotels.

THE AUTHOR'S CHOICE

Gran Hotel Ciudad de México (Map pp108–10; ☎ 1083-7700; ghciudaddemexico@yahoo.com. mx; 16 de Septiembre 82; r/ste US$99/115; P) Just off the Zócalo, this circa 1900 hotel is a fiesta of Mexican art nouveau. Relax on plush settees in the spacious lobby, listen to songbirds in their giant cages and gawk at the stained glass canopy high overhead. Suites offer extraordinary views of the Zócalo, while standard rooms look out on stately 16 de Septiembre. Buffet breakfasts are a specialty of the rooftop restaurant.

Accommodations are described here first by neighborhood and then by price range.

In general, the best cheap and moderately priced rooms are in the areas west of the Zócalo, near the Alameda Central and Plaza de la República. These are sometimes in charming old colonial or Porfiriato-era buildings with high ceilings and attractive balconies. Several hostels geared to international budget travelers provide another economical option.

Mid-range accommodations (US$30 to US$75 for a double room) provide comfortable, if sometimes small, rooms in multistory buildings with restaurants and bars. They often trade character for modern convenience. Hotels in this category are concentrated in the Plaza de la República and Roma neighborhoods, though they're found all over town. Note that places with the word 'garage' on the sign generally cater to short-term tryst-seeking guests, but these 'love motels' can be good-value options.

Top-end hotel rooms run from US$75 up to the sky and range from comfortable medium-sized, tourist-oriented hotels to modern luxury high-rises for business travelers. Top-end places are most densely concentrated in the Zona Rosa and the Polanco district.

Centro Histórico   Map pp108–10

Despite recent investment and improvements in the Historic Center, accommodations remain surprisingly affordable. Most of the suitable places are on Av 5 de Mayo and the streets to its north and south. The nearest metro stations are Allende or Zócalo, unless otherwise noted.

BUDGET

Hostel Catedral (Map p109; ☎ 5518-1726; www.hostel catedral.com; República de Guatemala 4; dm HI members/ nonmembers US$11/13, r US$27; ✕ 🖳) Right behind the cathedral, HI-Mexico's flagship operation is a modern, efficient 204-bed hostel in a refurbished neo-colonial building. Rooms have polished wood floors and lockers and hold from four to six people. Everything you need is here, including an Internet center, laundry facility, pool table and travel agency, and the top-floor guest kitchen opens onto a terrace with sublime views over the cathedral plaza. Rates include breakfast at the laidback ground-level café.

Hotel Isabel (Map p109; ☎ 5518-1213; www.hotel -isabel.com.mx; Isabel la Católica 63; s/d US$18/23, with shared bathroom US$11.50/13; 🖳 ; metro Isabel la Católica) A longtime choice for budget travelers, this grand, old hotel in the heart of the Centro has a colonial air with its plant-laden balustrades around a sun-drenched courtyard. Enormous rooms have high ceilings, sturdy balconies and well-scrubbed bathrooms, and there's a decent, moderately priced restaurant. Rooftop rooms are smaller but have excellent views.

Hostal Moneda (☎ 5522-5821, 800-221-72-65; www.hostalmoneda.com.mx; Moneda 8; dm from US$10, r US$25; ✕ 🖳) Just a stone's throw from the Zócalo, this converted hotel is a humbler, more casual affair than its HI counterpart, with some rooms painted by travelers in a creative mood. There are 100 beds in double and triple rooms and four- to six-person dormitories, along with laundry facilities, luggage storage and a roof garden café where breakfast (included in price) is served. There's an airport pick-up service (US$11) and daily tours to the Basílica de Guadalupe and Teotihuacán (US$16, plus admission fees).

Hostal Virreyes (☎ 5521-4180; www.hostalvirreyes .com.mx in Spanish; Izazaga 8; dm HI members/nonmembers US$9/10, r $28; 🖳 ; metro Salto del Agua) An enormous old hotel, the Virreyes is a convenient base for the Historic Center, with laundry service, a small kitchen, and various terraces and lounge areas. Dorm rooms have 10 bunks with lockers and *azulejo* bathrooms. The lobby lounge doubles as a nightclub. Rates include a light breakfast at the adjoining restaurant.

Hotel Habana (☎ 5518-1589; República de Cuba 7; s/d US$20/27) Habana is excellent value, with 40 well-maintained, decent-sized units in pastel shades with touches of Talavera tile. Be aware, however, that the streets can turn mean after dark.

Hotel Montecarlo (☎ 5518-1418; Uruguay 69; s/d US$18/20, with shared bathroom US$15/18) When DH Lawrence stayed here, it probably looked much the same as it does today. Sunlit lounge areas with potted palms and ancient furniture, and austere rooms with high ceilings complete the sense of preservation, though a new paint job and zealous cleaning staff keep it from feeling rundown.

Hotel Zamora (☎ 5512-8245; Av 5 de Mayo 50; s/d US$13/19, with shared bathroom US$9.50/15) Absolutely no frills here, but it's clean, friendly and cheap, with hot showers and a safe. If you can, get a front room: the balconies over 5 de Mayo are worth the price alone.

Hotel Washington (☎ 5512-3502; 5 de Mayo 54 at La Palma; s/d US$18/22) Tidy and cordial, the recently renovated Washington is a less basic alternative to the next-door Zamora.

Hotel Principal (☎ 5521-1333; Bolívar 29; s/d US$17/24, with separate bathroom US$7.50/9.50; 🖳) This old standby with budget travelers boasts a terrific location but could use some renovation. Large, plain rooms, arranged around a plant-filled court, have high ceilings and clean, tiled bathrooms.

MID-RANGE

Hotel Catedral (☎ 5518-5232; www.hotelcatedral.com; Donceles 95; s/d US$34/48; 🅿 🖳) Of the 120 wellkept rooms at this oft-recommended hotel, those at the rear of the fifth and sixth floor afford the best cathedral vistas. There's a splendid rooftop terrace and a reasonable restaurant off the lobby.

Hotel Gillow (☎ 5510-0791; hgillow@prodigy.net .mx; Isabel la Católica 17 at 5 de Mayo; s/d US$38/50; 🖳) A 1960s elegance pervades the lobby, where uniformed bellboys escort you to spacious carpeted rooms, some with great balconies.

Hotel Capitol (☎ 5512-0460; Uruguay 12; s/d US$32/37; 🖳 ; metro San Juan de Letrán) Though not luxurious, this friendly establishment offers clean, simple rooms around a central hall with fountain. A few have balconies overlooking Uruguay, while suites come with Jacuzzis.

Hotel Azores (☎ 5521-5220; www.hotelazores.com; República de Brasil 25; s/d from US$23/28) Just off the Plaza Santo Domingo, the recently modernized Azores offers a great location and standard mid-range amenities, including a comfy lobby bar. Exterior units have picture windows overlooking the street activity, which quietens down considerably after hours.

Hotel Roble (☎ 5522-7830; www.hotelroble.com.mx; Av Uruguay 109; s/d US$23/30) Two blocks south of the Zócalo, this modern if charmless option is at the lower end of the middle range. Adjoining is an American-style coffee shop.

TOP END
Hotel Majestic (☎ 5521-8600; www.majestic.com.mx; Av Madero 73, r US$130; ste from US$170; P ☒ ☐; metro Zócalo) A Best Western hotel, the venerable Majestic dominates the west side of the Zócalo. About a third of its 85 rooms overlook the vast plaza, and the rooftop restaurant boasts the best views around. Its lobby is a colonial fantasy of woodwork and Talavera tile.

Hotel Ritz (☎ 5518-1340; hotelritzdf@hotelritzdf.com; Av Madero 30; r US$80; ☐) The Ritz, 3½ blocks west of the Zócalo, caters to business travelers and north-of-the-border tour groups. Its 120 attractively furnished rooms feature large bathrooms. The standard rate includes breakfast; substantial discounts are often available.

Alameda Central & Around Map pp108–10
Hotels in this area are easily accessed from Metro Bellas Artes or metro Juárez unless otherwise noted.

BUDGET
Hotel Toledo (☎ 5521-3249; López 22; s/d US$17/20) This cozy older place has medium-sized, slightly worn rooms, all with TVs, phones and street views.

MID-RANGE
All lodgings listed in this category include restaurants.

Hotel Monte Real (☎ 5518-1149; www.hotelmonte real.com.mx; Revillagigedo 23; s/d US$45/50; P) Just a block from the Alameda, the Monte Real is a modern family-run place whose recently remodeled rooms include ceiling fans and phones. A bar and restaurant are on site and they can arrange for babysitters.

Hotel Bamer (☎ 5521-9060; hbamer@prodigy.net .mx; Av Juárez 52; s/d US$49/54; ☒ ☐) Many of the Bamer's large, comfortable rooms have fantastic views of the park. The cafeteria serves reasonably priced breakfasts and lunches.

Also recommended:

Hotel Fleming (☎ 5510-4530; hotelfleming@prodigy .net.mx; Revillagigedo 35; s/d US$30/39; P)

Hotel Marlowe (☎ 5521-9540; www.hotelmarlowe .com.mx in Spanish; Independencia 17; s/d US$45/58; P ☒ ☐)

TOP-END
Hotel de Cortés (☎ 5518-2181, 800-509-2340; www .hoteldecortes.com.mx; Av Hidalgo 85; r/ste US$131/205; metro Hidalgo) Behind the austere tezontle façade is a charming Best Western hotel. Originally built in 1780 as a monks' hospice, it has comfortable rooms with colonial décor touches. Small windows look out on the courtyard where *marimbas* (xylophone-type instruments) accompany traditional dance performances nightly.

Hotel Sheraton Centro Histórico (☎ 5130-5252; www.sheraton.com/centrohistorico; Av Juárez 70; r US$310-351; P ☒ ☒ ☐ ☒) Part of the Alameda redevelopment project, this just-unwrapped hotel/convention center is worth the money if you want to spend it. All the rooms are above the 10th floor and have breathtaking views; some suites feature Jacuzzis overlooking the Alameda and Bellas Artes. Beds come with big fluffy pillows and comforters. Bathroom sinks are set in elegant wooden tables, the tubs in polished golden granite.

Plaza de la República & Around   Map pp108–10
Though less convenient, this mainly residential area a few blocks west of the Alameda is relatively tranquil and unpretentious and boasts a number of reasonably priced lodgings. The closest metro station to this area is Revolución.

BUDGET
Casa de los Amigos (☎ 5705-0521; www.casadelos amigos.org; Mariscal 132; dm US$8, d US$20, s/d with shared bath US$10/18; ☒) A Quaker center supporting various community service projects, the Casa offers basic lodging to visitors working for social change. It's a good place to meet people with an informed interest in Mexico and Central America.

A two-night minimum stay is required, along with the completion of a brief questionnaire (email responses OK). The 45-bed guesthouse has single-sex dormitories and private rooms. (Note that the listed room rates are suggested donations.) There's a library, guest kitchen and a US$2 breakfast served Monday to Friday. Morning meditation, Spanish conversation and cultural chats are available to guests, who may volunteer to staff the Casa for a reduced room rate.

Hotel Oxford (☎ 5566-0500; Mariscal 67; s/d US$10/15) Situated behind the Museo San Carlos, the Oxford is an art-deco structure with rounded balconies overlooking Plaza Buenavista and ancient rooms and corridors. Rooms are spacious and many have king-size beds. If it's seedy charm you're after, the Oxford's bar will do nicely, and they'll send up drinks until 4am.

MID-RANGE

Almost all of the following places have convenient if unremarkable on-site restaurants serving 'international' cuisine.

Hotel Mayaland (☎ 5566-6066; Antonio Caso 23; s/d US$32/42; P ⬛) A business-oriented hotel with a Maya motif, this is one of the better deals around, offering well-maintained rooms and efficient service.

Hotel Jena (☎ 5097-0277; Terán 12 at Mariscal; r from US$58; P ⬛ ⬛) Towering above the neighborhood, this modern monolith is a short walk from Paseo de la Reforma. Its 120-plus rooms are among the most luxurious in the middle range.

Hotel Sevilla (☎ 5566-1866; www.sevilla.com.mx; Serapio Rendón 124; s/d US$30/39, 'modern' s/d US$45/55; P ⬛ ⬛) Opposite the Jardín del Arte this oft-recommended business-oriented hotel is divided into 'traditional' and 'modern' sections. The latter are air-conditioned and some have views of the Monumento a la Madre (Monument to Motherhood) across the way.

Hotel New York (☎ 5566-9700; Édison 45; s/d US$28/47; P) A few blocks northeast of Plaza de la República, this is an upscale option in a zone crammed with cut-rate hotels. Rates include breakfast and four Sky channels.

Palace Hotel (☎ 5566-2400; Ramírez 7; s/d US$32/46; P) A large, circa-1960s establishment just south of the plaza, the Palace has simple, cozy rooms, some with broad balconies.

Hotel Prim (☎ 5592-4600; www.hotelprim.com; Versalles 46; s/d US$43/49, ste US$57; P) The hulking Prim does not present an attractive façade, but it's decent value and a short walk from Reforma, the Zona Rosa or Colonia Roma. The junior suites are the best deal: they

have cozy living rooms, huge beds and two bathrooms.

The following three lodgings are all on Serapio Rendón, across the way from the Sevilla. What they lack in character they make up for in convenience, comfort and price. Be aware that nearby Parque Sullivan transforms into a busy prostitution market by night.

Hotel Astor (☎ 5148-2644; hotel.astor@mexico.com; Antonio Caso 83 at Serapio Rendón; s/d US$35/45; ⬛ P) The slickest of the trio, with Jacuzzis in some rooms.

Hotel Mallorca (☎ 5566-4833; Serapio Rendón 119; s/d from US$25/32; P) Doubles come in two sizes here.

Hotel Compostela (☎ 5566-0733; Sullivan 35 at Serapio Rendón; traditional/modern r US$35/42; P)

TOP END

Hotel Imperial (☎ 5705-4911; www.hotelimperial.com.mx; Reforma 64; r US$150; ⬛ ⬛) A national historic monument, this elegant hotel was built in 1902 as then-dictator Porfirio Díaz' private residence. During the 1940s it served as the US embassy; it was also the Hotel Francis for a time, named after the wife of famous Mexican comedian Mario Moreno 'Cantinflas.' With its distinctive symmetry and golden cupola, it is surely Paseo de la Reforma's most handsome structure, and its lush interior and elegantly appointed rooms are equally impressive.

Hotel Sevilla Palace (☎ 5566-8877; www.sevillapalace.com.mx; Paseo de la Reforma 105; r from US$125; ⬛ ⬛ ⬛) Crystal elevators soar above a central atrium, a 23rd-floor deck provides a paradisiacal pool and palapa setting, and the bar features evening entertainment with downtown views. For luxury lodging, the Sevilla Palace doesn't mess around. The two towers contain 413 spacious rooms and suites with all executive amenities.

Hotel Casa Blanca (☎ 5705-1300; www.hotel-casablanca.com.mx; Lafragua 7; s/d US$67/86; ⬛ ⬛ ⬛ ⬛) Here's a five-star hotel with all the trimmings for much less than the chains. Though recently renovated, it retains a '60s-modern ambience and a pink color scheme in its 270 rooms. Bonus: a rooftop pool with adjacent lounge.

Zona Rosa & Around   Map pp112–13

Accommodations right in the glitzy Pink Zone are expensive, but a couple of popular mid-range places are nearby (book ahead). Many of the top-end options offer discounts for walk-ins. Insurgentes and Sevilla are the nearest metro stations.

BUDGET

Las Dos Fridas Hostel (☎ 5286-3849; www.2fridas hostel.com; Hamburgo 301; dm/s/d per person with shared bathroom US$12/25/17; 🖳) This cozy little hostel is in a quiet area between the Zona Rosa and Chapultepec Park. It has four- and five-bed dorms, private rooms and 24-hour access. Amenities include a well-equipped kitchen, laundry facilities, TV room, telephone and fax access, and free breakfast. Discounts are offered for ISIC members or longer stays.

Hostel Mansión Havre (☎ 5533-1271; Havre 40; dm US$11,d/ste US$27/35; 🖳) Occupying a Porfiriato-style mansion, this cheerful establishment has 84 spaces in 12 rooms with two to eight beds, plus lockers, a guest kitchen and a TV lounge. Private rooms and suites (TV and kitchen) are suitable for families.

MID-RANGE

Casa González (Map p112; ☎ 5514-3302; J_Ortiz_Moore@hotmail.com; Río Sena 69; s/d from US$35/44) Guests appreciate the homey atmosphere at this family-run guesthouse, a 500m walk north of the Zona Rosa. Modestly decorated rooms with hardwood floors are in two older houses. Home-cooked meals are available in the dining room, and French and English are spoken. It's perfect for those staying several nights, and good value. No sign marks the Casa: ring the bell to enter.

Hotel María Cristina (☎ 5703-1212; Río Lerma 31; r/ste US$66/86; 🅿 🖳) This colonial-style gem boasts baronial public rooms, a patio with a fountain and an annex bar, all set amid manicured lawns. The rooms aren't as charming, but they're comfortable enough.

Hotel Bristol (☎ 5208-1717; www.hotelbristol.com .mx; Plaza Necaxa 17; s/d/ste from US$56/66/75; 🅿 ☒ ☒ 🖳) A good-value option in a pleasant location, the Bristol offers 140 large, comfy rooms, some with fine views. Management is helpful, and there's a decent on-site restaurant/bar.

Hotel del Ángel (☎ 5533-1032; Río Lerma 154; s/d US$60/73; 🅿 ☒ ☒) It's not the Sheraton, but the views of the Ángel from some of these rooms are just as impressive. After hours, have a cocktail in the 11th floor lounge.

Hotel Del Principado (☎ 5533-2944; Londres 42; s/d US$41/50; 🅿) On a quiet street near the Zona

Rosa, the Principado has bright, decent-sized rooms and eager-to-please staff.

TOP END

Four Seasons Hotel (☎ 5230-1818; www.fourseasons .com; Paseo de la Reforma 500; r US$290-450; 🅿 ☒ ☒ 🖳 🖳) Rooms overlook a charming courtyard at this colonial-style classic. An elegant restaurant, art gallery, 24-hour room service and open-air pool and spa make for a very pleasant stay.

Suites Hotel Reforma (☎ 5207-3074; www.reforma 374.com; Paseo de la Reforma 374; ste US$100-220; 🖳) These tastefully furnished suites have shiny tile floors and attractive views of Reforma, and they're equipped to prepare an elegant dinner. Discounts are available for extended stays.

María Isabel-Sheraton Hotel (☎ 5242-5555, in the US 800-325-3535; www.sheraton.com; Paseo de la Reforma 325; r US$285; 🅿 ☒ ☒ 🖳 🖳) This large, older hotel looking out on the Angel of Independence remains the primary base for business-people, journalists and embassy personnel. The 755 reasonably sized rooms and suites are in two sections, with remodeled units in the 'towers' area. There's a rooftop pool, fitness centers, two tennis courts, a couple of eating and drinking options, and mariachis nightly.

Condesa & Roma

BUDGET

Hostel Home (Map pp114-15; ☎ 5511-1683; www.hostel home.com.mx; Tabasco 303; dm members/nonmembers US$8/9; 🖳 ; metro Sevilla, six blocks away) A member of the HI-Mexico group, this small, friendly hostel is in a Porfiriato-era building on a quiet, tree-lined street. It accommodates 20 people in four separate-sex dorms sharing two bathrooms.

Hotel Embassy (Map pp114-15; ☎ 5208-0859; Puebla 115; s/d US$25/28; 🅿 ; metro Insurgentes) Despite the low price tag, this has a luxurious sheen – king-size beds, headboard TV remotes, modern art, big bathrooms.

MID-RANGE

Hotel Park Villa (Map pp116-17; ☎ 5515-5245; General Gómez Pedraza 68; s/d US$48/64; 🅿 ; metro Juanacatlán) Across from Bosque de Chapultepec, this affordable lodging is close to Condesa. Rooms have details like hand-painted designs over the headboards. Secluded behind an arched gateway, the colonial-style building remains quiet except for an occasional roar – that would be one of the lions in the adjacent restaurant/zoo.

Hotel Milán (Map pp114-15; ☎ 5584-0222; Álvaro Obregón 94; s/d US$35/40; **P** **🖳**) This decent older hotel is often recommended for its comfortable rooms and friendly staff, and it has a good street-view restaurant.

Hotel Parque Ensenada (Map pp114-15; ☎ 5208-0052; www.hotelensenada.com.mx in Spanish; Álvaro Obregón 13, cnr Morelia; s/d from US$53/57; **❌** **🖳**) This business hotel has standard and 'executive' rooms and a Wings coffee shop.

Casa de la Condesa (Map pp114-15; ☎ 5574-3186; Plaza Luis Cabrera 16; r with 1 bed US$47, ste with 1/2 beds US$76/87; **🖳**) Despite the name, this attractive guesthouse is in Colonia Roma. It offers suites with kitchenettes for business travelers on extended stays. The location, overlooking Plaza Luis Cabrera, is a plus; get a balcony room if possible. The Casa is often full, so book ahead.

Hotel Roosevelt (Map pp114-15; ☎ 5208-6813; Insurgentes Sur 287; s/d US$33/47; **P**) Just two blocks from Parque México, the gateway to Condesa, and down the street from Little Cuba's dance clubs, the Roosevelt is well-placed for night owls, though Insurgentes traffic could get on your nerves.

Hotel Puebla (Map pp114-15; ☎ 5525-3689; Puebla 36; s/d US$30/35; **P**) This modern lodging has cordial staff and is convenient to both the Zona Rosa and Centro.

TOP END

La Casona (Map pp114-15; ☎ 5286-3001; www.hotellacasona.com.mx in Spanish; Durango 280; r US$160; **❌**; metro Sevilla) Each of the 29 rooms is uniquely appointed at this boutique hotel in an early-20th-century mansion in a fairly busy neighborhood. Rates include breakfast in the patio.

Polanco   Map pp116–17

North of Bosque de Chapultepec, this area has some of the best business accommodations and a couple of excellent boutique hotels.

Casa Vieja (☎ 5282-0067; www.casavieja.com; Eugenio Sue 45; ste US$351-456; **P** **❌** **❌** **🖳**) Possibly the city's prettiest hotel, this charmingly restored old house has suites named after Mexican painters with museum-quality *artesanías* and furnishings. You'll find equipped kitchens, stereos and impeccable service.

A small rooftop restaurant serves Mexican dishes. Ask about seasonal discounts.

Camino Real México (☎ 5263-8888; www.caminoreal.com; Calz Mariano Escobedo 700; r US$275; **P** **❌** **❌** **🖳** **🖳**) This hotel's reputation is built on bold architecture and displays of art.

Habita Hotel (☎ 5282-3100, www.hotelhabita.com; Av Presidente Masaryk 201; ste US$351-456; **P** **❌** **❌** **🖳** **🖳**) Glass, metal, stone and natural fabrics in gray and white tones define this ultra-trendy little luxury hotel, with Polanco's hottest bar.

Hotel Polanco (☎ 5280-8082; Edgar Allan Poe 8; s/d US$100/110; **P** **❌** **❌** **🖳**) Near the business hotel district, the Polanco is more intimate and quieter than the others, with modest rooms and efficient service.

W Mexico City Hotel (☎ 9138-1800; www.whotels.com; Campos Elíseos 252; r US$370-425; **P** **❌** **❌** **🖳** **🖳**) Opened in late 2003, the stylish W features wireless Internet and a *temazcal* (indigenous Mexican steambath). In the Zona Hotelera, along the north side of Chapultepec Park, this is the best of four high-rise international luxury chains offering quality rooms, restaurants, business services and park views.

Basílica Area   Map pp104–5

Hotel La Villa (☎ 5577-4442; Calz de Guadalupe 677; s/d US$18/26; **P**) Spotless rooms and friendly management make this the best lodging in the area. Simple rooms with TV wrap round a little courtyard occupied by birds and turtles.

Terminal Norte   Map pp104–5

Hotel Brasilia (☎ 5587-8577; hbrasilia@prodigy.net.mx; Av de los Cien Metros 4823; s/d US$25/37) A seven-minute walk south of the northern bus terminal, this modern block has 200 decent rooms, a restaurant and bar.

EATING

The capital offers eateries for all tastes and budgets, from taco stalls to the most exclusive restaurants. Some of the best places are cheap; some of the more expensive ones are well worth the extra money.

The center is a good area to sample *chiles en nogada*, *mole poblano* or other traditional Mexican fare, while Condesa, Polanco and Roma offer plenty of European, Asian and Argentine restaurants in addition to Mexican venues.

THE AUTHOR'S CHOICE

La Fonda del Hotentote (Map pp108-10; ☎ 5522-1025; Cruces 40-3; dishes US$6-12; ☽ lunch Sun-Fri) In the wholesale paper district southeast of the Palacio Nacional, the Fonda brings a touch of class to classic Mexican cuisine without putting on airs. Upstairs is a traditionally decorated salon; the kitchen resembles a set from *Como Agua Para Chocolate*. The food is beautifully presented and attentively served. Standouts include red snapper tamales, nopales in *chile guajillo* sauce, and Pollo Tocotlán – chicken steamed in maguey leaves with aromatic herbs. Desserts are equally enticing. There's a picaresque mural behind the bar, which serves a variety of tequilas with homemade sangrita.

Those on a budget will find literally thousands of restaurants and holes in the wall serving a *comida corrida* (set lunch) for as little as US$2.50. Market buildings are good places to look for these while *tianguis* (indigenous people's markets) customarily have an eating section offering tacos, *barbacoa*, quesadillas and so on.

The city is also laced with modern chain restaurants whose predictable menus make a sound, if unexciting, fallback. Branches of **VIPS**, **Sanborns**, **Toks**, **Wings** and Californian restaurants serve US-style coffee shop fare and Mexican standards with main dishes in the US$4 to US$7 range. Some branches of these are shown on this chapter's maps. International chains, from KFC to Starbucks, are well represented, too.

Centro Histórico   Map pp104–5

Half the fun of eating in the center is basking in the atmosphere of some extraordinary colonial buildings. For places to eat overlooking the Zócalo, see p150.

BUDGET

Tacos La Canasta (Uruguay 80, near 5 de Febrero; tacos US$0.35; ☽ 10am-6pm) These bite-sized tacos are filled with things like potatoes, refried beans, *chicharrón* and mole (just the sauce), and arranged in a big basket. A couple of pails contain the garnishes: spicy guacamole and marinated carrot chunks and chilies.

Mercado San Camilito (adjacent to Plaza Garibaldi; pozole US$3.25; ☽ 24hr; metro Garibaldi) The block-long building contains over 70 kitchens serving Jalisco-style *pozole*, a broth brimming with hominy kernels and pork, served with a variety of garnishes such as radishes and oregano. (Specify *maciza* if pig noses and ears fail to excite you.) Also served is *birria*, a soulful goat stew, and *tepache*, a fermented pineapple drink.

Café El Popular (☎ 5518-6081; Av 5 de Mayo 52; breakfast & set lunches US$2-3; ☽ 24hr) An amazing number of people squeeze into this tiny split-level café, west of the Zócalo. Fresh pastries and good combination breakfasts (fruit, eggs, *frijoles* and coffee) are the main attractions. *Café con leche* (US$1) is served *chino* style (ie you specify the strength).

Café La Blanca (☎ 5510-9260; Av 5 de Mayo 40; 3-course lunches US$4.75) White-coated waiters and orange upholstery set the tone for this 1960s relic, offering hearty breakfasts and daily lunch specials. Sit at the U-shaped counter or grab a table by the window for people-watching over a cappuccino (US$1.25). Be sure to sample the *tamales de nata* – sweet with a hint of anise.

Vegetariano Madero (☎ 5521-6880; Av Madero 56; 4-course lunches US$4; ☽ 8am-7pm) Despite the minimally signed entrance, there's a lively restaurant upstairs where a pianist plinks out old favorites as you dine. The meatless menu is better than average: there are tasty variations on Mexican standards. Balcony seating lets you observe the street activity. Nearby is a more modern, street-level branch, **Restaurante Vegetariano** (☎ 5521-1895; Mata 13).

Taquería Beatriz (Bolívar 49; tacos US$1; ☽ 9am-5pm; metro San Juan de Letrán) This unassuming hole-in-the-wall has served up outstanding tacos for nearly a century. *Rajas* (sliced peppers), mole, *chicharrón* in salsa and other items are skillfully stuffed into handmade tortillas.

La Casa del Pavo (☎ 5518-4282; Motolinía 40; turkey tortas US$2; metro Allende) People come to this greasy spoon for the tortas (turkey and salt cod), served with chilies and marinated carrots.

A couple of the better Mexican chains are also found here:

El Charco de las Ranas (☎ 5510-0363; Uruguay 43; taco platters US$3; ☽ 8am-8pm Mon-Sat; ℗ ; metro San Juan de Letrán) Sleek, modern purveyor of tacos and quesadillas.

SQUARE MEALS: EATING AROUND THE ZÓCALO

Perhaps the quintessential Mexico City experience is dining or sipping cocktails overlooking the vast Zócalo with the Mexican tricolor waving proudly over the scene. Three hotels on the west side of the plaza offer abundant buffet breakfasts, although the food isn't as spectacular as the vista. If it's not too busy you can enjoy the view for the price of a drink.

Restaurante Terraza (☎ 5521-8600; Av Madero 73; breakfast US$15, buffet lunch Sat & Sun US$18) The widest-range views can be enjoyed from this restaurant on the top of the Hotel Majestic.

Restaurante El Mirador (☎ 1083-7700; Av 16 de Septiembre 82; breakfast US$8.75) The rooftop terrace restaurant of the Gran Hotel Ciudad de México is narrower than the Majestic's but also offers a sweeping panorama.

Restaurante El Balcón del Zócalo (☎ 5521-2121; 5 de Mayo 61; breakfast from US$9.50, main courses US$7-11) The Holiday Inn's terrace restaurant is within touching distance of the cathedral.

La Casa de las Sirenas (Map pp108-10; ☎ 5704-3225; República de Guatemala 32; main courses US$12-15, desserts US$3.75; ⊙ 1-6pm Mon, 1-11pm Tue-Fri, 8am-8pm Sat & Sun) Ensconced in a 17th-century home behind the cathedral, La Casa de las Sirenas has less awesome views, but its excellent *alta cocina mexicana* more than compensates. Dinner on the terrace might start with mushrooms in chipotle, followed by a succulent sesame sea bass and flan de elote for dessert. And to drink? Some 250 varieties of tequila (US$3.75 to US$20 a shot) are served in the Salones Tequila downstairs. Las Sirenas also makes a calm place for breakfast, far from the madding Zócalo crowd.

Potzollcalli (☎ 5521-4253; Av 5 de Mayo 39; pozole & antojitos US$3.50-5) Specializing in Guerrero and Jalisco-style *pozole*.

MID-RANGE & TOP END

Restaurante Danubio (☎ 5512-0912; Uruguay 3; 6-course lunches US$11, main courses US$5-11; ⊙ 1-10pm; metro San Juan de Letrán) This elegant operation has been specializing in seafood since the 1930s; prawns and Portuguese grilled sardines are standouts. The excellent lunch (available 1pm to 5pm only) includes fish and meat courses, plus coffee and liqueur.

Los Girasoles (☎ 5510-0630; Tacuba 8A; starters from US$4, main courses US$8-10.50; ⊙ 1pm-midnight Tue-Sat, 1-9pm Sun & Mon; P) Beside the Museo Nacional de Arte, this is one of the best restaurants specializing in *alta cocina mexicana*. Recipes are either traditional or innovative, but all have a very Mexican flavor. You might start with *crema de tres quesos* (three-cheese soup) and follow up with Sonoran ranch-style beef medallions with chipotle.

Restaurante Al-Andalus (☎ 5522-2528; Mesones 171; dishes US$7-10; ⊙ 9am-6pm; metro Pino Suárez) Al-Andalus offers tasty Lebanese cuisine upstairs in a grand colonial home. The Plato Libanés (US$10) lets you sample hummus and baba gannouj, among other Middle Eastern treats.

Gallos Centenario (☎ 5512-6868; República de Cuba 79; starters US$3-7, main courses US$7-15; ⊙ 1:30pm-midnight Mon-Sat, 1:30-6pm Sun; P) Worth visiting for the décor alone, the 16th-century building is extravagantly adorned with crockery, painted furniture, antique photos and lots of brass roosters. Mole, served over chicken or *arrachera* (skirt steak), is a specialty with three kinds from Oaxaca plus the traditional Puebla variety, accompanied by tamales. Downstairs is an equally atmospheric tequila salon.

Hostería Santo Domingo (☎ 5526-5276; Domínguez 72; dishes US$7-12; P) Cooking meals since 1860, this hugely popular (though not touristy) restaurant has an elegant, festive atmosphere, enhanced by chamber music. Stone archways border dining rooms on two levels. The menu is classic Mexican; it's famous for its enormous *chiles en nogada* (US$12), an Independence Day favorite, which is served here year-round.

Restaurante Chon (☎ 5542-0873; Regina 160; US$6-12; ⊙ noon-6pm) Pre-Hispanic fare is the specialty of this cantina-style restaurant. Sample *escamoles* (ant larvae), maguey worms (in season), grasshoppers, wild boar or armadillo in a mango sauce.

Café de Tacuba (☎ 5518-4950; Tacuba 28; 5-course lunch US$14, main courses US$7-11; P) Before the band there was the restaurant. Way before. The Porfiriato-era fantasy of colored tiles, brass lamps and oil paintings has served *antojitos* since 1912. The food is overrated, but the atmosphere is just right for a plate of *pambazos* or tamales with hot chocolate.

Alameda Central & Around   Map pp104–5

BUDGET

Taquería Tlaquepaque (☎ 5521-3082; Independencia 4; 3 tacos US$2-5; ⏱ 8-3am Sun-Thu, until 4am Fri-Sat) This is a clean, bustling place where bow-tied waiters will serve you up dozens of taco variations.

Churrería El Moro (☎ 5512-0896; Eje Central Lázaro Cardenas 42; hot chocolate or café con leche with 4 churros US$3; ⏱ 24hr; metro San Juan de Letrán) A fine respite from the Eje Central crowds, El Moro manufactures long, slender deep-fried *churros*, just made to be dipped in thick hot chocolate. It's a popular late-night spot, per-fect for winding down after hours.

Café Trevi (☎ 5512-3020; Colon 1 at Dr Mora; breakfast US$2-4, set meals US$4.50; ⏱ 8am-11:30pm) This Italian/Mexican restaurant facing the Alameda's west side serves breakfasts until noon and has a six-course *comida corrida*, plus pastas and personal pizzas.

Mi Fonda (☎ 5521-0002; López 101; ⏱ noon-5pm) Working-class *chilangos* line up for their share of paella valenciana, made fresh daily and patiently ladled out by women in white bonnets. Jesús from Cantabria in Spain oversees the proceedings.

MID-RANGE

Santa Fe Café (☎ 5518-7754; Av Juárez 76; breakfast US$7-10, lunch/dinner US$9-12; ⏱ 8am-11pm Sun-Thu, until 12:30am Fri-Sat; ⓟ 🔊) Upstairs in the Parque Alameda shopping mall with nice vistas of the Alameda Central, this slick, American-style eatery offers microbrews from its suburban beer factory.

Hong King (☎ 5512-6703; Dolores 25-A; dishes US $5-7; ⏱ noon-10:30pm) This is the most popular restaurant in Mexico City's small China-town. It has set Cantonese meals (US$6 to US$13, minimum two people) and menus in Chinese, Spanish and English. À la carte dishes include some vegetarian offerings such as the tofu with veggie stir-fry.

El Regiomontano (☎ 5518-0196; Luis Moya 115; grilled goat US$14.50; ⏱ 11am-10pm) The sign on the window says 'Baby goats very young kids' and there they are, splayed on stakes and grilling over a circle of coals, *norteño*-style. A single platter serves two.

Both the **Cloister Café** (☎ 5518-2265; US$4-6) at the Museo Franz Mayer and the more upscale **Café del Palacio** (☎ 5512-0807; US$7-10) at Bellas Artes offer sandwiches, salads and pastries between exhibits.

Zona Rosa & Around   Map pp112–13

While the Zona Rosa is packed with places to eat and drink, the culinary offerings tend to disappoint, with one notable exception: the abundance of authentic Asian restaur-ants aimed primarily at the neighborhood's growing Korean community. Fast-food junkies can get their fix on Génova between Hamburgo and Liverpool, with all the major franchises.

BUDGET

Delicity (☎ 5514-2506; Liverpool 170; noodles US$5) This little Korean kitchen serves big bowls of ramen and other Asian noodle dishes. The friendly owner speaks a little English.

Beatricita (☎ 5511-4213; Londres 190D; lunch US$4-5; ⏱ 10am-6pm Mon-Sat) This popular lunchtime destination has a solid *comida corrida* and friendly service. Friday is *pozole* day.

MID-RANGE

Fonda El Refugio (☎ 5525-8128; Liverpool 166; dishes US$8-10; ⏱ 1-11pm Mon-Sat, 1-10pm Sun; ⓟ) Your best bet for Mexican fine dining in the Zona Rosa, the Fonda serves regional specialties such as moles and *escamoles* (ant larvae) in a charming old house.

U Rae Ok (☎ 5511-1233; Hamburgo 232; dishes US$6-18; ⏱ noon-11pm Mon-Sat) This simple up-stairs locale is the best reason to come to the Zona Rosa. Although there are other good Korean restaurants, U Rae Ok has the best *bul-go-gi* (grilled marinated beef) and *chigae* (hearty soup), as well as the best prices.

Restaurante Vegetariano Yug (☎ 5533-3296; Varsovia 3; comida corrida US$4.50, buffet lunch US$5.50; ⏱ 7am-9pm Mon-Fri, 8:30am-8pm Sat, 1-8pm Sun) Just south of Reforma, Yug is downtown's best vegetarian restaurant. Local office workers head upstairs for the generous lunch buffet, served from 1pm to 5pm, with a plethora of great salads and fresh whole-wheat bread.

Konditori (☎ 5511-2300, ext 218; Génova 61; dishes US$5.25-10; ⏱ 7am-11:30pm) This Scandinavian café is a favorite along the Pink Zone's main pedestrian thoroughfare. Some people make a special trip here for the weekend brunch (US$9.50), accompanied by live jazz.

El Campirano (☎ 5533-3370; Londres 188; buffet US$8.50; ⏱ 1-6:30pm Mon-Sat, 7-10pm Thu-Fri) The buffet here is quite a spread, with various salads, nopales and *chiles en nogada*. On the hot table you'll find *cazuelas* sizzling with fish and meat moles, *pipianes* and salsas.

MEXICO CITY

TOP END

Les Moustaches (☎ 5533-3390; Río Sena 88; main dishes US$13-20; ☺ 1-11:30pm Mon-Sat; P) This is one of the city's most sophisticated and formal French restaurants, with tables in an elegant patio. Start off with pâté de foie gras, then choose from beef filet Roquefort, osso buco or yellowfin tuna. For dessert, there are tempting crêpes and soufflés.

At the Reforma end of Génova and along traffic-free Copenhague, you'll find several mid-to-top end eateries serving mostly steaks, pastas and Spanish fare. Recommended places include **La Góndola** and **Buenos Aires Grill** on Génova and **El Perro de Enfrente** on Copenhague.

Condesa   Map pp114–15

La Condesa has become the hub of the eating-out scene, and dozens of informal, bistros and cafés, many with sidewalk tables, compete for space along several key streets. Cuisines from all over the globe are represented here. Most higher-end Condesa restaurants offer valet parking for around US$2 (though you may wonder how they manage it).

BUDGET

Taquería El Güero (☎ 5286-4495; Amsterdam 135, cnr Michoacán; tacos US$1; ☺ 9am-4pm Mon-Fri, 9am-2pm Sat) This hole in the wall near Parque México has a staggering selection of taco fillings (guisados), from squash blossoms to sardines to Swiss chard, all attractively arrayed in dozens of clay casseroles and casually crammed into homemade tortillas by the wise-cracking güero the place is named after. Garnished with cactus leaves, crumbly goat's cheese or whatever works, a couple of these tacos will leave you stuffed.

El Tizoncito (☎ 5211-5139; Tamaulipas 122, cnr Campeche; tacos from US$0.70; ☺ noon-3:30am Sun-Thu, until 4:30pm Fri-Sat) The original branch of the city-wide chain has been going for close to 40 years. Staff claim to have invented tacos al pastor, and half the fun is watching the grillmen deftly put them together. If there are no seats, try the bigger location two blocks east on Campeche.

El Figonero (☎ 5211-9951; Campeche 429, cnr Cuernavaca; set lunch US$3; ☺ 8:30am-5pm Mon-Sat) In the midst of all the trendiness is this great little neighborhood place, offering a comida corrida that's a bit more creative than usual.

Show up before 3pm to avoid the lunchtime rush.

El Califa (☎ 5271-7666; Altata 22, cnr Alfonso Reyes; tacos US$1.50-3; ☺ 1:30pm-3:30am) This very popular taquería on Condesa's southern edge puts its own spin on the classic Mexican snack. Tables are set with a palette of savory salsas in sturdy clay bowls.

MID-RANGE & TOP END

Condesa's culinary heart is the intersection of Av Michoacán, Vicente Suárez and Atlixco. After 8pm the following four places are often filled to capacity and getting a table means waiting around for a while.

Fonda Garufa (☎ 5286-8295; Michoacán 93; pastas US$6-8, main courses US$8-15; ☺ 1pm-midnight Mon, 8am-midnight Tue-Wed, 8-1am Thu-Sat, 8am-11pm Sun; P) Serves a big range of good pasta, vegetarian brochettes and salads, plus seafood and other grills.

Mama Rosa's (☎ 5211-1640; Atlixco 105; pizzas US $7-10; P) Has wood-oven pizzas named after rock stars and topped with things like squid and huitlacoche (corn fungus).

Café La Gloria (☎ 5211-4180; Vicente Suárez 41; pastas & salads US$4-6, main courses US$7-9; ☺ 1pm-1am; P) This hip bistro with an international clientele specializes in salads and pastas.

La Buena Tierra (☎ 5211-4242; Atlixco 94, cnr Michoacán; breakfast combos US$5-8, sandwiches US$5-6; P) A natural café with fresh-baked bread, herbal medicinal teas and all kinds of juices and smoothies.

María del Alma (Map pp114-15; ☎ 5553-0403; Cuernavaca 68, Condesa; starters US$4-6, main courses US$7-12; ☺ 1:30-11pm Mon-Fri, until 1:30am Sat, 6pm Sun; P) Outside Condesa's center of activity, María del Alma serves Tabasco cuisine in a rambling California colonial home; the patio is filled with plants and chirping birds. Start off with a tropical fruit margarita, then sample southeastern specialties like tamales de chia and shark quesadillas. Savory seafood dishes highlight the menu, often laced with seasonal fruit sauces.

El Zorzal (☎ 5273-6023; Alfonso Reyes 139, cnr Tamaulipas; steaks US$9-15, pastas US$5.50-7; ☺ 1:30-11pm; P) This is the best of many options for Argentinean fare, with great imported cuts, as well as fresh pastas and generous salads. The parrillada (US$26), a mixed grill served on a chopping board, feeds at least two.

La Sábia Virtud (☎ 5286-6480; Tamaulipas 134B; main courses US$7-8; P) Nouvelle cuisine from

Puebla is lovingly presented at this cozy spot. Mole is prepared in the classic Santa Clara convent style or the restaurant's own *verde* version.

Restaurante Shalala (☎ 5286-5406; Tamaulipas 73, cnr Alfonso Reyes; Sushi from US$2; noodle & rice dishes US$8; ☉ 1-11pm Mon-Sat, 1-8pm Sun; **P**) This is a long-standing Japanese deli noted for its authenticity (owner Hiroshi is a Tokyo native) and casual atmosphere. Standouts include the tempura and *negitoro don* (fresh tuna with sesame oil served on a bed of rice).

Creperie de la Paix (☎ 5286-0049; Michoacán 103, cnr Vicente Suárez; crêpes US$3-6; **P**) On a busy corner, this place does sweet and savory crêpes.

Nevería Roxy (Montes de Oca 89, cnr Av Mazatlán; scoops from US$0.70, banana splits US$3; ☉ 11am-9pm Apr-Oct, 11am-8pm Nov-Mar) For dessert, try the old-fashioned Roxy which makes fresh ice cream on-site (another branch is at Tamaulipas 161 at Alfonso Reyes).

Neve e Gelato (☎ 5256-3345; Cuernavaca 124, cnr Michoacán; scoops from US$1.50; ☉ 10:30am-10pm) Offers to-die-for Italian ice cream and the best espresso around.

For a more tranquil setting, several good restaurants and cafés can be found along Amsterdam and Av México, the two roads that encircle Parque México.

Bistrot Mosaico (☎ 5584-2932; Michoacán 10; starters US$4-9, main courses US$9-16; ☉ noon-11:30pm Mon-Sat, noon-5:30pm Sun; **P**) French owner Francois Avernin opened this unpretentious bistro just west of Av Insurgentes as an alternative to his pricier Polanco restaurant, Champs Elysées. It's trendy for a reason: the service is stellar, the salads fresh and varied, the wines well-chosen. Picnickers can stock up on pâté and escargots at the deli counter.

Bistrot Rojo (☎ 5211-3705; Amsterdam 71; starters US$6-7, main courses US$8-12; ☉ 2pm-midnight Mon-Thu, 2pm-1am Fri-Sat, 2-6pm Sun; **P**) Rojo is an intimate low-lit French-style bistro with an emphasis on fresh seafood (shellfish-stuffed raviolis, shrimp sandwiches, salmon carpaccio). The desserts will knock your socks off.

Don Keso (☎ 5211-3806; Amsterdam 73, cnr Parras; baguettes & salads US$3-4; ☉ 10am-midnight Mon-Wed, 10-2am Thu-Sat, 1-9pm Sun) Across from Rojo is this cozy, reasonably priced hangout with great baguettes, salads and cocktails. Crowds rush in for the good value *comida corrida*.

La Casbah (☎ 5564-6826; Amsterdam 194; main courses US$8-10; ☉ 2-10pm Tue-Sat, 2-6pm Sun; **P**) For Moroccan cuisine, head for the Casbah, with

authentic couscous, tajines and *bastellas* (a pastry filled with meat or vegetables).

Roma   Map pp114–15
BUDGET
Mercado Medellín (btwn Medellín & Monterrey) The market features an extensive eating area with cheap and filling *comidas corridas*, as well as several excellent seafood restaurants. Enter from Coahuila.

El 91 (☎ 5208-1666; Valladolid 91; dishes US$3-8; ☉ 2-7pm Sun-Thu, 2-10pm Fri) Lunch is served to piano accompaniment at this homey, three-story restaurant/bar with balcony seating. Rather than the usual four-course *comida*, they offer a different menu daily, with a long list of homemade soups and main dishes. Across the street is the more rustic sister site, El 96.

Taquería El Jarocho (☎ 5574-7148; Manzanillo 26, cnr Tapachula; tacos US$1.50; ☉ Mon-Sat 8am-10pm, 9am-4pm Sun) Scrambled eggs in salsa verde, cactus leaves with shrimp cakes, and brains *a la mexicana* are among the two dozen taco fillings served at this long-standing Roma snack bar. Get two tacos for the price of one from 8am to 9:30am and 7pm to 10pm.

Hamburguesas (cnr Morelia & Colima; burgers US$1.50; ☉ 10am-midnight) This unassuming street stall does a roaring trade in hamburgers *a la parrilla* (charcoal-broiled), garnished with lettuce, tomatoes and chilies, though it's been known to move on at a moment's notice.

Non Solo Panino (☎ 5264-0094; Guanajuato 102 at Plaza Luis Cabrera; sandwiches & salads US$2.50-5; ☉ 12:30pm-12:30am Mon-Sat; **P**) The plaza's dancing fountains make a lovely backdrop for these Italian sandwiches, stuffed with things like mozzarella, pesto and smoked salmon.

Los Bisquets Obregón (☎ 5584-2802; Álvaro Obregón 60; breakfast US$3-4, antojitos US$3.50-5; **P** ⌘) The flagship branch of this city-wide chain overflows most mornings; fortunately there are a couple more nearby. *Chilangos* flock here for the *pan chino* (Chinese bakery pastries) and café con leche, dispensed from two pitchers, Veracruz style.

La Michoacana (Puebla 160; scoops from US$0.50; ☉ 10am-10pm) From humble origins in Tocumbo, Michoacán, this popsicle chain now boasts more than 1000 branches in Mexico City alone. All ice cream and ices are made on site; try a *mango con chile paleta de agua* (spicy mango popsicle).

MID-RANGE & TOP END

Contramar (☎ 5514-3169; Durango 200; starters US$5-9, main courses US$11-13; ⌚ 1:30-6:30pm; P) Fresh seafood, simply prepared, has made this stylish spot a Roma hit. The house specialty is tuna fillet Contramar style – split, swabbed with red chili and parsley sauces, and grilled to perfection.

La Tecla (☎ 5525-4920; Durango 186A; starters US$2.50-4.50, main courses US$5.50-9.50; ⌚ 1:30pm-midnight Mon-Sat, 1:30-6pm Sun; P) Creative variations on Mexican ingredients draw crowds to this cozy, reasonably priced restaurant near the Plaza Madrid. Check out the fish fillets stuffed with *huitlacoche* or fettuccine in *mole poblano* sauce.

El Discreto Encanto de Comer (☎ 5511-3860; Orizaba 76; main courses US$9.50-22; ⌚ 1:30-6pm Mon-Wed & Sat, 1:30-11pm Thu & Fri; P) Francophile Porfirio Díaz would have surely appreciated the classic French cuisine served at this ritzy establishment, discreetly ensconced in an early 20th-century home.

Polanco & Bosque de Chapultepec

BUDGET & MID-RANGE

Klein's (☎ 5281-0862; Av Presidente Masaryk 330B; prices from US$5; ⌚ 7am-1am; P) Though not strictly Jewish, this place serves breakfasts, *antojitos*, tortas, and meat, fish and chicken dishes with kosher accompaniments.

La Estrella de Galicia (☎ 5280-7737; Dumas 7; tapas US$5-8; ⌚ 1pm-1:30am Mon-Sat, 1pm-midnight Sun; P) Spanish beer and tapas combine well in this casually elegant setting.

For other moderately priced fare in Polanco, head for Av Presidente Masaryk between Dumas and France; a string of sidewalk cafés lines the south side of the street.

La Parrilla Suiza (☎ 5538-8015; cnr Ave Presidente Masaryk & Arquímedes; tacos from US$1.70; ⌚ noon-midnight) For hungry meat eaters, the mixed grills and tacos are a good economical choice at La Parilla Suiza, on the traffic circle 600m northwest of the Museo Nacional de Antropología. It gets packed at lunchtime when a *comida* is served.

TOP END

Rincón Argentino (☎ 5254-8775; Av Presidente Masaryk 177; dishes US$28-55; ⌚ 12:30-11:30pm, 12:30-10:30pm Sun; P) This Argentine eatery has a well-deserved reputation for the best steaks in town.

La Hacienda de los Morales (☎ 5096-3054; Vázquez de Mella 525; dishes US$25-50; ⌚ 1pm-midnight; P) Excellent Mexican and international dishes, with some particularly good fish choices, are served in and around spacious rooms and pretty gardens in this onetime colonial country hacienda. Reservations are advisable, and dress is formal for dinner (though not for lunch).

Chez Wok (☎ 5281-3410; Tennyson 117; dishes US$14-66; ⌚ 1:30-11pm Mon-Sat, 1:30-4:30pm Sun; P) Chinese dishes at Chez Wok are much more sophisticated than most in Mexico. The atmosphere is formal and reservations are recommended.

Villa María (☎ 5203-1398; Homero 704; dishes US $8-15; ⌚ 1:30pm-midnight Mon-Sat, 1:30-7pm Sun; P) This popular place serves traditional Mexican ingredients with nouveau touches and presentations.

Within Bosque de Chapultepec's 2a Sección are two elegant lakeside restaurants: **El Lago** (☎ 5515-9585; on Lago Mayor; main courses US$15-26; ⌚ 7:30am-noon, 1:30-11:30pm Mon-Sat, brunch 10:30am-4:30pm Sun), with *alta cocina mexicana*; and **Restaurante del Bosque** (☎ 5515-4652; on Lago Menor; main courses US$12-16; ⌚ 8am-6pm), with weekend buffet breakfast and lunch.

San Ángel Map p111

BUDGET

Bazar Sábado (Plaza San Jacinto 11; quesadillas US$1.50; ⌚ 9am-6pm Sat) For a break from shopping, grab one of the delicious quesadillas in a handmade tortilla in the plaza of the market building. There's also a breakfast (US$10) and lunch buffet (US$18), but better options are outside.

Mamá Rumba (☎ 5550-8099; Plaza San Jacinto 23; comida corrida US$4.50; ⌚ 1:30-6:30pm Wed-Sun) At the lower end of Plaza San Jacinto, you can get a four-course Cuban meal accompanied by soft, live music in the late afternoon. After 11pm it's a hot spot for Cuban dance music (see p162). Nearby are a couple of other reasonable *comida* places.

MID-RANGE & TOP END

Fonda San Ángel (☎ 5550-1641; Plaza San Jacinto 3; dishes US$8-15; ⌚ 8am-midnight Mon-Sat, 9am-10pm Sun; P) Facing the plaza, this attractive restaurant has an abundant weekend brunch buffet and serves creative dishes with Mexican elements such as the tasty salmon with chipotle sauce.

San Ángel Inn (☎ 5616-1402; Diego Rivera 50; dishes US$8-18; ☒ 1pm-1am Mon-Sat, until 9pm Sun; P) To dine in style, head for the San Ángel Inn, near the Estudio Diego Rivera. This is an ex-hacienda with a flowery courtyard and gardens, transformed into a restaurant serving Mexican and European cuisine. Even if you don't want to splurge for dinner, you can enjoy the gardens and architecture while having a drink in the bar; the margaritas and martinis are renowned for their size and quality. There's a US$2 table charge.

Saks (☎ 5616-2208; Plaza San Jacinto 9; dishes from US$7; ☒ 8am-6pm Sun-Wed, 8am-midnight Thu-Sat; P) At this mostly vegetarian restaurant you can enjoy tasty breakfasts with a half liter of juice, fresh yogurt and fruit, sweet rolls, and a choice of eggs and other dishes at pleasant outdoor tables. Later, choose from vegetarian specialties such as chilies stuffed with corn-fungus and goat cheese (US$9) or attractive salmon, steak or chicken options (US$9 to US$12).

Cluny (☎ 5550-7350; Av de la Paz 57; dishes US$7-12; ☒ 1pm-midnight Mon-Sat, 12:30-11pm Sun; P) Cluny serves up a scrumptious variety of crêpes both savory and sweet. Be prepared to wait for a table in the evening. You'll find it in the Centro Comercial Plaza del Carmen.

Coyoacán
Map p119
BUDGET
El Tizoncito (☎ 5554-7712; Aguayo 3; tacos from US$0.70; ☒ noon-2:30am Mon-Thu, noon-3:30am Fri-Sat) This is a branch of the popular taco chain that originated in Condesa.

Chamorros Coyoacán (☎ 5659-0340; Madrid 29; main dishes US$2.50-5.50; ☒ 1-6pm Mon-Sat) Office workers fill this barn-like structure at lunchtime. There's a long list of *guisados*, but most patrons order the *chamorros* (US$6), Flintstone-size joints of pork, and stuff the morsels into homemade tortillas.

Fonda El Morral (☎ 5554-0298; Allende 2; breakfast US$4-6.50, antojitos US$3-5.50) This large restaurant with tiled arches is good for a traditional breakfast or evening tamales and chocolate, served in clay mugs. *Barbacoa* is featured on weekends.

Nieves de Coyoacán (Plaza Hidalgo 31; scoops from US$1.50; ☒ 11am-11pm) This obligatory weekend stop has homemade ice cream and popsicles in flavors ranging from corn to Nescafe.

Coyoacán's best churros are found at **Churros Allende** (Map p119; Allende 38; from US$1; ☒ 9pm-midnight). Get in line for a bag – cream-filled or straight up – then stroll over to El Jarocho for coffee (see Drinking, p159).

For hearty inexpensive fare, head for the markets.

Mercado de Antojitos (Higuera, cnr Plaza Hidalgo & Caballo Calco) This market has all kinds of snacks, including deep-fried quesadillas, *pozole*, *esquites* (boiled corn kernels served with a dollop of mayo), tamales and *flautas*.

Tostadas Coyoacán (☎ 5659-8774; Allende btwn Malintzin & Xicoténcatl; tostadas US$1-2.50; ☒ noon-6pm) Inside Coyoacán's main market, 2½ blocks north of Plaza Hidalgo, is one of the best places to eat anywhere in town. Here an attractive array of platters will stop hungry visitors in their tracks. Tostadas are piled high with things like ceviche, marinated octopus and pig's feet, mushrooms and shredded chicken.

MID-RANGE & TOP END
El Jardín del Pulpo (☎ 5659-2807; cnr Allende & Malitzin; cocktails US$3.50-7, fish dishes US$8-10; ☒ 10am-6pm) Fresh fish platters, shrimp and oyster cocktails and *caldos* (broths) are served at this locale, taking up a corner of the main market. Everyone sits on benches at long tables.

Entre Vero (☎ 5659-0066; Jardín del Centenario 14C; pastas US$8.50, steaks US$11.50-14; ☒ 11am-11pm) This excellent Uruguayan restaurant with candlelit sidewalk tables serves up a variety of grilled meats and pastas. The *matambre de pollo* (chicken breast wrapped around a spinach and mild chili filling) is a very good choice.

Los Danzantes (☎ 5658-6054; Jardín del Centenario 12; dishes US$8-12) Los Danzantes puts a contemporary spin on Mexican cuisine with dishes like *huitlacoche*-stuffed raviolis and squash blossom salad. You'll also find mezcal cocktails and cigars from San Andrés in Veracruz.

DRINKING
Cafés, bars and cantinas are all major social venues on the capital's landscape. Recent arrival Starbucks is a latecomer to a long-standing café tradition fueled by beans from Veracruz, Oaxaca and Chiapas. Coyoacán in particular is jammed with java joints. The bar scene is extraordinarily lively with a high degree of specialization, from Irish

pubs to martini clubs. Colonia Condesa has exploded recently to become the city's hottest (and priciest) bar-hopping locale. Cantinas, Mexico's pubs, are traditionally a male domain but women are welcome nowadays (see opposite).

Prices for drinks vary quite a bit, but generally beers are around US$2 to US$3, and mixed drinks range from US$4 to US$10.

Centro Histórico Map pp108–10
CAFÉS & JUICE BARS

Jugos CanCun (☎ 5518-5255; Independencia 56; juices US$1.50-3, sandwiches US$2-3; ☿ 7am-9pm) This brightly colored juice bar squeezes all sort of fruit and vegetable combinations; it also does salads, tortas and homemade root beer.

Take a coffee break at any of these charming downtown locales.

Café del Passaje (☎ 5521-0683; Pasaje Iturbide; ☿ 9am-9pm Mon-Sat) Nice journal writing spot on traffic-free Gante.

Café del Río (☎ 5510-2250; Donceles 86; ☿ 9am-8pm Mon-Sat) A cozy hangout with espresso served in tiny China cups, good pastries and burritos.

La Selva Café (☎ 5521-4111; Bolívar 31) Branch of the Chiapas coffee distributor in the stunning patio of a colonial building.

BARS

La Gioconda (☎ 5518-7823; Mata 18; ☿ noon-11pm Mon-Wed, noon-2am Thu-Sat) Dark and light draft beer are served in this hip, popular meeting place, run by a British-Mexican couple. There's live jazz Friday evening.

Bar Mancera (☎ 5521-9755; Carranza 49; ☿ 10am-10pm Mon-Fri) Next door to the Legislative Assembly of the DF, this darkly atmospheric haunt seems preserved in amber since the 1920s, when it was last remodeled.

Plaza de la República Area Map pp108–10
Café Gran Premio (☎ 5535-0934; Antonio Caso 72 at Sadi Carnot; café con leche US$1.25) A long-standing java house with a neighborhood feel, the Gran Premio does a rich *café lechero* and has a case full of good pastries.

Condesa Map pp114–15
CAFÉS

Café La Selva (☎ 5211-5170; Vicente Suárez 38) The Mexican Starbucks serves organic coffee from Chiapas, produced by a group of small-scale indigenous coffee growers. The

Condesa branch is the hippest place in town for a coffee break.

BARS

Condesa's thriving bar scene is a recent phenomenon, and new places are popping up (and shutting down) all the time. The following are relatively well-established and filled beyond capacity Thursday through Saturday evenings.

Mitote (☎ 5211-9150; Amsterdam 53; ☿ 8pm-2am Tue-Sat) Mitote (Náhuatl for 'ruckus'), a lively little neighborhood joint near Parque España, lives up to its name. Owner Walter works the quirkily decorated lounge like a good host. If you're hungry, there are tasty tapas.

T Gallery (☎ 5211-7942; Saltillo 39; ☿ 10-2am Mon-Sat) A bohemian, multi-generational crowd settle down in the velvet plush sofas and funky furniture (much of it created by British owner Tina) for conversation or a game of backgammon along with a cup of tea or a draft beer.

Billar Américo (☎ 5553-5138; Av Michoacán 78; tables per hr US$4) Not an exclusively male domain by any means, Condesa's billiard hall is as trendy as some of its bars and restaurants, and there's usually some good soul or jazz playing.

Barracuda (☎ 5211-9480; Av Nuevo León 4A at Av Sonora; ☿ 7pm-2am Wed-Sat) A pioneer of Mexico City's martini craze, this ultra-cool lounge serves numerous variations of the cocktail (US$7 to US$8) along with tasty Asian-influenced cuisine (booths are reserved for dining).

Hookah Lounge (☎ 5264-6275; Campeche 284; cover US$1.50; ☿ 5pm-2am) Moroccan tapestries and pillows set the tone for this North African fantasy augmented by house music. Bring friends and share a water pipe (from US$9), available in a bewildering array of flavors.

Rexo (☎ 5553-5337; Saltillo 1 at Av Nuevo León; ☿ 1:30pm-2am Tue-Sat, 1pm-1am Sun-Mon) Perennially hip and often packed, Rexo offers a dining area where you can rise above the crowds and enjoy excellent Mediterranean food.

The former Cine Plaza Condesa, at the confluence of Tamaulipas and Nuevo León, has been reborn as a major bar zone, earning itself a reputation as a haven for *fresas* (literally 'strawberries,' a derogatory term for upper-class young women).

WELCOME TO THE CANTINA

Cantinas are Mexico's pubs. Some are humble, others swanky; some serve full meals, others just drinking snacks. What they all have in common is a simple design and a relaxed atmosphere. The days of men-only establishments are long gone, and it's not unusual to see a pair of women chatting over a Corona. There's usually a TV showing some sporting event. Tables are basic, with a slot on the legs for drinks, leaving room for dominoes. Troubadours often rove the premises, belting out boleros for a few pesos.

Beer and *copas nacionales* (rum, tequila) are the most popular drinks but it's OK to just order a soft drink. *Botanas* (drinking snacks, from roasted peanuts to sardine salad) are generally served with a drink; you pay for the drink only. The idea is to get you to drink more, but it still turns out to be a good deal, especially where the botanas are great. Waiters, often clad in an apron and bow tie, tend to be respectful, even reverent, but not reluctant to chat. Following are some of Mexico City's favorite cantinas.

Note: Don't even think about using a credit card in a cantina.

El Nivel (Map pp108-10; ☎ 5522-9755; Moneda 2; ☻ noon-midnight Mon-Sat) The country's first cantina proudly displays its license (No 1), dating from 1855. Inside the building that once housed the hemisphere's first university, it's within shouting distance of the Palacio Nacional. Since its opening, every Mexican president except Vicente Fox has stopped in for a *trago*.

La Ópera Bar (Map pp108-10; ☎ 5512-8959; Av 5 de Mayo 10; ☻ 1pm-midnight Mon-Sat, 1-5:30pm Sun) Two blocks east of Bellas Artes, this ornate early-20th-century watering hole only opened its doors to women in the 1970s. Booths of dark wood and a massive bar are all original. A hole in the ceiling is said to have been made by Pancho Villa's bullet.

El Centenario (Map pp114-15; ☎ 5553-4454; Vicente Suárez 42; ☻ noon-midnight Mon-Sat) An enclave of tradition in the heart of trendy Condesa, this little gem is jammed most evenings.

Los Portales de Tlaquepaque (Map pp108-10; ☎ 5518-6344; Bolívar 56) Sharing a funky downtown block with a number of other straightforward saloons, this two-story operation has the best-stocked bar and liveliest atmosphere.

Salón Corona (Map pp108-10; ☎ 5512-9007, Bolívar 24) Punks and suits crowd this boisterous, no-frills bar, in business since 1928. Amiable staff serve up *tarros* (mugs) of light or dark *cerveza de barril* (draft beer) and bottles of almost every known Mexican beer for US$2 each.

La Guadalupana (Map p119; ☎ 5554-6253; Higuera 14; ☻ 1pm-midnight) Beyond the swinging doors is a long narrow salon decorated with bullfighting memorabilia. Serving drinks for over seven decades, it breathes tradition, down to the blasé waiters in white coats. There are botanas and tortas as well as heartier fare.

La Polar (☎ 5546-5066; Guillermo Prieto 129, San Rafael) Any evening, someone is bound to be celebrating something at this sprawling beer hall, at least until the *birria* (succulent goat stew) runs out. Mariachis and norteño combos compete with the chatter.

El Viena (Map pp108-10; ☎ 5512-0929; República de Cuba 2E; ☻ 1pm-3am) The city's only gay cantina is a friendly place attracting a varied crowd, from truck drivers to journalists, and the jukebox is terrific.

Pata Negra (☎ 5211-5563; Tamaulipas 30; ☻ 1:30pm-2am) One of the friendliest places, this tapas bar attracts a clean-cut 20s to 30s crowd.

Cafeina (☎ 5212-0090; Av Nuevo León 73; ☻ 1pm-2am) This sleek combination of café and bar has antique armchairs and a narrow terrace, a good vantage point for gawking at gorgeous arrivals over a latte or Cafeini (espresso martini). A DJ works the room from a central module (Sunday is '80s night).

Celtics (☎ 5211-9081; Tamaulipas 36; ☻ 1:30pm-2am Mon-Sat) An Argentinean-run facsimile of an Irish pub, Celtics has become extraordinarily popular. A bottle of Guinness will set you back US$6, a draft Sol US$4. The soundtrack is more U2 than Chieftains; bands play on Monday night.

Cinna Bar (☎ 5286-8456; Av Nuevo León 67; ☻ 7pm-midnight Sun-Mon, 7pm-2am Tue-Sat) Cinna is another scene-making bar/restaurant/lounge. Behind its red plexiglass windows, an ambitious 30-something set sip martinis at the bar or nibble pan-Asian cuisine in the raised dining area.

Polanco
Map pp116–17

Though not as cutting edge as Condesa, this well-heeled neighborhood gets quite lively after dark.

Área (☎ 5282-3100; Av Presidente Mazaryk 201; ☺ 7pm-1am Mon-Sat) Atop the Hotel Habita is one of the most popular and unique bars in town. Covered only by a large tent top with a classy fireplace, it has great views, videos projected on the adjacent building, and no cover charge.

La Martinera (☎ 5281-7235; France 120; ☺ noon-1:30am) In Plaza Masaryk, between France and Lafontaine, is this hip spot for sipping martinis with friends.

Bar Fly de París (☎ 5282-2906; Av Presidente Mazaryk 393; admission US$10; ☺ 10pm-3am Tue-Sat) In the same complex as La Martinera, this place jumps to live Cuban sounds.

Dubliner (☎ 5250-8105; Calz Mariano Escobedo 434; ☺ noon-12:30am Mon-Wed, noon-3am Thu-Sat, 1-11:30pm) If you're hankering for a pint of Guinness, this is where the local Irish community gathers – and a lot of other people too.

Roma
Map pp114–15

CAFÉS
Enanos de Tapanco (☎ 5564-2274; Orizaba 161, cnr Querétaro; ☺ 8am-11:30pm Mon-Fri, 9am-11:30pm Sat, 3:30-10:30pm Sun) Possibly Mexico City's coolest café, 'The Dwarves of the Loft' also functions as an art gallery. Great cappuccinos and quiches are served, and there's always choice jazz on the stereo. There's live music Friday and storytelling Tuesday evening.

Café de Carlo (☎ 5525-6015; Orizaba 115; closed Sun) Coffee connoisseurs head for this unassuming sidewalk café, with an aromatic roaster and vintage espresso machine.

BARS
La Bodeguita del Medio (☎ 5553-0246; Cozumel 37; ☺ 1pm-2am Tue-Sat, 1pm-midnight Sun & Mon) The walls are scribbled with verses and messages at this lively branch of the famous Havana joint. Have a *mojito*, a Cuban concoction of rum and mint leaves (US$3.25), along with a plate of rice and beans.

D'Alfredos (☎ 5584-1412; Álvaro Obregón 112, cnr Orizaba; ☺ 1pm-midnight Mon-Sat) A fun supper club with an unapologetically kitschy decor, D'Alfredos features a Hammond organ trio from 3pm onward – anyone can grab the mike if the spirit moves them.

La Hija de los Apaches (☎ 5511-0071; Av Cuauhtémoc 39; ☺ 9am-9:30pm Mon-Sat) This is the place to get *pulque*, the traditional Mexican beverage made from the fermented sap of the agave. The viscous white liquid comes in a variety of flavors – coconut, pineapple, tomato and guava, to name a few – and is sprinkled with cinnamon. This working-class *pulquería* has long been a haunt of professional boxers.

Lamm (☎ 5514-8501; Álvaro Obregón 99; ☺ until 2am Mon-Wed, until 3am Thu-Sat) In the evening the open-air restaurant of the Casa Lamm turns into a modern lounge where a sophisticated, smartly dressed set congregate until the wee hours. There's live *música cubana* and jazz Tuesday and Wednesday.

Zona Rosa & Around
Map pp112–13

The Pink Zone can seem pretty sleazy with so many dark-suited bouncers and touts trying to lure business into strip joints, but there are plenty of fully clothed establishments, too.

CAFÉS
Auseba (☎ 5511-3769; Hamburgo 159B; snacks US$1.50-3; ☺ 8am-10:30pm Mon-Sat, 11am-10:30pm Sun) A good place to relax with a pot of tea or cup of coffee, Auseba has glass cases filled with enticing cakes and large windows for watching the pedestrian pageant on Hamburgo.

Sanborns Cafe (☎ 5207-9760; Londres 149; sandwiches & antojitos US$5-10; ☺ 24hr) This Sanborns is a busy after-partying coffee and gathering place.

Starbucks (☎ 5525-9167; Paseo de la Reforma 325 in Pasaje Manhattan Deli) This was the first provider of Seattle's java juice to set up in Mexico City – right next to the US Embassy.

BARS
Cantina Las Bohemias (☎ 5207-4384; Londres 142 at Amberes; ☺ 1:30pm-1:30am Mon-Sat) This bright, jolly place is popular with the after-work crowd. Both women and men gossip over their beer to live *norteño* sounds.

Yuppie's Sports Cafe (☎ 5533-0919; Génova 34; main dishes US$8-18; ☺ 11-1:30am) If you want to catch the big game while you're in town, be sure to make a reservation to save a place. Besides big screen TVs, the elegant stained glass and polished chrome makes this an attractive place even to a nonsports fan.

Bar Milán (☎ 5592-0031; Milán 18; ☯ 9pm-3am Thu-Sat) Tucked away on a quiet backstreet, this casual hangout is the closest you can get to riding the metro at rush hour, with a college crowd jamming two narrow rooms. Purchase beer tickets, then make your way over to the cactus-trimmed bar. The soundtrack ranges from classic rock to Café Tacuba; don't be surprised if the crowd spontaneously bursts into chorus.

Coyoacán   Map p119
Café El Jarocho (☎ 5554-5418; Av Cuauhtémoc 134 at Allende; ☯ 6-1am) This immensely popular joint churns out US$0.60 cappuccinos for long lines of java hounds. As there's no seating inside, people have their coffee standing in the street or sitting on curbside metal benches. The branch just around the corner makes great tortas, and both branches have terrific doughnuts. Another **El Jarocho branch** (☎ 5659-9107; Av México 125) is conveniently located near Viveros park.

ENTERTAINMENT
There's so much going on in Mexico City on any given evening, it's hard to keep track. *Tiempo Libre* (www.tiempolibre.com .mx in Spanish), the city's comprehensive what's-on magazine, will help you sort it all out. Published Thursday, it covers live music, theater, movies, dance, art and nightlife, with lots of family options as well as gay venues. Another useful guide is *DF*, a bimonthly with an English-language insert. *Primera Fila*, a Friday section of the *Reforma* newspaper, has information on all sorts of entertainment.

Ticketmaster (☎ 5325-9000; www.ticketmaster.com .mx in Spanish) sells tickets for all the major venues via Internet, phone or from any of these outlets.
Auditorio Nacional (Map pp116-17; Paseo de la Reforma 50; ☯ 11am-6pm)
Liverpool Centro (Map pp108-10; Venustiano Carranza 92; ☯ 10am-8pm Mon-Sat, 11am-7pm Sun); Polanco (Map pp116-17; Mariano Escobedo 425; ☯ 11am-8:30pm) Also see Shopping (p166).
Mixup Centro Histórico (Map pp108-10; Av Madero 51; ☯ 10am-9pm Mon-Sat, 11am-8pm Sun); Zona Rosa (Map pp112-13; Génova 76; ☯ 9am-9pm)

Cinemas
Mexico City is a banquet for moviegoers. Just about everything is projected here and ticket prices are low: around US$4, with many movie houses offering discounts on Wednesday. Except for children's fare, movies are in their original language, with Spanish subtitles. *Reforma* and *La Jornada* have comprehensive daily listings, including addresses of the cinemas.

The following multiplexes have mostly Hollywood fare, with the odd Mexican hit.
Cine Diana (Map pp112-13; ☎ 5511-3236; Paseo de la Reforma 423, facing La Diana Cazadora)
Cinemex Real (Map pp108-10; ☎ 5257-6969; Colón 17; metro Hidalgo)
Cinemex Palacio (Map pp108-10; ☎ 5512-0348; Iturbide 123)

There are other theaters offering a more eclectic program.
Lumiere Reforma (Map pp112-13; ☎ 5514-0000; Río Guadalquivir 104)
Cinemex Casa de Arte (Map pp116-17; ☎ 5280-9156; France 120, Polanco)

In addition, several repertory cinemas cater to film buffs.
Cineteca Nacional (Map p119; ☎ 1253-9390; www .cinetecanacional.net in Spanish; Av México-Coyoacán 389; tickets US$3) Thematically focused film series are shown on six screens, with at least one for Mexican cinema. There are cafés and bookstores at the center of the complex, 700m east of metro Coyoacán. In November the Cineteca hosts the Muestra Internacional de Cine, Mexico City's international film festival.
Centro Cultural Universitario (Map pp104-5; ☎ 5622-7003, Av Insurgentes Sur 3000; tickets US$3) UNAM has two cinemas.
Salon Cinematográfico Fósforo (Map pp108-10; ☎ 5702-4454, ext 218; San Ildefonso 43; tickets US$2) Inside the Antiguo Colegio de San Ildefonso (p124).
Cinematógrafo del Chopo (Map pp108-10; ☎ 5535-0447; Dr Atl 37, Colonia Santa María La Ribera; tickets US$3)

Dance, Classical Music & Theater
Orchestral music, opera, ballet, contemporary dance and theater are all abundantly represented in the capital's numerous theaters. Museums, too, serve as performance venues, including the **Museo de la Secretaría de Hacienda y Crédito Público** (p123) and the **Museo Universitario del Chopo** (Map pp108-10; ☎ 5553-2186; www.chopo.unam.mx in Spanish; González Martínez 10). The national arts council (Conaculta) provides a rundown at its website (www .cnca.gob.mx in Spanish) and in Friday's *La Jornada*.

Palacio de Bellas Artes (Map pp108-10; ☎ 5512-2593; Av Hidalgo 1; box office ☯ 11am-7pm) The Orquesta Sinfónica Nacional and prestigious opera and dance companies perform in the palace's ornate theater, while chamber groups appear in the recital halls. It's most famous, though, for the **Ballet Folclórico de México** (tickets US$22-37; ☯ 8:30pm Wed, 9:30am & 8:30pm Sun), a two-hour festive blur of costumes, music and dance from all over Mexico. Tickets are usually available the day of the show at the Palacio or from Ticketmaster (see p159).

Centro Cultural Universitario (Map pp104-5; ☎ 5622-6954; www.agendacultural.unam.mx in Spanish; Av Insurgentes Sur 3000) Ensconced in the woodsy southern section of the national university campus, the cultural center comprises five theaters, including the Sala Nezahualcóyotl, home of the UNAM Philharmonic; the Teatro Alarcón, which puts on plays; and the Sala Miguel Covarrubias, a contemporary dance venue. See p134 for directions.

Centro Nacional de las Artes (CNA; Map p119; ☎ 1253-9400, ext 1035; www.cenart.gob.mx in Spanish; Río Churubusco 79) This sprawling cultural complex/art institute has events across the artistic spectrum, many free. From metro General Anaya (Línea 2), exit on the east side of Calz de Tlalpan, walk north to the corner and turn right.

Centro Cultural del Bosque (Map pp116-17; ☎ 5280-8771, ext 433; cnr Paseo de la Reforma & Campo Marte; box office ☯ noon-3pm & 5-7pm Mon-Fri & prior to events) This complex behind the Auditorio Nacional features six theaters, including the **Teatro de la Danza**, dedicated to modern dance. On Saturday and Sunday afternoons, children's plays and puppet shows are staged.

If your Spanish is up to it, you might sample Mexico City's lively theater scene. The website www.mejorteatro.com.mx (in

---

GAY & LESBIAN MEXICO CITY

The Zona Rosa is the focus of the gay scene.

BGay BProud Café México (Map pp112-13; ☎ 5208-2547; Amberes 12-B; ☯ 11am-11pm) Stop by BGay BProud to meet people, check out the free literature and catch up on news of the local community. *Homópolis* magazine, available free in some clubs, and www.sergay.com.mx (in Spanish) have useful information on gay life in Mexico City.

El Almacén (Map pp112-13; ☎ 5207-0727; Av Florencia 37A, Zona Rosa; cover Thu-Sun US$5; ☯ 5pm-3am) This casual, low-lit bar is one of the Pink Zone's longest-established. Downstairs is the men-only **El Taller** (The Workshop), an industrial-themed disco. The cover lets you into both places.

Cabaré-Tito (www.cabaretito.com in Spanish) Neón (Map pp112-13; ☎ 5514-9455; Plaza del Ángel, Londres 161, Local 20-A; cover Thu & Sun US$3, Fri & Sat US$5; ☯ 6pm-3am); Fusión (Map pp112-13; ☎ 5207-2554; Londres 117-bis; cover Thu & Sun US$3, Fri & Sat US$5, ☯ 4pm-2am); Metal (Map pp114-15; ☎ 5511-4460; Av Insurgentes Sur 226; cover Fri & Sat US$5, Sun US$3; ☯ 8pm-4am Fri-Sat, 4pm-2am Sun) The success of this youth-oriented cabaret/disco has spawned two more branches. The original, now called Neón, appeals to young adult males and has electronic music; while Fusión attracts an adolescent set and favors Latin pop. Both stage female-impersonator shows at around midnight. At Metal, the newest flavor, Friday and Sunday are reserved for lesbians.

Butterflies (Map pp108-10; ☎ 5761-1861; Izazaga 9, Centro Histórico; cover US$7 incl two drinks; ☯ 9pm-4am Tue-Sun) Just outside metro Salto del Agua, Butterflies is an airplane-hangar-sized space that still gets densely packed, with five bars, a snack bar and elaborately choreographed stage shows. It's fun for straights, too, as long as you don't mind crowds, thick smoke and loud loud music.

Enigma (Map pp114-15; ☎ 5207-7367; Morelia 111; cover US$5-6; ☯ 9pm-4am Wed-Sun) Just off Ávaro Obregón on Roma's east end, Enigma has a mirror ball, crowded dance floor and continuous Latin pop for its predominately lesbian clientele.

Bar Oasis (Map pp108-10; ☎ 5521-9740; República de Cuba 2-G, Centro; ☯ 3pm-1am Sun-Thu, 3pm-3am Fri & Sat) Next to El Viena (p157), this disco has an entertaining show featuring lip-synching trannies.

Living (Map pp114-15; ☎ 5584-7468; www.living.com.mx; Orizaba 146, Roma; cover US$12; ☯ 11pm-4am Fri & Sat) Housed in a sprawling Porfiriato mansion, Living is one of the hottest spots for a 20-something crowd. There's a spectacular sound and light display and a variety of shows from strippers to acrobatic acts.

Spanish) covers the major venues. Performances are generally Thursday to Sunday evenings with weekend matinees.

Teatro Blanquita (Map pp108-10; ☎ 5510-1203; Eje Central Lázaro Cárdenas 16, Centro; tickets US$8-15; metro Bellas Artes) Classic variety theater.

Centro Cultural Telmex (Map pp114-15; ☎ 5514-2300; Cuauhtémoc, cnr Puebla, Colonia Roma; tickets US$15 35; metro Cuauhtémoc) Flashy Broadway-style productions.

Bar El Hábito (Map p119; ☎ 5659-1139; www.elhabito .com.mx in Spanish; Madrid 13, Coyoacán; metro Coyoacán) Cabaret with liberal doses of irreverent comedy and great music.

Live Music
The variety of music is impressive, with traditional Mexican, Cuban, folk, jazz, rock and other styles being played in concert halls, clubs, bars, museums, on public transportation and on the street. The 'Espectáculos Nocturnos' and 'Espectáculos Populares' sections in *Tiempo Libre* cover events.

Free concerts take place most weekends on the Zócalo. Coyoacán is another good bet most evenings and all day Saturday and Sunday. Musicians, comedians and mimes turn its two central plazas into a big open-air party.

CONCERTS
Auditorio Nacional (Map pp116-17; ☎ 5280-9250; www.auditorio.com.mx in Spanish; Paseo de la Reforma 50) Major gigs by Mexican and visiting rock and pop artists take the stage at the 10,000-seat national auditorium.

Salón 21 (Map pp116-17; ☎ 5255-1496; Andrómaco 17, cnr Moliere; cover varies) A warehouse-sized venue for touring salsa stars as well as rock, world and other performers. With excellent sound, wall-length bar and dance floor for thousands, this is one of Mexico's most cutting-edge clubs.

Teatro de la Ciudad (Map pp108-10; ☎ 5510-2942; Donceles 36; metro Allende) Built in 1918 and recently reopened, this lavishly restored 1500-seat hall gets some of the more interesting touring groups.

Teatro Metropolitan (Map pp108-10; ☎ 5510-1045; Independencia 90; metro Juárez) Artists as diverse as Café Tacuba, Pat Metheny and Cachao López have played this mid-sized hall.

MARIACHIS
Five blocks north of the Palacio de Bellas Artes, **Plaza Garibaldi** (Map pp108-10) is where the city's mariachi bands gather. Outfitted in fancy costumes, they tootle their trumpets, tune their guitars and stand around with a drink until approached by someone who'll pay for a song (about US$10) or whisk them away to entertain at a party.

Plaza Garibaldi gets going by about 8pm and stays busy until around midnight. For food, try the Mercado San Camilito north of the plaza.

El Tenampa (Map pp108-10; ☎ 5526-6176; north side of plaza; ✆ 1pm-3am) You can wander and listen to the mariachis, then stop here. Graced with murals of the giants of Mexican song and enlivened by its own mariachis, the festive cantina is an obligatory visit.

ROCK
The **Tianguis Cultural del Chopo** (p165) has a stage set up at its north end every Saturday afternoon for young and hungry alternative, metal and punk bands.

Dada X (Map pp108-10; ☎ 5113-0903; www.dadax .com.mx in Spanish; Bolívar 31, cnr 16 de Septiembre; free to US$10, depending on event) Black-clad youth gravitate toward this downtown space on the upper floor of a magnificent colonial building. The varied program includes cult films, poetry readings and live music, which might be anything from ska to electronica.

Multiforo Alicia (Map pp114-15; ☎ 5511-2100; Av Cuauhtémoc 91; cover US$5; ✆ 8pm-2am Fri & Sat) Behind the graffiti-scrawled façade is Mexico City's premier rock club. A suitably dark, smoky, seatless space, the Alicia stages up-and-coming punk, surf and ska bands, who hawk their music at the downstairs record store.

JAZZ
Papa Beto (Map pp112-13; ☎ 5592-1638; www.papa beto.com in Spanish; Villalongín 196H, Colonia Cuauhtémoc; cover US$8; ✆ 1st/2nd set 9pm/11pm Tue-Sat) Opened in 2003 by a Japanese expatriate to highlight local talent, this bistro is the best place in town to hear jazz.

Blu (Map p111; ☎ 5616-4791; Av de La Paz 57, San Ángel; cover $7, free with food order or bar seating; ✆ 7pm-1am Tue-Sat) Jazz accompanies dinner and martinis at this expansive, ultra-stylish lounge inside the Centro Commercial Plaza del Carmen. It's a good place to start the evening as the music is over by midnight.

Atrio (☎ 5264 3039; Orizaba 127, Colonia Roma; ✆ Tue-Sun 1pm-1am) Some stellar jazz talents

MEXICO CITY

take the stage Tuesday evenings at this cultural space; other nights you might hear flamenco guitar or chamber music.

Nightclubs

LATIN DANCE

The city's many aficionados have a whole circuit of clubs and *salones de baile* to choose from. Even if you don't dance salsa, merengue or cumbia you'll enjoy just listening to the great music and watching the experts on the dance floor.

You might learn a few steps at the **Plaza de Danzón** (Map pp108-10), northwest of La Ciudadela near metro Balderas. Couples crowd the plaza every Saturday afternoon to do the danzón, an elegant though complicated Cuban step that infiltrated Mexico in the 19th century. Lessons in danzón and other steps are given from 11am to 2pm.

At the following clubs, it's customary to go in a group and share a bottle of rum or tequila (around US$50, including mixers).

Salón Los Ángeles (☎ 5597-5181; Lerdo 206; cover US$3.50; ☼ 6-11pm Tue & Sun) 'Those who don't know Los Ángeles don't know Mexico' reads the marquee, and for once the hyperbole is well-deserved. Cuban music fans won't want to miss the outstanding orchestras who play here nor the incredibly graceful dancers who fill the vast floor. Particularly on Tuesday evening, when an older crowd comes for *danzones*, it's like the set of a period film. Two blocks south of metro Tlatelolco, Salón Los Ángeles is in a rough area so take a taxi.

Cuban dance clubs abound in Colonia Roma, particularly near the intersection of Av Insurgentes and Medellín.

El Gran León (Map pp114-15; ☎ 5564-7110; Querétaro 225; cover US$5; ☼ 9pm-3:30am Wed-Sat) This club hosts the city's finest Cuban *son* ensembles. Two or three groups take the tropical stage nightly. Unescorted (and escorted) women should expect to be invited up on the tightly packed dance floor.

Mamá Rumba (cover US$6; ☼ 9pm-3am Thu-Sat) Roma (Map pp114-15; ☎ 5564-6920; Querétaro 230, cnr Medellín); San Ángel (Map p111; ☎ 5550-8099; Plaza San Jacinto 23) Down the street from El Gran León, Mamá Rumba features contemporary salsa, attracting a younger, upscale crowd. Reserve ahead for a table. The southern branch, on San Ángel's central plaza, is just as much fun.

Mi Bohío (Map pp114-15; ☎ 5214-0544; Av Insurgentes Sur 300; ☼ 9pm-3:30am Thu-Sat, 2:30pm-midnight Sun) After dancing, go around the corner to relax with a *mojito* at this cozy Cuban shack, with combos from the island.

La Palapa (Map pp114-15; ☎ 5219-6718; Durango 6; ☼ 4pm-3am Thu-Sat, 4-9pm Wed & Sun) More excellent *soneros* (musicians who play Cuban *son*, the original Afro-Cuban dance style) play at this mock beach hut near metro Cuauhtémoc. Locals combine a seafood lunch with the entertainment.

TECHNO & ELECTRONICA

Wednesday to Saturday from about 11pm are the happening times.

El Colmillo (Map pp108-10; ☎ 5592-6114; Versalles 52; cover US$10) Mexican and Euro DJs crank the volume to coccyx-crunching levels at this hallucinogenic hangout. Gyrate to deep house, trip hop, psychedelic trance etc; the cocktail list is equally varied. There's live jazz in the more subdued upstairs lounge.

Pervert Lounge (Map pp108-10; ☎ 5518-0976; Uruguay 70-5; cover US$8.50; metro Isabel la Católica) A magnet for 20- to 30-year-old hipsters, the garage-like space offers kitschy decor, two turntables and some very large speakers.

Rioma (Map pp114-15; ☎ 5584-0613; Av Insurgentes Sur 377; cover US$10) A 1960s bar converted into a cutting-edge lounge, Rioma pulls in a sexy 20-something crowd who dance the night away to *punchis punchis* (Mexican slang for electronic music). DJs don't start until well after midnight.

ROCK & POP

La Bodega (Map pp114-15; ☎ 5511-7390; Popocatépetl 25, cnr Amsterdam; cover after 9pm US$6; ☼ 1pm-1am Mon-Sat) A great club – actually two or three in one – where you can eat, drink, dance and unwind. The cheerfully cluttered old house has a cabaret, **El Bataclán**, with excellent jazz, folk and comedy (separate cover US$12 to US$14). Meanwhile, top-notch Cuban *son* combos occupy rooms on both floors.

Cafebrería El Péndulo (www.pendulo.com in Spanish; cover US$12-18; ☼ shows from 9:30pm) Condesa (Map pp114-15; ☎ 5286-9493; Av Nuevo León 115); Zona Rosa (Map pp112-13; ☎ 5208-9728; Hamburgo 126) Leading Mexican *trovadores* play at this Condesa café/bookstore and at the Zona Rosa branch.

La Planta de Luz (Map p111; ☎ 5616-4761; www.plantadeluz.com in Spanish; Av Revolución y Río Magdalena, San Ángel; cover US$10-25; ☼ 9pm-3am Wed-Sat) This attractive supper club inside Plaza Loreto features popular songsters alternating with musical comedy revues by club owner/raconteur German Dehesa.

Hexen-Café (Map pp114-15; ☎ 5514-5969; www .hexen-cafe.com in Spanish; Jalapa 104, Colonia Roma; free to US$7, depending on event; shows ⏰ 8:30pm Thu-Sat) This pocket of German culture has an eclectic performance program, ranging from a cappella baroque to pop opera.

Bar Fly de París (Map pp116-17; ☎ 5282-2906; Av Presidente Masaryk 393; cover US$10; ⏰ 10pm-3am Tue-Sat) Cuban rhythms energize this lively nightspot in the Plaza Masaryk shopping mall.

Sports

SOCCER

The capital stages two or three *fútbol* (soccer) matches in the national Primera División almost every weekend of the year. There are two seasons: January to June and August to December. Mexico City has four teams: América, nicknamed Las Águilas (the Eagles), Las Pumas of UNAM, Cruz Azul and Atlante. The newspaper *Esto* has the best coverage.

The biggest match of all is El Clásico, between América and Guadalajara, filling the Estadio Azteca with 100,000 flag-waving fans – an occasion surprising for the friendliness between rival fans. This is about the only game of the year when you should get tickets in advance.

Tickets (US$7.50 to US$20 for regular season games) are usually available at the gate right up to game time, or from Ticketmaster (see p159). There are several stadiums that host games.

LUCHA LIBRE (MEXICAN WRESTLING)

Violence, torture and extreme cruelty are on display in Mexico's capital three nights a week. Lucha libre, the Mexican version of pro wrestling, serves up this antisocial behavior as popular entertainment. Laden with myth, charged with aggression and chock-full of hilarious theatrics, it can be an amusing spectacle.

Mexico City's two wrestling venues, the 17,000 seat **Arena de México** (Map pp108-10; Dr Lavista 197, Colonia Doctores; ☎ 5588-0266; tickets US$5-10; ⏰ 8:30pm Fri) and the smaller **Arena Coliseo** (Map pp108-10; República de Perú 77; ⏰ 7:30pm Tue, 5pm Sun) are taken over by a circus atmosphere each week, with roving vendors selling beer, sandwiches and wrestlers' masks. There are three or four bouts, building up to the most formidable match-ups. Sporting day-glo tights, flaming masks and rippling biceps, and taking names like Tarzan Boy, Violencia, Virus, Satánico and Super Crazy, the flamboyant *luchadores* play up their superhero and supervillain personae. After being ushered in by bikini-clad babes, the stars go at each other in teams or one-on-one. Though more a display of acrobatics and theatrical histrionics than an actual competition, their antics can be pretty impressive and not without bodily risk. Wrestlers catapult off the rope and launch into somersaults, en route to pouncing on their opponent. It's not unusual to see a pair of combatants, locked in an embrace, hurtle into the crowd. The predominantly working-class fans are happy to suspend their disbelief and enter the fray, with grandma shaking her fist and shouting, 'Kill him!'

Perhaps the sense of catharsis comes from witnessing an acting out of the unresolved struggle Mexicans observe on a daily basis in the political and social arenas – with the good guys winning for a change. Lucha libre (free fight) means anything goes, and referees seem more like props than arbiters. The scenario invariably pits 'craftsmen' *(técnicos)* against 'rulebreakers' *(rudos)* in a mythic face-off between good and evil. The *rudos* usually wear black and engage in dirty tactics, not hesitating to grab a nearby piece of furniture to pummel an opponent. They usually get the upper hand early on, only to be pounded mercilessly by the *técnicos* in a stunning reversal toward the end of the match.

For seven decades, the Consejo Mundial de Lucha Libre has provided a forum for lucha libre's popular heroes, who generally come from the city's rougher barrios. As with any sport, certain figures have loomed large. Undoubtedly the sport's most charismatic figure was Santo, who hid his real identity behind a silver mask until his death in 1984. Santo consolidated his presence in popular culture by crossing over into cinema during Mexico's golden age of B movies, battling zombies and martians on the screen. Another lucha libre star, Super Barrio, went into politics, becoming a standard bearer for the leftist PRD.

Estadio Azteca (Map pp104-5; ☎ 5617-6080; www
.esmas.com/estadioazteca in Spanish; Calz de Tlalpan 3665)
Home of América; kickoff is at noon on Sunday. Take the
Tren Ligero from metro Tasqueña to Estadio Azteca station.
Estadio Olímpico (Map pp104-5; ☎ 5528-9800; www
.pumasunam.com.mx in Spanish; Av Insurgentes Sur 3000,
Ciudad Universitaria) Home of the Pumas; games start at
noon on Sunday. See p134 for directions.
Estadio Azul (Map pp104-5; ☎ 5563-9525; www.cruz
-azul.com.mx in Spanish; Indiana 255, Colonia Noche
Buena) Cruz Azul home games kick off at 5pm on Saturday.
Southbound Av Insurgentes buses pass by the stadium,
which is next door to the Plaza México bullring.

BASEBALL
Mexico City has one team in the Liga Mexicana de Béisbol, the Diablos Rojos. During
the March to September season, they play
every other week at the **Foro Sol** (Map pp104-5;
☎ 5639-8722; cnr Av Río Churubusco & Viaducto Piedad;
tickets US$1.50-7; ☼ 6:30pm Tue-Wed & Fri, 4pm Thu
& Sat, noon Sun). From Puebla station, on metro
Línea 9, it's a 15-minute walk to the ball-
park.

BULLFIGHTS
If you're not put off by the very concept, a
corrida de toros is quite a spectacle, from
the milling throngs and hawkers outside
the arena to the pageantry and drama in
the ring itself.

One of the largest bullrings in the world,
Monumental Plaza México (Map pp104-5; ☎ 5563-
3961; Rodin 241, Colonia Noche Buena) is a deep
concrete bowl holding 48,000 spectators.
It's a few blocks west of Av Insurgentes (get
off at Eje 6 Sur) or a 10-minute walk from
metro San Antonio.

From November to March, professional
fights are held at the Monumental on Sunday from 4pm. From June to September,
junior matadors fight young bulls. Six bulls
are fought in an afternoon, two each by
three matadors.

The cheapest seats, less than US$4, are
in the Sol General section – the top tiers
on the sunny side of the arena. Seats in
the Sombra General section, on the shady
side, cost slightly more. The best seats are in
the Barreras, the seven front rows, and cost
US$43. Between the Barreras and General
sections are the Primer (1er) Tendido, then
the Segundo (2o) Tendido.

Except for the biggest *corridas*, tickets are
available up to the killing of the third bull,

though the best seats may sell out early.
You can buy advance tickets from 9:30am
to 2pm and 3:30pm to 7pm Saturday, and
from 9:30am onward Sunday.

For more on bullfights, see p55.

HORSE RACES
Hipódromo de las Américas (Map pp104-5; ☎ 5387-
0600; www.hipodromo.com.mx in Spanish; Av Industria
Militar, Colonia Residencial Militar; general admission $1.50,
mezzanine US$2; ☼ 3-8:30pm Fri-Sun) If you have a
hankering to bet, head for the Hipódromo
to watch the ponies run. The season runs
from February to November, with eight to
10 races per afternoon. Pick up a program,
study the stats and place your bets. There
are five restaurants and a cantina on the
premises.

From either metro Cuatro Caminos or
Tacuba stations on Línea 2, catch a 'Puerta 3'
pesero and ask to be let off at the racetrack.

SHOPPING
In most stores, and certainly in department stores and malls, prices are fixed and
marked. If you explore the public markets
and street markets, it's common to negotiate a bit on the price, especially if you
are planning to buy more than one item.
Before you start, think about what price
you consider fair and what you are willing
to pay, then offer that or something a little
lower.

Markets
Mexico City's markets are worth visiting, not
just for their extraordinarily varied contents,
but also for a glimpse of the frenetic business conducted within. Besides the major
ones listed here, neighborhood markets (indicated by 'Mi Mercado' signs) also make
for an interesting wander. See opposite for a
description of weekly street markets.
Mercado Insurgentes (Map pp112-13; Londres btwn
Florencia & Amberes, Zona Rosa; ☼ 9:30am-7:30pm
Mon-Sat, 10am-4pm Sun; metro Insurgentes) Packed with
crafts – silver, textiles, pottery, leather and carved wooden
figures – but you'll need to bargain to get sensible
prices.
Centro de Artesanías La Ciudadela (Map pp108-10;
Balderas at Dondé; ☼ 10am-6pm; metro Balderas) A favorite destination for good stuff from all over Mexico. Worth
seeking out are Oaxaca *alebrijes* – whimsical representations
of animals in wood (local 6, northernmost aisle, near Balderas
entrance); guitars from Paracho (local 64 off central patio);

and Huichol beadwork (local 163, off Dondé at parking entrance). Prices are generally fair even before you bargain.

Mercado de Artesanías San Juan (Map pp108-10; Ayuntamiento, cnr Buen Tono; ☺ 9am-7pm Mon-Sat, 9am-4pm Sun; metro San Juan de Letrán) Four blocks east of La Ciudadela, with similar goods and prices. Part of the Mercado San Juan complex, noted for its local and specialty foods.

La Lagunilla (Map pp108-10; Rayón cnr Allende) Enormous complex comprised of three buildings: Building No 1 contains clothes and fabrics, No 2 food, and No 3 furniture.

Mercado La Merced (Anillo de Circunvalación, cnr General Anaya) Occupies four whole blocks dedicated to the buying and selling of daily needs; photogenic food displays. Metro Merced exits into the market. See p142 for details of adjacent Sonora market.

Mercado de Jamaica (Map pp104-5; Guillermo Prieto cnr Congreso de la Union, Colonia Jamaica; metro Jamaica) Huge and colorful flower market.

MARKET DAY

Street markets in Mexico City date back to pre-Hispanic times when vendors from far and wide hawked foods, pottery and textiles laid out on the plaza of Tlatelolco. Today a visit to a tianguis (from the Nahua *tianquiztli*) is still an adventure of colors, textures, smells, tastes and sounds. Some tianguis are spontaneous and anarchic, but most have varying levels of official and unofficial organization, even allocating numbered spots for vendors. In most neighborhoods you'll find a tianguis at least once a week selling the freshest fruit and vegetables and vendors shouting out '¿Que le damos, mi reina?' (What can we give you, my queen?) Tianguis generally set up by 10am and pack up around 5pm or 6pm.

Saturday

Tianguis Cultural del Chopo (Map pp104-5; Nepomuceno Rosseins, east of the old train station; Colonia Buenavista; metro Buenavista) Densely populated countercultural gathering place; two aisles of stalls hawking CDs, videos and paraphernalia, with an emphasis on metal and hardcore. Concerts are staged at the north end.

Plaza del Arte (Map p111; Plaza del Carmen & Plaza San Jacinto, San Ángel) Two plazas of paintings and sculptures.

Sunday

Jardín del Arte (Map pp112-13; btwn Sullivan & Villalongín) Also known as the Sullivan Market; large selection of paintings and art supplies and some food.

Plaza del Ángel (Map pp112-13; btwn Amberes & Florencia, Zona Rosa) Antique silverware, jewelry, furniture and art.

Parque Pushkin (Map pp114-15; cnr Álvaro Obregón & Cuauhtémoc, Roma; metro Cuauhtémoc) Filled with fresh and prepared foods, new and used clothes; it seems like the whole neighborhood comes out for barbacoa or carnitas. Also open Wednesday.

Saturday & Sunday

Tianguis del Oro (btwn Insurgentes & Plaza Cibeles, Roma) The street clothing market for those with a bit more money, and for the best deal in town on Argentinean steaks.

Bazar de la Roma (cnr Alvaro Obregón & Parque Ignacio Chávez, Colonia Roma & Doctores) Used and antique items, large and small; books, radios, posters, art and furniture.

Bazar Artesanal de Coyoacán (Map p119; Plaza Hidalgo, Coyoacán) Handmade hippie jewelry and indigenous crafts; jugglers, fortune-tellers, candles and incense.

Tepito (Héroe de Granaditas, btwn Eje 1 Oriente & Reforma; metro Garibaldi or Lagunilla) Maze of street-side stalls spreading east from La Lagunilla with something for everyone, including clothes, pirated CDs, household goods and electronics. Also known as the Thieves Market for its black market goods and pickpockets. Look for antiques and bric-a-brac along Paseo de la Reforma.

Tuesday

Tianguis de Pachuca (Pachuca btwn Veracruz & Juan Escutia, Condesa; metro Chapultepec) An enormous selection of fruits and vegetables, as well as regional and seasonal items.

Shops

The well-heeled residents of Mexico City shop in modern malls with designer clothing stores, toy shops, cosmeticians and cinemas. Among the more accessible are **Plaza Loreto** (Map p111) between Altamirano and Río de la Magdalena in San Ángel; **Plaza Insurgentes**, on Av Insurgentes at San Luis Potosí at the edge of Colonia Roma, **Plaza Coyoacán** near metro Coyoacán; and **Plaza Molière** (Map pp116-17), at Molière and Horacio in Polanco.

Fonart (www.fonart.gob.mx in Spanish) Mixcoác (Map pp104-5; ☎ 5563-4060; Av Patriotismo 691; ☼ 9am-8pm Mon-Sat, 10am-7pm Sun); Alameda (Map pp108-10; ☎ 5521-0171; Av Juárez 89 ; ☼ 10am-7pm); Reforma (Map pp112-13; ☎ 5328-5000, ext 5423; Paseo de Reforma 116; ☼ 10am-7pm, Mon-Fri, 10am-6pm Sat) The government-run handicrafts store sells wares from around the country, from Olinalá lacquered boxes to Teotitlán del Valle blankets, as well as all sorts of pottery and glassware. Prices are fixed and fair. The largest store is in Mixcoác, but the more convenient Alameda Central branch has nice items, too.

Bazar Sábado (Map p111; Plaza San Jacinto 11, San Ángel; ☼ 10am-7pm Sat) The bazaar is a showcase for some of Mexico's best handcrafted jewelry, woodwork, ceramics and textiles. Prices are high but so is quality. Artists and artisans also display work in Plaza San Jacinto itself, and in nearby Plaza del Carmen. Between the two plazas are some interesting boutiques and antique shops, many open daily, including the **Casa del Obispo** (Map p111).

CENTRO HISTÓRICO

Mexico City's most upscale department stores, **El Palacio de Hierro** (Map p108-10; ☎ 5729-9905; Av 20 de Noviembre 3) and **Liverpool** (Map pp108-10; ☎ 5133-2800, Venustiano Carranza 92), have major branches downtown.

The streets south, west and north of the Zócalo are lined with stores specializing in everyday goods, from shoes to screws. You'll find clusters of shops selling similar items on the same street. You'll find photography supplies around the intersection of República de Brasil and Donceles; sports gear and backpacks on Venustiano Carranza west of Bolívar; and bridal gowns on República de Chile, north of Tacuba. Shoes are available on Av 16 de Septiembre, Pino Suárez and 20 de Noviembre; and electric guitars and other instruments along Bolívar south of Repúb-

lica de El Salvador. Hundreds of computer stores huddle in the **Plaza de la Computación y Electrónica** (Map pp108-10) on Eje Central Lázaro Cárdenas, south of Uruguay.

Tucked away in the backstreets are some special items.

Artesanos de Carretones (Carretones 5; ☼ 9am-2pm Mon-Sat) Handblown glass factory with stacks of plates, vases and wine glasses; west of Mercado Merced.

Discos Sonorámico (Map pp108-10; ☎ 5521-5323; Rep del Salvador 40) Salsa, Cuban and other Latin CDs.

Dulcería de Celaya (☼ 10:30am-7pm) Centro (Map pp108-10; ☎ 5521-1787; Av 5 de Mayo 39); Colonia Roma (Map pp114-15; ☎ 5207-5858; Colima 143) Traditional candy store operating since 1874 with candied fruits, sugared almonds and crystallized strawberries; worth stopping by just to look at the ornate old building.

Hoja Real (Map pp108-10; ☎ 5518-5200; Uruguay 12) Cigars from San Andrés, Veracruz.

La Europea (Map pp108-10; ☎ 5512-6005; Ayuntamiento 25) Big selection of reasonably priced tequilas and Mexican wines.

Palacio de las Máscaras (Map pp108-10; ☎ 5529-2849; Allende 84; ☼ 11am-6pm Mon-Sat) More than 5000 masks from all over the country; Lagunilla market area.

ZONA ROSA   Map pp112–13

This area has a variety of boutiques aimed at tourists. Between Génova and Florencia are a couple of arcades with access from Hamburgo or Londres. **Plaza La Rosa** is a good place to start if you're after clothes. **Plaza del Ángel** has a number of classy antique and art shops; more are strung along Amberes and Estocolmo.

POLANCO   Map pp116–17

Designer clothing houses line Av Presidente Masaryk in the blocks west of France. More boutiques can be found in the **Pasaje Polanco** and the nearby streets.

GETTING THERE & AWAY

Note that all passenger train services from Mexico City have been discontinued.

Air

Aeropuerto Internacional Benito Juárez (Map pp104-5; ☎ 5571-3600; www.aicm.com.mx in Spanish), 6km east of the Zócalo, is Mexico City's only passenger airport. See p967 for information on international and domestic flights. See opposite for airlines serving Mexico City.

The single terminal is divided into six salas (halls):

Sala A1 Domestic arrivals.
Sala A2 Check-in for Aeroméxico, Mexicana and Aero California; Hotel Marriott access.
Sala C Check-in for Aviacsa.
Sala D Check-in for Azteca and Magnicharter.
Sala E3 International arrivals.
Sala F Check-in for international flights.

The terminal has loads of shops and facilities, including numerous *casas de cambio*; **Tamibe** (☎ 5726-0578) in Sala E3 stays open 24 hours. Peso-dispensing ATMs on the Cirrus and Plus networks are easily found.

Telmex card phones and Internet terminals abound; cards are available from shops and machines. Car rental agencies and luggage lockers (open 24 hours; US$5 for up to 24 hours) are in Salas A1 and E3.

Direct buses to Cuernavaca, Querétaro, Toluca and Puebla depart from outside Sala D (see p168).

AIRLINE OFFICES
Aero California (Map pp112-13; ☎ 5207-1392; Paseo de la Reforma 332, Zona Rosa)
Aeromar (☎ 5133-1111, 800-237-66-27; airport)
Aeroméxico (☎ 5133-4000) Juárez (Map pp108-10; Paseo de la Reforma 80); Zona Rosa (Map pp112-13; Paseo de la Reforma 445)
Air Canada (☎ 9138-0280, 800-719-28-27; 13th fl, Blvd Ávila Camacho 1, Colonia Lomas de Chapultepec)
Air France (Map pp116-17; ☎ 2122-8282, 800-006-77-00; 8th fl, Jaime Balmes 8, Los Morales)
Alitalia (Map pp112-3; ☎ 5533-1240, 800-012-59-00; 6th fl, Río Tíber 103, Colonia Cuauhtémoc)
American Airlines (Map pp112-3; ☎ 5209-1400; Paseo de la Reforma 314, Zona Rosa)
Aviacsa (☎ 5716-9004, 800-006-22-00; airport)
Avianca (Map pp112-3; ☎ 5566-8550, 800-705-79-00; Paseo de la Reforma 195)
British Airways (Map pp116-17; ☎ 5387-0300; 14th fl, Jaime Balmes 8)
Continental Airlines (Map pp116-17; ☎ 5283-5500, 800-900-50-00; Andrés Bello 45, Polanco)
Copa Airlines (Map pp112-3; ☎ 5592-3535; Paseo de la Reforma 412)
Delta Airlines (Map pp112-3; ☎ 5279-0909, 800-902-21-00; Paseo de la Reforma 381)
Iberia (Map pp108-10; ☎ 5130-3030; Paseo de la Reforma 24)
Japan Air Lines (Map pp112-3; ☎ 5242-0150, 800-024-01-50; Paseo de la Reforma 295)
KLM/Northwest (Map pp116-17; ☎ 5279-5390; 11th fl, Andrés Bello 45, Polanco)

Lineas Aéreas Azteca (Map pp112-3; ☎ 5716-8989, 800-229-83-22; Niza 17, Zona Rosa)
Lufthansa (Map pp116-17; ☎ 5230-0000; Paseo de las Palmas 239, Colonia Lomas de Chapultepec)
Magnicharter (Map pp108-10; ☎ 5141-1351; Donato Guerra 9, cnr Bucareli)
Mexicana (☎ 5448-0990, 800-502-20-00) Juárez (Map pp108-10; Juárez 82 at Balderas); Zona Rosa (Map pp112-13; Paseo de la Reforma 312 at Amberes); Los Morales (Map pp116-17; Pabellón Polanco, Av Ejército Nacional 980)
United Airlines (Map pp112-13; ☎ 5724-8775; Hamburgo 213, Zona Rosa)

Bus
Mexico City has four long-distance bus terminals, basically serving the four compass points: Terminal Norte (north), Terminal Oriente (called TAPO, east), Terminal Poniente (west) and Terminal Sur (south). All terminals have baggage check services or lockers (US$1 to $5 per item), as well as tourist information modules, newsstands, card phones, post offices, Internet, ATMs and snack bars. For directions to the bus stations, see p173.

There are also buses to nearby cities from Mexico City airport (see p167).

For trips up to five hours, it usually suffices to go to the bus station, buy your ticket and go. For longer trips, many buses leave in the evening and may well sell out, so buy your ticket beforehand.

One helpful resource is **Ticketbus** (☎ 5133-2424, 800-702-8000; www.ticketbus.com.mx), an agency with outlets around town that reserves and sells tickets for more than a dozen bus lines out of all four stations. For ADO-GL, UNO and ETN, Ticketbus offers purchase by phone or Internet with Visa or MasterCard (plus US$3 service fee per ticket). Below are some key Ticketbus locations, open 9am or 10am to 2:30pm and 3:30pm to 7pm or 8pm Monday to Friday, and 9am or 10am to 2pm or 3pm Saturday.

Guerrero (Map pp108-10; Buenavista 9; metro Revolución)
Centro Histórico (Map pp108-10; Isabel la Católica 83E; metro Isabel la Católica)
Condesa (Map pp114-15; Tlaxcala 193; metro Chilpancingo)
Polanco (Map pp116-17; Av Presidente Masaryk; metro Polanco)
Roma Norte (Map pp114-15; Puebla 46; metro Cuauhtémoc)
Roma Norte (Map pp114-15; Mérida 156; metro Hospital General)
Reforma (Map pp112-13; Paseo de la Reforma 412)
Across from La Diana Cazadora.

MEXICO CITY

BUSES FROM MEXICO CITY

Destination	Journey	Terminal in Mexico City	Class	Bus Company	No Daily Departures	Price
Acapulco	5hr	Sur	executive	Estrella de Oro	6	US$37
			deluxe	Estrella de Oro	16	US$24
			executive	Turistar	4	US$37
			1st	Futura	39	US$24
		Norte	1st	Futura	8	US$24
Bahías de Huatulco	13-15hr 14hr	Oriente (TAPO)	deluxe	Cristóbal Colón Plus	1	US$56
			1st	Cristóbal Colón	1	US$42
		Norte	1st	ADO	1	US$42
		Sur	1st	Futura	2	US$42
Campeche	16hr	Oriente (TAPO)	deluxe	ADO-GL	1	US$70
			1st	ADO	3	US$63
		Norte	1st	ADO	1	US$63
Cancún	24hr	Oriente (TAPO)	deluxe	ADO-GL	1	US$100
			1st	ADO	3	US$84
		Norte	1st	ADO	1	US$84
Chetumal	18hr	Oriente (TAPO)	1st	ADO	3	US$68
Chihuahua	18hr	Norte	1st	Transportes Chihuahuenses	18	US$84
			1st	Ómnibus de México	10	US$84
Ciudad Juárez	25hr	Norte	1st	Transportes Chihuahuenses	18	US$105
			1st	Ómnibus de México	10	US$105
Cuernavaca	1¼hr	Sur	deluxe	Pullman de Morelos	31	US$6
			1st	Pullman de Morelos	every 15min to midnight	US$5
		Airport	1st	Pullman de Morelos	26	US$9
Guadalajara	7hr	Norte	deluxe	ETN	20	US$47
			1st	Primera Plus	28	US$37
			1st	Futura	20	US$35
		Poniente	deluxe	ETN	5	US$47
Guanajuato	5hr	Norte	deluxe	ETN	9	US$29
			1st	Primera Plus	11	US$23
Matamoros	14hr	Norte	1st	Transportes del Norte	7	US$59
Mazatlán	15hr	Norte	deluxe	Turistar	4	US$68
			1st	Elite	13	US$63
Mérida	18hr	Oriente (TAPO)	deluxe	ADO-GL	1	US$83
			1st	ADO	3	US$71
		Norte	1st	ADO	2	US$71
Mexicali	38hr	Norte	1st	Elite	19	US$118
			1st	Transportes del Pacífico	19	US$103
Monterrey	11hr	Norte	deluxe	Turistar	10	US$83
			1st	Futura/Transportes del Norte	19	US$53
			1st	Omnibus	8	US$53

Destination	Journey	Terminal in Mexico City	Class	Bus Company	No Daily Departures	Price
Morelia	4½hr	Poniente	deluxe	ETN	26	US$25
			1st	Autovías	every 30 min to 1am	US$19
		Norte	1st	Primera Plus	19	US$19
Nogales	34hr	Norte	1st	Elite	7	US$111
			1st	Transportes del Pacífico	2	US$98
Nuevo Laredo	15hr	Norte	deluxe	Turistar	5	US$92
			1st	Futura/Transportes del Norte	14	US$68
Oaxaca	6½hr	Oriente (TAPO)	deluxe	UNO	6	US$41
			deluxe	ADO-GL	7	US$30
			1st	Cristóbal Colón	3	US$26
				ADO	16+	US$26
		Sur	1st	Cristóbal Colón	3	US$26
		Norte	1st	ADO	4	US$26
Palenque	13hr	Oriente (TAPO)	1st	ADO	2	US$50
		Norte	1st	ADO	1	US$50
Papantla	5hr	Norte	1st	ADO	7	US$14
Pátzcuaro	5hr	Poniente	1st	Autovías	10	US$22
		Norte	1st	Primera Plus	2	US$26
Puebla	2hr	Oriente (TAPO)	deluxe	Estrella Roja	23	US$9
			deluxe	ADO-GL	22	US$9
			1st	Estrella Roja	50	US$8
			1st	ADO	46	US$8
		Norte	1st	ADO	38	US$8
		Sur	1st	Cristóbal Colón	16	US$8
		Airport	deluxe	Estrella Roja	42	US$12
Puerto Escondido	15hr	Sur	1st	Cristóbal Colón	1	US$42
			1st	Futura	1	US$38
		Norte	1st	ADO	1	US$42
Puerto Vallarta	13hr	Norte	1st	Futura	4	US$60
Querétaro	3hr	Norte	deluxe	ETN	27	US$18
			1st	Primera Plus	58	US$14
			1st	Futura/Elite	17	US$13
		Airport	1st	Primera Plus	18	US$18
San Cristóbal de Las Casas	15hr	Oriente (TAPO)	deluxe	UNO	1	US$90
			deluxe	Maya de Oro	1	US$65
			1st	Cristóbal Colón	3	US$55
			1st	Altos	1	US$51
		Norte	deluxe	Maya de Oro	1	US$65
San Luis Potosí	5-6hr	Norte	deluxe	ETN	18	US$32
			1st	Primera Plus	8	US$26
			1st	Futura/Elite	20	US$24
San Miguel de Allende	4hr	Norte	deluxe	ETN	4	US$21

Destination	Journey	Terminal in Mexico City	Class	Bus Company	No Daily Departures	Price
San Miguel de Allende *(continued)*			1st	Primera Plus	3	US$17
			1st	Autovías	2	US$17
			2nd	Herradura de Plata	22	US$14
Tapachula	17hr	Oriente (TAPO)	deluxe	UNO	1	US$91
			deluxe	Cristóbal Colón Plus	2	US$67
			1st	Cristóbal Colón	5	US$57
		Sur	1st	Cristóbal Colón	1	US$57
Taxco	2½hr		deluxe	Estrella de Oro	2	US$8
		Sur	1st	Futura	15	US$8
			1st	Estrella de Oro	5	US$7.50
Teotihuacán	1hr	Norte	2nd	Autobuses Teotihuacán	48	US$2.50
Tepoztlán	1hr	Sur	1st	Cristóbal Colón	every 10min to 11pm	US$4.50
			1st	Tres Estrellas	every 15min to 10pm	US$4.50
Tijuana	42hr	Norte	1st	Elite	19	US$131
Toluca	1hr	Poniente	deluxe	ETN	27	US$4
			2nd	Flecha Roja	every 10 min to 11:30pm	US$3
		Airport	deluxe	TMT Caminante	17	US$8
Tula	2hr	Norte	1st	AVM	23	US$4
Tuxtla Gutiérrez	15hr	Oriente (TAPO)	deluxe	UNO	1	US$84
			deluxe	Maya de Oro	3	US$61
			1st	Cristóbal Colón	4	US$52
			1st	ADO	2	US$52
		Norte	1st	ADO	1	US$52
Uruapan	6-7hr	Poniente	deluxe	ETN	7	US$32
			1st	Autovías	8	US$26
		Norte	1st	Primera Plus	5	US$26
Veracruz	5½hr	Oriente(TAPO)	deluxe	UNO	5+	US$35
			deluxe	ADO-GL	17+	US$25
			1st	ADO	18	US$22
			2nd	AU	18+	US$18
		Norte	1st	ADO	7	US$22
Villahermosa	10hr	Oriente(TAPO)	deluxe	UNO	1+	US$69
			deluxe	ADO-GL	3	US$51
			1st	ADO	17	US$44
		Norte	deluxe	ADO-GL	1	US$51
			1st	ADO	6	US$44
Xalapa	4½hr	Oriente (TAPO)	Deluxe	UNO	5+	US$25
			Deluxe	ADO-GL	8+	US$18
			1st	ADO	21	US$16
		Norte	1st	ADO	3	US$16
Zacatecas	8hr	Norte	1st	Ómnibus de México	17	US$37
Zihuatanejo	9hr	Sur	executive	Estrella de Oro	1	US$47
			deluxe	Estrella de Oro	4	US$32
			1st	Futura	6	US$34
		Poniente	1st	Autovías	2	US$33

Note: + indicates additional departures on weekends

For a number of major destinations you have a choice of terminals, thus avoiding the need to travel across town for connections. Oaxaca, for example, is served by TAPO, Sur and Norte terminals.

See p168 for a list of daily services from Mexico City to various destinations. More information can be found in other town and city sections of this book. It's all subject to change, of course.

Check schedules by phoning the bus lines or by visiting their (sometimes functional) websites.

ADO Group (☎ 5133-2424; www.ticketbus.com.mx) Includes ADO, ADO-GL, UNO, Cristóbal Colón, Maya de Oro, AU.
Autovías, Herradura de Plata (☎ 5277-7761)
Estrella Blanca Group (☎ 5729-0707) Includes Futura, Elite, Turistar.
Estrella de Oro (☎ 5549-8520; www.estrelladeoro .mx in Spanish)
Estrella Roja (☎ 5130-1800; www.estrellaroja.com.mx in Spanish)
ETN (☎ 5089-9200)
Primera Plus, Flecha Amarilla (☎ 5567-7176; www .primeraplus.com.mx in Spanish)
Omnibus de México (☎ 5567-5858; www.omnibusde mexico.com.mx in Spanish)
Pullman de Morelos (☎ 5549-3505; www.pullman .com.mx in Spanish)

TERMINAL NORTE   Map pp104–5
The largest of the four terminals, the **Terminal Central de Autobuses del Norte** serves points north, including cities on the US border, plus some points west (Guadalajara, Puerto Vallarta), east (Puebla, Veracruz) and south (Acapulco, Oaxaca). Over 30 different bus companies have services here. Deluxe and 1st-class counters are mostly in the southern half of the terminal. Luggage-storage services are at the far south end (open 24 hours) and in the central passageway; the latter section also contains a hotel booking agency.

TERMINAL ORIENTE   Map pp104–5
Terminal de Autobuses de Pasajeros de Oriente, usually called TAPO, serves points east and southeast, including Puebla, Veracruz, Yucatán, Oaxaca and Chiapas. Bus line counters are arranged around a rotunda with a restaurant and Internet terminals at the center. There's an ATM outside the AU counters and luggage lockers in Tunnel 3 beside Estrella Roja.

TERMINAL SUR   Map p119
Terminal Central de Autobuses del Sur serves Tepoztlán, Cuernavaca, Taxco, Acapulco, and other southern destinations, as well as Oaxaca, Huatulco, Puebla and Ixtapa-Zihuatanejo. Estrella de Oro (Acapulco, Taxco) and Pullman de Morelos (Cuernavaca) counters are on the right side of the terminal, Cristóbal Colón and Tres Estrellas (Tepoztlán) on the left. In Sala 1, you'll find a left luggage service, agents booking Acapulco hotels and an ATM amid some kiddie rides.

TERMINAL PONIENTE   Map pp104–5
Terminal Poniente de Autobuses is the place for most buses heading to the state of Michoacán and shuttle services running to nearby Toluca. In addition, ETN offers service to Guadalajara.

Car & Motorcycle

Touring Mexico City by car is strongly discouraged, unless you have a healthy reserve of stamina and patience. Even more than elsewhere in the country, traffic rules are seen as suggested behavior. Red lights may be run at will, no-turn signs are ignored and signals are seldom used. On occasion you may be hit by the bogus traffic fine, a routine means for traffic cops to increase their miserly salaries. Nevertheless, you may want to rent a car here for travel outside the city. Avoid parking on the street; most mid-range and top-end hotels have guest garages.

DRIVING RESTRICTIONS
To help combat pollution, Mexico City operates its Hoy No Circula (Don't Drive Today) program, banning many vehicles from being driven in the city between 5am and 10pm on one day each week. The major exceptions are cars of 1993 model or newer (supposedly less polluting), which have a *calcomanía de verificación* (verification hologram sticker) numbered 0. This sticker is obtained under the city's (reportedly corrupt) vehicle pollution assessment system.

For other vehicles (including foreign-registered ones), the last digit of the license plate number determines the day when they cannot circulate. Any car may operate on Saturday and Sunday.

Day	Prohibited last digits
Monday	5, 6
Tuesday	7, 8
Wednesday	3, 4
Thursday	1, 2
Friday	9, 0

For further information on the driving restriction program visit www.sima.com.mx.

RENTAL

Car rental firms have offices at the airport and in the Zona Rosa. Rates generally start at about US$50 per day, but you'll often do better by booking ahead via Internet.

Avis (Map pp112-13; ☎ 5511-2228; Paseo de la Reforma 308)

Thrifty (Map pp112-13; ☎ 5207-1100; Paseo de la Reforma 322)

ROADSIDE ASSISTANCE

The Green Angels (*Ángeles Verdes*) can provide assistance from 8am to 8pm. Phone ☎ 5250-8221 and tell them your location. For more information, see p980.

ROUTES IN & OUT OF THE CITY

Whichever way you come in, once past the last *caseta* (toll booth) you enter a no-man's land of poorly marked lanes, and traffic suddenly gets heavier and more chaotic. These *casetas* are also the points from which 'Hoy No Circula' rules take effect.

North

From Querétaro, the last toll booth is at Tepotzotlán. About 12km south, signs indicate a right-hand turnoff for Chapultepec, a little-used toll road. The preferred route into town is to continue south, following signs for Satélite and the Periférico. Beyond the skyscraper sculptures marking the gateway to Satélite, take the 'Rio San Joaquín' exit to the right, north of the enormous dome of the Toreo arena. Shortly after you exit, the ramp curves left over the Periférico. Keep right as you go over, then follow signs for Av Thiers and Reforma. Thiers leads right into Río Misisipi, which intersects Reforma at La Diana roundabout. Turn left for the Zona Rosa and Centro Histórico, or continue straight ahead for Colonia Roma.

Leaving the city, the simplest option is to take Reforma to the west end of Chapulte-pec Park where you can pick up the Periférico northbound.

From Pachuca, Hidalgo and northern Veracruz, the inbound route is one of the easiest, if not less chaotic, since the highway feeds into Av Insurgentes. Follow signs for the Centro Histórico and Zona Rosa. Crossing Reforma, the Zona Rosa is to the right, the Centro Histórico and Alameda Central to the left. Leaving the city this way, take Insurgentes north. This is also the route to Teotihuacán.

West

Coming from Toluca, after passing the high rises of Santa Fe, the road becomes Av Constituyentes. Don't take the exit for Reforma. Constituyentes passes under the Circuito Interior near the eastern end of Bosque de Chapultepec. Turn left after the underpass to pick up the Circuito, then follow signs for Reforma to get to the Zona Rosa and downtown. Or, continue straight ahead on Juan Escutia (Eje 2 Sur) right into Condesa. Heading west out of the city, take Av Chapultepec to Constituyentes, then follow the signs for the cuota or libre to Toluca.

East

From Puebla, the highway eventually feeds traffic left into Ignacio Zaragoza. Stay on Zaragoza for about 10km, then move left and follow signs for Río Piedad and Viaducto Alemán. From the Viaducto, exits access all the key areas. Exit at Viaducto Tlalpan to reach the Zócalo. Av Monterrey goes through Colonia Roma and the Zona Rosa.

Coming out of the airport, head south along Blvd Puerto Aéreo. After you cross Zaragoza, watch for signs to Río Piedad and Viaducto Alemán.

Heading for Puebla, Oaxaca or Veracruz, take the Viaducto Alemán east to Av Zaragoza and follow signs for Oaxaca until it joins the Puebla highway.

South

After the last caseta on the autopista from Cuernavaca, continue straight, taking a right exit for Calz Tlalpan. (Some signs are hidden behind trees.) Calz Tlalpan eventually feeds into Pino Suárez which ends at the Zócalo. For Colonia Roma, there's a left exit shortly after crossing the Viaducto Alemán. Leaving town, take Insurgentes or

Tlalpan south to join up with the Cuernavaca highway. Watch for a Y where signs point left for the autopista.

GETTING AROUND

Mexico City has an inexpensive, easy-to-use metro and an equally cheap and practical bus system plying all the main routes. Taxis are plentiful, but some are potentially hazardous (see p120).

Obvious though it may sound, always look both ways when crossing streets. Some one-way streets have bus lanes running counter to the flow of traffic, and traffic on some divided streets runs in the same direction on both sides.

To/From the Airport

The metro is convenient to the airport, though hauling luggage amid rush-hour crowds can be a Herculean task. Authorized taxis provide a painless, relatively inexpensive alternative.

METRO

The airport metro station is Terminal Aérea, on Línea 5 (yellow). It's 200m from the terminal: leave by the exit at the end of Sala A (domestic arrivals) and continue in the same direction, past the taxi stand, to the station. To the city center, follow signs for 'Dirección Politécnico'; at La Raza (seven stops away) change for Línea 3 (green) toward 'Dirección Universidad.' Metro Hidalgo, at the west end of the Alameda, is three stops south; it's also a transfer point for Línea 2 (blue) to the Zócalo. To get to the Zona Rosa from the airport, take Línea 5 to Pantitlán, the end of the line. Change for Línea 1 (pink) and get off at metro Insurgentes.

Going to the airport, take the Av Aeropuerto Municipal exit on the Dirección Politécnico side, and proceed directly to the terminal.

TAXI

Steer clear of street cabs outside the airport. Safe and reliable 'Transporte Terrestre' taxis, recognizable by their yellow doors and airplane logos, are controlled by a fixed-price ticket system.

Purchase taxi tickets from booths labeled 'Sitio 300' (those labeled 'ProTaxi' sell tickets for Suburban van taxis), located in Sala E3 (international arrivals), on your left as you exit customs, and near the Sala A1 (domestic arrivals) exit. Fares are determined by zones (shown on a map next to the booth). A ride to the Zócalo or Alameda Central is US$10, to the Zona Rosa or Plaza de la República US$12. One ticket is valid for up to four passengers and luggage that will fit in the trunk.

Taxi stands for the Sitio 300 taxis are outside Salas A1 and E1. Porters may offer to take your ticket and luggage the few steps to the taxi, but hold on to the ticket and hand it to the driver. Drivers won't expect a tip for the ride, but will of course welcome one.

To reserve a Transporte Terrestre taxi to the airport call ☎ 5571-9344; fares are slightly higher in this direction.

To/From the Bus Terminals

The metro is the fastest and cheapest way to any bus terminal, but it's tricky to maneuver through crowded stations and cars. Taxis are an easier option, but avoid street cabs outside the terminals. Fortunately, all terminals have ticket booths for 'taxis autorizados,' with fares set by zone (US$1 to US$1.50 surcharge from 9pm or 10pm to 6am.) To ensure you get an authorized taxi, an agent at the exit will assign you a cab. Ignore hustlers who tell you there are no authorized cabs left, or who try to take your ticket before you reach the taxi.

TERMINAL NORTE

Metro Línea 5 (yellow) stops at Autobuses del Norte, just outside the terminal. To the center, follow signs for 'Dirección Pantitlán,' then change at La Raza for Línea 3 (green) toward 'Dirección Universidad.' (The La Raza connection is a six-minute hike through a 'Tunnel of Science' with a planetarium.)

The taxi kiosk is in the central passageway; a cab for up to four people to the Alameda or Zócalo costs US$6.50, to the Zona Rosa US$5.

Across the road from the terminal, trolleybuses marked 'Central Autobuses del Sur' head south along Eje Central Lázaro Cárdenas, passing near the Alameda Central. The safest way across is through the metro station. From the center to the Terminal Norte, trolleybuses marked 'Central Autobuses del Norte' head north on Eje Central.

TERMINAL ORIENTE (TAPO)

This bus terminal is located next door to metro San Lázaro. To the center or Zona Rosa, take Línea 1 (pink) toward 'Dirección Observatorio.'

The authorized taxi booth is at the top (metro) end of the main passageway from the rotunda. The fare to the Zócalo is US$4; to the Zona Rosa, it's US$5.

ADO Group's deluxe bus lines (UNO, ADO-GL and Maya de Oro) run a shuttle service, called Citibus, to/from area hotels and to the airport. There are six departures from Monday to Friday to the Hotel del Ángel (p147) and eight to the airport (fewer on weekends). Purchase tickets (US$3.50) at TAPO or the hotel. Contact Ticketbus (p167) for schedules and other pick-up locations.

TERMINAL SUR

Terminal Sur is a two-minute walk from metro Tasqueña, the southern terminus of Línea 2 which stops at the Zócalo. For the Zona Rosa, transfer at Pino Suárez and take Línea 1 to Insurgentes (Dirección Observatorio). Going to the terminal, take the 'Autobuses del Sur' exit, which leads upstairs to a footbridge. Descend the last staircase on the left and cross the road to the terminal.

Authorized taxis from Terminal Sur cost US$7 to the Zona Rosa, US$8 to the Historic Center. Ticket booths are by the main exit and in Sala 3.

'Central Autobuses del Norte' trolleybuses run north from Terminal Sur along Eje Central Lázaro Cárdenas to the Palacio de Bellas Artes, then on to the Terminal Norte. From the terminal's main exit, go left and you'll find the trolleybuses waiting on the far side of the main road. From the city center to Terminal Sur, catch a 'Central Autobuses del Sur' trolleybus on the Eje Central.

TERMINAL PONIENTE

Observatorio metro station, the eastern terminus of Línea 1 (pink), is a couple of minutes' walk across a pedestrian bridge/market. A taxi ticket to the Zona Rosa costs US$6; to the Zócalo it's US$7.

Bicycle

Though not a common form of transportation in Mexico City except by delivery boys, bicycles are a viable way to get around and often quicker and more pleasant than riding on overcrowded, recklessly driven buses. It's also a convenient way to explore the city's nooks and crannies. The terrain is flat and the weather generally mild. Although careless drivers and potholes can make DF cycling an 'extreme sport,' if you stay alert and keep off the major thoroughfares, it's manageable. Keep an eye out for oblivious pedestrians and car doors that open unexpectedly; drivers rarely signal.

The city is working on a *ciclopista*, an extensive bike trail that follows the old bed of the Cuernavaca railroad. Currently it extends from Av Ejército Nacional in Polanco through Bosque de Chapultepec, skirting the Periférico freeway from La Feria to Av San Antonio, with several steep bridges overpassing the freeways. It is planned to eventually reach the Morelos border. Another path skirts Paseo de la Reforma from the Auditorio Nacional to the Museo Rufino Tamayo. Follow the red stripe.

You can rent bicycles at **Taller de Bicicletas Orozco** (Map pp114-15; ☎ 5286-3582; Av México 13C; ✔ 10:30am-8pm Tue-Sun), at Parque México in Condesa. Prices are US$2.50 per hour, US$13 per day (ID required), or a better rate for longer periods.

Bus, Pesero & Trolleybus

Mexico City's thousands of buses, peseros (also called micros or minibuses) and trolleybuses operate from around 5am to 8pm or 9pm daily; only a few run all night, notably those along Av Insurgentes and Paseo de la Reforma. This means you'll get anywhere you need to by bus and/or metro during the day but will probably have to take a few taxis after hours.

Peseros are generally gray and green minibuses, though sturdier light green vehicles and full-size buses plastered with ads have been phased in on some lines. Owned by private bus companies, they run along fixed routes, often starting or ending at metro stations, and will stop to pick up or drop off at virtually any street corner. Route information is randomly displayed on a series of cards attached to the windshield. Fares are US$0.20 for trips of up to 5km, US$0.25 for 5km to 12km and US$0.35 for more than 12km. The larger peseros along Av Insurgentes charge a base fare of US$0.30. Add 20% to all fares between 10pm and 6am.

Municipally operated full-size orange buses (labeled 'RTP') and electrically powered trolleybuses only pick up at bus stops, unlike the peseros; fares are US$0.20 (exact change only) regardless of distance traveled.

Some of the more useful routes are listed here. You'll find information on services to other points around the city in the relevant sections of this chapter.

'Autobuses del Sur' & 'Autobuses del Norte' trolleybus: Eje Central Lázaro Cardenas between north and south bus terminals (stops at Plaza de las Tres Culturas; Plaza Garibaldi; Bellas Artes/Alameda; metro Hidalgo)

'Metro Sevilla–P Masaryk' pesero: Between Colonia Roma and Polanco via Av Álvaro Obregón and Av Presidente Masaryk (stops at metro Niños Héroes; Av Insurgentes; metro Sevilla; Leibnitz; metro Polanco)

'Indios Verdes–San Ángel' bus or pesero: Av Insurgentes between north of town and San Ángel (stops at metro Indios Verdes; metro Buenavista/Tianguis del Chopo; Paseo de la Reforma; metro Insurgentes; Parque México/Condesa)

'Metro Tacubaya–Balderas–Escandón' pesero: Between Centro Histórico and Condesa, westbound via Puebla, eastbound via Durango (stops at Ayuntamiento at Plaza San Juan; metro Balderas; metro Insurgentes; Parque España; Av Michoacán; metro Tacubaya)

'Metro Hidalgo–La Villa' bus or pesero: Paseo de la Reforma between Auditorio Nacional or metro Chapultepec and Basílica de Guadalupe (stops at Zona Rosa; Av Insurgentes; Alameda/metro Hidalgo; Plaza Garibaldi; Plaza de las Tres Culturas)

Metro

The metro system offers the quickest way to get around Mexico City. About 4.7 million people ride the metro on an average weekday, making it the world's third-busiest subway, after those of Moscow and Tokyo. It has 175 stations and more than 200km of track on 11 lines. Trains arrive every two to three minutes during rush hours. At US$0.20 a ride, including transfers, it's also the world's cheapest subway.

All lines operate from 5am to 12:30am weekdays, 6am to 12:30am Saturday, and 7am to 12:30am Sunday. Platforms and cars can become alarmingly packed during rush hours (roughly 7:30am to 10am and 3pm to 8pm). At these times the forward cars are reserved for women and children, and men may not proceed beyond the 'Solo Mujeres y Niños' gate.

With such crowded conditions, it's not surprising that pickpocketing occurs, so watch your belongings.

Nevertheless, the metro is easy to use. Signs reading 'Dirección Pantitlán,' 'Dirección Universidad' and so on name the stations at the ends of the metro lines. Check a map for the direction you want. Buy a *boleto* (ticket), or several, at the *taquilla* (ticket window), feed it into the turnstile, and you're on your way. When changing trains, look for 'Correspondencia' (Transfer) signs. Maps of the vicinity around each station are posted near the exits.

Taxi

Mexico City has several classes of taxi. The cheapest are the cruising street cabs, mostly Volkswagen Beetles but also Nissans and other Japanese models. These should be avoided due to the risk of assaults (see p120). If you must hail a cab on the street, check that it has actual taxi license plates: numbers begin with the letter L (for *libre*, or free), and a green stripe runs along the bottom. Check that the number on them matches the number painted on the bodywork. Also look for the *carta de identificación* (also called the *tarjetón*), a postcard-sized ID card that should be displayed visibly inside the cab, and ensure that the driver matches the photo. If you find a cab does not pass these tests, get another one.

In libre cabs, fares are computed by taxímetro (meter), which should start at 4.8 to 5.8 pesos (US$0.45 to US$0.55). The total cost of a 2km or 3km ride in moderate traffic – say, from the Zócalo to the Zona Rosa – should be US$2 to US$2.50. Between 11pm and 6am, add 20%.

A radio taxi costs two or three times as much, but the extra cost adds an immeasurable degree of security. Their plates begin with S – for *sitio* (taxi stand) – and bear an orange stripe. When you phone, the dispatcher will tell you the cab number and the type of car. Hotels and restaurants should be willing to call a reliable cab for you.

Radio taxi firms, available 24 hours, include the following (you need not tip drivers unless they've provided some special service):

Servitaxis (☎ 5516-6020)
Super Sitio 160 (☎ 5271-9146, 5271-9058)
Taxi-Mex (☎ 9171-8888, 5634-9912)
Taxis Radio Unión (☎ 5514-8124)

Around Mexico City

CONTENTS

Some of Mexico's best things to see and do are within a day's travel of the capital. Many of them, such as the ancient city of Teotihuacán or the picturesque town of Tepoztlán, can easily be visited as day trips. Other destinations, such as the colonial cities of Puebla and Taxco, have so many attractions that you should plan to spend at least one night. Another fascinating option is a circular tour around the capital. The roads circumnavigating the Distrito Federal are not as good as those going to and from it, but this option is still quite feasible, either on local buses or in your own vehicle.

Geographically, the whole area is elevated. South of Mexico City, the Cordillera Neovolcánica, with Mexico's highest volcanoes, runs from Pico de Orizaba in the east to Nevado de Toluca in the west (and continues as far west as Colima). North of this range is the Altiplano Central (Central Plateau). This topographic diversity offers a variety of landscapes, from dramatic gorges to fertile plains, fragrant pine forests and snow-capped peaks. The altitude makes for a very pleasant climate, cooler and less humid than the lowlands, with rain falling in brief summer downpours. Geologically, it remains an active area, with still-smoking volcanoes and natural hot springs.

Despite the rich historical heritage, this is the heart of modern Mexico, with industrial plants and up-to-date transport and urban infrastructure. On weekends many getaways cater to crowds of visitors from the capital. Generally, this means that there are ample facilities available during the week, and if a place is crowded it won't be with foreigners.

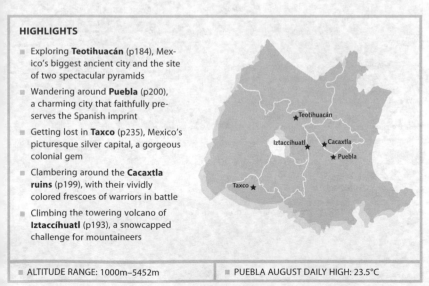

HIGHLIGHTS

- Exploring **Teotihuacán** (p184), Mexico's biggest ancient city and the site of two spectacular pyramids

- Wandering around **Puebla** (p200), a charming city that faithfully preserves the Spanish imprint

- Getting lost in **Taxco** (p235), Mexico's picturesque silver capital, a gorgeous colonial gem

- Clambering around the **Cacaxtla ruins** (p199), with their vividly colored frescoes of warriors in battle

- Climbing the towering volcano of **Iztaccíhuatl** (p193), a snowcapped challenge for mountaineers

★ Teotihuacán
Iztaccíhuatl ★ ★ Cacaxtla
★ Puebla
Taxco ★

- ALTITUDE RANGE: 1000m–5452m
- PUEBLA AUGUST DAILY HIGH: 23.5°C

AROUND MEXICO CITY

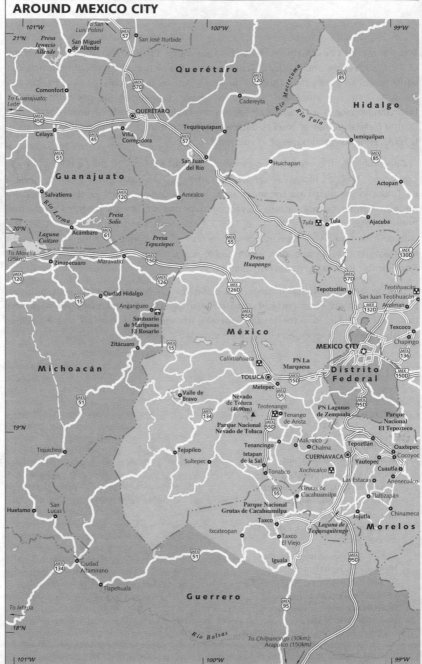

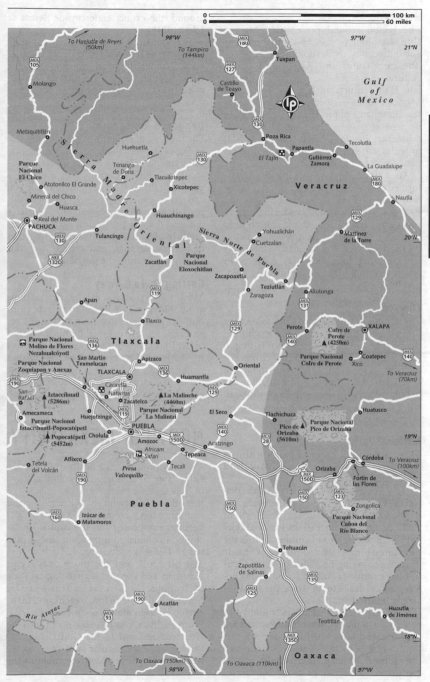

History

The region around present-day Mexico City was home to a succession of important indigenous civilizations (notably Teotihuacán, Toltec and Aztec) and was a cultural and economic crossroads. By the late 15th century, all but one of central Mexico's states were dominated by the Aztecs. Remnants of pre-Hispanic history can be seen at many archaeological sites and museums; Puebla's Museo Amparo (p203) provides an excellent overview of the region's history and cultures.

After the conquest, the Spanish transformed central Mexico, establishing ceramic industries at Puebla, mines at Taxco and Pachuca, and haciendas producing wheat, sugar and cattle. The Catholic church used the area as a base for its missionary activities and left a series of fortified monasteries and imposing churches. Today, most towns retain a central plaza surrounded by colonial buildings.

Climate

The altitude outside Mexico City makes for a very pleasant climate, cooler and less humid than the lowlands, with most rain falling in brief summer downpours. Snow covers the high peaks (*nevados*) for several months a year (November through March), but the populated areas in the foothills continue to enjoy mild climates while cross-country skiers glide about up in the clouds.

National Parks

There are several national parks within a day's drive of Mexico City, yet most of them are delightfully crowd-free.

Near Texcoco **Molino de Flores Nezahualcóyotl** (p195) preserves a pulque hacienda and a little known archaeological site. North of Pachuca, the rock formations inside **El Chico** (p191) attract legions of climbers while the pine forests make for cool hiking. Outside Tlaxcala, towering La Malinche is the focus of hikers inside **La Malintzi** (p200). Another steep ascent leads to an Aztec pyramid inside **El Tepozteco** (p219).

Only experienced climbers should approach the summits in **Iztaccíhuatl-Popocatépetl** (p193) – and only when they are not off-limits – but the foothills outside Amecameca offer some fine hiking. Alternatively, anyone can drive right up to, or cross-country ski around, the extinct crater inside **Nevado de Toluca** (p248).

For something a bit tamer, try camping in **Lagunas de Zempoala** (p235) near Cuernavaca. Perhaps the most popular of all the parks near the capital is **Grutas de Cacahuamilpa** (p244), a staggering network of huge caverns.

Dangers & Annoyances

For the tens of millions of people who live in Popocatépetl's shadow, possible evacuations due to volcanic eruptions are a constant possibility. Earthquakes are also a persistent threat. That said, there's little you can do to avoid or prepare for these unpredictable natural phenomena. Mexico's national disaster prevention agency (Cenapred) has learned much from the tragedies of the last decades, and experts are constantly monitoring the possibilities.

Getting There & Away

Most visitors arrive at the destinations around Mexico City by bus or private automobile. There are minor airports in the region, but for international flights it's easiest to use the express bus services that go direct from Mexico City's airport to the region's major cities. Within the region, it can be handy to have a car to reach out-of-the-way attractions. With enough patience, however, you can get almost anywhere by bus.

NORTH OF MEXICO CITY

Two main routes head north from Mexico City. Hwy 57D skirts the colonial town of Tepotzotlán, swings northwest past the turnoff for Tula (with its Toltec ruins) and continues to Querétaro (p633). Hwy 130D beelines northeast from the capital to Pachuca, a colonial mining town that is capital of Hidalgo state. Hwy 132D branches east off 130D past the old monastery at Acolman and the vast archaeological zone of Teotihuacán, then cuts across a starkly beautiful plateau before reaching Tulancingo, Hidalgo state's second largest city. From Pachuca, routes snake north into the Huasteca and east to the Gulf Coast, traversing some spectacular landscapes as the fringes of the Sierra Madre tumble to the coastal plain.

TEPOTZOTLÁN

☎ 55 / pop 42,000 / elevation 2300m

About 40km north of Mexico City, just beyond its urban sprawl, Tepotzotlán has a pleasant central plaza. Its primary attraction is the **Museo Nacional del Virreinato** (National Museum of the Viceregal Period; ☎ 876-02-45; Plaza Hidalgo 99; admission US$3.50; ✆ 9am-6pm Tue-Sun), which is comprised of the restored Jesuit **Iglesia de San Francisco Javier** and the adjacent **monastery**.

Among the fine art and folk art gathered here are silver chalices, pictures created from inlaid wood, porcelain, furniture and fine religious statues and paintings. Don't miss the **Capilla Doméstica**, whose Churrigueresque main altarpiece is thick with mirrors. To get to the Iglesia de San Francisco Javier, turn to the right after you enter the museum, go down the hall and then downstairs.

The church, an extreme example of Churrigueresque architecture, was originally built from 1670 to 1682; elaborations carried out in the 18th century made it one of Mexico's most lavish places of worship. The façade is a phantasmagoric array of carved saints, angels, people and plants, while the interior walls and the Camarín del Virgen adjacent to the altar are covered with a circus of gilded ornamentation.

Tepotzotlán's highly regarded Christmas *pastorelas* (**nativity plays**) are performed inside the former monastery in the weeks before December 25. Tickets, which include Christmas dinner and *piñata* smashing, can be purchased via **Ticketmaster** (☎ 5225-9000; www.ticketmaster.com.mx in Spanish) and at La Hostería de Tepotzotlán.

Sleeping

While Tepotzotlán is primarily geared to day-trippers, several good hotels await overnight guests.

Hotel Posada San José (☎ /fax 5876-0835; Plaza Virreinal 13; r US$17, with view US$23-34) On the zócalo's south side, this colonial-style hotel has a good restaurant and 14 lovely rooms with TV and private bath.

Posada del Cid (☎ 5876-0064; Av Insurgentes 12; s/d US$11/15; P) This no-frills hotel is 500m from the zócalo on the way to the autopista. The 14 rooms are clean and cheap and they don't smell bad. Rates rise a bit on weekends.

Hotel Posada del Virrey (☎ /fax 5876-1864; Av Insurgentes 13; s/d with TV US$23/32; P) Opposite

Posada del Cid is a brighter, more comfortable option. It has clean, colorful rooms on two arcaded levels. A few rooms even have Jacuzzis.

Eating

La Hostería de Tepotzotlán (☎ 5876-0243/1646; Plaza Virreinal 1; mains US$5-8; ✆ 12:30-6pm Tue-Sun) In a pretty courtyard within the monastery museum, this café serves hearty soups and original main courses.

Three popular restaurants with touting waiters await you under the arcades on the zócalo's north side: **Los Virreyes** (☎ 5876-0235), **Montecarlo** (☎ 5876-0586) and **Casa Mago** (☎ 5876-0229). All serve Mexican traditional favorites at slightly inflated prices – soup and salad US$4 to US$5, mains US$8 to US$15 – you're paying for the festive ambience, heightened by roving *ranchero* bands playing Mexican-style country music. Adjacent to Hotel Posada San José, **Restaurant-Bar Pepe** (☎ 5876-0520; mains US$6-10; ✆ 8am-9pm) is similarly priced but smaller and more intimate.

Cheaper fare is available at the market behind the Palacio Municipal, where **food stalls** serve fine *pozole* (soup or thin stew of hominy, meat, vegetables and chilies), quesadillas and fresh juices all day long.

Getting There & Away

Tepotzotlán is 1.5km west of the first tollbooth on Hwy 57D from Mexico City to Querétaro.

From Mexico City's Terminal Norte station, Autotransportes Valle de Mezquital buses stop at the tollbooth every 15 minutes en route to Tula. From there, take a local bus (US$0.30) or taxi (US$2.25), or walk along Av Insurgentes. You can also take a colectivo to Tepotzotlán from Mexico City's Rosario metro station (US$0.80). Returning 'Rosario' buses depart from Av Insurgentes opposite Posada San José.

TULA

☎ 773 / pop 26,000 / elevation 2060m

The probable capital of the ancient Toltec civilization stood 65km north of what is now Mexico City. Though less spectacular than Teotihuacán, Tula is still an absorbing site, best known for its fearsome 4.5m-high stone warrior figures. The modern town has a refinery and cement works on its outskirts, but the center is pleasant enough.

History

Tula was an important city from about AD 900–1150, reaching a peak population of 35,000. Aztec annals tell of a king called Topiltzin – fair-skinned, long-haired and black-bearded – who founded a Toltec capital in the 10th century. There's debate about whether Tula was this capital, though.

The Toltecs were mighty empire-builders to whom the Aztecs looked back with awe, claiming them as royal ancestors. Topiltzin was supposedly a priest-king dedicated to peaceful worship (which included sacrifices of animals only) of the feathered serpent god Quetzalcóatl. Tula is known to have housed followers of the less likable Tezcatlipoca (Smoking Mirror), god of warriors, witchcraft, life and death; worshiping Tezcatlipoca required human sacrifices. The story goes that Tezcatlipoca appeared in various guises in order to provoke Topiltzin. As a naked chili-seller, he aroused the lust of Topiltzin's daughter and eventually married her; as an old man, he persuaded the sober Topiltzin to get drunk.

Eventually, the humiliated leader left for the Gulf Coast, where he set sail eastward on a raft of snakes, promising one day to return and reclaim his throne. (This caused the Aztec emperor Moctezuma much consternation when Hernán Cortés arrived on the Gulf Coast in 1519.) The conventional wisdom is that Topiltzin set up a new Toltec state at Chichén Itzá in Yucatán, while the Tula Toltecs built a brutal, militaristic empire that dominated central Mexico.

Tula was evidently a place of some splendor – legends speak of palaces of gold, turquoise, jade and quetzal feathers, of enormous corn cobs and colored cotton that grew naturally. Possibly its treasures were looted by the Aztecs or Chichimecs.

In the mid-12th century, the ruler Huémac apparently moved the Toltec capital to Chapultepec after factional fighting at Tula, then committed suicide. Tula was abandoned in the early 13th century, seemingly after violent destruction by the Chichimecs.

Orientation & Information

The Zona Arqueológica (Archaeological Zone) is 2km north of the town center. The main street is Zaragoza, which runs from the outskirts to the zócalo. There are a couple of banks with ATMs on Juárez, a block-long pedestrian street off the zócalo.

Sights

TOWN CENTER

The fortress-like **church** on Zaragoza was part of the 16th-century fortified monastery of San José. Inside, its vault ribs are picked out in gold. Off the zócalo on the library wall is a **mural** of Tula's history.

ZONA ARQUEOLÓGICA

The old settlement of Tula covered nearly 16 sq km and stretched to the modern town's far side, but the present focus is the **ruins** (admission US$3; ⏰ 10am-5pm) of the main ceremonial center, perched on a hilltop with good views over rolling countryside.

About half a kilometer from the entrance, there's a **museum** (signs are in Spanish only) displaying pottery and large sculptures. After another 700m, you'll reach the center of the ancient city. At the site, there are explanatory signs in English, Spanish and Náhuatl.

The I-shaped ball court **Juego de Pelota No 1**, a copy of an earlier one at Xochicalco, is the first large structure you'll reach from the museum. Researchers believe its walls were decorated with sculpted panels that were removed under Aztec rule.

Also known as the temple of Quetzalcóatl or Tlahuizcalpantecuhtli (Morning Star), **Pirámide B** can be scaled via steps on its south side. At the top of the stairway stand the remains of two columnar roof supports that once depicted feathered serpents with their heads on the ground and their tails in the air.

The four basalt warrior-telamones at the top and the pillars behind supported the temple's roof. Wearing headdresses, butterfly-shaped breastplates and short skirts held in place by sun disks, the warriors hold spear-throwers in their right hands, and knives and incense bags in their left. The telamon on the left side is a replica of the original, now in Mexico City's Museo Nacional de Antropología (p129). The columns behind the telamones depict crocodile heads (which symbolize the Earth), warriors, symbols of warrior orders, weapons and Quetzalcóatl's head.

On the pyramid's north wall are some of the carvings that once surrounded the structure. These show the symbols of the warrior orders: jaguars, coyotes, eagles eating hearts, and what may be a human head in Quetzalcóatl's mouth.

Now roofless, the **Gran Vestíbulo** (Great Vestibule) extends along the front of the pyramid, facing the plaza. The stone bench carved with warriors originally ran the length of the hall, possibly to seat nobles and priests observing ceremonies in the plaza.

Near Pirámide B's north side is the **Coatepantli** (Serpent Wall), 40m long, 2.25m high and carved with rows of geometric patterns and a row of snakes devouring human skeletons. Traces remain of the original bright colors with which most Tula structures were painted.

Immediately west of Pirámide B, the **Palacio Quemado** (Burnt Palace) is a series of halls and courtyards with more low benches and relief carvings, one showing a procession of nobles. It was probably used for meetings or ceremonies.

The **plaza** in front of Pirámide B would have been the scene of religious and military displays. At its center is the *adoratorio*, a ceremonial platform. On the plaza's east side, **Pirámide C** is Tula's biggest structure but remains largely unexcavated. To the west is **Juego de Pelota No 2**, central Mexico's largest ball court at more than 100m in length.

Sleeping

Hotel Casa Blanca (☎ 732-11-86; casablancatuley@ yahoo.com.mx; Pasaje Hidalgo 11; s/d US$13/19; **P**) On a narrow pedestrian street behind the Singer store on Hidalgo, this is Tula's best budget place. The bright, clean and quiet rooms are a great deal (US$4 more with TV). Parking access is via Zaragoza.

Hotel Lizbeth (☎ 732-00-45; www.tulaonline.com /hotellizbeth; Ocampo 200; s/d/ste US$32/36/50; **P**) This modern hotel, 1½ blocks from the bus station (turn right at the station entrance), has clean, comfortable rooms and free parking.

Hotel Sharon (☎ 732-09-76; hotel_sharon@hotmail .com; Callejón de la Cruz 1; s/d/ste from US$32/43/75; **P**) This ultramodern place at the turnoff to the Zona Arqueológica is Tula's top hotel.

Eating

Restaurant Casablanca (☎ 732-22-74; Hidalgo 114; mains US$4-10) This large, clean restaurant near the cathedral features a traditional buffet-style lunch and decent, reasonably priced meals.

Fonda Naturística Maná (Pasaje Hidalgo; mains US$1-3) Adjacent to Hotel Casa Blanca, this family-run vegetarian hole-in-the-wall is great for towering veggie burgers, fruit salads, juices and other meatless fare, both liquid and solid.

Getting There & Away

Tula's bus depot is on Xicoténcatl, three blocks from the cathedral. First-class Ovnibus buses go to/from Mexico City's Terminal Norte (US$4, 1¼ hours, every 40 minutes) and to/from Pachuca (US$3.75, 1¾ hours, hourly). Autotransportes Valle de Mezquital runs 2nd-class buses (US$3.25) to the same destinations every 15 minutes. Flecha Amarilla has daily service to Guanajuato, León, Morelia and Querétaro.

Getting Around

If you arrive in Tula by bus, the easiest way to get to the Zona Arqueológica is to catch a taxi (US$2.25) from outside the depot. From the center, 'Actopan' microbuses (US$0.40) depart from 5 de Mayo and Zaragoza and pass within 100m of the site entrance.

ACOLMAN
☎ 957 / pop 4000 / elevation 2250m
Beside Hwy 132D, 32km north of Mexico City, you'll see what look like battlements surrounding the **Ex-Convento de San Agustín Acolman**. The historic building, with its massive walls, colonnaded courtyards and carved stonework, contains many frescoes. The adjacent **Iglesia de San Agustín**, built between 1539 and 1560, has a spacious Gothic interior and one of Mexico's earliest plateresque façades. The old monastery now houses a **museum** (☎ 957-16-44; admission US$2.75; ☒ 9am-6pm) with artifacts and paintings from the early Christian missionary period. It's a pleasant stop on the way to or from Teotihuacán.

Buses go to Acolman (US$1.50) from Mexico City's Indios Verdes metro station. It's not far from Teotihuacán; if there's no convenient bus you can get a taxi for around US$4. Frequent colectivos (US$0.50) also make the journey from Av Guerrero in San Juan Teotihuacán.

TEOTIHUACÁN

☎ 594 / pop 22,000 / elevation 2300m

If there's a must-see attraction near Mexico City, it's the archaeological zone Teotihuacán (teh-oh-tih-wah-*kan*), 50km northeast of Mexico City in a mountain-ringed offshoot of the Valle de México. Site of the huge Pirámides del Sol y de la Luna (Pyramids of the Sun and Moon), Teotihuacán was Mexico's biggest ancient city and the capital of what was probably Mexico's largest pre-Hispanic empire. (See p32 for an outline of its importance.) A day here can be awesome, if you don't let the hawkers get you down.

The city's grid plan was developed in the early part of the 1st century AD, and the

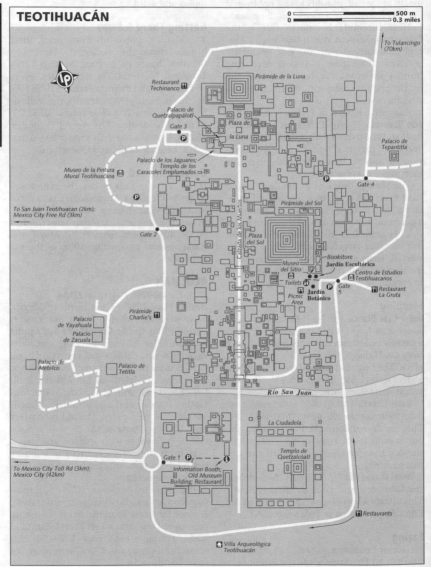

TEOTIHUACÁN

0 _____ 500 m
0 _____ 0.3 miles

To Tulancingo (70km)

Restaurant Techinanco

Pirámide de la Luna

Palacio de Quetzalpapálotl

Gate 3

Plaza de la Luna

Palacio de Tepantitla

Palacio de los Jaguares; Templo de los Caracoles Emplumados

Museo de la Pintura Mural Teotihuacana

Gate 4

To San Juan Teotihuacan (2km); Mexico City Free Rd (3km)

Pirámide del Sol

Calzada de los Muertos

Gate 2

Plaza del Sol

Bookstore
Jardín Escultórica

Museo del Sitio

Centro de Estudios Teotihuacanos

Toilets

Jardín Botánico

Gate 5

Restaurant La Gruta

Pirámide Charlie's

Picnic Area

Palacio de Yayahuala

Palacio de Zacuala

Palacio de Atetelco

Palacio de Tetitla

Río San Juan

La Ciudadela

To Mexico City Toll Rd (3km); Mexico City (42km)

Gate 1

Templo de Quetzalcóatl

Information Booth; Old Museum Building; Restaurant

Restaurants

Villa Arqueológica Teotihuacán

Pirámide del Sol was built – over an earlier cave shrine – by AD 150. The rest of the city was built between about AD 250 and 600. Social, environmental and economic factors hastened its decline and eventual collapse in the 8th century AD.

The city was divided into quarters by two great avenues that met near La Ciudadela (the Citadel). One, running roughly north–south, is the famous Calz de los Muertos (Avenue of the Dead) – so called because the later Aztecs believed the great buildings lining it were vast tombs, built by giants for Teotihuacán's first rulers. The major buildings are typified by a *talud-tablero* style, in which the rising portions of stepped, pyramid-like buildings consist of both sloping *(talud)* and upright *(tablero)* sections. They were often covered in lime and colorfully painted. Most of the city was made up of residential compounds, some of which contained elegant frescoes.

Centuries after its fall, Teotihuacán remained a pilgrimage site for Aztec royalty, who believed that all of the gods had sacrificed themselves here to start the sun moving at the beginning of the 'fifth world,' inhabited by the Aztecs. It remains an important pilgrimage site: thousands of Mexicans flock to the pyramids each year to celebrate the vernal equinox (March 21) and soak up the mystical energies that they believe converge here.

Orientation

Though ancient Teotihuacán covered more than 20 sq km, most of what there is to see now lies along nearly 2km of the Calz de los Muertos. Buses arrive at a traffic circle by the southwest entrance (Gate 1); four other entrances are reached by the ring road around the site. There are parking lots and ticket booths at each entrance. Your ticket allows you to reenter at any of them on the same day. The Museo del Sitio (site museum) is just inside the main east entrance (Gate 5).

Information

An **information booth** (☎ 956-02-76; ☒ 9am-4pm) is just near the southwest entrance (Gate 1). Free site tours by authorized guides (in Spanish only) may be available here if a sizable group forms.

Crowds at the **ruins** (admission US$3.50; ☒ 7am-6pm) are thickest from 10am to 2pm, and it's busiest on Sunday, holidays and around the vernal equinox. Most of the year, you should bring a hat and water; you may walk several kilometers, and the midday sun can be brutal. Because of the heat and the altitude, take it easy while clambering around the expansive ruins. Afternoon rain showers are common from June to September.

Numerous tours run from Mexico City. **Bestours** (☎ 55-5514-3080; Hamburgo 182, Colonia Juárez, Mexico City; tours US$33) runs several daily excursions with English-speaking guides, including transport and admission.

Sights

CALZADA DE LOS MUERTOS

Centuries ago the 'Avenue of the Dead,' the axis of the site, must have seemed incomparable to its inhabitants, who saw its buildings at their best. Gate 1 brings you to the avenue in front of La Ciudadela. For 2km to the north, the avenue is flanked by former palaces of Teotihuacán's elite and other major structures such as the Pirámide del Sol. At the northern end stands the Pirámide de la Luna.

LA CIUDADELA

The large, square complex called the Citadel is believed to have been the residence of the city's supreme ruler. Four wide walls, 390m long, topped by 15 pyramids, enclose a huge open space of which the main feature, toward the east side, is a pyramid called the **Templo de Quetzalcóatl**. The temple is flanked by two large, ruined complexes of rooms and patios, which may have been the city's administrative center.

The fascinating feature of the Templo de Quetzalcóatl is the façade of an earlier structure (from around AD 250–300), which was revealed by excavating the more recent pyramid that had been superimposed on it. The four surviving steps of this façade (there were originally seven) are adorned with striking carvings. In the *tablero* panels the sharp-fanged feathered serpent deity, its head emerging from a necklace of 11 petals, alternates with a four-eyed, two-fanged creature often identified as the rain god Tláloc but perhaps more authoritatively considered to be the fire serpent, bearer of the sun on its daily journey across the sky. On the sloping panels are side views of the plumed serpent.

MUSEO DEL SITIO

Continuing north along Calz de los Muertos toward the pyramids, a path to the right on the other side of the river leads to the **site museum**, just south of the Pirámide del Sol. It makes a refreshing stop midway through the site. Around the building, there's the Jardín Escultórica (a lovely sculpture garden with Teotihuacán artifacts), the Jardín Botánico (botanical garden), public toilets, a snack bar, picnic tables and a bookstore.

The museum is thematically divided with explanations in Spanish and English. There are excellent displays of artifacts, fresco panels and an impressive large-scale model of the city set under a transparent walkway, from where the real Pirámide del Sol can be viewed through a wall-size window.

CENTRO DE ESTUDIOS TEOTIHUACANOS

Situated just outside the east entrance (Gate 5), this research center is home to the interesting, INAH-sponsored **Museo Manuel Gamio** (☎ 965-15-99; admission free; ⏲ 7am-4pm Mon-Fri, 9am-4pm Sat & Sun), which presents bimonthly cultural exhibitions such as explorations of the history of pulque, complete with a full-scale replica of a traditional pulquería. There are also infrequent live music and theater programs in the open-air theater behind the museum.

PIRÁMIDE DEL SOL

The world's third-largest pyramid, surpassed in size only by the pyramid of Cholula (p211) and Egypt's Cheops, stands on the east side of Calz de los Muertos. The base is 222m long on each side, and it's now just over 70m high. The pyramid was built around AD 100, from 3 million tons of stone, brick and rubble without the use of metal tools, pack animals or the wheel.

The Aztec belief that the structure was dedicated to the sun god was validated in 1971, when archaeologists uncovered a 100m-long underground tunnel leading from near the pyramid's west side to a cave directly beneath its center, where they found religious artifacts. It's thought that the sun was worshiped here before the pyramid was built and that the city's ancient inhabitants traced the very origins of life to this grotto.

At Teotihuacán's height, the pyramid's plaster was painted bright red, which must have been a radiant sight at sunset. Climb the pyramid's 248 steps for an inspiring overview of the ancient city.

PALACIO DE TEPANTITLA

Teotihuacán's most famous fresco, the worn **Paradise of Tláloc**, is in the Tepantitla Palace, a priest's residence 500m northeast of Pirámide del Sol. The mural flanks a doorway in a covered patio in the building's northeast corner. The rain god Tláloc, attended by priests, is shown on both sides. On the right of the door appears his paradise, a garden-like place with people, animals and fish swimming in a mountain-fed river. To the left of the door, tiny human figures are engaged in a unique ball game. Frescoes in other rooms show priests with feather headdresses.

PIRÁMIDE DE LA LUNA

The Pyramid of the Moon, at the north end of Calz de los Muertos, is not as big as the Pirámide del Sol, but it's more gracefully proportioned. Its summit is nearly the same height, because it's built on higher ground. It was completed around AD 300.

The Plaza de la Luna, in front of the pyramid, is a handsome arrangement of 12 temple platforms. Some experts attribute astronomical symbolism to the total 13 (made by the 12 platforms plus the pyramid), a key number in the day-counting system of the Mesoamerican ritual calendar. The altar in the plaza's center is thought to have been the site of religious dancing.

PALACIO DE QUETZALPAPÁLOTL

Off the Plaza de la Luna's southwest corner is the Palace of the Quetzal Butterfly, where it's thought a high priest lived. A flight of steps leads up to a roofed portico with an abstract mural and, just off that, a well-restored patio with columns carved with images of the quetzal bird or a hybrid quetzal butterfly.

The **Palacio de los Jaguares** (Jaguar Palace) and **Templo de los Caracoles Emplumados** (Temple of the Plumed Conch Shells) are behind and below the Palacio de Quetzalpapálotl. On the lower walls of several of the chambers off the patio of the Palacio de los Jaguares are parts of murals showing the jaguar god in feathered headdresses, blowing conch shells and apparently praying to the rain god Tláloc.

The Templo de los Caracoles Emplumados, entered from the Palacio de los Jaguares patio, is a now-subterranean structure of the 2nd or 3rd century AD. Carvings on what was its façade show large shells – possibly used as musical instruments – decorated with feathers and four-petal flowers. The base on which the façade stands has a green, blue, red and yellow mural of birds with water streaming from their beaks.

MUSEO DE LA PINTURA MURAL TEOTIHUACANA

On the ring road between Gates 2 and 3, this impressive **museum** (guided tours ☎ 958-20-81; admission free with site ticket, parking US$2; ❉ 10am-6pm) showcases murals from Teotihuacán as well as reconstructions of murals you'll see in the ruins. Explanations of the modern exhibits are in Spanish only, but the museum is definitely worth a stop.

PALACIO DE TETITLA & PALACIO DE ATETELCO

Another group of palaces lies west of the site's main area, several hundred meters northwest of Gate 1. Their many murals, discovered in the 1940s, are often well-preserved or restored and perfectly intelligible. Inside the sprawling Tetitla Palace, no fewer than 120 walls have murals, with Tláloc, jaguars, serpents and eagles among the easiest figures to make out. Some 400m west is the Atetelco Palace, whose vivid jaguar or coyote murals – a mixture of originals and restorations – are in the Patio Blanco (White Patio) in the northwest corner. Processions of these creatures in shades of red perhaps symbolize warrior orders.

About 100m further northeast are Zacuala and Yayahuala, a pair of enormous walled compounds that probably served as communal living quarters. Separated by the original alleyways, the two structures are made up of numerous rooms and patios but few entranceways, perhaps to discourage unwanted guests.

Sleeping

BUDGET & MID-RANGE

The town of San Juan Teotihuacán, 3km west of the Pirámide del Sol, features several economical overnight options.

Hotel Posada Sol y Luna (☎ 956-23-68; Jiménez Cantú 13; d/ste from US$35/40; P) At the east end of town, closer to the pyramids, is this superior-value hotel with attentive English-speaking staff, an optional breakfast in the restaurant and 16 comfortable rooms, including a few Jacuzzi suites.

Hotel Posada Teotihuacán (☎ 956-04-60; Canteroco 5; s/d US$17/22) Two blocks east of the central plaza, this friendly, ever-expanding place on the way to Posada Sol y Luna offers clean rooms with TVs.

Hotel Quinto Sol (☎ 956-18-81; www.hotelquintosol.com.mx in Spanish; Av Hidalgo 26; s/d/ste from US$49/58/66; P ☎) This modern hotel has luxurious rooms and Jacuzzi suites with every amenity, including hairdryers, coffeemakers, phones and cable TV. The breakfast buffet (US$7) will keep you going all day.

Motel Quinto Sol (behind Hotel Quinto Sol; r/ste US$32/41; P ☎) The anonymous drive-in motel offers clean, modern rooms, each with one king-size bed, above private garages. The suites have Jacuzzis and you can use Hotel Quinto Sol's pool.

Trailer Park Teotihuacán (☎ 956-03-13; teotipark@prodigy.net.mx; López Mateos 17; tent sites per person US$4.50, full RV hookups US$10, dm US$10) You can camp here on a peaceful street behind a 16th-century Jesuit church. The grassy park has 24/7 hot showers and plans for new dormitory beds.

TOP END

Villa Arqueológica Teotihuacán (☎ 956-09-09, in Mexico City 55-5836-9020; www.teotihuacaninfo.com; r/f US$60/119; P ☎) This Club Med–run property, at the south end of the road that encircles the ancient city, has small yet charming rooms with all the features. There's also a heated pool, tennis court, billiards table and bar-restaurant.

Eating

Except for the rank of dusty numbered eateries along the ring road on the southeast side of the archaeological site, meals are pricey in the vicinity of the ruins. The most convenient place is on the 3rd floor of the **old museum building** just east of Gate 1, where there's a restaurant with views of La Ciudadela.

Restaurant Techinanco (☎ 958-23-06; ring road opposite Pirámide de la Luna; mains US$2-7; ❉ 10am-5:30pm) This friendly home-cooking eatery focuses its energy in the kitchen, rather than touting for customers, and thus is the best

PULQUERÍAS: THE ORIGINAL MEXICAN WATERING HOLE

Before the discotheque, before the leather seats of a hotel lounge, before even the venerated cantina, Mexico had *pulquerías*. Named for the drink they served, these seedy hovels were the working class' favorite drinking spot for the better part of 400 years, before better quality liquors and refrigeration forced them into the obscurity in which they languish today.

When the Aztecs ruled Mexico, pulque, made from the maguey plant, was used only in rituals and by the elite. Its production was strictly controlled and drunkenness was severely punished. When the Spanish arrived, pulque hit the streets, almost literally. The milky, low-alcohol brew was sold from makeshift stands that were open on all sides and covered with a shingled roof. The method of service was just as primitive: purveyors would ladle the drink from large basins or open barrels into a waiting patron's earthenware cup. As the day wore on, and the mood of the patrons got rowdier, these cups would be smashed against the ground once the contents were drained.

Pulquerías defined street life in the popular neighborhoods for much of the 17th and 18th centuries. They were the meeting spots where people would go to unwind after a hard day's work. Heavy boozing led to spontaneous eruptions of music and dancing. Food stands were set up to feed the drinkers. Fights were common, as were public displays of affection between lovers.

This behavior alarmed authorities and, almost from the outset, efforts were made to curtail the debauchery (Mexico's first recorded liquor laws were written in 1529). One inspector general reported that pulquerías were 'the real center and originating point of all the crimes and public sins which overwhelms this numerous population.' One measure called for the pulquerías to be enclosed in four walls, which brought protests from those who feared that once hidden from sight, the behavior would only worsen.

Another law prohibited members of the opposite sex from imbibing with each other. There were also attempts to limit the kinds of pulque sold, stemming from the belief that certain blends of roots and herbs had more damaging effects on the consumer. None of these measures proved to have any lasting effect. There were too many men who became very wealthy from pulque production, and this ensured a healthy flow of bribes to corrupt officials whenever tighter regulations compelled such action.

choice for miles around. It serves a limited menu of authentic homemade moles and other savory traditional dishes. The *mole de huitlacoche* (corn fungus mole, freshest in August and September), *caldo de hongos* (mushroom soup) and *huarache con carne asada* (grilled beef sandwich) are all divine. Ask ebullient owner Emma (aka Maya) about her curative massage (from US$30) or call 24 hours in advance to arrange a *temazcal* (indigenous Mexican steambath) for up to 15 people (around US$200).

Restaurant La Gruta (☎ 956-01-04; www.lagruta .com.mx; 75m east of Gate 5; mains US$5-15; ☯ 11am-7pm) Gourmet meals have been served in this huge, cool natural cave for a century; Porfirio Díaz (Mexican president for 33 years prior to the Mexican Revolution) ate here in 1906. The authentic food's quite good and fairly priced. On weekend afternoons, there's live music and folkloric ballet (cover US$1.50).

Pirámide Charlie's (ring road south of Gate 2; mains US$5-20; ☯ 11am-7pm) Undeniably a tour bus tourist trap, this place has its menu in four languages and serves savory but overpriced soup, chicken, beef and seafood dishes.

Getting There & Away

Autobuses México-San Juan Teotihuacán runs buses from Mexico City's Terminal Norte to the ruins every 20 minutes during the day (US$2, one hour). The ticket office is at the terminal's north end. Make sure your bus is going to 'Los Pirámides,' not to the nearby town of San Juan Teotihuacán.

Buses arrive and depart from the traffic circle near Gate 1, also making stops at Gates 2 and 3. Return buses are more frequent after 1pm. The last bus back to the capital from the traffic circle leaves around 6:30pm. Some terminate at Indios Verdes metro station in the north of Mexico City, but most continue to Terminal Norte.

But the authorities' efforts to quash Mexicans' love of pulque were most hampered by one simple fact. The royal treasury was raking in money from the taxes charged on the sale of pulque, especially toward the end of the 18th century when revenues from silver and gold were diminishing. During this time, taxes on pulque rose steadily, doubling in the 20-year period ending in 1784. The excessive taxes did accomplish the stated goal of reducing consumption – at least legally. But bootleggers, selling illegal and untaxed pulque, did very well indeed during this period.

More worrying for the last of the Spanish colonial administrators was that pulquerías would become the seat of rebellion, where dangerous ideas of independence could circulate among the common people. A new law was passed in 1811 (about a year after the rebellion against the Spanish Crown began) that prohibited pulque consumption. As a result, drinking went underground and clandestine pulquerías thrived.

Truth be told, patrons were not so concerned with making revolution as they were with getting drunk, gambling, dancing and making out in back corners. Besides that, the ability of the colonial viceroy to enforce any measures was undermined by the fact that he was losing the war to the rebelling Mexican forces. As a result, by 1821, when the Spanish finally gave up, pulquerías were more numerous than ever. Following Mexican independence, pulque consumption rose on a per capita basis, and by 1864 there was one pulquería for every 410 residents! Significantly, the government restricted their locations to neighborhoods outside the city center, a factor that may have contributed to pulque's eventual demise.

In the meantime, other drinks such as beer brought by German immigrants and the more potent mezcal and tequila began to gain greater popularity and supplant pulque as the intoxicant of choice. True pulque is homemade, not bottled, and therefore not viable for large-scale commercial production. While pulque is still available today in certain parts of central Mexico, it's clear that the glory days of pulque have gone.

In a way, the demise of the pulquería is a loss for Mexico. As you sit in a bar, listening to pre-recorded music instead of a live group of local musicians, sipping the beer that tastes the same wherever you order it, from a glass that will be washed and used again instead of smashed against the floor, you can't help but feel a certain misty sense of nostalgia for the days when pulquerías ruled Mexico's social scene.

Getting Around

To get to the pyramids from San Juan Teotihuacán, take any combi (US$0.30) labeled 'San Martín' departing from Av Hidalgo beside the central plaza. Combis returning to San Juan stop at Gates 1, 2 and 3.

PACHUCA

☎ 771 / pop 287,000 / elevation 2426m

Untouristed Pachuca, capital of Hidalgo state (population 2.3 million), is 90km northeast of Mexico City. It's grown rapidly in the past decade, and brightly painted houses climb the dry hillsides around the town. Pachuca has a few interesting sights, and is a good departure point for trips north and east into the dramatic Sierra Madre Oriental.

Silver was found nearby as early as 1534, and the mines of Real del Monte, 9km northeast, still produce substantial amounts of ore. Pachuca was also the gateway through which *fútbol* (soccer) entered Mexico, brought by

miners from Cornwall, England, in the 19th century. Further evidence of the Cornish influence, the savory meat pies known as *pastes* (pasties) are sold all over town.

Orientation

The rectangular Reloj Monumental (Clock Tower), built between 1904 and 1910 to commemorate the independence centennial, overshadows the north end of Pachuca's Plaza de la Independencia (zócalo), which is flanked by Av Matamoros on the east and Av Allende on the west. Guerrero runs parallel to Av Allende 100m to the west. About 700m to the south, both Guerrero and Av Matamoros reach the modern Plaza Juárez.

Information

Banks There are ATMs around Plaza de la Independencia.
Café Internet (cnr Hidalgo & Leandro Valle; per hr US$1) Offers Internet access two blocks east of the zócalo's southeast corner.

State Tourism Authority (☎ 800-718-26-00; www
.hidalgo.gob.mx) Contact by phone or Internet, as it lacks
a public office.

Tourist Module (☎ 715-14-11; Plaza de la Independencia; ☽ 10am-6pm) Irregularly staffed tourist office in
the clock tower's base; has small free city maps.

Sights

CENTRO CULTURAL DE HIDALGO

The Ex-Convento de San Francisco is now
the **Hidalgo Cultural Center** (cnr Hidalgo & Arista;
admission free; ☽ 10am-6pm Tue-Sun), which embodies two museums and a gallery, theater,
library and several lovely plazas. It's two
blocks east and four long blocks south of
Plaza Juárez. Upstairs, the **Museo Nacional
de la Fotografía** (admission free; ☽ 10am-6pm Tue-
Sun) displays early photographic technology
and selections from the 1.5 million photos
in the Instituto Nacional de Antropología
e Historia (INAH) archives. The images –
some by Europeans and Americans, many
more by pioneer Mexican photojournalist
Agustín Victor Casasola – provide fascinating glimpses of Mexico from 1873 to the
present.

MUSEO DE MINERÍA

Two blocks southeast of the zócalo, the **Mining Museum** (Mina 110; admission US$1.50, camera US$2,
video US$5; ☽ 10am-2pm & 3-6pm Wed-Sun) provides
a good overview of the mining industry that
shaped the region. Well-displayed photos
depict conditions in the mines from the
early years to the present. Also on display
are headlamps, miner's shrines and old
mining maps. Half a block east of Av Matamoros, it has hourly guided tours (in Spanish) with a 20-minute English-language
video program.

LOOKOUT POINTS

For jaw-dropping views, catch a 'Mirador'
bus (US$0.30) from Plaza de la Constitución
a few blocks northeast of the zócalo to the
mirador on the road to Real del Monte. Even
better views can be had from the **Cristo Rey
monument** on Cerro de Santa Apolonia
north of town.

Sleeping

Hotel de los Baños (☎ 713-07-00; Av Matamoros 205;
s/d US$20/25) Half a block southeast of the zó-
calo, this hotel has a restaurant and skylight
over a handsome enclosed courtyard. The

56 rooms vary in size and quality, but all
have cable TV, phones and clean baths.

Hotel Noriega (☎ 715-15-55; Av Matamoros 305;
s/d US$14/16; P) A block south of Hotel de
los Baños, this colonial-style hotel has a
leaf-covered courtyard, stately staircase
and decent restaurant. Have a look at a few
rooms, though, before checking in – some
are tiny and claustrophobic, while others
are large and airy. TV is US$2 extra and
overnight parking behind the hotel costs
US$1.50.

Hotel Emily (☎ 715-67-18; www.hotelemily.com
.mx; Plaza Independencia; s/d/ste US$33/38/44; P) On
the zócalo's south side, the modern Emily
has large comfortable rooms, some facing
a back patio, others with balconies on the
plaza.

Hotel Ciro's (☎ 715-40-83; www.hotelciros.com in
Spanish; Plaza Independencia 110; s/d/ste US$32/35/45;
P) Run by the same family as Emily, Ciro's
is on the opposite side of the plaza. The
building is very different, but the style and
quality of the rooms are similar.

Gran Hotel Independencia (☎ 715-05-15; Plaza
Independencia 116; s/d US$28/32; P) The Independ-
encia occupies an imposing building on the
zócalo's west side but is much less impressive inside, with big but bare rooms. Rates
are a couple of dollars higher on Friday and
Saturday night.

Eating

Pasties are available all over town, including
the bus station. Baked in pizza ovens, they
contain a variety of fillings probably never
imagined by Cornish miners, such as *mole
verde* (sauce made with green tomatos)
beans, pineapple and rice pudding. Especially popular are **Pastes Kiko's**, adjacent to
Gran Hotel Independencia; and **Pastes San
Juan** (Fernando Soto). The **grocery store** (Av Matamoros 205), adjacent to Hotel de Los Baños, is
a good spot to pick up tamales, tortas and
take-out chicken.

Mi Antiguo Café (Matamoros 15; breakfast US$4-5.50)
This charming café on the zócalo's east side
serves crêpes, tasty Mexican breakfasts and
good espresso.

Mina La Blanca Restaurant Bar (☎ 715-19-64; Av
Matamoros 201; mains US$4-8) Facing the zócalo's
southwest corner, this atmospheric place
serves 'authentic' pasties, filled with potatoes, leeks, parsley, ground beef and black
pepper. Decorated with stained-glass panels

of mining scenes, the cavernous dining hall also offers set breakfasts, salads and seasonal regional antojitos such as *gusanos de maguey* (maguey cactus worms).

Getting There & Away

From Pachuca, there's daily 1st-class service to the following places: Mexico City (US$5, 1¼ hours, every 15 minutes); Poza Rica (US$9, five hours, seven daily); and Tampico (US$24, eight hours, two daily). Buses serving destinations closer to Pachuca are nearly all 2nd-class; these frequently go to/from Tula, Tulancingo and Tamazunchale, while several go daily to/from Huejutla de Reyes and Querétaro.

Getting Around

The bus station is several kilometers southwest of downtown, beside the road to Mexico City. Green-striped colectivos marked 'Centro' take you to Plaza de la Constitución (US$0.30), a short walk from the zócalo; in the reverse direction, you can hop on along Av Allende. The trip by taxi costs in the vicinity of US$2.

AROUND PACHUCA

Three scenic roads climb into the forested, sometimes foggy Sierra Madre. **Hwy 105** heads north to Huejutla de Reyes (p654) and Tampico (p646). **Hwy 85** – the Pan-American Hwy – goes via Actopan and Ixmiquilpan to Tamazunchale and Ciudad Valles in the Huasteca (p646). **Hwy 130** goes east to Tulancingo and Poza Rica (p657).

Parque Nacional El Chico
☎ 771

Nine kilometers north of Pachuca, a road branches northwest (left) off Hwy 105 and snakes 20km to the picturesque old mining town of **Mineral del Chico**, inside El Chico National Park. The park has pine forests with lovely walks, spectacular rock formations (popular with climbers), and rivers and stocked ponds for fishing.

Río y Montaña Expediciones (☎ in Mexico City 55-5292-5032, toll-free in Mexico 866-900-9092; www.rio ymontana.com) organizes three-day expeditions to El Chico for groups of eight or more persons. The company supplies all climbing and camping equipment, but you must arrange your own transportation to the park.

SLEEPING & EATING

La Cabaña del Lobo (☎ in Mexico City 55-5776-2222; s/d US$78/39) Five kilometers from Hwy 105 (on the road toward Mineral del Chico) is a right turn that leads 1.2km by bumpy dirt road to La Cabaña. It's in a remote valley ringed by pine-covered mountains. The hotel features a row of cozy rooms with clean baths and hot water overlooking a restaurant and campfire/playground area. Some of the rooms have fireplaces – it can be chilly up here.

In Mineral del Chico there are a couple of nice hotels near the plaza. These places fill up fast on weekends, but are empty during the week.

Hospedaje El Chico (☎ 715-47-41; Corona del Rosal 1; s/d US$27/35) Ring the bell to the right of the Casa Brisa shop to access these 10 squeaky clean and comfortable rooms, each holding up to four people. Rates are per bed, not per person.

Hotel Posada del Amanacer (☎ 715-01-90; www .hotelesecoturisticos.com.mx in Spanish; Morelos 3; r Sun-Thu US$61, Fri & Sat US$76) This 11-room adobe structure has spacious rooms on two levels beside a lovely patio. It's a peaceful getaway without phones or TV. Fireplaces cost US$10 extra, full meal plans are available for US$40 per person and children under 12 stay free. Low-season rates are 25% less and all rates include guided hiking and bicycling tours into the park.

The same chain also runs the fancier **Hotel El Paraíso** (☎ 715-56-54; r Sun-Thu from US$65, Fri & Sat from US$80), down the hill from Posada del Amanacer; and the more basic **Hotel Real del Monte** (☎ 715-56-59; r Sun-Thu from US$40, Fri & Sat from US$60) in Mineral del Monte.

There are several **campgrounds** (per tent US$2, plus per person US$0.50) with rudimentary facilities between Km 7 and Km 10 of the road to Mineral del Chico, plus a **trailer park** (full-hookups US$9) just inside the park entrance gate.

GETTING THERE & AWAY

From Pachuca, colectivos (US$0.75) depart frequently from Galeana (west of the market, through an arch labeled 'Barrio el Arbolito'). Flecha Roja runs 2nd-class buses to Mineral del Chico (US$1, one hour, three daily) from Pachuca's bus station.

Hwy 105

Two kilometers past the park turnoff for Parque Nacional El Chico, **Mineral del Monte** (aka Real del Monte) was the scene of a miners' strike in 1776 – commemorated as the first strike in the Americas. Most of the town was settled in the 19th century, after a British company took over the mines. **Mine tours** (☎ 715-27-63; tours US$9) descend 150m into abandoned workings on weekends. The field opposite the Dolores mine was the first place in the country where soccer was played. Cornish-style cottages line many of the steep cobbled streets, and there is an English cemetery nearby. Flecha Roja buses leave Pachuca's bus terminal for Mineral del Monte (US$0.50, 30 minutes, every 30 minutes).

Eleven kilometers north of Mineral del Monte is a turnoff east to **Huasca** (or Huasca de Ocampo), which has a 17th-century church, *balnearios* (bathing places) and a variety of local crafts. Some old haciendas have been converted into attractive hotels. Nearby is a canyon with a waterfall and imposing basalt columns.

At **Atotonilco el Grande**, 34km northeast Pachuca, there's a 16th-century fortress-monastery and a balneario beside some hot springs. Market day is Thursday.

The highway then descends to Metzquititlán, in the fertile Río Tulancingo valley. For information about other places along this route, see Huejutla de Reyes and South of Huejutla (p654).

Actopan

☎ 772 / pop 26,000 / elevation 2400m

Actopan, 37km northwest of Pachuca on Hwy 85, has one of the finest of Hidalgo's many 16th-century fortress-monasteries, the well-preserved **Convento de San Nicolás de Tolentino**, founded in 1548. Its church has a lovely plateresque façade and a single tower showing Moorish influence. Mexico's best 16th-century frescoes are in the cloister: hermits are depicted in the Sala De Profundis, and saints, Augustinian monks and a meeting between Fray Martín de Acevedo (an important early monk at Actopan) and two indigenous nobles (Juan Inica Actopa and Pedro Ixcuincuitlapilco) are shown on the stairs. To the left of the church, a vaulted *capilla abierta* (open chapel) is also adorned with frescoes.

Wednesday is **market day** in Actopan, and has been for at least 400 years. Local handicrafts are sold, along with regional dishes such as barbecued lamb, which is wrapped

in maguey leaves and pit roasted. Several water parks in the area allow **camping** and provide secure RV parking.

PAI (Pachuca-Actopan-Ixmiquilpan) runs 1st-class buses from Pachuca to Actopan (US$2, 20 minutes, every 15 minutes). There is also a frequent 2nd-class service from Mexico City's Terminal Norte.

Ixmiquilpan

☎ 759 / pop 33,000 / elevation 1700m

The arid Mezquital Valley is a modern-day ethnic enclave; about half of Mexico's 350,000 Otomí people, descendents of ancient inhabitants, live in Hidalgo. The valley's commercial hub and former Otomí capital is Ixmiquilpan, 75km northwest of Pachuca on Hwy 85.

The valley is well known for Mexico's finest *ayates*, cloths which are woven from *ixtle* (the fiber of the maguey cactus). Traditional Otomí women's dress is a *quechquémitl*, an embroidered shoulder cape worn over an embroidered cloth blouse.

The busy Monday **market** is the best place to find Otomí crafts such as miniature musical instruments made of juniper wood with pearl or shell inlay, colorful drawstring bags or embroidered textiles. The rest of the week, you can go to the nearby community of El Nith (east of Ixmiquilpan) to find such items. Combis depart from Jesús del Rosal near the market; taxis make the trip around US$3.

Ixmiquilpan's **monastery** was founded by Augustinians in the mid-1500s. The church's nave, crowned by a huge Gothic vault, is unusual for a band of frescoes depicting indigenous warriors in combat. These show a clash between soldiers in Aztec military garb and scantily clad warriors using obsidian swords. Experts speculate the murals were painted by Mexica artists as propaganda against Chichimec invaders.

PAI runs 1st-class buses from Pachuca to Ixmiquilpan (US$3.75, 1½ hours, every 15 minutes).

Hwy 130

Just 46km east of Pachuca is the city of **Tulancingo** (population 99,000; elevation 2140m), which was briefly the Toltec capital before Tula. There's a Toltec pyramid at the foot of a cliff at **Huapalcalco**, 3km north. Market day is Thursday.

The Otomí village of **Tenango de Doria** is a rugged 40km northeast of Tulancingo by sometimes impassable roads. The residents make cotton fabric colorfully embroidered with plants and animals. In **Huehuetla**, 50km northeast of Tulancingo, there is one of the few communities of the tiny Tepehua indigenous group, who embroider floral and geometric patterns on their *enredos* (wraparound skirts) and *quechquémitls*.

Beyond Tulancingo, Hwy 130 descends toward Huauchinango (p658).

EAST OF MEXICO CITY

Toll road 150D speeds east to Puebla across a high, dry region studded with volcanic peaks, including Popocatépetl, Iztaccíhuatl and La Malinche. The mountains offer scope for anything from pleasant alpine strolls to demanding technical climbs – though Popocatépetl remains off-limits due to recent volcanic activity. Just north of the highway, the tiny state of Tlaxcala (population 1 million) features a charming capital and relics from a rich pre-Hispanic and colonial history.

Puebla is one of Mexico's best preserved colonial cities, a pivot of its history and a lively modern metropolis with much to see and do. Nevertheless, the state of Puebla is predominantly rural, home to approximately half a million indigenous people. This indigenous presence helps give Puebla a rich handicraft output, including pottery, carved onyx, and fine handwoven and embroidered textiles.

From Puebla you can continue east on Hwy 150D, past Mexico's tallest peak, Pico de Orizaba (p686), and descend from the highlands to the coast of Veracruz state. Alternatives are to swing north on Hwy 140 toward the remote Sierra Norte de Puebla, or wend your way to the Gulf Coast via Xalapa (p665), or take the scenic Hwy 135D south across the mountains to the state and city of Oaxaca.

POPOCATÉPETL & IZTACCÍHUATL

Mexico's second and third highest mountains, Popocatépetl (po-po-ka-*teh*-pet-l) and Iztaccíhuatl (iss-ta-*see*-wat-l), form the eastern rim of the Valle de México, 72km southeast of Mexico City and 43km west of Puebla. While the craterless Iztaccíhuatl is dormant,

Popocatépetl in recent years has spouted plumes of gas and ash, forced the evacuation of 25,000 people, and spurred experts to issue warnings to the 30 million people who live within striking distance of the volcano. Vulcanologists were continuing to watch Popo with concern at the time of writing.

After explosions of the 5452m volcano Popocatépetl – which is Náhuatl for 'Smoking Mountain' – sent 5000 tons of hot ash into the sky, soldiers evacuated 16 nearby villages on December 22, 1994. Popo, as the volcano is called locally, has been occasionally spewing ash since then. In the first few months of 2001, several eruptions sent ash up to 8km into the atmosphere. Smaller eruptions were observed in February 2003.

The federal **National Disaster Prevention Center** (Cenapred; ☎ 24/7 hotline 5205-1036; www.cenapred.unam.mx in Spanish) keeps an eye on volcanic activity via variations in gas emissions and seismic intensity, and advises the public about potential dangers.

Historically, Popo has been relatively kind. It has had 20 eruptive periods during the past 600 years, but none has caused a major loss of life or property. It has been over a thousand years since Popo delivered a really big blast, but experts don't discount the possibility of one now, and it is for this reason that Mexican authorities are not allowing anyone on the mountain except scientists monitoring its activity.

Iztaccíhuatl (White Woman), 20km north of Popo summit to summit, remains open to climbers and is perhaps all the more fetching because of her neighbor's unpredictable outbursts. Legend has it that Popo was a warrior who was in love with Izta, the emperor's daughter. As the story goes, Izta died of grief while Popo was away at war. Upon his return, he created the two mountains, laid her body on one and stood holding her funeral torch on the other. With some imagination, Izta does resemble a woman lying on her back. From the Mexico City side, you can, if the sky's clear, make out four peaks from left to right known as La Cabeza (the Head), El Pecho (the Breast), Las Rodillas (the Knees) and Los Pies (the Feet).

Amecameca

☎ 597 / pop 31,000 / elevation 2480m

From the Mexico City side, the town of Amecameca, 60km by road east of the city, is the key staging post for an Izta climb. But with a pair of volcanoes as a backdrop for the town's everyday activities and a few 16th-century churches, it makes an interesting destination in itself. There are ATMs around the plaza. The best way to get around town is by bicycle-taxi (US$0.35). There is a lively daily **market** next to the church.

The **Santuario del Sacromonte**, 90m above Amecameca to the west, is an important pilgrimage site built over a cave that was the retreat of the Dominican friar Martín de Valencia in the early 16th century. It makes a delightful walk with awesome views of the town spread out beneath the volcanoes. Go through the arch on the plaza's southwest side and walk down Av Fray Martín two blocks until you see the stairs ascending the hill on the right. From there, follow the stations of the cross uphill to the sanctuary.

Facing the plaza's southwest corner, **Hotel San Carlos** (☎ 978-07-46; Plaza de la Constitución 10; s/d US$8.50/17) has 33 clean, comfortable rooms that cost US$5 more with TV.

From Mexico City's TAPO, the 2nd-class Volcanes bus line runs to/from Amecameca (US$2, 1¼ hours, every 15 minutes) and Cuautla. From Amecameca's bus station, turn right and walk two blocks to the plaza.

Hiking

Izta's highest peak is **El Pecho** (5286m), and all routes to it require a night on the mountain. Between the staging point at La Joya parking lot and Las Rodillas, there is a shelter hut that can be used during an ascent of El Pecho. On average, it takes five hours to reach the hut from La Joya, another six hours from the hut to El Pecho, and six hours back to the base.

Before making the ascent, all climbers should contact the **Parque National Iztaccíhuatl-Popocatépetl** (☎ /fax 597-978-38-29/30; http://izta popo.conanp.gob.mx; Plaza de la Constitución 9B; ☺ 9am-6pm Mon-Fri, 9am-3pm Sat), on the southeast side of Amecameca's zócalo. To arrange permission, call the office ahead or submit a form available online. Technically, you do not need permission to climb Izta, but if you're starting from Amecameca, you'll need the permit to pass the military checkpoint near **Paso de Cortés**, in the saddle approximately halfway between Popo and Izta. Alternatively, you can depart from the village of

San Rafael, 8km north of Amecameca, a longer and more rigorous climb.

If you'd rather not climb Izta but would still like to spend a day enjoying the mountain scenery, Paso de Cortés has plenty of lower-altitude trails through pine forests and grassy meadows; some offer breathtaking glimpses of the nearby peaks. Trails begin about 2km beyond the Altzomoni Lodge at the La Joya parking lot. Again, you need to arrange for a permit, which may be available on Sundays at the checkpoint. Colectivos departing from Amecameca's plaza for Paso de Cortés cost US$2.75. Taxis departing from in front of the national park office will take you to La Joya (40 minutes) and back for around US$30.

Shelter is available at Paso de Cortés' visitors center and at **Altzomoni Lodge** (beds per person US$2) nearby. The lodge is by a microwave station roughly halfway between the visitors center at the Paso de Cortés and La Joya. Bring bedding and drinking water. All visitors must pay a new US$1 per day park entrance fee.

CLIMATE & CONDITIONS

It can be windy and well below freezing any time of year on Izta's upper slopes, and it is nearly always below freezing near the summit at night. Ice and snow are fixtures here; the average snow line is 4200m. The best months for ascents are October to February, when there is hard snow for crampons. The rainy season (April to September) brings with it the threat of whiteouts, thunderstorms and avalanches.

Anyone can be affected by altitude problems, including life-threatening altitude sickness. Even Paso de Cortés (3650m), the turnoff for Izta, is at a level where you should know the symptoms (see p989).

GUIDES

Iztaccíhuatl should be attempted by experienced climbers *only*, and because of hidden crevices on the ice-covered upper slopes, a guide is highly recommended.

Mario Andrade (☎ 55-5875-0105; mountainup@ hotmail.com; PO Box M-10380, México DF, Mexico), an English-speaking, Mexico City–based guide, has led many Izta ascents. His fee for leading climbers up Iztaccíhuatl is US$350 for one person; the per-person price goes down for groups. The cost includes transportation from Mexico City to Izta and back, lodging and the use of rope. In Amecameca, **José Luis Ariza** (☎ 597-978-13-35), a member of the rescue squad Búsqueda y Salvamento who has scaled peaks throughout Latin America, leads climbers up Izta's peak year-round. He charges US$100 for one person and US$50 for each additional person (transportation and equipment rental cost extra).

TEXCOCO & AROUND
☎ 595 / pop 109,000 / elevation 2778m

Some of Diego Rivera's finest mural work can be found at the agriculture school of the **Universidad Autónoma de Chapingo** just outside Texcoco, 67km east of Mexico City via Hwy 136. The former hacienda is now part of the university's administration building. Inside the **Capilla Riveriana** (admission US$3; ☾ 10am-3pm Mon-Fri, 10am-5pm Sat & Sun), sensual murals intertwine images of the Mexican struggle for agrarian reform and the Earth's fertility cycles. One of the 24 panels covering the chapel's walls and ceiling depicts buried martyrs of reform symbolically fertilizing the land and thus the future.

From Mexico City, take a local bus from metro Zaragoza or a direct bus from TAPO to downtown Texcoco where there are 'Chapingo' combis. From the main entrance, the hacienda is just at the end of the tree-lined path.

Also worth visiting is the **Parque Nacional Molino de Flores Nezahualcóyotl**, 3km east of Texcoco. Established in 1585 as the region's first wheat mill, the Molino later served as a *pulque* hacienda before being expropriated by the government in 1937. Today many of the original buildings are in ruins, but some have been partly restored. Works of local artists are exhibited in the *tinacal* where pulque was processed. A walk past the main buildings will take you to an unusual little church built into the side of a gorge, accessible on one side by a hanging bridge. To get to the park, hop a 'Molino de Flores' combi from downtown Texcoco.

About 5km further east from the Molino, the little known but interesting archaeological site **Baños de Nezahualcóyotl** contains the remains of temples, a palace, fountains, spring-fed aqueducts and baths built by the Texcocan poet-king, Nezahualcóyotl. He was perhaps the only Mesoamerican ruler to observe a type of monotheistic religion, worshiping an abstract god with feminine and masculine qualities. The site is on a hilltop with a view (when the pollution isn't bad) as far as Xochimilco. To get here, take a 'Tlamincas' combi from downtown Texcoco, or from the right fork just outside the national park's entrance, and get off at the sign pointing to the site. From there, it's a 1km walk to the summit.

TLAXCALA
☎ 246 / pop 79,000 / elevation 2252m

About 120km east of Mexico City and 32km north of Puebla, this quiet colonial town is the capital of Tlaxcala state, Mexico's smallest. It makes a pleasant day trip from either city.

History
In the last centuries before the Spanish conquest, numerous small warrior kingdoms (*señoríos*) arose in the Tlaxcala area. Some of them formed a loose federation that managed to stay independent of the Aztec empire as it spread from the Valle de México in the 15th century. The most important kingdom seems to have been Tizatlán, now on the edge of Tlaxcala city.

When the Spanish arrived in 1519, the Tlaxcalans fought fiercely at first, but then became Cortés' staunchest allies against the Aztecs (with the exception of one chief, Xicoténcatl the Younger, who tried at least twice to rouse his people against the Spanish and is now a Mexican hero). The Spanish rewarded the Tlaxcalans with privileges and used them to help pacify and settle Chichimec areas to the north. In 1527 Tlaxcala became the seat of the first bishopric in Nueva España, but a plague in the 1540s decimated the population and the town never played an important role again.

Orientation
Two central plazas meet at the corner of Independencia and Muñoz. The northern one, surrounded by colonial buildings, is the zócalo, called Plaza de la Constitución. The other, Plaza Xicohténcatl, has a crafts market on weekends.

Information
Banamex Has an ATM on the southwest side of Plaza Xicohténcatl.
Banorte Has an ATM on the plaza's southeast corner.

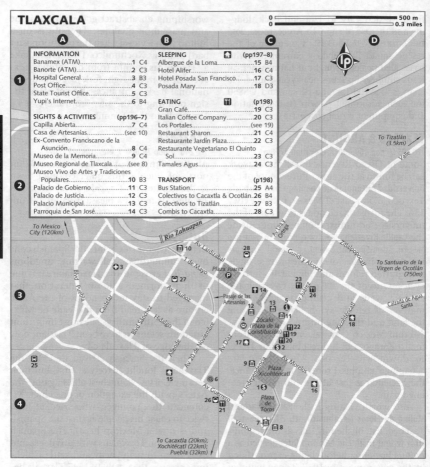

TLAXCALA

0 — 500 m
0 — 0.3 miles

INFORMATION
Banamex (ATM)..............................1 C4
Banorte (ATM)................................2 C3
Hospital General.............................3 B3
Post Office......................................4 C3
State Tourist Office........................5 C3
Yupi's Internet................................6 B4

SIGHTS & ACTIVITIES (pp196–7)
Capilla Abierta................................7 C4
Casa de Artesanías....................(see 10)
Ex-Convento Franciscano de la
   Asunción.....................................8 C4
Museo de la Memoria....................9 C4
Museo Regional de Tlaxcala.......(see 8)
Museo Vivo de Artes y Tradiciones
   Populares...................................10 B3
Palacio de Gobierno.....................11 C3
Palacio de Justicia........................12 C3
Palacio Municipal..........................13 C3
Parroquia de San José..................14 C3

SLEEPING (pp197–8)
Albergue de la Loma.....................15 B4
Hotel Alifer...................................16 C4
Hotel Posada San Francisco........17 C3
Posada Mary..................................18 D3

EATING (p198)
Gran Café......................................19 C3
Italian Coffee Company...............20 C3
Los Portales..............................(see 19)
Restaurant Sharon.......................21 C4
Restaurante Jardín Plaza.............22 C3
Restaurante Vegetariano El Quinto
   Sol...23 C3
Tamales Agus................................24 C3

TRANSPORT (p198)
Bus Station....................................25 A4
Colectivos to Cacaxtla & Ocotlán.26 B4
Colectivos to Tizatlán..................27 B3
Combis to Cacaxtla......................28 C3

To Tizatlán
(3.5km)

To Mexico
City (120km)

Río Zahuapan

To Santuario de la
Virgen de Ocotlán
(750m)

Zócalo
(Plaza de la
Constitución)

Plaza Juárez

Pasaje de las
Artesanías

Plaza
Xicohténcatl

Plaza
de
Toros

To Cacaxtla (20km);
Xochitécatl (22km);
Puebla (32km)

State Tourist Office (☎ 465-09-60/68, 800-509-65-57; www.tlaxcala.gob.mx/turismo; cnr Av Juárez & Av Lardizabal; tours incl transport US$2; ☉ 9am-6pm Mon-Fri, 10am-6pm Sat & Sun) The English-speaking staff run guided tours of the city and most of the outlying areas on Saturday and Sunday, with departures from Hotel Posada San Francisco at 10:15am.

Yupi's Internet (cnr Días & Guerrero; per hr US$1; ☉ 8am-8pm) Well-run place with fast connections.

Sights
ZÓCALO
The spacious, shady main plaza is one of Mexico's best looking. The 16th-century Palacio Municipal, a former grain storehouse, and the Palacio de Gobierno take up most of its north side. Inside the latter there are vivid

murals of Tlaxcala's history by Desiderio Hernández Xochitiotzin. The 16th-century building on the plaza's northwest side is the **Palacio de Justicia**, the former Capilla Real de Indios, constructed for the use of indigenous nobles. The handsome mortar bas-reliefs around its doorway depict the seal of Castilla y León and a two-headed eagle, symbol of the Hapsburg monarchs who ruled Spain in the 16th and 17th centuries. Near the zócalo's northwest corner is the pretty brick, tile and stucco **Parroquia de San José**.

EX-CONVENTO FRANCISCANO DE LA ASUNCIÓN
This former monastery is up a steep, shaded path from the southeast corner of Plaza

Xicohténcatl. Built between 1537 and 1540, it was one of Mexico's earliest monasteries, and its church – the city's cathedral – has a beautiful Moorish-style wooden ceiling. Next to the church is the **Museo Regional de Tlaxcala** (☎ 462-02-62; admission US$3, camera or video US$3; ☯ 10am-5pm Tue-Sun).

Just below the monastery, beside the 19th-century bullring, is a **capilla abierta**, which is unique for the Moorish style of its three arches.

MUSEO VIVO DE ARTES Y TRADICIONES POPULARES

This **popular arts museum** (☎ 462-23-37; Blvd Sánchez 1; admission US$0.75; ☯ 10am-6pm Tue-Sun) has displays on Tlaxcalan village life, weaving and pulque-making, sometimes with demonstrations. Next door the handicrafts at the **Casa de Artesanías** are also worth a look.

MUSEO DE LA MEMORIA

This **museum** (☎ 466-07-92; Plaza Xicohténcatl 3; admission US$1, video $3; ☯ 10am-5pm Tue-Sun) takes a multimedia approach to Tlaxcala's history. Exhibits on indigenous government, agriculture and contemporary festivals are well presented, though explanations are in Spanish only.

SANTUARIO DE LA VIRGEN DE OCOTLÁN

This is one of Mexico's most spectacular churches, and an important pilgrimage site owing to the belief that the Virgin appeared here in 1541 – her image stands on the main altar in memory of the apparition. The classic Churrigueresque façade features white stucco 'wedding cake' decorations contrasting with plain red tiles. During the 18th century indigenous Mexican Francisco Miguel spent 25 years decorating the altarpieces and the chapel beside the main altar.

The church is on a hill 1km northeast of the zócalo. Walk north on Av Juárez for three blocks, then turn right onto Zitlalpopocatl, or catch a 'Ocotlán' colectivo from near the corner of Av Guerrero and Av Independencia.

TIZATLÁN

These are the scant remains of Xicoténcatl's palace. Under a shelter are two altars with some faded frescoes of the gods Tezcatlipoca (Smoking Mirror), Tlahuizcalpantecuhtli (Morning Star) and Mictlantecuhtli (Under-world). The Templo San Esteban, next to the ruins, has a 16th-century Franciscan *capilla abierta* and frescoes of angels playing instruments. The site is on a hill 4km north of the town center; take a 'Tizatlán Parroquia' colectivo from the corner of Blvd Sánchez and Av Muñoz.

Courses

Estela Silva's Mexican Home Cooking Program

(☎ /fax 522-468-09-78; www.mexicanhomecooking.com; courses US$900) offers an intimate five-day cooking course with hands-on instruction in the preparation of classic Mexican dishes. The bilingual lessons focus on Puebla cuisine and take place in the Talavera-tiled kitchen of fun-loving Silva's hacienda-style home, which is in the small village of Santiago Tlacochcalco, about 10km south of Tlaxcala. Tuition includes all meals and lodging in comfortable double rooms with fireplaces and private baths. Mycologists should inquire about the Mushroom Tour that takes students foraging with local experts in late August or early September.

Festivals & Events

On the third Monday in May, the figure of the **Virgin of Ocotlán** is carried from its hilltop residence to other churches, attracting crowds of believers and onlookers. Throughout the month, processions commemorating the miracle attract pilgrims from around the republic.

The neighboring town of Santa Ana Chiautempan hosts the **Feria Nacional del Sarape** (National Sarape Fair) for two weeks on either side of July 26 to correspond with the celebration of its patron saint's day.

Sleeping

Hotel Alifer (☎ 462-56-78; www.hotelalifer.com in Spanish; Av Morelos 11; s/d US$28/37; P) The cheery hillside Alifer has clean carpeted rooms with TVs and phones. The hotel is less than two blocks from the zócalo, but the last 50m stretch is a steep climb. It also has a good restaurant for breakfast.

Albergue de la Loma (☎ 462-04-24; Av Guerrero 58; s/d US$19/24; P) This modernish hotel, at the top of 61 steps, has big, carpeted rooms with tiled bathrooms, some with good city views.

Posada Mary (☎ 462-96-55; Xicohténcatl 19; s/d with bathroom US$9/16; P) Tlaxcala's cheapest option is a basic but clean and friendly concrete crash pad down a dark street.

Hotel Posada San Francisco (☎ 462-60-22; www .posadasanfrancisco.com; Plaza de la Constitución 17; s/d/ste US$73/82/119; P ⚈) On the zócalo's south side in a restored 19th-century mansion, the full-service San Francisco is the classiest place in town, with a couple of restaurants, tennis courts, billiards and an inviting pool.

Eating

There's a row of places under the arcades on the zócalo's east side with live music on weekends. **Restaurante Jardín Plaza** (☎ 462-28-91; mains $3-8) is the best of the bunch, with an espresso machine and regional food served in a pleasant indoor/outdoor setting. **Gran Café** and **Los Portales** serve popular dinner buffets (US$8) featuring a wide variety of traditional dishes. The **Italian Coffee Company** (drinks $1-3) offers decent espresso and sandwiches, as well as desserts and a variety of gourmet teas.

Restaurant Vegetariano El Quinto Sol (☎ 466-18-57; Av Juárez 12; mains US$3-4) For healthy snacks and meals, try this popular place. It features fresh salads, veggie burgers, hearty breakfasts and a large variety of juices. The fixed-price meals here are good value.

Tamales Agus (Av Juárez 25; snacks from US$0.30) Across the street from El Quinto Sol, this tiny place serves delicious mole and salsa verde tamales along with assorted *atole* drinks.

Restaurant Sharon (Av Guerrero 14; 3 tacos US$2.75; ⚇ 1-7pm Sun-Fri) For scrumptious tacos, try this clean, unpretentious hole-in-the-wall.

Shopping

Embroidered capes and *huipiles* (sleeveless tunics) from Santa Ana Chiautempan, carved canes from Tizatlán, amaranth candies from San Miguel del Milagro and other local handicrafts are sold on weekdays along the **Pasaje de las Artesanías**, which forms an arc northeast of the Muñoz/Allende intersection.

Getting There & Away

Tlaxcala's sprawling **bus station** is 1km west of the plazas. For Mexico City's TAPO, Autobuses Tlaxcala-Apizaco-Huamantla (ATAH) operates its 1st-class 'expresso' buses (US$6.50, two hours, every 20 minutes) and 'ordinario' buses (US$3.75, 2½ hours,

hourly). ATAH has a new Veracruz service (US$12, five hours, four daily). Second-class Flecha Azul buses rumble to Puebla (US$1, every 10 minutes).

Getting Around

Most colectivos (US$0.30) at the bus station go to the town center. From the center to the bus station, catch a blue-and-white colectivo along the east side of Blvd Sánchez.

CACAXTLA & XOCHITÉCATL

The hilltop ruins at Cacaxtla (ca-*casht*-la) feature well-preserved, vividly colored frescoes showing, among many other scenes, nearly life-size jaguar and eagle warriors engaged in battle. The ruins were discovered in 1975 when a group of men from the nearby village of San Miguel del Milagro, in search of a reputedly valuable cache of relics, dug a tunnel and came across a mural.

The much older ruins at Xochitécatl (so-chi-*teh*-catl), 2km away, include an exceptionally wide pyramid as well as a circular pyramid. A German archaeologist led the first systematic exploration of the site in 1969, but it wasn't until 1994 that the pyramids were opened to the public. The two archaeological sites, approximately 32km northwest of Puebla and 20km southwest of Tlaxcala, are among Mexico's most interesting.

Though both sites can be toured without a guide, explanatory signs (in English and Spanish) tend to be either sketchy or overly technical. A good, if rushed, alternative is to join a Sunday tour (US$2) conducted by the **Tlaxcala tourist office** (p196) departing from Hotel Posada de San Francisco in Tlaxcala. It may be possible to hire a guide at the sites between Thursday and Sunday.

History

Cacaxtla was the capital of a group of Olmeca-Xicallanca or Putún Maya, who first came to central Mexico as early as AD 450. After the decline of Cholula (which they may have helped bring about) in around AD 600, they became the chief power in southern Tlaxcala and the Puebla valley. Cacaxtla peaked around AD 650–950 before being abandoned by AD 1000 in the face of possibly Chichimec newcomers.

Two kilometers west of Cacaxtla, atop a higher hill, the ruins of Xochitécatl predate Christ by a millennium. Just who first occupied the area is a matter of dispute, but experts agree that whereas Cacaxtla primarily served as living quarters for the ruling class, Xochitécatl was chiefly used for gory ceremonies to honor Quecholli, the fertility god. That isn't to say Cacaxtla didn't hold similar ceremonies; the discovery of the skeletal remains of more than 200 mutilated children attest to Cacaxtla's bloody past.

Cacaxtla

From the parking lot, which is opposite the **site entrance** (admission US$3.50, camera US$3; ☉ 10am-5pm), it's a 200m walk to the ticket office, museum, shop and restaurant.

From the ticket office, it's another 600m downhill to the main attraction – a natural platform 200m long and 25m high called the **Gran Basamento** (Great Base), which is now under a huge metal roof. Here stood Cacaxtla's main civic and religious buildings and the residences of its ruling priestly classes. At the top of the entry stairs is an open space called the **Plaza Norte**. From here, you will follow a clockwise path around the ruins until you reach the **murals**.

Archaeologists have yet to determine the identity of the muralists; many of the symbols found here are clearly from the Mexican highlands, and yet a Mayan influence from southeastern Mexico appears in all of them. The combined appearance of Mayan style and Mexican-highlands symbols in a mural is unique to Cacaxtla and the subject of much speculation.

Before reaching the first mural you come to a small patio whose main feature is an **altar** fronted by a small square pit in which numerous human remains were discovered. Just beyond the altar, along the complex' west edge, you'll find the **Templo de Venus**, which contains two anthropomorphic figures in blue – a man and a woman – wearing jaguar skin skirts. The temple's name is attributed to the appearance of numerous half-stars around the female figure, which are associated with the planet Venus.

On the opposite side of the path toward the Plaza Norte, the **Templo Rojo** (named for the amount of red paint used) contains four murals, only one of which is currently visible. Its vivid imagery is dominated by a row of corn and cacao crops whose husks contain human heads.

Facing Plaza Norte's north side is the long **Mural de la Batalla** (Battle Mural), dating from before AD 700. It shows two groups of warriors, one wearing jaguar skins and the other bird feathers, engaged in ferocious battle. The Olmeca-Xicallanca (the jaguar-warriors with round shields) are clearly repelling invading Huastecs (the bird-warriors with jade ornaments and deformed skulls).

At the end of the Mural de la Batalla, turn left and climb the steps to see the **second major mural group**, to your right behind the fence. The two main murals, from approximately AD 750, show a figure in a jaguar costume and a black-painted figure in a bird costume (who is believed to be the Olmeca-Xicallanca priest-governor) standing upon a plumed serpent.

Xochitécatl

From the parking lot at the **site entrance** (admission US$3; ☉ 10am-5pm Tue-Sun), follow a path around to the circular Pirámide de la Espiral. On top there's a cross planted by a neighboring village long before they knew the hill contained a pyramid. The path passes three other pyramids – the lowest in stature is Basamento de los Volcanes, the next is the mid-size Pirámide de la Serpiente and the last is the quite large Pirámide de las Flores.

Because of its outline and the materials used, archaeologists believe the circular **Pirámide de la Espiral** was built between 1000 and 800 BC. Its form and location high atop a hill suggest it may have been used as an astronomical observation post or as a temple to Ehecatl, the wind god.

Only the base of the **Basamento de los Volcanes** pyramid remains, and it's made of materials from two periods. Cut square stones were placed over the original stones, visible in some areas, and then stuccoed over. The colored stones used to build Tlaxcala's municipal palace appear to have come from this site.

The **Pirámide de la Serpiente** gets its name from a large piece of carved stone with the head of a snake at one end. Its most interesting feature is the huge pot found at its center, carved from a single boulder that was hauled from another region. Researchers surmise it was used to hold water.

Experts speculate that rituals honoring the fertility god were held at the **Pirámide de las**

Flores, due to the discovery of several sculptures and the remains of 30 sacrificed infants. Near the pyramid's base – Latin America's fourth widest – is a pool carved from a massive rock, where the infants were believed to have been washed before being killed.

Getting There & Away

The Cacaxtla site is 1.5km uphill from a back road between San Martín Texmelucan (near Hwy 150D) and Hwy 119, which is the secondary road between Puebla and Tlaxcala. By car from Tlaxcala, turn west off Hwy 119 just south of town. A sign 1.5km west of the village of Nativitas points to Cacaxtla and to the nearby village of San Miguel del Milagro.

By public transport from Tlaxcala, take a 'San Miguel del Milagro' colectivo from the corner of Av 20 de Noviembre and Av Lardizabal, which will drop you off about 500m from Cacaxtla. Alternatively, a 'Nativitas–Texoloc–Tlaxcala' colectivo, which departs from the same corner, goes to the town of Nativitas, 3km from Cacaxtla; from there, catch a 'Zona Arqueológica' colectivo directly to the site. Flecha Azul buses go direct from Puebla's CAPU to Nativitas. Between Cacaxtla and Xochitécatl, take a taxi (US$3), or hike the 2km.

LA MALINCHE

The long, sweeping slopes of this dormant 4460m volcano, named after Cortés' indigenous lover and interpreter, dominate the skyline northeast of Puebla.

The main route to the summit is from Hwy 136; turn southwest at the 'Centro Vacacional Malintzi' sign. Before you reach the center, you must register at the entrance of the **Parque Nacional La Malintzi** (✿ 24hr).

Centro Vacacional IMSS Malintzi (☎ 246-462-40-98, in Mexico City 55-5639-5698) has cabins (weekday/weekend US$40/46 up to six people, or US$65/75 up to nine people). This resort, run by the Mexican Social Security Institute, has woodsy grounds and fine views of the peak. Cabins come with fireplaces, kitchens and basic accommodations. The center charges US$1 per person for day visits. Those not staying at the center can park here for US$3.

Not far above the center, the road becomes impassable by car. Then it's 1km by footpath, through trees initially, on to a

ridge from where it's an arduous five-hour round-trip hike to the top. Hikers should take precautions against altitude sickness (see p989). La Malinche is snowcapped only a few weeks each year.

There are buses (8am, noon and 4pm) to the Centro Vacacional (US$1, three daily) from downtown Apizaco, at the corner of Av Hidalgo and Aquiles Serdán, in front of the Comex store. Apizaco can be reached via frequent buses from Tlaxcala, Huamantla or Puebla.

HUAMANTLA

☎ 247 / pop 44,000 / elevation 2500m

This quaint town dates from 1534 and is a national historic monument. Two of the most notable buildings are the 16th-century **Ex-Convento de San Francisco** and the 17th-century baroque **Parroquia de San Luis Obispo de Tolosa**. The **Museo de Títere** (☎ 472-10-33; Parque Juárez 15; ✿ 10am-2pm & 4-7pm Tue-Sat, 10am-3pm Sun), the national puppet museum, opposite the church, is a fun stop for the young at heart.

During the first couple of weeks of August, Huamantla celebrates its annual **feria**. The day before the feast of the Assumption (August 15), locals cover the town's streets with beautiful carpets made of flowers and colored sawdust. The Saturday following this event, there is a 'running of the bulls,' similar to that in Pamplona, Spain – but much more dangerous, because there is nothing to hide behind and the bulls charge from two directions!

Rates nearly double during Huamantla's feria, for which rooms are booked well in advance.

Hotel Mesón del Portal (☎ 472-26-26; Parque Juárez 9; s/d US$15/20) Facing the central plaza, this basic place has cheery rooms with cable TV.

Hotel Cuamanco (☎ 472-22-09; Carretera 136, Km 146.5; s/d US$15/19) A couple of kilometers east of town, this surprisingly tasteful three-star motel has 20 clean, sizable rooms, some of which have balconies overlooking the surrounding fields.

Oro and Suriano run frequent buses from Puebla and ATAH runs frequent buses from Tlaxcala.

PUEBLA

☎ 222 / pop 1.35 million / elevation 2162m

Few Mexican cities preserve the Spanish imprint as faithfully as Puebla. There are more

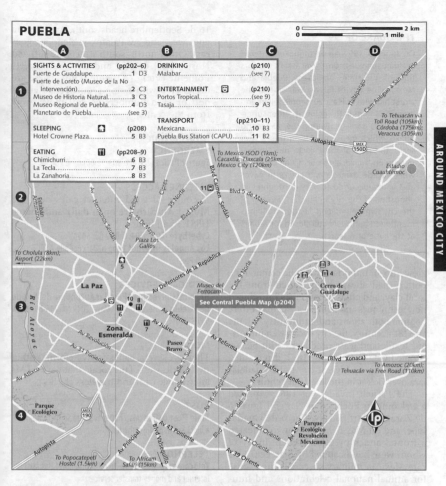

PUEBLA

SIGHTS & ACTIVITIES	(pp202–6)	**DRINKING**	(p210)
Fuerte de Guadalupe	1 D3	Malabar	(see 7)
Fuerte de Loreto (Museo de la No			
Intervención)	2 C3	**ENTERTAINMENT**	(p210)
Museo de Historia Natural	3 C3	Portos Tropical	(see 9)
Museo Regional de Puebla	4 D3	Tasaja	9 A3
Planetario de Puebla	(see 3)		
		TRANSPORT	(pp210–11)
SLEEPING	(p208)	Mexicana	10 B3
Hotel Crowne Plaza	5 B3	Puebla Bus Station (CAPU)	11 B2
EATING	(pp208–9)		
Chimichurri	6 B3		
La Tecla	7 B3		
La Zanahoria	8 B3		

AROUND MEXICO CITY

---

than 70 churches and, in the historic central area alone, a thousand colonial buildings – many adorned with the *azulejos* (painted ceramic tiles) for which the city is famous. The Centro Histórico was inscribed by Unesco as a World Heritage Site in 1987. Located on the Veracruz–Mexico City route, and set in a broad valley with Popocatépetl and Iztaccíhuatl rising to the west, Puebla has always played a leading role in national affairs.

Strongly Catholic, *criollo* and conservative, its people *(poblanos)* maintained Spanish affinities longer than most in Mexico. In the 19th century their patriotism was regarded as suspect, and today Puebla's Spanish-descended families have a reputation among other Mexicans for snobbishness. Nevertheless, it's a lively city with much to see and do. The historic center, where a great deal of conservation and restoration has taken place, has a prosperous modern dimension too, with its share of fancy boutiques. The Cerro de Guadalupe is a peaceful retreat from city noises, as well as the site of a celebrated Mexican military victory and a clutch of museums.

History

Founded by Spanish settlers in 1531 as Ciudad de los Ángeles with the aim of surpassing the nearby pre-Hispanic religious center of Cholula, the city became known as Puebla de los Ángeles eight years later and quickly

THE QUAKE OF '99

On June 15, 1999, an earthquake centered in Huajuapan de León, Oaxaca, sent tremors through the states of Oaxaca, Puebla and México. The city of Puebla was one of the worst hit, with at least 20 people killed and many buildings in the colonial center suffering serious damage. During the 40-second quake, which measured 6.9 on the Richter scale, the roof of the Palacio del Ayuntamiento on the zócalo's north side caved in, while façade damage and cracks in naves and vaults occurred to varying degrees in almost all of the city's churches. Several of the city's museums and historic buildings mentioned here were still closed for repairs at the time of research.

grew into an important Catholic center. Fine pottery had always been crafted from the local clay, and after the colonists introduced new techniques and materials, Puebla pottery became both an art and an industry. By the late 18th century, the city became an important textile and glass producer. With 50,000 people living in Puebla by 1811, it remained Mexico's second-biggest city until Guadalajara overtook it in the late 19th century.

The French invaders of 1862 expected a welcome in Puebla, but General Ignacio de Zaragoza fortified the Cerro de Guadalupe, and on May 5, his 2000 men defeated a frontal attack by 6000 French, many of whom were handicapped by diarrhea. This rare Mexican military success is the excuse for annual national celebrations and hundreds of streets named in honor of Cinco de Mayo. No one seems to remember that the following year the reinforced French took Puebla and occupied the city until 1867.

Orientation

At the city's center is the spacious, shady zócalo, with the cathedral on its south side. The majority of places to stay, eat and visit are within a few blocks of here. The area of smart, modern restaurants and shops along Av Juárez, 2km west of the zócalo, is known as the Zona Esmeralda.

The crucial intersection for the complicated naming system of Puebla's grid plan of streets is the northwest corner of the zócalo. From here, Av 5 de Mayo goes north, Av

16 de Septiembre heads south, Av Reforma goes west and Av Palafox y Mendoza goes east. Other north–south streets are suffixed Norte (Nte) or Sur, and west–east streets Poniente (Pte) or Oriente (Ote). These are designated with rising sequences of either odd or even numbers as you move away from the center.

Information

EMERGENCY
Tourist Police (☎ 800-903-92-00)

INTERNET ACCESS
A couple of good Internet cafés near the Museo Amparo are open daily and charge US$1.35 an hour.
Cyberbyte (Map p204; Calle 2 Sur 505B)
Los Angeles Internet (Map p204; cnr Calle 2 Sur & Av 9 Pte)

MEDICAL SERVICES
Hospital Universidad Popular Autónoma del Estado de Puebla (Hospital UPAEP; Map p204; ☎ 246-60-99; Av 5 Pte 715)

MONEY
There are several banks on Av Reforma within two blocks west of the zócalo that have ATMs and change cash and travelers checks.

POST
Main Post Office (Map p204; Av 16 de Septiembre) Half a block south of the cathedral.

TELEPHONE
Telecomm (Map p204; Av 16 de Septiembre) Has fax, Internet and money transfer services.

TOURIST INFORMATION
Municipal Tourist Office (Map p204; ☎ 246-18-90; www.puebla.gob.mx in Spanish; Portal Hidalgo 14; ☺ 9am-8pm Mon-Fri, 9am-5pm Sat & Sun) Friendly, English-speaking office conveniently located on the zócalo's north side.
State Tourist Office (Map p204; ☎ 246-12-85; www.turismopuebla.com.mx in Spanish; Av 5 Ote 3; ☺ 9am-8:30pm Mon-Sat, 9am-2pm Sun) Faces the cathedral yard. Staffed by English speakers.

Sights

ZÓCALO   Map p204
Puebla's central plaza was a marketplace where hangings, bullfights and theater took place before it acquired its current garden-

like appearance in 1854. The nearby arcades date from the 16th century. The plaza fills with entertainers (mostly clowns) on Sunday evening, when Restaurant Royalty's street-side tables (p208) are especially popular.

CATEDRAL   Map p204

The cathedral, whose image appears on the 500 peso bill, occupies the entire block south of the zócalo. It blends severe Herreresque-Renaissance style and early baroque. Building began in 1550 but most of it took place under bishop Juan de Palafox in the 1640s. At 69m the towers are the country's highest. The cathedral's bells are celebrated in the traditional rhyme *Para mujeres y campanas, las poblanas* – 'For women and bells, Puebla's (are best).'

CASA DE LA CULTURA   Map p204

Occupying the entire block facing the south side of the cathedral, the former bishop's palace is a classic 17th-century brick-and-tile building that now houses government offices, including the state tourist office and the **Casa de la Cultura** (☎ 232-12-27; Av 5 Ote 5; ☑ 10am-8pm). In the courtyard are a nice café and a good bookstore. The bulletin boards in Casa de la Cultura's hallways are a great place to find announcements for local musical and theater events. Upstairs is the **Biblioteca Palafoxiana** (☎ 246-31-86; www .bpm.gob.mx in Spanish; ☑ 10am-5pm Tue-Sun), with thousands of rare books, including the 1493

Nuremberg Chronicle with more than 2000 engravings.

MUSEO AMPARO   Map p204

This excellent modern **museum** (☎ 246-42-10; Calle 2 Sur 708; adult/student US$1.50/0.75, free Mon; ☑ 10am-6pm Wed-Mon), housed in two linked colonial buildings, is a must-see. The first has eight rooms with superb pre-Hispanic artifacts, which are well displayed with explanations (in English and Spanish) of their production techniques, regional and historical context, and anthropological significance. Crossing to the second building, you enter a series of rooms rich with the finest art and furnishings from the colonial period from all over Mexico.

An audiovisual system (headset rental US$1) offers information about the pre-Hispanic area in Spanish, English, French, German and Japanese. Two-hour guided group tours are offered in English (US$23) on request, and free 1½ hour tours are given at noon on Sunday. The museum has a library, a cafeteria, Talavera gift shop and a good bookstore.

MUSEO POBLANO DE ARTE
VIRREINAL   Map p204

Inaugurated in 1999, this top-notch **museum** (☎ 246-58-58; Calle 4 Nte 203; admission US$1.50, incl Museo Casa del Alfeñique; ☑ 10am-5pm Tue-Sun) is housed in the 17th-century Hospital de San Pedro (the galleries were once wings of the

---

PUEBLA ARTS

Alfeñique & Poblano Architecture

In the 17th century, local tiles – some in Arabic designs – began to be used to fine effect on Puebla church domes and, with red brick, on Puebla façades. In the 18th century, *alfeñique* – elaborate white stucco ornamentation named after a candy made from egg whites and sugar – became popular. Throughout the colonial period, the local gray stone was carved into a variety of forms to embellish many buildings. Also notable is the local indigenous influence, best seen in the prolific stucco decoration of buildings such as the Capilla del Rosario in Puebla's Templo de Santo Domingo (p205) and the Tonantzintla village church of Templo de Santa María (p215).

Talavera Tiles

Puebla's colorful hand-painted ceramics, known as Talavera (after a town in Spain), take many forms – plates, cups, vases, fountains and tiles. Designs show Asian, Spanish-Arabic and Mexican indigenous influences. Before the conquest, Cholula was the region's most important town, and it had artistic influence from the Mixtecs to the south. The colorful glazed Mixteca–Cholula–Puebla pottery was the finest in the land when the Spanish arrived; Moctezuma, it was said, would eat off no other. Today, the finest Puebla pottery of all is the white ware called *majolica*.

AROUND MEXICO CITY

CENTRAL PUEBLA

INFORMATION		
Banamex (ATM)................................1	B3	
Banamex (ATM)................................2	B2	
Bancomer (ATM)........................(see 1)		
Banorte (ATM)...........................(see 5)		
Cyberbyte..3	B3	
Hospital UPAEP...............................4	A2	
HSBC (ATM).....................................5	B2	
HSBC (ATM).....................................6	B3	
Los Angeles Internet.......................7	B3	
Municipal Tourist Office..................8	B3	
Plazuela de los Sapos.....................9	B3	
Post Office....................................10	B3	
State Tourist Office.......................11	B3	

SIGHTS & ACTIVITIES	(pp202–6)	
Barrio del Artista..........................12	C3	
Biblioteca Palafoxiana..............(see 13)		
Casa de la Cultura.........................13	B3	
Casa de los Muñecos......................14	B3	
Catedral..15	B3	
Ex-Convento de Santa Monica...16	C1	
Ex-Convento de Santa Rosa.........17	B1	
Iglesia de la Compañía..................18	C3	
Museo Amparo...............................19	B3	
Museo Bello...................................20	B2	
Museo Casa del Alfeñique.............21	C3	
Museo de Arte Popular		
Poblano...............................(see 17)		
Museo de la Revolución...............22	C2	
Museo Poblano de Arte Virreinal.23	C3	
Teatro Principal............................24	C3	
Templo de San Francisco..............25	D2	
Templo de Santo Domingo............26	B2	
Trolley Tour of Puebla..............(see 72)		

SLEEPING 🛏	(pp206–8)	
Gilfer Hotel...................................27	B3	
Gran Hotel San Agustín.................28	A2	
Hotel Aristos.................................29	A2	
Hotel Colonial...............................30	B3	
Hotel del Portal............................31	B3	
Hotel Imperial..............................32	C2	
Hotel Lastra..................................33	D1	
Hotel Palace..................................34	B3	
Hotel Posada San Pedro................35	B3	
Hotel Puebla Plaza........................36	B3	
Hotel Real del Parián....................37	C3	
Hotel Royalty...............................38	B3	
Hotel San Miguel..........................39	A2	
Hotel Teresita...............................40	A3	
Hotel Virreyes...............................41	A2	
Mesón Sacristía de		
Capuchinas........................42	C3	
Mesón Sacristía de la		
Compañía..........................43	C3	

EATING 🍴	(pp208–9)	
Café Aroma...................................44	A2	
Café Plaza.....................................45	B3	
El Santuario Restaurant.........(see 42)		
El Vegetariano..............................46	A2	
Fonda de Santa Clara....................47	A2	
Fonda de Santa Clara....................48	B3	
Fonda La Mexicana........................49	B3	
Food Court....................................50	B2	
La Poblana....................................51	B3	
La Poblanita & Late-Night Food		
Stands...................................52	B3	
La Zanahoria.................................53	B3	
Restaurant La Princesa.................54	B3	

Restaurant Royalty..................(see 38)		
Restaurant Sacristía.................(see 43)		
Sanborns......................................55	B2	
Super Tortas Puebla......................56	A3	
Tacos Tony....................................57	B3	
Tepoznieves..................................58	B3	
VIPS..59	B3	
Vittorio's......................................60	B3	

DRINKING 🍷	(p209)	
La Batalla.....................................61	C3	
La Bella..62	B3	
La Boveda................................(see 62)		
La Serenata..................................63	B3	

ENTERTAINMENT 🎭	(p210)	
Casanova Bar................................64	C3	
El Convento de las Carolinas		
Café.....................................65	C3	
La Bella Epoca/Xperimental.........66	B3	
Librería Cafetería Teorema...........67	A2	

SHOPPING 🛍	(p210)	
Barrio de Analco...........................68	C3	
El Parián Crafts Market.................69	C3	
La Central.....................................70	C2	
Patio de los Geranios...............(see 13)		
Talavera Uriarte...........................71	A2	

TRANSPORT	(pp210–11)	
Buses to Africam Safari.................72	B3	
Buses to Cerro de Guadalupe &		
CAPU....................................73	C3	
Colectivos to CAPU........................74	A2	
Colectivos to Cholula...................75	A1	

Parque
Ecológico
Revolución
Mexicana

hospital). One gallery displays temporary exhibits on the art of the vice-regal period (16th to 19th centuries); another has temporary exhibits of contemporary Mexican art; and the last houses a fascinating permanent exhibit on the hospital's history, including a fine model of the building. There's also a library and an excellent bookstore, with many art and architecture books in English.

CASA DE LOS MUÑECOS   Map p204
The tiles on the House of Puppets on Calle 2 Nte, near the zócalo's northeast corner, caricature the city fathers who took the house's owner to court because his home was taller than theirs. Inside is the **Museo Universitario** (☎ 246-28-99; Calle 2 Nte 2; admission US$0.50; ✆ 10am-5pm Tue-Sun), which tells the story of education in Puebla.

IGLESIA DE LA COMPAÑÍA   Map p204
This **Jesuit church** (cnr Av Palafox y Mendoza & Calle 4 Sur) with a 1767 Churrigueresque façade is also called Espíritu Santo. Beneath the altar is a tomb said to be that of a 17th-century Asian princess who was sold into slavery in Mexico and later freed. She was supposedly responsible for the colorful China Poblana costume – a shawl, frilled blouse, embroidered skirt, and gold and silver adornments. This costume became a kind of 'peasant chic' in the 19th century. But *china* also meant maidservant, and the style may have come from Spanish peasant costumes.

One of the building's towers fractured and a cupola collapsed during the 1999 earthquake. Next door the 16th-century **Edificio Carolino**, now the main building of Universidad Autónoma de Puebla, was also severely damaged by the quake.

MUSEO CASA DEL ALFEÑIQUE   Map p204
This **house** (☎ 232-42-96; Av 4 Ote 416; admission US$1.50, incl Museo Poblano de Arte Virreinal; ✆ 10am-5pm Tue-Sun) is an outstanding example of the 18th-century decorative style *alfeñique*. The museum exhibits 18th- and 19th-century Puebla household paraphernalia such as China Poblana gear, paintings and furniture.

TEATRO PRINCIPAL & BARRIO DEL ARTISTA   Map p204
The **theater** (☎ 232-60-85; Av 8 Ote at Av 6 Nte; ✆ 10am-5pm) dates from 1759, making it one of the oldest in the Americas – sort of. It

went up in flames in 1902 and was rebuilt in the 1930s. You can go inside only if it's not in use. Nearby is the **Barrio del Artista** (Calle 8 Nte, btwn Aves 4 Nte & 6 Nte), which has open studios where you can meet artists and buy their work.

TEMPLO DE SAN FRANCISCO   Map p204
The north doorway of the **San Francisco church** (14 Ote, east of Blvd Héroes del 5 de Mayo) is a good example of 16th-century plateresque; the tower and fine brick-and-tile façade were added in the 18th century. Structural damage occurred in the 1999 quake. In a glass case in the church's north chapel is the body of San Sebastián de Aparicio, a Spaniard who came to Mexico in 1533 and planned many of the country's roads before becoming a monk. His body attracts a stream of worshipers.

MUSEO DE LA REVOLUCIÓN   Map p204
This **house** (☎ 242-10-76; Av 6 Ote 206; admission US$1, free Tue; ✆ 10am-5pm Tue-Sun) was the scene of the first battle of the 1910 revolution. Betrayed only two days before a planned uprising against Porfirio Díaz' dictatorship, the Serdán family (Aquiles, Máximo, Carmen and Natalia) and 17 others fought 500 soldiers until only Aquiles, their leader, and Carmen were left alive. Aquiles, hidden under the floorboards, might have survived if the damp hadn't provoked a cough that gave him away. Both were subsequently killed. The house retains its bullet holes and some revolutionary memorabilia, including a room dedicated to female revolutionaries. Tours are available in Spanish, English and German.

TEMPLO DE SANTO DOMINGO   Map p204
Santo Domingo (cnr Av 5 de Mayo & Av 4 Ote) is a fine church, and its **Capilla del Rosario** (Rosary Chapel), south of the main altar, is a real gem. Built between 1650 and 1690, it has a sumptuous baroque proliferation of gilded plaster and carved stone with angels and cherubim popping out from behind every leaf. See if you can spot the heavenly orchestra.

EX-CONVENTO DE SANTA ROSA & MUSEO DE ARTE POPULAR POBLANO   Map p204
This 17th-century **ex-nunnery** (☎ 232-92-40; enter at Av 14 Pte 305; admission US$1, free Tue; ✆ 10am-5pm Tue-Sun) houses an extensive collection of

Puebla state handicrafts. You must join one of the hourly tours with a guide, who may try to rush you through the fine displays of traditional indigenous costumes, pottery, onyx, glass and metal work. Tours are in Spanish, but there are occasionally English-speaking guides available. *Mole poblano* is said to have originated in the ex-convent's kitchen (see 'Original Puebla Tastes,' p208).

MUSEO BELLO   Map p204
This **house** (Av 3 Pte 302; admission US$1.25, free Tue; ☼ 10am-5pm) is filled with the diverse art and crafts collection of a 19th-century industrialist family. There is exquisite French, English, Japanese and Chinese porcelain, and a large collection of Puebla Talavera. Tours are available in Spanish and English. This museum was closed for earthquake repairs at the time of writing.

CERRO DE GUADALUPE   Map p201
The hilltop park, 2km northeast of the zócalo, contains the historic forts of Loreto and Guadalupe and the Centro Cívico 5 de Mayo, a group of museums. Good views, relatively fresh air and eucalyptus woods add to the appeal. Take a 'Plaza de Loreto' bus (US$0.30) north on Blvd Héroes del 5 de Mayo.

The **Fuerte de Loreto**, at the west end of the hilltop, was one of the Mexican defense points on May 5, 1862, during the victory over the invading French. Today, it houses **Museo de la No Intervención** (admission US$2.75; ☼ 10am-5pm Tue-Sun), which has displays of uniforms and documents relating to the French occupation of Mexico.

A short walk east of the fort, beyond the domed auditorium, are the **Museo Regional de Puebla** (☎ 235-97-20; admission US$3; ☼ 10am-5pm Tue-Sun), which traces human history in the state; **Museo de Historia Natural** (☎ 235-34-19; admission US$2; ☼ 10am-5pm Tue-Sun); and the pyramid-shaped **Planetario de Puebla** (☎ 235-20-99; admission US$2.50), which shows IMAX movies as well as light shows. At the east end of the hilltop is **Fuerte de Guadalupe** (admission US$2.75; ☼ 9am-6pm Tue-Sun), which also played a part in the 1862 battle.

Tours
The **State Tourist Office** (p202) operates trolley tours (US$3.25) of the Centro Histórico that depart every half hour daily except Monday from the zócalo's south side.

Festivals & Events
Starting in late April, the month-long **Feria de Puebla** celebrates the state's cultural and economic achievements, while in June the **Festival del Mole Poblano** fetes culinary triumphs at several of the city's storied eateries.

Sleeping
Despite Puebla's abundance of hotels (easily recognizable by the illuminated red 'H' signs over their doors) the most economical options tend to fill up fast. Budget hotels, with six managed by the same company, are concentrated along the streets west of the cathedral. The near-monopoly diminishes competition and means that upkeep isn't always what it should be in the cheapest places. Mid-range and top-end options are much better value.

BUDGET
Hotel Teresita (Map p204; ☎ 232-70-72; Av 3 Pte 309; s/d US$17/20) The central Teresita has carpeted rooms with good beds and cable TV. Pay slightly more for one with two beds or windows facing the street.

Gran Hotel San Agustín (Map p204; ☎ 232-50-89; Av 3 Pte 531; s/d with breakfast US$19/25; **P**) A block west of Hotel Teresita, the San Agustín has a cheap restaurant and small, rather stuffy rooms with TVs and unreliable fluorescent lighting.

Hotel San Miguel (Map p204; ☎ 242-48-60; Av 3 Pte 721; s/d US$21/28) Just up the street from the San Agustín, the San Miguel has 65 clean, respectably sized rooms with TVs. Parking is unavailable, but you're entitled to a discount at a garage on the next block.

Hotel Virreyes (Map p204; ☎ 242-48-68; Av 3 Pte 912; s/d US$9/11, with bathroom US$14/18; **P**) The Virreyes is a bit rundown and not entirely bug-free, but unfortunately it's the center's best ultra-budget option. It has large, clean rooms with wood-beamed ceilings along two wide balconies.

Hotel Real del Parián (Map p204; ☎ 246-19-68; Av 2 Ote 601; s/d/tr US$12/14/20) Just south of the Parián crafts market, this friendly place may be brightly painted but the large rooms are rough around the edges. If possible, choose a room with a balcony; the interior rooms are stuffier. There's a laundry sink on the roof and a bar with a loud jukebox downstairs.

Popocatepétl Hostel (☎ 892-29-31/32, in Mexico City 55-5396-6988; www.hostelsofmexico.net in Spanish;

Calle 3 A Sur 5946, Colonia El Cerrito; dm/d US$9.50/17; 🖳) This new full-service HI affiliate is several kilometers south of the center but is reachable on public transit. From the bus station, walk three blocks on Blvd Norte to Plaza Los Gallos, then catch bus No 31 for a 20-minute ride to Villa Encantada and walk along Encino for a few minutes.

MID-RANGE

Hotel Colonial (Map p204; ☎ 246-41-99, 800-013-00-00; www.colonial.com.mx; Calle 4 Sur 105; s/d/tr/f US$41/50/58/64; 🖳) Facing the university, this well-run hotel has 70 lovely rooms. Originally part of a Jesuit monastery, the hotel retains a hearty colonial atmosphere despite extensive renovations. Most rooms are big and tiled, many have bathtubs and all have TVs and phones. Half of the rooms have colonial décor and half are modern – upstairs exterior rooms are best. There's a coin-op laundry and great sunset views on the roof, plus free WiFi Internet access on the top floor – perfect excuses to ask for a ride in the antique 1895 French elevator. This hotel is often full of foreign exchange students, so reserve ahead.

Hotel Imperial (Map p204; ☎ 242-49-80, 800-874-49-80; www.travelbymexico.com/pueb/imperial in Spanish; Av 4 Ote 212; s/d US$30/43, executive s/d US$35/48; 🅿 🖳) The Imperial caters to your every need, offering free basic breakfast and dinner, laundry service, a business center, a pool table and *golfito* (a two-hole golf course). Of the 65 comfortable rooms, the Imperial charges more for stylish carpeted units in the newer 'executive' wing.

Hotel Puebla Plaza (Map p204; ☎ 246-31-75, 800-926-2703; www.hotelpueblaplaza.com in Spanish; Av 5 Pte 111; s/d US$30/44; 🅿) Just west of the cathedral, this attractively remodeled hotel offers rooms with wood-beamed ceilings, colonial-style furniture, tiled baths and TVs.

Hotel Royalty (Map p204; ☎ 242-47-40, 800-638-99-99; www.hotelr.com in Spanish; Portal Hidalgo 8; s/d/ste US$41/53/67-74) Facing the zócalo's north side, the 45-room Royalty is another friendly, well-kept colonial-style place. The carpeted rooms are colorful and comfortable, and all are blessed with satellite TV.

Hotel Aristos (Map p204; ☎ 232-05-65; www.aristos hotels.com; Av Reforma 533; r from US$69; 🅿 ❌ 🈂) This big, fancy five-star place has a spa, gym, sauna and heated pool. The 152 user-friendly rooms aren't particularly spacious,

but rates drop to around US$45 from Friday to Sunday.

Gilfer Hotel (Map p204; ☎ 246-06-11; www.gilfer hotel.com.mx; Av 2 Ote 11; s/d/ste US$39/53/71; 🅿 🖳) The modern, central Gilfer caters to business travelers, offering 92 comfortable rooms with satellite TV, phones and safes.

Hotel Palace (Map p204; ☎ 232-24-30; www.travel bymexico.com/pueb/palace; Av 2 Ote 13; s/d US$38/50) Next door to the Gilfer, this is yet another pleasant and centrally located business traveler favorite. The 60 recently remodeled rooms have cable TV and parking costs US$4 extra.

Hotel del Portal (Map p204; ☎ 246-02-11; fax 232-31-94; Palafox y Mendoza 205; s/d US$41/50, with balcony US$44/55) This outwardly colonial hotel, half a block east of the zócalo, has a modern interior. The 100 rooms on offer are modest but well-appointed – the exterior ones with balconies merit the extra cash.

TOP END

Mesón Sacristía de Capuchinas (Map p204; ☎ 232-80-88, in Mexico 800-712-40-28, in the US 877-278-80-18; www.mesones-sacristia.com in Spanish; Av 9 Ote 16; r US$160-200; 🅿) The stylish renovation of an aristocratic 16th-century residence near the Museo Amparo resulted in this delightful antique-meets-avant-garde hideaway where everyone is treated like royalty. The décor in the six spacious suites is simple yet elegant, the high-vaulted ceilings are wood beamed, and, since the owners are antique dealers, all furnishings are for sale. Its 30-seat, reservation-only **El Santuario Restaurant** delivers contemporary takes on classic international cuisine; breakfast in bed (included in rates) is divine.

Mesón Sacristía de la Compañía (Map p204; ☎ 242-35-54, in Mexico 800-712-40-28, in the US 877-278-80-18; www.mesones-sacristia.com in Spanish; Calle 6 Sur 304; r US$160-200; 🅿) In the heart of the charming Barrio de los Sapos, this 18th-century retreat blends modern comfort with rustic colonial splendor. The small but splendid rooms and spacious suites are furnished with dramatic antiques (all for sale) such as wooden prison doors. Downstairs, there's an intimate piano bar, Talavera salon and the fine Restaurant Sacristía (see p209) serving typical poblano cuisine. The only possible drawback is the typical live music that plays in the courtyard until late. Rates include breakfast, and service is attentive and personalized.

Hotel Posada San Pedro (Map p204; ☎ 246-50-77, 800-712-28-08; Av 2 Ote 202; r/ste US$91/134; P 🏊) A block off the zócalo, this tastefully decorated hotel has a restaurant, bar and quiet courtyard. The 76 large rooms are comfortable if not elegant and special rates often start around US$65, including breakfast.

Hotel Lastra (Map p204; ☎ 235-97-55; Calz de los Fuertes 2633; r from US$79; P) The 51-room Lastra, 2km northeast of the zócalo on Cerro de Guadalupe, boasts a peaceful location, good views, easy parking and a pleasant garden. Rooms come in various shapes and sizes but all are comfortable.

Hotel Crowne Plaza (Map p201; ☎ 248-60-55, 800-226-76-00; www.crowneplazapuebla.com.mx; Blvd Serdán 141; r/ste from US$182/214; P ✖ 🖥 🏊) Geared toward business travelers, this luxury chain property is 3km northwest of the center. Its 216 clean, well-appointed rooms surround a courtyard pool.

Eating

Half the pleasure of eating here is having a wander around the sidewalk tables, browsing the menus and seeing what catches your fancy.

RESTAURANTS
Near the Zócalo

Restaurant La Princesa (Map p204; ☎ 232-11-95; Portal Juárez 101; mains US$2-7) This no-frills dining hall on the zócalo's west side is packed at lunchtime thanks to its five-course set meals (US$6) and fresh tropical fruit drinks.

Vittorio's (Map p204; ☎ 232-79-00; Morelos 106; mains US$5-15) This Italian-run restaurant is one of the zócalo's culinary highlights. The pizzas are good, there's sidewalk seating and staff claim to have Mexico's biggest collection of knives.

Restaurant Royalty (Map p204; ☎ 242-47-40; Portal Hidalgo 8; mains US$4-11) On the zócalo's north side, this smart place has a breakfast buffet and outdoor tables where you can watch the world go by for the price of a cappuccino. It also has tasty fish and meat dishes.

There are a couple of reliable coffee shops inside architecturally notable department stores just north of the zócalo:

Sanborns (Map p204; Av 2 Ote 6)

VIPS (Map p204; Calle 2 Nte 8)

Zona Esmeralda

The upscale stretch of Av Juárez between Paseo Bravo and the La Paz area has lots of slick, international-style restaurants.

La Tecla (Map p201; ☎ 246-60-66; Av Juárez 1909; mains US$4-8; ⏰ 1:30pm-2am Mon-Sat, 1:30-6pm Sun) Near Calle 21 Sur, La Tecla offers an enticing array of *alta cocina mexicana* in a stylish setting. Try the *filete tecla*, a tender steak with a white *huitlacoche* (corn smut fungus) sauce and graced with Roquefort cheese.

ORIGINAL PUEBLA TASTES

Mole poblano, which is found on almost every Puebla menu and imitated throughout Mexico, is a spicy sauce with a pinch of chocolate usually served over turkey (pavo or guajolote) or chicken – a real taste sensation if well prepared. Supposedly invented by Sor (Sister) Andrea de la Asunción of the Convento de Santa Rosa for a viceroy's visit, it traditionally contains fresh chile, chipotle (smoked, dried jalapeño), pepper, peanuts, almonds, cinnamon, aniseed, tomato, onion, garlic and, of course, chocolate.

A seasonal Puebla dish, available in July, August and September, is chiles en nogada, said to have been created in 1821 to honor Agustín de Iturbide, the first ruler of independent Mexico. Its colors are those of the national flag: large green chilies stuffed with dried fruit and meat are covered with a creamy white walnut sauce and sprinkled with red pomegranate seeds.

A substantial poblano snack is the cemita, a sesame roll filled with beef or pork and/or chiles rellenos or white cheese and seasoned with the essential herb pápalo…sort of a super torta.

Camotes are sticks of sweetened sweet potato paste flavored with various fruits. You can also buy sweet potatoes in a different form from Puebla's distinctive camote vendors. They wheel around a wood-burning stove with an ear-shattering whistle not unlike a steam engine. Inside are roasted sweet potatoes and plantains that you can eat plain or garnished with sugar and lechera (sweetened condensed milk).

From March through June keep an eye out for escamoles (ant larvae) and gusanos de maguey (maguey worms) – once ingested, they can be a savory surprise.

Chimichurri (Map p201; ☎ 249-15-34; cnr Calle 27 Sur & Av Juárez; mains US$5-20; ☯ 1:30pm-2am Mon Sat, 1:30-6pm Sun) This sleek Argentine bar-restaurant with live piano music specializes in big steaks and pastas.

POBLANO SPECIALTIES
Centro Comercial La Victoria's upper-level **food court** (Map p204) is a cheap place to sample Puebla specialties like mole and *cha-lupas* (tostada topped with meat, chilies, beans, cheese…whatever!) in a market-style setting. At night don't miss the opportunity to sample authentic snacks at food stands like **La Poblanita** (Av 5 Pte at Av 16 de Septiembre; mains US$1), where *huitlacoche* and a dozen other authentic *gordita* fillings are available until midnight.

Restaurant Sacristía (Map p204; ☎ 242-45-13; Calle 6 Sur 304; mains US$6-8; ☯ 8am-11:30pm Mon-Sat, 8am-6pm Sun) The award-winning restaurant in the delightful colonial patio of the Mesón Sacristía de la Compañía (see p207) is an elegant place for a cocktail in the intimate Confesionario bar or a meal of authentic poblano cuisine. Live traditional music begins nightly at 9pm.

Fonda de Santa Clara (Map p204; ☎ 242-26-59, Calle 3 Pte 307; mains US$6-10; ☯ 8am-10pm; P) This tour group favorite is a popular place to try typical poblano food. Standbys include chicken mole and enchiladas. Note that the *mixiote* (lamb stew served with guacamole) is cooked in bundles of wax paper, rather than the customary maguey-leaf – indicative of how tradition is falling by the wayside. Service is friendly but brisk and the menu is bilingual. There's another **branch** (Map p204; ☎ 246-19-52; Calle 3 Pte 920) a bit further from the center with the same menu and a more festive atmosphere.

Fonda La Mexicana (Map p204; ☎ 232-67-47; Av 16 de Septiembre 706; mains US$4-8; ☯ 10am-8pm) This unassuming restaurant serves a great *mole poblano* plus a US$4 set lunch and other good-value Puebla specialties.

La Poblana (Map p204; Av 7 Ote 17; mains US$1-2; ☯ 10am-6pm) Around the corner from Museo Amparo, this cubbyhole dishes up authentic Puebla *cemitas* (see 'Original Puebla Tastes,' opposite) in a dozen varieties.

VEGETARIAN
El Vegetariano (Map p204; ☎ 246-54-62; Av 3 Pte 525; mains US$2-4; ☯ 7:30am-9pm) The nonsmoking Vegetariano has a decent set lunch, Sunday buffet and lengthy menu of meatless dishes like chiles rellenos, *nopales rellenos* (stuffed cactus paddles) and *enchiladas suizas,* all of which come with salad, soup and a drink. Its sister restaurant, **La Zanahoría** (Map p204; Av 5 Ote 206), has the same menu and hours. There's another branch on Av Juárez in the Zona Esmerelda.

CHEAP EATS & SNACKS
Tacos Tony (Map p204; Av 3 Pte 149; tacos US$1-2; ☯ 9am-9pm) Follow your nose to get a *pan árabe* taco (with pita bread instead of tortillas), stuffed with seasoned pork sliced from a trio of enormous grilling cones.

Super Tortas Puebla (Map p204; ☎ 298-25-05; Av 3 Pte 311; tortas US$1.50-3) The tabletops at this place are set with dishes of marinated chilies, carrots and onions to spice up your super sandwich. Call for delivery.

Tepoznieves (Map p204; Av 3 Pte at Calle 3 Sur; mains US$1.50-2.50) Puebla's top traditional ice-cream shop features free samples for the asking and a long list of exotic, must-try flavors like fig with mezcal and mango with chili.

Café Aroma (Map p204; ☎ 232-60-77; Av 3 Pte 520; mains from US$1; ☯ 9am-9pm Mon-Sat) Opposite El Vegetariano, this is the spot for good coffee and light snacks. Beans are roasted on-site and sold in bulk. There are only six tables and they're usually occupied.

Café Plaza (Map p204; ☎ 237-25-05; Av 3 Pte 145; mains US$3-7; ☯ 8am-9pm) Just off the zócalo, this café serves light meals and also brews a mean cup of java from a fresh-ground blend of Coatepec, Sierra de Puebla and Chiapas beans.

Drinking
At night, mariachis lurk around **Callejón de los Sapos** – Calle 6 Sur between Avs 3 and 7 Ote – but they are being crowded out by the bars on nearby **Plazuela de los Sapos**. Tables at these bars, especially **La Bella** (Map p204), are crowded every night of the week. Many of these become live music venues after dark (also see following Live Music section). **La Batalla** (Map p204) favors karaoke and thumping dance music, while **La Boveda** (Map p204) and **La Serenata** (Map p204), a large hall with a good sound system, feature rock 'n' roll bands. The best bet is to wander around, compare the two-for-one drink specials and see what gets your booty shaking.

Malabar (Map p201; ☎ 248-55-39; cnr Av Juárez & Chipilo; cover US$5, women free after 7:30pm) In the Zona Esmeralda, the slick Malabar offers ladies free drinks on Wednesday from 8pm to 9:30pm.

Entertainment

Check with the tourist offices and Casa de la Cultura for the latest scoop on cultural events. You can pick up the weekly *La Vagonera* (US$1) food and entertainment guide at a tourist office.

LIVE MUSIC

Librería Cafeteria Teorema (Map p204; ☎ 242-10-14; Av Reforma 540; cover US$2) This bookstore-cum-café fills up in the evenings with a mixed arty/student/professor crowd. There's a variety of live music most nights from 9:30pm to 1am.

El Convento de las Carolinas Café (Map p204; ☎ 242-76-53; Av 3 Ote 403; cover US$1-2) This intimate café near Callejón de los Sapos serves up live jazz, folk, blues…and karaoke just to keep things interesting. Popular with students from the nearby university.

La Bella Epoca/Xperimental (Map p204; Av 5 Ote 209; cover US$2) Hosts live music most nights, ranging from dub, reggae and drum-n-bass to Gothic and live metal.

Casanova Bar (Map p204; ☎ 246-42-37; Av 3 Ote 615A) This cellar-like bar-café used to host live music but was undergoing a transformation during our last visit that seemed to suggest that it would emerge as a slick disco/nightclub.

NIGHTCLUBS

In the **Zona Esmeralda**, there are a number of cinemas, trendy discos and *antros* (music bars) on Av Juárez near Blvd Norte. Current Friday and Saturday night hotspots include the disco **Tasaja** (Map p201; ☎ 249-56-06; Av Juárez 2921; no cover) and **Portos Tropical** (Map p201; cover US$2-3) next door for salsa and merengue; these places get going after 9pm.

Shopping

Quite a few shops along Av 18 Pte, west of Ex-Convento de Santa Mónica, sell pretty Puebla ceramics. The big pieces are expensive, delicate and difficult to transport, but you can buy a smaller hand-painted Talavera tile for US$3 to US$5, or a plate for approximately US$10.

Talavera Uriarte (Map p204; ☎ 232-15-98; Av 4 Pte 911; www.uriartetalavera.com.mx; ☺ 9am-6pm Mon-Fri, 10am-5pm Sat, 11am-4pm Sun) Few Talavera shops make pottery on site anymore, but Uriarte still does, and has a factory and showroom. Free factory tours are given at 11am, noon and 1pm Monday to Friday, or earlier by appointment.

Patio del los Geranios (Map p204; Av 7 Ote side, Casa de la Cultura) Indigenous textiles and pottery can be found at this state-run handicraft shop.

El Parián crafts market (Map p204; btwn Calles 6 & 8 Nte & Avs 2 & 4 Ote) Local Talavera, onyx and trees of life are on offer, as well as the sorts of leather, jewelry and textiles that you find in other cities. Some of the work is shoddy, but there is also some good stuff and prices are reasonable.

Antique shops dominate Callejón de los Sapos, and on Sunday the Plazuela de los Sapos is the site of a lively outdoor antiques market. It's great for browsing, with a wonderful variety of old books, furniture, bric-a-brac and junk.

Also on Sunday, there is a major **market** (Map p204; Barrio de Analco, east side of Blvd Héroes del 5 de Mayo) where flowers, sweets, paintings and other items are sold.

Along Av 6 Ote east of Av 5 de Mayo, a number of shops sell traditional Puebla sweets such as *camotes* (candied sweet potato sticks) and *jamoncillos* (bars of pumpkin seed paste). Stay away if you're afraid of bees!

Getting There & Away

AIR

Aeropuerto Hermanos Serdán (PBC; ☎ 232-00-32), 22km west of Puebla on the Cholula–Huejotzingo road, has flights to/from Guadalajara and Tijuana by Aero California; to/from León and Mexico City by Aeromar; and daily to/from Mexico City and Monterrey with Aeroméxico.

BUS

Puebla's **Central de Autobuses de Puebla** (Map p201; CAPU; ☎ 249-72-11; cnr Blvds Norte & Carmen Serdán) is about 4km north of the zócalo and 1.5km off the autopista. There's a left-luggage facility, a phone office, an ATM, a tourist information kiosk, a restaurant and various shops.

Most buses to/from Puebla use Mexico City's TAPO, with half-hourly service also available to Terminal Norte. The 130km trip takes about two hours. Three bus lines have frequent services: ADO GL, a luxury service, runs direct buses every half hour (US$8.75); AU, a 2nd-class service, offers direct trips every 12 minutes (US$6.25); and Estrella Roja has 1st-class buses leaving every 20 minutes (US$7.50) and 2nd-class buses every 10 minutes (US$6.25). Estrella Roja also runs buses to Mexico City airport (US$11.50) hourly from 3am to 8pm.

There's daily service from Puebla to just about everywhere in the south and east of Mexico:

Cuernavaca Oro (US$12, 3½hr, 4 deluxe daily; US$11, 3½hr, 8 1st-class daily; US$9, hourly 2nd-class)

Oaxaca UNO (US$55, 4½hr, 1 deluxe daily); ADO GL (US$22, 2 deluxe daily; US$20, 7 1st-class daily; US$15, 3 2nd-class daily)

Tampico (US$25, 11hr, 1 deluxe daily; US$20, 11hr, 7 1st-class daily)

Tuxtla Gutiérrez UNO (US$78, 13hr, 1 deluxe daily); Cristóbal Colón (US$46, 13hr, 3 1st-class daily)

Veracruz ADO GL (US$17, 3½hr, 7 deluxe daily; US$16, 3½hr, 8 1st-class daily; US$14, 4½hr, hourly 2nd-class)

Villahermosa UNO (US$60, 8hr, 1 deluxe daily); ADO GL (US$42, 8hr, 1 deluxe daily; US$38, 8hr, 4 1st-class daily)

Xalapa (US$9, 3hr, 9 1st-class daily; US$8, hourly 2nd-class 7:15am-7:30pm)

Frequent colectivos to Cholula (US$0.50, 30 minutes) leave from the corner of Av 6 Pte and Calle 13 Nte in Puebla.

CAR & MOTORCYCLE

Puebla is 123km east of Mexico City by a fast autopista, Hwy 150D (tolls total about US$9). East of Puebla, 150D continues to Córdoba (negotiating a cloudy, winding 22km descent from the 2385m Cumbres de Maltrata en route) and Veracruz.

Getting Around

Most hotels and places of interest are within walking distance of the zócalo. From the bus station, take a taxi to the city center (US$3.25 ticket from the kiosk, US$4.25 after 10pm – beware of overpriced touts); or exit the station at the 'Autobuses Urbanos' sign and go up a ramp leading to the bridge over Blvd Norte. On the other side of the bridge, walk west (toward VIPS) and stop in front of the Chedraui supermarket. From there, you can catch a No 40 combi to Av 16 de Septiembre, four blocks south of the zócalo. The ride takes 15 to 20 minutes.

From the city center to the bus station, catch any northbound 'CAPU' colectivo from Blvd Héroes del 5 de Mayo at Av Palafox y Mendoza, three blocks east of the zócalo, or from the stop on the corner of Calle 9 Sur and Av Reforma. All city buses and colectivos cost US$0.30.

AFRICAM SAFARI

One of Mexico's best places to see both native and exotic wildlife is this drive-through safari park (☎ 281-70-00; www.africamsafari.com.mx in Spanish; Km 16.5 on road to Presa Valsequillo; adult/child US$9/8.50; ⏰ 10am-5pm). More than 3000 animals – among them rhinoceroses, bears and tigers – live in spacious 'natural' settings, and you can view them up close from within your car, a taxi or an Africam bus. It's best to visit first thing in the morning, when the animals are most active. **Estrella Roja** (☎ 273-83-00) runs daily round-trip buses from CAPU to Africam (adult/child US$12/11), including admission and a four-hour tour of the park. Similarly priced tours also depart from Puebla's zócalo from Tuesday to Sunday at 11:30am and 2:30pm (and occasionally at night).

CHOLULA

☎ 222 / pop 76,000 / elevation 2170m

Ten kilometers west of Puebla stands the widest pyramid ever built, Pirámide Tepanapa – the Great Pyramid of Cholula. By the 4th century AD, it measured 450m along each side of the base and 65m high, making it larger in volume than Egypt's Pyramid of Cheops. Now overgrown and topped by a church, it's difficult to even recognize the huge grassy mound as a pyramid. The town of Cholula is fairly unimpressive, but the University of the Americas, with many foreign students, adds a cosmopolitan touch, and there's a hearty nightlife. The nearby villages of Tonantzintla and Acatepec have splendid churches.

History

Between around AD 1 and 600, Cholula grew into an important religious center, while powerful Teotihuacán flourished 100km to the northwest. The Great Pyramid was built over several times. About AD 600, Cholula fell to the Olmeca-Xicallanca, who built nearby Cacaxtla. Sometime between AD 900 and 1300, Toltecs and/or

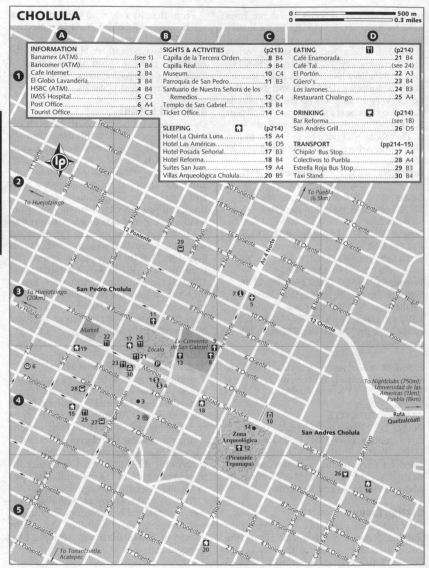

CHOLULA

INFORMATION	
Banamex (ATM)...............................(see 1)	
Bancomer (ATM)...................................**1** B4	
Cafe Internet...**2** B4	
El Globo Lavandería.............................**3** B4	
HSBC (ATM)..**4** B4	
IMSS Hospital.......................................**5** C3	
Post Office..**6** A4	
Tourist Office.......................................**7** C3	

SIGHTS & ACTIVITIES	**(p213)**
Capilla de la Tercera Orden...............**8** B4	
Capilla Real..**9** B4	
Museum...**10** C4	
Parroquia de San Pedro......................**11** B3	
Santuario de Nuestra Señora de los	
Remedios...**12** C4	
Templo de San Gabriel......................**13** B4	
Ticket Office.......................................**14** C4	

SLEEPING	**(p214)**
Hotel La Quinta Luna........................**15** A4	
Hotel Las Américas............................**16** D5	
Hotel Posada Señorial.......................**17** B3	
Hotel Reforma....................................**18** B4	
Suites San Juan..................................**19** A4	
Villas Arqueológica Cholula..............**20** B5	

EATING	**(p214)**
Café Enamorada.................................**21** B4	
Café Tal...(see 24)	
El Portón...**22** A3	
Güero's..**23** B4	
Los Jarrones......................................**24** B3	
Restaurant Chialingo.........................**25** B4	

DRINKING	**(p214)**
Bar Reforma.......................................(see 18)	
San Andrés Grill................................**26** D5	

TRANSPORT	**(pp214–15)**
'Chipilo' Bus Stop..............................**27** A4	
Colectivos to Puebla........................**28** A4	
Estrella Roja Bus Stop.......................**29** B3	
Taxi Stand..**30** B4	

Chichimecs took over, and it later fell under Aztec dominance. There was also artistic influence from the Mixtecs to the south.

By 1519 Cholula's population had reached 100,000, and the Great Pyramid was already overgrown. Cortés, having made friends with the nearby Tlaxcalans, traveled here at Moctezuma's request. Aztec warriors set an ambush, but unfortunately for them, the Tlaxcalans tipped off Cortés about the plot and the Spanish struck first. Within one day, they killed 6000 Cholulans before the city was looted by the Tlaxcalans. Cortés vowed to build a church here for each day of the year, or one on top of every pagan temple, depending on which legend you prefer.

Today there are 39 – far from 365 but still plenty for a small town.

The Spanish developed nearby Puebla to overshadow the old pagan center, and Cholula never regained its importance, especially after a severe plague in the 1540s decimated its indigenous population.

Orientation

Buses and colectivos drop passengers off two or three blocks north of the zócalo. Two long blocks to the southeast, the pyramid with its domed church on top is a clear landmark.

Information

Banks (Facing zócalo's south side) Change cash and have ATMs.

Cafe Internet (2 Sur 502; per hr US$1.50)

El Globo Lavandería (5 Ote 9; ⏰ 8:30am-3pm & 5-7pm Mon-Fri, 9am-3pm Sat) Charges around US$1 per kilo (minimum 3kg) for machine wash-and-dry.

IMSS Hospital (4 Nte btwn 10 & 12 Ote) Run by the Social Security Institute.

Tourist Office (☎ 247-31-16; cnr 12 Ote & 4 Nte; ⏰ 10am-5pm Mon-Fri, 10am-3pm Sat & Sun) Helpful office with free town maps.

Sights

ZÓCALO

The **Ex-Convento de San Gabriel** (aka Plaza de la Concordia), along the east side of Cholula's wide zócalo, includes three fine churches. On the left, as you face the ex-convent, is the Arabic-style **Capilla Real**, which dates from 1540 and has 49 domes (almost half of which were damaged during the 1999 earthquake). In the middle is the 19th-century **Capilla de la Tercera Orden**, and on the right is the **Templo de San Gabriel**, founded in 1530 on the site of a pyramid.

ZONA ARQUEOLÓGICA

Probably originally dedicated to Quetzalcóatl, Cholula's Pirámide Tepanapa is topped by the **Santuario de Nuestra Señora de los Remedios**. It's a classic symbol of conquest, but possibly an inadvertent one as the church may have been built before the Spanish knew the mound contained a pagan temple. The earthquake sent deep fractures through the church structure, but the pyramid suffered no damage. You can climb to the church by a path from the pyramid's northwest corner (no charge).

The **Zona Arqueológica** (admission US$3; ⏰ 9am-6pm Tue-Sun) comprises the excavated areas around the pyramid and the tunnels underneath. Enter via the tunnel on the north side. The small **museum** (Calz San Andrés; admission free with site ticket), across the road from the ticket office and down some steps, has the best introduction to the site – a large cutaway model of the pyramid mound showing the various superimposed structures.

Several pyramids were built on top of each other in various reconstructions. Over 8km of tunnels have been dug beneath the pyramid by archaeologists to penetrate each stage. From the tourist access tunnel, a few hundred meters long, you can see earlier layers of the building. Guides at the tunnel entrance charge around US$7 for a one-hour tour or US$3 for a 15-minute tour of just the tunnels; a few speak English. You don't need a guide to follow the tunnel through to the structures on the south and west sides of the pyramid, but they can be useful in pointing out and explaining various features as nothing is labeled.

The access tunnel emerges on the pyramid's east side, from where you can take a path around to the **Patio de los Altares** (Great Plaza) on the south side. This was the main approach to the pyramid, and it's ringed by platforms and unique diagonal stairways. Three large stone slabs on its east, north and west sides are carved in the Veracruz interlocking-scroll design. At its south end is an Aztec-style altar in a pit dating from shortly before the Spanish conquest. On the mound's west side is a reconstructed section of the latest pyramid, with two earlier exposed layers.

Tours

Trolley tours (tours US$3.50; ⏰ 11am Tue-Sun) of Cholula depart from Puebla's zócalo.

Festivals & Events

Of Cholula's many festivals, one of the most important is the **Festival de la Virgen de los Remedios**, which is celebrated the week of September 1 with daily traditional dances on the Great Pyramid. In the weeks that follow, Cholula's **regional feria** is held. On both the **spring** and **fall equinoxes**, a Quetzalcóatl ritual is reenacted in town with poetry, sacrificial dances, fireworks displays and music performed on pre-Hispanic instruments.

On **Shrove Tuesday**, masked Carnaval dancers reenact a battle between French and Mexican forces in Huejotzingo (weh-hot-*sin*-goh), 14km northwest of Cholula on Hwy 190.

Sleeping

Cholula is an easy day trip from Puebla, but there is accommodation if you'd rather stay the night.

Hotel Posada Señorial (☎ 247-03-41; Portal Guerrero 5; s/d US$29/34) In the shopping arcade off the plaza's west side, this modern retreat has large rooms with phones, TVs and rustic wooden furniture.

Suites San Juan (☎ 247-02-78; 5 Sur 103; s/d US$25/37; P) Half a block southwest of the main market, the San Juan has large, clean rooms with TVs and enormous beds; windows face a noisy street.

Hotel Las Américas (☎ 247-09-91; 14 Ote 6; s/d US$16/21; P ♨) Three blocks east of the pyramid, the sprawling 100-room Las Américas is a bit removed from the action, but offers a restaurant, a pleasant courtyard garden, and clean and comfortable rooms with private bathrooms and cable TV.

Hotel Reforma (☎ 247-01-49; s/d US$17/22; P) Midway between the zócalo and the pyramid, the Reforma is Cholula's oldest hotel. The dozen rooms are quite decent and have hot water and private bathrooms, but size and features vary. Parking costs an extra US$2.

Villa Arqueológica Cholula (☎ 273-79-00; www.clubmedvillas.com/cholula; 2 Pte 601; r Mon-Wed US$60, Thu-Sun US$69, ste US$119; P ♨) This quaint 54-room Club-Med property is within walking distance (across a few fields of flowers) of the pyramid. Rooms are simple but well done and it has lush gardens, tennis courts and a good restaurant. Nonguests can use the pool for US$5.

Hotel La Quinta Luna (☎ 247-89-15; www.laquintaluna.com; 3 Sur 702; r/ste US$141/164; P ☐) Cholula's finest hotel occupies a 17th-century mansion and blends colonial architecture with contemporary art (on sale) and modern amenities such as flat-screen TVs, DVD players and in-room Internet. The six luxurious rooms all face the garden patio, where international cuisine stars in the private restaurant.

Eating

All places on and around the zócalo are open from around 9am to midnight daily.

Café Enamorada (mains US$2-5) Facing the zócalo at Portal Guerrero's south corner, this café is one of the most popular places in town. It has live music most nights (when minimum consumption is US$8) and serves decent doses of the usual: sandwiches, tacos and quesadillas.

Los Jarrones (mains US$3-8) Underneath the plaza's attractive arcade, Los Jarrones serves set breakfasts and good-value regional dishes.

Café Tal (snacks US$2-4) Next door to Los Jarrones is a popular place for coffee or a snack, perfect for watching the action on the plaza.

Güero's (Av Hidalgo 101; mains US$3-9) Opposite the zócalo, this cheerful hangout is decorated with antique photos of Cholula. Hearty Mexican favorites on the menu include *pozole*, *cemitas* and quesadillas, all served with a delicious *salsa roja*.

El Portón (Av Hidalgo 302; set menu US$3.75; ☒ 10am-6pm) A block west of the zócalo, the Portal is popular for its set menu, which typically includes a choice of three soups, a main course (chicken, beef or vegetables), coffee and dessert.

Restaurant Chialingo (☎ 247-28-31; 7 Pte 113; mains US$5-10; ☒ 1-9pm) A few short blocks away from the zócalo, this fancier place overlooks a lovely courtyard and specializes in salads, steaks and seafood.

Drinking

Bar Reforma (cnr Av 4 Nte & Calz San Andrés) Adjacent to Hotel Reforma, Cholula's oldest drinking spot is a classic, smoky corner hangout with swinging-doors and freshly prepared sangrias and iceless margaritas. It's popular with the college crowd after 9pm.

On Calle 14 Pte, east of the pyramid, there are several bars and discos, including the **San Andrés Grill** (cnr Calles 14 Pte & 16 de Septiembre). This quiet area comes alive around 10pm Thursday to Saturday.

Entertainment

Warehouse-like *antros* and discos, including **Rocka**, **El Alebrije** and **La Adelita**, are clustered near the university exit of the 'Recta,' as the Cholula-Puebla highway is known.

Getting There & Away

Frequent colectivos to Puebla (US$0.50, 20 minutes) leave from the corner of Calles 5 Pte and 3 Sur. Estrella Roja runs frequent buses between Mexico City's TAPO and Puebla (US$3.75) that stop in Cholula on Calle 12 Pte.

TONANTZINTLA & ACATEPEC

The interior of Tonantzintla's **Templo de Santa María** (7am-2pm & 4-8pm Mon-Fri, 7am-8pm Sat & Sun) is among Mexico's most exuberant. Under the dome, the surface is covered with colorful stucco saints, devils, flowers, fruit, birds and more – a great example of indigenous artisanship applied to Christian themes. Tonantzintla celebrates the **Festival de la Asunción** (Festival of the Assumption) on August 15 with a procession and traditional dances.

The **Templo de San Francisco** (7am-2pm & 4-8pm) in Acatepec, 1.5km southeast of Tonantzintla, dates from about 1730. The brilliant exterior is beautifully decorated with blue, green and yellow Talavera tiles set in red brick on an ornate Churrigueresque façade.

Autobuses Puebla-Cholula runs 'Chipilo' buses from the Puebla bus station to Tonantzintla and Acatepec. In Cholula, pick them up on the corner of Calle 7 Pte and Blvd Miguel Alemán. Between the two villages you can either walk or wait for the next bus.

SIERRA NORTE DE PUEBLA

The mountains covering much of remote northern Puebla state rise to over 2500m before falling away to the Gulf coastal plain. Despite deforestation, it's beautiful territory, with pine forests and, at lower altitudes, semitropical vegetation. Sierra Norte handicrafts are sold in markets at Cuetzalan, Zacapoaxtla, Teziutlán, Tlatlauquitepec and elsewhere.

The Sierra Norte is home to many of Puebla state's approximately 400,000 Nahua indigenous people. The Nahua are Mexico's largest indigenous group and more of them live in Puebla than in any other state. Another 200,000 Nahua live in western parts of Veracruz state. The Nahua language (Náhuatl) was spoken by the Aztecs and, like the Aztecs, the Nahua were probably of Chichimec origin. Traditional Nahua women's dress consists of a black wool *enredo* (waist sash) and embroidered blouse and *quechquémitl* (shoulder cape). The Nahua are Christian but often also believe in a pantheon of super-

natural beings, including *tonos* (people's animal 'doubles') and witches who can become blood-sucking birds and cause illness.

Cuetzalan

233 / pop 5000 / elevation 980m
The commercial center of a lush coffee-growing region, colonial Cuetzalan is famed for its Sunday market that attracts scores of indigenous people in traditional dress.

ORIENTATION & INFORMATION

The main road into town from the south passes a bus depot before ending 100m later at the zócalo. The center is on a hillside; from the zócalo most hotels and restaurants are uphill. Children will offer to guide you around for a small fee. No English is spoken at the humble **tourist office** (331-00-04; Hidalgo; 9am-4pm Wed-Sun), west of the zócalo, but it has town maps. **Banamex** (Alvarado) has an ATM.

SIGHTS & ACTIVITIES

Two towers rise above town: the tall Gothic spire of the zócalo's **Parroquia de San Francisco** and the tower of the **Santuario de Guadalupe** to the west, with unusual decorative rows of clay vases. There's a regional **museum** opposite Posada Jaqueline.

Two lovely waterfalls called **Las Brisas** are 4km and 5km northeast of town. Catch a colectivo behind the Parroquia de San Francisco heading for the village of San Andrés, or walk along the dirt road that begins just west of the bus depot, keeping to the right when it forks, until you come to San Andrés. There, at least one child will offer to take you to the falls for US$2.50. You should accept, as there are many trails in the forest and no signs to the falls. Bring bathing gear as the **natural pools** under the falls are enticing. Some of the area's 32km network of caves can be explored at **Atepolihui**, accessible from the village of San Miguel, a half-hour walk from the end of Hidalgo.

FESTIVALS & EVENTS

A **traditional dance festival** in mid-July attracts groups from around the region. For several lively days around October 4, Cuetzalan celebrates both the festival of **San Francisco de Assisi** and the **Feria del Café y del Huipil** (Festival of Coffee and Huipiles).

SLEEPING

Posada Jaqueline (☎ 331-03-54; 2 de Abril 2; s/d US$10/16) On the zócalo's uphill side, Jaqueline's 21 basic but large and clean rooms are the best value in town.

Hotel Posada Cuetzalan (☎ 331-01-54; Zaragoza 10; s/d US$32/42; 🐾) Just 100m from the zócalo, this hotel has a restaurant, two lovely interior courtyards and 37 rooms with blue walls, TVs and lots of lightly stained wood.

Hotel La Casa de la Piedra (☎ 331-00-30; García 11; s/d/ste US$33/42/55; 🅿) Two blocks below the zócalo, the House of the Stone is the nicest place in town. The renovated yet rustic old house has fine wood floors and large picture windows. The two-level suites accommodate up to four people and offer views of the valley; dowstairs rooms have double beds.

Several places near Cuetzalan are designed for maximum appreciation of the area's beautiful landscapes.

Taselotzin (☎ 331-04-80; www.laneta.apc.org/mas eualsiua/hotel1.htm; dm/s/d US$8/17/30; 🅿) Just outside Cuetzalan on the Puebla road, this *albergue* is run by local Nahua craftswomen. It has five cozy cabins, as well as dormitory-style lodging amid peaceful gardens. The restaurant serves traditional local dishes.

Centro Vacacional Ecologico Metzintli (☎ 249-04-72, in Mexico City 55-1055-3507/08; www.metzintli .com in Spanish; r US$37, cabins US$55-64; 🅿) About 1km from the town center on the road to Yohualichán, this vacation center has lovely rooms and rustic cabins. The grounds include a soccer field and basketball court. Horses are available for rent.

EATING & DRINKING

Restaurant Yoloxochitl (☎ 331-03-35; 2 de Abril; mains US$1.50-3) Opposite Posada Jaqueline, this charming restaurant has a lovely view. It offers salads, antojitos and meat dishes. In season, mushrooms are served pickled in chipotle sauce.

La Terraza (☎ 331-06-62; Hidalgo 33; mains US$2-7) The Terrace is the best of several inviting restaurants along Hidalgo. It offers an assortment of salads, pastas and seafood.

Bar El Calate (☎ 331-05-66; Morelos 9B; drinks from US$0.50) On the zócalo's west side, this is a great place to try homemade alcoholic drinks made from coffee, limes and berries, as well as *yolixpán* (a medicinal herbal liqueur).

Restaurant Peña Los Jarritos (☎ 331-05-58; Plazuela López Mateos 7; mains US$3-7) This lively place hosts Saturday night *peñas* featuring regional dishes and drinks, *quetzal* dancers, local *huapango* bands and *voladores* (literally 'fliers,' the Totonac ritual in which men, suspended by their ankles, whirl around a tall pole). Reservations are recommended.

GETTING THERE & AWAY

First-class ADO buses (US$9.50, 4 hours) leave Puebla for Cuetzalan at 3pm, and Cuetzalan for Puebla at around 5:30am. Second-class Vía buses (US$8.50) make the same run hourly from 6am to 7:30pm, with the last bus to Puebla at 5:30pm. All services run daily except Sunday, when service is less frequent. Buy your return tickets early. Autotransportes Mexico-Texcoco runs 1st-class buses (US$13, 5½ hours, six daily) to/from Mexico City's TAPO.

Yohualichán

About 8km from Cuetzalan by cobblestone road, this **pre-Hispanic site** (admission US$3; 🕑 8am-5pm) has niche pyramids similar to El Tajín. The site is adjacent to Yohualichán's town plaza. To get here, board any colectivo (US$0.30) out of Cuetzalan from the end of Hidalgo. Get off when it stops beside the blue sign with an image of a pyramid on it. The site is a half-hour walk from this turnoff.

SOUTHERN PUEBLA

The main route from Puebla to Oaxaca is Hwy 135D, a modern toll road that turns south off Hwy 150D, 83km east of Puebla. Tolls total US$17 from Puebla to Oaxaca. Two older roads, Hwys 150 and 190, ramble through southern Puebla state toward Oaxaca.

Hwy 150

Heading east from Puebla, this road parallels Hwy 150D, but it's slower and more congested. Second-class buses stop at the towns en route. **Amozoc** (population 52,000), 17km from Puebla, produces pottery and many of the fancy silver decorations worn by *charros* (Mexican cowboys). **Tepeaca** (population 24,000), 38km from Puebla, has a big Friday market and a 16th-century Franciscan monastery. The village of **Tecali**, 11km southwest of Tepeaca, is an onyx carving center.

Tehuacán

☎ 238 / pop 223,000 / elevation 1640m

Modern Tehuacán, just east of Hwy 135D and 120km southeast of Puebla, is a pretty town with a fine zócalo. It's a nice pit stop on the way to Oaxaca, but otherwise doesn't see many foreign visitors.

ORIENTATION & INFORMATION

The main road into town coming from Puebla, Av Independencia, passes by the ADO bus station before reaching the north side of Parque Juárez – the zócalo. The main north–south road is Av Reforma.

Essential services and the city's most popular restaurants can be found around the zócalo. There's a sleepy **tourist information kiosk** (☯ 10am-2pm & 4-7pm) on the zócalo's northwest corner. **Internet** (Reforma Nte 217; per hr US$0.75), next door to Hotel Monroy, offers Internet access.

SIGHTS

The town is best known for its mineral water, which is sold in bottles all over Mexico; there are free tours of the **Peñafiel plant** (tours ☯ 9am-noon & 4-6pm Sat-Thu; Av José Garcia-Crespo s/n), 100m north of the Casas Cantarranas hotel (see Sleeping & Eating). Just up the road, competitor **Garci-Crespo** (tours ☯ 10am-4pm; Av José Garcia-Crespo s/n) offers tours of its underground springs.

The high, dry Tehuacán Valley was the site of some of Mexico's earliest agriculture. By 7000–5000 BC, people were planting avocados, chilies, cotton and corn. Pottery, the sign of a truly settled existence, appeared around 2000 BC.

The **Museo del Valle de Tehuacán** (admission US$1.25; ☯ 10am-5pm Tue-Sun), three blocks northwest of the zócalo inside the imposing Ex-Convento del Carmen cultural complex, explains in Spanish some of the archaeological discoveries and exhibits tiny preserved corn cobs thought to be among the first ever cultivated.

FESTIVALS & EVENTS

October 15 is the start of the two-week **La Matanza** festival, when goats are slaughtered en masse. *Mole de cadera* is the regional specialty that results from the carnage (you'll find it year-round at Restaurant Danny Richard, opposite Ex-Convento del Carmen).

SLEEPING & EATING

Hotel Monroy (☎ 382-04-91; Reforma Nte 217; s/d US$18/23) Opposite the convent, the no-frills Monroy maintains clean and spacious rooms.

Bogh Suites Hotel (☎ 382-34-74; Calle 1 Nte 102; s/d/ste US$26/31/50; Ⓟ) Off the zócalo's northwest side, the Bogh has small but attractive rooms with TVs, phones and fans. Fourth floor rooms (no elevator) are a bit cheaper.

Hotel México (☎ 382-24-19; http://hotelmexico .hypermart.net; cnr Reforma Nte & Independencia Pte; s/d US$39/45; Ⓟ ⓧ) This central hotel is quite tranquil with 86 large, comfortable rooms, several courtyards and a good restaurant.

Casas Cantarranas (☎ 383-49-22; hotelcc@prodigy .net.mx; Garci-Crespo 2215; s/d/ste US$60/72/120; Ⓟ ⓧ) This good-value resort features spacious gardens, a restaurant, spa, gym and 55 fine rooms with every amenity.

GETTING THERE & AWAY

ADO (Independencia 137) runs 1st-class buses to/from Puebla (US$6, two hours, every 30 minutes), service to/from Mexico City (US$12, four hours, hourly), a 6:30pm bus to Veracruz (US$11, 4½ hours, daily) and buses to Oaxaca (US$12, three hours, two daily).

Hwy 190

Hwy 190 swings 31km southwest from Puebla to colonial **Atlixco** (population 86,000), known for its avocados, colorful Tuesday and Saturday markets, cool mineral springs, and near-perfect climate. It's also known for its weeklong **Atlixcáyotl festival** of traditional indigenous culture in September, which culminates in a spectacular dance display by groups from all parts of Puebla state on the last Sunday of the month. Another 36km brings you to **Izúcar de Matamoros** (population 42,000), which also has therapeutic balnearios but is best known for ceramic handicrafts.

SOUTH OF MEXICO CITY

Heading south from Mexico City, Hwy 95 and toll Hwy 95D climb to more than 3000m from the Valle de México into refreshing pine forests, then descend to Cuernavaca, capital of Morelos state and longtime popular retreat from Mexico City. On the way, Hwy 115D branches southeast to

Tepoztlán, nestled beneath high cliffs, and to balnearios at Oaxtepec and Cuautla.

Morelos is one of Mexico's smallest and most densely populated states. Valleys at different elevations have a variety of microclimates, and many fruits, grains and vegetables have been cultivated here since pre-Hispanic times. The archaeological sites at Cuernavaca, Tepoztlán and Xochicalco show signs of the agricultural Tlahuica civilization and the Aztecs who subjugated them. In the colonial era, most of the state was controlled by a few families, including descendants of Cortés. Their palaces and haciendas can still be seen, along with churches and monasteries from as early as the 16th century. Unsurprisingly, the *campesinos* of Morelos became fervent supporters of the Mexican Revolution, and local lad Emiliano Zapata is the state's hero.

South of Cuernavaca, spurs of Hwy 95D go to the remarkable silver town of Taxco and to the industrial city of Iguala, both in mountainous Guerrero state. The Iguala branch continues south as Hwy 95 to Chilpancingo (p501) and Acapulco (p486). Locals claim they can drive the 400km between Mexico City and Acapulco via the Hwy 95D expressway (tolls around US$40) in under three hours. The alternative sections of free road are heavily used, slow and dangerous. Driving at night in Guerrero is inadvisable because cars are sometimes stopped and robbed. The route from Iguala to Ixtapa via Hwys 51 and 134 is said to be particularly risky.

TEPOZTLÁN

☎ 739 / pop 15,000 / elevation 1701m

Eighty kilometers south of Mexico City, Tepoztlán (Place of Copper) sits in a valley surrounded by high, jagged cliffs. It was the legendary birthplace, more than 1200 years ago, of Quetzalcóatl, the omnipotent serpent god of the Aztecs. The town retains indigenous traditions, with many older people still speaking Náhuatl, and younger generations now learning it in secondary school. Now something of an international hippie venue, Tepoztlán attracts writers, artists and astrologers, who, encouraged by UFO sightings, claim the place has a creative energy, as well as more conventional weekenders from Mexico City. A few years ago, developers proposed an enormous

golf club resort, but locals who feared their water supplies would be threatened protested against it successfully.

Orientation & Information

Everything here is easily accessible on foot, except the clifftop Pirámide de Tepozteco 2.5km away. Street names change in the center of town; for example, Av 5 de Mayo becomes Av Tepozteco north of the plaza.

There are plenty of card phones around town. On the plaza's west side, Bancomer has an ATM. Friendly **Internetepoz** (Av Revolución 22; per hr US$1) offers online access. There's no official tourist office, but the knowledgeable archaeology museum staff (see below) can answer most questions.

Sights

EX-CONVENTO DOMÍNICO DE LA NATIVIDAD

This **monastery** (☉ 10am-5pm Tue-Sun) and the attached church were built by Dominican priests between 1560 and 1588. The plateresque church façade has Dominican seals interspersed with indigenous symbols, floral designs and various figures including the sun, moon and stars, animals, angels and the Virgin Mary.

The monastery's arched entryway is an elaborate **mural** of pre-Hispanic history and symbolism composed of 60 varieties of seeds. Every year, during the first week of September, local artists create a new mural.

The 400-year-old complex is undergoing a major decade-long restoration. Some 4500 sq meters of murals from the 16th and 17th centuries have been meticulously restored. Upstairs, the cells of the west wing house a **museum** covering the region's natural history, economy, religion and social organization.

MUSEO ARQUEOLÓGICO CARLOS PELLICER

This **archaeology museum** (☎ 395-10-98; González 2; admission US$1; ☉ 10am-6pm Tue-Sun) behind the Dominican church has a small but interesting collection of pieces from around the country, donated by Tabascan poet Carlos Pellicer Cámara. The objects on display here are lively and vibrant, with an emphasis on human figures, but also including some animals. The stone fragments depicting a pair of rabbits – the symbol for Ometochtli, one

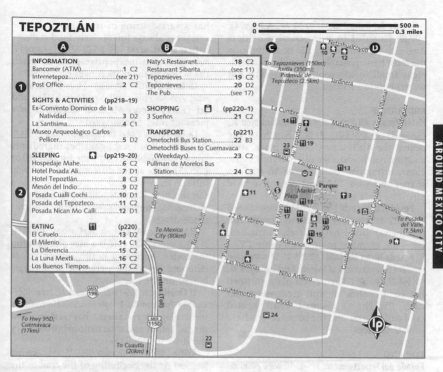

TEPOZTLÁN

INFORMATION	
Bancomer (ATM).........................1	C2
Internetepoz........................(see 21)	
Post Office..............................2	C2

SIGHTS & ACTIVITIES	(pp218–19)
Ex-Convento Dominico de la	
Natividad..............................3	D2
La Santisima............................4	C1
Museo Arqueológico Carlos	
Pellicer................................5	D2

SLEEPING	(pp219–20)
Hospedaje Mahe.......................6	C2
Hotel Posada Ali........................7	D1
Hotel Tepoztlán........................8	C3
Mesón del Indio........................9	D2
Posada Cualli Cochi..................10	D1
Posada del Tepozteco..............11	C2
Posada Nican Mo Calli..............12	D1

EATING	(p220)
El Ciruelo...............................13	D2
El Milenio................................14	C1
La Diferencia...........................15	C2
La Luna Mextli........................16	C2
Los Buenos Tiempos................17	C2

Naty's Restaurant....................18	C2
Restaurant Sibarita.............(see 11)	
Tepoznieves............................19	C2
Tepoznieves............................20	D2
The Pub.............................(see 17)	

SHOPPING	(pp220–1)
3 Sueños...............................21	C2

TRANSPORT	(p221)
Ometochtli Bus Station............22	B3
Ometochtli Buses to Cuernavaca	
(Weekdays)..........................23	C2
Pullman de Morelos Bus	
Station................................24	C3

---

of the 400 pulque gods – were discovered at the Tepozteco pyramid site.

PIRÁMIDE DE TEPOZTECO

The 10m-high **Pyramid of Tepozteco** (admission US$2.75; ⊗ 9am-5:30pm) was built on a cliff 400m above Tepoztlán in honor of Tepoztécatl, the Aztec god of the harvest, fertility and pulque. It's accessible by a steep path beginning at the north end of Av Tepozteco; the 2km one-way walk can take as little as half an hour or up to 1½ hours and may be too strenuous for some. At the top, you may be rewarded with a panorama of Tepoztlán and the valley, depending on haze levels. Hiking boots or at least good tennis shoes are recommended.

Festivals & Events

Tepoztlán is a festive place, with many Christian feasts superimposed on pagan celebrations. On the five days preceding Ash Wednesday (46 days before Easter Sunday), **Carnaval** features the colorful dances of the Huehuenches and Chinelos with feather headdresses and beautifully embroidered costumes. On **September 7** an all-night cele-

bration takes place on Tepozteco hill near the pyramid, with copious consumption of pulque in honor of Tepoztécatl. The following day is the **Fiesta del Templo**, a Catholic celebration featuring theater performances in the Náhuatl language and the re-creation of the seed mural on the monastery's entrance arch. The holiday was first intended to coincide with, and perhaps supplant, the pagan Tepoztécatl festival, but the pulque drinkers get a jump on it by starting the night before.

Sleeping

It can be difficult to find decent inexpensive accommodations during festivals and on weekends. Nicer places that cater mainly to weekend crowds from Mexico City will discount rates by up to 25% during the week.

BUDGET

Hospedaje Mahe (☎ 395-32-92; Paraíso 12; r US$32, with shared bathroom US$19; P ⊠) This simple six-room place is the best, if a bit dank, budget choice. There's a ping pong table, a guayaba tree and laundry possibilities, and the friendly owners live downstairs.

Mesón del Indio (☎ 395-02-38; Av Revolución 44; r US$20) Guarded by a hyperactive hairless dog with a permasmile, the basic Indio is the most basic passable option in town with eight small moldy rooms (each with hot water) beside a garden.

MID-RANGE

Hotel Posada Ali (☎ 395-19-71; Netzahualcóyotl 2C; r US$28-43, ste US$55-73; P ☂) North of the center, the Ali is a very homey place, with a sitting room and a small pool. Its 13 spacious, attractive rooms come in various shapes and sizes; the most expensive have king-size beds and cable TV.

Posada Cualli Cochi (☎ 395-03-93; Netzahualcóyotl 2; s US$35, d US$38-43; P) Next to Posada Ali, this newer hotel has sparsely furnished, clean but cramped rooms with cable TV.

Posada Nican Mo Calli (☎ 395-31-52; www.travel bymexico.com/todo/nican in Spanish; Netzahualcóyotl 4A; r US$68-87; P ☂) The newest place in town has eight rooms, all with great views and cable TV. There's a squash court, heated pool and Jacuzzi, and the larger rooms have private terraces.

TOP END

Posada del Tepozteco (☎ 395-00-10; www.posadadel tepozteco.com; Paraíso 3; r/ste from US$140/169; P ☂) This gorgeous hotel was built as a hillside hacienda in the 1930s and has lovely, well-manicured grounds, two solar-heated pools, an attractive restaurant-bar, La Sibarita, and terraces with spectacular views across town. It has 20 well-done rooms, and the airy suites come with private spa baths. Rates are discounted by US$20 from Sunday to Thursday.

Posada del Valle (☎ 395-05-21; www.posadadel valle.com.mx; Camino a Mextitla 5; r Mon-Thu only US$80, weekend spa packages for 2 US$370; P ☂) Posada del Valle has quiet, romantic rooms and a good Argentine restaurant. The weekend package includes two nights at the hotel, breakfast, massages and a visit to the *temazcal* (indigenous Mexican steambath). Children under 16 are not allowed. It's 2km east of town (take Av Revolución east and follow signs the final 100m to the hotel).

Eating & Drinking

If fine dining is your goal, arrive on the weekend. During the week many of the nicer restaurants are closed. Av Revolución has a varied string of restaurants and the market is always full of lively food stalls.

Naty's Restaurant (☎ 395-02-67; Av Revolución 7; mains US$3-7) An inexpensive place to watch the action in the market over breakfast.

La Luna Mextli (☎ 393-11-14; Av Revolución 16; mains US$5-10) This combo restaurant, bar and art gallery serves Mexican standards in a pleasant interior courtyard.

La Diferencia (Isabel La Catolica s/n; mains US$4-9; ☽ 1-9pm Fri-Mon) Fresh, gourmet ingredients and a reasonably-priced wine list (US$10 to US$25) make all the difference at this lively little French-inspired bistro. Tuck into a serrano ham baguette, chocolate fondue or vichyssoise soup and save room for a homemade dessert.

El Milenio (cnr Av Tepozteco & La Cumbre; mains US$1-3) This vegetarian café is a nice place to stop for coffee, juice or a healthy snack before climbing up to the pyramid, or a veggie burger on the way down.

El Ciruelo (☎ 395-19-37; Zaragoza 17; mains US$7-12; ☽ 1-7pm Mon-Thu, 1-11pm Fri & Sat) Tepoztlán's most elegant restaurant-bar serves good pizzas, salads and international dishes. Try the steak in tequila sauce.

Axitla (☎ 395-05-19; mains US$6-15; ☽ 10am-7pm Wed-Sun) At the beginning of the trail to the archaeological site, Axitla offers abundant portions of fine Mexican and international cuisine, and a jungle-like setting.

Tepoznieves (Av Revolución; scoops US$1-2) This ice-cream emporium scoops out 70 heavenly flavors, including exotics like cactus and pineapple-chili. It's an obligatory stop and has a couple of other branches (and many imitators), including one at Av Tepozteco 8 on the road to the pyramid.

Los Buenos Tiempos (☎ 395-05-19; Av Revolución 10; mains US$1-3) This cozy café serves light meals and slings Tepoz' best espresso. Try the homemade strudel.

The Pub (☎ 395-15-96; Av Revolución 10, 2nd fl; mains US$4-8) This central bar and restaurant is the only real nightlife option, with a singing Irish owner and occasional live Celtic music.

Shopping

On Saturday and Sunday, Tepoztlán's market stalls sell a mélange of handicrafts, including *sarapes* (blanketlike shawls), carvings, weavings, baskets and pottery. Shops in the adjacent streets also have interesting wares (some from Bali and India) at up-scale prices. A popular local craft product is miniature villages carved from the cork-like spines of the *pochote* tree. The lively local market day is Wednesday.

3 Sueños (upstairs at Av Revolución 22; 🕑 11am-6pm most days) This gringo-run shop sells pieces of work by local artists and craftspeople, as well as secondhand clothing, jewelry and books in English, German and most romance languages.

Getting There & Away

Pullman de Morelos runs 1st-class buses to/from Mexico City's Terminal Sur (US$4.50, one hour, hourly 5am to 8pm); buses arrive and depart at Av 5 de Mayo 35 near the southern entrance to town. Frequent buses to Oaxtepec (US$1, 15 minutes) and Cuautla (US$1.25, 15 minutes) depart from Hwy 95D tollbooth just outside town. Pullman de Morelos runs free combis between the 5 de Mayo terminal and the gas station near the autopista entrance; from there, walk down the left (exit) ramp to the tollbooth.

Ometochtli direct and 'ordinario' buses run to Cuernavaca (US$1, 45 minutes, every 10 minutes 5am to 9pm). The terminal is on the road south of town on the way to the autopista. From Monday to Friday you can catch the bus on the corner of Galeana and Av Tepozteco downtown.

If you're driving north from Cuernavaca on Hwy 95D, don't get off at the 'Tepoztlán' exit, which will put you on the slow federal highway. Instead, take the exit marked 'Cuautla/Oaxtepec.'

OAXTEPEC

☎ 735 / pop 6000 / elevation 1360m

In Oaxtepec (wahs-teh-*pec*) the 1.2 sq km **Centro Vacacional Oaxtepec** is a balneario with numerous pools and sulfur springs. The giant park is divided into two areas: a privately run **aquatic amusement park** (PAO; ☎ 356-01-01; www .pao.com.mx in Spanish; adult/child US$10/5; 🕑 10am-6pm Mon-Fri, 9am-8pm Sat & Sun) with a wave pool and giant slides; and a **recreational center** (☎ 356-01-01; adult/child US$4/2; 🕑 8am-6pm), operated by the Mexican Social Security Institute (IMSS) and open to the general public, with pools, a stadium, restaurants and a funicular. It's worth a visit, especially if you're traveling with kids.

Sleeping

Centro Vacacional IMSS Oaxtepec (☎ 356-01-01/02-02, 800-523-50-08, in Mexico City 55-5639-4173; www .imss.gob.mx/vacaciones in Spanish; camping adult/child US$5.50/2.75, r low/high season from US$22/29) For overnight stays, this government-run complex has campgrounds, five-person cabins and a hotel. With reservations, there's a 50% discount on admission to the aquatic amusement park. If you don't have a reservation, stop by the office adjacent to the complex entrance to see what's available. Tents rent for US$6 and room rates rise a bit on weekends and holidays.

Hacienda Cocoyoc (☎ 356-22-11, in Mexico City 55-5550-2202; www.cocoyoc.com.mx; Carretera 113 Km 32.5; r/ste from US$110/170; P 🐕) This 17th-century hacienda, 3km southwest of Oaxtepec, was an important sugar refinery until Zapata declared war on all sugar plantations during the revolution. Today it's a refreshing resort and spa with impeccable service, restaurants, horseback riding, tennis and a nine-hole golf course. A few suites here even have private pools.

Getting There & Away

Oaxtepec is just north of Hwy 115D, 100km south of Mexico City. Cocoyoc is 3km south of the Oaxtepec turnoff. Frequent 1st-class buses go from the capital's Terminal Sur to Oaxtepec's bus station beside the entrance to the springs complex (US$6.50, 1½ hours). There are also buses from Tepoztlán, Cuernavaca, Cuautla and Puebla. Taxis and combis to Cocoyoc also depart from outside the complex' entrance.

CUAUTLA

☎ 735 / pop 142,000 / elevation 1290m

The balnearios at Cuautla (*kwout*-la) and its pleasant year-round climate have been attractions since the time of Moctezuma, who reputedly enjoyed soaking in the sun and sulfur springs. These days, however, the city is spread out and uninspiring, though the center is pleasant enough.

José María Morelos y Pavón, one of Mexico's first leaders in the independence struggle, used Cuautla as a base, but the royalist army besieged the city from February to May 1812. Morelos and his army were forced to evacuate when their food gave out. A century later, Cuautla was a center of support for Emiliano Zapata's revolutionary

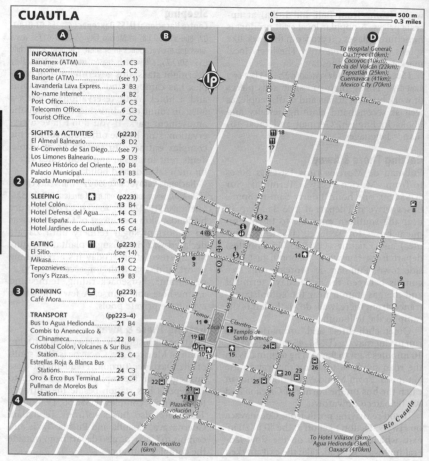

CUAUTLA

INFORMATION
Banamex (ATM)..........................1 C3
Bancomer..................................2 C2
Banorte (ATM).....................(see 1)
Lavandería Lava Express..........3 B3
No-name Internet.....................4 B2
Post Office................................5 C3
Telecomm Office.......................6 C3
Tourist Office............................7 C2

SIGHTS & ACTIVITIES   (p223)
El Almeal Balneario....................8 D2
Ex-Convento de San Diego......(see 7)
Los Limones Balneario..............9 D3
Museo Histórico del Oriente...10 B4
Palacio Municipal....................11 B3
Zapata Monument...................12 B4

SLEEPING 🏠   (p223)
Hotel Colón.............................13 B4
Hotel Defensa del Agua..........14 C3
Hotel España..........................15 C4
Hotel Jardines de Cuautla......16 C4

EATING 🍴   (p223)
El Sitio..............................(see 14)
Mikasa....................................17 C2
Tepoznieves............................18 C2
Tony's Pizzas..........................19 B3

DRINKING 🍷   (p223)
Café Mora...............................20 C4

TRANSPORT   (pp223–4)
Bus to Agua Hedionda.............21 B4
Combis to Aneneculco &
    Chinameca..........................22 B4
Cristóbal Colón, Volcanes & Sur Bus
    Station................................23 C4
Estrellas Roja & Blanca Bus
    Stations..............................24 C3
Oro & Erco Bus Terminal..........25 C4
Pullman de Morelos Bus
    Station................................26 C4

To Hospital General;
Oaxtepec (10km);
Cocoyoc (10km);
Tetela del Volcán (22km);
Tepoztlán (25km);
Cuernavaca (41km);
Mexico City (70km)

To Hotel Villasor (3km);
Agua Hedionda (3km);
Oaxaca (410km)

To Aneneculco
(6km)

---

army. Now, every April 10, the Agrarian Reform Minister lays a wreath at Zapata's monument in Cuautla, quoting the revolutionary's principles of land reform.

Orientation

Cuautla spreads north to south roughly parallel to the Río Cuautla. The two main plazas – Plaza Fuerte de Galeana, more commonly known as the Alameda, and the zócalo – are along the main avenue, whose name changes from Av Insurgentes to Batalla 19 de Febrero, then to Galeana, Los Bravos, Guerrero and Ordiera, on its way through town.

The zócalo has arcades with restaurants on the north side, a church on the east, the Palacio Municipal on the west and the Hotel Colón on the south. Bus lines have separate terminals in the blocks east of the plaza.

Information

Banks Around the plazas; have ATMs.

Computación de Cuautla (Batalla 19 de Febrero; per hr US$1) Offers Internet access.

Hospital General (☎ 353-61-93; Reforma) North of town, near the Autopista México.

Lavandería Lava Express (cnr Dr Hiedras & Niño Artillero; US$2.25 for 3.5kg load)

No-name Internet (cnr Niño Artillero & Bollas; per hr US$1) Offers Internet access.

Tourist Office (☎ 352-52-21; 🕙 9am-8pm) On the platform of the old train station, housed in the 16th-century Ex-Convento de San Diego. A wellspring of information, well stocked with literature and a good map of town.

Sights

Mexico's only **steam-powered train** (adult/child US$0.50/0.20) departs from the old railroad station (in the Ex-Convento de San Diego), where in 1911 presidential candidate Francisco Madero embraced Emiliano Zapata. The train does a circuit of Cuautla on Saturday and Sunday after 5pm.

The former residence of José María Morelos, off the plaza's southwest side, houses the **Museo Histórico del Oriente** (☎ 352-83-31; Callejón del Castigo 3; admission US$2.25, free Sun; ☼ 9am-6pm Tue-Sun). Each room covers a different historical period with displays of pre-Hispanic pottery, good maps and early photos of Cuautla and Zapata.

Plazuela Revolución del Sur is one of Cuautla's loveliest plazas. In its center stands an imposing **Zapata monument**, underneath which lie the rebel's remains.

Cuautla's best-known *balneario* (spa) is riverside **Agua Hedionda** (Stinky Water; ☎ 352-00-44; end of Av Progreso; adult/child US$3/1.50; ☼ 7am-5:30pm). Waterfalls replenish two lake-sized pools with sulfur-scented 27°C waters. To reach the complex, take an 'Agua Hedionda' bus (US$0.50) from Plazuela Revolución del Sur.

Other *balnearios* worth visiting include **El Almeal** (adult/child US$2.50/1.50; ☼ 9am-6pm) and **Los Limones** (Centinela 14; adult/child US$2.75/2.25; ☼ 8:30am-6:30pm). Both of these balnearios are served by the same spring (no sulfur) and have pleasant wooded grounds.

Sleeping

Hotel España (☎ 352-21-86; 2 de Mayo 22; s/d US$16/19; P) Half a block east of Hotel Colón, the España has 30 spacious rooms with hot water.

Hotel Colón (☎ 352-29-90; Portal Guerrero 48; s/d US$9/13) Facing the main plaza, the Colón's 22 rooms are basic but clean and nice enough for the price. The restaurant downstairs is popular with locals.

Hotel Jardines de Cuautla (☎ 352-00-88; 2 de Mayo 94; s/d US$14/18; P 🅰) Opposite the Cristóbal Colón bus terminal, this hotel has a garden and 41 clean, modern rooms with private bathrooms. It's convenient but unfortunately quite a bit of noise intrudes from the busy streets below.

Hotel Defensa del Agua (☎ 352-16-79; Defensa del Agua 34; s/d US$28/37; P 🅰) Two blocks east of the Alameda, this hotel surrounds a small garden with two small pools. Its pleasant colonial-style rooms have cable TV, phones and ceiling fans. Avoid rooms with windows facing the street.

Hotel Villasor (☎ 352-65-21; villasor@mail.cem-sa.com.mx; Av Progreso; s/d US$37/49; P 🅰) If you're only visiting Cuautla for Agua Hedionda, this hotel and spa, a stone's throw from the balneario, is the place to stay. Comfortable modern rooms come with TVs, fans and phones.

Eating & Drinking

The Alameda has several pleasant outdoor cafés that serve sandwiches, coffee, milkshakes and ice cream.

Tony's Pizzas (☎ 352-04-02; Portal Matamoros 6; mains US$4-12) On the zócalo, Tony's has a variety of pies plus cocktails, burgers and pasta.

El Sitio (Defensa del Agua 34A; mains US$5-11, set lunch US$5) Hotel Defensa del Agua's restaurant is an elegant alternative to the cafés, with salads, meat and seafood dishes. Its popular set lunch features exotic local options.

Café Mora (2 de Mayo 91; drinks US$0.75-1.50; ☼ 10am-3pm & 5-8pm Mon-Sat) Opposite Hotel Jardines de Cuautla, this aromatic café does Cuautla's finest espresso.

Mikasa (☎ 352-51-02; Obregón 12; mains US$3.50-7; ☼ 11am-10pm) This place serves a wide variety of Japanese dishes including sushi, udon and teriyaki. Check the raw fish display before ordering – it's far from fine cuisine, but it's among the best you'll find in these parts.

Tepoznieves (Obregón 9E; scoops US$1-2) Next door to Mikasa, this heavenly ice creamery has dozens and dozens of delicious tastes (some acquired); ask for a free sample of one with chili or alcohol.

Getting There & Away

Cristóbal Colón, a 1st-class line, and Sur and Volcanes, both 2nd-class, share a bus station at the eastern end of 2 de Mayo. Pullman de Morelos (Máximo Bravo 53D) is across the street, with 1st-class service to Tepoztlán (US$1.50) and Oaxtepec (US$1.25) every 15 minutes from 9am to 9pm. A block west is the Estrella Roja (2nd-class) and Estrella Blanca terminal; an elevated restaurant separates the two lines. A block south is the Oro and Erco station (cnr 2 de Mayo & Mongoy). Useful services include:

Cuernavaca Estrella Roja (US$3, 1¼hr, every 20-30min 5am-7:30pm)

Mexico City (TAPO) Volcanes or Sur (US$3, 2½hr, every 30min, via Amecameca)
Mexico City (Terminal Sur) Colón, Estrella Roja or Pullman de Morelos (US$5.50, 1¾hr, every 15min)
Oaxaca Sur (US$16, 7hr, 11:30pm daily)
Puebla Estrella Roja (US$8, 2½hr, every 15min 6am-7pm); Oro (US$8, 2½hr, hourly 6am-7pm)

AROUND CUAUTLA

The road south of Cuautla leads through some significant territory of the revolutionary period, where General Emiliano Zapata (see below) was born, fought and met his death at the hands of treacherous federalists. North of Cuautla, off Hwy 115 to Amecameca, a road heads east along the southern slopes of the active volcano Popocatépetl (see p193), passing an extraordinary series of small towns with magnificent monasteries. Here you will get a good glimpse of how traditional ways of life go on, apparently undisturbed by their proximity to the smoking behemoth.

TETELA DEL VOLCÁN

☎ 731 / pop 8000 / elevation 2220m

This village 22km east of Hwy 115 is one of several built around Augustinian monasteries on Popo's southern slopes. From the outside of Tetela's 16th-century **Ex-Convento de San Juan Bautista**, there are majestic views of the monastery crowned by the volcano. Like other villages in Popo's vicinity, Tetela has a notable military presence standing by, should an evacuation be necessary. There's a civil protection headquarters off the plaza, keeping residents posted on the latest volcanic activity.

¡QUE VIVA ZAPATA!

A peasant leader from Morelos state, Emiliano Zapata (1879–1919) was the most radical of Mexico's revolutionary leaders, fighting for the return of hacienda land to the peasants with the cry *'¡Tierra y Libertad!'* (Land and Freedom). The Zapatista movement was at odds both with the conservative supporters of the old regime and their liberal opponents. In November 1911 Zapata disseminated his Plan de Ayala, calling for restoration of all land to the peasants. After winning numerous battles (some in association with Pancho Villa) against government troops in central Mexico, he was ambushed and killed in 1919. The following route traces some of Zapata's defining moments.

Ruta de Zapata

In Anenecuilco, 6km south of Cuautla, what's left of the adobe cottage where Zapata was born, on August 8, 1879, is now a **museum** (Av Zapata; donation requested; ☯ 8am-9pm) featuring photographs of the rebel leader. Outside is a mural by Roberto Rodríguez Navarro that depicts Zapata exploding with the force of a volcano into the center of Mexican history, sundering the chains that bound his countrymen.

About 20km south of Anenecuilco you will find the **Ex-Hacienda de San Juan Chinameca**, where in 1919 Zapata was lured into a fatal trap by Colonel Jesús Guajardo following the orders of President Venustiano Carranza, who was eager to dispose of the rebel leader and consolidate the post-revolutionary government. Pretending to defect to the revolutionary forces, Guajardo set up a meeting with Zapata, who arrived at Chinameca accompanied by a guerrilla escort. Guajardo's men gunned down the general before he crossed the abandoned hacienda's threshold.

The hacienda, with a small **museum** (Cárdenas; donation requested; ☯ 9:30am-5pm), is on the left at the end of the town's main street, where there's a statue of Zapata astride a rearing horse. The exhibits (photos and newspaper reproductions) are pretty meager, but you can still see the bullet holes in the walls.

From Chinameca, Hwy 9 heads 20km northwest to Tlaltizapán, site of the **Cuartel General de Zapata** (Guerrero 67; donation requested; ☯ 9am-5pm Tue-Sun), the revolutionary forces' main barracks. It contains relics from General Zapata's time, including the bed where he slept, his rifle (the trigger retains his fingerprints) and the outfit he was wearing at the time of his death (they are riddled with bullet holes and stained with blood).

From Cuautla, yellow 'Chinameca' combis traveling to Anenecuilco and Chinameca (US$0.50) leave from Garduño and Matamoros every 10 minutes.

A fine place to stay is the English-speaking **Albergue Suizo** (☎ 357-00-56; cnr Morelos & Allende; s/d US$10/15). This tall brick hotel is approached by the first left after you go through Tetela's entryway arches. The hotel's interior is austere, but friendly staff make it cozy. The large rooms have a view (though not of Popo) and spacious bathrooms with hot water. Popo can be glimpsed through a wall of windows around the top-level dining room.

On the way to Tetela in Ocuituco there's a new HI-affiliated hostel, **Quinta La Joya** (☎ 357-03-88, in Mexico City 55-5544-3193; albjoya@yahoo.com; dm US$8).

A 15-minute drive east of Tetela, on the way to Hueyapan, is the pristine **Río Amatzinac**, where you can hike over stone bridges and along an old cobblestone road.

In Cuautla, microbuses to Tetela (US$0.75, 40 minutes) depart from near the Estrella Roja station.

CUERNAVACA

☎ 777 / pop 350,000 / elevation 1480m

With a mild climate, Cuernavaca (kwehr-nah-*vah*-kah) has been a retreat from Mexico City since colonial times. It attracts the wealthy from Mexico and abroad, many of whom have stayed on to become temporary or semipermanent residents. A number of their residences have become attractions in themselves, now housing museums, hotels and fine restaurants. As the local population grows and more and more visitors come, Cuernavaca is losing some of its charm and acquiring the problems that people from the capital try to escape – crowds, traffic, smog and crime. Mexico City's elite are now just as likely to go to Acapulco or Miami for the weekend, but many still maintain magnificent properties in Cuernavaca's suburbs.

Much of Cuernavaca's elegance is hidden in colonial courtyards, and is largely inaccessible to the casual visitor. A stroll through the lively zócalo costs nothing, but allow some extra pesos to enjoy the ambience at some of the better restaurants. It's also worth visiting for the famed Palacio de Cortés, and nearby balnearios and pre-Hispanic sites. Longer-term visitors often enroll at one of the numerous Spanish-language schools.

History

The people settling in the valleys of modern Morelos around AD 1220 developed a highly productive agricultural society based at Cuauhnáhuac (Place at the Edge of the Forest). Later, the dominant Mexica (Aztecs) called them 'Tlahuica,' which means 'people who work the land.' In 1379 a Mexica warlord conquered Cuauhnáhuac, subdued the Tlahuica and required them to pay an annual tribute that included 16,000 pieces of amate bark paper and 20,000 bushels of corn. The tributes payable by the subject states were set out in a register the Spanish later called Códice Mendocino in which Cuauhnáhuac was represented by a three-branched tree; this symbol now appears on the city's coat of arms.

The Mexica lord's successor married the daughter of the Cuauhnáhuac leader, and from this marriage was born Moctezuma I Ilhuicamina, the great 15th-century Aztec king who was a predecessor of Moctezuma II Xocoyotzin encountered by Cortés. The Tlahuica prospered under the Aztecs, themselves dominating small states to the south and trading extensively. Their city was also a learning and religious center, and archaeological remains suggest they had a considerable knowledge of astronomy.

When the Spanish arrived, the Tlahuica were fiercely loyal to the Aztecs. In April 1521 they were finally overcome and Cortés torched the city. Destroying the city pyramid, Cortés used the stones to build a fortress-palace on the pyramid's base (see Palacio de Cortés, p227). He also erected the fortress-like Catedral de la Asunción from the rubble. Soon the city became known as Cuernavaca, a more Spanish-friendly version of its original name.

In 1529 Cortés received his somewhat belated reward from the Spanish crown when he was named Marqués del Valle de Oaxaca, with an estate that covered 22 towns, including Cuernavaca and 23,000 indigenous Mexicans. After he introduced sugar cane and new farming methods, Cuernavaca became a Spanish agricultural center, as it had been for the Aztecs. Cortés' descendants dominated the area for nearly 300 years.

With its pleasant climate, rural surroundings and colonial elite, Cuernavaca became a refuge for the rich and powerful. One of these was José de la Borda, the 18th-century Taxco silver magnate. His lavish home was later a retreat for Emperor Maximilian and Empress Carlota. Cuernavaca also attracted

AROUND MEXICO CITY

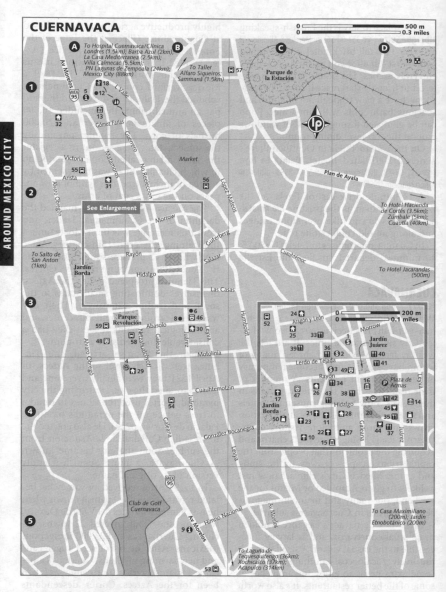

artists and writers, and achieved literary fame as the setting for Malcolm Lowry's 1947 novel, *Under the Volcano*.

Orientation

The zócalo (aka Plaza de Armas) is the heart of the city. Most budget hotels and important sites are nearby. The various bus lines use different terminals, most within walking distance of the zócalo.

Hwy 95D, the toll road, skirts the city's east side. If you're driving from the north, take the Cuernavaca exit and cross to Hwy 95 (where you'll see a statue of Zapata on horseback). Hwy 95 becomes Blvd Zapata as you descend south into town, then Av

Morelos; south of Av Matamoros, Morelos is one-way, northbound only. To reach the center, veer left and go down Matamoros.

Information

BOOKSTORES

Sanborns (cnr Juárez & Abasolo) Department store with good bilingual newsstand.

INTERNET ACCESS

There are several Internet cafés just east of the zócalo on Gutenberg.

Copy@net (Av Morelos 178; per hr US$1.50; ☺ 8am-9pm Mon-Sat, 11am-5pm Sun) Air-conditioned.

LAUNDRY

Nuevo Tintorería Francesa (Juárez 1; US$1 per kilo; ☺ 9am-7pm Mon-Fri, 9am-2:30pm Sat)

MEDICAL SERVICES

Hospital Cuernavaca/Clínica Londres (☎ 311-24-82; Cuauhtémoc 305 at 5 de Mayo) In Colonia Lomas de la Selva, 1km north of town.

POST

Main post office (south side Plaza de Armas; ☺ 8am-6pm Mon-Fri, 9am-1pm Sat)

TELEPHONE

Telecomm (south side Plaza de Armas) Next to post office.

TOURIST INFORMATION

On weekends there's an information booth in the cathedral and other information kiosks scattered around town.

Municipal Tourist office (☎ 318-75-61; www.cuernavaca.gob.mx in Spanish; Av Morelos 278; ☺ 10am-8pm) Near entrance to Pasillo de la Barranca.

State Tourist Office (☎ 314-38-72; www.morelostravel.com; Av Morelos 187; ☺ 8am-5pm Mon-Fri) Inconveniently located, understaffed; not very helpful.

Sights & Activities

PLAZA DE ARMAS & JARDÍN JUÁREZ

Cuernavaca's zócalo (Plaza de Armas) is flanked on the east by the **Palacio de Cortés**, on the west by the **Palacio de Gobierno** and on the northeast and south by a number of restaurants.

It's the only main plaza in Mexico without a church, chapel, convent or cathedral overlooking it. Adjoining the northwest corner is the smaller **Jardín Juárez**, with a central gazebo designed by tower specialist Gustave Eiffel. Roving vendors sell balloons, ice cream and corn on the cob under the trees, which fill up with legions of cacophonous grackles at dusk.

PALACIO DE CORTÉS

Cortés' imposing medieval-style fortress stands at the Plaza de Armas' southeast end. Construction of this two-story stone palace was accomplished between 1522 and 1532, and was done on the base of the pyramid that Cortés destroyed, still visible from various points on the ground floor. Cortés resided here until he returned to Spain in 1540. The palace remained with Cortés' family for most of the next century, but by the 18th century it was being used as a prison, and during the Porfirio Díaz era it became government offices.

Today the palace houses the **Museo Regional Cuauhnáhuac** (admission US$3; ☺ 9am-6pm Tue-Sun), with two floors of exhibits highlighting Mexican history and cultures. On the ground floor, exhibits focus on pre-Hispanic cultures, including the local Tlahuica and their relationship with the Aztec empire.

Upstairs, exhibits cover events from the Spanish conquest to the present. On the balcony is a fascinating mural by Diego Rivera, commissioned in the mid-1920s as a gift to the people of Cuernavaca by Dwight Morrow, the US ambassador to Mexico. From right to left, scenes from the conquest up to the 1910 revolution emphasize the cruelty, oppression and violence that have characterized Mexican history.

JARDÍN BORDA

These **gardens** (☎ 318-82-50; Av Morelos 271; admission US$1.25, free Sun; ☺ 10am-5:30pm Tue-Sun) were created in 1783 for Manuel de la Borda, as an addition to the stately residence built by his father, José de la Borda, the Taxco silver magnate. From 1866 the house was the summer residence of Emperor Maximilian and Empress Carlota, who entertained their courtiers in the gardens.

From the entrance at Av Morelos 271, you can tour the house and gardens to get an idea of how Mexico's aristocracy lived. In typical colonial style, the buildings are arranged around courtyards. In one wing, the **Museo de Sitio** has exhibits on daily life during the empire period, and original documents with the signatures of Morelos, Juárez and Maximilian.

Several romantic paintings on the walls of the **Sala Manuel M Ponce**, a recital hall near the entrance, show scenes of the garden in Maximilian's time. One of the most famous paintings of the collection depicts Maximilian in the garden with La India Bonita, the 'pretty Indian' who was to become his lover.

The **gardens** are formally laid out on a series of terraces, with paths, steps and fountains, and they originally featured a botanical collection with hundreds of varieties of ornamental plants and fruit trees. The vegetation is still exuberant, with large trees and semitropical shrubs, though there

is no longer a wide range of species. Because of a city water shortage, the fountains have been turned off, which greatly diminishes the gardens' aesthetic appeal. You can hire a little row boat for US$2 an hour. A café near the entrance serves cake and *empanadas*.

Beside the house is the **Parroquia de Guadalupe**, also built by José de la Borda, and dedicated in December 1784.

RECINTO DE LA CATEDRAL

Cuernavaca's cathedral stands in a large high-walled *recinto* (compound) on the corner of Av Morelos and Hidalgo (the entrance gate is on Hidalgo). Like the Palacio de Cortés, the cathedral was built on a grand scale and in a fortress-like style, as a defense against the natives and to impress and intimidate them. Franciscans started work under Cortés in 1526, using indigenous labor and stones from the rubble of Cuauhnáhuac; it was one of Mexico's earliest Christian missions. The first construction was the **Capilla Abierta de San José**, an open chapel on the cathedral's west side.

The cathedral itself, the **Templo de la Asunción de María**, is plain and solid, with an unembellished façade. The side door, which faces north to the compound's entrance, shows a mixture of indigenous and European features – the skull and crossbones above it is a symbol of the Franciscan order. Inside are frescoes discovered early in the 20th century. Cuernavaca was a center for Franciscan missionary activities in Asia, and the frescoes – said to show the persecution of Christian missionaries in Japan – were supposedly painted in the 17th century by a Japanese convert to Christianity.

The cathedral compound also holds two smaller churches. On the right as you enter is the **Templo de la Tercera Orden de San Francisco**, which was commenced in 1723; its exterior was carved in 18th-century baroque style by indigenous artisans, and its interior has ornate, gilded decorations. On the left as you enter is the 19th-century **Capilla del Carmen**, where believers seek cures for illness. Mass in English is given here at 9:30am on Sunday.

MUSEO ROBERT BRADY

Robert Brady (1928–86), an American artist and collector, lived in Cuernavaca for 24 years. His home, the **Casa de la Torre** (☎ 316-85-

54; Netzahualcóyotl 4; admission US$2.75; ⊙ 10am-6pm Tue-Sun), was originally part of the monastery within the Recinto de la Catedral. Brady had it extensively renovated and decorated with paintings, carvings, textiles, antiques and decorative and folk arts he'd acquired in his world travels. Now a museum, it's a short walk from the zócalo. There are several paintings by well-known Mexican artists, including Tamayo, Kahlo and Covarrubias, but the main attraction is the sheer size and diversity of the collection and the way it is arranged with delightful combinations and contrasts of styles, periods and places.

SALTO DE SAN ANTÓN

This 41m **waterfall** (⊙ 10am-6pm), surrounded by lush vegetation, is about 1km west of the Jardín Borda. A walkway is built into the cliff face so you can pass behind the falls, where there are a few picnic tables. The village of San Antón, above the falls, is a traditional center for pottery. The Ruta 4 bus (marked 'Salto') goes from the corner of Abasolo and Av Morelos directly to the entrance.

MUSEO DE MEDICINA TRADICIONAL Y HERBOLARIA

In Cuernavaca's suburbs, 1.5km southeast of the center, **Casa Maximiliano** was once a rural retreat for the Emperor Maximilian, where he would meet his Mexican lover. It was called La Casa del Olvido (the House of Forgetfulness), because Maximilian 'forgot' to include a room for his wife here. He did remember to include a small house in the back for his lover, which is now a **museum of traditional herbal medicine** (Matamoros 200, Colonia Acapatzingo; admission free; ⊙ 9am-5pm). Surrounding the museum, the **Jardín Etnobotánico** has a well-curated collection of herbs and medicinal plants from around the world. To get here, catch a Ruta 6 'Jardines' bus from the corner of Av Morelos and Degollado. Catch the return bus on 16 de Septiembre behind the garden.

PIRÁMIDE DE TEOPANZOLCO

This small **archaeological site** (☎ 314-40-46/48; cnr Río Balsas & Ixcateopan; admission US$3; ⊙ 9am-5.30pm) is in Colonia Vista Hermosa. There are actually two pyramids, one inside the other. You can climb on the outer base and see the older pyramid within, with a double staircase leading up to the remains of a

pair of temples. Tlahuicas built the older pyramid more than 800 years ago; the outside one was under construction by the Aztecs when Cortés arrived and was never completed. The name Teopanzolco means 'Place of the Old Temple,' and may relate to an ancient construction to the west of the current pyramid, where artifacts dating from around 7000 BC have been found as well as others with an Olmec influence.

Several other smaller platform structures surround the double pyramid. Near the rectangular platform to the west a tomb was discovered, containing the remains of 92 men, women and children mixed with ceramic pieces. They are believed to be victims of human sacrifice in which decapitation and dismemberment were practiced.

No buses go directly to the entrance. Catch a Ruta 4 'Barona' bus at the corner of Degollado and Guerrero, get off at Río Balsas, turn right and walk four blocks; or take a taxi to the site.

OTHER ATTRACTIONS

The great Mexican muralist David Alfaro Siqueiros had his *taller* (workshop) and home in Cuernavaca from 1964 until his death in 1974. The **Taller Alfaro Siqueiros** (☎ 315-11-15; Venus 52; admission free; ⊙ 10am-5pm Tue-Sun) is in Fraccionamiento Jardines de Cuernavaca. On display are four murals left unfinished at the artist's death and some mementos of his life.

The **Museo Fotográfico de Cuernavaca** (☎ 312-70-81; Gómes Farias 1; admission free; ⊙ 10am-5pm Tue-Sun) has a few early maps and photographs of the city. It's in a cute little 1897 building called El Castillito (Little Castle), 1km north of the zócalo. By the fountain at the foot of Gómes Farias is the entrance to the **Pasillo de la Barranca** (⊙ 8am-6pm), a walkway that follows a deep gorge bursting with flowers and butterflies, well below the roar of traffic. There are a few waterfalls along the 500m trail, which emerges by the arches at the corner of Guerrero and Gómez Farías.

Festivals & Events

In the five days before Ash Wednesday (late February or early March), a colorful **Carnaval** celebration features street performances by the Chinelo dancers of Tepoztlán, parades, art exhibits and more. The **Feria de la Primavera** (Spring Fair) in late March and early April includes cultural and artistic events, concerts and a beautiful exhibit of the city's spring flowers.

Sleeping

Accommodations in Cuernavaca don't offer great value. Cheap places tend to be depressingly basic while mid-range ones are scarce

and charmless. Top-end hotels, of course, are wonderful but expensive. On weekends and holidays, the town fills up with visitors from Mexico City, so phone ahead if possible.

BUDGET

The cheapest acceptable places (all with private bathroom, unless otherwise noted) are

---

LANGUAGE COURSES IN CUERNAVACA

Many foreigners come to Cuernavaca to study Spanish. The best schools offer small-group or individual instruction, at all levels, with four to five hours per day of intensive instruction plus a couple of hours' conversation practice. Classes begin each Monday, and most schools recommend a minimum enrollment of four weeks, though you can study for as many or as few weeks as you want.

Tuition fees vary from US$140 to US$300 per week for small group classes, usually payable in advance. You may get a discount outside the peak months of January, February, July, August and December; some schools offer discounts if you stay more than four weeks. Most schools also charge a nonrefundable one-time enrollment fee of US$75 to US$100.

The schools can arrange for students to live with a Mexican family to experience 'total immersion' in the language. The host families charge about US$20 per day with shared room and bathroom, or about US$25 per day with private room and bathroom; the price includes three meals daily. The schools can often help with hotels too. Recommended schools:

CALE – Center of Arts & Languages (☎ 313-06-03; www.gl.com.mx/cale; Nueva Tabachin 22B, Colonia Tlaltenango) Former students cite CALE's personalized approach to learning as its best asset.

Cemanahuac Educational Community (☎ 318-64-07; www.cemanahuac.com; Apartado 5-21) Emphasis is on language acquisition and cultural awareness.

Center for Bilingual Multicultural Studies (☎ 317-10-87, in the US 800-932-2068; www.bilingual -center.com; San Jerónimo 304) Accredited by the Universidad Autónoma del Estado de Morelos and affiliated with more than 100 foreign universities.

Cetlalic Alternative Language School (☎ 313-26-37; www.cetlalic.org.mx) Emphasis is on language learning, cultural awareness and social responsibility. Offers specials gay and lesbian programs.

Cuauhnáhuac Spanish Language School (☎ 312-36-73; www.cuauhnahuac.edu.mx; Av Morelos Sur 123) Helps students earn university language credits and members of the business and medical communities develop language interests.

Encuentros Comunicación y Cultura (☎ 312-50-88; www.learnspanishinmexico.com; Morelos 36, Colonia Acapantizingo) Program focuses on professionals and travelers wanting to learn Spanish.

Experiencia – Centro de Intercambio Bilingüe y Cultural (☎ 312-65-79, in the US 888-397-8363; www.experiencia.com; Leyva 200, Colonia Las Palmas) Intercambio program offers two-hour, twice-weekly conversational exchanges between Mexican and international students. Also in Tepoztlán.

IDEAL Latinoamerica (☎ 311-75-51; www.ideal-l.com) Program immerses students in Spanish language and Mexican culture while respecting the individual's pace and style of learning.

Instituto de Idiomas y Cultura en Cuernavaca (ICC; ☎ 317-04-55; www.idiomaycultura.com) A different teacher each week gives students exposure to different voices and personalities.

Prolingua Instituto Español Xochicalco (☎ 318-42-86; Hidalgo 24, Colonia Acapantzingo) Program helps develop conversational fluency while building awareness of Mexican culture, history and traditions through lectures.

Spanish Language Institute (SLI; ☎ 311-00-63; www.sli-spanish.com.mx; Bajada de La Pradera 208) Cultural courses include Mexican customs and Latin American literature.

Universal Centro de Lengua y Comunicación (☎ 318-29-04; www.universal-spanish.com) Mixes language study with visits to local communities and visits from local politicians, scholars and community leaders.

Universidad Autónoma del Estado de Morelos (☎ 316-16-26; www.uaem.mx in Spanish; Rio Pánuco 20, Colonia Lomas del Mirador) The university's Centro de Lengua, Arte e Historia para Extranjeros uses a communicative approach augmented by audio, video and print source materials.

on Aragón y León between Av Morelos and Matamoros – a strip worked by a handful of sex workers.

Hotel América (☎ 318-61-27; Aragón y León 14; s/d US$13/22) The top of the cheapie heap is basic but squeaky clean. Rooms come with hot water. TVs cost US$3 extra and there's one cheaper room without a private bathroom.

Hotel Iberia (☎ 314-13-24; Rayón 7; s/d US$19/24; P) The Iberia is a longtime foreign student favorite. Rooms are cramped and basic but all have cable TV and it's only a short walk to the zócalo. Bigger rooms upstairs are worth the few extra pesos.

Hotel Colonial (☎ 318-64-14; Aragón y León 17; s/d with bathroom US$15/24) Up the street from Hotel América, the rooms here are pleasant with most facing a cute garden. Two people sharing one bed is slightly cheaper and upstairs rooms are the best.

Hotel Las Hortensas (☎ 318-52-65; Hidalgo 13; s/d with bathroom US$19/24) A block from the zócalo, Las Hortensas has tiny, dark rooms. The rooms are clean enough, but price and location are the only reasons to stay here. Single number 23 on the roof is bright and breezy.

Villa Calmecac (☎ 310-21-03; info@turismoalternativo.org; Zacatecas 114, Colonia Buenavista; dm with breakfast US$18; P) This HI-affiliated hostel is very pleasant though 7km from the center. Made of adobe and wood, the building is equipped with rainwater-collection and sewage-recycling devices and surrounded by organic gardens. The included breakfast is an all-natural buffet and the bunk beds are in rustic-style rooms. It's 800m west of the Mexico City autopista. From the town center, it's a 20-minute ride on a Ruta 1, 2 or 3 bus from the corner of Av Morelos and Degollado. Zacatecas is two blocks past the Zapata monument on the left. Visitors must check in before 9pm.

MID-RANGE

La Casa Azul B&B (☎ 314-21-41; www.tourbymexico.com/lacasaazul; Arista 17; s/d with breakfast US$38/49; P 🖳 🖳) Finally, a mid-range charmer in the city center. The 19th-century Blue House, once a part of the Guadalupe Convent, has been thoughtfully updated and has nine comfortable rooms (a few with bathtubs) with modern amenities. The owner is a delight, the setting is tranquil and the décor is classic Mexican.

La Casa Mediterranea B&B (☎ 317-11-53; www.lacasamediterranea.com; Acacias 207, Colonia La Pradera; s/d with breakfast US$28/40; P 🖳) Tired of staying in impersonal, run-down hotels? Try this comfortable, seven-room family residence that's a 3km uphill walk from the center (US$2 taxi). The helpful owners have been hosting foreign language students for years and offer discounts for longer stays.

Hotel Juárez (☎ 314-02-19; Netzahualcóyotl 19; r US$28; 🖳) Next to the cathedral (with bells ringing all night long), the Juárez offers 12 simple but spacious and airy rooms with 24-hour hot water, plus a pool encircled by a lawn.

Hotel Papagayo (☎ 314-17-11; hotelpapagayo@prodigy.net.mx, Motolinía 13; s/d US$38/48, ste US$43-55; P 🖳) Welcome to Miami Beach: this sprawling place has 77 funky 1950s rooms with fans and TVs, two swimming pools, a leafy playground (bordered by mango trees) and plenty of parking. Rates include breakfast and complimentary lounge music on weekends.

TOP END

Las Mañanitas (☎ 314-14-66, in Mexico City 800-221-52-99, in the US 888-413-91-99; www.lasmananitas.com.mx; Linares 107; ste Sun-Thu US$233-479, Fri & Sat US$270-520; P 🖳) Renowned for its private gardens where peacocks strut around while the guests enjoy the heated pool, this is one of Mexico's finest small hotels and has been included in several World's Best listings. The 21 rooms range from cozy terrace suites to the master fireplace suite with a full living room. Its restaurant (see p232) is also justly famous.

Hotel Hacienda de Cortés (☎ 316-08-67; www.hotelhaciendadecortes.com in Spanish; Plaza Kennedy 90; s/d/ste from US$79/100/115; P 🖳) Built in the 17th century by Martín Cortés, who succeeded Hernán Cortés as Marqués del Valle de Oaxaca, the Hacienda de San Antonio Atlacomulco was renovated in 1980 to become this hotel. It has 23 luxurious suites, each with its own terrace and garden. There's a swimming pool built around old stone columns. In Atlacomulco, 4km southeast of the center, it's worth visiting even if you're not a guest, if only to stroll the lovely grounds or have lunch underneath the restaurant's magnificent colonial arches.

Hotel Posada María Cristina (☎ 318-57-67, 800-713-74-07; www.maria-cristina.com; Juárez 300; r/ste from

US$135/170; (P) (🏊)) This 16th-century estate is one of Cuernavaca's longtime favorites, with 20 tastefully appointed rooms in a nicely restored colonial building, a charming *alta cocina* restaurant, lovely hillside gardens, and an inviting pool and Jacuzzi.

Hotel Jacarandas (☎ 315-77-77, in Mexico City 55-5544-3098; www.jacarandas.com.mx; Cuauhtémoc 133; r/ste from US$150/285; (P) (🏊)) Rooms at the Jacarandas are not very large or fancy, but the rambling grounds are graced with lots of trees, gardens and three pools at varying temperatures. It's 2km east of the center in Colonia Chapultepec.

Eating

For a simple, healthy snack of yogurt with fruit, *escamochas* (a kind of fruit salad), corn on the cob or ice cream, visit one of the booths at the Jardín Juárez gazebo, then eat your treat on one of the park's many benches. Opposite Jardín Juárez along Galeana, the greasy joints that hang out signs shouting their cheap offerings are best avoided.

BUDGET

Jugos Chely's (Galeana; mains US$1-3; 🕐 7am-9pm) Opposite Jardín Juárez, Chely's has fresh fruit juice combos such as *zanayogui* (carrot and orange) and *toronjil* (grapefruit, pineapple and parsley), as well as breakfast, burgers and antojitos.

Cafeona (☎ 318-27-57; Morrow 6; drinks & snacks US$1-4; 🕐 8am-9pm Mon-Sat) This little corner of Chiapas in Morelos is a cool hangout, decorated with Chiapan crafts and serving organic coffee, as well as cheap beer, cocktails, pies, tamales and fruit salads with granola. Drop by to browse its small gift shop or check out its live music and event schedule.

El Barco (☎ 314-10-20; Rayón 5F; mains US$2-4; 🕐 11am-midnight) This popular place serves Guerrero-style *pozole* (shredded pork and hominy in delicious broth) from a clean, tiled kitchen with plenty of clay pottery. Small or large bowls are served with oregano, chili, chopped onions and limes. Specify *maciza* unless you want your soup to include bits of fat. For refreshment, there are pitchers of ice-cold *agua de jamaica*, beer and various tequilas.

MID-RANGE

Restaurant y Cafeteria Los Arcos (☎ 312-15-10; Jardín de los Héroes 4; set lunch US$4.50, mains US$3-9)

On the south side of Plaza de Armas, 'The Arches' is a popular meeting place among the international student crowd. Grab a seat at its outdoor tables, sip a coffee or a soda and watch the action on the plaza. The varied bilingual menu has something for everyone and is not too expensive. There's a separate seafood menu and live salsa music (and dancing in the aisles) on weekends.

Gastronomía Gourmet Vienés (☎ 318-40-44; Lerdo de Tejada 4; mains US$4-10, set lunch US$8.50; 🕐 2-9pm) Vienés offers middle-European dishes, such as knackwurst with sauerkraut and German fried potatoes. It also serves the best cakes, cream puffs and chocolate-rum truffles this side of Austria and a robust bottomless mug of coffee.

Trattoria Marco Polo (☎ 318-40-32; Hidalgo 30; mains US$5-10, pizza US$5-25; 🕐 1-10:30pm Sun-Thu, 1pm-midnight Fri & Sat; (P)) This lively trattoria has homemade pasta and a decent wine list and tosses superior pizzas, from single-serving to family-size pies. There's a perfect view of the cathedral compound from the balcony and breezy courtyard tables out back.

Gaucho Infiel (Las Casas 2; mains US$5-10) Just south of Jardín Juárez, Plazuela del Zacate funnels into a quaint pedestrian alley, which is where you'll find this lively Argentine place that does thick charcoal-grilled steaks and *parrilladas* (meat and sausage assortments that feed two) and not much else.

La Parroquia (☎ 318-58-20; Guerrero 102; mains US$4-8) On Jardín Juárez' east side, this is a favorite with Cuernavaca's older crowd. Come here for the location – the traditional Mexican food is nothing special.

La Universal (☎ 318-59-70; cnr Gutenberg & Guerrero; mains US$4-9) The Universal occupies a strategic position on the corner of the two central plazas, with tables under an awning facing the Plaza de Armas. Like La Parroquia, this popular place is all about location. The people-watching is great but the food is only average.

TOP END

Restaurant Las Mañanitas (☎ 314-14-66; Linares 107; mains US$15-30; 🕐 1-5pm & 7-11pm; (P)) For an indulgence, try one of Mexico's best and most famous restaurants at the hotel (see p231) of the same name. Choose between tables inside the mansion or on the terrace where you can watch peacocks and flamingos wander around the emerald-green garden among fine modern sculptures. The menu, presented tableside on a large blackboard, changes daily and features dishes from around the world. The bar overlooking the garden is a romantic place for a cocktail. Reservations are recommended.

Gaia (☎ 312-36-56; Blvd Juárez 102; mains US$10-20; ☉ 1pm-midnight Mon-Sat, 1-8pm Sun; ℗) In a mansion that once belonged to actor Mario Moreno (Cantinflas), this creative restaurant blends Mediterranean and Mexican ingredients into some fabulous dishes. The walls have been torn down to provide diners with a view of the pool, the bottom of which is adorned with a mosaic designed by Diego Rivera.

La India Bonita (☎ 318-69-67; Morrow 115; mains US$6-13; ☉ 8:30am-10:30pm Tue-Fri, 9am-10pm Sat, 9am-8pm Sun) This lovely courtyard restaurant in the former US ambassador's home (aka Casa Mañana, as in 'it will be finished tomorrow') delivers tasty, traditional Mexican cuisine. House specialties include chicken mole, chicken breast stuffed with squash flowers and *huitlacoche* sauce and a platter with seven different tacos. Saturday evening features live folkloric ballet from 7pm and on Sunday there's an elaborate buffet brunch spread.

Drinking

Plazuela del Zacate and adjacent alley Las Casas come alive in the evening with many bars featuring live music. **Bar Eclipse** has performers on two levels, folk on the bottom and rock on top. As the name implies, **El Romántico** is a venue for ballad singers.

La Estación Zócalo (☎ 312-13-37; cnr Blvd Juárez & Hidalgo) Opposite the Palacio de Cortés, this popular bar attracts a younger crowd with blaring loud rock music and two brightly colored, but dimly lit dance floors.

Entertainment

Hanging around the central plazas is always a popular activity, especially on Sunday from 6pm, when open-air concerts are often staged. The **Jardín Borda** (p228) hosts recitals (tickets US$5.50) most Thursdays at 7pm.

DISCOS

The better discos charge a cover of at least US$5; women are usually admitted free on Friday and Saturday nights. Some discos enforce dress codes, and the trendier places post style police at the door.

Barba Azul (☎ 311-55-11/55; Prado 10; ☉ Fri & Sat 10pm-late; ℗) in Colonia San Jerónimo with fab indoor gardens, and **Kaova** (☎ 318-43-80; Av Morelos 241; ☉ Wed, Fri & Sat 10pm-late; ℗) are two of the most popular places. Glitzy **Sammaná** (☎ 313-47-27; Plan de Ayala 708; ☉ 9pm-5am Wed-Sat) is another local favorite.

Tropical **Zúmbale** (☎ 322-53-48; Bajada de Chapultepec 13A; ☉ 9pm-5am Thu-Sat), 6km east of the center, is the hotspot for dancing to live salsa music.

Since public transport is sparse after hours, a taxi is the best way to get to the clubs. The fare to Zúmbale or Sammaná from the center of town should be no more than US$4.

THEATER

If your Spanish is up to it, you might sample Cuernavaca's theater scene.

Cine Teatro Morelos (☎ 318-10-50; Av Morelos 188; tickets from US$2) Morelos' state theater hosts a variety of cultural offerings, including quality film series, plays and dance performances.

Teatro Ocampo (☎ 318-63-85; Jardín Juárez 2) On Jardín Juárez' west side, this theater stages contemporary plays; a calendar of cultural events is posted at its entrance.

WRESTLING

Arena Isabel (☎ 318-59-16; cnr Juárez & Abasolo; adult/child US$4.50/2.75) Are you ready to rumble? Less highbrow diversions go down here in the form of *lucha libre* (wrestling). Peep at the good-vs-evil line-ups on posters pasted up around town.

Shopping

Cuernavaca has no distinctive handicrafts, but if you crave an onyx ashtray, a leather belt or some second-rate silver, try the **souvenir stalls** (south of Palacio de Cortés) or the Fonart outlet in Jardín Borda.

Getting There & Away
BUS

Quite a few bus companies serve Cuernavaca. The main lines operate five separate long-distance terminals:

Estrella de Oro (EDO; Av Morelos 900) (

Estrella Roja (ER; cnr Galeana & Cuauhtemotzin)

Flecha Roja & Estrella Blanca (FR & EB; Av Morelos 503, btwn Arista & Victoria)

Pullman de Morelos (PDM; cnr Abasolo & Netzahual-cóyotl & Casino de la Selva) Two stations northeast of the center.

Daily 1st-class buses from Cuernavaca:

Acapulco EDO (US$18, 4hr; hourly; US$20, 4hr; hourly deluxe); FR (US$20, 4hr; 7 daily)

Chilpancingo EDO (US$10, 2hr, 5 daily); FR (US$10, 2hr, 7 daily)

Cuautla ER (US$3, 1¼hr, every 20-30min 5am-7:30pm)

Grutas de Cacahuamilpa FR (US$3, 2hr, 6 daily)

Mexico City (Terminal Sur) PDM (US$5, 1¼hr, deluxe every 15min 5am-7:30pm, from downtown terminal; US$5.50, 1¼hr, 'ejecutivo' every 25min, from Casino de la Selva); FR (US$5, 1¼hr, frequent) Reserve one or two days in advance, if possible.

Mexico City Airport PDM (US$9, 2hr; hourly, from Casino de la Selva) Tickets may be purchased at PDM downtown terminal.

Oaxtepec ER (US$2.50, 1hr, every 15min)

Puebla ER (US$11, 3¾hr, hourly)

Taxco FR (US$3.75, 1½hr, 15 daily); EDO (US$3.50, 1½hr, 5 daily)

Tepoztlán (US$1.25, 30min, every 15min 6am-10pm) From the local bus terminal at the city market.

Toluca FR (US$4, 2½hr, every 30min)

Zihuatanejo EDO (US$26, 7hr; 2 daily, at 8:20pm & 10:20pm)

CAR & MOTORCYCLE

Cuernavaca is 89km south of Mexico City, a 1½-hour drive on Hwy 95 and a one-hour trip on the toll Hwy 95D (around US$7). Both roads continue south to Acapulco; Hwy 95 goes through Taxco, and Hwy 95D is more direct and much faster (around US$37).

Getting Around

You can walk to most places of interest in central Cuernavaca. Local buses (US$0.35) display their destinations on their windshields. Many local buses and those to nearby towns leave from the southern corner of the city market. Taxis go to most places in town for under US$4.

To get to the Estrella de Oro bus terminal, 1km south of the center, take a Ruta 20 bus down Galeana; in the other direction, catch any bus heading up Av Morelos. Ruta 17 buses head up Av Morelos and stop within one block of the Pullman de Morelos terminal at Casino de la Selva. The rest of the bus terminals are within walking distance of the zócalo.

AROUND CUERNAVACA

Many places can be visited on day trips from Cuernavaca, on the way north to Mexico City or south to Taxco.

Xochicalco

Atop a desolate plateau 15km southwest of Cuernavaca as the crow flies but about 38km by road is the ancient ceremonial center of **Xochicalco** (☎ 777-379-74-16; admission US$3.50; ◷ 9am-5pm), one of central Mexico's most important archaeological sites. In Náhuatl, the language of the Aztecs, Xochicalco (so-chee-*cal*-co') means 'Place of the House of Flowers.' It was inscribed as a Unesco World Heritage Site in 1999.

Today it's a collection of white stone ruins covering approximately 10 sq km, many yet to be excavated. They represent the various cultures – Toltec, Olmec, Zapotec, Mixtec and Aztec – for which Xochicalco was a commercial, cultural or religious center. When Teotihuacán began to weaken around AD 650-700, Xochicalco began to rise in importance, achieving its maximum splendor between AD 650 and 850 with far-reaching cultural and commercial relations. Around AD 650, a congress of spiritual leaders convened here, representing the Zapotec, Mayan and Gulf Coast peoples, to correlate their respective calendars.

The site's most famous monument is the **Pirámide de Quetzalcóatl** (Pyramid of the Plumed Serpent). Archaeologists have surmised from its well-preserved bas-reliefs that astronomer-priests met here at the beginning and end of each 52-year cycle of the pre-Hispanic calendar. Xochicalco remained an important center until around 1200, when its excessive growth caused a fall similar to that of Teotihuacán. Signs at the site are in English and Spanish, but information appearing beside displays at the impressive **museum** 200m from the ruins is in Spanish only.

GETTING THERE & AWAY

Take a 'Cuautepec' bus (US$0.70) from the local bus station near the Cuernavaca market. It will drop you off at the site entrance. The buses run every half hour. The last bus back to town leaves around 6pm. Alternatively, Pullman de Morelos runs buses every 40 minutes that will drop you off within

4km of the site. Flecha Roja runs buses by the same intersection every two hours. From there, you can walk (uphill) or catch a taxi (if you're lucky enough to find one).

Laguna de Tequesquitengo

This lake, 37km south of Cuernavaca, is a popular location for aquatic sports, particularly waterskiing. Hotels, restaurants and other facilities are around the lakeshore. Nearby are several of Morelos' famous balnearios – often natural springs that have been used as bathing and therapeutic places for hundreds of years.

Hotel Hacienda Vista Hermosa (☎ 734-345-53-61, in Mexico City 55-5662-4916/18; r without/with meals US$139/189; P ﹩) This hotel, 2km north of the lake, was a cane-alcohol refinery in the 16th century. Accommodations are in 105 rooms, some of which retain their original colonial-era furniture, which are set amid some 80,000 sq meters of lush gardens and palm-lined pathways. Nonguests can use the pool and sports facilities for US$5 per day.

Pullman de Morelos runs buses from Cuernavaca to the town of Tequesquitengo (US$2.50, 1½ hours, five daily), on the lake's southeast edge.

Las Estacas

Set amid botanical gardens with plenty of flowers near the town of Tlaltizapán, **Balneario Las Estacas** (☎ 734-345-00-77, in Mexico City 55-5563-2428; www.lasestacas.com; adult/child under 1.25m tall US$12/7.50; ﹩ 8am-6pm) is designed for relaxation in nature. You can swim in numerous pools or in a cool, clear river, replenished by underground springs. There's scuba diving equipment for hire and diving classes are offered. Visit during the week if you're seeking tranquility.

Fuerte Bambú (informes@lasestacas.com; dm adult/child US$22/18, trailer hookup US$21, s/d US$77/103) This is Las Estacas' HI-affiliated hostel and resembles a jungle village. It features a row of cool, well-ventilated adobe/reed houses. There are three bunk beds in each of the houses. Spacious bathhouses are adjacent to the villas. Other accommodations include a 14-room hotel and a cluster of four-person, palm-thatched huts, or you can camp. The fee for any of these options includes park admission. Rates are 10% to 25% lower during the week and reservations are encouraged.

GETTING THERE & AWAY

Combis from Jojutla (50 minutes south of Cuernavaca by frequent Pullman de Morelos buses) go directly to the park entrance (US$0.70). By car, take the Cuautla exit off the Mexico City-Acapulco autopista, then take Hwy 138 east to Yautepec. From there head south on Hwy 2 toward Tlaltizapán and follow the signs.

Parque Nacional Lagunas de Zempoala

Only 25km (an hour's drive) northwest of Cuernavaca by winding roads is a group of seven lakes high in the hills. Some of them are stocked with fish for anglers (the season is mid-February to mid-October), and the surrounding forest offers pleasant walks and camping (park admission free). Departing every half hour from Cuernavaca, Flecha Roja buses to Toluca make a stop at the park.

TAXCO

☎ 762 / pop 90,000 / elevation 1800m

The old silver-mining town of Taxco (*Tass-co*), 160km southwest of Mexico City, is a gorgeous colonial antique, and one of Mexico's most picturesque and pleasant places. Clinging to a steep hillside, its narrow cobblestone streets twist between well-worn buildings and open unexpectedly onto pretty plazas and reveal enchanting vistas at every corner. Unlike many Mexican towns from the colonial era, it has not become surrounded by industrial suburbs. Combis and VW taxis scurry through the labyrinth like ants on an anthill. And few streetscapes are defaced with rows of parked cars, because there's simply no room for them.

The federal government has declared Taxco a national historical monument, and local laws help protect the colonial-style architecture. Old buildings are preserved and restored wherever possible, and any new buildings must conform to the old in scale, style and materials – check out the colonial Pemex station. Though Taxco's silver mines are almost exhausted, handmade silver jewelry is one of the town's main industries. There are hundreds of silver shops, and visiting them is an excellent excuse to wander the streets.

History

Taxco was called Tlachco (meaning 'place where ball is played') by the Aztecs, who

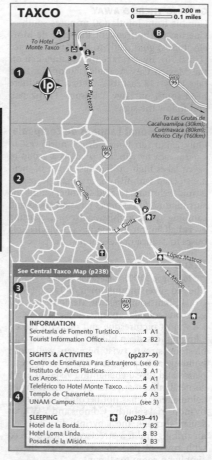

TAXCO

```
0                200 m
0                0.1 miles
```

INFORMATION
Secretaría de Fomento Turístico............1 A1
Tourist Information Office....................2 B2

SIGHTS & ACTIVITIES   (pp237–9)
Centro de Enseñanza Para Extranjeros..(see 6)
Instituto de Artes Plásticas....................3 A1
Los Arcos...4 A1
Teleférico to Hotel Monte Taxco............5 A1
Templo de Chavarrieta.........................6 A3
UNAM Campus...............................(see 3)

SLEEPING   🏠 (pp239–41)
Hotel de la Borda...............................7 B2
Hotel Loma Linda...............................8 B3
Posada de la Misión............................9 B3

the highway at the north end of present-day Taxco. The hacienda has gone through several metamorphoses and now houses the Instituto de Artes Plásticas and a branch of the Universidad Nacional Autónoma de México's Spanish-language institute.

The prospectors quickly emptied the first veins of silver from the hacienda and left Taxco. Further quantities of ore were not discovered until two centuries later, in 1743. Don José de la Borda, who had arrived in 1716 from France at the age of 16 to work with his miner brother, accidentally uncovered one of the area's richest veins. According to a Taxco legend, Borda was riding near where the Templo de Santa Prisca now stands when his horse stumbled, dislodged a stone and exposed the precious metal.

Borda went on to make three fortunes and lose two. He introduced new techniques of draining and repairing mines, and he reportedly treated his indigenous workers better than those working in other colonial mines. The Templo de Santa Prisca was the devout Borda's gift to Taxco. He is remembered for the saying 'Dios da a Borda, Borda da a Dios' (God gives to Borda, Borda gives to God).

His success attracted more prospectors, and new silver veins were found and emptied. With most of the silver gone, Taxco became a quiet town with a dwindling population and economy. In 1929 an American professor and architect named William (Guillermo) Spratling arrived and, at the suggestion of then US ambassador Dwight Morrow, set up a small silver workshop as a way to rejuvenate the town. (Another version has it that Spratling was writing a book in Taxco and resorted to the silver business because his publisher went broke. A third has it that Spratling had a notion to create jewelry that synthesized pre-Hispanic motifs with art deco modernism.) The workshop evolved into a factory, and Spratling's apprentices began establishing their own shops. Today there are more than 300 silver shops in Taxco.

Orientation

Taxco's twisting streets may make you feel like a mouse in a maze, and even maps of the town look confusing at first, but you'll learn to find your way around – in any case, it's a nice place to get lost. The zócalo (aka Plaza Borda) is the heart of the town, and

dominated the region from 1440 until the Spanish arrived. The colonial city was founded by Captain Rodrigo de Castañeda in 1529 with a mandate from Hernán Cortés. Among the town's first Spanish residents were three miners – Juan de Cabra, Juan Salcedo and Diego de Nava – and the carpenter Pedro Muriel. In 1531 they established the first Spanish mine in North America.

The Spaniards came searching for tin, which they found in small quantities, but by 1534 they had discovered tremendous lodes of silver. That year the Hacienda El Chorrillo was built, complete with water wheel, smelter and aqueduct – the remains of which form the old arches (Los Arcos) over

Sanborns Restaurant (p124), Casa de Azulejos
(House of Tiles)

Marionettes, Centro de Artesanías la
Ciudadela (p164), Mexico City

Brass model of the ancient Aztec island city of Tenochtitlán (p122), Mexico City

Cable car, Taxco (p235)

Religious shop, Mercado La Merced (p165),
Mexico City

Colorfully painted *trajinera* (gondola), canals of Xochimilco (p132)

its church, the Parroquia de Santa Prisca, is a good landmark.

Hwy 95 becomes Av de los Plateros beyond the remains of the old aqueduct (Los Arcos) at the north end of town, then winds its way around the east side of central Taxco. Both bus stations are on Av de los Plateros. La Garita branches west from Av de los Plateros opposite the Pemex station, and becomes the main thoroughfare through the middle of town. It follows a convoluted route, more or less southwest (one-way only) to Plaza Borda, changing names to Juárez along the way. Past the plaza, this main artery becomes Cuauhtémoc, and goes down to Plazuela de San Juan. Most essentials are along or nearby this La Garita–Juárez–Cuauhtémoc route. Several side roads go east back to Av de los Plateros, which is two-way and therefore the only way a vehicle can get back to the north end of town. The basic combi route is a counterclockwise loop going north on Av de los Plateros and south through the center of town.

Information

INTERNET ACCESS
Cybercafés come and go here like the clouds, but most charge around US$1 an hour and open around 10am to 11pm daily.

Net X Internet (Map p238; Ruíz de Alarcón 11)
Zona Virtu@l (Map p238; Hidalgo 18)

LAUNDRY
Lavandería Los Pinos (Map p238; ☎ 627-24-87; Ex-Rastro)

MONEY
There are several banks with ATMs around the town's main plazas.

POST
Main post office (Map p238; Av de los Plateros 382; ☾ 8am-4pm Mon-Fri, 9am-1pm Sat) South end of town, with branch at Palacio Municipal.

TELEPHONE
There are card phones near Plaza Borda and in most hotel lobbies; cards are sold at hotels, banks and stores.

TOURIST INFORMATION
Secretaría de Fomento Turístico (Map p236; ☎ 622-22-74/79; Av de los Plateros; ☾ 9am-8pm) In Centro de Convenciones de Taxco at north end of town.

Helpful English-speaking staff arrange guided tours of Taxco (US$30 for groups up to 10).
Tourist Information Office (Map p236; ☎ 622-07-98; Av de los Plateros) Nongovernmental office 1km further south, functions primarily to arrange city tours; its knowledgeable English- (and French- and German-); speaking staff can answer most questions.

The Flecha Roja bus station also has a helpful tourist information booth with free city maps.

Sights & Activities

PARROQUIA DE SANTA PRISCA   Map p238
On Plaza Borda, this **church** of rose-colored stone is a baroque treasure; its Churrigueresque façade is decorated with elaborately sculpted figures. Over the doorway, the oval bas-relief depicts Christ's baptism. Inside, the intricately sculpted, gold-covered altarpieces are equally fine Churrigueresque pieces.

The local Catholic hierarchy allowed Don José de la Borda to donate this church to Taxco on the condition that he mortgage his personal mansion and other assets to guarantee its completion. It was designed by Spanish architects Diego Durán and Juan Caballero and constructed between 1751 and 1758, and it nearly bankrupted Borda.

MUSEO GUILLERMO SPRATLING   Map p238
This three-story archaeology and history **museum** (☎ 622-16-70; Delgado 1; admission US$3.25; ☾ 10am-6pm Tue-Sat, 9am-3pm Sun) is directly behind Templo de Santa Prisca. Pre-Hispanic art exhibits on the two upper floors include jade statuettes, Olmec ceramics and other interesting pieces, mostly from the private collection of William Spratling.

MUSEO DE ARTE VIRREINAL   Map p238
One of Taxco's oldest colonial homes is commonly known as **Casa Humboldt**, though the German explorer and naturalist Friedrich Heinrich Alexander von Humboldt stayed here for only one night in 1803. The restored building now houses a colonial religious art **museum** (☎ 622-55-01; Ruiz de Alarcón 12; adult/child US$1.50/0.50; ☾ 10am-6:45pm Tue-Sat, 10am-3:45pm), with a small but well-displayed collection, labeled in English and Spanish. An interesting exhibit describes restoration work on the Templo de Santa Prisca, during

which some fabulous material was found in the basement.

CASA BORDA (CENTRO CULTURAL TAXCO)

Built by José de la Borda in 1759, the **Casa Borda** (☎ 622-66-34; east side of Plaza Borda; admission free; ⏰ 10am-5pm Tue-Sun) now serves as a cultural center exhibiting sculpture, painting and photos by Guerrero artists. However, the building is the main attraction. Due to the unevenness of the terrain, the rear window looks out on a precipitous four-story drop, even though the entrance is on the ground floor. The good bookstore next door stocks a few English-language Lonely Planet guides.

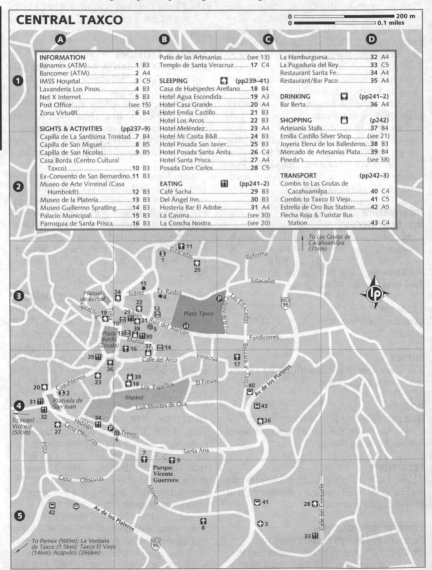

CENTRAL TAXCO

0 _____ 200 m
0 _____ 0.1 miles

INFORMATION
Banamex (ATM).............................1 B3
Bancomer (ATM)..........................2 A4
IMSS Hospital................................3 C5
Lavandería Los Pinos.................4 B3
Net X Internet..............................5 B3
Post Office.............................(see 15)
Zona Virtu@l................................6 B4

SIGHTS & ACTIVITIES (pp237-9)
Capilla de La Santísima Trinidad...7 B4
Capilla de San Miguel.................8 B5
Capilla de San Nicolas................9 B5
Casa Borda (Centro Cultural
    Taxco)...................................10 B3
Ex-Convento de San Bernardino..11 B3
Museo de Arte Virreinal (Casa
    Humboldt)..............................12 B3
Museo de la Platería..................13 B3
Museo Guillermo Spratling........14 B3
Palacio Municipal.......................15 B3
Parroquia de Santa Prisca.........16 B3

Patio de las Artesanías.............(see 13)
Templo de Santa Veracruz.........17 C4

SLEEPING (pp239-41)
Casa de Huéspedes Arellano.....18 B4
Hotel Agua Escondida...............19 A3
Hotel Casa Grande.....................20 A4
Hotel Emilia Castillo...................21 B3
Hotel Los Arcos..........................22 B3
Hotel Meléndez...........................23 A4
Hotel Mi Casita B&B...................24 B3
Hotel Posada San Javier.............25 B3
Hotel Posada Santa Anita..........26 C4
Hotel Santa Prisca......................27 A4
Posada Don Carlos......................28 C5

EATING (pp241-2)
Café Sacha..................................29 B3
Del Ángel Inn.............................30 B3
Hostería Bar El Adobe................31 A4
La Casona..............................(see 30)
La Concha Nostra..................(see 20)

La Hamburguesa........................32 A4
La Pagaduría del Rey.................33 C5
Restaurant Santa Fe...................34 A4
Restaurant/Bar Paco..................35 A4

DRINKING (pp241-2)
Bar Berta.....................................36 A4

SHOPPING (p242)
Artesanía Stalls..........................37 B4
Emilia Castillo Silver Shop......(see 21)
Joyería Elena de los Ballesteros...38 B3
Mercado de Artesanías Plata....39 B4
Pineda's.................................(see 38)

TRANSPORT (pp242-3)
Combis to Las Grutas de
    Cacahuamilpa...........................40 C4
Combis to Taxco El Viejo............41 C5
Estrella de Oro Bus Station.........42 A5
Flecha Roja & Turistar Bus
    Station.....................................43 C4

MUSEO DE LA PLATERÍA   Map p238

The small **silver museum** (Patio de las Artesanías Bldg, Plaza Borda; admission US$1; ☺ 10am-6pm Tue-Sun) exhibits some superb examples of the silversmith's art and outlines (in Spanish) its development in Taxco. Included are some classic designs by William Spratling. Notice the very colorful, sculptural combinations of silver with semiprecious stones – a feature of much local silverwork and a link with pre-Hispanic stone-carving traditions.

To get to the recently renovated museum, enter the Patio de las Artesanías building on the corner of Plaza Borda; on your left as you face Santa Prisca, turn left and go to the end of the hall and down the stairs.

TELEFÉRICO & MONTE TAXCO   Map p236

From the north end of Taxco, near Los Arcos, a Swiss-made **cable car** (round-trip adult/child US$2.75/1.75; ☺ 8am-7pm) ascends 173m to the Hotel Monte Taxco resort (p241), affording fantastic views of Taxco and the surrounding mountains. To find it, walk uphill from the south side of Los Arcos and turn right through the Instituto de Artes Plásticas gate.

Courses

The **Centro de Enseñanza Para Extranjeros** (CEPE; Map p236; ☎ 622-34-10; www.cepetaxco.unam.mx; UNAM campus; courses from US$450), a branch of the Universidad Nacional Autónoma de México (UNAM), offers six-week Spanish language courses in the Ex-Hacienda El Chorrillo. Advanced students may take additional courses in Mexican art history, geography and literature. Fees cover one language course and two culture/history courses, and CEPE can arrange lodging with local host families.

Next door, the **Escuela Nacional de Artes Plasticas** (☎ 622-36-90; enap_taxco@yahoo.com.mx; Instituto de Artes Plásticas) offers arts workshops from US$135 per month or US$800 per semester.

Festivals & Events

Try to time your visit to Taxco during one of its annual festivals, but do be sure to reserve a hotel room in advance. During Semana Santa, in particular, visitors pour into the city.

Fiestas de Santa Prisca & San Sebastián – The festivals of Taxco's two patron saints are celebrated on January 18 (Santa Prisca) and January 20 (San Sebastián),

when people parade by the entrance of the Templo de Santa Prisca with their pets and farm animals in tow for an annual blessing.

Jueves Santo – On the Thursday before Easter, the institution of the Eucharist is commemorated with beautiful presentations and street processions of hooded penitents, some of whom flagellate themselves with thorns as the procession winds through town.

Jornadas Alarconianas – In memory of Taxco-born playwright Juan Ruiz de Alarcón, a cultural festival takes place in the summertime (check with the tourist office for exact dates). Taxco's convention center, plazas and churches all host concerts and dance performances by internationally renowned performing artists. Other concerts take place inside the Grutas de Cacahuamilpa (see p244).

Día del Jumil – This unusual festival celebrates a savory local beetle (the *jumil*) on the first Monday after Day of the Dead on November 2. Traditionally, the entire town climbs Cerro de Huixteco on the Día del Jumil to collect *jumiles*, bring picnic baskets and share food and camaraderie. Many families come early and camp on the hill over the preceding weekend. The celebration is said to represent the *jumiles* giving energy and life to the people of Taxco for another year.

Feria de la Plata – The weeklong national silver fair is held during the last week in November or the first week in December (check with the tourist office for exact dates). Competitions are held in various categories (such as statuary and jewelry), and some of Mexico's best silverwork is on display. Other festivities include organ recitals in Santa Prisca, rodeos, burro races, concerts and dances.

Las Posadas – From December 16 to 24, nightly candlelit processions pass through Taxco's streets singing from door to door. Children are dressed up to resemble various Biblical characters, and at the end of the processions, they attack piñatas.

Sleeping

Taxco's hotels tend to be pricier than elsewhere in central Mexico, but they are generally so appealing that they're good value anyway. Few places have on-site parking, but most have a deal (US$3 to US$5 for 24 hours) with the central Plaza Taxco lot.

BUDGET

Casa de Huéspedes Arellano (Map p238; ☎ 622-02-15; Los Pajaritos 23; dm US$10, s/d/tr with shared bathroom US$13/20/26) Next to the silver market, this popular place has 15 simple but clean rooms and two shared showers. It's a family-run place with terraces for sitting and a rooftop laundry sink. To find it, walk down the alley on the south side of Santa Prisca until you reach a staircase descending to your right. Follow it past the stalls to a flight of stairs to your left; it's 32 steps down on the left.

Hotel Posada Santa Anita (Map p238; ☎ 622-07-52; hpsta54@hotmail.com; Av de los Plateros 320; s/d US$20/29; P) Near the Flecha Roja bus station, this hotel has 25 small, quiet rooms. TV costs a couple of dollars extra. Go for a rooftop room for good views.

Hotel Casa Grande (Map p238; ☎ 622-09-69; casagrande@prodigy.net.mx; Plazuela de San Juan 7; s/d US$15/23, with shared bathroom US$11/19) Occupying the upper level of the former mining court building, the Big House has 26 basic but clean rooms around an inner courtyard. Beware: the one shared bathroom is both tiny and dirty. Rooms can be noisy; adjacent La Concha Nostra (p241) hosts loud live music on Saturday. TV costs an extra US$4 and laundry facilities are available.

MID-RANGE

Hotel Posada San Javier (Map p238; ☎ 622-31-77; posadasanjavier@hotmail.com; Estacadas 32; s/d/f from US$32/35/46; P ▣) One of Taxco's most attractive places to stay at any price. Though centrally located, it's peaceful, with a lovely, large enclosed garden around a big swimming pool. Many of its 18 comfortable, high-ceilinged rooms come with terraces with private views. Good-value family-size apartments with living rooms and kitchens fetch up to US$60. Reservations are highly recommended.

Hotel Los Arcos (Map p238; ☎ 622-18-36; losarcoshotel@hotmail.com; Ruiz de Alarcón 4; s/d/ste US$31/36/51) This former 17th-century monastery retains a wonderful courtyard, lounging areas, a spectacular rooftop terrace and lots of character. The 26 rooms are all clean and spacious.

Hotel Mi Casita B&B (Map p238; ☎ 627-17-77; www.mycasita.com; Altos de Redondo 1; s/d/ste with breakfast US$46/55/64) In a charming old family house, this enticing new six-room B&B offers great views of the cathedral at most every turn. The comfortable rooms, including two suites, feature original hand-painted bathroom tiles and some have private terraces. Off-season rates are US$5 less and children are not welcome.

Hotel Santa Prisca (Map p238; ☎ 622-09-80; htl_staprisca@yahoo.com; Cena Obscuras 1; s/d/ste US$28/41/57; P) On Plazuela de San Juan's south side, the elegant Santa Prisca features a quiet interior patio and a pleasant restaurant. Some

rooms have private terraces. The parking lot is reached through a tunnel at the hotel's uphill end.

Hotel Emilia Castillo (Map p238; ☎ /fax 622-13-96; hotelemilia@hotmail.com; Ruiz del Alarcón 7; s/d US$32/37) Owned by a famous family of silver workers, this updated place opposite Hotel Los Arcos has colonial charm at reasonable prices. Don't miss the rooftop terrace. There's a shop downstairs displaying the family's unique silver designs.

Posada Don Carlos (Map p238; ☎ 622-00-75; Calle del Consuelo 8; r from US$55; P ▣) This hotel has eight tastefully appointed rooms, six with balconies offering superb views. There's a small pool on a terrace facing town. The hill to the hotel is a tough climb – take a taxi for US$1.50.

Hotel Victoria (☎ 622-00-04; www.victoriataxco.com in Spanish; Carlos Nibbi 5-7; s/d/ste US$46/50/73; P ▣ ▣) For a taste of old-time Taxco, try this sprawling place that dominates the town's southern hills. It retains the feel of a colonial village wrapped around a bend in the mountainside, complete with cobblestone streets and little overgrown nooks.

Hotel Agua Escondida (Map p238; ☎ 622-07-26; www.aguaescondida.com; Plaza Borda 4; s/d US$49/62; P ▣) Right on the zócalo, the Agua Escondida has a couple of pools on a high terrace and a basement garage. The 65 comfy if sterile rooms (some remodeled, some not) have Mexican furnishings, TVs and phones.

Hotel Loma Linda (Map p236; ☎ 622-02-06; www.hotellomalinda.com; Av de los Plateros 52; s/d/tr US$33/39/46, high season r US$50; P ▣) A kilometer north of town at a bend in the highway, the motel-style Loma Linda is perched on the edge of a vast chasm. The back rooms have vertigo-inducing views of a lush green valley. There's a restaurant, heated pool, easy parking and cable TV in all rooms.

Hotel Meléndez (Map p238; ☎ 622-00-06; Cuauhtémoc 6; s/d US$30/35) This is an older place with pleasant terrace sitting areas and a good location between the Plazuela de San Juan and Plaza Borda. Because of its location, however, quite a bit of street noise penetrates the 33 rooms.

TOP END

Posada de la Misión (Map p236; ☎ 622-00-63, 800-008-29-20; www.posadamision.com; Cerro de la Misión 32; s/d with breakfast & dinner US$135/155; P ▣ ▣) This luxurious colonial-style hotel within walking distance of the center is a superior option to other in-town hotels. Most of its large rooms feature private terraces with fine views, and two-bedroom suites have fireplaces and kitchenettes. Overlooking the large pool is one of the classiest restaurants in town, El Mural, and a mosaic mural of the Aztec emperor Cuauhtémoc designed by Mexican artist Juan O'Gorman.

Hotel Monte Taxco (☎ 622-13-00, 800-980-0000; www.montetaxco.com.mx; Lomas de Taxco; r/ste US$109/199; P ✕ ⚊) Way up on top of the mountain that it's named after, this five-star resort is considered Taxco's most fabulous place to stay, but magnificent views and nicer rooms can be had elsewhere for less. It can be reached by car, taxi or teleférico. Quoted rates, which rise on weekends, include use of the pool but not of the hotel's tennis courts, nine-hole golf course, under-equipped gym or steam baths. There are also restaurants, bars, a disco and a state-run handicrafts shop.

Hotel de la Borda (Map p236; ☎ 622-02-25; www .hotelborda.com; Cerro del Pedregal 2; r/ste from US$85/150; P ⚊) This sprawling four-star mission-style complex is perched on a hill, with a pool and a large dining room. Service is good but the spacious rooms, some with panoramic city views, are a bit faded and less elegant than you'd expect in this range.

Eating & Drinking

A noteworthy local delicacy are *jumiles*, 1cm-long beetles that migrate annually to the Cerro de Huixteco (the hill behind Taxco) to reproduce. They begin to arrive around September; the last ones leave by January or February. During this time, the *jumiles* are a great delicacy for the people of Taxco, who eat them alone or mixed in salsa with tomatoes, garlic, onion and chilies, or even alive, rolled into tortillas. In season, you can buy live *jumiles* in the market; Restaurant Santa Fe serves traditionally-prepared *salsa de jumil*.

CAFÉS & QUICK EATS
Café Sacha (Map p238; ☎ 628-51-50; Ruiz de Alarcón 1A; mains US$2-6; �8am-midnight) This cozy little upstairs bohemian café serves a variety of international snacks and vegetarian dishes. It's a great place to breakfast or hang out over coffee or a cocktail.

La Hamburguesa (Map p238; ☎ 622-09-41; Plazuela de San Juan 5; mains US$1.50-3; �8am-midnight Thu-Tue) For late-night snacks, try this place on the west side of Plazuela San Juan. It has burger-and-fries combos and excellent enchiladas.

RESTAURANTS & BARS
Hostería Bar El Adobe (Map p238; ☎ 622-14-16; Plazuela de San Juan 13; mains US$4-10) This place has a less captivating view than its neighbors but lovely interior décor. Specialties include garlic soup with shrimp and Taxco-style *cecina* (salted strip steak) with diced chicken and sliced poblano chilies.

Restaurant/Bar Paco (Map p238; ☎ 622-00-64; Plaza Borda 12; mains US$6-13; �noon-11:30pm) Overlooking Plaza Borda through large picture windows, Paco's is great for people-watching. The food is good too, but you pay for the view. Try the delicious mole enchiladas. The bar hosts live music on Friday and Saturday evenings.

Del Ángel Inn (Map p238; ☎ 622-55-25; Muñoz 4; mains US$5-15; �8am-10:30pm) On the left side of the Santa Prisca, the Del Ángel has a spectacular rooftop terrace bar. It's definitely tourist-oriented but the food isn't bad. The set lunch (US$8.50) consists of fresh bread with herbed butter, soup, a main course and dessert. Main courses include salads, pastas and Mexican dishes.

La Casona (Map p238; ☎ 622-10-71; Muñoz 4; mains US$4-9; �8am-8pm) Next door to the Del Ángel, La Casona has similar fare for a little less, as well as an excellent balcony with a view down Taxco's hillsides.

Restaurant Santa Fe (Map p238; ☎ 622-11-70; Hidalgo 2; mains US$3-7) Often recommended by locals, the Santa Fe serves good food at fair prices, though service can be brusque. It offers set breakfasts, a hearty four-course *comida corrida* (US$5.50) and *pozole* daily from 4pm.

La Concha Nostra (Map p238; ☎ 622-79-44; Plazuela de San Juan 5; mains US$3-7; �8-1am) This laid-back bar-restaurant inside the Casa Grande Hotel serves pizza, salads and various snacks until late. From the balcony, you can watch the action on Plazuela San Juan. Live rock music shakes the house every Saturday night.

Bar Berta (Map p238; Cuauhtémoc; drinks US$2-4) Just off the Plaza Borda at the beginning of Cuauhtémoc, this is a fine place for a drink. Hemingway would have felt at home here, with its simple green tables on two

AROUND MEXICO CITY

levels and bullfight posters on the walls. Papa would have started with the house specialty, a Berta, which is tequila, honey, lime and mineral water.

FINE DINING

Taxco's top two restaurants are on hills facing the city center and are best reached by taxi. Also recommended is Posada de la Misión's **El Mural** (p240).

La Ventana de Taxco (☎ 622-05-87; Paraje del Solar; mains US$8-15; **P**) South of town, this restaurant specializes in Italian food. Its *piccata lombarda* (veal sautéed in a lemon, butter and parsley sauce) is superb.

La Pagaduría del Rey (Map p238; ☎ 622-00-75; Colegio Militar 8; mains US$6-12; ⏱ 1:30-9:30pm Tue-Sun; **P**) In Barrio Bermeja, a short taxi ride from the center, is this equally fine place. It offers salads, pastas and classic Mexican dishes. It's also a great place to sip a drink and admire the view.

Shopping

SILVER

With over 300 shops selling silverwork, the selection is mind-boggling. Look at some of the best places first, to see what's available, then try to focus on the things you're really interested in, and shop around for those. If you are careful and willing to bargain a bit, you can find wonderful pieces at reasonable prices.

Most shops are both *menudeo* and *mayoreo* (retail and wholesale); to get the wholesale price you will have to buy 1kg of silver.

The price of a piece is principally determined by its weight; the creative work serves mainly to make it salable, though items with exceptional artisanship command a premium. If you're serious about buying silver, find out the current peso-per-gram rate and weigh any piece before you agree on a price. All silver shops have scales, mostly electronic devices that should be accurate. If a piece costs less than the going price per gram, it's not real silver. Don't buy anything that doesn't have the Mexican government '.925' stamp, which certifies that the piece is 92.5% sterling silver (most pieces also bear a set of initials identifying their workshop of origin). If a piece is too small or delicate to stamp, a reputable shop will supply a certificate confirming its purity. Anyone who is discovered selling forged .925 pieces is sent to prison.

The shops in and around Plaza Borda tend to have higher prices than those out of the center, but they also tend to have more interesting work. The shops on Av de los Plateros are often branches of downtown shops, set up for the tourist buses that can't make it through the narrow streets.

Several shops are in the **Patio de las Artesanías** building on the Plaza Borda. **Pineda's** (Map 238; ☎ 622-32-33; Muñoz 1) is justly famous; a couple of doors down, **Joyería Elena de los Ballesteros** (Map p238; ☎ 622-37-67; Muñoz) is another worthwhile shop. The tableware on display in the showroom of **Emilia Castillo** (Map p238; ☎ 622-34-74; Ruiz de Alarcón 7), inside Hotel Emilia Castillo, is a unique blend of porcelain and silver.

For quantity rather than quality, see the stalls in the **Mercado de Artesanías Plata** (Map p238; ⏱ 11am-8pm), which have vast quantities of rings, chains and pendants. The work is not as well-displayed here, but you just might uncover something special.

OTHER CRAFTS

It's easy to overlook them among the silver, but there are other things to buy in Taxco. Finely painted wood and papier-mâché trays, platters and boxes are sold along Calle del Arco, on the south side of Santa Prisca, as well as wood carvings and bark paintings. Quite a few shops sell semiprecious stones, fossils and mineral crystals, and some have a good selection of masks, puppets and semi-antique carvings.

Getting There & Away

Taxco has two long-distance bus terminals, both on Av de los Plateros. First-class Flecha Roja and Futura buses and deluxe Turistar buses, as well as several 2nd-class lines, use the terminal at Av de los Plateros 104, which offers luggage storage. The Estrella de Oro (1st-class) terminal is at the south end of town. Combis (US$0.35) pass both terminals every few minutes and will take you up the hill to Plaza Borda. Buy tickets early for buses out of Taxco as it can be hard to get a seat.

There are several daily long-distance departures (*directo* unless otherwise stated):

Acapulco Estrella de Oro (US$11, 4-5hr, 6 daily); Turistar (US$12.50, 4-5hr, 4 daily)

Chilpancingo Estrella de Oro (US$6, 2-3hr, 6 daily); Turistar (US$7, 2-3hr, 4 daily)

Cuernavaca Estrella de Oro (US$3.75, 1½hr, 3 daily); Estrella Blanca (US$3.75, 1½hr, hourly 6am-7pm)

Iguala Various 2nd-class operators (US$1, 45min, every 10min)

Ixtapan de la Sal Turistar (US$2.50, 1½hr, 3 daily); Tres Estrellas (US$3.25, 1½hr, every 40min, from Flecha Roja terminal)

Mexico City (Terminal Sur) Estrella de Oro (US$7.50, 2½-3hr, 5 daily); Futura (1st-class US$7.50, deluxe US$8.50, 2½-3hr, hourly 5am-8pm)

Toluca Turistar (US$6, 3hr, 3 daily); Tres Estrellas (US$6, 3hr, every 40min, from Flecha Roja terminal)

Getting Around

Apart from walking, combis (white Volkswagen minibuses) and taxis are the most popular ways of getting around Taxco's steep, winding streets. Combis (US$0.35) are frequent and operate from 7am to 8pm. 'Zócalo' combis depart from Plaza Borda, go down Cuauhtémoc to Plazuela de San Juan, then head down the hill on Hidalgo. They turn right at Morelos, left at Av de los Plateros and go north until La Garita, where they turn left and return to the zócalo. 'Arcos/Zócalo' combis follow basically the same route except that they continue past La Garita to Los Arcos, where they do a U-turn and head back to La Garita. Combis marked 'PM' for 'Pedro Martín' go to the south end of town, past the Estrella de Oro bus station. Taxis cost US$1 to US$1.50 for trips around town.

The Plaza Taxco shopping center has a large parking garage (US$1 an hour, with cheaper 24-hour rates via most hotels). Access is off Av de los Plateros via Estacadas. An elevator takes you up to the shopping center, on Ruiz de Alarcón next door to the Casa Humboldt.

AROUND TAXCO
Taxco El Viejo

Taxco's original site was 12km south at Taxco El Viejo, where the indigenous Tlahuica mined tin and silver deposits, which were later heavily exploited by the Spaniards. Today, the area's principal attraction is a pair of ranches north and south of Taxco El Viejo where silver is crafted in peaceful settings.

EX-HACIENDA SAN JUAN BAUTISTA

Just south of Taxco El Viejo, this former hacienda was one of seven silver-refining facilities established around Taxco during the region's first silver boom. Today it houses the Universidad Autónoma de Guerrero's **School of Earth Sciences**, and is worth exploring for its lovely, poinsettia-lined patios and remnants of its former use.

Enter through an archway on the left side of the highway, then turn left and downhill past some new school buildings. An architectural innovation of the facility was the intra-wall conduits for transporting water from the main aqueduct to the tanks in the patios, where mercury was added to extract silver (a process that polluted extensive groundwater sources). The building also contains the university's **mineralogy museum**.

RANCHO SPRATLING

Although William Spratling died in 1967, his former **workshop** (☎ 762-622-60-50; 🕑 8am-5pm Mon-Sat), just south of the Ex-Hacienda San Juan Bautista, continues to produce some of Mexico's finest silver and employs the same handcrafted methods and classic designs that make Spratling pieces collectibles. The former Spratling ranch is well-maintained and a new generation of artisans adhere to Spratling's standards under the guidance of maestro Don Tomás, one of Spratling's principal workers for many years.

Visitors are encouraged to enter the workshop and see how fine silver is crafted. Also on the premises is a showroom displaying work designed by Spratling; a second room features new designs by Don Tomás' apprentices. Prices are in US dollars.

RANCHO CASCADA LOS CASTILLO

The Castillo family's metal **workshops** (☎ 622-19-88; www.silverzeal.com; 🕑 8am-6pm Mon-Fri, 8am-3pm Sat) are on these lovely ranch grounds, off the highway north of Taxco El Viejo. On the way to the workshops, through rambling gardens, there is a **museum** displaying the antiquities collection of Antonio Castillo, who was a master craftsman and contemporary of William Spratling. Inside the workshops, craftspeople create unique silver, copper, tin and *alpaca* (nickel silver) objects. There is no shop on the premises, but you can buy their products online or in town at the shop in front of Posada de la Misión (p240).

GETTING THERE & AWAY

Taxco El Viejo is 25 minutes south of Taxco on Hwy 95. From Taxco, catch any of the frequent 2nd-class buses heading for Iguala at the Flecha Roja terminal, or a combi to Taxco El Viejo from just north of Taxco's IMSS hospital. To visit all three destinations, you could get off at the Rancho Spratling, walk back up the highway to the Ex-Hacienda San Juan Bautista (500m), then catch a bus back toward Taxco and get off at the Rancho Cascada Los Castillo. From there, take any bus or combi heading north to return to Taxco.

Parque Nacional Grutas de Cacahuamilpa

The **Cacahuamilpa caverns** (cave tours adult/child US$3/2, parking US$1; ☉ 10am-7pm, last ticket sold at 5pm) are a beautiful natural wonder of stalactites, stalagmites and twisted rock formations, with huge chambers up to 82m high. Thirty kilometers northeast of Taxco, they are well worth visiting.

You must tour the caves with a guide, through 2km of an illuminated walkway. Many of the formations are named for some fanciful resemblance – 'the elephant,' 'the champagne bottle,' 'Dante's head' and so on – and the lighting is used to enhance these resemblances. Much of the guide's commentary focuses on these – geological information (and guides' English) is minimal. After the two-hour tour, you can return to the entrance at your own pace.

From the cave entrance, a path goes down the steep valley to Río Dos Bocas, where two rivers emerge from the caves. The pretty walk down and back takes 30 minutes.

Tours depart from the visitors center every hour on the hour from 10am to 5pm. An English-speaking guide might be available for large groups. There are restaurants, snacks and souvenir shops at the visitors center.

GETTING THERE & AWAY

From Taxco, blue-striped combis (US$2, one hour) depart every hour or two from in front of the Flecha Roja bus terminal and go right to the visitors center. Alternatively, you can take any bus heading for Toluca or Ixtapan de la Sal, that get off at the 'Grutas' crossroads and walk 1km down to the entrance. The last combis leave the site around 5pm on Monday to Friday and 6pm on Saturday and Sunday; after this you might be able to catch a bus to Taxco at the crossroads but it's an expensive taxi ride.

WEST OF MEXICO CITY

The main road west from the capital, Hwy 15D, goes to Toluca, which has a pleasant center, an interesting museum and several art galleries. There are ruins nearby, and some of the surrounding villages are known for their handicrafts. The countryside to the east, south and west of Toluca is scenic, with pine forests, rivers and a huge volcano. Valle de Bravo is a lakeside resort and colonial gem 70km west of Toluca. Two highways head south from Toluca: Hwy 55 passes handicraft centers, impressive pyramids and spas at Ixtapan de la Sal and Tonatico, then continues on to Taxco; toll Hwy 55D is the fast route to Ixtapan de la Sal.

TOLUCA

☎ 722 / pop 475,000 / elevation 2660m

Toluca, 64km west of Mexico City, is 400m higher than the capital, and the extra altitude is noticeable. The eastern outskirts are an industrial area, but the colonial-era city center has attractive plazas and lively arcades. Its cultural sites include a number of museums and art galleries.

Toluca was an indigenous settlement from at least the 13th century; the Spanish founded the city in the 16th century after defeating the Aztecs and Matlazincas who lived in the valley. It became part of the Marquesado del Valle de Oaxaca, Hernán Cortés' personal Mexican estates. Since 1830 it has been capital of the state of México, which surrounds the Distrito Federal on three sides like an upside-down U.

Orientation

The main road from Mexico City becomes Paseo Tollocan, a dual carriageway, as it approaches Toluca. On reaching the city's east side, Paseo Tollocan bears southwest and becomes a ring road around the city center's southern edge. The bus station and the large Mercado Juárez are 2km southeast of the city center, just off Paseo Tollocan.

The vast Plaza de los Mártires, with the cathedral and Palacio de Gobierno, marks

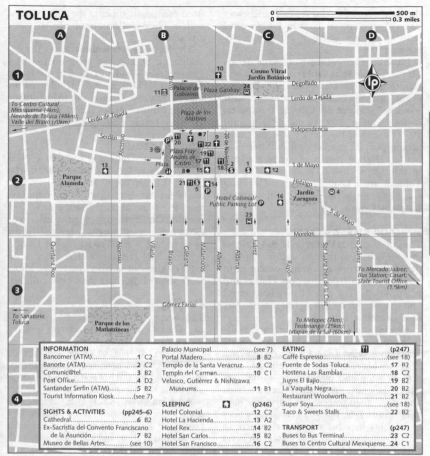

TOLUCA

0 ─────── 500 m
0 ─────── 0.3 miles

INFORMATION		Palacio Municipal.....................(see 7)	EATING 🍴 (p247)
Bancomer (ATM)...........................1 C2		Portal Madero.................................8 B2	Caffé Espresso.........................(see 18)
Banorte (ATM)..............................2 C2		Templo de la Santa Veracruz......9 C2	Fuente de Sodas Toluca...........17 R2
Comunic@tel.................................3 B2		Templo del Carmen....................10 C1	Hostería Las Ramblas...............18 C2
Post Office....................................4 D2		Velasco, Gutiérrez & Nishizawa	Jugos El Bajío...........................19 B2
Santander Serfin (ATM)..............5 B2		Museums..................................11 B1	La Vaquita Negra......................20 B2
Tourist Information Kiosk........(see 7)			Restaurant Woolworth..............21 B2
		SLEEPING 🏠 (p246)	Super Soya..............................(see 18)
SIGHTS & ACTIVITIES (pp245–6)		Hotel Colonial............................12 C2	Taco & Sweets Stalls................22 B2
Cathedral.....................................6 B2		Hotel La Hacienda......................13 A2	
Ex-Sacristía del Convento Franciscano		Hotel Rex...................................14 B2	TRANSPORT (p247)
de la Asunción.........................7 B2		Hotel San Carlos........................15 B2	Buses to Bus Terminal..............23 C2
Museo de Bellas Artes.............(see 10)		Hotel San Francisco...................16 C2	Buses to Centro Cultural Mexiquense...24 C1

the town center. Most of the life, however, is a block south in the pedestrian precinct, which is surrounded by arcades lined with shops and restaurants. The pleasant Parque Alameda is three blocks to the west along Hidalgo.

Information

Banks There are many with ATMs near Portal Madero.
Comunic@tel (Bravo; per hr US$1.10; 🕙 8:30am-9:30pm) Offers long-distance phone calls and Internet service.
Sanatorio Toluca Hospital (☎ 217-78-00; Peñaloza 233) Southwest of the center along Paseo Tollocan.
Santander Serfin (cnr Hidalgo & Matamoros) Changes cash and traveler's checks.
State Tourist Office (☎ 212-59-98; cnr Urawa & Paseo Tollocan) In the Edificio de Servicios Administrativos 2km

from center. English-speaking staff. Inconvenient, but good state and town maps are available.
Tourist Information Kiosk (Palacio Munipal) Helpful kiosk.

Sights

CITY CENTER

The 19th-century **Portal Madero**, running 250m along Av Hidalgo, is lively and bustling, as is the arcade along the pedestrian street to the east. A block north, the big, open expanse of **Plaza de los Mártires** is surrounded by fine old government buildings; the 19th-century **cathedral** and the 18th-century **Templo de la Santa Veracruz** are on its south side. The octagonal-shaped building in the plaza beside the cathedral was once the sacristy of the Convento Franciscano de la Asunción, which stood here until the 19th century. Today it is used as a city meeting hall.

Immediately northeast of Plaza de los Mártires is the **Plaza Garibay**; at the east end stands the unique **Cosmo Vitral Jardín Botánico** (Cosmic Stained-Glass Window Botanical Garden; cnr Juárez & Lerdo de Tejada; adult/child US$1/0.50; ☉ 10am-6pm Tue-Sun). Built in 1909 as a market, and until 1975 the site of the weekly *tianguis* (indigenous people's market), the building now houses 3500 sq meters of lovely gardens, lit through 48 stained-glass panels by the Tolucan artist Leopoldo Flores. On Plaza Garibay's north side is the 18th-century **Templo del Carmen**.

MERCADO JUÁREZ & CASART

The gigantic **Juárez Market** (cnr Fabela & 5 de Mayo; ☉ daily) is behind the bus station. On Friday villagers from all around swarm in to buy and sell fruit, flowers, pots, clothes and plastic goods. The market may be colorful and chaotic, but it's not a great place to buy local handicrafts.

Nearby, you'll find quality arts and crafts in more peaceful surroundings at the state crafts store, **Casart** (Casa de Artesanía; ☉ 10am-7pm). There's a big range, and the crafts sold here are often top-end pieces from the villages where the crafts are made. Prices are fixed and higher than you can get with some haggling in markets, but you can gauge prices and quality here before going elsewhere to buy. Craftspeople, such as basket weavers from San Pedro Actopan, often work in the store. Honey cookies from Sultepec and Tejupilco are baked on the premises.

CENTRO CULTURAL MEXIQUENSE

The impressive **State of México Cultural Center** (Blvd Reyes Herdes 302; admission US$2, free Sun; ☉ all museums 10am-6pm), 4.5km west of the city center, comprises three very good museums and a library.

The **Museo de Culturas Populares** has superb examples of the traditional arts and crafts of México state, with some astounding trees of life, whimsical Day of the Dead figures and a fine display of charro equipment – saddles, sombreros, swords, pistols, ropes and spurs.

The **Museo de Antropología e História** features top-notch exhibits on the state's history

from prehistoric times to the 20th century, with a good collection of pre-Hispanic artifacts.

The **Museo de Arte Moderno** traces the development of Mexican art from the late-19th-century Academia de San Carlos to the Nueva Plástica, and includes paintings by Tamayo, Orozco and many others. 'Centro Cultural' buses (US$0.50) go along Lerdo de Tejada, passing Plaza Garibay.

OTHER MUSEUMS

The ex-convent buildings adjacent to Plaza Garibay house Toluca's **Museo de Bellas Artes** (☎ 215-53-29; Degollado 102; admission US$1; ☉ 10am-6pm Tue-Sat, 10am-3pm Sun), which has paintings from the colonial period to the early 20th century. On Bravo, opposite the Palacio de Gobierno, are **art museums** devoted to the work of José María Velasco, Felipe Gutiérrez and Luis Nishizawa. The latter is an artist of Mexican-Japanese parentage whose work shows influences from both cultures.

Sleeping

The cheapest places don't have on-site parking. The lot on Matamoros charges US$5.50 for the night (9pm to 8am).

Hotel Rex (☎ 215-93-00; Matamoros Sur 101; r from US$20) The rooms here, some facing the arcade, have TVs and hot water. They're small and basic but acceptable.

Hotel San Carlos (☎ 214-43-36; hotelsancarlos@prodigy.net.mx; Portal Madero 210; s/d US$23/28) Opposite the Rex, this friendly place is a bit shabby but is clean and has 100 rooms with large bathrooms. Kick down US$4.50 extra for a king-size bed.

Hotel La Hacienda (☎ 214-36-34; Hidalgo Pte 508; s/d US$19/32; P) Half a block east of Parque Alameda, the 19 rooms here are overpriced, but most are decent with cable TV and colonial touches like wood-beam ceilings.

Hotel Colonial (☎ 215-97-00; Hidalgo Ote 103; s/d US$32/37; P) For true colonial ambience, try this hotel just east of Juárez. It has spacious, well-maintained rooms around an interior courtyard. Rates include free parking in the lot on Juárez.

Hotel San Francisco (☎ 213-44-15; Rayón Sur 104; s/d US$41/49; P) The San Francisco has comfortable modern rooms and luxury pretensions, including a glass-walled elevator shaft for viewing the slick skylit atrium restaurant.

Eating & Drinking

Toluqueños love to snack, and you can join them in the arcades around the Plaza Fray Andrés de Castro, beside the cathedral. Stalls selling authentic *tacos de Obispo* (a sausage from Tenancingo) are easily found because there are crowds of people flocking around them. The contents of these arm-width sausages – barbecued chopped beef spiced with *epazote,* almonds and raisins – are stuffed into tortillas and sold in large quantities. Other stalls sell candied fruit and *jamoncillos* and *mostachones* (sweets made of burned milk). Most eateries are open from around 8am to 9pm.

Jugos El Bajío (mains US$1-2) This place, in the arcade opposite the Templo de la Santa Veracruz, does good tortas, fruit cocktails and fresh fruit juices.

Fuente de Sodas Toluca (mains US$1-3) Around the corner from Jugos El Bajío, this café is exactly the same in design and menu.

La Vaquita Negra (mains US$1.50-2) On the northwest corner of the arcades, this place with green and red sausages hanging over the counter serves first-rate tortas. Don't forget to garnish your heaping sandwich with pickled peppers and onions, which are also sold in jars.

Caffé Espresso (☎ 215-54-43; 20 de Noviembre 109D; mains US$1-2) This relaxing hangout serves espresso and hot and cold cappuccinos. There are pastries for breakfast and live music most evenings.

Super Soya (mains US$1-2) Adjacent to Caffé Espresso, this popular spot serves tortas and heaping, semihealthy fruit and ice-cream concoctions.

Hostería Las Ramblas (☎ 215-54-88; 20 de Noviembre 107D; mains US$2-5) On the pedestrian mall is one of Toluca's best and most atmospheric places to eat or drink. It serves a variety of tasty antojitos, including *sopes, mole verde* and *sesos* (brains) a la mexicana.

Restaurant Woolworth (cnr Hidalgo & Galeana; mains & set meals US$3-6; ☺ 7am 8:30pm Mon-Sat, 9am-8pm Sun) Opposite Hotel San Carlos, Woolworth dishes up large set breakfasts with unlimited free (but bland) coffee refills.

Getting There & Away

Toluca's **bus station** (Berriozábal 101) is 2km southeast of the center. Ticket offices for many destinations are at the gate entrances, or right on the platforms. There are fre-quent departures to Querétaro (gate 2), Morelia (gate 5), Valle de Bravo (gate 6), Chalma and Malinalco (gate 9), Metepec (platform 10) and Cuernavaca, Taxco and Ixtapan de la Sal (platform 12).

In Mexico City Toluca buses use the Terminal Poniente. The 1st-class TMT line (US$3.25, 1 hour) runs buses between the two cities every five minutes from 5:30am to 10pm. From Toluca TMT has hourly direct service to the Mexico City airport from 4am to 10pm.

Getting Around

'Centro' buses go from outside the bus station to the town center along Lerdo de Tejada; 'Terminal' buses go from Juárez in the center to the bus station (US$0.50). Taxis from the bus station to the city center cost around US$4. Taxis around town are considerably cheaper.

AROUND TOLUCA
Calixtlahuaca

This **Aztec site** (admission US$2.75; ☺ 10am-5pm) is 2km west of Hwy 55, 9km northwest of Toluca. It's partly excavated and restored. The site has some unusual features, such as a circular pyramid that supported a temple to Quetzalcóatl and Calmecac, believed to have been a school for the children of priests and nobles. You can catch a bus in front of Suburbia (near Mercado Juárez) in Toluca that goes to within a short walk of the site.

Metepec

☎ 722 / pop 167,000 / elevation 2610m
Basically a suburb of Toluca, 7km to the south on Hwy 55, Metepec is the center for producing elaborate and symbolic pottery *árboles de la vida* (trees of life) and Metepec suns (earthenware discs brightly painted with sun and moon faces). A number of shops along the **Corredor Artesanal**, on Comonfort south of Paseo San Isidro, sell *árboles de la vida*. Prices range from US$5 for a miniature up to US$125 for a meter-high tree. Just north of Paseo San Isidro is the **Corral Artesanal**, a series of small shops along an arcade selling local crafts, and a restaurant.

The **potters' workshops** (*alfarerías*) are spread all over town; there's a map painted on the wall of the triangular **tourism office** in

AROUND MEXICO CITY

front of the Cerro del Calvario that shows their locations.

The workshop of **Beto Hernández** (Altamirano 58) is itself a work of art with fountains, altars, and designs embedded in the cobblestone walkway, and a sort of chapel built around the lavishly decorated kiln. Within the various display rooms are some amazing trees, many unpainted, at reasonable prices. The most elaborate and expensive trees are in the front gallery.

A few doors down, the workshop of **Adrián Luis González** (Altamirano 212) is equally remarkable; the floor of the upstairs gallery is adorned with butterflies and suns made by González. A fascinating genealogical tree shows members of the González family (Adrián himself is near the top) with their accoutrements. The tree demonstrates the process of its own creation, with subsequent levels at different stages of production – from unbaked clay at the bottom to a bright paint finish at the top.

A pleasant **hike** with great views can be made to the top of **Cerro del Calvario**, a hill decorated with a huge pottery mural.

Frequent 2nd-class buses reach Metepec from the Toluca bus station.

NEVADO DE TOLUCA

The extinct volcano Nevado de Toluca (aka Xinantécatl), 4690m high, lies across the horizon south of Toluca. A road runs 48km up to its crater, which contains two lakes, El Sol and La Luna. The earlier you reach the summit, the better the chance of clear views. The summit area is snowy (*nevado*) from November to March, and sometimes good for cross-country skiing, but the **Parque Nacional Nevado de Toluca** is closed during the heaviest snows.

Buses on Hwy 134, the Toluca–Tejupilco road, will stop at the turnoff for Hwy 10 to Sultepec, which passes the park entrance 8km to the south. On weekends it should be possible to hitch a ride the 29km from the junction of Hwys 134 and 10 to the crater. Taxis from Toluca will take you to the top for around US$30, or there and back (including some time for you to look around) for US$50. Be sure to pick a newer taxi; the road up is very rough and dusty.

From the park entrance, a road winds 3.5km up to the main gate at an area called **Parque de los Venados** (car/truck US$1/1.50;

8am-5pm, last entrance 3pm). From there it's a 17km drive along an unsurfaced road up to the crater. Six kilometers from the crater, there's a gate, shelter and a café. From that point, the crater can also be reached by a 2km hike via **Paso del Quetzal** (US$0.20 fee), a very scenic walking track. Dress warmly; it can be very cold at the top.

Sleeping & Eating

You can stay at any of the following places. Tent and car camping (around US$2 per person) is permitted by the first two.

Posada Familiar (r with shared bathroom per person US$5) This basic and much used but clean place in Parque de los Venados has 11 rooms with hot showers. There's a kitchen without utensils and a common area with a fireplace. Bring extra blankets.

Albergue Ejidal (dm US$3.50) This community-run hostel has 64 bunk beds (sleeping bag required), hot water and a large dining area with a huge fireplace. Before you go up, ask the attendant in the Parque de los Venados or someone at Posada Familiar to open it up for you. It's 2km further up.

The basic **state-run shelter** (dm US$1.50), near the summit (at 4050m), has foam mattresses but no bathrooms.

On weekends, food is served at stalls in the Parque de los Venados and at the gate near the summit. During the week, bring your own food and water.

VALLE DE BRAVO

☎ 726 / pop 27,000 / elevation 1800m
About 70km west of Toluca, Valle de Bravo (www.valledebravo.com.mx in Spanish) was a quiet colonial-era village in the hills until the 1940s, when it became a base for construction of a dam and hydroelectric station. The new 21 sq km lake gave the town a waterside location and it was soon a popular weekend and holiday spot for the wealthy. Nevertheless, this vibrant country community still retains its colonial charm. All essential services are available around the main plaza (zócalo), a 10-minute walk uphill from the water.

Sailing on the lake is the main activity here – there are hour-long **cruises** (US$2-2.50 per person) by *colectivo* boat. You can rent a private boat for US$25 to US$35 per hour. Waterskiing, horseback riding and hang gliding are also popular.

You can hike and camp in the hills around town, which attract monarch butterflies from December to March. A climb up the rock promontory La Peña, northwest of the center, provides a view of the whole lake.

The annual **Festival de las Almas**, which is held during the last week in October, is an international arts and culture festival that attracts music and dance groups from all over Latin America.

Sleeping & Eating

The town's budget hotels are a cut above those found elsewhere.

Posada Familiar Los Girasoles (☎ 262-29-67; Plaza Independencia 1; s/d US$24/33) The simple, clean rooms have small bathrooms and TVs.

Posada Casa Vieja (☎ 262-03-18; Juárez 101; s/d from US$28/37; P) This hotel is good value, with pleasant rooms (most with TV) facing an idyllic patio with a fountain and chirping birds. There's parking in the courtyard, but the entranceway is a tight squeeze.

Centro Vacacional ISSEMYM (☎ 262-00-04; Independencia 404; d/ste/f US$39/49/74; P 🏊) Just above the market, this is a colorful holiday center for state workers but it also accepts other guests. Featuring several pools and some other recreational facilities, it's a good deal.

There are scores of cafés and restaurants around the zócalo and near the pier, but the nicer places only open Friday to Sunday.

Los Veleros (☎ 262-32-79; Salitre 104; mains US$6-12; ☑ closed Tue) Specializing in seafood, Los Veleros is in an elegant adobe brick building with tables on a balcony overlooking a large garden.

For ambience, have a drink and/or a light meal at the floating lakefront restaurant-bars **La Balsa Avándaro** (☎ 262-25-53; mains US$6-9) and **Los Pericos** (☎ 262-05-58; mains US$6-9; ☑ 8am-10pm Thu-Tue).

Getting There & Away

The bus terminal is on 16 de Septiembre. Autobuses Zinacantepec runs hourly 2nd-class *directos* until 5:30pm to Mexico City's Terminal Poniente (US$7.50, 3 hours), all of which make a stop near Toluca's terminal. There is also frequent service to Zitácuaro (US$3.75). If you're driving between Toluca and Valle de Bravo, the southern route via Hwy 134 is quicker and more scenic.

TEOTENANGO

Tenango de Arista, 25km south of Toluca on Hwy 55, is overlooked from the west by the large, well-restored hilltop ruins of **Teotenango** (admission US$1.25, free Wed; ☑ 9am-5pm Tue-Sun), a Matlazinca ceremonial center dating from the 9th century. The site is quite extensive – several pyramids, plazas and a ball court – and has great views. The **Museo Arqueológico del Estado de México**, near the entrance, has Teotenango pottery and sculpture, as well as a section devoted to the prehistory of the region.

From Toluca's bus station, buses run every 10 minutes to the center of Tenango; from here you can walk to the site in 20 to 30 minutes or take a taxi (US$1.25).

Driving from Toluca on Hwy 55, pass the toll highway and turn right into Tenango; signs show you where to make a right turn on to a road that passes closest to the ruins.

MALINALCO

☎ 714 / pop 7000 / elevation 1740m

One of the few reasonably well-preserved Aztec temples stands above beautiful but little-visited Malinalco, 22km east of Tenancingo. The **Aztec site** (admission US$3; ☑ 9am-5:30pm Tue-Sun) is 1km west of the town center, approached by a well-maintained footpath with signs about the area in Spanish, English and Náhuatl. The views over the valley from the summit have inspired legions of painters. There's a new state-run **Universidad Autónoma del Estado de México museum** (admission US$1, free Wed; ☑ 10am-6pm Tue-Sun) of history and archaeology near the site entrance and the good Cafe La Fé next door.

The Aztecs conquered this area in 1476 and were still building a ritual center here when they were themselves conquered by the Spanish. El Cuauhcalli, thought to be the Temple of Eagle and Jaguar Warriors, where sons of Aztec nobles were initiated into warrior orders, survived because it is hewn from the mountainside itself. Its entrance is carved in the form of a fanged serpent.

Malinalco also has a well-restored 16th-century **Augustinian convent**, fronted by a tranquil tree-lined yard. Impressive frescoes done with paint made from flowers and herbs adorn its cloister. The **tourist office** (☎ 147-01-11; ☑ 9am-3pm Mon-Sat) is uphill from the plazas inside the Palacio Municipal. There's an ATM on Hidalgo, on the convent's north side.

Sleeping

Like other destinations near Mexico City, Malinalco is geared toward weekend visitors, which means you'll have no trouble finding a room Sunday to Thursday nights but your dining options may be limited. Conversely, weekend hotel reservations are recommended.

Hotel Marmil (☎ 147-09-16; Progreso 67; s/d/f US$19/28/33; P ⟨⟩) In the mustard-colored building near the north entrance into town, the Marmil is Malinalco's best place to stay. The 28 standard rooms have large comfy beds and nonguests can use the pool for US$1.50.

El Asoleadero (☎ 147-01-84; cnr Aldama & Comercio; r from US$20; P ⟨⟩) A couple of blocks uphill from the plaza, this new and very blue place has 15 big, clean rooms with private bathrooms and good down-valley views over the monastery.

Villa Hotel (☎ 147-00-01; Guerrero 101; s/d US$19/32, with shared bathroom US$7.50/16) On the plaza's south side, the friendly Villa has 15 rooms: the basic ones with cliff views share a single bath while more elegant ones with better beds face the plaza.

Hotel Las Cabañas (☎ 147-01-01; Progreso 1; cabins per person US$16; P ⟨⟩) Just north of the Marmil in a semiwoodsy area, Las Cabañas has 20 slightly run-down country cabins, each with two bedrooms, a fireplace and a kitchen with refrigerator and gas stove.

Eating

Malinalco has many good restaurants serving a wide variety of cuisines, but only a few of the fancy ones are open during the week. There are, however, plenty of places patronized by locals around the plaza that are open daily. On a hot day, don't miss the **Malinalli Nieves** ice-cream stand on the plaza.

Las Palomas (☎ 147-01-22; Guerrero 104; mains US$3-8; ⟨⟩ closed Mon) This elegant place has a tiled country kitchen at the front, citrus and mango trees on the patio and a palapa bar. Its reasonably priced menu consists of all-natural Mexican originals, with healthy, creative salads, meat dishes and trout dishes.

Los Placeres (☎ 147-08-55; west side of plaza; mains US$4-8; ⟨⟩ Fri-Sun) On the plaza's west side, this is an excellent choice, with a laid-back atmosphere, good music and great views in back. Its varied menu features hearty breakfasts with good coffee and tea, bagels with cheese or salmon, original salads, crêpes and exotic specials.

Le Chef (☎ 147-04-01; Morelos 107; mains from US$2-8) Behind the convent, this is a double restaurant: one serves pizzas, the other serves French cuisine with a strong Mexican flavor. The gregarious French owner/chef has at least seven delicious ways of making trout.

Beto's (☎ 147-03-11; Morelos 8; mains US$3-7; ⟨⟩ noon-8pm Tue-Sun) Opposite Le Chef, this bar serves seafood, including shark *empanadas* and terrific shrimp cocktails.

Getting There & Away

You can reach Malinalco by bus from Tenancingo or from the Toluca bus station. From Mexico City's Terminal Poniente, there are direct buses at 5:10pm and 5:50pm; alternatively, take one of many buses to Jajalpa (en route to Tenancingo), then get a local bus. By car from Mexico City, turn south at La Marquesa and follow the signs to Malinalco.

Direct buses back to Mexico City depart around 5:10pm daily. There is a frequent colectivo service to Tenango, from where you can catch a Toluca or Mexico City bus.

CHALMA

One of Mexico's most important shrines is in the village of Chalma, 10km east of Malinalco. In 1533 an image of Christ, El Señor de Chalma, miraculously appeared in a cave to replace one of the local gods, Oxtéotl, and proceeded to stamp out dangerous beasts and do other wondrous things. The Señor now resides in Chalma's 17th-century church. The biggest of many annual pilgrimages here is for **Pentecost** (the seventh Sunday after Easter) when thousands of people camp, hold a market and perform traditional dances.

Tres Estrellas del Centro runs hourly 2nd-class buses from Toluca to Chalma (US$2.75). A number of companies run 2nd-class buses from Mexico City's Terminal Poniente. There is also frequent bus service from Malinalco.

IXTAPAN DE LA SAL

☎ 721 / pop 17,000 / elevation 1880m

The spa town of Ixtapan features a kind of giant curative water park, the **Balneario,**

Spa y Parque Acuático Ixtapan (☎ 143-30-00; adult/child US$13/5.50; ⊙ spa 8am-7pm, aquatic park 9am-6pm), combining thermal water pools with waterfalls, water slides, a wave pool and a miniature railway. It's unashamedly a tourist town, but it's worth a stop if you want to take the waters or give your kids a fun day.

Hotels are clustered along Juárez south of the aquatic park, with a good range of lodging.

About 5km further on Hwy 55 is **Tonatico** with its own water park, the **Balneario Municipal Tonatico** (adult/child US$3.75/2.25; ⊙ 7am-6pm). It's about a 10th of the size of Ixtapan de la Sal's and consequently more relaxed. There is an economical hotel on the grounds. At the south end of town is a spectacular **waterfall** (El Salto).

From the bus terminal on Hwy 55, between Ixtapan and Tonatico, Tres Estrellas del Centro runs frequent buses to Toluca (US$3.25), Taxco (US$3.50) and Cuernavaca (US$4). There is also an hourly service to Mexico City (US$7) via autopista until 6pm daily. Buses to/from the terminal go up and down Juárez in Ixtapan (US$0.30); taxis charge US$1.25.

Heading north to Toluca, toll Hwy 55D parallels part of Hwy 55, bypassing Tenango and Tenancingo. Going south to Taxco, you could pass on the Grutas de la Estrella, but the Grutas de Cacahuamilpa (see p244) are a must.

Baja California

Some people like to take Baja slowly, working their way without haste down the Transpeninsular Hwy and into an enchanting desert landscape of mesquite, ocotillo, cholla, cenizo and sage. Others gravitate to the water: they kayak, surf, dive, snorkel, fish, sail and bask under a big Mexican sun. Some less fortunate souls fly into one of Baja's resort towns for a scant few days of vacation; you'll see them standing on the beach in Cabo San Lucas with a margarita in their hand, wistfully trying to figure out how to prolong their visit. Pity them not. By any measure, a little Baja is better than no Baja at all, and just a few days still makes for a trip and a half.

Even today, traveling the length of Baja on the Transpeninsular Hwy by car is a dicey proposition. Completed as recently as 1972, this narrow and winding two-lane road will challenge the driver and reward the passenger with marvelous scenery all along the way. Forests of towering Cordón cacti, in an endless variety of shapes and sizes, provide foreground to far-off mountains and the intermittent flash of shocking blue sea. Few who have made the journey will deny that it is one of the planet's great driving adventures. But be warned: those that leave the pavement need a vehicle that knows how to rough it!

From space, Baja is one of the most ostentatious geological features on earth. The 1300km-long peninsula – the fourth longest in the world – is flanked by more than 3200km of coastline. The Pacific coast is a veritable superhighway for whales who, like us, find Baja's special qualities worthy of a return visit.

To the east is the rugged beauty and fish-rich waters of the Sea of Cortez, inspiration to writers John Steinbeck and Edward Abbey and home to 875 fish species and 30 species of marine mammals. Wherever your journey takes you, Baja's wide-open frontier and its more civilized charms will capture your imagination and hold you in its sway.

BAJA CALIFORNIA

HIGHLIGHTS

- Strolling the waterfront malecón in **La Paz** (p284) as the big Baja sun drops into the bay
- Making the acquaintance of whales at **Laguna Ojo de Liebre** (p274) as they arrive after a 9700km journey from the Bering Sea
- Trekking by muleback into the **Sierra de San Francisco** (p276), where Cochimí masterpieces adorn the walls of caves
- Kayaking, diving or snorkeling in the marine-rich waters of the Sea of Cortez near **Loreto** (p280), Baja's water-sports paradise
- Living the good life on the beaches and in the nightclubs of **Cabo San Lucas** (p292), the quintessential party town

Laguna Ojo de Liebre
Sierra de San Francisco
Loreto
La Paz
Cabo San Lucas

ALTITUDE RANGE: 0m–3046m	LA PAZ AUGUST DAILY HIGH: 35°C

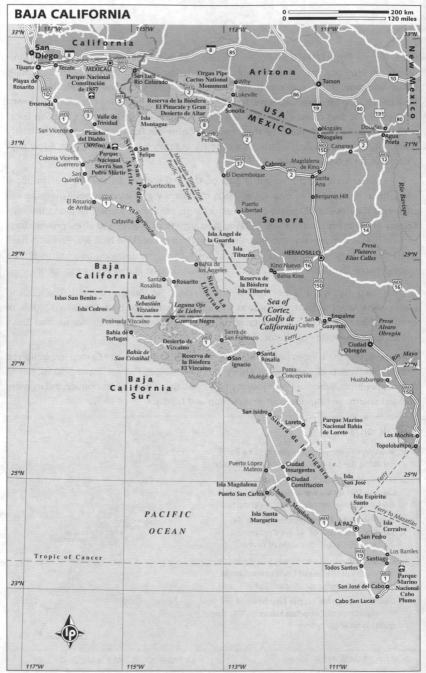

BAJA CALIFORNIA

0 ———— 200 km
0 ———— 120 miles

33°N
117°W   115°W   113°W   111°W

California

San Diego
8
Tijuana
Tecate   MEXICALI
2D
Playas de Rosarito
1D
Parque Nacional Constitución de 1857   San Luis Río Colorado
Ensenada
1
MEX
3   Valle de Trinidad
San Vicente   Isla Montague   8
MEX
31°N   Picacho del Diablo (3095m)   San Felipe
Colonia Vicente Guerrero   Parque Nacional Sierra San Pedro Mártir
San Quintín
El Rosario de Arriba   1   Puertecitos
Cataviña   Carr Transpeninsular

Organ Pipe Cactus National Monument   Why   Arizona
Lukeville   Tucson
86
Reserva de la Biósfera El Pinacate y Gran Desierto de Altar   Sonoíta   USA   19
MEXICO
Puerto Peñasco   2   Nogales   80   191
Nogales   80
2   Cananea   Agua Prieta
Caborca   Magdalena de Kino   Santa Ana   12
37   El Desemboque   2   Benjamin Hill   Río Bavíspe

Puerto Libertad   Sonora   14

Baja California

Isla Ángel de la Guarda   Presa Plutarco Elías Calles
Isla Tiburón
29°N   Bahía de los Ángeles   HERMOSILLO   16
Santa Rosaliíto   Rosarito   Kino Nuevo   16
Reserva de la Biósfera Isla Tiburón   Bahía Kino
Islas San Benito   Bahía Sebastián Vizcaíno   Laguna Ojo de Liebre   15D
Isla Cedros   Sea of Cortez (Golfo de California)   Empalme   Presa Alvaro Obregón
Península Vizcaíno   Guerrero Negro   San Carlos   Guaymas
Bahía de Tortugas   Sierra de San Francisco   Ferry   Ciudad Obregón
27°N   Bahía de San Cristóbal   Desierto de Vizcaíno   1   Santa Rosalía   Río Mayo
Reserva de la Biósfera El Vizcaíno   San Ignacio   Punta Concepción   Huatabampo
Mulegé   15D

Baja California Sur

San Isidro   Loreto
Parque Marino Nacional Bahía de Loreto
Los Mochis
Topolobampo
25°N   Puerto López Mateos   Ciudad Insurgentes   Isla San José   Ferry
Isla Magdalena   Ciudad Constitución   Isla Espíritu Santo   Ferry to Mazatlán
Puerto San Carlos   Llano de Magdalena   1   LA PAZ   Isla Cerralvo
PACIFIC   Isla Santa Margarita   19   San Pedro
OCEAN   Los Barriles
Santiago
Tropic of Cancer   1   Parque Marino Nacional Cabo Plumo
23°N   Todos Santos
San José del Cabo
Cabo San Lucas

History

Until Europeans first arrived in the 16th century, upward of 48,000 mobile hunter-gatherers lived on the peninsula; today you can still see their remarkable murals in caves and on canyon walls. Permanent European settlement failed to reach the peninsula until the Jesuit missions of the 17th and 18th centuries. The missions soon collapsed as indigenous people fell prey to European diseases, but ranchers from the mainland, miners and fisherfolk settled when foreigners built port facilities and acquired huge land grants in the 19th century. During US prohibition, Baja became a popular south-of-the-border destination for gamblers, drinkers and other 'sinners.' Today, Baja continues its growth in economic power, population and popularity as a tourist destination. Young in comparison with the rest of Mexico, it is still a kind of frontier state, imbued with the energy, creativity and pioneer spirit that goes along with this.

Climate

Baja is famous for its sunny skies and warm temperatures, but the peninsula actually has a surprising range of climates, from

BAJA BIODIVERSITY

From the mangrove swamps and bays of the Pacific coast, up and over the pine-covered central mountains, to the especially isolated Sea of Cortez, Baja California is home to a variety of life forms scarcely matched elsewhere. With a little luck, a pair of binoculars and a field guide or two, any traveler can hope to encounter many of the following plants and wildlife:

- Blue-footed booby – the boobies fly in formation in saltwater settings; each member of a booby squadron will obediently slash into the water after the leader. Why do they do this? One hazards to guess that they are all after the same fish!

- Blue whale – the largest creature *ever* to live on planet earth enjoys the marine-rich waters of the Sea of Cortez even more than you do.

- Boojum tree – perhaps the most unusual plant in Baja, this tree loses its leaves in the dry season and regains them within a few days of rain. It looks like an inverted carrot with a fingerlike set of branches, and attains a height of 20m.

- Brown pelican – these guys are everywhere along the coast, performing marvelous maneuvers and diving spearlike into the briny foam.

- Caracara – an imposing black-and-white carrion-eating falcon with a pink face patch, the caracara is omnipresent along the west coast of Baja California.

- Cardón – this, the largest cactus on earth, grows up to 20m high. Resembling gargantuan candelabras, the cardón is majestic beyond belief.

- Gray whale – each year Baja's west coast is the destination for thousands of gray whales on leave from the Arctic (p274).

- Man O'War bird – commonly called the fragata, this famous flier soars above the rocky cliffs of eastern Baja like a juvenile pterodactyl. In mating season, the male's bubblegum-pink balloon throat stuns potential mates.

- Ocotillo – Like the boojum tree, this thorny shrub is drought-deciduous. When it blooms shortly after a rain, the pollen from its scarlet flowers burns the eyes.

- Phainopepla – the 'silky flycatcher,' related to the American cedar waxwing, is gun-metal black with white wing patches.

- Toloache – commonly known by its scientific name, *datura*, this member of the tomato family was famously painted by Georgia O'Keeffe, and has long been used for medicinal and hallucinogenic properties. It contains atropine, a common ingredient of nerve gas. (Too much is too much.)

For more information, see *A Field Guide to Mexican Birds* by Roger Peterson or *Baja California Plant Field Guide* by Norman C Roberts.

subtropical to high desert. Thanks to the cool waters of the Pacific, the air temperature along the west coast and the cape region is comfortable all year. Along the Sea of Cortez or in Mexicali, it's a different story. Here, in the summer, you will be reminded of the meaning of the word 'hot.'

Dangers & Annoyances

Most of Baja's cities and towns are mellow places with little violent crime. The streets of Tijuana, however, require a degree of alertness on the part of the traveler, particularly after dark.

By and large, the sanitation standards in Baja are higher than in other parts of Mexico. The traveler's main concern should be with personal safety when enjoying potentially hazardous outdoor sports and traversing the notoriously sketchy roads.

Transport

Most of the travel to Baja is from the USA. There are six official border crossings from the US state of California to Baja. At any crossing, Mexican authorities will issue and stamp tourist cards and process car permits.

Since there are no direct flights from overseas into Baja airports, travelers from abroad must change planes in the US or Mexico City. Three domestic air carriers and several smaller ones connect Baja's larger towns with mainland Mexico. Ferries from Santa Rosalía and La Paz connect Baja California to mainland Mexico by sea.

Air-conditioned buses operate daily between towns all along the peninsula. Car travel is usually more convenient than bus travel and often the only way to reach isolated towns, villages, mountains and beaches.

NORTHERN BAJA

The northernmost part of the state of Baja California is referred to as La Frontera. The region includes the border towns of Tijuana and Tecate and extends down south to San Quintín. La Frontera corresponds roughly to the area colonized by the Dominicans, who established nine missions north of El Rosario from 1773 to 1821. Many view its cities and beaches as hedonistic enclaves, but Tijuana and Mexicali are major manu-

facturing centers, and Mexicali's Río Colorado hinterland is a key agricultural zone.

TIJUANA

☎ 664 / pop 1.27 million

Over the years Tijuana has been given somewhat of a bad rap. It's true that vice continues to be a tenacious menace around Av Revolución, and it's also true that many inebriated visitors pay good money to be photographed sitting upon a zebra-striped donkey holding a sign that reads 'Sitting on My Ass!' Unseemly, all of it. But there has always been another side of Tijuana: it's the place where two markedly different cultures stare eye to eye across a permeable cultural border. This ever-changing give-and-take exchange has resulted in a fascinating, vibrant city that is distinctly Mexican and unique.

These days there's talk of a Tijuana renaissance. The city's universities, office buildings, housing developments, shopping malls and industries mark it as a fast-growing city of increasing sophistication. And on the streets, young Tijuanans are shrugging off the city's reputation as a cultural wasteland and elevating its anomalies into art. Witness the rise of Nortec music: with its hybrid blend of techno dance rhythms melded with the traditional sounds of norteño music – think souped-up tuba and accordion with a break beat – Tijuana now has a sound all its own.

Filmmakers, fashion designers and visual artists have taken the DJs' lead, and suddenly TJ has a new creative movement.

At the end of WWI Tijuana had fewer than 1000 inhabitants, but it soon drew US tourists for gambling, greyhound racing, boxing and cockfights. During the war and through the 1950s, the US government's temporary *bracero* program allowed Mexicans to alleviate labor shortages north of the border. These workers replaced Americans who were stationed overseas in the military and caused Tijuana's population to increase to 180,000 by 1960. Growth has brought severe social and environmental problems – impoverished migrants still inhabit hillside dwellings of scrap wood and cardboard. On the rise, however, is a large and stable middle class. Tijuana has had its share of well-publicized crimes that have put it in the spotlight and have furthered its reputation as a dangerous travel destination. It is still a safe place to visit, but exercise caution when traveling at night or in isolated areas.

Orientation

Tijuana is south of the US border post of San Ysidro, California, 19km south of downtown San Diego. Tijuana's central grid consists of north–south *avenidas* and east–west *calles* (most of the latter are referred to by their numbers more frequently than their names). South of Calle 1a, Av Revolución (La Revo) is the main commercial center.

East of the Frontón Palacio Jai Alai, La Revo's major landmark, Tijuana's 'new' Zona Río commercial center straddles the river. Mesa de Otay, to the northeast, has another border crossing, the airport, *maquiladoras* (foreign-owned assembly-plant operations), neighborhoods and shopping areas.

Information

BOOKSTORES

Librería El Día (☎ 684-09-08; Blvd Sánchez Taboada 10050) Spanish-language media with a cultural bent.
Sanborns (☎ 688-14-62; Av Revolución 1102 at Calle 8a) This department store has a large selection of US and Mexican newspapers and magazines.

EMERGENCY

Fire Department (☎ 068)
Police (☎ 066)
Tourist Assistance hotline (☎ 078)

IMMIGRATION

Mexican tourist cards are available 24 hours a day at the San Ysidro–Tijuana border in the **immigration office** (☎ 682-64-39). They are also available – although less dependably – at a small office in the main bus terminal (Central Camionera; p262).

INTERNET ACCESS

SpaceNet (Calle 5a 8280; per hr US$1.50) 24hr access via a speedy connection.

INTERNET RESOURCES

www.seetijuana.com Tijuana's tourism site.

LAUNDRY

Lavamaticas 'Danny' (☎ 638-50-69; Av Constitución 1821; ☿ 7am-10pm) Self and wash-and-fold service.

MEDICAL SERVICES

Hospital General (☎ 684-00-78; Av Padre Kino, Zona Río) Northwest of the junction with Av Rodríguez.

MONEY

Everyone accepts US dollars, but countless *casas de cambio* (money changers) keep long hours. Travelers heading south or east by bus can use the *casa de cambio* at the Central Camionera. Most banks have ATMs.

POST

Central post office (☎ 684-00-78; Cnr Av Negrete and Calle 11a)

TOURIST INFORMATION

Cotuco (Comité de Turismo y Convenciones or Committee on Tourism & Conventions) head office (☎ 684-05-37; convistj@omnitec.com; Suite 201, Paseo de los Héroes 9365; ☿ 9am-6pm Mon-Fri); pedestrian border entrance visitors center (☎ 683-49-87; h 9am-5pm Mon-Sat, 8am-3pm Sun); Av Revolución visitors center (☎ 685-22-10; Av Revolución btwn Calle 3a & Calle 4a; ☿ 10am-4pm Mon-Thu, Fri-Sun 10am-7pm); airport visitors center (☎ 683-82-44; airport baggage claim; ☿ Mon-Sun 8am-3pm).
Secure office (Secretaría de Turismo del Estado; ☎ 973-04-24, 973-04-30; Plaza Viva Tijuana; ☿ 8am-8pm Mon-Fri, 9am-1pm Sat-Sun) has a friendly, English-speaking staff.

Dangers & Annoyances

It has always been easy to get into trouble in Tijuana. If you have come to party, keep in mind that La Revo is filled with unsavory characters who are well-practiced at relieving revelers of their *dinero* (money).

Drinking on the streets is against city ordinance and heavy fines are regularly imposed on offenders. Mexico plays hardball with casual drug users; the possession of even a few grams of contraband can result in eight years or more in prison.

Coyotes and *polleros* – people smugglers – congregate along the river west of the San Ysidro crossing. After dark, avoid this area and Colonia Libertad, east of the crossing.

Sights & Activities

South of Calle 1a, **La Revo** (Av Revolución) is the heart of Tijuana's tourist area. Every visitor braves at least a brief stroll up this raucous avenue of crowded discos, fine restaurants, seedy bars with bellowing hawkers, brash taxi drivers and tacky souvenir shops.

Until 1998 jai alai tournaments were held at the **Frontón Palacio Jai Alai**. The oddly attractive building, built over two decades from 1926 to 1947, remains a landmark and centerpiece for La Revo.

BAJA CALIFORNIA

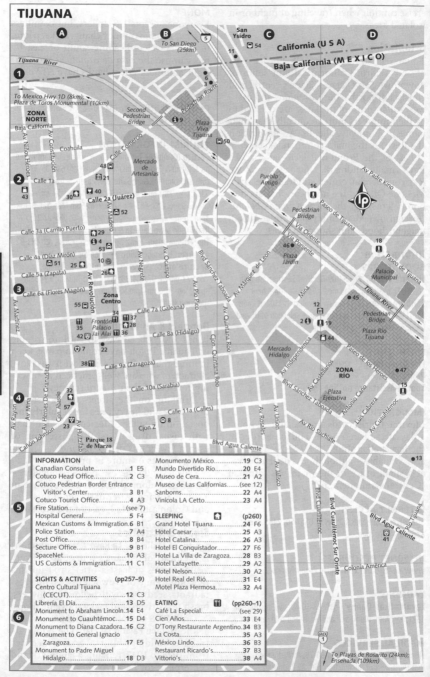

TIJUANA

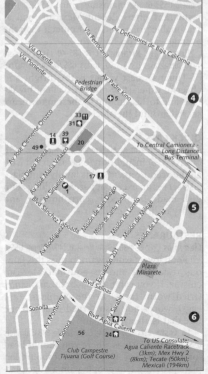

A modern landmark, Tijuana's **Centro Cultural Tijuana** (CECUT; ☎ 687-96-00; www.cecut.gob.mx; cnr Paseo de los Héroes & Av Independencia) is a cultural center of which any comparably sized city north of the border would be proud. It houses an art gallery, the **Museo de las Californias** (US$2; 🕙 10am-7pm Tue-Sun), a theater and the globular **Cine Omnimax** (programs from US$3.75; 🕙 1-9pm Tue-Fri, 10am-9pm Sat & Sun).

Vinícola LA Cetto (LA Cetto winery; ☎ 685-16-44; Cañón Johnson 2108; 🕙 10am-5:30pm Mon-Fri, 10am-4pm Sat), southwest of Av Constitución, offers tours and tasting for a modest charge. With vineyards in the fertile Valle de Guadalupe between Tecate and Ensenada, LA Cetto produces a range of tasty varietals, as well as sparkling wines and a decent brandy.

Leave any expectations at the door and you might actually enjoy a visit to Tijuana's **Museo de Cera** (wax museum; ☎ 688-24-78; Calle 1a 8281; US$1.50; 🕙 Mon-Sun 10am-7pm). On view are about 90 waxen figures including an uncanny Frida Kahlo and a really bad Elvis.

Considered one of the most beautiful courses in Mexico, the **Club Campestre Tijuana** (Tijuana Country Club; ☎ 681-78-55; off Blvd Agua Caliente near the racetrack) has a decent par-72, 6200m, 18-hole course. For 18 holes you'll pay US$21 on Monday, Tuesday, Thursday and Friday; the price doubles on Wednesday and on the weekend.

Tijuana for Children
If Av Revolución is too intense for the kiddies, consider taking them to the American-style amusement park **Mundo Divertido Río** (☎ 634-32-13; Av José Velasco 2578; 🕙 noon-9pm Mon-Fri, 11am-10pm Sat-Sun) for miniature golf, a huge video arcade, batting cages, rides and, naturally, the essential snack bar.

Festivals & Events
As Tijuana's reputation as a cultural center continues to grow, so does its annual calendar of cultural events. These and other listings can be found online at www.seetijuana.com.
International Dance Festival January.
Folkloric Dance Festival Tepeg Notu April.
Mexican Food Festival September.
International Seafood Festival October.
Tequila Festival October.
Hispanic American Guitar Festival November.

BAJA CALIFORNIA

Sleeping

Tijuana has a wealth of accommodations in all categories, from the really seedy to the truly luxurious. Most of Tijuana's cheapest accommodations cannot be recommended, as they do not meet basic standards of safety or cleanliness.

BUDGET

Hotel Lafayette (☎ 685-39-40; Av Revolución 926; s/d US$21/27) Perhaps downtown's most popular budget hotel is the Lafayette, above Café La Especial. The rooms overlooking the cacophonous Av Revolución are not tranquil havens; request one in the back.

Hotel Catalina (☎ 685-97-48; Calle 5a 2039; s/d US$18/26) This clean and secure hotel, a block away from Av Revolución, is comparable to the Lafayette but without the cacophony.

MID-RANGE

Hotel La Villa de Zaragoza (☎ 685-18-32; Av Madero 1120; s/d US$40/49, ste US$72; P ⊠ ⊠) Rooms at this modern and excellent hotel, directly behind the Frontón, include TV and telephone. There's laundry, childcare and room service, and also a good restaurant.

Hotel El Conquistador (☎ 681-79-55; fax 686-13-40; Blvd Agua Caliente 10750; s/d US$62/67; P ⊠ ⊠) This four-star Zona Río hotel has spacious, nice-looking rooms with cable TV, and a distinctive restaurant dedicated to Don Quijote.

Motel Plaza Hermosa (☎ 685-33-53; Av Constitución 1821; s/d US$31/41; P) This quiet hotel offers bright pink rooms with TV and fan. (To clarify, the entire hotel is pink!)

Hotel Nelson (☎ 685-43-03; Av Revolución 721; d US$42) The friendly Nelson Hotel is a long-time favorite for its central location and tidy, carpeted rooms. Rooms come with color TV, a view and the less-than-soothing sounds of La Revo. Its eponymous bar has incredibly cheap daily drink specials.

Hotel Caesar (☎ 685-16-06; fax 685-34-92; Av Revolución 827; s/d US$35/45) Hotel Caesar's long reign is evoked by the vintage bullfight posters and photographs that adorn its walls. The rooms are small and clean, and the restaurant (now a sports bar) claims to have created the Caesar salad in 1924.

TOP END

Hotel Real del Río (☎ 634-31-00; Av Velasco 1409A; s/d US$78/85, ste US$168; P ⊠ ⊠ ⊠) Utterly de-

void of character, the modern and efficient Real del Río makes up for it by providing excellent service and well-appointed, comfortable rooms.

Grand Hotel Tijuana (☎ 681-70-00; www.grandhoteltijuana.com; Blvd Agua Caliente 4500; s & d US$140, ste from US$282; P ⊠ ⊠ ⊠) The two 23-story buildings that include the luxurious Grand Hotel Tijuana also have a shopping mall, offices, restaurants, convention facilities, and an adjacent golf-course.

Eating

Tijuana's cuisine scene is one of the city's big surprises. You'll find everything from traditional *antojitos* (small plates of basic regional fare) to Mexican haute cuisine, prepared at a high level of quality. Don't fear the hot dog wrapped in bacon and smothered in diced cabbage and peppers – it's waiting for you at the corner.

CAFÉS

Café La Especial (☎ 685-66-54; Av Revolución 718; dinners US$3-6) A mainstay since 1952, this restaurant offers decent Mexican food at reasonable prices and is far quieter than the average eatery on La Revo.

Restaurant Ricardo's (☎ 685-40-31; Av Madero 1410; breakfasts US$3-5.50, tortas US$2.75-4.50) One of Tijuana's best values is this bright and cheerful diner-style place. Excellent breakfasts and tortas, among the best in town, are served around the clock.

QUICK EATS

Mexico Lindo (cnr Av Madero and Hidalgo; tacos US$1, dinners US$3-5) In addition to tacos served with all the accoutrements, this family-run place also serves an excellent *pozole*, a filling soup dish made from pork, corn hominy, and plenty of lime and cilantro.

RESTAURANTS

Cien Años (☎ 634-30-39; Av Velasco 1407; dinner US$9-15) Food lovers won't want to miss this famous restaurant and its gourmet Mexican cuisine. If you can't stomach the *chinicuiles* (fried worm tacos) or the *escamoles* (ant eggs), worry not: also served is less-exotic fare that is always brilliant.

La Costa (☎ 685-31-24; Calle 7a No 8131; dinners US$12-30) La Costa is where you should head for seafood. For US$34, the combination plate provides two people with a huge platter of crab, shrimp, lobster, octopus and fish fillet.

D'Tony Restaurante Argentino (☎ 685-50-77; Cnr Av Madero & Calle 7a; dinners US$7.50-23.50, wines US$15-42) For an elegant meal with impeccable service, try D'Tony for pastas, seafood and, of course, steaks prepared the Argentine way.

Vittorio's (☎ 685-17-29; Av Revolución 1687; pizzas US$5-13.50, pastas US$7-9.50) For years this comfortable Italian restaurant has been serving generous portions of reasonably priced pizza and pasta.

Drinking

The majority of Tijuana's ostentatious drinking establishments cater to a tourist crowd intent on pickling their hearty young livers. Look to the hotel bars if you just want to sip a Tecate (Mexican beer) without a Britney wanna-be dancing on the bar and upsetting your dish of peanuts. Most self-respecting Tijuana hipsters wouldn't be caught dead on La Revo; you'll find them imbibing in the Zona Río at Plaza Fiesta, where you'll also encounter a dozen or so restaurants and bars.

Rowdy Av Revolución is the place for 'upside-down margaritas' and ear-splitting music: try the **Hard Rock Café** (☎ 685-02-06; Av Revolución 520). For a sense of the nightlife away from the craziness of La Revo, try the bars **Ah Jijo** or **La Azotea**, which are among the interesting nightlife spots at the Plaza Fiesta.

Entertainment

When the sight of revelers stumbling down Av Revolución abruptly wears thin as a source of entertainment, you'll know it is time to take in some of the city's diverse sporting and cultural offerings. Entertainment listings are readily available online at www.seetijuana.com.

BULLFIGHTING

Some of the world's best matadors perform at Tijuana's two bullrings on Sunday afternoons from May to September .

Ten kilometers west of the city at Playas de Tijuana, the **Plaza de Toros Monumental** (Av Pacífico 1) is the only bullring in the world with a view of the sea. **El Toreo de Tijuana** (Blvd Agua Caliente 100) is the other bullring. Tickets cost $14 to US$70 and are sold at each bullring on the day of the event, or at the **El Toreo de Tijuana ticket office** (☎ 686-15-10 , 686-12-19; 🕙 10am-5pm Wed-Sun during the season). If you feel

that the sight of large mammals being slain by swords will upset your sensibilities, you should probably give this attraction a pass. Schedules for both rings can be found at www.bullfights.org.

DISCOS

Most fancier discos are in the Zona Río, such as the kitschy **Baby Rock** (☎ 634-24-04; Av Diego Rivera 1482), which charges a cover of US$10 on Saturday night.

DOG RACING

At the historic **Agua Caliente Racetrack** (☎ 633-73-00; Agua Caliente 12027), you can watch greyhounds chase that elusive electric rabbit every day of the week and of course you can bet on the proceedings. Races are held Monday, Wednesday Thursday and Friday at 7:45pm, Saturday and Sunday at 1pm, and Tuesday at 2pm and 7:45pm. To get there, catch the red and white 'La Mesa' route taxi on Calle 4a at Av Revolución

LIVE PERFORMANCES

The theater at the **Centro Cultural Tijuana** is the city's apex of drama, dance, and musical performance with several events scheduled each month.

If you want to witness the tuba played with wild abandon, then you might be in luck at the banda/norteño venue **Las Pulgas** (☎ 685-95-94; Av Revolución 1127), which generally charges US$3.75 and frequently admits women free of charge.

Shopping

Jewelry, Mexican blankets, wrought-iron furniture, baskets, silver, blown glass, pottery and leather goods are available in stores on Av Revolución and Av Constitución; at the **Mercado Municipal** on Av Niños Héroes between Calles 1a and 2a; and also at the sprawling **Mercado de Artesanías** just south of Comercio (Calle 1a) along Av Ocampo.

The **Mercado Hidalgo** (Blvd Taboada and Av Independencia) is where locals come to buy spices, dried chilies, exotic produce, fresh tortillas and seasonal specialties made from Aztec grains.

Getting There & Away

AIR

Aero California (☎ 684-21-00; Plaza Río Tijuana) Flies to La Paz and serves many mainland destinations from Mexico City northward.

BAJA CALIFORNIA

Aerolíneas Internacionales (☎ 684-07-27; Vía Poniente 4246, Plaza Jardín, Zona Río) Flies to mainland destinations from Hermosillo to Mexico City.
Aeroméxico (☎ 683-84-44, 684-92-68; Local A 12-1, Plaza Río Tijuana, Paseo de los Héroes & Av Independencia) Serves many mainland Mexican destinations, and has non-stop flights to La Paz and flights to Tucson and Phoenix, both via Hermosillo.
Aeropuerto Internacional Abelardo L Rodríguez (☎ 683-24-18) Is in Mesa de Otay, east of downtown.
Mexicana (☎ 634-65-66; Av Diego Rivera 1511, Zona Río) Flies daily to Los Angeles (but not from Los Angeles) and also serves many mainland Mexican cities.

BUS

About 5km southeast of downtown, the main bus terminal is the **Central Camionera** (☎ 626-17-01), where Elite and Crucero offer 1st-class buses with air-con and toilets. Destinations on mainland Mexico include Guadalajara (US$89, 36 hours) and Mexico City (US$133, 40 hours). All lines stop at major mainland destinations. Autotransportes del Pacífico, Norte de Sonora and ABC operate mostly 2nd-class buses to mainland Mexico's Pacific coast and around Baja California. ABC's Servicio Plus resembles Elite's and Crucero's. **ABC** (☎ 683-56-81) offers buses to Ensenada (US$8.50/7.50 1st/2nd-class, 1½ hours), Guerrero Negro (US$42, 13 hours), La Paz (US$87, 22 hours), Loreto (US$68, 17 hours), Mexicali (US$15/13 1st/2nd-class, 2½ hours), San Felipe (US$25.50, six hours), and Tecate (US$3.75, 1½ hours).

Tijuana has two bus departure locations near the border crossing that might prove more convenient than the outlying Central Camionera. **Suburbaja** (☎ 688-00-82), **Elite** (☎ 621-29-82) and the US-based **Greyhound** (☎ 688-19-79) use the handy downtown **Antigua Central Camionera** (☎ 686-06-95; Av Madero & Calle 1a). Suburbaja buses leave for Tecate every 20 minutes (US$3, 1½ hours); these are local buses that make many stops. Greyhound buses leave every hour for Los Angeles (US$20, four hours). Elite has four first-class buses each day to Mexico City (US$133, 40 hours) and Guadalajara (US$89, 32 hours).

From **Plaza Viva Tijuana** near the border, ABC offers inexpensive Ensenada buses. Buses leave every 30 minutes between 6am and 9:30pm for US$7.50 one-way, US$12 roundtrip. Next door, **Estrellas del Pacífico**

(☎ 683-50-22) has 1st-class buses leaving each hour for Guadalajara (US$89, 32 hours) and other mainland destinations.

Between 8am and 9pm, Mexicoach runs frequent buses (US$2) from its **San Ysidro terminal** (☎ 619-428-9517; 4570 Camino de la Plaza) to the **Terminal Turístico** (☎ 685-14-70; Av Revolución 1025), between Calle 6a and Calle 7a.

Between 5:40am and 9:50pm, buses leave from the **San Diego Greyhound terminal** (☎ 619-239-3266, 800-231-2222 in the USA; 120 West Broadway, San Diego) and stop at **San Ysidro** (☎ 619-428-1194; 799 East San Ysidro Blvd), en route to Tijuana's Antigua Central Camionera bus terminal or the Central Camionera. Fares to both locations are US$5 one-way, US$8 roundtrip.

TROLLEY

San Diego's popular **light-rail trolley** (☎ 619-233-3004) runs from downtown San Diego to San Ysidro every 15 minutes from about 5am to midnight (US$2.50). From San Diego's Lindbergh Field airport, city bus No 992 goes directly to the Plaza America trolley stop in downtown San Diego, across from the Amtrak depot.

CAR & MOTORCYCLE

The San Ysidro border crossing, which is a 10-minute walk from downtown Tijuana, is open 24 hours, but motorists may find the Mesa de Otay crossing (also open round the clock) less congested; it's 8km to the east of San Ysidro.

For rentals, agencies in San Diego are the cheapest option, but most of them allow rentals only as far as Ensenada. **California Baja Rent-A-Car** (☎ 619-470-7368), in Spring Valley, California, 32km from downtown San Diego and 24km from San Ysidro, is a good option if you plan to continue driving beyond Ensenada.

Getting Around
BUS & TAXI

For about US$0.40, local buses pretty much go everywhere, but the slightly pricier route taxis are much quicker. To get to the Central Camionera take any 'Buena Vista', 'Centro' or 'Central Camionera' bus from Calle 2a, east of Av Constitución. For a quicker and more convenient option, take a gold-and-white 'Mesa de Otay' route taxi from Av Madero between Calles 2a and 3a (US$0.80).

To get to the airport, take any 'Aeropuerto' blue and white bus from the street just south of the San Ysidro border taxi stand (about US$0.40); from downtown, catch it on Calle 5a between Avs Constitución and Niños Héroes. Sharing can reduce the cost of a taxi (about US$12 if hailed on the street).

Tijuana taxis lack meters, but most rides cost about US$5 or less. However, beware of the occasional unscrupulous taxi driver.

AROUND TIJUANA

A 30-minute drive south from Tijuana on Highway 1 is the beach resort town of Playas de Rosarito, which becomes glutted with party-goers from October to April but is fairly quiet the rest of the year. (Don't plan on frolicking in the ocean here; it's rarely warm enough.) One and a half hours to the east is the sleepy but fast-growing town of Tecate, home of a certain eponymous brewery of some renown.

Playas de Rosarito
☎ 661 / pop 56,000

South of Tijuana, the valley of Rosarito marks the original boundary between mainland California and Baja California. The town of Playas de Rosarito dates from 1885, but the Hotel Rosarito (now the landmark Rosarito Beach Hotel) and its long, sandy beach pioneered local tourism in the late 1920s. These days, the town has taken on a distinctly Hollywood sheen: Fox Studios Baja, built in 1996 for the filming of *Titanic,* has since served as a primary filming location for *Pearl Harbor* and, most recently, *Master and Commander: The Far Side of the World.*

Rosarito's main street – the noisy commercial strip of Blvd Juárez (part of the Carretera Transpeninsular, Hwy 1) – has many good restaurants and affordable accommodations.

The amphitheater at the beachfront **Parque Municipal Abelardo L Rodríguez** contains Juan Zuñiga Padilla's impressive 1987 mural *Tierra y Libertad* (Land and Liberty).

From downtown Tijuana, route taxis for Playas de Rosarito leave from Av Madero between Calles 3a and 4a (US$2). You can also catch a shuttle from the Terminal Turístico on Av Revolución between Calles 6a and 7a (US$10 roundtrip); they leave every two hours between 9am and 7pm.

Tecate
☎ 665 / pop 57,000

Tecate resembles more of a mainland Mexican village than a border town, but hosts several popular tourist events, such as bicycle races. Its landmark **Cuauhtémoc Moctezuma Brewery** (☎ 654-94-78; Hidalgo & Obregón; tours ☺ noon & 3pm, Mon-Fri) produces two of Mexico's best-known beers, Tecate and Carta Blanca, but *maquiladoras* drive the local economy.

For lodging, the best value in town is offered by **Motel La Hacienda** (☎ 654-12-50; Av Juárez 861; d US$42; P ☒ ☒), which has clean, carpeted rooms and a lovely flower-festooned courtyard.

Tecate is 55km east of Tijuana by Hwy 2, the east–west route linking Tijuana and Mexicali. The border crossing, open 6am to midnight daily, is less congested than either Tijuana or Mesa de Otay.

ENSENADA
☎ 646 / pop 245,000

On Bahía de Todos Santos 108km south of the border, Ensenada is the most sophisticated and well-rounded of the northern coastal towns. It's a fairly wealthy city with great civic pride, evident in the generously designed public areas – rather than hotels – that line the waterfront. Ensenada enjoys great popularity among tourists; about four million of them descend upon the city each year, including 350,000 arriving by cruise ship from southern California. Most visitors are drawn to Av López Mateos, a clean, nicely landscaped and pedestrian-oriented artery lined with interesting shops, cafés and restaurants with sidewalk seating, and many hotels. Outdoor activities such as fishing and surfing are popular, and Ensenada is the locus of Baja's wine industry.

In colonial times, Ensenada de Todos los Santos occasionally sheltered Acapulco-bound galleons returning from Manila, but the first permanent settlement was established in 1804. The discovery of gold in 1870 at Real del Castillo, 35km inland, brought a short-lived boom. Ensenada was capital of Baja territory from 1882 to 1915, but the capital shifted to Mexicali during the revolution. After the revolution the city catered to 'sin' industries until the federal government outlawed gambling in the 1930s.

ENSENADA

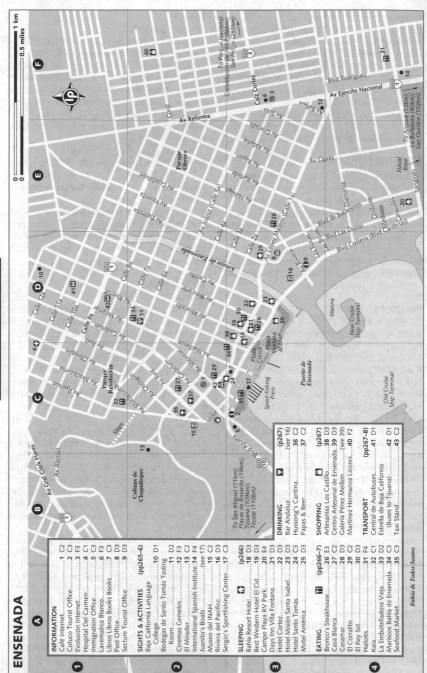

BAJA CALIFORNIA

Bahía de Todos Santos

0 ————— 1 km
0 ————— 0.5 miles

To San Miguel (11km);
Playas de Rosarito (19km);
Tijuana (109km);
Tecate (110km)

To Parque Nacional
Constitución de 1857 (86km);
San Felipe (251km)

To Airport (12km);
La Bufadora (40km);
San Quintín (192km)

Orientation

Near the water, hotels and restaurants line Blvd Costero, also known as Blvd Cárdenas. Av López Mateos (Calle 1a) parallels Blvd Costero for a short distance inland (north). The tourist district is between Av Ryerson and Av Castillo.

North of town, Hwy 3 heads northeast to Tecate; at the southeast edge of town it leads east toward Ojos Negros and Parque Nacional Constitución de 1857 (Laguna Hanson) before continuing south to the Valle de Trinidad and San Felipe.

Information

BOOKSTORES
Libros Libros Books Books (☎ 178-84-48; Av López Mateos 690) Good selection of books in Spanish and English.

EMERGENCY
Municipal Police (☎ 060 or 176-43-43)
State Police (☎ 061 or 176-36-36)

IMMIGRATION
Immigration office (☎ 174-01-64; Blvd Azueta 101; ⏱ 8:30am-1pm for document delivery, 1-3pm for document pickup) Open daily. Pick up a tourist card here if you haven't already got one and you're heading further south.

INTERNET ACCESS
Café Internet (☎ 175-70-11; Av López Mateos 582; per hr US$2)
Evolución Internet (☎ 177-24-20; Plaza Bahía shopping center, Cnr Calz Cortez & Av Reforma; per hr US$2) Macintosh only.

INTERNET RESOURCES
www.enjoyensenada.com Ensenada's tourism site.

LAUNDRY
Lavematica Blanco (☎ 176-25-48; Plaza Bahía shopping center, Cnr Calz Cortez & Av Reforma)

MEDICAL SERVICES
Hospital Del Carmen (☎ 178-34-77; Cnr Av Obregón and Calle 11)

MONEY
Most banks and *casas de cambio* are near the intersection of Av Ruiz and Av Juárez. There are numerous ATMs throughout Ensenada.

POST
Main post office (Av López Mateos at Club Rotario)

TOURIST INFORMATION
Cotuco tourist office (☎ 178-24-11; cotucoe@telnor .net; Blvd Costero 540; ⏱ 9am-5pm Sun-Tue, 9am-7pm Wed-Fri) Dispenses maps, brochures and current hotel information.
Secure tourist office (☎ 172-30-22; Blvd Costero 1477; ⏱ 8am-8pm Mon-Fri, 9am-1pm Sat-Sun) Carries similar information as the Cotuco office.

Sights

Opened in the early 1930s as Hotel Playa Ensenada, the extravagant **Riviera del Pacífico**, a Spanish-style former casino on Blvd Costero, is rumored to have been a regular haunt of Al Capone. It now houses a small **museum** (Museo de Historia de Ensenada; ☎ 177-05-94; admission US$1; ⏱ 9am-5pm Mon-Sun) and the Bar Andaluz, and offers retrospective film showings and art exhibitions. A small museum shop sells books on the history of Ensenada and historic bills and coins.

For an informative introduction to Baja's wine industry, **Bodegas de Santo Tomás** (☎ 178-33-33; Av Miramar 666; tour US$5; ⏱ 8am-5pm) holds tours of its cellars and wine tastings hourly from 10am to 1pm and at 3pm daily. Sample their signature big red: the award-winning 2000 Cabernet.

Built in 1886 by the US-owned International Company of Mexico, Ensenada's oldest public building houses the **Museo del INAH** (Instituto Nacional de Antropología e Historia, ex-Aduana Marítima de Ensenada; ☎ 178-25-31; Av Ryerson 1; admission free; ⏱ 9am-5pm Mon-Fri), a historical/cultural museum.

Atop the Colinas de Chapultepec, **El Mirador** offers panoramic views of the city and Bahía de Todos Santos. Climb or drive up Av Alemán from the western end of Calle 2a in central Ensenada to this highest point in town.

Activities

The beach at **San Miguel**, 11 km to the north of town, has a wonderful right to left break and often hosts **surfing** contests. For something a little less predictable, head west of Ensenada by boat to the **Islas de Todos Santos**, where you'll find a legendary spot called *El Martillo* (the hammer) with swells rising 4m to 5m. Boats run out to the breaks every day; check at the harbor.

Ensenada is known the world over for its excellent **sport fishing**. Most charter companies also offer **whale watching** tours from late December to March. The following options are well-regarded and both on the sport-fishing pier off El Malecón.

Juanito's Boats (☎ 174-09-53; www.sailorschoice.com /juanitos)

Sergio's Sportfishing Center & Marina (☎ 178-21-85; www.sergios-sportfishing.com)

Courses

The following language schools offer similar immersion programs with home-stay opportunities.

International Spanish Institute (☎ 176-01-09; www.sdro.com/spanishinstitute; Blvd Rodríguez 377)

Baja California Language College (☎ 174-17-21; www.bajacal.com; Av Riveroll 1287)

Festivals & Events

The events listed below constitute a tiny sample of the 70-plus sporting, tourist and cultural happenings that take place each year. Dates change, so contact tourist offices for details.

Carnaval Mardi Gras celebration, late February to early March.

Baja 500 Off-road car race, early June.

Fiesta de la Vendimia Wine harvest, mid-August.

Fiestas Patrias Mexican independence days, mid-September.

Mexican Surf Fiesta Grand finals of local surf competition, mid-October.

Fiesta del Tequila Last week in October.

Sleeping

Although Ensenada has many hotels, demand can exceed supply at times, particularly on weekends and in summer. Rates vary both seasonally and between weekdays and weekends, making it difficult to categorize hotels by price.

BUDGET

Campo Playa RV Park (☎ 176-29-18; Cnr Blvd Las Dunas & Sanginés; tent sites US$13, trailer sites with/without hookups US$20/16) Close to downtown, this place offers secure grounds with shady sites and well-maintained facilities.

   Motel América (☎ 176-13-33; Av López Mateos 1309; s/d US$25/32; **P**) This friendly motor lodge offers clean, simple rooms with fans; many have kitchenettes.

MID-RANGE

Hotel Misión Santa Isabel (☎ 178-33-45; hmision@ telnor.net; Blvd Cárdenas 1119; s/d from US$55/75; **P**

☒ ☒) Built in 1924 to resemble one of Baja's lost missions, this striking hotel offers clean, comfortable rooms decorated with tasteful tile work.

   Hotel Cortez (☎ 178-23-07; fax 178-39-04; Av López Mateos 1089; s/d US$70/80; **P** ☒ ☒) This large, family-friendly hotel has a gym, a basketball court, and a popular bar and restaurant.

   Days Inn Villa Fontana (☎ 178-34-34; www.villa fontana.com.mx; Av López Mateos 1050; d/ste with Jacuzzi US$52/130; ☒ ☒) Lacking in style but efficiently run, this hotel has tidy, comfortable rooms with views and cable TV. Prices increase by 20% on Friday and Saturday.

   Hotel Santo Tomás (☎ 178-15-03; hst@bajainn .com; Blvd Costero 609; d US$80; **P**) At the entrance to downtown Ensenada, this hotel has spacious rooms with satellite TV. Rates increase by 15% on Friday and Saturday.

TOP END

Best Western Hotel El Cid (☎ 178-24-01; www.mex online.com/elcid.htm; Av López Mateos 993; s/d US$72/98; **P** ☒ ▢ ☒) This four-star hotel has unique rooms, an outstanding restaurant and a lively bar featuring Cuban music on weekends. Prices include continental breakfast.

   Bahía Resort Hotel (☎ 178-21-03; www.hotel bahia.com.mx; Av López Mateos 850; s/d US$60/90; **P** ☒ ☒) If your idea of fun is to relax by the pool sipping a potent margarita this place is for you. The pleasant rooms have balconies, many with views of the port.

Eating

Ensenada has eateries ranging from corner taco stands to places serving the best of Mexican and international cuisine. Seafood lovers, in particular, will leave sated and smiling.

CAFÉS & QUICK EATS

El Corralito (☎ 178-23-70; Av López Mateos 627; breakfasts US$2.50-4, dinners US$4.50-8.50) This modest café offers good-value combination plates, steaks and seafood; it's also an economical place to get a quality tequila.

   At the **seafood market** near the sport-fishing piers on the Malecón running parallel to Blvd Costero, check out the impressive display of just-caught fish and then step across the sidewalk for a fish or shrimp taco with the works: you know it's fresh.

Casa Blanca (☎ 174-03-16; Av Ruiz 254; plates US$7) The Casa Blanca serves tasty, traditional fixed-price lunches.

RESTAURANTS

Haliotis (☎ 176-37-20; Delante 179; dinners US$12-18) Situated east of Av Ejército, this is a good option for seafood – the restaurant's name means 'abalone' (not 'bad breath').

Casamar (☎ 174-04-17; Blvd Cárdenas 987; dinners US$8-12, lobster US$26) This family-owned restaurant features elegant seafood dining and a full bar which offers great views of the port. Try the signature dish, *Fillet Casamar* (sea bass stuffed with seafood and spinach covered with clam sauce).

El Rey Sol (☎ 178-17-33; Av López Mateos 1000; dinners US$15-20) This venerable Franco-Mexican institution has elegant French food and homemade bread and pastries made fresh daily.

La Embotelladora Vieja (☎ 178-16-60; Cnr Av Miramar & Calle 7a; dinners US$11-15; closed Sun) Huge wooden casks and other rustic features grace the dining hall of this former wine-aging warehouse. The delicious *filet mignon Embotelladora*, marinated in port, is a decadent treat.

Bronco's Steakhouse (☎ 178-48-92; Av López Mateos 1525; dinners US$15) Carnivores will be well taken care of at this family-style steakhouse. If you're feeling excessive, consider *La Tradicional*, with sausage, chicken, steak and tripe all on one plate.

Kaia (☎ 178-22-38; Av Moctezuma 479; dinners US$15-20) This cozy, romantic Basque restaurant has a special ambience, and the food is exquisite. Try the *Cabicucho* fish with a salsa of mushrooms and chocolate.

Mariscos Bahía de Ensenada (☎ 178-10-15; Av Riveroll 109; dinners US$10, lobster US$25) Popular with the locals, this excellent inexpensive seafood restaurant has a nonsmoking section, an extensive kids menu, and a scrumptious *Caldos Mixto* (mixed seafood soup).

Drinking

On weekends, most bars and cantinas along Av Ruiz are packed from noon to early morning. If it's not your scene, head for one of the many quality hotels and fine restaurants where you're likely to find a laid-back spot to sip a top-shelf tequila.

Hussong's Cantina (☎ 178-32-10; Av Ruiz 113) the oldest and perhaps liveliest cantina in the Californias has been serving tequila since 1892. It's also a raucous palace of Mariachi music.

Papas & Beer (☎ 174-01-45; Cnr Av López Mateos & Av Ruiz) is a wildly popular restaurant and nightclub; it's not unusual to see partiers dancing on the tables in the middle of the afternoon.

For a complete change in ambience, visit the cultured **Bar Andaluz** (☎ 177-17-30) inside the Riviera del Pacífico (p265), where having a drink is an exercise in nostalgia. You can almost visualize Lana Turner sipping a martini at the polished walnut bar.

Entertainment

Entertainment opportunities in Ensenada are primarily of the drinking, eating, shopping and sporting variety. If you find yourself hungover, over-fed, shopped-out and weary, a movie might be just the ticket. **Cinemas Gemelos** (☎ 176-36-16; Cnr Av López Mateos & Av Balboa) has recent Hollywood fare, often dubbed into Spanish.

Shopping

Galería Pérez Meillon (☎ 171-61-27; Blvd Costero 1094), in the Centro Artesanal de Ensenada, sells authenticated pottery from the Paipai and Mata Ortiz. Also for sale are baskets woven from aromatic materials such as sage by the Kumiai people. Taxco silver is available at **Artesanías Los Castillo** (☎ 178-29-62; Av López Mateos 815). **Martínez Hermanos Licores** (☎ 177-39-08; Coral 768 at Av Revolución) is known for the widest tequila selection in the surrounding area with over 400 brands on the shelves. Sorry, no tasting.

Getting There & Away

AIR

Primarily a military airport, **Aeropuerto El Ciprés** (☎ 177-45-03) is just south of town off the Transpeninsular.

The only regularly scheduled flights serving Ensenada are by **Aerocedros** (☎ 177-35-34), which flies to Guerrero Negro and Isla Cedros (p275).

BUS

Ensenada's **Central de Autobuses** (☎ 178-66-80; Av Riveroll 1075) is 10 blocks north of Av López Mateos. **Elite** (☎ 178-67-70) serves mainland Mexican destinations as far as Guadalajara (US$86, 36 hours) and Mexico City (US$117, 44 hours). **ABC** (☎ 178-66-80) is the main peninsular carrier, and offers buses to Guerrero Negro (US$36, 10 hours), La Paz (US$85, 20 hours), Mexicali (US$21/17 1st/2nd-class, four hours), San Felipe (US$17, four hours),

Tecate (US$6.50, two hours) and Tijuana (US$9/8 1st/2nd-class, 1½ hours).

Estrella de Baja California (☎ 178-85-21; Riveroll 861) goes to Tijuana (US$8, 1½ hours) hourly from 5am to 9am, and at 11am, 2pm, 4pm and 6pm. Make sure to specify whether you want to go to the Tijuana's main terminal or to the border ('La Línea').

Getting Around

The main taxi stand is at the corner of Avs López Mateos and Miramar; taxis also congregate along Av Juárez. Most fares within the city cost around US$4 to US$8.

The asking price for a taxi trip to the airport is US$15 for one to four passengers.

Ensenada's main avenues are well served by buses and vans; most routes are designated by street name and charge US$0.50.

AROUND ENSENADA

The impressive **La Bufadora**, a magnificent tidewater blowhole on the craggy shores of the Pacific 40km south of Ensenada, periodically sends a jet of water 30 meters into the sky. To get there, drive south on the Transpeninsular and enter the town of Maneadero and head west at the junction. From here the road meanders through farmlands and skirts rocky shorelines and craggy cliffs. Alternately, you can catch a taxi at the taxi stand in Ensenada (US$10 per person, minimum four).

PARQUE NACIONAL CONSTITUCIÓN DE 1857

From Ojos Negros, east of Ensenada at Km 39 on Hwy 3, a 43km dirt road climbs to the Sierra de Juárez and Parque Nacional Constitución de 1857. Its highlight is the marshy, pined **Laguna Hanson** (also known as Laguna Juárez, 1200m). The lake abounds with migratory birds from August to November.

Camping is pleasant, but livestock have contaminated the water, so bring your own. Firewood is scarce along the lake but abundant in the hills. Only pit toilets are available. Nearby granite outcrops offer stupendous views but tiring ascents through dense brush and massive rock falls – beware of ticks and rattlesnakes. Technical climbers will find short but challenging routes.

The park is also accessible by a steeper road east of Km 55.2, 16km southeast of the Ojos Negros junction.

PARQUE NACIONAL SIERRA SAN PEDRO MÁRTIR

In the Sierra San Pedro Mártir, east of San Telmo and west of San Felipe, Baja's most notable national park comprises 650 sq km of coniferous forests, granite peaks exceeding 3000m and deep canyons cutting into its steep eastern scarp. The elusive desert bighorn sheep inhabits some remote areas of the park, along with bobcats, coyotes and eagles.

Camping areas and hiking trails are numerous, but maintenance is limited; carry a compass and a topographic map, along with cold- and wet-weather supplies, canteens and water purification tablets. Below 1800m, beware of rattlesnakes.

Observatorio Astronómico Nacional (☎ 554-54-70; ◷ 11am-1pm Sat only, call for reservations) is Mexico's national observatory. It's 2km from the parking area at the end of the San Telmo road. Even if you don't make it inside the observatory, you're sure to enjoy the jaw-dropping view of the multicolored desert mountains receding all the way to the Pacific to the west. To the east you can see the Sea of Cortez and, on a clear day, all the way to the Mexican mainland.

To reach San Pedro Mártir from San Telmo de Abajo, watch for the sign just south of Km 140 on the Transpeninsular (Hwy 1), about 52km south of San Vicente. A graded dirt road climbs 80km to the east through an ever-changing desert landscape, affording satisfying vistas all along the way. The road is relentlessly washboarded but passable to most passenger vehicles. In the spring when the snow is melting, be advised that you may have to cross a river along the way.

MEXICALI

☎ 686 / pop 588,000

Bustling Mexicali, capital of the state of Baja California, is a prosperous agricultural and industrial center. Some have said that its charms are subtle. Most travelers breeze through on their way south to San Felipe or east to Sonora and mainland Mexico, but those who stay are welcomed by several good restaurants and hotels. Mexicali enjoys excellent cultural and educational facilities and, unlike its neighbors Tijuana and San Felipe, is reluctant to pander to tourists. This ultimately makes the city all the more interesting. A day here spent wandering the

Dusk over La Paz (p284), Baja California Sur

Apartments, La Paz (p286)

Centro Cultural Tijuana
(CECUT; p259)

Plastic pink flamingoes for sale, Tijuana (p256)

Fiesta Americana Hotel (p444),
Puerto Vallarta

Carnaval dancers, Mazatlán (p418)

Clavadista (cliff diver), Acapulco (p486)

historic streets alongside the border reveals as much about mainland California as it does about Baja.

In the summer, the blazingly hot weather threatens to melt the soles of your shoes into the pavement. The denizens of Mexicali, however, seem undaunted: as the flavored ice vendors go into high gear, the rest of the population makes minor adjustments and goes about its business.

Orientation

Mexicali straddles the Río Nuevo, south of Calexico, California. Most of the historic center's main streets parallel the border. Av Madero passes through the central business district of modest restaurants, shops, bars and budget hotels. The diagonal Calz López Mateos heads southeast through newer industrial and commercial areas and becomes Hwy 2 (to Sonora). Many of Mexicali's hotels and restaurants are in the Zona Hotelera, which runs along Calz Sierra and Calz Juárez (which becomes Hwy 5 to San Felipe).

Information

BOOKSTORES
Librería Alethia (☎ 552-57-76; Altamirano 420A) Good selection of books on Mexican history, archaeology, anthropology and literature.

EMERGENCY
Asistencia Turística (☎ 078)
Cruz Roja (☎ 066)

INTERNET ACCESS
DirectNet Internet Cafe (☎ 554-55-68; Calz Sierra 820; per hr US$3.50, second hr free)
La Señal Internet (☎ 552-28-05; Plaza La Cachanilla mall, Calz López Mateos; per hr US$4)

INTERNET RESOURCES
www.mexicaliturismo.com Mexicali's tourism site.

MEDICAL SERVICES
On Av Reforma and Av Obregón near the US border are many health care providers offering quality services at a fraction of the cost north of the border.
Hospital México-Americano (☎ 552-23-00; fax 552-29-42; Av Reforma 1000) On the corner of Calle B near the border.

MONEY
Casas de cambio are abundant and keep long hours, while banks offer exchange services

Monday to Friday mornings only. Most banks in Mexicali and Calexico have ATMs. Bancomer is on Azueta at Av Madero; Banamex on Altamirano at Av Tejada.

POST
Main post office (Av Madero; ☼ 7am-6:30pm Mon-Fri, 8am-3pm Sat-Sun) Near Morelos.

TELEPHONE & FAX
Both pay phones and *cabinas* (call offices; mostly in pharmacies, but also in other small businesses) are common.

TOURIST INFORMATION
Mexican Tourism and Convention Bureau
(☎ 557-25-61; Cnr Calz López Mateos & Camelias; ☼ 8am-6pm Mon-Fri) Similar offerings are available at this office, opposite the Teatro del Estado 3km southeast of the border.
Secure tourist office (☎ 566-12-77; Calz Montejano 1, Zona Hotelera; ☼ 8am-8pm Mon-Fri, 9am-1pm Sat) Patient, bilingual staff and plenty of information about regional attractions and events.

Sights & Activities

The country's largest Chinatown, **La Chinesca**, is south of Calz López Mateos, centered on Av Juárez and Altamirano; the nearby **Plaza Constitución** is a good place to hear *banda* groups rehearse in the late afternoon (hence its nickname: **Plaza del Mariachi**).

Most of Mexicali's historic buildings are northeast of Calz López Mateos. **Catedral de la Virgen de Guadalupe**, corner of Av Reforma and Morelos, is the city's major religious landmark. Now the rectory of the Universidad Autónoma de Baja California, the former **Palacio de Gobierno**, built between 1919 and 1922, interrupts Av Obregón just east of Calle E.

The **Centro de Estudios Culturales – Museo UABC** (☎ 554-19-77; educativos@uabc.mx; Cnr Av Reforma & Calle L; admission free; ☼ 9am-6pm Tue-Fri, 10am-4pm Sat-Sun) is a modest eight-room place that features exhibits on geology, paleontology, human evolution, colonial history and photography.

To escape the summer heat, consider a visit to the **Ciudad Deportiva municipal pool** (☎ 568-30-25; Sports City Complex; ☼ 6am-1pm, 2-9pm). Before you can enter, you must submit to a glancing medical check and pay a US$4 membership fee, in addition to a US$1 per hour usage fee.

BAJA CALIFORNIA

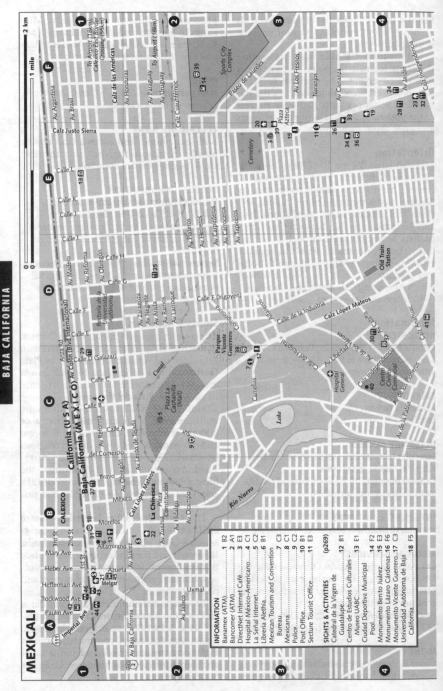

MEXICALI

BAJA CALIFORNIA

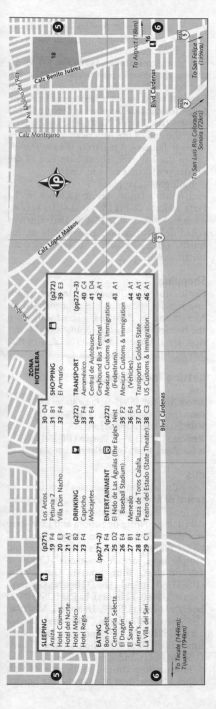

Festivals & Events

From September to October, Mexicali's cultural and historical institutions switch into high gear for the annual **Fiesta del Sol** (Festival of the Sun) to commemorate the city's founding in 1903. Events include concerts, art exhibits, a crafts exposition, theatrical performances and parades.

Sleeping

Lodging options are clustered around the border and in the zona hotelera. In general, they are less expensive than in Tijuana, but if you don't fancy sleeping in a hotel whose reception has iron bars on the windows, you're going to have to pay for it.

Araiza (☎ 564-11-00; www.araizainn.com.mx; Calz Juárez 2220; d US$117; P 🍴 ☐ 🛋) This recently expanded, family-friendly deluxe hotel has well-appointed rooms, two excellent restaurants, a gym, tennis courts and a convention center.

Hotel del Norte (☎ 552-81-01; Av Madero 205; s/d US$43/49; 🍴 ☐) The most pleasant of the border options, the landmark Hotel del Norte has 52 carpeted rooms, some with color TV.

Hotel Regis (☎ 566-34-35; fax 566-88-02; Calz Juárez 2150; s/d US$38/49; P 🍴) In the Zona Hotelera, the motor lodge–style Hotel Regis offers immaculate rooms with TV and phone.

Hotel Cosmos (☎ 568-11-55; Calz Sierra 1493; s/d with breakfast US$43/48; P 🍴) This popular motel offers TV, phone, and a restaurant. Make reservations because it fills up early.

Hotel México (☎ 554-06-69; Av Lerdo de Tejada 476; s/d US$25/28, rooms with Jacuzzis US$35; P 🍴) Mexicali's best budget option is this hotel between Altamirano and Morelos. The small but clean rooms have a TV and private bathroom.

Eating

Mexicali's up-and-coming image is reflected in the wide variety of quality restaurants throughout the city.

Bon Appétit (☎ 565-60-16; Calz Juárez 1142; breakfast US$5.50-7, dinners US$6-15) This cosmopolitan café offers wholesome vegetarian options and Franco–Italian cuisine.

Petunia 2 (☎ 552-69-51; Av Madero 436; breakfast US$4.50, lunch US$5) Convenient to the border, this cheerful place has a breezy dining room and good, inexpensive Mexican breakfasts and lunches.

Jinera's (☎ 566-01-11; Calz Juárez 1342; dinners US$5-10) Jinera's is the place to go for lovingly prepared central Mexican food, including exotic dishes. Don't miss the *Nopales Rellenos* (stuffed cactus) or the *Quesadillas de Chapulines* (grasshoppers).

Cenaduría Selecta (☎ 552-40-47; Av Arista 1510; dinners US$6-11) An institution since 1945, Cenaduría Selecta packs them in for its beloved antojitos and mole dishes.

El Sarape (☎ 554-22-87; Bravo 140; dinners US$5-10.50) This raucous, traditional Mexican restaurant features nightly mariachi music and a menu that will delight carnivores.

La Villa del Seri (☎ 553-55-03; Cnr Av Reforma & Calle D; dinners US$15-19) A great choice for a splurge, this place specializes in Sonoran beef. It also has excellent seafood, pastas and antojitos.

Villa Don Nacho (☎ 566-34-35; Calz Juárez 2150; breakfast US$5.50-8, dinners US$6.50-9) Adjacent to the Hotel Regis, this squeaky-clean establishment serves soups, salads, pasta and Mexican specials.

El Dragón (☎ 566-20-20; Calz Juárez 1830; dinners US$5-12) Housed in a neon-flanked pagoda, this large restaurant specializes in seafood and Cantonese cuisine.

Los Arcos (☎ 556-08-86; Av Calafia 454; dinners US$7-15) This is Mexicali's most popular seafood restaurant; it's near the Plaza de Toros in the Centro Cívico-Comercial.

Drinking

Night owls intent on shaking their bones until the mariachis go home should head for the zona hotelera and its growing selection of late-night diversions.

Molcajetes (☎ 556-07-00; Calz Montejano 1100A; ☽ 1pm-2am) Molcajetes is a good restaurant with a popular bar scene after 10pm.

Capricho (☎ 564-66-11; Calz Juárez 1840; ☽ 1pm-2am Sun-Wed, 1pm-4am Thu-Sat) Capricho is a lively, cavernous bar with an excellent tequila selection and decent pizza. Rock bands perform on Thursday through Saturday nights.

Entertainment

The ultramodern **Teatro del Estado** (☎ 554-64-18; Calz López Mateos & Parque Vicente Guerrero), just north of Compresora, presents a variety of local and visiting cultural performances year-round.

A raucous dance club that really draws a crowd is **Menealo** (☎ 557-03-95; 1100 Calz Monte-

jano; ☽ 9pm-4am Thu-Sat, closed Sun-Wed). Thursday is Salsa and Merengue night; lessons are offered from 8pm to 11pm.

Starting in October, **Las Águilas** (☎ 567-51-29; www.aguilasdemexicali.com.mx/aguilas; Calz Cuauhtémoc; tickets US$7-10), Mexicali's professional baseball team, hosts other teams from the Liga Mexicana del Pacífico at El Nido de Las Águilas (the Eagles' Nest). The season lasts from the end of the American World Series through January. A taxi from the zona hotelera to the ballpark, about 5km east of the border post, costs around US$6.

Bullfights take place two or three times each month from May to October in the **Plaza de Toros Calafia** (☎ 557-38-64; Cnr Av Calafia & Calz Independencia; US$8-26 at the gate). Current schedule information is available at the tourist offices or online at www.mexicali turismo.com.

Shopping

Curio stores selling cheap leather goods and kitschy souvenirs are concentrated on Melgar and Av Reforma, a short walk from the border. For a more sophisticated selection, try **El Armario** (☎ 568-19-06; Calz Sierra 1700, Suite 1A, Plaza Azteca mall).

Getting There & Away

AIR

Aeroméxico (☎ 557-25-51; Pasaje Alamos 1008D, Centro Cívico Comercial) Flies to La Paz, Mexico City, Mazatlán and other mainland points.

Mexicana (☎ 553-59-20; Obregón 1170) Flies daily to Guadalajara, Mexico City and intermediate points.

BUS

Long-distance bus companies leave from the **Central de Autobuses** (☎ 557-24-15; Calz Independencia), near Calz López Mateos. Autotransportes del Pacífico, Norte de Sonora and Elite serve mainland Mexican destinations, while ABC serves the Baja peninsula. Destinations and sample fares include Ensenada (US$20/18 1st/2nd-class, four hours), Guadalajara (US$87/80 1st/2nd-class, 32 hours), Guerrero Negro (US$60, 12 hours), La Paz (US$108, 24 hours), Loreto (US$87, 18 hours), Mazatlán (US$66/60 1st/2nd-class, 24 hours), Mexico City (US$128/113 1st/2nd-class, 42 hours), San Felipe (US$14, 2½ hours), and Tijuana (US$19/14 1st/2nd-class, 2½ hours).

From a stop on the south side of Calz López Mateos, near Melgar and the border,

Transportes Golden State (☎ 553-61-69) goes to Los Angeles (US$33, five hours) and intermediate points five times each day between 6am and 10:30pm. The Calexico, California, stop is at Church's Fried Chicken, 344 Imperial Av.

In Calexico, **Greyhound** (☎ 760-357-1895; 121 1st St) is directly across from the border. Daily there are five departures to Los Angeles (US$30/58 one-way/roundtrip), four to San Diego (US$20/32 one-way/roundtrip) and four to Tucson (US$46/82 one-way/roundtrip).

CAR & MOTORCYCLE

The main Calexico–Mexicali border crossing is open 24 hours. Vehicle permits are available at the border, as are tourist cards for those traveling beyond Ensenada or San Felipe. US and Mexican authorities have opened a second border complex east of downtown to ease congestion. It's open 6am to 10pm.

Getting Around

Cabs to **Aeropuerto Internacional General Rodolfo Sánchez Taboada** (☎ 553-67-42), 18km east of town, cost US$16 but may be shared.

Most city buses start from Av Reforma, just west of Calz López Mateos; check the placard for the destination. Local fares are about US$1.

A taxi to the Centro Cívico-Comercial or Zona Hotelera from the border averages about US$5; agree on the fare first.

SAN FELIPE

☎ 686 / pop 14,500

This once-tranquil fishing community on the Sea of Cortez (Golfo de California), 200km south of Mexicali, suffers blistering summer temperatures, roaring motorcycles, firecrackers, real-estate speculators and aggressive restaurateurs who practically yank patrons off the sidewalk. In spite of all this, travelers keep coming back. Perhaps it's San Felipe's beautiful location, nestled between the dramatic Desierto del Colorado and the Sea of Cortez. Or its white sand beach, or the epic sport fishing, or the balmy winters. If this sounds like prime kick-back territory to you, then your margarita glass need never be empty.

Bancomer (160 Av Mar de Cortez; ⏱ 8:30am-4pm Mon-Fri, 10am-2pm Sat) exchanges traveler's checks and has an ATM. Head to **The Net** (☎ 577-16-00; Plaza Canela 1; per hr US$5) for Internet access.

San Felipe has plenty of breezy seafood restaurants facing the beach, and a variety of places to sleep including RV parks, motor lodges and large resort town–style hotels. For accommodations, a good budget choice is the **Motel Pescador** (☎ 577-29-91; Av Mar de Cortez 101; d US$40; P ✂), which has basic rooms and is convenient to the beach. A family-friendly mid-range option is the **Costa Azul Hotel** (☎ 577-15-48; Cnr Av Mar de Cortez & Calle Ensenada; d US$82; P ✂ ✂); here up to two children can stay for free. **El Nido Seafood and Steak** (☎ 577-10-28; Av Mar de Cortez 3485; dinners US$8-20; closed Wed) serves well-prepared seafood and *carne asada* (grilled beef) in a rustic stone building.

By Hwy 5, San Felipe is 2½ hours from the Mexicali border crossing. At the **bus terminal** (☎ 577-15-16; Av Mar Caribe), just south of Calle Chetumal, **ABC** operates buses to Ensenada (US$19, four hours), Mexicali (US$14, 2½ hours), and Tijuana (US$30, 5½ hours).

AROUND SAN FELIPE

Though paved, the 85km road from San Felipe to the village of **Puertecitos** is in a fairly constant state of disrepair. Here is the starting point for a rugged southbound alternative to the Transpeninsular, but it should not be attempted unless you are driving a stalwart 4WD. For years the road has been slated to be paved, but these plans have yet to materialize.

SOUTHERN BAJA

As you travel across the 28th parallel and into the state of Baja California Sur, you pass into territory more aligned with mainland Mexico than with the northern lands of La Frontera. Baja's colonial and historical heritage is more palpable here, as seen in its well-preserved or restored mission churches and modest plazas.

South of the 28th parallel, the hour changes; Mountain time (to the south) is an hour ahead of Pacific time (to the north). Here you also enter the 25,000 sq km Reserva de la Biósfera El Vizcaíno, Latin America's largest protected area, not including those linked to others. It sprawls from the Península Vizcaíno across to the Sea of

Cortez and includes the major gray-whale calving areas of Laguna San Ignacio and Laguna Ojo de Liebre, and the Sierra de San Francisco, with its pre-Hispanic rock art.

Beyond Guerrero Negro and the desolate Desierto de Vizcaíno, the oasis of San Ignacio augurs the semitropical gulf coast between Mulegé and Cabo San Lucas. Paralleling the gulf, the Sierra de la Giganta divides the region into an eastern subtropical zone and a western zone of elevated plateaus and dry lowlands.

The southernmost part of the peninsula contains the city of La Paz and areas to its south including the popular resorts of Los Cabos. Los Cabos refers to the towns of San José del Cabo and Cabo San Lucas, as well as to the Los Cabos Corridor (the strip of beaches and luxury resorts that lines the coastline between the two towns).

GUERRERO NEGRO

☎ 615 / pop 11,000

The gateway to the state of Baja California Sur, Guerrero Negro's main draw is the nearby **Laguna Ojo de Liebre** (known in English as Scammon's Lagoon), which annually becomes the mating and breeding ground of California gray whales. Each year, the whales migrate 9700km from the Bering Sea to the lagoon, where they chill out in numbers sometimes exceeding 1500 from mid-December through March.

Orientation & Information

The town comprises two distinct sectors: a disorderly strip along Blvd Zapata, west of the Transpeninsular, and an orderly company town further west, run by Exportadora de Sal (ESSA). Nearly all accommodations, restaurants and other services are along Blvd Zapata; Guerrero Negro does not utilize street numbers.

There's a Banamex with an ATM at the far end of the commercial district on Blvd Zapata, just at the start of the company town.

To get online, your only option is **Compu .net** (☎ 157-21-58; Blvd Zapata about halfway down the strip; per hr US$2.50; ☯ 9am-10pm).

Guerrero Negro's only medical facility is the **Clínica Hospital IMSS** (☎ 157-04-33; Blvd Zapata), located where the road curves southwest.

Whale-Watching

Guerrero Negro travel agencies arrange whale-watching trips on Laguna Ojo de

---

CALIFORNIA GRAY WHALES

Along with the mysterious spawning runs of salmon up the great rivers and streams of the Pacific Northwest, the migration of the great gray whales from Siberian and Alaskan waters to the lagoons of Baja is one of the world's most amazing animal events. Sliding majestically along the shore – at the stately clip of 5km to 7km per hour – the whales will have swum 6250km to 9700km before reaching the sanctuary of Baja's warm and protected shallow waters. There, in calving grounds such as Ojo de Liebre (Scammon's Lagoon) southwest of Guerrero Negro and Laguna San Ignacio southwest of San Ignacio, 700kg calves will draw their first breath and begin learning the lessons of the sea from their ever-watchful mothers.

Peak months to see mothers and calves in the lagoons are February to early April, but the official whale-watching season begins December 15 and lasts until April 15. During the later days of their stay in Baja, the calves will have grown strong enough to slip the parental guidance of their leviathan moms. This can result in a curious calf swimming directly up to a rolling panga boat to have its snout scratched and petted – an awesome close encounter. After two to three months in these sheltered waters and a near doubling in their birth weight, the calves will follow their mothers back to the open sea to begin the three-month glide home to their rich feeding grounds in the frozen north. And the following year, they will return.

If you've got *ballena* (whale) fever, one of these destinations will provide a cure:

■ **Laguna Ojo de Liebre** (Scammon's Lagoon) (above)

■ **Laguna San Ignacio** (p277)

■ **Puerto López Mateos** (p283)

■ **Puerto San Carlos** (p283)

Liebre's shallow waters, where visitors are guaranteed to view whales in their natural habitat. **Malarrimo Eco Tours** (☎ 157-01-00; www .malarrimo.com; Blvd Zapata), at the beginning of the strip, offers four-hour tours for adults/children at US$45/35. A bit further south *pangueros* (boatmen) from Ejido Benito Juárez take visitors for whale-watching excursions for about US$30/25.

Sleeping

The whale-watching season can strain local accommodations; reservations are advisable from January through March.

Malarrimo Trailer Park (☎ 157-22-50, fax 157-01-00; www.malarrimo.com; Cnr Blvd Zapata & Guerrero; tent/RV sites US$5 per person/10-14; **P**) This camping site, at the eastern entrance to town, has 45 camping sites with full hookups, plenty of hot water and clean toilets.

Cabañas Don Miguelito (☎ 157-22-00; www.mal arrimo.com; cnr Blvd Zapata & Guerrero; d US$40-52; **P**) This comfortable hotel has a lot more ambience than the other options in town.

Motel Las Ballenas (☎ /fax 157-01-16; cnr Victoria Sánchez & Casillas; s/d US$18/25; **P**) The cheerful Motel Las Ballenas offers a good value, with hot water and color TV in each of its 14 rooms.

Hotel El Morro (☎ 157-04-14; Blvd Zapata; s/d US$28/31; **P**) On the north side of Blvd Zapata, this hotel has 36 comfortable, basic rooms.

Eating

Cafeteria del Motel El Morro (☎ 157-04-14; Blvd Zapata; dinners US$4-6) Adjacent to the Hotel El Morro, this place serves up inexpensive Mexican fare, including a near perfect Chile Relleno.

Malarrimo (☎ 157-01-00; cnr Blvd Zapata & Guerrero; dinners US$10-15) Specializing in seafood, both as *antojitos* and as sophisticated international dishes, the Malarrimo serves good food and generous portions.

About 8km south of Guerrero Negro, a good graded road leads 25km west to the Campo de Ballenas (Whale Watching Camp) on the edge of the lagoon. Here a US$5 parking fee includes the right to camp, and the *ejido* (communal landholding) runs a simple but good restaurant.

Getting There & Away

Guerrero Negro's airport is 2km north of the state border, west of the Transpeninsular.

The Aeroméxico subsidiary **Aerolitoral** (☎ 157-17-45; Blvd Zapata), on the north side of Blvd Zapata near the Pemex station, flies Tuesday, Thursday and Saturday to Hermosillo connecting to mainland Mexican cities.

Aerocedros (☎ 157-16-26; Blvd Zapata) flies to Isla Cedros and Ensenada Monday, Wednesday and Friday.

The **bus station** (☎ 157-06-11; Blvd Zapata) is served by ABC and Autotransportes Águila. Destinations include Ensenada (US$33, nine hours), La Paz (US$50, 11 hours), Loreto (US$27, six hours), Mulegé (US$19, four hours) and Tijuana (US$45, 11 hours).

SAN IGNACIO

☎ 615 / pop 2000

The lush village of San Ignacio is a welcome sight after the scrub brush and dense cacti of the vast Desierto de Vizcaíno. Drawn by the town's plum location and mellow charms, travelers have made San Ignacio *the* jumping-off point for whale-watching excursions to Laguna San Ignacio and trips to the spectacular pre-Hispanic rock art sites in the Sierra de San Francisco (p276).

Jesuits located the Misión San Ignacio de Kadakaamán in this soothing oasis in 1728, planting dense groves of date palms and citrus trees, but it was Dominicans who supervised construction of the striking church (finished in 1786) that still dominates the cool, laurel-shaded plaza. With lava-block walls nearly 1.2m thick and surrounded by bougainvillea, this is one of Baja's most beautiful churches.

Most services are around the plaza, including public telephones, but there is no bank. International calls can be made from the Hotel La Pinta.

Sleeping

For such a small town, San Ignacio has a rather surprising number of accommodation choices tucked away beneath its swaying palms.

BUDGET

Motel La Posada (☎ 154-03-13; Av Carranza 22; d US$25; **P**) Southeast of the plaza, La Posada has six clean, spartan rooms with showers. It's a bit difficult to find: take Av Hidalgo east from the plaza, turn right at Ciprés, then turn left onto Venustiano Carranza.

Rice & Beans RV Park (☎ 154-02-83; RV sites US$20; P) Rice and beans – the most basic of meals – is an apt name for this spartan RV park just off the Transpeninsular west of town. The real reason to come here is the on-site **restaurant** with its cantina ambience and well-prepared seafood dishes for US$6 to US$13.

MID-RANGE & TOP END

Ignacio Springs Bed & Breakfast (☎ 154-03-33; 500m from the highway on the road into town; d yurts US$50-60; P ✖ ✖ ✖) Sleeping in an air-conditioned yurt nestled in a palm grove by a river can be a charming reprieve from the heat of the desert. With kayaks and good river swimming, this kid-friendly place can also arrange trail riding and generous breakfasts and dinners. Only one of the yurts has private bath, the others are served by a clean, pleasant bath house. Backpackers may shack up in a communal tent for US$20.

Hotel La Pinta (☎ 154-03-00; s/d US$69, Dec-Mar US$77; P ✖ ✖) This service-oriented hotel one mile south of Hwy 1 on the paved road to San Ignacio offers well-appointed rooms surrounding a large courtyard. The restaurant serves local beef, good *antojitos* and seafood (US$8 to US$10).

Ricardo's Hotel (☎ 154-02-83; d US$50; P ✖) In the same complex as Rice & Beans RV Park, this is a squeaky-clean hotel offering satellite TV and two queen-sized beds per room.

Eating

Most of San Ignacio's eateries are run by the hotels and RV parks. One exception is **Rene's** (☎ 154-01-96; one block south of the plaza; dinners US$5-9), where you'll find reasonably-priced antojitos and seafood dishes, and friendly, attentive service.

Getting There & Away

Buses pick up passengers at the San Lino junction outside of town. You can catch northbound ABC buses in front of the Pemex station. Tijuana-bound buses leave at 6am, 7am, 8am and 9am. On the other side of the highway at the Mercado Rovi, Águila buses travel south at 7am and 10am.

AROUND SAN IGNACIO
Sierra de San Francisco

From Km 118 on the Transpeninsular, 43km northwest of San Ignacio, a graded but poorly consolidated road climbs east to Sierra de San Francisco, the gateway to the Desierto Central's most spectacular pre-Hispanic rock art. In recognition of its cultural importance, the Sierra de San Francisco has been declared a United Nations Educational, Scientific and Cultural Organization (UNESCO) World Heritage site, and is thus a protected archaeological zone under the auspices of the Instituto Nacional de Antropología (INAH). It is also part of the Reserva de la Biósfera El Vizcaíno.

Cueva del Ratón, about 2.5km before San Francisco, is the most accessible site. Excursions to Cueva del Ratón require hiring a guide (US$5 to US$9 for four people, in addition to a US$3 ticket fee and US$3 for each camera brought along). Guides can be hired through the **Instituto Nacional de Antropología e Historia** (INAH; ☎ 154-02-22; adjacent to the Misión San Ignacio on the plaza; ◷ 8am-3pm Mon-Sat).

If you are lucky enough to make the journey into the dramatic Cañón San Pablo, you will encounter sites that are better preserved. At **Cueva Pintada**, Cochimí painters and their predecessors decorated high rock overhangs with vivid red and black representations of human figures, bighorn sheep, pumas and deer, as well as with more abstract designs. **Cueva de las Flechas**, across Cañón San Pablo, has similar paintings, but the uncommon feature of arrows through some of the figures is the subject of serious speculation. One interpretation is that these paintings depict a period of warfare. Similar opinions suggest that they record a raid or an instance of trespass on tribal territory or perhaps constitute a warning against such trespass. One researcher, however, has hypothesized that the arrows represent a shaman's metaphor for death in the course of a vision quest.

The awesome mule-back descent of Cañón San Pablo requires at least two days, preferably three. Excursions to Cañón San Pablo involve hiring a guide with a mule through INAH for US$15 per day, plus a mule for each individual in the party for US$12 per day, and an additional pack animal for each person to carry supplies. Visitors should also provide food for the guide. The costs can add up fast, so be sure to get an itemized schedule of fees before departing. If you wish to leave the logistics to a tour operator, Kuyima (see following) will arrange the three day trip for US$270 to US$440 per person per day, depending on the size of the group.

The best season for visiting is early spring, when the days are fairly long but temperatures are not yet unpleasantly hot. Backpacking is permitted, but you still must hire a guide and mule.

Laguna San Ignacio

Along with Laguna Ojo de Liebre and Bahía Magdalena, Laguna San Ignacio is one of the Pacific coast's major winter whale-watching sites, with three-hour excursions costing around US$40 per person. **Kuyima** (☎ 154-00-70; www.kuyima.com; Morelos 23), a cooperative based at the east end of the plaza in San Ignacio, can arrange transport and accommodations. The 65km drive to the campsite (where cabins are also available) takes about two hours over rough roads.

SANTA ROSALÍA
☎ 615 / pop 12,000

With its clapboard houses made with imported timber, the copper town of Santa Rosalía was once populated by French copper barons working for the Campañía del Boleo in the 1880s. From the colonial charm of the Hotel Francés to the prefabricated church here that was designed by Alexandre Gustave Eiffel, Santa Rosalía still retains the singular ambience of a unique Franco-Mexican exchange. Where else in Baja can you get a decent baguette? For southbound travelers, Santa Rosalía offers the first glimpse of the Sea of Cortez after a long, dry crossing of the Desierto de Vizcaíno.

Orientation & Information

Central Santa Rosalía nestles in the canyon of its namesake *arroyo* (stream), west of the Transpeninsular, but French administrators built their houses on the northern Mesa Francia, now home to municipal authorities and the historic Hotel Francés. Santa Rosalía's narrow avenidas run east–west, while its short calles run north–south; one-way traffic is the rule. Plaza Benito Juárez, four blocks west of the highway, is the town center.

Travelers bound for Mulegé, which has no banks, should change US cash or traveler's checks here, where Banamex also has an ATM. The post office is at Avenida Constitución at Calle 2. Hotel del Real, on the exit road from town, has long-distance cabinas.

Sights

Designed and erected for Paris' 1889 World's Fair, disassembled and stored in Brussels, intended for West Africa, Gustave Eiffel's prefabricated **Iglesia Santa Bárbara** was finally shipped here when a Compañía del Boleo director signed for its delivery to the town in 1895. Many travelers agree that the church is interesting more as an early example of prefabricated architecture than for its beauty.

Built in 1885 by the French to house the offices of the Boleo Company, the **Museo Histórico Minero de Santa Rosalía** (US$1.25; ⏰ 8am-7pm) watches over the town and the rusting copper works from its perch on the hill near the Hotel Francés. The commanding wooden edifice now houses a museum about copper mining and cultural exchange in the area.

Sleeping

Of all the towns in central Baja, Santa Rosalía has perhaps the best variety of well-priced accommodation choices, from the historic to the picturesque.

BUDGET

Hotel del Real (☎ 152-00-68; Av Montoya; rooms US$25/30; 🛏) This old hotel has recently added a new wing of tidy new rooms with two beds. Along the front of the building is large veranda, suitable for roller-skating or vegetating.

Las Palmas RV Park (☎ 152-01-09; Km 192, Transpeninsular; tent/RV sites US$8/12) South of town, Las Palmas has grassy sites with hot showers, clean toilets and laundry. Adjacent is a swimming pool that charges US$3 per person.

MID-RANGE & TOP END

Hotel Francés (☎ 152-20-52; Cousteau 15; s/d US$48/51; 🛏) Built in 1886, this charmingly musty historic hotel has rooms with high ceilings, cloth-covered walls and charming stained wood details. On site is a restaurant open Monday to Saturday for breakfast and lunch.

Hotel Las Casita (☎ 152-30-23; Transpeninsular; d US$45; 🅿 🛏) Santa Rosalía's newest hotel,

3km south of town, has only five rooms, but each is tastefully appointed and affords private balconies and sublime views of the sea from the queen-sized beds. A hot tub rounds out its charms.

Hotel El Morro (☎ 152-04-14; Transpeninsular; s/d US$32/38, d with sea views US$44; P ✖ ⛱) With balconies overlooking the water, this atmospheric hacienda-style hotel, 3.5km south of town, continues to sustain high standards.

Eating

Taco stands are numerous and of high quality along Av Obregón, most charging US$0.80 for a fish taco.

Cenaduría Gaby (☎ 152-01-55; Calle 5 No 3; antojitos US$3-4.50) This restaurant, just north of Obregón, serves reasonably priced tacos, antojitos, and a delicious *Caldo de Res* (beef stew).

Playa Negra (☎ 152-06-85; on the malecón; breakfast US$4, dinners US$6-14) South of downtown, this waterfront restaurant serves sumptuous seafood as well as steak, chicken and pizza.

Panadería El Boleo (☎ 152-03-10; Obregón 30) Since 1901, this has been an obligatory stop for the rare find of good French bread in Baja. Also on board is a mouth-watering display of Mexican sweet breads. A loaf of French bread costs about US$0.25. Find it between Calles 3 and 4.

Getting There & Around

AIR

Aereo Servicio Guerrero (☎ 15-152-31-81) has flights every day but Wednesday and Sunday to Guaymas on the Mexican mainland for US$75. The ticket office, on the highway 300m south of the ferry terminal on the opposite side of the street, offers free transport to the airport.

BOAT

The new passenger/auto ferry *Santa Rosalía*, operated by Operadora Rotuaria del Noreste, sails to Guaymas at 8pm Tuesday and Friday, arriving at 7am; the return ferry from Guaymas sails at 8pm Monday and Thursday, arriving at 6am. Strong winter winds may cause delays.

The ticket office is at the **ferry terminal** (☎ 152-12-46 in Santa Rosalía, 622-222-02-04 in Guaymas; ✆ 8am-2pm, 4-8pm Mon-Sat), on the highway. Passenger fares are US$46 for seats

and US$116 to US$166 for cabins. Advance reservations are recommended. Vehicle rates vary with vehicle length. See the accompanying chart for vehicle fares.

Vehicle	Length	Rate
car or pickup	up to 5m	US$150
	5-7m	US$280
	7-10m	US$500
car with trailer	up to 15m	US$800
motorcycle	–	US$83

Before shipping any vehicle to the mainland, officials require a vehicle permit. Vehicle permits are not obtainable in Santa Rosalía, so get them in Tijuana, Ensenada, Mexicali or La Paz.

BUS

At least six buses daily in each direction stop at the **bus terminal** (☎ 152-14-08), which is in the same building as the ferry terminal on the highway just south of the entrance to town. Destinations include the following: Ensenada (US$50, 12 hours), Guerrero Negro (US$14, three hours), La Paz (US$34, eight hours), Loreto (US$13, three hours), Mulegé (US$8, one hour), San Ignacio (US$5, one hour), San José del Cabo (US$47, 12 hours) and Tijuana (US$59, 14 hours).

MULEGÉ

☎ 615 / pop 3000

Beyond Santa Rosalía, the Transpeninsular hugs the eastern scarp of the Sierra de la Giganta before winding through the Sierra Azteca and dropping into Mulegé, a laidback subtropical oasis. The village straddles the palm-lined Arroyo de Santa Rosalía (Río Mulegé), 3km inland from the gulf. Divers also flock to Mulegé, and the coast stretching to the north and south afford dozens of outstanding dive sites.

Most services, including the post office, are on or near Jardín Corona, the town plaza. Mulegé has no bank, but merchants change cash dollars or accept them for payment. To get online try **Prodigy Infinito** (☎ 153-03-77; per hr US$2; ✆ 9am-10 pm Mon-Sat), just off the plaza.

Sights

Across the highway, near the south bank of the arroyo, the hilltop **Misión Santa Rosalía de**

Mulegé was founded in 1705, completed in 1766, and abandoned in 1828. A short path climbs to a scenic overlook of the palm-lined arroyo.

The former territorial prison is now the **Museo Mulegé** (Barrio Canenea; admission free; ⏱ 8:30am-3pm Mon-Fri), overlooking the town. Its eclectic holdings include objects from the Mission de Santa Rosalía and prehistoric artifacts.

Diving

Mulegé's best diving spots can be found around the Santa Inés Islands (north of town) and just north of Punta Concepción (south of town). **Cortez Explorers** (☎ 153-05-00; Moctezuma 75A; www.cortez-explorer.com; ⏱ 10am-1pm, 4-7pm Mon-Sat) offers diving instruction and excursions, snorkel equipment rental and bike rental. Book trips one day in advance. Prices for scuba-diving/snorkeling excursions are US$60 to US$80/35 per person. There's a US$120/80 minimum for the scuba/snorkeling charters.

Sleeping

Mulegé's lodging options are limited in number but of great variety.

Casa de Huéspedes Manuelita (☎ 153-01-75; Moctezuma; s/d US$15/20, with air-con US$24) This budget hotel is basic but decent and has hot showers.

Hotel Las Casitas (☎ 153-00-19; Madero 50; s/d US$25/30; 🏊) Beloved Mexican poet Alán Gorosave once inhabited this well-run hotel near Martínez, perhaps inspired by its beautiful courtyard shaded by a well-tended garden of tropical plants.

Hotel Hacienda (☎ 153-00-21; hotelhacienda_mulege@hotmail.com; Madero 3; d US$36; 🏊 🍽) The oldest hotel in town, the atmospheric Hacienda offers rooms with twin beds, fridge, and a small pool.

Hotel Terrazas (☎ 153-00-09; Calle Zaragoza; d/t US$35/45; 🏊) This hotel has clean, basic rooms, a sunny common area on the roof and an open-air kitchen and barbecue for use by guests. Ask about the 20% discount for backpackers who promise not to turn on the air-con!

Hotel Cuesta Real (☎ 153-03-21; Km132 Transpeninsular; d US$45, RV hookups/camping US$15/$10; 🏊 🍽) This new place, south of town, offers quiet, clean rooms and privileged access to the Río Mulegé as it empties into the sea (thus making it a good choice for kayakers). The grounds also boast a pleasant restaurant.

Eating & Drinking

They roll up the sidewalks early in Mulegé, so dine expediently and get some sleep! Alternatively, you can always hit a bar. Or, you can hit the other bar.

Los Equipales (☎ 153-03-30; Moctezuma; lunch & dinner US$5-15) Just west of Zaragoza, this restaurant and bar has outstanding, well-priced meals and balcony seating.

Asadero Ramón (Cnr Madero & Romerio Rubio; tacos US$1) This place offers the closest the humble taco will ever get to haute cuisine, with various fillings and a cornucopia of tasty condiments at reasonable prices.

Las Casitas (☎ 153-01-19; Madero 50; antojitos US$6, seafood US$10-15) In its namesake hotel, try this place for antojitos and a few seafood dishes, served on the shady patio.

El Mezquite (Zaragoza) On the plaza, this is the rowdiest bar in town, with sweaty mariachis one night and a DJ playing the latest regional grooves the next. It's open until 3am.

Getting There & Away

Mulegé has no bus terminal. Buses going north and south stop at the Y-junction ('La Y Griega') on the Transpeninsular at the western edge of town. Northbound buses to Santa Rosalía (US$6.50, one hour) make two stops in the late afternoon at 4:30pm and 6pm; to continue northward you must transfer there. Six southbound buses pass daily to destinations including Loreto (US$8, two hours) and La Paz (US$ 29, seven hours).

AROUND MULEGÉ
Cañon La Trinidad

For a day trip to the beautiful Trinity Canyon to see the pre-Hispanic cave paintings, 29km southwest of town via a challenging dirt road, your best bet is with Mulegé native Salvador Castro of **Mulegé Tours** (☎ 153-02-32; excursions US$40 per person/day). To access the caves, light swimming is required. Rendered in shades of ochre and rust, the paintings feature shamans, manta rays, whales, and the famous Trinity Deer, which leaps gracefully from the walls of the cave as arrows pass harmlessly over its head.

Beaches

Mulegé is a gateway to some of Baja's most accessible pristine beaches. As you travel south from town there is a quick succession of pull-offs to *playas* with and without facilities, where you can string up a hammock and watch the pelicans dive-bomb the fish. A little exploring might reveal that hidden gem. The following spots, listed in north-to-south order, are the most easily accessible.

Playa Concepción Km111-12. The home of EcoMundo kayaking and natural history center.

Playa Koko Km110-111. This less-visited beach has palapas but no services.

Playa El Burro Km108-9. This popular beach has large palapas for US$7, and Bertha's Restaurant and Bar (☎ 615-155-40-55).

Playa Coyote Km107-8. A busy RV park makes this place occasionally overcrowded.

Playa Buenaventura Km94-95. Restaurant and hotel, with beach camping and cabañas.

LORETO

☎ 613 / pop 11,000

With a history that goes back nearly 12,000 years, Loreto is considered by anthropologists to be the oldest human settlement on the Baja Peninsula. It's the site of the first permanent European settlement in the Californias. In 1697 Jesuit Juan María Salvatierra established the peninsula's first permanent mission at this modest port some 135km south of Mulegé. These days, Loreto has settled into its reputation as Baja's water-sports paradise. It's home to Parque Marino Nacional Bahía de Loreto, with 2065 sq km of shoreline, ocean and offshore islands protected from pollution and uncontrolled fishing.

Orientation

Loreto has an irregular street plan. Most hotels and services are near the landmark mission church on Salvatierra, while the attractive malecón (waterfront boulevard) is ideal for evening strolls. The Plaza Cívica is just north of Salvatierra, between Madero and Davis.

Information

Loreto's **Municipal Department of Tourism** (☎ 135-04-11; turismoloreto@hotmail.com; ☼ 8am-3pm Mon-Fri), on the west side of the Plaza Cívica, has a good selection of brochures and flyers. The office of the **Parque Nacional Bahía de Loreto**

(☎ 135-04-77; ☼ 9am-1pm Mon-Sat), alongside the marina, is where you pay the US$6 entrance fee to the park. The staff at the marine park office is a good source of information for all water activities in the area.

Bancomer, at Salvatierra and Madero, has an ATM and changes US cash and traveler's checks Monday to Friday.

The **post office** (☼ 8am-3pm Mon-Fri) is on Deportiva, north of Salvatierra.

Several businesses along Salvatierra have long-distance cabinas, but they charge for international collect calls.

Centro de Salud (☎ 133-00-39; Salvatierra 68; ☼ 24hr) is a 24-hour health clinic.

To get online, head to the **Internet Café** (☎ 135-08-02; Madero; US$3 1hr; ☼ 9am-8pm Mon-Fri, 9am-5pm Sat), next to Café Olé.

Sights & Activities

The **Misión Nuestra Señora de Loreto**, dating from 1697, was the first permanent mission in the Californias and the base for the expansion of Jesuit missions up and down the Baja peninsula. Alongside the church, INAH's revamped **Museo de las Misiones** (☎ 135-04-41; Cnr Salvatierra & Misioneros; admission US$3; open 9am-1pm and 1:45-6pm Tue-Fri) chronicles the settlement of Baja California.

Loreto is a world-class destination for all types of outdoor activities; a number of outfitters cover the range from **kayaking** and **diving** along the reefs around Isla del Carmen to **horseback riding, hiking** and **mountain biking** in the Sierra de la Giganta.

Baja Outpost (☎ 135-12-29; www.bajaoutpost.com; Blvd López Mateos), between Jordán and Hidalgo, a well-run outfitter, offers diving, snorkeling, biking, and kayaking expeditions in addition to accommodations (p281).

Las Parras Tours (☎ 135-10-10; www.lasparrastours .com; Madero 16) offers diving, kayaking, biking and hiking trips to Misión San Francisco Javier (p282). For sport fishing, try locally-owned **Arturo Sportfishing** (☎ 135-07-66; arturosport@loretoweb.mx; Av Hidalgo), near the intersection with Romanita.

Sleeping

Most of Loreto's accommodation choices are on or near the picturesque malecón.

BUDGET

RV Park El Moro (☎ 135-05-42; Rosendo Robles 8; RV sites US$12, s/d US$30/40) Half a block from the

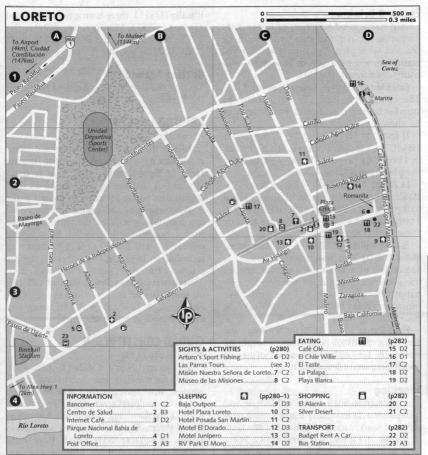

LORETO

To Airport (4km), Ciudad Constitución (147km)

To Mulegé (134km)

Sea of Cortez

Unidad Deportiva (Sports Center)

Marina

Plaza Cívica

Romanita

Paseo de Mayorga

Baseball Stadium

To Mex Hwy 1 (2km)

Río Loreto

Av Hidalgo

SIGHTS & ACTIVITIES	(p280)
Arturo's Sport Fishing	6 D2
Las Parras Tours	(see 3)
Misión Nuestra Señora de Loreto	7 C2
Museo de las Misiones	8 C2

INFORMATION	
Bancomer	1 C2
Centro de Salud	2 B3
Internet Café	3 D2
Parque Nacional Bahía de Loreto	4 D1
Post Office	5 A3

SLEEPING	(pp280–1)
Baja Outpost	9 D3
Hotel Plaza Loreto	10 C3
Hotel Posada San Martín	11 C2
Motel El Dorado	12 D2
Motel Junípero	13 C3
RV Park El Moro	14 D2

EATING	(p282)
Café Olé	15 D2
El Chile Willie	16 D1
El Taste	17 C2
La Palapa	18 D2
Playa Blanca	19 D2

SHOPPING	(p282)
El Alacrán	20 C2
Silver Desert	21 C2

TRANSPORT	(p282)
Budget Rent A Car	22 D2
Bus Station	23 A3

BAJA CALIFORNIA

beach, the friendly Park El Moro has 12 sites with full hookups, clean facilities and comfortable rooms.

Hotel Posada San Martín (☎ 135-11-07; Cnr Juárez & Davis; s/d US$20/30; ☒) The best value in town, this hotel has large rooms and a great location near the plaza. Rooms without aircon are US$15.

MID-RANGE & TOP END

Baja Outpost (☎ 135-11-34; Blvd López Mateos; rooms US$65, cabañas $86; ℗ ☒) This place specializes in activities such as scuba diving and kayaking (p280), but it also has beautiful rooms and romantic cabañas on offer. Although it's located directly off the busy *Malecón* between Jordán and Av Hidalgo,

after a few hours here you'll feel like you're in the jungle.

Hotel Plaza Loreto (☎ 135-02-80; fax 135-08-55; www.hotelplazaloreto.com; Av Hidalgo 2; s/d US$51/62; ☒) This well-run hotel is central and attractive; the appealing bar has well-priced drink specials.

Motel Junípero (☎ 135-01-22; Av Hidalgo; s/d US$30/40; ☒) Overlooking the mission and the town plaza, this family-run hotel has large rooms with refrigerators and a spacious balcony.

Motel El Dorado (☎ 135-15-00; Cnr Av Hidalgo and El Pipila; s/d US$45/50; ☒) One of the newest accommodation choices in town, this pleasant motel offers 11 spacious, comfortable rooms with satellite TV and laundry service.

Eating & Drinking

Loreto has a good selection of restaurants preparing the regional standards: excellent seafood with plenty of lime and cilantro, washed down by a potent margarita or a fruity *agua fresca*. Dig in!

Café Olé (☎ 135-04-96; Madero 14; dinners US$2-5) The inexpensive Café Olé is the place to stop for breakfast and good, basic Mexican lunches.

El Taste (☎ 135-14-89; Cnr Juárez & Zapata; dinners US$8-18) This restaurant serves the best steak in Loreto: be prepared to eat well, because the plates are *gigante*.

La Palapa (☎ 135-11-01; Av Hidalgo; dinner US$5-15) Can't get enough mariachi music? Head to the festive La Palapa, between Blvd López Mateos and El Pipila, for a seafood feast or some of that fiery cactus juice.

El Chile Willie (☎ 135-06-77; Blvd López Mateos; dinners US$5-12) This waterfront restaurant is something of a Loreto institution. Besides the good food, come for the two-for-one happy hours from 4pm to 7pm, or the live music on Friday and Saturday nights. Wear your dancing shoes.

Playa Blanca (☎ 135-11-26; Cnr Av Hidalgo & Madero; seafood dinners US$7-19) Try this atmospheric restaurant for top-notch seafood dishes or a well-prepared filet mignon.

Shopping

The pedestrian mall between Madero and Independencia has many shops selling jewelry and souvenirs. Try **El Alacrán** (☎ 135-00-29; Salvatierra 47) for varied handicrafts. For a large selection of sterling silver jewelry of good quality from the Taxco mines, visit **Silver Desert** (☎ 135-06-84; Salvatierra 36).

Getting There & Away

Aeropuerto Internacional de Loreto (☎ 135-04-54) is served by only one international airline. **Aero California** (☎ 135-05-00) has daily nonstop flights to La Paz and Los Angeles. **Aerolitoral** (☎ 135-09-99), also with an office at the airport, flies daily to and from La Paz.

Loreto's **bus station** (☎ 135-07-67) is near the convergence of Salvatierra, Paseo de Ugarte and Paseo Tamaral. Northbound buses pass through starting at 2:30pm; those heading south leave from 8am. Destinations include Guerrero Negro (US$28, six hours, one daily), La Paz (US$21, five hours, six daily), Mexicali (US$87, 18 hours, one daily), Santa Rosalía (US$13, three hours, two daily), and Tijuana (US$73, 15 hours, two daily).

The car-rental agency **Budget** (☎ 135-10-90) is on Av Hidalgo near the malecón.

Getting Around

Taxis to the airport, 4km south of Loreto off the highway, cost US$10.

AROUND LORETO

About 2km south of Loreto on the Transpeninsular is the junction for the rugged 35km mountain road to remote **Misión San Francisco Javier de Viggé-Biaundó**. The drive is spectacular but challenging. Depending on road conditions, passenger cars can usually make it. After enjoying the beautifully-preserved mission, take a walk on the path behind to find a magnificently gnarled 300-year-old olive tree, planted at the time of the mission's founding in 1699. On December 3, pilgrims celebrate the saint's fiesta at this mission.

Restaurant Palapa San Javier (meals US$2-5), on the main street just before the mission, serves simple fare, cold sodas and beer, and offers simple accommodations.

CIUDAD CONSTITUCIÓN
☎ 613 / pop 39,000

Like Guerrero Negro, Ciudad Constitución is a hub for travelers who wish to cavort with whales. Most travelers find little of interest in this agricultural town, but it's very convenient to the major whale-watching centers of Puerto San Carlos (p283) and Puerto López Mateos (p283), which have only limited accommodations. Most services are within a block or two of the north–south Transpeninsular, commonly known as Blvd Olachea.

Ciudad Constitución has no *casas de cambio,* but three banks on Blvd Olachea change US dollars or traveler's checks: Banca Serfin at the corner of Galeana, Banamex at the southwestern corner of Mina, and Bancomer on Pino Suárez just west of Blvd Olachea. All have ATMs.

The **post office** (☎ 132-05-84; ☾ 8am-3pm Mon-Fri) is on Galeana just west of Blvd Olachea. For phone service, try the cabinas on the east side of Blvd Olachea between Matamoros and Mina.

Access the Internet at **LaBaja.net** (☎ 132-28-44; Blvd Olachea; per hr US$2; ☾ 9am-9pm Mon-Sat), across from Banamex.

Taxis line up on Blvd Olachea adjacent to the Plaza Zaragoza.

Sleeping

Overall, Ciudad Constitución's lodging options are a bit grumpy, running the gamut from the plain to the merely decent. At the north end of town, near the junction of the highway to Puerto López Mateos, **Manfred's RV Trailer Park** (☎ 132-11-03; tent/RV sites US$10/14; 🐕) has spacious, shady sites in a lush garden setting. The **Hotel Conquistador** (☎ 132-27-45; Bravo 161; s/d US$33/41; 🐕) is somewhat dark and formal, but the adjacent restaurant serves good, economically-priced meals. **Hotel Conchita** (☎ 132-02-66; Olachea 180 at Hidalgo; s/d US$17/23; 🐕) has basic rooms with TV. Near Blvd Olachea, **Hotel Maribel** (☎ 132-01-55; Guadalupe Victoria 156; s/d US$32/34; 🐕) is more expensive, but the rooms are just as spartan.

Eating

Constitución's many taco stands on Blvd Olachea have the cheapest eats with tacos costing around US$1. A particularly good one is **Taquería Karen** (Cnr Blvd Olachea & Hidalgo). **Estrella del Mar** (☎ 132-09-55; Blvd Olachea), near the monument at the eastern entrance to town, serves quality seafood meals for US$5 to US$10. **El Taste** (☎ 132-67-71; Blvd Olachea), also near the monument, is the most pleasant restaurant in town, serving thick-cut steaks and a variety of seafood dishes including a delicious *brocheta de ostión* (oyster).

Getting There & Away

At the **bus terminal** (☎ 132-03-76; cnr Zapata & Juárez), southbound long distance buses leave twice daily for La Paz, and head north in the evening. Destinations include La Paz (US$12, 2½ hours, two daily), Mexicali (US$82, 19 hours, one daily), Puerto López Mateos (US$4, 45 minutes, two daily), Puerto San Carlos (US$3, 45 minutes, two daily) and Tijuana (US$68, 19 hours, one daily).

AROUND CIUDAD CONSTITUCIÓN
Puerto López Mateos
☎ 613 / pop 2400

Shielded from the open Pacific by the offshore barrier of Isla Magdalena, Puerto Adolfo López Mateos is one of Baja's best whale-watching sites. During the season,

the narrow waterway that passes by town becomes a veritable *ballena* cruising strip. Curva del Diablo (The Devil's Bend), 27km south of town, is reported to be the best viewing spot. Three-hour *panga* (skiff) excursions cost about US$55 per hour for up to six people and are easy to arrange.

Free **camping**, with pit toilets only (bring water), is possible at tidy Playa Soledad, which is near Playa El Faro 1 mile east of town (turn left at the water tower). The only other accommodations in Puerto López Mateos are at the small but tidy **Posada Ballena López** (s/d US$14/18).

Besides a couple of so-so taco stands, López Mateos has only a smattering of decent restaurants. **Restaurant California** (☎ 131-52-08; meals US$5-8) is a decent restaurant across from the church. At the entrance to town, **La Ballena Gris** serves seafood.

Puerto López Mateos is 34km west of Ciudad Insurgentes by a paved road; watch for hazardous potholes. **Autotransportes Águila** has buses from Ciudad Constitución (US$4) at 12:45pm and 7:15pm daily; return service to Constitución leaves at 6:30am and 2:30pm.

Puerto San Carlos
☎ 613 / pop 3800

On Bahía Magdalena, 56km west of Ciudad Constitución, Puerto San Carlos is a deepwater port and fishing town. The *ballenas* arrive in January to calve in the warm lagoon and the town turns to its attention to both whales and travelers. From January through March, *pangueros* take up to six passengers for whale-watching excursions for US$50 per hour.

With several hotels and restaurants to choose from, San Carlos is a good choice from which to base your whale-watching adventure. Accommodations can be tougher to find during the high season, but free camping is possible north of town on the public beach. There are no toilets at the beach. Another budget option is the **Motel Las Brisas** (☎ 136-01-52; Puerto Madero; s/d US$14/16), which has rooms that are basic and dark but clean and inexpensive.

The **Hotel Brennan** (☎ 136-02-88; Puerto La Paz; s/d US$30/40) strikes just the right balance with intimate rooms and plentiful patio space. With similar amenities, the **Hotel Alcatraz** (☎ 136-00-27; Puerto Acapulco; s/d US$30/35) offers

25 comfortable rooms with satellite TV, parking and laundry service.

At the Hotel Alcatraz is the town's best eatery: the **Restaurant Bar El Patio** (☎ 136-00-17; lunch & dinner US$5-15) with – you guessed it – patio seating and – you guessed it – seafood. Not to be outdone, **Mariscos Los Arcos** (Puerto La Paz; tacos US$2, dinners US$5-14) has tremendous shrimp tacos and seafood soup and a full breakfast menu.

From a small house on Calle Puerto Morelos, Autotransportes Águilar runs buses at 7:30am and 1:45pm daily to Ciudad Constitución (US$3) and La Paz (US$15). This is the only public transport from Puerto San Carlos.

LA PAZ
☎ 612 / pop 161,000
There are few finer places to watch a Baja sunset than on La Paz' splendid palm-lined malecón. The capital of Baja California Sur is a peaceful place with beautiful beaches, a handful of colonial buildings, and any number of outdoor activities to choose from. Its port of Pichilingue receives ferries from the mainland ports of Topolobampo and Mazatlán.

Hernán Cortés established Baja's first European outpost near La Paz, but permanent settlement waited until 1811. US troops occupied the city during the Mexican–American War (1846–48). In 1853 the quixotic American adventurer William Walker proclaimed a 'Republic of Lower California,' but he soon left under Mexican pressure. After Walker's fiasco La Paz settled down. It had a rich pearl industry but that pretty nearly disappeared during the revolution of 1910 to 1920.

Orientation
As you approach La Paz from the southwest, the Transpeninsular becomes Abasolo as it runs parallel to the bay. Four blocks east of 5 de Febrero, Abasolo becomes Paseo Obregón, leading along the palm-lined malecón in the direction of Península Pichilingue.

La Paz' grid makes basic orientation easy, but the center's crooked streets and alleys change names almost every block. The city's heart is Jardín Velasco (Plaza Constitución), three blocks southeast of the tourist pier.

Information
BOOKSTORES
Libros Libros Books Books (☎ 122-14-10; Constitución 195) Stocks books in English and Spanish.
Museo Regional de Antropología e Historia (p286) Museum store with good selection of Spanish-language books on Baja California and mainland Mexico.

EMERGENCY
Fire Department (☎ 068)
Police (☎ 060)
Red Cross (☎ 066)
Tourist Police (☎ 122-59-39)

IMMIGRATION
Airport immigration office (☎ 124-63-49;
⌚ 7am to 11pm daily)
Immigration office (☎ 122-04-29; Paseo Obregón;
⌚ 8am-8pm Mon-Fri, 9am-3pm Sat)

INTERNET ACCESS
Espacio Don Tomás (☎ 128-55-07; Paseo Obregón; per hr US$2; ⌚ 7am-11pm) Near Constitución. Web access, local art, and information.

INTERNET RESOURCES
www.vivalapaz.com La Paz' official tourism site.

LANGUAGE SCHOOLS
Centro de Idiomas, Cultura y Comunicación
(☎ 125-75-54; www.cicclapaz.com; Cnr Madero & Legaspi) Offers intensive Spanish classes and will help coordinate homestay lodging.

LAUNDRY
La Paz Lava (☎ 122-31-12; Cnr Ocampo & Mutualismo) Self-service machines and delivery service to hotels or homes.

MEDICAL SERVICES
Hospital Salvatierra (☎ 122-14-96; Bravo) Between Licenciado Verdad and Ortiz de Dominguez.

MONEY
Most banks (many with ATMs) and casas de cambio are on or around 16 de Septiembre.

POST
Main post office (Cnr Constitución & Revolución;
⌚ 8am-3pm Mon-Fri, 9am-1pm Sat)

TOURIST INFORMATION
Coordinación Estatal de Turismo information booth (☎ 124-01-03; Paseo Obregón; 8am-8pm Mon-Sat) Between Bravo and Rosales.

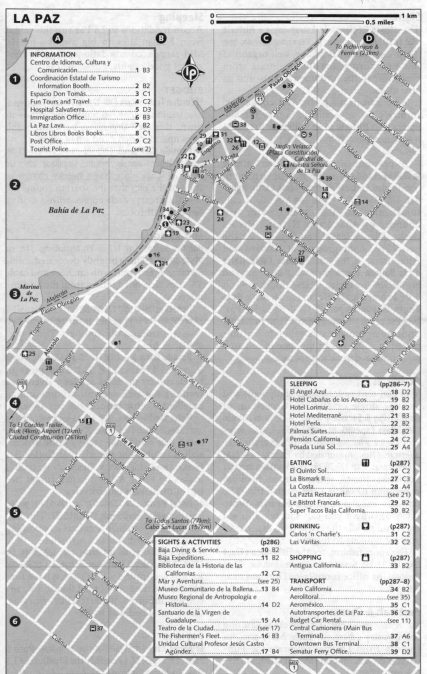

LA PAZ

0 — 1 km
0 — 0.5 miles

INFORMATION
Centro de Idiomas, Cultura y
Comunicación..........................1 B3
Coordinación Estatal de Turismo
Information Booth....................2 B2
Espacio Don Tomás....................3 C1
Fun Tours and Travel..................4 C2
Hospital Salvatierra...................5 D3
Immigration Office.....................6 B3
La Paz Lava...............................7 B2
Libros Libros Books Books...........8 C1
Post Office.................................9 C2
Tourist Police.........................(see 2)

Bahía de La Paz

*Marina
de
La Paz*

*To El Cordón Trailer
Park (4km); Airport (12km);
Ciudad Constitución (261km)*

*To Pichilingue &
Ferries (23km)*

Jardín Velasco
(Plaza Constitución)
Catedral de
Nuestra Señora
de La Paz

*To Todos Santos (77km);
Cabo San Lucas (157km)*

BAJA CALIFORNIA

SLEEPING   (pp286–7)
El Angel Azul...........................18 D2
Hotel Cabañas de los Arcos.....19 B2
Hotel Lorimar..........................20 B2
Hotel Mediterrané....................21 B2
Hotel Perla..............................22 B2
Palmas Suites..........................23 B2
Pensión California....................24 C2
Posada Luna Sol......................25 A4

EATING   (p287)
El Quinto Sol...........................26 C2
La Bismark II...........................27 C3
La Costa..................................28 A4
La Pazta Restaurant.............(see 21)
Le Bistrot Francais...................29 B2
Super Tacos Baja California.......30 B2

DRINKING   (p287)
Carlos 'n Charlie's...................31 C2
Las Varitas..............................32 C2

SHOPPING   (p287)
Antigua California....................33 B2

TRANSPORT   (pp287–8)
Aero California.........................34 B2
Aerolitoral.............................(see 35)
Aeroméxico.............................35 C1
Autotransportes de La Paz........36 C2
Budget Car Rental..................(see 11)
Central Camionera (Main Bus
Terminal)................................37 A6
Downtown Bus Terminal..........38 C1
Sematur Ferry Office................39 D2

SIGHTS & ACTIVITIES   (p286)
Baja Diving & Service...............10 B2
Baja Expeditions......................11 B2
Biblioteca de la Historia de las
Californias.............................12 C2
Mar y Aventura.....................(see 25)
Museo Comunitario de la Ballena....13 B4
Museo Regional de Antropología e
Historia.................................14 D2
Santuario de la Virgen de
Guadalupe.............................15 A4
Teatro de la Ciudad..............(see 17)
The Fishermen's Fleet...............16 B3
Unidad Cultural Profesor Jesús Castro
Agúndez.................................17 B4

Sights

The **Museo Regional de Antropología e Historia** (☎ 122-01-62; Cnr 5 de Mayo & Altamirano; admission free; ☎ 9am-6pm Mon-Sun) is a large, well-organized museum chronicling the peninsula from prehistory to the revolution of 1910 and its aftermath.

Across from the Jardín Velasco, La Paz' former Casa de Gobierno is now the **Biblioteca de la Historia de las Californias** (Cnr Madero & Av Independencia; ☎ 8am-3pm Mon-Fri), a history library.

A sprawling concrete edifice, the **Teatro de la Ciudad** is the most conspicuous element of the **Unidad Cultural Profesor Jesús Castro Agúndez** (☎ 125-02-07; ☽ 8am-3pm Mon-Fri), a cultural center that takes up most of the area bounded by Altamirano, Navarro, Héroes de la Independencia and Legaspi. At the periphery of the grounds at Navarro and Altamirano is the small **Museo Comunitario de la Ballena** (Community Whale Museum; admission free; ☽ 9am-1pm Tue-Sat). A few blocks west on 5 de Febrero and Serdán, the **Santuario de la Virgen de Guadalupe** (☎ 122-15-18) is La Paz' biggest religious monument. The building, undergoing a major renovation to be completed in 2005, was at the time of research an impressive work in progress.

Activities

You can rent water sports equipment and arrange single or multiday excursions at **Baja Diving & Service** (☎ 122-18-26; Paseo Obregón 166); **Baja Expeditions** (☎ 125-38-28; www.bajaex .com; Cnr Bravo & Paseo Obregón); or several other agencies. Recommended by kayakers is **Mar y Aventuras** (☎ 122-70-39; www.kayakbaja.com; Cnr 5 de Febrero & Topete), where you can book an expedition or outfit a self-guided trip. The one-day excursion to Isla Espíritu Santo (US$75), where you can snorkel with sea lions and paddle the coast, is an experience you are unlikely to forget.

For sport fishing, try the **Fishermen's Fleet** (☎ 122-13-13; david@lapaz.cromwell.com.mx; Paseo Obregón). Its office is on Paseo Obregón near Allende.

Festivals & Events

La Paz' pre-Lent Carnaval is among the country's best. In early May, *paceños* (person from La Paz) celebrate the Fundación de la Ciudad (Hernán Cortés' 1535 landing).

Sleeping

Accommodations in La Paz run the gamut from budget digs to big swanky hotels. Mid-range accommodations here are varied and of good quality.

BUDGET

El Cordón Trailer Park (☎ 124-00-78; Km 4 Transpeninsular; tent/RV sites US$10/14) Southwest of downtown, this well-organized park offers full hookups, electricity and small palapas.

Pensión California (☎ 122-28-96; fax 122-23-98; pensioncalifornia@prodigy.net.mx; Degollado 209; s/d US$13/18) This place has a quirky charm in spite of the fact that the spartan rooms are slightly dreary; each comes with a ceiling fan and bathroom.

MID-RANGE

Palmas Suites (☎ 122-46-23; Mutualismo 314; ste US$40-50; ☒) These brightly decorated, comfortable apartments with kitchens and cable TV provide a quiet retreat from the bustling malecón.

Hotel Lorimar (☎ 125-38-22; Bravo 110; s/d US$20/ 27 or US$40; ☒) This old favorite offers two classes of rooms, old and new. The rooms are small but homey.

Posada Luna Sol (☎ 120-70-39; Cnr 5 de Febrero & Topete; s/d US$35/50; ℗ ☒) This pleasant hotel, run by the folks at Mar y Aventuras (earlier), has well-decorated rooms and an excellent rooftop terrace with bay view.

Hotel Mediterrané (☎ 125-11-95; www.hotelmed .com; Allende 36B; s/d US$70/80; ☒ 🖳) This friendly hotel has somewhat stuffy, white stucco-walled rooms, but the adjacent Coffee Bar Greco and La Pazta Restaurant (p287) makes up for it. A night here includes free use of the kayaks and bicycles.

Hotel Perla (☎ 122-07-77; fax 125-53-63; perla@ lapaz.cromwell; Paseo Obregón 1570; d US$78) This historic service-oriented hotel has a swimming pool, restaurant, bar and nightclub.

Hotel Cabañas de los Arcos (☎ 122-27-44; fax 125-43-13; Rosales & Mutualismo; d/cabañas US$72/95) Rooms set around a lush garden have fireplaces, thatched roofs, tiled floors, TV, aircon and minibars. If you feel like splurging, this is not a bad way to go.

TOP END

El Ángel Azul (☎ 125-51-30; Cnr Av Independencia & Prieto; d from $95; ☒) Possibly the loveliest of La Paz' lodging options, El Ángel Azul offers elegantly-appointed rooms and beautifully-landscaped grounds in a historic building. Prices include breakfast.

Eating

La Paz' restaurant scene has become increasingly sophisticated over the past 10 years, and now offers much more than the typical antojitos and seafood.

El Quinto Sol (☎ 122-16-92; Cnr Av Independencia & Domínguez; breakfast US$3-4) In addition to healthy breakfasts and meat-substitute dishes for lunch and dinner, this vegetarian restaurant also sells health foods, fresh breads, teas and tonics.

Le Bistrot Francais (☎ 125-60-80; bistrot@prodigy .net.mx; Esquerro 10; breakfast US$4-6, dinner $8-10) The crêpes and fresh salads that are served up in the shaded courtyard of this French-run establishment are especially good.

Super Tacos Baja California (Cnr Arreola & Mutualismo; tacos US$1-2) The delicious fish and shrimp tacos at this popular stand are served with freshly-made salsas.

La Costa (☎ 122-88-08; Cnr Topete & Navarro; dinners US$7-10, lobster US$20) Many travelers report that La Costa offers some of the best seafood in Baja, and that's saying a lot. The menu is replete with delicious choices such as *chile rellenos* stuffed with crab.

La Bismark II (☎ 122-48-54; Cnr Degollado & Altamirano; antojitos US$7, seafood US$12-25) Removed from the touristy malecón, this place is an authentic Mexican seafood mecca serving generous platters.

La Pazta Restaurant (☎ 125-11-95; Allende 36B; dinner US$8-12) In the Hotel Mediterrané, La Pazta has moderately priced Italian and Swiss specials, including perhaps the only fondue in Baja.

Drinking

The following watering holes are within stumbling distance of the Malecón, where many travelers have been known to practice their drunken sailor routine.

Las Varitas (☎ 125-20-25; Av Independencia 111; admission US$4; ☺ 9pm-3am Tue-Sun) Featuring live music, this is where the local hipsters come to party.

Carlos 'n Charlie's (☎ 122-92-90; Cnr Paseo Obregón & 16 de Septiembre; admission US$4) This boozy nightspot has a popular restaurant, abundant patio seating and a raucous upstairs disco.

Shopping

Local stores that cater to tourists have plenty of junk and a smattering of good stuff.

Antigua California (☎ 125-52-30; Paseo Obregón 220) This place features a wide selection of crafts from throughout the country.

Getting There & Away

AIR

Aeroméxico (☎ 122-00-91; Paseo Obregón btwn Hidalgo & Morelos) has flights every day but Sunday between La Paz and Los Angeles, and daily flights to Tijuana and mainland Mexican cities. **Aerolitoral**, at the same address and phone number, flies daily to Loreto and Tucson.

Aero California (☎ 125-10-23; Paseo Obregón 55 and at the airport) operates daily nonstop flights to Los Angeles and Tijuana and to mainland Mexican destinations, including Los Mochis (for the Copper Canyon Railway), Mazatlán and Mexico City.

BOAT

Ferries to Mazatlán and Topolobampo leave from the **ferry terminal** at Pichilingue, 23km north of La Paz. The Mazatlán ferry is operated by **Sematur** (☎ 125-23-46; www.ferry sematur.com.mx; Cnr Prieto & 5 de Mayo, La Paz). Since 2003, **Baja Ferries** (☎ 125-75-43; www.bajafer ries.com) has been operating the La Paz–Topolobampo line; tickets and information can be obtained in La Paz at **Fun Tours and Travel** (☎ 124-23-46; Cnr Reforma & Prieto). Tickets for both Sematur and Baja Ferries can also be obtained in Pichilingue.

The ferry to Mazatlán departs at 3pm daily, arriving at 8:30am the following day; return ferries leave Mazatlán at 2:30pm to arrive in La Paz at 9am. Passenger fares are US$66 in salón (numbered seats), US$87 in turista (two- to four-bunk cabins with shared bath), US$170 in cabina (two bunks with private bath), and US$220 in especial (suite).

The Topolobampo ferry sails at 4pm Monday through Friday, arriving at 9pm the same night. On Saturday night it departs at midnight, arriving at 5am Sunday morning. The return ferry leaves at 12am Sunday through Friday, arriving at 5am. Passenger fares are US$58 in salón; cabina passengers pay the same rate with an additional US$71 fee for a group of up to four.

Vehicle rates – which are paid in addition to passenger fares – vary with vehicle length.

Vehicle	Length	La Paz–Mazatlán (Sematur)
car	5m or less	US$202
	5.01-6m	US$303
	6.01-7m	US$354
	7.01-8m	US$404
	8.01-9m	US$455
motorcycle	–	US$100

Vehicle	Length	La Paz–Topolobampo (Baja Ferries)
car	5m or less	US$170
	5.01-9m	US$328
motorcycle	–	US$50

Before shipping any vehicle to the mainland, officials require a vehicle permit. You can obtain a permit at **Banjército** (☼ 9am-1:30pm Mon-Sat, 9am-12pm Sun), at the ferry terminal.

BUS
The **Central Camionera** (main bus terminal; Cnr Jalisco & Héroes de la Independencia) is served by **ABC** (☎ 122-30-63) and **Autotransportes Águila** (☎ 122-42-70). Buses leave for Cabo San Lucas (US$11, three hours, six Autotransportes Águila buses daily), Ciudad Constitución (US$11, two hours, one ABC bus daily), Ensenada (US$85, 18 hours, four ABC buses daily), Guerrero Negro (US$50, 11 hours, one ABC bus daily), Loreto (US$21, five hours, two ABC buses daily), Mulegé (US$29, six hours, four ABC buses daily), San Ignacio (US$40, nine hours, four ABC buses daily), San José del Cabo (US$12, three hours, frequently), Tijuana (US$94, 22 hours, two ABC buses daily), and Todos Santos (US$6, two hours, six Autotransportes Águila buses daily).

Águila also operates the **Downtown Terminal** (☎ 122-78-98; Cnr malecón & Av Independencia), where two buses leave daily for Playa Tecolote (US$2.50, 1½ hours) and six for Pichilingue (US$1.50, one hour).

Buses by **Autotransportes de La Paz** (☎ 122-7-51; Prieto & Degollado) leave for Todos Santos (US$6, two hours), Cabo San Lucas (US$9, 2½ hours) and San José del Cabo (US$9, three hours) eight times daily, from 6:45am to 7:45pm.

Getting Around
The government-regulated minivan service **Transporte Terrestre** (☎ 125-11-56) charges US$14 per person to or from the airport. Private taxis cost approximately US$18, but they may be shared. See the Bus section (earlier) for information on transport to Pichilingue and Tecolote.

Car-rental rates start around US$60 per day. **Budget** (☎ 125-47-47; Cnr Paseo Obregón & Bravo) is one of several agencies.

AROUND LA PAZ
Beaches
On Península Pichilingue, the beaches nearest to La Paz are **Playa Palmira** (with the Hotel Palmira and a marina), **Playa Coromuel** and **Playa Caimancito** (both with restaurant-bars, toilets and *palapas*, or thatched roof shelters). **Playa Tesoro**, the next beach north, has a restaurant.

Camping is possible at **Playa Pichilingue**, 100m north of the ferry terminal, and it has a restaurant and bar, toilets and shade. The road is paved to **Playa Balandra** and **Playa Tecolote**. Balandra is problematic for camping because of insects in the mangroves, but it's one of the more beautiful beaches, with an enclosed cove. Lovely Playa Tecolote has plenty of private spots for car camping and two beachfront restaurants. **Playa Coyote**, on the gulf, is more isolated. Stay alert: thieves have reportedly broken into campers' vehicles in all these areas, especially the more remote ones.

LOS BARRILES
☎ 624 / pop 600
South of La Paz, the Transpeninsular brushes the gulf at Los Barriles, where brisk westerlies, averaging 20 to 25 knots, descend the 1800m cordillera. Naturally enough, this is Baja's windsurfing capital. Keep in mind that from April to August the winds really die down, and windsurfing becomes pretty much impossible.

Several fairly good dirt roads follow the coast south. Beyond Cabo Pulmo and Bahía Los Frailes, they are rough but passable for vehicles with good clearance. However, the road continuing south beyond Cabo Pulmo and Bahía Los Frailes is impassable for RVs and difficult for most other vehicles, particularly after rainstorms.

Martín Verdugo's Beach Resort (☎ 141-00-54; 20 de Noviembre; tent/RV sites US$12/15, d US$50-60) is a crowded 'resort' offering hot showers, full hookups, laundry and a sizable paperback book exchange. Some rooms have their own kitchenettes.

Hotel Los Barriles (☎ 141-00-24; losbarrileshotel@ prodigy.net.mx; s/d US$50/62) is a laid-back place offering clean, comfortable rooms. It rents out scuba, snorkeling and windsurfing gear.

Tío Pablo (☎ 143-03-30) has a good pizza menu and filling Mexican plates, but many people come for the 28oz (840g) 'beltbuster steak.' Tío's Tienda next door is a general-goods store.

RESERVA DE LA BIÓSFERA SIERRA DE LA LAGUNA

South of where the Transpeninsular and Hwy Mexico 19 meet, the precipitous heart of the Cape Region begins. Here, the uninterrupted wilds of the lush and rugged Sierra de la Laguna is a draw for stalwart backpackers. Foothill villages provide access to unique interior mountains and steep canyons.

Tranquil **Santiago**, 10km south of the junction for La Rivera and 2.5km west of the Transpeninsular, once witnessed a bloody Pericú indigenous revolt against the Jesuits. **Cañón San Dionisio**, about 25km west of Santiago, is the northernmost of three major east-west walking routes across the sierra; the others are **Cañón San Bernardo**, west of Miraflores, and **Cañón San Pedro**, west of Caduaño, which is about 10km south of Santiago. The terrain is difficult and unpredictable, and should only be attempted by experienced hikers. For more information, see Walt Peterson's *Baja Adventure Book*.

Just south of the plaza in Santiago, **Casa de Huéspedes Palomar** (☎ 612-122-0604; tent sites US$7, s/d US$30/60) has basic rooms amid fruit-tree covered grounds. Palomar's restaurant is well-known for its seafood, and its English-speaking owner is a good source of information on the Sierra de la Laguna.

SAN JOSÉ DEL CABO

☎ 624 / pop 34,000

In San José del Cabo, a quiet, laid-back atmosphere prevails. Despite its growth as a major tourist resort, it remains one of the most pleasant destinations in Baja with its narrow streets, Spanish-style buildings and shady plazas.

Orientation

San José del Cabo consists of San José proper, about 1.5km inland, and a zona

hotelera of large beachfront hotels, condos and time-shares. Linking the two areas, just south of shady Plaza Mijares, Blvd Mijares is a gringolandia of restaurants and souvenir shops.

Information

The office of the **Secretaria Municipal de Turismo** (☎ 142-29-60, ext. 150; Transpeninsular; ⌚ 8am-5pm Mon-Sat), just north of Gonzáles Conseco, has a stock of brochures and maps on hand.

Several *casas de cambio* keep long hours. Banks pay better rates but keep shorter hours. **Bancomer** (Cnr Zaragoza & Morelos), cashes traveler's checks and has an ATM.

The **post office** (Blvd Mijares; ⌚ 8am-6pm Mon-Fri, 9am-12pm Sat) is north of González Conseco.

The Internet café **Trazzo Digital** (☎ 142-03-03; Zaragoza; US$2.50 per half hr), near Hidalgo, has a fast connection and large monitors.

Libros Libros Books Books (☎ 142-44-33; Blvd Mijares 41) stocks books in English and Spanish.

The Fiesta de San José, on March 19, celebrates the town's patron saint.

Sights & Activities

The colonial-style **Iglesia San José** – built on the site of the 1730 Misión San José Del Cabo – faces the spacious Plaza Mijares.

Between raids on Spanish galleons, 18th-century pirates took refuge at the freshwater **Arroyo San José**, now a protected wildlife area replenished by a subterranean spring.

A palm-lined *Paseo del Estero* (pedestrian trail) parallels Blvd Mijares all the way to the Zona Hotelera.

The beaches at the south end of Blvd Mijares (known as Playa de California) have a mean riptide and are not good for swimming. The best beaches for swimming are along the road to Cabo San Lucas. **Playa Santa Maria** at Km 13 is one of the nicest beaches in Los Cabos.

Victor's Sportfishing (☎ 142-10-92; Hotel Posada Real, Paseo San José) arranges fishing excursions and sells and rents out tackle. Fisherfolk at **Pueblo La Playa**, a small fishing community about 2.5km east of the junction of Juárez and Blvd Mijares, arrange similar trips; ask them in the late afternoon as they cut up the day's catch on the beach.

Sleeping

During the peak winter months, it's a good idea to make advance reservations.

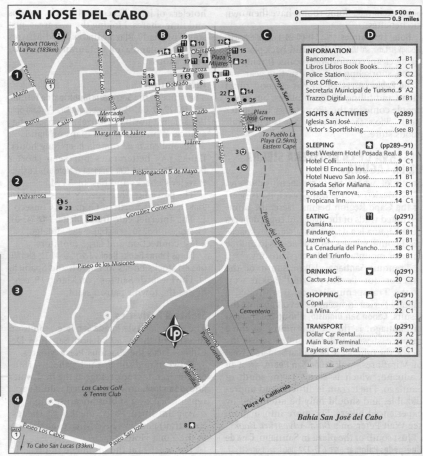

SAN JOSÉ DEL CABO

0 ———— 500 m
0 ———— 0.3 miles

BAJA CALIFORNIA

BUDGET

Free camping is possible at **Pueblo La Playa**, east of the center.

Hotel Nuevo San José (☎ 146-99-67; Cnr Obregón & Guerrero; s/d US$15/25; ☒) This backpackers' favorite has bright, spacious rooms, some with air-con.

MID-RANGE

Hotel Colli (☎ 142-07-25; Hidalgo; d US$38; ☒) Cozy, tidy rooms and a sunny patio characterize this family-run hotel, near Zaragoza.

Posada Señor Mañana (☎ 142-04-62; Obregón 1; d US$34-42; ☒) This casual hotel overlooking the arroyo just north of Plaza Mijares offers rooms of many styles and a community kitchen.

Posada Terranova (☎ 142-05-34; fax 142-09-02; Cnr Degollado & Doblado; d US$55) This inviting hotel also has a good restaurant.

Tropicana Inn (☎ 142-23-11; www.tropicanacabo .com; Blvd Mijares 30; d/ste US$74/122; ☒ ☒) This charming place has spacious rooms with satellite TV and a big, bucolic courtyard. Prices increase by 20% from October to April.

Hotel El Encanto Inn (☎ 142-03-88; www.elencanto inn.com; Morelos 133; d US$74-90, ste US$95-138; ☒ ☒) One of the most intimate in town is this hacienda-style inn with a beautifully landscaped garden and well-decorated rooms.

TOP END

Best Western Hotel Posada Real (☎ 142-01-55; fax 142-04-60; Paseo San José; d from US$112; ☒ ☒ ☒)

Ocean-view rooms are in a tasteful three-floor structure wrapped around a stately cactus garden. Prices increase by 30% from October to April.

Eating

Most restaurants are in Plaza Mijares and its side streets, and quality is very high.

Jazmín's (☎ 142-17-60; Cnr Morelos & Zaragoza; breakfast US$5, dinner US$9-13). The comfortable Jazmín's serves good food all day long and has excellent but unobtrusive service.

The clean **Mercado Municipal** (Ibarra), between Coronado and Castro, has numerous stalls offering simple and inexpensive but good, filling meals.

Pan del Triunfo (☎ 142-57-20; Cnr Morelos & Obregón) An excellent bakery with delicious pastries, baguettes and whole-grain loaves of bread for around US$1 to US$2 each.

La Cenaduría del Pancho(☎ 145-54-70; Zaragoza 10; dinners US$6-13) This restaurant operates out of a stately 150-year-old residence and offers the excellent combination of rooftop dining, a good view and exceptional fare.

Damiana (☎ 142-04-99, Plaza Mijares 8; dinners US$15) A romantic seafood restaurant is in a restored 18th-century house.

Fandango (☎ 142-22-26; Obregón 19; dinners US$12-15) A festive place offers creative Mexican and Pacific Rim cuisine in a relaxed setting.

Drinking

Noisy nightlife doesn't dominate San José the way it does Cabo San Lucas. **Cactus Jacks** (☎ 142-56-01; Cnr Blvd Mijares & Juárez) hosts the occasional live band.

Shopping

San José del Cabo has a wide range of shops to appeal to the interior decorator in you. Many of the best ones are on Blvd Mijares.

Copal (☎ 142-30-70; Plaza Mijares 10) On the east side of Plaza Mijares, Copal has an interesting assortment of crafts, jewelry, rugs and masks.

La Mina (☎ 142-37-47; Blvd Mijares 33C) This shop sells gold and silver jewelry in an imaginative setting.

Getting There & Away

AIR

All airline offices are at **Los Cabos airport** (☎ 146-50-13), which serves both San José and Cabo San Lucas.

Aero California (☎ 146-52-52) Flies daily to/from Los Angeles and Guadalajara.

Aeroméxico (☎ 146-50-97) Flies daily to/from San Diego and to many mainland Mexican destinations, with international connections via Mexico City.

Alaska Airlines (☎ 146-51-06) Flies to/from Los Angeles, Phoenix, San Diego, San Francisco and San Jose, California (USA).

American (☎ 146-53-00) Flies daily to Los Angeles and Dallas.

Continental Airlines (☎ 146-50-50, 800-900-5000 in the USA) Flies to/from Houston and, during the high season, Newark.

Mexicana (☎ 142-65-02) Flies daily to Los Angeles and to mainland destinations such as Mexico City, Guadalajara and Mazatlán.

BUS

From the main **bus terminal** (☎ 142-11-00; González Conseco), east of the Transpeninsular, buses depart for Cabo San Lucas (US$2, 30 minutes, frequent departures), La Paz (US$11, three hours, frequent departures), Loreto (US$33, eight hours, one daily), Ensenada (US$96, 22 hours, one daily), Tijuana (US$105, 24 hours, one daily), and Pichilingue's ferry terminal (US$11, 3½ hours, three daily).

CAR & MOTORCYCLE

Offering car rental, **Dollar** (☎ 142-01-00, 142-50-60 at the airport) is on the Transpeninsular just north of the intersection with González Conseco. Also try **Payless Car Rental** (☎ 142-55-00; Blvd Mijares), between Doblado and Coronado.

Getting Around

It is required by law for taxi drivers to display a sanctioned price list. The official, government-run company **Aeroterrestre** (☎ 142-05-55) runs bright yellow taxis and minibuses to Aeropuerto Internacional Los Cabos, 10km north of San José, for about US$12. Local buses from the main bus terminal to the airport junction cost less than US$2, but taking one means a half-hour walk to the air terminal.

LOS CABOS CORRIDOR

West of San José, all the way to Cabo San Lucas, a string of luxury resorts lines the once-scenic coastline. Along this stretch of the Transpeninsular, commonly referred to as 'the Corridor,' there are choice **surfing beaches** at Km 27, at Punta Mirador near

Hotel Palmilla, and at Km 28. The reefs off Playa Chileno are excellent for diving, and experienced surfers claim that summer reef and point breaks at Km 28 (popularly known as Zipper's) match Hawaii's best.

The best beaches for swimming are along the road to Cabo San Lucas. **Playa Santa Maria** at Km 13 is one of the nicest beaches in Los Cabos.

CABO SAN LUCAS
☎ 624 / pop 41,000
Cabo San Lucas has become a mecca for both the fishing and golfing crowd, as well as for younger Americans who see it as the quintessential party town, ideal for a weekend getaway or bachelor party. There's certainly no lack of things to do here, from beautiful beaches and water sports to an endless string of bars and nightclubs. The fracas quickly subsides, however, if you leave the strip and walk into Cabo's neighborhoods. Here you will find the streets unpaved and the pace unhurried.

Orientation
Northwest of Cárdenas, central Cabo has a fairly regular grid, while southeast of Cárdenas, Blvd Marina curves along the Harbor Cabo San Lucas toward Land's End (or 'Finisterra'), the tip of the peninsula where the Pacific Ocean and the Sea of Cortez meet. Few places have street addresses, so you will need to refer to the map to locate them.

Information
BOOKSTORES
Libros Libros Books Books (☎ 105-09-54; Plaza de la Danza, Blvd Marina) Books in English and Spanish.

EMERGENCY
Fire (☎ 068)
Police (☎ 060)
Red Cross (☎ 066)

IMMIGRATION
Immigration office (☎ 143-01-35; Cnr Cárdenas & Gómez Farías; ☺ 9am-1pm Mon-Sat)

INTERNET ACCESS
Café Cabo Mail (☎ 143-77-97; Plaza Arámburo, Cnr Cárdenas & Zaragoza; per hr US$8)
InternetPuntoCom (☎ 144-41-90; Cnr Vicario & 20 de Noviembre; per hr US$2.50)

INTERNET RESOURCES
www.aboutcabo.net A useful site for visitors.

MEDICAL SERVICES
AmeriMed American Hospital (☎ 143-96-70; Blvd Cárdenas near Paseo de la Marina)

MONEY
Several downtown banks cash traveler's checks and have ATMs, including the following places:
American Express (☎ 143-57-88; Plaza Bonita; ☺ 9am-6pm Mon-Fri; 9am-1pm Sat)
Banca Serfin (Cnr Cárdenas & Zaragoza)

POST
Main post office Blvd Cárdenas near 20 de Noviembre; ☺ 8am-4pm Mon-Fri)

TOURIST INFORMATION
Cabo has no government-sanctioned tourist offices or information booths, but there are many time-share sellers on Blvd Marina who distribute town maps and happily provide information (along with an aggressive sales pitch).

Sights
The **Casa de Cultura** houses a theater and has a small park and a mirador. Built into the one hill in downtown Cabo, the mirador is surrounded by landscaped gardens and offers a view of all of Cabo. It is a peaceful retreat from the craziness of Cabo. The entrance is on Niños Héroes.

For sunbathing and calm waters **Playa Médano**, in front of the Hacienda Beach Resort on the Bahía de Cabo San Lucas, is ideal. **Playa Solmar**, on the Pacific, has a reputation for dangerous breakers. Nearly unspoiled **Playa del Amor** shouldn't be missed; near Land's End, it is accessible by boat.

Activities
Among the best **diving** areas are Roca Pelícano, the sea lion colony off Land's End, and the reef off Playa Chileno, at Bahía Chileno east of town. At most shops, two-tank dives cost around US$60, introductory courses around US$80 and full-certification courses US$375 to US$450. Rental equipment is readily available. **Land's End Divers** (☎ 143-22-00) is on the marina at the Plaza Las Glorias. **Cabo Acuadeportes** (☎ 143-01-17), in front of the Hacienda Beach Resort, is

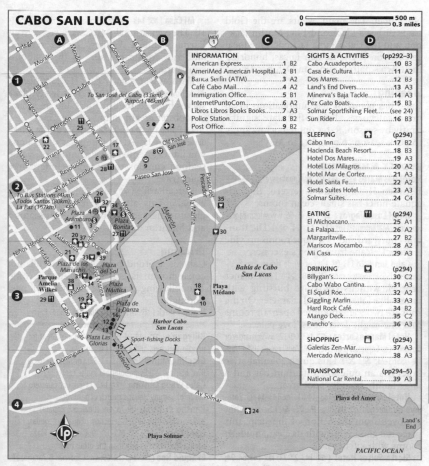

CABO SAN LUCAS

INFORMATION	
American Express	1 B2
AmeriMed American Hospital	2 B1
Banca Serfin (ATM)	3 A2
Café Cabo Mail	4 A2
Immigration Office	5 B1
InternetPuntoCom	6 A2
Libros Libros Books Books	7 A3
Police Station	8 B2
Post Office	9 B2

SIGHTS & ACTIVITIES	(pp292–3)
Cabo Acuadeportes	10 B3
Casa de Cultura	11 A2
Dos Mares	12 B3
Land's End Divers	13 A3
Minerva's Baja Tackle	14 A3
Pez Gato Boats	15 B3
Solmar Sportfishing Fleet	(see 24)
Sun Rider	16 B3

SLEEPING	(p294)
Cabo Inn	17 B2
Hacienda Beach Resort	18 B3
Hotel Dos Mares	19 A3
Hotel Los Milagros	20 A2
Hotel Mar de Cortez	21 A3
Hotel Santa Fe	22 A2
Siesta Suites Hotel	23 A3
Solmar Suites	24 C4

EATING	(p294)
El Michoacano	25 A1
La Palapa	26 A2
Margaritaville	27 B2
Mariscos Mocambo	28 A3
Mi Casa	29 A3

DRINKING	(p294)
Billygan's	30 C2
Cabo Wabo Cantina	31 A3
El Squid Roe	32 A2
Giggling Marlin	33 A3
Hard Rock Café	34 B2
Mango Deck	35 C2
Pancho's	36 A3

SHOPPING	(p294)
Galerías Zen-Mar	37 A3
Mercado Mexicano	38 A3

TRANSPORT	(pp294–5)
National Car Rental	39 A3

BAJA CALIFORNIA

the largest water-sports outfitter. In addition to diving excursions, it also offers snorkel, canoe and kayak trips, as well as windsurfing, sailing and waterskiing.

Minerva's Baja Tackle (☎ 143-12-82; www.minervas.com; Cnr Madero & Blvd Marina) offers charter boats and tackle. Sportfisher 31ft and 33ft boats can take five or six people for US$465 and US$500 per day. The **Solmar Sportfishing Fleet** (☎ 143-06-46; www.solmar.com; Solmar Suites hotel, at the end of Av Solmar) offers similar trips, charging from US$295 for a 26ft boat to US$750 for a 42-footer.

Tours

Dos Mares (☎ 143-89-71, Plaza Las Glorias) runs three-hour, glass-bottomed boat tours to Playa del Amor, near Land's End (US$10). Departures take place every hour from 9am to 5pm. It also offers three snorkeling tours a day to Santa Maria (US$35).

From the Plaza Las Glorias dock, **Pez Gato I** and **Pez Gato II** (☎ 143-37-97) offer two-hour sunset sailings on catamarans (child/adult US$15/30), and segregate their clientele into 'booze cruises' and 'romantic cruises.' Sunset dinner cruises are available on the **Sun Rider** (☎ 143-22-52). The boats leave at 5:30pm from the Plaza Las Glorias dock (adults US$40); reservations required.

Festivals & Events

Cabo San Lucas is a popular staging ground for fishing tournaments in October and

November. The main events are the Gold Cup, Bisbee's Black and Blue Marlin Jackpot, and the Cabo Tuna Jackpot. One local celebration is Día de San Lucas, honoring the town's patron saint, on October 18.

Sleeping

Cabo has plenty of accommodations in all price categories. Prices fluctuate significantly by season. Rates quoted below apply to peak season (November to May).

BUDGET & MID-RANGE

Hotel Dos Mares (☎ 143-03-30; Zapata; s/d US$35/45). Between Hidalgo and Guerrero, this adequate hotel has small, clean rooms.

Hotel Los Milagros (☎ 143-45-66; www.losmilagros .com.mx; Matamoros 116; d US$72; 🖳 🛋) The tranquil courtyard and 11 unique rooms provide a perfect escape from Cabo's excesses.

Cabo Inn (☎ 143-08-19; Cnr 20 de Noviembre & Vicario; d US$58; rooftop rooms US$90; 🖳) This former brothel, with its courtyard bursting with jungle-like foliage, has real character. On the roof are two well-appointed open-air rooms that one might describe as 'love palaces.'

Hotel Mar de Cortez (☎ 143-00-32; www.mardecortez.com; Cnr Cárdenas & Guerrero; old/new rooms US$49/59, ste US$63-73; 🛋 🖳) This quiet, colonial-style hotel has an outdoor restaurant-bar and a large family-friendly pool area.

Hotel Santa Fe (☎ 143-44-01; fax 143-44-03; Zaragoza cnr Obregón; ste US$80; P 🖳 🛋) Somewhat removed from the action of the strip, this place is a good value with its clean, modern rooms with kitchens.

Siesta Suites Hotel (☎ 143-27-73; fax 143-64-94; Cnr Zapata & Guerrero; s/d US$49/55; 🖳) This hotel has clean suites, each with a small kitchen.

TOP END

Hacienda Beach Resort (☎ 143-06-63; www.hacienda cabo.com; Paseo de la Marina; d from US$210, cabañas from US$315; P 🖳 🛋) On Playa Médano, the Hacienda is a class act with its fountains, tropical gardens and many amenities. There are garden patio rooms and beach cabañas.

Eating

Cabo's culinary scene features a great variety of eateries, from humble taco stands to gourmet restaurants.

El Michoacano (Vicario; tacos US$1) This pork palace, between Obregón and Carranza, has the best *carnitas* tacos in town.

Mi Casa (☎ 143-19-33; Cabo San Lucas; dinner US$21-31) The sensational Mi Casa, across from Parque Amelia Wilkes, serves refined, authentic Mexican dishes in their vibrant courtyard.

Mariscos Mocambo (☎ 143-21-22; Cnr Vicario & 20 de Noviembre; dinners US$9-17) This lively place serves huge seafood platters and an amazing lobster cream soup.

La Palapa (☎ 143-08-88; Zaragoza & Niños Héroes; dinners US$12-15) At the popular La Palapa you'll find attentive service and good-value seafood combos that even include a free margarita.

Margaritaville (☎ 143-00-10, Plaza Bonita; dinners US$10-25) This attractive restaurant serves gigantic margaritas alongside great seafood and Mexican dishes.

Drinking

Cabo is a proud party town, and alcohol consumption is encouraged all day long. The following places are all open well past midnight.

Mango Deck (☎ 143-09-01; Playa Médano) Party atmosphere and generous drink specials.

Billygan's (☎ 143-04-02; Playa Médano) Great for people-watchers and a sunset margarita.

Giggling Marlin (☎ 143-11-82; Cnr Matamoros & Blvd Marina) Wildly popular bar in the center.

Cabo Wabo Cantina (☎ 143-11-88; Cnr Guerrero & Madero) Sammy Hagar's church of hard rock.

Pancho's (☎ 143-09-73; Cnr Hidalgo & Zapata) It claims Mexico's largest selection of quality tequilas.

Hard Rock Café (☎ 143-37-79; Cárdenas at Plaza Bonita Mall) Less rowdy than the other bars.

El Squid Roe (☎ 143-12-69; Cnr Cárdenas & Zaragoza) The place to go if you need to dance on a table.

Shopping

Cabo's most comprehensive shopping area is the sprawling Mercado Mexicano, corner of Madero and Hidalgo, containing dozens of stalls with crafts from all around the country.

Galerías Zen-Mar (☎ 143-06-61; Cárdenas), between Matamoros and Ocampo, offers Zapotec weavings, bracelets and masks, as well as traditional crafts from other mainland indigenous peoples.

Getting There & Away

AIR

The closest airport is Los Cabos, north of San José del Cabo (p291).

BUS

Long-distance bus service to and from Cabo is provided by **Águila** (☎ 143-78-80; Hwy 19), which is located at the Todos Santos crossroad, north of downtown. Destinations include La Paz (US$11, 2½–four hours depending on route, eight daily), Loreto (US$32, eight hours, four daily), Tijuana (US$105, 24 hours, three daily), Todos Santos (US$5, one hour, four daily) and San José del Cabo (US$5, one hour, four daily).

From a small terminal near the Águila station, **Autotransportes de La Paz** (Cnr 5 de Febrero & Hidalgo) has eight buses daily to La Paz (US$10, 2½ hours).

Numerous car-rental agencies have booths along Blvd Marina and elsewhere in town. **National** (☎ 143-14-14), at Blvd Marina and Matamoros, offers rentals starting at US$60 per day.

Getting Around

The government-regulated **airport minibus** (☎ 146-53-93), costing US$14 per person, leaves every two hours from Plaza Las Glorias, 10am to 4pm. For US$60, shared taxis are another option. Cabs are plentiful but not cheap; fares within town average about US$4 to US$6.

TODOS SANTOS

☎ 612 / pop 3800

Over the past 20 years, Todos Santos has witnessed an invasion from the north as well-heeled New Mexico artists, organic farmers and even some Hollywood types have snapped up property and put down roots. On first glance the town seems to have retained its village character, but its chic galleries, restaurants and boutiques have made Todos Santos the bohemian capital of Baja.

Todos Santos' newly-found prosperity does not reflect its history. Founded in 1723 but nearly destroyed by the Pericú rebellion in 1734, Misión Santa Rosa de Todos los Santos limped along until its abandonment in 1840. In the late 19th century Todos Santos became a prosperous sugar town with several brick *trapiches* (mills), but depleted aquifers have nearly eliminated this thirsty industry.

Orientation & Information

Todos Santos has a regular grid, but residents rely more on landmarks than street names for directions. The plaza is surrounded by Márquez de León, Legaspi, Av Hidalgo and Centenario.

Todos Santos lacks an official tourist office, but **El Tecolote** (☎ 145-02-95), an English-language bookstore at the corner of Juárez and Av Hidalgo, distributes a very detailed town map and a sketch map of nearby beach areas.

The **Banorte** (Cnr Juárez & Obregón) exchanges cash and travelers checks and has an ATM.

The **post office** (Heróico Colegio Militar) is between Av Hidalgo and Márquez de León. There's an Internet café (☎ 145-02-03; Av Hidalgo; per hr US$5) in the Los Adobes de Todos Santos restaurant, between Juárez and Heróico Colegio Militar.

Sights

Scattered around town are several former *trapiches* (mills), including **Molino El Progreso**, at what was formerly El Molino restaurant, and **Molino de los Santana**, on Juárez opposite the hospital. The restored **Teatro Cine General Manuel Márquez de León** is on Legaspi, facing the plaza.

Housed in a former schoolhouse, the **Casa de la Cultura** (☎ 145-00-51; Juárez; admission free; ☺ 8am-6pm Mon-Fri, 10am-1pm Sat-Sun), near Topete, is home to some interesting nationalist and revolutionary murals dating from 1933. Also on display is an uneven collection of artifacts evoking the history of the region.

Festivals & Events

Todos Santos' two-day Festival de Artes (Arts Festival) is held in late January. At other times it's possible to visit local artists in their home studios.

Sleeping

Motel Guluarte (☎ 145-00-06; Cnr Juárez & Morelos; s/d US$22/30; ℗ ☎) This good budget option has small rooms with refrigerators, and a common balcony.

B&B Las Casitas (☎ 145-02-55; www.mexonline .com/lascasitas.htm; Rangel; s/d/ste US$52/67/78 include breakfast) This Canadian-run B&B, between Obregón and Hidalgo, has a superb breakfast, breezy attractive rooms and inexpensive tent sites.

The Todos Santos Inn (☎ 145-00-40; todossantos inn@yahoo.com; Legaspi 33; d US$90-130) This 19th-century building has been converted into a swanky hotel with gorgeous interiors and an excellent restaurant.

Eating

Taco stands, along Heróico Colegio Militar between Márquez de León and Degollado, offer fish, chicken, shrimp or beef cheaply.

Caffé Todos Santos (☎ 145-03-00, Centenario 33; breakfast US$5-9, dinners US$9-17) Coffee-conscious travelers can consume cappuccinos with savory pastries or enticing fruit salads here. For dinner, it's well-prepared Mexican favorites.

Las Fuentes (☎ 145-02-57; Degollado at Heróico Colegio Militar; antojitos US$5-10, seafood US$15). This moderately priced restaurant, in a bougainvillea-shaded patio with three refreshing fountains, has delicious antojitos and seafood specialties.

Café Santa Fe (☎ 145-03-40; Centenario 4; dinners US$15-25). If you're up for a splurge, look no further. The plaza-front Santa Fe started the cuisine scene in Todos Santos, and it's considered by many to be one of the premier restaurants in Baja. In preparing the Italian food, the chefs take full advantage of local organic farms.

Shopping

Galería de Todos Santos (☎ 145-05-00; Legaspi 33) Contemporary artworks by Mexican and North American artists.

Manos Mexicanas (☎ 145-05-38; Cnr Topete & Centenario) Wide selection of well-designed jewelry and artesanías.

Getting There & Away

At least six buses daily go to La Paz (US$5.50, 1½ hours) and to Cabo San Lucas (US$5.50, 1½ hours,) from the bus stop at Heróico Colegio Militar and Zaragoza.

Northwest Mexico

CONTENTS

The word is out about northwest Mexico and its expansive desert vistas, world-famous canyons and historic colonial towns. Many of its attractions are within a few days drive from the US border, so it's no wonder that an ever-increasing number of travelers are lingering longer in the great Desierto Sonorense (Sonoran Desert) and on its remote beaches. This chapter covers the northwestern state of Sonora, as well as portions of Chihuahua and Sinaloa, including the spectacular Barranca del Cobre (Copper Canyon) in the Sierra Madre Occidental and the Ferrocarril Chihuahua al Pacífico, or Copper Canyon Railway, the railroad that runs through it.

Once considered a wasteland, the 5000 sq-mile Sonoran Desert has come to be recognized as an ecological treasure. These lands, which span from southern Arizona throughout the state of Sonora and across the Gulf of California to Baja, are a place of biological riches and silent expanses. Anyone who has seen the desert wildflowers bursting from the once-parched turf after a summer rain can appreciate why proposals to protect these lands as a transnational Sonoran Desert National Park have gained momentum on both sides of the border. Visitors to the desert metropolis of Hermosillo and the beach towns San Carlos and Bahía Kino can take refuge from the blistering desert heat and enjoy dining, drinking and dipping.

Not to be missed, Copper Canyon is actually a system of more than 20 canyons, nine of which are deeper than the Grand Canyon in Arizona. As you descend into its gorgeous gorges via train or trail you will know that you making one of Mexico's great scenic journeys. It is by equal measures a cultural journey: to encounter the cliff- and cave-dwelling Tarahumara native people is to come face to face with one of the last vestiges of aboriginal culture in North America.

The state of Sonora, like its northern neighbor Arizona, does not observe daylight savings time.

HIGHLIGHTS

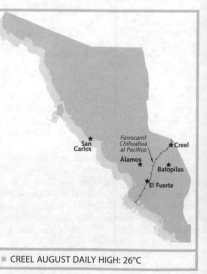

- Diving or snorkeling in the marine-life–rich waters near the scenic desert resort town of **San Carlos** (p312)
- Strolling down picturesque cobbled streets in the colonial towns of **Álamos** (p313) and **El Fuerte** (p322)
- Riding the **Ferrocarril Chihuahua al Pacífico** (p322) through some of the world's most breathtaking canyon scenery
- Exploring the Copper Canyon by foot, bicycle, horseback or thumb from the traveler's hub of **Creel** (p329)
- Reaching the end of the road in **Batopilas** (p335), a mining town deep in the heart of canyon country and home to a mysterious cathedral

- ALTITUDE RANGE: 0m–2400m
- CREEL AUGUST DAILY HIGH: 26°C

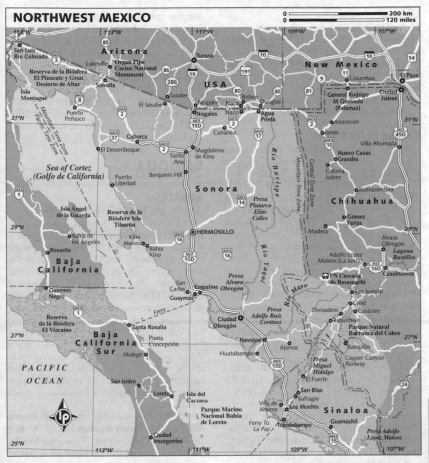

NORTHWEST MEXICO

History

The lands that stretch south from modern day Nogales have served as a gateway to Mexico ever since the first explorers passed this way some 30,000 years ago. The Pimas – who are direct descendants of those early visitors – established an elaborate system of irrigation that transformed the desert into fruitful agricultural lands. The region's colonial history dates from 1687 when the Italian Jesuit missionary Father Eusebio Francisco Kino began establishing missions and making inroads with the indigenous peoples, ultimately tying their destinies to the rest of New Spain.

In the 19th century, the coastal waters of the Sea of Cortez were witness to naval battles large and small, with most of the action centered on the port jewel of Guaymas, as various world powers challenged Mexico's fledgling independence and coveted its mineral wealth. Between Guaymas and Ciudad Obregón is the ancestral home of the fiercely independent Yaqui tribe, which aggressively resisted the forces of colonialism up until its last rebellion in 1901. The nomadic Seris of the central Sonoran coastal and desert lands fought a losing battle for their way of life, which was more suited for fishing and hunting than for Christianity or agricultural pursuits, and by the 1930s their numbers had dwindled to 300. Known today for their dark, polished wood carvings, the Seri population is steadily increasing.

Climate

In the Desierto Sonorense the summers are extremely hot, the winters benign. Spring and Fall are similar to the seasons that precede them. The best time to visit the Copper Canyon region is after the summer rains, when the rivers are swift and the flowers abundant. Spring – as it should be – is pleasant throughout the canyons.

Getting There & Away

Hwy 15, Mexico's principal Pacific coast highway, begins at the border town of Nogales, Sonora, opposite Nogales, Arizona, about 1½ hours south of Tucson. This is one of the most convenient border crossings between western Mexico and the USA. From Nogales, Hwy 15/15D heads south through the Desierto Sonorense for about four hours to Hermosillo and then cuts over to the coast at Guaymas, about 1½ hours south of Hermosillo. From Guaymas the highway parallels the beautiful Pacific coast for about 1000km, finally turning inland at Tepic (see p429) and heading on to Guadalajara and Mexico City. There are regular toll booths along Hwy 15 (including two between Nogales and Hermosillo, each charging US$11 per car).

The Nogales border crossing is the quickest and easiest route in this region. All of the following crossings are on Mexican Hwy 2, and have frequent bus services from the Mexican side to places deeper into Mexico (though possibly not on the US side between San Luis Río Colorado and Yuma).

San Luis Río Colorado (West of Nogales and 42km southwest of Yuma, Arizona; ☉ 24hr)

Agua Prieta (130km east of Nogales opposite Douglas, Arizona; ☉ 24hr)

Sonoita (357km west of Nogales opposite Lukeville, Arizona, immediately south of Organ Pipe Cactus National Monument; ☉ 8am to midnight)

Naco (90km east of Nogales, opposite Naco, Arizona; ☉ 24hr)

Getting Around

Nogales, Hermosillo and Los Mochis are the primary hubs for bus travel. Buses of all classes ply the cities and towns along Hwy 15 with great frequency, making it possible to travel from northwest Mexico to destinations throughout the mainland or to the USA with ease. Many travelers begin their journey through the Copper Canyon at Los

Mochis, traveling northeast by train on the Ferrocarril Chihuahua al Pacífico. Others do the trip in reverse, beginning in Chihuahua.

At Topolobampo, near Los Mochis, ferries arrive from and depart for La Paz in Baja California Sur, at midnight, from Sunday through to Friday nights. The major airports for the region are at Hermosillo, which has several flights to/from the USA, and Los Mochis, which serves several mainland destinations.

SONORA

NOGALES

☎ 631 / pop 168,800 / elevation 1170m

Like its border-city cousins Tijuana, Ciudad Juárez and Nuevo Laredo, Nogales is a major transit point for goods and people traveling between the USA and Mexico. On the northern side of the border in Arizona, its smaller US counterpart is also named Nogales. (The name means 'walnut trees,' of which precious few are evident today.)

Nogales presents an easier introduction to Mexico than do the larger border cities. Nogales has everything they have – curio shops overflowing with Mexican handicrafts, trinkets and souvenirs, Mexican restaurants, cheap bars and plenty of liquor stores and pharmacies – but all on a much smaller scale.

On the Arizona side, the small **Pimería Alta Historical Society Museum** (☎ 520-287-4621; 136 N Grand Ave; admission free; ☉ noon-4pm Mon-Thu, 10am-4pm Fri-Sun), at the intersection of Grand Ave and Crawford St one block from the border crossing, has interesting exhibits on the history of Nogales.

Orientation

The commercial section of Nogales is only a few blocks wide, being hemmed in on either side by hills. The main commercial street is Obregón, two blocks west of the border crossing, which eventually runs south into Mexico's Hwy 15. Almost everything you'll need is within walking distance of the border crossing.

Information
IMMIGRATION

If you are heading further south into Mexico, pick up a Mexican tourist permit at the

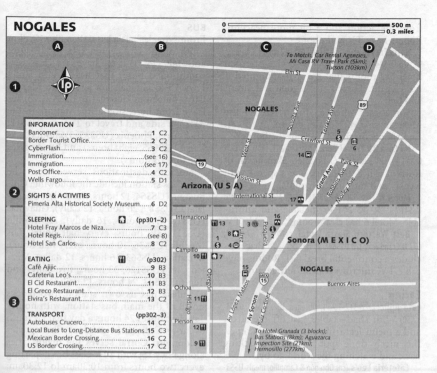

NOGALES

0		500 m
0		0.3 miles

To Motels, Car Rental Agencies,
Mi Casa RV Travel Park (5km);
Tucson (103km)

NOGALES

Arizona (U S A)

Sonora (M E X I C O)

NOGALES

Buenos Aires

INFORMATION
Bancomer...**1** C2
Border Tourist Office..............................**2** C2
CyberFlash...**3** C2
Immigration.......................................(see 16)
Immigration.......................................(see 17)
Post Office...**4** C2
Wells Fargo..**5** D1

SIGHTS & ACTIVITIES
Pimería Alta Historical Society Museum......**6** D2

SLEEPING (pp301–2)
Hotel Fray Marcos de Niza.....................**7** C3
Hotel Regis...(see 8)
Hotel San Carlos....................................**8** C2

EATING (p302)
Café Ajijic..**9** B3
Cafetería Leo's.....................................**10** B3
El Cid Restaurant..................................**11** B3
El Greco Restaurant..............................**12** B3
Elvira's Restaurant................................**13** C2

TRANSPORT (pp302–3)
Autobuses Crucero................................**14** C2
Local Buses to Long-Distance Bus Stations..**15** C3
Mexican Border Crossing.......................**16** C2
US Border Crossing...............................**17** C2

To Hotel Granada (3 blocks);
Bus Stations (8km); Aguazarca
Inspection Site (21km);
Hermosillo (277km)

immigration office in the large, modern, white building at the border crossing, on the west side of the big white arches. The tourist permit is also available at the vehicle checkpoint 21km south of the border, and if you're driving, it is more convenient to get it there at the same time as your vehicle permit (see p970). However, buses don't stop there, so if you're traveling by bus, be sure to pick up your permit at the immigration office. Both offices are open 24 hours a day.

INTERNET ACCESS
Cyber Flash (Internacional 67; per hr US$1.50; 10am-10pm Sun-Sat)

MONEY
There are plenty of *casas de cambio*, where you can change US dollars to pesos or vice versa, on both sides of the border crossing. On the Mexican side, dollars and pesos are used interchangeably.

Bancomer on Campillo between Juárez and Obregón has an ATM. On the US side there's a Wells Fargo Bank with ATM at the corner of Grand Ave and Crawford St.

POST
Mexican post office (Cnr Juárez & Campillo; 9am-3pm Mon-Fri)
US post office (300 N Morley Ave; 9am-5pm Mon-Fri) Three blocks north of border crossing.

TOURIST INFORMATION
Border tourist office (312-06-66; 9am-5pm Sun-Mon) Beside the border immigration office, this station dispenses information about Sonora and beyond.
Checkpoint tourist office (Km 21, Hwy 15) Those driving south may find this office, which dispenses the same information, more convenient.

Sleeping
Hotel San Carlos (312-13-46; Juárez 22; s/d US$32/40; P) A stone's throw from the border, the well-priced San Carlos offers very clean, nondescript rooms.

Hotel Regis (312-51-81; Juárez 34; s/d US$38/40;) Similar to the San Carlos in quality, the Regis has bright rooms and helpful service.

Hotel Granada (312-29-11; cnr López Mateos & González; s/d US$38/41;) Seven blocks south of the border crossing, the Granada is further from the action and a bit more peaceful. Rooms have TV and phone.

Hotel Fray Marcos de Niza (☎ 312-16-51; Campillo 91; s/d US$44/49; P 🏠) This service-oriented hotel has rooms that are well-appointed if not elegant. There's also a good restaurant and bar.

Sometimes when all the hotels on the Mexican side of Nogales are full, you can find rooms on the US side of the border.

Mi Casa RV Travel Park (☎ 520-281-1150; 2901 N Grand Ave; RV sites US$16) Located 5km north of town at exit 8, this park offers spaces with weekly and monthly discounts.

Motel 6 (☎ 520-281-2951; 141 W Mariposa Rd; s/d US$41/54; P 🏠 🏠) Predictable and affordable, Motel 6 has clean rooms and cable TV.

Best Western Siesta Motel (☎ 520-287-4671; 673 N Grand Ave; s/d US$64/72; P 🏠 🏠) Price includes a continental breakfast. Rooms have cable TV, microwaves and refrigerators.

Eating

Café Ajijic (☎ 312-30-31; Obregón 182; mains US$4-12.50) With shady tables just off the street and a menu featuring *antojitos* and crepes, this nicely done spot is good for kicking back and watching the world go by.

Cafeteria Leo's (cnr Obregón & Campillo; meals US$3-6) Bright, clean and cute, and good for economical meals. The food is tasty and fast.

Parador Restaurant (Hotel Granada, cnr López Mateos & González; mains US$4-7; 🕑 7am-midnight) This little restaurant has a good selection of Mexican-style breakfasts, beef dishes and antojitos.

Elvira's Restaurant (☎ 312-47-73; Obregón 1; mains US$6-16) Elvira's serves Mexican and international dishes in a cheerful setting.

El Greco Restaurant (☎ 312-43-58; Obregón 152; mains US$7-29) Excellent food that is only slightly undermined by the corny décor. Menu items range from chile rellenos to lobster thermidor. Enter via the stairs at the rear of the shop on the corner of Pierson.

El Cid Restaurant (☎ 312-15-00; Obregón 124; mains US$7-33). El Cid is similar to El Greco in menu and price, but more traditional in appearance. But they have something El Greco doesn't – frogs' legs! Enter via the stairs at the rear of a shopping arcade.

Getting There & Away

AIR

The nearest airport is in Tucson, Arizona, about 100km (1½ hours) north of Nogales.

BUS

From Nogales' **main bus station** (Hwy 15), 8km south of the city center, **Elite** (☎ 313-16-03) and **TAP** (☎ 313-16-06) have 1st-class air-conditioned buses that head south along Hwy 15 to Guadalajara and on to Mexico City. **Autobuses Crucero** (☎ 313-54-24) buses leave from here, stop at the station on the Arizona side and travel to Tucson (US$12, 1½ hours), Phoenix (US$25, 3½ hours), Las Vegas (US$65, eight hours) and Los Angeles (US$63, 13 hours).

Mexican destinations served from the main bus station include the following: Chihuahua (US$54, 12 hours, five daily), Guadalajara (US$89, 26 hours, 12 daily), Guaymas (US$18, five hours, 16 daily), Hermosillo (US$12, 3½ hours, every half hour), Los Mochis (US$36, 10 hours, every half hour), Mazatlán (US$63, 16 hours, 12 daily), Mexico City (US$128, 33 hours, five daily) and Tepic (US$82, 24 hours, 12 daily).

Tufesa has its own station, two blocks north of the main bus station, with hourly 1st-class buses 24 hours a day that go south as far as Culiacán. Next door, Transportes Baldomero Corral serves the major cities along Hwy 15; with a 1st-class bus departing every two hours from 10:30am to 12:30am; stops include Hermosillo (US$12, 3½ hours) and Álamos (US$29, nine hours). It also has six daily buses to Phoenix (US$29, three hours).

From Nogales, Arizona, **Autobuses Crucero** (☎ 520-287-5628; 35 N Terrace Ave), a block from the border crossing, has hourly buses for Tucson (US$9, one hour) and Phoenix (US$22, three hours), and there's a daily afternoon bus that goes to Las Vegas (US$62, nine hours). Here you can also hop on one of the six daily buses headed for Hermosillo (US$18, four hours).

CAR & MOTORCYCLE

Approaching Nogales, Arizona, from Tucson, the left lanes go to central Nogales. The right lanes, which go to the Mariposa border crossing outside the city, are the quickest way to enter Mexico. Both border crossings are open 24 hours a day. As you approach Nogales, you'll see plenty of signs for Mexican auto insurance, which you'll need if you're bringing a vehicle into Mexico.

Temporary vehicle import procedures are dealt with at the Aguazarca inspection site at the 21km point on the highway south of Nogales. See p970 for more on bringing a vehicle into Mexico and on simplified procedures for those who are only visiting Sonora.

Enterprise Rent-A-Car (☎ 520-281-0425; 800-325-8007; 1831 N Grand Ave) allows you to take its rental vehicles to Mexico. You can pick up the vehicle in either Nogales or Tucson (including the Tucson airport), and must return it where you got it. **Hertz** (☎ 520-287-2012; 800-654-3131; 1012 N Grand Ave) also rents out vehicles for trips into Mexico from either Tucson or Nogales.

On the Arizona side of Nogales, several attended lots near the border crossing offer parking for US$5.50 per day.

With more than 11,000 vehicles crossing into the US at Nogales each day, getting through the border quickly when heading north requires luck, or perhaps some foresight. The US Dept of Homeland Security posts estimated wait times online at http://apps.cbp.gov/bwt.

Getting Around

For the bus station, city buses marked 'Central' or 'Central Camionera' depart every 20 minutes from 6:30am to 8pm from a corner on Av López Mateos, two blocks south of the border crossing (US$0.30). Everything else you'll need in Nogales is within easy walking distance of the border crossing. Taxis wait on either side of the border crossing, but are not allowed to cross it.

NORTHERN SONORA

On the northeast coast of the Sea of Cortez (Golfo de California), **Puerto Peñasco** (population 30,000) is a popular destination for travelers with trailers and RVs, making tourism an even more profitable industry than the shrimping and fishing for which this small town is also known. About a 1½-hour drive south of the Sonoita border crossing, this is southern Arizona's nearest beach.

Growing rapidly, Puerto Peñasco has many good hotels, motels, trailer parks and restaurants, and a marina. Fishing, surfing, scuba diving, kayaking and yacht cruises are popular activities. English is widely spoken and local businesses are as keen to take US dollars as pesos.

Puerto Peñasco's **tourist office** (☎ 638-383-61-22; Blvd Juárez 320B; ⏲ 9am-5pm Mon-Fri, 9am-2pm

Sat) can help with activities and accommodations. In the USA, **Rocky Point Reservations** (☎ 602-439-9004; 800-427-6259) also arranges stays in Puerto Peñasco.

Northwest of Puerto Peñasco is the **Reserva de la Biósfera El Pinacate y Gran Desierto de Altar**, a reserve containing several extinct volcanic craters, a large lava flow, cinder cones, a cinder mine and vast sand dunes. To get there, travel 45km northeast of Puerto Peñasco on Hwy 8; the white ranger station is impossible to miss. Be sure to register before entering the park. Until 1993 part of the reserve formed the Parque Nacional El Pinacate, a title still sometimes used.

The small town of **Cananea**, on Hwy 2 about halfway between Santa Ana and Agua Prieta, is a mining town that is not of much note today, but it is significant in Mexican history because the miners' revolt that broke out here on June 1, 1906, near the end of the rule of Porfirio Díaz, helped to precipitate the Mexican Revolution. Displays in the small town **museum** tell the story of the strike.

HERMOSILLO

☎ 662 / pop 566,400 / elevation 238m

Many travelers simply pass through Hermosillo, a prosperous agricultural center and the capital of the Sonora state, about 280km south of Nogales. Those that linger discover a bustling place where commerce is king.

Each night at twilight, however, the blackbirds take possession of the town: they fly in great numbers around the dramatic rock formations that rise from the city center, and roost in the trees of picturesque Plaza Zaragoza.

Hermosillo was founded in 1700 by Juan Bautista Escalante for the resettlement of indigenous Pima. Many of its streets and avenues acknowledge the city's debt to the revolutionary heroes that were born here, including General Alvaro Obregón.

Located smack dab in the middle of the Desierto Sonorense, Hermosillo naturally gets unbearably hot in summer, but the rest of the year it's quite pleasant. If you're passing through at the end of April, you might catch the Exposición Ganadera (Sonora state fair), lasting 10 days.

Orientation

Hwy 15 enters Hermosillo from the northeast and becomes Blvd Francisco Eusebio

HERMOSILLO

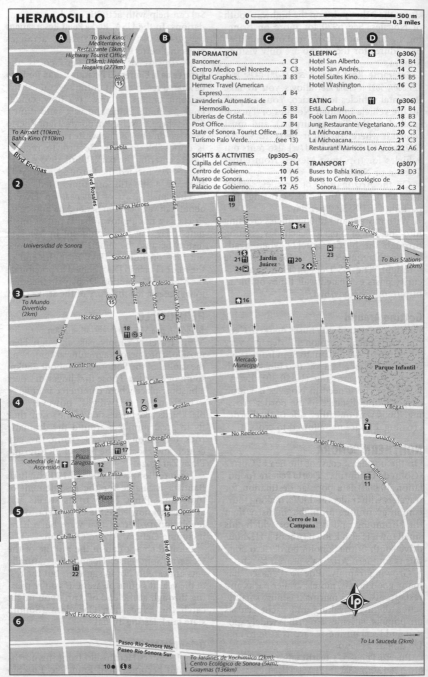

0 ——————————————— 500 m
0 ——————————————— 0.3 miles

INFORMATION
Bancomer...................................1 C3
Centro Medico Del Noreste......2 C3
Digital Graphics.......................3 B3
Hermex Travel (American
Express)...............................4 B4
Lavandería Automática de
Hermosillo...........................5 B3
Librerías de Cristal..................6 B4
Post Office..............................7 B4
State of Sonora Tourist Office...8 B6
Turismo Palo Verde............(see 13)

SIGHTS & ACTIVITIES (pp305–6)
Capilla del Carmen...................9 D4
Centro de Gobierno................10 A6
Museo de Sonora....................11 D5
Palacio de Gobierno................12 A5

SLEEPING (p306)
Hotel San Alberto..................13 B4
Hotel San Andrés...................14 C2
Hotel Suites Kino...................15 B5
Hotel Washington...................16 C3

EATING (p306)
Está...Cabral.........................17 B4
Fook Lam Moon......................18 B3
Jung Restaurante Vegetariano..19 C2
La Michoacana........................20 C3
La Michoacana........................21 C3
Restaurant Mariscos Los Arcos..22 A6

TRANSPORT (p307)
Buses to Bahía Kino................23 D3
Buses to Centro Ecológico de
Sonora................................24 C3

Kino, a wide street lined with orange and laurel trees. Blvd Kino continues west through the city, curves southwest and becomes Rodríguez, then Rosales as it passes through the city center, then Vildosola before becoming Hwy 15 again south of the city. The major business and administrative sections of Hermosillo lie on either side of Blvd Rosales and along Blvd Encinas, which transects the city center from northwest to southeast. The Periférico, once a beltway around Hermosillo, has become practically an inner loop due to the city's rapid expansion.

Both tourist offices (see following) offer a good free city map. Many of the city's nicer hotels and restaurants also hand out copies of the map.

Information

BOOKSTORES
Librerías de Cristal (☎ 213-71-97; Serdan 178) Wide selection of books in Spanish.

EMERGENCY
Police (☎ 066)
Red Cross (☎ 214-0010)
Tourist emergency assistance (☎ 01-800-623-79-00)

INTERNET ACCESS
Digital Graphics (Pino Suárez 171; per hr US$1.50; ☻ 9am-9pm Mon-Fri, 10am-8pm Sat, closed Sun)

LAUNDRY
Lavandería Automática de Hermosillo (cnr Yañez & Sonora; ☻ 8am-8pm Mon-Sat, 8am-2pm Sun)

MEDICAL SERVICES
Centro Medico Del Noreste (☎ 217-45-21; Colosio 23 Ote; ☻ 24hr) Medical care day or night.

MONEY
Banks and *casas de cambio* are scattered along Hermosillo's Blvds Rosales and Encinas. The American Express agent, **Hermex Travel** (☎ 213-44-15), is on the corner of Blvd Rosales and Monterrey.

POST
Main post office (cnr Blvd Rosales & Serdán; ☻ 8am-4pm Mon-Fri, 9am-1pm Sat)

TOURIST INFORMATION
Both of the following offices have information on all Sonora.

Highway tourist office (Hwy 15 at the checkpoint 15km north of Hermosillo; 8am-3pm Mon-Fri)
State of Sonora tourist office (☎ 217-00-76, 800-476-6672 in the USA; www.sonoraturismo.gob.mx; Edificio Sonora Norte, 3rd fl, Comonfort & Paseo Canal; ☻ 8am-5pm Mon-Fri) Parking here can be a challenge.

TRAVEL AGENCIES
Hermex Travel (☎ 213-44-15; cnr Blvd Rosales & Monterrey)
Turismo Palo Verde (☎ 213-47-01; Hotel San Alberto, cnr Blvd Rosales & Serdán)

Sights & Activities
Hermosillo's **Plaza Zaragoza** is home to the lovely **Catedral de la Ascensión**, also called the Catedral Metropolitana. On the east side, the gray-and-white **Palacio de Gobierno** has a courtyard with colorful, dramatic murals depicting episodes in the history of Sonora.

The **Cerro de la Campana** (Hill of the Bell) is the most prominent landmark in the area and an easy point of reference night or day. The panoramic view from the top is beautiful and well worth the walk or drive to get up there. Hugging the east side of the hill, the **Museo de Sonora** (☎ 217-27-14; Jesús García s/n; admission US$3, free Sun & holidays; ☻ 10am-5pm Tue-Sat, 9am-4pm Sun) has fine exhibits on the history and anthropology of Sonora. The building – the former Sonora state penitentiary – is one of the most interesting in Hermosillo (particularly if you have an unholy love of dungeons). To get there, it's an easy walk, or you can take local bus No 8 ('La Matanza') from the corner of Elías Calles and Garmendia to the museum entrance.

The **Centro Ecológico de Sonora** (☎ 250-12-25; admission US$2; ☻ 8am-5pm Tue-Sun) is a zoo and botanical garden with plants and animals of the Desierto Sonorense and other ecosystems of northwest Mexico. There is also an **observatory** (admission US$1; ☻ 7:30-11pm Fri & Sat) with telescope viewing sessions. The center is about 5km south of central Hermosillo, past the Periférico Sur and just off Hwy 15. The 'Luis Orcí' local bus departs every 10 minutes from the west side of Jardín Juárez and heads south on Blvd Rosales, stopping at a gate about 500m from the entrance. Ask the driver where to get off, as there are no signs.

Hermosillo for Children
Hermosillo boasts a couple of enjoyable recreation parks with miniature golf, boats,

bathing pools and other activities for children and adults: **Mundo Divertido** (☎ 260-35-05; Blvd Colosio 653; ☻ 1-8pm Mon-Fri, noon-9pm Sat & Sun) and **La Sauceda** (☎ 212-05-09; Blvd Serna; admission US$0.80; ☻ 10am-4pm Tue-Sun), east of Cerro de la Campana.

Sleeping

If you spend a night here in summer, do yourself a favor and make sure that the air-con works!

BUDGET & MID-RANGE

Hotel Washington (☎ 213-11-83; Noriega 68 Pte; s/d US$16/18) Hotel Washington has a cheerfully decorated lobby, vending machines and free coffee. On the whole the rooms are basic, large and clean, but some are a little dark and stuffy and the air-con is temperamental.

Hotel Suites Kino (☎ 213-31-31; www.hotelsuites kino.com; Pino Suárez 151 Sur; s US$40-43, d US$42-45, ste US$44-50; P ✄ ☎) This well-run hotel has perfectly adequate rooms, a decent restaurant and an on-site travel agency. 'Plus' rooms are larger and have desks and bigger TVs.

Hotel San Alberto (☎ 213-18-40; cnr Blvd Rosales & Serdán; s/d US$33/35; P ✄ ☎) With its lobby full of moldering safari trophies, the San Alberto has the feeling of a hotel whose time has past. Although it's a little rough around the edges, it's still decent value with amenities including a travel agency and a bookstore.

Hotel San Andrés (☎ 217-30-99; sanandres@infosel .net.mx; Oaxaca 14; s/d/ste US$37/40/45; P ✄) The Hotel San Andrés, a block from Jardín Juárez, has a restaurant, a bar and 80 modern rooms around a pleasant courtyard.

TOP END

Many of Hermosillo's better hotels and motels are strung along Blvd Kino in the northeast corner of the city. Among these are the following:

Araiza Inn (☎ 210-27-17; Blvd Kino 353; s/d US$68/90; P ✄ ☎) Convenient to the airport, with gym, restaurant and lounge.

Fiesta Americana (☎ 259-60-00; Blvd Kino 369; s/d/ste from US$132/190/258; P ✄ ✄ ☎) Spacious luxurious rooms and many amenities.

Eating

Hermosillo's cuisine scene is not going to blow your mind, but there are a few excellent choices for the discerning palate.

There are cheap food stalls in **Mercado Municipal**, on Matamoros between Elías Calles and Monterrey, but some of the cheapest food in Hermosillo can be bought from the hot-dog carts on many street corners. The hot dogs are surprisingly good, especially when piled high with all the local fixings.

For a cool fruit salad, yogurt with fruit, ice cream, fruit or vegetable juice or other cold drinks, check out the many branches of **La Michoacana**. The two bordering Jardín Juárez, open till 9pm, are convenient for getting snacks to take out on the plaza.

Está...Cabral (☎ 213-74-74; cnr Velazco & Allende; antojitos US$1-3.50, specials US$3.50-4.50; ☻ 5pm-midnight) This large, open-air café occupies the interior of a stately ruined building. With live music every night, it may be the coolest eatery in town.

Jardines de Xochimilco (☎ 250-40-89; Obregón 51; dinner special US$23; ☻ 11am-9pm) Hermosillo's best-known restaurant, it serves the beef for which Sonora is famous and also has mariachi bands. The dinner special for two is a memorable feast. The restaurant is in Villa de Seris, an old part of town just south of the center. Drive or come in a taxi at night, as the neighborhood is dark and somewhat remote from the center. If you are driving, look for signs on Blvd Rosales just south of Paseo Rio Sonora. Reservations are advised in the evening.

Jung Restaurante Vegetariano (☎ 213-28-81; Niños Héroes 75D; breakfast/dinner buffets US$7.50/8.50, mains US$2.50-4.50) This clean and cheerful vegetarian restaurant and health food store has a vast, reasonably priced menu.

Restaurant Mariscos Los Arcos (☎ 213-22-20; Michel 43; mains US$6-12) This pleasant restaurant is famous for its large variety of seafood dishes, including a sensational *caldos mixtos* (seafood stew) and several dishes inspired by Chinese cuisine.

Also recommended:

Mediterraneos Restaurante (214-91-29; Nayarit 208; mains US$6.50-16) This Italian place has a pleasant patio and well-prepared fare.

Fook Lam Moon (☎ 212-25-45; Blvd Rosales 91; mains US$6-12) Authentic Mandarin cuisine.

Shopping

If you always wanted to buy a pair of cowboy boots and a 10-gallon hat, you'll probably find what you want in Hermosillo. The city has one of the best selections of cowboy gear in Mexico; start your search on Matamoros near Jardín Juárez. Ironwood carvings made by the Seri people are another distinctive product of the region and are sold in front of the post office and at other places around town.

Getting There & Away

AIR

The airport, about 10km from central Hermosillo on the road to Bahía Kino, is served by Aero California, Aerolitoral, Aeroméxico, America West, and Mexicana. Daily direct flights, all with connections to other centers, go to Chihuahua, Ciudad Juárez, Ciudad Obregón, Culiacán, Guadalajara, La Paz, Los Angeles, Los Mochis, Mexicali, Mexico City, Monterrey, Phoenix, Tijuana and Tucson.

BUS

From the **main bus terminal** (☎ 213-44-55; Blvd Encinas), 2km southeast of the city center, 1st-class service is offered by Crucero, Elite, Estrella Blanca (EB), Transportes del Pacífico (TP), Transportes Norte de Sonora (TNS) and others. Other companies have separate terminals nearby – Transportes Baldomero Corral (TBC) is next door. Across the street is Tufesa, and about a block west of Blvd Encinas is Estrellas del Pacífico (EP). Services to many destinations depart around the clock. Daily 1st-class departures include the following:

Guadalajara (US$63-72, 23hr) Frequent buses from the main bus terminal via Los Mochis, Mazatlán and Tepic.
Guaymas (US$5-6, 1¾ hr) Frequent buses by most companies.
Los Angeles (US$74, 15hr, 3 Crucero)
Mexico City (US$97-110, 30-33 hr) Frequent buses from the main bus terminal.
Nogales (US$12, 4hr) Frequent buses by most companies.
Phoenix (US$39, 8hr, 5 Crucero, 4 TBC)
Puerto Peñasco (US$13, 6½hr, 4 TBC)
Tijuana (US$38-41, 13hr) Frequent buses by most companies.
Tucson (US$26, 5½ hr, 5 Crucero, 5 TBC)

Second-class buses to Bahía Kino depart from the AMH and TCH bus terminal in central Hermosillo, on Sonora between González and Jesús García, 1½ blocks east of Jardín Juárez. They depart hourly from 5:30am to 11:30am and from 3:30pm to 6:30pm (US$7, two hours).

Getting Around

Local buses operate from 5:30am to 10pm daily (US$0.40). To get to the main bus terminal, take any 'Central,' 'Central Camionera' or 'Ruta 1' bus from Juárez on the east side of Jardín Juárez. A taxi to the airport costs US$8 to US$10.

BAHÍA KINO

☎ 740 / pop 4000
Named for Father Eusebio Kino, a Jesuit missionary who established a small mission here for the indigenous Seri people in the late 17th century, the bayfront town of Kino, 110km west of Hermosillo, is divided into old and new parts that are as different as night and day.

Kino Viejo, the old quarter on your left as you drive into Kino, is a dusty, run-down fishing village. Kino Nuevo, on your right, is basically a single beachfront road stretching about 8km north along the beach, lined with the holiday homes and retreats of wealthy gringos and Mexicans. It's a fine beach with soft sand and safe swimming. From around November to March the 'snowbirds' drift down in their trailers from colder climes. The rest of the time it's not crowded – but it's always a popular day outing for families from Hermosillo escaping the city. The beach has many palapas providing welcome shade.

The **Museo de los Seris** (admission US$0.60; ☺ 8am-3pm Tue-Fri), about halfway along the beachfront road in Kino Nuevo, has illuminating exhibits about the Seri, the traditionally nomadic indigenous people of this area. There's a Seri artesanías shop next door. Seri ironwood carvings are sold in both Kino Nuevo and Viejo.

Sleeping & Eating

KINO NUEVO

Prices in Kino tend to be considerably higher than in Hermosillo. There are plenty of palapas all along the beach – you could easily string up a hammock and camp out under one of these for free. Most of the following places offer weekly and monthly discounts.

La Playa RV & Hotel (☎ 242-02-74; trailer sites with hookup US$18, ste US$86; P ⊠) This beach-front establishment has innovative trailer sites with enclosures and excellent beachfront rooms with kitchenettes.

NORTHWEST MEXICO

Kino Bay RV Park (☎ 242-02-16; tent/trailer sites US$15/20; P) At the far north end of Kino Nuevo, opposite the beach at the end of the bus line, this clean, attractive and well-equipped park has 200 tent or trailer spaces with full hookups.

Posada Santa Gemma (☎ 242-00-26; sites US$20, bungalows US$120; P ❀) Also on the beach, the Santa Gemma offers tent and trailer spaces without hookups as well as bungalows; prices seem to be negotiable.

Hotel Posada del Mar (☎ /fax 242-01-55; s/d/ste from US$38/45/45-66; ❀ ❀) This hotel is across the road from the beach. It's a little worn around the edges, but still a decent value.

Various places to eat – all specializing in fresh seafood, of course – lie along the beachfront road and in some of the hotels. **Restaurant La Palapa** (☎ 242-02-10), **Pargo Rojo** (☎ 242-02-05) and **Taco Bar** (☎ 242-02-10) are all recommended.

KINO VIEJO

On the beach is **Islandia Marina** (☎ 242-00-81; tent/trailer sites US$10/15, bungalows US$50-60; P) This is a trailer park with tent and trailer spaces, plus eight free-standing self-contained bungalows. Beachfront bungalows cost more; bring your own bed linen and dishes.

A block away, the pricey, air-conditioned **Restaurant Marlin** and **Roberto's** are popular

restaurants. Other small open-air eateries, serving fresh barbecued fish or tacos, are dotted around Kino Viejo.

Getting There & Away

Buses to Hermosillo leave from Kino Nuevo roughly every hour on the half hour, with the last bus departing from Kino Nuevo at 7:15pm and Kino Viejo at 7:30 pm. If you come at a busy time (on a Sunday, for example, when lots of families are there) and you want to get the last bus of the day, catch it at the first stop, on the north end of Kino Nuevo, while there is still space. Be aware that this is the only public transportation in Kino; there are no local buses or taxis.

If you're driving, you can make the trip from Hermosillo to Bahía Kino in about an hour. From central Hermosillo, head northwest out of town on Blvd Encinas and just keep going.

GUAYMAS

☎ 622 / pop 101,000

Guaymas, Sonora's main port, is inextricably linked to the sea. Visitors are reminded of this as they stroll the streets that ring the impressive natural harbor, where myriad fishing boats return home each afternoon to unload the day's catch. Some of this fresh seafood invariably will end up on your plate

---

THE SERIS

The Seris are the least numerous indigenous people in Sonora, but one of the most recognized due to their distinctive handicrafts. Traditionally a nomadic people living by hunting, gathering and fishing – not agriculture, as was prevalent among many other indigenous groups in Mexico – the Seris roamed along the Sea of Cortez from roughly El Desemboque in the north to Bahía Kino in the south, and inland to Hermosillo.

The Seris are one of the few indigenous peoples who do not work for outsiders, preferring to live by fishing, hunting and handicrafts. Their most famous handicrafts are their ironwood carvings of animals, humans and other figures. Other important traditional handicrafts, including pottery and basketry, are no longer as important. The Seris were once one of the very few peoples in the world who were nomadic and also made pottery.

Though the Seris are no longer strictly nomadic, they still often move from place to place in groups; sometimes you can see them camped at Bahía Kino, or traveling up and down the coast. You will also see Seris in Hermosillo, where some sell ironwood carvings outside the post office. Many, though, live far from modern civilization on the large, protected Isla Tiburón (which belongs to the Seris) or in other inconspicuous places along the Sonora coast, and they still maintain many of their old traditions reflecting the rhythms of living between the desert and the sea.

A visit to the Museo de los Seris in Kino Nuevo is rewarding. The exhibits encompass the Seris' distinctive clothing, their traditional houses with frames of ocotillo cactus, their musical instruments and handicrafts, and their nomadic social structure and nature-based religion.

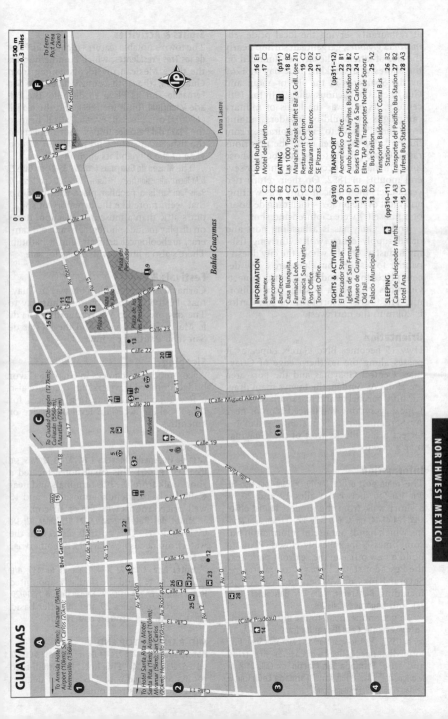

GUAYMAS

INFORMATION	
Banamex	1 C2
Bancomer	2 C2
BanCrecer	3 B2
Casa Blanquita	4 C2
Farmacia León	5 C1
Farmacia San Martin	6 C2
Post Office	7 C3
Tourist Office	8 C3

SIGHTS & ACTIVITIES	(p310)
El Pescador Statue	9 D2
Iglesia de San Fernando	10 D1
Museo de Guaymas	11 D1
Old Jail	12 B2
Palacio Municipal	13 D2

SLEEPING	(pp310–11)
Casa de Huéspedes Martha	14 A3
Hotel Ana	15 D1
Hotel Rubí	16 E1
Motel del Puerto	17 C2

EATING	(p311*)
Las 1000 Tortas	18 B2
Mariachi's Steak Buffet Bar & Grill	(see 21)
Restaurant Canton	19 D2
Restaurant Los Barcos	20 D2
SE Pizzas	21 C1

TRANSPORT	(pp311–12)
Aeroméxico Office	22 B1
Autobuses Los Mayitos Bus Station	23 B2
Buses to Miramar & San Carlos	24 C1
Elite, TAP & Transportes Norte de Sonora Bus Station	25 A2
Transportes Baldomero Corral Bus Station	26 B2
Transportes del Pacífico Bus Station	27 B2
Tufesa Bus Station	28 A3

at restaurants serving the local pride: *camarones gigantes*, gargantuan shrimp nearly the size of kittens. The city was founded on the shores of a sparkling blue bay in 1769 by the Spaniards at the site of Yaqui and Guaymenas indigenous villages. In the 19th century, its bay was the locus of military campaigns by would-be invaders ranging from the US Navy to French pirates. From the ranks of the latter came the notorious rascal Gaston Raousset de Bourbon, whose forces managed to occupy Guaymas for several months in 1852. On their return two years later, the Mexican army was waiting, and most of the pirates – including de Bourbon himself – were captured and shot.

Today Guaymas is a bustling port and naval supply center with a thriving fishing industry. On the whole, the city doesn't pander to visitors, but there are a few decent places to stay and eat. A ferry connects Guaymas with Santa Rosalía, Baja California. The tourist resort town of San Carlos is 20km to the northwest.

Orientation

Hwy 15 becomes Blvd García López as it passes along the northern edge of Guaymas. Central Guaymas and the port area are along Av Serdán, the town's main drag, running parallel to and just south of García López; everything you'll need is on or near Av Serdán. García López and Serdán intersect a few blocks west of the Guaymas map's extents.

Information

The **main post office** (Av 10; ☉ 9am-3pm Mon-Fri, 9am-1pm Sat), between Calles 19 and 20, is a short walk from the modest **tourist office** (☎ 224-41-14; cnr Av 6 & Calle 19; ☉ 9am-3pm Mon-Fri), which hands out useful information but sometimes is inexplicably closed. Plans to build a new office in the seafront park near the Pescador statue have yet to materialize. Several banks on Av Serdán have ATMs, including **BanCrecer** (Calle 15), **Bancomer** (Calle 18), and **Banamex** (Calle 20).

To get online, head to the giftshop-cum-Internet café **Casa Blanquita** (cnr Calle 19 & Av 11; per hr US$1; ☉ 9am-9pm Mon-Sat, 9am-3pm Sun). For long-distance calls, two casetas are tried and true: **Farmacia San Martín** (cnr Calle 21 & Av Rodríguez; ☉ 8am-11pm) and **Farmacia León** (cnr Av Serdán & Calle 19; ☉ 8am-6pm).

Sights & Activities

The town's notable features include the **Plaza de los Tres Presidentes**, which commemorates the three Mexican presidents hailing from Guaymas; the 19th-century **Iglesia de San Fernando** and its Plaza 13 de Julio; the **Palacio Municipal** (built in 1899); and the **old jail** (1900). For a pleasant evening stroll, head to the **Plaza del Pescador** to pay your respects to the fisherman statue and to take in a good view of the city and its environs.

The **Museo de Guaymas** (☎ 222-55-27; cnr Calle 25 & Av Iberri; admission free; ☉ 8am-2pm & 3:30-6pm Mon-Fri, 9am-1pm Sat) is a peculiar place with holdings that seem more like the inventory of someone's attic than a museum collection. Items on display include photographs and old cameras, archeological artifacts, and a bathtub. There's also a library with books for sale.

Festivals & Events

Carnaval is celebrated in a big way in Guaymas. Festivities occur on the Thursday to Tuesday preceding Ash Wednesday. Día de la Marina is on June 1; and the Fiestas de San Juan Bautista on June 24.

Sleeping

Accommodation choices in Guaymas favor budget-minded travelers, but there are also a few good (if uninteresting) choices for those seeking a certain level of service or amenities.

BUDGET

Casa de Huéspedes Martha (☎ 222-83-32; Av 9; US$13/15; [P] [X]) This small hotel, located a short walk from the bus terminals and near Calle 13, has a friendly atmosphere and 15 well-priced rooms with fan or air-con.

Motel del Puerto (☎ 222-24-91; Yañez 92; s/d US$20/26; [P] [X]) This no-frills motel near the waterfront needs new carpets, but otherwise is adequate.

Hotel Ana (☎ 222-30-48; Calle 25 No 135; d/tr US$20/25; [P] [X]) and the similarly-appointed **Hotel Rubi** (☎ 224-01-69; Av Serdán s/n; s/d US$19/20; [X]), between Calles 29 and 30, offer basic, clean rooms set around courtyards.

MID-RANGE & TOP END

Hotel Santa Rita (☎ 224-14-64; cnr Av Serdán & Calle 9; s/d US$26/31; [P] [X]) This hotel has small tiled rooms and a patio that is several degrees cooler than the street outside.

Motel Santa Rita (☎ 224-19-19; Av Serdán 590 Pte; s/d US$40/50; P ⚡ ▣) Situated in the next block from the Hotel Santa Rita, this three-story motel is somewhat cheerful; its retro-style diner (prices US$5 to US$10) has vinyl-clad booths and bright green doors. Prices include complimentary breakfast.

Armida Hotel (☎ 224-30-35; Carretera Internacional Salida Norte; r US$48, ste US$71-91; P ⚡ ▣) Rooms in this well-run hotel on the northern edge of town have refrigerators, satellite TV, balconies or terraces, and bathtubs. There's also a café and the El Oeste steak house.

Eating

As in most Mexican towns, Guaymas supports a market, which has stalls where you can sit down to eat for cheap. It's a block south of Av Serdán, on Av Rodríguez between Calles 19 and 20, and opens at around 5am.

SE Pizzas (Av Serdán near Calle 20; prices from US$2.75) has an all-you-can-eat pizza and salad buffet and the beer's cheap too. Watching the mad rush for pizza is also a good form of entertainment (unless you're very hungry). Next door, **Mariachi's Steak Buffet Bar & Grill** (cnr Calle 20 & Av Serdán; prices US$3.50) serves an ample buffet. **Las 1000 Tortas** (Av Serdán btwn Calles 17 & 18; prices from US$2) is a good snack shop serving tortas and hamburgers. **Restaurant Canton** (Av Serdán btwn Calles 20 & 21; prices from US$2.50) offers inexpensive Chinese fare as well as some Mexican dishes.

For a seafood feast, make a beeline for the popular seafront **Restaurant Los Barcos** (cnr Av 11 & Calle 22; prices US$4-11). In an enormous palapa you can sample the seafood for which Guaymas is famous or enjoy a sumptuous steak, seafood cocktail or salad.

Getting There & Away

AIR

The airport is about 10km northwest of Guaymas on the Hwy to San Carlos. **Aeroméxico**, with an office in town (☎ 222-01-23; cnr Av Serdán & Calle 16) offers direct flights to the Baja California destinations of La Paz, Loreto and Santa Rosalía, and to Hermosillo, where you can catch connecting flights to other destinations. Its office is on the corner of Av Serdán and Calle 16. **America West** (☎ 221-22-66) offers three direct flights to Phoenix each week.

BUS

Guaymas has five small bus stations, all on Calle 14; about two blocks south of Av Serdán. Elite, TAP (Transportes y Autobuses del Pacífico) and Transportes Norte de Sonora share a terminal at the corner of Calle 14 and Av 12; Transportes del Pacífico is opposite. All these have far-ranging northbound and southbound routes departing hourly, 24 hours.

Transportes Baldomero Corral (TBC), beside Transportes del Pacífico, goes hourly to Hermosillo, Nogales, Ciudad Obregón and Navojoa, and also has a daily bus (3:45pm) direct to Álamos. Autobuses Los Mayitos, between Avs 10 and 12, operates hourly buses north to Hermosillo and south to Navojoa, 7am to 9pm. Tufesa, at the corner of Av 10, has hourly buses heading north to Nogales, afternoon buses to Hermosillo, and bi-hourly buses south to Culiacán. All run 1st-class buses, though Transportes del Pacífico and Tufesa also have 2nd-class buses. Trip times and 1st-class fares include Álamos (US$9, four hours; TBC only), Guadalajara (US$52 to US$63, 20 hours), Hermosillo (US$3.50 to US$6, 1¾ hours), Los Mochis (US$10 to US$15, five hours), Mazatlán (US$36 to US$45, 11 hours), Mexico City (US$90 to US$116, 28 hours), Navojoa (US$7 to US$9, three hours), Nogales (US$5 to US$16, five hours), Tepic (US$55 to US$60, six hours) and Tijuana (US$42 to US$48, 15 hours).

BOAT

Overnight ferries connect Guaymas with Santa Rosalía, Baja California. The new passenger/auto ferry *Santa Rosalía*, operated by Operadora Rotuaria del Noreste, departs at 8pm on Monday and Thursday and arrives in Santa Rosalía at 7am. Ferries depart Santa Rosalía at 8pm on Tuesday and Friday and arrive in Guaymas at 7am. Strong winter winds may cause delays.

The ticket office is at the **ferry terminal** (☎ 222-02-04 in Guaymas, 615-152-12-46 in Santa Rosalía; ☎ 10am-2pm & 4-8pm Mon-Sat) on Av Serdán at the east end of town. Vehicle reservations are accepted by telephone a week in advance. Passenger tickets are sold at the ferry office on the morning of departure, or a few days before. Make reservations at least three days in advance and, even if you have reservations, arrive early at the ticket office. Passenger fares are US$46 for seats and US$116 to US$166 for cabins. Advance reservations are recommended. See p277 for vehicle fares.

Getting Around

To get to the airport, catch a bus from Av Serdán heading to Itson or San José, or take a taxi (around US$10). Local buses run along Av Serdán frequently between 6am and 9pm daily (US$0.40). Several eastbound buses stop at the ferry terminal; ask for 'transbordador.'

AROUND GUAYMAS

The closest beach is **Miramar**, on the Bahía de Bacochibampo about 5km west of Guaymas. It's not a big tourist destination like San Carlos, but it does have an interesting industry – pearl farming.

Hotel Playa de Cortés (☎ 221-12-24; Bahía de Bacochibampo; RV sites US$24, r US$80-124, ste US$100-124; P ⊠ ⊛) This classic beachfront hotel affords a stunning view of the bay and a good alternative to the downtown Guaymas scene or the touristy excess of San Carlos. It has 120 big, clean rooms and an excellent restaurant, plus a 90-space trailer park with full hookups and access to all hotel facilities. 'Miramar' buses head west on Av Serdán (starting from between Calles 19 and 20) every 30 minutes between 7am and 8pm (US$0.50).

San Carlos

☎ 622 / pop 1400

On Bahía San Carlos, about 20km northwest of Guaymas, San Carlos is a beautiful desert-and-bay landscape presided over by the dramatic twin-peaked Cerro Tetakawi. From around October to April, the town is full of *norteamericanos* and their trailers; the rest of the year it's quiet, except for a flurry of Mexican tourists in July and August.

San Carlos has two marinas: Marina San Carlos, which is in the heart of town, and the newer Marina Real at Algodones, which is in the northernmost sector of town. San Carlos is bursting with outdoor activities such as snorkeling, diving, sailing, fishing, kayaking, mountain biking, motorcycling, horseback riding and golfing. If it's sandy beaches you are after, San Carlos may disappoint as the accessible public shoreline is mostly rocky and difficult to reach. The

view from the *mirador* (lookout) is spectacular, especially at sunset.

INFORMATION

San Carlos has a helpful bilingual **tourist office** (☎ 226-02-02; hdtours@prodigy.net.mx; ⏱ 9am-5pm Mon-Fri, 9am-2pm Sat), in the Edificio Hacienda Plaza on Blvd Manlio Beltrones, the main road into San Carlos. Here you can also purchase tickets for the Ferry Santa Rosalía. The town's most reliable place to get online is **Gary's Internet Connection** (☎ 226-07-92; Blvd Manlio Beltrones, Km10; per hr US$5; ⏱ 9am-6pm Mon-Sat).

ACTIVITIES

It would be a shame to come to San Carlos and not take advantage of the many outdoor or water sport opportunities. The following companies lead snorkeling, wildlife, fishing and scuba excursions, and also provide scuba certification, outfitting and rentals:

Blue Water Sports (☎ 227-01-71; www.desertdivers .com; beachside at the San Carlos Plaza Hotel, Algodones)

El Mar Diving Center (☎ 226-04-04; www.elmar.com; Blvd Manlio Beltrones 263)

Gary's Dive Shop (☎ 226-00-49; www.garysdiveshop .com; Blvd Manlio Beltrones Km10)

FESTIVALS & EVENTS

Annual events include Carnavalito, which is held the week following the Carnaval celebration in Guaymas; a skydiving exhibition in March; a women's fishing tournament in May; an international fishing tournament in July; the Labor Day fishing tournament in September; a sailboat competition in October; and golf tournaments throughout the year.

SLEEPING & EATING

As a fledgling resort town, San Carlos has plenty of excellent RV parks and mid-range accommodations. Budget travelers – as is often the case in such places – are faced with slim pickings.

Best Western Hacienda Tetakawi (☎ 226-02-20; on the road to San Carlos 10km west of Hwy 15; sites US$10/15, r US$60, ste US$70-80; P ⊠ ⊛) This hotel, with its plum location facing the Sea of Cortez, provides an excellent alternative to the heavily touristed strip in San Carlos proper. Campers at the adjacent trailer park can use all the hotel's facilities.

El Mirador RV Park (☎ 227-02-13; www.elmirador rv.com; RV sites day/week US$22/140; ☻) This park, overlooking Marina Real, has great views, many amenities and 90 spaces. For some reason, they don't allow tent camping.

Posada del Desierto (☎ 226-04-67; ste US$34-38 for up to 4 people; P ☻) The Posada del Desierto, San Carlos' most economical hotel, overlooks Marina San Carlos. It has seven basic air-conditioned studio apartments with kitchen; cheaper weekly and monthly rates are available. To find it, follow signs to Hotel Marinaterra and keep going. At the convenience store, turn right.

Motel Creston (☎ 226-00-20; Blvd Manlio Beltrones Km 10; s/d US$45/50; P ☒ ☻) This well-run motor lodge has large rooms and retro charm.

Hotel Fiesta San Carlos (☎ 226-02-29; Blvd Manlio Beltrones Km 8.5; s/d US$38/45, including breakfast) This is a popular hotel with a swimming pool, restaurant, palapa bar, and beachfront rooms with balconies. (They are a little over-zealous with the industrial cleanser.)

San Carlos Plaza Hotel, Resort & Convention Center (☎ 227-00-77; fax 227-00-98; Mar Bermejo Norte No 4, Algodones; r US$203-242, ste US$247-1054; P ☒ ☒ ☐ ☻) This big beachfront hotel has a pool, Jacuzzi, two restaurants, a bar and an incredibly expensive presidential suite. The 1970s architecture and design hasn't aged well.

Good restaurants in San Carlos include the **San Carlos Grill** (☎ 226-05-09; Plaza Comercial San Carlos; mains US$6-14), which serves a variety of seafood and Mexican dishes; **Piccolo's** (☎ 226-05-03; Blvd Manlio Beltrones Km 10; mains US$6-14), an Italian restaurant; **Rosa's Cantina** (☎ 226-10-00; Blvd Manlio Beltrones Km 9.5; mains US$4-12), serving Mexican favorites and big breakfasts; and **El Bronco** (☎ 226-11-30; Creston 178; mains US$4.50-20), a steakhouse serving Sonoran beef. For seafood, where better than **San Carlos Mariscos Esterito** (Bahía San Carlos, across from the old marina; dinners US$3.50-8), an open-air palapa on a scenic estuary where you can bird-watch from your table?

GETTING THERE & AROUND

Buses to San Carlos from Guaymas run west along Av Serdán (starting from between Calles 19 and 20) from 5:30am to 10pm. Return buses leave San Carlos between 6:30am and 11pm. Buses run every 20 minutes (US$0.90).

NAVOJOA

☎ 642 / pop 100,000

Navojoa, 194km from Guaymas, is a mundane place. However, it is a significant hub for those heading to the picturesque town of Álamos, 53km east on Hwy 13.

Hwy 15D becomes Av Pesqueria as it passes through town; most of the bus stations are on the cross streets Guerrero or Allende. Navojoa has five bus stations within six blocks. Transportes del Pacífico, Transportes Norte de Sonora and Elite each have hourly 1st-class buses, 24 hours a day, going north and south on Hwy 15D.

Second-class buses to Álamos depart from the Transportes Baldomero Corral (TBC) station, on the corner of Guerrero and No Reelección, every half hour between 6am and 3pm, and hourly between 3:30pm and 10:30pm (US$2, one hour). TBC also has 1st-class service, including 12 daily buses north to Hermosillo (US$14, five hours), nine daily buses to Nogales (US$26, eight hours), and five daily buses to Tucson (US$35, 11 hours) and Phoenix (US$50, 13 hours).

ÁLAMOS

☎ 647 / pop 10,000 / elevation 432m

In Álamos, the façades of colonial mansions line the narrow cobbled streets, concealing courtyards lush with bougainvillea. Set in the forested foothills of the Sierra Madre Occidental 53km east of Navojoa, this serene town is replete with beautifully-restored colonial buildings. From Andalucía in southern Spain, 17th-century architects brought a Moorish sensibility to bear in numerous buildings throughout the town; as you walk down its cobbled streets you will see why Álamos has been declared a national historic monument.

The town's charms have proven irresistible to a community of American retirees and creative types, who over the past 30 years have snapped up many decaying colonial buildings to renovate and convert to hotels and restaurants. Now comprising a significant percentage of the town population, the well-heeled expats entertain each other in their enclosed courtyards, remaining largely segregated from their Mexican neighbors. The upside of all this for the traveler, of course, is that there is a wide range of choices in quality lodgings.

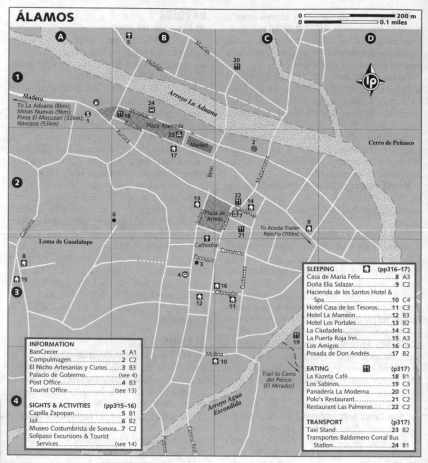

ÁLAMOS

INFORMATION	
BanCrecer	1 A1
Compulmagen	2 C2
El Nicho Artesanías y Curios	3 B3
Palacio de Gobierno	(see 4)
Post Office	4 B3
Tourist Office	(see 13)

SIGHTS & ACTIVITIES	(pp315–16)
Capilla Zapopan	5 B1
Jail	6 B2
Museo Costumbrista de Sonora	7 C2
Solipaso Excursions & Tourist Services	(see 14)

SLEEPING	(pp316–17)
Casa de María Felix	8 A3
Doña Elia Salazar	9 C2
Hacienda de los Santos Hotel & Spa	10 C4
Hotel Casa de los Tesoros	11 C3
Hotel La Mansión	12 B3
Hotel Los Portales	13 B2
La Ciudadela	14 C2
La Puerta Roja Inn	15 A3
Los Amigos	16 C3
Posada de Don Andrés	17 B2

EATING	(p317)
La Kazeta Café	18 B1
Los Sabinos	19 C3
Panadería La Moderna	20 C1
Polo's Restaurant	21 C2
Restaurant Las Palmeras	22 C2

TRANSPORT	(p317)
Taxi Stand	23 B2
Transportes Baldomero Corral Bus Station	24 B1

Álamos is on the border of two large ecosystems: the great Desierto Sonorense to the north and the lush tropical jungles of Sinaloa to the south. Nature-lovers are attracted by the area's 450 species of birds and animals (including some endangered and endemic species) and over 1000 species of plants. Horseback riding, hunting, fishing, hiking and swimming are popular activities.

From mid-October to mid-April, when the air is cool and fresh, norteamericanos arrive to take up residence in their winter homes and the town begins to hum with foreign visitors. Quail and dove hunting season, from November to February, also attracts many visitors. Mexican tourists come in the scorching hot summer months of July and August, when school is out. At other times you may find scarcely another visitor.

History

In 1540 this was the campsite of Francisco Vázquez de Coronado, future governor of Nueva Galicia (the colonial name for much of western Mexico), during his wars against the indigenous Mayo and Yaqui (the Yaqui resisted all invaders until 1928). If he had known about the vast amounts of gold and silver that prospectors would later find, he would have stayed.

In 1683 silver was discovered at Promontorios, near Álamos, and the Europa mine was opened. Other mines soon followed and Álamos became a boom town of more than 30,000, one of Mexico's principal 18th-century mining centers. Mansions, haciendas, a cathedral, tanneries, metalworks, blacksmiths' shops and later a mint were built. El Camino Real (the King's Hwy), a well-trodden Spanish mule trail through the foothills, connected Álamos with Culiacán and El Fuerte to the south.

After Mexican independence, Álamos became the capital of the newly formed province of Occidente, a vast area including all of the present states of Sonora and Sinaloa. Don José María Almada, owner of the richest silver mine in Álamos, was appointed as governor.

During the turmoil of the 19th century and up to the Mexican Revolution, Álamos was attacked repeatedly, both by rebels seeking its vast silver wealth and by the fiercely independent Yaqui. The years of the revolution took a great toll on the town. By the 1920s, most of the population had left and many of the once-beautiful haciendas had fallen into disrepair. Álamos became practically a ghost town.

In 1948 Álamos was reawakened by the arrival of William Levant Alcorn, a Pennsylvania dairy farmer who bought the 15-room Almada mansion on Plaza de Armas and restored it as the Hotel Los Portales. Alcorn brought publicity to the town and made a fortune selling Álamos real estate. A number of norteamericanos crossed the border, bought the crumbling old mansions for good prices and set about the task of lovingly restoring them to their former glory. Many of these people still live in Álamos today.

Orientation

The paved road from Navojoa enters Álamos from the west and leads to the green, shady Plaza Alameda, with outdoor cafés at either end where you can get a drink and sit and watch the world go by. The market is at the east end of Plaza Alameda; the other main square, Plaza de Armas, is two blocks south of the market.

The Arroyo La Aduana (Customs House Stream, which is usually dry) runs along the town's northern edge; the Arroyo Agua Escondida (Hidden Waters Stream, also usually dry) runs along the southern edge. Both converge at the east end of town with the Arroyo La Barranca (Ravine Stream), which runs, dryly, from the northwest.

Information

BOOKSTORES

Books about Álamos, and a variety of other books in English, are available at **El Nicho Artesanías y Curios** (cnr Juárez & Parroquia) behind the cathedral, at the gift shop of the Hotel Casa de los Tesoros, and at Los Amigos B&B. *A Brief History of Álamos* is an excellent source of information on the town. *The Stately Homes of Álamos* by Leila Gillette tells stories of many of the town's old homes. *The Álamos Guide* by BK Hamma and Donna McGee has tons of practical information for visitors as well as potential residents.

INTERNET ACCESS

Compulmagen (Morelos 39; per hr US$1; 7:30am-10:30pm Mon-Sat)

MONEY

BanCrecer (Madero 37; 9am-2pm Mon-Fri for money exchange) This bank also has an ATM.

POST

Post office (Palacio de Gobierno, Juárez; 9am-3pm Mon-Fri)

TOURIST INFORMATION

Tourist office (428-04-50; Juárez 6; 8am-3pm) Under the Hotel Los Portales on the west side of Plaza de Armas.

Sights & Activities

The **cathedral** is the tallest building in Álamos and also one of its oldest – construction lasted from 1786 to 1804 on the site of an early 17th-century adobe Jesuit mission. Legend relates that every family in Álamos contributed to the construction of the church. Inside, the altar rail, lamps, censers and candelabra were fashioned from silver, but were all ordered to be melted down in 1866 by General Ángel Martínez after he booted out French imperialist troops from Álamos. Subterranean passageways between the church and several of the mansions – probably built as escape routes for the safety of the rich families in time of attack – were blocked off in the 1950s.

The **Museo Costumbrista de Sonora** (428-00-53; Plaza de Armas; admission US$1; 9am-6pm Wed-Sun), on the east side of the plaza, is a fine little museum with exhibits on the history and traditions of the people of Sonora. Special attention is paid to mining's influence on Álamos and the fleeting prosperity it created.

Atop a small hill on the south side of town, **El Mirador** offers a privileged view of Álamos and its environs. To get there, take the walking trail that ascends from the Arroyo Agua Escondida next to Los Sabinos restaurant. Alternatively, you can walk up on paved roads that ascend from the left side of Juarez south of the Plaza de Armas.

Craig Leonard (☎ 428-01-42) offers Río Mayo rafting trips from December to March. **Felipe Acosta** (☎ 428-01-82), who runs a hunting lodge, offers bird-watching or bird-hunting trips and horseback riding. Another option for riding is **Caballos de Álamos** (☎ 428-09-26), which offers guided, half- and full-day rides to La Aduana and other area attractions.

Tours

The **Home & Garden Tour**, sponsored by Los Amigos de la Educación, starts at 10am Saturday in front of the museum. The tour costs US$10 and is given from around mid-October to mid-May.

At other times, Álamos' tour guides can take you to some of the homes. Álamos has six professional tour guides. Ask at the tourist office; a two-hour tour costs around US$9 per person. One-hour tours of the superb **Hacienda de los Santos** (see opposite) take place at 2pm daily for US$5.

Solipaso Excursions & Tourist Services (☎ /fax 428-04-66; www.solipaso.com; Cárdenas 15) offers nature tours including trips on the Río Mayo and Sea of Cortez and to the former silver mining town of La Aduana. It also leads bird-watching, hiking and historical tours from October through May, and operates La Ciudadela hotel (see following).

Festivals & Events

The Festival Dr Alfonso Ortíz Tirado, a high-quality cultural festival held the last 10 days of January, attracts thousands of visitors each year. The fiesta of the Virgen de Concepción, the town's patron saint, is December 8. Singing competitions are held December 4 to 14. Traditional *posadas* (processions) begin on December 16 and continue to Christmas Eve.

Sleeping

Out of all the towns in northwest Mexico, Álamos has the most interesting and attractive accommodations. With the exception of the Posada de Don Andrés, the hotels in the mid-range and top end categories inhabit restored colonial buildings and offer discounts during the summer months.

BUDGET

Acosta Trailer Rancho (☎ 428-02-46; fax 428-02-79; cnr 5 de Mayo & Guadalupe Posada; tent/trailer sites US$6/8-15, r US$58; ☒) About 1km east of the town center, the Acosta has 20 sites with full hookups, barbecue areas, shady trees and two swimming pools. It also has eight comfy rooms (for up to three people). The surrounding woods are a bird-watcher's paradise.

Doña Elia Salazar (☎ 428-01-44; Rosales 67; d & tr US$20) rents out rooms in her well-maintained home, offering a nice alternative to the excesses of the prettified mansions. The tourist office keeps a list of other *casas particulares* (private homes) that rent out rooms.

MID-RANGE

La Ciudadela (☎ 428-04-66; www.solipaso.com; Cárdenas 15; r US$75-125, 'dungeon' room US$40) An elegant guesthouse just off Plaza de Armas, this was the first jail in Álamos and is one of its oldest buildings. One of the four rooms is expandable to a two-room suite. It also has a secluded casita in the back.

Posada de Don Andrés (☎ 428-11-10; Rosales 24; d/tr US$46/58; ☒) One of the few Mexican-run hotels in town, this well-priced and welcome addition to Álamos' lodging scene is run by Jorge Álvarez Ramos, an artist and musician whose works are displayed throughout the place and whose friends sometimes come in the early evenings to make music.

La Puerta Roja Inn (☎ 428-01-42; www.lapuerta rojainn.com; Galeana 46; r US$65-75 including breakfast, casita with kitchen US$50; ℗) This gorgeous 150-year-old home is filled with wacky art and pleasing aromas emanating from the kitchen. The proprietor, a seasoned expat who welcomes pets and children, is a talented cook who serves famous breakfasts and lunches. The four rooms are colorful and beautifully appointed.

Casa de María Felix (☎ 428-09-29; www.casade mariafelix.com; Galeana 41; r US$69-92; ☒ ☎) This zealously-decorated place is built among the ruins of the original homestead of film icon María Felix, 'Mexico's Marilyn Monroe.' Children and pets are welcome.

Hotel Los Portales (☎ 428-02-11; Juárez 6; s/d US$30/60) The restored mansion of the Almada family, on the west side of Plaza de Armas, is the least impressive of Álamos' Spanish colonial buildings – but still a fine place.

TOP END

Hotel Casa de los Tesoros (☎ 428-00-10; www.tesoros -hotel.com; Obregón 10; d & tr US$92-120; 🏊) Formerly an 18th-century convent, this is now a handsome hotel with a swimming pool, cozy bar and courtyard restaurant with weekend entertainment. All rooms have fireplaces, and most have three beds, making it a good choice for families.

Los Amigos (☎ 428-10-14; www.alamosmexico .com/losamigos; Obregón 3; s/d US$75/87 including continental breakfast; 🏊) Los Amigos is a B&B, cafe, gallery and bookstore all in one small, 200-year-old restored colonial building. It rents out three large rooms and has a small pool and a sizable book exchange. Those on a budget are allowed to camp on the roof (US$5, US$10 with cot).

Hotel La Mansión (☎ 428-02-21; Obregón 2; r US$85-96) The beautiful La Mansión has rooms with king-size beds and chimneys around a sunny courtyard.

Hacienda de los Santos Hotel & Spa (☎ 428-02-17, toll-free from the US 800-525-4800; www.hacienda delossantos.com; Molina 8; r US$230-1000; 🏊 🍴) The most luxurious hotel in Álamos, the Hacienda de los Santos has three swimming pools, a gym, spa treatments, restaurant, bar and beautiful courtyards (see following).

Eating

Some of the cheapest food can be had at the food stalls in and around the market.

Panadería La Moderna (Macías s/n; bread & pastries US$0.50) Across the Arroyo La Aduana on the north edge of town, this is Álamos' favorite bakery. The best time to come is around 1pm, when the baked goods emerge from the outdoor oven.

La Kazeta Café, a simple snack bar on the west end of Plaza Alameda, is a nice place to watch the people.

Restaurant Las Palmeras (☎ 428-00-65; Cárdenas 9; meals US$3.50-8) This place on the north side of Plaza de Armas is a town favorite. The food is tasty, the prices are good, and

the dining rooms are spacious and warm in feeling. The diverse dessert menu is icing on the cake.

Polo's Restaurant (☎ 428-00-01; Zaragoza 4; mains US$5-9; ☻ 7am-9pm) The food and prices here are comparable to those at Las Palmeras, and some dishes – such as steaks – are superior. What it lacks is atmosphere.

Los Sabinos (dinners US$3-7.50) This place, on the edge of Arroyo Agua Escondida, consists of a few tables on a family's front porch. It offers a variety of *antojitos* (light dishes such as quesadillas or tostadas) and seafood or meat dishes.

The restaurant/bar at the **Hacienda de los Santos** (see earlier) serves breakfast, lunch, dinner and Sunday brunch, and a trio provides music every evening. Reservations are required. At **Hotel Casa de los Tesoros** (see earlier), you can dine in the air-conditioned restaurant, on the courtyard, or in the cozy bar. Indigenous dances are performed Saturday nights in winter; there's live dinner music all other evenings in winter, but only on Saturday in summer.

Shopping

Occupying a former silk factory behind the cathedral, **El Nicho Artesanías y Curios** (cnr Juárez & Parroquia) is a fascinating shop brimming with antiques, curios, folk art and handicrafts from all over Mexico.

A *tianguis* (flea market) is held from about 6am to 2pm Sunday beside the Arroyo La Aduana on the north side of town.

Getting There & Away

Access to Álamos is via Hwy 13 from Navojoa. Transportes Baldomero Corral and other bus companies have frequent service to Álamos (p313).

Álamos' Transportes Baldomero Corral bus station is on the north side of Plaza Alameda. Buses depart for Navojoa (US$2, one hour) at 4am, half-hourly from 6am to 12:30pm, hourly from 12:30pm to 6:30pm and at 9:15pm. A bus to Phoenix departs nightly at 9:15pm (US$52, 14 hours).

There's a taxi stand on the east end of Plaza Alameda, opposite the market.

AROUND ÁLAMOS

El Chalatón, a park about 2km southwest of town, is popular for swimming in summer. About 10km east of town, **Arroyo de**

Cuchujaqui has a delightful swimming hole and is enjoyable for fishing, camping and bird-watching. **Presa El Mocuzari** is also good for swimming, camping and fishing, with abundant largemouth bass, bluegill and catfish. Take the turnoff on the Navojoa-Álamos road, about 20km west of Álamos; the reservoir is about 12km from the turnoff.

Several small historic villages near Álamos make interesting day excursions. Check out **Minas Nuevas**, about 9km from Álamos on the Navojoa-Álamos road; the bus to Navojoa will drop you off there for US$0.70. La Aduana, the mine that once made Álamos rich, is also worth a visit. You can visit all these places on your own, or the tourist office can arrange a guide to take you.

Casa La Aduana Gourmet Restaurant & Inn (☎ 642-482-25-25; www.casaladuana.com; d/ste with breakfast US$65/85, d/ste with breakfast & dinner US$100/120, meals US$16-25) In La Aduana, on the plaza in front of the church, this inn has rustic rooms with fireplaces, but the real reason to come here is the lauded restaurant specializing in international gourmet meals. Allow about two hours for a four-course meal; reservations recommended. Closed in May and June.

LOS MOCHIS

☎ 668 / pop 207,000

Many travelers pass through Los Mochis (Place of Turtles), because it's the western terminus of the famous Ferrocarril Chihuahua al Pacífico (Chihuahua-Pacific Railway), which runs through the Barranca del Cobre (Copper Canyon) region. Topolobampo, 24km southwest of Los Mochis, is the mainland terminus of a ferry (departures at midnight) which runs services to La Paz, Baja California.

Los Mochis is a modern city without much history. It was founded in 1903 by American Benjamin Johnston, who established sugarcane plantations and a sugar factory here. Although without remarkable tourist attractions, its streets are alive with the hustle and bustle of an up-and-coming, predominantly middle class Mexican city. Grab a refreshing *raspado* (shaved ice with fruit syrup) and a bench on Blvd Castro and watch the wheels of commerce turn, with an expression befitting of one who has time for such things.

Orientation

The streets are laid out on a grid. The main street through the city, running southwest from Hwy 15D directly into the center of town, changes names from Calz López Mateos to Leyva as it enters the center. If you are coming from Topolobampo, you will enter the city center on Blvd Castro, another major artery. Some blocks in the center are split by smaller streets (not shown on the Los Mochis map) running parallel to the main streets.

Information

INTERNET ACCESS

Two good places from which to email your boss to announce that you're never coming home:

Hugo's Internet Café (Leyva 537; per hr US$1.25; 🕑 8am-9pm Mon-Sat)

Tito Café Internet (Blvd Castro 337; per hr US$1; 🕑 10am-10pm Mon-Sat)

LAUNDRY

Lavamatic (Allende 228 Sur; 🕑 7:30am-7pm Mon-Sat, 8am-1pm Sun)

MONEY

Banks are dotted around the city center. Some will not cash traveler's checks.

Bital (cnr Independencia & Leyva; 🕑 9am-5pm Mon-Fri) Will cash traveler's checks.

Bancomer (cnr Leyva & Juárez) Has an ATM.

Servicio de Cambio (Obregón 423 & Leyva 271) *Casas de cambio*, which have longer opening hours than banks.

Viajes Araceli (☎ 812-20-84; www.viajesaracely.com; Obregón 471A Pte) Amex agency.

POST

Post office (Ordoñez btwn Zaragoza & Prieto; 🕑 8am-3pm Mon-Fri, 8am-noon Sat)

TELEPHONE

Telephone/fax casetas (Leyva btwn Obregón & Hidalgo and Allende near Hidalgo) Both offer discounts after 8pm.

TOURIST INFORMATION

Tourist office (☎ 816-20-15; tursina@prodigy.net.mx; 🕑 9am-4pm Mon-Fri) On the ground floor of the large government building on Allende at Ordoñez. Very helpful.

Sights & Activities

Plazuela 27 de Septiembre is a pleasant plaza which has shady trees and a gazebo. It's

NORTHWEST MEXICO

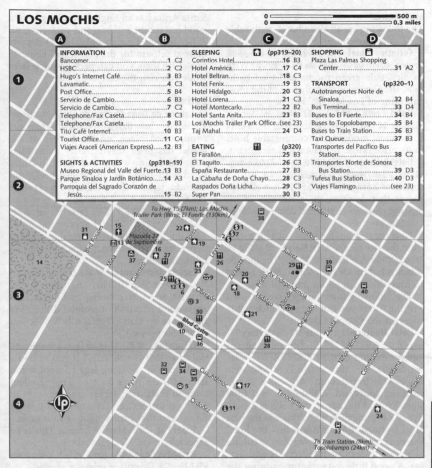

LOS MOCHIS

INFORMATION	
Bancomer	1 C2
HSBC	2 C2
Hugo's Internet Café	3 B3
Lavamatic	4 C3
Post Office	5 B4
Servicio de Cambio	6 B3
Servicio de Cambio	7 C2
Telephone/Fax Caseta	8 C3
Telephone/Fax Caseta	9 B3
Tito Café Internet	10 B3
Tourist Office	11 C4
Viajes Araceli (American Express)	12 B3

SIGHTS & ACTIVITIES	(pp318–19)
Museo Regional del Valle del Fuerte	13 B3
Parque Sinaloa y Jardín Botánico	14 A3
Parroquia del Sagrado Corazón de Jesús	15 B2

SLEEPING	(pp319–20)
Corintios Hotel	16 B3
Hotel América	17 C4
Hotel Beltran	18 C3
Hotel Fenix	19 B3
Hotel Hidalgo	20 C3
Hotel Lorena	21 C3
Hotel Montecarlo	22 B2
Hotel Santa Anita	23 B3
Los Mochis Trailer Park Office	(see 23)
Taj Mahal	24 D4

EATING	(p320)
El Farallón	25 B3
El Taquito	26 C3
España Restaurante	27 C3
La Cabaña de Doña Chayo	28 C3
Raspados Doña Licha	29 C3
Super Pan	30 B3

SHOPPING	
Plaza Las Palmas Shopping Center	31 A2

TRANSPORT	(pp320–1)
Autotransportes Norte de Sinaloa	32 B4
Bus Terminal	33 D4
Buses to El Fuerte	34 B4
Buses to Topolobampo	35 B4
Buses to Train Station	36 B3
Taxi Queue	37 B3
Transportes del Pacífico Bus Station	38 C2
Transportes Norte de Sonora Bus Station	39 D3
Tufesa Bus Station	40 D3
Viajes Flamingo	(see 23)

in front of the **Parroquia del Sagrado Corazón de Jesús**, on the corner of Obregón and Mina. With their brilliant white façade and graceful tower, the church and the plazuela make a lovely couple. **Parque Sinaloa y Jardín Botánico**, a large park and botanical garden, is behind and to the left of the big Plaza Las Palmas shopping center at the intersection of Blvds Castro and Rosales. There is also a small museum, the **Museo Regional del Valle del Fuerte** (cnr Blvd Rosales & Obregón; admission US$0.50, free on Sunday; ☺ 10am-1pm & 4-7pm Tue-Sat, 10am-1pm Sun), which has somewhat static exhibits (Spanish language only) on the history and culture of northwest Mexico. At the entrance is a small bookstore.

Sleeping
BUDGET
Pitch a tent or park an RV at **Los Mochis Trailer Park** (☎ 812-68-17; fax 812-00-46; Calz López Mateos; tent/rv sites US$14/18; P) The park, 1km west of Hwy 15D, has 120 spaces with full hookups. You can reserve and pay at the **Trailer Park office** (☎ 812-00-21; Hidalgo 419C Pte), on the ground floor of the Hotel Santa Anita; the office entrance is around the corner from the hotel entrance.

Hotel Hidalgo (☎ 818-34-53; hhidalgo@lmm.megared.net.mx; 2nd floor, Hidalgo 260 Pte; s/d US$21/24, r with fan US$16; P 🕸) Between Zaragoza and Prieto, the Hidalgo has small and somewhat basic rooms. Watch your head on the stairway.

MID-RANGE

The following are all clean hotels with cable TV in the rooms.

Corintios Hotel (☎ 818-22-24; 800-690-30-00; Obregón 580 Pte; s/d US$57/64, ste US$71-98; 🐱) With its airy, pale green rooms and tiled bathtubs, the Corintios is easily one of the most charming of Los Mochis' hotels.

Hotel Fenix (☎ 812-26-23; Flores 365 Sur; s/d US$27/32; 🐱) Recently remodeled, the Fenix is the most modern and comfortable hotel in its price range. It has a small restaurant.

Hotel Beltran (☎ 812-07-10; fax 815-71-00; Hidalgo 281 Pte; s/d US$34/40; 🐱) Hotel Beltran, on the corner of Zaragoza, has 55 clean, well-kept rooms that don't smell as strongly of industrial cleanser as the rest of the hotels in Los Mochis do.

Near the new bus terminal but a long walk from the city center is **Taj Mahal** (☎ 818-70-95; Obregón 400 Ote; d/ste US$51/71; 🐱 🖳) The outside is tacky, but inside the rooms are clean and comfortable, with phone and bathtubs.

The following three hotels have enclosed parking where you can leave a vehicle while you visit the Copper Canyon.

Hotel Montecarlo (☎ /fax 812-18-18; Flores 322 Sur; s/d US$25/30; P 🐱) A cheerful blue colonial building at the corner of Av Independencia, the Montecarlo is an old-style place with basic rooms around a sunny enclosed courtyard. Although it is a little worn around the edges, the hotel is evocative of a bygone time when this was the best hotel in town. Rumor has it that the hotel bar once counted as its regulars a coterie of notable Mexican intellectuals and artists. A good little restaurant rounds out the offerings to make this the most interesting mid-range lodging option in town.

Hotel Lorena (☎ 812-02-39; Obregón 186 Pte; s/d US$26/31; P 🐱) This adequate hotel, on the corner of Prieto, has impressively wide hallways and an inexpensive upstairs restaurant, open for breakfast from 7am to 11am.

Hotel América (☎ 812-13-55; fax 812-59-83; Allende 655 Sur; s/d US$35/41; P 🐱) Between Blvd Castro and Cuauhtémoc, the Hotel América has clean, nondescript rooms and a little restaurant. Rooms at the rear are quieter.

TOP END

Hotel Santa Anita (☎ 818-70-46; fax 812-00-46; santa anita@mexicoscoppercanyon.com; cnr Leyva & Hidalgo; s/d US$112/129, ste US$140; P 🐱) The overpriced Santa Anita has an English-speaking staff, a good restaurant and bar, and a travel agent. A bus for hotel guests only (US$7) departs daily at 5:15am for the Ferrocarril Chihuahua al Pacífico; you can park a vehicle here while you visit the canyon.

Eating

La Cabaña de Doña Chayo (☎ 818-54-98; Obregón 99 Pte; prices from US$1.50; 🕙 9-1am) This air-conditioned place, on the corner of Allende, has been serving tasty quesadillas and handmade carne and flour tortillas filled with *carne asada* (grilled beef) and *machaca* (spiced shredded dried beef) since 1963. Call and it will deliver.

El Taquito (☎ 817-23-95; Leyva 333 Sur; dishes US$2.75-6; 🕙 24hr; 🗙) The economical El Taquito, located between Hidalgo and Independencia, has retro booths and a varied bilingual menu.

España Restaurante (☎ 812-22-21; Obregón 525 Pte; mains from US$7-16) This restaurant serves Spanish and international cuisine, including a good selection of seafood dishes. Try the house specialty, Paella a la Valenciana (US$9.50/person).

El Farallón (☎ 812-12-73; cnr Flores & Obregón; seafood dinners US$7-11, sushi US$5-7) If you've had a hankering for bullfrog legs (c'mon, admit it), this is the place for you. This excellent seafood restaurant serves creative sushi in addition to Mexican favorites, and it has a liquor cart that comes right to your table.

Super Pan (cnr Blvd Castro & Zaragoza) This is an especially good Mexican bakery.

Raspados Doña Licha (cnr Allende & Juárez; prices US$1.25-1.50) This place serves *raspados*.

Getting There & Away

AIR

The airport is about 12km southwest of the city, on the road to Topolobampo. Daily direct flights (all with connections to other cities) are offered by **Aeroméxico/Aerolitoral** (☎ 815-25-70; at the airport) to Chihuahua, Hermosillo, La Paz, Los Cabos and Mazatlán. **Aero California** (☎ 818-16-16; at the airport) flies to Ciudad Obregón, Culiacán, Guadalajara, Hermosillo, La Paz, Mexico City and Tijuana.

BOAT

Ferries go from nearby Topolobampo to La Paz, Baja California Sur. They leave at midnight on Sunday through Friday. Tick-

ets are sold at the **Baja Ferries** office (www
.bajaferries.com.mx) at the ferry terminal in
Topolobampo (p321).

BUS

Los Mochis is on Hwy 15D; several major
bus lines offer hourly buses heading north
and south, 24 hours a day. Elite, Futura,
Turistar, TAP (Transportes y Autobuses del
Pacífico) and Transportes Chihuahuenses
(all 1st class) share a large new **bus terminal**
(☎ 815-00-62; cnr Blvd Castro & Constitución) several
blocks east of the center. Other 1st-class bus
lines have their own terminals. **Transportes
Norte de Sonora** (☎ 812-03-41) is on Degollado
at Juárez. **Transportes del Pacífico** (☎ 812-57-49)
is on Morelos between Zaragoza and Leyva.
All serve the same destinations.

Distances, times and 1st-class fares include the following: Guadalajara (US$40 to
US$46, 13 hours), Guaymas (US$12.50 to
US$15, five hours), Hermosillo (US$17.50
to US$22, seven hours), Mazatlán (US$23
to US$28, six hours), Mexico City (US$70 to
US$85, 23 hours), Navojoa (US$6 to US$7,
two hours), Nogales (US$30 to US$36, 11
hours), Tepic (US$35 to US$40, 11 hours),
and Tijuana (US$50 to US$56, 19 hours).

Tufesa (☎ 818-22-22) is on Zapata between
Juárez and Morelos. It only goes north to
Nogales and south to Culiacán and has
fewer buses. **Autotransportes Norte de Sinaloa**
(☎ 818-03-57), on the corner of Zaragoza and
Ordoñez, has 2nd-class buses going south
to Culiacán and Mazatlán.

The second-class buses (US$1/2, 45 min-
utes) to central Topolobampo/ the ferry terminal leave from Cuauhtémoc at the corner
of Prieto. Departures are every 30 minutes
between 6am and 8pm. Second-class buses
to El Fuerte (US$4.50, two hours) leave
from the corner of Zaragoza on the same
block of Cuauhtémoc. Departures are at
7:30am, 9am, 10:30am, 11:30am, 12:30pm,
2:30pm, 3:25pm, 3:45pm, 4:30pm, 4:45pm,
5:30pm, 6pm, 7:30pm and 8pm.

TRAIN

The **train station** in Los Mochis is 8km east of
the center on Serrano. The ticket window is
open from 5am to 7am daily for the morning's departures toward the Copper Canyon
and Chihuahua. Tickets are also sold inside
the office (☎ 824-11-51; fax 824-11-67; ⏰ 9am-
5:30pm Mon-Fri, 9am-12:30pm Sat & 9-11:30am Sun).

You can buy primera express (1st class)
tickets up to one week in advance of travel.
Tickets for clase económica (economy class)
trains are sold an hour before the train departs, or the day before. You can also purchase
tickets for either class one day in advance
through **Viajes Flamingo** (☎ 812-16-13; www.mex
icoscoppercanyon.com) at Hotel Santa Anita. It
sells tickets for both classes of travel plus a
5% fee, and another 5% service charge for
credit cards.

The primera express train leaves Los Mochis at 6am, clase económica at 7am. See
p324 for fares and detailed schedules.

Getting Around

Nearly everything of interest to travelers in
Los Mochis is within walking distance of
the city center.

Taxis queue up on Obregón adjacent to
Plazuelita 27 de Septiembre. A taxi to the
airport costs approximately US$12. One de-
pendable provider is **EcoTaxi** (☎ 817-11-05).

'Estación' buses to the train station
(US$0.40, 20 minutes) depart every five min-
utes between 5:30am and 8:30pm from Blvd
Castro, between Zaragoza and Prieta. You
can take the bus to get to the station for
the clase económica train, which departs
at 7am, but for the 6am primera express
departure it is probably safer to fork out
US$9 for a taxi to get to the station in plenty
of time. If arriving in Los Mochis by train,
you can catch a group taxi to the city center
for US$4.

TOPOLOBAMPO

☎ 668 / pop 7300

Topolobampo, 24km southwest of Los Mochis, is the terminus for a ferry route to/from
La Paz, Baja California. Mexicans love to
come here to eat fresh seafood (both in town
and at Playa El Maviri), go to the beach and
enjoy the town's natural surroundings.

For lodging, the only game in town is
the **Hotel Marina** (☎ 862-01-00; Albert K Owen 33 Pte;
r US$35), a new, comfortable hotel with a large
pool and restaurant. It's easy to find; just
follow the signs to the town center.

A 20-minute bus ride from Topolobampo
is **Playa El Maviri**, a popular beach with plenty
of seafood restaurants. Everyone recommends the *pescado zarandeado* (charcoal-
grilled fish wrapped in foil). On the way
to Playa El Maviri, you pass the **Cueva de los**

Murciélagos (Cave of Bats); you cannot enter this protected area, but it's beautiful to see the bats emerging at sunset and returning at sunrise.

Inexpensive *lanchas* (small motorized boats) will take you from either Topolobampo or Playa El Maviri to some beautiful natural spots that attract large populations of the animals they are named for. **Isla de Pájaros** is home to hundreds of birds, and **Santuario de Delfines** is a dolphin sanctuary. Other spots include **Playa Las Copas**, **Isla Santa María** with dunes where you can camp, and **Isla El Farallón** with seals and sea lions.

Ferry tickets are sold the day of departure by **Baja Ferries** (☎ 862-10-03; www.bajaferries .com; Topolobampo ferry terminal, Cerro de las Gallinas s/n; ☽ 9am-10pm Sun-Fri) Seats are US$58 in salón; cabina passengers pay the same rate with an additional US$71 fee for a group of up to four. Passenger ferries leave at 12am Sunday through Friday, arriving in La Paz at 5am. Returning ferries leave La Paz Monday through Friday at 4pm, arriving in Topolobampo at 9pm the same night, and on Saturday at midnight, arriving at 5am Sunday morning. See p284 for vehicle fares.

Viajes Flamingo (☎ 815-61-20; Leyva 121 Sur, Los Mochis) sells tickets up to a month in advance.

BARRANCA DEL COBRE (COPPER CANYON)

The name Barranca del Cobre (Copper Canyon) refers specifically to the awe-inspiring canyon of the Río Urique, southeast of the village of Divisadero, and generally to this and more than 20 nearby canyons carved out of the Sierra Tarahumara by at least six different rivers. Together, these canyons are four times larger than Arizona's Grand Canyon. Nine of them are deeper than it is. At an altitude of only 500m, the canyons' deepest point (Barranca de Urique, depth 1879m) has a subtropical climate, while the peaks high above are 2300m above sea level and home to conifers and evergreens. One of Mexico's most numerous indigenous peoples, the Tarahumara, still retains a traditional lifestyle here (see 'The Tarahumara').

The most popular way to see the canyons is by riding the Ferrocarril Chihuahua al Pacífico (Chihuahua-Pacific Railway, also known as the Copper Canyon Railway), which travels between Los Mochis near the Sea of Cortez and Chihuahua in the interior of northern Mexico. There are several stops in the Barranca del Cobre area.

Creel (p329), approximately eight hours from Los Mochis, is probably the best place in the Barranca del Cobre region to break the journey and explore the canyon. It's only a small town but it has several economical places to stay and plenty of tours and things to do.

Between Los Mochis and Creel, the charming town of El Fuerte is a good alternative starting point for your journey. Once in the canyons, overnight stays are possible at Cerocahui, Urique, Posada Barrancas and Divisadero, allowing you 24 hours before the train passes by again – time enough to get a closer look and explore the canyons.

Many travelers prefer to visit the area in spring or autumn, when the temperatures are not too hot at the bottom of the canyon (as in summer), or too cold at the top (as in winter).

A particularly good time to visit is late September and October (after the summer rains), when the vegetation is still green. Things dry up February to June, but you can still see some wildflowers.

FERROCARRIL CHIHUAHUA AL PACÍFICO (COPPER CANYON RAILWAY)

Many travelers consider the Ferrocarril Chihuahua al Pacífico to be among the world's most scenic rail journeys. A considerable feat of engineering, it has 36 bridges and 87 tunnels along 655km of railway line, connecting the mountainous, arid interior of northern Mexico with the Pacific coast. It was opened in 1961 after taking many decades to build. The major link between Chihuahua and the coast, the line is used heavily by passengers and for shipping freight. The beauty of the landscape it traverses – one of sweeping vistas, sheer canyon walls, flowing waterfalls and high desert plains – has made it one of the country's prime tourist excursions as well.

The Ferrocarril Chihuahua al Pacífico (CHEPE, which is pronounced *che*-pe) operates two trains: the first-class primera ex-

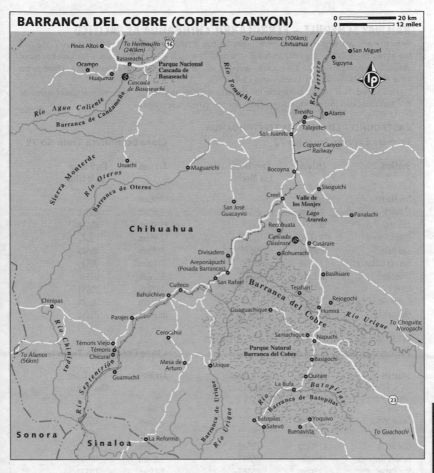

BARRANCA DEL COBRE (COPPER CANYON)

press, which costs twice as much but makes fewer stops and has a restaurant, bar and reclining seats; and the cheaper and slower clase económica, which has food provided by vendors and a snack bar. Cars on both trains have air-con and heating. It takes about 14 hours to make the trip on the primera express, and at least two hours longer on the clase económica, which stops frequently along the way.

If you're heading toward Los Mochis from Chihuahua, consider taking the primera express, as the clase económica, which runs later and is often late, and passes much of the best scenery (between Creel and Loreto) after dark, especially in winter when the sun sets earlier. Heading in the other

direction, you should be able to see the best views on either train, unless the clase económica is excessively delayed.

The majority of the good views are on the right side of the carriage heading inland (east), while the left side is best for trips going to the coast (west). Passengers often congregate in the vestibules between cars (where the windows open) to take photos.

Between Los Mochis and El Fuerte, the train passes through flat, gray farmland. Shortly after El Fuerte, it begins to climb through fog-shrouded hills speckled with dark pillars of cacti. It passes over the long Río Fuerte bridge and through the first of 87 tunnels about three hours after leaving Los Mochis. It cuts through small canyons and

RAILWAY SCHEDULE – FERROCARRIL CHIHUAHUA AL PACÍFICO

Both the primera express and clase económica trains run every day. Trains tend to run late and the times given below are only an ideal schedule. The clase económica train, which makes more stops, is virtually never on time, often arriving at the end of the line around 1am. There is no time change between Los Mochis and Chihuahua.

This schedule is only a guideline for departure times and fares. Check with a travel agent or the train stations in the originating cities for the latest schedules.

EASTBOUND – LOS MOCHIS TO CHIHUAHUA

Station	Primera Express Train No 73 Arrives	Fare from Los Mochis	Clase Económica Train No 75 Arrives	Fare from Los Mochis
Los Mochis	6:00am	–	7:00am	–
El Fuerte	7:26am	US$22	8:40am	US$10
Témoris	10:11am	US$36	11:35am	US$18
Bahuichivo	11:12am	US$43	12:45pm	US$22
San Rafael	12:05pm	US$48	1:40pm	US$25
Posada Barrancas	12:25pm	US$50	2:10pm	US$25
Divisadero	12:35pm	US$51	2:25pm	US$26
Creel	2:14pm	US$60	4:05pm	US$31
Cuauhtémoc	5:25pm	US$80	7:45pm	US$44
Chihuahua	7:50pm	US$112	10:25pm	US$56

WESTBOUND – CHIHUAHUA TO LOS MOCHIS

Station	Primera Express Train No 74 Arrives	Fare from Chihuahua	Clase Económica Train No 76 Arrives	Fare from Chihuahua
Chihuahua	6:00am	–	7:00am	–
Cuauhtémoc	8:15am	US$23	9:25am	US$12
Creel	11:26am	US$52	1:00pm	US$26
Divisadero	12:45pm	US$62	2:30pm	US$31
Posada Barrancas	1:20pm	US$63	3:05pm	US$31
San Rafael	1:30pm	US$64	3:15pm	US$32
Bahuichivo	2:32pm	US$70	4:35pm	US$34
Témoris	3:30pm	US$77	5:35pm	US$38
El Fuerte	6:16pm	US$100	8:42pm	US$49
Los Mochis	7:50pm	US$112	10:25pm	US$56

hugs the sides of cliffs as it climbs higher and higher through the mountains of the Sierra Tarahumara. The highlight of the ride is when the train stops at Divisadero and you get your first and only glimpse of the actual Barranca del Cobre.

If you're traveling only between Creel and Chihuahua, you may prefer to take the bus, as it's quicker and the schedule is more convenient.

Tickets

Primera express tickets can be purchased up to one week in advance, while tickets for clase económica trains can only be purchased one day in advance. You can usually be pretty sure of getting a ticket a day or two before your departure, though you should allow longer than this for travel during Semana Santa, July or August, or at Christmas.

For a same-day primera express ticket, it's prudent to go to the ticket office by 5am. Tickets also can be bought on the train, but you run the risk that they might be sold out. Alternatively, the Viajes Flamingo travel agency (p320) at Hotel Santa Anita in Los Mochis sells tickets for both classes of travel plus a 5% fee, and another 5% service charge for credit cards.

Chihuahua train station (☎ 614-439-72-12; ticket window ☒ 5-7am & 9am-6pm Mon, Wed & Fri; 5-6am & 9am-6pm Tue & Thu; 5-6am & 9am-noon Sat & Sun)

Los Mochis train station (☎ 668-824-11-51; ticket window ☒ 5-7am & 9-5:30pm Mon-Fri; 5-7am & 9am-12:30pm Sat; 5-7am & 9-11:30am Sun)

EL FUERTE

☎ 698 / pop 11,000 / elevation 180m

El Fuerte (The Fort) is a picturesque colonial town notable for its colonial ambience and Spanish architecture. Many travelers find El Fuerte to be a good alternative to Los Mochis as a starting or ending point for a trip on the Ferrocarril Chihuahua al Pacífico.

Founded in 1564 by the Spanish conqueror Francisco de Ibarra, El Fuerte was an important Spanish settlement throughout the colonial period. For more than three centuries, it was a major farming and commercial center and trading post on El Camino Real, the Spanish mule trail between Guadalajara to the southeast, the mines of Álamos to the north and the Sierra Madre Occidental to the northeast. In 1824 El Fuerte became the capital of the state of Sinaloa, a title it retained for several years.

The **Palacio Municipal**, **plaza**, **church** and **Hotel Posada del Hidalgo** are El Fuerte's most notable features. You can get a great view of the town, the Río Fuerte and surrounding area by walking up the small **mirador** hill behind the Posada del Hidalgo, just off the plaza. At the top, there's a **replica of the original fort** for which El Fuerte was named. Excursions around El Fuerte include a three-hour round-trip (on your own or with a guide) to a set of petroglyphs. El Fuerte's two reservoirs (Domínguez and Hidalgo) are excellent for bass fishing.

Bancomer (cnr Constitución & Juárez; ☒ 8:30am-4pm Mon-Fri), one block off the plaza, cashes traveler's checks and has an ATM. To get online, albeit by a very slow connection, try **Cibercafé Portales** (per hr US$1) located just off the plaza on Degollado.

Sleeping

Unlike the Sonoran town of Álamos, El Fuerte has yet to fully mine its colonial charms for tourist dollars. Happily, this means a good choice of well-priced, quality accommodations.

At time of research, El Fuerte's first hostel was nearing completion: **Casa Pascola** (☎ 893-10-68; José Morelos 510; per hr US$20 with continental breakfast) has small simple rooms, a communal kitchen, and shared bathroom and showers.

Hotel La Herradura (☎ 893-01-35; Montesclaros s/n; s/d US$30/35; ☒) Only a stone's throw from the church, this new hotel is clean and well-run, with plenty of hot water.

Río Vista Lodge (☎ 893-04-13; Cerro de las Pilas s/n; s/d US$35/50; ☐ ☒) This quirky hotel, at the top of the mirador, does indeed have a lovely view of the river. Once the stables for the original fort, the Río Vista now has varnished stone walls covered with art and curios, and a small open-air restaurant frequented by travelers and hummingbirds alike.

Posada Don Porfirio (☎ 893-00-44; Juárez 104; s/d US$35/45; ☐ ☒) Conveniently located near the plaza, the Posada Don Porfirio has a copacetic courtyard and several pleasant rooms with high ceilings.

Hotel Hacienda San Francisco (☎ /fax 893-00-55; Obregón 201; s/d US$58/68) Located 2½ blocks from the plaza, this place has a timeless ambience and attractive rooms encircling a colorful courtyard full of flowers and caged birds.

There are several upscale lodging options in El Fuerte; chief among them is the **Hotel Posada del Hidalgo** (☎ 893-11-92; hotelposadadel hidalgo@prodigy.net; cnr Hidalgo & 5 de Mayo; s/d US$110/120; ☒ ☒). The rich silver-mining Almada family of Álamos had strong connections in El Fuerte. In 1890 Rafael Almada built an opulent mansion, which is now this hotel. It's in the center of El Fuerte behind the church. It has beautiful interior gardens, restaurant/bar and 50 rooms. Reservations can be made at Hotel Santa Anita in Los Mochis (see p319).

Eating

Langostino (crayfish) and *filete de lobina* (fillet of bass) are El Fuerte specialties.

Restaurant El Supremo (cnr Rosales & Constitución; mains US$2-7) One block off the plaza, this pleasant and inexpensive restaurant is family-run (in fact, the family sometimes runs through the restaurant).

El Mesón del General (☎ 893-02-60; Juárez 202; mains US$4-9) This bright restaurant – a favorite of El Fuerte locals and a former residence of revolutionary Don Pablo Valenzuela – serves specialties from the river and sea and six styles of *pulpo* (octopus).

Restaurante Diligencias (☎ 893-15-03; 5 de Mayo 101; mains US$4-9) This new restaurant serves fresh black bass stuffed, grilled, breaded or as a *ceviche* (raw fish marinated in lime or lemon juice). Also on hand are plenty of *langostino* and shrimp dishes. The only caveat is that tour buses often feed their noisy masses here.

There's also an opulent restaurant at **Hotel Posada del Hidalgo** (see p325).

For less expensive fare, try one of the many taco stands on 16 de Septiembre at Juárez near the bus stop.

Getting There & Around

In El Fuerte, buses to Los Mochis (US$4.50, two hours, 78km) depart every half hour between 6am and 7pm, from the corner of Juárez and 16 de Septiembre.

The train station is a few kilometers east of town. The official departure time for the eastbound primera express is 7:26am; clase económica leaves at around 8:40am. The westbound primera express leaves at 6:16pm and clase económica at 8:42pm. Tickets are sold on board. You can take a taxi to the station for about US$4.

CEROCAHUI

☎ 635 / pop 500 / elevation 1600m

Cerocahui, about 16km from the Bahuichivo train stop, is a picturesque village in a valley with apple and peach orchards and fir and madrone trees. Its pretty yellow-domed church, **San Francisco Javier de Cerocahui**, was founded in 1680 by the Jesuit Padre Juan María de Salvatierra. Today, Cerocahui is an *ejido* (communal landholding) dedicated to forestry. It boasts a few quality lodging options for different budgets, an orphanage for Tarahumaran children and an atmosphere of repose. While there is not a lot to do in Cerocahui proper, the surrounding countryside is an excellent place for bird-watching; over 168 species of birds have been spotted here. Hikers will enjoy

---

THE TARAHUMARA

More than 50,000 indigenous Tarahumara live in the Sierra Tarahumara's numerous canyons, including the famous Barranca del Cobre (Copper Canyon). Isolated within this formidable topography, the Tarahumara retain many of their traditions; many still live in caves and log cabins (some of these dwellings can be seen near Creel) and they subsist on very basic agriculture of maize and beans.

The Tarahumara are well known for their eye-catching traditional apparel, especially the women, who wear full, pleated skirts and blouses made of brightly colored, patterned fabric. The men wear loincloths and ample, long-sleeved shirts also made from bright fabric. Both men and women wear the traditional sandals – now made from tire tread and leather straps.

They are also famous for running long distances. Running is so significant to the Tarahumara's culture that in their own language they call themselves Rarámuri – 'those who run fast.' Traditionally, the Tarahumara hunted by chasing down and exhausting deer, then driving the animals over cliffs to be impaled on wooden sticks strategically placed at the bottom of the canyon. Today, they run grueling footraces of 160km (or more), without stopping, through rough canyons, kicking a small wooden ball ahead of them.

A tradition of quite a different sort is the *tesquinada*, a raucous gathering in which they consume copious amounts of tesquino, a potent maize beer.

Catholic missionaries have made some progress improving living conditions for the Tarahumara, but they haven't been entirely successful in converting them to Catholicism. Many of the Tarahumara attend church services, but continue to worship their ancestral gods, particularly Raiénari, the sun god and protector of men, and Mechá, the moon god and protector of women. Sorcerers are as important as Catholic priests and are the only members of the Tarahumara permitted to consume peyote, a hallucinogen derived from a small cactus. They often take peyote in order to perform a bizarre dance to cure the sick.

the gentle hills and interesting limestone outcroppings, or a memorable 8km round-trip hike to **Cerocahui Falls**.

Any of the hotels here can arrange trips into the canyon. There is a restaurant in town on the plaza.

Sleeping & Eating

Hotel Raramuri (s/d US$12/18) This small hotel on the far side of the church is clean, and is pretty popular with backpackers. The newer rooms on the bottom floor are graced with a balcony that looks over the schoolyard and its free-form mid-morning soccer games. The hotel doesn't have a phone, but you can contact it through the town **caseta** (☎ 456-06-19).

Hotel Plaza (s/d US$17/25) Filling a need for additional economical accommodations in Cerocahui, Hotel Plaza is a friendly new hotel just off the plaza; it has 11 tidy, comfortable rooms. Contact the hotel via the town caseta.

Hotel Misión (s/d US$162/238 including all meals) This former hacienda, with bar, restaurant, gardens and a small vineyard, is the oldest and best-known hotel in Cerocahui. The rooms here – all with fireplace – are certainly adequate and comfortable, but not really worth the price. Reservations are made at the **Hotel Santa Anita** (☎ 668-818-70-46) in Los Mochis.

Hotel Paraíso del Oso (☎ 614-421-33-72 in Chihuahua, 800-844-3107 from the USA; www.mexicohorse .com; s/d US$105/161 including meals, campsite/dorm beds US$5/10) Named after a nearby rock formation resembling a cartoon bear in a porkpie hat, Paraíso del Oso occupies a peaceful and picturesque spot 5km north of Cerocahui village. The scene here is one that emphasizes eco-tourism and cultural exchange. Camping sites are next to the river; campers may shower and arrange meals at the hotel. There is one dorm room with eight beds. The management can arrange horseback or hiking trips as far as Batopilas.

Margarita's Cerocahui Wilderness Lodge (s/d US$150/190 including all meals) This luxurious hotel, on a cliff about a 25-minute drive from Cerocahui, offers spectacular views. The brightly painted rooms have electricity but are lit with kerosene lamps for ambiance. Reservations must be made in advance through **Hotel Margarita's Plaza Mexicana** (☎ 635-456-02-45) in Creel.

Getting There & Away

All the hotels except Raramuri and the Hotel Plaza will pick you up at the Bahuichivo train station. If you're going to the Raramuri you can catch a ride with one of the other hotels' buses, or pick up a free ride by thumb. The daily minibus from Bahuichivo to Urique may drop you off in Cerocahui if it's not too full (see p327).

URIQUE

☎ 635 / elevation 550m

This village, at the bottom of the impressive Barranca de Urique, is also accessed from the Bahuichivo train stop and is a good base for all kinds of canyon hikes lasting anywhere from one to several days. The two- to three-day hike between Batopilas and Urique is a popular trek.

Urique has only a few accommodations choices. All three of these hotels can see to it that you are fed.

Hotel Cañón de Urique (☎ 456-60-24; Principal s/n; s/d US$10/15) This hotel, often recommended by travelers, is nothing fancy but it provides a good value. Inquire at the **Restaurante Gran Cañón de Urique** across the street from the hotel, where you can also get simple meals starting at 6am.

Hotel Estrella del Río (☎ 456-60-03; r US$30) This hotel has spacious, bright rooms with electric fans, plenty of hot water and a privileged view of the Río Urique. Inquire about rooms at Restaurant Plaza, across from the plaza.

Hotel Barrancas de Urique (☎ 456-60-76; Principal 201; r US$30) Urique's new, eager-to-please accommodation and dining choice is this tidy establishment, on the main road at the edge of the river. Rooms have fans and television and the restaurant has chicken and fish.

When he is in town, the personable Keith from America also rents out rooms and has a camping area at his ranch at the edge of town on the road to Guadalupe.

A minibus heads down to Urique from Bahuichivo train station once a day after the last train passes the station (around 5pm). The jarring ride (US$10, three hours) makes a breathtaking descent into the Barranca de Urique, the deepest of the canyons. It departs for the return trip at around 8am, so plan on staying for two nights. Alternatively, you may be able to arrange transportation with your hotel in Urique.

AREPONÁPUCHI (POSADA BARRANCAS)

☎ 635 / elevation 2220m

About 5km southwest of Divisadero, Posada Barrancas station is next to Areponápuchi, the only village on the train line that is right on the rim of the canyon. Often referred to as Arepo, this village has magnificent views of the canyon and several places to stay, and is a good point for going into the canyon by foot, car or horseback. As in Creel, most of the hotels will organize any kind of canyon trip you would like, be it a hike to the rim of the canyon, halfway or all the way down to the Río Urique. In Arepo, however, the guides are more flexible and it is easier to find one willing to accommodate your personal preferences and itinerary.

Sleeping & Eating

Lucy González (☎ 578-30-15) rents out rooms in Arepo, with TV, carpet and private hot bath, for US$35 per day. You will very likely find her at the Divisadero train station selling food; if you get off there, she'll make sure you get a ride to Arepo.

Cabañas Díaz (☎ 578-30-08; 1-3-person cabaña with shared/private bath US$30-60, 3-5-person cabaña with private bath US$70, large room with 8 bunks US$70, meals US$5; **P**) The Díaz family is probably best suited to arrange custom trips for groups of more than a few people. Their guest lodge is known for its hospitality, delicious meals and tranquil, relaxing atmosphere. If no one from the family comes to meet the train, just walk down the main road into the village until you see the sign on the right (about 10 minutes).

Copper Canyon Trailhead Inn (☎ 578-30-07; r US$25, dm US$5) The inn offers several small basic rooms, a bunkhouse right on the trail to the Río Urique, good meals in the home adjacent to the inn and guide services (apparently to anywhere in the Barrancas) that are very competitive in price. To find it, walk from the station to town and turn left at the shop.

Cabañas Arepo Barrancas (☎ 578-30-46; r US$35 with breakfast) A reader-recommended place offering basic rooms with two beds and a cozy restaurant. The guide services offered here are competitive in price. Call in advance to arrange transportation from the station.

Cabañas Portales (☎ 578-30-42; r US$30) Slightly less welcoming is this place, which also offers basic rooms with fireplaces and two beds to accommodate up to four people. You will find it near the highway on the road leading into town. Meals are available by arrangement.

Hotel Posada Barrancas (s/d US$70/84; **P**) This hotel, at the train stop, is just a five-minute walk from the viewpoint. Breakfast is included; other meals can be purchased at Hotel Posada Mirador's (p328) spectacular dining room. Accommodations reservations are made at the **Hotel Santa Anita** (☎ 668-818-70-46) in Los Mochis.

Hotel Mansión Tarahumara (☎ 614-415-47-21 in Chihuahua; mansion@buzon.online.com.mx; s/d US$120/175 incl all meals; **P** 🏊) Near the train station, this place is also known as El Castillo because it looks like a medieval stone castle. It has a variety of cozy, rustic cabins. The hotel has a Jacuzzi, pool, bar and restaurant, and small private lake. In the summer, prices decrease by about 25%.

Hotel Posada Mirador (www.mexicoscoppercanyon.com; s/d US$162/238; **P**) Perched on the rim of the canyon, the Posada Mirador has 51 luxury rooms and suites – all with private terraces and magnificent views. Reservations are made at the **Hotel Santa Anita** (☎ 668-818-70-46) in Los Mochis.

Getting There & Away

See p322 for information on getting to Posada Barrancas by train. Buses between San Rafael and Creel will drop you off in Areponápuchi at the highway entrance (p333). The bus is much faster and cheaper than the train, but the center of town is a couple of kilometers from the highway and there are no taxis in town.

DIVISADERO

elevation 2240m

About seven hours out of Los Mochis, the train stops for 15 minutes at Divisadero for an excellent view of the Barranca del Cobre. For the rest of the trip, the train runs through pine forests skirting the edge of canyons, but not close enough to see down into them. The viewpoint at Divisadero is the first and only chance you'll get to see into the 1760m-deep canyon from the train. This will also probably be the first time you will see some of the Tarahumara people who inhabit the canyon. When the train pulls into the station, the place springs into action. The Tarahumara appear, to display and sell their handicrafts to visitors, and several snack stalls compete to sell tempting tacos and tasty Tarahumaran fare from makeshift oil drum stoves burning aromatic pine wood.

Hotels in Divisadero organize short trips into the canyon, but you can arrange a far better deal yourself with one of the Tarahumara who meet the train to sell handicrafts and food. If you hire a guide, you must have your own food for the trip; there are two restaurants and some snack stalls, but no stores in Divisadero. Your guide will lead you 1000m down to the Río Urique. Carry enough water for the descent and be prepared for a change in climate from cool – Divisadero is 2240m high – to warm and humid near the river. Autumn is the best time to come; flash floods and suffocatingly high temperatures are a problem in summer. You can spend more time here if you switch from a primera express to clase económica train, which is roughly two hours behind. Be aware that you will need two separate tickets to do this. Alternatively, you could make the short walk or hitch a ride to Areponápuchi, where there are several well-priced lodging options.

Next to the viewpoint, **Hotel Divisadero Barrancas** (☎ 614-415-11-99 in Chihuahua; s/d US$174/210 incl meals) has 52 luxurious rooms, all with views of the canyon. Rates are substantially lower in the summer. The restaurant/bar, with a spectacular view, is open to the public. The hotel will arrange guided tours into the canyon.

Buses between San Rafael and Creel will drop you off at Divisadero (see Getting There & Around in the Creel section for more information). For information on getting to Divisadero by train, see the p322.

CREEL

☎ 635 / pop 5000 / elevation 2338m

Creel, a pleasant small town surrounded by pine forests and interesting rock formations, is many travelers' favorite stop on the Ferrocarril Chihuahua al Pacífico. Its many hotels and guesthouses are brimming with travelers gearing up for excursions into the canyon, and thus it is a great place to meet like-minded people, exchange information, and stock up on maps and staples. From here you can catch a bus to Batopilas, a village 140km away deep in the heart of the Tarahumara canyon country, or arrange transport and guides to just about any place in the Barranca del Cobre. Creel is also a regional center for the Tarahumara people. You will see many Tarahumara in traditional dress, and numerous shops selling Tarahumara handicrafts.

Its high elevation means Creel can be very cold, even snowy, especially in winter. In summer, the cool air and piney aroma from the town's surrounding forests are a welcome relief from the heat of the tropical coastal lowlands or the deserts of northern Mexico.

Orientation

Creel is a very small town. Most things you need, including many hotels and restaurants, are on Av López Mateos, the town's main street, which leads south from the town plaza, where there are two churches, the post office, the bank and the Artesanías Misión shop. The train station is one block north of the plaza. Across the tracks are a couple more hotels and restaurants and the bus station.

Av Gran Visión is the highway through town; it heads northeast to Chihuahua and southeast to Guachochi, passing Lago Arareko and Cusárare. There is a paved road that runs southwest from Creel through Divisadero and on to San Rafael. Av López Mateos and Av Gran Visión intersect a couple of kilometers south of the center of town.

A large map of Creel is posted on the outside wall of Tarahumara Tours, on the main plaza. Maps of the surrounding area, including a series of topographical maps of the canyons, are sold at the Artesanías Misión shop. This shop also sells a number of fine books about the Barranca del Cobre and the Tarahumara, in Spanish and English.

Information

INTERNET ACCESS

CompuCenter (Av López Mateos 33; per hr US$2)

LAUNDRY

Best Western – The Lodge at Creel (⏰ 9am-6pm Mon-Sat) Laundry open to the public.

MEDICAL SERVICES

Clinica Santa Teresa (☎ 456-01-05; ⏰ 24hr) Behind Casa Margarita.

CREEL

0 — 200 m
0 — 0.1 miles

INFORMATION
3 Amigos.....................................1 D2
Banca Serfin...............................2 D1
Bank.....................................(see 7)
Clinica Santa Teresa.....................3 D1
CompuCenter.............................4 D2
Divisas La Sierra..........................5 D3
Divisas La Sierra..........................6 D1
Post Office..................................7 C1

SIGHTS & ACTIVITIES (p330)
Casa de las Artesanías del Estado de
   Chihuahua y Museo....................8 D1
Casa del Artesano Indígena......(see 12)
Church......................................9 D1
Church....................................10 D1
Complejo Ecoturístico Arareko
   Office...................................11 D2
Museo de Paleontología.............12 D2
Papelería de Todo......................13 D2
Tarahumara Tours.....................14 D2
Umarike Expediciones................15 C1

SLEEPING (pp331–2)
Best Western – The Lodge at
   Creel....................................16 D3
Cabañas Berti's.........................17 D2
Cabañas Sierra Azul...................18 D2
Casa de Huéspedes Pérez...........19 D1
Casa Margarita..........................20 D1
Hotel Korachi...........................21 C1
Hotel Los Pinos.........................22 D2
Hotel Los Valles........................23 D2
Hotel Margarita's Plaza
   Mexicana.............................24 D2
Hotel Nuevo.............................25 C1

To Chihuahua
(250km)

Train Station

To Cabañas Montebello (1.5km);
Complejo Ecoturístico Arareko
(7.5km); Lago Arareko (7.5km);
Divisidero (50km);
San Rafael (92km)

Cristo Rey

Plaza

Plaza

Cuesta

Batopilas

Elfido Batista

To Villa Mexicana (1km);
Hotel Pueblo Viejo (1km);
El Adventurero (1km)

Hotel Parador de la Montaña....26 D2
La Posada de Creel......................27 C2
Motel Cascada Inn.....................28 D2

EATING (p332)
El Caballo Bayo........................29 D3
Hospital Para Crudos.................30 C1
Pastelarte.................................31 C2
Restaurant Estela......................32 D3
Restaurant La Cabaña................33 D2
Restaurant Los Valles................34 D2
Restaurant Lupita......................35 D2
Restaurant Sierra Madre........(see 16)
Restaurant Verónica..................36 D2

DRINKING (p333)
Tío Molcas.................................37 D2

SHOPPING (p333)
Artesanías Misión Shop..............38 C1
Creel Café & Dog Orphanage.....39 D1

TRANSPORT (p333)
Autotransportes Noroeste Bus
   Station..................................40 C1
Buses to Batopilas.................(see 22)
Estrella Blanca Bus Station........41 C1

MONEY

Banca Serfin (🕙 9am-4pm Mon-Fri) On the plaza.
It changes money. The ATM here – the only one in
town – is prone to go offline for days at a time, so it
may be a good idea to arrive with a quantity of extra
cash just in case.

Divisas La Sierra (Av López Mateos 59) Changes US
dollars and traveler's checks.

POST

Post office (🕙 9am-3pm Mon-Fri)

TELEPHONE

Papelería de Todo (Av López Mateos; 🕙 9am-8pm)

TOURIST INFORMATION

Information about local attractions is available from the tour operators, most of the
places to stay, and the Artesanías Misión
shop. There is fierce competition for tour
business, so ask around and compare prices
to ensure that you are getting impartial
information.

3 Amigos Canyon Expeditions (☎ 456-00-36; Av
López Mateos 46) A good outlet for unbiased information,
it provides a good map of the town.

Sights & Activities

The **Casa de las Artesanías del Estado de Chihuahua y Museo** (☎ 456-00-80; admission US$1; 🕙 9am-
1pm & 3-6pm Tue-Fri, 10am-1pm Sat, 9am-1pm Sun),
overlooking the plaza, contains excellent
exhibits with texts in English on Tarahumara culture and crafts. Don't miss it.

The **Museo de Paleontología** (US$1; 🕙 9am-8pm,
closed Wed), on the smaller plaza, is less impressive. It has a hodgepodge of exhibits on Chihuahuan history, ranging from fossils and
rocks to antiques and Mennonite artifacts.

This is prime horseback-riding country,
and many of Creel's nearby attractions can
be enjoyed from horseback.

Norbert Padillo of **El Adventurero** (☎ 456-05-
57; elaventurero@hotmail.com; next to the Hotel Pueblo
Viejo) is an English-speaking guide with a
stable of well-behaved horses that love to
gallop. Seven horse tours from two to eight
hours in length are offered, ranging in price
from US$12 to US$48 per person.

Tours

Most of Creel's hotels offer tours of the surrounding area, with trips to canyons, rivers,

hot springs, waterfalls and other places. Trips range from a seven-hour tour to Río Urique, at the bottom of the Barranca de Urique, passing several indigenous villages, to an eight-hour excursion to Mennonite settlements in Cuauhtémoc, including a visit to a Mennonite cheese factory and lunch at a Mennonite home (see p357 for more on the Mennonites). See pp334–5 for information on other tour destinations.

Tarahumara Tours (☎ 456-00-65), with an office on the plaza, offers all the same tours and guide services as the hotels, often at better prices. There's also **Umarike Expediciones** (☎ 456-02-48; www.umarike.com.mx; cnr Villa & Cristo Rey), which offers guided hiking and mountain bike tours, rock climbing excursions and instruction. It rents out mountain bikes and camping gear, and offers maps and information for do-it-yourself trips. As the office is often closed, try making contact via the website or phone.

All tours require a minimum number of people. The easiest place to get a group together is often at Casa Margarita p331, but any hotel will organize a tour if there are enough people wanting to go, usually four or five. Most hotels don't require that you be a guest in order to go on a tour. Expect to pay US$11/25 per person for a half/full-day tour, but shop around – the pricier hotels tend to have more expensive tours. If you take any tour from Casa Margarita, it includes a box lunch. One or more destinations may be combined on the same tour.

You could also hire your own guide. Expect to pay around US$25 per person, per day. Inquire at the office of the Complejo Ecoturístico Arareko on Av López Mateos, the Tarahumara Tours office on the plaza, or ask around at the hotels.

If you have your own transport you can do many of these excursions on your own. While there are no car-rental outlets in Creel, it is possible to procure a vehicle. **The 3 Amigos Canyon Expeditions** (☎ 456-05-46; Av López Mateos 46) offers self-guided tour packages (US$100 per day for up to five people) that includes use of a double-cab Nissan truck, a healthy lunch, maps and travel information. For independent souls this is a good alternative to the typical regimented tour, and for a group it is comparable in price. (If you're cruising for some kissing in the canyon, ask about their 'romance package.')

Sleeping

Creel offers all sorts of lodging experiences, from rental homes to dorm-style bunks.

BUDGET

Creel is a budget traveler's dream, with more low-priced accommodation choices than you can shake a walking stick at.

The most popular place in this category is **Casa Margarita** (☎ 456-00-45; Av López Mateos 11; mattress on fl US$5, dm US$7, s/d US$20/30). With a variety of accommodations and prices – from beds in cramped dorms to nicer private rooms – Casa Margarita is a great place to meet other travelers. All prices here include both breakfast and dinner; everyone gathers at the table to eat together. It runs a variety of tours daily, which there is some pressure to join. It rents out bicycles, has laundry service, and promises to open a long-awaited juice bar, Internet café and lounge in the near future.

Roomier and more attractive than Margarita's dorms – and also quieter – is **Casa de Huéspedes Pérez** (☎ 456-00-47; Flores 257; dm US$8), which has one- to six-person log-walled rooms with wood stove heating. Also on the premises is a communal kitchen and Café Luly, which serves rather nice espresso in the morning.

Cabañas Berti's (☎ 456-05-51; Av López Mateos 31; s/d US$15/22; P) The simple but cozy rooms here come with either a heater or fireplace.

La Posada de Creel (☎ 456-01-42; Av Ferrocarril s/n; s/d US$15/18, with shared bath US$7 per person) The rooms at this creaky old hotel are attractive in a small, dark kind of way.

About 7km south of Creel, **Complejo Ecoturístico Arareko**, with an office in Creel (☎ 635-456-01-26; Av López Mateos) offers camping and lodging near Lago Arareko (see p333).

Villa Mexicana (☎ 456-06-65; www.vmcoppercanyon.com; Prolongacion López Mateos s/n; tent sites US$10 per person, RV sites with no/partial/full hookups US$10/15/20; 4/6-person cabins US$50-85/75-150; P) This new, well-equipped campground is on the south side of Creel, about a 15-minute walk from the center of town; head south on López Mateos and just keep going. Cheaper weekly and monthly rates are available. Facilities include a communal kitchen, baths, restaurant, bar, small shop, laundry and tours.

Hotel Pueblo Viejo (☎ 456-05-38; fax 456-02-95; s/d with breakfast US$60/70; dinners US$6; P) Nestled at the base of the hills behind Villa Mexicana,

NORTHWEST MEXICO

the family-friendly Pueblo Viejo features several cabins in various sizes and styles, from log cabin to fortress, which together resemble a small town. All cabins have a heater, water cooler, coffee maker and bath. It will pick up guests at the train station.

Cabañas Sierra Azul (☎ 456-01-11; Av López Mateos 29; tr/q US$20/25) This new hotel has clean rooms each with two queen-sized beds. If you fill them up with four people, you will be saving quite a bit of money. Inquire at the small grocery store called Abarrotes Pérez on Av López Mateos.

Hotel Los Pinos (☎ 456-00-44; López Mateos 39; s/d US$23/27) The Hotel Los Pinos has aging but tidy rooms with heaters, plus off-street parking.

MID-RANGE

Hotel Los Valles (☎ 456-00-92; Elfido Batista s/n; s/d US$20/30, ste to sleep 4-8 US$11 per person) Another newcomer, this squeaky-clean hotel has attractive rooms with TV and heaters. The suite is large and a good value.

Hotel Korachi (☎ 456-00-64; Villa 16; s/d/tr US$16/22/33, cabaña-style s/d/tr US$26/32/43) Across the tracks from the plaza, this hotel has simple rooms and cozy old-style cabañas with woodstoves. It also has seven rustic **country houses** in the countryside, 2km from Creel. Each can hold up to eight people.

Hotel Nuevo (☎ 456-00-22; fax 456-00-43; Villa 121; s/d US$25/55, cabaña-style rooms US$75) Across from the train station, the Nuevo offers both standard rooms as well as large, log-and-stone cabaña-style rooms.

Cabañas Montebello (☎ 625-837-69-20; Av Gran Visión s/n; s/d/tr US$30/35/40) This quiet, scenic hotel on the edge of town at the crossroads to Divisadero has copacetic rooms, each with two beds and private bath. Also available are family-friendly houses, all economically priced.

Hotel Margarita's Plaza Mexicana (☎ 456-02-45; Elfido Batista s/n; s/d US$38/48; P) The family that runs the Casa Margarita also runs this comfortable hotel, a block from López Mateos. It has a restaurant, bar and 26 spacious rooms, with TV, around a courtyard. Prices here include breakfast and a three-course dinner.

Motel Cascada Inn (☎ 456-02-53; Av López Mateos 49; r/tr US$50/53; P) The Cascada Inn has a restaurant, a lively bar, and 32 rooms each with TV and two double beds.

TOP END

Hotel Parador de la Montaña (☎ 456-00-23; Av López Mateos 44; r US$63, tr/q US$74/84; P) This well-run hotel offers spacious rooms with tiled floors, high ceilings, TV and heaters. There is also a good restaurant.

Best Western – The Lodge at Creel (☎ 456-00-71; in the USA 800-528-1234; www.thelodgeatcreel.com; Av López Mateos 61; cabins US$106, ste US$166; P X) This attractive hotel offers spacious, comfortable, self-contained wooden cabins, each with gas woodstove, two double beds and TV. The honeymoon suite comes with a private Jacuzzi and kitchenette. Also available are spa services.

Eating

Plenty of restaurants are on Av López Mateos in the few blocks south of the plaza. Most are open from around 7:30am to 10pm daily. **Restaurant Verónica** and **Restaurant La Cabaña** are both popular, serving steak, seafood and Mexican dishes for US$4 to US$9. The casual **Restaurant Lupita** (meals US$3-4.50) is less expensive and popular with locals. Homey **Restaurant Estela** serves good, economical meals in the same price range.

Pastelarte (Av Ferrocarril; per hr US$0.50-3), a new pastry and coffee shop is a pleasant place to while away an hour while you're waiting for that train whistle to blow. Here you can get perhaps the town's best cup of coffee and delicious cake and cookies.

Hospital Para Crudos (meals US$2.25-5.50) Next to the tracks just south of the train station, Hospital Para Crudos specializes in hangover remedies like *menudo* (soup made of tripe, hominy and chilies), hence the name. It also has burritos and other snack food.

Restaurant Los Valles (Av López Mateos; meals US$2-7) This new place on the main drag at the corner of Batista serves excellent *carne asada* and Mexican specialties in generous portions.

El Caballo Bayo (Av López Mateos; meals US$2-10) This popular eatery has a bilingual menu that features huge steaks, salads, fajitas, and accommodating service.

Restaurant Sierra Madre (Best Western – The Lodge at Creel; mains US$3.50-15) For more upscale dining, try this attractive place, with good food and a full bar. It serves breakfasts, pizza, and a full-on dinner including soup, salad, main course and dessert. Bottles of wine here cost US$9 to US$15.

Drinking

As Creel's status as a traveler's mecca continues to grow, its nightlife is starting to pick up. **Tío Molcas** (Av López Mateos 35), with its wood-heated bar in a back room, is the coziest of Creel's drinking establishments. For fresh margaritas, including one made from tamarind, head to **El Caballo Bayo** (Av López Mateos). The **Motel Cascada Inn** (Av López Mateos) has a spacious second-floor bar that keeps late hours for its mix of locals and travelers. Pool balls may be sunk at the bar at **Best Western – The Lodge at Creel** (Av López Mateos 61).

Shopping

Many shops in Creel sell Tarahumara handicrafts, including baskets, colorful dolls, wood carvings, violins, flutes, archery sets, pottery, clothing and more. Prices are very reasonable.

The **Artesanías Misión** shop, on the north side of the plaza, is the best place to buy handicrafts. All of the store's earnings go to support the Catholic mission hospital, which provides free medical care for the Tarahumara. If you would like to support individual Tarahamarans directly, then buy straight from the vendors who are working the sidewalks.

For something completely different, visit the **Creel Café and Dog Orphanage**. This funky establishment, located next to Casa Margarita, offers a book exchange, camping supplies, dried foods, and all sorts of information about Creel and its environs. All proceeds go to feed local children (or any hungry soul) via a daily sidewalk kitchen, and to support a casual street dog orphanage.

Getting There & Around

BUS

Travel between Creel and Chihuahua may be more convenient via bus rather than train, as the trip is shorter and the schedule more flexible. The Estrella Blanca bus station, across the tracks from the plaza, has nine daily buses to Chihuahua (US$17, 4½ hours), passing through San Juanito (US$2.50, 45 minutes), La Junta (US$8, two hours) and Cuauhtémoc (US$11, three hours) on the way. From Chihuahua, you can catch an onward bus to many mainland destinations.

Estrella Blanca also has three daily buses to San Rafael ($4, 1½ hours) via Divisadero

(US$3, one hour) and Posada Barrancas (Areponápuchi; US$3, one hour). They depart Creel daily at 11am, 3pm and 6pm. Autotransportes Noroeste, just north of Estrella Blanca, has departures for San Rafael (US$4) at 10:30am and 6:30pm and buses to Chihuahua (US$17) at 9:15am, 11:30am and 3pm.

A bus to Batopilas (US$16, five hours) leaves from outside the Hotel Los Pinos on López Mateos, two blocks south of the plaza, at 7:30am Tuesday, Thursday and Saturday, and at 9:30am Monday, Wednesday and Friday.

CAR & MOTORCYCLE

Now there's a paved road all the way from Creel to Divisadero and on to San Rafael. From San Rafael, if you have a sturdy 4WD vehicle, you could go all the way to El Fuerte in the dry season (March to May is the best time) via Bahuichivo, Mesa de Arturo, La Reforma and Choix, crossing the Colosio reservoir in a two-vehicle ferry. Or you could go from San Rafael to Álamos via Bahuichivo, Témoris and Chinipas, crossing the Río Chinipas. Both of these roads are very rough; assaults have also occurred on these roads.

TRAIN

Creel's train station is half a block from the main plaza. The westbound primera express train departs Creel at 11:26am and clase económica at 1pm; the eastbound trains depart at 2:14pm and 4:05pm. However, they are usually late. Check the board inside the train station for the estimated times of arrival that day. See p324 for schedule and ticket information.

BICYCLE

Several places rent out bicycles, and the surrounding countryside has many places accessible by pedal power.
Umarike Expediciones Half/full day US$11.50/17. Prices include map, helmet and tool kit.
Complejo Ecoturístico Arareko office Hour/day US$2.25/22.
Casa Margarita Full day US$8.
Creel Café Full day US$5.
3 Amigos Half/full day US$5/10.

AROUND CREEL

The area around Creel is rich in natural wonders, with everything from waterfalls to hot springs to rocks shaped like frogs only a day's hike, bike ride or drive from town. Local guides offer a variety of tours, some of which you can do on your own with a bicycle or even on foot. However, do not walk into the countryside by yourself: at least one woman has been assaulted while walking to Lago Arareko alone.

As for the Ferrocarril Chihuahua al Pacífico, east of Creel it goes through **Cuauhtémoc**, the center of northern Mexico's Mennonite population, and ends at **Chihuahua**, the capital of the state of Chihuahua. See p337 for information on these places.

Complejo Ecoturístico Arareko

An excellent local hike (or drive) is to the **Complejo Ecoturístico Arareko** (admission US$1.75), a Tarahumara *ejido* (communal landholding), and home to about 400 families. Here you'll find 200 sq km of pine forest with waterfalls, hot springs, inhabited caves and other rock formations. There are also deep canyons, farmlands, villages and **Lago Arareko**.

About 7km southeast of Creel, the lake is an easy hike or drive south along the road to Cusárare; hitchhiking is also relatively easy. A few caves inhabited by Tarahumara can be seen along the way. The lake is surrounded by boulders and pine forests; there's also an old log cabin, which was used as a set for the filming of the Mexican movie *El Refugio del Lobo* (Refuge of the Wolf).

There's a **campground** on the northeast shore of Lago Arareko. It has sites with barbecue pits, picnic areas, water and bathrooms for US$1.50 per person.

The *ejido* also operates two lodges.

Albergue de Batosárachi (dm/d US$10/20) This lodge, 1km south of Lago Arareko, has three rustic cabins with bunk beds or individual rooms, and hot showers; you can cook in the communal kitchen or arrange to have meals prepared. It can accommodate 70 people.

Cabaña de Segórachi (d US$25) This place, on the south shore of Lago Arareko, is more luxurious than Albergue de Batosárachi, and includes the use of a rowboat and other amenities. It holds 15 people.

You can make reservations for both of the lodges and arrange to rent bikes or boats for excursions on the lake at Complejo Ecoturístico Arareko's **office** (☎ 635-456-01-26), which can be found on Av López

Mateos in Creel. It will pick up lodge guests at the train or bus station.

To get to the *ejido* from Creel, head south on Av López Mateos and veer left off Av López Mateos, passing the town cemetery on your left. About 1.5km south of town there's a gate where the US$1.75 entrance fee is charged and you're given a map and printed information about the *ejido*. Continue straight ahead; caves and farmlands will appear on both sides of the road before you eventually arrive at the small Tarahumara village of **San Ignacio**, where there's a 400-year-old mission church.

Visitors often get lost trying to reach the lake from this point (the map isn't the best). Here's how to do it: from San Ignacio, continue straight ahead past the church, taking the trail up the hill. At the top of the hill, take the trail straight ahead through the next valley, and you'll come to the lake. If you do get lost, remember that the highway is running parallel to you, on your right (west); it's an easy hitch back to Creel.

Valle de los Monjes

The vertical rock formations found in this valley gave rise to its traditional Tarahumara name of Bisabírachi, meaning the Valley of the Erect Penises. The valley, also sometimes called the Valley of the Gods, is 9km from Creel and is considered a day trip by horse, although it is also possible to go by foot. To get there, walk to San Ignacio (see earlier) and ask there for the way. There is a US$0.50 entry fee. Alternatively, it's easy to arrange for transport from San Ignacio from a local into the Valle. Along the way you'll pass a couple other valleys named after the rock formations found there: Valle de las Ranas (Valley of the Frogs) and Valle de los Hongos (Valley of the Mushrooms). Tour operators can either rent out horses or tell you where to get them.

Cascada Cusárare

The 30m-high Cusárare waterfall is 22km south of Creel, near the Tarahumara village of Cusárare (place of eagles). Tour operators in Creel offer a four- to five-hour tour that involves going 22km by car, stopping at Lago Arareko on the way, and then hiking 2.5km to the waterfall. To do it yourself, if you're coming from Creel, don't take the first turnoff you see on your right where large signs point to the waterfall – this entrance leaves you with a longer, less interesting hike to reach the falls. Continue on for about another 5km, passing the sign to Cusárare village pointing off to your left, until you reach a small, inconspicuous sign pointing to your right saying 'Cascada Cusárare – Cusárare Waterfall.' Turn here, follow the road until you reach the small shop and park at the Copper Canyon Sierra Lodge. The waterfall (entrance US$1.75) is about a 40-minute walk along the river, on an easy-to-follow trail. You could camp here too, beside the river.

The rustic **Copper Canyon Sierra Lodge** (☎ 635-456-00-36, 800-776-3942 in the USA; per hr US$60 per person, incl meals) is a classic no-tech mountain lodge with beamed ceilings, pot-belly stoves, kerosene lamps and no electricity. Meals – and copious margaritas – are served in a fine old dining room with a grand fireplace.

Loyola Museum

In the Tarahumaran village of Cusárare, you can visit the brand new **Loyola Museum** (admission US$1.50; ☎ 10am-4:30pm Tue-Sun), an institution dedicated to the preservation of centuries-old paintings that were heretofore moldering in regional churches and missions. All of the 46 works on display – including an impressive 18th-century 12-panel series depicting the life of the Virgin Mary – have been restored recently for display in the museum's new building adjacent to the restored church.

Recohuata Hot Springs

These small natural hot springs are about 35km southwest of Creel at the bottom of Barranca Tararecua. A popular seven-hour tour from Creel begins with a 1½-hour truck ride and then a scenic hike down 607m into the canyon to the hot springs (entrance US$1.75).

CASCADA DE BASASEACHI

Basaseachi Falls, 140km northwest of Creel, is a dramatic 246m-high waterfall (the highest in Mexico), especially spectacular in the rainy season. It takes all day to visit the falls – a bumpy three-hour drive, then about two hours walking down, half an hour at the waterfall, three hours walking up again, and a bumpy three-hour return ride. If you're

up for it, it's worth it. If you're not up for the walk down into the canyon, you can still enjoy views of the falls and the canyon from up on the rim.

Rancho San Lorenzo (☎ 614-421-26-56) has several large cabins and an attractive camping area a five-minute walk from the falls. It also offers climbers access to first-class rock with more than 50 routes from 6m to 500m, along with equipment rentals.

BATOPILAS

☎ 649 / pop 1200 / elevation 495m

If you are lucky enough to make it down the bumpy, twisting road to Batopilas, a serene 19th-century silver-mining village 140km south of Creel, you can be satisfied that you have made your way deep into canyon country. The journey from Creel to Batopilas is a thrilling ride from an altitude of 2338m at Creel to 495m at Batopilas, with dramatic descents and ascents through several canyons, climates and vegetative zones. Batopilas' climate is distinctly warmer and more tropical than Creel's. Here you are surrounded by stands of tropical fruit trees rather than Creel's cool-loving pine forests.

There is a map of the town painted inside El Zaguán Bar, across the alleyway from El Quinto Patio, showing the locations of some interesting sites such as the ruins of Hacienda San Miguel and some abandoned mines. (If you decide to explore the mines, do not go in without a flashlight as there are some deep holes you'll want to avoid.)

Most tour operators offer a two-day excursion from Creel to Batopilas. But if you don't have two days to spare to visit Batopilas, a tour to **La Bufa** lets you experience some of that spectacular scenery in one day, with plenty of stops along the way. The nine-hour tour takes you 105km from Creel through five spectacular canyons to the viewpoint at La Bufa, overlooking the town of the same name in a canyon 1750m deep, with a cool river at the bottom.

History

In the 18th and 19th centuries the silver mines of Batopilas became known as among the richest in Mexico, but it wasn't until a former mayor of Washington, DC arrived on the scene with his modernizing ways that the Batopilas mines realized their full potential. Alexander Shepherd, having been ousted from elected office due to unproven corruption charges, moved his family to town in 1880 to form the Batopilas Mining Company, which would extract more than 567 million grams of silver over 40 years. Shepherd also brought technological advances to this once-sleepy pueblo; his hydroelectric plant made Batopilas only the second city in Mexico to have electricity, and he also built an aqueduct that is in use to this day. One of the most striking sights in town is the ruins of Shepherd's **Hacienda San Miguel**; it presides over the town from across the river, cloaked in perpetually blooming bougainvillea.

Activities

Batopilas is a great starting point for many short and long treks; any hotel can help arrange **canyon trips**. An interesting hike is to the beautiful Catedral Perdida (Lost Cathedral) at **Satevó**. It's a mystery why such an elaborate cathedral was built in a remote, uninhabited canyon where there has never been a sizable settlement. It was built so long ago that its origins are lost in the distant past. Satevó is 8km from Batopilas via a dirt road that runs beside the river.

Local guide Arturo Aguilar is well regarded for the excursions he leads to local points of interest including the Peñasquito mine and Mesa de la Yerbabuena, a Tarahumaran village with an amazing view. Inquire for him at La Casa Monse (see below).

The two- to three-day trek to the town of Urique is also very popular.

Sleeping & Eating

Hotel Mary (s/d US$10/15) Opposite the church, this place – with its simple rooms and good little restaurant – is a favorite with budget travelers. A single caveat: it can be a little noisy due to the bar next door.

La Casa Monse (☎ 456-90-27; Main Plaza; s/d US$10/18) More intimate is the Casa Monse, with a communal kitchen and its shady patio. Monse will cook Tarahumaran meals for you 'if you're intelligent.'

Hotel Juanita's (☎ 456-90-43; on Main Plaza; s/d US$20/35) This clean and comfortable hotel has rooms decorated with a simple flair, and its courtyard overlooking the river is a great place to watch the bats at dusk.

Real de Minas (☎ 456-90-45; cnr Guerra & Ochoa; r US$45) Real de Minas has eight brightly decorated rooms around a lovely courtyard, and a portico decorated with an impressive collection of Mexican kitsch.

La Hacienda Río Batopilas (☎ 635-456-02-45 in Creel; r/tr US$80/90 including all meals) This beautiful new hotel has 10 luxurious rooms decorated with tile and stained-glass windows. The rooms are lit with oil lamps for atmosphere. It's on the road from Creel, about a 10-minute walk from Batopilas. Make your reservations in advance through the Hotel Margarita's Plaza Mexicana in Creel.

El Quinto Patio (Hotel Mary; prices US$1-4.50) This unassuming restaurant serves inexpensive, flavorful meals.

El Puente Colgante (The Hanging Bridge; ☎ 456-90-23; mains US$4-8.50) Near the bridge at the far end of the plaza, this restaurant serves a delicious seasoned steak and rainbow trout stuffed with seafood. There is also a bar serving drinks on a bucolic patio.

Restaurant Clarita (main street; meals US$3.50) The Clarita serves good basic meals, and also is home to the town phone caseta. It also offers the cheapest accommodations in town (US$4 with shared bath).

Getting There & Away

The bus to Creel (US$16, five hours, 140km) departs from the plaza in Batopilas at 5am Monday to Saturday. On Tuesday, Thursday and Saturday the bus goes all the way from Batopilas to Chihuahua (US$34, eight hours, 396km).

Central
North Mexico

CONTENTS

Central
North Mexico

While most travelers just breeze through the Central North – which includes much of the state of Chihuahua, the entire state of Durango and a tiny part of Coahuila – the region has plenty to keep you there. Most striking is its intense desert landscape, with the surreal, magenta mountains of the Sierra Madre Occidental hugging earth that starts out a deep red in the north and fades into a sandy beige north of Torreón. The dustiness finally gives way to verdant fields of corn, cotton and lush trees on the outskirts of the city of Durango. The area also boasts plenty of attractions for history and archaeology buffs, including museums about the revolutionary hero Pancho Villa as well as the ruins of Paquimé and Cuarenta Casas – remnants of once-flourishing settlements of northern Mexico's indigenous people.

For such an unhyped region, you'll find plenty that locals are proud of – and discover that the object of pride can change in just a half-day of travel. In Durango, for example, it's the scorpion, and you'll find images of the creature emblazoned on flags, T-shirts and keychains everywhere you go. In Parral it's Pancho Villa, who has soared far beyond hero status for the proud folks who are a bit obsessed with him here. Chihuahua loves its railroad and its Chihuahuas (although there are actually none here to speak of), while Nuevo Casas Grandes loves its Paquimé-style pottery. And you'll love it all too.

Perhaps most inviting to travelers, however, is the exceptional lack of tourists in the region. While Juárez gets plenty of Texan residents hopping the border for nights of clubbing, and the city of Chihuahua sees a trickle of moneyed foreigners passing through to board the deluxe Copper Canyon railroad trains, most of the Central North is sleepy. The towns, usually rough and rundown rather than spruced up for the benefit of visitors, are full of local cowboys, families and merchants simply going about their business. And this makes visits all the more pleasurable, as it gives you the chance to interact with the region's best asset of all: the warm and welcoming local people.

HIGHLIGHTS

- Visiting Chihuahua's **Museo de la Revolución Mexicana** (p351), housed in Pancho Villa's former headquarters

- Staying in the wonderfully kitschy **Hotel Acosta** (p358) in friendly Hidalgo del Parral

- Shopping for cowboy boots in **Chihuahua** (p349), followed by evening snacks and cocktails al fresco at **La Casa de los Milagros** (p355)

- Strolling through Durango's beautiful **Plaza de Armas** (p362)

- Exploring the pre-Hispanic **cliffside dwellings** (p348) around mountainous Madera

- ALTITUDE RANGE: 1145m–2092m

- AUGUST DAILY HIGH: 30°C

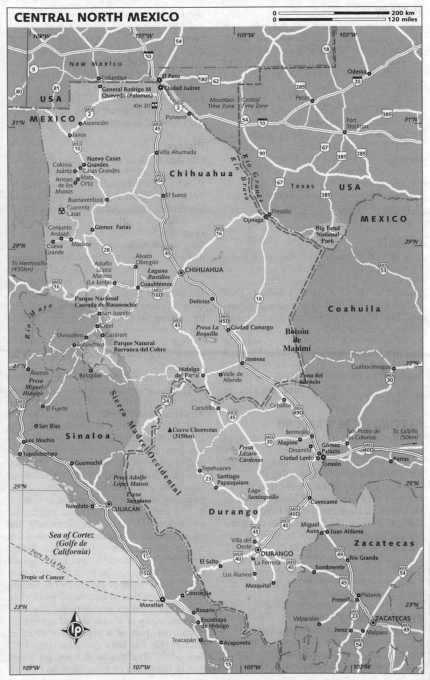

HISTORY

This region of Mexico was the subject of fierce battles during the Revolution, giving rise to Pancho Villa's División del Norte. As you travel through the area, you'll find that Villa is the most popular hero in these parts. You'll see evidence of early-20th-century influence lingering, too – especially at Nuevo Casas Grandes, the site of a no-longer-active railway station that has served the Rio Grande, Sierra Madre and Pacific Railway Companies at various times through history. But the history is much more ancient and vast here, as evidenced by the ruins of Paquimé and Cuarenta Casas – remnants of once-flourishing settlements of Mexico's indigenous and highly sophisticated peoples.

CLIMATE

The state of Chihuahua – the main focus of this chapter – is Mexico's largest; and the Desierto Chihuahuense (Chihuahuan Desert) is North America's largest. That makes for an awfully huge swath of sandy, arid land (though its western side is broken up by the Sierra Madre, which forms plenty of fertile valleys). The entire region is hot and dry, with an average rainfall of less than 102cm and an average temperature of 28°C. Durango's a bit wetter, with average temps going as high as 28°C in June and 13°C in January.

GETTING THERE & AROUND

Excellent bus service makes traveling around this region easy – Omnibus, Estrella Blanca and Chihuahuenses companies all have frequent service connecting the major cities and many towns, including Parral, Nuevo Casas Grandes and Madera. Stick to the Mexican buses, too, when heading into the region from the US: you can cross the border into Ciudad Juárez by foot (or taxi for about US$20 from the El Paso airport), catch a local bus to the major bus depot and then continue on from there. Direct bus journeys – as well as flights – from the US tend to be more costly.

CIUDAD JUÁREZ

☎ 656 / pop 1.2 million / elevation 1145m

Ciudad Juárez is a grimy, noisy, booming border town – the second busiest port of entry on the US–Mexico border, actually. It's inextricably linked with El Paso, its American neighbor just across the Rio Grande, which brings plenty of day-trippers over for cheap dental work, bargain shopping and under-21 drinking at bustling watering holes, including a throng of gay nightclubs. Travelers do not linger here, but use the city's excellent bus and road connections as a starting point for exploration further south – or north into the US, for that matter.

History

During the Mexican Revolution, Juárez had a strategic importance beyond its small size. Pancho Villa stormed the town on May 10, 1911, forcing the resignation of the dictator Porfirio Díaz. After the February 1913 coup against legitimately elected President Francisco Madero, Villa sought refuge in El Paso before recrossing the Rio Grande with just eight followers to begin the reconquest of Mexico. Within months, he had recruited and equipped an army of thousands, La División del Norte. In November he conquered Juárez for a second time – this time by loading his troops onto a train, deceiving the defenders into thinking it was one of their own, and steaming into the middle of town in a modern version of the Trojan-horse tactic.

Later on in the 20th century, another sort of Trojan horse moved in to town: factories. After the implementation of Nafta (North American Free Trade Agreement) in the mid-1990s, industry mushroomed in the city, as US manufacturers took advantage of low-cost labor in Mexico and markets grew on both sides of the border. With 13 industrial parks and more than 360 *maquiladoras* (assembly plants, usually foreign-owned) pumping out electronic goods and automotive parts, the area became a magnet for job-seeking Mexicans. Unfortunately, the employment and population explosion was taking place in a city which lacked the infrastructure to handle it, and now a sprawl of shanty towns creeps from the city's outskirts, many without electricity or running water. In another tragic turn, more than half of the workers drawn to the city were women, many of whom wound up victims of murder, part of a mysterious string of killings that has been going on since 1993 (see p342). The deaths did not get attention in the media or from Mexican officials

CIUDAD JUÁREZ

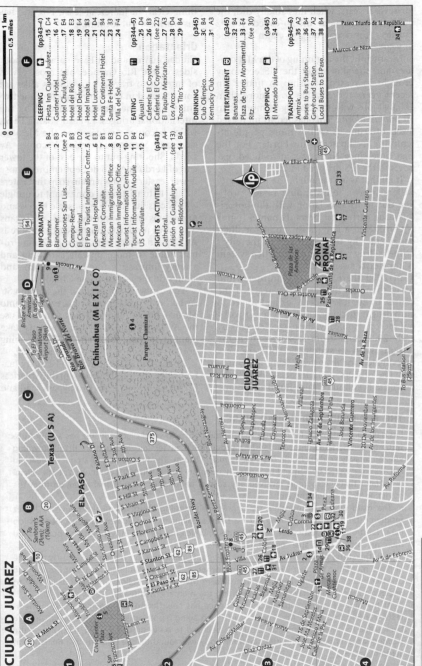

for several years; when they finally did, the publicity sadly made the so-called 'Juárez murders' the area's biggest claim to fame in years.

Meanwhile, the beginning of the 21st century and the slowing of the US economy brought increased hardship to Juárez. In recent years the city has lost more than 100,000 jobs with the closing of more than 30 *maquiladoras*. This has led to increased levels of crime as well as more people attempting to slip across the border. For the first time since Nafta was introduced, exports to the US dropped in 2002.

If all that wasn't enough, the border city suffers from a longstanding image problem due to its association with the notorious drug cartel that bears its name. Juárez is considered a key transit point for illicit drugs entering the US. Much of the city's crime is drug related and the justice system is hopelessly swamped.

In 2000 there were 183 murders, and fewer than half the cases even reached the courts. By 2001, President Fox had vowed to curb drug trafficking, labeling it 'a war without mercy.' Ironically, the biggest success by early 2004 came from looking within the system, when 13 state police officers were investigated for drug trafficking and murder. The officers' commander fled, and the outcome is still uncertain. But it made one thing clear: in Juárez, at least, Fox still has his work cut out for him.

Orientation

Ciudad Juárez and El Paso sprawl on both sides of the Rio Grande, but most places of interest to travelers and locals alike are concentrated in the central areas of the two cities, along the streets connected by the international bridges: El Paso's Santa Fe St, which becomes Av Juárez on the Mexican side; and Stanton St, which becomes Av Lerdo. Shooting out to the east of the lower end of Lerdo is Av 16 de Septiembre, whose newer, eastern end is a main strip that caters strictly to tourists who don't want to mingle with locals; its supply of upscale hotels and nightclubs draws mostly Mexican Texans who have money to burn. North of here is Av Lincoln, which runs through Zona Pronaf, home to more upscale shopping and a fairly impressive fine arts museum, and alongside the large Parque Chamizal.

You can walk across either the Stanton St/ Av Lerdo or Santa Fe St/Av Juárez bridge into Mexico, but to return on foot you must use the Av Juárez bridge. By car, you must take Stanton St going south and Av Juárez going north – the vehicle toll is US$2 each way.

About 4km east of the Santa Fe St/Av Juárez bridge, the toll-free Bridge of the Americas (Cordova Bridge) leads to a bypass road and

---

THE 'FEMINICIDES' OF CIUDAD JUÁREZ

Besides being infamous for its drug cartels, the border town of Ciudad Juárez has another disturbing claim to fame: the brutal serial murders (dubbed 'feminicides') of more than 100 young women, mainly workers in the city's many *maquiladoras*. The first corpse, of a poor 13-year-old girl, was discovered beaten and strangled in an empty lot back in 1993. But it wasn't until several years later that the murders received any sort of national or international attention from the media or Mexican government.

The main woman responsible for aggressively turning attention on the crimes is Juárez resident Ester Chávez; also joining her has been a Chihuahua city women's group called Justicia Para Nuestras Hijas (Justice for Our Daughters), which has formed in response to bodies found more recently in other areas of Chihuahua state.

Still, the string of killings has yet to be solved. Popular opinion among Mexicans is that the girls are murdered for their valuable organs; others believe they've been victims of groups who use the bodies for rituals; and still more believe that Mexican police, who have been slow to respond to the crimes, have been committing the murders themselves.

At the time of writing, no sufficient evidence has been found to support any of the theories. According to a recent *New Yorker* article, two aging hippie-artists living in Chihuahua have been jailed for one of the murders, but are believed to be victims of a setup. In any case, the murders are still being committed: another body was found on the outskirts of Chihuahua in September 2003.

Hwy 45D, which goes south to Chihuahua. Even further east, the Zaragoza toll bridge entirely avoids both El Paso and Juárez.

Information

CONSULATES

Mexico in El Paso (☎ 915-533-8555; 910 East San Antonio Ave; ☒ 8:15am-1pm)
US in Ciudad Juarez (☎ 613-1655; Av Lopez Mateos 924 Nte; ☒ 8am-4:45pm)

EMERGENCY

Fire, ambulance & police (☎ 060)

IMMIGRATION

Tourist cards (for those who need them – see p963) are available at the Mexican immigration offices at the ends of the Stanton St bridge and the Bridge of the Americas.

INTERNET ACCESS

Internet cafés are somewhat of a new phenomenon in Juárez; the few that do exist offer just a couple of terminals.
Compu-Rent (☎ 615-52-21; Av 16 de Septiembre 71; pre hr 15 pesos) This cool exception to the rule offers 24 computers and a hip young vibe.

MEDICAL SERVICES

General Hospital (☎ 613-15-71; Paseo Triunfo de la República 2401) Head here for walk-ins.

MONEY

Businesses in Ciudad Juárez generally accept US currency. Banks are clustered along Av 16 de Septiembre, with most open 9am to 5pm Monday to Friday.
Comisiones San Luis (☎ 614-20-33; cnr Juárez & 16 de Septiembre) This *casa di cambio* changes traveler's checks, as does the one at the bus station.

POST

Main post office (cnr Lerdo & Peña; ☒ 8am-5:30pm Mon-Fri, 9am-12:30pm Sat)

TOURIST INFORMATION

El Paso Tourist Information Center (☎ 915-544-0061; cnr Santa Fe St & Main Dr; ☒ 8:30am-5pm)
State Tourist Center (☎ 13-49-39; ☒ 9am-9pm) This state-run center sits in the Parque Chamizal, and offers information on everything from hotels and transportation to organized tours.
Tourist Information Center (☎ 611-31-74; Av de las Américas 2551; ☒ 9am-9pm) Bilingual staff; stocks a variety of brochures.

Tourist Information Module (☎ 629-33-40; cnr Villa & Guerrero; ☒ Mon-Fri, hours erratic) This small brick building that once served as a control point for metals exports is a more conveniently located information module. It offers many of the same materials as the main office.

Dangers & Annoyances

Juárez is notorious as a major port of entry into the US for illicit drugs. Most visitors will remain oblivious to mob activities linked with the drug trade and you'd be very unlucky indeed to get caught up in something nasty. That said, there is an alarmingly high crime rate in Ciudad Juárez; several innocent bystanders, including Americans, have been killed in drug-related shootings in public places in daylight.

The streets around the Av Juárez and Av Lerdo bridges are teeming with seedy, aggressive energy. The main drag along Juárez until it meets Av 16 de Septiembre is fairly well lit and always bustling, but potentially dangerous after dark. Women traveling solo may feel intimidated along this stretch at night. Remain vigilant, use taxis to get around after dark and don't stray into unlit side streets away from the main drag.

Sights

Other than watching the hustle and bustle along Juárez and in the markets, there's not a heck of a lot in the way of attractions.

The grand **Cathedral** (cnr Av 16 de Septiembre & Guerrero; ☒ 6:30am-10pm), built in 1935 and restored in 1976, is in the central Plaza de Armas. It has gorgeous stained-glass windows and an impressive neoclassical façade.

The conical **Museo de Arte e Historia** (☎ 616-74-14; cnr Av Lincoln & Anillo Pronaf; ☒ 10am-6pm Tue-Sun) is an architectural curiosity. Located within the Pronaf area, it houses colorful, eclectic exhibits on Mexico's pre-Hispanic civilizations as well as creations by local and national artists.

Museo Histórico (☎ 612-4707; cnr Av Juárez & Av 16 de Septiembre; admission free; ☒ 9am-5pm Tue-Sun), in the city's grand old customs building, has rather flat and unimpressive exhibits (in Spanish only) of local art and regional history.

Sleeping

Juárez accommodations are nothing to get excited about – it's either cheapo flops or sterile chains, for the most part.

BUDGET

Hotel Deluxe (☎ 615-00-82; Av Lerdo 300 Sur; s/d $22/28; ⊠) While this bare-bones budget spot may be sorely misnamed, it's gay-friendly, popular with Mexican tourists and conveniently located just a block east of the area's bustling gay nightclubs.

Gardner Hotel (☎ 915-532-3661; epihostl@whc .net; 311 E Franklin; dm US$17 for HI members, plus US$2 for sheets; d US$45) Those who don't care to spend the night in Juárez can choose this top budget option that's just over the border in El Paso. It offers both four-bed dorms and single rooms with cable, and is a switch from the string of characterless chains that huddle near the El Paso airport.

MID-RANGE

Hotel Chula Vista (☎ 617-12-07; Paseo Triunfo de la República 3555; s/d US$32/42; P ⊠ ⊠) Among the scores of roadside inns east of the center, this place is one of the better deals. It includes a restaurant, bar and spacious comfortable rooms with two double beds and color TVs, and smaller single rooms in an older wing by the highway.

Villa del Sol (☎ 617-24-24; Triunfo de la República 339; s & d US$52; P ⊠ ⊠) At the east end of Triunfo de la República is this classy hotel. Amenities include a large pool, satellite TV and a good restaurant; rooms are slightly cheaper on weekends.

Hotel del Río (☎ 615-55-25; Av Juárez 488 Nte; s/d US$25/33) A few blocks down from the northbound bridge, this hotel may be the best-kept secret in town. It's easy to miss the staircase leading up to the establishment's 18 neat, cozy rooms.

Plaza Continental Hotel (☎ 615-00-84; hotelcon@ avantel.net; Av Lerdo 112 Sur; s & d US$42; ⊠) You'll be charmed by the ornate chandeliered lobby and funky all-night diner, and the dim carpeted rooms are indeed a step up from basic accommodations down the block.

Hotel Impala (☎ 615-04-91; Av Lerdo 670 Nte; s/d with breakfast US$36/38) Right over the border near the Stanton St bridge is this old standby, with clean rooms and firm beds. It has a restaurant and a jovial lobby that's usually sporting a character or two.

Santa Fe Hotel (☎ 615-15-58; Av Lerdo 675 Nte; s/d $33/35; ⊠) The rooms in this cheery, spotless hotel have cable and – best of all – tile floors rather than the dreaded industrial carpeting.

TOP END

Hotel Lucerna (☎ 629-99-00; Paseo Triunfo de la República 3976; r Mon-Fri US$90, Sat & Sun US$72; P ⊠ ⊠ ⊠ ⊠) Catering to Juárez' business-class travelers – hence the cheaper rates on weekends – this luxurious option is definitely worth the extra 40 bucks if you just can't take another small, no-frills room. The poolside restaurant, palm-studded gardens and classy lounge areas make the seediness of Av Juárez seems far, far away.

Fiesta Inn Ciudad Juárez (☎ 686-07-00; Paseo Triunfo de la República 3451; s/d US$78/110; P ⊠ ⊠ ⊠ ⊠) Yes, it's part of a hotel chain, but the spiffy, business-class rooms – not to mention the satellite TV, large pool and restaurant-lounge – offer a welcome change from Juárez' less-than stellar alternatives.

Eating

Cafeteria El Coyote (☎ 614-25-71; Av Lerdo 118 Sur; mains US$5; ⊗ 24hr) Next to the Plaza Continental Hotel, this American-diner–style, central café is very convenient for breakfast, lunch or a late-night snack after the clubs have closed. There's also a branch on Av Juárez Norte at Av Colon, near the bridge.

El Taquíto Mexicano (Cristóbal Colón 190; 3 tacos US$1.50; ⊗ 11-2am) You'll find awesome tacos at this small eatery right off the main drag of Av Juárez. For just US$1.50 you'll get three tacos stuffed with beef, chicken or pork, and all the salsa, cilantro (coriander) and hot peppers you can swallow at the well-stocked fixings bar. Grab a stool at one of the long counters and take your pick of amusements: the soccer game on the wall-mounted TV or the parade of tipsy revelers coming in for a late-night refueling.

Tacos Tito's (intersection of Villa, de la Peña & Av Juárez) More cheap, excellent tacos – wrapped in fresh tortillas grilled right before your eyes – can be had at this roadside stall, grouped with several others, all of which are quite popular with the locals.

Ajuua!! (☎ 616-69-35; Ornelas 162 Nte; mains US$7-15; ⊗ 8-1am Sun-Thu, 8-2am Fri-Sat) Though there are touristy gimmicks, this cavernous restaurant-bar offers tasty versions of all the predictable classics, from excellent *chiles rellenos* to bowl-sized glasses of frozen margaritas. Plus, it's fun to watch the large tables of Mexican–Texan tourists thrill over the rowdy, flirtatious mariachi band.

Los Arcos (☎ 616-86-08; Paseo Triunfo de la República 2220; mains US$6-12) While eating fish in the middle of a desert may feel just plain wrong, you can catch some fine smoked marlin tacos and fresh fish fillets at this festive spot, a popular place for locals to hold celebratory dinners.

Drinking

It would be wise to steer clear of the grimy strip of bars and discos along Juárez late at night, as most cater to folks from north of the border who have no respect for the city beyond its cheap alcohol.

Kentucky Club (Av Juárez 643) If your curiosity gets the better of you, pick the Kentucky Club over the others. Its polished wood bar is a fine place to sip a margarita – even if its claim to inventing the cocktail does sound like a dubious publicity ploy.

Club Olímpico (☎ 615-57-42; Av Lerdo 210) This watering hole has no dancing or entertainment – just a mellow, mixed crowd of local gays and straights who are happy enough with the jukebox and the laid-back bartenders.

Entertainment

Bananas (cnr Peña & Corona) This gay nightclub – one of four on the block – has a hip, young vibe, its dance floor packed with hip, friendly boys from the 'hood and from Texas, starting at about midnight.

Plaza de Toros Monumental (☎ 613-16-56; Paseo Triunfo de la República) Juárez' bullfighting season is April to August. Events at the Plaza Monumental typically begin at 6pm Sunday. Off-track betting on the fighting (and on horse-racing in the area) is available at the Juárez Turf Club, a block from the Juárez bridge.

Ritz (cnr Peña & Lerdo) Earnest, old-school drag shows are the main draw on weekends at this gay nightclub, which draws a mixed clientele of both women and men.

Shopping

El Mercado Juárez (cnr Av 16 de Septiembre & Melgar; ◯ 9am-8pm) This massive, high-ceilinged market has an unfortunate mall-like quality, but its merchandise – baskets, blankets, jewelry, cheese and more – is affordable, and much of it is of good quality. The hawkers are mellower than they first appear, making pitches that come on strong but

quickly become half-hearted as you pass by their stands.

Getting There & Away

AIR

The best option for international arrivals and departures is the El Paso International Airport (ELP) where flights from major US cities including New York, Los Angeles and Chicago are half the price of those to Juárez.

The Juárez airport (Aeropuerto Internacional Abraham González) is just east of Hwy 45D, about 18km south of the center of town. Direct flights are available to/from Mexico City, Chihuahua, Guadalajara, Mazatlán and Tijuana. Flights to most other major cities go via Chihuahua or Mexico City. The main Mexican carriers are Aeroméxico and Aero California.

BUS

The Juárez bus station (Central de Autobuses) is on Teófilo Borunda, about 25 minutes southeast from town and accessible by local bus or taxi. For information on getting there, see p346. There are several destinations with daily departures:

Chihuahua (US$32, 5hr, 3 deluxe daily; US$23, 5hr, frequent 1st-class services)

Mexico City (US$116, 24hr, frequent 1st-class services) To Terminal Norte.

Nuevo Casas Grandes (US$14, 4hr, hourly 1st-class services)

Frequent 1st-class buses also go to Durango, Monterrey, San Luis Potosí and Zacatecas. Autobuses Americanos buses going direct to US cities (eg Albuquerque, Dallas and Denver) are generally cheaper than Greyhound from El Paso.

The **El Paso Greyhound station** (☎ 915-532-2365) has its main entrance on Santa Fe St between Av Overland and Av San Antonio. Several buses a day travel to Los Angeles (US$45, 16 hours), Chicago (US$99, 34 hours), Miami (US$99, 35 hours), New York (US$99, 48 hours) and other major US cities.

CAR & MOTORCYCLE

If you're driving into the Mexican interior, you must obtain a vehicle permit (see p970). The only place to do so in the Ciudad Juárez area (even if you're heading in another direction) is at the major customs checkpoint at Km 30 on Hwy 45D south.

Beyond the checkpoint, the highway to Chihuahua is in good condition but it comes with a US$10 toll. Hwy 2 to Nuevo Casas Grandes branches west at a traffic circle 25km south of town.

For liability and vehicle insurance coverage while in Mexico, compare the policies of these companies in El Paso: **Sanborn's** (☎ 915-779-3538; 2401 E Missouri Av) or **AAA** (☎ 915-778-9521; 1201 Airway Blvd).

TRAIN

El Paso's **Amtrak station** (☎ 915-545-2247; 700 San Francisco) is three blocks west of the Civic Center Plaza. Trains run three times a week to Los Angeles (US$96, 15 hours), Chicago (US$123, 48 hours), Miami (US$138, 48 hours) and New York (US$204, 60 hours).

Getting Around

Local buses to the Juárez bus station leave from Guerrero just west of Villa. Catch a blue-striped 'C Camionera' bus or a green-top 'Permisionarios Unidos' bus (US$0.40); it's a 25-minute trip. From the bus station to the town center, turn left and go out to the highway; any bus labeled 'Centro' will drop you near the cathedral. Inside the bus station, a booth sells tickets for authorized taxis into town (US$7.75).

From the El Paso bus station to the Juárez bus stations, hourly buses run for US$5. Autobuses Twin Cities runs a shuttle service between the Juárez and El Paso downtown areas; the blue vans depart from the corner of Villa and Galeana every 10 minutes (US$0.30). A taxi over the border from the El Paso airport costs $30, or you can catch one of the frequent Border Jumper trolleys from the El Paso Civic Center, in the center of downtown, accessible by public buses from the airport. In Ciudad Juárez, taxis from the Av Juárez area (where they are plentiful) to the pricier hotels toward Pronaf cost about US$8.

NUEVO CASAS GRANDES & CASAS GRANDES

☎ 636 / pop 55,000 / elevation 1463m

Nuevo Casas Grandes, a four-hour bus trip southwest of Ciudad Juárez, is a sleepy, prosperous country town with wide streets and a vibe similar to that of dusty small towns in the US West. The people, a mix of working folk, farming families and Mormon settlers whose presence dates back to the late 19th century, are unhurried and friendly. But the only real draw is for archaeology fans, who come in trickles to see the ruins of Paquimé, in the nearby residential village of Casas Grandes.

Information

You'll find banks (ATMs at Banamex and Bancomer), several *casas de cambio* and a post office clustered within blocks of 5 de Mayo and Constitución (Constitución is the street with railway tracks down the middle). For Internet and email, try **Paquinet** (☎ 694-66-66; Minerva 101; per hr US$3).

Sights

The **Centro Cultural Paquimé: Museo de las Culturas del Norte & Paquimé Ruins** (☎ 692-41-40; admission to museum & ruins US$4, video US$3.25; ☼ 10am-5pm Tue-Sun) are what give Casas Grandes (Big Houses) its name. The crumbling adobe remnants are from what was the major trading settlement in northern Mexico between AD 900 and 1340. Partially excavated and restored, the networks of eroded walls now resemble roofless mazes. Unfortunately, you're no longer allowed to wander within them, as the passageways have been chained off to protect the walls from damage. So circling around the rebuilt walls can seem a bit like visiting a boring, low-key theme park, except to the archaeology-inclined.

But the Paquimé people have a fascinating history, as they were a flourishing civilization with significant ties to the pre-Hispanic cultures of Arizona and New Mexico as well as other parts of Mexico. The structures here are similar to Pueblo houses of the US Southwest, with distinctive T-shaped door openings. Timber beams set into the walls supported roofs and upper floors, and the largest dwellings had up to three levels. While the walls are all that now exist in the ruins, mini samples of entire homes can be seen in the museum.

Despite the fortifications, Paquimé was invaded, perhaps by Apaches, in 1340. The city was sacked, burned and abandoned, and its great structures were left alone for more than 600 years. The site was partially excavated in the late 1950s, and subsequent exposure to the elements led to erosion of the walls until their restoration some years later.

The Paquimé were great potters and produced pieces from black clay as well as cream-colored earthenware with striking red, brown or black geometric designs. View the fine examples in the museum. But if you're interested in buying locally made pottery in the Paquimé style, skip the gift shop in favor of the small shop near the site's entrance, run by the Ortiz family, where you'll find all sizes of vases and bowls for incredibly reasonable prices (from about US$30 for small items to $175 for larger ones.)

Sleeping

Las Guacamayas B&B (☎ 692-41-44; maytelujan@msn .com; near entrance of Paquimé site; s/d with breakfast US$40/50; **P**) Offering the only accommodations worth getting excited about for miles around, this precious hostel/café sits snuggled on the edge of the small Casas Grandes village. While there is absolutely nothing around except small houses and the Paquimé ruins, the pink, adobe-style building has all you need: 11 charming rooms with tile floors, a lovely garden area with a hammock, and breakfast served in the owner's kitchen. It's about a 15-minute hike from the bus stop in Casas Grandes; when you get to the site's entrance, follow the convoluted signs for 'Hostal y Galeria de Arte y Café La Tertulia y Las Guacamayas B&B.'

Hotel Hacienda (☎ 694-10-46; hotelhacienda@pa quinet.com.mx; Av Juárez 2603; s/d US$57/67; **P** ✗ ❄ ❧) The Hacienda, 1.5km north of Nuevo Casas Grandes on Hwy 10, is the best option in or near Nuevo Casas Grandes, offering a garden courtyard, swimming pool, restaurant and comfortable air-conditioned rooms. The hotel also organizes guide services to the ruins.

Hotel California (☎ 694-11-10; fax 694-08-34; Constitución 209; s/d $29/34; ❄) This friendly hotel in the heart of town is an excellent choice, offering clean, air-conditioned rooms – with no carpets!

Motel Piñón (☎ 694-06-55; Av Juárez 605; s/d US$38/ 42; **P** ❄ ❧) On Juárez as you enter town from the north, this motor lodge features scruffy, air-conditioned rooms which reflect a faint and cheesy attempt to incorpo-

rate Paquimé motifs into the décor. There's a restaurant offering cheap breakfasts, an outdoor pool and a dimly lit bar. See the bartender, Mauricio, for driving tours of Paquimé, Mata Ortiz (see p348) and other area attractions.

Hotel Juárez (☎ 694-02-33; Obregón 110; s/d US$10/ 12) Most budget travelers stay at this dingy place, just south of 5 de Mayo and a stone's throw from the bus station. There's no heating or air-con (although some rooms have a fan), but for one or two nights it's tolerable.

Eating & Drinking

Constantino (☎ 694-10-05; cnr Juárez & Minerva; main dishes US$6; ☾ 7am-midnight) Located just north of the main plaza, the Constantino is popular with locals all day and serves fresh, tasty meals.

Dinno's Pizza (☎ 694-33-54; cnr 5 de Mayo & Obregón; main dishes US$6; ☾ noon-9pm) In addition to its good pizzas, this clean and popular place offers Szechuan-style dishes and good, strong coffee that the locals love.

Chuchy (☎ 694-07-09; Constitución 202; tortas US$2; ☾ 9am-8pm Mon-Sat) Chuchy's classic lunch counter is the perfect place to enjoy cheap, filling fare, from tortas to fries – plus a side of warm chat with Chuchy, the friendly old-timer who has owned the place for two decades.

Tortas Candela (Obregón, directly across from bus station; tortas US$1.50; ☾ 9am-9pm) This tiny, brightly-lit sandwich shop churns out extremely fresh, home-baked rolls stuffed with pork, cheese, creamy avocado and plenty of hot peppers.

Getting There & Away

Daily buses run to/from Ciudad Juárez (US$14, four hours), Chihuahua (US$18, 4½ hours) and Madera (US$17, four hours). Other daily buses run to Cuauhtémoc, Monterrey and Zacatecas.

Driving south to Madera, turn right onto Hwy 28 at Buenaventura. This road climbs through scenic mountains dotted with oaks and short stubby cacti on its way to Zaragoza and Gómez Farías before arriving at Madera. It's best driven in daylight.

Getting Around

Nuevo Casas Grandes is compact enough to walk everywhere within the town, unless you're staying at Hotel Hacienda, where you can get a taxi to take you into the center of town for about US$3. To reach the ruins, take a 'Casas Grandes/Col Juárez' bus from Constitución in the center of Nuevo Casas Grandes; they run every half hour during the day. The 8km journey takes about 15 minutes (US$0.50). You will be let off at the picturesque main plaza of Casas Grandes, and from there signs direct you to the ruins, a 15-minute walk. An alternative is to select one of the many local taxis, which queue up at 5 de Mayo and Constitución in Nuevo Casas Grandes and charge about US$8 to take you to Paquimé.

AROUND NUEVO CASAS GRANDES

Trips to the west and south of Nuevo Casas Grandes take in some interesting little towns, cool forests and several archaeological sites. Most can be reached by bus, but to see the ancient rock carvings in the rugged **Arroyo de los Monos**, 35km to the south, you will need a vehicle with good clearance.

A good day trip could include the Mormon village of **Colonia Juárez** and the **Hacienda de San Diego** (a 1902 mansion owned by the Terrazas family, who controlled most of pre-revolutionary Chihuahua state).

The journey to mountain-flanked **Mata Ortiz**, 30km south of Nuevo Casas Grandes, culminates with a long stretch of unpaved roads. It's an internationally renowned center for the production of pottery using materials, techniques and decorative styles like those of the ancient Paquimé culture. Juan Quezada, credited with reviving the Paquimé pottery tradition, is the most famous of the village's 300 potters; the best can command US$1000 per piece.

There are two hotels in teensy Mata Ortiz, both offering full board: the **Posada de las Ollas** (☎ 636-698-64-10; s/d US$39/59) and the more expensive and luxurious **Hotel del Adobe** (☎ 636-694-62-83; s/d US$45/75). It may be possible to find cheaper accommodations in **private homes**.

Visit www.ortizpots.com or www.mataor tizpottery.com for tour information. Some of the myriad companies offering tours to Mata Ortiz, either alone or as part of a larger itinerary, include **Baja's Frontier Tours** (☎ 800-726-7231, Tucson, AZ; www.bajasfrontierstours .com), which runs three-day visits to town, and **Cultural Arts Tours & Workshops** (☎ 323-344-

9064; Los Angeles), which arranges walking tours and pottery classes in town.

One bus a day makes the journey from Nuevo Casas Grandes to Mata Ortiz (US$3.75, 1½ hours), departing at 4pm from the market and returning the next morning at 8am. Try bargaining with mellow taxi drivers in Nuevo Casas Grandes to take you instead, but most are reluctant to make the 'long' drive – curious, considering there is barely any taxi business within the town itself!

MADERA & AROUND

☎ 652 / pop 15,600 / elevation 2092m

In the sierra south of Nuevo Casas Grandes, the Madera area is lush with mighty pine trees, salmon-colored cliffs, waterfalls and a wealth of archaeological sites.

Sights
CUARENTA CASAS

The existence of cliff dwellings at **Cuarenta Casas** (Forty Houses; admission US$1; ☉ 9am-3pm) was known to the Spaniards as early as the 16th century, when explorer Álvar Núñez Cabeza de Vaca wrote in his chronicles, '…and here by the side of the mountain we forged our way inland more than 50 leagues and found 40 houses.'

The number may have been exaggerated: about a dozen adobe apartments are carved into the west cliffside of a dramatic canyon at La Cueva de las Ventanas (Cave of the Windows); it's the only cave accessible to the public, although others can be viewed from the visitors' hut. Last occupied in the 13th century, Cuarenta Casas is believed to have been an outlying settlement of Paquimé, perhaps a garrison for defense of commercial routes to the Pacific coast. Though the site is not as well preserved as the dwellings at Casas Grandes, its natural setting and the hike required to get there make it a worthy outdoor excursion.

Cuarenta Casas is 43km north of Madera via a good paved road through pine forest. From the turnoff, a dirt road leads 1.5km to the entrance, where a trail descends into the Arroyo del Garabato and climbs the western slopes to the cave. Signs in English, Spanish and Tarahumara provide historical background along the way. The 1.5km hike isn't easy and takes about 80 minutes round-trip. Expect freezing temperatures in winter and be off the premises by 3pm.

From Madera, an 11:30am bus (US$4.50) goes by Cuarenta Casas en route to the town of Largo. In the reverse direction, it stops at the site at around 4pm, allowing just enough time to make a day trip from Madera.

SITES WEST OF MADERA

About 66km west of Madera, **Cueva Grande** sits behind a waterfall during the rainy season; inside the cave are some ancient adobe buildings in the architectural style of the Mogollón culture, closely associated with Paquimé. More of these cliff dwellings can be seen at **Conjunto Anasazi**, about 35km west of Madera by the same road; a strenuous 4km ascent is required. In the same area as the cliff dwellings is the **Puente Colgante** (Suspension Bridge) over the Río Huápoca, and some **thermal springs**.

The unpaved road to Cueva Grande should be attempted with a 4WD vehicle only; try to find a local guide to take you from Madera. **Motel Real del Bosque** (see below) offers guided van excursions that take in the Conjunto Anasazi, Cueva Grande and other points west for US$22 per person (minimum of eight participants). Or you may be able to find English-speaking taxi drivers at the taxi stand opposite the bus station in Madera starting at about US$50.

Sleeping & Eating

Motel Real del Bosque (☎ 572-05-38; s & d US$39; **P** ✖) This, the nicest place in town, is on the highway coming in from Chihuahua. The motel's rooms are spacious and carpet-free, and its operators conduct tours of the ruins and natural attractions in the area.

Hotel María (☎ 572-03-23; cnr Calle 5 & 5 de Mayo; s/d US$22/25) The rooms here are cramped but comfortable, and second-floor rooms are airier and nicest; the small restaurant has excellent Mexican breakfasts.

Parador de la Sierra (☎ 572-02-77, cnr Calle 3 & Independencia; s/d US$23/27) Large wood-paneled rooms here come with heaters and face a secluded courtyard. The next-door disco can make sleep difficult.

El Mexicano Restaurant (cnr Calle 3 & Guerrero; mains US$4-7) This friendly place offers cheap, filling meals of seafood, steak and Mexican food.

Getting There & Away

Madera's bus station is located on Calle 5. Second-class buses run to/from Cuauhté-moc (US$11, hourly, two hours), Chihuahua (US$17, hourly, three hours), Nuevo Casas Grandes (US$18, two daily, two hours) and Ciudad Juárez (US$33, three daily). The winding, scenic cliff road linking Madera and Nuevo Casas Grandes should not be driven at night.

CHIHUAHUA

☎ 614 / pop 688,200 / elevation 1455m

Chihuahua is a peaceful city, unfettered by the trappings of major tourism. It has some beautiful parks and plazas, excellent restaurants, a bustling market and a fine collection of cultural offerings. The bulk of foreigners use the metropolis only as an overnight stop at the start or finish of the Copper Canyon Railway, though, so the folks you'll encounter most will be the locals – a pleasing mix of professionals, working-class, students and dapper ranch-eros decked out in Wranglers and brightly colored cowboy boots.

This capital city of Mexico's largest state, Chihuahua, is a prosperous one, as evidenced by the fine colonial buildings that dot the city's center and the newer suburbs and industries that sprawl around the edges. Its main attractions are Pancho Villa's old house, Quinta Luz, and the museum of the Mexican Revolution that now occupies it, along with the main market, visited early in the morning by Mennonites and colorfully attired Tarahumaras.

History

The name Chihuahua literally means 'dry and sandy zone' in the indigenous Nahua language, and that's a good description for the landscape around the city. From the first few Spanish settlers it grew in size to become both an administration center for the surrounding territory and a commercial center for cattle and mining interests. In the War of Independence, rebel leader Miguel Hidalgo fled here, only to be betrayed, imprisoned by the Spaniards and shot. President Benito Juárez made Chihuahua his headquarters for a while when forced to flee northward by the French troops of Emperor Maximilian. The city also served as a major garrison for cavalry guarding vulnerable settlements from the incessant raids of the Apaches, until the tribe was subdued by the legendary 'Indian fighter,' Colonel Joaquín Terrazas.

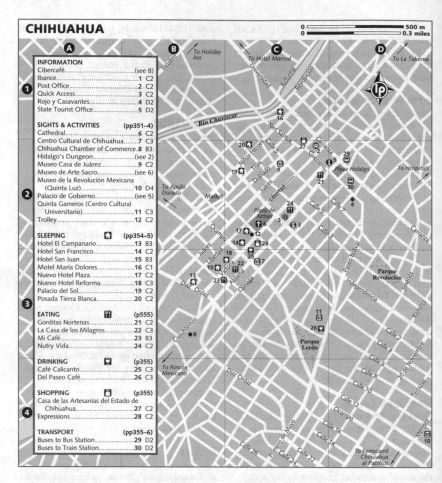

CHIHUAHUA

| 0 | 500 m |
| 0 | 0.3 miles |

INFORMATION
Cibercafé	(see 8)
Ibance	1 C2
Post Office	2 C2
Quick Access	3 C2
Rojo y Casavantes	4 D2
State Tourist Office	5 D2

SIGHTS & ACTIVITIES (pp351–4)
Cathedral	6 C2
Centro Cultural de Chihuahua	7 C3
Chihuahua Chamber of Commerce	8 B3
Hidalgo's Dungeon	(see 2)
Museo Casa de Juárez	9 C2
Museo de Arte Sacro	(see 6)
Museo de la Revolución Mexicana (Quinta Luz)	10 D4
Palacio de Gobierno	(see 5)
Quinta Gameros (Centro Cultural Universitario)	11 C3
Trolley	12 C2

SLEEPING (pp354–5)
Hotel El Campanario	13 B3
Hotel San Francisco	14 C2
Hotel San Juan	15 B3
Motel María Dolores	16 C1
Nuevo Hotel Plaza	17 C2
Nuevo Hotel Reforma	18 C3
Palacio del Sol	19 C2
Posada Tierra Blanca	20 C2

EATING (p555)
Gorditas Nortenas	21 C2
La Casa de los Milagros	22 C3
Mi Café	23 B3
Nutry Vida	24 C2

DRINKING (p355)
| Café Calicanto | 25 C3 |
| Del Paseo Café | 26 C3 |

SHOPPING (p355)
| Casa de las Artesanías del Estado de Chihuahua | 27 C2 |
| Expressions | 28 C2 |

TRANSPORT (pp355–6)
| Buses to Bus Station | 29 D2 |
| Buses to Train Station | 30 D2 |

The Porfirio Díaz regime brought railways to Chihuahua and helped consolidate the wealth of the huge cattle fiefdoms – one family held lands the size of Belgium.

After Pancho Villa's forces took Chihuahua in 1913 during the Mexican Revolution, Villa established his headquarters here. He had schools built and arranged other civic works, contributing to his status as a local hero. A statue of Villa graces the intersection of Universidad and División del Norte.

Orientation

Most areas of interest in Chihuahua are within a dozen blocks of the central Plaza de Armas – sometimes requiring a long walk or quick taxi ride. Independencia, running approximately northwest–southeast, divides the downtown and serves as a sort of 'zero' point for addresses. Streets parallel to it ascend by odd numbers (Calle 3, 5, 7 etc) heading northeast, and by even numbers heading southwest.

Information

EMERGENCY

Police (☎ 429-33-82) To report a crime or other nonemergency, you can also call this direct police line.

Police, fire & ambulance (☎ 060)

INTERNET ACCESS

Cibercafé (Cámara de Comercio de Chihuahua; Cuauhtémoc 1800; per hr US$3.25; ⌚ 8:30am-7:30pm Mon-Fri,

CHIHUAHUAS

So what's the connection between Chihuahua and those nervous, yipping little dogs? The puny pups – popular house pets averaging about 10cm to 20cm and 2kg in size – were first discovered in this area of Mexico about 100 years ago. While their exact origins are a mystery, it's widely believed that they first came from Asia or Egypt, and were introduced into Mexico by Spanish settlers. The canines were once thought to be indigenously Mexican because of similar creatures depicted in ancient Toltec and Aztec art and described by explorers, but there exists no archaeological evidence to support this belief. Those beasts, say experts, must have been rodents that disappeared from Mexico not long after the Spanish conquest in the 16th century.

9am-1pm Sat) This stone-and-glass structure houses a small Internet café.

Quick Access (☎ 415-33-77; Aldama 109; access per hr US$1.30; ☽ 8am-8pm Mon-Fri, 9am-7pm Sat, 9-2am Sun) This small, 3rd-floor Internet café offers fast hookups at five terminals, plus web camera and scanner services.

LEFT LUGGAGE
The Chihuahua bus station (for information, see p355) has locked baggage storage for US$0.30 per hour.

MEDICAL SERVICES
Hospital Central (☎ 415-90-00; Rosales 3302)
Hospital Clínica del Centro (☎ 416-00-22; Ojinaga 816, Colonia Centro)
Hospital Clínica del Parque (☎ 439-79-14; Rodríguez)

MONEY
Most of the larger banks are around the Plaza de Armas and most are open 9am to 5pm Monday to Friday. You'll find *casas de cambio* on Aldama southwest of the cathedral. **Ibance** (☎ 416-30-30; Aldama 8, ☽ 8am-8pm Mon-Sat) changes traveler's checks, while the nearby Banco Bital has a foreign exchange service.

POST
Palacio Federal (Juárez btwn Guerrero & Carranza; ☽ 8am-6pm Mon-Fri, 9am-1pm Sat).

TELEPHONE
Telmex pay phones, which can be operated with calling cards purchased at newsstands, are plentiful around the city.

TOURIST INFORMATION
State Tourist Office (☎ 410-10-77, 800-849-52-00; cturismo@buzon.chihuahua.gob.mx; ☽ 8:30am-6pm Mon-Fri, 10am-5pm Sat & Sun) On the ground floor of the Palacio de Gobierno, this information outlet has an extraordinarily helpful, English-speaking staff and a wide array of brochures.

TRAVEL AGENCIES
Rojo y Casavantes (☎ 415-58-58; Guerrero 1207 at Allende; ☽ 9am-6pm Mon-Fri, 9am-noon Sat) This friendly, full-service agency can assist you with bus, train and airplane tickets and provide tourist information on other areas in Mexico.

UNIVERSITIES
Universidad de Chihuahua (☎ 439-15-30; Av Escorza 900) The neighborhood surrounding this 48-year-old university is alive with intellectual young folk; programs range from political science to agriculture. There's also an impressive art museum, not on the campus (see Quinta Gameros, p352).

Sights
CATHEDRAL
Chihuahua's main Plaza de Armas, with its mass of pigeons, shoe shiners and loafing local men, is far from the prettiest plaza in Mexico. But the towers of its majestic **cathedral** (☽ 10am-8pm) at least lend the area a heavenly air. Construction, which began in 1726, was not completed until 1789 because of frequent raids by indigenous tribes. Its marvelous baroque façade contrasts with the simpler interior, featuring 16 columns and a small cupola. On the southeast side is the entrance to the small **Museo de Arte Sacro** (☎ 413-63-04; admission US$1; ☽ 10am-2pm & 4-6pm Mon-Fri), which displays 38 religious paintings from the 18th century. The painters represented were among the founders of Mexico City's first art schools, notably the Academia de San Carlos.

MUSEO DE LA REVOLUCIÓN MEXICANA (QUINTA LUZ)
Housed in the mansion and former headquarters of Pancho Villa, the **Museum of the Mexican Revolution** (☎ 416-29-58; Calle 10; admission US$1; ☽ 9am-1pm & 3-7pm Tue-Sat, 9am-5pm Sun) is a

must-see, not only for history buffs but for anyone who can appreciate a good made-for-Hollywood story of crime, stakeouts and riches.

After his assassination in 1923, a number of Villa's 'wives' (a hilariously long list is displayed at the ticket counter) filed claim for his estate. Government investigations determined that Luz Corral de Villa was the *generalísimo's* legal spouse; the mansion was awarded to her and became known as Quinta Luz (*quinta* means villa or country house). When Luz died in 1981, the government acquired the estate and made it a museum. Inside are rooms with their original furnishings, a veritable arsenal of weaponry, historical documents and some exceptional photographs of the revolution and its principals. The accompanying explanations are in Spanish, but you don't

need narratives to understand most of the offerings – especially the bullet-riddled black Dodge that Villa was driving when he was murdered, on morbid display in the back courtyard.

You can walk to the museum from the city center or take any bus designated 'Avaloz' or 'Juárez' running southeast on Ocampo. Get off the bus at the corner of Méndez, cross the street and walk downhill on Méndez for two blocks. Or visit as part of the city's trolley tour (see Trolley Turístico, p354), in which case you'll be dropped off at the museum entrance.

QUINTA GAMEROS

Manuel Gameros started building this gorgeous art nouveau **mansion** (☎ 416-66-84; cnr Bolívar & Calle 4; adult/child US$2.50/1.25; ⏱ 11am-2pm & 4-7pm Tue-Sun) in 1907 as a wedding present

---

PANCHO VILLA: BANDIT-TURNED-REVOLUTIONARY

Although best known as a hero of the Mexican Revolution, for much of his adult life Francisco 'Pancho' Villa was a murderous thief more given to robbing and womanizing than to any noble cause. Born Doroteo Arango on June 5, 1878, in the village of La Coyotada in rural Durango, the future revolutionary legend lived the rather unremarkable childhood of a typical peasant boy who later found work on a farm. That peaceful life took an abrupt turn on September 22, 1894, when 16-year-old Doroteo took the law into his own hands.

Accounts of what happened that day vary, but the popular version involves an alleged affront to the honor of his 12-year-old sister, Martina: Doroteo was returning from work in the fields when he came upon the landowner attempting to abduct Martina. Doroteo ran to a cousin's house, took a pistol down from a wall, then ran down the landowner and shot him. Fearing reprisal, Doroteo took to the hills and abandoned his baptismal name, calling himself Francisco Villa. 'Pancho,' as his associates called him, spent the next 16 years as a bandit and cattle thief, variously riding with three vicious gangs.

Although the life of Pancho Villa the Revolutionary is well documented, his years as a bandit are obscured by contradictory claims, half-truths and outright lies. But one thing is certain: although an outlaw and ever the bully, Villa detested alcohol, and the sight of excessive drinking made his blood boil. In his *Memorias*, Villa gleefully recalled how he once stole a magnificent horse from a man who was preoccupied with getting drunk in a cantina.

Long after his outlaw years, Pancho Villa became uncharacteristically mum whenever the subject of his criminal past came up. By 1909, at age 31, Villa had bought a house in Chihuahua and was running a peaceful, if not entirely legitimate, business trading in horses and meat from dubious sources. That spring, Chihuahua's revolutionary governor Abraham González began recruiting men to break dictator Porfirio Díaz' grip on Mexico, and among the people he lobbied was Villa. González knew about Villa's past, but he also knew that he needed men like Villa – natural leaders who knew how to fight – if he ever hoped to depose Díaz. Thus, González encouraged Villa to return to marauding, but this time for a noble cause: agrarian reform. The idea appealed to Villa, and a year later he joined the revolution.

Villa had no trouble finding men to fight beside him against federal troops, who had been taught only to march in perfect step and fire in volleys. The army knew nothing about how to deal with these mobs of men who, armed with hand bombs and rifles, attacked one minute and disappeared the next. When rebels under Villa's leadership took Ciudad Juárez in May 1911, Díaz

for his fiancée. By the time it was finished four years later, she had fallen in love with the architect, the Colombian Julio Corredor Latorre, and decided to marry him instead. Despite the wistful feeling this story will elicit when you see the place, the upstairs galleries, holding the **Centro Cultural Universitario** (the Universidad de Chihuahua's art collection), offer some cultural comfort.

PALACIO DE GOBIERNO
This handsome, 19th-century **palace** (cnr Aldama & Guerrero; free; ☺ 8am-8pm) features colonnades of arches surrounding the classic courtyard, and murals showing the history of Chihuahua cover the walls. Be sure to climb one of the wide staircases to the top and look down at the colorful bustle of visitors and government employees. On one side of the courtyard is a small room

with a flickering eternal flame marking the place where Hidalgo was shot.

HIDALGO'S DUNGEON
The cell in which Hidalgo was held prior to his execution is beneath the post office in what is now the **Palacio Federal** (Juárez btwn Guerrero & Carranza; admission US$0.50; ☺ 9am-6:30pm Tue-Sun). The entrance to the building is on Juárez – look for the cracked eagle's head inscribed 'Libertad.' The creepy quarters contain Hidalgo's crucifix, pistol and other personal effects, and a plaque recalls the verses the revolutionary priest dedicated to his captors in his final hours.

MUSEO CASA DE JUÁREZ
The home and office of Benito Juárez during the period of French occupation now houses this **museum** (☎ 410-42-58; Juárez 321;

---

resigned. Francisco Madero, a wealthy liberal from the state of Coahuila, was elected president in November 1911.

But Madero was unable to contain the various factions fighting for control throughout the country, and in early 1913 he was toppled from power by one of his own commanders, General Victoriano Huerta, and executed. Pancho Villa fled across the US border to El Paso, but within a couple of months he was back in Mexico, one of four revolutionary leaders opposed to Huerta. Villa quickly raised an army of thousands, the División del Norte, and by the end of 1913 he had taken Ciudad Juárez (again) and Chihuahua. His victory at Zacatecas the following year is reckoned to be one of his most brilliant. Huerta was finally defeated and forced to resign in July 1914. With his defeat, the four revolutionary forces split into two camps, with the liberal Venustiano Carranza and Álvaro Obregón on one side and the more radical Villa and Emiliano Zapata on the other, though the latter pair never formed a serious alliance. Villa was defeated by Obregón in the big battle of Celaya (1915) and never recovered militarily.

But before their fighting days were over, Villa's soldiers would go down in history for, among other things, being one of the few forces ever to invade the United States. Angered by troop support provided to Obregón by the US government in the battle of Celaya, and by the refusal of American merchants to sell them contraband despite cash advances for goods, in 1916 the Villistas ravaged the town of Columbus, New Mexico, and killed 18 Americans. The attack resulted in the US sending 12,000 soldiers into Mexico to pursue the invaders, but the slow-moving columns never did catch Villa's men.

In July 1920, after 10 years of revolutionary fighting, Villa signed a peace treaty with Adolfo de la Huerta, who had been chosen as the provisional president two months earlier. Villa pledged to lay down his arms and retire to a hacienda called Canutillo, 80km south of Hidalgo del Parral, for which the Huerta government paid 636,000 pesos. In addition, Villa was given 35,926 pesos to cover wages owed to his troops. He also received money to buy farm tools, pay a security guard and help the widows and orphans of the División del Norte.

For the next three years, Villa led a relatively quiet life. He bought a hotel in Parral and regularly attended cockfights. He installed one of his many 'wives,' Soledad Seañez, in a Parral apartment, and kept another at Canutillo. Then, one day while he was leaving Parral in his big Dodge touring car, a volley of shots rang out from a two-story house. Five of the seven passengers in the car were killed, including the legendary revolutionary. An eight-man assassin team fired the fatal shots, but just who ordered the killings remains a mystery.

admission US$0.50; ⊗ 9am-7pm Tue-Sun), which maintains an 1850s feel and exhibits documents signed by the great reformer as well as a replica of the carriage he used while in Chihuahua.

CENTRO CULTURAL DE CHIHUAHUA

Formerly a private home, this **center** (Aldama 430; ⊗ 10am-2pm & 4-7pm Tue-Sun) features intricate ironwork imported from New Orleans, a glass-domed patio, a small permanent exhibit on Paquimé pottery, and frequent cultural events and concerts.

TROLLEY TURÍSTICO

Chihuahua is in the midst of a new tourism campaign, and with it has come one of those silly trolleys (cnr Libertad & Plaza de Armas; tours US$3; ⊗ 9am-1pm & 3-7pm) that can be seen in tourist cities all over the world. This not being a tourist city, though, the trolley wasn't having much luck corralling passengers when this author was in town. In the meantime, you can use your trolley ticket all day long to visit Chihuahua's main attractions while boarding and disembarking whenever you please. Since none of the stops are too far away from each other, it's not a necessary tour to make. But if you're in a hurry to get a quick peek at everything, a ride on the loop takes about half an hour.

Sleeping

Chihuahua has a vast range of options for everyone's budget; just be warned that, while cheap spots do have a cheap feel, the luxury hotels are a tad scruffier than the sophisticated traveler may be accustomed to – just as in much of the rest of the country.

BUDGET

Hotel San Juan (☎ 410-00-35; Victoria 823; s/d US$10/13; P) This scruffy backpackers' flophouse, with a lovely tiled patio entrance and lively tavern, is good value – as long as you don't mind a bleak and dingy room with a flimsy lock on the door. Single women may feel uncomfortable in the long, dark hallways, and amid the male vibe.

Nuevo Hotel Reforma (☎ 410-03-47; Victoria 809; s/d US$13/15) The Reforma's dreary rooms are on par with those of its San Juan neighbor, but with some slightly different setbacks – terribly thin mattresses and rank-smelling quarters. But it is quiet, and does have overhead fans, a fairly grand lobby and a cozy cafeteria serving cheap meals all day long.

Nuevo Hotel Plaza (☎ 415-58-34; Calle 4 No 206; s/d US$9/10; ✕) Chihuahua's least expensive option is this faded and battered hotel, directly behind the cathedral. Rooms aren't bad for the price, with central air-con, ample hot water and lots of what once was polished wood.

Motel María Dolores (☎ 410-47-70; Niños Héroes 917; s/d US$19/21; P ✕) At the corner of Calle 9, the motel's basic but modern and air-conditioned rooms are a very good deal and fill up quickly.

MID-RANGE

Apolo Dorado (☎ 416-11-00; hapolo@prodigy.net.mx; Calle 14 No 321 at Teófilo Borunda; s/d US$42/45; ✕) This brand-new conversion of an old hotel was not yet open to visitors at press time. But if its former location, the elegant Hotel Apolo – with its Greco-Roman lobby and old-fashioned rooms – is any indication, it'll be a charming choice.

Hotel El Campanario (☎ 415-45-45; Díaz Ordaz; s/d US$47/50; ✕) A fine choice with large comfortable rooms, El Campanario is your standard type of spot that lacks style but is in a good, central location.

Posada Tierra Blanca (☎ 415-00-00; Niños Héroes 100; s/d US$45/48; P ✕ ⊛) This large motor-lodge-style place has stuffy but clean rooms, a nice outdoor pool and friendly staff, though its neighborhood can get slightly dicey after dark.

TOP END

Hotel San Francisco (☎ 416-75-50; hsanfco@chihuahua .podernet.com.mx; Victoria 409; r Fri-Sun US$75, Mon-Thu US$85; P ✕ ✕ ▣) It's well-worth the extra 30 bucks that it costs to stay in this luxury inn – especially on weekends, when rates are lowest. Sitting behind the cathedral and within walking distance of the market and good eateries, it's in a perfect location, and has all the high-end amenities, from satellite TV to a touristy restaurant and cocktail lounge. Best of all is the massive flock of tiny sparrows who migrate at sunset to the telephone wires just in front of Victoria, lending an eerily beautiful vibe to your stay.

Palacio del Sol (☎ 416-60-00; palacio@infosel.net .mx; Independencia 116; r Fri-Sun US$125, Mon-Thu US$95; P ✕ ✕ ▣) Yes, it's a hideous monstrosity from the outside – a white cement high-rise looming over the low-level city like some kind of urban prison. But the rooms are positively luxurious and the doting service is not so bad either.

Holiday Inn Hotel & Suites Chihuahua (☎ 439-00-00; suites@holidaychih.com; Escudero 702; s & d US$135-250; P 🗙 🗙 🖵 🗷) Unfortunately, the city's classiest option is part of the Holiday Inn conglomerate. But if you're a Copper Canyon rider seeking a tranquil escape – with a deluxe suite, spa and private, well-groomed grounds – you'll find it here, in the hills overlooking downtown.

Eating

Mi Café (☎ 410-12-38; Victoria 1000; mains US$5) This classic American-style diner caters both to travelers and local cowboys, serving up excellent breakfasts of egg platters and coffee at big, comfy booths.

La Casa de los Milagros (☎ 437-06-93; Victoria 812; mains US$6; ☽ 8am-2pm, 5pm-late) A variety of local hipsters flock to this stylish café for live music on weekends. But Milagros, housed in a beautiful old mansion and featuring high ceilings, tiled floors, local artwork and an open-roofed courtyard, is an excellent choice for lunch, dinner or drinks on any day of the week. The light-fare menu features a huge selection of coffee drinks, fresh salads and hearty *antojitos*, such as quesadillas filled with *huitlacoche*.

Nutry Vida (Aldama 117 at Calle 3, mains US$3) This natural-foods store, featuring a small café with several tables, is a vegetarian's paradise. You'll find delicious veggie burgers, salads, homemade yogurts, fresh-squeezed juices and a variety of vegan baked goods to eat in or take out.

Rincón Mexicano (☎ 411-14-27; Av Cuauhtémoc 2224, mains US$10; ☽ 8pm-midnight) You'll find occasional live music, excellent service, classic *comidas* and a festive ambience in the form of brightly tiled fireplaces, ochre walls and gleaming floors at this dinner spot. Menu highlights include grilled black bass, a succulent T-bone steak with chipotle gravy, enchiladas with three types of mole sauce and some amazing *huitlacoche* quesadillas.

Gorditas Norteñas (Aldamas 709; mains US$1.50; ☽ noon-4:30pm) This casual counter eatery is a don't-miss spot for tasty, cheap, fresh and filling gorditas, stuffed with treats from cheese and sliced hot peppers to spicy shredded pork.

Drinking

Hotel San Juan (see Sleeping, opposite) The bar edging the front courtyard of the San Juan hotel has divey character, a friendly vibe and entertainment in the form of norteño troubadours.

Café Calicanto (☎ 410-44-52; Aldama 411; ☽ 4pm-1am Sun-Thu, 4pm-2am Fri & Sat) Enjoy live jazz and folk music, top-shelf cocktails, light snacks and a young trendy crowd on the tree-lined patio of this intimate café.

Del Paseo Café (☎ 410-32-00; Paseo Bolívar 411, Colonia Centro; ☽ 4pm-late) Located along the wide Paseo Bolívar near the university, this bar and eatery has a little something for everyone: live music on weekends, a bustling outdoor patio, luscious cocktails, a good wine list and a full menu, offering everything from salads and tacos to steaks and desserts.

Shopping

Cowboy-boot shoppers should make a beeline to Libertad between Independencia and Díaz Ordaz, where stores jammed with a flashy selection of reasonably priced rawhide, ostrich, lizard and alligator boots line the avenue. There are some other good buying options:

Casa de las Artesanías del Estado de Chihuahua (☎ 437-12-92; Juárez 705; ☽ 9am-7pm Mon-Fri, 9am-5pm Sat & Sun) Paquimé pottery, Urique baskets and Tarahumara clothing are reasonably priced at this state-run shop with a market ambience, across from the post office.

Expressions (Victoria 412; ☽ 9am-6pm) Sure, this boutique is a touristy one, but the brightly colored T-shirts, emblazoned with fun, cartoonish graphics of Chihuahuas and cows and designed by a local artist, are the cutest souvenirs in town.

Getting There & Away

AIR
Chihuahua's airport has five flights a day to Mexico City and daily flights to Los Angeles and to major cities in northern Mexico.

BUS
The bus station on Av Aeropuerto contains restaurants, a luggage storage facility and a telephone caseta. Chihuahua is a major center for buses in every direction:
Ciudad Juárez (US$23, 5hr, hourly 1st-class)
Creel (US$17, 5hr, hourly 2nd-class)

Cuauhtémoc (US$6, 1½hr, 1st-class every 30min)
Durango (S$37, 9hr, frequent 1st-class)
Hidalgo del Parral (US$13, 3hr, frequent 1st-class;
US$9, 3hr, 5 2nd-class daily)
Madera (US$17, 3hr, hourly 2nd-class)
Mexico City (US$92, 18-22hr, frequent 1st-class)
To Terminal Norte.
Nuevo Casas Grandes (US$18.50, 4½hr; 6 1st-class
daily; US$16, 7 2nd-class daily)
Zacatecas (US$52, 12hr, frequent 1st-class)

Other buses go to Mazatlán, Ojinaga,
Monterrey, Saltillo, San Luis Potosí, Torreón and Tijuana. Omnibus Americanos
departs daily for Phoenix, Los Angeles, Albuquerque and Denver.

TRAIN
Chihuahua is the northeastern terminus
of the Chihuahua al Pacífico line for Barranca del Cobre (Copper Canyon) trains.
The train station to get to and from other
cities, including Juarez and México, is different from the Copper Canyon railroad,
and is located about 15 km north of the
central tourist area, near the intersection
of Méndez and Calle 24. Tickets are sold
from 5am to 7am and 9am to 6pm Monday, Wednesday and Friday; 5am to 6am
and 9am to 6pm Tuesday and Thursday;
5am to 6am and 9am to noon Saturday and
Sunday.

The air-conditioned primera express, No
74, departs daily at 6am for the 14-hour run
through the canyon country to Los Mochis.
Train No 73 from the coast supposedly arrives in Chihuahua at 7:50pm but is usually
late. The fare is US$112 each way. The clase
económica train, No 76, leaves Chihuahua
daily at 7am and takes at least two hours
longer. Though not as luxurious as the 1st-
class train, it's quite comfortable and air-
conditioned. This train in turn has two fare
categories: turista for US$56 and subsidio
for much less but available only to locals
with identification. For more information
on the trains and stops along the way, see
p322.

Getting Around
The bus station is a half-hour ride east
of town along Av Pacheco. To get there,
catch a 'Circunvalación 2 Sur' bus on Carranza across the street from Plaza Hidalgo
(US$0.40). From the bus stop in front of

the station, the 'Circunvalación Maquilas'
bus goes back to the center.

For the Chihuahua al Pacífico station,
take a 'Cerro de la Cruz' bus on Carranza at
Plaza Hidalgo, get off at the prison (it looks
like a medieval castle), then walk behind the
prison to the station.

A taxi stand on Victoria near the cathedral charges standard rates to the train
station (US$3.25), bus station (US$5) and
airport (US$10).

CUAUHTÉMOC
☎ 625 / pop 89,500 / elevation 2010m
West of Chihuahua, Cuauhtémoc is a center
for the Mennonite population of northern
Mexico. From the town's west end, Hwy 65
runs north through the principal Mennonite zone, with entrances to the numbered
campos (villages) along the way.

Information
Cumbres Friessen (☎ 582-54-57; info@divitur.com
.mx; Calle 3 No 466; 4½hr tours US$25 per person) Travel
agency conducting tours in English that include visits to a
local cheese-maker and to traditional Mennonite homes
and schools.
Logi-Q Computación (on the plaza; per hr US$3.50;
🕑 9am-2pm & 3:30-7pm Mon-Fri, 9am-3pm Sat)
Small café providing Internet connections.

Sleeping & Eating
Hotel San Francisco (☎ 582-31-52; Calle 3 No 132;
s/d with breakfast US$10/11; P 🐾) This serious
bargain offers spotless, modern rooms.

Motel Tarahumara Inn (☎ 581-19-19; www.tara
humarainn.com in Spanish; Av Allende 373; s & d US$55;
P ✖ 🐾) This is a very comfortable hotel
with clean, surprisingly unstuffy rooms
with tile floors, plus parking, a restaurant,
bar and small gym on the premises.

Restaurant El Duff (☎ 582-44-61; Hwy 65, Km 11;
mains US$4) You can sample home-cooked
Mennonite dishes such as *kilge* (noodles
with lots of cream and smoked ham) at this
restaurant outside town.

Rancho Viejo (☎ 582-43-60; Av Guerrero 303; mains
US$7) If you'd prefer good ol' Mexican food
to the Mennonite options, choose from
shrimp, beef and other traditional options
at this homey eatery and pub.

Getting There & Away
Cuauhtémoc is 1½ hours by bus (US$6) or
3½ hours by train from Chihuahua. By car,

THE MENNONITES

In villages around Cuauhtémoc, you're bound to encounter one of the following curious images: Mennonite men in baggy overalls selling big blocks of cheese on public buses or women in American Gothic dresses and black bonnets speaking a dialect of old German to blonde children. And you may wonder how they got there.

The Mennonite sect, founded by the Dutchman Menno Simonis in the 16th century, maintains a code of beliefs that, from the start, put it at odds with several governments of the world. Members take no oaths of loyalty other than to God and they eschew military service. And so, persecuted for their beliefs, the Mennonites moved from Germany to Russia to Canada – and to post-revolutionary Mexico, where thousands settled in the 1920s.

Traditionally, these towering figures lead a Spartan existence, speak little Spanish, and marry only among themselves, though their refusal to use machinery has been long forgotten; horse-and-buggy transport has been replaced by tractors and pickup trucks.

The Mennonite villages, called *campos* and numbered instead of named, are clustered along route 65, a four-lane highway heading north from Cuauhtémoc's western approach. It feels more like Iowa than Mexico here, where wide unpaved roads crisscross the *campos* through vast corn-fields interrupted by the occasional farm building and suburban-type dwellings.

And the cheese? It's *queso menonito*, the Mennonites' best-known product, which is also sold in many Cuauhtémoc shops.

head west via La Junta to the spectacular Cascada de Basaseachi waterfalls; for more information, see p322.

HIDALGO DEL PARRAL

☎ 627 / pop 110,400 / elevation 1652m

Parral is a pleasantly mellow little town, with a bustling main street, so-so restaurants and friendly residents – its courteous drivers even come to complete halts for pedestrians! Its biggest claim to fame is that it's the town where Pancho Villa was murdered on July 20, 1923 (see 'Pancho Villa: Bandit-Turned-Revolutionary,' pp352–3). A hero to the *campesinos* of the state of Chihuahua, Villa was buried in Parral, with 30,000 attending his funeral. (The story has a sordid postscript: shortly after the general's burial, his corpse was beheaded by unknown raiders.) In 1976, Villa's body was moved to Mexico City.

Founded as a mining settlement in 1631, the town took the 'Hidalgo' tag later but is still commonly called just 'Parral.' Throughout the 17th century, enslaved indigenous people mined the rich veins of silver, copper and lead from La Negrita mine, whose installations still loom above town but are no longer in use.

Orientation

With its narrow, winding one-way streets, Parral can be confusing at first – but it's also small enough to learn in a day. Two main squares, Plaza Principal and Plaza Guillermo Baca, are roughly in a line along the north side of the river, linked by busy Av Herrera (also called Mercaderes). The bus station at the east end of town is connected to the center of town by Av Independencia, which ends at the Hidalgo monument.

Information

Cámara Nacional de Comercio (☎ 522-00-18; Colegio 28; ☒ 9am-1pm & 3-7pm Mon-Fri, 9am-1pm Sat) is a small storefront that functions as a tourist office, distributing maps and brochures.

For financial needs, there are banks and *cambios* around Plaza Principal, including Bancomer, which has an ATM.

Infosel (Herrera 26, through Iris sewing shop; ☒ 9:30am-1pm & 4-7:30pm Mon-Fri, 10am-1pm Sat, per hr US$2) is the place for fast Internet connections.

The main bus station has left luggage facilities for US$3 per hour, although attendants, who keep unpredictable hours, are often nowhere to be found.

Sights

MUSEO FRANCISCO VILLA Y BIBLIOTÉCA

Pancho Villa was shot and killed from this building at the west end of town in 1923, and a star just outside the entrance marks the precise spot where he took the fatal bullet. These days it houses the **Pancho Villa Museum and Library** (cnr Juárez & Av Maclovio Herrera;

⊙ 9am-4pm, but sometimes randomly closed), with a small collection of photos, guns and memorabilia. The museum becomes a focal point every year in late July during the Jornadas Villistas festival, when townsfolk reenact his assassination with guns blazing. The following day, a cavalcade of some 300 riders descend on Parral on horseback after a six-day journey from the north, recalling Villa's famous marathons.

SANTUARIO DE FÁTIMA
This 1953 **church** (Calle Jesús García), located on a hill just beside the town's Prieto mine, was built from chunks of local gold, silver, zinc and copper ore, which sparkle in the thick walls. The congregation sits on short pillar-type stools rather than pews. Hours are unpredictable, so you may only get to see the façade.

Sleeping
Hotel Acosta (☎ 522-02-21; Barbachano 3; s/d US$23/28; ✗) This hotel is centrally located, extremely friendly, spic-and-span clean and great value. It also has the most character, with museum-quality '50s touches – from the big Pepsi cooler in the mint-green lobby to the bright linoleum floors in the rooms – that have been frozen in time by the third-generation owner, Doña Acosta. Be sure to check out the view of Plaza Principal from the roof.

Hotel Fuentes (☎ 522-00-16; coadriana@infosel .net.mx; Mercaderes 79; s/d US$15/17; ✗) The cheapest decent place is the Fuentes, recognizable by its pink stone façade, opposite the cathedral. The rooms off the cheerful lobby are all clean and basic; they vary in size, and some offer TV and air-conditioning.

Hotel Los Arcos (☎ 523-05-97; Pedro de Lille 5; s/d US$ 40/45; ✗ ✗) Although it's a bit far from the center of town, this hotel is a stone's throw from the bus station, making it perfect for late-night arrivals. It features a lovely lobby and cozy, clean rooms set around an elegant, flowering courtyard.

Motel El Camino Real (☎ 523-02-02; cnr Av Independencia & Pedro de Lille; s & d US$45; P ✗ ✗) Also close to the bus station and a trek from town is this comfortable motor lodge, offering a parking lot, small gym and a restaurant. The rooms are clean but boringly standard; unless you need a safe parking area, go with the nearby Hotel Los Arcos instead.

Eating & Drinking
Restaurant Turista (☎ 523-41-00; Hotel Turista, Plaza Independencia 12; breakfast US$4) This friendly eatery whips up big, tasty plates of *huevos mexicanos*.

Restaurant La Fuente (cnr Coronado & Benítez; mains US$6) Happy yellow walls and big front windows add to the warm ambience at this local favorite, where you'll find no-nonsense dishes including steak, chicken, crispy French fries and a fine plate of *chiles rellenos*.

La Michoacana (Ramírez 2; ice-cream cone US$0.75; ⊙ 9am-9pm) Teens gather nightly at this open-air parlor, which serves creamy homemade ice cream in rich flavors including coffee, caramel, mint and prune.

J Quissime Bar & Grill (☎ 523-34-44; Independencia; mains US$7) Boasting perhaps Parral's most festive atmosphere, J Quissime is also one of the few places open after 10pm (until about midnight). Located just opposite Motel El Camino Real, it's decorated with Tarahumara paraphernalia and offers so-so Mexican, steak and fish dishes.

Restaurant Bar Calipso (☎ 522-90-66; Paseo Gómez Morín 1; mains US$7) This slightly upscale, popular spot features international specialties, from steak to sushi.

Café La Prieta (☎ 522-88-06; Calle del Cerro 32) Sitting on a hill that overlooks the town, this cheerful nightspot offers various coffees, beers and antojitos for an average of US$2 a plate.

Getting There & Around
The bus station, on the southeast outskirts of town, is most easily reached by taxi (US$3); it's about a 15-minute walk. Regular 1st-class buses run to Chihuahua (US$13, three hours) and Durango (US$23, six hours). Frequent 2nd-class buses head to Valle de Allende (US$1.25, 30 minutes) from Independencia, near the bus station, opposite the hospital.

AROUND HIDALGO DEL PARRAL
The road east to Jiménez goes through dry, undulating country, but just south of this road, the village of **Valle de Allende** is lush with trees and surrounded by green farmland. The stream through the valley is fed by mineral springs that start near **Ojo de Talamantes**, a few kilometers west, where there's a small bathing area.

Canutillo, 80km south of Parral and just over the border of the state of Durango, is where Pancho Villa, a Durango native, spent the last three years of his life (see 'Pancho Villa: Bandit-Turned-Revolutionary,' pp352–3). His former hacienda, attached to a 200-year-old church, is now a slightly dilapidated museum with the unwieldy title of Museo Gráfico de la Revolución Mexicana. It houses a mediocre collection of photos, guns and various personal artifacts, but the surrounding scenery is beautifully rural. You can get dropped off here on a bus heading from Hidalgo del Parral to Durango or take a slow, infrequent local bus from Plaza Guillermo Baca; otherwise, you'll need to drive.

TORREÓN

☎ 871 / pop 517,000 / elevation 1150m

Tell any Chihuahua local that you're headed to Torreón, and they'll no doubt wrinkle their nose and offer this warning: *'Es feo.'* Sure, the metropolis is an off-putting mess of modern sprawl. But dig just below its surface and you'll find that it boasts an attractive central plaza and some good eateries, and makes a good base for exploring the surrounding desert region. For a panoramic view, take a taxi up to the **Cerro del Cristo de las Noas** lookout. The Christ statue, flanked by TV antennas, is the second-tallest in the Americas.

The 1910 battle for Torreón was Pancho Villa's first big victory in the Mexican Revolution, giving him control of the railways that radiate from the city. Villa waged three more battles for Torreón over the next few years. During one, his troops – in their revolutionary zeal – slaughtered some 200 Chinese immigrants.

Orientation

Torreón is located in the state of Coahuila and is part of the contiguous cities of Gómez Palacio and Ciudad Lerdo (both in Durango); all three together are known as La Laguna. Torreón itself fans out east of the Río Nazas, with the central grid lying at the west end of town and the Plaza de Armas at the west end of the grid. Avs Juárez and Morelos extend east from the plaza, past the main government plaza and, east of Colón, past several large shaded parks. The Torreón bus station is 6km east of the center on Av Juárez.

Information

The modern **Protursa tourist office** (☎ 732-22-44; promotos@prodigy.net.mx; Paseo de la Rosita 308D; 9am-2pm & 4-7pm Mon-Fri, 9am-2pm Sat), 5km east of the center, hands out maps and guides of Torreón and the region. Some staff members speak English.

You'll find Internet cafés around the Alameda park; most are open daily and charge about US$2.50 per hour.

Dangers & Annoyances

The city center can be fairly seedy after dark, particularly along Morelos, so be careful if walking around after about 9pm.

Sights

Pancho Villa's Torreón escapades are documented in the tiny **Museo de la Revolución** (cnr Múzquiz & Constitución; donations suggested; 10am-2pm Tue-Sun), beside the bridge to Gómez Palacio. Built in the 19th century to regulate the irrigation canal for a cotton plantation, the building now houses an unruly collection of photos, cannonballs, swords, posters and other memorabilia pertaining to the revolution.

Festivals & Events

Feria del Algodón (Cotton Fair) starts in late August and has a little of everything: charro singers, games, rides, a circus, regional food specialties, prize livestock and – the best reason to attend – an enormous beer garden with room for thousands.

Sleeping

Hotel Galicia (☎ 716-18-19; Cepeda 273; s & d US$13) This cheap and basic inn is a study in faded elegance, with tiled halls, stained glass and battered furniture.

Hotel del Paseo (☎ 716-03-03; fax 716-08-81; Morelos 574; s/d US$26/31;) The Paseo, offering pleasant rooms with firm beds, is a major step up in price and quality from the Galicia.

Hotel Calvete (☎ 716-15-30; fax 712-03-78; www.hotelcalvete.com.mx in Spanish; cnr Juárez & Corona; s/d from US$40/45; P) This hotel is a big white block, featuring spacious air-conditioned rooms with large balconies, plus an on-site restaurant downstairs and parking across the street.

Paraíso Del Desierto Grand Hotel (☎ 721-24-24; Blvd Independencia 100 Pte; s & d from US$90; P) This full-scale luxury hotel has an onsite restaurant and gym, plus basic, plush rooms with coffeemakers and data ports; more expensive quarters come with mini bars, full kitchens, fireplaces and hot tubs.

Camino Real Ejecutivo Torreón (☎ 750-99-85; Blvd Independencia 3595; r US$85; P ☒ ☒ ☐) Torreón's newest hotel, located near the airport, offers the finest in business-class amenities, with swanky, stylish rooms featuring high-speed Internet access, glass-door showers and marble desks.

Eating & Drinking

Restaurant Del Granero (☎ 712-91-44; Morelos 444 Pte; mains US$4; ☉ 8am-9pm) Vegetarians and carnivores alike will love this airy café, which serves delicious whole-wheat gorditas, burritos and fresh salads. Next door is a **bakery** doing whole-wheat versions of standard Mexican pastries.

Casa Alameda (☎ 712-68-88; Guerra 205; mains US$8) For Spanish and Mexican meals or snacks in a relaxed pub-style setting, try this roomy, bright place across the street from the Alameda park.

Getting There & Around

There are bus stations in both Torreón and Gómez Palacio, and long-distance buses will stop at both or transfer you from one to the other without charge if you've paid for a ticket to one or the other. Buses depart regularly for Chihuahua (US$28, six hours), Durango (US$16, 3½ hours), Mexico City (US$64, 14 hours), Saltillo (US$19, three hours) and Zacatecas (US$21, six hours). Taxis are the best way to get from the Torreón bus station to downtown (about US$2.50).

The tolls on the highway to Durango total US$25. To Saltillo, Hwy 40D costs US$16; most vehicles take the slightly slower free road. Drivers, pay attention as you near the sprawling city of Torreón no matter which direction you approach from, as the highways, signs and traffic patterns get increasingly confounding the closer you get.

AROUND TORREÓN

The deserts north of La Laguna are starkly beautiful, with strange geological formations around **Dinamita** and many semiprecious stones for gem hunters. Further north, the village of **Mapimí** was once the center of an incredibly productive mining area and served the nearby Ojuela mine between periodic raids by local Cocoyomes and Tobosos tribes. Benito Juárez passed through Mapimí in the mid-19th century during his flight from French forces. The house where he stayed, near the northwest corner of the Mapimí plaza, is now a small **history museum** (☉ closed Wed) displaying some very good sepia photos of Ojuela in its heyday.

At the end of the 19th century, the Ojuela mine supported an adjacent town of the same name with a population of over 3000. Today a cluster of abandoned buildings clings to a hillside as a silent reminder of Ojuela town's bonanza years. A spectacular 300m-long suspension bridge, the **Puente de Ojuela**, was built over a 100m-deep gorge to carry ore trains from the mine. You can walk across the bridge, fortified with 5cm steel cables, to the mine entrance. A **site guide** (suggested fee US$5) will accompany you through the 800m tunnel, and you'll emerge at a point that affords good views of the Bermejillo area.

To reach Mapimí from Torreón, go 40km north on Hwy 49 to Bermejillo, then 35km west on Hwy 30. It's easiest to get there with your own transport, but **Agencia Contraste** (☎ 871-715-20-51; Miguel Alemán 128, Torreón) arranges tours of the town and mines. From Torreón's bus station, Autobuses de la Laguna 2nd-class buses depart every half hour for Mapimí (US$3.25). To visit Puente de Ojuela, get off 3km before Mapimí, at a shop selling rocks and minerals. From there, a narrow road winds 7km up to the bridge. The walk takes about an hour, but you may be able to hitch a ride. Four kilometers from the turnoff, the road narrows further as the surface becomes cobblestoned and more suitable for hiking than driving.

At Ceballos, 130km north of Torreón, a rough road goes 40km east to the **Zona del Silencio**, so called because conditions in the area are said to prevent propagation of radio waves. Peppered with meteorites, the Zona is also believed to be a UFO landing site. The mysterious overtones associated with the region were amplified after a NASA test rocket crashed there during the 1970s. The ensuing search for the craft by US teams was of course veiled in secrecy, giving rise to all manner of suspicions. The Zona del Silencio is in the **Reserva de la Biósfera Bolsón de Mapimí**, a desert biosphere reserve dedicated to the study of arid-region plants and animals, including a very rare tortoise. This is a remote area with rough roads.

DURANGO

☎ 618 / pop 439,500 / elevation 1912m

Durango is a mellow, pleasant cowboy town with a delightful Plaza de Armas, fine colonial architecture, warm locals and a great selection of hotels and restaurants.

Founded in 1563 by conquistador Don Francisco de Ibarra and named after the Spanish city of his birth, the city is just south of the Cerro del Mercado, one of the world's richest iron ore deposits; this was the basis for Durango's early importance, along with gold and silver from the Sierra Madre. Other local industries include farm-ing, grazing, timber and paper – as well as the movie business, as evidenced by the collection of locations for westerns just outside the city.

Note that as you cross the border between Chihuahua and Durango, you enter into a different time zone; Durango is one hour ahead of Chihuahua.

Orientation

Durango is a good town to walk around in, and most of the interesting places to see and stay are within a few blocks of the two main squares, the Plaza de Armas and the Plaza IV Centenario. For some greenery, go to the extensive Parque Guadiana on the west side of town.

DURANGO

0 ____ 500 m
0 ____ 0.3 miles

INFORMATION	
Bancomer	1 B3
El Cactus.com	2 B3
State Tourist Office	3 A3

SIGHTS & ACTIVITIES	(p362)
Catedral Basílica Menor	4 B3
Museo de Arqueología de Durango Ganot-Peschard	5 B4
Museo de Cine	(see 3)
Palacio de Gobierno	6 B4
Teatro Ricardo Castro	7 B3

SLEEPING	(pp362–3)
Hotel Ana Isabel	8 C3
Hotel Buenos Aires	9 B3
Hotel Casablanca	10 B4
Hotel Gobernador	11 D3
Hotel Posada San Jorge	12 B3

Hotel Posada Santa Elena	13 A3
Hotel Roma	14 B3

EATING	🍴 (p363)
Corleone Pizza	15 B3
Cremería Wallander	16 A3
El Zocabón	17 B4
Eli-Bano	18 A4
Fuente de Sodas	(see 17)
Gorditas Gabino	19 B3
La Peña Café Cultural	20 B3
Restaurant Bar 1800	(see 12)
Samadhi Vegetarian	21 B3

SHOPPING	🛍 (p363)
Mercado Gómez Palacio	22 C3

TRANSPORT	(pp363–4)
Buses to Bus Station	23 B3

To Bus Station; Villa del Oeste; Villa Deportiva Juvenil (4km)

To Parque Guadiana (1km)

To Post Office; American Express (500m); Villa Deportiva Juvenil; Viajes Clatur SA de CV; Hospital General (1km)

Blvd Pescador

Pereyra

Gómez Palacio

Gabino Barreda

Coronado

Serdán

Negrete

Independencia

Hidalgo

Zaragoza

Martínez

Constitución

Juárez

Madero

Pasteur

Progreso

Zarco

Carlos León de la Peña

Saavedra

Av 20 de Noviembre

Florida

Plaza de Armas

5 de Febrero

Victoria

Patoni

Jardín San Antonio

Pino Suárez

Plaza IV Centenario

Mascareñas

Santa María

Park

Plazuela Baca Ortiz

Av Colón

Acequia Grande

To Los Alamos; La Ferrería

Information

American Express (☎ 817-00-23; Av 20 de Noviembre 810 Ote; ☺ 9am-7pm Mon-Fri & 10am-5pm Sat) Cashes traveler's checks.

Banks Several banks with ATMs as well as *cambios* on the west side of the Plaza de Armas.

El Cactus.com (☎ 825-64-43; Constitución 101 Sur; per hr US$1; ☺ 8am-9pm Mon-Sat) Cheerful Internet café with eight terminals and several laptop hook-up stations. Directly across the street from the Hotel Posada San Jorge.

Hospital General (☎ 813-00-11; cnr 5 de Febrero & Apartado) For emergencies or walk-in medical care.

Main Post Office (20 de Noviembre at Roncal; ☺ 8am-6pm Mon-Fri & 9am-noon Sat)

State Tourist Office (☎ 811-11-07; turismor@prodigy .net.mx; Florida 1006; ☺ 10am-7pm) A storefront tourist office and small café, which doubles as the state film board and film museum. Has friendly staff, some of whom speak English.

Viajes Clatur SA de CV (☎ 813-39-17; Av 20 de Noviembre 333A Ote) Can hook you up with bus or airplane reservations.

Sights

Catedral Basílica Menor (Av 20 de Noviembre; ☺ 8am-7pm), constructed between 1695 and 1750, has an imposing baroque façade that gives way to a vast Byzantine interior, with fine sculptures and paintings on the altars and carved wood choir stalls.

The **Plaza de Armas** is one of the loveliest in this region – spotless and shaded, filled with fountains and intricately carved wooden benches, and dominated by a domed kiosk. It's not far from the market, and is a great place to sit and people watch, especially in late afternoon, when groups of teens gather to goof around after school lets out.

The grand, balcony-topped baroque **Palacio de Gobierno** (5 de Febrero; ☺ 9am-6pm) has colorful murals depicting the history of the state. It was built on the estate of a Spanish mine owner and expropriated by the government after the War of Independence.

In its century of existence, the striking, neoclassical stone **Teatro Ricardo Castro** (Av 20 de Noviembre & Martínez; ☺ 10am-7pm) has served as a cinema and boxing arena. The entrance is brimming with decorative carvings and the French interior has gorgeous lighting fixtures, historical murals and a Frederic Chopin medallion in its central balcony.

Museo de Cine (☎ 813-39-17; Florida 1006; admission US$0.50; ☺ 10am-7pm) offers a pretty low-budget display, but if you can't make it out

to the actual film sets, this tiny museum gives a good overview of how the area has been used in westerns, including *A Man Called Horse* (1969) and *Pat Garrett and Billy the Kid* (1972), starring Bob Dylan.

Museo de Arqueología de Durango Ganot-Peschard (Zaragoza 315 Sur; admission US$0.50, free Tue; ☺ 10am-6pm Tue-Fri, 11am-7pm Sat & Sun), opened in 1998, is an innovative visual feast presenting the archaeological record of the region's indigenous cultures, from prehistoric times to the Spanish conquest. Highlights include a photographic exhibit on rock paintings and an interesting section demonstrating the archaeological method. All descriptions are in Spanish.

Sleeping

BUDGET

Hotel Buenos Aires (☎ 812-31-28; Constitución 126 Nte; s/d US$11/13) In the center of town, the Buenos Aires has tidy little rooms, some with bathrooms and hot water; undergoing renovations at time of writing, some of the hotel's dingy, dusty qualities are expected to disappear.

Hotel Ana Isabel (☎ 813-45-00; 5 de Febrero 219 Ote; s/d US$21/29; ☒) Just a stone's throw east of León de la Peña, the rooms here are quaint if stuffy; some have balconies over an indoor courtyard. It's an excellent budget option.

Hotel Roma (☎ 812-01-22; 20 de Noviembre 705 Pte; www.hotelroma.com.mx; s/d US$25/28; ☒) The friendly Roma is in a large century-old building on the opposite corner from the Teatro Ricardo Castro. The rooms here are small but in pretty good shape, and feature tiled tubs, soft beds and access to a lovely roof garden

Villa Deportiva Juvenil (☎ 818-70-71; Colegio Militar; dm US$4, plus US$2 deposit) Durango's cheapest digs, offering clean dorm beds and not much else, can be found at this youth hostel, 400m south of the bus station.

MID-RANGE

Hotel Posada San Jorge (☎ 813-32-57; fax 811-60-40; Constitución 102 Sur; s/d US$35/40; ☒) In a handsome 19th-century building with large rooms that encircle a courtyard restaurant, this is one of Durango's finest hotels – and still a major bargain. It offers colonial-style rooms and junior suites, the latter with sofas and walk-in closets – and all with cable TV and small balconies. The restaurant is popular with hip locals, and the grand stairway and bold mural leading to the sleeping quarters are welcoming sights at the end of a long day of sightseeing.

Hotel Posada Santa Elena (☎ 812-78-18; Negrete 1007 Pte; s/d US$35/40; ✗) Friendly, small and quiet, this hotel is a find. It features 10 tastefully furnished rooms, some with their own little courtyard.

Hotel Casablanca (☎ 811-35-99; www.hotelcasablancadurango.com; 20 de Noviembre 811 Pte; s/d US$53/58; ✗ ✗) A block west of the Hotel Roma, it offers large well-appointed, carpeted rooms with big TVs and small coffeemakers.

TOP END

Hotel Gobernador (☎ 813-19-19; fax 811-14-22, 20 de Noviembre 257 Ote; s & d US$120; P ✗ ✗ ⊡ ✗) The Gobernador is the best hotel in town, featuring a swimming pool, grandly landscaped grounds, a banquet hall and an elegant restaurant. The cushy rooms provide the works. It's the only non-chain luxury hotel in town.

Eating & Drinking

Durango boasts plenty of good restaurants – and will provide a thrill for those craving a bit of variety.

Corleone Pizza (cnr Constitución 110 Nte & Serdán; pizzas US$6) You'll find groups of hipsters, cozy booths, aromatic red sauce, a small wine selection and a European feel inside this dimly lit parlor.

Cremería Wallander (☎ 813-86-33; Independencia 128 Nte; prices from US$3) This is a good place to stock up for a picnic or bus journey; you'll find locally made yogurt, honey and granola, plus extraordinary tortas made with special German cold cuts and Mennonite cheese on fresh-baked rolls.

El Zocabón (☎ 811-80-83; 5 de Febrero 513; ☯ 7:30am-11pm; mains US$5) This large, pleasant café with a friendly staff makes a good spot for breakfast, serving big mugs of fresh steaming coffee and well-prepared egg dishes. Next door, **Fuente de Sodas** is an old-fashioned sit-down ice-cream parlor, serving excellent frozen and baked treats.

Eli-Bano (☎ 813-40-04; Hidalgo 310 Sur; mains US$7) Fans of Middle Eastern cuisine should head for this place, where you will find typical appetizers like hummus, tabbouleh and stuffed grape leaves.

Gorditas Gabino (☎ 812-11-92; Constitución 100A Nte; gorditas US$0.75, mains US$5) This excellent meal or snacking option is bustling with trendy youngsters and big families, all savoring the huge, delicious gorditas stuffed with avocados, shredded beef in salsa verde and other tasty fillings.

La Peña Café Cultural (☎ 825-81-05; Martinez 208; cocktails US$3; ☯ 7pm-2am Thu-Sun) You'll find quality live music, an extensive selection of rums and tequilas, snacks including quesadillas and guacamole, a warm and gay-friendly vibe – and even occasional AA gatherings! – in this happy, bustling tavern.

Restaurant Bar 1800 (☎ 811-03-25; Constitución 102 Sur; mains US$8-13) In an elegant courtyard of the Hotel Posada San Jorge (see Sleeping, opposite), this restaurant serves outstanding Mexican food, steaks, seafood and chicken dishes, and offers a daily salad bar. The succulent steaks (US$10) are simply delicious – very tender and served with a variety of fillings – and the bar scene is hopping.

Samadhi Vegetarian (Negrete 403 btwn Madero & Victoria; veggie comida US$4) Any herbivore will feel right at home in this small store-front, dotted with just a few tables and brightly painted chairs. It offers a rotating menu del día, with delicious elements including pozole, tamales, soy chorizo and lentil soup. You can also buy tofu and soy milk to go – a real find in these parts!

Shopping

Mercado Gómez Palacio (cnr Av 20 de Noviembre & Pasteur) You'll find just about everything in this jumbled maze of stalls, including cheap tacos, T-shirts, scorpion key chains, cowboy hats, dried herbs, fresh produce and cheeses, leather saddles, CDs and housewares.

Getting There & Away

Good bus connections are available from Durango to many of the places that travelers want to go:

Chihuahua (US$37, 9hr, 6 1st-class daily)
Hidalgo del Parral (US$23, 6hr, 9 1st-class daily)
Mazatlán (US$36, 7hr, 3 deluxe daily; US$27, 7hr, 10 1st-class daily; US$24, 7hr, 6 2nd-class daily)
Mexico City (US$77, 12hr, 1 deluxe daily; US$57, 12hr, 7 1st-class daily) To Terminal Norte.
Torreón (US$16, 3½hr, frequent 1st-class; US$14, 3½hr, 8 2nd-class daily)
Zacatecas (US$18, 4hr, frequent 1st-class; US$14, 4hr, 5 2nd-class daily)

Getting Around

The bus station is on the east side of town; white Ruta 2 buses departing from the far side of the parking lot will get you to the Plaza de Armas for US$0.30. Taxis, which are metered, charge about US$2.25 to the center.

To reach the bus station from downtown, catch a blue-striped 'Camionera' bus from 20 de Noviembre beside the plaza. Get off at the intersection of Colegio Militar (a major thoroughfare), then go left toward the Villa monument and take the overpass across Pescador.

AROUND DURANGO
Movie Locations

The clear light and stark countryside once made Durango a popular location for Hollywood movies. Around 120 films have been shot in the area – mostly westerns, including John Wayne vehicles and films by directors John Huston and Sam Peckinpah. While the golden era of the sets here ended well over two decades ago, they do appear to be undergoing a renaissance, as a number of Mexican TV series are in the works. Be sure to check with the tourist office before going out to the sets, as they may be off limits during production.

Villa del Oeste (off Hwy 45; admission US$0.50; open 11am-7pm Sat & Sun) is 12km north of Durango. After its use in a number of westerns, the 'main street,' known locally as Calle Howard, was left undisturbed. When not in production, it's a souvenir-drenched theme park that's open to visitors. To get there, take a 2nd-class bus for Chupaderos from the bus station (US$1, every half hour) and tell the driver to drop you at Villa del Oeste. To get back to Durango, just flag down any passing bus headed toward the city. Note that opening hours are changeable so it's best to check with the tourist office in Durango before heading out there.

The small village of **Chupaderos**, 2km north of Villa del Oeste, offers a fascinating look at a former set, now overtaken by the unfazed residents. It's a nice, sleepy, cactus-strewn place to spend a quiet afternoon.

To the southwest of Durango is **Los Álamos** (☑ daily), a '1940s town' where *Fat Man and Little Boy* was filmed in 1989; the movie, about the making of the first A-bomb, starred Paul Newman. To get there, take Blvd Arrieta south of town and stay on it for about 30km, past dramatic mesas and a steep river gorge. Watch for a rusty sign on the right announcing the turnoff for the set. From there it's another 1.5km over a rough road. Buses are not an option.

Museo de Arte Guillermo Ceniceros

Originally a British-built ironworks, the Ferrería de las Flores was converted into an **art museum** (☎ 618-826-03-64; La Ferrería; admission US$0.50; ☑ 10am-6pm Tue-Sun) in 1998 to display the work of Durango native Guillermo Ceniceros. Profoundly influenced by his teacher, the formidable muralist David Alfaro Siqueiros, Ceniceros developed his own method of visual expression. Mysterious landscapes and feminine figures are his preferred subjects. La Ferrería is 4km southwest of Durango on the way to Los Álamos. Regular 'Ferrería' buses depart from the Plazuela Baca Ortiz in the center of town.

En Route to Mazatlán

The road west from Durango to the coastal city of Mazatlán (see p412) is particularly scenic, with a number of worthwhile natural attractions. In the vicinity around **El Salto**, you can trek to waterfalls, canyons and forests. About 160km from Durango is a spectacular stretch of road called **El Espinazo del Diablo** (which means the Devil's Backbone).

You enter a new time zone when you cross the Durango–Sinaloa state border; Sinaloa is one hour behind Durango.

Northeast Mexico

Though enormous in size and occupying almost 15% of Mexican territory – stretching nearly 1000km from north to south and 500km from east to west – the states of Nuevo León, Tamaulipas and Coahuila are often overlooked by tourists in search of impressive pre-Hispanic ruins, charming colonial towns or pretty palm-fringed beaches. What northeast Mexico offers instead is a geography unlike anywhere else in Mexico, and a unique emerging culture.

Geographically, the deserts of northeast Mexico are the southern extension of the Great Plains of the USA and Canada, impressive for their stark, rugged beauty and sheer expanse. The Rio Grande (Río Bravo del Norte to Mexicans), vital for irrigation in this arid region, is not much more than a trickle at some points, the victim of overdevelopment. The coastal areas have remote beaches, lagoons and wetlands, home to diverse marine life and a winter stopover for many migratory birds. Inland, numerous winding roads climb to the eastern and northern edges of the Sierra Madre Oriental, offering spectacular scenery and a refreshing highland climate.

Culturally, northeast Mexico and the south-central USA comprise a frontier of epic proportions. There is so much Mexican influence in southern Texas that Spanish seems to be more widely spoken there than English, while cities such as Monterrey, the capital of Nuevo León, represent the most Americanized parts of Mexico. Spend at least a few days here and you will be rewarded with a glimpse into a vibrant and complex culture, where imports and exports refer to more than just goods and labor.

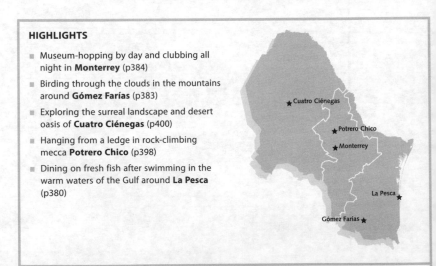

HIGHLIGHTS

- Museum-hopping by day and clubbing all night in **Monterrey** (p384)
- Birding through the clouds in the mountains around **Gómez Farías** (p383)
- Exploring the surreal landscape and desert oasis of **Cuatro Ciénegas** (p400)
- Hanging from a ledge in rock-climbing mecca **Potrero Chico** (p398)
- Dining on fresh fish after swimming in the warm waters of the Gulf around **La Pesca** (p380)

★ Cuatro Ciénegas

★ Potrero Chico

★ Monterrey

La Pesca ★

Gómez Farías ★

| ■ ALTITUDE RANGE: 0m–3810m | ■ MONTERREY AUGUST DAILY HIGH: 36°C |

NORTHEAST MEXICO

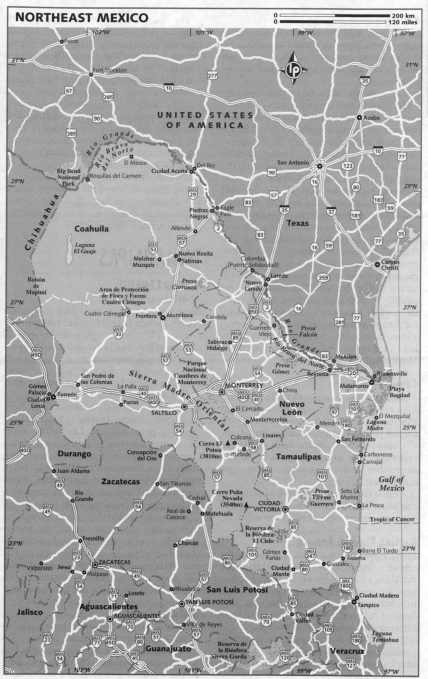

0 — 200 km
0 — 120 miles

103°W 101°W 99°W 97°W

Pecos
31°N   31°N
Fort Stockton
67   277
10
285
90
UNITED STATES   Austin
385   OF AMERICA
35
Rio Grande
Rio Bravo
del Norte   El Mosco   San Antonio   10   77
Big Bend   Ciudad Acuña   Del Rio   123
29°N   National   Boquillas del Carmen   90   16   80   29°N
Park   57
Chihuahua   MEX   183   59
29   181
Eagle   35
Coahuila   Piedras   Pass   83   Texas   77   35
Negras   MEX
Allende   2   Corpus
MEX   83   16   59   Christi
Laguna   53   Nueva Rosita   77
El Guaje   Melchor   Sabinas   Colombia
27°N   Bolsón   Muzquiz   (Puente Solidaridad)   27°N
de   Laredo   359
Mapimí   Area de Protección   Presa   Nuevo
de Flora y Fauna   Carranza   Laredo   281   77
Cuatro Ciénegas   MEX
Cuatro Ciénegas   Frontera Monclova Candela   85D   Rio   Presa
MEX   Guerrero   Grande   Falcón
30   MEX   Viejo   83   McAllen
Sabinas   53   54   Reynosa 2D Brownsville
MEX   Hidalgo   Presa   MEX
49D   San Pedro de   Parque   54   Gómez   101 Playa
Gómez   las Colonias   Nacional MONTERREY   China   Bagdad
Palacio   La Paila MEX Cumbres de MEX   El Mezquital
25°N   Ciudad Torreón 40 Monterrey 40D 40   Nuevo León 97 180 Laguna 25°N
Lerdo   MEX   El Cercado   Mendez   Madre
Parras   40D   Montemorelos   San Fernando
MEX   SALTILLO
Durango   54   Linares
MEX   Galeana   58   Carboneras
40D   Concepción Cerro El Iturbide Tamaulipas 101 Carvajal
Juan Aldama   del Oro Potosí
(3810m)   85   Gulf of
MEX   Mexico
49   Zacatecas San Tiburcio MEX   Presa
Rio   57   Soto La Vicente La Pesca
MEX   Grande   Cedral Cerro Peña   Marina Guerrero
45   MEX   Nevada   CIUDAD   Tropic of Cancer
54   Real de (3540m) VICTORIA   MEX
23°N   Catorce Matehuala   85   23°N
Fresnillo   Reserva de   180 Barra El Tordo
MEX   Charcas   la Biósfera   247
23   El Cielo Gómez   80 Aldama
Valparaíso Jerez ZACATECAS   101 Farias Ciudad Gonzalez
MEX   Malpaso MEX   Ahualulco 80   Mante
54   49   MEX   San Luis Potosí 57   MEX   Ciudad Madero
Jalisco   71 Loreto   80   85   Tampico
Aguascalientes SAN LUIS POTOSÍ Ciudad
MEX   AGUASCALIENTES   70   Valles 105 Laguna
23   70   Villa de Reyes MEX   Tamiahua
MEX MEX MEX 57   Reserva de   180D
71 45D 80 Guanajuato la Biósfera 120   Veracruz 127
54   Sierra Gorda
103°W   101°W   99°W   97°W

History

It was here that the two great colonizing movements, Spanish from the south and Anglo-Saxon from the north, confronted each other and displaced the indigenous peoples.

The area was slow to be developed by early Spanish settlers in the late 16th century because of the difficult conditions and absence of precious metals. Once Mexico achieved its independence from Spain, the region was plagued by border disputes with its neighbor to the north, including the conflict over the status of Texas. The war between Mexico and the USA (1846–48) officially established the nations' borders, but they were porous from the start.

As a result of its location and the discovery of petroleum, coal and natural gas, the region began to emerge as an industrial leader in the late 19th century. Today, money and resources surge back and forth across the border. The Texas economy especially is largely dependent on Mexican labor while American investment is integral for the maquiladoras (assembly-plant operations, usually foreign-owned), that are so key to the threatened economy of northern Mexico.

Climate

The geographic diversity of northeast Mexico – expansive deserts, remote coastal areas and the highlands of the Sierra Madre Oriental – produces similar climatic variation.

Coastal areas along the Gulf of Mexico experience the largest amounts of rain in September and are generally warm and humid year round.

August is the warmest month while winter can bring the occasional 'norther' with cold temperatures and sometimes even snow.

Getting There & Around

Many travelers enter Mexico at one of the region's five main border crossings from the USA, and take one of the several routes heading south as quickly as possible to get to what is seen as the 'real' Mexico. Millions of others drop across the 1000km of international border for short trips.

Scenic Hwy 2, the Carretera Ribereña, paralleling much of the Rio Bravo on the Mexican side, runs between Ciudad Acuña and Matamoros.

The main toll highways running south from the Texas border are Hwy 57, bypassing most mountainous areas, from Piedras Negras to Saltillo and eventually to Mexico City; Hwy 85, also known as the Pan American Hwy beginning at Nuevo Laredo and passing through Monterrey and Ciudad Victoria; and Hwy 40, running southwest from Reynosa to Monterrey, Saltillo and eventually the Pacific coast. Smaller Hwy 180 goes south from Matamoros, continuing all the way down the gulf coast through Tampico and Veracruz.

It's convenient and easy to catch a bus on the Mexican side of the border to almost any destination in the region and further afield, while numerous international air carriers service Monterrey.

TAMAULIPAS

NUEVO LAREDO

☎ 867 / pop 329,000

More foreign tourists enter Mexico through Nuevo Laredo than any other town on the northeast border, though numbers were in decline at the time of research due to sporadic violence between rival drug cartels fighting over the same turf. In general, however, it's Nuevo Laredo's reputation rather than your safety that is at risk. Roughly halfway between San Antonio, Texas and Monterrey, Nuevo Laredo is a convenient crossing point because Laredo, its sister city across the river is also a fast-growing commercial center. It's not historical sites, attractive architecture or laid-back charm that draws visitors, but the number of restaurants, bars and souvenir shops catering to day-trippers from the USA. Most accept US currency and quote prices in dollars. 'Across the water,' in Laredo, are supermarkets, motels and fast-food joints, all staffed with Spanish-speaking workers. The two cities share the only professional baseball team that has two home stadiums in two different countries, Los Dos Laredos.

History

In 1836 Texas seceded from Mexico and became an independent republic. From 1839 to 1841 the Rio Grande valley, and much of what is now northeastern Mexico, chafing at the Mexican government's authoritari-

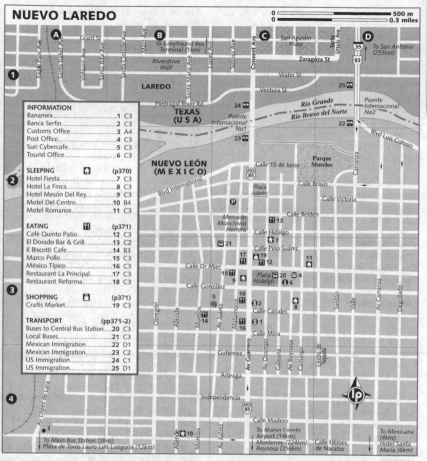

NUEVO LAREDO

INFORMATION	
Banamex.................................1	C3
Banca Serfin..........................2	C3
Customs Office......................3	A4
Post Office............................4	C3
Suri Cybercafe......................5	C3
Tourist Office.......................6	C3

SLEEPING	(p370)
Hotel Fiesta..........................7	C3
Hotel La Finca.......................8	C3
Hotel Mesón Del Rey.............9	C3
Motel Del Centro..................10	B4
Motel Romanos.....................11	C3

EATING	(p371)
Café Quinto Patio..................12	C3
El Dorado Bar & Grill.............13	C2
Il Biscotti Cafe......................14	B3
Marco Pollo...........................15	C3
México Típico........................16	C3
Restaurant La Principal...........17	C3
Restaurant Reforma...............18	C3

SHOPPING	(p371)
Crafts Market........................19	C3

TRANSPORT	(pp371–2)
Buses to Central Bus Station...20	C3
Local Buses...........................21	C3
Mexican Immigration..............22	D1
Mexican Immigration..............23	C2
US Immigration......................24	C1
US Immigration......................25	D1

anism and inability to defend its frontiers, also declared itself a separate republic. This was the Republic of the Rio Grande, with its capital at Laredo. However, it was dissolved after a number of skirmishes with the Mexican army.

The US annexation of Texas in 1845 precipitated the Mexican-American War, with the Rio Grande subsequently becoming the border between the USA and Mexico. Mexicans established a new town, Nuevo Laredo, south of the river. Until the first fully serviceable bridge was built in 1889 at a cost of $150,000, small boats navigated their way between the two inextricably linked communities and countries. Fires and periodic flooding, the worst in 1954, destroyed this

bridge and its replacement. Nuevo Laredo now collects more in tariffs and customs revenue than any other Mexican port of entry. The maquiladora industry is still the largest employer despite the exodus of a number of factories searching for even cheaper labor elsewhere.

Orientation

Two international bridges link the two Laredos. You can walk or drive over Puente Internacional No 1 – there's a small toll of US$0.50 for pedestrians and US$2 for vehicles. This bridge leaves you at the north end of Av Guerrero, Nuevo Laredo's main thoroughfare, which stretches for 2km (one way going south). Northbound traffic heading for Puente Internacional No 1 is directed via Av López de Lara on the western side of the city.

Puente Internacional No 2 is for vehicles only. It is preferred by drivers bypassing Nuevo Laredo's center, as it feeds directly into Blvd Luís Colosio, skirting the city to the east. On the US side, Interstate 35 goes north to San Antonio.

A third international bridge, the Puente Solidaridad, crosses the border 38km to the northwest. It enables motorists who are in a hurry to bypass Laredo and Nuevo Laredo altogether.

Plaza Hidalgo is seven blocks from Puente Internacional No 1, with a kiosk in the middle, the Palacio Federal on the east side, and a few hotels and restaurants around it.

Information

EMERGENCY
City Police (☎ 711-39-30)
Emergency Medical Aid (☎ 712-00-49)

IMMIGRATION
Both international bridges have Mexican immigration offices at the southern end where you can get your tourist card, if you plan to go further south into Mexico. You have to go to the *aduana* (customs) office in town to get a vehicle permit (see p372).

INTERNET ACCESS
Suri Cybercafe (Canales 3112; per hr US$2; ☺ 10am-9pm Mon-Fri, 11am-7pm Sat) A few blocks southwest of Plaza Hidalgo.

MONEY
Most *casas de cambio* will not change traveler's checks but most businesses will accept them with a purchase, and the main Mexican banks should change them. Businesses also accept US currency, but the exchange rate can be low. Banca Serfin and Banamex on Av Guerrero have ATMs.

POST
Post office (Camargo; ☺ 8am-6pm Mon-Fri, 8am-2pm Sat) Located behind the government offices on the east side of plaza.

TOURIST INFORMATION
Tourist office (☎ 712-73-97; www.nuevolaredo.gob .mx; ☺ 8am-8pm Mon-Fri) Located on the ground floor of the Palacio Federal on the east side of Plaza Hidalgo.

Maps and brochures for Nuevo Laredo and other nearby destinations are available.

Festivals & Events
Nuevo Laredo holds an agricultural, livestock, industrial and cultural fair September 6 to 22. The founding of Nuevo Laredo in 1848 is celebrated June 13 to 15 with music, baseball games and bullfights.

Sleeping
All the hotels listed here have air-con, a necessity during Nuevo Laredo's blistering summers, and TV with cable, though reception and service tends to vary. You'll find the international chain hotels and a few more upmarket places heading south, near several strip-malls, past where Guerrero turns into Reforma.

Hotel Fiesta (☎ 712-47-37; Av Ocampo 559; r US$36; ✖) Don't let the shabby exterior fool you, the rooms at the friendly Fiesta are large and clean and just a short walk to both Plaza Hidalgo and the bridge.

Motel Romanos (☎ 712-23-91; Dr Mier 2420; s/d US$25/32; ✖) Three short blocks east of the plaza, the lobby of the Motel Romanos is Greek-temple kitsch. While the front-desk staff may not be so inviting, the rooms and hallways are kept spotless.

Hotel La Finca (☎ 712-88-83; Av Reynosa 811; s/d US$27/31; P ✖) The centrally located La Finca, south of González, is slightly more welcoming than the Romanos and has spacious and clean basic rooms; however, the air-con can be loud.

Motel Del Centro (☎ 712-13-10; Héroes de Nacataz 3330; s/d US$39/56; P ✖ ✖) One wing wraps around a swimming pool, a nice place to hang out, especially if there is water in the pool. The small carpeted rooms are not in top shape. Breakfast included.

Hotel Santa María (☎ 715-88-70; Reforma 4446; r US$79; P ✖ ✖ ▣ ✖) The Santa María caters to business travelers and has all the amenities you'd expect, including a restaurant and piano bar. It's one of the first top-end places you come to heading south out of town.

Hotel Mesón Del Rey (☎ 712-63-60; Av Guerrero 718; s/d US$33/41; P ✖) The Mesón Del Rey, on the west side of the plaza, features spacious, though slightly dirty rooms and chilly central air-con. The entrance to the hotel's parking lot is on González.

Eating & Drinking

There are numerous eating possibilities, though the places on Av Guerrero, just south of the bridge, can be overpriced tourist joints.

Restaurant Reforma (☎ 712-62-50; Av Guerrero 718; mains US$4-8; ✵) Connected to the hotel of the same name, Reforma combines several good qualities. an extensive Mexican menu, a modern dining area decorated with local paraphernalia and attentive waitstaff.

Il Biscotti Caffe (☎ 712-33-79; Canales 3147, cnr Morales; breakfasts US$3, mains US$4; ☽ 8am-4pm Mon-Fri, 8am-2pm Sat; ✵) The wood-paneled Il Biscotti is a casual and comfortable spot to enjoy a meal or to relax with one of their specialty coffee drinks (US$2.50).

México Típico (☎ 712-15-12; Guererro 934; mains US$5-12; ✵) A popular spot for visitors north of the border and local businesspeople. Smartly dressed waiters serve, as the name suggests, typical Mexican fare, including *cabrito* (roasted young goat) in an elegant setting.

El Dorado Bar & Grill (☎ 712-00-15; cnr Belden & Av Ocampo; starters US$3-7, mains US$7-20; ✵ Ⓟ) Five blocks south of the bridge, this place has been a haunt for southern Texans since opening in 1922 as the casino-restaurant 'El Caballo Blanco.' It still harbors a significant number of gringos, attracted more to its familiar style and its relative sophistication – the waiters wear white jackets – than anything remarkable about the quality of its cuisine. In addition to soft-shell crabs and frog's legs, the El Dorado offers a variety of border favorites such as cabrito; all at about US$16.

Café Quinto Patio (☎ 712-13-06; cnr Dr Mier & Av Ocamp; mains US$3.50) During the day when it is busy and filled with regulars, Quinto Patio is a pleasant spot for good enchiladas and *lonches* (rolls stuffed with avocado, ground beef or eggs). At night, the harsh lighting makes the barely furnished dining area less welcoming.

Restaurant La Principal (☎ 712-13-01; Av Guerrero 624; mains US$8-11, parrillada for 2 US$33) For authentic *norteño* fare, check out La Principal, half a block north of the plaza; look for goats roasting over coals in the window. The popular restaurant offers all the cabrito variations – a substantial order of *pierna* comes with salsa, salad, tortillas and beans.

Marco Pollo (☎ 712-87-00; cnr Dr Mier & Matamoros; mains US$4-10) Charcoal-grilled chicken is the main attraction at this fast-food-style restaurant, which has overhead fans and tiled tables. A whole chicken (US$8) is served with salsa and tortillas. Large pizzas (US$10) are also offered.

Sports

Plaza de Toros Lauro Luis Longoria (☎ 712-71-92; Av Monterrey 4101; general admission sun/shade US$7/14) Two or three bullfights each month are held here, near Anáhuac, around 13km from the international bridge. Most are on Sundays and the season generally lasts from February to October.

Shopping

There's a crafts market on the east side of Av Guerrero half a block north of the main plaza. There is also Mercado Monclovio Herrera on the west side of Av Guerrero, between Hidalgo and Belden, where you'll find an assortment of T-shirts, silver, rugs, liquor, hats, leather and pottery.

Getting There & Away

AIR

Nuevo Laredo airport is off the Monterrey road, 14km south of town. **Mexicana** (☎ 719-28-15; Av Alvaro Obregon 3401), on the corner of Paseo Colón, has direct flights twice a day to/from Mexico City. Several airlines, including Continental and American Airlines, fly daily from Laredo, Texas to Mexico City, Houston and Dallas.

BUS

Nuevo Laredo's bus station is 3km south of Puente Internacional No 1 on Anáhuac. First- and 2nd-class buses serve every city in northern Mexico. Daily services from Nuevo Laredo include the following:

Ciudad Victoria (US$31, 7hr, 6 1st-class)
Guadalajara (US$60, 13hr, 3 1st-class)
Matamoros (US$20, 6hr, 6 1st-class)
Mexico City (US$97, 14hr, 3 deluxe; US$68, 14hr, 8 1st-class) To Terminal Norte.
Monclova (US$13, 4hr, 5 1st-class)
Monterrey (US$15, 3hr, 1st-class every half-hour; US$12, 3hr, 2nd-class)
Reynosa (US$15, 4hr, 8 1st-class)
Saltillo (US$20, 4½ hr, hourly 1st-class; US$17, 4½ hr, 2 2nd-class)
San Luis Potosí (US$48, 10hr, hourly 1st-class; US$40, 10hr, 4 2nd-class)
Zacatecas (US$40, 8hr, 6 1st-class)

Buses also go to Aguascalientes, Durango, Guadalajara and Querétaro, and to major cities in Texas.

There are also direct buses to cities in Mexico from the Laredo, Texas **Greyhound terminal** (☎ 956 723-4324; Salinas Av 610), but these are more expensive than services from Nuevo Laredo. You can sometimes use these buses to go between Laredo and Nuevo Laredo bus stations, but you have to ask the driver (it's less hassle and often quicker just to walk over the international bridge).

CAR & MOTORCYCLE

For a vehicle permit you must go to the **customs office** (cnr Av López de Lara & Héroes de Nacataz; ☯ 24hr). From Puente Internacional No 1, turn right onto Blvd Internacional and follow the 'vehicle permit' signs. After about 10 blocks, bear left onto Av López de Lara and into the left lane. Just past the train station on your left is a low, white wall labeled 'Importación Temporal de Vehículos Extranjeros'; swing around to the other side of the Blvd at the traffic circle, pull in at the entrance and park. The low building left of the parking lot entrance houses an immigration office and customs bureau. The office is always open and should issue a permit without hassle if your papers are in order (see p970).

The route south via Monterrey is the most direct to central Mexico, the Pacific Coast and the Gulf Coast. An excellent toll road, Hwy 85D, is fast but expensive (tolls total US$18 to Monterrey). The alternative free road (Hwy 85) is longer, rougher and slower. Hwy 2 is a rural road following the Rio Grande to Reynosa and Matamoros.

Getting Around

Frequent city buses (US$0.40) make getting around Nuevo Laredo simple enough. Many buses go down Av Guerrero from the plaza; 'Carr–Central' buses, with an aquamarine stripe, go to the main bus station. To get from Puente Internacional No 1 to the nearest bus stop, go two blocks on Blvd Internacional to Av Juárez, then left five blocks to Pino Suárez. From the bus station, local buses go back into town.

A taxi to the bridge from the bus station will cost about US$5, and about a dollar more in the reverse direction.

Public parking is readily available in Nuevo Laredo – there are a few lots around

the tourist district just over the border; try west on Victoria and on Juárez heading south. There's a secure parking garage four blocks south of the bridge on Victoria, west of Av Guerrero (US$1.50 per hour).

REYNOSA

☎ 899 / pop 447,000

Reynosa is one of northeast Mexico's most important industrial towns, with oil refineries, petrochemical plants, cotton mills, distilleries and maquiladoras. Over 200 companies, many with brand name recognition in the USA, employing nearly 70,000 workers, occupy the industrial parks outside the city center. Pipelines from here carry natural gas to Monterrey and into the USA.

As a commercial border crossing, Reynosa rivals Matamoros, but is less important than Nuevo Laredo. It has good road connections into Mexico and Texas, but most travelers will probably find one of the other crossings more direct and convenient. Across the Rio Grande is the town of McAllen.

The tourist trade is geared to short-term Texan visitors, with restaurants, nightclubs, bars and bawdier diversions; however, it's easy to ignore this part of town if you want. Reynosa is more manageable and less intimidating than Nuevo Laredo but not nearly as charming as Matamoros.

Reynosa was founded in 1749 as Villa de Nuestra Señora de Guadalupe de Reynosa, 20km from its present location – flooding forced the move in 1802. Reynosa was one of the first towns to rise up in the independence movement of 1810, but little of historical interest remains.

Orientation

Reynosa's central streets are laid out on a grid pattern, between the Rio Grande and the Canal Anzalduas. The Plaza Principal, on a rise a few blocks southwest of the Puente Internacional, is the site of the town hall, banks, hotels, a movie theater and a modern church.

South of the plaza, on Hidalgo, is a pedestrian mall lined with shops and cafés, extending to Gigante at the southern edge of the grid. Between the bridge and the center lies the Zona Rosa, with restaurants, bars and nightclubs.

If you're leaving Mexico, follow the signs to the Puente Internacional. Avoid the maze

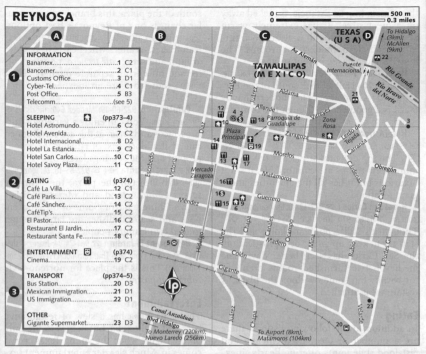

REYNOSA

of streets in the industrial zone south of the canal.

Information

US and Mexican immigration bureaus are at their respective ends of the bridge, and there's another Mexican post in the Reynosa bus station. Get a tourist card stamped at either Mexican post if you're proceeding beyond Reynosa deeper into Mexico.

You can change traveler's checks at **Banamex** (Guerrero btwn Hidalgo & Juárez). The main banks have ATMs, some dispensing US dollars as well as pesos, and there are several *casas de cambio* along Zaragoza near the bridge.

The **post office** (cnr Díaz & Colón; 9am-4pm Mon-Fri, 9am-1pm Sat) is adjacent to a Telecomm office.

Internet connections are US$1 per hour at **Cyber-Tel** (Zaragoza 608; 10am-9:30pm).

Festivals & Events

The festival of **Nuestra Señora de Guadalupe**, on December 12, is the town's major event. Pilgrims start processions a week before and

there are afternoon dance performances in front of the church. Reynosa's feria is held from late July to early August.

Sleeping

BUDGET

These two hotels are near the Puente Internacional and are fairly basic, but are of better value than the budget hotels closer to the center.

Hotel Avenida (922-05-92; Zaragoza Ote 885; s/d US$26/30) Just two blocks away from the plaza and a short walk to the bridge, Hotel Avenida has clean, well-maintained rooms that surround a pleasant courtyard.

Hotel Internacional (922-23-18; exportadores@ aol.com; Zaragoza 1050 Ote; s/d US$25/30) Nearby Avenida, this place is slightly larger and institutional looking.

MID-RANGE

There are a few good-quality hotels around the center. International chains and business hotels are further outside of town.

Hotel La Estancia (922-00-77; Guerrero 735; s/d US$36/41;) By far the best value in town, the unassuming La Estancia, is tucked away on a quiet street. It has extremely warm and cheerful rooms with well-matched furniture and clean, modern bathrooms. The long, bright hallway is kept spotless.

Hotel Savoy Plaza (☎ 922-00-67; Juárez 860 Nte; r US$44; P) Half a block south of the Parroquia de Guadalupe, the modern Savoy Plaza is a good choice though the compact rooms are not as inviting as La Estancia's.

Hotel Astromundo (☎ 922-56-25; astromundo@infosel.net.mx; Juárez 675 Nte; s/d US$66/75; P) The top downtown place is the Astromundo. Its rooms are comfortable; it's not luxurious but it has all the amenities and a great location.

Hotel San Carlos (☎ 922-12-80; hsancarlos@micros.com.mx; Hidalgo 970 Nte; s/d US$45/50; P) Though it's still a popular choice and the staff try to keep up an air of sophistication, the San Carlos has seen better days. The medieval-style furnished rooms aren't fit for royalty but some overlook the plaza. A restaurant is attached.

Eating

In addition to the following listings, there are a number of taco, fried-chicken and fast-food style joints offering hearty, inexpensive fare on and around the pedestrian mall on Hidalgo.

Café La Villa (☎ 922-02-67; cnr Zaragoza & Hidalgo; breakfast US$4, mains US$4.50-7;) The formal back room of La Villa is decorated like a castle banquet hall while the more casual front is like a Paris café. The design schemes may be centuries apart but the menus are the same: tacos, enchiladas and the rest. Both sections are charming and pleasant and importantly have air-conditioning.

El Pastor (☎ 922-41-91; Juárez 710 Nte; mains US$7-12;) El Pastor is the place for centrally located high-end dining. Waiters are formally attired and the interior is plush and elegant. There's a nice courtyard. Buffet breakfast is served every day from 7am to 11:30pm. Meat dishes, including *cabrito*, dominate the menu. Seafood offerings are in the works.

Café Sánchez (☎ 922-16-65; Morelos 575 Ote; breakfast US$3.50, mains US$3.50-7; 7am-7pm;) A popular spot with locals, Sánchez has lots of egg dishes, the usual Mexican fare and a cool interior.

Café Paris (☎ 922-55-35; Hidalgo 815; breakfast US$2.25-3.25, mains US$3.25-8;) Half a block

south of the plaza, this branch of the popular chain is one of Reynosa's best options, featuring breakfasts and scrumptious Mexican dishes. Waiters wheel carts of pastries around and serve *café lechero*, pouring coffee and milk from separate pitchers. Their tasty sandwiches are an inexpensive lunch (US$1.75).

CaféTips (☎ 922-60-19; Méndez 640; meals US$3; 6am-10pm) You can enjoy a variety of burritos, tacos and *tortas* at this air-conditioned café, half a block east of Hidalgo. Service is prompt and the servings large.

Restaurant Santa Fe (☎ 922-85-16; Zaragoza 690; dishes US$5.50-9) On the plaza, the Santa Fe serves Chinese food and Mexican dishes with a Chinese flavor. Some of the chicken, pork and seafood dishes are large enough to feed two hungry people.

Restaurant El Jardín (☎ 961-74-94; Juárez; dishes US$8; 7am-11pm Mon-Thu, 7am-noon Fri & Sat, 7am-10pm Sun) This is the place for norteño-style *cabrito al pastor*.

Entertainment

The Zona Rosa has a slew of restaurants, bars and nightclubs, but comes to life only on the nights when the young Texas crowd comes in. Much sleazier entertainment (exotic dancing and prostitution) is the rule at 'boys' town, a few kilometers west, just beyond where Aldama becomes a dirt road.

Getting There & Away

AIR

Reynosa's airport, Aeropuerto General Lucio Blanco, is 8km out of town, off the Matamoros road. There are daily Aeroméxico flights direct to/from Mexico City and Guadalajara. Several other small airlines operate here, such as **Aerolíneas Internacionales** (☎ 926-73-00), which flies to and from Aguascalientes and Tijuana. Aeroméxico and Aerolíneas both operate out of Reynosa.

BUS

The bus station is on the southeastern corner of the central grid, opposite the parking lot of the Gigante supermarket. Buses run to almost anywhere you'd want to go in Mexico. Daily service from Reynosa include the following:

Aguascalientes (US$48, 12hr, hourly 1st-class)
Ciudad Victoria (US$21.75, 4½hr, 5 or more 1st-class)
Guadalajara (US$78.50, 15hr, 8 1st-class)

Matamoros (1st/2nd class US$6/5.75, 2hr, every 2hr)
Mexico City (US$77, 14hr, 4 1st-class) To Terminal Norte.
Monterrey (US$14, 3hr, 1st-class every 2hr)
Saltillo (US$17, 5hr, 5 1st-class)
San Luis Potosí (US$33, 10hr, a few 1st-class)
Tampico (US$27, 7hr, a few 1st-class)
Torreón (US$34, 9hr, 9 1st-class)
Zacatecas (US$41, 10hr, 2 1st-class)

First-class buses also serve Chihuahua, Ciudad Juárez, Durango, Puebla, Querétaro, Veracruz and Villahermosa. Second-class buses serving mainly local destinations are also available. There are also direct buses to Houston (US$25), San Antonio (US$25), Austin (US$30) and Dallas (US$40) daily and to Chicago twice a week (US$105).

The nearest Texas transportation center, McAllen, is 9km from the border. **Valley Transit Company** (☎ 956-686-5479 in McAllen) runs buses between the McAllen and Reynosa bus stations every 30 minutes between 6am and 10pm (US$2). In Reynosa, tickets can be purchased at the Greyhound counter at the bus station.

Coming from McAllen, if you don't want to go all the way to the Reynosa bus station, get off on the US side of the bridge and walk over it into Reynosa.

CAR & MOTORCYCLE

East of the bridge, there's an *aduana* (customs) office that can issue car permits. To get there, turn left up Av Alemán after clearing immigration, and follow the yellow arrows. Take the first left after the Matamoros turnoff; the entrance is at the end of the street.

Going west to Monterrey (220km), the toll Hwy 40D is excellent and patrolled by Green Angels; the tolls total US$18. (The less direct, toll-free Hwy 40 follows roughly the same route.) Hwys 97 and 180 south to Tampico are two-lane, surfaced roads, but not too busy. Hwy 101 branches off Hwy 180 to Ciudad Victoria and the scenic climb to San Luis Potosí. If you want to follow the Rio Grande upstream to Nuevo Laredo, Hwy 2 is not in bad shape, but it's quicker to travel on the US side. Side roads off Hwy 2 reach a number of obscure border crossings and the Presa Falcón (Falcon Reservoir), as well as Guerrero Viejo, a town that was submerged after the dam's construction in 1953, and moved to its cur-

rent site at Nueva Ciudad Guerrero, 33km to the southeast. It's a smooth 40-minute drive east to Matamoros via the toll Hwy 2D, which begins just past Reynosa airport (US$4.50).

Getting Around

Battered yellow microbuses rattle around Reynosa. From the international bridge to the bus station, catch one of the Valley Transit Company coaches coming from McAllen with 'Reynosa' on the front (US$1.75).

To get from the bus station to the town center, turn left after exiting the bus station and go half a block, then cross the Gigante parking lot to the bus stop on Colón. Take one of the buses labeled 'Olmo' (US$0.40).

Taxis between the bus station and the bridge should not cost more than US$5. Expect to pay around US$15 for a taxi ride to/from the airport.

MATAMOROS

☎ 868 / pop 405,000

Matamoros is an energetic place, with many shops and restaurants targeting day-trippers from the other side of the border. With a few excellent hotels and restaurants, and a nearby beach, it's easily the border town that most closely resembles a vacation destination.

The city is no historical monument, but there is more evidence of the past here than in most border towns, and the charming town center, with its church and plaza, looks typically Mexican. South of the central area is a broad circle of newer industrial zones. Matamoros also is a commercial center for a large agricultural hinterland.

First settled during the Spanish colonization of Tamaulipas in 1686 as Los Esteros Hermosas (The Beautiful Estuaries), the city was renamed in 1793 after Padre Mariano Matamoros. In 1846, Matamoros was the first Mexican city to be taken by US forces in the Mexican-American War; Zachary Taylor then used it as a base for his attack on Monterrey. During the US Civil War, when sea routes to the Confederacy were blockaded, Matamoros transshipped cotton out of Confederate Texas, and supplies and war material into it.

Orientation

Matamoros lies across the Rio Grande from Brownsville, Texas. The river is spanned by

NORTHEAST MEXICO

MATAMOROS

0 ——————— 500 m
0 ——————— 0.3 miles

INFORMATION
Banca Afirme.................................1 C2
Bancomer......................................2 C2
Banorte...3 C2
Galaxy Ciber Café.......................4 C2
Internet Infinitum........................5 B2
Post Office....................................6 B3
Scotiabank Inverlat.....................7 C2
Telecomm..............................(see 6)
Tourist Bureau.............................8 C1
US Consulate................................9 C1

SIGHTS & ACTIVITIES   (p377)
MACT...10 C1
Museo Casamata.........................11 D2

SLEEPING   (pp377–8)
Best Western Hotel Plaza
    Matamoros................................12 B2
Hotel Autel Nieto.......................13 B2
Hotel Colonial.............................14 B2
Hotel Majestic.............................15 B2
Hotel Ritz.....................................16 B2
Hotel Roma..................................17 B2

EATING   (p378)
Café Latino..................................18 C2
Café Paris.....................................19 C2
Los Norteños...............................20 B2
Restaurant Los Faroles..............21 B2
Restaurant Louisiana..................22 B2
Transpatio Bar & Grill.................23 C2

ENTERTAINMENT
Teatro de la Reforma.................24 C2

TRANSPORT   (pp378–9)
Aero California............................25 C2
Bus Station..................................26 C3
Combi Vans to Playa Bagdad...27 B2

---

a bridge with border controls at each end. The Rio Grande is a disappointing trickle in this area, as most of its water has been siphoned off upstream for irrigation.

From the southern end of the bridge, Obregón winds around toward the town's central grid, 1.5km to the southwest.

Information

EMERGENCY
Police (☎ 060)
Red Cross (☎ 12-00-04)

IMMIGRATION
The Mexican border post waves most pedestrians through on the assumption that they are here just for a day's shopping or eating, but some cars will get the red light to be checked. If you're planning to proceed further south into Mexico, go to the immigration office and ask for a tourist card and have it stamped before you leave Matamoros.

INTERNET ACCESS
Galaxy Ciber Café (Abasolo 74; per hr M$15) Between Calle 5 and 6.

Internet Infinitum (Calle 9; per hr M$10) Between Matamoros and Abasolo.

MONEY
Several banks on Plaza Hidalgo have ATMs; Banca Afirme, Banorte and Scotiabank Inverlat will also change cash or traveler's checks. Often you get a better rate for cash in the exchange houses around the central area, but few change traveler's checks.

In Brownsville, there are exchange houses on International Blvd, which is the road running straight north from the international bridge. Some are open 24 hours a day.

POST
Post office (cnr Calle 11 & Río Bravo) Situated 1km south of the center.

TOURIST INFORMATION
Brownsville Chamber of Commerce (☎ 956-542-4341; info@brownsvillechamber.com; 1600 E Elizabeth St; ⏱ 8am-5pm Mon-Fri) About 300m east of the bridge. Good if you need maps, brochures or printed giveaways on Matamoros.

Tourist bureau (9am-1pm & 3-7pm) An informal and not especially helpful place. Found in the green and white shack on Obregón further away from town from the MACT.

Sights

MUSEO CASAMATA

This **fort** (cnr Guatemala & Degollado; admission free; 8am-4pm Tue-Fri, 9am-2pm Sat & Sun) dates from 1845. One of a series of walls and fortifications built in the 19th century to defend the city, it was the scene of fighting in the Mexican-American War. It now contains memorabilia of the Mexican Revolution, early photos of Matamoros and some ill-assorted miscellany. Explanations are in Spanish only.

MUSEO DE ARTE CONTEMPORANEO DE TAMAULIPAS

Originally dedicated to the development of local artists in the late '60s, then rechristened as the Corn Museum in the '80s, **MACT** (813-14-99; cnr Calle 5 & Constitution; admission US$1.25, free Wed; 10am-2pm & 3-6pm Tue-Sat) opened its doors once again in 2002 with the mission of promoting visual artists in Tamaulipas. The building itself is a work of art, an example of the type of modernist architecture found in public buildings in Monterrey.

PLAYA BAGDAD

Matamoros' beach, formerly known as Playa Lauro Villar, adopted the name of Bagdad from a town at the mouth of the Rio Grande that prospered during the US Civil War, but later succumbed to floods, hurricanes and military attacks. It's 37km east of Matamoros on Hwy 2, with a wide stretch of clean sand and a few beachside seafood restaurants. The water is warm and fairly clean and if you close your eyes you can almost ignore the cars parked on the beach. Blue, ramshackle combi vans heading to Playa Bagdad leave from Calle 10 on the east side of Plaza Allende (US$2.20, 1½ hours). Trips are hourly during the summer months but otherwise the vans leave only when full and even then depend on a last-minute roll call to determine whether enough passengers want the beach rather than another destination. Claim a seat early; otherwise you will have to stand, compete for scarce elbow room and struggle to keep your head from further damaging the roof. Ask the driver to estimate return trip times or you will have to rely on benevolent drivers to make it back to Matamoros.

Festivals & Events

The **Expo Fiesta Matamoros**, held every year from late June to early July, features an amusement park, handicrafts displays and popular entertainers.

The **International Autumn Festival**, in October, is the occasion for a variety of cultural events, from chamber music concerts to traditional dance displays. Many are performed in the beautifully restored Teatro de la Reforma.

Sleeping

There are a couple of basic options near the center of town for less than US$20 a double. It's worth spending just a little more money on one of the several excellent mid-range options also in the center.

BUDGET

Hotel Majestic (813-36-80; Abasolo 131; s/d with fan US$14/16) Less dispiriting than Hotel México next door, this family-run place has small but clean rooms with firm beds. There's no air-con but it's the best budget option in the center of town.

MID-RANGE & TOP-END

There's no shortage of excellent choices within a few blocks of each other.

Hotel Colonial (816-66-06; www.hcolonial.com; cnr Calle 6 & Matamoros; r US$43; P X) An absolute jewel, the Colonial has been masterfully refurbished. Relax under the stars in the brick-lined courtyard out front. Inside, the hallways and bathrooms are beautifully tiled and Mexican-themed artwork adorns the bedroom walls.

Hotel Roma (813-61-76; www.hotelfroma.com; Calle 9 1420; r US$36; P X) Under the same management as the Best Western Plaza Matamoros across the street, the Roma has none of the bells and whistles of its sister hotel. It does have modern, comfortable and secure rooms.

Hotel Ritz (812-11-90; www.ritzhotel.org; Matamoros 612; r US$50; P X) Geared more for the business traveler, the Ritz offers a gym, fax and laundry services, a sports bar and a car rental agency. The rooms are small but lovely, with Talavera-tiled furniture. Breakfast is included.

Best Western Plaza Matamoros (☎ 816-16-96; www.bestwestern.com/mx/hotelplazamatamoros; cnr Calle 9 & Bravo; r US$55; P ✗ ☐) The Hotel Plaza Matamoros has all the creature comforts and a handsome restaurant/atrium. Rooms in the back are especially plush.

Best Western Gran Hotel Residencial (☎ 813-94-40; www.bestwestern.com; Obregón 249; s & d US$72; P ✗ ☐ ☒) Matamoros' top hotel, 1.2km south of the international bridge, has 120 air-conditioned rooms, with terraces surrounding pleasant gardens and a few swimming pools.

Hotel Autel Nieto (☎ 813-08-57; autelnieto@hot mail.com; Calle 10 1508; s/d US$28/36; P ✗) Autel Nieto, between Bustamante and Bravo, has large, old-fashioned rooms, with cable TV, phone, and laundry services. It's an old place that doesn't look like much from the outside, but it's a good deal at this price.

Eating & Drinking

Besides a couple of fashionable eateries similar to establishments found in Mexico City and another cosmopolitan cities, Matamoros has plenty of cheap stand-bys around the pedestrian plaza.

Transpatio Bar & Grill (☎ 812-62-33; 2nd fl, Calle 6 181; mains US$8; ☯ noon-2am; P ✗) Dine on fish, pasta and traditional Mexican dishes surrounded by brick walls, mod booths and avant-garde paintings. Margaritas (US$4) and other drinks are mixed up at the bar. There's live music Saturday nights and a DJ Friday evenings in the cozy 1st-floor outdoor courtyard. Downstairs, Aroma's Café (part of same complex) keeps up the stylish vibe serving up breakfasts (US$5) and creative coffee drinks, smoothies and shakes like the delicious Moka Oreo (US$3).

Café Latino (☎ 816-90-93; Morelos 84; mains US$4; ☯ 8am-11pm Mon-Fri, 10am-11pm Sat; ✗) The creative kitchen at equally fashionable Café Latino dishes up empanadas, salads and even a shrimp hamburger.

Café Paris (☎ 816-03-10; González 125; breakfast US$2.50, mains US$2.25-5.50; ✗) This large, many-boothed operation is usually packed in the morning. A tempting variety of pastries are brought around on carts; coffee and hot milk are poured separately for café lechero. There are breakfast specials and Mexican antojitos (snacks, such as tacos and enchiladas).

Restaurant Los Faroles (☎ 812-11-90; cnr Calle 7 & Matamoros; mains US$5.50-10; ☯ 7am-11pm; P ✗) Across the street from the Hotel Ritz which it is part of, Los Faroles has an American-style Mexican menu. Portions of main dishes like fajitas or filet mignon are large and there's a breakfast buffet.

Restaurant Louisiana (☎ 812-10-96; Bravo 807; sandwiches US$4.50, mains US$8-11; P ✗) This elegant restaurant offers entrées including rib-eye steak with mushrooms (US$10), quail and shish kebab. Except for the frog's legs, however, there's no Cajun food on the menu.

Los Norteños (☎ 813-00-37; Matamoros 109; mains US$4.50, cabrito US$11; ☯ 8am-midnight; ✗) For authentic northern-Mexican cuisine, head for Los Norteños. A cantina-style restaurant with a bar, simple tables and attentive waiters, it offers cabrito al pastor, served with salad, tortillas and frijoles charros (cowboy beans).

Shopping

The 'new market,' or Mercado Juárez, occupies the blocks bordered by Calles 9 and 10, and Abasolo and Matamoros. A lot of the stuff on sale is second-rate but there's plenty of variety. Prices are 20% to 30% higher than the cheapest markets further south, but you can bargain vendors down a bit.

Getting There & Away

AIR

Matamoros has an airport 17km out of town on the road to Ciudad Victoria. **Aeroméxico** (☎ 812-24-60) and **Aero California** (☎ 812-22-00; Calle 5 1306; ☯ 9am-8pm Mon-Fri, 10am-6pm Sat & Sun) fly daily to Mexico City with a stop in Ciudad Victoria.

BUS

Both 1st- and 2nd-class buses run from the bus station on Canales, near the corner of Guatemala. The station has a 24-hour restaurant, a post office, left-luggage service and a telephone office (which also sells city maps).

Daily service from Matamoros include the following:

Ciudad Victoria (US$16, 4hr, 6 1st-class)
Mexico City (US$76, 15hr, 1 deluxe; US$65, 15hr, 7 1st-class; US$58, 15hr, 2 2nd-class) To Terminal Norte.
Monterrey (US$20, 5hr, frequent 1st-class)
Reynosa (US$7.50, 2hr, hourly 1st-class; US$5.50, 2hr 5 2nd-class)

Saltillo (US$23, 7hr, frequent 1st-class)
Tampico (US$23, 7hr, frequent 1st-class)
Torreón (US$39, 9hr, 8 1st-class)

Buses go to many other destinations including Chihuahua, Durango, Guadalajara, San Luis Potosí, Tijuana, Veracruz and Zacatecas. **Greyhound** (☎ 816-66-15, 800-550-6210 in USA) runs daily buses to Houston and Atlanta, and **El Expreso Bus Company** (☎ 813-79-72) has daily departures to points throughout the southeast USA.

You can get buses from the Brownsville, Texas, bus station direct to several cities inside Mexico, but they cost more than from Matamoros, and they might take up to two hours to get over the international bridge and through customs and immigration. It's quicker to walk across the bridge and take local transport to the Matamoros bus station.

Facing the USA from the north end of the international bridge, go left (west) on Elizabeth, then two blocks south on 12th for the **Brownsville bus station** (☎ 956-546-7171; 1134 East Saint Charles). There are buses to all the major cities in Texas, and connections to other US cities.

CAR & MOTORCYCLE

Driving across the bridge to/from Brownsville costs US$1.60. At the Mexican end there is a turnoff immediately before the customs building; pull in there to obtain your temporary vehicle permit. To cancel your permit on the way out, turn left through the opening in the median before you reach the toll booth, then park in the lane beside the customs building.

The main routes on into Mexico are Hwy 180 south to Tampico and Hwy 101 southwest to Ciudad Victoria and into the Bajío region (see following for more information on Hwys 180 and 101). These unfrequented two-lane roads are both in fair condition and free of tolls. Officials at various checkpoints will want to see your tourist card and vehicle permit, and might check your vehicle for drugs or firearms. You can also go west to Monterrey via Reynosa.

Getting Around

Matamoros is served by small buses called maxi-taxis, which charge US$0.50 to anywhere in town. You can stop them on any street corner. Ruta 2 maxi-taxis pass by the bus station on Calle 1 and go to the center of town. From the international bridge, regular taxis are on the right side of Obregón, maxi-taxis on the left beyond the taco stalls. Ruta 3 maxi-taxis go to the bus station. Alternatively, you could catch a free city tour bus in front of the García crafts shop on Obregón near the bridge. Every half hour between 9am and 6pm, the service shuttles visitors from the bridge to Mercado Juárez and back.

Taxis from the bus station to the bridge or center of town cost about US$6.

SOUTH OF MATAMOROS

For its first 183km, the 500km Hwy 180 to Tampico is the same road as Hwy 101 to Ciudad Victoria. Most of the highway runs 30km to 40km inland, crossing unspectacular lowlands where sugarcane is the chief crop, though there are some more scenic stretches where the outliers of the Sierra Madre Oriental come close to the coast. Budget and mid-range hotels are found in **San Fernando** (137km from Matamoros), **Soto La Marina** (267km) and **Aldama** (379km). Side roads go east to the coast, most of which consists of lagoons separated from the gulf by narrow sand spits. The longest is the **Laguna Madre**, extending some 230km along the northern Tamaulipas coast. (The lagoon dried up in the mid-20th century, forcing many to leave the area. When a 1967 hurricane replenished it, the area was resettled by *veracruzanos*.) The lagoons, sand dunes and coastal wetlands support a unique ecosystem, with many bird species and excellent fishing.

About 20km south of Matamoros, just past the airport, a side road crosses marshland for 60km before reaching **El Mezquital**, a small fishing village with a lighthouse and beach on the long thin spit of land that divides the Laguna Madre from the Gulf. From San Fernando, 120km further south, a road leads to **Carboneras**, another small fishing village facing the lagoon. There's not much here, but you might be able to get a boat out to the lagoon barrier island, where porpoises can sometimes be seen. Food and gas are available, but there are no rooms for rent in either El Mezquital or Carboneras.

From Soto La Marina, about 130km south of San Fernando, Hwy 70 heads east for

50km, paralleling the Río Soto La Marina, to La Pesca (see below). Further south, a 45km road runs east from Aldama, through the eastern fringes of the Sierra de Tamaulipas, to **Barra del Tordo**, another fishing village with a beach and good sport fishing. Facilities include budget and mid-range hotels, restaurants and a campground.

LA PESCA
☎ 835 / pop 1500

If coming directly from the USA or a Mexican city to the north, La Pesca feels satisfyingly worlds apart – it maintains the ramshackle and relaxed air of an ordinary fishing village. You'll drive right through if you're not careful. There's a long, wide beach, Playa La Pesca, 6km east of town. It has shady palapas and two seaside restaurants at one end, and is usually deserted during the day. The Río Soto La Marina and the Laguna Morales have abundant rainbow trout, kingfish, sea bass, porgy and sole. Most of the hotels can arrange boat rentals with fishing guides for around US$65 a day. A fishing tournament for sea bass takes place in November.

One of the world's most endangered sea turtles, the Kemp's ridley, digs its nests on the beaches from Tampico north to La Pesca from March to July. The Tamaulipas state environmental authority has a **turtle center** (☎ 834-312-60-18 in Ciudad Victoria for information), 800m north of the main beach, dedicated to the species' preservation at La Pesca, the northern limit of the turtles' nesting grounds. Visitors are educated about protection efforts and offered a firsthand glimpse of the hatching process during the months of peak activity.

There are no banks or ATMs and most places do not accept credit cards. You can purchase a phone card to make long distance calls but sometimes the entire town can run out.

The **Rivera del Río** (☎ 327-06-58; s/d US$27/37; P ⊠ ⊠) is by far the best place to stay in town. Heading north out of town, look to your right for the sign and turnoff. The rooms are large and plain but the real surprise is the unexpectedly well-maintained grounds and the lovely swimming pool perched over the river. Fishing and self-catering facilities are also available here. There is a good **restaurant** (☺ Thu-Sun) attached serving trout and sea bass dishes (US$8). On your left, just before the Rivera del Río turnoff, the rooms of the ordinary **Hotel Titanic** (r US$18; P ⊠) will do if the Rivera del Río is full and you want to stay in town. The bathroom toilets are seatless.

The nondescript village also has a few grocery stores and taco stands. For table service, try **Restaurant Yary** (mains US$4) and **El Barco del Capitain Axel** (☎ 327-07-15; seafood mains US$5). The latter is just before the bridge before you enter La Pesca proper and accepts some credit cards. After a day at the beach, unwind with drinks and a meal at **Posada Restaurant** (seafood mains US$6), next to the lighthouse at Playa la Pesca.

There are more than half a dozen riverside hotels along the approach to La Pesca, all featuring piers with lights for night-fishing and grills for cooking your catch. Designed for family weekends, most places charge around US$45 for a two- or three-bed room, but will reduce rates for solo travelers during the week. These are really only feasible if you have your own transportation.

Transportes Tamaulipecos De La Costa runs nine buses a day between Ciudad Victoria's bus terminal and Playa La Pesca (US$9, 3½ hours). You also can catch any of these buses from Soto La Marina's central plaza, an hour from La Pesca (US$2).

CIUDAD VICTORIA
☎ 834 / pop 300,000

About 40km north of the Tropic of Cancer, the capital of Tamaulipas state is a clean and pleasant city. It's around 310km south of Matamoros and Reynosa, well served by buses in every direction, and a good spot to break a journey between central Mexico and the Texas border. A late-afternoon stroll around Plaza Hidalgo is a great way to stretch the legs and tap into the lethargy of this laid-back place. With the Sierra Madre forming an impressive backdrop to the city, there's just enough altitude to moderate the steamy heat of the coastal plains or the Rio Grande valley.

Orientation
Three highways converge at Ciudad Victoria, and a ring road allows through traffic to move between them without entering the city itself. The center is laid out in a grid pattern. The north–south streets have both

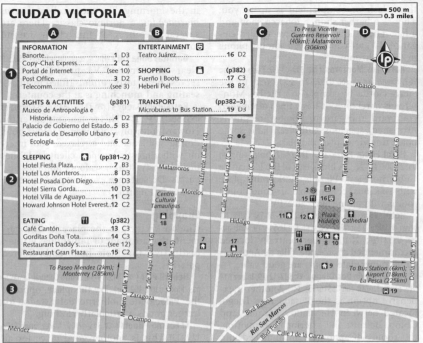

CIUDAD VICTORIA

0 —————— 500 m
0 ————————— 0.3 miles

INFORMATION
Banorte.....................................1 D3
Copy-Chat Express....................2 C2
Portal de Internet.................(see 10)
Post Office................................3 D2
Telecomm............................(see 3)

SIGHTS & ACTIVITIES (p381)
Museo de Antropología e
  Historia..................................4 D2
Palacio de Gobierno del Estado..5 B3
Secretaría de Desarrollo Urbano y
  Ecología.................................6 C2

SLEEPING (pp381–2)
Hotel Fiesta Plaza.....................7 B3
Hotel Los Monteros...................8 D3
Hotel Posada Don Diego............9 D3
Hotel Sierra Gorda...................10 D3
Hotel Villa de Aguayo...............11 C2
Howard Johnson Hotel Everest..12 C2

EATING (p382)
Café Cantón.............................13 C3
Gorditas Doña Tota...................14 C3
Restaurant Daddy's.............(see 12)
Restaurant Gran Plaza..............15 C2

ENTERTAINMENT
Teatro Juárez...........................16 D2

SHOPPING (p382)
Fuerño I Boots..........................17 C3
Heberli Piel...............................18 B2

TRANSPORT (pp382–3)
Microbuses to Bus Station........19 D3

To Presa Vicente
Guerrero Reservoir
(40km); Matamoros
(306km)

Abasolo

To Paseo Méndez (2km);
Monterrey (285km)

To Bus Station (6km);
Airport (18km);
La Pesca (225km)

numbers (Calle 7, Calle 8 etc) and names
(Díaz, Tijerina etc). Most of the shops are
on Hidalgo, from the central market to the
Centro Cultural Tamaulipas. The Río San
Marcos, a small trickle for much of the
year, separates the city center from neighborhoods that are steadily creeping up the
mountainside to the south.

Information

For internet access, check out **Copy-Chat Express** (202 Calle 9; per hr M$10) and **Portal de Internet**
(per hr M$10; 10am-11pm) next to Hotel Sierra
Gorda on Hidalgo. The main post office is
on Morelos, northeast of the plaza in the
Palacio Federal building.

Sights & Activities

Ciudad Victoria has no compelling tourist attractions, but there is the **Museo de
Antropología e Historia** (318-18-31; Matamoros;
admission free; 9:30am-7pm Mon-Fri), one block
north of Plaza Hidalgo, run by the University of Tamaulipas. It's a grab bag of mammoth bones, indigenous artifacts, colonial
memorabilia, revolutionary photos and one

vintage carriage. It's a measure of the scarce
foot traffic that the attendant on duty is
likely to greet you with a warm and somewhat surprised welcome.

Ciudad Victoria also has some interesting public buildings, such as the **Palacio de
Gobierno del Estado** (Juárez), between Calles
15 and 16, and the **Teatro Juárez**, facing the
north side of the Plaza Hidalgo, both with
large murals. The **Paseo Méndez** has plenty of
greenery, and a couple of **public pools** (admission US$1; 7am-10pm). There is an entrance
to Paseo Méndez on Calle 17 (Madero)
between Berriozabal and Carrera Torres.

About 40km northeast of Ciudad Vic-
toria, **Presa Vicente Guerrero** is a huge reservoir that attracts Mexicans and US citizens
for bass fishing.

Sleeping

There are plenty of good choices within a
few blocks of Plaza Hidalgo.

Hotel Sierra Gorda (312-20-10; Plaza Hidalgo
990; s/d US$36/41;) This somewhat ba-
roque hotel on the south side of Plaza
Hidalgo has lots of different styles. Whether

they clash or complement is up to you. There's a barber shop, a tobacco shop and a bar. The unique rooms have a faded elegance, TV, air-con and even a house phone in the bathroom.

Hotel Los Monteros (☎ 312-03-00; Plaza Hidalgo 962; r with fan/air-con US$22/23; 🔀) Next to the Sierra Gorda, by comparison, the Los Monteros is barebones. It has a fine colonnaded courtyard and garden. Rooms are simply furnished, spacious and clean, and some boast fine views over the plaza.

Hotel Fiesta Plaza (☎ 312-78-77; Juárez 401; s/d US$27/30; ℗ 🔀). A block east of the Palacio de Gobierno, Fiesta Plaza is a welcoming place with spacious, comfortable air-conditioned rooms with phone and cable TV.

Hotel Villa de Aguayo (☎ 312-78-18; Calle 10, btwn Hidalgo & Morelos; s/d with fan US$16/19, with air-con US$21/24; 🔀) Another centrally located recommended choice, the Villa de Aguayo's large immaculate rooms are good value.

Hotel Posada Don Diego (☎ 312-12-79; Juárez 814 Ote; r with fan/air-con US$16/18; 🔀) Another inexpensive option is the Posada Don Diego, located between Hermanos Vázquez and Colón. Because the exterior is so inviting, the rooms disappoint – mismatched and extra furniture are haphazardly scattered about.

Howard Johnson Hotel Everest (☎ 318-70-70; http://howard-johnson-everest.com; Colón 126; r US$120; ℗ 🔀 🔀 🖳 🖳) This tall structure on the west side of the plaza has luxurious, modern rooms (those in front have balconies with excellent plaza views). Ask about discount specials, as there are often promotions. The hotel features an indoor pool and a parking garage.

Eating

There's a surprising dearth of restaurants near Plaza Hidalgo. You'll find more choices, including international chains, north of the center.

Restaurant Gran Plaza (Morelos 202; mains US$3; 🕑 24hr) Lots of good food at cheap prices – you may end up at the Gran Plaza more than once. Lunch specials are a bargain: fish soup, filet of fish, rice, french fries, salad, desert and chips (US$3).

Café Cantón (☎ 312-16-43; Colón 114; breakfast US$3, other meals US$2.50-5) This modest café has very good coffee and stick-to-your-ribs breakfasts – perhaps that's why it's packed

in the morning. Try the excellent *huevos machacados,* a norteño classic. There are several members of this chain around town.

Gorditas Doña Tota (Hidalgo; gorditas from US$0.50) Near the corner of Vázquez, Doña Tota serves cheap, tasty *gorditas* (filled tortillas); seating and munching is at the counter.

Restaurant Daddy's (☎ 312-67-84; Colón 126; mains US$5.50-11; ℗ 🔀) This restaurant, under the Howard Johnson Hotel Everest, offers hotel dining ambience and a relaxed, cool interior with a mostly business clientele. Dishes include tasty steaks, seafood, *antojitos* and pastas. Desserts are excellent and there are menus in English.

Shopping

Ciudad Victoria is the place to find garments that are made of Tamaulipas leather, distinctive for their hand-embroidered patterns.

Heberli Piel (☎ 312-19-54, Centro Cultural Tamaulipas, Pino Suárez 402 Sur) Try this place, opposite the Palacio de Gobierno del Estado, for leather goods, particularly clothing.

El Fuerno I Boots (☎ 315-47-09; Juarez, btwn Calle 12 & 13) This is another good place for all your cowboy needs. There are a few locations around town.

For an assortment of handicrafts and local sweets have a browse through the informal market stalls in front of the Centro Cultural Tamaulipas building and around the market, east of Plaza Hildago.

Getting There & Away
AIR

The airport, Aeropuerto Nacional General Pedro J Méndez, is east of town off the Soto La Marina road. There are flights to Matamoros and Mexico City with **Aero California** (☎ 315-18-50) and to Mexico City with **Aeromar** (☎ 316-96-96).

BUS

The bus station, on the east side of town near the ring road, has a left-luggage service. Frequent 1st-class buses run to Ciudad Mante (US$7, 2½ hours), Guadalajara (US$41, nine hours), Matamoros (US$16, 4¼ hours), Monterrey (US$16, 3¾ hours), Reynosa (US$16, four hours), Saltillo (US$22, 4½ hours), San Luis Potosí (US$18, 5½ hours) and Tampico (US$12, four hours), and two a day leave for Mexico City's Terminal Norte (US$45, 10 hours)

Second-class buses leave Ciudad Victoria for La Pesca at least every two hours (US$9, 3½ hours) and there are frequent services south to Gómez Farías (US$6, 1½ hours), for those wanting to visit Reserva de la Biósfera.

CAR & MOTORCYCLE

From Ciudad Victoria, you can go southeast to Tampico for the Huasteca region or the Gulf Coast, or take one of the steep roads heading west ascending into the Sierra Madre Oriental. For San Luis Potosí, take Hwy 101 southwest – an incredibly scenic route. For Mexico City, Hwy 85 south, via Ciudad Mante and Ciudad Valles, is the most direct route.

Getting Around

From the bus station to the center of town, take a Ruta 25 bus, which goes down Bravo, three blocks north of Plaza Hidalgo (US$0.40). In the other direction, microbuses labeled 'Palmas' depart from Blvd Balboa at the bridge over the Río San Marcos. Taxis charge around US$3 for the same trip, or from Plaza Hidalgo to the tourist office.

RESERVA DE LA BIÓSFERA EL CIELO

☎ 832 / pop 3500

A reserve of 1440 sq km, El Cielo covers a range of altitudes on the slopes of the Sierra, and is a transition zone between tropical, semi-desert and temperate ecosystems, marking the northern limit for a number of tropical species of plants and animals. Most of the massive logging operations were shut down in 1975, but it wasn't declared an international biosphere reserve by the UN until 1987. Forty varieties of orchids can be found here, mostly within the cloud forest zone between 800m and 1400m. The reserve is also habitat to half the bird species in Mexico and 40 kinds of bats. When warm gulf moisture crosses the lowlands and hits the mountains, it rises creating the striking cloud cover, while higher up it condenses and turns to rain.

Though you don't need a permit to enter the reserve with your own vehicle, Tamaulipas' **Secretaría de Desarrollo Urbano y Ecología** (☎ 834-315-55-80; dirrec_nat@terra.com.mx; Garza 475;

⊗ 9am-6pm Mon-Fri) in Ciudad Victoria recommends you register with it beforehand as a safety measure. However, this is no easy feat and it's more convenient to register in the village of Gómez Farías; look for the Police Commander's office in the Palacio Municipal near the plaza. The Casa de Piedra (see below) can also arrange guides, some English-speaking and with ornithological expertise, and transport to the reserve, and has a shop with food and hiking supplies.

Several tracks, once used by loggers, take off from **Gómez Farías**, which is technically just outside the reserve, 11km up a side road off Hwy 85, about 100km south of Ciudad Victoria and 40km north of Ciudad Mante. One arduous trail climbs 10km (over an hour by truck) to the village of **Alta Cima** (860m), the starting point for hikes into the cloud forest. **San José** (1400m) is another 4km and **El Elefante** (1640m) 6km further up the same track. Be aware the way is very rough; non-4WD vehicles are at risk.

Some outdoor enthusiasts rave enthusiastically about the hiking, fishing, rafting and crystal-clear water at a handful of spots along tributaries of the Río Sabinas. Turn off the road heading back to the highway from Gómez Farías to find El Nacimiento and Poza Azul.

Sleeping & Eating

There are two real lodging options in Gómez Farías. **Casa de Piedra** (☎ 236-21-96; www.tourbymexico.com/elcielo_casadepiedra; Hidalgo; s/d US$36/46; Ⓟ), just 150m past the plaza, blends perfectly into its dramatic setting. It's difficult to leave this mountain refuge, especially if you stay in the marvelously snug room with a balcony perched over a mountain ravine. Breakfast is included. The excellent restaurant prepares tasty chicken mole (US$4).

Hotel Posada Campestre (☎ 236-22-00; www.posadaenelcielo.com; Hidalgo; r US$36) is a little further down the same road, and while it doesn't have Casa de Piedra's character, the rooms, which have bunk-beds, are neat and orderly. Besides a few small grocery stores and the Casa de Piedra, food is scarce in Gómez Farías. For a quick lunch of tacos and enchiladas try Karlitas in the plaza.

Accommodations are sort of an afterthought at **Rancho el Huasteco** (☎ 312-22-01, 317-27-70; 8-10-person cabins US$111, camping US$5.50), which is located in a lovely forest setting down a turnoff before you reach Gómez Farías proper. The owner can organize plenty of activities in the area such as three-hour kayaking trips (US$39), fishing (US$11 for three fish), abseiling (rappelling) and mountain biking.

To fully appreciate how isolated and pristine the reserve is, spend a night or two in the mountains. The two-story **Hotel Alta Cima** (☎ 831-254-61-17; r for up to 3/6 people US$27/46) in the village of the same name, is the least primitive, with simple but agreeable rooms. Just across from the hotel, **La Fe** (☺ 8am-6pm), run by the women's cooperative of Alta Cima, cooks up basic but filling meals.

A little further up the road is **El Pino** (1-2-person cabins US$14, 6-person cabins US$46), a group of low-slung dormitory-style buildings run by the men's cooperative of Alta Cima.

Canindo Research Station (☎ 831-254-59-30; cabins per person US$12), just before you reach the village of San José, about another hour on the extremely rough road past Alta Cima, is another rustic choice offering cots with mattresses. Solar panels provide sporadic electricity. Cabins here can accommodate 36 people, call beforehand to book and bring your own food.

Getting There & Away

From Ciudad Mante, Lumux buses go directly to Gómez Farías. Frequent buses also go directly from Ciudad Victoria (US$5.75, 1½ hours). You might be able to find someone in Gómez Farías to take you into the cloud forest by 4WD vehicle; it costs about US$85 for a truckload of up to 10 passengers.

NUEVO LEÓN

It was the crown's search for silver and slaves, and the church's desire to proselytize, that brought the Spanish to this sparsely inhabited region. In 1579, Luis de Carvajal was commissioned to found Nuevo León. He set up abortive settlements in Monterrey and Monclova. It was not until 1596 and 1644, respectively, however, that the Spanish established themselves at those sites, with help from native Mexicans from Tlaxcala and other areas to the south. In the late 17th century, Nuevo León and Coahuila were the starting points for Spanish expansion into Texas.

Silver was never found, but ranching slowly became viable around the small new towns, despite the raids by hostile Chichimecs from the north that continued into the 18th century. Nuevo León had an estimated 1.5 million sheep by 1710.

As the 19th century progressed and the railways arrived, ranching continued to expand and industry developed, especially in Monterrey. By 1900, Nuevo León had 328,000 inhabitants.

MONTERREY

☎ 81 / pop 3.3 million

Monterrey, capital of Nuevo León, is Mexico's second-biggest industrial center and third-biggest city. It's perhaps the most Americanized city in Mexico, and parts of it, with leafy suburbs, 7-Eleven convenience stores and giant air-conditioned malls, look just like suburbs in Texas or California. Industry and commerce drive Monterrey, and its pursuit of profit also seems more American than Mexican.

The city's historic center was ambitiously given a makeover in the mid-1980s, with a series of linked plazas and gardens, a pedestrian precinct on the west side and a historical zone on the east. Jagged mountains, including the distinctive saddle-shaped Cerro de la Silla (1288m), make a dramatic backdrop for the city, and provide opportunities for some worthwhile side trips; the surrounding countryside contains caves, canyons, lakes and waterfalls.

Most travelers bypass Monterrey in their haste to get to other parts of Mexico, but the city truly is a fascinating mixture of old and new, industry and style, tradition and efficiency. There's a lot to see here, particularly if you like modern art and architecture. The city is also a good place to party, with a buzzing nightlife scene in the Barrio Antiguo, the old part of town.

For budget travelers, Monterrey's disadvantage is that lodging is expensive and the cheaper places are mainly in an unattractive area outside the city center. The character of the city changes dramatically with the weather; the smog, humidity and rain can be bad, but you are just as likely to find fresh breezes, blue skies and clear, dry desert air.

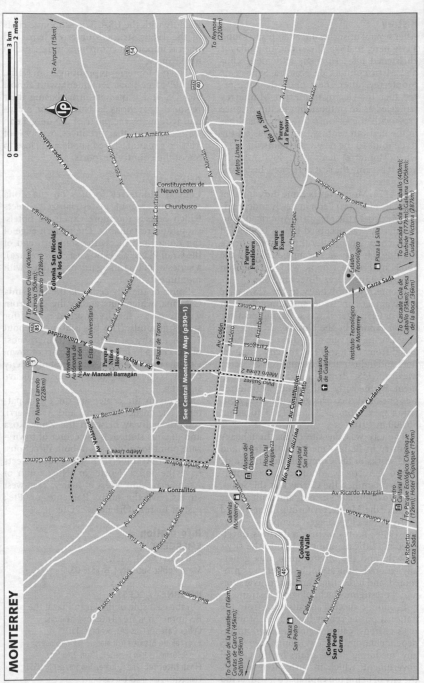

MONTERREY

To Airport (15km)

To Reynosa (220km)

Av Las Américas

Av Alemán

Río La Silla

Parque La Pastora

Av Llvas

Av Cavazos

Paseo de las Américas

Av Félix Cañón

Av Ruiz Cortines

Constituyentes de Nuevo Leon

Churubusco

Av Díaz de Berlanga

Colonia San Nicolás de los Garza

Av López Mateos

To Potrero Chico (40km);
Chipola (50km);
Nuevo Laredo (228km)

Av Nogala Sur

Av Ciudad de los Ángeles

Parque Fundidora

Parque España

Av Chapultepec

Av Revolución

Av Garza Sada

Plaza La Silla

Estadio Tecnológico

To Cascada Cola de Caballo (40km);
Iturbide (77km); Galeana (205km);
Ciudad Victoria (287km)

Estadio Universitario

Av Universidad

Parque Niños Héroes

Plaza de Toros

See Central Monterrey Map (p390–1)

Av Colón

Madero

Av Gómez

Zaragoza

Aramberi

To Nuevo Laredo (228km)

Universidad Autónoma de Nuevo León

Av A Reyes

Av Manuel Barragán

Guerrero

Metro Línea 2

Pino Suárez

Av Constitución

Santuario de Guadalupe

Av Prieto

Instituto Tecnológico de Monterrey

To Cascada Cola de Caballo (35km); Presa del la Boca (36km)

Av Bernardo Reyes

Metro Línea 1

Av Velázquez

Av Simón Bolívar

Dlano

Peña

Av Lázaro Cárdenas

Av Rodrigo Gómez

Av Lincoln

Av Ruiz Cortines

Museo del Obispado

Hospital Muguerza

Hospital San José

Río Santa Catarina

Av Gonzalitos

Av Frías

Paseo de los Leones

Galerías Monterrey

Av Ricardo Margáin

Av Gómez Morin

Centro Cultural Alfa

To Parque Ecológico Chipinque (12km); Hotel Chipinque (19km)

Av Roberta

To Parque Ecológico Chipinque

Colonia del Valle

Tikal

Av Gómez Morin

Av Roberto Garza Sada

Paseo de la Victoria

Blvd Gómez

Paseo de la Victoria

Plaza San Pedro

Calzada del Valle

Av Vasconcelos

Colonia San Pedro Garza

To Cañón de la Huasteca (16km); Grutas de García (45km); Saltillo (85km)

History

After several unsuccessful attempts to found a city here, in 1596 Diego de Montemayor christened his 34-person settlement Ciudad Metropolitana de Nuestra Señora de Monterrey, after the Conde de Monterrey, then the viceroy of Mexico. Monterrey struggled as an outpost, but its importance grew with the colonization of Tamaulipas in the mid-8th century, since it was on the trade route to the new settlements. In 1777, when Monterrey had about 4000 inhabitants, it became the seat of the new bishopric of Linares.

In 1824, Monterrey became the capital of the state of Nuevo León in newly independent Mexico. In the Mexican–American War, Monterrey was occupied by US troops led by Zachary Taylor after three days of fierce fighting. The city was occupied again in the 1860s by French troops, who were driven out by Benito Juárez' forces in 1866.

Monterrey's proximity to the USA gave it advantages in trade and smuggling: in the US Civil War it was a staging post for cotton exports by the blockaded Confederates. During the rule of Porfirio Diaz, which lasted from 1876 to 1910, the city's railway lines and industrial tax exemptions attracted Mexican, US, British and French investment. By the early 20th century Monterrey was one of Mexico's biggest cities; its population grew from 27,000 in 1853 to about 80,000 in 1910.

The city was the site of the first heavy industry in Latin America – the iron and steel works of the Compañía Fundidora de Fierro y Acero de Monterrey. Two intermarried families, the Garzas and the Sadas, came to dominate business and built a huge empire (the Monterrey Group) that owned many of the city's biggest companies. After the 1940s, scores of new industries developed but little planning went into the city's growth, and the environment was generally ignored. Education, however, was promoted, and today there are four universities and a prestigious technological institute.

Economic success and distance from the national power center have given Monterrey's citizens, called *regiomontanos*, an independent point of view. Monterrey resents any 'meddling' in its affairs by the central government, which in turn often accuses the city of being too capitalist or, worse, too friendly with the USA. The economic crisis of the 1980s struck Monterrey hard and several important companies were close to bankruptcy.

Today Monterrey is profiting from Nafta, the 1994 free-trade agreement, with almost 500 US and Canadian firms basing their regional operations in Nuevo León's capital. It remains the pillar of a Nuevo León state economy that produces over 9% of Mexico's manufactured goods and close to 6% of the country's exports.

Orientation

Central Monterrey focuses on the Zona Rosa, an area of pedestrianized streets which houses the more expensive hotels, shops and restaurants. The eastern edge of the Zona Rosa meets the southern end of the Gran Plaza (also known as Macroplaza), a series of plazas and gardens studded with monuments.

South of the city center is the Río Santa Catarina, which cuts across the city from west to east – the dry riverbed is used for sports grounds. The bus station is about 2.5km northwest of the city center; most of the cheap lodging is in this part of town. Colonia del Valle, 6km southwest of the city center, is one of Monterrey's most exclusive suburbs.

Streets in the center are on a grid pattern. The corner of Juárez and Aramberri, roughly halfway between the Zona Rosa and the bus station, is the center of town – zero point for addresses in both directions. North of Aramberri, north–south streets have the suffix 'Norte' or 'Nte'; south of Aramberri, 'Sur.' West of Juárez, east–west streets have the suffix 'Poniente' or 'Pte'; east of Juárez, 'Oriente' or 'Ote.'

Information

EMERGENCY

Red Cross (☎ 8375-1212)
State Public Security (☎ 8328-0606)

INTERNET ACCESS

On the east side of the Gran Plaza, the public library has free Internet access.
Cyber Café (Dr Coss 843; per hr M$15)
Evertek de Mexico (cnr Madero & Pino Suárez; ⏱ 9:30am-7:30pm Mon-Sat, 10am-2pm Sat)
Flash Internet (2nd fl, Juárez 164 Sur; per hr US$2) Connections are quick but expensive.

Internet Zone (Emilio Carranza 919; per hr M$30) Between Morelos and Hidalgo.

Ships 2000 (Escobedo 819; per hr US$2) Well situated near the Zona Rosa.

Ships Video (Washington 249; per hr M$20) Southeast corner of Plaza Alameda.

INTERNET RESOURCES
Convention & Vistors Bureau of Monterrey
(☎ 800-832-03-00; www.ocvmty.com.mx) Loads of useful information on hotels, museums and restaurants.

MEDICAL SERVICES
Hospital Muguerza (☎ 8399-3400; Hidalgo 2525)
Hospital San José (☎ 8347-1010; Morones Prieto 3000 Pte)

MONEY
Numerous city-center banks will change cash, though some do not handle traveler's checks. Almost all have ATMs. Exchange houses are clustered along Ocampo between E Carranza and Escobedo, on the western side of Plaza Zaragoza.

Amex (☎ 8318-3300; Av San Pedro 215 Nte; ☼ 9am-6pm Mon-Fri, 9am-1pm Sat) Amex traveler's checks are changed at rates superior to most banks, with no commission.

POST
Post office (Washington btwn Zaragoza & Zuazua; ☼ 9am-7pm Mon-Fri, 9am-1pm Sat) North of Gran Plaza.

TOURIST INFORMATION
Infotur (☎ 8345-0870, 800-832-22-00 in USA; www .monterrey-mexico.com; 3rd fl, Edificio Elizondo Paez, 5 de Mayo 525 Ote, ☼ 9am-6:30pm Mon-Fri) The staff speak fluent English, are knowledgeable about Monterrey and the state of Nuevo León and have lots of leaflets and maps. They can also tell you about upcoming cultural events and entertainment in the city.

There also two small tourist information offices at the bus station which are OK for basic stuff.

TRAVEL AGENCIES
Aventur (☎ 335-14-35; Av San Pedro, Col de Valle)
Gema (☎ 8125-8900; Bernardo Reyes 5700; ☼ 8am-6pm Mon-Fri, 9am-1pm Sat & Sun) Group transportation and entrance to Grutas de García (US$8) and Cola de Caballo (US$7) and tours of the city with stops at various museums.
Geo Ecoaventura (☎ 8374-5271; www.geoaventura .com.mx; Alamillo 302)
Turimex (☎ 8369-6472) Same services and prices as Gema.

Sights & Activities
GRAN PLAZA
A city-block wide and a kilometer long, this great swath of open space – carved out in the 1980s by the demolition of several entire city blocks – is a controversial piece of redevelopment. Many regard it as a grandiose monument to Monterrey's ambition. The once-desolate space has been softened by greenery and offers well-planned vistas of the surrounding mountains. Enclosed by the best of the city's old and new architecture, the area provides respite from the urban bustle and helps manage traffic problems with underpasses and extensive underground parking lots.

Though the overall size of the Gran Plaza could have been overwhelming, it actually comprises a series of smaller spaces, interspersed with buildings, monuments, sculptures, fountains, trees and gardens – there are no vast expanses of unrelieved pavement. At the very southern end, nearest the Río Santa Catarina, the **Monumento Homenaje al Sol** is a tall sculpture on a traffic island that faces the **Palacio Municipal**, a modern building raised up on concrete legs.

The monument occupies the south side of **Plaza Zaragoza**, which itself comprises the southern third of the Gran Plaza. The semi-formal space is often busy with people walking through, having lunch or listening to music from the covered bandstand. Facing the southeast corner of Plaza Zaragoza is the **Museo de Arte Contemporáneo** (Marco; ☎ 8342-4820; www.mtyol.com/marco; cnr Zuazua & Raymundo Jardón; admission US$3.25, free Wed; ☼ 10am-6pm Tue-Sun, 10am-8pm Wed), with its gigantic black dove sculpture by Juan Soriano. Inside, its idiosyncratic spaces are filled with water and light and major exhibitions of work by contemporary Mexican and Latin American artists. Just north of Marco is the baroque façade of the **cathedral**, built between 1635 and 1770. The south bell tower was not completed until 1899. Facing the cathedral across the plaza is the 19th-century Palacio Municipal, which now houses the **Museo Metropolitano de Monterrey** (☎ 8344-1971; Zaragoza Sur; admission free; ☼ 10am-6pm Tue-Sun). This museum has several upstairs galleries featuring the work of contemporary painters and sculptors. North of the museum, new and old buildings flank the east end of **Morelos**, a bustling pedestrian mall.

The centerpiece of Plaza Zaragoza is the stunning **Faro del Comercio** (Beacon of Commerce), a tall, flat, orange concrete slab designed by the architect Luis Barragán in his love-it-or-hate-it-but-you-can't-ignore-it style. If you're lucky you'll see green laser beams from the top sweep over the city at night.

Across Padre Mier is the **Fuente de la Vida** (Fountain of Life) with Neptune riding a chariot. North of here, the modern **Teatro de la Ciudad** and **Congreso del Estado** buildings face each other from the east and west sides of the plaza. Further north again, the **Biblioteca Central** (State Library) and the **Palacio de Justicia** (Courthouse) stand on either side of the **Parque Hundido** (Sunken Garden), a favorite spot for couples.

North again and down some steps, is the **Explanada de los Héroes** (Esplanade of the Heroes), also called the Plaza Cinco de Mayo, with statues of national heroes in each corner. It's the most formal and traditional of the spaces in the Gran Plaza and looks like a standard Plaza de Armas with the 1908 neoclassical **Palacio de Gobierno** on its north side. From the steps of the building you can look back down the length of the Gran Plaza to the south side of the river and toward the hills beyond. Behind the Palacio de Gobierno, a small park faces the 1930s **post office** and federal government building, providing yet another architectural contrast.

Just east of the Explanada de los Héroes is yet another wide open space, the **Plaza 400 Años**. Graced with fountains and pools, it serves as a grand entryway to the **Museo de Historia Mexicana** (☎ 8345-9898; www.museohistoriamexicana.org.mx; Plaza 400 Años; admission US$1.25 Wed-Sat, US$0.75 Sun, free Tue; 🕑 11am-8pm Tue-Sun), a 1994 addition to the Gran Plaza. The museum presents an exhaustive chronological survey of Mexican history, dividing its vast subject matter into four periods: Ancient Mexico, the Colonial Era, the 19th Century and Modern Mexico. There's also an area on rainforest ecology. Creatively designed and displayed, the museum appeals to kids and adults, with interactive exhibits on the Mayan calendar and pre-Hispanic math, a number of touch-screen computer terminals, and excellent models of all the major pre-Conquest cities. All explanations are in Spanish only but English tours can be arranged by phoning in advance. A nice café with a few computers for Internet access (free for customers) is on the lower floor.

Bordering the Plaza 400 Años to the southeast is the Paseo Santa Lucia, a canal-side promenade with restaurants, which is popular with weekend strollers.

ZONA ROSA

This is the area of top hotels, restaurants and shops just west of Plaza Zaragoza. It's bounded roughly by Morelos to the north, Zaragoza to the east, Hidalgo to the south, and E Carranza to the west. Two of the streets are pedestrian-only and it's usually a bustling place; it's a pleasure to walk around, window-shop or find a place to eat or drink.

BARRIO ANTIGUO

This is the old neighborhood, east of the Gran Plaza, and it's one of the few parts of Monterrey where you can admire traditional architecture. It has become a rather trendy area of art galleries, antique shops, cafés and restaurants. On Friday and Saturday nights, streets are closed to traffic and it becomes a major party zone with an excellent assortment of bars and clubs.

PARQUE ALAMEDA

Occupying eight city blocks a kilometer northwest of the city center, this lovely park offers fountains, paths and tall shade trees in pleasant contrast to the surrounding chaos of the city. It's a venue for occasional Sunday morning children's concerts.

CERVECERÍA CUAUHTÉMOC

This complex is in the gardens of the **old Cuauhtémoc brewery** (Av Alfonso Reyes 2202), 1km north of the bus station. Brought to you by the maker of Bohemia, Carta Blanca and Tecate beer, it now features a baseball hall of fame, brewery tours and free beer! Take Metro Line 2 to General Anaya and walk back south along Av Alfonso Reyes.

The **Salón de la Fama** (☎ 8328-5815; www.salondelafama.com.mx; admission free; 🕑 9:30am-6pm Mon-Fri, 10:30am-6pm Sat & Sun) has photos, memorabilia, and facts and figures on Mexican baseball. It features many Mexican players who made the big leagues in the USA, and some Americans whose careers made more headway south of the border. You can also test your throwing arm and batting skills – albeit with a Wiffle ball.

Brewery tours (☎ 8328-5355 for reservation; tours free; ☺ 9am-5pm Mon-Fri, 9am-2pm Sat) are given hourly. Tours in English are given in the morning by prior reservation or anytime on Saturday. Or you can join one of the many school groups for tours in Spanish. It's fun. The kids are unfailingly polite but of course less interested in how hops become beer than in trying to touch the controls. There is a very pleasant outdoor garden, a nice place to sit even if you don't partake of the free mug of Carta Blanca.

MUSEO DEL VIDRIO

Two blocks north of Av Colón, on the grounds of the former Vitro factory and corporate offices, this **museum** (☎ 8863-1070; www.museodelvidrio.com; Magallanes 517; admission US$1; ☺ 9am-6pm Tue-Sun) focuses on the history, manufacture and artistic use of glass in Mexico. Among the interesting exhibits are a set of 18th-century pulque glasses and a reproduction of a 19th-century stained-glass workshop. Another gallery for temporary exhibits of glass art is in a restored warehouse opposite the plant where beer and Coke bottles are made; samples of fine glasswork are sold in the gallery shop. Call ahead to schedule a tour in English.

PARQUE NIÑOS HÉROES

A botanical garden, an aviary, a lake and several museums are among the recreational and cultural facilities in this large **park** (admission US$1), north of the city center between Av Alfonso Reyes and Av Manuel Barragán. Most impressive is the permanent collection of paintings and sculpture found at the **Pinacoteca de Nuevo León** (☎ 8331-5462; admission free; ☺ 10am-6pm Tue-Sun), showing the outstanding work of the state's artists since colonial times.

Kids will enjoy the **Museo de la Fauna y Ciencias Naturales** (☎ 8351-7077; admission US$0.50; ☺ 9am-6pm), featuring life-sized dioramas of stuffed wildlife in its 'natural' habitats, from Saharan Africa to the Arctic. Enter the park from Av Alfonso Reyes, about 5km north of the city center.

MUSEO DEL OBISPADO

The **former obispado** (bishopric palace; ☎ 8346-0404; Verguer; admission US$3.25; ☺ 10am-5pm Tue-Sun), on a hill 2.5km west of the Zona Rosa, gives fine views of the city and surrounding

mountains, smog permitting. Initiated in 1787 on the orders of the bishop of Linares (who did not live to see its completion three years later), the building has an admirable churrigueresque façade. Now it's a small historical museum with various colonial and revolutionary relics.

PARQUE FUNDIDORA

Once a symbol of industrial success and development, the smokestacks and furnaces of this former **steel factory complex** (☎ 8343-4143; www.parquefundidora.org; ☺ 6am-11pm; Ⓟ) a few kilometers east of downtown now mark another stage in Monterrey's history. A successful example of urban renewal, the extensive grounds house a dizzying array of facilities for art, business and recreation. The following is only an abbreviated list: convention center, theater, art gallery, outdoor concert hall, art-house film center, Formula 1 racetrack, Parque Sesamo, two hotels, and a hostel (see p392). You can jog or bicycle on the tree-lined park paths.

CENTRO CULTURAL ALFA

This **cultural complex** (☎ 8303-0002; www.planetarioalfa.org.mx; Av Roberto Garza Sada 1000; admission US$6.75; ☺ 3-7pm Tue-Fri, 11:30am-8pm Sat & Sun) off Av Gómez Morín in Colonia del Valle is sponsored by the Alfa industrial group. It's well worth the trip. The main building, which looks like a water tank tipping over, has floors that are devoted to computers, astronomy, physics, Mexican antiquities and temporary exhibitions. The scientific displays have lots of educational hands-on exhibits, and everything is labeled (in Spanish only). In the center of the building is the planetarium and an Omnimax cinema.

Outside is the Jardín Prehispánico, with replicas of some of the great Mexican archaeological finds. **El Universo**, a superb glass mural, was created by Rufino Tamayo for the headquarters of the Alfa group, but was considered so beautiful that a special building was constructed to display it to a wider audience. It's in the Pabellón building, which resembles a covered wagon.

Special buses go every hour from the southwest corner of Parque Alameda, at the intersection of Washington and Villagrán (every half hour on Sunday); the last bus back to central Monterrey departs from the planetarium at 9pm.

CENTRAL MONTERREY

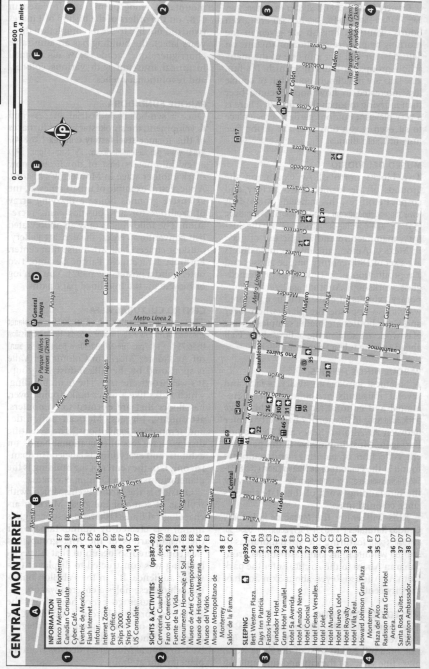

INFORMATION

Banco Mercantil de Monterrey....1	E7
Canadian Consulate.....................2	E8
Cyber Café................................3	E7
Evertek de Mexico.....................4	C3
Flash Internet...........................5	D5
Infotur....................................6	E6
Internet Zone...........................7	D7
Post Office...............................8	E6
Ships 2000..............................9	E7
Ships Video............................10	C5
US Consulate..........................11	B7

SIGHTS & ACTIVITIES (pp387–92)

Cervecería Cuauhtémoc..........(see 19)	
Faro del Comercio...................12	E8
Fuente de la Vida....................13	E7
Monumento Homenaje al Sol...14	E8
Museo de Arte Contemporáneo..15	E8
Museo de Historia Mexicana....16	F6
Museo del Vidrio......................17	E3
Museo Metropolitano de	
Monterrey...............................18	E7
Salón de la Fama......................19	C1

SLEEPING ▢ **(pp392–4)**

Best Western Plaza..................20	E4
Days Inn Patricia.....................21	D3
Fastos Hotel...........................22	C3
Fundador Hotel.......................23	E7
Gran Hotel Yamallel.................24	E4
Hotel 5a Avenida.....................25	E3
Hotel Amado Nervo..................26	C3
Hotel Colonial.........................27	D7
Hotel Fiesta Versalles...............28	C6
Hotel Jolet.............................29	C7
Hotel Mundo...........................30	C3
Hotel Nuevo León....................31	C3
Hotel Royalty.........................32	D7
Hotel Villa Real.......................33	C4
Howard Johnson Gran Plaza	
Monterrey...............................34	E7
Plaza del Arco.........................35	C3
Radisson Plaza Gran Hotel	
Ancira....................................36	D7
Santa Rosa Suites.....................37	D7
Sheraton Ambassador................38	D7

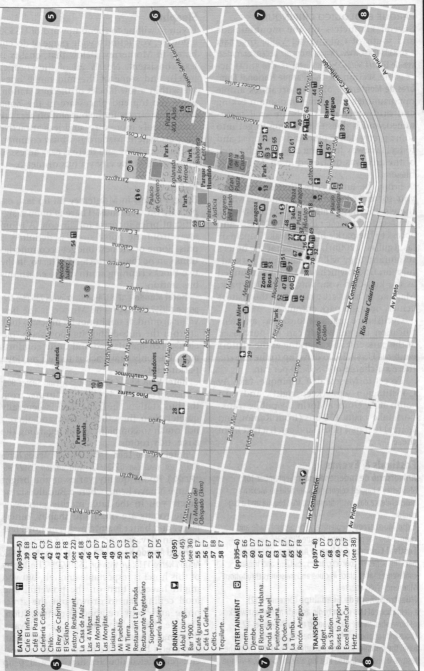

PARQUE ECOLÓGICO CHIPINQUE

Several kilometers up the mountainside and south of Colonia del Valle, this **park** (☎ 8303-0000; www.chipinque.org.mx; pedestrian/cyclist/vehicle US$1/1.50/6; ☉ 6am-8pm) is the most accessible section of the **Parque Nacional Cumbres de Monterrey**, offering urbanites ample opportunities for hiking, mountain biking and bird-watching. Trails are well maintained, and it doesn't take long to get into some pretty dense pine and oak forest and to feel far away from the city, though much of the area was destroyed in an April 1998 blaze.

From the entrance, a 7km drive brings you to the Meseta de Chipinque where there's the **Hotel Chipinque** (☎ 800-849-46-81; www.hotelchipinque.com; r US$131; P ⊠ ⊠) and access to the park's highest peak, Copete de las Águilas (2200m). If you eat at the hotel's restaurant, they will validate your park admission ticket which will then be refunded at the kiosk on your way out of the park. Maps and snacks are available at the visitors center, near the park entrance.

Cyclists are required to display an identification badge, which can be purchased at the park entrance. Parking at the visitors center is US$2.25; to drive up to the *meseta*, there's a charge of US$5.50 per car.

To get to Meseta de Chipinque, take Av Constitución west (keep right), and turn south at Av Gómez Morín. By public transport, take a ruta 130 bus (from Ramón and Juárez) to 'Los Tubos,' and catch a taxi from there.

Festivals & Events

Aniversario de Independencia (September 16) Monterrey's biggest celebrations are held on Mexico's independence day, with fireworks, free tequila and a big parade.

Expo Monterrey (September) The annual trade and cultural fair happens in the Parque Niños Héroes.

Festival Cultural del Barrio Antiguo (Late November) This series of concerts, art expositions and literary conferences takes place in clubs and museums throughout Monterrey's old quarter.

Nuestra Señora de Guadalupe (December 12) Celebrations of this event begin as early as the last week of November. In the days leading up to December 12, thousands of pilgrims head for the Santuario de Guadalupe, the pyramid-shaped structure south of the river. The festival is also celebrated in a big way in Abasolo, a village off the Monclova road.

Sleeping

If you're willing to spend upward of US$50 a double, you'll find a wide range of decent hotels in Monterrey. Below that, quality is less consistent. Nearly all of the cheaper hotels, and some of the mid-range ones, are within a few blocks of the bus station, while the top-end places are in the Zona Rosa. The streets in the bus station area are undoubtedly more dirty and less attractive than elsewhere. Madero is a busy commercial thoroughfare and there is easy access to other parts of the city via bus or metro.

BUDGET

Budget hotels in Monterrey fill up fast, especially on weekends. There is often a significant price increase for air-con. A room away from the noisy street is definitely a plus. Some of the best budget accommodations can be found on Amado Nervo, in the two blocks running south of the enormous bus station.

Hotel Mundo (☎ 8374-6850; Reforma 736 Pte; 1/2-person r US$22/25; ⊠) The Mundo is the best value around. It might not be much to look at from the outside but its rooms are spacious, well maintained and quite comfortable. The only drawback is there's no hotel parking lot.

Hotel Villa Real (☎ 8375-0355; Pino Suárez 806; 1-2-person r US$27; P ⊠) Slightly further from the bus station, the Villa Real is generally quieter than the other places, and there's not much to complain about regarding the large, tidy rooms.

Hotel Nuevo León (☎ 8374-1900; Amado Nervo 1007; s/d with fan US$23/32, with air-con US$27/46; P ⊠) Room quality varies at the bright orange Nuevo León, where a Buddha statue greets you in the faux marble entryway. Some rooms are small and shabby, others larger and better maintained. The hotel features an elevator and a parking garage.

Hotel Amado Nervo (☎ 8375-4632; fax 8372-5488; Amado Nervo 1110; s/d with fan US$18/22) The lobby of this hotel is respectable enough, but you might have to turn on the powerful and loud ceiling fan to drown out the street noise and your neighbors' conversation. Despite this and the ramshackle hallways, the small rooms with TV are kept clean and aren't bad for the price. There are several remodeled doubles that are a step-up in quality.

Villas Parque Fundidora (☎ 8355-7370; Madero 3500 Ote; dm with fan & shared bathroom US$5.50) Monterrey's cheapest accommodations are at this youth hostel designed for large student groups but open to individual travelers. East of the center beside the rusting smokestacks of the old foundry, the squat, white building features several dormitory rooms, the largest of which has 36 bunk beds (and one TV). Breakfast is included. You must call ahead during office hours to reserve: 8am to 1:30pm and 3pm to 11pm Monday to Friday. To get there, take a Ruta 2 bus along Madero, and tell the driver to let you off at 'Parque Acero.'

MID-RANGE

Most places in the bus-station area offer reduced rates on weekends.

Days Inn Patricia (☎ 8375-0750; www.daysinn .com; Madero 123 Ote; r US$43; ❄) The Patricia is a quantum leap in comfort and quality from the nearby budget options. It has a lobby-restaurant and is a modern, air-conditioned place, although the rooms are without much character.

Plaza del Arco (☎ 8372-4050; www.plazadelarco .com; Pino Suárez 935; r US$48; P ❄) An art-deco style standout, this all-white hotel is a surprise amid the otherwise ordinary buildings around Madero. The design scheme is applied in the modern rooms as well.

Best Western Plaza (☎ 8125-4800; www.bwplaza monterrey.com; Madero 250 Ote; r US$53; P) This place is similar in style to the Patricia – it also has a lobby-restaurant, as well as fax and laundry services. The elegant rooms have plush carpeting, polished wood, big comfortable beds and variable air-con. The parking lot entrance is on Galeana.

Fastos Hotel (☎ 8372-3250; www.fastoshotel.com .mx; Av Colón 956 Pte; r US$53; P ❄) In contrast to the surrounding area (it's opposite the bus station), the Fastos is a classy and comfortable hotel. Elegant, air-conditioned rooms each feature a pair of large, firm beds. Breakfast included.

Gran Hotel Yamallel (☎ 8375-3500; www.hotel yamallel.com.mx; Zaragoza 912 Nte; r US$40; P ❄) This towering hotel is modern in style and offers a parking garage, a restaurant, satellite TV and majestic views over the city from the upper floors. Some of the rooms are quite small so you should ask to see a few.

Hotel 5a Avenida (Quinta Avenida; ☎ 8375-6565; hotel5aavenida@terra.com.mx; Madero 243 Ote; s/d US$37/42; P ❄) This place has good, clean rooms on the smallish side with TV and phone; some have fine views. The rooms look a lot better than the foyer. Downstairs Restaurant York offers a buffet breakfast.

All the following hotels are located on the west side of the Gran Plaza (except the Fundador, which is on the east).

Fundador Hotel (☎ 8343-6464; hotelfundador@ prodigy.net.mx; Montemayor 802; r with/without air-con US$45/39; P ❄) Resting on its laurels as the sole lodging option in the Barrio Antiguo, the Fundador is a convenient place to stumble home after a late night in the neighborhood. This huge old-style place has a great central courtyard but the rooms are lackluster. Somewhere in the maze-like interior are an old-school bar and restaurant. The entrance to the hotel is on the corner of Montemayor and Matamoros.

Hotel Jolet (☎ 8150-6500; joletmty@prodigy.net.mx; Padre Mier 201 Pte; r US$53; P ❄) Well located, just on the edge of a busy commercial area, the Jolet is a gray-and-glass hulk covering almost an entire block. The lobby and carpeted rooms are more refined.

Hotel Royalty (☎ 8340-2800; www.royaltyhotel .com; r US$58; P ❄ ❅) The Royalty is a popular choice for local businesspeople and meetings. Rooms are not quite as nice as those at the Jolet, but there is a small outdoor pool and breakfast is included.

Hotel Colonial (☎ 8380-6800; reservaciones@hotel colonial.mty.com; Hidalgo 475 Ote; r US$53; ❄) Everything is white and shiny at the Colonial, which fronts Plaza Hidalgo and is a block from the Gran Plaza. Unfortunately the modern rooms are not as large or fancy as you'd expect. Local telephone calls are included in the tariff. Weekend specials are available and breakfast is included.

Howard Johnson Gran Plaza Monterrey (☎ 8380-6000, 800-832-4000; www.hojomonterrey.com .mx; Morelos 574 Ote; r US$66; P ❆ ❄ ❑ ❅) Though it lacks the style of its neighbors, this hotel fronting the Plaza Zaragoza is one of the more popular mid-range places, especially for American businesspeople. Its 198 rooms, many with views of the Gran Plaza, have all the modern conveniences, including a direct line to Domino's Pizza and a microwave oven for heating up your order.

Hotel Fiesta Versalles (☎ 8340-2281; hfv@nl1.tel mex.net.mx; Ramón 360 Pte; s/d US$43/52) Just south of the Parque Alameda, this friendly place is good value. Its air-conditioned rooms are spacious and attractively furnished. There's a café and a travel agency downstairs, and a parking lot across the street. Weekend specials might be available.

TOP END

At all of these downtown accommodation options you can expect restaurants and bars, and carpeted rooms with air-con, heater, TV and phone. Note that most places have weekend specials.

Radisson Plaza Gran Hotel Ancira (☎ 8150-7023, 800-830-60-00; www.hotel-ancira.com; Ocampo 443 Ote; r US$255; P X X ☐ ☎) Even if you're not a newlywed or on a business expense account, you should check out the Radisson. For atmosphere, nothing rivals this hotel in the center of the action on the corner of Escobedo and Plaza Hidalgo. It's been around since 1912, and it's said that Pancho Villa once rode into the lobby, which now has shops, a piano player, a restaurant and hovering waiters. It has big rooms and plenty of old-fashioned elegance, plus an equally nice small outdoor pool.

Sheraton Ambassador (☎ 8380-7000; monterrey .sheraton@sheraton.com; Hidalgo 310 Ote; r US$162; P X X ☐) Across the street from Hotel Royalty, facing the dry river bed and the highway that runs along it, this is the one of Monterrey's premier luxury hotels, with 239 rooms and suites.

Santa Rosa Suites (☎ 8342-4200; www.santarosa .com.mx; Escobedo 930 Sur; ste US$90; P X ☎) Much more intimate than the other top-end hotels, the Santa Rosa is also found on the Plaza Hidalgo. The lobby is small but the 'English'-style suites are quite large; each has a separate living and dining area. Breakfast included.

Eating

There are several suburbs with excellent dining options, including the posh Colonia del Valle to the west. A few of the recommended are La Habana (Thai), Tempu (Japanese) and La Catarina (gourmet Mexican).

BUS STATION AREA

There are a number of fast-food restaurants and inexpensive taco outlets.

Mi Pueblito (☎ 8375-3756; Madero; mains US$3; ☒ 24hr; ☒) An especially good spot for dinner if you're staying in this neighborhood, where choices are limited, modern and clean Mi Pueblito cooks up filling Mexican standards.

Fastory Restaurant (☎ 8372-3250; Av Colón 956; breakfast US$3.25-5.50, mains US$5-8; ☒ 24hr; ☒ P) This all-night restaurant in the Fastos Hotel offers Mexican food and coffee-shop standards in a bland but reassuring setting with prompt service. Dishes on offer include spaghetti bolognese (no trimmings) and enchiladas. Breakfast is also available.

Cafetería Coliseo (☎ 8375-5778; Av Colón; breakfast US$1.75-3.25, mains US$3-5.50; ☒ 24hr) Next to the bus station, this reasonably priced and personable café offers fresh juices and *licuados* (fruit drinks), sandwiches and a variety of homemade *guisados* (stews). Ask the knowledgeable waiters any transportation questions.

ZONA ROSA

Almost every block of the Zona Rosa seems to have at least one restaurant or café.

Mi Tierra (Morelos; mains US$3.25) West of E Carranza, on the pedestrian mall, Mi Tierra serves up tasty mole dishes in a casual atmosphere.

Restaurant La Puntada (Hidalgo 123 Ote; mains US$3; ☒ closed Sun; ☒) This ever-popular restaurant – a cross between a diner and a cafeteria – has a long list of Mexican items, as well as T-bone steak.

Chilo (Hidalgo 121; combo meals US$4) Look for the sign of the smiling cactus directly across from La Puntada, where portions are larger and service is quicker.

Las Monjitas (☎ 8344-6713; Escobedo 903; mains US$3.25-6.75, specials US$5.50-6.75) For good Mexican fare in a bizarre setting, try this restaurant just above Plaza Hidalgo, where the waitresses are dressed as nuns. There's another branch at the corner of Morelos and Galeana.

Luisiana (☎ 8343-1561; Hidalgo 530 Ote; mains US$; ☒ P) Tuxedoed waiters and all the trappings of high-end dining are available at Luisiana. The menu is eclectic and the quality of food and level of service is high. Try the grand marnier crepes or baked ice-cream for dessert.

Restaurante Vegetariano Superbom (☎ 8345-2663; 2nd fl, Padre Mier 300; buffet US$6.75, daily special

US$5; 8am-5pm Sun-Fri;) Vegetarians will find a haven here – the buffet lunch is excellent.

Taquería Juárez (8340-1956; Galeana 123 Nte; mains US$2.50; 10:30am-11pm Thu-Tue) Watch your *flautas*, tacos and enchiladas being prepared by at least 10 white-capped women behind a long window at this veritable *antojito* factory. An order of five items, combined according to your preference, is served with guacamole and salad.

BARRIO ANTIGUO

A stroll around the Antiguo is the best way to find a place to eat that is to your liking. Prices can be expensive and there might be a wait on weekend nights as the cafés and restaurants here are very popular.

Café el Infinito (8989-5252; Raymundo Jardón 904 Ote; mains US$4-8; 8-1am;) Trendy in a bohemian way, laid-back but sophisticated, Infinito gets our vote as the coolest, friendliest spot in the Antiguo for a meal or drink. The exposed sandstone walls here are adorned with sketches of naked bodies and rows of books. The Oaxacan pizza and the delicious fruit frappés – try the Jamaican Limon – are recommended. Live music and films are periodically on tap in the back room.

La Casa de Maíz (8340-4332; Abasolo 870; mains US$5;) The Casa prepares a variety of corn-based snacks from southern Mexico, including *memelas*, *tlacoyos* and *molotes*. All are creatively presented and served in healthy portions. Be sure to order a pitcher of refreshing *agua de fruta*.

Café El Paraíso (8344-6616; Morelos 958; mains US$3-5.50; 9am-midnight Mon-Wed, 9-2am Thu-Sat, 4:30pm-midnight Sun;) A great spot to stop for a meal before hitting the bars and clubs in the Antiguo, this café offers filling meals of nachos, salads and crepes, but fajitas are the specialty of the house. Come here for the food and drinks not the décor. On Saturday nights beers are two for the price of one.

El Siciliano (8675-5784; Morelos 1076 Ote; pizzas US$9, mains US$9-12; 1pm-midnight Mon-Sat, 1-6pm Sun;) On the eastern edge of the Barrio Antiguo, quaint El Siciliano does a great stuffed calamari (US$9) and risotto (US$11). There's a good wine selection as well.

El Rey del Cabrito (8345-3232; cnr Dr Coss & Constitución; mains US$9-12;) Somewhat of

a landmark, as much for its hunting-lodge-kitsch interior, than for the quality of its food, this vast dining hall is at the southern edge of the Barrio Antiguo near Marco. Your cabrito (US$11) arrives at the table still sizzling on a bed of onions, with a large salad and tortillas.

Drinking

Café La Galería (8342-5071; Morelos 902) A popular café/bar, Galería has a funky tribal vibe. The young and beautiful quaff cocktails from a huge menu, with delights such as Ticket to Fly and Astronaut (US$5)…you get the picture.

Café Iguana (8343-0822; Montemayor 927 Sur; admission US$5.50) More a space than a room, the Iguana features comfortable lounging areas inside and out, modern and ancient art and cutting-edge DJs.

Tequilarte (8340-4003; Padre Mier 817 Ote) Beautifully displayed bottles of tequila line the shelves of the elegant front room. In the back is a superbly designed space full of colors and light with a few tables. Down some tequila and a meal while being serenaded by music on weekends.

Celtics (8989-0410; Raymundo Jardón 839; 1pm-2am) The façade may be Roman temple, but the beautifully designed bar is all Irish. A more mature crowd frequents Celtics, where international and Mexican beers are on tap. For a spectacular view of the city and mountains, take your drinks and food upstairs to the bi-level rooftop patio.

Akbal Lounge (8340-4332; Abasolo 870 Ote) Upstairs from La Casa de Maíz, Akbal is a dim, cozy bar with an industrial décor setting, where the town's style-cats plant themselves on sofas, chairs and cushions. After a few drinks it isn't difficult to lose yourself to the sexy, soulful beats in the background.

Bar 1900 (8150-7000; Radisson Plaza Gran Hotel Ancira, Ocampo 443 Ote) The Zona Rosa has this elegant after-hours cabaret/bar inside the Ancira hotel. Sedate in comparison to venues in the Barrio Antiguo, it's good for a quiet drink.

Entertainment

The 1997 release of *Mucho Barato*, the band Control Machete's first album, marked the beginning of Monterrey's rise to national and international musical prominence with a burgeoning scene defined only by an openness to experimentation and a playful delight in the mixing of every imaginable sound and genre. Partly because of the city's proximity to the USA and the technology afforded by its relative wealth, band members are more likely to cite Twisted Sister and the Beastie Boys as influences rather than traditional norteño rhythms. Groups like Plastilina Mosh, Molotov, Zurdok, Kinky, El Gran Silencio and Genitallica all call Monterrey home and when not touring can be seen live in clubs in the Barrio Antiguo frequented by Monterrey's affluent younger set. On weekend nights, the neighborhood is very much the center of action – join the club-hopping crowds along Padre Mier east of Dr Coss. The establishments named here are but a few of the nightspots.

La Tumba (☎ 8345-6860; Padre Mier 827 Ote; admission US$5.50) This excellent coffeehouse has continuous live folk music and there's a quiet area for chilling where you don't have to pay the admission.

Rincón Antiguo (☎ 8379-8299; Raymundo Jardón 1006) Norteño groups perform thumping beats with big cowboy hats and boots to match.

El Rincón de la Habana (☎ 8342-0689; Morelos 887 Ote; admission US$7; ☑ 8:30pm-2:30am Thu-Sat) Regulars and novices dance to Cuban-style salsa.

Djembe (Hidalgo 229; ☑ 12:30pm-2am) For bohemian flavor in the Zona Rosa, head to Djembe, which showcases folk artists and singer-songwriters.

Fonda San Miguel (☎ 8342-6848; Morelos 924 Ote; admission US$5.50; ☑ 10pm-late Thu & Fri, 9pm-late Sat) The young, wealthy and good-looking flock to this throbbing club with a big stage, a good sound system and rock by popular bands. There's no cover if you come before 11pm on some nights.

La Orden (☎ 8344-2251; Dr Coss 837; admission US$11; ☑ 10pm-4:30am Fri & Sat) Classic big-city clubbing, complete with deafening music and sardine-packed dance floor.

Monterrey also has numerous cinemas and an active cultural life including concerts, theater and art exhibitions. The tourist office can tell you what's happening, and posters listing events are placed in strategic spots around town.

Fuenteovejuna (☎ 8344-4002; Morelos 1011; ☑ café 6pm-2am) An experimental theater, avant-garde film center and café, Fuenteovejuna, draws a young artsy set.

Plaza de Toros Lorenzo Garza (☎ 8374-0450; Alfonso Reyes 2401 Nte, Colonia del Prado) During bullfight season, March to August, *corridas* are held here at 5pm on Sunday.

The professional soccer season is from August to May. Games are played over the weekend at either the **Estadio Tecnológico** (☎ 8358-2000) at the Instituto Tecnológico de Monterrey, home of the Monterrey club (nicknamed the Pandilla Rayada, 'Striped Gang'), or the **Estadio Universitario** (☎ 8376-0524), home of the Tigres (Universidad de Nuevo León).

Estadio de Béisbol Monterrey (☎ 8351-0209; Parque Niños Héroes) Monterrey's Sultanes baseball team plays from March to August near the university. Check the newspaper *El Norte* for further details.

There are occasional *charreadas* in which *charros* (cowboys) appear in all their finery to demonstrate their skills. Contact Infotur (see Tourist Information, p387) for current venues.

Shopping

Monterrey has a number of interesting shops with quality handicrafts from different parts of Mexico.

Tienda Carápan (☎ 8345-4422; www.carapancrafts center.com; Hidalgo 305 Ote; ☑ 9am-7pm Mon-Sat) Across the street from the Sheraton Ambassador is Tienda Carápan where an extensive array of high-quality pottery, silver jewelry, hand-embroidered tablecloths and the like are on display. Overly solicitous staff make it somewhat difficult to browse in peace.

Tikal (☎ 8335-1740; Río Missouri 316 Pte, Colonia del Valle; ☑ 9am-7pm Mon-Fri, 9am-6pm Sat). There are no bargains here, but some of the items are reasonably priced given their quality.

The two main markets downtown, Mercado Colón and Mercado Juárez, are large, bustling places that sell everyday items. The wealthier *regiomontanos* prefer to shop at one of the big air-conditioned malls. These include **Plaza la Silla** (☎ 8369-1777; Av Garza Sada), south of the city center; **Plaza San Pedro** (Humberto Lobo 520), southwest in the suburb of San Pedro; or **Galerías Monterrey** (☎ 8348-4989; Av Insurgentes 2500), west of town.

Getting There & Away

AIR

There are direct flights, usually daily, to all major cities in Mexico and connections to just about anywhere else. Connections to most international destinations are best made through Houston.

Airline offices include the following:

Aero California (☎ 8345-9700)
Aeromexico (☎ 8343-5560)
American Airlines (☎ 8340-3031)
Aviacsa (☎ 8153-4300)
Continental Airlines (☎ 8369-0838)
Mexicana (☎ 8356-6611)
United Airlines (☎ 8356-9582)

BUS

Monterrey's huge bus station (Central de Autobuses) occupies three blocks along Av Colón, between Villagrán and Rayón. It's a small city unto itself, with restaurants, pay phones, an exchange office, a 24-hour left-luggage service (US$0.40 an hour) and ticket desks strung out along its whole length. First-class lines include **Sendor** (☎ 8375-0014), **Ómnibus de México** (☎ 8375-7063), and **Futura** (☎ 8318-3737); deluxe service is provided by **Turistar** (☎ 8318-3737). **Autobuses Americanos** (☎ 8375-0358) is the line for Texas destinations. Daily service from Monterrey include the following:

Aguascalientes (US$46, 8hr, 1 deluxe; US$35, 8hr, frequent 1st-class)
Chihuahua (US$62, 12hr, 2 deluxe; US$50, 12hr, frequent 1st-class)
Ciudad Victoria (US$18, 4hr, hourly 1st-class; US$16, 4hr, frequent 2nd-class)
Durango (US$52, 9hr, 4 deluxe; US$39, 9hr, 9 1st-class)
Guadalajara (US$67, 12hr, 3 deluxe; US$50, 12hr, 7 1st-class)
Matamoros (US$22, 4½h, frequent 1st-class)
Mexico City (US$79, 11hr, 8 deluxe; US$59, 11hr, 9 1st-class) To Terminal Norte.
Nuevo Laredo (US$25, 2½hr, 4 deluxe; US$17, 2½hr, frequent 1st-class; US$13, 2½hr, frequent 2nd-class)
Reynosa (US$15.50, 3hr, frequent 1st-class; US$13, 3hr, 2 2nd-class)
Saltillo (US$6.75, 1¾hr, 1 deluxe; US$5, 1¾hr, frequent 1st- & 2nd-class)
San Luis Potosí (US$43, 7hr, 3 deluxe; US$31, 7hr, frequent 1st-class; US$24, 7hr, frequent 2nd-class)
Tampico (US$48, 7¼hr, 2 deluxe; US$33, 7¼hr, frequent 1st-class)
Torreón (US$30, 4hr, 5 deluxe; US$23, 4hr, frequent 1st-class)
Zacatecas (US$27, 6hr, frequent 1st-class; US$22, 6hr, 7 2nd-class)

First-class buses also serve Acapulco, Ciudad Juárez, Mazatlán, Puebla and Querétaro, and there are six buses a day to the remote border towns of Piedras Negras (US$33) and Ciudad Acuña (US$36). Greyhound buses serve US destinations including Laredo, San Antonio (US$30), Dallas (US$43) and Houston (US$34).

CAR & MOTORCYCLE

Alal (☎ 8340-7611; Hidalgo 426 Ote)
Avis (☎ 8190-6673)
Budget (☎ 8369-0819) Have branches at the airport and in town as well.
Excell RentaCar (☎ 8340-8684; Hidalgo 400 Sur)
Hertz (☎ 8369-0822)
Sultana Internacional (☎ 8344-6363; Escobedo 1011 Sur)

Getting Around

TO/FROM THE AIRPORT

Monterrey airport is off Hwy 54 to Ciudad Alemán, about 15km northeast of the city center. A taxi costs around US$20 from one of the downtown hotels, or via **radio taxi service** (☎ 8372-4370, 8372-4371). From the airport you can purchase a ticket for an authorized taxi at a booth in the arrivals area.

There is no public transportation that serves the airport directly. However, if money is tight, look for any Pescaría bus with 'airport' indicated on the windshield (US$0.50) on Villagrán, just around the corner from Cafetería Coliseo and the bus station. It will drop you off on the airport access road from where you can flag down a taxi (US$2) for the remaining few kilometers.

BUS

Frequent buses (US$0.40) go almost everywhere in Monterrey, but often by circuitous routes. The following routes might be useful:

Bus station to center No 18, from the corner of Amado Nervo and Reforma, goes down Juárez to the edge of the Zona Rosa – get off at Padre Mier, Hidalgo or Ocampo.

Center to bus station No 1 (blue) can be picked up on Juárez at Padre Mier. It takes you to Av Colón, within two blocks of the bus station.

Center to Museo del Obispado No 4 (red and black) goes west along Padre Mier. For the Obispado, get off when the bus turns left at Degollado, walk up the hill and turn left, then take the first right (a 10-minute walk).

Center to Del Valle/San Pedro Ruta 131 (orange) from the corner of Juárez and Hidalgo goes to the big traffic circle in Colonia del Valle, then heads west along Av Vasconcelos.

Center to Instituto Tecnológico Take No 1 (San Nicolás-Tecnológico) from the corner of Hidalgo and Pino Suárez.

CAR & MOTORCYCLE

There are large parking lots underneath the Gran Plaza, charging only US$2 for the whole night. Another lot, just east of the bus station off Av Colón, is US$7 for 24 hours.

METRO

Monterrey's Metro is a sensible alternative for getting around town. Its very simple plan consists of two lines: the elevated Línea 1 runs east to west in the north of the city, primarily going to outlying residential areas; and the underground Línea 2 runs north to south from near the Cuauhtémoc brewery (General Anaya station), past the bus station (Cuauhtémoc), and down to the Zona Rosa (Padre Mier) and the Gran Plaza (Zaragoza). The Metro's two lines cross at the intersection of Av Colón and Cuauhtémoc, where the giant overhead Cuauhtémoc Metro station is located.

It's US$0.50/0.90 for a one-way/return journey anywhere on the network; tickets are dispensed from machines at the sta-tion entrances and can be purchased for multiple trips. The Metro runs from 5am to midnight daily. There are ATMs at many station entrances.

AROUND MONTERREY

A number of sights near Monterrey are easily accessible in your own vehicle, and somewhat less accessible by bus.

Grutas de García

An illuminated, 2.5km route leads through 16 chambers in this **cave system** (☎ 81-8347-1533; admission US$5.50; ⊙ 9am-5pm) discovered by a parish priest in 1843. It is located 1100m up in the Sierra El Fraile. The caves, reached by a 700m funicular railway, are 50 million years old, with lots of stalactites and stalagmites, as well as petrified seashells. Of course, it's hot and muggy inside but the view from the top is worthwhile. Admission includes the funicular ride and a tour.

This is a popular weekend outing. On Saturday and Sunday mornings, Transportes Villa de García runs buses directly to the caves from local platforms 17 to 19 in the Monterrey bus station, returning in the afternoon. On other days the same line runs frequent buses to Villa de García, 9km from the caves (US$0.60); taxis (US$10 round-trip) go the rest of the way. Driving from Monterrey, take Hwy 40 toward Saltillo. After 22km a sign points the way to the caves; turn right and go another 18km to the base of the funicular.

No matter how you get to the caves, it might make sense to spend the night in the

---

SCALING THE POTRERO CHICO

Crags, spires, steep cliff faces. If you like hanging from these, then climbing the awe-inspiring verti-cal limestone walls of Potrero Chico is a must. Arguably among the 10 best places in the world for learning rock climbing, Potrero Chico is only 1½ hours north of Monterrey, near the town of Hidalgo. Climbs range from 30m to 300m, with a range of features that will challenge both beginners and experienced climbers. Expert tuition is available on-site for all levels.

The big walls of the canyon currently support about 600 different routes (some requiring an overnight stay) with more being added all the time. Although routes have been established in the Potrero for over 30 years, it owes its current status to a group of American climbers who have been developing the area since 1990, opening many of the new routes and setting up accommodations and an excellent website www.elpotrerochico.com.mx.

Near the canyon is Rancho Cerro Gordo, where you can camp for US$4 a night. There are also two casitas, which have modern facilities and are very comfortable. They are priced at US$25 (sleeps up to four people) and US$35 (sleeps up to eight people).

From Monterrey a taxi will cost about US$40, or you can catch a 'Mina' bus ($2) to Hidalgo.

lovely little town of Villa de García. A block or so from the plaza is the whitewashed walls of the unique and beautiful **Posada De La Villa** (☎ 8283-1942; Juan de Dios Treviño 103; r for up to 4 people US$36). There's a great little courtyard that gets lots of sun depending on the time of day and each of the six antique-furnished rooms have heaps of character. For a different, but no less appealing atmosphere **Los Vientos de Garcia** (☎ 8348-8714; Escobedo Sur 109; ste US$46; P ⊠ ⛱) has a rooftop bar, pool out back, and five large, warm suites with living rooms and mini kitchens. There's a good restaurant as well.

Cañón de la Huasteca

About 20km west of Monterrey's city center, this **canyon** (☎ 81-8331-6785, admission per person/vehicle US$0.50/1; ⛱ 9am-6pm) is 300m deep and has some dramatic rock formations, as well as cliffside drawings (evidence of its prehistoric inhabitants). The town of Santa Catarina is at one end of the canyon and a playground is in the middle, somewhat reducing its attraction as a wilderness area. Reach the mouth of the canyon by taking a Ruta 206 bus, labeled 'Aurora,' from the corner of Ramón and Cuauhtémoc in Monterrey. If driving, take Av Constitución west out of the city center.

Cascada Cola de Caballo

Six kilometers up a rough road from El Mercado, a village 35km south of Monterrey on Hwy 85, you'll find the **Horsetail Falls** (admission US$2.75; ⛱ 9am-7pm). The site has its share of hawkers and food stalls, but it's quite pretty and attracts a lot of picnickers. Horses and donkeys can be hired for the last kilometer to the falls (US$4.50). Further up the valley, vegetation flourishes on the slopes of the sierra. Autobuses Amarillos runs frequent buses to El Cercado from the Monterrey bus station (US$2); you'll have to catch a local bus from there to the falls.

COAHUILA

The state of Coahuila is large, mostly desert and sparsely populated. The border crossings into Coahuila from Texas are less frequently used than those further southeast in Tamaulipas, because the road connections into Mexico and the USA are not as convenient for most travelers. Yet the remoteness and the harsh, arid landscape will appeal to some, and the state capital, Saltillo, is definitely worth a visit. For information about the western part of the state, including the city of Torreón (p359) and the Zona del Silencio (p360), see the Central North Mexico chapter (p337).

The Spanish came to Coahuila in search of silver, slaves and souls. The region was explored by the Spanish as early as 1535 and the state capital, Saltillo, was founded 42 years after, but incessant attacks by indigenous Chichimecs and, later, Apaches discouraged widespread settlement until the early 19th century. In 1800, Coahuila still had fewer than 7000 people. A few big landowners came to dominate the area. In southeast Coahuila, one holding of 890 sq km was bought from the crown for US$33 in 1731, and grew to 58,700 sq km by 1771, becoming the Marquesado de Aguayo, protected by a private cavalry.

After 1821, in the early years of independence, Coahuila and Texas were one state of the new Mexican republic, but Texas was lost after the Mexican-American War. As the 19th century progressed, ranching grew in importance, helped by the arrival of railways. By 1900, Coahuila had 297,000 inhabitants. In the 20th century, a steel foundry was established in Monclova, giving Coahuila a major industrial center.

Besides the main border-crossing points below, there a few 'unofficial' crossings including Boquillas del Carmen. From Big Bend National Park, Texas, small boats can ferry you across the river. It's another one and half km to the small town from which transportation to other parts of Mexico are extremely limited.

CIUDAD ACUÑA

☎ 877 / pop 121,000

Ciudad Acuña, across from the US town of Del Rio, is a fairly busy border crossing, open 24 hours a day, with the border town standard nightlife. A number of Hollywood films, including *El Mariachi*, were filmed here. Check out **Crosby's** (☎ 772-20-20; Hidalgo 195) and **Lando's** (☎ 772-59-75; Hidalgo 290) for good Mexican cuisine.

About 20km upriver, the **Presa de la Amistad** (Friendship Reservoir) is a joint Mexican–US water management project, offering good fishing and boating facilities. From Ciudad Acuña to Saltillo it's an eight-hour bus ride (US$29) on good two-lane roads

PIEDRAS NEGRAS

☎ 878 / pop 133,000

The border crossing between Piedras Negras and the US town of Eagle Pass is a major commercial route. Piedras Negras attracts quite a few short-term visitors from Texas. There's a crafts shop in the old San Bernardino mission that features work from all over Mexico, and the *casa de cultura* has occasional displays of Mexican art, music and dance.

Legend has it that Piedras Negras is the birthplace of the nacho, said to have been invented by Don Ignacio (Nacho) Anaya, a bar owner, to satisfy the snacking needs of his patrons from both sides of the border. The town holds its **International Nacho Festival** in early October.

Most of the hotels are located on Av Carranza, which runs into Allende and the city center. Hwy 57 goes southeast to Allende, Sabinas and Monclova and continues to Saltillo, about seven hours away by bus (US$26).

MONCLOVA

☎ 866 / pop 196,000

Not an attractive city, Monclova nevertheless offers a convenient stopover for those on their way to the Cuatro Ciénegas protected area. The city's Altos Hornos iron and steel works (Ahmsa), founded in 1944, is one of the largest in Mexico. Monclova struggled with Saltillo for political prominence as the capital of Coahuila and Texas until the latter gained its independence.

The **Monclova tourist office** (☎ 636-27-30; promotorac@prodigy.net.mx; Blvd Harold Pape 455; 🕑 9am-noon & 4-7pm Mon-Fri, 9am-1pm Sat) can give you excellent maps of the area between Monclova and Cuatro Ciénegas, promoted as La Ruta del Desierto.

There are several decent, inexpensive hotels near the bus station, including the **Hotel San Agustín** (☎ 633-11-04; V Carranza 311; s/d US$18/23; ❄) directly across the street. Right around the corner is the **Hotel San Cristóbal** (☎ 633-20-83; Cuauhtémoc 223; s/d US$20/25; P ❄).

The main bus terminal is on V Carranza, two blocks west of the plaza, with 1st- and 2nd-class service to/from Ciudad Acuña (US$18, five hours), Mexico City (US$56, 16 hours), Monterrey (US$11, three hours), Nuevo Laredo (US$13, four hours), Piedras Negras (US$15, four hours), Saltillo (US$11, three hours) and Torreón (US$16, five hours). Second-class buses to Cuatro Ciénegas depart every two hours (US$4, two hours).

Hwy 57 runs south to Saltillo (192km) and north to Piedras Negras (256km). About 25km south of Monclova, Hwy 53 branches southeast to Monterrey (195km; there are no fuel stations on this highway). Hwy 30 heads west for 82km to Cuatro Ciénegas, then southwest to Torreón.

CUATRO CIÉNEGAS

☎ 869 / pop 9000

In this valley in the middle of the Desierto Chihuahuense (Chihuahuan Desert), a network of underground springs forms rivers and numerous crystalline pools, creating the conditions for a desert habitat of extraordinary biological diversity. The Galapagos-like isolation of the area also contributes to the existence of dozens of endemic species, including several kinds of turtles and eight kinds of fish. Because of the fragility of the ecosystem, in 1994 federal authorities created the **Área de Protección de Flora y Fauna Cuatro Ciénegas**, an 843-sq-km protected area. Some of the pools have been set aside as recreational spots, ideal for swimming and snorkeling. Within the clear blue waters of these desert aquariums, you can observe a wide variety of small fish, as well as organisms called *estromatolitos,* formed by calcified algae colonies, which biologists believe are akin to the planet's first oxygen-producing forms of life.

Equally impressive is the area called **Las Arenales**, where glistening white sand dunes, formed by the crystallization of gypsum in the nearby Laguna Churince, create an eerily beautiful effect against a backdrop of six mountain ranges ringing the valley. Mining companies continue to excavate the valuable gypsum, which along with agriculture and livestock grazing threaten this unique environment's survival. The sleepy town of Cuatro Ciénegas is a good base for exploration of the reserve. The town is the birthplace of Venustiano Carranza, a participant in the overthrow of Porfirio Díaz and later president of Mexico. It has several points of historical interest, adobe-style architecture, as well as a few hotels and restaurants. There's a bank with an ATM on the corner of Zaragoza and Escobedo, one block north of the plaza.

Visiting the Reserve

Access to the reserve is south of town along Hwy 30. Though it's possible to explore on your own, the desert tracks are minimally labeled. Authorized guides will escort you through the reserve (US$20), but you'll need your own vehicle. A good alternative is to arrange a tour through the Cuatro Ciénegas **tourist office** (☎ 696-05-74; www.rutadeldesierto.com; Morelos 103; day tour US$50, up to 15 people) or ask at Hotel Plaza (see following).

A **visitors center** (Poza Las Tortugas; 🕙 9am-5pm Tue-Sun) 7km south of town has maps and illustrated explanations, in Spanish, of the relevant natural phenomena. In the reserve area there are over 170 cerulean pools, or *pozas*, some up to 13m deep. **Poza La Becerra** (☎ 696-05-74 for information; adult/child US$4/2), about 16km from the visitors center and closest to the highway, is set up as a recreational facility with a diving pier, bathrooms and showers. Swimming amid the desert landscape is a marvelous experience. Though the water temperature can get as high as 32°C (90°F) in summer, cooler water spouts up from spring sources. Wearing suntan lotion is prohibited when swimming in the *pozas*. You can get a bus here from town.

You can also swim at the peaceful **Río Los Mezquites**, cooler than the *pozas*, with some

shady palapas and picnic areas along the banks. Access to the river is 6.5km south of town: turn left at the blue swimmer sign and go another 1.5km on an unpaved track. There's a nice white sand beach at **Las Playitas**, the largest lake in the valley. Swimming is prohibited at **Poza Azul**, a fish and turtle sanctuary.

The entrance to Las Arenales is left of the Poza La Becerra; it's about a 4.5km drive from the highway turnoff. Reaching heights of 13m, the white dunes here are spotted with low desert brush, and you'll come across evidence of coyotes, rabbits, roadrunners and scorpions. Summer temperatures can be extreme, so bring plenty of water and avoid midday excursions.

Sleeping & Eating

You may set up a tent within the protected area at Río Los Mezquites or Poza La Becerra. There are two hotels in Cuatro Ciénegas proper and a third on the way to Monclova.

Hotel Plaza (☎ 696-00-66; Hidalgo 202; s/d US$37/47; P 🛞) If you're in the area, don't pass up this colonial-style place, just a block from the plaza, with its high ceilings, comfy beds and beautiful, warmly painted rooms. The attached restaurant **La Casona** (breakfast US$3; mains US$4) matches the hotel for ambience and quality.

Hotel Ibarra (☎ 696-01-29; Zaragoza 200; s/d US$18/27; P) Not nearly as nice as the Plaza,

---

PRICKLY DESERT TREASURE

Cactus paddles have been eaten by indigenous people in Mexico for thousands of years. While the juicy fruit of the *nopal* species tastes like a Fig Newton and connoisseurs experiment with dishes like *nopalitos con camarón* (cactus with shrimp), it has always been at the center of Mexican culture, pictured on the crest of the Mexican flag and a potent symbol for the ancient Aztecs whose capital was named Tenochtitlán, or 'Home of the Cactus People.'

But today, the home of the cactus is being threatened by a number of culprits including over-irrigation and the little-known practice of cactus smuggling. A multimillion-dollar industry caters to cactophiles in Europe, Japan, Sweden and the USA, Illegally harvesting and shipping out hundreds of the over-345 species found in northern Mexico every year.

Stymied by stiffer law enforcement in the deserts of the American southwest, poachers have turned to the sparsely populated and biologically diverse Desierto Chihuahuense of northern Mexico. The plants, some 50 to 100 years old, are valuable to landscapers, nurseries and hobbyists, while in Mexico they serve as food for the enormous variety of desert mammals, and homes for birds and insects. If the problem isn't addressed, environmentalists worry that some types of cacti, plants that have given succor to humans through their medicinal and psychotropic properties, are in danger of being poached out of existence.

the Ibarra, directly across from the Santander Serfin bank, nevertheless is not a bad second option. Rooms are large and clean.

Motel Santa Fe (☎ 696-04-25; Blvd Juárez; s/d US$28/36; ℗ 🐾) Along the approach from Monclova, about 4km out of town, this motel is a good deal for large, comfortable rooms if you don't mind the racket made by the air-con unit.

El Doc (☎ 696-04-26; Zaragoza 103; mains US$3-8). The only other game in town for a good sit-down meal is El Doc, on the east side of the plaza.

Getting There & Away

The bus terminal occupies the south side of the plaza. There is an hourly 2nd-class service to/from both Monclova (US$4, one hour) and Torreón (US$12, 3½ hours). Several buses a day journey to Saltillo (US$13) and each of the nearest border crossings at Ciudad Acuña (US$19) and Piedras Negras (US$18).

SALTILLO

☎ 844 / pop 591,000 / elevation 1599m

Set high in the arid Sierra Madre Oriental, Saltillo was founded in 1577, making it the oldest city in the northeast. It has a quiet central area with a small-town feel, making it a popular destination, though there are extensive new suburbs and major industries on the city's outskirts. A large student population adds energy and a progressive feel. The city, with its lovely colonial buildings, temperate climate, great restaurants and dignified hotels, embodies what most travelers are seeking from a small city – a relaxing place to observe and experience northern Mexican life. It's on the main routes between the northeast border and central Mexico, making it an ideal spot to break a journey.

In the late 17th century, Saltillo was the capital of an area that included Coahuila, Nuevo León, Tamaulipas, Texas and 'all the land to the north which reaches toward the pole.'

History

The first mission was established here in 1591 as a center for the education and religious conversion of the local indigenous populations. Native Tlaxcalans were brought to help the Spanish stabilize the area, and they set up a colony beside the Spanish one at Saltillo.

Sometime-capital of the state of Coahuila (and Texas after Mexican independence) the city was occupied by US troops under Zachary Taylor during the Mexican–American War in 1846. At Buenavista, south of Saltillo, the 20,000-strong army of General Santa Anna was repulsed by Taylor's force, a quarter the size, in the decisive battle for control of the northeast during that war.

President Benito Juárez came to Saltillo during his flight from the invading French forces in 1864, and the city was occupied once again by foreign troops before being freed in 1866. During the Porfiriato, agriculture and ranching prospered in the area, and the coming of the railway helped trade and the first industries in the city. Monterrey, however, was by this time quickly overtaking Saltillo in both size and importance.

These days Saltillo is still a center for a large livestock and agricultural area, and in recent decades it has expanded to include automobile and petrochemical plants.

Orientation

Saltillo spreads over a large area, but most places of interest are located in the blocks around the two central plazas. Periférico Echeverría, a ring road, enables traffic to bypass the inner-city area.

The junction of Hidalgo and Juárez, at the southeast corner of the plaza, serves as a dividing point for Saltillo's street addresses, with those located to the south suffixed 'Sur,' those to the east 'Ote' (Oriente), and so on.

The bus station is on the south side of town, on Periférico Echeverría Sur – a 10-minute bus ride from the center.

Information

EMERGENCY
Police (☎ 414-10-37)
Red Cross (☎ 414-33-33)
University of Saltillo Hospital (☎ 412-30-00; Madero 1291)

INTERNET ACCESS
Cyberbase (Padre Flores 159; per hr M$12)
Link Café (Obregón 108; per hr M$13)

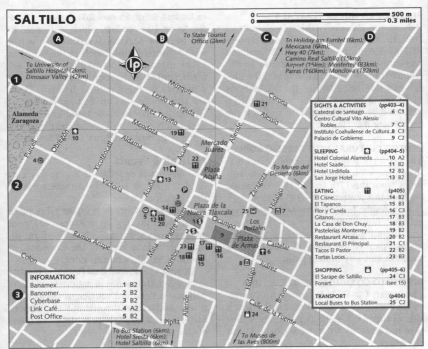

SALTILLO

0 — 500 m
0 — 0.3 miles

To State Tourist Office (2km)

To University of Saltillo Hospital (2km); Dinosaur Valley (42km)

To Holiday Inn Eurotel (6km); Mexicana (6km); Hwy 40 (7km); Camino Real Saltillo (15km); Airport (15km); Monterrey (83km); Parras (160km); Monclova (182km)

Alameda Zaragoza

Múzquiz

Lerdo de Tejada

Pérez Treviño

Mendoza

Obregón

Purcell

Aldama

Xicoténcatl

Victoria

Acuña

Corona

Alessio

Mercado Juárez

Plaza Acuña

Allende

To Museo del Desierto (6km)

Ramos Arizpe

Colón

Padre Flores

Ocampo

Plaza de la Nueva Tlaxcala

Los Portales

Zaragoza

Hidalgo

Plaza de Armas

Castelar

Mina

Morelos

Juárez

Hidalgo

Bravo

Allende

Calle de la Fuente

Pipila

To Bus Station (6km); Hotel Siesta (6km); Hotel Saltillo (6km)

To Museo de las Aves (800m)

SIGHTS & ACTIVITIES	(pp403–4)
Catedral de Santiago..................6	C3
Centro Cultural Vito Alessio Robles.................................7	C2
Instituto Coahuilense de Cultura..8	C3
Palacio de Gobierno..................9	C2

SLEEPING	(pp404–5)
Hotel Colonial Alameda..........10	A2
Hotel Saade...........................11	B2
Hotel Urdiñola........................12	B2
San Jorge Hotel......................13	B2

EATING	(p405)
El Cisne..................................14	B2
El Tapanco.............................15	B3
Flor y Canela.........................16	C3
Gitanos..................................17	B3
La Casa de Don Chuy.............18	B3
Pastelerías Monterrey.............19	B2
Restaurant Arcasa...................20	B3
Restaurant El Principal............21	C1
Tacos El Pastor.......................22	B3
Tortas Locas...........................23	B3

SHOPPING	(pp405–6)
El Sarape de Saltillo................24	C3
Fonart................................(see 15)

TRANSPORT	(p406)
Local Buses to Bus Station.......25	C2

INFORMATION	
Banamex..............................1	B2
Bancomer............................2	B2
Cyberbase............................3	B2
Link Café.............................4	A2
Post Office...........................5	B2

MONEY

You can change cash and traveler's checks at the banks near the Plaza de la Nueva Tlaxcala (all have ATMs). There are *casas de cambio* on Victoria, open until 6pm Monday to Friday, until 1pm on Saturday.

POST

The post office is centrally located at Victoria 223 Pte, a few doors from the Hotel Urdiñola.

TOURIST INFORMATION

In the old train station on the corner of Blvd Coss and Acuña, about 1.5km north of downtown, the **state tourist office** (☎ 412-51-22; www.saltillomexico.org; ☺ 9am-7pm Mon-Fri, 9am-noon Sat, 10am-6pm Sun) has abundant handouts including multiple-map guides to every region in the state.

TRAVEL AGENCIES

Both of the following companies offer a variety of services including day and overnight tours, rafting, rappelling, hiking, bird-watching etc.

Desert Adventures (☎ 871-732-22-44; www.desert-adventures.com)

Extrematour (☎ 415-77-57; www.extrematour.com)

Sights
CATEDRAL DE SANTIAGO

Built between 1745 and 1800, Saltillo's cathedral dominates the plaza and has one of Mexico's finest churrigueresque façades, with columns of elaborately carved pale gray stone. It's particularly splendid when lit up at night. Inside, the transepts are full of gilt ornamentation – look for the human figure perched on a ledge at the top of the dome.

PALACIO DE GOBIERNO

Facing the plaza are the state government headquarters. You are free to wander into this elegant 19th-century building. A mural in its 2nd-floor passageway traces Coahuila's history and depicts its historical figures, most prominently Venustiano Carranza, who, as governor of the state during the Revolution, launched a revolt against the provisional president Victoriano Huerta.

PLAZA DE LA NUEVA TLAXCALA

Behind the Palacio is this plaza, built in 1991 to commemorate the fourth centennial of Saltillo's foundation. A sculpted scene on its southern end alludes to the colonization of Coahuila. Allende, the plaza's east side, once divided the two sections of the old town – to the east was the section occupied by the Spaniards, to the west the area where the Tlaxcalans lived.

CENTRO CULTURAL VITO ALESSIO ROBLES

The book collection of the eponymous historian, now estimated at over 13,000 volumes from the 17th to the 19th centuries, anchors this **museum** (☎ 412-88-45; cnr Hidalgo & Aldama; admission free; ⊗ 10am-6pm Tue-Sun). Two galleries house temporary art exhibitions and there's a striking mural of the city's history painted on the walls surrounding the light and airy indoor patio.

INSTITUTO COAHUILENSE DE CULTURA

This **gallery** (☎ 410-20-33; cnr Juárez & Hidalgo; admission free; ⊗ 9am-6pm Tue-Sun), on the south side of the plaza, exhibits paintings, sculpture and crafts by artists from Coahuila and elsewhere.

ALAMEDA ZARAGOZA

Full of shady trees and pathways, this park has a playground and is a favorite spot for young couples. Live music is sometimes on tap on weekends. A pond at the southern end has an island shaped like Mexico. It is reached by going west down Victoria from behind the Palacio de Gobierno.

MUSEO DEL DESIERTO

Deserts cover up to 50% to 60% of Mexican territory, and this world-class **museum** (☎ 410 -66-33; www.museodeldesierto.org; Pérez Treviño 3745; adult/student or senior US$4/2; ⊗ 10am-5pm Tue-Sun), dedicated to the study of the Desierto Chihuahuense, the largest in North America, deserves a visit. Of the four pavilions, the most interesting deals with dinosaur fossils, many found in 'Dinosaur Valley' located 42km from Saltillo. There's also a botanical garden here that has 400 species of cactus on display.

MUSEO DE LAS AVES

A few blocks south of the plaza you'll find this **museum** (☎ 414-01-67; www.museodelasaves.org; cnr Hidalgo & Bolívar; admission US$1, free Sat; ⊗ 10am-6pm Tue-Sat, 11am-6pm Sun), which is devoted to the birds of Mexico. It's definitely worth a visit. Mexico ranks sixth in the world in avian diversity. Most of the exhibits are birds stuffed and mounted in convincing dioramas of their natural habitat. There are special sections on nesting, territoriality, birdsongs, navigation and endangered species. Over 670 bird species are displayed, along with bird skeletons, fossils and eggs.

Festivals & Events

The **Aniversario de Saltillo** is a nine-day cultural festival in late July commemorating the city's foundation.

Día del Santo Cristo de la Capilla takes place in the week leading up to August 6. Dance groups from around Coahuila perform on the esplanade in front of the cathedral, in honor of Saltillo's patron saint.

During the **International Festival of the Arts** in October, thousands of national and international artists and musicians perform in towns and cities throughout the region. Saltillo sees a large share of the more high-profile acts.

Sleeping

Since there are a few good-value places around the main plaza there's no real reason to stay near the bus station unless you're just looking for a bed.

BUDGET & MID-RANGE

Hotel Urdiñola (☎ 414-09-40; Victoria 251; s/d with fan US$31/35; P) The excellent Urdiñola offers heaps of character and great value. There's a sparkling white lobby with a wide sweeping stairway and a stunning stained-glass window. Large, airy rooms face a long courtyard with pleasant gardens.

Hotel Colonial Alameda (☎ 410-00-88; www.hotel colonialalameda.com; Obregón 222; r US$69; P ☒) This hotel is an excellent choice. The Spanish colonial-style building features 21 large, elegant, rooms each containing a pair of huge beds.

San Jorge Hotel (☎ 412-22-22; Acuña 240; s/d US$39/44; P ☒) Not as impressive as the Colonial Alameda, but still good, is this modern well-maintained establishment with a restaurant, a small rooftop swimming pool and comfortable rooms (some with terrific views).

Hotel Siesta (☎ 417-07-24; Echeverría 239; r US$24, larger r US$33) A decent option towards the budget end, this place is across the road from the bus station. Airy, upstairs rooms have good light and come with fan and TV.

Hotel Saltillo (☎ 417-22-00; Echeverría 249; r US$33) Beside the Siesta stands the Saltillo, beckoning visitors with its neon lights. It's a friendly place featuring modern, clean rooms with color TV, phone and ceiling fan. The hotel's 24-hour restaurant specializes in seafood.

Hotel Saade (☎ 412-91-20; www.hotelsaade.com; Aldama 397; s/d US$29/34; (P)) This large place in the heart of the city may look and feel like a hospital but it's rooms are OK. Fans are available on request.

TOP END

There are several four- and five-star hotels, aimed at business-class travelers, along the highways heading north and east from Saltillo.

Holiday Inn Eurotel (☎ 415-10-00; eurotel@prodigy .net.mx; V Carranza 4100; r Mon-Fri US$145, Sat & Sun US$77; (P) (X) (X) (X)) The Holiday Inn is located on Hwy 40 to Monterrey just south of the Carranza monument. It has all the modern luxuries; we consider weekend deals a bargain.

Camino Real Saltillo (☎ 438-00-00; www.camino real.com; Los Fundadores 2000; r Mon-Fri US$232, Sat & Sun US$118; (P) (X) (X) (X)) This classy establishment is as good as it gets in Saltillo, with two restaurants and lovely outdoor gardens. The weekend deals bring room prices within reach of most mortals.

Eating & Drinking

There are cheap eating stalls with outdoor seating in front of Mercado Juárez, overlooking Plaza Acuña.

Pastelerías Monterrey (Perez Treviño 401) Try this place for fresh-baked pastries.

El Cisne (☎ 414-68-17; Victoria 178; paninis US$4; (Y) restaurant 8am-9pm, bar 9pm-1:30am Thu-Sat; (X)) Stained glass and original paintings by local artists make this restored 19th-century house the perfect setting for a meal or just to sip one of the 40 different kinds of coffee drinks on offer. On weekend nights, enjoy live music outside in the equally exquisite courtyard.

Gitanos (☎ 410-37-95; 2nd fl, Juarez 259; mains US$4-9; (Y) 8:30-2am Mon-Sat) With a somewhat bizarre mixture of fake coconut trees, tacky statues and yellow walls, this eclectically decorated loft-space serves good continental breakfasts (US$3) and steak entrées (US$9). A narrow balcony overlooks the street and square.

Flor y Canela (☎ 414-31-43; Juárez 257; sandwiches US$3; (Y) 8:30am-9:30pm Mon-Fri, 4-9:30pm Sat & Sun; (X)) Another pleasant spot for coffee and a light meal, Flor y Canela is just below Gitanos.

El Tapanco (☎ 414-43-39; tapanco@prodigy.net.mx; Allende 225; mains from US$13) If you're looking for fine cuisine in splendid surroundings try the Tapanco. You can dine alfresco on the back patio or be serenaded inside by the piano player. The menu features a tempting array of salads, seafoods, pastas and crepes – the *huitlacoche* crepes are superb.

La Casa de Don Chuy (☎ 414-97-62; Allende 160; steak/seafood dishes US$9/12; noon-12am Mon-Sat, 1-6pm Sun) Similar to El Tapanco, this elegant restaurant offers courtyard dining in style – it's a favorite with tourists and a bit cheaper than its neighbor.

Restaurant Arcasa (☎ 412-64-24; Victoria 251; breakfast US$3.25, sandwiches US$2.25, Mexican dishes US$3.25; (X)) Next to the Hotel Urdiñola, Arcasa is a big, bright place with an extensive menu.

Restaurant El Principal (☎ 414-33-84; Allende 702; cabrito dishes US$7-12, steak dishes US$11; (X)) Norteño-style cabrito is the specialty at this family-style restaurant, four blocks down the hill from Plaza Acuña. It offers assorted goat parts displayed in the window, steaks and attentive service. There are two other Principals less centrally located.

Tortas Locas (☎ 414-42-26; Allende 146; sandwiches US$1.50-4; (Y) noon-10pm Tue-Sat, noon-9pm Sun) Almost 30 different kinds of sandwiches – enough said.

Tacos El Pastor (cnr Padre Flores & Aldama; 4 tacos US$1.75) On the southwest corner of Plaza Acuña, this busy place prepares tasty *tacos al pastor* (grilled spiced pork carved off a meter-high cone) and *tacos de lengua* (beef tongue).

Shopping

Saltillo used to be so famous for its serapes that a certain type was known as a 'Saltillo' even if it was made elsewhere in Mexico. These days the local workshops have stopped making classic all-wool serapes and seem to be obsessed with jarring combinations of bright colors. But you can still get ponchos and blankets in more 'natural' colors, some of which are pure wool.

El Sarape de Saltillo (☎ 414-96-34; Hidalgo 305; ☷ 9am-1pm & 3-7pm Mon-Sat) You can see serapes and other handicrafts at this shop, a couple of blocks up the hill from the cathedral. Wool is dyed and woven on treadle looms inside the shop.

Other places worth a look include the Mercado Juárez, next to Plaza Acuña, which also has a selection of serapes, as well as hats, saddles and souvenirs; and Fonart on Allende, just south of Juárez, a branch of the government-run crafts shop with a variety of pottery, textiles and jewelry from around Mexico.

Getting There & Away

AIR

Mexicana (☎ 488-07-70; Europlaza Mall, Venustiano Carranza 4120), with an office at the airport, has flights between Mexico City and Saltillo. **Continental Airlines** (☎ 488-13-14) flies to/from Houston.

BUS

Saltillo's modern bus station is on the ring road at Libertad. First-class lines have ticket desks to the right end of the hall as you enter; 2nd-class is to the left.

Lots of buses serve Saltillo but few start their journeys here. This means that on some buses, 2nd-class ones in particular, you often can't buy a ticket until the bus has arrived and they know how much room there is for new passengers. You'd be better off taking a 1st-class bus. The 1st-class lines include Transportes del Norte and Ómnibus de México, while Transportes Frontera and Línea Verde are 2nd-class; Turistar is the deluxe bus line. Daily departures include the following:

Aguascalientes (US$30, 7hr, 14 1st-class)
Durango (US$25, 8hr, 4 1st-class)
Guadalajara (US$44, 10hr, 15 1st-class)
Matamoros (US$23, 7hr, 13 1st-class)
Mexico City (US$65, 10hr, 2 deluxe; US$54, 10hr, 9 1st-class; US$48, 10hr, 2 2nd-class) To Terminal Norte.
Monterrey (US$7, 1½hr, 3 deluxe; US$5, 1½hr, frequent 1st-class)
Nuevo Laredo (US$20, 4hr, 8 1st-class)
Parras (US$7, 2½hr, 9 2nd-class)

San Luis Potosí (US$26, 6hr, frequent 1st-class; US$24, 6hr, 2 2nd-class)
Torreón (US$19, 3½hr, frequent 1st-class; US$14, 3½hr, frequent 2nd-class)
Zacatecas (US$22, 5hr, 10 1st-class; US$20, 5hr, 7 2nd-class)

Buses also go to Chihuahua, Ciudad Acuña, Ciudad Juárez, Mazatlán, Monclova, Morelia, Piedras Negras, Reynosa, Querétaro and Tijuana. Autobuses Americanos has services to Chicago, Dallas, Houston and San Antonio.

CAR & MOTORCYCLE

Saltillo is a junction of major roads. Hwy 40 going northeast to Monterrey is a good four-lane road, with no tolls until you reach the Monterrey bypass. Going west to Torreón (277km), Hwy 40D splits off Hwy 40 after 30km, becoming an overpriced toll road (US$16). Hwy 40 is free and perfectly all right.

Hwy 57 goes north to Monclova (192km), penetrating the dramatic Sierra San Marcos y Pinos at Cima de la Muralla (a butterfly migration zone in the summer months), and onward to Piedras Negras (441km). Going south to Mexico City (852km), Hwy 57 climbs to over 2000m, then descends gradually along the Altiplano Central to Matehuala (260km) and San Luis Potosí (455km), through barren but often scenic country. To the southwest, Hwy 54 crosses high, dry plains toward Zacatecas (363km) and Guadalajara (680km).

Getting Around

The airport is 15km northeast of town on Hwy 40; catch a 'Ramos Arizpe' bus along Xicoténcatl (US$0.40) or a taxi. To reach the city center from the bus station, take minibus No 9 (US$0.30), which departs from Libertad, the first street on the right as you leave the station. To reach the bus station from the center, catch a No 9 on Aldama between Zaragoza and Hidalgo. Taxis between the center and the bus station cost US$3.50.

If you have the time, a convenient way to see the sights is the tourist trolley (US$2) which makes the rounds from Friday to Sunday. You can get on and off at any of the 14 stops, which include the cathedral and the major museums.

PARRAS

☎ 842 / pop 32,000 / elevation 1580m

Parras, 160km west of Saltillo off the Torreón road, is an oasis in the Desierto de Coahuila. Underground streams from the sierra come to the surface here as springs. These are used to irrigate the grapevines (*parras*) for which the area is famous and giving the town its full name – Parras de la Fuente. It seems smaller than it is, and the pleasant climate and subdued pace warrant a stop.

An obelisk on Calle Arizpe honors Francisco Madero, an important leader in the Mexican Revolution, who was born in Parras. US and French troops occupied the town during their respective interventions in 1846 and 1866.

Orientation & Information

The few restaurants, hotels and shops are mostly found within a short walking distance of the bus station and Plaza Zaragoza.

The Parras **tourist office** (☎ 422-02-59; www.parrascoahuila.com.mx; ☽ 10am-1pm & 3:30-7pm) is on the roadside 3km north of town. You can withdraw pesos and dollars at the **Bancomer** (cnr Reforma & Ramos Arzipe).

Visit **Computo y Linea** (Allende 306; per hr M$12; ☽ 9am-2:30pm & 4-8:30pm) or **Cafe Internet** (Arzipe 121; per hr M$10; ☽ 9am-9pm Mon-Sat) for Internet access.

Sights

The first winery in the Americas was established at Parras in 1597, a year before the town itself was founded. The winery, now called **Casa Madero** (☎ 422-00-55; www.madero.com.mx; admission free; tours 9am-4pm), is about 4km north of town in San Lorenzo on the road going to the main highway. Tours are conducted in Spanish and last about an hour; you can buy quality wine and brandy on-site.

The town has an old aqueduct, some colonial buildings, and three *estanques* (large pools where water from the springs is stored) that are great for swimming. The **Iglesia del Santo Madero**, on the southern edge of town, sits on the plug of an extinct volcano. Expansive views reward those who make the steep climb.

An important manufacturer of *mezclilla* (denim), Parras is a good place to buy jeans. Its fig, date and nut orchards provide the basis for delectable fudgy sweets, on sale around town.

Festivals & Events

The grape fair, the **Feria de la Uva**, goes on for most of the month of August, featuring parades, fireworks, horse races, religious celebrations on the Día de la Asunción (August 15), and traditional dances by descendants of early Tlaxcalan settlers.

Sleeping

Hostal El Farol (☎ 422-11-13; hostalelfarol1@prodigy.net.mex; Ramos Arzipe 301; r US$67; ℗ ��) An unexpected oasis in the middle of town, the El Farol is a well-preserved gem. Extremely spacious, wood-paneled rooms surround a shaded colonial-style courtyard. The bedrooms are furnished with meticulous attention to period detail and the bathrooms are large and modern. Reduced rates apply Sunday to Thursday.

Hotel Posada Santa Isabel (☎ 422-05-72; Madero 514; r US$32; ℗) The Santa Isabel's rooms don't measure up to the graceful and tranquil courtyard. The quality of the rooms varies but while some beds sag, all are clean, and it's the best value in this price-range.

Hotel La Siesta (☎ 422-03-74; Acuña 9; s/d US$16/20) The Siesta, around the corner from the bus station, is the best budget option in town. The rooms and beds are smaller than the Santa Isabel but the lobby and courtyard are inviting.

Rincón del Montero (☎ 422-05-40; www.rincondelmontero.com; r or cabins US$95; ℗ ⓢ) A few kilometers north of town is this resort with golf, tennis, swimming and horseback riding. Approaching from the north, turn left off the main road just below the tourist information module.

Eating & Drinking

Restaurant El Farol (breakfast US$3, mains US$4-8; ☽ 7:30am-11pm; ⓧ ℗) El Farol the restaurant is as hospitable as the hotel. There's a bar with TVs, and a courtyard with tables. An order of tortilla soup (US$2.50) and enchiladas (US$4.50) make for a satisfying meal.

Restaurant Posada (breakfast US$3, mains US$4.50) If the hotel of the same name is vacant, you'll probably have the leafy courtyard dining area to yourself. Mexican standards are available at affordable prices.

There are a couple of economical restaurants on Reforma, between Arzipe and Madero, including **El Tiburón** (Reforma 17) and **Chávez** (Reforma 19). Both serve decent, inexpensive Mexican (US$4) and the latter dishes up pizza (US$9) as well.

Getting There & Away

Only 2nd-class buses serve Parras; there are nine daily to/from Saltillo (US$7, 2½ hours) A 1st-class bus from Saltillo or elsewhere might drop you at La Paila, about halfway between Saltillo and Torreón. From La Paila you can find local transport. There are five buses daily to/from Torreón (US$9, 2½ hours) to the west, bordering the state of Chihuahua. If you want to head to Cuatro Ciénegas without having to backtrack to Saltillo, you can catch a bus to San Pedro Las Colonias (US$6, 1½ hours) and then a 1st-class bus from there to Cuatro Ciénegas (US$17, two hours). Parras is easy to reach by car; turn off the highway at La Paila and go 27km south.

Central Pacific Coast

Picture yourself on a beach, any beach, doing anything. That beach exists on Mexico's central Pacific coast. Whatever you want from an ocean-side vacation, it's awaiting you, somewhere between Mazatlán and Acapulco. Between the stillness of seaside lagoons and earthquake-inducing nightclubs, ultra-luxury resorts and ramshackle fishing villages, fast-food chains and hidden homemade treats - it's there.

It doesn't matter if you seek exhilaration or decompression. You can snorkel, surf, sail, ride horses, scuba dive, explore lagoons by boat, mountain bike along ocean cliffs and drink yourself silly (all in one day if you want). Or you can soak up the sun and read a book before indulging in the best spa treatment or full body massage of your life. In many places you can do both, making the central Pacific coast a great destination for families and groups with people who want to do different things on their vacation.

Whether you have a couple of days, several months or years to spend on the coast, you won't find yourself bored or disappointed. You can always hop over to another town or beach because, with or without your own transportation, this is a pretty easy region to get around. And it's packed with hidden treasures like dirt roads that lead to the most unbelievable deserted beaches.

Mexico's central Pacific coast is a land of pristine bays, isolated beaches, infinite wildlife and mega-resorts. But at the end of the day you will inevitably find yourself falling in love with the people. It is truly amazing that after decades of heavy tourism they are still so friendly. And the food – it's fabulously fresh, wonderfully spiced and truly unforgettable.

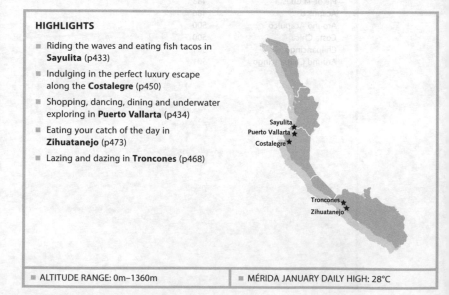

HIGHLIGHTS

- Riding the waves and eating fish tacos in **Sayulita** (p433)
- Indulging in the perfect luxury escape along the **Costalegre** (p450)
- Shopping, dancing, dining and underwater exploring in **Puerto Vallarta** (p434)
- Eating your catch of the day in **Zihuatanejo** (p473)
- Lazing and dazing in **Troncones** (p468)

Sayulita
Puerto Vallarta
Costalegre

Troncones
Zihuatanejo

- ALTITUDE RANGE: 0m–1360m
- MÉRIDA JANUARY DAILY HIGH: 28°C

HISTORY

People have been living along Mexico's Pacific coast for over 4000 years, but it wasn't until the 1940s that archeologists actually started studying the area. What they found were underground burial chambers in Nayarit, Jalisco and Colima that date back to 1900 BC. Similar tombs have been found only in Colombia and Ecuador, which suggests there was maritime exchange between the two continents around that time.

Based on the sculptures found around the Río Balsas in Guerrero state, it is believed that the cultures from that area were in contact with the Olmecs from the gulf side of Mexico. Artifacts in Guerrero, Nayarit, Jalisco, Colima and Michoacán suggest that much of the coast was connected to Teotihuacán culture as well.

The Spanish arrived in Mexico in 1519, and soon traveled to Acapulco, Zihuatanejo, Puerto Vallarta and Manzanillo. By 1565 Acapulco was an established port link in the trade route between Asia and Europe.

It was not until the middle of the 1950s and '60s that tourism really hit the coast, starting in Acapulco and Mazatlán with Puerto Vallarta soon to follow. Since Nafta was enacted in 1994, more and more foreigners have bought into and developed land along the coast, most noticeably around Puerto Vallarta.

CLIMATE

It's hot, really hot, and wet from May through early November. Hurricanes usually hit in September and October and tourists hit in December. The high-tourist season understandably coincides with the cooler, dry season from late November to late April.

DANGERS & ANNOYANCES

Mexico's central Pacific coast is *tranquilo* with little crime. Michoacán is associated with drug smuggling and occasional carjacking, so there are lots of checkpoints along the roads throughout the state. Acapulco is the grittiest of the coastal cities, where you might find glue-sniffing kids hovering in empty lots behind plush hotels. But for travelers, Acapulco is hardly dangerous.

Avoid driving at night; there are no road lights, many people drive without headlights, check points are more difficult to get through and animals wait for their death in the middle of the road.

However, the most likely danger you'll encounter are powerful undertows that can make swimming deadly. Heed local warnings and swim with caution. Otherwise, kick back; you're on vacation.

GETTING THERE & AROUND

There are plenty of direct international flights from USA and Canada to Acapulco, Zihuatanejo, Puerto Vallarta and Mazatlán. The Playa de Oro international airport between Manzanillo and Barra de Navidad is popular but requires a bit more land travel before you can start sipping margaritas.

It's long been popular to drive to Mexico's Pacific coast from the United States and Canada. It's all toll roads between the border and Mazatlán making it an easy approach. But past Mazatlán the road gets patchy and you'll oscillate between smooth pavement and shock-busting potholes. There are several opportunities to travel inland from the coast. Guadalajara, Pátzcuaro and Morelia are most popular.

Bus travel in this region is easy and surprisingly comfortable, almost luxurious. The buses serve nearly every community, large or small, but nicer buses serve bigger towns. First-class buses all have air-con, comfortable seats, cleanish bathrooms, TVs and other high-class comforts.

If you are traveling by private car or RV, you'll find that the rugged coast means slow-going twists and turns, which means speed is not an option. The good thing about going slow is that you'll have plenty of time to prepare for the unpredictably placed *topes* (speed bumps) and common potholes, and you'll be able to enjoy the fantastic scenery.

MAZATLÁN

☎ 669 / pop 340,000

Just 13km south of the Tropic of Cancer, Mazatlán is the largest port on Mexico's Pacific coast as well as a major beachside resort. It's only partly manicured, with insular resorts lining the coast north of the gritty port, where the air is thick, the streets dirty and the buildings crumbling. Mazatlán has long catered to cruise liners with cheap knick-knack stores, an abundance of

MAZATLÁN

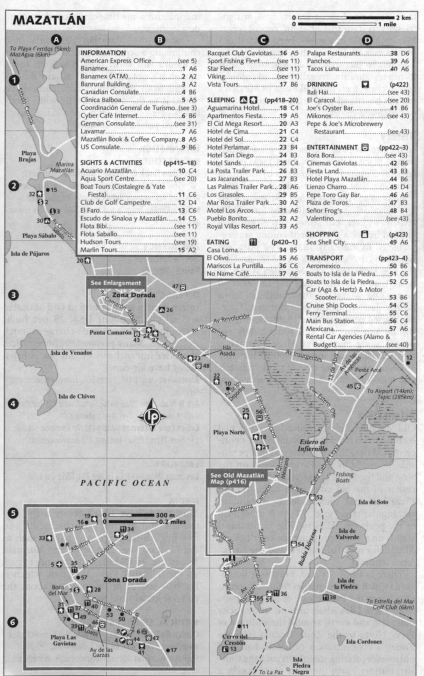

0 — 2 km
0 — 1 mile

A   **B**   **C**   **D**

To Playa Cerritos (5km);
MazAgua (6km)

INFORMATION
American Express Office............(see 5)
Banamex....................................1 A6
Banamex (ATM)..........................2 A2
Banrural Building........................3 A2
Canadian Consulate....................4 B6
Clinica Balboa............................5 A5
Coordinación General de Turismo..(see 3)
Cyber Café Internet....................6 B6
German Consulate...................(see 31)
Lavamar.....................................7 A2
Mazatlán Book & Coffee Company..8 A5
US Consulate..............................9 B6

SIGHTS & ACTIVITIES   (pp415–18)
Acuario Mazatlán.....................10 C4
Aqua Sport Centre..................(see 20)
Boat Tours (Costalegre & Yate
  Fiesta)....................................11 C6
Club de Golf Campestre...........12 D4
El Faro.....................................13 C6
Escudo de Sinaloa y Mazatlán...14 C5
Flota Bibi...............................(see 11)
Flota Saballo.........................(see 11)
Hudson Tours........................(see 19)
Marlin Tours............................15 A2

Racquet Club Gaviotas....16 A5
Sport Fishing Fleet........(see 11)
Star Fleet....................(see 11)
Viking.........................(see 11)
Vista Tours...................17 B6

SLEEPING   (pp418–20)
Aguamarina Hotel.........18 C4
Apartmentos Fiesta.......19 A5
El Cid Mega Resort.......20 A3
Hotel de Cima.............21 C4
Hotel del Sol..............22 C4
Hotel Perlamar...........23 B4
Hotel San Diego.........24 B3
Hotel Sands...............25 C4
La Posta Trailer Park....26 B3
Las Jacarandas..........27 B3
Las Palmas Trailer Park..28 B6
Los Girasoles.............29 B5
Mar Rosa Trailer Park...30 A2
Motel Los Arcos.........31 A6
Pueblo Bonito............32 A2
Royal Villas Resort......33 A5

EATING   (pp420–1)
Casa Loma................34 B5
El Olivo....................35 A6
Mariscos La Puntilla....36 C6
No Name Café...........37 A6

Palapa Restaurants.............38 D6
Panchos.............................39 A6
Tacos Luna.........................40 A6

DRINKING   (p422)
Bali Hai............................(see 43)
El Caracol.........................(see 20)
Joe's Oyster Bar................41 B6
Mikonos............................(see 43)
Pepe & Joe's Microbrewery
  Restaurant......................(see 43)

ENTERTAINMENT   (pp422–3)
Bora Bora..........................(see 43)
Cinemas Gaviotas...............42 B6
Fiesta Land.......................43 B3
Hotel Playa Mazatlán.........44 B6
Lienzo Charro....................45 D4
Pepe Toro Gay Bar.............46 A6
Plaza de Toros..................47 B3
Señor Frog's.....................48 B4
Valentino..........................(see 43)

SHOPPING   (p423)
Sea Shell City....................49 A6

TRANSPORT   (pp423–4)
Aeromexico.......................50 B6
Boats to Isla de la Piedra....51 C6
Boats to Isla de la Piedra....52 C5
Car (Aga & Hertz) & Motor
  Scooter........................53 B6
Cruise Ship Docks..............54 C6
Ferry Terminal...................55 C6
Main Bus Station...............56 C4
Mexicana........................57 A6
Rental Car Agencies (Alamo &
  Budget).....................(see 40)

CENTRAL PACIFIC COAST

Playa
Brujas

Marina
Mazatlán

Isla de Pájaros

Isla de Venados

Isla de Chivos

PACIFIC OCEAN

Playa Sábalo

Zona Dorada

Punta Camarón

Av Revolución

Av Insurgentes

Isla Asada

Av del Mar

Av de los Deportes

Playa Norte

Av Ejército Mexicano

Estero el Infiernillo

See Old Mazatlán
Map (p416)

Zaragoza
Carrasco
Paseo Olas Altas
Serdán

Av Ejército Mexicano

Av Néjera

Badía Dársena

Fishing Boats

Isla de Soto

Isla de Valverde

Isla de la Piedra

To Estrella del Mar
Golf Club (6km)

To Airport (14km);
Tepic (285km)

Perez Arcé

23 de Abril

Av de las Armenas

Circ Estero Ote

Cerro del
Crestón

Isla Cordones

Isla
Piedra
Negra

To La Paz

0 — 300 m
0 — 0.2 miles

Río Ibis

Albatros

Av Las Gaviotas

Zona Dorada

Boca
del Mar

Av Camarón Sábalo

Av Laguna

Av Loaiza

Av de las
Garzas

Playa Las
Gaviotas

taxis, over-sized mega-resorts and gringo-friendly restaurants. But in recent years Mazatlán's old town has been revitalized by the remodeling of the Ángela Peralta Theater. In fact, today old Mazatlán, with its hip restaurants, art galleries and colonial architecture, feels more like one of Mexico's famous heartland cities than a bustling port or beachside resort.

History
In the pre-Hispanic times Mazatlán (which means 'place of deer' in Náhuatl) was populated by Totorames, who lived by hunting, gathering, fishing and agriculture. On Easter Sunday in 1531, a group of 25 Spaniards led by Nuño de Guzmán officially founded a settlement here, but almost three centuries elapsed before a permanent colony was established in the early 1820s. The port was blockaded by US forces in 1847, and by the French in 1864, but Mazatlán was little more than a fishing village for the next 80 years. 'Old' Mazatlán, the traditional town center, dates from the 19th century. Tourists started coming in the 1930s, mainly for fishing and hunting, and some hotels appeared along Playa Olas Altas, Mazatlán's first tourist beach, in the 1950s. From the 1970s onward, a long strip of modern hotels and tourist facilities had spread north along the coast.

Orientation
Old Mazatlán, the city center, is best reached by bus or taxi from the bus station. It's concentrated near the southern end of a peninsula, bounded by the Pacific Ocean on the west and the Bahía Dársena on the east. The center of the old city is the cathedral, on Plaza Principal, surrounded by a standard rectangular street grid. At the southern tip of the peninsula, El Faro (The Lighthouse) stands on a rocky prominence, overlooking Mazatlán's sportfishing fleet and the La Paz ferry terminal.

There is a bus-covered, beachside boulevard (which changes names frequently) running along the Pacific side of the peninsula from Playa Olas Altas, around some rocky outcrops, and north around the wide arc of Playa Norte to the Zona Dorada (Golden Zone), a concentration of hotels, bars and businesses catering mainly to package tourists. Further north there are more hotels, a marina and some time-share condominium developments.

East of the Mazatlán peninsula (and comprising a separate municipality), Isla de la Piedra is a short boat ride from town, though it's not really an island any more – landfill from the airport construction has joined it to the mainland. The wide, sandy beach here is lined with open-sided, palm-thatched palapa restaurants.

Information
BOOKSTORES
Mazatlán Book & Coffee Company (Map p413; ☎ 916-78-99; Av Camarón Sábalo s/n; ☾ 9am-6pm Mon-Sat) Across from Hotel Costa de Oro. Has used books in English for sale and trade. Decent coffee is also available.

EMERGENCY
Fire Department (☎ 981-27-69)
Police (☎ 060)

INTERNET ACCESS
Internet cafés are plentiful in Old Mazatlán and all charge about US$1.25 per hour; places in the Zona Dorada charge as much as US$2.75. Many private telephone offices also offer Internet service. All places listed below have air-con.
AhorraNet (Map p416; Flores 508) Friendly reliable service.
Art & Web.com (Map p416; Sixto Osuna 15) Popular with students and offers cheap phone calls.
Cyber Café Internet (Map p413; Av Camarón Sábalo; ☾ 8am-11pm) Pricey but fast, hip and convenient.

LAUNDRY
Lavamar (Map p413; La Loaiza 214; US$5 per kilo)

MEDIA
Most hotels have stacks of city maps, restaurant and activity advertisements and free English-language newspapers such as *Pacific Pearl*, *Welcome Digest* and *Mazatlán Interactivo*. In Old Mazatlán be sure to pick up the bilingual *Viejo Mazatlán*, which is the best source of information about the cultural life around town.

MEDICAL SERVICES
Clínica Balboa (Map p413; ☎ 916-79-33; www.tourist medicalassist.com; Av Camarón Sábalo 4480; ☾ 24hr) English is spoken at this well regarded walk-in medical clinic.

MONEY

Banks, most with ATMs, and *casas de cambio* are plentiful in both old and new Mazatlán. There are Bancomer and Banamex branches near Plaza Principal (Map p416) and a **Banamex** (Map p413; Av Camarón Sábalo) in the Zona Dorada. **American Express** (Map p413; ☎ 913-06-00; Centro Comercial Balboa, Av Camarón Sábalo s/n) is in the Zona Dorada.

POST

Main post office (Map p416; Juárez on the east side of Plaza Principal)

TELEPHONE

Computel (Map p416; Serdán 1510; ☺ 7am-9pm) Air-conditioned, friendly and helpful with telephone, fax and limited Internet services.

Telecomm (Map p416; Juárez s/n, next to post office; ☺ 8am-7pm Mon-Fri, 9am-1pm Sat) Quiet pay phones in private cabins, fax and Internet service.

Cheap Internet phone calls are available at many Internet cafés as well.

TOURIST INFORMATION

Coordinación General de Turismo (Map p413; ☎ 916-5160/65; Av Camarón Sábalo s/n, 4th fl, Banrural building; www.sinaloa-travel.com in Spanish; ☺ 9am-6pm Mon-Fri, 9am-2pm Sat) Helpful with information about deals at hotels as well as what to see and do in Mazatlán and Sinaloa state.

Sights

Most people come to Mazatlán to sit on the beach, sportfish, snorkel and get a tan. But Mazatlán actually has plenty of out-of-the-sun attractions as well. Old Mazatlán is the cultural heart of the city with several impressive, well-curated museums, contemporary galleries, colonial architecture and historic monuments.

OLD MAZATLÁN   Map p416

The heart of Old Mazatlán is the large 19th-century **cathedral** (cnr Juárez & 21 de Marzo) with its high, yellow twin towers and beautiful statues inside. Built from 1875 to 1890, it faces **Plaza Principal**, which has lush trees and a bandstand. The unremarkable **Palacio Municipal** is on the west side of the Plaza Principal.

A couple of blocks southwest of Plaza Principal is the lovely tree-lined intimate **Plazuela Machado** (cnr Av Carnaval & Constitución). This is the heart of the restored area of arts

galleries, cafés and restaurants, accented by the **Teatro Ángela Peralta** (☎ 982-44-46; www.teatroangelaperalta.com in Spanish; Av Carnaval 47), half a block south of the plaza. The theater was built in 1860, and reopened in 1992 after a five-year restoration project. Cultural events of all kinds are presented here (see Entertainment, p422), and the opulent interior is open for viewing most days. It's surrounded by historic buildings and attractive sidewalk cafés, restaurants and bars.

West of the center, **Playa Olas Altas** is an intimate crescent-shaped beach in a small cove where Mazatlán's tourism began in the 1950s. Signs on the faded '50s hotels facing along the seafront road, Paseo Olas Altas, commemorate some of the area's first visitors like writer Jack Kerouac and photographers Tina Modotti and Edward Weston. From here you can see two of the town's many seafront monuments: the **Escudo de Sinaloa y Mazatlán** (Sinaloa and Mazatlán Shield) at the southern end of the cove and the small **Monumento al Venado** (Monument to the Deer) at the north end (a tribute to the city's Náhuatl name).

Further north, around the rocky outcrop called **Cerro de la Nevería** (Icebox Hill) is the **Monumento a la Continuidad de la Vida** (Monument to the Continuity of Life), featuring two naked humans and a group of dolphins. Also along here is the platform from which the **cliff divers** *(clavadistas)* plunge into the ocean swells below. There's no fixed schedule, but you're mostly likely to see the divers perform around lunchtime on weekends and holidays.

Paseo Olas Altas continues around another rocky promontory, where the cannons of the old fort point out to sea past one of Mazatlán's best surf breaks. Changing its name to Av del Mar, the seafront road heads towards **Playa Norte**, a sunset fishing spot for pelicans and other birds, by passing the **Monumento al Pescador** (Monument to the Fisherman), another of Mazatlán's nude statues.

At the south end of the peninsula, a particularly prominent rocky outcrop provides the base for **El Faro**, 157m above sea level and supposedly the second-highest lighthouse in the world (after one at Gibraltar). You can climb up there for a spectacular view of the city and coast. The hill, called Cerro del Crestón, was once an island, but a causeway built in the 1930s now joins it to the mainland. Mazatlán's sportfishing fleet, the ferry to La Paz and some of the tourist boats (see Tours, p418) dock in the marina on the east side of the causeway.

MUSEUMS
Map p416

The **Museo Arqueológico** (☎ 981-14-55; Sixto Osuna 76; admission US$2.25; ☺ 10am-4pm Mon-Sat, 10am-3pm Sun) is an interesting little archaeological museum with changing exhibits, usually artifacts from around Sinaloa state and a selection of historical photos of Mazatlán. There are some signs in English. Opposite, the small **Museo de Arte** (☎ 985-3502; cnr Sixto Osuna & Carranza; admission free; ☺ 10am-7pm Tue-Sun) has permanent and changing exhibits of work by Mexican artists (all signs in Spanish).

Also worth a peek is the **Machado Museo Casa** (Constitución 79; admission US$2; ☺ 10am-6pm), a beautifully restored 19th-century house filled with a collection of French and Austrian furniture, clothing and other antiques. Some exhibits are in English.

BEACHES & ZONA DORADA
Map p413

Mazatlán has 16km of sandy beaches stretching north from Old Mazatlán to beyond the Zona Dorada. Playa Norte begins just north of Old Mazatlán and arcs toward **Punta Camarón**, a rocky point dominated by the conspicuous white walls and turrets of the Fiesta Land nightclub complex. The traffic circle here marks the southern end of the Zona Dorada, an unashamed tourist

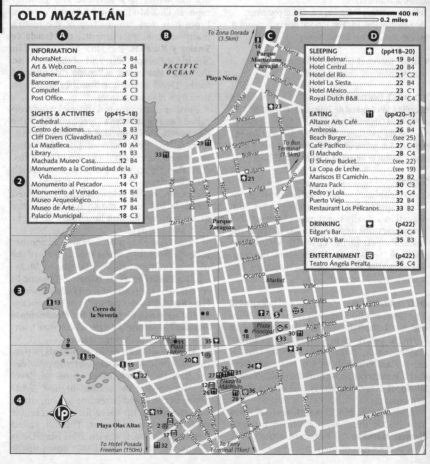

OLD MAZATLÁN

0 ——— 400 m
0 ——— 0.2 miles

To Zona Dorada (3.5km)

PACIFIC OCEAN

Playa Norte

INFORMATION
AhorraNet................................1 B4
Art & Web.com.........................2 B4
Banamex..................................3 C3
Bancomer.................................4 C3
Computel.................................5 C3
Post Office...............................6 C3

SIGHTS & ACTIVITIES (pp415–18)
Cathedral.................................7 C3
Centro de Idiomas....................8 B3
Cliff Divers (Clavadistas)..........9 A3
La Mazatleca..........................10 A4
Library...................................11 B3
Machada Museo Casa..............12 B4
Monumento a la Continuidad de la Vida.................................13 A3
Monumento al Pescador..........14 C1
Monumento al Venado............15 B4
Museo Arqueológico...............16 B4
Museo de Arte........................17 B4
Palacio Municipal....................18 C3

SLEEPING (pp418–20)
Hotel Belmar..........................19 B4
Hotel Central..........................20 B4
Hotel del Río..........................21 C2
Hotel La Siesta.......................22 B4
Hotel México..........................23 C1
Royal Dutch B&B.....................24 C4

EATING (pp420–1)
Altazor Arts Café.....................25 C4
Ambrosia.................................26 B4
Beach Burger.....................(see 25)
Café Pacífico..........................27 C4
El Machado.............................28 C4
El Shrimp Bucket................(see 22)
La Copa de Leche................(see 19)
Mariscos El Camichín..............29 B2
Marza Pack.............................30 C3
Pedro y Lola...........................31 C4
Puerto Viejo............................32 B4
Restaurant Los Pelícanos........33 B2

DRINKING (p422)
Edgar's Bar.............................34 C4
Vitrola's Bar...........................35 B3

ENTERTAINMENT (p422)
Teatro Ángela Peralta.............36 C4

Parque Martiniano Carvajal

To Bus Terminal (1.5km)

Cerro de la Nevería

Plaza Principal

Plaza Hidalgo

Plazuela Machado

Parque Zaragoza

Playa Olas Altas

To Hotel Posada Freeman (150m)

To Ferry Terminal (1km)

precinct of hotels, restaurants, bars and souvenir shops. The fanciest hotels face the fine beaches of **Playa Las Gaviotas** and **Playa Sábalo**, which extends north of the Zona Dorada. 'Sábalo-Centro' buses pass along all of these beaches.

North of Playa Sábalo, large-scale work continues on the extensive **Marina Mazatlán**. Other resort hotels and new condominium developments line the beaches north of the marina – **Playa Brujas** (Witches' Beach) and, further north, **Playa Cerritos**.

ISLANDS   Map p413

Three rocky islands are clearly seen from Mazatlán's beaches – **Isla de Chivos** (Island of Goats) is on the left, and **Isla de Pájaros** (Island of Birds) is on the right. In the middle, **Isla de Venados** (Deer Island) has been designated a natural reserve for protection of native flora and fauna; petroglyphs have also been found on the island. Secluded beaches on the island are wonderful for a day trip, and the clear waters offer great snorkeling. Boats depart from the Aqua Sport Centre at **El Cid Mega Resort** (☎ 916-34-68; www.elcid.com; Av Camarón Sábalo s/n). The trip lasts five hours and includes food and drinks for US$42.

ISLA DE LA PIEDRA   Map p413

Stone Island is actually a long, thin peninsula whose tip is opposite the south end of the city. Its beautiful, long, sandy beach is bordered by coconut groves, and a row of palapa restaurants, some of which have music and dancing on Sunday afternoons and holidays, when the beach is popular with locals. Good surf breaks offshore, and some very cheap accommodations make it popular with surfers. It is possible to camp here (see Sleeping, p419).

To get to Isla de la Piedra, take a small boat from one of two docks. The embarcadero Playa Sur is near the ferry terminal (boats leave 7am to 6pm), and boats from there will drop you at a jetty just a short walk from the Isla de la Piedra beach. The other dock is further north, near the end of Av Nájera (boats leave 5am to 8pm), and boats from there will take you to the village on Isla de la Piedra, slightly further from the beach (a *pulmonía* taxi will take you right to the beach for US$2). Boats depart every 10 minutes or so to the island (US$1 round-trip).

Activities

GOLF & TENNIS

There's golf at the **Club de Golf Campestre** (Map p413; ☎ 980-15-70; www.estrelladelmar.com; Hwy 15), east of town; the **Estrella del Mar Golf Club** (☎ 982-33-00; Isla de la Piedra), south of the airport by the coast; and **El Cid Mega Resort** (Map p413; ☎ 913-33-33; Av Camarón Sábalo s/n), north of the Zona Dorada.

Play tennis at the **Racquet Club Gaviotas** (☎ 913-59-39; cnr Ibis & Bravo) in the Zona Dorada, at El Cid resort and at almost any of the large hotels north of the center.

SPORTFISHING

Mazatlán is world famous for its sportfishing – especially for marlin, swordfish, sailfish, tuna and *dorado* (dolphinfish). It's an expensive activity (around US$350 for a day in a boat with three people fishing), though small-game fishing is less expensive, especially with a group of five or six. All operators should offer tag-and-release options. For the winter high season, make fishing reservations as far in advance as you can.

There are several established big-game fishing operators based at the boat dock on the peninsula:

El Cid Mega Resort (Map p413; ☎ 916-24-68 ext 6598, 800-525-19-25; www.elcid.com)
Flota Bibi (Map p413; ☎ 981-36-40; www.bibifleet.com)
Flota Saballo (Map p413; ☎ 981-27-61)
Star Fleet (Map p413; ☎ 982-26-65; www.starfleet.com.mx)
Viking (Map p413; ☎ 986-34-84)

WATER SPORTS

The **Aqua Sport Centre** (Map p413; ☎ 916-24-68, ext 6598; El Cid Mega Resort) is the place to go for water sports, including scuba diving, water-skiing, catamaran sailing, parasailing, boogie boarding and riding the 'big banana.' Water-sports equipment can also be hired on the beaches in front of most of the other large beachfront hotels.

The best surf breaks are the right hander at Punta Camarón, and 'Cannons,' the left off the point near the old fort on Paseo Olas Altas, as well as the breaks off Isla de la Piedra.

Courses

Centro de Idiomas (Map p416; ☎ 985-56-06; Domínguez 1908; www.go2mazatlan.com/spanish; 2hr/5hr classes per week US$130/160) charges registration fees from US$100 to US$140 depending on how far in advance you register. The center offers Spanish courses from Monday to Friday with a maximum of six students per class. You can begin any Monday and study for as many weeks as you like; registration is every Saturday morning from 9am to noon. There are discounts if you sign up for four weeks. Homestays (shared/private room US$142/160 per week) can be arranged with a Mexican family and include three meals a day (30-day advance notice required).

Mazatlán for Children

Between the center and the Zona Dorada, the **Acuario Mazatlán** (Map p413; ☎ 981-78-15; Av de los Deportes s/n; adult/child US$5/2.25; ♥ 9:30am-5:30pm), a block inland from Playa Norte, has 52 tanks with 250 species of fresh and saltwater fish and other creatures. Sea lion and bird shows are presented four times daily.

North of the marina, **MazAgua** (☎ 988-00-41; Entronque Habal-Cerritos s/n; admission US$8.50; ♥ 10am-6pm Mar-Dec) is a family aquatic park with water toboggans, a wave pool and other entertainment. The 'Cerritos-Juárez' bus takes you there from anywhere along the coastal road.

Tours

LAND TOURS

Many companies offer a variety of tours in and around Mazatlán. Prices are about the same from company to company for the same tours: a three-hour city tour (US$20); a colonial tour to the foothill towns of Concordia and Copala (US$32); and a tequila factory tour that includes the village of La Noria (US$30). If you make reservations, by calling or having a travel agent book for you ahead of time, they will pick you up from your hotel. Paying in pesos yields a better deal. Recommended agencies:

Hudson Tours (Map p413; ☎ 913-17-64; www.hudson tours.com; Ibis 502, Apartamentos Fiesta) Smaller more personalized tours including shopping and spearfishing.
Marlin Tours (Map p413; ☎ 913-53-01; Av Camarón Sábalo 1504, Local 113; www.toursinmazatlan.com; ♥ office 8:30am-6pm) Friendly and long-standing.
Vista Tours (Map p413; ☎ 986-83-83; Av Camarón Sábalo 51, Local 2 & 3; www.vistatours.com.mx) Bigger range to choose from, including Cosalá and the San Ignacio Missions.

BOAT TOURS

As well as trips to **Isla de Venados** (see Islands, p417), several boats do three-hour sightseeing trips, mostly leaving from the marina near El Faro at 11am (US$11 including hotel transfers). Two-hour sunset cruises, sometimes called 'booze cruises,' include hors d'oeuvres and an open bar (US$19 to US$23). To find out what's going on, look for flyers around town, talk to a tour agent or call the operators of boats such as **Costalegre** (Map p413; ☎ 982-31-30; Calz Joel Montes Camarena 7) and **Yate Fiesta** (Map p413; ☎ 981-71-54; Calz Joel Montes Camarena s/n).

Festivals & Events

Mazatlán has one of Mexico's most flamboyant **Carnaval** celebrations. For the week leading up to Ash Wednesday (the Wednesday 46 days before Easter Sunday), Mazatlán goes on a nonstop partying spree. People from around the country (and beyond) pour in for the music, dancing and general revelry. Be sure to reserve a hotel room in advance. The party ends abruptly on the morning of **Ash Wednesday**, when Roman Catholics go to church to receive ash marks on their foreheads for the first day of Lent.

A *torneo de pesca* (fishing tournament) for sailfish, marlin and *dorado* is held in mid-May and mid-November. Golf tournaments and various cultural festivals are held throughout the year; the tourist office has details.

On December 12 the day of the **Virgen de Guadalupe** is celebrated at the cathedral. Children come in colorful costumes.

Sleeping

Mazatlán's most luxurious hotels front the beaches north of the Zona Dorada, where the mid-range hotels rule. Most budget options are south of the Zona Dorada and in the center overlooking Playa Olas Altas. The following prices are for high season; lower rates may be available from May through October, or for longer stays.

BUDGET

Several of the hotels on Playa Olas Altas enjoyed their heyday in the 1960s and while they are clean and welcoming, they're also a bit faded.

Hotel del Río (Map p416; ☎ 982-44-30; Juárez 2410; s/d US$9/11, r with air-con US$17; P ♥)

This mariachi hangout in a working-class neighborhood close to the beach is a long-time traveler favorite. Limited English is spoken and cable TV is available for US$2 more.

Hotel Perlamar (Map p416; ☎ 985-33-66; cnr Av del Mar & Isla Asada; r US$11, with air-con & TV US$19; ⓟ ✖) Off the main drag a few kilometers south of the Zona Dorada, this little lemon yellow hotel is cheaply built and cheaply priced. Rooms are crowded but modern.

Hotel Central (Map p416; ☎ 982-18-66; Domínguez 2; r US$26; ⓟ ✖) Making up in creature comforts for what it lacks in architectural charm, the Hotel Central is a well-kept, well-run place. Fully equipped with cable TV and mini-fridges, it's popular with Mexican business travelers.

Hotel México (Map p416; ☎ 981-38-06; hotelmex@ starmedia.com; México 201; s/d US$9/14) With colorful tiled floors, dusty curtains and rustic bathrooms, this family-run cheapie still has some colonial charm. Just a block from the beach, it's a good deal.

Las Jacarandas (Map p413; ☎ 984-11-77; Av del Mar 2500; r US$17, with view, air-con & TV US$34; ⓟ ✖ ✖) Tacky brick arches adorn this unfinished reddish block of modern rooms. It's a few hundred meters from the nightlife and has a full range of rooms.

Hotel San Diego (Map p413; ☎ 983-57-03; www .hotelsandiego.tripod.com; cnr Av del Mar & Ave Buelna; r US$23-34; ⓟ ✖ ✖) Spitting distance from the nightlife, the San Diego offers clean, pleasant, economical rooms with air-con and TV.

Hotel Belmar (Map p416; ☎ 985-11-12/13; Paseo Olas Altas 166 Sur; s/d US$23/27, with view, air-con & TV US$28/32; ✖ ✖) Even the 'renovated' portions of this totally faded 1960s classic don't make up for the rough edges. Ocean views from private balconies are striking, but the pool is permanently murky and other maintenance has clearly been deferred. The bar is where the action is.

Tent camping is possible under the palapas on Isla de Piedra, but the mainland is focused on serving the RV community. The following places offer weekly and monthly discounts.

Mar Rosa Trailer & RV Park (Map p413; ☎ /fax 913-61-87; mar_rosa@pacificpearl.com; Av Camarón Sábalo 702; sites US$13-25; ☙ Nov-Apr only) It lacks sufficient shade but the location is hard to beat. Prices reflect distance from the sea.

Other recommendations:

La Posta Trailer Park (Map p413; ☎ 983-53-10; Av Buelna 7; sites US$17; ▯ ✖) This place offers more services (broadband Internet, coin-op laundry and a covered party area) than comfort.

Las Palmas Trailer Park (Map p413; ☎ 913-53-11; Av Camarón Sábalo 333; sites US$16) Tucked between a couple of high-rises, it's semishaded.

MID-RANGE

Not every room in a mid-range hotel has air-con, so be sure to ask for it if you want it. The rooms and apartments in this price bracket are a great deal for families.

Royal Dutch B&B (Map p416; ☎ 981-43-96; roydutch@mzt.megared.net.mx; Constitución 627; s/d US$45/65; ✖) Choose from three lovingly and tastefully decorated rooms in this cozy 130-year-old colonial home in old town. Run by a Mexican-Dutch couple, prices include full European breakfast and 5pm tea time. This place is a true treasure in a world of impersonal hotels.

Hotel La Siesta (Map p416; ☎ 981-26-40, 800-711-52-29; www.lasiesta.com.mx in Spanish; Paseo Olas Altas 11 Sur; r US$32, with view US$51; ✖) La Siesta has a lush courtyard of overgrown plants and creaking stairways covered by worn Astroturf. All 51 spacious and tidy rooms have cable TV and a touch of character. Air-conditioning, however, is via a dated centralized system.

Hotel Sands (Map p413; ☎ 982-00-00; www.sands arenas.com in Spanish; Av del Mar 1910; r US$47, with view US$57; ⓟ ✖ ✖) With life-sized cartoon characters around the pool this is *the* place for kids. Rooms are spotless, modern and large and come with satellite TV and refrigerator. Best of all, the beds are firm.

Los Girasoles (☎ 913-52-88; fax 913-06-86; Av Gaviotas 709; apt US$50-59) In a pleasant residential area, these comfortable, spacious and sparkling-clean apartments share a well-tended pool and are worth the somewhat inconvenient location.

Hotel del Sol (Map p413; ☎ 985-11-03; Av del Mar 800; r US$25, with kitchen US$37; ⓟ ✖ ✖) Slowly undergoing superficial renovations, the Del Sol has basic, worn but clean rooms, a small pool and friendly management. Bigger rooms with kitchens are a good deal for families.

Hotel de Cima (Map p413; ☎ 985-74-00, 800-696-06-00; Av del Mar 48; r from US$28; ⓟ ✖ ✖) The paint is peeling in most of the rooms at this wannabe fancy hotel. It's clean and has a tunnel to the beach but it's only a tiny step up from the budget options. Don't pay a peso more than the semipermanent promotional rate.

Other recommendations:

Apartamentos Fiesta (Map p413; www.hudsontours .com; Ibis 502; apt from US$35) Good value apartments around a leafy garden.

Motel Los Arcos (Map p413; ☎ /fax 913-50-66; mlarcos@prodigy.net.mx; Playa Gaviotas 214; r from US$65) Comfortable, spacious and clean rooms on the beach.

TOP END

Rooms at Mazatlán's top end hotels can be reserved quite economically as part of a holiday package – see your travel agent or poke around online.

Aguamarina Hotel (Map p413; ☎ 981-70-80; www .aguamarina.com; Av del Mar 110; r/ste US$87/119; P ⊠ ⊠ ⌨) Although the pool fronts busy Av del Mar, it's still a nice place to sunbathe. The rooms aren't fancy but the service is top notch and there's a travel agency and restaurant-bar on the grounds. Discount rates (starting from US$55) are often available.

Hotel Posada Freeman (☎ 888-800-96-19; www .mazatlan.com.mx/freeman; Olas Altas 79 Sur; r/ste US$75/ 150; P ⊠ ⊠ ⌨) If you want a view of the ocean, fancy lobby and luxury amenities, Posada Freeman is the only place to stay. Originally built in 1949 and recently renovated to its original glory, it's got character and extra comfort.

El Cid Mega Resort (Map p413; ☎ 913-33-33; www .elcid.com.mx; Av Camarón Sábalo s/n; r/ste US$80/230; P ⊠ ⊠ ⌨ ⌨) Mega resort? This is a 1068-room, 2.9 sq km mini-city that has it all – seven pools, several dive shops, restaurants, travel agencies, kids' areas, gyms and more. If you want to get away from it all and keep vacation easy but entertaining, this is the place. It's best to reserve ahead of time to get the best deal; discounts are abundant.

Pueblo Bonito (Map p413; ☎ 914-37-00; www .pueblobonito.com; Av Camarón Sábalo 2121; ste US$130-270; P ⊠ ⊠ ⌨ ⌨) Overlooking a nearly private stretch of sandy beach, this upscale hotel has an elegant colonial façade, fantastic pool and all the facilities you'd expect at the top end.

Royal Villas Resort (Map p413; ☎ 916-61-61, 800-696-70-00; www.royalvillas.com.mx; Av Camarón Sá-

balo 500; ste US$187-$690; P ⊠ ⊠ ⌨ ⌨) The Royal Villas pyramid is better looking on the inside with fabulous rooms that sleep at least four. They all have kitchens and dining rooms, balconies and comfortable décor.

Eating

Mazatlán is famous for fresh seafood – the shrimp is especially fantastic. Also try *pescado zarandeado*, a delicious charcoalbroiled fish stuffed with onion, celery and spices. A whole kilo, feeding two people well, usually costs around US$10, while shrimp runs at US$6 to US$12 per dish. Standard Mexican meat and chicken dishes are available at most places too, and generally cost much less than seafood.

The most centrally located supermarket is **Marza Pack** (Map p416; cnr Serdán & Ángel Flores).

OLD MAZATLÁN   Map p416

In the heart of Old Mazatlán, Plazuela Machado is a delightful space with old Mexican tropical ambience. It's sublime in the evening when music plays, kids frolic, the plaza is softly lit and cool drinks, snacks and meals at outdoor tables help create a very romantic atmosphere.

Altazor Arts Café (☎ 981-55-59; Constitución 519; snacks US$2-4; ⏰ 9-1am Mon-Sat, 4pm-1am Sun) Live music starts at 9pm at this popular, romantically lit cultural spot. Baguette sandwiches, pancakes and rich coffee are just a few of the simple treats available. Breakfast is lovely and movies are screened on Wednesday night.

Ambrosia (☎ 985-03-33; Sixto Osuna 26; mains US$4-7; ⏰ 11am-11pm; ⊠) This vegetarian delight has one of the largest and most creative menus going. Choose from tofu with *huitlacoche* (corn fungus) sauce, veggie *pozole* (a hearty stew) and salads galore. It's a simple place with good wine, good music and good coffee.

Beach Burger (☎ 981-43-56; Constitución 513; burgers US$2-4; ⏰ noon-midnight) If you like hamburgers, you won't be able to resist this southern-California-style joint. Beach Burger is a flowered-shirt and flip-flop sort of place with substantial servings. Delivery service available.

Pedro y Lola (☎ 982-25-89; Av Carnaval 1303; mains US$7-15) Named after the glamorous Mexican singers Pedro Infante and Lola Beltrán, this popular sidewalk restaurant-bar serves seafood, burgers and toned-down Mexican favorites. Good for both big groups or romantic couples. Beware: menu prices do not include tax.

Café Pacífico (☎ 981-39-72; Constitución 501; mains US$4-9; ☻ 10am-2am; 🞮) A bar, café or restaurant, depending on your needs, the Pacífico has been a mainstay on Plazuela Machado for years, thanks to its solid food, stiff drinks and friendly service.

El Machado (☎ 981-13-75; Sixto Osuna 34; mains US$4-10; ☻ 10am-midnight) The popular outdoor tables here are the perfect place for a couple of cold beers or an enormous margarita and a tasty fish taco or three.

Around the seafront, along Paseo Claussen and Paseo Olas Altas, assorted restaurant-cum-bars specialize in seafood and cold drinks. Most have outdoor tables, or open-sided seating areas.

Mariscos El Camichín (☎ 985-01-97; Paseo Claussen 97; mains US$5-11; ☻ 11am-10pm) Facing Playa Norte, this popular open-air patio restaurant serves delicious seafood under a cool palapa roof.

Restaurant Los Pelícanos (☎ 982-43-45; cnr Paseo Claussen & Uribe; mains US$4-7; ☻ 10am-6pm) Basic, fresh and cheap, this small open-air thatched-roof place makes some of the tastiest seafood in Mazatlán. Sea views and breezes make it the gem of Playa Norte.

La Copa de Leche (☎ 982-57-53; Paseo Olas Altas 122; mains US$5-15) This sidewalk restaurant-bar is popular with the local gentry for breakfast, a filling and economical *comida corrida*, a snack, a drink or an evening coffee.

Puerto Viejo (☎ 928-82-26; Paseo Olas Altas 25; mains US$3-7; ☻ 11am-11pm Sun-Thu, 11-1am Fri & Sat) This super casual, inexpensive seafood restaurant and watering hole is popular with locals and expats, especially at sunset and in the evening, when the sea breeze comes through the open sides. Local bands play here weekend nights.

El Shrimp Bucket (☎ 981-63-50; Paseo Olas Altas 11; mains US$6-20; 🞮) Opened in 1963, the ever-popular Bucket was the first of the international chain of Carlos Anderson restaurants. It has a large and varied menu, sidewalk tables and an air-conditioned interior. Live music on weekends.

ZONA DORADA & AROUND   Map p413
Zona Dorada restaurants cater mainly to the tourist trade.

Tacos Luna (Av Camarón Sábalo 400 block; tacos US$0.75; ☻ noon-midnight) Something of an oversized taco stand with an extra-large grill and a whole lot of plastic chairs, this is the place to chow down local-style. Burgers, quesadillas and other grilled staples are well worth the lack of air-con or ocean breeze.

El Olivio (☎ 916-30-23; Av Las Gaviotas 205; mains US$ 2-10; 🞮) This upscale café and deli serves gourmet sandwiches, stiff coffee, crêpes, incredible salads, omelets and has plenty of vegetarian options. Double check the check before you pay.

Casa Loma (☎ 913-53-98; Av Las Gaviotas 104; mains US$8-17; ☻ 1:30-10:30pm; 🞮) Some say Casa Loma is the best restaurant in Mazatlán. Escape the tourist scene and enjoy a sophisticated and high-quality meal in a homey atmosphere.

Panchos (☎ 914-09-11; Av Loaiza 408/1B; mains US$5-17; ☻ 7am-midnight) Overlooking Playa Las Gaviotas, Panchos is the perfect place for a tasty Mexican or American breakfast, light lunch, sunset snack or big dinner. It's pricey but super-clean and the food is high quality.

No Name Café (☎ 913-20-31; Av Loaiza 417; mains $5-15; ☻ 8-1am; 🞮) With a huge norteamericano-mexicano menu, this US-style sports bar with 'the best damn ribs you'll ever eat,' a mile-long drink list, big screens and a tropical patio keeps a loyal clientele.

Señor Frog's (☎ 985-11-10; Av del Mar s/n; mains US$6-20; ☻ noon-1am; 🞮) Halfway between the Zona Dorada and the center is a Mazatlán landmark, and another link in the Carlos Anderson chain. The food is OK (perhaps overpriced), but Frog's is mainly a party place (and merchandizing gimmick).

**FERRY TERMINAL & ISLA
DE LA PIEDRA**   Map p413
Mariscos La Puntilla (☎ 982-88-77; Flota Playa Sur s/n; mains US$5-15; ☻ 10am-7pm) Popular with Mexican families on the weekends, this open-air seafood specialist has a relaxed atmosphere and reliably good food. It's near the Isla de la Piedra ferries, on a small point with a view across the water.

Stroll along the beach on Isla de la Piedra and enjoy choosing where to eat. Check what's on offer at the open kitchens under the palapas. It's hard to beat a fresh barbecued fish and a cold beer as you wiggle your toes in the sand.

CENTRAL PACIFIC COAST

Drinking

Edgar's Bar (Map p416; cnr Serdán & Escobedo) For a taste of authentic Mazatlán, grab a pint or two at Edgar's, which has been a mainstay since 1949. It's well lit, adorned with original photographs, has a jukebox and welcomes women.

The **Bali Hai** bar, **Pepe & Joe's Microbrewery Restaurant** and **Mikonos** are all in the Fiesta Land complex (Map p413). Also see Nightclubs section (following).

Joe's Oyster Bar (Map p413; ☎ 983-53-33; Av Loaiza 100; cover US$5) Just 500m north of Fiesta Land, behind Hotel Los Sábalos, this beachfront bar is fine for a quiet drink until early evening, but it goes ballistic after 11pm when it's packed with college kids dancing on tables, chairs and each other.

Vitrolas's Bar (Map p416; www.vitrolasbar.com; Frias 1608; ☯ 5pm-1am Tue-Sun) For something more elegant, try this new gay bar in a beautifully restored building decorated with antiques. It's romantically lit, the bar is brass-edged and overall it's more button down than mesh muscle shirt.

Entertainment

No one will be bored in Mazatlán, with plenty of entertainment on offer. Choose from a full range of drinking and dancing spots, including a selection of gay venues, or take it easy at the movies. If you're looking for something a bit more refined, try the theater in the city's center.

CINEMAS

Check the local daily newspapers *El Sol del Pacífico* and *El Noroeste* for movie listings.

Cinemas Gaviotas (Map p413; Av Camarón Sábalo s/n; admission US$3, Wed US$1.50; ☒) This modern, six-screen movie house shows recent releases, some dubbed into Spanish and some with original English soundtrack and Spanish subtitles.

CULTURAL EVENTS

Teatro Ángela Peralta (Map p416; ☎ 982-44-46; www.teatroangelaperalta.com in Spanish; Carnaval 47) Old Mazatlán has become a buzzing little world of art and cultural events and the Teatro is the nucleus of the scene. Events of all kinds – movies, concerts, opera (Mazatlán has its own opera company), theater and more – are presented at this historic theater; a kiosk on the walkway in front of

the theater announces current and upcoming cultural events here and at other venues around town.

If you get a chance, try to hear a rousing traditional *banda sinaloense* – a boisterous brass band unique to the state of Sinaloa and especially associated with Mazatlán.

NIGHTCLUBS & DISCOS

Fiesta Land (Map p413; ☎ 984-17-77; Av del Mar s/n) The incongruous white castle on Punta Camarón, at the south end of the Zona Dorada, is a nightlife fun zone where several of Mazatlán's major venues are concentrated. There's a central ticket office with information about what's on at each venue. Nothing gets bumpin' until after midnight. Only in the lowest of low seasons do these places close their doors during the week; normally they pump the music nightly from 9pm to 4am. Cover charges usually don't kick in until after 11pm.

Valentino (Map p413; ☎ 984-16-66; in Fiesta Land; cover US$6-8; ☒) Well-dressed Mexican and foreign tourists, especially the 20- and 30-somethings, flock here for the dim lighting and limited range of pop, rap, disco and house music.

Bora Bora (Map p413; ☎ 984-16-66; in Fiesta Land; cover US$6) It's not clear if this beachfront bar is popular for its sand volleyball court, swimming pool, beachside dance floor or its lax policy on dancing on the bar.

Several hotels have nightclubs, music and dancing, though most are pretty sedate.

El Caracol (Map p413; ☎ 913-33-33; in El Cid Mega Resort; Av Camarón Sábalo s/n; cover $4-14; ☒) The cover here depends on the number of drinks included for the night. El Caracol attracts an upmarket crowd with throbbing techno music and fantastic lighting.

Hotel Playa Mazatlán (Map p413; ☎ 913-44-44; Av Loaiza 202; ☯ 7pm-midnight; ☒) This posh hotel's beachside restaurant-bar attracts the 30s-and-up crowd for dancing under the stars.

Señor Frog's (Map p413; ☎ 985-11-10; Av del Mar s/n; ☯ noon-1am; ☒) This is wild party central for the teens and 20-somethings, with loud music and a jam-packed dance floor.

Pepe Toro Gay Bar (Map p413; ☎ 914-41-76; www .pepetoro.com; Av de las Garza 18; ☯ Thu-Sun; ☒) This colorful and lively gay club attracts a fun-loving mixed crowd. On Saturday night there's a transvestite strip show at 1am. Staff also spin a good mix of danceable grooves.

FIESTAS MEXICANAS
Hotel Playa Mazatlán (Map p413; ☎ 913-44-44; Av Loaiza 202; admission US$26; ⏰ 7 10:30pm Tue, Thu & Sat; 😊) One of Mazatlán's few places where package tourists can get a dose of packaged Mexican culture is this hotel, where a Fiesta Mexicana (Mexican Party) features a buffet dinner, open bar, folkloric floor show and live Latin dance music. You can call the hotel for reservations or reserve at a travel agency.

SPORTS
Plaza de Toros (Map p413; Av Buelna) The Plaza de Toros, just inland from the Zona Dorada traffic circle, hosts bullfights from Christmas to Easter; the 'Sábalo-Cocos' bus will drop you there. Tickets for bullfights are available from travel agencies, major hotels, the Bora Bora shop beside Valentino disco and the **Salón Bacanora** (☎ 986-91-55; beside Plaza de Toros).

Charreadas (rodeos) are held at the **Lienzo Charro** (Map p413; ☎ 986-35-10; Peréz Arcé s/n in Colonia Juárez).

Shopping
Most of your tourist shopping needs will be met in the Zona Dorada, where plenty of clothes, pottery, jewelry and craft stores are located. Wander along Av Loaiza and you're sure to find something to bring home. Check out the strip mall on the streetside of Pancho's (see Eating, p421) for mass-produced cheapies. **Sea Shell City** (Map p413; Av Loaiza 407) is packed with an unbelievable assortment of you know what.

For something that's a bit more local, hop on a bus heading east to the Tianguis de Juárez (Juárez Flea Market), which is held every Sunday starting at 5am; the ride takes 20 minutes. You can't buy snake oil, but you can come close – snake skins, bootleg CDs, used clothes, housewares, tools, hamsters, taco stands and other Mexican treats are for sale.

Getting There & Away
AIR
The **Mazatlán international airport** (MZT; ☎ 928-04-38) is 20km southeast of the city. **America West** (☎ 981-11-84; Airport) flies direct to Phoenix and **Mexicana** (Map p413; ☎ 982-77-22; Av Camarón Sábalo, near Las Gaviotas) flies to Los Angeles. There are also offices in town for **Aero**

California (☎ 913-20-42; Airport) and **Aeroméxico** (Map p413; ☎ 982-34-44; Av Camarón Sábalo 310).

BOAT
Sematur (☎ 981-70-20/21, 800-728-95-33; www.ferry sematur.com.mx in Spanish; ⏰ ticket office 8am-3:30pm) operates ferries between Mazatlán and La Paz in Baja California Sur (actually to the port of Pichilingue, 23km from La Paz). The ferry to Pichilingue usually departs at 2:30pm (you should be there with ticket in hand at 2pm) daily except some Saturdays and the day before some holidays from the terminal at the southern end of town. Occasionally, the ferry carries cargo only, and doesn't take passengers. Tickets are sold from two days in advance until the morning of departure. See p287 for schedule and fare details.

BUS
The **Central de Autobuses** (main bus station; Map p413; Av de los Deportes, just off Av Ejército Méxicano) is three blocks inland from the northern end of Playa Norte, and ringed by inexpensive hotels. It's a full service station with a tourist module, phone offices, authorized taxi stands and left luggage service. All bus lines operate from separate halls in the main terminal. Local buses to small towns nearby (such as Concordia, Copala and Rosario) operate from a smaller terminal, behind the main terminal. There are several daily long-distance services:

Durango Elite (US$32, 7hr, 3 ejecutivo daily); Futura (US$24, 7hr, 7 1st-class daily)

Guadalajara Elite (US$36, 8hr, 2 ejecutivo daily); Futura (US$28, 8hr, 6 1st-class daily); TAP (US$24, 8hr, hourly 2nd-class)

Mexico City Elite (US$67, 17hr, 2 ejecutivo daily); Futura (US$63, 17hr, 6 1st-class daily); TAP (US$55, 17hr, frequent 2nd-class) To Terminal Norte.

Puerto Vallarta Elite (US$27, 8hr, 1st-class service at 4pm daily) Or take a bus to Tepic, where buses depart frequently for Puerto Vallarta.

Tepic Elite (US$13, 5hr, 5 1st-class daily); TAP (US$12, 5hr, 2nd-class at least hourly)

To get to San Blas (290km), go first to Tepic then get a bus from there. This involves some backtracking, but the alternative (getting off the bus at Crucero San Blas, and waiting there for a local bus to San Blas) is not safe. Travelers have been accosted at Crucero San Blas.

CAR & MOTORCYCLE

Shop around for the best rates, but don't expect to find much under US$50 per day. There are several rental agencies in town:

Aga (Map p413; ☎ 981-35-80; Av Camarón Sábalo 312)

Alamo (Map p413; ☎ 913-10-10; Av Camarón Sábalo 410)

Budget (Map p413; ☎ 913-20-00; Av Camarón Sábalo 402)

Hertz (Map p413; ☎ 913-60-60; Av Camarón Sábalo 314)

Getting Around

TO/FROM THE AIRPORT

Colectivo vans and a bus operate from the airport to town, but not from town to the airport. Taxis are about US$19.

BUS

Local buses run daily from 5:30am to 10:30pm. Regular white buses cost US$0.35; while Urban Pluss air-con green buses cost US$0.75. A useful route for visitors is the Sábalo-Centro, which travels from the market in the center to Playa Norte via Juárez, then north on Av del Mar to the Zona Dorada and further north on Av Camarón Sábalo. Another is Playa Sur, which travels south along Av Ejército Méxicano near the bus station and through the city center, passing the market, then to the ferry terminal and El Faro.

To get into the center of Mazatlán from the bus terminal, go to Av Ejército Mexicano and catch any bus going south (to your right if the bus terminal is behind you). Alternatively, you can walk 500m from the bus station to the beach and take a 'Sábalo-Centro' bus heading south (left) to the center.

MOTOR SCOOTERS

Various companies on Av Camarón Sábalo in the Zona Dorada rent out motor scooters – you'll see the bikes lined up beside the road. Prices are somewhat negotiable – anywhere from US$9 per hour to US$28 per day. You need a driver's license to hire one; a car license from any country will do.

PULMONÍAS & TAXIS

Mazatlán has a special type of taxi called a pulmonía, a small open-air vehicle similar to a golf cart – usually a modified VW. There are also regular red-and-white taxis and green-and-white taxis called 'eco-taxis' that have rates from US$2.25 to US$5 for trips around town. Pulmonías can be slightly cheaper (or much more expensive)

depending on your bargaining skills, time of day and whether there is a cruise ship in port or not.

AROUND MAZATLÁN

Several small, picturesque colonial towns in the Sierra Madre foothills make pleasant day trips from Mazatlán. **Concordia**, founded in 1565, has an 18th-century church with a baroque façade and elaborately decorated columns. Hot mineral springs are nearby. The village is known for its manufacture of high-quality pottery and hand-carved furniture. It's about a 45-minute drive east of Mazatlán; head southeast on Hwy 15 for 20km to Villa Unión, turn inland on Hwy 40 (the highway to Durango) and go another 20km.

Also founded in 1565, **Copala**, 40km past Concordia on Hwy 40, was one of Mexico's first mining towns. It still has its colonial church (1748), colonial houses and cobblestone streets.

Rosario, 76km southeast of Mazatlán on Hwy 15, founded in 1655, is another colonial mining town. Its most famous feature is the gold-leaf altar in its church, Nuestra Señora del Rosario.

In the mountains north of Mazatlán, **Cosalá** is a beautiful colonial mining village that dates from 1550. It has a 17th-century church, a historical and mining museum in a colonial mansion on the plaza, and two simple but clean hotels. Attractions nearby include **Vado Hondo**, a *balneario* (bathing place) with a large natural swimming pool and three waterfalls, 15km from town; **La Gruta México**, a large cave 18km from town; and the **Presa El Comedero** reservoir, 20km from town, with rowboats available for hire for fishing. To get to Cosalá, go north on Hwy 15 for 113km to the turnoff (opposite the turnoff for La Cruz de Alota on the coast) and then go about 45km up into the mountains.

Buses to all these places depart from the small bus terminal at the rear of the main bus station in Mazatlán. Alternatively, there are tours (see Tours p418).

SANTIAGO IXCUINTLA

☎ 323 / pop 18,000

Santiago Ixcuintla is mainly of interest as the jumping-off point for Mexcaltitán. It's not a tourist town but there are a couple of hotels near the market. **Hotel Casino** (☎ 235-08-50; cnr Ocampo & Rayón; s/d US$21/23; P ✖) is a pleasant, modern hotel with helpful owners.

Turn off Hwy 15 63km northwest of Tepic; Santiago Ixcuintla is about 7km west of the turnoff. Buses to Santiago Ixcuintla leave frequently from Tepic. From Mazatlán you must take a 2nd-class bus to Penas where frequent local buses go to Ixcuintla. Combis from Santiago Ixcuintla to La Batanga (the departure point for boats to Mexcaltitán) depart from the Terminal de Taxis Foráneos, three blocks north of the market, at 7am, 10am, noon and 2pm. The trip costs US$1.50 one way. Transportes del Pacífico also runs 2nd-class buses to La Batanga (US$2, one hour, 37km).

MEXCALTITÁN
☎ 323 / pop 1100
A small, ancient island village, Mexcaltitán is believed to be the original homeland of the Aztec people and was originally called Aztlán (Place of Egrets). Supposedly the Aztecs (also known as Mexica) left here around 1116 to begin the generations-long migration that eventually led them to Tenochtitlán (modern Mexico City) around 1325. It's also known as the 'Venice of Mexico' because at the end of the rainy season (September to November) the lagoon rises, water flows through the streets between the raised cement sidewalks, and all travel is done in canoes.

Tourism has scarcely touched the tiny, oval island. All telephones on the island go through one operator with a **switchboard** (☎ 232-02-11) in her living room. Mexcaltitán has one hotel, plenty of eateries and a small museum, making it a pleasant place to visit for a night.

To get there you must take a *lancha* (fast outboard boat) through a large mangrove lagoon full of fish and birds (and mosquitoes – bring repellent!)

Sights & Activities
The **Museo Aztlán del Origen** (admission US$0.50; ⏰ 9am-2pm & 4-7pm), on the northern side of the plaza, is small but enchanting. Among the exhibits are many interesting ancient objects and a fascinating long scroll, the Códice Ruturini, telling the story of the peregrinations of the Aztec people, with notes in Spanish.

You can arrange for **boat trips** on the lagoon for bird-watching, fishing and sightseeing – every family has one or more boats.

Festivals & Events
Semana Santa is celebrated in a big way here. On Good Friday a statue of Christ is put on a cross in the church, then taken down and carried through the streets. The **Fiesta de San Pedro Apóstol**, celebrating the patron saint of fishing, is on June 29. Statues of St Peter and St Paul are taken out into the lagoon in decorated lanchas for the blessing of the waters. Festivities start around June 20, leading up to the big day.

Sleeping & Eating
Hotel Ruta Azteca (☎ 232-02-11, ext 128; Venecia 5; s/d US$10/15) is almost charming in an ultra-rustic way. **Restaurant Alberca** (☎ 232-02-11, ext 128; mains US$5) is an east-shore restaurant specializing in shrimp and is only accessible by a rickety wooden walkway. It has a fabulous view of the lagoon as do several other seafood restaurants on the island.

Getting There & Away
From Santiago Ixcuintla, take a bus, taxi or colectivo to La Batanga, a small wharf where lanchas depart for Mexcaltitán. Colectivo lanchas' arrival and departure times are coordinated with the bus schedule. The boat journey takes 15 minutes and costs US$1 per person. If you miss the colectivo lancha you can hire a private lancha for US$5, between 8am and 6pm.

SAN BLAS
☎ 323 / pop 9000
The tranquil fishing village of San Blas, 70km northwest of Tepic, was an important Spanish port from the late 16th to the 19th century. The Spanish built a fortress here to protect their *naos* (trading galleons) from marauding British and French pirates. Today's visitors come to enjoy isolated beaches, abundant birdlife and tropical jungle reached by riverboats.

San Blas has the amenities of a small beach resort, but retains the character of a small Mexican village. The reason it hasn't been developed as a major resort is likely because of the proliferation of *jejenes* (sand flies), tiny gnat-like insects with huge appetites for human flesh; their bites will leave you with an indomitable itch. Abundant mosquitoes compete with the *jejenes* for your blood. During daylight hours they're not too active, but around sunset they appear from nowhere to attack. Use insect repellent, and check the screens in your hotel room. (Certain times seem to be relatively free of insects – if you find these warnings exaggerated, count yourself lucky.)

Orientation

San Blas sits on a tongue of land situated between Estuario El Pozo and Estuario San Cristóbal, with Playa El Borrego on the Pacific Ocean on the southern side. A 36km paved road connects San Blas with Hwy 15, the Tepic–Mazatlán road. This road goes through town as Av Juárez, the town's main east–west street. At the small zócalo it crosses Batallón de San Blas (Batallón for short), the main north–south street, which heads south to the beach. Everything in town, including the bus station on the zócalo, is within easy walking distance.

Information

Agencia de Cambio (Av Juárez s/n; ☾ 8am-2pm Mon-Sat) Prefers US dollars to any other currency.

Banamex (Av Juárez s/n) Has an ATM.

Cyber Met Alpha & Omega (Canalizo 4) One of several Internet places where you can connect for US$1.50 per hour.

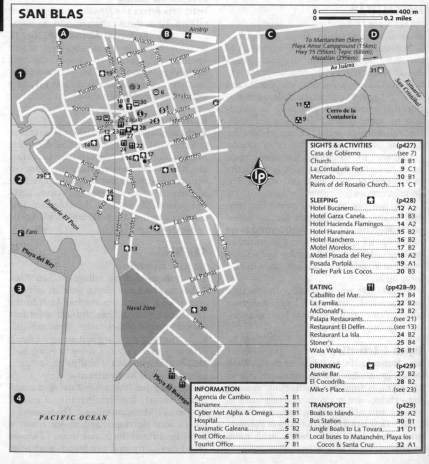

Lavamatic Galeana's (Batallón de San Blas s/n; load of laundry US$4.50)

Post office (Sonora at Echeverría) Isn't far from the public telephone-lined zócalo.

Tourist Office (☎ 285-00-05, 285-03-81; Casa de Gobierno, east side of the Zócalo; ☺ 9am-3pm Mon-Fri) This super-basic tourist office has a few maps and brochures about the area and the state of Nayarit. If the right person is working they can recommend guides and boat operators for specialized tours.

Sights & Activities

Although the beaches dominate here, everyone loves the boat tours through the estuaries where birds and wildlife abound.

BOAT TRIPS

A boat trip through the jungle to the freshwater spring of **La Tovara** is a real San Blas highlight. Small boats (maximum 13 passengers) depart from the *embarcadero* (jetty). Boats go up Estuario San Cristóbal to the spring, passing thick jungle vegetation and mangroves; you'll see exotic birds, turtles and perhaps a few crocodiles. Bring your swimsuit to swim at La Tovara; there's a restaurant there too.

For a few dollars more, you can extend the trip from La Tovara to the **Cocodrilario** (crocodile nursery), where reptiles are reared in captivity for later release in the wild. For a group of up to four people, it costs US$24 to go to La Tovara (3½ hours) and US$31 to the Cocodrilario (four hours). Each extra person costs US$6/9 to La Tovara/Cocodrilario. Shorter boat trips to La Tovara can be made from near Matanchén village, further up the river; they take an hour less and are a few dollars cheaper.

A five-hour bird-watching trip up the Estuario San Cristóbal to the **Santuario de Aves** (Bird Sanctuary), can be arranged at the same embarcadero by the bridge. Other boat trips depart from a landing on Estuario El Pozo. They include a trip to **Piedra Blanca** to visit the statue of the Virgin; to **Estero Casa Blanca** to gather clams; to **Isla del Rey** just across from San Blas; and to **Playa del Rey**, a 20km beach on the other side of Isla del Rey. It's not advisable for women to go to Playa del Rey alone.

You can make an interesting trip further afield to **Isla Isabel** (US$55 for four people), also called Isla María Isabelita, four hours northwest of San Blas by boat. Permission is required to visit the island and a couple of days is needed to appreciate it. The island is a bird-watcher's paradise, with colonies of many species and a volcanic crater lake. It's only about 1.5km long and 1km wide, with no facilities, so you need to be prepared for self-sufficient camping. For trips to Isla Isabel, ask at the Hotel Garza Canela or at the boat landing on Estuario El Pozo.

BEACHES

The beach closest to town is **Playa El Borrego**, at the end of Azueta. It's a wide, sandy surf beach with a few palapa restaurants; Stoner's (see Eating, p429) rents out surfboards, boogie boards and bikes. The surf here can be treacherous in some conditions – beware of rip currents and heed locals' warnings.

The best beaches are southeast of town around Bahía de Matanchén, starting with **Playa Las Islitas**, 7km from San Blas. To get there, take the road toward Hwy 15, and turn off to the right after about 4km. This paved road goes east past the village of Matanchén, where a dirt road goes south to Playa Las Islitas. The road continues on to follow 8km of wonderfully isolated beach. Further on, **Playa Los Cocos** and **Playa Miramar**, also popular for surfing, have palapas under which you can lounge and drink fresh coconut milk. Santa Cruz, about 16km from San Blas along the same road, has a pebble beach and simple accommodations.

A few times a year, when the swell and tides are right (usually in September and October), the world's longest surfable waves curl into Matanchén Bay – 1.7km according to the *Guinness Book of Records*.

CERRO DE LA CONTADURÍA

Just west of the bridge over Estuario San Cristóbal, the road passes the Cerro de la Contaduría. Climb up and see the ruins of the 18th-century Spanish **La Contaduría Fort and del Rosario church** (admission US$0.70); there's a fine view from the top.

Festivals & Events

Every year on January 31 the anniversary of the death of **Father José María Mercado** is commemorated with a parade, a march by the Mexican navy and fireworks in the zócalo. Mercado lived in San Blas in the early 19th century and helped Miguel Hidalgo with the independence movement by sending him a set of old Spanish cannons from the village.

On February 3 festivities for **San Blas**, the town's patron saint, are an extension of those begun on January 31, with dance and musical presentations. **Carnaval** is celebrated the weekend before Ash Wednesday. The **Virgen de Fátima** is honored on May 13. The **Día de la Marina** is celebrated on June 1 with burro races on the beach, sporting events, dances and partying.

Sleeping

San Blas has plenty of very reasonably priced hotels, but only the Hotel Hacienda Flamingos is noteworthy.

BUDGET

Hotel Ranchero (☎ 285-08-92; Batallón de San Blas 102; r US$16, without bath $11) Basic and friendly, this popular place has eight rooms and a communal kitchen for guests.

Posada Portolá (☎ 285-02-85; Paredes 118; bungalows US$19) The few recently remodeled family-sized bungalows with kitchens are a much better deal than the older, worn originals. All rooms are spacious.

Hotel Bucanero (☎ 285-01-01; Av Juárez 75; s/d US$12/17; P 🐾) This place has seen better days; the linen is clean, but bathrooms are missing tiles and the visibility in the pool is about six inches. It has character and a lively weekend disco next door.

Motel Morelos (Batallón 108; r US$16) is stark but homey, with rooms around a central courtyard.

Tent campers should be prepared for the swarms of insects, especially at sunset. There are a couple of options:

Trailer Park Los Cocos (☎ 285-00-55; Azueta s/n; tent/RV sites US$12/14) Pleasant, grassy and very-green with just enough trees.

Playa Amor (Playa Los Cocos; tent/RV sites US$7.50/13) A 15-minute drive from town, it's attractive and on the beachfront with sunset views and few mosquitoes.

MID-RANGE & TOP-END

Hotel Hacienda Flamingos (☎ 285-09-30; www.san blas.com.mx; Av Juárez 105; s/d US$49/60; 🐾 🔊) This superbly restored colonial gem is the classiest and best deal in town. All of the spacious rooms around the quaint courtyard have been tastefully modernized with coffeemakers and TVs. The swimming pool is surrounded by a pleasant, green garden.

Hotel Haramara (Guerrero 66; apt US$55-64; P 🐾) These sparklingly clean, new apartments located around a stark parking lot are a very good deal for parties of four who plan on staying a while. Kitchens are full-size, sitting areas are ample and mattresses are firm. If no one is around ring the bell across the street.

Hotel Posada del Rey (☎ 285-01-23; www.san blasmexico.com/posadadelrey; Campeche 10; s/d US$28/33; 🐾 🔲 🔊) Clean, modern rooms surround a cozy courtyard with a swimming pool. It's a family run business with a low-key but friendly atmosphere. There is a small bar and restaurant in the high season.

Hotel Garza Canela (☎ 285-01-12; www.garzacanela .com; Paredes 106 Sur; s/d/ste US$100/128/182; P 🐾 🔊) Modern, professional and comfortable, the Garza Canela is a reliable top-end choice. Standard rooms are spacious and decorated in colonial style, while the suites are enormous and contemporary with frosted glass and marble floors. It's also home to the best restaurant (see Restaurant El Delfin, below) and gift shop in town.

Eating

San Blas is a casual town with casual restaurants, all serving fresh seafood.

Restaurant El Delfin (☎ 285-01-12; at Hotel Garza Canela; mains US$7-15; 🐾) This colorfully decorated restaurant serves an impressive array of rich, gourmet dishes. Choose from items like green salad with kiwi, anise accented fish or cumin peppered shrimp. Desserts are magnificent and the international wines are reasonably priced.

McDonald's (☎ 285-04-32; Av Juárez 36; mains US$4-8) No relation to the burger chain, this old travelers' hangout serves filling food at reasonable prices.

Wala Wala (☎ 285-08-63; Av Juárez 94; mains $5-8; 🕑 closed Sun) This cheerfully decorated restaurant serves inexpensive, tasty, home-style meals. It's mostly basic Mexican and pasta with a few specialties such as lobster and *pollo con naranja*.

Restaurant La Isla (☎ 285-04-07; cnr Paredes & Mercado; mains US$5-8; 🕑 2-9pm Tue-Sun; 🐾) Fresh seafood is well done at this sea-shell clad, family-run restaurant. Don't let the décor dissuade you.

La Familia (☎ 285-02-58; Batallón de San Blas 16; mains US$ 4-8) Decorated in a bottom-of-the-sea spirit, this family restaurant asks moderate prices for wonderful seafood and Mexican dishes.

If you're looking to eat where the waves crash, head to Playa El Borrego where palapas line the beach. **Caballito del Mar** (Playa El Borrego; mains US$4-7) cooks up remarkably sophisticated seafood dishes and **Stoner's** (Playa El Borrego; mains US$3.50-5.50) is a traveler hangout with good music, lots of hammocks and well-prepared Western food (including vegetarian).

Drinking

It's a pretty, tranquil, little place, but San Blas does have more than one watering hole to choose from. **El Cocodrilo** (Av Juárez 6; ☺ 5:30-10:30pm) attracts gringos in the evening, **Mike's Place** (Av Juárez 36, above McDonald's) has live music and the **Aussie Bar** (Av Juárez 34) is an upstairs pool room and bar, frequented by surfers, travelers and local youth.

Getting There & Around

The little **bus station** (cnr Sinaloa & Canalizo) is served by Estrella Blanca 2nd-class buses. For many destinations to the south and east, it may be quicker to go to Tepic first.
Guadalajara (US$16, 5hr, 7am daily)
Mazatlán (US$11, 4½hr, 12:30pm daily) Or go via Tepic – but don't go to the highway and wait at Crucero San Blas for a Mazatlán bus, as it's not a safe place to wait.
Puerto Vallarta (US$9, 3½hr, 5 daily)
Santiago Ixcuintla (US$2.25, 1hr, hourly)
Tepic (US$3.75, 1hr, frequently)

Buses also depart from the corner of Sinaloa and Paredes several times a day, serving all the villages and beaches on Bahía de Matanchén, including Matanchén, Playa Las Islitas, Aticama, Playa Los Cocos, Playa Miramar and Santa Cruz, at the far end of the bay.

Taxis will take you around town and to nearby beaches – a good option with two or more people. Rent bicycles from Wala Wala restaurant for about US$1 per hour.

TEPIC

☎ 311 / pop 272,000 / elevation 920m
Tepic is the bustling capital of Nayarit. It's where Hwy 15/15D meets the start of Hwy 200; from here Hwy 15/15D turns inland toward Guadalajara and Mexico City, while Hwy 200 runs southwest to the coast. Local time is one hour behind Puerto Vallarta and Guadalajara in the neighboring state of Jalisco.

Many travelers pass through the outskirts of Tepic without stopping off. But it doesn't take long to visit the city, and there are a few things of interest, including a large neo-Gothic cathedral and several museums. Indigenous Huicholes are often seen here, wearing their colorful traditional clothing, and Huichol artwork is sold on the street and in several shops. Tepic's climate is noticeably cooler than on the coast.

Orientation

Plaza Principal, with the large cathedral at the eastern end, is the heart of the city. Av México, the city's main street, runs south from the cathedral to Plaza Constituyentes, past banks, restaurants, the state museum and other places of interest. The bus station is on the southeastern side of the city with plenty of buses serving the center. Peripheral roads allow traffic to pass through Tepic without entering the city center.

Information

The **state tourist office** (☎ 216-56-61, 212-08-36; www.turismonayarit.gob.mx; cnr Puebla Nte & Nervo Pte; ☺ 9am-8pm) is a great resource with free maps and extensive information about everything in Tepic and the state of Nayarit. The **Secretaría de Turismo** (☎ 214-80-71; Ex-Convento de la Cruz de Zacate, Av México s/n; ☺ 8am-8pm), 2km south of the center, is less convenient but just as helpful.

Banks and casas de cambio line Av México Nte between the two plazas.

The **post office** (Durango Sur s/n) is not next to **Telecomm** (Av México 50 Nte), which offers the usual phone and fax services. Post and Telecomm offices, and card phones, are also in the bus station.

You can access the Internet at **Cafetería La Parroquia** (Nervo 18; per hr US$1.50) or **@net.com** (Av México Sur s/n, Plaza Milenio; per hr US$1).

Sights

The large **cathedral** on Plaza Principal was dedicated in 1750; the towers were completed in 1885. Opposite the cathedral is the **Palacio Municipal** (city hall), where colorfully dressed Huicholes sell handicrafts under the arches at very reasonable prices. On Av México, south of the plaza, look inside the Palacio de

Gobierno and the Cámara de Diputados to see some impressive and colorful **murals**.

The 18th-century **Templo y Ex-Convento de la Cruz de Zacate** (cnr Calz del Ejército & Av México) is about 2km south of the cathedral. It was here in 1767 that Father Junípero Serra organized his expedition that established the chain of Spanish missions in the Californias; you can visit the room where he stayed, but there's not much else to see. In the southwest section of the city is the large **Parque Paseo de la Loma**.

The **Museo Regional de Nayarit** (☎ 212-19-00; Av México 91 Nte; admission US$3; ☙ 9am-7pm Mon-Fri, 9am-3pm Sat) displays a variety of exhibits on pre-Hispanic times including ancient tomb artifacts, as well as colonial painting and Huichol culture. The **Casa y Museo Amado Nervo** (☎ 212-29-16; Zacatecas 284 Nte; admission free; ☙ 9am-2pm Mon-Fri, 10am-2pm Sat) celebrates the life of the poet Amado Nervo, who was born in this house in 1870. The **Casa Museo Juan Escutia** (☎ 212-33-90; Hidalgo 71 Ote; admission free; ☙ 9am-2pm & 4-7pm Mon-Fri) was the home of Juan Escutia, one of Mexico's illustrious Niños Héroes (child heroes), who died in

1847 at age 17 defending Mexico City's Castillo de Chapultepec from US forces. Opposite, the **Casa de los Cuatro Pueblos** (☎ 212-17-05; Hidalgo 60 Ote; admission free; ☙ 9am-2pm & 4-7pm Mon-Thu, 9am-1pm Fri & Sat) displays contemporary popular arts of the Nayarit's Huichol, Cora, Nahua and Tepehuano peoples, including clothing, yarn art, weaving, musical instruments, ceramics and beadwork.

Aramara (☎ 216-42-46; Allende 329 Pte; admission free; ☙ 9am-2pm & 4-7pm Mon-Sat, 10am-3pm Sun) is another museum of visual arts. The **Museo Emilia Ortiz** (☎ 212-26-52; Lerdo 192 Pte; admission free; ☙ 9am-7pm Mon-Sat) honors the painter Emilia Ortiz and her work.

Sleeping

The cheapest hotels are near the bus station. There's a good selection of more comfortable hotels in the center.

Hotel Tepic (☎ 213-17-77; fax 210-05-45; Dr Martinez 438 Ote; s/d US$9/11) This hotel around 1km from the center has 85 small, clean rooms; add US$1.75 for TV.

Hotel Cibrian (☎ 212-86-98; Nervo 163 Pte; s/d US$15/19) This central hotel has clean, bright

---

TEPIC

0 ————— 400 m
0 ————— 0.2 miles

Bravo Poniente
Zaragoza Poniente
Amado Nervo Poniente
Lerdo Poniente
Hidalgo Poniente
Zapata Poniente
Morelos Poniente
Allende Poniente
Abasolo Poniente
Mina Poniente
Mercado Poniente
Durango Sur

Río Mololoa
Puebla Nte
Zaragoza Oriente
Amado Nervo Oriente
Plaza Principal
Market
Zaragoza Oriente
Guerrero
Plaza
Lerdo Oriente
Hidalgo Oriente
Zapata Oriente
Morelos Oriente
Allende Oriente
Abasolo Oriente
Sanchez Norte
San Luis Potosi Oriente
Plaza Constituyentes
Av Juárez

León Norte
Querétaro Norte
Durango Norte
México Norte
Veracruz Norte
Zacatecas Norte
Querétaro Sur
México Sur
Zacatecas Sur

To Aramara
(1km); Parque la
Alameda (1km);
Stadium (1.3km)

To Hotel Tepic (1km);
Bus Station (1km);
Airport (12km); Laguna
Santa María del Oro (58km)

Parque Paseo de La Loma

To Templo y Ex-Convento
de la Cruz de Zacate (1.5km);
Trailer Park Los Pinos (5km);
Puerto Vallarta (168km)

Volcán Ceborucco (98km); Guadalajara (216km)

rooms with TV, telephone and enclosed parking.

Hotel Ibarra (☎ 212-32-97; Durango 297 Nte; s/d US$23/25) Smallish but comfortable rooms, cable TV, telephone, parking and good service make this place popular with business travelers on a budget.

Hotel Sierra de Alica (☎ 212-03-22; hotelsierra dealica_h@hotmail.com; Av México 180 Nte; s/d US$23/40; (P)(X)) Just a block south of the cathedral, the standard rooms at this hotel have ceiling fans, phones, cable TV and exterior windows and are good value. Air-con rooms are slightly bigger.

Hotel Fray Junípero Serra (☎ 212-25-25; www .frayjunipero.com.mx in Spanish; Lerdo 23 Pte; s/d/ste US$49/54/64) Rooms in this modern hotel have all the facilities you'll need, and some have a view over the plaza.

Hotel Real de Don Juan (☎ /fax 216-18-88; Av México 105 Sur; r/ste US$58/78) Though it looks old and has some character, this hotel is thoroughly modern. It's possibly the best place to stay in downtown Tepic.

Trailer Park Los Pinos (☎ 213-12-32; Blvd Tepic-Xalisco 150; RV sites US$12, bungalows US$16) About 5km south of town, this park offers 18 bungalows, all with kitchens, and 27 trailer spaces with full hookups.

Eating & Drinking

Tepic has a good selection of vegetarian restaurants, but their local specialties are shrimp based.

Quetzalcóatl (☎ 212-99-66; León 224 Nte; mains under US$4; ☯ closed Sun) A friendly, inexpensive vegetarian restaurant with a pretty courtyard, relaxing music and tasteful décor.

Cafetería La Parroquia (Nervo 18; snacks US$1-3.50) On the northern side of the plaza, upstairs under the arches, this place is very pleasant for breakfasts, drinks and inexpensive light meals, and it does good coffee.

Cafetería y Restaurant Diligencias (☎ 212-15-35; Av México 29 Sur; mains US$2-4) Popular with locals for its *comida corrida*, Diligencias serves up quality coffee, snacks and full meals all day long.

El Trigal (☎ 216-40-04; Veracruz 112 Nte; mains under US$3) This inexpensive vegetarian restaurant has tables in an attractive courtyard. Offerings include wholemeal quesadillas, veggie burgers and an excellent *menú del día*.

La Gloria (☎ 217-04-22; cnr Lerdo & Av México; mains US$5-9) With live music and tables on a balcony overlooking the plaza, La Gloria is an especially enjoyable place for an evening meal. The menu is a little more adventurous than the average, and includes a selection of fresh seafood.

Getting There & Away

AIR

Tepic's **airport** (TPQ; ☎ 214-18-50) is in Pantanal, a 20-minute drive from Tepic, going toward Guadalajara. **Aero California** (☎ 214-23-20) and **Aeroméxico** (☎ 213-90-47) offer direct flights to Mexico City and Tijuana, with connections to other centers. Both airlines have offices at the airport.

BUS

The bus station is on the southeastern outskirts of town; local buses marked 'Central' and 'Centro' make frequent trips between the bus station and the city center. The bus station has a cafeteria, left-luggage office, shops, post office, tourist information, card phones, a Telecomm office and an ATM.

The main bus companies are Elite, Futura, Estrella Blanca and Ómnibus de México (all 1st-class), Transportes del Pacífico (1st- and 2nd-class) and TNS (2nd-class). Departures include the following:

Guadalajara (US$19, 3hr, frequent 1st-class; US$17, 3hr, frequent 2nd-class)
Ixtlán del Río (US$5, 1hr, 6 daily) Take an Ómnibus de México bus toward Guadalajara that is not *por autopista*.
Mazatlán (US$14, 4½-5hr, hourly 1st-class; US$12, 4½-5hr, hourly 2nd-class)
Mexico City (US$48, 10-11hr, hourly 1st-class; US$46, 10-11hr, hourly 2nd-class) To Terminal Norte.
Puerto Vallarta Elite (US$12, 3½hr, 1st-class 9pm daily); Transportes del Pacífico (US$10, 3½hr, hourly 2nd-class services 3am-10pm)
San Blas TNS (US$2.75, 1¼hr, hourly 6am-7pm)
Santiago Ixcuintla TNS (US$2.75, 1½hr, half-hourly 5:30am-8pm)

Getting Around

Local buses operate from around 6am to 9pm (US$0.30). Combis operate along Av México from 6am to midnight (US$0.30). There are also plenty of taxis.

AROUND TEPIC
Laguna Santa María del Oro

Idyllic Laguna Santa María del Oro (elevation 730m), surrounded by steep, forested mountains, is in a volcanic crater 2km around and thought to be over 100m deep. The clear, clean water takes on colors ranging from turquoise to slate. You can take some very pleasant walks around the lake and in the surrounding mountains, seeing numerous birds (some 250 species) and butterflies along the way. You can also climb to an abandoned gold mine, cycle, swim, row on the lake, kayak, or fish for black bass and perch. A few small restaurants serve fresh lake fish.

Koala Bungalows & RV Park (in Santa Maria del Oro; ☎ 327-244-02-37; tent/trailer/bungalow per person US$5/10/43) is an attractive, peaceful park with a restaurant, campsites and well-maintained bungalows in several sizes (with cheaper monthly rates). It's owned and operated by a friendly Englishman, who's an excellent source of information about the lake.

To get there, take the Santa María del Oro turnoff about 40km from Tepic along the Guadalajara road; from the turnoff it's about 10km to Santa María del Oro, then another 8km from the village to the lake. Buses to the lake depart from in front of the bus station in Tepic three times daily (US$2, one hour). Alternatively, buses to the village of Santa María del Oro depart from the bus station in Tepic every half-hour; from there you can take another bus (or a taxi) to the lake.

Volcán Ceboruco

This sleeping volcano, with a number of old craters, interesting plants and volcanic forms, has several short, interesting walks at the top. The 15km cobblestone road up the volcano passes lava fields and *fumaroles* (steam vents), with plenty of vegetation growing on the slopes. The road begins at the village of Jala, 7km off the highway from Tepic to Guadalajara; the turnoff is 76km from Tepic, and 12km before you reach Ixtlán del Río.

CHACALA
☎ 327

The tiny coastal fishing village of Chacala, about 1½ hours north of Puerto Vallarta and 10km west of Las Varas on Hwy 200, is a rustic fishing village on an amazingly beautiful little cove. Its kilometer of sandy beach is backed by lush green slopes and edged by rugged black rocks at either end. Camping is possible at several of the beachside palapas, but there are also some unique accommodations to choose from. The closest ATM and Internet service is in Las Varas.

The mama of Chacala bay, **Mar de Jade** (☎ 294-11-63; www.mardejade.com; Playa Chacala s/n; s/d US$90/120, ste US$110/140) is a bed and breakfast, retreat/workshop center, spa, Spanish school, organic farm, arts center and home for doctors doing a couple weeks of residency at a clinic run by the owner, Dr Laura del Valle. The result is a relaxing atmosphere in the company of some very interesting people. Three generous, healthy meals are included and mealtime is something of a thought exchange. Yoga and meditation are typical morning activities. Discounts are occasionally available for work-exchange and folks participating in workshops.

Majahua (☎ in Mexico City 5514-2983; www.majahua.com; Playa Chacala s/n; ste US$91-137) is an earthy eco-lodge with five beautifully designed rooms, a fantastic outdoor restaurant and spa services. It's just up the road from Mar de Jade.

Folks interested in getting to know locals should check out **Techos de Mexico** (☎ 275-02-82; www.playachacala.com/techos.htm; r US$21-40), a series of seven homes with room for up to four people. Rooms are separate from the host home, updated but basic and some come with kitchen.

For Chacala, get off a Puerto Vallarta–Tepic bus at Las Varas (US$16) and take a collective taxi from there (US$2, 15 minutes). A private taxi from Puerto Vallarta will set you back about US$55.

RINCÓN DE GUAYABITOS
☎ 327 / pop 3000

On the coast about 60km north of Puerto Vallarta, Rincón de Guayabitos ('Guayabitos' for short) is a tailor-made beach resort town catering to Mexican holidaymakers and winter visitors from Canada and other cold places. It's nothing fancy and shows its weathered age. It gets overrun during Semana Santa, Christmas, and the July and August school holidays. Weekends are busy, but the beautiful beach is practically empty the rest of the week. Activities include swimming, fishing, horseback riding and hiking up to the cross on the hill for the fine view. You can also take a boat out to Isla Islote, where you can rent snorkeling gear and eat in the restaurant. Boats do whale-watching trips from November to March.

Orientation & Information
Rincón de Guayabitos is just west of Hwy 200. At the northern entrance to town, a high water tower is a distinctive landmark; turn into town here, follow the curve around, and you'll be on Guayabitos' main street, Av del Sol Nuevo, lined with shops, restaurants and hotels. More restaurants and hotels are along the beach, two blocks over – they're reached by side streets as there's no road along the waterfront.

Near the water tower, the **Delegación de Turismo** (☎ 274-06-93; Av del Sol Nuevo s/n) provides information about the local area and the state of Nayarit. Guayabitos has a post office, but for Internet access, locals go to La Peñita de Jaltemba, a larger and less touristy town a couple of kilometers north on Hwy 200.

Sleeping
Most hotels in Rincón de Guayabitos are mid-range places pitched at Mexican families, offering bungalows with kitchen facilities and accommodations for two, four or more people.

Hotel Posada la Misión (☎ 274-03-57; Retorno Tabachines 6; r US$41, bungalows US$51; P ⊠ ⊡) There's a colonial theme going here, with beautiful tiles lining open halls in front, great sea views out the back, and a pretty, amoeba-shaped pool in the middle. Rooms are nice and quaint, and bungalows have balconies.

Villas Buena Vida (☎ 274-02-31; www.villasbuena vida.com; Retorno Laureles s/n; r US$64, ste US$91-119; P ⊠ ⊡) This luxurious hotel is a great place to splash out, with its beachfront swimming pool and balconies overlooking the ocean. Villas sleep one to four people; suites sleep five to six people.

Other recommendations:

Posada Jaltemba (☎ 274-01-65; cnr Av Sol Nuevo & Retorno Laureles; s/d US$30/50, bungalows US$38-85; P ⊠ ⊡) Variety of accommodations.

Paraíso del Pescador Trailer Park & Bungalows (☎ 274-00-14; paraisodelpescador@hotmail.com; Retorno Ceibas; tent & RV sites US$17, r US$55, ste US$110, 4-/8-person bungalows US$55/165) Stark and basic, but right on the beach.

Eating
Many eateries along Av del Sol Nuevo serve up ice cream, coffee, pizza and barbecued chicken.

Beto's (☎ 274-05-75; Av del Sol Nuevo s/n; mains US$4-9) In a block with several other restaurants, Beto's stands out for its fine seafood.

Rincón Mexicano (☎ 274-06-63; cnr Cedro & Retorno Laureles; mains US$6-11; ⊠ closed Wed) Attached to the beachfront Hotel Estancia San Carlos, this restaurant has a lunch and dinner menu with barbecue ribs, interesting beef dishes and imaginative meals such as shrimp in mango and red-wine sauce.

Getting There & Away
Second-class buses coming from Puerto Vallarta (US$6, 1½ hours) or Tepic (US$7, two hours) may drop you on the highway at Rincón de Guayabitos, but sometimes they don't stop here. A couple of kilometers toward Tepic, La Peñita is a sure stop. Colectivo vans operate frequently between La Peñita and Guayabitos (US$0.50, 10 minutes) or you can take a taxi (US$3).

AROUND RINCÓN DE GUAYABITOS
There are many pleasant little beach towns south of Rincón de Guayabitos that make good day trips from either Guayabitos or Puerto Vallarta; they all have places to stay and eat. Visit places like **Playa Los Ayala** (Km 96), about 2km south of Guayabitos, **Lo del Marco** (Km 108) and **San Francisco** (Km 118).

SAYULITA
☎ 329 / pop 1600
Sayulita is still low-key, but it has definitely been discovered and can feel crowded at times. The beautiful sandy beach, lined by homes and places to stay, is popular with surfers, especially novice surfers. There's are a couple of surf shops, two comfortable campgrounds and plenty of tasteful B&Bs. Places to eat range from cheap fish tacos on the street to full gourmet Mediterranean dinners on white linen. In addition to playing in the waves, boat trips, horseback riding, trekking and kayaking are all possible with a little help from operators on the main street.

Note that there's a time difference between Sayulita, which is in Nayarit state, and Puerto Vallarta, which is in Jalisco

(Nayarit is one hour behind Jalisco). There are no banks, casas de cambio or ATMs in Sayulita and most businesses are closed from May through November.

Information

Lava Zone (north side of plaza; load of laundry US$4) Offers self or full service laundry.

Sayulita Properties (☎ 291-30-76; Delfín 9; www .sayulitaproperties.com; ☻ 8am-8pm) Has tourist and rental information and Internet service (US$3.25).

Telephone office (Marlín s/n) Tiny office hiding inside the Bungalows Arbolitos office.

Sleeping

The following prices are for the winter high-season.

Bungalows Aurinko (☎ 291-31-50; www.sayulita -vacations.com; cnr Marlín & Revolución; 1-/2-bedroom bungalows US$68/106) Smooth riverstone floors, open-air kitchens, exposed raw beams and well appointed décor make this a very memorable place to stay. Huichol art adorns the walls while Oaxacan linen cover the beds.

Bungalows Las Gaviotas (☎ 291-32-18; Gaviotas 12; tr US$28, bungalow for 6 US$55; P) Friendly, basic and family-run, Las Gaviotas shows its years but it's only half a block from the beach.

Villa Amor (☎ 291-30-10; www.villaamor.com; villas US$58-292; ☙) Villa Amor's original villas have open showers, pipework sinks, integrated live trees, fabulous views and some have plunge pools. Newer rooms in a four-story building visible from anywhere on the beach are still comfortable but lack the same level of uniqueness.

El Camarón (Del Palmar s/n; sites/huts per person US$3.25) This grassy, kick-back spot, on the beach north of town, is the heart of the scene for young surfers and hippies. Basic structures with palapa roofs and damp mattresses are available for those without a tent. Beware: many come for a day and end up staying for months.

Sayulita Trailer Park & Bungalows (☎ 390-27-50; sayupark@prodigy.net.mx; Miramar s/n; tent & trailer sites with hookup US$12, bungalows US$23-60) Palm-shaded and right on the beach, this park has a restaurant, snack bar and ping-pong table to entertain guests.

Youth Hostel (cnr Navarette & Caracol; per person US$11) More of a crash-pad than a full-service hostel, this crumbling little building still houses many a budget traveler.

Eating & Drinking

There are plenty of simple cafés near the plaza and lively palapas on the beach that offer inexpensive food. Do try the super-popular, super-cheap taco stands in town; they are a gastronomic highlight.

Sayulita Fish Taco (east side of plaza; tacos from $0.50) American owner Albert spent years perfecting his recipe for this tiny, very popular stand.

Rollie's (Revolución 58; breakfast US$3.50-5; ☻ 8am-noon) This is *the* place for breakfasts. Rollie and friends lovingly serve Western breakfasts with an occasional Mexican twist. Choose music from Rollie's collection, or sing along with him.

Don Pedro's (☎ 275-02-29; Marlín 02; mains $5-12) This long-time favorite upscale palapa serves Westernized Mexican downstairs in a casual setting and gourmet Mediterranean fair in a fine dining atmosphere upstairs.

Getting There & Around

Sayulita is about 35km north of Puerto Vallarta just west of Hwy 200. Ten buses per day operate between Sayulita and the Puerto Vallarta bus terminal (US$2, one hour); otherwise, any 2nd-class bus headed north from Puerto Vallarta will drop you at the turnoff.

PUERTO VALLARTA

☎ 322 / pop 166,000

Formerly a quaint seaside village, Puerto Vallarta (or PV) has been transformed into a world-famous resort city hosting millions of visitors every year, nearly half of them from other countries. Some of the most beautiful beaches, secluded and romantic just a few years ago, are now dominated by giant luxury mega-resorts. Tourism – Vallarta's only industry – has made it a bilingual city, with English almost as commonly spoken as Spanish. But the cobblestone streets, old-fashioned white adobe buildings and red-tile roofs still make Vallarta one of Mexico's most picturesque coastal cities. If the pretty town and white-sand beaches aren't enough, you can venture out on cruises, horseback rides, dive trips and day tours, explore shops and art galleries, and enjoy numerous restaurants and a vibrant nightlife.

Puerto Vallarta stretches around the sparkling blue Bahía de Banderas (Bay of

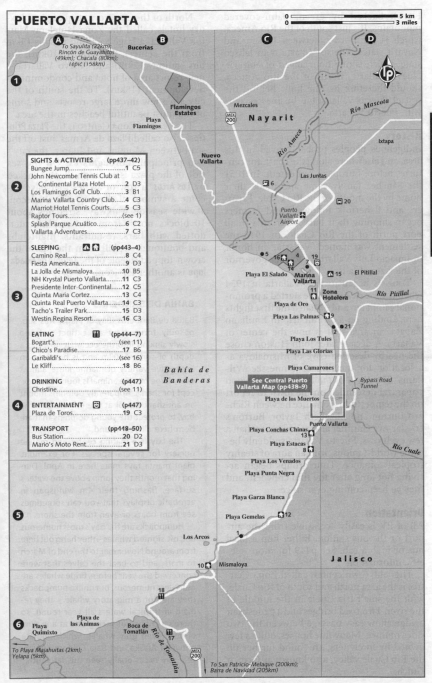

PUERTO VALLARTA

See Central Puerto Vallarta Map (pp438–9)

0 — 5 km
0 — 3 miles

To Sayulita (22km);
Rincón de Guayabitos
(49km); Chacala (80km);
Tepic (158km)

Bucerías

**Flamingos
Estates**

**Playa
Flamingos**

Mezcales

Nayarit

MEX 200

Río Mascota

Ixtapa

**Nuevo
Vallarta**

Las Juntas

6

**Puerto
Vallarta
Airport**

20

Río Ameca

16 4 19
14 7
**Marina
Vallarta**

15 **El Pitillal**

Playa El Salado

**Zona
Hotelera** 11

Río Pitillal

Playa de Oro

Playa Las Palmas 9

Playa Los Tules 2 21

Playa Las Glorias

Playa Camarones

**Bahía de
Banderas**

Playa de los Muertos

**Bypass Road
Tunnel**

Puerto Vallarta

Playa Conchas Chinas 13

Playa Estacas 8

Río Cuale

Playa Los Venados

Playa Punta Negra

Playa Garza Blanca

Playa Gemelas 12

Los Arcos 1

Jalisco

10 **Mismaloya**

18

**Playa
Quimixto**

**Playa de
las Ánimas**

**Boca de
Tomatlán** 17

Río de Tomatlán

MEX 200

To Playa Majahuitas (2km);
Yelapa (5km)

To San Patricio-Melaque (200km);
Barra de Navidad (205km)

SIGHTS & ACTIVITIES	(pp437–42)
Bungee Jump	1 C5
John Newcombe Tennis Club at	
Continental Plaza Hotel	2 D3
Los Flamingos Golf Club	3 B1
Marina Vallarta Country Club	4 C3
Marriot Hotel Tennis Courts	5 C3
Raptor Tours	(see 1)
Splash Parque Acuático	6 C2
Vallarta Adventures	7 C3

SLEEPING	(pp443–4)
Camino Real	8 C4
Fiesta Americana	9 D3
La Jolla de Mismaloya	10 B5
NH Krystal Puerto Vallarta	11 C3
Presidente Inter-Continental	12 C5
Quinta Maria Cortez	13 C4
Quinta Real Puerto Vallarta	14 C3
Tacho's Trailer Park	15 D3
Westin Regina Resort	16 C3

EATING	(pp444–7)
Bogart's	(see 11)
Chico's Paradise	17 B6
Garibaldi's	(see 16)
Le Kliff	18 B6

DRINKING	(p447)
Christine	(see 11)

ENTERTAINMENT	(p447)
Plaza de Toros	19 C3

TRANSPORT	(pp448–50)
Bus Station	20 D2
Mario's Moto Rent	21 D3

Flags), backed by green, palm-covered mountains. It's just south of the Río Ameca, which is the border between Jalisco and Nayarit states. Puerto Vallarta is in Jalisco state, which is one hour ahead of Nayarit. Nuevo Vallarta, north of the Río Ameca, should therefore be one hour behind the rest of Puerto Vallarta but businesses sync with Puerto Vallarta.

History

Indigenous peoples probably lived in this area, and elsewhere along the coast, for centuries before European settlement. In 1851 the Sánchez family came and made their home by the mouth of the Río Cuale. Farmers and fisherfolk followed, and farmers began shipping their harvests from a small port north of the Río Cuale. In 1918 the settlement was named 'Vallarta,' in honor of Ignacio Luis Vallarta, a former governor of the state of Jalisco.

Tourists began to visit Vallarta in 1954 when the Mexicana airline started a promotional campaign and initiated the first flights here, landing on a dirt airstrip in Emiliano Zapata, an area that is now the center of Vallarta. A decade later John Huston chose the nearby deserted cove of Mismaloya as a location for the film of Tennessee Williams' *The Night of the Iguana*. Hollywood paparazzi descended on the town to report on the tempestuous romance between Richard Burton and Elizabeth Taylor. Burton's co-star Ava Gardner also raised more than a few eyebrows. Puerto Vallarta suddenly became world-famous, with an aura of steamy tropical romance. Tour groups began arriving not long after the film crew left, and they've been coming ever since.

Orientation

All of PV is easily accessible from the airport or the bus station. Either hop a local bus or grab a cab. See p449 for more specific information.

The 'old' town center, called Zona Centro, is the area north and south of Río Cuale, with the small Isla Cuale in the middle of the river. Two road bridges and a pedestrian bridge allow easy passage between the two sides of town. Many fine houses, quite a few owned by foreigners, are found further up the Río Cuale valley, also known as Gringo Gulch.

North of the city are: a strip of giant luxury hotels called the Zona Hotelera; Marina Vallarta, a large yachting marina (9km from the center); the airport (10km); the bus station (12km) and Nuevo Vallarta, a new resort area of hotel and condominium development (18km). To the south of the city are a few more large resorts and some of the most beautiful beaches in the area.

The heart of Zona Centro is the **Plaza Principal**, also called Plaza de Armas, just off the sea between Morelos and Juárez, the city's two principal thoroughfares. On the sea side of the plaza is an amphitheater backed by **Los Arcos**, a row of arches that have become a symbol of the city. The Malecón, a wide seaside walkway, stretches about 10 blocks north from the amphitheater, dotted with bars, restaurants, nightclubs and boutiques. Uphill from the plaza, the crown-topped steeple of the **Templo de Guadalupe** is another PV icon.

BAHÍA DE BANDERAS

Bahía de Banderas (Bay of Flags) was supposedly formed by an extinct volcano slowly sinking into the ocean. It now has a depth of some 1800m and is home to an impressive variety of marine life – almost every large marine animal is found here, except for sharks. Apparently dolphins mount an antishark patrol at the entrance to the bay, to protect the young dolphins that are born here all year round.

The bay is a mating center and marine nursery for several species. For example, giant manta rays mate here in April. During that month they jump above the water's surface, flashing their 4m wingspan in acrobatic displays that you can sometimes see from boats or even from the shore.

Humpbacks are the bay's most numerous and oft-sighted whales – they hang out here from around November to the end of March to mate, and to bear the calves that were conceived the year before. Bride whales are much less numerous, but unlike humpbacks they are not a migratory whale – they remain in tropical waters all year round, so there's a chance of seeing one at any time of year. Even gray whales, which migrate between Alaska and Baja California every year, are occasionally seen this far south.

South of the river, the **Zona Romántica** is another tourist district with smaller hotels, restaurants and bars. It has the only two beaches in the city center: **Playa Olas Altas** (which doesn't actually have 'high waves,' despite the name) and **Playa de los Muertos** (Beach of the Dead), which takes its strange name from a fierce fight there sometime in the distant past.

City traffic has been reduced dramatically by the opening of a bypass road *(libramiento)* on the inland side of the city center, diverting traffic away from the center.

Information

BOOKSTORES

A Page in the Sun Bookshop-Café (Map pp438-9; ☎ 222-36-08; cnr Olas Altas & Diéguez; ❧ 8am-midnight) Buys and sells used English-language books, and serves great coffee.

Libros Libros Books Books (Map pp438-9; ☎ 222-7105; 31 de Octubre 127) Has a good selection of magazines and books (including Lonely Planet guides) in English.

EMERGENCY

Police (☎ 222-01-23)

INTERNET ACCESS

Numerous places offer Internet access with rates ranging from US$1 to US$2 per hour in the air-conditioning.

@ciber Sea Cafe (Map pp438-9; cnr Abasolo & Juárez; per hr US$1; ❧ 10am-midnight) Quiet, fast and inexpensive.

Storba's Caffe (Map pp438-9; east of Plaza Principal, 2nd fl; per hr US$1.50) Fast, relaxed but hot.

Vallart@ Millenium (Map pp438-9; Madero s/n; per hr US$2) Popular for its air-con.

Virtual Reality (Map pp438-9; F Rodríguez s/n; per hr US$2) Cheap phone calls and Internet access.

LAUNDRY

There are many laundries around town, all of which are closed Sunday and charge less than US$4 per load.

Lavandería Blanquita (Map pp438-9; Madero 407A)
Lavandería Elsa (Map pp438-9; Olas Altas 385)
Lavandería Púlpito (Map pp438-9; Púlpito 141)

MEDIA

Vallarta Today (www.vallartatoday.com) is a better daily English-language newspaper than its competition, the weekly *PV Tribune*. Both are free. *Vallarta Lifestyles* magazine and *Vallarta Voice* are published by the same company (www.virtualvallarta.com)

and are dominated by real estate ads and information. The *Gay Guide Vallarta* booklet has tons of information and a helpful map for finding gay-friendly businesses.

MONEY

Although most businesses in Vallarta accept US dollars as readily as they accept pesos, their exchange rates suck. There are several banks around Plaza Principal, most of them have ATMs.

Vallarta has many casas de cambio; it pays to shop around, since rates differ. Their rates are slightly less favorable than the banks, but the longer opening hours and faster service may make using them worthwhile. Look for them on Insurgentes, Vallarta and the Malecón. There's also an **American Express** (Map pp438-9; ☎ 223-29-55; cnr Morelos & Abasolo) in town.

POST

Main post office (Map pp438-9; Mina 188)

TELEPHONE & FAX

Telecomm (Map pp438-9; Hidalgo 582; ❧ 8am-7pm Mon-Fri, 9am-noon Sat & Sun) Offers fax as well as phone service. Pay phones (card only) are plentiful everywhere in town.

TOURIST INFORMATION

Vallarta's municipal **tourist office** (Map pp438-9; ☎ 223-25-00, 680-80-89; Juárez s/n, in Municipal bldg; ❧ 8am-4pm Mon-Fri) has multilingual tourist literature, free maps and friendly bilingual staff. A good website is www.puertovallarta .net, sponsored by the visitors bureau and tourist board.

For pre-arrival information for gay visitors, the Gay Guide Vallarta website (www .gayguidevallarta.com) is a complete directory of gay businesses. Their printed booklet with a map of gay businesses is readily available around town and at **Club Paco Paco** (Map pp438-9; ☎ 222-18-99; www.pacopaco.com; Vallarta 278), which has long been the informal tourist office for the gay community.

Sights & Activities

Any activity you associate with tropical ocean and wild jungle exists in Puerto Vallarta. From zipping through treetops to swimming with the dolphins to bungee jumping to dirt biking to whale-watching, PV really does have it all. Snorkeling,

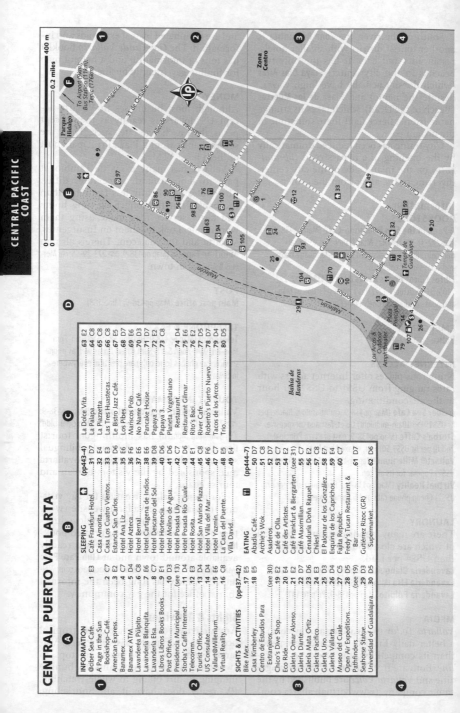

CENTRAL PUERTO VALLARTA

CENTRAL PACIFIC COAST

INFORMATION	
@iber Sea Cafe	1 E3
A Page in the Sun Bookshop-Café	2 C7
American Express	3 E2
Banamex	4 C7
Banamex ATM	5 D4
Lavandería Pulpito	6 C8
Lavandería Blanquita	7 E6
Lavandería Elsa	8 C7
Libros Libros Books	9 E1
Post Office	10 D3
Presidencia Municipal	(see 13)
Storba's Caffe Internet	11 D4
Telecomm	12 E3
Tourist Office	13 D4
US Consulate	14 D4
Vallart@Millenium	15 E6
Virtual Reality	16 C8

SIGHTS & ACTIVITIES	(pp437–42)
Bike Mex	17 E5
Casa Kimberley	18 E5
Centro de Estudios Para Extranjeros	(see 30)
Chico's Dive Shop	19 E2
Eco Ride	20 E4
Galería Omar Alonso	21 E2
Galería Dante	22 D7
Galería Mata Ortiz	23 D6
Galería Pacífico	24 E3
Galería Uno	25 D3
Galería Vallarta	26 D4
Museo del Cuale	27 C5
Open Air Expeditions	28 D5
Pathfinders	(see 19)
Seahorse Statue	29 D3
Universidad de Guadalajara	30 D5

SLEEPING	(pp443–4)
Café Frankfurt Hotel	31 D7
Casa Amorita	32 E4
Casa Los Cuatro Vientos	33 E3
Estancia San Carlos	34 D6
Hotel Ana Liz	35 F6
Hotel Azteca	36 F6
Hotel Bernal	37 E6
Hotel Cartagena de Indios	38 E6
Hotel Descanso del Sol	39 D8
Hotel Hortencia	40 D6
Hotel Molino de Agua	41 D6
Hotel Posada Lily	42 C7
Hotel Posada Río Cuale	43 D6
Hotel Rosita	44 E1
Hotel San Marino Plaza	45 C8
Hotel Villa del Mar	46 F6
Hotel Yazmín	47 D7
La Casa del Puente	48 E5
Villa David	49 E4

La Dolce Vita	63 E2
La Palapa	64 C8
La Piazzetta	65 C8
Las Tres Huasteca	66 C8
Le Bistro Jazz Café	67 E5
Los Pibes	68 D7
Mariscos Polo	69 E6
No Name Café	70 D3
Pancake House	71 D7
Papaya 3	72 E2
Papaya 3	73 C8
Planeta Vegetariano	74 D4
Restaurant Gilmar	75 E6
Rito's Baci	76 E2
River Cafe	77 D5
Roberto's Puerto Nuevo	78 D7
Tacos de los Arcos	79 D4
Trio	80 D5

EATING	(pp444–7)
Abadía Café	50 D7
Archie's Wok	51 C8
Asaderos	52 D7
Café de Olla	53 C7
Café de los Artistes	54 E2
Café Frankfurt & Biergarten	(see 31)
Café Maximilian	55 C8
Cenaduría Doña Raquel	56 E2
Chiles!	57 D8
El Palomar de los González	58 E7
Esquina de los Caprichos	59 E4
Fajita Republic	60 C7
Fredy's Tucan Restaurant & Bar	61 D7
Gutiérrez Rizoc (GR) Supermarket	62 D6

To Airport (5km); Bus Station (11km); Tepic (176km)

Zona Centro

Parque Hidalgo

Bahía de Banderas

Los Arcos & Outdoor Amphitheater

Plaza Principal

Temple de Guadalupe

400 m
0.2 miles

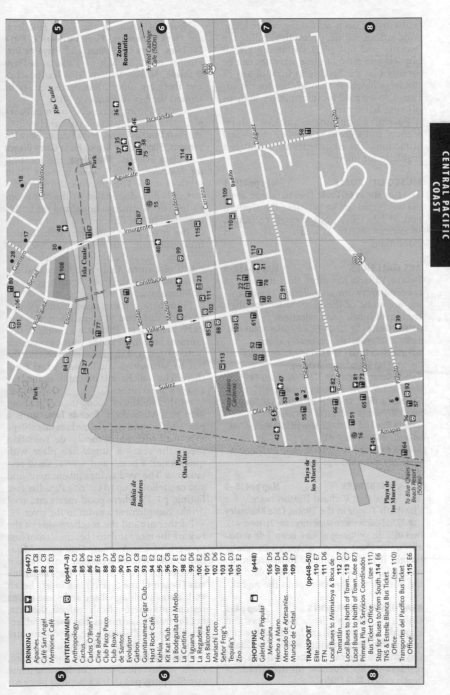

DRINKING (p447)
Apaches	81 C8
Café San Angel	82 C8
Memories Café	83 D3

ENTERTAINMENT (pp447–3)
Anthropology	84 C5
Cactus	85 D6
Carlos O'Brian's	86 E2
Cine Bahía	87 E6
Club Paco Paco	88 D7
Club Roxy	89 D6
de Santos	90 E2
Evolution	91 D7
Garbos	92 C8
Guantanamera Cigar Club	93 E3
Hard Rock Café	94 E2
Kahlúa	95 E2
Kit Kat Klub	96 C8
La Bodeguita del Medio	97 E1
La Cantina	98 E2
La Iguana	99 D6
La Regadera	10C E2
Los Balcones	101 D5
Mariachi Loco	102 D6
Señor Frog's	103 D7
Tequila's	104 D3
Zoo	105 E2

SHOPPING (p448)
Galería Arte Popular	
Mexicana	106 D5
Hecho a Mano	107 D4
Mercado de Artesanías	108 D5
Mundo de Cristal	109 E7

TRANSPORT (pp448–50)
Elite	110 E7
ETN	111 D6
Local Buses to Mismaloya & Boca de	
Tomatlán	112 D7
Local Buses to North of Town	113 C7
Local Buses to North of Town	(see 87)
Primera Plus & Servicios Coordinados	
Bus Ticket Office	(see 111)
Stop for Buses to/from South	114 E6
TNS & Estrella Blanca Bus Ticket	
Office	(see 110)
Transportes del Pacífico Bus Ticket	
Office	115 E6

scuba diving, deep-sea fishing, waterskiing, windsurfing, sailing, parasailing, riding the 'banana' and just plain swimming are all popular and most of these activities can be arranged on the beaches in front of any of the large hotels or through the tourist office. Also see p442 for information on firms offering activity trips.

Puerto Vallarta also has amazing natural scenery and a growing number of cultural attractions. The art galleries are definitely a highlight for many.

MUSEO DEL CUALE   Map pp438–9

The tiny **Museo del Cuale** (Paseo Isla Cuale s/n; admission free; 🕙 9am-5pm Tue-Sat), near the western end of Isla Cuale, has a small collection of ancient objects, as well as changing art exhibitions.

ART GALLERIES   Map pp438–9

Puerto Vallarta has more than its share of contemporary fine art galleries. The following are some of the best known for their consistent quality and selection:

Galería Dante (☎ 222-24-77; www.galleriadante.com; Badillo 269) Paintings and contemporary sculpture.

Galería Mata Ortiz (☎ 222-74-07; Cárdenas 268A) Very small but fine collection of pottery.

Galería Omar Alonso (☎ 222-55-87; Vicario 249) Mostly antique and contemporary photography.

Galería Pacífico (☎ 222-19-82; Aldama 174) Open since 1987, with an emphasis on local painters.

Galería Uno (☎ 222-09-08; Morelos 561) Mexican fine art in all mediums since 1971.

Galería Vallarta (☎ 222-01-90; Juárez 263) Paintings by Mexico's most collected painters.

CASA KIMBERLEY   Map pp438–9

The house that Richard Burton bought for Elizabeth Taylor in the 1960s, **Casa Kimberley** (☎ 222-13-36; www.casakimberley.com; Zaragoza 445; tours US$7.50; 🕙 9am-6pm) has been left virtually untouched since an American family bought it in 1990. Guided tours are informal and if you fall in love with the place and the host family, you can spend the night.

BEACHES & EXCURSIONS   Map p435

Only two beaches, Playa Olas Altas and Playa de los Muertos, are handy to the city center; they're both south of the Río Cuale. Gay men hang out at the southern end of Playa de los Muertos, on the stretch of beach called **Blue Chairs**.

North of town, in the Zona Hotelera, are **Playa Camarones**, **Playa Las Glorias**, **Playa Los Tules**, **Playa Las Palmas** and **Playa de Oro**. Further north, at Marina Vallarta, is **Playa El Salado**. Nuevo Vallarta also has beaches and there are others, less developed, right around the bay to Punta de Mita.

South of town, accessible by minibuses plying the superbly scenic coastal Hwy 200, are **Playa Conchas Chinas**, **Playa Estacas**, **Playa Los Venados**, **Playa Punta Negra**, **Playa Garza Blanca** and **Playa Gemelas**. **Mismaloya**, the location for *The Night of the Iguana*, is about 12km south of town. The tiny cove, formerly deserted, is now dominated by the 303-room La Jolla de Mismaloya hotel, and the buildings used in the film, on the southern side of the cove, have now been transformed into restaurants. Mismaloya has a few tourist attractions and a pleasant beach but isn't much of a town. Only minibuses that say 'Mismaloya' on the front actually go as far as Mismaloya.

From here you can head inland along a riverside dirt road to areas where you can swim in the river. There are a couple of restaurants here too. Having your own vehicle is the easiest way to get here; if you take the bus to Mismaloya you'll need a taxi from there. The walk back is downhill all the way and is a pleasant stroll.

Further southwest along the coast, about 4km past Mismaloya, **Boca de Tomatlán** is a peaceful, less commercialized seaside village in a small cove where the Río de Tomatlán meets the sea – a jungle-like place with quiet water, a beach and several small restaurants. The road swings inland here, and you can follow it up to Chico's Paradise (see Eating, p447), where good meals and cool drinks complement a swim in the river.

Further around the southern side of the bay are the more isolated beaches, from east to west, of Las Ánimas, Quimixto, Majahuitas and Yelapa, accessible only by boat (see Getting Around, p449). **Playa de las Ánimas** (Beach of the Spirits) is a lovely beach with a small fishing village and some **palapa** restaurants offering fresh seafood. **Quimixto**, not far from Las Ánimas, has a waterfall accessible by a half-hour hike, or you can hire a pony on the beach to take you up.

Playa Majahuitas is home to the secluded, rustic yet luxurious resort of the same name (see Sleeping, p444). It's a popular place for weddings, honeymoons and folks trying to get away from their laptops, hair driers and cell phones.

Yelapa, furthest from town, is one of Vallarta's most popular cruise destinations. This picturesque cove is crowded with tourists, restaurants and parasailing operators during the day, but empties out when the tourist boats leave in the late afternoon. Electricity recently reached the charming village at Yelapa and a sizable population of foreign high-season residents is steadily increasing. There are several comfortable places to stay the night here.

DIVING & SNORKELING

The most spectacular spots for diving and snorkeling are **Los Arcos** (Map p435), the rocky islands in the bay just south of town (now a protected ecological zone); and **Islas Marietas** at the entrance to the bay, which are surrounded by impressive reefs, underwater caves, tunnels and walls. Dolphins, whales and giant manta rays are often sighted between December and April.

Vallarta has several diving and snorkeling operators. **Chico's Dive Shop** (Map pp438-9; ☎ 222-18-95; www.chicos-diveshop.com; Paseo Díaz Ordaz 772; 2-tank dive trips US$83-100, PADI open-water certification US$300) is the biggest outfit, with the most offices around town, and usually offers hard-to-beat discounts. **Vallarta Adventures** (snorkeling US$60, 2-tank dive trips US$85-110, PADI open-water certification US$370) has 'golden palm' instructors (see Tours, p442).

DEEP-SEA FISHING

Deep-sea fishing is popular all year, with a major international sailfish tournament held every November. Prime catches are sailfish, marlin, tuna, red snapper and sea bass. The tourist office can recommend fishing operators for the type of trip you have in mind.

See p449 for information on hiring private yachts and lanchas for snorkeling and fishing trips.

DOLPHIN- & WHALE-WATCHING

At the dolphin center of **Vallarta Adventures** (see Tours, p442) you can choose from different levels of swimming with the dolphins for US$60 to US$240.

Dolphins are present in the Bahía de Banderas all year round, so if you go out on a boat you're likely to see some. Whale-

watching trips operate from December to March, when humpback whales are in the bay mating, bearing young and caring for new calves. Open Air Expeditions is a popular operator; Vallarta Adventure also does whale-watching trips (see Tours, p442).

BIKE TOURS

Bike Mex (Map pp438-9; ☎ 223-16-80; Guerrero 361) and **Eco Ride** (Map pp438-9; ☎ 222-79-12; www.ecoride mex.com; Miramar 382) both offer mountain bike tours with experienced bilingual guides, tailored to your level of fitness and experience. Bike Mex is the more established of the two with a better collection of bikes, but Eco Ride is more popular with youthful risk-takers.

HORSEBACK RIDING

The tourist offices keep a list of horseback riding operators. Some established operators, not far from town, are **Rancho El Charro** (☎ 224-01-14), **Rancho Ojo de Agua** (☎ 224-06-07) and **Rancho Palma Real** (☎ 221-12-36) – they will provide transportation from your hotel. Costs are around US$10 per hour, or US$85 for a full-day excursion, including lunch. At Mismaloya, **Rancho Manolo** (☎ 228-00-18) offers three-hour horseback trips from Mismaloya beach up a jungle trail, and longer nine-hour mountain trips.

GOLF & TENNIS

Golf courses north of the city include the exclusive **Marina Vallarta Country Club** (Map p435; ☎ 221-01-71; Paseo de la Marina s/n), just north of Marina Vallarta; and the less fancy **Los Flamingos Golf Club** (Map p435; ☎ 298-06-06; Hwy 200 s/n), 13km north of town.

Most of the large luxury hotels have tennis courts; phone them to reserve a court. The **John Newcombe Tennis Club** (Map p435; ☎ 224-43-60 ext 500) is at the Continental Plaza Hotel in the Zona Hotelera. The **NH Krystal** (Map p435; ☎ 224-02-02) and **Marriott Hotel** (Map p435; ☎ 221-00-04) both have courts available, and there are plenty of others.

BUNGEE JUMPING

The **bungee jump** (Map p435; ☎ 228-0670; www.val larta-action.com) is a platform jutting out over the sea cliffs, about 9km south of Puerto Vallarta on the road to Mismaloya. Make the 40m plunge between 10am and 6pm daily (US$55).

OFF-ROAD DRIVING

Pathfinders (Map pp438-9; ☎ 222-18-75; Paseo Díaz Ordaz 772), at Chico's Dive Shop, arranges three-hour dune buggy trips (US$110) on rough roads, riverbeds and the nearby hills, 'for the road warrior in all of us.' **Raptor Tours** (Map p435; ☎ 228-0670; www.vallarta-action.com), based at the bungee jump, does seven-hour excursions on similar terrain (US$200).

WATER PARK

Kids will enjoy **Splash Parque Acuático** (Map pp438-9; ☎ 297-07-08; Carr Tepic Km 155; admission US$9), which has 12 water slides, a lazy river swimming pool and a daily dolphin show.

CRUISES

A host of daytime, sunset and evening cruises are available in Vallarta, some emphasizing beach visits and snorkeling stops, some in sail boats and others that are accurately described as 'booze cruises.' The most popular ones are the cruises to Yel-apa and Las Ánimas beaches (US$25 to US$40); other cruises go to the Islas Marietas (US$60) further out. The tourist office or any travel agency can tell you which cruises are operating, details of where they go, what they offer (many include meals, open bar, live music and dancing) and what they cost.

The **Marigalante** (☎ 223-08-75; www.marigalante .com.mx) is a reproduction Spanish galleon that does daytime cruises from 9am to 5pm (US$59) and an evening cruise from 6pm to 11pm (US$68) that culminates in a mock pirate attack on the Malecón. On Thursday **Diana Tours** (☎ 222-15-10) does a gay and lesbian cruise, with plenty of food, drink and snorkeling (US$70).

If you just want to visit the beaches, a cheaper way to get there is by water taxi (see Getting Around, p449).

Courses

Centro de Estudios Para Extranjeros (CEPE; Map pp438-9; ☎ 223-20-82; www.cepe.udg.mx; Libertad 105-1) Courses start at US$93 for a week of basic tourist Spanish to US$431 for a month of university credit courses. The center is associated with the Universidad de Guadalajara and can arrange homestays with local families; some of its courses have a focus on Mexican culture and history. There are also language sessions offered for children.

Tours

The tourist offices and travel agents can set you up with city tours, jungle tours, bicycle tours, horseback riding tours and archaeological tours, among others. Several tour companies specialize in nature and outdoor tours.

Vallarta Adventures (Map p435; ☎ 297-12-12; www.vallarta-adventures.com; Av Las Palmas 39, Nuevo Vallarta) offer Canopy Adventures (US$65), Swimming with the Dolphins (US$130) and romantic dinner shows on a private beach (US$70); these guys do it all and they do it with humor, enthusiasm and professionalism.

Open Air Expeditions (Map pp438-9; ☎ 222-33-10; www.vallartawhales.com; Guerrero 339) offers whale-watching (US$78), bird-watching (US$53 to US$78), hiking (US$53) and customized tours.

Festivals & Events

As in the rest of Mexico, **Semana Santa** is the busiest holiday of the year. Hotels fill up and hundreds (or thousands) of excess visitors camp out on the beaches and party.

The **Fiestas de Mayo**, a city-wide fair with cultural and sporting events, concerts, carnival rides and art exhibits, is held throughout May.

A big, international fishing tournament is held each year in mid-November; dates vary according to the phase of the moon, which must be right for fishing.

Since 1995 Puerto Vallarta's culinary community has hosted a **gourmet food festival** in mid-November.

The **Día de Santa Cecilia** (November 22) honors the patron saint of mariachis, with all the city's mariachis forming a musical procession to the Templo de Guadalupe in the early evening. They come playing and singing, enter the church and sing homage to their saint, then go out into the plaza and continue to play. During the entire day one or another group of mariachis stays in the church making music.

All Mexico celebrates December 12 as the day of honor for the country's religious patron, the **Virgen de Guadalupe**. In Puerto Vallarta the celebrations are more drawn out, with pilgrimages and processions to the cathedral both day and night from November 30 until the big bash on December 12.

Sleeping

Vallarta has a good selection of accommodations for every budget. The following prices are for the December to April high season; cheaper prices are available the rest of the year. For accommodations at the very busiest times – Semana Santa or between Christmas and New Year's – be sure to book ahead.

BUDGET

Vallarta's cheapest lodgings are south of the Río Cuale, particularly along Madero. All rooms come with fan and private bath.

Hotel Villa del Mar (Map pp438-9; ☎ 222-07-85; Madero 440; s/d US$16/21) Good-sized rooms here are basic and worn but clean. Nicer rooms with private balconies with chairs and flowering plants cost a bit more.

Hotel Azteca (Map pp438-9; ☎ 222-27-50; Madero 473; s/d US$17/21, d with kitchen & TV US$33) A bit far from the action, but a bit nicer than her neighbors, the Azteca has an intimate courtyard, friendly management and pleasant rooms.

Hotel Bernal (Map pp438-9; ☎ 222-36-05; Madero 423; s/d US$12/17) This budget travelers' standby has dark, basic, cleanish, fan-cooled rooms around a courtyard.

Hotel Cartagena de Indios (Map pp438-9; ☎ 222-69-14; Madero 428; s/d US$15/20, with air-con US$26/30) Single rooms are tiny here where the rooms come with desks. Rooms with a balcony are brighter but cost more.

Other recommendations:

Hotel Ana Liz (Map pp438-9; ☎ 222-17-57; Madero 429; s/d US$15/18) Acceptable, inexpensive.

Hotel Hortencia (Map pp438-9; ☎ 222-24-84; Madero 336; s/d US$15/20, with air-con, refrigerator & TV US$29/33; 🌣) Crowded but clean.

Camping is available at **Tacho's Trailer Park** (Map p435; ☎ 224-21-63; Camino Nuevo al Pitillal s/n; tent/ RV sites US$17; 🌣).

MID-RANGE

The following places are a considerable step up from the budget options in price, comfort and ambience.

Café Frankfurt Hotel (Map pp438-9; ☎ 222-34-03; www.hotelfrankfurt.com; Badillo 300; RV sites US$16, r US$26, cabañas US$35, apt US$36-50; P 🌣) This friendly, family-oriented hotel set around an overgrown tropical garden is good value and monthly rates are available. The RV park is really only a small parking lot and there is a beer garden downstairs.

Hotel Posada Lily (Map pp438-9; ☎ 222-00-32; Badillo 109; s/d US$23/37; 🌣) Although it lacks a lobby, the Lily has the ultimate location – half a block from the beach. Remodeled rooms are crowded but they have refrigerators, TV and, for an extra few dollars, air-con – some have balconies with fine views.

Hotel Yazmín (Map pp438-9; ☎ 222-00-87; Badillo 168; s/d US$30/34, with air-con US$35/37; 🌣) This oft-recommended hotel is clean and friendly, with courtyard gardens. There are lots of restaurants nearby, and it's just a block from Playa de los Muertos.

Estancia San Carlos (Map pp438-9; ☎ /fax 222-54-84; Constitución 210; 1-/2-bedroom apt US$50/69; P 🌣 🄳) All apartments have fully-equipped kitchens and private balconies. Monthly rates are an even better deal.

Hotel Posada Río Cuale (Map pp438-9; ☎ /fax 222-04-50; Serdán 242; s/d US$46/52; 🌣 🄳) This pleasant hotel has a swimming pool with a poolside restaurant and bar.

Hotel Rosita (Map pp438-9; ☎ 222-10-33; www.hotel rosita.com; Paseo Díaz Ordaz 901; s/d from US$35/40, ste US$146; 🌣 🄳) If you want to be beachside and stumbling distance from the central PV nightlife, the Rosita is a pretty good deal. Cheaper street-side rooms are noisy and a bit outdated, but there are more pleasant rooms on offer.

Casa Los Cuatro Vientos (Map pp438-9; ☎ 222-01-61; www.cuatrovientos.com; Matamoros 520; d/ste US$55/69 with breakfast; 🄳) The cute but dated rooms overlook the garden patio restaurant below.

Paco's Paradise (☎ 227-21-89; paradise@pacopaco .com; Hotel Descanso del Sol, Suárez 583; dm/ste US$30/59) Accessible by boat only, this rustic (no electricity) getaway on 80,000 sq m of wilderness with a private beach, is quite a deal, but it's for gay men and women only. Groups leave from Club Paco Paco (see p448) at 11am daily.

Hotel Descanso del Sol (Map pp438-9; ☎ 222-52-29; paradise@pacopaco.com; Suárez 583; r/ste US$65/110; 🌣 🄳) Although the views are stunning, this hotel for gay men is a hike or taxi ride up the hill. The rooftop bar is a blast with many shirtless men at sunset. Rooms are tidy, trim and well-dressed, and some have kitchenettes.

TOP END

Puerto Vallarta's top end is largely dominated by the large and luxurious chains. The following very special, small and stylish places are a great alternative if you're looking for something more intimate.

Casa Amorita (Map pp438-9; ☎ 222-49-26; www.casa amorita.com; Iturbide 309; r with full breakfast US$95; ☒) Overlooking the cathedral, this beautiful four-room B&B is the home of hostess and breakfast-chef extraordinaire Rita Love and Maya, her beloved rottweiler. The spotless rooms are thoughtfully decorated but not overdone, and come with their own private balconies and Rita's own homemade soap. The Venetian tile pool and rooftop terrace add to the ambience.

Quinta María Cortez (Map p435; ☎ 221-53-17, in the US 888-640-8100; www.quinta-maria.com; Sagitario 132; r with full breakfast US$100-235; ☒) About 3km south of central Vallarta lies the area's most atmospheric place to stay. Seven spacious, romantic suites, all different sizes, are furnished with antiques and eclectic décor. Most come with kitchen, fireplace and sea views. Definitely reserve in advance.

Quinta Real Puerto Vallarta (Map p435; ☎ 226-66-88, in the US 800-457-4000; www.mexicoboutique hotels.com/qrvallarta; Pelicanos 311, Marina Vallarta; Master/Grand Class ste with full breakfast US$200/240; ☒ ☒ ☒ ☒ ☒) From the welcome cocktail to the gorgeous course-side pool, the Quinta Real offers everything the most exclusive place in town should. All 80 rooms are tastefully accented by original designs by Sergio Bustamante and the lobby has subtle hints of Asia. The only drawback here is that the hotel isn't on the beach, but the private beach club and discounted green fees make up for that.

Majahuitas (☎ 800-508-7923; Playa Majahuitas; casita US$326) Peaceful, primitive and elegantly luxurious, this un-electrified, phone-less getaway is about as far from 'regular' life as one can get. There are only eight, open-air 'casitas' on this secluded white-sand beach, making it extremely romantic. Playa Majahuitas is only reachable by boat from Boca de Tomatlán so you'll need to make reservations.

La Casa del Puente (Map pp438-9; ☎ 222-07-49; casadelpuente@yahoo.com; Libertad s/n; apt US$81) This intimate guesthouse with two apartments and one large room is spacious and pleasant with a cooling river breeze. It's a bit hidden behind the Restaurant La Fuente del Puente. Mollie Muir, the owner, is an entertaining hostess full of fascinating local information.

Villa David (Map pp438-9; ☎ 223-03-15; www.villa davidpv.com; Galeana 348; r/ste with full breakfast US$93/109; ☒ ☒) This low-key, unique and totally gay villa is a wonderful alternative to more crowded places near Playa Olas Altas. Rooms are spacious with colonial-style décor. Views from the rooftop are extraordinary.

Blue Chairs Beach Resort (☎ 222-50-40; www .bluechairs.com; Almendro 4; r US$102-165; ☒ ☒) All of the rooms at this hotel for gay men have balconies, the décor is tasteful and socializing is more than encouraged. This full-service resort has bars and restaurants on the beach and roof, with pool on roof as well. Kitchenettes are available.

Although the following five-star and Grand Tourism hotels have hundreds of rooms and do mostly package tours – which can be arranged by travel agents everywhere for rates considerably lower than the 'walk-in' rates quoted here – they still provide a notably high level of service and comfort.

Hotel San Marino Plaza (Map pp438-9; ☎ 222-30-50; www.hotelsanmarino.com; Gómez 111; r incl 3 meals US$160; ☒ ☒ ☒ ☒) Central and family friendly

NH Krystal Puerto Vallarta (Map p435; ☎ 224-02-02; www.nh-hotels.com; Av Las Garzas s/n, Zona Hotelera; r from US$140; ☒ ☒ ☒ ☒)

Fiesta Americana (Map p435; ☎ 224-20-10; www .fiestaamericana.com; Paseo de las Palmas s/n, Zona Hotelera; r from US$ 135; ☒ ☒ ☒ ☒)

Westin Regina Resort (Map p435; ☎ 226-11-00; www.westinpv.com; Paseo de la Marina Sur 105, Marina Vallarta; r from US$150; ☒ ☒ ☒ ☒)

Camino Real (Map p435; ☎ 221-50-00; www.pvr -caminoreal.com; Carretera 200, Km 3.5; r from US$135; ☒ ☒ ☒ ☒)

Presidente Inter-Continental (Map p435; ☎ 228-05-07; www.ichotelsgroup.com; Carretera 200 Km 8.5; r from US$136; ☒ ☒ ☒ ☒)

La Jolla de Mismaloya (Map p435; ☎ 226-06-60; www.lajollademismaloya.com; Bahía de Mismaloya; ste from $250; ☒ ☒ ☒ ☒)

Eating

SOUTH OF RÍO CUALE Map pp438–9

Some of the tastiest and cheapest food in town comes from the **taco stands** along Madero in the early evening. There are also several small, economical, family-run restaurants along Madero. Most other restaurants south of the Cuale cater to Mexican and foreign tourists, and Badillo in particular has emerged as Puerto Vallarta's 'restaurant row,' offering an excellent choice.

Fredy's Tucan Restaurant & Bar (☎ 222-08-36; cnr Badillo & Vallarta; mains US$3-4.50; ☷ 8-2:30am; ☒) Fredy's Tucan focuses on breakfast and that is what they do best, but the coffee could be better.

Pancake House (☎ 222-62-72; Badillo 289; mains US$3-5; ☷ 8am-2pm; ☒) You may have to wait in line here because the amazing array of pancakes and other breakfast goodies have made this place more than popular. The food is good in a diner kind of way, but coffee fans should skip the free refills and buy themselves an espresso.

Café de Olla (☎ 223-16-26; Badillo 168A; mains US$4-7; ☷ closed Tue) This small, busy, very pleasant tourist-oriented restaurant serves good traditional Mexican food.

Abadía Café (☎ 222-67-20; Badillo 252; mains US$14-20; ☷ 6-11pm, closed Tue; ☒) This super-stylish, air-conditioned café has a varied menu of well-prepared, pricey, but unique dishes like the house favorite, duckling breast in Chiapas coffee sauce.

Roberto's Puerto Nuevo (☎ 222-62-10; Badillo 284; mains US$8-17; ☷ noon-11:30pm; ☒) Ever-popular Roberto's serves fine Italian cuisine and fresh seafood.

Café Frankfurt & Biergarten (☎ 222-34-03; cnr Badillo & Constitución; mains US$8-12) Cold German beers and decent German food are served in a tropical garden with tropical birds.

Las Tres Huastecas (cnr Olas Altas & F Rodríguez; mains US$3-7; ☷ 7am-6pm) For delicious Mexican favorites in a homey atmosphere at local prices, this is the place. If you're lucky, soft guitar music may be played at the table next to you.

Archie's Wok (☎ 222-04-11; F Rodríguez 130; mains US$8-12; ☷ 2-11pm Mon-Sat) The setting is elegant but urban. The menu changes but it's always Asian fusion cuisine, with savory fish in rich tropical sauces the highlight. There's live music Thursday through Sunday.

El Palomar de los Gonzáles (☎ 222-07-95; Aguacate 425; mains US$10-20; ☒) The superb view over the city and bay is a big draw at this hillside restaurant, especially at sunset. Jumbo shrimp and fillet steak are specialties. It's a steep climb up here, so get a taxi or work up an appetite.

Gutiérrez Rizoc (GR; cnr Constitución & Serdán; ☷ 6:30am-11pm; ☒) For self-catering or a small indulgence, visit this well-stocked air-conditioned supermarket on the southern side of the Río Cuale.

Red Cabbage Café (☎ 223-04-11; Rivera del Río 204A; mains US$8-18; ☷ 5-11pm; ☒) The atmosphere is casual, with fabulous eclectic and bohemian artwork; the food is serious *alta cocina mexicana*. Make reservations in the high season.

La Palapa (☎ 222-52-25; Púlpito 103; mains US$12-36) Pan-seared scallops with mango chutney over risotto and mussel sauce is just one example of the delicacies on the menu at this elegant beachside palapa. It's an upscale crowd in casual attire.

Café Maximillian (☎ 222-50-58; Olas Altas 380B; mains US$5-15; ☷ 8am-midnight Mon-Sat; ☒) Fabulous coffees, desserts, snacks and meals, all with an Austrian flavor. Popular for evening drinks and the setting is upscale.

Other recommendations:

Asaderos (Badillo s/n; meals US$8) All-you-can-eat meat.

La Piazzetta (☎ 222-06-50; cnr Olas Altas & Gómez; mains US$5-7; ☷ 1pm-midnight Wed-Mon) Good service, decent pizza.

Chiles! (Púlpito 122; mains US$4-6; ☷ 11am-6pm Mon-Sat) High-end hamburger joint, high season only.

Restaurant Gilmar (☎ 222-39-23; Madero 418; mains US$4-8) Tasty Mexican dishes and seafood at reasonable prices.

Fajita Republic (☎ 222-31-31; cnr Badillo & Suárez; mains US$6-12; ☷ 1pm-midnight) Substantial Mexican, American and seafood dishes.

Mariscos Polo (Madero 362; mains US$7-12) Long-time seafood specialist.

ISLA CUALE   Map pp438–9

The riverside setting of the restaurants on the island makes for a romantic and relaxing dining experience.

Le Bistro Jazz Café (☎ 222-02-83; www.lebistro .com.mx; Isla Río Cuale 16A; mains US$8-16; ☷ 9am-midnight; ☒) Popular for breakfast, lunch, dinner and dessert, the Jazz Café has scrumptious cuisine, pleasant jazz recordings and beautiful tropical scenery. It's a bit formal but there isn't a dress code.

River Cafe (☎ 223-07-88; Isla Río Cuale 4; mains US$10-20; ☷ 9am-midnight; ☒) Imaginative seafood dishes are a highlight of this well-regarded and delightfully situated restaurant. Try shrimp with pecans and orange sauce, or the yummy shellfish salad.

NORTH OF RÍO CUALE   Map pp438–9

Just north of the river, the **Mercado de Artesanías** has simple stalls upstairs serving typical Mexican market foods. The blocks further north have numerous upmarket shops, nightclubs and restaurants.

Planeta Vegetariano Restaurant (☎ 222-30-73; Iturbide 270; buffet US$6; ☽ 11:30am-10pm Mon-Sat) Readers, locals and *Bon Appétit* magazine all agree: this all-you-can-eat vegetarian buffet does amazing things with tofu.

Cenaduría Doña Raquel (Vicario 131; mains US$3-5; ☽ 6-11:30pm Mon & Wed-Fri, 2-10:30pm Sat & Sun) You can smell the richness of the traditional Mexican basics served in this local haven from a block away. Friendly atmosphere and friendly prices.

Esquina de los Caprichos (☎ 222-09-11; cnr Miramar & Iturbide; tapas under US$4; ☽ noon-10pm Mon-Sat) This Spanish-Mexican tapas hole-in-the-wall serves delicious garlic-heavy gazpacho, buttery grilled scallops and much more. It's a small, stark setting, but entertaining and popular.

Rito's Baci (☎ 222-64-48; Domínguez 181; mains US$7-12; ☽ 1-11:30pm) Authentic, delicious Italian flavors in a quaint, simple setting make this *the* place in town for pastas, pizzas, salads and seafood. Reservations suggested. Phone for free delivery within the city.

Trio (☎ 222-42-28; Guerrero 264; mains US$13-18; ☽ 6-11:30pm; ☒) Trio is an elegant European-style restaurant-bar-bistro operated by two European chefs who creatively design a seasonal menu. Everything is rich and delicious, especially the desserts.

Café des Artistes (☎ 222-32-28; Sánchez 740; mains US$10-22; ☽ 6-11:30pm; ☒) With fine views over the town, this distinguished restaurant has a romantic ambience to match its exquisite French cuisine. Local seafood is featured in many of the dishes, such as grilled swordfish in green tomato sauce, or tuna in sesame seeds with wasabi mousse. Reservations are recommended.

Papaya 3 (☎ 223-16-92; Abasolo 169 & Olas Altas 485; mains US$4-8; ☽ 8am-10:30pm Mon-Sat, 9am-5pm Sun) The large menu of vegetarian salads, soups, pastas and Mexican dishes will satisfy any craving, but servings are a bit small.

Paseo Díaz Ordaz, the street fronting the Malecón, is thick with restaurants and bars, many with upstairs terraces and views of the bay. Prices are considerably higher than in other parts of the city. The following popular nighttime venues serve decent meals:

La Dolce Vita (☎ 222-38-52; Paseo Díaz Ordaz 674; mains US$7-10; ☽ noon-2am; ☒) Often crowded spot for wood-fired pizzas.

> **FRUIT IN A BAG**
>
> You'll see them in many parts of Mexico, in the city or on the beach: small cart vendors selling juicy slices of mango, cucumbers and jicama, or cut squares of watermelon and papaya. Each fruit or vegetable is brightly presented in a clear plastic bag or cup (with a fork or toothpick stuck on the top), tempting you to stop, drop some spare change and take a quick refreshing snack. How can you resist?
>
> You can often also choose a mixed bag of fruit, or ask the vendor to make you a particular combination of fruits (this may up the price by a few cents, though). The price depends on quantity of fruit in the bag and popularity of the town with tourists. Expect to pay from US$0.60 to US$1.50, with US$1.25 as the common denominator. For an extra savory kick, have the vendor add some salt, lime juice and chili powder to your bag – this may sound a bit unconventional at first, but one taste of sweet mango with the opposing flavors of salt and chili and you might just get hooked. Plus, not many bugs can survive the double-whammy of chili and lime. Hopefully your taste buds and tummy can, though.

No Name Café (☎ 223-25-08; cnr Morelos & Mina; mains US$5-20; ☽ 8-1am; ☒) Restaurant and sports bar serving all-American favorites; phone for free delivery.

Tacos de los Arcos (Zaragoza 120; tacos US$1) Clean, established and economical.

ELSEWHERE   Map p435

North of town, the top-end hotels in the Zona Hotelera and Marina Vallarta all have top-end restaurants. Recommended places:

Bogart's (☎ 224-02-02, ext 2077; Av Las Garzas s/n) At NH Krystal Puerto Vallarta (p444), gourmet international cuisine.

Garibaldi's (☎ 226-11-50, ext 4419; Paseo de la Marina Sur 105) At Westin Regina Resort (p444), fine seafood in a beachfront setting.

South of town, there are several places notable for lush tropical locations. All cater to tourists and get crowded at lunchtime when tour groups arrive.

Le Kliff (☎ 224-09-75; Carretera 200, Km 17.5; mains US$10-26; ☽ noon-11pm) Dramatic setting and super seafood menu – try the tequila jumbo shrimp.

Chico's Paradise (☎ 222-07-47; Carretera 200, Km 20; mains US$7-16; ☻ 10am-6pm) Accessible by car or bus. Rustic riverside palapas with decent food and a lot of action.

Drinking

Start your day in the artsy, relaxed **Café San Angel** (Map pp438-9; ☎ 223-21-60; Olas Altas 449; coffee US$3-4; ☻ 7-1am) with a strong coffee, sweet smoothie or a tasty pastry. For a down-to-earth, low-key night, head upstairs to **Memories Café** (cnr Mina & Juárez; ☻ 7pm-midnight).

Entertainment

Dancing and drinking are Vallarta's main forms of nighttime entertainment. At night people stroll the Malecón, where they can choose from romantic open-air restaurant-bars and discos with riotous reveling. Entertainment is often presented in the amphitheater by the sea, opposite Plaza Principal. Softly lit Isla Cuale is a quiet haven for a romantic promenade in the early evening.

NIGHTCLUBS & DISCOS

Along the Malecón are a bunch of places where teen and 20-something tourists get trashed and dance on tables. On a good night, they all stay open until 5am. You can see from the street which one has the most action. Usually there's no cover charge, but drinks are on the expensive side, except during the 'happy hours,' which can be any time from 5pm to 11pm. Mainstays include **Carlos O'Brian's** (Map pp438-9; ☎ 222-14-44; Paseo Díaz Ordaz 786; ☻), **Kahlúa** (Map pp438-9; ☎ 222-24-86; cnr Paseo Díaz Ordaz & Abasolo) and the **Zoo** (Map pp438-9; ☎ 222-49-45; Paseo Díaz Ordaz 638; ☻).

If you're looking for live music, **La Bodeguita del Medio** (Map pp438-9; ☎ 223-15-85; cnr Paseo Díaz Ordaz & Allende; ☻ 11-2:30am) has live Cuban music, stiff mojitos and decent food. Otherwise, check the **Hard Rock Café** (Map pp438-9; ☎ 222-55-32; Paseo Díaz Ordaz 652).

Young locals drink and dance to loud Latin music at **La Cantina** (Map pp438-9; Morelos 700), or drink and do karaoke at **La Regadera** (Map pp438-9; Morelos 664). Super chic is **de Santos** (Map pp438-9; ☎ 223-30-52; Morelos 771; ☻ 6pm-4am).

South of the Río Cuale, a wider variety of nightspots caters to a more diverse clientele, and drink prices are generally lower than on the Malecón.

Club Roxy (Map pp438-9; Vallarta 217) Live rock, blues and reggae classics for everyone.

Cactus (Map pp438-9; cnr Vallarta & Cardenas) Friendly simple, drinking hole with a jukebox.

Kit Kat Klub (Map pp438-9; ☎ 223-00-93; Púlpito 120; ☻) Ultra-hip dinner show spot with wicked martinis.

Señor Frog's (Map pp438-9; ☎ 222-51-71; cnr Vallarta & Carranza; ☻) Youthful tabletop dancing and blaringly loud music.

Evolution (Map pp438-9; ☎ 222-03-91; Vallarta 399; cover $25; ☻) Cover includes all the drinks you can handle.

North of the city, some large resort hotels have bars and nightclubs, but they're usually low-energy, high-priced affairs. To cut the cost of the cover charge, look for discount coupons offered by time-share touts.

Christine (Map p435; ☎ 224-69-90; Av Las Garzas s/n; cover US$5-16; ☻) At the NH Krystal Puerto Vallarta (p444), this flashy disco is livelier than most places in the area, but you'll need good clothes and good moves to cut it on the dance floor here.

BULLFIGHTS

Bullfights are held at 4pm on Wednesday from November to May, in the Plaza de Toros opposite the marina.

CIGAR CLUBS

Guantanamera Cigar Club (Map pp438-9; ☎ 223-25-07; Corona 186B; ☻ 10am-10pm Mon-Sat; ☻) For PV's classiest cancer enhancer try the Guantanamera, the most widely recommended place to have your cigars rolled to order, or to buy pre-rolled Cubanos. You can enjoy them on the spot with a drink in the comfortable lounge.

CINEMAS

Cine Bahía (Map pp438-9; cnr Insurgentes & Madero; admission US$3.50; ☻) For less frenetic evening entertainment, catch a movie in air-con at Cine Bahía. Recent releases are often shown in English with Spanish subtitles.

FIESTAS MEXICANAS

These folkloric shows give tourists a crash course in not-very-contemporary Mexican culture.

La Iguana (Map pp438-9; ☎ 222-01-05; Cárdenas 311; admission US$33; ☻ 7-11pm Thu-Sun; ☻) Said to be the original of this much-copied tourist entertainment, the deal here includes a Mexican buffet, open bar, live music, folkloric dances, mariachis, cowboy rope tricks, bloodless cockfights and a piñata.

Some of the big resort hotels also do Fiesta Mexicana nights, including the **NH Krystal Puerto Vallarta** (Map p435; ☎ 224-02-02 ext 2091; Las Garzas s/n; admission US$45; shows Tue & Sat 7pm; 🔀).

MARIACHIS
Two places present regular mariachi music. One attracts mostly tourists; the other is mainly for Mexicans.

Tequila's (Map pp438-9; ☎ 222-57-25; Galeana 104; 🔀) This upstairs restaurant-bar features live mariachi music every night except Monday, starting around 7:30pm.

Mariachi Loco (Map pp438-9; ☎ 223-22-05; cnr Cárdenas & Vallarta; cover US$3; 🔀) Usually attracting an enthusiastic all-Mexican crowd, this restaurant-bar presents an entertaining (if slightly amateur) show of music, comedy and mariachi every night at 6:30pm and 10:30pm. It's a great bit of local color, but you'll need good Spanish to enjoy it.

Shopping
Markets have the best prices but you'll have to hunt for quality. Otherwise, PV is a haven for shoppers, with many shops and boutiques selling fashionable clothing, beachwear and crafts from all over Mexico. If you're looking for the best, head to the art galleries (see p440) as well as the following places.

GAY PUERTO VALLARTA

The gay scene is huge in PV, with accommodations, tours, cruises and a variety of nightspots all catering to the gay market.

Club Paco Paco (Map pp438-9; ☎ 222-18-99; Vallarta 278; ☾ noon-6am) This popular bar-disco is the place for contacts and information on Puerto Vallarta's thriving gay scene. It's also a lot of fun, with regular floor shows, strippers and drag acts.

Other recommendations:

■ **Garbo** (Púlpito 142; 🔀) Chic piano and jazz bar.

■ **Apaches** (Map pp438-9; ☎ 222-52-35; Olas Altas 439; ☾ closed Sun; 🔀) Slick martini bar with yummy appetizers.

■ **Los Balcones** (Map pp438-9; ☎ 222-46-71; Juárez 182; 🔀) Bar and disco with weekend strip and drag shows.

■ **Anthropology** (Map pp438-9; Morelos 101; 🔀) Best strip show daily.

Mercado de Artesanías (Map pp438-9; ☎ 223-09-25; A Rodríguez 260) Everything from Taxco silver, sarapes and huaraches to wool wall-hangings and blown glass.

Galería Arte Popular Mexicana (Map pp438-9; ☎ 222-69-60; Libertad 285) Inexpensive assortment of local crafts.

Hecho a Mano (Map pp438-9; ☎ 223-14-) Fabulous selection of Mexican-made furniture and home décor.

Mundo de Cristal (Map pp438-9; ☎ 222-41-57; Insurgentes 333) Incredible selection of hand-blown glass.

Getting There & Away
AIR
Puerto Vallarta's international airport (Map p435) is on Hwy 200 about 10km north of the city. **Aeroméxico** (☎ 224-27-77) flies to Guadalajara, León, Los Angeles, Mexico City and Tijuana. **Alaska Airlines** (☎ 221-13-50) flies to Los Angeles, San Francisco, Seattle and Phoenix. **America West** (☎ 221-13-33) flies to Phoenix, **American Airlines** (☎ 221-17-99) flies to Dallas, **Continental** (☎ 221-10-25) flies to Houston and Newark, and **Mexicana** (☎ 224-89-00) flies to Chicago, Denver, Guadalajara and Mexico City.

BUS
Vallarta's long-distance bus station (Map p435) is just off Hwy 200, about 12km north of the city center and a kilometer or two north of the airport.

Most intercity bus lines have offices south of the Río Cuale, where you can buy tickets without having to make a trip to the station. They include Elite, TNS and Estrella Blanca, on the corner of Badillo and Insurgentes; ETN, Primera Plus and Servicios Coordinados, at Cárdenas 268; and Transportes del Pacífico, at Insurgentes 282.

Buses depart from the main bus station and most buses heading south will usually pick up passengers at offices in town.

Daily departures from the main terminal include the following:

Barra de Navidad Primera Plus (US$15, 3½-4hr, 6 1st-class daily; US$12, 3½-4hr, 9 2nd class daily) Also same buses as to Manzanillo.

Guadalajara ETN (US$37, 5hr, 11 deluxe daily); Futura, Transportes del Pacífico & Primera Plus (US$29, 5hr, frequent 1st-class services)

Manzanillo Primera Plus, Elite & Autocamiones Cihuatlán (US$17-18, 5hr, 7 1st-class daily); Estrella Blanca (US$15, 5hr, 5 2nd-class daily)

Mazatlán Transportes del Pacífico (US$27, 8hr, 4 daily) Or take a bus to Tepic, where buses depart frequently for Mazatlán.

Mexico City ETN (US$80, 12-13hr, 1 deluxe daily); Elite, Futura, Transportes del Pacífico & Primera Plus (US$60, 12-13hr, hourly 1st-class) To Terminal Norte.

Rincón de Guayabitos (US$5, 1½hr) Same buses as to Tepic.

San Blas TNS (US$10, 3½hr, 2nd-class 10am & 12:15pm daily)

San Patricio–Melaque (US$14, 3½-4hr, 7 1st-class daily; US$10, 3½-4hr, regular 2nd-class) Also same buses as to Manzanillo.

Sayulita Transportes del Pacífico (US$2, 1hr, 10 2nd-class daily)

Tepic Transportes del Pacífico (US$10, 3½hr, frequent 2nd-class daily)

CAR & MOTORCYCLE

To rent a vehicle you must be at least 25 years old and hold a valid driver's license (a foreign one will do). If you don't have a credit card you'll have to pay a large cash deposit. Rates vary, so it pays to shop around, but you can count on at least US$40 per day not including a deposit.

Mario's Moto Rent (Map p435; ☎ 229-81-42; Av Ascencio 998), opposite the Sheraton Buganvilias hotel, rents out trail bikes and motor scooters at US$38 for 12 hours, and US$48 for 24 hours.

Getting Around

TO/FROM THE AIRPORT

Colectivo vans operate from the airport to town, but not from town to the airport. The cheapest way to get to/from the airport is on a local bus for US$0.30. 'Aeropuerto,' 'Juntas' and 'Ixtapa' buses from town all stop right at the airport entrance; 'Centro' and 'Olas Altas' buses go into town from beside the airport entrance. A taxi from the city center costs around US$6. From the airport to the city, taxis ask as much as US$13, but shouldn't be more than US$8 for most parts of the city.

BOAT

In addition to taxis on land, Vallarta also has water taxis to beautiful beaches on the southern side of the bay that are accessible only by boat.

Water taxis departing from the pier at Playa de los Muertos head south around the bay, making stops at Playa Las Ánimas (25 minutes), Quimixto (30 minutes) and Yelapa (45 minutes); the round-trip fare is US$28 for any destination. Boats depart at 10am,

11am and 4pm, and return mid-afternoon (the 4pm boat returns in the morning).

A water taxi also goes to Yelapa from the beach just south of Hotel Rosita, on the northern end of the Malecón, departing at 11:30am Monday to Saturday (US$14 one-way, 30 minutes).

Cheaper water taxis to the same places depart from Boca de Tomatlán, south of town, which is easily reachable by local bus. Water taxis to Playa Las Ánimas (15 minutes), Quimixto (20 minutes) and Yelapa (30 minutes) depart from here daily at 10:30am and 11:30am, 1pm, 2pm, 4pm and 5:30pm, or more frequently if enough people want to make the trip; the one-way fare is US$8 to any destination (double for round-trip).

Private yachts and lanchas can be hired from the southern side of the Playa de los Muertos pier. They'll take you to any secluded beach around the bay; most have gear aboard for snorkeling and fishing. Lanchas can also be hired privately at Mismaloya and Boca de Tomatlán, but they are expensive.

BUS

Local buses that are marked 'Ixtapa' and 'Juntas' go to the bus station; 'Centro' and 'Olas Altas' buses run into town from beside the bus-station parking lot. A taxi between the center and the bus station costs US$5 to US$8.

Local buses operate every five minutes from 5am to 11pm, on most routes and cost US$0.35. Plaza Lázaro Cárdenas at Playa Olas Altas is a major departure hub. Northbound local bus routes also stop in front of the Cine Bahía, on Insurgentes near the corner of Madero.

Northbound buses marked 'Hoteles,' 'Aeropuerto,' 'Ixtapa,' 'Pitillal' and 'Juntas' pass through the city heading north to the airport, the Zona Hotelera and Marina Vallarta; the 'Hoteles,' 'Pitillal' and 'Ixtapa' routes can take you to any of the large hotels north of the city.

Southbound 'Boca de Tomatlán' buses pass along the southern coastal highway through Mismaloya (US$0.45, 20 minutes) to Boca de Tomatlán (US$0.75, 30 minutes). They depart from Constitución near the corner of Badillo every 10 minutes from 6am to 10pm.

TAXI

Cab prices are regulated by zones; the cost for a ride is determined by how many zones you cross. Always determine the price of the ride before you get in.

COSTALEGRE BEACHES & RESORTS

South of Puerto Vallarta, the stretch of Mexico's Pacific coast from Chamela to Barra de Navidad is blessed with many fine beaches. Tourism promoters and developers refer to this shoreline as the 'Costalegre' (Happy Coast) or the 'Mexican Riviera.'

Due to increased development, several pristine hideaways along here have effectively been commandeered by private interests, notwithstanding federal laws prohibiting privatization of the shoreline. Thankfully, many beaches remain publicly accessible.

From north to south they include (with kilometer numbers as measured from the Hwy 80/200 junction just outside San Patricio–Melaque): the sheltered **Playa Pérula** (Km 76), at the northern end of tranquil 11km-long Bahía de Chamela; the once-untouched **Playa Chamela** (Km 72), where tourism is slowly creeping in; pristine **Playa Negrito** (Km 64), at the south end of Bahía de Chamela; **Playa Careyes** and **Playa Careyitos** (Km 52), where endangered hawksbill sea turtles are making a comeback with the help of local activists; deserted white-sand **Playa Tecuán** (Km 33), 10km off the highway near an abandoned resort; **Playa Tenacatita** (Km 30), with crystal clear snorkeling waters and a large mangrove lagoon with good bird-watching and the wide-open 10km-long **Playa Boca de Iguanas** (Km 19), both on Bahía Tenacatita; sheltered **Playa La Manzanilla** (Km 13), marking the southern end of public access to Bahía Tenacatita; and pleasant **Playa Cuastecomates**, 3km west of San Patricio–Melaque.

PERFECT HONEYMOON GETAWAYS

If you're looking for breathtaking natural beauty, unforgettable luxury and absolute tranquility for your honeymoon, look no further. The Costalegre is home to some of the world's most romantic beachside resorts and the following are some of our favorites, listed from north to south.

Hotelito Desconocido (☎ 322-222-25-26; www.hotelito.com; La Cruz de Loreto; r US$350, ste US$480-640) Love for nature and luxury are in the air at this world of unforgettable rustic comfort. As the sun sets, the candles are lit and the evening orchestra of frogs, birds and cicadas begins, you'll find yourself drunk with relaxation. Take a dip in the saltwater pool before cuddling between the ever-so-smooth sheets in your lagoon-side bungalows on stilts. In the morning simply raise a flag and the staff will bring you coffee in bed. The Hotelito is 90km south of Puerto Vallarta.

Las Alamandas (☎ 322-285-55-00; www.alamandas.com; Carretera 200, Km 83.5; r US$430-850, ste US$860-1500) Celebrities love this ultra-sexy, ultra-romantic getaway. Start with a welcome cocktail followed by oceanfront, side-by-side massages. Have a gourmet picnic on the private mile-long beach before exploring the 284 square meters of tropical jungle. Snuggle beside your own beach bonfire before unwinding with a bottle of champagne in your ocean-view Jacuzzi. Las Alamandas is just over two hours south of Puerto Vallarta near the dusty village of Quémaro.

El Careyes Beach Resort & Spa (☎ 315-351-00-00; www.mexicoboutiquehotels.com/thecareyes; Carretera 200 Km 43; ste US$425-845) A bottle of champagne and an overflowing fruit basket will welcome you to your flower-filled suite with private, ocean-view plunge pool after a complimentary cocktail. Relax together to the sounds of the tranquil bay on the sheltered, pillow-piled outdoor beds. Enjoy massages before indulging in a sunset dinner at La Lantana, the on-site restaurant with a menu of 'food of the sea gods' as interpreted by renowned Mexican chef Patricia Quintana.

El Tamarindo Golf Resort & Spa (☎ 315-351-50-32; www.mexicoboutiquehotels.com/thetamarindo; Carretera 200, Km 7.5; villas US$420-629) El Tamarindo is the ultimate in romantic locations, with three secluded beaches on 8 sq km of breathtaking wilderness, 28 gorgeous and private bungalows with plunge pools, and poolside beds. Oceanside massage palapas and double spa-treatment rooms make relaxing together effortless. El Tamarindo also has one of the world's most stunning and empty golf courses – think skinny dipping between birdies. El Tamarindo is only 7km north of Melaque.

See www.mexicoboutiquehotels.com for more honeymoon-worthy properties throughout Mexico.

SAN PATRICIO–MELAQUE

☎ 315 / pop 8000

Known by most as Melaque (may-*lah*-kay), this kick-back beach resort on the Bahía de Navidad hasn't lost its old Mexico charm.

Originally two foreign-owned haciendas – San Patricio (on the east side) and Melaque (on the west) – stood side by side here, with the dividing line running between them where López Mateos is today. Settlements gradually grew around the haciendas and eventually merged into today's sleepy town.

Besides being a popular vacation destination for Mexican families and a low-key winter hangout for snowbirds (principally Canadians), the town is famous for its weeklong **Fiesta de San Patricio** (St Patrick's Day Festival) in March.

The crumbling ruins of the Casa Grande Hotel are an imposing reminder of the 1995 earthquake and subsequent *maremotos* (tidal waves) that severely damaged the region.

Orientation

Everything in Melaque is within walking distance. Most hotels, restaurants and public services are concentrated on or near east–west Gómez Farías, which runs parallel to the beach, and north–south López Mateos, the main Hwy 200 exit. Building numbers on Gómez Farías and some other streets are not consecutive – refer to the map for locations. Barra de Navidad is 5km southeast of Melaque via Hwy 200 or 2.5km by walking 30 to 45 minutes along the beach.

Information

Barra de Navidad's tourist office (see p454) has some basic information on Melaque. **Banamex** (Gómez Farías s/n) has an ATM and will change US and Canadian dollars; traveler's checks are changed from 9am to noon only. **Casa de Cambio Melaque** (Gómez Farías s/n, Pasaje Comercial 11) changes cash and traveler's checks.

The **post office** (Orozco, near Corona) is conveniently open regular hours. **Telecomm** (Morelos 53; ✆ 9am-2:30pm Mon-Fri) offers the usual fax and phone services. See the map for other telephone casetas. **Ciber@Net** (Pasaje Comercial 27A, Gómez Farías; ✆ 9:30am-2:30pm & 4-8pm Mon-Sat) and **El Navegante** (Gómez Farías 48; ✆ 9am-2:30pm & 5-9pm

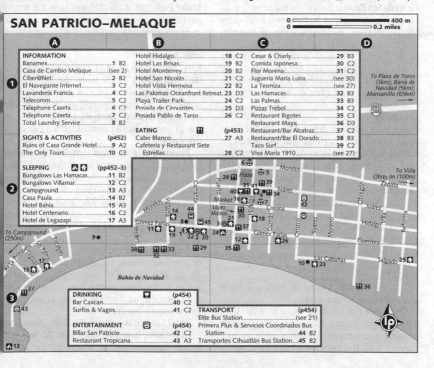

SAN PATRICIO–MELAQUE

INFORMATION	Hotel Hidalgo..................18 C2	Cesar & Charly..................29 B3
Banamex..................1 B2	Hotel Las Brisas..................19 B2	Comida Japonesa..................30 C2
Casa de Cambio Melaque..........(see 2)	Hotel Monterrey..................20 B2	Flor Morena..................31 C2
Ciber@Net..................2 B2	Hotel San Nicolás..................21 C2	Juguería María Luisa..........(see 30)
El Navegante Internet..................3 C2	Hotel Vista Hermosa..................22 B2	La Tesmiza..................(see 27)
Lavandería Francia..................4 C2	Las Palomas Oceanfront Retreat..23 D3	Las Hamacas..................32 B3
Telecomm..................5 C2	Playa Trailer Park..................24 C2	Las Palmas..................33 C2
Telephone Caseta..................6 C2	Posada de Cervantes..................25 D3	Pizzas Trebol..................34 C2
Telephone Caseta..................7 C2	Posada Pablo de Tarso..................26 C2	Restaurant Bigotes..................35 C3
Total Laundry Service..................8 B2		Restaurant Maya..................36 D3
	EATING 🍴 (p453)	Restaurant/Bar Alcatraz..................37 C2
SIGHTS & ACTIVITIES (p452)	Cabo Blanco..................27 A3	Restaurant/Bar El Dorado..................38 B3
Ruins of Casa Grande Hotel........9 A2	Cafetería y Restaurant Siete	Taco Surf..................39 C2
The Only Tours..................10 C3	Estrellas..................28 C2	Viva María 1910..................(see 27)
SLEEPING 🏠🛏 (pp452–3)		
Bungalows Las Hamacas..........11 B2		
Bungalows Villamar..................12 C2		
Campground..................13 A3		
Casa Paula..................14 B2		
Hotel Bahía..................15 B3		
Hotel Centenario..................16 C2		
Hotel de Legazapi..................17 A3		

DRINKING 🍸 (p454)		
Bar Caxcan..................40 C2	**TRANSPORT** (p454)	
Surfos & Vagos..................41 C2	Elite Bus Station..................(see 21)	
	Primera Plus & Servicios Coordinados Bus	
ENTERTAINMENT 🎭 (p454)	Station..................44 B2	
Billar San Patricio..................42 C2	Transportes Cihuatlán Bus Station...45 B2	
Restaurant Tropicana..................43 A3		

To Plaza de Toros (3km); Barra de Navidad (5km); Manzanillo (65km)

To Villa Obregón (100m)

Bahía de Navidad

Mon-Sat, 9am-2:30pm Sun) have air-conditioned Internet access for US$2.25 per hour.

Total Laundry Service (Gómez Farías 26) and **Lavandería Francia** (Juárez btwn Hidalgo & Guzmán; ☽ 9am-10pm) both charge around US$1 per kilo.

Sights & Activities

Melaque is the perfect place to simply relax and take it easy. The main activities are swimming, lazing on the beach (or beachcombing), watching pelicans fish at sunrise and sunset, climbing to the mirador (lookout) at the bay's west end, prowling the plaza and public market, or walking to Barra de Navidad. A *tianguis* (indigenous people's market) is held every Wednesday starting around 8am; it's on Orozco two blocks east of the plaza.

For mountain bike and kayak rentals and excursions, go to **The Only Tours** (☎ 355-67-77; Las Cabañas 26), which runs popular snorkeling tours (US$19) and Colima tours (US$35).

Festivals & Events

Melaque's biggest annual celebration is the **Fiesta de San Patricio** honoring the town's patron saint. A week of festivities – including all-day parties, rodeos, a carnival, music, dances and nightly fireworks – leads up to St Patrick's Day (March 17), which is marked with a mass and the blessing of the fishing fleet. Take care when the *borrachos* (drunks) take over after dark.

Sleeping

Rates vary greatly depending on the season. Prices are highest during Mexican school holidays in July, August, December and at Semana Santa, and are not much lower between November and May when the gringos roll in. The following prices are for November through May. You can get discounts for staying a week or longer anytime of year. Bungalows here are apartments with kitchens, where kids stay for no extra charge.

BUDGET

All of the budget places in Melaque have discounts for longer stays.

Casa Paula (☎ 355-50-93; Vallarta 6; s/d US$14/19) This simple home has four basic rooms around a courtyard. Staying here is like staying with the sweetest grandma ever.

Bungalows Villamar (☎ 355-50-05; Hidalgo 1; s/d US$16/18) The *estilo californiano* Villamar has five spacious but worn garden bungalows, a pool and a beachfront terrace. It's popular with norteamericanos since owner Roberto speaks English.

Hotel Hidalgo (☎ 355-50-45; Hidalgo 7; s/d US$17/20) The Hidalgo has a courtyard, communal kitchen and simple rooms. Upstairs rooms are brighter.

Hotel Centenario (☎ 355-63-08; Corona 38; s/d/tr US$10/19/28) Above the market, the Centenario has nine mostly bright, old-style rooms – look at a few before settling in.

Hotel San Nicolás (☎ 355-50-66; Gómez Farías 54; r US$14) This crashpad is popular with youthful Mexicans and foreigners alike. Its rugged but street-facing rooms have private balconies with ocean views.

The Ejidal beachfront **campground** (west end of Av La Primavera; sites US$2) is becoming more formal, with someone officially collecting fees. But it still doesn't have any facilities; most of the nearby *enramadas* (palapa restaurants) charge a nominal fee for showers and bathroom usage. Otherwise, beachfront **Playa Trailer Park** (☎ 355-50-65; Gómez Farías 250; tent/RV sites US$7/17) is where repeat, long-timers make their reservations months in advance.

MID-RANGE

Hotel Bahía (☎ 355-68-94; Legazpi 5; s/d US$23/33; ▣) Just half a block from the beach, this family-run place is one of Melaque's best deals. It's clean, very well maintained and has a communal open-air kitchen. One of the 21 rooms has a private kitchen but costs the same.

Posada Pablo de Tarso (☎ 355-51-17; Gómez Farías 408; r US$43, bungalows from US$59; P ▣ ▣) The bungalows lack the air-conditioning that has been added to the other rooms at this pleasant posada. The lush courtyard, colonial style furnishing, covered parking and lovely beachfront pool make this a very good deal.

Posada de Cervantes (☎ /fax 355-65-74; posadade cervantes@hotmail.com; Salgado 132; bungalows US$66-72; ▣ ▣) This well-decorated, intimate home-away-from-home has ultra-friendly management and lovely sitting areas. Bungalows are a bit crammed.

Hotel Las Brisas (☎ /fax 355-51-08; Gómez Farías 9; s/d US$30/41, bungalows from US$58; ▣ ▣) Las Brisas has one of the nicest pools in the neighborhood, outdoor communal cooking facilities, friendly staff and a small library. All rooms have fridge, air-con and TV.

Hotel de Legazpi (☎ 355-83-97; hotel@delegazapi .com; Las Palmas 3; r US$37, with kitchen US$43; P ▧) Right on the beach, the Legazpi has bright, if a bit worn, rooms. It's very popular for the rooms with ocean views; they cost the same but are hard to get.

Bungalows Las Hamacas (☎ 355-51-13; Gómez Farías 13; d/q US$33/60; P ▧) Beachfront Las Hamacas has chipping paint, and worn but big rooms with full kitchens.

Other recommendations:

Hotel Monterrey (☎ 355-50-04; hotelmonterrey@ prodigy.net.mx; Gómez Farías 27; r US$30, bungalows US$37; P ▧) Shabby overall, but the rooms with sea views are a steal.

Hotel Vista Hermosa (☎ 355-50-02; Gómez Farías 23; r US$39, bungalows for 4 US$73) Rooms vary from crammed to extra large.

TOP-END

Las Palomas Oceanfront Retreat (☎ /fax 355-53-45; www.tomzap.com/lapaloma.html; Las Cabañas 13; studios US$72-98; ▧ ▧) All of the unique, comfortable studios here are tastefully decorated, and most have terraces with fabulous ocean views. The lush gardens, beachside pool, Jacuzzi, complimentary breakfast, small library, communal kitchen and art studio make an extended stay here extremely tempting. Reservations are a must, especially if you're interested in any of the drawing, painting or mask-making classes.

Eating

From 6pm to midnight, food stands serve inexpensive Mexican fare a block east of the plaza along Juárez; a tummy-full of *carne asada* (grilled beef) costs about US$3. Lots of eateries await along Corona in the two market alleys on either side of López Mateos, and several good, cheap places surround the plaza.

Taco Surf (Juárez s/n; tacos US$0.35; ☑ 6pm-midnight) What makes these the best tacos in town is either the fresh pounded tortillas, assortment of condiments on the table or perfect juiciness of the grilled meats.

Flor Morena (Juárez s/n; mains $1.50-3; ☑ 6-11pm Tue-Sun) You may have to wait to get a seat in this tiny, all-women run place, but it's worth it. Everything is made fresh, there are plenty of vegetarian options and even

the house specialty, shrimp pozole (hearty hominy stew), costs less than US$3.

Restaurant Maya (Obregón 1; www.restaurantmaya .com; mains US$7-14; ☑ 6-11pm Tue-Sun & 11am-3pm Sat & Sun) The menu changes regularly but the quality at this Asian-fusion hotspot is consistently excellent. Dinners include a range of gourmet salads, grilled meats and fish with exotic sauces, and there are appetizers like tequila lime prawns. Western favorites like eggs benedict and rich omelets with Brie rule the brunch menu.

Juguería María Luisa (cnr López Mateos & Corona; snacks US$1-3) María Luisa whips up fresh fruit and vegetable juices, *licuados,* yogurt and granola, tortas and good burgers.

Restaurant/Bar Alcatraz (cnr López Mateos & Gómez Farías; mains US$6-9; ☑ 2-10:30pm Fri-Wed) This small, cheerful upstairs restaurant serves seafood, kebabs and burgers under a lofty palapa. The chateaubriand (US$15) serves two.

Comida Japonesa (cnr López Mateos & Corona; mains US$3.50-6.50; ☑ 11am-5pm Tue-Sat) Ridiculously popular with locals and visitors alike, this little market eatery cooks and rolls up teriyaki, gyoza, sushi, curry dishes and generous lunch specials with quality ingredients.

Restaurant Bigotes (south end of López Mateos; mains US$5-10; ☑ 8am-9pm) Seafood is the specialty at this pleasant beachfront palapa; try the *huachinango a la naranja* (red snapper à l'orange) or *camarones al cilantro* (cilantro shrimp). The two-for-one happy hour (2pm to 8pm) is popular.

Other recommendations:

Cafetería y Restaurant Siete Estrellas (☎ 355-64-21; López Mateos 49; mains US$2-7; ☑ 7am-midnight) Inexpensive Mexican dishes; free delivery available.

Pizzas Trebol (☎ 355-63-84; cnr Juárez & Guzmán; pizzas US$3-10; ☑ 10am-10:30pm) Just pizza with free delivery.

Cesar & Charly (south end of Carranza; mains US$4-11; ☑ 7am-10pm) Beachfront with a variety of inexpensive dishes, including healthy options.

A row of pleasant palapa restaurants (mains US$4 to US$11) stretches along the beach at the west end of town (see the map for locations). **Cabo Blanco** is a favorite with both locals and visitors alike; nearby **Restaurant La Tesmiza** and **Viva María 1910** are also good places. A bit closer to town, the fancier **Restaurant/Bar El Dorado** has live music on Friday and Saturday nights. Nearby, **Las Palmas** and **Las Hamacas** are a bit cheaper.

Drinking

Surfos & Vagos (Juárez s/n) Second-floor, open palapa, rocks to an agreeable beat and has a pool table and board games.

Bar Caxcan (cnr López Mateos & Juárez) The new kid in town thumps out techno beats, has a pool table, an extended happy hour and attracts mostly young men.

Entertainment

On the beach at the west end of town, **Restaurant Tropicana** hosts a dance for local teens on Sunday afternoon. On Sunday night locals gather in the plaza to snack, socialize and enjoy the balmy evening air. In summer keep an eye out for the arrival of the **circus**.

Billar San Patricio (cnr Juárez & Orozco; 11am-11pm) This pool hall attracts gregarious men and charges US$1.50 for a table.

During the winter and spring, **corridas de toros** (bullfights) occasionally liven up the Plaza de Toros off Hwy 200 near the Barra turnoff. Watch for flyers promoting **charreadas** (Mexican rodeos), and keep an ear out for cruising, megaphone-equipped cars scratchily announcing **béisbol** games and **fútbol** (soccer) matches.

Getting There & Away

AIR

For information on the nearest airport to Melaque, see p457.

BUS

Melaque has three bus stations. Transportes Cihuatlán and Primera Plus/Servicios Coordinados are on opposite sides of Carranza at the corner of Gómez Farías. Both have 1st- and 2nd-class buses and ply similar routes for similar fares. Buses trundling out of these stations serve the following destinations:

Barra de Navidad (US$0.30, 10min, every 15min 6am-9pm) or take any southbound long-distance bus.

Guadalajara (US$20, 5-7½hr, 10 1st-class daily; US$17, 5-7½hr, 12 2nd-class daily)

Manzanillo (US$4, 1-1½hr, 10 1st-class daily; US$3.50, 1-1½hr, 2nd-class at least hourly 3am-11:30pm)

Puerto Vallarta (US$14, 3½-5hr, 2 1st-class daily; US$12, 3½-5hr, 17 2nd-class daily)

The 1st-class Elite bus station is a block east on Gómez Farías. Two buses daily go to Puerto Vallarta (US$13, 3½ hours), then continue up the coast and on to Tijuana.

Elite's southbound buses go to Manzanillo, where many more southbound buses depart from.

Local buses for Villa Obregón and Barra de Navidad (US$0.40, 15 to 20 minutes) stop near the plaza by the Paletería Michoacán every 15 minutes.

TAXI

A taxi between Melaque and Barra should cost no more than US$4.50, or as little as US$3, depending on how well *tu hablas espanglish.*

BARRA DE NAVIDAD

☎ 315 / pop 4000

Barra de Navidad (usually simply called 'Barra') is squeezed onto a sandbar between Bahía de Navidad and the Laguna de Navidad, around the bay from San Patricio-Melaque. Local surfers prefer Barra to Melaque since Barra's waves are bigger, especially in January. The Grand Bay Hotel's marina is a popular yacht port from November to May.

Orientation

Legazpi, the main drag, runs parallel to the beach. Veracruz, the town's other major artery and the highway feeder, runs parallel to Legazpi before merging with it at the southern end of town, which terminates in a finger-like sandbar. Buses drop passengers at offices on Legazpi.

Information

The regional **tourist office** (/fax 355-51-00; www.costalegre.com; Jalisco 67) has information about more than just Barra, free maps and runs an information kiosk on the jetty during the high tourist season.

Barra has an air-conditioned **Banamex ATM** (Veracruz s/n). You can change money at **Vinos y Licores Barra de Navidad** (Legazpi s/n; 8:30am-11pm), or at the more official **casa de cambio** (Veracruz 212).

The **post office annex** (cnr Sinaloa & Mazatlán; 9am-2:30pm Mon-Fri) is the place to send snail mail.

Telecomm (Veracruz 212-B; 9am-3pm Mon-Fri) and **Mini-Market Hawaii** (Legazpi at Sonora; noon-10pm) have telephone and fax services. See the map for caseta locations.

Ciber@Money (Veracruz 212-C; 9am-2pm & 4-7pm Mon-Fri, 9am-6:30pm Sat) has a decent Internet connection and charges US$3 per hour for access, while **Internet Centro** (Veracruz s/n; ⏰ noon-9pm Mon-Fri, 10am-3pm Sat) only charges US$2 an hour.

Both **Lavandería Jardín** (Jalisco 71; ⏰ 9am 2pm & 4-7pm Mon-Fri, 9am-noon Sat) and **Lavandería Mat's** (☎ 355-65-78; Legazpi 62-A; ⏰ 9am-7pm Mon-Fri, 9am-2pm Sat) charge US$3.50 for a minimum load of four kilos.

You can exchange, but not buy, books at **Beer Bob's Book Exchange** (Tampico 8; ⏰ noon-3pm Mon-Fri).

Activities

The beach is Barra's prime attraction.

Surfboards, body boards, snorkeling gear, kayaks, bicycles, cars and apartments can be rented from **Crazy Cactus** (☎ 355-60-99; Jalisco 8; ⏰ 9:30am-6pm Mon-Sat). **Nauti-Mar dive shop** (☎ 355 57 91; Veracruz 204) rents out outfits for all manner of aquatic sports.

The **Sociedad Cooperativa de Servicios Turísticos** (Veracruz 40; ⏰ 7am-8pm) offers a variety of boat excursions, ranging from half-hour trips around the lagoon (US$14 per boat) to all-day jungle trips to Tenacatita (US$137 per boat). One popular tour heads across the lagoon to the village of Colimilla (US$11). Prices (good for up to eight people) are posted at the open-air lagoonside office. The cooperative also offers fishing, snorkeling and diving trips.

For a short jaunt out on the water, you could also catch a water taxi from a

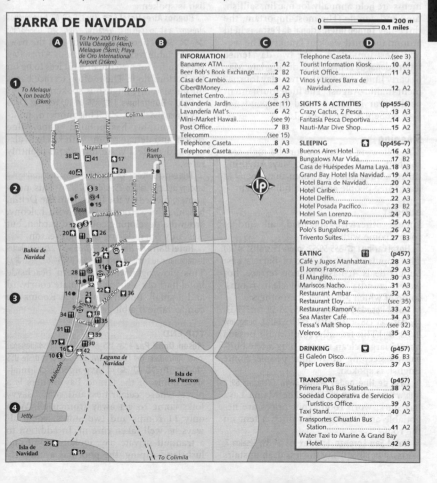

BARRA DE NAVIDAD

0 — 200 m
0 — 0.1 miles

To Hwy 200 (1km);
Villa Obregón (4km);
Melaque (5km); Playa
de Oro International
Airport (26km)

To Melaqui
(on beach)
(3km)

Zacatecas

Colima

Nayarit

Boat
Ramp

Bahía de
Navidad

Laguna de
Navidad

Isla de
los Puercos

Jetty

Isla de
Navidad

To Colimila

INFORMATION	
Banamex ATM	1 A2
Beer Bob's Book Exchange	2 B2
Casa de Cambio	3 A2
Ciber@Money	4 A2
Internet Centro	5 A3
Lavandería Jardín	(see 11)
Lavandería Mat's	6 A2
Mini-Market Hawaii	(see 9)
Post Office	7 B3
Telecomm	(see 15)
Telephone Caseta	8 A3
Telephone Caseta	9 A3
Telephone Caseta	(see 3)
Tourist Information Kiosk	10 A4
Tourist Office	11 A3
Vinos y Licores Barra de Navidad	12 A2

SIGHTS & ACTIVITIES	(pp455–6)
Crazy Cactus, Z Pesca	13 A3
Fantasía Pesca Deportiva	14 A3
Nauti-Mar Dive Shop	15 A3

SLEEPING ⭐	(pp456–7)
Buenos Aires Hotel	16 A3
Bungalows Mar Vida	17 B2
Casa de Huéspedes Mama Laya	18 A3
Grand Bay Hotel Isla Navidad	19 A4
Hotel Barra de Navidad	20 A2
Hotel Caribe	21 A3
Hotel Delfín	22 A3
Hotel Posada Pacífico	23 B2
Hotel San Lorenzo	24 A3
Meson Doña Paz	25 A4
Polo's Bungalows	26 A2
Trivento Suites	27 B3

EATING 🍴	(p457)
Café y Jugos Manhattan	28 A3
El Jorno Frances	29 A3
El Manglito	30 A3
Mariscos Nacho	31 A3
Restaurant Ambar	32 A3
Restaurant Eloy	(see 35)
Restaurant Ramon's	33 A2
Sea Master Café	34 A3
Tessa's Malt Shop	(see 32)
Veleros	35 A3

DRINKING 🍷	(p457)
El Galeón Disco	36 B3
Piper Lovers Bar	37 A3

TRANSPORT	(p457)
Primera Plus Bus Station	38 A2
Sociedad Cooperativa de Servicios Turísticos Office	39 A3
Taxi Stand	40 A2
Transportes Cihuatlán Bus Station	41 A2
Water Taxi to Marine & Grand Bay Hotel	42 A3

nearby dock and head over to the Grand Bay Hotel on Isla de Navidad or Colimilla (US$1 round-trip; see Getting There & Around, p457).

If a serious deep-sea fishing expedition is what you have in mind, pass on the lanchas and check out **Z Pesca** (☎ 355-60-99; crazycactusmx@yahoo.com; Jalisco 8, at Crazy Cactus) or **Fantasía Pesca Deportiva** (☎ 355-68-24; fantasia1@terra.com.mx; Legazpi 213), both of which have better boats and equipment. A six-hour all-inclusive (except beer) trip costs US$100 to US$200 depending on the size of the boat and number of fisherfolk.

Festivals & Events

Big-money international fishing tournaments are held annually for marlin, sailfish, tuna and *dorado*. The most important, the three-day **Torneo Internacional de Pesca**, is held around the third week in January. The second most important is the two-day **Torneo Internacional de Marlin**, held during late May or early June, with another two-day tournament in mid-August. The final tournament of the year is held around Independence Day on September 15 and 16.

Sleeping

The following prices are for the high season between November and May. Anything called a bungalow is a room that sleeps at least three people and has a full kitchen.

BUDGET

Unless otherwise specified, all budget rooms come with a fan.

Hotel Caribe (☎ 355-59-52; Sonora 15; s/d US$14/19) The popular Caribe is one of Barra's best budget deals. It has a rooftop terrace, hot water, laundry service and clean rooms, some of which are larger than others.

Hotel Posada Pacífico (☎ 355-53-59; fax 355-53-49; Mazatlán 136 at Michoacán; s/d US$14/21, bungalow US$33; P) This friendly, comfortable posada has 25 large, clean rooms, plus a few bungalows sleeping up to four people. Some English is spoken.

Casa de Huéspedes Mama Laya (Veracruz 69; r with/without bathroom US$23/14) The Mama Laya has stark, worn rooms, but prices are negotiable and you can also pitch a tent on the roof.

Hotel San Lorenzo (☎ /fax 355-51-39; Sinaloa 7, near Mazatlán; r US$23) Try the less drab upstairs

rooms at bright orange San Lorenzo if all the other budget hotels in town are full.

MID-RANGE

Hotel Delfín (☎ 355-50-68; www.hoteldelfinmx.com; Morelos 23; r US$46, apt with breakfast US$64; P 🖥 🖵) The Delfín is one of Barra's best hotels with large, pleasant rooms that open onto shared balconies, a grassy pool area and exercise room. Discounts are available for longer stays but repeat customers fill the place in winter. Don't show up after 10pm when no one is around to let you in.

Bungalows Mar Vida (☎ 355-59-11; www.tomzap.com/marvida.html; Mazatlán 168; apt US$55; ✂ 🖵) The fine little Mar Vida has five newly remodeled studio apartments and some English is spoken.

Buenos Aires Hotel (☎ /fax 355-69-67; hotelbuenosairesmx@yahoo.com.mx; Veracruz 209; s/d US$43/46; ✂ ✂ 🖵) There is no smoking in the new, comfortable rooms at the Buenos Aires. Pay US$9 more for air-con, or a bit less to be on the bottom floor. The rooftop terrace bar is for guests only. English is spoken.

Polo's Bungalows (☎ 355-64-10; Veracruz 174 & 210; r from US$35; P ✂) This modern, luxurious complex has popular, good-value rooms and deluxe rooms with kitchen, air-con and cable TV. Inquire about monthly rates.

Trivento Suites (☎ /fax 355-53-78; arturomadrigal@prodigy.net.mx; Jalisco 75; s/d US$28/36) This newcomer, owned by the folks from the Delfín, has nice, new rooms, some with balcony, around a developing courtyard garden, but it is only open during the high season.

Hotel Barra de Navidad (☎ 355-51-22; www.hotelbarradenavidad.com; Legazpi 250; s/d US$54/62; ✂ 🖵) This glowingly white, modern beachside hotel harbors a shaded, intimate courtyard and a small, but inviting pool. Rooms are comfortable if a bit generic.

TOP END

Mesón Doña Paz (☎ 355-6441; www.mesondonapaz.com; Rinconada del Capitán s/n; Isla Navidad; d/ste US$ 210/320; P ✂ 🖵 🖵) This gorgeous colonial-style home of the Grand Bay owners is a place where celebrities and other savvy folks come to get away from it all. With only 11 rooms and two suites, you'll always be well taken care of. In addition to a tranquil private bay, lookout point and lush landscaping, the pool has a uniquely natural feel. Guests here have access to all Grand Bay facilities.

Grand Bay Hotel Isla Navidad (☎ 355-50-50; fax 355-60-71; www.wyndham.com; Rinconada del Capitán s/n, Isla Navidad; r/ste from US$170/320; P ⬚ 🖳 ⬚) This super-luxury resort is magnificent and very large. Golf, tennis and other packages can be booked online.

Eating

Several of Barra's many good restaurants are on the beachfront with beautiful sunset views, and others overlook the lagoon. Simple, inexpensive little indoor-outdoor places line Veracruz in the center of town. However, most are open only in the high season.

Restaurant Ambar (cnr Veracruz, Jalisco & Legazpi s/n; mains US$6-15; ☒ 8am-noon & 5pm-11pm high season only) This upstairs treasure serves imaginatively prepared crêpes (in addition to other French favorites) under a high palapa roof. The food and wine here are high quality. Check out the seaside location with an Italian focus too.

Restaurant Ramon's (☎ 355-64-35; Legazpi 260; mains US$5-11; ☒ 7am-11pm) This casual and friendly palapa restaurant serves excellent fish tacos among other local and gringo favorites.

Other recommendations:

Tessa's Malt Shop (cnr Veracruz & Jalisco; ☒ 9am-11pm Mon-Sat; mains US$3-5) Thick sweet malts, shakes and sundaes.

Cafe y Jugos Manhattan (Legazpi s/n; ☒ 8:30am-1pm Wed-Mon) Fabulous breakfast in a quaint setting.

El Jorno Frances (Sinaloa 18-D; ☒ 8am-2pm) Fresh baked breads and cappuccino.

At several other good beachfront places near the corner of Legazpi and Yucatán, full dinners cost US$7 to US$15. **Mariscos Nacho** features a wide selection of breakfasts and seafood, and it proudly proclaims itself *'el rey del pescado asado'* ('king of grilled fish'). The **Sea Master Café** (cnr Legazpi & Yucatán) is another decent bar and grill. Nearby, also with fine views overlooking the lagoon on Veracruz, are **Restaurant Eloy, Veleros** (☎ 355-58-38; Veracruz 64; mains US$5-12; ☒ noon-10pm) and **El Manglito** (Veracruz s/n; mains $6-9; ☒ noon-7pm).

Drinking

Adjacent to Hotel Sands, **El Galeón** (☒ Nov-Easter) is a disco with a popular poolside bar.

The daily happy hour (4pm to 6pm) includes use of the pool. Happy hour at **Piper Lovers Bar** (Legazpi 154A; www.piperlover.com) runs 5pm to 6pm and 9pm to 10pm daily year-round; loud live music often follows in high season.

Getting There & Around
AIR

Barra de Navidad and Melaque are served by Playa de Oro International Airport (ZLO), 25km southeast on Hwy 200, which also serves Manzanillo. To get to town from the airport, take a taxi (US$23, 30 minutes), or take a bus 15km to Cihuatlán and a cheaper taxi from there. For flight details, see p462.

BOAT

Water taxis operate on demand 24 hours a day from the dock at the southern end of Veracruz, offering service to the Grand Bay Hotel (US$1), the marina, the golf course and Colimilla. Also see p455 for information on boat tours.

BUS

The long-distance buses stopping at San Patricio–Melaque (see p454) also stop at Barra De Navidad (15 minutes before or after). Transportes Cihuatlán's station is at Veracruz 228; Primera Plus is almost opposite (look to the right); Elite is just around the corner on Gómez. Elite only stops in Melaque (see p454).

In addition to the long-distance buses, colorful local buses connect Barra and Melaque (US$0.40, every 15 minutes, 6am to 9pm), stopping in Barra at the long-distance bus stations (buses stopping on the southbound side of the road loop round Legazpi and back to Melaque).

TAXI

Catch taxis from the official stand (cnr Veracruz and Michoacán) to ensure the best price.

MANZANILLO

☎ 314 / pop 103,000

The 'little apple' is an industrial city and major port of call dominated by shipping piers, train tracks and a bustling central district. Away from the center, fine beaches ring nearby Bahía de Santiago and Bahía de Manzanillo, and the lagoons surrounding town offer good bird-watching. As the new swordfish sculpture on the plaza suggests, deep-sea fishing is very popular here too. In fact, boosters call Manzanillo the 'World Capital of Sailfish' – more than 300 *pez vela* were caught here during a three-day fishing tournament in 1957.

Orientation

Manzanillo extends 16km from northwest to southeast. The resort hotels and finest beaches begin at Playa Azul, across the bay from Playa San Pedrito, the closest beach to the center. Further around the bay is the Península de Santiago, a rocky outcrop holding Las Hadas Resort and Playa La Audiencia. Just west of the peninsula, Bahía de Santiago is lined with three excellent stretches of sand: Playas Santiago, Olas Altas and Miramar. Just west of Playa Miramar are Laguna de Juluapan and Playa La Boquita.

Central Manzanillo is bound by Bahía de Manzanillo to the north, the Pacific Ocean to the west and Laguna de Cuyutlán to the south. Av Morelos, the main drag, runs along the north edge of town center,

beside the sea. At its east end it meets Av Niños Héroes, which leads to Hwy 200. The city center begins at the zócalo (also known as the *jardín central*) and continues south along Av México, a major artery. The east–west streets crossing Av México change names on either side of it.

Information

Banks Several banks with ATMs are scattered around the city center.

HSBC (Av México s/n) Open regular hours if you need to exchange currencies.

Computel (Map p460; Av Morelos 144 & Av México 302; 7am-10pm) Has long-distance telephone and fax service. Public telephones are plentiful around the center.

Internet Alaska (Map p460; ☎ 332-79-27; Madero 423; per hr US$1) Offers fast connections in a comfortable atmosphere.

Internet Online (Map p460; Carrillo Puerto 223; per hr US$1.75; closed Sun) Also fast connections and comfort.

Lavandería Lavimatic (Map p460; cnr Madero near Dominguez; US$0.75 per kg; closed Sun) Within walking distance of the center.

Municipal Tourist Office (Map p460; ☎ 332-10-02, ext 247; www.manzanillo.com.mx; 9am-7pm)

MANZANILLO

0		4 km
0		2 miles

To Airport (25km), Barra de Navidad (50km); Puerto Vallarta (275km)

MEX 200

To Minatitlán (50km)

MEX 200D (toll)

Miramar

Laguna de Juluapan

Playa Olas Altas

Playa Miramar

Playa La Boquita

Santiago

Playa Santiago

Salahua

Playa de Oro

Bahía Cenicero

Bahía de Santiago

Playa La Audiencia

Playa La Escondida

Laguna de las Garzas

Península de Juluapan

Península de Santiago

Playa Azul

Bahía de Manzanillo

Playa Las Brisas

MEX 200

Laguna de San Pedrito

MANZANILLO

See Central Manzanillo Map (p460)

Laguna de Cuyutlán

To Cuyutlán (35km); Armería (40km); Guadalajara (320km)

INFORMATION
State Tourist Office.....................1 C1

SIGHTS & ACTIVITIES (p459)
Las Hadas Golf Course...............2 C1
Neptune's Diving & Sports
 Center.....................................3 C1
Plaza Pacifico.......................(see 4)
Underworld Scuba.....................4 C1

SLEEPING (pp459–61)
Brisas del Mar Hotel & Villas.....5 C2
Club Maeva................................6 B1
Hotel Anita................................7 B1
Hotel Brillamar.......................(see 7)
Hotel La Posada.........................8 C2
Hotel Marlyn..........................(see 7)
Hotel Playa de Santiago.........(see 7)
Hotel Sierra Manzanillo............9 C1
Hotel Villa La Audiencia..........10 B2
Las Hadas Golf Resort &
 Marina..................................(see 9)

EATING (p461)
Carnes y Tacos Julio................11 B1
Colima Bay Café......................12 C2
Comercial Mexicana
 Supermarket.......................(see 13)
Juanito's...............................(see 11)
Manos Morenos......................13 C1

ENTERTAINMENT (p461–2)
Hacienda Guacho....................14 C1
Nautilus..................................15 C2
Olé Olé....................................16 C2
Teto's Bar...............................17 C2
Vog Disco.............................(see 15)

TRANSPORT (p462)
Bus Station..............................18 C2
ETN Bus Station........................19 B1

Operates a sidewalk tourist information desk in front of the Presidencia Municipal.

Post Office (Map p460; Galindo 30)

State Tourist Office (Map p458; ☎ 333-22-77/64; Blvd Miguel de la Madrid 1294; www.visitacolima.com.mx; ⊙ 9am-2pm & 5pm-7:30pm Mon-Fri, 10am-2pm Sat) A bit hard to find; it also has offices in the new bus station too.

Telecomm (Map p460; Presidencia Municipal) Offers fax service.

Tourist police Stationed behind the Presidencia Municipal.

Sights & Activities

MUSEO UNIVERSITARIO DE ARQUEOLOGÍA
Map p460

The University of Colima's **archaeological museum** (☎ 332-22-56; Niños Héroes at Glorieta San Pedrito; admission US$1.25; ⊙ 10am-2pm & 5-8pm Tue-Sat, 10am-1pm Sun) presents interesting objects from ancient Colima state and other parts of Mexico. The university art gallery is opposite.

BEACHES

Playa San Pedrito, 1km northeast of the zócalo, is the closest beach to town. The next closest stretch of sand, spacious **Playa Las Brisas**, caters to a few hotels. **Playa Azul** stretches northwest from Las Brisas and curves around to Las Hadas and the best beaches in the area: **La Audiencia**, **Santiago**, **Olas Altas** and **Miramar**. Miramar and Olas Altas have the best surfing and bodysurfing waves in the area; surfboards can be rented at Miramar. Playa La Audiencia, lining a quiet cove on the west side of Peninsula de Santiago, has more tranquil water and is popular for waterskiing and other noisy motorized water sports.

Getting to these beaches from the town center is easy: local buses marked 'Santiago,' 'Las Brisas' and 'Miramar' head around the bay to San Pedrito, Salahua, Santiago, Miramar and beaches along the way and take 40 minutes. 'Las Hadas' buses take a more circuitous, scenic route down Peninsula de Santiago. These buses pick-up passengers from local bus stops, along the length of 21 de Marzo, and from the main bus station, every 10 minutes from 6am to 11pm. Fares (pay the driver) are US$0.30 to US$0.60, depending on how far you're going.

WATER SPORTS

Snorkeling, scuba diving, windsurfing, sailing, waterskiing and deep-sea fishing are all popular around the bay.

Susan and Carlos have more than 35 years of diving experience between them at **Underworld Scuba** (Map p458; ☎ 333-06-42; www.divemanzanillo.com; Santiago Peninsula, Plaza Pacífico). Their complete PADI dive center charges US$62 for two tank dives, including equipment, or US$272 for PADI certification.

Another good choice is **Neptune's Diving & Sports Center** (Map p458; ☎ 334-30-01; www.neptunesdiving.com; Hwy 200, Km 14.8), which offers similar dives, costs and services. It also does night dives and snorkeling trips.

Festivals & Events

In early February a **sailing regatta** ends with celebrations at Las Hadras – coming from San Diego, Alta California, in any even-numbered years and from Puerto Vallarta in odd-numbered years.

The **Fiestas de Mayo** celebrate Manzanillo's anniversary with sporting competitions and other events over the first 10 days in May. Here, as elsewhere in Mexico, the **Fiesta de Nuestra Señora de Guadalupe** is held December 1–12 in honor of Mexico's revered manifestation of the Virgin Mary.

Sailfish season is from November to March, with marlin, red snapper, sea bass and tuna also plentiful. The biggest international tournament is held in November, with a smaller national tournament in February.

Sleeping

Central Manzanillo is safe, with the town's best cheap options within a block or two of the zócalo. There are more places in the squalid area a few blocks south of the city center. Around the bay, where the better beaches are, hotels are more expensive; Playa Santiago, half an hour away by bus, is the exception.

BUDGET

Hotel Colonial (Map p460; ☎ 332-10-80, 332-06-68; Bocanegra 100; s/d US$19/23; P ✗) Whether you're a mid-range or budget traveler, this is the best deal in town. Priced like a budget option, the Colonial offers quality mid-range amenities and comfort. All rooms have air-con, a bit of character and new, comfortable bedding.

Hotel San Pedrito (Map p460; ☎ /fax 332-05-35; hotelsanpedrito@hotmail.com; Teniente Azueta 3; r US$20; P ✗ ⊛) Both beachfront and close to downtown, this hotel has a full range of rooms from the dank and musty with fans to spacious and bright with kitchen and air-con; look at more than one before choosing. From the zócalo, walk 15 leisurely minutes east along the Malecón, or catch a local bus and get off at the archaeology museum.

All other budget options have worn but bearable rooms.

Hotel Emperador (Map p460; ☎ 332-23-74; Dávalos 69; s/d US$11/12.50) Half a block from the zócalo, this simple but clean refuge has some top-floor rooms that are brighter than the rest. The hotel's restaurant is good and is one of the cheapest in town.

Hotel Flamingos (Map p460; ☎ 332-10-37; Madero 72; s/d US$12/16) Some of the rooms here can be musty; try for one with two beds and an outside window.

Hotel Miramar (Map p460; ☎ 332-10-08; Juárez 122; s/d US$12/16) This stark, old place has worn rooms with saggy mattresses but they're reasonably clean.

Hotel Anita (Map p458; ☎ 333-01-61; r US$26) This is the cheapest place on Playa Santiago, with endless remodeling efforts and 36 large, faded rooms.

MID-RANGE

Brisas del Mar Hotel & Villas (Map p458; ☎ 334-11-97; hecluna@prodigy.net.mx; Playa las Brisas; d/villa US$44/46; P ⊠ ☎) The beautiful, generous suites and villas at Brisas del Mar are all modern and colorfully decorated. They're beachside and within walking distance to some action.

Hotel Villas La Audiencia (Map p458; ☎ 333-08-61; Santiago Peninsula near Playa Audiencia; r/ villas from US$54/92 P ⊠ ☎) A bit far from the beach, this moderately priced hotel is good value, especially for families. All the villas come with a kitchen, air-con and satellite TV.

The following hotels overlooking Playa Santiago are a winding 15-minute walk (or five-minute bus ride) from Santiago town, down the road leading off Hwy 200 past the ETN bus station. The hotels perch on a bluff overlooking the beach, and all have beachfront swimming pools; the Marlyn and Playa de Santiago also have restaurant/bars.

Hotel Marlyn (Map p458; ☎ 333-01-07, in Guadalajara 33-3613-8411; d/ste from US$46/64; ⊠ ☎) Rates depend on views and amenities.

CENTRAL MANZANILLO

0 — 400 m
0 — 0.2 miles

Bahía de Manzanillo

To Lookout
Naval Base

Playa San Pedrito

To Hwy 200 (5km);
Bus Station (8km);
Santiago (12km);
Airport (35km)

Old Train Station

To Hwy 200 (5km);
Armería (45km); Colima
(100km); Lázaro
Cárdenas (312km)

Laguna de Cuyutlán

Hotel Brillamar (Map p458; ☎ 334-11-88; r/bungalows from US$37/ 64; 🐾 🖳) All breezy rooms come with air-con and TV, and bungalows have a kitchen.

Hotel Playa de Santiago (Map p458; ☎ 333-02-70; hoplasan@bay.net.mx; r US$55; 🖳) Good family rate with two children under 10 staying free; private sea-view balconies are amazing.

TOP END

Most of Manzanillo's upmarket hotels are on or near the beaches outside the city center. Many sprawl along the beach side of the main road near Playa Azul.

Hotel La Posada (Map p458; ☎ /fax 333-18-99; www.hotel-la-posada.info; Cárdenas 201; s/d US$58/78; P 🖳) Right on the beach, this friendly, oh-so-pink posada has helpful staff and spacious rooms with Mexican architectural touches. However, the neighborhood needs some attention and it's not within walking distance to anything.

Manzanillo also has plenty of all-inclusive resorts that are best booked ahead of time. Among the best are the following:

Las Hadas Golf Resort & Marina (Map p458; ☎ 331-01-01; www.brisas.com.mx; Av Vistahermosa s/n, Playa Audiencia; r from US$180; P ✕ 🐾 🖳 🖳) Ultra-posh, 220-room Arabian-style complex.

Hotel Sierra Manzanillo (Map p458; ☎ /fax 333-20-00; www.sidek.com.mx in Spanish; Av de la Audiencia 1, Playa Audiencia; s/d US$147/177; P ✕ 🐾 🖳 🖳) Grand but stark with gorgeous ocean views.

Club Maeva (Map p458; ☎ 331-08-75, in the US & Canada 800-466-2382; www.clubmaeva.com; Playa Miramar; per person $149; P ✕ 🐾 🖳 🖳) Absolute mega-resort; rates include unlimited food and drink, water sports and entertainment.

Eating

Several good, down-to-earth options are on the zócalo, while chain and chain-like spots line Hwy 200 around the bay.

Restaurante Chantilly (Map p460; ☎ 332-01-94; Juárez 44; mains US$3-10) This crowded *cafetería* and *nievería* has reasonably priced meals and snacks, plus a generous *comida corrida*, genuine espresso and good ice cream.

Los Candiles (Map p460; ☎ 332-10-80; Hotel Colonial, Bocanegra 100; mains US$4-11) The Hotel Colonial's restaurant opens onto a pleasant patio, features surf-and-turf fare and has a full bar and sports dominating the satellite TV.

Restaurant Emperador (Map p460; ☎ 332-23-74; Hotel Emperador, Dávalos 69; mains US$2-5) Good, cheap and simple, this intimate ground-

floor restaurant is popular with locals and budget travelers. Highlights here are the set breakfasts and the meat-and-seafood *comida corrida*.

A **market-style dining hall** (Map p460; cnr Madero & Cuauhtémoc; mains US$2-5; 🕑 7am-6pm) has a number of inexpensive food stalls that you can choose from.

Many more restaurants are spread out around the bay all the way past the plaza in Santiago.

Manos Morenos (Map p458; ☎ 333-03-20; Carretera 200, Km 11; mains US$6-13) Choose from fish with mango sauce or chicken with *huitlacoche* sauce or keep it simple with crêpes or a generous salad at this palapa with a golf-course view.

Colima Bay Café (Map p458; ☎ 333-11-50; Carretera 200 Km 6.5, Playa Azul; mains US$7-16; 🕑 2pm-1am) This super-fun Mexican restaurant feels like Carlos 'n' Charlie's but isn't. Service is professional, DJ music is thumpin' and portions are more than generous.

Comercial Mexicana Supermarket (Map p458; Plaza Manzanillo, Km 10.5; 🕑 8am-10pm Sun-Thu, 8am-11pm Fri-Sat) This mega-market has an incredible selection of prepared and unprepared foods. Just look for the pelican symbol and large building.

Carnes y Tacos Julio (Map p458; ☎ 334-00-36; Carretera 200, Km 14.3; mains US$4-11; 🕑 8am-midnight) Savory grilled meat is the specialty at this lively place, but breakfast, pasta and other tourist-friendly fare won't disappoint.

Juanito's (Map p458; ☎ 333-13-88; Carretera 200, Km 14.3; mains US$3.50-8) Juanito's is a popular mid-range gringo hangout with sports on the satellite TV.

Entertainment

If you're in town on a Sunday evening, stop by the zócalo, where multiple generations come out to enjoy an ice cream and the warm evening air. On the most atmospheric of nights, a band belts out traditional music from the gazebo, and every night around sunset you can hear the cacophony of the resident *zanates'* (blackbirds) bombing squad – don't stand under any electrical wire for too long. Behind the doors of the **Bar Social** (Map p460; cnr Av 21 de Marzo & Juárez; 🕑 noon-midnight Mon-Sat) is a world frozen in the past; it's not scary, but it is odd.

Tourist nightlife starts in Playa Azul, with theme discos like **Vog** (Map p458; ☎ 333-18-75;

Carretera 200 Km 9.2; women/men cover US$10/15; 🕑 Fri & Sat nights) and **Nautilus** (Map p458; ☎ 334-33-31; Carretera 200, Km 9.5; cover US$15; 🕑 Fri & Sat nights) and continues northwest around the bay. Near the Hotel Fiesta Mexicana, **Teto's Bar** (Map p458; ☎ 333-19-90; Carretera 200 Km 8.5) offers live music and dancing. **Olé Olé** (Map p458; Carretera 200 Km 7.5) is the place to dance to live salsa music.

Near Las Hadas in Santiago, **Hacienda Guacho** (Map p458; ☎ 334-19-69; Playa Santiago) features carne asada and dance music. On Playa Miramar, **Club Maeva** (Map p458; ☎ 335-05-96) houses the Disco Boom Boom and the casual Solarium Bar with a pool table; phone for reservations.

Getting There & Away
AIR
Playa de Oro International Airport (ZLO) is 35km northwest of Manzanillo's Zona Hotelera on Hwy 200. Aero California, Aeromar and Mexicana all fly direct to/from Mexico City. Aerolitoral (under Aeroméxico) flies to/from Guadalajara, Ixtapa, Monterrey and Puerto Vallarta. Aero California and Alaska both fly to/from Los Angeles. America West flies to/from Phoenix during the high season.

BUS
Manzanillo's new, airport-like, full-service *Centro Camionera* (bus station; Map p458) is northwest of the center near Playa Las Brisas, just off Blvd Miguel de la Madrid (Hwy 200). It's an organized place with two tourist offices, phones, eateries and left luggage. **ETN** (☎ 334-10-50) offers deluxe and 1st-class service from its own terminal near Santiago at Carretera 200, Km 13.5. Daily departures include:

Armería Autobuses Nuevo Horizonte, Rojos de Colima & Autotransportes del Sur de Jalisco (US$2.50, 45min, 2nd-class services at least hourly)

Barra de Navidad Flecha Amarilla (US$4.50, 1-1½hr, 10 1st-class daily; US$3.50, 1-1½hr, 2nd-class at least hourly 4:30am-midnight)

Colima ETN (US$6.50, 1½-2hr, seven deluxe daily); Primera Plus (US$5, 1½-2hr, 4 1st-class daily); Autobuses Nuevo Horizonte & Autotransportes del Sur de Jalisco (US$4.25, 1½-2hr, 2nd-class every half-hour 2am-10pm)

Guadalajara Primera Plus & ETN (US$23, 4½-8hr, frequent 1st-class daily); Transportes Cihuatlán & Autotransportes del Sur de Jalisco (US$14-18, 4½-8hr, 19 2nd-class daily)

Lázaro Cárdenas Elite (US$21, 6hr, 1st-class at 2am & 6am daily); Autotransportes del Sur de Jalisco & Galeana (US$15, 6hr, 6 2nd-class daily)

Mexico City ETN (US$65, 12hr, 1st-class at 7:30pm daily); Primera Plus (US$53, 12hr, at 7pm daily) To Terminal Norte.

Puerto Vallarta Elite (US$18.50, 5-6½hr, 1st-class at 4pm, 7:30pm & 9:30pm daily); Transportes Cihuatlán (US$19, 5-6½hr, 1st-class at 8am daily); Transportes Cihuatlán (US$16, 5-6½hr, 9 2nd-class daily)

San Patricio–Melaque (1-1½hr, same as to Barra de Navidad)

ETN also offers daily service to the airport in Guadalajara (US$24).

Getting Around
Transportes Turísticos Benito Juárez (☎ 334-15-55) shuttles door-to-door to/from Playa de Oro airport. The fare is US$22 for private service (one or two people) or US$8 per person when three or more people share the ride. A taxi from the airport to Manzanillo's center or most resort hotels costs US$18 to US$22.

Local buses heading around the bay to San Pedrito, Salahua, Santiago, Miramar and beaches along the way depart every 10 minutes from 6am to 11pm from the corner of Madero and Domínguez, the corner of Juárez and 21 de Marzo near the zócalo, and from the main bus station. Fares (pay the driver as you board) are US$0.30 to US$0.60, depending on how far you're going.

Taxis are plentiful in Manzanillo. From the bus station buy a pre-paid ticket for a collective taxi to ensure the best price. From the bus station, a cab fare is around US$2 to the zócalo or Playa Azul, US$6 to Playa Santiago and US$9 to Playa Miramar. Agree with the driver on the price before you get into the cab.

CUYUTLÁN & EL PARAÍSO
☎ 313
The small, black-sand-beach resort towns of Cuyutlán (population 1000) and El Paraíso (population 300) are popular with Mexicans but see very few norteamericanos. They're both pretty shabby and offer little to do besides laze on the beach. Cuyutlán has a better selection of hotels, but the beach is less crowded and more tranquil in El Paraíso.

Orientation & Information
Cuyutlán is at the southeastern end of Laguna de Cuyutlán, 40km southeast of Manzanillo and 12km west of Armería. Sleepy El

Paraíso is 6km southeast of Cuyutlán along the coast, but 12km by road.

Most of Cuyutlán's tourist facilities are clustered near the beach. If you arrive in town by bus you'll be dumped off on Hidalgo, on the east side of the zócalo. Walk four blocks toward the ocean on Hidalgo and you'll land right in the middle of the beachfront hotel and restaurant area.

Cuyutlán has a post office (El Paraíso does not), but neither town has a bank; for this you'll have to visit Armería. Both towns have public telephones and long-distance casetas near their zócalos.

Sights & Activities

Cuyutlán is known for its **ola verde** (green wave), appearing just offshore in April and May. It's supposedly caused by little green phosphorescent critters, but it's the subject of much local debate. **Centro Tortuguero** (☎ 328-86-76; admission US$2; ☉ 8:30am-5:30pm) is a beachside turtle sanctuary and environmental education center 4km toward Paraíso.

Cuyutlán lies near the *salinas* (salt ponds) at the southeast end of Laguna de Cuyutlán. In an old wooden warehouse a block north of the plaza, there's free, but uninspiring **Museo de Sal**; retired salt workers who act as caretakers appreciate donations.

Good **surfing** can be found 3km south of El Paraíso near Boca de Pascuale.

Sleeping & Eating

The beachfront accommodations here are cheaper than they are at other coastal resorts. The high season here is Christmas and Semana Santa, when Cuyutlán's hotels are booked solid by Mexican families. Rates quoted here are therefore for the off-season, unless otherwise noted.

CUYUTLÁN

You can camp on the empty sands on either side of the hotels – when in doubt, ask the closest palapa owner for permission. Several of the beachfront enramadas rent showers.

As you approach the beach on Hidalgo, you'll cross Veracruz one block before the pedestrian-only beachfront Malecón, which is where Cuyutlán's best budget hotels survive. Several other hotels and beachfront seafood restaurant/bars lie a block or two to either side.

Hotel Morelos (☎ 326-40-13; Hidalgo 185 at Veracruz; without/with meals US$12/22 per person; ☒) Rather old school, the Hotel Morelos has 35 clean, spacious rooms (some remodeled, check a few), hot water and a decent, if greasy, restaurant.

Hotel Fénix (☎ /fax 326-40-82; Hidalgo 201 at Veracruz; US$11 per person) One block off the beach, Fenix boasts breezier, brighter 2nd-floor rooms that are worth the extra pesos. The downstairs bar and open-air restaurant can get loud at night.

Hotel María Victoria (☎ 326-40-04; Veracruz 10; US$16 per person; ℗ ☒) Right on the beach, Cuyutlán's most luxurious hotel has a seaview restaurant that serves fresh typical Mexican fare.

Hotel San Rafael (☎ 326-40-15; Veracruz 46; r interior/exterior US$19/28; ☒) Next to the María Victoria, the remodeled San Rafael's most inviting rooms have sea views and share a large balcony.

EL PARAÍSO

None of the hotels in El Paraíso offer much more than crumbling, grubby cement cells for their guests. The nicest place in town, **Hotel Paraíso** (☎ 322-10-32; r US$23; ℗ ☒) has 60 decent rooms and is to the left of the T-intersection at the entrance to town.

Otherwise, you can camp on the beach or string up a hammock at one of El Paraíso's beachfront enramadas. All the enramadas serve basically the same food at similar prices; expect to spend US$5 to US$10 per person for a full, fresh meal.

Getting There & Away

Cuyutlán and Paraíso are connected to the rest of the world through Armería, a dusty but friendly little service center on Hwy 200, 46km southeast of Manzanillo and 55km southwest of Colima. From Armería a 12km paved road heads west past orchards and coconut plantations to Cuyutlán; a similar road runs 8km southwest from Armería to El Paraíso.

To reach either place by bus involves a transfer in Armería. Two bus lines – Sociedad Cooperativa de Autotransportes Colima Manzanillo and Autotransportes Nuevo Horizonte – have offices and stops just off Armería's main street. They both operate 2nd-class buses to Manzanillo every half hour from 5am to 12:30am (US$2.50,

45 minutes) and to Colima every half hour from 5:45am to 10:30pm (US$2.50, 5 minutes). Buses go every 20 minutes to Tecomán (US$0.70, 25 minutes), where you can connect with buses heading southeast on Hwy 200 to Lázaro Cárdenas and elsewhere. Just a couple of doors down from the local bus stops, Flecha Amarilla runs frequent 2nd-class buses to Mexico City and Guadalajara. Across the street, Autotransportes del Sur de Jalisco serves Colima and Manzanillo.

Buses to Cuyutlán and El Paraíso depart from Armería's market, one block north and one block east of the long-distance bus depots. To Cuyutlán, they depart every half hour from 6am to 7:30pm (US$0.75, 20 minutes). To El Paraíso, they go every 45 minutes from 6am to 7:30pm (US$0.65, 15 minutes).

No buses shuttle directly between Cuyutlán and El Paraíso. To go by bus, you must return to Armería and change buses again. It's not as difficult as it sounds, but taxis are also available to link any of the towns directly. Approximate cab fares are: Cuyutlán to Armería (US$6), El Paraíso to Armería (US$4) and Cuyutlán to El Paraíso (US$5).

MICHOACÁN COAST

Much improved Hwy 200 hugs the shoreline most of the way along the beautiful 250km coast of Michoacán, one of Mexico's most beautiful states. The route passes dozens of untouched beaches – some with wide expanses of golden sand, some tucked into tiny rocky coves, some at river mouths where quiet estuaries harbor multitudes of birds. Several have gentle lapping waves that are good for swimming, while others have big breakers suitable for surfing. Many of the beaches are uninhabited, but some have small communities. Mango, coconut, papaya and banana plantations line the highway, while the green peaks of the Sierra Madre del Sur form a lush backdrop inland.

Beaches

At the Michoacán–Colima border, **Boca de Apiza**, deposited at the mouth of the Río Coahuayana, is a mangrove-lined beach with many competing seafood enramadas; turn off Hwy 200 at the town of Coahuayana. Kilometer markers begin counting down from Km 231 at the state border.

Twenty kilometers south, after the highway meets the coast, **San Juan de Alima** (Km 209) is popular with surfers and has many beachfront restaurants and several modern hotels.

A short distance down the coast, **Las Brisas** (Km 207) is another beachside community with places to stay. Still further along, **Playa La Ticla** (Km 183) is another surfing beach with beachfront cabañas for rent.

The next stop is **Faro de Bucerías** (Km 173), known for its clear, pale-blue waters, yellow sand and rocky islands. It's a good spot for camping, swimming and snorkeling, and the local Nahua community prepares fresh seafood.

Further along, white-sand **Playa Maruata** (Km 150) is one of Michoacán's most beautiful beaches, with clear turquoise waters. This is the principal Mexican beach where black sea turtles lay their eggs; these and other species of sea turtles are set free here each year by conservation programs. Camping and discreet nude bathing are possible, and services include rustic cabañas and some palapas serving fresh seafood.

Further south, **Pichilinguillo** (Km 95) is in a small bay, good for swimming. Further still are beautiful unsigned **Barra de Nexpa** (Km 56), popular with surfers; **Caleta de Campos** (Km 50), on a lovely little bay; **La Soledad** (Solitude), a very beautiful, tranquil little beach; and **Las Peñas**, another good surfing beach. **Playa Azul**, 24km northwest of Lázaro Cárdenas, is another laid-back beach community that is easy to visit and has surfable waves.

Barra de Nexpa

☎ 753 / pop 50

At Km 55.5, just north of Puente Nexpa bridge and 1km from the highway down a mostly cobbled road, lies the small community of Nexpa. The salt 'n' pepper bar of sand here, and a good number of healthy waves – which build up and curl sharply in the mornings – are all that's necessary to bring in surfers from around the world. An inland lagoon empties out at the southern end of the sometimes stony 3km beach, with decent swimming there and beyond. Rustic cabañas, good campsites and some decent restaurants add comfort to the mix, and the very laid-back feel completes the recipe for a peaceful stay. Keep an eye out for scorpions, though.

Pablo's Palapa, near Chichos restaurant, repairs and rents surfboards. There's a larger surf shop in the nearby service town of Caleta de Campos (below); a taxi will take you there for about US$3.25.

SLEEPING & EATING

Rio Nexpa Rooms (☎ 531-52-55 in Caleta de Campos; www.surf-mexico.com/sites/nexpa; r US$19; P) This beautifully crafted Southeast Asian style palapa about 200m inland along the river, has four comfortable rooms with three full-sized beds and a loft. There's a shared kitchen, lagoon-side garden area and tranquil communal sitting room.

Gilberto's Cabañas (cabañas for 4 US$15-28, tent/ RV sites US$3/9; P) Gilberto's offers a variety of cabañas, some more rustic than others, some with kitchen, and most with hammocks. There's a communal kitchen and shower block for campers/RVs, and Gilberto offers taxi service to Caleta. Look for Gilberto's sign on the right side as you enter town.

Restaurant Chicho (cabañas US$14-23; mains US$3-10) has good food, good views and basic cabañas for rent. It's just south of the well-signed and always crowded **La Isla Restaurant** (r US$11-20; mains $3-12). Both are within eyeshot of the store at Gilberto's Cabañas. Gringos gather at La Isla in the morning for the serve-yourself coffee. There's also a casual book exchange and taxi service available.

Caleta de Campos

☎ 753 / pop 2000

A friendly little town on a bluff overlooking a lovely azure bay, 'Caleta' (Km 50) is a quiet place, but since it's a regional service center it has a pair of good, clean hotels and several friendly, satisfying places to eat. Caleta's paved main drag has all the essentials, including a telephone caseta, late-night taquerías and torta shops, a pharmacy and several grocery stores. Just off the main drag, near Hotel Yuritzi, is the area's best surf shop, **Surf y Espuma** (☎ 531-52-55; per day gear rentals $6-9), which sells and rents gear. The southern side of the bluff has perfect waves for novice surfers.

Hotel Yuritzi (☎ 531-50-10; www.hotelyuritzi.com in Spanish; Corregidora 10; s/d US$22/28, with air-con US$33/42; P ✕ ﹩) is modern, well maintained and comfortable, and is preferred by business travelers and families.

Hotel Los Arcos (☎ 531-50-38; s/d US$14/19, with air-con & hot water US$35; P ✕), toward the ocean at the end of the main drag, is a bit rundown, but the owners are friendly and the bird's eye view of the Bahía de Bufadero's blowhole is stunning.

First-class Ruta Paraíso and 2nd-class Galeana buses depart from Caleta for Lázaro Cárdenas every 25 minutes from 5am to 7pm (US$3, 1½ hours). In Lázaro Cárdenas, these buses depart from the Galeana terminal on Av Lázaro Cárdenas. A taxi between Caleta de Campos and Nexpa costs around US$3.25; it's a bit less to the Nexpa turnoff on Hwy 200.

Playa Azul

☎ 753 / pop 3500

Playa Azul is a sleepy, dusty, little beach resort backed by lagoons that are fed by tributaries of the Río Balsas. Mexican families fill the hotels during Semana Santa and the Christmas holidays, making the prices rise and reservations necessary. The rest of the time it's quiet, with a negligible trickle of foreign travelers enjoying the long beach and surfable waves. A strong undertow, however, makes swimming touch-and-go; also beware of stray stingrays on the sand. Swimming is better (when it's not mosquito season) at Laguna Pichi, a couple of kilometers east along the beach, where boat trips take visitors to view the plants, birds and other animals that inhabit the surrounding mangrove forest.

ORIENTATION & INFORMATION

Playa Azul is so small and everything is so close that there's little need for street names. Basically, five main streets run parallel to the beach. The beachside street, usually referred to as the Malecón, is officially named Zapata. Heading inland, the next four streets are Carranza, Madero, Independencia and Justo Sierra, in that order.

Independencia is the first north–south street as you enter town from the highway. This is where combis and buses drop off and pick up passengers. The beach is three blocks straight ahead. A few blocks east (left as you face the sea) is a mostly cement, wind-blown plaza. Almost everything you need is somewhere between the plaza and intersection at the entrance to town. A long row of seafood enramadas stretches along the coast.

The **post office** (Madero) is at the northwest corner of the plaza. Telecomm, with fax and telex service, is in the same building (different entrance). There are several telephone casetas around town and public card phones at most hotels.

ACTIVITIES

For swimming, pools provide a safer alternative to the turbulent ocean. Behind Hotel Playa Azul, **Balneario Playa Azul** (Malecón; admission US$1.50, free to Hotel Playa Azul guests; ☼ 10am-6pm Sat & Sun) has a large swimming pool, a water slide and a restaurant/bar. Hotel Playa Azul also has a courtyard pool with a poolside restaurant (see Sleeping & Eating, below).

A few kilometers southeast down the beach, **Laguna de Pichi** makes a good excursion; lanchas can be hired for lagoon tours, and the estuary is good for swimming and bird-watching. You can walk there in half an hour or take a taxi (US$3).

SLEEPING & EATING

You can string up a hammock at most of the beachfront enramadas; ask permission from the family running the restaurant, who probably won't mind if you eat there once or twice. A couple of enramadas provide public toilets and showers. Otherwise there are a couple of reasonable hotels, all with private bathrooms, in town.

Hotel Costa de Oro (Madero s/n; s/d US$14/19; P ☼) Don't let the scummy pool turn you off to this friendly, very basic budget option near the plaza. Most rooms are clean with warm water and nearly new mattresses.

Hotel María Isabel (☎ 536-00-16; Madero s/n; s US$14-32, d US$23-42; P ☼ ☼) On the far (east) side of the plaza, Hotel María has a variety of clean, spacious rooms with a range of amenities.

Hotel Playa Azul (☎ 536-00-24/91; Carranza s/n; r US$40, with air-con & TV US$55; RV sites US$17; P ☼ ☼) The upmarket, 73-room Playa Azul has a small trailer park and enjoyable rooms around a garden courtyard with an inviting pool. The poolside **Las Gaviotas restaurant/bar** (mains US$7-15; ☼ 7:30am-10:30pm) is a good bet for anything from pizza to pozole; if you eat or drink here, you can use both the hotel's pool and the adjacent Balneario Playa Azul.

Playa Azul's beachfront enramadas prepare a tasty selection of fresh seafood at competitive prices – the fanciest are to the right as you face the beach. Try the regional specialty, *pescado relleno,* a fried fillet of fish stuffed with shrimp, octopus and sundry seafood.

Locals recommend two small family restaurants, **Restaurant Galdy** and **Restaurant Familiar Martita**, both on the market street near Madero, around the corner from Hotel Playa Azul. Both serve fresh-squeezed juices and good cheap grub (*comida corrida* US$3.25).

GETTING THERE & AWAY

Combis run every 10 minutes from 5am to 9pm, between Playa Azul and Lázaro Cárdenas (US$1.25, 30 minutes, 24km). They enter Playa Azul and follow Carranza, dropping you off anywhere along the way. In Playa Azul, catch combis on Carranza or as they loop back on Independencia.

Intercity buses don't pass through Playa Azul; they will drop you off 7km to the north at the Hwy 200 junction in La Mira (3.5km east of Playa Azul). To skip Lázaro Cárdenas and go from Playa Azul to Caleta de Campos or beyond, catch the northbound bus at La Mira.

Taxis between Playa Azul and Lázaro Cárdenas cost around US$10.

LÁZARO CÁRDENAS

☎ 753 / pop 78,000

The significant port of Lázaro Cárdenas is Michoacán's largest coastal city. Originally named Melchor Ocampo, its name was changed in 1970 to honor Lázaro Cárdenas, Michoacán's reform-minded governor (1928–32) and Mexico's president (1934–40), who is most famous for nationalizing foreign (mostly US) oil assets during his tenure.

An industrial city, Lázaro has nothing of real interest to travelers – but since it's the terminus of several bus routes, travelers do pass through. Reasons to stop here include changing buses, stocking up on provisions, and heading 24km west to Playa Azul (see p465). If you must spend the night here, you'll find several adequate hotels near the bus stations.

Orientation & Information

The eponymous main drag, Av Lázaro Cárdenas, caters to travelers' needs. Near the bus terminals along Lázaro Cárdenas, the town center is a busy commercial area with travel agencies and banks, including **Banamex** (9am-1pm Mon-Fri) and **Bancomer** for money exchange and ATM. Internet access and long-distance phone service is available next door to Hotel Reyna Pio (below) for US$1.50 per hour.

The state-run **Tourist Office** (532-15-47; Nicolás Bravo 475) is in front of Hotel Casablanca (below), four blocks northwest of the Galeana bus station and a block east of Av Lázaro Cárdenas. It has free city and regional maps.

Sleeping & Eating

There are many more places to stay here in Lázaro than those listed. The following have long been reliable and recommended options:

Hotel Reyna Pio (532-06-20; Corregidora 78; s/d US$17/21;) A comfortable, smallish hotel at the corner of 8 de Mayo, a block east of Av Lázaro Cárdenas.

Hotel Viña del Mar (532-04-15; Javier Mina 352; s/d US$19/24;) Half a block west of Av Lázaro Cárdenas, with a small courtyard swimming pool and plain rooms with air-con, TV and phone.

Hotel Casablanca (537-34-80; Nicolás Bravo 475; s/d US$32/47;) Business-minded luxury a block east of Av Lázaro Cárdenas.

Many cheap restaurants cluster around the bus terminals. Locals recommend **Restaurant El Tejado** (Lázaro Cárdenas s/n, btwn Corregidora & Javier Mina; mains $4.50-10) for an ample, economical meal. If you're tired of Mexican, **Restaurant Kame** (537-26-60; 1 block south of Estrella Blanca bus terminal; lunch US$4.50) is an authentic Japanese eatery with a variety of delicious, multi-course set meals.

Getting There & Away

AIR

The Lázaro Cárdenas airport is 6km east of the center – five minutes by taxi (US$3.50) or colectivo (US$0.50). Aeromar flies to/from Mexico City; Aero Cuahonte flies to/from Uruapan, Morelia and Guadalajara; and Aeroméxico flies to/from Mexico City, Monterrey, Tijuana and Veracruz.

BUS

Lázaro has four bus terminals, all within a few blocks of each other. **Galeana** (532-02-62) and **Parhikuni** (532-30-06), with services northwest to Manzanillo and inland to

Uruapan and Morelia, share a **terminal** (Lázaro Cárdenas 1810, cnr Constitución de 1814). Opposite, Autobuses de Jalisco, La Línea, Vía 2000 and Sur de Jalisco share a **terminal** (537-18-50; Lázaro Cárdenas 1791) and serve the same destinations, plus Colima, Guadalajara and Mexico City.

Estrella Blanca's terminal (532-11-71; Francisco Villa 65), two blocks west behind the Galeana terminal, is also home base for Cuauhtémoc and Elite. From here buses head southeast to Zihuatanejo and Acapulco; up the coast to Manzanillo, Mazatlán and Tijuana; and inland to Uruapan, Morelia and Mexico City. The **Estrella de Oro terminal** (532-02-75; Corregidora 318) is two blocks southwest of Estrella Blanca, and serves Acapulco, Cuernavaca, Mexico City and Zihuatanejo.

Buses from Lázaro Cárdenas include:

Acapulco Estrella Blanca (US$16, 6-7hr, 12 1st-class daily; US$10, 6-7hr, hourly 2nd-class service); Estrella de Oro (US$15, 6-7hr, 1st-class service at 6:30am daily; US$12, 6-7hr, hourly 2nd-class service)

Caleta de Campos Galeana (US$3.50, 1½hr, 2nd-class every 30min 6:20am-8pm)

Colima Autobuses de Jalisco & La Línea (US$20, 4-6½hr); Sur de Jalisco (US$19, 4-6½hr) Same buses as to Guadalajara.

Guadalajara Autobuses de Jalisco/La Línea 'Plus' (US$32, 9-11hr, service at 10:30am daily; US$30, 9-11hr, 1st-class at 12:15pm daily); Sur de Jalisco (US$22.50, 9-11hr, 2nd-class at 2:30am, 7am & 5pm daily)

Manzanillo Estrella Blanca (US$20, 6-7hr, 1st-class at 1:30pm & 11:40pm daily); Galeana (US$14.50, 6-7hr, 4 2nd-class daily); Sur de Jalisco (US$14, 6-7hr, 2nd-class at 2:30pm & 5:30pm daily) Or take Sur de Jalisco's Tecomán bus (US$12, 5½hr, hourly) and then a frequent local bus from there.

Mexico City Vía 2000 (US$42, 12hr, 2 1st-class daily) To Terminal Poniente.

Mexico City Estrella Blanca (US$34, 10-11hr, 3 1st-class daily); Estrella de Oro (US$35, 10-11hr, 1st-class at 5:50am, 9:50am, 7pm, 8pm & 9pm daily) To Terminal Sur.

Morelia Vía 2000 (US$25, 4-8hr, 3 1st-class daily); Galeana/Parhikuni 'Plus' (US$23, 4-8hr, 12 1st-class daily); Estrella Blanca (US$22, 4-8hr, 1st-class daily); Galeana/Parhikuni ((US$19, 4-8hr, 14 2nd-class daily)

Puerto Vallarta Estrella Blanca (US$34, 11-12hr, 12:10pm daily)

Uruapan (US$12-17, 3-6hr) Same buses as to Morelia.

Zihuatanejo (US$4-7, 2-3hr) Same buses as to Acapulco.

Combis to Playa Azul via La Mira trawl Av Lázaro Cárdenas every 10 minutes from 5am to 9pm (US$1.25, 30 minutes, 24km), stopping to rebait outside the Autobuses de

CENTRAL PACIFIC COAST

Jalisco terminal, opposite Galeana. A taxi between Lázaro Cárdenas and Playa Azul costs US$10 to US$12.

TRONCONES, BAHÍA MANZANILLO & MAJAHUA

☎ 755 / pop 400

A 25-minute drive or one-hour bus ride northwest of Zihuatanejo, Playa Troncones is a beach on the open sea with several beachfront seafood restaurants. It's a popular outing for Zihuatanejo families and home to a growing number of gringo expats. Just to the north is Playa Manzanillo, which lines Bahía Manzanillo – a lovely little bay. And just north of the bay is the quiet little fishing village of Majahua.

Orientation & Information

The one-burro village of Troncones, 100m inland from the beach, has just two roads: the 3km paved road coming in from Hwy 200, and another dirt track stretching along the beach for 5km. The village surrounds the end of the paved road, but most of what you'll probably be looking for is along the unpaved beachfront road. Where the road coming in from the highway meets the sea, the Burro Borracho is 1km to the left, the Casa de la Tortuga 1.5km to the right (north), Playa Manzanillo is 3.5km north of that, and Majahua is a 10-minute walk past Playa Manzanillo. From Majahua, another dirt road (rough in wet season) leads to Hwy 200 near Km 32.

Internet access isn't cheap, but it's available at the Inn at Manzanillo Bay (see Sleeping, p469) for US$8 per hour and at Jaguar Tours (see Activities, below) for US$6 per hour. The folks at Casa Canela & Canelita (see Sleeping, p469) will do your laundry for US$1.25 per kilo. There's good prearrival information available online at www.troncones.com.mx.

Activities

Jaguar Tours (☎ 553-28-62; www.jaguartours.net; 🕑 closed Sun), opposite Casa de la Tortuga (p469), runs a range of tours from cave and canopy adventures (US$50) to sea turtle observation (US$130 for four) and surf tours (US$175). Staff also rent out surfboards (US$14) and mountain bikes (US$14).

SCORPIONS

Many travelers never even see one, but *alacranes* – or scorpions – are a common and dangerous pest in many parts of Mexico. There are over 200 species of this particular arachnid worldwide, all of them poisonous to some degree (though only seven can actually kill a human being). Their habitat ranges widely, from high desert areas to low tropical coastlines.

In Durango scorpions are collected by the thousands and turned into attractive knick-knacks like keychains, paperweights and napkin holders. But across other parts of Mexico, the little beasts aren't seen in quite the same light. Scorpions sting over 200,000 people and kill hundreds of children in the country every year, and intense extermination programs have successfully been implemented to limit the populations of this 'national pest.'

Scorpions are often seen on the floors, walls or even ceilings of old dwellings, such as wooden beach cabañas, though they also favor trash heaps and rock piles. They often like to hide out in dark, enclosed spaces such as your hiking boots, backpack, clothes and even bed sheets. If staying in rustic abodes, shake out your footwear, clothing and packs – especially when they've been lying on the ground. Hands and feet are the body parts most often pricked, so don't reach into strange rocky crevices indiscriminately. You shouldn't get overly paranoid, but be aware that the little creatures could lurk in some surprising places.

Young children and feeble elderly folk are most affected by stings. If you're a healthy adult (and not especially allergic to insect bites or stings) you should survive an encounter, though you may experience intense pain, convulsions, sweating, difficulty swallowing, rolling eyes, nausea and heart palpitations. Get yourself to a Mexican clinic quickly; they should have an excellent antivenin serum readily available, which starts working within 20 minutes or so after application.

But remember that scorpions aren't all bad – they feed on a variety of insects, including cockroaches! In places where there are many scorpions, cockroach populations are low. So if you're lucky enough to see one of these critters, think twice before descending the boot.

Playa Troncones has several world-class **surfing** breaks; it's best to get out in the morning, before 11am when the breeze picks up, or around sunset when the surf gets glassy. Troncones Point is popular, and there are at least 20 other surfing spots, good for beginning to advanced surfers, along the coast within 20km. Saladita, 7km from Troncones, has an awesome half-mile left-hand break.

There's good **snorkeling** at Manzanillo Point, at the north end of Troncones. Other **water activities** in the area include fishing, sea kayaking, body-boarding, horseback riding, hiking, bird-watching and turtle-watching – you can observe sea turtles laying their eggs here in the sand on moonlit nights. Relaxing on the beach is another major 'activity.'

Sleeping

While still a sleepy hideaway, Troncones has been experiencing a gringo-backed building boom since the *ejidos* (communal landholding) went up for public sale in December 1995. Troncones' pristine 5km shoreline now boasts more than 80 beachfront rooms, and Playa Manzanillo and Majahua appear poised to follow a similar development trajectory. Reservations are necessary almost everywhere in Troncones during the high season (November through April). Prices the rest of the year can be as much as 50% lower than those listed below. But beware, most business owners aren't around in the low season.

Quinta d'Liz (☎ 553 2914; www.playatroncones.com; d with breakfast US$28) These six beachfront, simple but stylish bungalows are popular with 20-somethings. The best deal in town.

Walking from town along the beach road south you'll come to the following:

La Puesta del Sol (☎ 553-28-18, in the US 323-913-0423; www.troncones.com.mx/puestadelsol; r US$30-55, ste US$75-130) This attractive four-room, three-story palapa offers a variety of rooms – from a simple 'surfers' room' to a super-luxurious penthouse apartment.

Casas Canela & Canelita (☎ 553-28-00; www .tronconestropic.com/canela.html; r/house US$35/100) Although it's not right on the beach, this two-building garden property is an affordable, comfortable option. Casa Canela, the house in front, sleeps six, and has a large kitchen and hammock-strewn front porch. Casa Canelita is a duplex with rooms that can be rented individually and share a kitchen and terrace.

Down the northern stretch of the unpaved beachfront road, from nearest to furthest, are the following:

Casa Ki (☎ 553-28-15; www.casa-ki.com; bungalows US$75-185) Ed and Ellen Weston's charming B&B retreat includes a variety of oceanview rooms and a thoughtfully furnished main house with a full kitchen.

Casa de la Tortuga (☎ 553-28-62; www.troncones .com.mx/tortuga; r without/with bathroom US$45/65) Owned and operated by the gregarious man who put Troncones on the gringo map, this modest B&B has six comfortable rooms that can be rented individually or together. There's a large round dining table conducive to social breakfasts and an attractive beachside patio and self-service beer bar.

Casa Delfín Sonriente (☎ 553-328-03, in the US 831-688-6578; www.casadelfinsonriente.com; r US$65-119; ⌦ ⌦) This Spanish-Mediterranean-style seaside B&B villa offers a variety of well-furnished accommodations, some with aircon. All units have access to the swimming pool, artists' workshop and communal master kitchen.

Inn at Manzanillo Bay (☎ 553-28-84; www.man zanillobay.com; bungalows US$112; ℗ ⌦) This upscale surf-resort has eight well-appointed thatched-roof bungalows around a beautiful pool within earshot of a classic point break.

Hacienda Edén (☎ 553-28-02; www.edenmex.com; r US$65-85, bungalows US$85-95) On tranquil Playa Manzanillo, 3.5km north of Troncones town, this beachfront bed and breakfast has four lovely bungalows, 10 beautifully decorated rooms, a gourmet restaurant and a full bar. The friendly proprietors, Eva and Jim, are gracious hosts.

Anita LaPointe, owner of the **Tropic of Cancer** (see Eating & Drinking, p470) beach club, manages several properties in Troncones, and, with a bit of time, can set you up with anything from an affordable room to a luxurious house. Drop her an email or stop by to let her know what you're after.

Other recommendations:

Miscelánea Jasmín (s/d US$14/19) Behind the in-town abarrotes shop, has decent rooms with bathrooms.

El Burro Burracho (www.burroborracho.com; r US$60) Several new bungalows have been added to this old favorite.

Eating & Drinking

The cheapest dining options are in Troncones and Majahua. Both towns have several taco stands where you can eat well for under US$3, as well as a few beachfront enramadas where US$10 goes a long way. Good Mexican-owned beachfront restaurants include **Costa Brava**, north of the T-intersection just across the bridge, and nearby **Doña Nica's Enramada**, just south of the T-intersection.

Tropic of Cancer (www.tronconestropic.com; mains US$4-9; ☺ closed Tue) A few shuffles further south of Doña Nica's, this restaurant/bar, run by Quebecois expat Anita LaPointe, is a popular spot with a few hard-to-get rooms for rent.

Burro Borracho (mains US$5-10) Further south, the Burro Borracho is a happening beachfront restaurant/bar with excellent burgers and seafood and occasional sports on the tube. The Burro is also Troncones' main information center and hosts a wonderful folkloric show on Sunday night at 8pm.

At the south end of Bahía Manzanillo, you'll find **Restaurant Playa Manzanillo** (aka María's; mains US$3-7), a traditional Mexican seafood enramada; and the **Inn at Manzanillo Bay** (mains US$7-12), which serves Thai-style fried shrimp tacos – as well as gringo-inspired gourmet takes on traditional Mexican dishes.

La Cocina del Sol (mains $4-9) Further north at Hacienda Edén, the renowned La Cocina del Sol is run by Mexican-food aficionado Christian, and is open for all meals (one dinner seating only, at 6:30pm, reservations recommended). On Sunday there's breakfast and a barbecue. Keep your eye out for Christian's new casual **Cafe Cocina del Sol**, near the bridge close to town.

In Majahua **Marta** has an ideal bayside location and makes a *machaca* ($4) like no other in all of Mexico – it's a must for adventurous eaters.

Getting There & Away

If you're driving to Troncones from Ixtapa or Zihuatanejo, head northwest on Hwy 200 toward Lázaro Cárdenas. Just north of Km 30 you'll see the marked turnoff for Troncones; follow this winding paved road 3km west to the beach.

There are no direct buses from Ixtapa or Zihuatanejo, but 2nd-class buses heading northwest toward Lázaro Cárdenas or La Unión will let you off at the turnoff for Troncones. In Zihua, buses heading for Lázaro Cárdenas depart from the long-distance bus terminals; in La Unión, buses heading for Ixtapa and Zihuatanejo depart from the lot a couple of blocks east of the market. Ask to be let off at the Troncones turnoff (US$1, 30 minutes to 60 minutes).

A microbus shuttles between Hwy 200 and Troncones every half hour or so in the morning and evening, and every hour or so around siesta time (US$0.50). We found it safe and easy to hitch from the turnoff into Troncones, and also vice versa, but locals note that you'll probably have better luck and more success flagging down a bus on Hwy 200 for the return trip to Zihua during daylight hours. If someone offers, ride to Pantla, halfway to Zihua, then catch a micro or 2nd-class bus (both US$1.25) from there.

A taxi from Ixtapa or the Zihua airport to Troncones costs around US$35/50 one-way/round-trip. Taxis from Zihua to Troncones can be bargained down to around US$23/40 one-way/round-trip, and taxis from Troncones back to Zihua can be even cheaper.

IXTAPA

☎ 755 / pop 1500

Not so long ago, Ixtapa (eeks-*tah*-pah) was a coconut plantation and nearby Zihuatanejo was a sleepy fishing village. Then in 1970, Fonatur – the Mexican government tourism-development organization that conceived Cancún – decided that the Pacific coast needed a Cancún-like resort. After many focus groups, Fonatur sagely selected Ixtapa, 210km northwest of Acapulco, for its resort complex. Proximity to the USA, an average temperature of 27°C, tropical vegetation and fine beaches were its criteria. Fonatur bought the coconut plantation, paved streets, dug reservoirs, strung electrical lines and rolled out the red carpet for hotel chains.

Today, Ixtapa boasts a string of luxurious resort hotels that are spread out along Bahía del Palmar; Club Med and some fine beaches are further west beyond Punta Ixtapa. It's a beautiful spot, but many travelers cringe at the purpose-built glitz targeted primarily at gringos and a growing Mexican middle class.

Information

The state-run **Sefotur Tourist Office** (☎ 553-19-67; ☺ 8am-8:30pm Mon-Fri, 8am-3pm Sat) is in Plaza Los Patios, opposite the Hotel Presidente Inter-Continental. The **tourist police station** (☎ 553-20-08; Centro Commercial La Puerta) is nearby. Note: Ixtapa has several offices and sidewalk kiosks offering tourist information. They may provide free maps and answer queries, but their ultimate purpose is to promote time-share schemes.

Ixtapa has banks and casas de cambio where you can change US dollars and traveler's checks. **American Express** (☎ 553-08-53; ☺ 9am-6pm Mon-Fri, 9am-2pm Sat) is at NH Krystal Ixtapa.

The town doesn't have a post office, but you can drop mail at big hotels. The **Telecomm** (☺ 9am-3pm Mon-Fri) office is behind Sefotur.

Sights & Activities
BEACHES

Ixtapa's big hotels line **Playa del Palmar**, a long, broad stretch of white sand that's often overrun by parasail and jet-ski out-fits. Be very careful if you swim here: the large waves crash straight down and there's a powerful undertow. The west end of this beach, just before the entrance to the lagoon, is locally called **Playa Escolleras** and is favored by surfers.

Further west, heading past the marina, are **Playa San Juan**, **Playa Casa Blanca** and **Playa Cuatas**. These small, beautiful beaches are among the best beaches in the area. Unfortunately, they've all been effectively privatized by new developments; unless you can gain access by skiff or helicopter, you're probably out of luck, since the Mexican public-access law appears to have been overlooked here.

To the west, past Punta Ixtapa, are **Playa Quieta** and **Playa Linda**, both popular with locals. From Playa Linda's pier, boats run every half hour (if there are enough passengers) to **Isla Ixtapa**, which is just offshore and has four beaches good for **snorkeling**; you can rent gear there for about US$5 a day. The round-trip boat ride (five minutes each way) costs US$3; boats operate from 8am to 5pm daily.

ACTIVITIES

Bicycling is a breeze along a 15km *ciclopista* (bicycle path) that stretches from Playa Linda, north of Ixtapa, practically into Zihuatanejo. Bicycles can be rented in Ixtapa (see Getting There & Around, p473).

Scuba diving is a popular pastime in the area's warm clear waters. NAUI-affiliated **Zihuatanejo Scuba Center** (☎ 554-21-47; www.divemexico.com) offers daily morning and afternoon dives at more than 30 dive sites. The company's Ixtapa office is in the Centro Comercial Ixtapa. See p476 for other recommendations.

The **Ixtapa Club de Golf Palma Real** (☎ 553-10-62) and the **Marina Ixtapa Golf Club** (☎ 553-14-10) both have 18-hole courses, tennis courts and swimming pools. Children will enjoy the **mini-golf** near Ixtapa's Cine Flamingos. There's a **yacht club** (☎ 553-11-31; Porto Ixtapa) beside the Ixtapa Marina. **Horseback riding** is available on Playa Linda (see Beaches, p471).

Kid-stuff is the specialty of the NH Krystal Ixtapa's **Krystalitos Children's Club** (☎ 553-03-33; child 4-12 yrs US$13; ☉ 10am-5pm). Drop your children off at 10am to enroll; they'll be fed breakfast and lunch, enjoy fun activities all day long and receive a club T-shirt and hat. The club is open to everyone, not just guests of the hotel.

Magic World (☎ 553-13-59; admission US$4; ☉ 10:30am-5:30pm Fri-Sun), an aquatic park beside the Hotel Ixtapa Palace, has rides, water slides, toboggans and other amusements.

Next to Carlos 'n' Charlie's, the new **Delfiniti Project Dolphinarium** (☎ 553-27-07; www.delfiniti.com; 20/45min US$75/150) offers visitors the chance to swim with and learn about dolphins. Daily sessions start at 10am, noon and 4pm.

Sleeping

Ixtapa's resorts are all top-end, costing upwards of US$150 a night in the winter high season (mid-December to Easter) and just a bit less the rest of the year. If you want to stay in Ixtapa, try arranging a package deal through a travel agent, including airfare from your home country, or check online. Otherwise, Zihuatanejo's accommodations are cheaper.

Among the hotels in Ixtapa – all with top-notch amenities – are the **Barceló Ixtapa Beach Resort** (☎ 553-18-58; www.barcelo.com), **NH Krystal Ixtapa** (☎ 553-03-33; www.nh-hotels.com),

Riviera Beach Resort (☎ 553-10-66; www.riviera.com.mx) and **Las Brisas** (☎ 553-21-21; www.brisas.com).

Ixtapa resorts with all-inclusive rates include **Club Med** (☎ 553-00-40; www.clubmed.com), **Hotel Presidente Inter-Continental** (☎ 553-00-18; www.icontinental.com) and **Qualton Club** (☎ 552-00-80; www.qualton.com).

Eating

Ixtapa has plenty of restaurants in addition to those in the big hotels.

Carlos 'n' Charlie's (☎ 553-00-85; Paseo del Palmar s/n; mains $6-14), **Señor Frog's** (☎ 553-02-72; Blvd Ixtapa s/n; mains $6-13) and **Señor-Itto** (☎ 553-02-72; Blvd Ixtapa s/n; mains $7-15) deliver decent meals and good times. Itto's has an all-you-can-eat fest on Saturday from 2:30pm to 5pm. The latter two are side by side in the Centro Comercial, opposite the Presidente Inter-Continental; Carlos 'n' Charlie's is further west, by Hotel Posada Real.

Beccofino (☎ 553-17-70; Veleros Lote 6, Ixtapa Marina Plaza; mains US$14-28; ☉ 9am-11pm) Indoor-outdoor Beccofino enjoys a good reputation for delicious Italian cuisine, especially seafood. Several other good restaurants ring the marina.

Villa de la Selva (☎ 553-03-62; Paseo de la Roca Lote D; mains US$14-30; ☉ 6:30-11:30pm) Reservations are a must at this elegant Mexican–Mediterranean restaurant in the former home of Mexican president Luis Echeverría. The cliffside villa overlooks the ocean (sunsets are superb), near the Las Brisas hotel.

Entertainment

All the big hotels have bars and nightclubs, and most also have discos. The best disco is NH Krystal Ixtapa's **Christine** (☎ for reservations 553-04-56), with no cover on Monday. The Barceló Ixtapa Beach Resort's **Sanca Bar** is popular for dancing to Latin music. The best lobby bar is at **Las Brisas**. **Liquid** is in Ixtapa's Centro Comercial. Also popular in Ixtapa are **Carlos 'n' Charlie's** and **Señor Frog's**, lively chain restaurant/bars with dancing.

Behind Señor Frog's in the Centro Comercial Ixtapa, the restaurant-bar **Los Mandiles** (☎ 553-03-79) has popular Bongo's disco upstairs.

Inside the Magic World aquatic park is the newer **Millenium disco** (☎ 553-27-10; Paseo de las Garzas s/n; ☉ Wed-Sat).

At the top of a 25m-high lighthouse, **El Faro** (☎ 553-10-27; Marina Ixtapa) is a great bar for watching the sunset and also has music and dancing.

Several of Ixtapa's big hotels hold evening 'Fiestas Mexicanas,' which typically include a Mexican buffet and open bar, entertainment (traditional Mexican dancing, mariachis and cockfighting demonstrations), door prizes and dancing; the total price is usually US$33 to US$40. The **Barceló Ixtapa Beach Resort** holds fiestas year-round; in the high season several other hotels, including the **Dorado Pacífico** (☎ 553-04-76), also present fiestas. The **Riviera Beach Resort** (☎ 553-10-66) holds a weekly show with a pre-Hispanic theme; **Club Med** presents a variety of international theme shows. Reservations can be made directly or through travel agents.

Ixtapa's relatively new and plush **Cine Flamingos** (☎ 553-24-90; admission US$4), behind the tourist office and opposite the Plaza Ixpamar and mini-golf, screens two films nightly, usually in English with Spanish subtitles.

Shopping

If your idea of a fun activity is shopping, head to Ixtapa's Tourist Market, opposite the Barceló Ixtapa Beach Resort. It's packed with everything from tacky T-shirts to silver jewelry and hand-painted pottery.

Getting There & Around

For information on getting to Zihuatanejo, the essential stop for getting to Ixtapa, see p482. Private colectivo vans provide transportation from the airport to Ixtapa for US$6 per person, but not in the other direction. A taxi to the airport costs US$10 to US$12 from Ixtapa.

Local 'Directo' and 'B Viejo' buses run frequently between Ixtapa and Zihua, a 15-minute ride. They depart every 15 minutes from 6am to 11pm (US$0.50). In Ixtapa, buses stop all along the main street, in front of all the hotels. In Zihua, buses depart from the corner of Juárez and Morelos. Buses marked 'Zihua–Ixtapa–Playa Linda' continue through Ixtapa to Playa Linda (US$0.65), stopping near Playa Quieta on the way, and operate from 7am to 7pm.

Cabs are plentiful in Ixtapa. You should always agree on the fare before climbing into the cab. Prices between Zihua and Ixtapa are around US$4. If you can't hail a taxi on the street, call **Radio Taxi UTAAZ** (☎ 554-33-11).

Ixtapa has several places renting motorbikes (around US$40 per hour), including **Fun On Wheels** (☎ 553 02 59), in the Centro Comercial Los Patios. Most of these places also rent mountain bikes for around US$3.50/20 per hour/day. You'll probably need a driver's license and credit card to rent.

ZIHUATANEJO

☎ 755 / pop 58,000

Like its sister city Ixtapa, cacophonous Zihuatanejo (see-wah-tahn-*nay*-ho) is quite touristy. Nevertheless, it retains an easygoing, coastal ambience, and its setting on a beautiful bay with several fine beaches makes it a gratifying place to visit. Small-scale fishing is still an economic mainstay; if you stroll down by the pier early in the morning, you can join the pelicans in greeting successful fisherfolk and inspecting the morning's catch. Needless to say, seafood is superb here.

Orientation

Though Zihua's suburbs are growing considerably, spreading around Bahía de Zihuatanejo and climbing the hills behind town, in the city's center everything is compressed within a few blocks. It's difficult to get lost; there are only a few streets and they're clearly marked. Ixtapa, 8km northwest, is easily reached by frequent local buses or by taxi. At press time, Zihua's street-numbering scheme was changing: new blue metal number plates were posted around town but hadn't officially been adopted yet. New numbers are given here wherever they were available.

Information

EMERGENCY

Hospital (☎ 554-36-50; Av Morelos near Mar Egeo)
Police (☎ 554-20-40, 060)
Tourist Police (☎ 554-22-07)

INTERNET ACCESS

Zihuatanejo is crawling with Internet cafés, and competition is fierce. Several other places have air-con but charge significantly more for slower service. The following places charge US$1 per hour.
Chachito.com (Ejido 16; ☯ 10am-midnight Mon-Sat, 10am-9pm Sun) Crowded with only four computers.
Internet@ (cnr Álvarez & 5 de Mayo) Air-con, comfortable and low-key.
Zihua@.com (Ejido 17; ☯ closed Sun) Small with a decent connection.

LAUNDRY

Lavandería Express (☎ 554-43-93; González 35 & Cuauhtémoc 37A) Free pickup/delivery; US$4.50 for 3kg.

MONEY

Zihuatanejo has many banks and *casas de cambio* where you can change US dollars and traveler's checks. **Bancomer** (cnr Juárez & Bravo), **Santander Serfin** (cnr Juárez & Bravo), **Banorte** (cnr Juárez & Ejido) and **Banamex** (cnr Ejido & Guerrero) all have air-conditioned ATMs and keep normal business hours. A less busy Banamex ATM is inside **Farmapronto** (Juárez 12).

Casa de Cambio Guiball (Galeana 4; ⏱ 8am-9pm) offers slightly less favorable rates than banks but is open longer hours.

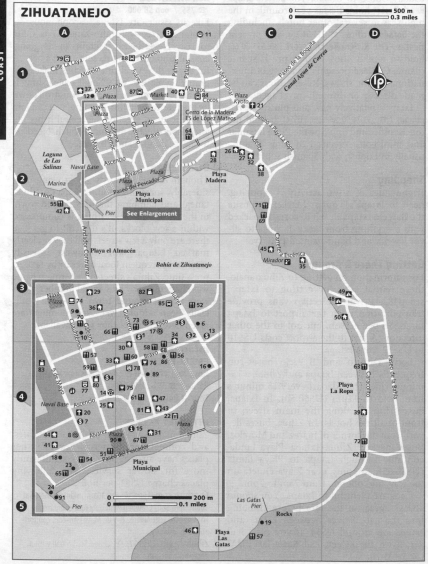

POST

Post Office (off Morelos) Well signed but still hard to find. Several other places in town also sell stamps.

TELEPHONE & FAX

Long-distance telephone and fax services are available at several telephone *casetas*, including two on the corner of Galeana and Ascencio. Public Lada telephones are all around town. **Telecomm** (inside the post office; ☻8am-6pm Mon-Fri, 9am-1pm Sat) has a fax service.

TOURIST INFORMATION

The **Muncipal Tourist Office** (☎ /fax 553-19-68; www.ixtapa-zihuatanejo.com; Zihuatanejo Pte s/n, Colonia La Deportiva; ☻8am-4pm Mon-Fri) is upstairs in the *Ayuntamiento* (City Hall), 2km northeast of the town center (local buses between Ixtapa and Zihuatanejo stop out front). During the high season it operates a **tourist kiosk** (Álvarez s/n; ☻9am-8pm) in the heart of town that offers free information, maps and brochures.

TRAVEL AGENCIES

Various agencies provide travel services and arrange local tours. Two of Zihua's biggest agencies are **Turismo Internacional del**

Pacífico (TIP; ☎ 554-75-10/11; cnr Juárez & Álvarez) and **América-Ixtamar Viajes** (☎ 554-35-90; cnr Cuauhtémoc & Bravo).

Sights & Activities

MUSEO ARQUEOLÓGICO DE LA COSTA GRANDE

At the east end of Paseo del Pescador, this small **archeology museum** (☎ 554-75-52; admission US$0.50; ☻ closed Mon) houses exhibits on the history, archaeology and culture of the Guerrero coast, with Spanish captions; a free English-language brochure has translations.

BEACHES

Waves are gentle at all Bahía de Zihuatanejo's beaches. If you want big ocean waves, head west toward Ixtapa.

Playa Municipal, in front of town, is the least appealing swimming beach on Bahía de Zihuatanejo. **Playa Madera** is a pleasant five-minute walk from Playa Municipal along a concrete walkway (popular with young couples in the evening) around the rocky point.

Walk over the hill along the steep Carretera Escénica for another 15 to 20 minutes from Playa Madera, past the mirador, and you'll reach the broad, 2km expanse of **Playa La Ropa**, bordered by palm trees and seafood restaurants. It's a pleasant walk, with the road rising up onto cliffs offering a fine view over the water. One of Zihua's most beautiful beaches, La Ropa is great for swimming, parasailing, waterskiing and sand-soccer. You can also rent sailboards and sailboats.

Opposite Zihuatanejo, **Playa Las Gatas** is a protected beach, crowded with sunbeds and restaurants. It's good for snorkeling (there's some coral) and as a swimming spot for children, but beware of sea urchins. According to legend, Calzontzin, a Tarascan chief, built a stone barrier here in pre-Hispanic times to keep the waves down and prevent sea creatures from entering, making it a sort of private swimming pool. Beach shacks and restaurants rent snorkeling gear for around US$5 per day.

Boats to Playa Las Gatas depart frequently from the Zihuatanejo pier from 8am to 5pm daily. Tickets (US$3.25 round-trip) are sold at the ticket booth at the foot of the pier; one-way tickets can be bought on board. Or you can reach Playa Las Gatas by walking around the bay from Playa La Ropa; a road takes you half the way, then scramble up and down slippery rocks for 15 to 20 minutes before reaching the Las Gatas pier.

Between Zihuatanejo and Ixtapa, **Playa Majahua** is accessible via a road serving a new hotel zone there, similar to Ixtapa. The beach, facing the open sea, has large waves and similar conditions to Ixtapa.

A boat goes to **Isla Ixtapa** (p471) from the Zihuatanejo pier, but only when there are eight passengers or more. It departs at 11am and leaves the island at around 4pm. The cruise takes an hour each way (US$11 round-trip).

About 10km south of Zihuatanejo, halfway between town and the airport, **Playa Larga** has big waves, beachfront restaurants and horseback riding. Nearby **Playa Manzanillo**, a secluded white-sand beach reachable by boat from Zihuatanejo, is said to offer the best snorkeling in the area. Between these two beaches is **Playa Riscalillo**. To reach Playa Larga, take a 'Coacoyul' combi (US$0.65) from Juárez opposite the market and get off at the turnoff to Playa Larga;

another combi will take you from the turnoff to the beach.

SNORKELING & SCUBA DIVING
Snorkeling is good at Playa Las Gatas and even better at Playa Manzanillo, especially in the dry season when visibility is best. Marine life is abundant here due to a convergence of currents, and the visibility can be great – up to 35m. Migrating humpback whales pass through from December to February; manta rays can be seen all year, but you're most likely to spot them in summer, when the water is clearest, bluest and warmest. Snorkel gear can be rented at Playa Las Gatas for around US$5 per day.

The same beaches also have dive operators, who will take you diving for US$50/75 for one/two tanks, or give you scuba lessons in the quiet water. Based in Playa Las Gatas, **Carlo Scuba** (☎ 554-35-70; www.carloscuba.com; Playa Las Gatas) offers a variety of PADI courses.

Zihua's most professional dive outfit is the NAUI-affiliated **Zihuatanejo Scuba Center** (☎ 554-21-47; www.divemexico.com), offering daily morning and afternoon dives at more than 30 dive sites. The company's home base is Hotel Paraíso Real (see Sleeping, p478) on Playa La Ropa.

Conveniently located in town, **Buceo Nautilus Divers** (☎ 554-91-91; www.nautilus-divers .com; Álvarez s/n) does all of the usual dives and certification as well.

Snorkeling trips are made by boat to Playa Manzanillo, about an hour's ride south from Zihuatanejo. Zihuatanejo Scuba Center takes snorkeling trips there. Or you can hire a boat at the foot of the Zihuatanejo pier, stop at Playa Las Gatas to rent snorkeling gear, and off you go.

SPORTFISHING
Sportfishing is also popular. Sailfish are caught here year-round; seasonal fish include blue or black marlin (March to May), roosterfish (September to October), wahoo (October), mahimahi (November to December) and Spanish mackerel (December).

Three fishing cooperatives are based near Zihuatanejo's pier: the **Sociedad Cooperativa de Lanchas de Recreo y Pesca Deportiva del Muelle Teniente José Azueta** (☎ 554-20-56, 044-755-559-52-79), at the foot of the pier; **Servicios Turísticos Acuáticos de Zihuatanejo Ixtapa** (☎ 554-41-62; Paseo del Pescador 6) and **Sociedad**

Cooperativa Benito Juárez (☎ 554-37-58; Paseo del Pescador 20-2). Any of these can arrange deep-sea fishing trips, from around US$150 for up to four people including equipment. Alternatively, you can walk along the pier and negotiate, as chatting it up in a friendly lazy style will certainly yield the best deal here. French and English are spoken at **Whisky Water World** (☎ 554-01-47; www .zihuatanejosportfishing.com; Paseo del Pescador 20).

Tours

Most travel agencies offer a wide array of tours (see Travel Agencies, p475). Interesting possibilities include: the pre-Hispanic La Soledad de Maciel archaeological zone, also called La Chole, 20km southeast of Zihua; Pantla, a brick-making center on Hwy 200 a half hour northwest of Zihuatanejo; and Petatlán (p483), a colonial town on Hwy 200 a half hour southeast of Zihuatanejo.

A couple of sailboat cruises tour local waters and can include snorkeling as part of the package.

Tristar (☎ 554-26-94, 554-82-70; www.tristarsailing .com) is a 67ft trimaran based in Bahía de Zihuatanejo that offers a couple of different excursions. The 'Sail & Snorkel' trip (US$55, 10am to 2:30pm) goes outside the bay for brief snorkeling (gear-rental US$5) at Playa Manzanillo, about an hour's cruise away. The trip includes lunch, an open bar, flying from the spinnaker and a great party. The 2½-hour sunset cruise (US$45, 6pm to 8:30pm) heads around the bay and out along the coast of Ixtapa. Add US$3 for transportation to/from any hotel in Ixtapa. Reservations are required; private charters are also available.

Nirvana (☎ 554-59-15), a 65ft Australian-built wooden cutter, offers day-sailing trips (US$70) including snorkeling, swimming, sailing and lunch, as well as sunset cruises (US$50 with snacks and open bar) and private charters. Ring ahead for reservations.

Sleeping

Zihuatanejo has a good selection of reasonably priced places to stay. But during the high season many hotels here fill up, so phone ahead to reserve a room; if you don't like what you get, you can always look for another room early the next day. The busiest times of year are Semana Santa and the week between Christmas and New Year; at these times you must reserve a room and be prepared to pony up extra pesos. Tourism is much slower and rates are often negotiable from mid-April to mid-December. Most places in Zihua will offer 10% to 20% (negotiable) off rack rates for longer stays, if asked. The following prices are for the high season.

BUDGET

The budget hotels listed here are in central Zihuatanejo and have rooms with fans.

Hotel Raúl Tres Marías (☎ 554-21-91, 554-25-91; r3mariasnoria@yahoo.com; La Noria 4; s/d US$25/30) Across the lagoon footbridge, this clean place is many a frequent visitor's home away from home. Many of its spacious rooms (with cold-water showers and portable fans) open onto large shared terraces. The wooden shuttered windows do let in quite a bit of noise.

Angela's Hotel & Hostel (☎ 554-50-84; www .zihuatanejo.com.mx/angelas; Ascencio 10; dm/d US$7/13; 🖳) Friendly, convenient and helpful, this hostel is hard to beat. Rooms are dark and crowded, but there is a shared kitchen and Internet service (US$1 per hour) available.

Hotel Casa Aurora (☎ 554-36-92; www.zihuatanejo .com.mx/aurora; Bravo 60; s/d US$19/28, with air-con US$33/43; 🍴) Upstairs rooms are the way to go at the well-kept Casa Aurora, which is more like a mid-range option. There are also bungalows available on Playa La Ropa.

Casa de Huéspedes Miriam (☎ 554-39-86; Nava 17; per person US$8; P) This old-timer is slowly seeing improvements in its spacious, clean fan-only rooms with cold-water showers.

Hotel Ulises (☎ 554-37-51; Armada de México 9; s/d US$12/15) Across from the sleepy Club Naval, this family-run hotel has 16 crowded, basic rooms with hot water bath. Upstairs rooms are brighter.

Other recommendations:

Hotel Lari's (☎ 554-37-67; Altamirano 28; s/d US$14/23; P) TV and off-street parking.

Hotel Posada Coral (☎ 554-54-77; cnr Los Mangos & Las Palmas; s/d US$14/17) Near the main market, basic if a bit noisy.

Casa de Huéspedes La Playa (☎ 554-22-47; Álvarez 6-7; per person US$9) Bottom-of-the-barrel hotel, usually full with repeat visitors.

Camping is available in Playa La Ropa at two small, basic trailer parks – actually just the backyards of a couple of friendly families. Both offer spaces for tents (US$4) and trailers (from US$10, depending on size). Compare the two to see which will best meet your needs.

Trailer Park Los Cabañas (☎ 554-47-18) Four spaces in the Cabaña family's backyard; no water hookups.

Trailer Park La Ropa (☎ 554-60-30) Unsigned and hard to find, beside the Mercado de Artesanías, behind Marisquería Mary's.

MID-RANGE

Central Zihuatanejo has several mid-range lodgings that provide easy access to banks, restaurants and other services. A five-minute walk east from the center on quiet Eva S de López Mateos, the Playa Madera area has several good places to stay. Most are bungalows with full kitchens, and all have large terraces offering fine views of the bay.

Hotel Palacios (☎ /fax 554-20-55; Adelita s/n; s/d US$42/51, with air-con US$55; **P** **✕** **≋**) Overlooking the east end of Playa Madera, pleasant Hotel Palacios is a family place with a swimming pool and beachfront terrace. Low-season rates are cheaper (around US$30 to US$50) but don't include breakfast.

Hotel Paraíso Real (☎ 554-38-73; www.dive mexico.com; southern end of Playa La Ropa; r US$70-145; **P** **✕** **≋**) This ecologically conscious hideaway offers both garden and beachfront rooms. Operated by Zihuatanejo Scuba Center, the hotel also offers lodging-and-dive packages and some good low-season student deals.

Bungalows Allec & Sotelo (☎ 554-63-07; bun _allec@hotmal.com; López Mateos 13; bungalows US$55-100; **✕**) Under new ownership, these bungalows have experienced a facelift and offer a range of options for two to six people. Side-by-side, both have views and access to Playa Madera.

Hotel Catalina (☎ 554-20-32; www.catalina-beach -resort.com; northern end of Playa La Ropa; r US$55-105, bungalows US$135) On a hill overlooking Playa La Ropa, this place features one of Zihuatanejo's most beautiful settings. It's a well-loved old favorite with a variety of rooms, fabulous restaurant/bar and wonderful staff. Children under 12 stay for free.

Posada Citlali (☎ 554-20-43; Guerrero 4; s/d US$28/33) This pleasant older posada features terrace sitting areas around a leafy courtyard. The rooms have hot water and are clean and comfortable. Credit cards are accepted.

Hotel Imelda (☎ 554-76-62; hotelimelda@cdnet .com.mx; González 70; s/d/tr US$46/55/64; **P** **✕** **≋**) The popular Imelda has two swimming pools, enclosed parking and a high-season restaurant/bar. The rooms are crammed but clean and have cable TV and air-con.

Bungalows Pacíficos (☎ /fax 554-21-12; bungpaci@ prodigy.net.mx; López Mateos s/n; bungalows US$50-70) Swiss owner and long-time Zihua resident, Anita Hahner has six older bungalows with ample sea-view terraces and fully equipped kitchens. Anita can help you find anything from good restaurants to the best bird-watching spots.

Hotel Amueblados Valle (☎ 554-20-84; fax 544-32-20; Guerrero 33; 1-bed/2-bed apt US$40/60) This apartment-style hotel is a good deal, with five large, airy units equipped with everything you need, including full kitchens. Three-bedroom apartments are also available. Ask owner Luis about other Playa La Ropa apartments, which may be cheaper, especially for longer stays.

Hotel Raúl Tres Marías Centro (☎ 554-67-06; Álvarez 52; r US$44; **P** **✕**) Upstairs from Garrobo's restaurant, this hotel has simple but clean rooms that are cheaper by the week. French and English are spoken.

Hotel Susy (☎ 554-23-39; cnr Guerrero & Álvarez; s/d US$28/37; **P**) Just a block from Playa Municipal and within walking distance of everything else, the Susy is a pleasant, if crammed, in-town option.

Hotel Ávila (☎ 554-20-10; fax 554-85-92; Álvarez 8; r US$48, with view US$64; **P** **✕**) Fronting Playa Municipal, the Ávila has terraces overlooking the bay and large, well-equipped rooms with air-con, fan and cable TV.

Hotel Casa Bravo (☎ 554-25-48; Bravo 12; s/d with air-com US$23/33; **✕**) This remodeled hotel has clean, pleasant rooms with cable TV; some have air-con. Traffic can make exterior rooms noisy, but interior rooms are darker.

TOP END

If you seek luxury and Ixtapa doesn't suit your taste, Playa La Ropa has a few lovely luxury hotels.

La Casa Que Canta (☎ 554-70-30, in Mexico 800-710-93-45; www.lacasaquecanta.com; Carretera Escénica s/n; ste from US$360; **P** **✕** **▭** **≋**) Perched on the cliffs between Playa Madera and Playa La Ropa, this incredible, award-winning luxury hotel has reddish adobe-style walls and thatched awnings that are also visible all around the bay. It's also where part of *When a Man Loves a Woman* with Meg Ryan and Andy Garcia was filmed.

Villa del Sol (☎ 554-22-39, in the US & Canada 888-389-2645; www.hotelvilladelsol.net; northern end of Playa La Ropa; r from US$260; (P) ⊠ 🐾 💻 🏊) Luxury and style abound at this gorgeous all-inclusive resort. Children under 14 are not allowed in winter.

Hotel Brisas del Mar (☎ 554-21-42; www.hotel brisasdelmar.net; López Mateos s/n; ste US$104-131; 🐾 💻 🏊) This attractive red adobe-style hotel has a large swimming pool, a beach-front restaurant and a hill-top bar with fine views of the bay. All suites come with exquisite ocean-view terraces; some also have refrigerators and coffeemakers. There are a few cheaper rooms without view.

Owen's Las Gatas Beach Club (☎ 554-83-07; fax 554-47-62; www.lasgatasbeachclub.com; bungalows US$100) Seven large freestanding bungalows sit on peaceful grounds at the edge of the bay where you'll hear only the rhythmic sound of the surf and the sea breezes rustling through the palms. The unique bungalows are made of natural building materials, and some sleep up to eight people.

Bungalows Ley (☎ 554-45-63, 554-40-87; bunga lowsley@prodigy.net.mx; López Mateos s/n; 1-bed/2-bed bungalows US$85-170; 🐾) These well-kept, spacious bungalows aren't luxurious but they are good value with unbeatable views and beach access, and they're within easy walking distance of town.

Eating

Guerrero is famous for its pozole (see 'Holy Pozole!,' below) which is on most menus in town (especially on Thursday) and is well worth a try.

HOLY POZOLE! *Danny Palmerlee*

When it comes to flavor, heartiness, healthiness, and getting the most meal for your money, few Mexican dishes can top *pozole*, a hearty stew whose definitive ingredient is hominy (hulled and dried corn kernels prepared by boiling in water). Pozole is eaten throughout Mexico, but it's especially popular in Jalisco, Michoacán, Nayarit, Colima, and – more than anywhere else – Guerrero. In Guerrero, every Thursday is pozole day – called *jueves pozolero* – when restaurants big and small cook up giant batches, and folks migrate to their favorite eateries to relax over a bowl of soup.

The word 'pozole' comes from the Náhuatl 'pozolli,' meaning 'foam' or 'froth.' The word was probably used to describe the foam created when treating corn kernels with lime and water, the traditional process used to remove the skins from the kernels, allowing the kernels to expand into the soft, easily digestible hominy. Now pozole is a rich stew with many variations, but usually prepared with pork, and, perhaps, a few vegetables for good measure.

Eating pozole is an art – and a very personal one – that is taken quite seriously. A proper bowl of pozole is served with side-plates of colorful garnishing (sometimes called *botanas*) which, at the very least, should include avocado, diced onion, sliced radishes, oregano, chili powder and lemon or lime – all of which are carefully added to the soup, according to one's taste, and stirred in gently. A good restaurant will always serve a few fried tortillas and *chicharrones* (fried pork skins) on the side as well.

The traditional pozole served on Thursday in Guerrero is *pozole verde* (green pozole) which is a bit richer than another popular variation, *pozole blanco* (white pozole). Many people who haven't tried pozole before prefer the milder *pozole blanco*, so choose accordingly if both are on the menu.

The best part about pozole is that it's usually pretty cheap, and one bowl will surely fill you up. In markets and small *cenadurías* (family-style dinner restaurants), where pozole is often at its best, a bowl will cost no more than US$2!

Zihuatanejo is loaded with restaurants that serve pozole every night of the week, so you don't have to wait until Thursday to indulge. Our favorite is **Cenaduría Antelia** (p480) or, for something a little more gourmet, the excellent **Tamales y Atoles Any** (p480).

Perhaps the grandest of all *pozolerías* (restaurants specializing in pozole) is **Pozolería Los Cazadores** (p497) in Acapulco. If you make it down there, stop in on a Thursday or Saturday evening (the only days it's open) and you'll see just how serious pozole can be.

Tiretas (slivers of raw fish marinated with onion, green chili and vinegar and served with soda crackers and *chile picante*) are Zihua's specialty, but you won't find them on many menus – look for them at carts near the bus stations, or request them at any beachfront enramada. A hearty inexpensive breakfast or lunch is also available in the **market** (Juárez btwn Nava & Gonzáles). **Comercial Mexicana supermarket** is behind the Estrella Blanca bus station. **La Reina Panadería y Pastelería** (Paseo de la Boquita 15A) is Zihua's reigning queen of baked goods.

PASEO DEL PESCADOR

Seafood here is fresh and delicious; many popular (if touristy) fish restaurants run parallel to Playa Municipal. The following are the best options from west to east.

La Sirena Gorda (☎ 554-26-87; Paseo del Pescador 90; mains US$4-15; ☒ closed Wed) Closest to the pier, the Fat Mermaid is a casual open-air place famous for its seafood tacos, plus delicious burgers, shrimp and traditional Mexican dishes.

Casa Elvira (☎ 554-84-25; Paseo del Pescador 8; mains US$8-20) This longtime favorite is known for its outstanding seafood, though it also turns out some delicious meat and chicken dishes and has a long list of tasty soups.

Café Marina (Paseo Pescador, west side of plaza; pizzas US$5-10; ☒ closed Sun & May-Nov) Tiny Café Marina tosses good pizzas, bakes fabulous chocolate cake (US$3.50) and has an English-language book exchange.

Just east of the basketball court on Paseo del Pescador, insistent touts will no doubt invite you into **Mariscos Los Paisanos** (mains US$7 to US$16) and **Tata's** (mains US$7 to US$18). Both are decent seafood spots with popular happy hours. At either one you can sit inside or at shaded beachfront tables with fine views of the bay.

CENTRAL ZIHUATANEJO – INLAND

Many good inexpensive options lie a couple of blocks from the beach.

Garrobo's (☎ 554-67-06; Álvarez 214; mains US$8-18) Below Hotel Raúl Tres Marías Centro, Garrobo's is a popular post-fishing hangout. Try the house specialty paella (US$17).

Cenaduría Antelia (☎ 554-30-91; Bravo 14 at Andador Pellicer; all under US$2) This family-style open-air eatery has been dishing out superb *antojitos Mexicanos* (traditional Mexican snacks) and desserts since 1975. The beer is always cold, the TV is always on, and the social atmosphere spills out into the alley on balmy evenings. Tuck into a *chile-verde tamal* (US$0.50) or a bursting bowl of the *muy rico pozole* (US$1.50).

Tamales y Atoles Any (☎ 554-73-73; Ejido 15 at Guerrero; mains US$3-6; ☒ closed Sun) Friendly owners Any and José deserve a big post-meal *'buen provecho'* for their excellent offerings. The faux-rustic décor, with a high palapa roof, is colorful and inviting, and the menu features an amazing variety of reasonably priced dishes, including huge piping-hot tamales (US$1 to US$2), sweet atoles and traditional regional Mexican antojitos. Phone for free delivery. Every Thursday is a pozole fiesta.

Gondwana (☎ 554-60-16; Galeana 15; mains US$7-11; ☒ closed Sun) This stylish, British-owned curry restaurant prepares outstanding madras, korma and balti curries in one of the most handsome kitchens in town. Other dishes that you'll want to sink your teeth into include the tikka kebabs, mouthwatering spicy coconut mushrooms (US$5.50) and the avocado fan with walnut-apple salad (US$4.40). You will be hard pressed to find Indian food this good anywhere else on the coast.

Los Braceros (☎ 554-48-58; Ejido 21; mains US$3-10; ☒ 8:30-1am) Los Braceros specializes in grilled and skewered meat and veggie combinations, and you can watch your selection being prepared at the sidewalk grill. There are 30 combinations to choose from and many other tasty meat dishes, with more than 100 items on the menu. Mini, double-tortilla pork tacos (US$0.35) attract many late-night diners.

Restaurant Acacio (Galeana 21; mains US$2.50-5; ☒ 10am-midnight Mon-Sat) This simple little seafood eatery with shaded streetside tables, is one of the best places in town to get authentic *tiretas*; they're prepared fresh daily with the catch of the day. There are plenty of other seafood dishes on the menu too, all at unbeatable prices.

Cafetería Nueva Zelanda (☎ 554-23-40; Cuauhtémoc 23-30; mains US$3-7) Step back in time at this spotless, popular diner and café with entrances on Cuauhtémoc and Galeana. It's best for breakfast, everything is available *para llevar* (to go) and they steam a decent cappuccino.

Panificadora El Buen Gusto (Guerrero 8A) This delightful little bakery makes mouthwatering chicken mole empanadas (US$1.25) on Tuesday. The open-air café next door has an espresso machine.

Il Paccolo (Pacco's; Bravo 22 near Guerrero; pizzas US$6-9; ☼ 4pm-midnight) Pacco's super-cheesy lasagna (US$6.50), the most authentic this side of the Sierra Madre, is delicious. Other options include pizza, pasta, meats and seafood. The ambience is low-key and the bar is friendly.

Fonda Económica Susy (Bravo 18; mains US$2-3.50) Susy serves up some of the cheapest, good food in town, including a dependable *comida corrida*. *Telenovela* (soap opera) devotees gather around the TV at the late-night **taquería** next door.

JJ's Grill (☎ 554-83-80; Guerrero 6; mains US$7-12; ☼ 11-2am) JJ's is a gringo haven with a popular restaurant, sports bar and pool tables. The food is classic American, including giant burgers, filet mignon sandwiches, grilled tuna steak and clam chowder.

Casa Puntarenas (La Noria, near Hotel Raúl Tres Marías; ☼ 8:30-11am & 6-9pm Dec-Mar) Across the lagoon from town, this simple, family-run eatery has a relaxed atmosphere and attracts a steady crowd with its hearty portions of good, cheap Mexican food.

Pollos Locos (☎ 554-40-44; Bravo 15; mains US$3-8; ☼ 1-11pm) This simple open-air place serves inexpensive wood-grilled chicken and other meats.

AROUND THE BAY

Restaurant Kau-Kan (☎ 554-84-46; Carretera Escénica 7; mains US$13-20; ☼ 6pm-midnight) High on the cliffs this renowned, gourmet, chic restaurant enjoys stellar views. Making a selection is exhausting when faced with choices like stingray in black butter sauce, sautéed octopus and grilled beef paillard.

La Casa Que Canta (☎ 554-70-30; Carretera Escénica s/n; dinner from US$60; ☼ 6:30-10:30pm) The most expensive place in town is this intimate, open-air, multilevel patio in the luxury hotel (see Sleeping, p478). Of course, the food is the highlight. Reservations are required.

Puesta del Sol (☎ 554-83-42; Carretera Escénica s/n; mains US$10-20; ☼ closed Mon) Reservations are highly recommended in high season at this romantic restaurant. Hanging on the cliffs between Playa Madera and Playa La Ropa, Puesta del Sol (Spanish for 'sunset')

offers spectacular bay views and stunning sunset vistas.

On Playa La Ropa, **Rossy's** (☎ 554 40-04; mains US$8-11), **La Perla** (☎ 554-27-00; mains US$7-11) and **La Gaviota** (☎ 554-38-16; mains US$7-18) are all good seafood restaurants. On Playa Las Gatas, **Chez Arnoldo's** and **Owen's Las Gatas Beach Club** (see Sleeping, p479) also feature fresh seafood.

Drinking
For big-time nightlife, head to Ixtapa. Zihuatanejo is all about being mellow.

Many beachfront bars have an extended happy hour. **Tata's** and **Mariscos Los Paisanos** (see Eating, p480), side by side on Zihuatanejo's Playa Municipal, attract jolly sunset crowds.

Jungle Bar (cnr Ascencio & Ramírez; ☼ noon-late) Bob your head to the kick-back bass on the stereo at this street-side bar with a gregarious, English-speaking staff and cheap drinks. It's a good place to meet others (locals and travelers alike) and get the lowdown on town.

Hotel Catalina (☎ 554-20-32; Playa La Ropa; ☼ 3-11pm, happy hour 6-8pm) Tucked into the hillside over Playa La Ropa, the Catalina (see Sleeping, p478) is a great spot to watch the sunset. Its relaxed bar affords a magnificent view over the whole bay.

Ventaneando (Guerrero 24) Across the street from Club D'Latino, Ventaneando is a popular 'canta baile bar' that attracts a steady crowd of karaoke-loving local teens.

Cafe Zihuatanejo (Cuauhtémoc 48; ☼ closed Sun) has fresh-brewed locally grown organic coffee, whole beans by the kilo and good conversations at tiny sidewalk tables.

Entertainment
Club D'Latino (cnr Bravo & Guerrero) Zihuatanejo's only real discothèque, Club D'Latino is an open-air street-corner bar serving cheap draft Corona.

Zihua's only cinema is **Cine Paraíso** (Cuauhtémoc near Bravo; admission US$2.25). It shows two films nightly, usually in English with Spanish subtitles.

For something that's far from tame, check out the transvestite show at the **Safari Club** (☎ 554-00-24; La Laja s/n; ☼ Fri-Sun).

Shopping
Mexican handicrafts, including ceramics, *típica* clothing, leatherwork, Taxco silver,

wood carvings and masks from around the state of Guerrero are all in abundance.

Zihuatanejo's **Mercado Turístico La Marina** (5 de Mayo) has the most stalls. A few more are in the **Mercado Municipal de las Artesanías** (González near Juárez).

El Jumil (☎ 554-61-91; Paseo del Pescador 9) This friendly artesanías shop (in the block west of the basketball court) specializes in authentic guerrerense masks. Guerrero is known for its variety of interesting masks, and El Jumil stocks museum-quality examples, many starting from around US$15. English is spoken and the owners are a good source of local information.

Coco's Cabaña (☎ 554-25-18; cnr Guerrero & Álvarez) Next door to Coconuts restaurant, Coco's Cabaña stocks an impressive selection of handicrafts from all over Mexico.

Several shops along Cuauhtémoc sell Taxco silver. **Alberto's** (☎ 554-21-61; Cuauhtémoc 12 & 15) and **Pancho's** (☎ 554-52-30; Cuauhtémoc 11) have the best selection of quality pieces.

Getting There & Away
AIR
The Ixtapa/Zihuatanejo **international airport** (☎ 554-20-70) is 19km southeast of Zihuatanejo, a couple of kilometers off Hwy 200 heading toward Acapulco. **Aero Cuahonte** (☎ 554-39-88) flies to Lázaro Cárdenas, Morelia and Uruapan. **Aeroméxico** (☎ 554-20-18/19, airport 554-22-37, 554-26-34; Álvarez 34) flies to Guadalajara, Los Angeles, Mexico City and Oaxaca. **Alaska** (☎ 554-84-57) flies to Los Angeles and San Francisco, **America West** (☎ 800-235-92-92) flies to Phoenix, **Continental** (☎ 554-42-19) flies daily to Houston, and **Mexicana** (☎ 554-22-08/9, airport 554-22-27; Guerrero 22 & Hotel Dorado Pacífico, Ixtapa) flies to Guadalajara and Mexico City.

BUS
Both long distance bus terminals are on Hwy 200 about 2km south of the town center (toward the airport). The **Estrella Blanca terminal** (☎ 554-34-76/77), called the Central de Autobuses, runs 1st-class Elite, Futura, Plus and Cuauhtémoc bus services. **Estrella de Oro** (☎ 554-21-75) has its own smaller terminal, across a side road from Estrella Blanca, a couple of hundred meters nearer town. Buses include:

Acapulco Estrella Blanca (US$9-11, 4hr, 1st-class hourly 5am-9:30pm; US$7, 4hr, 2nd-class hourly); Estrella de Oro (US$9, 4hr, 3 1st-class daily; US$8.50, 4hr, 2nd-class hourly 5:30am-5pm)

Lázaro Cárdenas Estrella Blanca (US$4-5, 2hr, 11 1st-class 1am-9:30pm; US$3.50, 2hr, 2nd-class hourly 9am-10pm); Estrella de Oro (US$4, 2hr, 2nd-class hourly 6:30am-8pm)

Manzanillo Estrella Blanca (US$20, 8hr, 1st-class at 10:20am)

Mexico City Estrella Blanca (US$35, 10hr, 1st-class at 6:45pm) To Terminal Norte.

Mexico City Estrella Blanca (US$47, 8-9hr, deluxe 'Ejecutivo' at 10:30pm); Estrella de Oro (US$47, 8-9hr, deluxe 'Diamante' at 9:15pm; US$33, 8-9hr, 10 1st-class daily); Futura (US$35, 8-9hr, 5 1st-class daily) To Terminal Sur.

Petatlán Estrella Blanca (US$1.50, 30min, 1st-class every half hour 3.45am-11.20pm) Estrella de Oro (US$1.50, 30min, 2nd-class hourly 5:30am-6pm) Most buses to Acapulco also stop in Petatlán. Or take a local bus (US$1.25, 30min) from the bus lot a couple of blocks east of the market in Zihuatanejo.

Puerto Escondido Estrella Blanca (US$26, 12hr, hourly 1st-class)

Manzanillo-bound buses continue to Puerto Vallarta (US$46, 14 hours, 718km) and Mazatlán (US$75, 24 hours, 1177km); the noon bus goes all the way to Tijuana (US$156).

CAR & MOTORCYCLE
There are several car rental companies in Ixtapa and Zihuatanejo:

Alamo (☎ 553-02-06 at Centro Comercial Los Patios, Ixtapa; ☎ 554-84-29 at airport)

Budget (☎ 554-48-37 at Centro Comercial Ambiente, Local 10, Ixtapa; ☎ 554-48-37 airport)

Econo Franquicia (☎ 554-78-07 at airport)

Europcar (☎ 553-10-32 at Centro Comercial Los Patios, Ixtapa)

Hertz (☎ 554-22-55 at Bravo 37, Zihuatanejo; ☎ 554-25-90 at airport)

Rent-A-Car (☎ 553-10-88 at Centro Comercial La Puerta, Local 1)

Thrifty (☎ 553-00-18 ext 4156 at Hotel Presidente Inter-Continental; ☎ 544-57-45 at airport)

Getting Around
TO/FROM THE AIRPORT
The cheapest way to get to the airport is via a public 'Coacoyul' colectivo (US$0.50) with a plane on the windshield, departing from Juárez near González between 6am and 9pm. Private colectivo vans provide transportation from the airport to Ixtapa or Zihua (US$5.50 per person), but they don't offer service to the airport. A taxi to the airport costs US$7 from Zihua.

BUS

Local 'Directo' and 'B Viejo' buses run between Ixtapa and Zihua every 15 minutes from 6am to 11pm (US$0.50, 15 minutes). In Zihua, buses depart from the corner of Juárez and Morelos. In Ixtapa, buses stop all along the main street, in front of all the major hotels. Buses marked 'Zihua–Ixtapa–Playa Linda' continue through Ixtapa to Playa Linda (US$0.50), stopping near Playa Quieta on the way; they operate from 7am to 7pm.

The 'Correa' route goes to the Central de Autobuses from 6am to 9:30pm (US$0.40). Catch it on Juárez at the corner of Nava.

'Playa La Ropa' buses head south on Juárez and out to Playa La Ropa every half hour from 7am to 8pm (US$0.70).

'Coacoyul' colectivos heading toward Playa Larga depart from Juárez near the corner of González, every five minutes from 6am to 10pm (US$0.50).

TAXI

Cabs are plentiful in Zihuatanejo. Always agree on the fare before getting in. Approximate sample fares (from central Zihua) include: US$3.50 to Ixtapa, US$2.50 to Playa La Ropa, US$5 to Playa Larga and US$1.50 to the Central de Autobuses. If you can't hail a taxi streetside, ring **Radio Taxi UTAAZ** (☎ 554-33-11).

SOUTH OF IXTAPA & ZIHUATANEJO
Barra de Potosí
☎ 755

A 40-minute drive southeast of Zihuatanejo, Barra de Potosí is a popular daytrip area with a long, sandy, open-sea beach (beautiful, but dangerous for swimming) and another beach on a large lagoon with good swimming. You can take boat trips, rent a canoe and paddle around the estuary (good bird-watching) or go horseback riding or hiking on local trails.

Seafood restaurants line the beach – try the *pescado a la talla* (broiled fish fillets) or *tiretas*, both local specialties.

Casa del Encanto (☎ 556-81-99; www.casadel encanto.com; d US$60) is a knockout B&B with the sort of private yet open-air rooms that blend interior with exterior to keep things as cool and relaxed as possible. Candles provide the only nighttime light. There are four spacious rooms, all with bathrooms

and mosquito nets and plenty of books around to flip through. It's on the main road in the village.

Hotel Barra de Potosí (☎ 554-34-45, 554-70-60; www.hotelbarradepotosi.com; s/d US$37/55; P ☒ ☒), right on the beach, has a child-filled swimming pool and a variety of comfy rooms.

To get here, head southeast on Hwy 200 toward Acapulco; turn off at the town of Los Achotes, 25km from Zihua, and head for the sea, another 10km. Any bus heading to Petatlán (see p482) will drop you at the turnoff. Tell the driver you're going to Barra de Potosí; you'll be let off where you can meet a minibus going the rest of the way. The total cost is about US$2.50 if you go by bus; a taxi from Zihua costs US$35/45 one-way/round-trip (negotiable).

Petatlán
☎ 758 / pop 18,000

A colonial town half an hour southeast of Zihua, Petatlán (Km 209) is best known for its Santuario Nacional del Padre Jesús de Petatlán, a large, modern church attracting pilgrims from near and far. Gold is sold cheaply from many shops beside the church. Petroglyphs and other pre-Hispanic artifacts are displayed in the town center. During Semana Santa there's a traditional fair with food, music and handicrafts exhibitions. Petatlán's religious festival is held on August 6.

Petatlán is on Hwy 200, 32km southeast of Zihua heading toward Acapulco. See p482 for bus information.

La Barrita
☎ 758

La Barrita (Km 187) is a shell-size village on a beautiful beach an hour southeast of Zihua off Hwy 200. Not many tourists stop here, but if you're a surfer you might want to check the break 3km north at **Loma Bonita**. Several restaurants have rooms for rent, including **Restaurant Maritoña** (r US$7) and **Las Peñitas** (s/d/cottage US$7/11/30). Second-class buses heading south from Zihua or north from Acapulco will drop you at La Barrita.

PIE DE LA CUESTA
☎ 744 / pop 400

Ten kilometers northwest of Acapulco, Pie de la Cuesta is a narrow 2km strip of land bordered by a wide beach and the ocean on one side and by the large, freshwater Laguna de Coyuca on the other. Known for its relaxed beach scene, Pie de la Cuesta is quieter, more rustic, closer to nature and much more peaceful than neighboring Acapulco. However, swimming in the surf can be dangerous due to a riptide and the shape of the waves; each year a number of people drown here. Laguna de Coyuca, three times as large as Bahía de Acapulco, is better for swimming; in the lagoon are the islands of Montosa, Presido and Pájaros, which is a bird sanctuary.

Pie de la Cuesta has many oceanfront restaurants specializing in seafood, and it's a great place for watching the sunset. The only nightlife is the billiards parlor, so if you're looking for excitement you're better off in Acapulco. Waterskiing is popular on Laguna de Coyuca; several waterskiing clubs provide the equipment (US$42 per hour). Boat trips on the lagoon, where Sylvester Stallone filmed *Rambo*, are also an option. Negotiate for your own launch any time, or take one of the regularly scheduled colectivos (US$5 per person). You can

also go horseback riding on the beach for around US$11 an hour.

Sleeping

Accommodations are less expensive and more intimate in Pie de la Cuesta than in Acapulco. You can easily check out the 15 or so hotels that line the single, 2km road. Every hotel provides safe parking. All rooms have private bathrooms unless otherwise specified and prices are high-season rates.

BUDGET

Hotel Parador de los Reyes (☎ 460-01-31; Calz Pie de la Cuesta 305; per person US$7; P ☒) This clean, economical choice is right beside the road and has a small courtyard swimming pool.

Villa Roxana (☎ 460-32-52; Calz Pie de la Cuesta 302; s/d US$19/23, with kitchen US$28; P) Villa Roxana is an attractive and spotlessly clean place, with nice gardens with plenty of shaded hammocks, a small swimming pool, a restaurant and bar, and attractively furnished rooms. Guests should note that Villa Nirvana's facilities are off-limits to Roxana's

PIE DE LA CUESTA

0 _____ 500 m
0 _____ 0.3 miles

To Playa Lucas Camping (4km); Quinta Erika (6km)

Military Base

Laguna de Coyuca

Boats

MEX 200

PACIFIC OCEAN

SIGHTS & ACTIVITIES	
Arched Entrance	1 D3
Billiards Parlor	2 D2
Club de Ski Acuario	3 B1
Club de Ski Chuy	4 B2
Club Náutico Cadena Ski	5 B2
Colectivo Boat Launch	6 C2
Restaurant Sunset Club de Ski	7 A1

SLEEPING	(pp484–5)
Acapulco Trailer Park & Mini-Super	8 B2
Acapulco Trailer Park & Mini-Super	9 B1
Bungalows María Cristina	10 B2
Hotel & Restaurant Casa Blanca	11 B2
Hotel & Restaurant Tres Marías	12 B2
Hotel Casa de Huéspedes	13 D3
Hotel Parador de los Reyes	14 C2
Hotel Quinta Blancas	15 C3
Trailer Park Quinta Dora	16 A1
Trailer Park Quinta Dora	17 A1
Villa Nirvana	18 C3
Villa Roxana	19 C2

EATING	(pp485–6)
Coyuca 2000	(see 21)
Restaurant Bar El Zanate	20 C2
Restaurant/Bar Rocío	(see 13)
Ricardito's Cevichería	21 B2

DRINKING	(pp485–6)
Steve's Hideout/ El Escondite	22 C2

TRANSPORT	(p486)
Pie de la Cuesta/San Isidro/Pedregoso Buses to/from Acapulco	23 D2

guests. Check out both places before deciding which one suits your needs.

Camping is much easier here than in Acapulco. Discounts for long stays are available.

Acapulco Trailer Park & Mini-Super (☎ 460-00-10; RV sites US$9-19) Beachside with big spaces, clean facilities, friendly management and just enough shade, this is the nicest campground in the whole Acapulco area. Prices depend on amenities and proximity to the crashing waves.

Trailer Park Quinta Dora (☎ 460-11-38; RV sites US$8) Quite overgrown with uninviting bathrooms and showers, the Quinta Dora is a less appealing option. But it does have a bar and restaurant.

Four kilometers north of Pie de la Cuesta, **Playa Luces Camping** (☎ 444-42-77; playaluces@hotmail.com; Playa Luces; tent sites US$14, RV sites US$22-27; P ⬛) is a 110-space landscaped campground with trailer spaces that have full hookups. Amenities here include a large beachfront swimming pool, a restaurant/bar, children's playgrounds and laundry and Internet service (US$2 per hour). The 'Pie de la Cuesta – Playa Luces' bus stops at the gate upon request.

MID-RANGE

Quinta Erika (☎ /fax 444-41-31; www.quintaerika.de.vu; Playa Luces; r with breakfast US$50; P) Six kilometers northeast of Pie de la Cuesta at Playa Luces, this small, lagoonside, quality lodging is one of the region's best places to relax for a few days. Quinta Erika takes pride in being quiet, restful and attentive. Reservations are strongly suggested. German, Spanish and a little English are spoken.

Villa Nirvana (☎ 460-16-31; www.lavillanirvana.com; rear Calz Pie de la Cuesta 302; r/cottages US$28/46; P ⬛ ⬛) Villa Nirvana's friendly American owners have thoughtfully decorated, landscaped and expanded this cheerful beachfront property. Rooms are comfortable and decorated with local crafts. A beachside swimming pool, pleasant open-air restaurant (breakfast only) and bar, and complimentary (but limited, please) Internet access round out the good-value offering. Villa Nirvana is just behind Villa Roxana, but has its own driveway.

Hotel Casa de Huéspedes & Restaurant Rocío (☎ 460-10-08; Calz Pie de la Cuesta s/n; s/d US$28/37;

P) Félix López, the resident bartender, chef and guitarist, provides music and good times at this beachfront hotel/restaurant/bar. Newer oceanside rooms with large balconics cost the same as other doubles.

Hotel & Restaurant Tres Marías (☎ 460-01-78; Calz Pie de la Cuesta s/n; r US$46; P ⬛ ⬛) Long-established Tres Marías is popular with local businessmen and their families for its good rooms with king-size beds. Its seaside restaurant is said to have some of the best food in the area, but some complain that service is lax.

Bungalows María Cristina (☎ 460-02-62; Calz Pie de la Cuesta s/n; r/bungalows US$28/59) Run by English-speaking Enrique and his friendly family, this is a clean, well-tended, relaxing place with a barbecue and hammocks overlooking the beach. The large bungalows have kitchens and sleep five or six people.

Hotel & Restaurant Casa Blanca (☎ 460-03-24; casablanca@acanet.com.mx; Calz Pie de la Cuesta s/n; r with air-con US$43; P ⬛ ⬛) This well-tended beachfront place has a new pool and its restaurant retains a homey atmosphere.

Hotel Quinta Blancas (☎ 460-03-12/13; Calz Pie de la Cuesta 307; s/d US$19/38, with air-con US$46; P ⬛ ⬛) Air-con has been added to this sprawling, spiffed-up hotel. Rooms and grounds lack charm but are comfortable enough.

Eating & Drinking

Restaurants here are known for fresh seafood. Plenty of open-air places front the beach, though some close early in the evening. Most of the hotels and guesthouses have restaurants, as do many of the water-skiing clubs. Food prices tend to be higher here than in Acapulco, so it may be worth bringing some groceries and getting a room with kitchen access, as many local families do on Saturday and Sunday.

Coyuca 2000 (mains US$2-7) About halfway down to the military base, this locally owned place serves good traditional Mexican fare and exhibits a special flair with seafood.

Ricardito's Cevichería (mains US$2-5) Near Coyuca 2000 and lagoonside, Ricardito's Cevichería does wonders with marinated *mariscos* (seafood).

Restaurant Bar El Zanate (mains US$2-4) In a pinch, this roadside restaurant serves a filling *comida corrida*.

Steve's Hideout/El Escondite (snacks US$1-2)
Across the street from El Zanate, around
the lagoon at the end of the dirt road, Steve's
is built on stilts over the water, and is better
for drinks than grub.

Getting There & Away

From Acapulco, take a 'Pie de la Cuesta'
bus on La Costera across the street from the
post office near the zócalo. Buses go every
15 minutes from 6am until around 8pm;
the bumpy, roundabout 35- to 50-minute
ride costs US$0.40. Buses marked 'Pie de la
Cuesta – San Isidro' or 'Pie de la Cuesta –
Pedregoso' stop on Hwy 200 at Pie de la
Cuesta's arched entrance; those marked 'Pie
de la Cuesta – Playa Luces' continue all
the way along to Playa Luces, 6km further
along toward Barra de Coyuca. VW microbus colectivos (US$0.40) continue on from
Barra de Coyuca back out to Hwy 200.

Colectivo taxis to Pie de la Cuesta operate 24 hours along La Costera, and elsewhere in Acapulco's old town, and charge
US$1.25 one-way. A taxi from Acapulco
costs anywhere from US$6 to US$10 one-
way (more after dark), but typically you'll
pay only US$4.50 to US$6 to return to
Acapulco, since the cabbies hate to go home
empty-handed.

ACAPULCO

☎ 744 / pop 640,000

Acapulco is the granddaddy of Mexican
coastal resorts. Commerce and tourism are
the city's primary industries and have been
since the Spanish conquistadors pioneered
trade routes between Europe and Asia in
the early 16th century. Today, the name
Acapulco evokes images of golden beaches,
towering resort hotels, glitzy nightlife and
La Quebrada's daredevil, swan-diving *clavadistas* (cliff divers).

Acapulco is a fast-growing city of dual
personalities. Around the curve of Bahía
de Acapulco stretches an arc of beautiful
beaches, luxury hotels, jet-set discos, air-
conditioned shopping plazas and restaurants with trilingual menus (many French
Canadians come here). Just inland is a
none-too-glamorous commercial center
with crowded sidewalks, congested traffic and ranks of constantly honking taxis
and colorful customized buses menacing
pedestrians.

Throughout the year you can expect average daytime temperatures of 27°C to 33°C
and nighttime temperatures of 21°C to 27°C.
Afternoon showers are common from June
to September but rare the rest of the year.

History

The name 'Acapulco' is derived from ancient Náhuatl words meaning 'where the
reeds stood' or 'place of giant reeds.' Archeological finds show that when the Spanish
discovered the Bay of Acapulco in 1512,
people had already been living in the area
for some 2000 years.

Port and shipbuilding facilities were
quickly established by the Spanish because
of the substantial natural harbor and in
1523 Hernán Cortés, Juan Rodríguez Vil-
lafuerte and merchant Juan de Sala joined
forces to finance an overland trade route
between Mexico City and Acapulco. This
route, known as the 'Camino de Asia,' was
the principal trade route between Mexico
City and the Pacific; the 'Camino de Europa,' from Mexico City to Veracruz on the
Gulf Coast, completed the overland leg of
this route between Asia and Spain.

Acapulco became the only port in the
New World authorized to receive *naos*
(Spanish trading galleons) from China
and the Philippines. During the annual
springtime Acapulco Fair, lasting up to two
months after the galleons arrived from Manila, traders converged on Acapulco from
Mexico City, Manila and Peru.

By the 17th century trade with Asia was
flourishing, and English and Dutch pirate
ships were thriving in the Pacific and along
the coastlines of mainland Mexico and Baja
California. To fend off freebooters, the
Fuerte de San Diego was built atop a low
hill overlooking Bahía de Acapulco. It was
not until the end of the 18th century that
Spain permitted its American colonies to
engage in free trade, ending the monopoly
of the *naos* and the Manila–Acapulco trade
route. The *naos* continued trading until the
early 19th century.

Upon gaining independence Mexico severed most of its trade links with Spain and
Spanish colonies, and Acapulco declined
as a port city. It became relatively isolated
from the rest of the world until a paved road
linked it with Mexico City in 1927 (look for
the older green signs along La Costera). As

Mexico City flourished, its citizens began vacationing on the Pacific coast. A new international airport was built, Hollywood filmed a few flicks here, and by the '50s Acapulco was becoming a glitzy jet-set resort.

Orientation

Acapulco occupies a narrow coastal sliver along the 11km shore of Bahía de Acapulco (aka Bahía de Santa Lucía). Accessible via Hwy 200 from the east and west and by Hwy 95 and Hwy 95D from the north, it's 400km south of Mexico City and 240km southeast of Ixtapa and Zihuatanejo. Street signs are as scarce as safe crosswalks, and building numbers are erratic and often obscured or unused, but inquiring on the street will eventually lead you to your destination. As in most Spanish colonial cities, the cathedral and adjacent zócalo dominate the heart of the old central commercial district.

Acapulco can be divided into three parts: Old Acapulco (which promoters once called 'Acapulco Tradicional' and now call 'Acapulco Náutico') is the western (old) part of the city; Acapulco Dorado heads around the bay east from Playa Hornos; and Acapulco Diamante is a newer luxury resort area 18km southeast of Acapulco proper, between Bahía de Acapulco and the airport. Tourism is more low key in Pie de la Cuesta (p483), 10km northwest of Acapulco off Hwy 200.

At Bahía de Acapulco's west end, the Península de las Playas juts south and east from Old Acapulco. South of the peninsula is Isla de la Roqueta. From Playa Caleta on the south edge of the peninsula, Av López Mateos climbs west and then north to Playa La Angosta and La Quebrada before curling east back toward the city center.

Playa Caleta also marks the beginning of Acapulco's principal bayside avenue, Av Costera Miguel Alemán – often called 'La Costera' or 'Miguel Alemán.' From Playa Caleta, La Costera traverses the Península de las Playas and then hugs the shoreline all the way around the bay to Playa Icacos and the naval base at the eastern end of Bahía de Acapulco. Most of Acapulco's hotels, restaurants, discos and points of interest are along or near La Costera. Just after the naval base, La Costera becomes La Carretera Escénica (Scenic Highway), which rejoins the main route of Hwy 200 after 9km. Hwy 200 then leads south toward Puerto Marqués and the airport.

Information

BOOKSTORES

For its size, Acapulco is woefully lacking good bookstores. However, there are several worth a visit:

Comercial Mexicana (Map pp488-9; La Costera s/n) Major American magazines in English. Several branches.

La Tienda (Map p490; Fuerte de San Diego museum) City's best Spanish-language academic section plus a limited selection in English.

Sanborns (Map pp488-9; ☎ 484-20-44; La Costera 3111) Stocks a larger selection than the location near the zócalo.

Wal-Mart (Map pp488-9; La Costera s/n) Limited English-language selection.

EMERGENCY

Cruz Roja (Red Cross; ☎ 485-59-12) Provides ambulance service.

Locatel (☎ 481-11-00) Operated by Sefotur, 24-hour hot line for all types of emergencies.

Tourist police (☎ 485-04-90)

IMMIGRATION

Migración (Immigration Office; Map pp488-9; ☎ 484-90-14/21; cnr La Costera & Elcano; ☺ 8am-2pm Mon-Fri)

INTERNET ACCESS

It's impossible to walk more than a few blocks without passing a cybercafé in Acapulco's major hotel districts – Internet places now outnumber discos. Most places with online access are run by friendly younger folks, have quick connections, stay open late and charge just under US$1 per hour.

Big M@sternet (Map p490; Hidalgo 6) Family-run with air-con inside a small shopping center.

Cafe Internet (Map p490; Hidalgo 8; ☺ 9am-1am) Popular but not service oriented.

GDS Internet (Map p490; Mina 3-C) Lots of computers, lots of teenage boys.

SGD Internet (Map p490; Galeana 13; ☺ 10am-11pm)

LAUNDRY

Lavandería Lavadín (Map p490; ☎ 482-28-90; cnr La Paz & Iglesias) Pickup and delivery service for about US$3.

Lavandería Azueta (Map p490; ☎ 546 69 49; Azueta 14-A; US$1 per kilo wash & dry) Below Hotel Paola.

MONEY

Many places in Acapulco are eager to change your money. Omnipresent banks give the best rates. Conspicuous casas de cambio pay a slightly lower rate, but are open longer hours and are less busy than banks; shop around, as rates vary. Banks and casas de cambio cluster around the zócalo and line La Costera. Hotels will also change money, but their rates are usually extortionate. There's also an **American Express** (Map pp488-9; ☎ 435-22-00; La Costera 121, Hotel Continental Plaza; ☒ 9am-6pm Mon-Fri, 9am-1pm Sat).

POST
Main post office (Map p490; ☎ 483-53-63; La Costera 125, Palacio Federal)
Post office (Map pp488-9; cnr Cuauhtémoc & Massieu, at Estrella de Oro bus station) Around the corner from main bus station entrance, with a Western Union office.

TELEPHONE & FAX
Long-distance calls can be made from Telmex card phones – plentiful throughout the city – or from private telephone casetas (with signs saying '*larga distancia*'). There are many casetas near the zócalo and along La Costera.
Caseta Alameda (Map p490; west side of the zócalo) Telephone and fax services.
Telecomm (Map pp488-9; ☎ 484-69-76; La Costera 125 at main post office) Fax, telephone and limited Internet service.

TOURIST INFORMATION
The following offices in the Centro de Convenciones all provide tourist information and assistance.
Procuraduría del Turista (Map pp488-9; ☎ /fax 484-45-83; La Costera 4455; ☒ 8am-10pm) In the yellow building out front, this government dispenser of visitor information also sells tickets for local attractions and for bus and air travel for less than travel agencies. It also provides free medical care and money exchange.
Casa Consular (Map pp488-9; ☎ /fax 481-25-33; La Costera 4455; ☒ 9am-3pm Mon-Fri) The Casa Consular office provides consular assistance to visitors of all nationalities.
State tourist office (Map pp488-9; Sefotur; ☎ 484-24-23; sefotur@yahoo.com; La Costera 4455; ☒ 9am-3pm & 6-8pm Mon-Fri, 9am-3pm Sun)

Sights
Acapulco may not have a wealth of colonial architecture but it does have an interesting history and culture off the beach. The history museum at the San Diego fort, the mask museum and the cliff divers are country highlights, not just highlights for the city.

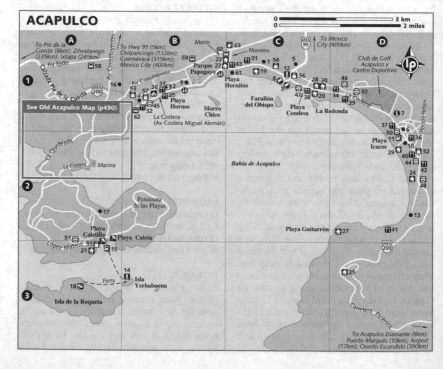

FUERTE DE SAN DIEGO **Map p490**

This beautifully restored pentagonal fort was built in 1616 atop a hill just east of the zócalo. Its mission was to protect from marauding Dutch and English buccaneers the Spanish *naos* (galleons) conducting trade between the Philippines and Mexico. It must have been effective because this trade route lasted until the early 19th century. Apparently the fort was also strong enough to forestall the takeover of the city for four months by independence leader José María Morelos y Pavón in 1812.

After a 1776 earthquake damaged most of Acapulco, the fort had to be rebuilt. It remains basically unchanged today, having been recently restored to top condition by the Instituto Nacional de Antropología e Historia (INAH). The panorama of Acapulco you'll get from the fort is free and worth the trip alone.

The fort is now home to the **Museo Histórico de Acapulco** (☎ 482-38-28; admission US$3, free Sun; 9:30am-6:30pm Tue-Sun), which has fascinating exhibits detailing the city's history, with Spanish and English captions. When skies are clear during the high season, the museum puts on an evening light show (8pm Friday and Saturday).

CASA DE LAS MÁSCARAS **Map p490**

This lovely **mask museum** (admission by donation; 10am-4pm Tue-Sun) is near the fort on the pedestrian portion of Morelos, just downhill past the parking lot through the fort's front entrance gate. It has an amazing collection of masks from around Mexico with an especially impressive display of high quality masks by modern artists. Signs are in Spanish, but if you're thinking about buying a Mexican mask, come here first to learn where to shop and what to look for.

LA QUEBRADA CLIFF DIVERS **Map p490**

The famous *clavadistas* (cliff divers) of **La Quebrada** (☎ 483-14-00; admission US$2.25, children under 9 yrs free; shows at 12:45pm, 7:30pm, 8:30pm, 9:30pm & 10:30pm) have been dazzling audiences since 1934, swan diving with graceful finesse from heights of 25m to 35m into the narrow ocean cove below. Understandably, the divers pray at a small shrine

INFORMATION
Aerolíneas Internacionales....(see 19)
Aeroméxico....(see 4)
American Airlines....1 C1
American Express....(see 43)
ATM....(see 43)
ATM....(see 60)
Banamex ATM....(see 33)
Banamex ATM....(see 4)
Banamex....2 B1
Bancomer ATM....(see 52)
Bital ATM....(see 4)
Canadian Consulate....3 C1
Casa Consular....(see 7)
Comercial Mexicana....4 B1
Comercial Mexicana....5 C1
Comercial Mexicana....6 D1
French Consulate....(see 7)
Mexicana....(see 43)
Migración (Immigration Office)....(see 36)
Netherlands Consulate....(see 61)
Pemex Gas Station....(see 56)
Pemex Gas Station....(see 4)
Post Office....(see 60)
Procuraduría de la Turista....7 D1
State Tourist Office....(see 7)
Swedish Consulate....(see 42)
Telecomm....(see 60)
US Consulate....8 C1

SIGHTS & ACTIVITIES (pp488–93)
Acapulco Scuba Center....(see 20)
AJ Hackett Bungee....(see 20)
Bodega Aurrera....9 B1
Casa de la Cultura....10 D2
Centro de Convenciones....(see 7)
CICI & Acapulco Mágico....11 D2
Delfines Paradise....(see 20)
Diana Statue (La Diana)....12 C1
Icacos Naval Base....13 D2
La Capilla Submarina (Underwater Chapel)....14 B3
La Gran Plaza....(see 43)
Mágico Mundo Marino....15 A3
Shotover Jet....(see 8)
Unidad Deportiva Acapulco....16 A1
Yacht Club....17 A2
Zoo....18 A3

SLEEPING (pp493–5)
Costa Club Acapulco....19 C1
Fiesta Americana Condesa....20 C1
Hotel Boca Chica....21 A3
Hotel del Valle....(see 22)
Hotel Jacqueline....22 B1
Hotel Ritz....23 B1
Hyatt Regency Acapulco....24 D2
Las Brisas....25 D3
Playa Suave Trailer Park....26 B1
Radisson Resort....27 D2
Romano Palace Hotel....28 C1
Suites Selene....29 D2
Youth Hostel K3....30 C1

EATING (pp495–7)
100% Natural....31 C1
100% Natural....32 B1
100% Natural....33 B1
Carlos 'n' Charlie's....34 D1
El Amigo Miguel....35 B1
El Fogón....36 D2
Fersato's....(see 36)
Marina Club Sushi & Oyster Bar....(see 21)
Mariscos Pipo's....37 D1
Pancho's....38 C1
Sam's Club....(see 5)
Sanborns....39 D1
Sanborns....40 D2
Señor Frog's....41 D2
VIPS (24-hours)....42 D2
VIPS....43 C1
VIPS....(see 39)

ENTERTAINMENT (pp497–8)
Andromedas....44 D2
Baby'O....(see 52)
Copacabana....45 B1
Demas....46 D1
Disco Beach....47 C1
El Alebrije....48 D2
Enigma....(see 25)
Factory Demas....49 D1
Hard Rock Cafe....50 D1
Nina's....(see 50)
Picante....(see 46)
Planet Hollywood....(see 50)
Plaza de Toros....51 A2
Relax....(see 46)
Salon Q....(see 40)
Tropicana....(see 45)

SHOPPING (pp498–9)
100% Mexico....52 D2
Centro Comercio Plaza Bahía....(see 19)
Mercado Central....53 B1
Mercado de Artesanías Dalia....54 C1
Mercado de Artesanías La Caletilla....55 A3
Mercado de Artesanías La Diana....56 C1
Mercado de Artesanías Noa Noa....57 B1
Mercado de Artesanías Papagayo....(see 4)
Wal-Mart....(see 42)

TRANSPORT (pp499–500)
Alamo Rent-A-Car....(see 40)
Avis....(see 61)
Budget Rent-A-Car....(see 8)
Estrella Blanca 1st-Class Bus Station (Central Ejido)....58 A1
Estrella Blanca 1st-Class Bus Station (Central Papagayo)....59 B1
Estrella de Oro Bus Station....60 B1
Hertz....61 C1
Local Bus Stops....62 B1
Pemex Gas Station....63 C1
Saad Rent-A-Car....(see 52)

CENTRAL PACIFIC COAST

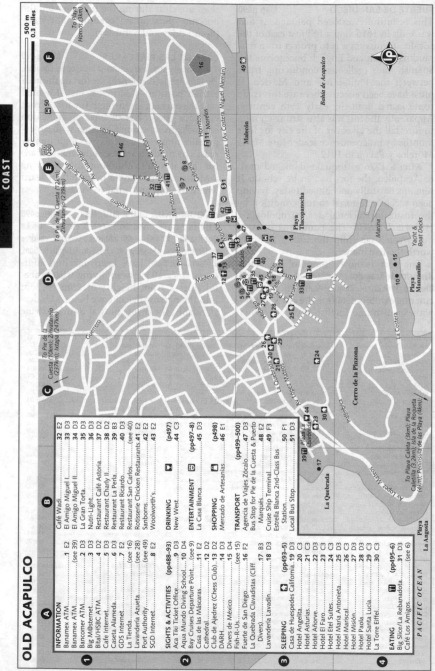

OLD ACAPULCO

before leaping over the edge, as did Elvis Presley in the 1963 flick *Fun in Acapulco*. At least three divers perform each time, and you're allowed to stay for more than one show. To get to La Quebrada (the Ravine), either walk up the hill from the zócalo on La Quebrada or take a taxi. La Quebrada is also an excellent place to watch the sunset.

The aerial view of the divers you get from La Perla restaurant/bar (see Eating, p497) comes at a price. The cover price while the diving's going on, including two drinks, is US$15, with meals costing twice that.

CENTRO DE CONVENCIONES Map pp488–9

Acapulco's **convention center** (☎ 484-71-52, 484-70-98; La Costera 4455) is a huge complex with a permanent crafts gallery (Galería de Artesanías), temporary special exhibitions, a large plaza, theaters and concert halls. Also here are the tourist offices, Casa Consular and Locatel. A Fiesta Mexicana is held several evenings each week (see Entertainment, p497). Phone the center to ask about current offerings.

CASA DE LA CULTURA Map pp488–9

Set around a garden just southeast of CICI down La Costera, this **complex** (☎ 484-23-90, for schedules 484-38-14; La Costera 4834; ☉ 10am-6pm Mon-Fri, 10am-3pm Sat) houses an innovative art gallery, a handicrafts shop and the free **Salon de Fama de los Deportistas de Guerrero** (Hall of Fame of Guerrero Athletes). It also has an open-air theater in addition to an indoor auditorium.

BEACHES

Visiting Acapulco's beaches tops most visitors' lists of must-dos. The beaches heading east around the bay from the zócalo – **Playas Hornos**, **Hornitos**, **Condesa** and **Icacos** – are the most popular. The high-rise hotel district begins on Playa Hornitos, on the east side of Parque Papagayo, and heads east from there. City buses constantly ply La Costera, making it easy to get up and down this long arc of beaches.

Playas Caleta and **Caletilla** are two small, protected beaches beside one another in a cove on the south side of Peninsula de las Playas. They're especially popular with families with small children, as the water is very calm. All buses marked 'Caleta' heading down La Costera go there. The Mágico Mundo Marino aquarium (see p493) sits on a tiny point of land separating the two beaches; boats go regularly from there to Isla de la Roqueta.

Playa La Angosta is in a tiny, protected cove on the west side of the peninsula. From the zócalo it takes about 20 minutes to walk there. Or you can take any 'Caleta' bus and get off near the Hotel Avenida, on La Costera, just one short block from the beach.

Further afield are other good beaches, including Puerto Marqués and Playa Revolcadero (p500) and Pie de la Cuesta (p483).

ISLA DE LA ROQUETA Map pp488–9

In addition to a popular (crowded) beach and snorkeling and diving possibilities, Isla de la Roqueta has a severely underfunded **zoo** (admission US$0.60; ☉ 10am-5pm) with some exotic cats (pumas, jaguars, leopards etc) and other jungle critters in small cages. You can rent snorkeling gear, kayaks and other water-sports equipment on the beach.

From Playas Caleta and Caletilla, boats make the eight-minute one-way trip every 20 minutes or so (US$3 round-trip). The

---

CHASING SUNSETS

All those beaches stretching around the Bahía de Acapulco, and not a single sunset – over the water anyway. If you're achin' to watch the sun sink slowly into the sea, you'll have to pick your spot carefully. First off, think Old Acapulco. The only place you can sit on the sand (within the city limits) and watch the sun set on the water is Playa La Angosta (see above), a sliver of a beach on the Península de las Playas. Plaza La Quebrada, where the divers perform, is another great spot – arrive early for the 7:30pm dives in the summer and you'll catch the sunset too. One of the finest views of all is at the small Sinfonía del Mar (Symphony of the Sea), a stepped plaza built on the edge of the cliffs just south of La Quebrada. Its sole purpose is giving folks a magical view. If you really feel like chasing the sunset, you should head over to Pie de la Cuesta (p483), about a half-hour's ride northwest of Acapulco. It's long, wide beach and hammock-clad restaurants are famous for spectacular sunsets.

alternative is a glass-bottomed boat that makes a circuitous trip to the island, departing from the same beaches but traveling via **La Capilla Submarina** (the Underwater Chapel), a submerged bronze statue of the Virgen de Guadalupe – visibility varies with water conditions. Round-trip fare is US$5; the trip takes about an hour, depending on how many times floating vendors accost your boat. You can alight on the island and take a later boat back, but find out when the last boat leaves, usually around 5:30pm.

Activities

As one might expect, Acapulco's activities are largely beach based. There are non-beach things to do, but generally everything is in the spirit of mega-vacation with once-in-a-lifetime adventure and/or adrenaline rush promised. For activities like scuba diving, you should shop around and choose an outfit you feel most comfortable with.

WATER SPORTS

Just about everything that can be done on, or below, the water is done in Acapulco. On the Bahía de Acapulco, waterskiing, boating, 'banana-boating' and parasailing (paracaída) are all popular activities. To partake in any of these, walk along the Zona Dorada beaches and look for the usually orange kiosks run by **FADAP**, the local cooperative. They charge US$7 for snorkel gear, US$19 for a five-minute parasailing flight, US$28 for a jet ski ride and US$47 for one hour of waterskiing. The smaller Playas Caleta and Caletilla have sailboats, fishing boats, motorboats, pedal boats, canoes, snorkel gear, inner tubes and water bicycles for rent.

For a fast, white-knuckle boat ride on the Río Papagayo, contact **Shotover Jet** (Map pp488-9; ☎ 484-11-54/55/56; www.shotoverjet.com; La Costera 121, Hotel Continental Emporio Acapulco). The four-hour trip costs US$55, including transportation time (all included in the price), with about 35 minutes spent rocketing down the river at about 80kmh. (Bird-watching on speed.)

Though Acapulco isn't quite a scuba destination in itself, there are some decent dive sites nearby if you're itching to get wet. Several outfitters offer quality services. **Acapulco Scuba Center** (Map pp488-9; ☎ 484-67-47; www.acapulcoscuba.com; La Costera 101),

below AJ Hacket Bungee , has PADI and NAUI certified instructors and offers several certification courses and guided day trips. All prices include a guide, gear, boat and refreshments. Prices range from US$60 for a beginning level dive, to US$350 for a five-day PADI open water certification. A guided, two-tank dive for experienced divers costs US$70.

Aqua Mundo Diving School (Map p490; ☎ 482-10-41; La Costera 100) offers instruction only and is certified by FMAS (Federación Mexicana de Actividades Subacuáticas, a government certification similar to PADI). Classes are in shallow ocean and cost US$38 each.

The best **snorkeling** is off Isla de la Roqueta (p491), though Playas Caleta and Caletilla also have some decent spots; gear can be rented onsite at both places.

Sportfishing is very popular in Acapulco and several companies offer six- to seven-hour fishing trips; book at least a day in advance and figure on a 6am or 7am departure time. **Aqua Mundo** (above), **Divers de México** (Map p490; ☎ 482-13-98; eililee1999@infosel.com; La Costera 100) and **Fish-R-Us** (Map p490; ☎ 487-87-87, 482-82-82; www.fish-r-us.com; Costera 100) all offer fishing trips. The cost for a six-hour trip aboard a four- to six-line boat is around US$250 (for the entire boat). If you don't have a group large enough to cover the boat, both Fish-R-Us and Divers de Mexico can usually add one or two people to an existing group for US$55 to US$70 per person. The local fishing cooperative **DARH** (Map p490; ☎ 482-96-81, 480-04-65; Costera 211), facing Playa Tlacopanocha on the Malecón, offers trips for six to eight people for US$200.

OTHER SPORTS

The **Unidad Deportiva Acapulco** (Map pp488-9; ☎ 486-10-33; Chiapas s/n, Colonia Progreso; admission stadium track/pool US$0.30/1; ☼ noon-6pm Tue, 9am-6pm Wed-Sun) has an Olympic-size pool, children's pool, gymnasium, stadium, sports courts and grass fields.

For tennis, try **Club de Golf Acapulco** (☎ 484-65-83), **Club de Tenis Hyatt** (☎ 469-12-34), **Villa Vera Racquet Club** (☎ 484-03-34), **Hotel Panoramic** (☎ 481-01-32) or **Fairmont Acapulco Princess Hotel** (☎ 469-10-00).

Acapulco also has gyms, squash courts and other recreational facilities. The tourist office has information on sports in Acapulco.

CRUISES

Various boats and yachts offer cruises, which depart from the Malecón (Map p490) near the zócalo. Cruises (from US$20 low season) are available day and night; they range from multilevel boats with blaring salsa music and open bars to yachts offering quiet sunset cruises around the bay. All take basically the same route – they leave from the Malecón, go around Peninsula de las Playas to Isla de la Roqueta, pass by to see the cliff divers at La Quebrada, cross over to Puerto Marqués and then come back around Bahía de Acapulco.

The **Hawaiano** (☎ 482-21-99, 482-07-85), the **Fiesta** and **Bonanza** (☎ 482-20-55), and the large **Aca Tiki** (☎ 484-61-40) catamaran are all popular; you can make reservations directly or through travel agencies and most hotels.

Acapulco for Children

Acapulco is very family friendly with many fun options designed for children, but fun for adults too.

PARQUE PAPAGAYO   Map pp488–9

This large **amusement park** (☎ 485-71-77; La Costera btwn Morín & El Cano; admission free; ☻ 8am-8pm, rides operate 3-10pm) is full of tropical trees and provides access to Playas Hornos and Hornitos. Its attractions, for both kids and adults, include a roller-skating rink, skateboard area, a lake with paddleboats, a children's train, quadricycles, mechanical rides, animal enclosures with deer, rabbits, crocodiles and turtles, an aviary, a restaurant/bar and a hill affording an excellent view. A 1.2km 'interior circuit' pathway is good for jogging. There are entrances on all four sides of the park.

CICI   Map pp488–9

The **Centro Internacional de Convivencia Infantil** (CICI; ☎ 484-82-10; La Costera 101; admission US$5.50; ☻ 10am-6pm) is a family water-sports park on the east side of Acapulco. Dolphin, seal and diving shows are presented several times daily; there's also an 80m-long water toboggan, a pool with artificial waves, a small tide-pool aquarium and the Sky Coaster ride, which simulates the La Quebrada cliff-diving experience. Children who are two years and up pay full price, plus you'll need to rent a locker (US$1), and an inflatable ring (US$2) to use the toboggan.

Another attraction here is **Acapulco Mágico** (☎ 481-02-94, 484-19-70), where visitors can swim with dolphins for US$55 for 20 minutes or US$100 for an hour. Phone ahead for reservations.

Any local bus marked 'CICI,' 'Base' or 'Puerto Marqués' will take you there.

MÁGICO MUNDO MARINO   Map pp488–9

This **aquarium** (☎ 483-12-15; admission adult/child 3-12 yrs US$2.75/1.50; ☻ 9am-6pm) stands on a small point of land between Playas Caleta and Caletilla. Highlights include a sea lion show; the feeding of crocodiles, turtles and piranhas; swimming pools; water toboggans; and an oceanographic museum.

Festivals & Events

Probably the busiest time of year for tourism in Acapulco is **Semana Santa**, when there's lots of action in the discos, on the beaches and all over town.

The **Tianguis Turístico** (www.tianguisturistico.com.mx), Mexico's major annual tourism trade fair, is held the second or third week in April. The **Festivales de Acapulco**, held for one week in May, feature Mexican and international music at venues around town.

International film festivals include the **Festival de Cine Negro** (Black Film Festival), held in early June; and the weeklong **Festival de Cine Francés** (French Film Festival) in late November. The festival for Mexico's favorite figure, the **Virgen de Guadalupe**, is celebrated all night on December 11 and all the following day; it's marked by fireworks, folk dances and street processions accompanied by small marching bands. The processions converge at the cathedral in the zócalo, where children dressed in costumes congregate.

Sleeping

Acapulco has more than 30,000 hotel rooms in all categories. Rates vary widely by season; high season is from the middle of December until the end of Easter, with another flurry of activity during the July and August school holidays. At other times of year you can often bargain for a better rate, especially if you plan to stay a while. During Semana Santa or between Christmas and New Year's Day, it's essential to book ahead. The following prices are for the high season.

BUDGET

Most of Acapulco's budget hotels are concentrated around the zócalo and on La Quebrada. Hotels up near Plaza La Quebrada enjoy more breeze than those near the zócalo.

Hotel Asturias (Map p490; ☎ /fax 483-65-48; La Quebrada 45; s/d US$11/16, with air-con US$23/33; P ❄ ☑) Deservedly popular, this friendly, family-run hotel is super clean and well tended, with pleasant rooms on a courtyard, cable TV in the lobby, a small swimming pool and a book exchange.

Youth Hostel K3 (Map pp488-9; ☎ 481-31-11/13; La Costera 116; www.k3acapulco.com; dm/r with continental breakfast US$15/45; ❄ ☐) If you're wanting to hook up with young, outgoing travelers, K3 is the place. It's rather industrial with stark, sterile rooms, but it offers every service travelers need and the patio and game room provide ample space for socializing.

Hotel Añorve (Map p490; ☎ 482-32-6; Juárez 17; per person US$14) Humble, clean and pleasantly pink, this hotel boasts hot water, friendly management and new tiles in the bathrooms.

Hotel Paola (Map p490; ☎ 482-62-43; Azueta 16; s/d US$11/16) The positively pink Paola is clean and family-run. Outside rooms have small private balconies, the interior rooms are quieter, and all are outfitted in pastels.

Hotel Santa Lucía (Map p490; ☎ 482-04-41; Av López Mateos 33; per person US$9) Don't be turned off by the gated entry at this well-secured, clean, family-run place. The no-frills rooms are a good value at this price. Rooms in the back are less noisy.

Hotel Maria Antonieta (Map p490; ☎ 482-50-24; Azueta 17; per person US$9) Maria Antonieta is a good but cavernous place near the zócalo with reasonably quiet rooms and a communal kitchen.

Hotel Angelita (Map p490; ☎ 483-57-34; La Quebrada 37; s/d US$9/14) The Angelita has a bit of grandma in the air with plastic flowers and a friendly group of motherly folks hanging out in the front sitting room.

Casa de Huéspedes California (Map p490; ☎ 482-28-93; La Paz 12; per person US$14) The California attracts a motley crew of single men. The courtyard is inviting but cleanliness in the rooms is variable. English and some French are spoken.

Hotel El Faro (Map p490; ☎ 482-13-65; La Quebrada 83; per person US$9) On Plaza La Quebrada, the old El Faro has large, rundown rooms and unreliable hot water. Its strongest feature is the large communal balcony facing the ocean with a fabulous sunset view.

La Torre Eiffel (Map p490; ☎ 482-16-83; Inalámbrica 110; hoteltorreeiffel@hotmail.com; s/d US$11/16; P ☑) Despite the rumors, the aged Torre Eiffel still stands tall with new paint and new management. Rooms aren't all spacious and some of the mattresses sag, but the new color TVs, thumping techno beats and huge balconies with sitting areas facing the sea keep it popular.

Hotel Mariscal (Map p490; ☎ 482-00-15; La Quebrada 35; r US$16) Having lost its luster, the Mariscal tries to make up for the dusty corners by putting TVs in the bare-bones rooms and hot showers in bathrooms with seatless toilets.

Like most places along the Pacific coast, camping in Acapulco is primarily designed for RVs.

Playa Suave Trailer Park (Map pp488-9; ☎ 485-18-85; La Costera 276; sites US$21) Through the entrance on Vasco Núñez de Balboa, between Mendoza and Malaespina, is this well-hidden urban park convenient to the rest of town. The 38 cement covered spots are open all year round.

Trailer Park Diamante (☎ 466-02-00; Copacabana 8, Fraccionamiento Playa Diamante; sites US$15; ☑) This lush, green park is tough to find – turn at the 'Construama' sign. It's 3km from the beach but the pools keep a regular stream coming back every year.

MID-RANGE

Most of the high-rise hotels along La Costera tend to be expensive. But there are some good deals in older places around town. A few places near CICI and Playa Icacos offer rooms with fully equipped kitchens.

Hotel Boca Chica (Map pp488-9; ☎ 483-67-41; www.acapulco-hotelbocachica.com; Playa Caletilla; r/ste from US$60/73; P ❄ ☑) There's a hint of original Acapulco in the air at this family-run, landmark hotel tucked into the rocks at the end of Playa Caletilla. It has got a private ocean cove for snorkeling, diving, boating and evening swimming. Rooms are comfortable with views of Isla de la Roqueta, Playa Caletilla or the garden. Don't miss out on the open-air, seaside Marina Club Sushi & Oyster Bar (see Eating, p497).

Suites Selene (Map pp488-9; ☎ /fax 484-36-43; suitesselene@hotmail.com; Colón 175; ste with/without view US$55/45; (P) (✕) (⌖)) One door from the beach, Selene is a great option. It's especially good value for anyone planning to stay a while and cook for themselves. Rooms show a bit of age and the Astroturf is faded, but the pool is pleasant and the location is tough to beat.

Hotel Misión (Map p490; ☎ 482-36-43; Valle 12; per person US$23; (P)) Near the zócalo, Acapulco's oldest hotel is a relaxing colonial place with stylish but basic rooms with tiles and heavy Spanish furniture. The best of the courtyard-side rooms are upstairs. Both continental breakfast (US$3) or complete breakfast (US$6) are available.

Hotel Etel Suites (Map p490; ☎ 482-22-40/41; Cerro de la Pinzona 92; ste/apt from US$55/91; (P) (✕) (⌖)) High atop the hill overlooking Old Acapulco, this friendly hotel's good-value, spotless suites and apartments have expansive terraces with views of La Quebrada and the bay. Amenities include full kitchens, two swimming pools and well-manicured gardens. It is recommended, especially for larger groups.

Romano Palace Hotel (Map pp488-9; ☎ 484-77-30, 800-212-23-00; La Costera 130; r US$55) One of the more economical hotels is the 22-story Romano Palace, whose luxurious, if a bit gauche, rooms have private balconies and floor-to-ceiling windows with great bayfront views; ask for an upper-story room.

Hotel Ritz (Map pp488-9; ☎ 482-66-77, 800-715-40-54; Massieu s/n; r US$46-73; (P) (✕) (⌖)) Half a block from Playa Hornitos, this six-story, well-worn hotel has 81 motel-style rooms with air-con, cable TV, carpet and private terraces overlooking the swimming pool.

Hotel Jacqueline (Map pp488-9; ☎ 485-93-38; Morín 205 at La Costera; r US$46; (✕)) On the east side of Parque Papagayo, near La Costera and popular Playa Hornitos, the humble Jacqueline has 10 rooms around a pleasant little garden. All rooms have air-con and cable TV.

Hotel del Valle (Map pp488-9; ☎ 485-83-36/88; Espinosa 8; r with fan/air-con US$43/52; (P) (⌖)) Next to the Jacqueline, the del Valle has comfortable rooms, a small swimming pool and communal kitchens (US$6.50 surcharge per day). The nearest street sign indicates Morín (which actually starts a block north).

TOP END
Acapulco has numerous deluxe 'grand tourism' and ultraluxe 'special category' hotels

to choose from. Many of the luxury hotels are in the newer Acapulco Diamante zone, east of Puerto Marqués, and beachfront along La Costera; the original high-rise zone begins at the eastern end of Parque Papagayo and curves east around the bay. Off-season package rates and special promotions, which can be less than half the standard holiday rack rates, dip as low as US$129 per night for double occupancy – ask reservation agents for special deals. During the high season, the sky is truly the limit and nothing goes for less than US$200 per night without reservations.

There are several impressive special category hotels:

Camino Real Acapulco Diamante (☎ /fax 435-10-10/20, in the US 800-722-6466; www.caminoreal.com; Carretera Escénica, Km 14; (P) (✕) (⌖))

Fairmont Acapulco Princess (☎ 484-21-24, in the US 800-441-1414; www.fairmont.com; Playa Revolcadero s/n; (P) (✕) (✕) (⌖) (⌖))

Fairmont Pierre Marqués (☎ 466-05-66, in the US 800-469-1000; www.fairmont.com; Villa 741, Playa Revolcadero s/n; (P) (✕) (✕) (⌖) (⌖))

Hyatt Regency Acapulco (Map pp488-9; ☎ 469-1234, in Mexico 800-005-00-00, in the US 800-233-1234; www.acapulco.hyatt.com; La Costera 1; (P) (✕) (✕) (⌖) (⌖))

Las Brisas (Map pp488-9; ☎ 469-69-00, in Mexico 800-227-47-47, in the US 800-223-6800; www.brisas.com.mx; Carretera Escénica s/n; (P) (✕) (⌖))

There are also several noteworthy grand tourism hotels:

Costa Club Acapulco (Map pp488-9; ☎ 485-90-50, 800-712-20-00; La Costera 123; (P) (✕) (⌖) (⌖))

Fiesta Americana Condesa (Map pp488-9; ☎ 484-28-28; www.fiestaamericana.com; La Costera 97; (P) (✕) (⌖) (⌖))

Radisson Resort (Map pp488-9; ☎ 446-65-65; www.radisson.com; Costera Guitarrón 110; (P) (✕) (⌖) (✕))

Vidafel Mayan Palace (☎ 466-23-93; fax 466-00-38; Costera de las Palmas 1121; (P) (✕) (⌖) (⌖))

Villa Vera Hotel Spa (☎ 484-03-33; fax 484-74-79; Lomas del Mar 35; (P) (✕) (✕) (⌖) (⌖))

Eating
OLD ACAPULCO   Map p490
Emerging from the zócalo's west side, Juárez has at least a dozen inexpensive, casual restaurants. For eat-in or takeout rotisserie-roasted chicken, head for 5 de Mayo, where there are four places side by side, plus a **Mr Taco** joint across the street.

El Amigo Miguel (☎ 485-77-64, 483-69-81; Juárez 31 & Azueta 7; mains US$4-10) This cheery open-air restaurant is one of the busiest, featuring cheap and delicious seafood. Miguel has two restaurants opposite one another, on the same corner, with other branches around town. Several other good seafood places are nearby.

Big Slice/La Rebanadota (north side of plaza; ⊙ 9-1am; mains US$2-5) This place is popular for its tasty, economical food and attractive tables both out on the plaza (which is great for people-watching) and inside where it is air-conditioned. Specialties include pizza, pasta and salads, and the 'big slices' are gigantic.

Restaurant San Carlos (Juárez 5; mains US$3-6) An open-air patio, good traditional Mexican fare and an ample atmosphere.

Restaurant Café Astoria (Plaza Álvarez, Edificio Pintos 4C; snacks US$1.50-4) Hidden away at the back of the zócalo, this café has outdoor tables in a shady, semiquiet spot just east of the cathedral.

La Gran Torta (☎ 483-84-76; La Paz 6; set lunch US$3) Popular with local families, the Big Torta serves up hearty breakfasts, good espresso, a sizable *comida corrida* and very tasty tortas.

Nutri-Light (Hidalgo 1; snacks US$1-2.50) For juices, empanadas, tortas and other light snacks, this bright, friendly little place has it all.

Restaurant Charly II (Carranza s/n; tacos US$2) Around the corner from Café Astoria, on the pedestrian alley of Carranza, economical Charly II has shady sidewalk tables.

Restaurant Ricardo (☎ 482-11-40; Juárez 9; set lunch US$3) A couple of doors further from the zócalo, Ricardo's is a popular restaurant with locals for its cheap set meals and robust café con leche.

Café Wadi (☎ 482-09-14; Mina 18; coffee US$1-2; ⊙ closed Sun) This is a great morning stop for excellent fresh-roasted espresso drinks before hitting the nearby artisans market.

Sanborns (☎ 482-61-67; cnr Escudero & La Costera; mains US$4-8) Near Woolworth's, Sanborns also has an air-conditioned restaurant serving Mexi-American fare; there are a couple more locations along La Costera.

Woolworth's (☎ 482-23-45; Escudero 250; mains US$3-8) This department store has an air-conditioned restaurant which is popular with locals for its good-value meal deals.

Café Los Amigos (La Paz 10; mains US$3-5) This is *the* spot for North American eggs and bacon in the company of many hungry gringos devouring tasty set breakfasts. Have eggs (however you want them), toast with jam, OJ, beans or potatoes, and a bottomless cup of coffee, all for US$3.

LA COSTERA   Map pp488-9

Dozens of restaurants line La Costera heading east toward the high-rise hotels; most specialize in fresh seafood or flashy gimmicks.

Fersato's (☎ 484-39-49; La Costera 44; mains US$4-12) Opposite the Casa de la Cultura, this long-standing family establishment features delicious Mexican food.

Mariscos Pipo's (☎ 484-01-65; cnr La Costera & Nao Victoria; mains US$5-18; ⊙ 1-9:30pm) Near Plaza Canadá, Pipo's used to be known as one of Acapulco's best marisquerías, but it's far from the best value on the beach; the combination seafood cocktail (US$14/17 small/large) might feed two.

VIPS (☎ 486-85-74; Gran Plaza, cnr La Costera & Massieu; mains US$4-10; ⊙ until 2am Fri & Sat) The Mexican version of Denny's is a big, bright, air-conditioned place, more popular with locals than tourists. There are a couple more locations along La Costera, including one at Playa Icacos that's open 24 hours.

Carlos 'n Charlie's (☎ 484-00-39; La Costera 112; mains US$6-15; ⊙ 1pm-midnight) Carlos Anderson's chain place isn't cheap, but it sends the tourists home happy after a night of rowdy music and a quirky bilingual menu.

Señor Frog's (☎ 446-57-34; Carretera Escénica 28, Centro Comercial La Vista; mains US$5-17; ⊙ 1pm-1am) On the east side of Bahía de Acapulco, this famously boisterous place has great views and less great food.

Pancho's (☎ 484-10-96; La Costera 109; mains US$6-14; ⊙ 6pm-midnight) This open-air restaurant is reasonably priced and serves tasty Mexican and international meals, especially grilled and barbecued meats.

Many other open-air beachfront restaurant/bars are opposite the Romano Palace Hotel. Stroll along, browse the posted menus, and take your pick.

Health-conscious **100% Natural** (☎ 485-52-79; La Costera 200, 34 & 112; mains US$2-7) chain outlets, serving mid-range, mostly vegetarian fare, are found throughout Acapulco; there are several along La Costera. The one at La Costera 200 is open 24 hours.

Another chain, **El Fogón** (☎ 484-50-79; La Costera 10; mains US$4-9) serves its traditional Mexican dishes at several La Costera branches. Many fast food chains also litter La Costera, especially near the east end.

ELSEWHERE

Some of the best eating experiences are a little more difficult to find, but well worth the work.

Pozolería Los Cazadores (☎ 482-51-29; cnr Calle 6 & Av Mexico, Colonia Cuauhtémoc; pozole US$2-5; ☒ 2pm-midnight Thu & Sat) Get ready for an off-the-beaten track Mexican eating experience. In a residential area north of the zócalo, Los Cazadores attracts hordes of people for its renowned pozole. The full-serving *botana* (a side plate of avocado, tortilla chips, lemon, fried pork rinds, quesadillas, cheese, a stuffed chili and more) is enough for two bowls of pozole and a must if you want to enjoy your soup properly. Admittedly it isn't the most gourmet pozole in town, but the dining experience is incomparable, especially when folks take to the floor to dance off their meal. The bands kick in around 4pm. A taxi from the zócalo costs around US$3.

Marina Club Sushi & Oyster Bar (Map pp488-9; ☎ 483-63-88; Hotel Boca Chica, Playa Caletilla; mains US$5-15; ☒ 12:30-2:30pm & 7:30pm-midnight) Only ultra-fresh fish hits the plates and grill here. Chocolate clams from Baja are flown in daily and other fish is limited to what local fishermen are catching, which keeps the quality sushi tasty. Thai specialties are expected to hit the menu soon. If dinner isn't for you, come by for a relaxing drink beneath the high palapa roof.

Restaurant La Perla (Map p490; ☎ 483-11-55; Plaza Las Glorias Hotel, Plazoleta La Quebrada 74; dinner show US$32; ☒ 7-11pm) This scenic restaurant has a nightly à la carte meal on candlelit terraces under the stars; it's expensive, but the unbelievable view of the *clavadistas* (see La Quebrada Cliff Divers, p489) makes for a memorable evening.

SELF-CATERING

The huge air conditioned **Comercial Mexicana**, **Bodega Aurrera** and **Bodega Gigante** combination supermarkets and big-box discount department stores are along La Costera between the zócalo and Parque Papagayo. Another **Comercial Mexicana** is opposite CICI.

Sam's Club and yet another **Comercial Mexicana** are on Hwy 95, just inland from the La Diana traffic circle. **Wal-Mart**, on the east end of the city, has a pharmacy and is open 24 hours. **Costco** is further east.

Drinking

New West (Map p490; ☎ 483-10-82; La Quebrada 81) Out near La Quebrada, this popular local bar has a sawdust floor, a mechanical bull (fun to watch, painful to ride), beer on tap, rodeo videos and a jukebox blaring norteño, banda, tejano and a smattering of US country 'n' western hits.

Entertainment

Acapulco's active nightlife rivals its beaches as the main attraction. Much of it revolves around discos and nightclubs, with new ones continually opening up to challenge the old.

DANCE, MUSIC & THEATER

As an alternative to the discos, most of the big hotels along La Costera have bars with entertainment, be it quiet piano music or live bands.

Centro de Convenciones (Map pp488-9; ☎ 484-71-52; La Costera s/n; show plus dinner only/open bar & dinner US$23/48; ☒ 7-10pm Mon, Wed & Fri) The convention center presents a Fiesta Mexicana three nights a week, featuring regional dances from many parts of Mexico, mariachis, the famous Papantla voladores and a rope performer.

Other theaters at the Centro de Convenciones present plays, concerts, dance and other cultural performances, as does the **Casa de la Cultura** (Map pp488-9; ☎ 484-23-90, 484-38-14); phone or stop by for current schedules. **Parque Papagayo** (☎ 485-71-77, 485-96-23) also sometimes hosts alfresco events.

NIGHTCLUBS & DISCOS

Most of the discos open around 10pm and have a cover charge of at least US$10, which sometimes includes an open bar. You can identify the most popular of-the-moment places by comparing the length of the VIP lines.

Palladium (☎ 446-54-90; Carretera Escénica s/n, Las Brisas; cover US$20-25) Hailed by many as the best disco in town, the Palladium attracts the younger crowd by playing a range of hip-hop, house, trance, techno and other base-heavy beats. Dress up and expect to wait in line.

Enigma (☎ 446-57-11; Carretera Escénica s/n, Las Brisas; cover US$20-25) This Egyptian-extravaganza with waterfalls, lightshows and endless house and techno music has outstanding views and attracts an energetic crowd.

Baby'O (Map pp488-9; ☎ 484-74-74; La Costera 22; cover US$14-30) Always popular, Baby'O has a laser light show, Wednesday theme nights and spins a pop-heavy set that attracts a young crowd.

Andromedas (Map pp488-9; ☎ 484-88-15/16; cnr La Costera & La Fragata Yucatán; cover US$23) Totally sexy in a nautical theme, this popular disco pumps out techno-pop, but most people come to see the nearly-nude mermaids in the aquariums.

El Alebrije (Map pp488-9; ☎ 484-59-02; La Costera 3308; cover US$23) This disco/concert hall bills itself as 'one of the largest and most spectacular discos in the world.' Less spectacular than big, it's usually packed. The music is a middle-of-the road mix of Latin and rock.

Salon Q (Map pp488-9; ☎ 484-32-52, 481-01-14; La Costera 23; cover from US$23) Cover at this 'catedral de la salsa' includes an open bar. Nightly entertainment includes Latin rhythms, impersonators and live music; reservations are recommended. Discounts for groups are available.

Disco Beach (Map pp488-9; ☎ 484-8230; La Costera s/n, Playa Condesa) This popular disco is in the line of beachfront restaurant/bars opposite the Romano Palace Hotel, right on Playa Condesa.

Hard Rock Cafe (Map pp488-9; ☎ 484-66-80; La Costera 37; ☽ noon-2am) It's hard to miss the Hard Rock. Just west of CICI, the chain's Acapulco branch has live music from 11pm to 1:30am.

Planet Hollywood (Map pp488-9; ☎ 484-42-84; La Costera 2917; ☽ noon-2am) Planet Hollywood has dancing from around 11pm.

If discos aren't your thing, there are other options around town.

Nina's (Map pp488-9; ☎ 484-24-00; La Costera 41; cover US$20-25) For live Latin music (salsa, cumbia, cha cha cha, merengue) and a heated dance floor, Nina's is the best place in town.

Tropicana and **Copacabana** (Map pp488-9; Playa Hornos; minimum consumption US$4.50) are next door to each other. They're two fast routes out of the glitzy disco scene and into the world of norteña, ranchera and banda, the most popu-

lar music styles in Mexico (country stuff despised by the most fashionable clubbers). But they're great if you want a party.

GAY VENUES
Acapulco has an active gay scene with several gay bars and clubs.

Demas (Map pp488-9; Piedra Picuda 17, behind Carlos & Charlie's) Only men, weekend shows.

Factory Demas (Map pp488-9; Av de los Deportes 10) Up the street opposite Hotel Galeana.

Picante (Map pp488-9; Piedra Picuda 16, behind Carlos 'n' Charlie's)

Relax (Map pp488-9; Lomas del Mar No 4; ☽ Thu-Sat nights) Men and women welcome.

Also worth checking out are the transvestite shows at **La Casa Blanca** (Map p490; cnr La Paz & Iglesias; ☽ 7pm Thu-Sat).

CINEMAS
Acapulco has several cinemas – at least three front La Costera, and several more are scattered around town. Show times are listed in the *Acapulco Novedades* and *Sol de Acapulco* newspapers.

BULLFIGHTS
Bullfights are held at the Plaza de Toros (Map pp488–9), southeast of La Quebrada and northwest of Playas Caleta and Caletilla, every Sunday at 5:30pm from December to March; tickets are sold at the **bullring ticket office** (☎ 482-11-82, 483-95-61) after 4:30pm and at travel agencies. The 'Caleta' bus passes near the bullring.

Shopping
100% Mexico (Map pp488-9; ☎ 486-28-45; www.100 mexico.com; La Costera 127, Local 17; ☽ 10am-4pm & 5-8pm Wed-Mon) For high quality crafts from around Mexico, visit this Fonart shop.

Mercado de Artesanías (Map p490; btwn Cuauhtémoc & Vicente de León at Parana) Bargaining is the rule at this 400-stall mercado, Acapulco's main craft market. It's paved and pleasant, and is a good place to get better deals on everything that you see in the hotel shops – serapes, hammocks, jewelry, huaraches, clothing and T-shirts. Other artisan markets (all on Map pp488–9), include the **Mercados de Artesanías Papagayo, Noa Noa, Dalia** and **La Diana**, all on La Costera, and **Mercados de Artesanías La Caletilla** at the west end of Playa Caletilla.

Mercado Central (Map pp488-9; Diego H de Mendoza s/n) Several blocks north of the Costera on the east side of the street is this sprawling indoor-outdoor market where you'll find everything from peat moss and piñatas to chainsaws and child-salvation booths (not to mention sandals, T-shirts, leather goods, food products and souvenirs). Any eastbound 'Pie de la Cuesta' or 'Pedregoso' marked bus will drop you in front; when the sidewalk turns to tarp-covered stalls, you know you're there.

Getting There & Away

AIR

Acapulco has a busy **airport** (☎ 466-94-34) with many international flights, most connecting through Mexico City or Guadalajara – both short hops from Acapulco. **Aerolíneas Internacionales** (Map pp488-9; ☎ 486-56-30, 486-00-02; La Costera 127, Local 9) flies to Cuernavaca, **Aeroméxico/Aerolitoral** (Map pp488-9; ☎ 485-16-25/00; La Costera 286) to Guadalajara and Mexico City, and **America West** (☎ 466-92-75; Airport) to Phoenix. **American Airlines** (Map pp488-9; ☎ 481-01-61; La Costera 116, Plaza Condesa, Local 9) flies to Dallas, **Continental Airlines** (☎ 466-90-46; Airport) to Houston, **Mexicana** (Map pp488-9; ☎ 486-75-85; La Costera 1632, La Gran Plaza) to Mexico City, and **Northwest** (☎ 800-900-08-00; Airport) to Minneapolis (one Saturday flight, December to April).

BUS

There are two major 1st-class long-distance bus companies in Acapulco: Estrella de Oro and Estrella Blanca. The tiny, air-conditioned **Estrella de Oro terminal** (Map pp488-9; ☎ 485-93-60; cnr Av Cuauhtémoc & Massieu) has free toilets and a Banamex ATM. Estrella Blanca has two 1st-class terminals: **Central Papagayo** (Map pp488-9; ☎ 469-20-80; Av Cuauhtémoc 1605) just north of Parque Papagayo; and **Central Ejido** (Map pp488-9; ☎ 469-20-28/30; Av Ejido 47). Estrella Blanca also has a **2nd-class terminal** (Map p490; ☎ 482-21-84; Av Cuauhtémoc 97) that sells tickets for all buses, but only has departures to nearby towns. Estrella Blanca tickets are also sold at several agencies around town, including **Agencia de Viajes Zócalo** (☎ 482-49-76; La Costera 207, Local 2) a couple of blocks east of the zócalo.

Both companies offer frequent services to Mexico City, with various levels of luxury; journey durations depend on whether they use the faster autopista (Hwy 95D) or the old federal Hwy 95.

Chilpancingo Estrella de Oro (US$5, 1½-3hr, 1st-class or Plus every 1-2 hours 5:30am-midnight); Futura (US$5, 1½-3hr, 4 daily); Estrella Blanca (US$6, 1½-3hr, 1 Ejecutivo daily, from Central Papagayo; US$4.50, 2nd-class every half hour 5am-7pm, from 2nd-class terminal)

Cuernavaca Estrella de Oro (US$19, 4-5hr, 3 Primera daily; US$20, 4-5hr, 3 Plus daily; US$15, 4-5hr, 3 hourly 2nd-class); Estrella Blanca (US$18, 4-5hr, 7 Primera daily; US$20, 4-5hr, 1 Plus daily; US$21, 4-5hr, 1 Futura daily, from Central Ejido; US$22, 4-5hr, 3 Futura daily, from Central Papagayo)

Iguala Estrella de Oro (US$11, 3hr, 13 Primera daily; US$9, 3½hr, Ordinario/2nd-class hourly 6am-8:30pm); Estrella Blanca (US$10, 3½hr, 17 Primera daily, from Central Ejido)

Mexico City Estrella de Oro (US$24, 6hr, 1 Plus daily; US$24, 6hr, 9 Futura daily); Estrella Blanca (US$37, 6hr, 1 Ejecutivo daily, from Central Papagayo; US$23, 6hr, 2 Económico daily; US$37, 6hr, 2 Futura daily, from Central Ejido) To Terminal Norte.

Mexico City Estrella de Oro (US$25, 5hr, 20 Plus daily; US$26, 5hr, 5 Crucero daily; US$37, 5hr, 6 Diamante daily); Futura (US$24, 5hr, at least hourly 7am-midnight); Estrella Blanca (US$37, 5hr, 4 Ejecutivo daily, from Central Papagayo; US$25, 5hr, 5 Primera & 8 Futura daily, from Central Ejido) To Terminal Sur.

Puerto Escondido Estrella Blanca (US$17.50, 7hr, 3 Primera daily, from Central Ejido; US$15,8-10hrs, hourly Economica daily from Centro Papagayo)

Taxco Estrella de Oro (US$11, 4hr, 3 Primera daily); Estrella Blanca (US$13, 4hr, 4 Primera daily, from Central Ejido)

Zihuatanejo Estrella Blanca (US$9, 4-5hr, 3 Primera daily; US$10.50, 4-5hr, 15 Primera Plus daily; US$11, 4-5hr, 1 Futura at 6:30pm, from Central Papagayo); Estrella de Oro (US$8, 4-5hr, 2nd-class hourly 5am-5:30pm)

CAR & MOTORCYCLE

Many car rental companies rent Jeeps as well as cars; several have offices at the airport as well as in town, and some offer free delivery to you. Shop around to compare prices. Rental companies include:

Alamo (Map pp488-9; ☎ 484-33-05, 466-94-44; La Costera 2148)

Avis (Map pp488-9; ☎ 466-91-90, 462-00-75; La Costera 139C)

Budget (Map pp488-9; ☎ 481-24-33, 466-90-03; La Costera 93, Local 2)

Hertz (Map pp488-9; ☎ 485-68-89; La Costera 137)

Saad (Map pp488-9; ☎ 484-34-45; La Costera 28) Local rentals only.

Getting Around

TO/FROM THE AIRPORT

Acapulco's airport is 23km southeast of the zócalo, beyond the junction for Puerto Marqués. Arriving by air, buy a ticket for transportation into town from the colectivo desk before you leave the terminal; it's about US$8 per person for a lift directly to your hotel.

Leaving Acapulco, phone **Móvil Aca** (☎ 462-10-95) or **Shuttle** (☎ 462-10-95) 24 hours in advance to reserve transportation back to the airport. They'll pick you up 90 minutes before your flight for domestic flights or two hours before your flight for international flights; the cost is US$8 per person. Taxis from the center to the airport cost around US$20 if hailed in the street; 'hotel rates' are higher.

BUS

Acapulco has a good city bus system (especially good when you get an airbrushed beauty with a bumping sound system). They operate from 5am to 11pm daily and cost US$0.35 to US$0.45. From the zócalo area, the bus stop opposite Sanborns department store on La Costera, two blocks east of the zócalo, is a good place to catch buses – it's the beginning of several bus routes so you can usually get a seat. There are several useful city routes:

Base-Caleta – from the Icacos naval base at the southeast end of Acapulco, along La Costera, past the zócalo to Playa Caleta.

Base-Cine Río-Caleta – from the Icacos naval base, cuts inland from La Costera on Av Wilfrido Massieu to Av Cuauhtémoc, heads down Av Cuauhtémoc through the business district, turning back to La Costera just before reaching the zócalo, continuing west to Playa Caleta.

Puerto Marqués-Centro – from opposite Sanborns, along La Costera to Puerto Marqués. **Zócalo-Playa Pie de la Cuesta** – from opposite Sanborns, to Pie de la Cuesta; Buses marked 'Playa' or 'Luces' go all the way down the Pie de la Cuesta beach road; those marked 'San Isidro' or 'Pedregoso' stop at the entrance to Pie de la Cuesta.

TAXI

Blue and white VW cabs are as plentiful as they are noisy in Acapulco, and taxi drivers are happy to take gringos for a ride, especially for fares higher than the official rates. Ask locals the going rate for your ride and agree on the fare with the cabby before you climb in.

AROUND ACAPULCO

The cove at **Puerto Marqués**, 18km southeast of Acapulco, is much smaller than Bahía de Acapulco. You get a magnificent view of Bahía de Acapulco as the Carretera Escénica climbs south out of the city. Puerto Marqués' calm surf is good for waterskiing and sailing. Frequent 'Puerto Marqués' buses run along Acapulco's La Costera every 10 minutes from 5am to 9pm (US$0.30).

Heading out toward the airport past Puerto Marqués, **Playa Revolcadero** is the long, straight beach of the new Acapulco Diamante luxury tourism developments. Waves are large and surfing is popular here, especially in summer, but a strong undertow makes swimming dangerous. Horseback riding along the beach is also popular.

During Semana Santa, the Passion of Christ is acted out in the town of **Treinta**, 30km northeast of Acapulco; the Acapulco tourist office has details.

COSTA CHICA

The coast of Guerrero is known as the **Costa Grande** (Big Coast) from Acapulco northwest to the border of Michoacán, and as the **Costa Chica** (Small Coast) from Acapulco southeast to the less-traveled Oaxacan border.

On Hwy 200, 60km (about an hour) east of Acapulco, **San Marcos** is an unremarkable town, but it provides essential services. Similarly small **Cruz Grande** is on Hwy 200 about 40km further east.

Almost three hours southeast of Acapulco, **Playa Ventura** is a pristine beach with soft white and gold sand, clear water, a number of simple beachfront seafood restaurants and basic places to stay. From Playa Ventura you can walk about 1km to another good beach, **Playa La Piedra**. Horseback riding is available. On most maps, Playa Ventura is labeled **Juan Álvarez**. To get there from Acapulco, first take a bus heading southeast on Hwy 200 from Acapulco to **Copala** (US$4.50, two hours, 120km). Buses depart from Estrella Blanca's 2nd-class terminal on Av Cuauhtémoc every half hour from 3:30am to 7pm. In Copala, camionetas and microbuses depart for Playa Ventura every half hour (US$1.25, 30 minutes, 13km).

Marquelia, 20km east of Copala on Hwy 200, is another town providing essential services, including several inexpensive hotels. From Marquelia you can take a combi (US$0.40) to the nearby **Playa La Bocana**, where the Río Marquelia meets the sea and forms a lagoon. Another beach, **Playa Las Peñitas**, is 5km from La Bocana. The same buses that depart from

Acapulco for Copala also continue to Marquelia (US$1.75, 2½ hours, 140km).

Punta Maldonado, also referred to as El Faro, is a more remote Costa Chica beach. On a small bay fine for swimming, the tiny hamlet of Punta Maldonado has some seafood restaurants on the beach and one small hotel, which unfortunately is none too beautiful. To reach Punta Maldonado, take a camioneta from Cuajinicuilapa (aka 'Cuaji'), a small town on Hwy 200, some 200km southeast of Acapulco. Camionetas depart hourly from Cuaji (US$1.75, 45 minutes), or you can take a taxi. Second-class buses from Acapulco to Cuaji depart hourly from 3:30am to 6:30pm (US$10, five hours, 200km) from Estrella Blanca's Central Ejido terminal.

CHILPANCINGO

☎ 747 / pop 152,000 / elevation 1360m

Chilpancingo, capital of the state of Guerrero, is a university city and agricultural center. It lies on Hwys 95 and 95D, 130km north of Acapulco and 270km south of Mexico City. As an administrative center, it's a rather nondescript place between the much more compelling destinations of Taxco and Acapulco.

Murals in the former **Palacio Municipal** showing the 1813 Congress of Chilpancingo are the only remaining signs of the city's important place in Mexico's history. In the spring of 1813, rebel leader José María Morelos y Pavón encircled Mexico City with his guerrilla army and demanded a congress in Chilpancingo. The congress issued a Declaration of Independence and began to lay down the principles of a new constitution. Their achievements, however, were short-lived – Spanish troops breached the circle around Mexico City and recaptured most of the state of Guerrero, including Chilpancingo. Morelos was tried for treason and executed by firing squad.

The state-operated **tourist office** (☎ 472-95-66; Moisés Guevara 8) hands out information on the town, the region and the state of Guerrero.

Sleeping & Eating

Hotel El Presidente (☎ 472-97-31; Calle 30 de Agosto 1; s/d/ste US$23/32/38; P ⊠) The tidy, modern Presidente is only a block from the bus station and is visible from the highway and the bus terminal.

Hotel Cárdenas Madero (Madero 13 at Abasolo; s/d US$11/15) In the heart of the downtown action, this female run place has basic rooms in an old building. Most rooms have TV and there are some cheaper rooms without bathrooms.

Hotel El Presidente has a popular midrange restaurant/bar, and several other cheaper places are visible from the bus station. Just east of the bus terminal, the lively public market's upstairs fondas are cheap places to fuel up if you're waylaid here – don't miss the pork specialties and pozole with *chicharrones* (pork rinds) on Thursday.

Getting There & Away

Chilpancingo is served by the bus companies **Estrella Blanca** (☎ 472-06-34) and **Estrella de Oro** (☎ 472-21-30). Buses operate to/from Acapulco (US$5, 1½ hours), Chilapa (US$2, 45 minutes), Iguala (US$3.50, 1½ hours), Mexico City (US$21, 3½ hours) and Taxco (US$7.50, two hours).

AROUND CHILPANCINGO
Chilapa

The itty-bitty town of Chilapa, 45 minutes east of Chilpancingo by 2nd-class bus, holds a traditional market every Sunday, starting very early in the morning. Market day has almost a pre-Hispanic feel; indigenous people pour out of the hills, and all types of foodstuffs, handicrafts and animals are on display. Many vendors from this market cart their leftover wares to Acapulco on Monday. Virgen de Guadalupe devotees shouldn't miss the church clock; at noon daily Juan Diego emerges from the Virgen and showers the plaza below with flowers.

Olinalá

The tiny, remote town of Olinalá is famous throughout Mexico for its beautiful lacquered boxes and other locally produced lacquered woodcraft. Linaloe, the fragrant wood used to make the boxes, grows in this area. Olinalá is waaaay up in the mountains (altitude 1350m) and not often visited. If you do make it here, you'll find simple hotels around the plaza and a few places to eat. Second-class buses from Chilpancingo to Tlapa will drop you at the crossroads for Olinalá (4½ hours); then catch another bus (3rd-class, one more hour) to Olinalá.

Western Central Highlands

Some of the most rewarding and down-to-earth travel in Mexico is right here in the friendly highlands of Jalisco, Michoacán and Colima. Visit exciting and gracious Guadalajara, capital of Jalisco and Mexico's second-largest metropolis; Morelia, the fine capital of Michoacán; the Santuario Mariposa Monarca, a special reserve for the monarch butterfly; Pátzcuaro, a captivating colonial town and soul of Michoacán's indigenous Purépecha culture; and Volcán Paricutín, the cone that rose almost overnight in 1943 from Michoacán's lush countryside. In addition, the region's little-visited backcountry beckons explorers with its rugged landscapes, fertile valleys, timeless villages and even more scenic volcanoes, such as the snowy Volcán Nevado de Colima or the actively puffing Volcán de Fuego.

WESTERN CENTRAL HIGHLANDS

HIGHLIGHTS

- Exploring and eating out in cosmopolitan **Guadalajara** (p505), birthplace of mariachi music, tequila and *charreadas* (Mexican rodeos)

- Checking out distinguished **Morelia** (p542), capital of Michoacán that boasts colonial architecture, fine food, Spanish courses and a lively student population

- Visiting the Santuario Mariposa Monarca (**Monarch Butterfly Reserve**, p550), the fluttering winter resort for millions of migratory butterflies

- Relaxing in **Pátzcuaro** (p552), a beautiful and peaceful highland town and the soul of the Purépecha people

- Trekking up the extinct volcanic peak of **Nevado de Colima** (p541) or the still-steaming **Volcán Paricutín** (p568)

- ALTITUDE RANGE: 550m–4240m
- AVERAGE TEMPERATURE: 21°C

HISTORY

The western central highlands were remote from the country's pre-Hispanic empires, though a fairly advanced agricultural village society flourished in parts of the region as early as 200 BC. In the 14th to 16th centuries AD, the Tarascos of northern Michoacán developed a major pre-Hispanic civilization with its capital at Tzintzuntzan, near Pátzcuaro. The zenith of the Tarascan empire coincided with the Aztec empire, but the Tarascos always managed to fend off Aztec attacks. West of the Tarascos – and occasionally at war with them – was the Chimalhuacán confederation of four indigenous kingdoms, in parts of what are now Jalisco, Colima and Nayarit states. To the north were Chichimecs, whom the Aztecs regarded as barbarians.

Colima, the leading Chimalhuacán kingdom, was conquered by the Spanish in 1523, but the region as a whole was not brought under Spanish control until the 1529–36 campaigns of Nuño de Guzmán, who tortured, killed and enslaved indigenous people from Michoacán to Sinaloa in his pursuit of riches, territory and glory. Guzmán was appointed governor of most of what he had conquered, but eventually his misdeeds caught up with him and in 1538 he was sent back to Spain. These territories came to be called Nueva Galicia and retained some autonomy from the rest of Nueva España until 1786.

A rebellion in Jalisco in 1540 set that area aflame in what is known as the Mixtón War; it was ended the next year by an army led by the Spanish viceroy. Guadalajara was established in its present location in 1542, after three earlier settlements were abandoned in the face of attacks by hostile indigenous groups.

The region developed gradually, with ranching and agriculture as mainstays, and Guadalajara (always one of Mexico's biggest cities) became the 'capital of the west.' The church, with help from the enlightened bishop Vasco de Quiroga, fostered small industries and handicraft traditions in its effort to ease the poverty of the indigenous people.

In the 1920s Michoacán and Jalisco were hotbeds of the Cristero rebellion by Catholics against government antichurch policies. Lázaro Cárdenas of Michoacán, as state governor (1928–32) and then as Mexican president (1934–40), instituted reforms that did much to abate antigovernment sentiments.

CLIMATE

The climate is pleasantly warm and dry most of the year, with a distinct rainy season from June to September (when some 200mm of rain per month falls in most of the area). At lower altitudes, like the areas near Uruapan and Colima, temperature and humidity rise, and tropical plants abound. In higher-altitude places, such as Pátzcuaro, winter nights can get chilly.

TRANSPORT

All major cities in the western central highlands (Guadalajara, Colima, Morelia, Pátzcuaro and Uruapan) are well-connected by bus from outside the region. Guadalajara and Morelia have regular flights from many other cities in Mexico, as well as the United States.

GUADALAJARA

☎ 33 / pop 4 million / elevation 1540m

Playing second fiddle only to Mexico City, Guadalajara is a surprisingly manageable and friendly metropolis. In the Centro Histórico (historic center) many attractive pedestian streets and plazas are dotted with gushing fountains, leafy shrubs, relaxing benches and occasional sculptures. The city's residents (nicknamed *tapatíos*, which also refers to anyone Jalisco-born) stroll around peacefully in this renovated downtown, which is full of beautiful and elegant old buildings as well as fashionable shops. And when they tire of the noise and congestion, nearby suburbs like Zapopan, Tlaquepaque and Tonalá – formerly separate communities that have retained their small-town charm – become popular weekend jumps for visits or shopping trips.

Guadalajara's major contributions to the Mexican lifestyle include tequila, mariachi music, the broad-rimmed sombrero (hat), *charreadas* (rodeos) and the Mexican Hat Dance. It's also western Mexico's largest industrial center and claims a healthy share of museums, galleries, festivals, historic buildings, nightlife and culture. As a traveler to this remarkable city, you'll find plenty of entertainment.

HISTORY

Guadalajara was established on its present site only after three settlements elsewhere had failed. In 1532, Nuño de Guzmán and 63 Spanish families founded the first Guadalajara near Nochistlán (now in Zacatecas state), naming it after Guzmán's home city in Spain. Water was scarce, the land was hard to farm and the indigenous people were hostile, so in 1533 Captain Juan de Oñate ordered the settlement moved to the pre-Hispanic village of Tonalá, today a suburb of Guadalajara. Guzmán, however, disliked Tonalá and in 1535 had the settlement moved to Tlacotán, northeast of the modern city. In 1541 this was destroyed by a confederation of indigenous tribes led by the chief Tenamaxtli. The surviving colonists wearily picked a new site in the valley of Atemajac beside San Juan de Dios Creek, which ran where Calz Independencia is today. The new Guadalajara was founded by Oñate on February 14, 1542, near where the Teatro Degollado now stands.

Guadalajara prospered, and in 1560 was declared the capital of Nueva Galicia province. The city quickly grew into one of colonial Mexico's most important population centers and the heart of a rich agricultural region. It also was the starting point for Spanish expeditions and missions to western and northern Nueva España – and as far

GUADALAJARA

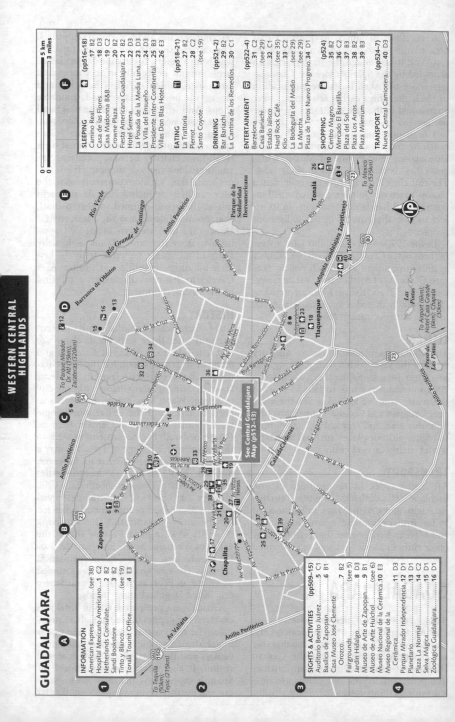

INFORMATION

American Express.....................(see 38)
Hospital Mexicano Americano.....1 C2
Netherlands Consulate.................2 B2
Sandi Bookstore..........................3 B2
Tinto y Blanco.........................(see 19)
Tonalá Tourist Office.................4 E3

SIGHTS & ACTIVITIES (pp509–15)

Auditorio Benito Juárez................5 C1
Basílica de Zapopan....................6 B1
Casa Museo José Clemente
  Orozco...................................7 B2
Fairgrounds...............................(see 5)
Jardín Hidalgo............................8 D3
Museo de Arte de Zapopan.........9 B1
Museo de Arte Huichol..............(see 6)
Museo Nacional de la Cerámica..10 E3
Museo Regional de la
  Cerámica...............................11 D3
Parque Mirador Independencia..12 D1
Planetario................................13 D1
Plaza La Normal........................14 C2
Selva Mágica...........................15 D1
Zoológica Guadalajara...............16 D1

SLEEPING (pp516–18)

Camino Real............................17 B2
Casa de las Flores....................18 D3
Casa Madonna B&B..................19 C2
Crowne Plaza...........................20 B2
Fiesta Americana Guadalajara....21 B2
Hotel Serena.............................22 D3
La Posada de la Media Luna.....23 D3
La Villa del Ensueño.................24 D3
Presidente Inter-Continental......25 B3
Villas Don Blas Hotel................26 E3

EATING (pp518–21)

La Trattoria...............................27 B2
Pierrot....................................28 B2
Santo Coyote.........................(see 19)

DRINKING (pp521–2)

Bar Bariachi.............................29 B2
La Cantina de los Remedios......30 C1

ENTERTAINMENT (pp522–4)

Barzelona.................................31 C2
Casa Bariachi........................(see 29)
Estadio Jalisco..........................32 C1
Hard Rock Café......................(see 35)
Kilo..33 C2
La Bodeguita del Medio..........(see 29)
La Marcha.............................(see 29)
Plaza de Toros Nuevo Progreso..34 D1

SHOPPING (p524)

Centro Magno...........................35 B2
Mercado El Baratillo.................36 C2
Plaza del Sol...........................37 B3
Plaza Los Arcos.......................38 B2
Plaza Milenium.......................39 B3

TRANSPORT (pp524–7)

Nueva Central Camionera..........40 D3

See Central Guadalajara Map (pp512–13)

away as the Philippines. Miguel Hidalgo, a leader in the fight for Mexican independence, set up a revolutionary government in Guadalajara in 1810 but was defeated near the city in 1811, not long before his capture and execution in Chihuahua. The city was also the object of heavy fighting during the War of the Reform (1858–61) and between Constitutionalist and Villista armies in 1915.

By the late 19th century Guadalajara had overtaken Puebla as Mexico's second-biggest city. Its population has mushroomed since WWII, and now the city is a huge commercial, industrial and cultural center and the communications hub for a large region.

ORIENTATION

Guadalajara's large twin-towered cathedral, at the heart of the city, is edged by four lovely plazas. The plaza east of the cathedral, Plaza de la Liberación, extends two blocks to the Teatro Degollado, also a city landmark. This whole area, along with a few surrounding blocks, is known as the Centro Histórico.

East of Teatro Degollado, the Plaza Tapatía pedestrian precinct extends half a kilometer to the Instituto Cultural de Cabañas, another historically significant building. Just south of Plaza Tapatía is Mercado Libertad, a huge three-story market covering two city blocks.

Calz Independencia is a major north–south central artery. From Mercado Libertad, it runs south to Parque Agua Azul and the Antigua Central Camionera (Old Bus Terminal), still used by short-distance regional buses. Northward, it runs to the zoo and other attractions. Don't confuse Calz Independencia with Calle Independencia, the east–west street one block north of the cathedral.

In the city center, north–south streets change names at Av Hidalgo, the street running along the north side of the cathedral.

About 20 blocks west of the cathedral, the north–south Av Chapultepec is Guadalajara's Zona Rosa, a smart area with modern office blocks, a few fancy shops and some fine restaurants. The long-distance bus terminal is the Nueva Central Camionera (New Bus Terminal), approximately 9km southeast of the city center past the suburb of Tlaquepaque.

INFORMATION
Bookstores

A fair selection of books and magazines in English is available in the gift shops of most major hotels and at many of the larger bookstores.

El Libro Antiguo (Map pp512-13; ☎ 3126-3865; Suárez 86; ✆ 10am-8pm Mon-Sat) place for a small selection of used English paperbacks. They trade books in also.

Sanborns (Map pp512-13; ☎ 3613-6264; downstairs, cnr 16 de Septiembre & Juárez; ✆ 7:30am-10pm)

Sandi Bookstore (Map p506; ☎ 3121-4210; sandibooks@sandibooks.com; Av Tepeyac 718; ✆ 9:30am-7pm Mon-Fri, 9:30am-2pm Sat & Sun) About 1km west of Av López Mateos, this bookstore has an extensive travel section, including many Lonely Planet guides. They also carry a wide selection of magazines, maps and other books, all in English.

Cultural Centers

Alianza Francesa (Map pp512-13; ☎ 3825-5595; www.alianzafrancesa.org.mx/guadalajara; Cotilla 1199; ✆ 9am-1pm & 4-8pm Mon-Fri, 9am-12:30pm Sat) Offers francophiles classes, movies and a library – all French-oriented, of course.

Internet Access

Several places around the central area offer Internet access for US$1.25 per hour.

Centro de Computación (Map pp512-13; 2nd fl, Moreno 509; ✆ 10:30am-10pm) Closer to the center than Micronet.

Micronet (Map pp512-13; Juárez 811; ✆ 9am-midnight) Ten blocks west of center.

Laundry

For clean duds you'll have hike southwest of the center a few blocks to the closest **lavandería** (Map pp512-13; Aldama 125). Full service costs US$3.75 per machine load and takes about three hours to wash and dry. Self-service is US$2.50 per load.

Media

The Spanish-language *Público*, the city's most prominent daily newspaper, offers exhaustive entertainment listings on Friday (see p522). *Guadalajara Reporter* (www.guadalajarareporter.com) caters to expats living in the region, including Lago de Chapala and Puerto Vallarta. *Guadalajara Weekly* is a free but not very informative visitor newsletter, available at the tourist office and some hotels. Many of the newsstands in central Guadalajara sell English-language periodicals.

Medical Centers

Hospital Mexico Americano (Map p506; ☎ 3641-3141; Colomos 2110) About 3km northwest of the center.

Money

Banks are plentiful in Guadalajara and almost all of them have ATMs. **HSBC** (Map pp512-13; ⏰ 8am-7pm Mon-Fri, 8am-3pm Sat) tends to keep the longest hours.

The *casas de cambio* (money changers) on López Cotilla, in the few blocks east of 16 de Septiembre, offer competitive exchange rates, quicker service and longer hours than banks. They're very eager, so try not to get dragged in.

American Express (Map p506; ☎ 3818-2319; Av Vallarta 2440; ⏰ 9am-6pm Mon-Fri, 9am-1pm Sat) is in the small Plaza Los Arcos shopping center, way west of center.

Post

Main post office (Map pp512-13; cnr Carranza & Indepenencia)

Telephone

There aren't many calling offices in Guadalajara; the cheapest way to dial home is to buy a Telmex phone card (look for the signs outside stores selling them) and then find a reasonably quiet public phone.

Tourist Offices

State tourist office (Map pp512-13; ☎ 3668-1600, 800-362-22-00; Morelos 102 or Paseo Degollado 105; ⏰ 9am-8pm Mon-Fri, 9am-1pm Sat & Sun) This excellent office can be reached from either Morelos or Paseo Degollado. The English-speaking staff offer information on Guadalajara and the state of Jalisco.

Tourist information booth (Map pp512-13; ⏰ 9:30am-2:30pm & 5-7:30pm Mon-Fri, 10am-12:30pm Sat & Sun) In the Palacio de Gobierno, just inside the entrance facing the Plaza de Armas. Information booths are provided around the central area too, especially during cultural events and festivals.

WALKING TOUR

Guadalajara's Centro Histórico is laid out on a grand and orderly plan, with most of its buildings and plazas occupying entire blocks. The arrival of the automobile made the area less walkable (and it's now more difficult to fully appreciate the heroic proportions of the center than in bygone years) but the many remaining pedestrian malls make hours of strolling a enjoyable

pastime. Plans are afoot to pedestrianize more streets; keep your fingers crossed, but don't hold your breath.

The **Plaza de Armas** was the hub of the city in colonial times and is a logical place to begin a walking tour. The roof of its fine central bandstand is attractively supported by bronze art nouveau ladies. Free concerts of Jaliscan music often take place here evenings (see p523). Make your first stop the **Palacio de Gobierno** (**1**; see opposite), which takes up the whole block east of the plaza.

Next head half a block north on Avenida 16 de Septiembre from the plaza's northwest corner to enter the ungainly **cathedral** (**2**; see opposite). When you've seen enough of the interior, cross the busy avenue to Plaza de los Laureles, named for its many laurel trees. The plaza has a pleasant clamshell fountain and affords the best exterior views of the cathedral; try to imagine the avenue filled with horsedrawn carriages in place of the hurtling buses.

Crossing Avenida Hidalgo diagonally from the northwest corner of the plaza will take you to the ornate **Templo de La Merced** (**3**), which was built in 1650; inside are several fine large paintings, crystal chandeliers and lots of gold decoration. Then you can head east to the **Presidencia Municipal** (City Hall; **4**), which was built between 1949 and 1952 but looks much older. Above its interior stairway is a somewhat frightening mural by Gabriel Flores depicting the founding of Guadalajara.

As you continue east on Hidalgo each of the following sites occupies its own block on the north side of the avenue. In order, they are the vaguely Greco-Roman **Plaza de los Jaliscenses Ilustres** (**5**); the precious old **Museo Regional de Guadalajara** (**6**; p510); the **Palacio Legislativo** (**7**), where the state congress meets, distinguished by massive stone columns in its interior courtyard; and the **Palacio de Justicia** (State Courthouse; **8**), built in 1588 as part of the Convento de Santa María, Guadalajara's first nunnery. A 1965 mural by Guillermo Chávez, depicting Benito Juárez and other legendary Mexican lawmakers, graces the interior stairway. The next block east holds the fairly unremarkable **Templo de Santa María de Gracia** (**9**), which served as the city's first cathedral (1549–1618).

You may have been looking longingly at the *south* side of Hidalgo in this stretch.

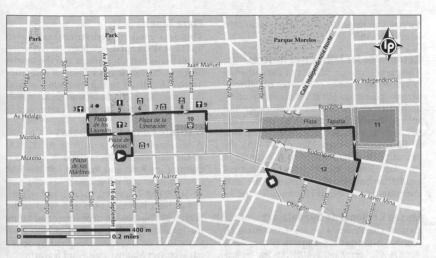

Well by all means, head back to **Plaza de la Liberación**, a lively and impressive space created by a 1980s urban renovation project involving the demolition of two whole blocks of colonial buildings (the redevelopment is still a source of controversy). The plaza's east end is dominated by the hulking **Teatro Degollado** (**10**; p510); if you've timed it right, have a look inside the theater.

Now prepare for the real walking part of the tour. Lengthy **Plaza Tapatía** sprawls to the east for more than 500m from behind Teatro Degollado, affording plenty of opportunities for window-shopping, snacking and people-watching all the way. When you hit the other end you can rest on one of several wonderfully whimsical bronze sculpture/benches and prepare to enter the **Instituto Cultural de Cabañas** (**11**; p510) complex.

Finally, swing south through **Mercado Libertad** (**12**; p524), a good spot for a cheap lunch, to the last point on the tour: Plaza de los Mariachis. Catch some tunes. Set a spell.

SIGHTS & ACTIVITIES
Palacio de Gobierno

This impressive structure housing state government offices is on the east side of Plaza de Armas. The **palacio** (Map pp512-13; Av Corona btwn Moreno & Morelos; ☼ 9am-8pm) was finished in 1774 in a combination of styles: a mix of simple, neoclassical features and riotous churrigueresque decorations. Its most interesting artistic feature is the huge portrait of Miguel Hidalgo in José Clemente Orozco's

1937 mural over the interior stairway. An angry Hidalgo, brandishes a torch in one fist while the masses struggle at his feet. In this mural Orozco also comments on the pressing issues of his time: communism, fascism and religion. Another Orozco mural in the ex-Congreso (former Congress Hall) upstairs depicts Hidalgo, Benito Juárez and other figures important in Mexican history.

Cathedral

Guadalajara's twin-towered **cathedral** (Av 16 de Septiembre btwn Morelos & Hidalgo; ☼ 8am-8pm, closed during mass) is the city's most famous symbol and most conspicuous landmark. Begun in 1558 and consecrated in 1618, it's almost as old as the city itself. Up close you can see that, like the Palacio de Gobierno, the cathedral is a stylistic hodgepodge, but one that doesn't hold entirely together. The exterior decorations, some of which were completed long after the consecration, are in churrigueresque, baroque, neoclassical and other styles. The towers date from 1848; they're much higher than the originals, which were destroyed in an earthquake in 1818. The interior includes Gothic vaults, Tuscany-style pillars and 11 richly decorated altars given to Guadalajara by King Fernando VII of Spain (1784–1833). The glass case nearest the north entrance is a very popular reliquary containing the hands and blood of the martyred Santa Inocencia. In the sacristy, which an attendant can open for you on request, is *La Asunción de la*

Virgen, painted by Spanish artist Bartolomé
Murillo in 1650.

Rotonda de los Jaliscenses Ilustres

The plaza on the north side of the cathedral
is ringed by bronze sculptures of Jalisco's
favorite characters (20 at last count): writers,
architects, revolutionaries, a composer and
others. Some of them are buried beneath the
Rotonda de los Jaliscienses Ilustres (Rotunda
of Illustrious Jaliscans; Map pp512–13), the
round pillared monument in the center of
the plaza. Before the city establishment got
egalitarian and added a woman to the mix,
the rotunda was 'de los Hombres Ilustres.'

Museo Regional de Guadalajara

East of the Rotonda de los Jaliscienses Ilustres, this must-see **museum** (Map pp512-13;
☎ 3614-9957; Liceo 60; admission US$3, free Sun; ⏰ 9am-
5:40pm Tue-Sat, to 5pm Sun) has an eclectic collection covering the history and prehistory of
western Mexico. Displays in the ground-floor
natural history section include the skeleton of
a woolly mammoth, and the archaeological
section has many fine artifacts of ceramic,
silver, gold and other materials. Upstairs
are galleries of colonial paintings, a history
gallery covering the area since the Spanish
conquest and an ethnography section with
displays about indigenous life in Jalisco,
and about *charros* (Mexican cowboys). The
museum building is the former seminary of
San José, a late-17th-century baroque structure with two stories of arcades and several
courtyards holding hidden delights, some
of which can only be viewed from above; be
sure to wander everywhere.

Teatro Degollado

The imposing neoclassical-style **Teatro Degollado** (Map pp512-13; ☎ 3614-4773; Degollado btwn Hidalgo
& Morelos; admission free; ⏰ for viewing 12:30-2:30pm
Mon-Fri) was begun in 1856, inaugurated 30
years later and has been reconstructed several
times since. Over the columns on its front is a
frieze depicting Apollo and the Nine Muses.
The five-tiered theater's interior is decorated
with red velvet and gold and is crowned by
a Gerardo Suárez mural based on the fourth
canto of Dante's *Divine Comedy.* The theater
hosts frequent performances of music, dance
and drama, and is sometimes open for viewing at 10am, depending on the Guadalajara
Philharmonic's rehearsal schedule.

Plaza Tapatía

This is a modern pedestrian mall (Map
pp512–13) comprising shops, restaurants,
street performers, fountains and the tourist
office. It extends half a kilometer east from
Teatro Degollado to the Instituto Cultural
de Cabañas. Calz Independencia passes
underneath it at about its midpoint.

Instituto Cultural de Cabañas

A huge neoclassical gem (Map pp512–13)
at the east end of Plaza Tapatía houses a
cultural institute and **museum** (☎ 3668-1640;
Cabañas 8; admission US$1, free Sun; ⏰ 10:15am-5:45pm
Tue-Sat, 10:15am-2:45pm Sun), theater and school.
It was built between 1805 and 1810 as the
Hospicio Cabañas, an orphanage and home
for invalids founded by Bishop Don Juan
Cruz Ruiz de Cabañas. Designed by Spanish architect Manuel Tolsá and featuring 23
separate courtyards, the complex continued
to serve mainly as an orphanage for over
150 years, often housing up to 3000 children at a time. At one time or another it has
also served as an insane asylum, military
barracks and jail.

Between 1936 and 1939 José Clemente
Orozco painted murals in the main chapel.
They are the institute's main attraction and
widely regarded as Orozco's finest works.
Most notable is *El Hombre de Fuego* (Man
of Fire) in the dome; it's been the subject of
widely varying interpretations. Fifty-three
other frescoes cover the walls and ceiling of
the chapel, which is furnished with benches
on which you can lie back and look straight
up. A small book in English and Spanish,
*The Murals of Orozco in the Cabañas Cul-
tural Institute,* on sale at the main entrance,
gives some information about the artist and
the murals.

The complex was declared a Unesco
World Heritage Site in 1997. Tours in English and Spanish are available. The museum
features a permanent exhibition of more
than 100 Orozco drawings (mostly sketches
for his on-site murals) and paintings, plus
temporary exhibitions of painting, sculpture
and engraving. The institute also hosts dance
festivals, drama performances and concerts.

Plaza de los Mariachis

Plaza de los Mariachis, near the intersection
of Av Javier Mina and Calz Independencia
Sur, is arguably the birthplace of mariachi

music. It's more like a short pedestrian street than a plaza, but you can't miss the outdoor tables, where people sit, eat and drink while wandering mariachis offer their musical services – for about US$5 per song. Unfortunately the plaza attracts some unpleasant types after dark, so it's probably unwise to linger after 9pm.

Colonial Churches

In addition to churches mentioned previously, central Guadalajara holds a dozen other churches, some quite impressive.

The **Santuario de Nuestra Señora del Carmen** (Map pp512–13), facing the small plaza on the corner of Juárez and 8 de Julio, is a lovely church, with lots of gold decoration, old paintings and murals in the dome. On the corner of 16 de Septiembre and Blanco, the **Templo de Aranzazú** (Map pp512–13), built from 1749 to 1752, has three ornate churrigueresque golden altars. Beside it is the less showy **Templo de San Francisco** (Map pp512–13), built two centuries earlier.

Museo de la Ciudad

History buffs will appreciate this **museum** (Map pp512–13; ☎ 3658-3706; Independencia 684; admission US$0.40, free Sun; ☼ 10am-5:30pm Tue-Sat, 10am-2:30pm Sun), which offers a well-displayed collection of artifacts and photos depicting Guadalajara's history. Exhibition rooms fringe an old courtyard, and the labels are in Spanish. Cultural events are occasionally held here.

Universidad de Guadalajara & Templo Expiatorio

West of the city center, where Juárez meets Federalismo, is shady **Parque Revolución** (Map pp512–13) Three blocks further west at Juárez 975 is the **Paraninfo** (Theater Hall), one of the main buildings of the University of Guadalajara (Map pp512–13). Inside, the stage backdrop and dome feature large, powerful murals by Orozco. In the back of the same building is the **Museo de las Artes** (Map pp512–13; ☎ 3134-1664; admission free; ☼ 10am-6pm Tue-Sun), which has occasional exhibits of modern art.

The next block south is the gothic **Templo Expiatorio** (Map pp512–13; ☼ 7am-11pm), accented by tall, fluted stone columns and 15m-high stained-glass windows. Look up toward the ceiling in front of the small golden altar and be amazed.

Casa-Museo José Clemente Orozco

During the 1940s, the great *tapatío* painter and muralist José Clemente Orozco (1883–1949) lived and worked in this **house** (Map p506; ☎ 3616-8329; Aurelio Aceves 29; admission free; ☼ 9am-5pm Mon-Fri). Personal effects, photographs, documents, a mural and a few paintings are on display.

Parque Agua Azul

About 20 blocks south of the city center, **Parque Agua Azul** (Map pp512–13; Calz Independencia Sur; adult/child US$0.40/0.20; ☼ 10am-6pm Tue-Sun) is a large verdant park offering pleasant relief from the city hubbub. There are lots of benches on which to rest, so bring a good book or your sweetie. The grassy and tree-filled areas feature an orchid house, butterfly house, aviary and children's playground. The orchids are at their best in October, November, April and May. Bus No 60 (or any marked 'Agua Azul') heading south on Calz Independencia will drop you here from the city center.

The **Casa de las Artesanías de Jalisco** (☎ 3619-4664; Calz Gallo 20; 10am-6pm Mon-Fri, 10am-5pm Sat, 10am-3pm Sun) displays handicrafts and arts from all over Jalisco, and almost everything is for sale. Prices are reasonable enough, and there are some excellent-quality *artesanías* to choose from.

Zoológico Guadalajara, Selva Mágica & Planetario

The zoo, Selva Mágica children's amusement park and planetarium are near one another on the northern outskirts of the city. Trolleybus R600 and buses No 60 and 62A (marked 'Zoológico'), heading north on Calz Independencia, drop you close by.

The **Zoológico Guadalajara** (Map p506; ☎ 3674-4230; www.zooguadalajara.com.mx; Paseo del Zoológico 600; adult/child US$3/1.50; ☼ 10am-5:30pm Wed-Sun) is a large, older zoo with two pyramid-shaped aviaries, a snake house, a children's petting zoo and a train that will take you around if you don't feel like walking. The north end of the site provides a view of the Barranca de Oblatos.

Beside the zoo is **Selva Mágica** (☎ 3674-0138, off Calz Independencia Nte; US$2-8 depending on the attractions package; ☼ 10am-5:30pm), a children's amusement park with a dolphin-and-seal show, a trained-bird show and mechanical rides.

CENTRAL GUADALAJARA

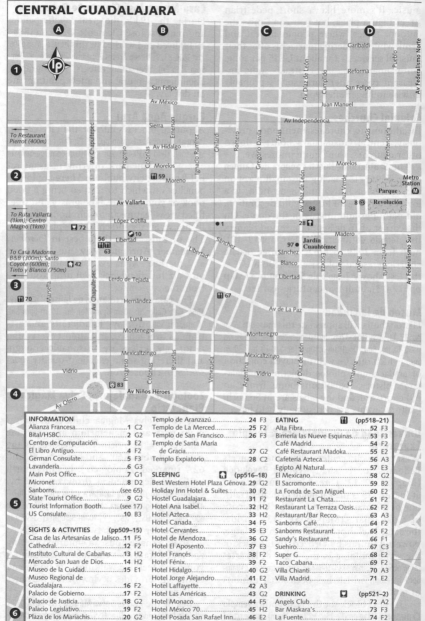

WESTERN CENTRAL HIGHLANDS

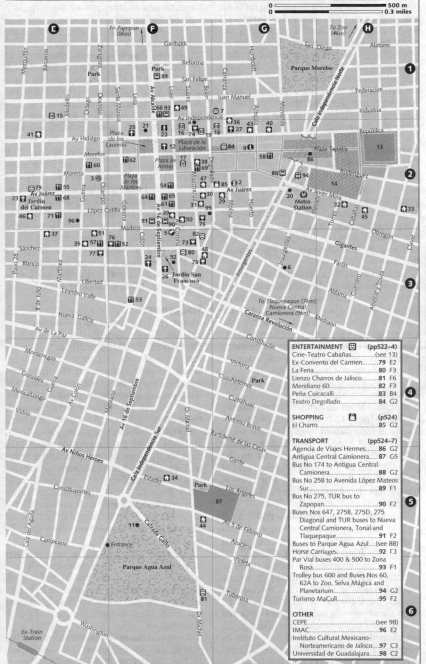

ENTERTAINMENT (pp522–4)
Cine-Teatro Cabañas.............(see 13)
Ex-Convento del Carmen.......**79** E2
La Feria.................................**80** F3
Lienzo Charros de Jalisco.....**81** F6
Meridiano 60........................**82** F3
Peña Cuicacalli....................**83** B4
Teatro Degollado..................**84** G2

SHOPPING (p524)
El Charro.............................**85** G2

TRANSPORT (pp524–7)
Agencia de Viajes Hermes.......**86** G2
Antigua Central Camionera.....**87** G5
Bus No 174 to Antigua Central
  Camionera............................**88** G2
Bus No 258 to Avenida López Mateos
  Sur.....................................**89** F1
Bus No 275, TUR bus to
  Zapopan..............................**90** F2
Buses Nos 647, 275B, 275D, 275
  Diagonal and TUR buses to Nueva
  Central Camionera, Tonal and
  Tlaquepaque..........................**91** F2
Buses to Parque Agua Azul....(see 88)
Horse Carriages.....................**92** F3
Par Vial buses 400 & 500 to Zona
  Rosa....................................**93** F1
Trolley bus 600 and Buses Nos 60,
  62A to Zoo, Selva Mágica and
  Planetarium..........................**94** G2
Turismo MaCull.......................**95** F2

OTHER
CEPE...................................(see 98)
IMAC....................................**96** E2
Instituto Cultural Mexicano-
  Norteamericano de Jalisco....**97** C3
Universidad de Guadalajara......**98** C2

If you exit the zoo via its parking lot (well east and south of its pedestrian entrance), you're about a five-minute walk from the **planetarium** (☎ 3674-4106; Anillo Periférico 401; admission US$1; ☼ 9am-7pm Tue-Sun). It has exhibits on astronomy, space, airplanes, the body and other science-related topics, as well as an antique car museum with some great American dinosaurs from the 1950s. Planetarium shows (US$0.75) are held roughly every two hours starting at 10am.

Barranca de Oblatos & Cascada Cola de Caballo

To see this impressive 670m-deep canyon, take trolleybus R600 north on Calz Independencia to its terminus at Parque Mirador Independencia (about 12 blocks past the zoo entrance). Or take Bus No 60, also northbound on Calz Independencia. You can also peek at the canyon from inside the zoo.

In the canyon, the Cola de Caballo (Horse Tail) waterfall flows all year but is most impressive during the summer rainy season. For a view of the falls (which you can't see from Parque Mirador Independencia), take a local bus from the city center north on Alcalde about 10 blocks to Plaza La Normal. From there get an Ixcatan bus and ask to be let off at Parque Mirador Dr Atl.

Zapopan

About 8km from downtown, on the northwestern edge of Guadalajara, the suburb of Zapopan (population 944,000) holds some attractions of note. Its helpful **tourist police** (☎ 3110-0754) can usually be found on the plaza in front of the basilica, or due east of it along Paseo Tepitzintli, a pleasant pedestrian street (head straight out the basilica's front door).

The **Basílica de Zapopan** (Map p506) built in 1730, is home to Nuestra Señora de Zapopan, a tiny statue of the Virgin visited by pilgrims from near and far. Throughout the year the statue makes a tour of other churches in Jalisco, eventually reaching Guadalajara. On October 12, during the Fiestas de Octubre, the statue is taken from Guadalajara's cathedral and returned to Zapopan amid much merrymaking; the occasion draws hundreds of thousands of pilgrims. The Virgin receives a new car each year for the procession, but the engine is never turned on (thus remaining 'virginal'); instead, the car is hauled along by ropes.

To the right of the basilica entrance, the small **Museo de Arte Huichol** (Wixarica; Map p506; ☎ 3636-4430; Plaza de las Américas; ☼ 9:30am-1:30pm & 3-6pm Mon-Sat, 10am-3pm Sun) sells Huichol handicrafts and exhibits many colorful yarn paintings and other fine examples of Huichol arts and crafts. The worthwhile **Museo de Arte de Zapopan** (MAZ; ☎ 3816-2575; www.mazmuseo.com; cnr Paseo Tepitzintli & Andador 20 de Noviembre; admission with/without ISIC card US$0.50/1; ☼ 10am-6pm Tue-Sun) is one block east of Plaza de las Américas. It's a modern, well-curated museum, whose temporary exhibitions have included a small but fine selection of works by Diego Rivera and Frida Kahlo, and a whimsical showing of Anthony Browne prints that saw the top floor covered with turf, sticks, stones and sand.

Bus No 275 Diagonal and the turquoise TUR bus marked 'Zapopan,' heading north on 16 de Septiembre or Alcalde, stop beside the basilica; the trip takes 20 minutes.

Tlaquepaque

About 7km southeast of downtown Guadalajara, Tlaquepaque ('tlah-keh-PAH-keh,' population 473,000) is an important center for arts and ceramics production. In colonial times it was one of the first stops along the long road to Mexico City, and the Guadalajara gentry built substantial mansions here in the 19th century. Many of these mansions have now been renovated into stylish restaurants, galleries and B&Bs, and the charming plaza is graced with small benches, flowers, monuments and a fountain. Pedestrian streets are popular with locals for long lunches, and steer tourists into fancy shops full of ceramics, bronze figures, handmade glassware, embroidered clothing and many other beautiful items from all over Mexico. Restaurants are especially busy for Sunday lunch.

Get some help at the Tlaquepaque **tourist office** (☎ 3635-1532; turismotlaquepaque@hotmail.com; Juárez 238; ☼ 9am-6pm Mon-Fri). Spaced out along Independencia and around El Parián are a few tourist booths, open daily more or less from 10am to 5pm, that also dispense information.

The good **Museo Regional de la Cerámica** (Map p506; ☎ 3635-5404; Independencia 237; admission free; ☼ 10am-6pm Mon-Sat, 10am-3pm Sun) surrounds a shady courtyard and has many well-displayed exhibits showing the different types and styles of ceramic work made in Tlaquepaque and elsewhere. Some pieces are amazing.

An excellent display of prize-winning ceramics is housed at the **Museo Pantaleón Panduro** (☎ 3639-5646; Sánchez 191; admission free; ☾ 10am-6pm Tue-Sat, 10am-3pm Sun). Competition winners from all over Mexico are nicely exhibited, and many come from Tonalá.

To get to Tlaquepaque, take buses No 275 Diagonal, 275B or 647 (US$0.35). The turquoise TUR bus marked 'Tonala' has air-con and is more comfortable (US$0.60). All these buses leave central Guadalajara from 16 de Septiembre and Madero. The trip takes about 20 minutes. As you near Tlaquepaque, watch for the brick bridge and then a traffic circle. Get off at the next stop. Up the street a little, on the left, is Calle Independencia, which will take you to the heart of Tlaquepaque.

Tonalá

This busy suburb (population 347,000) is about 13km southeast of downtown Guadalajara, beyond Tlaquepaque. You could say Tonalá is Tlaquepaque's less sophisticated but more ample country cousin. There aren't many upscale art shops nestled in renovated mansions here, nor any fancy pedestrian streets or elegant courtyard restaurants serving cutting-edge cuisine. What you will find, however, are countless shopfronts, stores and factories selling much of the glassware and ceramics found in Tlaquepaque and in other parts of Guadalajara. Wholesale buyers from all over the world come to shop here for bargain merchandise. The wide range of choices can be astounding.

On Thursday and Sunday most of the town becomes a huge street market that covers dozens of streets and alleys and takes hours to explore. Not only ceramics and glass are sold; you can also find many wood, metal, papier-mâché and textile handicrafts, plus plenty of tasty treats to keep you going. As a wise shopper, try to check out some factory stores, since some of the best crafts are found here at the source. The tourist office can help you locate them (though you'll need to speak some Spanish). In the market itself you'll also find many bargains, but

be sure to examine all pieces very carefully since many of them are seconds.

The **Tonalá tourist office** (Map p506 ☎ 3284-3092; Tonaltecas 140; ☾ 9am-3pm Mon-Fri), on the main drag in the Casa de Artesanos, gives out maps and information.

The **Museo Nacional de la Cerámica** (Map p506; ☎ 3635-5404; Constitución 104; admission free; ☾ 9am-5pm Tue-Fri, 9am-3pm Sat & Mon) houses an excellent though eclectic array of pots from all over Mexico, but they could be better displayed. Other attractions in Tonalá are several old churches and a *charreada*, starting between 4pm and 5pm Saturday.

To get to Tonalá, take bus No 275 Diagonal or 275D (both US$0.35). The turquoise TUR bus marked 'Tonala' has air-con and is more comfortable (US$0.60). All these buses leave Guadalajara's from 16 de Septiembre and Madero. The trip takes about 45 minutes. As you enter Tonalá, get off on the corner of Av Tonalá and Av Tonaltecas, then walk three blocks north on Tonaltecas to the tourist office (in the Casa de Artesanos). From the Casa de Artesanos, it's three blocks east and two blocks north to the Plaza Principal.

COURSES

A number of schools in Guadalajara teach language and cultural courses.

CEPE (Map pp512-13; ☎ 3616-4399; www.cepe.udg.mx; Universidad de Guadalajara, Apartado Postal 1-2130, Guadalajara, Jalisco 44100) Registration US$100; five weeks' tuition two to six hours per day US$322 to US$965. Private lessons US$22 per hour. Homestays or other lodging available. The Universidad de Guadalajara is the second-largest university in Mexico and Guadalajara's most established language school. Its Centro de Estudios para Extranjeros (Foreign Student Studies Center), or CEPE, offers 10 levels of intensive five-week Spanish-language courses. Workshops in topics such as folkloric dance, guitar and singing are also available, as are special cultural events and excursions to other parts of Mexico.

IMAC (Map pp512-13; ☎ 3613-1080; www.spanish-school.com.mx; Guerra 180) Registration fee US$50. The Instituto Mexicano–Americano de Cultura (IMAC) offers one- to 52-week courses. You can choose to study from one to four hours per day, and weekly rates depend on how long you study. Check their website for a complete listing of course prices, including homestays. Music and dance classes are also available, as are cultural excursions.

Instituto Cultural Mexicano-Norteamericano de Jalisco (Map pp512-13; ☎ 3825-5838; www.instituto cultural.com.mx; Díaz de León 300) This cultural institute teaches five levels of Spanish and charges US$450 for six weeks of instruction (9am to midday Monday to Friday). One week costs US$80. Cultural activities are offered twice a week, and homestays are available.

TOURS

Panoramex (☎ 3810-5057; www.panoramex.com.mx; Federalismo Sur 944) This company offers numerous tours with English-, French- and Spanish-speaking guides. Book tours at the tourist office. They leave from Jardín San Francisco at 9.30am. Standard offerings include the following:

Tour No 1 (5hr; US$12.50; Mon-Sat) Visits some of the main sights of Guadalajara and Tlaquepaque.

Tour No 2 (6hr; US$16.50; Tue, Thu & Sun) Visits Chapala and Ajijic.

Tour No 3 (6½hr; US$19; Mon, Wed, Fri & Sat) Visits the town of Tequila, including the agave fields and a tequila distillery.

FESTIVALS & EVENTS

Several major festivals are celebrated in Guadalajara and its suburbs. They include the following:

Feria de Tonalá Annual handicrafts fair in Tonalá, specializing in ceramics, is held the week before and the week after Semana Santa.

Fiestas de Tlaquepaque Tlaquepaque's annual fiesta and handicrafts fair takes place mid-June to the first week of July.

Fiesta Internacional del Mariachi In late August and early September, mariachis come from everywhere to hear, play and celebrate the latest sounds.

Fiestas de Octubre Beginning with a parade on the first Sunday in October, the October Fiestas, lasting all month, are Guadalajara's principal annual fair. Free entertainment takes place from noon to 10pm daily in the Benito Juárez auditorium at the fairgrounds (5km north of the center), while elsewhere around the city are livestock shows, art and other exhibitions and sporting and cultural events. On October 12 a religious element enters the festivities with a procession from the cathedral to Zapopan carrying the miniature statue of the Virgin of Zapopan (see Zapopan, p514).

Feria Internacional del Libro This is one of the biggest book promotions in Latin America; last week of November and first week of December.

SLEEPING

As always, prices go up during holidays. Ask for discounts if staying more than a few days.

Budget

Guadalajara has some decent budget options, but they're spread out in pockets over the city. Some are well-located near the center, however.

Hotel Posada San Rafael Inn (Map pp512-13; ☎ 3614-9146; sanrafael@avantel.net; López Cotilla 619; s/d from US$18/24; P ⬛) Most rooms here are quiet but dim, and set around a nice, homey covered patio. The renovated rooms cost more but come with TV and a few modern touches.

Posada San Pablo (Map pp512-13; ☎ 3614-2811; posadasanpablo@prodigyy.net.mx; Madero 429; s/d US$24/28, with shared bathroom US$11.50/16; P) There's almost a hostel-like feel here, with spacious rooms, a common kitchen and a grassy garden area. Prices vary with your budget.

Hostel Guadalajara (Map pp512-13; ☎ 3562-7520; www.hostelguadalajara.com; Maestranza 147; dm with/without ISIC card US$10.50/11.50; ⬛) Six large, tiled dorm rooms and one private room (US$24 for two people, US$30 for three) all share bathrooms, a rather simple kitchen and large common spaces. It's centrally located and pleasant enough, but the beds are springy and it can be noisy. Bring a lock for the lockers.

Hotel Las Américas (Map pp512-13; ☎ 3613-9622; Hidalgo 76; s/d from US$15/17) On a whole, this central place is surprisingly bright and quiet considering its unfortunate location (a noisy, busy street). Rooms are a fair deal and come with TV and fan.

Hotel Hidalgo (Map pp512-13; ☎ 3613-5067; Hidalgo 14; r US$6-8.50, with shared bathroom US$4.50) On a street with all the charm of a freeway off-ramp, these run-down digs give new meaning to the word 'basic.' You won't get a cheaper bed this close to center.

Southeast of Mercado Libertad there's a cluster of budget hotels. This part of town is a bit rough and not especially pleasant, but you can find a cheap room here when every other place is full.

Hotel Azteca (Map pp512-13; ☎ 3617-7465; Javier Mina 311; s/d US$19/24; P) There's a wide range of rooms here, with the best and brightest ones facing the back. Inside rooms are dark, and there are also side rooms both quiet and bright. All have TV and fan; it's a good budget choice.

Hotel Ana Isabel (Map pp512-13; ☎ 3617-7920; Javier Mina 164; s/d US$18/20) Three stories of small, dark rooms are planted around a modest hallway patio. Its business card advertises this place as a 'moral' one, so be careful who you invite in.

Hotel México 70 (Map pp512-13; ☎ 361/-99/8; Javier Mina 230; s/d US$15/16) The bigger outside rooms with balconies are much better than the dark inside ones. Mexico hosted the World Cup in 1970; ask the receptionist why they've never won it. TV is US$2 extra.

There are several cheap accommodation options near the Antigua Central Camionera (Old BusTerminal).

Hotel Canada (Map pp512-13; ☎ 3619-4014; fax 3619-3110; Estadio 77; s/d from US$11/12.50; ℗) Here you can choose from many types of rooms, both old and renovated. All are good and clean, though some can be small. Still, it's friendly enough and TV is included.

Hotel Monaco (Map pp512-13; ☎ 3619-0018; 5 de Febrero 152; s/d US$10/11.50) Halls are cold, but rooms are basic, good, and come with TV and solid beds. Get one away from the noisy street.

Way over in Tlaquepaque there are these options:

La Posada de la Media Luna (Map pp512-13; ☎ 3635-6054; http://lamedialuna.tripod.com; Juárez 36; s/d US$24/28) Just east of El Parián is this nice budget hotel, offering 18 good small rooms. Most surround the sunny second-floor terrace. It's an affordable stay, especially since it includes breakfast.

Villas Don Blas Hotel (☎ 3683-2588; www.tonala .gob.mx/donblas; Cerrada Altimira 10; r from US$17; ℗) If you'd like to sleep in Tonalá, this good budget choice has nice, comfortable and surprisingly stylish rooms fringing a central well. Some 'villas' come with kitchen and sleep up to 10.

Mid-Range

Hotel El Aposento (Map pp512-13; ☎ 3614-1612; www .elaposento.com; Madero 545; s/d US$52/62; ℗ 🍴 🖥) Large, gorgeous and well-appointed rooms are set around a lovely open courtyard filled with plants and a small fountain. It's an elegant stay, with breakfast and constant background musak included in the deal.

Hotel San Francisco Plaza (Map pp512-13; ☎ 3613-8954; fax 3613-3257; Degollado 267; s/d US$41/44; ℗ 🍴)

Hotel San Fransisco Plaza's beautifully airy, plant-and-fountain-filled tropical courtyard is surrounded by dark but good spacious rooms. It's a nicely done hotel where you'll be quite comfortable.

Posada Regis (Map pp512-13; ☎ 3614-8633; posada regis@usa.net; Corona 171; s/d US$22/29) In a funky old mansion, this hotel sports large rooms with high ceilings, original details and a spacious central patio. Downsides are noisy street-facing rooms, spotty plumbing and the annoying security buzzer.

La Rotonda (Map pp512-13; ☎ 3614-1017; Liceo 130; s/d US$50/61; ℗) Most rooms are fixed around a sweet little covered courtyard filled with tables. Some rooms are larger than others, and those inside aren't too bright. King-sized beds available.

Hotel Francés (Map pp512-13; ☎ 3613-1190; www .hotelfrances.com, Maestranza 35; r from US$52; ℗) This is the oldest hotel in town (1610), but rooms vary and some aren't so nice inside – peek at a few. The arched stone courtyard (now a bar) was originally used to keep horses. Toss back enough drinks and you can still hear them neigh.

Hotel Cervantes (Map pp512-13; ☎ 3613-6846; Sánchez 442; s/d from US$57/62; ℗ 🛇 🖭) A marble lobby with open restaurant greets you up front, and while the rooms are modern and comfortable, they aren't luxurious. The hotel has five floors and 100 rooms with many amenities.

Hotel Roma (Map pp512-13; ☎ 3614-8650, 800-368-26-00; romaresv@hotmail.com; Juárez 170; r from US$62; ℗ 🛇 🖥 🍴 🖭) This central hotel has fairly modern and decent rooms, the upper ones boasting good views. There's also a rooftop pool.

Hotel Jorge Alejandro (Map pp512-13; ☎ 3658-1051; Hidalgo 656; s/d US$26/32; ℗) Twenty tastefully decorated rooms with carpet, TV and fan greet you at this former convent. The rooms here are pleasant and new, but the showers don't have curtains.

Hotel Laffayette (Map pp512-13; ☎ 3615-0252, 800-362-22-00; ventas@laffayette.com.mx; Av de la Paz 2055; r from US$72; ℗ 🛇 🖥 🍴 🖭) Located west of center in the Zona Rosa, which is home to Guadalajara's better restaurants. The lobby here is gloomy but elegant, and the rooms small but brightly decorated. The hotel caters to wealthy businesspeople and rates rise to US$84 Monday through Thursday. Ask for discounts.

Hotel Serena (Map p506; ☎ 3600-0910; fax 3600-0015; Antigua Carretera Zapotlanejo 1500; r US$38; ℗ 🖳 ✕ 🚰) Across the entrance from the Nueva Central Camionera (New Bus Terminal), this hotel offers tiny rooms you can barely swing a cat in – unless you dish out for the suites (US$70). At least there's a couple of pools, and regular discounts (ask) make it a better deal.

Top End

Casa Madonna B&B (Map p506; ☎ 3615-6554; www .casamadonna.com.mx; Lerdo de Tejada 2308; r US$105-140; ✕) For something different in Guadalajara, check out this 'boutique' hotel. Five rooms and suites come brightly decorated and are comfortable though not luxurious. It's intimate, however, and breakfast is of course included. The best suite is upstairs.

Holiday Inn Hotel & Suites (Map pp512-13; ☎ 3613-1763; holidaycentro@prodigy.net.mx; Juárez 211; r from US$110; ℗ ✕ 🖳 ✕) Are your parents paying? Get them to stay here. Rooms are very nice, and some suites come with kitchenettes and Jacuzzi. There are fancy stores in the small lobby, with the breakfast area just above. Rates drop to US$92 from Friday to Sunday.

Best Western Hotel Plaza Génova (Map pp512-13; ☎ 3613-7500, 800-362-24-00; www.hplazagenova.com; Juárez 123; r from US$89; ℗ ✕ 🖳 ✕) It's well-located, decent and comes with the typical amenities, but don't expect luxury. Call the 800 number for special rates.

Hotel de Mendoza (Map pp512-13; ☎ 3613-4646, 800-361-26-00; www.demendoza.com.mx; Carranza 16; r from US$115; ℗ ✕ 🖳 ✕ 🚰) Originally built as a convent to the nearby church of Santa María de Gracia, this refurbished hotel now offers 104 decent but unexceptionally modern rooms with many amenities. Call the 800 number for special rates.

Hotel Fénix (Map pp512-13; ☎ 3614-5714, 800-361-11-00; www.holahoteles.com.mx; Corona 160; r from US$87; ℗ ✕ 🖳) This place has big, fairly bright rooms, some with balconies and views. It caters to business travelers and gives discounts at quiet times.

Hotel Casa Grande (Map p506; ☎ 3678-9000; www .casagrande.com.mx; r from US$143; ℗ ✕ 🖳 ✕ 🚰) Located right at the airport, this business-oriented hotel has all the amenities, and the rooms are very comfortable. If you're flying out you can blow your leftover pesos on a suite, which comes with Jacuzzi.

Fiesta Americana Guadalajara (Map p506; ☎ 3825-3434, 800-504-50-00; www.fiestamericana.com; Aceves 225; r from US$160; ℗ ✕ 🖳 ✕ 🚰) Way out on Av Lopéz Mateos Norte, the Fiesta Americana is one of Guadalajara's finest hotels and caters mainly to corporate executives. Almost 400 fine rooms on 22 floors are offered, along with a complete range of services including meeting rooms, gym, tennis courts and 24-hour room service. Families and travelers are also welcome, with babysitting services and shops right on the premises.

Other hotels in this class, and also far outside the center, include the following:

Camino Real (Map p506; ☎ 3134-2424, 800-901-23-00; www.caminoreal.com/guadalajara; Vallarta 5005; ℗ ✕ 🖳 ✕ 🚰)

Crowne Plaza (Map p506; ☎ 3634-1034, 800-365-55-00; www.crowneplaza.com.mx; López Mateos Sur 2500; ℗ ✕ 🖳 ✕ 🚰)

Presidente Inter-Continental (Map p506; ☎ 3678-1234; www.intercontinental.com; Av López Mateos Sur at Moctezuma; ℗ ✕ 🖳 ✕ 🚰)

Suburban Tlaquepaque has some wonderful places to stay.

Casa de las Flores (Map p506; ☎ 3659-3186; www .casadelasflores.com; Santos Degollado 175; r US$88-100; ✕) Four blocks south of the main plaza, this charming paradise is lovingly tended by friendly hosts, Stan Singleton and José Gutiérrez. Just a handful of spacious, comfortable and tasteful rooms surround a flower-filled courtyard harboring plenty of intimate patios in which to relax. Common areas (as well as the rooms) are dotted with local artesanías, and the good breakfasts are a treat.

La Villa del Ensueño (Map p506; ☎ 3635-8792; www .mexonline.com/ensueno.htm; Florida 305; s/d from US$76/88; ℗ ✕ 🖳 ✕ 🚰) Seven blocks northwest of the main plaza, this pleasant villa offers a variety of accommodation, including two-bedroom units. The pool, gardens, shaded patios and bar make it a good place to relax, even though the place is located on two sides of the street and the feel is a bit resorty. A buffet breakfast is included.

EATING

Most eateries in the center of town serve up standard Mexican fare, with higher prices buying better atmosphere rather than more creative dishes. Guadalajara's best restaurants are scattered around the suburbs, so you'll have to make an extra effort to sample the city's finer cuisine.

Centro Histórico & Around

All fancy hotels sport equally fancy restaurants. The ones at Hotel Francés and Hotel de Mendoza are magnificent old dining rooms, beautifully done up.

Restaurant La Chata (Map pp512-13; ☎ 3613-0588; Corona 126; mains US$3.75-7) Quality food and large portions keep a legion of loyal patrons happy, as do the friendly and efficient service. Their specialty is a *platillo jalisciense*: chicken, potatoes, soup, an enchilada and a *flauta*; they also serve up *pozole* (hominy soup) and *chiles rellenos*. Chips and salsa come complementary.

Café & Restaurant Madoka (Map pp512-13; ☎ 3613-0649; Martínez 78; mains US$2.75-6) This classic, old-style hangout attracts mostly men, but is comfortable for women as well. It's popular for coffee, ice-cream and the *menu del día* (US$4.25). Bring lots of conversation, and check out the guys playing dominoes.

Café Madrid (Map pp512-13; ☎ 3614-9604; Juárez 264; mains US$2.50-5) A Guadalajara favorite, the Madrid sizzles up hamburgers, meat and Mexican dishes, along with breakfast. Professional waiters in white coats offer brisk service, and the unfussy décor includes red booths.

La Fonda de San Miguel (Map pp512-13; ☎ 3613-0809; Guerra 25; mains US$9-15; ⏰ 8am-midnight Mon-Sat, 8am-6pm Sun) This romantic restaurant is set around a lush courtyard filled with hanging metal stars, colorful furniture and squawking parrots. Food is good but not exceptional, though there is live music (and buffets) on weekends.

Villa Madrid (Map pp512-13; ☎ 3613-4250; López Cotilla 553; mains US$2.25-5; ⏰ 11:30am-9pm Mon-Fri, to 8pm Sat) This casual corner eatery is popular for its healthy menu of sandwiches, salads, yogurt, *licuados* and juices. Meat dishes are also served.

Alta Fibra (Map pp512-13; ☎ 3613-6980; Sánchez 370B; ⏰ closed Sun) For exclusively meat-free fare, this vegetarian restaurant is nearby.

Egipto Al Natural (Map pp512-13; ☎ 3613-6277; Sánchez 416; ⏰ closed Sun) This is another vegetarian restaurant nearby Villa Madrid. Both these vegetarian places are cheap and have large, somewhat impersonal dining rooms. They're open mainly for lunch.

Sanborns Restaurant (Map pp512-13; ☎ 3603-1862; cnr 16 de Septiembre & Juárez; mains US$4-8; ⏰ 7:30am-midnight Sun-Thu, to 1am Fri & Sat) Like other Sanborns restaurants, this place is popular with well-dressed locals who come for the squeaky-clean surroundings and to see waitstaff wearing ersatz traditional dress. The menu holds no surprises, though.

Sanborns Café (Map pp512-13; ☎ 3613-6283; Juárez 305; mains US$4-8; ⏰ 7-1am Sun-Thu, 24-hr Fri & Sat) Right across from Sanborns Restaurant, this less-fancy café has the same menu and almost looks like a branch of the US restaurant chain Denny's. Booths and serene music make it a popular standby, and it has long hours.

Sandy's Restaurant (Map pp512-13; ☎ 3614-4236; Alcalde 118; mains US$5-8) A pleasant, airy balcony helps the lunch buffet (US$4.50) go down easy. The breakfast buffet is even less. It's a modern chain, so prices and food are similar at other branches.

El Mexicano (Map pp512-13; ☎ 3658-0345; Morelos 79; mains US$8.50-10.50) This festive, gym-size eatery comes complete with a young woman greeting you at the door. It's a good place for large groups, and serves big barbecued meat dishes and plenty of drinks. Live music is played most nights.

Taco Cabana (Map pp512-13; ☎ 3613-1539; Moreno 250; mains US$3.75-6) With loud music and loud locals, this is a great place for cheap tacos and beer, or you can order seviche and steak. Free snacks arrive soon after your butt hits the seat, though you may have to fend off peddlers. Be patient with the service.

Restaurant La Terraza Oasis (Map pp512-13; ☎ 3613-8285; Morelos 435; mains under US$3; ⏰ 1-10pm) This no-frills, industrial-like cafeteria has outdated furniture, but it's really cheap. Hamburgers, steaks, chicken dishes and even cigarettes are on the menu – these are probably to accompany the nightly live music (from 6pm).

The Mercado Libertad (Map pp512–13), just east of the city center, has scores of food stalls serving the cheapest eats in town. Smaller Mercado Corona, at Hidalgo and Zaragoza, is similar. Sensitive stomachs beware: the hygiene at these markets is 'adventurous.' For cheap hotel-room picnics there's a **Super G supermarket** (Map pp512-13; cnr Juárez & Martínez; ⏰ 8am-11pm).

Plaza de las Nueve Esquinas

Half a dozen blocks south of the center is this small, untouristy, triangular block where several small streets intersect. It's a little neighborhood popular with eateries specializing in *birria*, a delicious meat stew.

Birriería las Nueve Esquinas (Map pp512-13; ☎ 3613-6260; Colón 384; mains US$3.75-6) This friendly, homey restaurant serves up great food in an airy little dining room. The open kitchen has beautiful tiled surfaces, and out of it comes some very tasty *barbacoa de borrego* (tender baked lamb) and *birria de chivo* (goat stew).

Zona Rosa & Around

Guadalajara's Zona Rosa is basically the few blocks around Av Chapultepec north and south of Av Vallarta. It's home to the city's best cuisine; note however, that some of the fanciest restaurants are closed on Sunday. To get here, catch the westbound Par Vial 400 or 500 bus from Independencia and Alcalde. Taxis should cost around US$2.75 (negotiate).

Cafetería Azteca (Map pp512-13; ☎ 3825-5599; Chapultepec 201; mains US$2.25-5) This casual and breezy eatery sits on a busy corner, and in its leather chairs you feast on inexpensive burgers and Mexican specialties while watching the world zoom by on the busy avenue. The *menu del día* is US$3.75.

Restaurant/Bar Recco (Map pp512-13; ☎ 3825-0724; Libertad 1981; mains US$8-10.50; ☽ 1-11:30pm Mon-Sat, 1-9:30pm Sun; ℗) A menu of classy Italian dishes (the lasagne is excellent), seafood (try the sea bass in beer batter) and meat dishes are on offer at this elegant restaurant located in an old mansion. The white-jacketed waiters treat you right.

Suehiro (Map pp512-13; ☎ 3826-0094; Av de la Paz 1701; ☽ 1:30-6pm & 7:30-11pm Mon-Sat, 1:30-7:30pm Sun; ℗) Great Japanese food is either cooked or sliced here, and you'll be rubbing elbows with Guadalajara's finest bluebloods. Dining areas surround a beautifully manicured garden with a stream, which adds peace to your sushi. Bring deep pockets.

El Sacromonte (Map pp512-13; ☎ 3825-5447; Moreno 1398; mains US$8-14; ☽ 1pm-midnight Mon-Sat; ℗) One of the best restaurants in town, this festive eatery offers creative cuisine in an airy courtyard setting. Metal handicrafts decorate the walls, soft music trembles in the air, and there's live music on some afternoons and evenings.

Villa Chianti (Map pp512-13; ☎ 3630-2250; José Guadalupe Zuño 2152; mains US$8.50-12.50; ☽ 1pm-midnight

Mon-Sat; ℗) This fancy restaurant is located in a gorgeous old mansion surrounded by gardens – dine inside or out on the terraces. Alta cocina Italiana, along with some fusion dishes, are on the menu. The wine list is extensive, and you should make reservations.

Tinto y Blanco (Map p506; ☎ 3615-9535; Francisco Javier Gamboa 235; mains US$9-15; ☽ 1:30pm-1:30am Mon-Sat; ℗) A limited menu of international dishes is cooked up here, and there's plenty of wine by the glass or bottle (as the name suggests). Décor is elegant and intimate, so bring a date.

Pierrot (Map p506; ☎ 3630-2087; Justo Sierra 2355; mains US$9-16; ☽ 1:30pm-midnight Mon-Sat; ℗) Up-scale French cuisine is served in this pretty vine-covered building, and the sophisticated air-con atmosphere is nice. Nibble on escargots and crêpes suzette, wash them down with fine wine and finish with a luscious dessert. Service is good.

Santo Coyote (Map p506; ☎ 3615-5248; López Cotilla 1589; mains US$10-18; ☽ 1-11pm; ℗) This monster restaurant takes up a whole block, and inside you'll find tropical gardens, *palapa* dining pavilions and good (if pricey) seafood and meat dishes. There's even a small waterfall in one corner. Décor is beautifully done, but this is a place for the (rich) masses.

La Trattoria (Map p506; ☎ 3122-1817; Niños Héroes 3051; mains US$6-10; ☽ 1pm-midnight) It's a hike out, but large serves and reasonable prices make this Italian place one of the most popular in Guadalajara. Well-prepared dishes include pastas, meats and seafood. The antipasto bar (US$5) is excellent, and a green salad bar comes with mains. Reservations are crucial after 9pm, especially on weekends. To get here, take bus No 51 A or B, or a taxi.

Tlaquepaque

Just southeast of the main plaza, El Parián is a block of little restaurant-bars with plenty of tables crowding a lively inner courtyard. There are so many different businesses that all the tables mesh together, but just pick a spot that appeals. You'll get plenty of help from overly eager waiters ready to pounce on the undecided. This courtyard is best on weekends, when lots of folks come to sit, drink and enjoy live (and loud) mariachi music. Don't plan on eating dinner here, as food quality is not a priority.

There are plenty of high-quality dining choices in town. Just double-check the hours, since many close early.

Casa Fuerte (☎ 3639-6481; Independencia 225; mains US$6 17; ☿ 12:30pm-midnight) With tables set in a beautiful leafy patio, this long-popular restaurant serves thoughtfully-prepared versions of classic Mexican favorites. Try the *torta de elote colonial* (US$4.25), a delicious corncake appetizer, the tender *el dorado* steak (US$12) or the tamarind shrimp (US$17). Live music fills the air during the afternoon.

Mariscos Progreso (☎ 3639-6149; Progreso 80; mains US$7-14; ☿ 11am-8pm) Nibble ceviche, oysters, grilled shrimp or a fish fillet in an attractive covered courtyard setting. The menu is mostly seafood, though a few meat dishes appear as well. Come early, because this place closes at 8pm.

Adobe (☎ 3657-2792; Independencia 195; mains US$8-12; ☿ 11:30am-7pm) Located behind its crafts and furniture showroom, this upscale restaurant serves tasty and visually artistic gourmet dishes. The airy atmosphere is very relaxed, with natural-style décor and cheesy live music. The generous salads are excellent.

Café San Pedro (☎ 3639-0616; Juárez 85; coffees under US$3; ☿ 9am-11pm) This hip and modern café sits under the arches across the street from El Parián, steaming up a tasty variety of cappuccinos, espressos and hot chocolates. Nibble on the good-looking pastries also.

DRINKING

The historic center has a few bars serving snacks, drinks and sometimes live music.

La Maestranza (Map pp512-13; ☎ 3613-2085; Maestranza 179; ☿ 10-2:30am) Decorated with a vast array of bullfighting memorabilia, this upscale cantina attracts lots of 20- and 30-somethings with its cheap beer (pitchers US$9), salty snacks and lively Mexican music (live on Wednesday nights).

Los Carajos (Map pp512-13; ☎ 3126-7951; Morelos 79; ☿ 1pm-midnight Mon-Thu, to 3am Fri & Sat) Sitting pretty above El Mexicano restaurant is this casual bar, which seems to cater to larger groups. If you're hungry they've got plenty of food, and if you're thirsty well... that's not a problem either. Live music plays on weekends.

La Fuente (Map pp512-13; Suárez 78; ☿ 8:30am-11pm Mon-Thu, to midnight Fri & Sat) For a great, very local and even raunchy hangout, there's no beating La Fuente. Grab a drink and pretend to sing along – raucous live music plays from 2:30pm to 9:30pm daily (longer on weekends). It's a mostly older male joint, though women frequent too. Come for the cultural experience.

Hotel Francés (Map pp512-13; ☎ 3613-1190; Maestranza 35; ☿ noon-midnight) The lobby piano bar at this hotel is a sedate and rather stuffy option, but it's certainly stylish and a musical trio provides nightly music. Drink up in the marble courtyard and take in the old-class feel.

Outside the center are some of the hippest watering holes.

La Cantina de los Remedios (Map p506; ☎ 3817-4410; Av Américas 1462) was being remodeled at the time of research, but will probably be a nightlife magnet when it opens.

Bar Bariachi (Map p506; ☎ 3616-9180; Vallarta 2308; ☿ 6pm-3am Mon-Sat) Casa Bariachi's smaller cousin offers women all-the-tequila-you-can-drink nights on Tuesdays. Think any men show up to watch? Crowded leather chairs and dark atmosphere prevail, though the upstairs balcony tables are nice. Live mariachi music plays nightly from 9:30pm on. If you get bored, go next door to La Bodeguita del Medio (p523).

Gay & Lesbian Venues

Guadalajara's gay scene is alive and kicking, but you gotta know where to look.

La Prisciliana (Map pp512-13; ☎ 3562-0724; Sánchez 394; ☿ 5pm-1:30am) This wonderfully relaxed, often tranquil bar offers intimacy in a fabulous old colonial building. Sometimes things get rowdy and there's a drag show, but usually you can just sit back and chat. Grab a stool at the bar if you're alone. Lesbians are welcome, but don't seem to stay late here.

Los Caudillos (Map pp512-13; ☎ 3613-5445; cnr Sánchez 407; ☿ 5pm-3am) Diagonally across from La Prisciliana, and also on the 2nd storey of an old house, this loud and smoky disco offers flashing lights and a small dance floor. Both gay and straight folks can be found carefully checking each other out. There's no cover charge.

Bar Maskara's (Map pp512-13; ☎ 3614-8103; Maestranza 238; ☿ 2pm-3am) Skimpily-clad trannies, dancing on the bar, liven up shows no end on Wednesday, Friday and Sunday nights.

Maybe that's why it's so hot and steamy inside. Go to the 2nd floor for a more quiet atmosphere. There's no cover charge, and on Wednesdays beers are three for one all day.

Angels Club (Map pp512–13; ☎ 3615-2525; López Cotilla 1495B; admission US$8; ۞ 9pm-5am Fri & Sat) A glittery upscale disco/bar, Angels features modern lines, Latin techno sounds and go-go rounds. A mixed gay/straight clientele perch on dainty acrylic tables or lounge in the beanbag room. Security is heavy, so leave the Uzi at home. The cover includes one drink.

Sexy's Bar (Map pp512–13; ☎ 3658-0062; Degollado 273; ۞ 5pm-3am) Don't let the boring front restaurant turn you off: the action happens in the back. Here it's dark, loud and full of wallflowers looking wistfully at the small dance floor. Trannie singers croon nightly at this very casual and quirky spot. There's no cover charge, but on Saturday nights the minimum consumption is US$2.75.

ENTERTAINMENT

Guadalajara is in love with music of all kinds, and live performers can be heard any night of the week. Theaters, cinemas, discos and bars are also plentiful. If you're into drinking and dancing, ask around for the current hotspots, because style can be fickle.

For entertainment info, stop by the tourist office and check out its weekly schedule of events; the bilingual staff will find something to suit your fancy. Also, check out the Friday edition of the daily newspaper *Público*; its entertainment insert, *Ocio*, includes a cultural-events calendar for the coming week and is the place to look for information on restaurants, movies, exhibits and the club scene. *Occidental* and *Informador*, also Spanish-language dailies, have entertainment listings, as does the weekly booklet *Ciento Uno*.

Popular venues hosting a range of drama, dance and music performances include the **Teatro Degollado** (Map pp512–13; ☎ 3613-1115) and the **Instituto Cultural de Cabañas** (Map pp512–13; ☎ 3668-1640), both downtown cultural centers, as well as the **Ex-Convento del Carmen** (Map pp512–13; ☎ 3614-7184; Juárez 638).

Ballet Folklórico

It's a good idea to call and double-check performance times.

Ballet Folklórico de la Universidad de Guadalajara (☎ 385-8888; seats US$3-19) The university's folkloric dance troupe stages grand performances at the Teatro Degollado at 8.30pm Thursday and 10am Sunday.

Ballet Folklórico del Instituto Cultural de Cabañas (☎ 3668-1640 ext 1004; seats US$4.50) Performances are given here at 8.30pm every Wednesday.

Cinema

Big shopping centers like **Plaza del Sol** (Map p506; Av López Mateos Sur), **Plaza Milenium** (Map p506; Av López Mateos Sur) and **Centro Magno** (Map p506; Av Vallarta 2425) have the best multiscreens, ideal for the latest US 'blow-it-up' flick. Several other cinemas show international films and classics. Check *Ocio* (in the daily *Público*) or other local newspapers.

Alianza Francesa (Map pp512–13; ☎ 3825-5595; www.alianzafrancesa.org.mx/guadalajara; López Cotilla 1199) Shows French films.

Cine-Teatro Cabañas (Map pp512–13; ☎ 3617-4322; Instituto Cultural de Cabañas) Come here for more cultural offerings.

Mariachis

Pay your respects to the mariachi tradition in its home city. The Plaza de los Mariachis, just east of the historic center, is a good place to sit and drink beer while being regaled by these passionate Mexican bands. Be careful if you linger here after about 9pm, however, as the adjacent neighborhood to the east is a bit rough.

Most tourists now get their mariachi experience in one of the sanitized venues provided for the purpose.

La Feria (Map pp512–13; ☎ 3613-7150; Corona 291; mains US$6-10; ۞ 2pm-3am) Traditional and modern mariachi music plays nightly at this festive restaurant/entertainment venue, a former mansion. It's a bit touristy and popular with loud groups, but can be enjoyable. Reservations necessary on weekends.

Casa Bariachi (Map p506; ☎ 3616-9900; Vallarta 2221; mains US$6-12; ۞ 1pm-3am Mon-Sat) This brightly decorated, barnlike restaurant/bar has a great atmosphere, with colorful cutout paper hanging from the ceiling, romantic lighting and leather chairs. Big margaritas and lots of mariachis start the fun at 3:30pm daily. Casa Bariachi is located on happening Ruta Vallarta (a popular section of Av Vallarta), about a 10-minute taxi ride west of center. Its nearby brother Bar Bariachi (p521), just a few doors away, also plays mariachi music every night.

Way over in Tlaquepaque, the El Parián quadrangle highlights a courtyard mariachi gazebo surrounded by hundreds of tables.

Nightclubs & Discos

Some of Guadalajara's trendiest nightspots are outside the center. Discos here attract young, affluent locals who dress to impress. No track shoes or jeans, please.

La Marcha (Map p506; ☎ 3615-8999; Vallarta 2648; ◷ 11pm-5am Wed, Fri & Sat) The young, rich and gorgeous feel right at home here on fashionable Ruta Vallarta, bopping to the techno beat and sipping expensive drinks – though there are occasional open bars until 1am. And if you tire of the DJ music, 'cue' up for a pool table. Cover for men: US$15 until 1am, US$7 after 1am. Cover for women: free before midnight; US$11.50 after midnight.

Klio (Map p506; Av Américas 318; ◷ 10pm-5am Wed, Fri & Sat) Currently the hippest disco in town. The well-dressed masses line up outside, so look good and play up your exoticness. Once inside there's barely enough room to stand (let alone dance), it's too loud for chit-chat, and it's too dim to see much. It may also be too smoky to breathe, so just grab an expensive cocktail. Or come early and drink free from 10pm to 2am. Cover for men: US$15 until 2am, US$8 after 2am. Women: free before 2am, US$8 after 2am.

Barzelona (Map p506; ☎ 3817-6076; Av Américas 1462; ◷ 10:15pm-5am Wed, Fri & Sat) Here's another exclusive club where you really need to look slick. Inside, the bowl-like setting is dark and loud, with good and sometimes extravagant shows (like trapeze) three times nightly. Barzelona is in a cluster of nightspots so if you don't like it there are other nearby options. Cover for men/women US$7/2.75 Fri, US$7/7 Sat, US$22/5 (including 6 drinks) Sun. Taxis here cost US$6.

Meridiano 60 (Map pp512-13; ☎ 3613-8489; Maestranza 223; ◷ 8pm-3am Wed & Thu, 8pm-4am Fri & Sat) This smallish downtown nightspot, sporting a jungly theme, attracts a young crowd. Live Brazilian, reggae and rock – all Mexican style – play nightly. There's a restaurant upstairs if you're hungry, or throw all caution to the wind and just drink: the house cocktail is a *mamada* (US$8.50), a giant frothy cauldron of rum, beer, vodka, lemon juice and *jarabe* (sweet syrup). To sniff out this place, look for the rhino head outside. Cover US$6 Friday and Saturday.

Other Live Music

State and municipal bands present free concerts of typical *música tapatía* in the Plaza de Armas at 6:30pm on most Tuesdays, Thursdays and Sundays, and on other days as well during holiday seasons.

MARIACHIS

Not many images capture the heart and soul of Mexico better than a spirited group of proud-faced mariachis. Handsomely decked out in broad-rimmed sombreros and brightly matching *charro* suits, their traditional Mexican ballads entertain folks at crowded town plazas, festive wedding parties and noisily packed restaurants. Even doe-eyed sweethearts nuzzling on a park bench can get that special serenade.

Some historians contend that 'mariachi' is a corruption of the French word *mariage* (marriage) and that the name stems from the time of the French intervention (1861–67). Others say that the word arose from festivals honoring the Virgin Mary, and was probably derived from the name María with the Náhuatl diminutive '-chi' tacked on. It could also have come from the name of the stage upon which *jarabes* (folk dances) were performed. But whatever the root of its name, the music is known to have originated in Jalisco, in a region south of Guadalajara.

Back in the early 20th century mariachi bands were made up of only stringed instruments such as violins, guitars and a harp, and their repertoire was limited to traditional *tapatío* melodies. Today, however, most mariachi bands belt out their melodramatic tunes on three violins, two trumpets, a guitar, a *guitarrón* (deep-pitched bass) and a *vihuela* (high-pitched guitar). The exact number of violins, guitars and trumpets can vary quite a bit. Most of their broad repertoire of favorite Mexican ballads involves love, betrayal or machismo themes.

To check out some venues for this music see Mariachis, p522. Or just keep an eye out for these roving jukeboxes on any Mexican street; if you're feeling sentimental they'll stop and play you a tune, but just make sure you agree on a price first.

Peña Cuicacalli (Map pp512-13; ☎ 3825-4690; Niños Héroes 1988; admission US$5-12) This popular *peña* (folk-music club) presents a varied program of contemporary Mexican and Latino folk ballads, called *trova*, and other Latin sounds, jazz, comedy and more. Pick up their schedule at the tourist office.

La Bodeguita del Medio (Map p506; ☎ 3630-1620; Vallarta 2320; mains US$8; ☯ 1pm-2am) The writing is on the walls: this place plays some hoppin' Cuban tunes. With 'graffiti' as décor, you can enjoy a restaurant upstairs and bar downstairs, while live music rocks the place inside out most nights. It's on Ruta Vallarta, right next to Bar Bariachi.

Instituto Cultural Mexicano Norteamericano de Jalisco (Map pp512-13; ☎ 3825-5666; www.instituto cultural.com.mx; Díaz de León 300) Classical music concerts and recitals are often hosted here.

Hard Rock Café (Map pp512-13; ☎ 3616-4564; Vallarta 2425; admission US$5 Tue; ☯ 11-1:30am) It's more like a restaurant (burgers and Tex-Mex US$7 to US$10.50), and the slick décor's no surprise, but this popular spot has live rock music most nights. Look for it inside the Centro Magno shopping center.

Sport
BULLFIGHTS & CHARREADAS
Plaza de Toros Nuevo Progreso (Map p506; ☎ 3637-9982; north end of Calz Independencia; admission US$3-25) The bullfighting season is October to March, and the fights are held on select Sundays starting at 5pm. A couple of fights will almost certainly take place during the October fiestas; the rest of the schedule is sporadic. Check at the bullring or tourist office.

Lienzo Charros de Jalisco (Map pp512-13; ☎ 3619-0515; Dr Michel 572; admission from US$3) *Charreadas* are held at noon most Sundays in this ring behind Parque Agua Azul. *Charros* come from all over Jalisco and Mexico to show off their skills. *Escaramuzas* (cowgirls) also compete in daring displays of their sidesaddle riding.

SOCCER
Fútbol is Guadalajara's favorite sport. The seasons are from August to December and from January to May or June. The city usually has at least three teams playing in the national top-level primera división: Guadalajara (Las Chivas), the second most popular team in the country after América of Mexico City; Atlas (Los Zorros); and Universidad Autónoma de Guadalajara (Los Tecos).

Estadio Jalisco (Map p506; ☎ 3637-9800; Siete Colinas 1772; admission US$2-12). The teams play at stadiums around the city, but this main venue (seating 65,000) has hosted several World Cup matches. Contact the stadium or tourist office for schedule information. Really big games cost more.

SHOPPING
Handicrafts from Jalisco, Michoacán and other Mexican states are available here in Guadalajara. The Casa de las Artesanías de Jalisco, just outside Parque Agua Azul, has a good selection (see p511).

Tlaquepaque and Tonalá, two suburbs less than 15km from Guadalajara's center, are major producers of handicrafts and furniture. See p514 for more information.

Mercado Libertad (Map pp512-13; Mercado San Juan de Dios; cnr Javier Mina & Calz Independencia) This huge general market has three floors of stalls selling everything of which you can think. It's open every day.

Mercado El Baratillo This popular Sunday flea market stretches blocks in every direction on and around Javier Mina. To get there, take a Par Vial bus east along Hidalgo.

El Charro (Map pp512-13; ☎ 3614-7599; Juárez 148) If you ever wanted to play Mexican cowboy (or cowgirl), this is the place to check out. The Mariachi suit you've always wanted is here, too. Several similar (and cheaper) shops are on Juárez to the east.

Guadalajara's most prosperous citizens prefer to shop at one of the big shopping centers west of the city center, such as **Centro Magno** (Map p506; Av Vallarta 2425), about 2km west of center; **Plaza del Sol** (Map p506; Av López Mateos Sur), about 7km southwest of center; and **Plaza Milenium** (Map p506; Av López Mateos Sur), about 7.5km southwest of center. To get to these malls, take bus No 258 going west from San Felipe and Alcalde or TUR 707 going west on Juárez.

GETTING THERE & AWAY
Air
Guadalajara's **Aeropuerto Internacional Miguel Hidalgo** (Map p530; ☎ 3688-5504) is 17km south of downtown, just off the highway to Chapala. Inside are ATMs, money exchange and many car rental booths. Surprisingly, there's no tourist office in the terminal.

A multitude of airlines offer direct flights to more than 20 cities in Mexico and about

10 cities in the US and Canada, as well as one-stop connections to many other places.

Airlines that serve Guadalajara include the following:

Aero California (☎ 3616-2525; Av Vallarta 2440, Colonia Arcos Vallarta)

Aeroméxico (☎ 3614-5400; Rincón de las Acacias 122, Colonia Rinconada del Sol, Zapopan)

Air France (☎ 3630-3707; Av Vallarta 1540-103, Colonia Americana)

American Airlines (☎ 3616-4402; Av Vallarta 2440, Colonia Arcos Vallarta)

Aviacsa (☎ 3616-8500; Av México 3201, Colonia Vallarta San Jorge)

Continental (☎ 3647-4251; Moctezuma 3515L-6G, Colonia Astral Plaza, Zapopan)

Delta (☎ 3630-3530; López Cotilla 1701, Colonia Americana)

Mexicana (☎ 3641-5352; Mariano Otero 2353, Colonia Verde Valle)

United Airlines (☎ 3616-7993; Av Vallarta 2440, Colonia Arcos Vallarta)

Bus

Guadalajara has two bus terminals. The long-distance bus terminal is the Nueva Central Camionera (New Bus Terminal; Map p506), a large modern V-shaped terminal that is split into seven separate *módulos* (mini-terminals). Each *módulo* has ticket desks for a number of bus lines, plus restrooms, cafeterias and sometimes 'left luggage' services. The Nueva Central Camionera is 9km southeast of the Guadalajara city center, past Tlaquepaque.

Buses travel to and from just about everywhere in western, central and northern Mexico. The same destination can be served by several companies in several different *módulos*, making price comparisons difficult and time-consuming since the *módulos* are quite spread out. If you don't mind traveling in 1st-class, however, you can check schedules and even buy your ticket right in central Guadalajara. Try **Turismo MaCull** (Map pp512-13; ☎ 3614-7014; López Cotilla 163; ❧ 9:30am-7pm Mon-Fri, 9:30am-1pm Sat) or **Agencia de Viajes Hermes** (☎ 3617-3330; Calz Independencia Norte 254; ❧ 9:30am-7:30pm Mon-Sat). Both agencies sell only 1st-class bus tickets, which should cost about the same as at the Nueva Central Camionera.

The companies suggested following have the most frequent departures to the cities indicated.

Barra de Navidad (Autocamiones de Cihuatlán, US$21, 5½hr, 6 daily from Módulo 3; Primera Plus US$21, 5½hr, 6 daily from Módulo 1)

Colima (Primera Plus/Servicios Coordinados, US$14, 3hr, 24 daily from Módulo 1)

Guanajuato (Primera Plus, US$19-23, 4hr, 10 daily from Módulo 1)

Mexico City (Primera Plus, US$39, 7-8hr, 24 daily from Módulo 1; Ómnibus de México,US$36, 7-8hr, 11 daily from Módulo 6) To Terminal Norte.

Morelia (Primera Plus, US$20, 4hr, 8 daily from Módulo 1; La Línea, US$18-20, 4hr, 6 daily from Módulo 2)

Puerto Vallarta (Pacífico, US$25, 5hr, 20 daily from Módulos 3 & 4; Futura/Elite, US$28, 5hr, 16 daily from Módulos 3 & 4)

Querétaro (Primera Plus, US$23, 5½hr, 11 daily from Módulo 1)

San Miguel de Allende (Primera Plus, US$28, 5hr, 3 daily from Módulo 1)

Tepic (Elite/Futura (US$17, 3hr, 8 daily from Módulo 3; Ómnibus de México, US$17, 3hr, 20 daily from Módulo 6)

Uruapan (Primera Plus, US$16-18, 4½hr, 8 daily from Módulo 1)

Zacatecas (Ómnibus de México (US$22, 5hr, 25 daily from Módulo 6)

For deluxe buses to many of these destinations (at considerably higher fares), try ETN, Módulo 2. Their waiting room is downright plush.

Guadalajara's other bus terminal is the Antigua Central Camionera (Old Bus Terminal; Map pp512–13), about 1.5km south of the cathedral near Parque Agua Azul. From here 2nd-class buses serve destinations roughly within 75km of Guadalajara. There are two sides: Sala A is for destinations to the east and northeast; Sala B is for destinations northwest, southwest and south. Some destinations are served by both sides, however. There's a US$0.05 charge to enter the terminal, which offers a left-luggage service in Sala B and lots of food stalls.

Autotransportes Guadalajara–Chapala buses depart Sala A every half hour from 6am to 9pm for Chapala (US$3, 50 minutes), Ajijic (US$3, 55 minute) and San Juan Cosalá (US$3, one hour). Rojo de Los Altos buses depart from Sala B every 15 or 20 minutes from 5:30am to 9pm for Tequila (US$3, 1¾ hours) via Amatitán (US$2, 1¼ hours).

Bus No 616 connects the Nueva Central Camionera with the Antigua Central Camionera.

Car & Motorcycle

Guadalajara is 535km northwest of Mexico City and 344km east of Puerto Vallarta. Highways 15, 15D, 23, 54, 54D, 80, 80D and 90 all converge here, combining temporarily to form the Periférico, a ring road around the city.

Guadalajara has many car rental agencies. Several of the large US companies are represented, but you may get a cheaper deal from a local company. Agencies include:

Auto Rent de Guadalajara (☎ 3825-1515)
Budget (☎ 3613-0027, 800-700-17-00)
Dollar (☎ 3826-7959, 3688-5659)
Hertz (☎ 3688-5633, 800-654-30-30)
National (☎ 3614-7994, 800-227-73-68)
Quick Rent A Car (☎ 3614-6006, 3614-2247)

Train

The only train serving Guadalajara is the Tequila Express – a tourist excursion to the nearby town of Tequila (see p527).

GETTING AROUND
To/From the Airport

The airport is 17km south of Guadalajara's center, just off the highway to Chapala. To get into the center on public transport, walk outside the airport and head to the bus stop in front of Hotel Casa Grande, about 50m to the right. A local bus marked 'Zapote' (US$0.40, 25 minutes) runs every 20 minutes or so from 6am to 9pm and after about half an hour winds up at the Antigua Central Camionera. From here many buses go to the center. If you're lucky you can catch the more comfortable 'Atasa' bus (US$1), which runs hourly from 9am to 5pm. It also winds up at the Antigua Central Camionera.

Taxis to the center cost US$14.50. Buy tickets inside the airport.

To get to the airport from Guadalajara's center, take bus No 174 to the Antigua Central Camionera and then an 'Aeropuerto' bus (every 20 minutes, 6am to 9pm) from the stop where the 174 drops you.

To/From the Bus Terminals

To reach the city center from the Nueva Central Camionera, take any bus marked 'Centro' (US$0.35). For more comfort, however, catch a turquoise-colored TUR bus (US$0.60). These should be marked 'Zapopan' – don't take the ones marked 'Tonalá,' as these go away from Guadalajara's center. Taxis to the center cost around US$7, but you may have to bargain.

To reach the Nueva Central Camionera from the city center, take bus Nos 275B, 275 Diagonal or any TUR bus marked 'Tonalá.' These are frequent and leave from 16 de Septiembre and Madero. Many buses run from the Antigua Central Camionera to the center. From the center, bus No 174 going south on Calz Independencia will get you back to the Antigua Central Camionera.

Bus No 616 runs between the two bus terminals.

GUADALAJARA BUS ROUTES		
Destination	**Bus**	**Route or stop**
Antigua Central Camionera	No 174	south on Calz Independencia
Nueva Central Camionera	No 275B, 275 Diagonal or TUR (marked 'Tonalá')	at 16 de Septiembre and Madero
Parque Agua Azul	any bus marked 'Agua Azul'	south on Calz Independencia
Zoo, Selva Mágica and Planetarium	Nos 60 and 62A , or Trolleybus R600	north on Calz Independencia
Av López Mateos Sur	No 258 at San Felipe and Alcalde,	or TUR 707 west on Juárez
Tlaquepaque	No 275B, 275 Diagonal, 647 or TUR (marked 'Tonalá')	at 16 de Septiembre and Madero
Tonalá	No 275D, 275 Diagonal or TUR (marked 'Tonalá')	at 16 de Septiembre and Madero
Zapopan	No 275 or TUR (marked 'Zapopan')	north on 16 de Septiembre or Alcalde
Zona Rosa	Par Vial buses 400 & 500	at Calle (not Calz!) Independencia and Alcalde

WESTERN CENTRAL HIGHLANDS

Bus

Guadalajara has a comprehensive city bus system, but be ready for crowded, rough rides. On major routes, buses run every five minutes or so from 6am to 10pm daily; they cost US$0.35. Many buses pass through the center of town, so for an inner suburban destination you'll have a few stops to choose from. The routes diverge as they get further from the city center, and you need to know the bus number for the suburb you want. Some bus route numbers are followed by an additional letter indicating which circuitous route they will follow in the outer suburbs.

The TUR buses, painted a distinctive turquoise color, are a more comfortable alternative on some routes. They have air-con and plush seats. The fare is US$0.60. If they roar past without stopping, they're full; this can happen several times in a row during rush hour. It's enough to drive you crazy.

The tourist office has a list of the many bus routes in Guadalajara and can help you figure out how to get anywhere you want to go. The table shown here lists some of the most common suburban destinations, the buses that go to those destinations, and suggestions on where to catch the buses in the Centro Histórico.

Horse Carriages

For that romantic touch, you can hire a horse carriage for US$14 per half hour, US$21 per hour. There's a carriage stand right at Jardín San Francisco (Map pp512–13).

Metro

The subway system has two lines that cross the city. Stops are marked around town by a 'T' symbol. The subway is quick and comfortable enough, but doesn't serve many points of visitor interest. Línea 1 stretches north–south for 15km all the way from the Periférico Nte to the Periférico Sur. It runs more or less below Federalismo (seven blocks west of the city center) and Av Colón. You can catch it at Parque Revolución, on the corner of Av Juárez.

Línea 2 runs east–west for 10km below Avs Juárez and Mina.

Taxi

Cabs are plentiful in the city center. All Guadalajara taxis now have meters, but many taxi drivers would rather quote a flat fee for a trip. Generally it's cheaper to go by the meter. If you're quoted a flat fee and feel it's inflated, bargain.

Typical fares from the city center at the time of writing were: US$2.50 to the Antigua Central Camionera; US$3 to Parque Agua Azul; US$3 to Centro Magno; US$5 to Zapopan; US$6 to Plaza del Sol; US$6.50 to Tlaquepaque or the zoo; US$7 to the Nueva Central Camionera; US$7.50 to Tonalá; US$13 to the airport and US$34 to Chapala. Settle the fare before you get into the taxi.

AROUND GUADALAJARA

Guadalajara has some worthwhile day or weekend trips. Lago de Chapala, 40km to the south, offers pretty lake scenery and a few towns with much slower paces and distinctly different feels from the big city. The liquor-producing town of Tequila, to the northwest, needs no introduction. And further south and west, Jalisco's Zona Montaña is home to several small, charming mountain towns that are ideal for exploration.

So, if you tire of the rattling urban vibes of Guadalajara, hop on a bus and zoom away from it all – and get ready to experience some fascinating new adventures.

ZAPOTLANEJO
pop 28,000

There's not much historical or architectural interest in this town, which lies some 30km east of Guadalajara. If you're in need of some clothing, however, this is *the* place to visit. Hundreds of vendors sell all manner of inexpensive clothing from storefront after storefront, all lined up down several blocks. Don't expect high-quality goods, though some may exist here and there. Most of the clothes sold here are made in Mexico, and some are shipped abroad.

Buses arrive half-hourly from Guadalajara's Nueva Central Camionera (US$2, half an hour). They stop at the plaza; the main clothing street is just a block past the church.

TEQUILA
☎ 374 / pop 25,000 / elevation 1219m

The town of Tequila, 50km northwest of Guadalajara, has been home to the liquor of the same name since the 17th century. Fields of blue agave, the cactuslike plant from which tequila is distilled, surround the town. You can almost cop a buzz just breathing the heavily scented air that drifts from the town's distilleries.

If you come by bus its last stop will probably be on Gorjón. Continue on foot in the same direction (west) a block or two and turn right at the church to reach the main plaza. The plaza's western boundary is Calle Ramón Corona. La Rojeña distillery is just across this street from the southwest corner of the plaza.

The biggest show in town is **La Rojeña** (☎ 742-13-82; cnr Corona & José Cuervo; tours with/without ISIC US$3/6, child under 12 & adult over 59 free; ⏱ 10am-3pm Mon-Sat, noon-1pm Sun), which produces José Cuervo tequila, and lots of it. Cuervo's hourly tours include samples of the product, as do those of most of the other distilleries in the area.

The **Museo Nacional del Tequila** (☎ 742-24-10; Corona 34; adult/child under 11 US$1.50/0.75; ⏱ 10am-

TEQUILA

In ancient times, indigenous Mexicans used the plant we call blue agave (*Agave tequilana weber*) as a source of food, cloth and paper. They even used it as a torture instrument, thrusting the long, needlelike tips of the plant's leaves into their victims' flesh (and, when paying penance to the gods, into their own). Today, the blue agave is known more widely as the source of Mexico's national drink: tequila.

To ensure quality control, the Mexican government allows blue agave to be grown only in the state of Jalisco and in parts of Nayarit, Michoacán, Guanajuato and Tamaulipas states. It is here, and nowhere else in Mexico, distillers say, that conditions are right for the blue agave to produce a good-tasting tequila. At any given moment more than 100 million tequila agaves are in cultivation within this designated territory.

In some ways the production of tequila has changed little since the drink was invented near Guadalajara hundreds of years ago. The blue agaves are still planted and harvested by hand, and the heavy pineapple-like hearts from which the alcohol is derived are still removed from the fields on the backs of mules.

When planted, the agave heart is no bigger than an onion. Its blue-gray, swordlike leaves give the plant the appearance of a cactus, although it is more closely related to the lily. By the time the agave is ready for harvesting, eight to 12 years after planting, its heart is the size of a beach ball and can weigh up to 150kg.

The harvested heart, called a *piña*, is chopped to bits, fed into ovens and cooked for up to three days. After cooking, the softened plants are shredded and juiced. The juice, called *aguamiel* (honey water) for its golden, syrupy appearance, is then pumped into fermentation vats, where it is usually mixed with yeast. Premium tequilas, in order to bear the 100% agave label, can add nothing else legally. Lesser tequilas add sugar and sometimes flavoring and/or coloring agents. By law the mixture can contain no less than 51% agave if it is to be called tequila.

There are four varieties of tequila. Which is best is a matter of personal opinion. White or silver (*blanco* or *plata*) tequila is not aged, and no colors or flavors are added (though sugar may be). The gold variety (*oro*) also is not aged, but color and flavor, usually caramel, are added. Tequila *reposado* (rested) has been aged from two to 11 months in oak barrels. Tequila *añejo* (aged) has spent at least one year in oak barrels.

Tequila's increasing popularity resulted in a shortage of blue agave plants in the official growing region in recent years. This dearth resulted in higher retail prices for the liquor and even cases of *piña*-rustling. Many producers quietly removed the '100% agave' designation from their labels and began adding sugar to eke out the precious aguamiel.

It's rumored that some began using agave shipped in from outside the official region, and even used maguey species other than blue agave (maguey is the Spanish word for agave and covers the whole genus).

With the price of *piñas* sky-high, everybody and her sister has been rushing to plant agave crops. These poorly regulated, amateur farmers, using nontraditional methods, could result in an overabundance of sub-standard raw material in the near future.

5pm Tue-Sun) is opposite the Cuervo complex and half a block south. It's very well done, with photos, exhibits, tequila apparatus (including a huge vat) and good explanations (all in Spanish) of the mechanics and history of the industry. There's also a display case with dozens of brands of tequila (some of which are on sale in the shop).

About 4½ blocks further south (Corona changes names – bear slightly right) is the big, white **Perseverancia distillery** (☎ 742-02-43, Francisco Javier Sauza Mora 80; tours US$3.50; ☺ 11am-4pm Mon-Fri, 11am-2pm Sun), producer of Sauza tequila.

The **Tequila Express** (☎ 33-3880-9099 in Guadalajara; adult/child 6-12 US$62/38) departs Guadalajara's train station, located a couple blocks south of Parque Agua Azul, at 11am Saturday (with occasional Friday and Sunday departures). The diesel loco heads to Amatitán, 39km (1½ hours) from Guadalajara and home to the venerable Herradura distillery, which still employs traditional methods and apparatus. Ticket prices include a tour of the distillery, a mariachi show, snacks, lunch and an open bar with mucho tequila; you roll back into Guadalajara by 8pm. Book at least four days ahead; you can do this in Guadalajara at Morelos 395.

Do-it-yourselfers can reach Tequila on Rojo de los Altos buses that leave every 15 minutes from Sala A of Guadalajara's Antigua Central Camionera (US$3, 1¾ hours). Tequila Plus buses (same price but usually a bit quicker and more comfy) depart Sala B hourly on the half hour.

CHAPALA
☎ 376 / pop 20,000 / elevation 1560m
Mexico's largest natural lake, Lago de Chapala, lies 40km south of Guadalajara. Though picturesque, the lake suffers from significantly declining levels; towns that were once by the shore now overlook a swath of sand and marshy grass several hundred meters wide. Guadalajara and Mexico City's water needs exceed the flow into the lake, and whatever does make it here is often polluted with fertilizers that nourish water hyacinth, a decorative but fast-growing invasive plant that clogs the lake's surface. Still, the area's near-perfect climate and lovely countryside have attracted thousands of part- or full-time residents from the USA and Canada, many who are retirees. And in 2003 a deluge of

rain over central Mexico pumped extra water into Lago de Chapala, upping lake levels and delighting the local population.

One of the largest settlements on the lake, Chapala took off as a resort when president Porfirio Díaz vacationed here every year from 1904 to 1909. DH Lawrence wrote most of *The Plumed Serpent* at Zaragoza 307, now a beautiful villa. The Templo de San Francisco, at the lake end of Av Madero (the main street), figures in the book's final pages. Today Chapala is a non-descript, modern and touristy town that gets busier when Guadalajarans visit on weekends, but it also caters to its more permanent expat population. In September 2003 the lake was about 1km away from town, though this will change with the seasons.

Information
Chapala's **tourist office** (☎ 765-31-41; upstairs, Madero 407; ☺ 9am-7pm Mon-Fri, 9am-1pm Sat & Sun) is somewhat helpful. **Libros de Chapala** (☎ 765-25-34; Madero 230A; ☺ 9am-4pm Mon-Sat, 9am-2pm Sun), opposite the plaza, has a few English novels, guidebooks and magazines.

Sights
At the foot of Av Madero, near the dry pier, are a small park and some souvenir stalls. There's also a covered crafts market about 400m east along Paseo Corona. Further east, the expansive **Parque La Cristiania** has a big swimming pool, a playground and nice picnic lawns. Enter from Av Cristiania, off Ramón Corona, the road east around the lake.

A small booth at the pier sells boat tickets to **Isla de los Alacranes** (Scorpion Island), 6km from Chapala, which has some restaurants and souvenir stalls but isn't all that interesting. A round-trip, with 30 minutes on the island, costs US$20 per boatload; for one hour it's US$26. **Isla de Mezcala**, 15km from Chapala, has the ruins of a fort and other buildings. Mexican independence fighters heroically held out there from 1812 to 1816, repulsing several Spanish attempts to dislodge them and finally winning a full pardon from their enemies. A three-hour roundtrip boat ride (including wait) costs a whopping US$95, though you might be able to negotiate it down to US$70 if you deal with individual boat owners. It's about a 1km walk down to the water from the

WESTERN CENTRAL HIGHLANDS

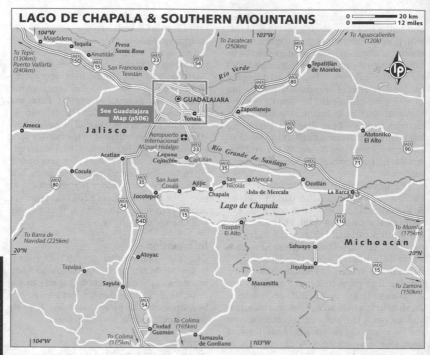

LAGO DE CHAPALA & SOUTHERN MOUNTAINS

pier, but if you buy advance tickets you might be able to get a ride to the shore.

Sleeping

Hotel Las Palmitas (☎ 765-30-70; Juárez 531; s/d/tw US$15/18/23) Chapala's cheapest digs have 15 basic but acceptable budget rooms with TV, set around a simple courtyard.

Mi Casa es tu casa (☎ 765-50-59; Guerrero 19A; s/d US$35/40) This US-run place offers six dark and small but comfortable rooms. There is a simple, sunny rooftop area and Mi Casa's owner (a mind/body/spiritual counselor) encourages quiet relaxation. Kitchen use is limited.

Lake Chapala Inn (☎ 765-47-86, 800-501-9446 in US & Canada; www.mexonline.com/chapalainn.htm; Paseo Ramon Corona 23; r US$59; P X ☎) Four large, gorgeous rooms greet you at this elegant inn. There's also a common living room and wonderful covered terrace overlooking the marshy lakeside. Breakfast is included.

Quinta Quetzalcóatl (☎ 765-36-53; www.chapala living.com; Zaragoza 307; r US$76-117; P ☎) The luxurious grounds are a paradise, and the unique rooms beautifully decorated with

Mexican crafts. This is where DH Lawrence wrote *The Plumed Serpent*, and you can ponder in his study. Stone paths lead to the small pool with Jacuzzi. Reservations required; credit cards incur a 5% fee.

Eating

East along Paseo Corona, a whole school of fish restaurants cast for customers to flop at tables overlooking what used to be the lake. Despite the distant view, it's still pleasant to sit here, and prices remain reasonable. Just be aware most of the finned critters probably come from fish farms – considering the state of the lake this isn't such a bad idea.

Av Madero's sidewalk restaurants provide menus in English and have high standards of cleanliness.

Café Paris (☎ 765-53-43; Madero 421; mains US$2.75-7) Good for breakfast and snacks, this casual place often has expats sitting in its inside booths, sidewalk tables or upstairs terrace.

Restaurant Superior (☎ 765-21-80; Madero 415) This is a similar expats magnet, just down the street.

El Árbol de Café (☎ 765-39-08; Hidalgo 236) On the busy highway leading to Ajijic, this small coffeeshop has good coffee, cakes, and fruit and yogurt plates – *if* you catch them open (hours are sporadic).

Getting There & Away
From Guadalajara's Antigua Central Camionera, Autotransportes Guadalajara-Chapala buses depart Sala A every half hour from 6am to 9pm (US$3, 50 minutes). Once you get to Chapala's bus terminal, it's a 10-minute walk down Av Madero to the dry pier. There are no long-distance services from Chapala's bus terminal; you must return to Guadalajara for these.

Buses connect Chapala and Ajijic every 20 minutes from 7am to 10pm (US$0.60, 15 minutes).

AJIJIC
☎ 376 / pop 13,000 / elevation 1550m
Seven kilometers west and much more charming than Chapala, Ajijic (ah-hee-*heek*) is a pretty little town of cobbled streets and some brightly painted houses. It's home to a sizable colony of Mexican, US and Canadian artists. The lakeshore isn't as far away here as in Chapala, though there's still a wide marshy strip out there. On Sundays Mexican families flock to the water for picnics and fun. Usually the town is fairly tranquil, except during the nine-day Fiesta de San Andrés, at the end of November, and over Easter, when a reenactment of Christ's trial and crucifixion is staged over three days.

The bigger buses will drop you on the highway at the top of Colón, the main street, which leads two blocks down to the main plaza and four more blocks down to the lake. The chapel on the north side of the plaza, two blocks down, dates from the 18th century and possibly even earlier. A handful of small galleries and some upmarket crafts shops lie on and off Colón.

Information
There's no tourist office in Ajijic, but the **Lake Chapala Society** (☎ 776-11-40; www.lakechapala society.org; 16 de Septiembre 16A; ☷ information office 10am-2pm Mon-Sat), which provides many services for expats, can help with some local information. Travelers are welcome to browse in the library, but only members have borrowing privileges. **Bancomer**

(☷ 8:30am-4pm Mon-Fri) and its ATM are on the plaza. If your threads are filthy head to the **lavandería** (Morelos 24A; per load US$2.75; ☷ 9:30am-2pm & 3-7pm Mon-Sat) off the northwest corner of the plaza.

Sleeping
Laguna B&B (☎ 766-11-74; www.lagunamex.com; Zaragoza Ote 29; r US$30; P) Four good rooms come with comfortable beds (some king-size) and colorful décor. A nice common living room and good breakfast add to the appeal. Prices drop to US$25 from April to September.

Mis Amores (☎ 766-46-40; www.misamores.com; Hidalgo 22B; r US$63) Twelve beautiful, colorful and romantic rooms with TV and fridge are set around a small but lush, tropical garden. All are artistically different from each other and very comfortable. The restaurant out front is good. Breakfast is included. Rates jump to US$76 from October to February.

La Nueva Posada (☎ 766-14-44; nuevaposada@ laguna.com.mx; Donato Guerra 9; s/d from US$54/61; P ☲) This immaculate, wonderfully decorated inn has large comfortable rooms with either terraces or balconies. Breakfast is included. The pool is tiny but surrounded by a patio full of plants, and there's also a great grassy garden. Rooms with lake view cost more; there is a 10% discount for cash. Villas are available.

Hotel Estancia (☎ 766-07-17; duransky@hotmail .com; Morelos 13; s/d US$33/38) Clean, simple and nicely-done rooms come with TV and surround a flowery courtyard on two levels. It's family-run, and there's a great rooftop terrace. Breakfast is included.

Hotel Italo (☎ 766-22-21; marianabrandi60@hotmail .com; Guadalupe Victoria 8; s/d US$23/29) If you're seeking good, no-nonsense budget rooms you'll find them here. They'll be renovating, though, so prices may rise and Jacuzzis may appear. 'Apartments' are also available and rented by the week or month. Visit the rooftop terrace for a nice view of the nearby lake.

Hotel Ajijic Plaza Suites (☎ 766-03-83; www .ajijichotel.com; Colón 33; r US$40-50) This US-run place has 10 simple but good suites, lined up along a garden path and stocked with TV and fridge. There's a pool/bar area out back, and a spa is in the works. Breakfast is included. It's good to reserve three to six months in advance, especially for January and February.

Eating & Drinking

Bruno's (☎ 766-16-74; Carretera Ote 20; mains US$7-13; ☼ 12:30-3pm & 5:30-8pm Mon-Sat) Enormously popular with expats, this intimate Canadian-run eatery grills up some of the best meats around the lake. Creative stir-frys, Italian dishes and salads are also very good.

B-Natural Deli & Salads (☎ 766-46-21; Colón 29; mains US$3.50-5; ☼ noon-10pm Tue-Sat, noon-6pm Sun) Vegetarians will adore this courtyard spot. Select your own lettuce, toppings and dressings from a wide array of choices. Hearty soups, sandwiches and fruit shakes are also on the menu, and portions are large.

El Sabor de Oaxaca (☎ 766-44-68; Av Plaza del Sol 25; ☼ 9:30am-2pm & 6-9pm) Across from the church, this small café serves Oaxacan coffees (US$0.75 to US$2.25), espresso, capuccino and mocha frappés, along with pastries.

Tom's Bar (☎ 766-12-50; Constitución 32; ☼ 10am-midnight Mon-Fri, 10-1am Sat & Sun) This Canadian-run watering hole is an expat magnet, with sports on the tube and welcome spaces in which to chat (including a courtyard). Some food, plus many drinks, are available.

Down near the pier are some restaurants that cater to tourists and expats. **Los Telares** (☎ 766-06-66; Morelos 6) and **Ajijic Grill** (☎ 766-24-58; Morelos 5) have popular courtyards. Their food is generally OK but sometimes the cooks miss the bullseye.

Getting There & Around

From Guadalajara's Antigua Central Camionera, Autotransportes Guadalajara-Chapala buses depart Sala A every half hour from 6am to 9pm (US$3, 55 minutes). These buses drop you on the highway at Colón. There are direct buses back to Guadalajara every half hour from 5.30am to 7:30pm (US$3). These are marked 'directo' and leave from the tiny Autotransportes Guadalajara-Chapala bus office on the highway, No 2A. Non-direct buses to Guadalajara go through Chapala. There are no long-distance services from Ajijic; you must return to Guadalajara for these.

Buses connect Chapala and Ajijic every 20 minutes from 7am until 10pm (US$0.60, 15 minutes); these stop on the highway.

SAN JUAN COSALÁ

☎ 387 / pop 3000 / elevation 1560m

At San Juan Cosalá, 10km west of Ajijic, there's a **thermal spa** (admission US$8; ☼ 8:30am-7pm) in an attractive lakeside setting. The spa has its own natural geyser and several swimming pools.

Hotel Balneario San Juan Cosalá (☎ 761-02-22; La Paz 420; s/d US$63/65; ℗) is a huge, well-run complex offering nice, clean rooms with big bathrooms and fridges. Spacious grounds sport Jacuzzis and a sauna. Next door, the more intimate **Hotel Villa Bordeaux** (☎ 761-04-94; ℗) has identical prices and is run by the same management.

Buses from Ajijic run every 20 minutes and cost US$0.60.

ZONA MONTAÑA

South of Lago de Chapala, the mountainous region of Jalisco known as the Zona Montaña has become a popular weekend getaway for Guadalajarans. They come, sometimes by the hordes, to enjoy the rural landscapes, cute colonial villages and local sweets, fruit preserves and dairy products.

Tapalpa

☎ 343 / pop 15, 480 / elevation 2100m

Once a mining town, Tapalpa has now become a bit touristy, and on weekends and holidays attracts a gaggle of upperclass Guadalajarans. It's still a sweet little thing, however, daintily perched on the slopes of the Sierra Tapalpa about 130km southwest of Guadalajara. There's an impressive church, nice plaza, cobbled streets and quaint old buildings with balconies and red-tiled roofs. Wonderful walking can be found in the surrounding area, which features pine forests, fishing streams and **Las Piedrotas**, some impressive rock formations 5km north of town. You can walk along a country road to these rocks, passing a funky old paper mill, or take a taxi (US$5, but negotiate). **El Salto**, a fine 105m-high waterfall, is about 13km south of town.

There's a tiny **tourist office** (☎ 432-06-50; ☼ 9am-4pm Mon-Fri, 10am-2pm Sat & Sun) on the plaza.

Accommodation is available at a dozen hotels and guesthouses, though they can all be full on weekends and holidays. The dark, basic and sometimes musty **Hotel Tapalpa** (Matamoros 35; s/d US$14/19) is the cheapest digs, and it's right on the plaza. **Casa de Maty** (☎ /fax 432-01-09; Matamoros 69; r Sun-Thu US$69, Fri & Sat US$92) is almost next door and the complete opposite, with luxurious rooms and gardens. In between in value and comfort are the fair-deal **Posada El Carretero** (☎ 432-00-49; Yañez 12; r US$29), right off the plaza, and **Las Margaritas** (☎ 432-07-99; 16 de Septiembre 81; r from US$43), which has a handful of pleasant rooms and villas a few blocks up the hill.

Food is good here in Tapalpa. Sample tasty *tamales de acelga* (chard-filled tamales), sold at the cheap food stalls next to the church. Another scrumptious dish is *borrego al pastor* (grilled lamb), done very nicely at **El Puente** (☎ 432-04-35; Hidalgo 324). This casual yet large restaurant is next to the river, three blocks down from the church; look for the smoky grill outside.

Hourly buses run to Tapalpa from Guadalajara's Antigua Central Camionera (US$6, 3½ hours).

Mazamitla

☎ 382 / pop 8765 / elevation 2240m
Another good base for visiting the mountains is tranquil Mazamitla, south of Lago de Chapala and 132km by road from Guadalajara. This is a tidy town of cobbled streets, tiled roofs and whitewashed buildings. Everywhere in town you'll see small storefronts selling homemade fruit preserves and cheeses, and on Mondays there's a small lively **market** (☙ 8am-3pm) on Juárez. About 5km south of town is the leafy park **Los Cazos** (admission US$0.50; ☙ 9am-5pm), which harbors the 30m waterfall El Salto. A taxi here costs US$3.50.

Mazamitla's **tourist office** (☎ 538-02-30; ☙ 9am-3pm Mon-Fri, 10am-2pm & 4-6pm Sat, 10am-4pm Sun) is to the right side of the church as you face the church.

There are a few sleeping options in town. Right at the plaza, **Posada Alpina** (☎ 538-01-04; Reforma 8; s/d Mon-Thu US$11.50/23, Fri-Sun US$17/25) has nice patios and good but small modern rooms with cable TV.

Also close to the plaza is **El Cortijo Azul** (☎ 538-00-68; Juárez 10; s/d US$12.50/21) offering just four dark, unpretentious, womb-like rooms (one with fireplace) around a nice courtyard.

Unique and friendly **Hotel Cabañas Colina de los Ruiseñores** (☎ cellular 01-333-4941-210; Allende 50; s/d US$14/29) is a wonderfully rustic place offering comfortable, tree-house-like rooms and walkways (most on the ground) with creative wood accents everywhere.

For eats, try **Posada Mazamitla** (☎ 538-06-08; Hidalgo 2; mains US$3.50-5; ☙ 8:30am-6pm), a pleas-ant patio restaurant that on Sundays serves the town's landmark dish *El Bote* (a stew of meats, vegetables and *chiles serranos* in a base of *pulque* – a milky, frothy liquid fermented from the maguey plant).

Another venerable restaurant is **El Troje** (☎ 538-00-70; Galeana 53; mains US$5-7; ☙ 10am-7pm), at the edge of town across from Pemex. It serves mostly steak and shrimp dishes, along with plenty of mixed drinks.

Fifteen buses run daily from Guadalajara's Nueva Central Camionera (US$6, three hours). They stop three blocks north of the plaza. From Colima there are five buses daily (US$8, 2¾ hours). These stop at the market, just a block west of the plaza. There are also daily buses to/from Zamora, Morelia and Manzanillo.

Ciudad Guzmán (Zapotlán el Grande)

☎ 341 / pop 62,400 / elevation 1500m
This pleasant-enough city claims the 'largest plaza in Jalisco,' which may well be true. The **Sagrado Corazón**, a 17th-century church, along with the more modern neo-classical cathedral, huddle in one corner of the plaza.

There are many arcades, and in the center of the plaza is a stone gazebo with a homage to famous Mexican muralist José Clemente Orozco painted on its ceiling. Indeed, Ciudad Guzmán is the birthtown of Orozco, and some of his original carbon illustrations and lithographs can be seen at the small **Museo Regional de las Culturas de Occidente** (Dr Ángel González 21; admission US$2.25; ☙ 9:30am-5:30pm Tue-Sun). There's also a nice recreational lake, Laguna de Zapotlán, just north of town. The adventure traveler, however, might see Ciudad Guzmán as the closest convenient base to Volcán Nevado de Colima (p541). This lofty mountain is about 25km (as the vulture flies) southwest of the city.

Get centered at the **tourist office** (☎ 413-53-13 ext 107; Lázaro Cárdenas 80; ☙ 8:30am-3pm Mon-Fri). It's located upstairs in the big yellow building.

Plant roots at **Zapotlán Hotel & Villas** (☎ 412-00-40; http://mx.geocities.com/zapotlan_hotel_villas; Federico del Toro 61; s/d from US$20/22; ☏ ☐ ☒). A nice swimming pool, tennis court and gym make this a great deal for thrifty jocks, and other perks include a location right on the plaza, decent rooms with TV and breakfast.

Nearby, the **Flamingos Hotel** (☎ 412-0203; Federico del Toro 133; s/d/tw from US$10/12.50/16; ☏)

offers simple but adequate budget rooms in wells that can get noisy (TVs blare – and rooms with TV cost more).

For something fancier try **Tlayolan Hotel** (☎ 412-33-17; Javier Mina 35; s/d/tw from US$13/17/24), with small, clean and modern rooms. TV costs more; suites are available.

There are many restaurants around the plaza. Behind the cathedral is the market and the city's cheapest eats.

Ciudad Guzmán's bus terminal is about four blocks west of the plaza. There are almost-hourly buses to Guadalajara (US$7 to US$8, two hours) and Colima (US$5-6, one hour). Buses to El Fresnito, the closest village to Volcán Nevado de Colima, run mostly in the mornings (US$1, 15 minutes, nine daily). There are three buses daily to Tapalpa (US$4, two hours). For car rentals, try **Pilot Renta Autos** (☎ 412-20-29; Federico del Toro 325).

INLAND COLIMA

The tiny (5191 sq km) state of Colima offers a widely varied landscape, from tall volcanoes in its northern fringes to shallow lagoons near the Pacific coast. The climate is similarly diverse: cool in the highlands and hot along the coast. This section deals with the upland area of the state; the narrow coastal plain, including the beach resorts of Manzanillo, Cuyutlán and Paraíso, is covered in the Central Pacific Coast chapter (p409).

Colima, the semitropical state capital, is a small, little-visited but pleasant city. Overlooking it from the north are two spectacular volcanoes: the active, constantly steaming Volcán de Fuego (3820m), and the extinct, snowcapped Volcán Nevado de Colima (4240m). Both can be reached relatively easily if you have a taste for adventure and a not-too-tight budget, though access to the Volcán de Fuego is usually barred for safety reasons.

The state's main agricultural products are coconuts, limes, bananas and mangoes. Its biggest industry is mining – one of Mexico's richest iron deposits is near Minatitlán.

History

Pre-Hispanic Colima was remote from the major ancient cultures of Mexico. Seaborne contacts with more distant places might have been more important: legend says one king of Colima, Ix, had regular treasure-bearing visitors from China.

Colima produced some remarkable pottery, which has been found in over 250 sites, mainly tombs, dating from about 200 BC to AD 800. The pottery includes a variety of figures, often quite comical and expressive. Best known are the rotund figures of hairless dogs, known as Xoloitzcuintles (see The Colima Dog, p536).

Archaeologists believe the makers of the pottery lived in villages spread around the state. The type of grave in which much of the pottery was found, the shaft tomb, occurs not only in the western Mexican states of Colima, Michoacán, Jalisco and Nayarit, but in Panama and South America as well.

When the Spanish reached Mexico, Colima was the leading force in the Chimalhuacán indigenous confederation that dominated Colima and parts of Jalisco and Nayarit. Two Spanish expeditions were defeated by the Colimans before Gonzalo de Sandoval, one of Cortés' lieutenants, conquered them in 1523. That same year he founded the town of Colima, the third Spanish settlement in Nueva España, after Veracruz and Mexico City. The town was moved to its present site, from its unhealthy original lowland location near Tecomán, in 1527.

COLIMA

☎ 312 / pop 126,000 / elevation 550m

Colima lives at the mercy of nature's whims. Volcán de Fuego, clearly visible 30km to the north, has had nine major eruptions in the past four centuries. Of even greater concern are earthquakes; the city has been hit by a series of them over the centuries, the most recent major one in January 2003 – today you can still see the occasional crumbled building site, waiting to be reconstructed. Because of these devastating natural events, Colima has few colonial buildings, despite having been the first Spanish city in western Mexico.

Still, Colima remains a pleasant city graced by several attractive plazas. It's only 45km from the coast, but quite a bit cooler and less humid. There are a number of interesting things to do in town, though some sights are eight or 10 blocks from the city center – buff up your walking shoes. And some great daytrips around the city await the adventurous.

Orientation

Three plazas constitute the heart of Colima, with Plaza Principal at the center of things. Portal Medellín is the row of arches on the north side, with Portal Morelos on the south side. Jardín Quintero is behind the cathedral, while Jardín Núñez is three blocks further east. Street names change at Plaza Principal (also known as Jardín Libertad). Colima's bus terminal is some 2km east of the city center, on the Guadalajara–Manzanillo road.

Information

You can change money at numerous banks and *cambios* around the city center; most

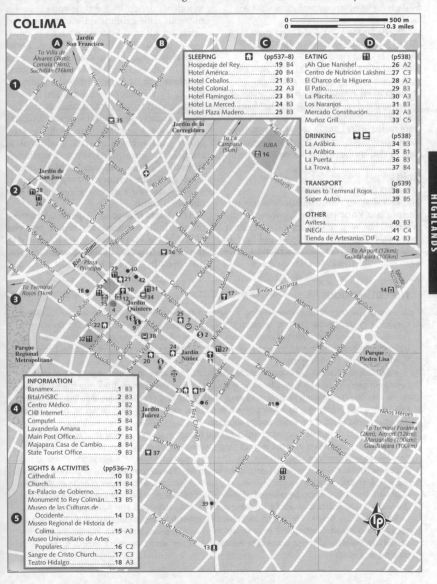

COLIMA

0 — 500 m
0 — 0.3 miles

To Villa de Álvarez (3km); Comala (9km); Suchitlán (16km)

To La Campana (5km)

To Airport (12km); Guadalajara (100km)

To Terminal Rojos (3km)

To Terminal Foránea (2km); Airport (12km); Manzanillo (100km); Guadalajara (100km)

Parque Regional Metropolitano

Parque Piedra Lisa

Niños Héroes

banks have ATMs. **Majapara Casa de Cambio**
(cnr Juárez & Morelos; ⌚ 8:30am-7pm Mon-Sat) will
take travelers checks. Many other money
changers are nearby.

Centro Médico (Herrera 140; ☎ 312-40-45)

Cl@ Internet (Hidalgo 6; per hr US$1.50; ⌚ 9am-
10:30pm) Check your spam here.

Computel (Morelos 234; ⌚ 7:30am-10pm) With
telephone and fax services, can hook you up with folks
back home.

Lavandería Amana (☎ 314-48-41; Domínguez 147-A;
US$3 for 3kg; ⌚ 8am-9pm Mon-Sat, 8am-3pm Sun)
Come here to sud up your duds.

Main post office (Madero 247; ⌚ 8am-5:30pm Mon-
Fri) Send 'wish-you-were-here' postcards.

Prestigio travel agency (☎ 313-10-11; Prestigio 7A;
⌚ 9am-8pm Mon-Fri, 9am-5pm Sat, 9am-1pm Sun) Can
make flight arrangements.

State tourist office (☎ 312-43-60; www.visitacolima
.com.mx; cnr Hidalgo & Ocampo; ⌚ 8:30am-8pm Mon-Fri,
10am-2pm Sat) In a domed white building on a corner.

Sights
AROUND PLAZA PRINCIPAL
The **cathedral**, or Santa Iglesia, on the east
side of Plaza Principal (also known as Jardín
Libertad) has been rebuilt several times since
the Spanish first erected a cathedral here in
1527. The most recent reconstruction dates
from just after the 1941 earthquake.

Next to the cathedral is the **Ex-Palacio
de Gobierno**, built between 1884 and 1904.
Local artist Jorge Chávez Carrillo painted
the murals on the stairway to celebrate the
200th anniversary of the birth of independence hero Miguel Hidalgo, who was once
parish priest of Colima. The murals depict
Mexican history from the Spanish conquest
to independence. By the time you get here a
museum with exhibits on archaeology and
works by Alfonso Michel may have opened.

On the south side of the plaza, **Portal
Morelos** is a handsome colonnade shading
outdoor tables. The **Museo Regional de Historia
de Colima** (☎ 312-92-28; Portal Morelos 1; admission
US$2.75; ⌚ 9am-6pm Tue-Sat, 5-8pm Sun) is well
worth a visit to see ceramic vessels and figurines (mostly people and adorable Xoloitzcuintle dogs) unearthed in Colima state.
Other permanent displays include masks,
textiles, costumes, basketry and shellwork
from the Colima coast, and exhibits on the
19th- and 20th-century history of the state.
There's also an impressive reconstruction
of a shaft tomb.

The **Teatro Hidalgo** (cnr Degollado & Independencia) was built in neoclassical style between
1871 and 1883 on a site originally donated to
the city by Miguel Hidalgo. The theater was
destroyed by the earthquakes of 1932 and

THE COLIMA DOG

One thing you may notice while visiting a museum or souvenir shop in Colima is the cute and
curious dog statues called Xoloitzcuintles (sho-lo-itz-*kuint*-lehs), or *itzcuintles* (itz-*kuint*-lehs).
Though they were not confined only to this part of Mexico, so many of these shiny, red-clay
figures have been uncovered by archaeologists in Colima state that they've become known as
'Colima dogs' to English speakers.

Xoloitzcuintle statues, produced from AD 200 to AD 900, were modeled after some of the first
canines in pre-Hispanic Mexico. Often these figures are just standing on their four thick legs, but
sometimes they're dancing joyfully with each other or sitting on their haunches smiling quizzi-
cally. It can be surprising how many poses and comical expressions the crafters of these figures
have bestowed upon their short, pudgy subjects.

The Aztecs believed that Xoloitzcuintles helped human souls reach their final resting place in
the afterworld, explaining why the statues (and the dogs themselves) have been found in tombs.
Even their name confirms this – 'Xolotl' was the Aztec god who guided souls in the afterlife, and
'itzcuintle' is the Náhuatl word for dog. But even in life, Xoloitzcuintles were important to pre-
Hispanic Mexicans. The dogs were believed to possess mystical curative powers and people often
slept with them, hoping to be relieved of their ailments. This may be why they were also part of
the ancient diet, a fact that would explain their charming rotundity and hairlessness.

Today the clay figures are prized by collectors, often fetching thousands of dollars each at
auction. And Xoloitzcuintles still exist in the flesh as the purebred Mexican Hairless. It's now
one of the oldest and rarest domesticated canines in the world, so don't expect to see them
on a menu anymore.

1941, and reconstruction was undertaken in 1942. In late 2003 the theater was again being renovated; during your tenure in town it may only be open for special events.

MUSEO DE LAS CULTURAS DE OCCIDENTE

The **Museum of Western Cultures** (☎ 313-06-08 ext 15; cnr Calz Galván & Ejército Nacional; admission US$1.50; ☺ 9am-7:30pm Tue-Sun), a little over 1km east of the city center. The well-lit museum exhibits hundreds of pre-Hispanic ceramic vessels, figurines and musical instruments from Colima state, with explanations in Spanish. Most impressive are the human figures and Xoloitzcuintle dogs, but the wide variety of other figures includes mammals, reptiles, fish and birds, depicted with a cartoonlike expressiveness that would make Disney proud.

MUSEO UNIVERSITARIO DE ARTES POPULARES

The **University Museum of Popular Arts** (☎ 312-68-69; cnr Barreda & Gallardo; admission US$1, free Sun; ☺ 10am-2pm & 5-8pm Tue-Sat, 10am-1pm Sun) is about 900m north of Plaza Principal in the Instituto Universitario de Bellas Artes (IUBA). It displays folk art from Colima and other states, with a particularly good section of costumes and masks used in traditional Colima dances. Other fascinating exhibits include textiles, ceramics, models and furniture.

Adjacent to the museum, the interesting **Taller de Reproducciones** is a workshop making reproductions of ancient Coliman ceramic figures. Some of these figures may be on sale at the museum shop, which stocks an assortment of inexpensive folk-art souvenirs.

PARKS

The **Parque Regional Metropolitano**, on Degollado a few blocks southwest of the city center, has a small sad zoo, a swimming pool, a café and a forest with an artificial lake. You can rent bikes to explore the forest paths, or rowboats to cruise the lake.

East of the city center on Calz Galván, **Parque Piedra Lisa** is named after its locally famous Sliding Stone. Legend says that visitors who slide on this stone will some day return to Colima, either to marry or to die.

LA CAMPANA

This **archaeological site** (☎ 313-49-46; Av Tecnológico s/n; admission US$2, free Sun; ☺ 9am-5pm Tue-Sun)

dates from as early as 1500 BC and is easily accessible by a No 7 or No 22 bus from the city center. It's about 5km north of town. Several low, pyramid-like structures have been excavated and restored, along with a small tomb you can look into and a space that appears to be a ball court (very unusual in western Mexico). The structures seem to be oriented due north toward Volcán de Fuego, which makes an impressive backdrop. A taxi from Colima costs US$4.

Festivals & Events

Many masked dances are performed at fiestas in Colima state. The Museo Universitario de Artes Populares has a good display of the masks and costumes worn by the dancers, and plenty of information on the subject. The following festivals take place in or very near Colima city:

Ferias Charro (Taurinas San Felipe de Jesús) For 10 days in late January and early February, this celebration honors the Virgen de la Candelaria (February 2) and takes place in Villa de Álvarez, about 5km north of the city center. Each day of the festival except Tuesday and Friday, a large crowd parades through the streets accompanied by giant *mojigangos* (caricature figures of the village's mayor and wife) and groups of musicians. They start at Colima's cathedral and go to Villa de Álvarez where the celebrations continue with food, music, rodeos and bullfights.

Feria de Todos los Santos (Feria de Colima) The Colima state fair (late October and early November) includes agricultural and handicraft exhibitions, cultural events and carnival rides.

Día de la Virgen de Guadalupe From about December 1 to the actual feast day, on December 12, women and children dress in costume to pay homage at the Virgin's altar in the cathedral. In the evenings *mañanitas* (traditional songs) are sung, and Jardín Quintero (behind the cathedral) fills with busy food stalls.

Sleeping

Hotel Plaza Madero (☎ 330-28-95; Madero 165; s or d US$43, tw US$52; P ☺) Strangely located inside a small shopping mall, this pleasant and relatively new place is quiet at night (when the mall shuts down). Rooms are colorful and great; those facing the street are brighter.

Hotel Ceballos (☎ 312-44-44; www.hotelceballos .com; Portal Medellín 12; r from US$87; P ☺ ☐ ☎) On the north side of Plaza Principal is this stately five-star hotel. It's been the past home to three state governors. The 63 nicely remodeled rooms come with high ceilings, and some have French windows opening onto small balconies. The least expensive rooms are pretty tight, though.

Hospedajes del Rey (☎ /fax 313-36-83; Rey Colimán 125; s or d US$25, tw US$34; **P**) The good modern rooms at this more intimate hotel have cable TV and fan, but those with two beds are a better size. They'll ask for a US$10 deposit – don't forget to ask for it back!

Hotel América (☎ 312-74-88; hamerica@prodigy .net; Morelos 162; r/ste from US$61/81; **P** 🛇 🖵 🖳) The suites here are nicest, and overlook the hotel's small fountain garden. Standard rooms straddle maze-like outdoor halls and scream for a remodel; they're downright plain-looking. There's a fancy restaurant.

Hotel La Merced (☎ 312-69-69; Hidalgo 188; s/d US$15/19; **P**) The best rooms (old-colonial style, but dark) are way in the back, behind the parking lot. Avoid the ones fringing the driveway. Rooms come with TV and fan, and some are generously sized.

Hotel Flamingos (☎ 312-25-25; Av Rey Colimán 18; s/d US$17/20; **P**) Here's a good budget choice. Old but bright rooms come with solid beds, tiled floors, balconies and TVs. The rooms on the 4th floor even have views, but those facing west bake in the afternoon sun.

Hotel Colonial (☎ 313-08-77; Medellín 142; s/d from US$11.50/17) Both old and new rooms are available here, though the cheaper ones are darker. It's a good deal, with small grassy areas softening the rough edges a bit.

Eating

Many small restaurants around Plaza Principal offer good simple fare – try Restaurants El Patio or La Placita. Mercado Constitución, south of Plaza Principal a couple blocks, has cheap food stalls serving juices, *pozole* and other meals.

¡Ah Qué Nanishe! (☎ 314-21-97; Calle 5 de Mayo 267; mains US$3.75-6; 🕑 1:30pm-midnight Wed-Mon) The name of this restaurant means 'How delicious!,' and the Oaxacan specialties here are indeed good. Order *moles* (thick sauces made with countless spices or chocolate) or *chapulines* (crunchy fried grasshoppers). It's worth the walk from center.

El Charco de la Higuera (☎ 313-01-92; Jardín de San José s/n; mains US$3.75-6) Around the corner from ¡Ah Qué Nanishe!, this peaceful restaurant faces Jardín de San José. The menu is pretty standard, with the usual Mexican soups, *antojitos* and grills, but the outdoor tables and

the lively atmosphere make it an enjoyable place to nibble your hunger pangs away. Breakfast runs from US$2.25 to US$6.

Centro de Nutrición Lakshmi (☎ 312-64-33; Madero 265; light meals & snacks under US$3; 🕑 8am-9:30pm Mon-Sat, 6-9:30pm Sun) This self-service natural-foods café serves healthy vegetarian fare like soy burgers and natural yogurt products. It caters more to take-out, but there are a few tables around a courtyard. You can also buy whole-wheat breads.

Muñoz Grill (☎ 314-94-94; Calz Galván 207; mains US$7-10.50; 🕑 1pm-midnight Tue-Sun) If you seek large portions of grilled meat, this is your paradise. The several sauces that come with your carnal order, including *chimichurri* (a tangy parsley/olive oil/garlic sauce), must be sampled. The covered outdoor patios are relaxing, the service is attentive and there's live music at 9pm from Wednesday to Sunday.

Los Naranjos (☎ 312-00-29; Barreda 34; mains US$4.50-7) This upscale spot offers pleasant seating (there's a nice patio out back) and tasty food. The breakfast selection is good, with plenty of coffee choices to keep you buzzed up.

Drinking

Colima is basically a quiet city, but there are a few things you can do in the evening – hanging around the plaza, lingering over coffee or beer, is a well-practiced pastime here. To help with the relaxed mood, the state band plays in Plaza Principal every Thursday and Sunday at around 7pm.

La Arábica (☎ 314-70-01; Barreda 4; coffee US$0.75-1.50; 🕑 8am-2pm & 5:30-9:30pm Mon-Sat) Great espresso, cappuccinos and lattes are whipped up in this tiny space – it's mostly take-out, since there are just a few stools to sit on. There's another **branch** (Herrera 263; 🕑 8am-2:30pm Mon-Sat), just a little bigger, north of the center.

La Trova (☎ 314-11-59; Revolución 363; 🕑 8pm-2am Tue-Sun) Also a restaurant, this casual 'bar bohemio' offers up a varied selection of live music nightly. Tables are set up around a small intimate courtyard, and there are plenty of liquids to imbibe.

La Puerta (☎ cellular 312-103-45-89; 27 de Septiembre 135; 🕑 6pm-2am Tue-Sun) Check out the local characters at this relatively long-running nightspot. If you luck out you'll hit stripper night, or open bar night. Otherwise there's a juke box, football table and lots of *botanas* (snacks) and drinks.

Getting There & Around

Both **Aeromar** (☎ 313-55-88) and **Aero California** (☎ 314-48-50) serve Mexico City daily, while only Aero California zooms to Tijuana several times a week. Colima's airport is near Cuauhtémoc, 12km northeast of the city center off the highway to Guadalajara (a taxi will cost US$8).

Colima has two bus terminals. The main long-distance terminal is Terminal Foránea, 2km east of the city center at the junction of Av Niños Héroes and the city's eastern bypass. There's a luggage keep (open 6am to 10pm daily). To get to Colima's center from this terminal, hop on a Ruta 4 bus (taxis US$1.50). For the return trip catch the same Ruta 4 bus on 5 de Mayo or Zaragoza. Destinations include the following:

Ciudad Guzmán (US$4.50-5.50, 1-2hr, 25 daily)
Guadalajara (US$11-17, 2½-3½hr, 65 daily)
Manzanillo (US$4.50-7, 1½-2hr, 41 daily)
Mexico City (US$24-63, 10-15hr, 7 nightly) To Terminal Norte.

Colima's second bus terminal, serving local towns, is Terminal Suburbana (or Terminal Rojos), about 1.5km west of Plaza Principal. Many buses run to Colima's center from this terminal (taxis US$1.25). Any bus marked 'Rojos' going north on Morelos will take you to the terminal. Destinations from here include Comala (US$0.50, 15 minutes, every 15 minutes), Manzanillo (US$3.50 to US$4.50, 1¾ hours, every 30 minutes), Tecomán (US$19 to US$2.25, 45 minutes, every 20 minutes) and Armería (US$2 to US$2.50, 45 minutes, every 30 minutes).

Taxi fares within town are US$1 to US$1.50. And if you want to rent a car to explore Colima's surrounding volcanoes and villages, try **Super Autos** (☎ 312-07-52; Coliman 382). The cheapest ride will cost you US$38 per day, but it'll be little more than a motorcycle with shell.

AROUND COLIMA
Comala

☎ 312 / pop 8000 / elevation 600m
Nine kilometers north of Colima is this darling little town, with great views of the nearby twin volcanoes, Fuego and Nevado. Comala is known for its fine handicrafts, especially wood furniture. It's not so small that there isn't an Internet café or *casa de cambio*, however.

The town's leafy plaza has a fine white gazebo, pretty flowering trees and a cute church with a mix of architectural styles. Under the arches along one side of the plaza are some inviting *centros botaneros*, which are bars where minors are allowed (but not served alcohol) and where each beverage is accompanied by a free snack. They're open from about noon to 6pm. On weekends, many people come to Comala just to hang out at these joints.

About a 30-minute walk from town is the small but good **Museo Alejandro Rangel Hidalgo** (☎ 315-60-28; admission US$1; ⏰ 10am-2pm & 3:30-7pm Tue-Fri, 10am-6pm Sat, Sun & holidays), in the Ex-Hacienda Nogueras. Hidalgo was a designer, painter and illustrator with a fine collection of pre-Hispanic artifacts, now very nicely displayed in this museum. To get here, walk 400m along Calle Degollado (it's left of the church). Turn left at the T-intersection, go 1km, then turn right at the next T-intersection and go another 1km. You can also take a bus (US$0.35, leaves from behind church) or a taxi (US$1.50).

Comala buses leave from Colima's Terminal Rojos (US$0.50, 15 minutes, every 15 minutes). Buses back to Colima depart from Comala's plaza.

Suchitlán

☎ 318 / pop 3200 / elevation 1200m
Small and hilly Suchitlán, 7km northeast of Comala, has quaint cobbled streets dotted with stray dogs and chickens. The village is famous for its animal masks and witches. The masks are carved in the village and worn by dancers in the traditional Danza de los Morenos, which takes place here during Semana Santa. This dance commemorates the legend that dancing animals enabled the Marys to rescue Christ's body, by distracting the Roman guards. You can ask around for the homes of the mask makers (try Erminio Candelario), who often have masks for sale.

Take a break at **Restaurant Portales de Suchitlán** (☎ 395-44-52; Galeana 10; mains US$3.50-5; ⏰ 8:30am-6:30pm Tue-Sun). They serve killer handmade corn tortillas and little plates of snacks (including rabbit), along with some alcoholic beverages. It's at the southwest corner of the plaza (which is 1km east from the highway) and popular with locals and tourists alike; pleasant tables are set around a garden and covered patio, and parrots provide a squawking background.

Buses to Suchitlán leave half-hourly from Colima's Terminal Rojos (US$0.75, 45 minutes).

Mahakua & Around

From Suchitlán the road winds about 8.5km north to **El Jacal de San Antonio** (😀 Sat, Sun & holidays), a restaurant where tables under big palapas have an unsurpassed view of Volcán de Fuego. It's worth a stop for lunch.

Do you need a place to crash and have lots of money to burn? Try **Mahakua** (Hacienda de San Antonio; ☎ 312-313-44-11; www.mahakua.com; s/d US$1095/1225; 🅿 🏊), a few kilometers further up the road. This fabulously restored hacienda is now a working ranch and coffee farm, still producing its own excellent brew. The grounds are accented by expansive manicured gardens buzzing with hummingbirds, and the hallways and common spaces will make you feel like royalty. Twenty-five suites are beautifully furnished with elegant tapestries, antiques and original artworks. You can play tennis, swim in the gorgeous 35m pool, try your hand at croquet or take in the surrounding countryside on a tour. All gourmet meals, alcoholic beverages and most activities are included. Make reservations; the guard won't let you in without them.

Lagunas La María & Carrizalillos

North of the hacienda, the road continues about 1.5km to the tiny pueblo of La Becerra. Turn right here and after 1km you'll reach the entrance to **Laguna La María** (☎ 312-320-88-91; admission US$0.75), a lovely green lake surrounded by lush hills – it's a popular weekend picnic spot. You can camp (US$0.75; showers available) or stay in one of the simple rooms with kitchen and TV (US$29 to US$72). RV hookups cost US$19. There's also a restaurant, rowboat rentals and soccer field. Ask about the caves in the area (about US$4 for guide). Book ahead during holiday times.

Two buses run daily from Colima's Terminal Rojos to La Becerra (US$1.25, one hour, departures at 6:30am and 1:25pm), but you'll have to walk the 1km to the lake.

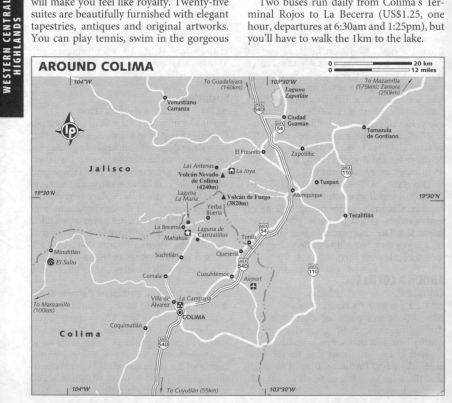

AROUND COLIMA

Getting to **Laguna de Carrizalillos** (☎ 312-320-95-96; admission US$0.50; ◷ 9am-6pm Wed-Sun) requires backtracking down the highway 6km from La Becerra and heading east 3½km along the road to Quesería. It also has picnic tables (US$1.50), camping (US$3.75) and cabañas (US$11.50-17), but isn't as nice as La María. However, you can rent horses (US$3.50 per half-hour) and boats (US$2.25 to US$4.50 per hour). There's also a restaurant. Three buses, marked 'Naranjal,' run daily from Colima's Terminal Rojos (US$1.50, one hour).

Parque Nacional Volcán Nevado de Colima

This national park, straddling the border of Colima and Jalisco, includes two dramatic volcanoes: the still-active Volcán de Fuego and the inactive Volcán Nevado de Colima. Ciudad Guzmán (p533) is a good base for exploring the area.

VOLCÁN DE FUEGO

Overlooking Colima from the north, 30km from the city as the crow flies, is the steaming Volcán de Fuego (Volcano of Fire, 3820m). It has erupted 30 times in the past four centuries, with a big eruption about every 70 years. A major burp in 1913 spelled the end of one cycle of activity, then another began in the 1960s. Some 3km of new lava emerged in 1998, and in 1999 the fireworks started up again. In 2002 and again in 2003 the volcano was hot and bothered enough to prompt the evacuation of nearby pueblo Yerbabuena. You can reach Yerbabuena (now almost a ghost village) in your own vehicle, but it's unlikely you'll get past the military post guarding the dirt road to the volcano. Information on the current condition of the volcano is posted (in Spanish) on the University of Colima's website www.ucol.mx/volcan.

There's another more accessible long dirt track on the east side of the volcano, but you probably won't be able to get right up to the volcano – just a safe distance away. You may also need a 4WD vehicle, though the track is sometimes kept in good condition as a fire access road. Call Ciudad Guzmán's tourist office (p533); they may be able to provide details.

To get to this dirt track from Colima, take highway 54D (the *cuota* or toll road,

US$8) toward Guadalajara, about 45 minutes, and after the stinky mill town of Atenquique get off at the first exit ('Tuxpan'). Backtrack through Atenquique (you'll now be on the free road, highway 54) and keep an eye out for the landmark parabolic church. Go 2.5km uphill past the church, to Km 56, and turn right onto the dirt track at the 'RMO Cerro Alto-Telmex' sign. The longer but cheaper approach is to take the free road, highway 54, all the way north to Km 56, turning left at the 'RMO Cerro Alto-Telmex' sign.

VOLCÁN NEVADO DE COLIMA

The higher and more northerly peak of Nevado de Colima (4240m) is accessible for most of the year. Remnants of a pine forest cover most of Nevado, and alpine desert appears at the highest altitudes. Wildlife frolicking in the area include deer, wild boar, coyotes and even mountain lions. For climate information you can dial (☎ 341-412-39-97, 341-412-20-25) in Ciudad Guzmán; for volcano information in Spanish check out www.zapotlan.com/patronato nevado/guia.htm.

The best months for climbing this volcano are the dry winter months of September through February. Keep in mind, however, that temperatures from December to February can get down to zero centigrade. Snowfall is always possible on the upper slopes – *nevado* means 'snow-covered.' The park's winter hours are 7am to 6pm (no cars up after 2pm). The summer rainy season is from July to September, when park hours are longer.

To access the volcano with your own car (2WD is OK in the dry winter season), take highway 54D (the *cuota* or toll road, US$8) north from Colima for about 45 minutes, and get off at the Tuxpan exit. Or take the free highway 54 north about 1½ hours to Km 63. At the roundabout, follow the 'Guadalajara libre/Colima cuota' sign and cross over the white and yellow bridge; then follow the 'Guadalajara libre' sign. You'll parallel highway 54D for 10 minutes, then cross over it. Head towards Ciudad Guzmán; just before you reach the town, turn left onto the El Grullo road. After 8.5km, on the left, you'll see the gravel road marked 'Nevado de Colima.' After winding about 17.5km (45 minutes) you'll reach Puerto

Las Cruces, where you'll sign in and be asked for a small donation. Drive another 1.5km to the free 3500m La Joya shelter. If staying here to acclimatize (a good idea) bring a sleeping bag and food; there's a spring but bring water just in case. About 4km beyond here is the end of the road, and the top is a 90-minute hike up. Remember to sign out at Puerto Las Cruces on your way down the mountain.

Driving up this volcano on the relatively good dirt road means that you'll be ascending to a high altitude very quickly. If you or any in your party feels lightheaded or dizzy, they may be suffering from *mal de montaña* (altitude sickness). That person should descend as quickly as possible, as this condition can be potentially fatal. For more on this health problem, see the Health chapter (p989).

If you don't have your own wheels, consider calling on Spanish-speaking **Aristeo 'El Indio' Rodríguez** (☎ 414-70-30; Carretera Atenquique 112). He lives in El Fresnito, the pueblo at the base of the volcano, and hangs out at an *abarrotes* (small grocery store). It's on the right, in a blue-and-white building as you enter town; look for the Corona Extra sign. Aristeo charges US$76 roundtrip (with three to four hours waiting time) to transport up to four people; each extra person after that is US$10. To get to El Fresnito, take a frequent bus from Colima's main bus terminal to Ciudad Guzmán (US$4.50 to US$5.50, one to two hours depending on which highway). From there, take another bus to El Fresnito (10p, 15 minutes, nine daily). Most buses to El Fresnito depart in the morning.

The Colima tour company **Azteca tours** (☎ 314-64-37; www.aztecatours.com; Av Fernando 533) charges about US$60 per person, including hotel pickup and snacks, for comfortable transport to either of the volcanoes (eight to nine hours roundtrip). Tours leave only once or twice a week, so plan ahead.

INLAND MICHOACÁN

Michoacán is a beautiful state studded by the Cordillera Neovolcánica, the volcanic range that gives the region both fertile soils and a striking mountainous landscape. Along a 200km stretch of the cordillera

across the northern part of Michoacán you can explore a number of fascinating destinations. These include the spectacular Reserva Mariposa Monarca (Monarch Butterfly Reserve), the handsome state capital of Morelia, the enchanting colonial town of Pátzcuaro, the very Mexican city of Uruapan (with its miniature tropical national park) and the famous Volcán Paricutín, a short distance beyond Uruapan.

The name Michoacán is an Aztec word meaning 'Place of the Masters of Fish.' Northern Michoacán once had extensive lakes, but most were drained for farmland during the colonial period. Traditional 'butterfly' nets are still used on Lago de Pátzcuaro, although nowadays the catch is more tourists' pesos than fish.

MORELIA

☎ 443 / pop 569,000 / elevation 1920m
Morelia lies 315km west of Mexico City and 278km southeast of Guadalajara. The capital of Michoacan is a well-preserved colonial city – the historic center is a Unesco World Heritage Site – with a large cathedral, an important university, an active cultural scene and some language schools offering Spanish courses. And yet despite its picturesque buildings and active demeanour, Morelia isn't overly touristy. Some foreigners who've made it here have discovered this city is a good place for an extended visit.

Morelia was one of the first Spanish cities in Nueva España, officially founded in 1541, although a Franciscan monastery had been in the area since 1537. The first viceroy, Antonio de Mendoza, named it Valladolid after the Spanish city of that name, and he encouraged families of Spanish nobility to move here. The families remained and maintained Valladolid as a very Spanish city, at least architecturally, until 1828. By that time Nueva España had become the independent republic of Mexico, and the city had been renamed Morelia in honor of local hero José María Morelos y Pavón, a key figure in Mexico's independence movement.

Many of Morelia's downtown streets are lined with colonial buildings, and it still looks nearly as Spanish as it did before independence. City ordinances require that all new construction in the city center be done in colonial style with arches, baroque façades

MORELIA

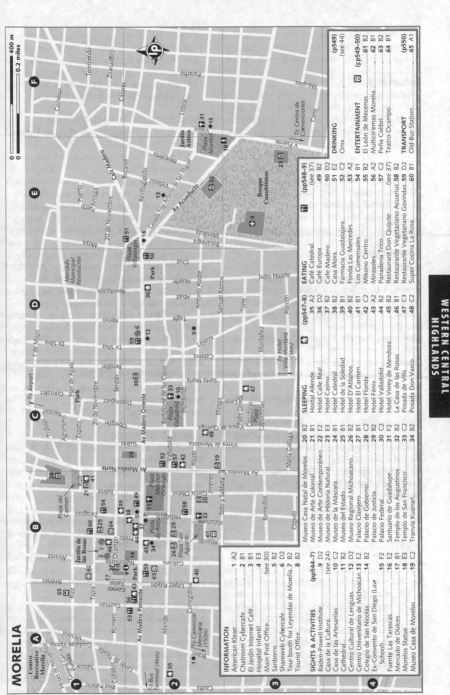

and walls of pink stone. A good number of streets remain fairly narrow, but unfortunately they often get congested with traffic.

Orientation

Morelia's imposing cathedral is the soul of the city and a major landmark. East–west streets change their names at the cathedral while north–south streets change names at Madero.

The elegant row of arched verandas facing the Plaza de Armas (or *zócalo*) is commonly called Portal Hidalgo; the arches on Abasolo facing the west side of the plaza are called Portal Matamoros.

Morelia's bus terminal is about 4km northwest of center.

Information

Banks and ATMs are plentiful in the *zócalo* area, particularly on and near Madero.

American Klean (Bravo 200; self-service load US$4, 15 pieces full service US$5.50; ☼ 9am-7pm Mon-Fri, 8am-6pm Sat, 8am-3pm Sun) Let your clothes mingle with the local threads at this laundry.

Chatroom Cybercafe (Nigromante 132A; per 5-30min US$1) Has good connections.

El Jardín Internet Café (Prieto 157; per hr US$1.50; ☼ 10:30am-2pm & 4:30-9:30pm) Another Internet place with good connections.

Main post office (Madero Ote 369) Pick up care packages from home here.

Sanborns (☎ 317-84-72; cnr Av Madero Pte & Zaragoza; ☼ 7:30am-midnight) If you're in need of maps or English magazines and novels, look no further than this bookstore.

Tourist office (☎ 312-80-81, 800-450-23-00; cnr Madero Pte & Nigromante; ☼ 9am-7pm Mon-Fri, 9am-2pm & 5-7pm Sat, 9am-2pm Sun) Offers basic tourist information.

Hospital Star Médica (☎ 322-77-00, Virrey de Mendoza 2000) Good for slight indigestion - or worse.

Sights

CATHEDRAL

The cathedral dominating the *zócalo* took more than a century to build, from 1640 to 1744. Architecturally, it is a combination of Herreresque, baroque and neoclassical styles. Its twin 70m-high towers, for instance, have classical Herreresque bases, baroque midsections and multicolumned neoclassical tops. Inside, much of the baroque relief work was replaced in the 19th century with more balanced and calculated neoclassical pieces. Fortunately, one

of the cathedral's interior highlights was preserved: a sculpture of the Señor de la Sacristía made from a dried corn paste and topped with a gold crown from the 16th-century Spanish king, Felipe II. There's also a very large organ with 4600 pipes.

MUSEO REGIONAL MICHOACANO

Just off the *zócalo*, the **Michoacán Regional Museum** (☎ 312-04-07; Allende 305 & Abasolo; admission US$3, free Sun; ☼ 9am-7pm Tue-Sat, 9am-4pm Sun) is housed in the late-18th-century baroque palace of Isidro Huarte. The museum displays a great variety of pre-Hispanic artifacts, colonial art and relics, contemporary paintings by local artists and exhibits on the geology, flora and fauna of the region. A highlight is the mural on the stairway by Mexican painter Alfredo Alce. The mural is in halves: the right half portrays people who have had a positive influence on Mexico, while the left half *mostly* portrays those who have had a negative influence (find the bad guys).

The **Palacio de Justicia**, across Abasolo from the museum, was built between 1682 and 1695 to serve as the city hall. Its facade is a chunky and eclectic but well-done mix of French and baroque styles. The stairway in the courtyard has a dramatic mural by Agustín Cárdenas showing Morelos in action. A museum might be open here by the time you arrive.

MUSEO DEL ESTADO

The **Michoacán State Museum** (☎ 313-06-29; Prieto 176; admission free; ☼ 9am-8pm Mon-Fri, 9am-7pm Sat & Sun) has good information about this interesting state. Downstairs is devoted to the history of Michoacán from prehistoric times to the first contact between the Tarascos and the Spanish. Upstairs, the story continues to the present, with exhibits on many aspects of modern life in Michoacán including clothing, handicrafts and agriculture. Ask about the program of free cultural events such as regional music, dance and artesanías.

MORELOS SITES

José María Morelos y Pavón, one of the most important figures in Mexico's struggle for independence from Spain, was born in the house on the corner of Corregidora and García Obeso on September 30, 1765. Two centuries later, the house (which dates from the 1650s) was declared a national monument and made into the **Museo Casa Natal de Morelos** (Morelos Birthplace Museum; ☎ 312-27-93, Corregidora 113; admission free; ⏱ 9am-8pm Mon-Fri, 9am-7pm Sat & Sun). Morelos memorabilia fill two rooms; a public library, auditorium and projection room occupy the rest of the house. An eternal torch burns next to the projection room. Free international films and cultural events are held at the museum (see p549).

In 1801 Morelos bought the Spanish-style house on the corner of Av Morelos and Soto y Saldaña. Today it's the **Museo Casa de Morelos** (Morelos House Museum; ☎ 313-26-51; Morelos Sur 323; admission US$2.25, free Sun; ⏱ 9am-7pm), with exhibits on Morelos' life and his role in the independence movement. There are also some nice period antiques, including liturgical items.

Morelos studied at the **Colegio de San Nicolás** (cnr Madero Pte & Nigromante), one block west of the *zócalo*. The Colegio later became the foundation for the Universidad Michoacana and is still used by the university. Upstairs, the Sala de Melchor Ocampo is a memorial room to another Mexican hero, a reformer and governor of Michoacán. Preserved here are Ocampo's library and a copy of the document he signed to donate his library to the college, just before being shot by firing squad on June 3, 1861. Visitors can enter the university buildings Monday to Friday during term time.

PALACIO CLAVIJERO & MERCADO DE DULCES

From 1660 to 1767, the Clavijero Palace was home to the Jesuit school of St Francis Xavier. After the Jesuits were expelled from Spanish dominions, the building served variously as a warehouse, prison and seat of the state legislature. In 1970 it was completely restored and renovated for use as state government offices. The majestic main patio has imposing colonnades and pink stonework.

Be sure to visit the arcade on the western side of the palace to taste some of the goodies on sale in the **Mercado de Dulces** (Sweets Market; ⏱ 9am-10pm). Some folksy Michoacán handicrafts and souvenirs are also sold in the arcade, but for high-quality handicrafts you'll do better at the Casa de las Artesanías.

CASA DE LA CULTURA & AROUND

Three blocks north of the cathedral, in baroque buildings that were once a church and convent, the impressively large complex of the Casa de la Cultura hosts dance and music performances, films and art exhibitions. Stop by for a free monthly brochure describing cultural events in the city. Inside, the **Museo de la Máscara** (☎ 313-13-20; Av Morelos Nte 485; admission free; ⏱ 10am-2pm & 4-8pm Mon-Fri, 10am-6pm Sat & Sun) has masks from around Mexico, each labeled with the ethnic group and the particular dance it's associated with.

South of Plaza del Carmen, the **Museo de Arte Colonial** (☎ 313-92-60; Juárez 240; admission free; ⏱ 9am-8pm Mon-Fri, 10am-2pm & 4:30-7pm Sat & Sun) contains 18th-century religious paintings, lots of gruesome crucifixes, an exhibit on how cornpaste figures are made and an interesting ivory Christ with Asian features (which possibly arrived on a treasure ship from the Philippines).

CASA DE LAS ARTESANÍAS

The **House of Handicrafts** (☎ 312-12-48; Plaza Valladolid; ⏱ 9am-8pm Mon-Sat, 9am-1pm Sun) occupies the Ex-Convento de San Francisco, attached to the Templo de San Francisco, three blocks east of the *zócalo*. Arts and handicrafts from all over Michoacán are displayed and sold; they're expensive but some of the best you'll see anywhere in the state. Upstairs, small shops represent many of Michoacán's towns, with craftspeople demonstrating how the specialties of their area are made. You'll find guitars from Paracho, copperware from Santa Clara del Cobre, lacquerware, weaving and much more. The shops keep individual hours, which may vary somewhat from those listed.

FUENTE LAS TARASCAS & EL ACUEDUCTO

At the east end of Madero Ote, nine blocks from the cathedral, the *fuente* (fountain) spouts from a tray of fruit supported by three bare-breasted Tarascan women. The original fountain here vanished mysteriously in 1940, and this replacement was installed in the 1960s. Adjacent Plaza Villalongín has another fine fountain.

El Acueducto (the Aqueduct) runs for several kilometers along Av Acueducto and makes a couple of bends around Plaza Villalongín. The aqueduct was built between 1785 and 1788 to meet the city's growing water needs. Its 253 arches make an impressive sight, especially at night when they are illuminated by floodlights.

PLAZA MORELOS & AROUND

Running roughly east from the Fuente Las Tarascas, the cobbled Calz Fray Antonio de San Miguel is a broad and elegant pedestrian promenade lined by fine old buildings. It leads about 500m to Plaza Morelos, an irregular but finely proportioned space surrounding the landmark **Estatua Ecuestre al Patriota Morelos**, a statue of Morelos on horseback trotting to battle. Sculpted by the Italian artist Giuseppe Ingillieri between 1910 and 1913, this makes a fine focal point in this very attractive area.

On the northeast edge of the plaza, the **Santuario de Guadalupe** is a delightfully overdone baroque church built from 1708 to 1716; the mauve-and-gold interior (including the psychedelic rotunda with yellow windows) dates from 1915. Beside the church, the **Ex-Convento de San Diego** was built in 1761 as a monastery and now houses the law school of the Universidad Michoacana. Check the elaborate façade, and look inside to see the bronze fountain.

The aqueduct delineates the south side of the plaza, and on the other side of that is the **Bosque Cuauhtémoc**, a large park with lots of trees, children's amusements and a couple of museums. The **Museo de Arte Contemporáneo** (☎ 312-54-04; Acueducto 18; admission free; ⏰ 10am-8pm Mon-Fri, 10am-6pm Sat & Sun) is a French-style 19th-century building housing changing exhibitions of contemporary art. There's a bookstore with video and art supplies, and a cafeteria. The small **Museo de Historia Natural** (☎ 312-00-44; Av Ventura Puente 23; admission free; ⏰ 10am-9pm), on the east side of the park, has displays of stuffed, dissected and skeletal animals, along with deformed human fetuses and freaky pickled animals. Bring a strong stomach.

CENTRO DE CONVENCIONES

This **convention center** (☎ 314-61-50), about 1.5km south of center, holds several places of interest. You can reach it on the Ruta Roja (red) combi heading east on Tapia or 20 de Noviembre.

Inside the complex are a **planetario** (planetarium; ☎ 314-24-65; admission US$2), with 164 projectors simulating stars on a dome 20m in diameter (show times are 9pm Tuesday to Friday, and 1pm, 5pm and 7pm Saturday and Sunday), and a nearby **Orquidario** (Orchid House; ☎ 314-62-02; admission US$0.45; ⏰ 9am-6pm

Mon-Fri, 10:30am-3pm & 4-6pm Sat & Sun), which exhibits nearly 3000 species of wild and hybrid orchids. The best months for flowering are April, May and October; Sometimes there are orchid expositions during these months (call).

PARQUE ZOOLÓGICO BENITO JUÁREZ

The **zoo** (☎ 314-04-88; Calz Juárez s/n; admission US$1; ⏰ 10am-5pm) is 3km south of the *zócalo*. It's a mostly pleasant place with lions and tigers and bears (oh my) in naturalistic habitats. The wolves and hyenas could use more space, though. Other animals include sea lions, giraffes, elephants, lots of birds, and reptiles. Gravel paths make it hard for strollers, but kids may enjoy the lake with rowboats for hire, a small train and playground.

The Ruta Guinda and Ruta Rosa combi, or the Santa María bus (white with blue-and-grey stripes), all heading south on Nigromante, will drop you off at the zoo entrance.

Courses

Several schools in Morelia offer Spanish-language and Mexican-culture courses.

Centro Cultural de Lenguas (☎ 312-05-89; www.ccl.com.mx; Madero Ote 560) Group lessons US$180 per week, private lessons US$280 per week. This centrally located school offers Spanish-language courses running from two weeks, four hours daily (three hours of classroom work and, if desired, an hour spent on workshops related to Mexican history, literature and culture). Living with Mexican families is encouraged (US$18 to US$20 per day, including all meals) and organized by the school.

Baden-Powell Institute (☎ 312-40-70; www.baden-powell.com; Alzate 565) Private lessons US$13 per hour, group lessons US$165 per week (four hours per day). This small, well-run and affordable school offers courses in Spanish language, as well as Mexican politics, cooking, culture, guitar playing and folk dancing. Lodging with a Mexican family is US$22 per day, including three meals.

Centro Universitario de Michoacán (☎ 317-14-01; becky_alfaro@hotmail.com; Calz Fray Antonio de San Miguel 173) Intensive courses cost US$250 per week; there's a discount after two weeks. In a large colonial building, this school offers courses in Spanish language and Mexican culture. Classes run four hours daily in groups of five or fewer students. Family living costs about US$20 a day.

Tours

Tranvía Kuanari (☎ 314-94-56; Loaiza 132) offers three different loop tours of the city in imitation antique trolley cars, which depart from the Hotel Virrey de Mendoza. Tours cost US$3.50, US$5 and US$7 and take from 50 minutes to two hours. Departures depend on the tour and day; check beforehand for exact schedules.

Leyendas de Morelia is an interesting tour (US$7) that leaves at 8pm Tuesday to Saturday from the Hotel de la Soledad. It covers some major sites in the center along with an underground crypt (two hours). For more information check at the hotel or the tour's info booth in the Plaza de Armas.

For tours to places outside the city, ask the tourist office to recommend an authorized guide or tour company. One recommended company is **Mex Mich Guías** (☎ 320-11-57; www.mmg.com.mx), which provides personalized tours and transport to many area destinations, including the Monarch Butterfly Reserve.

Festivals & Events

As well as the usual Mexican celebrations, Morelia's many annual festivals include the following:

Feria de Morelia Morelia's major fair, running for three weeks in mid-May, sports exhibits of handicrafts, agriculture and livestock from around Michoacán, plus regional dances, bullfights and fiestas. The anniversary of the founding of Morelia in 1541 is celebrated on May 18 with fireworks, displays of historical photos and more.

Feria de Órgano This international organ festival is held during the first two weeks of the Feria de Morelia.

Festival Internacional de Música The International Music Festival occurs the last week of July and first week of August.

Cumpleaños de Morelos Morelos' birthday is celebrated on September 30 with a parade, fireworks and more.

Día de la Virgen de Guadalupe The Day of the Virgin of Guadalupe is celebrated on December 12 at the Templo de San Diego; in the preceding weeks, typical Mexican foods are sold on the pedestrian street Calz Fray Antonio de San Miguel.

Feria Navideña The Christmas Fair, with traditional Christmas items, foods and handicrafts from Michoacán, is celebrated from approximately December 1 to January 6.

Sleeping

As elsewhere, rates can rise about 20% during the holidays, especially December and January.

BUDGET

Hostal Allende (☎ 312-22-46; www.hostels.com.mx; Allende 843; s/d from US$11/19, dm US$8) The sex-segregated dorms here only hold four; most rooms are private. There's a small common kitchen, leafy courtyard in which to hang and a blue-yellow color scheme. Rooms are simple and clean, and the cheapest ones are pretty small. Ten percent discount with HI or ISIC card.

Hotel El Carmen (☎ 312-17-25; fax 314-17-97; Ruíz 63; s/d from US$17/24; **P**) This place is a winner, offering tastefully furnished rooms with TV, a pretty lobby and peaceful location. There are wood accents and the whole ambience is comfortable and clean.

Hotel Colonial (☎ 312-18-97; 20 de Noviembre 15; s/d from US$12/15) A good budget find, this 25-room colonial-style hotel offers large street-facing rooms with high beamed ceilings and small balconies; however, they catch a lot of traffic noise. Interior rooms are dark and quieter. Some baths are musty, so smell around a bit. TV costs US$6 more.

Hotel Fénix (☎ 312-05-12; Madero Pte 537; s/d US$10.50/13; **P**) The Fénix has dark and basic but spacious rooms with saggy mattresses. It's in a great location and well-priced for shoestringers.

Posada Don Vasco (☎ 312-14-84; posada_don_vasco@hotmail.com; Vasco de Quiroga 232; s/d US$19/22) This colonial-style hotel has decent carpeted rooms with TV and small baths. The lower ones are dark; look at a few, as it's a good deal if you get one of the better ones. There's also a nice stone courtyard with sitting areas and plants.

Posada de Villa (☎ 312-72-90; Padre Lloreda 176; s/d US$19/22; **P**) No-nonsense tiled rooms here are spacious and sport a tiny bit of personality, but don't get much light. It's friendly, though, and the apartments are good for families (US$33).

MID-RANGE

Hotel Casino (☎ 313-13-28, 800-450-21-00; www.hotelcasino.com.mx; Portal Hidalgo 229; r from US$60; **P ▢**) Well-located on the north side of the *zócalo*, this Best Western hotel has 48 decent rooms with carpet and cable TV.

Those facing the street have balconies with views of the *zócalo*; the interior rooms overlook a covered courtyard with tables.

Hotel Valladolid (☎ 312-00-27; fax 312-45-63; Portal Hidalgo 245; r US$48) Simply done but comfortable and attractive rooms are available here, but the central location of this colonial-style hotel (on the zócalo) is the best feature. Continental breakfast included.

Hotel D'Atilanos (☎ 312-01-21; cbias@prodigy.net.mx; Corregidora 465; s/d US$25/38) Some personality can be found at this colonial-style hotel, but ground-floor rooms are dark, most are average at best, and management is tepid. Fluorescent lighting doesn't improve things much.

Hotel Florida (☎ 312-18-19; www.unimedia.net.mx.hotelflorida.com; Morelos Sur 161; s/d US$24/36) The good, carpeted rooms with cable TV are a fair deal at this well-located hotel, but there's not much charm. It's a decent value at this price range, though.

Hotel Catedral (☎ 313-04-06; hotel_catedral@infosel.net.mx; Zaragoza 37; r US$57; P) Within ringing distance of the cathedral, this attractive colonial-style hotel offers 45 acceptable rooms fringing a nicely decorated, covered courtyard. Try for a room with balcony, out front.

Hotel Calle Real (☎ 313-28-56, 800-451-5500; www.hjmorelia.com.mx; Av Madero Ote 766; r from US$75; P 🖳 😵) This Howard Johnson hotel offers what you'd expect from a HoJo: 64 quiet, very comfortable rooms with all the amenities. There are views from the 2nd floor, and a courtyard restaurant in front. It's located eight blocks east of center, near Bosque Cuauhtémoc.

TOP END

Hotel de la Soledad (☎ 312-18-88, 800-716-01-89; www.hsoledad.com; Zaragoza 90; s/d from US$73/82; P) Popular with honeymooners, this gorgeous, well-located colonial hotel has beautiful courtyards and unique rooms of all different sizes. The historical building has been a carriage house, a convent and a private mansion. It's a peaceful stay that might take you back in time.

Hotel Virrey de Mendoza (☎ 312-49-40; www.hotelvirrey.com; Madero Pte 310; r from US$124; P 🖳) Above the elegant lobby are truly elegant, very comfortable rooms finely furnished with antiques and crystal chandeliers. It's one of the classiest places in town and a

former mansion. In case you're a fan, Salma Hayek once rested here.

La Casa de las Rosas (☎ 312-45-45; www.lacasadelasrosas.com; Prieto 125; r from US$200; P 🖳) This is one of the most romantic stays in Michoacán. Four gorgeous and immaculate rooms and suites offer fine details like gauzy curtains around stone bathtubs, beautiful wood floors, period furniture and antique-looking rugs. It's like a little paradise in the middle of Morelia. Breakfast is included in the price.

Hotel Villa Montaña (☎ 314-02-31; www.villamontana.com.mx; Patzimba 201; r from US$150) Some 3km south of the city center, in one of Morelia's swankiest suburbs, is this elegant hotel. Even the standard rooms are spacious and come with fireplace. The lush grounds, heated swimming pool and tennis court aren't bad either, and the terrace bar sports grand views. If you want the best in town with all the services to boot, come lay your head here.

Eating

Dulces morelianos – delicious sweets made mainly of milk and sugar – are a local product. Another specialty is *gazpachos*, a snack made of chopped jicama, mango and pineapple or papaya, with cheese, chile, lime and salt. Delicious!

Café Europa (☎ 317-07-20; Portal Galeana 143; mains US$2-7; ⌚ 8am-11pm) Sleek, chic and not for the meek, this modern, Euro-like café serves up elegantly prepared munchies along with a great selection of tasty coffees (US$1 to US$2.25). Salads, sandwiches, crêpes and pastries can all be daintily nibbled.

Panadería Trico (☎ 313-42-32; 2nd fl, Valladolid 8; mains US$2.75-5) Excellent soups, salads and sandwiches, along with a stunning view of the cathedral, make this 2nd-floor restaurant a treat. Below is their popular bakery and deli.

Super Cocina La Rosa (cnr Tapia & Prieto; mains under US$4; ⌚ 8:30am-4:30pm) Popular for its filling *comida corrida*, this unpretentious family restaurant has a changing daily menu.

Fonda Las Mercedes (☎ 312-61-13; Guzmán 47; mains US$7-14; ⌚ 1:30-11:30pm Mon-Sat, 1:30-6pm Sun) This place has table in an intimate covered courtyard with potted palms, and also in a stone hall with atmospheric lighting. The international menu offers a good choice of pasta, crêpes, meats and seafood.

Mirasoles (☎ 317-57-75; Madero Pte 549; mains US$7-17; ⏱ 1-11pm Mon-Sat, 1-6pm Sun) This beautiful and classy restaurant offers Michoacán specialties; or alternatively, sample the Argentine parrilla with *chimichurri*. Chilean, French and California wines are poured.

Mikono Centro (☎ 312-40-44; Madero Pte 402; mains US$6-10) For something different, get your sushi, sashimi or maki-roll fix here. Remember you're about 200km from the ocean, but at least the cooks look half-Japanese (a good sign).

Los Comensales (☎ 312-93-61; Zaragoza 148; mains US$5-8) A more reasonably priced spot is this pleasant courtyard restaurant. The Mexican menu includes *antojitos*, seafood, steak or sizzling paella. The US$5.50 *menú del día* is served until 6pm.

Restaurante Vegetariano Acuarius (☎ 317-11-68; Hidalgo 75; meals under US$3.50; ⏱ 9am-5pm) In a peaceful, colorful courtyard, this no-frills place offers US$3 breakfasts and juices under US$2. The daily *comida corrida* is posted outside.

Restaurante Vegetariano Govindas (☎ 313-13-68; Madero Ote 549; mains under US$3.50; ⏱ 10:30am-5pm) This small upstairs café serves basic but tasty-looking breakfast and lunch specials of soy burgers, salads, soups and vegetarian versions of Mexican dishes.

On the north side of the zócalo, under the arches of Portal Hidalgo, is a row of restaurants and sidewalk cafés open from 8am to 11pm daily. These include **Café Catedral** (☎ 312-32-89; Portal Hidalgo 213) and **Restaurant Don Quijote** (☎ 313-13-28; Portal Hidalgo 229).

On the south side of Plaza Villalongín the pleasant **Café Madero** (☎ cellular 044-443-325-28-81; Av Madero Ote 880) does a good line in coffee, ice-cream and light breakfasts (and offers Internet) while nearby **Casa Mora** (☎ 317-39-59; Villalongín 42) sits in a nice courtyard and serves pizza, salads and sandwiches.

Plaza San Agustín (cnr Abasolo & Corregidora) One block south of the zócalo, this plaza has food stalls and tables under the covered arches running around three of its sides. The vendors serve all manner of Mexican meals, snacks and taste treats from approximately 3pm until 1am daily. It's an entertaining and economical place to eat.

Comercial Mexicana (⏱ 8am-10pm), near the intersection of Bravo & Manuel Muñiz, is more than a supermarket: find anything from WD40 to pyjamas to take-out food, along with your basic supermarket items. It's located southwest of center. For 24-hour convenience, **Farmacia Guadalajara** (cnr Av Morelos Sur & Valladolid) stocks some canned goods and snacks.

Drinking

Wet your whistle at **Onix** (☎ 317-82-90; Portal Hidalgo 261; ⏱ 8:30am-midnight Sun-Thu, 8-1am Fri-Sat). Their large beverage selection includes the *skorppio* (drowned scorpion included in drink). Flavored margaritas and martinis are other house specialties. It's an ultra fancy modern restaurant-bar, so bring your good-looking date, dress up and find a table back near the metal-and-stone waterfall.

Entertainment

Being a university town as well as the capital of one of Mexico's most interesting states, Morelia has a lively cultural life. Stop by the tourist office or the Casa de la Cultura for *Cartelera Cultural*, a free weekly listing of films and cultural events in and around Morelia, published every Monday. Daily newspapers *El Sol de Morelia*, *La Voz de Michoacán* and *El Cambio de Michoacán* have cultural sections with events notices and theater and cinema ads.

International film series are presented by various cinema clubs, with admission often free. Venues are the Museo Regional Michoacano, the Casa Natal de Morelos and the Casa de la Cultura. For recent-release movies, check **Multicinemas Morelia** (cnr Gómez Farías & Tapia).

The Casa Natal de Morelos also presents free talks and cultural events Fridays at 7pm. At the Museo del Estado, regional dances, music, stories and exhibitions from the state of Michoacán are presented most Wednesdays at 7.30pm. For theater, check what's on at the **Teatro Ocampo** (☎ 312-37-34; cnr Ocampo & Prieto) or **Teatro Morelos** (☎ 314-62-02; cnr Camelinas & Ventura Puente), part of the Centro de Convenciones complex 1.5km south of center.

For live music, the longstanding **Peña Colibrí** (☎ 312-22-61; Galeana 36; admission US$2.75-4.50; ⏱ 6pm-12:30am Mon-Fri, to 1am Sat) offers a dark, comfortable atmosphere in which to enjoy various styles of Latin music including trova, samba, rumbaflamenca and Cuban. Snacks, dinner and drinks are available.

El León de Mecenas (☎ 314-74-18; Abasolo 325; admission US$2.25-10; ⏱ 6pm-2am Mon-Sat) gives

WESTERN CENTRAL HIGHLANDS

you blues, jazz, trova, flamenco or even Mexican folk music. It has a good rustic ambience and also serves refreshments.

Getting There & Around

AIR

The **Francisco J Múgica Sirport** (☎ 317-14-11) is 27km north of Morelia, on the Morelia-Zinapécuaro highway. Plenty of flights are available to cities in Mexico, and limited flights serve cities elsewhere in North America.

Airlines servicing Morelia include the following:

Aeromar (☎ 324-67-77; Hotel Fiesta Inn, Pirindas 435)
Aeroméxico (☎ 324-27-75; Av Camelinas 5030-18 local C, Plaza Morelia)
AeroCuahonte (☎ 315-39-69; at the airport)
Mexicana (☎ 324-38-08; Hotel Fiesta Inn, Pirindas 435)

Taxis to the airport cost US$15; there are no public buses.

BUS & COMBI

Morelia's bus terminal is about 4km northwest of center, near the football stadium. It's separated into three *módulos* (smaller terminals) which correspond to 1st-, 2nd- and 3rd-class buses. To get here, take a Ruta Cafe 2 (brown) combi going west on Corregidora. Taxis from the center cost US$2.75. Destinations include the following:

Guadalajara (ETN, US$25, 3½-5hr, 8 daily)
Guanajuato (Servicios Coordinados, US$10, 4hr, 2 daily)
Lázaro Cárdenas (Parhikuni, US$26-34, 7hr, 14 daily)
León (Primera Plus, US$12, 3½-4hr, 15 daily; Flecha Amarilla, US$10.50, 3½-4hr, 20 daily)
Mexico City (Primera Plus, US$20, 4¾hr, hourly) To Terminal Norte.
Mexico City (ETN, US$24, 4hr, 27 daily; Autovías, US$20, 4hr, 24 daily) To Terminal Poniente.
Pátzcuaro (Parhikuni, US$3.25, 1¼hr, 3 daily; Flecha Amarilla, US$2.50, 1¼hr, half-hourly until 6pm; Purhépecha, US$2.50, 1¼hr, every 15min until 9pm)
Querétaro (ETN, US$14, 3-4hr, 1 daily; Primera Plus, US$11, 3-4hr, 15 daily; Servicios Coordinados, US$10, 3-4hr, 8 daily)
Uruapan (ETN, US$14, 1½-2hr, 2 daily; Parhikuni, US$8, 35 daily; Primera Plus, US$8, 1½-2hr, 6 daily; Flecha Amarilla, US$6, 1½-2hr, half-hourly until 6pm)
Zamora (Primera Plus, US$10, 2½hr, 4 daily)
Zitácuaro (Autovías, US$8, 3hr, 7 daily)

Around town, small combis and buses operate from 6am until 10pm daily (US$0.35).

Combi routes are designated by the color of their stripe: Ruta Roja (red), Ruta Amarilla (yellow), Ruta Guinda (pink), Ruta Azul (blue), Ruta Verde (green), Ruta Cafe (brown) and so on. Ask the tourist office for help with bus and combi routes.

TAXI

Taxis are plentiful in the city center; the average ride costs about US$2, or a little more to outer areas like the Centro de Convenciones.

CAR & MOTORCYCLE

To rent a car, call **Hertz** (☎ 313-53-28), **Budget** (☎ 314-70-07) or **Alamo** (☎ 324-29-22). Discuss the price, and expect to pay over US$60 per day.

SANTUARIO MARIPOSA MONARCA

In the easternmost part of Michoacán, straddling the border of México state, lies this 160-sq-km **Monarch Butterfly Reserve** (admission US$2; ☼ 9am-6pm mid-Nov–Mar). Every autumn, from late October to early November, millions of monarch butterflies arrive in these forested Mexican highlands for their winter hibernation. They'll have flown from the Great Lakes region of the US and Canada, over 4000km. At night and in the early morning the butterflies cluster together, covering whole fir trees and weighing down the branches. As the day warms up, they begin to flutter around like gold and orange snowflakes, descending to the humid forest floor for the hottest part of the day. By midafternoon they might cover the ground completely, like a brilliant living carpet.

Later on in the warm spring temperatures of March, the butterflies reach their sexual maturity and mate – abdomen to abdomen, with the males flying around carrying the females underneath. The exhausted males die shortly afterward, and the pregnant females fly north to Texas, Florida and other sites in the southeastern US. There they lay their eggs in milkweed bushes, then die themselves. The eggs hatch into caterpillars that feed on the milkweed, then make cocoons and emerge in late May as a new generation of monarch butterflies. These young monarchs flutter to the Great Lakes region, where they themselves breed, so that by mid-August yet another generation is ready to start the long trip south to central Mexico. It takes from three to five generations of butterflies to complete the entire roundtrip journey between Canada and Mexico.

In January 2002 an unusually severe storm struck central Mexico, dumping more than 100mm of rain on the butterfly sanctuaries, followed by freezing temperatures. A vast number of butterflies perished in the fatal combination of wet and cold conditions, especially in areas where illegal logging had depleted forest cover. The death toll was estimated at over 250 million insects, possibly even up to a half-million. Survival of the migratory monarch looked grim, but to everyone's surprise 200 to 500 million butterflies returned to make 2003 a banner year.

The Santuario Mariposa Monarca is ecologically significant enough to have been decreed a Reserva de la Biosfera, giving it protected status – at least in theory. Illegal logging in up to 60% of reserve lands has severely damaged the butterflies' habitats. It's difficult to change traditions, as local farmers cut down the precious wood, plant corn and allow their livestock into butterfly territory. Some organizations are trying to change these patterns, offering local communities incentives to protect their forests. For more information (and a chance to help) check out www.michoacanmonarchs .org and www.wwf.org.mx/monarch_con servation.php.

Visiting the Reserve

The reserve allows visitors from around mid-November through March, but exact opening dates vary year to year depending on weather, temperatures and the butterflies' migration patterns. At the beginning or end of the season it's best to ask for information at the Morelia or Mexico City tourist office before heading all the way out here.

Two of the reserve's five sanctuaries are open to visitors. The Sierra Chincua sanctuary is about a half-hour's drive north of Angangueo, while the much more popular El Campanario (or El Rosario) sanctuary lies above the small village of El Rosario and about a 45-minutes drive from Angangueo.

Angangueo (see p551) is relatively close to both sanctuaries and the most popular base for visits to the reserve. However, it's also possible to do a day trip from Morelia. The easiest and most expensive way is with

an organized tour (see p547). To get there by yourself, you'll need a very early start. First take a bus to Zitácuaro (US$8, from Morelia three hours, seven daily) and then another to Angangueo (US$1.25, 1¼ hours, every 15 minutes).

Here, at the village's *auditorio* (auditorium) or outside hotels, you can hire a *camioneta* (truck; US$33 for up to 10 to 12 people with two hours' waiting time) which takes 45 bumpy minutes to reach the El Campanario sanctuary entrance. You'll have a steep uphill walk of about 3km to 4km to where the butterflies will be.

In January and February you won't have to walk as far (maybe 30 minutes) because more butterflies are around. In November and December fewer butterflies have arrived, so your walk may take up to an hour. Try to get back to Angangueo before 6pm for the return to Morelia.

Reaching the El Campanario sanctuary from Angangueo is also possible by cheaper local bus, but you'll have to spend the night in Angangueo. Take the 8:30am bus from Angangueo to the village of El Rosario (US$1.50, one hour; there are also buses at 2pm and 7pm). Ask to get off at the *crucero*, or intersection, where you'll walk 20 minutes to the reserve entrance, then 3km to 4km to the butterflies, depending on the season. Return buses to Angangueo pass by the crucero around 8am, noon and 5pm. Miss them and you'll be walking 1½ hours back down to the main road, where you can catch frequent buses to Angangueo.

Trucks aren't as keen to take folks to the less-visited Sierra Chincua sanctuary, and there's no local bus here. It's a long walk from the entrance to the butterfly colonies, which can be difficult to find.

Angangueo

☎ 715 / pop 5000 / elevation 2980m

Angangueo is an old mining town that still extracts some lead and silver from the rugged hillsides. It's spread out along a single main street (variously called Nacional and Morelos) with the Plaza de la Constitución and two churches at the uphill end. The town is enjoyable to stroll around, and a miner monument offers good views.

A **tourist office** (☎ 156-00-01; ◷ 10am-8pm Sep-Apr) is just downhill from the plaza. Its hours are shorter during slower times.

The cheapest hotel in Angangueo is **Casa de Huéspedes Juárez** (☎ 156-00-23; Nacional 15; s/d from US$11.50, tw US$23), which has clean and basic rooms fringing a pleasant, flowery garden.

Across the street is **El Paso de la Monarca** (☎ 156-01-87; Nacional 20; s/d US$12.50/19), a bit more claustrophobic but with still acceptable budget rooms, some with views.

Require more comfort? Try **Albergue Don Bruno** (☎ 156-00-26, 55-5512-4918 in Mexico City; www.donbruno.web1000.com; Morelos 92; s/d from US$62/76). It's a beautiful place with good colorful and modest rooms (some with fireplace), and prices here fall 50% during non-butterfly season.

Restaurants in town include **Los Geranios** (mains US$10-20; ⏲ 7am-10pm), at the Albergue Don Bruno and boasting mountain views, and **Los Arcos** (Plaza de la Constitución 5A; mains under US$5), an economical and friendly eatery near the plaza.

To get to Angangueo from Morelia, the fastest way is to first take a bus to Zitácuaro (US$8, three hours, seven daily) and then another to Angangueo (US$1.25, 1¼ hours, every 15 minutes).

To get to Angangueo from Mexico City's Terminal Poniente, take Autobuses México-Toluca-Zinacantepec's 2nd-class bus (US$9, 3½ hours, five daily). They also have buses to Zitácuaro (US$8, three hours, 21 daily), from where there are frequent local buses heading to Angangueo. Other companies with buses servicing Zitácuaro include 2nd-class Autobuses de Occidente (US$8, half-hourly) and 1st-class Autovías (US$9, half-hourly).

PÁTZCUARO

☎ 434 / pop 49,000 / elevation 2175m

Lovely Pátzcuaro, nestled in the heart of Purépecha country, is the crown jewel of highland Michoacán. The town's colonial center is filled with serene plazas, impressive churches, pretty cobbled streets and tiled adobe buildings painted white and reddish-brown. It's a beautiful place in which to explore or relax for a few days.

Central Pátzcuaro focuses on the fine Plaza Vasco de Quiroga (popularly known as Plaza Grande) and the smaller but busier Plaza Gertrudis Bocanegra (popularly known as Plaza Chica) one block further north, with the town market on its west side. The city center is fairly flat, but some streets climb steeply to the basilica just east of the plazas. It's a very walkable city, and most points of interest are easily reached on foot.

Just 3km to the north lies scenic Lago de Pátzcuaro, ringed by traditional Purépecha villages and dotted with a few islands. One of these islands – Isla Janitzio – is Mexico's biggest magnet during early November's Día de Muertos. At this time Mexicans from all over the country descend here in hordes, though plenty of tourists also come for Christmas, New Year's and Semana Santa. Make advance reservations and bring warm clothes in winter – you're in the high country here.

History

Pátzcuaro was the capital of the Tarasco people from about AD 1325 to 1400. Then, after the death of King Tariácuri, the Tarascan state became a three-part league comprising Pátzcuaro, Tzintzuntzan and Ihuatzio. The league repulsed Aztec attacks, but was friendly to the Spanish, who first came to the area in 1522. However, the Spanish then returned in 1529 under Nuño de Guzmán, a conquistador of legendary cruelty.

Guzmán's inhumanity to the indigenous people was so severe that the Catholic Church and the colonial government sent Bishop Vasco de Quiroga, a respected judge and cleric from Mexico City, to clean up the mess Guzmán left. Quiroga, who arrived in 1536, established a bishopric (based initially at Tzintzuntzan, then, from 1540, at Pátzcuaro) and pioneered village cooperatives based on the humanitarian ideas of Sir Thomas More's Utopia.

To avoid dependence on Spanish mining lords and landowners, Quiroga successfully encouraged education and agricultural self-sufficiency in the villages around Lago de Pátzcuaro, with all villagers contributing equally to the community. He also helped each village develop its own craft specialty. The utopian communities declined after his death in 1565, but the crafts traditions continue to this day. Not surprisingly, Tata Vascu, as the Tarascos called Quiroga, is highly venerated for his accomplishments. You'll notice that streets, plazas, restaurants and hotels all over Michoacán are named after him.

Orientation

Central Pátzcuaro focuses on Plaza Vasco de Quiroga (better known as Plaza Grande) and Plaza Gertrudis Bocanegra (better known as Plaza Chica).

Ahumada heads north out of town toward the old Morelia-Uruapan highway, 2km away. Lago de Pátzcuaro is another half kilometer further north from the highway.

The bus terminal lies on a ring road on the southwest side of town, about 2km from the city center.

Information

Several banks in the center will change your money; all have ATMs.

Cambio Numismática del Lago (Iturbe 30; 9:30am-7pm Mon-Fri, 9:30am-2:30pm Sat & Sun) Has slightly lower rates, but you won't have to wait in line.

Consultorio Médicos del Centro (342-45-33; Navarrete 44-A)

Icser (Portal Morelos 64) Around the corner from Meganet; charges the same but has slower waves (connections).

Lavandería San Francisco (Terán 16; 3kg US$3.75; 9am-9pm Mon-Sat) Spin your threads here.

Meganet (Mendoza 8; per hr US$1.25) Surf the Internet without getting too wet.

Municipal tourist office (342-02-15; Portal Hidalgo 1; 9am-3pm & 4-7pm Mon-Sat, 9am-3pm Sun) On the west side of Plaza Grande.

Post office (Obregón 13; 9am-3pm Mon-Fri, 9am-1pm Sat) Send love letters from here.

PÁTZCUARO

INFORMATION	
Banco Bital/HSBC	1 C3
Bancomer	2 C3
Cambio Numismática del Lago	3 C3
Consultorio Médicos del Centro	4 B4
Icser	5 C3
Lavandería San Francisco	6 B4
Meganet	7 B3
Municipal Tourist Office	8 B4
Post Office	9 C2
State Tourist Office	10 C3

SIGHTS & ACTIVITIES	(pp554–5)
Basílica de Nuestra Señora de la Salud	11 D3
Biblioteca Gertrudis Bocanegra	12 C3
Casa de los Once Patios	13 C4
Ex-Colegio Jesuita	14 C4
Museo de Artes Populares	15 C4
Teatro Emperador Caltzontzin	16 C3
Templo de la Compañía	17 C4
Templo del Sagrario	18 C4
Templo El Santuario	19 B3
Templo San Francisco	20 B4
Templo San Juan de Dios	21 B4

SLEEPING	(pp556–7)
Casa Brunson B&B	22 C4
Gran Hotel	23 C3
Hostal del Valle	24 D3
Hotel de la Concordia	25 C3
Hotel Fiesta Plaza	26 C3

Hotel Los Escudos	27 B4
Hotel Mansión Iturbe	28 C3
Hotel Mesón del Gallo	29 C4
Hotel Misión San Manuel	30 B4
Hotel Posada de la Salud	31 D3
Hotel San Agustín	32 C3
Hotel San Gabriel	33 B4
Hotel Valmen	34 C4
La Casa Encantada	35 C4
Mesón de San Antonio	36 D3
Posada de la Basílica	37 C3
Posada de los Ángeles	38 C2
Posada Mandala	39 C3

EATING	(pp557–8)
Casa de las Once Pizzas	40 C4
El Patio	41 C4
El Primer Piso	42 C4
Food Stalls	43 C3
La Puerta Roja	44 C3

Mandala	(see 39)
Merza Pack	45 C3
Priscilla's	46 B3
Restaurant Doña Paca	47 C3
Restaurante Don Rafa	48 C3

DRINKING	(p558)
Campanario Bar	(see 30)
El Sotano	49 D3
El Viejo Gaucho	50 C3

SHOPPING	(p558)
Mercado de Artesanías	51 C3

TRANSPORT	(p559)
Buses to Bus Terminal	52 C3
Buses to Lake	53 C3

OTHER	
CELEP Language School	54 B4

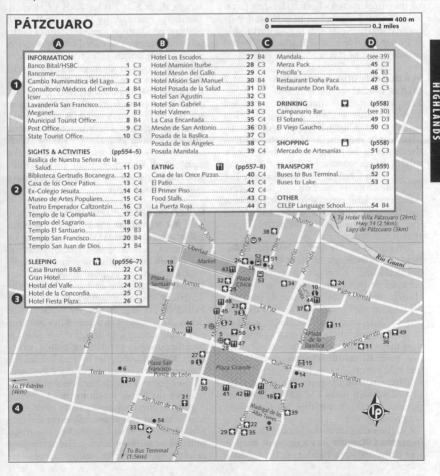

State tourist office (☎ 342-12-14; Calle Buena Vista 7; ☉ 9am-2pm & 4-7pm Mon-Sat, 9am-2pm Sun) Sits just downhill of the basilica.

Sights

PLAZA VASCO DE QUIROGA (PLAZA GRANDE)

Pátzcuaro's wide and well-proportioned main plaza is one of the loveliest in Mexico. A tall statue of Vasco de Quiroga gazes benignly down from the central fountain. The plaza is ringed by trees and flanked by portales that form part of the facades of 17th-century buildings. Originally grand mansions, these buildings are now mostly used as hotels, restaurants and shops. The sides of the plaza are named (independently of the street names) Portal Hidalgo (west side), Portal Aldama (south side) and Portal Matamoros (east side). The north side is Portal Allende east of Iturbe and Portal Morelos west of Iturbe.

PLAZA GERTRUDIS BOCANEGRA (PLAZA CHICA)

Pátzcuaro's second main plaza is named after a local heroine who was shot by firing squad in 1818 for her support of the independence movement. Her statue adorns the center of the plaza, and she looks like a mighty tough woman.

The town's **market** bustles away on the west side of the plaza. You can find everything from fruit, vegetables and fresh lake fish to herbal medicines, crafts, and clothing, including the region's distinctive striped shawls and sarapes.

On the north side of the plaza, the **Biblioteca Gertrudis Bocanegra** (☎ 342-54-41; admission free; cnr Lloreda & Títere; ☉ 9am-7pm Mon-Fri, 10am-1pm Sat) occupies the 16th-century former San Agustín church. A large, colorful Juan O'Gorman mural covering the rear wall depicts the history of Michoacán from pre-Hispanic times to the 1910 revolution. The library's opening days may vary throughout the year.

A small **Mercado de Artesanías** operates on the side street next to the library. Crafts sold here include grotesque Tócuaro masks, carved wooden forks and knives from Zirahuén. Quality is variable but the prices are good.

On the west side of the library, the **Teatro Emperador Caltzontzin** was a convent until it was converted to a theater in 1936. Movies and occasional cultural events are presented here.

BASÍLICA DE NUESTRA SEÑORA DE LA SALUD

Two blocks east of Plaza Chica is this impressive church, built atop a pre-Hispanic ceremonial site. Vasco de Quiroga originally intended it to be the centerpiece of his Michoacán community. The building you see today wasn't completed until the 19th century and is only the central nave of the original design. Quiroga's tomb, the Mausoleo de Don Vasco, is just to the left inside the main west doors.

Behind the altar at the east end stands a much revered figure of the Virgin, Nuestra Señora de la Salud (Our Lady of Health). The image was made by Tarascos in the 16th century, on Quiroga's request, from a corn-cob-and-honey paste called *tatzingue*. Soon after, people began to experience miraculous healings, and Quiroga had the words 'Salus Infirmorum' (Healer of the Sick) inscribed at the figure's feet. Ever since, pilgrims have come from all over Mexico to ask this Virgin for a miracle. Many make their way on their knees across the plaza, into the church and along its nave. Walk up the stairs behind the image to see the many small tin representations of hands, feet, legs and so on that pilgrims have offered to the Virgin.

MUSEO DE ARTES POPULARES

This **folk art museum** (☎ 342-10-29; cnr Enseñanza & Alcantarillas; admission US$3.50; ☉ 9am-7pm Tue-Sat, 9am-3pm Sun) is housed in a spacious old colonial building. On this site in 1540, Quiroga founded the original Colegio de San Nicolás, arguably the first university in the Americas. The institution was later moved to Valladolid (as Morelia was then called), and much of the present structure dates from the early 18th century. In fact, the whole lot is superimposed on pre-Hispanic stone structures, some of which can be seen behind the museum courtyards. Look also for the tasteful use of cows' knuckle bones as decorations between the flagstones on the floor.

Among the rotating exhibits of Michoacán arts and crafts you might see delicate white lace shawls, striking feather 'paintings' or hand-beaten copperware. The permanent displays (none well lit, sadly) include one

WESTERN CENTRAL HIGHLANDS

of the best collections of lacquerware in the country, and a room set up as a typical Michoacán kitchen, with a tremendous brick oven and a full set of ceramic and copper utensils.

TEMPLO DE LA COMPAÑÍA & OTHER CHURCHES

Built in the 16th century, the **Templo de la Compañía** (cnr Lerín & Alcantarillas) and the adjacent plain white building became a Jesuit training college in the 17th century. The church is still in use and houses some relics from Vasco de Quiroga. The college building fell into ruin after the expulsion of the Jesuits. Restored in the early 1990s, it is now used for cultural and community activities.

Pátzcuaro has several other old churches of interest, including del Sagrario, San Juan de Dios, San Francisco and El Santuario.

CASA DE LOS ONCE PATIOS

This 'House of the 11 Courtyards' is a fine rambling edifice built as a Dominican convent in the 1740s. (Before that, the site held one of Mexico's first hospitals, founded by Vasco de Quiroga.) Today the house is a warren of small artesanías shops, each specializing in a particular regional craft. Look for copperware from Santa Clara del Cobre, straw goods from Tzintzuntzan and musical instruments from Paracho, as well as gold-leaf-decorated lacquerware, hand-painted ceramics and attractive textiles.

In some shops you can see the artisans at work. Most shops are open from 10am to 7pm daily, with a lunch break in the afternoon.

EL ESTRIBO

El Estribo, a lookout point on a hill 4km west of the town center, offers a magnificent view of the entire Lago de Pátzcuaro area. It takes up to an hour to get there on foot but only a few minutes in a vehicle. Either way, you take Ponce de León from the southwest corner of Plaza Grande and follow the signs. It's best to do this on a Saturday or Sunday, when lots of people are walking the trails – this can be an isolated spot.

Courses

Centro de Lenguas y Ecoturismo de Pátzcuaro (CELEP; ☎ 342-47-64; www.celep.com.mx; Navarrete 50) Two-week language course US$278; language and culture programs US$433. CELEP offers courses in two-week blocks (though one- and three-week programs are also available). Courses involve four hours of classes Monday to Friday, and the cultural programs include activities Monday, Wednesday and Friday. Accommodation and meals with local families can be arranged for US$20 per day.

Tours

Several tour guides operate around the Pátzcuaro area. Here are just a couple.

Miguel Ángel Núñez (☎ 344-01-08; casadetierra@ hotmail.com) Based in Erongarícuaro on the west side of the lake, Miguel Ángel offers tours of Pátzcuaro, the lakeside villages and other destinations in Michoacán. He'll even take visitors to Guanajuato, Mexico City or the coast. In his tours, Miguel Ángel emphasizes native culture, archaeology, colonial history, art and architecture, and rural tourism. He speaks English and some German, and provides transport. Tour prices depend on the destination, but local tours are US$19 per person.

Rafaela Luft (☎ 342-19-47; ☎ cellular 01-44-33-00-52-42; rluft@ml.com.mx) Rafaela Luft, an art restorer, does three-hour walking tours of Pátzcuaro for US$10 per person (one to five people). For a group larger than five, the cost drops to US$8 per person. Shorter Pátzcuaro walks are also available. Rafaela's other tour destinations in the region include Tzintzuntzan, Tupátaro (with its amazingly painted church), Morelia, Oponguio (a *mezcal*-producing village) and Tingambato (pre-Hispanic ruins).

Festivals & Events

Pátzcuaro and especially Isla Janitzio are at the heart of Mexico's Day of the Dead celebrations (see When the Dead Return p58, and The Purépecha & Day of the Dead p556). It's an exciting, festive and at times stressful time to be here, with car-clogged streets, drunken revelers and basically just too many people everywhere. To avoid crowds, check out the local festivities at some of the smaller villages around the lake (though the nice cemetery at Tzintzuntzan is also a popular tourist magnet). To *really* avoid the cemetery crowds, go after 3am. Isla Janitzio is insanely crowded all night long, however.

Other interesting events in Pátzcuaro include:

Pastorelas These dramatizations of the journey of the shepherds to see the infant Jesus are staged in Plaza Grande on several evenings around Christmas. *Pastorelas indígenas*, on the same theme but including mask dances, enact the struggle of angels against the devils that are trying to hinder the shepherds. These *pastorelas* are held in eight villages around Lago de Pátzcuaro on different days between December 26 and February 2. Rodeos and other events accompany them.

Semana Santa Easter week is full of events in Pátzcuaro and the lakeside villages: Palm Sunday processions in several places; Viacrucis processions on Good Friday morning, enacting Christ's journey to Calvary and the crucifixion itself; candlelit processions in silence on Good Friday evening; and, on Easter Sunday evening, a ceremonial burning of Judas in Plaza Grande. There are many local variations.

Nuestra Señora de la Salud On December 8, a colorful procession to the basilica honors the Virgin of Health. Traditional dances are performed, including Los Reboceros, Los Moros, Los Viejitos and Los Panaderos.

Sleeping

During holidays and festivals, especially Día de Muertos, secure reservations way in advance and expect most hotel prices to skyrocket 25% to 100% or more.

BUDGET

Hotel Valmen (☎ 342-11-61; Padre Lloreda 34; s/d US$10/17) One of the best budget deals in town, the friendly Valmen offers simple, clean and unpretentious rooms with nicely tiled halls. Rooms vary, so peek until you find one that fits. Rates remain the same during holidays.

Hotel Posada de la Salud (☎ 342-00-58; posada delasalud@hotmail.com; Serrato 9; s/d US$19/24) Well-kept and a great deal, this sparkling place has 15 small but clean courtyard rooms.

Posada de los Ángeles (☎ 342-24-40; Títere 16; s/d/tw US$21/24/33) This is a good find, with very nice rooms next to a pleasant and flowery patio out back. Rates are higher on weekends, however.

Hotel Posada de la Rosa (☎ 342-08-11; Portal Juárez 29; s/d US$24/29, with shared bathroom US$13/14) Homely rooms are cheap, decent and set around a plain upstairs patio. The location's great, however.

Hotel Mesón del Gallo (☎ 342-14-74; www.mex online.com/mesondelgallo.htm; Dr Coss 20; s/d US$18/29; **P**) 'Suites' cost the same as regular rooms at this OK hotel, though they aren't terribly special. Still, it's decent value, though rates rise to US$27/45 for high seasons.

THE PURÉPECHA & DAY OF THE DEAD

About 125,000 Purépecha people inhabit the region extending from Lago de Pázcuaro to west of Uruapan. You may notice them especially in Pátzcuaro itself and in the almost pure indigenous villages fringing the lake.

The Purépecha are direct descendants of the Tarascos (or Tarascans), who emerged around Lago de Pátzcuaro in about the 14th century and established Tzintzuntzan as the center of their empire. The Tarascos developed western Mexico's most advanced pre-Hispanic civilization while continually repelling Aztec domination. They might have originated from the more northerly, nomadic Chichimecs, but neither the modern Purépecha language nor the old Tarasco language has any established links to any other tongue (though connections with languages such as Zuni, from the US Southwest, and Quechua, from Peru, have been suggested).

The old Tarascos were noted potters, metalsmiths and weavers, and many Purépecha villages still specialize in these crafts – a legacy of Vasco de Quiroga, the bishop who salvaged these people from the brutalization of the Nuño de Guzmán. (In fact, today some Purépecha consider the term 'Tarasco' pejorative, since the Spanish called them that). The modern Purépecha also maintain some of the country's most vital and ancient religious traditions: Día de Muertos (Day of the Dead) observances around Lago de Pátzcuaro are particularly famous.

Best known of these – and attracting an overwhelming number of sightseers – are the events at Isla Janitzio, culminating in a parade of decorated canoes late in the evening on November 1. Many events, including parades, crafts markets, dancing, ceremonies, exhibitions and concerts, are held in Pátzcuaro and nearby villages on the days before and after Día de Muertos. In Jará-cuaro, dance groups and musicians stage a traditional contest of their skills in the village square on the evening of November 1. If you're going to be around during this time, make reservations way in advance and be prepared for a cultural treat.

For the camping option, see Hotel Villa Pátzcuaro.

MID-RANGE

Mesón de San Antonio (☎ 342-25-01; alfredriom01@prodigy.net.mx; Serrato 33; s/d/tw US$29/38/38) Simple but tastefully decorated rooms surround the quaint old courtyard at this friendly place. Some rooms are cavernous, and come with fireplace. Beds are good, ceilings are high and it's fairly quiet.

Posada Mandala (☎ 342-41-76; matiasag@hotmail.com; Lerín 14; r US$24-33) Four attractive and comfortable rooms greet you here, along with an excellent vegetarian restaurant that's open only during high season. Two downstairs rooms share a bathroom and are cheaper, but the two upstairs rooms (one composed of two separated spaces) have a nice balcony and views.

Hotel Los Escudos (☎ 342-01-38; hescudos@ml.com.mx; Portal Hidalgo 73; s or d US$45, tw US$67; P) This well-kept and historical hotel offers 30 gorgeous rooms with pretty tiled baths; two surrounding flowery courtyards provide peace. Some of the larger rooms have lofts and fireplaces, and the location's great.

Hotel Misión San Manuel (☎ 342-13-13; Portal Aldama 12; s or d US$48, tw US$67) A wonderful old-world feel permeates this former monastery, which now offers 42 nice old high-ceilinged rooms, some with fireplace and partial carpeting. There's a cute patio in the back.

Hostal del Valle (☎ 342-05-12; www.hostaldelvalle.com; Lloreda 27; s/d US$32/41; P) Descend to the unusual but attractive lobby area – it feels like a huge living room – and check out the nicely decorated rooms, as some are nicer than others (number 9 is especially great). Prices are 20% higher on weekends, and astronomical during the holidays.

Hotel Fiesta Plaza (☎ 342-52-80; www.hotelfiestaplaza.com; Plaza Chica 24; r US$62; P) Beautiful colonial courtyards and plenty of sitting areas surround the 60 good rooms with cushy beds, good lighting and pleasant bathrooms.

Posada de la Basílica (☎ 342-11-08; www.mexonline.com/posadabasilica.htm; Arciga 6; r US$49-78; P) Opposite the basilica, this colonial hotel offers beautiful large rooms (king-size beds available) around an attractive courtyard overlooking the town's red-tile roofs. Most rooms have fireplaces, and some come with balcony and a view. The restaurant here is good.

Hotel Villa Pátzcuaro (☎ 342-07-67; www.villapátzcuaro.com; Av Lázaro Cárdenas 506; tent sites per person US$6, trailer sites up to US$14, r US$33-41; ☒) Two kilometers north of the center is this friendly and pleasant hotel with grassy camping grounds. Great rooms have TV and fireplace. Any bus to the lake will drop you here.

Hotel de la Concordia (☎ 342-00-03; Portal Juárez 31; s/d/tw US$24/40/43; P) Well-priced for its location, this atmospheric hotel has pleasant high-ceilinged rooms with TV. The 2nd-floor restaurant faces Plaza Chica.

Hotel San Gabriel (☎ 342-50-70; Navarrete 57; s or d US$29, tw US$48, P) If you're not looking for quaint colonial surroundings, consider this: 20 spacious and modern rooms with cable TV come with soft beds and are good value.

Gran Hotel (☎ 342-04-43; www.mexonline.com/granhotel.htm; Plaza Chica 6; s/d US$33; P) The small but serviceable rooms here come with cable TV and are good, clean and well-located. If you're lucky you'll encounter the friendly receptionist.

TOP END

Casa Brunson B&B (☎ 342-39-03; www.mexonline.com/casabrunson.htm; Dr Coss 13; r US$95-130) Just three decadent rooms, including an elegant suite with huge bathtub, surround the beautiful and well-tended gardens at this B&B. A full breakfast is served on the patio. Reservations are required, and there is also a two-night minimum stay. No kids under 16.

La Casa Encantada (☎ 342-34-92; www.lacasaencantada.com; Dr Coss 15; r US$75-155) This pleasant, US-run B&B offers three modest rooms and one spacious apartment, along with a comfortable living room and covered outdoor kitchen. Breakfast is self-service continental, and two small dogs and a parrot roam the leafy patios. Reservations are a good idea.

Hotel Mansión Iturbe (☎ 342-03-68; www.mexonline.com/iturbe.htm; Portal Morelos 59; r US$89-110; P) This posh hotel exudes colonial elegance with its high ceilings, polished wood floors and antique furnishings. Modern amenities and charming patios add to your luxurious experience, as does a fabulous library upstairs. The 14 rooms vary, so ask to see a couple. Prices include breakfast, welcome cocktail and free use of bicycles.

Eating

One Pátzcuaro specialty is the small *pescado blanco* ('white fish'), traditionally caught on Lago de Pátzcuaro using 'butterfly' nets. The taste is nothing special, though, and these days *pescado blanco* is as likely to come from a fish farm (most of Pátzcuaro's wastewater pours untreated into the lake). Another specialty, *sopa Tarasca*, is a rich tomato-based soup with cream, dried chili and bits of crisp tortilla. You can also nibble *corundas* – tamales with a little pork, bean and cream filling.

El Patio (☎ 342-04-84; Plaza Grande 19; mains US$6-8) Thoughtful presentation, tasty food, good service and pleasant décor makes this place a winner. Try the *chuleta de puerco adobada* (marinated pork chop) or delicious *sopa Tarasca*. Occasionally there's live traditional music.

La Puerta Roja (☎ 342-58-59; Buena Vista 9; mains US$7-10; ☽ 1-10pm Tue-Sun) When you tire of Mexican fare, try this great new Spanish restaurant. Tasty tapas are US$3.50 per dish, or taste the rabbit or seafood offerings. There's paella on weekends.

Priscilla's (☎ 342-57-08; Ibarra 15; mains US$7-14; ☽ 1:30-10:30pm) Located at the posh La Casa de Los Sueños, this fancy place serves up a variety of international dishes such as lasagna al prosciutto, fish-filled nopals and cheese fondue. It comes with an excellent reputation.

Restaurant Doña Paca (☎ 342-03-68; Portal Morelos 59; mains US$6-10; ☽ 8:30am-noon & 1:30-9pm Mon-Sat, to 6pm Sun) Inside the Hotel Mansión Iturbe, the upscale but darkish Doña Paca is one of Pátzcuaro's best hotel restaurants. There's also a café with tables out on the sidewalk. Food and service are good, and it's open early for breakfast.

Mandala (☎ 342-41-76; Lerín 14; mains US$4; ☽ closed Tue) Homemade pastas and other vegetarian treats await at this pleasant eatery, though it's only open during high season months – December to January, April to May, July to August, and late October to early November.

El Primer Piso (☎ 342-01-22; Plaza Grande 29; mains US$8-10; ☽ 1:30-10pm Mon & Wed-Sat, 1:30-8pm Sun) This old standby specializes in *chiles en nogada* (chiles in a sweet creamy white sauce), though some claim standards have slipped. At least its 2nd-floor balcony offers a romantic setting.

Posada de la Basílica (☎ 342-11-08; Arciga 6; mains US$5-10) The view is fabulous and the food quite tasty at this upscale joint – but they tack on an automatic 10% service charge to your bill. Thick tablecloths and heavy ceramic plates are a nice touch.

Restaurante Don Rafa (☎ 342-03-68; Mendoza 30; mains US$3.75-8.50) A standard for regional food, this place might claim to have invented *sopa Tarasca* (perhaps only half right). The food and service are fine, but the spaces are almost too narrow.

Casa de las Once Pizzas (☎ 342-00-62; Plaza Grande 33; pizzas US$3-6; ☽ noon-10pm) Choose one of their combos, or make up your own. For pizza in Mexico it's not bad, and the medium pie feeds you and a pal. If you're lucky they'll offer you two kinds of Worcestershire sauce.

The market on Plaza Chica has a tasty choice of inexpensive food stalls serving everything from fruit juices to tacos to tortas to *caldo de res* (a rich beef stew). It's a penny-pincher's delight. For supermarket treats, check out **Merza Pack** (Mendoza 24; ☽ 7am-9:45pm).

Drinking

You don't have a whole lot of options when it comes to nightlife in Pátzcuaro. You can down a few at the airy sidewalk tables of **Campanario Bar** (Plaza Grande 14; ☽ 3-11pm), and there's also the loud, underground (literally) youth magnet **El Sótano** (Serrato 31; ☽ 5:30pm-2am Wed-Sun). For something more cultural, however, try the restaurant **El Viejo Gaucho** (☎ 342-03-68; Iturbe 10; admission US$2.25; ☽ 6-11pm Tue-Sat). Good folk music starts around 9pm at this small venue; they're sometimes closed Tuesday and Wednesday.

Shopping

The Casa de los Once Patios is a good place to seek Michoacán crafts, but you can also try the main market and the Mercado de Artesanías, both next to Plaza Chica. On Friday mornings a ceramics market, with pottery from different villages, is held in Plaza San Francisco.

Around the lake and in the Pátzcuaro area are several villages that make great destinations for avid shoppers. If you're serious about your task and want some help, ring **Kevin Quigley** (☎ 342-59-62; mananawood@ml.com.mx), a friendly American based in Ihuatzio.

He knows plenty about the area's crafts, and offers guided shopping trips for US$20 per person (including transport).

Getting There & Around

Pátzcuaro's bus terminal is about 1.5km southwest of the town center. It has a cafetería, telephones and a left-luggage service (open 7am to 9pm daily).

To catch a bus heading to the center, walk outside the terminal, turn right (going past the fenced lot) and at the corner take any bus marked 'Centro' (US$0.35). Taxis cost US$1.50 to US$1.75 (US$0.50 surcharge after 11pm).

Buses back to the terminal (marked 'Central') leave from the northeast corner of Plaza Chica. Buses to the boat pier (marked 'Lago') also leave from near here. These local buses run from about 6am to 10pm daily.

Destinations from Pátzcuaro include the following:

Erongarícuaro (US$0.75, 35min, every 15min 6am-8:30pm)
Guadalajara (US$14-18, 4½hr, three daily)
Lázaro Cárdenas (US$16, 7hr, hourly 6am-6.30pm)
Mexico City (to Terminal Poniente US$23, 5-5½hr, hourly; to Terminal Norte US$19-23, 5-5½hr, 4 daily)
Morelia (US$2.50-3.25, 1hr, every 15min 7am-9pm)
Quiroga (US$1, 35min, every 15min 5.30am-7pm)
Santa Clara del Cobre (US$0.50, 30min; every 15min 6am-8:30pm)
Tzintzuntzan (US$0.75, 20min, every 15min 5:30am-7:30pm)
Uruapan (US$2.50-3.25, 1hr, every 20min 5:45am-8:30pm)
Zirahuén (US$0.75, 50min, 5 daily)

AROUND PÁTZCUARO

Lago de Pátzcuaro

Just 3km from central Pátzcuaro, this serene body of water is punctuated with a few small islands. Streams feeding the lake, however, are being diverted at such an unsupportable rate that Lago de Pátzcuaro may cease to exist in 50 years. Pollution is also a serious problem, as raw sewage flows unfiltered into the water (though a new sewer system is currently being finished). Still, it's a pleasant destination and quite scenic as a whole.

To get to the *muelle* (dock), take a bus (marked 'Lago') from Pátzcuaro's Plaza Chica. The touristy dock is lined with cheap fish restaurants and souvenir shops. The ticket office is about 50m down, on the right side.

Isla Janitzio is heavily devoted to tourism, and on weekends and holidays becomes a popular Mexican destination. But it's still worth seeing, even when crowded, since folks are happy to be visiting and in doing so lend a festive air to the whole experience. During Día de Muertos, however, the island becomes *completely* overrun with people – to the point of dangerous overcrowding – and queues for boats can be crushingly hellish. Consider yourself warned.

The island's pathways are interesting to explore and eventually wind their way to the top, where a 40m-high **statue** (admission US$0.50) of independence hero José María Morelos y Pavón stands. It's so large that it's easily visible from the mainland. Inside the statue is a set of murals depicting Morelos' life. You can climb all the way up to his wrist for a panoramic view.

Other things to do here include eating at the many fish restaurants and checking out the many souvenir shops. The **Hotel Terhúnukua** (☎ 342-04-38; r US$14) has small, modest rooms (some with views) and is 50m straight up from the dock. There are no cars on the island.

Roundtrip boat rides to Janitzio are US$2.75 and take 25 minutes each way; they leave when full (about every 30 minutes; more frequent on weekends).

The small *frijole*-shaped **Isla Yunuén** is green, tranquil and has a strong Purépecha community. If you want to stay for the night, check out **Cabañas de Yuñuen** (☎ 434-342-44-73; www.yunuen.com; cabañas US$33-190). Nine romantic and very comfortable wood cabañas sleep from two to 16 people, and all come with TV and kitchenette.

Roundtrip boat rides to Yunuén are US$13 for one to four people; try to hook up with others if you're by yourself. They leave when full, so you may have to wait around a bit.

Lakeside Villages

There are some interesting day trips to the villages surrounding Lago de Pátzcuaro. All these villages can be reached by local transport from Pátzcuaro's bus terminal. To save some time you can take a 'Lago' bus from Plaza Chica, get off anywhere between the Posada de Don Vasco and highway 14, then wait by the roadside for a bus heading to your village. This is less pleasant and certain than waiting at the bus terminal, however. Buses to Ihuatzio run directly from Plaza Chica.

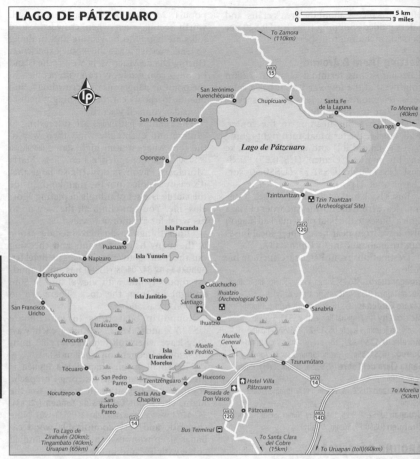

LAGO DE PÁTZCUARO

Buses (and *servicio mixto:* four-door pickups with benches in back) run between the villages, so you can visit several in one day. Transport between Quiroga and Erongarícuaro is infrequent, however, so traveling between the two may be quicker by returning to Pátzcuaro.

IHUATZIO

Lying 14km from Pátzcuaro, Ihuatzio was capital of the Tarascan league after Pátzcuaro (but before Tzintzuntzan). Today it's just a plain little village where everyone knows everyone else, until *you* walk into town.

The largish, partially restored **Ihuatzio archaeological site** (admission US$2.25; ☺ 10am-5pm)

lies 1.1km up the hill from the village's small plaza. Walking the cobbled road during the rainy season is delightful, particularly in September, when the riot of colorful flowers is at its brightest. The Tarascan ruins' main feature is an open ceremonial space 200m long with two pyramid-like structures at its west end. Climbing the pyramids is forbidden, but you can walk to the top of the restored wall to their left (south) side for views of the fields you came up through, the surrounding mountains and the distant Morelos statue on Isla Janitzio. Two carved stone coyotes were found at the site; one is in the National Archeological Museum in Mexico City, the other graces the belltower of Ihuatzio's church.

A good stay here is **Casa Santiago B&B** (☎ 434-342-59-62; www.geocities.com/theothermexico; s/d with shared bathroom US$40/60), 1.5km west of Ihuatzio just off the road to Cucuchucho. A vibrant US-Purépecha couple offer just a few simple and intimate rooms in their attractive housing compound, which is not for everyone – it's located way out in the country and services are limited (there's currently only one bath). If you want to experience the countryside and a small local village, however, it's a good choice.

TZINTZUNTZAN

The interesting little town of Tzintzuntzan ('tseen-TSOON-tsahn') is about 15km north of Pátzcuaro. You can visit impressive buildings from both the pre-Hispanic Tarasco empire and the early Spanish missionary period. Along the highway through town (Av Lázaro Cárdenas), craftspeople sell a variety of straw goods (a local specialty), ceramics and other Michoacán artesanías, including a fabulous selection of enormous stone carvings.

Tzintzuntzan is a Purépecha name meaning Place of Hummingbirds. It was the capital of the Tarascan league at the time of invasions by the Aztecs (who were repulsed) in the late 15th century and by the Spanish in the 1520s. The Purépecha chief came to peaceable terms with Cristóbal de Olid, leader of the first Spanish expedition in 1522. But this did not satisfy Nuño de Guzmán, who arrived in 1529 in his quest for gold and had the chief burned alive. This barbaric act is depicted on the O'Gorman mural in Pátzcuaro's Biblioteca Gertrudis Bocanegra.

Vasco de Quiroga established his first base here when he reached Michoacán in the mid-1530s, and Tzintzuntzan became the headquarters of the Franciscan monks who followed him. The town declined in importance after Quiroga shifted his base to Pátzcuaro in 1540.

On the west (lake) side of Av Cárdenas lies the **Ex-Convento de San Francisco**, a religious complex constructed partly with stones from the Tarascan site up the hill, which the Spanish demolished. Here Franciscan monks began the Spanish missionary effort in Michoacán in the 16th century. The olive trees in the churchyard are said to have been brought from Spain and planted by Vasco de Quiroga; they're believed to be the oldest olive trees in the Americas.

Straight ahead as you walk into the churchyard is the still-functioning **Templo de San Francisco**, built for the monks' own use. The old monastery's lovely cloister, to the left of the *templo*, was undergoing a total restoration at last pass, of both the structure and its decorative elements – including a set of faded murals around the galleries of both floors and Mudejar-patterned wooden ceiling ornamentation in each of the four ground-floor corners.

Toward the right rear corner of the complex stands the church built for the Purépechas, the **Templo de Nuestra Señora de la Salud**. This contains El Santo Entierro de Tzintzuntzan, a much-revered image of Christ. For most of the year he lies in a *caja de cristal* (glass coffin). When devout worshipers swore they saw his feet pushing against the end of the coffin, an extension was added to it. US banknotes sent by believers living abroad are attached to the extension, including a $2 bill and at least one 20. On Good Friday, following an elaborate, costumed passion play, the image is removed from its coffin and nailed to the large cross that usually leans against an inside wall of the church; being a Cristo de Goznes (hinged Christ), his arms can be extended and his legs crossed. After being taken down from the cross, the image is paraded through town until dark, when it is returned to the church. Penitents come from all over, some in chains or carrying crosses, some crawling on their knees. Thousands of candles are placed in the church for an all-night wake.

In the enclosed yard beside this church is an old open chapel (parts of it date to the 16th century), the **Capilla Abierta de la Concepción**, in whose foundation you can clearly see carved stones from the Tarascan site.

Head out the monastery's front gate, across the highway and up the hill. Turn left when you reach the upper paved road and walk to the entrance (700m in all) of the **Tzintzuntzan archeological site** (Las Yácatas; US$2.75; ☷ 10am-5pm), an impressive group of five round-based temples. Known as *yácatas* (thus the site's former official name), they sit on a large terrace of carefully fitted stone blocks. Some of the stones in their bases bear petroglyphs. You're not allowed to climb the *yácatas*, but the hillside location affords great views of the town, lake and surrounding mountains. The small **museum** at the site's entrance is worth a peek as well.

QUIROGA

Quiroga lies 7km northeast of Tzintzuntzan. In existence since pre-Hispanic times, the town is named after Vasco de Quiroga, who was responsible for many of its buildings and handicrafts. These days Quiroga has few original old buildings, but it's a great place to shop for *artesanías*. Every day seems like a huge market, with hundreds of shops selling brightly painted wooden products, leatherwork, wool sweaters, sarapes and much more.

On the first Sunday in July, the Fiesta de la Preciosa Sangre de Cristo (Festival of the Precious Blood of Christ) is celebrated with a long torchlight procession. The procession is led by a group carrying an image of Christ crafted from a paste made of corncobs and honey.

ERONGARÍCUARO

A pretty 18km trip from Pátzcuaro, Erongarícuaro (or 'Eronga') is one of the oldest settlements on the lake. It's a peaceful little town where you can enjoy strolling along streets still lined with old Spanish-style houses. French artist André Breton (1896–1966) lived here for a time in the 1950s, visited occasionally by Diego Rivera and Frida Kahlo. Breton made the unusual wrought-iron cross in the forecourt of the church. The fine old seminary attached to the church has some very nice gardens out back – look for the traditional Purépecha *troje* house.

Downhill from the plaza on Urueta Carrillo, **Muebles Finos Artesanales** (☎ 344-02-07; www.mfaeronga.com; ◷ tours 9am-6pm Mon-Fri) is run by a US couple and produces some amazingly beautiful and quirky hand-painted furniture. Custom orders are taken.

On January 6, the **Fiesta de los Reyes Magos** (Festival of the Magic Kings) is celebrated with music and dance.

TÓCUARO

Some of Mexico's finest mask makers live in this sleepy, one-bus-stop town 10km from Pátzcuaro. You wouldn't know it, though, as there are no traditional shopfronts. Behind closed doors, many families are involved in the craft, but only a handful produce the highest-quality masks.

To find Tócuaro's most famous mask maker, Juan Orta Castillo, walk up the street (Morelos) from the bus stop. After you pass Hidalgo, it's the first house on your left (look for the sign). He's open 9am to 9pm daily. Tócuaro's other highly regarded mask makers include Gustavo Orta, Felipe de Jesus Orta and Felipe Anciola. Ask around town and look for their signs.

One thing you won't find is a bargain – quality mask making is a recognized art, and a fine mask takes many hours to make. The best ones are wonderfully expressive, realistic and surrealistic, but they'll cost hundreds of dollars.

Santa Clara del Cobre
☎ 434 / pop 12,000 / elevation 2180m

Santa Clara del Cobre (also called Villa Escalante), about 15km south of Pátzcuaro, was a copper-mining center from 1553 onward. Though the mines are closed, this nice little town still specializes in copperware, with dozens of workshops crafting objects from the ore.

The small **Museo del Cobre** (☎ 343-02-54; Morelos 262; admission US$0.20; ◷ 10am-3pm & 5-7pm Tue-Sat, 10am-4pm Sun) exhibits an impressive collection of copper bowls and other containers, but lacks any display labels. If you're here in August, ask them about the two-week-long **Feria del Cobre** (Copper Fair), held each during this month; exact dates vary.

Buses from Pátzcuaro take 30 minutes and leave every 15 minutes from 6am to 8:30pm (US$0.50)

Lago de Zirahuén
☎ 353 / pop 2300 / elevation 2240m

Smaller than Lago de Pátzcuaro, but much deeper and cleaner, this pretty blue lake lies about 20km southwest of Pátzcuaro. Right on its shoreline is the colonial town of Zirahuén, a peaceful spot for a day trip or for camping. It's a popular weekend destination for Mexicans.

The *muelle general* (main dock), a block down from the main plaza, has some shack restaurants and cheap souvenir stalls. Boat excursions from here run on weekends only. Weekday excursions from other docks along the lake are possible, but don't come cheap.

You have several options for staying at this lake. Camping is free along the grassy lakeshore right before getting into town, or try the organized sites at grassy **Los Cedritos** (☎ 41-33; cabañas from US$34, tent sites per person US$5). Other choices include rickety **Cabañas Rústicas** (☎ 342 02-80 in Pátzcuaro; cabanas US$19-29), a 15-minute walk from town; fancy **Las Cabañas de Zirahuén** (☎ 353-40-41; cabañas from US$82); and good-value **Casa Familiar** (☎ 41-17; r from US$29), right across the street from Las Cabañas de Zirahuén. Prices rise on weekends and high seasons (which vary widely), so call ahead to confirm prices.

Five buses arrive daily from Pátzcuaro (US$0.75, 50 minutes).

URUAPAN

☎ 452 / pop 231,000 / elevation 1620m

When the Spanish monk Fray Juan de San Miguel arrived here in 1533, he was so impressed with the Río Cupatitzio and the lush vegetation surrounding it that he gave the area the Purépecha name Uruapan ('oo-roo-AH-pahn'), which means 'a time when a plant bears flowers and fruit simultaneously.' We tend to translate it as 'Eternal Spring.' Uruapan is 500m lower in altitude than Pátzcuaro and much more humid and warm.

Fray Juan had a large market square, hospital and chapel built, and he arranged streets in an orderly checkerboard pattern. Under Spanish rule, Uruapan quickly grew into a productive agricultural center, and today it's renowned for high-quality avocados (*aguacates*), coffee, fruit and chocolate. It bills itself as the 'Capital Mundial del Aguacate' (see Holy Guacamole! The Amazing Avocado, below) and has an avocado fair in November. The town's craftspeople are famed for their hand-painted cedar lacquerware, particularly trays and boxes.

Uruapan is a very traditional 'Mexican' city retaining some colonial ambience.

HOLY GUACAMOLE! THE AMAZING AVOCADO

Explore the regions surrounding Uruapan and you may realize that avocados are big business here. Mexico is the world's largest producer of the fruit, with the majority grown in Michoacán state – especially around Uruapan. It's estimated that the region produces over one billion kilos of avocados annually, with only about 5% – including the best fruit – being exported. That's still a lot of guacamole crossing borders.

Avocados were thought to have originated in Mexico, Central America and the Andes region. The word 'avocado' comes from the Spanish 'aguacate,' which came from 'ahuacatl,' the Náhuatl word for testicle. The rich and sensuous fruit do indeed hang languidly in pairs, resembling a part of the male anatomy. The Aztecs even considered the fruit to have a special aphrodisiac quality, and would ban young women from strolling outdoors when avocados were being harvested.

Today there are over 100 kinds of avocados. The Hass variety, however, is by far the most popular, accounting for about 80% of worldwide consumption. Commercial trees are produced by grafting (since production is faster and quality superior this way) rather than by seeding, and are currently being grown in a wide variety of temperate regions such as California, South Africa, the Dominican Republic, Israel, Brazil and of course Mexico. Mature avocado trees can produce up to 400 fruit annually and live for some 200 years.

The avocado is a wonderfully adaptable fruit enjoyed all over the globe. It's cut into soups in Ecuador, puréed into drinks in the Philippines, mashed into sushi rolls in California and blended into ice-cream in Brazil. You can stuff it, batter it or cream it, all the while taking advantage of its high fiber, cholesterol-lowering abilities and anti-oxidant benefits. Just remember to use it in moderation, as a good-sized avocado can pack over 300 calories! And if you're lucky enough to have access to a tree, keep in mind that those rock-hard avocados don't start ripening until *after* you pick them.

Finally, if you're adventurous or just unlucky enough to hate the avocado's taste, try experimenting with mashed avocados in a facial (as a moisturizer) or rubbed into your hair (for shine). Or use as a paste to treat itchy, red skin caused by eczema or dermatitis. What more could you ask from one of nature's most perfect fruit?

Attractive red-tile roofs top a few stucco buildings and a lush hillside surrounds the city. The splendid little national park, Parque Nacional Eduardo Ruiz, is just a 15-minute walk from the town center. You can also visit the remarkable volcano Paricutín, 35km to the west.

Orientation

Uruapan's heart is its long main plaza. Practically everything of interest to travelers is within walking distance of here.

Note that street names change often in Uruapan, both at the plaza and at various other points. And the portales facing the plaza are named independently of the streets; Portal Degollado is the east side of the plaza, while Portal Carrillo and Portal Matamoros run along the south side. The north portal is Portal Mercado.

Information

Several banks (with ATMs), along with a few *cambios*, are near the central plaza, especially on Cupatitzio in the first two blocks south of the plaza.

Casa del Turista (☎ 524-06-67; www.uruapan.gob.mx; Carranza 44; ☻ 9am-7:30pm) The municipal tourist office.

Ciberplanet (Art 123 No 12; ☻ 10am-9pm Mon-Fri, to 11pm Sat) Offers you the Internet.

Delegación de Turismo (☎ 524-71-99; Juan Ayala 16; ☻ 9am-2pm & 4-7pm Mon-Sat) The state tourist office is a couple of blocks northwest of the plaza.

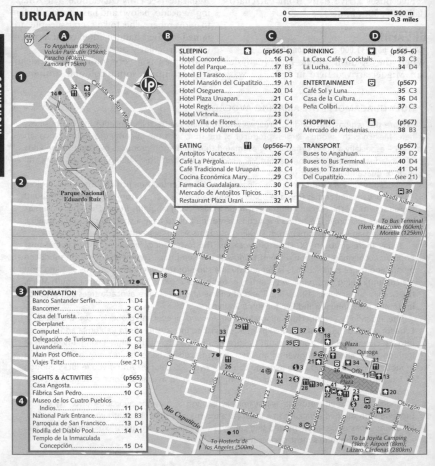

URUAPAN

0 ——— 500 m
0 ——— 0.3 miles

SLEEPING	(pp565–6)
Hotel Concordia	16 D4
Hotel del Parque	17 B3
Hotel El Tarasco	18 D3
Hotel Mansión del Cupatitzio	19 A1
Hotel Oseguera	20 D4
Hotel Plaza Uruapan	21 C4
Hotel Regis	22 C4
Hotel Victoria	23 D4
Hotel Villa de Flores	24 C4
Nuevo Hotel Alameda	25 D4

EATING	(pp566–7)
Antojitos Yucatecas	26 C4
Café La Pérgola	27 C4
Café Tradicional de Uruapan	28 C4
Cocina Económica Mary	29 C3
Farmacia Guadalajara	30 C4
Mercado de Antojitos Típicos	31 D4
Restaurant Plaza Urani	32 A1

DRINKING	(pp565–6)
La Casa Café y Cocktails	33 C3
La Lucha	34 D4

ENTERTAINMENT	(p567)
Café Sol y Luna	35 C3
Casa de la Cultura	36 C4
Peña Colibrí	37 C3

SHOPPING	(p567)
Mercado de Artesanías	38 B3

TRANSPORT	(p567)
Buses to Angahuan	39 D2
Buses to Bus Terminal	40 D4
Buses to Tzaráracua	41 D4
Del Cupatitzio	(see 21)

INFORMATION	
Banco Santander Serfin	1 D4
Bancomer	2 D4
Casa del Turista	3 C4
Ciberplanet	4 C4
Computel	5 C4
Delegación de Turismo	6 C3
Lavandería	7 D4
Main Post Office	8 C4
Viajes Tzitzi	(see 21)

SIGHTS & ACTIVITIES	(p565)
Casa Angosta	9 C3
Fábrica San Pedro	10 C4
Museo de los Cuatro Pueblos Indios	11 C4
National Park Entrance	12 B3
Parroquia de San Francisco	13 D4
Rodilla del Diablo Pool	14 A1
Templo de la Inmaculada Concepción	15 D4

Parque Nacional
Eduardo Ruiz

To Angahuan (35km);
Volcán Paricutín (35km);
Paracho (40km);
Zamora (115km)

To Bus Terminal
(1km); Pátzcuaro (60km);
Morelia (125km)

To Hostería de
los Angeles (500m)

To La Joyita Camping
(3km); Airport (8km);
Lázaro Cárdenas (280km)

Hospital Fray Juan de San Miguel (☎ 524-44-47; Mazatlán 75)

Lavandería (cnr Carranza & Garcia; ⏱ 9am-2pm & 4-8pm Mon-Sat) Bubble up your threads here.

Main post office (Ocaranza 22; ⏱ 8am-2pm Mon-Fri)

Viajes Tzitzi (☎ 523-34-19; Ocampo 64; ⏱ 9:30am-2pm & 4-7:30pm Mon-Fri, 9:30pm-2pm Sat) Beside the entrance to Hotel Plaza Uruapan; sells ETN and Primera Plus bus tickets.

Sights

MUSEO DE LOS CUATRO PUEBLOS INDIOS

In the Huatápera, an old colonial building near the northeast corner of the central plaza, is this tiny **museum** (☎ 524-34-34; admission free; ⏱ 9:30am-1:30pm & 3:30-6pm Tue-Sun). This courtyard building was one of the institutions established in the 1530s under the auspices of Vasco de Quiroga, and reputedly the first hospital in the Americas. The decorations around the doors and windows were carved by Purépecha artisans in a Mudejar style. The museum itself is only one room, and showcases some nice lacquerware, ceramics and gourd crafts of the surrounding region. Future plans call for the museum's expansion.

PARQUE NACIONAL EDUARDO RUIZ

This lovely tropical **park** (the west end of Independencia; admission US$1; ⏱ 8am-6pm) is only 1km west of the central plaza. It follows the lushly vegetated banks of the Río Cupatitzio from its source at the Rodilla del Diablo pool, at the park's north end. Legend has it that the devil knelt here and left the mark of his knee. Many paths guide a shady stroll down the gorge, over bridges and past waterfalls and fountains – the park is famous for its water features. Boys dive into the river's deepest pools and ask for coins.

FÁBRICA SAN PEDRO

This great old **textile factory** (☎ 524-06-77; telaresuruapan@prodigy.com.mx; Miguel Treviño s/n; tours 7am-7pm) is a late-19th-century factory now operated by Telares Uruapan. High-quality, hand-loomed and hand-dyed bedspreads, tablecloths and curtains, among other things, are made here from pure cotton and wool. The original 100+-year-old machines are still used – this place is essentially a working museum of the industrial revolution. It's run by a fascinating US couple who've lived in Uruapan for decades. Call

ahead for a tour (by appointment only) and see the entire weaving process from cotton bale to finished tablecloth.

CASA ANGOSTA

Only those tourists seeking the tacky will appreciate this **'world's narrowest house'** (Carrillo Puerto 50C; admission US$0.50; ⏱ 9am-5pm Sat & Sun). The one in Amsterdam is actually narrower, but this one might be worth a curious peek. It's three-stories high and 1.40m wide, and a private residence so hours may vary. Search for it carefully: blink and you might miss it.

Festivals & Events

Semana Santa Palm Sunday is marked by a procession through the city streets. Figures and crosses woven from palm fronds are sold after the procession. A major crafts competition takes place on this day, and a weeklong exhibition/market of Michoacán handicrafts fills up the central plaza; prices get lower as the week goes on.

Día de San Francisco St Francis, the patron saint of Uruapan, is honored with colorful festivities on October 4.

Festival de Coros y Danzas Around October 17 and 18, the Choir & Dance Festival is a contest of Purépecha dance and musical groups.

Festival del Cristo Rey On the last Sunday of October, an evening procession parades an image of Christ over the town's winding streets, which are covered in murals made of flower petals or colored sawdust.

Feria del Aguacate For two weeks in November, the Avocado Fair is a big event, with bullfights, cockfights, concerts and agricultural, industrial and handicraft exhibitions.

Sleeping

BUDGET

Hotel del Parque (☎ 524-38-45; Independencia 124; s/d US$15/20; P) Very handy to the national park, but 6½ blocks west of the central plaza, this friendly place is still the most pleasant of Uruapan's cheap lodgings. The 14 plain rooms have cable TV and are clean and spacious. There's also a rear patio area where you can wash small amounts of laundry.

Hotel Oseguera (☎ 523-98-56; fax 524-29-05; Degollado 2; s/d from US$7/10) Twenty-nine basic, dark but spacious rooms with minimal furniture and no views greet you here. TV costs US$2.75 extra.

La Joyita (☎ 523-03-64; Estocolmo 22; tent sites per person US$5.75) This camping park is 1½ blocks east of Paseo Lázaro Cárdenas at the southern end of town. It has a lawn area for tents, a barbecue and 24-hour hot water in the showers.

MID-RANGE

Hotel Villa de Flores (☎ 524-28-00; Carranza 15; s/d US$28/34) One of the better deals in town, this well-run hotel has an excellent location and good rooms with cable TV. All surround leafy outdoor patios. Try for one in back, on the upper floor; rooms here are bigger and brighter.

Hotel El Tarasco (☎ 524-15-00; hoteltarasco@ hotmail.com; Independencia 2; s/d US$50/57; **P** 🖳 🚇 🗷) This modern hotel offers up some very nice, comfortable and carpeted rooms with good bathrooms and views. It's a good deal in this price range, especially with its pool with small waterfall.

Hotel Victoria (☎ 524-66-11, 800-420-39-00; www .hotelvictoriaupn.com.mx; Cupatitzio 11; s/d US$50/57; **P** 🖳 🚇 🗷) Not quite as good as the Tarasco, this hotel nevertheless offers 80 decent, fairly-modern mid-range rooms. Some have balconies, and the street isn't overly noisy.

Hotel Regis (☎ 523-58-44; hotelregis@intermatsa .com.mx; Portal Carrillo 12; s/d US$27/36; **P**) The doorstep is right on the plaza, and the colorful rooms worn but OK. There's a clean indoor patio and interesting décor.

Hotel Concordia (☎ 523-04-00; www.hotelconcordia .com.mx; Portal Carrillo 8; s/d/ste US$33/44/64; **P**) Three floors of antiseptic hallways and dark unmemorable rooms, are on offer here. The four large suites face out over the plaza and are pleasant, but much more wallet-thinning. King-size beds are available.

Nuevo Hotel Alameda (☎ 523-41-00; fax 523-36-45; 5 de Febrero 11; s/d US$27/34; **P** 🗷) Barebones, budget and bleak, but pretty much bearable without breaking the bank.

TOP END

Hotel Mansión del Cupatitzio (☎ 523-21-00; www .mansioncupatzio.com; Calz Rodilla del Diablo 20; s/d US$94/112, ste from US$135; **P** 🚇) This hacienda-style place at the north end of Parque Nacional Eduardo Ruiz is the most pleasant hotel in Uruapan. Gorgeous rooms, lovely grounds and all the services you could wish for are at your fingertips.

Hotel Plaza Uruapan (☎ 523-35-99; www.hotel plazauruapan.com.mx; Ocampo 64; s/d from US$64/80; **P** 🖳 🗷) Catering mainly to business travelers, this hotel has 120 good rooms with lots of amenities. There's also a business center, meeting rooms and gym. Exterior rooms have great views through floor-to-ceiling windows. Call for possible discounts.

Eating

Several places on the south side of the plaza serve good breakfasts, economical *comidas corridas* and adequate à la carte meals for dinner.

Café La Pérgola (☎ 523-50-87; Portal Carrillo 4; mains US$3.75-8) This place cooks up soups, salads, sandwiches and regional food. Food is tasty and service good. It's also kid-friendly.

Cocina Económica Mary (☎ 524-73-39; Independencia 59; mains under US$3; 🕑 8.30am-5.30pm Mon-Sat) This well-patronized, family-run place serves a delicious home-style meal of soup followed by a choice of several main courses from *bistek con papas* to *tortas de brócoli*, plus a drink. Plan your meal ahead though; it closes early and isn't open Sunday.

Hostería de los Ángeles (☎ 523-13-62; Caracol 30; mains US$6.50-10; **P**) A wonderful old-world ambience (including a replica painting of a 17th century church in Tupátaro) helps the *filete relleno de huitlacoche* (US$7) and paella (served only on Sundays) go down well. Also on the Spanish–Mexican fusion menu are seafood, meats and crêpes. This restaurant is located south of town across the river, three blocks south of the García bridge (then turn left on Caracol).

Antojitos Yucatecos (☎ 524-61-52; Carranza 37; mains under US$5; 🕑 5:30-11pm Tue-Fri, 1-11pm Sat & Sun) Try the tasty *sopa de lima* (US$1.75) at this small eatery, along with other delicious dishes from Yucatán – *tacos cochinita pibil* is one of the most typical. The menu's pretty succinct, but highly recommended.

Restaurant Plaza Urani (☎ 524-86-98; Calz Rodilla del Diablo 13; mains US$6-8.50; 🕑 9:30am-7pm; **P**) The shady, open-air tables at this riverside restaurant are mighty pleasant after a long walk through the national park. It's located opposite Hotel Mansión del Cupatitzio, at the park's northern exit. The specialty is fresh *trucha arco iris* (rainbow trout), though meat dishes are also on tap.

Café Tradicional de Uruapan (☎ 523-56-80; Carranza 5B; snacks & breakfast under US$4; 🕑 8am-10:30pm) Sip caffeine with Uruapan's elite: this dark, wood-detailed womb has good breakfasts, snacks, cakes and a large selection of strong gourmet coffees (and teas).

Right on the plaza, the **Mercado de Antojitos Típicos** (Constitución s/n; 🕑 8am-11pm) offers adventurous diners dozens of cheap food stalls serving authentic Michoacán dishes. You'll have to head one block north into the market to find the big square where these stalls are located. For 24-hour convenience, there's the ubiquitous **Farmacia Guadalajara** (Carranza 3).

Drinking
La Lucha (☎ 524-03-75; García Ortiz 20; coffees US$3; 9am-9pm Mon-Sat) Sit back in the solid wooden furniture and enjoy a good, strong cup of java at this standard café, half a block north of the central plaza.

La Casa Bar (☎ 524-36-11; Revolución 3; 4-11pm) Offering fancy coffees (US$1 to US$5) and cocktails (US$3.50), this hip joint caters to patrons who like it dark and moody. Appetizers are available, or bring your own date.

Entertainment
You might find one or two things to do after dark besides lingering over coffee or going to church.

Peña Colibrí (☎ 519-01-94; Independencia 18; 6pm-2am) The intimate atmosphere is dark here; settle under an arch or right in front of the small stage. Live music such as *canto nuevo* or *trova Cubana* plays daily from 9:30pm on; cover charges depend on the day (Monday free, Tuesday to Thursday US$2, Friday to Saturday US$3.50 to US$3.75).

Casa de la Cultura (García Ortiz 1) Half a block north of the plaza, this place hosts exhibitions, occasional concerts and other events. Check with the tourist office to see what's cooking during your stay in Uruapan.

Café Sol y Luna (☎ 524-42-21; Independencia 15A; 10am-11pm) More bar than café, this bohemian hot spot is popular with the student crowd. It serves cocktails, snacks and good coffee, and even offers an Internet connection. Live music starts things rolling Thursday to Saturday nights from 9pm (US$1 to US$2.25 cover).

Shopping
Local crafts such as lacquered trays and boxes can be bought at the Mercado de Artesanías, opposite the entrance to Parque Nacional Eduardo Ruiz. The town market, which stretches more than half a kilometer up Constitución from the central plaza to Calz Juárez, is also worth a browse. Check out Telares Uruapan (see Fábrica San Pedro, p565) for quality textiles.

Getting There & Around
Uruapan's bus terminal is 3km northeast of central Uruapan on the highway to Pátzcuaro and Morelia. It has a telephone caseta, cafetería and left luggage (open 7am to 11pm daily). Destinations include the following:

Angahuan (US$1.25, 1hr, every 1-2hr)
Colima (6-8hr, 2 daily 10:30am US$14 & 9:45pm, US$18) More connections via Zamora or Guadalajara.
Guadalajara (US$13-22, 4½hr, 30 daily)
Lázaro Cárdenas (US$15-17, 4hr, 16 daily)
Mexico City (US$22-27, 7hr; 8 daily) To Terminal Norte.
Mexico City (US$27-33, 5½hr, 15 daily) To Terminal Poniente.
Morelia (US$6-10, 2hr, every 20min)
Paracho (US$1.25, 1hr, every 20min)
Pátzcuaro (US$3-3.25, 1hr, every 20min)
Zamora (US$5.50-8.50, 2hr, 25 daily)

Local buses marked 'Centro' run from the just outside the bus terminal to the plaza (US$0.35). If you want a taxi, buy a ticket from the taquilla inside the station (US$1.75). For the return trip catch a 'Central Camionera' bus from the south side of the plaza.

If you need your own wheels (US$72 per day) to explore Uruapan's surroundings, try the car rental agency **Del Cupatitzio** (☎ 523-11-81, ☎ cellular 044-452-500-69-19; autorent@prodigy.net .mx), at the Hotel Plaza Uruapan.

AROUND URUAPAN
Cascada de Tzaráracua
Ten kilometers south of Uruapan is the popular 30m Tzaráracua **waterfall** (admission US$0.75, cars US$0.50 extra). To see it up close, however, you'll have to huff and puff 557 sometimes slippery stone steps down into a small valley. Hiring one of the many horses in the touristy parking lot will cost US$6 roundtrip; the price is the same for one way back up.

There's a 20-minute hike upstream from Tzaráracua to the smaller but lovelier Tzararacuita. Getting here is much more 'adventurous' and may require waterproof sandals, as the trail is less maintained and even hazardous at times. Still, you'll see few people. To get here, follow the steep muddy track beyond the Tzaráracua bridge, and after about 10 minutes turn right at the stone outcropping.

Hourly buses to Tzaráracua depart from in front of the Hotel Regis, on the south side of Uruapan's main plaza (US$0.35). Taxis cost US$5.

WESTERN CENTRAL HIGHLANDS

Tingambato

The **ruins** (admission US$2.75; ☼ 10am-5pm) of this ceremonial site that flourished from about AD 450 to AD 900 are near the village of the same name, about 30km from Uruapan on the road to Pátzcuaro. They show Teotihuacán influence and date from well before the Tarascan empire. Also known by its older name Tinganio, the compact, tidy complex includes a ball court (rare in western Mexico), an 8m-high stepped pyramid and an underground tomb where a skeleton and 32 skulls were found. A small museum has photos of the excavation work and some pieces recovered from tombs.

Galeana Purhépecha buses to Morelia (via the free road) leave from Uruapan's terminal every 20 minutes and stop in Tingambato town (US$0.75, 30 minutes). The ruins are about a 15-minute walk downhill on Calle Juárez, the last street on the Uruapan side of town.

Paracho

☎ 423 / pop 16,000 / elevation 2220m

Paracho, 40km north of Uruapan on highway 37, is a small Purépecha town famous for its high-quality, handmade stringed instruments. It's worth visiting if you want to buy a guitar, violin, cello or traditional Mexican stringed instrument at a very reasonable price. You can also attend free guitar concerts by first-rate musicians and watch some of the country's best luthiers at work. The liveliest time to come is during the annual **Feria Nacional de la Guitarra** (National Guitar Fair), a weeklong splurge of music, dance, exhibitions, markets and cockfights in early August.

One of two places guitar-lovers shouldn't miss is **Expo Cuerdas** (20 de Noviembre s/n; ☼ 11am-4pm), in the Casa de la Cultura on the southeast corner of the main plaza. It has historical photos of Paracho on display as well as old and new guitars of all sorts (classical, Hawaiian, steel-string and even some electrics), violins, *guitarrones* and *vihuelas*. The new ones are for sale, and range from inexpensive (but good) to top-dollar pieces made of exotic woods, some with carving and elaborate inlay. Most include a good-quality case in the price.

The other must-see, about two blocks southeast, is the **Centro para la Investigación y el Desarrollo de la Guitarra** (CIDEG; ☎ 525-01-90; cnr Nicolás Bravo & Hidalgo; admission free; ☼ 9am-1pm & 3-6pm Mon-Fri, 9am-1pm Sat). It's a guitar museum, with good exhibits on the history of music, instrument-making and related subjects. Among the displays are various miniature instruments and a couple of beautifully decorated guitars. CIDEG hosts free guitar concerts in its auditorium on the last Friday of every month.

Many buses from Uruapan to Zamora stop in Paracho. Galeana Ruta Paraíso 2nd-class buses leave Uruapan every 15 minutes (US$1.25, one hour) and will often make flag stops on Uruapan's Calz Juárez at Venustiano Carranza, eliminating your having to backtrack to the terminal. Get off at the official bus stop in Paracho.

Zamora

☎ 351 / pop 124,000 / elevation 1560m

Zamora is about 115km northwest of Uruapan and 190km southeast of Guadalajara. It's a pleasant town in the center of a rich agricultural region known for its strawberries and potatoes. Zamora's delicious *dulces* (sweets) are also famous, and on sale at numerous stalls in the market.

Founded in 1574, Zamora has an inordinate number of churches, including the so-called **Catedral Inconclusa**, started in 1898 and still not quite finished. Ask a local, however, and she's likely to say '*pero falta poco!*' (but it's almost done!). There are a few hotels in the town's center, which is just a short bus or taxi ride from the bus terminal.

Fifteen kilometers southeast of town at Tangancícuaro is the spring-fed, tree-shaded **Laguna de Camécuaro**, a lovely spot for drivers to stop and picnic.

Zamora is something of a regional transport hub, and its bus terminal has regular connections to Guadalajaraf (US$10.50, 2¼ hours), Colima (US$13, 4½ hours), Uruapan (US$7, two hours), Pátzcuaro (US$6, two hours) and Morelia (US$4.50, 2½ hours).

VOLCÁN PARICUTÍN

On the afternoon of February 20, 1943, a Purépecha farmer, Dionisio Pulido, was plowing his cornfield some 35km west of Uruapan when the ground began to shake and swell and spurt steam, sparks and hot ash. The farmer tried at first to cover the moving earth, but when that proved futile, he fled. A volcano started to rise from the spot. Within a year it had risen 410m above the surrounding land and its lava had engulfed the Purépecha villages of San Salvador Paricutín and San Juan Parangaricutiro. No one was hurt: the lava flow was gradual, giving the villagers plenty of time to evacuate.

The volcano continued to spit lava and fire and to increase in size until 1952. Today its large black cone stands mute, emitting gentle wisps of steam. Near the edge of the 20-sq-km lava field, the top of San Juan's church protrudes eerily from the sea of solidified, black lava. It's the only visible trace of the two buried villages.

An excursion to Paricutín from Uruapan makes a fine day trip, to see San Juan's church engulfed in a jumble of black boulders and/or to climb the volcanic cone. At 2800m, the volcano is not memorably high – the much bigger Tancítaro towers to the south – but it's interesting and fairly easy to access. If you want to do it in one day from Uruapan, as most people do, start early.

Angahuan & Around

☎ 452 / Angahuan pop 3000 /
Angahuan elevation 2693m

Angahuan is the nearest town to the volcano. It's a typical Purépecha town with wooden houses, dusty streets, more horses than cars and loudspeakers booming out announcements in the Purépecha language. Amuse passing locals by greeting them with a 'natz evansco' (buenos días) or 'natz susco' (buenas tardes).

SIGHTS

On the main plaza is the 16th-century **Iglesia de Santiago Apóstol**, with some fine carving around its door done by a Moorish stonemason who accompanied the early Spanish missionaries here.

The ruined **Templo San Juan Parangaricutiro** church is a one-hour walk from where the bus lets you off on the highway. At the bus stop you'll be mobbed by guides with horses, but you don't really need a guide (US$10 per person with horses and guide; half with just a walking guide – negotiate!). If you prefer to take the nice walk, just say 'no gracias' and cross the highway, heading down the street framed by the wire arch. After 10 minutes turn right at the main

plaza, then after 200m bear left at the fork (note the satellite dish). Keep following this road, which eventually leads out of town and to a dirt parking lot (where there are more horses and guides). The easy trail, flanked by barbed-wire fences and covered in hoof tracks, starts down from here.

Getting around the church site is surprisingly difficult, as the walls are filled with, and surrounded by, huge boulders of black volcanic rock. The missing tower was not a casualty of the volcano – it was never completed.

If you have a 4WD car you can drive practically all the way to the church – there's a dirt parking lot (and shack restaurants) near the base of the lava field in which the church is buried. You may get charged for parking.

SLEEPING

Cuartos Familiares (Camino al Paricutín s/n; r US$19-24; (P)) There aren't many sleeping options in Angahuan, but this is a good and friendly one. Four simple and pleasant rooms come with fireplace and bath. Look for it on the road to the ruined church, about 1km from the bus stop; the green sign ('Cuartos Familiares/estacionamento') and building are hard to miss. Unfortunately, they didn't have a telephone at research time so scoring a room is hit or miss.

Centro Turístico de Angahuan (Las Cabañas; ☎ 523-39-34; Camino al Paricutín s/n; camping per person US$2.75, dm US$10, cabañas from US$29; (P)) This low-key 'tourist' complex offers food, accommodation (camping, dorms, simple cabañas) and some information about the volcano. If you're not staying here there's a US$0.75 admission charge to enter the complex, but on slow days the fee isn't collected. The restaurant (mains US$3.75 to US$6, open 9am to 6pm daily) has a minimal menu and sometimes shows an interesting video about the eruption. A lookout point here provides good views of the lava field, the protruding San Juan church tower and the volcano itself. If it's clear you can even glimpse Colima's volcanoes. If you're not staying here it's not really worth going into this complex (unless you want to use the restrooms).

GETTING THERE & AWAY

Angahuan is 32km from Uruapan. Galeana 2nd-class buses leave the Uruapan bus terminal for Angahuan every 30 minutes from

5am to 7pm (US$1.25, one hour). Alternatively, flag down a Los Reyes, Sicuicho or Charapan bus on Calz Juárez (at Venustiano Carranza) in Uruapan; this will save you a trip to the bus terminal.

Buses back to Uruapan run every 15 minutes until about 7pm, but a few may run much less frequently until 9pm. Double-check this information before getting stuck in Angahuan for the night.

Climbing Paricutín
BY HORSE

As soon as you alight at Angahuan's bus stop, guides with horses will offer you their services to the ruined church (see Templo San Juan Parangaricutiro, p569) or volcano. If you want to go to the volcano on horseback, you can start negotiating right here; it should cost about US$38 for one person and US$57 for two people. You can also walk a half-hour to the dirt parking lot just beyond Angahuan; there are more horses and guides here, but prices are the same.

Some guides are young boys, with very little experience, poor equipment, little Spanish and zero English. Make sure you deal with the actual person who will be guiding you, and don't agree to go with someone who isn't able to look after himself. Smart guides bring something to eat and drink.

The trip to the volcano is 14km round-trip and takes about six hours (of which you'll spend four in the saddle), so your butt will get sore. You'll have to climb up the last few hundred meters as the horses can't negotiate the steep scree; bring good hiking shoes.

BY FOOT

If you'd rather walk to the volcano, you'll most likely still need a guide (about US$19 for one person, US$24 for two). There are two ways up: the walking trail and the horse trail. You can do a loop and take in both – this should take about seven to eight hours.

On the more interesting walking trail it's very easy to get lost (and many travelers do), because it leads you into a disorienting pine forest full of small side tracks created by wood gatherers and tree planters. A compass may help. The beginning of this trail starts at the dirt parking lot about a half-hour from the bus stop (see Templo San Juan Parangaricutiro, p569).

After this walking trail winds a few hundred meters through the confusing pine forest, go a little beyond and cross a dirt road, picking up the trail on the other side. Within 30m you should pass through a gate, and soon afterward the path begins to slope upward considerably. The trail weaves through thickets where wildflowers bloom much of the year. After about 30 minutes of hiking, there's a basic campsite and then the woods open to a barren lava field. The path to the crater, over jagged black rock, is marked occasionally with splashes of paint.

About 150m from the summit, the rock gives way to a sandy ash and you'll see steam rising from fumaroles on knolls to the left of the trail. A narrow 40m trail links the main trail to the knolls, which are worth visiting. They are covered with bright yellow, sulfurous rock that is quite striking amid the surrounding black lava. You can see steam rising from the crevices around you.

The lip of the crater has two high points. Beneath the northern lip, on the outside of the cone, is a dust slide that is fun to bound down at a fast, high-stepping walk. This brings you down near the flat, dusty horse trail that returns via the ruined church, which is worth seeing. To return the way you came, pass on the dust slide. Using the walking trail most people need 3½ or four hours to reach the summit, and another three hours for the return trip (and remember the trailhead is a half-hour's walk from the bus stop).

To walk along the longer, less-steep and less-interesting horse trail, head out from the ruined church (see Templo San Juan Parangaricutiro, p569). The trail follows a road past some farms, then narrows and passes through brush before reaching an open, sandy area. From here a 15-minute walk brings you to the foot of the volcano, and 25-minute steep ascent puts you at the top.

It's a good idea to bring some food and water from Uruapan as there's none on the route and only a limited selection available in Angahuan.

Northern Central Highlands

CONTENTS

In the highlands northwest of Mexico City the Spanish extracted most of the silver and other precious metals fundamental to their colonial ambitions – and they built some of the country's most magnificent cities with the silver's great fortunes. The most spectacular of these cities are Guanajuato and Zacatecas, which along with Potosí in Bolivia were the Americas' major silver-producing centers. San Miguel de Allende, Querétaro and San Luis Potosí retain a wealth of colonial architecture, and boast lively arts and entertainment scenes. It's a highly rewarding region to visit, the distances are not huge and the landscape between the cities is always impressive.

The flatter, more fertile land, forming an arc from Querétaro through León to Aguascalientes, is known as the Bajío (ba-*hee*-o), and has long been one of Mexico's major agricultural zones. From colonial times, the Bajío fed and supplied the mining towns, and it formed an important transport corridor to Mexico City. Bajío cities have developed as industrial centers, though many of them retain a colonial core and have an important place in Mexico's history. It was here the movement for independence from Spain began in 1810, and thus the region is known as La Cuna de la Independencia (the Cradle of Independence). The town of Dolores Hidalgo, where the uprising started, and nearby places like San Miguel de Allende, Querétaro and Guanajuato are full of key sites from this historic movement.

This chapter encompasses the states of Zacatecas, Aguascalientes, Guanajuato and Querétaro, and most of San Luis Potosí state. Eastern San Luis Potosí state is covered in the Central Gulf Coast chapter.

HIGHLIGHTS

- Exploring the sublime cathedral, superb museums and subterranean nightclub in an abandoned mine in **Zacatecas** (p581), a stylish silver city

- Discovering the magic, stark mountains and fine Italian cuisine in **Real de Catorce** (p603), a miraculous ghost town re-awakening from a long slumber

- Luxuriating in expat chic, exuberant fiestas, top-notch food and super artsy shopping in smart **San Miguel de Allende** (p631)

- Wandering the crooked cobbled alleyways of **Guanajuato** (p615), a rollicking student city with a very quixotic festival

- Meandering along Hwy 120 through the **Sierra Gorda** (p641), a remote region of Unesco World Heritage sites

- ALTITUDE RANGE: 760m–2756m
- AUGUST DAILY HIGH: 25°C

HISTORY

The northern central highlands were inhabited by fierce seminomadic tribes known to the Aztecs as Chichimecs. They resisted Spanish conquest longer than other Mexican peoples but were ultimately pacified in the late 16th century. The wealth subsequently amassed by the Spanish was at the cost of many Chichimecs, who were used as slave labor in the mines.

Criollo resentment of the Spanish-born colonists' stranglehold on power coalesced in Querétaro and sparked the 1810 rebellion (see p41). The region's revolutionary tendencies resurfaced in 1910 when Francisco Madero released his Plan de San Luis Potosí. The 1917 signing of Mexico's constitution in Querétaro cemented the region's leading role in Mexican political affairs.

CLIMATE

A fairly dry, temperate upland region stretches northwest from Mexico City and comprises the southern part of the Altiplano Central (Central Plateau). Further north on the plateau, the dry northern semideserts, which don't get too hot because of their altitude, begin in southern San Luis Potosí and Zacatecas states.

NATIONAL PARKS & RESERVES

From the distinctive rock formations of Sierra de Órganos (p585) to the diverse

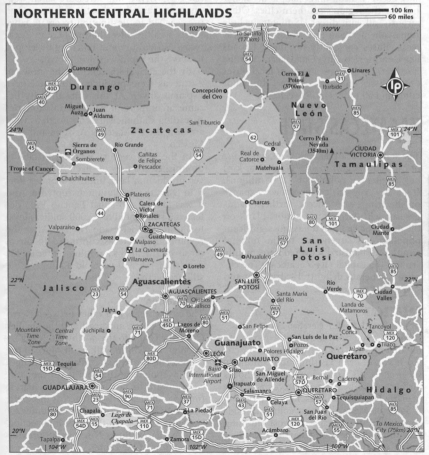

NORTHERN CENTRAL HIGHLANDS

cological zones within the Reserva de la Biosfera Sierra Gorda (p641), the region is bookended by little-explored ecosystems that reward the considerable efforts required to reach them.

DANGERS & ANNOYANCES

Major flooding throughout the low-lying Bajío region in mid-2003 rerouted traffic and led to the declaration of several states of emergency. Infrequent natural disasters aside, the highlands are one of the country's safest and most hassle-free regions to visit.

GETTING THERE AND AWAY

Aeropuerto International del Bajío, halfway between León and Silao, is the major hub for the region's southern cities. Other airports, all with direct US flights, include Aguascalientes, San Luis Potosí and Zacatecas. Buses constantly ply the toll roads between Mexico City, Guadalajara and the northern silver cities. Frequent local buses of all classes efficiently connect the major cities and all points in between.

ZACATECAS STATE

The state of Zacatecas (zak-a-tek-as) is one of Mexico's largest in area (73,252 sq km) but smallest in population (1.37 million). It's a dry, rugged, cactus-strewn expanse on the fringe of Mexico's northern semi-deserts, with large tracts almost blank on the map. The fact that it has any significant population is largely due to the mineral wealth the Spanish discovered here, mainly around the capital city Zacatecas. The climate is generally delightful – dry, clear and sunny, but not too hot.

ZACATECAS

☎ 492 / pop 116,000 / elevation 2445m

If you've come from the north, welcome to the first of Mexico's justly fabled silver cities. If you've been visiting more southerly silver cities, it's worth coming a few hours further north, because Zacatecas is a particularly beautiful and fascinating city.

Some of Mexico's finest colonial buildings, including perhaps its most stunning cathedral, cluster along narrow, winding streets at the foot of a spectacular rock-topped hill called Cerro de la Bufa. A state capital and university city, Zacatecas is sophisticated for its size, and though it's popular with Mexican and European visitors, its off-center location insulates it from hordes of tourists.

History

Indigenous Zacatecos – one of the Chichimec tribes – had mined local mineral deposits for centuries before the Spanish arrived; it's said that the silver rush here was started by a Chichimec gifting a piece of the fabled metal to a conquistador. The Spaniards founded a settlement in 1548 and started mining operations that sent caravan after caravan of silver off to Mexico City. While some treasure-laden wagons were raided by hostile tribes, enough ore reached its destination to create fabulously wealthy silver barons here in Zacatecas. Agriculture and ranching developed to serve the rapidly growing town.

By the early 18th century, the mines of Zacatecas were producing 20% of Nueva España's silver. At this time the city became an important base for missionaries spreading Catholicism as far north as what are now the US states of Arizona and New Mexico.

In the 19th century political instability diminished the flow of silver. Although silver production later improved under Porfirio Díaz, the revolution disrupted it. And it was here in 1914 that Pancho Villa defeated a stronghold of 12,000 soldiers loyal to President Victoriano Huerta. After the revolution, Zacatecas continued to thrive on silver. It remains a mining center to this day, with the 200-year-old El Bote mine still productive.

Orientation

The city center is in a valley between Cerro de la Bufa to the northeast and the smaller Cerro del Grillo to the northwest. Most attractions are within walking distance of the center. The two key streets are Av Hidalgo, running roughly north–south, with the cathedral toward its north end; and Av Juárez, running roughly east–west across the south end of Av Hidalgo. Av Hidalgo becomes Av González Ortega south of its intersection with Av Juárez. Buses Nos 7 and 8 provide a good tour of the center.

ZACATECAS

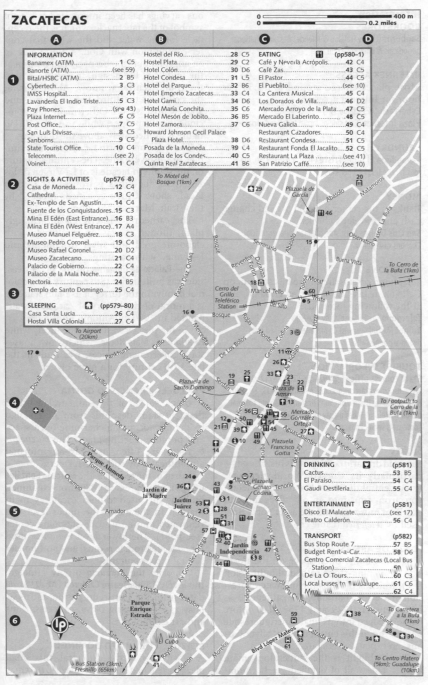

0   400 m
0   0.2 miles

INFORMATION
Banamex (ATM).........................1 C5
Banorte (ATM)....................(see 59)
Bital/HSBC (ATM)......................2 B5
Cybertech................................3 C3
IMSS Hospital............................4 A4
Lavandería El Indio Triste............5 C3
Pay Phones.........................(see 43)
Plaza Internet............................6 C5
Post Office..............................7 C5
San Luis Divisas........................8 C5
Sanborns.................................9 C5
State Tourist Office...................10 C4
Telecomm..........................(see 2)
Voinet...................................11 C4

SIGHTS & ACTIVITIES (pp576-8)
Casa de Moneda.......................12 C4
Cathedral...............................13 C4
Ex-Templo de San Agustín.........14 C4
Fuente de los Conquistadores.....15 C3
Mina El Edén (East Entrance)......16 B3
Mina El Edén (West Entrance).....17 A4
Museo Manuel Felguérez...........18 C3
Museo Pedro Coronel................19 C4
Museo Rafael Coronel...............20 D2
Museo Zacatecano....................21 C4
Palacio de Gobierno.................22 C4
Palacio de la Mala Noche..........23 C4
Rectoría.................................24 B5
Templo de Santo Domingo.........25 C4

SLEEPING (pp579-80)
Casa Santa Lucía......................26 C4
Hostal Villa Colonial.................27 C4

Hostel del Río..........................28 C5
Hostel Plata............................29 C2
Hotel Colón............................30 D6
Hotel Condesa........................31 C5
Hotel del Parque.....................32 B6
Hotel Emporio Zacatecas..........33 C4
Hotel Gami.............................34 D6
Hotel María Conchita...............35 C6
Hotel Mesón de Jobito.............36 B5
Hotel Zamora..........................37 C6
Howard Johnson Cecil Palace
   Plaza Hotel..........................38 D6
Posada de la Moneda................39 C4
Posada de los Condes...............40 C5
Quinta Real Zacatecas..............41 B6

EATING (pp580-1)
Café y Nevería Acrópolis...........42 C4
Café Zas................................43 C5
El Pastor................................44 C5
El Pueblito........................(see 10)
La Cantera Musical..................45 C4
Los Dorados de Villa................46 D2
Mercado Arroyo de la Plata......47 C5
Mercado El Laberinto...............48 C5
Nueva Galicia.........................49 C4
Restaurant Cazadores..............50 C4
Restaurant Condesa.................51 C5
Restaurant Fonda El Jacalito......52 C5
Restaurant La Plaza............(see 41)
San Patrizio Caffé...............(see 10)

DRINKING (p581)
Cactus...................................53 B5
El Paraíso...............................54 C4
Gaudi Destilería......................55 C4

ENTERTAINMENT (p581)
Disco El Malacate................(see 17)
Teatro Calderón......................56 C4

TRANSPORT (p582)
Bus Stop Route 7....................57 B5
Budget Rent-a-Car...................58 D6
Centro Comercial Zacatecas (Local Bus
   Station)..............................59 C5
De La O Tours.........................60 C3
Local buses to Guadalupe..........61 C6
Mini......................................62 C4

NORTHERN CENTRAL HIGHLANDS

Information

BOOKSTORES
Sanborns (cnr Av Hidalgo & Allende) Best international periodicals & book selection.

INTERNET ACCESS
Most places charge around US$1.50 per hour for Internet access.
Cybertech (Av Hidalgo 771)
Plaza Internet (East side of Jardin Independencia)

LAUNDRY
Lavandería El Indio Triste (Tolusa 826) Wash, dry & fold service US$1.25 per kilo.

MONEY
Banks in the center have ATMs and change cash and traveler's checks.
San Luís Divisas (East side of Plaza Independencia) Changes cash dollars.

TELEPHONE
Telephone *casetas* are in the bus station, on Callejón de las Cuevas, off Av Hidalgo, and at the following locations.
Telecomm (Av Hidalgo at Av Juárez)
Voinet (Av Hidalgo s/n) Cheap Internet-based long-distance phone calls.

TOURIST INFORMATION
State tourist office (☎ 924-05-52, 800-712-40-78; www.turismozacatecas.gob.mx; Av Hidalgo 403; ☯ 9am-8pm Mon-Sat, 10am-7pm Sun) Upstairs in an old colonial building. Helpful & has plenty of brochures (in Spanish). Some staff speak English.

Sights
Set amid dry, arid country, this historic city – particularly its Unesco World Heritage-listed central district – has much to detain you, from trips into an old silver mine to excellent museums and the ascent of la Bufa itself by *teleférico* (cable car).

PLAZA DE ARMAS
This plaza is the open space on the north side of the pink-stone cathedral (admission free), which is perhaps the ultimate expression of Mexican baroque. The cathedral was built between 1729 and 1752, just before baroque edged into its final churrigueresque phase. And in this city of affluent silver barons, no expense was spared.

The highlight is the stupendous main façade. This wall of detailed yet harmoni-ous carvings has been interpreted as a giant symbol of the tabernacle, which is the receptacle for the wafer and the wine that confer communion with God. A tiny figure of an angel holding a tabernacle can be seen at the middle of the design, the keystone atop the round central window. Above this, at the center of the third tier, is Christ, and above Christ is God. Other main statues include the 12 apostles, while a smaller Virgin figure is immediately above the doorway.

The south and north façades, though simpler, are also very fine. The central sculpture on the southern façade is of La Virgen de los Zacatecas, the city's patroness. The north façade shows Christ crucified, attended by the Virgin Mary and St John.

The cathedral's interior is disarmingly plain, though it was once adorned with elaborate gold and silver ornaments and festooned with paintings.

The **Palacio de Gobierno** on the plaza's east side was built in the 18th century for a colonial family. In the turret of its main staircase is a mural of the history of Zacatecas state, painted in 1970 by Antonio Rodríguez.

On the plaza's west side, the lovely white **Palacio de la Mala Noche**, which now houses state government offices, was built in the late 18th century for a mine owner.

PLAZUELA FRANCISCO GOITIA
A block south of the cathedral a broad flight of stairs descends from Av Hidalgo to Tacuba, forming a charming open space and popular meeting place. The *plazuela*'s terraces are often used as an informal amphitheater by street performers.

North of the *plazuela*, the **Mercado González Ortega** is an impressive 1880s iron-columned building that used to hold Zacatecas' main market. In the 1980s the upper level was renovated into an upscale shopping center (see p581). The lower level was once used for *bodegas* (storage rooms) and now houses several hip restaurants.

Opposite the *plazuela* on Av Hidalgo, the lovely 1890s **Teatro Calderón** (☎ 922-81-20) dates from the Porfiriato period and is as busy as ever staging plays, concerts, films and art exhibitions.

PLAZUELA DE SANTO DOMINGO
A block west of the cathedral, this small plaza is reached from the Plaza de Armas

by a narrow lane, Callejón de Veyna, and is dominated by the **Templo de Santo Domingo**. Although the church is done in a more sober baroque style than the cathedral, it has some fine gilded altars and a graceful horseshoe staircase. Built by the Jesuits in the 1740s, the church was taken over by Dominican monks when the Jesuits were expelled in 1767.

The **Museo Pedro Coronel** (☎ 922-80-21; Plaza de Santo Domingo s/n; US$2; ☯ 10am-5pm Fri-Wed) is housed in a 17th-century former Jesuit college beside Santo Domingo. Pedro Coronel (1923–85) was an affluent Zacatecan artist who bequeathed his collection of art and artifacts from all over the world, as well as much of his own work. The collection includes 20th-century prints; drawings and paintings by Picasso, Rouault, Chagall, Kandinsky and Miró; some entertaining Hogarth lithographs; and fine ink drawings by Francisco de Goya (1746–1828). The pre-Hispanic Mexican artifacts seem to have been chosen as much for their artistic appeal as their archaeological importance, and there's an amazing collection of masks and other ancient pieces from all over the world. It all adds up to one of provincial Mexico's best art museums.

CALLES DR HIERRO & AUZA

Dr Hierro, leading south from Plazuela de Santo Domingo, and its continuation Auza, are quiet, narrow streets. About 100m from Plazuela de Santo Domingo is the Casa de Moneda, which housed Zacatecas' mint (Mexico's second biggest) in the 19th century. A bit further along is the **Museo Zacatecano** (☎ 922-65-80; Dr Hierro 301; US$1.50; ☯ 10am-5pm Wed-Mon), largely devoted to Huichol art.

Another 100m south is the **Ex-Templo de San Agustín**, built for Augustinian monks in the 17th century. During the 19th-century anticlerical movement, the church became a casino. Then, in 1882, it was purchased by American Presbyterian missionaries who destroyed its 'too Catholic' main façade, replacing it with a blank white wall. In the 20th century the church returned to Catholic use. Today it hosts art and cultural exhibitions. The adjoining former monastery is now the seat of the Zacatecas bishopric. The church's finest feature is the plateresque carving of the conversion of St Augustine over the north doorway.

The street ends at **Jardín Juárez**, a tiny but charming park. The Universidad Autónoma de Zacatecas' administrative headquarters are housed in the neoclassical **Rectoría** building on its west side.

MINA EL EDÉN

The **Edén Mine** (☎ 922-30-02; tours adults/child US$2.50/1.50; ☯ every 15min 10am-6pm), once one of Mexico's richest, is a must-see because of the dramatic insight it provides into the region's source of wealth and the terrible price paid for it. Digging for fabulous hoards of silver, gold, iron, copper and zinc, the enslaved indigenous people, including many children, worked under horrific conditions. At one time up to five people a day died from accidents or diseases like tuberculosis and silicosis.

El Edén was worked from 1586 until the 1950s. Today the fourth of its seven levels is open to visitors. The lower levels are flooded. An elevator or miniature train takes you deep inside Cerro del Grillo, the hill in which the mine is located. Then guides – who may or may not speak some English – lead you along floodlit walkways past deep shafts and over subterranean pools.

The mine has two entrances. To reach the higher one (the east entrance), walk 100m southwest from Cerro de Grillo *teleférico* station; from this entrance, tours start with an elevator descent. To reach the west entrance from the town center, walk west along Avenida Juárez and stay on it after its name changes to Torreón at the Alameda. Turn right immediately after the IMSS hospital (bus No 7 from the corner of Av Hidalgo goes up Av Juárez and past the hospital) and a short walk will bring you to the mine entrance where tours begin with a descent on the narrow-gauge railway.

For information about Disco El Malacate, the mine's nighttime alter ego, see the Entertainment section, p581.

TELEFÉRICO

Zacatecas' most exhilarating ride, and the easiest way to summit Cerro de la Bufa, is the Swiss-built **cable car** (☎ 922-01-70; adult/child/senior US$2/1.50/1; ☯ 10am-6pm) that crosses high above the city from Cerro del Grillo. It's a short walk east from Mina El Edén (east entrance) to the *teleférico*'s

Cerro del Grillo station. Alternatively, huff up the steep steps of Callejón de García Rojas, which lead straight to the *teleférico* from Genaro Codina. Cars depart every 15 minutes (except when it's raining or when winds exceed 60km/h), and the trip takes seven minutes.

CERRO DE LA BUFA

The most appealing of the many explanations for the name of the hill that dominates Zacatecas is that 'bufa' is an old Spanish word for wineskin, which is certainly what the rocky formation looks like. The views from the top are superb, and there's an interesting group of monuments, a chapel and a museum up there.

The small **Museo de la Toma de Zacatecas** (☎ 922-80-66; US$1.50; ☾ 10am-5pm) commemorates the 1914 battle fought on the hill's slopes in which the revolutionary División del Norte, led by Pancho Villa and Felipe Ángeles, defeated President Victoriano Huerta's forces. This gave the revolutionaries control of Zacatecas, which was the gateway to Mexico City. The museum features descriptions of the battle and contemporary newspaper cuttings, all in Spanish.

La Capilla de la Virgen del Patrocinio, adjacent to the museum, is named after the patron saint of miners. Above the altar of this 18th-century chapel is an image of the Virgin said to be capable of healing the sick. Thousands of pilgrims flock here each year around September 8, when the image is carried to the cathedral.

Just east of the museum stand three imposing equestrian **statues** of the victors of the battle of Zacatecas – Villa, Ángeles and Pánfilo Natera. A path behind the statues leads to La Bufa's rocky **summit**, where there are marvelous views on all sides. The hill is topped by a metal cross that is illuminated at night.

From the right of the statues, a path along the foot of the rocky hilltop leads to the **Mausoleo de los Hombres Ilustres de Zacatecas**, with the tombs of Zacatecan heroes from 1841 to the present.

An exciting and convenient way to ascend la Bufa is by *teleférico* (see p576). More strenuously, you can walk up (start by going up Calle del Ángel from the cathedral's east end). To reach it by car, take Carretera a la Bufa, which begins at Av López Velarde beside the university library, a couple of

kilometers east of the center. A taxi costs US$4. All three routes end at the monuments, chapel and museum. Just above the *teleférico* station, the quaint round building is a **meteorological observatory**.

You can return to town by the *teleférico* or by a footpath leading downhill from the statues.

MUSEO DE ARTE ABSTRACTO MANUEL FELGUÉREZ

This art **museum** (☎ 924-37-05; cnr Colón & Seminario; US$2; ☾ 10am-5pm Wed-Mon) is a couple of blocks west of Tolosa, up some steep *callejones* (alleys). It specializes in abstract art, particularly the work of Zacatecan artist Manuel Felguérez, but also includes paintings, sculptures and installations by other artists; it's a varied and stunning collection. The building itself, originally a seminary, was later used as a prison, and has been renovated to create some remarkable exhibition spaces. There's also a popular café.

MUSEO RAFAEL CORONEL

The **Museo Rafael Coronel** (☎ 922-81-16, cnr Abasolo & Matamoros; adult/senior US$2/1; ☾ 10am-5pm Thu-Tue), imaginatively housed in the ruins of the lovely 16th-century ex-Convento de San Francisco, houses Mexican folk art collected by the Zacatecan artist Rafael Coronel, brother of Pedro Coronel and son-in-law of Diego Rivera. The highlight is the astonishing, colorful display of over 2000 masks used in traditional dances and rituals. Also on display are pottery, puppets, pre-Hispanic objects and sketches by Rivera.

MUSEO FRANCISCO GOITIA

The **Museo Francisco Goitia** (☎ 922-02-11; Estrada 102; US$2; ☾ 10am-5pm Tue-Sun) displays work by several major 20th-century Zacatecan artists. Set in a fine former governor's mansion, above the pleasant Parque Enrique Estrada, it's well worth the short walk. Francisco Goitia (1882–1960) himself made some evocative paintings of indigenous people. There's also a striking Goitia self-portrait. Other artists represented include Pedro Coronel, Rafael Coronel and Manuel Felguérez.

Tours

A couple of agencies run city tours and excursions to nearby places of interest. Typical offerings include a four-hour city tour including the mine and the *teleférico* (US$13); four-hour trips to Guadalupe (US$13); and a six-hour excursion to the archaeological site of La Quemada and the town of Jerez (US$16). The tourist office can recommend agencies, including:

De La O Tours (☎ 922-34-64; Tolosa 906A)
Viajes Mazzocco (☎ 922-89-54; Fátima 115)

Festivals & Events

La Morisma – Usually held on the last weekend in August. Features the most spectacular of many mock battles staged at Mexican fiestas commemorating the triumph of the Christians over the Muslims (Moors) in old Spain. Rival 'armies' parade through the streets in the mornings, then, accompanied by bands of musicians, enact two battle sequences, one around noon & another in the afternoon, between Lomas de Bracho & Cerro de la Bufa. One sequence portrays a conflict between Emperor Charlemagne & Almirante Balam, king of Alexandria. The other deals with a 16th-century Muslim rebellion. Surprise: the enactments develop over the festival's three days & both culminate in Christian victory on Sunday.

Feria de Zacatecas – Annual fair during the first three weeks in September. Renowned matadors fight famous local bulls; *charreadas* (rodeos), concerts, plays, film festivals & agricultural & craft shows are staged; & on September 8 the image of La Virgen del Patrocinio is carried to the cathedral from its chapel on Cerro de la Bufa.

Festival Internacional de Teatro de Calle – In mid-October, drama takes to the streets in this vibrant weeklong celebration of street theater.

Sleeping

Zacatecas' cheap lodgings tend to be in extreme contrast to the stately beauty of its colonial architecture. Mid-range and top-end hotels hike their rates in high season. At other times you may be able to get a discount on the prices listed here.

BUDGET

The cheapest central places don't have parking, but public lots charge about US$1 per night. Cheapies further out on Blvd López Mateos suffer much street noise but have parking, phones and cable TV. All places except the hostels have private bathroom.

Hostel Villa Colonial (☎ /fax 922-19-80; www .hostels-zacatecas.com; cnr 1 de Mayo & Callejón Mono Prieto; dm/d US$8/18; 💻) This lively, family-run HI-affiliate is *the* rendezvous point for shoestring travelers. Dorms have four beds and a few new rooms have private bathroom. Amenities include kitchen, laundry, a cable

TV/DVD lounge, bar, rooftop patio, book exchange and free bus terminal pickup. It makes up for what it lacks in space with hospitality and its central location. English and French are spoken and the owners often take guests out on the town.

Hostel Plata (☎ 925-17-11; www.hostels-zacatecas .com; 2nda de Margaritas 105; dm/d US$8/18; P) Zacatecas' newest hostel is an easy walk from the cathedral, but you must first check in at Hostel Villa Colonial. Dorms have six beds and it's just as amicable, if a bit less lively, than its sister location.

Hostal del Río (☎ 924-00-35; Av Hidalgo 116; s/d US$18/20) Often full, this 10-room hotel has a great location, some character and an assortment of clean, comfortable rooms. Some rooms overlook the street while downstairs dwellings are dungeon-like.

Hotel Zamora (☎ 922-12-00; hotel_zamora@terrra .co.mx; Plazuela Zamora 303; s/d US$14/17) All rooms have minimal facilities at the cheapest central hostelry. The best rooms overlook Plazuela Zamora while the cheapest ones are small and gloomy.

Other recommendations:
Hotel Gami (☎ 922-80-05; Blvd López Mateos 309; s/d US$17/23; P) Small, pleasant rooms. Rates are per bed (not per person) so it's a bargain for those willing to share.
Hotel Colón (☎ 922-89-25; Blvd López Mateos 106; s/d US$19/21; P) A pleasant walk from the center of town. Rooms are reasonably sized & well kept.
Hotel María Conchita (☎ 922-14-94; Blvd López Mateos 401; s/d US$15/18; P) Modern place with clean rooms. Superior top floor rooms are worth extra charge.

MID-RANGE

All these places have in-room phones and TVs (mostly cable or satellite).

Casa Santa Lucia (☎ 924-49-00; Av Hidalgo 717; low/high r from US$69/119; P) This former bishop's residence straddles the mid- and upper-ranges, depending on the season, and is an easy stroll from the cathedral. It's small and appealing with a comfortable, rustic character.

Hotel Condesa (☎ 922-11-60; www.visitezacatecas .com; Av Juárez 102; s/d US$37/43) Centrally located and recently renovated, the Condesa has 60 rooms around a covered courtyard. Nearly all have exterior windows and a few have balconies; those facing northeast have fine views of La Bufa.

Posada de la Moneda (☎ 922-08-81; posadadel moneda@hotmail.com; Av Hidalgo 413; s/d/ste US$34/50/70)

An imposing old building and a perfect location near the cathedral make this one of Zacatecas' most attractive three-star hotels. The spacious rooms are comfortable and nicely decorated, though they lack old-fashioned charm.

Howard Johnson Cecil Palace Plaza Hotel (☎ 922-33-11, 800-440-4000; www.hj.com.mx; Blvd López Mateos s/n; r from US$59; P 🐾 🖵 🖳) This recently upgraded, 126-room plain-Jane franchise member attracts business travelers with frequent promo rates, its fitness center and executive floor business center.

Posada de los Condes (☎ 922-10-93; Av Juárez 107; s/d US$23/28) Opposite Hotel Condesa, this colonial building is three centuries old, but a modernization stripped most evidence of its age from the interior. The carpeted rooms are modern and well kept, though few have exterior windows.

Motel del Bosque (☎ 922-07-45; www.hoteles delbosque.com.mx; Paseo Díaz Ordaz s/n; r from US$41; P) This motoring-friendly lodge on the northwest side of town is ideal if you don't want to deal with driving in the congested center; you can walk to town in 10 minutes, but the 15-plus-minute climb back is much harder! The quiet, comfortable rooms tend toward rundown but come with all modern conveniences, and some have great views. Full RV hookups in the slanted parking lot cost US$14.

TOP END

Hotel Mesón de Jobito (☎ /fax 924-17-22, 800-021-00-40; www.mesondejobito.com; Jardín Juárez 143; r/ste from US$167/192; P 🐾 🖵) Several restored buildings have been incorporated into this superb luxury hotel. The 53 finely decorated rooms, two excellent restaurants, bar and lobby are all rich with charm and historic character and the service exemplifies attentive.

Quinta Real Zacatecas (☎ 922-91-04, 800-714-41-57; www.quintareal.com; Rayón 434; ste from US$195; P 🐾 🐾) The 49-room Quinta Real is one of Mexico's most fetching hotels, spectacularly situated around the country's oldest (now retired) bullring. The El Cubo aqueduct runs across the property and past the elegant restaurant (see p581). The least expensive rooms are spacious, very comfortable master suites.

Hotel Emporio Zacatecas (☎ 922-61-83, 800-800-61-61; www.hotelesemporio.com; Av Hidalgo 703; r/ste

US$120/145; P 🐾 🐾) Superbly located in a renovated colonial building facing the Plaza de Armas, the Emporio's 115 rooms have modern furnishings but lack colonial charm. The upstairs restaurant has a great view of the cathedral.

Eating

Many restaurants serve local specialties featuring ingredients like *nopal* (cactus paddle) and pumpkin seeds. Locally produced wine can also be good. You might also like to try *aguamiel* (honey water), a nutritional drink derived from the maguey cactus. In the morning, look around Av Hidalgo for burros (donkeys) carrying pottery jugs of the beverage.

AROUND AVENIDAS HIDALGO & JUÁREZ

It's a pleasure to walk these lively streets, comparing the many excellent eateries. There are lots of mid-range possibilities serving well-prepared Mexican standards, as well as plenty of greasy fast food.

Café y Nevería Acrópolis (☎ 922-12-84; cnr Av Hidalgo & Plazuela Candelario Huizar; mains US$4-8) Near the cathedral, this well-situated café is popular with locals and visitors for excellent coffee, delicious cakes and light meals.

El Pueblito (☎ 924-38-18; Av Hidalgo 403D; mains US$4-7; 🕙 1-11pm Wed-Mon) Located below the tourist office, El Pueblito offers local Zacatecan specialties and tasty renditions of standard Mexican dishes. It has bright decor, light entertainment and an enjoyable atmosphere.

San Patrizio Caffé (☎ 922-43-99; Av Hidalgo 403C; drinks & snacks US$1-2.50) Below the tourist office, the nicest café in town boasts relaxing courtyard seating, light snacks, Illy espresso, fancy teas and an array of Italian sodas.

Nueva Galicia (☎ 922-80-46; Plazuela Francisco Goitia 102; mains US$5-10) Half restaurant, half bar, this smart place overlooking Plazuela Goitia offers a good choice of breakfasts, plus well-prepared pasta, meat and seafood dishes with a Spanish touch. There's live music Friday and Saturday nights.

Los Dorados de Villa (☎ 922-57-22; Plazuela de García 1314; mains US$4-7; 🕙 3pm-1am) A homey local favorite for quality traditional Mexican specialties like *pozole verde* (hominy soup with pork and green salsa).

La Cantera Musical (☎ 922-88-28; Tacuba 2; mains US$5-9) In the old storerooms below Mercado

González Ortega, the Musical Quarry has classic and truly delicious Mexican food. It's a fun, if touristy, place with an open kitchen and live music most nights. Set breakfasts are under US$5, and full meals, snacks and drinks are dispensed all day long.

Restaurant Cazadores (☎ 924-22-04; Callejón de la Caja 104; mains US$6-10) 'Hunters' has a very meaty menu and is decorated with animal trophy heads. The main attraction, though, is the location, upstairs overlooking lively Plazuela Goitia – request a window seat.

Café Zas (☎ 922-70-89; Av Hidalgo 201; mains US$3-5) Popular, clean and friendly, Café Zas serves decent breakfasts, *antojitos* (appetizers) and substantial meat and chicken meals.

JARDÍN INDEPENDENCIA & AROUND

Restaurant La Plaza (☎ 922-91-04; Rayón 434, in Quinta Real Zacatecas; mains US$10-20) The Quinta Real's elegant dining room is especially memorable for its outlook to the aqueduct and bullring, as well as for its refined ambience and superb Continental cuisine. It's also a good choice for a formal breakfast or a cocktail in what used to be the bull-holding pen. Reservations recommended.

Restaurant Fonda El Jacalito (☎ 922-07-71; Juárez 18; mains US$4-8) This bright, airy place is the best choice on Av Juárez, offering set breakfasts from US$4, a good *comida corrida* and tasty versions of traditional favorites.

El Pastor (☎ 922-16-35; Independencia 214; mains US$2-4) This friendly, family-run restaurant facing Jardín Independencia dishes out charcoal-roasted chicken, tortilla chips and salad. Pay a little more for chicken mole and rice.

Restaurant Condesa (☎ 922-11-60; Juárez 102; mains US$3-6) Attached to Hotel Condesa, this standard eatery is a convenient choice for an inexpensive breakfast or lunch.

SELF-CATERING & QUICK EATS

There are two central produce markets. Mercado El Laberinto's main entrance is on Av Juárez and budget eateries abound nearby. A bit to the southeast, Mercado Arroyo de la Plata is entered from the curved street Arroyo de la Plata.

Drinking

Gaudi Destilería (☎ 922-14-33; Mercado González Ortega Local 8) On the street level of the market's east side, this cave-like drinking den is popular with a young and stylish crowd, especially on Thursday and Friday nights.

Cactus (☎ 922-05-09; Av Hidalgo 111-13; US$3 Fri & Sat; ☾ 9pm-3am Mon-Sat) This enjoyable video-and-billiards bar is most popular for drink specials on Wednesday and music and dancing on Friday and Saturday until late.

El Paraíso (☎ 922-61-64; cnr Hidalgo & Plazuela Goitia) This smart bar in the southwest corner of the Mercado González Ortega attracts a friendly, varied, mostly 30s clientele; it's most busy on Friday and Saturday.

Entertainment

Pick up a free copy of the monthly Agenda Cultural at the tourist office. The **Teatro Calderón** (☎ 922-81-20) is the top venue for cultural events. Check the Eating section (p580) for restaurants that host live music.

Disco El Malacate (☎ 922-30-02; Dovali s/n; US$5; ☾ 9:30pm-2:30am Thu-Sat) Get down in a gallery of the Mina El Edén (see p576) to a mix of Latin and US hits with a big mixed crowd of locals and domestic and international tourists. The essential Zacatecas nightlife experience, it really gets going after midnight. Space is limited, so phone ahead to reserve a table – or risk getting left out of the shaft, so to speak.

Shopping

Zacatecas is known for silver, fine leather and colorful sarapes. Try along Arroyo de la Plata and in the indoor market off this street. The more upmarket Mercado González Ortega is the place to look for silver jewelry, local wines and leather *charrería* (rodeo) gear – boots, saddles, chaps, belts, sarapes and more.

FOR WHOM THE HORN TOOTS

Zacatecas has a tradition of *callejoneadas* – a custom from Spain in which a group of professional musicians in costume leads a crowd of revelers through the city, drinking wine, singing and telling stories along the way. In Zacatecas it's usually horn players leading the parade. There doesn't seem to be a regular schedule but during fiestas and on some weekends *callejoneadas* set off around 8pm from the **Teatro Calderón** (see p581). You can join in for free; ask for details at the tourist office

---

NORTHERN CENTRAL HIGHLANDS

The Zacatecas silversmithing industry is being revived in a number of workshops at the **Centro Platero** (☎ 899-09-94; ⏲ 9am-6pm Mon-Fri, 10am-3pm Sat), a few kilometers east of town at the 18th-century ex-Hacienda de Bernardez on the road to Guadalupe. Tour companies (see p578) can arrange visits to these workshops, or you can make your own way there by taxi.

Getting There & Away

AIR
Zacatecas' airport is 20km north of the city. Mexicana flies direct daily to/from Mexico City and Tijuana and weekly to/from Chicago and Los Angeles. Aero California flies from Zacatecas to Mexico City, Morelia and Tijuana.

AIRLINE OFFICES
Aero California (☎ 925-24-00; at airport)
Mexicana (☎ 922-74-29; Av Hidalgo 408)

BUS
Zacatecas' main bus station is on the southwest edge of town, 3km from the center. Many buses are *de paso* (stopping here en route between other cities). The station has a luggage checkroom, pharmacy and telephone *casetas*. The old bus station (Centro Comercial Zacatecas) is on Blvd López Mateos and handles only a few local destinations, such as Fresnillo and Villanueva (for La Quemada).

Aguascalientes (US$7.50, 2hr, 1st-class frequent daily; US$5-6.50, 2hr, half-hourly, 2nd-class Estrella Blanca daily)
Durango (US$16, 4½-6 hours, 13 1st-class Ómnibus de México daily; US$16, 4½-6 hours, 6 2nd-class Estrella Blanca daily)
Fresnillo (US$3, 1-1½hr; hourly 1st-class Futura daily; US$2.75, 1-1½hr, hourly 2nd-class Estrella Blanca & Camiones de los Altos daily)
Guadalajara (US$21, 4hr; hourly 1st-class Ómnibus de México & Chihuahuenses daily; US$18, 4hr, hourly 2nd-class Estrella Blanca & Rojo de los Altos daily)
Guanajuato Take a León bus & change there for Guanajuato
León (US$13, 3hr, 10 1st-class Ómnibus de México & Chihuahuenses daily)
Mexico City (US$49, 6-8hr, 1 deluxe daily; US$37, 6-8hr; 16 1st-class Futura, Chihuahuenses & Ómnibus de México daily) To Terminal Norte.
Monterrey (US$25, 5hr, 9 1st-class Transportes del Norte daily; US$21, 5hr, 10 2nd-class Estrella Blanca & Rojo de los Altos daily)

San Luis Potosí (US$9.50, 3hr, 12 1st-class Futura & Ómnibus de México daily; US$9, 3hr, 15 2nd-class Estrella Blanca daily)

There are also frequent buses to Jerez and Torreón and several a day to Chihuahua, Ciudad Juárez, Saltillo and Nuevo Laredo.

CAR & MOTORCYCLE
Budget (☎ 922-94-58; López Mateos 202) Next to Hotel Colón.
Lloguer (☎ 922-34-07; Héroes de Chapultepec 119) Discounts for local hotel guests.

Getting Around
The cheapest way between the center and the airport is via **combi** (☎ 922-59-46; US$5). Taxis charge around US$15.

Bus route No 8 from the bus station (US$0.30) runs directly to the cathedral. Heading out of the center, they go south on Villalpando. Bus route No 7 runs from the bus station to the corner of Avs González Ortega and Juárez. Taxis from the bus station to the center cost around US$2.

GUADALUPE
☎ 492 / pop 85,000
About 10km east of Zacatecas, Guadalupe has an historic former monastery with an impressive church that still attracts pilgrims, and one of Mexico's best colonial art collections. Stroll around the quaint plaza to browse the antiques and handicrafts shops between bites at a café or ice creamery.

The **Convento de Guadalupe** was established by Franciscan monks in the early 18th century as an apostolic college. It developed a strong academic tradition and was a base for missionary work in northern Nueva España until the 1850s. The convent now houses the **Museo Virreinal de Guadalupe** (☎ 923-23-86; Jardín Juárez s/n; US$3, free Sun; ⏲ 10am-4:30pm), with many paintings by Miguel Cabrera, Juan Correa, Antonio Torres and Cristóbal Villalpando. The art is almost entirely religious – lots of saints, angels and bloody crucifixions. The building itself has a wonderful medieval feeling, and visitors can see part of the library and step into the choir on the church's upper floor, with its fine carved and painted chairs. From the choir area you can look down into the beautifully decorated 19th-century **Capilla de Nápoles** on the church's north side.

Beside Museo Virreinal, the free **Museo Regional de Historia** (☎ 923-23-86; ⏰ 10am-4:30pm) has a good bookstore and giftshop and a limited number of exhibits on the state's history.

The town holds a cultural festival at the end of September and its annual fair during the first two weeks of December, focused on the **Día de la Virgen de Guadalupe** (December 12).

From Zacatecas, Transportes de Guadalupe buses run to Guadalupe every few minutes (US$0.25, 20 minutes); catch one at the bus stop on Blvd López Mateos opposite the old bus station. Get off at a small plaza in the middle of Guadalupe where a 'Museo Convento' sign points to the right, along Madero. Walk 250m along Madero to Jardín Juárez, a sizable plaza. The museums are on the left side of the plaza. To return to Zacatecas, catch the bus where you disembarked.

FRESNILLO & PLATEROS

☎ 493 / Fresnillo pop 100,000

Fresnillo is an unexciting town 58km north of Zacatecas, beside the highway to Durango and Torreón. The village of Plateros, 5km northeast, is home to the Santuario de Plateros, one of Mexico's most visited shrines. If you're interested in Mexican Catholicism, you might find the shrine worth visiting. Otherwise, give both towns a miss.

Orientation

Fresnillo's bus station is on Ébano, 1km northeast of the town center on local bus No 3. Direct buses to Plateros depart Fresnillo's bus station hourly. If you need to go into Fresnillo for a meal or a room, you'll find it's a higgledy-piggledy place with three main plazas. The most pleasant of the three is Jardín Madero with the colonial church on its north side.

Santuario de Plateros

Pilgrims flock to this 18th-century church's altar to see El Santo Niño de Atocha, a quaint image of the infant Jesus wearing a colonial pilgrim's feathered hat. A series of rooms to the right of the church entrance is lined with thousands of *retablos* (altarpieces) giving thanks to Santo Niño for all manner of miracles. Some older ones go back to WWII, while others recall traffic accidents, muggings and medical operations. More recent ones include copies of school

reports and academic records. The surrounding streets are lined with stalls selling gaudy religious artifacts – Santo Niño souvenirs especially.

Sleeping

There are a few hotels in Plateros for pilgrims planning a 6am mass, but they aren't very restful. Fresnillo is a better overnight option. Opposite Fresnillo's bus terminal, **Hotel Lirmar** (☎ 932-45-98; Durango 400; s/d US$14/19) is a fairly modern place with clean, comfortable rooms.

A block south of Av Juárez and a block west of Av Hidalgo in central Fresnillo, **Hotel Maya** (☎ 932-03-51; Ensaye 9; s/d US$14/17) has bright, fairly clean rooms with TV. Three blocks east of Jardín Hidalgo, **Hotel Casa Blanca** (☎ 932-00-14; García Salinas 503; s/d US$27/32) caters to business travelers.

Getting There & Around

Fresnillo is well served by long-distance buses, though many are *de paso*. Frequent 1st-class buses serve Durango (US$12, 3¼ hours), Torreón (US$18.50, five hours) and Zacatecas (US$2.50, one hour); 2nd-class buses are even more frequent.

To Plateros, buy a ticket at the Parques Industriales counter in Fresnillo's bus station for an hourly 2nd-class bus (US$0.60). Local No 6 buses (US$0.50) also go to Plateros from Emiliano Zapata, 2½ blocks east of Jardín Madero.

JEREZ

☎ 494 / pop 38,000

A small country town 30km southwest of Zacatecas, Jerez has some fine 18th- and 19th-century buildings that testify to the wealth that silver brought to even the lesser towns of the Zacatecas region. Jerez holds a lively 10-day Easter fair starting on Good Friday featuring *charreadas*, cockfights and other rip-snorting family fun.

Orientation & Information

Jardín Páez, the pleasant main plaza, has an old-fashioned gazebo and plenty of trees, birds and benches. The **tourist office** (☎ 945-68-24; Guanajuato 28) is two blocks north. Efficient Inbox Cybercafé (Salinas 2A), a block north, charges US$1.50 per hour. Several banks (with ATMs) and card phones are around the plaza.

Sights

The 18th-century Parroquia de la Inmaculada Concepción and the 19th-century Santuario de la Soledad have fine stone carvings. Go one block south from Jardín Páez' southeast corner, then one block east for the church, or one block west for the shrine. Just past the shrine, on Jardín Hidalgo's north side, is the beautiful 19th-century Teatro Hinojosa.

Sleeping & Eating

There are a couple of good places to rest your head near the plaza and several eateries dish out cheap standards like chicken, *bistec* (steak) and beans. Half a block north of the plaza's northeast corner, **Posada Santa Cecilia** (☎ 945-24-12; Constitución 4; s/d US$21/24) occupies an old but renovated building and offers modern comforts in appealing rooms. The best of several cheapies on the plaza is **Hotel Plaza** (☎ 945-20-63; Plaza Principal Sur 8; s/d US$8.50/13), with small, bare, clean rooms with bathroom and TV (on request). East of town on the road to Zacatecas, the modern **Leo Hotel** (☎ 945-20-01; www.leohotel.com; Calzada La Suave Patria s/n; r from US$49; P ♨) is the fanciest place around, with a heated pool, disco and a cinema next door.

Getting There & Around

The Jerez turnoff is near Malpaso, 29km south of Zacatecas on the Zacatecas–Guadalajara road. The Zacatecas–Jerez line runs 2nd-class buses from Zacatecas' bus station to Jerez (US$2.75) every 30 minutes. There are also services by Ómnibus de México and Estrella Blanca/Rojo de los Altos. Jerez' bus station is on the east side of town, 1km from the center along Calz La Suave Patria. 'Centro-Central' buses (US$0.25) run to/from the center. There are also several daily services to/from Fresnillo (US$2).

LA QUEMADA

The impressive **ruins** (☎ 922-60-85; US$3; ☯ 10am-3:30pm) of La Quemada stand on a hill overlooking a broad valley 45km south of Zacatecas, 2km east of the Zacatecas–Guadalajara road. They're also known as Chicomostoc, once thought to be the place of that name where the Aztecs halted during their legendary wanderings toward the Valle de México. The remote and scenic setting makes the ruins well worth the trip from Zacatecas.

The **site museum** (US$0.75; ☯ 10am-4pm) has fascinating archaeology exhibits and is an interesting piece of architecture in itself. Both the museum and the site have explanatory labels in English as well as Spanish.

La Quemada was inhabited between about AD 300 and AD 1200 and probably peaked between AD 500 and AD 900 with as many as 15,000 people. From around AD 400 it was part of a regional trade network linked to Teotihuacán (see p32), but fortifications suggest that La Quemada later tried to dominate trade in this region. Traces of a big fire indicate that its final downfall was violent.

Some of the ruins can be seen atop the hill to the left as you approach from the Zacatecas–Guadalajara road. Of the main structures, the nearest to the site entrance is the **Salón de las Columnas** (Hall of the Columns), probably a ceremonial hall. A bit further up the hill are a ball court, a steep offerings pyramid and an equally steep staircase leading toward the site's upper levels. From the upper levels of the main hill, a path leads westward to a spur hilltop with the remains of a cluster of buildings called **La Ciudadela** (the Citadel). A stone wall, probably built for defensive purposes late in La Quemada's history, spans the slopes to the north.

Getting There & Away

From Zacatecas' old bus station, board a 2nd-class bus for Villanueva (US$2.75) and ask to be let off at 'las ruinas'; you'll be deposited at the Restaurant Las Siete Cuevas. Walk 2km along the paved road going east to the site. Returning to Zacatecas, you may have to wait a while before a bus shows up – don't leave the ruins too late. Ómnibus de México and Rojo de los Altos have regular service from Zacatecas' 1st-class bus station to Villanueva and Guadalajara, and these may also stop at the La Quemada turnoff. You can also do an organized tour (US$16) from Zacatecas (see p578).

SOMBRERETE

☎ 433 / pop 19,000

Looking like something from a Western movie, Sombrerete is an archetypical old Mexican town, its timeworn buildings and traditional streets almost totally intact. The first settlements here were in the 1550s, and mines began extracting minerals that financed a rich legacy of churches, mansions and public buildings.

Opposite the cathedral, the soporific **municipal tourist office** (☎ 935-00-88; Hidalgo s/n) doesn't see many tourists, but the staff can answer questions (in Spanish). Next door, the small **Museo de la Ciudad** (Hidalgo 207; US$0.75; ☯ 10am-4pm Mon-Sat) has folksy but well-displayed history exhibits.

Bathrooms have been added and electricity installed, but everything else about **Gran Hotel Hidalgo** (☎ 935-00-98; Hidalgo 135; s/d US$5.50/11, with bathroom & cable TV US$12/19) is straight out of the 19th century, from the tiled courtyard to the high ceilings. It's on the main drag adjacent to the bus company offices.

Sombrerete's bus station is not far from the town center, and numerous buses stop here between Zacatecas and Durango. If you're driving, the main street is just south of Hwy 45.

PARQUE NACIONAL SIERRA DE ÓRGANOS

High on the western edge of Zacatecas state, the Organ Range is named for its distinctive rock formations, some of which resemble organ pipes. The clear sky and striking high desert scenery make an ideal backdrop for western movies: *Cisco Kid*, *The Guns of San Sebastian* and *The Sons of Katie Elder* all filmed scenes here. The area was declared a national park (US$1.25) in 2000, and a visitors center is in the works. There are a few picnic areas and campsites, but no other facilities, and no year-round water source. Most people come on a day-trip and some good hikes are possible (carry water and wear a hat), but you really need your own transport.

To get here, turn north off Hwy 45 about 15km west of Sombrerete, follow the dirt roads for 10km until you see rocky formations on your left, then take the next left to the park entrance.

AGUASCALIENTES STATE

The state of Aguascalientes (population 1 million) is one of Mexico's smallest. It was originally part of Zacatecas; according to tradition, a kiss planted on the lips of dic-

tator Santa Anna by the attractive wife of a prominent local politician brought about the creation of a separate Aguascalientes state.

Industry is concentrated in and around the capital city, also called Aguascalientes, but the rest of the state is primarily agricultural, growing corn, beans, chilies, fruit and grain on its fertile lands. The state's ranches produce beef cattle as well as bulls, which are sacrificed at bullfights countrywide.

AGUASCALIENTES

☎ 449 / pop 630,000 / elevation 1800m

Named for its hot springs, this prosperous industrial city has a few handsome colonial buildings in the well-planned central area. Aguascalientes also has several modern shopping malls and a very modern bullring. If you're interested in Mexican art, the museums devoted to José Guadalupe Posada and Saturnino Herrán justify a visit. Even by Mexican standards, Aguascalientes is a very friendly town.

History

Before the Spanish invasion, a labyrinth of catacombs was built here, so the first Spaniards called it La Ciudad Perforada – the perforated city. Archaeologists have little understanding of the tunnels, which are off-limits to visitors.

Conquistador Pedro de Alvarado arrived in 1522 but was driven back by the Chichimecs. A small garrison was founded here in 1575 to protect Zacatecas–Mexico City silver convoys. Eventually, as the Chichimecs were pacified, the region's hot springs sparked the growth of a town; a large tank beside the Ojo Caliente springs helped irrigate local farms that fed hungry nearby mining districts.

The city's industries began with processing agricultural products into textiles, wine, brandy, leather and preserved fruits, but now include a huge Nissan plant just south of town. Today, more than half of the state's population lives in the city.

Orientation

Aguascalientes is pancake flat and easy to get around. The center of town is Plaza de la Patria, surrounded by some pleasant pedestrian streets. Shops, hotels, restaurants and some fine buildings are within a few blocks.

AGUASCALIENTES

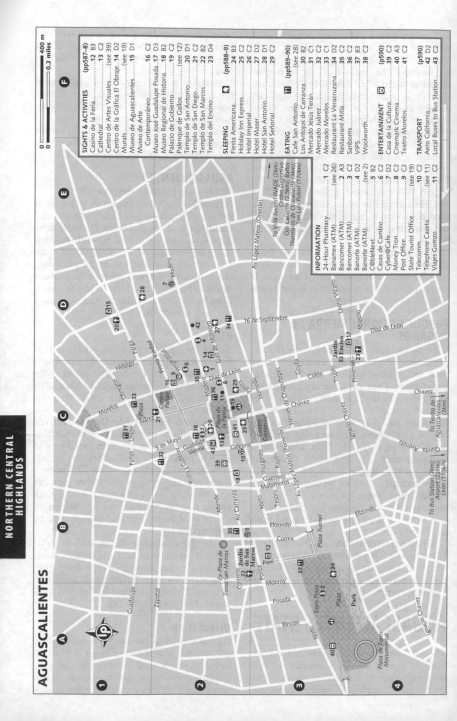

0
0   400 m
                            0.2 miles

SIGHTS & ACTIVITIES	(pp587–8)
Casino de la Feria.................	12 B3
Cathedral..............................	13 C2
Centro de Artes Visuales........	(see 39)
Centro de la Gráfica El Obraje.	14 D2
Murals...................................	(see 19)
Museo de Aguascalientes........	15 D1
Museo de Arte	
Contemporáneo..................	16 C2
Museo José Guadalupe Posada.	17 D3
Museo Regional de Historia.....	18 B2
Palacio de Gobierno...............	19 C2
Palenque de Gallos................	(see 12)
Templo de San Antonio...........	20 D1
Templo de San Diego..............	21 C2
Templo de San Marcos............	22 B2
Templo del Encino.................	23 D4

SLEEPING	(pp588–9)
Fiesta Americana...................	24 B3
Holiday Inn Express................	25 C2
Hotel Imperial......................	26 C2
Hotel Maser.........................	27 D2
Hotel San Antonio.................	28 D1
Hotel Señorial......................	29 C2

EATING	(pp589–90)
Cafe San Antonio..................	(see 28)
Los Antojos de Carranza.........	30 B2
Mercado Jesús Terán..............	31 C1
Mercado Juárez.....................	32 C2
Mercado Morelos...................	33 C1
Restaurant La Veracruzana......	34 D2
Restaurant Mitla...................	35 C2
Sanborns.............................	36 C2
VIPS....................................	37 B3
Woolworth...........................	38 C2

ENTERTAINMENT	(p590)
Casa de la Cultura.................	39 C2
Cinemark Cinema..................	40 A3
Teatro Morelos....................	41 C2

TRANSPORT	(p590)
Aero California.....................	42 D2
Local Buses to Bus Station......	43 C2

INFORMATION	
24-Hour Pharmacy.................	1 C2
Banamex (ATM).....................	(see 26)
Bancomer (ATM)....................	2 A3
Bancomer (ATM)....................	3 C2
Banorte (ATM)......................	4 D2
Banorte (ATM)......................	(see 2)
C@bleNext...........................	5 B2
Casas de Cambio....................	6 C2
Cyber@Cafe.........................	7 D2
Money Tron..........................	8 C2
Post Office...........................	9 C2
State Tourist Office................	(see 19)
Telecomm...........................	10 C2
Telephone Caseta..................	(see 11)
Viajes Gomzo.......................	11 C2

Av Chávez/5 de Mayo is the main north–south artery; it passes through a tunnel beneath Plaza de la Patria. Av López Mateos, the main east–west artery, is a couple of blocks south of the plaza.

Information

BOOKSTORES
Casa Terán (☎ 994-10-09; Rivero y Gutiérrez 110; ☯ 9am-9pm Mon-Sat) Good bookstore & Mexican cultural center with a patio café.

INTERNET ACCESS
Most places charge around US$1 an hour.
C@bleNext (Correa 139)
CyberCafé (Madero 402)

MEDICAL SERVICES
24-Hour Pharmacy (Madero s/n)

MONEY
Banks with ATMs are common around Plaza de la Patria and Expoplaza. *Casas de cambio* cluster on Hospitalidad, opposite the post office.
Money Tron (Montoro s/n; ☯ 9am-4pm Mon-Fri) Exchange house half a block east of the plaza with drive-thru window.

TELEPHONE
Telecomm (Galeana 102)

TOURIST INFORMATION
State tourist office (☎ 915-95-04, 800-949-49-49; www.aguascalientes.gob.mx; in Palacio de Gobierno; ☎ 9am -8pm) Free city maps.

TRAVEL AGENCIES
Viajes Gomzo (☎ 916-54-13; Montoro 114)

Sights & Activities

PLAZA DE LA PATRIA
The well-restored 18th-century baroque cathedral, on the plaza's west side, is more magnificent inside than outside. Over the altar at the east end of the south aisle is a painting of the Virgin of Guadalupe by Miguel Cabrera. There are more works by Cabrera, colonial Mexico's finest artist, in the cathedral's *pinacoteca* (picture gallery); ask a priest to let you in.

Facing the cathedral's south side is **Teatro Morelos**, scene of the 1914 Convention of Aguascalientes, in which revolutionary factions led by Pancho Villa, Venustiano Carranza and Emiliano Zapata tried unsuccessfully to mend their differences. Busts of these three, plus one of Álvaro Obregón, stand in the foyer, and there are a few exhibits upstairs.

On the plaza's south side, the red and pink stone **Palacio de Gobierno** is Aguascalientes' most noteworthy colonial building. Once the mansion of colonial baron Marqués de Guadalupe, it dates from 1665 and has a striking courtyard with a mural by the Chilean artist Osvaldo Barra. This depicts the 1914 convention, pointing out that some of its ideas were crystallized in Mexico's still-governing 1917 constitution – including the eight-hour workday. Barra, whose mentor was Diego Rivera, also painted the mural on the far (south) wall, a compendium of the economic and historic forces that forged Aguascalientes (look for the depiction of the Mexico-USA border being drawn).

MUSEUMS & CHURCHES
The fascinating **Museo José Guadalupe Posada** (☎ 915-45-56; Jardín El Encino s/n; US$1, free Sun; ☯ 11am-6pm Tue-Sun) is beside Jardín El Encino. Aguascalientes native Posada (1852–1913) was in many ways the founder of modern Mexican art. His engravings and satirical cartoons during the Porfiriato dictatorship broadened the audience for art in Mexico, drew attention to social problems and inspired later artists like Diego Rivera. Posada's hallmark is the *calavera* (skull or skeleton), and many of his *calavera* engravings have been widely reproduced. Less well known are his engravings of current events for periodicals; the series on executions by firing squad conveys the violence of the revolutionary period. The museum has a large collection of Posada prints, each displayed alongside the original etched zinc plate so you can appreciate the demands of the printmaker's art. There's also a permanent exhibition of work by Posada's predecessor Manuel Manilla (1830–90), and temporary exhibitions of works by other Mexican artists.

The **Templo del Encino** (☯ 11am-1pm & 5-7pm Mon-Fri), beside the Posada museum, contains a black statue of Jesus that some believe is growing. When it reaches an adjacent column, a worldwide calamity is anticipated. The huge 'Way of the Cross' murals are also noteworthy. The shady plaza outside makes a nice picnic spot.

The handsome neoclassical **Museo de Aguascalientes** (☎ 915-90-43; Zaragoza 507; US$1.25, free Sun; ☙ 11am-6pm Tue-Sun) houses a permanent exhibition of work by Saturnino Herrán (1887–1918), another great Mexican artist born in Aguascalientes. In a graphic style reminiscent of French art nouveau, his portraits and illustrative work depict Mexican people and places with great technical skill and sensitivity. The very sensual sculpture *Malgretout* on the patio is a fiberglass copy of the marble original by Jesús Contreras.

Opposite the museum, **Templo de San Antonio** is a crazy quilt of architectural styles built around 1900 by self-taught architect Refugio Reyes. San Antonio's interior is highly ornate, with huge round paintings and intricate decoration highlighted in gold.

The **Museo de Arte Contemporáneo** (☎ 918-69-01; cnr Morelos & Primo Verdad; US$1, free Sun; ☙ 11am-6pm Tue-Sun) is a modern museum displaying recent products of Aguascalientes' artists – it's well worth a look. Nearby, the **Centro de la Gráfica El Obraje** (☎ 994-00-74; Montoro 222; ☙ 10am-8pm Tue-Sun) is a workshop-studio-gallery for printmakers and graphic designers that hosts free bimonthly exhibitions.

The **Museo Regional de Historia** (☎ 916-52-28; Carranza 118; US$2.75, free Sun; ☙ 10am-7pm Tue-Sun) was designed by Refugio Reyes as a family home. It has several rooms of exhibits on Aguascalientes' history from the big bang to the *revolución*. It's only really worth checking out if you are a Mexican history aficionado. There are a couple of nice cafés nearby on the same street.

EXPOPLAZA & AROUND
Half a kilometer west of Plaza de la Patria, via Av López Mateos or Nieto, Expoplaza is a modern shopping center with a few cafés and a modern 10-screen cinema (tickets US$2). On the mall's south side, the wide and somewhat soulless pedestrian promenade comes alive during the annual Feria de San Marcos (see p588). At its west end, the mammoth Plaza de Toros Monumental is notable for its modern-colonial treatment of traditional bullring architecture.

On Expoplaza's east side, **Pani** runs two blocks north to the 18th-century **Templo de San Marcos** and the shady **Jardín de San Marcos**, the center of extensive urban restoration project. Keep an eye out here for hip new cafés and restaurants. The **Palenque de Gallos**, in the **Casino de la Feria** building on Pani, is the city's cockfighting arena. Near the northeast corner of Jardín de San Marcos, the **Ex-Plaza de Toros San Marcos**, the old bullring, is now a school for aspiring matadors.

HOT SPRINGS
It's no surprise that a town called Aguascalientes has geothermally-heated springs. The best known are at **Centro Deportivo Ojo Caliente** (☎ 970-06-98; Carretera San Luis Potosí Km 1; US$2.25; ☙ 7am-7pm Wed-Fri in summer, 7am-8pm in winter), on the city's east edge. Take bus No 12 along Av López Mateos. The large pool and other smaller pools have warmish water; the hot water is in private pools (from US$3.50). The large parklike grounds have tennis, volleyball and squash courts and a restaurant.

Nearby, the **Baños Termales de Ojocaliente** (☎ 970-07-21; Tecnológico 102; US$2.75; ☙ 8am-7pm) are less sporty and more elegant, and worth seeing for the restored 1808 architecture.

Tours
El Tranvía, an imitation double-decker trolley car, offers three different routes through the city, including a guided visit to the Palacio de Gobierno, (six times daily, except Monday, between 10am and 6pm). Get information and tickets (adults/child US$2.25/1.35) at the state tourist office (see p587).

Festivals & Events
Mexico's biggest annual state fair, **Feria de San Marcos**, centers around Expoplaza and routinely attracts a million visitors with exhibitions, bullfights, cockfights, rodeos, free concerts and an extravaganza of cultural events, including an international film festival. The fair starts in mid-April and lasts nearly a month. The big parade takes place on the saint's day, April 25.

During **Festival de las Calaveras**, from October 25 to November 4, Aguascalientes celebrates Día de los Muertos (Day of the Dead) with an emphasis on the symbolism of *calaveras* (skeletons), as depicted by local artist Posada in the 19th century.

Sleeping
Prices skyrocket during the Feria de San Marcos and accommodations are completely booked for the fair's final weekend;

residents run a lucrative homestay service at this time. Ask around at the fair or tourist office if you're stuck.

BUDGET

Hotel San Antonio (☎ 915-93-41; 916-33-20; Zaragoza 305; s/d US$14/19; Ⓟ) It's tough to beat this clean, courteous motel, especially if you are driving. The 24-7 drive-thru reception window is strict about not admitting 'couples without luggage'. There's cable TV and the beds are firm but the echoing engine noise from the enclosed courtyard parking lot can make it tough to sleep in.

Hotel Maser (☎ 915-35-62; Montoro 303; s/d US$11/15; Ⓟ) The Maser has helpful management and 47 simple but clean rooms around a covered inner courtyard. The enclosed parking is free but a bit tight and TV costs a couple of extra dollars.

Villa Juvenil INADE (☎ 970-08-63; cnr Av Circunvalación Ote & Jaime Nunó; dm US$4; Ⓟ Ⓡ) This youth hostel, 3km east of the center on the ring road, mainly hosts youth groups, but travelers can crash here in a pinch. The hostel has 72 beds in clean separate-sex dormitories. Bus No 20 from the bus station or the red bus east along Av López Mateos will take you to Av Circunvalación; walk north 200m to the hostel.

Overnight dry RV camping is possible at the **Centro Deportivo Ojo Caliente** (see Sleeping, p588) if you pull in before the gate closes at 8pm.

MID-RANGE

Hotel Señorial (☎ 915-16-30/14-73; Colón 1041; s/d US$19/28) This friendly, 40-year-old, family-run hotel has 32 reasonable rooms with cable TV and phone. There's a variety of rooms, some with balconies.

Hotel Imperial (☎ 915-16-64; 5 de Mayo 106; r from US$29) The well-located Imperial is a fine-looking building outside, though the lobby is unimpressive. The basic rooms are spacious, modern and clean, with fan, TV and phone. Interior rooms are darker, quieter and cheaper than the exterior ones, some of which have balconies and plaza views.

TOP END

Holiday Inn Express (☎ 916-16-66, 800-009-99-00; Nieto 102; hiexp@ags.acnet.net; r/ste from US$96/112; ✕ Ⓡ) The historic center's most comfortable option has 89 rooms with all modern

conveniences, and full facilities for business travelers. Discounts of 25% are available some weekends.

Fiesta Americana (☎ 918-60-10; www.fiestaamericana.com; Laureles s/n, Colonia Las Flores; r from US$139; Ⓟ ✕ Ⓧ Ⓛ Ⓡ) This luxury chain hotel has 192 rooms and all the amenities, including a fitness center and inviting pool. Weekend rates start around US$90 for two and include brunch.

Some recommended luxurious resort-style hotels near the industrial zone on the outskirts of the city include:

Quinta Real Aguascalientes (☎ 978-58-18; www.summithotels.com; Av Aguascalientes Sur 601; ste US$175-220; Ⓟ ✕ Ⓧ Ⓛ Ⓡ)

Hotel Las Trojes (☎ 973-00-06, 800-288-91-99; www.hotellastrojes.com.mx; cnr Zacatecas & Colosio; r from US$80; Ⓟ ✕ Ⓧ Ⓡ)

Eating

AROUND PLAZA DE LA PATRIA

Sanborns (☎ 915-20-24; Madero 101; mains US$4-9; ◷ 7:30am-1am; ✕) Above Sanborns department store in the restored Hotel Francia building, this dependable restaurant is popular with well-to-do locals for a snack, drink or a meal. On offer are fixed-price breakfasts and lunches, as well as a choice of à la carte Mexican dishes.

Restaurant Mitla (☎ 916-61-57; Madero 220; mains US$5-10) This large, clean and pleasant restaurant has been going since 1938. It's popular with locals and welcomes foreigners. There's a choice of good-value set breakfasts, four-course set lunches (US$4.50) and a variety of well-prepared local specialties. It's a good place to linger over coffee or a drink.

Restaurant La Veracruzana (☎ 915-44-38; Hornedo 402; mains US$1.50-3; ◷ 8:30am-5pm Mon-Sat) This small, simple, family-run restaurant does solid home-style cooking at rock bottom prices: the four-course *comida corrida* (US$2.75) is a bargain and the *frijoles* are some of the Mexico's best.

Woolworth (☎ 918-41-98; 5 de Mayo 122; mains US$4-7; ✕) Straightforward Woolworth has good-value (if bland) breakfasts until noon, Westernized Mexican standards, *pozole* (shredded pork in broth) every day and padded, diner-style booths.

NEAR EXPOPLAZA

There's a good selection of mid-range eateries on Av Carranza and the pedestrian street Pani going south to Expoplaza, which has many bars and fast food options.

Los Antojos de Carranza (☎ 953-23-31; Carranza 301; mains US$4-8; 🕸) This is a smart place where you can get breakfast, a big salad and well-prepared regional meat, poultry and fish dishes. It's also a good spot for a drink, and sometimes has live music or sports events on TV.

VIPS (☎ 918-42-61; Centro Comercial Expoplaza; mains US$4-9; 🕸) Inside Expoplaza shopping center is yet another link in the reliable, if unremarkable, chain of Mexi-American restaurants.

SELF-CATERING & QUICK EATS
Fresh produce is available in three markets near Plaza de la Patria: Mercado Juárez, Mercado Jesús Terán and Mercado Morelos. Quite a few quick-bite places around and north of the plaza cater to shoppers and local workers.

Entertainment
Pani, the pedestrian street between the Expoplaza and Jardín de San Marcos, is lively most evenings, with a good selection of bars and lively restaurants.

The trendy nightspots are out in the suburbs; **Centro Comercial Galerias** (☎ 912-66-12; Independencia 2351) is a shopping mall with several bars and discos, including the popular **El Reloj**. Grab a cab for either **Metro** (Aguascalientes s/n) a hot, very yellow disco on the north side of town, or **Pervert** (Madero s/n), an underground club on the eastside spinning cutting-edge electronica.

In a fine 17th-century building, the **Casa de la Cultura** (Carranza near Galeana) hosts art exhibitions, concerts, theater and dance events. The **Teatro Morelos** (Plaza de la Patria) and the **Teatro de Aguascalientes** (Chávez at Aguascalientes), south of the center, both stage a variety of cultural events. Free concerts, dance and theater are presented some Sunday lunchtimes in the courtyard of **Museo José Guadalupe Posada** (see p587).

Getting There & Away
AIR
Aéropuerto Jesús Terán (☎ 915-81-32) is 26km south of Aguascalientes off the road to Mexico City. Aeroméxico/Aerolitoral has daily direct Mexico City, Monterrey, San Luis Potosí, San Antonio (Texas) and Ti-

juana flights, plus direct flights to/from Los Angeles. Aero California and Aerolíneas Internacionales both serve Mexico City and Tijuana.

AIRLINE OFFICES
Aero California (☎ 915-24-00; Madero 319)
Aerolíneas Internacionales (☎ 915-85-05; Av Las Américas 110)
Aeroméxico/Aerolitoral (☎ 916-13-61/62; Madero 474)

BUS
The Central Camionera is 2km south of the center on Av Circunvalación Sur (aka Av Convención). It has a post office, card phones, a cafétería and luggage storage. Daily departures include:
Guadalajara (US$20, 2½-4hr, 4 deluxe ETN daily; US$15, 2½-4hr, hourly 1st-class daily)
Guanajuato (US$12, 3hr, 1st-class *de paso* Primera Plus 8pm daily; US$9, 3hr, 2nd-class Flecha Amarilla 6:45am daily) More frequent services from León.
León (US$6.50, 2hr, hourly 1st-class Primera Plus daily)
Mexico City (US$42, 6hr, 8 deluxe ETN 1st-class daily; US$31, 6hr, hourly Futura & Ómnibus de México daily; US$27, 6hr, 5 2nd-class Flecha Amarilla daily) To Terminal Norte.
San Luis Potosí (US$11, 3hr, 14 1st-class Futura daily; US$8.50, 3hr, hourly 2nd-class Estrella Blanca daily)
Zacatecas (US$7.50, 2hr, 13 1st-class Ómnibus de México & Futura daily; US$6, 2hr, half-hourly 2nd-class Rojo de los Altos daily)

There's also frequent service to Ciudad Juárez, Monterrey, Morelia and Torreón, plus at least two buses daily to San Miguel de Allende (US$12).

Getting Around
Most places of interest are within easy walking distance of each other. Regular city buses (US$0.30) run 6am to 10pm; red buses (US$0.40) are more comfortable and follow the same routes.

Bus Nos 3, 4 and 9 (marked 'Centro' or '5 de Mayo') run from the bus station to the city center. Get off at the first stop after the tunnel under Plaza de la Patria: on 5 de Mayo or Rivero y Gutiérrez. From the city center to the bus station, take any 'Central' bus on Moctezuma opposite the cathedral's north side, or around the corner on Galeana.

Within town and to the bus station, the standard taxi fare is US$2; to the airport it's about US$8.

SAN LUIS POTOSÍ STATE

The state of San Luis Potosí (poh-toh-*see*; population 2.35 million) contains two of the most interesting destinations between Mexico City and the US border: the mountain ghost town of Real de Catorce and the city of San Luis Potosí itself, a major colonial town steeped in history.

Most of the state is high and dry, with little rainfall. The exception is its eastern corner, which drops steeply to the tropical valleys near the Gulf coast (see p647).

Before the Spanish conquest, western San Luis Potosí was inhabited by warlike hunters and gatherers known as Guachichiles, the Aztec word for 'sparrows,' after their widespread custom of wearing only loincloths and, sometimes, pointed headdresses resembling sparrows' heads.

Christian missionaries entered the state in the 1570s and 1580s, but it was the discovery of silver in the Cerro de San Pedro that really awakened Spanish interest in the region. San Luis Potosí city was founded near these deposits in 1592, and Tlaxcalans, Tarascans and Otomíes were imported to work the mines and cattle ranches.

In the 18th century the area had a reputation for maltreatment of indigenous people. This was partly because a number of parishes were transferred from the Franciscans, who had done their best to protect indigenous people, to other clergy. Appalling labor conditions and discontent over expulsion of the Franciscans (who ran the best schools in Mexico and managed their estates relatively well) culminated in an uprising in 1767.

Under Spanish reforms in 1786, the city of San Luis Potosí became capital of a huge area covering the modern states of San Luis Potosí, Tamaulipas, Nuevo León, Coahuila and Texas. This lasted only until Mexican independence, and in 1824 the state of San Luis Potosí was formed with its present area.

Today it's a fairly prosperous state. The northern silver mines are some of Mexico's richest, and gold, copper, lead and zinc are also extracted. Agriculture (corn, beans, wheat and cotton) and ranching are other major sources of wealth, as is industry, which is concentrated in the capital.

SAN LUIS POTOSÍ

☎ 444 / pop 652,000 / elevation 1860m

The state capital was a major colonial city and has been a mining center, a seat of governments-in-exile and a revolutionary hotbed. Today its main importance is as a regional capital and industrial center. Flat and laid out in an orderly grid, San Luis is less spectacular than colonial cities like Guanajuato and Zacatecas, but its historic heart has fine buildings, congenial pedestrian areas, expansive plazas and a general air of elegance. It's also a university town, with cultural attractions and an active nightlife. Don't be put off by the industrial outskirts – San Luis is lovely in the middle.

History

Founded in 1592, 20km west of the silver deposits in the Cerro de San Pedro hills, San Luis is named Potosí after the immensely rich Bolivian silver town of that name, which the Spanish hoped it would rival.

Yields from the mines began to decline in the 1620s, but the city was well enough established as a ranching center to remain the major city of northeastern Mexico until overtaken by Monterrey at the start of the 20th century.

It was known in the 19th century for its lavish houses and imported luxury goods. San Luis was twice the seat of President Benito Juárez' government during the 1860s' French intervention. In 1910 in San Luis the dictatorial president Porfirio Díaz jailed Francisco Madero, his liberal opponent, during that year's presidential election. Freed after the election, Madero hatched his Plan de San Luis Potosí (a strategy to depose Díaz), announcing it in San Antonio, Texas in October 1910. The plan declared the recent election illegal, named Madero provisional president and designated November 20 as the day for Mexico to rise in revolt.

Orientation

Central San Luis stretches from the Alameda park in the east to Plaza de los Fundadores and Plaza San Francisco in the west. Within this triangle are two more main plazas, Plaza del Carmen and the Plaza de Armas. Hotels and restaurants concentrate in this central area, with most cheaper lodgings near the old train station. An upscale commercial strip stretches some 3km west from Plaza de los Fundadores along Av Carranza.

Information

INTERNET ACCESS

Most places charge around US$1 per hour.

Café Cibernetico (Av Carranza 416) Fast connections, good coffee.

Café Plaza Internet (south side Plaza de Armas, 2nd floor)

Fox Cyber Café (Iturbide 355)

LAUNDRY

Lavandería (5 de Mayo 870) 3kg loads for US$2.75.

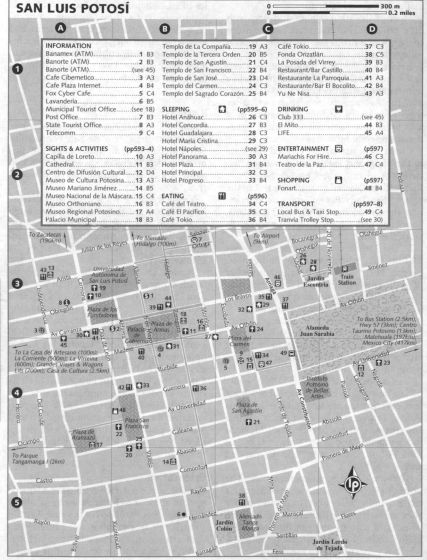

SAN LUIS POTOSÍ

INFORMATION		
Banamex (ATM)..................1	B3	
Banorte (ATM)....................2	B3	
Banorte (ATM)...............(see 45)		
Cafe Cibernetico.................3	A3	
Cafe Plaza Internet.............4	B4	
Fox Cyber Cafe...................5	C4	
Lavandería.........................6	B5	
Municipal Tourist Office........(see 18)		
Post Office.........................7	B3	
State Tourist Office.............8	A3	
Telecomm..........................9	C4	
SIGHTS & ACTIVITIES	(pp593–4)	
Capilla de Loreto...............10	A3	
Cathedral.........................11	B3	
Centro de Difusión Cultural...12	D4	
Museo de Cultura Potosina...13	A3	
Museo Mariano Jiménez.......14	B5	
Museo Nacional de la Máscara...15	C4	
Museo Orthoniano..............16	B3	
Museo Regional Potosino.....17	A4	
Palacio Municipal...............18	B3	
Templo de La Compañía........19	A3	
Templo de la Tercera Orden...20	B5	
Templo de San Agustín.........21	C4	
Templo de San Francisco.......22	B4	
Templo de San José.............23	D4	
Templo del Carmen.............24	C3	
Templo del Sagrado Corazón...25	B4	
SLEEPING	(pp595–6)	
Hotel Anáhuac...................26	C3	
Hotel Concordia.................27	B3	
Hotel Guadalajara..............28	C3	
Hotel María Cristina...........29	C3	
Hotel Nápoles...................(see 29)		
Hotel Panorama.................30	A3	
Hotel Plaza......................31	B4	
Hotel Principal..................32	C3	
Hotel Progreso..................33	B4	
EATING	(p596)	
Café del Teatro.................34	C4	
Café El Pacífico................35	C3	
Café Tokio.......................36	B4	
Café Tokio.......................37	C3	
Fonda Orizatlán................38	C5	
La Posada del Virrey...........39	B3	
Restaurant/Bar Castillo........40	B4	
Restaurante La Parroquia......41	A3	
Restaurante/Bar El Bocolito...42	B4	
Yu Ne Nisa......................43	A3	
DRINKING		
Club 333.........................(see 45)		
El Mito............................44	B3	
LIFE...............................45	A4	
ENTERTAINMENT	(p597)	
Mariachis For Hire..............46	C3	
Teatro de la Paz...............47	C4	
SHOPPING	(p597)	
Fonart............................48	B4	
TRANSPORT	(pp597–8)	
Local Bus & Taxi Stop..........49	C4	
Tranvía Trolley Stop...........(see 30)		

MONEY

Banks with ATMs are scattered around the Plaza de Armas and Plaza de los Fundadores. Several *casas de cambio* are along Morelos.

Banamex (cnr Obregón & Allende) Like other banks, changes cash & traveler's checks

TELEPHONE

There are many card phones in the center.

Telecomm (south side Plaza del Carmen)

TOURIST INFORMATION

Municipal tourist office (☎ 812-27-70; www .ayuntamientoslp.gob.mx; east side of Plaza de Armas, in Palacio Municipal; ☎ 8am-7pm Mon-Fri, sometimes 10am-2pm Sat & Sun)

State tourist office (☎ 812-99-39; www.visita sanluispotosi.com; Obregón 520; ☎ 8am-8pm Mon-Fri, 9am-1pm Sat) Has maps & brochures with lots of ideas for getting off the beaten track in San Luis Potosí state.

TRAVEL AGENCIES

Grandes Viajes (☎ 817-60-04; gviajes@infosel.net.mx; Carranza 1077; ☎ 9am-2pm & 4-6pm Mon-Fri, 10am-1pm Sat) American Express agent, 1km west of Plaza de los Fundadores.

Wagons Lits (☎ 813-04-18; Carranza 1026) Good for flight arrangements.

Sights

PLAZA DE ARMAS & AROUND

Also known as Jardín Hidalgo, this plaza is the city's central square. It's fairly quiet as traffic is channeled away from it.

The three-nave baroque **cathedral**, built between 1660 and 1730, is on the plaza's east side. Originally it had just one tower; the northern tower was added in the 20th century. The marble apostles on the façade are replicas of statues in Rome's San Juan de Letrán Basilica. The interior, remodeled in the 19th century, has a Gothic feel, with sweeping arches carved in pink stone; the leaf motif on the arches is repeated in blue and gold on the ceiling.

Beside the cathedral, the 19th-century **Palacio Municipal** is a stocky building with powerful stone arches. Finished in 1838, it was the home of Bishop Ignacio Montes de Oca from 1892 to 1915. In the rear of the building's patio is a stone fountain carved with the heads of three lions. The city's coat of arms in stained glass overlooks a double staircase.

Behind the cathedral, the **Museo Othoniano** (☎ 812-74-12; Av Othón 225; US$0.30; ☎ 10am-2pm & 4-6pm Tue-Sun) is the birthplace of celebrated Mexican poet Manuel José Othón (1858–1906). The 19th-century home is furnished in period style and exhibits include some of Othón's manuscripts and personal effects.

The neoclassical **Palacio de Gobierno**, built between 1798 and 1816, lines the plaza's west side. Numerous important Mexicans have lodged here, but its most illustrious occupant was Benito Juárez – first in 1863 when he was fleeing from invading French forces, then in 1867 when he confirmed the death sentence on French puppet emperor Maximilian. In the upstairs rooms that Juárez occupied are various historical artifacts, including a life-size model of Juárez with Princess Inés de Salm-Salm kneeling before him. Salm-Salm, an American who had married into Maximilian's family, came to San Luis in 1867 to make one last plea for his life. The palace is open during business hours; go left at the top of the stairs and ask a custodian to open the Salón de Juárez.

PLAZA DE LOS FUNDADORES & AROUND

The busy Founders' Plaza (aka Plaza Juárez) is where the city was born. On the north side is a large building housing offices of the Universidad Autónoma de San Luis Potosí. It was probably on this site that Diego de la Magdalena, a Franciscan friar, started a small settlement of Guachichiles around 1585. The building, which has a lovely courtyard, was constructed in 1653 as a Jesuit college.

To the west of these offices is the **Templo de la Compañía**, built by the Jesuits in 1675 with a baroque façade. A little further west is the **Capilla de Loreto**, a Jesuit chapel from 1700 with unusual twisted pillars.

Northwest of the plaza, the **Museo de Cultura Potosina** (☎ 812-18-33; Arista 340; adult/child US$0.50/0.30; ☎ 10am-2pm & 4-6pm Tue-Fri, 10am-2pm Sat-Sun) has models and dioramas explaining the city's history, mainly for children.

PLAZA SAN FRANCISCO & AROUND

Dominated by its namesake church's bulk, this quiet square is one of the city's most fetching.

The interior of the 17th- and 18th-century **Templo de San Francisco** was remodeled in the 20th century but the sacristy (the priest's dressing room), reached by a door to the right of the altar, is original and has a fine dome and carved pink stone. The **Sala De Profundis**, through the arch at the south end of the sacristy, has more paintings and a carved stone fountain. A beautiful crystal ship hangs from the main dome.

Along the street to the west of Templo de San Francisco, the **Museo Regional Potosino** (☎ 814-35-72; Galeana 450; US$2.50, free Sun; ⏰ 10am-7pm Tue-Sat, 10am-5pm Sun) was originally part of a Franciscan monastery founded in 1590. The ground floor has exhibits on pre-Hispanic Mexico, especially the indigenous people of the Huasteca. Upstairs is the lavish **Capilla de Aranzazú**, an elaborate private chapel for the monks, constructed in the mid-18th century.

The small **Templo de la Tercera Orden** and **Templo del Sagrado Corazón**, both formerly part of the Franciscan monastery, stand together at the plaza's south end. Tercera Orden was finished in 1694 and restored in 1960. Sagrado Corazón dates from 1728–31.

A couple of blocks south and west of the plaza, the free **Museo Mariano Jiménez** (Museo de las Revoluciones; ☎ 814-73-93; 5 de Mayo 610; ⏰ 10am-2pm & 4-6pm Tue-Fri, 9am-3pm Sat, 10am-2pm Sun) covers some of the most dramatic events in Mexican history. It has a rebellious theme and a good account of indigenous resistance to the Spanish conquest.

PLAZA DEL CARMEN

Plaza del Carmen is dominated by San Luis' most spectacular structure, the churrigueresque Templo del Carmen (1749–64). On the vividly carved stone façade, hovering angels show the touch of indigenous artisans. The Camarín de la Virgen, with a splendid golden altar, is to the left of the main altar inside. The entrance and roof of this chapel are a riot of small plaster figures.

Near the church, the neoclassical **Teatro de la Paz** (1889–94) contains a concert hall and exhibition gallery as well as a theater. Posters announce upcoming events (see Entertainment, p597).

The **Museo Nacional de la Máscara** (National Mask Museum; ☎ 812-30-25; Plaza del Carmen; US$0.50; ⏰ 10am-2pm & 5-7pm Tue-Sat, 10am-2pm Sun) is a distinguished 19th-century neoclassical building on the plaza's south side. Inside, 2000 ceremonial masks from all over Mexico are displayed with explanations of the dances

and rituals in which they are used. Look for the *gigantes* (papier-mâché giants).

ALAMEDA & AROUND

The **Alameda Juan Sarabia** marks the eastern boundary of the downtown area. It used to be the vegetable garden of the monastery attached to the **Templo del Carmen**. Today it's a large, attractive park with shady paths.

Inside the **Templo de San José**, facing the Alameda's south side, is the image of El Señor de los Trabajos, a Christ figure attracting pilgrims from near and far. Numerous *retablos* (altarpieces) around the statue testify to prayers answered in finding jobs, regaining health and passing exams.

The **Instituto Potosino de Bellas Artes** (☎ 822-12-06; cnr Av Universidad & Constitución; gallery ⏰ 10am-2pm & 4-8pm Mon-Fri), a modern building in 'neo-indigenous' architectural style, hosts art exhibitions and performances. Two blocks east, the **Centro de Difusión Cultural** (☎ 812-43-33; cnr Av Universidad & Negrete; galleries ⏰ 10am-2pm & 5-8pm Tue-Sun) is another interesting example of modern Mexican architecture, with a shape inspired by a spiral sea shell. Inside, art galleries show changing contemporary exhibitions.

Just over the railway bridge east of the Alameda is the **Centro Taurino Potosino**, comprising the 7000-seat Plaza de Toros (Bullring) and the **Museo Taurino** (☎ 822-15-01; cnr Universidad & Triana; ⏰ 11am-2pm & 5:30-8pm Tue-Sat), a bullfighting museum displaying intricately decorated matador suits, historical posters, stuffed bulls' heads and more. The museum is only open on days when there are bullfights.

PARQUE TANGAMANGA I

This 3.3-sq-km **park** (Blvd Diagonal Sur), 2km southwest of the center, has a planetarium, outdoor theater, amusement park and acres of green open spaces. The **Museo de las Culturas Populares** (☎ 817-29-76; US$0.25; ⏰ 9am-4pm Tue-Sun) exhibits typical crafts and clothing from around the state, with some good pieces for sale. To get to the park, take a southbound 'Perimetral' bus, or Bus No 25 or 26, from the Alameda's west end.

Tours

The **Tranvía** (☎ 814-22-26), an imitation of an antique trolley, does a one-hour loop (US$3.75) around the historic center, starting from Hotel Panorama (see p595). A few of the drivers speak English; ask when you purchase tickets.

Festivals & Events

Semana Santa – Holy Week is celebrated with concerts, exhibitions & other activities; on Good Friday morning Christ's passion is reenacted in the barrio of San Juan de Guadalupe, followed by a silent procession through the city.

Festival Internacional de Danza – This national festival of contemporary dance is held in the last two weeks of July.

Feria Nacional Potosina – San Luis' National Fair, normally in the last two weeks of August, includes concerts, bullfights, rodeos, cockfights & agricultural shows.

Día de San Luis Rey de Francia – On August 25 the city's patron saint, St Louis IX, King of France, is honored as the highlight of the Feria Nacional. Events include a large parade with floats & *gigantes* (papier-mâché giants).

Sleeping

You'll enjoy San Luis more if you choose a hotel in the pedestrianized center, away from the traffic and among the attractive architecture.

BUDGET

Hotel Plaza (☎ 812-46-31; Jardín Hidalgo 22; r US$20-23) In an 18th-century building, the city's original hotel has loads of character. The rooms at the front, with balconies overlooking the Plaza de Armas, are the best and cost a bit more. Others open onto two upstairs patios and are stuffier and more worn.

Hotel Principal (☎ 812-07-84; principal_hotelslp@hotmail.com; Sarabia 145; s/d US$14/19) Three blocks east of the central plazas, the Principal has 18 reasonable rooms and a convenient location.

Hotel Progreso (☎ 812-03-66; Aldama 415; r US$21-25) The 51-room Progreso may have a good location and art nouveau statues overlooking the lobby but it suffers deferred maintenance issues. The spacious rooms were once modernized but retain their high ceilings. In its day it was probably an elegant place but on weekends it suffers from noisy nearby nightclubs – request a room away from the street.

Near the old train station, a couple of places provide inexpensive accommodations and off-street parking.

Hotel Anáhuac (☎ 812-65-05; Xóchitl 140; s/d US$22/26; P) The amiable Anáhuac has 78 clean, freshly-painted rooms that vary in size, outlook and the presence of cable TV.

Hotel Guadalajara (☎ 812-46-12; Jiménez 253; s/d US$23/25; P) Facing a small plaza off a pedestrian street, the Guadalajara has enclosed parking (overnight US$1 extra) and 33 clean, comfortable, well ventilated rooms with fan and cable TV.

MID-RANGE

Hotel Panorama (☎ 812-17-77, 800-480-01-00; www.hotelpanorama.com.mx; Av Carranza 315; s/d US$53, with heat & air-con US$63; P ✕ 🖳 🗳) The 126 comfortable rooms at this smart, service-oriented hotel opposite the Plaza de los Fundadores all have floor-to-ceiling windows. Superior rooms on the south side have private balconies overlooking the pool. The marble-clad lobby and piano bar make it a favorite with business travelers.

Hotel María Cristina (☎ 812-94-08; www.mariacristina.com.mx; Sarabia 110; s US$46, d US$49-61; P 🖳) A short block northwest of the Alameda, the modern María Cristina caters to business travelers with a restaurant and bright, carpeted rooms with cable TV, fan and phone. Some rooms enjoy superb city views.

Hotel Nápoles (☎ 812-84-18; hnapoles@clinker.net; Sarabia 120; s/d/ste US$39/44/56; P) Next door to the María Cristina, the three-star Nápoles has similar facilities at slightly lower prices but isn't as good value.

Hotel Concordia (☎ 812-06-66, 800-711-13-18; concrdia@prodigy.net.mx; cnr Av Othón & Morelos; s/d US$39/44; P) The modernized Concordia occupies an old building; its 94 carpeted rooms all have cable TV and other amenities. Exterior rooms are nicer than interior ones.

TOP END

There are several upscale places that are east of the city fronting the highway near the bus station.

Hotel Real de Minas (☎ 818-26-16, 800-480-39-00; www.realdeminasdesanluis.com; Carretera 57 Km 426.6; r/ste US$100/119; P ✕ 🖳 🗳) The best of the big hotels outside of the center has landscaped grounds, a 24-hour restaurant and 170 rooms with satellite TV. The chain offers heavily discounted (up to 50% off) promo rates when it's not full of conventioneers.

Hotel María Dolores (☎ 816-36-86, 800-480-16-00; Carretera 57 Km 1; s/d US$82/91; P ✕ 🗳) Opposite the bus station, the modern, motel-style María Dolores has a nightclub, bar, restaurant and 213 fully equipped rooms. Rack rates are often cut in half, making it a good deal.

Eating

One local specialty is *tacos potosinos* – tacos stuffed with chopped potato, carrots, lettuce and loads of *queso blanco* (white cheese), then smothered in *salsa roja*. For the lowdown on SLP's upscale eateries, ask the tourist office for the booklet *Guía de Restaurantes*, which includes many interesting options outside the city center.

CITY CENTER

La Posada del Virrey (☎ 812-32-80; Jardín Hidalgo 3; mains US$4-10). On Plaza de Armas' north side, the former home of Spanish viceroys dates from 1736 and has been a popular restaurant with the local gentry for the last few decades. Some lunchtimes, live music plays in the attractive covered courtyard. Breakfast specials are available as well as a set lunch and generous surf-and-turf meals, though most of the menu is unadventurous Mexican fare.

Restaurante La Parroquia (☎ 812-66-81; Av Carranza 303; mains US$5-8) A popular place with *potosinos*, this restaurant has big windows looking onto Plaza de los Fundadores. It offers a four-course *comida corrida* and many à la carte dishes, including *cabrito* (kid) and *enchiladas potosinas*. A huge buffet spread appears at breakfast on Saturday and Sunday.

Yu Ne Nisa (☎ 814-36-31; Arista 350-60; mains US$2.50-5; ⏰ 9:30am-6pm Mon-Sat, store until 8:30pm) This small vegetarian restaurant and health food shop offers healthy snacks – sandwiches, gorditas and soyburgers – plus mouth-watering smoothies. It also does a full set lunch for US$4.

Restaurante/Bar El Bocolito (☎ 812-76-94; Guerrero 2; mains US$2.50-6.50) An interesting option with friendly atmosphere is this restaurant facing charming Plaza San Francisco. It serves up huge platters of Huasteca-style food, with dishes like *gringa* and *mula india*, which are combinations of meats fried up with herbs, onion, chili, tomato and green pepper topped off with melted cheese. It also offers cheap breakfasts, tasty tacos and a US$4 set lunch. It's a cooperative venture benefiting young indigenous students and features live music Thursday to Saturday from 9pm.

Café El Pacífico (☎ 812-54-14; Av Constitución 200; mains US$3-4; ⏰ 24-7) This classic diner is popular with families and unemployed mariachis for inexpensive meals, coffee or desert. The booths are comfy, the flowers are plastic and the menu has the usual *antojitos* and Mexican mains – avoid the pasta. No alcohol served after midnight.

Café del Teatro (☎ 814-07-33; Villaries 205; mains US$4-7; ⏰ 11am-midnight) Beside Teatro de la Paz, this quirky, inexpensive place is good for a coffee, a meal, a drink or all three. It's also a regular live music venue.

Fonda Orizatlán (☎ 815-67-86; Hernández 240; mains US$5-9) Eight blocks south of the center, Fonda Orizatlán is locally renowned for its first-class Huasteca-style cuisine. Thursday, Friday and Saturday nights feature folkloric dances and a buffet spread appears all day Sunday.

Restaurant/Bar Castillo (☎ 812-29-57; Madero 125-45; mains US$2-6) Side by side café, bakery and bar, the Castillo is a small, cozy, spot half a block west of the Plaza de Armas. You can get a big breakfast, with eggs, beans and salad, set lunches and Mexican mains for dinner.

Café Tokio (☎ 814-61-89; cnr Zaragoza & Guerrero; mains US$3-5) This bright and sizable café has no trace of Japanese influence. Rather, it serves up Mexican and fast-food standards, and is popular for a cheap set lunch or late night snack. The original location (☎ 812-58-99; Othón 415; ✖) faces the Alameda and is popular for ice cream or coffee after a stroll in the park.

AV CARRANZA

There's a growing selection of both hip and upscale restaurants west of the center along Av Carranza ('La Avenida').

La Corriente (☎ 812-93-04; Av Carranza 700; mains US$5-10; ⏰ 8am-midnight Mon-Sat, 8am-6pm Sun) One of the most attractive restaurants in town, La Corriente is 400m west of Plaza de los Fundadores, at the start of the La Avenida strip. It specializes in regional and ranch-style food, presented in an elegant dining room or delightful plant-filled courtyard. A good four-course set lunch (US$4) is served Monday to Saturday and sometimes there's music in the evenings.

La Virreina (☎ 812-37-50; Av Carranza 830; mains US$7-12; ⏰ 1pm-midnight) A long-established gourmet favorite, the Virreina has a classic menu of international and Mexican dishes, award-winning desserts and an excellent reputation.

Entertainment

San Luis has quite an active cultural scene. Ask in the tourist office about what's on and keep your eye out for posters. The free monthly Guiarte booklet and posters detail cultural attractions.

The hottest nightspot in the center of town, **El Mito** (☎ 814-41-57; cnr Jardín Hidalgo & Hidalgo; US$5; ☎ 9pm-2am Fri-Sat) attracts the young and the beautiful with full blast pop, Latin and dance sounds. It's periodically closed by the authorities – a great recommendation in itself.

Within walking distance of the center on Av Carranza, it's hard to miss the lines behind the velvet rope outside side-by-side **Club 333** and **Life**. Other popular discos, bars and music venues are further west along Av Carranza or in malls like the **Centro Comercial Mexicano** on the northwest edge of town. It's best to take a cab here.

The neoclassical, 1500-seat **Teatro de la Paz** (☎ 812-52-09) presents something most nights and Sunday around noon. The **Orquesta Sinfónica** (☎ 814-36-01; tickets US$9) brings symphony to the theater in September and October. Concerts, theater, exhibitions and cultural events are also presented at places like the **Teatro de la Ciudad**, an open-air theater in Parque Tangamanga I, and the **Casa de la Cultura** (☎ 813-22-47; Carranza 1815), 2½km west of Plaza de los Fundadores.

Shopping

The main shopping district is between the Plaza de Armas and the Mercado Hidalgo. A few blocks further northeast is the larger, interesting Mercado República. Milky sweets are a local specialty and can be found in the markets and at shops along Av Carranza.

Fonart (☎ 812-39-98; Plaza San Francisco 6; ☼ 9am-2pm & 4-7:30pm, from 10am Sat & Sun) Like other shops in the government-run chain, this outlet has a good selection of quality handicrafts from all over Mexico.

La Casa del Artesano (☎ 814-89-90; Av Carranza 540) For more local products try this shop full of potosino pottery, masks, woodwork and canework.

Getting There & Away

AIR

Aéropuerto Ponciano Arriaga (☎ 822-23-96) is 10km north of the city off Hwy 57. Aeromar serves San Antonio, Texas and Mexico City and Monterrey several times daily. Aerolitoral offers direct service to/from Guadalajara and Monterrey. Aero California flies direct to Mexico City, Tijuana and Bajía airport (León).

AIRLINE OFFICES

Aero California (☎ 811-80-50; at airport)
Aerolitoral (☎ 822-22-29; at airport)
Aeromar (☎ 817-79-36; Carranza 1030)

BUS

The **Terminal Terrestre Potosina** (TTP; ☎ 816-45-96; Carretera 57 s/n), 2½km east of the center, is a hub with deluxe, 1st-class and some 2nd-class services. Facilities include card phones, a telephone *caseta*, 24-hour luggage storage and two cafés.

Daily departures include:
Guadalajara (US$29, 5-6hr, 8 deluxe ETN daily; US$21, 5-6hr, 12 1st-class Transportes del Norte daily; US$19, 5-6hr, 8 2nd-class Estrella Blanca daily)
Guanajuato (US$12.50, 4hr, 5 2nd-class Flecha Amarilla daily)
Matehuala (US$10, 2½hr, hourly 1st-class Sendor daily; US$9, 2½hr, hourly 2nd-class Estrella Blanca daily)
Mexico City (US$32, 5-6hr; 16 deluxe ETN daily; US$26, 5-6hr, frequent 1st-class Primera Plus & Ómnibus de México daily; US$21, 5-6hr, 8 2nd-class Flecha Amarilla daily) To Terminal Norte.
Monterrey (US$28, 6hr, hourly 1st-class Futura daily; US$26, 6hr, 12 2nd-class Estrella Blanca daily)
Querétaro (US$16, 2½-3½hr, 3 deluxe ETN daily; US$13, 2½-3½hr, hourly 1st-class Futura & Ómnibus de México daily; US$10, 2½-3½hr, 2nd-class Flecha Amarilla daily)
San Miguel de Allende (US$10, 4hr, 6 1st class Flecha Amarilla daily)
Tampico (US$26, 7-8hr, 2 1st-class Oriente, Ómnibus de México or Futura daily; US$24, 7-8hr,14 2nd-class Vencedor or Oriente daily)
Zacatecas (US$9.50, 3hr, hourly 1st-class Ómnibus de México daily; US$8.50, 3hr, 2nd-class Estrella Blanca daily)

Daily buses go to Aguascalientes, Ciudad Juárez, Ciudad Valles, Ciudad Victoria, Chihuahua, Dolores Hidalgo, León, Morelia, Nuevo Laredo, Saltillo, and Torreón.

CAR & MOTORCYCLE

Budget (☎ 822-24-82; Av Carranza 1040B)
Hertz (☎ 812-82-29; Obregón 670)

Getting Around

Taxis charge around US$11 for the half-hour trip to/from the airport.

NORTHERN CENTRAL
HIGHLANDS

To reach the center from the bus station, exit, turn left, take the footbridge over the busy road, and take any 'Centro' bus. No 5, 'Central TTP,' is the most direct. A convenient place to get off is on the Alameda, outside the train station. A booth in the bus station sells taxi tickets (US$2) to the center.

From the center to the bus station, take any 'Central TTP' bus southbound on Av Constitución from the Alameda's west side. City buses run 6:30am to 10:30pm. The basic *blanco* (white) buses cost US$0.35; the better ones, in various colors, cost US$0.40. For places along Av Carranza, catch a 'Morales' or 'Carranza' bus in front of the train station.

SANTA MARÍA DEL RÍO

Forty-eight kilometers south of San Luis Potosí, just off the highway to Mexico City, this picturesque town (population 12,000) is known for its excellent handmade rebozos (shawls) and inlaid woodwork. The rebozos are usually made of synthetic 'silk' thread called artisela, in less garish colors than in many Mexican textile centers. You can see and buy them at the Escuela del Rebozo on the central Plaza Hidalgo, and in a few private workshops. A Rebozo Fair is held each year in the first half of August.

MATEHUALA

☎ 488 / pop 78,000 / elevation 1600m

The only town of any size on Hwy 57 between Saltillo and San Luis Potosí, Matehuala ('ma-te-WAL-a') is an unremarkable but pleasant and prosperous place high on the Altiplano Central. It was founded in the 17th century but has little left in the way of colonial charm. Most travelers just use it to get to Real de Catorce (see p599).

Hwy 57 bypasses the town to the east. There is a large parabolic 'arch of welcome' at each end of town – the arches are something of a Matehuala trademark. One wonders, did they come before or after the infamous fast food chain?

Orientation & Information

Central Matehuala lies between two plazas: the shady Plaza de Armas and the bustling Placita del Rey 300m to the north, with its new concrete cathedral. Cheaper hotels and the town's restaurants are in this area. Between the center and Hwy 57 is the shady Parque Vicente Guerrero.

The bus station is just west of the highway, 2km south of the center. To walk to the center, turn left out of the bus station and go straight along Av 5 de Mayo for 1½km, then turn left on Insurgentes for a few blocks to reach the Plaza de Armas.

The English-speaking **tourist office** (☎ 882-50-05), on the highway at Motel El Dorado, is a fount of information about San Luis Potosí state.

All essential services (ATMs, phones, Internet, etc) are easily found around the main plazas.

Sleeping

The following three hotels are in town.

Hotel María Esther (☎ 882-07-14; Madero 111; s/d US$19/22; P) The best rooms at this family-run favorite face the plant-filled second patio out back behind the restaurant. It's a block north and a block west of Placita del Rey.

Hotel Matehuala (☎ 882-06-80; Bustamante & Hidalgo; s/d US$20/24) This is the most atmospheric place, with high ceilings and dark rooms, set around a large, covered courtyard. It's somewhat overpriced but convenient for buses to Real de Catorce and they may give a discount. It's half a block north of the Plaza de Armas.

Hotel Álamo (☎ 882-00-17; Guerrero 116A; s/d US$11/15) Much more modern and slightly brighter than Hotel Matehuala, the family-run Álamo is half a block east of the Plaza de Armas and is also convenient for buses to Real de Catorce.

Several '60s-style motels dot Hwy 57 as it passes Matehuala.

Las Palmas Midway Inn (☎ 882-00-01/02; Carretera 57 Km 617; trailer sites US$23, s/d US$54/61; P ☒ ☒) Family-oriented Las Palmas has nice rooms around landscaped gardens with a pool, mini-golf and a level trailer park with full hookups.

El Dorado (☎ 882-01 74; Carretera 57 Km 614; s/d US$26/31, with TV & air-con US$32/43; P ☒) Across the highway, El Dorado has fewer frills and thus better-value rooms.

Eating

Restaurant Santa Fe (☎ 882-07-53; Morelos 709; mains US$3-6) Facing shady Plaza de Armas, this long-standing local favorite is big, clean and reasonably priced, with generous portions of good plain food. Breakfast is inexpensive and the US$4 set lunch is generous.

Restaurant Fontella (☎ 882-02-93; Morelos 618; mains US$2.50-4) Just north of the plaza, the relaxed Fontella does a solid, four-course *comida corrida* (US$3.25) and has interesting regional dishes. The fresh fruit salad makes a healthy breakfast.

Getting There & Around

Frequent 1st- and 2nd-class buses head north and south, but Matehuala is midroute so they may not have seats available. Daily departures include:

Mexico City (US$35, 7½-8hr, 8 1st-class *directo* daily; US$30, 7½-8hr, frequent 2nd-class *de paso* daily) To Terminal Norte.

Monterrey (US$18, 5hr, 14 1st-class daily; US$15, 5hr, frequent 2nd-class daily)

Saltillo (US$15, 3hr, 3 1st-class daily; US$12, 3hr, frequent 2nd-class daily)

San Luis Potosí (US$10, 2hr, hourly 1st-class daily; US$9, 2 hr, frequent 2nd-class daily)

Infrequent beige buses marked 'Centro' run from the bus station to the town center; buses marked 'Central' go the other way. Depending on your load, it can be quicker to walk. A taxi costs about US$2.50.

TO/FROM REAL DE CATORCE

Sendor runs 1st-class buses from Matehuala's bus station to Real de Catorce (US$4, two hours) at 8am, 10am, noon, 2pm and 5:45pm, with an extra weekday departure at 6am; the bus can be caught in town about 15 minutes later on Guerrero, a little east of and across the street from Hotel Álamo. During festivals and holidays, buses to Real may be full. Upon arrival in Matehuala, ask if you need to buy a ticket to Real in advance, and whether you can catch the bus in town the next day. If you buy a round-trip ticket, note the time stated for the return journey; readers have reported difficulty getting on a bus at a different time.

REAL DE CATORCE

☎ 488 / pop 1500 / elevation 2756m

This reawakening ghost town radiates magic. High on the fringes of the Sierra Madre Oriental, it was a wealthy silver-mining town of 40,000 people until early last century. Not long ago, it was nearly deserted, its cobblestone streets lined with crumbling buildings,

its mint a ruin and a few hundred people eking out an existence from the annual influx of pilgrims, and old mine tailings.

Recently, Real has begun to attract trendier residents – well-to-do Mexicans and gringos looking for an unusual retreat. Artists have set up shop in restored old buildings, and filmmakers love the light in the surrounding hills. The cast and crew of *The Mexican*, including Julia Roberts, Brad Pitt and Gene Hackman, took over town for a few months in 2000. One day Real may become another Taxco or San Miguel de Allende, but thankfully it still has a ways to go.

The Huichol people, who live 400km away on the Durango-Nayarit-Jalisco-Zacatecas borders, believe that the deserts around Real are a spiritual homeland called Wirikuta, where their peyote and corn gods live. Every May or June the Huichol make an annual pilgrimage here for rituals involving peyote (see 'Huichol Visions', p600). This hallucinogenic cactus has great cultural and spiritual significance, and its indiscriminate use by foreigners is regarded as offensive, even sacrilegious. There is also a concern that if too many peyote buttons are taken to meet tourist demands, the Huichol will have increasing difficulty obtaining what they need for ceremonial purposes.

You can make a day-trip to Real de Catorce from Matehuala, but it's worth staying longer to explore the surrounding hills and soak up the unique atmosphere.

History

Real de Catorce translates as 'Royal of 14': the '14' probably comes from 14 Spanish soldiers killed here by indigenous resisters around 1700. The town was founded in the mid-18th century, and the church built between 1783 and 1817. The original name, Villa Real de Minas de Nuestra Señora de la Limpia Concepción de Guadalupe de los Álamos de Catorce, was shortened...for some reason.

The mines had their ups and downs. During the independence war (1810–21) some of the shafts were flooded, and in 1821 and 1822 an Englishman, Robert Phillips, made a yearlong journey from London to Catorce bringing a 'steam machine' for pumping the water out of the mines.

Real de Catorce reached its peak in the late 19th century when it was producing an estimated US$3 million in silver a year. It had a bullring and shops selling European luxury goods. A number of opulent houses from this period still stand. The dictator Porfirio Díaz journeyed here from Mexico City by train, mule-carriage and horseback in 1895 to inaugurate two mine pumps purchased from California.

HUICHOL VISIONS

The remote Sierra Madre Occidental, in and around the far north of Jalisco, is the home of the Huichol, one of Mexico's most distinctive and enduring indigenous groups. Even in pre-Hispanic times the Huichol were an independent people, one of the few groups that were not subjugated by the Aztecs, Toltecs or any of the other dominant kingdoms. Traditionally, they lived by hunting deer and cultivating scattered fields of corn in the high valleys.

The arrival of the Spanish had little immediate effect on the Huichol, and it wasn't until the 17th century that the first Catholic missionaries reached the Huichol homelands. Rather than convert to Christianity, the Huichol incorporated various elements of Christian teachings into their traditional animist belief systems. In Huichol mythology, nature's elements assume a personal as well as a supernatural form. Gods become personalized as plants, totem animal species and natural objects, while their supernatural form is explored in religious rituals. For example, rain is personified as a snake, thus visions of snakes can indicate when rain might be expected.

Every year the Huichol leave their isolated homeland and make a pilgrimage of some 400km across Mexico's central plateau to what is now northern San Luis Potosí state. In this harsh desert region, they seek out the mezcal cactus (*Lophophora williamsii*; often called peyote cactus), a small, well-camouflaged plant that scarcely grows above ground level. The rounded 'buttons' on the top of the cactus contain peyote, a powerful hallucinogenic drug (whose chief element is mescaline) that is central to the Huichol's rituals and complex spiritual life. Most of the buttons are collected, dried and carried back to the tribal homelands, but a small piece is eaten on the spot, as a gesture to the plant. Small amounts of peyote help to ward off hunger, cold and fatigue (good for visits with the in-laws!), while larger amounts are taken on ritual occasions, such as the return from the annual pilgrimage. In particular, peyote is used by shamans whose visions inform them about when to plant and harvest corn, where to hunt deer or how to treat illnesses.

The Huichol resisted absorption into the mine and ranch economy of colonial Mexico, and only a few migrated to the growing urban areas in the 19th century. They have not generally intermarried with other indigenous groups or with the mestizo population, most retain the Huichol language and many still take part in the annual pilgrimages and peyote rituals. Some Huichol do seasonal work on the coastal plantations, and many speak Spanish as well as their own language, but mostly they exist on the margins of the modern market economy. Development of a unique artistic style has brought new recognition to Huichol culture and provided many Huichol people with a source of income.

Traditionally, the main Huichol art forms were telling stories of the supernatural and making masks, ritual items and colorful, detailed geometric embroidery. In the last few decades, the Huichol have been depicting their myths and visions graphically, using brightly colored beads or yarn pressed into a beeswax-covered substrate. Beadwork generally uses abstract patterns and is often done on wooden bowls, animal skulls or masks. The 'yarn pictures' are notable for their wealth of symbolism and surreal imagery. The mouth of a deer might be linked by wavy lines to a crescent moon, combining with other shapes to form an eagle, all surrounded by a circular design representing the sun. Fluid designs and brilliant colors interweave in psychedelic style. Snakes, birds and rabbits often appear, along with ritual items like feathers, candles, drums and, of course, peyote cactus.

Huichol artwork is sold in craft markets, shops and galleries in most big cities and tourist resorts. If you buy from a market stall, there's a decent chance that the artist will be there to explain the various elements of a picture; often the story is written on the back. Prices are usually fixed, and the Huichol don't like to haggle. Huichol art is expensive compared with some souvenirs, but it takes a long time to produce, and each piece is unique. To see the best work, visit one of the specialist museums in Zapopan (near Guadalajara), Tepic, Puerto Vallarta or Zacatecas.

NORTHERN CENTRAL HIGHLANDS

Just why Real became a ghost town within three decades is a bit of a mystery. Some locals claim that during the revolution (1910–20) *bandidos* hid out here and scared off other inhabitants. The state tourist guidebook explains, perhaps more plausibly, that the price of silver slumped after 1900.

Orientation

The bus from Matehuala drops you off after passing through the 2.3km Ogarrio tunnel. If you arrive in a car, leave it in the dusty parking area at the far end of the tunnel – local kids will promise to watch it all day for a few pesos. Or, they'll pester you to hire them as guides or to take you to a place to stay. Walk a few steps up from the parking lot to Lanzagorta, a stony street heading west through a row of shops, past the church to the center of town.

Information

Surf www.realdecatorce.net for a good overview of the town. There's a tourist office (Constitución s/n) at the Palacio Municipal.

There are card phones around the plaza and a telephone office on Plaza Hidalgo's east side. Sótano Real (cnr Constitución & Morelos) and Venus CaféNet (Lanzagorta s/n) both charge US$1.75 for dial-up Internet access. Mini Super San Francisco (Ramón Corona s/n) changes cash dollars when they have pesos on hand, but don't count on it – there's no ATM here.

Sights & Activities

LA PARROQUIA

The charmingly timeworn *parroquia* (parish church), the **Templo de la Purísima Limpia**, is an impressive neoclassical building. The attraction for thousands of Mexican pilgrims is the reputedly miraculous image of St Francis of Assisi on one of the side altars. A cult has grown up around the statue, whose help is sought in solving problems and cleansing sins.

Walk through the door to the left of the altar to find a roomful of **retablos** (altarpieces). These small pictures usually depict some life-threatening situation from which St Francis has rescued the victim, and they

REAL DE CATORCE

0 —————— 200 m
0 —————— 0.1 miles

INFORMATION
Pay Phone...............................1 A2
Sotano Real.............................2 B2
Telefone Caseta.......................3 B2
Tourist Office...........................4 B2
Venus CafeNet.........................5 B3

SIGHTS & ACTIVITIES (pp601–2)
Galería Vega M57.....................6 A2
Mini Super San Francisco........7 A3
Museo Parroquial.....................8 B3
Palenque de Gallos..................9 A2
Sleepy Billard Hall...............(see 1)
Templo de la Purísima...........10 B3

SLEEPING (pp602–3)
Casa de Huéspedes La
  Providencia..........................11 C3
Casa de Huéspedes San
  Francisco..............................12 A2
El Corral de Conde..................13 B2
Hospedaje Familiar..................14 B2
Hostal Alcazaba.......................15 A1
Hotel & Restaurant El Real......16 B3
Hotel Ruinas del Real..............17 A2
Hotel San Juan........................18 A2
Mesón de Abundancia.............19 B3
Quinta La Puesta del Sol.........20 A1
Rincón Magico..........................21 A1

EATING (pp603–4)
El Cactus Café.........................22 A2
Eucalipto..................................23 A2

ENTERTAINMENT (pp603–4)
Cine Club Ogarrio....................24 B2

SHOPPING (p604)
Callejon Artesanal Wirikuta.....25 B3

TRANSPORT (p604)
4WDs to Estación Catorce...(see 26)
Horses for Hire........................26 A3
Jeeps to Estación Catorce.......27 A3

include a brief description of the incident and some words of gratitude. Car accidents and medical operations are common themes. *Retablos* have become much sought after by collectors and are sometimes seen in antique shops. Many of those on sale have been stolen from churches – talk about bad karma.

Underneath the church, behind an old door on Lanzagorta, is the small **Museo Parroquial** (cnr Lanzagorta & Reyes; US$0.25; ☺ infrequently & weekends only), containing photos, documents and other miscellanea rescued from the crumbling town. Count yourself lucky if you find it open.

CASA DE LA MONEDA

Opposite the church's façade, the old mint made coins for a few years in the 1860s, but now houses a **silver workshop** and is occasionally used for art exhibitions and community classes. It's in bad repair but restoration appears to be underway.

PLAZA HIDALGO

Further west along Lanzagorta, past the church and mint, this small **plaza** is terraced into the hillside. It dates from 1888 and originally had a fountain in the middle, where the small rotunda now stands. It's a beautiful little space, with a sleepy barpoolroom on the north side that's straight out of a western movie.

GALERIA VEGA M57

Real's biggest **art gallery** (Zaragoza 3; ☺ 11am-4pm Sat & Sun) hosts exhibitions of work in a variety of media in a restored colonial building. You might see a giant mobile in the courtyard, an installation in one of the spaces and displays of modern jewelry in another.

PALENQUE DE GALLOS & PLAZA DE TOROS

A block northwest of the plaza lies a monument to the town's heyday – a **cockfighting ring** (admission US$0.20) built like a Roman amphitheater. It was restored in the 1970s and sometimes hosts theater or dance performances. Follow Zaragoza/Libertad north to the edge of the town where the restored bullring is used for soccer practice; the **panteón** (cemetery; ☺ 9am-5pm Wed-Mon) across the street is free and also worth a look.

HORSEBACK RIDING & HIKING

Numerous trails lead out into the stark and stunning countryside around Real. The most popular guided trail ride is the three-hour trip to **Montaña Sagrada** (Sacred Mountain), a big hill that offers wonderful views. Another good trip is to the **Pueblo Fantasmo** (Ghost Town). Guides and people with horses congregate every morning around Plaza Hidalgo. Rates are around US$5 an hour or a negotiable US$50 for two people for a full day, including horses and a guide. Jeep trips and guided hiking trips can also be arranged. For best results, ask your hotel to suggest a guide.

If you prefer to **hike** or **trek** by yourself, you can simply wander out from Real in almost any direction. But be prepared with water, a hat and strong footwear; it's unforgiving country.

Festivals & Events

Real is usually very quiet, but Semana Santa and Christmas are big events, and the **Fiesta de San Francisco** is huge. Between September 25 and October 12, 150,000 pilgrims come to pay homage to the figure of St Francis of Assisi in the town's church. Many of them just come for the day, by the busload to the Ogarrio tunnel, and from there on rickety horse-drawn carts. Thousands stay in the town too, filling every lettable room, and also sleeping rough in the plazas. The streets are lined with stalls selling religious souvenirs and food, while the town's trendy Italian restaurants close for a month. Tourists who desire the ghost town experience should keep well away during this period. The **Festival del Desierto** cultural festival begins the second week in September and features folkloric music and dance performances in towns all around the region.

Sleeping

During Semana Santa, July/August, the Fiesta de San Francisco and Christmas–New Year, all places fill up early and prices may double.

BUDGET

Several cheap *casas de huéspedes* (homes converted into simple guest lodgings) cater mainly to pilgrims; kids in the parking area can lead you to the more obscure ones. It can be very cold here in winter in the cheapest digs; bring a sleeping bag or request extra blankets.

Casa de Huéspedes San Francisco (Terán s/n; s/d US$9/14, r with shared bathroom US$9) Just uphill from Plaza Hidalgo, the friendly, family-run San Francisco has a few small, basic rooms. The best ones upstairs with balcony and private bathroom are worth the extra pesos. The shared facilities get nasty during festivals, when they are open to the public.

Hotel San Juan (cnr Constitución & Zaragoza; s/d US$14/17) A 'new' hotel in an old building, the quiet, family-run San Juan has small, rustic but clean rooms, some with a nice outlook over Plaza Hidalgo.

Rincón Magico (Libertad at Zaragoza; s/d US$14/28) This basic, simpático spot is cheaper by the week and has a bar and patio with expansive valley views.

Hospedaje Familiar (☎ 887-50-09; Constitución 21; d US$22, s/d with shared bathroom US$9/14) As the name suggests, this place provides 'family lodgings,' mostly for pilgrims. The rooms are small and plain, but clean, and they may discount rates during slow periods.

Casa de Huéspedes La Providencia (Lanzagorta 19; s/d US$15/19) The closest place to the tunnel has very ordinary, tiny rooms that aren't great value. If there aren't many visitors in town, ask for a discount. The best rooms have fine views down the valley while one cheaper cell downstairs shares a bathroom with nonguests. The attached restaurant does a decent *comida corrida* for US$2.50.

MID-RANGE

Some very inviting upmarket accommodations await in old buildings, newly restored.

Mesón de Abundancia (☎ 887-50-44; Lanzagorta 11; s/d/f US$33/46/69) This 19th-century bank building has been renovated and is now run as a hotel and restaurant by a Swiss-Mexican couple. All 11 rooms are large, quaint and decorated with local crafts. Three have balconies and great views. Rates rise US$10 to US$20 on weekends and holidays. There's a good **restaurant** (see p603) and it's the only place in town that accepts credit cards.

Hostal Alcazaba (☎ 887-50-75; vayssa31@hotmail .com; Libertad (Zaragoza 33); r from US$40) Real's newest mid-range option is scenically situated (the name means 'well protected high place') opposite the cemetery. The five cozy *casitas* (villas) have private bathroom and kitchen and share terraces and panoramic views. Ask friendly owner Pedro about discounts for stays of longer than three nights.

Hotel Ruinas del Real (☎ 887-50-65/66; cnr Lerdo & Libertad; s/d US$50/59, ste from US$79) Real's best-known boutique hotel, in a wonderfully rebuilt stone building, is on the west side of town, a couple blocks uphill from Plaza Hidalgo. The rooms are colorful, spacious and well-decorated. The spacious Roberts and Hackman suites (as in Julia and Gene) have fireplaces, tubs and Jacuzzis.

Hotel El Real (☎ 887-50-58; hotelreal@yahoo.com; Morelos 20; s/d US$32/41; 🖳) Another restored building houses this comfortable place with well-decorated but crowded bedrooms on three floors around an open courtyard. Some have views over the town and the hills. There's a good restaurant and English, German and French are spoken.

El Corral del Conde (☎ 887-50-48; cnr Morelos & Constitución; s/d/f with breakfast & TV US$32/46/55) The 11 spacious stone-walled rooms here are straight out of a medieval castle, though they're tastefully furnished and very comfortable.

Quinta La Puesta del Sol (☎ 887-50-10; Libertad s/n; s/d/ste with breakfast US$28/39/45; 🅿) On the road to the bullring, this rambling modern hotel lacks old-world charm but has a superb view down the valley. Amenities include satellite TV, covered parking and a restaurant.

Eating, Drinking & Entertainment

Food stalls around the plaza and along Lanzagorta serve standard Mexican snacks, while several restaurants compete (with each other and with the better hotels) to do the best Italian cuisine. **Hotel El Real's restaurant** (see Sleeping, p603; mains US$5-10; ⏲ 8am-9pm) serves good Italian, vegetarian and Mexican food.

El Cactus Café (☎ 887-50-56; Plaza Hidalgo; mains US$3-7.50) On the plaza's west side, this cheery eatery is run by an Italian cook and his Mexican wife. You'll feel like you're eating in a friend's rustic kitchen while sharing family-style wooden tables and lingering over a glass of wine. It's nonsmoking, the bread and pasta are homemade and there are plenty of good Mexican and veggie options.

Eucalipto (Constitución at Libertad; mains US$5-10) Eucalipto also does excellent Italian and international dishes. It's warm and romantic at night when its exposed stone walls are dimly lit.

The bar and fireplace at the restaurant part of **Mesón de Abundancia** (see Sleeping, p603; mains US$4-10) create a wonderful atmosphere, and the Italian-Mexican meals are very good.

Cine Club Ogarrio (cnr Morelos & Constitución; US$1.50) screens movies every Friday night and kids flicks on Sunday morning.

Shopping

As more of the itinerant artists who flock in during the high season to hawk their wares set up shop here permanently, the selection and quality of jewelry, silverwork and organic beauty products continues to improve. Check the Callejón Artesanal Wirikuta street market and shops along the main drags for locally-produced handicrafts.

Getting There & Away

See Getting There & Away in Matehuala (p604) for bus details. Confirm the return bus schedule upon arrival.

If driving, from Hwy 57 north of Matehuala turn off to Cedral, 20km west on a mostly paved road. After Cedral, you turn south to reach Catorce on what must be one of the world's longest cobblestone streets. It's a slow but spectacular zigzag drive up a steep mountainside. The Ogarrio tunnel (US$1 per vehicle) is only wide enough for one vehicle; workers stationed at each end with telephones control traffic. You may have to wait a while for traffic in the opposite direction to pass. If it's really busy, you'll have to leave your car at the tunnel entrance and continue by pick-up, cart or whatever.

Vintage Jeep Willys leave Real around noon (and on demand) downhill from the plaza along Allende for the rough but spectacular descent to the small hamlet of Catorce de 14 (US$2.25, 1 hour). From there, buses head to San Tiburcio, where there are connections for Saltillo and Zacatecas.

GUANAJUATO STATE

The state of Guanajuato (population 4.85 million) has historically been one of Mexico's richest. After silver was found in Zacatecas, Spanish prospectors combed the rugged lands north of Mexico City and were rewarded by discoveries of silver, gold,

iron, lead, zinc and tin. For two centuries up to 40% of the world's silver was mined in Guanajuato. Silver barons in Guanajuato city enjoyed opulent lives at the expense of indigenous people who worked the mines, first as slave labor and then as wage slaves.

Eventually the well-heeled criollo class of Guanajuato and Querétaro states began to resent the dominance of Spanish-born colonists. After the occupation of much of Spain by Napoleon Bonaparte's troops in 1808 and subsequent political confusion in Mexico, provincial criollos began – while meeting as 'literary societies' – to draw up plans for rebellion.

The home of a member of one such group in Querétaro city was raided on September 13, 1810. Three days later a colleague, parish priest Miguel Hidalgo, declared independence in the town of Dolores (later named Dolores Hidalgo). After Dolores, San Miguel de Allende was the next town to fall to the rebels, Celaya the third and Guanajuato the fourth. Guanajuato state is proud to have given birth to Mexico's most glorious moment and is often visited almost as a place of pilgrimage.

In addition to the quaint colonial towns of Guanajuato and San Miguel, Guanajuato state has several important industrial centers. It's also a fertile agricultural state – the strawberries that are grown around Irapuato are famous. And it's still an important source of silver, gold and fluorspar. In the late 1990s the state thrived under its PAN (National Action Party) governor, Vicente Fox Quesada, with Mexico's lowest unemployment rate and an export rate three times the national average. Fox was chosen as the PAN candidate for the 2000 presidential election, and his gubernatorial record was a key factor in his victory.

GUANAJUATO

☎ 473 / pop 78,000 / elevation 2017m

Gorgeous Guanajuato is crammed onto the steep slopes of a ravine, with narrow streets twisting around the hillsides and disappearing into a series of tunnels. This impossible topography was settled in 1559 because the silver and gold deposits that were found here were among the world's richest. Much of the fine architecture built from this wealth remains intact, making Guanajuato a living monument to a prosperous, turbulent past; the city was inscribed as a Unesco World Heritage site in 1988.

But it's not only the past that resounds in Guanajuato's narrow cobbled streets. The University of Guanajuato, known for its arts programs, enrolls over 20,000 students, giving the city a youthful vibrancy and cultural life that are as interesting as the colonial architecture and exotic setting. The city's cultural year peaks in October with the Festival Internacional Cervantino (see p611).

History

One of the hemisphere's richest silver veins was uncovered in 1558 at La Valenciana mine and for 250 years the mine produced 20% of the world's silver. Colonial barons benefiting from this mineral treasure were infuriated when King Carlos III of Spain slashed their share of the wealth in 1765. The king's 1767 decree banishing Jesuits from Spanish dominions further alienated both the wealthy barons and the poor miners, who held allegiance to the Jesuits.

This anger was focussed in the War of Independence. In 1810 rebel leader Miguel Hidalgo set off the independence movement with his Grito de Independencia (Cry for Independence) in nearby Dolores (see 'Miguel Hidalgo: ¡Viva Independence!' in the Dolores Hidalgo section, p618). Guanajuato citizens joined the independence fighters and defeated the Spanish and loyalists, seizing the city in the rebellion's first military victory. When the Spaniards eventually retook the city they retaliated by conducting the infamous 'lottery of death,' in which names of Guanajuato citizens were drawn at random and the 'winners' were tortured and hanged.

Independence was eventually won, freeing the silver barons to amass further wealth. From this wealth arose many of the mansions, churches and theaters that make Guanajuato one of Mexico's most handsome cities.

Orientation

Guanajuato's center is quite compact, with a few major streets and lots of tiny *callejones* (alleys). It's ideal for walking, but tricky to drive around. The main street, running roughly west–east, is called Juárez from the Mercado Hidalgo to the basilica on Plaza de la Paz. East of the basilica, this street continues as a pedestrian street called Obregón to the Jardín de la Unión (the city's main plaza), then continues further east as Sopeña.

Roughly parallel to Juárez/Obregón is another long street, running from the Alhóndiga to the university, and bearing the names 28 de Septiembre, Pocitos and Lascuraín de Retana along the way. Hidalgo (aka Cantarranas) parallels Sopeña and is another important street. Once you know these streets you can't get lost – just walk downhill until you find one of them. You can, however, have a great time getting lost among the maze of crooked *callejones* winding up the hills from the center.

Traffic on these main arteries is one-way, traveling east to west. Vehicles (including public buses) going west to east must use the main underground roadway, Subterránea Padre Miguel Hidalgo, a one-way route along the dried-up Río Guanajuato riverbed. (The river was diverted after it flooded the city in 1905.) At least eight other tunnels have been constructed to cope with increasing traffic. The Tunel Noreste Ingeniero Ponciano Aguilar and Tunel Santa Fe, running one-way east to west, enable vehicles to bypass the city center altogether.

Surrounding central Guanajuato is the winding Carretera Panorámica, offering great views of the town and surrounding hills.

Information

INTERNET ACCESS

Quite a few places offer Internet access for around US$1.25 an hour.

CyberCenter (Pasaje de los Arcos) Cramped, loud & smoky but fast.

Español Universal (Cantaranas s/n) Good coffee & Tampico-style tacos & tamales at café.

Rede Guanajuato (Alonso 70B; ☯ 9am-8pm)

LAUNDRY

Lavandería Automática Internacional (Doblado 28; ☯ 10am-8pm Mon-Sat) 3kg load for US$3.65.

Lavandería del Centro (Sopeña 26; ☯ 9am-8:30pm Mon-Fri, 9am-4pm Sat) US$2.25 per kilo or US$4.25 for up to five kilos.

MONEY

Banks along Av Juárez change cash and traveler's checks (some only until 2pm), and have ATMs. Banorte, opposite the tourist office, is convenient and relatively quick.

NORTHERN CENTRAL HIGHLANDS

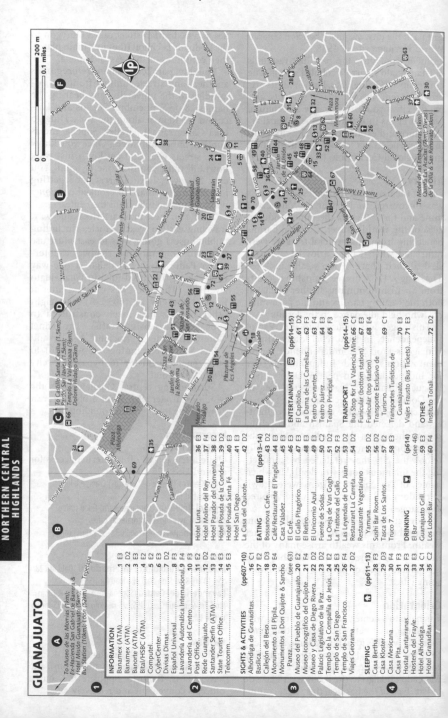

Divisas Dimas (Juárez 33A; ⊗ 9:30am-8pm Mon-Sat)
Convenient *casa de cambio* with decent rates.
Viajes Georama (☎ 732-51-01; Plaza de la Paz 34)
American Express agent , doesn't exchange traveler's
checks.

TELEPHONE & FAX
Pasaje de los Arcos, an alley off the south side
of Obregón near the tourist office, has card
phones in reasonably quiet surroundings.
Computel (Ayuntamiento 25) Opposite post office, with
fax & Internet.
Telecomm (cnr Sopeña & Rincón del Arte)

TOURIST INFORMATION
State tourist office (☎ 732-19-82, 800-714-10-86;
www.guanajuato-travel.com, www.guanajuato.gob.mx;
Plaza de la Paz 14; ⊗ 9am-5pm Mon-Fri, 10am-5pm Sat,
10am-2pm Sun) Friendly staff, mostly English-speaking,
with free city maps & brochures (in Spanish & English).

Sights
CENTRAL PLAZAS
A wander around the beautiful main plazas,
the bustling hubs of Guanajuato's social life,
is a good introduction to Guanajuato's historic center. Starting from the east, pretty
Jardín de la Unión, surrounded by restaurants
and shaded by trees, is the social heart of
the city. The elegant **Teatro Juárez** sits on its
southeast corner. Walk west on Obregón to
Plaza de la Paz, the small triangle beside the
basilica, surrounded by the former homes
of wealthy silver lords.

Meander west and south along the curv-
ing Av Juárez to **Plazuela de los Ángeles**, where
the steps and ice-cream stands are popular
gathering spots for students. The Callejón
del Beso (see p607) is just a few meters
uphill from here.

Continue on Juárez to the handsome
Jardín de la Reforma, behind the row of classical columns. This leads on to **Plaza San Roque**,
where *entremeses* (theatrical sketches) are
performed during the Cervantino festival
(see p611). Nearby is the pleasant, shady
Plazuela de San Fernando. These three linked
spaces form a superbly picturesque detour
northwest of Av Juárez.

Further west on Av Juárez is the bustling
area in front of Mercado Hidalgo. A block
north, **Plaza Alhóndiga** is a usually empty
space with wide steps leading up to the Alhóndiga. From there, head back east along
28 de Septiembre (which changes names

several times), past museums and the university, and a few twists and turns, to **Plaza
del Baratillo** with its Florentine fountain. A
right turn and a short block south from
there will bring you back to Jardín de la
Unión, where tourists and well-to-do locals
congregate in the late afternoon, along with
buskers, shoe shiners and snack vendors.

TEATRO JUÁREZ & OTHER THEATERS
The magnificent **Teatro Juárez** (☎ 732-01-83;
Sopeña s/n; US$1.50; ⊗ 9am-1:45pm & 5-7:45pm Tue-Sun
when no performances are scheduled) was built between 1873 and 1903 and inaugurated by the
dictator Porfirio Díaz, whose lavish tastes
are reflected in the plush red and gold interior. The outside is festooned with columns,
lampposts and statues; inside the impression
is Moorish, with the bar and lobby gleaming
with carved wood, stained glass and precious
metals. The steps outside are a popular place
to watch the scene on the plaza.

The **Teatro Principal** (☎ 732-15-23; Hidalgo s/n)
and **Teatro Cervantes** (☎ 732-11-69; Plaza Allende s/n)
are not as spectacular as Teatro Juárez, but
they all host a full schedule of performances
during the Cervantino festival, and less regular shows at other times. Statues of Don
Quixote and Sancho Panza grace the small
Plaza Allende, in front of Teatro Cervantes.

CALLEJÓN DEL BESO
The narrowest of the many narrow alleys
that climb the hills from Guanajuato's main
streets is the **Alley of the Kiss**, where the balconies of the houses on either side of the alley
practically touch. In a Guanajuato legend,
a fine family once lived on this street, and
their daughter fell in love with a common
miner. They were forbidden to see each
other, but the miner rented a room opposite, and the lovers exchanged furtive *besos*
(kisses) from these balconies. Of course the
romance was discovered and the couple
met a tragic end. From the Plazuela de los
Ángeles on Av Juárez, walk about 40m up
Callejón del Patrocinio and you'll see the
tiny alley to your left.

ALHÓNDIGA DE GRANADITAS
The site of the first major rebel victory in
Mexico's War of Independence is now a
history and **art museum** (☎ 732-11-12; 28 de Septiembre; US$3, free Sun, video camera US$3; ⊗ 10am-2pm
& 4-6pm Tue-Sat, 10am-3pm Sun).

The Alhóndiga was a massive grain and seed storehouse built between 1798 and 1808. In 1810 it became a fortress for Spanish troops and loyalist leaders. They barricaded themselves inside when 20,000 rebels led by Miguel Hidalgo attempted to take Guanajuato. It looked as if the outnumbered Spaniards would be able to hold out. Then, on September 28, 1810, a young miner named Juan José de los Reyes Martínez (aka El Pípila), under orders from Hidalgo, tied a stone slab to his back and, thus protected from Spanish bullets, set the gates ablaze. While the Spaniards choked on smoke, the rebels moved in and took the Alhóndiga, killing most of those inside. (El Pípila probably perished in the battle, but some versions of the story have it that he lived to a ripe old age.)

The Spaniards later took their revenge: the heads of four leaders of the rebellion – Aldama, Allende, Jiménez and Hidalgo himself, who was executed in Chihuahua – were displayed on the four outside corners of the Alhóndiga from 1811 to 1821. The metal cages in which the heads hung are now exhibited inside, and the hooks can still be seen outside. The Alhóndiga was used as a prison for a century, beginning in 1864; it became a museum in 1967. The museum's historical sections cover Guanajuato's pre-Hispanic past, its great flood of 1905 and modern times. There's also a fine art gallery. Don't miss Chávez Morado's dramatic murals of Guanajuato's history on the staircases.

MUSEO Y CASA DE DIEGO RIVERA
Diego Rivera's birthplace is now a **museum** (☎ 732-11-97; Pocitos 47; adult/student US$1.50/0.50; ✆ 10am-7pm Tue-Sat, 10am-3pm Sun) honoring the painter. Rivera and a twin brother were born in the house in 1886 (his twin died at the age of two), and lived here until the family moved to Mexico City six years later.

In conservative Guanajuato, where Catholic influence prevails, the Marxist Rivera was *persona non grata* for years. The city now honors its once blacklisted son with a small collection of his work. The first floor contains the Rivera family's 19th-century antiques and fine furniture. On the 2nd and 3rd floors are portraits of peasants and indigenous people, a nude of Frida Kahlo and sketches for some of Rivera's memorable murals. There's a good giftshop downstairs

and the upper floors also host temporary exhibitions of work by Mexican and international artists.

MUSEO ICONOGRÁFICO DEL QUIJOTE
The excellent and surprisingly interesting **museum** (☎ 732-67-21; Doblado 1; US$2; ✆ 10am-6:30pm Tue-Sat, 10am-2:30pm Sun) fronts the tiny plaza in front of the Templo de San Francisco. Every exhibit relates to Don Quixote de la Mancha, the notorious Spanish literary hero. Enthusiasts find it fascinating to see the same subject depicted in so many different media by different artists in different styles. Paintings, statues, tapestries, even chess sets, clocks and postage stamps all feature the quixotic icon and his bumbling companion Sancho Panza.

UNIVERSIDAD DE GUANAJUATO
The **University of Guanajuato**, whose ramparts are visible above much of the city, is on Lascuraín de Retana one block up the hill from the basilica. It's considered one of Mexico's finest schools for music, theater, mine engineering and law. Some of the buildings originally housed a large Jesuit seminary, but the distinctive multistory white and blue building with the crenellated pediment dates from the 1950s. The design was controversial at the time, but it's now recognized as a successful integration of a modern building into a historic cityscape.

MUSEO DEL PUEBLO DE GUANAJUATO
Located beside the university, this **art museum** (☎ 732-29-90; Pocitos 7; US$1.50; ✆ 10am-6:30pm Tue-Sat, 10am-2:30pm Sun) has a collection ranging from colonial to modern times. The museum occupies the former mansion of the Marqueses de San Juan de Rayas, who owned the San Juan de Rayas mine. The private church upstairs in the courtyard contains a powerful mural by José Chávez Morado.

BASILICA & OTHER CHURCHES
The **Basílica de Nuestra Señora de Guanajuato**, on Plaza de la Paz, a block west of Jardín de la Unión, contains a jewel-covered image of the Virgin, patron of Guanajuato. The wooden statue was supposedly hidden from the Moors in a cave in Spain for 800 years. Felipe II of Spain gifted it to Guanajuato in thanks for the wealth it provided to the crown.

Other fine colonial churches include the **Templo de San Diego**, opposite the Jardín de la Unión; the **Templo de San Francisco**, on Doblado; and the large **Templo de la Compañía de Jesús**, on Navarro, which was completed in 1747 for the Jesuit seminary whose buildings are now occupied by the University of Guanajuato.

FUNICULAR

This incline **railway** (Plaza Constancia s/n; US$1/2 one-way/roundtrip; 🕑 9am-10pm Mon-Sat, 10am-9pm Sun) inches up the slope behind the Teatro Juárez to a terminal and scenic bar near the El Pípila monument. The modern track and the terminals both seem a little incongruous in this ancient town, but it's a scenic trip for visitors, and a great boon for those who live in steep hillside suburbs south and west of the center.

MONUMENTO A EL PÍPILA

The **monument** to El Pípila honors the hero who torched the Alhóndiga gates on September 28, 1810, enabling Hidalgo's forces to win the first victory of the independence movement. The statue shows El Pípila holding his torch high over the city. On the base is the inscription *Aún hay otras Alhóndigas por incendiar* ('There are still other Alhóndigas to burn').

It's worth going up to the statue for the magnificent view over the city; you can climb up inside the statue (one peso) to about shoulder level but the view is just as good from the terraces at its feet. Two routes from the center of town go up steep, picturesque lanes. One goes east on Sopeña from Jardín de la Unión, then turns right on Callejón del Calvario (you'll see the 'Al Pípila' sign). Another ascent, unmarked, goes uphill from the small plaza on Alonso. If the climb is too much for you, the 'Pípila-ISSSTE' bus heading west on Juárez will let you off right by the statue, or you can ride up in the funicular.

MUSEO DE LAS MOMIAS

The famous **Museum of the Mummies** (☎ 732-06-39; Camino a las Momias s/n; adult/child US$2.25/1.75, cameras/videos US$0.75/1.75; 🕑 9am-6pm daily) at the *panteón* (cemetery) is a quintessential example of Mexico's obsession with death. Visitors from all over come to see scores of corpses disinterred from the public cemetery.

The first remains were dug up in 1865, when it was necessary to remove some bodies from the cemetery to make room for more. What the authorities uncovered were not skeletons but flesh mummified with grotesque forms and facial expressions. The mineral content of the soil and extremely dry atmosphere had combined to preserve the bodies in this unique way.

Today more than 100 mummies are on display in the museum, including the first mummy to be discovered, the 'smallest mummy in the world,' a pregnant mummy and plenty more. Since space is still tight in the cemetery, bodies continue to be exhumed if the relatives can't pay the upkeep fees. It takes only five or six years for a body to become mummified here, though only 1% or 2% of the bodies exhumed are 'display quality' specimens. The others are cremated.

In the same building as the Museo de las Momias, the **Salón de Culto a la Muerte** is a series of hokey horror-show exhibits that you can see for an extra US$1.

The complex is on the western edge of town, a long walk or a 10-minute ride from Av Juárez on any 'Momias' bus.

MINA & TEMPLO LA VALENCIANA

For 250 years **La Valenciana mine** (☎ 732-05-70/80; US$1; 🕑 8am-7pm), on a hill overlooking Guanajuato 5km north of the center, produced 20% of the world's silver, in addition to quantities of gold and other minerals. Shut down after the Mexican Revolution, the mine reopened in 1968 and is now run by a cooperative. It still yields silver, gold, nickel and lead, and you can see the ore being lifted out and miners descending the immense main shaft, 9m wide and 500m deep. Guides (ask for an English-speaker) will show you around the compound (they expect a tip), though you can't go inside the mine.

On the main road near the mine is the magnificent **Templo La Valenciana** (aka Iglesia de San Cayetano). One legend says that the Spaniard who started the mine promised San Cayetano that if it made him rich, he would build a church to honor the saint. Another says that the silver baron of La Valenciana, Conde de Rul, tried to atone for exploiting the miners by building the ultimate in churrigueresque churches.

Whatever the motive, ground was broken in 1765, and the church was completed in 1788. Templo La Valenciana's façade is spectacular, and its interior dazzles with ornate golden altars, filigree carvings and giant paintings.

Just downhill behind the church, the **Bocamina Valenciana** (☎ 732-05-70; adult/child US$2/1; ☺ 10am-6pm) is another section of mine shaft that's open to visitors.

To get to La Valenciana, take a 'Cristo Rey' or 'Valenciana' bus (every 15 minutes) from the bus stop on Alhóndiga just north of 28 de Septiembre. Get off at Templo La Valenciana, then cross the road and follow the signs to the mine entrance.

GALERAS DE LA INQUISICIÓN

On the road to La Valenciana, the old **Hacienda del Cochero** (☎ 733-01-39; Calle de la Cochera 11; adult/child US$2.25/US$1; ☺ 10am-7pm) has a tourist trap in its cellars. Allegedly used as torture chambers during the Inquisition, the cellars now contain scarecrowlike dummies being tormented on reproduction racks, wheels and iron maidens. The rote tour commentary is sometimes in English.

EX-HACIENDA SAN GABRIEL DE BARRERA

Built at the end of the 17th century, this was the grand hacienda of Captain Gabriel de Barrera, whose family was descended from the first Conde de Rul of the famous La Valenciana mine. Opened as a museum in 1979, the **hacienda** (☎ 732-06-19; Camino Antiguo a Marfil Km 2.5; US$2, camera US$2, video US$2.50; ☺ 9am-6pm) has been magnificently restored with period European furnishings.

The large grounds, originally devoted to processing ore from La Valenciana, were converted in 1945 to beautiful terraced gardens with pavilions, pools, fountains and footpaths – a lovely and tranquil retreat from the city.

The house and garden are 2.5km west of the city center. Take one of the frequent 'Marfil' buses heading west on Juárez and ask the driver to drop you at Hotel Misión Guanajuato.

PRESAS DE LA OLLA & SAN RENOVATO

In the hills at the east end of the city there are two small reservoirs with a green park between them and a lighthouse on the hill above. It's a popular family park on Sunday, when you can bring a picnic and hire rowboats. The rest of the week it's quiet and peaceful, though not especially scenic. Any eastbound 'Presa' bus, from the underground stop down the steps at the southwest corner of the Jardín de la Unión, will take you here.

Courses

Guanajuato is a university town and has an excellent atmosphere for studying Spanish. Group classes average around US$5 per hour and private lessons average US$10 an hour. Schools can arrange homestays with meals for US$15 to US$20 per day. Additional costs to ask about include registration and/or placement test fees, and costs for excursions and extracurricular activities.

Academia Falcón (☎ /fax 731-07-45; www.academia falcon.com, Paseo de la Presa 80) Well-established institute with two to five students per class. Registration is every Saturday morning.

Escuela Mexicana (☎ 732-50-05; www.escuelamexi cana.int.com.mx; Sóstenes Rocha 28) Small school with classes in Spanish (grammar, conversation, literature) & other topics from pre-Hispanic art to business culture. Homestay & on-site accommodation (see Sleeping, opposite) available.

Instituto Tonali (☎ 732-73-52; Juárez 4) Spanish classes at all levels, dance & craft programs.

Universidad de Guanajuato (UGTO; ☎ 732 00-06 ext 8001; www.ugto.mx/idiomas/spanish.htm; Lascuraín de Retana 5) Summer Spanish courses, plus classes in Mexican & Latin American culture; sessions begin in early June & early July. Also offers a range of semester-long courses in language & culture, beginning in January & July.

Tours

Several agencies offer similar tours of Guanajuato's major sights (usually in Spanish). You can reach all the same places on local buses, but if your time is limited a tour may be useful.

Transporte Exclusivo de Turismo (☎ 732-59-68; cnr Juárez & 5 de Mayo), in a kiosk, and **Transportes Turísticos de Guanajuato** (☎ 732-21-34; cnr Obregón & El Truco), below the front courtyard of the basilica, both offer Guanajuato Colonial tours, which include the mummies, La Valenciana mine and church, the Pípila monument and the Carretera Panorámica. Trips (US$6.50, three hours) depart up to three times daily. Longer tours go to Cristo Rey (US$7.50) or make an eight-hour circuit through Dolores Hidalgo and San

Miguel de Allende (US$14). Night tours (US$10, five hours) take in Guanajuato's views and nightspots and the street parties called *callejoneadas* (see Entertainment, p614).

Festivals & Events

BAILE DE LAS FLORES

The **Flower Dance** takes place on the Thursday before Semana Santa (Holy Week). The next day, mines are open to the public for sightseeing and celebrations. Miners decorate altars to La Virgen de los Dolores, a manifestation of the Virgin Mary who looks after miners.

FIESTAS DE SAN JUAN Y PRESA DE LA OLLA

The **Festivals of San Juan** are celebrated at the Presa de la Olla park in late June. The 24th is the big bash for the saint's day itself, with dances, music, fireworks and picnics. Then on the first Monday in July, everyone comes back to the park for another big party celebrating the opening of the dam's floodgates.

DIA DE LA CUEVA

Cave Day is a country fair held on July 31, when locals walk to a cave in the nearby hills, to honor San Ignacio de Loyola, and enjoy a festive picnic.

FIESTA DE LA VIRGEN DE GUANAJUATO

This **festival**, on August 9, commemorates the date when Felipe II gave the people of Guanajuato the jeweled wooden Virgin that now adorns the basilica.

FESTIVAL INTERNACIONAL CERVANTINO

Guanajuato's **arts festival** (www.festivalcervantino.gob.mx) is dedicated to the Spanish writer Miguel Cervantes, author of Don Quixote. In the 1950s the festival was merely *entremeses* (theatrical sketches) from Cervantes' work performed by students. It has grown to become one of Latin America's foremost arts extravaganzas. Music, dance and theater groups arrive from around the world, performing work that nowadays may have nothing whatsoever to do with Cervantes. (A recent festival included Argentine orchestras, Australian writers, Nigerian dancers, Polish drama and new Japanese cinema.) The festival lasts two to three weeks starting around the second

week of October. If your visit coincides with the festival, you shouldn't – and won't be able to – miss it.

While some events are held in the Teatro Juárez and other theaters, the most spectacular *entremeses*, with galloping horses and medieval costumes, are performed in the historic settings of Plaza San Roque and Plaza Alhóndiga.

Many events, in fact some of the biggest, are free. The festival opens at Plaza Alhóndiga – arrive a couple hours early if you want a seat. On Saturday and Sunday, when Guanajuato's population swells to many times its normal size, there's music – from children's ensembles to rock/hip-hop bands – on practically every corner.

Cervantino events are organized into morning, afternoon and evening sessions, for which tickets range from US$7 to US$25. Tickets and hotels should be booked in advance. Advance tickets are available through **Ticketmaster** (www.ticketmaster.com.mx). In Guanajuato, buy tickets from the ticket office on the southeast side of Teatro Juárez (not in the theater ticket office).

Sleeping

Prices given here are for the summer season. They may be lower in other months, but may be even higher at Christmas, Semana Santa and during the Cervantino Festival. The classiest in-town address is Jardín de la Unión, where several venerable hotels have rooms, bars and restaurants facing the lively but traffic-free plaza. Browse www.hotelesguanajuato.com for a thorough accommodations overview.

BUDGET

Casa Kloster (☎ 732-00-88; Alonso 32; dm/s/d with shared bathroom US$9/11/19) The classic backpackers' choice is near all the action, a short block down an alley from the basilica. Birds and flowers grace the sunny courtyard, and well-tended rooms are clean and comfortable. Those facing the street can be noisy. Larger rooms cost slightly more. It's a relaxed, friendly place, but don't leave valuables lying around. Arrive early because it's often booked.

Casa de Pita (☎ 732-15-32; www.casadepita.com; Cabecita 26, near Plaza Mexiamora; r with shared bathroom from US$9 per person, from US$11 with private bathroom, full apt US$41; ☐) The 10 rooms at the colorful

300-year-old guesthouse of gregarious, motherly Senora Valtierra share an authentic Mexican kitchen and a terrace with good city views. Rates include a simple breakfast. Guests who appreciate the quiet and privacy end up taking advantage of the long-term rates.

Casa Bertha (☎ /fax 732-13-16; casaberthagto@ hotmail.com; Tamboras 9; r with shared bathroom from US$10 per person, apt with kitchen from US$13 per person) This family-run *casa de huéspedes*, a few minutes east of the Jardín de la Unión, is a maze of 10 doubles and three family-size apartments, all with cable TV. It's a homey, well kept and central labyrinth, with modern bathrooms and a rooftop terrace with views over the town. Walk up the street beside the Teatro Principal to Plaza Mexiamora. Head straight uphill, take the first right, then turn left and follow the path to the door directly ahead.

Casa Mexicana (☎ 732-50-05; www.escuelamexi cana.int.com.mx; Sóstenes Rocha 28; r with shared bathroom US$9 per person, with private bathroom US$12 per person; ⌨) Smallish rooms are centered around a courtyard at this clean, friendly, family-run place connected to the Escuela Mexicana language school (see p610). The bar next door is popular with language students and locals looking to practice their English.

Other recommendations:

Hotel Alhóndiga (☎ 732-05-25; Insurgencia 49; s/d US$16/22; P) Family-run with clean, comfortable not quite 'colonial' rooms with color TV; some have small private balconies.

Hotel Granaditas (☎ 732-10-39; Av Juárez 109; s/d US$14/23) A bit gloomy but the best of the older hotels near Mercado Hidalgo. Upsides are some friendly staff & clean rooms with hot water & TV (on request).

Hotel Posada de la Condesa (☎ 732-14-62; Plaza de la Paz 60; s/d US$13/19) Cheap, central lodgings. Rooms are passably clean, but they're worn & can be noisy. Large group rooms have balconies; others are dark, without windows or ventilation. If you must stay right in the center, the price is OK for the better rooms but too much for poor ones. The bar next door can be loud but fun.

MID-RANGE

Hotel San Diego (☎ 732-13-00; www.hotelerasandiego .com; Jardín de la Unión 1; r from US$70) The four-story San Diego has 55 comfortable rooms and suites (for up to eight), a rooftop terrace and subterranean sports bar. Superior rooms with balconies cost the same as interior rooms.

Hotel Molino del Rey (☎ 732-22-23; mach1@ avantel.net; cnr Campanero & Belaunzaran; s US$23-28, d

US$40) An easy stroll from the center, the 'King's Mill' is notable for its quiet, convenient location. Its 35 rooms are set around a pretty patio, though housekeeping standards are variable and some rooms are nicer than others. A small ground floor restaurant serves tasty, inexpensive meals.

Hostal Cantarranas (☎ 732-51-44; fax 732-17-08; Hidalgo 50; r US$27-45) A short hop from the Jardín, the Singing Frog is an old building with eight pleasant and bright but crowded rooms, mostly apartments. The apartments have two to four beds, a kitchen, sitting room, TV and phone. The carpet downstairs tends toward dank (try for something on the upper floors) but the rooftop terrace is a sunny hangout. The bar next door faces a small plaza and runs happy hour all day.

Hostería del Frayle (☎ /fax 732-11-79; Sopeña 3; s/d US$54/75; P) A block from the Jardín, this historic hotel – it was built in 1673 as the Casa de Moneda – has 37 attractive but dark rooms with high wood-beamed ceilings, satellite TV and other comforts. Service is friendly and the thick adobe walls keep things quiet.

Motel de las Embajadoras (☎ 731-01-05; cnr Embajadoras & Paseo Madero; s/d low US$32/45, high US$42/59; P) If you're driving and want to avoid the congested center, this motel has plenty of parking and is only five minutes uphill from the center on an 'Embajadoras' or 'Presa' bus. The restaurant/bar is elegant but inexpensive, and the lovely courtyard is full of plants, trees and birds. Clean, comfortable rooms have color TV and phone.

Hotel Parador del Convento (☎ 732-25-24; hpconv@prodigy.net.mx; Calz de Guadalupe 17; r from US$47; P) A steep five-minute walk up behind the university, this former hostel has converted its simple carpeted rooms into comfy private accommodations with cable TV.

TOP END

Some quaint old buildings in various parts of town have been restored as small boutique hotels. The road to La Valenciana has several posh places with lofty locations. Other upmarket places are in Marfil, a 15-minute drive or bus ride west of town.

Hotel Posada Santa Fé (☎ 732-00-84; www.posada santafe.com; Jardín de la Unión 12; s/d US$59/71, exterior d from US$97; P ⌨) Overlooking the Jardín, this storied 1862 mansion has 47 comfortable rooms, though they're not as classy as the elegant lobby might suggest (the location is this place's best feature). Don't miss the rooftop Jacuzzi and check their website for multiple-night promo packages. It's the only place on the plaza with on-site parking.

Hotel Luna (☎ 732-97-25; Jardín de la Unión 6; r from US$75, exterior d from US$88, ste from US$109) Another handsome building facing the plaza, this 100 year old hotel has been completely restored and modernized. Rooms combine contemporary facilities with old-style charm. Rates include breakfast but don't reflect a 10% cash-discount.

Quinta Las Acacias (☎ 731-15-17, 800-710-89-38 in Mexico, 888-497-41-29 in USA; www.quintalasacacias.com .mx; Paseo de la Presa 168; ste with breakfast US$195-250; P 🖵 🖳 🖥) This new nine-suite hideaway combines attentive service and intimate luxury in a former 19th-century French colonial summer residence. Caged parakeets warble in the patio while sheets are turned down and a delightful plate of local cookies appears. Master suites are appointed with oversize beds and Talavera tiles; modern amenities include hydromassage tubs and portable phones. Each suite is thoughtfully decorated with folk art from a different Mexican state. In the morning, you'll wake up to the waft of housebaked biscuits served with homemade jams.

La Casa del Quixote (☎ /fax 732-39-23; Pocitos 37; ste low/high season US$80/112) This small eight-room retreat is built into a steep hillside overlooking town. The large, comfortable rooms are a real delight. All rooms have kitchenettes and living rooms, most have bathtubs and half have brilliant views.

Castillo Santa Cecilia (☎ 732-04-85, 800-012-08-58; castillostacecilia@hotmail.com; Camino a La Valenciana Km 1; r/ste US$117/149; P 🖳) This large stone building looks like a castle, and the lobby, dining room and bars all aim for a medieval ambience. The rooms have all the modern amenities, and there are tennis courts, a good restaurant and wine bar. Renovated standard rooms are worth the extra US$9.

Parador San Javier (☎ 732-06-26, 800-714-73-25; hpsjgto@redes.int.com.mx; Plaza Aldama 92; s/d/ste US$82/91/105; P 🖳 🖥) Opposite Castillo Santa Cecilia, this Disneyesque Howard Johnson property offers attentive service and comfortable accommodations in a restored ex-hacienda setting. The majority of rooms, however, are in a modern, high-rise wing where the interior color scheme is decidedly non-colonial.

La Casa de Espíritus Alegres (ex-Hacienda La Trinidad; ☎ /fax 733-10-13; www.casaspirit.com; Real de Marfil s/n; r with breakfast US$135-155; P) This attractive B&B, run by a Californian artist, has enough pieces to fill a Mexican folk arts museum. The well-restored 18th-century hacienda has lush gardens and eight individually decorated rooms with fireplaces and private outdoor sitting areas. Children are not allowed. Adjacent is the highly-touted gourmet restaurant Chez Nicole.

Hotel Misión Guanajuato (☎ 732-39-80, 800-900-38-00; www.hotelesmision.com.mx; Camino Antiguo a Marfil Km 2.5; r/ste US$119/181; P 🖳 🖥) This chain hotel has a restaurant, bar, heated pool, tennis courts and 160 luxury rooms. It's west of the city beside the ex-Hacienda San Gabriel de Barrera (see p607). There's a free shuttle service to and from the center.

Eating

For fresh produce and local sweets, the Mercado Hidalgo is a five-minute walk west of the main plaza on Juárez.

JARDÍN DE LA UNIÓN & AROUND

The hotels on the west side of the **Jardín de la Unión** (see p611) have good upscale restaurants where you can enjoy the atmosphere of the plaza. At the tables outside **Posada Santa Fé**, well-prepared *antojitos* cost US$5 to US$9, and steak dishes run US$7 to $10; allow extra for wandering musicians. Adjacent, the **Hotel Luna** (mains US$8-10) restaurant also has a bar, outdoor tables and a good, if uninspired, Mexican selection. At the Jardín's southwest corner, **Hotel San Diego** (mains US$6-10) has an elegant upstairs restaurant with balcony tables overlooking the plaza; the breakfast specials and the *comida corrida* are the best values here. On the southeast side of the Jardín, several simple places offer quick eats like pizza slices, hamburgers and ice cream.

Café/Restaurante El Pingüis (☎ 732-14-14; Jardín de la Unión 21; mains US$1.50-3; 🕒 8:30am-9:30pm) Facing the Jardín, this unpretentious café is consistently one of the most popular places in town. The menu mixes Mexican and fast-food standards, with good coffee, egg dishes, enchiladas, big sandwiches and a solid *comida corrida* (US$3.50).

Truco 7 (☎ 732-83-74; El Truco 7; mains US$2-6) This intimate, artsy café-restaurant-gallery attracts a loyal mixed crowd of students, travelers and teachers with delicious food and a great atmosphere. Set lunches are inexpensive and the breakfast and dinner choices are more imaginative than in most places. Background music includes jazz, blues and classical.

El Café (☎ 732-25-66; Sopeña 10; mains $3-7) This popular hangout is the place to socialize al fresco over cocktails or a light meal. There are more tables under umbrellas across the street, alongside Teatro Juárez.

El Retiro (☎ 732-06-22; Sopeña 12; mains US$3-7) This lively traditional restaurant-bar attracts a regular crowd with a good *menú del día* for US$4 and live music Wednesday through Friday evenings from 9pm.

El Gallo Pitagórico (☎ 732-94-89; Constancia 10; mains US$6-11) South of the Jardín, up the steep path behind Templo San Diego, this romantic restaurant is in a bright blue building with wonderful city views. The fine Italian cuisine includes assorted antipasti, rich minestrone and a range of pastas. It's well worth the walk. Service is good, the music is classical and most of the wines are imported.

La Trattoria del Gallo (☎ 736-67-26; Sopeña 3; mains US$5-9; ☺ 1-11pm) The owners of El Gallo Pitagórico present a menu of mid-priced Italian dishes, including an excellent pizza and pasta selection, in a less formal setting. There's a fun 1950s motorcycle racing theme.

El Unicornio Azul (☎ 732-07-00; Plaza Baratillo 2; mains US$1-3; ☺ closed Sun) Mainly a health food store, the Blue Unicorn has a few tables where you can linger over a yogurt and fruit breakfast or a soyburger, or get wholemeal cookies and other healthy baked goods to go.

Casa Valadez (☎ 732-11-57; Jardín de la Unión 3; cnr Sopeña; mains US$6-10) Opposite Teatro Juárez, this cavernous but upmarket restaurant serves economical breakfasts and a good value *comida corrida* – despite the cheesy live organ music, it's never empty.

AV JUÁREZ & AROUND

Tasca de Los Santos (☎ 732-19-98; Plaza de la Paz 23; mains US$5-9) This place opposite the basilica has outdoor tables on picturesque Plaza de la Paz for tapas, paella and other Spanish specialties. It's a bit pricey but worth it for the authentic flavors and European ambience.

Sushi Bar Room (☎ 732-01-79; Av Juárez 25A; mains US$3-8; ☺ 2-10:30pm Mon-Thu, 2-11:30pm Fri & Sat) Not the greatest sushi and teppanyaki you'll ever taste, but it's a hip and admirable attempt and a good change from the usual Mexican fare.

Restaurant La Carreta (☎ 732-43-58; Av Juárez 96; mains US$2-4) Trust your nose: La Carreta does a good version of the standard *pollo al pastor* (grilled chicken) and *carne asada* (grilled beef), both served with large portions of rice and salad. The grill out front keeps it warm inside on cold days.

Fuente de Sodas (Juárez 120; snacks US$1-2) This classic sandwich and juice bar is good for a quick *licuado*, fruit salad or *torta*.

Restaurante Vegetariano Yamuna (Callejón de Calixto 20; lunch US$3-4; ☺ 2-4pm Tue-Sun) Just uphill from Plazuela de los Ángeles, this peaceful place serves a tasty set lunch of *comida hindu*. It also sometimes rents out cheap beds upstairs.

PLAZUELA SAN FERNANDO

This little plaza is home to an ever-changing slate of hip hangouts and is delightful in the evening, for a drink, a snack or a meal.

La Oreja de Van Gogh (☎ 732-69-03; Plazuela San Fernando 24; mains US$3-7) Van Gogh's Ear has Vincentish murals inside, congenial tables outside, cheap breakfast and cheap beer at the 5pm happy hour. The menu features burgers and your favorite Mexican dishes.

Other pleasant places here with sidewalk seating include **Bossanova Café** and **Las Leyendas de Don Juan**.

Drinking

Guanajuato Grill (☎ 732-02-85; Alonso 4) This casual disco and drink spot is frequented by affluent, energetic students who like loud dance music. It's packed after midnight on Friday and Saturday. On quieter nights they pull in the patrons with drink specials from 9pm to 10pm.

Los Lobos Bar (Doblado 2) This hard-rockin' dive next to the Corona distributor draws a golden oldies crowd and sometimes features classic-rock cover bands.

Entertainment

Every evening, the **Jardín de la Unión** comes alive with tourists and others crowding the outdoor tables, strolling, people-watching and listening to the street musicians. The state band and other groups give free concerts in the gazebo some evenings from 7pm.

NIGHTCLUBS & DISCOS

El Bar (☎ 732-56-66; Sopeña 10; ☼ 10pm-late Tue-Sat) Upstairs above El Café, this popular, friendly place swings to salsa music, attracting a mixed but mostly young crowd. Good dancers will feel right at home. Others can ask about Thursday evening salsa classes.

El Capitolio (☎ 732-08-10; Plaza de la Paz 62; ☼ 9pm-3am Tue-Sat) Another disco blasting techno and dance music to big weekend crowds, Capitolio heavily promotes its karaoke and cheap drink deals but manages a slightly more stylish ambience than the nearby Guanajuato Grill.

La Dama de las Camelias (☎ 732-75-87; Sopeña 32) For Latin sounds and a dose of dirty dancing in an artsy, gay-friendly atmosphere, check out La Dama, playing live and recorded salsa, flamenco, *danzón*, *son cubano* and Andean music.

CALLEJONEADAS

On Friday, Saturday and Sunday evenings around 8pm (daily during festivals), **callejoneadas** (or *estudiantinas*) depart from in front of San Diego church on the Jardín de la Unión. The *callejoneada* tradition is said to have come from Spain. A group of professional songsters and musicians, dressed in traditional costumes, starts up in front of the church, a crowd gathers, then the whole mob winds through the ancient alleyways of the city, playing and singing heartily. On special occasions they take along a burro laden with wine; at other times wine is stashed midpoint on the route. Stories and jokes are told between songs, though these are unintelligible unless you understand Spanish well. It's good fun and one of Guanajuato's most enjoyable traditions, even if it's become a bit touristy. There's no cost except a small amount for the wine you drink. Tour companies and others try to sell you tickets for the *callejoneadas*, but you don't need them!

PERFORMING ARTS

Guanajuato has three fine theaters, the 100-year-old **Teatro Juárez** (☎ 732-01-83; Sopeña s/n), **Teatro Principal** (☎ 732-15-23; Hidalgo s/n) and **Teatro Cervantes** (☎ 732-11-69; Plaza Allende s/n), none far from the Jardín de la Unión. Check their posters to see what's on. International films are screened in several locations, including the Teatro Principal, Teatro Cervantes and Museo y Casa de Diego Rivera (see p607).

The **Viva la Magia** program runs every weekend from March to September, with Guanajuato's theaters hosting a variety of music, dance and literary events on Thursday, Friday and Saturday evenings. The tourist office has details of what's on each week.

Getting There & Away

AIR

Guanajuato is served by the Aeropuerto Internacional del Bajío, which is about 30km west of Guanajuato, halfway between León and Silao. See the León section (p617) for detailed flight information.

BUS

Guanajuato's Central de Autobuses is way out on the southwest outskirts of town. It has a tourist office, card phones, restaurant and luggage checkroom. Deluxe and 1st-class bus tickets can be bought in town at **Viajes Frausto** (☎ 732-35-80; Obregón 10). Daily departures include:

Dolores Hidalgo (US$3.50, 1hr, 2nd-class Flecha Amarilla every 20min, 5:30am-10:20pm daily)
Guadalajara (US$24, 4hr, 6 deluxe ETN; US$20, 4hr, 8 1st-class Primera Plus daily; US$17, 4hr, 8 2nd-class Flecha Amarilla daily)
León (US$4.50, 1hr, 6 deluxe ETN daily; US$3, 1hr, 7 1st-class Primera Plus daily; US$2.50, 1hr, 2nd-class Flecha Amarilla or Flecha de Oro every 15min, 5:30am-10:20pm daily)
Mexico City (US$29, 4½hr; 9 deluxe ETN daily; US$23, 4½hr; 11 1st-class Primera Plus daily; US$21, 4½hr, 3 1st-class Futura or Ómnibus de México daily) To Terminal Norte.
San Luis Potosí (US$11.50, 4hr, 2 1st-class Flecha Amarilla daily)
San Miguel de Allende (US$8.50, 1½hr, 2 deluxe ETN daily; US$6.50, 1½hr 3 1st-class Primera Plus daily; US$5, 1½hr, 9 2nd-class Flecha Amarilla daily)

There are also hourly 2nd-class Flecha Amarilla buses to Celaya, plus three to Querétaro. For Morelia, catch an Irapuato bus and change there.

Getting Around

A taxi to Bajío international airport will cost about US$25. A cheaper option is a frequent bus to Silao, and a taxi from there (US$9).

'Central de Autobuses' buses run constantly between the bus station and city center up to midnight. From the center, you can catch them heading west on Juárez, or on the north side of the basilica. A taxi costs US$3.

You won't want a car in town, but if you want one to explore the surrounding area, try **Lloguer** (☎ 733-36-90).

City buses (US$0.30) run from 5am to 10pm. The tourist office is very helpful with bus information. Taxis are plentiful in the center and charge about US$2 for short trips around town.

LEÓN

☎ 477 / pop 1.07 million / elevation 1854m

The industrial city of León, 56km west of Guanajuato, is a big bus interchange point and a likable enough place if you need to stay overnight. From the 16th century it became the center of Mexico's ranching district, providing meat for the mining towns and processing hides into essential tack for the early mining days. León is still famous for its leather goods, though fashion footwear now outsells fancy saddles. The city's other products include steel, textiles and soap.

Orientation & Information

The heart of the city is the wide main Plaza de los Mártires del 2 de Enero (aka Plaza Principal), a well-groomed pedestrian space with the Palacio Municipal on its west side. The adjoining Plaza de los Fundadores and several nearby streets are also traffic-free

and full of shoe shops, food vendors, cafés and restaurants.

A board in Plaza Principal shows a big map of the city center, and a nearby **information booth** is staffed sporadically. You could also try calling the **regional tourism office** (☎ 763-44-01/02, 800-716-53-66; www.leon -mexico.com; Vasco de Quiroga 101). Lively **La Monarca Internet Café & Bar** (5 de Mayo 103, 2nd fl; ☺ 9am-midnight) has balconies overlooking the plaza and slow connections for US$2 per hour; to find the entrance in the evening, follow your nose and look for long lines approaching the woman selling *rico* tamales in the entryway. **Mexicana** (☎ 714-95-00; López Matos 308) has an in-town office but most other airline offices are at Bajío airport. Other essentials like banks and card phones are around the plazas.

Sights

Shopping and walking around León's historic heart are the main attractions; look for fine buildings like the **Casa de Cultura** (☎ 714-33-50), facing Plaza de los Fundadores. The big, twin-towered, baroque **Catedral Basílica** (cnr Obregón & Hidalgo) is a block northeast of the Casa de Cultura. The neoclassical 1869 **Teatro Doblado** (☎ 716-43-01; cnr Aldama & Moreno) still stages concerts, dance and drama. The free **Museo de la Ciudad** (☎ 714-50-22; Aldama 134; ☺ 9:30am-2:30pm & 5-7:30pm Tue-Sat, 9:30am-2:30pm Sun) exhibits contemporary work by local artists.

Festivals & Events

In January/February, the **Guanajuato State Fair** attracts millions of visitors with agricultural displays, music, dancing, carnival rides and bullfights. Hundreds of shoemakers display their wares in the **Centro de Exposiciones** (Conexpo; ☎ 771-25-00; cnr López Mateos & Francisco Villa) during the fair. Like Guanajuato, León also celebrates a Cervantino cultural festival, starting mid-October. If you happen to be in the area, the annual **Festival del Globo** hot air balloon gathering in mid-December is worth craning your neck for.

Sleeping & Eating

The Centro Histórico has several hostelries at various standards. There are many cheap hotels near the bus station on Calle La Luz (walk to the right from the station's main exit – La Luz is the first cross-street).

CRISTO REY: MEXICO'S GEOGRAPHIC HEART

Cristo Rey (Christ the King) is a 20m bronze statue of Jesus erected in 1950 on the summit of the Cerro de Cubilete, 15km west of Guanajuato on a side road off the road to Templo La Valenciana, and is said to be the exact geographical center of Mexico. For religious Mexicans there is a special significance in having Jesus at the heart of their country, and the statue is a popular attraction for Mexicans visiting Guanajuato.

Tour agencies offer 3½-hour trips to the statue (see p610), but you can go on your own for US$3.50 roundtrip by an Autobuses Vasallo de Cristo bus from Guanajuato's bus station. Buses depart nine times between 6am and 6pm on weekdays, with additional buses on weekends and holidays. From the bus station it is possible to see the statue up on the hill in the distance.

Hotel Fundadores (☎ 716-17-27; fax 716-66-12; Ortiz de Domínguez 218; s/d US$17/19) A block west of Plaza Principal, the two-star Fundadores offers clean, comfortable rooms with TV, phone and few frills.

Hotel Rex (☎ 714-24-15; 5 de Febrero 104; s/d with breakfast US$24/28, with air-con US$41/48; P ✕) The three-star Rex has spacious, carpeted 'traditional' (read: worn) rooms, and more expensive renovated air-con rooms with bathroom.

Howard Johnson Hotel Condesa (☎ 713-11-20; www.hj.com.mx; Portal Bravo 14; r/ste US$69/101; P ▣) On the main plaza's east side, this corporate favorite has comfortable rooms and frequent half-off discounts. The busy restaurant has pool tables, live music, outdoor tables and a popular buffet lunch (US$7.50).

Hotel Fiesta Americana (☎ 713-60-40; www.fiesta americana.com.mx; López Mateos Ote 1102; r from US$139; P ✕ ▣) This is the most luxurious of the several top-end hotels on López Mateos, the boulevard that runs east from the center and becomes Hwy 45 to the airport.

Restaurant Cadillac (☎ 716-84-07; Hidalgo 107; mains US$3.50-7) On a pedestrian street north of the plazas, the Cadillac is decorated with Hollywood posters. The set lunch (US$4) is a good value, and it serves tasty American and Mexican favorites until late at night.

Panteón Taurino (☎ 713-49-69; Calz de los Héroes 408; mains US$6-9). For something different, try this restaurant-bar-museum where you eat off the gravestones of ex-bullfighters. The walk is dark at night, so it's best to catch a cab.

Shopping

For quality shoes, browse the dozens of shops around the center, or the main leather district near the bus station. Just south of the bus station, **Plaza del Zapato** and **Plaza Piel** (cnr López Mateos & Hilario Medina) are shopping malls devoted entirely to footwear and leather goods. Ordinary-looking shops on La Luz and Hilario Medina can have extraordinary leather bargains.

Getting There & Away

AIR

Aeropuerto Internacional del Bajío is 20km southeast on the Mexico City road. Aerolitoral, Aeroméxico, American, Continental and Mexicana offer direct flights to Acapulco, Guadalajara, Mexico City, Monterrey, Puerto Vallarta and Tijuana, plus a host of cities in the USA.

BUS

The **Central de Autobuses** (Blvd Hilario Medina s/n), just north of Blvd López Mateos 1½km east of the city center, has a cafétería, left luggage, money exchange, Telecomm office and card phones. There are regular services to just about everywhere in northern and western Mexico.

Guanajuato (US$4.50, 1hr, 6 deluxe ETN daily; US$3, 1hr, 9 1st-class Primera Plus daily; US$2.50, 1hr, 2nd-class Flecha Amarilla every 10min daily)

Mexico City (US$31, 5hr, 14 deluxe ETN daily; US$25, 5hr, hourly 1st-class Primera Plus daily; US$23, 5hr, hourly

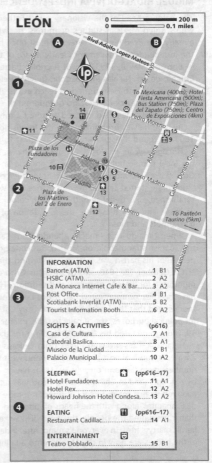

LEÓN

0   200 m
0   0.1 miles

2nd-class Herradura de Plata or Flecha Amarilla daily) To Terminal Norte.

San Miguel de Allende (US$12.50, 2¼hr, 2 deluxe ETN daily; US$10, 2¼hr, 2 1st-class Primera Plus daily)

Getting Around

There's no bus service from Bajío airport to central León – a taxi costs about US$14. The closest long-distance bus station to the airport is in Silao; a taxi there from the airport will cost about US$9.

From the bus station, turn left (south) and walk 150m to López Mateos, where 'Centro' buses (US$0.40) go west to the city center. To return to the bus station, catch a 'Cen-tral' bus east along López Mateos, two blocks north of Plaza Principal. A taxi between the center and the bus station costs US$3.

DOLORES HIDALGO

☎ 418 / pop 53,000 / elevation 1955m

Dolores is where the Mexican independence movement began in earnest. Here, at 5am on September 16, 1810, Miguel Hidalgo, the parish priest, rang the bells to summon people to church earlier than usual and issued the Grito de Dolores, also known as the Grito de Independencia. His precise words have been lost to history but they boiled down to 'Long live Our Lady of Guadalupe! Death

---

MIGUEL HIDALGO: ¡VIVA INDEPENDENCE!

The balding head of the visionary priest Father Miguel Hidalgo y Costilla is familiar to anyone who's ogled Mexican statues or murals. He was, it seems, a genuine rebel idealist, who had already sacrificed his own career at least once before that fateful day in 1810. And he launched the independence movement clearly aware of the risks to his own life.

Born on May 8, 1753, son of a criollo hacienda manager in Guanajuato, he studied at the Colegio de San Nicolás in Valladolid (now Morelia), earned a bachelor's degree and, in 1778, was ordained a priest. He returned to teach at his alma mater and eventually became rector. But he was no orthodox cleric: Hidalgo questioned the virgin birth and the infallibility of the pope, read banned books, gambled, danced and had a mistress.

In 1800 he was brought before the Inquisition. Nothing was proven, but a few years later, in 1804, he found himself transferred as priest to the hick town of Dolores.

Hidalgo's years in Dolores show that he was interested not only in the religious welfare of the local people but also in their economic and cultural welfare. Somewhat in the tradition of Don Vasco de Quiroga of Michoacán, founder of the Colegio de San Nicolás where Hidalgo had studied, he started several new industries. Silk was cultivated, olive groves planted and vineyards established, all in defiance of the Spanish colonial authorities. Earthenware building products such as bricks and roof tiles were the foundation of the ceramics industry that today produces fine glazed pots and tiles.

When Hidalgo met Ignacio Allende from San Miguel, they shared a criollo discontent with the Spanish stranglehold on Mexico. But Hidalgo's standing among the mestizos and indigenous people of his parish was vital in broadening the base of the rebellion that followed.

On October 13, 1810, shortly after his Grito de Independencia, Hidalgo was formally excommunicated for 'heresy, apostasy and sedition'. He answered by proclaiming that he never would have been excommunicated had it not been for his call for Mexican independence and furthermore stated that the Spanish were not truly Catholic in any religious sense of the word, but only for political purposes, specifically to rape, pillage and exploit Mexico. A few days later, on October 19, Hidalgo dictated his first edict calling for the abolition of slavery in Mexico.

Hidalgo led his growing forces from Dolores to San Miguel, Celaya and Guanajuato, north to Zacatecas, south almost to Mexico City and west to Guadalajara. But then, pushed northward, their numbers dwindled and on July 30, 1811, having been captured by the Spanish, Hidalgo was shot by a firing squad in Chihuahua. His head was returned to the city of Guanajuato, where his army had won its first major victory. It hung in a cage for 10 years on an outer corner of the Alhóndiga de Granaditas, along with the heads of independence leaders Allende, Aldama and Jiménez. Rather than intimidating the people, this lurid display kept the memory, the goal and the example of the heroic martyrs fresh in everyone's mind. After independence the cages were removed, and the skulls of the heroes are now in the Monumento a la Independencia in Mexico City.

to bad government and the *gachupines!*' ('*Gachupines*' was a derisive term for the Spanish-born overlords who ruled Mexico.)

Hidalgo, Ignacio Allende and other conspirators had been alerted to the discovery of their plans for an uprising in Querétaro, so they decided to launch their rebellion immediately from Dolores. After the Grito they went to the lavish Spanish house on the plaza, today the Casa de Visitas, and captured the local representative of the Spanish viceroy and the Spanish tax collector. They freed the prisoners from the town jail and set off for San Miguel at the head of a growing band of *criollos, mestizos* and *indígenas*.

Today, Hidalgo is Mexico's most revered hero, rivaled only by Benito Juárez in the number of civic monuments dedicated to him. Dolores was renamed in his honor in 1824. Visiting Dolores Hidalgo has acquired pilgrimage status for Mexicans, though it's not the most attractive town. If you're interested in the country's history, it's worth a day trip from Guanajuato or San Miguel de Allende, or a stop between them.

Orientation & Information
Everything of interest is within a couple of blocks of the Plaza Principal, which is a couple blocks north of the bus station.

The **tourist office** (☎ 182-11-64; ☼ 10am-3pm & 5-7pm Mon-Fri, 10am-6pm Sat & Sun) is on the Plaza Principal's north side, in the Presidencia Municipal. The staff can answer, in Spanish, any questions about the town.

Cash and traveler's checks can be changed at several banks around the plaza (they all have ATMs). There are some *casas de cambio* too. **Comunidad Virtu@l** (Hidalgo s/n; ☼ 9am-10pm) has fast Internet connections for US$1 an hour. Card phones are outside the tourist office and at the Flecha Amarilla bus station.

Sights
PLAZA PRINCIPAL & AROUND
The **Parroquia de Nuestra Señora de Dolores**, the church where Hidalgo issued the Grito, is on the north side of the plaza. It has a fine 18th-century churrigueresque façade. Some say that Hidalgo uttered his famous words from the pulpit, others that he spoke at the church door to the people gathered outside.

Adjacent the church is the **Presidencia Municipal**, which has two colorful murals on the theme of independence. The plaza contains a **statue of Hidalgo** (in Roman garb, on top of a tall column) and a tree that, according to a plaque beneath it, was a sapling of the tree of the Noche Triste (Sad Night), under which Cortés is said to have wept when his men were driven out of Tenochtitlán in 1520.

The **Casa de Visitas**, on the plaza's west side, was the residence of Don Nicolás Fernández del Rincón and Don Ignacio Díaz de la Cortina, the two representatives of Spanish rule in Dolores. On September 16, 1810, they became the first two prisoners of the independence movement. Today, this is where Mexican presidents and other dignitaries stay when they come to Dolores for ceremonies.

MUSEO DE LA INDEPENDENCIA NACIONAL
The **National Independence Museum** (☎ 182-08-09; Zacatecas 6; US$1, free Sun & under 13; ☼ 9am-5pm) has few relics but plenty of information on the independence movement. It charts the appalling decline in Nueva España's indigenous population between 1519 (an estimated 25 million) and 1605 (1 million), and identifies 23 indigenous rebellions before 1800 as well as several criollo conspiracies in the years leading up to 1810. There are vivid paintings, quotations and details on the heroic last 10 months of Hidalgo's life.

MUSEO CASA DE HIDALGO
Miguel Hidalgo lived in this **house** (☎ 182-01-71; cnr Hidalgo & Morelos; US$3, free Sun & under 13; ☼ 10am-6pm Tue-Sat, 10am-5pm Sun) when he was Dolores' parish priest. It was here, in the early hours of September 16, 1810, that Hidalgo, Ignacio Allende and Juan de Aldama conspired to launch the uprising against colonial rule. It is now something of a national shrine. One large room is devoted to a collection of memorials to Hidalgo. Other rooms contain replicas of Hidalgo's furniture and independence movement documents, including the order for Hidalgo's excommunication.

Festivals & Events
Dolores is the scene of major **Día de la Independencia** (September 16) celebrations, when the Mexican president often officiates. The **Fiestas Patrias** festivities start September 6 and the subsequent slate of cultural celebrations often doesn't end until November.

Sleeping

Most visitors stay here just long enough to see the church and museums and enjoy an ice cream on the plaza. Accommodations can fill up during special events and holiday weekends; at other times you may get a discount on listed prices.

Posada Cocomacán (☎ 182-60-86; www.posada cocomacan.com; Plaza Principal 4; s/d US$28/37) The positively pink Cocomacán is the best place on the plaza. It has a good courtyard restaurant, rooftop terrace bar and 38 clean rooms with TV, phones and good ventilation.

Hotel Posada Hidalgo (☎ /fax 182-04-77; hotel posadahidalgo@hotmail.com; Hidalgo 15; s/d US$28/33; P 🖳) This comfortable, modern hotel is conveniently located between the bus stations and the Plaza Principal. It's well managed and super clean, though somewhat sterile. Rates include use of steam baths downstairs (US$3), which are open to the public.

Posada Dolores (☎ 182-06-42; Yucatán 8; s/d US$6.50/11, with bathroom US$11/14) This basic, friendly *casa de huéspedes* has the cheapest rooms in town, though they're pretty small. Pay a few pesos more for larger, renovated rooms with TV.

Hotel El Caudillo (☎ 182-01-98; cromero@prosat.net .mx; Querétaro 8; s/d US$17/28; P) Opposite the east side of the church, El Caudillo has 32 carpeted rooms with cable TV. The rooms are clean, but a bit cramped. Their on-site disco, Cesar's, goes off Thursday through Saturday.

Eating & Drinking

Dolores is famous not only for its historical attractions but also for its ice cream. On the plaza's southwest corner you can get cones (US$0.50 to US$1.50) in a variety of unusual, fast-melting flavors including mole, *chicharrón* (fried pork skin), avocado, corn, cheese, honey, shrimp, whiskey, tequila and a dozen tropical fruit flavors. The **Fruti Yoghurt** (Hidalgo s/n) fruit stand is a fresh and healthful alternative. Also look for the delicious locally made dulces (sweets) at street stalls and in the markets.

El Carruaje Restaurant (☎ 182-04-74; Plaza Principal 8; mains US$3-9) This cavernous Mexican place caters to day-tripping families with its US$6 set lunch, live music at night and a big US$8.50 weekend buffet.

Restaurant El Delfín (☎ 182-22-99; Veracruz 2; mains US$4-8; ⏲ 9am-7pm) For surprisingly good seafood, check out this pleasant place one block east of the plaza. The fare here includes fish dishes, seafood soup and large shrimp servings.

Restaurant Plaza (☎ 182-02-59; Plaza Principal 17B; mains US$4-10) This good family restaurant does filling Mexican breakfasts, pasta, enchiladas and other *antojitos*, and a four-course set lunch (US$6).

Restaurant Libertadores (in Hotel El Caudillo; mains US$4-9) Hotel El Caudillo's restaurant/bar is cool and pleasant. À la carte breakfasts are inexpensive and there's a good selection. It's often open when most other eateries are closed and it brews good coffee.

DOLORES HIDALGO

INFORMATION	
Banamex (ATM)	1 D2
Bancomer (ATM)	2 D1
Banorte (ATM)	3 D2
Bital/HSBC (ATM)	4 C1
Comunidad Virtu@l	5 C2
Post Office	6 D2
Presidencia Municipal	7 D1
Telecomm	(see 6)
Tourist Office	(see 7)

SIGHTS & ACTIVITIES	(p619)
Casa de Visitas	8 C1
Museo Casa de Hidalgo	9 C2
Museo de la Independencia Nacional	10 C1
Parroquia de Nuestra Señora de Dolores	11 D1
Templo de la Tercera Orden	12 D2

SLEEPING	(p620)
Hotel El Caudillo	13 D1
Hotel Posada Hidalgo	14 C2

Posada Cocomacán	15 D1
Posada Dolores	16 C1

EATING	(p620)
El Carruaje Restaurant	17 D2
Fruti Yoghurt	18 C2
Ice Cream Stands	19 D1
Restaurant El Delfín	20 D2
Restaurant Libertadores	(see 13)
Restaurant Plaza	21 D2

TRANSPORT	(p621)
Herradura de Plata & Pegasso Plus Bus Station	22 C2
Primera Plus & Flecha Amarilla Bus Station	23 C2

0 ———— 200 m
0 ———— 0.1 miles

To San Felipe (50km)
To San Miguel de Allende (40km); San Luis de la Paz (58km)
To Guanajuato (56km)
Río Batan
Jardín de los Compositores

NEIL SETCHFIELD

Flower seller, Guadalajara (p505)

JEFF GREENBERG

Neoclassical Teatro Degollado (p510),
Guadalajara

CHRISTIAN ASLUND

Festive decorations for Día de Muertos
(Day of the Dead; p558)

Iglesia del Sagrario (Church of the Shrine; p555), Pátzcuaro

JOHN NEUBAUER

Festival Internacional Cervantino (p611), Guanajuato

Cactus pots, San Miguel de Allende (p621)

Hotel Quinta Real Zacatecas (a former bullring; p580), Zacatecas

Shopping

Ceramics, especially Talavera ware (including tiles), have been the signature handicraft of Dolores ever since Padre Hidalgo founded the town's first ceramics workshop in the early 19th century. A number of shops sell these and other craft items. If you've got wheels, stop by the ceramics workshops along the approach roads to Dolores. An increasing number of workshops make 'antique,' colonial-style furniture.

Getting There & Away

Nearly all buses to/from Dolores are 2nd-class. The Primera Plus/Flecha Amarilla station is on Hidalgo, 2½ blocks south of the plaza. Herradura de Plata/Pegasso Plus use a small station on Chiapas at Yucatán. Daily departures include:

Guanajuato (US$3.50, 1hr, 2nd-class Flecha Amarilla every 20min 5:20am-9pm daily)

Mexico City (US$20, 5hr, 1st-class Pegasso Plus noon daily; US$16, 5hr, 2nd-class Herradura de Plata or Flecha Amarilla every 40min, 5:30am-9pm daily) To Terminal Norte.

San Miguel de Allende (US$2, 45min; half-hourly 2nd-class Flecha Amarilla or Herradura de Plata every 20min, 5:15am-9pm)

There are also regular 2nd-class connections to Querétaro (US$5.25), León (US$6) and San Luis Potosí (US$7.50).

SAN MIGUEL DE ALLENDE

☎ 415 / pop 63,000 / elevation 1840m

A charming colonial town in a beautiful setting, San Miguel is well known for its large expatriate community. The influx began in the 1940s, when artists, writers and other creative types came to San Miguel's Escuela de Bellas Artes. From the 1950s onwards, US citizens in particular came to study at the Instituto Allende. Several thousand foreigners have retired here permanently, many others overwinter here and hundreds more come for crash courses in Spanish. Since it was rated one of the world's top 20 places to retire, the town has lost much of its bohemian character, real estate offices outnumber art galleries and English is widely spoken.

For all the foreign influence (and partly because of it), San Miguel has preserved its lovely old buildings and quaint cobbled streets, often with unexpected vistas over the plains and distant hills. To protect its charm, the Mexican government has declared the entire town a national monument. Locals are especially fond of festivals, fireworks and parades, making the place even more colorful. It's easy for visitors to feel at home here, the restaurants and bars are many and varied, and every other luxury is available, though budget lodging can be in short supply.

San Miguel has two peak visitor periods. The main one is from mid-December to the end of March, when many *norteamericanos* fly south for the winter, and there's another influx from June to August. San Miguel has an agreeable climate and superbly sharp light, which attracts artists. It's cool and clear in winter, and warm and clear in summer, with occasional thunderstorms and heavy rain.

History

The town, so the story goes, owes its founding to a few hot dogs. These hounds were dearly loved by a courageous barefooted Franciscan friar, Juan de San Miguel, who started a mission in 1542 near an often-dry river 5km from the present town. One day the dogs wandered off from the mission, later found reclining at the spring called El Chorro south of the present town. This site was so superior that the mission was moved.

San Miguel was then central Mexico's most northern Spanish settlement. Tarascan and Tlaxcalan allies of the Spanish were brought to help pacify the local Otomí and Chichimecs. San Miguel barely survived the fierce Chichimec resistance, until in 1555 a Spanish garrison was established to protect the new road from Mexico City to the silver center of Zacatecas. Spanish ranchers settled in the area, and it grew into a thriving commercial center known for its knives, textiles and horse tack. It also became home to some of Guanajuato's wealthy silver barons.

San Miguel's favorite son, Ignacio Allende, was born here in 1779. He became a fervent believer in the need for Mexican independence and a leader of a Querétaro-based conspiracy that set December 8, 1810, as the date for an armed uprising. When the plan was discovered by authorities in Querétaro on September 13, a messenger rushed to San Miguel and delivered the news to Juan de Aldama, another conspirator. Aldama sped north to Dolores where, in the wee hours of September 16, he found Allende at the house of the priest Miguel Hidalgo, also one of the coterie.

SAN MIGUEL DE ALLENDE

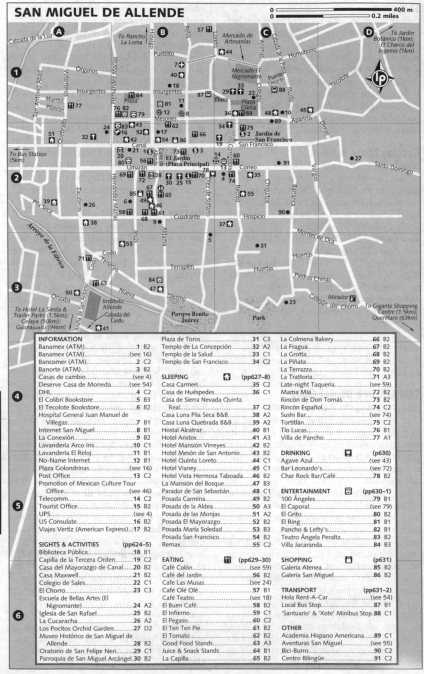

INFORMATION
Banamex (ATM)...........................1 B2
Banamex (ATM)......................(see 16)
Bancomer (ATM).......................2 C2
Banorte (ATM)...........................3 B2
Casas de cambio.....................(see 4)
Deserve Casa de Moneda.......(see 54)
DHL..4 C2
El Colibrí Bookstore...................5 B3
El Tecolote Bookstore................6 B2
Hospital General Juan Manuel de
  Villegas...................................7 B1
Internet San Miguel...................8 B1
La Conexión...............................9 B2
Lavandería Arco Iris.................10 C1
Lavandería El Reloj..................11 B1
No-Name Internet....................12 B1
Plaza Golondrinas..................(see 16)
Post Office...............................13 C2
Promotion of Mexican Culture Tour
  Office..................................(see 46)
Telecomm................................14 C2
Tourist Office...........................15 B2
UPS..(see 4)
US Consulate...........................16 B2
Viajes Vertiz (American Express)..17 B2

SIGHTS & ACTIVITIES   (pp624–5)
Biblioteca Pública....................18 B1
Capilla de la Tercera Orden......19 C2
Casa del Mayorazgo de Canal...20 B2
Casa Maxwell...........................21 B2
Colegio de Sales......................22 C1
El Chorro.................................23 C3
Escuela de Bellas Artes (El
  Nigromante)...........................24 A2
Iglesia de San Rafael...............25 B2
La Cucaracha...........................26 A2
Los Pocitos Orchid Garden.......27 D2
Museo Histórico de San Miguel de
  Allende..................................28 B2
Oratorio de San Felipe Neri......29 C1
Parroquia de San Miguel Arcángel..30 B2

Plaza de Toros........................31 C3
Templo de La Concepción........32 A2
Templo de la Salud..................33 C1
Templo de San Francisco.........34 C2

SLEEPING   (pp627–8)
Casa Carmen...........................35 C2
Casa de Huéspedes..................36 C1
Casa de Sierra Nevada Quinta
  Real......................................37 C2
Casa Luna Pila Seca B&B.........38 B2
Casa Luna Quebrada B&B.........39 A2
Hostal Alcatraz........................40 B1
Hotel Aristos............................41 A3
Hotel Mansión Virreyes............42 B2
Hotel Mesón de San Antonio....43 B2
Hotel Quinta Loreto.................44 C1
Hotel Vianey............................45 C1
Hotel Vista Hermosa Taboada...46 B2
La Mansión del Bosque............47 B3
Parador de San Sebastián.........48 C1
Posada Carmina......................49 B2
Posada de la Aldea..................50 A3
Posada de las Monjas...............51 A2
Posada El Mayorazgo...............52 B2
Posada María Soledad..............53 B2
Posada San Francisco..............54 B2
Remax....................................55 C2

EATING   (pp629–30)
Café Colón...........................(see 59)
Café del Jardín........................56 B2
Cafe Las Musas....................(see 24)
Café Olé Olé............................57 B1
Café Teatro..........................(see 18)
El Buen Café............................58 B2
El Infierno...............................59 C1
El Pegaso.................................60 C2
El Ten Ten Pie..........................61 B2
El Tomato................................62 B2
Good Food Stands...................63 A3
Juice & Snack Stands...............64 B2
La Capilla................................65 B2

La Colmena Bakery..................66 B2
La Fragua................................67 B2
La Grotta.................................68 B2
La Piñata.................................69 B2
La Terrazza..............................70 B2
La Trattoria..............................71 A3
Late-night Taquería..............(see 59)
Mama Mía...............................72 B2
Rincón de Don Tomás..............73 B2
Rincón Español........................74 C2
Sushi Bar.............................(see 74)
Tortitlán..................................75 C2
Tío Lucas.................................76 B1
Villa de Pancho.......................77 A1

DRINKING   (p630)
Agave Azul...........................(see 43)
Bar Leonardo's.....................(see 72)
Char Rock Bar/Café..................78 B2

ENTERTAINMENT   (pp630–1)
100 Ángeles............................79 B1
El Caporal............................(see 79)
El Grito...................................80 B2
El Ring....................................81 B1
Pancho & Lefty's.....................82 B1
Teatro Ángela Peralta...............83 B2
Villa Jacaranda........................84 B3

SHOPPING   (p631)
Galería Atenea.........................85 B2
Galería San Miguel..................86 B2

TRANSPORT   (pp631–2)
Hola Rent-A-Car....................(see 54)
Local Bus Stop.........................87 B1
'Santuario' & 'Xote' Minibus Stop..88 C1

OTHER
Academia Hispano Americana...89 C1
Aventuras San Miguel............(see 55)
Bici-Burro...............................90 C2
Centro Bilingüe.......................91 C2

A few hours later Hidalgo proclaimed rebellion from his church. By that evening, San Miguel as well as Dolores was in rebel hands. Its local regiment had joined forces with the band of insurgents arriving from Dolores. San Miguel's Spanish population was locked up and Allende was only partly able to restrain the rebels from looting the town. After initial successes, Allende, Hidalgo and other rebel leaders were captured in 1811 in Chihuahua. Allende was summarily executed, Hidalgo four months later. When Mexico finally achieved independence in 1821 they were recognized as martyrs, and in 1826 the town was renamed San Miguel de Allende.

The Escuela de Bellas Artes was founded in 1938 and the town started to take on its current character when David Alfaro Siqueiros began mural-painting courses that attracted artists of every persuasion. The Instituto Allende opened in 1951, also attracting foreign students. Many were US citizens seeking to escape the conformity of post-WWII USA. Neal Cassady, hero of Jack Kerouac's *On the Road*, died here in 1968, allegedly walking along the railroad tracks, but another version is that he overdosed at a house in town.

Orientation

The Plaza Principal, called the Jardín, is the town's focal point. The Gothic-like spires of the *parroquia* (parish church) beside the Jardín can be seen from far and wide. The central area is small and straightforward and most places of interest are within easy walking distance of the Jardín. Most streets change names at the Jardín. Canal/San Francisco, on its north side, and Umarán/Correo, on the south side, are the main streets.

Information

See www.portalsanmiguel.com for a good overview of the town.

BOOKSTORES & LIBRARIES

Biblioteca Pública (Insurgentes 25; ☽ 10am-2pm & 4-7pm Mon-Fri, 10am-2pm Sat) The public library functions as cultural center with an emphasis on children's activities. Has an excellent collection of books in English and Spanish plus general reference books, novels & magazines. On-site Café Teatro is a great place for tea.

El Colibri (☎ 152-07-51; Diez de Sollano 30) Paperbacks, magazines and art books in English and Spanish.

El Tecolote (☎ 152-73-95; Jesús 11; ☽ Tue-Sat 10am-6pm, Sun 10am-2pm) Many titles in English and Spanish.

INTERNET ACCESS

Internet (Hidalgo 23) No-name place; US$2 per hour.

Internet San Miguel (☎ 154-46-34; Reloj 30 & Mesones 57; ☽ 9am-9pm Mon-Sat, 10am-6pm Sun) English-speaking staff, good coffee & fastest connection in town for US$3 per hour.

LAUNDRY

Laundromats charge around US$3.75 to wash and dry up to four kilos.

Lavandería Arco Iris (Pasaje Allende, local N) Inside arcade off Mesones

Lavandería El Reloj (☎ 152-38-43; Reloj 34A)

MEDIA

The informative weekly bilingual (English/Spanish) newspaper, *Atención San Miguel* (US$0.65) is full of local news, housing ads and yoga, Spanish, art and dance class schedules. You can buy it at the public library and elsewhere. The same sorts of things are advertised on notice boards in the Biblioteca Pública, the Escuela de Bellas Artes and the language schools. Also look for the free *Arcángel City* arts and culture tabloid.

MONEY

There are several banks with ATMs in the couple of blocks east of the Jardín.

Deserve Casa de Moneda (☽ 9am-7pm Mon-Fri, 9am-5pm Sat) Exchange office inside Posada San Francisco.

POST

Main post office (cnr Correo & Corregidora) Mexpost express mail next door; DHL, FedEx & UPS all nearby on Correo.

TELEPHONE & FAX

Card phones are plentiful in the center, and there's a *caseta* at the bus station.

La Conexión (☎ 152-16-87; Aldama 3; ☽ 9am-7pm Mon-Sat, 10am-2pm Sun) One of several places offering mail forwarding, Internet access & phone message services.

Telecomm (Correo 16) Telephone *caseta* two doors from post office.

TOURIST INFORMATION

Tourist office (☎ 152-65-65; www.sanmigueldeallende .gob.mx; Plaza Principal s/n; ☽ 10am-5pm Mon-Fri, 10am-2pm Sat & Sun) Adjacent to the Iglesia de San Rafael. Grab maps of the town & printed brochures in English & Spanish.

TRAVEL AGENCIES

Viajes Vertiz (☎ 152-18-56; Hidalgo 1A; ☽ 9am-2pm & 4-6:30pm Mon-Fri, 10am-2pm Sat) American Express agent, sells domestic & international air tickets.

Sights

PARROQUIA DE SAN MIGUEL ARCÁNGEL

The parish church's pink 'wedding cake' towers dominate the Jardín. These strange pinnacles were designed by indigenous stonemason Zeferino Gutiérrez in the late 19th century. He reputedly based the design on a postcard of a Belgian church and instructed builders by scratching plans in the sand with a stick. The rest of the church dates from the late 17th century. In the chapel to the left of the main altar is the much-revered image of the *Cristo de la Conquista* (Christ of the Conquest), made in Pátzcuaro from cornstalks and orchid bulbs, probably in the 16th century. Irish visitors will be pleased to find a statue of St Patrick. The adjacent **Iglesia de San Rafael** was founded in 1742 and has undergone Gothic-inspired alterations.

MUSEO HISTÓRICO DE SAN MIGUEL DE ALLENDE

Near the *parroquia* is the house where Ignacio Allende was born, now the **history museum** (☎ 152-24-99; Cuna de Allende 1; US$3; ☎ 10am-4pm Tue-Sun). Exhibits relate the interesting history of the San Miguel area, with special displays on Allende and the independence movement. A Latin inscription on the façade reads 'Hic natus ubique notus,' which means 'Here born, everywhere known'. Another plaque points out that the more famous independence hero, Miguel Hidalgo, only joined the movement after being invited by Allende.

CASA DEL MAYORAZGO DE CANAL

This historic **house**, one of San Miguel's most imposing old residences, now houses Banamex offices. It's a handsome neoclassical structure with some late baroque touches. The original entrance is at Canal 4 and retains beautiful carved wooden doors.

TEMPLO DE SAN FRANCISCO

San Francisco church (cnr San Francisco & Juárez) has an elaborate late-18th-century churrigueresque façade. An image of St Francis of Assisi is at the top. There's a free **museum** (☎ 152-09-47; ☷ 10am-2pm Mon-Fri) of religious painting in the old convent beside the church.

CAPILLA DE LA TERCERA ORDEN

The **Chapel of the Third Order** was built in the early 18th century and, like San Francisco church, was part of a Franciscan monastery

complex. The main façade shows St Francis and symbols of the Franciscan order.

ORATORIO DE SAN FELIPE NERI

This multitowered and domed 18th-century **church** is near the east end of Insurgentes. The pale pink main façade is baroque with an indigenous influence. A passage to the right of this façade leads to the east wall, where a doorway holds the image of *Nuestra Señora de la Soledad* (Our Lady of Solitude). You can see into the cloister from this side of the church.

Inside the church are 33 oil paintings showing scenes from the life of San Felipe Neri, the 16th-century Florentine who founded the Oratorio Catholic order. In the east transept is a painting of the Virgin of Guadalupe by leading colonial painter Miguel Cabrera. In the west transept is a lavishly decorated 1735 chapel, the Santa Casa de Loreto. It's a replica of a chapel in Loreto, Italy, legendary home of the Virgin Mary. If the chapel doors are open you can see tiles from Puebla, Valencia and China on the floor and walls and gilded cloth hanging. Behind the altar, the *camarín* has six elaborately gilded baroque altars. In one is a reclining wax figure of San Columbano; it contains the saint's bones.

TEMPLO DE LA SALUD

This **church**, with a blue and yellow tiled dome and a big shell carved above its entrance, is just east of San Felipe Neri. The façade is early Churrigueresque. The church's paintings include one of San Javier by Miguel Cabrera. San Javier (St Francis Xavier, 1506–52) was a founding member of the Jesuits.

COLEGIO DE SALES

This was once a college, founded in the mid-18th century by the San Felipe Neri order. It's adjacent to the **Templo de La Salud**, which was once part of the same college. Many of the 1810 revolutionaries were educated here. Spaniards were locked up here when the rebels took San Miguel.

TEMPLO DE LA CONCEPCIÓN

The splendid **Church of the Conception** has a fine altar and several magnificent old oil paintings. Painted on the interior doorway are a number of wise sayings to give pause to those entering the sanctuary. The church was begun in the mid-18th century; its dome, added in the late 19th century by the versatile Zeferino Gutiérrez, was possibly inspired by pictures of Les Invalides in Paris.

ESCUELA DE BELLAS ARTES

The **School of Fine Arts** (Centro Cultural Nigromante; ☎ 152-02-89; Hernández Macías 75; admission free; 🕙 9am-8pm) is housed in the beautiful former monastery of La Concepción church, which was converted into a fine-arts school in 1938. It's officially named the Centro Cultural Ignacio Ramírez, after a leading 19th-century liberal thinker. His nickname was El Nigromante (The Sorcerer), and the center is also commonly called by this name.

One room in the cloister is devoted to an unfinished mural by Siqueiros, done in 1948 as part of a mural painting course for US war veterans. Its subject – though you wouldn't guess it – is the life and work of Ignacio Allende. (The light switch is to the right of the door just before you enter.)

INSTITUTO ALLENDE

This large 1736 **complex** (Ancha de San Antonio 20) with several patios and an old chapel was originally the home of the Conde Manuel de la Canal. Later it was used as a Carmelite convent, eventually becoming an art and language school in 1951 (see Courses, below). Above the entrance is a carving of the Virgin of Loreto, patroness of the Canal family.

MIRADOR & PARQUE JUÁREZ

One of the best views over the town and surrounding country is from the **mirador** (overlook) southeast of town. Take Callejón del Chorro, the track leading directly downhill from here, and turn left at the bottom, to reach El Chorro, the spring where San Miguel was founded. Today it gushes out of a fountain built in 1960, and there are still public washing tubs here. A path called Paseo del Chorro zigzags down the hill to the shady Benito Juárez Park.

BOTANICAL GARDENS

The large **Jardín Botánico El Charco del Ingenio** (☎ 154-47-15; off Antiguo Camino Real a Querétaro; US$2; open sunrise-sunset), devoted mainly to cacti and other native plants of this semiarid region, is on the hilltop 1.5km northeast of town. It's a wildlife and bird sanctuary and thus a lovely place for a walk, particularly in the early morning or late afternoon, though women alone should steer clear of its more secluded parts. Pathways range along the slope above a reservoir and a deep canyon.

The direct approach to the garden is to walk uphill from Mercado El Nigromante along Homobono and Cuesta de San José, then fork left up Montitlan past the Balcones housing development, from where signs point the way to the main entrance.

Alternatively, a 2km vehicle track leads north from the Gigante shopping center, 2.5km east of the center on the Querétaro road. Gigante can be reached on 'Gigante' buses from the bus stop on the east side of Jardín de San Francisco. A taxi to the gardens from the center costs about US$2.50.

Closer to town, the orchid garden **Los Pocitos** (Santo Domingo 38; closed Sun) is home to 2000 plants covering 230 species. It's at its best in February, March and April.

GALLERIES

Galería San Miguel (☎ 152-04-54; Plaza Principal 14; 🕙 9am-2pm & 4-7pm Mon-Sat) and **Galería Atenea** (☎ 152-07-85; Jesús 2; 🕙 10am-2pm & 4-8pm Fri-Wed, noon-2pm Thu) are two of the best and most established commercial art galleries. **Escuela de Bellas Artes** and **Instituto Allende** (p626) stage art exhibitions year-round. Other galleries advertise in *Atención San Miguel*.

Activities

See Tours (p626) for agencies that rent out bicycles and scooters and offer other enticing active options.

Posada de la Aldea (see Sleeping, p627) opens its **swimming pool** (☎ 152-10-22; Ancha de San Antonio 15; US$2.50) to nonguests most days, but it's more enjoyable to visit the balnearios (bathing spots) in the surrounding countryside (see Around San Miguel, p632).

Rancho La Loma (☎ 152-21-21; rancholaloma@ hotmail.com; Carretera Dolores Hidalgo s/n; horses per hr US$30) rents horses and can arrange instruction and guides.

Courses

Several institutions offer Spanish courses, with group or private lessons, and optional classes in Mexican culture and history. There are also many courses in painting, sculpture, ceramics, music, and dance. Most private lessons start around US$10 an hour;

group and long-term rates are much lower. Most courses are available year-round, except for a three-week break in December.

Instituto Allende (☎ 152-01-90; www.instituto-allende.edu.mx; Ancha de San Antonio 20) Offers courses in fine arts, crafts and Spanish. Arts courses can be joined at any time and usually entail nine hours of attendance a week. Spanish courses begin every four weeks and range from conversational to total impact (maximum six students per class).

Academia Hispano Americana (☎ 152-03-49; www.ahaspeakspanish.com; Mesones 4) This place runs courses in the Spanish language and Latin American culture. The cultural courses are taught in elementary Spanish. One-on-one language classes, for any period you like, are also available. The school arranges homestays with Mexican families with a private room and three meals per day for around US$20 per day.

Escuela de Bellas Artes (☎ 152-02-89; Hernández Macías 75) Offers courses in art, dance, crafts and music. Most are given in Spanish and cost around US$95 a month, plus materials. Registration is at the beginning of each month. Some classes are not held in July, and there are none in August.

Other organizations offering Spanish instruction include:

Centro Bilingüe (☎ 152-54-00; www.geocities.com/centrobilingue; Correo 46)

Warren Hardy Spanish (☎ 154-40-17, 152-47-28; www.warrenhardy.com; San Rafael 6)

Tours

An English-language tour of the loveliest private homes and gardens in San Miguel begins at noon every Sunday from the Biblioteca Pública. Tickets go on sale at 11am. The cost is US$16 for the two-hour tour, with three different houses visited weekly. Saturday tours of nearby ranches, haciendas and ruins are also offered, in aid of a disabled children's school; contact **El Centro de Crecimiento Zamora** (☎ 152-00-18) for details.

Promotion of Mexican Culture (☎ 152-01-21, 866-355-9655 in USA; www.pmexc.com; Cuna de Allende 11; walking tours US$10-15, bus tours US$55) This company conducts two-hour historical walking tours of central San Miguel, plus a variety of day tours by bus. Stop by their office in Hotel Vista Hermosa Taboada (see p629) for a brochure.

Aventuras San Miguel (☎ 152-64-06; aventurasma@yahoo.com; Recreo 10; tours US$30 per day for groups of 3 or more; office ☽ 9am-2pm Mon-Sat) Rents scooters and conducts hiking, biking, camping and horseback riding trips, as well as small group trips to many destinations in central Mexico.

Bici-Burro (☎ 152-15-26; www.bici-burro.com; Hospicio 1; trips US$40-70) Bici-Burro conducts all-inclusive guided mountain bike tours for groups of two or more. Popular trips include five- or six-hour excursions to Atotonilco or Pozos. It also rents bikes (US$20 per day).

Festivals & Events

Since San Miguel is so well endowed with churches and patron saints (it has six), it also enjoys a multitude of festivals each month. You'll probably learn of some by word of mouth – or via firework bursts – while you're here.

Blessing of the Animals – Happens in several churches, including the *parroquia*, on January 17.

Allende's Birthday – On January 21 various official events celebrate this occasion.

Cristo de la Conquista – The image of Christ in the *parroquia* is feted on the first Friday in March, with scores of dancers in elaborate pre-Hispanic costumes & plumed headdresses.

San Patricio – March 17 sees a parade, but celebrations are more saintly than in cities with an Irish tradition.

Semana Santa – Two weekends before Easter pilgrims carry an image of the Señor de la Columna (Lord of the Column) from Atotonilco, 11km north, to San Miguel's church of San Juan de Dios on Saturday night or Sunday morning. During Semana Santa itself, the many activities include the lavish Procesión del Santo Entierro on Good Friday & the burning or exploding of images of Judas on Easter Day.

Fiesta de la Santa Cruz – This unusual, rather solemn festival has its roots in the 16th century. It happens on the last weekend in May at Valle del Maíz, 2km from the center of town. Oxen are dressed in lime necklaces & painted tortillas, & their yokes festooned with flowers & fruit. One beast carries two boxes of 'treasure' (bread & sugar) & is surrounded by characters in bizarre costumes on horses or donkeys. A mock battle between 'Indians' & 'Federales' follows, with a wizard appearing to heal the 'wounded' & raise the 'dead'.

Corpus Christi – This movable feast in June features dances by children in front of the *parroquia*.

Chamber Music Festival – The Escuela de Bellas Artes sponsors an annual festival of chamber music in the first two weeks of August.

Fiestas Patrias – Two months of cultural programs kicks off in mid-August; check with the tourist office for a full event schedule.

San Miguel Arcángel – Celebrations honoring the town's chief patron saint are held around the third Saturday of September. There are cockfights, bullfights & *pamplonadas* (bull-running) in the streets. The party kicks off at 5am with an *alborada*, an artificial dawn created by thousands of fireworks around the cathedral, but the hub of a general town party is provided by traditional dancers from several states who meet at Cruz del Cuarto, on the road to the train station. Wearing bells, feather head-dresses, scarlet cloaks & masks, groups walk in procession to the *parroquia* carrying flower offerings called *xuchiles*, some playing armadillo-shell lutes. Dances continue over a few days & include the Danza Guerrero in front of the *parroquia*, which represents the Spanish conquest of the Chichimecs.

San Miguel Music Festival – This largely classical music festival presents an almost daily program with Mexican & international performers throughout the second half of December. Most concerts are at the fine Teatro Ángela Peralta (see p630).

Sleeping

The better-value places are often full; reserve ahead if possible, especially during high seasons. Many hotels offer discounts to long-term guests. If you decide to stay a while, there are plenty of houses, apartments and rooms to rent (see Long Term Accommodations, p628).

BUDGET

Hostal Alcatraz (☎ 152-85-43; Reloj 54; dm from US$8.50; 🖵) San Miguel's only HI-affiliated hostel is centrally located and appealing, with TV room and shared kitchen. Dorms are single-sex.

Villa de Pancho (☎ 152-12-47; Quebrada 12; dm US$7.50, s/d/tr from US$11/17/22) Above his eponymous restaurant, jovial Pancho has a couple of shared-bath rooms that rent for US$45 per week or US$165 per month. Same-day machine laundry service costs about US$1 per kilo.

Posada El Mayorazgo (☎ 152-13-09; Hidalgo 8; s/d US$19/21) A comfortable, central choice with modern rooms around a sunny courtyard, plus a kitchenette apartment suitable for four adults.

Casa de Huéspedes (☎ 152-13-78; Mesones 27; s/d US$14/23) This clean, pleasant upstairs hostelry has seven renovated rooms, two apartments and a rooftop terrace with good views. The two kitchenette units cost the same and you might negotiate a discount for a longer stay or at off-peak times.

Parador de San Sebastián (☎ 152-70-84; Mesones 7; r/tr US$22/25; 🅿) This central place is clean, quiet and quaint. Compare one of the newer, smallish rooms to one of the older ones around the courtyard with a fireplace before settling in.

Hotel Vianey (☎ 152-45-59; Aparicio 18; r from US$14) The Vianey has a sunny terrace and small, plain but good-value rooms around a plant-filled courtyard.

Posada María Soledad (☎ 152-28-98; Hernández Macías 114; s/d US$17/23) A few blocks from the center on a pretty street, the smallish, dark but recently updated rooms here vary in quality; all have TV but the cheapest ones share a bathroom.

Lago Dorado KDA Trailer Park (☎ 152-23-01; sites US$10) Near the reservoir south of town, the KDA has a lounge, laundry and 80 shady, level spaces with full hookups. From town, take the Celaya road, then after 3km turn right at Hotel Misión de los Ángeles and continue another 3km toward the lake.

Hotel & Trailer Park La Siesta (☎ 152-02-07; Carretera Celaya 2km; www.hotellasiesta.com; sites US$11; 🚐) This big grassy lot behind Hotel La Siesta is 2km south of town. It has 58 spaces with full hookups, showers and shares the pool with the hotel, which charges US$50 per night for basic doubles.

MID-RANGE

Posada de las Monjas (☎ 152-01-71; www.posadalas monjas.com; Canal 37; s/d from US$30/37; 🅿) This welcoming family-run monastery-turned-motel remains one of San Miguel's better values. The 65 carpeted rooms are comfortable and nicely decorated, and the bathrooms all have slate floors and hand-painted tiles. Rooms in the newer section out back are in better shape than those in the castle-like old section and just as charming. Numerous terraces give lovely views over the valley. Restaurant, bar and laundry service are available, but readers warn against the breakfast. Rates are more for larger rooms and those with fireplaces.

Posada San Francisco (☎ 152-00-72; www.nafta connect.com/hsanfrancisco; Plaza Principal 2; r from US$66; 🅿 🖵) The San Francisco is great value for its perfect location facing the Jardín and for its classic colonial courtyard. Most of the spacious, modern, comfortable rooms have bathtubs but they are not especially charming. Valet parking costs US$4 per day and there's a sidewalk café that's good for people-watching.

Hotel Quinta Loreto (☎ 152-00-42; hqloreto@cyber matsa.com.mx; Loreto 15; s/d US$34/37; P 🏊) This motel-style place is a longtime expat favorite. The 38 pleasant rooms, some with small private patio, are spread around large, leafy grounds. Many rooms are recently renovated, TV is available for an extra charge and the restaurant (open for breakfast and lunch) receives rave reviews. Stays of a week or longer net a 10% a discount. Reservations recommended.

Hotel Mesón de San Antonio (☎ 152-05-80; msanantonio@cibermatsa.com; Mesones 80; r/ste US$49/58; 🏊) Centrally located, this basic hotel has modern rooms around an attractive courtyard with a lawn and a small pool. Rates include breakfast and cable TV.

Hotel Mansión Virreyes (☎ 152-08-51; mansion virreyes@prodigy.net.mx; Canal 19; s/d/tr US$48/63/90; P) This colonial place half a block from the Jardín has 22 rooms (some renovated, some not) around two courtyards and a restaurant-bar in the rear patio. There's a nice terrace and rates include breakfast.

Posada Carmina (☎ 152-04-58; www.posadacar mina.com; Cuna de Allende 7; s/d/ste from US$44/54/70) Close to the Jardín, this former colonial mansion boasts large, attractive rooms, tiled bathrooms and amenities like phones and TV. There's a pleasant restaurant-bar in the leafy courtyard.

La Mansión del Bosque (☎ 152-02-77; www .infosma.com/mansion; Aldama 65; s/d US$35-50/65-100) Opposite Parque Benito Juárez, this long-running guesthouse has 23 unique rooms that haven't changed much since 1968. They are all comfortable and well-maintained, with decent furniture and original art. Rates are higher in winter and July/ August, when the breakfast and dinner meal plan (US$20) is mandatory. It's popular with Instituto Allende attendees so reserve well in advance.

Posada de la Aldea (☎ /fax 152-10-22; www.nafta connect.com/hotellaaldea; Ancha de San Antonio 15; r/ste US$68/83; P 🏊 💻) Opposite the Instituto Allende, this modern hotel has wide lawns, a rustic courtyard, a tennis court and 66 large, well-equipped, carpeted rooms.

Hotel Vista Hermosa Taboada (☎ 152-00-78; Cuna de Allende 11; r from US$30) The Vista Hermosa has 15 uninspiring carpeted rooms with double beds and five apartments with TV.

Hotel Aristos (☎ 152-03-92, in USA 800-527-47-86; www.aristoshotels.com; Calzada del Cardo 2; r/ste US$69/128; P 🏊) On spacious grounds behind the Instituto Allende, the Aristos has tennis courts, a heated pool and modern if worn rooms. The carpet is a bit dank downstairs but upstairs rooms have terraces. Readers have reported poor food and lax service.

TOP END

Casa de Sierra Nevada Quinta Real (☎ 152-70-40, 800-500-40-00 in Mexico, 800-457-40-00 in USA & Canada; www.quintareal.com; Hospicio 35; r/ste from US$200/300; P 🏊) The most luxurious place in town has 33 units in five converted colonial mansions. It has a heated outdoor pool, day spa, two fine award-winning restaurants, views over the town, superbly appointed rooms and flawless service.

Casa Carmen (☎ 152-08-44; www.infosma.com/casa carmen; Correo 31; s/d US$60/80) Centrally located in a charming colonial home, Natalie Mooring's B&B has 11 rooms with high-beamed ceilings, set around a pleasant courtyard with a fountain, flowers and orange trees. Rates include a delicious breakfast and lunch in the elegant dining room.

Other recommendations:

Casa Luna B&B (☎ /fax 152-11-17; www.casaluna .com; Pila Seca 11 & Quebrada 117; r with breakfast US$135-176) Two delightfully restored & uniquely decorated colonial homes; check online photos to choose your room.

Guadiana B&B (☎ 152-49-48; www.hoteldeallende .com; Mesquite 11, Colonia Guadiana; s/d with breakfast US$55/73) Ten rooms in a new Mediterranean-style home, an easy 1km walk from the plaza.

LONG-TERM ACCOMMODATIONS

Thinking to stay in San Miguel for more than a few weeks? Consider renting a house or apartment. Many lovely, fully furnished homes are only used for a few weeks a year, usually in winter, and are otherwise available for rent. Rates start around US$400 a month for a decent two-bedroom house. Housesitting is another possibility. Check the notice boards and flyers around town, scan the ads in the free papers or contact one of the following local real estate offices:

Casas de San Miguel (☎ 152-44-16)

Century 21 (☎ 152-18-42; www.century21mexico.com; Jesús 18)

Remax (☎ 152-73-63; www.realestate-sma.com; Recreo 14)

Eating

San Miguel's eateries serve a startling variety of quality international cuisine. For thrifty travelers, there are plenty of more traditional options that cater to loyal crowds of local families.

BUDGET

Near the Jardín, several inexpensive places cater mostly to visitors.

Tortitlán (☎ 152-33-76; Juárez 17; mains US$2-5; ☻ 9am-7pm Mon-Sat, 10am-5pm Sun) There's much more than heaping sandwiches at this locally popular diner. Try to contain yourself while watching tacos, meats and burgers get grilled up in the open kitchen – cruel, but great marketing! – or phone for free delivery.

El Infierno (☎ 152-23-55; Mesones 25; mains US$4-7) The Infierno will do a full meal of soup, chicken, veggies and fries, but the main attraction here is the take-out chicken.

Café Colón (Mesones 25; set meals US$2-3; ☻ 8am-5pm) Adjacent to El Infierno, this café is popular with locals for its cheap set breakfasts and lunches.

Villa de Pancho (☎ 152-12-47; Quebrada 12; set lunch US$3-4; ☻ 9am-9pm) A cheerful little place offering basic breakfasts, savory set lunches and cheap beers.

La Piñata (☎ 152-20-60; cnr Jesús & Umarán; mains US$3-5; ☻ 9am-8pm Wed-Mon) The convivial Piñata is popular for juices, breakfasts, salads and sandwiches.

El Ten Ten Pie (☎ 152-71-89; Cuna de Allende 21; mains US$3-6; ☻ 9am-midnight) This diminutive family-run hangout serves up home-style Mexican cooking with superb chili sauces. Try the inexpensive set lunch (US$5.50), or *antojitos* like the tasty cheese and mushroom tacos. Breakfast is great, the bar is full and there are always veggie options.

El Tomato (☎ 154-60-57; Mesones 62; mains US$3-6; ☻ 9am-9pm Mon-Sat) For something healthy, visit the Tomato, where light meals include pasta, whole wheat sandwiches and salads, and feature fantastically fresh and tasty ingredients like lettuce you can really taste. There are also fresh squeezed juices, and the set lunch (US$5.50) is a good value. The only drawback is that it isn't non-smoking.

MID-RANGE

There are several lively places facing the Jardín, where you pay a premium for the roaming musicians and ringside location.

Rincón de Don Tomás (☎ 152-37-80; Portal de Guadalupe 2; mains US$6-9) This good restaurant has a solid menu of classic Mexican dishes like *chiles en nogada* and *gorditas* using handmade tortillas.

Café del Jardín (☎ 152-50-06; Portal Allende 2; mains US$5-10; ☻ 7am-midnight) This café isn't a great value for a full meal, but is a convenient pit stop for ice cream, coffee, cakes or late-night snacks.

La Terrazza (☎ 152-01-51; Correo s/n; mains US$5-10) Near the tourist office, balcony tables at La Terrazza and some other eateries overlook the Jardín. It's often crowded with people who come to see people, though the food is ordinary and the prices quite high. Adjacent, beware the soggy pizza by the slice.

El Buen Café (☎ 152-58-07; Jesús 23; mains US$4-7; ☻ 9am-8pm Mon-Sat) Apart from the good coffee, this unpretentious place does healthy breakfasts, Mexican specialties and sweet homebaked goodies, each with an unexpected twist. Think ginger pancakes with homemade applesauce or thick oatmeal topped with blackberries and crème brûlée.

El Pegaso (☎ 152-13-51; Corregidora 6; mains US$4-9; ☻ 8:30am-10pm Mon-Sat) Begin your day at this casual local favorite with fruit, eggs Benedict, fresh bread and coffee. For lunch, nosh on fancy sandwiches like smoked turkey or salmon with cream cheese. For dinner, there's an intriguing mix of Mexican, Italian and Asian-inspired dishes, plus decadent desserts. Between bites, browse the intriguing assortment of dangling handicrafts.

Mama Mía (☎ 152-20-63; Umarán 8; mains US$5-10; ☻ 8am-late) This San Miguel institution has a restaurant, several bars, a disco and a live music venue. The restaurant, in a leafy courtyard, features a wide range of dishes, with pastas, well-prepared steak and seafood. Breakfasts are the best deal, it's most popular at night (see Drinking & Entertainment, p630).

Rincón Español/Sushi Bar (☎ 152-29-84; Correo 29; mains US$6-10; ☻ noon-11pm) This long-standing place has traditional Mexican and Spanish dishes, which tend toward the pricey side but are worth it if you come in the evening when flamenco dancers perform. The set lunch is (US$5) is also good. If you aren't in the mood for paella, check out their sushi bar next door.

Café Olé Olé (☎ 152-08-96; Loreto 66; mains US$5-10; ☻ 1-11pm) This friendly family-run café near the market is brightly decorated with bullfighting memorabilia. It's been eternally popular for its grilled chicken and beef, and its special chicken fajitas.

TOP END

When money is no object, San Miguel is one of the country's best places to take a break from the lard and savor some fine cuisine.

La Capilla (☎ 152-06-98; Cuna de Allende 10; café US$6-11, mains US$15-20; ☽ 1-11pm Wed-Mon) The location – beneath the *parroquia* – is unique, the atmosphere is magic and the food superb at this stylish restaurant, offering 'tastes from Mexico and around the world'. Downstairs, the classy café-bar, an elegant place for drink, hosts live acoustic music.

La Grotta (☎ 152-37-90; Cuadrante 5; mains US$7-12 Wed-Mon) The Grotto claims to serve Mexico's best pizza – a number of places make this claim, but here it's supported with a truly excellent product. The pasta is also good, and the homemade Italian desserts are delicious.

Tío Lucas (☎ 152-49-96; Mesones 103; mains US$8-13; ☽ noon-midnight) This US-style steakhouse is known for its beef and also serves a good range of soups and salads; the Caesar is recommended. Happy hour runs from 6pm to 8pm weekdays and there's live blues or jazz nightly.

La Fragua (☎ 152-11-44; Cuna de Allende 3; mains US$10-15; ☽ 6pm-2am) This is a long popular courtyard restaurant-bar, with live music nightly and happy hour from 6pm to 8pm. It's more popular as a bar than a restaurant, but it's still an enjoyable place to try a Continental take on Mexican fare.

La Trattoria (☎ 152-38-90; Zacateros at Codo; mains US$7-15) The Trattoria does a good range of Italian and vegetarian dishes, and is one of the nicest places near the Instituto Allende.

SELF-CATERING & QUICK EATS

There are some excellent bakeries around town – don't miss **La Colmena** (Reloj 21; ☽ closed Sun). Snack carts on the Jardín offer cheap, tasty Mexican fare like *elotes* (steamed corn ears), hamburgers, hot dogs, fresh fruit salads and tamales. Reliable juice stands front the small plaza off Insurgentes, and the *taquería* on Mesones, just uphill from El Infierno, stays open late.

Downhill toward Instituto Allende, on the corner of Ancha San Antonio and tree-shaded Calle Nueva, several food stands

assemble in the evenings, selling ice cream, tacos and other cheap snacks. They're very clean, the tastes are a treat and the experience is delightful.

Mercado El Nigromante, with all the usual produce stands and market eateries, is only four blocks from the Jardín but light years away from the gringo scene.

Drinking

Mama Mía (☎ 152-20-63; Umarán 8; cover US$3-5; ☽ 8pm-2am or 3am) The main bar at this perennially popular place features live rock (Friday to Saturday) or South American music (Thursday). At night the restaurant attracts an older crowd for live folk music on the patio. Up front, Bar Leonardo's shows big-screen sports, and the terrace bar upstairs offers a fine view of the town. Serious nightlife gets going around 11pm.

Agave Azul (☎ 152-51-51; Mesones 80; cover US$3; 11pm-1am or later) Hotel Mesón de San Antonio's restaurant morphs into a full-fledged bar after the 5pm to 8pm happy hour. Live music kicks in around 9pm, when the long tequila list begins to look tempting. On Sunday, the NFL takes over the TV.

Char Rock Bar/Café (☎ 152-73-73; upstairs at Correo & Diez de Sollano) This café has live bands doing classic rock covers from 10pm daily and a 6pm to 9pm happy hour to get the students in early, but later on it's mostly an older crowd who appreciate the great views.

Entertainment

Every evening at sunset, the Jardín hosts a free concert of birdsong as the trees fill with twittering, whistling and preening birds, while the paths (lookout below!) fill with people doing much the same. These days, gray-haired gringos can outnumber flirting teenagers, but it's a delight to be there, as the air cools and the fragrance of flowers and food stalls floats across the plaza.

Several restaurants double as drinking, dancing and entertainment venues. Most of the action is on Thursday, Friday and Saturday nights, but during holidays some places will have live nightly music. The fabled Beat dive **La Cucaracha** (Zacateros 22) has closed its storied doors, but rumors persist about it possibly resurfacing somewhere.

For more formal entertainment, check *Atención San Miguel* for what's on. The **Escuela de Bellas Artes** (see Courses, p625) hosts a variety of cultural events, many in English; check its notice board for a current schedule. Built in 1910, the elegant **Teatro Ángela Peralta** (☎ 152-22-00; cnr Mesones & Hernández Macías) often hosts local productions.

CINEMA

Villa Jacaranda Cine/Bar (☎ 152-10-15; Aldama 53; tickets US$5.50) projects recent releases of US movies on a big screen at 7:30pm daily. Entry includes a drink and popcorn. The Biblioteca Pública (see Information, p623) screens quality videos in the evening Tuesday to Saturday.

NIGHTCLUBS & DISCOS

El Ring (☎ 152-19-98; Hidalgo 25; cover US$3-6; ☺ 10pm-3am Thu-Sat, nightly in high season) This flashy place is San Miguel's most popular club, blasting a mix of Latin, US, and European dance music. After midnight it's usually packed with young Mexicans and foreigners.

El Grito (☎ 152-00-48; Umarán 15; ☺ 10pm-2am Thu-Sat) An oversized face shouts above the doorway of this upscale disco opposite Mama Mía.

Pancho & Lefty's (☎ 152-19-58; Mesones 99; cover US$3-5; 8pm-3am Wed, Fri & Sat) A young, affluent, hard-drinking crowd flocks here for live, loud rock, blues and DJ techno and disco nights.

100 Ángeles (☎ 152-59-37; Mesones 97; cover US$3-5; ☺ 10pm-4am Fri-Sat) This disco/dance club is San Miguel's premier gay and lesbian venue (everyone is welcome), with a '70s ambience from the music to the glitter ball. Next door, **El Caporal** bar has a small stage for acoustic music and comedy acts.

Shopping

San Miguel has one of Mexico's biggest and best concentrations of craft shops, with folk art and handicrafts from all over the country. Local crafts include tinware, wrought iron, silver, brass, leather, glassware, pottery and textiles. Prices are not low, but quality is high and the range of goods is mind-boggling.

Casa Maxwell (☎ 152-02-47; Canal 14) This rambling store offers a tremendous array of decorative and household goods. There are many, many more within a few blocks, especially on Canal, San Francisco and Zacateros.

The **Mercado de Artesanías** is a collection of handicraft stalls in the alleyway between Colegio and Loreto; prices are lower than in San Miguel's smarter shops, but the quality

varies. The **Mercado El Nigromante** sells fruit, vegetables and assorted goods, mostly to the local community.

The biggest weekly outdoor market on Tuesday beside the Gigante shopping center, 2.5km east of the center on the Querétaro road. Take a 'Gigante' or 'Placita' bus (10 minutes) from the Jardín's east side.

Getting There & Away

AIR

The nearest tarmac is Aeropuerto Internacional del Bajío, between León and Silao (see León, p617, for flight information). Mexico City's airport is served by many more direct (usually cheaper) flights than Bajío but the latter, around 1½ hours away by private car, is more convenient for San Miguel.

A few agencies provide transport to/from Bajío, if there are enough passengers. Try **PMC Tours** (☎ 152-01-21); **Aventuras San Miguel** (☎ 152-64-06) or **Viajes Vertiz** (☎ 152-18-56). Alternatively, take a bus to Silao and get a taxi from there to the airport. For Mexico City airport, get a bus to Querétaro, and a bus direct to the airport from there.

BUS

The small Central de Autobuses is on Canal, 1km west of the center. ETN, Primera Plus and Pegasso Plus tickets can be bought in-town at **PMC Tours** (☎ 152-01-21; Cuna de Allende 11). Daily departures include:

Celaya (US$2.75, 1¼hr; 2nd-class Flecha Amarilla every 15min daily)

Dolores Hidalgo (US$2, 1hr; 2nd-class Flecha Amarilla or Herradura de Plata every 40min, 7am-8pm daily)

Guadalajara (US$33, 6hr, 2 deluxe ETN daily; US$27, 6hr, 4 1st-class Primera Plus daily; US$24, 6hr, 2nd-class Servicios Coordinados, 7:50pm daily)

Guanajuato (US$8.50, 1-1½hr, 2 deluxe ETN daily; US$6.50, 1-1½hr, 4 1st-class Primera Plus daily; US$5, 1-1½hr, 1 1st-class Ómnibus de México daily; US$4.50, 1-1½hr, 10 2nd-class Flecha Amarilla daily)

León (US$12.50, 2¼hr; 2 deluxe ETN daily; US$12, 1 1st-class Primera Plus; US$9, 2¼hr , 2 2nd-class Servicios Coordinados daily)

Mexico City (US$21, 3½-4hr, 4 deluxe ETN daily; US$17, 3½-4hr, 2 1st-class Primera Plus, 2 1st-class Herradura de Plata daily; US$14, 3½-4hr, 2nd-class Herradura de Plata semidirect every 10min, 7am-8pm daily) To Terminal Norte.

Querétaro (US$6.50, 1hr, 3 deluxe ETN daily; US$3.50, 1hr, 2nd-class Flecha Amarilla or Herradura de Plata every 40min, 7am-8pm daily)

Other 1st-class buses serve Aguascalientes, Monterrey and San Luis Potosí. Americanos buses depart for Texas and Chicago at 5:30pm daily.

CAR & MOTORCYCLE
If you need a car for more than a few days, it may be worth going to Querétaro, or at least contacting rental agencies there. The only San Miguel–based agency is **Hola** (☎ 152-01-98), inside Posada San Francisco. Prices start around US$60 per day for a manual-transmission VW Beetle. Reserve at least a week ahead, especially during the high season.

Getting Around
Via bus from Bajío airport, you must make a connection in León. Taxis charge around US$60 one-way.

Local buses (US$0.30) run 7am to 9pm daily. 'Central' buses run every few minutes between the bus station and the town center. Coming into town these go up Insurgentes, wind through the town a bit and terminate on the corner of Mesones and Colegio. Heading out of the center, you can pick one up on Canal. A taxi between the center and the bus station costs around US$2, as do most trips around town.

SANTUARIO DE ATOTONILCO

Turning west off the Dolores Hidalgo Hwy 11km north of San Miguel and going 3km will bring you to the hamlet of Atotonilco, dominated by its sanctuary founded in 1740 as a spiritual retreat. Ignacio Allende married here in 1802. Eight years later he returned with Miguel Hidalgo and a band of independence rebels en route from Dolores to San Miguel to take the shrine's banner of the Virgin of Guadalupe as their flag.

Today a journey to Atotonilco is a goal of pilgrims and penitents from all over Mexico, and the starting point of an important and solemn procession two weekends before Easter, in which the image of the Señor de la Columna is carried to the church of San Juan de Dios in San Miguel. Inside, the sanctuary has six chapels and is vibrant with statues, folk murals and other paintings. Restoration is ongoing. Traditional dances are held here on the third Sunday in July.

AROUND SAN MIGUEL DE ALLENDE
Hot Springs
Natural hot springs near San Miguel have been developed as *balnearios*, with swimming pools where you can soak in mineral waters amid pleasant surroundings. The *balnearios* are accessed via the highway north of San Miguel – take a Dolores Hidalgo bus from the San Miguel bus station, or a 'Santuario' minibus (half-hourly) from the bus stops on Puente de Umarán, off Colegio and opposite the Mercado El Nigromante. These buses will stop out front, or within walking or hitching distance, of all the main *balnearios*. Returning to town, hail a bus along the highway. Taxis (around US$8 each way) are another option; you can ask the driver to return for you at an appointed time. Most places are crowded with local families on weekends but *muy tranquilo* during the week.

The most popular balneario is **Taboada** (☎ 152-08-50; US$3.25; ◷ 7:30am-6pm Wed-Mon), 8km north then 3¼km west down a signposted cobblestone road. It has a large lawn and three swimming pools: one Olympic-size with warm water, a smaller pool for children, and a thermal spa that gets quite hot. A snack kiosk and a bar provide refreshments. Hourly 'Xote' minibuses, departing from Puente de Umarán, will get you within 1½km of Taboada. Jump off where the bus turns off the Taboada side road and walk the remaining 15 minutes to the hot springs.

Nearby, the family-oriented **Balneario Xote** (☎ 614-58-89; www.xoteparqueacuatico.com; adult/child US$3.75/1.75; ◷ 9am-6pm) water park is 3½km off the highway down the same cobblestone road as Taboada. At the next turnoff beside the highway to Dolores Hidalgo is **Santa Verónica** (adult/child US$3.25/3; ◷ 9am-6pm Sat-Thu).

Next up, **Escondido Place** (☎ 185-20-22; US$4.50; ◷ 8am-6:30pm) has two warm outdoor pools and three connected indoor pools, each progressively hotter. The picturesque grounds have plenty of picnicking space, and there's a kiosk for drinks and snacks. It's 10km from San Miguel all told, 1km up a gravel road (a 15-minute walk) off the road to Dolores Hidalgo.

Nine kilometers from San Miguel, **Parador del Cortijo** (☎ 152-17-00; US$6.75; ◷ 9am-6pm) is a hotel-restaurant with a thermal pool, massages and private bathroom.

Just past Parador del Cortijo at Km 9.5, **La Gruta** (☎ 185-20-99; US$4.50; ◷ 8am-5pm) has three small pools where a thermal spring is channeled. The hottest is in a cave entered through a tunnel, with water gushing from the roof, lit by a single shaft of sunlight.

Pozos

☎ 412 / elevation 2305m

Less than a hundred years ago, Mineral de Pozos was a flourishing silver- and copper-mining center of 50,000 people, but as the minerals played out the population dwindled and abandoned houses, mine workings and a large but unfinished church. Now visitors enjoy exploring the crumbling buildings and touring the surrounding area by horseback or mountain bike. You can also visit workshops that produce replicas of pre-Hispanic musical instruments like deerskin drums and rainmakers, which are used to accompany traditional dances in local fiestas.

Two inviting, aesthetically pleasing B&Bs-cum-galleries await side-by-side facing the sleepy main plaza.

Casa Mexicana Hotel (☎ 293-00-14; www.casamexi canahotel.com; Jardín Principal 2; r from US$80; P) This 100-year-old hacienda was Pozos' first place to be converted to tourist lodging, and it was very well done. The unique, multilevel rooms – each with its own Picasso lithograph – are elegant and spacious. One has a tree growing inside; others have great views. Also here is **Isadora's**, a new tapas bar with live music in high season. Credit cards accepted.

Casa Montana (☎ 293-00-32; www.casamontana hotel.com; Jardín Principal 4A; r/ste US$90/115) A total renovation has turned this antique stone building into a comfortable B&B, restaurant and art gallery featuring haunting B&W photos by American Jack Spencer.

Pozos is 14km south of San Luis de la Paz, a detour east of Hwy 57. To get here by bus from San Miguel, go first to Dolores Hidalgo, then to San Luis de la Paz and then take a third bus to Pozos. By car it's about 45 minutes from San Miguel. **Aventuras San Miguel** runs day-trips to Pozos from San Miguel and **Bici-Burro** does it as a bike tour (see Tours in San Miguel, p626).

QUERÉTARO STATE

Querétaro (population 1.52 million) is primarily an agricultural and ranching state. Industry has developed around Querétaro city and San Juan del Río. The state also turns out opals, mercury, zinc and lead. Apart from Querétaro city, with its fine colonial architecture, there are other areas worth visiting, like pretty Tequisquiapan with its thermal springs. In the state's northeast corner, the rugged edge of the Sierra Madre has little-visited archaeological sites, and a dramatic road descending to old mission towns on the fringe of the Huasteca.

QUERÉTARO

☎ 442 / pop 580,000 / elevation 1762m

Querétaro's museums and colonial architecture may be less spectacular than those of Guanajuato or Zacatecas, but it's a lively, undiscovered city. It's prettiest at night when many of its buildings are floodlit, and wandering the streets and plazas is a real pleasure. It especially warrants a visit if you're interested in Mexico's history, in which it has played an important role. Today, it's said to be one of Mexico's cleanest cities and its historic center was inscribed as a Unesco World Heritage Site in 1996 in recognition of its colonial monuments and unique street plan.

History

The Otomí founded a settlement here in the 15th century that was soon absorbed by the Aztecs, then by Spaniards in 1531. Franciscan monks used it as a missionary base not only to Mexico but also to what is now the southwestern USA. In the early 19th century, Querétaro became a center of intrigue among disaffected criollos plotting to free Mexico from Spanish rule. Conspirators, including Miguel Hidalgo, met secretly at the house of Doña Josefa Ortiz (La Corregidora), who was the wife of Querétaro's former *corregidor* (district administrator).

When the conspiracy was uncovered, the story goes, Doña Josefa was locked in her house (now the Palacio de Gobierno) but managed to whisper through a keyhole to a coconspirator, Ignacio Pérez, that their colleagues were in jeopardy. Pérez galloped off to inform another conspirator in San Miguel de Allende, who in turn carried the news to Dolores Hidalgo, where on September 16, 1810, Padre Hidalgo issued his famous Grito, the call to arms that initiated the War of Independence.

In 1867 Emperor Maximilian surrendered to General Escobedo, Benito Juárez'

QUERÉTARO

To Aeroméxico &
Turismo Beverly;
Cerro de las
Campanas (1km)

To San Miguel de
Allende (63km); Dolores
Hidalgo (110km); San Luis
Potosí (204km)

To Celaya
(52km)

To Olé Spanish
Language School
(100m)

To IBI Bar (2km); OUI
(3km); Mexicana Bus
Station (5km); Mexico
City (220km)

To Airport
(7km)

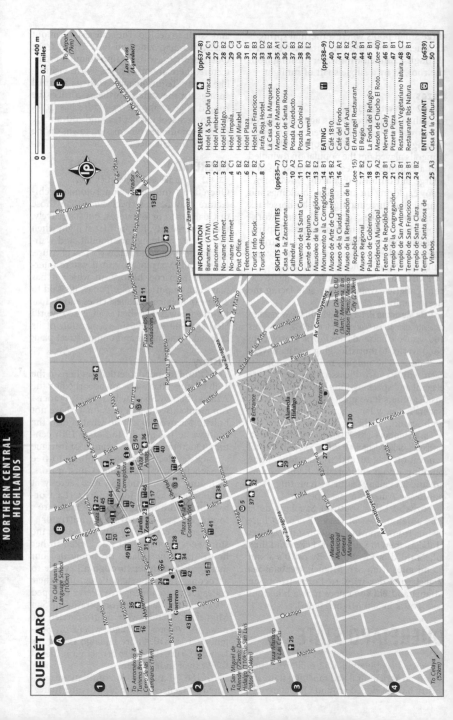

NORTHERN CENTRAL
HIGHLANDS

general, here, after a siege lasting nearly 100 days, and was executed by firing squad.

In 1917 the Mexican constitution – still the basis of Mexican law – was drawn up by the Constitutionalist faction in Querétaro. The PNR (which later became the PRI, the Institutional Revolutionary Party) was organized in Querétaro in 1929, and it dominated Mexican politics for the rest of the 20th century.

Orientation

The historic center is fairly compact, with *andadores* (pedestrian streets) linking a number of lively plazas – it makes for pleasant strolling. The heart of things is Jardín Zenea, the main plaza, with Av Corregidora, the main downtown street, running along its east side. The Plaza de Armas (aka Plaza de la Independencia) is two blocks east, and the small Plaza de la Corregidora is a block north. The shady Alameda, a few blocks south, is popular for picnicking, jogging, strolling and relaxing in general. Madero/5 de Mayo is the boundary between north–south and east–west street addresses.

Information

The **tourist office** (☎ 212-25-36/36-50, 800-715-17-42; www.mqro.gob.mx; Pasteur Norte 4; 🕐 8am-8pm Mon-Fri, 9am-8am Sat & Sun) has city maps and brochures.

There are several banks with ATMs around Jardín Zenea. *Casas de cambio* are along Juárez and Colón. The American Express agent is **Turismo Beverly** (☎ 216-15-00; Tecnológico 118), which also books airplane tickets.

Telecomm (Allende Norte 4) has Internet and money order services. There are card phones on Jardín Zenea, Plaza de Armas and elsewhere around the center. Handy no-name Internet places are at Libertad 32 and Carranza 9; both charge around US$1 per hour.

Sights

TEMPLO DE SAN FRANCISCO

This impressive **church** fronts Jardín Zenea. Pretty colored tiles on the dome were brought from Spain in 1540, around the time construction of the church began. Inside are some fine religious paintings from the 17th, 18th and 19th centuries.

MUSEO REGIONAL

The **Museo Regional** (☎ 212-20-31; cnr Av Corregidora & Jardín Zenea; US$3; 🕐 10am-7pm Tue-Sun) is beside Templo de San Francisco. The ground floor holds exhibits on pre-Hispanic Mexico, archaeological sites, Spanish occupation and the state's various indigenous groups.

Upstairs there are exhibits on Querétaro's role in the independence movement, post-independence history and many religious paintings. The table at which the Treaty of Guadalupe Hidalgo was signed in 1848, ending the Mexican-American War, is on display, as is the desk of the tribunal that sentenced Maximilian to death.

The museum is housed in part of what was once a huge monastery and seminary. Begun in 1540, the seminary became the seat of the Franciscan province of San Pedro y San Pablo de Michoacán by 1567. Building continued until at least 1727. The tower was the city's highest vantage point, and in the 1860s the monastery was used as a fort both by imperialists supporting Maximilian and by the forces who finally defeated him in 1867.

MUSEO DE ARTE DE QUERÉTARO

Adjacent the Templo de San Agustín, **Querétaro's art museum** (☎ 212-23-57; Allende Sur 14; US$1.50, free Tue; 🕐 10am-6pm Tue-Sun) occupies a splendid baroque monastery built between 1731 and 1748. There are angels, gargoyles, statues and other ornamental details all over the building, particularly around the stunning courtyard.

The ground-floor display of 16th- and 17th-century European painting traces interesting influences, from Flemish to Spanish to Mexican art. On the same floor you'll find 19th- and 20th-century Mexican painting, a collection of 20th-century Querétaro artists and a hall for temporary exhibitions. The top floor has more art, from 16th-century mannerism to 18th-century baroque. There's a good bookstore and giftshop.

MUSEO DE LA CIUDAD

Inside the old prison that held Maximilian, the 11-room **City Museum** (☎ 212-47-02; Guerrero Nte 27; US$0.65, students free; 🕐 11am-7pm Tue-Sun) has some quite good contemporary art, and not terribly interesting displays on the city's recent history. It's also worth checking out the new **Museo de la Restauración de la Republica** (Guerrero Nte 23) next door.

TEATRO DE LA REPÚBLICA

This lovely old **theater** (☎ 212-03-39; cnr Juárez & Peralta; ⏰ 10am-2pm & 5-8pm Tue-Sun) was where a tribunal met in 1867 to decide the fate of Emperor Maximilian. Mexico's constitution was also signed here on January 31, 1917. The stage backdrop lists the names of its signatories and the states they represented. In 1929, politicians met in the theater to organize Mexico's ruling party, the PNR (now the PRI, the Institutional Revolutionary Party).

PALACIO DE GOBIERNO (CASA DE LA CORREGIDORA)

Doña Josefa Ortiz' home, where she informed Ignacio Pérez of the plans to arrest the independence conspirators, occupies the Plaza de Armas' north side. Today the building is the state government building. The room where Doña Josefa was imprisoned is upstairs, over the entrance – it's now the governor's conference room. The building can be visited during normal office hours, but there's not much to see.

CONVENTO DE LA SANTA CRUZ

Ten minutes' walk east of the center is one of the city's most interesting sights. The **monastery** (☎ 212-03-35; cnr Acuña & Independencia; donation requested; ⏰ 9am-2pm Tue-Fri, 9am-4:30pm Sat) was built between 1654 and about 1815 on the site of a battle in which a miraculous appearance of Santiago (St James) had led the Otomí to surrender to the conquistadors and Christianity. Emperor Maximilian had his headquarters here while under siege in Querétaro from March to May 1867. After his surrender and subsequent death sentence, he was jailed here while awaiting the firing squad. Today it's used as a religious school.

A guide will provide insight into the Convento's history and artifacts, which include an ingenious water system and unique colonial ways of cooking and refrigeration. The guide will also relate several of the site's miracles, including the legendary growth of a tree from a walking stick stuck in the earth by a pious friar in 1697. The thorns of the tree form a cross. Tours are given in English or Spanish.

ACUEDUCTO & MIRADOR

Walk east along Independencia past Convento de la Santa Cruz then fork right along Ejército Republicano, and you come to a **mirador** with a view of 'Los Arcos,' Querétaro's emblematic 1.28km **aqueduct**, with 74 towering arches built between 1726 and 1735. The aqueduct runs along the center of Av Zaragoza and still brings water to the city from 12km away.

Across the street from the mirador is the **Mausoleo de la Corregidora**, the resting place of Doña Josefa Ortiz (La Corregidora) and her husband, Miguel Domínguez de Alemán. Behind the tomb is a shrine with pictures and documents relating to Doña Josefa's life.

OTHER CENTRAL SIGHTS

Plaza de la Corregidora is dominated by the **Monumento a la Corregidora**, a 1910 statue of Doña Josefa Ortiz bearing the flame of freedom.

A block west of Jardín Zenea is the **Fuente de Neptuno** (Neptune's Fountain), designed by noted Mexican neoclassical architect Eduardo Tresguerras in 1797. Adjacent, the 17th-century **Templo de Santa Clara** has an ornate baroque interior. On Madero at Ocampo is the rather plain 18th-century **cathedral**. Hidalgo, which runs parallel to Madero two blocks north, is lined with many fine mansions.

At the intersection of Arteaga and Montes is the 18th-century **Templo de Santa Rosa de Viterbos**, Querétaro's most splendid baroque church, with its pagodalike bell tower, unusual exterior paintwork, curling buttresses and lavishly gilded and marbled interior. The church also boasts what some say is the earliest four-sided clock in the New World.

Other notable colonial churches include the **Templo de San Antonio** (Peralta at Corregidora Norte) with two large pipe organs, elaborate crystal chandeliers and several oil paintings; and the **Templo de la Congregación** (Pasteur Norte at 16 de Septiembre) with beautiful stained-glass windows and a splendid pipe organ.

The **Casa de la Zacatecana** (☎ 224-07-58; Independencia 59; US$2; ⏰ 11am-7pm) is a finely restored 17th-century home with its own murder mystery – look for the skeletons in the basement. The main attraction is the collection of 18th- and 19th-century furniture and decorations.

CERRO DE LAS CAMPANAS

A good 35-minute walk from the center, the **Hill of the Bells** was the site of Maximilian's execution. The emperor's family constructed a chapel here. Today the area is a park, with a statue of Benito Juárez, a café and the **Museo del Sitio (Siege) de Querétaro** (☎ 215-20-75; US$0.10; 🕑 10am-2pm, 3:30-6pm). Hop on a westbound 'Tecnológico' bus on Zaragoza at Alameda Hidalgo and get off at the Ciudad Universitaria.

Courses

Olé Spanish Language School (☎ 214-40-23; www.ole.edu.mx; Escobedo 32) offers a range of courses with homestay options and extracurricular programs.

Tours

Guided two-hour city center walking tours (US$2), in English or Spanish, leave the tourist office up to six times daily, depending on demand. **Queretour** (☎ 223-08-33; Velázquez 5, Colonia Pathé) runs city tours (US$14) and longer trips to regional attractions.

Festivals & Events

Querétaro's Feria Internacional, one of Mexico's biggest state fairs, happens the first two weeks of December. While it focuses on livestock, it also covers industry, commerce, artistry and entertainment.

Sleeping

BUDGET

Jirafa Roja Hostel (☎ 212-48-25; 20 de Noviembre 72; dm from US$9) A short walk from the historic center, the fun-loving Red Giraffe is Querétaro's only HI-affiliated hostel. The young owners, rooftop terrace and lively nightlife nearby all add up to a likely party. There's space for 20 in doubles and 3- and 4-bed rooms and plans for another 20 beds in the historic center.

Mesón de Matamoros (☎ 214-03-75; Matamoros 10; s/d US$22/24) Well positioned on a lively little pedestrian street, this inviting *posada* has 25 pleasant rooms around an enclosed courtyard, with several cafés and bistros nearby.

Hotel San Francisco (☎ 212-08-58; Corregidora Sur 144; s/d US$14/17) This three-story, no-frills place has a restaurant and lots of smallish but decent rooms, all with cable TV.

Posada Colonial (☎ 212-02-39; Juárez Sur 19; s/d US$9/10, with bathroom US$19/20) Some of the rooms here are very basic while others have extras like TV and a private bathroom.

Villa Juvenil (☎ 223-31-20; Ejército Republicano s/n; dm US$3; P) The single-sex dorms at this 'youth village' are only open seasonally. The 10pm curfew, cold water, morning-only showers and location in the back of a sports complex a 1km walk east of the center make it a good choice only at a pinch. Dorms and bathrooms are clean, and guests can use the kitchen, pool and gym.

MID-RANGE

Hotel Hidalgo (☎ 212-00-81; www.hotelhidalgo.com.mx; Madero Pte 11; s/d US$24/28; P) A few doors off the Jardín Zenea, the three-star Hidalgo was Querétaro's first hotel. Rooms vary greatly in size and appeal. The cheapest rooms are pokey; larger rooms with two beds cost more and the largest can hold up to seven people. They all have private bathroom and some upper-floor rooms have small balconies.

Hotel Plaza (☎ 212-11-38; Juárez Nte 23; s/d from US$23/26) The respectable Plaza has 29 tidy, comfortable, charm-free rooms. Some have French doors and balconies facing the Jardín, offering plenty of light, air and noise for a few more pesos.

Posada Acueducto (☎ 224-12-89; Juárez Sur 64; s/d/tr US$23/32/46) The 15 clean, remodeled rooms here are well-kept and colourful, with fan and cable TV. The best rooms have private balconies. Children under 12 stay free.

Hotel Impala (☎ 212-25-70; www.hotelimpala.com.mx; Colón 1; s/d/ste US$32/40/77; P) This modern four-star hotel opposite Alameda Hidalgo has 114 carpeted, business-friendly rooms with cable TV and phone. Some rooms have park views; interior rooms are quieter and bright enough. Rooms vary – check first. Readers suggest avoiding rooms ending in '28'.

Hotel Amberes (☎ 212-86-04; hamberes@prodigy.net.mx; Corregidora Sur 188; s/d/tr US$37/46/54; P) Another business-traveler favorite facing the Alameda, the Amberes is a bit older but smarter with remodeled air-con rooms for US$10 extra.

Hotel Mirabel (☎ 214-35-35, 800-401-39-00; www.hotelmirabel.com.mx; Av Constituyentes Ote 2; s/d/ste US$59/80/91; P) More demanding business travelers prefer the slicker Mirabel. The comfy carpeted standard rooms (some with park views) have air-con and there's room service, a travel agency and babysitting.

TOP END

La Casa de la Marquesa (☎ 212-00-92; www.lacasadelamarquesa.com; Madero 41; r/ste from US$135/155; P) For something extraordinary, try this magnificent 1756 baroque-Mudéjar mansion filled with lavish period furnishings, carved stonework, tiles and frescoes (some original). The 25 singular suites have names such as Alhambra and Maximiliano y Carlota, with style to match. Rates include continental breakfast and welcome cocktail. Slightly less expensive rooms are in a separate building, Casa Azul, a couple of doors west on the corner of Madero and Allende. The Imperial Suite (US$280) is unforgettable. Children under 12 are not admitted.

Doña Urraca Hotel & Spa (☎ 238-54-00, 800-021-71-16 in Mexico, 877-278-80-18 in USA; www.dona urraca.com.mx; 5 de Mayo 117; r/ste from US$190/235; P ✗ ⚑ 🖳) Ready for some pampering? Rates at this contemporary hideaway include two spa treatments. The 24 spacious, full-featured suites are lavished with fine touches like bathrobes and handmade herbal soaps. There's a gym, heated pool and outdoor Jacuzzi and restaurant's wine cellar morphs into a romantic private dining room for two. Go on, spoil yourself!

Mesón de Santa Rosa (☎ 224-26-23; Pasteur Sur 17; r/ste from 119/165; P ⚑) On the Plaza de Armas, Mesón de Santa Rosa is a finely restored 17th-century building built around three patios: one with a heated pool, one with a fountain and one with a restaurant. The 21 elegant, modernized rooms are each unique but all come with a minibar and satellite TV.

Eating

Plaza de la Corregidora and Plaza de Armas are ringed by restaurants with outdoor tables and a vibrant evening atmosphere. Most of them offer live music and post their menus out front; stroll around and take your pick. The surrounding pedestrian streets have many mid-range restaurants and cafés catering to shoppers and workers.

PLAZA DE LA CORREGIDORA

La Fonda del Refugio (☎ 212-07-55; Plaza de la Corregidora 26; mains US$6-9; ☾ 1pm-2am) This refuge has a pretty standard menu, with chicken dishes and steaks, and special nights for *pozole* and *parrillada* (barbecue). After 8pm Thursday to Saturday there's live music.

El Regio (☎ 214-12-75; Plaza de la Corregidora & 16 de Septiembre; mains US$5-10; ☾ 8-3am) El Regio has a similar setup to La Fonda del Refugio, serving well-prepared Mexican standards at breezy outdoor tables.

Pizzeta Pizza (☎ 212-40-33; 16 de Septiembre 14; mains US$4-9; ☾ noon-11pm) Pizzeta is Plaza de la Corregidora's most economical option, with a good range of meat and veggie pizzas.

Nevería Galy (5 de Mayo 20; mains US$1.50) This Querétaro institution is known for its homemade ice cream. Specialties include *nieve de limón* (lemon sorbet) with mineral water, cola or red wine.

PLAZA DE ARMAS

Plaza de Armas has a handful of more upscale restaurants that have indoor and outdoor tables.

Mesón de Chucho El Roto (☎ 212-42-95; Libertad 60; mains US$5-10) The most popular place boasts *alta cocina mexicana* and offers interesting variations on classic Mexican dishes and regional specialties like *tacos de flor y huitlacoche* (squash flower and corn fungus tacos). There's a good wine list and you can linger over a drink.

Café 1810 (☎ 214-33-24; Andador Libertad 60; mains US$4-8) Café 1810 is slightly cheaper than its neighbor Chucho and has a more standard menu of Mexican and international dishes; try the local specialty *enchiladas queretanas* (fried enchiladas with chili sauce, cheese and onions).

ELSEWHERE

Casa Azul Café (☎ 212-00-92; cnr Madero & Allende; mains US$4-9; ☾ 7am-5pm) La Casa de la Marquesa's attractive courtyard bistro boasts a gurgling fountain, fine food and a good upscale *comida corrida* (US$7.50).

Café del Fondo (☎ 212-09-05; Pino Suárez 9; everything under US$2.50; ☾ 7:30am-10pm) This relaxed, rambling alternative hangout is popular with chesshead punks and newpaper-reading elderstatesmen. You can get a set breakfast with eggs, *frijoles*, bread roll, juice and house-roasted coffee, snacks or a four-course *comida corrida* with plenty of choices.

El Arcángel Restaurant (☎ 212-65-42; southwest cnr of Jardín Guerrero; mains US$3-7; ☾ 8am-10pm) For a power breakfast or a slow-paced four-course set lunch (US$7), join local businessfolk at this old-fashioned place with a pleasant patio.

Restaurante Ibis Natura (☎ 244-22-12; Juárez 47 Nte; mains US$2-4; ☾ 8am-9:30pm) Vegetarians and natural-food fans will enjoy the good-value *comida corrida* (US$3.25) or the soyburgers with mushrooms and cheese.

Restaurante Vegetariano Natura (☎ 214-10-88; Vergara 7; mains US$1.50-3.50; ⏱ 8am-9pm Mon-Sat) On a quiet pedestrian street, this nonsmoking vegetarian cubbyhole serves set breakfasts, salads and a good value three-course *comida corrida* (US$3.25).

Entertainment

Querétaro has cultural activities befitting a state capital and university city. Sit in the Plaza Principal any Sunday evening with local families enjoying concerts; the state band performs from 7pm to 9pm, sometimes with dancers. A callejoneada kicks off from the Plaza de Armas at 8pm Saturday in summer. The **Casa de la Cultura** (☎ 212-56-14; 5 de Mayo 40) sponsors concerts, dance, theater and art events; stop by during office hours to pick up the monthly schedule.

Most of the fashionable bars and nightclubs are in the suburbs, outside the historic center. Check the entertainment section of Friday's *Diario de Querétaro*, or ask the tourist office to suggest some happening nightspots. There's a slew of bars, clubs and discos along Av Constituyentes (get a taxi), the city's eastern ring road, south of the aqueduct.

The disco **QIU** (☎ 213-72-39; Av Constituyentes 1192) is perennially popular. Another reliable hotspot is the **JBJ Bar** (☎ 213-43-07; Blvd Bernardo Quintana 109), which has live music on weekends. Other suburban clubs that are worth seeking out include **Foreplay** and **El Alebrije**.

Getting There & Away

AIR

The modern John Ingeniero F Espinoza Gutierrez International Airport is 8km northeast of the center, a 15-minute colectivo (US$4.50) or taxi ride (US$8). Aeroméxico and Mexicana run regular flights to/from Mexico City and Monterrey, while Aerolitoral has a couple daily flights to/from Guadalajara. Aeromar also has some services.

In-town airline offices include **Aeroméxico** (☎ 215-64-74; Tecnológico 100, Colonia Carrizal) and **Mexicana** (☎ 246-00-71; Bernardo Quintana 4100, Colonia Alamos).

BUS

Querétaro is a hub for buses in all directions; the modern Central Camionera is 5km southeast of the center. There's one building for deluxe and 1st-class (labeled A), one for 2nd-class (B) and another for local buses (C). Facilities include a café, telephone *casetas*, shops and luggage storage. Daily departures include:

Guadalajara (US$29, 4½-5½hr, 8 deluxe ETN daily; US$22, 4½-5½hr, 10 1st-class Primera Plus & 4 Ómnibus de México daily; US$21, 4½-5½hr, 7 2nd-class Flecha Amarilla & 10 Oriente daily)

Guanajuato (US$8.50, 2½-3hr; 2 1st-class Ómnibus de México daily; US$7.50, 2½-3hr, 4 2nd-class Flecha Amarilla daily) Also catch frequent buses to Irapuato, from where buses frequently leave for Guanajuato.

Mexico City (US$19, 2½-3hr, deluxe ETN every ½hr 5am-10pm daily; US$14, 2½-3hr, 1st-class Primera Plus every 20min 6am-8pm daily; US$13, 2½-3hr, 5 1st-class Ómnibus de México daily; US$11, 2½-3hr, 2nd-class Flecha Amarilla, many direct, daily; US$11, 2½-3hr, 2nd-class Herradura de Plata every 15min daily) To Terminal Norte.

Mexico City (US$10, 4hr, frequent (every fivemin) 2nd-class Herradura de Plata daily) To Terminal Poniente.

Mexico City Airport (US$18, 3hr, 18 1st-class Aeroplus daily)

Morelia (US$10-11, 3-4hr, 21 1st-class Primera Plus/ Servicios Coordinados daily; US$9, 3-4hr, 8 2nd-class Flecha Amarilla daily)

San Luis Potosí (US$16, 2½hr, 3 deluxe ETN daily; US$13, 2½hr, 22 1st-class Primera Plus/Servicios Coordinados daily; US$10, 2½hr, hourly 2nd-class Flecha Amarilla daily)

San Miguel de Allende (US$6.50, 1hr; 3 deluxe ETN daily, US$3.50, 1hr, 2nd-class Herradura de Plata or Flecha Amarilla every 40min, 6am-10pm daily)

Tequisquiapan (US$2.25, 1hr, half-hourly from 7am-9pm 2nd-class Flecha Azul daily)

CAR & MOTORCYCLE

If you want a car to explore the Sierra Gorda, English-speaking **Express Rent-a-Car** (☎ 242-9028; www.queretaro-express.com) has competitive rates. **Auto Rentals del Bajío** (☎ 214-23-39) and **Golf's** (☎ 212-11-47) are also worth checking.

Getting Around

Once you have reached the city center, you can easily visit most sights on foot. City buses (US$0.40) run from 6am until 9pm or 10pm but can be infuriatingly slow. They leave from an open lot outside the bus station; turn right from the 2nd-class terminal, left from the 1st-class side. Several routes go to the center including Nos 8 and 19, which both go to the Alameda Hidalgo then up Ocampo. Newer Transmetro buses (US$0.45) are quicker. For a taxi, get a ticket first from the bus station booth (US$2.75 for up to four people).

For the bus station from the center, take city bus No 19, No 25 Zaragoza, or No 36 or any other saying 'Terminal de Autobuses' heading south on the east side of the Alameda Hidalgo.

TEQUISQUIAPAN

☎ 414 / pop 28,000 / elevation 1880m

This small town ('teh-kees-kee-AP-an'), 70km southeast of Querétaro, is a quaint weekend retreat from Mexico City or Querétaro. It used to be known for its thermal springs – Mexican presidents came here to ease their aches and tensions. Local industries now use most of the hot water, but there are still some delightful cool-water pools, some set in pretty gardens at attractive hotels. It's a pleasure to simply stroll the streets, lined with brilliant purple bougainvillea and colorful colonial buildings. Tequis is sometimes playfully abbreviated TX, pronounced 'teh-kees'.

Orientation & Information

The bus station is a vacant lot southwest of town, a 10-minute walk along Niños Héroes from the center. The **tourist office** (☎ 273-02-95; east side Plaza Principal; ☉ 9am-5pm Wed-Sun) has town maps and info on Querétaro state. On the plaza's southeast side, Bancomer has an ATM.

Sights & Activities

The Plaza Principal is surrounded by *portales* (arcades), overlooked by the 19th-century **Templo de Santa María de la Asunción**.

The **main market**, on Ezequiel Montes, and **Mercado de Artesanías** (Crafts Market) on Carrizal, are a couple of blocks away through little lanes. The large, verdant **Parque La Pila** is a short distance past the Mercado de Artesanías along Ezequiel Montes.

Most hotel swimming pools are for guests only; an exception is Hotel Neptuno's **cool pool** (admission US$2.75; ☉ 8am-6pm daily Apr-Oct, 8am-6pm Sat & Sun only Nov-Mar). Other *balnearios* are just north of town along Hwy 120.

Look for migratory birds at the **Santuario de Aves Migratorios La Palapa** by the dam at the north end of the lake just south of town; it's on the right if you approach Tequis from San Juan del Río. Other things you can do here include horseback riding, tennis and golf (ask at the tourist office or your hotel).

Festivals & Events

The **Feria Internacional del Queso y del Vino** (International Wine and Cheese Fair), from late May to early June, attracts people from far and wide for tastings, music and rodeo. Tequis is a tranquil place to enjoy the **Fiestas Patrias** on either side of Independence Day (September 16).

Sleeping

The best budget options are the posadas along Moctezuma. Demand is low Monday to Thursday, when you may be able to negotiate a discount.

Posada San Francisco (☎ 273-02-31; posadasanfrancisco@hotmail.com; Moctezuma 2; s/d US$32/36; ℗ ☒) Well-traveled, English-speaking owner Juan Pablo and his French wife are thoughtfully restoring his family's century-old retreat. The 11 rooms all have cable TV and a few have bathtubs. Out back, there's a large garden and pool, watched over by a statue of a nymph.

Posada Tequisquiapan (☎ 273-00-10; Moctezuma 6; s/d US$21/35; ☒) This hotel has pretty gardens and a splendid grotto-like pool. Rooms are spacious, with cable TV.

Hotel/Balneario Neptuno (☎ 273-02-24; Juárez Oriente 5; s/d US$28/46; ☒) Two blocks east of Plaza Principal, the Neptuno has a big pool and lots of rooms, including larger family rooms.

Hotel La Plaza (☎ 273-00-56; www.tequisquiapan .com.mx/la_plaza; Juárez 10; r US$35-65; ℗ ☒) Facing the plaza, this hotel has a restaurant, sports bar and a choice of 15 rooms and suites of varying size.

Hotel El Relox (☎ 273-00-66; Morelos Pte 8; r from US$100; ℗ ☒) This sprawling 110-room complex, 1½ blocks north of the plaza, is set in extensive gardens with a restaurant, several pools, gym, tennis courts and private thermal pools (26°C to 38°C).

Eating

The cheapest place for a snack or meal is the rear of the main market, where clean *fondas* (food stalls) cluster under awnings in the patio from 8am to 8pm. Fancier restaurants around the plaza specialize in long lunches for large family groups.

K'puchinos (☎ 273-10-46; Morelos 4; mains US$4-9) With indoor and outdoor tables, this place on the plaza's west side is good for set lunch (US$7) or dinner. The menu is standard Mexican fare, with well-prepared mains, pastas, *antojitos* and a big coffee selection.

El Sabor Italiano (mains $3-5), off the plaza inside the Santa Clara ice creamery, has great risotto and a nice covered patio seating.

Getting There & Around

Tequis is 20km northeast on Hwy 120 from the larger town of San Juan del Río, which is on Hwy 57. A local bus (US$0.30) from outside the bus station to the Mercado will let you off on Carrizal, a two-minute walk northeast of the Plaza Principal.

Buses to/from Tequis are all 2nd class. Flecha Azul runs half hourly 5:30am to 7pm to Querétaro (US$2.25, 1 hour); Flecha Amarilla has connections to/from Mexico City's Terminal Norte (US$11, 2½-3 hours).

NORTHEAST QUERÉTARO STATE

Those heading to/from northeast Mexico, or with a hankering to get off the beaten track, might consider following Hwy 120 northeast from Tequisquiapan over the scenic Sierra Gorda to the lush Huasteca (see Central Gulf Coast chapter, p647). It's possible to get to most places on the way by bus, but it's much easier with your own transport.

Highway 120

Heading north from Tequis, you pass dusty **Ezequiel Montes** and then the winery **Cavas de Freixenet** (☎ 441-277-01-47; www.freixenetmexico.com.mx; tours ☽ 11am-3pm), where you can see wine being made by *método champenoise* during free 40-minute tours.

The next big town is **Cadereyta**, 38km from Tequis. On the east edge of town, signs point to the **Quinta Fernando Schmoll** (☽ 10am-5pm), a botanical garden with over 4400 varieties of cactus.

After another 38km there's a turnoff going east to **San Joaquín**. Follow the good but very winding road from the turnoff for 32km through the rugged mountains; stay on that road through San Joaquín, and continue a few steeply climbing kilometers to the little-visited archaeological site of **Ranas** (US$3; ☽ 9am-4pm), with well-built walls and circular steps incorporated into a steep hillside. There are ball courts and a small hilltop pyramid. Dating from as early as the 8th century, the site is appealing for its

rugged forest setting. San Joaquín has basic lodgings and eateries.

Continuing north on Hwy 120, the road winds up to 2300m at **Pinal de Amoles** and makes several dramatic ups and downs (and 860 turns!) before reaching **Jalpan** at 760m. The attractive town centers on the **mission church**, constructed by Franciscan monks and their indigenous converts in the 1750s. The **Museo de la Sierra Gorda** (☎ 441-296-01-65; Fray Junípero Serra 1; US$0.50; ☽ 10am-4pm) explores the region's pre-Hispanic cultures, and the mission-building period.

On the plaza opposite the church, **Hotel María del Carmen** (☎ 441-296-03-28; Independencia 8; s/d US$23/28; P ☷) has clean, comfortable rooms, with air-con for US$10 more.

On the plaza's west side, the attractive **Hotel Misión Jalpan** (☎ 441-296-02-55, 800-623-10-04; www.hotelesmision.com.mx; Fray Junípero Serra s/n; r from US$72; P ☷ ☲) has a good restaurant and all the comforts of home. Package deals start around US$45 per person.

SIERRA GORDA MISSIONS

In the mid-18th century, Franciscans established four other beautiful missions in this remote region, inscribed as a Unesco World Heritage site in 2003. Their leader Fray Junípero Serra went on to found the California mission chain. The churches have been restored and are notable for their colorful façades carved with symbolic figures. Going east from Jalpan on Hwy 120, there are missions at **Landa de Matamoros** (1760–68); **Tilaco** (1754–62), 10km south of the highway; and **Tancoyol** (1753–60), 20km north of the highway. The other mission is 35km north of Jalpan on Hwy 69 at **Concá** (1754–58).

RESERVA DE LA BIÓSFERA SIERRA GORDA

Northwest of Jalpan, the 3830-sq-km **Sierra Gorda Biosphere Reserve** has a 240-sq-km core that covers a range of altitudes and is notable for the diversity of its ecological systems, from subtropical valleys to high deserts to coniferous forests. **Contact Promotur** (☎ 442-212-89-40; www.promoturqueretaro.com.mx; Independencia 77, Querétaro) for details about guided camping and hiking trips throughout the Sierra Gorda.

NORTHERN CENTRAL HIGHLANDS

642

Central
Gulf Coast

CONTENTS

Maybe it's the humid fecundity of the Central Gulf Coast that gives its inhabitants their slow, sultry smiles. Possibly it's the European influence that imbued them with reserved graciousness, and Afro-Caribbean culture that dissolved music into their veins. But whatever the subtle alchemy, the diverse residents of this region are as warmly welcoming as its lush landscape.

Shot through with rivers and waterfalls, this coastal crescent shelters Mexico's highest peak and one of its deepest karst pits. Nestled within this natural beauty lies an array of human-made structures: the niched pyramids of El Tajín, brightly-painted colonial edifices, and even surrealist stairways spiraling towards the sky. And the sounds of the Gulf Coast are not limited to squawking birds gathering in the plazas at dusk, but are layered with *jarocho* guitars and bouncy marimbas, raucous laughter and cathedral bells.

Long after Hernán Cortés first planted his boot on the sand of Veracruz, foreign travelers are rediscovering this slice of Mexico. The rhythm of a journey here can be regulated to anyone's pulse rate, from adrenaline-crazy to the sometimes-lazy. For the former, opportunities range from summiting the icy Pico de Orizaba, to rafting rapids, to diving offshore in Veracruz. The latter might find their bliss sprawling on a quiet beach, sampling the local *huachinango a la veracruzana*, or lifting a cool margarita glass to their lips. Besides these varied pleasures are the region's unburied treasures, like the immense Olmec heads in Xalapa's archaeological museum, or the birds to be spotted from jungle or rooftop. Whatever you do, you won't be able to avoid soaking up the sunny smiles of the folks you meet on the journey.

HIGHLIGHTS

- Time-traveling Mexican civilization at the **Museo de Antropología** (p665), Xalapa
- Climbing the **Pico de Orizaba** (p686), North America's third-highest peak
- Sipping a michelada under the **zócalo's portales** (p670) in Veracruz
- Exploring the mysterious, jungle-bound ruins of **El Tajín** (p660)
- Soaking up surrealism and soothing rainforest air in **Xilitla** (p653)

■ ALTITUDE RANGE: 0m–5611m ■ VERACRUZ AUGUST DAILY HIGH: 28.4°C

CENTRAL GULF COAST

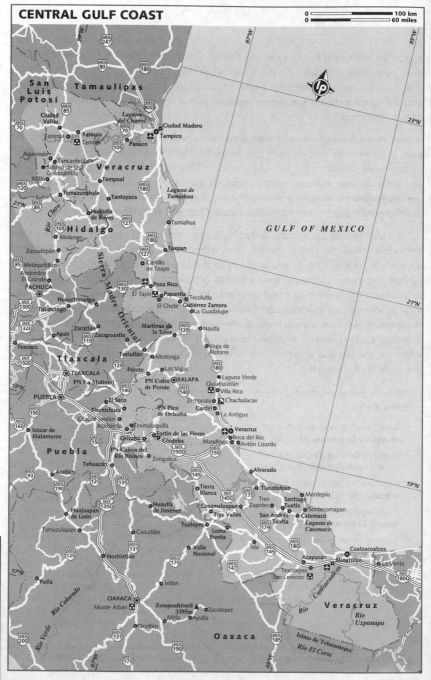

CENTRAL GULF COAST

0 | 100 km
0 | 60 miles

HISTORY
Olmec

The Olmecs, Mesoamerica's earliest known civilization, built their first great center around 1200 BC at San Lorenzo, in southern Veracruz. They prospered there until about 900 BC, when their city was apparently violently destroyed. Subsequently, La Venta in neighboring Tabasco served as the main Olmec center until around 600 BC, when it too seemingly met a violent end. Olmec culture lingered for several centuries at Tres Zapotes, Veracruz, gradually being subsumed by other influences.

Classic Veracruz

After the Olmec decline, the Gulf Coast centers of civilization moved west and north. El Pital, whose ruins were discovered in the early 1990s, was a large city about 100km northwest of Veracruz port. Existing from about AD 100 to 600, it had links with Teotihuacán and may have been home to more than 20,000 people.

The Classic period (AD 250 to 900) saw the emergence in central and northern Veracruz of several politically independent power centers sharing a religion and culture. Together they're known as the 'Classic Veracruz' civilization. Their hallmark is a unique style of carving, with curving and interwoven pairs of parallel lines. This style appears on three types of mysterious carved stone objects, which are probably connected with the civilization's important ritual ball game. They are the U-shaped *yugo,* representing a wooden or leather belt worn in the game; the long paddle-like *palma;* and the flat *hacha,* shaped somewhat like an ax head. The latter two, often carved in human or animal forms, are thought to represent items attached to the front of the belt. Hachas may also have been court markers.

The most important Classic Veracruz center, El Tajín (p660), was at its height over the period AD 600 to 900. Other main centers were Las Higueras, near Vega de Alatorre, close to the coast south of Nautla; and El Zapotal, near Ignacio de la Llave, south of Veracruz port. Classic Veracruz sites show Mayan and Teotihuacán influences. These cultures exported cotton, rubber, cacao and vanilla to central Mexico, influencing developments in Teotihuacán, Cholula and elsewhere.

Totonac, Huastec, Toltec & Aztec

By AD 1200, when El Tajín was abandoned, the Totonacs were establishing themselves from Tuxpan in the north to beyond Veracruz in the south. North of Tuxpan, the Huastec civilization, another web of small, probably independent states, flourished from AD 800 to 1200. The Huastecs were Mexico's chief cotton producers. As skilled stone carvers, they also built many ceremonial sites.

During this time, the war-like Toltecs, who dominated much of central Mexico in the early post-Classic age, moved into the Gulf Coast area. They occupied the Huastec Castillo de Teayo between AD 900 and 1200. Toltec influence can also be seen at Zempoala (p663), a Totonac site near Veracruz port. In the mid-15th century, the Aztecs subdued most of the Totonac and Huastec areas, exacting tributes of goods and sacrificial victims and maintaining garrisons to control revolts.

Colonial Era

When Cortés arrived on the scene in April 1519, he made Zempoala's Totonacs his first allies against the Aztecs by telling them to imprison five Aztec tribute collectors and vowing to protect them against reprisals. Cortés set up his first settlement, Villa Rica de la Vera Cruz (Rich Town of the True Cross), north of modern Veracruz port. Then he established a second settlement at La Antigua, where he scuttled his ships to prevent desertion before advancing to Tenochtitlán, the Aztec capital. In May 1520 he returned to Zempoala and defeated a rival Spanish expedition sent to arrest him.

All the Gulf Coast was in Spanish hands by 1523. New diseases, particularly smallpox, decimated the indigenous population. Veracruz harbor became an essential trade and communications link with Spain and was vital for anyone trying to rule Mexico, but the climate, tropical diseases and threat of pirate attacks inhibited the growth of coastal Spanish settlements.

19th & 20th Centuries

The population of Veracruz city actually shrank in the first half of the 19th century. In the second half, under dictator Porfirio Díaz, Mexico's first railway (1872) linked Veracruz to Mexico City, propelling the development of some industries.

In 1901 oil was discovered in the Tampico area, and by the 1920s the region was producing a quarter of the world's oil. Although that proportion eventually declined, new oil fields were found in southern Veracruz, and in the 1980s the Gulf Coast still held well over half of Mexico's reserves and refining capacity.

CLIMATE

The Central Gulf Coast region is generally warm and humid, hotter along the coast, wetter in the foothills – the hottest and the wettest of all in the southeast. Two-thirds or more of the rain falls between June and September. Veracruz city receives about 1650mm of rain annually. From April to October it features temperatures well over 30°C, falling into the teens at night only from December to February. Tuxpan and Tampico, on the north coast, are a bit drier. Coatzacoalcos, in the southeast, gets more than three meters (!) of rain a year.

DANGERS & ANNOYANCES

Though crime is not much of a problem in this region, travelers should remain wary of petty theft in hotel rooms or pickpocketing in crowded market areas.

Mosquitos along the Central Gulf Coast carry dengue fever, especially in central and southeastern Veracruz. Baste yourself generously with mosquito repellent.

GETTING THERE & AROUND

Veracruz port has the region's main airport, with flights from Mexico City, Monterrey, Reynosa and Villahermosa. Within the region, Tampico and Poza Rica are short hops from here. From the US, Continental has direct flights into Tampico and Veracruz from their Houston, Texas hub.

Aerolitoral flies between Monterrey, Poza Rica, Reynosa and Veracruz, with connections to Villahermosa.

Frequent 1st-class buses go just about everywhere within the region and link the main cities here with Monterrey, Mexico City, Puebla and Oaxaca. The main company serving this area is ADO, with a superdeluxe fleet (UNO) and a deluxe fleet (ADO GL) as well as normal 1st-class buses. Greyhound buses run between the US and Mexico through their Mexican affiliates. Routes include Brownsville to Tampico.

The Central Gulf Coast region's highways are generally in great shape, but the ubiquitous *topes* (speedbumps) may get you down. If you don't expect to go speeding through the countryside, you'll be primed to enjoy the lush landscape as you bump on by.

TAMPICO & THE HUASTECA

Industrial, developed Tampico contrasts sharply with the verdant Huasteca, inland where the coastal plain meets the fringes of the Sierra Madre Oriental. Spread over southern Tamaulipas, eastern San Luis Potosí, northern Veracruz and small corners of Querétaro and Hidalgo, the Huasteca is named after the Huastec people, who have lived here for about 3000 years.

Heading inland from the Huasteca, four steep, winding routes cross the sierra: Hwy 70, from Ciudad Valles to San Luis Potosí; Hwy 120, from Xilitla toward Querétaro; Hwy 85, from Tamazunchale to Ixmiquilpan (near which you can turn off toward Querétaro, Pachuca and Mexico City); and Hwy 105, from Huejutla to Pachuca and on to Mexico City via Hwy 85.

TAMPICO & CIUDAD MADERO

☎ 833 / Tampico pop 295,000,
Ciudad Madero pop 182,000

At the southern tip of Tamaulipas state, a few kilometers upstream from the Río Pánuco's mouth, Tampico remains Mexico's busiest port – a tropical place where cantinas stay open late and the sweaty market constantly bustles. Mexican families flock to the wide beaches of Ciudad Madero, to the north, but foreign visitors will be more interested in Tampico's artfully redeveloped Plaza de la Libertad, surrounded by 19th-century French-style buildings. And although prices are inflated by the oil business, you don't have to hunt too hard for bargain accommodations and seafood.

History

In the 1530s a mission was established in Tampico to convert the Huastecs to Christianity. The town was destroyed by pirates in 1684 but was refounded in 1823 by families from Altamira, to the north. After the 1901 discovery of oil in the area, Tampico suddenly became the world's biggest oil port – rough, tough and booming. Although the city experienced its heyday in the 1920s, the oil and its profits were under foreign control until 1938, when the industry was nationalized by President Lázaro Cárdenas following a strike by Tampico oil workers.

Mexico's 1970s and 1980s oil boom took place further down the coast, but the Tampico–Ciudad Madero area remains important. Pipelines and barge fleets bring oil from fields north and south, on- and offshore, to the area's refineries and harbor. Ciudad Madero remains the headquarters of the powerful oil workers' union, the STPRM.

Orientation

Set in a marshy region near the mouth of the Río Pánuco, Tampico is ringed by several lakes, including Laguna del Chairel and Laguna del Carpintero. You'll cross numerous small estuaries as you approach the city from the north or west. Going south, the spectacular Puente Tampico (Tampico Bridge) crosses the Río Pánuco to Veracruz state.

Downtown Tampico centers on two attractive plazas. The zócalo, or Plaza de Armas, features a grand rotunda and a 20th-century cathedral on its north side. One block south and one block east is the elegant Plaza de la Libertad, with balconied buildings on three sides. Hotels and restaurants of all grades are within a few blocks of these two plazas.

South and east of Plaza de la Libertad is a dodgy area frequented by prostitutes and clients, containing the market, erstwhile train station and riverside docks. Those wishing to avoid unsavory attention should steer clear after dark, particularly in the unlit streets around the market and waterfront.

Addresses on these east–west streets will usually have the suffix 'Ote' (Oriente; east) or 'Pte' (Poniente; west), while those on north–south streets are 'Nte' (Norte; north) or 'Sur' (south). The dividing point is the junction of Colón and Carranza, at the zócalo's northwest corner.

Ciudad Madero's center is about 8km northeast of central Tampico. Industrial zones extend east from there to Playa Miramar, on the Gulf of Mexico.

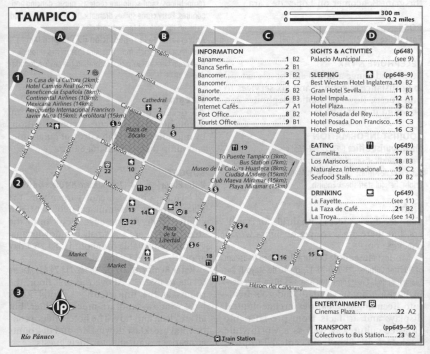

TAMPICO

0 — 300 m
0 — 0.2 miles

INFORMATION		
Banamex	1	B2
Banca Serfin	2	B1
Bancomer	3	B2
Bancomer	4	C2
Banorte	5	B2
Banorte	6	B3
Internet Cafés	7	A1
Post Office	8	B2
Tourist Office	9	B1

SIGHTS & ACTIVITIES		(p648)
Palacio Municipal		(see 9)

SLEEPING		(pp648–9)
Best Western Hotel Inglaterra	10	B2
Gran Hotel Sevilla	11	B3
Hotel Impala	12	A1
Hotel Plaza	13	B2
Hotel Posada del Rey	14	B2
Hotel Posada Don Francisco	15	C3
Hotel Regis	16	C3

EATING		(p649)
Carmelita	17	B3
Los Mariscos	18	B3
Naturaleza Internacional	19	C2
Seafood Stalls	20	B2

DRINKING		(p649)
La Fayette		(see 11)
La Taza de Café	21	B2
La Troya		(see 14)

ENTERTAINMENT		
Cinemas Plaza	22	A2

TRANSPORT		(pp649–50)
Colectivos to Bus Station	23	B2

To Casa de la Cultura (2km);
Hotel Camino Real (6km);
Beneficencia Española (8km);
Continental Airlines (10km);
Mexicana Airlines (14km);
Aeropuerto Internacional Francisco
Javier Mina (15km); Aerolitoral (15km)

Obregón
Altamira
Carranza
Cathedral
Plaza de Zócalo
Díaz Mirón
Olmos
20 de Noviembre
Colón
Madero
Juárez
Aduana
Plaza de la Libertad
López de Lara
Altato
Serdán
Portes Gil
Héroes del Cañonero

Inés de la Cruz
Mendez
La Paz
Esteya
Market
Market
Río Pánuco
Train Station

To Puente Tampico (3km);
Bus Station (7km);
Museo de la Cultura Huasteca (8km);
Ciudad Madero (15km);
Club Maeva Miramar (15km);
Playa Miramar (15km)

CENTRAL GULF COAST

Information

EMERGENCY
Fire (☎ 212-12-22)
Police (☎ 214-32-49)

INTERNET ACCESS
Internet Cafés (20 de Noviembre, btwn Carranza & Obregón; per hr US$0.75-1; ☯ 9am-10pm) Several air-conditioned places with decent connections.

LEFT LUGGAGE
Find 24-hour left luggage lockers at the Tampico bus station.

MEDICAL SERVICES
Beneficencia Española, AC (☎ 213-23-63; Hidalgo 3909) Find quality medical care at this hospital.
Centro Médico de Tampico (☎ 214-03-60; Altamira 423 Pte)

MONEY
Numerous banks are scattered around the central plazas. All have 24-hour ATMs and exchange cash before midday, but they may not accept traveler's checks. Your most reliable bet for changing traveler's checks is at the giant Bancomer on López de Lara.

POST
Post Office (☎ 212-19-27; Madero 309)

TELEPHONE & FAX
Many mid-range and top end hotels extend long-distance telephone and fax services to non-guests. Rows of public telephones can be found in both plazas.

TOURIST INFORMATION
Main Tourist Office (☎ 229-27-65; dir. proecoyturistica@tampico.gob.mx; 3rd flr, Palacio Municipal, Plaza de Armas; ☯ 8am-3pm Mon-Fri) Some of the bright, helpful staff speak English.

Sights
Tampico doesn't teem with thrills for travelers, but there are a couple of sights worth checking out.

Modest **Museo de la Cultura Huasteca** (Museum of Huastec Culture; ☎ 210-22-17; cnr 10 de Mayo & Sor Juana Inés de la Cruz; admission free; ☯ 10am-5pm Mon-Fri, 10am-3pm Sat), in Ciudad Madero's Instituto Tecnológico, features archaeological displays and artifacts from pre-Hispanic Huastec culture, as well as a worthwhile bookstore. It's 8km from central Tampico;

take a 'Boulevard' bus (US$0.50) north on Alfaro and ask for 'Tecnológico de Madero.'

On the first floor of Tampico's **Casa de la Cultura** (☎ 219-06-63; Aguirre 105; admission free; ☯ 9am-7pm Mon-Fri), there's an archaeological museum housing Huastecan artifacts and art exhibitions.

The 10km-long **Playa Miramar** is about 15km from downtown Tampico. The beach is wide and reasonably clean, and the lukewarm water is clear, if not crystalline. A long line of simple restaurants features mariscos and margaritas, and each joint rents out shady palapas on its stretch of sand. On holidays and weekends the beach is crowded with families filling every palapa and hawkers selling coconuts, cold beer and seashell souvenirs. At other times the stretch can be deserted. From central Tampico, take a 'Playa' bus (US$0.50) or colectivo (US$2) north on Alfaro.

Festivals & Events
Semana Santa (week preceding Easter Sunday) Activities at Playa Miramar include regattas, fishing and windsurfing competitions, sand-sculpture contests, music, dancing and bonfires. Petty crime spikes dramatically during this period, so be on the lookout for pickpockets.
Aniversario de la repoblación de Tampico (April 12) Features a procession from Altamira that passes through the zócalo here at Tampico, celebrating the city's refoundation in 1823.

Sleeping
All decent downtown places may fill up during holidays, so secure accommodations by mid-afternoon. Rates drop at quiet times and jump during Semana Santa.

BUDGET
Hotel Plaza (☎ 214-17-84; Madero 204 Ote; s & d US$18; 🖳) Though by no means gargantuan, the Plaza's rooms are immaculately kept and comfy. Some rooms have views onto the street, and there's a small bar downstairs. Parking is available for about US$3.75 a day at nearby Hotel Colonial.

Hotel Regis (☎ 212-02-90; fax 212-74-65; Madero 603 Ote; s/d US$22/25) Above the first floor, the rooms at the unpretentious Hotel Regis have windows and are much brighter, but all are clean and tidy. The hotel offers a continental breakfast downstairs and discounts at nearby restaurants for their guests.

MID-RANGE

Mid-range hotels have air-con, hot water, cable TV and phones.

Hotel Posada Don Francisco (☎ /fax 219-28-35; Díaz Mirón 710 Ote; s/d US$24/33; P ✖) With wrought-iron details and colorful walls, this well-maintained inn has quiet rooms. Plants keep guests company in the common sitting areas, and the restaurant-bar downstairs offers reasonably priced Mexican dishes.

Hotel Posada del Rey (☎ 214-10-24; fax 212-10-77; Madero 218 Ote; s/d US$27/33; ✖) The Posada del Rey has a prime location on the Plaza de la Libertad, featuring homey rooms and warm, sociable common areas. Rooms on the plaza share a wide balcony, but beware of ancient, frighteningly loud air-con in some rooms.

Gran Hotel Sevilla (☎ 214-38-33; recepcion@gran hotelsevilla.com.mx; Héroes del Cañonero 304 Pte; s & d US$52; ✖ ✖) With a slick interior and well-appointed rooms, the Sevilla is an excellent deal for the price. Room rates include breakfast, which you'll want to savor on the fabulous terrace overlooking the Plaza de la Libertad.

Or try these mid-range places:

Hotel Impala (☎ 212-09-90, 800-570-09-00; fax 212-06-84; Díaz Mirón 220 Pte; s/d US$39/52; P ✖) Included with room rates are a breakfast buffet, helpful management and gleaming, attractive rooms.

Best Western Hotel Inglaterra (☎ 219-28-57, 800-715-71-23; beweingl@prodigy.net.mx; Díaz Mirón 116 Ote; s & d US$63; P ✖ ✖ ✖) All the modern conveniences you'd expect, and bathtubs too.

TOP END

Hotel Camino Real (☎ 213-88-11; Hidalgo 2000; s/d from US$129/161; P ✖ ✖ ✖) Ten minutes from the airport along the suburban strip mall of Av Hidalgo, the Camino Real is Tampico's most luxurious hotel. It boasts a large pool, spacious rooms and bungalows facing a tropical garden-courtyard. Bonuses include the fitness center, child care services and airport shuttle.

Club Maeva Miramar (☎ 230-02-02, 800-849-19-87, in the USA 888-739-0113; www.maevamiramar.com.mx; Blvd Costero s/n, Playa Miramar; s/d US$222, all-inclusive; P ✖ ✖ ✖) Out by the beach, the Maeva Miramar is a large resort hotel whose enormous rooms come with all the comforts. All-inclusive room rates cover all meals and beverages, live entertainment and access to a private strip of beach. Check the website for discounts off the rack rates.

Eating

Tampico's seafood is fresh and plentiful. Or try the *carne asada tampiqueña*, a local specialty – steak marinated in garlic, oil and oregano and usually served with guacamole, strips of chili and corn chips.

Inexpensive comedores and restaurants stay open late around the zócalo and to the east; the further east you go, the cheaper and seedier they get. A row of **seafood stalls** on Olmos south of the plaza offers great cocteles and other treats for around US$4.

Carmelita (☎ 214-25-22; Héroes del Cañonero 500 Ote; comida corrida US$2-2.75; ☽ 9am-8pm Mon-Sat) The unassuming, breezy Carmelita serves tasty items ranging from pozole to menudo to mole – and teeny tamales (US$0.50).

Naturaleza Internacional (☎ 212-49-79; Aduana 107 Nte; breakfast buffet US$4; ☽ 8am-8pm) Stop by Naturaleza for fresh juices, vegetarian *comida corrida* or the breakfast buffet with items like whole-grain rolls stuffed with avocado, fresh cheese, sprouts and other juicy veggies. Mock meat features in many of the Mexican dishes.

Los Mariscos (☎ 214-08-12; Héroes del Cañonero 409-C Ote; fish dishes US$6.50-9; ☽ 11am-10pm) As the name implies, good seafood is the house specialty at this cavernous place. Non-marine antojitos are also served here, along with a decent selection of cocktails and beer.

Drinking

The best places to kick it with a cold one are the hotel restaurants **La Troya** at Hotel Posada del Rey and **La Fayette** at Gran Hotel Sevilla (see Sleeping, earlier). Both have terraces with wrought-iron railings overlooking the park and street action.

La Taza de Café (☎ 219-04-20; Madero 303; ☽ 9:30am-8:30pm Mon-Sat) La Taza is a secluded place to chill, off the busy street. It has a mellow ambience, great espresso and handicrafts that run less to the Huastecan and more to the *jipiosa* (hippie-esque).

Cinemas Plaza (☎ 214-24-39; Colón 100 Sur) Sometimes shows recent American exports subtitled in Spanish.

Getting There & Away

AIR

Aeropuerto Internacional Francisco Javier Mina is 15km north of downtown.

From Tampico, **Aerolitoral** (☎ 228-08-56; Aeropuerto Internacional Francisco Javier Mina; ☽ 9am-6pm) flies to Monterrey, Poza Rica, Reynosa and Veracruz, with connections to Villahermosa; **Mexicana** (☎ 228-36-62; Universidad 700-1; 🕒 9am-6pm) offers daily flights to Mexico City. **Continental** (☎ 800-900-50-00; Hidalgo 4503, Edificio Chairel Desp. 205; 🕒 9am-6:30pm Mon-Fri) operates flights between Tampico and Houston, Texas.

BUS

Tampico's bus station is seven annoying kilometers from downtown on Rosalio Bustamente. Facing the station is a long row of taco stalls, but there's no restaurant inside. Nor can you sit anywhere until you've bought a ticket and are admitted to the departure lounges.

First-class buses run to most major towns north of Mexico City and down the Gulf Coast:

Matamoros (US$25, 7hr, 10 daily)
Mexico City (US$26, 10hr, at least 9 daily) To Terminal Norte.
Monterrey (US$30, 7½hr, at least 10 daily)
Nuevo Laredo (US$43, 11hr, 4 daily)
Poza Rica (US$14, 5hr, at least 12 daily)
San Luis Potosí (US$25, 8hr, 6 daily)
Tuxpan (US$11, 3½hr, at least 12 daily)
Veracruz (US$25, 9½hr, 20 daily)

Deluxe and 2nd-class services also run to most of these destinations.

Long-distance 1st-class buses also go to Reynosa, Soto la Marina, Villahermosa and Xalapa. Towns in the Huasteca are mostly reached by 2nd-class local buses. The quickest options are probably Vencedor for Ciudad Valles and Tamazunchale, and Autobuses Blancos for Huejutla.

CAR & MOTORCYCLE

Hwy 180 north of Tampico is a good four-lane divided highway for about 80km, then it's two-lane northeast to Aldama or northwest on Hwy 81 to Ciudad Victoria. Heading south from Tampico, Hwy 180 soars across the Puente Tampico and continues down to Tuxpan. It's an adequate two-lane road, but avoid driving it at night.

If you want a car to explore the Huasteca, contact one of the several rental agencies that are located at Aeropuerto Internacional Francisco Javier Mina:

Avis (☎ 228-05-85)
Budget (☎ 227-18-80)
Dollar (☎ 227-25-75)

Getting Around

Tampico's colectivo taxis are large, old US cars with destinations painted on the doors. They're inexpensive but slower than taxis, with frequent stops.

Transporte Terrestre (☎ 228-45-88) runs colectivo combis from the airport to anywhere in Tampico–Ciudad Madero for about US$6 to US$7, depending on distance.

Taxi tickets from the bus station to the city center cost US$3. A little cheaper, colectivo taxis wait outside the station. From the city center to the bus station, take a 'Perimetral' or 'Perimetral-CC' colectivo (US$0.50) from Olmos, a block south of the zócalo.

CIUDAD VALLES & AROUND

☎ 481 / pop 106,000 / elevation 71m

Ciudad Valles – or simply 'Valles' – is a convenient motorist stop and a practical base for trips into the Huasteca. The town lies just south of the halfway point between Monterrey and Mexico City, at the intersection of Hwy 85 (the Pan-American) and Hwy 70 (running east–west from Tampico to San Luis Potosí).

Orientation & Information

Hwy 85, called Blvd México–Laredo in town, curves north–south through the city. To reach the main plaza, head six blocks west on Av Juárez or Av Hidalgo. Hwy 70 bypasses town on the south side.

The main bus station is at the southern edge of town on Hwy 85 (Carr Nacional México–Laredo). A small, helpful **tourist booth** (🕒 8am-2pm Mon-Fri, 8am-1.30pm Sat) is on the west side of Hwy 85, about 250m north of the bus station. East of the plaza, downtown, the main drags of Hidalgo and Abasolo have several banks with 24-hour ATMs, Internet cafés and local 2nd-class bus stops.

Sights & Activities

While Valles itself is pleasant enough, the more appealing attractions await in the surrounding countryside. They're most easily reached by car, but local buses can get you there...eventually.

TAMUÍN

The important Huastec ceremonial center of **Tamuín** (admission free; 🕒 7am-6pm) flourished from AD 700 to 1200. Today it's one of the few Huastec sites worth visiting, though it's nothing spectacular. The only cleared part of the 170,000-sq-meter site is a plaza with platforms made of river stones. Look for a low bench with two conical altars, extending from a small platform in the middle of the plaza. The bench has the faded remains of some 1000-year-old frescoes believed to represent Quetzalcóatl.

Southwest of that site are two unrestored pyramids on private property, and further southwest is Puente de Dios (God's Bridge), a notch in a ridgeline on the horizon. At the winter solstice, around December 21-22, you can stand on the main Tamuín platform and watch the sun set into the Puente de Dios, with the pair of pyramids exactly between them, all aligned with the Río Tampaón.

To get to the ruins, go to the town of Tamuín, 30km east of Ciudad Valles on Hwy 70. A kilometer or so east, turn south from the highway down a road marked 'Zona Arqueológica' and 'San Vicente.' Follow it roughly south for 5km to another 'Zona Arqueológica' sign, then head west 800m.

Frequent buses between Tampico and Ciudad Valles go through Tamuín. The Vencedor window in town sells tickets for local buses (US$0.50) to the ruins; you'll have to walk the last 800m up the trail.

WATERFALLS & SWIMMING SPOTS

Many rivers flow eastwards from the well-watered slopes of the sierra, forming cascades, waterfalls and shady spots for cool swims. One of the nicest areas is around Tamasopo, 5km north of Hwy 70, 55km west of Ciudad Valles. **Cascadas de Tamasopo** has good swimming and a beautiful natural arch.

The **Cascadas de Micos** are north of Hwy 70, a few kilometers west of Ciudad Valles. They're not so good for swimming, but rental canoes are available on weekends.

Another fun place to get wet is **Coy Parque Acuático** (☎ 382-41-59; Carr Valles-Tamazunchale, Km 35; admission US$5.50; ☒ 9am-6pm Sat & Sun). From April to August it's open daily. On Hwy 85 south of town, the park features water slides and a swimming pool. For more information, stop by the Ciudad Valles tourist information booth.

TANINUL

To reach this small village, head south off Hwy 70 between Ciudad Valles and Tamuín. The turnoff is marked by a sign for Hotel

Taninul (see Sleeping, below), a minor hot springs resort. Next to the hotel, the lovely **Museo Lariab** (☎ 382-00-00; admission US$1; ☒ 9am-3pm Tue-Sun) has well-presented exhibits on the Huasteca, ancient and contemporary.

Sleeping

It's usually a snap to find a place to sleep in downtown Valles.

BUDGET

Hotel Piña (☎ /fax 382-01-83; hotel_pina@yahoo .com.mx; Av Juárez 210; s/d US$18/25, with air-con & TV US$22/33; ☒ ☒) Two blocks east of the plaza, this well-run budget hotel features spotless rooms and bathrooms. Doors seem a bit flimsy, but there's a safe at the front desk. Off-street parking and helpful staff make this a good budget choice.

Hotel Rex (☎ 381-04-11; hotelrex@avantel.net; Av Hidalgo 418; s/d US$22/30; ☒ ☒) Comparable in amenities to the Piña, the Rex is 3½ blocks east of the plaza on busy Av Hidalgo.

MID-RANGE

Hotel Valles (☎ 382-00-50; hotelvalles@prodigy.net .mx; Blvd México-Laredo 36 Nte; s/d US$47/66, trailer sites US$8.50; ☒ ☒ ☒) 500m north or so of downtown Valles is this delightful tropical garden hotel, with stone buildings, a big swimming pool and two excellent restaurants onsite. All rooms are large and air-conditioned; newer ones are fancier. The campground offers trailer sites with full hookups.

Hotel Misión Ciudad Valles (☎ 382-00-66, 800-900-38-00; www.hotelesmision.com.mx; Blvd México-Laredo 15 Nte; s/d US$37/47; ☒ ☒ ☒) Small but comfy rooms at this hotel are bright and happy, with a staff to match. A wide garden with animal topiaries leads to the pool area, and the atmosphere is peaceful and relaxed.

Hotel San Fernando (☎ 382-22-80; fax 382-01-84; Blvd México-Laredo 17 Nte; s/d US$35/41; ☒ ☒ ☒) A well-run place embellished with cheerful, generic art, rooms at the San Fernando are fine and clean. Downstairs, there's Internet access 24 hours a day, even for nonguests.

Hotel Taninul (☎ 388-01-43; taninul@avantel.net; s/d US$48/66; Carr Valles-Tampico Km 15; ☒ ☒ ☒) This resort offers hot mineral springs and moderately luxurious accommodations. Set within a tropical forest reserve, the grounds are a peaceful place to stay for travelers with their own vehicles – located 15km east of Valles, public transportation to Taninul is a hassle.

Eating & Drinking

Some of the best places to eat are the hotel restaurants. Hotel Piña's **La Troje** (dishes US$3-6; 8am-11pm) does US and Mexican standards for around US$3. At Hotel Valles, **El Bosque Steak House** (dishes US$5-12; noon-11pm) does great things with beef; while pleasant **La Palapa** (dishes US$3-12; 8am-10pm) serves up a variety of salads, cocktails and typical regional fare.

Other worthwhile recommendations:
Bonanza (382-48-20; Blvd México-Laredo 19 Nte; buffet US$6.50; 24hr) Satisfy insomniac cravings at Bonanza, where the menu offers Mexican selections at all hours.
Tortas Don Max (381-60-06; Av Juárez 227; tortas US$2-3; 11am-9pm) At the In-N-Out of Valles, your torta is grilled to order in the busy open kitchen.

Getting There & Away

BUS

East of Hwy 85 on the way to Tamazunchale and Mexico City, the user-friendly bus terminal offers card phones and a left-luggage room. A booth sells taxi tickets to the center of town for US$1.75. Many buses are de paso (a bus that started its journey somewhere else but is stopping to let off and take on passengers).

Daily 1st-class buses depart from Ciudad Valles to several destinations:
Matamoros (US$27, 10hr, 11 daily)
Mexico City (US$31, 10hr, 8 daily) To Terminal Norte.
Monterrey (US$29, 8hr, 18 daily)
San Luis Potosí (US$17, 5hr, at least one hourly)
Tampico (US$8.50, 2½hr, at least 12 daily)

Second-class buses run more frequently and cost about 10% less; local routes have buses going to Pachuca, Ciudad Victoria, Tamazunchale and Xilitla.

CAR & MOTORCYCLE

Hwy 70 west of Valles is spectacular as it climbs the Sierra Madre towards San Luis Potosí (262km) on the Altiplano Central. It's a twisting road, and you can get stuck behind slow trucks and buses, so don't count on doing it in a hurry. East to Tampico, Hwy 70 is in worse condition but is straighter and faster. Going south, Hwy 85 heads to Tamazunchale and then southwest toward Mexico City. You can also continue east from Tamazunchale to Huejutla, circling the Huasteca back to Tampico.

AQUISMÓN & AROUND

482 / pop 1800 / elevation 137m
The mellow Huastec village of Aquismón – 45km south of Ciudad Valles and 5km up a side road west of Hwy 85 – holds its colorful market on Saturday but is a slow-paced haven any day of the week. **Video Liz** (Av Juárez 12; per hr US$1; 9am-7pm Mon-Sat) has Internet access and video games to boot.

Mexico's second-deepest pit, the **Sótano de las Golondrinas** (Pit of the Swallows; admission US$1; dawn-dusk), is a 376m-deep, roughly cone-shaped cave 13km southwest of Aquismón. It's home to tens of thousands of swifts that fly out en masse just after sunrise and return at dusk. You'd be wise to hire your own camioneta (4WD truck) and driver – about US$20 round-trip – for the bumpy journey up the rough mountain road. The drive takes about an hour, and a five-minute hike from the road takes you through a Tenec village to the mouth of the cave.

About 30km north of Aquismón (allow 1½ hours from Aquismón), the **Cascada de Tamul** plunges 105m into the pristine Río Santa María. Alternatively, you can reach the falls from Tanchachin, south of Hwy 70, by a 2½-hour river trip – this option is unavailable during flooding, when the falls can be up to 300m wide.

The bustling town of **Tancanhuitz**, called 'Ciudad Santos' on highway signs, is in the heart of the area inhabited by modern-day Huastecs. It's in a narrow, tree-covered valley about 5km southeast of Aquismón, 3km east of Hwy 85. A lively market takes place on Sunday, and pre-Hispanic Huastec remains can be seen near Tampamolón, a few kilometers east.

Tancanhuitz and Aquismón are the centers for the lively festivals of San Miguel Arcángel (September 28 & 29) and the Virgen de Guadalupe (December 12). Huastec dances performed include Las Varitas (Little Twigs) and Zacamsón (Small Music), which both imitate the movements of wild creatures. In its full version, the Zacamsón dance has more than 75 parts, danced at different times of the day and night. At festivals, much drinking of sugarcane alcohol accompanies the performances.

A short stroll from Aquismón's plaza, **Hotel La Mansión** (368-00-04; Carmona 16; s & d US$14, with air-con US$23;) is surrounded by trees, with small, spic-and-span rooms.

Voladores (p659), Papantla

JEFFREY N BECOM

JAMES LYON

Olmec head (p665), San Lorenzo

Cathedral, Veracruz (p673)

JAMES LYON

DAN HERRICK

Garlic seller, Central de Abastos
(p720), Oaxaca City

Local shopkeeper, Teotitlán del Valle (p727),
Oaxaca City

BILL W

Gilded stucco ceiling, Santo Domingo (p797), Oaxaca City

JEFFREY

The simple **Hotel San Cosme** (cnr Zaragoza & Av Juárez; s/d US$10/14; [P]) is right off the plaza, with an open terrace and some rooms with mountain views. Some toilets are seatless, but all rooms are bright and tidy.

Family-run restaurants serving good, inexpensive regional fare can be found around Aquismón's plaza.

Buses from Ciudad Valles or Xilitla can drop you at the crossroads of Hwy 85; taxis (US$2.75) can take you the last 5km to Aquismón.

XILITLA

☎ 489 / pop 5700 / elevation 1151m

On the slopes of the Sierra Madre Oriental, diminutive Xilitla (he-*leet*-la) boasts a 16th-century church and mission, a temperate climate and a rainforest with abundant bird life, wild orchids, stunning waterfalls, caves and walking trails.

Xilitla's most famous attraction is **Las Pozas** (The Pools; admission US$2; ☯ 9am-sunset) – a bizarre concatenation of concrete buildings, bridges, pavilions, sculptures and spiral stairways leading nowhere. This surreal fantasy of Sir Edward James (see box below) is a magical place – a child's dream, but a parent's nightmare: guardrails are nonexistent, and one false step can lead to a nasty end.

Skillfully cast by local workers in the 1960s and 1970s, the concrete and reinforcing rod is beginning to deteriorate in the jungle environment. Swimming holes and waterfalls make this a popular weekend picnic spot, but it can be deserted during the week. Las Pozas is a 25 minute walk east of Xilitla, or a short 2km drive through the jungle; colectivos (US$2) leave frequently from the road behind the church and market.

Built by Edward James' friend Plutarco Gastelum, the wonderfully winding **Posada El Castillo** (☎ 365-00-38; fax 365-00-55; Ocampo 105; s/d US$40/95; [≋]) was formerly a mansion and is now a guesthouse that provides comfortable, unconventional accommodations. The beguilingly pretty posada has unique rooms within a tropical garden haven. Having recently changed management, we can only hope that El Castillo will retain its beautiful atmosphere.

Those entranced enough by Las Pozas can stay there in simple **cabañas** (☎ 365-03-67; cabañas US$25-68; [P] [≋]) scattered throughout the estate. Each has a unique view of the surrounding jungle; all have private bathrooms. Downsides include slippery moss-covered walkways and some musty interiors, so scope out a few before settling in. The café here is open daily from 10am to 6pm.

In an attractive stone building, **Hotel Guzmán** (Corregidora 208; s & d US$14-18) has clean, comfortable rooms with cable TV and fans.

EDWARD JAMES: AN ENGLISH ECCENTRIC

Born in 1907, Edward James was rumored to be the illegitimate grandson of King Edward VII. Educated at Eton and Oxford, James was well endowed with money, charm and social connections. He bankrolled the publication of poems by John Betjeman, supported Dylan Thomas for a short time and sponsored a ballet so his own wife could play the lead.

Haunted by women who tormented him (his mother considered him a social nuisance, while his wife wanted everything to do with his money and nothing to do with him), James entered a period of depression after the breakup of his marriage in the early 1930s. He moved from England to mainland Europe and became absorbed in surrealist art. He collected Picassos, was a patron of Magritte and commissioned work by Dalí.

As WWII threatened, James moved to the USA and visited Mexico for the first time. In 1945 he discovered Xilitla and was besotted by the exotic plants and birds of the rainforest. Initially he devoted himself to cultivating local orchids, but when a freak snowfall destroyed his collection in 1962, he turned to a more enduring medium. With the help of his Mexican friend Plutarco Gastelum, he hired local workers to craft giant, colored, concrete flowers beside his idyllic jungle stream.

For the next 17 years, James and Gastelum created ever larger and stranger structures, many of which were never finished. James died in 1984, making no provision to maintain his creation, which is already decomposing into another Mexican ruin. As Salvador Dalí reputedly said: 'Edward James is crazier than all the surrealists put together. They pretend, but he is the real thing.'

Restaurant Cayo's (☎ 365-00-44; Alvarado 117; dishes US$3.50-8; ☽ 9am-9pm) serves up hearty regional classics accompanied by huge valley and mountain views, a jukebox full of romantic ballads and a familial atmosphere. Down the street, **La Casa Vieja Café** (Hidalgo 101; dishes US$4-9; ☽ 9am-9pm Sat & Sun) has dark wood furnishings and some fortifyingly strong coffee that you can sip with your meal.

Run by a co-op of Nahua women, **La Flor de Café** (☎ 365-03-76; Hidalgo 215; comida corrida US$2; ☽ 6:30am-9pm) makes delicious meals from locally cultivated food. This comedor provides a community gathering place, where folks can bring their own food or partake of the café's seasonal aguas frescas, tasty tamales and egg-and-veggie creations.

Xilitla can be reached from Ciudad Valles, Tampico or Querétaro on Vencedor's comfortable 2nd-class buses. Hwy 120, heading west to Jalpan then southwest toward Querétaro, is an exciting route through the Sierra Gorda (see p641). Southeast of Xilitla, Hwy 85 veers through Tamazunchale before climbing steeply to Ixmiquilpan (see p191), then continues to Pachuca. This is the most direct route from the Huasteca to Mexico City. It's a steep but scenic route over the Sierra Madre. Start early to avoid mist and fog.

HUEJUTLA DE REYES
☎ 789 / pop 34,000

On the northern edge of Hidalgo state in the semitropical lowlands, Huejutla is a cheery town with a wacky, huge central plaza. Its 16th-century fortress-monastery was built when this area was frontier territory and foreign newcomers were subject to attack by indignant indigenous folks. The big Sunday market attracts many Nahua people from outlying villages.

Several banks with 24-hour ATMs are clustered off the plaza around Morelos and Hidalgo. On Morelos, a block up from Cuautémoc, is an Internet café open until midnight daily.

Hotel Oviedo (☎ 896-05-59; Morelos 12; s/d US$14/18; P ☒) is a smashing deal, featuring clean, elegantly furnished rooms with TV and windows facing a central courtyard. Polished wood furniture and friendly management give a homey feel.

A way up the street, **Hotel Posada Huejutla** (☎ 896-03-03; Morelos 32; s & d US$29; P ☒ ☒) has

flagstone walkways, a Spanish-style fountain and a poolside view of the neighboring cliff face. In this peaceful atmosphere, the rooms come with air-con, phones, TV and patio seating.

Enjoy some tiny tacos while Huejutla's street life passes by the perky **Refrequería La Gloria** (Hidalgo, on the plaza; tacos US$0.50, fruit juice US$0.75; ☽ 9am-9pm Mon-Sat).

SOUTH OF HUEJUTLA

Hwy 105 rolls through lush, hilly farmland near Tampico, but south of Huejutla it climbs into the lovely Sierra Madre Oriental. It's a tortuous, foggy road to Pachuca. On the way you'll pass old monasteries at **Molango** and **Zacualtipán**.

The highway then leaves the Sierra Madre and drops several hundred meters to scenic **Metzquititlán**, in the fertile Río Tulancingo Valley. The village of **Metztitlán**, 23km northwest up the valley, sports a fairly well preserved monastery. It was the center of an Otomí state that the Aztecs couldn't conquer.

Back on Hwy 105, an 800m climb up from the Tulancingo Valley, about 100km by road, brings you to **Atotonilco El Grande**, 34km from Pachuca (see p191).

NORTHERN VERACRUZ

Between the coast and southern end of the Sierra Madre Oriental, the northern half of Veracruz is rolling plains. The Laguna de Tamiahua stretches 90km along the coast, separated from the Gulf of Mexico by a series of sandbars and islands. It shelters isolated though sometimes polluted beaches along the coast and offers fishing and birding. The major archaeological attraction is El Tajín, usually reached from Papantla.

Although your vehicle may be stopped and searched at army checkpoints along this coast, the soldiers are usually courteous to tourists.

TUXPAN
☎ 783 / pop 75,000

Tuxpan (sometimes spelled Túxpam) is a fishing town and minor oil port near the mouth of the Río Tuxpan, 300km north of Veracruz and 190km south of Tampico. With a wide river and nothing much to do, the town is a pleasant stop for resting and refueling. Playa Norte, the beach 12km to the east, is popular with vacationing Mexicans, though it's no idyllic seaside resort.

Orientation & Information

The downtown area, on the Río Tuxpan's north bank, spreads six blocks upstream from the high bridge spanning the river. The riverfront road, Blvd Reyes Heroles, passes under the bridge and runs east to Playa Norte. A block inland from Blvd Reyes Heroles is hotel-heavy Av Juárez. Parque Reforma, at Juárez' west end, serves as the heart of downtown and is popular in the evening.

Tuxpan's **tourist office** (☎ 834-01-77; ground flr, Palacio Municipal; ☼ 9am-8pm Mon-Sat) offers basic maps and tourist brochures. There are card phones in Parque Reforma, and ATM-endowed banks stand nearby. North of Juárez, find the post office several blocks up on Mina, and Internet cafés along Zapata.

Sights & Activities

Other than the small museums, there isn't much to see around Tuxpan.

The recently refurbished **Museo Arqueológico** (Parque Reforma; admission free; ☼ 9am-1pm & 4-7pm Mon-Fri), on the west side of the park, exhibits Totonac and Huastec artifacts.

On the river's south side, the **Museo de la Amistad México-Cuba** (Mexican-Cuban Friendship Museum; Obregón s/n; donation requested; ☼ 8am-7pm) commemorates Fidel Castro's 1956 stay in Tuxpan. After planning the Cuban revolution here, he sailed for Cuba with 82 comrades in a converted private yacht. The museum has a yellowing collection of maps, B&W photos and displays on José Martí and Ché Guevara. To get there, take one of the small boats (US$0.25) across the river, walk several blocks south to Obregón, then turn right. The museum is at the end of Obregón, just before you reach the river again.

Tuxpan's beach, **Playa Norte** – is a wide strip stretching 20km north from the Río Tuxpan's mouth, 12km east of town. Its beauty is diminished by a power station 2km north of the river mouth, but the water and sand are fairly clean and, apart from holidays and weekends, it's almost empty.

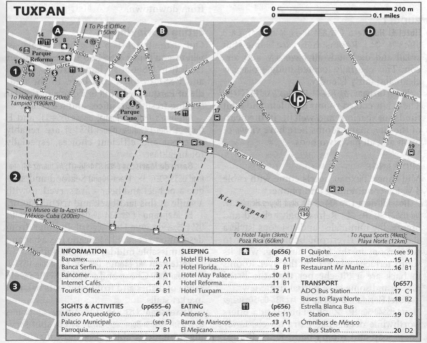

TUXPAN

INFORMATION		SLEEPING 🏠	(p656)	El Quijote	(see 9)
Banamex	1 A1	Hotel El Huasteco	8 A1	Pastelísimo	15 A1
Banca Serfín	2 A1	Hotel Florida	9 B1	Restaurant Mr Mante	16 B1
Bancomer	3 A1	Hotel May Palace	10 A1		
Internet Cafés	4 A1	Hotel Reforma	11 B1	TRANSPORT	(p657)
Tourist Office	5 A1	Hotel Tuxpam	12 A1	ADO Bus Station	17 C1
				Buses to Playa Norte	18 B2
SIGHTS & ACTIVITIES	(pp655–6)	EATING 🍴	(p656)	Estrella Blanca Bus	
Museo Arqueológico	6 A1	Antonio's	(see 11)	Station	19 D2
Palacio Municipal	(see 5)	Barra de Mariscos	13 A1	Ómnibus de México	
Parroquia	7 B1	El Mejicano	14 A1	Bus Station	20 D2

To Post Office (150m)

To Hotel Riviera (20m); Tampico (190km)

To Museo de la Amistad México-Cuba (200m)

To Hotel Tajín (3km); Poza Rica (60km)

To Aqua Sports (4km); Playa Norte (12km)

CENTRAL GULF COAST

Palapas serve seafood and sell souvenirs. Local buses (US$0.75, 25 minutes) marked 'Playa' leave every 20 minutes from the south side of Blvd Reyes Heroles and drop you at the south end of the beach.

Aqua Sports (☎ 837-02-59; Carr Tuxpan-La Barra Km 8.5; 4-6 dives from US$175 per person; ☽ 9am-6pm), around 4km from downtown, is an established scuba-diving operation. For groups of six or so, they offer dive trips to the nearby reefs or Isla de Lobos. They can also arrange fishing trips, water-skiing and windsurfing.

Festivals & Events
A big fishing tournament brings hundreds of visitors to Tuxpan in late June or early July. Festivities for the **Assumption** (August 15) continue for a week with folk-dancing contests, bullfights and fireworks.

Sleeping
As usual along the coast, accommodations here can be full during holidays and summer, but discounts may be available at other times. A few cheap hotels and campsites are available at Playa Norte.

BUDGET
Hotel El Huasteco (☎ 834-18-59; Morelos 41; s & d US$18-26; ☒) Rooms here are somewhat small and dark, but all have TV and air-con. This centrally located budget place is clean and fairly friendly.

Hotel Tuxpam (☎ 834-41-10; Mina 2; s/d US$21/24) These fan-cooled rooms are plain and a bit tired, but spacious and well lit. In the heart of the city, many rooms here have views of town and all have two beds.

MID-RANGE
Mid-range Tuxpan hotels come with cable TV, air-conditioning and phone.

Hotel Riviera (☎ 834-53-49; Blvd Reyes Heroles 17; s/d US$29/34; P ☒) Refreshingly relaxed and breezy, the minimalist and spacious Riviera stands on the riverfront boulevard. Try to get a room in the front building, with its sunny terrace looking onto the river. Rooms in back are a bit cheaper than the listed prices, and some have partial river views.

Hotel Florida (☎ 834-02-22; fax 834-06-50; Juárez 23; s/d US$40/50; P ☒ ☒) The Florida offers worthwhile details like extra towels, fancy floral soap and roomy bathrooms. Rooms

are big, and the more expensive ones come with river views. The helpful and attentive staff are a bonus here.

Hotel Reforma (☎ 834-02-10; hotelreforma@prodigy.net.mx; Av Juárez 25; s/d US$54/63; P ☒ ☒) The sparkly Reforma has smallish rooms with nice wooden furniture and marble countertops in the bathrooms. A courtyard with a colonial fountain brightens the interior, while sunny views of town offset the lack of river vistas.

Hotel May Palace (☎ 834-88-81; fax 834-88-82; Av Juárez 44; s/d US$52/60; P ☒ ☒ ☒) Bonuses at this hotel include in-room fridges, king size beds and a pool on the wooden roof deck with an expansive view of the river and town. Though a bit worn around the edges, this is a good higher-end choice.

TOP END
Hotel Tajín (☎ 834-22-60; misiontajin@prodigy.net.mx; Carr a Cobos Km 2.5; s & d US$74; P ☒ ☒) Undergoing renovation at the time of research, the Tajín's pool, spacious rooms and on-site entertainment venues should be looking good by the time you arrive. The downside is its location – across the river, removed from downtown.

Eating & Drinking
Out at the beach is a long line of palapas, where you'll pay US$4.50 for fish soup or fresh fish, US$6 for a large shrimp cocktail and US$1.25 for a cold beer. In the middle of Parque Reforma is a circle of tiendas serving fresh fruit, juices and ice cream.

Antonio's (Hotel Reforma; dishes US$4-11) and **El Quijote** (Hotel Florida; dishes US$4-9) are reliably excellent and efficient choices, especially for breakfast.

Barra de Mariscos (☎ 834-46-01; Av Juárez 44; seafood US$3.50-7; ☽ 11am-10pm) Seafood and sangría – or beef and beer – are served up with a smile at this laid-back and friendly joint.

El Mejicano (☎ 834-89-04; Morelos 49; buffet US$4.25; ☽ 8:30am-11pm Tue-Sat) Popular from desayuno to cena, El Mejicano has a bar and an unmissable midday bargain buffet.

Restaurant Mr Mante (Av Juárez 8; dishes US$3-7; ☽ 11am-9pm) Cheap and sociable, with a wide range of dishes and front-row seats to street market stalls.

Pastelísimo (☎ 834-20-14; Arteaga 42; pastries US$2.25; ☽ 9am-8pm Tue-Sun) A sweet spot serving fresh, delectable cakes and coffee.

Getting There & Around

Book 1st-class buses out of Tuxpan as far ahead as possible, as all are de paso and only a limited number of seats are reserved for passengers boarding here. You might have to take a 2nd-class bus to Poza Rica and a 1st-class one from there. The modern ADO (1st-class) station, on Rodríguez half a block north of the river, is also used by UNO deluxe buses.

Ómnibus de México (ODM; 1st-class) is under the bridge on the north side of the river. Estrella Blanca, on the corner of Constitución and Alemán, two blocks east of the bridge, runs regular 2nd-class service for about 10% less than ADO; Turistar, Futura, ABC Blanco, and Coordinados offer a few 1st-class buses from here. Daily departures:

Matamoros ADO (US$39, 11hr; 2 daily) Also several 2nd-class services.

Mexico City UNO (US$27, 4hr, 1 daily); ADO (US$17, 4hr, 16 daily); ODM (US$17, 4hr, 7 daily) To Terminal Norte.

Papantla ADO (US$3.50, 1½hr, 7 daily)

Poza Rica ADO (US$3.50, 45mins, at least hourly; 2nd-class every 20 minutes)

Tampico ADO (US$12.50, 3½hr, 26 daily; 2nd-class every 30 minutes)

Veracruz ADO (US$15.50, 5½hr, 15 daily)

Villahermosa ADO (US$44, 12hr, 4 daily)

Xalapa ADO (US$16, 5½hr, 7 daily)

Covered launches (US$0.25) ferry passengers across the river.

AROUND TUXPAN

Tamiahua, 43km north from Tuxpan by paved road, is at the southern end of Laguna de Tamiahua. It has a few seafood-shack restaurants, and you can rent boats for fishing or trips out to the lagoon's barrier island. From Tuxpan take a 1st-class ODM bus (US$1.50) or a more frequent 2nd-class bus.

Castillo de Teayo, 23km up a bumpy road west off Hwy 180 (the turnoff is 18km from Poza Rica), was one of the southernmost points of the Huastec civilization from about AD 800. Beside its main plaza is a steep, 13m-high restored pyramid topped by a small temple. It's in Toltec style and was probably built during that civilization's domination of the area, sometime between AD 900 and 1200.

Around the base of the pyramid are some stone sculptures that have been found in the surrounding area. Some of these are in Huastec style, while others are thought to be the work of Aztecs who controlled the area briefly before the Spanish conquest.

POZA RICA

☎ 782 / pop 172,000

Congested and polluted, the oil city of Poza Rica is at the junction of highways 180 and 130. You might have to change buses here, but it's not worth staying the night.

If you do get stuck, there's the convenient **Auto Hotel Los Arcos** (☎ 822-16-00; fax 823-92-10; Puebla 308; s & d US$23; P), a block from the bus station. Though parked cars are concealed within green-curtained carports and rooms can be rented by the six-hour chunk (US$14), it's a clean, respectable enough place.

Alternatively, choose the pleasingly reliable **Best Western Hotel Poza Rica** (☎ 822-01-12; fax 823-20-32; cnr Kehoe & 10 Ote; s/d US$66/73; P), downtown.

The main Poza Rica bus station, on Puebla east off Blvd Lázaro Cárdenas, has 2nd-class and some 1st-class buses. Most 1st-class buses leave from the adjoining ADO building, including departures to Mexico City (Terminal Norte; US$13, five hours, at least one hourly), Pachuca (US$9, four hours, at least two daily), Papantla (US$1, 30 minutes, at least one hourly throughout the day and evening), Tampico (US$14, five hours, at least one hourly), Tuxpan (US$3, 45 minutes, at least one hourly) and Veracruz (US$12, five hours, about one hourly).

For El Tajín, take one of Transportes Papantla's frequent buses to Coyutla (US$1) and ask to get off at the turnoff marked 'Desviación El Tajín,' about 30 minutes from Poza Rica. From the turnoff, the entrance to El Tajín is a pleasant 500m stroll down the road. Buses to El Chote, Agua Dulce or San Andrés by Autotransportes Coatzintla and other 2nd-class companies also go past the Desviación El Tajín.

POZA RICA TO PACHUCA

The 200km Poza Rica–Pachuca road, Hwy 130, is the direct approach to Mexico City from the northern part of Veracruz state. This scenic, misty route climbs up to the Sierra Madre, across the semitropical north of Puebla state and into Hidalgo. The area's population has a high proportion of Nahua and Totonac indigenous people.

Huauchinango, roughly halfway between Poza Rica and Pachuca, is the center of a flower-growing area. You'll also find embroidered textiles in the busy Saturday market. A weeklong flower festival, known as the *feria*, includes traditional dances and reaches its peak on the third Friday in Lent. This is a fascinating time to visit the town. **Acaxochitlán**, 25km west of Huauchinango, has a Sunday market; specialties include fruit wine and preserved fruit.

The traditional Nahua village of **Pahuatlán** is the source of many of the cloths you'll see around central Mexico, woven with multicolored designs of animals and plants. Reach it by turning north off Hwy 130, about 10km past Acaxochitlán. A spectacular dirt road winds several hundred meters down to the village, which holds a sizable Sunday market. About half an hour's drive beyond Pahuatlán is **San Pablito**, an Otomí village where colorfully embroidered blouses abound.

Hwy 130 climbs steeply to Tulancingo, in the state of Hidalgo. See p191 for details on the rest of this route to Pachuca.

PAPANTLA
☎ 784 / pop 49,000 / elevation 196m

Set on a hillside, Papantla is the perfect base for visiting El Tajín as well as a laid-back, happy destination in its own right. The zócalo is delightful on Sunday evenings, when half the town is out dancing and smooching.

Some Totonacs still wear traditional costume here – men in loose white shirts and trousers, women in embroidered blouses and *quechquémitls*. Because the town is in the center of a vanilla-growing region, a fresh, sweet aroma pervades the area.

Orientation & Information
Papantla lies just off Hwy 180, which runs southeast from Poza Rica. The center of town is uphill from the main road. From the zócalo, uphill (facing the cathedral) is south, and downhill is north.

To get to the town center from the ADO bus station, turn left as you go out, then follow Av Carranza a couple of hundred meters west to Calle 20 de Noviembre. Turn left and climb 20 de Noviembre past the Transportes Papantla bus terminal and market to the zócalo. The **tourist office** (☎ 842-0026; Palacio Municipal; ☽ 9am-3pm & 6-9pm Mon-Fri) is hidden away on the ground floor of the Palacio Municipal, opposite the cathedral on 16 de Septiembre, a block uphill from the zócalo.

There's a fast connection at the **Internet café** (per hr US$1; ☽ 8:30am-10:30pm; ☒) on the west end of the plaza, upstairs next to La Hacienda restaurant (see Eating, opposite). To get to the **post office**, take the street west of the church, then right on 16 de Septiembre. Walk four blocks, going left at the fork; you'll find the post office on your left.

Sights
Officially called Parque Téllez, the **zócalo** is terraced into the hillside below the Iglesia de

---

PLAIN VANILLA

Vanilla is sexy. What's not seductive about the planet's only known edible orchid – an aphrodisiac, a spice second only to saffron as the most expensive in the world, a coveted pod once used to pay taxes to the Aztecs?

Now so commonplace that it connotes the bland and unoriginal, the sweetly fragrant yellow orchid known as *vanilla planifolia* was first cultivated by the Totonacs, who believed that vanilla was a gift from the gods and carefully guarded their methods of curing the pods. Mixed with cacao and other spices, vanilla is the historically overlooked but equally valued ingredient of *xocolatl*, the Aztec concoction that introduced chocolate to the rest of the world.

Still precious in value, real vanilla can take up to three years to cultivate and cure, and due to its expense and popularity, many products – from paint to perfumes to ice cream – incorporate synthetic vanilla flavor rather than the real thing.

But if you lust for the real thing, Papantla celebrates its Festival de Vainilla (Vanilla Festival; see Festivals & Events, opposite) on June 18. Local hotels can arrange visits to vanilla plantations; you'll catch the orchids blooming in April and May, and harvest time in early December. In the markets in town, you can pick up vanilla pods, extracts and liqueurs throughout the year.

la Asunción. Beneath this Franciscan cathedral, a 50m-long mural facing the square depicts Totonac and Veracruz history. A serpent stretches along most of the mural, linking a pre-Hispanic stone carver, El Tajín's Pirámide de los Nichos and an oil rig.

At the top of the hill towers Papantla's **volador monument**. This 1988 statue portrays a volador musician playing his pipe as preparation for the four fliers to launch themselves into space. To reach the monument, take the street heading uphill from the southwest corner of the cathedral yard; at the end of the road, hang a left. Spanish inscriptions around its base give an explanation of the ritual. The spot serves as Lovers' Point on weekend nights.

On the edge of town on the road to El Tajín, the humble **Museo de Cultura Totonaca** (16 de Septiembre; admission US$1.50; 9am-6pm Mon-Sat) has exhibits on Totonac culture from pre-Hispanic times to the present. The Spanish-speaking Totonac guides give detailed explanations and can answer questions. White micros from 16 de Septiembre can get you here for a couple of pesos.

Festivals & Events

The fantastic **Corpus Christi festival**, in late May and early June, is the big annual event. In Papantla it's a celebration of Totonac culture, and the town is swamped for the parades, dances and other cultural events. The main procession is on the first Sunday; voladores fly two or three times a day, and costumed performers do traditional dances.

Papantla's other major celebration is the **Festival de Vainilla** (Vanilla Festival) on June 18, featuring indigenous dancers, gastronomical delights sold in street stalls and vanilla products galore.

Sleeping

Papantla has several good mid-range hotels. All of these places offer rooms with TVs and air-con.

Hotel Tajín (842-01-21; fax 842-10-62; Núñez 104; s/d US$26/39, with air-con US$42/55;) Look for the Hotel Tajín's pinkish façade several meters east of the zócalo mural's left end. Easily the coziest and most charming place in town, the Hotel Tajín has well-kept quarters. Rooms in front have balconies overlooking the town and surrounding hillsides.

Hotel Provincia Express (842-16-45; hotprovi@prodigy.net.mx; Enríquez 103; s & d US$30-44;) Facing the plaza, the Provincia has bright, spacious quarters. Light sleepers should avoid the rooms with appealing little balconies facing the plaza.

Hotel Totonacapán (842-12-20; cnr 20 de Noviembre & Olivo; s/d US$23/25;) A quiet place a few blocks downhill from the zócalo, this hotel has roomy elevators and wide, wood-paneled doors opening onto sparse – but large and comfy – rooms with cable TV.

Hotel Pulido (842-10-79; Enríquez 205; s & d US$15-32;) The simple, fan-only rooms here are slightly grungy but make an OK budget option. Find it 250m east from the downhill side of the zócalo.

Eating

Papantla's pleasing eateries, which include one vegetarian venue, are attractively priced.

Plaza Pardo (842-00-59; Enríquez 103 Altos; dishes US$3.50-6; 7:30am-11:30pm) Upstairs on the downhill side of the zócalo, Plaza Pardo has balcony tables with a terrific view of the cathedral and volador monument. Breakfasts here are the best in town, but it's also the perfect place for beers in the evening.

La Hacienda (Reforma 100 Altos; US$3-6; 7:30am-11:30pm) For a different angle on the hilltop volador, try La Hacienda. The friendly staff bring the usual antojitos and a mean flan.

Restaurant Sorrento (Enríquez 105; dishes US$2.50-4; 7:30am-midnight-ish) Dig into good, economical Mexican fare and watch the burros swing by the Sorrento.

Shayā Michān (16 de Septiembre 104 & Nuñez 204; comida corrida US$2.75; 9am-10pm Mon-Sat) Everything on the vegetarian set menu at family-run Shayā Michān is made fresh daily. The huge meal – an excellent deal – includes courses like *nopales rellenos* (stuffed cactus) and comes with a jug of agua fresca. The addresses indicate different entrances to the same restaurant.

Shopping

As Mexico's leading vanilla-growing center, Papantla offers quality vanilla extract, vanilla pods and *figuras* (pods woven into the shapes of flowers, insects or crucifixes). Try the regional vanilla liquor or vanilla-infused cigarettes. **Mercado Hidalgo**, at the northwest corner of the zócalo, has some pretty

Totonac costumes, good baskets and vanilla souvenirs. **Mercado Juárez**, at the southwest corner opposite the cathedral, sells mainly food.

Getting There & Away

Few long-distance buses stop at Papantla's quaint station. Most are de paso, so book your bus out of town as soon as possible. If desperate, go to Poza Rica and get one of the much more frequent buses from there. ADO is the only 1st-class line serving Papantla. The main 2nd-class alternative, costing about 10% less than ADO and with much slower, older vehicles, is Transportes Papantla (TP), with slow, old vehicles. ADO destinations:

Mexico City (US$14, 5hr, 6 daily) To Terminal Norte.
Poza Rica (US$1, 30mins, about one hourly) TP every 15 minutes.
Tampico (US$15, 5½hr, 3 daily)
Tuxpan (US$3, 1½hr, 3 daily)
Veracruz (US$11, 4hr, 8 daily)
Xalapa (US$12, 4hr, 10 daily)

White microbuses (US$1, hourly) make the 30-minute drive to El Tajín from 16 de Septiembre, the street on the uphill side of the cathedral. Those marked 'El Tajín' on their fronts will take you to the parking lot at the entrance to El Tajín.

EL TAJÍN

Among verdant hills a few kilometers from Papantla lies the peaceful site of El Tajín – Totonac for 'thunder,' 'lightning' or 'hurricane,' all of which can happen here in summer. The ancient Totonacs may have occupied El Tajín in its later stages, but most of it was built before that civilization became important. It is the highest achievement of Classic Veracruz civilization, about which little is known.

El Tajín was first occupied about AD 100, but most of what's visible was built around AD 600 or 700. The years AD 600 to 900 saw its zenith as a town and ceremonial center. Around AD 1200 the site was abandoned, possibly after attacks by Chichimecs, and lay unknown to the Spaniards until about 1785, when an official found it while looking for illegal tobacco plantings.

Among El Tajín's special features are rows of square niches on the sides of buildings, numerous ball courts, and sculptures

depicting human sacrifice connected with the ball game. The archaeologist who did much of the excavation here, José García Payón, believed that El Tajín's niches and stone mosaics symbolized day and night, light and dark, and life and death in a universe composed of dualities, though many are skeptical of this interpretation. Despite extensive reconstruction in 1991, El Tajín retains an aura of mystery.

Information

The **Tajín site** (admission US$3.50; 🕙 8am-6pm) covers about 10 sq km, and you need to walk a few kilometers to see it all. There's little shade and it can get blazingly hot, especially in the middle of the day – a water bottle and hat are highly recommended.

Bordering the parking lot are stalls selling food and handicrafts. The visitors center has a restaurant, souvenir shops, a left-luggage room, an information desk and an excellent museum with a model of the site. Exhibits are labeled in English and Spanish. Those seeking more information should look for the book *Tajín: Mystery*

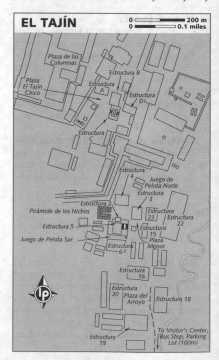

EL TAJÍN

0 — 200 m
0 — 0.1 miles

Plaza de las Columnas
Plaza El Tajín Chico
Estructura A
Estructura B
Estructura D
Estructura C
Estructura 4
Juego de Pelota Norte
Estructura 3
Estructura 2
Pirámide de los Nichos
Estructura 23
Estructura 22
Estructura 5
Juego de Pelota Sur
Estructura 6
Plaza Menor
Plaza 15
Estructura 16
Estructura 20
Plaza del Arroyo
Estructura 18
Estructura 19
To Visitor's Center, Bus Stop, Parking Lot (100m)

and Beauty, by Leonardo Zaleta, sometimes available (in English, French, German and Spanish) at the souvenir shops.

Sights

Two main parts of the site have been cleared and restored: the lower area, containing the Pirámide de los Nichos (Pyramid of the Niches); and, uphill, a group of buildings known as 'El Tajín Chico' (Little Tajín). Most features of the site are known by the labels used in a 1966 INAH survey, with many called simply 'Estructura' (Structure) followed by a number or letter.

PLAZA MENOR

Beyond the unremarkable Plaza del Arroyo you come to the Plaza Menor (Lesser Plaza), part of El Tajín's main ceremonial center, with a low platform in the middle. A statue on the first level of Estructura 5, a pyramid on the plaza's west side, represents either a thunder-and-rain god who was especially important at El Tajín, or Mictlantecuhtli, a death god. All of the structures around this plaza were probably topped by small temples, and some were decorated with red or blue paint.

JUEGO DE PELOTA SUR

Some 17 ball courts have been found at El Tajín. The Juego de Pelota Sur (Southern Ball Court), between Estructuras 5 and 6, dates from about 1150 and is the most famous of the courts owing to the six relief carvings on its walls depicting various aspects of the ball-game ritual.

The panel on the northeast corner (on the right as you enter the court from the Plaza Menor) is the easiest to make out. At its center, three ballplayers wearing knee pads are depicted carrying out a ritual postgame sacrifice: one player is about to plunge a knife into the chest of another, whose arms are held by the third. A skeletal death god on the left and a presiding figure on the right look on. Another death god hovers over the victim.

The central north wall panel depicts the ceremonial drinking of pulque – a figure holding a drinking vessel signals to another leaning on a pulque container. Quetzalcóatl sits cross-legged beside Tláloc, the fanged god of water and lightning. The panel at the northwest corner of the same wall is

thought to represent a ceremony that preceded the ball game. Two players face each other, one with crossed arms, the other holding a dagger. Speech symbols emerge from their mouths. To their right is a figure with the mask of a coyote, the animal that conducted sacrificial victims to the next world. The death god is on the right.

The southwest corner panel seems to show the initiation of a young man into a band of warriors associated with the eagle. A central figure lies on a table; to the left, another holds a bell. Above is an eagle-masked figure, possibly a priest. The central south wall panel, another pulque-drinking scene, shows Tláloc squatting as he passes a gourd to someone in a fish mask who appears to be in a pulque vat. On the left is the maguey plant, from which pulque is made. Maguey is not native to this part of Mexico, which points to influences from central Mexico (possibly Toltec) at this late stage of El Tajín. On the southeast corner panel, a man offers spears or arrows to another, perhaps also in the eagle-warrior initiation ceremony.

PIRÁMIDE DE LOS NICHOS

The 35-sq-meter Pyramid of the Niches is just off the Plaza Menor by the northwest corner of Estructura 5. The six lower levels, each surrounded by rows of small square niches, climb to a height of 18m. The wide staircase on the east side was a late addition, built over some of the niches. Archaeologists believe that there were originally 365 niches, suggesting that the building may have been used as a kind of calendar. The insides of the niches were painted red and their frames blue. The only similar known building, probably of earlier date, is a seven-level niched pyramid at Yohualichán near Cuetzalán, 50km southwest of El Tajín.

EL TAJÍN CHICO

The path north toward El Tajín Chico passes the Juego de Pelota Norte (Northern Ball Court), which is smaller and older than the southern court but also bears carvings on its sides.

Many of the buildings of El Tajín Chico have geometric stone mosaic patterns known as 'Greco' (Greek); similar patterns are found in decorations at Mitla (Oaxaca), a later site. The main buildings, probably

9th century, are on the east and north sides of Plaza El Tajín Chico. Estructura C, on the east side, with three levels and a staircase facing the plaza, was initially painted blue. Estructura B, next to it, was probably home to priests or officials. Estructura D, behind Estructura B and off the plaza, has a large lozenge-design mosaic and a passage underneath.

Estructura A, on the plaza's north side, has a façade like a Mayan roof comb, with a stairway leading up through an arch in the middle. This corbeled arch, its two sides jutting closer to each other until they are joined at the top by a single slab, is typical of Mayan architecture, and its presence here is yet another oddity in the confusing jigsaw puzzle of pre-Hispanic cultures.

Uphill to the northwest of Plaza El Tajín Chico is the as-yet-unreconstructed Plaza de las Columnas (Plaza of the Columns), one of the site's most important structures. It originally housed an open patio inside, with adjoining buildings stretching over the hillside to cover an area of nearly 200m by 100m. Most of this area is heavily overgrown and fenced off with 'no access' signs. Some reassembled columns are displayed in the museum at the visitors center.

Voladores Performances

The Totonac voladores rite – traditionally carried out only once a year, but now performed almost daily for visitors – is a sort of slow-motion bungee jump from the top of a vertiginously tall pole. The rite begins with five men in richly decorated costumes climbing to the top of the pole. Four of them sit on the edges of a small, square frame at the top, arrange their ropes and then rotate the frame to twist the ropes around the pole. The fifth man dances on the tiny platform above them while playing a *chirimía*, a small drum with a flute attached. When he stops playing, the others fall backward in unison. Arms outstretched, they revolve gracefully around the pole and descend to the ground, upside-down, as their ropes unwind.

This ancient ceremony is packed with symbolic meanings. One interpretation is that it's a fertility rite and the fliers make invocations to the four corners of the universe before falling to the ground, bringing with them the sun and rain. It is also noted that each flier circles the pole 13 times, giv-

ing a total of 52 revolutions. The number 52 not only is the number of weeks in the modern year but also was an important number in pre-Hispanic Mexico, which had two calendars – one corresponding to the 365-day solar year, the other to a ritual year of 260 days. A day in one calendar coincided with a day in the other calendar every 52 solar years.

Totonacs carry out the exciting voladores rite most days from a 30m-high steel pole beside the visitors center. Performances are usually around noon, 2pm and 4pm; before they start, a Totonac in traditional dress requests donations (US$2) from the audience.

Getting There & Away

Frequent buses journey here from Papantla (see p660) and Poza Rica (see p657).

SOUTH OF PAPANTLA

Hwy 180 runs near the coast for most of the 230km from Papantla to Veracruz. Strong currents can make for risky swimming here.

Tecolutla

☎ 766 / pop 3800

This minor seaside resort has a relaxed, enjoyable atmosphere on holidays, when it's crowded with families and students. A wide, sandy, palm-fringed beach lines one side of town, and the mouth of Río Tecolutla is on the other. Launches make trips into the mangroves for fishing and wildlife watching. Prices for accommodations skyrocket during high season, quadrupling during Semana Santa.

A 15-minute stroll from the plaza, **Hotel Oasis** (☎ 846-02-75; Agustín Lara 8; s & d US$14-27; **P**) features large, simple, pretty rooms across from the bucolic beach. Upstairs rooms are bigger and get better breezes through their bamboo screens. The friendly managers can pick you up from the town center if you call ahead.

Hotel Posada del Conquistador (☎ /fax 846-02-81; cnr Obregón & Centenario; s/d US$19/22; **P** 🛇 🛋) is a great bargain, centrally located near the plaza and malecón. This comfortable posada boasts a cute pool, bright lime-green paint job and decorative tiles.

The small, marlin-mosaic swimming pool at **Hotel Posada Dora Emilia** (☎ 846-01-85; Hidalgo 45; s & d US$12-27; **P** 🛇 🛋) is surrounded by cheerful smallish rooms – more expensive ones have air-con. This place has a nice family vibe and friendly management. Down the street, the low-key **Hotel Álbatros** (☎ 846-00-02; cnr Hidalgo & Prieto; s & d US$14-35; 🔀) offers clean and bright rooms around a courtyard full of healthy plants.

Tecolutla abounds in cheap, good restaurants, and there are lots of busy taco stalls on the plaza. Near the plaza, **Merendero la Galera** (☎ 845-16-71; Obregón s/n; menúes económicos US$2.75-3.25; 🕙 8am-10pm) has a festive atmosphere, and everything is prepared fresh to order.

The road to Tecolutla branches off Hwy 180 at Gutiérrez Zamora. ADO and Transportes Papantla buses go to and from Papantla; in Gutiérrez Zamora, colectivos pick up passengers opposite the ADO station.

Costa Esmeralda

The 20km Emerald Coast sports a scattering of hotels and trailer parks along a strip between Hwy 180 and the dark, sandy beach. It's a popular summer and holiday spot but deserted most of the year. At the north end of the coast, **La Guadalupe** is an OK stop. Further south, hotels get more upscale and expensive; near the village of Casitas, check out the sparkly **Hotel Playa Paraíso** (☎ 232-321-00-44; Carr 180, Km 81; s & d US$40; P 🔀 🏊), with pool and attractive beach setting.

At the mouth of the Río Bobos, the small fishing town of **Nautla** dozes on the south side of a toll bridge. There's seafood at a couple of simple places near the brown beach.

Laguna Verde & Villa Rica

Mexico's controversial first nuclear power station is at Laguna Verde, about 80km north of Veracruz port on Hwy 180. The first unit began operating in 1989 and the second in 1996, but government plans for more reactors have been scrapped in the face of public protest. Concerns about the safety of this reactor have led to suggestions that it be replaced with natural-gas-powered generators.

Now just a fishing village, 69km north of Veracruz, Villa Rica is the probable site of the first Spanish settlement in Mexico. Here you can explore traces of a fort and a church on the Cerro de la Cantera or bask on a lovely beach. The nearby Totonac tombs of **Quiahuiztlán** are superbly situated on a hill overlooking the coast.

CENTRAL VERACRUZ

Hwy 180 echoes the curves of the coast, running past the ruins of Zempoala to Cardel, where a side road leads to the beach at Chachalacas and Hwy 140 branches west to Xalapa, the state capital. The countryside around Xalapa shelters appealing villages and dramatic river gorges that are increasingly popular for rafting expeditions. The very early colonial ruins at La Antigua are worth a stop on the way to the lively port of Veracruz, 35km south of Cardel. From Veracruz, Hwy 150D heads southwest to Córdoba, Fortín de las Flores and Orizaba, on the edge of the Sierra Madre.

CENTRAL COAST
☎ 296

North of the city of Veracruz lies the central coastal area, a popular vacation spot for beach-bound Mexican holidaymakers and home to the Totonac ruins of Zempoala.

Zempoala

The pre-Hispanic Totonac town of Zempoala (or 'Cempoala') holds a key place in the story of the Spanish conquest. Its ruins stand 42km north of Veracruz and 4km west of Hwy 180 in modern Zempoala. The turnoff is by a Pemex station 7km north of Cardel. Voladores regularly perform at the ruins, especially on holidays and on weekends, around 10am, noon and 2pm. Zempoala is most easily reached through Cardel – take a bus marked 'Zempoala' (US$1) from the Cardel bus station, or a taxi (US$6).

HISTORY

Zempoala became a major Totonac center after about AD 1200 and may have been the leader of a federation of southern Totonac states. It fell subject to the Aztecs in the mid-15th century; thus, many of the buildings are in Aztec style. The town boasted defensive walls, underground water and drainage pipes and, in May 1519 when the Spanish came, about 30,000 people. As Cortés approached the town, one of his scouts reported back that the buildings were made of silver – but it was only white plaster or paint shining in the sun.

Zempoala's portly chief, Chicomacatl, known to history as 'the fat cacique' from a description by Bernal Díaz del Castillo, struck an alliance with Cortés for protection against the Aztecs. But his hospitality didn't stop the Spanish from smashing his gods' statues and lecturing his people on the virtues of Christianity. Zempoalan carriers went with the Spaniards when they set off for Tenochtitlán in 1519. The nexr year, it was at Zempoala that Cortés defeated the Pánfilo de Narváez expedition, which had been sent out by Cuba's governor to arrest Cortés.

By the 17th century Zempoala had virtually ceased to exist. Its population, devastated by diseases, was reduced to eight families. Eventually the town was abandoned. The present town dates from 1832.

ZEMPOALA RUINS

After you enter Zempoala, take a right where a sign says 'Bienvenidos a Cempoala.' The main **archaeological site** (admission US$2.75; ⊙ 9am-5:30pm) is at the end of this cobbled road.

The site is green and lovely, with palm trees and a mountain backdrop. Most of the buildings are faced with smooth, rounded riverbed stones, but many were originally plastered and painted. A typical feature is battlement-like 'teeth' called almenas.

The **Templo Mayor** (Main Temple) is an 11m-high, 13-platform pyramid, originally plastered and painted. A wide staircase ascends to the remains of a three-room shrine on top (you're not allowed to climb it). In 1520 this was probably Pánfilo de Narváez' headquarters, which Cortés' men captured by setting fire to its thatched roof.

On their first visit to Zempoala, the conquistador and his men lodged in **Las Chimeneas**. The hollow columns in front of the main structure were thought to be chimneys – hence the name. A temple probably topped the seven platforms here.

There are two main structures on the west side. One is known as the Gran Pirámide or **Templo del Sol**, with two stairways climbing its front side to three platforms on top, in typical Toltec–Aztec style. It faces east and was probably devoted to the sun god. To its north, the **Templo de la Luna** has a rectangular platform and ramps in front, and a round structure behind, similar to Aztec temples to the wind god Ehecatl.

East of Las Chimeneas beyond the irrigation channel, you'll see a building on your right called **Las Caritas** (Little Heads), named

for niches that once held several small pottery heads. Three other structures formerly stood east of Las Caritas, in line with the rising sun. Another large wind-god temple, known as **Templo Dios del Aire**, is in the town itself – go back south on the site entrance road, cross the main road in town and then go around the corner to the right. The ancient temple, with its characteristic circular shape, is beside an intersection.

Chachalacas

A few kilometers northeast of Cardel, this unpretentious seaside 'resort' has miles of uncrowded beaches and some sand dunes north of town. Most accommodations are geared to family groups, and at peak times they ask about US$40 for a large room.

The amiable, family-run **Hotel & Restaurant Yoli** (☎ 962-53-31; Circuito de las Gaviotas; s & d US$18, with air-con US$27; ℗ ⊠) wins the Chachalacas best value award. Well-maintained, decent-sized rooms are comfortable and clean, and it's right across from the beach.

Chachalacas Hotel-Club (☎ 962-52-42, 800-508-96-36; chachalacas@prodigy.net.mx; s & d from US$69; ℗ ⊠ ⊠ ⊠) has luxurious rooms and on-site dining options. You're unlikely to find such a glut of wading pools elsewhere on the coast (they have 12!).

Several restaurants line up along the beach, generally charging around US$6 for fresh fish.

Cardel

pop 18,000

The area's main town, Cardel (José Cardel) is no more than a transit stop, unless you're an avid bird-watcher. Cardel is under the migration corridor of around 30 species of raptors, between August and November. For non-birders, there are banks, restaurants and Internet cafés around the plaza, and comfortable accommodations at **Bienvenido Hotel** (☎ 962-07-77; www.mdc.com.mx /bienvenido; Cardel Sur 1; s/d US$24/29; ℗ ⊠).

From the Veracruz bus station, regular 1st-class ADO buses to Cardel cost US$3; frequent 2nd-class AU buses cost US$2.

La Antigua

pop 900

Intriguing La Antigua is 2km east of the coastal Hwy 150 and 23km north of Veracruz. A Spanish settlement was established here near the mouth of Río Huitzilapan in 1525, after Villa Rica was abandoned and before Veracruz was founded. The picturesque ruined building was the 16th-century customhouse (commonly called the 'Casa de Cortés'). The Ermita del Rosario church, probably dating from 1523, is one of the oldest in the Americas. Riverside accommodations (mosquitoes!) are available at **Hotel La Malinche** (s/d US$14/27; **P** 🛎). Nearby, small seafood restaurants are popular with day-trippers from Veracruz.

XALAPA

☎ 228 / pop 396,000 / elevation 1427m

Cool and cultured, Xalapa is truly a capital city. Sometimes spelled 'Jalapa' (but always pronounced 'ha-*la*-pa'), this urban delight houses not only the government of Veracruz state but also the Universidad Veracruzana, a lively arts scene, a convivial café life and a sophisticated, chic population.

Visitors can enjoy Xalapa's rolling hills and terraced parks, revel in the cool mountain climate and fuel their explorations with some of the Gulf Coast's finest cuisine. The city's highlight, the superb anthropological museum, is a particularly welcome retreat on one of Xalapa's many misty, drizzly days, when the traffic noise and fumes grow too vile to bear.

You should allow a couple of days to get to know the city.

History

A pre-Hispanic town on this site became part of the Aztec empire around 1460, and Cortés and his men passed through in 1519. The Spanish town didn't take off until the annual trade fair of Spanish goods was first held here in 1720 (it ran until 1777). Today Xalapa is a commercial hub for the coffee and tobacco grown on the slopes, and the city is also well known for its flowers.

Orientation

The city center is on a hillside, with the plaza, Parque Juárez, more or less in the middle of things. Uphill is north. Xalapa's cathedral is on Enríquez, just east of the plaza. Many of the mid-range hotels and restaurants are a little to the east, on Enríquez and Zaragoza. CAXA, the bus station, is 2km east of the city center, and the unmissable anthropology museum is a few kilometers north.

Glossy tourist maps (US$2) are available at the Palacio Municipal tourist information booth.

Information

EMERGENCY

Fire (☎ 815-00-80)
Police (☎ 818-18-10)

INTERNET ACCESS

@lex Internet (☎ 841-17-49; Callejón Diamante 17; per hr US$1; 🕑 9am-11pm) Has a fast connection, in a side alley off Callejón Diamante.
Papelería (Gutiérrez Zamora 16; per hr US$1; 🕑 10am-5:30pm Mon-Fri) Has a speedy connection.

LAUNDRY

Most mid-range and top end hotels have laundry services, but lavanderías (US$1 per kilo) are plentiful around the city center.

MEDICAL SERVICES

Centro de Especialidades Médicas (☎ 814-46-24; Av Ruiz Cortines s/n; 🕑 8am-6pm) Hospital offering excellent medical care.

MONEY

Banks (Enríquez/Gutiérrez Zamora) Have 24-hour ATMs.
HSBC (Gutiérrez Zamora 36; 🕑 9am-2pm & 4-6pm Mon-Fri, 10am-2pm Sat) Offers quicker exchange services and has slightly longer hours than the banks.

POST

Post Office (cnr Gutiérrez Zamora & Leño)

TELEPHONE & FAX

Telecomm (Leño 70; 🕑 8am-7:30pm Mon-Fri, 9am-5pm Sat, 9am-noon Sun) Next to the post office.

TOURIST INFORMATION

Information Desk (☎ 815-07-08; Museo de Antropología; 🕑 9am-5pm Tue-Sun) Inside museum entrance.
Tourist Information Booth (☎ 842-12-00, ext 3025; Palacio Municipal; 🕑 9am-3pm Mon-Fri) Under the arches of the Palacio Municipal, facing Parque Juárez.

Sights & Activities

MUSEO DE ANTROPOLOGÍA

Veracruz University's gorgeous **Museum of Anthropology** (☎ 815-09-20; Av Xalapa s/n; admission US$3.75, children under 12 free; 🕑 9am-5pm Tue-Sun), devoted to the archaeology in the state, is one of Mexico's best museums. Its large collection includes seven huge Olmec heads (up to 3000 years old) and 2500 other superb artifacts. The spacious, bright layout

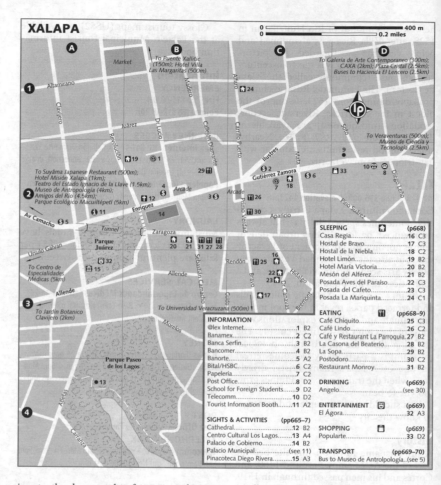

XALAPA

0 — 400 m
0 — 0.2 miles

To Puente Xallitic (150m); Hotel Villa Las Margaritas (500m)

To Galería de Arte Contemporáneo (300m); CAXA (2km); Plaza Cristal (2.5km); Buses to Hacienda El Lencero (2.5km)

To Veraventuras (500m); Museo de Ciencia y Tecnología (2.5km)

To Suyama Japanese Restaurant (500m); Hotel Misión Xalapa (1km); Teatro del Estado Ignacio de la Llave (1.5km); Museo de Antropología (4km); Amigos del Río (4.5km); Parque Ecológico Macuiltépetl (5km)

To Centro de Especialidades Médicas (5km)

To Jardín Botánico Clavijero (2km)

To Universidad Veracruzana (500m)

Parque Juárez

Parque Paseo de los Lagos

SLEEPING (p668)
Casa Regia 16 C3
Hostal de Bravo 17 C3
Hostal de la Niebla 18 C2
Hotel Limón 19 B2
Hotel María Victoria 20 B2
Mesón del Alférez 21 B2
Posada Aves del Paraíso 22 C3
Posada del Cafeto 23 C3
Posada La Mariquinta 24 C1

EATING (pp668–9)
Café Chiquito 25 C3
Café Lindo 26 C2
Café y Restaurant La Parroquia 27 B2
La Casona del Beaterio 28 B2
La Sopa 29 B2
Postodoro 30 C2
Restaurant Monroy 31 B2

DRINKING (p669)
Angelo .... (see 30)

ENTERTAINMENT (p669)
El Ágora 32 A3

SHOPPING (p669)
Popularte 33 D2

TRANSPORT (pp669–70)
Bus to Museo de Antropología .. (see 5)

INFORMATION
@lex Internet 1 B2
Banamex 2 C2
Banca Serfin 3 B2
Bancomer 4 B2
Banorte 5 A2
Bital/HSBC 6 C2
Papelería 7 C2
Post Office 8 D2
School for Foreign Students 9 D2
Telecomm 10 D2
Tourist Information Booth 11 A2

SIGHTS & ACTIVITIES (pp665–7)
Cathedral 12 B2
Centro Cultural Los Lagos 13 A4
Palacio de Gobierno 14 B2
Palacio Municipal .... (see 11)
Pinacoteca Diego Rivera 15 A3

---

is a textbook example of museum design. Unfortunately, information explaining the exhibits is available only in Spanish. Cameras are allowed, but you can't use a flash.

The exhibits occupy a series of galleries and courtyards descending a gentle slope. First you reach the Olmec material from southern Veracruz; the largest Olmec head here, 2.7m high, is from San Lorenzo. Another San Lorenzo head is pocked with hundreds of small holes, thought to be a deliberate mutilation at the time of San Lorenzo's fall. Apart from many more fine Olmec carvings, other museum highlights include an array of beautiful *yugos* and *hachas* from central Veracruz, murals from the Classic Veracruz center of Las Higueras, and

a collection of huge Classic-period pottery figures from El Zapotal. The lowest level displays examples of the codices that describe the first contact with Europeans.

The museum is on the west side of Av Xalapa, 4km northwest of the city center – look for the spacious gardens and the building with a fountain outside. To get there take a 'Tesorería-Centro-SEP' or 'Museo' bus (US$0.50) from in front of the Banorte on Av Camacho. To return, take a bus marked 'Centro.' Buses can be infrequent or full, so a taxi may be worth the US$1.50 fare.

CITY CENTER

The central **Parque Juárez** is like a terrace, with its elevated south side overlooking the valley below and snowcapped mountains in the distance. Tucked beneath the plaza is the **Pinacoteca Diego Rivera** (☎ 818 18 19; Herrera 5; admission free; 10am-6pm Tue-Sat). This cool little art museum houses a permanent exhibit of works from throughout Rivera's life. Rotating shows feature works by other Mexican artists. Reach the museum via the steps leading down from the west side of the plaza.

On the plaza's north side are the **Palacio Municipal** arcades. On the east side is the **Palacio de Gobierno**, the seat of the Veracruz state government. The Palacio de Gobierno sports a fine **mural** by Mario Orozco Rivera depicting the history of justice; it's above the stairway you'll reach from the eastern entrance on Enriquez.

Facing the Palacio de Gobierno across Enríquez is the unfinished **cathedral** (started in 1772), from where Revolución and Dr Lucio both lead up to the active area above the market. Further north, Dr Lucio crosses a deep valley via **Puente Xallitic**, a high, arched bridge.

GALERÍA DE ARTE CONTEMPORÁNEO

The state-run **Gallery of Contemporary Art** (☎ 818-04-12; Xalapeños Ilustres 135; admission US$0.50; 10am-7pm Tue-Sun) is in a fine renovated colonial building 1km east of the city center, just past Arteaga. It shows worthwhile temporary exhibitions.

MUSEO DE CIENCIA Y TECNOLOGÍA

The eclectic collection here includes old trains, assorted cars, airplanes, ecology displays and hands-on scientific exhibits. Thematic galleries cover the human body, earth sciences, water, transportation and space exploration. Exhibits are high quality and particularly excellent for children who can read Spanish. The **museum** (☎ 812-51-10; Av Vidal s/n; admission US$5 with IMAX theater; 9am-6pm Tue-Fri, 10am-7pm Sat & Sun) is in the southeast of town – take a Murillo Vidal bus (US$0.50) or a taxi (US$2).

PARKS

Just south of Parque Juárez is **Parque Paseo de los Lagos**, winding for 1km along either side of a lake. At its northern end is the **Centro Cultural Los Lagos** (☎ 812-12-99; Paseo los Lagos s/n; ccloslagos@yahoo.com.mx; admission US$1; 9am-3pm & 6-9pm Mon-Sun), a lovely, sophisticated escape

that hosts courses, concerts and temporary cultural exhibits. If you're lucky, you'll hear the strains of orchestras practicing as you stroll through the grounds.

On a hill in the north of the city, **Parque Ecológico Macuiltépetl** is the thickly wooded cap of an old volcano; the turnoff is about 200m south of the anthropology museum. Paths spiral to the top, which offers good views. At the summit, the small **Museo de la Fauna** (admission US$1; 11am-6pm Tue-Fri) has some tethered eagles, regionally endemic reptiles and a taxidermist's dream array of displays.

Southwest of the town center the attractive **Jardín Botánico Clavijero** (☎ 842-18-27; jbclavij@ecologia.edu.mx; Antigua Carr a Coatepec, Km 2.5; admission free; 9am-5pm) has a fine collection of subtropical plants.

WHITE-WATER RAFTING

Xalapa is the base for a number of adventure tourism operators, several offering rafting trips on nearby rivers.

Veraventuras (☎ 818-95-79, 800-712-65-72; www .veraventuras.com.mx in Spanish; Santos Degollado 81 Int 8; half-day trips from US$53) does trips ranging from a half-day on the Río Filo-Bobos to a three-day expedition on the class IV rapids of the Barranca Grande, on the upper reaches of Río Pescados. To find the company's office, go up the driveway and look for the building behind the parking lot. Another established rafting operator is **Amigos del Río** (☎ 815-88-17; www.esvirtual.com/amigosdelrio in Spanish; Chilpancingo 205; half-day trips from US$45).

Rafting trips usually require a minimum of four to eight participants, so it's a good idea to contact the operator ahead of time. Weekend trips offer the best chance of joining up with other people.

Courses

The Universidad Veracruzana's **Escuela para Estudiantes Extranjeros** (School for Foreign Students; ☎ 817/ 86 87; www.uv.mx/eee; Gutiérrez Zamora 25; courses from per hr US$20, per semester US$195) offers short-term programs in Spanish and Náhuatl languages, and Mexican culture.

Tours

BTT Xalapa (☎ 812-00-81; victoursxalapa_btt@hotmail .com; prices from US$20-60 per person) Daily tours of the city and excursions to nearby towns and archaeological and historical sites; some guides speak English.

Roy Dudley (☎ 812-05-55; roydudly@xal.megared.net
.mx; 3hr walking tour US$50 per person) A gringo expat
who has lived in Xalapa for 31 years, Roy can customize
trips in and around Xalapa.

Sleeping

BUDGET

Posada Aves del Paraiso (☎ /fax 817-00-37; p_aves
delparaiso@hotmail.com; Dr Canovas 4; s/d US$17/27) Big,
charming, fanless rooms here are named
after various birds. Rooms outfitted with
cable TV and nice furniture face a homey
courtyard on a quiet street.

Hostal de Bravo (☎ 818-90-38; Bravo 11; s/d US$17/19)
Set back from the street, Hostal de Bravo offers large, comfortable rooms with tall windows. The simple rooms that are surrounding
a peaceful, terracotta-tiled courtyard, are
spotless.

Hostal de la Niebla (☎ 817-21-74; www.delaniebla
.com; Gutiérrez Zamora 24; dm/ste US$11/44; P ☐)
Backpacker traditionalists should hit this
European-style hostel. Immaculate and spacious, with a bright kitchen, dining area and
terrace, this hostel offers perks like parking, 24-hour Internet access and a roomy
refrigerator.

Hotel Limón (☎ 817-22-04; fax 817-93-16; Revolución
8; s/d US$10/11) Noise-sensitive travelers, bring
your earplugs. The Limón's cheery, yellow-
tiled rooms may be miniscule, but they're
very clean and they're cheap. A winding staircase, narrow echo-chamber – er, courtyard –
and proximity to the cathedral give a vaguely
monastic feel.

MID-RANGE

Posada del Cafeto (☎ /fax 817-00-23; p_cafeto@xal
.megared.net.mx; Dr Canovas 8; s/d US$25/34) Sur-
rounding a garden courtyard, this secure,
cute posada has airy, fan-cooled rooms with
split bathrooms. A cozy café, tiled walkways and mellow atmosphere tempt guests
to linger here.

Mesón del Alférez (☎ 818-01-13; m_alferez@xal
.megared.net.mx; Sebastián Camacho 2; s/d US$39/45)
This unique place is housed in a renovated
old building oozing with character. Decorated with magnificent wooden furniture
and sculptures, the rooms are arranged
around a plant-filled courtyard. The atmospheric, skylit restaurant is open until 4pm
daily.

Posada La Mariquinta (☎ 818-11-58; laquinta@
xalapa.net; Alfaro 12; s/d from US$35/44; P) A guest-
house in an 18th-century colonial resi-
dence, La Mariquinta offers rooms, suites
and bungalows. Lodgings sit around a
lovely garden at this centrally located but
peaceful posada.

Hotel Villa Las Margaritas (☎ 840-08-86, 800-
719-43-67; www.villamargaritas.com in Spanish; Dr Lucio
186; s/d US$40/51; P ☒) A bit of a hike from
Xalapa's center, the goofily luxurious Villa
Las Margaritas is eminently comfortable,
with an amiable staff. Rooms have 'mega'
cable and tiled bathrooms with tubs.

Other possibilities:

Casa Regia (☎ 812-05-91; fax 817-25-35; Hidalgo 12;
s/d US$23/32) Comfortable, smallish rooms in a posada
with a dark, old-world feel.

Hotel María Victoria (☎ 818-60-11, 800-260-08-00;
fax 818-05-21; Zaragoza 6; s & d US$45, with king-size
bed US$54; P ☒) Boasting every convenience, this
otherwise sterile hotel offers some fabulous views of the
mountains and city.

TOP END

Hotel Misión Xalapa (☎ 818-22-22, 800-260-26-00;
lic_lissetgs@megared.net.mx; cnr Victoria & Bustamante;
s & d US$92; P ☒ ☒ ☒) The modern, 200-
room Misión lies 1km west of the city
center, 1½ blocks uphill from Av Camacho.
The complex holds bars, a pool, a restaurant and a good cafeteria. Most of the Misión
Xalapa's clientele are business travelers, as
it's the most upscale digs in town.

Eating

Xalapa has plenty of excellent, inexpensive
eateries, with one local specialty being *chiles
rellenos* (stuffed peppers). And where do
you think the jalapeño got its name?

La Casona del Beaterio (☎ 818-21-19; Zaragoza
20; dishes US$4-9; ☽ 8am-10pm) With tall arched
doors, tables around its foliage-filled courtyard and walls bearing photos of old Xalapa,
this stately restaurant occupies an old colonial home. Nibble pan dulce while awaiting
your breakfast, or try their delicious crêpes
or enchiladas.

Café Chiquito (☎ 812-11-22; Bravo 3; dishes US$2-8;
☽ 7:30am-10:30pm) Serving great meals all day
at reasonable prices, Café Chiquito has both
indoor and outdoor tables around a bricked
courtyard. Live local bands sometimes play
here in the evenings.

La Sopa (☎ 817-80-69; Callejón Diamante 3A; meals
US$2.50; ☽ 11:30am-11pm) The very popular La
Sopa offers a fine lunchtime *comida corrida*

and set menu in the evening. There's live music Friday and Saturday nights and a gregarious atmosphere anytime.

Café Lindo (☎ 817-35-15; Primo Verdad 21; dishes US$1-6; ☉ 10am-11pm) One of Xalapa's trendiest spots, just south of Enríquez/Gutiérrez Zamora, Café Lindo dishes out sandwiches and snacks, espresso and carnivore-friendly main courses. This sociable place has live music most weekend nights.

Postodoro (☎ 841-20-00; Primo Verdad 11; pizzas from US$4; ☉ 12:30pm-12:30am Mon-Sat, 1:30-10:30pm Sun) Come to Postodoro to curtail all your pasta, espresso, Chianti and gelato cravings; they also make a killer pizza.

Suyâma Japanese Restaurant (☎ 841-31-55; Camacho 54A; 10-piece sushi rolls from US$2.75; ☉ 2-11pm Mon-Sat, 2-6pm Sun) With loud music and an upscale atmosphere, Suyâma is a good place for groups. For their quality cuisine, there's a 100-peso minimum.

Tried-and-true institutions with great people-watching and hearty fare include:

Café y Restaurant La Parroquia (☎ 817-44-36; Zaragoza 18; dishes US$5-8; ☉ 7:30am-11pm) A good bet anytime, with efficient and courteous service.

Restaurant Monroy (☎ 817-86-53; Zaragoza 16; dishes US$5-8; ☉ 24hr) Antojitos around the clock and a four-course comida corrida at lunchtime – plus a smiley, family-run feel.

Drinking

You can sip espresso amongst the artsy-craftsy set on Callejón Diamante, where small cafés are plentiful. But if tea is your bag, try **Angelo** (☎ 817-61-71; Primo Verdad 21A; pot of tea US$2.25; ☉ 8am-9pm Mon-Sat), a quaint, tiny teahouse with intimate tables, sweet treats and an array of unusual teas.

Entertainment

For news of what's happening around town, scope out **El Ágora** (☎ 818-57-30; underneath Parque Juárez; ☉ 10am-10pm Tue-Sun, 9am-6pm Mon), the focus of Xalapa's busy arts scene. This arts center contains a cinema, theater, gallery, bookstore and café. For more entertainment listings, try checking the notice board in the Café La Parroquia.

The state theater, **Teatro del Estado Ignacio de la Llave** (☎ 818-08-34; cnr Ignacio de la Llave & Camacho; ☉ from 8pm) hosts performances by both the Orquesta Sinfónica de Xalapa and the Ballet Folklórico of the Universidad Veracruzana.

Like most big cities, Xalapa's nightlife options are ever-evolving; particularly popular are salsa clubs featuring live music. Check the tourist information booth in the Palacio Municipal – or your trendy, friendly waiter – for suggestions.

Shopping

Xalapa hipsters hang in Callejón Diamante, an alley lined with street vendors and small shops. For the folks back home, find gifts of hammered tin mirrors or body jewelry.

Also check out **Popularte** (☎ 841-12-02; populver@hotmail.com; Gutiérrez Zamora 38; ☉ 9am-6pm Mon-Sat). Handicrafts made locally and further afield – like *jaranas* (small eight-stringed guitars), weavings and jewelry – are marked with artisans' names.

Getting There & Away

As an inland transportation hub, Xalapa offers excellent connections throughout the state.

BUS

Xalapa's gleaming, modern, well-organized bus station, the **Central de Autobuses de Xalapa** (CAXA; ☎ 842-25-00; 20 de Noviembre), is 2km east of the city center. Deluxe service is offered by UNO and ADO GL, 1st-class service by ADO, and 2nd-class service by AU (many 2nd-class services are direct, and not much slower than 1st class).

Cardel (US$3, 1½hr, at least 16 1st-class daily; US$3, 1½hr, 2nd-class every 20 minutes 5:15am-7:15pm)

Mexico City (US$15, 5¼hr, at least 20 1st class daily; US$13, 5¼hr, 17 2nd class daily) To TAPO.

Papantla (US$12, 5hr, 8 1st class daily)

Puebla (US$9, 3¼hr, 9 1st class daily; US$8, 3¼hr, 14 2nd class daily)

Tampico (US$24, 10hr, 1st class at 10.30pm)

Veracruz (US$5, 2hr, 1st class every 20-30 minutes 5am-11pm; US$5, 2hr, 18 2nd class daily)

Villahermosa (US$28, 8½hr, 4 1st class daily)

Other places served by ADO include Acayucan, Campeche, Catemaco, Córdoba, Fortín de las Flores, Mérida, Orizaba, Poza Rica, San Andrés Tuxtla and Santiago Tuxtla. AU also goes to Salina Cruz.

CAR & MOTORCYCLE

For cheap car rentals, try **Kanguro** (☎ 817-78-78; Camacho 1350; from US$45 per day) or **Alsad** (☎ 817-70-46; Ignacio de la Llave 14; from US$45 per day).

Hwy 140 to Puebla is narrow and winding until Perote; the Xalapa-Veracruz road is very good. Going to the northern Gulf Coast, it's quickest to go to Cardel, then turn north on Hwy 180; the inland road via Tlapacoyan is scenic but slow.

Getting Around

For buses from CAXA to the city center, follow the signs to the taxi stand, then continue downhill to the big road, Av 20 de Noviembre. Turn right to the bus stop, from where any microbus or bus marked 'Centro' will take you within a short walk of Parque Juárez (US$0.50). For a taxi to the city center, buy a ticket in the bus station (US$2), then walk down the ramp and through the tunnel to the taxi stand. To return to the bus station, take a 'CAXA' bus east along Zaragoza.

AROUND XALAPA

The countryside around Xalapa has some dramatic landscapes with rivers, gorges and waterfalls, and some appealing old towns lie nearby.

Hacienda El Lencero

About 12km from Xalapa on the Veracruz highway, a signposted road branches off right for a few kilometers to the **Museo Ex-Hacienda El Lencero** (Carr Xalapa-Veracruz, Km 10; admission US$1.50, free Tue; 🕙 10am-6pm Tue-Fri). Well worth a visit, the former estate rests on land once granted to a soldier from the army of Cortés. One of the first inns between Mexico City and Veracruz was established here. One-time dictator General Antonio López de Santa Anna owned the property from 1842 to the mid-1850s; the hacienda, chapel and other buildings date mostly from this period. The grand, superbly restored house is furnished with fine period pieces, and the gardens and lake are delightful (the vast fig tree is said to be 500 years old).

From Xalapa, catch one of the regular 'Banderia' buses (US$2) from outside the Plaza Cristal shopping center.

El Carrizal

South of the Veracruz road, 44km from Xalapa, El Carrizal hot springs feed several sulfurous pools. The site also houses a restaurant and a spa-hotel. To speak to the resort area representative in Xalapa, contact 🕾 228-818-97-74, fax 228-818-96-80.

Coatepec & Xico

Coatepec (population 44,700), a charming colonial town 15km south of Xalapa, is known for its coffee and orchids. The María Cristina orchid garden, on the main square, is open daily. Xico (population 15,000) is a pretty colonial village, 8km south of Coatepec. From Xico it's a pleasant 2km walk to the photogenic 40m **Texolo waterfall**.

Buses go about every 15 minutes to Coatepec or Xico from Av Allende, about 1km west of central Xalapa (US$1).

Parque Nacional Cofre de Perote

The 4274m-high Cofre de Perote volcano is southwest of Xalapa but often obscured by mist. From the town of Perote, 50km west of Xalapa on Hwy 140, Calle Allende continues southwest to become a dirt road that climbs 1900m in 24km, finishing just below the summit. There's no public transportation here.

Valle Alegre

To reach this 'happy valley' take the highway toward Puebla and turn south after 15km, just west of Las Vigas. Follow the side road through El Llanillo to Tembladeras, where you'll find **Valle Alegre Hostel** (🕾 282-812-20-54, www.vallealegre.com.mx), with dorm accommodations and bungalows surrounded by an ecological reserve offering hiking and wildlife-watching possibilities. Call ahead for reservations and current prices. AU buses (US$3) leave daily from Xalapa's CAXA.

VERACRUZ

🕾 229 / pop 550,000

O heroic town! Festive, frenetic Veracruz revels in peripatetic mariachis, pleasingly aesthetic colonial buildings and a kinetic fervor that starts in its zócalo and pervades its denizens (*jarochos*). Bands flock to town during Carnaval, which stands as Mexico's biggest and wildest. Land and seashore offer you chances to cruise past historical attractions, to booze and party with locals or merely to snooze in a shaded plaza. In Veracruz, tropical hedonism is the norm.

Though tourists may take the city by storm, it retains an almost small-town charm – warm, vivacious and vibrant. Whatever form your visit takes, beware. You'd best believe that when the time comes to go, you may not want to leave.

History

The coast here was occupied by Totonacs, with influences from Toltec and Aztec civilizations. This mix of pre-Hispanic cultures can be seen at Zempoala (p663), 42km to the north. After the Spanish conquest, Veracruz provided Mexico's main gateway to the outside world for 400 years. Invaders and pirates, incoming and exiled rulers, settlers, silver and slaves – all came and went to make the city a linchpin in Mexico's history.

SPANISH CONQUEST & PIRATE RAIDS

Cortés made his first landing here at an island 2km offshore, which he named 'Isla Sacrificios' because of the remains of human sacrifices he found there. He anchored off another island, San Juan de Ulúa, on Good Friday (April 21), 1519, where he made his first contact with Moctezuma's envoys. Cortés founded the first Spanish settlement at Villa Rica, 69km north, but this was later moved to La Antigua, and finally to the present site of Veracruz in 1598.

Veracruz became the Spaniards' most important anchorage, and until 1760 it was the only port allowed to handle trade with Spain. Tent cities blossomed for trade fairs when the fleet from Spain made its annual arrival, but because of seaborne raids and tropical diseases (malaria and yellow fever were rampant) Veracruz never became one of Mexico's biggest cities.

In 1567 nine English ships under the command of John Hawkins sailed into Veracruz harbor, with the intention of selling slaves

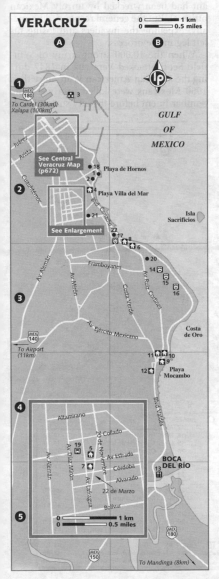

VERACRUZ

To Cardel (30km), Xalapa (100km)

GULF OF MEXICO

See Central Veracruz Map (p672)

Playa de Hornos
Playa Villa del Mar
Isla Sacrificios
See Enlargement

Costa de Oro

To Airport (11km)
Playa Mocambo

BOCA DEL RÍO

To Mandinga (8km)

CENTRAL GULF COAST

in defiance of the Spanish trade monopoly. They were trapped by a Spanish fleet, and only two of the ships escaped. One of them, however, carried Francis Drake, who went on to harry the Spanish in a long career as a sort of licensed pirate. The most vicious pirate attack of all occurred in 1683, when the Frenchman Laurent de Gaff, with 600 men, held the 5000 inhabitants of Veracruz captive in the town church with little food or water. De Gaff's men killed anyone who tried to escape, piled the Plaza de Armas with loot, got drunk, raped many of the women and threatened to blow up the church unless the people revealed their secret stashes. They left a few days later, much richer.

19TH & 20TH CENTURIES

In 1838 General Antonio López de Santa Anna, who had been routed in Texas two years earlier, fled Veracruz in his underwear under bombardment from a French fleet in the 'Pastry War' (the French were pressing various claims against Mexico, including that of a French pastry cook whose restaurant had been wrecked by unruly Mexican officers). But the general responded heroically, expelling the invaders and losing his left leg in the process.

When the 10,000-strong army of Winfield Scott attacked Veracruz in 1847 during the Mexican-American War, more than 1000 Mexicans were killed in a weeklong bombardment before the city surrendered.

CENTRAL VERACRUZ

0 — 400 m
0 — 0.2 miles

INFORMATION	
Banamex	1 A2
Banca Serfin	2 A2
Bancomer	3 A2
Banorte	4 B2
HSBC	5 A2
Netchatboys	6 A2
Post Office	7 B1
Telecomm	(see 7)
Tourist Office	8 B2

SIGHTS & ACTIVITIES	(pp673–5)
Altar a la Patria	9 C2
Baluarte de Santiago	10 C3
Casa Museo Salvador Díaz Mirón	11 B3
Faro Carranza	12 C2
Museo de la Ciudad de Veracruz	13 B3
Museo Histórico Naval	14 C2
Palacio Municipal	(see 8)
Pemex Building	15 C1
Tridente	16 D3

SLEEPING	(pp675–7)
Calinda Veracruz	17 A2
Fiesta Inn	18 D2
Hawaii Hotel	19 B2
Holiday Inn	20 A1
Hotel Amparo	21 A2
Hotel Colonial	22 A2
Hotel Concha Dorada	23 B2
Hotel Emporio	24 C2
Hotel Imperial	25 A2
Hotel México	26 B2
Hotel Oriente	27 B2
Hotel Ruiz Milán	28 B2
Hotel Sevilla	29 B2
Hotel Villa Rica	30 D3

EATING	(pp677–8)
Cocina Económica Veracruz	31 A3
El Rincón de la Trova	32 B3

Fish Market	33 B2
Gran Café de la Parroquia	34 B2
Gran Café del Portal	35 B2
La Estancia de Boca	36 B2
La Suriana 2	37 B2
Pardiñola's	38 B2

ENTERTAINMENT	(p679)
Centro Cultural Casa Principal	39 A2
La Casona de la Condesa	40 B3

TRANSPORT	(pp679–80)
Boats for Harbor Tours	41 C1
Buses to Mocambo & Boca del Rio	42 B2
Buses to San Juan de Ulúa	43 B2
Mexicana & Aerocaribe	44 A3

In 1859, during Mexico's internal Reform War, Benito Juárez' Veracruz-based liberal government promulgated the reform laws that nationalized church property and put education into secular hands. In 1861 when Juárez, having won the war, announced that Mexico couldn't pay its foreign debts, a joint French-Spanish-British force occupied Veracruz. The British and Spanish planned only to take over the customhouse and recover what Mexico owed them, but Napoleon III intended to conquer Mexico. Realizing this, the Brits and Spaniards went home, while the French marched inland to begin their five-year intervention.

Napoleon III's reign came to an end, however, and Veracruz again began to flower. Mexico's first railway was built between Veracruz and Mexico City in 1872, and, under the dictatorship of Porfirio Díaz, investment poured into the city.

In 1914, during the civil war that followed Díaz' departure in the 1910–11 revolution, US troops occupied Veracruz to stop a delivery of German arms to the conservative dictator Victoriano Huerta. The Mexican casualties caused by the intervention alienated even Huerta's opponents. Later in the civil war, Veracruz was for a while the capital of the reformist Constitutionalist faction led by Venustiano Carranza.

Orientation

The center of the city's action is the zócalo, site of the cathedral and Palacio Municipal. The harbor is 250m east, with the San Juan de Ulúa fort on its far side. Blvd Camacho ('El Boulevard') follows the coast to the south, past naval and commercial anchorages, to a series of grimy beaches. About 700m south of the zócalo along Av Independencia is Parque Zamora, circling a wide green space. Nearby is Mercado Hidalgo, the main market. The 1st- and 2nd-class bus stations are back to back, 2km south of Parque Zamora along Díaz Mirón.

Information

EMERGENCY

Fire (☎ 932-28-38)
Police (☎ 938-06-64)

INTERNET ACCESS

Netchatboys (Map p672; netchatboys@hotmail.com; Lerdo 369; per hr US$1; ⏰ 9am-8:30pm Mon-Fri, noon-8pm Sat) Lightning-fast Internet access available here and next door.

LEFT LUGGAGE

There's a 24-hour left luggage room at the 2nd-class bus station (see Buses, later).

MEDICAL SERVICES

Beneficencia Española (☎ 932-00-21; 16 de Septiembre 955) Hospital offering general medical services.
Hospital Regional (☎ 937-55-00; Diaz Mirón 165)

MONEY

A cluster of banks dominates the corner, a block north of the zócalo – they have ATMs and change traveler's checks.

POST

Main Post Office (Map p672; Plaza de la República 213; ⏰ 8am-4pm Mon-Fri, 9am-1pm Sat) A five-minute walk north of the zócalo.

TELEPHONE & FAX

Telecomm (Map p672; Plaza de la República 213; ⏰ 8am-7pm Mon-Fri, 9am-5pm Sat, 9am-noon Sun) Next to post office, offers public phone and fax services; there are Telmex card phones on the zócalo.

TOURIST INFORMATION

City & State Tourist Office (Map p672; ☎ 989-88-17; Palacio Municipal; ⏰ 9am-8pm Mon-Sat, 10am-6pm Sun) Offering maps, coupon books and cheesy brochures; staffers are super-sweet, some speak English.

Sights & Activities

ZÓCALO   Map p672

Veracruz' zócalo, also called the Plaza de Armas, Plaza Lerdo and Plaza de la Constitución, is the hub of the city for jarochos and visitors alike. It's a fine-looking place with *portales* (arcades), palm trees, a fountain, the 17th-century Palacio Municipal on one side and an 18th-century cathedral on another. The level of activity accelerates as the day progresses, from breakfast and coffee under the arches, through a leisurely lunch, to afternoon entertainment on an outdoor stage. In the evening, as the sweat cools off Veracruz bodies, the zócalo becomes a swirling, multifaceted party, with cool drinks and competing street musicians (see p679).

HARBOR & MALECÓN   Map p672

Veracruz' harbor is still busy, though oil ports such as Tampico and Coatzacoalcos now handle greater tonnages. The **Paseo del Malecón** (also called Insurgentes) is a pleasant waterfront walk; starting with the Plaza de las Artesanías opposite the zócalo, colorful souvenir stalls lining the Malecón sell a mind-boggling selection of seashell knickknacks and tacky T-shirts.

Stroll out along the Malecón and view the ships, cranes and ancient fortress across the water, or take a sightseeing boat trip (see p675) for a closer look. At the corner of Blvd Camacho are monuments to the city's defenders against the Americans in 1914 and to all sailors who gave their lives to the sea. The high-rise building here is an early example of modern Mexican architecture; built in 1940, it now houses Pemex offices and has some interesting murals.

Two blocks inland from the Malecón is the 1998 **Altar a la Patria**, a solemn obelisk beneath which are buried the remains of those who defended Veracruz during its numerous conflicts

FARO CARRANZA   Map p672
Facing the waterfront on the Malecón, the cream-colored **Faro Carranza** holds a lighthouse and navy offices. The Mexican navy goes through an elaborate parade in front of the building Monday mornings. Venustiano Carranza lived here during the revolution, in 1914 and 1915, and it was here that the 1917 Mexican constitution was drafted. A large statue of Carranza stands in front, and the pond at his feet houses the mother of all turtles. Exhibits on Carranza and his political struggles are in the Museo Histórico Naval.

SAN JUAN DE ULÚA   Map p671
This **fortress** (☎ 938-51-51; admission US$3.50; ⏰ 9am-4.30pm Tue-Sun) protecting Veracruz harbor was originally an island, but it's now connected to the mainland by a causeway. In 1518 the Spaniard Juan de Grijalva landed here during an exploratory voyage from Cuba. The next year Cortés also landed here, and it subsequently became the main entry point for Spanish newcomers to Mexico. The Franciscan chapel is thought to have been built in 1524 and the first fortifications in the 1530s, but most of what can be seen now was built progressively between 1552 and 1779.

The central part of the fortress, Fuerte San José, has also been a prison, most notoriously

during the Porfirio Díaz regime. Many inmates died of yellow fever or tuberculosis.

Today San Juan de Ulúa is an empty ruin of passageways, battlements, bridges and stairways. Guided tours are available in Spanish and, sometimes, English. To get there, take a 'San Juan de Ulúa' bus (US$0.50) from the east side of Plaza de la República. The last bus back to town leaves at 6pm.

BALUARTE DE SANTIAGO   Map p672
From the 16th to 19th centuries, central Veracruz was surrounded by a defensive wall that incorporated nine forts. The only one remaining is the **Baluarte (Bastion) de Santiago** (☎ 931-10-59; Canal s/n; admission US$3.50; ⏰ 10am-4.30pm Tue-Sun), built in 1526 beside a canal at what was then the waterfront. Inside is a small exhibit of pre-Hispanic gold jewelry known as 'Las Joyas del Pescador' (the Fisherman's Jewels). The name refers to some fabulous gold artifacts discovered by a fisherman in Veracruz harbor in 1976, but most pieces on display here come from other sources. The price covers admission to the fort interior, but you can walk around the outside battlements anytime for free.

ACUARIO DE VERACRUZ   Map p671
Veracruz' **aquarium** (☎ 931-10-20; www.acuariode veracruz.com; Blvd Camacho s/n; child/adult US$2.50/4.75; ⏰ 10am-7pm) is inside the Plaza Acuario shopping mall at Playa de Hornos, about 2km south of the city center. The most impressive exhibit is the huge, donut-shaped tank in which sharks, rays and giant turtles swim right around and over visitors. Numerous tanks and ponds house freshwater and saltwater fish species, reptiles and amphibians, river otters and even manatees.

MUSEUMS
Veracruz has an eclectic handful of museums around the city center.

Built as a school for naval officers in the 1890s, the **Museo Histórico Naval** (Map p672; ☎ 931-40-78; Arista 418; admission free; ⏰ 9am-5pm Tue-Sun; ♿) was handsomely restored before opening as a museum in 1997. The museum covers Mexico's maritime heritage and naval history. Along with rooms full of weapons and model ships, the museum holds beautifully presented – and guilt-inspiring, for Americans – exhibits on the US attacks on Veracruz in 1847 and 1914, and on revolutionary hero Venustiano Carranza, whose government-in-exile was based in Veracruz for a time. The displays are well laid out, but information is in Spanish only.

Once the home of celebrated poet Salvador Díaz Mirón (1853–1928), **Casa Museo Salvador Díaz Mirón** (Map p672; ☎ 989-88-00, ext 146; Av Zaragoza 322; admission free; ☽ 10am-8pm Mon-Fri, 10am-6pm Sat) is a center for literary and theatrical workshops. Some rooms upstairs are restored and decorated in late-19th-century style. There's not a whole lot to see, but with a little imagination, you can feel you're in the presence of greatness.

The **Museo de la Ciudad de Veracruz** (Veracruz City Museum; Map p672; ☎ 931-84-10; Av Zaragoza 39; admission US$2.75; ☽ 10am-6pm Tue-Sun) has fine displays and presentations ranging from the city's early history (particularly slavery) to the present.

BEACHES & LAGOONS   Map p671
In general, the further south you go, the cleaner the beaches get. Hence, few people venture into the water at Playa de Hornos, just south of the city center, or at Playa Villa del Mar, a little further south. The beaches are more acceptable 5km south of the city at **Costa de Oro** and 7km south at **Playa Mocambo**. Non-guests of the Hotel Playa Paraíso (p677) are welcome to use the beach for US$1/0.50 per adult/child.

Still further south, the road goes to **Boca del Río**, with popular seafood restaurants. Over the bridge, the coastal road continues to **Mandinga**, where you can hire a boat to explore the lagoons and **Antón Lizardo**. For details on getting yourself there, see p680.

DIVING & SNORKELING
The beaches near Veracruz may not be inviting, but there is good diving – including at least one accessible wreck – on the reefs near the offshore islands. Part of the area has been designated an underwater natural park. **Tridente** (Map p672; ☎ 931-79-24; tridente_ver@hotmail.com; Blvd Camacho 165A; diving trips from US$45 per person), a PADI dive school, arranges dive and snorkel trips from Veracruz and Antón Lizardo (45 minutes down the coast). For at least two people, you can do a day trip with two dives, a guide and equipment. Guides speak English, Spanish, French and even a little Russian. Other operations are a few blocks south of Tridente

on the boulevard; still more are based in Boca del Río and Antón Lizardo.

Club Amphibian (Map p671, ☎ 931-09-97; clubamphibian@ver.megared.net.mx; Blvd Camacho 1707; ☽ 9am-6pm Mon-Fri) is another outfit offering activity-based tours; in addition to diving and snorkeling trips, they also run hiking, rock-climbing and kayaking tours.

Tours
Boats from the Malecón offer hour-long **harbor tours** (US$5 per person; every 30 minutes; ☽ 7am-7pm). They leave when they're full, which may not happen often – or ever – in the slow season. Also leaving from the Malecón, streetcars (US$2) make a 40-minute circuit of the city's attractions.

Festivals & Events
Carnaval (February or March) – Veracruz busts out into a nine-day party before Ash Wednesday each year. Starting the previous Tuesday, colorful parades wind through the city daily, beginning with one devoted to the 'burning of bad humor' and ending with the 'funeral of Juan Carnaval.' Other events include fireworks, dances, salsa and samba music, handicrafts, folklore shows and children's parades. See the tourist office (p673) for a program of events.
Festival Internacional Afrocaribeño (last two weeks of July) – High point of the summer holiday season is the festival of Afro-Caribbean culture. Various Caribbean nations participate in academic forums, trade shows and business conferences, but the main attractions are the dance and music performances (many of them free), film screenings and art expositions.

Sleeping
Veracruz is most crazed at Carnaval, when the town is packed, hotels are booked weeks or months ahead, and prices soar. Other busy periods, when reservations are recommended, are Semana Santa, the summer from mid-July to mid-September, and the period from mid-November to mid-January. At other times, plenty of rooms are available at the low-season prices listed here.

It's convenient and fun to stay on or near the zócalo. The cheaper places are around here and near the bus stations, while the more expensive tend to be the resort hotels in the beach suburb of Mocambo.

BUDGET
Count on hot water, but check for adequate ventilation and a working fan at these budget hotels.

Hotel México (Map p672; ☎ 931-57-44; Morelos 343; s & d US$18) Just around the corner from the zócalo, the Hotel México has rooms with TV and fan. Maintenance varies dramatically between rooms, so take a look at several before committing. Interior rooms are dark and quieter than the sunny rooms facing traffic-heavy Av Morelos.

Hotel Sevilla (Map p672; Morelos 359; s & d US$23) Conveniently located on the edge of the zócalo action, the Sevilla has dark hallways and clean rooms with small balconies. Big, spare rooms have ceiling fan and TVs.

Hotel Amparo (Map p672; ☎ 932-27-38, Serdán 482; s & d US$11, with TV US$14) Dirt-cheap – but clean – the super-friendly Amparo is a simple place with fluorescent lighting and cheery yellow and aqua tiles. Rooms are mid-sized, with fans and small desks.

Hotel Villa Rica (Map p672; ☎ 932-48-54, Blvd Camacho 165; s/d US$18/27) Backpackers wanting to stay near the water should head to the unassuming Villa Rica. The rooms are small, tidy and breezy, with tiny tiled balconies and hallway sitting areas. Sit and chat awhile with the wry proprietor.

Hotel Impala (Map p671; ☎ 937-01-69; fax 935 1257; Orizaba 650; s & d US$23/29; P ⊠) Your peso packs some punch at the Impala, near the bus station: comfy rooms smell fresh and come with air-con, cable TV and phones.

Hotel Azteca (Map p671; ☎ /fax 937-42-41; 22 de Marzo 218; s/d US$18; ⊠) On the corner of Orizaba a couple of blocks from the bus station, the mellow and very yellow Azteca is a good deal. The clean, quiet rooms have air-conditioning, phone and TV.

MID-RANGE

Mid-range options in Veracruz range from elegant to characterless, but almost all offer good value. Air-con, cable TV, elevators and good water pressure are standard in this category.

The following places are in the vicinity of the zócalo area.

Hotel Imperial (Map p672; ☎ 932-12-04, 800-522-01-11; imperialver@prodigy.net.mx; Lerdo 153; s/d US$36/45; ⊠) With its elegant lobby and stained-glass ceiling, the Imperial is worth a visit just for a ride in the vintage elevator. Spacious rooms come with marble-floored bathrooms. It's a good spot to treat yourself, with old-fashioned ambience and all the modern comforts.

Hotel Colonial (Map p672; ☎ 932-01-93; hcolonial@ infosel.net.mx; Lerdo 117; s/d US$36/45, for new rooms US$48; ⊠) If you can get past the weirdly institutional lobby and indifferent staff, the perfect location and elegant furnishings here might appeal to you. Newer rooms are more luxurious, and the 5th- and 6th-floor terraces have tremendous views of the cathedral and Palacio Municipal.

Calinda Veracruz (Map p672; ☎ 931-22-33, 800-900-00-00; www.hotelescalinda.com.mx; cnr Av Independencia & Lerdo; s & d from US$55) The Calinda's beautiful corridors resemble those in Mughal palaces. The well-decorated rooms are surprisingly small, but pricier ones have balconies. There's a superb view from the rooftop pool.

Hotel Oriente (Map p672; ☎ /fax 931-24-90; Lerdo 20; s/d US$29/35, for 2 beds US$38; ⊠) The clean, smallish rooms with enormous beds feature cable TV and phones; outside rooms have balconies and are predictably noisier. The zócalo and Malecón are both a block's stroll away. Staff here are helpful and sweet.

Hotel Concha Dorada (Map p672; ☎ 931-29-96, 800-712-53-42; conchadorada@yahoo.com.mx; Lerdo 77; s/d US$25/32; ⊠) Attentive staff and spotless rooms make this comfortable place a great mid-range deal for this central location.

If you want to stay near the city seafront, consider these places.

Hotel Ruiz Milán (Map p672; ☎ 932-37-77, 800-221-42-60; ventas@ruizmilan.com.mx; cnr Paseo del Malecón & Farías; s/d from US$44/62; P ⊠ ⊠) Only six blocks from the city center, the Ruiz Milán has plush, colorful rooms with all the trimmings. Be sure to get a balcony room with a view of the harbor.

Hawaii Hotel (Map p672; ☎ 938-00-88; hawaii@ infosel.net.mx; Paseo del Malecón 458; s/d US$45/50; P ⊠ ⊠) Don't fall down in the Hawaii, where white marble dominates the landscape. Huge, cool rooms have refrigerators and more marvelous views of the Malecón and industrial cranes. Staff here have aloha spirit.

Hostal de Cortés (Map p671; ☎ 923-12-00, 800-112-98-00; www.hostaldecortes.com.mx; cnr Blvd Camacho & Las Casas; s & d US$55 with breakfast buffet; P ⊠ ⊠) About 2.5km south of the zócalo, this friendly hotel is located right across from the beach. Some of the motel-style rooms here have great seaview balconies, and there's a decent pool fringed with palms at lobby level.

There are several good mid-range places around Playa Mocambo:

Hotel Villas Santa Ana Inn (Map p671; ☎ /fax 922-47-57; Suárez 1314; s/d US$36/45, bungalows from US$64; P ☒ ☒) A short walk from Playa Mocambo, this inn is ideal for families, with a garden, pool and spacious suites decorated with Diego Rivera prints. The hotel faces the inland side of the Carr Veracruz-Boca del Río; look for the easily-missed first street on the right, a couple of hundred meters south of the traffic circle by Hotel Mocambo (below).

Hotel Bello (Map p671; ☎ 922-48-28, 800-715-74-97; www.hotelbello.com; Av Ruiz Cortines 258; s & d US$55; P ☒ ☒ ☒) Polished to a high gloss, the Hotel Bello has the shiny, happy staff to match. Comfortable tiled rooms facing the ocean or Carnaval parade route are within stumbling distance of Veracruz nightlife.

Hotel Lois (Map p671; ☎ 937-82-90, 800-712-91-36; www.hotellois.com; Av Ruiz Cortines 10; s & d US$68; P ☒ ☒) If you're into gaudy, Lois is the lady for you. The garish interior might hurt your eyes, but rooms are decked out with safes, minibars and bathtubs. It's in the middle of nightlife central, and the rooms on the north side have a good view of the Carnaval parade.

TOP END
Efficient service and plenty of gleam are the hallmarks of this price range.

Holiday Inn (Map p672; ☎ 932-45-50; hichvera@ prodigy.net.mx; Morelos 225; s & d from US$74; P ☒ ☒) Two blocks from the zócalo, the stylishly renovated Holiday Inn has a funky trapezoidal pool and comfortable rooms with all the modern conveniences. Beautiful ceramic sinks, painted details and wooden furniture set this place apart from flashier hotels.

Features of these higher-end city seafront hotels include business centers, conference rooms, upscale restaurants and gyms.

Fiesta Inn (Map p671; ☎ 923-15-00; fax 923-15-09; Figueroa 68; s/d US$125/135; P ☒ ☒ ☒) With a gorgeous pool bordered with palms, a bright lobby and beautiful suite-style rooms, the Fiesta Inn is a very solid top-end choice. Junior suites have kitchenettes with minifridges and coffeemakers. The location is quiet, the management excellent and the views amazing.

Hotel Emporio (Map p672; ☎ 932-00-20, 800-295-20-00; emporio@ver.megared.net.mx; Paseo del Malecón 244; s & d US$95; P ☒ ☒) Towering over the harbor, the slick Emporio features an outside elevator that soars above three swimming pools to a rooftop garden. The luxuries of a large 'standard' room include bathtub, hair dryer and separate faucet for drinking water.

The following luxury resorts around Playa Mocambo boast pools, gardens and private beaches.

Hotel Mocambo (Map p671; ☎ 922-02-00; 800-290-01-00; hmocambo@ifosel.net.mx; Av Ruiz Cortines 4000; s & d US$83; P ☒ ☒) This airy, sunny hotel is the original luxury resort in this area. Its all-encompassing nautical theme comes complete with creaky wooden stairways and steering-wheel window frames. Amenities include three sizable pools (two indoors) and tennis courts, and all rooms have ocean – or at worst, horizon – views. Playa Mocambo is a minute's walk from the foot of the terraced gardens.

Hotel Playa Paraíso (Map p671; ☎ 923-07-00, 800-715-48-18; www.playaparaiso.com.mx; Av Ruiz Cortines 3500; s & d US$113; P ☒ ☒ ☒) Smaller than its neighbors, the Playa Paraíso possesses a relaxed elegance. Rooms and suites have spacious bathrooms and safes, hairdryers and coffeemakers. Bungalows near the beach are older and a bit cheaper.

Hotel Puerta del Sol (Map p671; ☎ 989-05-04, 800-110-01-23; www.hotelpuertadelsolveracruz.com; Av Ruiz Cortines 3495; s & d US$105; P ☒ ☒ ☒ ☒) This swank, imposing place has 258 rooms with picturesque views. The hotel's beach club is open daily from 10am to 7pm, with free hourly shuttle, and its restaurant serves up live music every Thursday through Saturday. Standing above its own mall full of shops and fast food, the hotel is also next to Veracruz' World Trade Center and Plaza las Américas shopping mall.

Eating
Food in Veracruz is nothing short of wonderful. Veracruzana sauce, found on fish all over Mexico, is made from onions, garlic, tomatoes, olives, green peppers and spices. International cuisine is available – but with so much great, cheap Mexican fare around, why bother?

ZÓCALO AREA   Map p672
The cafés under the portales are as much for drinks and atmosphere as for food. During the day here, popular places serve lunches at outdoor café tables; at night, music is the

magnet. Saunter by and find one that appeals to you, or stop at any one with a free table. Typically, fish dishes cost US$6, seafood cocktails US$4 and beer around US$1.75.

Gran Café del Portal (☎ 931-27-59; cnr Av Independencia & Zamora; meals US$3-9; 🕑 7am-midnight) Years ago this spot was the site of a Veracruz institution known as the Gran Café de la Parroquia. After a change in ownership and moniker, it remains a cavernous, convivial café, and customers still request a refill of café lechero by clinking spoons on glasses. For food, try typical dishes such as fish veracruzana or steak tampiqueño. If you wish for peace and quiet, avoid this place: marimbas and mariachis set up residence here.

El Rincón de la Trova (☎ 918-54-25; Callejón de la Lagunilla 59; comida corrida US$2.50; 🕑 1-9pm Mon-Fri) Stop by for the excellent *comida corrida* at lunchtime, then come back in the evening for drinks and live music (Thursday through Saturday from 8pm to 3am). Look for Callejón de la Lagunilla between Serdán and Arista, two blocks south of the zócalo.

Pardiñolas (☎ 779-15-47; Zamora 138; dishes US$3-8; 🕑 11am-10pm) On the less hectic southeast side of the zócalo, Pardiñolas serves sea bass in 10 different ways – for more adventurous people, there's the seafood-stuffed plantain. The strains of marimba and norteño music waft in from across the plaza, not from across the table.

THE CRAFTY COUNTESS

Local myth has it that during the colonial era, a countess who made her home in Veracruz didn't take too well to her husband's protracted absences. To while away the time, she took lovers from among the city's lesser nobility – and, to preserve her reputation, had a set of tunnels built between the buildings she visited most often.

Fanciful as such proceedings may seem, they're probably more accurate than further tales that have the countess murdering the lovers who began to bore her. According to these stories, the tunnels served as escape routes from the crime scenes.

Rumor has it that tunnels still exist between the Palacio Municipal site and the cathedral, extending as far as the building presently housing the nightspot known as 'La Casona de la Condesa.'

La Estancia de Boca (☎ 932-32-75; guspein@hotmail.com; cnr Morelos & Juárez; dinners US$5-9; 🕑 11am-10pm) Come here to sample regional specialties like *molcajete* (US$7), the house special – a pre-Hispanic dish with tomatoes, garlic, onion and nopal. The relaxed and upscale atmosphere is enhanced by amiable, thoughtful waiters.

Cocina Económica Veracruz (☎ 31-00-80; cnr Zamora & Av Madero; comida corrida US$2; 🕑 11am-8pm) Two blocks southwest of the zócalo, this place is aimed at locals, not tourists. It serves cheap, basic, wholesome Mexican food at unbeatable prices.

HARBOR Map p672

Gran Café de la Parroquia (☎ 932-25-84; Farias 34; meals US$3-9; 🕑 6am-midnight) This vast restaurant-coffeehouse faces the harbor and has a very sociable ambience. The menu is similar to Gran Café del Portal's, and it gets as crowded. It's especially popular for breakfast, when the café con leche is in high demand.

Samborcito (☎ 931-43-88; 16 de Septiembre 700; dishes US$2-10; 🕑 7am-6pm) Packed with locals feasting on excellent gorditas, this is a Veracruz favorite.

La Suriana 2 (☎ 931-70-99; Av Zaragoza 286; dishes US$2-8; 🕑 11am-7pm) La Suriana has a friendly family feel and excellent seafood at budget prices – come here for cocteles, soup and the freshest of fish.

The top floor of the municipal **fish market** (Landero y Cos) is packed until early evening with comedores doing bargain fish filets and shrimp *al mojo de ajo*. Not for the faint of stomach, the market is heavy on atmosphere and fishy aromas.

DOWN THE COAST

Restaurants at Playa Mocambo tend to be pricey and boring. However, enjoying a seafood meal in the river-mouth village of Boca del Río, 10km south of Veracruz' center, is an indispensable part of a visit to Veracruz for many Mexicans – a long Sunday lunch is the favorite way to do it. **Pardiño's** (☎ 986-05-65; Zaragoza 127; dishes US$3-8; 🕑 11am-10pm), in the village center, is the best-known restaurant, but there are several more equally worthwhile ones along the riverside.

Mandinga, about 8km further down the coast from Boca del Río, is also known for its seafood (especially prawns) and has a clutch of small restaurants.

Entertainment

A café seat under the **zócalo portales** is a ringside ticket to some of the best entertainment in town. There you might witness, in two blinks, crazily dancing couples, families with out-of-control kids, cruising transvestites and vendors hawking SpongeBob balloons – to the accompaniment of wandering mariachis, marimba bands and guitarists vying to be heard above each other. Some evenings there are visiting musicians or dancers on a temporary stage. Sometimes you'll find whole groups of revelers going wild; other times it's all staid tourists sitting at their tables waiting for something to happen.

LIVE MUSIC

La Casona de la Condesa (Map p672; ☎ 933-54-51; Callejón de la Lagunilla 17; cover US$2.75, US$3.75 on Sat; ☼ 10pm-5am Tue-Sun) Those looking for a less teenybopper-oriented evening than is offered by the city's nightclubs might try La Casona, which offers great mixed drinks and solid live music every night it's open.

El Rincón de la Trova (see Eating, earlier; ☼ 8pm-3am, Thu-Sat), just down the alley from La Casona, attracts salsa lovers with live music and awesome cocktails Thursday through Saturday nights.

If you hanker for something more sedate, ask the tourist office for information on concerts and cultural events. Several central cinemas show recent-release movies. **Centro Cultural Casa Principal** (Map p672; ☎ 932-69-31; Molina 315; admission US$1; ☼ 10am-6pm Tue-Sun) hosts art exhibitions and cultural events.

NIGHTCLUBS & DISCOS

Popular with the under-30 set is the happening nightclub, bar and disco scene along waterfront Blvd Camacho near the junction with Av Ruiz Cortines.

Hotel Lois lobby bar (cocktails from US$2.75; ☼ from 10pm) The purple neon tower of Hotel Lois is the most conspicuous focus, and it attracts a well-dressed crowd with live music nightly.

Most of the discos in this area charge a cover of US$3 to US$10 and don't open until 10pm or 11pm. Women often get in cheaper, and Friday and Saturday nights are more expensive. During holiday times, the entire area becomes an outdoor party, with bars and snack stalls along Blvd Camacho, live loud music, and dancing in the streets.

There's a good collection of trendy spots:

Aquarius (Map p671; ☎ 922-77-07; Blvd Camacho 10; ☼ 2pm-4am Tue-Sun) No shorts or sandals, kids.

Big Fish (Map p671; ☎ 922-77-00; Blvd Camacho 10; cover US$3.75; ☼ 10pm-5am Thu-Sat) No cover on Thursdays.

Carioca (Map p671; ☎ 937-82-90; Hotel Lois; ☼ from 10pm) Know your pasos beforehand at this hip salsa club.

Carlos 'n' Charlie's (Map p671; ☎ 922-29-10; Blvd Camacho 26; no cover; ☼ 2pm-3am) Twenty- and 30-somethings hang here.

Kachimba (Map p671; ☎ 927-19-80; info@kachimba.com; cnr Blvd Camacho & Militar; cover US$7.50; ☼ from 8pm) Call ahead for reservations at this formal salsa club with live shows.

La Sobremesa (Map p671; ☎ 922-45-79; Blvd Camacho 9; cover US$5; ☼ from 6pm Tue-Sun) A busy stop for mixed drinks, cheap beer and dancing on tables.

Roka (Map p671; ☎ 937-64-80; Av Ruiz Cortines 8; cover US$5; ☼ from 10pm Thu-Sat)

Getting There & Away

Passenger train service to Veracruz is, sadly, no more.

AIR

Frequent flights between Veracruz and Mexico City are offered by Mexicana and Aeroméxico; the latter also flies to and from Tampico and Villahermosa, and Mexicana flies to Tampico and to Cancún via Mérida. Aerocaribe has direct flights to Minatitlán, with onward connections to Cancún and other destinations. Direct flights from Houston are offered by Continental.

Aerocaribe & Mexicana (Map p672; ☎ 932-22-42, 800-502-20-00; fax 932-86-99; cnr Serdán & 5 de Mayo; ☼ 9am-1:30pm & 4-7:50pm Mon-Fri, 9am-2:45pm Sat)

Continental (Map p671; ☎ 922-60-08; Av Ruiz Cortines 1600; ☼ 9am-6pm Mon-Sat)

BUS

Veracruz is a major hub, with good services up and down the coast and inland along the Córdoba–Puebla–Mexico City corridor. Buses to and from Mexico City can be heavily booked at holiday times.

The renovated bus station (Map p671) is about 3km south of the zócalo. The 1st-class/deluxe area fronts Av Díaz Mirón on the corner with Xalapa and, though modern, it's quite inconvenient for users. The waiting area has phones and a snack bar, but you might not be allowed in if you don't have a ticket. The left-luggage room closes at night, and the only alternative is to buy a token for an overpriced locker. Behind the 1st-class station, the 2nd-class side is entered from Av Lafragua. There's a 24-hour luggage room here. Daily departures include the following:

Acayucan (US$12, 3½hr, 16 1st-class daily; frequent 2nd-class)

Catemaco (US$7.50, 3½hr, 9 1st-class daily; 10 2nd-class directos)

Córdoba (US$6, 1¾hr, 29 1st-class daily; hourly 2nd-class directos)

Mexico City (US$22, 5½hr, 16 1st-class daily; at least 15 2nd-class daily) To TAPO.

Oaxaca (US$25, 7hr, 3 1st-class daily; 1 2nd-class directo)

Orizaba (US$7, 2½hr, 29 1st-class daily; at least 10 2nd-class directos)

Papantla (US$11, 4½hr, 6 1st-class daily; hourly 2nd-class)

Poza Rica (US$12, 5hr, 21 1st-class daily; hourly 2nd-class)

Puebla (US$15, 3½hr, 7 1st-class daily; at least 3 2nd-class directo)

San Andrés Tuxtla (US$7, 3hr, 15 1st-class daily; frequent 2nd-class)

Santiago Tuxtla (US$6, 2½hr, 11 1st-class daily; frequent 2nd-class)

Tampico (US$25, 9½hr, 17 1st-class daily)

Tuxpan (US$14, 5½hr, 11 1st-class daily)

Villahermosa (US$23, 7½hr, 14 1st-class daily)

Xalapa (US$5, 2hr, 1st-class every 20-30 min 6am-11.30pm; hourly 2nd-class)

Buses leaving Veracruz also go to Campeche, Cancún, Chetumal, Matamoros, Mérida and Salina Cruz.

CAR & MOTORCYCLE
Many car rental agencies have desks at the Veracruz airport. There are also some larger agencies scattered around town:

Avis (Map p671; ☎ 923-40-21; Howard Johnson Hotel, Blvd Camacho 1263; ◷ 9am-6pm Mon-Fri)

Dollar (Map p671; ☎ 935-88-08; fax 935-88-07; Bolivar 501B; ◷ 9am-6pm Mon-Fri)

Hertz (Map p671; ☎ 937-47-88; Hotel Costa Verde, Blvd Camacho 3797; ◷ 8am-7pm Mon-Fri, 9am-7pm Sat, 9am-1pm Sun)

Getting Around
Veracruz' airport is 11km southwest of town near Hwy 140. There's no bus service to or from town; taxis cost around US$12.

To get into the city center from in front of the 1st-class bus station, take a bus marked 'Díaz Mirón y Madero' (US$0.50). It will head to Parque Zamora then up Madero. For the zócalo, get off on the corner of Madero and Lerdo and turn right. Returning to the bus stations, pick up the same bus going south on 5 de Mayo. At the booth outside the 1st-class station you can buy a taxi ticket to the zócalo for US$2.50.

Buses marked 'Mocambo-Boca del Río' (US$1 to Boca del Río) leave every few minutes from the corner of Zaragoza and Serdán near the zócalo; it goes to Parque Zamora then down Blvd Camacho to Mocambo (20 minutes; for the beach, get off at Expover exhibition hall on Calzada Mocambo and walk down the street left of the Hotel Mocambo) and Boca del Río (30 minutes).

AU buses to Antón Lizardo stop at Boca del Río and Mandinga. They leave from the 2nd-class bus station every 20 minutes until 8:45pm; the last one back to town leaves around 8pm.

CÓRDOBA & FORTÍN DE LAS FLORES
☎ 271 / Córdoba pop 135,000, Fortín pop 20,000 / Córdoba elevation 924m, Fortín elevation 970m
Although Córdoba lacks big-ticket natural or cultural attractions, this proud colonial town is worth a stop for its atmosphere alone. About 125km west of Veracruz, the city lies in the foothills of Mexico's central mountains, surrounded by enticing, fertile countryside. Its inhabitants enjoy a cool, temperate climate, a laid-back lifestyle and some first-class cuisine.

In 1618, 30 Spanish families founded Córdoba in order to stop escaped African slaves from attacking travelers between Mexico City and the coast; consequently, the town is known as 'La Ciudad de los Treinta Caballeros' (City of the 30 Knights). Today it's a commercial and processing center for produce such as sugarcane, tobacco and coffee from the nearby hillsides and fruit from the lowlands.

Just west of Córdoba, **Fortín de las Flores** is a center for commercial flower production, though most of the color is confined to the nurseries and to private gardens. Peaceful Fortín is popular as a weekend retreat for the Mexico City middle class, but there's little for most travelers here.

Orientation

Córdoba's central Plaza de Armas sports fine 18th-century portales on three sides, with a row of busy cafés under the arches on the northeast. The city streets have numbers, not names. Avs 2, 4, 6 etc are northeast of the plaza; Avs 3, 5, 7 etc are southwest of the plaza. The Calles are at right angles to the Avenidas, with Calles 2, 4, 6 etc northwest of the plaza and the odd-numbered Calles to the southeast.

Fortín's big, open plaza, the Parque Principal, shelters the Palacio Municipal in the middle and a cathedral on the south side. It's 7km from central Córdoba, but the towns have grown into each other along Hwy 150.

Information

Banks Around the plaza; have 24-hour ATMs and change traveler's checks.

eWorld Ciber Café (☎ 714-19-63; Calle 4 No115; per hr US$1; ☼ 9am-10pm) Internet access.

Post Office (Av 3 s/n; ☼ 8am-4pm Mon-Fri, 9am-1pm Sat) Just northwest of the plaza.

Sanatorio Covadonga (☎ 714-55-20; www.sanatorio covadonga.com.mx in Spanish; Av 7 No 1610; ☼ 24hr) Provides urgent care at all hours.

Tourist Information (☎ 712-25-31; Palacio Municipal; ☼ 8:30am-8pm Mon-Fri, 8:30am-1pm Sat) On the northwest side of the plaza; friendly staff offer maps, brochures and a monthly schedule of activities, all in Spanish.

Sights & Activities

The **Ex-Hotel Zevallos**, built in 1687, is not a hotel but the former home of the condes (counts) of Zevallos. It's on the northeast side of Córdoba's Plaza de Armas, behind the portales. Plaques in the courtyard record that Juan O'Donojú and Agustín de Iturbide met here after mass on August 24, 1821, and agreed on terms for Mexico's independence. O'Donojú, the new viceroy, had concluded it was useless for Spain to try to cling to its colony; Iturbide, leader of the anti-imperial forces, was a former royalist general who had changed sides. Contrary to the Plan de Iguala, in which Iturbide and Vicente Guerrero had proposed a European monarch as Mexican head of state, O'Donojú and Iturbide agreed that a Mexican could hold that office. Iturbide went on to a brief reign as Emperor Agustín I. The building is now notable mainly for its excellent restaurants.

At the southeast end of Plaza de Armas, the sprawling late-18th-century church is **La Parroquia de la Inmaculada Concepción**, famous for its loud bells.

Just off the plaza, the **Museo de Antropología** (Calle 3 s/n; admission free; ☼ 9am-2pm & 4-8pm) has a modest but well-presented collection of originals and replicas of indigenous artifacts from around the area. Displays include a Classic Veracruz palma and some beautifully crafted personal ornaments.

Faraventuras runs trips to waterfalls, caves, underground rivers and other natural attractions in the area. Climbs on Pico de Orizaba, for a group of six people, will cost you around US$60 per person per day with

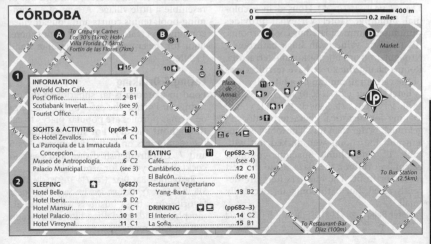

CÓRDOBA

0 — 400 m
0 — 0.2 miles

To Crepas y Carnes Los 30's (1km); Hotel Villa Florida (1.5km); Fortín de las Flores (7km)

Market

INFORMATION	
eWorld Ciber Café	1 B1
Post Office	2 B1
Scotiabank Inverlat	(see 9)
Tourist Office	3 C1

SIGHTS & ACTIVITIES	(pp681–2)
Ex-Hotel Zevallos	4 C1
La Parroquia de La Inmaculada Concepción	5 C1
Museo de Antropología	6 C2
Palacio Municipal	(see 3)

SLEEPING 🛏	(p682)
Hotel Bello	7 C1
Hotel Iberia	8 D2
Hotel Mansur	9 C1
Hotel Palacio	10 B1
Hotel Virreynal	11 C1

EATING 🍴	(pp682–3)
Cafés	(see 4)
Cantábrico	12 C1
El Balcón	(see 4)
Restaurant Vegetariano Yang-Bara	13 B2

DRINKING 🍷	(pp682–3)
El Interior	14 C2
La Sofia	15 B1

Plaza de Armas

To Bus Station (2.5km)

To Restaurant-Bar Díaz (100m)

CENTRAL GULF COAST

guide, equipment and food. A three-day expedition to the summit, with all equipment, accommodations and food, costs US$250 per person in a group of six. Contact the company at its head office in the **Xochítl travel agency** (☎ 713-16-95; http://communities.msn.com.mx /faraventuras in Spanish; cnr Av 3 Pte & Calle 2; 🕒 9am-5:30pm Mon-Fri) in Fortín de las Flores – just a couple of blocks from the plaza.

Festivals & Events

On the evening of Good Friday, Córdoba marks Jesus' crucifixion with a procession of silence, in which thousands of residents walk through the streets behind an altar of the Virgin. Everyone holds a lit candle, no one utters a word, and the church bells are eerily quiet.

April, May and June are the best months to see flowers blooming; Fortín's annual flower festival runs for a week in late April or early May.

Sleeping

Style and value typify Córdoba's hotels.

CÓRDOBA

Hotel Iberia (☎ 712-13-01; hoteliberiacordoba@hot mail.com; Av 2 No 919; s/d US$15/18, 2 beds US$24; P 🐶) Amiable management and details like arched brick window frames lend a cozy feel to the Iberia, the best budget deal in town. Small, modern rooms with cable TV and air-con are arranged around a courtyard.

Hotel Virreynal (☎ 712-23-77; fax 712-03-95; Av 1 No 309; s/d US$24/27; 🐶) Housed in a colonial building, Hotel Virreynal provides sumptuous, immaculate fan-cooled rooms. It's fantastic value, with huge bathrooms, wrought-iron ornamentation and terracotta. Rooms facing the street have terrific views of the cathedral, but can be a bit noisy.

Hotel Mansur (☎ 712-60-00; fax 712-69-89; Av 1 No 301; s/d US$29/32, 2 beds US$33; P 🐶) If you're looking for historical character, it doesn't get much better than this. The lobby is opulent and the rooms well decked out with cable TV and phone. Spacious common balconies overlook the plaza, as do the best rooms in front. The quarters here are decently sized, but bathrooms are decidedly small.

Hotel Bello (☎ 712-81-22; cnr Av 2 & Calle 5; s/d US$33/38; P 🐶) A sparkly choice, the newish,

tidy Hotel Bello has some lovely mountain views. Interior rooms are quieter, but all have small bathrooms with elegant showers.

Hotel Palacio (☎ 712-21-88; fax 712-60-78; Av 3 No 200; s/d US$24/33, with air-con US$34/38; P 🐶) This hotel though lacking in style, has spacious and clean rooms, where the air-con is whisper-quiet. Many upper rooms have wonderful views of Pico de Orizaba.

Hotel Villa Florida (☎ 716-33-33; vflorida@ver1 .telmex.net.mx, Av 1 No 3002; s/d US$83/110; P 🐶 🐶) Cockily aware that it's Córdoba's most upmarket option, the Villa Florida has a big pool, restaurant and lovely gardens with a fountain. Here's the rub: its location, 1.5km northwest of the center.

FORTÍN DE LAS FLORES

Hotel Posada Loma (☎ 713-06-58; posada66@prodigy .net.mx; Blvd Córdoba-Fortín Km 333; s/d US$55/59, bungalows from US$80; P 🐶 🐶) Treat yourself to a stay here. The rooms are good value in themselves, but the real draw is the park-like setting: gardens and terraces, birds and orchids. Breakfast in the restaurant, which offers a spectacular view of Pico de Orizaba, is unbeatable. An inviting pool and friendly management sweeten the deal. This attractive hotel is off the south side of Hwy 150, about 1km from central Fortín.

Gran Hotel El Pueblito (☎ 713-00-33; hotelpueb lito@hotmail.com; Av 2 Ote 505; s/d US$28/35; P 🐶 🐶) A slightly humbler option than the Posada Loma, this hotel is charming in its own right. The spacious, comfortable rooms are named, not numbered, and laid out to resemble a little village. A gem of a swimming pool, tennis courts and bougainvillea combine to create a delightful atmosphere. Look for the entrance between Calles 9 and 11 Nte.

Eating & Drinking

Food in Córdoba is far superior to the offerings in Fortín. The cafés under the Plaza de Armas portales are popular places to eat throughout the day. For fine seafood, try the restaurants on Calle 15 between Avs 5 and 7. Ultrafresh fish dishes and seafood cocktails are yours for around US$6.

Restaurant-Bar Díaz (☎ 714-37-90; Calle 15 No 516; US$1.50-9; 🕒 10:30am-7pm Tue-Sun) This local favorite does brisk business with a fun atmosphere and specialties like an avocado stuffed with mariscos.

El Balcón (Av 1 No 101; dishes US$6-10; ☸ from 5:30pm Mon-Sat, from 2pm Sun) Upstairs in the Ex-Hotel Zevallos building, El Balcón overlooks the plaza. The steaks are solid and the desserts delectable, and this balcony is the best seat in town.

Crepas Y Carnes Los 30's (☎ 712-33-79; Av 9 No 2004; crêpes US$2.50-5; ☸ 1pm-midnight) Though it's a good trek from the zócalo, at the corner of Calle 20, this place is worth the walk. You'll sit down to colorful décor, a party atmosphere and mouthwatering sweet and savory crêpes. Next door, they serve Sicilian pizza (US$5 to US$6) and delish Italian specialties.

Restaurant Vegetariano Yang-Bara (☎ 712-69-34; Av 5 No 100; veggie comida corrida US$1.75; ☸ 9am-7pm Mon-Sat) A humble veggie oasis, Yang-Bara does a cheap, healthy *comida corrida* and fresh juices.

Cantábrico (Calle 3 No 9; lunch buffet US$7.50-11; ☸ 11am-9pm) Slightly upscale in atmosphere, this is an excellent choice for quality cuisine. From 2pm to 6pm daily, the lavish lunch buffet is a great deal with soups, salads, entrées and desserts.

El Interior (☎ 727-17-17; Av 3 No 318, Int 2; coffee US$1.25; ☸ 9am-9pm Mon-Sat, 10am-8pm Sun) Hidden away in a shady arcade, this café and gift shop has new-agey books and luscious desserts on offer.

La Sofia (☎ 714-51-81; Av 5 s/n; ☸ 5pm-2am Mon-Sat) Near Calle 4, this bar makes a kick-ass michelada. It's an OK place to hang, with soccer on the tube and a non-cantina feel.

Getting There & Around
BUS
Córdoba's bus station, which has deluxe (UNO and ADO GL), 1st-class (ADO and Cristóbal Colón) and 2nd-class (AU) services, is at Av Privada 4, 2.5km southeast of the plaza. To get to the town center from the station, take a local bus marked 'Centro' or buy a taxi ticket (US$1.50). To Fortín de las Flores and Orizaba, it's more convenient to take a local bus (US$1.25) from Av 11 than to go out to the Córdoba bus station. As always, 2nd-class buses run more often to mid-range destinations, take longer and cost 10% less than the corresponding 1st-class service. Long-distance deluxe and 1st-class buses from Córdoba include the following departures:

Mexico City (US$18, 4½hr, about 1 hourly) To TAPO.
Oaxaca (US$20, 6hr, 2 daily)
Puebla (US$11, 3hr, at least 12 daily)
Veracruz (US$6, 2hr, at least 1 hourly)
Xalapa (US$9, 3½hr, about 15 daily)

In Fortín, local buses arrive and depart from Calle 1 Sur, on the west side of the plaza. A small ADO depot on the corner of Av 2 and Calle 6 has mainly de paso services to Mexico City, Veracruz, Puebla and Xalapa. UNO has two daily deluxe buses to Mexico City; ADO GL has one. Prices are more or less the same as those from Córdoba.

CAR & MOTORCYCLE
Córdoba, Fortín de las Flores and Orizaba are linked by toll Hwy 150D, the route which most buses take, and by the much slower Hwy 150. A scenic back road goes through the hills from Fortín, via Huatusco, to Xalapa.

ORIZABA
☎ 272 / pop 121,000 / elevation 1219m
Orizaba, 16km west of Córdoba, was founded by the Spanish to guard the Veracruz–Mexico City road. It retains a few colonial buildings and church domes, though much was lost in the 1973 earthquake. An industrial center in the late 19th century, its factories were early centers of the unrest that led to the unseating of dictator Porfirio Díaz. Today it has a big brewery and cement, textile and chemical industries.

Most foreign visitors use Orizaba only as a base for climbing Pico de Orizaba, one of Mexico's most spectacular volcanoes and its highest peak. But Orizaba's cool climate and café scene has its own appeal, and one jewel here is the excellent art museum.

Orientation
The central plaza is Parque Castillo, with the irregularly shaped Parroquia de San Miguel on its north side. Madero, a busy street bordering the plaza's west side, divides avenidas into Oriente (Ote; east) and Poniente (Pte; west). Av Colón, on the south side, is the boundary between the Norte and Sur calles. All of the other streets have numbers rather than names – check out the map to learn the strange logic of the system. Av Pte 7/Av Ote 6, three blocks south of the plaza, is the main east–west artery.

Information

Banks A couple of banks with ATMs are on Av Ote 2, a block south of the plaza.

Cruz Roja (☎ 725-05-50; Av Colón Ote 253; US$2.50 consultation fee; ⏱ 24hr) Provides medical care.

Cybercity (Av Ote 2; per hr US$1; ⏱ 8:30am-10pm Mon-Sat, 8:30am-6pm Sun) Internet access.

Post Office (Av Ote 2)

Tourist Office (☎ 726-58-61; dirturismori@hotmail .com; Palacio de Hierro; ⏱ 8am-9pm Mon-Fri, 8am-3pm Sat) Enthusiastic staff; just off the main plaza.

Sights

PARQUE CASTILLO

Although Orizaba's central plaza isn't as festive as one might wish, it does have some noteworthy attractions. The **Parroquia de San Miguel**, the big parish church on the park's north side, is mainly 17th century in style, with several towers and some Puebla-type tiles.

The **Palacio de Hierro**, off the northwest corner of the plaza, was the Belgian pavilion at the Paris International Exhibition in the late 19th century. Orizaba bought the prefabricated cast-iron and steel building for US$13,800 and had it dismantled, shipped to Mexico and reassembled as a town hall. Many municipal offices have been moved to the new Palacio Municipal on the west side of the river, but the renovated old building now holds the tourist office, some government chambers, a minuscule beer museum and a café.

MUSEO DE ARTE DEL ESTADO

The highlight of Orizaba is the **State Art Museum** (☎ 724-32-00; cnr Av Ote 4 & Calle Sur 25; admission US$1; ⏱ 10am-5pm Tue-Sun), at Calle Sur 25. This masterpiece is housed in a gorgeously restored colonial building dating from 1776 that has been at times a church, a hospital and a military base. The museum consists of several rooms, each of which adheres to a different theme. In one room, exquisite paintings depict key moments in the history of Veracruz state. Another has contemporary works by regional artists; still another depicts Veracruz through the eyes of travelers. There's also a respectable collection of 20th-century Mexican paintings and drawings.

Activities

The canyon beside the Hotel Fiesta Cascada (see following) features a beautiful waterfall emerging from dense forest, offering spectacular **hiking** possibilities. A forest-flanked trail begins a few meters west of the hotel and descends to the canyon floor, where it forks. To the left, the trail follows the river for several kilometers. To the right, it crosses a footbridge beside the waterfall and a small power station, then reaches a rough road that winds northwest into the mountains, through forest and farmland.

Looming over the Alameda park west of town, the **Cerro del Borrego** offers brilliant views if you get to the top very early, before the mist rolls in.

Turismo Aventura Desafío (☎ 725-06-96; Av Pte 3 No 586) arranges various adventure activities in nearby hills, mountains and canyons, including climbs of the Pico de Orizaba (p686). A one-day climb partway up the mountain and back costs about US$170 per person.

Sleeping

Hotel Arenas (☎ /fax 725-23-61; Av Nte 2 No 169; s/d US$12/17) The best budget value is this friendly, family-run hotel, with a central location and a quiet, plant-filled courtyard garden. Centrally located, its clean rooms come with cable TV – smell-check the bathrooms before check-in.

Grand Hotel de France (☎ 725-23-11; fax 725-44-44; Av Ote 6 No 186; s/d US$23/29, old rooms US$17/21; ⓟ ✷) Your peso goes a long way in this grand hotel, with thoughtfully decorated rooms surrounding a pleasant interior courtyard. Newer rooms are more attractive, but all are somewhat noisy, between the street traffic outside and the courtyard acoustics inside.

Hotel L'Orbe (☎ 725-50-33; fax 725-53-44; Av Pte 5 No 33; s/d US$27/32; ⓟ ✷) Enormous, spotless rooms render this hotel a great mid-range deal. The remodeled quarters feature aircon, cable TV and phones. Upstairs rooms have fab views of Pico de Orizaba.

Hotel Aries (☎ 725-35-20; Av Ote 6 No 263; s/d US$21/25; ⓟ ✷) Bright, comfortable rooms come with the usual modern amenities at this reasonably priced hotel. The halls are a bit dim, but the Aries is clean and friendly.

Hotel Fiesta Cascada (☎ 724-15-96; fax 724-55-99; Carr Puebla-Córdoba Km 275; s/d US$41/46, bungalows from US$44; ⓟ ✷ ▣) If you don't mind the long hike or taxi ride (head down Hwy 150D and look for two Pemex stations opposite each

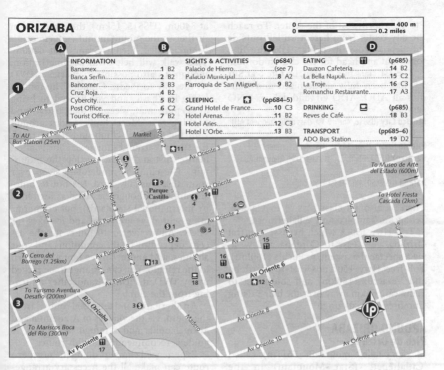

ORIZABA

INFORMATION	
Banamex	1 B2
Banca Serfin	2 B2
Bancomer	3 B3
Cruz Roja	4 B2
Cybercity	5 B2
Post Office	6 C2
Tourist Office	7 B2

SIGHTS & ACTIVITIES	(p684)
Palacio de Hierro	(see 7)
Palacio Municipal	8 A2
Parroquia de San Miguel	9 B2

SLEEPING	(pp684–5)
Grand Hotel de France	10 C3
Hotel Arenas	11 B2
Hotel Aries	12 C3
Hotel L'Orbe	13 B3

EATING	(p685)
Dauzon Cafetería	14 B2
La Bella Napoli	15 C2
La Troje	16 C3
Romanchu Restaurante	17 A3

DRINKING	(p685)
Reves de Café	18 B3

TRANSPORT	(pp685–6)
ADO Bus Station	19 D2

other, about 2km east of the center), consider staying here. The Cascada sits above a gorgeous canyon and has a pool, gardens and a private patch of rainforest. Charming, spacious rooms with minibar, TV and phone come at an unbeatable price.

Eating & Drinking

Some decent taco joints lie around the plaza, and the market, as always, offers cheap eats. In sedate Orizaba, many of the moderately priced restaurants close early.

Dauzon Cafetería (☎ 726-36-19; cnr Sur 5 & Av Colón; comida corrida US$2.50; ☒ 8am-9pm Mon-Thu, 8am-10pm Fri-Sun) If you can't stomach any more meat, head for this wonderful vegetarian restaurant and bakery. Wheat gluten posing as carne al pastor, or soy impersonating chorizo, is prepared fresh daily.

La Troje (☎ 725-08-05; Sur 5 No 225; comida corrida US$4; ☒ 11am-10pm) La Troje offers a dark, upscale atmosphere and an excellent five-course *comida corrida*. Mexican specialties are the order of the day.

La Bella Napoli (☎ 724-77-70; Sur 7 No 230; dishes US$5-11; ☒ 1:30pm-midnight Tue-Sun) Come here for superb Italian food and a festive atmosphere.

Romanchu Restaurante (☎ 725-25-85; cnr Av Pte 7 & Sur 4; Sun midday buffet US$9.50; ☒ 8am-11pm Mon-Sat, 8am-9:30pm Sun) A nonvegetarian paradise, the large and colorful Romanchu is popular for its exquisite beef dishes.

Mariscos Boca del Río (Av Pte 7 s/n; seafood US$5-7; ☒ noon-8pm Tue-Sun) Don't be deterred by its humble appearance: this is the best seafood restaurant in town. A few blocks west of the Romanchu, it offers large and economical shrimp, fish and squid dishes. An imposter restaurant of the same name lies north of the plaza.

Reves de Cafe (☎ 725-47-35; Sur 3 No 225; coffee US$1.25; ☒ 10:30am-10:30pm Mon-Sat, 5-10:30pm Sun) Warm up with some strong coffee at this café's low-key tables in its off-street courtyard.

Getting There & Around

Local buses from Fortín or Córdoba stop four blocks north and six blocks east of the town center, around Ote 9 and Nte 14. The AU (2nd-class) bus station is at Zaragoza

Pte 425, northwest of the center. To reach the city center from here, turn left outside the depot, cross the bridge, take the first fork right and head for the church domes.

The 1st-class bus station, on Ote 6 at Sur 13, has been fully modernized and handles all ADO, ADO GL and deluxe UNO services.

Mexico City (US$16, 4hr, 12 1st-class daily; frequent AU) To TAPO.

Puebla (US$9, 2½hr, 14 1st-class daily; frequent AU)

Veracruz (US$7, 2¼hr, 25 1st-class daily; frequent AU directo)

Xalapa (US$9.50, 4hr, 10 1st-class daily)

There is also 1st-class service to Oaxaca, Tehuacán, Tampico and Villahermosa.

Toll Hwy 150D, which bypasses central Orizaba, goes east to Córdoba and west, via a spectacular ascent, to Puebla (160km). Toll-free Hwy 150 runs east to Córdoba and Veracruz (150km) and southwest to Tehuacán, 65km away over the hair-raising Cumbres de Acultzingo.

AROUND ORIZABA
Pico de Orizaba

Mexico's tallest mountain (5611m), called 'Citlaltépetl' (Star Mountain) in the Náhuatl language, is 25km northwest of Orizaba. This dormant volcano has a small crater and a three-month snowcap. From the summit, in good weather, one can see Popocatépetl, Iztaccíhuatl and La Malinche to the west and the Gulf of Mexico 96km to the east. The only higher peaks in North America are Mt McKinley in Alaska and Mt Logan in Canada.

The most common route up Orizaba is from the north, using the small town of **Tlachichuca** as a base. Tlachichuca can be reached by white microbuses departing from the bus terminal in Ciudad Serdán (US$1, one hour). Serdán, in turn, can be reached from Puebla (US$3, two hours) or Orizaba (US$3.50, two hours). Infrequent AU buses also run directly between Tlachichuca and Puebla (US$4, four hours).

Unless you have navigation skills and a good map, and your group has some experience of snow- and ice-climbing techniques, you should not attempt this climb without a guide. Remember to allow several days for acclimatization beforehand. From Tlachichuca, take a taxi to Villa Hidalgo

at 3400m (US$15, 15km), then walk 10km further to the mountain hut *(refugio* or *albergue)* called 'Piedra Grande,' at 4200m. This walk will help with acclimatization, though it's also possible to charter a 4WD all the way to Piedra Grande. The refugio is big but basic, and you'll need to bring a sleeping mat, sleeping bag, stove and cooking gear. Most climbers start around 2am for the final climb and try to reach the summit around sunrise or shortly after, before mist and cloud envelop the mountain. The climb is moderately steep over snow that's usually hard. It's not technically difficult (though classified as 'extreme' by international standards), but crampons are essential, as are ropes and ice axes for safety. Allow five to 10 hours for the ascent, depending on the conditions and your abilities, and another three hours to return to the refugio. You can arrange to be picked up by 4WD at Piedra Grande after returning from the climb.

An alternative and less-used route is from the south, via the villages of Atzitzintla and Texmalaquilla and a refugio at 4750m. A guide is recommended for this route.

Experienced climbers doing the northern route can make all the necessary arrangements in Tlachichuca, but get maps well in advance. The 1:50,000 INEGI map is supposed to be the best, but it can be hard to obtain. Some specialist books on climbing in Mexico have adequate maps, including *Mexico's Volcanoes*, by RJ Secor. The best climbing period is October to March, with the most popular time being December and January.

In Tlachichuca, the Reyes family runs **Servimont** (☎ 245-451-50-09; www.servimont .com.mx; Ortega 1A), a climber-owned and climber-operated outfit that offers a wide range of trips up the mountain. Basic accommodations and good meals are available in a charming former soap factory that also serves as the company office. Servimont also acts as a Red Cross rescue facility and has an excellent reputation for safety. It's the longest-running operation in the area by far. Make reservations four months in advance. A three-day trip, including guide and rentals, costs approximately US$350 per person for a group of four or more.

Other guides also operate in Tlachichuca and you can book them in Orizaba and elsewhere. They may offer lower rates than Servimont, but a few have been known to cut corners when it comes to safety. It's even possible to make Pico de Orizaba trips from as far away as Oaxaca, where the adventure tourism firm Tierra Dentro (see p708) offers a range of trips lasting between four and six days for US$260 to US$620 per person.

If you're not staying with Servimont, you can hole up in Tlachichuca at the friendly and commodious **Hotel Gerar** (☎ 245-451-50-75; hotel_gerar@hotmail.com; Av 20 de Noviembre 200; s/d US$6/12; **P**). Staff can help with arranging guides and providing information. On the plaza, **La Casa Blanca** serves up a righteous steak for US$4.50.

Zongolica

A road leads 38km south from Orizaba to the mountain village of Zongolica, where isolated indigenous groups have unique styles of weaving. Buses leave Orizaba from Ote 3 between Nte 12 and Nte 14 every half-hour.

SOUTHEAST VERACRUZ

Southeast of Veracruz port is a flat, hot, wet coastal plain crossed by rivers and sheltering the serene port town of Tlacotalpan. South and southeast of Tlacotalpan is a hilly, green and fertile region known as Los Tuxtlas (*tooks*-tlahs), home to myriad lakes and waterfalls, as well as an agreeable climate. Mexican vacationers are attracted to Catemaco, a small lakeside resort, while the undeveloped coastline is increasingly popular with foreign visitors.

Los Tuxtlas is the western fringe of the ancient Olmec heartland, and Olmec artifacts can be observed at Santiago Tuxtla, Tres Zapotes and San Lorenzo. The basalt for the huge Olmec heads was quarried from Cerro Cintepec in the east of the Sierra de los Tuxtlas and then moved, probably by roller and raft, to San Lorenzo, 60km to the south.

The southeastern end of Veracruz state, bordering Tabasco and Chiapas, is home to oil metropolises such as Minatitlán and Coatzacoalcos, neither of which holds any attractions for visitors other than the fun of pronouncing their names.

TLACOTALPAN

☎ 288 / pop 9000 / elevation 10m

A tranquil, charming old town on the north bank of the wide Río Papaloapan, Tlacotalpan was a major port in the 19th century. Having preserved its broad plazas, colorful houses and cobbled streets, it received Unesco World Heritage status in 1998.

Information

For a helpful map of town, hit the **tourist office** (Palacio Municipal; 🕙 9am-3pm Mon-Fri), under the green and red portales facing Plaza Hidalgo. Around the corner toward the river, find the **post office** (🕙 8am-4pm Mon-Fri). A block south from the zócalo lies an **Internet café** (Alegre s/n; per hr US$1; 🕙 11am-11pm), and you can withdraw cash from a Scotiabank ATM next door to Posada Doña Lala (see following).

Sights

Enjoy idiosyncratically narrated tours of Tlacotalpan's mini-museums, starting with **Museo Salvador Ferrando** (Calle Alegre 6; admission US$1; 🕙 10:30am-5pm Tue-Sun), displaying assorted furniture and artifacts from the town's colonial history. Move on to **Casa Museo Agustín Lara** (Beltrán 6; admission US$1; 🕙 10am-5pm Mon-Sat), featuring memorabilia of Tlacotalpeño Agustín Lara (1900–70), a legendary and prolific musician, composer and Casanova. Locals may point you down the road to the **Mini-Zoológico Museo** (Carranza 25; donation US$1; 🕙 10am-5pm Mon-Sat), the home of Don Pío Barrán, who keeps several crocodiles and a range of artifacts including a locally excavated mastodon tooth and a sword supposedly belonging to Porfirio Díaz.

Move on to the pink **Casa de la Cultura Agustín Lara** (☎ 884-22-02; Carranza 43; 🕙 9am-5pm), where art exhibits, folkloric dance rehearsals and jarocho music lessons are free for visitors to observe; the gallery upstairs may exact an admission fee.

Festivals & Events

In late January and early February, Tlacotalpan's lively Candelaria festival features bull-running in the streets and an image of the Virgin floating down the river followed by a flotilla of small boats.

Sleeping

Prices triple or quadruple during the Candelaria holiday.

Hotel Posada Doña Lala (☎ 884-25-80; fax 884-25-81; Av Carranza 11; s & d US$23, with air-con US$33; P ⚒ ⚒) Near the river, the Doña Lala has the most personality of Tlaco's hotels, adorned with imaginative paintings and providing spotless, spacious rooms.

Hotel Reforma (☎ 884-20-22; Av Carranza 2; s & d US$27, with air-con US$32; P) Right off Plaza Zaragoza, this hotel is clean, cool, sunny and friendly.

Hotel Tlacotalpan (☎ 884-20-63; hoteltlacotalpan@tlaco.com.mx; Beltrán 35; s & d US$32-41; P ⚒ ⚒) Two blocks from the bus station, this low-key place has blue portales and rooms surrounding a simple courtyard.

Hotel Candelaria (☎ 884-31-20; Beltrán 66; s & d US$32-36; ⚒) Shiny as a newly minted peso, the Hotel Candelaria is comfortably housed in a modern building – front rooms have tiny balconies over the street.

For good eats, try **Restaurante Doña Lala** or one of the terrific open-air eateries (fresh seafood US$4-5) on the riverfront. In the center of town, a couple of lovely cafes face Plaza Hidalgo and the zócalo. Also around the plazas are artesanias shops selling local handicrafts such as crocheted lace and tiny chairs made from wood and leather.

Getting There & Around

Hwy 175 runs from Tlacotalpan up the Papaloapan valley to Tuxtepec, then twists and turns over the mountains to Oaxaca (320km). ADO offers service to Mexico City, Puebla, Xalapa and Veracruz, while Cuenca and Transportes Los Tuxtlas (TLT) buses cover local routes.

SANTIAGO TUXTLA

☎ 294 / pop 16,000 / elevation 180m

Santiago, founded in 1525, is a quiet valley town in the rolling green foothills of the volcanic Sierra de los Tuxtlas. Though a stopover in its own right, it's worth visiting mainly for the Olmec artifacts around town and at Tres Zapotes, 23km away.

ADO and AU buses arriving in Santiago drop you where Calle Morelos runs off the highway. Go south (downhill) down Morelos a little and the Transportes Los Tuxtlas office will be on your left; turn right (west) here onto Ayuntamiento to reach the museum, on the south side of the zócalo. The post office is also on the zócalo, as are banks that change traveler's checks.

The **Olmec head** in the zócalo is known as the 'Cobata head,' after the estate (west of Santiago) where it was found. Thought to be a very late or even post-Olmec production, it's the biggest known Olmec head and unique in that its eyes are closed.

The newly remodeled **Museo Regional Tuxteco** (☎ 947-10-76; admission US$3; ☯ 9am-6pm Mon-Sat, 9am-3pm Sun & holidays), on the plaza, exhibits Olmec stone carvings, including another colossal head (this one from Nestepec west of Santiago), a rabbit head from Cerro de Vigía and a copy of Monument F, or 'El Negro,' from Tres Zapotes, which is an altar or throne with a human form carved into it. Countless small tools and other artifacts are also on display here.

Santiago celebrates the festivals of San Juan (June 24) and Santiago Apóstol (St James; July 25) with processions and dances including the Liseres, in which the participants wear jaguar costumes. The dance costumes also come out the week before Christmas.

Because it's also a family home, **Hotel Morelos** (☎ 947-04-74; Obregón 12; s/d US$11/15, 2 beds US$18) is easy to miss – the entrance is almost opposite the Transportes Los Tuxtlas bus station, a block south of Ayuntamiento. The rooms are small, cozy and neat; some are brighter than others. All have cable TV, fans and private bath with hot water.

The modern **Hotel Castellanos** (☎ 947-02-00; fax 947-04-00; cnr 5 de Mayo & Comonfort; s/d US$23/25; ⚒ ⚒), in a circular building on the north side of the zócalo, is unbelievable value. It's a beautiful establishment with all the modern facilities – surprising for a town of this size. The charming, round rooms are complemented by a refreshing swimming pool and incredible views. The restaurant serves decent main courses for around US$3.50. Cheaper eateries line up on the south side of the zócalo.

If no convenient services are available out of Santiago Tuxtla, you can go first to San Andrés Tuxtla by the frequent but suspension-free TLT buses (US$0.75, 30 minutes) or less frequent Cuenca vehicles (US$0.75, 20 minutes).

All local and regional buses stop at the same station beside the main road. From Santiago, ADO has eight de paso buses a day going west to Veracruz (US$6.50, 2½ hours) via Alvarado, five a day going east to Coatzacoalcos (US$7.50, 2½ hours) via Catemaco (US$1.50, one hour), and four a day to Acayucan (US$5, two hours). Cuenca has three buses a day going to Tlacotalpan (US$4). Cheaper but less comfortable TLT buses depart every 10 minutes for San Andrés Tuxtla, Catemaco and Veracruz, and hourly for Acayucan. Colectivo taxis frequently leave Ayuntamiento for San Andrés Tuxtla (US$2.50).

TRES ZAPOTES
☎ 294 / pop 3500

The important late-Olmec center of Tres Zapotes is now just a series of mounds in maize fields, but there are many interesting finds displayed at the museum in the village of Tres Zapotes, 23km west of Santiago Tuxtla.

Tres Zapotes was occupied for over 2000 years, from around 1200 BC to AD 1000. It was probably first inhabited while the great Olmec center of La Venta (Tabasco) still flourished. After the destruction of La Venta (about 600 BC), the city carried on in what archaeologists regard as an 'epi-Olmec' phase – a period when the spark had gone out of Olmec culture, and other civilizations, notably Izapa, were adding their marks. Most of the finds are from this later period.

At Tres Zapotes in 1939, Matthew Stirling, the first great Olmec excavator, unearthed part of an interesting chunk of basalt. One side was carved with an epi-

Olmec 'were-jaguar,' the other with a series of bars and dots, apparently part of a date in the Mayan Long Count system. Stirling decoded the date as September 3, 32 BC, which meant that the Olmecs preceded the Maya; until then, the Maya were believed to have been Mexico's earliest civilization. Much debate followed, but later finds supported Stirling's discovery. In 1969 a farmer came across the rest of the stone, now called Stela C, which bore the missing part of Stirling's date.

At the **Museo de Tres Zapotes** (admission US$2.50; ⏰ 8am-6pm), the objects are arranged on a disappointingly small cross-shaped platform. On the far side is the Tres Zapotes head, dating from about 100 BC, which was the first Olmec head to be discovered in modern times; it was found by a hacienda worker in 1858. Opposite the head is Stela A, the biggest piece, with three human figures in the mouth of a jaguar. This originally stood on its end. To the right of Stela A are two pieces. One is a sculpture of what may have been a captive with hands tied behind his or her back. The other piece has a toad carved on one side and a skull on the other.

Beyond Stela A is an altar or throne carved with the upturned face of a woman, and beyond that, in the corner, is the less interesting part of the famous Stela C. (The part with the date is in the Museo Nacional de Antropología, but a photo of it is on the wall here.) The museum attendant is happy

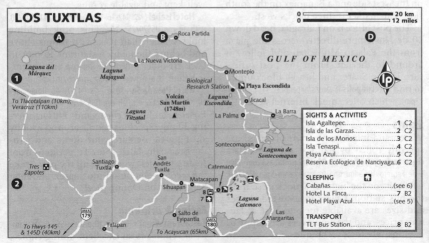

LOS TUXTLAS

0 _____ 20 km
0 _____ 12 miles

GULF OF MEXICO

Roca Partida

La Nueva Victoria

Laguna del Márquez

Laguna Majagual

Montepio

Biological Research Station

Playa Escondida

Volcán San Martín (1748m) ▲

Laguna Escondida

Jicacal

To Tlacotalpan (10km); Veracruz (110km)

Laguna Titzatal

La Palma

La Barra

Sontecomapan

Laguna de Sontecomapan

Tres Zapotes

Santiago Tuxtla

San Andrés Tuxtla

Catemaco

Sihuapan

Matacapan

Laguna Catemaco

Las Margaritas

To Hwys 145 & 145D (40km)

MEX 179

Talapan

Salto de Eyipantla

MEX 180

To Acayucan (65km)

SIGHTS & ACTIVITIES
Isla Agaltepec	1 C2
Isla de las Garzas	2 C2
Isla de los Monos	3 C2
Isla Tenaspi	4 C2
Playa Azul	5 C2
Reserva Ecológica de Nanciyaga	6 C2

SLEEPING
Cabañas	(see 6)
Hotel La Finca	7 B2
Hotel Playa Azul	(see 5)

TRANSPORT
TLT Bus Station	8 B2

to answer questions in Spanish or give a tour (be nice and tip him US$0.50 or so).

The road to Tres Zapotes goes southwest from Santiago Tuxtla; a 'Zona Arqueológica' sign points the way from Hwy 180. Eight kilometers down this road, you fork right onto a newly paved stretch for the last 15km to Tres Zapotes village. It comes out at a T-junction next to the Sitio Olmeca taxi stand. From here you walk to the left, then turn left again to reach the museum.

To get to Tres Zapotes, take a green-and-white taxi (US$1.75/10 colectivo/private) from Santiago Tuxtla. They leave from the Sitio Puente Real, on the far side of the pedestrian bridge at the foot of Zaragoza, the street going downhill beside the Santiago Tuxtla museum. Infrequent TLT buses (US$1.25) also make the trip.

SAN ANDRÉS TUXTLA

☎ 294 / pop 55,000 / elevation 300m

San Andrés is in the center of Los Tuxtlas, surrounded by countryside producing maize, bananas, beans, sugarcane, cattle and tobacco (the town is Mexico's cigar capital). San Andrés itself is active but not particularly interesting; however, several scenic geographical features are nearby, including the dormant Volcán San Martín (1748m).

Orientation & Information

The main bus station is on Juárez, 1km northwest of the plaza. The cathedral is on the plaza's north side, the Palacio Municipal on the west side and a Banamex on the south side. The market is three blocks west.

The post office is on Lafragua; head down 20 de Noviembre directly across the plaza from the Palacio Municipal and follow it around to the left. From the post office, turn left on Suárez and head a block uphill to find **Internépolis** (Suárez s/n; per hr US$1; ☉ 8am-11pm), which offers quick Internet access.

Sights

Watch and inhale as the *puros* (cigars) are speedily rolled by hand at the **Santa Clara cigar factory** (☎ 947-99-00; ventas@tabasa.com; Blvd 5 de Febrero 10; admission free; ☉ 8am-5pm Mon-Fri, 8-11am Sat), on the highway a block or so from the bus station. Cigars in assorted shapes and sizes are available for purchase at factory prices, and the employees are happy to demonstrate their technique.

Twelve kilometers from San Andrés, a 242-step staircase leads down to the **Salto de Eyipantla** (admission US$0.50), a 50m-high, 40m-wide waterfall. Follow Hwy 180 east for 4km to Sihuapan, then turn right down a dirt road to Eyipantla. Frequent TLT buses (US$1) make the trip, leaving from the corner of Cabada and 5 de Mayo, near the market.

The **Laguna Encantada** (or Enchanted Lagoon) rises in dry weather and falls when it rains. It occupies a small volcanic crater 3km northeast of San Andrés. A dirt road goes there but no buses do; travelers and locals report muggings in the area.

At Cerro del Gallo near **Matacapan**, just east of Sihuapan, is a pyramid in Teotihuacán style, dating from AD 300 to 600. It may have been on the route to Kaminaljuyú in Guatemala, the last Teotihuacán outpost.

Sleeping

Most of these hotels can be found right near the zócalo; to find them, turn right on Madero when you hit the plaza from Juárez.

Hotel Posada San Martin (☎ 942-10-36; Juárez 304; s & d US$25, 2 beds US$31; P 🏊 🍴) Midway between the bus station and the zócalo, this hacienda-style posada is a fabulous deal. Not only does it offer the usual conveniences, but also a pool in a peaceful garden, and pretty details like yellow-and-blue tiled sinks in the comfy rooms.

Hotel de los Pérez (☎ 942-07-77, 800-290-39-00; fax 942-36-46; Rascón 2; s/d US$26/35; P 🏊) Closer to the zócalo, the Hotel de los Pérez offers well-kept and sizable rooms.

Hotel Isabel (☎ 942-16-17; Madero 13; s/d US$15/20, with air-con US$20/25; 🏊) This pink building looks smaller than it is, with rooms above and behind the lobby restaurant. Rooms in back are older but more serene and charming than the newer ones in front.

Hotel Posada San José (☎ 942-10-10; Domínguez 10; s/d US$14/17, with air-con US$21/28; P 🏊) The Posada San José is cheap and central, offering 30 tidy, spacious rooms around a lobby sitting area. Be sure your doors and windows actually latch shut. To get here from Juárez, turn left when you hit the plaza, take the second right onto Pino Suárez, and then hang a left on Domínguez.

Eating & Drinking

Restaurant Winni's (Madero 10; dishes US$3-6; ☉ 8am-10pm) Winni's is an excellent dining choice, just down from the plaza. Options include soup, egg dishes and antojitos, as well as substantial main courses. Try 'Sabana Win nis,' a toothsome steak smothered with ham and melted cheese.

Restaurant & Cafetería del Centro (dishes US$4-5; ☼ 7am-midnight) Beneath the Hotel de los Pérez, this restaurant is good for American-style breakfasts, snacks and set meals; they whip up a mean burger.

Hotel del Parque (☎ 942-01-98; Madero 5; dishes US$5-8; ☼ 8am-midnight) The restaurant here has outdoor tables facing the plaza, where regular customers have enjoyed their evening coffee for years. The slightly overpriced food won't blow you away, but it's a reliable spot at any hour.

Café Tuxtlán (Madero s/n; ☼ 8am-2pm & 4-11:30pm Mon-Sat) This well-lit neighborhood café offers coffee and a few munchies. Off the busy zócalo area, it's a good place to meet the locals over a cuppa joe.

Getting There & Away

San Andrés is the transport center for Los Tuxtlas, with fairly good bus services in every direction – 1st-class with ADO and good 2nd-class with AU. TLT buses are old and bouncy, but because of their frequent departures they're often the quickest way of getting to local destinations. TLT buses leave from the corner of Cabada and Solana Nte, a block north of the market; they skirt the north side of town on 5 de Febrero (Hwy 180), and you can get on or off at most intersections. They charge 10% less than ADO buses.

Acayucan (US$4, 2¼hr, 9 1st-class daily; TLT every 10min)

Campeche (US$34, 12½hr, 2 1st-class nightly)

Catemaco (US$0.75, 20min, 14 1st-class daily; TLT every 10min)

Mérida (US$42, 15hr, 1st-class at 9.15pm daily)

Mexico City (US$28, 9hr, 3 1st-class nightly; 4 afternoon AU) To TAPO.

Puebla (US$22, 7hr, 3 1st-class nightly)

Santiago Tuxtla (US$0.75, 20min, at least 8 2nd-class daily; TLT every 10min)

Veracruz (US$7, 3hr, 22 1st-class daily; TLT every 10min)

Villahermosa (US$15, 6hr, 8 1st-class daily)

Xalapa (US$12, 5hr, 10 1st-class daily)

CATEMACO

☎ 294 / pop 24,000 / elevation 340m

This town on the western shore of beautiful Laguna Catemaco makes most of its living from fishing and from Mexican families who flood in during July and August and for Christmas, New Year and Semana Santa. It's one of the state's few real tourist towns, with hawkers bugging travelers right and left. The annual convention of *brujos* (witch doctors), held on Cerro Mono Blanco (White Monkey Hill), north of Catemaco, on the first Friday in March, has become more a tourist event than a supernatural one.

Orientation & Information

Catemaco slopes gently down to the lake. A **tourist information office** (Map p692; Municipalidad; ☼ 9am-3pm Mon-Fri) on the north side of the zócalo, offers very limited information, but staff can give you a simple map of town. The **post office** (Map p692; Cuauhtémoc s/n; ☼ 9am-6pm Mon-Fri, 9am-1pm Sat) is a few blocks west of the central plaza.

In the mall on the west side of the zócalo, **@ctual's Internet café** (Map p692; Boettinger s/n; per hr US$1; ☼ 8am-11pm) has flat-screen monitors and a superfast connection. **Bancomer** (Map p692; Boettinger) changes cash but not traveler's checks, usually in the mornings only. In a pinch, try the Hotel Los Arcos (p692), which sometimes changes American Express traveler's checks at disadvantageous rates. You'll find two ATMs on the north side of the zócalo and one at Bancomer.

Sights

Ringed by volcanic hills, **Laguna Catemaco** is roughly oval and 16km long. East of town are a few gray-sand beaches where you can swim in murky water.

The lake contains several islands; on the largest, Isla Tenaspi, Olmec sculptures have been discovered. **Isla de los Monos** (Monkey Island; Map p689), also called Isla de los Changos, holds about 60 red-cheeked *Macaca arctoides* monkeys, originally from Thailand. They belong to the University of Veracruz, which acquired them for research. Despite pleas from the university for the animals to be left alone, boat operators bring food so tourists can get close-up photos.

On the north shore of the lake lies the **Reserva Ecológica de Nanciyaga** (Map p689; ☎ 943-01-99; www.nanciyaga.com; Carr Catemaco-Coyame, Km 7; admission US$2.75; ☼ 9am-6pm). Dedicated to promoting 'responsible tourism,' it preserves a small piece of rainforest. A guided walk in

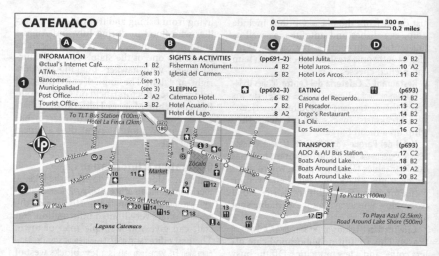

CATEMACO

INFORMATION	
@ctual's Internet Café	1 B2
ATMs	(see 3)
Bancomer	(see 1)
Municipalidad	(see 3)
Post Office	2 A2
Tourist Office	3 B2

SIGHTS & ACTIVITIES	(pp691–2)
Fisherman Monument	4 B2
Iglesia del Carmen	5 B2

SLEEPING	(pp692–3)
Catemaco Hotel	6 B2
Hotel Acuario	7 B2
Hotel del Lago	8 A2

Hotel Julita	9 B2
Hotel Juros	10 A2
Hotel Los Arcos	11 B2

EATING	(p693)
Casona del Recuerdo	12 B2
El Pescador	13 C2
Jorge's Restaurant	14 B2
La Ola	15 B2
Los Sauces	16 C2

TRANSPORT	(p693)
ADO & AU Bus Station	17 C2
Boats Around Lake	18 B2
Boats Around Lake	19 A2
Boats Around Lake	20 B2

Spanish includes the chance to sample mineral water and have a mini spa experience with mineral mud. Replicas of Olmec ruins are scattered around the site. It's interesting but a bit contrived – indeed, *Medicine Man*, a Sean Connery film, was shot here. It's possible to experience a **temascal** (sweat lodge; US$25 per person; 8pm Sat); call ahead to secure a spot. The reserve can be reached by *pirata* (pickup truck, US$0.75) or by boat.

Boats moored along the lakeside offer trips around the islands and across to the ecological reserve at Nanciyaga – the posted price for up to six people is US$40, or US$5.50 per person if you go as an individual.

Sleeping

Catemaco has lodging in all price ranges, all over the place. Air-con is standard in mid-range places.

BUDGET

Hotel Julita (Map p692; ☎ 943-00-08; Av Playa 10; s/d US$11/20) Near the waterfront just down from the zócalo, the Julita is a decent budget bargain, with cute, large rooms including fan and hot water. It's a bright and friendly family-run place with a relaxed feel.

Hotel Acuario (Map p692; ☎ 943-04-18; cnr Boettinger & Carranza; s/d US$11/18; P) Right by the zócalo, the clean Acuario sports small, plain quarters with the bathroom right there in the middle of the room! Watch out for uneven steps in the stairwell.

MID-RANGE

Hotel Los Arcos (Map p692; ☎ 943-00-03; www.arcos hotel.com.mx; Madero 7; s & d from US$36; P) Los Arcos has helpful staff, a swimming pool and lovely, comfortable rooms with common balconies. The drawback to this beautiful place is the thumping disco next door, which stops for no cranky guest.

Hotel Juros (Map p692; ☎ 943-00-84; Av Playa 14; s/d US$27/34, with air-con US$39; P) Renovated, air-con rooms at the Juros are large and pretty, and the rooftop pool has a great view of the lake and shoreline mountains.

Catemaco Hotel (Map p692; ☎ 943-02-03; hcate maco@yahoo.com.mx; Carranza 8; s/d US$29/33; P) On the north side of the zócalo, the Catemaco features a huge pool and not so huge rooms with cable TV. Balconies have views on the plaza, and some back rooms have mountain views. While the management is affable, it's not super value.

Hotel del Lago (Map p692; ☎ 943-01-60; fax 943-04-31; cnr Av Playa & Abasolo; s & d US$32; P) Rooms at this lakefront hotel are adequate, but you're paying more for the location than the amenities. Still, the small pool looks over the lake and the management is friendly.

Reserva Ecológica de Nanciyaga (Map p689; cabañas US$45-55, tent sites US$2.75) The ecological reserve (see p691) offers several simple cabins on an isolated lagoon. All have shared bath facilities. Rates are halved from Monday through Thursday and during low season. Basic tent sites are also available in La Jungla, an adjacent stretch of forest. The onsite café is open from 8am to 5pm and serves delicious, freshly-prepared – and mostly vegetarian – cuisine.

TOP END

Hotel La Finca (Map p689; ☎ 943-03-22, 800-523-46-22; www.lafinca.com.mx; Carr 180 Km 47; s & d US$91; P ✗ ✗ ⌘) The lakeside, four-star La Finca is 2km west of town on the Acayucan road. It's a stylish modern building with comfortable rooms, most with large balconies and lake views. Discounts off the rack rate are often available.

Hotel Playa Azul (Map p689; ☎ 943-00-01; www .playaazulcatemaco.com; s & d US$72, bungalows 137, trailer sites 11; P ✗ ⌘) Situated 2.5km east of town by the lake, this coral-colored hotel adjoins a patch of rainforest. Bright, air-conditioned rooms are surrounded by a garden and parking lot. Facilities include satellite TV, swimming pool, playground, restaurant and a discoteca.

Eating

The lake provides the specialties here: *tegogolo* (a snail reputed to be an aphrodisiac and best eaten in a sauce of chili, tomato, onion and lime), *chipalchole* (shrimp or crab claw soup), *mojarra* (a type of perch) and *anguilas* (eels). *Tachogobi* is a hot sauce sometimes served on mojarra; eels may come with raisins and hot chilies. Many eating spots tend to close early out of season.

Casona del Recuerdo (Map p692; ☎ 943-08-13; Aldama 4; dishes US$4 7; ✆ 11am 10pm) This cozy place features delightful balcony tables, friendly service and a flirtatious parrot, all in a beautiful garden-like setting. It serves superb seafood dishes.

Jorge's Restaurant (Map p692; ☎ 943-12-99; Paseo del Malecón s/n; dishes US$3-7; ✆ 9am-9pm) Offering local fish dishes, Jorge's is one of the two most popular and pleasant of Catemaco's many restaurants. It's right beside the lake, with a breezy garden eating area.

La Ola (Map p692; ☎ 943-00-10; Paseo del Malecón s/n; dishes US$3-8; ✆ 9am-9pm) Next door to Jorge's, La Ola is its prime competitor. The food is of a similarly high standard, and prices are virtually identical. The only difference is that La Ola seems to be patronized by a slightly older clientele.

Hotel Julita (Map p692; dishes US$4 6; ✆ 7am 8pm) Not far from the lakeside, this hotel (p692) has a budget restaurant with good fare.

Cruise by **El Pescador** and **Los Sauces** (Map p692; Paseo del Malecón s/n; dishes US$3-8; ✆ noon-10pm), two popular lakeside spots for eating, drinking and socializing after sunset.

Getting There & Away

Few long-distance buses reach Catemaco, so you may have to travel via San Andrés Tuxtla (12km west on Hwy 180) or Acayucan (80km south), taking the more frequent but less comfortable local buses to or from Catemaco. ADO and AU buses operate from a small terminal by the lakeside at the corner of Av Playa and Revolución. The local TLT buses pull up at the main road junction on the west side of town.

First-class buses run to several destinations including the following:

Acayucan (US$3.50, 1½hr, 4 daily)
Córdoba (US$13, 5hr, 5 daily)
Mexico City (US$29, 2hr, 8 daily) To TAPO.
Puebla (US$22, 6hr, 2 daily)
Santiago Tuxtla (US$1.25, 1hr, 10 daily)
Veracruz (US$7.50, 3½hr, 10 daily)
Xalapa (US$13, 5½hr, 5 daily)

To explore the villages and country east of the lake, where the mountain Santa Marta stands out, take a *pirata* (pickup truck) going to Las Margaritas (around US$2). They leave every hour or two from a corner five blocks north of the ADO station.

AROUND CATEMACO

About 4km northeast of Catemaco, the road forks. The section to the right follows the east side of the lake past the Reserva Ecológica Nanciyaga to Coyame and Las Margaritas; the road to the left is sealed and scenic as it goes over the hills toward the coast. At **Sontecomapan**, 15km from Catemaco, you can turn right (east) off the main road and go down to the lagoon side, where there are a few restaurants; stroll to the left for 100m to find the idyllic **Pozo de los Enanos** (Well of the Dwarves) swimming hole. Several **ejidos** (communal villages; ☎ 295-661-61-70) near here, including Sontecomapan, form an ecotourism network and can organize trips to local sights like waterfalls and archaeological sites. They also provide accommodations and meals for travelers; call ahead to make arrangements.

From the ejidos, you can rent boats for excursions into the mangroves around

Laguna de Sontecomapan. It's 20 minutes by boat to the mouth of the lagoon, where there's a beach near the fishing village of **La Barra**. There, you can stay at **Los Amigos** (☎ 294-943-01-01; www.losamigos.com.mx in Spanish; cabañas US$27; P). Soothing La Barra can also be reached by a side road from La Palma, 8km north of Sontecomapan.

The road is rough after Sontecomapan, but the countryside is lovely – mainly cattle ranches and rainforest, with green hills rolling down to the shore. About 5km past La Palma, a sign points down another rough side road to Playa Escondida. This takes you past **Jicacal**, a small, poor fishing village with a long gray-sand beach, one restaurant and some basic bungalows. **Playa Escondida** itself is about 4km from the main road. A reader-recommended hotel is the **Hotel Playa Escondida** overlooking the beach.

Back on the 'road' you pass a biological research station next to one of the few tracts of unspoiled rainforest on the Gulf Coast. A turnoff here leads to pretty Laguna Escondida, hidden in the mountains. The end of the road is at **Montepío**, where there's a picturesque beach at the river mouth, with two places to eat. **Posada San José** (☎ 294-942-10-10; s/d US$13/15, for air-con US$21/26; P) is a reasonably comfortable place to sleep.

Public transportation to Sontecomapan and beyond is by camionetas (pickup trucks with benches in the back), also called *piratas*. They leave Catemaco every half hour or so (when they're full) from 6am to 3pm, from the corner of Revolución and the Playa Azul road (from the northeast corner of the plaza, walk five blocks east and six blocks north, and look for vehicles congregating). The full 39km trip to Montepío, with numerous stops, takes about two hours and costs US$3.

ACAYUCAN

☎ 924 / pop 47,000

Animated Acayucan is at the intersection of where Hwy 180 (between Veracruz and Villahermosa) meets Hwy 185 (which goes south across the Isthmus of Tehuantepec to the Pacific coast). The east–west autopista (toll road), Hwy 145D, also passes nearby. You may have to change buses here, but try to avoid it, as it's an inconvenient stop. If you do get stuck here, don't fret: it's a cheerily busy junction town with plenty of opportunities to mingle with locals, who don't often see travelers.

The bus stations are on the east side of town. To reach the central plaza, walk uphill through the market to Av Hidalgo, turn left and walk six blocks. The plaza has a modern church on the east side and the town hall on the west. Several banks alongside the plaza have ATMs and change traveler's checks. A generic **Internet café** (Victoria s/n; per hr US$1; ⏱ 8:30am-10pm) provides access on the south side of the plaza.

In the evening, especially on weekends, Acayucan's central plaza fills with happily chattering schoolkids, romantically entwined couples, wizened town elders and solo pedestrians out for a stroll. It's the best place to strike up a conversation while sipping a cool drink.

Sleeping & Eating

Hotel Joalicia (☎ /fax 245-12-22; Zaragoza 4; s/d US$9/12.50, with air-con US$16/21; P) On the plaza's south side, the Joalicia is a tidy, decent budget place with nice staff. Rooms are decently sized and well maintained, and there's an elevator.

Hotel Arcos del Parque (☎ 245-65-06; fax 245-00-18; Hidalgo 804; s/d US$27/33; P) Fronting the plaza's north side, this sunny yellow place features sterile but large and comfortable rooms. There's a nice pool, making it a solid mid-range pick.

Hotel Kinaku (☎ /fax 245-04-10; Ocampo Sur 7; s/d US$36/41; P) At Acayucan's highest-end hotel, the big, modern rooms are an OK deal for the price; try to get one with a view of town. The fancy restaurant here, open 24 hours, has entrées for US$5 to US$9.

La Parrilla (dishes US$6-7; ⏱ 8am-10pm) For good antojitos and satisfying meals near the plaza, try La Parrilla at Hotel Arcos del Parque.

Los Tucanes Cafetería (snacks US$3-6; ⏱ 24hr) On the north end of the pedestrian alley a block west of the plaza, this cafetería is always full and a fun place for a bite.

Getting There & Away

Most 1st-class buses (ADO and Cristóbal Colón) are de paso, but the computerized reservation systems indicate if seats are available. UNO and ADO GL run a few deluxe services, while AU and Sur provide quite good 2nd-class service. All these companies operate from the same terminal on the lower side of the market. TLT provides very rough services to the Tuxtlas area from a terminal on the edge of the market, for 15% less than the 1st-class price. Travel times given below are by autopista where available, on a directo bus.

Catemaco (US$3.50, 1½hr, 1st-class at 4:50pm daily; frequent 2nd-class)
Juchitán (US$9, 3hr, 7 1st-class daily; US$6, 3hr, 2nd-class every 30min)
Mexico City (US$33, 7hr, 7 1st-class daily) To TAPO.
San Andrés Tuxtla (US$4, 2hr, 5 1st-class daily; frequent 2nd-class)
Santiago Tuxtla (US$3, 2¼hr, hourly 2nd-class)
Tapachula (US$2.75, 10hr, 4 2nd-class daily)
Tuxtla Gutiérrez (US$18, 8hr, 6 1st-class daily)
Veracruz (US$12, 3½hr, at least 15 1st-class daily)
Villahermosa (US$11, 3½hr, 13 1st-class daily)

The toll highway, 145D, passes south of town. Heading east, it's signposted to Minatitlán; heading west, toward Córdoba or Veracruz, it's marked to 'Isla' (referring to the inland town of Isla, not to any island). The tolls are expensive, costing more than US$30 to get to Córdoba.

Local buses run between the terminal and city center (US$0.50); a taxi costs about US$1.

SAN LORENZO

Near the small town of Tenochtitlán, 35km southeast of Acayucan, San Lorenzo was the first of the two great Olmec ceremonial centers. It had its heyday from about 1200 to 900 BC.

Ten Olmec heads and numerous smaller artifacts have been found here, but most of the finds are in museums elsewhere. Some heavy stone thrones, with figures of rulers carved in the side, were also found. Tools made from the black volcanic glass obsidian were imported from Guatemala or the Mexican highlands, and basalt for the heads and thrones was transported from the Sierra de los Tuxtlas. Such wide contacts, and the organization involved in building the

site, demonstrate how powerful the rulers of San Lorenzo were. Other features include an elaborate stone-pipe drainage system and evidence of cannibalism. During San Lorenzo's dramatic destruction, which occurred around 900 BC, most of the big carvings were mutilated, dragged on to ridges jutting out from the main platform of the site, and covered with earth.

The main structure was a platform about 50m high, 1.25km long and 700m wide, but now the San Lorenzo site is nothing more than a low hill. The **'museum'** (admission free; ☯ 8am-5pm) here is just two disappointingly tiny rooms of stone artifacts and a single large head.

Another site, **El Azazul**, is in the countryside about 7km further south. The hill here seems to have been a large pyramid but is completely overgrown. Halfway up it, under a shelter, are some remarkably well carved kneeling stone figures. They are said to be over 1000 years old, but they're in such good condition that it's hard to believe. Often there are people in the hut who will show you around in return for a tip of a few pesos.

Unless you're totally into archaeology it's not worth visiting these sites by public transportation. From Acayucan take a bus to Texistepec (south of the Minatitlán road), then take another bus to the town of Tenochtitlán (also called San Lorenzo–Tenochtitlán). Then take a local bus or taxi to the 'zona arqueológica' south of town, and look for the cream-colored buildings behind a chain-link fence on the left side of the road. The entire trip costs about US$7 and takes about three centuries (OK, 2½ hours, but who's counting by now?).

The Azazul site is virtually inaccessible by public transportation, but a taxi driver might consent to take you for about US$2. If you're driving, head 7km past the San Lorenzo museum and look for a road branching left and a hut on the right. Exploring these sites is much less traumatic with your own wheels.

Oaxaca State

CONTENTS

The rugged southern state of Oaxaca (wah-*hah*-kah) is a world away from central Mexico. It's separated by barriers of sparsely populated mountains that have always permitted Oaxaca to pursue its own destiny – though today their insulating effect is reduced by the spectacular, modern Hwy 135D traversing them from the north.

Oaxaca enjoys a slower, sunnier existence and a magical quality that has to do with its dry, rocky landscape, bright southern light and large indigenous population, which is the driving force behind the state's fine handicrafts and booming art scene.

The beautiful, colonial state capital, Oaxaca City, lies at the meeting point of the three Valles Centrales (Central Valleys), which are full of thriving village markets and spectacular ruins of pre-Hispanic towns such as Monte Albán, Mitla and Yagul. On Oaxaca's magnificent coast, Mexico's newest tourist resort is growing up on the lovely Bahías (Bays) de Huatulco, but travelers continue to enjoy a relaxed beach scene at longer-established beach spots such as Puerto Escondido, Puerto Ángel and Zipolite.

The dramatic backcountry of the region is increasingly accessible thanks to an exciting new wave of active-tourism ventures based in Oaxaca city.

The western two-thirds of the state are rugged and mountainous; the eastern third lies on the hot, low-lying Isthmus of Tehuantepec (Istmo de Tehuantepec). Oaxaca also has a thin plain along the Pacific coast and a low-lying north-central region bordering Veracruz state. This combination of temperate and tropical climatic zones and several mountain ranges gives Oaxaca spectacularly varied landscapes and greater biodiversity than any other Mexican state. Cloud forests and big stands of oak and pine grow in the highlands, while lower-lying areas and Pacific-facing slopes support deciduous tropical forest.

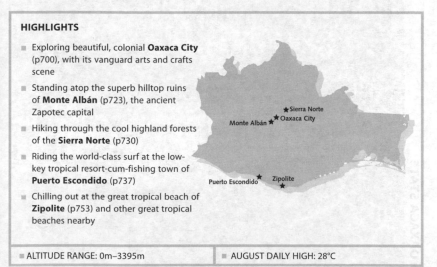

HIGHLIGHTS

- Exploring beautiful, colonial **Oaxaca City** (p700), with its vanguard arts and crafts scene

- Standing atop the superb hilltop ruins of **Monte Albán** (p723), the ancient Zapotec capital

- Hiking through the cool highland forests of the **Sierra Norte** (p730)

- Riding the world-class surf at the low-key tropical resort-cum-fishing town of **Puerto Escondido** (p737)

- Chilling out at the great tropical beach of **Zipolite** (p753) and other great tropical beaches nearby

★Sierra Norte

Monte Albán ★★Oaxaca City

Puerto Escondido ★   Zipolite ★

- ALTITUDE RANGE: 0m–3395m   ■ AUGUST DAILY HIGH: 28°C

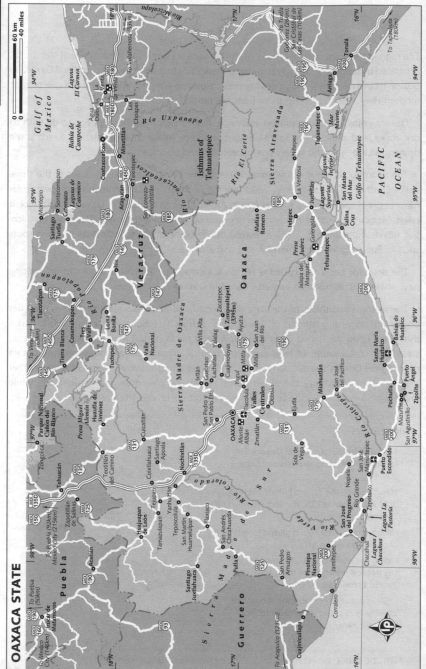

OAXACA STATE

0 ——— 60 km
0 ——— 40 miles

HISTORY
Zapotecs & Mixtecs

The Valles Centrales (Central Valleys) have always been the hub of Oaxacan life, and their pre-Hispanic cultures reached heights rivaling those of central Mexico. The hilltop city of Monte Albán here became the center of the Zapotec culture, which extended its control over much of Oaxaca by conquest, peaking between AD 300 and 700. Monte Albán declined suddenly; by about AD 750 it was deserted, as were many other Zapotec settlements in the Valles Centrales. From about 1200, the surviving Zapotecs came under growing dominance by the Mixtecs from Oaxaca's northwest uplands, renowned potters and metalsmiths. Mixtec and Zapotec cultures became entangled in the Valles Centrales before the Aztecs conquered them in the 15th and early 16th centuries.

Colonial Era

The Spaniards had to send at least four expeditions before they felt safe enough to found the city of Oaxaca in 1529. Cortés donated large parts of the Valles Centrales to himself and was officially named Marqués del Valle de Oaxaca. The indigenous population dropped disastrously. The population of the Mixteca region in the west is thought to have fallen from 700,000 at the Spanish arrival to about 25,000 in 1700. Rebellions continued into the 20th century, but the indigenous peoples never united to form a serious threat.

Juárez & Díaz

Benito Juárez, the great reforming leader of 19th-century Mexico, was a Zapotec. He served two terms as Oaxaca state governor before being elected Mexico's president in 1861 (see 'Benito Juárez,' p706).

Juárez appointed Porfirio Díaz, son of a Oaxaca horse trainer, as state governor in 1862, but Díaz rebelled against Juárez' presidency in 1871. Díaz went on to control Mexico with an iron fist from 1877 to 1910, bringing the country into the industrial age but also fostering corruption, repression and, eventually, the revolution. In Valle Nacional in northern Oaxaca, tobacco planters set up virtual slave plantations, most of whose 15,000 workers had to be replaced annually after dying from disease, beating or starvation. Indigenous lands were commandeered by foreign and mestizo coffee planters.

Oaxaca Today

After the revolution about 300 *ejidos* (peasant land-holding cooperatives) were set up, but land ownership remains a source of conflict today. With little industry, Oaxaca is one of Mexico's poorest states, and many Oaxacans leave home to work in the cities or the USA. The situation is made worse in some areas, notably the Mixteca, by deforestation and erosion. Tourism thrives in Oaxaca city and nearby villages and a few places on the coast, but underdevelopment still prevails in the backcountry.

CLIMATE

The Valles Centrales are warm and dry, with most rain falling between June and September. On the coast and in low-lying areas it's hotter and a bit wetter.

GETTING THERE & AROUND

Oaxaca city has good bus links with Mexico City and Puebla to the north, and a few daily services to/from Veracruz, Villahermosa, Tuxtla Gutiérrez and San Cristóbal de Las Casas. Services between the city and the state's main coastal destinations are fairly frequent though mostly 2nd-class. Plenty of buses (again mostly 2nd-class) also travel along coastal Hwy 200 into Oaxaca from Acapulco and Chiapas.

TOP OAXACA WEBSITES

- **Oaxaca's Forum** (http://bbs.oaxaca.com) Bulletin board where you can look for rented accommodations or shared transportation or just ask any old question.

- **Oaxaca's Tourist Guide** (http://oaxaca-travel.com) Photo-filled website with excellent background on anything from fine beaches and great buildings to regional recipes and biographies of famous Oaxacans. No up-to-date practical stuff, though.

- **Pacific Coast of Oaxaca** (www.tomzap.com) A mine of information about the coast, with a useful message board, 'Visitors' Comments.'

Several daily flights link Oaxaca city with Mexico City. Further flights go east to Tuxtla Gutiérrez, Tapachula, Villahermosa and beyond. Small planes hop over the mountains between Oaxaca city and the coastal resorts Puerto Escondido and Bahías de Huatulco, which you can also reach direct from Mexico City.

DANGERS & ANNOYANCES

Buses and other vehicles traveling isolated stretches of highway, including the coastal Hwy 200 and Hwy 175 from Oaxaca city to Pochutla, have occasionally been stopped and robbed. The best way to avoid risk is not to travel at night.

OAXACA CITY

☎ 951 / pop 260,000 / elevation 1550m

The state's capital and only large city has a colonial heart of narrow, straight streets, liberally sprinkled with lovely stone buildings. Oaxaca is relaxed but stimulating, remote but cosmopolitan. Its dry mountain heat, manageable scale, old buildings, broad shady plazas and leisurely cafés help slow the pace of life. At the same time, diverse Oaxacan, Mexican and international influences create a spark of excitement. The city has some first-class museums and galleries, arguably the best handicrafts shopping in Mexico, and a vivacious cultural, restaurant, bar and music scene. It's a capital of the modern Mexican art world and an increasingly popular location for Spanish-language courses or simply hanging out.

Head first for the zócalo and taste the atmosphere. Then ramble and see what markets, crafts, galleries, cafés, bars and festivities you run across. Allow time, if you can, for more than one trip out to the many fascinating places in the Valles Centrales and outlying mountain areas. Oaxaca is a jumping-off point for some great hiking, biking, birdwatching, climbing and other activities.

HISTORY

The Aztec settlement here was called Huaxyácac (meaning 'In the Nose of the Squash'), from which 'Oaxaca' is derived. The Spanish laid out a new town around the existing zócalo in 1529. It quickly became the most important place in southern Mexico.

Eighteenth-century Oaxaca grew rich from exports of cochineal, a red dye made from tiny insects living on the prickly pear cactus, and from the weaving of textiles. By 1796 it was probably the third-biggest city in Nueva España, with about 20,000 people (including 600 clergy) and 800 cotton looms.

In 1854 an earthquake destroyed much of Oaxaca city. It was decades later, under the presidency of Porfirio Díaz, before Oaxaca began to grow again; in the 1890s its population exceeded 30,000. Then in 1931 another earthquake left 70% of the city uninhabitable.

Oaxaca's major expansion has come in the past two decades, with tourism, new industries and rural poverty all encouraging migration from the countryside. The population of the city proper has almost doubled in 25 years, and together with formerly separate villages and towns it now forms a conurbation of perhaps 450,000 people.

ORIENTATION

Oaxaca centers on the zócalo and the adjoining Alameda de León plaza in front of the cathedral. Calle Alcalá, running north from the cathedral to the Iglesia de Santo Domingo (a universally known landmark), is mostly pedestrian-only.

The road from Mexico City and Puebla traverses the northern part of Oaxaca as Calz Niños Héroes de Chapultepec. The 1st-class bus station is situated on this road, 1.75km northeast of the zócalo. The 2nd-class bus station is almost 1km west of the center, near the main market, the Central de Abastos.

The blocks north of the zócalo are smarter, cleaner and less traffic-infested than those to the south. The commercial area occupies the blocks southwest of the zócalo.

Inegi (☎ 512-48-00; Zapata 316, Colonia Reforma; ⏰ 8:30am-8:30pm Mon-Fri) sells a great range of topographical maps covering Oaxaca, Chiapas and Tabasco states; you can also consult maps for free.

INFORMATION
Bookstores

Amate (Map p702; ☎ 516-69-60; Plaza Alcalá, Alcalá 307-2; ⏰ 10:30am-2:30pm & 3:30-7:30pm Mon-Sat) Probably the best English-language bookstore in all Mexico, stocking almost every Mexico-related title in print in English.

Librería Universitaria (Map p702; ☎ 516-42-43; Guerrero 108) This bookstore, located just off the zócalo, sells some English-language books about Oaxaca and Mexico.

Proveedora Escolar (Map p702; ☎ 516-04-89; Independencia 1001; ☒ 9am-8pm Mon-Sat) Has a great upstairs section devoted to history, literature, archaeology and anthropology (mostly in Spanish).

Emergency

Ceprotur (Centro de Protección al Turista; Map p702; ☎ 514-21-55; Murguía 206) This department in the tourist office is there to help tourists with any legal problems they may have; if you have a complaint, or if you've lost documents or had any of your belongings stolen, you can report it here.

Emergency services (☎ 066)

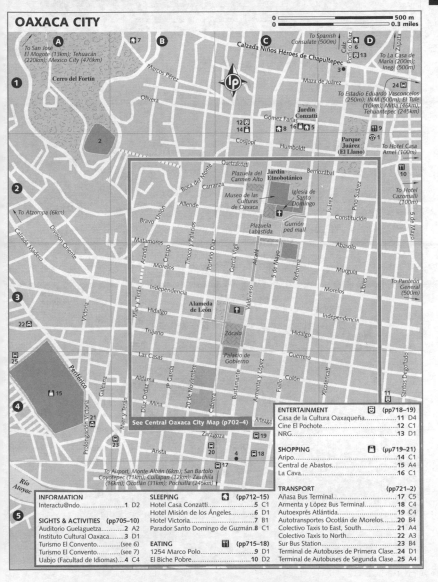

OAXACA CITY

0 — 500 m
0 — 0.3 miles

To San José
El Mogote (13km); Tehuacán
(220km); Mexico City (470km)

To Spanish
Consulate (500m)

To La Casa de
María (200m);
Inegi (500m)

Cerro del Fortín

Calzada Niños Héroes de Chapultepec

Marcos Pérez

Maza de Juárez

To Estadio Eduardo Vasconcelos
(250m); INM (500m); El Tule
(10km); Mitla (46km);
Tehuantepec (245km)

Olivera

Jardín
Conzatti

Gómez Farías

Cosijopí

Humboldt

Parque
Juárez
(El Llano)

To Hotel Casa
Arnel (100m)

Quetzalcóatl

Jardín
Etnobotánico

Plazuela del
Carmen Alto

Berriozábal

Boca del Monte

Carranza

Iglesia de
Santo
Domingo

To Hotel
Cazomalli
(100m)

Museo de las
Culturas
de Oaxaca

Allende

Bravo

Plazuela
Labastida

Gurrión
ped mall

Constitución

Matamoros

Abasolo

Morelos

Porfirio Díaz

García Vigil

5 de Mayo

Reforma

To Panteón
General
(500m)

Independencia

Hidalgo

Alameda
de León

Zócalo

Independencia

Trujano

Hidalgo

Las Casas

Palacio de
Gobierno

Guerrero

Aldama

JP García

20 de Noviembre

Cabrera

Bustamante

Armenta y López

Fiallo

Colón

Xicoténcatl

Santos Degollado

Mina

To Airport, Monte Albán (6km); San Bartolo
Coyotepec (11km); Cuilapan (12km); Zaachila
(16km); Ocotlán (31km); Pochutla (245km)

See Central Oaxaca City Map (p702-4)

Arteaga

Zaragoza

Arista

Río
Atoyac

ENTERTAINMENT (pp718-19)
Casa de la Cultura Oaxaqueña...........11 D4
Cine El Pochote.....................................12 C1
NRG...13 D1

SHOPPING (pp719-21)
Aripo...14 C1
Central de Abastos................................15 A4
La Cava...16 C1

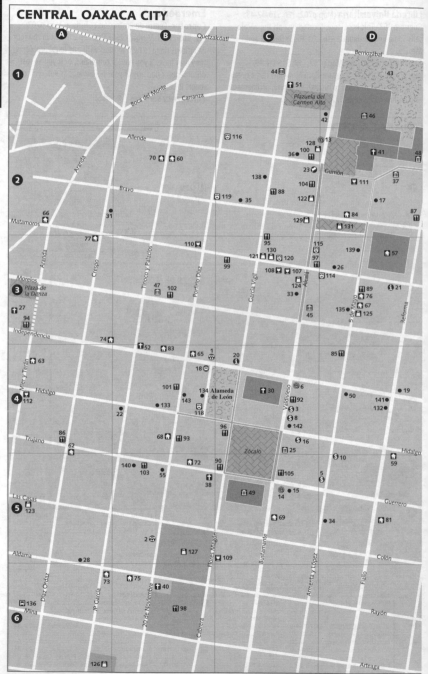

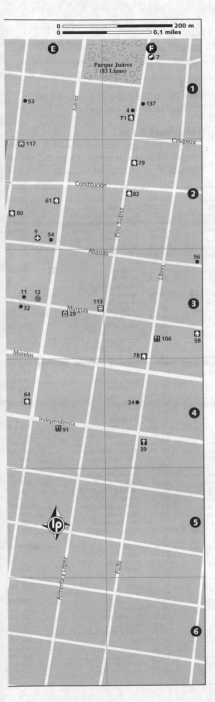

Immigration

INM (Instituto Nacional de Migración; ☎ 518-40-11; Pensamientos 104; ⏱ 9am-1:30pm Mon-Fri) Come here to extend a tourist card or replace a lost one. It's in Colonia Le Reforma in the north of town.

Internet Access

C@fe Internet (Map p702; Valdivieso 120; per hr US$1; ⏱ 8am-11pm Mon-Sat, 9am-10pm Sun) One block from the zócalo.

Fray-Net (Map p702; Murguía 309A; per hr US$0.50; ⏱ 9am-8pm Mon-Sat)

Inter@ctive Internet (Map p702; Alcalá 503; per hr US$0.60) Good connections.

Internet (Map p702; Guerrero 104; per hr US$1; ⏱ 7:30am-9pm) Just off the zócalo.

Laundry

Same-day wash-and-dry service is available at several laundries. All charge US$4.50 to US$5 for a 3.5kg (7.7lb) load.

Dommar Lavandería (Map p702; ☎ 501-20-92; Murguía 307; ⏱ 9am-9pm Mon-Sat, 11am-3pm Sun)

Super Lavandería Hidalgo (Map p702; cnr Hidalgo & JP García)

Libraries

Biblioteca Circulante de Oaxaca (Map p702; Oaxaca Lending Library; oaxlib.org; Pino Suárez 519; ⏱ 10am-1pm & 4-7pm Mon-Fri, 10am-1pm Sun) Sizable collection of books and magazines on Oaxaca and Mexico, in English and Spanish; two-month visitor membership (US$19 plus US$28 deposit) allows you to borrow books.

Instituto de Artes Gráficas de Oaxaca (Map p702; ☎ 516-69-80; Alcalá 507; ⏱ 9:30am-8pm) The excellent library here covers art, architecture, literature, botany, ecology and history.

Media

Notice boards (Map p702; Plaza Gonzalo Lucero, 5 de Mayo 412) Check these for ads for rental apartments, classes in everything from Spanish to yoga, and other interesting stuff. You'll also find useful notice boards in the language schools.

Oaxaca (www.go-oaxaca.com) Free monthly trilingual (English, French and Spanish) paper. Available at various places around town. Contains some interesting articles, useful practical information and small ads.

Oaxaca Times (www.oaxacatimes.com) Ditto but in English only.

Medical Services

Clínica Hospital Carmen (Map p702; ☎ 516-26-12; Abasolo 215; ⏱ 24hr) One of the town's best private hospitals, with emergency facilities and English-speaking doctors.

OAXACA STATE

Money

There are plenty of ATMs around the center, and several *casas de cambio* and banks will exchange US-dollar cash and traveler's checks. Try the following for some of the best rates.

Banamex (Map p702; ☎ 514-57-47; Valdivieso 116; ☯ 9am-4pm Mon-Fri)

Bital (Map p702; ☎ 516-19-67; cnr Armenta y López & Guerrero; ☯ 8am-7pm Mon-Sat)

Cecambio (Map p702; ☎ 504-14-81; Valdivieso 106)

Consultoria Internacional (Map p702; ☎ 514-91-92; Armenta y López 203C; ☯ 8:30am-7pm Mon-Fri, 9am-2pm Sat) Changes cash euros, yen, sterling, Canadian dollars and Swiss francs too.

Money Exchange (Map p702; Hidalgo 814; ☯ 8:30am-9pm Mon-Sat, 10am-6pm Sun) Changes cash euros too.

Post

Main Post Office (Map p702; Alameda de León; ☯ 8am-7pm Mon-Fri, 9am-1pm Sat)

Telephone & Fax

Telmex card phones are available around the zócalo and elsewhere. Many call offices are scattered around town.

ATSI (Map p702; 20 de Noviembre 402 & Independencia 603) Cheaper than pay phones for national long-distance calls and calls to Europe; both branches have fax service too.
Interactu@ndo (Map p702; Pino Suárez 804) Cheap calls to USA.

Tourist Information

Sedetur Independencia (Map p702; ☎ 516-01-23; Independencia 607; 🕑 8am-8pm); Murguía (Map p702; ☎ 576-48-28; Murguía 206; 🕑 8am-8pm); airport (🕑 8am-7pm) The Oaxaca state tourism department has three information offices in the city. Someone in attendance can usually speak English, but workers are often student volunteers with limited knowledge.

Travel Agencies

Turismo Joven (Map p702; ☎ 514-22-20; Alcalá 407, Local 19) Issues ISIC cards and sells student air fares and trips to Cuba and elsewhere.

DANGERS & ANNOYANCES

It's best not to go up on Cerro del Fortín, the hill with the Guelaguetza auditorium, except for special events such as the Guelaguetza. It's a well known haunt of robbers.

SIGHTS
Zócalo & Alameda   Map p702

Traffic-free, shaded by tall trees and surrounded by *portales* (arcades) with numerous cafés and restaurants, the zócalo is the perfect place to soak up the Oaxaca atmosphere. The adjacent Alameda, also traffic-free but without the cafés, is another popular local gathering place.

On the south side of the zócalo stands the **Palacio de Gobierno** (State Government Palace; admission free), whose stairway mural by Arturo García Bustos depicts famous Oaxacans and Oaxacan history. At the top of the mural are the heads of revolutionary Ricardo Flores Magón (left); Benito Juárez and his wife, Margarita Maza (center); and José María Morelos (right). Porfirio Díaz appears below Juárez, in blue, with a sword. At the bottom, toward the right, Vicente Guerrero's execution at Cuilapan is shown. The left wall shows ancient Mitla. At the center of the right wall is Juana Inés de La Cruz, the 17th-century nun and love poet.

Oaxaca's **cathedral**, begun in 1553 and finished (after several earthquakes) in the 18th century, stands just north of the zócalo. Its main façade, facing the Alameda, features fine baroque carving.

Around the Zócalo   Map p702

Fine carved façades adorn the colonial churches of **La Compañía** (cnr Trujano & Flores Magón) and **San Juan de Dios** (cnr Aldama & 20 de Noviembre). Iglesia de San Juan de Dios, a beautiful small church, dates from the 1520s and was Oaxaca's first cathedral. Its interior is adorned with many murals and paintings, with large canvases on the history of Christianity in Oaxaca, including the story of Juan Bautista and Jacinto de los Ángeles, the martyrs of Cajonos (a village in the Sierra Norte) who were beatified by Pope John Paul II in 2002. The 18th-century baroque **Templo de San Felipe Neri** (cnr Independencia & JP García) is where Benito Juárez and Margarita Maza were married in 1843; Maza was the daughter of Don Antonio Maza, who had taken in young Benito on his arrival in Oaxaca.

The 1903 **Teatro Macedonio Alcalá** (☎ 514-69-89; Independencia 900) is in the French style that was fashionable under Porfirio Díaz. It has a marble stairway and a five-tier auditorium that holds 1300 people.

Calle Alcalá   Map p702

Free of traffic and with most of its colonial-era stone buildings cleaned up and restored, **Calle Alcalá** makes a fine pedestrian route from the city center to the Iglesia de Santo Domingo, dotted with attractive shops, galleries, cafés and restaurants.

The **Museo de Arte Contemporáneo de Oaxaca** (MACO; ☎ 514-22-28; Alcalá 202; admission US$2; 🕑 10:30am-8pm Wed-Mon) occupies a lovely colonial house built around 1700. It exhibits contemporary art from Oaxaca, Mexico and around the world. Sometimes works by leading modern Oaxacan artists such as Rufino Tamayo, Francisco Toledo or Rodolfo Morales are on show.

Iglesia de Santo Domingo   Map p702

Four blocks north of the cathedral, **Santo Domingo** (cnr Alcalá & Gurrión; 🕑 7am-1pm & 4-8pm except during mass) is the most splendid of Oaxaca's churches. It was built mainly between 1570 and 1608, as part of the city's Dominican monastery. The finest artisans from Puebla and elsewhere helped with its construction. Like other big buildings in this earthquake-prone region, Santo Domingo has immensely thick stone walls. During the 19th-century wars and anticlerical movements it was used as a military stable and warehouse.

BENITO JUÁREZ

One of the few Mexican national heroes with an unambiguous reputation, Benito Juárez (1806–72) was born in the mountain village of Guelatao, 60km northeast of Oaxaca. His Zapotec parents died when he was three. At the age of 12, knowing only a few words of Spanish, he walked to Oaxaca and found work at the house of Antonio Salanueva, a bookbinder. Salanueva saw the boy's potential and decided to help pay for an education Juárez otherwise might not have received.

Juárez trained for the priesthood but abandoned it to work as a lawyer for poor villagers. He became a member of the Oaxaca city council and then of the Oaxaca state government. As state governor from 1848 to 1852, he opened schools and cut bureaucracy. The conservative national government exiled him in 1853, but he returned to Mexico in the 1855 Revolution of Ayutla that ousted General Santa Anna. Juárez became justice minister in Mexico's new liberal government. His Ley Juárez (Juárez Law), which transferred the trials of soldiers and priests charged with civil crimes to ordinary civil courts, was the first of the Reform laws, which sought to break the power of the Catholic Church. These laws provoked the War of the Reform of 1858 to 1861, in which the liberals eventually defeated the conservatives.

Juárez was elected Mexico's president in 1861 but had only been in office a few months when France, supported by conservatives and clergy, invaded Mexico and forced him into exile again. In 1866–67, with US support, Juárez ousted the French and their puppet emperor, Maximilian.

One of Juárez' main political achievements was to make primary education free and compulsory. He died in 1872, a year after being elected to his fourth presidential term. Today countless statues, streets, schools and plazas preserve his name and memory, and his sage maxim *'El respeto al derecho ajeno es la paz'* ('Respect for the rights of others is peace') is widely quoted.

Amid the fine carving on the baroque façade, the figure holding a church is Santo Domingo de Guzmán (1172–1221), the Spanish monk who founded the Dominican order. The Dominicans observed strict vows of poverty, chastity and obedience, and in Mexico they protected the indigenous people from other colonists' excesses.

The interior, lavish with gilded and colored stucco, has a magically warm glow during candlelit evening masses. Just inside the main door, on the ceiling, is an elaborate family tree of Santo Domingo de Guzmán. The church's main altarpiece dates only from the 1950s: its predecessor disappeared during the military occupation. The 18th-century Capilla de la Virgen del Rosario (Rosary Chapel), on the south side of the nave, is a profusion of yet more gilt.

Museo de las Culturas de Oaxaca   Map p702

The beautiful monastery buildings adjoining the Iglesia de Santo Domingo house the large and excellent **Museum of Oaxacan Cultures** (☎ 516-29-91; cnr Alcalá & Gurrión; admission US$3.50; ☯ 10am-8pm Tue-Sun), which takes you right through the history and cultures of Oaxaca state up to the present day. Explanatory material is in Spanish, but you can rent good audio guides in other languages for US$5. These buildings were used as military barracks for over 100 years until 1994, before being restored as a museum, which opened in 1998.

A lovely stone cloister serves as an antechamber to the museum proper. The museum emphasizes the direct lineage between Oaxaca's pre-Hispanic and contemporary indigenous cultures, illustrating continuity in such areas as crafts, medicine, food, drink and music. A video in one room shows members of each of the state's 15 indigenous peoples speaking their own languages. Other exhibits feature plenty of archaeological relics and colonial art. The greatest highlight is the Mixtec treasure from Tumba 7 at Monte Albán, in Sala 3. This treasure dates from the 14th century, when Mixtecs reused an old Zapotec tomb to bury one of their kings and his sacrificed servants. With the bodies they placed a hoard of beautifully worked silver, turquoise, coral, jade, amber, jet, pearls, finely carved jaguar and eagle bone and, above all, gold. The treasure was discovered in 1932 by Alfonso Caso.

Jardín Etnobotánico   Map p702

In the former monastic grounds behind the Iglesia de Santo Domingo, this **Ethnobotanic Garden** (☎ 516-76-15; cnr Constitución & Reforma; suggested donation US$14; tours in English 11am Tue & Thu, 4pm Sat, in Spanish 10am & 5pm Tue-Sat) features Oaxaca state plants. Though it has only been growing since the mid-1990s, it is already a fascinating demonstration of Oaxaca's biodiversity. Visits are by guided tour only, with a maximum of 18 people per tour.

Instituto de Artes Gráficas de Oaxaca   Map p702

The **Oaxaca Graphic Arts Institute** (IAGO; ☎ 516-69-80; Alcalá 507; admission free; ☯ 9:30am-8pm), almost opposite Santo Domingo, is in a beautiful colonial house donated by artist Francisco Toledo. It offers changing exhibitions of graphic art as well as a superb arts library.

Museo Casa de Juárez   Map p702

The house where Benito Juárez found work as a boy with bookbinder Antonio Salanueva (see 'Benito Juárez,' p706) is now the interesting little **Juárez House Museum** (☎ 516-18-60; García Vigil 609; admission US$2.75; ☯ 10am-7pm Tue-Sun), showing how simply the middle class of early-19th-century Oaxaca lived. The binding workshop is preserved, along with pictures and other memorabilia of Juárez.

Museo Rufino Tamayo   Map p702

This excellent **pre-Hispanic art museum** (☎ 516-47-50; Morelos 503; admission US$2.75; ☯ 10am-2pm & 4-7pm Mon & Wed-Sat, 10am-3pm Sun) was donated to Oaxaca by its most famous artist, the Zapotec Rufino Tamayo (1899–1991). The collection, housed in a fine 17th-century building, focuses on the aesthetic qualities of pre-Hispanic artifacts and traces artistic developments in preconquest times. It has some beautiful pieces and is strong on the Preclassic era and lesser-known civilizations such as those of Veracruz and western Mexico.

Basílica de la Soledad   Map p702

The image of Oaxaca's patron saint, the Virgen de la Soledad (Virgin of Solitude), resides in the 17th-century **La Soledad** (Independencia), 3½ blocks west of the Alameda. The church, with a richly carved baroque façade, stands where the image is said to have miraculously appeared in a donkey's

---

OAXACAN ART: THE NEW WAVE *Neil Pyatt*

Following the death of Rufino Tamayo in 1991, the chain of command in Oaxacan art was again upset in 2000 with the sad death of Rodolfo Morales from Ocotlán, a tireless portrayer of Oaxacan life and feeling. You can recognize most Morales paintings by their trademark child-like angel figures. The Oaxacan maestros who remain are Francisco Toledo, Luis Zárate and Sergio Hernández, who share a certain stereotypical imagery that is now being rejected by the most innovative of young Oaxacan painters as they strive for new styles and new directions.

Advanced commercially as well as artistically, young Oaxacans such as Demian Flores, Guillermo Olguín, Soid Pastrana and Luis Enrique Hampshire have spent lengthy periods of study abroad, which have helped to create international markets for their work. Their styles manage to combine modern thought with ancient forms of illustration, and they differ as much from each other as from their elder, supposedly higher-ranking predecessors.

Opening nights, preview showings, seminars and workshops occur regularly in Oaxaca and are well publicized. They provide the best way to keep up with the local, national and even international art scenes and their respective players. The Oaxacan nightlife and artistic communities are inextricably intertwined due to the size of the city and its self-styled role as a spiritual home to the strong hedonistic side of the Mexican personality, a relationship that continues to inspire the exceptionally creative resident population. In practical terms, this means most bars offer flyer and poster space to such events and will probably count at least one resident artist, writer or other knowledgeable party among their staff or regular clientele.

Neil Pyatt is an Oaxaca-based freelance writer who puts a psychology and anthropology background to use dissecting Mexican culture, in both English and Spanish, for a number of publications.

pack in 1543. The virgin was later adorned with enormous worldly riches – but lost her 2kg gold crown, a huge pearl and several hundred diamonds to thieves in the 1990s.

Galleries

At the forefront of contemporary Mexican art, Oaxaca attracts artists, art dealers and art buyers from far and wide. Some of the best Mexican art and photography is on show in its burgeoning number of commercial galleries (admission is free to all of them):

Arte Contemporáneo Manuel García (Map p702; ☎ 514-10-93; www.galeriamanuelgarcia.com; Portal Juárez 110; ☺ 10am-2pm & 4-8pm Mon-Sat) Great on avant-garde and multimedia stuff; on the west side of the zócalo.

Arte de Oaxaca (Map p702; ☎ 514-09-10; www.arte deoaxaca.com in Spanish; Murguía 105; ☺ 10am-3pm & 5-8pm Mon-Sat) Part of the Fundación Cultural Rodolfo Morales, set up in 1990 by Morales, a native of Ocotlán and one of Mexico's leading 20th-century artists, to promote the arts, heritage and social welfare of Oaxaca's Valles Centrales. The excellent gallery includes a room devoted to Morales' own work.

Bodega Quetzalli (Map p702; ☎ 514-62-68; Murguía 400; ☺ 10am-2pm & 5-8pm Mon-Sat) Sister space to Galería Quetzalli, leaning slightly more to the avant-garde.

Centro Fotográfico Álvarez Bravo (Map p702; ☎ 516-45-23; Murguía 302; ☺ 9:30am-8pm Wed-Mon) Puts on good photo exhibitions and has a library of photography books.

Galería Índigo (Map p702; ☎ 514-38-89; Allende 104; ☺ 10am-8:30pm Mon-Sat, noon-6pm Sun) Classy gallery with eclectic stock.

Galería Quetzalli (Map p702; ☎ 514-00-30; Constitución 104; ☺ 10am-2pm & 5-8pm Mon-Sat) Oaxaca's leading serious gallery, free of 'folklorism.' It handles the biggest names in Oaxacan art including Francisco Toledo, Luis Zárate and Sergio Hernández.

La Mano Mágica (Map p702; ☎ 516-42-75; www .casacerrosagrado.com; Alcalá 203; ☺ 10:30am-3pm & 4-7:30pm Mon-Sat) Chiefly a classy crafts gallery, the 'Magic Hand' also has some art, including prints by the likes of Tamayo and Toledo. See also Shopping, p719.

The **Museo de Arte Contemporáneo de Oaxaca** (MACO; Map p702; see also p705) is another place where you'll often see first-rank contemporary art.

ACTIVITIES

Several well-established outfits with an eco-logical and/or community ethic will send you hiking or biking in the mountains or valleys, spotting rare birds or lending a

hand to help the city's impoverished street children. For bird-watching, Turismo de Aventura Teotitlán in Teotitlán del Valle (see p727) is also recommended.

Bicicletas Bravo (Map p702; ☎ 516-09-53; www .bikeoaxaca.com; García Vigil 409; ☺ 9:30am-2:30pm & 4:30-7:30pm Mon-Sat) does easy-to-moderate half-day mountain bike trips in the Valles Centrales for around US$24 per person (minimum two). They rent bikes too (see Getting Around, p722).

Bicicletas Pedro Martínez (Map p702; ☎ /fax 514-59-35; www.bicicletaspedromartinez.com; Aldama 418), run by the amiable Pedro Martínez, a champion mountain biker, offers rides lasting from four hours to two days in the Valles Centrales and the Santiago Apoala area (see p735). Prices per person range from US$28 for a half-day trip to the Parque Comunal San Felipe on the northern fringe of the city to around US$200 for two-day bike-and-hike trips around Santiago Apoala. Trips include meals; most have a two-person minimum and on several rides there are discounts for five or more people. Pedro also does four-day Oaxaca–Puerto Escondido expeditions for around US$450. Keen bikers of all levels enjoy Pedro's trips. He rents bikes too (see Getting Around, p722).

Centro de Esperanza Infantil (Map p702; ☎ 501-10-69; www.oaxacastreetchildren.org; Crespo 308; ☺ 9am-7pm Mon-Fri, 10am-3pm Sat) is a center for street children that sponsors and cares for kids who are homeless or have to support their deeply impoverished families by selling chewing gum or shining shoes. Many are from the Triqui ethnic group and have fled political violence in western Oaxaca. The center has a dining room, library, computers, classrooms and kindergarten. The staff do a great job and welcome donations, sponsors and volunteers to help with meals, the on-site medical center and activities such as art, English and computer classes.

Expediciones Sierra Norte (Map p702; ☎ 514-82-71; www.sierranorte.org.mx in Spanish; Bravo 210; ☺ 9am-3pm & 4-7pm Mon-Fri, 9am-2pm Sat) This very well-run rural community organization offers walking, mountain biking and accommodations in the beautiful Sierra Norte, northeast of the city; see the Pueblos Mancomunados section, p736.

Tierra Dentro (Map p702; ☎ /fax 514-92-84; http: //welcome.to/tierradentro; Reforma 528B; ☺ 11am-8pm

Mon-Sat, 12:30-8pm Sun) offers rock climbing (one to two days, US$50 to US$90), bird-watching (six hours, US$40), hot-air ballooning (US$120), and a range of mountain bike and hiking trips. It also offers treks and ascents on Mexico's highest mountain, Pico de Orizaba (see p686), some of which are practicable even if you don't have high-altitude climbing experience (four to six days, US$260 to US$620).

Tierraventura (Map p702; ☎ 501-13-63; www.tierra ventura.com; Abasolo 217; ⏰ 10am-2pm & 5-8pm Mon-Sat), run by a multilingual Swiss and German couple, is friendly and very well organized. It takes groups of up to six on trips in the Valles Centrales, Sierra Norte, Mixteca, Pacific coast and elsewhere in the Oaxaca state. Some fairly remote destinations are included, and there's a focus on hiking, nature, crafts, meeting locals and traditional medicine, wherever possible working with local community tourism projects. On most trips, prices range between US$55 and US$70 per person per day.

COURSES
Language

Oaxaca has half a dozen popular and well-established language schools, and new ones are popping up all the time. All schools offer group instruction at a variety of levels, Monday to Friday, and most emphasize the spoken language. Most can also provide individual classes and a range of special subjects and packages. Textbooks and other materials are an additional cost at some schools: ask about this before signing up.

Many schools also offer extra activities such as dance, weaving or cooking classes, movies, tours and *intercambios* (meetings with local people for Spanish conversation), and they can also arrange accommodations for you, either in hotels, self-catering or with families. Family accommodation, where you will normally have your own room, costs around US$15 a day with breakfast, plus around US$4 extra if you take lunch and US$2 for dinner.

Amigos del Sol (Map p702; ☎ 514-34-84; www.mex online.com/amisol.htm; Libres 109; US$85 a week for 15hr) This is a small school, popular with travelers, with a maximum class size of five. Start any Monday or other weekday (go to the school at 8:45am). There's no minimum duration and no charge for registration or textbooks.

Becari Language School (Map p702; ☎ 514-60-76; www.becari.com.mx; Bravo 210; US$90/120/180 a week for 15/20/30hr) A medium-size school with maximum class size of five. Start any Monday morning. A US$70 registration fee is charged.

Español Interactivo (Map p702; ☎ 514-60-62; www .mexonline.com/esp-interactivo.htm; Armenta y López 311B; US$90/120/180/240 a week for 15/20/30/40hr) Small, central school with maximum class size of four; start any Monday; no registration fee.

OAXACA'S COMMUNITY MUSEUMS

Oaxaca state is in the forefront of Mexico's admirable community museums movement. Of the 60 or so villages around the country that have set up these small museums to foster their unique cultures and keep their archaeological and cultural treasures 'at home,' 17 are scattered around Oaxaca.

Museos Comunitarios de Oaxaca (Map p702; ☎ 562-02-50; Salón No 9, Edificio del Siglo XIX, Centro Cultural Santo Domingo, cnr Reforme & Constitución) has full information on these small but often fascinating museums. The office also offers organized trips for groups of 10 or more to four museum villages: Santa Ana del Valle (p728), San Martín Huamelulpan (p736), Santiago Suchilquitongo in the Valle de Etla, which has impressive archaeological relics, and San Pedro Huixtepec south of Zimatlán. For a cost per person of US$19 (US$37 for San Martín Huamelulpan, an overnight trip which includes a demonstration of traditional healing practices), the excursions include traditional local meals and visits to local artisans, archaeological sites and so on.

Other community museums within easy reach of Oaxaca are at Teotitlán del Valle (p727) and San José El Mogote (p734). If you're up for a bit of an off-the-beaten-track adventure, consider visiting the museums at Natividad in the Sierra Norte, with a recreation of an old gold mine; Cerro Marín near Valle Nacional, which tells the story of the villagers' struggle for rights to use their local spring; or San Miguel Tequistepec near Coixtlahuaca, with fascinating pre-Hispanic material in a restored 16th-century *cacique's* house. Simple accommodations are available at or near several of these outlying villages.

Instituto de Comunicación y Cultura (Map p702; ☎/fax 516-34-43; www.iccoax.com; Plaza Alcalá, Alcalá 307; US$130/160 a week for 15/20hr) Founded in 1986, ICC gives classes in groups of three to five, starting any Monday, with a US$50 registration fee. It emphasizes its teachers' qualifications and experience. Special courses are offered in business and medical Spanish, translation, Mexican literature and Spanish for children.

Instituto Cultural Oaxaca (Map p701; ☎ 515-34-04; www.instculturaloax.com.mx; Juárez 909; 'total-immersion' 4-week courses US$400) The Instituto Cultural's popular seven-hour-a-day program includes *intercambios* and workshops in arts, crafts and culture; many classes are held in the school's spacious gardens and terraces. It's possible to enrol for less than the full four weeks. There's a US$50 registration fee.

Soléxico (Map p702; ☎/fax 516-56-80; www.solexico .com; Abasolo 217; US$92/155 a week for 15/25hr for first 2 weeks, rates decrease thereafter) Professionally-run school with another branch in Playa del Carmen, enabling students to split their time between the two locations. Soléxico has a refined 12-level system and you'll be taught at the appropriate one even if you are the only person at that level. Fees include cooking and salsa classes, movies and social gatherings but not textbooks or the US$80 registration fee. Start any Monday. Soléxico offers the chance of volunteer work in local social projects.

Uabjo (Map p701; Universidad Autónoma Benito Juárez de Oaxaca; ☎/fax 516-59-22; Burgoa s/n; US$80 a week for 20hr) Uabjo is Oaxaca's university, and its Facultad de Idiomas (Languages Faculty) offers courses of one, two, three or four weeks, with an average eight students per class. You can also study Mexican history, art and literature and the Zapotec and Mixtec languages here.

Vinigúlaza (Map p702; ☎ 513-27-63; www.vinigulaza .com; Abasolo 503; US$45/67.50/90 a week for 10/15/20hr) Maximum class size at this competitively priced school is six people. Classes are conversation-based. Start any Monday.

Private tutors are not hard to find; check notice boards (see Media, p700) or ask at the schools. One-on-one instruction organized through schools costs US$10 to US$15 an hour.

Cooking

Several Oaxacan cooks regularly impart their secrets to those wanting to recreate special flavors back home. The following well-received classes are (or can be) held in English, and include market visits to buy ingredients.

El Jardín de los Sabores (Map p702; ☎ 516-57-04; www.lasbugambilias.com; Libres 205; 4hr class US$55 per person) Pilar Cabrera, owner of Café La Olla, gives classes from 10:30am to 2:30pm on Tuesday, Thursday and Saturday at her guesthouse in central Oaxaca, La Casa de los Sabores. Participants prepare and then eat a five-course meal, usually including some vegetarian dishes. The price is reduced if you attend more than one class, or if more than eight people attend.

La Casa de mis Recuerdos (Map p702; ☎ 515-56-45; www.misrecuerdos.net; Pino Suárez 508; classes US$45-65) Nora Gutiérrez, from a family of celebrated Oaxacan cooks, conducts classes for groups of up to eight at her family's charming B&B (see Sleeping, p712). You prepare a Oaxacan lunch (planned a couple of days ahead), then sit down to eat it. Price depends on the number of participants and what they want to cook. Vegetarian classes are available. La Casa de Mis Recuerdos also offers one-week cooking-class packages at US$450/750 for singles/doubles.

Seasons of My Heart (☎ 518-77-26; www.seasons ofmyheart.com; Rancho Aurora, AP 42 Admon 3, Oaxaca 68101; 1-day class US$75, 1-week course US$1695 incl hotel and meals) This cooking school at a ranch in the Valle de Etla is run by American chef and Oaxacan food expert Susana Trilling. It offers classes in Mexican and Oaxacan cooking, from one-day group sessions (most Wednesdays) to long-weekend and week-long courses, plus culinary tours around Oaxaca state.

TOURS

If you're short on time, a guided trip can save hassles and be lots of fun. A typical four-hour group trip to El Tule and Mitla or to Cuilapan and Zaachila, costs around US$10/14 per child/adult. Whole-day trips – for example to El Tule, Teotitlán del Valle, Mitla, Hierve El Agua and a mezcal distillery – are around US$17/23 (admission fees and meals are extra in both cases). Agencies with a wide choice of itineraries include the following:

Continental-Istmo Tours (Map p702; ☎ 516-96-25; Alcalá 201)

Turismo El Convento (www.oaxacaexperts.com) Camino Real Oaxaca (Map p702; ☎ 516-18-06; 5 de Mayo 300); Hotel Misión de los Ángeles (Map p701; ☎ 513-38-48; Calz Porfirio Díaz 102); Hotel Victoria (Map p701; ☎ 513-31-88; Lomas del Fortín 1)

Viajes Turísticos Mitla Hotel Rivera del Ángel (Map p702; ☎ 514-31-52; Mina 518); Hostal Santa Rosa (Map p702; ☎ 514-78-00; Trujano 201)

Some agencies are more specialized. **Rug Tours** (Map p702; ☎ 516 09 53; www.rugsoaxaca.com; García Vigil 409; US$10 per person) does half-day tours to the weaving village of Teotitlán del Valle, visiting at least six of Teotitlán's best weaving workshops.

FESTIVALS & EVENTS

All major national festivals are celebrated here, and Oaxaca has some unique fiestas of its own, the biggest and most spectacular being the **Guelaguetza** (http://guelaguetza-oax.com). It's held from 10am to 1pm on the first two Mondays after July 16 (unless July 18 is a Monday, in which case Guelaguetza is July 25 and August 1). This brilliant feast of Oaxacan folk dance takes place in the open-air Auditorio Guelaguetza (Map p701) on Cerro del Fortín. Thousands of people flock into Oaxaca for these and associated events, turning the city into a feast of celebration and regional culture (and a rich hunting ground for visiting pickpockets, so stay alert). On the appointed Mondays, known as Los Lunes del Cerro (Mondays on the Hill), magnificently costumed dancers from the seven regions of Oaxaca state perform a succession of dignified, lively or comical traditional dances, tossing offerings of produce to the crowd as they finish. The excitement climaxes with the incredibly colorful pineapple dance by women of the Papaloapan region, and the stately, prancing Zapotec Danza de las Plumas (Feather Dance), which reenacts, symbolically, the Spanish conquest.

Seats in the amphitheater (which holds perhaps 10,000) are divided into four areas called *palcos*. For Palcos A and B, the two nearest the stage, tickets (around US$32) go on sale about three months beforehand from tourist offices in Oaxaca. Nearer festival time they're also available at other outlets in the city. Tickets guarantee a seat, but you should arrive before 8am if you want one of the better ones. The two much bigger rear *palcos*, C and D, are free and fill up early – if you get in by 8am you'll get a seat, but by 10am you'll be lucky to get even standing room. Wherever you sit, you'll be in the open air, with no shelter, for hours, so equip yourself accordingly.

A number of towns and villages around Oaxaca now stage their own smaller Guelaguetzas on or near the same dates. They can make a refreshing change from the hub-bub and crowds of Oaxaca. Tlacochahuaya village has a particularly attractive site on a hillside overlooking the village.

Many other events have grown up around the Guelaguetza. Highlights include the **Desfile de Delegaciones** (on Saturday afternoons preceding Guelaguetza Mondays), a parade of the regional delegations through the city center; and the **Bani Stui Gulal** (on Sunday evenings preceding Guelaguetza Mondays), a vibrant show of music, fireworks and dance telling the history of the Guelaguetza, in the Plaza de la Danza by the Basílica de la Soledad. There's also a mezcal fair; and lots of concerts, exhibitions and sports events. Programs are widely available.

The origins of the Guelaguetza lie in pre-Hispanic rites in honor of maize and wind gods, held about the same time of year on Cerro del Fortín. After the Spanish conquest the indigenous festivities became fused with Christian celebrations for the Virgen del Carmen (July 16). Celebrations in something like their present form began in 1932, and the purpose-built amphitheater was opened in 1974. Guelaguetza is a Zapotec word meaning cooperation or exchange of gifts, referring to the tradition of people helping each other out at such times as weddings, births and deaths.

There are many other festivals throughout the year.

Fiesta de la Virgen del Carmen (a week or more before July 16) The streets around the Templo del Carmen Alto on García Vigil become a fairground and the nights are lit by processions and fireworks.

Blessing of Animals (about 5pm, August 31) Pets are dressed up and taken to the Iglesia de La Merced, on Independencia.

Día de Muertos (November 2) Day of the Dead is a big happening here, with associated events starting several days in advance. These include music and dance at the main cemetery, the Panteón General, on Calz del Panteón about 1.25km east of the zócalo. Some guesthouses and agencies arrange guided tours and excursions to village events.

Posadas (December 16-24) Nine night-time neighborhood processions symbolizing Mary and Joseph's journey to Bethlehem.

Día de la Virgen de la Soledad (December 18) Processions and traditional dances, including the Danza de las Plumas, at the Basílica de la Soledad.

Noche de los Rábanos (Night of the Radishes; December 23) Amazing figures carved from radishes are displayed in the zócalo.

Calendas (December 24) These Christmas-Eve processions from churches converge on the zócalo about 10pm, bringing music, floats and fireworks.

SLEEPING

The high seasons in Oaxaca are from mid-December to mid-January, a week each side of Easter and Día de Muertos, and from mid-July to mid-August. Many places, except those in the hardcore budget bracket, raise their prices by between 15% and 30% during these periods (dates vary from one establishment to another).

Budget

Oaxaca has more backpacker hostels than any other city in Mexico, and many budget hotels. Hostels in the following listings all have shared bathrooms and, unless stated, kitchens where you can cook up your own meals.

Hotel Casa Arnel (☎ 515-28-56; www.casaarnel .com.mx; Aldama 404; s/d from US$25/30, with shared bathroom US$12.50/25; 🖳) Family-run Casa Arnel is in quiet, cobbled Colonia Jalatlaco, five minutes' walk from the 1st-class bus station and 20 minutes northeast of the city center. The clean rooms surround a big, leafy courtyard. The ensuite rooms have been attractively remodeled with folksy decorative touches. Casa Arnel also offers a travel agency (village tours available), economical car rental, breakfast, library, Internet, laundry, a clothes-washing sink and a great roof terrace.

Hostel Luz de Luna Nuyoo (Map p702; ☎ 516-95-76; mayoraljchotmail.com; Juárez 101; dm US$5.50, hammock or tent per person US$4) This is a friendly, medium-sized hostel run by two young Oaxacan musician brothers. Separate bunk rooms for women, men and couples open on to a wide patio; you can hang a hammock or put up a tent on the roof terrace.

Hostal Paulina (Map p702; ☎ 516-20-05; www .paulinahostel.com; Trujano 321; dm US$7, d/tr/q US$17/25/33) Impeccably clean and efficiently run, this 96-capacity hostel provides bunk dorms for up to 11 people, and rooms holding one double bed and one pair of bunks, all with lockers. There's a US$1 discount if you have an HI or ISIC card. A neat, green little interior garden and a roof terrace add to the appeal. There's no kitchen or social area, but a breakfast café might be open by the time you get there.

Posada Margarita (Map p702; ☎ 516-28-02; Plaza de las Virgenes, Plazuela Labastida 115; s/d US$20/23, with shared bathroom US$12/15) The Margarita has 12 very plain but clean rooms, just a stone's throw from Calle Alcalá.

Magic Hostel (Map p702; ☎ 516-76-67; www.magic hostel.com.mx; Fiallo 305; dm US$5.50, s/d US$6.50/13; 🖳) Some love it, some hate it. The Magic is Oaxaca's social, party-scene hostel with plentiful sitting 'areas and a bar (open 8pm to 11pm) and roof lounge, but little care wasted on the rooms. There are 41 places in women-only and mixed dorms and 15 rooms holding up to eight people.

There are plenty of other recommended budget places:

Hostal Guadalupe (Map p702; ☎ 516-63-65; Juárez 409; dm US$5.50, d US$12) Small, very clean, tranquil hostel offering separate-sex bunk rooms and a particularly well equipped kitchen.

Hotel Posada El Chapulín (Map p702; ☎ 516-16-46; Aldama 317; s/d US$14/19; 🖳) Friendly small travelers' hotel, with roof terrace, TV and fans in rooms.

Hostal Santa Isabel (Map p702; ☎ 514-28-65, 516-74-98; hostalsantaisabeloax@hotmail.com; Mier y Terán 103; dm US$5, d US$11-13; 🖳) Relaxed, friendly hostel with room for about 40 in bunk dorms (one for women only) and varied bedrooms, around two patios with plants. It has lockers, and bicycles to rent at US$0.50 per hour.

Mid-Range

Oaxaca boasts some delightful mid-range hotels and B&Bs, many of them in colonial or colonial-style buildings.

Hotel Azucenas (Map p702; ☎ 514-79-18, 800-717-25-40, in US 877-780-1156, in Canada 877-343-8570; www.hotelazucenas.com; Aranda 203; s/d US$38/43) The Azucenas is a small, welcoming, Canadian-owned hotel in a beautifully restored colonial house. The 10 cool, white, tile-floored rooms are prettily designed, and a delicious buffet breakfast (US$3) is served on the lovely roof terrace. Some signs on the street still post its old name, Calle Unión.

Las Bugambilias (Map p702; ☎ /fax 516-11-65, in US 321-249-9422; www.lasbugambilias.com; Reforma 402; s US$39-60, d US$41-73, all with breakfast; ✷ ✗ 🖳) This delightful B&B, entered through Café La Olla, has nine rooms which are named after flowers and decorated with inspired combinations of folk and contemporary art. Some have air-conditioning and/or a balcony; all have tiled bathrooms and fans. A big treat here is the gourmet two-course Oaxacan breakfast. Further attractions include high-speed Internet connection, cheap international phone calls, a meditation room and a lovely roof terrace.

Hotel Las Golondrinas (Map p702; ☎ 514-32-98; lasgolon@prodigy.net.mx; Tinoco y Palacios 411; r US$32-45; ☒) Lovingly tended by friendly owners and staff, this fine small hotel has about 18 rooms that open out onto three beautiful, leafy patios. It's often full, so you should try to book ahead. None of the rooms are huge but all are tastefully decorated and immaculately clean. Good breakfasts (not included in room rates) are served in one of the patios.

Hotel Posada del Centro (Map p702; ☎ /fax 516-18-74; www.mexonline.com/posada.htm; Independencia 403; s/d US$29/33, large r US$42, s/d with shared bathroom US$15/20; ℗) Attractive, centrally situated Posada del Centro has two large, verdant patios where breakfast is available. The 22 rooms have fans and pleasing Oaxacan artisanry (though none have large windows), there's an ample roof terrace, and staff are young, bright and helpful.

Casa de la Tía Tere (Map p702; ☎ 501-18-45, 800-514-33-33; www.mexonline.com/tiatere.htm; Murguía 612; r incl continental breakfast US$50-55; ℗ 🖳 🗭) This B&B has 12 large, uncluttered rooms, and is one of the very few accommodations in central Oaxaca with a swimming pool. The pool sits between patches of lawn in the rear garden. Tía Tere also offers a large, clean kitchen and dining room for guests, free coffee and Internet, laundry service and low-cost phone calls. A top choice.

Hotel Las Mariposas (Map p702; ☎ 515-58-54; www.mexonline.com/mariposas.htm; Pino Suárez 517; s/d US$32/37, studio apt s/d US$41/46) Las Mariposas offers five studio apartments (with small kitchen) and half a dozen rooms, all set around pretty patios. All are large, spotlessly clean and simply but prettily decorated. It's a tranquil, friendly place.

Hotel Posada Catarina (Map p702; ☎ 516-42-70; Aldama 325; r US$32-41) Posada Catarina is on a busy street southwest of the zócalo, but inside it's welcoming, large and rambling, with two patios (one with a garden) and rooms that are traditional in style but modern in comfort, including phone and fan. A mix of contemporary and folk art decks the walls.

Parador San Miguel (Map p702; ☎ 514-93-31; www.mexonline.com/paradorsanmiguel.htm; Independencia 503; r US$55; ☒) One of the best of Oaxaca's new wave of modern hotels in traditional style, Parador San Miguel has 23 good-sized rooms with orange and green hues and pleasing wrought-iron and wooden touches. Each has a phone, safe, TV and either one king-size or two normal double beds. Also here is the good Restaurante El Andariego (see p715).

Hotel Cazomalli (☎ 513-86-05; www.hotelcazomalli.com; El Salto 104; r US$37; 🖳) The welcoming, family-run Cazomalli, decked with tasteful Oaxacan artisanry, is five minutes' walk from the 1st-class bus station, in quiet Colonia Jalatlaco. The 18 rooms all have safe, fan and hair dryer, and the roof terrace has lovely views. Breakfast is available.

Hostal Casa del Sótano (Map p702; ☎ /fax 516-24-94; hostal_casa_sotano@hotmail.com; Tinoco y Palacios 414; r US$39-44) This small, modern, colonial-style hotel is arranged along two lovely patios with fountains, little water gardens and pools. The clean, good-sized rooms have solid wooden furnishings, cable TV, phone and fan. Also here are a café with great views and a gallery selling work by some of Mexico's top artists.

La Casa de los Milagros (Map p702; ☎ 501-22-62; www.mexonline.com/milagros.htm; Matamoros 500C; r incl breakfast US$73-87; ☒) The 'House of the Miracles' is a beautiful, architect-modernized, century-old house with just three spacious rooms, all with king-size beds. The renovation makes inspired use of light, color and space. One room even has a garden inside its bathroom. There's a well-equipped kitchen for guests. Children under 12 are not allowed.

Hotel Las Rosas (Map p702; ☎ 514-22-17; Trujano 112; s/d US$32/36) Dependable Las Rosas offers clean, fan-cooled rooms with TV, on two levels around a broad courtyard. The entrance is up a flight of stairs from the street, just half a block from the zócalo.

La Casa de los Sabores (Map p702; ☎ 516-57-04; www.lasbugambilias.com; Libres 205; s/d incl breakfast US$49/55; ☒) Five folksy-featured, high-ceilinged rooms are on offer here, four of them around the patio in which owner Pilar Cabrera gives her thrice-weekly cooking classes (see p709). The breakfasts are large and gourmet. A roof terrace provides a change of scene. Children under six are not allowed here.

La Casa de María (☎ 515-12-02; http://oaxacalive.com/maria.htm; Belisario Domínguez 205, Colonia Reforma;

s/d incl continental breakfast US$36/46; (P)) Tucked behind a high wall in the north of town, this attractive guesthouse is an oasis of calm run by the lively, friendly María Díaz. The 16 comfortable, pretty rooms are set around two lovely garden areas. There's a roof terrace and a sitting room too. From the 1st-class bus station, it's four blocks north along Zapata, then half a block west along Belisario Domínguez.

Hotel Antonio's (Map p702; ☎ 516-72-27; fax 516-36-72; Independencia 601; s/d 1-bed US$23/28, r 2-bed US$32) Antonio's, half a block from the Alameda, has 18 bright, sizable rooms with phone and TV. The best are those above the courtyard restaurant.

Parador Santo Domingo de Guzmán (Map p702; ☎ /fax 514-21-71; www.paradorstodomingo.com.mx; Alcalá 804; s/d/tr/q US$59/64/68/73, per week US$330/358/383/408; (P) (🏊)) This apartment hotel, still comfortable though starting to show signs of wear, is 8½ blocks north of the zócalo. Each apartment has two double beds, a sitting room, bathroom, cable TV, safe, fan and well-equipped kitchen. There's hotel-style room service with clean sheets daily.

Hotel Francia (Map p702; ☎ 516-48-11; www .hotelfrancia.com.mx; 20 de Noviembre 212; r incl breakfast US$36) The century-old, 60-room Francia, one block from the zócalo, has been brightened up and its rooms are now cheerful though still moderately sized. They have fan, phone and TV. This is a clean, amiable place (and DH Lawrence stayed here).

Hotel Gala (Map p702; ☎ 514-22-51, 800-712-73-16; www.gala.com.mx; Bustamante 103; s/d incl American breakfast US$46/53) The rooms here are mostly good enough, all possessing phone and fan, but steer clear of the small interior ones in hot weather.

Hotel Principal (Map p702; ☎ 516-25-35; jdbrena@ spersaoaxaca.com.mx; 5 de Mayo 208; r US$35) The 17 rooms are sizable and set around a sunny courtyard, but they're bare, basic and overdue for an update.

Numerous rental apartments and houses are available. Check notice boards and the *Oaxaca* and *Oaxaca Times* papers (including their online editions – see p703) and the Spanish-language paper *Noticias*.

La Casa de Mis Recuerdos (see following) rents out two apartments (US$292/731 per week/month), as well as a bungalow (US$205/702 per week/month) and a house (US$819/3510 per week/month) in quiet Colonia Jalatlaco.

Top End

Top-end accommodations range from a converted convent to modern resort hotels.

Camino Real Oaxaca (Map p702; ☎ 501-61-00, in US & Canada 800-7-CAMINO; www.caminoreal.com/oaxaca; 5 de Mayo 300; s/d US$232/258; (P) (✕) (🏊) (🍴)) The Camino Real was created in the 1970s when the 16th-century Santa Catalina convent, four blocks northeast of the zócalo, was converted. The old chapel is a banquet hall, one of the five lovely courtyards contains an enticing swimming pool, and the bar is lined with books on otherworldly devotion. Beautiful thick stone walls help keep the place cool. The 91 rooms are well decorated in colonial styles. If you can, choose one upstairs and away from kitchen noise.

Casa de Sierra Azul (Map p702; ☎ 514-84-12; www .mexonline.com/sierrazul.htm; Hidalgo 1002; s/d US$86/107) The Sierra Azul is a 200-year-old house converted to a beautiful small hotel, centered on a broad courtyard with a fountain and stone pillars. The 14 good-sized, tasteful rooms have high ceilings, old-fashioned-style furnishings and good tiled bathrooms.

La Casa de mis Recuerdos (Map p702; ☎ 515-56-45; www.misrecuerdos.net; Pino Suárez 508; s incl breakfast US$40-65, d incl breakfast US$78-93; (✕)) A big Mexican breakfast in the family dining room is a feature of this charming, tastefully decorated guesthouse. Eight of the 10 rooms have private bathroom, the best overlook a central garden and a few are air-conditioned. There's a minimum stay of three nights. Prices fall a few dollars from August to late October and from March to May, except around Semana Santa.

Hotel Victoria (Map p701; ☎ 515-26-33; www.hotel victoriaoax.com.mx; Lomas del Fortín 1; r US$139, villa US$171, junior ste US$203; (P) (✕) (🏊) (🍴)) The Victoria stands on the lower slopes of Cerro del Fortín, surrounded by big gardens with tennis courts and an Olympic-size pool. Many of the 150 large, comfortable, bright rooms and suites have fine views over the city. The villas are large rooms with a terrace and bathtub in the area around the pool. The restaurant, overlooking the gardens, is excellent, with pasta, meat and fish mains costing from US$5.50 to US$11. The hotel runs a free shuttle to/from the city center several times daily; a taxi is US$2.50.

Hotel Misión de los Ángeles (Map p701; ☎ 502-01-00; www.misiondelosangeles.com; Calz Porfirio Díaz 102; r US$127; (P) (🍴) (🏊)) Also north of the center, the Misión de los Ángeles has 173 large rooms and suites in extensive tropical gardens, plus tennis courts, a large pool, bars, restaurant and a children's play area. Standard rooms all have two double beds, air-conditioning, TV and phone: the best overlook the pool area.

Parador del Domínico (Map p702; ☎ 513-18-12; dominico@infosel.net.mx; Pino Suárez 410; s/d US$90/103; ☒) This Best Western hotel has a lovely stone-columned patio bar. The 32 rooms are air-conditioned, with cable TV, a safe and a pleasant décor of wood, tiles and fabrics. There's a restaurant too.

Hotel Casa Conzatti (Map p701; ☎ 513-85-00, 800-717-99-74; Farías 218; r US$117; ☒ ☒ ☒) Casa Conzatti is classy and modern but colonial style. It faces a tranquil park, and has 45 bright, pleasing rooms.

Hotel Casa Antigua (Map p702; ☎ 501-12-40; www .hotelcasaantigua.com; 5 de Mayo 206; r US$107, junior ste

US$139; ☒ ☒) This small hotel has sober, comfortable rooms, two cool patios (one with restaurant, one with bar) and a roof terrace where you can enjoy fine views over breakfast or drinks.

EATING
On & Near the Zócalo   Map p702
All the cafés and restaurants beneath the zócalo arches are great spots for watching Oaxaca life, but quality and service vary.

El Asador Vasco (☎ 514-47-55; Portal de Flores 10A; mains US$7.50-12.50; ☒ noon-11:30pm Mon-Sat) Upstairs at the southwest corner of the zócalo, the Asador Vasco serves up good Oaxacan, Spanish and international food. It's strong on meat and seafood. For a table overlooking the plaza on a warm evening, book earlier in the day.

Terranova Café (☎ 514-05-33; Portal Juárez 116; mains US$5-7.50) One of the best places on the

---

COCINA OAXAQUEÑA

Good Oaxacan cooking is spicily delicious, and the seven traditional Oaxacan moles (sauces) are renowned. The moles are usually served over chicken or pork. Here are some of the Oaxaca specialties:

amarillo – a yellow-orange cumin and chili mole (with chicken)

chapulines – grasshoppers! They come fried, often with chili powder, onion and garlic. They're high in protein and good with a squeeze of lime. Vendors sell them from baskets in the zócalo and you can find them in food markets too – if you eat some, they say, you'll return to Oaxaca.

chíchilo – a dark, rich mole made with varied chilies

coloradito – a brick-red chili-and-tomato mole, usually served over pork or chicken

colorado – a dark red mole

manchamanteles – 'tablecloth-stainer': a mole made with pineapple and bananas

mole negro – the monarch of Oaxacan moles, sometimes called just mole oaxaqueño. A dark, spicy, slightly sweet sauce made with many ingredients including chilies, bananas, chocolate, pepper and cinnamon; usually served with chicken.

picadillo – spicy minced or shredded pork, often used for the stuffing in *chiles rellenos*

quesillo – Oaxacan stringy cheese

tamal oaxaqueño – a tamal with a mole and (usually) chicken filling

tasajo – a slice of pounded beef

tlayuda or **tlalluda** – a big crisp tortilla, traditionally served with salsa and chili but now topped with almost anything, making it into a kind of pizza

verde – a green mole made from beans, chilies, parsley and epazote (goosefoot or wild spinach)

Another Oaxacan favorite is chocolate. A bowl of steaming hot chocolate to drink, with sweet bread to dunk, is the perfect warmer when winter sets in 1500m above sea level. The mix to which hot milk or water is added typically contains cinnamon, almonds and sugar as well as ground-up cocoa beans. The area around the south end of Oaxaca's Mercado 20 de Noviembre has several shops specializing in this time-honored treat – and not just chocolate for drinking but also chocolate for moles, hard chocolate for eating, and more. You can sample chocolate with or without cinnamon, light or dark chocolate with varying quantities of sugar, and many other varieties at any of these places. And most of them have vats where you can watch the mixing.

zócalo, Terranova serves good breakfasts until 1pm (with a US$8 unlimited buffet on Sunday), and a big range of antojitos, baguettes, lunches and dinners.

El Sagrario (☎ 514-03-03; Valdivieso 120; mains US$4-9) This popular and reliable spot half a block north of the zócalo serves Mexican, Italian and international food on three floors.

La Primavera (☎ 516-25-95; Portal de Flores 1C; mains US$4-7; ☒ 7:30am-midnight) A fairly good zócalo restaurant with some vegetarian options. Three quesadillas with mushrooms, guacamole, the herb *epazote* and pumpkin flower cost US$4.25.

Mercado 20 de Noviembre (btwn 20 de Noviembre & Cabrera; mains US$1.75-3) Cheap *oaxaqueño* meals can be had in this market south of the zócalo. Most of the many small *comedores* here serve up local specialties such as chicken in *mole negro*. Pick a *comedor* that's busy – those are the best. Many stay open until early evening, but their food is freshest earlier in the day.

West of the Zócalo   Map p702

Restaurante El Naranjo (☎ 514-18-78; Trujano 203; soups & salads US$4.50, mains US$8-10; ☒ 1-10pm Mon-Sat) This excellent courtyard restaurant features fine *oaxaqueño* food with a modern touch. Owner/chef Iliana de la Vega picked up some imaginative ideas during years spent in Mexico City, and she's a great cook, though her innovations don't go down well with many locals, who find it hard to contemplate a mole made without lard – just the kind of thing that appeals so much to foreign visitors. Each of the seven Oaxacan moles is served one day of the week, with chicken breast or pork fillet. The *chiles rellenos*, with unusual fillings, is another fine choice.

Café Alex (☎ 514-07-15; Díaz Ordaz 218; breakfasts US$3.25-4.50; ☒ 7am-9pm Mon-Sat, 7am-noon Sun) Clean, busy Alex is well worth hunting out for great-value breakfasts, served until 12:30pm. Twenty deals are on offer and servings are generous: US$3.50 will buy you scrambled eggs with potatoes, ham and onion, plus beans, tortillas or bread, juice or fruit, and coffee or tea. There's usually a mixed Mexican and foreign crowd here, and service is quick.

Restaurante El Andariego (☎ 514-93-31; Independencia 503; menú del día US$3.25 or US$4.50, mains US$6.50-9.50) This bright restaurant at the front of the Parador San Miguel hotel is especially popular for its good-value four-course set lunches.

Restaurant Colonial (20 de Noviembre 112; lunch US$2.75; ☒ 8am-noon & 2-5pm Mon-Sat) The Colonial's 10 or so tables fill up with locals for the good-value four-course *comida corrida*, which includes soup, rice, a main course such as *pollo a la naranja* (chicken *à l'orange*), dessert and *agua de fruta*.

Fidel Pan Integral (20 de Noviembre 211; baked goods around US$1) Fidel is a brown-bread-lover's dream, even with wholegrain croissants.

Jardín Sócrates (Independencia; snacks up to US$1) For authentic local snacks, head to this shady little plaza by the Basílica de La Soledad. It's full of *neverías* (sorbet stands) and *dulcerías* (pastry and cake stands) hawking their delicious wares, and Oaxacans of all stripes come here to relax.

East of the Zócalo   Map p702

El Buen Gourmet (☎ 516-78-22; Independencia 1104; mains US$1.50-2) The straightforward Buen Gourmet turns out good, straightforward Mexican dishes like *chiles rellenos* and chicken in *mole poblano* at nice, straightforward prices. Soups and salads are under US$1.25.

North of the Zócalo

Restaurante Los Danzantes (Map p702; ☎ 501-11-84; Alcalá 403; mains US$8-11; ☒ 2:30-11:30pm) Innovative Mexican food in an avant-garde architect-designed setting makes Los Danzantes one of the most exciting places to eat in Oaxaca. A formerly derelict colonial patio now sports high adobe-brick walls, tall wooden columns and cool pools of water in an impeccably contemporary configuration, half open to the sky. Efficient and welcoming young staff serve up a short but first-class selection of food: you might start with *sopa de nopales con camarón* (prawn and prickly pear cactus soup) and follow it with a tender *arrachera* steak. Beware the innocuous-looking chili lying quietly beside the *arrachera*. It's a *chile de agua*, and it packs a major punch.

Café La Olla (Map p702; ☎ 516-66-68; Reforma 402; dishes US$2.50-9; ☒ 8am-10pm Tue-Sat, 9am-10pm Sun) This excellent café serves good wholegrain tortas, juices, salads, meat dishes and regional specialties, with plenty of vegetarian choices. It's a fine place for breakfast (US$2.50 to US$4.50), from light continental to full Oaxacan.

1254 Marco Polo (Map p701; ☎ 513-43-08; Pino Suárez 806; breakfasts US$2.50 3, mains US$6-11; ❤ 8am-6pm Wed-Mon) A popular breakfast and lunch spot opposite El Llano park, Marco Polo has a large garden dining area, attentive waiters and great food. The large breakfasts come with bottomless cups of coffee; from noon until closing, antojitos and oven-baked seafood are the main draws.

1254 Marco Polo (Map p702; ☎ 514-43-60; 5 de Mayo 103; breakfast US$2.50-3, mains US$6-11; ❤ 8am-10:30pm Mon-Sat) The downtown branch of 1254 Marco Polo has the same excellent menu and good service as the Pino Suárez branch.

Panini (Map p702; ☎ 501-20-36; Matamoros 200A; prices US$2.75-3.75; ❤ 9am-9pm Mon-Sat) This is a great little place to drop into for a fine ciabatta torta (with vegetarian varieties available), salad, sweet crêpe, carrot cake or walnut strudel. Good coffee too!

La Rústica (Map p702; ☎ 516-76-96; Murguía 101; pasta US$6-6.50, pizzas US$6-14; ❤ 1:30-10pm) Rústica's pizzas are generous and tasty – a *grande* should satisfy three. There are 29 sauces for pasta, and antipasti, salads and wine aplenty – and the location, upstairs on a corner of Alcalá, can't be beat.

Café La Antigua (Map p702; ☎ 516-57-61; Reforma 401; breakfasts & light meals US$3-4.50; ❤ 9:30am-11pm Mon-Sat) The tranquil Antigua serves great breakfasts, croissants, crêpes, cakes, salads, burgers and quality organic coffee from Oaxaca's southern mountains. What more could you ask? Unlimited coffee refills are on offer before noon and from 2pm to 6pm. There's also a full range of alcoholic drinks, and mellow guitar or keyboard music Wednesday to Saturday nights.

Hostería de Alcalá (Map p702; ☎ 516-20-93, Plaza Alcalá, Alcalá 307; mains US$7.50-12, wines from US$20) This courtyard restaurant is one of Oaxaca's classiest eateries. The steaks, at the top of the price range, are a specialty. For something more economical, try pasta or a salad (US$5 to US$6).

Café Los Cuiles (Map p702; ☎ 514-82-59; Plaza de las Virgenes, Plazuela Labastida 115; breakfasts US$2.50-3, salads, soups & snacks US$1.50-2) Los Cuiles is an excellent spot for breakfast, or for light eats at any time of day, with a handy central location and spacious lounge/gallery feel –

popular with travelers and local and foreign students.

Decano (Map p702; 5 de Mayo 210; prices US$3 -4.50) Decano satisfies a range of food needs from breakfast to a good *menú del día* or tasty light eats (*el super munchies*). In the evening it's a very popular spot for young *oaxaqueños* to down a drink or two. Decano has our favorite Oaxaca restaurant music collection.

Pizza Nostrana (Map p702; ☎ 514-07-78; Alcalá 501A; pasta US$5-6, pizzas from US$6.50; ❤ 1-11pm) This small Italian restaurant serves well prepared food, a stone's throw from the Iglesia de Santo Domingo. Choose from five types of pasta and 19 sauces. The *piccolo* (small) pizzas feed two. The entrance is on Allende, just off Alcalá.

La Brew (Map p702; ☎ 514-96-73; García Vigil 304; prices US$1-4; ❤ 8am-8pm Mon-Sat, 8am-2pm Sun) Come to American-owned La Brew for waffles, coffee, BLT sandwiches, yogurt and granola, homemade brownies and chocolate chip cookies.

Comala (Map p702; García Vigil 406; breakfasts & light meals US$2.75-5; ❤ 9am-11pm Mon-Sat) Recommended for the hungry is the excellent *hamburguesa de res* (US$5), a big, juicy, filling burger. Also see Drinking, p718.

Restaurant Flor de Loto (Map p702; ☎ 514-39-44; Morelos 509; mains US$3-4.50) Flor de Loto makes a reasonable stab at pleasing a range of palates from vegan to carnivore. The chicken brochette (US$4.50) is a large and very tasty choice. For vegetarians, the spinach pancakes and *vegetales al gratin* (vegetables with melted cheese) are both good. The US$4 *comida corrida* is a real meal.

Tlayudas Libres (Map p702; Libres 212; tlayudas around US$3; ❤ 9pm-4:30am; Ⓟ) Some assert that the best food in Oaxaca are the *tlayudas* prepared nightly by motherly cooks on an open-air streetside range here on Libres. The large, light, crisp, hot *tlayudas* are folded over frijoles, *quesillo*, and salsa if you want it. With a slice of *tasajo* and a refresco, they make a filling, tasty meal. Sit on benches around the cooking range or at tables in the adjacent building.

El Biche Pobre (Map p701; ☎ 513-46-36; Calz de la República 600; mains US$3.75-5; ❤ 9am-8pm Tue-Sun, 9am-6pm Mon) El Biche Pobre, 1.5km northeast of the zócalo, is an informal place serving a range of Oaxacan food at about a dozen tables, some long enough to stage lunch for a whole extended Mexican family. For an introduction to the local cuisine, you can't beat the US$5.50 *botana surtida*, a dozen assorted little items that add up to a tasty meal.

DRINKING

Café Del Jardín (Map p702; Portal de Flores 10) The Jardín, meeting place of local journalists and scribes, has a peerless position beneath the arches at the southwest corner of the zócalo. Its food is ordinary but the beer and *café latte* (US$2) are good.

Freebar (Map p702; Matamoros 100; ☽ 9pm-2am Mon-Sat) Freebar hosts a young and vibrant crowd which doesn't mind being rammed together to soak up beer and the atmosphere. Nicknamed *la pescera* (the goldfish bowl) with good reason.

Bar del Borgo (Map p702; Matamoros 100; ☽ 10am-11pm Mon-Sat) The Borgo complements its neighbors Freebar and La Tentación by serving a quiet-ish coffee or beer all day in a very small but neatly arranged space that looks out on to the street.

Comala (Map p702; García Vigil 406; ☽ 9am-11pm Mon-Sat) Comfortingly quiet though rarely empty, artsy, mildly bohemian Comala can accompany your snacks, coffee, beer or fancy juices (US$1.50 to US$2) with very good modern or classical music at any time of day.

Salón Central (Map p702; ☎ 514-20-42; Hidalgo 302; individuals/couples Fri & Sat US$3/5; ☽ 10pm-2am Wed-Sat) This great bar has a federal rather than a city license which means a closed-door policy and flexible closing times. You'll find a 20- and 30-something creative crowd in a good-looking bar with nightclub leanings, owned and regularly re-designed by one of Oaxaca's innovative young painters, Guillermo Olguín. The Central hosts rarely-seen live music acts and independent films and uses its wall space as an alternative gallery for celebrated and unheard-of artists alike. Extremely cool during the week, but Oaxaca-style networking fades into a dancey scene by the weekend.

La Divina (Map p702; ☎ 582-05-08; Gurrión 104; ☽ approx 5pm-1am Tue-Sun) Loud, busy La Divina, across the street from Santo Domingo, has a disco-esque interior and music from Spanish-language rock to house to English pop. A mixed-nationality crowd generates a warm atmosphere that spills out on to

the street if you're lucky. Drinks start at around US$1.75.

La Casa del Mezcal (Map p702; Flores Magón 209; ☽ 10-1am) Open since 1935, this is one of Oaxaca's oldest bars, 1½ blocks south of the zócalo. It's a cantina, but a safe one. One room has a large stand-up bar and shelves full of mezcal (US$1 to US$2.50 a shot); the other room has tables where *botanas* are served. Most but not all patrons are men.

La Cucaracha (Map p702; ☎ 501-16-36; Porfirio Díaz 301A; ☽ 7pm-2am Mon-Sat) A good place to make acquaintance with some classic Mexican beverages, this specialist bar stocks 40 varieties of mezcal and 100 of tequila, at around US$1.75 to US$5 a shot. Everyone's welcome, food is available, and there's live Latin music and a lively atmosphere on weekends.

ENTERTAINMENT

Thanks to its student and tourist populations, Oaxaca has a bright entertainment and cultural scene.

Cinema

Cine El Pochote (Map p701; ☎ 514-11-94, 516-69-80; García Vigil 817; admission free, donations accepted; ☽ screenings 6pm & 8pm Tue-Sun) El Pochote shows independent, art-house and classic Mexican and international movies in their original language with Spanish subtitles. There's usually a different theme each month.

Cultural Centers

The **Centro Cultural Ricardo Flores Magón** (Map p702; ☎ 514-62-93; Alcalá 302) and the **Casa de la Cultura Oaxaqueña** (Map p701; ☎ 516-24-83; www.rnet.com.mx in Spanish; Ortega 403) both stage varied musical, dance, theater and art events several evenings a week and a few mornings. These are largely non-touristic events and many of them are free; drop by to see the programs.

Guelaguetza Shows

If you're not lucky enough to be in Oaxaca for the Guelaguetza itself (see p711), it's well worth attending one of the regular imitations.

Camino Real Oaxaca (Map p702; ☎ 516-06-11; 5 de Mayo 300; admission US$27 incl dinner; ☽ 7pm Fri) The classy Camino Real hotel stages a highly colorful three-hour Guelaguetza show in what used to be a convent chapel. Extra shows are held on Monday and Wednesday in high season.

Casa de Cantera (Map p702; ☎ 514-75-85; Murguía 102; admission US$10.50; ☼ 8:30pm) A lively mini-Guelaguetza is staged here nightly, in colorful costume with live music. To make a reservation, phone or stop by during the afternoon. Food and drinks are available.

Hotel Monte Albán (Map p702; ☎ 516-27-77; Alameda de León 1; admission US$6.50; ☼ 8:30pm) This hotel presents a 1½-hour version nightly.

Sometimes there are free Guelaguetza shows at the **Centro Cultural Ricardo Flores Magón** (see earlier).

Live Music

Candela (Map p702; ☎ 514-20-10; Murguía 413; admission US$3-4; ☼ 1pm-2am Tue-Sat) Candela's writhing salsa band and beautiful colonial-house setting have kept it at the top of the Oaxaca nightlife lists for over a decade. Arrive fairly early (9:30pm to 10:30pm) to get a good table, and either learn to dance or learn to watch. Candela is a restaurant too, with a good lunchtime menú (US$4). Drinks start at around US$1.75.

El Sol y La Luna (Map p702; ☎ 514-80-69; Reforma 502; admission US$3.50; ☼ 6pm-1am Mon-Sat) El Sol y La Luna offers smooth Latin music, jazz or feature attractions from across the musical spectrum, starting around 9:30pm several nights a week. The setting is a colonial-style house and the crowd tends to be a refined one of dining couples and art lovers. Pasta, salads, crêpes, chicken and meat dishes cost between US$4.50 and US$8.

La Tentación (Map p702; ☎ 514-95-21; Matamoros 101; admission US$3; ☼ 9pm-2am Tue-Sun) A casual but erratic alternative to Candela, La Tentación puts on live salsa, merengue and cumbia Friday and Saturday, and some DJ nights mid-week. It's close to the zócalo and has a relaxed door policy.

Other places with regular live music include **La Cucaracha** (see Drinking, p718) and the trova den **La Parroquia** (Map p702; Bravo 216; ☼ approximately 9pm-1am several nights weekly).

Free **concerts** in the zócalo are given several evenings each week at 7pm, and at 12:30pm on Wednesday and Sunday, by the state marimba ensemble or state band.

Night Clubs & Discos

NRG (Map p701; Calz Porfirio Díaz 102; admission U$5-7; ☼ Wed-Sat 10:30pm-2:30am) The best of a fairly poor bunch of discos in middle-class Colonia Reforma, north of the center, NRG is your benchmark meat-market nightclub with flashing lights, pop music and special events to pull in the punters. It changes its name and look frequently but usually manages to squeeze in a semi-outdoor bar or similar architectural novelty. It's best to go at the weekend, or check out the huge boards outside to get the lowdown on the next event.

Club 502 (Map p702; ☎ 516-60-20; Porfirio Díaz 502; admission US$3; ☼ 11pm-dawn Thu-Sat) Oaxaca's most prominent and very central gay club offers the best house music in town. Thanks to its late license you can dance long into the early hours, and then some. Expect attention and attitude to start at the door which is opened from the inside once you've rung the bell.

SHOPPING

The state of Oaxaca has the richest, most inventive folk art scene in Mexico, and the city is its chief marketplace. You'll find the highest-quality crafts mostly in the smart

---

MEZCAL

Central Oaxaca state – especially around Santiago Matatlán and the Albarradas group of villages, south and east of Mitla – produces probably the best mezcal in Mexico (and therefore the world). Just like its cousin tequila, mezcal is made from the maguey plant and is usually better when *reposado* or *añejo* (aged). There are also some delicious *crema* varieties with fruit or other flavors.

Several Oaxaca shops southwest of the zócalo specialize in mezcal. Try **El Rey de los Mezcales** (Map p702; Las Casas 509) or look along Aldama, JP García or Trujano. Around US$11 will buy you a decent bottle but some US$4 mezcals are also fine. North of the zócalo, the fancy **Plaza del Mezcal** (Map p702; ☎ 514-90-57; Matamoros 103) features the Tobalá brand from San Bartolo Yelavina. Some bottles made fom wild agave cost up to US$40. For some export-quality mezcals from Santiago Matatlán (up to US$55), head to **La Cava** (☎ 515-23-35; Farías 212B; ☼ 10am-3pm & 5-8pm Mon-Sat), north of the center. It has a good selection of wines too.

stores on and near Alcalá, 5 de Mayo and García Vigil, but prices are lower in the markets. You may not pay more for crafts in the city than in the villages where most of them are made, but in the city a lot of your money may be going to intermediaries. Some artisans have grouped together to market their own products directly (see Craft Shops, following).

Oaxacan artisans' techniques remain pretty traditional – back-strap and pedal looms, hand-turning of pottery – but new products frequently appear in response to the big demand for Oaxaca crafts. The colorful wooden fantasy animals known as *alebrijes* were developed little more than a decade ago from toys that Oaxacans had been carving for their children for centuries.

Special crafts to look out for include the distinctive black pottery from San Bartolo Coyotepec; blankets, rugs and tapestries from Teotitlán del Valle; *huipiles* and other indigenous clothing from anywhere; the creative pottery figures made by the Aguilar sisters of Ocotlán; and stamped and colored tin from Oaxaca itself. Jewelry is also made and sold here, and you'll find pieces using gold, silver or precious stones, but prices are a bit higher than in Mexico City or Taxco. Many shops can mail things home for you.

Rugs or blankets with muted colors are less likely to have been made with synthetic dyes than some of the more garish offerings. There are various ways to assess the quality of a woven rug:

- Gently tug at the fibers to see how tightly it's woven.
- Rub your fingers or palm on it for about 15 seconds – if balls appear, the quality is poor.
- Crumple it up a bit, then spread it on the floor – the creases will disappear from good rugs.

Just as fascinating, in its way, as the fancy craft stores is Oaxaca's commercial area stretching over several blocks southwest of the zócalo. Oaxacans flock here, and to the big Central de Abastos market, for all their everyday needs.

Markets

Mercado Juárez (Map p702; btwn Florés Magón & 20 de Noviembre) This indoor market, a block southwest of the zócalo, concentrates on food (more expensive than the Central de Abastos) but also has flowers and some crafts, especially leatherwork.

Central de Abastos (Supplies Center; Map p702; Periférico) The vast main market, on the western edge of the city center, is a hive of activity every day, though Saturday is the biggest day. If you look long enough, you can find almost anything here. Each type of product has a section to itself, so you'll find 20 or so woven-basket sellers here, a dozen CD stalls there, and so on.

Mercado de Artesanías (Crafts Market; p702; cnr JP García & Zaragoza) A block southwest of Mercado 20 de Noviembre, this sizable indoor crafts market gets limited numbers of customers because it's slightly off the beaten track – so you may pick up some bargains. It's strong on pottery, rugs and textiles.

Mercado 20 de Noviembre (Map p702; btwn Cabrera & 20 de Noviembre) A block south of the Mercado Juárez, the 20 de Noviembre market is mainly occupied by comedores, but has a few inexpensive craft stalls on its west side.

Craft Shops

MARO (Map p702; ☎ 516-06-70; 5 de Mayo 204; 🕑 9am-8pm) This is a sprawling store with a big range of good crafts at good prices, all made by the 300 members of the MARO women artisans' cooperative around Oaxaca state. Whether you buy a stamped tin mirror or a wooden skeleton on springs, you know your money is going direct to the makers.

La Mano Mágica (Map p702; ☎ 516-42-75; www.casacerrosagrado.com; Alcalá 203; 🕑 10:30am-3pm & 4-7:30pm Mon-Sat) This store sells some wonderfully original and skilled crafts, including weavings by one of its owners, the Teotitlán del Valle master weaver Arnulfo Mendoza. Some Mendoza pieces go for thousands of dollars.

El Cactus (Map p702; ☎ 514-03-05; Alcalá 401) El Cactus is good for blankets and rugs.

Aripo (Map p701; ☎ 514-40-30; García Vigil 809; 🕑 9am-8pm Mon-Fri, 10am-6pm Sat, 11am-4pm Sun) Aripo, run by the Oaxaca state government, has a moderately sized stock of varied crafts including some beautiful textiles.

Casa de las Artesanías de Oaxaca (Map p702; ☎ 516-50-62; Matamoros 105; 🕑 9am-9pm Mon-Sat, 10am-8pm Sun) This store sells the work of 80 family workshops and crafts organizations from around Oaxaca state. Its patio is surrounded by several rooms full of varied crafts.

Corazón El Pueblo (Map p702; ☎ 516-69-60; Alcalá 307; ☷ 10:30am-2:30pm & 3:30-7:30pm Mon-Sat) A fine array of top-class work.

Oro de Monte Albán (Map p702; www.orodemonte alban.com) Plaza Alcalá (☎ 516-18-12; Alcalá 307); Casa Vieja (☎ 514-38-13; Alcalá 403); Alcalá 503 (☎ 516-42-24; Alcalá 503) This firm's goldsmiths produce high-class jewelry in gold, silver and semi-precious stones, including copies of pre-Hispanic jewelry and pieces inspired by colonial-era designs.

GETTING THERE & AWAY
Air

Direct flights to and from Mexico City (one hour) are operated by Mexicana four times daily and Aeroméxico three times (both around US$150 one-way) and Aviacsa once (US$100).

Aerocaribe has two daily flights to/from Tuxtla Gutiérrez (around US$150 one-way for the cheapest tickets), one of them continuing to/from Villahermosa (US$180), Mérida (US$200), Cancún (US$250) and Havana (US$400/640 one-way/return). Aviacsa has daily nonstop flights to and from Tapachula (US$160) and Acapulco.

For the spectacular half-hour hop over the Sierra Madre del Sur to Puerto Escondido and Bahías de Huatulco on the Oaxaca coast, Aerotucán (with a 14-seat Cessna) flies daily to/from both destinations, with fares to either around US$100 one-way. Aerovega flies a seven-seater daily to/from Puerto Escondido (US$90 one-way) and to/from Huatulco (US$100) with a minimum of three passengers.

AIRLINE OFFICES

Aerocaribe Centro (Map p702; ☎ 516-02-29; Fiallo 102); Airport (☎ 511-52-29)
Aeroméxico Centro (Map p702; ☎ 516-10-66; Hidalgo 513; ☷ 9am-6pm Mon-Sat)
Aerotucán Centro (Map p702; ☎ 501-05-30; Alcalá 201, Interior 204)
Aerovega Centro (Map p702; ☎ 516-49-82; aerovega@ prodigy.net.mx; Alameda de León 1; ☷ 9am-2pm & 5-8pm Mon-Fri, 9am-5pm Sat)
Aviacsa Centro (Map p702; ☎ 518-45-55; Pino Suárez 604); Airport (☎ 511-50-39)
Mexicana Centro (Map p702; ☎ 516-73-52; Fiallo 102); Airport (☎ 511-52-29)

Bus

Terminal de Autobuses de Primera Clase (1st-class Bus Station, Map p701; ☎ 515-12-48; Calz Niños Héroes de Chapultepec 1036) is 1.5km northeast of the zócalo. Also known as the Terminal ADO, it's used by UNO (deluxe service), Maya de Oro and ADO GL (executive), ADO, OCC/Cristóbal Colón (1st-class) and Sur, AU and Cuenca (*económico*). The **Terminal de Autobuses de Segunda Clase** (2nd-class Bus Station; Map p701; Las Casas) is 1km west of the zócalo; the main long-distance companies using it are **Estrella del Valle/Oaxaca Pacífico** (EV/OP; ☎ 516-54-29), **Fletes y Pasajes** (Fypsa; ☎ 516-22-70), and **Transportes Oaxaca-Istmo** (TOI; ☎ 516-36-64). Unless otherwise noted, buses mentioned here use one of these two main stations.

It's advisable to buy your ticket a day or two in advance for some of the less frequent services, including buses to San Cristóbal de Las Casas and the better services to the coast. **Ticket Bus** (20 de Noviembre Map p702; ☎ 514-66-55; 20 de Noviembre 103D; ☷ 8am-10pm Mon-Sat, 9am-4pm Sun; Valdivieso Map p702; ☎ 516-38-20; Valdivieso 2A; ☷ 8am-10pm Mon-Sat, 8am-9pm Sun), in the city center, sells tickets for UNO, Maya de Oro, ADO, OCC, Sur and AU buses throughout Mexico.

For the Oaxaca coast, as always, it's safest to travel in daylight. **Autoexprés Atlántida** (Map p701; ☎ 514-70-77; La Noria 101) runs 14-seat, air-conditioned Chevrolet Suburban vans nine times daily by the spectacular Hwy 175 to Pochutla (US$11, 6½ hours), the jumping-off point for Puerto Ángel, Zipolite, Mazunte and other nearby beaches. Also by Hwy 175, EV/OP runs *directo* 2nd-class buses at 10am, 2:30pm, 10:45pm and 11:15pm to Pochutla (US$8/8.50 by day/night) and Puerto Escondido (US$8.50/9, eight hours) from its **Armenta y López terminal** (Map p701; ☎ 514-09-28; Armenta y López 721), 500m south of the zócalo. From the 2nd-class bus station, EV/OP runs nine *ordinarios* to Pochutla (US$6.50) and Puerto Escondido (US$7), and buses to Santa Cruz Huatulco (7½ hours) at noon (US$8) and 10pm (US$10).

Cristóbal Colón (1st-class) runs four buses daily by the longer but less winding Salina Cruz route to Bahías de Huatulco (US$17 to US$20, 7½ hours). Three of them continue to Pochutla (US$18, 8½ hours) and Puerto Escondido (US$18, 10 hours).

Other services to Puerto Escondido (US$7.50 to US$8.50) go from the 2nd-class bus station by Transol, with 10 buses daily by highways 175 and 200, and **Estrella Roja del Sureste** (☎ 516-06-94), has six daily (eight-nine hours by the more direct but poorly paved Hwy 131).

Other daily bus departures from Oaxaca:

Mexico City (US$26-40, 6hr, 40 daily from 1st-class terminal; US$18, 6hr, 13 Fypsa) Most go to TAPO, and a few to Terminal Sur or Terminal Norte.

Puebla (US$19-22, 4½hr, 9 daily from 1st-class terminal; US$13, 4½hr, 10 Fypsa)

San Cristóbal de Las Casas (US$27-29, 12hr, 3 daily from 1st-class terminal)

Tapachula (US$22-33, 12hr, 3 daily from 1st-class terminal)

Tehuantepec (US$11, 4½hr, 14 daily from 1st-class terminal; US$7.50, 4½hr, 18 Fypsa; US$7.50, 4½hr, 13 TOI)

Tuxtla Gutiérrez (US$23-27, 10hr, 4 daily from 1st-class terminal; US$18, 10hr, 5 Fypsa)

Veracruz (US$25-28, 7hr, 4 daily from 1st-class terminal)

Villahermosa (US$32, 12hr, 3 daily from 1st-class terminal)

Car & Motorcycle

Hwy 135D branches south off the Mexico City–Veracruz highway, 150D, east of Puebla for a spectacular traverse of Oaxaca's northern mountains en route to Oaxaca city. Tolls from Mexico City to Oaxaca on highways 150D and 135D total US$26 (from Puebla, US$17); the trip takes about six hours. For some reason, the 135D is also numbered 131D for some stretches. The main toll-free alternative, via Huajuapan de León on Hwy 190, takes several hours longer.

Rental cars from major firms here start around US$60 with unlimited kilometers. The airport desks may come up with offers. Agencies include:

Alamo Centro (Map p702; ☎ 514-85-34; 5 de Mayo 203); Airport (☎ 511-62-20)

Budget (Map p702; ☎ 516-44-45; 5 de Mayo 315A); Airport (☎ 511-52-52)

Hertz Centro (Map p702; ☎ 516-24-34; Plaza de las Virgenes, Plazuela Labastida 115); Airport (☎ 511-54-78)

GETTING AROUND
To/From the Airport

Oaxaca airport is 6km south of the city, 500m off Hwy 175. Transporte Terrestre combis from the airport will take you to anywhere in the city center for US$2.25. A taxi costs about US$9.

You can book a combi seat from city to airport, a day or more ahead, at **Transportes**

Aeropuerto (Map p702; ☎ 514-43-50; Alameda de León 1G; ☙ 9am-2pm & 5-8pm Mon-Sat).

Bicycle

You can rent good mountain bikes at **Bicicletas Pedro Martínez** (Map p702; ☎ 514-59-35; Aldama 418; US$9.50 per day) or **Bicicletas Bravo** (Map p702; ☎ 516-09-53; García Vigil 409; US$11.50 per day). Bicicletas Bravo will give you four days for the price of three or seven days for the price of five. Both these firms offer bike tours too (see Activities, p708).

Bus

Most points of importance in the city are within walking distance of each other, but you might want to use city buses (US$0.30) to and from the bus stations.

From the 1st-class bus station, a westbound 'Juárez' bus will take you down Juárez and Ocampo, three blocks east of the zócalo; a 'Tinoco y Palacios' bus will take you down Tinoco y Palacios, two blocks west of the zócalo. To return to the bus station, take an 'ADO' bus north up Xicoténcatl or Pino Suárez, four blocks east of the zócalo, or up Díaz Ordaz or Crespo, three blocks west of the zócalo.

Buses between the 2nd-class bus station and the center pass slowly along congested streets, and it's almost as quick to walk. 'Centro' buses head toward the center along Trujano, then turn north up Díaz Ordaz. Going out to the 2nd-class bus station, 'Central' buses head south on Tinoco y Palacios, then west on Las Casas.

Car & Motorcycle

There are several guarded parking lots in the city center. **Estacionamiento Trujano** (Map p702; Trujano 219; ☙ 6am-11pm) charges US$2.75 for an overnight stay (8pm to 8am), and US$0.80 an hour from 8am to 8pm.

Taxi

A taxi anywhere within the central area, including the bus stations, costs US$2.50 to US$3.

VALLES CENTRALES

Three valleys radiate from the city of Oaxaca: the Valle de Tlacolula, stretching 50km east; the Valle de Etla, reaching about 40km

VALLES CENTRALES

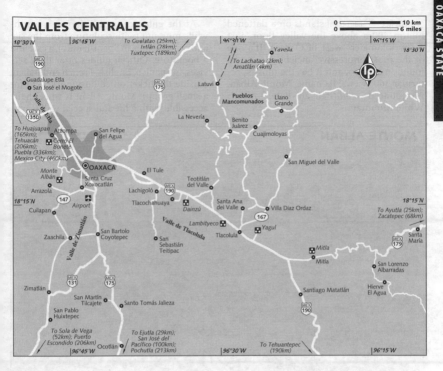

0 ___ 10 km
0 ___ 6 miles

north; and the Valle de Zimatlán, stretching about 100km south. In these Valles Centrales (Central Valleys), all within day-trip distance of Oaxaca city, you'll find much to fascinate – craft-making villages, pre-Hispanic ruins, and busy country markets. The people are mostly Zapotec.

Market Days

The markets are at their busiest in the morning, and most of them start to wind down in early afternoon. Following are the main ones:

Sunday Tlacolula
Tuesday Atzompa
Wednesday San Pedro y San Pablo Etla
Thursday Zaachila and Ejutla
Friday Ocotlán, Santo Tomás Jalieza and San Bartolo Coyotepec
Saturday Mitla

Getting There & Away

Most of the places in the Valle de Tlacolula, east of Oaxaca, are within walking distance of the Oaxaca–Mitla road, Hwy 190. Transportes Oaxaca-Istmo's buses to Mitla, every

few minutes from Gate 9 of Oaxaca's 2nd-class bus station, will drop you anywhere along this road. There are further services to some specific towns and villages. South from Oaxaca, Hwy 175 goes through San Bartolo Coyotepec, Ocotlán and Ejutla. Separate roads go to Monte Albán and to Cuilapan and Zaachila. Further details on bus services are given under the individual sites and villages.

An alternative to traveling by bus, costing twice as much (but still cheap!), is to take a colectivo taxi. These run to places north of Oaxaca (such as Atzompa and San José El Mogote) from Trujano on the north side of the 2nd-class bus station; and to places to the east, south and southwest (including El Tule, Teotitlán del Valle, San Bartolo Coyotepec, Ocotlán, Arrazola, Cuilapan and Zaachila) from Prolongación Victoria just east of the Central de Abastos market. They leave when they're full (five or six people).

MONTE ALBÁN

The ancient Zapotec capital of **Monte Albán** (☎ 951-516-12-15; admission US$3.50, under-13s &

over-60s free; 🕑 8am-6pm) stands on a flattened hilltop 400m above the valley floor, just a few kilometers west of Oaxaca. It's one of the most impressive ancient sites to be found in Mexico, and it has the most spectacular 360° views. Its name, Monte Albán, pronounced '*mohn*-teh ahl-*bahn*,' means White Mountain.

At the entrance to the site are a worthwhile museum (with sculpture from the site and explanations in Spanish only), a café and a bookstore. Official guides offer their services, in Spanish, English, French and Italian, outside the ticket office (around US$20 for a small group). Monte Albán is wheelchair-accessible, with a lift and special walkways.

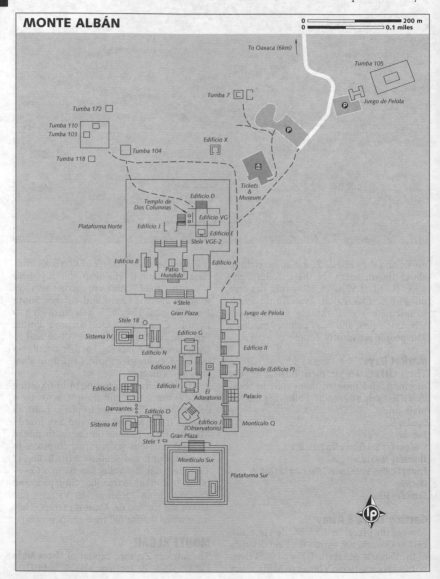

MONTE ALBÁN

History

The site was first occupied around 500 BC, probably by Zapotecs from the outset. It probably had early cultural connections with the Olmecs to the northeast.

Archaeologists divide Monte Albán's history into five phases. The years up to about 200 BC (phase Monte Albán I) saw the leveling of the hilltop, the building of temples and probably palaces, and the growth of a town of 10,000 or more people on the hillsides. Hieroglyphs and dates in a dot-and-bar system carved during this era may well mean that the elite of Monte Albán were the first to use writing and the written calendar in Mexico. Between 200 BC and about AD 300 (Monte Albán II) the city came to dominate more and more of Oaxaca. Buildings of this period were typically made of huge stone blocks and had steep walls.

The city was at its peak from about AD 300 to 700 (Monte Albán III), when the main and surrounding hills were terraced for dwellings, and the population reached about 25,000. Most of what we see now dates from this time. Monte Albán was the center of a highly organized, priest-dominated society, controlling the extensively irrigated Valles Centrales, which held at least 200 other settlements and ceremonial centers. Many Monte Albán buildings were plastered and painted red, and talud-tablero architecture indicates influence from Teotihuacán. Nearly 170 underground tombs from this period have been found, some of them elaborate and decorated with frescoes. Monte Albán's people ate tortillas, beans, squashes, chilies, avocados and other vegetarian fare, plus sometimes deer, rabbit and dog. Skulls with holes drilled, cut or scraped into them have been found in more than 20 burials here – thought to be evidence of medical treatments unique in ancient Mexico.

Between about AD 700 and 950 (Monte Albán IV), the place was abandoned and fell into ruin. Monte Albán V (AD 950–1521) saw minimal activity, except that Mixtecs arriving from northwestern Oaxaca reused old tombs here to bury their own dignitaries.

Gran Plaza

The **Gran Plaza**, about 300m long and 200m wide, was the center of Monte Albán. Its visible structures are mostly from the peak Monte Albán III period. Some were temples, others residential. The following description takes you clockwise around the plaza. Many of the structures in and around the plaza are cordoned off to prevent damage by too many visitors' feet.

The stone terraces of the deep, I-shaped **Juego de Pelota** (Ball Court), constructed about 100 BC, were probably part of the playing area, not stands for spectators. The **Pirámide** (Edificio P) was topped by a small pillared temple and was probably an observatory of some sort. From the altar in front of it came a well-known jade bat-god mask, now in Mexico City's Museo Nacional de Antropología (p128). The **Palacio** (Palace) has a broad stairway and, on top, a patio surrounded by the remains of typical Monte Albán III residential rooms. Under the patio is a cross-shaped tomb.

The big **Plataforma Sur** (South Platform), with its wide staircase, is still good for a panorama of the plaza. **Edificio J**, an arrowhead-shaped building constructed about 100 BC and riddled with tunnels and staircases (unfortunately you can't go inside), stands at an angle of 45 degrees to the other Gran Plaza structures and was an observatory. Figures and hieroglyphs carved on its walls record Monte Albán's military conquests of other towns.

Edificio O, at the front of **Sistema M**, a patio-temple-altar complex from the Monte Albán III phase, was added, like the front of Sistema IV to an earlier structure in an apparent attempt to conceal the plaza's lack of symmetry. (The rock mounds supporting the Plataforma Sur and Plataforma Norte are not directly opposite each other.)

Edificio L is an amalgam of the Monte Albán I building that contained the famous Danzante carvings and a later structure built over it. The **Danzantes** (Dancers), some of which are seen around the lower part of the building, are thought to depict leaders of conquered neighboring people. Carved between 500 and 100 BC, they generally have open mouths (sometimes down-turned in Olmec style) and closed eyes. Some have blood flowing where their genitals have been cut off. Hieroglyphs accompanying them are the earliest known examples of true writing in Mexico.

Sistema IV, the twin to Sistema M, combines typical Monte Albán II construction with overlays from Monte Albán III and IV.

Plataforma Norte

The **North Platform**, over a rock outcrop, is almost as big as the Gran Plaza. It was rebuilt several times over the centuries. Chambers on either side of the main staircase contained tombs, and columns at the top of the stairs supported the roof of a hall. Atop the platform is a ceremonial complex built between AD 500 and 800; it's composed of the **Patio Hundido** (Sunken Patio), with an altar at its center, **Edificios D**, **VG** and **E** (which were topped with adobe temples) and the **Templo de Dos Columnas**. **Stele VGE-2**, on the southern side of Edificio E, shows members of Monte Albán's ruling class around AD 800 – four women and a fifth figure represented by a jaguar.

Tombs

Most of Monte Albán's ancient tombs are usually closed to visitors to help their preservation. But if you're lucky you might be able to peer into one of the following.

TUMBA 104

Tomb 104, behind Plataforme Norte, dates from AD 500 to 700. Above its underground entrance is an urn in the form of Pitao Cozobi, the Zapotec maize god, wearing a mask of Cocijo, the rain god whose forked tongue represents lightning. The walls are covered with colorful Teotihuacán-style frescoes. The figure on the left wall is probably the Zapotec flayed god and god of spring, Xipe Tótec; on the right wall, wearing a big snake-and-feather headdress, is Pitao Cozobi again.

TUMBA 7

This tomb, just off the main parking lot, was built around AD 800, beneath a dwelling. In the 14th or 15th century it was reused by Mixtecs to bury a dignitary, two sacrificed servants, and one of the richest ancient treasure hoards in the Americas, the famed Mixtec treasure, now in the Museo de las Culturas de Oaxaca (p706).

TUMBA 105

Tomb 105, behind the Juego de Pelota Chica (Small Ball Court), features decaying Teotihuacán-influenced murals showing a procession of figures that may represent nine gods of death or night and their female consorts. It lies beneath one of Monte Albán's biggest palace-residences, built between AD 500 and 800.

Getting There & Away

Autobuses Turísticos (☎ 951-516-53-27) runs buses to the site from Hotel Rivera del Ángel, at Mina 518 in Oaxaca, a 10- to 15-minute walk southwest of the zócalo. The buses leave every half hour from 8:30am to 2pm, and at 3pm, 3:30pm and sometimes 4pm (details of the schedule change from time to time). The ride up takes 20 minutes. The US$2.25 fare includes a return trip at a designated time, giving you about two hours at the site. If you want to stay longer, you must hope for a spare place on a later return bus and pay a further US$1.25. Buses start back from Monte Albán every half-hour from 11am to 4pm and at 5pm and 6pm.

A taxi from Oaxaca to Monte Albán costs about US$7, but coming down you may have to pay more. Walking up from the city center takes about 1½ hours.

EL TULE

pop 6800 / elevation 1550m

The unremarkable village of El Tule, 10km east of Oaxaca along Hwy 190, draws crowds of visitors for one very good reason: **El Árbol del Tule** (The Tree of El Tule; admission US$0.30; ☻ 9am-5pm), which is claimed to be the biggest single biomass in the world. This vast *ahuehuete* (a type of cypress), 58m around and 42m high, dwarfs the 17th-century village church in whose churchyard it towers. You are extremely unlikely ever to see another tree trunk of such vast girth. Its age is equally impressive: the tree is officially reckoned to be between 2000 and 3000 years old.

Long revered by Oaxacans, the Árbol del Tule is now under threat from nearby new industries and housing which tap its water sources. Local campaigners are trying to win Unesco World Heritage status for the tree. They argue that the only long-term solution is integral protection of the 110-sq-km basin that supplies the tree's water, including reforestation in the mountains above and creation of a large green zone in the valley.

Autotransportes Valle del Norte buses go to El Tule (US$0.30, every 10 minutes) from the 2nd-class bus station in Oaxaca.

DAINZÚ

Twenty-one kilometers from Oaxaca along the Mitla road, a track leads 1km south to the small but interesting **ruins of Dainzú** (admission US$2.25, under-13s & over-60s free; ☻ 8am-6pm).

To the left as you approach you'll find the pyramid-like Edificio A, 50m long and 8m high, built about 300 BC. Along its bottom wall are some 50 bas-reliefs of feline figures, masks and heads, mostly related to the ball game. Among the ruins below Edificio A are a partly restored ball court from about AD 1000 and a sunken tomb (inside Edificio B) with its entrance carved with a representation of a crouching jaguar. Among the scrub at the top of the hill behind the site are more rock carvings similar to those of Edificio A, but you'll need a guide to find them. Ask the caretaker if you want help.

TEOTITLÁN DEL VALLE

☎ 951 / pop 4600 / elevation 1700m

This famous weaving village is 4km north of Hwy 190, about 25km from Oaxaca. Blankets, rugs and sarapes wave at you from houses and showrooms along the road into the village (which becomes Av Juárez as it approaches the center), and signs point to the central **Mercado de Artesanías**, where yet more are on sale. The variety of designs is enormous – from Zapotec gods and Mitla-style geometric patterns to imitations of paintings by Rivera, Picasso and Escher.

The weaving tradition here goes back to pre-Hispanic times: Teotitlán had to pay tributes of cloth to the Aztecs. Quality is still high, and traditional dyes made from cochineal, indigo and moss have been revived. Many shops have weavers at work and are happy to demonstrate how they obtain natural dyes. Teotitlán's most celebrated weaver, Arnulfo Mendoza (born 1954), sells work for thousands of dollars and has a large house overlooking the north end of the village. You can see fine examples of his work in his Oaxacan shop La Mano Mágica (p720).

Facing the Mercado de Artesanías on the central plaza is the **Museo Comunitario Balaa Xtee Guech Gulal** (☎ 524-41-23; admission US$0.50; ⏰ 10am-6pm Tue-Sun), a community museum with local archaeological finds and displays on local crafts and traditions. From the plaza, steps rise to a fine broad church yard with the handsome 17th-century **Templo de la Virgen de la Natividad** in one corner.

Turismo de Aventura Teotitlán (☎ 524-43-71; roque_antonio740@hotmail.com; Av Juárez 59) offers bird-watching, mountain biking or hiking trips and village tours, mostly with English-speaking guides, for US$30 to US$55. The

bird-watching trips with guide Roque Antonio Santiago get good reports.

Calle 2 de Abril No 12 (☎ 524 41 64; 2 de Abril 12; s/d incl breakfast US$28/55), a house belonging to friendly, English speaking Elena González, has weaving looms in the courtyard and three bright, clean upstairs rooms with private bathroom and hot water.

Restaurante Tlamanalli (☎ 524-40-06; Av Juárez 39; mains US$11, soups & desserts US$2.50-3.75; ⏰ 1-4pm Tue-Sun) serves top-class Oaxacan lunches; exhibits on weaving add to the interest.

Autotransportes Valle del Norte buses run to Teotitlán (US$0.70, 50 minutes, hourly from 7am to 9pm Monday to Saturday) from Gate 29 at Oaxaca's 2nd-class bus station; the last bus back to Oaxaca from the village leaves about 7pm. Alternatively, get any Mitla- or Tlacolula-bound bus to the signposted Teotitlán turnoff on Hwy 190 (US$0.70), then a colectivo taxi (US$0.40) to the village.

LAMBITYECO

This small **archaeological site** (admission US$2.25, under-13s & over-60s free; ⏰ 8am-6pm) is on the south side of the Mitla road, 29km from Oaxaca. Between AD 600 and 800, Lambityeco became a sizable Zapotec center of about 3000 people. Its interest today lies in two patios with striking sculptures. In the first are two carved stone friezes, each showing a bearded man holding a bone (a symbol of hereditary rights) and a woman with a Zapotec hairstyle. Both these couples, plus a third in stucco on a tomb in the patio, are thought to have occupied the building around the patio and to have ruled Lambityeco in the 7th century. The second patio has two heads of the rain god Cocijo. On one, a big headdress spreading above Cocijo's stern face forms the face of a jaguar.

TLACOLULA

pop 12,000 / elevation 1650m

This town 31km from Oaxaca holds one of the Valles Centrales' major markets every Sunday, when the area around the church becomes a packed throng. Crafts, foods and plenty of everyday goods are on sale. It's a treat for lovers of market atmosphere.

The interior of the domed 16th-century Capilla del Santo Cristo is a riot of golden, indigenous-influenced decoration comparable with the Capilla del Rosario in Santo

Domingo, Oaxaca. Carvings of martyrs can be seen carrying their heads under their arms. The church was one of several founded in Oaxaca by Dominican monks.

Transportes Oaxaca-Istmo and Fletes y Pasajes buses run to Tlacolula from Oaxaca's 2nd-class bus station (US$1, one hour, every few minutes).

SANTA ANA DEL VALLE
☎ 951 / pop 2250 / elevation 1700m
Santa Ana, 4km north of Tlacolula, is another village with a time-honored textile tradition. Today it produces woolen blankets, sarapes and bags. Natural dyes have been revived, and traditional designs – flowers, birds, geometric patterns – are still in use. On the central plaza are the richly decorated 17th-century **Templo de Santa Ana**, the **Museo Comunitario Shan-Dany** (☎ 562-70-00; admission US$1; 🕙 10am-2pm & 3-6pm), a community museum with exhibits on local textiles, archaeology and history and the Zapotec Danza de las Plumas; and a small **Mercado de Artesanías** (Crafts Market) with local textiles. There are a few textile workshops that you can visit, but you need to ask around.

Buses and minibuses run frequently from Tlacolula to Santa Ana until about 6pm.

YAGUL
The **ruins of Yagul** (admission US$2.75; 🕙 8am-5pm) are finely sited on a cactus-covered hill, 1.5km to the north of the Oaxaca–Mitla road. Unless you have a vehicle, you'll have to walk the 1.5km – but the ruins' setting makes the effort well worthwhile. The signposted turnoff is 34km from Oaxaca.

Yagul was a leading Valles Centrales settlement after the decline of Monte Albán. Most of what's visible was built after AD 750.

Patio 4, down to the left as you reach the main part of the site from the entrance, was surrounded by four temples. On its east side is a carved-stone animal, probably a jaguar. Next to the central platform is the entrance to one of several underground **Tumbas Triples** (Triple Tombs).

The beautiful **Juego de Pelota** (Ball Court) is the second biggest in Mesoamerica (after one at Chichén Itzá). To its west, on the edge of the hill, is **Patio 1**, with the narrow **Sala de Consejo** (Council Hall) along its north side.

The labyrinthine **Palacio de los Seis Patios** (Palace of the Six Patios) was probably the leader's residence. Its walls were plastered and painted red.

It's well worth climbing the **Fortress**, the huge rock that towers above the ruins. The path passes **Tumba 28**, made of cut stone. Several overgrown ruins perch atop the Fortress – and the views are marvelous.

MITLA
☎ 951 / pop 7500 / elevation 1700m
The stone 'mosaics' of ancient Mitla, 46km southeast of Oaxaca, are unique in Mexico. Today they are surrounded by a dusty modern Zapotec town.

Orientation
If you tell the bus conductor from Oaxaca that you're heading for *las ruinas*, you should be dropped at a junction signed 'Zona Arqueológica' soon after you enter Mitla (the bus station is 600m further east from this stop). For the ruins, go north along Av Morelos from your bus stop, and continue through the plaza toward the three-domed Iglesia de San Pablo, 850m beyond the plaza. The ticket office is behind this church.

Ruins
The **ruins** (☎ 568-03-16; admission to Grupo de la Iglesia & Grupo de las Columnas US$2.75; 🕙 8am-5pm) date almost entirely from the last two or three centuries before the Spanish conquest, when Mitla was probably the most important of Zapotec religious centers, dominated by high priests who performed literally heart-wrenching human sacrifices. Evidence points to a short period of Mixtec domination here in the 14th century, followed by a Zapotec reassertion before the Aztecs arrived in 1494. Somewhere beneath the town may be a great undiscovered tomb of Zapotec kings; the 17th-century monk Francisco de Burgoa wrote that Spanish priests found it but sealed it up. It's thought that each group of buildings we see at Mitla was reserved for specific occupants – one for the high priest, one for lesser priests, one for the king and so forth.

The **Grupo de las Columnas** (Group of the Columns), the major group of buildings, is just south of the Iglesia de San Pablo. It has two main patios, each lined on three sides by long rooms. Along the north side of the Patio Norte is the **Sala de las Columnas** (Hall of the Columns), 38m long with six thick columns. At one end of this hall, a passage leads to the additional **Patio de Mosaicos** (Patio of the Mosaics), with some of Mitla's best stonework. Each little piece of stone was cut to fit the design, then set in mortar on the walls and painted. The 14 different geometric designs at Mitla are thought to symbolize the sky, earth, feathered serpent and other important beings. Many Mitla buildings were also adorned with painted friezes.

In the Patio Sur are two underground tombs. The one on the north side contains the so-called **Columna de la Vida** (Column of Life) – if you put your arms around it, the number of hand widths between your fingertips is (absurdly) supposed to measure how many years of life you have left.

The **Grupo de la Iglesia** (Church Group) is similar to the Grupo de las Columnas but less well preserved. The church was built over one of the group's patios in 1590. The **Grupo del Arroyo** is the most substantial of the other groups. Remains of forts, tombs and other structures are scattered for many kilometers around.

Sleeping & Eating

Restaurant Doña Chica (☎ 568-02-25; Av Morelos 41; mains US$3.75-5; ☷ 10am-9pm) This homey, thatch-roofed restaurant is 100m from the bus stop (not the bus station) on the street leading to

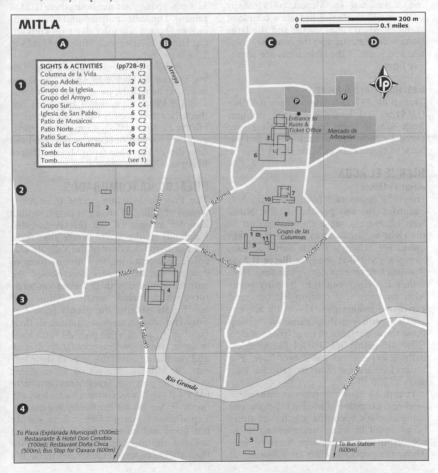

MITLA

0 ————————— 200 m
0 ————————— 0.1 miles

SIGHTS & ACTIVITIES	(pp728–9)
Columna de la Vida	1 C2
Grupo Adobe	2 A2
Grupo de la Iglesia	3 C2
Grupo del Arroyo	4 B3
Grupo Sur	5 C4
Iglesia de San Pablo	6 C2
Patio de Mosaicos	7 C2
Patio Norte	8 C2
Patio Sur	9 C3
Sala de las Columnas	10 C2
Tomb	11 C2
Tomb	(see 1)

Arroyo

Entrance to Ruins & Ticket Office

Mercado de Artesanías

Reforma

5 de Febrero

Grupo de las Columnas

Moctezuma

Nezahualcóyotl

Madero

5 de Febrero

Río Grande

Xicoténcatl

To Plaza (Explanada Municipal) (100m); Restaurante & Hotel Don Cenobio (100m); Restaurant Doña Chica (500m); Bus Stop for Oaxaca (600m)

To Bus Station (600m)

the center and ruins. Straightforward and delicious Oaxacan dishes (moles, enchiladas, *tasajo* etc) are prepared at ranges open for all to see and as clean, neat and inviting as everything else here. Good antojitos, soups and salads cost around US$2.25.

Restaurante & Hotel Don Cenobio (☎ 568-03-30; Av Juárez 3; mains US$5-7.50; 🕙 10am-6pm Wed-Mon) Set on the central plaza, this is the town's classiest eatery, serving mainly Oaxacan and Mexican fare in attractive surroundings with its own lily-filled garden, bar and pool. Mitla's first-ever quality hotel was due to be added to all this in 2004.

Shopping

Mitla's streets are sprinkled with shops selling local mezcal (see 'Mezcal,' p719). Many of them will invite you to taste a couple of varieties. Many other shops, and the large **Mercado de Artesanías** near the ruins, sell local textiles. Some of the tablecloths are attractive buys.

Getting There & Away

Transportes Oaxaca-Istmo buses to Mitla (US$1.50, 1¼ hours, every few minutes from 5am to 7pm) leave from Gate 9 of Oaxaca's 2nd-class bus station. The last bus back to Oaxaca leaves Mitla about 8pm.

HIERVE EL AGUA

elevation 1800m

Hwy 179 heads east from Mitla up into beautiful, sparsely populated hills. Nineteen kilometers out, a signpost points to the right to San Lorenzo Albarradas, 3km away. Six kilometers past San Lorenzo, along a good dirt road, is **Hierve El Agua** (The Water Boils; admission US$1; 🕙 9am-6pm). Here mineral springs run into bathing pools with an incredible clifftop location and expansive panoramas. The cliffs are encrusted with petrified minerals, giving them the appearance of huge frozen waterfalls. Altogether it's one of the weirdest bathing experiences you'll ever have. The waters here were used for irrigation as long ago as 1300 BC.

Hierve El Agua is a popular *oaxaqueño* weekend excursion. But check before you come that it's open: the site has at times been closed in recent years owing to an ownership dispute between local villages. Above the pools and cliffs are a number of

comedores (antojitos US$2-3) and half a dozen **cabañas** (per person US$7) providing accommodations in simple rooms with private bathroom. Also here (though temporarily closed at the time of research) is a **tourist yú'ù** (per person US$6.50), with bunks for half a dozen people and an equipped kitchen. You can make reservations for the *yú'ù*, one of several in and around the Valles Centrales, which are run by the Oaxaca state government, at the tourist offices in Oaxaca.

The area is dotted with maguey fields: San Lorenzo Albarradas, nearby San Juan del Río and the other 'Albarradas' villages produce some of Oaxaca's finest mezcal.

Viajes Turísticos Mitla in Oaxaca (see Tours, p710) runs two daily trips to Hierve El Agua, giving you three hours there (US$14 return). The same company and other agencies in Oaxaca also offer day trips combining Hierve El Agua with Mitla for US$25 to US$30 per person.

A Fypsa bus leaves Oaxaca's 2nd-class bus station for Hierve El Agua (US$3, two hours) at 8am daily, passing through Mitla about 9.15am. *Camionetas* (pickups) run from the street outside Mitla bus station to Hierve El Agua (US$2, 45 minutes) whenever they have six or seven people. On busy days there's also a bus from Mitla to Hierve El Agua (US$2) at noon.

PUEBLOS MANCOMUNADOS

The Pueblos Mancomunados (Commonwealth of Villages) are eight small, remote Zapotec villages in the thickly forested highlands of the Sierra Norte that form the northern boundary of the Valle de Tlacolula. For centuries, in a unique form of cooperation, the villages have pooled the natural resources of their 290-sq-km territory, which include extensive pine and oak forests, sharing the profits from forestry and other enterprises among all their families. In an effort to provide extra local income, stem a modern population decline and maintain sustainable uses of their forests, the villages have set up an excellent ecotourism program, **Expediciones Sierra Norte** (☎ 951-514-82-71; www.sierranorte.org.mx; Bravo 210, Oaxaca; 🕙 9am-3pm & 4-7pm Mon-Fri, 9am-2pm Sat). Expediciones Sierra Norte offers simple but good and comfortable lodgings, and walking and mountain-biking along more than 100km of scenic tracks and trails. It's a great way to experience this unique region of Oaxaca, completely different from the dry Valles Centrales or the tropical Pacific coast. Elevations range between 2200m and over 3200m, and the landscapes with their canyons, caves, crags, waterfalls and panoramic lookouts are spectacular. There's great natural diversity: over 400 bird species, 350 butterflies, all six Mexican wild cats (including the jaguar) and nearly 4000 plants have been recorded in the Sierra Norte. The variety of wildflowers here is astonishing. One highlight walk is the beautiful Latuvi-Lachatao canyon trail, which follows a pre-Hispanic track that connected Oaxaca's Valles Centrales with the Gulf of Mexico and passes through cloud forests festooned with bromeliads and hanging mosses. The villages themselves are mostly poor, simple and well cared for.

The trained local guides almost certainly will only speak Zapotec and Spanish but are knowledgeable about the plants, wildlife and ecology of these sierras. You can go without a guide, but if you do, be ready to get lost since trail marking is less than perfect. For accommodations and meals, each village has simple but comfortable cabañas (mostly with shared bathrooms with hot showers, some with fireplaces), a designated camping ground, and at least one comedor serving cheap and good local meals.

The best first step is to contact Expediciones Sierra Norte's office in Oaxaca, which has full information on trails, tracks, accommodations and how to prepare, and takes bookings for both guided and independent trips. The office also sells a very useful guide/map for US$4. Be ready for much cooler temperatures: in the Sierra Norte's higher, southern villages, it can freeze in winter. The rainiest season is from late May to September, but there's little rain from January to April.

Prices for visiting the Pueblos Mancomunados are: guide for up to five people US$11 per day; cabaña accommodation US$8.50 per person; camping US$3.25; bicycle rental (only in Benito Juárez, Cuajimoloyas and Llano Grande) US$14 per day; *huentzee* (contribution to maintenance costs) US$4.75 per visit. Fully organized trips including meals, accommodations and transportation are US$90 for two days, on foot or bike. Some adventure travel agencies, such as Tierraventura in Oaxaca (see p708), can take you to the Pueblos Mancomunados: this costs more but they take the work out of the planning, preparation and transportation.

The most common starting villages are Cuajimoloyas (elevation 3180m), Benito Juárez (2750m) and Llano Grande (2900m), which are at the higher, southern end of the Sierra Norte, so that walks or rides starting here will be more downhill than up. A good place to end up is Amatlán in the north, where the comfortable cabins have fireplaces. Nearby Lachatao is today almost a ghost village but has a huge 17th-century church, fruit of the riches produced by nearby colonial gold mines.

It's also possible simply to base yourself in one village and take local walks or rides from there, with or without guides. Some superb lookout points are accessible from the southern villages, such as the 3000m El Mirador, a 2.5km walk from Benito Juárez, or the 3280m Yaa-Cuetzi lookout, 1km from Cuajimoloyas. From Yaa-Cuetzi in clear weather you can see such distant mountains as Pico de Orizaba and Zempoaltépetl. Within a couple of hours' walk of Llano Grande you can reach Piedra Larga, a rocky crag with equally superb views, or the Cueva Iglesia, a cave and canyon hidden in the mountain forests.

Extra accommodations in Benito Juárez include a state-government–run self-catering **tourist yú'ù** (dm US$8.50, d US$17). You can reserve accommodation and guides through the village's helpful **ecotourism office** (☎ 954-545-99-94), and places in the *yú'ù* (a Zapotec word meaning house) can also be booked through the tourist offices in Oaxaca. A Sunday market is held each week beside Benito Juárez' 17th-century church.

Cuajimoloyas also has extra accommodations in the form of the **Hostal Yacuetzi**, with five rooms sharing one bathroom. You can reserve accommodations and guides through Cuajimoloyas' **ecotourism office** (☎ 951-514-06-01; Av Oaxaca 15). To reserve accommodation and guides at Llano Grande, contact the village's **Comité de Ecoturismo** (☎ 951-562-04-19).

Getting There & Away
Cuajimoloyas and Llano Grande have the best bus links with Oaxaca: five daily

buses (US$2, two hours to Cuajimoloyas; 2½ hours, US$2.50 to Llano Grande) from the 2nd-class bus station by **Flecha del Zempoaltépetl** (☎ 951-516-63-42). For Benito Juárez (US$2, two hours) and Latuvi (US$2.50, three hours), Transportes Ya'a-Yana buses leave from Calle Niño Perdido 306, Colonia Ixcotel, Oaxaca, at 4pm Tuesday, Friday and Saturday (5pm during the daylight saving period). The stop is next to a Pemex gas station on Hwy 190, a couple of kilometers east of the 1st-class bus station; taxi is the easiest way there from the city center. Returning to Oaxaca, the buses leave Latuvi at 4am and Benito Juárez at 5am on the same days. Another way to reach Benito Juárez is to take a Cuajimoloyas-bound bus to the Benito Juárez turnoff (*desviación de Benito Juárez*), 1¾ hours from Oaxaca, then walk 3.5km west along the unpaved road to the village.

Transportes Ya'a-Yana also runs buses from the same stop in Oaxaca at 4pm daily to Amatlán (US$2.25, 2¼ hours) and Lachatao (US$2.50, 2½ hours). Returning to Oaxaca, the buses leave Lachatao at 5am and Amatlán at 5:15am.

Unlike Oaxaca, the Pueblos Mancomunados do not observe daylight saving time – so triple-check all bus departure times for your return trip!

SAN BARTOLO COYOTEPEC
☎ 951 / pop 3000 / elevation 1550m
All the polished, black, surprisingly light pottery in hundreds of shapes and forms – candlesticks, jugs and vases, decorative animal and bird figures – that you find around Oaxaca comes from San Bartolo Coyotepec, a small village 11km south of the city. Look for the signs to the **Alfarería Doña Rosa** (☎ 551-00-11; www.go-oaxaca.com/dona_rosa.htm; Juárez 24; ☾ 9am-6:30pm), a short walk east off the highway. Several village families make and sell the *barro negro* (black ware), but it was Rosa Real Mateo (1900–80) who invented the method of burnishing it with quartz stones for the distinctive shine. Her family pottery workshop (*alfarería*) is the biggest in the village, and demonstrations of the process are given whenever a tour bus rolls in (several times a day). The pieces are hand-molded by an age-old technique using two saucers functioning as a rudimentary potter's wheel. Then they are fired in pit kilns; they turn black because of the

iron oxide in the local clay and because smoke is trapped in the kiln.

Buses to San Bartolo (US$0.50, 20 minutes) go every few minutes from the terminal at Armenta y López 721, 500m south of the Oaxaca zócalo.

SAN MARTÍN TILCAJETE & SANTO TOMÁS JALIEZA
The village of San Martín Tilcajete, 1km west of Hwy 175, 24km south of Oaxaca, is the source of many of the bright copal-wood *alebrijes* (animal figures) seen in Oaxaca. You can see and buy them in makers' houses, many of which have 'Artesanías de Madera' (Wooden Handicrafts) signs outside.

The women of Santo Tomás Jalieza, on the east side of Hwy 175, 2km south of the San Martín Tilcajete turnoff, weave high-quality textiles on back-strap looms; some of the detailed work on their cotton waist sashes (*fajas*), with pretty animal or plant designs, is very fine. There's a permanent **Mercado de Artesanías** (Crafts Market) in the village square, selling tablecloths, table mats and embroidered dresses as well as more traditional weavings. It opens daily but is busiest on Friday to coincide with the Ocotlán market. Colectivo taxis run from Ocotlán.

OCOTLÁN
☎ 951 / pop 13,000 / elevation 1500m
The sprawling Friday market in and around the central plaza of Ocotlán, 31km south of Oaxaca, dates back to pre-Hispanic times and is one of the biggest in the Valles Centrales. Ocotlán's most renowned artisans are the four Aguilar sisters and their families, who create whimsical, colorful pottery figures of women with all sorts of unusual motifs. The Aguilars' houses are together on the west side of the highway as you come into Ocotlán from the north – spot them by the pottery women on the wall. Most renowned are the family of **Guillermina Aguilar** (Prolongación de Morelos 430), who turn out, among other things, miniature Frida Kahlos.

Ocotlán was the hometown of artist Rodolfo Morales (1925–2001), who turned his international success to Ocotlán's benefit by setting up the **Fundación Cultural Rodolfo Morales** (☎ 571-01-98; Morelos 108; ☾ 10am-2pm & 4-8pm

Mon-Sat). This foundation's headquarters was Morales' own home: it has a lovely leafy patio but there's nothing special to do there unless you want to log on to the Internet (US$0.50 per hour).

Aside from providing Ocotlán with its first ambulance and planting 3500 jacaranda trees, the Morales foundation has undertaken the renovation of the handsome 16th-century church overlooking the main plaza, the **Templo de Santo Domingo**, which now sports beautiful, colorful paintwork inside and out. It has also turned the adjoining **Ex-Convento de Santo Domingo** (admission US$2; 9am-6pm), previously a dilapidated jail, into a first-class museum of popular and religious art which includes several of Morales' own canvases and a room of folk art dominated by the Aguilar sisters. Morales' ashes are interred here too.

Estrella del Valle/Oaxaca Pacífico runs buses to Ocotlán (US$1, 45 minutes, every few minutes from 5am to 9:30pm) from the terminal at Armenta y López 721 in Oaxaca. Autotransportes Ocotlán de Morelos operates a similar service from 6am to 8pm from its terminal on Cabrera.

SAN JOSÉ DEL PACÍFICO
☎ 951 / pop 500 / elevation 2750m
The small mountain village of San José del Pacífico, 102km south of Ocotlán (about 50 minutes past Miahuatlán), is just outside the Valles Centrales on Hwy 175 heading toward Pochutla and the coast. The scenery is spectacular and it's a good base for walks through the cool mountain pine forests to waterfalls and other goals. Guides (around US$5/10 per half/whole day) and information are available from the places to stay and from the *cuatrimoto* (four-wheel motorbike) rental place by the main road in the village. The San José area is also famed for its magic mushrooms.

The best place to stay is **Cabañas y Restaurante Puesta del Sol** (☎ 547-42-25, ☎ /fax 572-01-11; www.sanjosedelpacifico.com; r US$28, cabañas for 2/5 US$37/46; P), beside Hwy 175, 1km north of the village. The Puesta del Sol offers superb views and beautiful wooden rooms and cabañas set in spacious hillside grounds, all with hot showers. The cabañas have fireplaces too. The good restaurant here serves antojitos and omelettes for around US$2.50 and meat dishes for around US$3.50. Under

the same ownership and with a very similar restaurant menu, the **Rayito del Sol** (☎ 547-42-25, ☎ /fax 572-01-11; s/d with shared bathrooms US$6.50/11; P), beside the main road in the village, has plain but clean rooms and cold, shared showers.

If you want to get right off the beaten track try **Posada Yegoyoxi** (☎ 201-250-72-50; r/cabaña with shared bathrooms US$9.50/11) in the Zapotec village of San Mateo Río Hondo, 10km east of San José del Pacífico. It has rustic but cosy accommodations, hot water, a temazcal, horses for rent, and meals available as well as cooking facilities for guests. For transportation ask at the *cuatrimoto* place in San José. Omit the 951 area code if telephoning the Yegoyoxi number.

All Hwy 175 buses between Oaxaca and Pochutla stop at San José.

ARRAZOLA
pop 1000
Below the west side of Monte Albán and about 4km off the Cuilapan road, Arrazola produces many of the colorful copal alebrijes that are sold in Oaxaca. You can see and buy them in artisans' homes.

CUILAPAN
pop 11,000 / elevation 1570m
Cuilapan (sometimes spelt Cuilapam), 9km southwest of Oaxaca, is one of the few Mixtec villages in the Valles Centrales. It's the site of a beautiful, historic Dominican monastery, the **Ex-Convento Dominicano** (admission to cloister US$2.25; 9am-5:45pm), whose pale stone seems almost to grow out of the land.

In 1831 the Mexican independence hero Vicente Guerrero was executed at the monastery by soldiers supporting the rebel conservative Anastasio Bustamante, who had just deposed the liberal Guerrero from the Mexican presidency. Guerrero had fled by ship from Acapulco, but the ship's captain put in at Huatulco and betrayed him to the rebels. Guerrero was transported to Cuilapan to die.

From the monastery entrance you reach a long, low, unfinished church that has stood roofless since work on it stopped in 1560. Beyond is the church that succeeded it, which contains the tomb of Juana Donají (daughter of Cocijo-eza, the last Zapotec king of Zaachila). It's only open for mass, around 7am to 8am and 5pm to 6pm most days. Around the church's right-hand end is a two-story Renaissance-style cloister; some rooms have faded 16th- and 17th-century murals. A painting of Guerrero hangs in the small room where he was held, and outside stands a monument on the spot where he was shot.

Añasa (Bustamante 604), five blocks south of Oaxaca's zócalo, runs buses to Cuilapan (US$0.40, 20 minutes, every 15 minutes from 5:30am to 9pm).

ZAACHILA

☎ 951 / pop 12,000 / elevation 1520m

This part-Mixtec, part-Zapotec village, 4km beyond Cuilapan, has a busy Thursday market. Zaachila was a Zapotec capital from about 1400 until the Spanish conquest. Its last Zapotec king, Cocijo-eza, became a Christian with the name Juan Cortés and died in 1523. Behind the village church, which overlooks the main plaza, a sign indicates the entrance to the **Zona Arqueológica** (Archaeological Zone; admission US$2.25; ⏱ 9am-6pm), a small assortment of mounds where you can enter two small tombs used by the ancient Mixtecs. Both are in the same mound, near the ticket office. Tumba No 1 retains sculptures of owls, a turtle/man figure and various long-nosed skull-like masks. Tumba No 2 has no decoration but in it was found a Mixtec treasure hoard comparable with that of Tumba 7 at Monte Albán – and now in the Museo Nacional de Antropología (p128) in Mexico City. Mexican archaeologists Alfonso Caso and Ignacio Bernal were forced to flee by irate Zaachilans when they tried to excavate these tombs in the 1940s and 1950s. Roberto Gallegos excavated them under armed guard in 1962.

A fine place to eat is **Restaurante Típico La Capilla** (☎ 528-61-15; Carretera Oaxaca-Zaachila, Km 14; mains US$3.75-7.50; ⏱ 9am-7pm), 1km from Zaachila center on the Cuilapan road. Long wooden tables and benches are set around a large garden compound whose heart is the long range where cooks prepare top-quality Oaxacan antojitos and main dishes – moles, tasajo, chiles rellenos, lomo de puerco al horno (roast pork)… With plenty of space and even swings and slides to keep the kids happy, it's not surprising that the place gets packed with weekending Oaxacans on Sundays.

Añasa buses to Cuilapan (see p733) continue to Zaachila (US$0.40, 30 minutes from Oaxaca).

ATZOMPA

pop 14,000 / elevation 1600m

Atzompa, 6km northwest of Oaxaca, is one of the leading pottery-making villages in Valles Centrales. A lot of their very attractive, colorful work is sold at excellent prices in the **Mercado de Artesanías** (Crafts Market; Av Libertad 303), on the main street entering the village from Oaxaca. The restaurant at this market is good for a moderately priced snack or lunch.

From the church up in the village center, a 2.5km road (mostly dirt) leads south up **Cerro El Bonete**. The road ends a few minutes' walk from the top of the hill, which is dotted with unrestored pre-Hispanic ruins.

Choferes del Sur, at Gate 39 of Oaxaca's 2nd-class bus station, runs buses every few minutes to Atzompa (US$0.30). If driving yourself, follow Calz Madero northwest out of Oaxaca, turn left along Masseu (signposted 'Monte Albán') at a big intersection on the fringe of town, then go right at traffic signals after 1.5km.

SAN JOSÉ EL MOGOTE

Fourteen kilometers northwest of central Oaxaca on Hwy 190, a westward turnoff signposted to Guadalupe Etla leads 2km to the tiny village of San José El Mogote. Long ago, before Monte Albán became important, Mogote was the major settlement in Oaxaca. It was at its peak between 650 and 500 BC, and flourished again between 100 BC and AD 150, with a main plaza that was almost as big as Monte Albán's. The major surviving structures (partly restored) are a ball court and a sizable pyramid-mound on the village periphery. The interesting community museum, the **Museo Comunitario Ex-Hacienda El Cacique** (admission US$1; ⏱ 9am-1pm & 3-5pm), is in the former landowner's hacienda in the village center. If you find it closed, ask around for its encargado (keeper). A museum highlight is 'El Diablo Enchilado' (the Chilied Devil), a pre-Hispanic brazier in the form of a bright red grimacing face. The museum also has interesting material on the villagers' 20th-century struggle for land ownership.

Colectivo taxi is the simplest way to get to Mogote; see Valles Centrales Getting There & Away section, p723.

MIXTECA

The rugged, mountainous west of Oaxaca state (and adjoining bits of Puebla and Guerrero states) is known as the Mixteca, for its Mixtec indigenous inhabitants. It was from here in about the 12th century that Mixtec dominance began to spread to the Valles Centrales. The Mixtecs were famed workers of gold and precious stones, and it's said the Aztec emperor Moctezuma would only eat off their fine Mixteca–Puebla ceramics.

Today much of the Mixteca is overfarmed, eroded and deforested, and politics and business are dominated by mestizos. Many Mixtecs have to emigrate for work. Foreign visitors are not frequent here, though some guided trips are available from Oaxaca (see p708). You can visit the Mixteca in a long day trip from Oaxaca, but basic hotels or *casas de huéspedes* are available in Nochixtlán, Coixtlahuaca, Tamazulapan, Teposcolula and Putla, and better ones in Tlaxiaco and Huajuapan de León. In Huajuapan, a good, inexpensive choice is **Hotel Colón** (☎ 953-532-08-17; Colón; s/d US$13/18; P), a motel-style place with a courtyard surrounded by two floors of rooms. It's clean, green and friendly, and rooms have TV and fan.

Getting There & Away

First-class ADO buses run from Oaxaca to Nochixtlán (US$5, 1¼ hours, 10 daily). **Sur** (☎ 951-514-44-86; Periférico 1014), a good 2nd-class line with its terminal near Oaxaca's Central de Abastos market, leaves hourly from 6am to 8pm for Huajuapan de León (US$3.75, 2¾ hours) via Hwy 190, stopping at Nochixtlán (US$1.50, 1½ hours), Yanhuitlán (US$2, 1¾ hours) and Tejupan (US$2.75, 2¼ hours), and hourly from 6:30am to 7:30pm for Teposcolula (US$2.75, 2½ hours) and Tlaxiaco (US$3.75, three hours). Several buses a day head south from Tlaxiaco to Pinotepa Nacional.

For Coixtlahuaca, Fletes y Pasajes (Fypsa) runs from Oaxaca's 2nd-class bus station (US$6, 10 daily), or you can take a Huajuapan-bound bus to Tejupan, where colectivo taxis run to Coixtlahuaca. Santiago Apoala has a bus service three days a week to/from Nochixtlán. You can also reach Apoala by taxi or camioneta (pickup) from Nochixtlán.

Buses run from Mexico City's Terminal Oriente (TAPO) to several Mixteca towns.

SANTIAGO APOALA

This small village, 2000m above sea level in a beautiful green valley 40km north of Nochixtlán, is a great place to get off the beaten track.

The journey from Nochixtlán, by unpaved roads in poor condition, takes two hours. The scenery around Santiago is spectacular, with the 60m waterfall Cascada Cola de la Serpiente and the 400m-deep Cañón Morelos among the highlights. Several Oaxaca active-tourism agencies run trips here, typically of two days, with a three-hour walk through the canyon to the village on the first day, and a walk to the waterfall (where you can usually have a swim) the next day.

You can also do it independently: the village's **Comité de Turismo** (Tourism Committee; ☎ 55-5151-9154) has a comfortable three-room lodge, and there's the **Parador Turístico** (s/d US$7.50/15, 4-/8-person tents US$11/20). Reserve direct or try through the tourist offices in Oaxaca. Meals at the parador cost US$2.75 each (phone ahead to check availability and take a few supplies in any case), mountain-bike rental is US$2.50/9.50 per hour/day, and each group of up to five people has to pay a US$5 access charge. The tourism committee offers two-day packages including one night's lodging, guided hikes and four meals for between US$19 and US$23 per person. Accommodations and meals are also available in private homes at similar prices to the Parador.

YANHUITLÁN, COIXTLAHUACA & TEPOSCOLULA

The beautiful 16th-century **Dominican monasteries** (admission US$2.25 each; ☯ 10am-5pm) in these three Mixteca villages are among colonial Mexico's finest architectural treasures. Their restrained stonework fuses medieval, plateresque, Renaissance and indigenous styles. The one at Coixtlahuaca is perhaps the most beautiful of the group. Its church has a lovely rib-vaulted ceiling and pure Renaissance façade, beside which stands a graceful, ruined *capilla abierta* (open chapel), used for preaching to crowds of indigenous people. The weightier monastery at Yanhuitlán, designed to withstand earthquakes and serve as a defensive refuge, towers beside Hwy 190, 120km from Oaxaca. The cloister has an interesting little museum. The church contains valuable works of art, and a fine Mudéjar timber roof supports the choir. Teposcolula's monastery features a stately *capilla abierta* of three open bays, outside the monastery church.

TLAXIACO & AROUND

Tlaxiaco, a town of 14,000 people 43km south of Teposcolula on Hwy 125, was known before the Mexican Revolution as París Chiquita (Little Paris), for the quantities of French luxuries such as clothes and wine imported for its few rich families. Today the only signs of that elegance are the arcades around the main plaza and a few large houses with courtyards. The market area is off the southeast corner of the plaza – Saturday is the main day. Accommodations in central Tlaxiaco include **Hotel Del Portal** (☎ 953-552-01-54; Plaza de la Constitución 2; r US$20-25), on the main plaza, with big, clean rooms around a pleasant courtyard; and **Hotel México** (☎ 953-552-00-86; Hidalgo 13; s/d US$18/20, with shared bathroom US$8/9).

About 18km north of Tlaxiaco, just off Hwy 125 toward Teposcolula, is **San Martín Huamelulpan**, where the **Museo Comunitario Hitalulu** (☎ 015-201-59-05; Plaza Cívica; admission US$1; ☯ 11am-5pm Wed-Sun) focuses on traditional medicine (the practitioners here are renowned for their powers) and archaeology. Also well worth a visit is the Mixtec

archaeological site, located 500m from the village.

South of Tlaxiaco, Hwy 125, all paved, winds through the remote Sierra Madre del Sur to Pinotepa Nacional, on coastal Hwy 200. The major town is **Putla**, 95km from Tlaxiaco. Just before Putla is **San Andrés Chicahuaxtla**, in the small territory of the indigenous Triquis. The Amuzgo people of **San Pedro Amuzgos**, 73km south of Putla, are known for their fine *huipiles*.

NORTHERN OAXACA

Hwy 175, scenic but rough in parts, crosses Oaxaca's northern sierras to **Tuxtepec** (population 88,000), the main town in the low-lying Papaloapan region of far northern Oaxaca, which in culture and geography is akin to neighboring Veracruz. In the Sierra Mazateca west of Tuxtepec is **Huautla de Jiménez**, where (according to legend) the likes of Bob Dylan, the Beatles, Timothy Leary and Albert Hoffman (the inventor of LSD) used to go to trip on the local *hongos* (hallucinogenic mushrooms) under the guidance of María Sabina, Huautla's famed *curandera* (medicine woman). María Sabina died in 1985, but others follow in her footsteps and a trickle of foreigners still make their way to Huautla. Fresh mushrooms appear in the rainy season from June to August. Locals disapprove of mushroom-taking just for thrills.

PEOPLES OF OAXACA

Oaxaca's population of 3.6 million includes 15 indigenous groups, numbering somewhere between 1 million and 2 million people in total. Each group has its own language, but most also speak Spanish. Colorful traditional costumes are still in common use, and you'll notice a strong indigenous presence in the villages, markets and festivals. Indigenous land and housing are, however, usually the poorest in the state.

The approximately 500,000 Zapotecs live mainly in and around the Valles Centrales and on the Isthmus of Tehuantepec. You're sure to come into contact with them, though few obvious signs identify them. Most are farmers, but they also make and trade handicrafts, mezcal and other products. Many emigrate temporarily for work.

About 500,000 Mixtecs are spread around the mountainous borders of Oaxaca, Guerrero and Puebla states, with more than two-thirds of them in Oaxaca. The state's other large indigenous groups include 160,000 or so Mazatecs in the far north, 100,000 Mixes in the highlands northeast of the Valles Centrales, and 100,000 Chinantecs around Valle Nacional in the north.

In Oaxaca city you may well see Triquis, from western Oaxaca; the women wear bright red *huipiles* (sleeveless tunics). The Triquis are only about 15,000 strong and have a long history of violent conflict with mestizos and Mixtecs over land rights.

GUELATAO & IXTLÁN

☎ 951

On Hwy 175, 60km from Oaxaca, Guelatao village was the birthplace of Benito Juárez (see p706). By the pretty lake at the center of the village is a statue of the boy Benito as a shepherd. Among the adjacent municipal buildings are two statues of Juárez and a small exposition, the **Sala Homenaje a Juárez** (admission free; ☺ 9am-4pm Wed-Sun).

In the small town of Ixtlán, 3km beyond Guelatao on Hwy 175, is the baroque **Templo de Santo Tomás**, where baby Benito was baptized. Note this church's finely carved west façade. On Ixtlán's plaza you'll also find a community ecotourism venture, **Shiaa-Rua-Via** (☎ /fax 553-60-75; http://oaxaca.host.sk in Spanish), which offers cabaña accommodation and guided hikes and mountain-biking on a similar basis to the Pueblos Mancomunados, in similar Sierra Norte country.

The Cuenca line runs nine daily buses from Oaxaca's 1st-class bus station to Guelatao (US$2.75, 1½ hours) and Ixtlán (US$3, 1¾ hours). The companies **Benito Juárez** (☎ 951-516-57-76) and **Flecha del Zempoaltépetl** (☎ 951-516-63-42), US$1 cheaper, go 10 times daily from Oaxaca's 2nd-class bus station.

OAXACA COAST

A laid-back spell on the beautiful Oaxaca coast is the perfect complement to the inland attractions of Oaxaca City and the Valles Centrales. The trip down Hwy 175 from Oaxaca is spectacular: south of Miahuatlán you climb into pine forests, then descend into ever lusher and hotter tropical forest.

The once remote fishing villages and former coffee ports of Puerto Escondido and Puerto Ángel are now also informal tourist resorts. Puerto Escondido has famous surf and a lively travelers' scene, while Puerto Ángel is the hub for a series of wonderful beaches with limitless low-cost accommodations – among them the fabled Zipolite and its increasingly popular neighbor Mazunte. To the east, a bigger tourist resort has been developed on the lovely Bahías de Huatulco.

West of Puerto Escondido, nature lovers can visit the lagoons of Manialtepec and Chacahua, teeming with bird life, and hang out at Chacahua village.

The coast of Oaxaca is hotter and much more humid than the state's highlands. Most of the year's rain falls between June and September, turning everything green. From October the landscape starts to dry out, and by March many of the trees are leafless. May is the hottest month.

Note that the peak tourism seasons on this coast are from mid-December to mid-January, Semana Santa and the months of July and August when room prices often double. We give the prices that hold for most of the year (ie outside the peak periods).

The Oaxaca coast is an impoverished region apart from its few tourism honey pots. Be on your guard against theft in Puerto Escondido and the Puerto Ángel-Zipolite area.

PUERTO ESCONDIDO

☎ 954 / pop 40,000

Known to surfers since before paved roads reached this part of Oaxaca, Puerto Escondido (Hidden Port) remains relaxed and inexpensive with a lively travelers' scene. It has several beaches, a steadily improving range of accommodations, some excellent restaurants, plenty of cafés and a spot of nightlife. Several interesting ecotourist destinations are close by.

Any hint of breeze is a blessing in Puerto, and you're more likely to get one up the hill a little bit than down at sea level.

Orientation

The town rises above the small, south-facing Bahía Principal. Hwy 200, here called the Carretera Costera, runs across the hill halfway up, dividing the upper town – where buses arrive and most of the locals live and work – from the lower, tourism-dominated part. The heart of the lower town is El Adoquín, the pedestrianized section (from 5pm until late) of Av Pérez Gasga (*adoquín* is Spanish for paving stone). The west end of Av Pérez Gasga winds up the slope to meet Hwy 200 at an intersection with traffic signals, known as El Crucero.

Bahía Principal curves around at its east end to the long Playa Zicatela, the hub of the surf scene, with loads more places to stay and eat. About 1km west of El Crucero, the area above Playa Carrizalillo has a few new places to stay, restaurants and services.

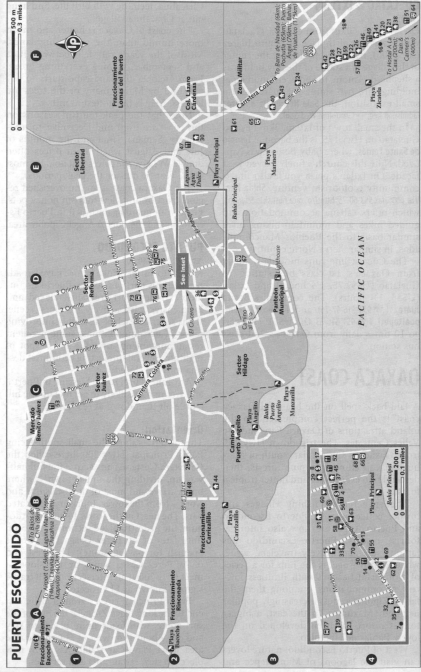

Information

BOOKSTORES

PJ's Book Bodega (Morro s/n, Zicatela) A large collection of new and used books in English and Spanish.

INTERNET ACCESS

Cofee Net (per hr US$2) Adoquín (Av Pérez Gasga s/n); Zicatela (Hotel Surf Olas Altas)

Hotel Acuario (Morro s/n, Zicatela; per hr US$1.50) Also see Sleeping, p741.

Servinet (Av Pérez Gasga 705; per hr US$2; 🕑 9am-midnight)

Un Tigre Azul (Av Pérez Gasga s/n; per hr US$2) Restaurant/bar with Internet access; see Drinking, p744.

LAUNDRY

Lavamática del Centro (Av Pérez Gasga 405A; 🕑 8am-8pm Mon-Sat, 8am-5pm Sun) Wash 3.5kg of clothes for US$1.30; complete wash and dry service costs US$1.30 per kg.

MEDIA

The free bimonthly paper **El Sol de la Costa** (www.puertoconnection.com), in Spanish and English, is full of information about what's on and what to do.

MONEY

Many hotels give a fair rate for dollars. The town's *casas de cambio*, named Money Ex-

change, open longer hours than its banks. There's a handy **Bital ATM** (El Adoquín), next door to Restaurant Los Crotos (p743). The following banks all have ATMs, will change US dollar traveler's cheques and cash US dollars:

Banamex (cnr Av Pérez Gasga & Unión; 🕑 9am-2pm Mon-Fri)

Bancomer (cnr 3 Poniente & 2 Norte; 🕑 9am-2pm Mon-Sat)

Banorte (Av Hidalgo 4; 🕑 9am-4pm Mon-Fri, 10am-4pm Sat)

Bital (cnr 1 Norte & 2 Poniente; 🕑 8am-7pm Mon-Sat)

The last three mentioned are in the upper part of town and their service may be quicker.

POST

Post Office (cnr Av Oaxaca & 7 Norte; 🕑 8am-3pm Mon-Fri) A 20- to 30-minute uphill walk from El Adoquín, but you can take a 'Mercado' bus or colectivo taxi up Av Oaxaca.

TELEPHONE & FAX

You'll find pay phones and a couple of telephone casetas on the Adoquín, and more pay phones along Calle del Morro on Zicatela.

TOURIST INFORMATION

Sedetur (☎ 582-01-75; cnr Carretera Costera & Blvd Juárez; ☼ 9am-2pm & 4-7pm Mon-Fri, 10am-2pm Sat) This office is about 2.5km west of the center on the road to the airport.

Tourist Information Kiosk (ginainpuerto@yahoo.com; cnr Av Pérez Gasga & Marina Nacional; ☼ 9am-2pm & 4-6pm Mon-Fri, 10am-2pm Sat) This very helpful place is at the west end of El Adoquín. Gina Machorro, the energetic, multilingual information officer usually found here, happily answers your every question.

TRAVEL AGENCIES

Viajes Dimar (☎ 582-15-51; Av Pérez Gasga 905B) You can buy air tickets here.

Dangers & Annoyances

Puerto has an up-and-down safety record. To minimize any risks, avoid isolated or empty places, and stick to well-lit areas at night (or use taxis). Take special care on the beach at Playa Zicatela and in the rocks area between Zicatela and Playa Marinero, and it's probably best to use the coastal walkway passing the lighthouse only in the mornings and with company.

Beaches

BAHÍA PRINCIPAL

The main town beach is long enough to accommodate restaurants at its west end, the local fishing fleet in its center and sun worshipers and young body-boarders at its east end (called Playa Marinero). Occasional flocks of pelicans wing in inches above the waves. Boats bob on the swell, and a few hawkers wander up and down. The smelly water entering the bay at times from the inaptly named Laguna Agua Dulce will put you off dipping away from Playa Marinero.

PLAYA ZICATELA

Long, straight Zicatela is Puerto's hip beach, with enticing cafés, restaurants and accommodations as well as the waves of the legendary 'Mexican Pipeline,' just offshore, which test the mettle of surfers from far and wide.

Nonsurfers beware: the Zicatela waters have a lethal undertow and are definitely not safe for the boardless. Lifeguards rescue several careless people most months (their base, the Cuartel Salvavidas, is in front of Hotel Surf Olas Altas).

BAHÍA PUERTO ANGELITO

The sheltered bay of Puerto Angelito, about 1km west of Bahía Principal, has two small beaches separated by a few rocks. Playa Manzanilla, the eastern one, is quieter because vehicles can't reach it.

Lanchas (fast, open, outboard boats) from the west end of Bahía Principal will take three or four people to Puerto Angelito for US$2.75 per person each way. The boat returns at an agreed pick-up time. By land, it's a 20- to 30-minute walk or a US$2 taxi ride from El Adoquín.

PLAYA CARRIZALILLO

Just west of Puerto Angelito, small Carrizalillo beach is in a rockier cove but is OK for swimming, snorkeling, body-boarding and surfing. It has a bar with a few palapas. *Lanchas* from Bahía Principal (about US$3.75 per person each way) will bring you here too. A path down from the cliff top immediately north of the beach also reaches the cove.

Activities

You can rent boards for surfing and body-boarding in a few places on Playa Zicatela. One is **Central Surf** (☎ 582-22-85; www.centralsurf shop.com; Morro s/n; per hr/day US$4/9 for body-board & fins, per hr/day US$5.50/13 for long boards), in the Hotel Acuario building. Central Surf also offers surfing lessons for US$27 per hour.

Lanchas from the west end of Bahía Principal will take groups of four out for about an hour's **turtle-spotting** (and, in winter, sometimes dolphin-spotting) for around US$30, with a dropoff at Puerto Angelito or Playa Carrizalillo afterwards.

Local marlin fishers and sailfishers will take two to four people **fishing** with them for three hours for US$84. Ask at the *lancha* kiosk at the west end of Bahía Principal. The price includes cooking some of the catch for you at one of the town's seafood restaurants.

Diving is another possibility. The San Andreas Fault begins not far out to sea from Zicatela. **Aventura Submarina** (☎ 582-23-53; Av Pérez Gasga 601A; one-/two-tank dive trips US$54.50 per person, Discover Scuba Diving US$68, 4-day open water certification course US$318) teaches diving courses and leads dive trips for all levels.

Horseback riding on Playa Zicatela looks fab. Ask the guys on the beach or arrange your rides through Beach Hotel Inés (p742).

Courses

Instituto de Lenguajes Puerto Escondido (☎ 582-20-55; www.puertoschool.com; Carretera Costera, Zicatela; 1/2 people per hr US$10/16) runs classes by experienced surfer/teacher Brian Vander Kooy right in the heart of surfing territory.

Festivals & Events

Semana Santa is a big week for local partying; a local surf carnival is held at this time. At least two international surf contests are held on Zicatela each year: the International Surfboard Contest in August, and the International Surfing Tournament in mid-November. National surfing championships happen on the last weekend of November.

November is a big month in other ways too: the Festival Costeña de la Danza, a fiesta of Oaxaca coastal dance, and a sailfish-fishing contest and art exhibitions all take place over the second and/or third weekends of the month.

Sleeping

The two main accommodation zones are the central Av Pérez Gasga area and the surf beach Playa Zicatela. But there are new places cropping up in Carrizalillo. In the peak seasons the most popular places will probably be full, especially on Zicatela. Your best chance of getting into a place you like, if you haven't booked ahead, is to ask early in the day, about 9am or 10am.

Several apartments and houses are available for short and long stays. Apartments start at US$400/800 a month in low/high season; houses overlooking the beach are around US$730/1750. Ask at the tourist information office on Av Pérez Gasga.

BUDGET

Budget accommodation options near the beaches are limited, but there are a few good-value places on Playa Zicatela and one at Playa Carrizalillo.

Hotel Buena Vista (☎ /fax 582-14-74; buenavista101@hotmail.com; Morro s/n; r US$23, with kitchen US$28) The plain, well-kept Buena Vista stands on the hillside, reached by a steep flight of steps from Calle del Morro. The 16 reasonably sized rooms all have one double bed and one single, mosquito screens or nets, and hot-water bathroom. Many have breezy balconies. Prices double in the high seasons.

Hotel Rockaway (☎ 582-06-68; fax 582-24-20; Morro s/n; s/d US$11/17; P ⊠) The popular Hotel Rockaway has 16 or so good, solid cabañas with showers, nets and fans, around a pool, plus a bar.

Las Olas (☎ 582-09-19; zazielucassen@hotmail.com; Morro 15; bungalows US$18, cabañas US$15) Las Olas has 12 good cabañas with cookers and rooms (called bungalows) with TV; each has attached bathroom, fan, screens and fridge.

Hostel Shalom (☎ 582-32-34; amital2000@yahoo.com; Blvd Juárez 4082, Rinconada, Carrizalillo; per person: hammock US$3, camping US$3.75, dm US$4.75, private room US$5; P ⊠) Accommodations fan out from an old house on a huge piece of treed land just five minutes from the steps down to Playa Carrizalillo. Run by a fun-loving young couple, this place has a bar/restaurant, common kitchen, lockers, a big swimming pool and surfboard rental.

Hostal A La Casa (☎ 580-37-88; alacasa55@hotmail.com; Las Brisas s/n; dm or private room incl breakfast per person US$6) This relaxed French-Canadian-owned hostel is only 200m from the beach, towards the end of Zicatela. A breezy dormitory with 20 beds (with mosquito nets) sits atop a breakfast bar, and a couple of private rooms. The inclusive breakfast is hearty. There are lockers, a pool table, cable TV, surfboard rental and laundry service.

There are a number of budget spots in the area around Av Pérez Gasga.

Hotel Mayflower (☎ 582-03-67; minnemay7@hotmail.com; Andador Libertad s/n; dm US$6, s/d US$17/18) The attractive, popular Mayflower, beside the steps leading down to El Adoquín from the east end of Merklin, has five fan-cooled dormitories with 32 places in all. Rates include filtered water and the use of a kitchen with fridge and microwave. The 16 pleasing single and double rooms have fan and bathroom. There are semi-open sitting areas, a billiard table, board games and a safety box.

Cabañas Pepe (☎ 582-20-37; Merklin 201; s/d US$12/14) Not far below El Crucero, friendly, family-run Pepe's is geared to backpackers and offers six rooms with two double beds, fan, nets and hot-water bathroom. Most are in good shape and four have superb views.

Hotel Naxhiely (☎ 582-30-75; Av Pérez Gasga 301; s/d US$14/19) This small hotel has 15 plain, smallish but good clean rooms with fan and TV. Security is good and there's a small cafeteria, and laundry service. Prices rise by about US$5 in high seasons.

Currently there is no trailer park in Puerto but plans are afoot to develop a new site on the highway behind Zicatela. Camping options are limited to Hostel Shalom (tents only). Campervans can be parked in the grounds of Hotel Arco Iris (below).

MID-RANGE

There's plenty of choice near the beaches. Zicatela is sublime but it can get hectic in high seasons.

Dan & Carmen's (☎ 582-27-60; www.casadany carmen.com; Jacaranda 14, Colonia Santa María; cabañas US$14, with garden view US$19, sea view US$23, big sea view US$28; P ⊠) This excellent place owned by the Cafecito folk (see following) offers 12 self-contained units with fully equipped kitchens and lovely Talavera-tiled bathrooms. Units vary in size from small 'cabañas' for one or two people to larger family rooms for three to four people, with terrace and views. There's a terrific extra-long lap pool. Reservations are essential.

Tabachín del Puerto (☎ 582-11-79; www.tabachin .com.mx; at end of short lane behind Hotel Santa Fe; r incl breakfast US$45-65; P ⊠) The American-owned Tabachín offers six gorgeous studio-rooms of various sizes, all with kitchen, air-con, TV and phone. Most have balcony access; décor and furniture range from folksy Mexican to classical fine art. The vegetarian breakfast, which includes organically grown coffee and fruits from the owners' farm in Nopala, is a feature here.

Hotel Arco Iris (☎ /fax 582-04-32; www.puerto connection.com/arco.html; Morro s/n; r US$55 or US$60; P ⊠) The attractive, colonial-style Arco Iris has 32 big, clean rooms with balconies or terraces, most looking straight out to the surf, plus a large pool and a good upstairs restaurant/bar open to the breeze. All rooms have two double beds and ceiling fans, and some have a kitchen. You can also park a camper in the sizable grounds.

Hotel Flor de María (☎ 582-05-36; www.mexon line.com/flordemaria.htm; 1a Entrada a Playa Marinero; r US$35-45; ⊠) A friendly Canadian couple run this good hotel on a lane behind Playa Marinero. The 24 ample rooms, around a columned patio, all have two double beds and safes and are very pretty, with individually painted murals and door panels. One or two rooms have sea views. Extras include a rooftop pool and bar and a good international restaurant.

Hotel Acuario (☎ 582-03-57; fax 582-10-27; Morro s/n; r US$33-58; P ⊠ ⊡ ⊠) The 30 or so accommodations here range from cramped rooms to wooden cabañas to spacious upstairs rooms with terrace and beach view. The more substantial bungalows have the most appealing interiors and have kitchens. All rooms have mosquito nets or netting. The pool area is inviting.

Beach Hotel Inés (☎ /fax 582-07-92; www.hotel ines.com; Morro s/n; r US$11-41; P ⊠ ⊠) German-run Inés has a range of cabañas, rooms with and without air-con, bungalows and suites; cabañas will take four or more people from US$37. At the center of things is a relaxed, shaded and popular pool area with a café serving good food. Horseback riding can be arranged here.

Bungalows Zicatela (☎ 582-07-98; www.bunga lowszicatela.com.mx; Morro s/n; s/d US$19/28, with air-con & view US$55; ⊠ ⊠) Next door to the Arco Iris, the Zicatela has a sociable pool and restaurant. All 40-odd accommodations are a good size, have mosquito-netted windows and are solidly built, even if they're squeezed a little tightly together. Most have kitchens. You'll pay double in the high seasons.

Bungalows Puerta del Sol (☎ 587-29-22; Morro s/n; s/d US$28/32; ⊠) Just east of Hotel Inés, this place has a good pool area with artistic flourishes, and 10 spacious, solidly built rooms, each with two double beds, fan, balcony and hammock.

Casas de Playa Acali (☎ 582-07-54; Morro s/n; r US$68, bungalows US$50, cabañas US$37; ⊠ ⊠) Acali provides wooden cabañas, each with one double and one single bed, and bungalows with two double beds and a kitchen. More expensive rooms on the hillside have air-con, kitchen and terrace. All accommodations have mosquito nets, fan and hot water.

There's a good range of places around Av Pérez Gasga too.

Hotel Paraíso Escondido (☎ 582-04-44; Unión 10; r US$54; ⊠ ⊠) Owned by a group of architects and designers, the Paraíso Escondido is a rambling whitewash-and-blue place decorated with tiles, pottery, stained glass and stone sculpture by well-known Mexican sculptors. The 20 clean though moderately sized rooms have air-con. It has an attractive restaurant/bar/pool area,

Hotel San Juan (☎ 582-05-18; Merklin 503; s/d US$17/23, r with air-con US$40; P ⊠ ⊠) The friendly San Juan, just below El Crucero, has 31 good, straightforward rooms. All have hot water, mosquito screens, cable TV and a security box; some have terraces and excellent views. The hotel also boasts a pool and a rooftop sitting area.

Hotel Hacienda Revolución (☎/fax 582-18-18; www.haciendarevolucion.com; Andador Revolución 21; r US$32) This decent place, on a flight of steps leading up from El Adoquín, has 11 attractive and spacious rooms around a garden-courtyard with a beautiful central fountain. Rooms have colorful paintwork and Talavera-tiled hot-water bathrooms; most have a patio and hammock.

Hotel Nayar (☎ 582-01-13; fax 582-03-19; Av Pérez Gasga 407; r with fan/air-con US$33/41; P ⬚ ⬚) The yellow-painted Nayar gets a good breeze in its wide sitting areas/walkways, and the 40 rooms have hot water and small balconies. Fifteen rooms have sea views. The pool is in a big garden by the entrance.

Hotel Loren (☎ 582-00-57, fax 582-05-91, Av Pérez Gasga 507; r with fan/air-con US$23/32; P ⬚ ⬚) A minute uphill from El Adoquín, this friendly, sky-blue-and-lobster-colored hotel has bare but spacious rooms. All have two double beds, cable TV and balconies, but not all catch a sea view. There are hammocks beside the pool. Prices double in the high seasons.

Hotel Rincón del Pacífico (☎ 582-00-56; rcon paci@prodigy.net.mx; Av Pérez Gasga 900; r US$23-28; ⬚) This hotel on El Adoquín has 20-odd big-windowed rooms with fan, TV and hot-water bathroom around a palm-filled courtyard. Staff are helpful and the hotel has a beachside café/restaurant.

Hotel Casa Blanca (☎ 582-01-68; Av Pérez Gasga 905; s/d US$21/28; ⬚) The friendly Casa Blanca is right at the heart of things on the inland side of El Adoquín, and it fills up with guests quickly. It has a small pool and 21 large rooms with fan; the best are streetside with balconies.

TOP END

Hotel Santa Fe (☎ 582-01-70; www.mexonline.com /hotelsantafe.htm; Morro s/n; s/d US$86/100, bungalows US$100/108; P ⬚ ⬚ ⬚) The Santa Fe, behind the rocky outcrop dividing Playa Marinero from Playa Zicatela, has 51 rooms attractively set around small terraces and a palm-fringed pool. Rooms vary in size and view, but good design, with a clever use of

tiles, makes most of them agreeable. Many have air-con. Also available are eight appealing bungalows with kitchens. The restaurant (see Eating, below) is a must.

Hotel Surf Olas Altas (☎ 582-23-15; ☎/fax 582-00-94; www.surfolasaltas.com.mx; Morro 310; r US$80-100; P ⬚ ⬚ ⬚) Zicatela's biggest hotel is a modern place with 60 rooms. It has less character than some of the smaller places but the rooms are spotless; most have two double beds and all have air-con and satellite TV. Only some rooms catch a sea view. There's a restaurant out front.

Villas Carrizalillo (☎ 582-17-35; www.villascarriz alillo.com; Av Carrizalillo 125, Carrizalillo; apt US$50-100) Sublimely perched on the cliffs above the small Bahía Carrizalillo, Villas Carrizalillo has apartments for two to six people, with fully equipped kitchens and private terraces. Some have stunning sea views. A path goes directly down to Playa Carrizalillo.

Eating

Puerto has some excellent eateries, a large proportion of them Italian thanks to the tide of Italian travelers drawn here by the movie *Puerto Escondido*. Many are at least partly open-air. You'll eat some of the freshest fish and seafood you've ever had. Tofu products, and a mind-boggling range of fruit and vegetable juices and milk and yogurt combos, make this a vegetarian's paradise.

UPPER TOWN

Mercado Benito Juárez (cnr 8 Norte & 3 Poniente; fish plates US$3.50, vegetarian plates US$2.25, lobster US$5) Several clean stalls in the expanded market in the upper part of town prepare good fare.

PLAYA ZICATELA

Sakura (Calle del Morro s/n; fish & seafood dishes US$5-12, rice & pasta dishes US$3-6) With a prime spot on the sands looking out to the surf break at Zicatela and terrific fresh ingredients, this Japanese-owned restaurant is heavenly. Pick from the list of sushi, tempura, tofu and teriyaki dishes, curries, rice and spring rolls. Watch out for the tongue-tingling ginger paste! The sushi and tofu *a la parrilla* (grilled) are sensational.

Carmen's Cafecito (☎ 582-05-16; Morro s/n; meals US$0.75-7; 🕓 7:30am-10pm) Carmen's, run by an inspired Mexican/Canadian couple, does a roaring trade morning, noon and night. Wicked pastries, croissants and cakes cost just US$0.75, coffee refills are free, and the wholemeal tortas (including a superb scrambled egg, ham, cheese and tomato creation) go for US$2.25. Homemade lunch and dinner dishes, including Mexican options, cost from US$4.50 to US$7. **El Cafecito**, next door, has the same owners and menu. There's another El Cafecito at Carrizalillo.

Hotel Santa Fe (☎ 582-01-70; Morro s/n; pasta US$6-8, red snapper or prawn dishes US$11-13, vegan dishes US$4) This airy and beautifully sited restaurant looks down on the west end of the Mexican pipeline. Sink into a comfy leather chair and choose from their extended list of delicious Mexican vegetarian, vegan and fish and seafood meals.

Restaurante El Jardín (☎ 582-23-15; Hotel Surf Olas Altas, Morro s/n; dishes US$3-7) This palapa restaurant has been through a few incarnations but currently has adopted the menu of former successful, long-standing vegetarian La Gota de Vida (The Drop of Life). Fish and seafood have been added to the food list but you can still eat old favorites like gado gado, hummus, many salad varieties, tofu and tempeh. There's also an extensive beverage and juice list.

La Galera (☎ 582-04-32; Hotel Arco Iris, Morro s/n; menu del día US$4, mains US$6-10) This restaurant has a good, open-air, upstairs setting, and tasty mixed Mexican/international fare. Main dishes focus on fish and meat though there are a few vegetarian choices including pastas and salads.

La Nueva Cuba (Morro s/n; tacos from US$3; ☯ 1pm-1am) This popular little hang-out at the far end of Zicatela specializes in simple Mexican-surfer style munchies, and mixed drinks like margaritas and cubas.

Zicatela has two or three small **grocery stores**, including a 24-hour store at Hotel Rockaway.

PLAYA MARINERO

Carmen's Panadería y Cafetería (1a Entrada a Playa Marinero; breakfasts around US$2; ☯ 7am-3pm Mon-Sat, 7am-noon Sun) This is a brilliant café for breakfast or lunchtime snacks, run by the same people as Carmen's Cafecito on Zicatela, and with an outdoor terrace overlooking tropical greenery. Breakfasts include big servings of fruit salad, yogurt and granola, or whole-wheat French toast with honey and lots of fruit. A bakery section sells excellent bread and baked goods.

AV PÉREZ GASGA

La Galería (☎ 582-20-39; mains US$4-10) At the west end of El Adoquín, La Galería is one of Puerto's best Italian spots, with art on the walls and good fare on the tables. The pasta dishes are original and tasty, and the jumbo mixed green salad is a real treat. You can breakfast here too.

Restaurant Junto al Mar (☎ 582-12-72; Av Pérez Gasga 600; mains US$4-9) On the bay side of El Adoquín (as its name implies), the Junto al Mar has a terrace overlooking the beach where attentive waitstaff serve up excellent fresh seafood. The squid dishes and the fish fillet *a la veracruzana* (tomato, onion and pepper sauce) get the thumbs up.

La Perla Flameante (mains US$5-9; ☯ 5pm-1am) This palapa restaurant overlooking the Adoquín receives steady praise for its excellent fish fillet dishes and sushi. Try the tuna in white wine sauce.

Restaurant Los Crotos (☎ 582-00-25; mains US$6-9) With romantic night lighting, Los Crotos serves similar fare to the Junto al Mar in an attractive setting almost on the sands of Playa Principal. Try the fish or seafood.

Baguettería Vivaldi (breakfasts & baguettes US$2.50-4) Vivaldi serves good breakfasts (named for German cities), baguettes on white or whole-wheat bread and crêpes, both sweet and savory (US$2.50 to US$3.50). There is a pleasant little courtyard for outdoor eating.

Restaurant Alicia (dishes US$2.25-9) The little Alicia, around the middle of El Adoquín, is good value, with multiple spaghetti variations, seafood cocktails and good fish dishes. It does cheap breakfasts and beer is cheap too!

Drinking

Barfly (Av Pérez Gasga, El Adoquín) This two-story bar with good music is the epicenter of the travelers' scene on the Adoquín and pulls in a hip crowd nightly.

Un Tigre Azul (Av Pérez Gasga, El Adoquín) This small laid-back restaurant/bar run by genial Ana Marquéz and her daughter Ana appeals to the alternative crowd.

Rival drinking dens with loud music on the Adoquín include **Terraza Bar**, **Wipe Out Bar** and **Los 3 Diablos**. **Tarros** (Marina Nacional), around the corner, is in the same league. Most of these hold two-for-one happy hours from 9pm to 10pm but don't expect much action before 11pm.

Casa Babylon (Morro s/n, Zicatela; ☺ 10:30am-2pm & 6pm-late) This cool little travelers' bar has board games and a big selection of second-hand books to sell or exchange.

A few bars overlooking the sea, such as **Restaurant Liza's** on Playa Marinero at the **Hotel Arco Iris** on Zicatela, have happy hours from about 5pm to 7pm to help you enjoy Puerto's spectacular sunsets.

Entertainment

El Son y La Rumba (☎ 582-10-30; Morro s/n; ☺ 9:30pm-late Tue-Sun) Almost on the sands at the Zicatela end of Playa Marinero, this friendly place hosts good live salsa several nights a week.

Tequila Sunrise (Marina Nacional; admission US$2; ☺ 10pm-late Tue-Sun) This disco, a block or so west of the Adoquín, is billed as 'hot' and sometimes lives up to this.

Restaurant Da Claudio (just off the Adoquín) The Italian-owned Da Claudio shows the 1992 Italian travel-and-crime movie *Puerto Escondido* at 8pm nightly. This film has attracted thousands of Italians and others to Puerto and is well worth seeing, even if it makes the place seem more remote than it really is.

Cinemar (Zicatela Sur; film showings at 5pm, 7pm & 9pm) Air-conditioned Cinemar, next to PJ's Book Bodega, shows films ranging from classics to latest general releases, in Spanish and English.

Shopping

The Adoquín is great for a browse – shops and stalls sell fashions from surf designers and from Bali, new-age and silver jewelry, souvenirs and classy crafts that are works of art. The Mall de Puerto, a complex with 47 shops, hotel and gardens, is being built just east of Baguettería Vivaldi (see p743).

Getting There & Away

AIR

Aerotucán (☎ 582-17-25; Puerto Escondido airport) and **Aerovega** (☎ 582-01-51; cnr Marina Nacional & El Adoquín) fly to/from Oaxaca. See the Oaxaca City section (p721) for details. **Aerocaribe** (☎ 582-20-24; Puerto Escondido airport) flies nonstop to/from Mexico City twice daily from Thursday to Monday (from US$125, 50 minutes).

BUS

At the time of research a new bus station was being built in the upper part of town between 3 and 4 Poniente, north of 9 Norte. Until it opens, travelers will have to use the bus terminals lower down, a couple of blocks about 1 Crucero. **Estrella Blanca** (EB, ☎ 582-00-86) is entered from 1 Oriente; **Estrella del Valle/Oaxaca Pacífico** (EV/OP; ☎ 582-00-50), **Transol** and **Estrella Roja Sur** (ERS; ☎ 582-08-75) are all located on Av Hidalgo; and **Cristóbal Colón** (☎ 582-10-73) is on 1 Norte. The only true 1st-class bus services are Colón's and a couple of the Estrella Blanca Mexico City runs.

It is advisable to book in advance for Colón buses and for the better services to Oaxaca. There are several daily departures to Oaxaca:

Via highways 200 & 175 (US$7.50/8.50 ordinario/directo, 6½-7½hr, 10 EV/OP daily; US$7.50-8.50, 6½-7½hr, 6 Transol daily)

Via Hwy 131 (US$7.50-8.50, 8-9hr, 6 ERS daily) This is a shorter route on poor roads.

Via highways 200 & 190 (US$18, 10-11hr, 1 Colón daily) The longest but smoothest route.

There are several daily departures to other destinations:

Acapulco (US$14/19 ordinario/semi-directo, 8-9½hr, 12 EB daily)

Bahías de Huatulco (US$5, 2½hr, 8 Colón daily; US$4/5 ordinario/semi-directo, 2½hr, 8 EB daily)

Pochutla (US$3, 1½hr, 8 Colón daily; US$2/4 ordinario/semi-directo, 1½hr, 8 EB daily; US$2, 1½hr, Servicio Mixto de Río Grande buses from El Crucero every 20mins from 5am-7pm)

Colón also runs two daily buses each to Tuxtla Gutiérrez (US$25, 12 hours), San Cristóbal de Las Casas (US$28, 14 hours) and one to Mexico City via highways 200 and 190 (US$42, 18 hours). EB goes to Mexico City (US$40, 12 hours) via Hwy 200, northwest from Puerto. Colón and EB go to Salina Cruz (US$9-10, five hours), and Colón runs to Juchitán (US$13, six hours).

Warning: keep a particularly close eye on your baggage when going to or from Acapulco and be sure to get a ticket for any bags placed in the baggage hold.

CAR & MOTORCYCLE

Budget (☎ 582-03-12; Blvd Juárez, Bacocho), opposite the tourist office, charges US$72 a day for its cheapest cars, including unlimited kilometers and insurance. **Alamo** (☎ /fax 582-30-03; Av Pérez Gasga 113) has similar prices.

Getting Around

The **airport** (☎ 582-04-92) is 4km west of the center on the north side of Hwy 200. A taxi costs around US$2.50, if you can find one (look on the main road outside the airport). Otherwise, colectivo combis (US$4 per person) will drop you anywhere in town. You should have no problem finding a taxi from town to the airport for about US$2.50.

Taxis and *lanchas* are the only available transportation between the central Av Pérez Gasga/Bahía Principal area and the outlying beaches if you don't want to walk. Taxis wait at each end of El Adoquín. The standard fare to Playa Zicatela is US$2.

AROUND PUERTO ESCONDIDO

Laguna Manialtepec

This lake, 6km long, begins 14km west of Puerto Escondido along Hwy 200. It's home to ibis, roseate spoonbills, parrots, pelicans and several species of hawk, falcon, osprey, egret, heron, kingfisher and iguana. The best months for observing birds are December to March, and they're best seen in the early morning. The lagoon is mainly surrounded by mangroves, but tropical flowers and palms accent the ocean side.

Several restaurants along the lake's north shore (just off Hwy 200) run boat trips on the lake. To reach these places from Puerto Escondido, take a Río Grande-bound microbus from 2 Norte just east of the Carretera Costera, in the upper part of town, leaving every half hour from 6am to 7pm (US$0.30).

Restaurant Isla del Gallo (halfway along lake; 2hr trip for up to 10 people US$31-41; colectivo service 8am-5pm in peak tourism periods per person US$6; kayak rental per hr US$5.50) offers shaded boat trips and the boatmen know their birds. Good grilled fish and seafood are available at the restaurant for US$5 to US$8.

Puesta del Sol (toward west end of lake; 2½hr trip for up to 5 people US$37; colectivo service per person US$6.50) is another recommended embarkation point. Fish and prawn dishes here cost US$5.50 to US$7.

A good guide speaking your language can greatly enhance your experience. Several four-to-five-hour options are available from Puerto Escondido.

Hidden Voyages Ecotours (☎ 954-582-15-51; www.wincom.net/~pelewing; Viajes Dimar, Av Pérez Gasga 905B; 5hr morning & 4hr sunset tours for 4-10 people Dec

1-Apr 1, per person US$35) offers highly recommended trips run by knowledgeable Canadian ornithologist Michael Malone.

Ana's Ecotours (☎ 954-582-29-54; Un Tigre Azul, Av Pérez Gasga; 4-hr trips per person US$32), run by Jamiltepeca Ana Márquez, an excellent, English-speaking local guide, provides enjoyable Manialtepec tours year-round. You can go in a motorized dug-out (minimum four people) or by kayak (minimum two people).

Bajos de Chila

The Mixtec ball game (pelota mixteca), a five-a-side team sport descended from the pre-Hispanic ritual ball game, is played at 3pm every Saturday in the village of Bajos de Chila, 10km west of Puerto Escondido along Hwy 200. If this living relic of Mexico's ancient culture sparks your curiosity, wander along and have a look. The playing field, called the *patio* or *pasador*, is easy to find in the village. Colectivos to Bajos de Chila (US$0.40, 15 minutes) leave about every 30 minutes from 2 Norte just east of the Carretera Costera, in the upper part of Puerto Escondido. For more on the ball game, see p56.

Barra de Navidad

The Los Naranjos and Palmazola coastal lagoons, near this village 6km southeast of Puerto Escondido along Hwy 200, offer another chance to get close to the abundant bird life of the Oaxaca coast – and to the local crocodile population. Villagers have formed a society to protect the lagoons and offer guided visits (US$12) lasting about 1¼ hours, including a half-hour boat ride, best in the early morning or late afternoon. Unaccompanied visits are not permitted. Barra de Navidad is a short walk south from Hwy 200 on the east side of the Río Colotepec bridge; take a 'La Barra' colectivo from the highway at the east end of Av Pérez Gasga in Puerto.

Other Destinations

The mainly Mixtec town of **Jamiltepec**, 105km west of Puerto Escondido on Hwy 200, holds a colorful Sunday market with many people in traditional clothing.

The town of **Nopala**, about 35km northwest of Puerto Escondido off Hwy 131, is set in the foothills of the Sierra Madre del

Sur in the indigenous Chatino region. You can visit organic coffee plantations and see ancient steles, and a display of local archaeology and Chatino culture in the Palacio Municipal. In winter, the owners of Tabachín del Puerto (p741) open the pleasant Posada Nopala there.

Ana's Ecotours (see earlier) offers day trips to these destinations for around US$34 per person, usually with a minimum of four people.

LAGUNAS DE CHACAHUA

Hwy 200, heading west from Puerto Escondido toward Acapulco, runs along behind a coast studded with lagoons, pristine beaches and prolific bird and plant life. The population in this region includes many descendants of African slaves who escaped from the Spanish.

The area around the coastal lagoons of Chacahua and La Pastoría forms the beautiful **Parque Nacional Lagunas de Chacahua**. Birds from Alaska and Canada migrate here in winter. Mangrove-fringed islands harbor roseate spoonbills, ibis, cormorants, wood storks, herons and egrets, as well as mahogany trees, crocodiles and turtles. El Corral, a mangrove-lined waterway filled with countless birds in winter, connects the two lagoons.

It's fun to get to Chacahua on your own (see p748); an independent day trip from Puerto Escondido is quite feasible.

Zapotalito

Sixty kilometers from Puerto Escondido, a 5km road leads south from Hwy 200 to Zapotalito, a small fishing village at the eastern end of La Pastoría lagoon. A few simple restaurants flank the lagoon. A cooperative here runs four-hour *lancha* tours of the lagoons, costing US$72 for up to 10 people. The trips visit islands, channels to the ocean and the fishing village of Chacahua, at the western end of the park.

The simplest one-way route from Zapotalito to Chacahua village is by a combination of colectivo *lancha* and camioneta (pickup), for US$3. You travel 15 minutes across the lagoon from Zapotalito to meet with a camioneta that will make the half-hour trip along the spit to Chacahua. *Lanchas* leave Zapotalito at 8:30am and 10:30am and 1:30pm, 3:30pm and 5:30pm

daily. Their departure point is 300m further around the shore beyond the *lancha* tours departure point. This route is adventurous but misses out on the delights of the Lagunas de Chacahua. Direct colectivo boats to Chacahua village (US$4 to US$8 per person, 25km, 45 minutes), which take you the full length of the lagoons, also leave from 300m beyond the *lancha* tours departure point, but they have no schedule: they leave when they have seven or eight passengers so you may have a long wait, and negotiating the price could be problematic. You should be able to return to Zapotalito by colectivo boat but you need to allow for waiting time. If this fails, take the last afternoon camioneta. Check its departure time before you settle in for the day!

Chacahua

Chacahua village straddles the channel that connects the west end of Chacahua lagoon to the ocean. The ocean side of the village, fronting a wonderful beach, is a perfect place to bliss out. The waves here can be good for surfers, but there are some strong currents; check where it's safe to swim. The inland half of the village contains a crocodile-breeding center with a sad-looking collection of creatures kept for protection and reproduction. Chacahua's croc population (not human-eating) has been decimated by hunters.

Tours

Several Puerto Escondido agencies offer good day trips, including **Hidden Voyages Ecotours** (US$37 per person; Thu only Dec-Mar) and **Ana's Ecotours** (US$37 per person, minimum 6; daily). See earlier for contact details.

Sleeping & Eating

Several places along the beach at Chacahua village offer basic cabañas. You can sling a hammock or camp for free if you eat at a particular establishment. However, this arrangement is not exactly secure, and some readers have complained of theft. There are no phone numbers and addresses for these places.

Restaurante Siete Mares (cabañas s/d US$7.50/11; main dishes US$5.50-7.50) The Siete Mares, at the west end of the beach, prepares phenomenal fish and seafood meals. It has some of Chacahua's better cabañas, 300m away along the beach, with two beds, fans, nets and clean bathrooms. The señora here will lock up your valuables.

Cabañas Los Almendros (r or cabañas US$9-31) The waters of the lagoon lap against this place, just two minutes' walk from the beach, run by a friendly young couple. It ain't luxury but is fine. There are three cabañas and a couple of other rooms – the upstairs cabaña is the pick of the bunch. The shared bathroom is acceptable.

Getting There & Away
From Puerto Escondido, you first have to get to the town of Río Grande, 50km west on Hwy 200. Río Grande–bound microbuses (US$1.50, one hour) leave 2 Norte just east of the Carretera Costera, in the upper part of Puerto Escondido, about every half hour. All Estrella Blanca buses between Puerto Escondido and Acapulco stop at Río Grande too. From the microbus stop in Río Grande, cross the road and get a colectivo taxi (US$1) to Zapotalito, 14km southwest. For information on getting from Zapotalito to Chacahua, see p747.

Chacahua village is linked to San José del Progreso, 29km north on Hwy 200, by a sandy track that is impassable in the wet season. Three camionetas travel this route daily (US$2.75) when possible.

PINOTEPA NACIONAL
☎ 954 / pop 23,000
This is the biggest town between Puerto Escondido (140km east) and Acapulco (260km west). To the southwest there's a fine beach, **Playa Corralero**, near the mouth of Laguna Corralero (from 'Pino' go about 25km west on Hwy 200, then some 15km southeast). You can stay in palapas at Corralero village; two camionetas run there daily from Pinotepa. Pinotepa is a good base for exploring the surrounding area's small towns and villages, famous for crafts such as wooden masks and traditional, colorful, embroidered garments.

Hotel Marissa (☎ 543-21-01; Av Juárez 134; s/d US$14/15, with air-con US$19/25; **P** **※**), half a block east of Pino's central plaza, this hotel has small, clean rooms with hot-water bathroom and fan.

Hotel Carmona (☎ 543-23-22; Porfirio Díaz 401; s/d US$16/22, with air-con US$23/32; **※** **※**), on the main road about 500m west of the main

plaza, is the best in Pino. Rooms have hot-water bathroom and TV.

All Estrella Blanca buses between Puerto Escondido and Acapulco stop at Pinotepa. From here it's three hours to Puerto Escondido (1st-class/ordinario US$6.50/4.50) and five to 6½ hours to Acapulco (1st-class/ordinario US$9/8.50). First-class Cristóbal Colón buses and 2nd-class Fletes y Pasajes buses travel north on Hwy 125 through the Mixteca, some reaching Oaxaca that way.

POCHUTLA
☎ 958 / pop 11,000
This bustling, sweaty market town is the starting point for transportation to the nearby beach spots Puerto Ángel, Zipolite, San Agustinillo and Mazunte. It also has the nearest banks to those places.

Orientation
Hwy 175 from Oaxaca runs through Pochutla as Cárdenas, the narrow north–south main street, and meets the coastal Hwy 200 about 1.5km south of town. Hotel Izala marks the approximate midpoint of Cárdenas. Long-distance bus stations cluster on Cárdenas around 300m to 400m south of the Izala. The main square, Plaza de la Constitución, is a block east of the Izala along Juárez.

Information
At least four banks – Scotiabank Inverlat, Bital and Bancomer, in south–north order on Cárdenas, and Banamex on Plaza de la Constitución – have ATMs, though it's quite possible to find none of the machines providing money at any given moment. Bital changes traveler's checks and US dollars from 8am to 7pm Monday to Friday, and 8am to 3pm Saturday. Bital also provides over-the-counter Visa-card cash advances (take your passport).

The **post office** (Cárdenas; ※ 8am-3pm Mon-Fri) is opposite Hotel Santa Cruz (see following). **Caseta Cybeltel** (Cárdenas 62; ※ 7am-10pm), almost opposite the Hotel Izala, offers 60 minutes' Internet access for US$1, plus long-distance telephone service.

Sleeping & Eating
Hotel Costa del Sol (☎ 584-03-18; fax 584-00-49; Cárdenas 47; s/d US$19/21; **P** **※**) Pochutla's best central hotel, 1½ blocks north of the Izala,

has a few artistic touches and some greenery. Rooms have pleasant tiled bathrooms, hot water and cable TV.

Hotel Izala (☎ 584-01-15; Cárdenas 59; s/d US$14/32, with air-con US$23/44; **P** **✗**) The Izala offers plain, clean rooms, with bathroom and cable TV, on two levels around a leafy courtyard.

Hotel Santa Cruz (☎ /fax 584-01-16; Cárdenas s/n; s/d US$9/11, with air-con US$14/19; **✗**) The Santa Cruz has simple, good-sized, adequate rooms with bathroom and fan. It's situated about 150m north of the main cluster of bus stations.

Restaurant y Marisquería Los Ángeles (Cárdenas s/n; mains US$4-9; ☼ 7am-8pm Mon-Sat) This little upstairs place near the Cólon bus station is recommended.

Getting There & Away

The three main bus stations, in north–south order near the south end of Cárdenas, are Estrella Blanca (EB, 2nd-class) on the west side of the street, Estrella del Valle/Oaxaca Pacífico (EV/OP, 2nd-class) on the east side, and Cristóbal Colón (1st-class) on the west side.

OAXACA

Oaxaca is 245km away by Hwy 175 (six to seven hours) or 450km by the better highways 200 and 190 (via Salina Cruz, nine hours). At the time of research Colón had two daily buses by the Salina Cruz route (US$17) – but schedules and routings are changeable. Thirteen or so daily EV/OP buses take Hwy 175 (ordinario/directo US$6.50/8.50). **Autoexprés Atlántida** (☎ 584-01-16; Hotel Santa Cruz, Cárdenas s/n) runs nine daily air-conditioned Chevrolet Suburban vans, taking up to 14 people, by Hwy 175 (US$11, 6½ hours). Vans leave Pochutla at 4am, 7:45am and 11am and 12:30pm, 2:30pm, 4pm, 5:30pm, 8:45pm and 11pm. You can reserve by phone and pay one hour beforehand.

PUERTO ÁNGEL & NEARBY COAST

Transportation services to the nearby coast change frequently. When things are going well, frequent buses, camionetas and colectivo taxis run along the paved road from Pochutla to Puerto Ángel, Zipolite, San Agustinillo and Mazunte between 7am and 7pm, usually starting at the EV/OP station or nearby on Cárdenas. At the time of writing, camioneta service through Puerto Ángel was suspended but frequent colectivo taxis going to Puerto Ángel (US$0.90, 13km, 20 minutes), Zipolite (US$1.50, 30 minutes), San Agustinillo (US$2, 40 minutes) and Mazunte (US$2, 45 minutes) were leaving from a stand on Cárdenas 200m north of the EB bus station. For Zipolite, San Agustinillo and Mazunte, camionetas leave frequently from beside Ferretería RoGa, on Cárdenas 300m north of the Hotel Izala. These go via San Antonio on Hwy 200 northwest of Mazunte (not via Puerto Ángel) and are quicker than the colectivo taxis for Mazunte (US$0.90, 30 minutes) and San Agustinillo (US$0.90, 35 minutes), though longer for Zipolite (US$1.25, 45 minutes).

In addition, a big old bus rattles between Pochutla and Mazunte (via Puerto Ángel) hourly from 7am to 7pm, and a few camionetas operate between Pochutla and Puerto Ángel (US$0.75, supposedly hourly). Private cabs cost US$5 to Puerto Ángel, US$8 to Zipolite and US$9 to San Agustinillo or Mazunte.

OTHER DESTINATIONS

Daily bus departures include:

Acapulco EB (US$22 semi-directo, 8-10hr, 5 daily)

Bahías de Huatulco Colón (US$2.25, 1hr, 8 daily); EB (US$2.25, 1hr, 5 daily); Sur (US$1.25, 1hr, every 40min, from outside Cólon); Transportes Rápidos de Pochutla (US$1.25, 1hr, buses every 15min 5:30am-8pm, from yard opposite EB)

Puerto Escondido Colón (US$3, 1½hr, 5 daily); EB (US$3 semi-directo, 1½hr, 4 daily); Sur (US$2.50, 1½hr, hourly 7:30am-7:30pm); Servicio Mixto de Río Grande (US$2, 1½hr, buses every 20min 5am-7pm, from Allende, one block south and half a block east of Hotel Izala)

San Cristóbal de Las Casas Colón (US$25, 11hr, 2 daily)

Tuxtla Gutiérrez Colón (US$21, 10hr, 2 daily)

Colón runs buses to Salina Cruz (US$8), Tehuantepec (US$9) and Juchitán (US$10). EB also serves Salina Cruz. Both of these companies go to Mexico City (US$35 to US$42).

PUERTO ÁNGEL

☎ 958 / pop 3000

The small fishing town, naval base and travelers' hangout of Puerto Ángel (*pwerr-toh ahn-hel*) straggles around a picturesque bay between two rocky headlands, 13km south of Pochutla. Many travelers prefer to stay out on the beaches a few kilometers west at Zipolite, San Agustinillo or Mazunte, but the marginally more urban Puerto Ángel is a good base too. It offers its own little beaches, some excellent places to stay and eat, and easy transportation to/from Zipolite.

Orientation

The road from Pochutla emerges at the east end of the small Bahía de Puerto Ángel. The road winds around the back of the bay, over an often-dry *arroyo* (creek) and up a hill. It then forks – right to Zipolite and Mazunte, left down to Playa del Panteón. The road is mostly called Blvd Uribe within the town.

Information

Banks Nearest banks are in Pochutla, but several accommodations and restaurants will change cash or traveler's checks at their own rates.

Casa Arnel (Internet access per hr US$1.50) See Sleeping, following.

Caseta Telefónica Lila (Blvd Uribe) Has Internet, phone and fax service.

Farmacia El Ángel (☎ 584-30-58; Vasconcelos) The *simpático* Dr Constancio Aparicio is a doctor recommended by foreign residents. He's based here mornings only.

G@l@p@gos (Blvd Uribe s/n; Internet access per hr US$1.50)

Gel@net (Vasconcelos 3; ⏰ 7am-10pm) Has telephone, fax and Internet (per hr US$1.50).

Post Office (Av Principal; ⏰ 8am-3pm Mon-Fri) East end of town.

Municipal Tourist Office (Blvd Uribe; ⏰ 4-8pm Mon-Fri) In a palapa-roofed building at the entrance to the pier; useful for transportation details.

Dangers & Annoyances

Theft and robbery can be a problem, especially on the Zipolite road.

Beaches

Playa del Panteón, on the west side of Bahía de Puerto Ángel is shallow and calm, and its waters are cleaner than those near the fishers' pier across the bay.

Half a kilometer up the road toward Pochutla, a sign points right along a path to **Playa Estacahuite** 700m away. The three tiny, sandy bays here are all good for snor-

PUERTO ÁNGEL

0 — 200 m
0 — 0.1 miles

INFORMATION	
Caseta Telefónica Lila	1 B2
Farmacia El Ángel	2 C3
G@l@p@gos	3 B2
Gel@net	4 C3
Post Office	5 D3
Tourist Office	6 C3

SIGHTS & ACTIVITIES	(p751)
Azul Profundo	7 A2
Byron Luna	8 A3

SLEEPING	(pp751-2)
Casa Arnel	9 B2
Casa de Huéspedes Gundi y Tomás	10 A2
El Almendro	11 C2
Hotel Cordelia's	12 A2
Hotel Puesta del Sol	13 A2
Hotel Soraya	14 C3
La Buena Vista	15 B1
La Posada Cañon Devata	16 A2
Penelope's	17 A2
Posada Rincón Sabroso	18 C2
Villa Serena Florencia	19 C2

EATING	(p752)
Beto's	20 A2
Casa de Huéspedes El Capy	21 A2
Other Beach Restaurants	(see 22)
Restaurante Susy	22 A3
Rincón del Mar	23 A2

TRANSPORT	(pp752-3)
Bus Stop	24 B2
Bus Stop	25 B2
Taxi Stand	26 C3

OTHER	
Naval Base	27 B2

To Zipolite (2.5km); Mazunte (5km); Puerto Escondido (64km)

To Playa Estacahuite (700m); Playa La Boquilla; Bahía de la Luna (7.5km); Pochutla (12.5km);

Playa Principal

Playa del Panteón

Bahía de Puerto Ángel

Pier

Beach Restaurants

La Playita

Blvd Uribe

Arroyo

Pilo Brilo

Azueta

Vasconcelos

Calle del Trio

Av Principal

keling, but watch out for jellyfish. A couple of shack restaurants serve good, reasonably priced seafood or spaghetti, and should have snorkels to rent.

The coast northeast of Estacahuite is dotted with more good beaches, none of them very busy. A good one is **Playa La Boquilla**, on a small bay about 5km out, site of the Bahía de la Luna accommodations and restaurant (p752). You can get there by a 3.5km road from a turnoff 4km out of Puerto Ángel on the road toward Pochutla. A taxi from Puerto Ángel costs US$4.50 each way, but it's more fun to go by boat – you can get a fisher to take a few people from Playa Panteón or from the pier across the bay for around US$11 per person, including a return trip at an agreed time.

Activities
Snorkeling and **fishing** are popular and you can go **diving** too. The drops and canyons out to sea from Puerto Ángel are suitable for very deep dives; another dive is to a ship wrecked in 1870.

Some of the café-restaurants on Playa del Panteón rent snorkel gear (US$2.75/6.75 per hour/day). **Byron Luna** (☎ 584-31-15; 3hr trips US$54 for 4-5 people) offers snorkeling and fishing trips to four beaches. Byron is great fun and enjoys spotting dolphins, orcas and turtles. Look for him at his home next to Restaurant Susy. **Azul Profundo** (☎ 584-31-09; azul_profundomx@hot:mail.com; Playa del Panteón; 4hr snorkeling trips per person US$10; fishing trips per person per hr US$31), run by friendly Chepe, offers snorkeling, fishing and dives at all levels. One-tank dives cost US$37, and two-tank dives US$64. A first-timer session costs US$37 and a seven-day PADI course US$328.

Sleeping
Places with an elevated location are more likely to catch any breeze. Mosquito screens are a big plus too. Some places have a water shortage.

La Posada Cañon Devata (☎ 584-31-37; www .posadapacifico.com; off Saenz de Barandas; s/d with fan US$20/31, 2-room units for 2 US$39-46, extra adult US$3; [P]) On a hillside behind Playa del Panteón, the friendly Cañon Devata has a variety of attractive accommodations scattered among foliage. Run by the ecologically minded López family, it's a good place for those seeking a quiet retreat. Fine Mexican and

vegetarian food, prepared in a super-clean kitchen, is available. There's a security box.

Casa de Huéspedes Gundi y Tomás (☎ 584-30-68; www.puertoangel-hotel.com; off Blvd Uribe; s/d US$11/14-20) Owned by Gundi, the same friendly German woman as El Almendro (below), this tranquil guesthouse has a variety of brightly decorated rooms, all with fans, mosquito nets and/or screens, and some off-beat artistic touches. Good food is available, including homemade bread, mainly vegetarian snacks, and fruit drinks. Dishes cost less than US$3. The main dining area and one clutch of rooms have outstanding views. There's a safe for valuables, an exchange service for cash or traveler's checks, and airport transportation.

La Buena Vista (☎ /fax 584-31-04; www.labuena vista.com; La Buena Compañía s/n; d US$35-48; extra person US$6) The 19 big rooms and five excellent mud-brick bungalows on this verdant property are kept scrupulously clean. All have private bathrooms with pretty Talavera tiles, fans, mosquito screens and breezy balconies with hammocks. Wood is cleverly used throughout. There's a good restaurant on an expansive terrace.

Hotel Puesta del Sol (☎ /fax 584-30-96; www .puertoangel.net; Bvd Uribe s/n; s/d with shared bathroom US$10/12, d with private bathroom US$14-26; [🖳]) The friendly German/Mexican-owned Puesta del Sol offers sizable, clean rooms with fans and screens. Some sleep up to six people. The more expensive ones have their own terraces and hot-water bathroom. The sitting room has a small library and satellite TV. Hammocks on a breezy terrace invite relaxation. Breakfast is available.

El Almendro (☎ 584-30-68; www.puertoangel hotel.com; off Bvd Uribe; s/d US$16/23) Set in a shady garden up a little lane a few meters past the Rincón Sabroso (p752) steps, El Almendro has six clean, brightly painted rooms, plus a bungalow for up to six people. From November to April, the 6pm to 7pm happy hour is followed by a barbeque dinner of marinaded meats or fish, salad from the salad bar and baked potatoes (US$5).

Penelope's (☎ 584-30-73; Cerrada de la Luna s/n; s/d US$17/28) Penelope's, with just four rooms, is set in a quiet, leafy neighborhood high above Playa del Panteón. It's just off the Zipolite road, clearly signposted a couple of hundred meters beyond the fork to Playa del Panteón. The clean, spacious rooms nave hot-water bathroom, fan and mosquito screens. There's an attractive terrace restaurant with economical meals prepared by the attentive owner.

Bahía de la Luna (☎ 584-61-86; www.totalmedia .qc.ca/bahiadelaluna in Spanish; Playa La Boquilla; s/d/tr from US$37/41/46; P) This Canadian-owned tropical hideaway out at gorgeous Playa La Boquilla (see p750), has attractive adobe bungalows set on a tree-filled hillside overlooking the beach. A five-person bungalow costs US$63, and there's a house (one-to-eight people) for US$164. It also has a good beachside restaurant-café with moderate prices. Inner development workshops in yoga, astrology, stress control and dream interpretation are offered here.

Hotel Cordelia's (☎ 584-31-09; Playa Panteón; s/d US$23/46; P) Cordelia's is a new hotel right in the middle of this lovely beach. Run by the same family as the Azul Profundo dive shop, it has eight fan-cooled rooms, four of which are spacious with good-sized Talavera-tiled bathrooms, and terraces overlooking the sea.

Casa Arnel (☎ /fax 584-30-51; www.oaxaca.com.mx /arnel; Azueta 666; s/d US$15/17; 🖵) Casa Arnel is along the lane past the market. Owned by the sister of Arnel from the popular Hotel Casa Arnel in Oaxaca, it has five clean, ample rooms with fan. *Refrescos*, coffee and tea are available, and there's a hammock area.

Villa Serena Florencia (☎ /fax 584-30-44; villa serenaoax@hotmail.com; Bvd Uribe s/n; s/d US$23/32, aircon US$3 extra) The Florencia has 13 pleasant but smallish rooms with fans and screens, all set off a couple of walkways. There's a cool sitting area.

Hotel Soraya (☎ 584-30-09; Vasconcelos s/n; s US$13-22, d US$18-27, s/d with air-con US$32/37; P 🌂) Overlooking the pier, the Soraya's 32 rooms with fan and TV are clean though a bit rundown and musty. All have a balcony and the more expensive have good views and hot-water bathroom. Admin is hip.

Posada Rincón Sabroso (☎ 584-30-95; Bvd Uribe s/n; s/d US$8/11) This greenery-shaded hotel is up a flight of stairs from the street. It has 10 plain, fan-cooled rooms with mosquito screens. The tiled terraces strung with hammocks are pretty and the views stunning.

Eating & Drinking

La Buena Vista (☎ /fax 584-31-04; La Buena Compañía s/n; breakfast US$3.75-4.25, dinner US$5.50-8.50; 🌂 Mon-Sat) Be sure to pre-book dinner out of the high seasons! On an airy terrace overlooking the bay, La Buena Vista's restaurant offers well-prepared Mexican and American fare, from hotcakes to *chiles rellenos* with a *quesillo* (Oaxacan cheese) filling. A barbeque and a brick pizza oven fill out the menu choices.

Posada Cañon Devata (☎ 584-31-37; off Saenz de Barandas; dinner US$9, in high season US$11; 🌂 breakfast 8:30am-noon, dinner from 7:30pm) Outsiders are welcome here. A good three-course dinner is served at long tables in a lovely palm-roofed, open-sided dining room. Fare is Mexican and whole-food vegetarian. Book early in the day.

Rincón del Mar (above walkway to Playa del Panteón; dishes US$2.25-6) This place has top views from its cliffside location, reached by steps up from the walkway. The food's good too. Don't miss the house specialty, *filete a la cazuela*, prepared with olives, peas, onions and tomatoes.

Villa Serena Florencia (☎ /fax 584-30-44; Bvd Uribe s/n; dishes US$2.25-7) This Italian restaurant, a reliable standby, manages to turn out good pasta dishes, salads, Mexican fare and pizzas. Breakfasts are inexpensive. You can sip a wine or a cocktail here too.

Beto's (Bvd Uribe s/n; fish fillets US$6.50, ceviche US$4.50) On the uphill stretch of Blvd Uribe, Beto's is a reliable, friendly and clean little place with a large terrace.

Casa de Huéspedes El Capy (☎ 584-30-02; Carretera Playa del Panteón; dishes US$2-5.50) This terrace restaurant with sea views is best in the cool of the evening. The long menu includes fish, shrimp, chicken, meat and salads.

The restaurants on Playa del Panteón offer fish and seafood for US$5 to US$11, plus cheaper fare such as *entomatadas* and eggs. Be careful about the freshness of seafood in the low season. The setting is very pretty after dark. **Restaurante Susy** (☎ 584-30-19) is one of the better beachside establishments.

You'll also find several economical places to eat on the main town beach, though none is very well frequented.

Getting There & Away

See p749 for details of transportation from Pochutla. A taxi to or from Zipolite costs US$0.65 colectivo, or US$3.75 for the whole cab (US$5 after dark and even more after

10pm or 11pm). You can find cabs on Blvd Uribe; there's a stand at the corner of Vasconcelos.

A taxi to Huatulco airport costs US$31, to Puerto Escondido airport US$42.

ZIPOLITE

☎ 958 / pop 800

The beautiful 1.5km stretch of pale sand called Zipolite, beginning about 2.5km west of Puerto Ángel, is fabled as southern Mexico's perfect place to lie back and do as little as you like, in as little as you like, for as little as you like (well, almost).

Once just a small fishing settlement with a few comedores, Zipolite has grown in recent years. Budget places to stay and eat now line nearly the whole beach, but most are still reassuringly ramshackle and wooden. Some have incredible conical thatched roofs.

Zipolite is as great a place as ever to take it easy, with a magical combination of pounding sea and sun, open-air sleeping, eating and drinking, unique scenery and the travelers' scene. It's the kind of place where you may find yourself postponing departure over and over again. The cluster of larger establishments toward the beach's west end is the hub of Zipolite for many, but there's plenty of room elsewhere if you want to really chill out.

Total nudity is more common at the west end of the beach.

Orientation

The eastern end of Zipolite (nearest Puerto Ángel) is called Colonia Playa del Amor, the middle part is Centro, and the area toward the western end (divided from Centro by a narrow lagoon-cum-creek) is Colonia Roca Blanca. The few streets behind the beach are mostly nameless; Av Roca Blanca, a block back from the beach in Colonia Roca Blanca, is the most prominent and is now fancily paved like the Adoquín in Puerto Escondido.

Information

Banks Nearest banks are in Pochutla, but some accommodations may cash US dollars.

Caseta Oceana (Av Roca Blanca) Has long-distance phone service.

Lavandería Yamile (US$1.25 a kilo same-day laundry service; ⏰ 10am-8pm Mon-Sat) On the main road east of Casa de Huéspedes Lyoban (see following).

Zipolnet (Internet per hr US$1.50; ⏰ 9am-9pm) Just round the corner from Av Roca Blanca; has Internet service and long-distance phone service.

Dangers & Annoyances

Beware: the Zipolite surf is deadly, literally. It's fraught with riptides, changing currents and a strong undertow. Locals don't swim here, and going in deeper than your knees can be risking your life. Most years several people drown here. Local voluntary lifeguards (*salvavidas*) have rescued many, but they don't maintain a permanent watch. If you do get swept out to sea, your best hope is to try to swim calmly parallel to the shore to get clear of the current pulling you outward.

Theft can be a problem here, and it's not advisable to walk along the Puerto Ángel–Zipolite road after dark.

Sleeping

Most Zipolite accommodations are right on the beach, where nearly every building rents small rooms, cabañas or hammocks. Wander along and pick one that suits you – it makes sense to choose one where your belongings can be locked up. Rooms here do not have private bathrooms unless stated.

El Alquimista (info@el-alquimista.com; west end Playa Zipolite; d US$28-32) Attached to one of Zipolite's best restaurants, this place has the five best rooms (three with views) on the beach. Each has bathroom, fan and mosquito net, contemporary lampshades and homespun textiles.

Solstice (www.solstice-mexico.com; Colonia Playa del Amor; dm without/with breakfast US$8/11, studio US$23, bungalow US$33, loft US$20) This excellent, friendly, Dutch-owned retreat, set back from the east end of the beach, specializes in yoga courses. Conical-roofed bungalows, studios and dorm accommodations are set around a central space; décor is bright and homey. Bathrooms have an Asian-style *mandi* for splashing water. The yoga room is large and inviting. Book ahead as there may be a group retreat.

Las Casitas (☎ 584-31-51; www.las-casitas.net; btwn Lo Cósmico & Shambala, west end Playa Zipolite; bungalows s US$11, d US$15-22, t US$26) These tasteful, solar-powered bungalows set 100m above El Alquimista have private bathrooms, kitchens and good views. Meals in the beautifully sited restaurant cost from US$20. Airport transportation can be arranged.

Lo Cósmico (www.locosmico.com/en/index.htm; west end Playa Zipolite; d cabañas US$9-19, extra person US$3, hammocks US$3) This place is truly cosmic! The far-out conical-roofed cabañas of Mexican/Swiss-owned Lo Cósmico are dotted around a tall rock outcrop near the west end of the beach. Each cabaña has a double bed, hammock, fan and net; the cheaper ones are a bit enclosed while the pricier ones have two floors and views. The hammock area is on a clifftop overlooking the beach. A security box is available and there's a good restaurant too!

Brisa Marina (☎ 584-31-93; brisamarina@prodigy .net.mx; Colonia Roca Blanca; d US$ 6.50-9, with bathroom US$9.50-17; P) Slap-bang in the center of things, this popular, three-story, American-owned place caters for a range of budgets. Out back in a wooden section are the cheaper rooms. More expensive rooms with bathroom and fan, some with views, occupy a concrete building fronting the beach – these have cemented-in safes, though there is also a common safe.

La Choza (☎ 584-31-90; www.geocities.com/lachoza .mx; Colonia Roca Blanca; r US$9, with bathroom US$14) La Choza is also large and substantial for Zipolite. The bare but decent rooms have fans and screens. A sea-front 'suite' (US$37) holds up to five people. There is 24-hour security and valuables can be locked away for you. Prices more than double at peak times. At the front is one of the beach's most popular restaurants.

El Eclipse (Colonia Roca Blanca; cabañas US$14-19) Rebuilt after Hurricane Pauline (1997) and again after a fire in 2001, this popular Mexican/Italian-run establishment offers cabañas with and without sea views. Don't miss the excellent restaurant.

Tao (☎ 584-31-95; www.geocities.com/zipolite_tao /Zipolite.html in Spanish; Colonia Roca Blanca; cabañas US$14-26) This popular, well-kept, rustic place has four upper-level cabañas with sea views and some acceptable ground-level rooms.

Casa de Huéspedes Lyoban (☎ 584-31-77; www .lyoban.com.mx; Colonia Playa del Amor; hammock US$4.75, s/d/tr US$9.25/14/18, d with private bathroom US$28) Young travelers love this place; it has basic, clean accommodations and a sociable bar-restaurant area with board games, pool table and library. The hammock price includes a blanket, a sturdy locker and shower usage.

Shambhala Posada (Casa Gloria; ☎ 584-31-53; www.cepulihtoa.com; west end Playa Zipolite; hammock US$2, s US$5.50, d US$7-9; P) The popular, long-established, ecologically run Shambhala climbs the hill at the west end of the beach, with great views back along it. Rooms have mosquito nets. The shared bathrooms are OK. Shambhala has a restaurant and a luggage room to keep your stuff safe; there's a meditation area.

Lola's (☎ 584-32-01; Colonia Playa del Amor; s/d US$11/14; P) Second from the east end of the beach, friendly Lola's has 25 reasonable rooms on two levels of a tiled-roof building. Rooms have private bathroom, fan and mosquito screens. There's also a popular restaurant.

Posada San Cristóbal (☎ 584-31-91; Colonia Roca Blanca; r US$9.50, with bathroom US$14) The San Cristóbal provides bare accommodations with double bed, net and fan, alongside a leafy garden. It has a reliable beachside restaurant.

Chololo's (☎ 584-31-59; www.prodigyweb.net.mx /genarino in Spanish; Colonia Playa del Amor; r US$13, with private bathroom US$14; P) Chololo's, with a new roof and just a few simple rooms, is the easternmost place on the beach. Its friendly Mexican and Italian hosts, Guille and Genaro, prepare good Mexican and Italian food – including pizzas cooked in a brick oven.

Cabañas Zipolite (☎ 584-32-13; Colonia Roca Blanca; s/d cabañas US$6.50/7.50) These ramshackle basic wooden accommodations with mosquito nets and shared bathrooms are next door to La Choza. There is a security box. Prices almost double at peak times.

Trailer Park Las Palmeras (Fernando's Camp Ground, Carretera Puerto Ángel-Zipolite; person, tent or vehicle US$2; P) This small park, beside the road from Puerto Ángel as you enter Zipolite, has a grassy plot edged with trees. Rates include electrical hookups, showers and toilets, water for washing and 24-hour caretaking.

Eating

Eating and drinking in the open air a few steps from the surf is an inimitable Zipolite experience. Most accommodations have a restaurant of some kind, and there are also some good independent places. Most of the best eateries are toward the west end of the beach and in the streets behind there.

El Eclipse (Colonia Roca Blanca; mains US$4.50-9; ☾ closed Tue) With candle-lit tables on the beach just west of La Choza, El Eclipse does very good Italian fare. Pasta and pizza cost US$4 to US$6, and seafood and meat a bit more. The friendly Italian hostess whips up a fresh pasta daily. There's wine too.

Buon Vento (on street btwn Av Roca Blanca & the main road; pastas US$3.50-4; ☺ 7am-midnight Thu-Tue) Sample inland Zipolite at this excellent Italian restaurant with good music and subtle vibes. The huge pasta list includes some delicious baked options. Wine costs US$4 to US$18 a bottle.

El Alquimista (west end Playa Zipolite; mains US$4-9) Popular El Alquimista is one of Zipolite's best, with a great site in the cove between Lo Cósmico and Shambhala. The very wide-ranging fare ranges from falafel tortas to good meat and chicken dishes. There's excellent espresso coffee.

La Choza (☎ 584-31-90; Colonia Roca Blanca; mains US$4.50-10) The beachside restaurant here has a wide-ranging menu and does most of it well, with generous servings. Choose grilled meat or fish.

Restaurant Posada San Cristóbal (☎ 584-31-91; Colonia Roca Blanca; dishes US$1.50-11) This popular place offers a wide variety of tasty food, from 20 breakfast items, including *pan francés* (French toast), to antojitos or salads to whole fish, prawns, octopus or chicken.

Pizzeria 3 de Diciembre (along the street opposite Buon Vento; prices US$3.75-5; ☺ 7pm-2am Wed-Sun) The 3 de Diciembre serves not only excellent pizzas but also good pastry pies with fillings such as cauliflower-and-parmesan or baked spinach. It's great for late-night munchies!

Restaurante 2 de Diciembre (back to back with Pizzeria 3 de Diciembre; mains US$5-7.50, wine US$12 a bottle) This local favorite serves fish or meat dishes and salads. Meat cuts are said to be excellent.

Lo Cósmico (west end Playa Zipolite; dishes US$3-5) Lo Cósmico, on the rocks near the end of the beach, has an open-air restaurant with good food from an impeccably clean kitchen. Especially tasty are the crêpes (sweet and savory) and salads.

Peter's Pan (on street btwn Av Roca Blanca & main road; breakfasts US$1.75-4; ☺ 7am-noon Mon-Sat Sep-Jun, 8am-1pm Jul-Aug) The breakfasts here, with fresh wholegrain or white bread from the bakery inside, go well with a visit to Zipolnet (p753) next door.

Piedra de Fuego (along the east of Peter's Pan; mains US$3.75-6, beers US$1; ☺ dinner only in low seasons) At this simple but excellent family-run place, you'll get a generous serving of fish fillet or prawns, served with rice, salad and tortillas. They have four cabañas too.

Drinking

Zipolite's beachfront restaurant-bars have unbeatable locations for drinks around sunset and after dark. Those toward the west end of the beach are generally the most popular – especially **El Alquimista** (see earlier), which plays cool music and serves cocktails as well as the usual beer, mezcal, etc. A swing seat at the bar is fun.

Entertainment

For slightly more active nightlife Zipolite has two open-air *discotecas*, where nothing much happens before midnight (nothing much may happen after midnight either, but you might as well have a look).

La Puesta (☺ 9:30pm-late Mon-Sat Oct-Apr, 9:30pm-late Wed-Sat May-Sep) is next door to Zipolnet in Colonia Roca Blanca; **Zipolipa's** (☺ 10pm-3am Fri-Sat, nightly in high seasons) opens onto the beach next to Casa de Huéspedes Lyoban.

Getting There & Away

See p749 for details on transportation from Pochutla and for transportation from Puerto Ángel. The camionetas from Pochutla via Mazunte and San Agustinillo terminate on the main road at the far west end of Zipolite (about 2km from the east end of the beach). Colectivo taxis from Puerto Ángel will go to the same spot too, but pass along the length of Zipolite en route, so are probably a better bet if you're heading for the east end of the beach.

After dark, a non-colectivo taxi is your only option for getting to Puerto Ángel or San Agustinillo (about US$5 from 6pm until about 10pm, more after that). There's a taxi stand opposite Zipolnet.

SAN AGUSTINILLO
☎ 958

West from Zipolite, other glorious beaches stretch almost unbroken all the way to Puerto Escondido. Long, straight Playa Aragón – in the Zipolite mold, but almost empty – stretches west from the headland at the west end of Zipolite to the tiny but expanding village of San Agustinillo. Footpaths behind Shambhala Posada cross the headland from Zipolite, or you can take the road that loops inland, then comes back down to San Agustinillo (4km from Zipolite).

San Agustinillo is set on a small curved bay, with waves that are perfect for **boogie-boarding** and often good for **body-surfing**. There are several relaxed little places to stay and a line of open-air beach comedores serving mainly seafood. You can rent surfboards and boogie-boards at **México Lindo y qué Rico!** (see Sleeping, below) for US$4.75 and US$2.75 an hour respectively; snorkel gear costs US$2 an hour. **Palapa Olas Altas** (see Sleeping, below) offers *lancha* trips at US$32 an hour (one to five people) for turtle-viewing (and occasionally dolphin-viewing) or fishing. Apapan, the bakery on the main drag, doubles as a laundry.

The coast between Zipolite and Puerto Escondido is a major sea turtle nesting ground. Until hunting and killing sea turtles was banned in Mexico in 1990, San Agustinillo was the site of a gruesome slaughterhouse (now demolished) where some 50,000 turtles were killed per year for their meat and shells.

Sleeping & Eating

México Lindo y qué Rico! (fafinyleila@latinmail.com; west end Playa San Agustinillo; r US$23-28; P) Fourth along from the west end of the beach, México Lindo's six rooms are among San Agustinillo's best – especially the breezy upstairs pair under the tall palapa roof. They're large, with room, fan, double bed and net and a few bright touches like tiled bathrooms and wooden doors. The owners, Fausto and Leila, are young, friendly and serve good food (main dishes US$4 to US$7), including pizzas from a brick oven.

Casamar (☎ 589-24-01; www.costachica.net/san_agustinillo; west end Playa San Agustinillo; r US$37-60; ☒) This friendly place is luxurious by San Agustinillo standards. Its three pretty rooms have salon and equipped kitchen, balcony and private hot-water bathroom. There's a small garden area with a little swimming pool.

Posada Doña Sol (san agustinillo@yahoo.com; main street San Agustinillo; r US$10-23) This unique small hotel established by an American-Mexican couple features an interior garden, the best equipped kitchen imaginable, and a colored glass feature wall. Rooms vary but most

have private hot-water bathroom and one has a kitchen. Owner/chef Ana cooks up a range of delectable dishes (US$7.50) from December to March.

Posada San Agustinillo (Playa Aragón; r US$13-26; P) This fairly unattractive, long, curved concrete block contains 15 excellent-value rooms, each with bathroom, fan, mosquito screens and delicious views.

Palapa Olas Altas (☎ 589-82-70; west end Playa San Agustinillo; r US$8.50-19; main dishes US$4.50-11) Olas Altas has 13 or so palatable rooms, one with sea views. A few have private bathroom while all have mosquito nets and fan. The beachside restaurant serves decent food.

Palapa de Evelia (west end Playa San Agustinillo; main dishes US$5.50-6.50; ☒ 10am-6pm) Evelia's, third along from the west end of the beach, does the best food on the beach, with straightforward but well-prepared fish and seafood, and great guacamole.

Apapan (main street, San Agustinillo; slice of chocolate pie US$1.25; 500g bread US$1.75) This Dutch-run bakery/café prepares breakfasts of wholemeal bread and rolls, fruit salad and yogurt, lunches of bread, salads and soup, sweet pies and pastries. It also sells wine.

Two places have stunning positions atop the steep slope backing Playa Aragón. Both can be reached by drivable tracks from the road or by paths up from the beach.

Rancho Cerro Largo (ranchocerrolargomx@yahoo.com; Playa Aragón; d cabañas incl breakfast & dinner US$64; P) This place has just a handful of superior, fan-cooled cabañas; the meals are excellent.

Rancho Hamacas (☎ 584-05-49; b_silva_mendez@hotmail.com; Playa Aragón; hammocks US$3.50, cabañas US$28; P) Further west on the hilltop from Rancho Cerro Largo, Rancho Hamacas has a couple of adobe cabañas with double bed, mosquito net, fridge and cooker. There's a separate patio for hammock-hanging. The owners make beautiful, strong hammocks (around US$100).

Getting There & Away

See p749 for information about transportation from Pochutla. Camionetas to or from Zipolite or Mazunte cost US$0.50.

MAZUNTE

☎ 958 / pop 450

Like San Agustinillo, Mazunte, 1km further west, grew up around the turtle industry.

When this was banned in 1990, many villagers turned to slash-and-burn cultivation, threatening nearby forests. Encouraged by a Mexico City–based environmental group, Ecosolar, in 1991 Mazunte declared itself an ecological reserve, attempting to preserve the environment while creating a sustainable economy. Projects included printing and natural cosmetics workshops, construction of ecological toilets and garbage separation. A key element was tourism, which the government-funded Centro Mexicano de la Tortuga, opened in 1994, was also intended to encourage. After Hurricane Pauline in 1997, which caused great damage at Mazunte, Ecosolar's influence waned, but by then the village was well established on the tourism map, and today it's a travelers' hangout almost as popular and hip as Zipolite. The waters of the fine, curving, sandy beach are generally safe, though the waves can be quite big.

Orientation & Information

The paved road running west from Zipolite to Hwy 200 passes through the middle of Mazunte. The Centro Mexicano de la Tortuga is beside this main road toward the east end of the village. Three sandy lanes run from the road to the beach (about 500m). The western one is called Camino al Rinconcito, as the west end of the beach is known as El Rinconcito. **Mazunet** (Camino al Rinconcito near main road; per hr US$1.50) offers Internet access.

Sights & Activities

The popular **Centro Mexicano de la Tortuga** (Mexican Turtle Center; ☎ 584-30-55; cmt_mazunte@hotmail.com; admission US$2; ☻ 10am-4:30pm Wed-Sat, 10am-2:30pm Sun) is a turtle aquarium and research center containing specimens of all seven of Mexico's marine turtle species, on view in fairly large tanks. It's enthralling to get a close-up view of these creatures, some of which are BIG! Visits are guided (in Spanish) and start every 10 to 15 minutes. Volunteers are accepted at the center for a minimum stay of one month.

Mazunte's natural cosmetics workshop and store, **Cosméticos Naturales** (☻ 9am-4pm Mon-Sat, 9am-2pm Sun), is by the main road toward the west end of the village. This small cooperative makes excellent shampoo and cosmetics from natural sources such as

maize, coconut, avocado and sesame seeds. It also sells organic coffee, peanut butter and natural mosquito repellents.

Aromatherapy massage and a range of adventure activities are available at **Cabañas Balamjuyuc** (see p758; full body massage per hr US$17). They will take small groups out on 2½-hour boat trips (US$14 per person) to see turtles and dolphins or for snorkeling. Surfboard rental, surfing and kayaking classes and trekking tours are offered too.

PUNTA COMETA

This rocky cape, jutting out from the west end of Mazunte beach, is the southernmost point in the state of Oaxaca and a fabulous place to be at sunset, with great long-distance views in both directions along the coast. You can walk there in 30 minutes over the rocks from the end of Mazunte beach, or take the Camino a Punta Cometa, a path that starts through the woods almost opposite the entrance to Cabañas Balamjuyuc (see p758).

PLAYA VENTANILLA

Some 2.5km along the road west from Mazunte, a sign points left to Playa Ventanilla, 1.2km down a dirt track. The settlement here includes a handful of simple homes, a couple of comedores and the palapa of **Servicios Ecoturísticos La Ventanilla** (1½hr lagoon tours adult/child US$3.75/2; ☻ 8:30am-4:30pm). Servicios Ecoturísticos is a local cooperative providing interesting canoe trips on a mangrove-fringed lagoon, the Estero de la Ventanilla, a few hundred meters along the beach. You'll see river crocodiles (there are about 200 in the lagoon), lots of water birds (most prolific during July and August) and, in an enclosure on an island in the lagoon, a few white-tailed deer. Servicios Ecoturísticos also offers three-hour horseback rides (US$13.50) to another lagoon further west.

A camioneta runs every two hours from Mazunte to Playa Ventanilla but frequent camionetas pass the turnoff, leaving you with the 1.2km walk. A taxi from Mazunte costs US$2.50.

Sleeping

Most places along Playa Mazunte (including restaurants) have basic rooms or cabañas, hammocks to rent and often tent space. Bathrooms are shared unless otherwise stated. Security can be a problem here. You'll find information on nearly all these places at www.costachica.net/mazunte.

Alta Mira (☎ /fax 584-31-04; www.labuenavista.com/alta_mira; Camino a Punta Cometa; d with private bathroom US$32-37; ℗) The Alta Mira is run by the people from La Buena Vista at Puerto Ángel, and its 10 rooms are Mazunte's classiest and comfiest, all with beautiful Talavera-tiled bathrooms, mosquito nets and terrace with hammock. They're strung beside steps leading down the hillside, and most catch some breeze and excellent views. Alta Mira is 500m up from Camino al Rinconcito (signposted). You can also get there by steps up from El Rinconcito beach. The restaurant serves breakfast and dinner, and there's a safety box.

Cabañas Balamjuyuc (http://perso.wanadoo.fr/balam in French; Camino a Punta Cometa; s/d US$9/18, d with view US$27; breakfast US$2.50, dinner US$6; ℗) Balamjuyuc is perched on a hilltop above the west end of the beach, with superb views. Next door to Alta Mira, about 400m from Camino al Rinconcito, it has the same approach routes including steps up from the beach. A friendly French couple manage this quiet tree-covered property, which uses solar electricity. The five cabañas are large, airy and mosquito-netted with pretty, tiled, shared bathrooms. Activities are offered (see p757).

Cabañas Ziga (far east end Playa Mazzunte; s/d with shared bathroom US$9/14, d/tr/q US$25/31/37; ℗) On a breezy beachside elevation a little west of the turtle center, Ziga has decent little rooms with terrace, hammock, fan and mosquito net, plus a good restaurant. There's a little flower garden.

Posada del Arquitecto (El Rinconcito; s & d cabañas US$13.50, with private bathroom US$23-26, hammocks US$3, hanging beds US$3.75) On a rocky outcrop near the west end of the beach, the friendly Italian-owned Posada del Arquitecto has 10 or so cabañas cleverly constructed around the natural features of the land, using predominantly natural materials. One cabaña has eight beds. A hammock and locker area is at the top of the property.

Restaurant Yuri (east end Playa Mazunte; s & d US$9-14, tr US$18, d cabañas US$13) Yuri's rooms and cabañas are plain but clean, adequate and with electricity. The restaurant's kitchen is super clean. There's a safety deposit box.

Palapa El Mazunte (middle Playa Mazunte; camping or hammock per person US$3, s/d cabañas US$6/9) This is one of the most popular spots along this part of the beach. The clean cabañas have electricity.

El Agujón (elagujonmazunte@yahoo.com.mx; El Rinconcito; s/d cabaña US$6.50/11; ℗) Friendly El Agujón, across the street from the Posada del Arquitecto, has 10 small, very rustic, clean cabañas on the hillside just above its restaurant.

Posada Lalo (inland from basketball courts on main street; camping or hammock per person US$2, tr per person US$4.75, r US$13; ℗) One of a few places along the street heading inland from the main road in the middle of Mazunte (and thus about 750m from the beach), Lalo's is a shady spot with friendly young owners. Its few simple rooms have mosquito nets and fans; the price includes kitchen usage.

Restaurant Omar (middle Playa Mazunte; camping per person US$2.50, hammock US$3, s/d/tr US$9/9/18) Omar is beside the end of the middle lane to the beach. The rooms have mosquito nets and one or two double beds.

Palapa El Pescador (middle Playa Mazunte; camping or hammock per person US$3, d cabañas US$14) This popular restaurant has a small tent/hammock area on the sand and a couple of clean upstairs cabañas with power.

Eating

Most places to stay are also places to eat. On the beach, most have similar prices.

Palapa El Pescador (dishes US$2-7) One of the best and most popular places, with fish, seafood and lighter eats such as quesadillas, tacos, fruit salad, eggs and tortas.

El Agujón (dishes US$2-7) Another good restaurant, with a very wide range from large and excellent French-bread tortas to crêpes, fish and, in the evening, pizzas.

Restaurante Bar Bella Vista (east end Playa Mazunte, near turtle museum; fish fillets US$4.50, spaghetti US$3.50) Belongs to Cabañas Ziga and with its elevated position catches a breeze.

La Dulce Vita (main road, east of Cosméticos Naturales; mains US$5-8) This Italian restaurant is well known for its excellent food.

La Empanada (west end, main road; sushi US$3-4, oriental rice dishes US$1-5; ⏲ from 5pm low seasons, 9am-late high seasons) Choose from a Mexican–Asian mix of delectable items including vegetable and fish sushi, all lovingly prepared by a young Mexican–American couple.

Palapa Restaurante Tania (west end, main road; comida corrida US$3.50, fish fillets US$3-5.50; vegetarian dishes US$2.50) This restaurant scores high marks for both its good-value food and hospitality.

Entertainment

La Barra de Mazunte (off Camino al Rinconcito; ☽ Fri & Sat only) Check out mellow La Barra, nestled deep among the trees on a minor track east of Camino al Rinconcito, if you're after late-night music and a spot of dancing.

Getting There & Away

See p749 for information about transportation from Pochutla. Camionetas between Mazunte and San Agustinillo or Zipolite cost US$0.40.

BAHÍAS DE HUATULCO

☎ 958 / pop 18,000

Mexico's newest big coastal resort is arising along a series of beautiful sandy bays, the Bahías de Huatulco (wah-*tool*-koh), 50km east of Pochutla. Until the 1980s this stretch of coast had just one small fishing village and was known to just a few lucky people as a great place for a quiet swim in translucent waters. Huatulco's developers appear to have learned some lessons from other modern Mexican resorts. Pockets of development are separated by tracts of unspoiled shoreline. The maximum building height is six stories, and no sewage goes into the sea. For now, Huatulco is still an enjoyable,

relatively uncrowded resort with a succession of lovely beaches lapped by beautiful water and backed by forest. You can have an active time here – agencies offer all sorts of energetic pursuits from rafting and horseback riding to diving and kayaking. Huatulco is not a place to stay long on a tight budget, however.

The Parque Nacional Huatulco, declared in 1998, protects 119 sq km of land, sea and shoreline west of Santa Cruz Huatulco but is under pressure as developers seek to open up new areas.

Orientation

A divided road leads about 5km down from Hwy 200 to La Crucecita, the service town for the resort. La Crucecita has the bus stations, market, most of the shops and the only cheap accommodations. One kilometer south, on Bahía de Santa Cruz, is Santa Cruz Huatulco, site of the original village (no trace remains), with some mainly plush hotels and a harbor. The other main developments so far are at Bahía Chahué with mainly mid-range hotels, 1km east of Santa Cruz; Tangolunda, 4km further east with most of the luxury hotels; and El Faro, near Playa La Entrega, 2.5km south of Santa Cruz.

The Huatulco bays are strung along the coast about 10km in each direction from Santa Cruz. From west to east, the main ones are San Agustín, Chachacual, Cacaluta, Maguey, El Órgano, Santa Cruz, Chahué, Tangolunda and Conejos.

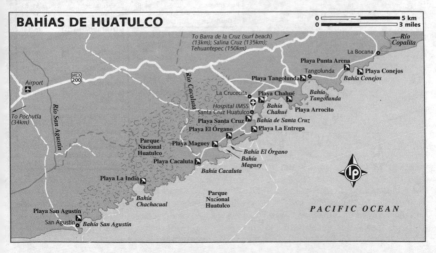

BAHÍAS DE HUATULCO

Bahías de Huatulco airport is 400m north of Hwy 200, 12km west of the turnoff to La Crucecita.

Information

INTERNET ACCESS

El Telefóno (Map p760; Av Bugambilia 501, La Crucecita; per hr US$1.50)

Porticos Internet Café (Map p760; cnr Gardenia & Tamarindo, La Crucecita; per hr US$2.75) Best coffee in town.

Turismo Conejo (Map p7600; Guamuchil 208, La Crucecita; per hr US$1)

LAUNDRY

Lavandería Estrella (Map p760; cnr Flamboyan & Carrizal, La Crucecita; 8am-9pm Mon-Sat) This laundry

will wash 3kg for US$3.25 with same-day pick-up, less for the following day.

MEDICAL SERVICES

The big hotels have English-speaking doctors on call.

Hospital IMSS (☎ 587-11-84; Blvd Chahué) Halfway between La Crucecita and Bahía Chahué; some doctors speak English.

MONEY

La Crucecita has several ATMs and banks, including the following:

Banamex ATM (Map p760; cnr Carrizal & Guamuchil)

Bancomer ATM (Map p760; Plaza Principal)

Bancrecer (Map p760; Av Bugambilia 1104) Changes cash and traveler's checks.

LA CRUCECITA

0 — 200 m
0 — 0.1 miles

INFORMATION
Bahías Plus................................1 B3
Banamex (ATM)..........................2 B3
Bancomer (ATM)........................3 B4
Bancrecer..................................4 A2
BITAL/HSBC...............................5 A2
Bital/HSBC..........................(see 20)
Casa de la Cultura.................(see 12)
El Telefóno................................6 B4
Internet...............................(see 20)
Lavandería Estrella....................7 B3
Porticos Internet Café................8 A3
Post Office.................................9 C3
Scotiabank (ATM)....................10 B3
Tourist Information Kiosk...........11 B3
Tourist Office...........................12 B4
Turismo Conejo...................(see 20)

SIGHTS & ACTIVITIES (pp761–3)
Copalita River Tours...............(see 24)
Park Entrances.........................13 C3
Park Entrances.........................14 B2
Parroquía de Nuestra Señora de
 Guadalupe.............................15 A3

SLEEPING (pp763–5)
Hotel Arrecife..........................16 A4
Hotel Busanvi I.........................17 B3
Hotel Flamboyant.....................18 A3
Hotel Jaroje.............................19 B4
Hotel Plaza Conejo....................20 B3
Hotel Posada Del Parque...........21 B4
Hotel Suites Begonias................22 B3
Misión de los Arcos...................23 A3
Posada Michelle.......................24 A2

EATING (p765)
Comedores..............................25 B3
El Patio....................................26 B3
Pizzería Don Wilo......................27 B3
Restaurant La Crucecita.............28 B4
Restaurant-Bar Oasis................29 B3
Tostados Grill.......................(see 21)

DRINKING (p766)
Heladería & Agua Zamora...........30 B3
La Crema.................................31 B3
La Selva...................................32 B3

ENTERTAINMENT (p766)
Billiards Bar.............................33 A3

SHOPPING (p766)
Plaza Oaxaca...........................34 B4
Shopping Mall..........................35 B3

TRANSPORT (pp766–7)
Budget....................................36 A3
Bus Stop............................(see 35)
Buses to Salina Cruz.................37 B2
Colectivo Taxi & Microbus
 Stop.....................................38 B3
Cristóbal Colón & Sur Bus
 Station.................................39 A2
Estrella Blanca Bus Station.......40 A2
Transportes Rápidos de
 Pochutla Bus Stop..................41 A1

To Hwy 200 (5km);
Aeropuerto (16km);
Pochutla (50km)

Parque Ecológico
Rufino Tamayo

Blvd Chahué

Blvd Chahué

Sabali

Pochote

Cardenal

Jazmin

Palo Verde

Palma Real

Ocotillo

Macuil

Macuhitle

Av Bugambilia

Guarumbo

Carrizal

Parque Ecológico
Rufino Tamayo

Av Oaxaca

Blvd Chahué

Guanacaste

Guamuchil

Priv
Tamarindo

Plaza
Principal

Flamboyan

Flamboyan

Chacah

Colorín

Canal

Cocotillo

Ceiba

Acacia

Laurel

To Hospital IMSS (200m);
Posada Chahué; Hotel
Posada Edén Costa (500m);
Bahía Chahué (1km);
Tangolunda (4km)

To Santa Cruz
Huatulco (1km)

Bital (Map p760; Av Bugambilia 1504; ⏳ 9am-7pm Mon-Sat) Changes cash and traveler's checks and has two ATMs, with another in Plaza Conejo.

There are further facilities in Santa Cruz Huatulco and Tangolunda:

Banamex (Map p761; Blvd Santa Cruz, Santa Cruz) Changes cash and traveler's checks and has ATM.

Bancomer (Map p761; Blvd Santa Cruz, Santa Cruz)

Bital ATM (Map p761; Blvd Juárez, front of Hotel Gala, Tangolunda)

POST

Post Office (Map p760; Blvd Chahué, La Crucecita) Four hundred meters east of the Plaza Principal.

TOURIST INFORMATION

Asociación de Hoteles de Huatulco (Map p761; ☎ 587-08-48; www.hotelshuatulco.com.mx; Hotel Castillo Huatulco, Santa Cruz; ⏳ 9am-3pm & 5-7pm Mon-Fri, 9am-2pm Sat) Also provides tourist information.

Municipal Information Kiosk (Map p760; Plaza Principal; ⏳ 9am-2pm & 4-7pm Mon-Fri, 9am-1pm Sat)

Municipal Tourist Office (Map p760; ☎ 587-18-71; turismohuatulco@hotmail.com; Av Bugambilia 201; ⏳ 9am-5pm Mon-Fri, 9am-1pm Sat) In the Casa de la Cultura.

Parque Nacional Huatulco (☎ 587-08-49; ⏳ 9am-1pm, 4-7pm Mon-Fri) In the port.

Sedetur (☎ 581-01-76; sedetur@oaxaca.gob.mx; Blvd Juárez s/n; ⏳ 9am-3pm & 5-7pm Mon-Fri, 9am-2pm Sat) The Oaxaca state tourist office is in Tangolunda, on the left as you arrive from the west.

TRAVEL AGENCY

Bahías Plus (☎ 587-02-16; Carrizal 704, La Crucecita) Can help with air tickets.

Sights & Activities

There's little to do in La Crucecita itself, but there are some exciting possibilities when you hit the stunning beaches or jungle hinterland. You can sail, snorkel, dive, kayak, surf, fish, raft, canoe, walk in the jungle, watch birds, ride horses, rappel, canyon, cycle, visit a coffee plantation or waterfalls, take a mud bath and more! Most half-day outings cost US$23 to US$33.

BEACHES

Huatulco's beaches are sandy with clear waters (though boats and jet skis leave an oily film here and there). Like the rest of

SANTA CRUZ HUATULCO

0 ————— 200 m
0 ————— 0.1 miles

INFORMATION	
Asociación de Hoteles de	
Huatulco	1 C1
Banamex	2 B2
Bancomer	3 B2
HSBC	4 C2
Officina Parque Nacional	
Huatulco	5 D2

SIGHTS & ACTIVITIES	(pp761-3)
Church	6 D3
Hurricane Divers	7 C3
Temazcal El Dexkite	8 D2

SLEEPING	(pp763-5)
Hotel Castillo Huatulco	9 C1
Hotel Marina Resort	10 D2
Hotel Marlin	11 B3

EATING	(p765)
Café Huatulco	12 C2
Jardín del Arte	(see 11)
Restaurant Ve El Mar	13 D3

ENTERTAINMENT	(p766)
Magic Tropic	14 B3

SHOPPING	(p766)
Mercado de Artesanías	15 C2
Snorkel Gear	(see 18)

TRANSPORT	(pp766-7)
Aerocaribe	16 C1
Aerotucán	(see 16)
Colectivo Taxi & Microbus Stop	17 C2
Lancha Tickets & Embarkation	18 C2
Private Taxi Stand	19 C2

To Chahué Hotels (500m);
Bahía Chahué (500m);
Plaza Chahué (700m);
La Crucecita (1km);
Tangolunda (3km)

To Playa La Entrega (2km);
Bahía Maguey (5km)

Blvd Santa Cruz

Tehuantepec

Monte Albán

Coyula

Pochutla

Ojitlán

Huatulco

Mitla

Plaza

Plaza

Harbor

Playa Santa Cruz

Bahía de Santa Cruz

Cruise Ship Pier

Mexico, all beaches are under federal control, and anyone can use them – even when hotels appear to treat them as private property. Some have coral offshore and excellent snorkeling, though visibility can be poor in the rainy season.

Lanchas will whisk you out to most of the beaches from Santa Cruz Huatulco harbor any time between 8am and 4pm or 5pm, and they'll return to collect you by dusk. Taxis can get you to most beaches for less money, but a boat ride is more fun. *Lancha* tickets are sold at a hut (Map p761) beside the harbor. Round-trip rates for up to 10 people include: Playa La Entrega (US$18), Bahía Maguey and Bahía El Órgano (US$46) and La India (US$73). Another possibility for a fun day is a 6½-hour, **seven-bay boat cruise** (US$23 per person; 🕙 11am-5pm) with an open bar.

At Santa Cruz Huatulco, the small **Playa Santa Cruz** is kept pretty clean but is inferior to most Huatulco beaches. It has an ugly, new, deep sea pier to accommodate cruise liners. **Playa La Entrega** lies toward the outer edge of Bahía de Santa Cruz, a five-minute *lancha* trip or 2.5km by paved road from Santa Cruz. This 300m-long beach, backed by a line of seafood palapas, can get crowded, but it has calm water and good snorkeling in a large area from which boats are cordoned off. 'La Entrega' means 'The Delivery': here in 1831, Mexican independence hero Vicente Guerrero was betrayed to his enemies by an Italian sea captain for 50,000 pieces of gold. Guerrero was taken to Cuilapan near Oaxaca and shot.

Some of the western bays are accessible by road. A 1.5km paved road diverges to **Bahía Maguey** from the road to La Entrega, about half a kilometer out of Santa Cruz. Maguey's fine 400m beach curves around a calm bay between forested headlands. It has a line of seafood palapas. There's good snorkeling around the rocks at the left (east) side of the bay. **Bahía El Órgano**, just east of Maguey, has a 250m beach. You can reach it by a narrow 10-minute footpath that heads into the trees halfway along the Santa Cruz–Maguey road. El Órgano has calm waters good for snorkeling, but it lacks comedores.

The beach at **Bahía Cacaluta** is about 1km long and protected by an island, though there can be undertow. Snorkeling is best around the island. Behind the beach is a la-goon with bird life. The road from Maguey to Cacaluta is paved except for the last section to the beach. There is a research station here investigating turtles and purple sea snails.

Bahía Chachacual, inaccessible by land, has a headland at each end and two beaches. The easterly Playa La India is one of Huatulco's most beautiful and is the best place for snorkeling.

Thirteen kilometers down a dirt road from a crossroads on Hwy 200, 1.7km west of the airport, is **Bahía San Agustín**. After 9km the road fords a river. The beach is long and sandy, with a long line of palapa comedores, some with hammocks for rent overnight. It's popular with Mexicans on weekends and holidays, but quiet at other times. Usually the waters are calm and the snorkeling is good (some of the comedores rent equipment).

A paved road runs to the eastern bays from La Crucecita and Santa Cruz, continuing eventually to Hwy 200. **Bahía Chahué** has a good beach and a new harbor at its east end. Further east, **Bahía Tangolunda** is the site of the major top-end hotel developments to date. The sea is sometimes rough here. Be wary of currents and be sure to heed the colored-flag safety system. Tangolunda has an 18-hole golf course too. Three kilometers further east is the long sweep of **Playa Punta Arena**, on Bahía Conejos. Around a headland at the east end of Bahía Conejos is the more sheltered **Playa Conejos**, unreachable by road. About 2km to 3km beyond Bahía Conejos, the road runs down to the coast again at **La Bocana**, at the mouth of the Río Copalita, where you'll find a handful of seafood comedores and another long beach stretching to the east.

The small fishing village of **Barra de la Cruz**, at the mouth of the Río Zimatán, has good surfing. Access is by a 1.5km-dirt road from Hwy 200, around 20km east of Santa Cruz. A taxi from La Crucecita costs about US$15 to the beach. Eastbound 2nd-class buses will drop you at the junction.

PARQUE ECOLÓGICO RUFINO TAMAYO   Map p760
This park on the edge of La Crucecita is composed mainly of natural vegetation, with some paved paths and tile-roofed shelters with benches.

SNORKELING & DIVING

You can rent snorkeling gear beside the *lancha* kiosk at Santa Cruz harbor for US$4.75 a day. At Playa Maguey you can rent a snorkel, mask and fins for US$4.50 a day. Tour guides will take you snorkeling for US$18-43.

Huatulco has around 13 dive sites. At least two companies will take you diving and offer instruction from beginner's sessions through to full certification courses:

Buceo Sotavento La Crucecita (Leeward Dive Center; Map p760; ☎ 587-21-66; buceosotavento@yahoo.com; Local 18 Interior, Plaza Oaxaca, Flamboyan); Tangolunda (☎ 581-00- 51) This excellent local company offers a range of options from a 4hr introduction (US$75) to full certification (5 days; US$335) or specialty night dives (US$65); they also do 2hr fishing trips for 1-6 people (US$80).

Hurricane Divers Santa Cruz (Map p761; ☎ 587-11-07; www.hurricanedivers.com; Playa Santa Cruz) A single dive is US$43; PADI programs cost US$84-354.

RAFTING

The Copalita and Zimatán Rivers near Huatulco have waters ranging from class 1 to class 4/5 in rafting terms. They're at their biggest in the rainy season, between July and November. Three La Crucecita outfits run rafting and kayaking trips:

Aventuras Piraguas (☎ 587-13-33, www.piraguas .com in Spanish; 4-hr trip US$35; full day US$75)

Copalita River Tours (Map p760; ☎ 587-05-35; raftingcopalita@hotmail.com; Posada Michelle, Gardenia 8; 4hr beginner or family outing per person US$33; longer, more challenging 6hr trip US$60)

Rancho Tangolunda (☎ 589-30-25; rafting trip per person level 1 or 2 US$40, level 3 or 4 US$75) You can choose to go upriver by horse and then come down it by raft (US$54).

HIKING

Aventuras Huatulco (☎ 587-16-95; Plaza de las Conchas, Tangolunda) Guided three-hour walks from Playa Maguey to Playa Cacaluta cost US$19.

Sleeping

Many places double their rates for Semana Santa, July to August and Christmas/New Year.

BUDGET

All these hotels are in La Crucecita.

Hotel Arrecife (Map p760; ☎ 587-17-07; hotel arrecife@hotmail.com; Colorín 510; s with fan US$19-25, d with fan US$23-28, with air-con US$32; ℗ 🅧 🅡) In a quiet, leafy neighborhood, the Arrecife ◾ a small pool and a good little restaurant. ◯ the 24 rooms, the best are sizable, with tw◾ double beds, air-con and balcony; others are small and open straight onto the street. All have cable TV and private hot-water bathroom, which in some cases is outside the room.

Hotel Jaroje (Map p760; ☎ /fax 583-48-01; jaroje .tripod.com.mx; Av Bugambilia 304; s/d US$19/23, d with air-con US$28; 🅧 🅡) Bright, fresh, three-story Jaroje has good-sized, pleasantly decorated rooms with cable TV. Prices include Internet use and continental breakfast.

Hotel Plaza Conejo (Map p760; ☎ 587-00-09; turis moconejo@hotmail.com; Guamuchil 208; s/d US$18/23; 🅡) This friendly hotel, in Plaza Conejo, half a block from Plaza Principal, has 10 tidy, bright, clean rooms with fan, telephone and TV, all off an interior patio. The ceramic basins have pretty floral designs and the lintels are hand painted. There's an Internet café too.

Hotel Busanvi I (Map p760; ☎ 587-00-56; Carrizal 601; s/d with air-con US$14/28; 🅧) The clean Busanvi I has plain, largish rooms with hot-water bathroom and TV (not cable). Beds are good, and the showers excellent! Two rooms have balconies.

MID-RANGE

There are mid-range hotels in La Crucecita, Santa Cruz, Chahué and Tangolunda.

The cheaper places in this category are in La Crucecita.

Hotel Flamboyant (Map p760; ☎ 587-01-13; flam boyhuatulco@prodigy.net.mx; Plaza Principal; r incl breakfast US$50; ℗ 🅧) This pink hotel has a pleasant courtyard, helpful staff, an attractive pool, its own restaurant and 70 rooms with air-conditioning. Décor is Oaxacan folksy. There is free transportation to Playa La Entrega.

Misión de los Arcos (Map p760; ☎ 587-01-65; www .misiondelosarcos.com; Gardenia 902; r with fan/air-con US$27/32, ste US$55-76; ℗ 🅧 🅡) This seven-year-old, 13-room, American-owned hotel is embellished by a touch of interior greenery. It has big, bright comfortable rooms, all decorated in simple white and beige, and a gym.

Hotel Suites Begonias (Map p760; ☎ 587-03-90; getosa@prodigy.net.mx; Av Bugambilia 503; s/d/tr US$24/28/32) The small Suites Begonias has comfortable two-room suites with two

...ble beds, TV, fan and pretty tiled bath-
...ms, opening on upstairs walkways.

Hotel Posada Del Parque (Map p760; ☎ 587-16-97;
...etosa@prodigy.net.mx; Flamboyan 306, Plaza Principal; s/d
incl continental breakfast US$23/27, with air-con US$28/32;
P ⊠) This hotel, which is under new man-
agement, has fairly comfortable and sizable
rooms. All have hot water, fan and satellite
TV. The restaurant out front is excellent.

Posada Michelle (Map p760; ☎ 587-05-35; Gar
denia 8; r with fan/air-con US$19/32; ⊠) The Mich-
elle is next to the Estrella Blanca bus station
and can be noisy until 9pm. But it's a friendly
place, and the dozen or so rooms are brightly decorated and have cable TV. There's a
little sitting area with hammocks.

Santa Cruz and Chahué's mid-range options are generally more luxurious than
those in La Crucecita.

Hotel Marlin (Map p761; ☎ 587-00-55; www.oaxaca
-mio.com/marlin.htm; Mitla 28; r US$46; P ⊠ ⊠)
The friendly French-owned Marlin offers tastefully decorated, colorful rooms
with TV, air-con and phone. It has a good
French–Mexican restaurant, the Jardín del
Arte (see following), and a small pool.

Posada Chahué (☎ 587-09-45; www.huatulco.com
.mx/posadachahue; Mixe 75; r US$62-80; P ⊠ ⊠)
Family-owned Posada Chahué, affiliated
with the Best Western group, is about 1km
east of La Crucecita and 500m from Playa
Chahué. Going down Blvd Chahué toward
Bahía Chahué, take the second turn to the
left (east) after the Pemex station. There
are 12 attractive, modern rooms, most
with two king-size beds, all with air-con,
fan, cable TV and safety box. A pool and
moderately priced restaurant are set in the
lawned garden.

Hotel Posada Eden Costa (☎ 587-24-80; www
.edencosta.com; Calle Zapoteco MZNA 27, Sector R –
Chahué; r US$37, ste with salon & kitchen US$72;
P ⊠ ⊠) Swiss- and Laotian-owned Eden
Costa, on the street behind Posada Chahué,
is a good recent addition to the Huatulco
scene, especially because of its attached,
cool Mambo Cafe (following). Rooms have
a bird theme; comforts include private
bathroom, cable TV and air-con.

TOP END
If what you want is a holiday in a top-end
Huatulco hotel, a package is your best bet. If
you're already in Mexico, ask a travel agent.
Around US$700 could buy two people re-

turn flights from Mexico City and three
nights in a top hotel. The price is usually
inclusive of food and drink.

Both Santa Cruz' and Chahué's top-end
choices are less expensive than those in
Tangolunda.

Hotel Castillo Huatulco (Map p761; ☎ 587-01-44;
Blvd Santa Cruz 303, Santa Cruz; r US$128; P ⊠ ⊠)
The colonial-style Castillo Huatulco has a
decent pool, a restaurant and 112 good-
sized, brightly decorated, air-conditioned
rooms, with TV. Transportation to the Castillo's beach club on Bahía Chahué is free.
The hotel also offers packages with the third
night for free.

Hotel Marina Resort (Map p761; ☎ 587-09-63; Tehuantepec 112; r US$84; P ⊠ ⊠) The 50-room
Marina Resort, on the east side of Santa
Cruz harbor, has three pools, a *temazcal*
and youthful managers.

Hotel Villablanca (☎ 587-06-06; www.villablanca
hotels.com.mx; cnr Blvd Juárez & Zapoteco, Chahué; r US$95,
ste from US$105; P ⊠ ⊠) This hotel, on the
main drag about 250m back from Playa
Chahué, has a large, clean pool and offers
air-conditioned rooms with soothing décor
and cable TV. Packages offer a third night
for free. Main dishes in its restaurant are
inexpensive.

Tangolunda is real top-end territory.
Promotional rates can cut prices in the
Zaashila, Barceló and Gala.

Quinta Real (☎ 581-04-28; www.quintareal.com;
Paseo Juárez 2; ste from US$204; P ⊠ ⊠) The ut-
terly gorgeous Quinta Real has a hilltop
position at the west end of Tangolunda.
Its 27 suites have Jacuzzi and ocean view;
some have fountain-fed private pools that
threaten to spill down the hillside to the
beach and main swimming pool area.

Camino Real Zaashila (☎ 581-04-60; www.camino
real.com/zaashila; Blvd Juárez 5; ste US$318-409; P
⊠ ⊠) Toward the east end of Tangolunda,
this tranquil, attractive hotel has a big pool
in lovely gardens. There are 120 rooms; of
these 41 come with their own small pool,
and of course, higher price!

Casa del Mar (☎ 581-02-03; Balcones de Tangolunda 13; ste US$91-133; P ⊠ ⊠) One kilo-
meter beyond the Zaashila is the elegant
and sensationally sited Casa del Mar, with
25 air-conditioned suites and a beautiful
pool and restaurant.

Barceló Resort (☎ 581-00-55; www.barcelo.com; Blvd
Juárez s/n; r from US$203; P ⊠ ⊠ ⊠) Between the

Quinta Real and the Camino Real Zaashila, the pinkish-toned Barceló has 375 rooms, 50 with ocean view. Its big pool sits in a beachside garden, and you'll find all the amenities you'd expect: restaurants, bars, tennis courts, gymnasium, water sports, shops and nightly mariachi entertainment.

Hotel Gala (☎ 583-04-00; www.galaresorts.com; Blvd Juárez s/n; r US$149, suites with all meals & drinks from US$195; P X) Next door to the Barceló, and strangely similar in color and architecture, the Hotel Gala has five pools, a disco, fitness center and 300 air-conditioned rooms. Prices include land and water sports and entertainment.

Eating

LA CRUCECITA & BAHÍA CHAHUÉ

Mambo Cafe (☎ 587-24-80; Calle Zapoteco MZNA 27, Sector R – Chahué; mains US$4.50-11, desserts US$4-7.50; Y closed Mon) This palapa-roofed restaurant is attached to the Hotel Posada Eden Costa in Chahué (see earlier). Here the Swiss French chef takes a stab at French, Thai, Italian, Vietnamese, Mexican and Oaxacan dishes. The Thai salad with prawns and bean sprouts is delicious. Quiche Lorraine, spring rolls and seafood lasagne are further tasty choices. Wines are available.

Restaurant-Bar Oasis (Map p760; ☎ 587-00-45; Flamboyan 211, Plaza Principal; mains US$3-11) The Oasis has good, moderately priced fare, from *tortas* to fish fillets or steaks. It does Oaxacan specialties and tries Japanese food too. The Oasis is popular for breakfast – the yogurt, fruit, granola and honey plate (US$3.75) will set you up for the day. Delicious local Pluma coffee is served.

Tostados Grill (Map p760; ☎ 587-02-19; Flamboyan 306, front Hotel Posada del Parque; breakfasts US$2.75-8, salads US$4, mains US$4.50-8) Owned by the same group as the Oasis, this little, mainly Italian restaurant, has some inspired dishes. The spinach salad with bacon is a good bet.

Pizzería Don Wilo (Map p760; ☎ 587-06-23; Plaza Principal; mains US$5-15) You could try one of their piping hot pizzas but the Oaxacan dishes, including tamales and tlayudas, are very popular. They do fish and steaks too.

Restaurant La Crucecita (Map p760; cnr Av Bugambilia & Chacah; dishes US$2-8; Y closed Tue) This in expensive spot is a block from the plaza. Its *sincronizadas a la mexicana* (US$4) make a good antojito. Tangy *licuados* with yogurt or milk are a specialty (US$2). Early in the

day, watch the chef prepare serious quantities of *salsa roja*.

El Patio (Map p760; ☎ 587-07-11, Flamboyan 24; breakfasts US$2.50-4.50, mains US$4.50-8.50) The attraction of this restaurant is the lovely garden patio with tables out back. Their breakfasts are good deals. The usual range of fish, seafood, chicken dishes and Oaxacan specialties are offered.

Mercado (market; cnr Av Bugambilia & Guanacastle; fish or shrimp platters US$4-5; enfrijoladas or entomatadas US$2.75) The very clean comedores here serve up good food.

SANTA CRUZ HUATULCO

Restaurant Ve El Mar (Map p761; ☎ 587-03-64; Playa Santa Cruz; mains US$6-11) Food at the eateries on Playa Santa Cruz is mostly average, but this place at the east end is an exception. The seafood is fine, and the *salsas picante* and the margaritas potent. Try a whole fish, an octopus or shrimp dish or, if you have US$18 to spare, lobster.

Jardín del Arte (Map p761; Hotel Marlin, Mitla 28; dishes US$2-9) This restaurant features international cuisine with a French touch. The bread is homemade. You can enjoy pizzas, crêpes, fish dishes or a sociable breakfast on the terrace.

Café Huatulco (Map p761; ☎ 587-12-28; Plaza Santa Cruz; coffees US$1.25-3, cakes US$3) This café in the plaza near the harbor serves good Pluma coffee in many different ways – the *capuchino frío* (cold cappuccino with a dollop of ice cream) is well worth a try.

TANGOLUNDA

The big hotels offer a choice of expensive bars, coffee shops and restaurants.

Casa del Mar (☎ 581-02-03; Balcones de Tangolunda 13; starters US$4-8, mains US$7-13.50) This restaurant with its great view and romantic setting is one of the best. Try the *tamal de pescado* (steamed corn dough stuffed with fish). Flambéed bananas to finish? Why not?

There are also a few medium to expensive restaurants along Tangolunda's two streets.

Restaurant La Pampa Argentina (☎ 581-01-75; Blvd Juárez s/n; dishes US$11-27) This is the place for a steak-out.

La Casa de la Nona (☎ 581-03-76; Blvd Juárez s/n; dishes US$4.50-12) This Italian–Argentine restaurant opposite the Barceló Resort offers well-priced pastas, pizzas and salads, steaks and grilled fish.

BEACHES

There are decent seafood palapas at Playas La Entrega, Maguey, San Agustín and La Bocana. A whole grilled *huachinango* (red snapper) will cost US$6 to US$9.

Drinking

La Crema (Map p760; ☎ 587-07-02; cnr Flamboyan & Carrizal, La Crucecita; ☽ 7pm-3am) This dark, moody bar pulls a cool crowd; you'll pay US$2.25 to US$3.75 for a shot of tequila.

La Selva (Map p760; ☎ 587-10-63; Av Bugambilia 601, La Crucecita) A laid-back, open-air bar overlooking Plaza Principal.

Heladería & Agua Zamora (Map p760; cnr Flamboyan & Av Bugambilia) Prepared here are some exquisite items to quench your thirst. Absolutely don't miss the Spanish *horchata*.

Entertainment

Santa Cruz and Chahué have a couple of nightspots.

Magic Tropic (Map p761; Mitla s/n, Santa Cruz; admission US$5.50; ☽ 11pm-4am Thu-Sat) Shake your bootie to salsa, tropical and merengue.

La Papaya (Blvd Juárez Mz 3, Lot 1, Chahué; admission US$9; ☽ 11pm-5am Thu-Sat) This successful venue, near the Mexicana office, appeals to the 18-25 age group.

La Mina (beneath Hotel Real Aligheri, Mixe 77, Chahué; admission US$5.50; ☽ 11pm-4am Thu-Sat) Get sweaty to disco, merengue and tropical music at this venue next door to Posada Chahué.

Noches Oaxaqueñas (☎ 581-00-01; Blvd Juárez s/n, Tangolunda; admission US$9; ☽ 8pm Tue, Thu & Sat) Noches Oaxaqueñas, beside the Tangolunda traffic circle, presents a Guelaguetza regional dance show. Drinks and/or dinner (US$7 to US$17) are extra.

There's a **billiards bar** (Map p760; cnr Gardenia & Guanacastle; ☽ 24hr) upstairs fronting La Crucecita's Plaza Principal.

Shopping

Mercado de Artesanías (Map p761) Santa Cruz' market has a wide range of beach gear and handicrafts, including some good jewelry and textiles.

La Crucecita is worth a good browse – some of the products that get down to its shops are of high quality.

La Crema (Map p760; ☎ 587-07-02; cnr Flamboyan & Carrizal, La Crucecita) An interesting 'alternative' boutique with artifacts and unique jewelry from Africa, Indonesia, Peru and India.

A new shopping mall has opened on the corner of Guamuchil and Carrizal.

Getting There & Away

AIR

Mexicana and its subsidiary Aerocaribe offer two to four flights daily to/from Mexico City (US$128 one way). Aerotucán (with a 14-seat Cessna) flies daily to/from Oaxaca, with fares around US$100 oneway. Aerovega flies a seven-seater daily to/from Oaxaca (US$100) with a minimum of three passengers. Cheap charters from Canada, the US and the UK are sometimes available.

Airline Offices

Aerocaribe Santa Cruz (Map p761; ☎ 587-12-20; Zona Comercial, Hotel Castillo Huatulco); Airport (☎ 581-90-30)

Aerotucán Huatulco Santa Cruz (☎ 587-24-27; Zona Comercial, Hotel Castillo Hutaulco)

Mexicana Chahué (☎ 581-90-08; Local 3, Plaza Chahué, Blvd Juárez); Airport (☎ 587-02-23)

BUS

The main bus stations are located on Gardenia in La Crucecita. Some buses coming to Huatulco are marked 'Santa Cruz Huatulco,' but they still terminate in La Crucecita. Make sure your bus is not headed to Santa María Huatulco, which is a long way inland.

First-class **Cristóbal Colón** (Map p760; ☎ 587-02-61; cnr Gardenia & Ocotillo) is four blocks from the plaza. Most of its buses are *de paso*. Sur buses pull up here too. **Estrella Blanca** (EB; Map p760; ☎ 587-01-03; cnr Gardenia & Palma Real) has *primera* services that are quick and fairly comfortable, and *ordinario* buses which are typical ordinario. Daily departures include the following:

Oaxaca (US$17, 8hr via Salina Cruz, 2 Colón overnight)

Pochutla Colón (US$2.25, 1hr, 6 daily); EB (US$1.75-2, 1hr, 7 daily); Transportes Rápidos de Pochutla (US$1.25, every 15min 6am-8pm, from the main road opposite Av Bugambilia)

Puerto Escondido Colón (US$5, 2½hr, 6 daily); Sur (US$3, 2½hr, 12 daily); EB (US$4.25-5, 2½hr, 5 daily)

Salina Cruz Colón (US$6, 2½hr, 8 daily); Sur (US$6, 2½hr, 2 daily); EB (US$7, 2½hr, 3 daily); Istmeño buses (US$5, 2½hr, hourly 4am-7pm, from cnr Blvd Chahaué & Carrizal)

Colón also runs a few buses to Tehuantepec, Juchitán, Tuxtla Gutiérrez, San Cristóbal de Las Casas (US$25) and Tapachula. EB goes to Acapulco (US$23). Colón and EB go to Mexico City (US$41 to US$47, 15 hours).

CAR & MOTORCYCLE
Advantage (☎ 581-00-00; Hotel Gala, Tangolunda) Rents Nissan Tsurus for around US$60 a day with unlimited kilometers, taxes and insurance, as well as 4X4 soft-top Trackers for US$66.

Budget (Map p760; ☎ 587-00-10; cnr Ocotillo & Jazmín, La Crucecita)

Getting Around
TO/FROM THE AIRPORT
Transportación Terrestre (☎ 581-90-14, 581-90-24) provides colectivo combis for US$7 per person from the airport to La Crucecita, Santa Cruz or Bahía Chahué and for US$8 to Tangolunda. Get tickets at the company's airport kiosk. For a whole cab at a reasonable price, walk just outside the airport gate, where you can pick one up for about US$10 to La Crucecita, Santa Cruz or Tangolunda, or US$14 to Pochutla. Even cheaper, walk 400m down to Hwy 200 and catch a microbus for US$0.60 to La Crucecita or US$1.25 to Pochutla. Those buses heading to La Crucecita may be marked 'Santa Cruz' or 'Bahías Huatulco' or something similar.

BUS & COLECTIVO
Colectivo taxis and a few microbuses provide transportation between La Crucecita, Santa Cruz Huatulco and Tangolunda. In La Crucecita catch them on the corner of Guamuchil and Carrizal, one block from the Plaza Principal. In Santa Cruz they stop by the harbor, and in Tangolunda at the traffic circle outside the Hotel Gala. Fares are the same in either type of vehicle: from La Crucecita to Santa Cruz US$0.40, and to Tangolunda US$0.60.

BICYCLE
Edgar Erasto Rojas (☎ 587-16-95; Aventuras Huatulco, Plaza Las Conchas, Tangolunda; bike rental 1hr US$3), opposite the Barceló Resort, rents mountain bikes and takes groups out cycling along the bays.

TAXI
Taxis are plentiful. From La Crucecita you pay around US$1.50 to Santa Cruz, US$2.25 to Tangolunda, US$6 to Bahía Maguey and US$9 to the airport.

ISTHMUS OF TEHUANTEPEC

Eastern Oaxaca is the southern half of the 200km-wide Isthmus of Tehuantepec (teh-wahn-teh-*pek*), Mexico's narrowest point. This is sweaty, flat country, but Zapotec culture is strong. If you spend a night or two here, you'll probably be agreeably surprised by the people's liveliness and friendliness. A new fast highway from Oaxaca to Salina Cruz may spur on the economic growth of the region.

Fifteen kilometers northeast of Juchitán, around La Ventosa (where Hwy 185 to Acayucan diverges from Hwy 190 to Chiapas), strong winds sweep down from the north and sometimes blow high vehicles off the road.

History & People
In 1496 the isthmus Zapotecs repulsed the Aztecs from the fortress of Guiengola, near Tehuantepec, and the isthmus never became part of the Aztec empire. Later there was strong resistance to the Spanish here.

Isthmus women are noticeably open and confident and take a leading role in business and government. Many older women still wear embroidered *huipiles* and voluminous printed skirts. For the numerous *velas* (fiestas), Tehuantepec and Juchitán women turn out in velvet or sateen *huipiles*, gold and silver jewelry (a sign of wealth), skirts embroidered with fantastically colorful silk flowers and a variety of odd headgear. Many isthmus fiestas feature the *tirada de frutas*, in which women climb on roofs and throw fruit on the men below!

TEHUANTEPEC
☎ 971 / pop 38,000
Tehuantepec is a friendly town, often with a fiesta going on in one of its barrios.

Orientation
The Oaxaca–Tuxtla Gutiérrez highway (190) meets Hwy 185 from Salina Cruz about 1km west of Tehuantepec. Hwy 190 then skirts the north edge of town. All Tehuantepec's bus stations, collectively known as La Terminal, cluster just off Hwy 190, 1.5km northeast of the town center.

al buses to/from Salina Cruz also p, more conveniently, where Hwy 190 asses the end of 5 de Mayo, a minute's walk from the central plaza. To reach the plaza from La Terminal on foot, follow Av Héroes until it ends at a T-junction, then turn right along Guerrero for four blocks to another T-junction, then go one block left along Hidalgo.

Information

Bancomer and **Bancafe** (5 de Mayo) South side of the market, both have ATMs.

Bital ATM (Romero) South off the plaza, next to the entrance to the Hotel Oasis.

El Clubo (Romero 64; per hr US$1) Internet café.

Interistmo (Ocampo 8; Internet access per hr US$0.80)

Isthmus Tourist Office (☎ 514-21-55; Carretera Transístmica 7 bis Altos; ☽ 9am-8pm Mon-Fri, 9am-2pm Sat) Oaxaca's state office, on Hwy 185 coming inland from Salina Cruz, near the junction with Hwy 190 to Oaxaca.

Santander Serfin (22 de Mayo; 9am-4pm Mon-Sat) North side of the plaza; will change traveler's checks and cash US dollars.

Sights

EX-CONVENTO REY COSIJOPÍ

This former Dominican monastery, on a short street off Guerrero, is Tehuantepec's **Casa de la Cultura** (Callejón Rey Cosljopí), holding classes and occasional exhibitions. Built in the 16th century, the monastery is named for the local Zapotec leader of the day (who paid for it) and features sturdy two-story construction around a central courtyard. It served as a prison before being restored in the 1970s.

GUIENGOLA

The hillside Zapotec stronghold of Guiengola, where king Cosijoeza rebuffed the Aztecs, is north of Hwy 190 from a turnoff about 11km out of Tehuantepec. A sign points to 'Ruinas Guiengola 7' just past the Km 240 marker. You can see the remains of two pyramids, a ball court, a 64-room complex known as El Palacio and a thick defensive wall. There are fine views over the isthmus.

To get there take a bus bound for Jalapa del Marqués from La Terminal. Get off at Puente Las Tejas, from which it's a walk of about 2½ hours. There are guides at Las Tejas. Start early, 6am or before, to take advantage of the morning cool.

MARKET

The dark, almost medieval market is on the west side of the plaza. It spills onto the surrounding streets and explodes with color at times like Day of the Dead when marigolds are for sale.

Sleeping

Guiexhoba (☎ 715-17-10; Carretera Panamericana Km 250.5; s/d US$32/42; P ☒ ☒) The best hotel in the vicinity is a new colonial-style building. Bright and cheerful outside, it has large and well-fitted rooms, though they're a little dark. The garden is strewn with big plant pots. There's a large covered swimming pool and a restaurant.

Hotel Donají (☎ 715-00-64; hoteldonaji@hotmail .com; Juárez 10; s/d with fan US$11/15, with air-con US$14/22; P ☒ ☒) The bright Donají is two blocks south of the east side of the central plaza, and has clean rooms with TV on two upper floors with open-air walkways. There's a small gym and a small pool.

Hotel Oasis (☎ 715-00-08; Ocampo 8; r with fan US$12/16, with air-con US$2; P) A block south of the plaza, the Oasis has 26 basic rooms, with warm showers, set around a courtyard with car parking.

Eating

Restaurant Guiexhoba (☎ 715-17-10; Carretera Panamericana Km 250.5; full breakfasts US$4.50; mains US$8-10) This four-star hotel restaurant is the slickest place to eat in Tehuantepec.

Restaurante Scarú (☎ 715-06-46; Leona Vicario 4; dishes US$3-10) Up a side street a block east of the Hotel Donají, the Scarú occupies an 18th-century house with a courtyard and colorful modern murals of Tehuantepec life. Sit beneath a fan, quaff a *limonada* and sample one of the many fish, seafood, meat and chicken dishes on offer. On weekends old-timers play a marimba.

Getting There & Away

The 245km trip from Oaxaca takes 4½ hours in a 1st-class bus. The road winds downhill for the middle 160km.

At La Terminal, Cristóbal Colón and ADO (1st-class) and Sur and AU (2nd-class) share one building. Many 1st-class buses are *de paso*, often in the wee hours. Colón runs 11 buses daily to Oaxaca (US$11) and a few each to Tuxtla Gutiérrez (US$12.50 – change there for San

Cristóbal de Las Casas), Bahías de Huatulco (US$7), Pochutla (US$9), Puerto Escondido (US$12), Mexico City (US$41) and Tapachula (US$19). ADO runs twice daily to Villahermosa (US$20). AU has a few buses to Veracruz (US$22, eight hours). Sur runs frequent buses to Arriaga.

Transportes Oaxaca-Istmo (TOI, 2nd-class), just east of Colón, has hourly buses to Oaxaca (US$7.50) around the clock, plus five to Tuxtla Gutiérrez (US$9) and some daytime services too.

Across the street from Colón are local buses to Juchitán (US$2, 30 minutes) and Salina Cruz (US$1.25, 25 minutes) They go at least every half hour during daylight hours.

Getting Around

A curious form of local transportation is the *motocarro* – a kind of three-wheel buggy in which the driver sits on a front seat while passengers stand behind on a platform. They congregate by the railway track behind the market.

SALINA CRUZ

☎ 971 / pop 74,000

Once an important railway terminus and port, then undermined by the cutting of the Panama Canal, Salina Cruz has revived as an oil pipeline terminal with a refinery. It's a windy city with a rough-and-ready feel, though a bit of sophistication is creeping in with the spoils of the oil trade.

Orientation & Information

Hwy 200 from Puerto Escondido and Pochutla meets the Salina Cruz–Tehuantepec road, Hwy 185, on the northern edge of Salina Cruz. Av Tampico runs 2km south from this junction to the center, with the combined bus station of Cristóbal Colón, ADO and AU just off Av Tampico on Laborista, seven blocks north of the center. Estrella Blanca is on the corner of Av Tampico and Frontera, four blocks north of the center. Sur has a bus station on 5 de Mayo, one block south of the central plaza.

Reaching the center, Av Tampico passes one block west of the wide, windy plaza. Banks with ATMs on the plaza or nearby Av Camacho (north from the plaza) include Banorte, Scotiabank and Bancomer. **Sonex**

Web (Av Camacho 306; per hr US$1.25) offers Internet access on the east side of the plaza.

Sights & Activities

Heading west toward Huatulco, only 30 and 45 minutes from Salina Cruz, there are a couple of great beaches which locals and those in the know frequent – **Playa Azul** and **Playa Cangrejo.** Take a camioneta heading west out of town. Istmeño buses to Huatulco ply this route too. Pick one up on Av Tampico. You can return the same way up until about 6pm after which traffic on the highway gets thin. Each beach is about 1km from the highway. There's a small settlement at Playa Azul.

Sleeping & Eating

Misión San José (☎ 714-22-15; Pacífico 9, Barrio Cantaranas; s/d US$37/46, ste US$100; 🖭) This new hotel, three blocks south of the plaza, heralds the gentrification of Salina Cruz. Rooms are off a long patio with palms. Décor is simple but striking with purple, ochre and yellow paint work, and carved wooden doors. A pool and restaurant were underway when we visited.

Hotel Posada del Jardín (☎ 714-01-62; Av Camacho 108; s with fan US$12-15, with air-con US$17-19, d with fan US$16-19, d with air-con US$21-24; 🅿 😠) Posada del Jardín, 1½ blocks north of the main plaza, has clean rooms with shower and TV, on two levels around a leafy courtyard. Its air-cooled café next door is excellent. Select from an international–Mexican menu (main dishes US$3 to US$4.50) and a long list of coffees and juices.

Hotel Costa Real (☎ 714-02-93; fax 714-51-11; Progreso 22; s/d/tr US$37/41/50; 🅿 😠) The modern Costa Real, two blocks north of the plaza, is a reasonable choice. The 40 carpeted, air-conditioned rooms have color TV. It also has a decent, light, airy restaurant (main dishes US$5.50 to US$9).

Viña del Mar (Av Camacho 110; dishes US$4-11) This bright, fan-cooled café with a big fake palm tree is a few doors north of the Posada del Jardín. Its specialty is fish and seafood; long lime juices (US$2) hit the spot.

Getting There & Away

Cristóbal Colón, ADO and Estrella Blanca run 1st-class buses. The Sur bus station, a block south of the plaza, sells all 1st-class tickets as well as its own.

Four to six Colón and four Estrella Blanca buses run daily to Bahías de Huatulco (US$6 to US$6.50, 2½ hours), Pochutla (US$8.50, 3½ hours) and Puerto Escondido (US$11.50, 5 hours). ADO has two to Huatulco (US$7). Colón also runs five buses to Oaxaca (US$11.50, five hours) and three to Tuxtla Gutiérrez (US$11.25, seven hours). For San Cristóbal de Las Casas, change in Tuxtla. There's 1st-class service to Tapachula (US$19.50, eight hours), Veracruz (US$25, eight hours), Villahermosa (US$21, nine hours) and Mexico City (US$37 to US$47, eight hours). Estrella Blanca goes to Acapulco (US$31, 13 hours).

Frequent local buses to Tehuantepec (US$1.25, 25 minutes) and Juchitán (US$2, one hour) leave from the corner of Av Tampico and Progreso, one block west and two north from the plaza. Sur ordinario buses also run to Tehuantepec (US$1) and Juchitán (US$2) every half-hour between 1:30pm and 6pm, then at 7pm and 8pm. Sur runs to Puerto Escondido, Pochutla and Huatulco too.

Getting Around

Local buses run along Av Tampico between the bus stations and town center. Going out to the bus stations, they're marked 'Refinería' or 'Refi.'

JUCHITÁN

☎ 971 / pop 67,000

Istmeño culture is strong in this friendly town, which is visited by few gringos.

Prolongación 16 de Septiembre leads into Juchitán from a busy intersection with traffic signals on Hwy 190, on the north edge of town. The main bus terminal is about 100m toward town from the intersection. The street curves left, then right, then divides into 5 de Septiembre (the right fork) and 16 de Septiembre (left). These emerge as opposite sides of the central plaza, Jardín Juárez, after seven blocks.

Information

There are two banks with ATMs on the Jardín. You can change traveler's checks and cash US dollars at **Bital** (16 de Septiembre 52; exchange services 9am-3pm Mon-Fri), 3½ blocks from the plaza. You'll find several Internet places on 16 de Septiembre. All charge US$1.25 an hour, including **Internet Caffe** (opposite Hotel Lopez Lena Palace; ☻ noon-2am).

Sights

Jardín Juárez is a lively central square. A thriving market on its east side spills into the surrounding streets. Here you can find traditional Isthmus women's costumes. The market comedores may have iguana on the menu.

Juchitán's **Lidxi Guendabiaani** (Casa de la Cultura; José F Gómez; admission free; ☻ 10am-3pm & 5-8pm Mon-Fri, 10am-2pm Sat), a block south of Jardín Juárez, has an interesting archaeological collection and an art collection with works by leading 20th-century Mexican artists, including Rufino Tamayo and *juchiteco* Francisco Toledo. It's set around a big patio beside the Iglesia de San Vicente Ferrer.

Sleeping & Eating

Hotel Santo Domingo del Sur (☎ 711-10-50; Carretera Juchitán-Tehuantepec s/n; s/d with air-con US$29/39; P ☒ ☒) Situated by the Hwy 190 crossroads, the popular Santo Domingo has decent rooms, a large garden with swimming pool, and a good restaurant (meals US$3 to US$14).

Hotel López Lena Palace (☎ 711-13-88; fax 711-13-89; 16 de Septiembre 70; s/d with air-con US$28/37, ste US$60; P ☒) The López Lena Palace, about halfway between the bus station and town center, has a mock Arabic exterior that suggests more luxury than actually exists. Nevertheless, rooms are reasonable, with comfy beds, and multichannel TV. The attached **Restaurant El Califa** (mains US$3-13) prepares some excellent dishes including lovely fresh salads and stuffed fish.

Casagrande Restaurant (☎ 711-34-60; prices US$5-16) This is the flashest eatery in town, in a pleasant covered courtyard with ceiling fans and tall plants, on the south side of Jardín Juárez. It offers all sorts of goodies, from regional dishes or pasta to seafood, served piping hot.

Café Santa Fé (☎ 711-15-45; Cruce de Carretera Transístmica; dishes US$4-8; ☻ 24hr) For cool air and good food, try this restaurant handily wedged between the main bus station and the highway. It does excellent breakfasts, with a breakfast buffet (US$7) on Sunday. The service, by white-coated waiters, is brisk.

Getting There & Away

Cristóbal Colón and ADO (1st-class) and Sur and AU (2nd-class) use the main bus terminal on Prolongación 16 de Septiembre. Frequent 2nd-class Istmeño buses to Tehuantepec (US$1.25, 30 minutes) and Salina Cruz (US$2, 1 hour) stop at the next corner south on Prolongación 16 de Septiembre during daylight hours. Fletes y Pasajes (FYPSA, 2nd-class) has its own terminal, separated from the main one by a Pemex station.

Many buses are *de paso* and leave in the middle of the night. To Oaxaca (US$8 to US$12, five-to-six hours) there are 13 Colón and four ADO buses daily, as well as FYPSA departures about hourly around the clock. Colón runs five daily buses to Bahías de Huatulco (US$8, four hours) and at least three each to Pochutla (US$10, five hours), Puerto Escondido, (US$13, seven hours), San Cristóbal de Las Casas (US$15, seven hours) and Tapachula (US$18, seven hours). Colón and FYPSA go several times daily to Tuxtla Gutiérrez (US$8 to US$13, five hours). Sur has frequent service to Acayucan (US$7, 3½ hours) and a bus to Huatulco at 2:30pm (US$7, four hours). ADO runs five buses to Villahermosa (US$19, seven hours) and one at 2am to Palenque. Colón and AU go to Mexico City (US$32 to US$39, 12 hours), Veracruz (US$12, eight hours) and Puebla (US$29, 10 hours).

Getting Around

'Terminal-Centro' buses run between the bus station and Jardín Juárez. A taxi costs US$1.50.

Tabasco & Chiapas

CONTENTS

The states of Tabasco and Chiapas have widely different appeal. Tabasco is largely flat, steamy well-watered lowland with little to detain the visitor apart from the moderately interesting archaeological sites of Parque La Venta and Comalcalco. The state's early historical heritage is undeniably impressive – Mesoamerica's first great civilization, the Olmecs, emerged in these verdant plains. But following this initial flourish, Tabasco settled into a lengthy stupor as a tropical backwater until recent decades, when its oilfields have brought prosperity and development.

Chiapas, by contrast, has terrific allure and enormous variety. Indeed it almost seems over-endowed with wonderful scenery: cool, mist-wrapped mountains and pine-forested peaks, plus extensive jungle reserves home to bountiful wildlife. But above all, Mexico's southernmost state is defined by the culture and customs of the Maya, both ancient and modern, for the descendents of the pyramid-builders remain in the region and give Chiapas a uniquely colorful indigenous identity.

Its attractions are compelling. San Cristóbal de Las Casas is a delight: a tranquil colonial town with a rich architectural heritage, and terrific cafés and restaurants, surrounded by traditional Maya villages. North of here are the spectacular turquoise Agua Azul waterfalls, and the jungle-clad Maya temples of Toniná and Palenque. East of Chiapas is the Lacandón Jungle, Mexico's largest rainforest, which envelopes a breathtaking lake, Laguna Miramar. The Lacandón forests fringe the Maya temples of Yaxchilán and Bonampak where you have a good chance of encountering toucans and howler monkeys. Close to the border with Guatemala, the lakes of the Lagos de Montebello region offer wonderful scenery in a more temperate alpine climate. Chiapas' steamy Pacific coastal region, El Soconusco, also has lagoons and mangroves to explore and the sleepy laid-back beach resort of Puerto Arista.

TABASCO & CHIAPAS

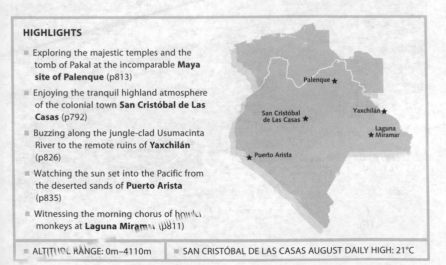

HIGHLIGHTS

- Exploring the majestic temples and the tomb of Pakal at the incomparable **Maya site of Palenque** (p813)
- Enjoying the tranquil highland atmosphere of the colonial town **San Cristóbal de Las Casas** (p792)
- Buzzing along the jungle-clad Usumacinta River to the remote ruins of **Yaxchilán** (p826)
- Watching the sun set into the Pacific from the deserted sands of **Puerto Arista** (p835)
- Witnessing the morning chorus of howler monkeys at **Laguna Miramar** (p811)

Palenque ★

San Cristóbal de Las Casas ★

Yaxchilán ★

Laguna ★ Miramar

★ Puerto Arista

■ ALTITUDE RANGE: 0m–4110m ■ SAN CRISTÓBAL DE LAS CASAS AUGUST DAILY HIGH: 21°C

History

Mesoamerica's first civilization was that of the Olmecs – sometimes called Mexico's 'mother culture.' Blossoming in western Tabasco from around 900 BC until 500 BC, after first emerging in San Lorenzo (in Veracruz), Olmec religion, art, astronomy and architecture matured at the settlement of La Venta in Tabasco, and was to deeply influence all Mexico's subsequent pre-Hispanic civilizations. The Olmecs established a trading network with villages along Chiapas' Pacific coast, and as far south as El Salvador.

Just east of Tabasco and Chiapas in the rainforests of northern Guatemala, another great civilization, the Maya, was thriving by around 200 BC. Little is currently known about late pre-Classic (300 BC–AD 250) Mayan history in Mexico, but the splendid Mayan city-states of Palenque, Yaxchilán and Toniná played a pivotal role in the Classic period (approximately AD 250–900). Dozens of other minor powers – including Bonampak, Comalcalco and Chinkultic – prospered during this time as Mayan culture reached a peak of artistic and cultural achievement during the 7th and 8th centuries. The exact causes of the Maya's rapid decline are still uncertain, but it is known that it followed a population explosion and a lengthy drought. After the Classic Mayan collapse, highland Chiapas came to be divided among a number of often-warring kingdoms.

TABASCO & CHIAPAS

Cortés disembarked on the Tabasco coast in 1519 and founded a settlement called Santa María de la Victoria, which was later moved inland and renamed Villahermosa de San Juan Bautista. However, Tabasco was largely ignored by the Spanish.

Chiapas' colonial history is quite distinct - for most of the Spanish era it was administered from Guatemala. Central Chiapas was brought under Spanish control by the 1528 expedition of Diego de Mazariegos, who defeated the dominant, warlike Chiapa people, many of whom jumped to their death in the Cañón del Sumidero rather than be captured. But new diseases arrived with the Spaniards, and an epidemic in 1544 killed about half its indigenous people.

The remoteness of the province of Chiapas from Guatemala meant there was little check on the excesses of the colonists against its native people, though some church figures, particularly Bartolomé de Las Casas (1474–1566), the first bishop of Chiapas, did fight for indigenous rights.

In 1822, newly independent Mexico unsuccessfully attempted to annex Spain's former Central American provinces (including Chiapas). But a year later a small military force under General Vicente Filísola managed to persuade Chiapas to join the Mexican union, and this was approved by a referendum in 1824.

After the Mexican Revolution, a succession of governors appointed by Mexico City, along with local landowners, maintained an almost feudal control over Chiapas. Periodic uprisings bore witness to bad government, but the world took little notice until January 1, 1994, when Zapatistas briefly occupied San Cristóbal de Las Casas and nearby towns by military force. Fighting for a fairer deal for indigenous peoples, the rebel army won widespread support but few concessions. From remote jungle bases they campaigned for democratic change and their rights, though the national Congress twice watered down progressive new legislation (see p793).

Tabasco also remained poor and isolated until recent decades, when the state's mineral riches, particularly petroleum, have brought great prosperity.

Climate

The rainy season is between May and October with the heaviest rainfall mostly in June, September and early October. During the rainy season the days often start dry and fairly bright, and there's usually a heavy downfall in the afternoon. Tabasco gets particularly heavy rainfall (about 1500mm annually). Between November and April, warm sunny days are the norm (if not the rule). The hottest months are April and May, when the fields turn a dusty brown before the onset of the rains.

Temperatures in Tabasco and Chiapas don't vary that much according to the season – altitude is a much more influential factor. All lowland areas (most of Tabasco, the Lacandón jungle, Palenque, the Usumacinta area and the Pacific coast) are hot and sticky the whole year round with daily highs above 30°C and punishing humidity. But away from these areas, in the centre of the region, the climate is less oppressive. In Los Altos – the central highlands of Chiapas, mostly 2000m to 3000m high – San Cristóbal de Las Casas has a very temperate climate, and evenings can get decidedly chilly between November and February.

Dangers & Annoyances

Since the 1994 Zapatista uprising, the army has been present in big numbers in Chiapas. Though the security situation has been volatile at times in parts of the state, things were generally much calmer by early 2004. You'll almost certainly see large numbers of troops on the move as you travel around Chiapas, but violent incidents have been extremely rare and have not involved tourists.

There are regular checkpoints on some routes, particularly the Carretera Fronteriza. Make sure your tourist card and passport are in order. If your visit extends beyond plain tourism (human-rights observation, for instance), ask in advance at a Mexican consulate or embassy about visa requirements.

In some remote areas outside San Cristóbal de Las Casas, unknown outsiders could be at risk because of local politico-religious conflicts. Similarly, some Zapatista-aligned villages (particularly around the fringes of the Montes Azules reserve) have ideologically opposed ecotourism trips like kayaking (see p793) in their region. Take local advice about where not to go. The far east of Chiapas is an area where many illegal drugs are smuggled into Mexico, and the area has a dangerous reputation for that reason.

When traveling by bus, take care of your belongings and don't accept food or drink from other passengers. At the time of writing we had not heard of any highway holdups for several years, but those who are driving themselves should always take soundings.

Having said all this, unpleasant incidents of any kind affecting travelers are extremely rare, and you're unlikely to have anything other than a trouble-free time in Chiapas.

There are no specific security issues concerning Tabasco.

Getting There & Away

Transport links with the rest of the country are relatively good, and the road network is currently being upgraded. At the time of writing new toll highways were due to open between Chiapa de Corzo and San Cristóbal de Las Casas, and between Tuxtla Gutiérrez and Coatzacoalcos.

The main airports are Villahermosa (see p782) and Tuxtla Gutiérrez (see p789) which both have daily flights to/from Mexico City and Mérida and Cancún. Tapachula (see p166) also has daily flights to/from Mexico City. At the time of research Palenque airport (see p822) was closed for improvements, though when it reopens flights should resume to/from Mérida, Tuxtla Gutiérrez, Cancún, Flores in Guatemala and probably Mexico City.

There are several swift daily bus links to/from Mexico City (see p167) and all the major cities of the region: Villahermosa, Tuxtla Gutiérrez, San Cristóbal de Las Casas and Tapachula, as well as Palenque and Comitán.

From Oaxaca (see p721) there are three daily buses each to Villahermosa, Tuxtla Gutiérrez, Tapachula and San Cristóbal. Getting to/from the Yucatán peninsula is straightforward, with fast daily buses connecting Palenque, Villahermosa and San Cristóbal de Las Casas with Mérida (see p804) and Cancún (see p782). There are also daily buses between Tulum (see p822) and Palenque.

There are several options to get to/from Guatemala. For details of the Ciudad Cuauhtémoc/La Mesilla road border crossing, see p834. The two main road border crossings near Tapachula (Talismán/El Carmen and Ciudad Hidalgo/Tecún Umán) and onward routes in Guatemala (and Central America) are covered on p840 and p838. River routes to Guatemala from Frontera Corrozal are covered on p826, from Benemérito Las Américas on p828; for the less popular Río San Pedro route via La Palma see p784.

Getting Around

Bus transport links are generally good. All cities and major towns in Tabasco and Chiapas are well connected with fairly fast, comfortable and reliable bus services. *Colectivo* taxis and minibuses offer an even speedier alternative on many major routes (including San Cristóbal de Las Casas to Tuxtla Gutiérrez).

TABASCO

Tabasco is not the most immediately appealing Mexican state, though if you're passing through there are a few interesting diversions. The state is rather sparsely populated, with two million people inhabiting 24,475 sq km.

The northern part of the state is predominantly flat, with numerous meandering rivers draining into the rich wetlands of the Gulf of Mexico; the topography changes to undulating hills as you near Chiapas.

VILLAHERMOSA

☎ 993 / pop 348,000 / elevation 12m

Villahermosa is anything but the 'beautiful city' that its name implies, but it's an important gateway and a key provincial center. Downtown is steamy, scruffy and crowded, and cultural and architectural attractions are pretty slim on the ground, though at least most of the central streets (the Zona Luz) are pedestrianized.

By contrast, oil money has pumped modernity and commerce into the sprawling outer districts – where you'll find glitzy shopping malls, luxury hotels and spacious parks.

There's little reason to linger long in Villahermosa, but to see everything you'll have to stay at least one night. Parque-Museo La Venta (which combines an Olmec archaeological museum and a zoo) is the city's chief attraction, though there's also Yumká, a kind of safari park outside the city, and the Museo Regional de Antropología.

Orientation

In this sprawling city you'll find yourself walking some distances in the sticky heat, and occasionally hopping on a minibus (*combi*) or taking a taxi. The bus station is a 20-minute walk from the Zona Luz, which extends north–south from Parque Juárez down to the Plaza de Armas, and is roughly bounded by Calle Hidalgo and the banks of the Río Grijalva.

Parque-Museo La Venta lies 2km northwest of the Zona Luz, beside Av Ruíz Cortines, the main east–west highway crossing the city. About 1km west of Parque-Museo La Venta is the Tabasco 2000 district, where you'll find modern commercial and government buildings.

Information

EMERGENCY

Police ☎ 066

INTERNET ACCESS

Cybercafés are very plentiful in Villahermosa, with at least a dozen in the Zona Luz alone. Rates are US$0.75 to US$1 per hour.

Millenium (Map p778; Sáenz 130)
Multiservicios (Map p778; Aldama 621C)

LAUNDRY

Lavandería Top Klen (Map p778; Madero s/n; per kg for next-day service US$1.50)

MEDICAL SERVICES

Hospital Cruz Roja Mexicana (Map p777; ☎ 315-55-55; Av Sandino 716) A short ride southwest of the Zona Luz.
Unidad Médica Guerrero Urgencias (Map p778; ☎ 314-56-97/98; 5 de Mayo 444; ☻ 24hr)

MONEY

Most banks in the Zona Luz have ATMs.
HSBC (Map p778; cnr Juárez & Lerdo de Tejada; ☻ 8am-7pm Mon-Sat)

POST & TELEPHONE

You'll find pay phones along Juárez.
Main Post Office (Map p778; Sáenz 131)

TOURIST INFORMATION

There are info desks at the entrance to Parque-Museo La Venta, inside the Museo de Historia and at the 1st-class (ADO) bus station.

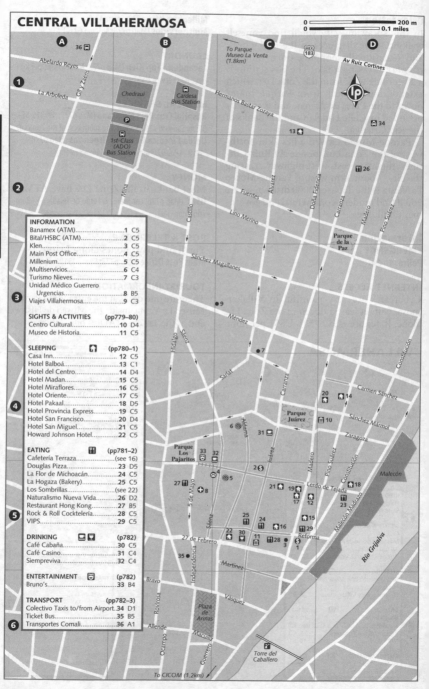

CENTRAL VILLAHERMOSA

0 ————————— 200 m
0 ————————— 0.1 miles

INFORMATION
Banamex (ATM).............................1 C5
Bital/HSBC (ATM).........................2 C5
Klen...3 C5
Main Post Office..........................4 C5
Millenium....................................5 C5
Multiservicios..............................6 C4
Turismo Nieves............................7 C3
Unidad Médico Guerrero
 Urgencias.................................8 B5
Viajes Villahermosa......................9 C3

SIGHTS & ACTIVITIES   (pp779–80)
Centro Cultural..........................10 D4
Museo de Historia......................11 C5

SLEEPING   (pp780–1)
Casa Inn....................................12 C5
Hotel Balboá..............................13 C1
Hotel del Centro.........................14 D4
Hotel Madan..............................15 C5
Hotel Miraflores.........................16 C5
Hotel Oriente.............................17 C5
Hotel Pakaal...............................18 D5
Hotel Provincia Express...............19 C5
Hotel San Francisco....................20 D4
Hotel San Miguel........................21 C5
Howard Johnson Hotel................22 C5

EATING   (pp781–2)
Cafetería Terraza....................(see 16)
Douglas Pizza............................23 D5
La Flor de Michoacán..................24 C5
La Hogaza (Bakery).....................25 C5
Los Sombrillas........................(see 22)
Naturalismo Nueva Vida..............26 D2
Restaurant Hong Kong................27 B5
Rock & Roll Cockteleria...............28 C5
VIPS...29 C5

DRINKING   (p782)
Café Cabaña..............................30 C5
Café Casino................................31 C4
Siempreviva...............................32 C4

ENTERTAINMENT   (p782)
Bruno's......................................33 B4

TRANSPORT   (pp782–3)
Colectivo Taxis to/from Airport...34 D1
Ticket Bus.................................35 B5
Transportes Comali.....................36 A1

State tourist office (Map p778; ☎ 316-36-33; www
.visitetabasco.com; Av de los Ríos & Calle 13, Tabasco 2000;
☒ 8am-9pm Mon-Fri, until 1pm Sat) To get there from
the Zona Luz, take a 'Fracc Carrizal' combi from Madero
just north of Parque Juárez, get off at the big traffic circle
surrounded by banks after you cross Av Ruíz Cortines, and
walk one block to the left along Av de los Ríos. Staff are
helpful and have a glut of glossy material.

TRAVEL AGENCIES
Both these agencies sell international and
domestic tickets and can arrange tours.
Turismo Nieves (Map p778; ☎ 314-18-88; reservaya@
turismonieves.com.mx; Sarlat 202)
Viajes Villahermosa (Map p778; ☎ 312-54-56; viajes
_vhsa@hotmail.com; Méndez 724)

Sights
Aside from Parque-Museo La Venta, Villahermosa's attractions are hardly abundant.
However, the pedestrianized Zona Luz is
an enjoyable place to explore, and its busy
lanes – full of salsa-blaring clothes stores –
buzz with life.

PARQUE-MUSEO LA VENTA
The fascinating outdoor **Parque-Museo La
Venta** (Map p777; ☎ 314-16-52; Av Ruíz Cortines;
US$2.75; ☒ sculpture trail 8am-4pm daily, zoo until 4pm
Tue-Sun) was created in the 1940s, when pet-
roleum excavation threatened the ancient
Olmec settlement of La Venta. Archaeolo-
gists moved the most significant finds, in-
cluding three of the colossal stone heads, to
Villahermosa.

The city of La Venta flourished in the
centuries between 900 and 500 BC on an
island near where the Río Tonalá runs into
the Gulf some 130km west of Villahermosa.
Danish archaeologist Frans Blom (see
p798) did the initial excavations in 1925,
and work was continued by archaeologists
from Tulane University and the University
of California. Matthew Stirling is credited
with having discovered, in the early 1940s,
five huge Olmec heads sculpted from basalt.
The largest weighs over 24 tons and stands
more than 2m tall. It's thought that the
Olmecs probably managed to move these
massive basalt heads from a quarry over
100km away in the Tuxtla mountains using
a system of sledges and river rafts.

Plan two to three hours for your visit. Independent guides charge US$16 to take one
to four people around the Parque; a site map

costs US$1. Snack stands and a little *cafetería*
provide sustenance. Be warned: the setting
in humid tropical forest means you really do
need to slap on the mosquito repellent.

Once inside, you come to the **zoo** first. It's
devoted to animals from Tabasco and nearby
regions: cats include jaguars, pumas, lynxes,
ocelots and there are white-tailed deer, spider monkeys, crocodiles and turtles, boa
constrictors, peccaries and plenty of colorful birdlife including green macaws, mealy
parrots and keel-billed toucans. There's an
informative display (in English and Spanish)
on Olmec history and archaeology as you
pass through to the sculpture trail.

A giant *ceiba* (the sacred tree of the Olmecs
and Mayas) marks the starting point of the
sculpture trail, forming an open-air museum,
which winds for 1km through dense tropical
foliage. All the exhibits are well labeled with
information in Spanish and English.

Perhaps the most impressive, in the order
that come to them, are Stele 3, which depicts
a bearded man with a headdress; Stele 9,
which represents an old warrior bearing the
claws of a harpy eagle; Altar 5, which depicts a figure carrying a child; the monkey-
faced Monument 56; and Monument 1, the
colossal head of a helmet-wearing warrior.
Along the way, many trees bear signs giving
their names and species, and animals that
pose no danger – such as coatis, squirrels
and black agoutis – roam freely.

Parque-Museo La Venta is 3km from
the Zona Luz. A 'Fracc Carrizal' combi
(US$0.50) from Madero, just north of
Parque Juárez in the Zona Luz, will drop
you at the corner of Paseo Tabasco and Av
Ruíz Cortines. Then walk 1km northeast
across Parque Tomás Garrido Canabal and
along the Malecón de las Ilusiones, a pleasant lakeside path, to the entrance. A taxi
from the Zona Luz costs US$1.50.

CICOM & MUSEO REGIONAL
DE ANTROPOLOGÍA
The Centro de Investigación de las Culturas
Olmeca y Maya (CICOM) is a complex of
buildings on the bank of the Río Grijalva,
1km south of the Zona Luz. Its centerpiece
is the **Museo Regional de Antropología Carlos
Pellicer Cámara** (Map p777; ☎ 312-63-44; Periférico
Carlos Pellicer; admission US$1.75; ☒ 9am-5pm Tue-Sun,
wheelchair access) named for the scholar and
poet responsible for salvaging the Olmec

TABASCO & CHIAPAS

artifacts displayed in the Parque-Museo La Venta. Besides the museum, the complex also holds a theater, research center and arts center. Though the museum building itself is pretty dilapidated, there are some interesting exhibits; however, all are poorly labeled, and in Spanish only.

It's best to begin on the upper level where exhibits outline Mesoamerica's many civilizations, from the oldest, Stone-Age inhabitants to the relatively recent Aztecs. After you've brushed up on the broad picture, the middle floor concentrates on Olmec and Mayan cultures including displays of masks and incense burners, and others devoted to the nearby Maya ruins of Comalcalco. Finally, on the ground floor there are some huge stone Olmec and Maya steles and sculptures, plus temporary exhibits.

CICOM is 1km south of the Zona Luz. You can walk there in about 15 minutes, or catch any 'CICOM' combi or microbus heading south on Madero.

MUSEO DE HISTORIA
The **History Museum** (Map p778; Juárez 402; US$0.50; 10am-8pm Tue-Sat, until 5pm Sun), is housed in a striking 19th-century building also known as La Casa de los Azulejos ('House of Tiles'). Though it deals with Tabasco history, it's the *azulejos* themselves that are the most interesting features here, covering the façade and most of the interior.

CENTRO CULTURAL
The stunning new **Culture Center** (Map p778; ☎ 312-54-73; Madero facing Parque Juarez; 10am-10pm) is housed in a modernist concrete-and-glass edifice. There are photographic and art exhibitions, Latin American films and a pleasant café area.

TORRE DEL CABALLERO
This lookout tower rising from the footbridge over the Río Grijalva near the city center affords medium-distance panoramas of the area, as well as potentially embarrassing encounters with young couples who come here for semi-secluded smooching.

TABASCO 2000
The Tabasco 2000 complex (Map p777), with its modern government buildings, convention center, fountains and chic boutiques in the Galerías Tabasco 2000 mall, is a

testimony to the prosperity oil has brought to Villahermosa. From the Zona Luz, take a 'Fracc Carrizal' combi from Madero just north of Parque Juárez.

Sleeping
BUDGET
Most inexpensive and mid-range hotels are in the Zona Luz. There are few inviting budget options. Keep street noise in mind when choosing a room, and consider splurging out extra for air-conditioning. As an oil town, Villahermosa has no shortage of luxury hotels; most offer heavily discounted weekend rates.

Hotel Oriente (Map p778; ☎ 312-01-21; fax 312-11-01; Madero 425; s/d US$15/22, with TV & air-con US$23/29;) Well-run, recently-renovated hotel where the pleasant rooms are kept spick-and-span, and the bathrooms (all are en suite) even have a little sparkle.

Hotel del Centro (Map p778; ☎ 312-59-61; Pino Suárez 209; s/d with fan US$16/20, with air-con US$20/24.50;) Slightly shambolic but acceptable basic-budget hotel where all the rooms have TV and bathroom.

Hotel San Francisco (Map p778; ☎ 312-31-98; Madero 604; s/d US$18/22;) The grubby hotel lobby looks uninviting, but the rooms are decent enough, and all come with air-con, bathroom and TV.

Hotel Balboá (Map p778; ☎ /fax 312-45-50; Hermanos Bastar Zozaya 505; s US$12, d with fan US$17, with air-con US$26; P) This hotel has basic but clean single and doubles rooms with fan, or better quality doubles upstairs with two beds; you pay extra for cable TV.

Hotel San Miguel (Map p778; ☎ 312-12-85; fax 312-14-26; Lerdo de Tejada 315; s/d/tr with fan US$11/14/17, with TV & air-con US$19/24/27;) On a pedestrianized street, this rambling hotel has largish, bare but functional rooms, all with shower.

MID-RANGE
Hotel Madan (Map p778; ☎ /fax 314-33-73; madan@intrasur.net.mx; Madero 408; r US$40-43;) Representing excellent value for money, the Madan has 40 well-presented, spacious rooms, nice wooden furniture and attractive bathrooms; the king-size beds are ample for a sumo wrestler.

Hotel Provincia Express (Map p778; ☎ 314-53-76; villaop@prodigy.net.mx; Lerdo de Tejada 303; s/d US$33/35;) Well-kept hotel with 50 bright rooms, which all have decent-quality beds, reading lights, air-con, cable TV and private bathroom.

Hotel Miraflores (Map p778; ☎ 312-00-22; www .miraflores.com.mx; Reforma 304; s/d/ste US$45/50/63; P ⬛) Set on a traffic-free street, the Miraflores' large, fairly sparse air-conditioned rooms have plenty of natural light, desks, balconies and cable TV, while the hotel boasts a café, restaurant and two bars.

Howard Johnson Hotel (Map p778; ☎ /fax 314-46-45; 800-201-09-09; www.hojo.com.mx; Aldama 404; s/d US$62, Fri & Sat US$42; ⬛ ⬛) The Howard Johnson is a well-established hotel in the heart of town, but though the accommodations are comfortable enough, some rooms suffer a degree of traffic noise – ask for one on the upper floor. The in-house restaurant (see below) is a good dining option.

Hotel Pakaal (Map p778; ☎ 314-46-48; Lerdo de Tejada 106; s/d US$32/36; ⬛) It's not first choice in this category, but this hotel has fair-sized air-conditioned rooms, all with cable and slightly bizarre color schemes.

TOP END

Casa Inn (Map p778; ☎ 358-01-02, 800-201-09-09; www .casainn.ws; Madero 418; r US$108 , US$53 Fri & Sat ⬛ ⬛ ⬛ ⬛) The Casa Inn is already the classiest downtown hotel, but ongoing renovations will add a pool and fitness center. All the modern rooms are comfortable, and come with writing desks and voicemail, and there are two restaurants and a bar.

Hotel Cencali (Map p777; ☎ /fax 315-19-99, 800-112-50-00; www.cencali.com.mx; cnr Av Juárez & Paseo Tabasco; r incl breakfast US$121, Fri & Sat US$62 ⬛ ⬛ ⬛ ⬛ ⬛) The Cencali boasts an excellent quiet location not far from Parque-Museo La Venta, and 120 attractive modern rooms with balconies and bathtubs. There's a great swimming pool in tropical gardens running down to the Laguna de las Ilusiones.

Best Western Hotel Maya Tabasco (Map p777; ☎ 314-11-11, 800-237-77-00; www.hotelmaya.com.mx; Av Ruíz Cortines 907; r US$108, ste US$148 ⬛ ⬛ ⬛ ⬛) Located 1km north of the Zona Luz, this business-orientated hotel has well-presented, though not huge, modern rooms and attractive gardens. There's a large pool, two bars, a restaurant, an ATM and free airport transfers.

Hyatt Regency Villahermosa (Map p777); ☎ 315-12-34; http://villahermosa.regency.hyatt.com; Av Juárez 106, Colonia LindaVista; r US$187, Fri & Sat US$88;

⬛ ⬛ ⬛ ⬛ ⬛) Villahermosa's smartest hotel has leisure facilities that include a large swimming pool and tennis courts, and there are several restaurants and a sports bar. All 207 luxuriously-appointed rooms and suites come with modem connections.

Eating

Taco joints and fast-food fryers are thick on the ground in the Zona Luz, particularly on Madero. This area's hotel and chain restaurants offer greater variety – for a few pesos more. More restaurants will open when the riverside development under construction on Malecón Madrazo is finished.

Naturalismo Nueva Vida (Map p778; ☎ 312-81-98; Carranza 318; comida corrida US$3; ☽ noon-4:30pm Mon-Fri) Family-run veggie *comedor*, open for lunch only, with a nutritious set menu that includes soup, salad, a main dish, a sweet and a drink.

Los Sombrillas (Map p778; Howard Johnson Hotel, Aldama 404; pasta from US$3.50, meat & fish mains from US$6; ☽ 7.30am-10pm; ⬛) Well-regarded, informal hotel restaurant with a good-value menu that includes delicious pasta Alfredo.

Douglas Pizza (Map p778; ☎ 312-76-76; Lerdo de Tejada 105; pizzas US$5-12; ☽ 4-11pm Mon-Sat, 2-9:30pm Sun; ⬛) Opposite Hotel Pakaal, this place serves up good pizzas with a wide assortment of toppings. There's a pleasant ambience, and pasta and salads too.

La Hogaza (Map p778; Juárez s/n; ☽ 8am-7pm) For food on the run this bakery really excels, with croissants, doughnuts, muffins, pizza, juices, and shelves of bread rolls.

VIPS (mains US$5-9; ⬛) Zona Luz (Map p778; ☎ 314-39-71; Madero 402; ☽ 8am-10pm); Ruíz Cortines (Map p777; ☎ 315-44-55; Av Ruíz Cortines 1503; ☽ 8am-10pm) This countrywide chain restaurant, popular with families, offers a menu of Mexican and international food in very clean surroundings. The Ruíz Cortines branch is near the Hyatt Regency Villahermosa.

Cafetería Terraza (Map p778; ☎ 312-00-22; Hotel Miraflores, Reforma 304; comida corrida US$5.50, mains US$7-9; ☽ 7.30am-10pm; ⬛) Reliable hotel café-restaurant, with filling portions of well-priced Mexican staples.

Restaurant Hong Kong (Map p778; ☎ 312-59-96; 5 de Mayo 433; mains from US$6; ☽ 12.30am-3pm, 7-10.30pm) Popular Chinese restaurant with tasty specials that include beef in yellow bean sauce and chow mein, plus good-value set meals from US$10.

La Flor de Michoacán (Map p778; Juárez s/n; 8am-7.30pm) Opposite La Hogaza, this place has delicious fresh juices, *licuados*, frozen yogurt and fruit cocktails.

Rock & Roll Coctelería (Map p778; ☎ 312-05-93; Reforma 307; seafood cocktails US$6-12; noon-10pm) A maelstrom of heat, swirling fans, a thumping jukebox and hard-drinking punters. Everyone's here for the *cócteles* (fish or seafood, tomato sauce, lettuce, onions and a lemon squeeze) and the cheap beer.

Outside the Zona Luz these places are well worth trying.

Karukay (Map p777; ☎ 316-40-80; Galerías Tabasco 2000 mall; per person US$5-7; 11am-8pm;) Good place to sample fairly authentic Japanese food with *yakisoba* for US$3 and tempura or sushi plates for US$6.

Restaurant Los Tulipanes (Map p777; ☎ 312-92-17; Periférico Carlos Pellicer 511; mains from US$7; 8am-10pm Mon-Sat, noon-6pm Sun;) Seafood and steaks are the specialties at this restaurant, which overlooks the Río Grijalva near the Museo Regional de Antropología. The Tabascan Sunday buffet (US$13.50 per head) here offers the perfect opportunity to gorge yourself silly.

Bougainvillea (Map p777; ☎ 315-12-34; Hyatt Regency Villahermosa; Av Juárez 106, Colonia Lindavista; mains US$7-12; noon-3pm, 6.30-10pm;) Bougainvillea is a very-well-thought-of hotel restaurant with an extensive menu of Mexican and international dishes.

Drinking   Map p778
Coffee-bar culture is sweeping through the Zona Luz, but you'll find the best brew at the venerable **Café Casino** on Juárez where Villahermosa's chattering classes gather to discuss the political issues of the day. **Café Cabaña**, at the southern end of Juárez, is another good bet for a caffeine kick, while **Siempreviva**, just west of the Parque Los Pajaritos on Lerdo de Tejada, is an art gallery with a pleasant courtyard café. The little café inside the **Centro Cultural** at Parque Juárez is air-conditioned.

Entertainment
Nightlife in the Zona Luz is very limited and pretty staid, with most of the 'action' confined to the hotels: on Madero, there's often live music at the bars inside the **Casa Inn** and **Hotel Madan** (see Sleeping, p780) For more of an alternative feel try **Bruno's**

(Map p778; cnr 5 de Mayo & Lerdo de Tejada) which is popular with artists, musicians and students. Outside the Zona Luz, you'll find more live music, usually with dancing, in the hotel bars of several hotel including the **Hyatt Regency** and **Cencali**. The **La Selva** bar (Map p777; Best Western Maya Tabasco;) is one of *the* places in town to dance to tropical Latin beats.

Teatro Esperanza Iris (Map p777; ☎ 314-42-10; Periférico Carlos Pellicer) This theater, just north of CICOM, often stages folkloric dance, theater, cinema and music performances.

Getting There & Away
AIR
Villahermosa's **Aeropuerto Rovirosa** (☎ 356-01-57) is 13km east of the center on Hwy 186. Nonstop or one-stop direct flights to/from Villahermosa include the following:

Cancún (Aerocaribe, daily)
Guadalajara (Aeroméxico & Mexicana, daily)
Houston, Texas (Continental, 4 weekly)
Mérida (Aviacsa, daily)
Mexico City (Aeroméxico, Mexicana, Aviacsa & Aero California; total 8 daily)
Monterrey (Aeroméxico & Mexicana, 2 each daily)
Oaxaca (Aerocaribe, daily)
San Antonio, Texas (Mexicana, 5 weekly)
Tuxtla Gutiérrez (Mexicana, Aerocaribe, daily)
Veracruz (Aeroméxico & Aerolitoral, 2 daily)

Airline offices in Villahermosa are at the following addresses:
Aero California (☎ 800-237-6225)
Aerocaribe (Map p777; ☎ 316-50-46; Local 9, Plaza D'Atocha Mall, Tabasco 2000)
Aeroméxico & Aerolitoral (Map p777; ☎ 312-15-28; CICOM, Periférico Carlos Pellicer 511-2)
Aviacsa (Map p777; ☎ 316-57-00; Local10, Plaza D'Atocha Mall, Tabasco 2000)
Mexicana (Map p777; ☎ 316-31-32; Locales 5 & 6, Plaza D'Atocha Mall, Tabasco 2000)

BUS
The 1st-class (ADO) **bus station** (Map p778; ☎ 312-76-92; Mina 297) is about 12 blocks north of the city center. It has a **luggage room** (per hr US$0.40; 7am-11pm) and a selection of cafés. Deluxe and 1st-class UNO, ADO and Cristóbal Colón buses run from here, as well as a few 2nd-class services. Though Villahermosa is an important transportation point, many buses serving it are *de paso*, so buy your onward ticket as early as

possible. Few destinations in Tabasco are served by this bus station; most local services leave from small independent bus and minibus terminals.

It's also possible to book 1st-class bus tickets in the city center at **Ticket Bus** (Map p778; ☎ 312-12-60; Independencia 309; ☽ 9am-9pm Mon-Sat), just north of the Plaza de Armas. They charge a commission of US$0.50 per ticket. Daily departures (most in the evening) include the following:

Campeche (US$17-22, 6 hr, 17 daily)
Cancún (US$40-60,12 hr, 10 daily)
Chetumal (US$24, 8 hr, 8 buses)
Mérida (US$24-44, 9 hr, 17 daily)
Mexico City (TAPO; US$43-63, 11 hr, 31 daily)
Oaxaca (US$32, 12 hr, 3 daily)
Palenque (US$5-6.50, 2½hr; 12 daily)
Playa del Carmen (US$38,12 hr, 8 daily)
San Cristóbal de Las Casas (US$13-14, 7 hr, 3 daily) Or go via Tuxtla Gutiérrez.
Tuxtla Gutiérrez (US$13-1, 6 hr, 6 daily)
Veracruz (US$22-35, 8 hr,16 daily)

CAR & MOTORCYCLE
Most rental companies have desks at the airport.
Dollar (Map p777; ☎ 315-80-88, Torre Empresarial, Paseo Tabasco 1203 & ☎ 314-44-66; Hotel Best Western Maya Tabasco)

Getting Around
A taxi from city to airport costs US$10 to US$13 (from airport to city US$15) and takes about 25 minutes. Alternatively, go to the road outside the airport parking lot and pick up a colectivo taxi into the city for US$1 per person. These terminate on Carranza half a block south of Ruíz Cortines, about 1km north of the Zona Luz. Take a 'Dos Montes' vehicle from there to return to the airport.

To get from the ADO bus station to the Zona Luz, take a 'Centro' combi (US$0.50) or a taxi (US$1.25). Alternatively it's a 15- to 20-minute walk via Lino Merino, Parque de la Paz and Carranza. From the Zona Luz to the ADO bus station, take a 'Chedraui' bus or combi north on Malecón Madrazo. Chedraui is a big store just north of the bus station.

Any taxi ride within the area between Av Ruíz Cortines, the Río Grijalva and Paseo Usumacinta costs US$1.25 to US$1.50. Combi rides within the same area are US$0.50.

YUMKÁ
Yumká (☎ 356-01-07; admission US$3.50, lake extra US$1.25; ☽ 9am-5pm), 18km east of Villahermosa (signposted 4km past the airport), is a Tabascan safari park. 'Yumká' is the legendary jungle-protecting spirit of the local indigenous Chontal people.

It's divided into jungle, savanna and lake zones – representing the state's three main ecosystems. Visits take the form of guided tours of the three areas (30 minutes each). In the jungle zone you pass by Tabascan species such as howler monkeys, jaguars (the big cats are enclosed), red macaws and toucans. The savanna is viewed from a tractor-pulled trolley. There is an African section with elephants, giraffes, zebras and hippos, and an Asian section with axis deer, antelope, buffalo and gaur (the largest ox in the world). You tour the lake by boat and should see plenty of birds, including herons and pelicans.

It's hardly a Kenya game drive, but Yumká's space and greenery offer a welcome break from the city. Drinks and snacks are available. A taxi from the Zona Luz costs US$16.

COMALCALCO
The Chontal Mayan city of **Comalcalco** (3km northeast of Comalcalco town; admission incl museum US$2.50; ☽ 10am-4pm) flourished during the late Classic period, between AD 500 and 900, when the region's agricultural productivity allowed population expansion. Comalcalcans traded the cacao bean with other Mayan settlements, and it is still the chief local cash crop.

Somewhat resembling Palenque in architecture and sculpture, Comalcalco is unique because it is built of bricks made from clay, sand and, ingeniously, oyster shells. Mortar was made with lime from the oyster shells. All the site's buildings have information panels in Spanish and English.

As you enter the ruins, you pass the great brick-built tiered pyramid of **Templo 1** – at its base there are remains of the stucco sculptures that once covered the building including the feet of a giant winged toad. Opposite Templo 1, the **acrópolis** complex soars over the entire site with views from its summit over a canopy of palm trees to the Gulf of Mexico. Opposite Templo 1, the crumbling profile of the **palacio** dominates the acrópolis, its twin-corbel arched galleries once Comalcalco's royal residence. Close by, there's a fine stucco carving-lined tomb vault, and the stepped profile of Templo 4. Although the west side of the acrópolis once held a crypt comparable to that of Palenque's Pakal, the tomb was vandalized centuries ago and the sarcophagus stolen.

Comalcalco's attractive site **museum** provides background in Spanish about the site, and has sculptures of a cormorant's head and stucco representations of a turtle and crocodile.

Getting There & Away

Air-conditioned minibuses operated by Transportes Comali leave from their office on Gíl y Zaens in Villahermosa, three blocks north of the main ADO bus terminal, every 20 minutes between 5am and 9pm; returning from their private terminal in Comalcalco town two blocks west of the central plaza. The 55km journey takes about an hour and costs US$2.25.

The ruins are about 3km from Comalcalco town. You can cover the distance by taxi (US$2.50) or by a Paraíso-bound combi. A few combis go right to the ruins, but most drop you at the entrance, from where it's a 1km walk. Excursions to Comalcalco offered by Villahermosa travel agents (see p779) cost from US$57 to US$85. The US$85 tour run by Villahermosa's Turismo Nieves also visits La Hacienda de la Luz, a nearby cacao plantation, and concludes with lunch and a lagoon trip at Paraíso, on the coast.

TO/FROM GUATEMALA VIA TENOSIQUE

It's possible to travel from Tabasco into Guatemala via the town of Tenosique and a river route along the Río San Pedro, though there are no longer any scheduled Fboat services. Most travelers opt for the quicker, cheaper route via Frontera Corozal in Chiapas (see p824), which passes close to the impressive ruins of Yaxchilán.

If you do decide to travel via Tenosique, there are 10 buses a day (US$8.50, 3½ hours) from Villahermosa's ADO bus station. From Tenosique, regular colectivo taxis (US$2) and combis (US$1.75) go to the village of La Palma (45 minutes) from where you'll have to charter a boat (around US$80, four hours) to El Naranjo in Guatemala. Minibuses leave El Naranjo every half hour (four hours) until 3pm for Santa Elena, near Flores.

Buses (US$2.50, 1½ hours), also leave Tenosique for the remote border post of El Ceibo, from where irregular boats depart for El Naranjo (around US$30, 1¼ hours). From El Ceibo the last bus returns at 5:30pm. There are no immigration facilities at El Ceibo or La Palma; you'll have to get your passport stamped at Tenosique or Palenque.

CHIAPAS

Chiapas is Mexico's most enigmatic state. It's a terrific place to visit, with wildly beautiful landscapes, rich indigenous culture, the colonial charm of San Cristóbal de Las Casas and an array of impressive archaeological ruins.

There are major banana- and coffee-growing regions along the fertile Soconusco. Chiapas is also blessed with natural resources including oil and gas, and generates vast hydroelectric power. Yet one-third of the homes in this resource-rich state do not have running water, and rates of illiteracy and child mortality are among the highest in Mexico. Most *chiapanecos* are very poor, and wealth is concentrated among a small oligarchy.

TUXTLA GUTIÉRREZ

☎ 961 / pop 456,000 / elevation 532m

Chiapas' state capital is a fairly mundane, modern city, though there are a couple of things worth stopping to see. Perhaps Mexico's best zoo (devoted to the fauna of Chiapas) is on the outskirts of town, and the jungle-clad 800m-deep Cañón del Sumidero is close by. However, both these trips could also be completed in a long day from San Cristóbal de Las Casas, which is only an hour away via a fast new highway.

Tuxtla Gutiérrez lies toward the west end of Chiapas' hot, humid central valley. Its name comes from the Náhuatl word *tuchtlan* (meaning 'where rabbits abound'), and from Joaquín Miguel Gutiérrez, a leading light in Chiapas' early-19th-century campaign to not be part of Guatemala. Tuxtla Gutiérrez was not an important city until it became the state capital in 1892.

TUXTLA GUTIÉRREZ

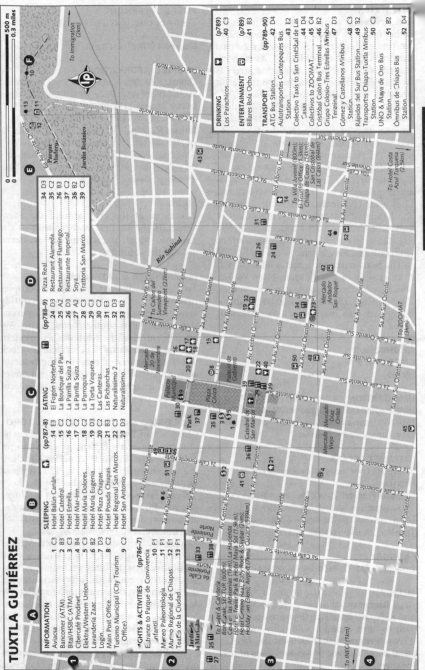

INFORMATION

Avixsa..	1 C3
Bancomer (ATM).......................	2 B3
Bital/HSBC (ATM).....................	3 C3
Cibercafé Prodinet...................	4 B4
Elektra/Western Union.............	5 C3
Lavandería Zaac.......................	6 B2
Login..	7 D3
Main Post Office......................	8 C2
Turismo Municipal (City Tourism Office)................................	9 C2

SIGHTS & ACTIVITIES (pp786-7)

Entrance to Parque de Convivencia Infantil...............................	10 F1
Museo Paleontología................	11 F1
Museo Regional de Chiapas.......	12 E1
Teatro de la Ciudad.................	13 F1

SLEEPING (pp787-8)

Hotel Balún Canán.....................	14 E3
Hotel Catedral.........................	15 C2
Hotel Estrella...........................	16 C2
Hotel Mar-Inn..........................	17 C2
Hotel María Dolores..................	18 C2
Hotel María Eugenia.................	19 D3
Hotel Plaza Chiapas..................	20 C2
Hotel Posada Chiapas...............	21 B3
Hotel Regional San Marcos........	22 C3
Hotel San Antonio....................	23 D3

EATING (pp788-9)

El Fogón Norteño.....................	24 D3
La Boutique del Pan..................	25 A2
La Parrilla Suiza 2....................	26 D3
La Parrilla Suiza.......................	27 A2
La Parroquia............................	28 C3
La Torta Vaquera.....................	29 C3
Las Canteras...........................	30 C2
Las Pichanchas........................	31 E3
Naturalíssimo 2........................	32 D3
Naturalíssimo...........................	33 B2
Pizza Real...............................	34 D3
Restaurant Alameda.................	35 C2
Restaurante Flamingo...............	36 B3
Restaurante Imperial................	37 A2
Soya..	38 C3
Trattoria San Marco.................	39 C3

DRINKING (p789)

Los Parachicos.........................	40 C3

ENTERTAINMENT (p789)

Billares Bola Ocho....................	41 B3

TRANSPORT (pp789-90)

ATG Bus Station.......................	42 D4
Autotransportes Cuxtepeques Bus Station..............................	43 E2
Colectivo Taxis to San Cristóbal de Las Casas...............................	44 D4
Colectivos to ZOOMAT.............	45 C4
Cristóbal Colón Bus Terminal.....	46 B2
Grupo Colosio-Tres Estrellas Minibus Terminal.....................	47 D3
Gómez y Castellanos Minibus Station..................................	48 C3
Rápidos del Sur Bus Station.......	49 32
Transportes Chiapa-Tuxtla Minibus Station..................................	50 C3
UNO & Maya de Oro Bus Station..................................	51 B2
Ómnibus de Chiapas Bus Station..................................	52 D4

TABASCO & CHIAPAS

Orientation

The city center is the Plaza Cívica, with the cathedral on its south side. The main east–west street, here called Av Central, runs past the north side of the cathedral. As it enters the city from the west, this same street is Blvd Dr Belisario Domínguez; to the east it becomes Blvd Ángel Albino Corzo.

East–west streets are called Avenidas and are named Norte or Sur, depending whether they're north or south of Av Central. North–south streets are Calles and are called Poniente (Pte) or Oriente (Ote), depending whether they're west or east of Calle Central. Each street name also has a suffix indicating whether it is east (Oriente, Ote), west (Poniente, Pte), north (Nte) or south (Sur) of the intersection of Av Central and Calle Central. So the address 2a Av Nte Pte 425 refers to No 425 on the western (Pte) half of 2a Av Norte.

The best source for maps is **INEGI** (☎ 613-17-83; 6a Av Sur Pte 670; ☒ 8:30am-4:30pm Mon-Fri), which is located southwest of the center. INEGI sells 1:25,000 and 1:50,000 maps of many parts of Chiapas and other Mexican states.

Information

EMERGENCY
☎ 060

IMMIGRATION
Instituto Nacional de Migración (☎ 614-32-88, 613-32-91; Libramiento Nte Ote; ☒ 9am-5pm Mon-Fri) This is 4km northeast of the center.

INTERNET ACCESS
There are over a dozen cybercafés in central Tuxtla.
Cibercafé Prodinet (2a Calle Pte Sur; per hr US$0.75; ☒ 9am-8pm Mon-Sat, noon-7pm Sun; ☒)
Login (2a Av Sur Ote 540B; per hr US$0.50; ☒ 8am-11pm Mon-Sat, 10am-7pm Sun; ☒)

LAUNDRY
Lavandería Zaac (2a Av Sur Ote 424; per 3kg US$2.75)

MONEY
Both **Bancomer** (cnr Av Central Pte & 2a Av Nte Pte) and **HSBC** (west side of Plaza Cívica) are open from 9am to 3pm Monday to Friday and have ATMs. **Western Union** (inside Elektra store, Calle Central Nte facing Plaza Cívica; ☒ 9am-9pm) does money transfers.

POST & TELEPHONE
Plenty of card phones are scattered around the plaza.
Main Post Office (1a Av Nte Ote, just off Plaza Cívica)

TOURIST INFORMATION
Airport (☒ 7.30am-5pm)
SECTUR (State Tourism Office; ☎ 800-280-35-00; Blvd Belisario Domínguez 250; ☒ 9am-9pm Mon-Fri, until 4pm Sat & Sun) It's 1.6km west of the center.
Turismo Municipal (City Tourism Office; ☎ 612-55-11 ext 214; Calle Central Nte & 2a Av Nte Ote; ☒ 8am-8pm Mon-Fri, until 4pm Sat) In the underpass at the northern end of Plaza Cívica. Helpful, informed staff and offers a free left-luggage service.

Sights

The heart of the city, around the Plaza Cívica, is the liveliest part of town in the daytime. Most attractions are scattered around the suburbs.

PLAZA CÍVICA & CATHEDRAL
Tuxtla's broad, lively main **plaza** occupies two blocks and is flanked by an untidy array of concrete civic and commercial structures. At its southern end, across Avenida Central, is the whitewashed modern **Catedral de San Marcos**. The cathedral's clock tower tinkles out a tune on the hour to accompany a kitsch merry-go-round of apostles' images that emerge from one of the structure's upper levels.

ZOOLÓGICO MIGUEL ÁLVAREZ DEL TORO
Chiapas, with its huge range of natural environments, claims the highest concentration of animal species in North America – including several varieties of big cat, 1200 types of butterfly and over 600 kinds of bird. About 180 of these species, many of them in danger of extinction, are in relatively spacious enclosures at Tuxtla's excellent **zoo** (☎ 614-47-65; El Zapotal; US$1.75; ☒ 9am-5pm Tue-Sun).

Recently remodeled, Zoológico Miguel Álvarez del Toro (ZOOMAT) has several innovative new features including a 'museum' of the zoo with information about the life of its conservationist founder Dr Miguel Álvarez del Toro. There are also exhibits about the creatures that have lived in the zoo over the years, including a monkey-eating harpy eagle (*águila arpia*).

Wildlife you can expect to see includes ocelots, jaguars, pumas, tapirs, red macaws, toucans, three species of crocodile, snakes and spider monkeys. To get there take a 'Cerro Hueco, Zoológico' colectivo (US$0.40) from the corner of 1a Calle Ote Sur and 7a Av Sur Ote. They leave every 20 minutes and take 20 minutes. A taxi is US$3.

PARQUE MADERO

This museum-theater-park area is 1.25km northeast of the city center. If you don't want to walk, take a colectivo along Av Central to Parque 5 de Mayo at the corner of 11a Calle Ote, then another colectivo north along 11a Calle Ote.

The modern **Museo Regional de Chiapas** (☎ 612-04-59; Calz de los Hombres Ilustres s/n; admission US$3; ☻ 9am-4pm Tue-Sun) has archaeological and colonial history exhibits, and costume and craft collections, all from Chiapas, plus temporary exhibitions. The neighboring **Teatro de la Ciudad** often has an interesting Latin American film to see. Also close by is the new **Museo Paleontología** (☎ 600-02-54; Calz de los Hombres Ilustres s/n; admission US$2.75; ☻ 10am-5pm Tue-Fri, 11am-5pm Sat & Sun), which has a small collection of dinosaur bones and fossils.

Parque Madero also contains the **Jardín Botánico** (Botanical Garden; admission free; ☻ 9am-6pm Tue-Sun) and a children's park, the **Parque de Convivencia Infantil** (admission free; ☻ 9am-8:30pm Tue-Fri, until 9:30pm Sat & Sun), which has a mini-train, mechanical rides, swings, climbing equipment and minigolf. You pay for the individual rides and activities.

Sleeping

Budget hotels congregate around the plaza. Most luxury and mid-range hotels are west of the center, and periodically offer discounted rates.

BUDGET

Hotel Posada Chiapas (☎ 612-33-54; 2a Calle Pte Sur 243; s/d US$9/16; ☐) An excellent budget choice, with small but attractive, brightly decorated rooms all with good beds, bathroom and fan set around a courtyard.

Hotel San Antonio (☎ 612-27-13; 2a Av Sur Ote 540; s/d US$8.50/14; ☐) Hotel San Antonio is run by friendly people, is well located for the San Cristóbal minibus terminal, and has clean, good-value rooms with fan and bathroom.

Hotel Plaza Chiapas (☎ 613-83-65; 2a Av Nte Ote 229; s/d US$14/16, TV extra US$5) This place has

a shiny lobby and a small restaurant. The rooms, all with fan and some with balcony, are clean and represent fair value.

Hotel Catedral (☎ 613-08-24; 1a Av Nte Ote 367; s/d/tr US$17/20/24; ☐) This hotel has decent, serviceable rooms with bathroom, fans, hot water and cable TV.

Northeast of the plaza is a cluster of unloved, basic places that will do for a night:

Hotel María Dolores (☎ 612-36-83; 2a Calle Ote Nte 304; s/d with bathroom US$7.50/9)

Hotel Estrella (☎ 612-38-27; 2a Calle Ote Nte 322; s/d without bathroom US$7/9)

Hotel Mar-Inn (☎ 612-57-83; 2a Av Nte Ote 347; s/d with fan & bathroom US$12/15)

Villa Juvenil Chiapas (☎ 613-54-78; Blvd Albino Corzo 1800; dm US$4) If price is a real issue, this is a grubby youth hostel nearly 2km east of Plaza Cívica. To get there from the city center, take a 'Ruta 1' colectivo along Av Central to the yellow footbridge – it's just before a statue of Albino Corzo.

La Hacienda Trailer Park (☎ 612-78-32; Blvd Belisario Domínguez 1197; trailer sites for 2 US$12, plus US$3.50 per extra person; ☐ ☒) This place is 3km west of Plaza Cívica, and has all hookups, a coffee shop and a tiny pool, but the park area is small and somewhat blighted by traffic noise.

MID-RANGE

Hotel Regional San Marcos (☎ 613-19-40; san marcos@chiapas.net; 2a Calle Ote Sur 176; s/d US$20/23, with ☒ US$25/29; ☐) A minute's walk from Plaza Cívica, this hotel has medium-size, fairly pleasant rooms with TV and private bathroom. Bright, flower-patterned furniture adds a little dash.

Hotel Costa Azul Turquesa (☎ 611-34-85; Libramiento Sur Ote 3722 ; r/ste US$42/61; ☐ ☒) Located on the southeast edge of the town with fine vistas of Chiapas' central valley, this elegant new hotel is set in spacious leafy grounds. Good-value stylish rooms, and the suites all have Jacuzzis.

Hotel Maya Sol (☎ 615-05-52, 800-112-42-63; www.hotelmayasol-chiapas.com; Blvd Belisario Domínguez 1380; s/d/ste US$62/69/93; ☐ ☒ ☒) Attractive upmarket motel, located 3km west of the plaza, with 64 modern, comfortable rooms all with air-con and cable TV. There's a small pool, restaurant and bar.

Hotel Bonampak (☎ 613-20-50; hotbonam@prodigy .net.mx; Blvd Belisario Domínguez 180; s/d US$62/69;

(P) (X) (R)) Almost opposite the state tourist office, 1.6km west of Plaza Cívica, the Bonampak has comfortable accommodations with cable TV, though avoid the noise-prone streetside rooms. It boasts a pool, travel agency and a copy of one of the famous Bonampak murals.

Hotel María Eugenia (☎ 613-37-67; heugenia@ prodigy.net.mx; Av Central Ote 507; r US$63-71; (X) (P)) This is the most comfortable downtown hotel, and has a good restaurant. Of the 83 airy, light rooms, all have either two double beds or a huge king-size and cable TV, and many have great views.

La Hacienda Hotel (☎ 612-78-32; Blvd Belisario Domínguez 1197; s/d rooms with fan US$38/46, with (X) US$53/62; (P) (R)) La Hacienda is 3km west of Plaza Cívica and has comfortable, spacious rooms and friendly management. Small pool, too.

Hotel Balún Canán (☎ 612-30-48; www.baluncanan .com.mx; Av Central Ote 944; s/d US$27/35; (P) (X)) The motel-style Balún Canán, 1km east of the center, has old-fashioned rooms with rickety furniture, bathroom and TV.

TOP END

Hotel Camino Real (☎ 617-77-77; www.caminoreal .com/tuxtla; Blvd Belisario Domínguez 1195; r US$195; (P) (X) (Q) (R)) The cutting-edge design of the five-star Camino Real rises like some contemporary castle of the hospitality industry above the west of the city. There's a spectacular interior, with a pool and waterfall in a large, verdant inner courtyard full of free-flying tropical birds. Commodious rooms come with all mod cons, and have wheelchair access. Facilities include a spa, tennis courts and a gym. Special rates sometimes offer doubles with breakfast for US$120.

Holiday Inn (☎ 917-10-00, 800-009-99-00; www.6c .com; Blvd Belisario Domínguez 1081; r US$99; (P) (X) (Q) (R)) This hotel, built in an attractive, modern Arabic style, is located 3km west of the center opposite the Plaza Crystal mall. The accommodations here are up to business-class standards, and there's a huge pool and a gym. Weekend rates sometimes drop to US$75.

Eating

There's plenty of choice in Tuxtla, though little gourmet cuisine. Local specialities include *chipilín* (a corn-based cheesy soup).

The first three places listed all have outdoor tables, and offer a peaceful setting behind the cathedral to enjoy your meal.

Trattoria San Marco (☎ 612-69-74; Callejón Ote Sur, Local 5; mains US$3.25-5.75, pizzas US$4-10.50) Snack on a sub, baguette or a salad, or delve into the extensive pizza menu. Also offers *papas al horno* (potatoes with filling) and delicious savory *crepas*.

La Parroquia (☎ 600-11-97; Callejón Ote Sur, Local 6; mains US$4-9) Next door to Trattoria San Marco, the Parroquia specializes in *a la parrilla* grills, from bacon to *filete mignon* and chorizo.

La Torta Vaquera (☎ 613-20-94; Callejón Ote Sur; snacks from US$0.50) This place is popular for coffee, tacos and *quesadillas*.

Restaurante Imperial (Calle Central Nte; snacks US$1-2, mains US$2.50-3, comida corrida US$3). Busy, efficient place facing the west side of Plaza Cívica and close to the 1st-class bus station. Offers a wholesome two-course comida corrida with lots of main-dish choice. Full breakfast menu too, and there's good drinking chocolate.

Restaurante Alameda (☎ 612-25-06; 1a Av Nte Pte 133; snacks US$1-2.25, mains US$2.50-3) Family-run place that's a great choice for inexpensive Mexican meals, and offers porridge or hotcakes for breakfast.

Naturalíssimo (☎ 613-53-43; 6a Calle Pte Nte 124; ☎ 613-96-48; Av Central Ote 525; breakfasts US$3-4.50, antojitos US$2-3.25, lunch US$4.50) Bright, cheery vegetarian Naturalíssimo offers healthy breakfasts, Mexican dishes like wholewheat *tortas* and *chilaquiles* and a tasty three-course lunch. The Av Central Ote branch also sells yogurt and ice cream.

Restaurante Flamingo (☎ 612-09-20; 1a Calle Pte Sur 17; mains US$4-11, comida corrida US$5.50; (X)) Located along a passage off a downtown street, this is a pleasingly formal restaurant. Tuck into a full hotcakes breakfast, a filling set lunch, or meat and fish dishes and marvel at the lollipop-pink and powder-blue paint job, which must have been the height of chic in 1962.

Pizza Real (☎ 614-71-51; 2a Av Sur Ote 557; comida corrida US$1) Opposite Hotel San Antonio, this *comedor* does a bargain-priced lunchtime set meal including rice and two other dishes. No pizzas, though!

Hotel María Eugenia (☎ 613-37-67; Av Central Ote 507; mains US$7-9) This hotel has a reliable restaurant that's particularly popular for its filling and economical comida corrida (US$4.50) and breakfast buffet (US$7).

Soya (☎ 613-36-16; Av Central Pte; ice cream US$0.75-1.75) A few blocks west of the center, Soya sells wholemeal breads, fresh yogurt and yogurt ice cream, for which you can select a range of toppings and fruits to be crushed into it.

La Boutique del Pan (☎ 613-35-17; Av Central Pte 961; snacks US$1-4) Excellent bakery, facing the Parque Jardín de la Marimba, with a bright, air-conditioned café section where you can sit down for a pastry, sandwich or coffee.

La Parrilla Suiza (☎ 614-44-74; Av Central Pte 1013; ☎ 612-20-41; Central Ote 731; tacos US$0.50, 2-person grills US$7; ☷ 4pm-4am) The Parrilla Suiza's two branches score highly for economical meat feasts.

Las Canteras (☎ 611-43-10; 2a Av Nte Pte 148; mains US$4.50-9) Set in what looks like the shell of an abandoned evangelical church, Las Canteras is decorated with local textiles, specializes in local cooking and has live marimba music. Try the *cochinito chiapaneco* or the excellent-value US$3.50 comida corrida.

Cafetería Bonampak (☎ 613-20-50; Hotel Bonampak, Blvd Belisario Domínguez 108; mains US$5-8) Deservedly popular, attractive and moderately priced hotel restaurant.

Las Pichanchas (☎ 612-53-51; Av Central Ote 837; mains US$3-8; ☷ noon-midnight) This courtyard restaurant, located six blocks east of Plaza Cívica, has a long menu of local specialties. Try the tasty *tamales*, or *chipilín*, a cheese-and-cream soup with a maize base, and leave room for the dessert *chimbos*, made from egg yolks and cinnamon. There's live marimba music, and Chiapas folkloric dance in the evening too.

El Fogón Norteño (☎ 611-38-61; Av Central Ote 784; grills for 2 US$7, salads US$1.75-2.50) Popular place offering a similar meat-munchers' menu to Parrilla Suiza across the street.

Drinking

Downtown there's little action after dark, but the bar **Los Parachicos** (☎ 613-19-40; cnr 1a Av Sur Ote & 2 Calle Ote Sur) is fine for a beer and they sometimes have live music, as does the bar on the upper level of **Trattoria San Marco** (see Eating opposite).

Entertainment

Popular, free marimba concerts are held from 7pm to 10pm Saturday and Sunday (and sporadically on other evenings when the weather's fine) in the Parque Jardín de la Marimba, a pleasant park beside Av Central Pte, eight blocks west of Plaza Cívica. If the weather's not so kind, check out the pool hall, **Billares Bola Ocho** (2a Calle Pte Sur s/n). Located two blocks west of the plaza, it's a hustlers' heaven.

Clubbers congregate in the 'Zona Dorada' zone west of the center along the Blvd Domínguez, where **Baby Rock** (☎ 615-14-28; Calz Emiliano Zapata 207), off Blvd Belisario Domínguez opposite the Camino Real hotel, and **Skybar** (☎ 615-29-57; Blvd Las Fuentes 101), just outside the Camino Real's main door, both play Latin and Western dance hits.

Shopping

Casa de las Artesanías de Chiapas (☎ 602-65-65; Blvd Belisario Domínguez 2035; ☷ 10am-8pm Mon-Sat, until 3pm Sun) This place, though an unhandy 2km west of Plaza Cívica, sells a good range of Chiapas crafts. There's also a very pretty Museo Etnográfico here, with exhibits on seven Chiapas indigenous groups.

Getting There & Away

AIR

Tuxtla's **Aeropuerto Francisco Sarabia** (☎ 612-29-20), also called Aeropuerto Terán, is 3km south of Hwy 190 from a signposted turn-off 5km west of Plaza Cívica. A taxi from the center to the airport costs US$6.

Aerocaribe flies to/from Mexico City, Oaxaca, Villahermosa, Veracruz, Tapachula, Palenque, Mérida, Cancún – all at least once daily. Aviacsa and Mexicana fly several times daily to/from Mexico City (US$174).

Airline offices include the following:
Aerocaribe City (☎ 602-56-49, Bvld Belisario Domínguez 1748); Airport ☎ 615-15-30)
Aviacsa City (☎ 611-20-00; Av Central Pte 160, just west of Plaza Cívica); Airport (☎ 671-52-46)
Mexicana City (☎ 602-57-71, Bvld Belisario Domínguez 1748); Airport (☎ 671-52-18)

BUS

There are numerous bus stations. The main terminal, **Cristóbal Colón** (☎ 612-51-22), is at 2a Av Nte Pte 268, two blocks west of the main plaza: Colón, Altos and ADO all operate from here. The 2nd-class line Rápidos del Sur (RS) is next door, and UNO and Maya 'e Oro deluxe services are across the street. There's no left luggage, but the city tourist office (see p786) will look after your gear, as will some stores on 2a Nte Pte: look for 'Se guardan maletas' or 'Se guardan equipaje' signs.

A new bus station has been projected for a site several kilometers east of the center near the Central de Abastos Libramiento Sur (Libramiento Sur Market) for years, but it may not come into operation during the lifetime of the book.

Most 2nd-class companies' terminals are east of the center.

Autotransportes Cuxtepeques (10a Calle Ote Nte at 3a Nte Ote)

Autotransportes Tuxtla Gutiérrez (ATG; 3a Av Sur Ote 712)

Fletes y Pasajes (FYPSA; 9a Av Sur Ote 1882)

Grupo Colosio-Tres Estrellas (2a Av Sur Ote 521)

Ómnibus de Chiapas (OC; 3a Av Sur Ote 884)

Note that all journey times between Tuxtla Gutiérrez and San Cristóbal de Las Casas depend on the route that is taken. By the time you read this all transport will probably be using the fast new toll highway (which cuts the journey time from two hours to one hour). All colectivo taxis and minibuses are already using the new highway. But if your bus uses the old road, add an hour to your journey time. Similarly, if you're heading to Palenque, Villahermosa or Mérida add an extra hour to the time indicated below.

Daily departures from Tuxtla include the following:

Comitán (US$8, 3½hr, 5 Maya de Oro; US$7, 3 Colón; US$5, 16 Cuxtepeques)

Mérida (US$41, 13 hr, 1 Maya de Oro; US$36, 1 Colón; US$27, 2 ATG)

Mexico City (US$80, 17 hr, 1 UNO; US$58, 4 Maya de Oro; US$51, 8 Colón/ADO) Most go to TAPO, a few to Norte.

Oaxaca (US$26, 10 hr, 1 Maya de Oro; US$22, 3 Colón; US$18, 8 FYPSA)

Palenque (US$12, 6 hr, 2 Maya de Oro; US$8-11, 7 Colón; US$9, 4 ATG)

Puerto Escondido (US$23, 11½hr, 2 Colón)

San Cristóbal de Las Casas (US$4.25-5.50, 1-1½hr; 9 Maya de Oro/UNO; US$3.50, 7 Colón; US$3, 6 ATG; US$3.25, frequent Colosio-Tres Estrellas minibuses; US$2.75, OC minibuses every 20 mins 6am to 6pm; US$3.75 frequent colectivo taxis from 3a Av Sur Ote 847)

Tapachula (US$26, 7½hr, 1 UNO; US$19, 6 Maya de Oro; US$16, 14 Colón; US$13, 31 RS)

Villahermosa (US$14, 7 hr, 2 Maya de Oro; US$13, 4 Colón; US$9, 3 ATG)

CAR & MOTORCYCLE

These rental companies also have desks at the airport:

Budget (☎ 615-06-83; Blvd Belisario Domínguez 2510)

Hertz (☎ 615-53-48; Hotel Camino Real, Blvd Belisario Domínguez 1195)

Getting Around

All colectivos (US$0.40) on Blvd Belisario Domínguez-Av Central-Blvd Albino Corzo run at least as far as the Hotel Bonampak and state tourist office in the west, and 11a Calle Ote in the east. Official stops are marked by 'parada' signs but they'll sometimes stop for you elsewhere. Taxi rides within the city cost US$1.75 to US$2.

CHIAPA DE CORZO

☎ 961 / pop 31,000 / elevation 450m

Chiapa de Corzo is an attractive colonial town with an easygoing, provincial air. Situated on the north bank of the broad Río Grijalva, it's 12km east of Tuxtla Gutiérrez, and is the main starting point for trips to the Cañón del Sumidero.

History

Chiapa de Corzo has been occupied almost continuously since about 1500 BC, though there is not much to see in the way of pre-Hispanic remains.

In the couple of centuries before the Spaniards arrived, the warlike Chiapa tribe had their capital, Nandalumí, a couple of kilometers downstream from present-day Chiapa de Corzo, on the opposite bank of the Grijalva. When Diego de Mazariegos invaded the area in 1528, the Chiapa, realizing defeat was inevitable, apparently hurled themselves by the hundreds – men, women and children – to their death in the canyon rather than surrender.

Mazariegos founded a settlement that he called Chiapa de Los Indios here, but quickly shifted his base to another new location, Villa Real de Chiapa (now San Cristóbal de Las Casas), where he found the climate and natives were more agreeable.

At Chiapa in 1863, liberal forces, organized by Chiapas state governor Ángel Albino Corzo, defeated conservatives supporting the French invasion of Mexico. The name of Corzo, who was also born in the town and died here, was added to the name Chiapa in 1888.

Orientation & Information

Everything revolves around, or just off, Chiapa's vast central plaza, named for Albino Corzo. Tuxtla Buses and minibuses stop on its north side. The Chiapa embarcadero for Cañón del Sumidero boat trips is two blocks south of the plaza along 5 de Febrero, the street on the plaza's west side.

The **tourist office** (5 de Febrero 11; ☼ 9am-2pm Mon-Sat) is just off the southwest corner of the plaza. **Banamex** (☼ 9am-2pm Mon-Fri, until 3pm Sat) is on the west side of the plaza and has an ATM. **Cyberparachico** (☼ 9am-9pm Mon-Sat), on the north side of the plaza, offers Internet access.

Sights

Impressive **arcades** frame three sides of the plaza, and a statue of General Corzo rises on the west side. **La Pila**, an elaborate castle-like colonial brick fountain in Mudéjar-Gothic style, said to resemble the Spanish crown, stands toward the southeast corner. Completed in 1562, and restored in 1944, locals claim it's the only example of this architectural style in the Americas.

The large **Templo de Santo Domingo de Guzmán**, one block south of the plaza, was built in the late 16th century by the Dominican order. Its adjoining convent is now the **Centro Cultural**, holding an exposition of the *grabado* (block printing) art of the Chiapa-born Franco Lázaro Gómez. This center's also home to the absorbing **Museo de la Laca** (☎ 616-00-55; Av Mexicanidad Chiapaneca 10; admission free; ☼ 10am-5pm), dedicated to the local craft specialty, lacquered gourds. There are pieces dating back to 1606 and even some from China, Japan and Thailand, where lacquerwork also evolved.

Festivals & Events

Chiapa's annual fiesta (January 9–21), the Fiesta de Enero, is one of Mexico's most extraordinary spectacles, including nightly dances involving cross-dressing young men, known as Las Chuntá. Blond-wigged, mask-toting Parachicos (actually conquistador-impersonators) parade on January 15, 17 and 20. A canoe battle and fireworks extravaganza follows on the final day.

Sleeping

Hotel Los Ángeles (☎ 616-00-48; fax 616-02-65; Plaza Albino Corzo; s/d with bathroom & fan US$16/18, with air-con US$21/23; P ⊠) This hotel, at the southeast corner of the plaza, has spotless rooms with hot water and TV; those on the upper level are more spacious.

Hotel La Ceiba (☎ 616-07-73; laceibachiapadecorzo@hotmail.com; Av Domingo Ruíz 300; s/d US$42/47; P ⊠ ⊠) La Ceiba, located two blocks west of the plaza, has an inviting pool and extensive gardens, and the 91 attractive rooms have fans and cable TV.

Posada Río Grijalva (☎ 616-07-59; Av Independencia 182B; d US$11; P) Three blocks southeast of the plaza, this basic place has four rooms, all with one double bed, fan and (very ensuite) bathroom.

Eating & Drinking

By the embarcadero are eight overpriced restaurants with near-identical menus, though the river views are nice. Near the market, across from the Museo de la Laca, are the standard ultra-cheap market *comedores* – try **El Asadero** for grilled meats. The best place for fresh fruit licuados, juices and ice cream is **La Michoacana** on the southeast corner of the plaza.

Comedor Díaz (Av Julián Grajales; mains US$2-2.50) Opposite Hotel Los Ángeles, this informal comedor has big portions of Mexican food.

Restaurant Los Corredores (☎ 616-07-60; 5 de Febrero at Madero; breakfast US$2.75, mains US$4.50-7) Facing the southwest corner of the plaza, it has good breakfasts, reasonably priced fish plates and lots of local specialities.

Restaurant Jardines de Chiapa (☎ 616-01-98; Madero 395; mains US$4.50-6.50) One block along Madero from Los Corredores, this large place is set around a garden patio. There's an extensive menu, including tasty *cochinito al horno*.

Restaurant El Campanario (☎ 616-03-90; Urbina 5; mains US$5-8) Half a block east of the plaza, this attractive restaurant has folksy décor and a plant-filled patio. The ambience is relaxed and the food list extensive, with plenty of fish, seafood and regional specialities like *pepito con tasajo*.

Getting There & Away

Minibuses from Tuxtla Gutiérrez to Chiapa de Corzo are run by Gómez y Castellanos, at 3a Av Sur Ote 380, and Transportes

Chiapa–Tuxtla, on 2a Av Sur Ote at 2a Ote Sur. Both services depart every few minutes from 5:30am to 10:30pm for the US$0.60, 20-minute trip, and will also stop at Embarcadero Cahuaré if you wish (see next).

Buses to/from San Cristóbal de Las Casas don't pass through central Chiapa de Corzo; most stop at a northeast gas station on Hwy 190. Microbuses (US$0.40) run between here and the top end of Chiapa's plaza.

CAÑÓN DEL SUMIDERO

The Cañón del Sumidero (Sumidero Canyon) is a spectacular fissure in the earth east of Tuxtla Gutiérrez. In 1981 the Chicoasén hydroelectric dam was completed at its northern end, damming the Río Grijalva which flows through the canyon, and creating a 25km-long reservoir. A new 'ecotourism' park with adventure activities opened here on the reservoir's banks in 2003.

The canyon can be viewed from a couple of *miradores* (lookout points) reached by road from Tuxtla; taxi drivers charge around US$25 for a two-hour round trip. However most people choose to see the canyon using one of the fast *lancha* **motorboats** (return trip US$11; ☺ 8am-4pm) that speed through the canyon between its towering sheer rock walls. It's about a two-hour return trip, and unfortunately most *lancheros* rush to get the journey over with as soon as possible.

Boat trips start in either Chiapa de Corzo or at the **Embarcadero Cahuaré**, 5km to the north along the road to Tuxtla. You'll rarely have to wait more than half an hour for a boat to fill up. Bring something to drink, something to shield you from the sun and, if the weather is not hot, a layer or two of warm clothing.

It's about 35km from Chiapa de Corzo to the dam. Soon after you pass under Hwy 190, the sides of the canyon tower an amazing 800m above you. Along the way you'll see a variety of birds – herons, egrets, cormorants, vultures, kingfishers – plus probably a crocodile or two. The boat operators will point out a couple of caves and a few odd formations of rock and vegetation, including one cliff face covered in thick, hanging moss resembling a giant Christmas tree, where in rainy periods water cascades down the 'branches.'

Soon after this, 40 minutes from Chiapa de Corzo, is the new **Parque Ecoturístico** (☎ 602-85-00; www.sumidero.com; adults & children over 6 US$14.50; ☺ 9:30am-5pm). This ecopark occupies a jungle-clad bank of the canyon, and offers a great base for a range of adventure sports – at a price. You have to pay extra to hire a kayak (per hour US$4.50) or mountain bike (US$3.50), rappel (US$3.50) or swing through the trees on a zip line (five turns are US$6). The large swimming pool, aviary, crocodile pools, minizoo (with jaguars and a puma) and jungle trails are gratis. You'll also find a café and a restaurant, which is just as well as visitors are not permitted to bring in their own food or drink.

Lanchas drop you off at the park embarcadero, and return regularly to Chiapa until 5pm. A return ticket costs US$11.

SAN CRISTÓBAL DE LAS CASAS

☎ 967 / pop 121,000 / elevation 2163m

From Tuxtla Gutiérrez you'll either travel here via serpentine Hwy 190, or a fast new toll highway that cuts the 85km trip from two hours to one. Both routes seem to climb endlessly into the clouds before descending into the temperate, pine-clad Valle de Jovel, where lies the beautiful colonial town of San Cristóbal (cris-*toh*-bal).

San Cristóbal has been a favorite travelers' haunt for decades. It's a pleasure to spend time here: exploring the cobbled streets and markets, visiting nearby indigenous villages and absorbing the unique, relaxed ambience. San Cristóbal has a bohemian, artsy, floating community of Mexicans and foreigners, a lively bar and music scene and wonderfully clear highland light. There's a terrific selection of accommodations at all price levels, and a cosmopolitan array of cafés and restaurants. All in all, it's easy to see why San Cristóbal is many people's favorite Mexican town.

History

Ancestors of the indigenous Maya people of the San Cristóbal area, the Tzotziles and Tzeltales, are thought to have moved to these highlands after the collapse of lowland Maya civilization, more than 1000 years ago. Diego de Mazariegos founded San Cristóbal as the Spanish regional base in 1528. For most of the colonial era San Cristóbal was a neglected outpost governed ineffectively from Guatemala. Its Spanish citizens made fortunes from wheat; the indigenous people lost their lands and suffered diseases, taxes and forced labor.

The church afforded some protection against colonist excesses. Dominican monks reached Chiapas in 1545 and mad' San Cristóbal their main base. The town is now named after one of them, Bartolomé de Las Casas, who was appointed bishop of Chiapas and became the most

THE ZAPATISTAS

On the day of NAFTA's Initiation (January 1, 1994), a previously unknown leftist guerrilla army, the Zapatistas, emerged from the woods to occupy San Cristóbal de Las Casas and other towns in Chiapas. Linking anti-globalization rhetoric with Mexican revolutionary sloganism their declared goal was to overturn a wealthy local oligarchy's centuries-old hold on land, resources and power and to fight to improve the wretched living standards of Mexico's indigenous people.

Though the Mexican army evicted the Zapatistas within days with about 150 people (mostly Zapatistas) killed in the fighting, the rebels retreated to hideouts on the fringes of the Lacandón Jungle. Here they launched a propaganda blitz – mainly fought via the Internet rather than direct military engagement. The Zapatistas' charismatic pipe-puffing Subcomandante Marcos (actually a former university professor named Rafael Guillén) rapidly became a cult figure. His articulate dispatches – delivered in mocking, humorous and often self-deprecating tones – demanded justice and reform. High-profile conventions against neoliberalism were held and international supporters flocked to Zapatista headquarters at La Realidad, 85km southeast of Ocosingo. Zapatista-aligned peasants took over hundreds of farms and ranches in Chiapas.

Politically, the San Andrés accords (on indigenous rights and autonomy) were reached between Zapatista and government negotiators in 1996. However, the governing PRI (Institutional Revolutionary Party) party never ratified these agreements and through 1997 and 1998, tension and killings escalated in Chiapas. After the Zapatistas set up autonomous municipalities, PRI-linked right-wing paramilitaries massacred 45 people in the village of Acteal in December 1997.

By 1999 an estimated 21,000 Zapatista-aligned villagers had fled their homes after the Mexican army soldiers (aided and abetted by paramilitaries) launched a campaign of intimidation.

Hopes of a fresh start rose in 2000 when two new non-PRI politicians were elected: as presidente Vicente Fox and, in Chiapas, state governor Pablo Salazar.

Early in 2001 the Zapatistas forced the issue of indigenous rights to top of the political agenda again via a 'Zapatour' journey from Chiapas to Mexico City. Two further attempts to make the necessary constitutional changes failed, however, as Congress watered down proposals; supporters of the status quo fearing the emergence of a mini-Mayan state outside the Mexican federation. After the second impasse in September 2002, the Zapatistas refused to participate in further talks and a period of silence ensued.

Parts of the Chiapas countryside remained tense. Occasional incidents propelled the unresolved conflict on to the news agenda, such as the Zapatista seizure of American-owned hotel Rancho Esmeralda near Ocosingo in February 2003. Thousands of army troops still patrolled the state, and in some areas paramilitary groups clashed with Zapatistas.

By this time some former supporters were expressing growing disillusionment with Marcos' increasingly isolationist stance. Zapatista political influence remained slight outside their own enclaves, with even Marcos recognizing the rebels' 'exasperating barrier of distrust' toward outsiders. Many questioned the Zapatistas' tussle with environmental group Conservation International over settlements inside the protected Montes Azules biosphere reserve. The Zapatistas also loudly denounced the concept of ecotourism, and detained kayakers in the south of the state.

In September 2003, signs of a more pragmatic, patient strategy appeared to be evident. Relatively low-key plans to celebrate the 10th anniversary of the 1994 uprising were announced, concentrating on raising money through a nationwide raffle, and dances and concerts in Chiapas rather than headline-grabbing political statements. And as the Zapatista leadership acknowledged, 'For 500 years the authorities have refused to listen to us. We have time on our side.' The main Zapatista-affiliated website is www.ezln.org, with further background available at www.global exchange.org and http://flag.blackened.net/revolt/mexico.html.

SAN CRISTÓBAL DE LAS CASAS

0 / 400 m
0 / 0.2 miles

INFORMATION
Banamex (ATM)...................1 B4
Bancomer............................2 B4
Cristóbal Colón Bus Station....(see 101)
Crisan Estación....................3 C4
Dr Roberto Lobato's Clinic........4 C3
General Hospital...................5 B5
La Pared.............................6 B4
Lacantún Money Exchange........7 B4
Lavandería La Rapidita............8 B4
Lavasor...............................9 C4
Lavomart............................10 D4
Librería Chilam Balam............11 B3
Libros Soluna......................12 C4
Main Post Office...................13 A4
Municipal Tourist Office..........14 B4
SECTUR.............................15 B4
Tr@vel Net.........................16 C3

SIGHTS & ACTIVITIES (pp797-9)
Astur.................................(see 1)
Café Museo Café..................17 C3
Cathedral...........................18 B4
Centro Bilingüe El Puente.........19 C4
Centro Cultural de los Altos......20 B2
Centro Cultural El Carmen........21 B5
Church..............................22 B4
Church..............................23 B2
Ex-Convento de la Merced......(see 34)
Explora.............................24 B3
Iglesia de San Cristóbal..........25 A5
Iglesia de Santa Lucía............26 B5
Iglesia El Cerrillo..................27 C3
Instituto Jovel.....................28 C3
Jardín de Orquídeas..............29 E4
Kanan-Ku Viajes...................30 B4
Los Pingüinos......................31 A4
Museo de las Culturas Populares de
    Chiapas.........................32 A4
Museo de Trajes Regionales Sergio
    Castro...........................33 A4
Museo del Ámbar de Chiapas....34 A4
Na Bolom..........................35 E2
Otisa................................36 C4
Templo & Ex-Convento de Santo
    Domingo.........................37 B2
Templo de la Caridad.............38 B3
Templo de San Francisco.........39 B4
Templo del Carmen...............40 B5
Torre del Carmen.................41 B5
Turística Chan-Balum............42 C4
Viajes Chincultik.................(see 46)
Zapata Tours......................(see 78)

SLEEPING (pp800-2)
Albergue Juvenil/Youth Hostel...43 C4
Backpackers Hostel................44 B2
Casa Dr Felipe Flores.............45 C4
Casa Margarita....................46 B4
El Paraíso..........................47 B3
Hotel Adriana......................48 B3
Hotel Casa Mexicana.............49 B3
Hotel Casavieja....................50 C3
Hotel Catedral.....................51 A4
Hotel El Cerrillo...................52 C3
Hotel Diego de Mazariegos.......52 B3
Hotel Flamboyant Español........54 B3
Hotel La Noria.....................55 B4
Hotel Lucella......................56 B5
Hotel Mansión de los Ángeles...57 C4
Hotel Plaza Central................58 B4
Hotel Posada del Barón...........59 C4
Hotel Santa Clara..................60 B4
Magic 61 A4
Mador San Juan de Dios..........62 D1
Posada Casa Real..................63 C4
Posada Doña Rosita..............64 C3

Posada Jovel.......................65 C3
Posada Las Casas..................66 D4
Posada San Cristóbal.............67 B4

EATING (pp802-3)
Cafetería del Centro 2...........(see 99)
Cafetería del Centro..............68 C4
El Edén.............................(see 47)
El Fogón de Jovel.................69 B3
El Gato Gordo......................70 C4
Emiliano's Moustache.............71 B4
Hamburguesas Juanito...........72 C4
La Alpujarra........................73 C4
La Casa del Pan....................74 C3
La Jungla...........................75 C4
La Paloma..........................76 B4
Los Merenderos....................77 B5
Madre Tierra.......................78 B5
Mayambé...........................79 D4
Naturalíssimo......................80 B3
Restaurant El Teatro..............81 B3
Restaurante El Sol................82 B6
Restaurante Margarita..........(see 46)
Restaurante Maya Pakal.........83 C4
Restaurante Tuluc................84 B4

DRINKING (p803)
Café La Selva......................85 B4
Hotel Ciudad Real Bar............86 B4

ENTERTAINMENT (p803)
Bar Las Velas......................87 C4
Bar Zapata Viva...................88 A4
Blue.................................89 B4
Circo................................90 B3
Creación............................91 B3
La Ventana........................(see 78)
Latino's.............................92 C4
Mr Sapo............................93 B4

SHOPPING (p804)
Casa de las Artesanías de Chiapas.94 B4
Casa del Jade......................95 B3
El Mono de Papel..................96 B4
La Galería.........................(see 76)
Lágrimos de La Selva.............97 B4
Nemizapata........................98 C4
Pasaje Mazariegos Mall..........99 C4
Sna Jolobil.........................100 B2

TRANSPORT (pp804-5)
ADO Bus Station..................101 B6
AEXA Bus Station.................102 B6
ATG Bus Station..................103 A6
Budget.............................104 A4
Colectivo Taxis to Comitán.......105 B6
Combis to Grutas de San
    Cristóbal.......................106 C6
Combis to San Juan Chamula....107 B2
Combis to Zinacantán............108 C2
Corazón de María Suburbans....109 C6
Dr Rodulfo Figueroa Bus
    Station..........................(see 101)
Ómnibus de Chiapas Bus
    Station..........................(see 102)
Optima.............................110 A
Suburbans to Comitán...........111 B6
Suburbans to Ocosingo..........112 B6
Taxis Jovel Colectivos to Tuxtla
    Gutérrez.........................113 B6
Ticket Bus.........................114 C4
Transportes Lacandonia Bus
    Station...........................115 B6
UNO Transportes Bus Station...(see 101)

OTHER
Pronatura..........................116 B5

prominent Spanish defender of indigenous people in colonial times. In modern times Bishop Samuel Ruiz, who retired in 1999 after a long tenure, followed very much in Las Casas' footsteps. He supported the oppressed indigenous people and earned the violent hostility of the Chiapas establishment for his pains.

San Cristóbal was the Chiapas state capital from 1824 to 1892 but remained relatively isolated until the 1970s, when tourism began to influence its economy. Another fairly recent change has been an influx of around 20,000 people who were expelled by village authorities from Chamula and other indigenous villages for turning Protestant under the influence of foreign missionaries. These people live in what locals call the Cinturón de Miseria (Belt of Misery), a series of squalid, violence-ridden, makeshift colonies around San Cristóbal's Periférico (ring road). Lacking work, schools and many basic amenities, these people represent a social time bomb for the beautiful colonial town they encircle. Most of the craft sellers around Santo Domingo church and the underage chewing-gum hawkers around town are drawn from their numbers.

The city of San Cristóbal was catapulted into the limelight on January 1, 1994, when Zapatista rebels selected it as one of four places in which to launch their revolution, seizing and sacking government offices in the town before being driven out within a few days by the Mexican army. Underlying social tensions remain, but San Cristóbal's future as a cultured, prosperous city looks secure, with a burgeoning tourist sector, booming property market and an increasingly affluent middle class.

Orientation

San Cristóbal is easy to walk around, with straight streets rambling up and down several gentle hills. A long *andador* (pedestrianized walkway) starts at the Templo Santo Domingo in the north, passes the cathedral and finishes at the Torre del Carmen. The Pan-American Hwy (190) runs through the southern part of town. Officially named Blvd Juan Sabines, it's more commonly called 'El Bulevar.'

Nearly all transportation terminals are on or just off the Pan-American. From the Cristóbal Colón bus terminal, it's six blocks north up Insurgentes to the central square, Plaza 31 de Marzo, which has the cathedral on its north side.

Information

BOOKSTORES & LIBRARIES

La Pared (Hidalgo 2; lapared9@hotmail.com) Stocks a superb choice of new and used books in English, with plenty of Mexico and Latin America subject matter as well as Lonely Planet guides. It's run by a friendly American, Dana Burton, who also trades used books.

Librería Chilam Balam (Utrilla 33) Lots of books on Mexican history, anthropology and literature in Spanish – and a few guidebooks in English.

Libros Soluna (Real de Guadalupe 13B) Has some books on Chiapas and Mexico in English, and many more in Spanish.

Na Bolom (Guerrero 33; ☺ officially 10am-4pm Mon-Fri) The more than 11,000 books and documents at Na Bolom (see p798) make up one of the world's biggest libraries on the Maya and their lands.

IMMIGRATION

Instituto Nacional de Migración (☎ 678-02-92; Diagonal El Centenario 30) On a corner with Pan-American Hwy, 1.2km west of the Cristóbal Colón bus station.

INTERNET ACCESS

San Cristóbal has at least two dozen cybercafés, most are very inexpensive (US$0.50 to US$0.90 per hour).

Crosan Estación (Av Belisario Domínguez s/n; per hr US$0.50; ☺ 7am-11pm)

Tr@vel Net (Paniagua 29A; per hr US$0.50)

LAUNDRY

Lavandería La Rapidita (Insurgentes 9) Offers a wash, dry and fold service within 2½ hours, or wash your own for less.

Charging US$3.50 to wash and dry 3kg of clothes:

Lavasor (Belisario Domínguez 8D)

Lavomart (Real de Guadalupe 70A)

MEDICAL SERVICES

Dr Roberto Lobato (☎ 678-77-77; Belisario Domínguez 17; per consultation US$23) Recommended by foreign residents, though he speaks very basic English.

Hospital (☎ 678-07-70) The general hospital is on Insurgentes.

MONEY

Banamex (Plaza 31 de Marzo; ☺ 9am-5:30pm Mon-Sat) Has an ATM and is efficient at currency exchange.

HSBC (Mazariegos s/n; ☯ 8am-7pm Mon-Sat, 10am-2pm Sun) Also has an ATM and is open the longest hours.

Outside bank hours (but at worse rates):
Lacantún Money Exchange (Real de Guadalupe 12A)
Viajes Chincultik (Casa Margarita, Real de Guadalupe 34)

TELEPHONE & POST
One of the cheapest places to call abroad is **La Pared** (see opposite); at the time of research calls to Europe, Israel and Australia cost US$0.70 a minute. Telmex card phones are at both ends of Plaza 31 de Marzo and in the Cristóbal Colón bus station.
Main post office (Ignacio Allende 5B)

TOURIST INFORMATION
Municipal tourist office (☎ 678-06-65; inside Palacio Municipal, Plaza 31 de Marzo; ☯ 8am-8pm Mon-Sat, 9am-3pm Sun)
State tourist office (☎ 678-65-70; Hidalgo 1B; ☯ 9am-8pm Mon-Sat; until 2pm Sun) This is usually the better-informed office, and has English-speaking staff and plenty of leaflets.

Sights
PLAZA 31 DE MARZO
The graceful main **plaza**, or *zócalo*, is surrounded by elegant colonial buildings and is a fine place to take in San Cristóbal's unique, unhurried highland atmosphere. Shoe shiners, newspaper vendors and *ambulantes* (walking vendors) gather around an elaborate iron bandstand.

The **cathedral**, on the north side of the plaza, was begun in 1528 but completely rebuilt in 1693. Its gold-leaf interior has a baroque pulpit and altarpiece, and the detailed stonework on the west façade has been attractively picked out in yellow, red and white paint.

The Hotel Santa Clara (see p801) on the plaza's southeast corner, was the house of Diego de Mazariegos, the Spanish conqueror of Chiapas. It's one of the few secular examples of plateresque style in Mexico.

TEMPLO & EX-CONVENTO DE SANTO DOMINGO
North of the center on 20 de Noviembre, the **Templo de Santo Domingo** is one of the most beautiful in San Cristóbal, especially when its pink façade catches the late-afternoon sun. The church and adjoining monastery were built between 1547 and 1560. The church's baroque frontage – on which can be seen

the double-headed Hapsburg eagle, symbol of the Spanish monarchy in those days - was added in the 17th century. The interior is lavishly gilded, especially the ornate pulpit.

Chamulan women and bohemian types from all over the world conduct a super-colorful daily crafts market around Santo Domingo and the neighboring Templo de La Caridad (built in 1712). You'll find local and Guatemalan textiles, woolen rugs and blankets, leather bags and belts, Zapatista dolls, hippie jewelry, *animalitos* from Amatenango del Valle and more.

The Ex-Convento (ex-monastery) attached to Santo Domingo contains two interesting exhibits. One is the showroom of **Sna Jolobil** (20 de Noviembre s/n; ☯ 9am-2pm & 4-6pm Mon-Sat), a cooperative of 800 indigenous women weavers from the Chiapas highlands. Here you can see very fine *huipiles*, hats, blouses, skirts, rugs and other woven items. Prices range from a few dollars for smaller items to over US$1000 for the best *huipiles* and ceremonial garments. The weavers of Sna Jolobil, which was founded in the 1970s to foster the important indigenous art of backstrap loom weaving, have revived forgotten techniques and designs, and developed dyes from plants, soil, bark and other natural sources.

Also in the Ex-Convento buildings, the **Centro Cultural de los Altos** (20 de Noviembre s/n; admission US$3, free Sun & holidays; ☯ 10am-5pm Tue-Sun) houses a moderately interesting museum, set round a courtyard. The lower floor is dedicated mainly to the history of San Cristóbal and the region, and exhibits an array of colonial-era ecclesiastical relics. Upstairs are Mayan ceramics and a room dedicated to the rustic tools of yesteryear. Explanatory material is in Spanish only.

TORRE, TEMPLO & CENTRO CULTURAL DEL CARMEN
The **Torre del Carmen** tower, at the southern end of the *andador* walkway on Hidalgo, was once the city's gateway. Built in Mudéjar style, the white arched structure, topped with a double bell tower, dates from 1680 and remains a city landmark. The baroque façade adjoining the tower to the east belongs to the **Templo del Carmen**, whose relatively sober interior contains hardwood paneling and a neoclassical altar.

Just west of the tower is the ex-convent building, now the **Centro Cultural El Carmen** (admission free; ⏰ 9am-6pm Tue-Sun) which hosts art and photography exhibitions – and the odd musical event – in a wonderful colonial building with large, peaceful gardens. There's a small café here too.

MERCADO MUNICIPAL

To get a real flavor of the region's indigenous character, visit San Cristóbal's busy municipal **market** (daily from around 7am to 5pm), eight blocks north of the main plaza between Utrilla and Belisario Domínguez. It's quite an assault on the senses, as vendors peer from behind pyramids of tomatoes and mangoes, and you'll find dozens of varieties of chiles as well as bloody butchers stalls and fly-plagued dried shrimp stands.

CENTRO DE DESARROLLO DE LA MEDICINA MAYA (CEDEMM)

The **Maya Medicine Development Center** (☎ 678-54-38; www.laneta.apc.org/omiech; Av Salomón González Blanco 10; admission US$1.75; ⏰ 10am-6pm Mon-Fri, until 5pm Sat & Sun) was founded by OMIECH, the Organization of Indigenous Doctors of Chiapas, which focuses on traditional Mayan medicine. For these practitioners, it's not a matter of pills and chemical formulae but of prayers, candles, incense, bones and herbs. An award-winning museum demonstrates how pulse readers, midwives, herbalists, prayer specialists and other traditional practitioners work, a medicinal plant garden and a *casa de curación*, where treatments including *limpias* (soul cleansings) are carried out. Herbal medicines are on sale too.

MUSEO DEL ÁMBAR DE CHIAPAS

Housed in the Ex-Convento de la Merced, the **Chiapas Amber Museum** (Mazariegos s/n; www.museodelambar.com.mx; admission US$0.90; ⏰ 10am-2pm & 4-7pm Tue-Sun) is very well laid out, and has some excellent amber exhibits. All things amber are explained in several languages and there are some exquisitely-carved items and insect-embedded pieces on display, and for sale. Chiapas amber, which comes in several shades including green and red, is known for its clarity and diverse colors.

MUSEO DE LAS CULTURAS POPULARES DE CHIAPAS

The **Popular Cultures Museum** (Mazariegos 37; admission by donation; ⏰ 9am-2pm & 5-8pm Tue-Sat) is across the road from the Amber Museum.

At the time of research it was only displaying temporary exhibits of paintings and photography.

MUSEO DE TRAJES REGIONALES SERGIO CASTRO

The privately-run **Museum of Regional Costumes** (☎ 678-42-89; Guadalupe Victoria 38; admission by donation) can only be visited by appointment, best made the day before you want to visit. This fascinating collection of indigenous costumes, and assorted curios including catapults, belongs to Sergio Castro, a Mother Teresa–type figure (but male and Mexican), who speaks several languages including English and Italian. Your donation goes towards supporting Mayan communities in Chiapas – one of Sergio's main projects is treating burns suffered by people sleeping too close to open fires.

CERRO DE SAN CRISTÓBAL & CERRO DE GUADALUPE

Two of the most prominent of the small hills around San Cristóbal are crowned by churches and offer fine views. **Cerro de San Cristóbal**, southwest of the center, is reached by steps up from Allende, while prettier **Cerro de Guadalupe**, topped by a church that Graham Greene described as a 'Soapbubble dome upon a rock,' is seven blocks east of the main plaza. It's not advisable to go up either after dark.

CAFÉ MUSEO CAFÉ

This combined café and **coffee museum** (☎ 678-78-76; http://members.es.tripod.de/cafemuseo cafe; MA Flores 10; admission free; ⏰ 9am-9pm Mon-Sat, 4-9pm Sun) is a venture of Coopcafé, a group of 15,000 small-scale, mainly indigenous, Chiapas coffee growers. The museum covers the history of coffee and its cultivation in Chiapas, indigenous coffee growing and organic coffee. The information is translated in English. You can taste some of that good organic coffee in the café and snacks and breakfasts (US$2.25 to US$3.50) are served too.

NA BOLOM

A visit to this lovely **19th-century house** (☎ 678-14-18; www.nabolom.org; Guerrero 33; view house only US$3, 1½-hour tour in English or Spanish US$4.50 ⏰ tours 11:30am, 4:30pm) is an intriguing experience. For many years Na Bolom was the home of Swiss anthropologist and photographer Gertrude (Trudy) Duby-Blom (1901–93), who with her Danish archaeologist husband Frans Blom (1893–1963) bought the house in 1950.

The couple shared a fascination for Chiapas. While Frans explored and surveyed ancient Mayan sites including Palenque, Toniná and Chinkultic, Trudy devoted much of her life to studying, photographing and trying to protect the scattered, isolated Lacandón people of eastern Chiapas and their jungle environment (see p825). Since her death Na Bolom has continued as a museum and institute for the study and preservation of Chiapas' indigenous cultures, under a board of trustees. The thrust of the Bloms' work is maintained through community and environmental programs in indigenous areas.

Na Bolom means 'Jaguar House' in the Tzotzil language (as well as being a play on its former owners' name). The house, visited by around 25,000 people a year, is full of photographs, archaeological and anthropological relics and books (see p796). Behind the house is an organic garden and tree nursery, and there's also an adjoining garden café and gift shop.

The house tour does provide a revealing insight into the lives of the Bloms, though the guides do tend to paint a slightly antiquated, romanticized picture of the Lacandones as 'noble savages.' The reality is that most Lacandones are now Presbyterian or evangelical churchgoers, and adherence to age-old cultural traditions is fast waning.

Na Bolom also offers guest rooms and meals (see p801 and p803), and takes volunteers for work on some of its programs.

JARDÍN DE ORQUÍDEAS
This pleasant **orchid garden** (☎ 674-62-52; Real de Guadalupe 153; admission by donation; ◷ 10am-6pm Tue-Sun) functions as a reproduction and resource center. It's an enjoyable place to stroll around, and you can see examples of orchids from five separate climate zones. There's also a very inexpensive café that serves snacks and drinks.

Courses
Instituto Jovel (☎ /fax 678-40-69; www.institutojovel .com; MA Flores 21; 5 days tuition & 7 days family accommodations individual US$240, group US$185; individual/group classes per hr US$11/7) Instituto Jovel employs professionally trained teachers and receives excellent reports from students. Most tuition here is one-to-one, with three hours' teaching a day. Group classes are only possible if other students at your level are also wanting to take a group class. Free *intercambio* is also offered.

Centro Bilingüe El Puente (☎ 678-37-23; centro elpuente@prodigy.net.mx; Real de Guadalupe 55; family accommodations per wk individual US$175, group US$160) The weekly rates include 15 hours of group instruction, or 12 hours one-to-one, and several hours of chat sessions. El Puente is aimed at travelers and has an attached café, Internet access and cinema, and hosts salsa classes.

Tours
For tours of indigenous villages around San Cristóbal, see p806. Agencies in San Cristóbal also offer tours further afield, often with guides who speak English, French or Italian. All the destinations can also be reached independently.

Some typical prices per person (usually with a minimum of four people):

Chiapa de Corzo & Cañón del Sumidero (not incl Parque Ecoturístico ecopark, US$20, 6-7 hr)

Lagos de Montebello, Chinkultic ruins, Amatenango del Valle, Grutas de San Cristóbal (US$23, 9 hr)

Palenque ruins, Agua Azul, Misol-Ha (US$33, 14 hr)

Toniná, Grutas de San Cristóbal (US$25, 12 hr)

Tour agencies include the following:

Astur (☎ 678-39-17; Portal Oriente B, Plaza 31 de Marzo)

Kanan-Ku Viajes (☎ 678-61-01; Niños Héroes 2C)

Otisa (☎ 678-19-33; www.otisatravel.com; Real de Guadalupe 3C)

Natutur (☎ 674-69-15; Calle Las Casas 8, Colonia la Isla; natutur@hotmail.com) Organizes 4-day excursions to Laguna Miramar by boat or truck (US$260 per person) and caving trips.

Turística Chan-Balum (☎ 678-76-56; Real de Guadalupe 26G)

Viajes Chincultik (☎ 678-09-57; agchincultik@prodigy .net.com; Real de Guadalupe 34) This agency employs accredited guides and generally provides good value.

Zapata Tours (☎ 674-51-52; www.zapatatours.com; above Restaurant Madre Tierra, Insurgentes 19)

Explora (☎ 678-42-95; www.ecochiapas.com; 1 de Marzo 30; 4-6 day jeep, raft & kayak trips per person US$195-375) offers excellent adventure trips in remote areas of Chiapas for groups of three to 12 people, stopping at Mayan ruins en route. Combined jeep and kayak trips involve overnight stays at remote ecolodges on the fringes of Selva Lacandona. Rafting trips follow the Lacanjá river (February to May) and La Venta river (July to October).

Festivals & Events

MARCH/APRIL

Semana Santa The crucifixion is acted out on Good Friday in the Barrio de Mexicanos in the northwest part of town.

Feria de la Primavera y de la Paz (Spring & Peace Fair) The Saturday afternoon is the start of the annual town fair with parades, bullfights and so on.

Anniversary of the town's founding (March 31) Sometimes these celebrations fall in the midst of it all too!

JULY

Feast of San Cristóbal (July 17 to 25) Look out for events marking this feast.

AUGUST

Ámbar Expo (www.expo-ambar.com.mx) Held annually in mid-August, includes exhibitions of particularly fine examples and contests for the best-carved pieces.

OCTOBER

Fiesta Barroco Late in the month, this is a lively cultural program with live music and theater.

Sleeping

Strong competition means that accommodations are generally very good value for money in San Cristóbal. There are many highly atmospheric places to stay. The following is just a selection as new hotels are opening all the time, often in attractive colonial buildings. Many places cut prices by around 15% to 20% outside high season.

BUDGET

You'll find most budget hotels are surprisingly pleasant and very affordable.

Posada Jovel (☎ 678-17-34; Paniagua 28; www.mundochiapas.com/hotelposadajovel; s/d with shared bath US$9.50/12, with bathroom US$12/16, annex rooms s/d with bathroom & TV US$18/24) Well-managed, secure Posada Jovel has an excellent selection of attractive accommodations, most with stripped wooden floors, bedside lights and highland blankets; while those in the annex over the road are larger and have private bathrooms. Flowers and posters of Chiapas brighten up the communal corridors, and there are two sun terraces, and a breakfast restaurant. Rates drop by 10% to 15% in low season.

Hotel Plaza Central (☎ 674-51-25; hostal_plaza central@latinmail.com; Paniagua 2; s/d US$4.50/11; 🖳)

Great new budget place set in a historic house in the center of town. There are 30 large, pleasant rooms, all with tables and shelves and most with nice private bathrooms; the shared facilities are spotless too. There's a sun terrace and a bar area, and a restaurant is planned.

Casa Margarita (☎ 678-09-57; agchincultik@prod igy.com; Real de Guadalupe 34; s/d US$15/19; 🖳) This ever-popular travelers' haunt has recently been refurbished and offers 28 tastefully-presented, clean rooms all with their own private bathroom and safe, set off by a pretty courtyard. There is an in-house travel agency and restaurant that are under the same ownership.

Hotel Posada del Barón (☎ /fax 678-08-81; hotel baron@hotmail.com; Belisario Domínguez 2; s/d with bath US$13/18) The Posada del Barón has 12 simple, good-value rooms with TV along a wood-pillared patio.

Posada Las Casas (☎ 678-28-82; Madero 81; pegede oro@hotmail.com; dm/s/d without bathroom US$3.50/7/11, with bathroom & TV US$11/15) This family-owned *posada* offers large, clean rooms on two floors along an open-air courtyard. There's a sun terrace and a kitchen for guests.

Posada Casa Real (☎ 678-13-03; Real de Guadalupe 51; s/d without bathroom US$4.50/9) Friendly, quiet place that's popular with women travelers, with eight clean rooms. There's a pleasant upstairs sitting area and the door is locked at 11pm.

Hotel Lucella (☎ 678-09-56; Insurgentes 55; s/d US$9/11, with bathroom US$11/13) The Lucella, opposite Santa Lucía church, is run by a friendly family and has simple, clean rooms around a patio. Prices drop by 25% in low season.

There are also several good hostels in town.

Magic Hostel (☎ 674-70-34; marquelia50@hotmail .com; Guadalupe Victoria 47; dm/s/d US$3.75/7.50/9) Excellent hostel, with a sociable atmosphere and clean, spacious 6- to 8-person dorms set round a large courtyard, plus six *cabañas*. The communal shower rooms are well looked after and there's a well-equipped kitchen, laundry, Internet access and safe.

Backpackers Hostel (☎ 674-05-25; Real de Mexicanos 16; dm or camping per person US$3.75; 🅿) Friendly, well-run hostel that has good dorm rooms with lockers, one reserved for women only, and very pleasant grassy grounds, with hammocks and plenty of space for campers. Guests get a free breakfast, Internet use and Spanish lessons too!

Posada Doña Rosita (☎ 678-09-23; posadadn_ros
ita@hotmail.com; Ejército Nacional 13; dm/s/d/tr
US$2.25/5/6/8) Hostel-style place run by a friendly señora
who also practices natural medicine. The rooms, most with
shared bathrooms, are plain but fairly clean. Breakfast
is just US$0.90, and there's a kitchen and a rooftop sun
terrace.

Albergue Juvenil (Youth Hostel; ☎ 678-76-55;
youth@sancristobal.com.mx; Juárez 2; dm with/without
bathroom US$3.75/3.25, d US$4) Offers bunk beds in
clean 6- to 8-person dorms, and doubles. Bathrooms are
spotless, and there's a kitchen, communal TV area, Internet
access and lockers available for US$0.40 per day.

Rancho San Nicolás (☎ 678-00-57; camping per person
US$3.50, trailer sites for 2 US$12; Ⓟ) This camping and trailer park, nearly 2km east of the
center on an eastward extension of León, is
a friendly place with grassy lawns, tall
trees, clean bathrooms, laundry and a central fireplace.

MID-RANGE

El Paraíso (☎ 678-00-85; hparaiso@mundomaya.com
.mx; 5 de Febrero 19; s/d US$32/42) This colonial-
style hotel set around a lovely courtyard
garden has real character, and represents excellent value. There are 10 large, elegantly-
decorated rooms, with high ceilings and
splendid bathrooms, most with stone-tiled
tubs and mosaic detailing. The in-house restaurant, El Edén, serves great Mexican and
Swiss cuisine (see p803).

Posada San Cristóbal (☎ 678-68-81; Insurgentes
3; s/d US$32/39; Ⓟ) Located just a block south
of the plaza, this posada has 10 large, airy
rooms around a courtyard and smaller
newer rooms at the rear; all have attractive
furnishings and TV.

Na Bolom (☎ 678-14-18; www.nabolom.org; Guerrero 33; s/d with bathroom US$40/49) This museum-
research institute (see p798) has 14 stylish
guest rooms, all with real period character, and some with log fires – Diego Rivera stayed in the Harvard room. Meals are
served in the house's stately dining room.
Its location, about 1km from the plaza, is a
drawback, however.

Hotel La Noria (☎ 678-68-78; Insurgentes 18A;
www.hotel-lanoria.com; s/d US$26/35) La Noria has
30 comfortable, brightly decorated, carpeted rooms, with attractive, tiled bathrooms and cable TV.

Hotel Santa Clara (☎ 678-11-40; www.estancias
coloniales.com; Insurgentes 1; s/d US$50/58) The his-

toric Santa Clara, on the main plaza, has
a selection of sizable rooms, though they
do vary in quality considerably so ask to
look first before you check in. There's a
restaurant, a bar/lounge and a courtyard
with caged red macaws. Some off-season
deals include breakfast.

Hotel Flamboyant Español (☎ 678-00-45; www
.hotelesflamboyant.com.mx; 1 de Marzo 15; s/d/ste US$52/
59/81; Ⓟ) This large hotel is set in a historic
building with comfortable rooms, all with
smart bathrooms, heating and TV. There's
a pretty garden with lots of trees, flowers
and birds. Graham Greene stayed here in
the 1930s.

Hotel Catedral (☎ 678-53-56; Guadalupe Victoria
21; hotelcatedral@prodigy.net.mx; s/d/ste US$53/64/75;
Ⓟ Ⓡ) Vast colonial-style hotel with 65
rooms and 18 suites on four levels around
a glass-covered courtyard. Most mod cons
are provided, and the suites have Jacuzzis,
though standards are not up to the five-
star status the hotel claims. There's a small
heated pool at the rear.

Hotel El Cerrillo (☎ /fax 678-12-83; Belisario
Domínguez 27; r with 1/2 beds US$23-28/36-39; Ⓟ)
Friendly El Cerrillo has a flowery glass-
covered courtyard and good-size, prettily
painted carpeted rooms with bathroom and
cable TV. There is a roof terrace, restaurant
and bar, too.

Hotel Casavieja (☎ /fax 678-68-68; www.casavieja
.com.mx; MA Flores 27; s/d/ste with bathroom US$50/61/67)
The Casavieja is set in a converted 18th-
century house, with 37 attractive, comfortable rooms and two suites arranged around
grassy, flower-filled courtyards There's a
neat restaurant too.

Hotel Adriana (☎ /fax 678-81-39; 1 de Marzo 29;
s/d with bathroom & TV US$27/39-47) The Adriana
has attractive, brightly-painted rooms situated around a pretty open courtyard.

Hotel Mansión de los Ángeles (☎ 678-11-73;
hotelangeles@prodigy.net.com; Madero 17; s/d with TV &
bathroom US$37/42; Ⓟ) Colonial-style building
with 20 pleasant rooms around two patios.
Indigenous costume prints add an attractive touch, and one patio contains a wood-
and-glass-roofed restaurant.

TOP END

Casa Dr Felipe Flores (☎ 678-39-96; www.felipe
flores.com; JF Flores 36; r with bathroom incl full breakfast
US$75-90) This wonderfully tranquil colo-
nial guesthouse has five immaculate guest

ooms, all with their own fireplaces, set off two flowery courtyards. The American owners have decorated the house with local artwork and furnishings, and the Mexican staff are welcoming and attentive. There are some terrific books to browse through in the commodious lounge area.

Hotel Casa Mexicana (☎ 678-06-98; www.hotel casamexicana.com; 28 de Agosto 1; s/d/ste US$67/87/118; P) Stylish and inviting, the Casa Mexicana exudes colonial charm. Great attention to detail is evident: witness the immaculate gardens, fountains, art, sculpture and monochrome photos. The accommodations are highly attractive, and there's a restaurant, bar and sauna.

Parador San Juan de Dios (☎ 678-11-67; Calz Roberta 16; villas US$65-185, ste US$130 & US$280; P) Stunning converted mansion with a choice of voluminous suites, furnished with oriental rugs and antiques, or stylishly decorated villas. In the beautiful lawned grounds there's a top-class restaurant with an inventive and expensive menu. Located on the northern edge of town, about 2km from the plaza.

Hotel Diego de Mazariegos (☎ 678-08-33; 5 de Febrero 1; r/ste US$64/74; P) This hotel occupies two handsome buildings either side of Utrilla just a block north of the plaza. The 77 rooms are a little old-fashioned but comfortable enough, and most have fireplaces. There's a café, bar and travel agent.

Eating

San Cristóbal offers a break from purely Mexican cuisine if you want; indeed, it's possible to find most kinds of global food, and there's plenty of choice for vegetarians.

REAL DE GUADALUPE AREA

Mayambé (☎ 674-62-78; Real de Guadalupe 66; mains US$3-5; 9am-10:30pm) Superb, very fairly priced courtyard restaurant with a highly innovative menu, developed by the well-traveled Mexican Sikh owners. Tuck in to delicious Indian and Thai curries, Greek and Lebanese treats including falafel and to-die-for *lassis* and juices. There's live music some evenings around the central fireplace, and Mayambé is also home to a bookshop (see p796) and has a few rooms to rent upstairs.

Cafetería del Centro (One, Real de Guadalupe 15; Two, Pasaje Mazariegos mall off Real de Guadalupe; mains US$4.50) Two friendly branches offering filling portions and decent breakfasts, and beers are a buck a pop.

Restaurante Margarita (☎ 678-09-57; Real de Guadalupe 34A; mains US$4-8) A broad choice of dependable, though a little pricey, food in a large family restaurant that has been serving travelers for decades.

La Jungla (Belisario Domínguez, south of Real de Guadalupe; snacks US$0.50-2.50) Hole-in-the-wall juice joint with inexpensive fruit-based breakfasts, juices and licuados, and filling tortas too.

INSURGENTES

Restaurante Tuluc (☎ 678-20-90; Insurgentes 5; breakfasts US$2.25-3, mains US$3-4; 6:30am-10pm) Tuluc, 1½ blocks south of the main plaza, consistently and efficiently serves up good food at reasonable prices.

Madre Tierra (☎ 678-42-97; Insurgentes 19; mains US$2.25-6; 8am-10pm) Madre Tierra offers a lovely patio and atmospheric dining room setting for an eclectic and appetizing vegetarian menu: wholesome soups, great sandwiches, salads and jacket potatoes. The breakfasts (US$2 to US$3.50) here are also superb.

Los Merenderos (Insurgentes s/n; mains US$1.75-2) The food stalls around the Mercado de Dulces y Artesanías serve up some of the cheapest meals in town.

Restaurante El Sol (Insurgentes 71; breakfasts US$2.25-3; mains US$4) El Sol is a small, unpretentious restaurant serving economical breakfasts, a good-value comida corrida and tasty chicken and beef dishes.

MADERO

El Gato Gordo (☎ 678-04-99; Madero 28; breakfasts & veg comida US$2-2.25; 9am-10:30pm Wed-Mon) Bargain-priced Gato Gordo rightly attracts budget travelers in droves. There's an unbeatable set menu, and excellent pasta, *crepas*, tortas and a great choice of beers.

Restaurante Maya Pakal (☎ 678-59-11; Madero 21A; mains US$2.75-4; 7am-11pm) There's a cluster of restaurants on Madero, but Maya Pakal's good prices and generous portions make it constantly busy. The Mexican dishes are best, and the three-course comida (US$3.75) and cheap breakfasts are popular too.

La Alpujarra (☎ 632-20-20; Madero 24; snacks US$1-1.50, pizzas US$2.75-7; 8am-11pm) Excellent little café run by an industrious Mexican

Muslim team. The menu includes flavorsome pastry *rollitos*, terrific tortas, pizzas and juicy juices.

HIDALGO & ROSAS
La Paloma (☎ 678 15-47; Hidalgo 3; mains US$4-11) Elegant, spacious restaurant with a glass atrium roof and greenery that includes bamboo and banana trees. The menu at Paloma is creative and varied with winsome pasta, beef, chicken and fish dishes, plus a few local specialities.

Emiliano's Moustache (☎ 678-72-46; Rosas 7; breakfasts and snacks US$1.75-3.50, mains US$3.50-6.50; ꖌ 9-1am) This large, enjoyable place specializes in tacos filled with combinations of meat, vegetable or cheese. Meat *filetes* also excel, and vegetarian possibilities exist here too (including veggie tacos, pasta with pesto and quiche). The set menu is only average, however.

NORTH OF THE CENTER
El Edén (☎ 678-00-85; inside El Paraíso hotel; mains US$7-9) Classy, comfortable hotel restaurant with a tempting European and Mexican menu that includes *sopa azteca* and succulent meat dishes. The signature dish (Swiss-style fondue) is ample for three.

La Casa del Pan (☎ 678-58-95; Dr Navarro 10; snacks & mains US$2.75-5.50; ꖌ 8am-10pm Tue-Sun) This attractive bakery-cum-restaurant offers lots of vegetarian fare: whole-wheat sandwiches, vegan salads, *hojaldres* (vegetable strudels), nachos and pizzas. Try the 'high-energy breakfast' of orange juice, fruit, yogurt, granola, organic Chiapas coffee and croissant or whole-grain bread.

Naturalíssimo (☎ 678-99-97; 20 de Noviembre 4; snacks US$2-3.50, mains US$4-5; ꖌ 7am-11pm) This health food store-cum-restaurant offers good breakfasts and set meals, snacks, and lush licuados and juices.

Na Bolom (☎ 678-14-18; www.nabolom.org; Guerrero 33; dinner US$9) For unique ambience, eat at Na Bolom. Guests sit at one long wooden table in the Bloms' old dining room. Most vegetables are organically grown in the garden. Dinner is at 7pm.

Restaurant El Teatro (☎ 678-31-49; 1 de Marzo 8; set menu US$6, mains 4.50-9; ꖌ 1-10pm Tue-Sun) The venerable old-fashioned Teatro's European-based menu includes chateaubriand, crêpes, fresh pasta and generous desserts, plus a few Mexican dishes.

Drinking
Café La Selva (☎ 678-72-43; Rosas 9; baguettes & snacks US$2.50-4) Attractive, slightly bijou café, with an open courtyard where you can choose from 39 different types of organic, indigenous-grown Chiapas coffee. For a slightly more sedate atmosphere than the clubs below, try **La Casa del Pan** (☎ 678-58-95; Dr Navarro 10; admission free or US$2; ꖌ 8am-10pm Tue-Sun) or the bars of **Hotel Santa Clara** (☎ 678-11-40; Insurgentes 1) and **Hotel Ciudad Real** (☎ 678-44-00; Plaza 31 de Marzo 10) on the main plaza.

For organic, Chiapas-grown coffee, try **Café Museo Café** (678-78-76; MA Flores 10; ꖌ 9am-9pm Mon-Sat, 4-9pm Sun).

Entertainment
Live music is big in San Cristóbal. Reggae is the most popular genre though bossa nova, jazz, *trova*, Cuban *son*, salsa and rock are also popular. Clubs tend to play a very eclectic mix of Latin dance, electro pop, rock, reggae and commercial techno.

Creación (☎ 678-66-64; 1 de Marzo; ꖌ 9:30am-11pm Mon-Sat) Perhaps the hippest bar in town, with modish Latin dance, chill-out sounds and live music most nights. Happy hour offers 2-for-1 beers and cocktails, and there's a daytime food (mains US$3) menu, Internet access and films upstairs.

Circo (☎ 678-56-63; 20 de Noviembre 7; admission free, weekends US$2; ꖌ 8pm-3am Mon-Sat) Bar-cum-club where the city's *salseros* gather to groove. There's live music after 10pm.

Latino's (☎ 678-99-27; Madero 23; admission free; closed Sun) The live Latin music here attracts a slightly older crowd; there's space to dance, and reasonably priced food.

Bar Las Velas (Madero 14; admission US$1.25; ꖌ 9pm-3am) This club attracts young locals and travelers alike. It plays a mix of Latin house, ska and reggae, and has a live band about 1am.

Other popular, no-entry-charge bar-clubs that are open Monday to Saturday from 9pm to 3am, and have live music and dancing include the following:
Bar Zapata Viva (☎ 678- 33-55; 5 de Mayo 2)
Blue (☎ 678-22-00; Rosas 2)
Mr Sapo (☎ 678-58-55; Diego de Mazariegos 19)

Several places show movies. For arthouse, alternative, Latin and some Hollywood films try **La Ventana** (Insurgentes 19; admission US$1.25), **Cinema El Puente** (☎ 678-37-23; Guadalupe 55; admission US$1.25) or **Creación** (see above).

TABASCO & CHIA

Shopping

The outstanding local *artesanías* are textiles such as huipiles, blouses and blankets: Tzotzil weavers are some of the most skilled and inventive in Mexico.

The heaviest concentration of **craft shops** is on Real de Guadalupe and along the *andador*, but there's also a huge range of wares at good prices at the busy daily **crafts market** around Santo Domingo and La Caridad churches. Next to Santo Domingo the showroom/shop of **Sna Jolobil** (20 de Noviembre s/n; ☺ 9am-2pm & 4-6pm Mon-Sat) has some of the finest textiles in Mexico. The **Casa de Las Artesanías de Chiapas** (cnr Niños Héroes & Hidalgo) also sells a good range of Chiapas crafts.

Another Chiapas specialty is **amber**, sold in numerous San Cristóbal shops. Amber, which is fossilized pine resin, is mined near Simojovel, north of San Cristóbal, but beware of plastic imitations: the real thing is never cold and never heavy. You'll find fine-quality amber at fair prices at **Lágrimos de la Selva** (Hidalgo 1C) and **El Árbol de La Vida** (Guadalupe 27). For jewelry, **La Galería** (Hidalgo 3) has a great selection in turquoise, amber, silver, gold and more. **Casa del Jade** (House of Jade; 16 de Septiembre No 16) is another classy jeweler's shop, with some exquisite jade artwork, and a 'museum' (US$3) with reproductions of ancient Olmec pieces (there's even a full-size replica of Pakal's tomb at Palenque).

For Zapatista-made and pro-Zapatista crafts and souvenirs head to **Nemizapata** (Real de Guadalupe 45). Subcomandante Marcos dolls in little black balaclavas and T-shirts are commonplace all over town. Several shops sell Zapatista videos, including **El Mono de Papel** (Libertad s/n).

Getting There & Away

AIR

San Cristóbal airport is located about 15km out of town on the Palenque road. At the time of research the only passenger flight was to/from Mexico City daily by **Aeromar** (☎ 674-30-03 at the airport). One-way fares start around US$180: Kanan-Ku Viajes (see p799) is one agency selling tickets. There are many more flights from Tuxtla Gutiérrez. A taxi to Tuxtla airport costs around US$35 and takes about 1¼ hours via the toll highway.

BUS, SUBURBAN & TAXI

There are around a dozen terminals; all of them are on or just off the Pan-American Hwy, except for a few serving nearby villages (see p805).

The main bus terminal for deluxe and 1st-class services (Cristóbal Colón, ADO, Altos, UNO) plus 2nd-class Transportes Dr Rodulfo Figueroa (TRF) buses is at the corner of Insurgentes and the Pan-American. Tickets for buses on all these lines are for sale at **Ticket Bus** (☎ 678-86-03; Belisario Domínguez 8C) in the center of town.

Transportes Lacandonia (TL), 2nd-class, is 150m west of Colón along the highway, and Autotransportes Tuxtla Gutiérrez (ATG), also 2nd-class, is just north of the highway on Allende.

AEXA (1st-class) and Ómnibus de Chiapas (2nd-class, OC) have a joint terminal on the south side of the highway, and various Suburban-type vans and colectivo taxi services have their depots on the highway in the same area. The Suburbans and colectivos run all day from 6am or earlier and leave when the vehicle is full. See the San Cristóbal de Las Casas map (pp794-5) for locations.

Note that journey times to Chiapa de Corzo and Tuxtla Gutiérrez depend on the route your transport takes (see p789). Daily departures from San Cristóbal include the following:

Cancún (US$42-50, 16 hr, 4 from Colón terminal; US$34, 2 ATG)

Chiapa de Corzo (1¼hr) Take a 2nd-class bus, van, or colectivo heading for Tuxtla Gutiérrez, but check first that it will let you off in Chiapa de Corzo.

Ciudad Cuauhtémoc (Guatemalan border; US$6.25, 2½hr, 6 Altos) Leave early if you want to get any distance into Guatemala the same day.

Comitán (US$3.50-4.50, 1 to 1½hr, 11 from Colón terminal) Other buses and Suburbans (US$3) and colectivo taxis (US$3.50) from south side of Pan-American Hwy.

Mérida (US$33-37, via Campeche 11 hr, 2 from Colón terminal)

Mexico City (TAPO; US$50-87, 19 hr, 7 from Colón terminal; US$44, 1 ATG)

Oaxaca (US$25-29, 12 hr, 3 from Colón terminal)

Ocosingo (US$3.25-4.25, 2 hr, 10 from Colón terminal; US$2.75, 4 AEXA; US$3, 4 ATG; US$1.75, 1 TL) Colectivo taxis (US$3.75) and Suburbans (US$2.75) from north side of Pan-American Hwy.

Palenque (US$6.50-9, 5 hr, 10 from Colón terminal; US$7, 4 ATG; US$6.25, 3 AEXA)

Puerto Escondido (US$2, 13 hr, 2 Colón)
Tuxtla Gutiérrez (US$3.50-5.50, 1-1½hr, 18 from Colón terminal; US$3, 8 ATG; US$3, 3 AEXA; US$2.75, OC every 20 min 6am-6pm) Colectivo taxis (US$3.75) by Taxis Jovel, Suburbans 4am-9pm (US$2.75) by Corazón de María and Tojtic Ocotal.
Villahermosa (US$13-14, 7 hr, 2 from Colón terminal; US$11, 4 ATG)

Buses of various classes from the Colón terminal also run to Tapachula, Bahías de Huatulco, Campeche, Chetumal, Playa del Carmen, Pochutla, Tulum and Veracruz.

If you're heading to Guatemala, Viajes Chincultik (see p799) runs a shuttle service (on Tuesday and Friday) to La Mesilla (US$20, 2½ hours), Quetzaltenango (US$40, 5½ hours), Panajachel (US$50, 7½ hours) and Antigua (US$60, 9½ hours).

CAR & MOTORCYCLE
Budget (☎ 678-31-00; Mazariegos 39 in Hotel Mansión del Valle) VW Beetles for US$52 per day on the same basis as those rented at Optima.
Optima (☎ 674-54-09; optimacar1@hotmail.com; Mazariegos 39-1) VW Beetles for US$42/240 per day/week including unlimited kilometers, insurance and taxes.

Getting Around
Combis go up Rosas from the Pan-American Hwy to the town center. Taxis cost US$1.50 within the town (after 11pm US$1.75).

Los Pingüinos (☎ 678-02-02; Ecuador 4B; www.bike mexico.com; office ☉ 10am-2:30pm, 3:30-7pm Mon-Sat) rent decent-quality mountain bikes with lock and maps for three hours/24 hours/week at US$6/8.50/41. You need to deposit some security such as your passport with them. Staff can advise on good and safe routes; they also conduct guided bicycle tours (see p809).

AROUND SAN CRISTÓBAL
The inhabitants of the beautiful Chiapas highlands are descended from the ancient Maya and maintain some unique customs, costumes and beliefs.

Weekly **markets** at the villages are nearly always on Sunday. Proceedings start very early, with people arriving from outlying settlements as early as dawn, and wind down by lunchtime.

Festivals often give the most interesting insight into indigenous life, and there are plenty of them. Occasions like **Carnaval** (late February/early March), for which Chamula

is famous, **Semana Santa**, **Día de Muertos** (November 2) and the **Día de La Virgen de Guadalupe** (December 12) are celebrated almost everywhere. At some of these fiestas much *posh*, an alcoholic drink made from sugarcane, is drunk and there are barrages of firecrackers.

During Carnaval, groups of minstrels stroll the roads in tall, pointed hats with long, colored tassels, strumming guitars and chanting.

Reserva Ecológica Huitepec
The entrance to **Huitepec Ecological Reserve** (self-guided visits US$1.50; ☉ 9am-3pm Tue-Sun) is about 3.5km from San Cristóbal, on the

---

RISE AND FALL

Many of the conservative, traditional indigenous *pueblos* around San Cristóbal have remained tense since the Zapatista uprising in 1994. The political, religious and social conflicts of this situation are complex, but if you do decide to explore this region it's essential to be respectful of local customs. Some of the more remote villages are extremely close-knit and can be suspicious of outsiders.

Some villages north of San Cristóbal including San Pedro Chenalhó, head of the municipality where the 1997 Acteal massacre took place, were quite edgy at the time of research.

San Juan Chamula, Zinacantán, Amatenango del Valle and San Andrés Larráinzar (a center of strong Zapatista support) were considered safe to visit at that time. In all cases, if you're going independently, make prior inquiries about security, and make sure that you get back to San Cristóbal well before dark. Walking or riding by horse or bicycle by day along the main roads to Chamula and Zinacantán should not be risky, but it's not wise to go wandering into unfrequented areas or down isolated tracks.

In some villages cameras are at best tolerated – and sometimes not even that. Photography is banned in the church and during rituals at San Juan Chamula, and in the church and churchyard at Zinacantán. You may put yourself in physical danger by taking photos without permission. If in any doubt at all, ask before taking a picture.

road to San Juan Chamula. Set on the slopes of Cerro Huitepec (2700m), the reserve covers terrain rising from evergreen oak woods to rare cloud forest rich with bromeliads. It has some 60 resident bird species and over 40 winter visitors. The self-guided trail is 2.5km long. If you're interested in plants, it's well worth taking a four-hour guided tour with the Tzotzil guide, Javier, who speaks some English and focuses on the medical and spiritual properties of plants. This tour costs US$9 per person (up to eight people), and you need to book one day before at **Pronatura** (☎ 967-678-50-00; Hidalgo 9; www.pronatura-chiapas.org) in San Cristóbal. Javier also gives four-hour early-morning bird tours.

San Juan Chamula
pop 3100 / elevation 2200m

The Chamulans are a fiercely independent people, and their village San Juan Chamula, 10km northwest of San Cristóbal, is the center for some unique religious practices. They put up strong resistance to the Spaniards in 1524 and launched a famous rebel-

lion in 1869, attacking San Cristóbal. Today they are one of the largest subgroups of the Tzotzil people, about 80,000 strong.

Local costume is highly distinctive. Most men wear loose homespun tunics of white wool (sometimes, in cool weather, thicker black wool), but cargo-holders – those with important religious and ceremonial duties – wear a sleeveless black tunic and a white scarf on the head. Chamula women wear fairly plain white or blue blouses and/or shawls and woolen skirts.

Outsiders are free to visit Chamula, though it's essential to respect local traditions. A big sign at the entrance to the village strictly forbids photography in the village church or anywhere where rituals are being performed. Nearby, around the shell of an older **church**, is the village **graveyard**, with black crosses for people who died old, white for the young, and blue for others. There's a small village museum, **Ora Ton** (admission US$0.60; ☼ 9am-6pm) near this old church too.

Starting at dawn on Sunday, people from the hills stream into San Juan Chamula for

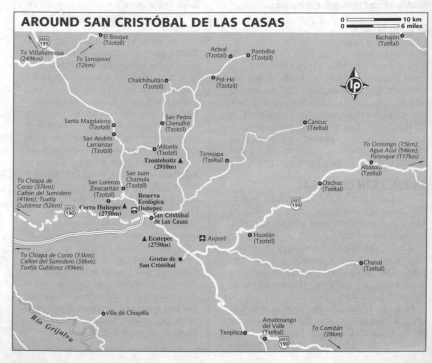

AROUND SAN CRISTÓBAL DE LAS CASAS

0 — 10 km
0 — 6 miles

the weekly **market** and to visit the church. Busloads of tourists also stream in, so you might prefer to come another day (though avoid Wednesday when the church is often all but deserted due to local superstitions). *Artesanías* (mainly textiles) are sold every day for the passing tourist trade.

The **Templo de San Juan**, Chamula's main church, white with a colorfully painted door arch, stands beside the main plaza. A sign tells visitors to obtain tickets (US$0.90) at the **tourist office** (⏰ 9am-6pm), at the side of the plaza, before entering the church. Do not wear a hat inside. Hundreds of flickering candles, clouds of incense and worshipers kneeling with their faces to the pine needle-carpeted floor make a powerful impression. Chanting *curanderos* may be rubbing patients' bodies with eggs or bones. Images of saints are surrounded with mirrors and dressed in holy garments. Chamulans revere San Juan Bautista (St John the Baptist) above Christ, and his image occupies a more important place in the church.

Christian **festivals** are interwoven with older ones here: the important **Carnaval** celebrations also mark the five 'lost' days of the ancient Mayan Long Count calendar,

---

INDIGENOUS PEOPLES OF CHIAPAS

Of the 4.2 million people of Chiapas, over one million are indigenous (mostly Mayan groups). At least nine languages are spoken in the state. Spanish is the idiom of commerce, most education and government in the cities. In the countryside in various parts of the state, indigenous peoples speak the Chol, Chuj, Lacandón, Mam, Tojolabal, Tzeltal, Tzotzil and Zoque languages. Although all are derived from ancient Mayan, most of these tongues are now mutually unintelligible, so local inhabitants use a second language such as Spanish or the fairly widely understood Tzeltal to communicate with other groups. The indigenous languages also define ethnic groups that have common beliefs, traditions and dress customs.

The indigenous people who travelers are most likely to come into contact with are the 500,000 or so Tzotziles, who mainly live in a highland area centered on San Cristóbal de Las Casas and stretching about 50km from east to west and 100km from north to south. Tzotzil clothing is among the most varied, colorful and elaborately worked in Mexico. It not only identifies wearers' villages but also marks them as inheritors of ancient Mayan traditions.

You may encounter the Tzeltales, who also number about 500,000, and inhabit the region between San Cristóbal and the Lacandón Jungle. Both groups are among Mexico's most traditional indigenous peoples. Their nominally Catholic religious life involves some distinctly pre-Hispanic elements and goes hand in hand with some unusual forms of social organization. Most of the people live in the hills outside the villages, which are primarily market and ceremonial centers.

Other Chiapas indigenous peoples include about 190,000 Choles, mainly in the north of the state, and some 42,000 Zoques in the northwest.

Chiapas' indigenous peoples are 2nd-class citizens in economic and political terms, living, on the whole, on the least productive land in the state. Some have emigrated to the Lacandón Jungle to clear new land, or to the cities in search of work. Their plight was the major reason for the 1994 Zapatista uprising.

But not everyone supports the Zapatistas, and violence between opposing indigenous factions has been an ugly side of the Zapatista upheaval. One series of revenge killings between pro-PRI and pro-Zapatista Tzotziles culminated in a 1997 massacre at the village of Acteal, in the municipality of Chenalhó, north of San Cristóbal. Some 45 people, mostly women and children, from Las Abejas (the Bees), a Catholic pacifist group sympathetic to the Zapatistas, were gunned down in a chapel by pro-PRI paramilitaries. As a result of this and other incidents, somewhere between 10,000 and 20,000 people fled their homes for refugee camps, chiefly in northern areas of Chiapas. In 2001, some started returning home, but the release from jail at the same time of some of the 34 men convicted of the Acteal massacre raised tensions again in the Chenalhó area.

Despite their problems, indigenous peoples' identities and self-respect survive. Traditional festivals, costumes, crafts and often ancient religious practices assist in this. These people generally remain suspicious of outsiders, and may resent interference, especially in their religious observances. But they also will be friendly and polite if treated with due respect.

which divided time into 20-day periods (18 of these make 360 days, leaving five to complete a year). Other festivals include ceremonies for **San Juan Bautista** (June 22–25, with up to 20,000 people gathering to dance and drink on the 24th) and the annual **change of cargos** (December 30 to January 1). Conflicts between adherents of traditional Chamulan 'Catholicism' and converts to Protestantism in the past couple of decades have resulted in the expulsion of many thousands of Chamulans from their villages, and they now inhabit the shanty-towns around San Cristóbal.

San Lorenzo Zinacantán
pop 3700 / elevation 2558m

The road to the orderly village of San Lorenzo Zinacantán, about 11km northwest of San Cristóbal, forks left off the Chamula road before descending into a valley. This is the main village of the Zinacantán municipality (population 45,000). Zinacantán people are Tzotzil, and the men of Zinacantán have distinctive pink tunics embroidered with flower motifs and may sport flat, round, ribboned palm hats. Zinacantán women wear pink or purple shawls over richly embroidered blouses.

A small **market** is held on Sundays until noon, and during fiesta times. The most important celebrations are for the festival of **La Virgen de La Candelaria** (August 7–11) and **San Sebastián** (January 19–22).

Zinacantecos are great flower growers and have a particular love for the geranium, which along with pine branches is offered in rituals performed to bring a wide range of benefits.

The village has two churches. The huge central **Iglesia de San Lorenzo** (admission US$0.40) was rebuilt following a fire in 1975. Photography is banned in the church and churchyard. The small thatched-roofed **Museo Sna Jsotz'** (admission US$0.20, ☺ 9am-5pm), three blocks below the central basketball court, is devoted to local culture and has some fine textiles and musical instruments.

Grutas de San Cristóbal
These **caves** (admission US$1.25; ☺ 8am-5pm) are in fact a single long cavern 9km southeast of San Cristóbal. The entrance is among pine woods, a five-minute walk south of the Pan-American Hwy. The first 350m or so of the

cave has a concrete walkway and are lit. The army took control of the land around the caves in September 2003, and though visitors were still welcome, check first with the tourist office in San Cristóbal (see p797).

To get there take a Teopisca-bound combi from the Pan-American Hwy, about 150m southeast of the Cristóbal Colón bus station, and ask for 'Las Grutas' (US$0.70).

Amatenango del Valle
pop 3400 / elevation 1869m

The women of this Tzeltal village, by the Pan-American Hwy 37km southeast of San Cristóbal, are renowned potters. Amatenango women wear fine white huipiles with red and yellow embroidery, wide red belts and blue skirts. Pottery here is still fired by a pre-Hispanic method, building a wood fire around the pieces rather than putting them in a kiln. In addition to everyday pots and jugs that the village has turned out for generations, young girls now find a ready tourist market with *animalitos* – little animal figures that are inexpensive but fragile. If you visit the village, expect to be surrounded within minutes by children selling these.

From San Cristóbal, take a Comitán-bound bus or combi.

Tours
Exploring the region with a good guide can open up doors and give you a feel for indigenous life and customs you could never gain alone. The following all offer well-received daily trips to local villages, usually San Juan Chamula and Zinacantán.

Alex & Raúl (☎ 967-678-37-41; alexraultours@yahoo.com .mx; 5-hr tours, per person US$9) Enjoyable and informative English or Spanish minibus tours. Alex, Raúl (and/or their colleague César) wait by San Cristóbal's cathedral at 9:30am daily. Tuesday and Sunday see trips to Tenejapa; visits to San Andrés Larraínzar (US$14) can also be arranged.

Viajes Chincultik (☎ 967-678-09-57; agchincultik@ prodigy.net.com; Casa Margarita, Real de Guadalupe 34; 5-hr trip US$10; with extension to San Andrés Larraínzar, US$14) Educative trips led by an English-, Spanish- and Tzotzil-speaking sociologist member of the family that runs the Casa Margarita.

Mercedes Hernández Gómez (5-6-hr trips, US$9) Mercedes waits just before 9am daily near the kiosk in San Cristóbal's main plaza, twirling a colorful umbrella. Her tours, traveling by minibus and on foot, have been popular for years. A fluent English-speaker who grew up in Zinacantán, she's a strong character and a knowledgeable (and loquacious) guide. On occasions she chastises participants for not concentrating properly.

Further village tours are offered by agencies including Astur, Kanan-Ku Viajes and Zapata Tours (see p799).

BICYCLE TOURS

Los Pingüinos (☎ 678-02-02; Ecuador 4B, San Cristóbal; www.bikemexico.com; office ☒ 10am-2:30pm, 3:30-7pm) Friendly English-, German- and Spanish-speaking folk at Los Pingüinos operate guided mountain-bike tours of 20km to 42km. Most trips are to little-visited, scenic country areas east of San Cristóbal, passing through cloud forests; one 25km route (four hours, US$20) crosses a limestone bridge. The trails are predominantly off-road but without long, hard gradients. Book one day or more ahead.

HORSEBACK RIDING

Almost any travel agency or place to stay in San Cristóbal can arrange a three- or four-hour guided ride to San Juan Chamula for US$8 to US$10. You might want to ask about the animals: are they horses or just ponies, fiery or docile, fast or slow? Rides with Viajes Chincultik at Casa Margarita have received good reports.

Getting There & Away

Transportation to most villages leaves from points around the Mercado Municipal in San Cristóbal. Check latest return times before you set out: some services wind down by lunchtime. Combis to San Juan Chamula (US$0.60) leave from Calle Honduras fairly frequently from 5am up to about 6pm; for Zinacantán, combis (US$0.80) and colectivo taxis (US$1) go at least hourly, 6am to 5pm, from a yard off Robledo.

OCOSINGO

☎ 919 / pop 29,000 / elevation 900m

Around the halfway mark of the 180km journey from San Cristóbal to Palenque, a trip that takes you down from cool, misty highlands to steamy lowland jungle, is the agreeable town of Ocosingo, a busy market hub for a large area. Ocosingo is only a few kilometers from the impressive Mayan ruins of Toniná, and also a jumping-off point for beautiful Laguna Miramar.

The market area, three blocks east downhill from the main plaza, is the liveliest part of town. Its Tianguis Campesino (Peasants' Market) is for farmers to sell their goods direct: they sit on the bare ground to do so.

Ocosingo saw the bloodiest fighting during the 1994 Zapatista rebellion, with about 50 rebels killed here by the Mexican army. The town has remained calm since then, but occasional land rights disputes have blown up in the region. In February 2003 Zapatista-affiliated villagers seized the nearby guesthouse Rancho Esmeralda (see p793).

Orientation & Information

Ocosingo spreads east (downhill) from Hwy 199, the San Cristóbal–Palenque road. Av Central runs down from the main road to the pleasant central plaza. Hotels, restaurants and services are within a few blocks.

Serfin bank, on Calle Central Nte, which runs off the plaza beside Hotel Central, changes cash US dollars and traveler's checks and has an ATM. Banamex on the plaza has another ATM. There are three cybercafés on Calle Central Nte just off the plaza, all charge US$0.90 per hour.

With few tourists, Ocosingo makes a good base for studying Spanish. For private tuition, the teacher **Rodolfo Gómez Trujillo** (☎ 673-06-14; rodolfogt@hotmail.com) receives good reports.

Sleeping

Hospedaje Esmeralda (☎ 673-00-14; www.rancho esmeralda.net; Calle Central Nte 14; s/d US$11/18, with bath US$13/22; **P**) Set up by the owners of the Rancho Esmeralda, this small welcoming guesthouse has five attractive rooms, all with bright bedcovers and fans. There's a snug bar area, good home-style cooking available, and excellent horse-riding excursions (US$20) can be arranged.

Hotel Central (☎ 673-00-24; Av Central 5; s/d US$12/16; **P**) This very neat little hotel has a prime location on the north side of the main plaza, and simple, spotless rooms with fan, bath and TV.

Other possibilities include:

Hotel Nak um (☎ 673-02-80; Calle Central Nte 19; s/d US$10/19; **P** ☒) Next to Hospedaje Esmeralda , with big bare rooms with TV and bathroom.

Hospedaje Las Palmas (Av 1 Nte; s/d with shared bath US$5.50/7.50) Family-run, one block west and one north from the plaza.

Hotel Tierra Maya (☎ 673 -09-17; hoteltierramaya@ hotmail.com; 2 Ote Sur 12; d with fan US$27 with air-con US$34; Ⓟ ✖️) Two blocks north, two blocks east of the plaza; new with comfortable rooms and a restaurant.

Eating

Ocosingo is known for its *queso amarillo* (yellow cheese), indeed the town's nickname is 'Los Quesos.' There are six main types, including 'de Bola' which comes in 1kg balls with an edible wax coating and a crumbly, whole-fat center.

Fábrica de Quesos Santa Rosa (☎ 673-00-09; 1 Ote Nte 11) For a taste, check out this cheese shop.

Las Delicias (☎ 673-00-24; Av Central 5; mains US$4-6.50) Set on Hotel Central's veranda overlooking the plaza, this reliable restaurant has big portions and good breakfasts.

Restaurant Esmeralda (☎ 673-00-14; Hospedaje Esmeralda; mains US$5) Offers healthy buffet breakfasts (US$3.75 to US$5) and dinner favorites include good goulash and pasta.

Restaurant Los Portales (Av Central 19; mains US$2.50-4.50; ⏱ 8am-6pm) A few doors east of Las Delicias, this is a straightforward place serving hearty soups, chicken, *milanesas* and egg dishes at good prices.

Pizzas El Desván (☎ 673-01-17; Av 1 Sur Ote 10; pizzas US$4.50-12) El Desván has plaza views and decent pizzas, steaks and breakfasts.

You can get a comida for US$1.50 at comedores in the **mercado** on Av Sur Ote.

Getting There & Away

Servicios Aéreos San Cristóbal (☎ 673-01-88; sasc_ ocosingo@hotmail.com) does small-plane charters from Ocosingo's airstrip, about 4km out of town along the Toniná road. Destinations include day trips to Bonampak and Yaxchilán (around US$140 a person for a return flight) or San Quintín near Laguna Miramar; see p812 (one way, per person US$45). Prices are based on four paying passengers.

The main Colón transportation terminal (which serves four 1st-class and TRF 2nd-class buses) is on Hwy 199, 600m west of the plaza; ATG (2nd-class buses) is next door, with AEXA 1st class buses opposite. Daily departures from Ocosingo include:

Palenque (US$4.50-6.50, 2¾hr, 14 1st class from Colón terminal; US$4.50, 4 ATG; US$4.50, 3 AEXA /OC)
San Cristóbal de Las Casas (US$3.50-4.50, 2 hr, 15 from Colón terminal; US$3, 4 ATG; US$2.75, 5 AEXA)
Tuxtla Gutiérrez (US$5-7.50, 3½hr, 12 from Colón terminal; US$5, 4ATG)

Colón and/or ATG also run buses to Campeche, Cancún, Chetumal, Mérida, Mexico City and Villahermosa.

TONINÁ

elevation 900m
The Mayan ruins of **Toniná** (ruins & museum US$3; ⏱ ruins 9am-4pm daily, museum until 5pm closed Mon), 14km east of Ocosingo, overlook a verdant pastoral valley and form an expansive and intriguing site. Built into a steep hillside, Toniná's towering ceremonial core comprises one of the Mayan world's most imposing temple complexes. The city has an interesting history, which is well explained in the neat site museum.

PLACE OF THE CELESTIAL CAPTIVES

The prelude to Toniná's heyday was the inauguration of the Snake Skull–Jaguar Claw dynasty in AD 688. The new rulers, ambitious and military-minded, contested control of the region with Palenque. In alliance with Calakmul (see p855), they constantly harassed their rival state from around AD 690, and captured at least three Palenque leaders. One, Kan-Xul II, probably had his head lopped off here around AD 720.

Toniná was at its most powerful in the decade following its devastation of Palenque in 730. It became known as the Place of the Celestial Captives, for in some of its chambers were held the captured rulers of Palenque and other Mayan cities, destined either to be ransomed for large sums or to be decapitated. A recurring image in Toniná sculpture is that of captives before decapitation, thrown to the ground with their hands tied.

Around AD 900 Toniná was rebuilt in a simpler, austere style. But Jaguar Serpent, in 903, was the last Toniná ruler of whom any record has been found. Classic Mayan civilization was ending here, as elsewhere, and Toniná has the distinction of having the last-ever recorded Long Count date, AD 909.

Toniná was not excavated until 1979.

Some explanatory signs near the site entrance explain Toniná's history and background, in Spanish.

The path from the entrance and museum crosses a stream and climbs to the broad, flat **Gran Plaza**. At the south end of the Gran Plaza is the **Templo de la Guerra Cósmica** (Temple of Cosmic War), with five altars in front of it. Off one side of the plaza is a ball court, which was inaugurated around 780 under the rule of the female regent Smoking Mirror. A decapitation altar stands beside it.

To the north rises the ceremonial core of Toniná, a seminatural hillside terraced into a number of platforms, rising to a height of 80m above the Gran Plaza. At the right-hand end of the steps rising from the first to the second platform is the entry to a **ritual labyrinth** of passages.

Higher up on the right-hand side is the **Palacio de las Grecas y de la Guerra** (Palace of the Grecas and War). The *greca* is a zigzag X-shape, possibly representing Quetzalcóatl. To the right is a rambling series of chambers, passages and stairways, believed to have been Toniná's administrative headquarters.

Higher again is Toniná's most remarkable sculpture, the **Mural de las Cuatro Eras** (Mural of the Four Eras). Created some time between AD 790 and 840, this stucco relief of four panels – the first, from the left end, has been lost – represents the four suns, or four eras of human history, in Mayan belief. At the center of each panel is the upside-down head of a decapitated prisoner. Blood spurting from the prisoner's neck forms a ring of feathers and, at the same time, a sun. In one panel, a dancing skeleton holds a decapitated head with its tongue out. To the left of the head is a lord of the underworld, who resembles an enormous rodent. This mural was created at a time when a wave of destruction was running through the Mayan world. The people of Toniná believed themselves to be living in the fourth sun – that of winter, mirrors, the direction north and the end of human life.

Near the middle of the same level you'll find a tomb with a stone sarcophagus. Up the next steps is the seventh level, with remains of four temples. Behind the second temple from the left, steps descend into the very narrow **Tumba de Treinta Metros** ('Thirty-Meter Tomb'), which is definitely not for the claustrophobic or obese!

Above here is the acropolis, the abode of the rulers of Toniná and site of its eight most important temples – four on each of two levels. The right-hand temple on the lower level, the **Templo del Monstruo de la Tierra** (Temple of the Earth Monster), has Toniná's best-preserved roof comb, built around AD 713.

The topmost level has four more temples. The tallest, the **Templo del Espejo Humeante** (Temple of the Smoking Mirror), was built by Zots-Choj, who took the throne in AD 842. In that era of the fourth and final sun and the direction north, Zots-Choj needed to raise this, Toniná's northernmost temple, higher than all the others, which necessitated a large, artificial northeast extension of the hill.

Getting There & Away

Combis to Toniná (US$1.25) leave from opposite the Tianguis Campesino in Ocosingo every 45 minutes from early morning on. The last one returns around 5pm.

LAGUNA MIRAMAR
elevation 400m

Ringed by rainforest, pristine Laguna Miramar, 130km west of Ocosingo, is one of Mexico's most remote and exquisite lakes. Thanks to a successful ecotourism project, it's possible to stay in a village, **Ejido Emiliano Zapata**, near its western shore.

Frequently echoing with the roars of howler monkeys, the 16-sq-km lake, located within the Montes Azules biosphere reserve, has a beautiful temperature all year and is virtually unpolluted. No settlement is permitted within 1km of its shore and motorboats are banned. Ejido life in Emiliano Zapata – a poor but well-ordered Mayan community – is fascinating too. It is forbidden to bring alcohol or drugs into the community.

Miramar is not an easy place to get to. If you do decide to go, try to visit outside the rainy period from late August to the end of October, when land access can be more difficult and foot trails muddy.

When you reach Emiliano Zapata, ask for the Presidente de la Laguna. Through him you must arrange and pay for the services you need – per day a guide is US$9, the overnight fee is US$3, a canoe is US$20. The village is a spread-out place of huts and a few concrete communal buildings, on a gentle slope running down to the Río Perlas – a beautiful bathing place.

The 7km walk from village to lake, through *milpas* (cornfields) and forest that includes *caoba* (mahogany) and the *matapalo* (strangler fig) trees, takes about 1½ hours. Apart from the incessant growls of howler monkeys *(saraguatos)*, you may hear jaguars at night. Other wildlife includes spider monkeys *(monos arañas)* and tapirs; birdlife includes macaws and toucans; butterflies are prolific too. Locals fish for perch *(mojarra)* in the lake, and will assure you that its few crocodiles are not dangerous. It takes about 45 minutes to canoe across to Isla Lacan-Tun, an island rich in overgrown, ruined remains of a pre-Hispanic settlement. The Chol-Lacantún people who survived here were unconquered by the Spanish until the 1580s. As the island is looked after by another village, you could be asked to pay an additional fee if you want to visit it.

Sleeping & Eating
At the lakeshore, camp or sling a hammock under a *palapa* shelter. A small guesthouse next to the Río Perlas in Ejido Emiliano Zapata, **Posada Zapata** (☎ 55-5150-5618; per bed US$5, hammock US$2.50) has six rooms, a hammock area, showers and lockers. Breakfast and dinner is available in villagers' homes.

Food supplies in Emiliano Zapata's stores are very basic; there are slightly better stocks and simple comedores in neighboring San Quintín.

Getting There & Away
Natutur (see p799) organizes four-day trips to Laguna Miramar for US$260 per person (minimum four people). This includes transportation by boat or jeep, food and drink and local guides. You can also get there yourself via Ocosingo: either in a tiny Cessna plane or by truck along a rough track to San Quintín. From the bus stop in San Quintín, walk five minutes along the airstrip and turn down a dirt road to the right, opposite a complex of military buildings. From here it's a 15- or 20-minute walk to the middle of Ejido Emiliano Zapata.

AIR
Servicios Aéreos San Cristóbal (see p810) planes leave Ocosingo most mornings for San Quintín. If you're at the airstrip by 9:30am you should get a place. The one-way fare is US$45. Return flight times are less reliable, but there's one most days.

BUS & TRUCK
From Ocosingo, four or five buses, microbuses or passenger-carrying trucks *(tres toneladas)* run between 9am and 11am daily to San Quintín from just south of the Tianguis Campesino. The 130km trip costs US$6.50 and takes around six hours (more in the rainy season) through an area known as Las Cañadas de Ocosingo, a Zapatista stronghold. Your documents may be checked at Mexican army (and possibly Zapatista village) checkpoints as you travel through; keep your passport and tourist card handy.

Vehicles head back from San Quintín to Ocosingo at 8am, 2pm and midnight.

AGUA AZUL, AGUA CLARA & MISOL-HA
These three stunning attractions – the turquoise cascades of Agua Azul, serene Río Shumulhá and the spectacular waterfall of Misol-Ha – are all short detours off the Ocosingo–Palenque road. (Note that during the rainy season, they may be less than stunning, as the water gets murky.)

All three are most easily visited in an organized day tour from Palenque, though it's possible, but not necessarily cheaper, to go independently too. There are accommodations at Misol-Ha.

In the past, the road between Ocosingo and Palenque has been the scene of highway robberies, though no incidents have been reported recently. However it's not advisable to be waiting around for transportation on Hwy 199 after about 5pm.

Agua Azul
The turnoff for these waterfalls is about halfway between Ocosingo and Palenque. Agua Azul is a breathtaking sight and it's easy to wallow away several blissful hours in its myriad tropical turquoise pools, which are separated by dazzling white waterfalls and surrounded by verdant jungle.

On holidays and weekends the place is thronged; at other times you'll have few companions.

The temptation to swim is great, but take extreme care. The current is deceptively

GREG ELMS

Harvesting maguey plants for mezcal (p719)

Hats, Ocotlán market (p732)

ALISON WRIGHT

RICHARD I'ANSON

Painted table top, San Martín
Tilcajete (p732)

Ex-Convento Domínicano (p733), Cuilapan

RICHARD I'ANSON

Maya woman, San Cristóbal de Las Casas (p792)

Bas-relief on El Palacio (p817), Palenque

Cascada Misol-Ha (p813), movie set for *Predator*

fast, and there are many submerged hazards like rocks and dead trees. Use your judgment to identify slower, safer areas. People do drown here.

The falls are in the territory of an **ejido** (admission per person on foot US$1.50, per car US$2). A paved road leads 4.5km down from Hwy 199 to a cluster of **comedores** (mains around US$3.25) near the main falls.

It's best not to stray too far from the main zone. Sadly, people have occasionally been robbed in isolated spots.

Agua Clara

About 8km after the Agua Azul turnoff, heading toward Palenque, another signed detour leads 2km by paved road to Agua Clara. Here the Río Shumulhá (or Tulijá) is a beautiful, broad, shallow expanse of turquoise water that's a delight to swim in (but test the current before choosing your spot). You can also take a stroll across a hanging footbridge, or ride a horse (per hour US$9), or in winter, rent a kayak (per hour US$3.25).

It's a delightfully tranquil spot, but be aware that there are proposals to build a large restaurant, guesthouse and gift shops here.

Misol-Ha

About 20km south of Palenque, the spectacular waterfall of Misol-Ha cascades 35m into a wonderful wide pool surrounded by lush tropical vegetation. It's a sublime place for a dip. A path behind the main fall leads into a cave with some smaller trickles of water. Misol-Ha is 1.5km off Hwy 199 and the turn is signposted. Admission is US$1.50 per person.

Centro Turístico Ejidal Cascada Misol-Ha (☎ 55-5329-0995 ext 7006; cabin US$15, with kitchen US$30). These great wooden cabins have bathrooms and mosquito netting. There's a restaurant nearby, open until 6pm.

Getting There & Away

Most Palenque travel agencies (see p815) offer daily trips to Misol-Ha and Agua Azul. Trips cost US$11 to US$13, and last between seven and nine hours, spending 30 to 60 minutes at Misol-Ha and two to three hours at Agua Azul. Admission fees and sometimes breakfast are included in the price. An air-conditioned van and/or

a side trip to Agua Clara can add a few pesos.

To do it independently, take a *camion eta* (pickup) from Cárdenas, off Juárez a block west of the Colón/ADO bus station in Palenque, or any 2nd-class bus along Hwy 199; they will drop you off at any of the three intersections. The fare to the Agua Azul junction (*crucero*) is US$2. From San Cristóbal, a Figueroa bus will take you to the Agua Azul junction for US$5.50.

The distances from the highway to Misol-Ha and Agua Clara are manageable on foot. For the 4.5km between the Agua Azul crucero and Agua Azul itself, there are camionetas for US$1. Check out times of camionetas going back to the crucero, as it's uphill in that direction.

A taxi from Palenque to Misol-Ha with a one-hour wait costs around US$25; to Agua Azul with a two-hour wait should be US$55.

PALENQUE

☎ 916 / pop 33,000 / elevation 80m

The ancient Mayan city of Palenque, with its superb jungle setting and exquisite architecture and decoration, is one of the marvels of Mexico. Modern Palenque town, a few kilometers to the east, is a sweaty, humdrum place with little attraction except as a base for visiting the ruins. El Panchán, just down the road, is not for everyone, but it's a well-known traveler hangout.

History

The name Palenque (Palisade) is Spanish and has no relation to the city's ancient name, which according to current theories was probably B'aakal (Bone). Palenque was first occupied around 100 BC, and flourished from around AD 630 to around 740. The city rose to prominence under K'inich Janaab' Pakal (generally known just as Pakal), who reigned from AD 615 to 683. Archaeologists have determined that Pakal is represented by hieroglyphics of sun and shield, and he is also referred to as Sun Shield (in Spanish, Escudo Solar). He lived to the age of 80.

During Pakal's reign, many plazas and buildings, including the superlative Templo de las Inscripciones (Pakal's own mausoleum), were constructed in Palenque. The structures were characterized by mansard roofs and very fine stucco bas-reliefs.

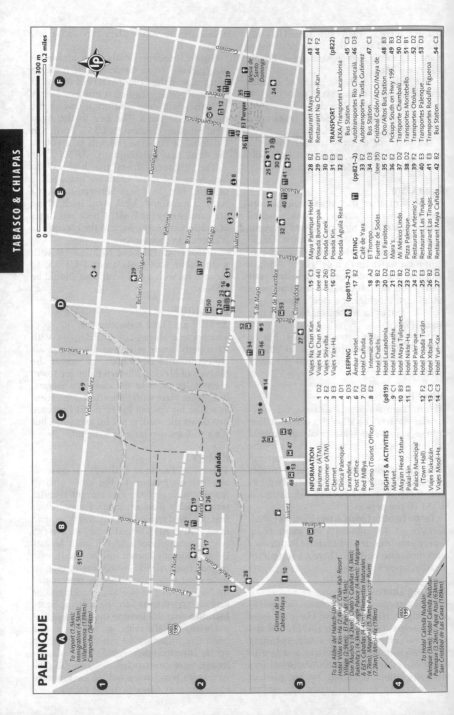

PALENQUE

La Cañada

To Airport (1.5km);
Immigration (4.5km);
Villahermosa (139km);
Campeche (364km)

To La Aldea del Halach-Uinic &
Hotel Villas Kin-Ha (2.4km); Chan-Kah Resort
Village (2.9km); El Panchán (4.1km);
Don Mucho's (4.2km); Chato's Cabañas (4.3km);
Rakshita's (4.3km); Jungle Palace (4.4km); Margarita
& Ed's Cabañas (4.4km); Elementos Naturales
(4.7km); Mayabell (5.7km); Palenque Ruins
(7.2km); Misol-Ha (19km)

To Hotel Calinda Nututun
Palenque (3km); Hotel Calinda Nututun
Palenque (3.2km); Agua Azul (63km);
San Cristóbal de Las Casas (189km)

Gloneta de
la Cabeza
Maya

MEX
199

MEX
199

Iglesia de
Santo
Domingo

0 — 300 m
0 — 0.2 miles

INFORMATION
Banamex (ATM)	**1** D2
Bancomer (ATM)	**2** E2
Cibernet	**3** E3
Clinica Palenque	**4** D1
Lavandería	**5** D3
Post Office	**6** F2
Red M@ya	**7** D2
Turismo (Tourist Office)	**8** E2

SIGHTS & ACTIVITIES (p819)
Market	**9** C1
Mayan Head Statue	**10** B3
Pakal-kin	**11** E3
Palacio Municipal (Town Hall)	**12** F2
Viajes Kukulcán	**13** C3
Viajes Misol-Ha	**14** C3
Viajes Na Chan Kan	**15** C3
Viajes Na Chan Kan	(see 44)
Viajes Shivalba	**16** D2
Viajes Yax-Ha	(see 26)

SLEEPING (pp819-21)
Ámbar Hostel	**17** B2
Hotel Cañada Internacional	**18** A2
Hotel Chatils	**19** B2
Hotel Lacandonia	**20** E2
Hotel Marznatha	**21** E3
Hotel Maya Tulipanes	**22** B2
Hotel Nikte-Ha	**23** D2
Hotel Palerque	**24** F3
Hotel Posada Tucán	**25** E3
Hotel Xibalba	**26** B2
Hotel Yun-Kax	**27** D3
Maya Palenque Hotel	**28** B2
Posada Bonampak	**29** D1
Posada Canek	**30** E3
Posada Kin	**31** E3
Posada Águila Real	**32** E3

EATING (pp821-2)
Café de Yara	**33** E2
El Trompo	**34** D3
Fuente de Sodas	(see 35)
Los Farolitos	**35** F2
Mara's	**36** E2
Mi México Lindo	**37** D2
Pizza Palenque	**38** D2
Restaurant Artemio's	**39** F2
Restaurant Las Tinajas	**40** E3
Restaurant Las Tinajas	**41** E3
Restaurant Maya Cañada	**42** B2
Restaurant Maya	**43** F2
Restaurant Na Chan-Kan	**44** F2

TRANSPORT (p822)
AEXA/Transportes Lacandonia Bus Station	**45** C3
Autotransportes Río Chancalá	**46** D3
Autotransportes Tuxtla Gutiérrez Bus Station	**47** C3
Cristobal Colón/ADO/Maya de Oro/Altos Bus Station	**48** B3
Pickups South on Hwy 199	**49** B3
Transporte Chambalú	**50** D2
Transportes Montebello	**51** B1
Transportes Ocosingo	**52** D2
Transportes Oxlum	**53** D3
Transportes Rodulfo Figueroa Bus Station	**54** B2

TABASCO & CHIAPAS

Pakal was succeeded by his son K'inich Kan B'alam II, who is symbolized in hieroglyphics by the jaguar and the serpent (and also called Jaguar Serpent II). Kan B'alam continued Palenque's political and economic expansion and artistic development. He completed his father's crypt in the Templo de las Inscripciones and presided over the construction of the Grupo de la Cruz temples, placing sizable narrative stone steles within each.

During Kan B'alam II's reign, Palenque extended its zone of control to the western bank of the Usumacinta river, but was challenged for regional control by the rival Mayan city of Toniná, 65km to the south. Toniná's hostility was probably the major factor in Palenque's brief hiatus after Kan B'alam's death in 702. Kan B'alam's brother and successor, K'an Hoy Chitam II, was captured by forces from Toniná and probably executed there. However Palenque recovered to enjoy a resurgence under Ahkal Mo' Naab' III, who took the throne in 721 and added many substantial buildings during a rule of perhaps 15 years.

After AD 900 Palenque was largely abandoned. In an area that receives the heaviest rainfall in Mexico, the ruins were soon overgrown.

The city remained unknown to the western world until 1746 when Mayan hunters revealed the existence of a jungle palace to a Spanish priest named Antonio de Solís. Later explorers claimed Palenque was a capital of an Atlantis-like civilization. One flamboyant character, the eccentric Count de Waldeck, who in his 60s lived atop one of the pyramids for two years (1831–33), even published a book with fanciful neoclassical drawings that made the city resemble a great Mediterranean civilization.

It was not until 1837 – when John L Stephens, an amateur archaeology enthusiast from New York, reached Palenque with artist Frederick Catherwood – that the site was insightfully investigated. And another century passed before Alberto Ruz Lhuillier, the tireless Mexican archaeologist, uncovered Pakal's hidden crypt in 1952.

Frans Blom, a mid-20th-century investigator, remarked: 'The first visit to Palenque is immensely impressive. When one has lived there for some time this ruined city becomes an obsession.' It's not hard to understand why.

Orientation

Hwy 199 meets Palenque town's main street, Juárez, at the Glorieta de la Cabeza Maya, an intersection with a large statue of a Maya chieftain's head, at the west end of the town. From here Juárez heads 1km east to the central square, El Parque. The main bus stations are on Juárez just east of the Mayan head statue.

A few hundred meters south of the Mayan head, the 7.5km road to the Palenque ruins diverges west off Hwy 199. This road passes the site museum after 6km, then winds on 1.5km to the main entrance to the ruins.

Information

EMERGENCY
Police ☎ 066

IMMIGRATION
Instituto Nacional de Migración (☎ 345-07-95; 6km north of town on Hwy 199; ◷ 8am-2pm & 6-8pm) Transportes Otolum or Transportes Palenque combis run there from their terminals on Allende.

INTERNET ACCESS
There are over a dozen cybercafés in town; rates are around US$0.90 an hour.
Cibernet (Independencia; ◷ 8am-11pm)
Red M@ya (Juárez 133; ◪)

LAUNDRY
Lavandería (5 de Mayo opposite Hotel Kashlan; 3kg wash & dry US$4) Same-day service if you drop off in the morning.

MEDICAL SERVICES
Clínica Palenque (☎ 345-15-13; Velasco Suárez 33; ◷ 9am-5pm) Dr Alfonso Martínez speaks English.

MONEY
Outside banking hours, try travel agents if you don't have a card for the ATMs at Bancomer or at Banamex, a block further west on Juárez.
Bancomer (Juárez s/n; ◷ 9am-noon Mon-Fri) Changes US dollars cash and US-dollar traveler's checks.

POST & TELEPHONE
Post office (Independencia at Bravo) You'll find card phones around El Parque.

TOURIST INFORMATION
Turismo (cnr of Juárez & Abasolo; ◷ 9am-9pm Mon-Sat, until 1pm Sun) Has reliable town and transportation information and a few maps.

Visiting the Ruins

Ancient **Palenque** (admission US$4; ☽ site 8am-5pm daily, museum 9am-4pm Tue-Sun) stands at the precise point where the first hills rise out of the Gulf Coast plain, and the dense jungle covering these hills forms an evocative backdrop to Palenque's outstanding Mayan architecture. The ruins are made up of some 500 buildings spread over 15 sq km, but only relatively few, in a fairly compact central area, have been excavated. Everything you see here was built without metal tools, pack animals or the wheel.

As you explore the ruins, try to picture the gray stone edifices as they would have been at the peak of Palenque's power: painted blood-red with elaborate blue and yellow stucco details embellishing their façades. The forest around these temples is home to toucans and ocelots, while you may hear howler monkeys, especially if you stay near the ruins.

Opening time is a good time to visit, when it's cooler and not too crowded and morning mist may still be wrapping the temples in a picturesque haze.

Bring sunscreen with you. Refreshments, hats and souvenirs (including quivers of arrows sold by Lacandones) are available from the hawker circus outside the entrance, and there are cafés here and at the museum.

Official site **guides** (2-hr tour for up to 7 people US$32) are available by the entrance. A Mayan guide association, **Guias e Interpretes Mayas**,

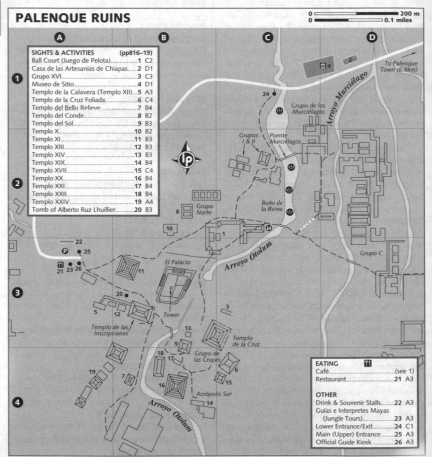

PALENQUE RUINS

0 — 200 m
0 — 0.1 miles

SIGHTS & ACTIVITIES	(pp816–19)
Ball Court (Juego de Pelota)	1 C2
Casa de las Artesanías de Chiapas	2 D1
Grupo XVI	3 C3
Museo de Sitio	4 D1
Templo de la Calavera (Templo XII)	5 A3
Templo de la Cruz Foliada	6 C4
Templo del Bello Relieve	7 B4
Templo del Conde	8 B2
Templo del Sol	9 B3
Templo X	10 B2
Templo XI	11 B3
Templo XIII	12 B3
Templo XIV	13 B3
Templo XIX	14 B4
Templo XVII	15 C4
Templo XX	16 B4
Templo XXI	17 B4
Templo XXII	18 B4
Templo XXIV	19 A4
Tomb of Alberto Ruz Lhuillier	20 B3

To Palenque
Town (6.8km)

Grupo de los
Murciélagos

Grupos
I & II

Puente
Murciélagos

Grupo
Norte

Baño de
la Reina

Grupo C

El Palacio

Arroyo Otolum

Tower

Templo de las
Inscripciones

Templo
de la Cruz

Grupo de
las Cruces

Acrópolis Sur

Arroyo Otolum

EATING	🍴
Café	(see 1)
Restaurant	21 A3

OTHER	
Drink & Souvenir Stalls	22 A3
Guías e Interpretes Mayas (Jungle Tours)	23 A3
Lower Entrance/Exit	24 C1
Main (Upper) Entrance	25 A3
Official Guide Kiosk	26 A3

also has a desk here and offers informative two-hour jungle tours (two people minimum, per person US$9) in Spanish that take in the outlying Templo Olvidado (Forgotten Temple).

An excellent place to read up on Palenque is the official website of some of the archaeologists who are working here: www.meso web.com/palenque.

Most people take a combi or taxi to the main (upper) entrance, see the major structures and a few outlying buildings then walk downhill to the museum, visiting minor ruins along the way. However, if you want to view Pakal's tomb (access inside the Templo de las Inscripciones is restricted) consider stopping first at the site museum and getting a permit early in the day.

Transporte Chambalú, on Allende at Hidalgo, and Transportes Palenque, Allende at 20 de Noviembre, operate combis to the ruins about every 15 minutes from around 6am to 6pm daily (US$0.70 one way). The vehicles will pick you up anywhere along the town-to-ruins road. A taxi from town to ruins costs US$4.50.

TEMPLO DE LAS INSCRIPCIONES GROUP

As you emerge through the trees from the entrance, a line of temples rising in front of the jungle on your right comes into view. Below them is the tomb of Mexican archaeologist Alberto Ruz Lhuillier, who discovered Pakal's tomb in 1952.

The first of these is Templo XII, called the **Templo de La Calavera** (Temple of the Skull) for the relief sculpture of a rabbit or deer skull at the foot of one its pillars. The second temple has little interest. Third is **Templo XIII**, containing a tomb of a female skeleton, colored red as a result of treatment with cinnabar, which was found in 1994. You can enter this Tumba de la Reina Roja (Tomb of the Red Queen) to see her sarcophagus. With the skeleton were found a malachite mask and about 1000 pieces of jade, but no inscriptions to tell who the 'queen' was. Some speculate, from resemblances to Pakal's tomb next door, that she was his wife.

The line of temples culminates in the **Templo de las Inscripciones** (Temple of the Inscriptions), perhaps the most celebrated burial monument in the Americas – the tallest and most stately of Palenque's buildings. Owing to inevitable damage to its murals from the humidity exuded by hordes of visitors, this temple is now only open on a restricted basis. Free permits can be obtained from the site museum (see p819) and it's only possible to view Pakal's tomb after 3pm.

Constructed on eight levels, the Templo de las Inscripciones has a central front staircase rising 25m to a series of small rooms. The tall roof comb that once crowned it is long gone, but between the front doorways are stucco panels with reliefs of noble figures. On the interior rear wall are the three panels with a long Mayan inscription, for which Ruz Lhuillier named the temple. The inscription, dedicated in AD 692, recounts the history of Palenque and the temple. Also at the top is the access to the slippery stairs leading down into the tomb of Pakal. Pakal's jewel-bedecked skeleton and jade mosaic death mask were removed to Mexico City, and the tomb was re-created in the Museo Nacional de Antropología (from where the priceless death mask was stolen in 1985), but the stone sarcophagus lid remains here. This carved slab depicts Pakal's rebirth as the Maize god, encircled by serpents, mythical monsters and glyphs recounting his reign. Stucco figures on the walls represent the nine lords of the underworld. Between the crypt and the staircase, a snakelike hollow ventilation duct connected Pakal to the realm of the living.

EL PALACIO

Diagonally opposite the Templo de las Inscripciones is the **Palace**, a large, complex structure divided into four main courtyards, with a maze of corridors and rooms. Its tower, restored in 1955, has remnants of fine stucco reliefs on the walls, but is not open to visitors. Archaeologists believe the tower was constructed so that Mayan royalty and priests could observe the sun falling directly into the Templo de las Inscripciones during the winter solstice.

The northeastern courtyard, the **Patio de los Cautivos** (Patio of the Captives), contains a collection of relief sculptures that seem disproportionately large for their setting: it's conjectured that they are representations of conquered rulers and were brought from elsewhere.

In the southern part of the complex, the extensive subterranean bathrooms included six toilets and a couple of sweat baths.

GRUPO DE LA CRUZ

Pakal's son Kan B'alam II was a prolific builder, and soon after the death of his father started designing the three temples of the Grupo de la Cruz (Group of the Cross). All three pyramid-shaped structures face inwards towards an artifical elevated plaza, just southeast of the Templo de las Inscripciones. They were all dedicated in 692 as a spiritual focal point for Palenque's triad of patron deities. The 'cross' carvings here symbolize the ceiba tree, which in Mayan belief held up the universe.

The **Templo del Sol** (Temple of the Sun), on the west side of the plaza, has the best-preserved roof comb at Palenque. Carvings inside, commemorating Kan B'alam's birth in AD 635 and accession in 684, show him facing his father. At least one guide at Palenque will have you believe that some of the carvings on the roof represent a Chinese dragon and the Buddha, and that all this stuff about Pakal, Kan B'alam and company is so much hocus-pocus. Others view this beautiful building as sure proof that Palenque's ancient architects were inspired by the same magic mushrooms as some modern-day travelers enjoy around here. Make up your own mind!

Steep steps climb to the **Templo de la Cruz** (Temple of the Cross), the largest and most elegantly proportioned in this group. The stone tablet in the central sanctuary shows the lord of the underworld smoking tobacco on the right, and Kan B'alam in full royal attire on its left. Behind is a reproduction of a panel depicting Kan B'alam's accession.

On the **Templo de la Cruz Foliada** (Temple of the Foliated Cross), the corbel arches are fully exposed, revealing how Palenque's architects designed these buildings. A well-preserved inscribed tablet shows a king (probably Pakal) with a sun shield emblazoned on his chest, corn growing from his shoulder blades and the sacred quetzal bird on his head.

ACRÓPOLIS SUR

In the jungle south of the Grupo de la Cruz is the **Southern Acropolis**, where archaeologists have focused their most recent excavations and recovered some terrific finds. You may find part of the area roped off. The Acrópolis Sur appears to have been constructed as an extension of the Grupo de la Cruz, with both groups set around what was probably a single long open space.

Templo XVII, between the Cruz group and the Southern Acropolis, contains a reproduction carved panel depicting a standing figure bearing a spear, probably Kan B'alam, with a bound captive kneeling before him.

In 1999, close to **Templo XIX**, archeologists made the most important Palenque find for decades: an 8th-century limestone platform with stunning carvings of seated figures and lengthy hieroglyphic texts that detail Palenque's origins. A reproduction has been placed inside Templo XIX now – the central figure on the long south side of the platform is the ruler K'inich Ahkal Mo' Naab' III, in whose reign this temple was dedicated. Also on view is a wonderful reproduction of a colorful tall stucco relief of the ruler's son, Upakal K'inich.

In **Templo XX**, a many-muraled tomb of an unknown personage was found in 1999. It's thought that this large temple was being extensively remodeled in late Classic times, though the work was never completed.

GRUPO NORTE

North of El Palacio are a **ball court** (juego de palota) and the handsome buildings of the Northern Group. Crazy Count de Waldeck (see p815) lived in the so-called **Templo del Conde** (Temple of the Count), constructed in AD 647.

NORTHEASTERN GROUPS

East of the Grupo Norte, the main path crosses Arroyo Otolum. Some 70m beyond the stream, a right fork will take you to **Grupo C**, a set of jungle-covered buildings and plazas on different levels, thought to have been lived in from about AD 750 to 800.

If you stay on the main path, you'll find it descends steep steps to a group of low, elongated buildings, thought to have been occupied residentially around AD 770 to 850. The path goes alongside the Arroyo Otolum, which here tumbles down a series of small falls known as the **Baño de la Reina** (Queen's Bath). It's not permitted to bathe here anymore.

The path continues to another residential quarter, the **Grupo de Los Murciélagos** (Bat Group), then crosses the **Puente Murciélagos** (Bat Bridge), a suspension footbridge across Arroyo Otolum.

Across the bridge and a bit further downstream, a path goes west to **Grupos 1 and 2**, a short walk uphill. These ruins, only partly uncovered, are in a beautiful jungle setting. The main path continues downriver to the road, where the museum is along to the right a short distance.

MUSEO DE SITIO
Palenque's Site Museum does a wonderful job of displaying finds from the site and interpreting Palenque's history. It includes a copy of the lid of Pakal's sarcophagus and recent finds from Templo XIX. Next door you'll find a pleasant café and a handicraft shop. The museum is closed on Mondays.

El Panchán
About 4.4km along the road to the ruins, **El Panchán** is a near-legendary travelers' hangout set in patch of dense rainforest; the trippy epicenter of Palenque's alternative scene, and home to a bohemian bunch of Mexican and Western residents and wanderers. Once ranchland, the area has now been reforested by the remarkable Morales family, one of whom heads the team of archaeologists working at Palenque ruins. There are several (fairly rustic) accommodations and a couple of restaurants in Panchán.

Tours
There are several different agencies in Palenque that offer transportation packages to Agua Azul, Agua Clara and Misol-Ha (see p813), to Bonampak and Yaxchilán (see p822), and to Flores in Guatemala via Frontera Corozal.

Agencies located in Palenque include the following:
Pakal-kin (☎ 345-11-97; viajespakal_kin@hotmail.com; 5 de Mayo 7)
Transporte Chambalú (☎ 345-08-67, Hidalgo at Allende)
Transportes Palenque (Allende at 20 de Noviembre)
Viajes Kukulcan (☎ 345-15-06; www.kukulcantravel.com; Juárez s/n)
Viajes Misol-Ha (☎ 345-22-71; www.palenquemx.com/viajesmisolha; Juárez 148)
Viajes Na Chan Kan (☎ 345-21-54; rosita_palenque@yahoo.com.mx; Hidalgo at Jiménez & Juaréz s/n)
Viajes Shivalba (☎ 345-04-11; www.palenquemx.com/shivalva; Merle Green 9, La Cañada)

Sleeping
The first choice to make is whether you want to stay in Palenque town, or at one of the places (including campgrounds) outside. Most places out of town are along the 7.5km road to the ruins including El Panchán (see above). Palenque town is scruffy and not particularly attractive, but if you stay here you'll have plenty of restaurants and services (like cybercafés and travel agents) close at hand.

Prices given here are for the high season, which at most establishments is from mid-July to mid-August, mid-December to early January, and Semana Santa. Rates at many mid-range and top-end places fall by up to 35% at other times.

BUDGET
The following places are located in Palenque town.

Posada Kin (☎ 345-17-14; Abasolo 1; s/d US$13/16) Welcoming posada with four floors of clean, light, decent-sized rooms; all have good beds, bathroom and ceiling fan. Breakfast is available for US$1.25.

Posada Bonampak (☎ 345-09-25; Belisario Domínguez 33; s/d US$5/6) This family-run place is a good budget bet. It has a quiet location, and basic but tidy, reasonable-sized rooms, with fan and attached tiled bathrooms, though there's no hot water.

Posada Canek (☎ 345-01-50; 20 de Noviembre 43; dm/r US$5/9) Posada Canek, southwest of El Parque, has functional dorms with shared showers and largish rooms with bathroom and fan. There's a safe for your valuables.

Hotel Yun-Kax (☎ 345-07-25; Corregidora 87; s/d with fan US$11/14, with air-con US$16/23; ❄) The Yun-Kax, between the bus stations and town center, has clean rooms with shower, arranged around a little patio. There's free water for guests.

Hotel Maranatha (☎ 345-10-07; 20 de Noviembre 19; r US$13-18) The Maranatha offers good-value, tile-floored rooms with fan, wardrobes, TV and bathroom, though the color schemes are a little bizarre.

Ámbar Hostel (☎ 345-10-08; ambarhostel2001@hotmail.com; Merle Green s/n; dm/s/d US$6/18/27) Set in the quiet, leafy La Cañada area, Ámbar has a couple of screened dorms with bunks and rooms with fan and bath. There's a kitchen, table tennis and a bar.

There are also some wonderful places on the road to the ruins. Many of these are clustered in El Panchán. All Panchán accommodations are signposted, and between 100m and 300m from the road (Panchán is 300m up a side track from Carr Palenque–Ruinas, 4.4km from town.)

Margarita&EdCabañas (☎ 341-00-63;edcabanas@ yahoo.com; El Panchán; cabañas s/d US$11/12-14, r with fan & bathroom US$12-23, with air-con US$27; **P** 🕸) Margarita and Ed, a welcoming Mexican-US couple, defy the odds and maintain scrupulously clean rooms in middle of the Panchán jungle, 4.7 km away. The rustic screened cabañas are also pleasant, and come with reading lights and private bathrooms. There's free drinking water for all.

Mayabell (☎ 345-01-25; mayabell82@hotmail.com; Carr Palenque-Ruinas Km 6; hammock space/camping US$2.75 per person, hammocks to rent US$1.25, small vehicle without hookups US$1, vehicle site with hookups US$12, treehouse US$8, r with bathroom & fan US$16-22 with air-con US$37; **P** 🕸 🐾) This spacious grassy site is just 400m from the site museum and has a plethora of different accommodations options, and a large heat-busting pool. Happy campers and hammock-heads share clean toilet and shower blocks. Rooms with air-con are very homey and comfortable; those with fan are basic. In the pleasant restaurant few items cost more than US$3.50. Lockers are US$0.90 a day, and a Maya-style steam bath is US$2.75. A taxi from town is US$3.25 by day and US$4.50 at night.

Chato's Cabañas (☎ 341-48-46; El Panchán; elpan chan@yahoo.com; cabañas US$11-13; **P** 🐾) Chato's wood cabins,4.6km away from Palenque, vary a little in design, but all have screened windows, hot-water bathrooms and fans, and some have nice little porches. There's a tiny pool too.

Jungle Palace (☎ 341-48-46;El Panchán;elpanchan@ yahoo.com; cabañas with fan, all shared showers US$7-9) Offers rudimentary screened cabins, many of which back onto a stream. Hammock-slingers pay just US$2 a night and lockers are US$0.90 per day, 4.7km from the town.

Rakshita's (www.rakshita.com; El Panchán; hammock US$2.75; dm/cabañas US$2.75/8-13) Rakshita's has a decent five-person dorm with shared bathroom facilities and simple cabañas (some have bathrooms) with fans and mosquito-netted windows. Guests can use the kitchen and plunge pool, and there's a meditation center and an inexpensive vegetarian restaurant here, 4.6 km from town.

Elementos Naturales (Carr Palenque-Ruinas Km 5; dm US$5.25, double cabañas US$13; **P**) It's 700m further from El Panchán to this calm spot with cabañas and palapa shelters scattered around grassy grounds. The dorms and cabañas have fan and electric light; the bathrooms are clean. Breakfast is included and they'll look after your valuables at the desk.

La Aldea del Halach-Uinic (☎ 345-16-93; Carr Palenque-Ruinas Km 2.7; aldea@mexico.com; s/d US$8/15; **P** 🕸) Some 4km from town, the Halach-Uinic has pleasant rustic palapa-roofed cabañas amid pretty gardens. Each hut has two screened beds, hammocks and a little porch. There's a small pool, clean shared toilets and showers, and a restaurant.

MID-RANGE

Hotel Lacandonía (☎ 345-00-57; Juárez at Allende; s/d US$22/33; 🕸) New hotel – smack in the center of town – whose tastefully presented light, airy accommodation all has stylish furnishings including wrought iron beds, reading lights and cable TV.

Hotel Posada Tucán (☎ 345-18-59; merisuiri@ hotmail.com; 5 de Mayo 5; r with fan US$23, with air-con US$31; 🕸) Posada Tucán has a breezy up-stairs location and attractive, clean and fair-sized rooms with fan, TV and nicely-tiled bathrooms. Prices drop by 30% outside high season.

Posada Águila Real (☎ /fax 345-00-04; 20 de Noviembre s/n; s/d with bathrooms and fan US$23/28, with air-con US$30/35; 🕸) Six attractive, well-priced spotless rooms with good quality beds and TV set around a little patio. There's a small café/restaurant and lounge area too.

Hotel Villas Kin-Ha (☎ 345-05-33; www.palenque .com.mx/kin-ha; Carr Palenque-Ruinas Km 2.7; r US$52-59; **P** 🕸 🐾) Kin-Ha offers pleasant thatched air-con casitas, with one king-size or two double beds, in pretty gardens that have a pool and open-sided palapa restaurant.

Hotel Cañada Internacional (☎ /fax 345-20-93; Juárez 1; r US$24-43; **P** 🕸 🐾) The Cañada Internacional has a small pool and comfortable rooms on four stories all with two beds (at least one a double) and TV. The more expensive rooms are bigger and newer, with air-con.

Hotel Chablis (☎ 345-08-70; Merle Green 7; r with one/two beds US$40/43; **P** 🕸) The Hotel Chablis enjoys a quiet location and offers well-presented, spacious rooms, all with air-con fan, TV and balcony.

Hotel Xibalba (☎ 345-04-11; shivalva@tnet.net.mx; Merle Green 9; s/d with fan & TV US$24/27, with air-con US$33/36; **P** **◯**) Opposite the Chablis is the 14-room Xibalba, with reasonably attractive rooms – though sizes vary – in two buildings. Guests can use the pool at the Maya Tulipanes, for a US$2.75 charge.

Hotel Nikte-Ha (☎ 345-05-97; Juárez 133; nikte_ha@hotmail.com; r US$23-32; **◯**) This place has 12 clean, modern rooms all with tiled floors, bathroom, air-con and TV.

Hotel Palenque (☎ /fax 345-01-88; htlpque@tnet.net.mx; 5 de Mayo 15; r with fan US$50, with **◯** US$62) Just east of El Parque, this is the town's oldest hotel, and little has been done to the weary-looking décor since its opening. The rooms, set around a garden courtyard, all hold up to four people and have TV, phone and free bottled water.

TOP END

Maya Palenque Hotel (☎ 345-07-80; hmayapal@tnet.net.mx, cnr Merle Green & Juárez; r/ste US$89/102; **P** **◯** **◯**) The Maya Palenque, part of the Best Western group, has very spacious aircon rooms with two double beds and balconies that enjoy plenty of natural light. There's a large pool in leafy gardens.

Hotel Maya Tulipanes (☎ 345-02-01; www.mayatulipanes.com.mx; Cañada 6; r US$69-77; **P** **◯** **◯** **◯**) Located in the La Cañada area, this hotel has large airy comfortable rooms – some with two huge double beds – plus modish bathrooms and air-con. There's a small pool and a restaurant.

Hotel Calinda Nututun Palenque (☎ 345-01-00; cnututun@tnet.net.mx, Carr Palenque-Ocosingo Km 3.5; r US$92; **P** **◯** **◯**) The Calinda, 3.5km south of town on the road to San Cristóbal, has motel-style buildings with large, comfortable, air-con rooms in spacious tropical gardens shaded by palm trees. There's a wonderful bathing spot in the Río Chacamax, which flows through the hotel property. However, the hotel restaurant is pretty ordinary.

Chan-Kah Resort Village (☎ 345-11-00; www.chan-kah.com; Carr Palenque-Ruinas Km 3.2; r/ste US$105/263; **P** **◯** **◯**) This resort on the road to the ruins, 4.5km from town, has handsome, well-spaced wood-and-stone cottages with generous bathrooms, ceiling fans and air-con. However, it's the stupendous Edenesque 70m stone-lined swimming pool and lush jungle gardens that are the real draw.

Service can be distracted, though, and it's rarely busy, except when tour groups block-book the place.

Eating & Drinking

Palenque is definitely not the gastronomic capital of Mexico, but there's an improving dining scene and prices are fair. The cheapest places are the *taquerías* along the eastern side of El Parque. Try **Los Farolitos** or neighboring **Fuente de Sodas** for a plate of tacos at around US$2.75.

Restaurant Las Tinajas (two branches on 20 de Noviembre; mains US$4-7.50; �9 7:30am-10pm) Gargantuan portions and home-style cooking make Las Tinajas a perennial travelers' favorite. All meals (except breakfast) start with a sinus-clearing dose of home-brewed salsa, and even the modestly priced *tacos filete* is enough for two. A new branch next door has more upmarket pretensions, concentrating on fish and seafood: try the *robalo a la veracruzana*.

Don Mucho's (☎ 341-48-46; El Panchán; mains US$3-4, snacks US$1.50-2.75) Ever-popular Don Mucho's in El Panchán has a very-good-value menu, with sandwiches and salads, and silly-but-tasty themed breakfasts – try *'cielo'* (heaven) or *'arco de iris'* (rainbow). The epic pizzas – cooked in a purpose-built Italian-designed wood-fired oven – must be the finest this side of Naples. There's live music here most nights.

El Trompo (☎ 345-18-81; Av Juárez s/n; tacos US$0.60-1.25, mains US$4-5.50) This refurbished, informal restaurant has a fish- and meat-based menu and also pulls 'em in with a 2-for-1 cocktail happy hour (5pm to 7pm).

Mi México Lindo (☎ 341-63-52; Av Hidalgo s/n; mains US$4.50-7; �9 7am-11pm) This is a large, recently opened restaurant that serves some of the most authentic Mexican food in town including great garlic-soaked *mojarra al ajillo*. Snacks and garlic-free breakfasts are available too.

Mara's (☎ 345-15-76; Juárez 1; mains US$5-8; �9 8am-10pm) Mara's has a prime location facing El Parque, some sidewalk tables and an abundance of whirring fans inside. The Mexican cuisine here is reliable.

Restaurant Maya (☎ 345-02-16, cnr Independencia & Hidalgo; mains US$4.50-8) The Maya has a similar menu and prices to Mara's, though the comidas corridas (US$2.75 to US$3.75) do offer good value.

Restaurant Na Chan-Kan (☎ 345-02-63; cnr Hidalgo & Jiménez; set meals US$2.75-4.50) Opposite the northeast corner of El Parque, Na Chan-Kan serves tasty two-course meals (soup, main dish and drink), *sincronizadas* and beers are US$1 each.

Restaurant Artemio's (☎ 345-02-63; Hidalgo 14; mains US$3-6.50) Family-run Artemio's serves pizzas, set menus from US$3 to US$4.50, breakfasts and a big range of *antojitos*.

Café de Yara (☎ 345-02-69; Hidalgo 66; snacks & breakfasts US$2-4, mains US$4-6; ❤ 8am-10:30pm) Efficient modern café that's good for breakfasts, spaghetti and salads. Also serves fine organic Chiapas coffee, with espresso, cappuccinos and lattes available.

Pizza Palenque (☎ 345-03-32; Juárez 168; pizzas US$4-7.50) The pizzas here won't win prizes, but they're filling and fairly priced. There's free delivery too.

Restaurant Maya Cañada (☎ 345-00-42; Merle Green s/n; mains US$5.50-12, ❤ 8:30am-10:30pm) Well-regarded, elegant La Cañada restaurant, with fine steaks and terrific seafood kebabs. It's open to the air and has a cool upstairs terrace.

Rakshita's (El Panchán; menú del día US$3) Located in El Panchán, vegetarian Rakshita's has a good set meal that changes daily, sometimes with an Indian or Middle Eastern flavor, depending who's cooking.

Getting There & Away

Palenque's airport, 2km north of the Maya head statue along Hwy 199, was undergoing renovations and was closed at the time of research. However it's likely that flights will resume to Mérida, Tuxtla Gutiérrez, Cancún, Flores in Guatemala and possibly Mexico City.

There have been occasional reports of theft on buses serving Palenque, especially night buses to/from Mérida. Take special care of your possessions, don't accept drinks from strangers and don't leave anything of value in the overhead rack or under the seats.

Westernmost of the main bus terminals on Juárez you will find the joint Cristóbal Colón/ADO/Maya de Oro/Altos 1st-class terminal. A block east is Autotransportes Tuxtla Gutiérrez (ATG, 2nd-class), and half a block further east, at Juárez 159, is the joint AEXA (1st-class), Transportes Lacandonia (TL, 2nd-class) and Cárdenas (2nd-class)

terminal; Transportes Rodulfo Figueroa (TRF) is opposite.

It's a good idea to buy your outward ticket a day in advance. Daily departures include the following:

Campeche (US$15-20, 5 hr; 4 from Colón terminal; US$14, 1 ATG)
Cancún (US$34-41, 13 hr, 5 from Colón, US$28, 1 ATG)
Mérida (US$23-24, 8 hr, 4 from Colón; US$18, 1 ATG)
Mexico City (TAPO & Norte; US$50,16 hr, 3 ADO)
Oaxaca (US$37, 15 hr, 1 ADO)
Ocosingo (US$4.50-6.50, 2¾hr, 9 from Colón; US$4.50, 4 TRF; US$4, 4 ATG; US$4.50, 5 AEXA)
Playa del Carmen (US$31-37, 12 hr, 4 from Colón)
San Cristóbal de Las Casas (US$6.50-9, 5 hr, 9 from Colón; US$6.50, 4 TRF; US$6, 4 ATG; US$6.50, 5 AEXA)
Tulum (US$31-35, 11 hr, 2 from Colón)
Tuxtla Gutiérrez (US$8-12, 6½hr, 9 from Colón; US$9, 4 ATG; US$9, 4 TRF; US$9, 5 AEXA).
Villahermosa (US$5-6.50, 2½hr, 12 from Colón)

For information on travel to or from Guatemala, see below.

Getting Around

In town, taxis wait at the northeast corner of El Parque and at the Colón/ADO bus station; they charge US$2 to the airport.

BONAMPAK, YAXCHILÁN & THE CARRETERA FRONTERIZA

The ancient Mayan cities of Bonampak and Yaxchilán, southeast of Palenque, are now much more accessible thanks to the Carretera Fronteriza, a paved road completed in 2000 which runs parallel to the Mexico–Guatemala border all the way round from Palenque to the Lagos de Montebello. Bonampak is 148km by road from Palenque; Yaxchilán is 173km by road then about 22km by boat down the Río Usumacinta.

Visiting this area independently doesn't necessarily work out cheaper than taking a tour from Palenque, but it allows you time to explore an intriguing region at leisure. You can cross into Guatemala at Frontera Corozal or Benemérito de las Américas.

This part of Mexico does not observe daylight saving time, so you should triple-check all transportation schedules! And don't forget insect repellent.

GETTING THERE & AWAY

Autotransportes Río Chancalá at 5 de Mayo 120 in Palenque runs combis to Frontera

Corozal (three hours, US$4.50) five times daily between 6am and 3pm, and to Benemérito (three hours, US$5) 13 times between 4.30am and 4.15pm. Transportes Montebello, on Velasco Suárez two blocks west of Palenque market, runs buses to Frontera Corozal (four hours, US$4.50) at noon, to Benemérito (four hours, US$5) nine times daily, and around the Carretera Fronteriza to Comitán (11 hours, US$14) four times per day. Both these companies, like the region they travel to but unlike the rest of Palenque, they tend to ignore daylight saving time in summer – meaning that by Palenque time, departures during that period are one hour after posted times.

All the above-mentioned services stop at San Javier (US$3.75, 2¼ hours), 140km from Palenque, where a side road branches to Bonampak and Lacanjá Chansayab. They also stop at Crucero Corozal, the intersection for Frontera Corozal, where there are comedores.

Numerous military checkpoints are dotted along the Carretera Fronteriza.

Bonampak

Bonampak's setting in dense jungle hid it from the outside world until 1946. Stories of how it was revealed are full of mystery and innuendo, but it seems that Charles Frey, apparently a young WWII conscientious objector from the US, and John Bourne, heir to the Singer sewing machine fortune, were the first outsiders to visit the site when Chan Bor, a Lacandón, took them there in February 1946. Later in 1946 an American photographer, Giles Healey – who had apparently fallen out with Frey and Bourne during an earlier expedition to film the Lacandones – was also led to the site by Chan Bor and found the Templo de las Pinturas with its famous murals. Frey drowned in 1949, when his canoe capsized on another expedition to Bonampak.

The site of **Bonampak** (admission US$3; 8am-5pm) spreads over 2.4 sq km, but all the main ruins stand around the rectangular Gran Plaza. Bonampak was never a major city, and spent most of the Classic period under Yaxchilán's sphere of influence. The most impressive surviving monuments were built under Bonampak's Chan Muwan II, who took the throne in AD 776. He was a nephew of the Yaxchilán ruler Itzamnaaj

B'alam II and was married to Yaxchilán royalty. The 6m-high **Stele 1** in the Gran Plaza depicts Chan Muwan holding a ceremonial staff at the height of his reign. He also features in **Steles 2 and 3** on the Acrópolis, which rises from the south end of the plaza.

However it's the astonishing frescoes inside the modest-looking **Templo de las Pinturas** (Edificio 1) on the Acrópolis steps that have given Bonampak its fame, and its name: Bonampak means 'Painted Walls' in Yucatecan Maya.

Diagrams outside the temple help interpret these murals, which have weathered badly since their discovery. (Early visitors even chucked kerosene over the walls in an attempt to bring out the colors.) Room 1, on the left as you face the temple, shows the consecration of an infant heir – probably Chan Muwan II's son – who is seen held in arms toward the top of the right end of the room's south wall, which faces you as you enter. Witnessing the ceremony are 14 jade-toting noblemen. The central Room 2 shows tumultuous battle scenes on its east,

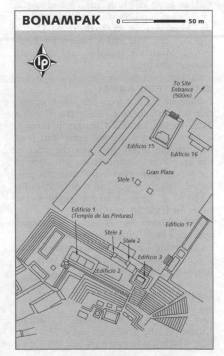

BONAMPAK   0 —— 50 m

To Site Entrance (500m)

Edificio 15

Edificio 16

Gran Plaza

Stele 1

Edificio 1 (Templo de las Pinturas)

Stele 3

Stele 2

Edificio 17

Edificio 3

Edificio 2

south and vault walls, while on the north wall, the torture (by fingernail removal) and sacrifice of prisoners, is presided over by Chan Muwan II in jaguar-skin battle dress. A severed head lies below him, beside the foot of a sprawling captive. Room 3 shows a celebratory dance on the Acrópolis steps by lords wearing huge headdresses, and on its east wall three white-robed women puncture their tongues in a ritual bloodletting. By one interpretation, the prisoner sacrifices, the bloodletting and the dance may all have been part of the ceremonies surrounding the new heir.

The infant prince probably never got to rule Bonampak, and the place was abandoned before the murals were finished, as Classic Mayan civilization imploded.

Refrescos and snacks are sold at a café at the Monumento Nacional Bonampak entrance, 9km before the ruins, and at a house by the archaeological site entrance.

SLEEPING

Camping Margarito (at Lacanjá Chansayab turnoff; camping per person US$1, hammock sites US$2, rented tents/hammocks per person US$2/3.25) This Lacandón-run camping ground, 9km from Bonampak, is the closest you can stay to the ruins. There's a grassy campsite and a palapa for hammocks. Meals are available, and there are showers and toilets.

GETTING THERE & AWAY

Bonampak is 12km from San Javier, a junction on the Carretera Fronteriza. The first 3km, to the Lacanjá Chansayab turnoff, is paved; the rest is good gravel/dirt road through the forest. Just past the start of the gravel/dirt section is the entrance to the Monumento Nacional Bonampak protected zone: here you can rent bicycles for US$0.90 an hour or take a combi to the ruins for US$7.50 round-trip.

A taxi from San Javier to Bonampak ruins and back, with time to visit the ruins, costs around US$12. You may have to wait a while at San Javier before one turns up, however. Hitching is possible.

Lacanjá Chansayab
pop 600 / elevation 320m
Just 12km from Bonampak is Lacanjá Chansayab, the largest Lacandón Maya village, which was founded around 1980. It's a

sprawling settlement, with an inviting river pool you can bathe in. The villagers here are now predominantly Presbyterian.

Villagers can guide you to Bonampak (around US$10) and to other places of interest in the nearby forests such as the little-explored Maya ruins of Lacanjá, the 2.5km-long Laguna Lacanjá or the Cascadas Lacanjá. A guide costs around US$18 for a five-hour hike. Wildlife you can hope to see includes coatis, toucans and macaws.

You may want to budget a few extra pesos for the pottery, wood carvings, seed necklaces, arrows and drums that the villagers sell.

SLEEPING & EATING

Several villagers have set up simple *campamentos* where you can pitch a tent and/or rent a hammock – look for their signs or ask for Carlos Cham Bor Kin, Kin Bor, Vicente or Manuel Chan Bor. It's around US$1 per person to pitch a tent and US$2 to rent a hammock under a shelter. Most places provide meals, or there's good food at the Campamento Río Lacanjá restaurant below.

Campamento Río Lacanja (☎ 55-5329-0995 ext 8055; 2km south of village entrance; cabins US$6.50, casitas US$30) These accommodations are a grade better than the others, though they are also more pricey. Basic wooden cabins stand near the jungle-shrouded Río Lacanjá, most with two bunks and all with mosquito nets, viewing deck and hammock. There's a clean, separate bathroom block. Newly-built, modern, spotless casitas have been constructed to a very high standard, each have two double beds and hot-water bathrooms. All **meals** (mains US$3-4) are available, **rafting** (per person US$45) and walking outings can be arranged. One trip includes a climb up a ceiba tree where a *mirador* offers amazing views over the jungle canopy.

GETTING THERE & AWAY

Lacanjá Chansayab is 6.5km by paved road from San Javier on the Carretera Fronteriza. A taxi is US$5 (US$1.25 colectivo) but you might have to walk or hitch.

Frontera Corozal
pop 5200 / elevation 200m
This riverside frontier town (formerly called Frontera Echeverría) is 16km by paved road from Crucero Corozal junction on the

Carretera Fronteriza. The Usumacinta, flowing swiftly between jungle-covered banks, forms the Mexico–Guatemala border here. Frontera Corozal is an essential steppingstone both to the ruins of Yaxchilán and for onward travel into Guatemala.

Long, outboard-powered launches come and go from the river embarcadero, below a cluster of wooden buildings that includes a few inexpensive **comedores**. Almost everything you'll need is on the paved main street leading inland from here – including the immigration office, where you should hand in/obtain a tourist card if you're leaving for/arriving from Guatemala.

The neat modern village **museum** (admission US$1.80; ☉ 8am-8pm), signposted just off the main street, has good examples of Chol Maya *traje* (clothing) and a few photographs by Trudy Blom (see p798). But

---

THE LACANDÓN JUNGLE & THE LACANDONES

The Selva Lacandona (Lacandón Jungle) in eastern Chiapas occupies just one quarter of 1% of Mexico. Yet it contains more than 4300 plant species, about 17% of the Mexican total; 450 types of butterfly, 42% of the national total; at least 340 birds, 32% of the total; and 163 mammals, 30% of the Mexican total. Among these are such emblematic creatures as the jaguar, red macaw, white turtle, tapir and harpy eagle, and the extremely rare Lacandonia schismatica flower.

This great fund of natural resources and genetic diversity is the southwest end of a 30,000-sq-km corridor of tropical rainforest stretching into northern Guatemala, Belize and the southern Yucatán. But the Selva Lacandona is shrinking fast: from around 15,000 sq km in the 1950s to an estimated size of between 3000 and 4500 sq km today. Most of the remaining jungle is in the eastern half of the Reserva de la Biósfera Montes Azules.

The 800 or so Lacandón Maya are thought to have reached the Selva Lacandona in the 18th century, and largely avoided contact with the outside world until the 1950s. Their language is related to Yucatecan Maya, and they call themselves Hach Winik, the True People.

Most live in the village of Lacanjá Chansayab (see p824) near Bonampak, where Presbyterianism is now the dominant religion. Najá, another Lacandón village about 50km further northwest, remains truer to Lacandón traditions. You will almost certainly encounter Lacandones at Palenque, where they sell quivers of arrows and are readily recognizable in their long white tunics with their long black hair cut in a fringe.

Other Chol and Tzeltal Maya have settled in the Lacandón Jungle near the reserve's eastern edge. These three groups today jointly administer an area of over 6000 sq km called the Comunidad Lacandona.

The first waves of settlers deforested the northern third of the Selva Lacandona by about 1960. Also badly deforested are the far eastern area called Marqués de Comillas, settled since the 1970s, and Las Cañadas, the heavily settled area between Ocosingo and the Montes Azules reserve. Many settlers found that the land here deteriorated fast after the jungle had been cleared. Plummeting yields resulted in *milpas* (cornfields) being converted to grassland for cattle ranching. The grass turned to weeds, leaving the settlers little better off than before. Struggling Las Cañadas settlers have always provided some of the Zapatistas' strongest support.

Traditional Lacandón agriculture, by contrast, makes it possible to live almost indefinitely off small areas of land. Leaving some plots fallow allows land to regenerate, and many varied crops are planted under a canopy of big trees. But these cultivation methods are now rare, like other traditional ways – few Lacandón now adhere to Mayan religion, and selling crafts to tourists has become a major income source for many.

The Montes Azules reserve has become something of a battleground between environmental groups and settlers in the last few years. According to Conservation International (CI), 10 new communities have been established illegally inside the reserve since 2000, despite its protected status. Around half these communities support the Zapatistas. The settlers accuse CI of 'biopiracy,' and claim the conservation group seeks to exploit the forests for the benefit of biotechnology giant Grupo Pulsar, a CI funder.

What's not in question is the ongoing destruction of the reserve and, as well, the lack of political will to act against it.

pride of place is reserved for the two very fine steles, both intricately carved on both sides, retrieved from the nearby site of Dos Caobas.

SLEEPING & EATING

Escudo Jaguar (☎ 55-3290-0993 ext 8059; www.chiapas tours.com.mx/escudojaguar; US$12-18, larger cabañas with private bath US$26-39; P), 100m back from the embarcadero, has 15 spotless pink thatched cabañas with fans and mosquito nets, and a good, if slightly pricey **restaurant** (main dishes US$4.50-6.50).

Nueva Alianza (☎ 55-5329-0995 ext 8061; per person US$4.50; P), about 250m from the embarcadero, is an excellent new budget place, with rooms in well-constructed wood cabins that have fans, mosquito nets and lights. There are also hammocks with nets (US$2.25), clean shared bathrooms and a decent **restaurant** (mains US$4).

GETTING THERE & AWAY

If you can't get a bus or combi direct to Frontera Corozal, get off at Crucero Corozal, 20 minutes southeast of San Javier on the highway, where taxis (US$2 per person colectivo, US$5.50 otherwise) and occasional buses run to Frontera Corozal.

At the time of research combis left Frontera Corozal for Palenque at about 5am, 9am, noon and 3pm, and a Transportes Montebello bus left at 3am. The last Palenque-bound combi passes Crucero Corozal about 5pm.

For Guatemala, fast river launches (*lanchas*) leave for Bethel, on the Guatemalan bank of the Usumacinta 40 minutes upstream, and for La Técnica, which is directly opposite Frontera Corozal. It's best to check timetables first at the *lancha* offices in the Escudo Jaguar, or at the Cooperativa Tikal Chilam (further up the main street from the embarcadero) where they also know the departure times of onward Guatemalan buses. A boat to Bethel for up to six people costs US$40; for seven to 10 people it costs about US$50. The launches can carry bicycles and even motorcycles. Buses from Bethel leave for Santa Elena, near Flores at 5am, noon, 2pm and 4pm (four hours, US$3.50). Bethel's pleasant **Posada Maya** (☎ 502-801-1799; s/d US$9/18) has camping, hammock space and cabañas on the banks of the Usumacinta.

Lanchas to La Técnica cost just US$0.70 per person, from where buses leave at 4am and 11am (five hours, US$4) to Flores.

Yaxchilán

Yaxchilán (admission US$3; ☺ 8am-4:45pm), shrouded in jungle, has a terrific setting above a horseshoe loop in the Usumacinta. This position, and its ability to control commercial trade enabled the city to prosper in Classic Maya times. Archaeologically, Yaxchilán is famed for its ornamented building façades and roof combs, and impressive stone lintels carved (often on their undersides) with conquest and ceremonial scenes. A flashlight is a help in exploring some parts of the site.

Another feature of these ruins is the howler monkeys that come to feed in some of the tall trees here. You'll almost certainly hear their roars, and you stand a good chance of seeing some. Spider monkeys, and occasionally red macaws, have also been sighted at the ruins in recent years.

Conquests and alliances made Yaxchilán one of the most important pre-Hispanic cities in the Usumacinta region. It peaked in power and splendor between AD 681 and 800 under the rulers Itzamnaaj B'alam II (Shield Jaguar II, 681–742), Pájaro Jaguar IV (Bird Jaguar IV, 752–768) and Itzamnaaj B'alam III (769–800). The city was abandoned around AD 810.

Yaxchilán's inscriptions tell more about its 'Jaguar' dynasty than is known of almost any other Mayan ruling clan. The rulers' names come from the hieroglyphs representing them: the shield-and-jaguar symbol appears on many Yaxchilán buildings and steles. Pájaro Jaguar IV's hieroglyph is a small jungle cat with feathers on its back and a bird superimposed on its head.

At the site, refrescos are sold at a shack near the river landing. There are information boards in three languages, including English, by most of the main monuments.

As you walk toward the ruins, a signed path to the right leads up to the **Pequeña Acrópolis**, a group of ruins on a small hilltop - you can visit this later. Staying on the main path, you soon reach the mazy passages of **El Laberinto** (Edificio 19), built between AD 742 and 752, during the interregnum between Itzamnaaj B'alam II and Pájaro Jaguar IV. Dozens of bats shelter under the structure's roof today. From this complicated two-level building you emerge at the northwest end of the **Gran Plaza**.

Though it's hard to imagine anyone here ever wanting to be hotter than they already were, **Edificio 17** was apparently a sweat house. About halfway along the plaza, **Stele 1**, flanked by weathered sculptures of a crocodile and a jaguar, shows Pájaro Jaguar IV in a ceremony that took place in 761. **Edificio 20**, from the time of Itzamnaaj B'alam III, was the last significant structure built at Yaxchilán; its lintels are now in Mexico City. **Stele 11**, now at the northeast corner of the Gran Plaza, was originally found in front of Edificio 40. The bigger of the two figures visible on it is Pájaro Jaguar IV.

An imposing stairway climbs from Stele 1 to **Edificio 33**, the best-preserved temple at Yaxchilán, with about half of its roof comb intact. The final step in front of the building is carved with ball-game scenes. There are splendid relief carvings on the undersides of the lintels. Inside is a decapitated statue of Pájaro Jaguar IV; he lost his head to treasure-seeking 19th-century timber cutters.

From the clearing behind Edificio 33, a path leads into the trees. About 20m along this, fork left uphill. Go left at another fork after about 80m, and in 10 minutes – mostly uphill – you reach three buildings on a hilltop: **Edificios 39, 40 and 41**. You can climb to the top of Edificio 41 for great views across the top of the jungle to the distant mountains of Guatemala.

GETTING THERE & AWAY

You can reach Yaxchilán by chartered plane from places including Ocosingo (see p810) or by boat from Frontera Corozal (see p826).

River launches take 40 minutes running downstream from Frontera Corozal, and one hour to return. Two operators in Frontera Corozal run trips (see p826). A round-trip, including about three hours at the ruins, costs around US$55 for up to four people, and US$88 for up to 10 with either company. Lanchas leave frequently until 1:30pm or so, and you should be easily able to hook up with other travelers or a tour group to share costs.

TABASCO & CHIAPAS

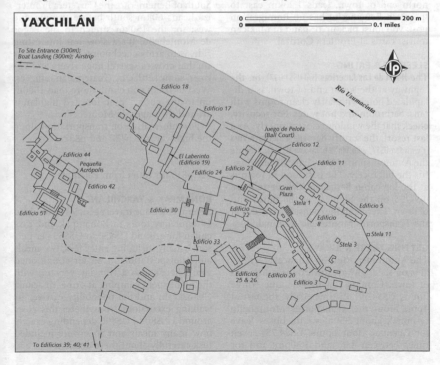

YAXCHILÁN

To Site Entrance (300m);
Boat Landing (300m); Airstrip

Río Usumacinta

Edificio 18

Edificio 17

Juego de Pelota
(Ball Court)

Edificio 12

Edificio 11

El Laberinto
(Edificio 19)

Edificio 23

Edificio 24

Edificio 44

Pequeña
Acrópolis

Edificio 42

Gran
Plaza

Stela 1

Edificio 5

Edificio 51

Edificio 30

Edificio
22

Edificio
8

Stela 11

Edificio 33

Stela 3

Edificios
25 & 26

Edificio 20

Edificio 3

To Edificios 39; 40; 41

0   200 m
0   0.1 miles

Benemérito de las Américas
pop 6400 / elevation 200m

South of Frontera Corozal you soon enter the area of far eastern Chiapas known as Marqués de Comillas (for its Spanish former landowner). After oil explorers opened tracks into this jungle region in the 1970s, land-hungry settlers poured in from all over Mexico. Now it's one of the most deforested parts of the Lacandón jungle. Cattle and logging have made many settlers rich, while others profit from drug smuggling – you may receive warnings about violence associated with this.

Benemérito de las Américas is the main town, located on the west bank of the Río Salinas, an Usumacinta tributary that forms the Mexico–Guatemala border here. It's a pretty forlorn place, with a good dose of 'Wild West' atmosphere, and no attractions except as a staging post. Plenty of Central Americans enter Mexico around these parts on their way to 'El Norte.'

The main street is a 1.5km-long stretch of the Carretera Fronteriza. A side street beside the Farmacia Arco Iris, toward the north end of town, leads 1.25km east to the river. Benemérito has no immigration post; you must pick up or hand in Mexican tourist cards at Frontera Corozal.

SLEEPING & EATING
The **Hotel de Las Américas** (s/d US$14/17), on the highway at the south end of town, is a dilapidated hotel with fairly clean rooms with fans, bathroom and hot water. For security, check that the windows close properly. As a last resort, the scruffy **Hospedaje Siempre Viva** (r with fan US$7, with fan & bathroom US$11), beside the Autotransportes Río Chancalá terminal, fits the bill nicely. The best food in town is at the log cabin **Restaurant Viejo Oeste** (mains US$3.75-5) on the highway at the north end of town. There's an inexpensive comedor at the Transportes Montebello terminal.

GETTING THERE & AWAY
The Autotransportes Río Chancalá terminal is on the highway, toward the north end of town. Combis run to Palenque (three hours, US$4.50) 12 times daily, the last at 4pm. From the Transportes Montebello terminal, about 350m south, buses leave for Palenque (four hours, US$4.75) seven times between 4am and 1.30pm, and for

Comitán (seven hours, US$9) via the Carretera Fronteriza four times between 5am and 12.45pm, with a couple of others going just to Ixcán and Chajul.

For Guatemala, you can hire a lancha for around US$150 to take you up the Río Salinas and Río de la Pasión to Sayaxché (Guatemala) in three to four hours. Sayaxché is a base for visiting the Mayan ruins of Ceibal, Aguateca and Dos Pilas and has lodgings and regular buses to Flores. On the way, there may be Guatemalan immigration checks at Pipiles, and you have the opportunity to stop to see more ruins at Pipiles and Altar de los Sacrificios. Cargo boats are cheaper (around US$8 per person) but are infrequent and take all day.

An alternative is to take a lancha a short distance downriver to Laureles on the Guatemalan side (colectivo US$1.50, especial US$10). From Laureles buses leave for El Subín (US$2.50, 2½ hours) where you could change for Sayaxché, and Flores.

Benemérito de las Américas to Lagos de Montebello
South of Benemérito, the Carretera Fronteriza heads 60km south before turning due west for the 150km stretch to the Lagos de Montebello. It's a slow but interesting ride, with army checkpoints every 50km or so, that crosses several huge rivers and villages, some settled by Guatemalan refugees. West of Ixcán you climb more than 1000m up to the cooler, pine-forested highlands around the Lagos de Montebello.

For information on transportation along the highway, see p822 and p832.

Tours
See p819 for tours from Palenque.

BONAMPAK & YAXCHILÁN
Several Palenque travel agencies have 13- to 14-hour day tours to Bonampak and Yaxchilán for around US$50 to US$55 per person, usually including entry fees, two meals and transportation in an air-conditioned van. There's also a two-day version, with the night spent camping at or near Lacanjá Chansayab, and the possibility of river or walking excursions from there: this costs around US$80 to US$90 depending exactly how many meals and so on are included (ask carefully about these details).

GUATEMALA
Palenque agencies offer transportation packages to Flores (near Tikal) for around US$28 (p819). Check carefully the details of what the agencies are offering: the deal usually includes an air-conditioned van to Frontera Corozal, river launch from there to either Bethel or La Técnica in Guatemala, and public 2nd-class bus on to Flores – 10 or 11 hours altogether. Some agencies include a visit to Bonampak for a few dollars more.

RAFTING & KAYAKING
Explora (see p799), based in San Cristóbal de Las Casas but also with a camp at Lacanjá Chansayab, offers trips along the rivers of the Lacandón Jungle.

Ecolodges
Two projects at remote *ejidos* in the southern Selva Lacandona aim to preserve the environment by providing local people with an income from non-destructive tourism.

LAS GUACAMAYAS
Las Guacamayas (☎ 55-5329-0995 ext 8004) is dedicated to the protection of the red macaw. Located on the edge of Reforma Agraria ejido, it's 40km southwest of Benemérito by unpaved road. The lodge receives few visitors, perhaps due to its remote location.

Howler monkeys, toucans and white-tailed deer also live in the 12-sq-km forest reserve here. Accommodations are in good-quality, well-kept divided cabins, costing US$18 for two people. It's best to phone first so the volunteers can purchase food for your stay. For further information try the Chiapas state tourist office in Tuxtla Gutiérrez (see p786) or Escudo Jaguar in Frontera Corozal (see p826).

To get here, take a combi from Palenque or Benemérito to Pico de Oro (four daily; from Palenque, four hours, US$6; from Benemérito, one hour, US$1), then a taxi to Reforma Agraria (about 20 minutes, US$5). In Reforma Agraria, ask for Don Germán Hernández.

ESTACIÓN IXCÁN
The solar-powered **Estación Ixcán** (☎ 55-5329-0995 ext 8050) ecolodge is wonderfully located beside the foaming Río Lacantún, at the southern tip of the Montes Azules Biosphere Reserve. At the time of research the lodge was closed for repair after serious storm damage, but it should be up and running again by the time you read this. They plan to resume offering guided jungle walks (by night as well as day), and there's also fine swimming, a library and videos. You stand a good chance of seeing howler monkeys (among other wildlife), and there are minor

---

THE USUMACINTA
Forming much of the border between Guatemala and Mexico, the Río Usumacinta is the largest river between Venezuela and Texas. It's estimated that it discharges 105 billion cubic meters of fresh water into the Gulf of Mexico each year.

The river is also lined with Mayan ruins, including two large cities – remote Piedras Negras on the Guatemalan bank and Yaxchilán in Mexico – plus over a dozen minor sites.

All these sites are threatened by long-standing plans drawn up by the Guatemalan and Mexican governments to dam the river. Mayanists, environmentalists and villagers have campaigned against this project for over two decades. The river, whose name American writer Christopher Shaw translates as 'Sacred Monkey River' in his excellent book about the Usumacinta, harbors 112 fish species, crocodiles and rare turtles, and flows through some of the remotest jungle in Mesoamerica.

In 2001 President Fox's grandiose Plan Puebla-Panama development program resurrected the scheme, recommending a dam at Boca del Cerro just west of Tenosique and smaller dams upstream to the southeast. The Inter-American Development bank undertook funding studies. One proposal involves a 100m dam that would flood half the site of Piedras Negras and would necessitate digging up the lower level temples of Yaxchilán and replacing them on higher ground. Tens of thousands of people would also have to be displaced from their homes.

You'll find more information about the Usumacinta at www.gomaya.com/dams and www.planeta.com.

TABASCO & CHIAPAS

Mayan ruins in the vicinity too. Prices may change but it was thought that camping will cost around US$10 per site, single/double mosquito-screened rooms US$32/51; meals will be around US$8 and guided excursions will cost between US$16 and US$51 for up to seven people.

The lodge is situated on the territory of Ejido Ixcán, which is just off the Carretera Fronteriza at Km 340, approximately 100km east of Tziscao. You can reach Ejido Ixcán by bus along the Carretera Fronteriza (see p828 and p832). Then it's a half-hour boat ride (US$45 for up to seven people) to the Estación.

You can get up-to-date information and make advance bookings (a week's notice is preferable) through **Conservation International**, (☎ /fax 961-602-90-32;luazqoaz@conservation.org; Blvd Comitán 191, Colonia Moctezuma, Tuxtla Gutiérrez).

COMITÁN
☎ 963 / pop 75,600 / elevation 1635m

Comitán is an agreeable town with colonial character, and possibly the cleanest streets in Mexico. Most travelers bypass the place on their way to or from Guatemala, but with a few minor yet interesting museums and archaeological sites (and the Lagos de Montebello an hour away) you could easily spend an enjoyable couple of days based here.

The first Spanish settlement here, San Cristóbal de los Llanos, was founded in 1527. Today it's officially called Comitán de

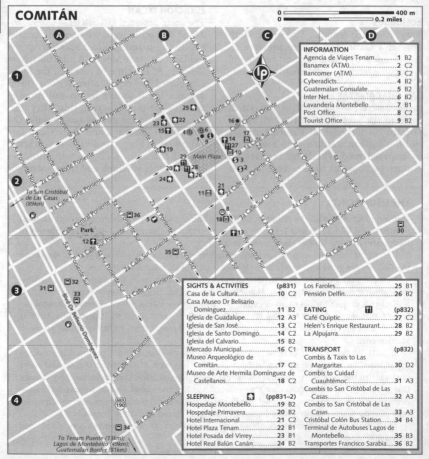

COMITÁN

0 _____ 400 m
0 _____ 0.2 miles

INFORMATION	
Agencia de Viajes Tenam	1 B2
Banamex (ATM)	2 C2
Bancomer (ATM)	3 C2
Cyberadicts	4 B2
Guatemalan Consulate	5 B2
Inter Net	6 B2
Lavandería Montebello	7 B1
Post Office	8 C2
Tourist Office	9 B2

SIGHTS & ACTIVITIES	(p831)
Casa de la Cultura	10 C2
Casa Museo Dr Belisario Domínguez	11 B2
Iglesia de Guadalupe	12 A3
Iglesia de San José	13 C2
Iglesia de Santo Domingo	14 C2
Iglesia del Calvario	15 B2
Mercado Municipal	16 C1
Museo Arqueológico de Comitán	17 C2
Museo de Arte Hermila Domínguez de Castellanos	18 C2

SLEEPING	(pp831–2)
Hospedaje Montebello	19 B2
Hospedaje Primavera	20 B2
Hotel Internacional	21 A3
Hotel Plaza Tenam	22 B1
Hotel Posada del Virrey	23 B1
Hotel Real Balún Canán	24 B2

Los Faroles	25 B1
Pensión Delfín	26 B2

EATING	(p832)
Café Quiptic	27 C2
Helen's Enrique Restaurant	28 B2
La Alpujarra	29 B2

TRANSPORT	(p832)
Combis & Taxis to Las Margaritas	30 D2
Combis to Cuidad Cuauhtémoc	31 A3
Combis to San Cristóbal de Las Casas	32 A3
Combis to San Cristóbal de Las Casas	33 A3
Cristóbal Colón Bus Station	34 B4
Terminal de Autobuses Lagos de Montebello	35 B3
Transportes Francisco Sarabia	36 B2

To San Cristóbal de Las Casas (89km)

Park

To Tenam Puente (13km); Lagos de Montebello (49km); Guatemalan Border (81km)

MEX 190

Domínguez, after Belisario Domínguez, a doctor who was a senator during the presidency of Victoriano Huerta. He spoke out in 1913 against Huerta's record of political murders and was then murdered himself.

Orientation & Information

Comitán is set on hilly terrain, with a beautiful broad main plaza. Hwy 190 passes through the west of town.

The **tourist office** (☎ 632-40-47; ☺ 8am-4pm), on the north side of the plaza, has fairly well-informed staff. **Bancomer** (☺ 9am-5pm Mon-Fri) on the southeast corner of the main plaza, does currency exchange and has an ATM. There's a central **post office** (Av Central Sur 45; ☺ Mon-Fri 9am-3pm) and card phones are dotted around the plaza's fringes.

Most cybercafés charge US$0.90 per hour. **Cyber@dicts** (Local 13B) and **Inter Net** (Local 12; ☺ 9am-2pm & 4-9pm), both on Pasaje Morales, have quick connections.

The laundry **Lavandería Montebello** (Av Central Nte 13A) charges US$1.50 per kilo for next-day service.

Museums

The **Casa de la Cultura**, on the southeast corner of the plaza, includes an exhibition gallery as well as an auditorium. Behind it is the **Museo Arqueológico de Comitán** (☎ 632-06-24; 1a Calle Sur Ote; admission free; ☺ 10am-5pm Tue-Sun), which has artifacts from the region's archaeological sites, including stele fragments from Chinkultic. The misshapen pre-Colombian skulls on display – deliberately 'beautified' by squeezing infants' heads between boards – make you wonder what kind of thoughts would have taken shape inside such distorted brains. There's wheelchair access.

Just south of the main plaza, **Casa Museo Dr Belisario Domínguez** (Av Central Sur 35; admission US$0.50; ☺ 10am-6:45pm Tue-Sat, 9am-12:45pm Sun), the martyr-hero's family home, provides fascinating insights into medical practices and the life of the professional classes in early-20th-century Comitán. One block further down this street is a neat little art museum, the **Museo de Arte Hermila Domínguez de Castellanos** (☎ 632-20-82; Av Central Sur 53; admission US$0.50; ☺ 10am-2pm & 4-6pm Mon-Fri, until 4pm Sat, until 1pm Sun), with paintings by many leading 20th-century Mexican artists, including Rufino Tamayo, Francisco Toledo and José Guadalupe Posada.

Tenam Puente

This minor Mayan **archaeological site** (admission free; ☺ 9am-4pm), 14km south of town, features three ball courts, a 20m tiered pyramid and other structures rising from a terraced, wooded hillside. It has a pleasant rural setting and good long-distance views from the topmost structures. Like Chinkultic (see p832) it was one of a set of fringe Maya settlements from the late Classic period (AD 600–900) that survived a century or two longer than lowland Chiapas sites such as Palenque and Yaxchilán.

A 5km-long paved road leads west to the site from Hwy 190, 9km south of Comitán. Transportes Francisco Sarabia buses leave every 45 minutes from 3a Av Pte Sur 8 between 9am and 6pm (US$0.90) to the site, or the village of Francisco Sarabia, 2km before Tenam Puente. The last bus returns at 4pm from the ruins. To head on to Chinkultic or Lagos de Montebello from Tenam Puente, flag down a combi or bus heading south on Hwy 190. A taxi costs US$11 return with an hour at the ruins.

Tours

Agencia de Viajes Tenam (☎ 632-16-54; www.viajes tenam.com; Pasaje Morales 8A) has tours to Tenam Puente, Chinkultic and Lagos de Montebello for US$18 per head (three-person minimum) and should also offer car hire by the time you read this.

Sleeping

There are plenty of good-value budget and mid-range hotels, though there's nothing in the luxury bracket.

BUDGET

Hospedaje Primavera (☎ 632-20-41; Calle Central Pte 4; s/d without bathroom US$6.50/8) This is one of Comitán's better cheap posadas with small, plain but clean rooms.

Hospedaje Montebello (☎ 632-35-72; 1a Calle Nte Pte 10; F_montebello@prodigy.net.mx; s/d without bathroom US$4.50/9, with bathroom US$5.50/11) Welcoming cheapie with large, tiled clean rooms around a courtyard. There's free drinking water.

Pensión Delfín (☎ 632-00-13; Av Central Sur 11; s/d with US$16/20; P) The Delfín, on the west side of the main plaza, has decent-size rooms, some with wood paneling and all with bathroom & TV.

MID-RANGE

Hotel Internacional (☎ 632-01-10; fax 632-01-12; Av Central Sur 16; r US$28-39; (P)) A block from the plaza, this excellent downtown hotel is great value considering the comfort levels and stylish décor offered. All the large rooms have two double beds, TV and attractive bathrooms, and there's a decent café/restaurant.

Hotel Posada del Virrey (☎ 632-18-11; hotel_del virrey@hotmail.com; Av Central Nte 13; s/d with TV US$22/25) The Virrey has 19 characterful though smallish rooms with reading lights and spotless tiled bathrooms around a pretty courtyard.

Los Faroles (☎ 632-02-20; 1a Av Ote Nte 16; s/d 22/28) This friendly place has five very spacious, attractive rooms, all with TV and bathroom, plus an apartment with a kitchen.

Hotel Real Balún Canán (☎ 632-10-94; fax 632-00-31; 1a Av Pte Sur 7; s/d with bathroom US$22/28; (P)) This hotel has small but comfortable rooms with TV and a bizarre, inauthentic Scottish-themed restaurant.

Hotel Plaza Tenam (☎ 632-04-36; Av Central Nte 8; s & d/tr US$23/32; (P)) This decidedly odd-looking hotel resembles an aircraft hangar. The refurbished rooms perched around an upstairs walkway are spacious if a bit soulless; all have private bathroom, TV and safe.

Eating & Drinking

La Alpujarra (☎ 632-20-00; Av Central Sur 3; snacks US$0.90-2.50, pizzas US$2.75-7) Excellent, efficient new place on the west side of the plaza with very flavorsome snacks – including pastry *rollitos* and home-made soups – plus good coffee and cakes, and terrific pizzas.

Helen's Enrique Restaurant (☎ 632-17-30; Av Central Sur 9; mains US$4-6.50 ☯ 8am-10pm) This long-running place close by on the plaza is a good choice for meat dishes: try the *brochete de carne con salsa de championes* (beef kebabs with mushroom sauce).

Café Quiptic (☎ 632-04-00; 1a Av Ote Sur s/n; breakfasts US$3, mains US$3.75-5.50) On the other side of the plaza, the elegant Quiptic is set under an impressive stone colonnade and run by indigenous coffee growers. It serves pricey but filling breakfasts plus superb organic coffee, *tortas,* salads, desserts and other light eats.

Getting There & Around

Comitán is 90km southeast of San Cristóbal along the Pan-American Hwy, and 83km from the Guatemalan border. The Cristóbal Colón bus station (deluxe, 1st class and 2nd class) is on the Pan-American Hwy, here named Blvd Dr Belisario Domínguez and called simply 'El Bulevar.' Minibuses and Suburban vans leave when full, approximately every 20 to 30 minutes.

Daily Colón bus terminal departures include the following:

Ciudad Cuauhtémoc (US$3.50, 1¼hr, 6 buses) also minibuses (US$3.25, 1hr) from El Bulevar between 1a and 2a Calle Sur Pte.

Mexico City (TAPO & Norte; US$54-67, 20hr, 7 buses)

San Cristóbal de Las Casas (US$3.50-4.50, 1½hr, 10 buses; US$3, 1hr, Suburban vans) From El Bulevar between 1a and 2a Calle Sur Pte.

Tapachula (US$9.50, 5½hr, 7 buses via Motozintla)

Tuxtla Gutiérrez (US$7-8, 3½hr, 7 buses; minibuses (3hr, US$6.50) From El Bulevar between 1a and 2a Calle Sur Pte.

Colón also serves Oaxaca, Palenque, Villahermosa, Playa del Carmen and Cancún.

Buses and combis to the Lagos de Montebello and along the Carretera Fronteriza go from a terminal at 2a Av Pte Sur 23. Combis and buses include the following:

Benemérito de las Américas (US$9, 7hr, 4)

Ixcán (US$5, 3hr, about 12)

Laguna Bosque Azul (US$1.75, 1hr, about every 20 min) Combis from 5:30am to 5:30pm.

Palenque (US$12,11hr, 2)

Tziscao (US$2, 1¼hr, 20 or more)

'Centro' microbuses, across the road from the Colón bus station, will take you to the main plaza for US$0.40. A taxi is US$1.50.

LAGOS DE MONTEBELLO

The temperate forest along the Guatemalan border southeast of Comitán is dotted with 59 small lakes of varied colors, the Lagos (or Lagunas) de Montebello. The area is very picturesque, refreshing and peaceful, and there's good swimming, hiking and biking. At the western edge of the lake district are the Mayan ruins of Chinkultic.

Orientation

The paved road to Montebello turns east off Hwy 190 just before the town of La Trinitaria, 16km south of Comitán. It passes Chinkultic after 30km, and enters the forest and the Parque Nacional Lagunas de Montebello 5km beyond. At the park entrance (no fee) the road splits. One road continues 3km north to end at Laguna Bosque Azul. The other heads east to the village of Tziscao (9km), beyond which it becomes the Carretera Fronteriza, continuing east to Ixcán and ultimately Palenque (see p828).

Chinkultic

These dramatically sited ruins (admission US$2.75; ⊙ 10am-5pm) lie 2km north of La Trinitaria-Montebello road. The access road is paved.

Chinkultic was a minor power that rose during the Classic Maya period, from around AD 591 to 897. Of the 200 mounds scattered over a wide area here, only a few have been cleared, but the site is worth a visit.

The ruins are split in two, on either bank of a stream. From the entrance, first take the path to the left, which curves around to the right below one of Chinkultic's biggest structures, E23, still covered in thick vegetation. The path reaches a grassy plaza with several weathered steles, some carved with human figures, and a long ball court on the right.

Return to the entrance, from which another path heads to the **Plaza Hundida** (Sunken Plaza), crosses the stream, then climbs steeply up to the **Acrópolis**, a partly restored temple atop a rocky escarpment. From the Acrópolis you have remarkable views over the surrounding lakes and forests and down into a cenote 50m below – into which the Maya used to toss offerings of pottery, beads, bones and obsidian knives.

The Lakes

From the park entrance gateway, one road heads straight ahead, passing the **Lagunas de Colores** – five lakes whose vivid hues range from turquoise to deep green. The first, on the right after about 2km, is **Laguna Agua Tinta**. Then on the left come **Laguna Esmeralda** and **Laguna Encantada**, with **Laguna Ensueño** on the right opposite Encantada. The fifth and biggest is **Laguna Bosque Azul**, on the left where the paved road ends. Here are gift shops, several basic comedores (with hygiene standards to match) and horses and boats to rent. There's also a cave-cum-shrine 800m ahead along a signposted path.

On the other road from the gateway, after about 3km a track leads 200m left to the bigger **Laguna de Montebello**, with a flat, open area along its shore where the track ends.

Three kilometers further along the Tziscao road another track leads left to the **Cinco Lagunas** (Five Lakes). Only four are visible from the road, but the second, **La Cañada**, on the right after about 1.5km, is one of the most beautiful Montebello lakes, nearly cut in half by two rocky outcrops. The track eventually reaches the village of San Antonio.

One km nearer to Tziscao from the Cinco Lagunas turnoff, a track leads 1km north to cobalt-blue **Laguna Pojoj**, with an island in the middle. **Laguna Tziscao**, on the Guatemalan border, comes into view on the right, 1km beyond the Laguna Pojoj turnoff. The junction for Tziscao village, a pleasant, spread-out place, is a little further, again on the right.

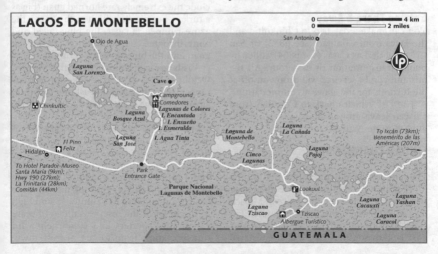

LAGOS DE MONTEBELLO

Sleeping & Eating

El Pino Feliz (☎ 963-102-10-89; Carr La Trinitaria-Lagos de Montebello Km 31.5; cabins per person US$4) The roadside 'Happy Pine' has simple wood cabins, reliable hot water and also provides excellent meals. The Alborres family here make you feel part of the family, though their accounting can be vague when toting up your bill. You can contact José Saenz, a guide who runs hiking trips (minimum three nights) here; he also rents fair-quality mountain bikes for US$8 per day.

In Tziscao village, 2km from the highway turnoff, the **Albergue Turístico** (also known as 'Hotel Tziscao'; ☎ 963-633-52-44; r with bathroom, cabaña US$6 per person) has a peaceful position right by the lakeshore, with extensive grounds that include a sandy beach with terrific views over the lake to the foothills of the Cuchumatanes in Guatemala. There are reasonable rooms, and nice rustic A-frame cabañas, or you can camp for US$1.75 per person. Restaurant meals are here too (US$2.25 to US$3.25).

Hotel Parador-Museo Santa María (☎ /fax 963-632-51-16; Carr La Trinitaria-Lagos de Montebello Km 22; r US$61) In a class of its own, the Santa María is a restored 19th-century hacienda, decorated with period furniture and art. Its chapel has been turned into a religious art museum. There are six guest rooms, a restaurant serving *chiapaneco* and international cuisine, and billiards in the bar. Watch for the sign 22km from La Trinitaria on the Montebello road. It's 2km from highway to hotel.

Getting There & Away

You can make a day trip to Chinkultic and the lakes from Comitán (see p832) or San Cristóbal de Las Casas (see p804) either by public transportation or as a tour. All the bus and combi services will drop you off at the turnoffs for the above accommodations.

The last vehicles back to Comitán from Tziscao leave around 5pm, and from Laguna Bosque Azul around 5.30pm.

CIUDAD CUAUHTÉMOC

pop 2200

The 'city' of Cuauhtémoc amounts to little more than a few houses and a comedor or two, but it's the last and first place in Mexico on the Pan-American Hwy (190). Comitán is 83km north, and the Guatemalan border post is 4km south at La Mesilla. Colectivo

taxis (US$0.50) ferry people between the two sides. There's a bank on the Guatemalan side of the border, and plenty of money changers loiter with intent on both sides. Guatemalan officials often ask for unofficial entry fees of a dollar or two to get through the border.

If you do get stuck at this border, **Hotel Mily's** at La Mesilla has decent doubles with fan, cable TV and bath for around US$15.

Frequent buses and combis run to and from Comitán (see p832); and fairly regularly to and from San Cristóbal (see p804).

From La Mesilla, buses leave for Huehuetenango (two hours, US$1.50) and Quetzaltenango (3½ hours, US$4) at least 20 times between 5:45am and 6pm. If there's no bus to your destination, take one to Huehuetenango, where you may be able to get an onward connection.

RESERVA DE LA BIÓSFERA EL TRIUNFO

The luxuriant cloud forests high in the remote El Triunfo Biosphere Reserve in the Sierra Madre de Chiapas are a bird-lovers' paradise and a remarkable world of trees and shrubs festooned with epiphytes, ferns, bromeliads, mosses and vines. The cool cloud forest is formed by moist air rising from the hot, humid lowlands to form clouds and rain on the uplands.

The Sierra Madre de Chiapas is home to more than 30 bird species that are nonexistent or rare elsewhere in Mexico, including the resplendent quetzal. Other birds here include the extremely rare horned guan (big as a turkey, but dwelling high in the trees), the azure-rumped tanager, the blue-tailed and wine-throated hummingbirds, the black guan and the blue-throated motmot.

Visits are controlled. Avoid the May-to-October wet season. For a permit and arrangements, contact – at least one month in advance – Jorge Uribe, Coordinador del Programa de Visitas Guiadas, Ecoturismo (☎ 961-612-1394; eco-triunfo@hotmail.com, jorgeuribe@hotmail.com; Reserva de la Biósfera El Triunfo, Av 4a Nte 143, Colonia El Centro, 29000 Tuxtla Gutiérrez, Chiapas).

There's a minimum group size of four, and a minimum cost of about US$180 per person. For that you get four nights at the basic Campamento El Triunfo, 1850m high in the heart of the reserve, guides who are expert bird-spotters and some help with transportation from/to the nearest town,

Jaltenango. Campamento El Triunfo is a three- to four-hour uphill hike (mules will take the baggage) from Finca Prusia, a coffee plantation near Jaltenango. Jaltenango is served by Autotranportes Cuxtepeques buses from Tuxtla Gutiérrez.

EL SOCONUSCO

Chiapas' steamy, fertile coastal plain is called the Soconusco. This strip – 15km to 35km wide – is hot and sweaty all year round, with serious rainfall from mid-May to mid-October. Rising from this plain, the steep, lushly-vegetated lower slopes of the Sierra Madre de Chiapas provide an excellent environment for coffee, bananas and other crops.

Tonalá

☎ 966 / pop 33,000 / elevation 45m

Tonalá, a dull steamy town on Hwy 200, is the jumping-off point for Puerto Arista. There's a helpful **tourist office** (☎ 663-27-87; cnr Hidalgo & 5 de Mayo; ⊗ 8am-7pm Mon-Fri, 9am-3pm Sat) on the main street (Hidalgo), two blocks east of the main plaza, Parque Esperanza. **Hotel Tonalá** (☎ 663-04-80; Hidalgo 172; s/d with fan US$13, with ✇ US$23; P) between the main plaza and the Colón bus station, is a good moderate-price choice if you get stuck here.

The Cristóbal Colón (deluxe and 1st-class) terminal is on Hidalgo 1km east of the main plaza. Rápidos del Sur (RS, 2nd-class) is at the opposite end of Hidalgo, six blocks east of the plaza.

Tapachula (US$9.50-11, 3hr, 11 from Colón; 32 RS)

Tuxtla Gutiérrez (US$7.50-8, 4 hr, 11 from Colón; 32 RS)

All Tapachula buses stop at Escuintla (US$6.25 to US$8, 2½ hours). Colón also runs buses to Mexico City, Oaxaca and Puerto Escondido. For Puerto Arista, a 20-minute ride away, combis and microbuses (US$0.80) leave from Juárez and 5 de Mayo, one block east of the market, until 6pm. Colectivo taxis (US$1.25) run as late as 7pm from Matamoros and 5 de Mayo, one block downhill from the RS terminal.

Puerto Arista

☎ 994 / pop 1000

The broad, sandy beach of Puerto Arista, 18km southwest of Tonalá, is a peaceful place that tends to grow on you the longer you stay. Initial impressions are not good –

the pot-holed shoreside lane is lined with a scruffy strip of palm-shack restaurants and crumbling, salt-bitten concrete hotels. However, once you're on the beach itself, gazing at the Pacific surf breaking onto an infinite expanse of sweeping gray sands, Puerto Arista's appeal becomes evident.

At weekends the peace is broken somewhat as a hundred or so chiapanecos cruise in from the towns (while during Semana Santa and Christmas they come by the thousands). The rest of the time, the most action you'll see is when a piglet breaks into a trot because a dog has gathered the energy to bark at it. You get through a lot of refrescos while you listen to the Pacific pound the shore.

The ocean is clean here, but take care where you go in. There's little undertow, but riptides (known as *canales*) can sweep you a long way out in a short time.

Puerto Arista's only real street, called interchangeably Matamoros or Zapotal, parallels the back of the beach. The road from Tonalá hits it at a T-junction by a lighthouse, the midpoint of town.

About 500m behind the beach hotels, the **Estero Prieto** is a treacle-colored mangrove estuary. Rare boat-billed herons are common here, and there are caimans, freshwater turtles and a few iguanas. You can paddle up here on a kayak; ask at Josés (see below).

A nice outing is to **Boca del Cielo**, a lagoonside village 15km southeast, where you can take a lancha across to a sandbar that's home to a few seafood comedores, between lagoon and ocean – almost suspended between water and sky. The road to Boca del Cielo turns southeast off the Puerto Arista–Tonalá road around 1km inland: combis from Tonalá run along it fairly frequently.

SLEEPING & EATING

There are plenty of places in both directions from the lighthouse. The following is just a selection, starting at the southeast end of town and moving northwest. On busy weekends some places raise their prices.

José's Camping Cabañas (☎ 600-90-48; camping per person US$2, s/d with shared showers US$7/11, r with bathroom US$18; P ✇) Follow the main beach road southeast for 800m, then turn left (inland) by Hotel Lucero. Run by a Canadian who's been living here for three decades, this is a welcoming place to stay. It has a small pool. Basic cabañas with mosquito

TABASCO & CHIAPAS

screens and fan (and a few more comfortable options) are dotted about an extensive coconut and citrus grove. The (powerful) shared showers and toilet block are kept immaculate. José enjoys socializing with his guests and provides filling meals (including vegetarian) choices: *robalo*, shrimp or snapper meals cost US$6, rice 'n' beans US$2.25. Kayak tours of the bird-rich estuary to the rear cost US$2.75 per person.

Cabañas Amazonia (☎ 600-90-50; camping per person US$2, cabañas US$9-11; P ♒) Next to José's, this attractive place has cute screened cabañas with small built-in bathrooms. There's a pool, and soccer and volleyball pitches. Meals costs US$2 to US$5.

Hotel Lucero (☎ 600-90-41; Matamoros 800; s/d/ste US$23/37/46; P ✂ ♒) This is the best midrange hotel in town. It doesn't front the beach, but does have comfortable, light airconditioned rooms with either one or two double beds; those on the top floor have a sea view. There's a pool and restaurant.

The next three places are clustered together just southeast of the lighthouse. All rooms are of similar quality and have bathrooms. The first, three-story **Hotel Lizeth** (☎ 600-90-38; r US$18/23, add US$5 for air-con; P ✂) has clean plain rooms (one to two double beds). Next door, the **Agua Marina** (☎ 600-90-18; r US$13/23 with air-con US$18/28; ✂) has 24 clean, functional rooms. **Restaurant Hospedaje Brisas del Mar** (☎ 600-90-47; r US$27-37; ✂) beachside of these two, has darkish, bare clean rooms with two double beds.

Hotel Arista Bugambilias (☎ 600-90-44; r/ste US$63/96; P ✂ ♒) About 900m northwest of these three, the Arista Bugambilias is the most expensive place, though its somewhat perfunctory rooms, with air-con and TV, are spacious but overpriced. There's a pool, restaurant and bar in beachfront gardens.

Reserva de la Biósfera La Encrucijada

This large biosphere reserve protects a 1448-sq-km strip of coastal lagoons, sandbars, wetlands, seasonally-flooded tropical forest and the country's tallest mangroves (some above 30m). The ecosystem is a vital wintering and breeding ground for migratory birds and harbors one of Mexico's biggest populations of jaguars. Other species include spider monkeys, turtles, crocodiles and caimans, boa constrictors, fishing eagles and lots of waterfowl – many in danger of extinction.

A ride in a *lancha* through the reserve takes you between towering mangroves and past palm-thatched lagoonside villages. Birding is good any time of year, but best during the November-to-March nesting season. Lanchas also serve Barra de Zacapulco, a small settlement on a sandbar between ocean and lagoon, with a handful of palapa comedores and a sea-turtle breeding center nearby.

The nearest town to the reserve is Acapetahua, 6km southwest of Escuintla.

Hotel El Carmen (☎ 918-647-00-62; Av Central, Acapetahua; r US$12; ✂), on Acapetahua's main street, has rooms with bathroom and TV. At the **Barra de Zacapulco comedores** you can camp or sling a hammock for US$2 per person. A big plate of fresh prawns with salad and tortillas costs around US$4.50.

To get here, take a bus along Hwy 200 to Escuintla, then get a colectivo taxi to Acapetahua (US$0.50, 6km). Beside the railway in Acapetahua, get a combi or bus to Embarcadero Las Garzas (US$1.25, 16km). These run about every 30 minutes.

From Embarcadero Las Garzas, a colectivo lancha to Barra de Zacapulco takes 25 minutes for US$3.25. The last lancha back to Embarcadero Las Garzas from Barra de Zacapulco may be as early as 3.30pm, and the last combi from Embarcadero Las Garzas to Acapetahua about 5pm. You can arrange three-hour private lancha tours from Embarcadero Las Garzas for around US$55.

TAPACHULA

☎ 962 / pop 192,000 / elevation 96m

Mexico's bustling southernmost city is a busy commercial center but has very limited appeal – other than as a gateway to Guatemala. However the surrounding area, dominated by the towering cone of Volcán Tacaná, has its attractions.

At the the Parque Hidalgo, the city's main plaza, you'll find the tourist office, banks, cathedral and museum. Bus stations and hotels are scattered around the central area.

Information

EMERGENCY

Hospital (Sanatorio Soconusco; ☎ 626-50-74, 4a Nte 68)
Police ☎ 066

IMMIGRATION

Imigración (☎ 626-91-02; Carr del Antiguo Aeropuerto Km 1.5; 9am-4:30pm Mon-Fri) 2.5km south of the center.

INTERNET ACCESS, POST & TELEPHONE

Pay phones and *casetas* are dotted around the Parque Hidalgo.

Infinitum (5a Pte 7; per hr US$0.60)

Post office (1a Ote s/n)

LAUNDRY

Tintorería 2000 (13a Ote 5D; next-day service per kg $1.40)

MONEY

Banorte (8a Nte 28; 9am-4pm Mon-Fri) Has an ATM.

Centro Cambiario Casa Santa (2a Nte 6, 8:30am-5:30pm Mon-Fri, until 3pm Sat)

TOURIST INFORMATION

City Tourist Office (626-14-85 ext 116; 8a Nte s/n; 8am-4pm Mon-Fri & 9am-noon Sat) West side of plaza.

Museo Arqueológico del Soconusco

The **Soconusco Archaeological Museum** (625-54-09; 8a Nte; admission free), facing Parque Hidalgo, was being renovated at the time of research, but will reopen with displays of Maya artifacts and stone sculptures from the nearby Izapa ruins.

Sleeping

BUDGET

All hotels listed here have attached bathrooms.

Hospedaje Las Américas (626-27-57; 10a Nte 47; s/d US$5.50/7.50-9) This pleasant cheapie has clean rooms with fan around a leafy patio.

Hospedaje Chelito (626-24-28; 1a Nte 107; s/d with fan & TV US$15/17 with US$20/24) A short walk

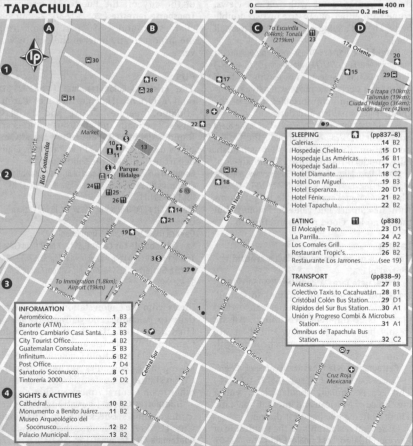

from the Cristóbal Colón bus station, Chelito has good-value, clean, spacious rooms.

Other budget options include the spotless **Hotel Diamante** (☎ 628-65-81; 2a Nte cnr 7a Pte; s/d 14/18 with fan) and the very basic **Hospedaje Sadai** (☎ 626-38-20; Callejón Domínguez 17; s/d US$7/9; P).

MID-RANGE

Galerías (☎ 626-44-48; 4a Nte 21; s/d US$33/40; P ⛏ ▢) Smart new place with eight large, comfortable air-con rooms, all with modem access and attractive bathrooms. There's a café here too.

Hotel Tapachula (☎ 626-60-60; www.hoteltapachula.com; 9a Pte 17; s/d/ste US$56/65/69; P ⛏ ▣) This new glass-fronted luxury hotel is the best address in town. Large, stylish, marble-floored rooms, some with volcano views, come with either queen-size or two double beds. There's a good restaurant and a small pool.

Hotel Fénix (☎ 625-07-55; www.fenix.com.mx; 4a Nte 19; s/d with fan US$17/22, with air-con US$28/46; ⛏) The Fénix has a selection of rooms, so look before you sleep. The most expensive rooms are spacious and comfortable; some of the cheaper are smallish and dark.

Hotel Esperanza (☎ /fax 625-91-35, 17a Ote 8; s/d incl breakfast US$23/28; ⛏) Opposite the Colón bus station, the Esperanza offers smallish, fairly modern rooms with TV and air-con.

Hotel Don Miguel (☎ 626-11-43; www.hoteldonmiguel.com.mx; 1a Pte 18; s/d/ste US$42/52/61; P ⛏) The Don Miguel's comfortable, bright rooms with air-con are fair value for money, but there's no lift. Good restaurant, though.

Eating

There's a good choice of places around the central plaza.

El Molcajete Taco (2a Nte 95; tacos US$0.50; ☾ 8am-2pm) Close to the Colón terminal, this small, very friendly, Mexican-American-owned place has 26 different taco fillings. All are freshly prepared every day, and there are vegetarian options like mushroom with cream cheese.

Restaurante Los Jarrones (Hotel Don Miguel; ☎ 626-11-43; breakfasts US$3.50-6.75, mains US$5.75-11.50; ⛏) This is a perennially popular place, with a big choice of Mexican and international fare. There's often a live band for dinner.

Of several restaurants on the south side of Parque Hidalgo, **Los Comales Grill** (☎ 626-24-05,

Portal Pérez; mains US$4.25-8; ☾ 24 hr) is the best; the menu also includes *antojitos*, good *caldo tlalpeño* and tasty steaks. A few doors down **Restaurant Tropic's** (Portal Pérez; antojitos US$1.75-3.50, mains US$3.50-6.75) is a cheaper option. Across the street from Los Comales, **La Parrilla** (☎ 626-40-62, 8a Norte 28; antojitos US$1.75-3.50; mains US$4.50-8. ☾ 7-12.30am) has another wide-ranging menu including *tacos bandidos* and great fruit salads.

Getting There & Around

AIR

Aviacsa (☎ 626-14-39; Central Nte 18) and **Aeroméxico** (☎ 800-021-40-10; Central Ote 4) both fly at least twice daily to/from Mexico City. One-way tickets cost around US$160.

Tapachula's airport is 20km southwest of the city off the Puerto Madero road. **Transporte Terrestre** (☎ 625-12-87), 2a Sur 68, charges around US$5 per person from the airport to any hotel in the city, or vice versa.

BUS

The **Cristóbal Colón terminal** (☎ 626-28-81), on 17a Oriente 1km northeast of Parque Hidalgo, operates deluxe and 1st-class buses. The main 2nd-class bus stations are Rápidos del Sur (RS) at 9a Pte 62, and Ómnibus de Tapachula (OT) at 7a Pte 5. Daily departures include the following:

Comitán (US$9.50, 6 hr, 7 from Colón) Via Motozintla.
Escuintla (US$3.25, 1 hr, 7 from Colón; US$1.50, 32 RS; US$1.50, 50 OT)
Mexico City (TAPO or Norte; US$57-88,18 hr, 12 from Colón)
Oaxaca (US$22-25, 12 hr, 3 from Colón)
San Cristóbal de Las Casas (US$12, 7 hr, 3 from Colón)
Tonalá (US$9.50-11.50, 4 hr, 9 from Colón; US$7, 32 RS)
Tuxtla Gutiérrez (US$16-26, 7 hr, 19 from Colón; US$13, 32 RS)

Buses from the Colón station also go twice-daily to Palenque, and daily to Bahías de Huatulco, Pochutla, Puerto Escondido, Cancún, Villahermosa and Veracruz.

To travel to and from Guatemala, the following three companies run buses from the Colón station to Guatemala City (and on to other main Central American cities):

Transportes Galgos (www.transgalgosinter.com.gt) runs services to/from Guatemala City (US$17, six hours, three daily). Its **Guatemala City terminal** (☎ 253-9131) is at 7a

Av 19-44, Zona 1. Galgos also runs buses to San Salvador (US$25, eight hours, two daily) via Escuintla in Guatemala.

Tica Bus (www.ticabus.com) leaves at 7am for Guatemala City (US$13, six hours) and San Salvador (US$21, 10 hours). You can buy tickets through to Choluteca, Honduras (US$36), Managua (US$45) and San José, Costa Rica (US$53) and Panamá (US$71) involving overnight stops. Tica's **Guatemala City terminal** (☎ 331-4279) is at 11a Calle 2-74, Zona 9.

For destinations in western Guatemala including Quetzaltenango, it's best to get a bus from the border (see p840).

AROUND TAPACHULA
Izapa

The Pre-Hispanic ruins at Izapa are important to archaeologists, and of real interest to the very dedicated. Izapa flourished from approximately 200 BC to AD 200, and its carving style (typically seen on tall slabs known as *steles*, fronted by round altars) shows descendants of Olmec deities, with their upper lips unnaturally lengthened. Mayan monuments in Guatemala are similar, and Izapa is thus considered an important 'bridge' between the Olmecs and the Maya.

Izapa is around 11km east of Tapachula on the Talismán road. There are three groups of **ruins** (per site US$0.50; ⊙ 8am-5pm Wed-Sun), each looked after by a caretaking family.

The northern part of the site is on the left of the road if you're coming from Tapachula: watch out for the low pyramid mounds. You'll also see a ball court and several carved steles and altars. The warden, whose home, piglets and chicks are all part of the site, has a basic information sheet in Spanish.

From the northern area, go back 700m toward Tapachula and take a signposted dirt road to the left. You'll pass houses with 2000-year-old sculptures lying in their gardens. After 800m you reach a fork with signs to Izapa Grupo A and Izapa Grupo B, each about 250m further. Grupo A has 10 very weathered stele-and-altar pairings around a field. Grupo B is a couple of grass-covered mounds and more stone sculptures, including three curious ball-on-pillar affairs.

Take a Unión y Progreso combi or microbus (US$0.70) from 5a Pte 53 in Tapachula; all pass the Colón bus terminal on 17 Ote.

Santo Domingo, Unión Juárez & Volcán Tacaná
☎ 962

Volcán Tacaná's dormant cone towers over the countryside north of Tapachula. Even if you're not interested in climbing its summit, two villages on its gorgeously verdant lower slopes make an attractive side trip, their cooler climate offering welcome relief from oven-baked Tapachula.

Santo Domingo (population 3700) lies 34km northeast of Tapachula amid coffee plantations. The splendid three-story wooden 1920s *casa grande* of the German immigrants who formerly owned the coffee plantation here has been restored as the **Centro Turístico Santo Domingo** (☎ 629-12-75; admission free), with a restaurant, video bar, small coffee museum and well-tended tropical garden.

Nine kilometers up the paved road beyond Santo Domingo, **Unión Juárez** (population 2600, elevation 1300m) is the starting point for ascents of Tacaná. Tapachula folk like to come up here on weekends and holidays to cool off and feast on *parrillada*, a cholesterol-challenging plate of grilled meat and a few vegetables.

The best months to climb Tacaná are late November to March. Guatemalans even hold a small food-and-drink market at the summit (which is on the Mexico-Guatemala border) over the Christmas holiday period.

There are two routes up the mountain from Unión Juárez. Neither requires any technical climbing, but you need to allow two or three days for either, plus time to acclimatize. Be prepared for extreme cold at the top. If you have a vehicle (preferably 4WD) the better option is first to drive 12km up to Chiquihuite. From there it's a three-hour walk to Papales, where you can sleep in huts for US$0.80. From Papales to the summit is about a five-hour ascent. If you're without a vehicle, the preferable route is via Talquián (about two hours' walk from Unión Juárez) and Trigales (five hours from Talquián). It's about a six-hour climb from Trigales to the summit.

It's a good idea to get a guide in Unión Juárez, especially for the Chiquihuite-Papeles route, which is harder to follow. Brothers Fernando and Diego Valera charge between US$30 and US$50 for most ascents: ask for them at the Hotel Colonial Campestre. Diego speaks passable English.

Another place to head for in the area is **Pico del Loro**, a parrot's-beak-shaped overhanging rock that offers fine panoramas. The rock is situated 5km up a driveable track that leaves the Santo Domingo-Unión Juárez road about halfway between the two villages.

La Ventana (the Window) is a lookout point over Guatemala and the valley of the Río Suchiate (which forms the border): it's about a 20-minute walk from the road, 2km below Unión Juárez. The turnoff is about 300m above the Km 27 marker. Or ask directions to the **Cascadas Muxbal** waterfalls, about one hour's walk from Unión Juárez.

SLEEPING & EATING

In Santo Domingo there are a couple of good options, and you'll find plenty of plenty of comedores and restaurants around Unión Juárez' plaza.

Hotel Santo Domingo (☎ 629-90-73; s/d with fan & bathroom US$15/21) A short walk from the Centro Turístico, Santo Domingo's old *Casa del Pueblo* is now a reasonable hotel.

Centro Turístico Santo Domingo (☎ 629-12-75; antojitos US$3, mains US$4-6) The restaurant here has some tables outside on the attractive multiple verandas.

Hotel Colonial Campestre (☎ 647-20-00; fax 647-20-15; s/d US$21/23; mains US$4-6.50) A block and a half below Unión Juárez' plaza, this place has spacious rooms with bath, TV, good views and a **restaurant** (parrillada for 2 US$13).

Hotel Aljoad (☎ 647-21-06; s/d US$11/21) Just north of Unión Juárez' plaza, Hotel Aljoad has clean tidy rooms around a large patio, all with hot-water bathrooms. Inexpensive meals are available too.

GETTING THERE & AWAY

From Tapachula you must first get to the small town of Cacahuatán, 20km north. Unión y Progreso microbuses (US$0.70, one hour) go every few minutes from 5a Pte 53, as do colectivo taxis (US$1.25, 30 minutes) from 10a Norte between 9a and 11a Pte. From where these services terminate in Cacahuatán, Transportes Tacaná combis head

on to Santo Domingo (US$0.60, 30 minutes) and Unión Juárez (US$0.70, 45 minutes).

Guatemalan Border Towns

It's 37km from Tapachula to the international border at Ciudad Hidalgo, opposite Ciudad Tecún Umán in Guatemala, the busiest (and most chaotic) of the two border crossings.

The other entry point is closer, 20km from Tapachula, at the Talismán bridge opposite El Carmen in Guatemala. Both crossings are open 24 hours and have money-changing facilities. The Guatemalan officials may ask for various (illegal) small charges as you go through.

GETTING THERE & AWAY

Combis run by Ómnibus de Tapachula head to Ciudad Hidalgo from 7a Pte 5 every 10 minutes between 5:30am and 8:40pm (US$0.90); it's a 30-minute ride. Rápidos del Sur buses from 9a Pte 62 in Tapachula cover the same route, leaving every 20 minutes from 5:40am to 6:30pm (US$1). In the opposite direction, combis and buses run from 7am to around 9pm.

Unión y Progreso combis leave for Talismán from 5a Pte 53 in Tapachula every few minutes, 5:30am to 10:30pm (US$0.80).

You can also catch combis to either border from the street outside the Cristóbal Colón bus station as they leave town. A taxi from Tapachula to Talismán takes 20 minutes and costs around US$7.

Frequent buses leave Ciudad Tecún Umán for Guatemala City (about five hours away) by the coastal slope route through Retalhuleu and Escuintla. From El Carmen there's a colectivo taxi service to Malacatán, on the road to Quetzaltenango (Xela). If you're heading for Lake Atitlán or Chichicastenango, you need to get to Quetzaltenango first, for which you can get buses at Retalhuleu or Malacatán.

Talimán is also convenient for Quetzaltengano in Western Guatemala, with direct buses until around 4pm, but other services here are less frequent.

Yucatán Peninsula

CONTENTS

The Yucatán Peninsula is divided into three Mexican states: Campeche occupies the west, Yucatán state takes up a pie slice of territory in the north, and the east belongs to Quintana Roo. It is the latter state that attracts the overwhelming majority of the peninsula's visitors. From spring-breakers to snowbirds, newlyweds to newly-retired, millions of travelers every year make the pilgrimage to Quintana Roo's resort mecca: Cancún. Vacationers are drawn by the Caribbean Coast's seductive lure...and understandably so; from its northern tip to the Belizean border, Quintana Roo is hemmed by a silky ribbon of white sand. And the offshore coral reefs (part of the earth's second-largest barrier shelf) offer some of the most spectacular diving and snorkeling sites in the world.

Much less traveled, but equally rich in natural beauty, are the neighboring states of Yucatán and Campeche. These states don't claim paradisiacal beaches, but they do boast expansive nature reserves that protect populations of rare animal and plant life. Also intriguing are the mysterious crystalline-water *cenotes* (pools, sinkholes) that accent the flat limestone landscape here. It is in Yucatán and Campeche too where you can explore the most ancient and fascinating archeological sites – the long-abandoned, ever-awesome Mayan cities of Chichén Itzá, Calakmul and Uxmal among them.

Each of the three states that comprise the peninsula maintains its own identity; however, what separates the peninsular states is much less significant than what unites them: culture. Geographically isolated from the rest of Mexico for centuries, the peninsula was able to successfully preserve its Mayan heritage. The majority of people living in the peninsula today are descendants of the great empire builders of the past and many preserve the customs of their ancestors, including language, cuisine, dress and religion. Yucatecans are known for their relaxed, dignified and giving character, and you'll find that your hosts generously return any warmth you extend.

HIGHLIGHTS

- Snorkeling Cozumel's magnificent **reefs** (p915)

- Topping the 120th step of Nohoch Mul Pyramid in **Cobá** (p932), catching a breath and having it taken away again by the view

- Hoping to spot a jaguar in **Reserva de la Biósfera Calakmul** (p853) but being distracted by the jungle's brilliant bird life instead

- Salsa dancing Sunday nights away in the streets of **Mérida** (p866)

- Wearing little and doing nothing on the soft-sand beaches of **Tulum** (p926)

- ALTITUDE RANGE: 0m–309m

- MÉRIDA AUGUST DAILY HIGH: 37°C

YUCATÁN PENINSULA

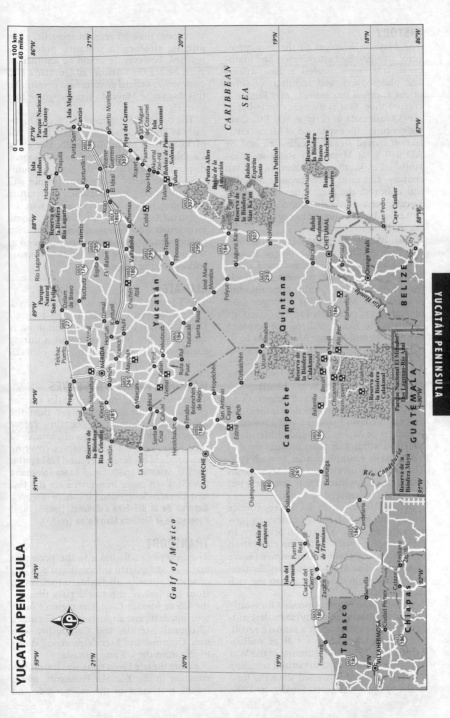

HISTORY

The Maya – inventors of the concept of zero; accomplished astronomers and mathematicians; sophisticated artists, writers and philosophers; and architects of some of the grandest monuments ever known – created their first settlements in (what is now) Guatemala as early as 900 BC. Over the centuries, the expansion of Mayan civilization moved steadily northward and by AD 550 great Mayan city-states were established in southern Yucatán. In the 9th century, and most likely because of political upheaval, the great cities of southern Yucatán were slowly abandoned, though by 850 new Mayan civilizations began to flourish in the north.

The last of the great Mayan capitals, Mayapán (p870), started to collapse around 1440 when the Xiú Maya and the Cocom Maya began a violent, protracted struggle for power. In 1540 Spanish conquistador, Francisco de Montejo the Younger (son of legendery conquistador Francisco de Montejo the Elder) utilized the tensions between the still-feuding Mayan sects to finally conquer the area. The Spaniards allied themselves with the Xiú against the Cocom, finally defeating the Cocom and gaining the Xiú as reluctant converts to Christianity.

Francisco de Montejo the Younger, along with his father, Francisco de Montejo the Elder and cousin (named…you guessed it, Francisco de Montejo) founded Mérida in 1542 and within four years brought most of the Yucatán Peninsula under Spanish rule. The Spaniards divided up the Mayan lands into large estates where the natives were put to work as indentured servants.

When Mexico won its independence from Spain in 1821, the new Mexican government used the Yucatecan territory to create huge plantations for the cultivation of tobacco, sugarcane and henequén (agave rope fiber). The Maya, though legally free, were enslaved in debt peonage to the rich landowners.

In 1847, after being oppressed for nearly 300 years by the Spanish and their descendants, the Maya rose up in a massive revolt, massacring whole towns full of ladinos (whites). This was the beginning of the War of the Castes, the most organized rebellion the Americas had witnessed since the time of the Spanish Conquest. Finally, in 1901, after more than 50 years of sporadic, often intense, violence, a tentative peace was reached; however, it would be another 30 years before the territory of Quintana Roo came under official government control. To this day some Maya do not recognize that sovereignty.

The commercial success of Cancún in the early 1970s led to the selling off of hundreds of kilometers of public beach along the Caribbean coast to commercial developers, displacing many small fishing communities. While many indigenous people still eke out a living by subsistence agriculture or fishing, large numbers now work in the construction and service industry. Some individuals and communities, often with outside encouragement, are having a go at ecotourism, opening their lands to tourists and/or serving as guides.

CLIMATE

The Yucatán Peninsula is hot and humid. The rainy season is mid-August to mid-October, when you'll get afternoon showers most days. The best time to visit is during the dryer, slightly cooler months between November and March.

NATIONAL PARKS & RESERVES

There are several national parks on the peninsula, some scarcely larger than the ancient Mayan cities they contain – **Parque Nacional Tulum** (p926) is a good example of this. National biosphere reserves covering thousands of hectares, surround **Río Lagartos** (p893), **Celestún** (p880) and **Banco Chinchorro** (p935). Even more impressive are the two vast Unesco-designated biosphere reserves: **Reserva de la Biósfera Calakmul** (p855) and **Reserva de la Biósfera Sian Ka'an** (p933).

TRANSPORT

The majority of flights into the peninsula arrive at Aeropuerto International de Cancún and virtually all flights into Cancún from the rest of the world pass through the US or Mexico City. The region's other four international airports are at Cozumel, Chetumal, Mérida, and Campeche, with only Cozumel and Mérida receiving direct flights from the US and Canada.

Before the late 1960s there was little infrastructure in the Yucatán Peninsula, which means that most of the main roads and

Fuerte de San Miguel (p848),
Campeche

Ballet Folklórico traditional dancers, Mérida
(p866)

Diving, Akumal (p925)

El Castillo (p885), Chichén Itzá

SCOTT E

Cenote Dzitnup (p890), Valladolid

Caribbean Sea, Isla Mujeres (p904)

JOHN NE

El Castillo ruins, Tulum (p926)

JOHN NEUBAUER

highways are relatively new, and the construction and expansion of highways, roads and thoroughfares (mostly to facilitate tourism) continues. Except in the downtown areas of Cancún and Mérida, car travel in the Yucatán is convenient and easy.

The bus system in the peninsula is reliable and inexpensive. First and 2nd-class buses will carry you safely and comfortably between all major cities and towns, and most sites in between. Buses run from the peninsula's major cities (Campeche, Cancún, Chetumal and Mérida) to most other parts of Mexico as well.

CAMPECHE STATE

Campeche is the first of the Yucatán Peninsula's three states that travelers hit when coming overland from other parts of Mexico but it's the least visited. However, Campeche is proudly preparing to take its place among Mexico's top tourist destinations, as rapid excavation, restoration and reconstruction work continues at many archaeological sites throughout the state. Visitors can enjoy the uncrowded Mayan archaeological sites of Edzná (p851), Calakmul (p855), and Chicanná (p855); the impressive walled city of Campeche (p845), with its colonial fortifications and architecture; and the Reserva de la Biósfera Calakmul (p855), Mexico's largest biosphere reserve.

The 56,000-sq-km state is largely flat, like other parts of the peninsula, but instead of light forest and brush, 30% of Campeche is covered with jungle. Marshlands, ponds and inlets are common along the state's coastline, which faces the dark and generally uninviting waters of the Gulf of Mexico.

CAMPECHE

☎ 981 / pop 198,000

In 1999 Unesco added the city of Campeche to its list of World Heritage Sites. Campechanos are rightly proud of this and are doing an excellent job of improving the colonial heart of the city, while retaining the best of the old. Many structures have been restored, repainted in their original pastel hues and, in some cases, reconstructed from scratch.

During Campeche's glory days, wealthy Spanish families built lavish mansions, many of which still stand. Two segments

of the city's famous wall have survived the times as well, as have no fewer than seven of the *baluartes* (bulwarks or defensive walls) that were built into it. Most impressive are the two formidable forts that still stand – cannons poised – as if ready to fire at a stray pirate vessel…or unlucky cruise ship.

Adding to Campeche's charm is its location on the Gulf of Mexico. Though the water is murky and uninviting for swimming, the broad waterfront boulevard provides the perfect place for cloud and sunset watching; add a thunderstorm rolling in off the Gulf and you have a sound-and-light show nonpareil.

History

Campeche was once a Mayan trading village called Ah Kin Pech (Lord Sun Tick) and was ruled by its fearless leader, Moch-Cuouh. The first Europeans – a Spanish expedition – landed on the shores of Ah Kin Pech in 1517. Moch-Cuouh granted to give the parched sailors water but warned them not to stay. When they didn't obey Moch-Cuouh and his men attacked the Spanish ship, killing everyone aboard. Over the next two decades other Spaniards attempted to conquer Moch-Cuouh's kingdom but met with the same success as their predecessors.

It wasn't until 1540, after Moch-Cuouh's death, that the Conquistadors – led by Francisco de Montejo the Younger – gained enough control over the region to establish a surviving settlement. They named it Villa de San Francisco de Campeche.

The small city soon flourished and became the major port of the Yucatán Peninsula. Locally grown timber and dyewoods were major exports to Europe. Gold and silver, mined in other regions, were also brought to Campeche for export. Such wealth did not escape the notice of pirates, who began to arrive only six years after the town was founded. For two centuries, they terrorized Campeche, attacking not only ships, but the port itself. They robbed citizens, raped women and burned buildings. In the most gruesome assault, in early 1663, various pirate hordes set aside their rivalries to converge as a single flotilla upon the city, where they massacred many of Campeche's citizens.

This tragedy finally spurred the Spanish monarchy to take preventive action, but it was not until five years later, in 1668, that

YUCATÁN PENINSULA

CAMPECHE

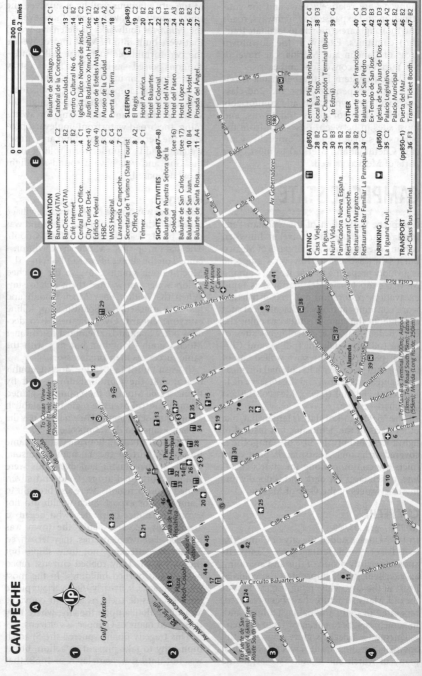

INFORMATION
Banamex (ATM).....................................1 C2
BanCrecer (ATM).................................2 B2
Café Internet......................................3 B2
Central Post Office.............................4 C1
City Tourist Desk..........................(see 14)
Edificio Federal..............................(see 4)
HSBC..5 C2
IMSS Hospital.....................................6 C4
Lavandería Campeche......................7 C3
Secretaría de Turismo (State Tourist
   Office)...8 A2
Telmex...9 C1

SIGHTS & ACTIVITIES   (pp847–8)
Baluarte de Nuestra Señora de la
   Soledad.....................................(see 16)
Baluarte de San Carlos..............(see 17)
Baluarte de San Juan......................10 B4
Baluarte de Santa Rosa..................11 A4

Baluarte de Santiago.......................12 C1
Catedral de la Concepción............13 C2
Inmaculada.......................................14 B2
Centro Cultural No 6........................15 C2
Jardín Botánico Xmuch Haltún..(see 12)
Museo de Estelas Maya...................16 B2
Museo de la Ciudad........................17 A2
Puerta de Tierra...............................18 C4

SLEEPING   (p849)
El Regis...19 C2
Hotel América..................................20 B2
Hotel Baluartes................................21 B2
Hotel Colonial..................................22 B2
Hotel del Mar...................................23 B1
Hotel del Paseo................................24 A3
Hotel López......................................25 B3
Monkey Hostel..................................26 B2
Posada del Angel..............................27 C2

EATING   (pp850)
Casa Vieja...28 B2
La Pigua...29 D1
Nutri Vida...30 B3
Panificadora Nueva España.............31 B2
Restaurant Campeche......................32 B2
Restaurant Marganzo......................33 B2
Restaurant-Bar Familiar La Parroquia..34 C2

DRINKING   (pp850)
La Iguana Azul..................................35 C2

TRANSPORT   (pp850–1)
2nd-Class Bus Terminal....................36 F3

Lerma & Playa Bonita Buses............37 C4
Local Bus Stop..................................38 D3
Sur Champotón Terminal (Buses
   to Edzná).......................................39 C4

OTHER
Baluarte de San Francisco................40 C4
Baluarte de San Pedro......................41 D3
Ex-Templo de San José.....................42 B3
Iglesia de San Juan de Dios.............43 D3
Palacio Legislativo............................44 A2
Palacio Municipal.............................45 B2
Puerta del Mar..................................46 B2
Tranvía Ticket Booth........................47 B2

work on the 3.5m-thick ramparts began. After 18 years of building, a 2.5km hexagon incorporating eight strategically placed *baluartes* surrounded the city. A segment of the ramparts extended out to sea so that ships literally had to sail into a fortress, easily defended, to gain access to the city.

Today the local economy is largely driven by shrimping and offshore petroleum extraction, and the prosperity brought by these activities has helped fund the downtown area's renovation.

Orientation

Though the bastions still stand, the city walls themselves have been mostly razed and replaced. Today Av Circuito Baluartes rings the city center just as the walls once did. Many of the streets making up the circuit are paved with stone taken from the demolished wall.

According to the compass, Campeche is oriented with its waterfront to the northwest, but be aware that locals giving directions usually follow tradition and convenience, which dictate that the water is to the west, inland is east.

A multilane boulevard with bicycle and pedestrian paths on its seaward side extends several kilometers in either direction along Campeche's shore, changing names a few times. The stretch closest to the city center is named Av Adolfo Ruiz Cortínez and is commonly referred to as *el malecón* (the seafront drive).

Information

EMERGENCY
Fire (☎ 060)
Police (☎ 816-36-35)
Red Cross (☎ 065)

INTERNET ACCESS
Café Internet (cnr Calles 10 & 61; per hr US$2) This air-conditioned Internet café has fast connections.

LAUNDRY
Lavandería Campeche (Calle 55 btwn 12 & 14; per load US$4) Fast service.

MEDICAL SERVICES
Hospital Dr Manuel Campos (811-11-42; Av Circuito Baluartes Norte btwn calles 14 & 16)
IMSS Hospital (☎ 816-52-02; cnr Av Circuito Baluartes Este & Av Central)

MONEY
Banks with ATMs can be found near Parque Principal.

PHONE
Telmex office (Calle 8, nr Calle 51)

POST
Central post office (☎ 816-21-34; cnr Av 16 de Septiembre & Calle 53)

TOURIST INFORMATION
City tourist desk (Calle 57 No 6; ☯ 9am-3:30pm & 6-9pm Mon-Fri) Northwest of the Centro Cultural Casa Número 6.
Secretaría de Turismo (☎ 816-67-67; Plaza Moch-Couoh; ☯ 9am-3pm & 6-9pm) Off Av Ruiz Cortínez, the Secretariat of Tourism office has good maps of the city and dispenses tourist magazines with information about what's going on around town and in the state.

Sights

Most of Campeche's historic sites are contained in the old city within the city walls and are easily accessible on foot.

OLD CITY CENTER
The **Baluarte de Nuestra Señora de la Soledad** (Calle 8 at Calle 57) holds the **Museo de Estelas Maya** (admission US$2.50; ☯ 8am-7:30pm Tue-Sun). Many of the Mayan artifacts here are badly weathered, but the precise line-drawing next to each stone shows you what the designs once looked like. You can take in the vista from the roof here as well.

Parque Principal, Campeche's main plaza, is the center of town and a pleasant place where locals go to sit and think, chat, smooch, plot, snooze, have their shoes shined or stroll and cool off after the heat of the day. Come for the concerts that are held here on Sunday evenings.

Construction of the grand **Catedral de la Concepción Inmaculada** (Parque Prinicpal), on the northeast side of the main plaza, began in 1650 but wasn't finished until two centuries later in 1850. Inside the black-and-white marble floor is especially dramatic, as is the carved ebony Holy Sepulcher decorated with a flock of stamped silver angels.

The 18th-century **Centro Cultural Casa Número 6** (Calle 57 on the southwest side of Parque Principal; admission free; ☯ 9am-9pm) is furnished with lovely period pieces; once inside it's easy (and fun) to imagine how the city's

YUCATÁN PENINSULA

high society lived back then. The center also contains several computer-interactive exhibits providing information about the main tourist attractions in the city and state of Campeche. Free (Spanish only) guided tours of the building are also available.

The **Baluarte de Santiago** (admission free; 9am-3pm & 5pm-8pm Mon-Fri, 9am-1pm & 4pm-8pm Sat, 9am-1pm Sun) houses a minuscule yet lovely tropical garden, the **Jardín Botánico Xmuch Haltún** with 250 species of tropical plants set around a lovely courtyard of fountains.

The **Baluarte de San Pedro** (admission free; 9am-3pm & 5pm-9pm) is in the middle of a complex traffic intersection at the beginning of Av Gobernadores. Within the bulwark is the **Exposición Permanente de Arte-sanías**, a regional crafts sales center.

Puerta de Tierra (Calle 59 at Circuito Baluartes Este; admission free; 8am-9pm) is a great stone fortress, built in 1732. It remains virtually intact; even the massive wooden door is original. There is an interesting little museum with an early 18th-century five-ton cannon in the entryway. Inside, portraits of pirates don the walls.

Baluarte de San Carlos (Calle 8 III Ave Circuito Baluartes Sur; admission free; 9am-2pm Mon, 8am-8pm Tue-Sat, 8am-2pm Sun) contains the modest **Museo de la Ciudad** (City Museum). There's a good scale model of the old city, historical photos, specimens of dyewood and the like. You can visit the dungeon, or escape to the roof for a breathtaking view of the sea.

The **Ex-Templo de San José** (Calles 10 & 63) is an absolute visual delight. The Jesuits built this baroque church in 1756. Its block-long façade is covered in striking blue and yellow Talavera tiles, and one spire is topped by a lighthouse complete with weather vane.

FUERTE DE SAN MIGUEL & MUSEO ARQUEOLÓGICO

Four kilometers southwest of Plaza Moch-Couoh, a road turns left off the malecón and climbs for about 600m to **Fuerte de San Miguel** (admission US$2.50; 9am-7pm Tue-Sat, 9am-noon Sun). This colonial fortress is now home to an excellent archaeological museum, where you can see objects found at the ancient Mayan sites of Calakmul, Edzná and Jaina, an island north of the city once used as a burial site for Mayan aristocracy.

Among the objects on display are stunning pieces of jade jewelry and exquisite vases,

masks and plates. The star attractions are the jade burial masks from Calakmul. Also displayed are stelae, weapons, arrowheads, seashell necklaces and clay figurines.

The fort is itself a thing of beauty. In mint condition, it's compact and equipped with a dry moat and working drawbridge, and it's topped with several cannons. The views are great too.

For US$0.50, 'Lerma' or 'Playa Bonita' buses depart from the market (at the northeast edge of the center) and travel counterclockwise most of the way around the *circuito* before heading down the *malecón*. Tell the driver you're going to the Fuerte de San Miguel. The turnoff for the fort, Av Escénica, is across from the old San Luis artillery battery. To avoid the strenuous walk from the coastal road up the hill (about 600m), you can take a taxi or the *tranvía* (trolley) – see p848.

Festivals & Events
There's no cost to attend any of the following festive performances:

Folk music and dancing From September to May the state tourism office sponsors free performances, which take place 7pm Saturday (weather permitting) at Plaza la República; and 8:30pm Thursday at the Centro Cultural Casa Numero 6.

Parque Principal Wednesday through Sunday nights there is always something going on at the Parque, be it jazz, rock, marimba groups or the Banda del Estado (State Band).

Tours
Three different tours by motorized *tranvía* depart daily from Parque Principal; buy tickets from the **Tranvía ticket booth** (per 45min US$8). Hourly between 9am and 9pm, the 'Tranvía de la Ciudad' heads off on a tour of the principal neighborhoods of the historic town center. On the same schedule, 'El Guapo' goes to the **Fuerte de San Miguel** and its twin on the north side of the city, the **Fuerte de San José**, which contains a modest maritime museum. You don't get enough time to take in the archaeological museum; if it's your goal, just use the tram to get there, then walk down the hill. The third tour departs at 9am and 5pm to the Fuerte de San José.

Servicios Turísticos Xtampak (812-64-85; xtampak@elfoco.com; Calle 57 btwn Calles 10 & 12; $25) This company offers archaeological tours to Edzná, Calakmul, and the various sites around Xpujil in eastern Campeche, among other places.

YUCATÁN PENINSULA

Monkey Hostel (☎ 811-65-00; cnr Calles 10 & 57) Offers shuttle service to Mayan sites Edzná and Kin-Há; Calakmul, Becán, Chicanná, and Xpuhil, and the Ruta Puuc sites.

Sleeping
BUDGET

Monkey Hostel (☎ 811-65-00; www.hostalcampeche .com; cnr Calles 10 & 57; dm US$8; ▯) It would be more aptly named Monkey Luxury Hostel. It occupies the upstairs of a grand old building directly overlooking the Parque Principal, and has a rooftop terrace with a bar and superb views of the park and cathedral. It has the usual hostel amenities: lockers, kitchen and laundry facilities, plus special perks like a book exchange, high speed Internet access (per hour US$1.50), and inexpensive bike rentals. A small breakfast is included in the price.

Hotel Colonial (☎ 816-22-22; Calle 14 No 122; r US$20, with air-con US$28; ▨) Hotel Colonial is popular with budget travelers. Housed in what was once the mansion of doña Gertrudis Eulalia Torostieta y Zagasti, former Spanish governor of Tabasco and Yucatán, the rooms have plenty of character, and surprisingly – considering its antique plumbing – good, hot showers.

MID-RANGE

Hotel América (☎ 816-45-88; Calle 10 No 252; r US$35, with air-con US$42; P ▨ ▯) Simple elegance characterizes this converted colonial home. The rooms are spacious and comfortable, each with two double beds, TV (not cable), and nice warm showers. The rooms with balconies are especially inviting, but especially noisy too. Extra perks include continental breakfast and free Internet access. This is one of the only hotels in the city center with parking.

Hotel del Paseo (☎ 811-01-00; www.hoteldelpaseo .8k.com; Calle 8 No 215; d US$48; ▨) Although the del Paseo is a distance from the center, it is located only a block from the ocean. The 48 like-new rooms here are very reasonably priced. and all have air-con, cable TV, phone and a balcony. The double beds are comfortable and the bathrooms spotless. There's a good restaurant and bar as well.

Hotel López (☎ 816-33-44; lopezh@elsitio.com; Calle 12 No 189; r US$40; ▨) Remodeled in 2003, the Hotel López has three floors of comfortable accommodations. The rooms, though small, are very clean and each one overlooks one of three tranquil courtyards.

Posada del Ángel (☎ 816-77-18; Calle 10 No 307; d US$27, with air-con US$35; ▨) This hotel, with its 14 clean (though minimally furnished) rooms is a great value. Plus it's centrally located directly across from the cathedral.

El Regis (☎ 816-31-75; Calle 12 No 148; r US$33; ▨) This two-story colonial home has seven rooms, all very large (which helps compensate for the miniscule bathrooms) and very clean; plus all are equipped with air-con and non-cable TV. The convenient central location makes this place an excellent deal.

TOP END

The following are considered to be Campeche's top hotels, but they are not luxury spots by any means, and are very conventional by all means.

Hotel Baluartes (☎ 816-39-11; www.baluartes.com .mx; Av 16 de Septiembre 128; d US$62; P ▨ ▯ ▨) You can't tell from its office-building façade, but this place is pretty stylish inside. Rooms are modern, beds are comfy, bathrooms are tiled and the air-con is strong. Get a room on one of the upper floors, the higher the better, with a good view of the sea or the city.

Ocean View (☎ 811-99-99; www.oceanview.com .mx; Av Pedro Sainz de Baranda at Joaquín Clausell; d US$67; P ▨ ▯ ▨) As the name suggests, this two-story hotel overlooks the ocean, (although only half the rooms actually have ocean views). It strives for international-businessman-sleek and achieves a sort of wannabe charm. The rooms are very comfortable and the staff extremely friendly. Continental breakfast, use of the gym, fast Internet access, airport transportation, and local calls are all free. Ocean View also features what few hotels in the Yucatán do: wheelchair-accessible rooms.

Hotel Del Mar (☎ 811-91-91; delmarcp@camp1 .telmex.net.mx; Av Ruiz Cortínez 51; r with city/sea view US$90/110; P ▨ ▨) This once-upon-a-time Ramada is still touted as *the* place to stay in town; however, its reputation is a bit inflated as are its prices. The Del Mar does have modern, comfortable, amenity-filled rooms though, and the views from the ocean-side ones are the best in the city. Creature comforts include a coffee shop, restaurant (with room service until 2am), bar and gym.

Eating

Most restaurants are in the city center, a close walk from any downtown hotel. While in town, be sure to try the regional specialty pan de *cazón*, which is dogfish – a small shark – cooked between layers of tortilla in a dark sauce. Another regional specialty is *camarones al coco*, consisting of shrimp rolled in ground coconut and fried. It's often served with marmalade and when done right tastes much better than it sounds.

La Pigua (☎ 811-33-65; Av Alemán 179A; mains US$7-13; ☻ noon-6pm) The bright blue entrance leads you into this pretty little restaurant considered by locals to be the best restaurant in town – no arguments here. The seafood menu is extensive and every item fresh and seasoned with regional flair. The *arroz con pulpo* (rice with squid) is particularly delicious, as is the shellfish-stuffed fish.

Casa Vieja (☎ 811-13-11; Calle 10 No 319 above the plaza; lunch & dinner mains US$8-12) The food is a good reason to come here, but the location's an even better one. The breezy terrace overlooking the plaza is the ideal place to enjoy a relaxed meal. Casa Vieja specializes in authentic Cuban cuisine as well as Campechean favorites with a twist (eg shrimp in papaya sauce).

Restaurant Marganzo (☎ 811-38-98; Calle 8 btwn Calles 57 & 59; breakfast US$3-5, mains US$5-10) This popular (especially with tourists) restaurant faces the Baluarte de Nuestra Señora. It serves good breakfasts and juices (carrot and beet among them), plus espresso drinks, and has an extensive seafood menu.

Restaurant Campeche (☎ 816-21-28; Calle 57; mains US$5-9; ☻ 6:30am-midnight) Opposite the Parque Principal, this place is in the building that saw the birth of Justo Sierra, founder of Mexico's national university. It's popular and offers a wide selection of dishes. It makes a convenient early morning or late-night stop.

Restaurant-Bar Familiar La Parroquia (Calle 55 No 8; breakfast US$4.50-5, mains US$5-7; ☻ 24hr) La Parroquia is the complete family restaurant/café hangout. Substantial and tasty breakfasts are served in the morning; lunches and dinners of traditional and regional dishes are offered the rest of the day and late into the night. Try the *ceviche* (seafood cocktail 'cooked' in lemon juice).

Nutri Vida (Calle 12 No 167; mains $4; ☻ closed Sun) Nutri Vida is a health-food store serving up healthy vegetarian treats such as fruit juices and salads. They also offer soy burgers and soy hotdogs.

Panificadora Nueva España (cnr Calles 10 & 59) This place has a large assortment of yummy, just-out-of-the-oven baked goods. For a treat try the *pan dulce* (sweet bread).

El Mercado (the main market) Just north of downtown outside the wall is El Mercado, where you can find fresh produce, and lots of food stands selling tasty treats like fresh fish tacos. It is open every day and meal prices at the food stands are US$2.50 to US$3.

Drinking

The best place to enjoy a drink is in the lush patio at **La Iguana Azul** (Calle 55), opposite La Parroquia, and at the bar at **Casa Vieja** (see Eating earlier) above the plaza. For good espresso drinks and healthy juice blends try **Restaurant Marganzo** (see Eating earlier).

Getting There & Away

AIR

The tiny airport is at the end of Av López Portillo (reached by Av Central), which is 3.5km southeast from Plaza Moch-Couoh. **Aeroméxico** (☎ 816-66-56) flies to Mexico City twice daily.

BUS

Campeche's **main bus terminal** (ADO; cnr Avs Patricio Trueba & Casa de la Justicia) is about 20 blocks south of Av Circuito Baluartes Este (note that Av Patricio Trueba is also known as Av Central). At the time of research the **2nd-class bus station** (cnr Avs Gobernadores & Chile) was 1.7km east of Plaza Moch-Cuouh – about 1.5km from most hotels. Note that the bus station may move to the same location as the main bus terminal.

Though most of its buses leave from the main terminal, **Sur** (Av República) has a terminal for buses to Champotón across from the Alameda (south of the market). Rural buses for Edzná and other parts depart from here as well.

There have been reports of theft on night buses, especially to Chiapas; keep a close eye on your bags.

Daily buses from Campeche include the following:
Bolonchén de Rejón (US$5, 3-4hr, four daily)
Cancún (US$27, 6hr, two direct 1st-class daily; US$22, 7hr, one 2nd-class via Mérida)

Chetumal (US$27, 9hr, 1 1st-class at noon; US$17, 9hr, 2nd-class at 8:15am & 10pm daily)

Edzná (US$2, 1½hr, 6am & 10am then hourly until 6pm) Buses leave from the Sur Champotón terminal. See p853 for further information.

Escárcega (US$8, 2½hr, 5 1st-class daily; US$6, 2½hr, many 2nd-class daily)

Hopelchén (US$3.50, 2hr, several 2nd-class daily)

Mérida (US$10, 2½-3hr, hourly 1st-class buses via Bécal; US$8, 2½-3hr, 2nd-class buses every 30 minutes until 7pm, via Bécal)

Mérida (US$7.50, 4hr, 5 2nd-class buses between 6am and 5pm via Uxmal)

Mexico City (TAPO) (US$65-78, 18hr, 4 1st-class buses & 1 deluxe daily)

Palenque (US$23, 5hr, 1 deluxe bus at midnight) For US$17-23, three 1st-class buses, some Villahermosa-bound, can drop you at Catazajá (the Palenque turnoff), 27km north of Palenque town.

San Cristóbal de Las Casas (US$33, 14hr, 1 deluxe at midnight)

Villahermosa (US$24, 6hr, 8 1st-class daily)

Xpujil (US$15, 6-8hr, 1 1st-class at noon; US$12, 6-8hr, 4 2nd-class daily, including one via Hopelchén)

CAR & MOTORCYCLE

Whether you're heading for Edzná, the long route (Highway 261) to Mérida, or the *via cuota* (toll road) going south, take Av Central and follow signs for the airport and Edzná. For the free slow route (Highway 180) south you can just head down the *malecón*.

For the nontoll, short route to Mérida head north on the *malecón*; it curves right eventually and hits the highway at a Pemex station.

Getting Around

Local buses all originate at the market. Most charge US$0.35 and go at least part-way around the Av Circuito Baluartes counterclockwise before heading to their final destinations. Ask a local where along the *circuito* you can catch the bus you want.

Taxis have set prices for destinations on a sign posted in the back seat, but agree on a price with the driver before you go; by the hour prices are US$7.75. The fare between the main bus terminal and the center is around US$2.50. Between the airport and the center should be US$7. *Colectivo* taxis from the airport charge about US$3 per person.

CAMPECHE TO MÉRIDA
Highway 180 (Short Route)

The *ruta corta* (short route) is the fastest way to get between the two cities, and it's the road most traveled by buses. If you'd prefer to go the long way via Kabah and Uxmal, ask for a seat on one of the less-frequent long-route buses. If you'd like to stop at one of the towns along the short route, catch a 2nd-class bus.

From Campeche it's 109km to **Bécal**, a center of the Yucatán Peninsula's Panama hat trade, just inside the border of Campeche state. Townsfolk have been making the soft, pliable hats, called *jipis*, since the mid-19th century. The jipis are woven from the fronds of the *jipijapa* palm tree; to keep the fibers moist and pliable the hat makers work in humid limestone caves. The caves – there's at least one on every block, generally reached by a hole in the ground in someone's backyard – are typically no larger than a bedroom. About 1000 of the town's 3000 adult residents make their living weaving hats. The hats cost from under US$10 to well over US$70, depending on quality. If you're shopping for one, be sure to visit the cooperative on the main street, a stone's throw from Bécal's dominating church. From Bécal it's 85km to Mérida.

Highway 261 (Long Route)

Most travelers take the long route from Campeche to Mérida in order to visit the various ruin sites on the way. It's often referred to as 'la Ruta Chenes,' for the *chenes* (wells) that give the region its name.

EDZNÁ

The closest major ruins to Campeche are about 53km to the southeast. **Edzná** (admission US$4; 8am-5pm) covered more than 17 sq km and was inhabited from approximately 600 BC to the 15th century AD. Most of the visible carvings date from AD 550 to 810. Though it's a long way from such Puuc Hills sites as Uxmal and Kabah, some of the architecture here has elements of the Puuc style. What led to Edzná's decline and gradual abandonment remains a mystery.

Beyond the ticket office is a *palapa* (thatched-roofed shelter) protecting carvings and stelae from the elements. A path from here leads about 400m through vegetation to the zone's big draw, the Plaza

YUCATÁN PENINSULA

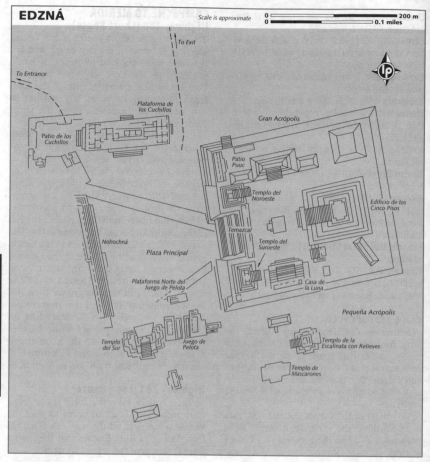

EDZNÁ

Scale is approximate

To Exit

To Entrance

Plataforma de los Cuchillos

Gran Acrópolis

Patio de los Cuchillos

Patio Puuc

Templo del Noroeste

Edificio de los Cinco Pisos

Temazcal

Nohochná

Plaza Principal

Templo del Suroeste

Plataforma Norte del Juego de Pelota

Casa de la Luna

Pequeña Acrópolis

Templo del Sur

Juego de Pelota

Templo de la Escalinata con Relieves

Templo de Mascarones

Principal (follow the signs for the Gran Acrópolis), which is 160m long, 100m wide and surrounded by temples. On your right as you enter from the north is the **Nohochná** (Big House), a massive, elongated structure that was topped by four long halls likely used for administrative tasks, such as the collection of tributes and the dispensation of justice. The built-in benches facing the main plaza were designed for spectators to view theatrical and ritual events.

Across the plaza is the Gran Acrópolis, a raised platform holding several structures, including Edzná's major temple, the 31m-high **Edificio de los Cinco Pisos** (Five-Story Building). It rises five levels from its vast base to the roofcomb and contains many

vaulted rooms. A great central staircase of 65 steps goes right to the top. Some of the weathered carvings of masks, serpents and jaguars' heads that formerly adorned each level are now in the *palapa* near the ticket office.

The current structure is the last of four remodels and was done primarily in the Puuc architectural style. Scholars generally agree that this temple is a hybrid of a pyramid and a palace. The impressive roofcomb is a clear reference to the sacred buildings at Tikal in Guatemala.

In the Pequeña Acrópolis to the south of the main plaza is the *palapa*-protected **Templo de Mascarones** (Temple of Masks), which features carved portrayals of the sun god,

Kinich-Ahau. The central motif is the anthropomorphic head of a Maya man whose face has been modified to give him the appearance of a jaguar.

From Campeche, dilapidated rural buses leave from outside the Sur Champotón terminal at 6am and 10am, then roughly hourly until 6pm (US$2, 55km, 1½ hours). Most drop you about 200m from the site entrance; ask before boarding. The last bus returning to Campeche passes near the site at about 2pm, so if you're coming here on a day trip from the city you'll want to catch one of the two early buses leaving Campeche. The bus schedules can vary slightly, so check the day before.

Coming from the north and east, get off at San Antonio Cayal and catch a bus 20km south to Edzná. If you're headed north on leaving Edzná, you'll have to depend on the occasional bus to get you to San Antonio Cayal, where you can catch a Ruta Chenes (Chenes Route) bus north to Hopelchén, Bolonchén de Rejón and ultimately Uxmal.

Coming by car from Campeche, take Av Central out of town and follow the signs to the airport and Edzná. If you drove to Edzná from the north and are headed to Campeche city, don't retrace your route to San Antonio Cayal; just bear left shortly after leaving the parking lot and follow the signs westward.

Tours (p848) of Edzná from Campeche start at about US$25 per person.

BOLONCHÉN DE REJÓN & XTACUMBILXUNAAN

Forty kilometers east of San Antonio Cayal is Hopelchén, where Highway 261 turns north; there's a Pemex station on the west side of town. The next town to appear out of the lush countryside is Bolonchén de Rejón, after 34km. Its local **festival of Santa Cruz** is held each year on May 3.

Bolonchén de Rejón is near the **Grutas de Xtacumbilxunaan** (admission US$2.25; 8am-6pm), pronounced Grutas de *shtaa*-koom-beel-shoo-*nahn*, is about 3km south of town. Lighted steps lead down to a barely visible *cenote* (sink hole, pool or cave river) beyond which a passage leads 100m further. There are few stalactites or stalagmites, but the climb back up to the green forest surrounding the cave is dramatic, and with future improvements the *cenote* may be visible.

Highway 261 continues north into Yucatán state to Uxmal (p871), with a side road leading to the ruins along the Ruta Puuc (p875).

ESCÁRCEGA TO XPUJIL

Hwy 186 heads due east across southern-central Campeche state, from grubby Escárcega through jungle to Xpujil and on to Chetumal – in Quintana Roo – a 273km ride. It passes several fascinating Mayan sites and through the ecologically diverse and archaeologically rich **Reserva de la Biósfera Calakmul**. The largest settlement between Escárcega and Chetumal – and the only one with accommodations – is Xpujil, on Highway 186 about 20km west of the Campeche–Quintana Roo border. The only gas station in the same stretch is about 5km east of Xpujil. There is no fee to be in the area.

Many of the numerous archaeological sites between Escárcega and Xpujil are being restored. The most historically significant is **Calakmul** (p855), which is also one of the most difficult to reach (60km from the highway and no buses). It, and most of the other sites in this section, can be visited by taxis hired in Xpujil or tours booked either through hotels in Xpujil or Campeche (see p848).

The predominant architectural styles of the region's archaeological sites are **Río Bec** (p854) and **Chenes** (p856). The former is characterized by long, low buildings that look as though they're divided into sections, each with a huge serpent or monster-mouth door. The façades are decorated with smaller masks, geometric designs (with many X forms) and columns. At the corners of the buildings are tall, solid towers with extremely small, steep, nonfunctional steps and topped by small false temples. Many of these towers have roofcombs. The Chenes style shares most of these characteristics except for the towers. (See p854 for specific details about the ruins.)

XPUJIL

The hamlet of Xpujil (pronounced shpu-*heel*) lies at the junction of east-west Highway 186 and Campeche Highway 261, which leads north to Hopelchén and eventually

Mérida. A good base from which to explore the area's sites, Xpujil is growing rapidly in anticipation of a tourist boom, however, it still has no bank or laundry, and the nearest gas station is 5km east of town. Several restaurants, a couple of hotels and a taxi stand are near the bus depot.

From the junction, the Xpuhil ruins are less than 1km west, Becán is 8km west, Chicanná is 12km west, Balamkú is 60km west, and the Calakmul ruins are 120km southwest.

Sights
XPUHIL

Xpuhil (admission US$3; ⊗ 8am-5pm), 'Place of the Cattails' in Mayan, flourished during the late classic period from AD 400 to 900, though there was a much earlier settlement here. The site's entrance is on the western edge of town on the north side of Highway 186, at the turnoff for the airport, less than 1km west of the junction.

One large building and three small ones have been restored. Estructura I in Grupo I, built about 760, is a fine example of the Río Bec architectural style, with its lofty towers. The three towers (rather than the usual two) have traces of the impractically steep ornamental stairways reaching nearly to their tops, and several fierce jaguar masks (go around to the back of the tower to see the best one). About 60m to the east is Estructura II, once an elite residence.

Xpuhil is a far larger site than may be imagined from these buildings. Three other structure groups have been identified, but it may be decades before they are restored.

Sleeping & Eating

Hotel y Restaurant Calakmul (☎ 983-871-60-29; cabins US$22, d with bath US$40) The Calakmul is about 350m west of the junction. Rooms at the back are large, modern and clean, with lots of tile. The **restaurant** (Meals $4-6; ⊗ 6am-midnight), serves decent food but at a…very…slow…pace.

El Mirador Maya (☎ 983-871-60-05; bungalow US$25, r US$35) About 1km west of the junction, this hotel has eight bungalows and two rooms. Each bungalow comes with a fan and two beds. The rooms are new and have air-con but are very small, and the air-con is poorly placed. There is a **restaurant** (Meals $4-6; ⊗ 6am-midnight) here as well.

Getting There & Around

Xpujil is 220km south of Hopelchén, 153km east of Escárcega and 120km west of Chetumal. Stopping in Xpujil are 11 buses daily to Escárcega (US$6), five to Campeche (US$14) and five to Chetumal (US$6). No buses originate in Xpujil, so you must hope you luck into a vacant seat on one passing through. The bus terminal is just east of the Xpujil junction, on the north side of the highway.

The Xpuhil ruins are within walking distance of Xpujil junction. You may be able to hitch a ride to the access roads for Becán, Chicanná and Balamkú, but for other sites you will need to hire a cab.

AROUND XPUJIL
Ruins
HORMIGUERO

Hormiguero (admission US$3; ⊗ 8am-5pm) is reached by heading 14km south from Xpujil junction, then turning right and heading another 8km west on a shoddily paved road. Hormiguero (Spanish for 'anthill') is an old site, with some buildings dating as far back as AD 50; however, the city flourished during the late classic period. Hormiguero has one of the most impressive buildings in the region. Entering the site you will see the 50m-long **Estructura II**, which has a giant Chenes-style monster-mouth doorway with much of its decoration in good condition. You'll also want to see **Estructura V**, 60m to the north; Estructura E-1, in the East Group, should be a sight once it is excavated.

RÍO BEC

The entrance to the collective farm Ejido 20 de Noviembre is 10km east of the Xpujil junction and signed 'Río Bec.' The unpaved *ejido* road south leads 5km to the collective itself and its U'lu'um Chac Yuk Nature Reserve. Look for the small store on the left side of the road, and ask there for guides to show you the various sites, which are about 13km further down the very rough road. There is no charge to enter the area, although the guides charge (US$10 to US$25) for their services. 'Río Bec' is the designation for an agglomeration of small sites, 17 at last count, in a 50-sq-km area southeast of Xpujil. It gave its name to the prevalent architecture style in the region. Of these many sites, the most interesting is certainly Grupo B, followed by Grupos I and N. The best example is Estructura I at Grupo B, a late classic building dating from around AD 700. Though not restored, Estructura I has been consolidated and is in a condition certainly good enough to allow appreciation of its former glory. At Grupo I look for Estructuras XVII and XI. At Grupo N, Estructura I is quite similar to the grand one at Grupo B.

The road is passable only when dry, and even then you need a high-clearance vehicle. The way is unsigned as well; you're best off hiring a guide whether you have a 4WD truck or not. A taxi to the *ejido* will charge around US$5 for drop-off service; negotiate waiting time. Though it looks closer on the map, access to Río Bec from the road to Hormiguero is all but impossible.

BALAMKÚ

Balamkú (admission US$3; 🕑 8am-5pm) is 60km west of Xpujil (88km east of Escárcega). Discovered in 1990, this small site's attractions are its frescoes, and an exquisite, ornate stucco frieze. Amazingly, much original color is still visible on both the frescoes and the frieze. You'll notice toads dominate the designs at Balamkú. These amphibians, not only at home on land and water, were considered to move easily between this world and the next as well. The toad was a revered spirit guide that helped humans navigate between earth and the underworld.

The frescoes are open to public viewing, but the frieze is housed in a locked building. The caretaker will open the door and even provide a flashlight tour upon request. (A tip is appreciated.)

CALAKMUL

Calakmul (admission US$3; 🕑 8am-5pm), which means 'Adjacent Mounds,' was first discovered by outsiders in 1931 by US botanist Cyrus Lundell. Mayanists consider Calakmul to be a site of vital archaeological significance. This historic site was once the seat of a nearly unrivaled superpower. It was even further-reaching in size – and often influence – than neighboring Tikal in Guatemala.

From about AD 250 to 695, Calakmul was the leading city in a vast region known as the Kingdom of the Serpent's Head. Its perpetual rival was Tikal, and its decline began with the power struggles and internal conflicts that followed the defeat by Tikal of Calakmul's king Garra de Jaguar (Jaguar Paw).

As at Tikal, there are indications that construction occurred over a period of more than a millennium. Beneath Edificio VII, archaeologists discovered a burial crypt with some 2000 pieces of jade, and tombs continue to yield spectacular jade burial masks; many of these objects are on display in Campeche city's Museo Arqueológico. Calakmul holds at least 120 carved stelae, though many are eroded.

So far only a fraction of Calakmul's 100-sq-km expanse has been cleared, and few of its 6500 buildings have been consolidated, let alone restored; however, exploration and restoration are ongoing.

Lying at the heart of the vast, untrammeled Reserva de la Biósfera Calakmul (one of the two Unesco-designated biosphere regions on the Yucatán Peninsula; Reserva de la Biósfera Sian Ka'an is the other) the ruins are surrounded by rainforest, which is best viewed from the top of one of the several pyramids. There are over 250 bird species living in the reserve and you are likely to at least see wild turkeys, parrots and toucans. The menagerie of other wildlife protected by the reserve includes jaguar, spider monkey, puma, ocelot and white-lipped peccary.

The turnoff to Calakmul is 59km west of Xpujil, and the site is 59km further south on a paved road. A toll of US$4 per car (more for heavier vehicles) and US$2 per person is levied at the turnoff from Highway 186, to fund the constant road maintenance. From the parking lot to the ruins is a 500m walk.

At the Semarnat post 20km from the highway, rangers allow **camping**; please pay a donation if you use the shower and toilets. They've built a small, screened *palapa* that can sometimes be rented.

Villas Puerta Calakmul (puertacalakmul@hotmail.com; cabins US$60-80) is a comfortable place, located about 300m east of the access road, just in from the highway. It has 15 tastefully decorated, fan-cooled cabins. The restaurant serves generous meals and low prices.

CHICANNÁ

Buried in the jungle almost 12km west of Xpujil and 500m south of the highway,

Chicanná (admission US$3; ⏰ 8am-5pm), 'House of the Snake's Jaws,' is a mixture of Chenes and Río Bec architectural styles. The city was occupied from about AD 300 to 1100.

Enter through the modern *palapa* admission building, then follow the rock paths through the jungle to Grupo D and Estructura XX (AD 830), which feature not one but two monster-mouth doorways, one above the other, and atop this a roofcomb.

A five-minute walk along the jungle path brings you to Grupo C, with two low buildings (Estructuras X and XI) on a raised platform; the temples bear a few fragments of decoration.

The buildings in Grupo B (turn right when leaving Grupo C) have some intact decoration as well, and there's a good roofcomb on Estructura VI.

Shortly beyond is Chicanná's most famous building, Estructura II (750 to 770) in Grupo A, with its gigantic Chenes-style monster-mouth doorway, believed to depict the jaws of the god Itzamná, Lord of the Heavens, creator of all things. If you photograph nothing else here, you'll want a picture of this, best taken in the afternoon.

Take the path leading from the right corner of Estructura II to reach nearby Estructura VI.

Formerly the Ramada, **Chicanná Ecovillage Resort** (☎ 981-811-91-91; chicanna@campeche.sureste .com; s/d US$98/110) is 500m north of the highway and directly across from the road to the ruins. Large, airy rooms with ceiling fans are grouped mostly four to a bungalow and set amid well-tended lawns. There's a pool, and the small dining room/bar serves decent but expensive meals.

The charming, super eco-friendly **Río Bec Dreams** (☎ 983-871-60-57; www.riobecdreams .com; Hwy 186 Km 142; cabanas US$25-50) offer rustic 'jungalows' surrounded by bromeliads and orchids, a restaurant, bar and gift shop.

BECÁN

Becán (admission US$3.50; ⏰ 8am-5pm), 8km west of Xpujil, sits atop a rock outcrop; a 2km moat snakes its way around the entire city to protect it from attack. (Becán – literally 'path of the snake' – is also the Mayan word for 'canyon' or 'moat.') Seven causeways crossed the moat, providing access to the city. Becán was occupied from 550 BC until AD 1000.

This is among the largest and most elaborate sites in the area. The first thing you'll come to is a plaza. If you walk keeping it to your left you'll pass through a rock-walled passageway and beneath a corbeled arch. You will reach a huge twin-towered temple with cylindrical columns at the top of a flight of stairs. This is Estructura VIII, dating from about AD 600 to 730. The view from the top of this temple has become partially obscured by the trees, but on a clear day you can still see structures at the Xpuhil ruins to the east.

Northwest of Estructura VIII is Plaza Central, ringed by 30m-high Estructura IX (the tallest building at the site) and the more interesting Estructura X. In early 2001, at X's far south side, a stucco mask still bearing some red paint was uncovered. It is enclosed in a wooden shelter with a window for viewing.

In the jungle to the west are more ruins, including the Plaza Oeste, which is surrounded by low buildings and a ball court. Much of this area is still being excavated and restored, so it's open to the public only intermittently.

Loop back east, through the passageway again, to the plaza; cross it diagonally to the right, climbing a stone staircase to the Plaza Sureste. Around this plaza are Estructuras I through IV; a circular altar (Estructura IIIA) lies on the east side. Estructura I has the two towers typical of the Río Bec style. To exit, you can go around the plaza counterclockwise and descend the stone staircase on the southeast side or go down the southwest side and head left.

YUCATÁN STATE

The state of Yucatán is a pie slice at the top of the Yucatán Peninsula. Until the development of Cancún in neighboring Quintana Roo, it was the peninsula's economic engine. While Quintana Roo's tourist-driven economy has surpassed Yucatán's in recent years, historically and culturally Yucatán remains paramount. Here you'll find the peninsula's most impressive Mayan ruins (Chichén Itzá and Uxmal), its finest colonial cities (Mérida and Valladolid) and two coastal communities internationally famous for their wild red flamingos.

As a tourist destination, traditional Yucatán complements commercial Quintana Roo extremely well, and travel between the two states is convenient and affordable. A high-speed highway served by numerous 1st-class buses links Cancún and Mérida, and the trip to one of Mexico's oldest cities following a visit to one of its most modern resorts is highly recommended.

MÉRIDA

☎ 999 / pop 690,000

Mérida, once the Mayan city of T'hó, has been the dominant metropolitan center in the Yucatán region since the Spanish Conquest. Today the capital of the state of Yucatán is a prosperous city of narrow streets, colonial buildings and shady parks. Mérida is the intellectual, arts and cultural center of the peninsula, and every night of the week some engaging event takes place: folkloric dances or music, theatrical performances, art openings and film showings. The city center is especially delightful on weekends when the streets are blocked to all but pedestrians, giving respite from the otherwise heavy, noisy, smoky traffic that generally plagues downtown.

There are hotels and restaurants of every class and price range and good transportation services to any part of the peninsula and the country. The city makes a good base for embarking on numerous excursions around the region.

History

Francisco de Montejo the Younger founded a Spanish colony at Campeche, about 160km to the south, in 1540. From this base he was able to take advantage of political dissension among the Maya, conquering T'hó (now Mérida) in 1542. By the end of the decade, Yucatán was mostly under Spanish colonial rule.

When Montejo's conquistadors entered defeated T'hó, they found a major Mayan settlement of lime-mortared stone that reminded them of Roman architectural legacies in Mérida, Spain. They promptly renamed the city and proceeded to build it into the regional colonial capital, dismantling the Mayan structures and using the materials to construct a cathedral and other stately buildings. Mérida took its colonial orders directly from Spain, not from

Mexico City, and Yucatán has had a distinct cultural and political identity ever since.

During the War of the Castes, only Mérida and Campeche were able to hold out against the rebel forces. On the brink of surrender, the ruling class in Mérida was saved by reinforcements sent from central Mexico in exchange for Mérida's agreement to take orders from Mexico City. Although Yucatán is certainly part of Mexico, there is still a strong feeling in Mérida and other parts of the state that the local people stand a breed apart.

Mérida today is the peninsula's center of commerce, a bustling city that has benefited greatly from the *maquiladoras* (assembly-plant operations) that opened in the 1980s and '90s and the tourism that picked up during those decades as well.

Orientation

The Plaza Grande, as *meridanos* call the main square, has been the city's center since Mayan times. Most of the services that visitors want are within five blocks of the square. Odd-numbered streets run east–west, and their numbers increase by twos going from north to south (for example, Calle 61 is a block north of Calle 63); even-numbered streets run north–south, and increase by twos from east to west.

House numbers may increase very slowly, and addresses are usually given in this form: 'Calle 57 No 481 x 56 y 58' (btwn Calles 56 and 58).

Information

BOOKSTORES

Arte Maya (Calle 57 btwn Calles 60 & 62) This bookstore has stack upon stack of used books, mostly paperbacks in English. They also have a two-for-one trade policy.

Librería Dante (☎ 928-26-11; Plaza Grande) There's a convenient branch next to La Via Olimpio; and a smaller branch on the corner of Calles 58 and 60. Librería Dante sells paperbacks in English, including some guidebooks. It also has an extensive selection on art and archaeology. (Look for John L Stephen's fascinating account *Incidents of Travel in Yucatán*. First published in 1843, it is now out of print but editions can sometimes be found here.)

EMERGENCY

Fire (☎ 924-92-42)
Police (☎ 925-20-34)
Red Cross (☎ 924-98-13)
Tourism Police (☎ 930-32-00)

MÉRIDA

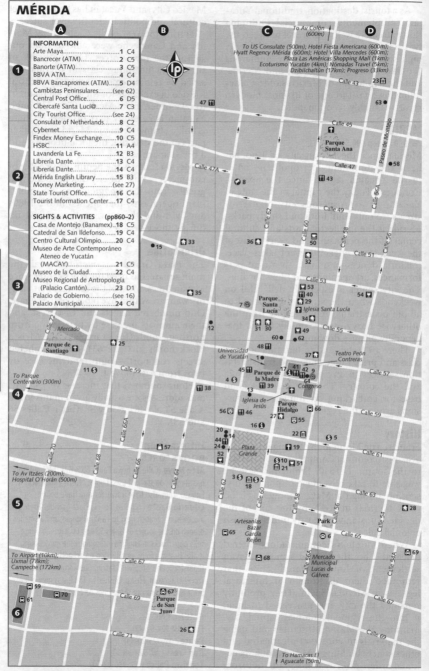

INFORMATION
Arte Maya...........................1 C4
Bancrecer (ATM)...................2 C5
Banorte (ATM)......................3 C5
BBVA ATM...........................4 C4
BBVA Bancapromex (ATM)......5 D4
Cambistas Peninsulares........(see 62)
Central Post Office.................6 D5
Cibercafé Santa Lucí@...........7 C3
City Tourist Office................(see 24)
Consulate of Netherlands........8 C2
Cybernet...............................9 C4
Findex Money Exchange........10 C5
HSBC...................................11 A4
Lavandería La Fe...................12 B3
Librería Dante......................13 C4
Librería Dante......................14 C4
Mérida English Library..........15 B3
Money Marketing...............(see 27)
State Tourist Office...............16 C4
Tourist Information Center....17 C4

SIGHTS & ACTIVITIES   (pp860–2)
Casa de Montejo (Banamex)..18 C5
Catedral de San Ildefonso.....19 C4
Centro Cultural Olimpio........20 C4
Museo de Arte Contemporáneo
  Ateneo de Yucatán
  (MACAY)............................21 C5
Museo de la Ciudad..............22 C4
Museo Regional de Antropología
  (Palacio Cantón)................23 D1
Palacio de Gobierno............(see 16)
Palacio Municipal.................24 C4

To Av Colón
(600m)

To US Consulate (500m); Hotel Fiesta Americana (600m);
Hyatt Regency Mérida (600m); Hotel Villa Mercedes (600m);
Plaza Las Américas Shopping Mall (1km);
Ecoturismo Yucatán (4km); Nómadas Travel (5km);
Dzibilchaltún (17km); Progreso (33km)

To Parque
Centenario (300m)

To Av Itzáes (200m);
Hospital O'Horán (500m)

To Airport (10km);
Uxmal (78km);
Campeche (172km)

To Hamacas El
Aguacate (50m)

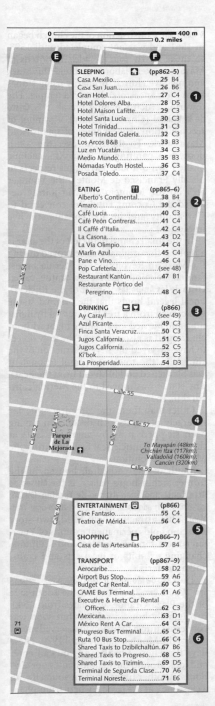

Calle 54 · Calle 52 · Calle 50A · Calle 50 · Parque de La Mejorada

To Mayapán (48km);
Chichén Itzá (117km);
Valladolid (160km);
Cancún (320km)

71

INTERNET ACCESS

There are so many Internet places around the city it's hard *not* to find one. A couple of those with cheap prices, decent connections and air-con include:

Cibercafé Santa Lucí@ (cnr Calles 62 & 55; per hr US$2)
Cybernet (Calle 57A btwn Calles 58 & 60; per hr US$2)

LAUNDRY

Lavandería La Fe (Calle 64 No 470 btwn Calles 55 & 57; per 3kg load US$4) Rates include a load to be washed and dried.

LIBRARIES

Mérida English Library (☎ 924-84-01; Calle 53 No 524 btwn Calles 66 & 68) This small library is a great resource; you are welcome to browse through the stacks, sit and read, and take a book or two on loan for a few days.

MEDICAL SERVICES

Hospital O'Horán (☎ 924-84-00; Av Itzaés) Near Parque Centenario, this is Mérida's largest hospital.

MONEY

Banks and ATMs are scattered throughout the city, especially near the Plaza Grande (see map for some locations).

For money changing, *casas de cambio* give good rates and have much faster service than banks. A couple of reputable choices include the following:

Cambistas Peninsulares (Calle 60 btwn Calles 55 & 57)
Money Marketing (Gran Hotel, Parque Hidalgo)

POST

Central Post Office (cnr Calles 65 & 56)

TOURIST INFORMATION

City Tourist Office (☎ 928-20-20; Plaze Grande, Calle 62; ◷ 8am-8pm)
State Tourist Office (☎ 930-31-03; Plaza Grande, Calle 61; ◷ 8am-9pm)
Tourist Information Center (☎ 924-92-90; Calles 60 & 57A; ◷ 8am-8pm) At the northeast edge of Parque de la Madre.

TRAVEL AGENCIES

Nómadas Travel (☎ 948-11-87; www.nomadastravel .com; Prolongacíon Paseo de Montejo 370) This agency is a bit out of the way, but worth the trip. They sell student discount tickets as well as the International Student Identity Card (ISIC). They also offer some of the lowest fares to Cuba. Take a cab or a northbound bus on Paseo de Montejo heading for Colonia Benito Juárez Norte.

YUCATÁN PENINSULA

Dangers & Annoyances

Guard against pickpockets, bag-snatchers and bag-slashers in the market district and in any crowd, such as at a performance.

It is likely that at least one or two (probably a lot more) individuals claiming to be official tour guides will approach you on the street and offer to show you the sights. Legitimate state and city guides do not solicit on the street. The imposters you meet may be able to give you a reasonable tour (for a more-or-less reasonable fee) but remember they are not government employees, and are considered by the tourism office to be 'pirates.'

At night, in the center or along the Paseo de Montejo, single women are perfectly safe and only in danger of being annoyed by unwanted attention; however, please beware: the area around the bus stations is not safe for women alone at night, nor are the hotels in that neighborhood (none of which are listed below).

Sights & Activities

PARQUE CENTENARIO

About 12 blocks west of the Plaza Grande, lies the large, verdant **Parque Centenario** (admission free; 6am-6pm Tue-Sun) bordered by Av de los Itzáes. The park's **zoo** (admission free; 8am-5pm Tue-Sun) features the fauna of Yucatán, as well as some exotic species. To get there, take a bus west along Calle 61 or Calle 65.

PLAZA GRANDE

This large but at times surprisingly intimate square is the most logical place to start a tour of Mérida. Also known as 'El Centro' (as in the center of town) or the Plaza Principal, the Plaza Grande was the religious and social center of the ancient Mayan city T'hó; under the Spanish it was the Plaza de Armas (parade ground), laid out by Francisco de Montejo the Younger. The plaza is surrounded by some of the city's most impressive and harmonious colonial buildings, and its carefully tended laurel trees provide welcome shade. On Sunday, hundreds of *meridanos* take their *paseo* (stroll) here. Various events take place around the plaza, based on weekly schedules.

On the plaza's east side, on the former site of a Mayan temple, is one of Mexico's oldest churches: **Catedral de San Ildefonso** (6am-noon & 4pm-7pm). Construction of the church began in 1561 and was not completed until 1598. In those nearly four decades, hundreds of Mayan workers labored to build this stark and massive church, primarily using stones from their ancestors' destroyed temple. The towering crucifix behind the altar is **Cristo de la Unidad** (Christ of Unity), a symbol of reconciliation between those of Spanish and Maya stock. To the right, over the south door, is a painting of Tutul Xiú, cacique of the town of Maní, paying his respects to his ally Francisco de Montejo the Younger at T'hó (de Montejo and Xiú jointly defeated the Cocom; Tutul Xiú converted to Christianity and his descendants still live in Mérida).

In the small chapel to the left of the altar is a replica (the original was destroyed during the Mexican Revolution) of Mérida's most famous religious artifact, a statue called **Cristo de las Ampollas** (Christ of the Blisters). Local legend holds that the original statue was carved from a tree that was hit by lightning and burned for an entire night without charring. It is also said to be the only object to have survived the fiery destruction of the church in the town of Ichmul (though it was blackened and blistered from the heat). The statue was moved to the Mérida cathedral in 1645.

Other than these, the cathedral's interior is largely plain, its rich decoration having been stripped away by angry peasants at the height of anticlerical feeling during the Mexican Revolution.

South of the cathedral, housed in the former archbishop's palace, is the **Museo de Arte Contemporáneo Ateneo de Yucatán** (MACAY; ☎ 928-31-91; admission US$2.50; 10am-6pm Wed-Mon). This attractive light-filled, two-story museum holds permanent exhibits of Yucatán's most famous painters and sculptors, changing exhibits of local arts and crafts, and a cafeteria.

The **Casa de Montejo** (Palacio de Montejo; 9am-5pm Mon-Fri, 9am-2pm Sat) is on the south side of the Plaza Grande and dates from 1549. It originally housed soldiers but soon was converted into a mansion that served members of the Montejo family until 1970. These days it shelters a bank, and you can enter and look around during the bank's opening hours. At other times, content yourself with a close look at the façade, where triumphant conquistadors with halberds hold their feet on the necks of generic barbarians (who are supposedly not Maya, though the association is inescapable). Also gazing across the plaza from the façade are busts of Montejo the Elder, his wife and his daughter.

Across the square from the cathedral is Mérida's **Palacio Municipal** (City Hall). Originally built in 1542, it was twice refurbished, in the 1730s and the 1850s. Just north, occupying the corner of the plaza is the **Centro Cultural Olimpo**, Mérida's municipal cultural center. Attempts to create a modern exterior for the building were halted by government order, to preserve the colonial character of the plaza. The ultramodern interior serves as a venue for music and dance performances, as well as other exhibitions. Schedules for these and frequent film showings are posted outside.

On the north side of the plaza, the **Palacio del Gobierno** (admission free; ⊙ 8am-9pm) houses the state of Yucatán's executive government offices (and one of its tourist information offices). It was built in 1892 on the site of the palace of the colonial governors. Inside are murals painted by local artist Fernando Castro Pacheco; completed in 1978, they were 25 years in the making and portray a symbolic history of the Maya and their interaction with the Spaniards.

CALLE 60

A block north of the Plaza Grande, just beyond shady Parque Hidalgo, rises the 17th-century **Iglesia de Jesús**, also called Iglesia de la Tercera Orden. Built by the Jesuits in 1618, this is the sole surviving edifice from a complex of buildings that once filled the entire city block. This church was built from the stones of a destroyed Mayan temple that once occupied the same site. Though the Spaniards systematically destroyed any carved surfaces on stones used for building, here a few traces of the past survive. On the west wall facing Parque Hidalgo, you can see two stones still bearing Mayan carvings.

North of the church is the large and lavish **Teatro Peón Contreras** (cnr Calles 60 & 57), built between 1900 and 1908, during Mérida's *henequén* heyday. Once inside it is easy to see the influence of the Italian architects who designed this theatre. The main staircase is made of pure Carrara marble, and frescoes by Italian artists adorn the dome.

Outside of performance hours, the guard may allow you in to see the theater.

Across Calle 60 from the theater is the main building of the **Universidad de Yucatán**. Though the Jesuits provided education to Yucatán's youth for centuries, the modern university was established in the 19th century by Governor Felipe Carrillo Puerto and General Manuel Cepeda Peraza.

A block north of the university is pretty little **Parque Santa Lucía** (Calles 60 & 55), with arcades on the north and west sides. When Mérida was a lot smaller, this was where travelers would get on or off the stagecoaches that linked towns and villages with the provincial capital. The **Bazar de Artesanías** (⊙ 11am Sun), the local handicrafts market, is held here.

PASEO DE MONTEJO

The **Paseo de Montejo** was an attempt by Mérida's 19th-century city planners to create a wide boulevard similar to the Paseo de la Reforma in Mexico City or the Champs Élysées in Paris. Though more modest than its predecessors, the Paseo de Montejo is still a beautiful, long, wide swath of green in an otherwise urban conglomeration of stone and concrete. Most tourists don't venture beyond the downtown area, but the Paseo de Montejo is where life for many *meridanos* (especially the middle and upper classes) begins.

Europe's architectural and social influence can be seen along the *paseo* in the fine mansions built by wealthy families around the end of the 19th century. The greatest concentrations of surviving mansions are north of Calle 37 – which is three blocks north of the Museo Regional de Antropología (see below) – and on the first block of Av Colón west of Paseo de Montejo.

MUSEO DE LA CIUDAD

The **City Museum** (Calle 61 btwn Calles 58 & 60; admission free; ⊙ 10am-2pm & 4pm-8pm Tue-Fri, 10am-2pm Sat-Sun) is small but worthwhile, with artifacts, exhibits and good photos of the city and region. Signs in English explain subjects such as Mayan traditions, history and the process of *henequén* production.

MUSEO REGIONAL DE ANTROPOLOGÍA

The great white Palacio Cantón houses the **Museo Regional de Antropología** (cnr Paseo de

Montejo & Calle 43; admission US$3; 8am-8pm Tue-Sat, 8am-2pm Sun). Construction of the mansion lasted from 1909 to 1911. Its owner, General Francisco Cantón Rosado (1833–1917), lived here for only six years before his death. Its splendor and pretension make it a fitting symbol of the grand aspirations of Mérida's elite during the last years of the Porfiriato, the period from 1877 to 1911 when Porfirio Díaz held despotic sway over Mexico.

The museum covers the peninsula's history since the age of mastodons. Exhibits on Mayan culture include explanations (many in Spanish only) of forehead-flattening, which was done to beautify babies, and other cosmetic practices such as sharpening teeth and implanting them with tiny jewels. If you plan to visit archaeological sites near Mérida, you can study the exhibits here – some with plans and photographs – covering the great Mayan cities of Mayapán, Uxmal and Chichén Itzá, as well as lesser-known sites such as Ek' Balam. There's also a good bookstore with many archaeological titles.

Mérida for Children

Parque Centenario (p860) is an oasis of green where you will enjoy the shade and kids will enjoy the (somewhat rundown) complex of playgrounds. Especially attractive to children is the park's **Zoo** (p860), which houses native monkeys, birds and reptiles. There are also pony rides, picnic areas and a small lake.

Mérida en Domingo (p866) is a super kid-friendly event that takes place every Sunday downtown.

Courses

Centro de Idiomas del Sureste (CIS; Calle 14 No 6; ☎ 926-11-55; www.cisyucatan.com.mx; 2 weeks tuition US$370, housing per week from US$135) This long-established Spanish-language school has three locations citywide. Courses begin every Monday year-round and run for a minimum of two weeks. The school provides home-stay accommodations.

Nómadas Spanish Workshop (☎ 944-33-76; www .nomadastravel.com; tuition per week US$79, housing per week US$42-135) At the time of research this new school run by the directors of Nómadas Youth Hostel was slated to open in late 2004. Housed in a modern facility in the north end of the city, students here will participate in small group, total immersion courses for minimum one-week programs. The school will offer accomodations at Nómadas Youth Hostel or with a local family.

Tours

City Tourist Office (☎ 928-20-20; Calle 60 at Plaza Grande; tours depart 9:30am) The City Tourist Office, housed in the Palacio Municipal, offers free daily guided walking tours of the historic center. They meet in front of the Palacio Municipal and depart from there.

Ecoturismo Yucatán (☎ 920-27-72; www.ecoyuc.com; Calle 3 No 235) The owners of this reputable outfit are passionate about both protecting and sharing the state's natural treasures. Their trips, which can be tailor-made to fit your interests, focus on archaeology, birding, natural history, biking and kayaking. Prices vary from one-day excursions (US$50) to ten-day jungle tours (US$1,400).

Nómadas Youth Hostel (☎ 924-52-23; www.nomad astravel.com; Calle 62 No 433) Nómadas offers low prices (about US$30) on a variety of organized tours, including Celestún Flamingo tour, Chichén Itzá, Uxmal and Kabah. They can also help you arrange do-it-yourself trips in your rented car or on public transportation. They will also assist in matching up travelers with sharing cars for group trips.

Festivals & Events

Carnaval February or March, prior to Lent. Features colorful costumes and nonstop festivities. It is celebrated with greater vigor in Mérida than anywhere else in Yucatán state.

Kihuic End February or beginning of March. A market that fills the Plaza Grande with handicrafts artisans from all over Mexico.

Cristo de las Ampollas September 22 to October 14. *Gremios* (guilds or unions) venerate the Cristo de las Ampollas (Christ of the Blisters) statue in the cathedral with processions.

Exposición de Altares November 1. Another big religious tradition, Exposición de Altares is when the Maya welcome the spirits of their ancestors with elaborate dinners outside their homes. Although this custom is more apparent in the countryside, Mérida observes it with elaborate festivities in the center of town from 11am until 11am the next day.

Sleeping

You get a lot of hotel for your money in Mérida, especially compared with room prices in the coastal resort towns. Prices fluctuate between low and high season (high season being roughly between mid-December through March), but not wildly like they do in Cancún or Playa del Carmen. When business is slow many places will discount, some without being asked. If you're arriving at the CAME bus terminal, check at the tourism desk for flyers offering hotel discounts. Wherever possible, high-season rates have been given here.

BUDGET

Nómadas Youth Hostel (☎ 924-52-23; www.nomad astravel.com; Calle 62 No 433; hammock or tent US$4, dm US$6, r US$13) This spacious, clean, extremely well-run hostel offers full use of the kitchen, hot showers and hand-laundry facilities. Continental breakfast is included in the price and Internet (US$1.50 per hour) is available. Nómadas also has a lively night-life: on Tuesdays and Fridays guests can enjoy live *Trova* (folk music), and free Salsa dance classes the rest of the week.

Hotel Trinidad Galería (☎ 923-24-63; Calle 60 No 456; s/d US$22/25; 🖭) Funky, fun and down-right silly, this is one of two hotels (the other listed below) run by Mexican artist Manolo Rivera. This former appliance showroom is now a showcase of eclectic artifacts, includ-ing fine original paintings and sculpture, as well as dolls and inflatable toys, all of which are tangled up in a labyrinth of vegetation. The rooms themselves are pretty small and dark, but the spacious patios and palm-shaded poolside area help make up for what the rooms lack.

Hotel Trinidad (☎ 923-20-33; www.hoteltrinidad .com; Calle 62 No 464 btwn Calles 55 & 57; dm US$8, r US$25-30; 🖭) This 19-room hotel centers around two lovely courtyards. Each unit is uniquely furnished with an artist's eye for décor and ambience. There's a small café here as well and guests are invited to use the pool at sister hotel Trinidad Galería.

MID-RANGE

Medio Mundo (☎ 924-54-72; www.hotelmediomundo .com; Calle 55 No 533; r with fan US$45-55, with fan & air-con US$60-65; 🖭 🖭) Ahh…this urban oasis exudes peace and tranquility. The owners (and gracious hosts) transformed this once-dilapidated home into a virtual *Architec-tural Digest* centerfold. The colors – from the paint on the walls to the flowers in the courtyard – have been orchestrated to evoke just the right mood, and every detail – including the quiet air con and not too soft, not-too-hard beds – has been attended to. What this hotel does not have are any distractions: no phone, no TV, no noise. Healthy breakfasts (US$8) and organic cof-fee are served at the poolside patio.

Luz en Yucatán (☎ 924-00-35; www.luzenyucatan .com; Calle 55 No 499; r US$40-60; 🖭 🖭) Two beers on arrival is the delightfully eccentric own-er's policy. Madeline – usually with parrot,

Godzilla, perched on her shoulder – will make you feel immediately at home. Each of the seven rooms that surround the court-yard and small pool is an original work dedicated to comfort and coziness; all are equipped with air-con and cable TV, and most with a small kitchenette. Special ser-vices offered upon request include: mas-sage, pedicure, yoga and Spanish lessons.

Casa Mexilio (☎ 928-25-05, 800-538-68-02 in the US; www.casamexilio.com; Calle 68 No 495 btwn Calles 57 & 59; r US$47-83; 🖭 🖭) The intimate Casa Mexilio is housed in a beautifully decorated 19th-century townhouse. Each of the eight rooms is uniquely named (ie, the Frida Kahlo Room) and adorned accordingly. The courtyard with pool and Jacuzzi is the perfect refuge from Mérida's busy streets. Rates include breakfast served in the period dining room.

Los Arcos B&B (☎ 928-02-14; www.losarcosmerida .com; Calle 66 btwn Calles 49 & 53; s/d US$65/85; 🖭 🖭) This gay-friendly B&B only has three rooms, so as a guest you virtually have this whole gorgeous home to yourself. There's a stun-ning garden and pool area and the owners invite you to share their extensive library of books and CDs too. You're also welcome to use the computer for short email checks. Your only concern here: whether to have breakfast served in your room or by the pool.

Gran Hotel (☎ 924-77-30; Calle 60 No 496 btwn Calles 59 & 61; s/d US$51/55; 🅿 🖭) Fidel Castro chose to stay here when he was in town. The charming Gran Hotel was built in 1901 and retains many delightful decorative flour-ishes. The 28 air-conditioned rooms have period furnishings; the most charming overlook Parque Hidalgo.

Hotel Maison Lafitte (☎ 923-91-59; www.maison lafitte.com.mx; Calle 60 No 472 btwn Calles 53 & 55; s/d US$68/72; 🅿 🖭 🖭 🖭) Simplicity and ele-gance characterize this three-story converted colonial home. The comfortable rooms sur-round a quiet courtyard with small swim-ming pool. A generous breakfast, served in the hotel's restaurant is included, as is half an hour's worth of free Internet access.

Casa San Juan (☎ 986-29-37; www.casasanjuan .com; Calle 62 No 545A btwn Calles 69 & 71; d US$45-55; 🅿 🖭) This pensión is housed in a lovingly restored colonial home. Some of the seven large rooms have air-con, all have mile-high ceilings and original woodwork. Breakfast is included. Parking per day costs US$2.

Posada Toledo (☎ 923-16-90; Calle 58 No 487 at Calle 57; d with fan/air-con US$35/45; P 🔀) This former mansion retains its regal air. The architecture and much of the furnishings (don't worry, not the beds) are straight out of the 19th century. The rooms vary greatly in size and noise level; you can ask to see a couple before making your choice. Breakfast is available in the grand dining room.

Hotel Santa Lucía (☎ 928-26-72; www.hotelsanta lucia.com.mx; Calle 55 No 508 btwn Calles 60 & 62; s/d US$36/40; 🔀 🕮) This pastel-pink colonial hotel across the street from Parque Santa Lucía is understandably a favorite among travelers. It has a small pool and all 51 rooms are clean and have TV and telephone.

Hotel Dolores Alba (☎ 928-56-50, 800-849-50-60; www.doloresalba.com; Calle 63 btwn Calles 52 & 54; r US$35, with air-con US$40; P 🔀 🕮) The Dolores Alba is a Mérida institution and excellent value. Rooms are around two large courtyards; all those in the new, modern wing are quite large and face the lovely, chlorine-free pool. The hotel has secure parking and is quiet, well managed and friendly.

TOP END

Hotel Villa Mercedes (☎ 924-90-00; www.hotelvilla mercedes.com.mx; Av Colón 500 at Calle 60; r from US$110; P 🔀 🕮 🕮) This refurbished mansion has been restored to its original Art Nouveau splendor. It's smaller (84 rooms) and more intimate (as mansions go) than its counterparts in this category. There's a pool, gym and business center.

Fiesta Americana Mérida (☎ 942-11-11, 800-343-78-21 in the US; www.fiestaamericana.com; Calle 56A No 451; r from US$150; P 🔀 🕮 🕮) This enormous, modern neocolonial luxury hotel is part of a complex housing shops, travel agencies, airline offices and restaurants. Though the official address doesn't indicate it, the hotel occupies a large stretch of Av Colón, on the northern edge of the colonial center.

YUCATECAN CUISINE – FOOD OF THE MAYA

Because of the region's long-time isolation from the rest of Mexico, Yucatecan cuisine derived its own distinct character. Its influences are primarily Mayan and European with flashes of Middle Eastern and Asian inspiration (see also the Food & Drink chapter, p84). While you are here be sure to try some of the standard favorites:

achiote – a paste ground from annatto seeds and mixed with lemon juice and spices.

frijol con puerco – Yucatecan-style pork and beans, topped by a sauce made with grilled tomatoes, and decorated with bits of radish, slices of onion and leaves of fresh *cilantro* (coriander leaves); served with rice.

huevos motuleños – 'eggs Motul style'; fried eggs atop a tortilla, garnished with beans, peas, chopped ham, sausage, grated cheese and a certain amount of spicy chili – high in cholesterol, fat and flavor.

papadzules – dipped in pumpkin seed sauce and tortillas stuffed with chopped hard-boiled eggs and topped with a light tomato sauce and pumpkin seed oil, or sauce made with squash or cucumber seeds.

pavo relleno – slabs of turkey meat layered with chopped, spiced beef and pork and served in a rich, dark sauce; the Yucatecan *faisán* (pheasant) is actually the *pavo* (turkey).

pibil – meat wrapped in banana leaves, flavored with achiote, garlic, sour orange, salt and pepper, traditionally baked in a barbecue pit called a *pib*; the two main varieties are *cochinita pibil* (suckling pig) and *pollo pibil* (chicken).

poc-chuc – tender pork strips marinated in sour orange juice, grilled and served topped with pickled onions.

puchero – a stew of pork, chicken, carrots, squash, potatoes, plantains and *chayote* (vegetable pear), spiced with radish, fresh *cilantro* and sour orange.

salbutes – Yucatán's favorite snack: a handmade tortilla fried then topped with shredded turkey, onion and slices of avocado.

sopa de lima – 'lime soup'; chicken broth with bits of shredded chicken, tortilla strips, lime juice and chopped lime.

venado – venison, a popular traditional dish, might be served as a *pipián* (stew) flavored with a sauce of ground squash seeds, wrapped in banana leaves and steamed.

Hyatt Regency Mérida (☎ 942-02-02; www.hyatt .com; Av Colón 344; r from US$160; P ⊠ ▢ ▩) Not far from the Fiesta Americana, the 17-story Hyatt is Mérida's most expensive hotel. It has 300 rooms, tennis courts, a gym and steam bath, and a great pool with swim-up bar.

Eating

BUDGET

Pop Cafetería (☎ 928-61-63; Calle 57 btwn Calles 60 & 62; breakfast US$3-5, mains US$4-6) The Pop is plain, modern and well cooled. It has tasty, cheap breakfast combinations and a good variety of Mexican dishes; try the chicken in mole or the delicious guacamole.

Marlín Azul (Calle 62 No 488 btwn Calles 57 & 59; mains US$5) Frequented by locals but rarely tourists, this small place serves cheap and yummy seafood; the *ceviche mixto* (a cocktail made from a variety of seafood and 'cooked' in lemon juice) is excellent.

Mercado Municipal Lucas de Gálvez (Calle 56; ☼ daily) The bustling market is full of small eateries. Upstairs joints have tables and chairs and more varied menus; main-course platters of beef, fish or chicken go for as little as US$1.50. Downstairs at the north end are some cheap *taquerías* where you sit on a stool at a narrow counter, while near the south end are *coctelerías* serving shrimp, octopus and conch cocktails.

MID-RANGE

Amaro (☎ 928-24-52; Calle 59 btwn Calles 60 & 62; mains US$6-10) Amaro is a romantic dining spot, especially at night. It's set in the courtyard of the house in which Andrés Quintana Roo – poet, statesman and drafter of Mexico's Declaration of Independence – was born in 1787. The restaurant has Yucatecan food and a good variety of vegetarian plates, as well as some continental dishes and pizzas.

La Casona (☎ 923-99-96; Calle 60 btwn Calles 47 & 49; mains US$5-11) This grand old house is the ideal setting for a cozy dinner. You may choose to sit outside in the lush courtyard or in one of the two dining rooms. They serve excellent Italian food as well as steak, seafood and Yucatecan specialties.

Café Lucia (☎ 928-07-40; Calle 60 No 474 btwn Calles 53 & 55; mains US$8-10) This quiet, chic gallery-restaurant features an impressive display of local and international artists' work. If you'd prefer to eat outside, there is seating across

the street in Parque Santa Lucia, an especially nice setting on weekends when local musicians play table-side *Trova*. The menu features seafood, steak and pasta, all of which are very good. Service is excellent.

Restaurant Kantún (☎ 923-44-93; Calle 45 btwn Calles 64 & 66; mains US$6-8; ☼ Thu-Sun) This family-run, neighborhood place serves some of the best seafood in town. Entrées are all prepared to order and superbly seasoned or sauced; try the *filete* Normanda, a fillet stuffed with smoked oysters and topped with anchovies.

Pane e Vino (☎ 928-62-28; Calle 62 btwn Calles 59 & 61; mains US$5-8; ☼ closed Mon) This cozy Italian Restaurant serves standard and tasty pizzas and pastas, most with vegetarian variations available.

Il Caffé d'Italia (☎ 925-94-52; Calle 57A btwn Calles 58 & 60; US$5-8) This is another good hang-out-and-watch-people place. The menu includes good breakfasts, strong coffee, and reasonable Italian fare for lunch and dinner.

La Vía Olimpo (☎ 923-58-43; Calle 62 btwn Calles 61 & 63; breakfast US$5; mains US$5-8) Olimpo is a trendy and popular restaurant-café on the west side of the Plaza Grande. It is open practically 24-7. They serve mostly soups, salads, sandwiches and breakfasts. Round-the-clock (slow) Internet access is available too.

Cafe Peón Contreras (Calle 60; breakfast US$5; pizzas US$7-10) A few steps north of Parque Hidalgo, this café has espresso drinks and a long, varied menu, including a combination plate of Yucatecan specialties.

TOP END

Alberto's Continental (☎ 928-53-67; Calle 64 at 57; mains US$10-20) Housed in a 1727 colonial home, Alberto's is rich in atmosphere. The floor is a mosaic of Cuban tiles. Mirrors, baroque religious artifacts and Mayan figurines line the walls, and Moorish arches frame the patio. The cuisine is mostly Middle Eastern and completely delicious. Specialties include kebabs, hummus, baba-ganoush and tabbouleh. The seafood, steak and chicken are also good. Try the dessert too if you can.

Restaurante Pórtico del Peregrino (☎ 928-61-63; Calle 57 btwn Calles 60 & 62; mains US$12-20) Several pleasant, traditional-style dining rooms (some air-conditioned) surround a small courtyard here. Yucatecan dishes are its forte, especially the *pollo pibil* (p84), but you'll find many continental dishes and a broad range of seafood and steaks as well.

Drinking

Ki'bok (☎ 928-55-11; Calle 60 btwn Calles 53 & 55) You may need to leave a trail of breadcrumbs to find your way back to the front door of this hip labyrinthine café/bar. There is an endless choice of nooks, crannies, patios, bridges and balconies from which to enjoy a drink; once you've decided where to sit then you get to choose what to order from the extensive menu…

Finca Santa Veracruz (☎ 924-24-50; cnr Calles 60 & 51) A good place to get great coffee. Many of their espresso drinks can be ordered straight up or a la mode; if ice-cream isn't enough, they're happy to add a shot of booze to your drink as well.

Jugos California (Plaza Mayor; Calle 63A, cnr Calle 58) On a sweltering Mérida afternoon this is the perfect place to stop for a tall glass of cool fruit juice. Every local fruit is juiced here (papaya, mamey, mango, guanabana). Combine a few flavors to create your own thirst-quenching concoction.

Entertainment

CULTURAL EVENTS

Mérida's cultural life is thriving and any night of the week offers an opportunity to take in a different musical or theatrical performance. Pick up a copy of *Yucatán Today* (available at any tourist office and most hotels) to check the schedule of current events.

Ballet Folklórico de la Universidad de Yucatán (University of Yucatán; Calle 60 at 57; adult US$2; ☯ 9pm) Every Friday night the university's folk dance troupe puts on an impressive and authentic performance of regional dances.

Centro Cultural Olimpio (☎ 928-20-20; Plaza Grande) There's something interesting – from films to concerts to art installations – scheduled nearly every night of the week.

Teatro Peón Contreras (cnr Calle 60 & 57) Features Mexican and international musical and dance performances. Check theater for current schedule of events.

Mérida en Domingo (Plaza Grande; ☯ 9am-9pm) 'Mérida on Sunday' is a lively fair that takes place every Sunday. The main plaza and Calle 60 – from the plaza to Parque Sant Lucia – are cordoned off and closed to

all but pedestrian traffic. Food and drink stands are set up, art activity booths are available for kids, there's a small flea market and used book exchange. From about 11am bands – jazz, folk, classical – play in front of the Palacio del Gobierno on the plaza. At around 7pm in Parque Hidalgo the live salsa music and dancing begin; on any given Sunday, as many as 500 *meridanos* may be dancing in the streets. You can sit in a sidewalk café and watch, or better yet, join in.

Noche Mexicana (☯ 9am-9pm) A free outdoor traditional Mexican music and dance performance that takes place every Saturday in the the park at the beginning of Paseo de Montejo. It is festive, fun and entertaining for all ages.

NIGHTCLUBS

La Prosperidad (☎ 924-14-07; Calle 56 at 53) A big *palapa* bar that features live rock, lots of beer and tasty *botanas* (snacks).

Mambo Café (☎ 987-75-33; Plaza Las Américas Shopping Mall) The always-crowded Mambo, approximately 1km north of town, has live salsa bands at weekends and DJ-spun disco, house and pop other nights.

Azul Picante (Calle 60 btwn Calles 55 & 57) This fun club features live latin pop and salsa music. Salsa dance lessons are offered on site too.

Ay Caray! (Calle 60 btwn Calles 55 & 57) This is a popular, trendy bar that features live (and loud) music – usually rock – most nights.

CINEMA

Mérida has several cinemas, most of which show some first-run Hollywood fare in English, with subtitles. **Teatro Mérida** (Calle 62 btwn Calles 59 & 61) often runs classic Hollywood and Mexican movies. **Cine Fantasio** (Parque Hidalgo) shows international and art films. **Cinepolis** (Plaza Las Américas Shopping Mall) is a big modern cineplex showing first-run Hollywood flicks, almost all in English with subtitles.

Shopping

Mérida is a fine place for buying Yucatecan handicrafts. Purchases to consider include traditional Mayan clothing such as the colorful embroidered *huipiles* (women's tunics), panama hats woven from palm fibers and of course the wonderfully comfortable Yucatecan hammocks.

Mercado Municipal Lucas de Gálvez (cnr Calles 56 & 56A at Calle 67; daily) Southeast of the Plaza Grande is Mérida's main market. The surrounding streets are all part of the large market district, lined with shops selling everything one might need. Guard your valuables in the market area. Watch for pickpockets, purse-snatchers and bag-slashers.

HANDICRAFTS

Casa de las Artesanías (Calle 63 btwn Calles 64 & 66; ⏰ 9am-8pm Mon-Sat, 10am-2pm Sun) This is a government-supported market for local artisans selling just about everything: earthenware, textiles, wicker baskets, sandals, wind chimes, ceramic dolls, vases, purses and pouches, figurines of Mayan deities and bottles of locally made liqueurs. Prices are fixed and reasonable; you can have a look at the stuff here, then try to bargain down independent sellers elsewhere, but it's often not worth the effort.

PANAMA HATS

Locally made panama hats are woven from *jipijapa* palm leaves in caves, where humid conditions keep the fibers pliable. Once exposed to the relatively dry air outside, the panama hat is surprisingly resilient and resistant to crushing. The Campeche town of Bécal is the center of the hat-weaving trade, but you can buy good examples in Mérida.

The best quality hats have a fine, close weave of slender fibers. The coarser the weave, the lower the price should be. Prices range from a few dollars for a hat of basic quality to US$80 or more for top quality. They can be found at the Casa de las Artesanías and elsewhere.

HAMMOCKS

'The Yucatán hammock is an honest hammock and does not play dirty tricks in the middle of night,' observed travel writer Michel Peissel in 1964. A well-made hammock is not only a fine alternative to a mattress; it is a fine work of art. Mérida is one of the best places to buy a Yucatecan hammock, but only if you know where to shop. Street vendors and many small shops sell tacky, uncomfortable, made-for-tourists renditions. The best place in town to shop for a quality hammock is at the reputable **Hamacas El Aguacate** (☎ 928-64-69; cnr Calle 58 at 73). If you want to venture out of town you

can go to the nearby village of Tixcocob (buses run from the Progreso bus terminal) and watch hammock makers at work. It is also a good place to find a well-crafted hammock at a fair price.

Getting There & Away
AIR

Mérida's modern airport is a 10km, 20-minute ride southwest of the Plaza Grande off Highway 180 (Av de los Itzáes). It has car rental desks, an ATM and a currency exchange booth, and a tourist office where staff can help with hotel reservations.

Most international flights to Mérida are connections through Mexico City or Cancún. Nonstop international services are provided by Aeroméxico (Los Angeles and Miami) and Continental (Houston). Scheduled domestic flights are operated mostly by smaller regional airlines, with a few flights by Aeroméxico and Mexicana.

AIRLINE OFFICES

Aerocaribe (☎ 928-67-90; www.aerocaribe.com; Paseo de Montejo 500B)

Aeroméxico (☎ 920-12-60; www.aeromexico.com; Hotel Fiesta Americana, Av Colón at Paseo Montejo)

Aviacsa Mérida (☎ 925-68-90; www.aviasca.com.mx; Hotel Fiesta Americana, Av Colón at Paseo Montejo)
Airport (☎ 946-18-50)

Continental Airlines (☎ 800-900-50-00; www .continental.com; at airport)

Mexicana (☎ 924-69-10; www.mexicana.com.mx; Paseo de Montejo 493)

BUS

Mérida is the bus transportation hub of the Yucatán Peninsula. Take care with your gear on night buses and those serving popular tourist destinations (especially 2nd-class buses); Lonely Planet has received many reports of theft on the night runs to Chiapas and of a few daylight thefts on the Chichén Itzá route and other lines.

Mérida has a variety of bus terminals, and some lines operate out of (and stop at) more than one terminal. Tickets for departure from one terminal can often be bought at another, and destinations overlap greatly among lines. Following are some of the stations, bus lines operating out of them and areas served.

Hotel Fiesta Americana (Av Colón), near Calle 56A, is a small 1st-class terminal on the west side of the hotel complex and is aimed at guests staying at the luxury hotels on Av Colón, far from the center. Don't arrive here by bus unless you'll be staying at the Fiesta, Villa Mercedes or Hyatt. ADO GL and Super Expresso have services between Mérida and Cancún, Campeche, Chetumal and Playa del Carmen.

Parque de San Juan (Calle 69 btwn Calles 62 & 64) is the terminus for shared taxis, vans and Volkswagen combis going to Dzibilchaltún Ruinas, Muna, Oxkutzcab, Petó, Sacalum, Tekax and Ticul.

Progreso (Calle 62 No 524) This is a separate terminal for Progreso-bound buses.

CAME bus terminal (☎ 924-83-91; Calle 70 btwn Calles 69 & 71) is Mérida's main terminal, seven blocks southwest of Plaza Grande. Come here for (mostly 1st-class) buses to points around the Yucatán Peninsula and well beyond (eg Campeche, Cancún, Mexico City, Palenque, San Cristóbal de Las Casas and Villahermosa). Lines include the more economical ADO and Altos (air-con and few stops, but no bathroom), and the deluxe lines ADO GL, Maya de Oro, Super Expresso and UNO (air-con, non-stop and bathrooms).

Terminal de Segunda Clase (Calle 69) Around the corner from CAME bus terminal, ATS, Mayab, Omnitur del Caribe, Oriente, Sur, TRP and TRT run mostly 2nd-class buses to points in the state and around the peninsula.

Terminal Noreste (Calle 67 btwn Calles 50 & 52) is the Noreste bus line's terminal; LUS uses it as well. Buses run from here to many small towns in the northeast part of the peninsula, including Tizimín and Río Lagartos, as well as frequent service to Cancún and points along the way, and small towns south and west of Mérida, including Celestún, Ticul and Oxkutzcab.

Destinations served from Mérida include the following:

Campeche – short route via Bécal (US$8, 2½-3½hr, frequent ADO 1st-class buses; US$7, ATS 2nd-class buses every 30 min until 7pm)

Campeche – long route via Uxmal (US$7.50, 4hr, 5 Sur 2nd-class buses between 6am-5pm)

Cancún (US$12, 4-6hr, 16 Oriente 2nd-class buses daily; US$17, 20 Super Expresso deluxe) Many other buses also travel to/from Cancún.

Celestún (US$3.50, 2hr, 15 2nd-class daily)

Chetumal (US$19, 6-8hr, 8 deluxe Omnitur del Caribe and Super Expresso; US$16, 3 Mayab 2nd-class)

Chichén Itzá (US$5, 2-2½hr, 3 Super Expresso & 16 Oriente 2nd-class) Some Cancún-bound buses stop at Chichén Itzá during the day, at night in nearby Pisté.

Cobá (US$11, 3½hr, 1 deluxe Super Expresso at 1pm; US$8, 1 Oriente bus at 5:15am)

Escárcega (US$14, 5½hr, 1 Altos 1st-class; US$16, 5 ADO 1st-class; US$13 many Sur 2nd-class)

Felipe Carrillo Puerto (US$12, 5½hr, 7 Mayab 2nd-class; US$13, 5 TRP 2nd-class)

Izamal (US$3, 1½hr, frequent Oriente 2nd-class)

Mayapán Ruinas (US$1.50, 2hr, 15 LUS 2nd-class) Buses leave from Terminal Noreste.

Mexico City (Nte) (US$77, 19hr, 1 ADO 1st-class at 12:05pm)

Mexico City (TAPO) (US$75, 20hr, 4 ADO 1st-class buses btwn 10am and 9:15pm)

Palenque (US$29, 8-9hr, 1 deluxe Maya de Oro; US$26, 3 ADO 1st-class; US$24, 1 Altos)

Playa del Carmen (US$20, 5-7hr, 10 deluxe Super Expresso)

Progreso (US$1.25, 1hr, every 20 minutes from 8am to 9pm) Buses depart from the Progreso bus terminal. For the same ticket price, shared taxis or vans (some with air-con) take off from a parking lot at Calle 60 between Calles 65 and 67.

Río Lagartos (US$6-8, 3-4hr, 3 Noreste 1st- & 2nd-class buses from 9am)

Ticul (US$3.50, 2hr, frequent 2nd-class Mayab) For US$2.75 there are also frequent minibuses (combis and vans) from Parque de San Juan.

Tizimín (US$8, 2½-4hr, several 1st-class Noreste; US$7, several 2nd-class Noreste) Shared taxis to Tizimín (US$7, 2-3hr) leave (when full) from Calle 65 near the corner of Calle 52.

Tulum (US$13, 4hr, deluxe Super Expresso via Cobá at 6:30am, 11am & 1pm) There is a 2nd-class service to Tulum, but it costs more and takes at least twice as long.

Tuxtla Gutiérrez (US$45, 13-16hr, 1 deluxe Maya de Oro at 9:30pm; US$37, 1 Altos at 7:15pm) You can change at Palenque or Villahermosa.

Valladolid (US$8.50, 2½-3½hr, frequent buses, including deluxe Super Expresso; US$6.50, frequent 2nd-class Oriente and ATS buses)

Villahermosa (US$30, 8-9hr, 10 ADO 1st-class; US$50, superdeluxe UNO at 9:30pm and 11pm; US$48, ADO GL at 5:30pm)

CAR & MOTORCYCLE

The optimal way to tour the many archaeological sites south of Mérida is by car; however, getting around town is definitely better done on foot or with public transportation. Most corners have traffic lights *and* traffic cops, one signaling you to go and the other to stop. Drivers are impatient, streets are narrow, and buses merciless, so hold off renting a car until you've seen most of Mérida, or at least gotten well oriented.

México Rent A Car (☎ 923-36-37; Calle 57A btwn Calles 58 & 60) offers rates the big-name agencies often can't touch, especially if you're paying cash. It's sometimes possible to get a VW Beetle for as little as US$25 a day, and long-term rentals can bring prices lower than that, even on higher-quality cars. Cars are in very good condition, and the friendly managers speak good English.

Several other agencies have branches at the airport as well as on Calle 60 between Calles 55 and 57, including **Budget** (☎ 928-66-59), **Executive** (☎ 923-37-32) and **Hertz** (☎ 924-28-34).

Getting Around

TO/FROM THE AIRPORT

Bus No 79 ('Aviación') travels between the airport and city center every 15 to 30 minutes until 9pm, with occasional service until 11pm. The half-hour trip (US$0.50) takes you via a very roundabout route; the best place to catch the bus is on Calle 70 just south of Calle 69, near the corner of the CAME terminal.

Transporte Terrestre (☎ 946-15-29) provides speedy service between the airport and the center, charging US$11 per carload (same price for hotel pick-up). A taxi from the center to the airport should run about US$8 (but you'll pay slightly more from the airport to the center).

BUS

Most parts of Mérida that you'll want to visit are within five or six blocks of the Plaza Grande and are thus accessible on foot. Given the slow speed of city traffic, particularly in the market areas, travel on foot is also the fastest way to get around.

City buses are cheap at US$0.40, but routes are confusing. Most start in suburban neighborhoods, meander through the city center and terminate in another distant suburban neighborhood. To travel between the Plaza Grande and the upscale neighborhoods to the north along Paseo de Montejo, catch the Ruta 10 at the corner of Calles 58 and 59, half a block east of the Parque Hidalgo, or catch a 'Tecnológico,' 'Hyatt' or 'Montejo' bus on Calle 60 and get out

at Av Colón. To return to the city center, catch any bus heading south on Paseo de Montejo that is displaying the destination sign 'Centro.'

TAXI

Taxis in Mérida are not metered. Rates are fixed, with an outrageous US$3 minimum fare, which will get you from the bus terminals to all downtown hotels. Most rides within city limits do not exceed US$5.50. Taxi stands can be found at most of the *barrio* parks, or call **Taximetro** (☎ 928-54-27); service is available 24 hours (dispatch fees are an extra US$1 to US$2).

SOUTH OF MÉRIDA
Hacienda Yaxcopoil

Hacienda Yaxcopoil (☎ 999-927-26-06; admission US$4; ☁ 8am-6pm Mon-Sat, 9am-1pm Sun) is on the west side of Highway 261, 33km southwest of central Mérida. A vast estate that grew and processed *henequén*, its numerous French Renaissance–style buildings have been restored and turned collectively into a museum of the 17th century. Frequent buses pass Yaxcopoil running between Mérida and Ticul.

SMALL WONDER

The Irish have leprechauns, Scandinavians have elves and Snow White has her dwarfs. In Mayan mythology the equivalent big-spirited, small-bodied inhabitants of the forest are called *aluxes* (a-LOOSH-es). These very clever, often mischievous little people are said to live in caves and make themselves seen only occasionally and usually to small children.

Aluxes hold an important position in Mayan legend and are believed to have the ability to travel between the human world and that of the spirits. Attributed with power for both assisting those who believe in them and wreaking havoc for those who don't, the Maya traditionally demonstrated their confidence in the *aluxes* by making offerings to the magical beings. Some farmers today – as their ancestors did for generations – leave gifts of food and drink to the *aluxes* in gratitude for the *aluxes'* help in aiding crops and bringing good luck to a family or community.

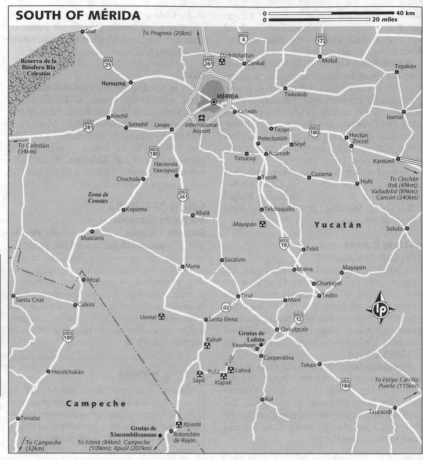

SOUTH OF MÉRIDA

Mayapán

The **Mayapán ruins** (admission US$3; ☼ 8am-5pm) are some 50km southeast of Mérida, on Yucatán state Highway 18. Though far less impressive than many Mayan sites, Mayapán is historically significant, its main attractions are clustered in a compact core, and visitors usually have the place to themselves.

Don't confuse the ruins of Mayapán with the Mayan village of the same name, some 40km southeast of the ruins, past the town of Teabo.

HISTORY

According to legend, Mayapán was supposedly founded by Kukulcán (Quetzalcóatl) in AD 1007. His dynasty, the Cocom, or-

ganized a confederation of city-states that included Uxmal, Chichén Itzá and many other notable cities. Despite their alliance, animosity arose between the Cocom of Mayapán and the Itzáes of Chichén Itzá during the late 12th century, and the Cocom stormed Chichén Itzá, forcing the Itzá rulers into exile. The Cocom dynasty emerged supreme in all of northern Yucatán.

Cocom supremacy lasted for almost 250 years, until the ruler of Uxmal, Ah Xupán Xiú, led a rebellion of the oppressed city-states and overthrew Cocom hegemony. The great capital of Mayapán was utterly destroyed and remained uninhabited ever after.

Struggles for power continued in the region until 1542, when Francisco de Montejo the Younger conquered T'hó and established Mérida. At that point the current lord of Maní and ruler of the Xiú people, Ah Kukum Xiú, proposed to Montejo a military alliance against the Cocom, his ancient rivals. Montejo accepted, and Xiú was baptized as a Christian, taking the name Francisco de Montejo Xiú. The Cocom were defeated and – too late – the Xiú rulers realized that they had signed the death warrant of Mayan independence.

THE SITE

The city of Mayapán was large, with a population estimated at 12,000; it covered 4 sq km, all surrounded by a great defensive wall. In the early 1950s and early '60s, archaeologists mapped over 3500 buildings, 20 *cenotes* and traces of the city wall. The late postclassic workmanship is inferior to that of the great age of Mayan art.

Among the structures that have been restored is the **Castillo de Kukulcán**, a climbable pyramid with fresco fragments around its base and, at its rear side, friezes depicting decapitated warriors. The **Templo Redondo** (Round Temple) is vaguely reminiscent of El Caracol at Chichén Itzá. Close by is Itzmal Chen, a *cenote* that was a major Mayan religious sanctuary. Excavation and restoration continue at the site.

GETTING THERE & AWAY

The Ruinas de Mayapán are just off Highway 18, a few kilometers southwest of the town of Telchaquillo. LUS runs 15 2nd-class buses between 5:30am and 8:00 pm from the Noreste terminal in Mérida (US$1.50, two hours) that will let you off near the entrance of the ruins.

Uxmal

Some visitors rank **Uxmal** (admission US$9 Mon-Sat, US$4 Sun; 🕑 8am-5pm), pronounced oosh-*mahl*, among the top Mayan archaeological sites. It certainly is one of the most harmonious and peaceful. Fascinating, well-preserved structures made of pink-hued limestone cover the wide area. Adding to its appeal is Uxmal's setting in the hilly Puuc region, which lent its name to the architectural patterns in this area. *Puuc* means 'hills,' and these, rising to about 100m, are the only ones in the northwest region of the otherwise flat peninsula.

HISTORY

Uxmal was an important city and its dominance extended to the nearby towns of Sayil, Kabah, Xlapak and Labná. Although Uxmal means 'Thrice Built' in Mayan, it was actually constructed five times.

That a sizable population flourished in this dry area is yet more testimony to the engineering skills of the Maya, who built a series of reservoirs and *chultunes* (cisterns) lined with lime mortar to catch and hold water during the dry season. First settled about AD 600, Uxmal was influenced by highland Mexico in its architecture, most likely through contact fostered by trade. This influence is reflected in the town's serpent imagery, phallic symbols and columns. The well-proportioned Puuc architecture, with its intricate, geometric mosaics sweeping across the upper parts of elongated façades, was strongly influenced by the slightly earlier Río Bec and Chenes styles.

The scarcity of water in the region meant that Chac-Mool, the rain god or sky serpent, was supreme in importance. His image is ubiquitous at the site in the form of stucco masks protruding from façades and cornices. There is much speculation as to why Uxmal was abandoned in about 900; drought conditions may have reached such proportions that the inhabitants had to relocate.

Rediscovered by archaeologists in the 19th century, Uxmal was first excavated in 1929 by Frans Blom. Although much has been restored, much has yet to be discovered.

INFORMATION

Parking is US$1 per car. The site is entered through the modern Unidad Uxmal building, which holds an air-conditioned restaurant, a small museum, shops selling souvenirs and crafts, an auditorium and bathrooms. Also here is Librería Dante, a bookstore that stocks an excellent selection of travel and archaeological guides and general-interest books about Mexico in English, Spanish, German and French; the imported books are very expensive.

The price of admission, if you retain the wristband-ticket, includes a 45-minute sound-and-light show, beginning at 8pm nightly in summer and 7pm in winter. It's in Spanish, but you can rent devices for listening to English, French, German or

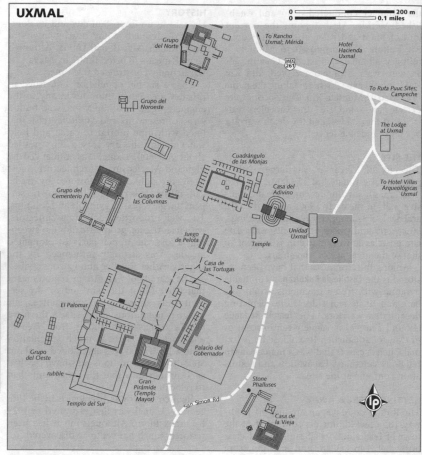

Italian translations (beamed via infrared) for US$2.75. Specify the language you need or it may not be broadcast. Cost for the show only is US$3.50, applicable toward the next day's site admission.

CASA DEL ADIVINO

This tall temple (the Magician's House), 39m high, was built on an oval base. The smoothly sloping sides have been restored; they date from the temple's fifth incarnation. The four earlier temples were covered in the rebuilding, except for the high doorway on the west side, which remains from the fourth temple. Decorated in elaborate Chenes style (which originated further south), the doorway proper forms the mouth of a gigantic

Chac-Mool mask. Climbing the structure is not allowed.

CUADRÁNGULO DE LAS MONJAS

The 74-room, sprawling Nuns' Quadrangle is west of the Casa del Adivino. Archaeologists guess variously that it was a military academy, royal school or palace complex. The long-nosed face of Chac-Mool appears everywhere on the façades of the four separate temples that form the quadrangle. The northern temple, grandest of the four, was built first, followed by the southern, then the eastern and then the western.

Several decorative elements on the façades show signs of Mexica, perhaps Totonac, influence. The feathered-serpent (Quetzalcóatl, or in Mayan, Kukulcán) motif along the top of the west temple's façade is one of these. Note also the stylized depictions of the *na* (Mayan thatched hut) over some of the doorways in the northern and southern buildings.

Passing through the corbeled arch in the middle of the south building of the quadrangle and continuing down the slope takes you through the **Juego de Pelota** (ball court). Turn left and head up the steep slope and stairs to the large terrace.

CASA DE LAS TORTUGAS

To the right at the top of the stairs is the House of the Turtles, which takes its name from the turtles carved on the cornice. The Maya associated turtles with the rain god, Chac-Mool. According to Mayan myth, when the people suffered from drought so did the turtles, and both prayed to Chac-Mool to send rain.

The frieze of short columns, or 'rolled mats,' that runs around the temple below the turtles is characteristic of the Puuc style. On the west side of the building a vault has collapsed, affording a good view of the corbeled arch that supported it.

PALACIO DEL GOBERNADOR

The Governor's Palace, with its magnificent façade nearly 100m long, has been called 'the finest structure at Uxmal and the culmination of the Puuc style' by Mayanist Michael D Coe. Buildings in Puuc style have walls filled with rubble, faced with cement and then covered in a thin veneer of limestone squares; the lower part of the façade is plain, the upper part festooned with stylized Chac-Mool faces and geometric designs, often latticelike or fretted. Other elements of Puuc style are decorated cornices, rows of half-columns (as in the House of the Turtles) and round columns in doorways (as in the palace at Sayil).

GRAN PIRÁMIDE

Though it's adjacent to the Governor's Palace, to reach the Great Pyramid without disobeying any signs you must retrace your route down the hillside and turn left before reaching the ball court.

The 32m-high pyramid has been restored only on its northern side. Archaeologists theorize that the quadrangle at its summit was largely destroyed in order to construct another pyramid above it. That work, for reasons unknown, was never completed. At the top are some stucco carvings of Chac-Mool, birds and flowers.

EL PALOMAR

West of the Great Pyramid sits a structure whose roofcomb is latticed with a pattern reminiscent of the Moorish pigeon houses built into walls in Spain and northern Africa – hence the building's name (the Dovecote, or Pigeon House). The nine honeycombed triangular 'belfries' sit on top of a building that was once part of a quadrangle. The base is so eroded that it is hard for archaeologists to guess its function.

CASA DE LA VIEJA

Off the southeast corner of the Palacio del Gobernador is a small complex, largely rubble, known as the Casa de la Vieja (Old Woman's House). In front of it is a small *palapa* sheltering several large phalluses carved from stone. Don't get any ideas; the signs here read 'Do Not Sit.'

SLEEPING & EATING

There is no town at Uxmal – only the archaeological site and several top-end hotels, so for cheap food you must head up or down the road a ways.

Camping Bungalows Sacbé (☎ 985-858-12-81, sacbebungalow@hotmail.com; tent sites per person US$3, dm US$6.50, d US$14-16; Ⓟ) These quiet, well-kept bungalows and campground are on the south side of the village of Santa Elena, 16km southeast of Uxmal and 8km north of Kabah. 'Sacbe' offers camping in a park-like setting, seven simple but pleasant and clean bungalows with spotless baths and a four-bed dorm with separate bath. Sacbé is convenient to the Ruta Puuc ruins, and the friendly owners speak French, English and Spanish, and serve good, cheap breakfasts. To get here, catch a southbound bus from Uxmal and ask the driver to let you off at the *campo de portivo* (sports field) beyond the Santa Elena turnoff.

B&B The Flycatcher Inn (www.mexonline.com /flycatcherinn.htm; d US$40; Ⓟ) Situated on the southeastern edge of Santa Elena, this lovely B&B offers three spacious, clean and comfortable rooms. A tropical breakfast is included in the price.

Rancho Uxmal (☎ 997-972-62-54; d US$25; P   ◓)
The friendly hotel has 23 basic, serviceable
guestrooms with good ventilation, a swimming pool and a shaded, welcoming restaurant serving three meals.

Hotel Villas Arqueológicas Uxmal (☎ 997-976-
20-20, 800-258-2633 in the US, 801 80 28 03 in France;
villauxm@sureste.com; d US$63; P   ✕   ◓) This is
an attractive Club Med-run hotel with a
swimming pool, tennis courts, a restaurant
and air-conditioned guestrooms, not far
from the ruins entrance.

The Lodge at Uxmal (☎ 997-976-21-02, 800-235-
4079 in the US; www.mayaland.com; d from US$150; P
 ✕   ◓) Mayaland Resorts' lodge, just opposite the entrance to the archaeological site,
is Uxmal's newest, most luxurious hotel.
There are two pools and a restaurant/bar.

Hotel Hacienda Uxmal (☎ 997-976-20-12, 800-235-
4079 in the US; www.mayaland.com; d US$40, with air-con
US$100; P   ✕   ◓) This is another Mayaland
Resort, 500m from the ruins and across the
highway. It originally housed the archaeologists who explored and restored Uxmal.
Wide, tiled verandas, high ceilings and a
beautiful swimming pool make this an exceptionally comfortable place to stay. The
fan-cooled rooms are in a more modest
annex.

Restaurant El Chac-Mool (☎ 996-20-25; mains
US$4) At the south entrance of Santa Elena,
this friendly place serves generous help-
ings of Yucatecan food with vegetarian
alternatives.

GETTING THERE & AWAY
Uxmal is 78km (1½ hours) from Mérida.
The inland route between Mérida and Campeche passes Uxmal, and most buses coming
from either city will drop you there, or at
Kabah or the Ruta Puuc turnoff. When you
want to leave, though, passing buses may be
full (especially Saturday and Monday).

ATS buses depart Mérida's Terminal de
Segunda Clase at 8am daily on a whirlwind
excursion (US$10) to the Ruta Puuc sites,
Kabah and Uxmal, heading back from Uxmal's parking lot at 2:30pm. This 'tour' is
transportation only; you pay all other costs.
The time spent at each site is enough to get
only a nodding acquaintance, though some
say the two hours at Uxmal is sufficient, if
barely.

Organized tours of Uxmal and other sites
can be booked in Mérida (p862).

If you're going from Uxmal to Ticul, first
take a northbound bus to Muna (US$0.50,
20 minutes) then catch one of the frequent buses from there to Ticul (US$0.80,
30 minutes).

Kabah

After Uxmal, Kabah (AD 750–950) was the
most important city in the region. The ruins
of **Kabah** (admission US$3; ☽ 8am-5pm), just over
23km southeast of Uxmal, are right astride
Highway 261. The guard shack/souvenir
shop (selling snacks and cold drinks) and
the bulk of the restored ruins are on the east
side of the highway.

On entering, head to your right to climb
the stairs of the structure closest to the
highway, **El Palacio de los Mascarones** (Palace
of Masks). The façade is an amazing sight,
covered in nearly 300 masks of Chac-Mool,
the rain god or sky serpent. Most of their
huge curling noses are broken off; the best
intact beak is at the building's south end.
These curled up noses may have given the
palace its modern Mayan name, Codz Pop
(Rolled Mat).

Once you're up to your ears in noses,
head around back to check out the two
restored **atlantes** (an atlas – plural 'atlantes' – is a male figure used as a supporting
column). These are especially interesting, as they're among the very few three-
dimensional human figures you'll see at a
Mayan site. One is headless and the other
wears a jaguar mask atop his head. A third

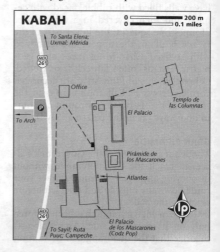

KABAH

0 ———— 200 m
0 ———— 0.1 miles

To Santa Elena;
Uxmal; Mérida

MEX
261

Office

P

To Arch

El Palacio

Templo de
las Columnas

Pirámide de
los Mascarones

Atlantes

MEX
261

To Sayil; Ruta
Puuc; Campeche

El Palacio
de los Mascarones
(Codz Pop)

atlas stands by the office near the entrance; the two others that were discovered here are in museums.

Descend the steps near the atlantes and turn left, passing the small **Pirámide de los Mascarones**, to reach the plaza containing **El Palacio**. The Palace's broad façade has several doorways, two of which have a column in the center. These columned doorways and the groups of decorative *columnillas* (little columns) on the upper part of the façade are characteristics of the Puuc architectural style.

Steps on the north side of El Palacio's plaza put you on a path leading a couple of hundred meters through the jungle to the **Templo de las Columnas**. This building has more rows of decorative columns on the upper part of its façade.

West of El Palacio, across the highway, a path leads up the slope and passes to the south of a high mound of stones that was once the **Gran Pirámide** (Great Pyramid). The path curves to the right and comes to a large restored **monumental arch**. It's said that the *sacbé* (cobbled and elevated ceremonial road) leading from here goes through the jungle all the way to Uxmal, terminating at a smaller arch; in the other direction it goes to Labná. Once, all of the Yucatán Peninsula was connected by these marvelous 'white roads' of rough limestone.

At present, nothing of the *sacbés* is visible, and the rest of the area west of the highway is a maze of unmarked, overgrown paths leading off into the jungle.

There's good, affordable lodging about 8km north of Kabah at **Camping Bungalows Sacbé** (p873) and **B&B The Flycatcher Inn** (p873).

Kabah is 101km from Mérida, a ride of about two hours (p874). Kabah gets particularly short shrift from the ATS excursion bus; about 25 minutes.

Buses will usually make flag stops at the entrance to the ruins. Many visitors come to Kabah by private car and may be willing to give you a lift, either back to Mérida or southward on the Ruta Puuc.

Ruta Puuc

Just 5km south of Kabah on Highway 261, a road branches off to the east and winds past the ruins of Sayil, Xlapak and Labná, ending at the Grutas de Loltún. This is the Ruta Puuc, and its sites offer some marvelous architectural detail and a deeper acquaintance with the Puuc Mayan civilization, which flourished roughly between AD 750 and 950.

See p874 for details on the ATS excursion bus, the only regularly scheduled public transport on the route. During the busy winter season it's usually possible to hitch rides from one site to the next; however, the best way year-round to appreciate the sites is by rented car.

SAYIL

The ruins of **Sayil** (admission US$3; ☾ 8am-5pm) are 4.5km from the junction of the Puuc Route with Highway 261.

Sayil is best known for **El Palacio**, the huge three-tiered building with a façade some 85m long-reminiscent of the Minoan palace on Crete. The distinctive columns of Puuc architecture are used here over and over, as supports for the lintels, as decoration between doorways and as a frieze above them, alternating with huge stylized Chac-Mool masks and 'descending gods.' Ascending the Palacio beyond its first level is not allowed.

Taking the path south from the palace for about 400m and bearing left, you come to the temple named **El Mirador**, whose roosterlike roofcomb was once painted a bright red. About 100m beyond El Mirador, beneath a protective *palapa*, is a stela bearing the relief of a fertility god with an enormous phallus, now badly weathered.

XLAPAK

From the entrance gate at Sayil, it's 6km east to the entrance gate at **Xlapak** (admission US$2.50; ☾ 8am-5pm), pronounced shla-*pak*. The name means 'Old Walls' in Mayan and was a general term among local people for ancient ruins.

If you're going to skip any of the Ruta Puuc sites, Xlapak should be it. The ornate **palace** at Xlapak is smaller than those at Kabah and Sayil, measuring only about 20m in length. It's decorated with the inevitable Chac-Mool masks, columns and colonnettes and fretted geometric latticework of the Puuc style. The building is slightly askew, looking as though it doesn't know which way to fall. There's not much else here.

LABNÁ

If Xlapak is the skippable Puuc site, **Labná** (admission US$3; 8am-5pm) is the one not to miss. Its setting on a flat, open area is unique in the region, and if no one has been through before you for a while, at each doorway you approach you're likely to startle groups of long-tailed mot-mots (clock birds) into flight. Between the birds and the vegetation growing atop the Palacio, you can almost imagine yourself one of the first people to see the site in centuries.

Archaeologists believe that at one point in the 9th century, some 3000 Maya lived at Labná. To support such numbers in these arid hills, water was collected in *chultunes*. At Labná's peak there were some 60 *chultunes* in and around the city; several are still visible. From the entrance gate at Xlapak, it's 3.5km east to the gate at Labná.

El Palacio, the first building you come to at Labná is one of the longest in the Puuc region, and much of its interesting decorative carving is in good shape. On the west corner of the main structure's façade, straight in from the big tree near the center of the complex, is a serpent's head with a human face peering out from between its jaws, the symbol of the planet Venus. Toward the hill from this is an impressive Chac-Mool mask, and nearby is the lower half of a human figure (possibly a ballplayer) in loincloth and leggings.

The lower level has several more well-preserved Chac-Mool masks, and the upper level contains a large *chultún* that still holds water. The view of the site and the hills beyond from there is impressive.

From the palace a limestone-paved sacbé leads to **El Arco Labná**, which is best known for its magnificent arch, once part of a building that separated two quadrangular court-yards. It now appears to be a gate joining two small plazas. The corbeled structure, 3m wide and 6m high, is well preserved, and the reliefs decorating its upper façade are exuberantly Puuc in style.

Flanking the west side of the arch are carved *na* with multitiered roofs. Also on these walls, the remains of the building that adjoined the arch, are lattice patterns atop a serpentine design. Archaeologists believe a high roofcomb once sat over the fine arch and its flanking rooms.

Standing on the opposite side of the arch and separated from it by the sacbé is a pyramid known as **El Mirador**, topped by a temple. The pyramid itself is largely stone rubble. The temple, with its 5m-high roof-comb, is well positioned to be a lookout, thus its name.

Grutas de Loltún

North and east of Labná 15km, an over-grown sign points out the left turn to the Grutas de Loltún, 5km further northeast. The road passes through lush orchards and some banana and palm groves, a refreshing sight in this dry region.

The **Loltún Caverns** (admission US$5.25; 9am-5pm), one of the largest and most interest-ing cave systems on the Yucatán Peninsula, provided a treasure trove of data for ar-chaeologists. Carbon dating of artifacts found here reveals that humans used the caves 2500 years ago. Chest-high murals of hands, faces, animals and geometric motifs were apparent as recently as 20 years ago, but so many people have touched them that scarcely a trace remains. Today, visitors to the illuminated caves see mostly natural limestone formations, some of which are quite lovely.

To explore the labyrinth, you must take a scheduled guided tour at 9:30am, 11am, 12:30pm, 2pm, 3pm or 4pm, but they may depart early if enough people are waiting, or switch languages if the group warrants it. The services of the English-speaking guides are included in the admission price.

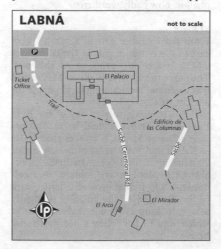

LABNÁ not to scale

P

Ticket Office

Trail

El Palacio

Sacbé (Ceremonial Rd)

Edificio de las Columnas

Sacbé

El Arco

El Mirador

GETTING THERE & AWAY

At the time of research, LUS had temporarily discontinued its service from the Noreste terminal in Mérida to the Grutas. Other buses run frequently between Mérida and Oxkutzcab (pronounced osh-kootz-kahb) via Ticul. Loltún is 7km southwest of Oxkutzcab, and there is usually some transportation along the road. *Camionetas* (pickups) and *camiones* (trucks) charge around US$1 for a ride. A taxi from Oxkutzcab may charge US$6 or so, one-way.

If you're driving from Loltún to Labná, turn right out of the Loltún parking lot and take the next road on the right, which passes Restaurant El Guerrero's driveway. Do not take the road marked for Xul. After 5km turn right at the T-intersection to join the Puuc Route west.

Ticul

☎ 997 / pop 27,000

Ticul, 30km east of Uxmal and 14km northwest of Oxkutzcab, is the largest town in this ruin-rich region. It has decent hotels and restaurants and good transportation. Although there is no public transportation to the Puuc Route from Ticul, it is possible to stay the night here and take an early morning bus to Muna, arriving there in time to catch a tour bus to the Puuc Route ruins (p878). Ticul is also a center for fine *huipil* weaving, and ceramics made here from the local red clay are renowned throughout the Yucatán Peninsula.

Because of the number of Mayan ruins in the vicinity from which to steal building blocks and the number of Maya in the area needing conversion to Christianity, Franciscan friars built many churches in the region that is now southern Yucatán state. Among them is Ticul's **Iglesia de San Antonio de Padua**, construction of which dates from the late 16th century. Although looted on several occasions, the church has some original touches, among them the stone statues of friars in primitive style flanking the side entrances and a Black Christ altarpiece ringed by crude medallions.

Saturday mornings in Ticul are picturesque: Calle 23 in the vicinity of the public market is closed to motorized traffic, and the street fills with three-wheeled cycles transporting shoppers between the market and their homes.

ORIENTATION & INFORMATION

Ticul's main street is Calle 23, sometimes called the Calle Principal, going from the highway northeast past the market and the town's best restaurants to the main plaza, or Plaza Mayor. A post office faces the plaza, as does a bank with ATM, and the bus terminal is less than 100m away. Catercorner to the Plaza Mayor is the recently built **Plaza de la Cultura**, which is all cement and stone but nevertheless an agreeable place to take the evening breeze, enjoy the view of the church and greet passing townspeople.

YUCATÁN PENINSULA

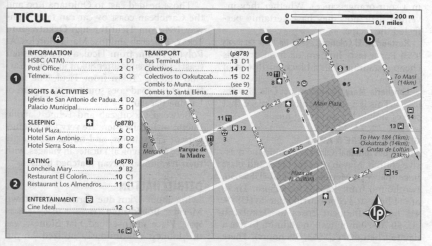

TICUL

0 ———— 200 m
0 ———— 0.1 miles

INFORMATION	
HSBC (ATM)	1 D1
Post Office	2 C1
Telmex	3 C2

SIGHTS & ACTIVITIES	
Iglesia de San Antonio de Padua	4 D2
Palacio Municipal	5 D1

SLEEPING 🏠	(p878)
Hotel Plaza	6 C1
Hotel San Antonio	7 D2
Hotel Sierra Sosa	8 C1

EATING 🍴	(p878)
Lonchería Mary	9 B2
Restaurant El Colorín	10 C1
Restaurant Los Almendros	11 C1

ENTERTAINMENT 🎭	
Cine Ideal	12 C1

TRANSPORT	(p878)
Bus Terminal	13 D1
Colectivos	14 D1
Colectivos to Oxkutzcab	15 D2
Combis to Muna	(see 9)
Combis to Santa Elena	16 B2

Calle 21
Calle 23
Main Plaza
Calle 25
El Mercado
Parque de la Madre
Plaza de la Cultura
To Maní (14km)
To Hwy 184 (1km); Oxkutzcab (14km); Grutas de Loltún (23km)

SLEEPING

Hotel San Antonio (☎ 927-19-83; cnr Calles 25A & 26; s/d US$24/30; P 🐾) The rooms in this new-kid-on-the-block hotel have comfortable beds, good air-con, TVs and telephones. The restaurant here is decent too.

Hotel Plaza (☎ 972-04-84; www.hotelplazayucatan .com; cnr Calles 23 & 26; r with fan/air-con US$30/35; P 🐾) This is considered the nicest hotel in town, although the newer Hotel San Antonio is better value. Rooms are very comfortable with good beds and bathrooms, and a large mango tree shades the courtyard. Air-conditioned rooms have telephone and cable TV.

Hotel Sierra Sosa (☎ 972-00-08; Calle 26 No 199A; s/d with fan US$14/18, with air-con US$19/22; 🐾) This clean and friendly hotel is just northwest of the plaza. Rooms in the back tend to be a little dark.

EATING

Ticul's lively market, **El Mercado** (Calle 28A btwn Calles 21 & 23) provides all the ingredients for picnics and snacks. It also has lots of those wonderful eateries where the food is good, the portions generous and the prices low.

Restaurant Los Almendros (Calle 23 No 207 btwn Calles 26A & 28; mains US$5-8) The original Almendros (now with fancier branches in Mérida and Cancún) specializes in hearty Yucatecan food. The original chefs at this restaurant are credited with having invented the now ever-favorite Yucatecan specialty *poc-chuc* (pork with tomatoes and onions in a sour-orange sauce). Whether they invented it or not, they have certainly perfected the recipe.

Restaurant El Colorín (Calle 26 No 199B; set meals US$3) For a tasty homemade meal, try this cheap restaurant, half a block northwest of the plaza.

Lonchería Mary (Calle 23 east of Calle 28; mains US$3-4) This is a clean, family-run place that serves simple but satisfying meals.

GETTING THERE & AWAY

Ticul's **bus terminal** (Calle 24) is behind the massive church. Mayab runs frequent 2nd-class buses between Mérida and Ticul (US$3.50, two hours) from 4:30am to 9:45pm. There are 11 buses to Felipe Carrillo Puerto (US$9, 4½ hours), frequent buses to Oxkutzcab (US$0.70, 20 minutes), in addition to five a day to Chetumal (US$13, 6½ hours). There

are also seven Mayab buses to Cancún each day (US$17, six hours), three of which also serve Tulum (US$12, eight hours) and Playa del Carmen (US$15, seven hours). **Super Expresso** has a less frequent 1st-class service to some of these destinations.

Colectivos (vans) depart from the intersection of Calles 24 and 25 between 5am and 7pm and head directly to Mérida's Parque de San Juan (US$1, 1½ hours). *Colectivos* for Oxkutzcab (US$0.80, 30 minutes) leave from Calle 25A on the south side of the church between 7am and 8:30pm.

Combis (vans or cars) going to Santa Elena (US$0.80, 20 minutes), the village between Uxmal and Kabah, depart from Calle 30 just south of Calle 25 between 6:15am and 7:45pm. They take Highway 02 and drop you to catch another bus northwest to Uxmal (15km) or south to Kabah (3.5km). You can also take a combi or bus to Muna (see later) on Highway 261 and another south to Uxmal (16km).

Ruta Puuc-bound travelers can catch one of the early-morning buses from Ticul to Muna and pick up the ATS tour bus (US$5) for Labná, Sayil, Xlapak, Kabah and Uxmal at 9am on its way from Mérida. It returns to Muna at 3pm. Any of the buses leaving Ticul between 6am and 8am for Muna (US$1) will get you there in time to catch the Ruta Puuc bus (all 2nd-class Mérida-bound buses stop in Muna). *Combis* for Muna (US$1) leave from in front of Lonchería Mary on Calle 23 near Calle 28.

Those headed east to Quintana Roo and the Caribbean coast by car can take Highway 184 from Ticul through Oxkutzcab to Tekax, Tzucacab and José María Morelos. At Polyuc, 130km from Ticul, a road turns left (east), which ends after 80km in Felipe Carrillo Puerto, 210km from Ticul. The right fork of the road goes south to the region of Laguna Bacalar.

Between Oxkutzcab and Felipe Carrillo Puerto or Bacalar there are very few restaurants or gas stations, and no hotels. Mostly you see small, typical Yucatecan villages, with their traditional Mayan thatched houses.

DZIBILCHALTÚN

Lying about 17km due north of downtown Mérida, **Dzibilchaltún** (admission US$6; 🕐 8am-5pm), Place of Inscribed Flat Stones, was the longest continuously utilized Mayan administrative and ceremonial city, serving the Maya from 1500 BC or earlier until the European conquest in the 1540s. At the height of its greatness, Dzibilchaltún covered 15 sq km. Some 800 structures were mapped by archaeologists in the 1960s; few of these have been excavated and restored.

Enter the site along a nature trail that terminates at the modern, air-conditioned **Museo del Pueblo Maya** (☉ 8am-4pm Tue-Sun), featuring artifacts from throughout the Mayan regions of Mexico, including some superb colonial-era religious carvings and other pieces. Exhibits explaining Mayan daily life and beliefs from ancient times until the present are labeled in Spanish and English. Beyond the museum, a path leads to the central plaza, where you will find an open chapel that dates from early Spanish times (1590–1600).

The **Templo de las Siete Muñecas** (Temple of the Seven Dolls), which got its name from seven grotesque dolls discovered here during excavations, is a 1km walk from the central plaza. It is most unimpressive but for its precise astronomical orientation: the rising and setting sun of the equinoxes 'lights up' the temple's windows and doors, making them blaze like beacons and signaling this important turning point in the year.

The **Cenote Xlacah**, now a public swimming pool, is more than 40m deep. In 1958 a National Geographic Society diving expedition recovered more than 30,000 Mayan artifacts, many of ritual significance, from the *cenote*. The most interesting of these are now on display in the site's museum. South of the *cenote* is **Estructura 44**, at 130m one of the longest Mayan structures in existence.

Parking costs US$1. Minibuses and *colectivo* taxis depart frequently from Mérida's Parque de San Juan, on Calle 69 between Calles 62 and 64, for the village of Dzibilchaltún Ruinas (US$0.80, 30 minutes), only a little over 1km from the museum.

PROGRESO

☎ 969 / pop 46,000

If Mérida's heat has you dying for a quick beach fix, or you want to see the longest wharf (7km) in Mexico, head to Progreso (also known as Puerto Progreso). Otherwise there's little reason to visit this dual-purpose port-resort town. The beach is fine, well groomed and long, but it's nearly shadeless and is dominated by the view of the wharf, giving it a rather industrial feel. Winds hit here full force off the Gulf in the afternoon and can blow well into the night. As with other Gulf beaches, the water is murky; visibility even on calm days rarely exceeds 5m. None of this stops *meridanos* from coming in droves on weekends, especially in the summer months. Even on spring weekdays it can be difficult to find a room with a view.

Progreso's street grid confusingly employs two different numbering systems 50 numbers apart. The city center's streets are numbered in the 60s (10s), 70s (20s) and 80s (30s). This text uses the high numbers. Even-numbered streets run east–west and decrease by twos eastward; odd ones decrease by twos northward. The **bus terminal** (Calle 79) west of Calle 82, a block north (toward the water) from the main plaza. It's six short blocks from the plaza on Calle 80 to the waterfront Malecón (Calle 69) and *muelle* (wharf); along the way are two banks, one with an ATM.

Sleeping & Eating

All hotels and restaurants listed are no more than a total of 11 blocks north and east of the bus station.

Casa Quixote (☎ 935-29-09; www.casaquixote.com; Calle 23 btwn Calles 48 & 50; r US$40-80; P ⊠ ⊠) It may be worth a trip to Progreso just to stay here. Once an aristocrat's summer home, this elegant yellow house a half a block from the beach is now a charming B&B. The Texan owners cook up healthy breakfasts (included) and invite you – and nonguests too – to their Saturday night barbeque.

Tropical Suites (☎ 935-12-63; cnr malecón & Calle 70; d with fan/air-con US$35/40; ⊠) This seaside hotel enjoys an excellent location and a certain dilapidated charm. There are 21 very simple but tidy and comfortable rooms, some with sea views.

Hotel Real del Mar (☎ 935-07-98; d with fan/air-con US$25/40; ⊠) Across the street from Tropical Suites, this place features 13 fairly worn but comfortable rooms with various configurations of beds and views. Wheelchair-accessible rooms available.

Restaurant Los Pelícanos (cnr malecón & Calle 70; mains US$5-15) Part of the Hotel Real del Mar, this restaurant has a *palapa*-topped terrace, sea views, a good menu and moderate prices. The grilled fish entrees are especially generous and tasty.

Le Saint Bonnet (☎ 935-22-99; malecón at Calle 78; mains US$5-8) This is where locals go for seafood. The fish is fresh and inexpensive.

Restaurant El Cordobes (Calle 80 & 81; mains US$4-8) On the plaza, this restaurant is housed in a 100-year-old building with lots of character. The food is decidedly Yucatecan and decidedly good.

Getting There & Away

Progreso is 33km due north of Mérida along a fast four-lane highway that's basically a continuation of the Paseo de Montejo. If you're driving, head north on the Paseo and follow signs for Progreso. For bus information see p867.

CELESTÚN

☎ 988 / pop 6200

Celestún is in the middle of a wildlife sanctuary abounding in resident and migratory waterfowl, with flamingos as the star attraction. It makes a good beach-and-bird day trip from Mérida, and it's also a great place to kick back and do nothing for a few days. Fishing boats dot the white-sand beach that stretches to the north for kilometers. Afternoon breezes cool the town on most days, though the winds can kick up sand and roil the sea, making the already none-too-clear water unpleasant for swimming.

Celestún is sheltered by the peninsula's southward curve, resulting in an abundance of marine life. It's a fine place to watch the sun set into the sea, and if you are from a west coast anywhere you'll feel perfectly oriented. If you're not from a west coast, all you need to know is that Calle 11 is the road into town (due west from Mérida), ending at Calle 12, the dirt road paralleling the beach along which lie most of the restaurants and hotels.

Flamingo Tours

The Reserva de la Biósfera Ría Celestún's 591 sq km are home to a huge variety of animal life, including a large flamingo colony.

Given the winds, the best time to see birds is in the morning, though from 4pm onward they tend to concentrate in one area after the day's feeding, which can make for good viewing. There are two places to hire a boat for bird-watching: from the bridge on the highway into town (about 1.5km from the beach), and from the beach itself.

The best months to see the flamingos are from March to September. Tours from the beach last 2½ to three hours and begin with a ride south along the coast for several kilometers, during which you can expect to see egrets, herons, cormorants, sandpipers and many other species of bird. The boat then turns into the mouth of the *ría* (estuary) and passes through a 'petrified forest,' where tall coastal trees once belonging to a freshwater ecosystem were killed by saltwater intrusion long ago and remain standing, hard as rock.

Continuing up the *ría* takes you under the highway bridge where the other tours begin and beyond which are the flamingos. Depending on the tide, the hour and the season, you may see hundreds or thousands of the colorful birds. Don't encourage your captain to approach them too closely; a startled flock taking wing can result in injuries and deaths (for the birds). In addition to taking you to the flamingos, the captain will wend through a 200m-long mangrove tunnel and go to one or both (as time and inclination allow) of the freshwater *cenotes* welling into the saltwater of the estuary, where you can take a refreshing dip.

Asking price for this type of tour is US$100 per boatload (up to six passengers). Boats depart from several beachside spots, including from outside Restaurant Celestún, at the foot of Calle 11. The restaurant's beachfront *palapa* is a pleasant place to wait for a group to accumulate.

Tours from the bridge, where there is a parking lot, ticket booth and a place to wait for fellow passengers, are cheaper. For US$40 per boat (again up to six passengers) plus US$2 per passenger, you get the latter part of the tour described earlier: flamingos, mangrove tunnel and spring. It's also possible to tour from the bridge south to the 'petrified forest' and back (also US$40), or combine the two (each lasts about 1¼ hours).

With either operation, bridge or beach, your captain may or may not speak English. English-speaking guides can be hired at the bridge; this may reduce the maximum possible number of passengers. Bring snacks, water and sunscreen for the longer tours, and cash for any of them. There is no bank in town, and neither credit cards nor traveler's checks are accepted by the tour operators.

Sleeping

Except for the first listing below, Celestún's hotels are all on Calle 12, within a short walk of one another. Try to book ahead if you want a sea view, especially Saturday and Sunday.

Eco-Paraíso Xixim (☎ 916-21-00; www.mexonline.com/eco-paraiso.htm; d US$175; P 🖘) This remote eco-resort is at the end of a dirt road 9km north of Celestún. Fifteen individual, lovely *palapas* are nestled between miniature coconut palms along a private 3-mile stretch of virgin beach. It could be considered just another luxury joint, but its eco-centric policies set it apart. All gray and black water is recycled and most of the energy is derived from solar panels. The surrounding natural environment is protected and respected, which allows turtles to safely breed here. Amenities include a very good restaurant, bar, pool, and guided ecotours. Check the website for less expensive, all-inclusive packages.

Eco Hotel Flamingos Playa (☎ 999-929-57-08 in Mérida; Calle 12; d US$28; 🖭 🖵 🖘) About three blocks north of Calle 11, the recently built Flamingos has decent rooms with air-con, fan, TV and purified water. There's a small beachside pool, a restaurant/bar, and Internet facilities.

Ria Celestún Hostel (☎ 916-21-70; www.home casa.net; cnr Calles 12 & 13; dm US$7; 🖵) This is a bright, clean, airy hostel. Guests share a full kitchen and a comfortable communal area with books, games and a TV. Internet access is available too, as are cheap bike rentals. The friendly owner and native to Celestún, Marcos, can arrange inexpensive tours of the area.

Hotel María del Carmen (☎ 916-21-70; Calle 12; d with fan/air-con US$22/30; 🖭) South of Calle 11, this hotel has 14 clean and pleasant beachfront rooms. Those on the upper floors have balconies facing the sea. The hotel serves breakfast in its little beachfront café.

Eating & Drinking

Celestún's specialties are crab, octopus and, of course, fresh fish. Service and decor vary from restaurant to restaurant, but the menus and prices are all very similar. Many restaurants have outdoor seating on the beach.

El Lobo (southwest edge of the plaza; breakfast & mains US$4-7) This Dutch-owned establishment serves especially good espresso drinks. It's also a good breakfast spot and a fine place for a meal of pizza or pasta.

La Playita (on the beach, just past the foot of Calle 11; mains US$5-7) This friendly restaurant offers large portions of fresh seafood. Try the *pescado en mojo de ajo* (grilled fish with butter and garlic sauce). It's delicious.

Restaurante Chivirico (cnr Calles 11 & 12; mains US$5-7) Come here for good food and a good laugh. English translations on the menu include 'fish to I wet of garlic' (fresh fish with garlic sauce), which is excellent. So is the crab salad.

Getting There & Away

Buses from Mérida head for Celestún (US$3.75, two hours) 15 times daily between 5am and 8pm from the Terminal Noreste (p868). The route terminates at Celestún's plaza, a block inland from Calle 12. Returning to Mérida, buses run from 5am to 8pm.

Nómadas Youth Hostel (p862) books day trips to see the flamingos for around US$40, leaving Mérida at 9am and returning at 5pm. They include transportation, guide, a boat tour and lunch.

By car from Mérida, the best route to Celestún is via the road out of Umán.

IZAMAL
☎ 988 / pop 14,500

In ancient times, Izamal was a center for the worship of the supreme Mayan god, Itzamná, and the sun god, Kinich-Kakmó. A dozen temple pyramids were devoted to these or other gods. It was probably these bold expressions of Mayan religiosity that inspired the Spaniards to build the enormous Franciscan monastery that stands today at the heart of this town.

Just under 70km east of Mérida, Izamal is a quiet, colonial gem of a town, nicknamed La Ciudad Amarilla (the Yellow City) for the yellow paint that brightens the walls of most buildings. It is easily explored on foot and makes a great day trip from Mérida.

Sights

When the Spaniards conquered Izamal, they destroyed the major Mayan temple, the Ppapp-Hol-Chac pyramid, and in 1533 began to build from its stones one of the first monasteries in the Western Hemisphere. Work on **Convento de San Antonio de Padua** (admission free; ✿ 6am-8pm) was finished in 1561. Under the monastery's arcades, look for building stones with an unmistakable mazelike design; these were clearly taken from the earlier Mayan temple.

The monastery's principal church is the **Santuario de la Virgen de Izamal**, approached by a ramp from the main square. The ramp leads into the **Atrium**, a huge arcaded courtyard in which the fiesta of the Virgin of Izamal takes place each August 15.

At some point, the 16th-century **frescoes** beside the entrance of the sanctuary were completely painted over. For years they lay concealed under a thin layer of whitewash until a maintenance worker who was cleaning the walls discovered them. Fire, started by a fallen candle, destroyed the church's original altarpiece. Its replacement, impressively gilded, was built in the 1940s. In the niches at the stations of the cross are some superb small figures.

In the small courtyard to the left of the church, look up and toward the Atrium to see the original sundial projecting from the roof's edge.

The best time to visit is in the morning, as the church is occasionally closed during the afternoon siesta.

Three of the town's original 12 Mayan **pyramids** have been partially restored so far. The largest is the enormous Kinich-Kakmó, three blocks north of the monastery. You can climb it for free.

Sleeping & Eating

Macan-Ché B&B (☎ 954-02-87; www.macanche.com; Calle 22 No 305; d US$28-55; 🐾) About three long blocks east of the monastery, this charming B&B has a cluster of cottages in a jungle setting, with 12 pretty rooms in all. The most expensive has air-con and a kitchenette. Rates include a big breakfast.

Hotel Canto (d US$15) Directly in front of the monestary, the Canto's location and price make it good value; however, the rooms, though tidy and colorfully painted, are a little on the musty side.

Restaurant Kinich-Kakmó (☎ 954-08-89; Calle 27 btwn Calles 28 & 30; mains US$4-8) This restaurant is casual and extremely friendly, offering fan-cooled patio dining beside a garden. It specializes in traditional Yucatecan food, and you can have an absolute feast for less than US$8.

Getting There & Away

Oriente operates frequent buses between Mérida and Izamal (US$2.75, 1½ hrs) from the 2nd-class terminal. There are buses from

---

DEEP MYSTERY

In a cataclysmic collision 65 million years ago, a huge meteor struck the area that is now the Yucatán Peninsula, leaving a 284km-wide crater on the land's surface. Millions of years later cracks formed just below the limestone surface of the crater's perimeter and rainwater began filling the cavities that these fissures created. Eventually the surface layer around the underground chambers began to erode and crumble, revealing the intricate vascular system of underground rivers and *cenotes* that lay beneath.

According to Mayan cosmology there are three levels of existence: heaven (which itself has several strata), earth and the nine-tiered underworld: Xibalba. The Maya viewed *cenotes* as entranceways into the after-worlds and they believed that anyone who was sacrificed to the *cenotes* as an offering to the gods would avoid Xibalba and go directly to heaven. (Direct access to heaven was also given to women who died in childbirth and soldiers killed in battle.)

In 2002 National Institute of Anthropology and History (INAH) in Mexico City began a six-year study of some of the Yucatán's nearly 3000 *cenotes*. The marine anthropologists are finding that not only subjects of sacrifice (usually virgins or captured enemy warriors) were thrown into the *cenotes'* depths but that as a sendoff to the other worlds, many dead – from the regal in full funerary finery to commoners – were also deposited in the watery graves of *cenotes*.

Today as many as 10,000 people a year visit the region's *cenotes* to swim, snorkel and dive. Anthropologists hope that so much activity in the *cenotes* won't disturb the evidence that may lay many meters below the water's crystalline surface.

Valladolid (US$3, two hours) as well. Coming from Chichén Itzá you must change buses at Hóctun. Izamal's bus terminal is just one block west of the monastery.

Other services from Izamal include buses to Tizimín (US$5, 2½ hrs) and Cancún (US$9, six hours).

Driving by car from the west, turn north at Hóctun to reach Izamal; from the east, turn north at Kantunil.

CHICHÉN ITZÁ

The most famous and best restored of the Yucatán Peninsula's Mayan sites, **Chichén Itzá** (Mouth of the Well of the Itzáes; admission US$9 Mon-Sat, US$4 Sun & hols; ☻ 8am-5:30 daily winter, 8am-6pm daily summer) will awe even the most jaded visitor. Many mysteries of the Mayan astronomical calendar are made clear when one understands the design of the 'time temples' here. Other than a few minor passageways, El Castillo is now the only structure at the site you're allowed to climb or enter.

At the vernal and autumnal equinoxes (20-21 March and 21-22 September), the morning and afternoon sun produces a light-and-shadow illusion of the serpent ascending or descending the side of El Castillo's staircase. Chichén is mobbed on these dates, however, making it difficult to get close enough to see, and after the spectacle, parts of the site are sometimes closed to the public. The illusion is almost as good in the week preceding and following each equinox, and is re-created nightly in the sound-and-light show year-round.

Heat, humidity and crowds can be fierce; try to spend the night nearby and do your exploration of the site (especially climbing El Castillo) either early in the morning or late in the afternoon.

History

Most archaeologists agree that the first major settlement at Chichén Itzá, during the late classic period, was pure Mayan. In about the 9th century, the city was largely abandoned for reasons unknown. It was resettled around the late 10th century, and Mayanists believe that shortly thereafter it was invaded by the Toltecs, who had migrated from their central highlands capital of Tula, north of Mexico City. Toltec culture was fused with that of the Maya, incorporating the cult of Quetzalcóatl (Kukulcán, in

Mayan). Throughout the city, you will see images of both Chac-Mool, the Mayan rain god, and Quetzalcóatl, the plumed serpent.

The substantial fusion of highland central Mexican and Puuc architectural styles makes Chichén unique among the Yucatán Peninsula's ruins. The fabulous El Castillo and the Plataforma de Venus are outstanding architectural works built during the height of Toltec cultural input.

The warlike Toltecs contributed more than their architectural skills to the Maya. They elevated human sacrifice to a near obsession, and there are numerous carvings of the bloody ritual in Chichén demonstrating this. After a Maya leader moved his political capital to Mayapán while keeping Chichén as his religious capital, Chichén Itzá fell into decline. Why it was subsequently abandoned in the 14th century is a mystery, but the once-great city remained the site of Mayan pilgrimages for many years.

Orientation

Most of Chichén's lodgings, restaurants and services are ranged along 1km of highway in the village of Pisté, to the western (Mérida) side of the ruins. It's 1.5km from the ruins' main (west) entrance to the first hotel (Pirámide Inn) in Pisté, or 2.5km from the ruins to Pisté village plaza, which is shaded by a huge tree. Buses generally stop at the plaza; you can make the hot walk to and from the ruins in 20 to 30 minutes.

On the eastern (Cancún) side, it's 1.5km from the highway along the access road to the eastern entrance to the ruins.

Information

Filming with a video camera costs US$3 extra; tripods are forbidden. Hold onto your wristband ticket; it gives you in-and-out privileges and admission to that evening's sound-and-light show. Parking costs US$1. Explanatory plaques are displayed in Spanish and English.

The main entrance is the western one, with a large parking lot and a big, modern entrance building, the **Unidad de Servicios** (☻ 8am-10pm). The Unidad has a small but worthwhile **museum** (☻ 8am-5pm) with sculptures, reliefs, artifacts and explanations of these in Spanish, English and French.

The **Auditorio Chilam Balam**, next to the museum, sometimes has video shows about

Chichén and other Mexican sites. The picture quality can be truly abominable, but the air-con is great. In the central space of the Unidad stands a scale model of the archaeological site, and off toward the toilets is an exhibit about excavations of the Sacred Cenote. Facilities include two bookstores with a good assortment of guides and maps;

a currency-exchange desk and, around the corner from the ticket desk, a free *guardería de equipaje* where you can leave your belongings while you explore the site.

The 45-minute **sound-and-light show** (without ruins ticket US$3; ☽ 8pm summer & 7pm winter) is performed beneath El Castillo (see later). If you don't have a ruins ticket the cost

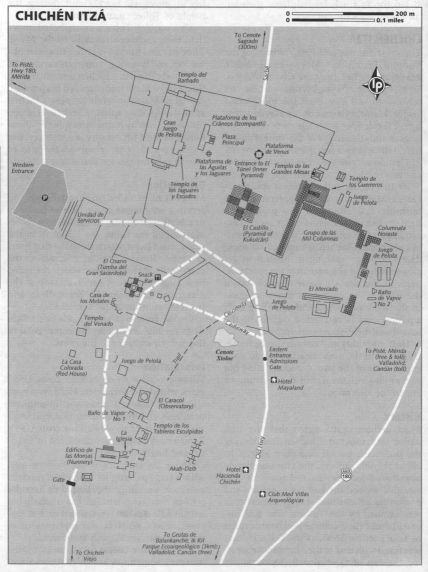

CHICHÉN ITZÁ

0 ——————— 200 m
0 ——————— 0.1 miles

To Cenote Sagrado (300m)

Sacbé

To Pisté; Hwy 180; Mérida

Templo del Barbado

Gran Juego de Pelota

Plataforma de los Cráneos (tzompantli)

Plaza Principal

Plataforma de Venus

Templo de las Grandes Mesas

Templo de los Guerreros

Western Entrance

Plataforma de las Águilas y los Jaguares

Entrance to El Túnel (Inner Pyramid)

Juego de Pelota

Templo de los Jaguares y Escudos

Columnata Noreste

Unidad de Servicios

El Castillo (Pyramid of Kukulcán)

Grupo de las Mil Columnas

Juego de Pelota

El Osario (Tumba del Gran Sacerdote)

Snack Bar

Casa de los Metates

El Mercado

Baño de Vapor No 2

Templo del Venado

Juego de Pelota

Causeway

Causeway

La Casa Colorada (Red House)

Juego de Pelota

Trail

Cenote Xtoloc

Eastern Entrance Admissions Gate

To Pisté; Mérida (free & toll); Valladolid; Cancún (toll)

El Caracol (Observatory)

Hotel Mayaland

Baño de Vapor No 1

Templo de los Tableros Esculpidos

La Iglesia

Edificio de las Monjas (Nunnery)

Akab-Dzib

Hotel Hacienda Chichén

Gate

Club Med Villas Arqueológicas

Old Hwy

MEX 180

To Chichén Viejo

To Grutas de Balankanché; Ik Kil Parque Ecoarqeológico (3km); Valladolid; Cancún (free)

YUCATÁN PENINSULA

is applicable toward the admission price for the following day. Devices for listening to English, French, German or Italian translations (beamed via infrared) rent for US$2.50. Specify the language you need or it may not be broadcast.

Visiting the Ruins
EL CASTILLO
As you approach from the turnstiles at the Unidad de Servicios into the archaeological zone, **El Castillo** (also called the Pyramid of Kukulcán) rises before you in all its grandeur. The first temple here was pre-Toltec, built around AD 800, but the present 25m-high structure, built over the old one, has the plumed serpent sculpted along the stairways and Toltec warriors represented in the doorway carvings at the top of the temple.

The pyramid is actually the Mayan calendar formed in stone. Each of El Castillo's nine levels is divided in two by a staircase, making 18 separate terraces that commemorate the 18 20-day months of the Vague Year. The four stairways have 91 steps each; add the top platform and the total is 365, the number of days in the year. On each façade of the pyramid are 52 flat panels, which are reminders of the 52 years in the Calendar Round.

To top it off, during the spring and autumn equinoxes, light and shadow form a series of triangles on the side of the north staircase that mimic the creep of a serpent (note the carved serpent's heads flanking the bottom of the staircase). The serpent ascends in March and descends in September.

The older pyramid inside El Castillo boasts a red jaguar throne with inlaid eyes and spots of jade, and it also holds a Chac-Mool figure. The entrance to **El Túnel** (11am-3pm & 4-4:45pm), the passage up to the throne, is at the base of El Castillo's north side. The dank air and steep, narrow stairway can make the climb a sweltering, slippery, claustrophobic experience.

GRAN JUEGO DE PELOTA
The great ball court, the largest and most impressive in Mexico, is only one of the city's eight courts, indicative of the importance the games held here. The court is flanked by temples at either end and bounded by towering parallel walls with stone rings cemented up high.

There is evidence that the ball game may have changed over the years. Some carvings show players with padding on their elbows and knees, and it is thought that they played a soccerlike game with a hard rubber ball, the use of hands forbidden. Other carvings show players wielding bats; it appears that if a player hit the ball through one of the stone hoops, his team was declared the winner. It may be that during the Toltec period the losing captain, and perhaps his teammates as well, were sacrificed. Along the walls of the ball court are stone reliefs, including scenes of decapitations of players.

The court's acoustics are amazing – a conversation at one end can be heard 135m away at the other, and a clap produces multiple loud echoes.

TEMPLO DEL BARBADO & TEMPLO DE LOS JAGUARES Y ESCUDOS
The structure at the northern end of the ball court, called the Temple of the Bearded Man after a carving inside of it, has some finely sculpted pillars and reliefs of flowers, birds and trees. The **Temple of the Jaguars and Shields**, built atop the southeast corner of the ball court's wall, has some columns with carved rattlesnakes and tablets with etched jaguars. Inside are faded mural fragments depicting a battle.

PLATAFORMA DE LOS CRÁNEOS
The **Platform of Skulls** (*tzompantli* in Náhuatl) is between the Templo de los Jaguares and El Castillo. You can't mistake it, because the T-shaped platform is festooned with carved skulls and eagles tearing open the chests of men to eat their hearts. In ancient days this platform held the heads of sacrificial victims.

PLATAFORMA DE LAS ÁGUILAS Y LOS JAGUARES
Adjacent to the *tzompantli*, the carvings on the **Platform of the Eagles and Jaguars** depicts those animals gruesomely grabbing human hearts in their claws. It is thought that this platform was part of a temple dedicated to the military legions responsible for capturing sacrificial victims.

CENOTE SAGRADO
A 300m rough stone road runs north (a five-minute walk) to the huge sunken well that

gave this city its name. The **Sacred Cenote** is an awesome natural well, some 60m in diameter and 35m deep. The walls between the summit and the water's surface are ensnared in tangled vines and other vegetation.

GRUPO DE LAS MIL COLUMNAS

Comprising the **Templo de los Guerreros** (Temple of the Warriors), **Templo de Chac-Mool** (Temple of Chac-Mool) and **Baño de Vapor** (Sweat House or Steam Bath), this group behind El Castillo takes its name (Group of the Thousand Columns) from the forest of pillars stretching south and east.

Structures are adorned with stucco and stone-carved animal deities. Archaeological work in 1926 revealed the Temple of Chac-Mool beneath the Temple of the Warriors. You can walk through the columns on its south side to reach the **Columnata Noreste** (Northeast Colonnade), notable for the 'big-nosed god' masks in its façade. Some have been reassembled on the ground around the statue. Just to the south are the remains of a Mayan sweat house, with an underground oven and drains for the water. The sweat houses were regularly used for ritual purification.

EL OSARIO

The Ossuary, otherwise known as the Bonehouse or the **Tumba del Gran Sacerdote** (High Priest's Grave), is a ruined pyramid southwest of El Castillo. As with most of the buildings in this southern section, the architecture is more Puuc than Toltec. It's notable for the serpent heads at the base of its staircases.

EL CARACOL

Called **El Caracol** (the Snail) by the Spaniards for its interior spiral staircase, this observatory is one of the most fascinating and important of all the Chichén Itzá buildings. Its circular design resembles some central highlands structures, although, surprisingly, not those of Toltec Tula. In a fusion of architectural styles and religious imagery, there are Mayan Chac-Mool raingod masks over four external doors facing the cardinal directions. The windows in the observatory's dome are aligned with the appearance of certain stars at specific dates. From the dome the priests decreed the times for rituals, celebrations, corn-planting and harvests.

EDIFICIO DE LAS MONJAS & LA IGLESIA

Thought by archaeologists to have been a palace for Mayan royalty, the so-called **Edificio de las Monjas** (Nunnery), with its myriad rooms, resembled a European convent to the conquistadors, hence their name for the building. The building's dimensions are imposing: its base is 60m long, 30m wide and 20m high. The construction is Mayan rather than Toltec, although a Toltec sacrificial stone stands in front of the building. A smaller adjoining building to the east, known as **La Iglesia** (the Church), is covered almost entirely with carvings.

AKAB-DZIB

On the path east of the Nunnery, the Puucstyle **Akab-Dzib** is thought by some archaeologists to be the most ancient structure excavated here. The central chambers date from the 2nd century. The name means 'Obscure Writing' in Maya and refers to the south-side annex door, whose lintel depicts a priest with a vase etched with hieroglyphics that have never been translated.

Grutas de Balankanché

In 1959 a guide to the Chichén ruins was exploring a cave on his day off when he came upon a narrow passageway. He followed the passageway for 300m, meandering through a series of caverns. In each, perched on mounds amid scores of glistening stalactites, were hundreds of ceremonial treasures the Maya had placed there 800 years earlier: ritual *metates* and *manos* (grinding stones), incense burners and pots. In the years following the discovery, the ancient ceremonial objects were removed and studied. Eventually most of them were returned to the caves, placed exactly where they were found.

The **Grutas de Balankanché** (admission US$5; 9am-5pm) are caverns 5km east of the ruins of Chichén Itzá and 2km east of the Hotel Dolores Alba on the highway to Cancún. Second-class buses heading east from Pisté toward Valladolid and Cancún will drop you at the Balankanché road. The entrance to the caves is 350m north of the highway.

Outside the caves you'll find a botanical garden (displaying native Yucatecan flora), a small museum, a sundries shop, and a ticket booth. The museum features large photographs taken during the exploration of the caves, and descriptions (in English,

Spanish and French) of the Mayan religion and the offerings found in the caves. Also on display are photographs of modern-day Mayan ceremonies called Ch'a Chaac, which continue to be held in all the villages on the Yucatán Peninsula during times of drought and consist mostly of praying and making numerous offerings of food to Chac-Mool.

Compulsory 40-minute tours (minimum six people, maximum 30) are accompanied by a recorded narration, which is difficult to hear and thus less dramatic than intended. English is at 11am, 1pm and 3pm; Spanish is at 9am, noon, 2pm and 4pm; and French is at 10am.

Be warned that the cave is unusually hot, and ventilation is poor in its further reaches. The lack of oxygen makes it difficult to draw a full breath until you're outside again.

Cenote Ik Kil

A little more than 3km east of the eastern entrance to the ruins is **Ik Kil Parque Ecoarqueológico** (☎ 985-851-00-00; adult/child US$4/2; ☺ 9am-5pm), whose *cenote* has been developed into a divine swimming spot. Small cascades of water plunge from the high limestone roof, which is ringed by greenery. A good buffet lunch runs an extra US$5. Get your swim in by no later than 1pm to beat the tour groups.

Sleeping

No matter what you plan to spend on a bed, don't hesitate to haggle in the off-season (May, June, September and October), when prices should be lower. Prices listed below are for high season.

Highway 180 is known as Calle 15A on its way through Pisté.

BUDGET

Pirámide Inn (☎ 985-851-01-15; www.piramideinn.com; Calle 15A No 30; tent sites per person US$4; P ⊠ ⊜) This is an agreeable hotel on the west side of Pisté that allows you to pitch a tent or hang a hammock under a *palapa*. You also get to enjoy the Pirámide Inn's pool and watch satellite TV in the lobby. Campers have use of tepid showers, clean shared toilet facilities and a safe place to stow gear.

Posada Olalde (☎ 985-851-00-86; Calle 6 btwn Calles 15 & 17; s/d US$15/20) Two blocks south of the highway by Artesanías Guayacán, this is

the best of Pisté's several small pensiones, offering seven clean, quiet and attractive rooms. There are four rustic bungalows on the premises as well, and the friendly manager speaks good English.

Posada Chac-Mool (☎ 985-851-02-70; Calle 15A; d US$37; ⊠) Just east of the Hotel Chichén Itzá on the opposite (south) side of the highway in Pisté, the Chac-Mool has basic doubles all with good air-con.

MID-RANGE

Club Med Villas Arqueológicas (☎ 985-851-00-34, 800-258-2633 in the US, 801 802 803 in France; www.clubmed.com; d US$75; P ⊠ ⊜) This is the only mid-range priced hotel next to the ruins, only 300m from the east entrance. It is an exact clone of the Club Med villas at Cobá and Uxmal except the beds are larger and the rooms are smaller. The grounds are lush and there's a relaxing poolside bar and good restaurant.

Hotel Dolores Alba (☎ 985-858-15-55; www.doloresalba.com; Hwy 180 Km 122; d US$40; P ⊠ ⊜) This hotel is across the highway from Cenote Ik Kil, just over 3km east of the eastern entrance to the ruins and 2km west of the Grutas de Balankanché. Its 40 air-conditioned rooms are simple but pleasingly decorated and face two inviting swimming pools. There's a restaurant, and staff will transport you to (but not from) the Chichén ruins.

Hotel Chichén Itzá (☎ 985-851-00-22; www.mayaland.com; Calle 15A No 45; d US$40-60; P ⊠ ⊜) On the west side of Pisté, this place has 42 pleasant rooms with tile floors and old-style brick-tile ceilings. Rooms in the upper range face the pool and nicely landscaped grounds. Breakfast is included.

Pirámide Inn (☎ 985-851-01-15; www.piramideinn.com; Calle 15A No 30; d US$45; P ⊠ ⊜) On the main street in Pisté, next to the eastern bus stop, stands this recently renovated hotel. All 42 rooms have air-con, and there's a book exchange and deep swimming pool. The restaurant serves international and vegetarian cuisine.

Stardust Inn (☎ 985-851-01-22; d US$37; P ⊠ ⊜) Next door to the Pirámide, the Stardust is slightly more worn than its neighbor, but it offers similar amenities: clean rooms, air-con and a swimming pool. There is also a site in back for tent and trailer camping.

TOP END

Hotel Mayaland (☎ 998-887-24-50, 800-235-4079 in the US; www.mayaland.com; d US$150, bungalows from US$200; P ⊠ ⊠) Less than 100m from the ruins' main entrance, this hotel was built around 1923 and is the most gracious in Chichén's vicinity, with multiple pools and restaurants and vast, green grounds. Both the rooms and the bungalows are beautifully decorated and very comfortable.

Hotel Hacienda Chichén (☎ 999-924-21-50 in Mérida, 800-624-8451 in the US; www.haciendachichen.com; d US$120-140; P ⊠ ⊠) About 200m further from the entrance, this is an elegant converted colonial estate that dates from the 16th century. It was here that the archaeologists who excavated Chichén during the 1920s lived. Their bungalows have been refurbished, new ones have been built and a swimming pool has been added.

Parque Ik Kil (☎ 998-851-00-00; bungalows US$100; P ⊠ ⊠) These new luxury bungalows are in the Ik Kil Parque Ecoarqueológico right next to Cenote Ik Kil. (p887). The spot is divine, but busloads of day-trippers take over the restaurant and *cenote* swimming hole in the afternoons.

Eating

The highway through Pisté is lined with more than 20 small restaurants. The cheapest are the market eateries on the main plaza opposite the huge tree. The others are arranged along the highway from the town square to the Pirámide Inn.

Restaurant Hacienda Xaybe'h (buffet lunch & dinner US$9) Set back from the highway opposite the Hotel Chichén Itzá (see Sleeping, earlier), this big restaurant has decent food. Diners can use its swimming pool for free.

El Carrousel (mains US$4-6) This is a popular local restaurant specializing in Yucatecan dishes, such as *sopa de lima* (lime soup) and *pollo pibil* (chicken wrapped in banana leaves).

Restaurant y Cocina Económica Chichén Itzá (mains US$3-4) This simple place serves good sandwiches, omelets and enchiladas.

Getting There & Away

A modern airport lies about 14km east of Pisté. At the time of research it had yet to receive other than local charter flights.

When all goes well, Oriente's 2nd-class buses pass through Pisté bound for Mérida (US$4.50, 2½ hours, hourly between 7:30am and 9:30pm). Oriente buses go to/from Valladolid (US$1.50, 50 minutes, hourly between 7:30am and 8:30pm) and Cancún (US$7, 4½ hours, hourly between 7:30am and 8:30pm). A bus travels to/from Chiquilá (US$7, four hours to reach Isla Holbox, one daily at 1:30am).

First-class buses depart Pisté for Mérida (US$6.25, 1¾ hours, twice a day at 2:30pm and 5pm); Cancún (US$12, 2½ hours, once a day at 4:30pm); and Cobá (US$5, 1½ hours, twice a day at 8am and 4:30pm); Tulum (US$7.50, 2½ hours, twice a day at 8am and 4:30pm) and Playa del Carmen (US$15, 3½ hours, twice a day at 8am and 4:30pm).

Shared vans to Valladolid (40 minutes, US$1.75) pass through town regularly.

Getting Around

Buses passing through Pisté stop near the east and west sides of town; during Chichén Itzá's opening hours they also stop at the ruins (check with the driver), and they will take passengers from town for about US$0.60 when there's room. For a bit more, 2nd-class buses will also take you to the Hotel Dolores Alba/Cenote Ik Kil and the Grutas de Balankanché (be sure to specify your destination when buying your ticket).

There is a taxi stand near the west end of town; the asking price to the ruins is US$2.75. There are sometimes taxis at Chichén's parking lot, but make advance arrangements if you want to be sure of a ride.

VALLADOLID

☎ 985 / pop 40,000

Valladolid is a relatively small, manageable to get around and affordable place. It has an easy pace of life, many handsome colonial buildings and several good hotels and restaurants. It's a fine place to stop and spend a day or three getting to know the real Yucatán, and it makes a good base from which to visit the surrounding area, including Chichén Itzá.

History

Valladolid was once the Mayan ceremonial center of Zací (pronounced sah-*kee*). The initial attempt at conquest in 1543 by Francisco de Montejo, nephew of Montejo

VALLADOLID

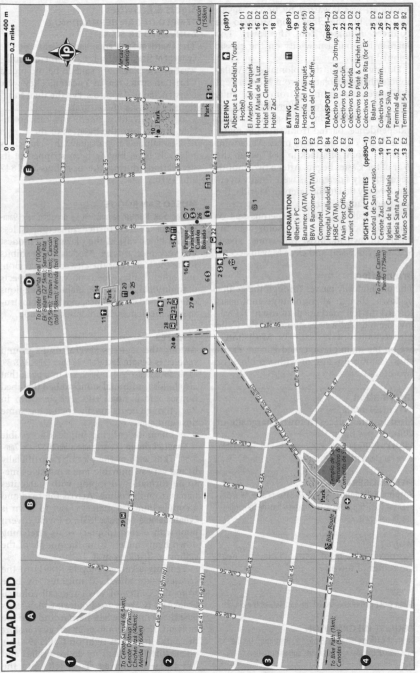

INFORMATION
@lbert's PC..............................**1** E3
Banamex (ATM).......................**2** D3
BBVA Bancomer (ATM)............**3** E2
Computel.................................**4** D3
Hospital Valladolid.................**5** B4
HSBC (ATM).............................**6** D2
Main Post Office.....................**7** E2
Tourist Office..........................**8** E2

SIGHTS & ACTIVITIES (pp890–1)
Catedral de San Gervasio.........**9** D3
Cenote Zací............................**10** E2
Iglesia de la Candelaria..........**11** D1
Iglesia Santa Ana...................**12** F2
Museo San Roque...................**13** E2

SLEEPING (p891)
Alberque La Candelaria (Youth
 Hostel)...............................**14** D1
El Mesón del Marqués.............**15** D2
Hotel María de la Luz.............**16** D2
Hotel San Clemente................**17** D3
Hotel Zací..............................**18** D2

EATING (p891)
Bazar Municipal......................**19** D2
Hostería del Marqués...........(see 15)
La Casa del Café-Kaffe............**20** D2

TRANSPORT (pp891–2)
Colectivo to Samulá & Dzitnup...**21** D2
Colectivos to Cancún..............**22** D2
Colectivos to Merida..............**23** D2
Colectivos to Pisté & Chichén Itzá..**24** C2
Colectivos to Santa Rita (for Ek'
 Balam)................................**25** D2
Colectivos to Tizmín...............**26** E2
Paulino Silva..........................**27** D2
Terminal 46............................**28** D2
Terminal 54............................**29** B2

the Elder, was thwarted by fierce Mayan resistance, but the Elder's son Montejo the Younger ultimately took the town. The Spanish laid out a new city on the classic colonial plan.

During much of the colonial era, Valladolid's physical isolation from Mérida kept it relatively autonomous from royal rule. The Maya of the area suffered brutal exploitation, which continued after Mexican independence. Barred from entering many areas of the city, the Maya made Valladolid their first point of attack in 1847 when the War of the Castes began. After a two-month siege, the city's defenders were finally overcome. Many fled to the safety of Mérida; the rest were slaughtered.

Today Valladolid is a prosperous seat of agricultural commerce, with some light industry thrown in. Most *vallisetanos* speak Spanish with a soft and clear Mayan accent.

Orientation

The old highway passes through the center of town, though all signs urge motorists toward the toll road north of town. To follow the old highway eastbound, take Calle 41; westbound, take Calle 39. Most hotels are on the main plaza, called Parque Francisco Cantón Rosado, or within a block or two of it.

Information

INTERNET ACCESS
Most Internet places in town charge about US$1.50 per hour.
@lbert's PC (Calle 43 No 200G; per hr US$1.20) A reliable place with fairly fast connections.

MEDICAL SERVICES
Hospital Valladolid (☎ 856-28-83; cnr Calles 49 & 52) Near the Convento de Sisal, the hospital handles emergencies 24 hours a day.

MONEY
Various banks, most with ATMs, are near the center of town.

POST
Main post office Located on the east side of the plaza.

TOURIST INFORMATION
Tourist office (☎ 856-18-65; 9am-8pm) On the east side of the plaza. It has maps and information.

Sights & Activities

TEMPLO DE SAN BERNARDINO & CONVENTO DE SISAL
The **Church of San Bernardino de Siena** and the **Convent of Sisal**, just under a kilometer southwest of the plaza, are said to be the oldest Christian structures in Yucatán. They were constructed in 1552 to serve the dual functions of fortress and church.

If the convent is open, you can go inside. Apart from the likeness of the Virgin of Guadalupe on the altar, the church is relatively bare, having been stripped of its decorations during the uprisings of 1847 and 1910.

MUSEO SAN ROQUE
Museo San Roque (admission by donation; 9am-9pm), this church turned museum, is less than a block east of the plaza. It is modest but very nicely done. Models and exhibits relate the history of the city and the region, and other displays focus on various aspects of traditional Mayan life, including religious offerings and ceremonies, masks and instruments, medicines, handicrafts and food.

CENOTES
Among the region's several underground *cenotes* is **Cenote Zací** (Calle 36 btwn Calles 37 & 39; admission US$0.50; 8am-5pm), set in a park that also holds traditional stone-walled thatched houses and a small zoo. People swim in Zací, though being mostly open it has some dust and algae.

A bit more enticing but less accessible is **Cenote Dzitnup** (Xkekén; admission US$2; 7am-6pm), 7km west of the plaza. It's artificially lit and very swimmable, and a massive limestone formation dripping with stalactites hangs from its ceiling. Across the road and a couple hundred meters closer to town is **Cenote Samulá** (admission US$1), a lovely cavern pool with *álamo* (poplar) roots stretching down many meters from the middle of the ceiling to drink from it.

Pedaling a rented bicycle (p891) to the *cenotes* takes about 20 minutes. By bike from the center of town take all-colonial Calle 41A (Calz de los Frailes), which leads past the Templo de San Bernardino and the convent. Keep them to your left as you skirt the park, then turn right on Calle 49. This opens into tree-lined Av de los Frailes and hits the old highway. Turn left onto the *ciclopista* (bike path) paralleling the road to Mérida. Turn left again at the sign for Dzitnup and continue for just under 2km; Samulá will be off this road to the right and Dzitnup a little further on the left.

Taxis from Valladolid's main plaza charge US$1 for the round-trip excursion to Dzitnup and Samulá, with an hour's wait (this is the locals' price; your rate may vary). You also can hop aboard a westbound bus; ask the driver to let you off at the Dzitnup turnoff, then walk the final 2km (20 minutes) to the site; or catch a *colectivo* taxi (US$1) from Calle 39 at Calle 44. Dzitnup has a restaurant and drinks stand.

Sleeping

El Mesón del Marqués (☎ 856-20-73; Calle 39 No 203; d US$50; [icons]) Long considered the best hotel in town, on the north side of the plaza. It has two colonial courtyards, a pool, good restaurant and guestrooms with air-con, ceiling fans and cable TV.

Ecotel Quinta Real (☎ 856-34-72; www.ecotelquin tareal.com.mx; Calle 40 No 160 btwn Calles 27 & 29; d from US$65; [icons]) Surrounded by an orchard – the only eco thing about it – this attractive neocolonial hotel has clean, comfortable and quiet rooms. There's a pool and tennis courts.

Hotel María de la luz (☎ 856-20-71; www.maria delaluzhotel.com; Calle 42 No 193; d US$33; [icons]) This is the best value in town. At the northwest corner of the plaza, this colonial house has comfortable rooms all with air-con and TVs. The pool is especially nice.

Hotel Zací (☎ 856-21-67; Calle 44 No 191; d with fan/air-con US$30/35; [icons]) This well-kept place has 48 rooms with mock-colonial decor and TVs, all situated around a quiet courtyard with a bar.

Hotel San Clemente (☎ 856-22-08; www.hotelsan clemente.com.mx; Calle 42 No 206; d US$35; [icons]) The San Clemente has a pool and 64 rooms with air-con, cable TV and decor nearly identical to Zací's (or vice vera). It's on the corner of the plaza, across from the cathedral.

Alberque La Candelaria (☎ 856-22-67, 800-800-26-25; Calle 35 No 201F; dm US$7-7.50, d US$17) This-HI affiliate is in a classic old house on the north side of the park across from Iglesia de la Candelaria. It has a full kitchen, self-service laundry area, a common area with cable TV, Internet access and a serene back area. There are 33 beds with private lockers

in single-sex rooms. The owners provide loads of information about the area and arrange tours.

Eating

Bazar Municipal (cnr Calles 39 & 40; set meals US$2-3) This is a collection of market-style cookshops at the plaza's northeast corner, popular for their big, cheap breakfasts. At lunch and dinner there are *comidas corridas* (set meals) – check the price before you order.

La Casa del Café-Kaffé (☎ 856-28-79; Calle 44; mains US$2-4) The best espresso in town is served here. They also have inexpensive breakfasts and light lunch and dinner fare.

Hotel María de la Luz (Calle 42 No 193; mains US$4-6) This hotel has breezy tables overlooking the plaza and serves a tasty and bountiful breakfast, and very good seafood entrees for lunch and dinner.

Hostería del Marqués (☎ 856-20-73; Calle 39 No 203; mains US$4-6) The best restaurant in town is in the Hotel El Mesón del Marqués. It serves delicious food in the beautiful and tranquil courtyard. Try the Yucatecan sampler dish for a taste of a variety of regional specialties.

Drinking & Entertainment

On Sundays from 8pm-9pm the municipal band or other local groups perform live music in the main plaza.

La Chispa de 1910 (☎ 856-26-68; Calle 41 No 201; 6pm-1am Mon-Thu, 5pm-3am Fri-Sun) Located a half-block from the main plaza, La Chispa is a lively bar and restaurant popular with young locals.

Getting There & Around

BICYCLE

Paulino Silva (Calle 44 btwn Calles 39 & 41; bike hire per hr US$0.50) is among a few places that rents bikes. The rental price includes a lock and map.

BUS

Valladolid has two bus terminals: the convenient **Terminal 46** (Calle 39 at Calle 46), two blocks from the plaza, and **Terminal 54** (Calle 37 at Calle 54) five blocks further northwest. All buses going through town stop at both terminals. Many 1st-class buses running between Cancún and Mérida don't go into town at all but drop passengers near the toll road's off-ramp. Free shuttles then take passengers into town.

The principal services are Oriente, Mayab and Expresso (2nd-class) and ADO and Super Expresso (1st-class).

Cancún (US$6-8, 2-3hr, frequent buses from 8:30am to 9:30pm)

Chetumal (US$12, 6hr, 5 Mayab 2nd-class buses)

Chichén Itzá/Pisté (US$1.75, 45min, 17 Oriente Mérida-bound buses 7:30am to 6pm) Buses stop near the ruins during the day.

Chiquilá – for Isla Holbox (US$6, 2½hr, 2nd-class at 1:30am)

Cobá (US$4, 1hr, 3 1st-class; US$2.50, 3 2nd-class)

Izamal (US$3.50, 2hr, 3 2nd-class)

Mérida (US$6-8, 2-3hr, frequent buses)

Playa del Carmen (US$11, 3-3½hr, 3 1st-class; US$6.25, 5 2nd-class)

Tizimín (US$2, 1hr, 12 buses)

Tulum (US$5, 2hr, 3 1st-class; US$4.50, 3 2nd-class)

COLECTIVOS

Often faster, more reliable and more comfortable than buses are *colectivos* – the shared vans that leave for various points as soon as their seats are filled. Direct services to Mérida (US$5, two hours) depart from Calle 39 just east of Calle 46; Cancún (US$6, two hours) buses depart from in front of the cathedral – confirm that the route is nonstop. *Colectivos* for Pisté and Chichén Itzá (US$1.50, 40 minutes) leave from Calle 46, north of Calle 39, and for **Tizimín** from the east side of the plaza at Calle 40.

It's possible to catch a *colectivo* from Calle 44 between Calles 35 and 47 in Valladolid for the village of Santa Rita (US$1), a 2km walk from Ek' Balam. A round-trip taxi ride from Valladolid with an hour's wait at the ruins will cost around US$20. Hostel La Candelaria (see Sleeping earlier) can arrange tours.

EK' BALAM

The turnoff for the fascinating archaeological site **Ek' Balam** (admission US$2.50; 8am-5pm) is due north of Valladolid, 17km along the road to Tizimín. Ek' Balam is another 10.5km east. There is usually someone at the site willing to act as a guide; tips are appreciated.

Vegetation still covers much of the area, but excavations and restoration continue to add to the sights, including an interesting ziggurat-like structure near the entrance, as well as a fine arch and a ball court.

Most impressive is the main pyramid – a massive, towering structure sporting a huge jaguar mouth with 360-degree dentition. At its base are stucco skulls, and to its right side are unusual winged human figures (some call them Mayan angels). From the top of the pyramid you can see pyramids at Chichén Itzá and Cobá.

For transport see p892.

TIZIMÍN

986 / pop 41,000

Travelers bound for Río Lagartos change buses in Tizimín, a ranching center. There is little to warrant an overnight stay, but the tree-filled Parque Principal is pleasant, particularly at sundown.

Both Bital, on the southwest side of Parque Principal, and Bancomer, at Calles 48 and 51, have ATMs.

Two great colonial structures – **Parroquia Los Santos Reyes de Tizimín** (Church of the Three Wise Kings) and its former **Franciscan monastery** (the ex-*convento*) – are worth a look.

The **Posada María Antonia** (863-23-84; Calle 50 No 408; r US$20), just south of the church, has 12 fairly basic air-conditioned rooms accommodating up to four people.

The **Tres Reyes** (863-21-06; cnr Calles 52 & 53; mains US$5-7) restaurant on the main square is a delightful surprise. The ranch-style food is very good, as is the friendly service.

Popular **Pizzería César's** (mains US$3-5), near the Posada María Antonia, serves pizza, pasta, sandwiches and burgers.

The **market** (8am-8pm), two blocks north of the church, has the usual inexpensive and tasty eateries.

Oriente (shared with Mayab, both 2nd-class only) and Noreste (1st- and 2nd-class) share a terminal on Calles 47 between Calles 46 and 48. Noreste's 1st- and 2nd-class terminal is around the corner on Calle 46.

Cancún (US$7-8, 3-3½hr, Mayab & Noreste buses between 3am & 8pm)

Izamal (US$5.25, 2½hr, Oriente bus at 5:15am, 11:20am & 4pm)

Mérida (US$7.50, 2¼hr, 10 1st-class Noreste between 4:30am & 6:30pm)

Río Lagartos (US$1, 1hr, 8 Noreste between 6am & 7:45pm) Some buses continue another 12km west to San Felipe (US$2).

Valladolid (US$2, 1hr, 7 Oriente between 5:30am & 7pm)

RÍO LAGARTOS

☎ 986 / pop 220

The largest and most spectacular flamingo colony in Mexico warrants a trip to this fishing village, 103km north of Valladolid, 52km north of Tizimín and lying within the Reserva de la Biósfera Ría Lagartos. The mangrove-lined estuary is also home to snowy egrets, red egrets, tiger herons, snowy white ibis, hundreds of other bird species and a small number of the crocodiles that gave the town its name (Alligator River).

The Maya knew the place as Holkobén and used it as a rest stop on their way to the nearby lagoons (Las Coloradas) from which they extracted salt. (Salt continues to be extracted, on a much vaster scale now.) Spanish explorers mistook the inlet for a river and the crocs for alligators, and the rest is history.

Flamingo Tours

The brilliant orange-red birds can turn the horizon fiery when they take wing. For their well-being, however, please ask your boat captain not to frighten the birds into flight. You can generally get to within 100m of flamingos before they walk or fly away. Depending on your luck, you'll see either hundreds or thousands of them.

The four primary haunts, in increasing distance from town, are Punta Garza, Yoluk, Necopal and Nahochín (all flamingo feeding spots named for nearby mangrove patches). Prices vary with boat, group size (maximum five) and destination. The lowest you can expect to pay is around US$40; a full boat to Nahochín runs to as much as US$65.

Ismael Navarro (☎ 826-00-00) and **Diego Núñez Martínez** (☎ 862-02-02) are licensed guides with formal training both as guides and naturalists. They offer extensive day tours as well as night excursions. (Crocodiles are a common nocturnal sight, and from May through September, sea turtles are easily spotted.) To reach them follow the signs for Restaurante-Bar Isla Contoy; you can ask for either of them at the restaurant.

Alternatively, you can negotiate with one of the eager men in the waterfront kiosks near the entrance to town. They speak English and will connect you with a captain (who usually doesn't).

Sleeping & Eating

Most residents aren't sure of the town's street names, and signs are few. The road into town is north–south Calle 10, which ends at the waterfront Calle 13.

Cabañas Dos Hermanos (☎ 862-01-46; cabins US$20) Near the school at the east edge of town, this comfortable place has four spacious cabañas with fans.

Posada Leyli (☎ 862-01-06; cnr Calles 14 & 11; d with bath US$20) Two blocks south of Calle 10, this place has six pleasant, fan-cooled rooms. La encargada (manager) often needs to be sought out; you can ask a neighbor or at the waterfront kiosks.

Hotel Villas de Pescadores (☎ 862-00-20; Calle 14; d US$35) This hotel is two blocks north of the Leyli, near the water's edge, and offers 12 very clean rooms, each with good cross-ventilation (all face the estuary), two beds and a fan. The owner rents bicycles and canoes as well; if he's not around, ask for his neighbor Benigno.

Restaurante-Bar Isla Contoy (Calle 19 at waterfront; mains US$4-6) This popular spot serves generous helpings of fresh fish – the shrimp-stuffed fillet is especially good. Isla Contoy is also a good place to meet other travelers and form groups for the boat tours.

Getting There & Away

Several buses run between Tizimín (US$2, one hour), Mérida (US$7, three to four hours) and Cancún (US$7, three to four hours). There are buses to San Felipe (US$1, 20 minutes) several times a day.

SAN FELIPE

This seldom-visited fishing village 12km west of Río Lagartos makes a nice day trip or overnight stay. Birding and the beach are the main attractions, both of which are just across the estuary at Punta Holohit.

Hotel San Felipe de Jesús (☎ 986-862-20-27; sanfelip@prodigy.net.mx; r US$25-35) To get to this friendly, clean and cleverly constructed hotel, turn left at the water and proceed 100m. Six of the 18 rooms are large and have private balconies and water views. All rooms have good cross-ventilation and are super bargains. The restaurant offers tasty seafood at low prices.

Six buses a day travel from Tizimín through Rio Largartos and continue to San Felipe (US$2, 1½ hours). You can also catch a bus directly to San Felipe from Río Lagartos (US$1, 20 minutes).

QUINTANA ROO

The state of Quintana Roo, Mexico's only Caribbean real estate, stretches north from the border with Belize to the extreme northeastern tip of the Yucatán Peninsula. Its barrier reef – the world's second largest – runs almost this entire distance, ending at Isla Mujeres. This and the other reefs along the coast, all bathed in crystal-clear Caribbean waters teeming with tropical fish, provide a profusion of excellent diving and snorkeling sites ranked among the world's best. Quintana Roo is also home to several impressive Mayan ruins and to resorts of every size and flavor.

Owing in part to its geographic isolation and the effects of the War of the Castes, the region did not have an official name until 1902, when it was given the status of territory and named after Andrés Quintana Roo, the poet-warrior-statesman who presided over the drafting of Mexico's constitution. In 1974, largely as a result of the development of Cancún, the territory achieved statehood.

CANCÚN

☎ 998 / pop 457,000

In the 1970s Mexico's tourism planners decided to take a gamble: they set out to duplicate the tourist sensation of Acapulco by designing a brand-new, world-class resort... from scratch. They scouted the Yucatán Peninsula's pristine Caribbean coast for the perfect location and found it: Cancún, a deserted spit of sugary sand just offshore from the tiny fishing village of Puerto Juárez. The government spent vast sums on landscaping, infrastructure and development, yielding straight, well-paved roads, potable tap water and palatial resorts strung along great swaths of white beaches. Soon the pace of hotel construction could barely keep up with the demand for rooms, and the tourist success of Cancún quickly surpassed that of Acapulco and that of the developers' most ambitious dreams.

Cancún's raison d'être is to attract tourists...and it does! Every year over two million people come here on a mission for sun, fun and diversion, and with the spectacular beaches, all-night clubs and opulent malls it is a mission easily accomplished. That is why every spring throngs of US university students descend on Cancún for Spring Break (usually during the week prior to, and the week following Easter). Their overwhelming numbers at this time of the year drive up both lodging prices and the blood pressure of locals.

Most visitors to the insular world of Cancún's beach resorts don't venture much past their hotel grounds; however, the real Cancún – not the Hollywood movie, the genuine place – can easily be found just minutes away from the hotel zone. Downtown Cancún has all the energy, bustle and livliness of any modern Mexican city. It also has comfortable accommodations and excellent restaurants and best of all it makes for a convenient base from which to explore the rest of the region.

Orientation

Cancún is actually made up of two very distinct areas: the downtown area, Ciudad Cancún; and the hotel zone, Zona Hotelera. These two sections of Cancún share little in common. Very few locals, except those who work in the service industry, spend time in the Zona Hotelera, and few tourists venture beyond the resorts to visit downtown.

On the mainland lies **Ciudad Cancún**, a planned city founded as the service center of the resort industry. The area of interest to tourists is referred to as 'el centro' ('downtown'). The main north–south thoroughfare is Av Tulum, a 1km-long tree-shaded boulevard lined with banks, shopping centers and restaurants.

There are quite a few nice, small hotels in the downtown area, many with swimming pools. Though not near the water, the beach is just a taxi or bus ride away from downtown accommodations.

The sandy spit of an island, Isla Cancún, is usually referred to as the **Zona Hotelera** (so-na oh-te-le-ra). Blvd Kukulcán, a four-lane divided avenue, leaves Ciudad Cancún and goes eastward out on the island several kilometers, passing condominium developments, several moderately priced hotels, some expensive larger ones and several shopping complexes, to Punta Cancún (Cancún Point) and the Centro de Convenciones (Convention Center).

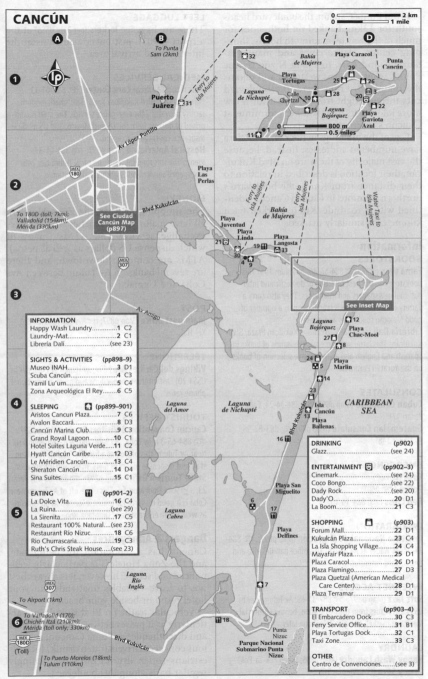

CANCÚN

0 — 2 km
0 — 1 mile

To Punta Sam (2km)

Ferry to Isla Mujeres

Puerto Juárez

Av López Portillo

To 180D (toll; 7km); Valladolid (154km); Mérida (330km)

See Ciudad Cancún Map (p897)

Blvd Kukulcán

MEX 180

MEX 307

Av Amigo

Playa Las Perlas

Playa Juventud

Playa Linda

Bahía de Mujeres

Ferry to Isla Mujeres

Ferry to Isla Mujeres

Water Taxi to Isla Mujeres

See Inset Map

Laguna Bojórquez

Playa Chac-Mool

Playa Marlin

Isla Cancún

Playa Ballenas

CARIBBEAN SEA

Laguna del Amor

Laguna de Nichupté

Laguna Cabra

Laguna Río Inglés

To Airport (1km)

To Valladolid (170); Chichén Itzá (210km); Mérida (toll only; 330km)

MEX 307

MEX 180D (Toll)

To Puerto Morelos (18km); Tulum (110km)

Blvd Kukulcán

Playa San Miguelito

Playa Delfines

Punta Nizuc

Parque Nacional Submarino Punta Nizuc

INSET MAP

Bahía de Mujeres

Playa Tortugas

Playa Caracol

Punta Cancún

Laguna de Nichupté

Calle Quetzal

Laguna Bojórquez

Playa Gaviota Azul

0 — 800 m
0 — 0.5 miles

INFORMATION
Happy Wash Laundry	1 C2
Laundry-Mat	2 C1
Librería Dalí	(see 23)

SIGHTS & ACTIVITIES (pp898–9)
Museo INAH	3 D1
Scuba Cancún	4 C3
Yamil Lu'um	5 C4
Zona Arqueológica El Rey	6 C5

SLEEPING (pp899–901)
Aristos Cancun Plaza	7 C6
Avalon Baccará	8 D3
Cancún Marina Club	9 C3
Grand Royal Lagoon	10 C1
Hotel Suites Laguna Verde	11 C2
Hyatt Cancún Caribe	12 D3
Le Méridien Cancún	13 C4
Sheraton Cancún	14 D4
Sina Suites	15 C1

EATING (pp901–2)
La Dolce Vita	16 C4
La Ruina	(see 29)
La Sirenita	17 C5
Restaurant 100% Natural	(see 23)
Restaurant Río Nizuc	18 C6
Rio Churrascaria	19 C3
Ruth's Chris Steak House	(see 23)

DRINKING (p902)
Glazz	(see 24)

ENTERTAINMENT (pp902–3)
Cinemark	(see 24)
Coco Bongo	(see 22)
Dady Rock	(see 20)
Dady'O	20 D1
La Boom	21 C3

SHOPPING (p903)
Forum Mall	22 D1
Kukulcán Plaza	23 C4
La Isla Shopping Village	24 C4
Mayafair Plaza	25 D1
Plaza Caracol	26 D1
Plaza Flamingo	27 D3
Plaza Quetzal (American Medical Care Center)	28 D1
Plaza Terramar	29 D1

TRANSPORT (pp903–4)
El Embarcadero Dock	30 C3
Ferry Service Office	31 B1
Playa Tortugas Dock	32 C1
Taxi Zone	33 C3

OTHER
Centro de Convenciones	(see 3)

YUCATÁN PENINSULA

From Punta Cancún, the boulevard heads south for 13km, flanked on both sides for much of the way by mammoth hotels, shopping centers, dance clubs and many restaurants and bars, to Punta Nizuc (Nizuc Point), where it turns westward and rejoins the mainland. From there, the boulevard cuts through light tropical forest for a few more kilometers to its southern terminus at Cancún's international airport.

Few of the buildings in the Zona Hotelera have numbered addresses. Instead, because the vast majority of them are on Blvd Kukulcán, their location is described in relation to their distance from Km 0, the boulevard's northern terminus in Ciudad Cancún, identified with a roadside 'Km 0' marker. Each kilometer is similarly marked.

Information

BOOKSTORES

Fama (Map p897; ☎ 884-56-86; Av Tulum 105) This bookstore has the best selection of domestic and international newspapers and magazines. They also carry a variety of books in various languages plus a number of good Mexican road maps and atlases.

Librería Dalí (Map p895; 2nd floor, Kukulcán Plaza, Blvd Kukulcán) This large bookstore has thousands of books in Spanish and English and an impressive selection of books on the Yucatán Peninsula.

CONSULATES

Cuban Consulate (Map p897; ☎ 884-34-23; Calle Pecari 17)

Guatemalan Consulate (Map p897; ☎ 883-82-96; Av Nader 148)

EMERGENCY

Fire (☎ 060)

Police (☎ 060)

Red Cross (☎ 884-16-16)

IMMIGRATION

Instituto Nacional de Migración (Map p897; ☎ 884-14-04; Av Náder at Av Uxmal) This office handles visa and tourist-card extensions.

INTERNET ACCESS

Soft Jazz (Map p897; ☎ 887-31-68; Av Tulum; per hr US$1.20) Across from the bus station, behind Comercial Mexicana market. See also Telephone later.

LAUNDRY

Happy Wash Laundry (Map p895; Paseo Pok-Ta-Pok)

Lava y Seca (Crisantemos 20)

LEFT LUGGAGE

There are baggage **lockers** (per 24hr US$5) at the airport (p903), just outside customs at the international arrival area.

MEDICAL SERVICES

American Medical Care Center (☎ 883-01-13; Plaza Quetzal, Blvd Kukulkan Km 8) This small, modern facility provides 24hr emergency service. The staff is comprised of doctors from the US and Mexico, and US medical insurance coverage is accepted.

Hospital Americano (Map p897; ☎ 884-61-33; Viento 15) This medical center off of Av Tulum has 24hr emergency service and English-speaking staff.

MONEY

The shopping malls in the Zona Hotelera all have major bank branches with money-exchange services and ATMs (many of which dispense US dollars as well as pesos). ATMs are common downtown, and there are several banks on Av Tulum between Avs Cobá and Uxmal.

POST

Main post office (Map p897; cnr Avs Sunyaxchén & Xel-Ha)

TELEPHONE

Vikings del Caribe (Map p897; Av Uxmal at Pino; per hr US$1.20) Fast Internet connections and good international phone rates

TOURIST OFFICES

Cancún Convention & Visitors Bureau (Map p897; ☎ 884-65-31; Av Cobá; 🕑 9am-2pm & 4-7pm Mon-Fri) Near Av Tulum, this office has a friendly English-speaking staff and dispenses plenty of fliers, maps and information.

State Tourism Office (Map p897; ☎ 884-80-73; Pecari 23; 🕑 9am-9pm Mon-Fri) This office off of Av Tulum near Cobá is a good resource for tourist information on Cancún as well as the entire state of Quintana Roo.

Dangers & Annoyances

Cancún has a reputation for being safe, and the Zona Hotelera is particularly well-policed and secure; however, it is always best not to leave valuables unattended in your hotel room or beside your beach towel.

Vehicular traffic on Blvd Kukulcán, particularly as it passes between the malls, bars and discotheques at Punta Cancún, is a serious concern. Drivers (often drunk) hit pedestrians (often drunk) on a frighteningly regular basis along this boulevard.

CIUDAD CANCÚN

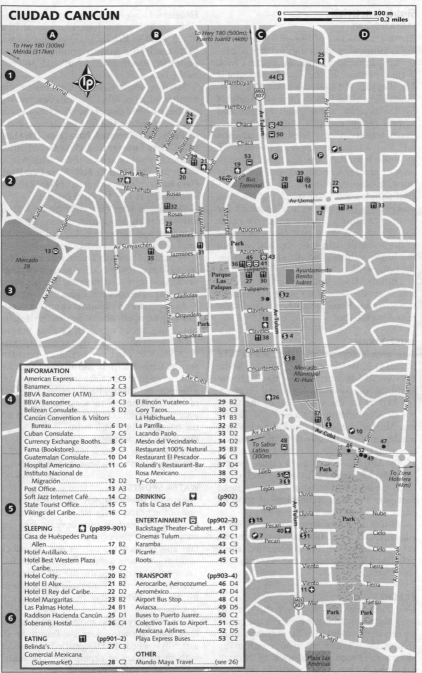

0   300 m
0   0.2 miles

INFORMATION

American Express	1 C5
Banamex	2 C3
BBVA Bancomer (ATM)	3 C5
BBVA Bancomer	4 C3
Belizean Consulate	5 D2
Cancún Convention & Visitors Bureau	6 D4
Cuban Consulate	7 C5
Currency Exchange Booths	8 C4
Fama (Bookstore)	9 C3
Guatemalan Consulate	10 D4
Hospital Americano	11 C6
Instituto Nacional de Migración	12 D2
Post Office	13 A3
Soft Jazz Internet Café	14 C2
State Tourist Office	15 C5
Vikings del Caribe	16 C2

SLEEPING 🏠 (pp899–901)

Casa de Huéspedes Punta Allen	17 B2
Hotel Antillano	18 C3
Hotel Best Western Plaza Caribe	19 C2
Hotel Cotty	20 B2
Hotel El Alux	21 B2
Hotel El Rey del Caribe	22 D2
Hotel Margaritas	23 B2
Las Palmas Hotel	24 B1
Raddison Hacienda Cancún	25 D1
Soberanis Hostal	26 C4

EATING 🍴 (pp901–2)

Belinda's	27 C3
Comercial Mexicana (Supermarket)	28 C2
El Rincón Yucateco	29 B2
Gory Tacos	30 C3
La Habichuela	31 B3
La Parrilla	32 B2
Lacando Paolo	33 D2
Mesón del Vecindario	34 D2
Restaurant 100% Natural	35 B3
Restaurant El Pescador	36 C3
Rolandi's Restaurant-Bar	37 D4
Rosa Mexicano	38 C3
Ty-Coz	39 C2

DRINKING 🍷 (p902)

Tatis la Casa del Pan	40 C5

ENTERTAINMENT 🎭 (pp902–3)

Backstage Theater-Cabaret	41 C3
Cinemas Tulum	42 C1
Karamba	43 C3
Picante	44 C1
Roots	45 C3

TRANSPORT (pp903–4)

Aerocaribe, Aerocozumel	46 D4
Aeroméxico	47 D4
Airport Bus Stop	48 C4
Aviacsa	49 D5
Buses to Puerto Juarez	50 C2
Colectivo Taxis to Airport	51 C5
Mexicana Airlines	52 D5
Playa Express Buses	53 C2

OTHER

Mundo Maya Travel	(see 26)

Sights & Activities

MAYAN RUINS

There are two sets of Mayan ruins in the Zona Hotelera, and though neither is particularly impressive, both are worth a look if time permits. In the **Zona Arqueológica El Rey** (Map p895; Blvd Kukulcán btwn Kms 17 & 18; admission US$3; ☉ 8am-5pm), on the west side of Blvd Kukulcán, are a small temple and several ceremonial platforms. The other, much smaller, site is **Yamil Lu'um** (admission free), atop a beachside knoll on the parklike grounds separating the Sheraton Cancún and Pirámides Cancún towers. Only the outward-sloping remains of the weathered temple's walls still stand, but the ruin makes for a pleasant venture, as much for its lovely setting as anything else. To reach the site visitors must pass through either of the hotels flanking it or approach it from the beach – there is no direct access from the boulevard.

The tiny Mayan structure and Chac-Mool statue on the beautifully kept grounds of the Sheraton Hotel are authentic and were found on the spot.

MUSEO INAH

The archaeological museum, **Museo INAH** (☎ 883-03-05; admission US$3.50; ☉ 9am-8pm Tue-Fri, 10am-7pm Sat-Sun), operated by the National Institute of Anthropology and History (INAH), is on the south side of the Centro de Convenciones in the Zona Hotelera. Most of the items – including jewelry, masks and intentionally deformed skulls – are from the postclassic period (AD 1200–1500). Also here are part of a classic-period hieroglyphic staircase (inscribed with dates from the 6th century) and the stucco head that gave the local archaeological zone its name of El Rey (the King).

Most of the informative signs are in Spanish only, but at the ticket counter you can get a fractured-English information sheet detailing the contents of the museum's 47 showcases.

BEACHES

Under Mexican law you have the right to walk and swim on every beach in the country except those within military compounds. In practice, it is difficult to approach many stretches of beach without walking through the lobby of a hotel, particularly in the Zona Hotelera. However, unless you look suspicious or unless you look like a local (the hotels tend to discriminate against locals, particularly the Maya), you'll usually be permitted to cross the lobby and proceed to the beach.

Starting from Ciudad Cancún in the northwest, all of Isla Cancún's beaches are on the left-hand side of the road (the lagoon is on your right). The first beaches are **Playa Las Perlas**, **Playa Juventud**, **Playa Linda**, **Playa Langosta**, **Playa Tortugas** and **Playa Caracol**; after rounding Punta Cancún, the beaches to the south are **Playa Gaviota Azul**, **Playa Chac-Mool**, **Playa Marlin**, the long stretch of **Playa Ballenas** and finally, at Km 17, **Playa Delfines**.

Delfines is about the only beach with a public parking lot; unfortunately, its sand is coarser and darker than the exquisite fine sand of the more northerly beaches.

Warning: Cancún's ambulance crews respond to as many as a dozen near-drownings per week. The most dangerous beaches seem to be Playa Delfines and Playa Chac-Mool.

As experienced swimmers know, a beach fronting on open sea can be deadly dangerous, and Cancún's eastern beaches are no exception. Though the surf is usually gentle, undertows can be powerful, and sudden storms (called *nortes*) can blacken the sky and sweep in at any time without warning. The local authorities have devised a system of colored pennants to warn beachgoers of potential dangers. Look for the pennants on the beaches where you swim:

Blue Normal, safe conditions
Yellow Use caution, changeable conditions
Red Unsafe conditions; use a swimming pool instead.

WATER SPORTS

For decent **snorkeling**, you need to travel to one of the nearby reefs. Resort hotels, travel agencies and various tour operators in the area can book you on day-cruise boats that take snorkelers to the barrier reef, as well as to other good sites within 100km of Cancún. To see the sparse aquatic life off Cancún's beaches, you can rent snorkeling equipment for about US$10 a day from most luxury hotels.

For **diving**, try **Scuba Cancún** (Map p895; ☎ 849-75-08; www.scubacancun.com.mx; Blvd Kukulcán Km 5), a family-owned, PADI-certified operation with many years of experience. The bilingual staff is safety oriented and environmentally aware, and they offer a variety of dive options (including *cenote* and night dives), as well as snorkeling and fishing trips, at reasonable prices.

Deep-sea fishing excursions (US$100, 4 hrs) can also be booked through a travel agent or one of the large hotels. Most of the major resorts rent **kayaks** (US$10 per day) and the usual water toys; a few make them available to guests free.

Cancún for Children

Couples usually come here before they have children or forget to bring them along once they do have them, but Cancún actually has a lot to offer kids – mainly the beach, sun and surf. The ocean playground here is endless and the waters are calm and shallow enough that even young children can be introduced to snorkeling. For specific kid-friendly venues, try one of the eco-parks **Xcaret** (p924) or **Xel-Há** (p925), south of Cancún. You may not enjoy the parks' contrived eco-theme, but kids seem to love it. Most hotels offer tours to these spots, or you can easily reach them by bus or car.

Tours

Most hotels and travel agencies work with companies that offer tours to surrounding attractions. Day trips to Chichén Itzá or Tulum, for example, cost about US$45 per person and include transportation, guide, admission cost and snacks.

Mundo Maya Travel (Map p897; ☎ 884-45-64; www .mayaworld.com; Av Cobá 5) Operates out of the lobby of Soberanis Hostel downtown. They offer professional tours at some of the lowest rates available.

Sleeping

As in other popular Yucatán Peninsula destinations, the rates of most Cancún hotels change with the tourist seasons, and every hotelier's idea of when these seasons is is slightly different. Rate changes occur more at mid-range and top-end establishments, though during Semana Santa (Easter Week) rates can rise at budget hotels as well. Broadly, Cancún's high season is from mid-December through March. All prices quoted here are for that high season unless otherwise specified; off-season rates can be significantly lower.

When business is slow, getting a significant discount can be as easy as showing

hesitation about a place. It's always worth asking for a *promoción* (discount), regardless of season.

BUDGET

All budget accommodations are downtown. 'Budget' is a relative term; prices in Cancún are higher for what you get than anywhere else in Mexico.

Casa de Huéspedes Punta Allen (Map p897; ☎ 884-02-25; www.puntaallen.da.ru; Punta Allen 8; d US$33-37; ✖) From Av Uxmal, walk south along Av Yaxchilán and take the first right, Punta Allen, to find this friendly family-run guesthouse. The ample rooms have bath and aircon. A light breakfast is included.

Hotel Cotty (Map p897; ☎ 884-05-50; Av Uxmal 44; www.hotelcotty.com; s/d US$34/38; Ⓟ ✖) Each of the 38 rooms here has a shower, aircon, cable TV, phone and two comfortable double beds. A full breakfast is included in the price and off-street parking is available too. Note: the 2nd-floor rooms at the rear get club noise from Av Yaxchilán.

Soberanis Hostal (Map p897; ☎ 884-45-64, 800-101-01-01; www.soberanis.com.mx; Av Cobá 5; dm US$12, d US$40; ✖ ▣) The Soberanis is excellent value. All rooms have strong air-con, comfortable beds, tile floors, and cable TV. It is primarily a hotel, with one four-bed dorm room available. Continental breakfast is included in the price. Internet service, phone center, activity room, tour and travel agencies, cafeteria and bar are all on site as well.

Las Palmas Hotel (Map p897; ☎ 884-25-13; Palmera 43; d US$28; ✖) Las Palmas has clean, cool rooms with comfy beds and TV. Good, cheap meals are also available.

Hotel El Alux (Map p897; ☎ 884-66-13; Av Uxmal 21; s/d US$28/37; ✖) The Alux has 35 spacious (though slightly dark) air-conditioned rooms, each with hot shower, phone and TV.

MID-RANGE

'Mid-range' in Cancún is a two-tiered category; the downtown area is much cheaper than the Zona Hotelera and only a short bus ride away from the Zona's beaches. The following hotels are downtown.

Hotel El Rey del Caribe (Map p897; ☎ 884-20-28; www.reycaribe.com; cnr Avs Uxmal & Náder; s/d US$50/60; Ⓟ ✖ ✖ ▣) Do yourself and the environment a favor and stay at this oasis of calm in the heart of the city. El Rey is a true eco-tel that composts, uses solar collectors and cisterns, gardens with gray water and even has a few composting toilets. The 25 suites have fully equipped kitchenettes, good showers comfy beds, cable TV and phones. There's a lush courtyard, a lovely small pool, a Jacuzzi and off-street parking. The shoes-off garden café serves healthy fruit-filled breakfasts and organic coffee. Massage, mud baths, reiki and early morning tai-chi sessions are also available.

Radisson Hacienda Cancún (Map p897; ☎ 881-65-00; www.radisson.cancun.com.mx; Av Nader 1; r from US$95; P ⚹ ⌨ ⚋) The Radisson offers all the amenities of the more expensive hotels in the Zona Hotelera with one exception: beachfront property. To make up for this, the hotel offers its guests free access and shuttle service to the Avalon Bay Beach Club. All 248 rooms in this hacienda-esque hotel have tile floors, cheerful décor and cable TV. There is a large pool in the lush patio area as well as a poolside bar and restaurant.

Hotel Best Western Plaza Caribe (Map p897; ☎ 884-13-77, 800-780-7234 in the US; www.hotelplazacaribe.com; Pino btwn Avs Tulum & Uxmal; d US$100; ⚹ ⚋) Directly across from the bus terminal, this franchise hotel offers 140 comfortable air-conditioned rooms with all the amenities. A pool and restaurant are on the premises.

Hotel Antillano (Map p897; ☎ 884-11-32; www.hotelantillano.com; Claveles 1; d US$65; ⚹ ⚋) Five blocks south of the bus terminal, just off Av Tulum, this pleasant hotel has a pool and 48 light and airy guestrooms with comfortable beds, telephones and cable TV.

Hotel Margaritas (Map p897; ☎ 884-93-33; cnr Av Yaxchilán & Av Jazmines; d US$85; ⚹ ⚋) This cheerful, friendly hotel has 100 bright and clean guestrooms all with phones and cable TV. There is a sunny pool patio and very good restaurant/bar.

The following mid-range hotels are in the Zona Hotelera.

Hotel Suites Laguna Verde (Map p895; ☎ 883-34-14; www.hotel-suites-laguna-verde-cancun.world-hotel-network.com; Paseo Pok-Ta-Pok Km 1; d US$80; P ⚹ ⚋) The spacious, clean comfortable rooms are equipped with kitchenettes, dining tables and a couch. There's a nice pool and a good restaurant. Though the hotel is not on the beach, guests have access to the nearby Fat Tuesday beach club.

Grand Royal Lagoon (Map p895; ☎ 883-27-49; www.grlafoon.com; Quetzal 8; r US$10; P ⚹ ⚋) This hotel, 100m off Blvd Kukulcán Km 7.7, has 36 air-conditioned rooms with cable TV; most have two double beds (some have kings). There's also a pool on the premises.

Sina Suites (Map p895; ☎ 883-10-17; Quetzal 33; ste US$106-143) Each of the 33 spacious suites here has a kitchen, two baths, two double beds, a separate living room (with a sofa bed) and satellite TV. Other amenities include a pool, bar and restaurant.

Aristos Cancún Plaza (Map p895; ☎ 885-33-33; www.aristoshotels.com; Blvd Kukulcán Km 20.5; r US$90; P ⚹ ⚋) Considering its beachfront location and amenities, this place offers one of the best values of the Zona's moderately priced digs. All rooms have marble floors, cable TV and balconies with sea or lagoon views. The hotel also has a restaurant and two pools.

Cancún Marina Club (Map p895; ☎ 849-49-99; Blvd Kukulcán 5.5; r US$110; P ⚹ ⚋) This popular hotel has a water-sports center, a very inviting pool and a pleasant restaurant/bar overlooking the lagoon. Among the 75 rooms, 10 are penthouses, two with Jacuzzis.

TOP END

All of these resorts are in the Zona Hotelera and border the Caribbean.

Avalon Baccará (Map p895; ☎ 883-20-77; www.avalonvacations.com; Blvd Kulkulcán Km 11.5; r from US$185; P ⚹ ⚋) This is Cancún's only boutique hotel and the only real choice for intimate accommodations on the beach. Each of the 34 rooms is beautifully decorated with Mexican furnishings, art and textiles, and each has a kitchenette, living room, dining area, and balcony with Jacuzzi. The highlight here is the artistically designed pool area next to the beach...and of course the beach itself.

Le Méridien Cancún (Map p895; ☎ 881-22-00, 800-543-4300 in the US; www.meridiencancun.com.mx; Blvd Kukulcán Km 14; r from US$365; P ⚹ ⌨ ⚋) This is one of the classiest hotels in Cancún and smaller (relatively) than the other cruise ship–sized resorts in the Zona Hotelera. Each room is warm and elegant and features a marble tiled bathroom with separate tub and walk-in shower. The onsite European spa offers an array of exotic treatments. If the pool, beach and tennis courts aren't enough, you can go windsurfing, scuba diving or horseback riding.

Hyatt Cancún Caribe (Map p895; ☎ 848-78-00, 800-633 7313 in the US; www.hyatt.com; Blvd Kukulcán Km 10.3; r from US$250; P ⊠ ▢ ⊠) The luxurious Hyatt has a range of accommodations among its 226 lovely guestrooms and suites. Multiple pools, restaurants and tennis courts are among the amenities here, and the location is prime beachfront.

Sheraton Cancún (Map p895; ☎ 883-19-88, 800-325-3535 in the US; www.sheraton.com/cancun; Blvd Kukulcán Km 12.5; r from US$170; P ⊠ ▢ ⊠) The Sheraton has tremendous appeal, from the elegant lobby to the immaculate gardens to the gorgeous tiled art in the restaurant. A real Mayan ruin sits on part of the resort's property.

Eating

The best selection of budget eats is available downtown, away from the big resorts. As with budget restaurants, the downtown area has a wider variety of middle-priced places than the Zona Hotelera. Though there are many establishments in this category in the Zona Hotelera, their prices sometimes reflect their location more than the quality of food.

BUDGET

Belinda's (Map p897; Tulipanes 23; breakfast US$3-4, mains US$4-5) This friendly café is the place to go for a delicious big breakfast. The Yucatecan lunches and dinners are very good too.

El Rincón Yucateco (Map p897; Av Uxmal 24; set meals US$3.50) Across from the Hotel Cotty, this place serves excellent yet inexpensive Yucatecan food, with good *comidas corridas*.

Ty-Coz (Map p897; ☎ 884-60-60; Av Tulum; sandwiches US$3-4; ✆ closed Sunday) This tidy café, popular with the local lunch crowd, is in a small shopping center across from the bus station, behind the Comercial Mexicana supermarket. Their specialty is tasty stuffed baguette and filled croissants. The espresso drinks are good too.

La Ruina (Map p895; Plaza Terramar; mains US$6.25) This place faces Blvd Kukulcán near Km 8.5. The highlights here are the delicious traditionally Mexican meals.

Restaurant Río Nizuc (Map p895; mains US$5-8) At the end of a short, nameless road near Blvd Kukulcán Km 22, this outdoor restaurant, which is flanked by mangroves, is a nice

place to settle in a chair under a *palapa* and watch convoys of snorkelers pass by. Fresh octopus, conch and fish are served in various ways.

Comercial Mexicana (Map p897; Cnr Avs Tulum & Uxmal) This centrally located supermarket has a good selection of produce, meet, cheese and bread. There is also an ATM on the premises.

MID-RANGE

Rosa Mexicano (Map p897; ☎ 884-63-13; Claveles 4; mains from US$10) A long-standing favorite, this is the place to go for unusual Mexican dishes in a pleasant *hacienda* atmosphere. Try the squid sautéed with three chilies or the shrimp in a *pipián* sauce (made of ground pumpkin seeds and spices).

Restaurant El Pescador (Map p897; ☎ 884-26-73; Av Tulipanes 28; mains US$7-12) Many locals insist this is the best seafood place in town. It's definitely popular and you will most likely have to wait for a table. Traditional Mexican dishes are served too and are considerably less expensive than the seafood fare.

Rolandi's Restaurant-Bar (Map p897; ☎ 883-25-27; Av Cobá 12; mains US$7-10) This attractive Italian eatery, between Avs Tulum and Náder just off the southern roundabout, serves elaborate pizzas, spaghetti plates and more substantial dishes of veal and chicken.

Mesón de Vecindario (Map p897; ☎ 884-89-00; Av Uxmal 23; mains US$7-9) Out of place but very cute, this chalet-looking restaurant specializes in fondue of all sorts as well as salads and pasta.

Gory Tacos (Map p897; Tulipanes 26; mains US$4-8) Don't let the name spoil your appetite; this *taquería* serves excellent tacos, burgers and vegetarian meals.

Restaurant 100% Natural Ciudad Cancún (Map p897; ☎ 884-36-17; Av Sunyaxchén nr Av Yaxchilán; mains US$4-10) Cancún (Map p895; ☎ 885-29-04; Plaza Kukulcán, Paseo Kukulcán Km 13; mains US$4-10) These branches are part of the healthfood restaurant chain serving fresh and frothy blended juice – a wide selection of yogurt-fruit-vegetable combinations – and pasta, fish and chicken dishes. There's a bakery on the premises.

La Parrilla (Map p897; ☎ 887-61-41; Av Yaxchilán 51; mains US$9-16) A bit of a tourist trap but popular with locals as well, this traditional Mexican restaurant is known for its grilled specialties. The mixed-grill plate is generous and includes chicken, shrimp, steak and lobster.

Rio Churrascaria (Map p895; ☎ 849-90-40; Blvd Kukulcán Km 3.5; mains US$8-15) This Brazilian-style grill serves fresh-off-the-skewer charcoal grilled meat. There is also an extensive salad bar that includes an array of seafood choices.

TOP END

La Habichuela (Map p897; ☎ 884-31-58; Margaritas 25; mains US$12-30) La Habichuela's dimly lit courtyard is full of romantic ambience. The house specialty, *habichuela* (string bean) soup is excellent as is the shrimp in tequila sauce. Save room for a taste of *Xtabentun* (Mayan anise and honey liqueur).

Lacando Paolo (Map p897; ☎ 887-26-27; Av Uxmal 35; mains US$10-30) Elegant but not fussy, this restaurant specializes in authentic southern Italian cuisine. The seafood pasta dishes are innovative, and service is excellent. For an alternative to a main meal, try their tapas bar.

La Sirenita (Map p895; ☎ 881-80-00; Blvd Kulkulcán Km 17; mains US$15-40) In the Hilton, you can dine right on the beach at this intimate restaurant. The cuisine is a sort of Mex-Asian fusion, featuring sushi and lots of other fresh seafood.

La Dolce Vita (Map p895; ☎ 885-01-61; Blvd Kukulcán Km 14.8; mains US$12-30; 🛇) Overlooking the lagoon, this is one of Cancún's fanciest Italian restaurants. It specializes in homemade pasta and fresh seafood dishes.

Ruth's Chris Steak House (Map p895; ☎ 883-33-01, Plaza Kukulcán, Paseo Kukulcán Km 13; steaks US$22-35) The Ruth's Chris chain is known internationally for its aged, corn-fed, USDA prime beef.

Drinking

On a hot day (ie every day) **Restaurant 100% Natural** (☎ 884-36-17 & 885-29-04), see Eating earlier, is the best place to quench your thirst with a healthy fresh-fruit smoothy.

Glazz (Map p895; ☎ 883-18-81; La Isla Shopping Village) This sleek, hip lounge serves every cocktail imaginable and then some.

Tatis la Casa del Pan (Map p897; ☎ 892-38-77; cnr Pecari & Av Tulum) This bakery café is a nice place to enjoy fresh-roasted coffee and espresso drinks.

Entertainment

CINEMA

In general Hollywood movies are shown in English with Spanish subtitles; however, English-language children's movies are usually dubbed in Spanish. Ticket prices run about US$4 for children and adults.

Cinemas Tulum (Map p897; ☎ 884-34-51; Av Tulum 10) This theater shows first-run Hollywood movies in English with Spanish subtitles, as well as foreign films and current Mexican releases.

Cinemark (Map p895; ☎ 883-56-03; La Isla Shopping Village) This cineplex shows only English-language, first-run Hollywood hits.

GAY & LESBIAN VENUES

Backstage Theater-Cabaret (Map p897; ☎ 887-91-06; Tulipanes 30) This place has terrific ambience and a joyful crowd. It features drag shows, strippers (male and female), fashion shows and musicals.

Karamba (☎ 884-00-32; cnr Azucenas & Av Tulum; 🕒 10:30pm-6am Tue-Sun) Above the Ristorante Casa Italiana, this nightclub is popular among cross-dressers and lesbians, and famous for its frequent drink specials.

Picante (Av Tulum 20) Set back from the street in the Plaza, Galeria shopping mall a few blocks north of Av Uxmal, Picante is mainly for talkers, not dancers.

NIGHTCLUBS

Much of the Zona Hotelera's nightlife is aimed toward a young crowd and is loud and booze-oriented (often with an MC urging women to display body parts). Most of the dance clubs charge around US$12 admission (some have open bar nights for about US$25); some don't open their doors before 10pm, and none are hopping much before midnight.

Coco Bongo (Map p895; ☎ 883-50-61; Blvd Kukulcán Km 9, Forum Mall) This club is a favorite with spring breakers – it's often a featured venue for MTV spring break coverage. The party starts early here with live entertainment (celebrity impersonators, clowns, dancers) and continues all night with live music and dancing (on the floor, on the stage, on the tables, on the bar…).

Dady'O (Map p895; ☎ 800-234-97-97; Blvd Kukulcán Km 9) Opposite the Forum Mall, this is one of Cancún's hottest dance clubs. The setting is a five-level black-walled faux cave with a two-level dance floor and zillions of laser beams and strobes, and the beat is pure disco.

Dady Rock (Map p895; Blvd Kukulcán Km 9) This steamy rock 'n' roll club with live music is next door to Dady'O. It attracts a slightly older, though no less subdued crowd than its neighbor.

La Boom (Map p895; Blvd Kukulcán Km 3.8) A varied and (relative to neighboring clubs) sophisticated selection of danceable tunes are featured here, all played at mega decibels.

Sabor Latino (☎ 892-19-16; cnr Avs Xcaret & Tankah) You can dance all night and into the morning at this ever-lively salsa club.

Roots (Map p897; ☎ 884-24-37; Tulipanes 26; ⊗ closed Sun) This relaxed venue features live jazz, reggae, salsa, rock and occasionally flamenco performers.

Shopping

Many of the malls in the Zona Hotelera are as massive and ornate as the neighboring hotels. Several major shopping malls along Blvd Kukulkán between approximately Km 8 and Km 13. Principal among them are: **Plaza Caracol** (☎ 883-29-61; Km 8.5); **Mayfair Plaza** (☎ 883-05-71; Km 8.5); **Forum Mall** (☎ 883-44-25; Km 9.5); **Plaza Flamingo** (☎ 883-29-45; Km 11.5); **La Isla Shopping Village** (☎ 883-50-25; Km 12.5); and **Plaza Kukulcan** (☎ 885-22-00; Km 13). Along with the usual mall fare (The Gap, Guess, Hugo Boss), there are a myriad of superchic boutiques selling everything from Colombian emeralds to Cuban cigars, all at exorbitant prices. Still, window-shopping in these chichi malls costs the same here as anywhere else and is a lot more fun – there's just so much not to buy.

Bargain hunting doesn't get much better downtown. For last-minute purchases before flying out of Cancún, try the **Mercado Municipal Ki-Huic** (Map p897; Av Tulum), north of Av Cobá, a warren of stalls and shops carrying a wide variety of souvenirs and handicrafts. It's a 100% tourist trap, so even hard bargaining may not yield the required results.

Getting There & Away

AIR

Cancún's international airport (☎ 886-00-49), about 8km south of the city center, is the busiest in southeastern Mexico. The best place to change money is the Bital bank just outside the domestic arrivals and departures area.

Between Mexicana and its subsidiaries Aerocaribe and Aerocozumel there is at least one flight daily to each of the following: Mexico City (US$120, two hours and 15 minutes), Oaxaca (US$180, 4 hrs), Tuxtla Gutiérrez (US$225, 3½ hours), Villahermosa (US$175, 3½ hours) and Veracruz (US$217, 4 hours). The airlines have a total of two flights daily to Chetumal (US$145, 50 minutes) and Mérida (US$115, 50 minutes), as well as daily flights to Cozumel (US$75, 20 minutes). They also fly twice daily to Havana, Cuba (US$290, two hours and 10 minutes).

Airline Offices

Aerocaribe & Aerocozumel (Map p897; ☎ 884-20-00; Av Cobá 5, Plaza América)

Aeroméxico (Map p897; ☎ 884-10-97; Av Cobá 80)

American Airlines (☎ 886-01-63, 800-904-60-00) At the airport.

Aviacsa (Map p897; ☎ 887-42-11; Av Cobá 37)

Aviateca (☎ 884-39-28) At the airport.

Continental (☎ 886-00-40, 800-900-50-00) At the airport.

Mexicana (☎ 881-90-90, 800-502-20-00; Av Cobá 39)

BOAT

Puerto Juárez, the port for passenger ferries to Isla Mujeres, is about 4km north of the center. Punta Sam, the dock for the slower car ferries to Isla Mujeres, is about 8km north of the center. See also p909 for further transport information.

BUS

Cancún's **bus terminal** (Map p897) occupies the wedge formed where Avs Uxmal and Tulum meet. Services are 2nd-class, 1st-class and any of several luxury options. Across Pino from the bus terminal, a few doors from Av Tulum, is the ticket office and miniterminal of **Playa Express** (Map p897; Pino), which runs shuttle buses down the Caribbean coast to Tulum and Felipe Carrillo Puerto at least every 30 minutes until early evening, stopping at major towns and points of interest along the way.

Following are some of the major routes serviced daily:

Chetumal (US$14-17, 5½-6½hr, frequent buses)

Chichén Itzá (US$11, 3-4hr, 1 Riviera bus at 9am; US$7.50, hourly Oriente buses from 5am to 5pm)

Felipe Carrillo Puerto (US$11, 3½-4hr, 8 Riviera buses; US$9, hourly 2nd-class Mayab buses)

Mérida (US$20, 4-6hr, 15 deluxe and 1st-class UNO, ADO GL & Super Expresso buses; US$12, hourly 2nd-class Oriente buses from 5am to 5pm)

YUCATÁN PENINSULA

Mexico City – TAPO (US$80, 24hr, 1 1st-class ADO; US$88, 2 deluxe ADO GL)
Mexico City – Terminal Nte (US$80, 24hr, 1 1st-class ADO)
Playa del Carmen (US$3.50, 45min-1¼hr, 1st-class Riviera every 15 minutes 5am to midnight; US$2.50, frequent 2nd-class buses)
Puerto Morelos (US$1.50-2, 40min, Playa Express every 30 minutes until 4:30pm) There are numerous other services.
Ticul (US$17, 6hr, 6 2nd-class Mayab buses)
Tizimín (US$7, 3-4hr, 9 2nd-class Noreste & Mayab buses)
Tulum (US$6, 2-2½hr, 7 1st-class Riviera; US$5, 2nd-class Playa Express every 30 minutes) There are numerous other services.
Valladolid (US$8, 2-3hr, many 1st-class ADO; US$6, 2nd-class Oriente buses)
Villahermosa (US$45, 12hr, 11 1st-class buses)

CAR & MOTORCYCLE

Alamo (☎ 886-01-79; www.goalamo.com), **Avis** (☎ 886-02-22; www.avis.com), **Budget** (☎ 886-00-26; www.drivebudget.com), **Dollar** (☎ 886-01-79; www.dollar.com), **Hertz** (☎ 886-01-50; www.hertz.com.mx) and **Thrifty** (☎ 886-03-93; www.thrifty.com), among other car rental agencies, have counters at the airport. You can often receive better rates if you reserve ahead of time, but it doesn't hurt to do some comparison shopping after arriving.

YUCATÁN PENINSULA

Getting Around

TO/FROM THE AIRPORT

If you don't want to pay US$40 for a taxi ride into town, there are a few options. Comfortable shared vans charging US$9 leave from the curb in front of the international terminal about every 15 minutes, heading for the Zona Hotelera via Punta Nizuc. They head into town after the island, but it can take up to 45 minutes to get downtown. If volume allows, however, they will separate passengers into downtown and Zona groups. To get downtown more directly and cheaply, exit the terminal and pass the parking lot to a smaller dirt lot between the Budget and Executive car rental agencies. There is a ticket booth there for buses (US$5) that leave the lot every 20 minutes or so between 5:30am and midnight. They travel up Av Tulum, one of their most central stops being across from the Chedraui supermarket on Av Cobá (confirm your stop with the driver as there are two Chedrauis in town). At time of research there were plans for a bus service between the airport and the main bus terminal (US$1.50).

If you follow the access road out of the airport and past the traffic-monitoring booth (a total of about 300m), you can often flag down a taxi leaving the airport empty that will take you for about US$5 to US$7.

To get to the airport you can catch the airport bus on Av Tulum just south of Av Cobá, outside the Es 3 Café, or a **colectivo** (per person US$3; 🕑 6am-9pm) from the stand in the parking area a few doors south; *colectivo* taxis leave when full. The official rate for private taxis from town is US$15.

Riviera runs buses to/from the airport to Playa del Carmen (US$7.25, 45 minutes to one hour, 11 express 1st-class buses between 7am and 7:30pm). Tickets are sold at a counter in the international section of the airport.

BUS

To reach the Zona Hotelera from downtown, catch any bus with 'R1,' 'Hoteles' or 'Zona Hotelera' displayed on the windshield as it travels south along Av Tulum or east along Av Cobá. The fare each way is US$0.60.

To reach Puerto Juárez and the Isla Mujeres ferries, catch a Ruta 13 (US$0.40, 'Pto Juárez' or 'Punta Sam') bus at the stop in front of Cinemas Tulum (next to McDonald's), on Av Tulum north of Av Uxmal.

TAXI

Cancún's taxis do not have meters. There is a sign listing official fares on the northeast outside wall of the bus terminal; if you can't refer to it you'll probably have to haggle. From downtown to Punta Cancún is US$8, to Puerto Juárez US$3.

ISLA MUJERES

☎ 998 / pop 12,000

Isla Mujeres (Island of Women) has a reputation as a backpackers' Cancún – a quieter island where many of the same amenities and attractions cost a lot less. That's not as true today – Cancún makes itself felt each morning as boatloads of tourists arrive for a day's excursion. But Isla Mujeres continues to offer good values, a popular sunbathing beach and plenty of diving and snorkeling sites. Though its character has changed, the island's chief attributes are still a relaxed

ISLA MUJERES

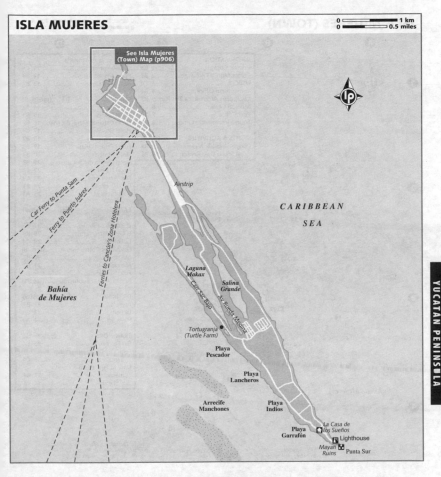

CARIBBEAN SEA

See Isla Mujeres (Town) Map (p906)

Car Ferry to Punta Sam

Ferry to Puerto Juárez

Ferries to Cancún's Zona Hotelera

Airstrip

Bahía de Mujeres

Laguna Makax

Salina Grande

Av Rueda Medina

Car Sec Bajo

Tortugranja (Turtle Farm)

Playa Pescador

Playa Lancheros

Arrecife Manchones

Playa Indios

Playa Garrafón

La Casa de los Sueños

Lighthouse

Mayan Ruins

Punta Sur

tropical social life and waters that are brilliant blue and bathtub warm.

History

Although many locals believe Isla Mujeres got its name because Spanish buccaneers kept their lovers there while they plundered galleons and pillaged ports, a less romantic but still intriguing explanation is probably more accurate. In 1517 Francisco Hernández de Córdoba sailed from Cuba to procure slaves for the mines there. His expedition came upon Isla Mujeres, and in the course of searching it the conquistadors located a stone temple containing clay figurines of Mayan goddesses. Córdoba named the island after the icons.

Today some archaeologists believe that the island was a stopover for the Maya en route to worship their goddess of fertility, Ixchel, on the island of Cozumel. The clay idols are thought to represent the goddess.

Orientation

The island is 8km long, 300m to 800m wide and 11km off the coast. The town of Isla Mujeres is at the island's northern tip, and the ruins of the Mayan temple are at the southern tip; the two are linked by Av Rueda Medina, a loop road that hugs the coast. Between Isla Mujeres and the ruins are a handful of small fishing villages, several saltwater lakes, a string of westward-facing beaches, a large lagoon and a small airport.

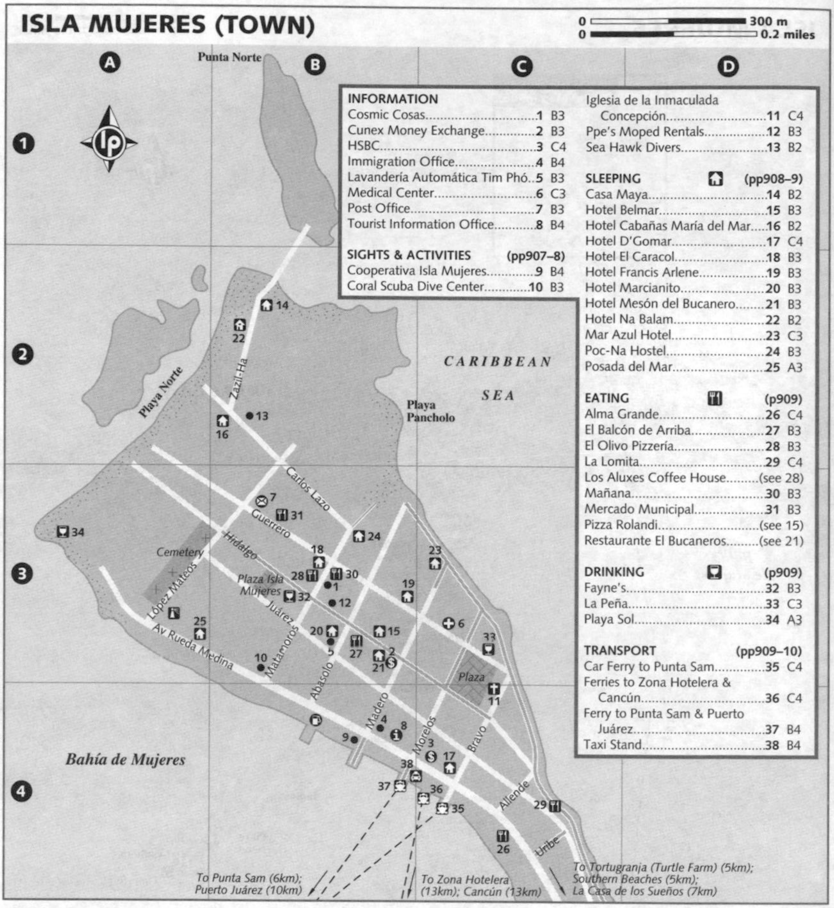

ISLA MUJERES (TOWN)
0 300 m
0 0.2 miles
INFORMATION
Cosmic Cosas 1 B3
Cunex Money Exchange 2 B3
HSBC 3 C4
Immigration Office 4 B4
Lavandería Automática Tim Phó 5 B3
Medical Center 6 C3
Post Office 7 B3
Tourist Information Office 8 B4
SIGHTS & ACTIVITIES (pp907–8)
Cooperativa Isla Mujeres 9 B4
Coral Scuba Dive Center 10 B3
Iglesia de la Inmaculada Concepción 11 C4
Ppe's Moped Rentals 12 B3
Sea Hawk Divers 13 B2
SLEEPING (pp908–9)
Casa Maya 14 B2
Hotel Belmar 15 B3
Hotel Cabañas María del Mar 16 B2
Hotel D'Gomar 17 C4
Hotel El Caracol 18 B3
Hotel Francis Arlene 19 B3
Hotel Marcianito 20 B3
Hotel Mesón del Bucanero 21 B3
Hotel Na Balam 22 B2
Mar Azul Hotel 23 C3
Poc-Na Hostel 24 B3
Posada del Mar 25 A3
EATING (p909)
Alma Grande 26 C4
El Balcón de Arriba 27 B3
El Olivo Pizzería 28 B3
La Lomita 29 C4
Los Aluxes Coffee House (see 28)
Mañana 30 B3
Mercado Municipal 31 B3
Pizza Rolandi (see 15)
Restaurante El Bucaneros (see 21)
DRINKING (p909)
Fayne's 32 B3
La Peña 33 C3
Playa Sol 34 A3
TRANSPORT (pp909–10)
Car Ferry to Punta Sam 35 C4
Ferries to Zona Hotelera & Cancún 36 C4
Ferry to Punta Sam & Puerto Juárez 37 B4
Taxi Stand 38 B4
Punta Norte
CARIBBEAN SEA
Playa Pancholo
Playa Norte
Zazil-Ha
Carlos Lazo
Guerrero
Hidalgo
Cemetery
Plaza Isla Mujeres
Juárez
López Mateos
Av Rueda Medina
Matamoros
Abasolo
Madero
Morelos
Bravo
Plaza
Allende
Uribe
Bahía de Mujeres
To Punta Sam (6km); Puerto Juárez (10km)
To Zona Hotelera (13km); Cancún (13km)
To Tortugranja (Turtle Farm) (5km); Southern Beaches (5km); La Casa de los Sueños (7km)

The best snorkeling sites and some of the best swimming beaches are on the island's southwest shore; the eastern shore is washed by the open sea, and the surf there is dangerous. The ferry docks, the town and the most popular sand beach (Playa Norte) are at the northern tip of the island.

Information

BOOKSTORES

Cosmic Cosas (Map p906; Matamoros 82) Just north of Hidalgo, this very cool little store buys, sells and trades mostly English-language books.

INTERNET ACCESS

Cosmic Cosas (see Bookstores earlier; per hr US$1.50) Speedy connections.

Laundry

Lavandería Automática Tim Phó (Juárez at Abasolo; per 3kg load US$3) Includes washing, drying and folding.

MEDICAL SERVICES

Medical Center (Guerrero btwn Madero & Morelos)

MONEY

Bital (Av Rueda Medina 3) across from the Zona Hotelera ferry dock has an ATM.

Cunex Money Exchange (Av Hidalgo at Av Madero) has good exchange rates.

POST

Post office (Guerrero at López Mateos)

TOURIST INFORMATION

Tourist Information Office (☎ 877-07-67; Av Rueda Medina btwn Madero & Morelos; ☯ 8am-8pm Mon-Fri, 9am-2pm Sat & Sun)

Sights & Activities

TORTUGRANJA (TURTLE FARM)

Three species of sea turtle lay eggs in the sand along the island's calm western shore. Although they are endangered, sea turtles are still killed throughout Latin America for their eggs and meat, both of which are considered a delicacy. In the 1980s, efforts by a local fisherman led to the founding of the **Isla Mujeres Tortugranja** (☎ 877-05-95; Carretera Sac Bajo Km 5; admission US$2; ☯ 9am-5pm), which protects the turtles' breeding grounds and places wire cages around their eggs to protect against predators. Hatchlings live in three large pools for up to a year, at which time they are tagged for monitoring and released. Because most turtles in the wild die within their first few months, the practice of guarding them until they are a year old greatly increases their chances of survival. Moreover, the turtles that leave this protected beach return each year, which means their offspring receive the same protection. The main draw here is several hundred sea turtles, ranging in weight from 150g to more than 300kg. The farm also has a small but good quality aquarium, displays on marine life and a gift shop. Tours are available in Spanish and English. The facility is easily reached by taxi (about US$3). If you're driving, biking or walking bear right at the unsigned 'Y' south of town.

MAYAN RUINS

At the south end of the island lie the severely worn remains of the **temple** (Map p905) dedicated chiefly to Ixchel, Mayan goddess of the moon and fertility. (This is the temple that Francisco Hernández de Córdoba's expedition came upon in 1517. The conquistadors found various clay female figures here; whether they were all likenesses of Ixchel or instead represented several goddesses is unclear.) In 1988 Hurricane Gilbert nearly finished the ruins off. Except for a still-distinguishable stairway and scattered remnants of stone buildings, there's little left to see other than the sea (a fine view) and, in the distance, Cancún. The ruins are beyond the lighthouse, just past Playa Garrafón. From downtown, a taxi costs about US$5.

BEACHES

Walk west along Calle Hidalgo or Calle Guerrero to reach the town's principal beach, **Playa Norte** (Map p906), sometimes called Playa Los Cocos or Cocoteros. The slope of the beach is gradual, and the transparent and calm waters are only chest-high even far from shore. Playa Norte is well supplied with bar/restaurants and can be crowded at times.

South of town 5km is **Playa Lancheros** (Map p905), the southernmost point served by local buses. The beach is less attractive than Playa Norte, but it sometimes has free musical festivities on Sunday. A taxi ride to Lancheros is US$2.

Another 1.5km south of Lancheros is **Playa Garrafón** (Map p905), with translucent water, colorful fish and little sand. Unfortunately the reef here has been heavily damaged by hurricanes and careless visitors. The water can be very choppy, sweeping you into jagged areas, so it's best to stay near shore. Avoid the overhyped Parque Natural and visit instead the **Hotel Garrafón de Castilla** (☎ 877-01-07; Carretera Punta Sur Km 6; admission US$2; ☯ 9am-5pm), which offers chairs, umbrellas, showers and baths with the entrance fee. Snorkeling gear is US$6 extra. It has a roped-off swimming area as well as a restaurant and snack bar. Locker and towel rentals are available too. Taxis from town cost about US$4.

DIVING & SNORKELING

Within a short boat ride of the island are a handful of lovely reef dives, such as Barracuda, La Bandera, El Jigueo and Manchones. A popular nonreef dive is the one to a cargo ship resting in 30m of water 90 minutes by boat northeast of Isla Mujeres. Known as **Ultrafreeze** (or El Frío) because of the unusually cool water found there, the site contains the intact hull of a 60m-long cargo ship.

At all the reputable dive centers you need to show your certification card, and you will be expected to have your own gear, though any piece of scuba equipment is usually available for rent. One reliable shop is **Coral Scuba Dive Center** (☎ 877-07-63; www.coral scubadivecenter.com; Matamoros & Av Rueda Medina; dives

US$30-100, snorkeling US$15). Another reliable place is friendly **Sea Hawk Divers** (☎ 877-02-96; abarran@prodigy.net.mx; Carlos Lazo; dives US$45-55, snorkeling US$20).

The fishermen of Isla Mujeres have formed a cooperative that offers snorkeling tours of various sites from US$14, including the reef off Playa Garrafón, as well as day trips to Isla Contoy (see also Poc-Na Hostel in Sleeping, following, and p910). You can book through its office, **Cooperativa Isla Mujeres** (☎ 877-02-74; Av Rueda Medina) in a *palapa* just steps away from the dock.

Sleeping

Each hotel seems to have a different high season; prices here are for mid-December through March, when you can expect many places to be booked solid by midday (earlier during Easter week). Some places offer substantially lower rates in low-season periods.

BUDGET

Poc-Na Hostel (Map p906; ☎ 877-00-90; www.pocna .com; cnr Matamoros & Carlos Lazo; tent sites per person US$6.50, dm US$9-12.50, d US$26-36; ☒ ☐) On 100m of beachfront property, this is the Club Med of hostels. There is a full beach restaurant/bar, a big, bright, airy *palapa*-roofed communal space plus a billiard and game room. There's live music every Saturday night and spontaneous festivities other days. Breakfast is included. Tents are provided for those who want to camp. Internet access is available for US$1.50 per hour. Bike rentals cost US$10 per day. Tours and activities are organized for every day of the week, including snorkeling excursions to Isla Contoy (US$35, including food and drink).

Hotel El Caracol (Map p906; ☎ 877-01-50; Matamoros btwn Hidalgo & Guerrero; d with fan/air-con US$25/35; ☒) This place offers 18 clean, well-furnished rooms with insect screens and tiled bathrooms; many have two double beds.

Hotel Marcianito (Map p906; ☎ 877-01-11; Abasolo 10; r US$30-35) The 'Little Martian' is a neat, tidy hotel offering 13 comfortably furnished, fan-cooled rooms.

MID-RANGE

Casa Maya (Map p906; ☎ 877-00-45; www.kasamaya .com.mx; Calle Zazil-Ha 129; d from US$6; ☒) This cheerful place has rooms and *cabañas* of different sizes and configurations (some

with air-con, some with fans), but all are clean and comfortable and most are bright and breezy. There's a communal lounge and guests are free to use the kitchen too. Best of all is its location fronting the calm and lovely Playa Secreto lagoon.

Mar Azul Hotel (Map p906; ☎ 877-01-20; Madero; d US$60; ☒ ☒) A block north of Guerrero right on the eastern beach, this hotel has a pool, restaurant and 91 nice, sizable rooms on three floors. All have balconies and most have wonderful sea views.

Posada del Mar (Map p906; ☎ 877-00-44; Av Rueda Medina 15; d US$70-85; ☒ ☒) This recently remodeled hotel was one of the island's first inns. It's simple, quiet and comfortable and just a block from the beach. The rooms are spacious and clean, and those in the main building have sea views and air-con. There's also a very attractive garden pool area.

Hotel Belmar (Map p906; ☎ 877-04-30; Hidalgo btwn Abasolo & Madero; d US$55-95; ☒) Hotel Belmar is above the Pizza Rolandi restaurant and is run by the same friendly family. All rooms are comfy, well kept, have cable TV and good air-con.

Hotel Mesón del Bucanero (Map p906; ☎ 877-02-10; www.bucaneros.com; Hidalgo btwn Abasolo & Madero; d US$30-75; ☒) Above El Bucanero restaurant, the charming rooms (most with air-con) all have TV and come with various combinations of beds, balcony, tub and fridge.

Hotel Francis Arlene (Map p906; ☎ 877-03-10; Guerrero 7; r with fan/air-con US$45/50; ☒) This homey hotel offers good-sized, comfortable rooms with fan and fridge. Most have a king bed or two doubles, and all have balconies, many with sea views.

Hotel D'Gomar (Map p906; ☎ 877-05-41; Av Rueda Medina btwn Morelos & Bravo; d with fan/air-con US$35/45; ☒) A friendly place facing the ferry dock, the D'Gomar has four floors of attractive, amply sized rooms with double beds, air-con and large tiled baths.

TOP END

La Casa de los Sueños (Map p905; ☎ 877-06-51; www.lossuenos.com; Carretera El Garrafón; d US$110-275; ☒ ☒) The nine-room 'Dream House' is pretty much that. This secluded B&B is nestled away on the south end of the island atop a bluff overlooking Bahia de Mujeres. The terraced rooms have breathtaking views. Most spectacular is the cliff-side pool, which appears to seamlessly merge with the sea. Breakfast is included, and smoking not allowed. Two pony-size Great Danes share the premises.

Hotel Na-Balam (Map p906; ☎ 877-02-79; www .nabalam.com; Calle Zazil-Ha; r from US$170; ☐ ☒) This hotel is situated on an ideal section of Playa Norte near the northern tip of the island. Most of the accommodations face the beach, while a few other thatched-roof units are across the street surrounding a garden with pool. All are decorated with simple elegance and numerous nice touches, and all have terraces or balconies with hammocks. The hotel offers yoga and meditation classes as well as massage services, two bars and an acclaimed restaurant.

Hotel Cabañas María del Mar (Map p906; ☎ 877-01-79; www.cabanasdelmar.com; cnr Carlos Lazo & Zazil-Ha; d US$110; ☒ ☒) Near Playa Norte, this hotel has 73 well-furnished rooms (all with balcony or terrace, many with sea or pool views and lovely tiled bathrooms), a large, lush courtyard and a restaurant and swimming pool. Rates include continental breakfast.

Eating

Most places to eat on the island are casual and relatively inexpensive, and the seafood, of course, is fresh and delicious.

Los Aluxes Coffee House (Map p906; Matamoros btwn Guerrero & Hidalgo; sandwiches US$4-5) The friendly Aluxes serves bagels with cream cheese, croissants, muffins, sandwiches and espresso drinks, including excellent iced mocha.

El Olivio Pizzería (Map p906; Matamoros btwn Guerrero & Hidalgo; pizza slices US$1.50) This pizzeria sells delicious slices of pizza, with just cheese or a variety of toppings, including seafood choices.

Mañana (Map p906; ☎ 877-04-30; cnr Matamoros & Guerrero; sandwiches US$2-5) This small, relaxed, indoor-outdoor café serves baguette sandwiches, coffee, juice blends and some Middle Eastern dishes.

Pizza Rolandi (Map p906; Hidalgo btwn Abasolo & Madero; mains US$7-10, pizzas US$6-10) Below the Hotel Belmar, the oh-so-popular Rolandi bakes very tasty thin-crust pizzas and calzones in a wood-fired oven. The menu also includes pasta, fresh salads, fish, good coffee and some Italian specialties.

Alma Grande (Map p906; Av Rueda Medina btwn Allende & Uribe; mains US$6-8) The Alma is a tiny, colorfully painted shack dishing up cocktails of shrimp, conch and octopus, heaping plates of delicious ceviche, and seafood soups.

La Lomita (Map p906; Juárez btwn Allende & Uribe; mains US$4-6) 'The Little Hill' serves good, inexpensive Mexican food. Seafood and chicken dishes predominate.

El Balcón de Arriba (Map p906; ☎ 877-05-13; Hidalgo; mains US$5-9) Just east of Abasolo, this is an airy, casual 2nd-floor eatery popular with tourists. El Balcón serves good fruit drinks, some veggie dishes and a large selection of seafood. Try the rich *camarones a la Reina* (shrimp in cream sauce) if you have friend who can help out.

Restaurante El Bucanero (Map p906; ☎ 877-01-26; Hidalgo btwn Abasolo & Madero; mains US$3-12) Below the Hotel Mesón del Bucanero, this fan-cooled, mostly outdoor restaurant has a pleasing ambience and a variety of alcoholic and nonalcoholic tropical shakes and drinks. The best deal is the *menú ejecutivo*: for about US$7 you can choose either a fish, meat or veggie dish, accompanied by soup, beans, rice and coffee.

Mercado Municipal (Map p906; Guerrero) At the town market, open daily, there are a couple of stalls serving simple but tasty and filling meals at the best prices on the island.

Drinking

The beach bar at Hotel Na Balam (see Sleeping earlier) is a popular spot Saturday and Sunday afternoons with live music, dancing and a three-hour-long happy hour.

Fayne's (Map p906; Hidalgo) Near Matamoros, Fayne's features live reggae, salsa and lots of dancing. If you work up an appetite on the dance floor, you can order some excellent Caribbean food here too.

La Peña (Map p906; Guerrero btwn Morelos & Bravo) Off the north side of the plaza, is this English-run club; it has a fun atmosphere, great music and best of all, an excellent sea breeze coming off the north shore.

Playa Sol (Map p906; Playa Norte) The Sol is a happening spot day and night with volleyball, a soccer area and good food and drinks at decent prices. It's a great spot for watching the sunset, and in high season bands play reggae, salsa, merengue and other danceable music.

Getting There & Away

There are four main points of embarkation to reach Isla Mujeres. The following description starts from the northernmost port and progresses southeast (p895). To reach Puerto Juárez or Punta Sam from downtown Cancún, catch a northbound bus on Av Tulum (US$0.40) displaying signs with those destinations.

PUNTA SAM

Punta Sam, about 7km north of Cancún center provides the only vehicle-carrying service to Isla Mujeres. The car ferries, which also carry passengers, take about an hour to reach the island. Departure times are 8am, 11am, 2:45pm, 5:30pm and 8:15pm from Punta Sam; from Isla Mujeres they are 6:30am, 9:30am, 12:45pm, 4:15pm and 7:15pm. Walk-ons and vehicle passengers pay US$1.50; cars cost US$19 vans US$24, motorcycles US$7.50 and bicycles US$6. If you're taking a car in high season, it's good to get in line an hour or so before departure time. Tickets go on sale just before the ferry begins loading.

PUERTO JUÁREZ

About 3km north of the Cancún city center is Puerto Juárez, from which express boats head to Isla Mujeres every 30 minutes from 6am to 8pm (US$4 one-way, 25 minutes), with a final departure at 9pm. Slower boats (US$2 one-way, 45 minutes) run roughly every hour from 5am to 5:30pm.

EL EMBARCADERO

The Shuttle departs from the Cancún dock at Playa Linda in the Zona Hotelera area approximately five times daily between 9:30am and 4:15pm, returning from Isla Mujeres at 12:30pm, 3:30pm and 5:15pm. The round-trip fare is US$15 and includes soft drinks. Show up at the terminal at least 20 minutes before departure so you'll have time to buy your ticket and get a good seat on the boat. It's the beige building between the Costa Real Hotel and the channel, on the mainland side of the bridge (Blvd Kukulcán Km 4).

PLAYA TORTUGAS

The **Isla Shuttle** departs Cancún's Zona Hotelera from the dock near Fat Tuesday's on Playa Tortugas beach (Km 6.35) at 9:15am, 11:30am, 1:45pm and 3:45pm, returning from Isla Mujeres at 10:15am, 12:30pm, 3:30pm and 6:30pm. The one-way fare is US$9 (40 minutes).

Getting Around

BUS & TAXI

By local (and infrequent) bus from the market or dock, you can get within 1.5km of Playa Garrafón; the terminus is Playa Lancheros. The owners of Cosmic Cosas bookstore can give you an idea of the bus's erratic schedule. Unless you're pinching pennies, you'd be better off taking a taxi anyway – the most expensive one-way trip on the island is under US$4. Taxi rates are set by the municipal government and are posted at the taxi stand just south of the ferry dock.

SCOOTER & GOLF CART

If you rent a scooter or 50cc Honda 'moped,' shop around, compare prices and look for new or newer machines in good condition with full gas tanks and reasonable deposits. Cost per hour is usually US$8 with a two-hour minimum, US$28 all day. Shops away from the busiest streets tend to have better prices, but not necessarily better equipment.

Many people find golf carts a good way to get around the island, and caravans of them can be seen tooling down the roads. They average US$12 per hour or US$35 per day. **Ppe's Moto Rent** (Map p906; ☎ 877-00-19; Hidalgo btwn Matamoros & Abasolo) is a good rental place for both scooters and golf carts.

BICYCLE

Cycling is an excellent way to get around the island. A number of shops rent bicycles for about US$2/7 an hour/day; most will ask for a deposit of about US$10.

David (☎ 044-998-860-00-75, Av Rueda Medina nr Abasolo) is reliable and has a good selection of bikes.

PARQUE NACIONAL ISLA CONTOY

From Isla Mujeres it's possible to take an excursion by boat to tiny, uninhabited Isla Contoy, a national park and bird sanctuary 25km north. Its dense foliage is home to more than 100 species, including brown pelicans, olive cormorants, wild turkey, brown boobies and red-pouched frigates, and it's subject to frequent visits by red flamingos, snowy egrets and white herons.

There is good snorkeling both en route to and just off Contoy, which sees about 1500 visitors a month. Bring mosquito repellent.

Daily visits to Isla Contoy are offered by the **Cooperativa Isla Mujeres** (☎ 877-02-74; Av Rueda Medina; adult US$40; ☼ tours 9am-5pm) The all-day tours include a light breakfast, lunch (including fish caught en route), drinks, stops for snorkeling (gear provided), and scientific information about the island.

ISLA HOLBOX

☎ 984 / pop 1600

Isla Holbox (hol-*bosh*) is a pristine beach site not yet overwhelmed by foreigners, though guesthouses and hotels (mostly Italian and Majorcan owned) are going up at a rapid pace. The island is 25km long and 3km wide, with seemingly endless beaches, tranquil waters and a galaxy of shells in various shapes and colors.

As part of the Yum Balam Reserve, the island is home to an array of protected flora and fauna species. From April to October over 400,000 flamingos visit the island. Dolphins are a common site year-round and during the summer months enormous and gentle whale-sharks swim the waters here. The only wildlife you won't enjoy encountering are the mosquitoes. Bring repellent and be prepared to stay inside for a couple of hours each evening.

The town of Holbox has sandy streets and few vehicles. Everything is within walking distance of the central plaza ('el Parque'), and locals will graciously give directions to visitors. You should know that there are no banks on the island and few places accept credit cards.

Sleeping

From budget to top-end, Holbox offers a variety of accommodations. Rates given here are for high season.

Note: some of the hotels pay taxi drivers to bring guests to them; don't let a driver's suggestion on where to stay sway you.

BUDGET

Posada Los Arcos (☎ 875-20-43; Juárez; d with fan/air-con US$20/3; ✖) This is the best budget option in town, with good-sized, bright rooms surrounding a central courtyard.

Posada d'Ingrid (☎ 875-20-70; d with fan/air-con US$25/35; ✖) This is a friendly place one block west and one block north of the parque. All rooms have hot water and TV.

MID-RANGE & TOP-END

All of the following accommodations are on the beach and all are fan-cooled.

Hotelito Casa Las Tortugas (☎ 875-21-19; www .holboxcasalastortugas.com; d US$45) Nestled between palms and flourishing bougainvillea, these lovely *palapa* units are bright, airy and, clean with comfy beds and tiled bathrooms. Some units have kitchenettes. There is a small café where the hospitable hosts serve breakfast, and a great shared common space – a sort of lookout hut – on the upstairs balcony with expansive sea views.

Posada Mawimbi (☎ 875-20-03; www.mawimbi .com.mx; d US$45) Next door to Las Tortugas, the Mawimbi shares much of the same charms as its neighbor, though the units are a little darker. Each room has a balcony, comfortable beds and a hammock and a few have kitchenettes. During summer months staff at Mawimbi guide whale-shark watching expeditions. They also organize dive trips – for expert divers only.

Resort Xaloc (☎ 875-21-60; www.holbox-xalocre sort.com; d US$120; ⚲) This intimate eco-resort is comprised of 18 individual palm-roofed *cabañas*. Each is rustic and romantic with tile floors, wood beamed ceilings, spacious bathrooms and big comfy beds, and all have porches with hammocks. There are two swimming pools, a restaurant and bar plus a small library and games room. Breakfast is included.

Villas Chimay (☎ 875-22-20; www.holbox.info/; d US$75) This Swiss-owned eco-getaway is 1km west of town on a secluded section of beach. There are seven cheery *palapa*-topped bungalows and a good restaurant/bar. The extremely eco-conscious and knowledgeable staff organize walking tours and kayaking trips.

Villas Delfines (☎ 884-86-06; www.holbox.com; d US$100) This charming place is an eco-tel that composts waste, catches rainwater and uses solar power. Its large beach bungalows are built on stilts, fully screened and fan-cooled. Meal plans are also available.

Eating & Drinking

The specialty on the island is seafood in general and lobster in particular. The restaurants in the beach hotels tend to be good but pricey; an exception is the **restaurant** (US$5-7) at Hotel Faro Viejo, which has a good menu and a prime right-on-the-beach location.

YUCATÁN PENINSULA

Pizzería Edelyn (el Parque; pizza US$4.50-15, mains US$4-8) This popular pizzeria serves pizza and a range of tasty seafood dishes.

La Peña Colibrí (el Parque; meals US$3-5) This cozy spot serves Mexican dishes with an international flair. Most weekends there is low-key live musical entertainment, often a flamenco dancer and an accompanying guitarist.

Jugos Y Licuados La Isla (el Parque) Next door to La Peña Colibrí (and owned by the same people), this little juice bar/café serves generous portions of fruit salad and freshly blended fruit drinks. It's also a good place for a strong cup of coffee.

Getting There & Away

There's a launch that ferries passengers (US$3.50, 25 minutes, eight times per day from 5am to 6pm winter and 6am to 7pm summer) to Holbox from the port village of Chiquilá. It is usually timed to meet arriving and departing buses. Three 2nd-class buses (two Mayab, one Noreste) leave Cancún daily for Chiquilá (US$6, 3½ hours, 8am, 12:30pm and 1:45pm). There are also Oriente buses that travel from Valladolid (US$6, 2½ hours, 1:30pm). Another way to go is to take a 2nd-class bus traveling between Mérida and Cancún to El Ideal, on Highway 180 about 73km south of Chiquilá. From there you can take a cab (about US$20) or catch one of the Chiquilá-bound buses coming from Cancún, which pass through El Ideal around 10:30am and 3:30pm. Schedules are subject to change; verify ahead of time.

If you're driving, you can either park your car in Chiquilá (US$2.50 per day) or try to catch the infrequent car ferry to Holbox. It doesn't run on a daily schedule, and you won't have much use for a car once you arrive.

PUERTO MORELOS

☎ 998 / pop 2800

Puerto Morelos, 33km south of Cancún, is a quiet fishing village known principally for its car ferry to Cozumel. It has some good hotels, and travelers who spend the night here find it refreshingly free of tourists. Scuba divers come to explore the splendid stretch of barrier reef 600m offshore, reachable by boat.

This small town centers around the main plaza. A Bital ATM is located at the

northeast corner of the plaza and diagonally across the plaza from the bank you will find Computips, an air-conditioned Internet place.

Two kilometers south of the turnoff for Puerto Morelos is the **Jardín Botánico Alfredo Barrera** (admission US$7; ⏲ 9am-5pm Mon-Sat), with 3km of trails through several native habitats. The orchids, bromeliads and other flora are identified in English, Spanish and Latin. Buses may be hailed directly in front of the garden.

Sleeping & Eating

Posada Amor (☎ 871-00-33; www.posadaamor.com; d US$30) The Amor is 100m southwest of the plaza and has been in operation for many years. The pleasant rooms are fan-cooled. It has a shady back area with tables, chairs and an abundance of plants. Meals are available too.

Hotel Hacienda Morelos (☎ 871-04-48; d US$68; P ✖ ⛱) On the waterfront, about 150m south of the plaza, the Morelos has 15 very appealing, breezy rooms with sea views, kitchenettes and air-con. There's also a pool and a good restaurant.

Rancho Libertad (☎ 871-01-81; www.rancholiber tad.com; d downstairs/upstairs US$70/80 P ✖) This mellow B&B, beyond the ferry terminal, is the best place in town and has 15 charming guestrooms in one- and two-story thatched bungalows. All rooms have private bath and good ventilation; some have air-con. There's a pleasing beach, and room rates include breakfast for two and use of bikes and snorkeling gear. Massage (and other bodywork) is available.

La Nueva Luna (☎ 871-05-13; Av Rojo Gómez; mains US$4-5; ⏲ closed Tue) This is the place to go for hearty sandwiches and healthy faux-meat veggie dishes like soy burgers, soy ham, soy hotdogs (and soy forth). This is also a good place to find out about yoga classes and spiritual retreats offered in and around town.

Mama's Bakery (☎ 845-68-10; dishes US$3-5) Mama's is a couple of blocks north of La Nueva Luna (see earlier). In addition to a variety of gourmet breads they serve brownies cakes and coffee, plus fruit juice blends and good breakfasts.

John Gray's Kitchen (☎ 871-06-55; Av Niños Héroes; mains US$9-12; ⏲ 6-10pm Mon-Sat) John cooks up some really delicious dinners. The ecclectic menu changes frequently and may include anything from Thai curry chicken to pork chops.

Getting There & Away

Playa Express and Riviera buses traveling between Cancún and Playa del Carmen drop you by the side of Highway 307. Some Mayab buses enter town.

The plaza is 2km from the highway. Taxis are usually waiting by the turnoff to shuttle people into town, and there's usually a taxi or two near the square to shuttle people back over to the highway. The official local rate is US$1.25 each way, for as many people as you can stuff in.

The **transbordador** (vehicle ferry; ☎ 871-06-14, 987-872-09-50 in Cozumel; per person/car with driver US$6/80) to Cozumel leaves Puerto Morelos most days at 5am, with an additional departure Sunday and Monday at 2pm. Other days a second departure occurs sometime between 10am and 4pm. All times are subject to change according to season or the weather; during high seas, the ferry won't leave at all. Unless you plan to stay awhile on Cozumel, it's really not worth shipping your vehicle. You must get in line at least two hours before departure and hope there's enough space. The voyage takes anywhere from 2½ to four hours. Departure from Cozumel is from the dock in front of the Hotel Sol Caribe, south of town along the shore road.

COZUMEL

☎ 987 / pop 70,000

Cozumel, 71km south of Cancún, is a teardrop-shaped coral island ringed by crystalline waters. It is Mexico's only Caribbean island and, measuring 53km by 14km, it is also the country's largest. Called Ah-Cuzamil-Peten (Island of Swallows) by its earliest inhabitants, Cozumel has been a favorite destination for divers since 1961, when a Jacques Cousteau documentary about its glorious reefs first appeared on TV. Today, no fewer than 100 world-class dive sites have been identified within 5km of Cozumel, and no less than a dozen of them are shallow enough for snorkeling.

History

Mayan settlement here dates from AD 300. During the postclassic period, Cozumel flourished as a trade center and, more importantly, a ceremonial site. Every Mayan

woman on the Yucatán Peninsula and beyond was expected to make at least one pilgrimage here to pay tribute to Ixchel – the goddess of fertility and the moon – at a temple erected in her honor at San Gervasio, near the center of the island.

At first Spanish contact with Cozumel (in 1518, by Juan de Grijalva and his men), there were at least 32 Mayan building groups on the island. According to Spanish chronicler Diego de Landa, Cortés sacked one of the Mayan centers a year later. He left the others intact, apparently satisfied with converting the island's population to Christianity. Smallpox introduced by the Spanish wiped out half of the 8000 Maya. Of the survivors, only about 200 escaped genocidal attacks by conquistadors in the late 1540s.

The island remained virtually deserted into the late 17th century, its coves providing sanctuary for several notorious pirates, including Jean Lafitte and Henry Morgan. In 1848 Mayans fleeing the War of the Castes began to resettle Cozumel. At the beginning of the 20th century the island's mostly *mestizo* population grew, thanks to the craze for chewing gum. Cozumel was a port of call on the chicle export route, and locals harvested chicle on the island. After the demise of chicle Cozumel's economy remained strong owing to the construction of a US air base during WWII.

When the US military departed, the island fell into an economic slump, and many of its people moved away. Those who stayed fished for a living until 1961, when Cousteau's documentary broadcast Cozumel's glorious sea life to the world. The tourists began arriving almost overnight.

Orientation

It's easy to make your way on foot around the island's only town, San Miguel de Cozumel. The waterfront boulevard is Av Rafael Melgar; along Melgar south of the main ferry dock (the 'Muelle Fiscal') is a narrow sand beach. The main plaza is just opposite the ferry dock. The airport is 2.2km north of town.

Information
BOOKSTORES

Fama (Av 5 Nte btwn Av Juárez & Calle 2 Nte) This bookstore carries books and periodicals in English and Spanish as well as some CDs.

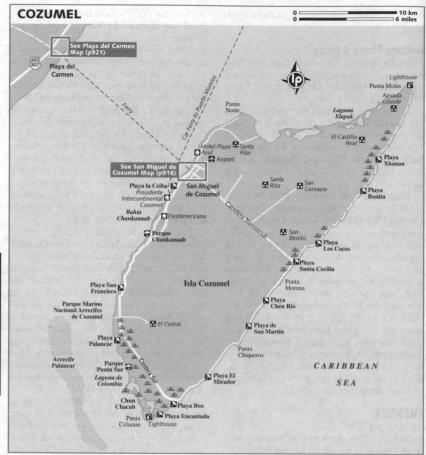

COZUMEL

See Playa del Carmen Map (p921)

Playa del Carmen

San Miguel de Cozumel

See San Miguel de Cozumel Map (p916)

Car Ferry to Puerto Morelos

Punta Norte

Hotel Playa Azul

Airport

Playa la Ceiba

Presidente Intercontinental Cozumel

Bahía Chankanaab

Fiestamericana

Parque Chankanaab

Playa San Francisco

Parque Marino Nacional Arrecifes de Cozumel

Isla Cozumel

Santa Rita

San Gervasio

El Castillo Real

Laguna Xlapak

Aguada Grande

Lighthouse
Punta Molas

Playa Xhanan

Playa Bonita

San Benito

Playa Los Cocos

Playa Santa Cecilia

Punta Morena

Playa Chen Río

Arrecife Palancar

Playa Palancar

Parque Punta Sur

Laguna de Colombia

Chun Chacab

Punta Celarain

El Cedral

Playa de San Martín

Punta Chiqueros

Playa El Mirador

Playa Box

Playa Encantada

Lighthouse

Costera Sur

Carretera Transversal

Santa Pilar

CARIBBEAN SEA

0   10 km
0   6 miles

MEX 307

Ferry

YUCATÁN PENINSULA

INTERNET ACCESS
Rockafé (Salas btwn Avs 15 & 20 Sur; per hr US$2)
This place is air-conditioned, serves snacks and has good connections.

LAUNDRY
Express Lavandería (Salas btwn Avs 5 & 10 Sur; per load US$6) Includes washing and drying.

MEDICAL SERVICES
Centro Médico de Cozumel (☎ 872-35-45; cnr Calle 1 Sur & Av 50 Nte) Come here for medical assistance or in case of emergency.

MONEY
For currency exchange, try any of the banks near the main plaza. Many have ATMs.

POST
Post office (Calle 7 Sur at Av Melgar)

TOURIST OFFICES
Tourist Information Booth (ferry dock; ✆ 8am-4pm Mon-Sat)
Tourist Information Office (☎ 872-75-63; Plaza del Sol, Main Plaza; ✆ 9am-3pm Mon-Fri)
Tourist Police Kiosk (Main Plaza; ✆ 9am-11:30pm)
The police are helpful with information and directions.

Sights
In order to see most of the island you will have to rent a bicycle, moped or car, or take a taxi. The following route will take you south from San Miguel, then counter-clockwise around the island. There are some

places along the way to stop for food and drink, but all the same it's good to bring water.

MUSEO DE LA ISLA DE COZUMEL

Before you go explore the island, check out the fine **Museo de la Isla de Cozumel** (Av Melgar btwn Calles 4 & 6 Nte; admission US$3; ☺ 9am-6pm). Exhibits present a clear and detailed picture of the island's flora, fauna, geography, geology and ancient Mayan history. Thoughtful and detailed signs in English and Spanish accompany the exhibits. It's a good place to learn about coral before hitting the water, and it's one not to miss before you leave the island. Hours may vary seasonally.

PARQUE CHANKANAAB

Parque Chankanaab (admission US$10; ☺ 6am-6pm) on the bay of the same name is a very popular snorkeling spot, though there's not a lot to see in the water beyond brightly colored fish and some deliberately sunken artificial objects. The beach is a beauty, though, and 50m inland is a limestone lagoon surrounded by iguanas and inhabited by turtles. You're not allowed to swim or snorkel there, but it's picturesque nevertheless. The beach is lined with *palapas* and fiberglass lounge chairs, and you can rent snorkeling and diving equipment or try out 'snuba' (diving with a helmet that requires no special training).

Dolphin and sea lion shows are included in the admission price. The grounds also hold a small archaeological park containing replica Olmec heads and Mayan artifacts, a small museum holding objects imported from Chichén Itzá, and a botanical garden with 400 species of tropical plants. Other facilities include a restaurant, bar and snack shops, as well as dressing rooms, lockers and showers (included in the admission fee). A taxi from town costs about US$10 one-way.

PLAYA PALANCAR

Palancar, about 17km south of town, is one of the island's nicest publicly accessible beaches. There's a **beach club** that rents hydro bikes, kayaks, snorkeing gear and sailboats, plus a restaurant and a dive operation. Nearby Arrecife Palancar (Palancar Reef) has some very good diving and snorkeling spots.

PARQUE PUNTA SUR

The southern tip of the island has been turned into the overpriced eco-park, **Parque Punta Sur** (☎ 872-09-14; admission US$10; ☺ 9am-5pm). Visitors board an open vehicle for the 3km ride to visit picturesque **Celarain lighthouse** and the small nautical museum at its base. Another vehicle carries visitors to **Laguna Colombia**, part of a three-lagoon system that is the habitat of crocodiles and many resident and migratory waterfowl. A pontoon-boat ride on the lagoon (US$3) gives you a chance to see more birds.

THE EAST COAST

The eastern shoreline is the wildest part of the island and highly recommended for beautiful seascapes. Unfortunately, except at **Punta Chiqueros**, **Playa Chen Río** and **Punta Morena**, swimming is dangerous on Cozumel's east coast because of riptides and undertows. There are a few small restaurants along the road serving seafood; most are expensive, but have great views of the sea.

PUNTA MOLAS

Beyond where the east coast highway meets the Carretera Transversal, intrepid travelers may take a poorly maintained, infrequently traveled road toward **Punta Molas**, the island's northeast point, accessible only by 4WD or on foot. About 17km down the road are the Mayan ruins known as **El Castillo Real**, and a few kilometers further is **Aguada Grande**. Both sites are quite far gone, their significance lost to time. In the vicinity of Punta Molas are some fairly good beaches and a few more minor ruins. If you head down this road be aware of the risk: if your vehicle breaks down, you can't count on flagging down another motorist for help.

The best camping spot along the road is Playa Bonita. Playa Xhanan isn't nearly as pretty, and there are no sandy beaches north of it.

Diving & Snorkeling

Cozumel is one of the most popular diving destinations in the world. Its diving conditions are unsurpassed for many reasons, chief among them is the fantastic year-round visibility (50m and greater) and jaw-droppingly awesome variety of marine life. Many of the dive sites are within the protected Parque Nacional Marino Arrecifes de

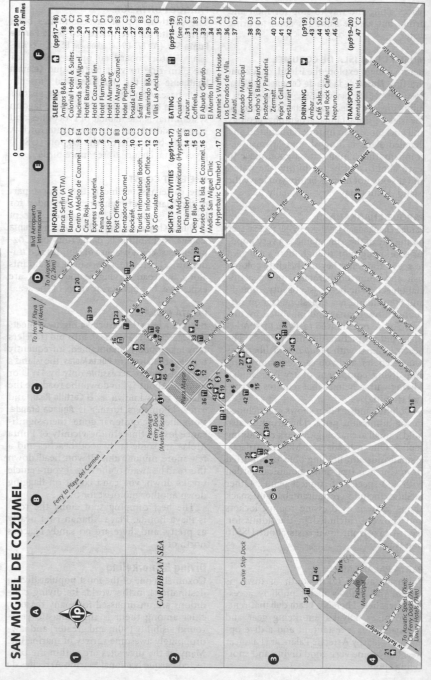

SAN MIGUEL DE COZUMEL

INFORMATION	
Banca Serfín (ATM)......................	1 C2
Banorte (ATM).............................	2 C2
Centro Médico de Cozumel........	3 E4
Cruz Roja...................................	4 C2
Express Lavandería.....................	5 C3
Fama Bookstore..........................	6 C2
HSBC..	7 C2
Post Office..................................	8 B3
Rentadora Cozumel.....................	9 C3
Rockafé.......................................	10 C3
Tourist Information Booth............	11 C2
Tourist Information Office............	12 C3
US Consulate...............................	13 D2

SIGHTS & ACTIVITIES	(pp914–17)
Buceo Médico Mexicano (Hyperbaric Chamber)..............	14 B3
Deep Blue...................................	15 C3
Museo de la Isla de Cozumel.......	16 C1
Médica San Miguel Clinic (Hyperbaric Chamber).........	17 D2

SLEEPING	(pp917–18)
Amigos B&B................................	18 C4
Colonial Hotel & Suites...............	19 C2
Hacienda San Miguel...................	20 D1
Hotel Barracuda.........................	21 A4
Hotel Cozumel Inn......................	22 C2
Hotel Flamingo..........................	23 D1
Hotel Marruang..........................	24 C2
Hotel Maya Cozumel..................	25 B3
Hotel Pepita...............................	26 C3
Posada Letty...............................	27 C3
Safari Inn....................................	28 B3
Tamarindo B&B...........................	29 D2
Villas Las Anclas........................	30 C3

EATING	(pp918–19)
Acuario...........................	(see 35)
Azucar..	31 C2
Coffeelia.....................................	32 B3
El Abuelo Gerardo......................	33 C2
El Morrito III..............................	34 D1
Jeannie's Waffle House...............	35 A3
Los Dorados de Villa...................	36 C2
Manati..	37 D2
Mercado Municipal Loncherías...	38 D3
Pancho's Backyard......................	39 D1
Pastelería y Panadería Zermatt...	40 D2
Pepe's Grill.................................	41 C2
Restaurant La Choza....................	42 C3

DRINKING	(p919)
Ambar...	43 C2
Café Salsa...................................	44 D2
Hard Rock Café...........................	45 C2
Neptuno.....................................	46 A3

TRANSPORT	(pp919–20)
Rentadora Isis............................	47 C2

Cozumel (Cozumel Reefs Marine National Park), declared in 1996.

There are scores of dive centers on Cozumel and dozens more in Playa del Carmen (p920). Prices vary, but in general, expect to pay about US$70 for a two-tank dive (less if you bring your own BCD and regulator), US$60 for an introductory 'resort' course and US$350 for PADI open-water-diver certification. Multiple-dive packages and discounts for groups or those paying in cash can bring these rates down significantly.

There are dozens of dive shops and instructors in Cozumel. Listed below are some of the most reputable ones. All are in downtown San Miguel. Some offer snorkeling and deep-sea fishing trips as well as dives and diving instruction.

Acuatic Sports (☎ 872-06-40; www.scubacozumel.com; cnr Av 15 Sur & Calle 21 Sur) Owner Sergio Sandoval has been diving for more than 30 years and is as enthusiastic as ever.

Deep Blue (☎ 872-56-53; www.deepbluecozumel.com; cnr Av 10 Sur at Salas) This PADI, NAUI, TDI and IANTD operation has very good gear and fast boats. Among others, they offer trips to Arrecife Cantarell when the eagel rays are congregating.

There are several hyperbaric chambers in San Miguel. Two reliable ones are: **Buceo Médico Mexicano** (☎ 872-14-30; Calle 5 Sur btwn Avs Melgar & 5 Sur); and **Cozumel Hyperbaric Research** (☎ 872-01-030; Calle 6 Nte btwn Avs 5 &10 Nte) in the Médica San Miguel clinic.

Snorkelers: all of the best sites are reached by boat. A half-day tour will cost US$30 to US$50, but you'll do some world-class snorkeling. For an impressive but less dramatic snorkeling experience you can walk into the gentle surf at Playa La Ceiba, Bahía Chankanaab, Playa San Francisco and elsewhere.

Sleeping

All hotel rooms come with private bath and fan. Prices in all categories are winter rates and may be much lower at other times of year. Whatever the season, if business is slow, most places are willing to negotiate prices.

BUDGET

Hotel Pepita (☎ 872-00-98; Av 15 Sur btwn Calles 1 Sur & Rosado Salas; d US$30; ✷) This is a friendly place with well-maintained rooms grouped around a garden. All have two double beds, refrigerators and air-con, and there's free morning coffee.

Hotel Cozumel Inn (☎ 872-03-14; Calle 4 Nte btwn Avs Melgar & 5 Nte; d with fan/air-con US$30/37; ✷ ⚭) This hotel has 30 decent rooms and a small swimming pool, well-maintained and pleasant rooms, all with comfortable beds and hot showers.

Hotel Marruang (☎ 872-16-78; Rosado Salas 440; r US$28) This hotel, entered via a passageway across from the municipal market, is simple and clean with well-screened fan-cooled rooms.

MID-RANGE

Amigo's B&B (☎ 872-38-68; www.bacalar.net; Calle 7 Sur btwn Avs 25 & 30 Sur; d US$70; ✷ ⚭) It's worth the hike from the center to enjoy one of the three well-appointed, cottage-style rooms here. All have air-con and full kitchenettes, and there's a huge garden with fruit trees and an inviting pool. Breakfast included. Book ahead.

Tamarindo B&B (☎ 872-36-14; www.cozumel.net/bb/tamarind; Calle 4 Nte 421; d from US$40) Near Av 20 Nte, five blocks from downtown, this is another out-of-the-way place but it's well worth it. Run by a Mexican architect and his French wife, this beautifully designed B&B holds five guest rooms, each one decorated with Mexican folk art and tasteful small touches. Each has cable TV and ample bathrooms and a couple have air-con. A big breakfast is included and there is an open air kitchenette and barbeque for guest use.

Villas Las Anclas (☎ 872-61-03; www.lasanclas.com; Av 5 Sur btwn Calles 3 & 5 Sur; d US$75; ✷) Lovely, roomy two-story suites with air-con and kitchenettes are clustered around a leafy garden. The excellent complimentary breakfasts are served in your suite.

Hotel Flamingo (☎ 872-12-64; www.hotelflamingo.com; Calle 6 Nte btwn Avs 5 Nte & Melgar; d US$40-60; ✷) This colorful hotel is charming and friendly. The spacious comfortable rooms (the best are the upstairs ones with air-con) surround a leafy courtyard where you can eat breakfast or have a drink. There is also a sundeck on the roof with nice views. Guests can rent bikes and snorkeling equipment.

Hacienda San Miguel (☎ 872-19-86; www.haciendasanmiguel.com; Calle 10 Nte btwn Av 5 & Melgar; r US$70; ✷) Built and furnished to resemble an old *hacienda,* this hotel seems a little out of place in its island habitat but has a lot of charm nonetheless. All rooms surround a park-like courtyard and all have air-con and fully equipped kitchenettes. Niceties include bathrobes and continental breakfast served in your room.

Hotel Barracuda (☎ 872-00-02; www.cozumel.net /hotels/barracuda/; Av Melgar 628; d US$75; ❌ 🖳) On the beach five blocks south of downtown, the Barracuda is a good spot for divers, snorkelers or anyone who wants to enjoy the water. There is a pier, diveshop, rinse tank and gear storage lockers on the premises. There's also a restaurant and Internet service. Most of the 52 rooms have sea views, all have air-con and small refrigerators.

Colonial Hotel & Suites (☎ 872-90-90; www.suites colonial.com; Av 5 Sur btwn Calles Rosado Salas & 1 Sur; r US$70) The Colonial is down a passageway off Av 5 Sur near Rosado Salas. It has studios and nice, spacious, one-bedroom suites (some sleep four people) with kitchenettes. All rooms have cable TV, fridge and air-con, and breakfast is included.

Safari Inn (☎ 872-01-01; www.aquasafari.com; Av Melgar at Calle 5; d US$45; ❌) This simple, very clean and friendly hotel is above Aqua Safari Dive Shop and across the street from the shop's pier. This is a nice place to stay for divers and nondivers alike. The rooms are big, beds are comfortable, showers are warm and the air-con cool. The streetside corner rooms have nice views and are particularly bright and breezy.

TOP END

Beginning several kilometers south of town are the big luxury resort hotels.

Presidente Intercontinental Cozumel (☎ 872-95-00; www.cozumel.interconti.com; Carretera a Chankanaab Km 6.5; r from US$200; P ❌ 🖳) This is one of the island's oldest luxury hotels and retains to this day all its original elegance and charm. It has a beach and 253 posh guestrooms, many with sea views, set amid tropical gardens and swimming pools. Wild iguanas roam the grounds.

Fiesta Americana (☎ 872-26-22, 800-343-7821 in the US; www.fiestamericana.com; Carretera a Chankanaab Km 7.5; r from US$125; P ❌ 🖳) This dive resort has plenty of gardens, a spectacular swimming pool, 172 mostly ocean-view rooms (with balconies, safes and full minibars) and 56 'Tropical Casitas' behind the main building.

Hotel Playa Azul (☎ 872-01-99; www.playa-azul .com; Carretera a San Juan Km 4; d from US$145; P ❌ 🖳) On its own pretty stretch of beach, this hotel north of town offers spacious and comfortable rooms; all of them have balconies with sea views. The hotel has bar, restaurant and gorgeous pool.

Eating
BUDGET

Cheapest of all eating places, with tasty food, are the little market *loncherías* next to the **Mercado Municipal** (Rosado Salas btwn Avs 20 & 25 Sur). All offer soup and a main course for around US$3, with a large selection of dishes available; ask about cheap *comidas corridas* not listed on the menu.

Coffeelia (Calle 5 Sur btwn Avs Melgar & 5 Sur; breakfast US$3-5) This is a meeting place for Cozumel's art community and the ambience is particularly relaxed. The menu includes quiches, good salads and vegetarian dishes, and premium organic coffee.

Pastelería y Panadería Zermatt (cnr Av 5 Nte & Calle 4 Nte; meals US$.50-2) Try this place for delicious baked goods including whole-wheat breads. They also serve excellent espresso drinks.

MID-RANGE

Los Dorados de Villa (☎ 872-01-97; Calle 1 Sur nr Av 5 Sur; mains US$4-10) The menu here is Mexican with an emphasis on regional dishes from Mexico City. They also have a selection of seafood dishes, all of which are fresh and satisfying.

El Abuelo Gerardo (Av 10 Nte btwn Av Juárez & Calle 2 Nte; mains US$6-12) The menu here is extensive (mostly Mexican) and includes seafood. Guacamole and chips are on the house.

Restaurant La Choza (☎ 872-09-58; cnr Salas & Av 10 Sur; mains US$8-12) This is an excellent and popular restaurant specializing in authentic regional cuisine. All entrées include soup.

Azucar (☎ 869-26-35; Salas 58 btwn Avs Melgar & 5 Sur; mains US$7-12) This cozy, dimly lit, chalet-looking restaurant specializes in fondue and wine. The service is especially friendly and attentive.

Jeannie's Waffle House (☎ 872-60-95; Av Melgar & Calle 11 Sur; breakfast US$3-7, sandwiches US$5-6) The sea views are great from the outdoor courtyard here. Jeannie's serves waffles (of course), hash browns, egg dishes, sandwiches and other light fare.

Acuario (☎ 872-60-95; Av Melgar & Calle 11 Sur; mains US$4-12) Jeannie's Waffle House by day, Acuario by night. The bustling breakfast joint transforms into a romantic dining spot in late afternoon. The menu is mostly Mexican with plenty of good seafood options.

El Morrito III (☎ 876-01-07; Calle 6 Nte btwn Avs Melgar & 5 Sur; mains US$4-10) This is a small family-run eatery, which serves good Mexican dishes, breakfasts and *licuados* (blended fruit drinks).

TOP END

Pepe's Grill (Av Melgar; mains US$20-25) Just south of Salas, this is traditionally considered Cozumel's finest restaurant and the prices reflect this reputation. It's mostly meat (steaks and prime rib), but there's also charcoal-broiled lobster (available at market price, typically around US$35).

Manatí (cnr Calle 8 Nte & Av 10 Nte; mains US$7-15) This pleasant New Age restaurant serves inventive cuisine. There's usually at least one veggie dish on the menu, as well as pasta, chicken and fish dishes, plus espresso drinks.

Pancho's Backyard (☎ 872-21-41; Av Melgar & Calle 8 Nte; mains US$10-17) This atmospheric restaurant is set in an intimate and handsomely decorated inner courtyard. The food (mostly seafood) is as good as the ambience.

Drinking

Ambar (Av 5 Sur btwn Calles 1 Sur & Salas; ⊙ closed Wed) This artistically decorated bar and lounge has a lovely garden area where you can enjoy a drink and a light snack. There's DJ-spun lounge and house music inside and live music on Saturdays.

Hard Rock Café (Av Melgar) Near the main ferry dock, the Hard Rock has live music most nights of the week. Go on, add another T-shirt to your collection!

Neptuno (cnr Av Melgar & Calle 11 Sur; ⊙ Thu-Sat) The only disco in town worth the title; it's huge and generally not crowded so there is lots of room to dance.

Getting There & Away

AIR

There are some direct flights from the US, but European flights are usually routed via the US or Mexico City. **Continental** (☎ 800-231-0856 in the US; www.continental.com) has direct flights from Newark and Houston. **Mexicana** (☎ 872-02-63) flies direct to Mexico City on Saturday and Sunday.

Aerocozumel (☎ 872-09-28), with offices at the airport, flies a few times daily between Cancún and Cozumel.

BOAT

Passenger ferries run from Playa del Carmen (p924), and vehicle ferries run from Puerto Morelos (p913).

Getting There & Around

AIR

The airport is about 2km north of town. You can take a van from the airport into town for about US$5 (slightly more to the hotels south of town), but you'll have to take a taxi (US$4.50 from town, US$9 to US$20 from southern hotels) to return to the airport.

TAXI

Fares in and around town are US$2 per ride; luggage may cost extra. Carry exact change. There is no bus service.

CAR & MOTORCYCLE

Rates for rental cars usually run US$35 (for a beat-up VW Beetle) to US$50 per day, all-inclusive, though you'll pay more during late December and January. There are plenty of agencies around the main plaza. **Rentadora Isis** (☎ 872-33-67; Av 5 Nte btwn Calles 2 & 4 Nte) rents cars, bicycles and scooters. If you rent, observe the law on vehicle occupancy. Usually only five people are allowed in a vehicle. If you carry more, the police will fine you.

Note that some agencies will deduct tire damage from your deposit, even if tires are old and worn. Be particularly careful about this if you're renting a 4WD for use on unpaved roads; straighten out the details before you sign.

There's a gas station on Av Juárez five blocks east of the main square.

Motorbikes are one way to tour the island on your own, and rental opportunities abound. The standard price is US$30 a day (US$20 in the off-season), with gas, insurance and tax included.

To rent, you must have a valid driver's license, and you must leave a credit card slip or put down a deposit (usually US$100). There is a helmet law and it is enforced (the fine for not wearing one is US$25), although most moped-rental people won't

YUCATÁN PENINSULA

mention it. Before you sign a rental agreement, be sure to request a helmet.

The best time to rent is first thing in the morning, when all the machines are there. Choose one with a working horn, brakes, lights, starter, rearview mirrors and a full tank of fuel; remember that the price asked will be the same whether you rent the newest machine or the oldest rattletrap.

Bring a towel to toss on the bike's seat when parked – the black plastic can get blisteringly hot in the sun. Keep in mind that you're not the only one unfamiliar with the road here, and some of your fellow travelers may be hitting the bottle. Drive carefully.

BICYCLE
Bicycles typically rent for US$5 to US$10 for 24 hours and can be a great way to get to Bahía Chankanaab and other spots on this flat island.

PLAYA DEL CARMEN
☎ 984 / pop 50,000

Only a decade ago Playa was still a relatively small fishing village. Travelers passed through here to catch the Cozumel-bound ferry but few lingered long in the sleepy town. As Cancún's popularity grew over the years, however, the number of travelers roaming this part of the Yucatán Peninsula increased dramatically, as did the number of hotels and restaurants serving them. Today Playa del Carmen is the fastest growing city in all of Mexico, and rivals Cancún as a preferred vacation destination.

What's to do in Playa? Hang out. Swim. Dive. Shop. Eat. Drink. Walk the beach. Get some sun. Listen to beach bands. Dance in clubs. In the evening, Playa's pedestrian mall, Quinta Av (5th Ave), is a popular place to stroll and dine, or drink and people-watch, or any combination of the above, though the number of restaurants and timeshare touts can be dismaying at times.

Nudity is tolerated on at least three beaches north of the town center. Never leave valuables unattended, especially on isolated stretches of beach. Run-and-grab thefts while victims are swimming or sleeping is common.

Orientation
Playa is laid out on an easy grid. The pedestrian stretch of Quinta Av (Fifth Avenue) is

the most happening street in town, especially along the pedestrian stretch.

Information

EMERGENCY
Police & Fire (☎ 060)

INTERNET ACCESS
Cibernet (Calle 8; per hr US$1.50) This air-conditioned place just east of Quinta Av has decent connections.

MEDICAL SERVICES
Centro de Salud (☎ 873-03-14; 15 Av nr Av Juárez)

MONEY
There are many banks with ATMs around town.

POST
Post office (cnr 15 Av & Av Juárez)

TOURIST OFFICES
Tourist Information Office (☎ 873-28-04; Av Juárez at 15 Av; ☼ 9am-9pm Mon-Sat, 9am-5pm Sun)
Tourist Police Kiosk (☎ 873-02-91; Main Plaza)

Diving & Snorkeling
Playa is one of the best places on the coast to dive and snorkel. If you like, you can grab a snorkel and mask and dive in right from the beach; however, the most spectacular underwater sites are at the offshore reefs. The following dive centers offer both scuba and snorkeling trips – including night excursions – to the reefs:
Abyss (☎ 873-21-64; www.abyssdiveshop.com; Calle 12; Blue Parrot Inn)
Dive Mike (☎ 873-09-69; www.divemike.com; Calle 8 btwn Quinta Av and the beach)
Phocea Caribe (☎ 873-12-10; www.phoceacaribedive .com; 1 Av btwn Calles 10 & 12)

Sleeping
Playa del Carmen has been developing and changing rapidly for several years. You can expect new hotels by the time you arrive, as well as a number of changes in the existing ones. Room prices in Playa – more so than anywhere else in the peninsula – are highly volatile and subject to change depending on how busy things are. The room prices given are for the busy winter tourist season (roughly January to March). Prices at many places can be up to 40% lower at most other times; however, hotel prices during the

apex of the tourist season – approximately December 20 to January 5 can jump as high as 40% above the prices listed below.

BUDGET

Posada Barrio Latino (☎ 873-23-84; www.posadabar riolatino.com; Calle 4 btwn 10 & 15 Avs; d with fan/air-con US$35/43; [P] [X]) This hotel offers 16 clean, pleasant rooms with good ventilation, tiled floors, ceiling fans and hammocks (in addition to beds). The friendly Italian owners speak English and Spanish and maintain strict security. Other amenities include off-street parking, bicycles for rent and a free safe for valuables.

Hotel Casa Tucán (☎ 873-02-83; Calle 4 btwn 10 & 15 Avs; d from US$25; [X]) This German/Texan-run hotel features 29 rooms; all are fan-cooled, a couple have kitchenettes and the cheapest share bathrooms. There is a swimming pool and the restaurant, in a pleasant tropical garden, serves good, affordable breakfasts.

Hotel La Ziranda (☎ 873-39-33, www.hotelziranda .com; Calle 4 btwn 15 & 20 Avs; r US$35) Constructed in late 2000, the Ziranda's two buildings have 15 nice rooms, all with balconies or terraces and two double beds or one king. The grounds are agreeably landscaped and the staff is friendly.

Playa Hostel (☎ 879-39-28; www.hostelworld.com; cnr Av 25 & Calle 8; dm US$9.50, d US$20) Two blocks south and one block west of the ADO bus station, this hostel is very well run, extremely clean and unusually quiet. There is

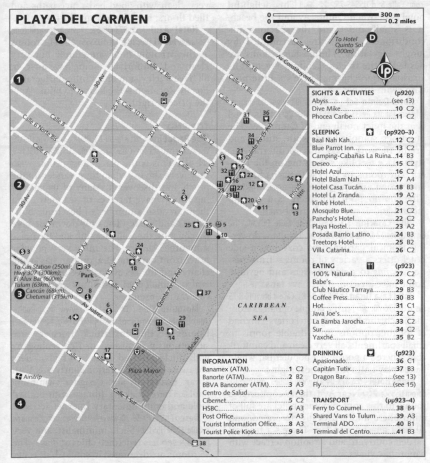

PLAYA DEL CARMEN

SIGHTS & ACTIVITIES	(p920)
Abyss	(see 13)
Dive Mike	10 C2
Phocea Caribe	11 C2

SLEEPING	(pp920–3)
Baal Nah Kah	12 C2
Blue Parrot Inn	13 C2
Camping-Cabañas La Ruina	14 B3
Deseo	15 C2
Hotel Azul	16 C2
Hotel Balam Nah	17 A4
Hotel Casa Tucán	18 B3
Hotel La Ziranda	19 A2
Kinbé Hotel	20 C2
Mosquito Blue	21 C2
Pancho's Hotel	22 C2
Playa Hostel	23 A2
Posada Barrio Latino	24 B3
Treetops Hotel	25 B2
Villa Catarina	26 C2

EATING	(p923)
100% Natural	27 C2
Babe's	28 C2
Club Náutico Tarraya	29 B3
Coffee Press	30 B3
Hot	31 C1
Java Joe's	32 C2
La Bamba Jarocha	33 C2
Sur	34 C2
Yaxché	35 B2

DRINKING	(p923)
Apasionado	36 C1
Capitán Tutix	37 B3
Dragon Bar	(see 13)
Fly	(see 15)

TRANSPORT	(pp923–4)
Ferry to Cozumel	38 B4
Shared Vans to Tulum	39 A3
Terminal ADO	40 B1
Terminal del Centro	41 B3

INFORMATION	
Banamex (ATM)	1 C2
Banorte (ATM)	2 B2
BBVA Bancomer (ATM)	3 A3
Centro de Salud	4 A3
Cibernet	5 C2
HSBC	6 A3
Post Office	7 A3
Tourist Information Office	8 A3
Tourist Police Kiosk	9 B4

CARIBBEAN SEA

To Hotel Quinto Sol (300m)

To Gas Station (250m); Hwy 307 (300km); El Alux Bar (600m); Tulum (63km); Cancún (68km); Chetumal (375km)

a large communal kitchen and a nice shared space with couches, hammocks and TV.

Camping-Cabañas La Ruina (☎ 873-04-05; Calle 2; tents & hammocks per person US$6; d US$18-25, with bath US$30-38; 🛏) Aptly named, this place is sort of a ruin, but it is the only place to (officially) camp in Playa. The rooms in the hotel are worn but clean and the showers are decent. You can pitch your tent or hang your hammock (they're available for rent) in a large lot on the beach. Some rooms have ceiling fans, some have air-con. The cheapest are bare, with no view; the more expensive face the beach.

MID-RANGE

Treetops Hotel (☎ 873-14-95; www.treetopshotel .com; Calle 8; d US$45-75; 🛏 🛏) This delightful hotel is between Quinta Av and the beach. It is small, quiet and the spacious air-conditioned rooms are surrounded by jungle vegetation. The upstairs rooms are nestled in the treetops lending Treetops its Crusoe-esque charm. There's a little pool with swim-up bar.

Hotel Quinto Sol (☎ 873-32-92; www.hotelquinto sol.com; Quinta Av 330; d US$75; 🛏 🛏) This hotel is at the quiet north end of Quinta Av. The buildings smooth-lined white stucco and bright tilework make this Mediterranean-style place feel like something on the Riviera. The rooms are large with big bathrooms and strong air-con; some are nonsmoking. There is no pool, but there is a rooftop Jacuzzi and easy access to the beach.

Villa Catarina (☎ 873-20-98; Calle Privada Nte btwn Calles 12 & 14; d US$75) Set amidst a flowering tropical garden, this cozy beach-side hotel offers a variety of rooms – from rustic *cabañas* to *palapa* towers and beyond. Some have air-con, most have fans.

Hotel Casa Tucan (☎ 873-02-83; Calle 4 btwn 10 & 15 Avs; d US$ 20-40; 🛏) Just a couple of blocks from the beach, this laid-back hotel offers a myriad of lodging options from double rooms to small apartments, all very clean and comfortable. There's a pool and a popular bar where bands play Latin music most nights.

Kinbé Hotel (☎ 873-04-41; www.kinbe.com; Calle 10; d from US$50; 🛏) Near Av 1, the 19 comfortable rooms in this contemporary hotel are full of atmosphere and artistically decorated, and all have air-con and fan. There's a tropical garden courtyard and a rooftop terrace with panoramic views.

Pancho's Hotel (☎ 873-22-22; www.panchoshotel .com; Quinta Av 217 at Calle 12; d US$70; 🛏 🛏) At the decadent heart of Quinta Av, Pancho's invokes the symbols of Mexican rebels: Pancho Villa, Marcos and Frida Kahlo to create its revolutionary-chic mood. Irony aside, the rooms are spacious and tastefully furnished. The showers are big and the king-size beds are firm and comfy. Each room has cable TV, ceiling fan and air-con. There's a small pool in the busy open-air lounge area (next to Frida Bar) that's more decorative than useable.

Hotel Balam Nah (☎ 873-21-17; www.hotelbalam nah.com; Calle 1 btwn Quinta Av & 10 Av; d with fan/air-con US$ 40/50; 🛏) Rooms in this three-story hotel surround a cool, green courtyard. Each is very clean with good beds, nice baths and tiled floors; most have a small fridge.

Hotel Azul (☎ 873-05-62; www.hotel-azul.com; Quinta Av btwn Calles 10 & 12; d US$55; 🛏) The rooms at this friendly hotel are simple but very clean and comfortable. Some have air-con, all have a television and a little refrigerator. For the location – the heart of Quinta Av – the price is right.

TOP END

Blue Parrot Inn (☎ 873-00-83, 888-854-4498 in the US; www.blueparrot.com; Calle 12; cabañas US$75, d US$145; 🛏 🛏) This is the place most people wish they were staying when they wander up the beach and discover it. Many of its charming rooms have terraces or sea views, and there are also a number of beachside bungalows and villas. (The only downside here is acoustics: the walls are thin and the noise sometimes thick.) The inn's very popular beachfront bar, The Dragon Bar, has swing chairs and the occasional live band. There is also a small pool, restaurant and Internet café on the premises.

Mosquito Blue (☎ 873-12-45; www.mosquitoblue .com; Quinta Av btwn Calles 12 & 14; d US$140; 🛏 🖥 🛏) Rooms at this luxurious hideaway are sumptuously furnished in rich mahogany with thick-pillowed sofas and beds. There are two cloistered interior courtyards with a bar, restaurant and designer swimming pools. There is also a library with billiard table and complimentary Internet access.

Deseo (☎ 879-36-20; www.hoteldeseo.com; Quinta Av & Calle 12; d US$130) Slick, minimalist, and very hip, Deseo has redefined chic for Playa. The 15 rooms are decorated in smoky blue tones with dark wood accents. Furnishings include little more than plush, barely-off-the-floor king-size beds and a claw-foot bathtub (in the middle of the room). An elevated platform supports the outside pool-lounge bar area, where more cushy beds are set up so guests can sun in the day or lounge at night by candlelight.

Baal Nah Kah (☎ 873-00-40; www.playabedand breakfast.com; Calle 12 btwn 1 & 5 Avs; d from US$85; 🛇) There are five guestrooms in this homey three-story B&B just a block from the beach. All the rooms are decorated in rustic Mexican decor with talavera tile and spacious bathrooms; some have air-con. On the second floor there is a huge, sun-filled communal room containing a small library and lots of space to relax. A generous breakfast is included in the cost and guests have full use of the big kitchen as well.

Eating

Java Joe's (Quinta Av btwn Calles 10 & 12; breakfast US$2-3) Joe's serves breakfast all day as well as sandwiches and excellent espresso drinks.

Coffee Press (Calle 2; breakfast US$3-4, lunch US$4) Near Quinta Av, this is another place for a caffeine fix, with a selection of gourmet coffees and teas. The breakfasts are excellent, and there's light lunch fare in the afternoon.

Hot (☎ 876-43-70; Calle 14 btwn Quinta & 10 Avs; breakfast US$4) Disregard the colours – bright red and yellow – that make this place look like a fast food chain. The baked goods – from banana bread to Kahlua brownies – are fresh out of the oven and scrumptious. The coffee is strong and the breakfast egg dishes, especially the chili cheese omelettes, are really good.

Yaxché (☎ 873-25-02; Calle 8 at Quinta Av; mains US$10-25) The cuisine here is authentically Mayan. Everything is exquisitely seasoned and the seafood dishes are delicious.

Sur (☎ 873-803-32-85; Quinta Av btwn Calles 12 & 14; lunch US$8-15, dinner US$10-25) This relaxed but refined Argentinean restaurant serves delicious grilled delicacies including meat and seafood. The pasta dishes are light and satisfying as are the salads. The wine menu is extensive.

Club Náutico Tarraya (Calle 2; mains US$4-7) This eatery at the beach is one of the few in town that dates from the 1960s. It continues to offer good food at decent prices.

100% Natural (cnr Quinta Av & Calle 10; mains US$4-9) Yes, it's a franchise, but the trademark fruit and vegetable juice blends, salads, chicken dishes and other healthy foods are delicious and filling, the green courtyard is inviting, and service is excellent.

Babe's (Calle 10 btwn Quinta & 10 Avs; mains US$5-9) Babe's serves fabulous Thai food, including a perfectly spiced, home-style *tom ka gui* (chicken and coconut-milk soup) brimming with veggies. Also recommended are the Vietnamese salad (with shrimp and mango), and smoked salmon wasabi noodles.

La Bamba Jarocha (Calle 10 btwn Quinta & 1 Avs; mains US$7-10) La Bamba is a good choice for seafood and Mexican dishes. The *ceviche* here is particularly fresh and tasty.

Drinking & Entertainment

There's a party scene along Quinta Av most nights.

El Alux (☎ 803-07-13; Av Juárez) There isn't anything like this bar is in a cave – a real cave – replete with stalactites, stalagmites, and natural freshwater pools. Pillows and sofa-like set ups are arranged wherever the wall and the floor accommodates. Candlelight adds to the subterranean mood…and detracts a little from the amount of available oxygen…but with a little tequila you won't notice.

Fly (Quinta Av at Calle 12) Part of the ultrachic Deseo hotel, Fly is definitely the trendiest – and probably most expensive – bar in town. The house DJ spins international club tunes all night long and beyond.

Apasionado (☎ 803-11-00; Quinta Av & Calle 14) This Latin Jazz club features excellent bands every night. The huge *palapa* roofed venue glows with candlelight and good vibes.

Dragon Bar (Calle 12 at the beach) The Blue Parrot Inn's open-sided *palapa* bar is legendary for its swing bar (where you sit in swings instead of bar stools), live music and all night dancing.

Capitán Tutix (Calle 4 at the beach) A band playing reggae, rock, calypso or salsa starts up most nights at this extremely popular open-air beach bar.

Getting There & Away

BUS

Playa has two bus terminals. **Terminal del Centro** (cnr Quinta Av & Av Juárez) is the older bus terminal, receiving all 2nd-class buses, and is opposite the main plaza. All Riviera buses leave from Terminal del Centro; buses to Cancún and its airport have a separate ticket counter, on the Av Juárez side. The 1st-class **ADO Terminal** (20 Av nr Calle 12) is several blocks north. A taxi to the main plaza from Terminal ADO will run at about US$1.25.

Cancún (US$3.50, 1hr, Riviera buses every 10 minutes)
Cancún International Airport (US$7, 45min-1hr, 9 direct Riviera buses btwn 7am & 7:30pm)
Chetumal (US$15, 5-5½hr, 12 Riviera buses; US$14, 11 2nd-class Mayab)
Chichén Itzá (US$16, 3½hr, 1 Riviera bus at 7:30am)
Cobá (US$4.50, 1½hr, 1 Riviera bus at 7:30am)
Mérida (US$20, 5-8hr, 9 1st-class Super Expresso)
Palenque (US$33-40, 10hr, 3 1st-class buses)
San Cristóbal de Las Casas (US$40-50, 16hr, 3 1st-class buses)
Tulum (US$3, 1hr, frequent Riviera & Mayab buses)
Valladolid (US$6.25-11, 2½-3½hr, frequent Riviera & Mayab buses)

COLECTIVO VANS

Shared vans head south to Tulum (US$2, 45 minutes) from Calle 2 near 20 Av about every 15 minutes from 5am to 10pm daily.

BOAT

Ferries to Cozumel run nearly every hour on the hour from 6am to 11pm (US$8 one-way). The open-air boat takes 45 minutes to an hour, while the air-conditioned catamaran leaving from the opposite side of the pier takes closer to half an hour (same ticket, same price, less frequent).

CAR & MOTORCYCLE

Sixty-eight kilometers south of Cancún, just off Highway 307, Playa del Carmen is an easy and direct drive from Cancún and the airport there. Other points south along the well-paved Highway 307 (including Tulum, 63km) are also easily reached from Playa by car.

Many of the major car-rental agencies have cars in Playa.

PLAYA DEL CARMEN TO TULUM
Xcaret

Once a precious spot open to all, **Xcaret** (☎ 984-871-52-00; admission adult/child US$50/25; ☾ 8:30am-10pm), pronounced shkar-*et*, is about 10km south of Playa del Carmen and is now a heavily Disneyfied 'ecopark.' There

are still Mayan ruins and a beautiful inlet on the site, but much of the rest has been created or altered using dynamite, jackhammers and other terraforming techniques. The park offers a *cenote* and 'underground river' for swimming, a restaurant, an evening show of 'ancient Mayan ceremonies' worthy of Las Vegas, a butterfly pavilion, a botanical garden and nursery, orchid and mushroom farms and a wild-bird breeding area.

Package tourists from Cancún fill the place every day and enjoy attractions and activities, such as swimming with captive dolphins.

Paamul

Paamul, 87km south of Cancún, is a de facto private beach on a sheltered bay. Like many other spots along the Caribbean coast, it has signs prohibiting entry to nonguests, but people still go (parking is limited).

The attractions here are the beach and the great diving. The sandy beach is fringed with palms, but it holds many small rocks, shells and spiked sea urchins in the shallows offshore, so take appropriate measures. The large RV park here is a favorite with snowbirds; the 'BC' license plates you see here are from British Columbia, not Baja California. There is also an attractive alabaster sand beach about 2km north.

Giant sea turtles come ashore here at night in July and August to lay their eggs. If you run across one during an evening stroll along the beach, keep a good distance away and don't shine a flashlight at it, as that will scare it off. Do your part to contribute to the survival of the turtles, which are endangered; let them lay their eggs in peace.

Scuba-Mex (☎ 984-873-10-66; www.scubamex.com) offers diving trips to any of 30 superb sites for a reasonable price and has dive packages and certification courses.

Paamul Hotel (☎ 984-875-10-51; www.paamul.com.mx; tent sites US$7, RV sites US$20, d cabaña US$70; P ✖) has 10 lovely, serene and spacious beachfront *cabañas*. Each *cabaña* has two beds, a ceiling fan, private bathroom with hot water and a veranda.

To reach Paamul by bus requires a 500m walk from the highway to the hotel and beach.

Xpu-Há

Pronounced shpoo-*ha*, this beach area about 95km south of Cancún extends for several kilometers. It's reached by numbered access roads (most of them private).

At the end of X-4 (Xpu-Há access road 4), this slightly weathered, very laid-back place, **Hotel Villas del Caribe** (☎ 984-873-21-94; cafedelmarxpuha@yahoo.com.mx; cabañas US$45, r US$55), sits on a lovely stretch of beach whose northern reaches are nearly empty. All rooms have a terrace or balcony and are very clean and quiet, with fans and good beds. The personable owners offer massage, yoga and meditation classes. There's a good restaurant on the premises with reasonable meal plans available.

Most other accommodations on the beach are all-inclusive resorts including **Copacabana** (☎ 984-875-18-00; www.hotelcopacabana.com; d US$100) and the wheelchair-accessible **Xpu-Ha Palace** (☎ 984-875-10-10; wwwpalaceresorts.com; US$125).

Akumal

Famous for its beautiful beach, Akumal (Place of the Turtles) does indeed see some sea turtles come ashore to lay their eggs in the summer, although fewer and fewer arrive each year thanks to resort development. Akumal is one of the Yucatán Peninsula's oldest resort areas and consists primarily of pricey hotels and condominiums on nearly 5km of wide beach bordering four consecutive bays.

Although increasing population is taking a heavy toll on the reefs that parallel Akumal, **diving** remains the area's primary attraction. Dive trips and deep-sea **fishing** excursions are offered by: **Akumal Dive Shop** (☎ 984-875-90-32; www.akumal.com). A one-tank dive costs US$30, night dives are US$55. Deep sea fishing trips cost US$100 per person for a two-hour excursion.

The hotel and restaurant **Que Onda** (☎ 984-875-91-01; www.queondaakumal.com; r from US$75) is set amid an expanse of greenery in a fairly residential area only 50m from Laguna Yal-kú. The six fan-cooled rooms have tiled floors and great beds; upstairs rooms have balconies. There is a lovely pool, free Internet access, bicycles and snorkeling equipment. The restaurant serves delicious homemade pasta.

On the beach, **Villa Las Brisas** (☎ 984-876-21-10; www.aventuras-akumal.com; r US$50-250) is an attractive, modern place with condos and a studio apartment – all under one roof.

The friendly owners speak English, Spanish, German, Italian and some Portuguese. The turnoff to get here is 2.5km south of the turnoff for Playa Akumal.

Just outside the entrance of Akumal is a minimarket that stocks a good selection of inexpensive food. **La Cueva del Pescador** (☺ breakfast, lunch & dinner; meals US$4-6), just inside the entrance, serves breakfast egg dishes and seafood lunch and dinner plates.

Xel-Há

Once a pristine natural lagoon brimming with iridescent tropical fish, **Xel-Há** (☎ 984-875-60-00; admission adult/child US$25/13; ☺ 9am-6pm), pronounced shell-ha, is now a private park with landscaped grounds, developed *cenotes*, caves, nature paths, several restaurants/bars and more. It's very touristy, but the lagoon is still beautiful and full of fish.

Most buses traveling between Playa and Tulum will drop you at the Xel-Há ticket booth (about 45km south of Playa del Carmen). On the way out you will either have to walk (under 1km) or take a taxi (there are plenty around) to the highway to flag a bus.

If driving, you will see very visible signs for the park posted along Highway 307; the entrance to the park is right off the highway.

Bahías de Punto Solimán

These two protected bays are one of the best kept secrets (don't tell anyone) on the coast. Located 123km south of Cancún and 11km north of Tulum (turn off Highway 307 at the big white signed exit reading Oscar y Lalo's), this area offers good wildlife watching, kayaking, excellent snorkeling and long, white swathes of palm-shaded beach. On the north bay sits **Oscar y Lalo's** (☎ 984-804-69-73; mains US$7-15), a spacious restaurant overlooking the water. The food is very good and comes in heaped portions. The owners also rent kayaks.

On the south bay (also known as Bahía de San Francisco) private homes – many very luxurious – line the road. Most of them rent for the week at well over US$1000. There are a couple – though still not cheap – exceptions to the rent-the-whole-house-for-a-bundle rule. **Casa Nah Uxibal** (www.vrbo.com; per night from US$90) rents four really lovely, light and airy beachfront units, all with tastefully tiled baths, kitchens and hammock-adorned porches. **Casa del Corazón** (www.locogringo.com; per night from US$150) rents three cozy, artistically furnished, fully equipped beach bungalows, all set amidst palms and shady vegitation just steps from the beach. Note that there's a three-night minimum stay.

Cenotes

On the west side of the highway south of Paamul are several *cenotes* (limestone sinkholes/caverns filled with water) you can visit (and usually swim in) for a price. A few kilometers south of Akumal is the turnoff for Cenote Dos Ojos, which provides access to the Nohoch Nah Chich cave system, the largest underwater cave system in the world. You can take guided snorkel and dive tours of some amazing underwater caverns, floating past illuminated stalactites and stalagmites in an eerie wonderland.

Hidden Worlds (☎ 984-877-85-35; www.hidden worlds.com.mx) is an American-run outfit offering three-hour snorkeling tours for US$40, and one-/two-tank dive tours for US$50/80. The snorkeling price includes flashlights, wet suit, equipment and transportation to the *cenotes* on a unique 'jungle mobile.' The drive through the jungle is a unique experience in itself, and the guides are very knowledgeable and informative. The diving tours are at 9am, 11am and 1pm daily; equipment rental costs extra. You don't need to make a reservation, but it never hurts to call.

These are cavern (as opposed to cave) dives and require only standard open-water certification. However, don't try doing it on your own. Cavern diving without an experienced guide (preferably one with cave certification) can be just as deadly as cave diving.

TULUM

☎ 984 / pop 7000

Tulum lies some 130km south of Cancún. Its main attractions are at the water's edge: Mayan ruins, beautiful beaches and a profusion of *cabañas* for rent. The area's foreign population has been steadily increasing as new hotels and restaurants (many Italian-owned) open in town and at the beach.

Orientation & Information

Traveling southbound towards Tulum, the first thing you reach is Tulum Crucero, the junction of Highway 307 and the old access road to the ruins. The new access road is 400m further south and leads another 600m to the ruins themselves. Another 1.5km south on the highway brings you to the Cobá junction; turning right (west) takes you to Cobá. The road to the left leads about 3km to the north–south road servicing the Zona Hotelera, the string of waterfront lodgings extending 10km south from the ruins. This road eventually enters the Reserva de la Biósfera Sian Ka'an (p933), continuing some 50km past Boca Paila to Punta Allen.

The town, sometimes referred to as Tulum Pueblo, flanks the highway (called Av Tulum through town) south of the Cobá junction. It has Telmex pay phones, numerous currency-exchange booths and one Bital bank with ATM. The post office is at the north end of town on the west side of Av Tulum. The Weary Traveler hostel (see Sleeping & Eating later) has several terminals with fast **Internet access** (per hr US$1.50). John, the friendly operator, also offers travelers' information, free valuables storage (recommended if you're staying out at the beach *cabañas*), free incoming phone calls and faxes (up to two pages), a big two-for-one book exchange and coffee and juice drinks for sale. The hostel is open 24 hours.

Savana's also offers Internet access (at a similar price), along with copier, fax and telephone services. It's about four blocks north of the Weary Traveler, and across the street.

Tulum Ruins

Tulum Ruins (admission US$4; ۞ 7am-5pm), though well preserved, the Tulum Ruins (officially named, though rarely referred to as Parque Nacional Tulum), would hardly merit rave reviews if it weren't for their setting. The grayish-tan buildings dominate a palm-fringed beach lapped by turquoise waters. Even on dark, stormy days, the majestic cliff-top ruins overlooking vast stretches of pristine beach are fit for the cover of a guide book. Just don't come to Tulum expecting anything comparable to the architecture at Chichén Itzá or Uxmal. The buildings here, decidedly Toltec in influence, were the product of a Mayan civilization in decline.

Tulum is a prime destination for tour buses. To best enjoy the ruins, visit them

TULUM RUINS

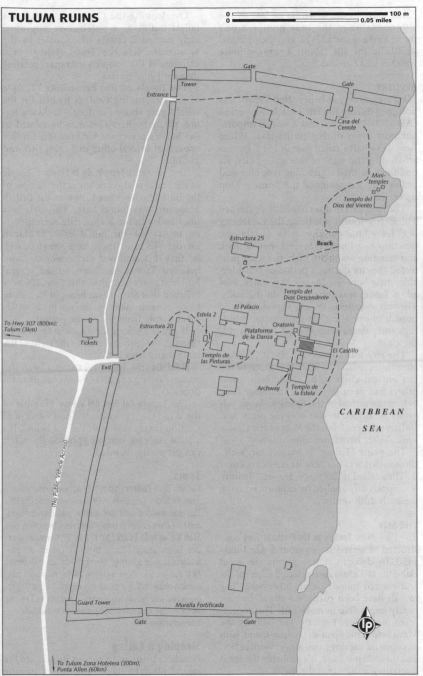

| 0 | 100 m |
| 0 | 0.05 miles |

Gate

Tower

Gate

Entrance

Casa del Cenote

Mini-temples

Templo del Dios del Viento

Estructura 25

Beach

To Hwy 307 (800m); Tulum (3km)

Templo del Dios Descendente

El Palacio

Estela 2

Oratorio

Tickets

Estructura 20

Plataforma de la Danza

El Castillo

Exit

Templo de las Pinturas

Archway

Templo de la Estela

CARIBBEAN SEA

(No Public Vehicle Access)

Guard Tower

Muralla Fortificada

Gate

Gate

To Tulum Zona Hotelera (300m); Punta Allen (60km)

YUCATÁN PENINSULA

either early in the morning or late in the afternoon, when the tour groups aren't there. Parking costs US$3, and the optional shuttle to the site (about a seven-minute walk) is US$2 round-trip.

HISTORY

Most archaeologists believe that Tulum was occupied during the late postclassic period (AD 1200–1521) and that it was an important port town during its heyday. When Juan de Grijalva sailed past in 1518, he was amazed by the sight of this walled city, its buildings painted a gleaming red, blue and yellow and a ceremonial fire flaming atop its seaside watchtower.

The ramparts that surround three sides of Tulum (the fourth side being the Caribbean Sea) leave little question as to its strategic function as a fortress. Several meters thick and standing 3m to 5m high, the walls protected the city during a period of considerable strife between Mayan city-states. Not all of Tulum was situated within the walls. The vast majority of the city's residents lived outside them; the civic-ceremonial buildings and palaces likely housed Tulum's ruling class.

The city was abandoned about 75 years after the Spanish conquest. It was one of the last ancient cities to be abandoned; most others had been given back to nature long before the arrival of the Spanish. Maya pilgrims continued to visit over the years, and Indian refugees from the War of the Castes took shelter here from time to time.

The name 'Tulum' is Mayan for 'wall,' though that was not how its residents knew it. They called it Zama, or 'Dawn.' 'Tulum' was apparently applied by explorers during the early 20th century.

THE SITE

The two-story **Templo de Las Pinturas** was constructed in several stages around AD 1400–1450. Its decoration was among the most elaborate at Tulum and included relief masks and colored murals on an inner wall. The murals have been partially restored but are nearly impossible to make out. This monument might have been the last built by the Maya before the Spanish conquest, and with its columns, carvings, two-story construction and the stela out front, it's probably the most interesting structure at the site.

Overlooking the Caribbean is Tulum's tallest building, a watchtower appropriately named **El Castillo** (the Castle) by the Spaniards. Note the Toltec-style serpent columns at the temple's entrance, echoing those at Chichén Itzá.

The **Templo del Dios Descendente** (Temple of the Descending God) is named for the relief figure above the door – a diving figure, partly human, that may be related to the Maya's reverence for bees. This figure appears at several other east coast sites and at Cobá.

The restored **Templo de la Estela** (Temple of the Stela) is also known as the Temple of the Initial Series. Stela 1, now in the British Museum, was found here. The stela was inscribed with the Mayan date corresponding to AD 564 (the 'initial series' of Mayan hieroglyphs in an inscription gives its date). At first this confused archaeologists, who believed Tulum had been settled several hundred years later than this date. It's now believed that Stela 1 was brought to Tulum from Tankah, 4km to the north, a settlement dating from the classic period.

If you're anxious for a look at the sea, go through the corbeled arch to the right of the temple and turn left.

El Palacio (the Palace) features a beautiful stucco carving of a diving god over its main doorway.

The **Templo del Dios del Viento** (Temple of the Wind God) provides the best views of El Castillo juxtaposed with the sea below. It's a great place for snapping photos, though it can get pretty crowded.

Tours

Cenote Dive Center (☎ 871-22-32; www.cenotedive .com; Av Tulum; Cave dives US$90, cave snorkeling US$30) This recommended outfit specializes in guided cavern tours and cave dives as well as cenote and cavern snorkeling trips.

Sian Ka'an Info Tours (☎ 871-24-99; www.siankaan .org; Tulum Crucero) Adjacent to Hotel El Crucero, this professional ecotour operation offers guided tours to Reserva de la Biósfera Sian Ka'an, including all-day excursions and evening birdwatching trips. All-day excursions cost US$80 per person and include transportation and snacks. Evening bird watching trips cost US$60 per person and include transportation.

Sleeping & Eating

Hotels in town and Crucero Ruinas are the logical place to stay if you're just passing through or only want to visit the ruins. If it is the beach you're after, the Zona Hotelera is a better choice. The following listings give high-season lodging rates. Off-season rates can be as much as 50% lower.

TULUM PUEBLO & NORTH

Hotel El Crucero (☎ 871-26-10; www.el-crucero.com; Tulum Crucero; dm US$7.50, d US$35, theme r US$50; 🅿 🔀 🖳) Just a limestone stone's throw away from the ruins, El Crucero's location is ideal and its value unbeatable. The hotel features three spotless dorm rooms, five nicely appointed double rooms and four large, kind of silly, very comfortable theme rooms (eg the Powder Puff Playroom) featuring whimsical murals and air-conditioning. There is an excellent and very popular restaurant/bar on site as well as a professional dive shop and an art gallery. Internet access and bike rentals are available and the beach is just a long walk/short bike ride away.

Weary Traveler (☎ 871-24-61; www.intulum.com; Av Tulum; s/d beds in dm US7.50/14, r US$20) The Weary is across from the bus terminal and one block south. The small but clean dorm rooms have two bunk beds, a fan, and bathroom with shower. There is a relaxing, shaded courtyard, several computers with fast Internet connections and a two-for-one book exchange. The hostel provides a free shuttle service to the beach, shows nightly videos and is home to very lively Sunday night barbeques, which always feature great food and usually live music.

L'Hotelito (☎ 871-20-61; Av Tulum; fan/air-con d US$55/65) Three blocks north of the bus station on the west side of the street, this nice Italian-run place has clean, quiet rooms. The upstairs rooms have good ventilation, the downstairs ones have air-con. The restaurant here serves good breakfasts, espresso drinks and Italian food at reasonable prices.

La Nave (east side of Av Tulum; mains US$5; 🕑 closed Sun) If you come here for breakfast, you'll be back for lunch and dinner. It's that good. Really. From the fresh baked bread to the wood-fired pizza, to the ceviche, everything is fresh and satisfying. Also the best place in town for coffee and espresso drinks.

El Tacontento (Av Tulum; mains US$3-6) Located on the corner a couple of blocks south from La Nave, this Mexican restaurant serves very tasty tacos, *ceviche* and fresh fish dishes.

San Francisco de Asís (Av Tulum) This large, very well-stocked supermarket is at the very north end of town at the junction of Av Tulum and the road to Cobá. If you are heading to the beach it's a good idea to stop by here first and stock up on food and supplies.

ZONA HOTELERA

Along the coastal road leading to Punta Allen (Carretera Tulum Ruinas – Boca Paila), which begins less than 1km south of the ruins, is a string of *cabaña* hotels. A few cater primarily to backpackers, and most have simple restaurants but no telephones. Of those places that have electricity, many shut it off at 9pm or 10pm.

The cheapest way to sleep here is to have your own hammock and mosquito net; if you don't, several of the inexpensive places rent them. Most places (even though they have nets over beds) aren't well screened against bugs; bring repellent. Few of the flimsy, primitive *cabañas* can be reliably secured. Thieves lift the poles in the walls to gain entrance, or burrow beneath through the sand, or jimmy the locks. At least one theft a month is reported. Never leave valuables unattended in a cabaña.

The following places are ordered north to south. As a rule, the further south you travel along the beachfront road, the more expensive (and secure) accommodations become. There are over forty hotels along this stretch of beach; listed below are but a few favorite establishments.

Cabañas El Mirador (☎ 879 60-19; cabañas with hammock/bed US$10/20; 🅿) This place is closest to the ruins. It has 28 cabins (half with sand floors), most with beds, some with hammocks. The beach is wide here and there's a decent restaurant with excellent views.

Zazil Kin (☎ 871-24-17; d US$18, with bath US$25-35; 🅿) At time of research ownership of this place, formerly Don Armando's, was changing hands. If things don't change under new management, this should remain the most popular inexpensive place on the beach. It's clean, secure and always lively. There's a good dive center, basketball court, ever-happening restaurant/bar and a nice stretch of beach.

Hotel Diamante K (☎ 871-23-76, www.diamantek.com; r US$25-55, with bath US$60-200; 🅿) This eco-hotel's lovely *cabañas* have suspended beds and a table for candles (the solar-generated electricity goes off at 11:30pm). The Diamante K has a small beach and a fine vegetarian restaurant and bar. It's often full even in the low season.

Cabañas Copal (☎ 871-24-81; www.cabanascopal .com; d US$35, with bath from US$65; ℗ ☐) This longtime budget spot, is now a chakra-cleansing, New Age retreat. The *cabañas* are lovely and overlook a clothing-optional stretch of beach. Amenities include a holistic spa, mystical *temezcal*, flotation chamber, yoga classes, restaurant/bar and Internet café.

Nohoch Tunich (☎ 871-22-71; cabañas US$35, with bath US$45, r US$45-65; ℗) This place offers both tidy, appealing hotel rooms with porches and electricity (until 11pm), and handsome thatch-and-board *cabañas* with wooden floors, very near the beach. There's a mini-market on the premises as well as a money-exchange desk.

Zamas (☎ 415-387-98-06; www.zamas.com; d US$80-145; ℗) Zamas' romantic *cabañas* all have terraces with two hammocks, 24-hour light, purified drinking water, big, private baths and two comfy beds with mosquito nets (you'll need 'em, as screens don't extend to the roof). The lovely and regionally acclaimed restaurant, Que Fresco, overlooks the rocks, sea and beach.

Maya Tulum (☎ 888-515-45-80; www.mayatulum .com; cabañas US$95-165; ℗) The focus is on meditation and spiritual growth at this place approximately 500m south of Zamas. There are three grades of *cabañas*, a gorgeous beach nearby, a huge tiled, *palapa*-roofed meditation and yoga room (massages available also) and a vegetarian restaurant.

Posada Margherita (www.posadamargherita.com; d US$70-140; ℗) This beautiful eco-friendly hotel has something virtually unheard of in the Yucatán: wheelchair access. The four ground-floor rooms are completely wheelchair accessible and the restaurant and other public areas have ramps or paths. Most impressive is the dive shop, which offers scuba for those with limited mobility. The six rooms here are tiled and bright with verandas or balconies. The beach is particularly wide and lovely and many locals consider the beachfront restaurant here to be the best around.

Nueva Vida (☎ 877-20-92; www.tulumnv.com; d US$110-260; ℗ ✕) This eco-retreat is secluded and tranquil, and fronts a spectacular, vast, sugary beach. As to not disturb the dunes,

the seven rustic *cabañas* are spread out in the lush jungle back from the shore and elevated on stilts two meters off the ground. All rooms have good beds, strong fans and warm showers; some are nonsmoking. The 24hr electricity is completely solar or wind generated. There's a nice family-run restaurant and breakfast is included in the rate.

Getting There & Around

You can walk from Tulum Crucero to the ruins (800m). The *cabañas* begin about 600m south of the ruins and can be reached by taxi from Tulum Pueblo; fares are fixed and cheap. At the center of town you'll see the large sign of the Sindicato de Taxistas, on which the rates are posted. To the ruins it's US$3, to most of the cabañas US$5.

The bus terminal is toward the southern end of town (look for the two-story building with 'ADO' painted on it in huge letters). When leaving Tulum, you can also wait at Tulum Crucero for a Playa Express or regular intercity bus. Following are some distances, travel times and prices for buses leaving Tulum. There are many buses daily to the following locales:

Cancún (US$5-6, 2hr)
Chetumal (US$9-11, 3½-4hr)
Chichén Itzá (US$7.25, 3hr)
Cobá (US$2.25, 45min)
Felipe Carrillo Puerto (US$4-5, 1¾hr)
Mérida (US$14, 7hr)
Playa del Carmen (US$3, 1hr)
Valladolid (US$4-5, 2hr) If you're headed for Valladolid, be sure your bus is traveling the short route through Chemax, not via Cancún.

GRAND CENOTE

A little over 3km from Tulum on the road to Cobá is Grand Cenote, a worthwhile stop on your way between Tulum and the Cobá ruins, especially if it's a hot day. You can **snorkel** (US$5) among small fish in the caverns here if you bring your own gear.

COBÁ

Among the largest of Mayan cities, Cobá, 50km northwest of Tulum, offers the chance to explore mostly unrestored antiquities set deep in tropical jungle.

History

Cobá was settled much earlier than Chichén Itzá or Tulum, and construction reached its peak between AD 800 and 1100. Archaeologists believe that this city once covered 50 sq km and held 40,000 Maya.

Cobá's architecture is a mystery; its towering pyramids and stelae resemble the architecture of Tikal, which is several hundred kilometers away, rather than the much nearer sites of Chichén Itzá and the northern Yucatán Peninsula.

Some archaeologists theorize that an alliance with Tikal was made through marriage to facilitate trade between the Guatemalan and Yucatecan Maya. Stelae appear to depict female rulers from Tikal holding ceremonial bars and flaunting their power by standing on captives. These Tikal royal females, when married to Cobá's royalty, may have brought architects and artisans with them.

Archaeologists are also baffled by the extensive network of sacbés (stone-paved avenues) in this region, with Cobá as the hub. The longest runs nearly 100km from the base of Cobá's great pyramid Nohoch Mul to the Mayan settlement of Yaxuna. In all, some 40 sacbés passed through Cobá, parts

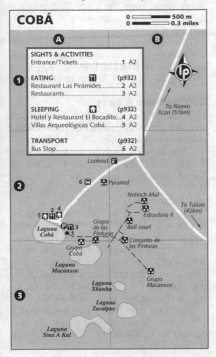

COBÁ

0 — 500 m
0 — 0.3 miles

SIGHTS & ACTIVITIES	
Entrance/Tickets.....................1 A2	

EATING	(p932)
Restaurant Las Pirámides............2 A2	
Restaurants..............................3 A2	

SLEEPING	(p932)
Hotel y Restaurant El Bocadito....4 A2	
Villas Arqueológicas Cobá.........5 A2	

TRANSPORT	(p932)
Bus Stop.................................6 A2	

To Nuevo Xcan (51km)

Lookout

6   Pyramid

Nohoch Mul

To Tulum (42km)

Estructura X

2 4
5   3   Grupo de las Pinturas   Ball court
Laguna Cobá   1
Grupo Cobá   Conjunto de las Pinturas

Laguna Macanxoc

Laguna Xkanha   Grupo Macanxoc

Laguna Zacalpuc

Laguna Sina A Kal

of the huge astronomical 'time machine' that was evident in every Mayan city.

The first excavation was by the Austrian archaeologist Teobert Maler in 1891. There was little subsequent investigation until 1926, when the Carnegie Institute financed the first of two expeditions led by Sir J Eric S Thompson and Harry Pollock. After their 1930 expedition, not much happened until 1973, when the Mexican government began to finance excavation. Archaeologists now estimate that Cobá contains some 6500 structures, of which just a few have been excavated and restored, though work is ongoing.

Orientation & Information

The small village of Cobá, 2.5km west of the Tulum–Nuevo Xcan road, has a small cheap hotel and several small, simple and low-cost restaurants. At the lake, turn left for the ruins, right for the upscale Villas Arqueológicas Cobá hotel.

The **Cobá ruins** (admission US$4; ⏰ 7am-6pm) has a parking lot charging US$1.50 per passenger car.

Be prepared to walk several kilometers on paths, depending on how much you want to see. Bring insect repellent and water; the shop next to the ticket booth sells both at reasonable prices, but there are no drinks stands within the site. Avoid the midday heat if possible. Most people spend around two hours at the site.

A short distance inside, at the Grupo Cobá, are **bicycles** (per day US$2.50). These are useful if you really want to get around the further reaches, and the breeze they create is cooling. If the site is crowded it's probably best to walk.

You may want to buy a book about Cobá before visiting the site – onsite signage and maps are minimal and cryptic. Guides near the entrance size you up and ask whatever they think you're worth, anywhere from US$8 to over US$65, depending on the length of the tour. They can be worth it, as they are up on the latest restoration work. Nohoch Mul pyramid is the only structure the public is allowed to climb.

Grupo Cobá

Walking just under 100m along the main path from the entrance and turning right brings you to the **Templo de las Iglesias**

(Temple of the Churches), the most prominent structure in the Cobá Group. It's an enormous pyramid, with views from the top of the Nohoch Mul pyramid and surrounding lakes (but climbing it is forbidden).

Back on the main path, you pass through the **juego de pelota** (ball court), 30m further along. It's been restored quite well.

Grupo Macanxoc

About 500m beyond the juego de pelota, the path forks. Going straight gets you to the **Grupo Macanxoc**, a group of stelae that bore reliefs of royal women who are thought to have come from Tikal. They are badly eroded, and it's a 1km walk; however, the flora along the way is interesting.

Conjunto de las Pinturas

Though it's signed to the left at the fork, if you're on foot you can reach the **Conjunto de las Pinturas** (Group of Paintings) by heading toward the Grupo Macanxoc a very short distance and turning left. The temple here bears traces of glyphs and frescoes above its door and remnants of richly colored plaster inside.

You approach the temple from the southeast. Leave by the trail at the northwest (opposite the temple steps) to see several stelae. The first of these is 20m along beneath a *palapa*. Here, a regal figure stands over two others, one of them kneeling with his hands bound behind him. Sacrificial captives lie beneath the feet of a ruler at the base. Continue along the path past another badly weathered stela and a small temple to rejoin the Nohoch Mul path and turn right.

Nohoch Mul

A walk of 800m more brings you to **Nohoch Mul** (Big Mound), also known as the Great Pyramid, built on a natural hill. Along the way is another ball court, at whose north end lie weathered stelae; the track then bends between piles of stones – a ruined temple – before passing Templo 10 and Stele 20. The exquisitely carved stela bears a picture of a ruler standing imperiously over two captives. Eighty meters beyond stands the Great Pyramid.

At 42m high, the Great Pyramid is the tallest Mayan structure on the Yucatán Peninsula. There are two diving gods carved over the doorway of the temple at the top (built in the postclassic period, AD 1100–1450), similar to the sculptures at Tulum. The view is spectacular!

Sleeping & Eating

There's no organized campground, but you can try finding a place along the shore of the lake, which is inhabited by crocodiles (local children can show you a safe swimming spot).

Hotel y Restaurant El Bocadito (☎ 985-852-00-52; r US$8-10) The hotel has very simple, fan-cooled rooms with private bath. The restaurant is very well run and serves a great *menú* (set meal). They'll store luggage while you visit the ruins. See also Getting There & Away later.

Villas Arqueológicas Cobá (☎ 998-858-15-27, 800-258-2633 in the US; d US$70) This Club Med hotel next to the lake has a swimming pool and mediocre restaurant to complement the air-conditioned rooms. It's a nice place to relax and the best value among the Villas Arqueológicas on the Yucatán Peninsula.

Restaurant Las Pirámides (mains US$5) A few doors down from the Club Med, this restaurant has good lake views and friendly service.

There are several small restaurants by the site parking lot, including **Restaurant El Faisán** and **Restaurant El Caracol**, both of which serve inexpensive meals (US$3.50 to US$6).

Getting There & Away

El Bocadito (see Sleeping & Eating, earlier) also serves as Cobá's bus terminal and colectivo taxi terminus.

There are six to eight buses daily between Tulum and Cobá (US$2.50, 45 minutes). Six of these also serve Playa del Carmen (US$4.50, 1½ hours). *Combis* between Cobá and Tulum charge US$5 per person. There is also bus service to Valladolid (US$2.50, one hour), Chichén Itzá (US$5, 1½ hours) and Mérida (US$11, 3½ hours).

A more comfortable but expensive way to reach Cobá is by taxi from Tulum Crucero. Find some other travelers interested in the trip and split the cost, about US$50 roundtrip, including two hours at the site.

The 31km road from Cobá to Chemax is arrow-straight and in good shape. If you're driving to Valladolid or Chichén Itzá this is the way to go.

TULUM TO PUNTA ALLEN

Punta Allen is at the end of a narrow stretch of land that reaches south nearly 40km from its start just below Tulum. There are some charming beaches along the way, with plenty of privacy, and most of the spit is within the protected, wildlife-rich Reserva de la Biósfera Sian Ka'an.

There are two ways to reach Punta Allen from Tulum. One is to take the unpaved, muffler-busting coastal road that goes directly to Punta Allen; the other is to go to the pier in Playón where boats leave regularly for Punta Allen.

If you are taking public transportation to Punta Allen you have a couple of options. A van (weather and road permitting) makes the trip from the taxi cooperative in the middle of Tulum Pueblo to Punta Allen at around 11:30am, taking 1½ to three hours (US$12). Alternatively you can take a bus to Puerto Carrillo Puerto and then a shared van from there to the pier in Playón (US$9, three hours). Water taxis from Playón (about US$3) run between 9am and 5pm – again, weather permitting.

By car the most direct – when the road is open – way to get to Punta Allen in on the coastal road. Though Punta Allen is only 40km away, the crater-sized potholes will slow you down considerably – especially when the holes are filled with water from recent rains, making it impossible to gauge their depth. Note also: no fuel is available on the beach-road route.

To reach Playón by car take the 'Vigía Chico' exit off Highway 307 (about 42 km south of Tulum) and drive another 42km (on an unpaved road, about two hours) to the boat landing.

Reserva de la Biósfera Sian Ka'an

Over 5000 sq km of tropical jungle, marsh, mangroves and islands on Quintana Roo's coast have been set aside by the Mexican government as a large biosphere reserve. In 1987 the United Nations appointed it a World Heritage Site – an irreplaceable natural treasure.

Sian Ka'an (Where the Sky Begins) is home to howler monkeys, anteaters, foxes, ocelots, pumas, crocodiles, eagles, raccoons, tapirs, *javelinas* (peccaries), giant land crabs, jaguars and hundreds of bird species, including *chocolateras* (roseate spoonbills)

and some flamingos. There are no hiking trails through the reserve; it's best explored with a professional guide.

Three Punta Allen locals with training in English, natural history, interpretation and birding conduct bird-watching, snorkeling and nature tours, mostly by boat, for about US$110 for five to six people: **Baltazar Madera** (☎ 984-871-20-01); **Marcos Nery**, reachable through the local telephone office (☎ 984-871-24-24); and **Chary Salazar** (enquire in town). The latter two are experts on endemic and migratory bird species, and Chary also does walking tours when she's around.

At the time of research a new eco-tel, **Boca Paila Camps** (☎ 984-871-24-99; www.siankaan .org; dm US$25, d US$65), 4 km from the entrance of the reserve on the Tulum–Punta Allen road – was about to open. The hotel, run by the Tulum-based ecology group Centro Ecológico Sian Ka'an (CESiaK), has 15 elevated, low-environmental-impact (solar power, compost toilets) *palapa* units. There is a restaurant and the staff offers tours of the surrounding reserve as well as kayak and bike rentals.

Punta Allen

Although it suffered considerable damage from the ferocious winds of Hurricane Gilbert in 1988, Punta Allen still sports a laid-back ambience reminiscent of the Belizean cayes. There's also a healthy reef 400m from shore that offers snorkelers and divers wonderful sights. Between the reef and the beach there's lots of sea grass; that's a turnoff to a lot of people, but it provides food and shelter for numerous critters and is one of the reasons the snorkeling and diving are so good.

The area is known primarily for its bone-fishing, and for that many people come a long way. The guides listed above, as well as cooperatives in town, do fishing trips for about US$200, including lunch. Some places, such as the Cuzan Guest House offer all-inclusive week-long packages of accommodations, boats, guides and meals for around US$3500 a week.

Tres Marías (d US$25) is a set of locally run, simple *cabañas* in the middle of town.

Fully furnished *cabañas* at **Posada Sirena** (☎ 984-878-77-95; www.casasirena.com; d US$30-40) have kitchens and hot-water showers.

Accommodations at **Cuzan Guest House** (☎ 983-834-03-58; www.flyfishmx.com; d US$40-80) are rustic but offer all the amenities you could need: 24-hour solar electricity, private baths with hot showers, comfortable beds and fans. The sand-floored *palapa* restaurant is open for three meals a day and serves, of course, very fresh seafood.

FELIPE CARRILLO PUERTO

☎ 983 / pop 21,000

Now named for a progressive governor of Yucatán, this crossroads town 95km south of Tulum was once known as Chan Santa Cruz, the rebel headquarters during the War of the Castes.

Carrillo Puerto offers the visitor little in the way of attractions, but it's a transit hub and the first town of consequence if you're arriving from the Mérida/Ticul/Uxmal area. There's a gas station on the highway and inexpensive air-conditioned accommodations.

History

By the spring of 1849 the Maya faced what appeared certain victory in the War of the Castes. Confident with their success and eager to get back to their lands to begin that year's planting, many put down their arms and returned home. The *ladinos* seized this reprieve to fortify their forces with new troops and weapons from Mexico City. By that summer the reinforced *ladino* army began to prevail, taking brutal revenge on Mayan communities throughout the north. Many Maya began to flee to the peninsula's southeast coast, seeking refuge in the relatively uninhabited region. Living in the jungle, the refugees banded together under the charismatic leadership of José María Barrera.

In 1850 Barrera and a group of his followers announced they had found a 'talking cross' erected by a *cenote* (*cenotes* were often considered shrines) in the woods. The cross told the Maya that they were the chosen people, and exhorted them to continue the struggle against the whites, assuring them victory if they did so. The Cruzob (followers of the cross) soon founded their own town: Chan Santa Cruz (Small Holy Cross) – which is today Felipe Carillo Puerto.

The oracular cross guided the Cruzob triumphantly in battle for years. In 1857 they conquered the fortress at Bacalar and

claimed for themselves all territory from Tulum to the Belizean border. From 1901 to 1915 Mexican troops occupied Chan Santa Cruz sending the Maya back into the jungle where they artfully and successfully engaged in guerrilla warfare. By 1915 the Mexicans retreated and the Chan Santa Cruz Maya reclaimed their city. In the 1920s a boom in the chicle market brought prosperity to the region, and heightened Mexico City's interest in the territory. After years of negotiation the Chan Santa Cruz Maya finally signed a peace treaty with Mexico and in 1930 came under Mexican rule.

Though the Cruzob no longer officially governed the region, many Maya continued to worship the talking cross. Many followers of the cult remained in or around Chan Santa Cruz, where they revere the cross to this day. While in town you may see followers of the cross visiting the **Santuario de la Cruz Parlante**, the *cenote* where the cross was kept, especially if you visit on May 3, the day of the Holy Cross.

Sights

The **Santuario de la Cruz Parlante** (Sanctuary of the Talking Cross) is five blocks west of the gas station on Highway 307. Because of its sacred importance, some townspeople don't readily welcome strangers into the sanctuary, especially those with cameras. The **Casa de Cultura** on the plaza has art exhibitions, workshops, and the occasional exhibit on the War of the Castes. Be sure to check the mural outside.

Sleeping & Eating

Hotel Esquivel (☎ 834-03-44; Calle 65 No 746; d with fan/air con US$17/22) The Esquivel is around the corner from the plaza and bus terminal. The rooms have tile floors and very clean bathrooms. Splurge on an air-con room if you can, the screens on the fan rooms aren't great.

El Faisán y El Venado (☎ 834-07-02; Av Juárez 7812; d US$22) The 30 air-conditioned rooms of this hotel feature private bath, firm mattresses, TV and ceiling fans. The adjoining **restaurant** (meals $3-5) has very good, reasonably priced food.

Restaurant 24 Horas (Av Juárez; mains US$3.50-5) This friendly restaurant is a few dozen meters south with food a bit cheaper than El Faisán's.

Getting There & Away
Most buses serving Carrillo Puerto are *de paso* ('in passing'; they don't originate there). The following services run to/from:

Cancún (US$10.50, 3½-4hr, 9 1st-class buses; US$8, hourly 2nd-class)

Chetumal (US$7.25, 2-3hr, 4 1st-class; US$6, 14 2nd-class)

Mérida (US$12, 5½hr, 11 2nd-class)

Playa del Carmen (US$7.50, 2½hr, 9 1st-class; US$6.25, hourly 2nd-class)

Ticul (US$9, 4½hr, 11 2nd-class) Change at Ticul or at Muna for Uxmal.

Tulum (US$4.75, 1¾hr, 9 1st-class; US$3.75, hourly 2nd-class)

Note that there are very few services such as hotels, restaurants or gas stations between Carrillo Puerto and Ticul, and there's no gas station between Carrillo Puerto and Chetumal.

COSTA MAYA
The coast south of the Reserva de la Biósfera Sian Ka'an to the small fishing village of **Xcalak** (shka-*lak*) is often referred to as the Costa Maya. Development of the area has been in fits and starts: Xcalak is now linked to Highway 307 by a paved road, and the town of Mahahual to the north has a cruise-ship pier and airport, though ships have had much difficulty docking, and the airport sees little traffic. Realtors' advertisements and 'Land for Sale' signs are abundant on the coastal road, but Mahahual and Xcalak remain for the moment relatively primitive parts of Mexico. There are very few services, and most residents have electricity only six hours a day.

Mahahual
This precious beach town faces slow but steady exploitation by developers and tourist operations. Cruise ships threaten to dock more frequently and all-inclusive resorts are being constructed north of town. For the time being, however, Mahahual retains its tranquility and charm and is still one of the most peaceful, mellow enclaves on the coast.

You will enjoy some of the best diving in the Caribbean off the coast here. The friendly and seasoned professional, Douglas Campell-Smith at **Blue Ha diving Center** (☎ 983-753-58-21; www.bluehadiving.com; Km 2.7),

offers a variety of diving and snorkeling classes and excursions.

Sleeping & Eating
There are a few places to stay right in town, but the best accommodations are at the beachside *cabañas* south of town, most of which are owned by eco-conscious expats.

Balamku Inn (www.balamku.com; Km 5.7; d US$65; 🖳) The gorgeous high-ceilinged *cabañas* all face the ocean. There is hot water, 24-hour electricity (solar powered), Internet access and a very good restaurant.

Travel'in (Km 5.8; dm US$7) Owned and lovingly run by inveterate backpackers, Justa and Adam, this is the perfect spot to pitch your tent, hang your hammock or enjoy a comfortable dorm bed. The food in the adjoining restaurant is homemade and yummy.

Kohun Beach (http://kohunbeach.o-f.com; Km 7; US$35) The three cozy *palapa* units are tucked under the palms just footsteps from the beach; each has tiled floors, hot water showers, 24-hour electricity and comfortable beds. This is an amazing deal.

Casa del Mar (Km 2; breakfast, mains US$3-5) This friendly German-run place serves breakfast, yummy baked goods, vegetarian dishes and coffee (including great cappuccino).

Xcalak
Xcalak's appeal lies in its quiet atmosphere, Caribbean-style wooden homes, swaying palms and pretty beaches. Another draw is the little-explored **Reserva de la Biósfera Banco Chinchorro**, the largest coral atoll in the Northern Hemisphere, 40km northeast. In addition to its many natural beauties, the atoll is a wreck diver's paradise. So many vessels have collided with the ring of islands that parts of it resemble a ship graveyard; many are easily snorkeled. The barrier reef is much closer and provides some very interesting diving and snorkeling opportunities.

Xcalak to Chinchorro (XTC) Dive Center (☎ 983-831-04-61; www.xcalak.com.mx), about 300m north of town on the coast road, offers dive and snorkel trips to the wondrous barrier reef just offshore, and they are the only outfit in the area with official permission to lead trips to Banco Chinchorro.

Sleeping & Eating
Hotel Caracol (d US$11) This six-room hotel offers decent rooms with fan and cold-water

private bathroom. Electricity is available from 6pm to 10pm. Look for the owner, Señora Mauricia Garidio, next door to the hotel. At time of research the owner of Restaurant Bar Xcalak Caribe (see later) was in the process of opening a campground. Enquire with Alan at the restaurant.

The following places are among a handful on the old coastal road leading north from town (most run by Americans or Canadians); rates given are the higher winter prices. All listed have purified drinking water, ceiling fans, 24-hour electricity (from solar or wind with generator backup), bikes and/or sea kayaks for guests' use, and private hot-water bathrooms. They all have lovely beaches and docks from which to swim or snorkel.

Hotel Tierra Maya (☎ 983-831-04-04; www.tierra maya.net; d US$85-95) This is a modern beachfront hotel 2km north of town. It features six lovely rooms (three quite large), each tastefully appointed and with many architectural details. Each of the rooms has mahogany furniture and a balcony facing the sea – the bigger rooms have small refrigerators. Air-con (available in some rooms) is US$10 extra per night. Meals are available at the pleasant **restaurant** (mains around US$11; ☽ dinner). Rates include a light buffet breakfast.

Casa Carolina (☎ 983-831-04-44; www.casacarolina .net; d US$85) Carolina is just up the road from Hotel Tierra Maya. Its four guestrooms have large balconies facing the sea, with hammocks. Each room has a kitchen with fridge, and the bathrooms try to outdo one another with their beautiful Talavera tile. All levels of scuba instruction (NAUI) are offered here, as well as recreational dives at the barrier reef.

Playa Sonrisa (☎ 983-838-18-72; www.playason risa.com; d US$75-95) 'All you need is a smile' is the motto here and many guests wear little else. The beach at this little resort is lovely and the long pier provides a perfect spot for swimming and sunning. The six guest rooms are bright and comfortable and the restaurant/bar is particularly homey.

Grocery trucks service the coast road, and there are a few small restaurants near the center of Xcalak that keep sporadic hours. **Lonchería Silvia** (meals US$3-5) is the most likely to be open, and it serves good fish dinners. **Restaurant Bar Xcalak Caribe** (one block south of the wharf and just across the street from the beach) serves delicious fried fish, *ceviche*, generous servings of lobster and cold beer (US$5 to US$15).

Getting There & Around

From Highway 307, take the signed turnoff for Mahahual. The turnoff is 68km south of Felipe Carrillo Puerto (1km south of Limones) and 46km north of Bacalar. About 55km east, a few kilometers before Mahahual, turn right (south) and follow the signs to Xcalak (another 60km).

Expect to be stopped at least once at a military checkpoint; they're only searching for contraband. The road passes through young mangroves and is frequented by diverse wildlife. Watch out for the usual herons and egrets, as well as jabirus, iguanas, peccaries and other critters.

Rickety Sociedad Cooperativa del Caribe buses depart Chetumal's main bus terminal for Xcalak (US$5.50, 200km, five hours, every day at 5am and 3pm). From Felipe Carrillo Puerto catch a bus to Limones; from there buses to Xcalak (US$4.25) depart at around 6:30am and 4:30pm. Buses depart Xcalak for Chetumal at 5am and 2pm and leave for Limones at around 8:30am and 6:30pm.

A taxi now works the town, serving the northern hotels for US$11 and can be hired for excursions to further destinations.

LAGUNA BACALAR

A large, clear, turquoise freshwater lake with a bottom of gleaming white sand, Laguna Bacalar comes as a surprise in this region of tortured limestone and scrubby jungle.

The small, sleepy town of Bacalar, just east of the highway, 125km south of Felipe Carrillo Puerto, is the only settlement of any size on the lake. It's noted mostly for its old Spanish fortress and its popular *balneario* (bathing place).

The fortress was built above the lagoon to protect citizens from raids by pirates and Indians. It served as an important outpost for the whites in the War of the Castes. In 1859 it was seized by Maya rebels, who held the fort until Quintana Roo was finally conquered by Mexican troops in 1901. Today, with formidable cannons still on its ramparts, the fortress remains an imposing sight. It houses a **museum** (admission US$1; ☻ 10am-6pm Tue-Sun) exhibiting colonial armaments and uniforms from the 17th and 18th centuries.

A divided avenue runs between the fortress and the lakeshore north a few hundred meters to the *balneario*. There are some small **restaurants** along the avenue and near the *balneario*, which is very busy on weekends.

Costera Bacalar & Cenote Azul

The road that winds south for several kilometers along the lakeshore from Bacalar town to *Cenote* Azul is called the Costera Bacalar (also known as Calle 1). It passes a few lodging and camping places along the way. *Cenote* Azul is a 90m-deep natural pool on the southwest shore of Laguna Bacalar, almost at the end of the end of the road and just 200m east of Highway 307. (If you're approaching from the north by bus, get the driver to let you off here.) There's a **restaurant** (meals US$6-10) overlooking the cenote.

Casita Carolina (☎ 983-834-23-34; www.casitacarolina.com; d US$25-45) This delightful place is about two blocks south of the fort. It has an expansive lawn leading down to the lake, five fan rooms and a deluxe *palapa* that sleeps up to four people. Kayaks are available for guests' use.

Los Coquitos (tent sites per person US$4.50) Only 700m south of the Hotel Laguna along the Costera is this very nice camping area on the lakeshore. Water and soft drinks are sometimes for sale, but it's best to bring your own food and water; the nearest meals are at the Hotel Laguna's restaurant.

Getting There & Away

Coming from the north by bus, have the driver drop you in Bacalar town, at the Hotel Laguna or at Cenote Azul, as you wish; check before you buy your ticket to see if the driver will stop.

Departures from Chetumal's minibus terminal on Primo de Verdad at Hidalgo (p940) to the town of Bacalar are about once an hour from 5am to 9pm (US$1.75, 45 minutes); some northbound buses departing from the bus terminal will also drop you near the town of Bacalar (US$1.50).

If you are driving, take Highway 307 north 25km and turn off at the exit marked Cenote Azul and Costera Bacalar.

CHETUMAL

☎ 983 / pop 130,000

Before the Spanish conquest, Chetumal was an important Mayan port for shipping gold, feathers, cacao and copper to the northern Yucatán Peninsula. After the conquest, the town was not actually settled until 1898. It was founded in order to put a stop to the illegal trade in arms and lumber carried on by the descendants of the War of the Castes rebels. Dubbed Payo Obispo, the town changed its name to Chetumal in 1936. In 1955 it was virtually obliterated by Hurricane Janet.

The rebuilt city is laid out on a grand plan with a grid of wide boulevards along which traffic speeds (be careful at stop signs).

Chetumal is the gateway to Belize. With the peso so low against the neighboring currency, Belizean shoppers frequently come to Chetumal.

Orientation & Information

Despite Chetumal's sprawling layout, the city center is easily manageable on foot, and it contains several hotels and restaurants. This is a big but very lightly touristed city.

EMERGENCY SERVICES

In case of emergency contact **Cruz Roja** (☎ 832-05-71; cnr Avs Independencia & Heroes de Chapultapec) or **Hospital Morelos** (☎ 832-45-95), northeast of Cruz Roja in the same block.

INTERNET ACCESS

Web Center (Efraín Aguilar btwn Avs Belice & de los Héroes; per hr US$1) Provides fast Internet access.

MONEY

There are several banks and ATMs around town, including a Bital ATM in the bus terminal.

POST

Post office (☎ 832-00-57; cnr Plutarco Elías Calles & 5 de Mayo)

TOURIST INFORMATION

Immigration office (☎ 832-63-53; Av de los Héroes; ☻ 9am-11pm Mon-Fri) On the left about four blocks north of Av Insurgentes (and the bus terminal). You can get tourist-card extensions here.

Tourist information kiosk (☎ 832-36-63; Av de los Héroes; ☻ 9am-2pm & 6-9pm Mon-Sat)

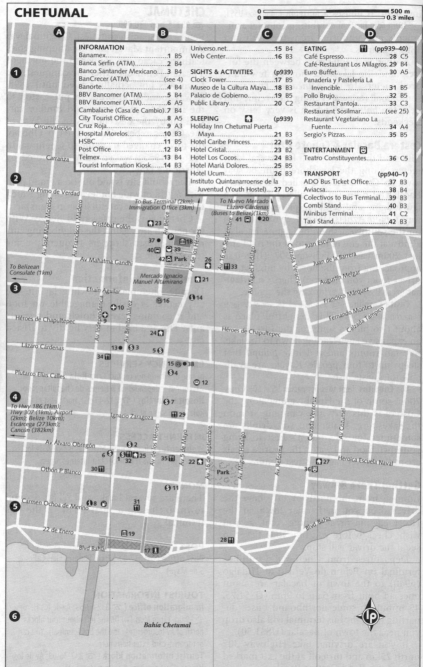

CHETUMAL

0 _____ 500 m
0 _____ 0.3 miles

INFORMATION
Banamex.....................................**1** B5
Banca Serfin (ATM)....................**2** B4
Banco Santander Mexicano.....**3** B4
BanCrecer (ATM)...................(see **4**)
Banorte......................................**4** B4
BBV Bancomer (ATM)..............**5** B4
BBV Bancomer (ATM)..............**6** A5
Cambalache (Casa de Cambio).**7** B4
City Tourist Office.....................**8** A5
Cruz Roja....................................**9** A3
Hospital Morelos.....................**10** B3
HSBC..**11** B5
Post Office...............................**12** B4
Telmex......................................**13** B4
Tourist Information Kiosk.......**14** B3

Universo.net.............................**15** B4
Web Center...............................**16** B3

SIGHTS & ACTIVITIES (p939)
Clock Tower..............................**17** B5
Museo de la Cultura Maya.....**18** B3
Palacio de Gobierno...............**19** B5
Public Library...........................**20** C2

SLEEPING (p939)
Holiday Inn Chetumal Puerta
  Maya......................................**21** B3
Hotel Caribe Princess.............**22** B5
Hotel Cristal.............................**23** B2
Hotel Los Cocos.......................**24** B3
Hotel Mariá Dolores................**25** B5
Hotel Ucum..............................**26** B3
Instituto Quintanarroense de la
  Juventud (Youth Hostel)....**27** D5

EATING (pp939–40)
Café Espresso...........................**28** C5
Café-Restaurant Los Milagros.**29** B4
Euro Buffet...............................**30** A5
Panadería y Pastelería La
  Invencible.............................**31** B5
Pollo Brujo...............................**32** B5
Restaurant Pantoja.................**33** C3
Restaurant Sosilmar...........(see **25**)
Restaurant Vegetariano La
  Fuente...................................**34** A4
Sergio's Pizzas.........................**35** B5

ENTERTAINMENT
Teatro Constituyentes............**36** C5

TRANSPORT (pp940–1)
ADO Bus Ticket Office.............**37** B3
Aviacsa......................................**38** B4
Colectivos to Bus Terminal.....**39** B3
Combi Stand.............................**40** B3
Minibus Terminal.....................**41** C2
Taxi Stand................................**42** B3

YUCATÁN PENINSULA

Sights

MUSEO DE LA CULTURA MAYA

Museo de la Cultura Maya (☎ 823-68-38; Av de los Héroes btwn Colón & Av Gandhi; admission US$5.50; 9am-7pm Tue-Thu & Sun, 9am-8pm Fri-Sat) is the city's claim to cultural fame – a bold showpiece designed to draw visitors from as far away as Cancún.

The museum is organized into three levels, mirroring Mayan cosmology. The main floor represents this world, the upper floor the heavens, and the lower floor the underworld. Though the museum is short on artifacts, the various exhibits (labeled in Spanish and English) cover all of the lands of the Maya and seek to explain their way of life, thought and belief. There are beautiful scale models of the great Mayan buildings as they may have appeared, replicas of stelae from Copán, Honduras, reproductions of the murals found in Room 1 at Bonampak and artifacts from sites around Quintana Roo. Ingenious interactive mechanical and computer displays illustrate the Mayas' complex numerical and calendrical systems.

The museum's courtyard (admission free) has salons for temporary exhibits of modern artists (such as Rufino Tamayo) and paintings reproducing Mayan frescoes. Just walk past the ticket window.

Sleeping

Holiday Inn Chetumal Puerta Maya (☎ 835-04-00; Av de los Héroes 171; d US$110;) The Holiday Inn is two blocks north of Hotel Los Cocos along Av de los Héroes, near the tourist information kiosk. Its comfortable rooms overlook a small courtyard with a swimming pool set amid tropical gardens; there's a restaurant and bar. This is the best in town.

Hotel Los Cocos (☎ 832-05-44; cnr Av de los Héroes & Calle Héroes de Chapultepec; d with air-con & TV US$68;) This hotel has a nice swimming pool, a guarded parking lot and a popular sidewalk restaurant. Rooms are good and have fridges.

Hotel Caribe Princess (☎ 832-09-00; Av Obregón 168; d US$40;) This quiet hotel is well run and nicely appointed. All rooms have air-con, phone and TV, and there's off-street parking.

Hotel María Dolores (☎ 832-05-08; Av Álvaro Obregón 206; d US$18;) This hotel, west of Av de los Héroes, is the best for the price. Beds

are a bit saggy, but some of the fan-cooled rooms are spacious, and there's off-street parking.

Hotel Ucum (☎ 832-07-11, 832-61-86, Av Mahatma Gandhi 167; d with fan/air-con US$20/25;) Hotel Ucum has lots of simple rooms around a central courtyard/parking area. There's a small pool and the hotel restaurant is inexpensive and good.

Instituto Quintanarroense de la Juventud (☎ 832-05-25; Heroica Escuela Naval; dm US$4, tent sites per person US$2) Off Calz Veracruz just past the eastern end of Av Obregón, this hostel is the cheapest place in town. It has single-sex dorms (four bunks to a room) and serves three meals a day, each for under US$3. The doors lock at 11pm but you can arrange to be let in later.

Eating & Drinking

Café-Restaurant Los Milagros (Calle Ignacio Zaragoza btwn Avs 5 de Mayo & de los Héroes; breakfast US$3-4, mains US$4-5) This place serves espresso and meals indoors and outdoors. It's a favorite with Chetumal's student and intellectual set.

Sergio's Pizzas (☎ 832-08-82; Av Álvaro Obregón 182; pizza US$4-18, mains US$5-15) Air-conditioned Sergio's has pizzas and cold beer in frosted mugs, plus Mexican and continental dishes and an extensive wine list. Sergio's also has a full bar with a somewhat lively crowd on the weekends.

Café Espresso (cnr 22 de Enero & Av Miguel Hidalgo; breakfast US$3-4, mains US$6-9) Open for breakfast and dinner. Try this café facing the bay for your coffee fix. It has an upscale ambience and a good selection of omelets and other breakfasts; the *huevos chetumaleños* (eggs, cheese, *chaya* – a spinachlike green – tomato and onion) are excellent. Dinner adds various cuts of meat to the menu.

Restaurant Sosilmar (Av Álvaro Obregón 206; mains US$4-6) Beneath the Hotel María Dolores, this bright and simple restaurant serves filling platters of fish or meat.

Pollo Brujo (Av Álvaro Obregón btwn Avs de los Héroes & Juárez; chicken US$4) This restaurant is west of the Sosilmar. You can buy a juicy roasted chicken and dine on it in the air-conditioned salon.

Restaurant Vegetariano La Fuente (Lázaro Cárdenas 222; meals US$4-5; Sun) La Fuente is a tidy vegetarian restaurant next to a homeopathic pharmacy. Here you can order a variety of faux meat dishes (made with wheat gluten) as well as refreshing fruit and veggie drinks.

Euro Buffet (Blanco btwn Avs Juárez & Othón P Independencia; ⊙ Sat & Sun) This is another great vegetarian find. Salads are the specialty and you can build your own. Priced by the kilo, a huge salad will run at less than US$3.

Restaurant Pantoja (cnr Av Mahatma Gandhi & 16 de Septiembre; mains US$3-5) The Pantoja is a family-run restaurant that opens early for breakfast and later provides *enchiladas* and other entrées.

Panadería y Pastelería La Invencible (Calle Carmen Ochoa de Merino) West of Av de los Héroes, this is a good pastry shop.The bread and rolls are always fresh and the pastries are light and tasty.

Mercado Ignacio Manuel Altamirano (meals US$2.50-3.50) Across from the Holiday Inn, the market has a row of small, simple eateries serving set meals.

Getting There & Away
AIR
Chetumal's small airport is about 2km northwest of the city center along Av Álvaro Obregón.

Aviacsa (☎ 832-77-65, 832-77-87 at the airport; Av Cárdenas at 5 de Mayo) flies to Mexico City.

For flights to Belize City (and on to Tikal) or to Belize's cayes, cross the border into Belize and fly from Corozal (p941).

BUS
The bus terminal is about 2km north of the center near the intersection of Avs Insurgentes and Belice. ADO, Sur, Cristóbal Colón, Omnitur del Caribe, Maya de Oro, Mayab and Novelo's, among others, provide service. The terminal has lockers, a bus information kiosk, ATM, post office, international phone and fax services, an exchange counter, cafetería and shops. East of the terminal is a huge San Francisco de Asís department store.

You can also buy ADO tickets and get information about most bus services at the **ADO office** (Av Belice), just west of the Museo de la Cultura Maya.

Many local buses, and those bound for Belize, begin their runs from the **Nuevo Mercado Lázaro Cárdenas** (Calz Veracruz) at Confederación Nacional Campesina (also called Segundo Circuito), about 10 blocks north of Av Primo de Verdad. From this market,

some Belize-bound buses continue to the long-distance terminal and depart from there 15 minutes later. Tickets can be purchased at the market, on board the buses or at the main terminal.

The **minibus terminal** (cnr Avs Primo de Verdad & Hidalgo), has services to Bacalar and other nearby destinations. Departures listed below are from the main bus terminal unless otherwise noted.

Bacalar (US$1.50, 45min, hourly minibuses; US$1.75, frequent Mayab buses) From the minibus terminal.

Belize City, Belize (US$7, 3-4hr, 20 1st-class; US$5.50, 20 2nd-class) Novelo's and Northern buses, depart from Nuevo Mercado between 4:30am and 6pm, some depart from main terminal 15 minutes later.

Campeche (US$20, 6½-9hr, 1 1st-class ADO at noon; US$16, 2 2nd-class)

Cancún (US$17, 5½-6½hr, frequent 1st-class; US$15, frequent 2nd-class)

Corozal, Belize (US$2.25, 1hr with border formalities, 2nd-class) See Belize City schedule.

Escárcega (US$11-13, 6hr, 9 buses btwn 4:15am & 10:30pm)

Felipe Carrillo Puerto (US$6-7, 2-3hr, frequent buses)

Flores, Guatemala (for Tikal) (US$36, 8hr, 5 1st-class Servicio San Juan & Mundo Maya buses btwn 6:20am & 2:30)

Mahahual (US$4, 4hr, 2nd-class buses at 4am, 6am & 3:15)

Mérida (US$19, 6-8hr, 8 deluxe Omnitur del Caribe & Super Expresso; US$16, 3 2nd-class Mayab)

Orange Walk, Belize (US$3.50, 2¼hr, frequent 1st-class; US$3, frequent 2nd-class) See Belize City schedule.

Playa del Carmen (US$12-15, 4½-6hr, frequent buses)

Ticul (US$13, 6hr, 6 buses)

Tulum (US$12, 3½-4hr, frequent buses)

Valladolid (US$12, 6hr, 2 2nd-class)

Veracruz (US$49, 16hr, 2 1st-class)

Villahermosa (US$26, 7-9hr, 5 buses)

Xcalak (US$5.50, 5hr, 2nd-class buses at 4am, 6am & 3:15pm)

Xpujil (US$4.75-5.75, 2-3hr, 9 buses)

Getting Around
Taxis from the stand at the bus terminal charge US$1.25 to the center (agree on the price before getting in; some will try to charge per person). You can try to avoid haggles by walking out of the terminal to the main road (Av Insurgentes), turning left (east), and walking a little over a block to the traffic circle at Av de los Héroes to hail a taxi. From here you can also catch the cheapest ride to the center (US$0.30), in an eastbound ('Santa María' or 'Calder-

itas') *combi*. The route will be circuitous. To reach the terminal from the center, head for the **combi & taxi stands** (Av Belice) behind the Museo de la Cultura Maya. By *combi* ask to be dropped off at the glorieta (traffic circle) at Av Insurgentes. Head left (west) to reach the terminal.

KOHUNLICH

The archaeological site of **Kohunlich** (admission US$3; 8am-5pm) is being aggressively excavated, though most of its nearly 200 mounds are still covered in vegetation. The surrounding jungle is thick, but the archaeological site itself has been cleared selectively and is now a delightful forest park. Drinks are sometimes sold at the site. The toilets are usually locked and 'under repair.'

These ruins, dating from the late preclassic (AD 100–200) and the early classic (AD 250–600) periods, are famous for the great **Templo de los Mascarones** (Temple of the Masks), a pyramid-like structure with a central stairway flanked by huge, 3m-high stucco masks of the sun god. The thick lips and prominent features are reminiscent

of Olmec sculpture. Of the eight original masks, only two are relatively intact following the ravages of archaeology looters.

The masks themselves are impressive, but the large thatch coverings that have been erected to protect them from further weathering obscure the view; you can see the masks only from close up. Try to imagine what the pyramid and its masks must have looked like in the old days as the Maya approached it across the sunken courtyard at the front.

A few hundred meters southwest of Plaza Merwin are the **Los 27 Escalones** (27 Steps), the remains of an extensive residential area, with photogenic trees growing out of the steps themselves.

The hydraulic engineering used at the site was a great achievement; 90,000 of the site's 210,000 sq meters were cut to channel rainwater into Kohunlich's once-enormous reservoir.

Getting There & Away

At the time of research, there was no public transportation running directly to Kohunlich. To visit the ruins without your own vehicle, you need to start early, taking a bus to the village of Francisco Villa near the turnoff to the ruins, then either hitching or walking the 8.5km to the site.

Better still, take a taxi from Chetumal to the ruins, have the driver wait for you, and then return. Round-trip taxi fare, with the wait, will cost about US$60 per party. Another means is to travel to Xpujil and book a tour from there.

To return by bus to Chetumal or head west to Xpujil or Escárcega you must hope to flag down a bus on the highway; not all buses will stop.

SOUTH TO BELIZE & GUATEMALA

Corozal, 18km south of the Mexico–Belize border, is a pleasant, sleepy farming and fishing town and an appropriate introduction to Belize. It has several hotels and restaurants catering to a full range of budgets.

Buses run directly from Chetumal's market to Belize City via Corozal and Orange Walk; all connect with buses to Melchor de Mencos in Guatemala. From there they continue onward to Flores, Tikal and points in Guatemala. There are also buses from Chetumal to Flores (Tikal is about an hour beyond Flores). See p940 for further transport details.

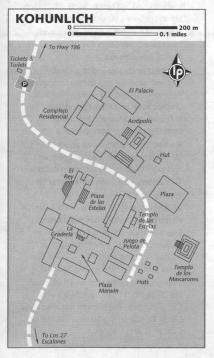

KOHUNLICH

0   200 m
0   0.1 miles

To Hwy 186

Tickets & Toilets

P

El Palacio

Complejo Residencial

Acrópolis

Hut

El Rey

Plaza de las Estelas

Plaza

Templo de los Estelas

La Gradería

Juego de Pelota

Plaza Merwin

Huts

Templo de los Mascarones

To Los 27 Escalones

YUCATÁN PENINSULA

Directory

ACCOMMODATIONS

Accommodations in Mexico range from hammocks and huts to hotels of every imaginable standard and world-class luxury resorts. This book categorizes accommodations as budget (where a typical room for two people costs under US$30, including taxes), mid-range (US$30 to $75) or top end (above US$75).

Recommended budget accommodations include camping grounds, hammocks, palm-thatched cabañas, backpacker hostels with dormitories, and economical hotels. These accommodations will be simple and with-out frills but generally clean. Hotel rooms, even in the budget range, will usually have a private bathroom containing hot shower, WC and washbasin. (In this book rooms are assumed to have private bathroom unless otherwise stated.)

Mid-range accommodations are chiefly hotels, ranging in comfort and atmosphere according to price, though in some areas of Mexico even US$35 can get you a cozy, attractively decorated room in a friendly

---

PRACTICALITIES

- Mexicans use the metric system for weights and measures.

- Most prerecorded videotapes on sale in Mexico (like the rest of the Americas and Japan) use the NTSC image registration system, incompatible with the PAL system common to most of Western Europe and Australia and the SECAM system used in France. Some PAL videos are available in Mexico, however.

- Electrical current is 110V, 60Hz, and most plugs have two flat prongs, as in the US and Canada.

- The best and most independent-minded national newspapers include *Reforma* and the left-wing *La Jornada*. (Except for a few local periodicals, Mexico has no widely distributed English-language newspapers.)

- For the online editions of about 300 Mexican newspapers and magazines, and links to dozens of Mexican radio and TV stations, visit www.zonalatina.com.

- Free-to-air TV is dominated by Televisa, which runs four of the six main national channels; TV Azteca has two (Azteca 7 and Azteca 13). Many viewers have multichannel cable systems such as Cablevision but switch to Televisa for news and soap operas (telenovelas).

- Two good noncommercial TV channels are Once TV (11 TV), run by Mexico City's Instituto Politécnico Nacional, and Canal 22, run by Conaculta, the National Culture & Arts Council.

small hotel. Some mid-range hotels will have swimming pools, restaurants, in-house travel agencies and other facilities. Many of the country's most appealing and memorable lodgings are in this bracket – small or medium-sized hotels, well cared for, with a friendly atmosphere and personal attention from staff. In some locations you can also find apartments, bungalows and more comfortable *cabañas* in this same price range.

Top-end hotels run from classy international hotels in cities to deluxe coastal resort-hotels and luxurious smaller establishments catering to travelers with a taste for comfort and beautiful design, and the funds to pay for them.

Tourism high seasons in most of Mexico are Semana Santa (the week before Easter and a couple of days after it), most of July and August, and the Christmas–New Year holiday period of about two weeks. Of course, there are local variations: in some places on the Pacific coast and the Yucatán Peninsula high season runs from Christmas right through to Easter. During the peak seasons, many mid-range and top-end establishments in tourist destinations raise their room prices by 20% to 50% above low-season rates. Budget accommodations are more likely to keep the same rates all year. Throughout this book we note major seasonal price changes and deviations from the normal seasonal pattern. We also note special deals, low weekend rates, off-season discounts and other ways you can cut costs.

In popular destinations at busy times it's best to reserve a room in advance, or go early in the day to secure a room. Growing numbers of places take bookings on websites or by email. Otherwise try by telephone or fax: if the place is not booked out, a simple phone call earlier in the day, to say what time you'll arrive, is sufficient. A few places are reluctant to take bookings, but don't worry: you'll always end up with a room somewhere.

Accommodation prices are subject to two taxes: IVA (value-added tax; 15%) and ISH (lodging tax; 2% in most states). Many budget and some mid-range establishments only charge these taxes if you require a receipt, and they quote room rates accordingly (ie not including taxes). Generally, though, IVA and ISH are included in quoted prices. In top-end hotels a price may often be given

as, say, 'US$100 *más impuestos*' (US$100 plus taxes), in which case you must add 17% to the figure. When in doubt, you can ask '*¿Están incluidos los impuestos?*' ('Are taxes included?'). To the best of our knowledge, prices in this book all include IVA and ISH, where payable.

Apartments

In some places you can find *apartamentos* with fully equipped kitchens designed for tourists. Some are very comfortable and they can be good value for three or four people. Tourist offices and ads in local papers (especially English-language papers) are good sources of information on these.

B&Bs

B&Bs, where they exist, are generally attractive, upmarket guesthouses, often aimed at North American tourists. They are usually comfortable and enjoyable places to stay.

Camping & Trailer Parks

Most organized campgrounds are actually trailer parks set up for RVs (camper vans) and trailers (caravans) but are open to tent campers at lower rates. Some are very basic, others quite luxurious. Expect to pay about US$5 to pitch a tent for two, and US$10 to US$20 for two people with a vehicle, using full facilities. Some restaurants and guesthouses in small beach spots will let you pitch a tent on their patch for a couple of dollars per person.

Campgrounds are most common along the coasts.

Casas de Huéspedes & Posadas

Cheap and congenial accommodations are often to be found at a *casa de huéspedes*, a home converted into simple guest lodgings. Good *casas de huéspedes* are usually family-run, with a relaxed, friendly atmosphere. A double room typically costs US$10 to US$20, though a few places are more comfy and more expensive.

Many *posadas* (inns) are like *casas de huéspedes*; others are small hotels.

Hammocks & Cabañas

You'll find hammocks and *cabañas* mainly in low-key beach spots in the south of the country. You can rent a hammock and a place to hang it – usually under a palm roof outside a small guesthouse or beach restaurant – for US$2 in some places, though it might reach US$10 on the more expensive Caribbean coast. If you have your own hammock, the cost comes down a bit. A hammock is often the most comfortable place to sleep in hot, southern areas. It's easy enough to buy hammocks in Mexico, especially in Oaxaca and Chiapas states and the Yucatán Peninsula. Mosquito repellent is handy if you're sleeping in a hammock.

Cabañas are basically huts with a palm-thatched roof. Some have dirt floors and nothing inside but a bed; others are deluxe, with electric light, mosquito nets, fans, fridge, bar and decor. Prices for simple *cabañas* range from US$10 to US$35. The most expensive ones are on the Caribbean where you'll find luxury *cabañas* costing over US$100.

Hostels

Hostels for international budget travelers now exist in many of the cities where such travelers congregate, especially in the center and southeast of the country. They provide dormitory accommodation for US$5 to US$12 per person, plus communal kitchens, bathrooms and living space. Aside from being cheap, they're generally relaxed, and are good places to meet other travelers. **HostelWorld** (www.hostelworld.com) has listings.

Some hostels are members of Mexico's Hostelling International affiliate **HI-Mexico** (www.hostellingmexico.com, www.hihostels.com), whose flagship is Hostel Catedral (p144) in Mexico City. There's a dollar or two off nightly rates for HI members at these places.

Hotels

Every Mexican town has its cheap hotels. There are clean, friendly, secure ones, and there are dark, dirty, smelly ones where you may not feel your belongings are safe. Decent double rooms with private hot shower are available for under US$25 in most of the country.

Mexico specializes in good mid-range hotels where two people can get a room with private bathroom, TV and perhaps air-con for US$30 to US$60. Often there's a restaurant and bar. You can expect these places to be pleasant, safe and comfortable. Among the most charming lodgings, in both the mid-range and the top end, are the many old mansions, inns, even convents, turned into hotels. Most of these are wonderfully atmospheric, with fountains gurgling in flower-bedecked stone courtyards. Some are a bit spartan (but relatively low in price); others have been modernized, and can be posh and expensive. These are probably the lodgings you will remember most fondly after your trip.

Mexico also has plenty of large, modern luxury hotels, particularly in the coastal resorts and largest cities. They offer the expected levels of luxury – with pools, gyms, bars, restaurants and so on – at expectedly lofty prices. If you like to stay in luxury but also enjoy saving some money, look for a Mexican hotel that's not part of an international chain.

Fortunately for families and small groups of travelers, many hotels in all price ranges have rooms for three, four or five people that cost not much more than a double.

In this book we use 'single' (abbreviated 's') to mean a room for one person, and 'double' ('d') to mean a room for two people. Mexicans sometimes use the phrase *cuarto sencillo* (literally, single room) to mean a room with one bed, but that bed may well be a *cama matrimonial* (double bed). Sometimes one person can occupy such a room for a lower price than two people; otherwise the price is the same. A *cuarto doble* often means a room with two beds, which may both be *camas matrimoniales*.

ACTIVITIES

You can hike, bike, climb, ride horses or watch wildlife in some of the country's most spectacular areas, and take part in most imaginable activities in, on and under the water along Mexico's coasts. This section gives a brief introduction to what you can do: for more detail, see the relevant destination sections of this book. Good Internet sources on active tourism in Mexico include **Planeta.com** (www.planeta.com) and **Mexico Online** (www.mexonline.com).

Climbing

Mexico's mecca for technical climbers is the limestone of Potrero Chico (p398), north of Monterrey, with 600 routes developed. Popocatépetl, the famous volcano east of Mexico City, has been off-limits for several years because of volcanic activity, but two other peaks in Mexico's central volcanic belt – Pico de Orizaba (p686), Mexico's highest, and Iztaccíhuatl (p194) – present fine challenges. Parque Nacional El Chico (p191) is another popular climbing locale. Guides are available for all these places. A good book is *Mexico's Volcanoes: A Climbing Guide* by RJ Secor. Conditions at high altitude are best from October to February.

Hiking

Trails in the Barranca del Cobre (Copper Canyon, p322), Parque Nacional Sierra San Pedro Mártir (p268) in Baja California, and Oaxaca's Pueblos Mancomunados (p730) are among the most popular and developed in Mexico. Other fine places for great hikes that don't require climbing skills include Parque Nacional El Chico (p191), the Reserva de la Biósfera El Cielo (p383), Real de Catorce (p602), Nevado de Toluca (p248), Laguna Santa María del Oro (p431), Volcán Paricutín (p570), Volcán Nevado de Colima (p541), La Malinche (p200), Volcán Tacaná (p839) and the lower slopes of Iztaccíhuatl (p194). A guide is a very good idea for many routes, as marking is incipient and walking alone across remote territory can be risky. The best seasons for hiking vary from place to place, but conditions at high altitude are usually best from October to February.

Horseback Riding

Locations for this increasingly popular activity include Valle de Bravo (p248), Álamos (p313), the Barranca del Cobre (Copper Canyon, p330), Real de Catorce (p602) and San Cristóbal de Las Casas (p809). Canter along the beaches at Puerto Vallarta (p441), Pie de la Cuesta (p483) and many other Pacific resorts.

Mountain Biking

You'll find mountain bikes available for excursions or guided trips of up to several days in places as diverse as Loreto (p280) in Baja California, the Barranca del Cobre (Copper Canyon, p330), Puerto Vallarta (p441), San Patricio-Melaque (p452), Oaxaca (p708) and San Cristóbal de Las Casas (p805). There's endless magnificent country to ride. See p974 for some tips on cycling in Mexico.

Water Sports

Most coastal resorts offer snorkel gear rentals and can arrange boat and fishing trips. Waterskiing, parasailing, jet skiing and 'banana' riding are widespread resort activities too. Always cast an eye over the equipment before taking off.

Inland are many *balnearios*, bathing places with swimming pools, often centered on hot springs in picturesque natural surroundings.

FISHING

There's lake and reservoir fishing inland, and lagoon, river and sea fishing along the Gulf and Caribbean coasts. Fanatics flock to Barra del Tordo (p380) and La Pesca (p380) in the northeast, and Punta Allen (p933) in the southeast. But it's sportfishing for marlin, swordfish, sailfish and tuna along the Pacific coast (p417) and Sea of Cortez (p280) for which Mexico is justly famous. Deep-sea charters are available in all of the major resort towns, and many of them now practice catch-and-release for billfish. The prime locations include Ensenada (p265), San Felipe (p893), Loreto (p280), La Paz (p286), San José del Cabo (p289), Cabo San Lucas (p292), San Carlos (p312), Mazatlán (p417), Puerto Vallarta (p441), Barra de Navidad (p455), Manzanillo (p457), Zihuatanejo (p476), Acapulco (p492), Puerto Escondido (p740) and Puerto Ángel (p751).

In general the biggest catches occur from April to July and from October to December. Fishing licenses (costing around US$11/22 per day/week) are required for fishing from boats in estuaries and on the ocean; charters usually include them, but you'll need your own if you hire a local fisher to take you out. Most towns have an *oficina de pesca* (fisheries office) that issues licenses.

KAYAKING, CANOEING & RAFTING

Mexico's many coastal lagoons and sheltered bays make magnificent waters for kayaks and canoes. There's equipment to rent at prime sites in Baja California, such as La Paz (p286), Cabo San Lucas (p292) and Loreto (p280) on the Pacific coast at places such as San Patricio-Melaque (p452), Barra de Navidad (p455), Barra de Potosí (p483), Acapulco (p492) and Bahías de Huatulco (p763); and on the Caribbean coast at Cancún (p898).

Xalapa (p667), capital of Veracruz state, where rivers fall dramatically from the Sierra Madre Oriental to the coastal plain, is the epicenter of white-water rafting, called *descenso de ríos* in Mexico. You can also raft at Bahías de Huatulco (p763) in Oaxaca from July to November and on some rivers in Chiapas (p799). Always use a reliable company with good equipment and experienced guides.

A Gringo's Guide to Mexican Whitewater by Tom Robey details 56 kayak, canoe and raft runs on 37 different rivers.

SNORKELING & DIVING

The Caribbean is world famous for its wonderful reefs and clear waters. Great diving locations include Isla Mujeres (p907), Playa del Carmen (p920), Cozumel (p915), Akumal (p925), Paamul (p924), Punta Allen (p933), Xcalak (p935) and the Banco Chinchorro coral atoll (p935). Most of these are good for snorkeling, too. Inland you can dive some of the Yucatán's famed *cenotes* (limestone sinkholes) near Akumal (p926).

The Pacific coast also has good spots. Strap on your tanks at Mazatlán (p417), Puerto Vallarta (p441), Barra de Navidad (p455), Manzanillo (p459), Zihuatanejo (p476), Puerto Escondido (p740) or Bahías de Huatulco (p763). There's top snorkeling at most of these sites, as well as Playa Tenacatita (p450), Playa Troncones (p468), Faro de Bucerías (p464) and Acapulco (p492).

In Baja California the top diving and snorkeling locales are Mulegé (p279), Loreto (p280), La Paz (p286) and Cabo San Lucas (p292). Mexico's most unusual snorkeling site has to be the lagoons of Cuatro Ciénegas (p400) – in the middle of the Chihuahuan Desert!

When renting diving equipment, try to make sure that it's up to standard. And beware of dive shops that promise certification after just a few hours' tuition. The websites of the international diving organizations **PADI** (www.padi.com) and **NAUI** (www.naui .com) enable you to search for the affiliated dive shops. The **FMAS** (www.fmas.org), also internationally recognized, is the Mexican equivalent of PADI and NAUI.

SURFING & WINDSURFING

The Pacific coast has some awesome waves. Among the very best are the summer breaks at spots between San José del Cabo and Cabo San Lucas in Baja California; the 'world's longest wave' on Bahía de Matanchén (p427), near San Blas; and the barreling 'Mexican Pipeline' at Puerto Escondido (p740). Other fine spots include Ensenada (p265), Sayulita (p433), Barra de Navidad (p455), Manzanillo (p459), Boca de Pascuale (p463), near El Paraíso, Playa La Ticla (p464), Barra de Nexpa (p464), Playa Azul (p465), Playa Troncones (p469), Saladita (p469), Ixtapa (p471), Playa Revolcadero (p500), near Acapulco, and Barra de la Cruz (p762), to

---

SAFETY GUIDELINES FOR DIVING

Before embarking on a scuba diving, skin diving or snorkeling trip, carefully consider the following points to ensure a safe and enjoyable experience:

- Possess a current diving certification card from a recognised scuba diving instructional agency (if scuba diving).
- Be sure you are healthy and feel comfortable diving.
- Obtain reliable information about physical and environmental conditions at the dive site (eg from a reputable local dive operation).
- Be aware of local laws, regulations and etiquette about marine life and the environment.
- Dive only at sites within your realm of experience; if available, engage the services of a competent, professionally trained dive instructor or dive master.
- Be aware that underwater conditions vary significantly from one region, or even site, to another. Seasonal changes can significantly alter any site and dive conditions. These differences influence the way divers dress for a dive and what diving techniques they use.
- Ask about the environmental characteristics that can affect your diving and how local trained divers deal with these considerations.

the east of Bahías de Huatulco...for starters. Most beach breaks receive some sort of surf all year, but wave season is really May to October/November. June, July and August are the biggest months for waves. You can rent surfboards in a few spots. Most airlines charge US$50 or more (each way) to carry your surfboard to Mexico.

Los Barriles (p288) is Baja California's windsurfing capital (September to March). Farther south, Puerto Vallarta (p437) and Manzanillo (p459) can be good too.

Wildlife & Bird-Watching

Observing Mexico's varied and exotic fauna is an increasingly popular and increasingly practicable pastime – see p77 for an introduction to what you can see and where.

BUSINESS HOURS

Stores (shops) are generally open from 9am or 10am to 7pm or 8pm Monday to Saturday. In the south of the country and in small towns some stores may close for siesta between 2pm and 4pm, then stay open till 9pm. Some don't open on Saturday afternoon. Stores in malls and coastal resort towns often open on Sunday. Supermarkets and department stores are usually open 9am or 10am to 10pm every day.

Offices have similar Monday to Friday hours to stores, with greater likelihood of the 2pm to 4pm lunch break. Government offices are usually not open to the public after lunch (their staff have much more important things to do). Offices with tourist-related business usually open on Saturday, too, from at least 9am to 1pm.

Typical restaurant hours are 7am or 8am (9am in central Mexico) to between 10pm and midnight. If a restaurant has a closing day, it's usually Sunday, Monday or Tuesday. Cafés typically open from between 8am and 10am to between 8pm, and 10pm daily. Bars are normally open daily, but each seems to have its own special pattern of hours.

Banks are normally open 9am to 5pm Monday to Friday, and 9am to 1am Saturday. In smaller towns they may close earlier or not open on Saturday. *Casas de cambio* (money exchange offices) are usually open from 9am or 10am to 6pm or 7pm daily, often with even longer hours in coastal resorts. Post offices typically open from 8am

or 9am to between 4pm and 6pm Monday to Friday, and 9am to 1pm Saturday.

In this book we only spell out opening hours where they do not fit the above parameters. See inside the front cover for further typical opening hours.

CHILDREN

Mexicans love children, and will affectionately call any child whose hair is less than jet black '*güeró/a*' (blondie). Children are welcome at all kinds of hotels and in virtually every café and restaurant.

The sights, sounds and colors of Mexico excite and stimulate most children, but many kids don't like traveling all the time; they're happier if they can settle into a place for a while and make friends. Try to give them time to get on with some of what they like doing back home. Children are also more easily affected than adults by heat, disrupted sleeping patterns and strange food. They need time to acclimatize and you should take extra care to avoid sunburn. Ensure you replace fluids if a child gets diarrhea (see p989).

Lonely Planet's *Travel with Children* has lots of practical advice on the subject, based on firsthand experience.

Documents for Under-18 Travelers

To prevent international child abduction, minors (people under 18) entering Mexico without one or both of their parents must be able to produce a notarized consent form signed by the absent parent or parents, giving permission for the young traveler to enter Mexico. Airlines flying to Mexico may refuse to board passengers not meeting this requirement. A form for this purpose is available from Mexican consulates. In the case of divorced parents, a custody document may be acceptable instead. If one or both parents are dead, or the traveler has only one legal parent, a notarized statement saying so may be required.

These rules are aimed primarily at visitors from the USA and Canada but may also apply to people from elsewhere. Contact a Mexican consulate to find out exactly what you need to do.

Practicalities

Cots for hotel rooms and high chairs for restaurants are available mainly in mid-range and top-end establishments. If you want a rental car with a child safety seat, the major international rental firms are the most reliable providers. You will probably have to pay a few dollars extra per day.

It's usually not hard to find an inexpensive baby-sitter if parents want to go out on their own – ask at your hotel. Diapers (nappies) are widely available, but if you are dependent on some particular cream, lotion, baby food or medicine, bring it with you. Public breast-feeding is not common and, when done, is done discreetly.

On flights to and within Mexico, children under two generally travel for 10% of the adult fare, as long as they do not occupy a seat, and those aged two to 11 normally pay 67%. Children under 13 pay half-price on many Mexican long-distance buses, and, if they're small enough to sit on your lap, they will usually go for free.

Sights & Activities

In some places, apart from the obvious beaches and swimming pools, you'll find excellent special attractions such as amusement parks, aquatic parks, zoos and aquariums. These tend to cluster in the cities – for example, Mexico City (p141), Guadalajara (p511), Mérida (p862) and Hermosillo (p305), and in coastal resorts such as Cancún (p899), Mazatlán (p418), Puerto Vallarta (p442), Acapulco (p493) and Ixtapa (p472). Other especially child-friendly attractions are Monterrey's Museo de Historia Mexicano (p388) and Museo de la Fauna y Ciencias Naturales (p389), the Africam Safari park near Puebla (p211) and the Centro Mexicano de la Tortuga at Mazunte (p757).

Kids don't have to be very old to enjoy activities such as snorkeling, riding bicycles, horses and boats, and watching wildlife (p944), or even – for some! – shopping and visiting markets. Cybernetically inclined kids will stay happy for US$1 an hour at Mexico's myriad Internet cafés. Archaeological sites are fun if the kids are into climbing pyramids and exploring tunnels (few aren't).

CLIMATE CHARTS

June to October are both the hottest and the wettest months across most of Mexico. For tips on the best seasons to travel, see p13.

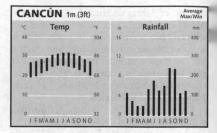

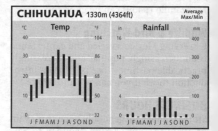

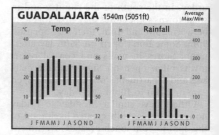

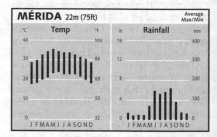

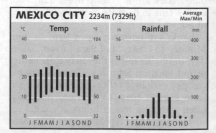

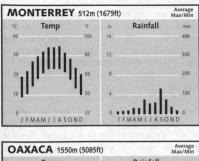

MONTERREY 512m (1679ft) — Average Max/Min — Temp / Rainfall

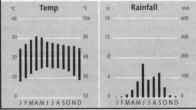

OAXACA 1550m (5085ft) — Average Max/Min — Temp / Rainfall

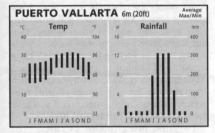

PUERTO VALLARTA 6m (20ft) — Average Max/Min — Temp / Rainfall

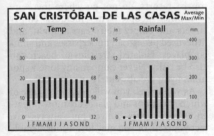

SAN CRISTÓBAL DE LAS CASAS — Average Max/Min — Temp / Rainfall

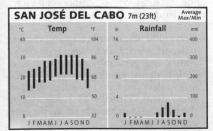

SAN JOSÉ DEL CABO 7m (23ft) — Average Max/Min — Temp / Rainfall

COURSES

Taking classes in Mexico can be a great way to meet people and get an inside angle on local life as well as study the language or culture. The country specializes in short courses in the Spanish language. In addition, Mexican universities and colleges often offer tuition to complement college courses you may be taking back home. For long-term study in Mexico you'll need a student visa; contact a Mexican consulate.

Good US sources on study possibilities in Mexico are the University of Minnesota's **Learning Abroad Center** (www.istc.umn.edu) and the **Council on International Educational Exchange** (www.ciee.org). There are also helpful links on the **Lonely Planet** website (www.lonelyplanet.com).

Cooking

Fans of Mexican food can learn from experts how to prepare delicious dishes at excellent cooking schools in Oaxaca (p710) and Tlaxcala (p197).

Language

Many of Mexico's most attractive cities are home to Spanish language schools, among them Cuernavaca, Guadalajara, Guanajuato, Mérida, Mexico City, Morelia, Oaxaca, Puerto Vallarta, San Cristóbal de Las Casas, San Miguel de Allende and Taxco (see city sections for more details). Some schools are private, some affiliated to universities.

Course lengths range from a few days to a year. In some places you can enroll on the spot and start any Monday. You may be offered accommodations with a local family as part of the deal. This can help your language skills as much as any formal tuition. In some schools, courses in art, crafts, indigenous languages or in-depth study of Mexico are also available.

Costs per week, with accommodations and meals included, can range from around US$160 to over US$400, depending on the city, the school and how intensively you study.

Useful information is available from the **National Registration Center for Study Abroad** (www.nrcsa.com).

CUSTOMS

Things that visitors are allowed to bring into Mexico duty-free include items for personal use such as clothing; a camera and video camera; up to 12 rolls of film or video-cassettes; a cellular phone; a portable computer; a CD or cassette player; medicine for personal use, with prescription in the case of psychotropic drugs; 3L of wine, beer or liquor; 400 cigarettes; and US$300 worth of other goods (US$50 if arriving by land).

The normal routine when you enter Mexico is to complete a customs declaration form (which lists duty-free allowances), and then place it in a machine. If the machine shows a green light, you pass without inspection. If a red light shows, your baggage will be searched.

DANGERS & ANNOYANCES

Mexico, especially its big cities and, above all, Mexico City, has a crime problem, but with a few precautions you can minimize danger to your physical safety. However, lone women and even pairs of women should be very cautious about going to remote beach spots, and everyone should be extremely careful with taxis in Mexico City.

Official information can make Mexico sound more alarming than it really is, but for a variety of useful information on travel to Mexico consult your country's foreign affairs department: **Australia** (☎ 1300-139-281; www.dfat.gov.au); **Canada** (☎ 800-267-8376; www.dfait-maeci.gc.ca); **UK** (☎ 0870-606-0290; www.fco.gov.uk); **USA** (☎ 202-647-5225; http://travel.state.gov). If you're already in Mexico, you can contact your embassy (p952). Keep an ear to the ground as you travel.

Highway Robbery

Bandits occasionally hold up buses, cars and other vehicles on intercity routes, especially at night, taking luggage or valuables. Sometimes buses are robbed by people who board as passengers. The best ways to avoid highway robbery are to not travel at night and to travel on toll highways as much as possible. Deluxe and 1st-class buses use toll highways, where they exist; 2nd-class buses do not. Hwy 200 along the Pacific coast between Ixtapa and Puerto Escondido has a bad reputation for highway robberies.

Theft & Robbery

Tourists are vulnerable to theft and robbery as they are considered wealthy by Mexican standards and are generally presumed to be carrying valuables. Pocket-picking and purse- or bag-snatching are risks in large cities, particularly Mexico City. Crowded buses, bus stops, bus stations, airports, the Mexico City metro, markets, packed streets and plazas, and anywhere frequented by large numbers of tourists, are all possible haunts of the thieves.

Pickpockets often work in teams: one or two of them may grab your bag or camera (or your arm or leg), and while you're trying to get free another will pick your pocket. Or one may 'drop' something as a crowd jostles onto a bus and as he or she 'looks for it,' a pocket will be picked or a bag slashed. The objective is to distract you. If your valuables are underneath your clothing, the chances of losing them are greatly reduced.

Robbery, or mugging, is less common than pocket-picking and purse-snatching, but more alarming and more serious: resistance may be met with violence (do *not* resist). Robbers may force you to remove your money belt, watch, rings etc. They may be armed. Usually they will not harm you: what they want is your money, fast. But there have been cases of robbers beating victims, or forcing them to drink large amounts of alcohol to extract credit card security numbers. Mexico City taxis, which are notorious for (sometimes violent) robberies, are especially dangerous if you take the wrong kind of cab (see p120).

To avoid being robbed in cities, even tourist resorts, do not go where there are few other people. This includes empty streets and empty metro cars at night, and little-used pedestrian underpasses and similar places. Isolated stretches of beach can also be risky. Never camp in any lonely spot unless you are absolutely sure it's safe.

As you travel, you will develop a sense of which situations and places are more threatening than others. But you must always protect yourself, or you may lose a considerable amount. To reduce your chances of becoming a victim, adhere to the following:

■ Leave most of your cash, traveler's checks, passport, jewelry, air tickets, credit cards, watch and perhaps your camera in a sealed, signed envelope in your hotel's safe, unless you have immediate need of these items. Virtually all hotels except the very cheapest provide safekeeping for guests' valuables.

- Leave valuables in a locked suitcase in your hotel room. It's often safer than carrying them on the streets of cities. Divide your funds into several stashes and keep them in different places.
- Carry a small amount of ready money – just enough for the outing you're on – in a pocket. If you have to carry valuables, keep them in a money belt, shoulder wallet or pouch underneath your clothing.
- Walk with purpose and be alert to people around you.
- Don't keep cash, credit cards, purses, bags or cameras in open view any longer than you have to. At ticket counters in bus stations and airports, keep your bag between your feet.
- Use ATMs only in secure locations, not those open to the street, and try to use them during working hours.
- Do not leave anything valuable-looking visible in a parked vehicle.
- Be careful about accepting food or drinks from strangers, especially in resort cities; there have been cases of drugging followed by robbery and assault, including sexual assault.
- Be wary of attempts at credit card fraud. One method is when the cashier swipes your card twice (once for the transaction and once for nefarious purposes). Keep your card in sight at all times.

DISABLED TRAVELERS

Mexico is not yet very disabled-friendly, though some hotels and restaurants (mostly towards the top end of the market) and some public buildings and archaeological sites now provide wheelchair access. Mobility is easiest in the major tourist resorts and the more expensive hotels. Bus transportation can be difficult; flying or taking a taxi is easier.

Mobility International USA (☎ 541-343-1284; www.miusa.org) advises disabled travelers on mobility issues and runs exchange programs (including in Mexico). Its website includes an international database of disability organizations with several Mexican organizations listed.

In the UK, **Radar** (☎ 020-7250-3222; www.radar .org.uk) is run by and for disabled people. Its excellent website has links to good travel and holiday-specific sites, as does Australia's **Acrod** (www.acrod.org.au).

Another excellent information source for disabled travelers is **Access-able Travel Source** (www.access-able.com).

DISCOUNT CARDS

The ISIC student card, the IYTC card for travelers under 26, and the ITIC card for teachers can help you obtain reduced-price air tickets to or from Mexico at student- and youth-oriented travel agencies bought outside and in Mexico. Reduced prices on Mexican buses and at museums, archaeological sites and so on are usually only for those with Mexican education credentials, but the ISIC, IYTC and ITIC cards will sometimes get you a reduction. The ISIC card is the most recognized. It may also get you discounts in a few hostel-type accommodations.

A Hostelling International card will save you US$1 or so in some hostels in Mexico. Take it along if you have one.

All these cards can be obtained in Mexico. One outlet is the youth/student travel agency **Mundo Joven** (www.mundojoven.com in Spanish), with offices in Mexico City and several other cities. You need proof of your student/teacher/youth status to obtain the ISIC/ITIC/IYTC card.

EMBASSIES & CONSULATES
Mexican Embassies & Consulates

The following are embassies unless otherwise noted. Updated details can be found at www .sre.gob.mx. Some Mexican embassy and consulate websites are very useful information sources on visas and similar matters.

Australia Canberra (☎ 02-6273-3963; www.embassyof mexicoinaustralia.org; 14 Perth Ave, Yarralumla, ACT 2600)

Belize Belize City (☎ 02-30-193; www.embamexbelize .gob.mx; 18 North Park St, PO Box 754)

Canada Ottawa (☎ 613-233-8988; www.embamexcan .com; 45 O'Connor St, Suite 1500, ON K1P 1A4); consulate in Montreal (☎ 514-288-2502; www.consulmex.qc.ca; 2055 rue Peel, bureau 1000, QC H3A 1V4); consulate in Toronto (☎ 416-368-2875; www.consulmex.com; Commerce Court West, 199 Bay St, Suite 4440, ON M5L 1E9); consulate in Vancouver (☎ 604-684-3547; www.consulmexvan.com; 710-1177 West Hastings St, BC V6E 2K3)

France Paris (☎ 01-53-70-27-70; www.sre.gob.mx/francia; 9 rue de Longchamp, 75116); consulate in Paris (☎ 01 42 86 56 20; 4 rue Notre Dame des Victoires, 75002)

Germany Berlin (☎ 030-269-323-332; www.embamex .de in Spanish; Klingelhöferstrasse 3, 10785 Berlin); consulate in Frankfurt-am-Main (☎ 069-299-8750; Taunusanlage 21, 60325)

Guatemala consulate in Ciudad Tecún Umán (☎ 776-8181; comexteu@terra.com.gt, 1a Av 4-01, Zona 1); Guatemala City (☎ 420-3433; www.sre.gob.mx/guatemala; 2a Av 7-57, Zona 10); consulate in Quetzaltenango (☎ 767-5542; mexicog@yahoo.com.mx; 21a Av 8-64, Zona 3)

Ireland Dublin (☎ 01-260-0699; www.sre.gob.mx /irlanda; 43 Ailesbury Rd, Ballsbridge, Dublin 4)

Italy consulate in Milan (☎ 02-7602-0541; info@mexico .it; Via Cappuccini 4, 20122); Rome (☎ 06-441151; www.sre.gob.mx/italia; Via Lazzaro Spallanzani 16, 00161)

Japan Tokyo (☎ 3-3581-1131; www.sre.gob.mx/japon; 2-15-1 Nagata-cho, Chiyoda-ku, 100-0014)

Netherlands The Hague (☎ 070-360-2900; http://emba mex-nl.com in Spanish; Burgemeester Patijnlaan 1930, 2585CB)

New Zealand Wellington (☎ 04-472-0555; www .mexico.org.nz; Level 8, 111 Customhouse Quay)

Spain consulate in Barcelona (☎ 93-201-1822; consulmex-barcelona.net; Paseo de la Bona-nova 55, 08017); Madrid (☎ 91-369-2814; www.sre.gob .mx/espana; Carrera de San Jerónimo 46, 28014)

UK London (☎ 020-7235-6393; www.embamex.co.uk; 8 Halkin St, SW1X 7DW)

USA Washington, DC (☎ 202-728-1600, www.sre.gob .mx/eua; 1911 Pennsylvania Ave NW, 20006)

MEXICAN CONSULATES IN THE USA

There are consulates in many other US cities, including the following:

Arizona Douglas (☎ 520-364-3107; www.consulmex douglas.com in Spanish); Nogales (☎ 520-287-2521); Phoenix (☎ 602-242-7398; www.sre.gob.mx/phoenix); Tucson (☎ 520-882-5595)

California Calexico (☎ 760-357-3863) Los Angeles (☎ 213-351-6800; www.sre.gob.mx/losangeles); Sacramento (☎ 916-441-3287; www.consulmexsacramento .com); San Diego (☎ 619-231-8414; www.sre.gob.mx /sandiego); San Francisco (☎ 415-392-6576; www.sre .gob.mx/sanfrancisco)

Colorado Denver (☎ 303-331-1110; www.consulmex -denver.com)

Florida Miami (☎ 786-268-4900; www.sre.gob.mx /miami); Orlando (☎ 407-422-0514)

Georgia Atlanta (☎ 404-266-2233; www.consulmex atlanta.org)

Illinois Chicago (☎ 312-855-1380; www.consulmex chicago.com in Spanish)

Massachusetts Boston (☎ 617-426-4181; www.sre .gob.mx/boston)

Michigan Detroit (☎ 313-964-4515; www.sre.gob.mx /detroit)

New Mexico Albuquerque (☎ 505-247-2139; www.users .qwest.net/~consulmexalb in Spanish)

New York New York (☎ 212-217-6400; www.consulmex ny.org)

Oregon Portland (☎ 503-274-1442; www.sre.gob.mx /portland)

Pennsylvania Philadelphia (☎ 215-922-4262)

Texas Austin (☎ 512-478-2866; www.onr.com/consul.mx in Spanish); Brownsville (☎ 956-542-4431; www.sre.gob .mx/brownsville); Dallas (☎ 214-252-9250; www.sre.gob .mx/dallas); Del Rio (☎ 830-775-2352); Eagle Pass (☎ 830-773-9255); El Paso (☎ 915-533-3644; www.sre.gob.mx /elpaso); Houston (☎ 713-271-6800; www.sre.gob.mx /houston); Laredo (☎ 956-723-0990; www.sre.gob.mx /laredo); McAllen (☎ 956-686-0243) San Antonio (☎ 210-227-9145; www.consulmexsat.org)

Utah Salt Lake City (☎ 801-521-8502)

Washington Seattle (☎ 206-448-3526; www.sre.gob .mx/seattle

Washington, DC Washington, DC (☎ 202-736-1000; consulwas@aol.com; 2827 16th St NW, 20009)

Embassies & Consulates in Mexico

Mexico City entries in the following selective list are for embassies or their consular sections; listings for other cities are consulates. Embassy websites are often useful sources of information about Mexico.

Australia (www.mexico.embassy.gov.au) Guadalajara (☎ 33-3615-7418; Río de la Plata 2593-5, Colonia Colomos Providencia) Mexico City (☎ 55-1101-2200; Rubén Darío 55, Polanco) Monterrey (☎ 81-8158-0791; Av Munich 195, Colonia Cuauhtémoc, San Nicolás de los Garza)

Belize Cancún (☎ 998-887-84-17; Av Náder 34 503B, Super-Manzana 2A) Chetumal (☎ 983-832-18-03; Av Armada de México 91, Colonia Campestre) Mexico City (☎ 55-5520-1274; embelize@prodigy.net.mx; Bernardo de Gálvez 215, Lomas de Chapultepec)

Canada Acapulco (☎ 744-484-13-05; Centro Comercial Marbella, Local 23) Cancún (☎ 998-883-33-60; Plaza Caracol II, 3er Piso, Local 330, Blvd Kukulcán Km 8.5, Zona Hotelera) Guadalajara (☎ 33-3616-5642; Hotel Fiesta Americana, Local 31, Aceves 225, Colonia Vallarta Poniente) Mazatlán (☎ 669-913-73-20; Hotel Playa Mazatlán, Loaiza 202, Zona Dorada) Mexico City (☎ 55-5724-7900, 800-706-29-00; www.canada.org .mx; Schiller 529, Polanco) Monterrey (☎ 81-8344-3200; Edificio Kalos, C1 fl, Local 108A, Zaragoza 1300 Sur) Oaxaca (☎ 951-513-37-77; Pino Suárez 700, Local 11B) Puerto Vallarta (☎ 322-293-00-98; Edificio Obelisco Local 108, Av Francisco Medina Ascencio 1951, Zona Hotelera) Tijuana (☎ 664-684-04-61; Gedovius 10411-101, Zona Río)

Cuba Cancún (☎ 884-34-23; Calle Pecari 17)

France Acapulco (☎ 744-481-25-33; Casa Consular, Centro Convenciones) Cancún (☎ 998-887-81-41; Av Bonampak 239 No 8, SM4) Guadalajara (☎ 33-3616-5516; López Mateos Nte 484) Mazatlán (☎ 669-985-12-28; Belisario Domínguez 1008 Sur, Colonia Centro) Mérida (☎ 999-925-22-91; Calle 33B No 528) Mexico City (☎ 55-9171-9700;

www.francia.org.mx; Campos Elíseos 339, Polanco) consulate in Mexico City (☎ 55-9171-9840; Lafontaine 32, Polanco) Monterrey (☎ 81-8346-1587; Hidalgo 2303 Pte, Colonia Obispado)

Germany Acapulco (☎ 744-484-18-60; Alaminos 26, Casa Tres Fuentes, Colonia Costa Azul) Cancún (☎ 998-884-18-98; Punta Conoco 36, SM24) Guadalajara (☎ 33-3613-9623; Corona 202) Mazatlán (☎ 669-914-93-10; Av Playa Gaviotas 212, Zona Dorada) Mexico City (☎ 55-5283-2200; www.embajada-alemana.org.mx; Lord Byron 737, Polanco) Monterrey (☎ 81-8378-6078; Proa Consultores SC, Río Rosas 400 Sur, Local 12, Planta Pista, Colonia Del Valle, Garza García)

Guatemala Cancún (☎ 883-82-96; Av Nader 148) Ciudad Hidalgo (☎ 969-698-01-84; 5a Calle Ote btw 1a & 3a Nte) Comitán (☎ 963-632-04-91; 1a Calle Sur Pte 26) Mexico City (☎ 55-5540-7520; embminex@minex.gob.gt; Av Explanada 1025, Lomas de Chapultepec) Tapachula (☎ 962-626-15-25; Calle Central Ote 42)

Ireland Mexico City (☎ 55-5520-5803; embajada@irlanda.org.mx; Cerrada Blvd Ávila Camacho 76, piso 3, Lomas de Chapultepec)

Italy Cancún (☎ 998-884-12-61; Alcatraces 39) Guadalajara (☎ 33-3616-1700; Av López Mateos Nte 790, 1st fl, Fraccionamiento Ladrón de Guevara) Mexico City (☎ 55-5596-3655; www.embitalia.org.mx; Paseo de las Palmas 1994, Lomas de Chapultepec) Monterrey (☎ 81-8378-2444; Prolongación Moralillo 109, Colonia Lomas del Valle, GarzaGarcía)

Japan Mexico City (☎ 55-5211-0028; Paseo de la Reforma 395)

Netherlands Acapulco (☎ 744-486-82-10; Hotel Qualton Club Acapulco, La Costera 159) Cancún (☎ 998-886-00-70; Aerocharter Martinair, Aeropuerto Cancún) Guadalajara (☎ 33-3673-2211; Av Vallarta 5500, Colonia Lomas Universidad, Zapopan) Mérida (☎ 999-924-31-22; Calle 64 No 418) Mexico City (☎ 55-5258-9921; www .paisesbajos.com.mx/f_explorer_esp.html; Av Vasco de Quiroga 3000, 7th fl, Santa Fe)

New Zealand Mexico City (☎ 55-5283-9460; kiwi mexico@compuserve.com.mx; Lagrange 103, 10th fl, Los Morales)

Spain Acapulco (☎ 744-435-15-00; Hotel El Cano, La Costera 75) Cancún (☎ 998-883-24-66; Blvd Kukulcán con Cenzontle, Lote 1, Edificio Oásis, Zona Hotelera) Guadalajara (☎ 33-3630-0450; Torre Sterling, mezzanine izquierdo, Francisco de Quevedo 117, Sector Juárez) Oaxaca (☎ 951-518-00-31; Calzada Porfirio Díaz 340, Colonia Reforma) Mexico City (☎ 55-5280-4383; www.mae.es /consulados/mexico/index.htm; Galileo 114, Polanco)

UK Acapulco (☎ 744-484-17-35; Casa Consular, Centro Internacional Acapulco, La Costera) Cancún (☎ 998-881-01-00; The Royal Sands, Blvd Kukulcán Km 13.5, Zona Hotelera) Guadalajara (☎ 33-3343-2296; Jesús de Rojas 20, Colonia Los Pinos 20, Zapopan) Monterrey

(☎ 81-8315-2049; Callejón de la Piedra 127, Colonia Las Lajas) Tijuana (☎ 664-686-53-20; Blvd Salinas 1500, Fraccionamiento Aviación Tijuana) Mexico City (☎ 55-5242-8500; www.embajadabritanica.com.mx; Río Lerma 71, Colonia Cuauhtémoc) consulate in Mexico City (☎ 55-5242-8523; Río Usumacinta 30)

USA Acapulco (☎ 744-469-05-56; Hotel Continental Plaza , La Costera 121, Local 14) Cabo San Lucas (☎ 624-143-3566; Blvd Marina y Pedregal 1, Local No 3) Cancún (☎ 998-883-02-72; Plaza Caracol II, 3rd fl, Local 320-323, Blvd Kukulcán Km 8.5) Ciudad Juárez (☎ 656-611-30-00; López Mateos 924 Nte) Guadalajara (☎ 33-3825-2700; Progreso 175) Hermosillo (☎ 662-217-2375; Av Monterrey 141) Ixtapa (☎ 755-553-21-00; Plaza Ambiente, office 9) Matamoros (☎ 868-812-44-02; Calle 1 No 2002) Mazatlán (☎ 669-916-58-89; Hotel Playa Mazatlán, Loaiza 202, Zona Dorada) Mérida (☎ 999-925-50-11; Paseo de Montejo 453) Mexico City (☎ 55-5080-2000; www.usembassy-mexico.gov; Paseo de la Reforma 305) Monterrey (☎ 81-8345-2120; Av Constitución 411 Pte) Nogales (☎ 631-313-48-20; San José s/n, Fraccionamiento Los Álamos) Nuevo Laredo (☎ 867-714-05-12; Allende 3330, Colonia Jardín) Oaxaca (☎ 951-514-30-54; Plaza Santo Domingo, Alcalá 407, Interior 20) Puerto Vallarta (☎ 322-223-00-69; Zaragoza 160) San Miguel de Allende (☎ 415-152-23-57; Hernández Macías 72) Tijuana (☎ 664-681-74-00; Tapachula 96, Colonia Hipódromo)

FESTIVALS & EVENTS

Mexico's many fiestas are full-blooded, highly colorful affairs that often go on for several days and add much spice to everyday life. In addition to the national festivals listed below, each town has many local saint's days, regional fairs, arts festivals and so on (see destination chapters for information on local festivals). There's also a national public holiday just about every month (see p954), often the occasion for yet further partying.

January

Día de los Reyes Magos (Three Kings' Day or Epiphany; January 6) This is the day that Mexican children traditionally receive gifts, rather than at Christmas. (But some get two loads of presents!)

February/March

Día de la Candelaría (Candlemas; February 2) Commemorates the presentation of Jesus in the temple 40 days after his birth; celebrated with processions, bullfights and dancing in many towns.

Carnaval (late February or early March) A big bash preceding the 40-day penance of Lent, it takes place during the week or so before Ash Wednesday (which falls 46 days before Easter Sunday). It's celebrated most festively in

Mazatlán, Veracruz and La Paz, with parades and masses of music, food, drink, dancing, fireworks and fun.

March/April

Semana Santa Holy Week starts on Palm Sunday (Domingo de Ramos). Particularly colorful celebrations are held in San Miguel de Allende, Taxco and Pátzcuaro; most of Mexico seems to be on the move at this time.

September

Día de la Independencia (Independence Day; September 16) Commemorates the start of Mexico's war for independence from Spain; the biggest celebrations are in Mexico City the evening before.

November

Día de Todos los Santos (All Saints' Day; November 1) & **Día de Muertos** (Day of the Dead; November 2) Every cemetery in the country comes alive as families visit graveyards to commune with their dead on the night of November 1 to 2 and the day of November 2, when the souls of the dead are believed to return to earth. The souls of dead children (*angelitos*, little angels) are celebrated the previous day, on All Saints' Day (see p58).

December

Día de Nuestra Señora de Guadalupe (Day of Our Lady of Guadalupe; December 12) A week or more of celebrations throughout Mexico leads up to this celebration of Mexico's religious patron – a manifestation of the Virgin Mary who appeared to an indigenous Mexican, Juan Diego, in 1531. Children are taken to church dressed as little Juan Diegos or indigenous girls. The biggest festivities are at the Basílica de Guadalupe in Mexico City.
Posadas (December 16-24) Nine nights of candlelit parades reenact the journey of Mary and Joseph to Bethlehem. More important in small towns than big cities.
Día de Navidad (Christmas Day; December 25) is traditionally celebrated with a feast in the early hours of December 25, after midnight mass.

FOOD

A few of the Eating sections in destination chapters of this book are divided into budget, mid-range and top end categories. We define a mid-range restaurant as one where a main dish at lunch or dinner costs between US$5 and US$10. Budget and top-end places are, respectively, less than US$5 and over US$10. For the full story on eating in Mexico, see the Food & Drink chapter (p82).

GAY & LESBIAN TRAVELERS

Mexico is more broad-minded about sexuality than you might expect. Gays and

lesbians do not generally maintain a high profile, but rarely attract open discrimination or violence. There are large gay communities and lively scenes in cities such as Puerto Vallarta (especially), Mexico City, Cancún, Mazatlán, Acapulco, Guadalajara and Ciudad Juárez. Discrimination based on sexual orientation has been illegal since 1999, and can be punished with up to three years in prison.

A good source of information is the **Gay Mexico Network** (www.gaymexico.net). It offers information on gay-friendly hotels and tours in Mexico. **Sergay** (www.sergay.com.mx), a Spanish-language magazine and website, is focused on Mexico City but with bar, disco and cruising-spot listings for the whole country. Also worth looking at is **PlanetOut** (www.planetout.com). *Gay Mexico: The Men of Mexico* by Eduardo David is a portrait of gay culture in Mexico.

HOLIDAYS

The chief holiday periods are Christmas–New Year, Semana Santa (the week leading up to Easter and a couple of days afterwards), and mid-July to mid-August. Transportation and tourist accommodations are heavily booked at these times. Banks, post offices, government offices and many shops throughout Mexico are closed on the following national holidays:
Año Nuevo (New Year's Day) January 1
Día de la Constitución (Constitution Day) February 5
Día de la Bandera (Day of the National Flag) February 24
Día de Nacimiento de Benito Juárez (anniversary of Benito Juárez' birth) March 21
Día del Trabajo (Labor Day) May 1
Cinco de Mayo (anniversary of Mexico's victory over the French at Puebla) May 5
Día de la Independencia (Independence Day) September 16
Día de la Raza (commemoration of mixed ancestry Mexicans) October 12
Día de la Revolución (Revolution Day) November 20
Día de Navidad (Christmas Day) December 25

At Easter, businesses usually close from Good Friday (Viernes Santo) to Easter Sunday (Domingo de Resurrección). Many offices and businesses close during major national festivals (see p953).

INSURANCE

A travel insurance policy to cover theft, loss and medical problems is a good idea. Some policies specifically exclude dangerous activities such as scuba diving, motorcycling and even trekking.

You may prefer a policy that pays doctors or hospitals directly rather than you having to pay on the spot and claim later. If you have to claim later, ensure you keep all documentation. Check that the policy covers ambulances or an emergency flight home. For further information on medical insurance, see p983.

For information on motor insurance see p970.

INTERNET ACCESS

Most travelers make constant use of Internet cafés (which cost around US$1 per hour) and free Web-based email such as **Yahoo** (www.yahoo.com) or **Hotmail** (www.hotmail.com).

To access a specific account of your own, you'll need to know your incoming (POP or IMAP) mail server name, your account name and your password. Get these from your ISP or network supervisor.

If you are traveling with a notebook or hand-held computer, be aware that your modem may not work once you leave your home country. The safest option is to buy a reputable 'global' modem before you leave home, or buy a local PC-card modem if you're spending an extended time in any one country. A second issue is the plug: Mexico uses 110V plugs with two flat prongs, like those found in the US. Third, unless you're sporting a completely wireless system, you'll have to hunt down a hotel room with a phone jack to plug into – or find a jack you can use somewhere else.

If you really want to travel with a laptop, consider using a local ISP, unless you use an international server with access numbers in Mexico (such as AOL or CompuServe). For more information on traveling with a portable computer, see www.teleadapt.com.

LEGAL MATTERS
Mexican Law

Many believe that Mexican law is based on the Napoleonic code, presuming an accused person is guilty until proven innocent.

The minimum jail sentence for possession of more than a token amount of any

THE LEGAL AGE FOR...
- drinking: 18
- driving: 18
- sex: 12

narcotic, including marijuana and amphetamines, is 10 years. As in most other countries, the purchase of controlled medication requires a doctor's prescription.

It's against Mexican law to take any weapon or ammunition into the country (even unintentionally) without a permit from a Mexican embassy or consulate.

Road travelers should expect occasional police or military checkpoints. They are normally looking for drugs, weapons or illegal migrants. Drivers found with drugs or weapons on board may have their vehicle confiscated and may be detained for months while their cases are investigated.

See p970 for information on the legal aspects of road accidents.

While the marriage age is 12, sex with someone under 18 is illegal if their consent was obtained by deception, such as a false promise of marriage.

Useful warnings on Mexican law are found in the **US Department of State website** (www.travel.state.gov).

Getting Legal Help

If arrested, you have the right to contact your embassy or consulate. Consular officials can tell you your rights, provide lists of local lawyers, monitor your case, make sure you are treated humanely, and notify your relatives or friends – but they can't get you out of jail. More Americans are in jail in Mexico than in any other country except the USA – about 450 at any one time. By Mexican law the longest a person can be detained by police without a specific accusation is 72 hours.

Tourist offices in Mexico, especially those run by state governments, can often help you with legal problems such as complaints or reporting crimes or lost articles. The national tourism ministry, **Sectur** (☎ 55-5250-0123, 800-903-92-00), offers 24-hour telephone advice.

If you are the victim of a crime, your embassy or consulate, or Sectur or state tourist offices, can give advice. In some cases, you may feel there is little to gain by going to the police, unless you need a statement to present to your insurance company. If you go to the police and your Spanish is poor, take a more fluent speaker. Also take your passport and tourist card, if you still have them. If you just want to report a theft for the purposes of an insurance claim, say you want to '*poner una acta de un robo*' (make a record of a robbery). This should make it clear that you merely want a piece of paper and you should get it without too much trouble.

If Mexican police wrongfully accuse you of an infraction (as they have often been known to do in the hope of obtaining a bribe), you can ask for the officer's identification, to speak to a superior or to be shown documentation about the law you have supposedly broken. You can also note the officer's name, badge number, vehicle number and department (federal, state or municipal). Pay any traffic fines at a police station and get a receipt, then make your complaint at Sectur or a state tourist office.

MAPS

GeoCenter, Nelles, ITM and the AAA (American Automobile Association) all produce good country maps of Mexico suitable for travel planning, available internationally for between US$5 and US$12. The map scales vary between 1:2,500,000 (1cm:25km) and 1:3,700,000 (1cm:37km). The GeoCenter map is recommended for its combination of relief (terrain) shading, archaeological sites, national parks, roads graded by quality and settlements graded by size. ITM also publishes good 1:1 million (1cm:10km) maps of some Mexican regions (including the Yucatán Peninsula and the Pacific coast). For information on road atlases, see p979.

Tourist offices in Mexico provide free city, town and regional maps of varying quality. Bookstores and newsstands sell commercially published ones. **Inegi** (Instituto Nacional de Estadística, Geografía e Informática; ☎ 800-490-42-00; www.inegi.gob.mx) publishes a large-scale map series covering all of Mexico at 1:50,000 (1cm:500m) and 1:250,000 (1cm:2.5km), plus state maps at 1:700,000 (1cm:7km). Most of these maps have been updated within the past decade, and they are well worth having if you plan to do any hiking or

back-country exploring. Inegi's Centros de Información in every Mexican state capital (listed on the website), and at least three outlets in Mexico City (see p99), sell these maps for US$4 to US$6 each.

MONEY

Mexico's currency is the peso, usually denoted by the '$' sign. Any prices quoted in US dollars will normally be written 'US$5,' '$5 Dlls' or '5 USD' to avoid misunderstanding. The peso is divided into 100 centavos. Coins come in denominations of five, 10, 20 and 50 centavos and one, two, five, 10 and 20 pesos. There are notes of 20, 50, 100, 200 and 500 pesos.

Since the peso's exchange value is sometimes unstable, in this book we give prices in US dollar equivalents. For exchange rates, see inside the front cover. For information on costs, see p14.

The most convenient form of money in Mexico is a major international credit card or debit card – preferably two or three of them, if you have them. Cards such as Visa, American Express and MasterCard can be used to obtain cash easily from ATMs in Mexico, and are accepted for payment by most airlines, car rental companies, travel agents, many upper mid-range and top-end hotels, and some restaurants and shops. Making a purchase by credit card normally gives you a more favorable exchange rate than exchanging money at a bank, and isn't subject to commission, but you'll normally have to pay a 'foreign exchange' transaction fee of around 2.5%. However, acceptance of cards is erratic in Mexico – American Express cards in particular are not accepted for payment by a significant number of Mexican businesses. Some holders of US-issued Visa cards have reported similar problems. Visa, Amex or MasterCard stickers on a door or window in Mexico do *not* necessarily mean that these cards will be accepted for payment there. If you're short of cash, you may find yourself having to go out and look for an ATM to pay your restaurant check.

As a backup to credit or debit cards, it's best to also take some traveler's checks and a little cash. US dollars are still the most easily exchangeable foreign currency in Mexico. In tourist areas you can even pay for some things in US dollars, though the exchange rate used will probably not be in your favor.

Euros, British pounds and Canadian dollars, in cash or as traveler's checks, are now accepted by most banks and some *casas de cambio* (exchange houses), but procedures for these currencies may be a little more time-consuming, and acceptance is less certain if you're away from main cities and tourist centers. Traveler's checks should be a major brand such as American Express or Visa. American Express traveler's checks are recognized everywhere.

For tips on keeping your money safe, see p950.

ATMs

ATMs (*caja permanente* or *cajero automático* in Spanish) are very common in Mexico, and are the easiest source of cash. You can use major credit cards and some bank cards, such as those on the Cirrus and Plus systems, to withdraw pesos from ATMs. The exchange rate that banks use for ATM withdrawals is normally more in your favor than the 'tourist rate' for currency exchange – though that advantage may be negated by extra handling fees, interest charges and other methods that banks have of taking your money away from you.

Banks & Casas de Cambio

You can exchange money and traveler's checks in banks or at *casas de cambio*. Banks go through a more time-consuming procedure than *casas de cambio,* and usually have shorter exchange hours (typically 9am to 5pm Monday to Friday and 9am to 1pm Saturday, or shorter hours in some smaller, sleepier towns). *Casas de cambio* can be found easily in just about every large or medium-size town and in many smaller ones. These places are quick and often open evenings or weekends, but some don't accept traveler's checks, whereas banks usually do.

Exchange rates vary a little from one bank or *cambio* to another. There is often a better rate for *efectivo* (cash) than for *documento* (traveler's checks).

If you have trouble finding a place to change money, particularly on a weekend, you can always try a hotel, though the exchange rate won't be the best.

International Transfers

Should you need money wired to you in Mexico, an easy and quick method is the 'Dinero en Minutos' (Money in Minutes) service of **Western Union** (☎ 800-325-6000 in the USA; www.westernunion.com). It's offered by thousands of bank branches and other businesses around Mexico, identified by black-and-yellow signs bearing the words 'Western Union Dinero en Minutos.' Your sender pays the money online or at a Western Union branch, along with a fee, and gives the details on who is to receive it and where. When you pick it up, take along photo identification. Sending US$500 online from California to Mexico, for example, costs US$25. Western Union has offices worldwide.

US post offices (☎ 888-368-4669; www.usps.com) offer reasonably cheap money transfers to branches of Bancomer bank in Mexico.

Taxes

Mexico's *impuesto de valor agregado* (IVA, value-added tax) is levied at 15%. By law the tax must be included in virtually any price quoted to you and should not be added afterward. Signs in shops and notices on restaurant menus often state '*IVA incluido.*' Occasionally they state instead that IVA must be added to the quoted prices.

Impuesto sobre hospedaje (ISH, lodging tax) is levied on the price of hotel rooms. Each Mexican state sets its own rate, but in most it's 2%. See p942 for further information on taxes on hotel rooms.

Tipping & Bargaining

In general, workers in small, cheap restaurants don't expect much in the way of tips, while those in expensive resorts expect you to be lavish in your largesse. Workers in the tourism and hospitality industries often depend on tips to supplement miserable basic wages. In resorts frequented by foreigners (such as Acapulco, Puerto Vallarta and Cancún) tipping is up to US levels of 15%; elsewhere 10% is usually plenty. If you stay a few days in one place, you should leave up to 10% of your room costs for the people who have kept your room clean (assuming they have). A porter in a mid-range hotel will be happy with US$1 a bag. Taxi drivers don't generally expect tips unless they provide some special service. Gas station attendants and car park attendants don't expect tips but appreciate them if offered (US$0.25 to US$0.50).

Room rates are pretty firm, though if you are going to stay a few nights you can attempt to bargain some prices down, especially in cheaper places and in the off-season. In markets bargaining is the rule, and you may pay much more than the going rate if you accept the first price quoted. You can also often bargain with drivers of unmetered taxis.

POST

An airmail letter or postcard weighing up to 20g costs US$0.80 to the US or Canada, US$1 to Europe or South America, and US$1.10 to the rest of the world. Items weighing between 20g and 50g cost US$1.30, US$1.50 and US$1.80 respectively. *Certificado* (registered) service costs an extra US$1.50. Mark airmail items 'Vía Aérea.' Delivery times (outbound and inbound) are elastic. An airmail letter from Mexico to the USA or Canada (or vice-versa) should take somewhere between four and 14 days to arrive. Mail to or from Europe may take between one and two weeks, for Australasia two to three weeks.

Post offices *(oficinas de correos)* are typically open from 8am or 9am to between 4pm and 6pm Monday to Friday, and 9am to 1pm Saturday. You can receive letters and packages care of a post office if they're addressed to the post office's *lista de correos* (mail list), as follows:

Jane SMITH (last name in capitals)
Lista de Correos
Correo Central
Acapulco
Guerrero 00000 (post code)
MEXICO

When the letter reaches the post office, the name of the addressee is placed on an alphabetical list that is updated daily and often pinned up on the wall. To claim your mail, present your passport or other identification. There's no charge, but many post offices only hold *lista* mail for 10 days before returning it to the sender. If you think you're going to pick mail up more than 10 days after it has arrived, have it sent to the following:

Jane SMITH
Poste Restante
Correo Central
Acapulco
Guerrero 00000 (post code)
MEXICO

Poste restante may hold mail for up to a month, but no list of what has been received is posted.

If you're sending a package internationally from Mexico, be prepared to open it for customs inspection at the post office; it's better to take packing materials with you, or not seal it until you get there. For assured and speedy delivery, you can use one of the more expensive international courier services, such as **UPS** (☎ 800-902-92-00; www.ups.com), **Federal Express** (☎ 800-900-11-00; www.fedex.com) or Mexico's **Estafeta** (☎ 800-903-35-00; www.estafeta.com). Packages up to 500g cost around US$25 to the US or Canada, or US$35 to Europe.

SHOPPING

Mexico's most exciting buys are the wonderful and amazingly varied regional handicrafts made predominantly by indigenous people. You can buy these *artesanías* in the villages where they are produced, or in stores and markets in urban centers. *Artesanías* stores in cities will give you a good overview of what's available and a basis for price comparisons. Places such as Mexico City, Guadalajara, Monterrey, San Miguel de Allende, Puerto Vallarta and Oaxaca have stores selling quality handicrafts from all over Mexico. A few cities have special markets devoted to crafts, but ordinary daily or weekly markets always sell crafts (everyday objects such as pots and baskets as well as more artistic regional specialities) too. The quality of market goods may not be as high as in stores, but you'll usually pay less; bargaining is expected in markets, whereas stores generally have fixed prices. Traveling out to craft-making villages gives you a chance to see artisans at work, and if you buy there you'll know that more of your money is likely to go to the artisans themselves and less to entrepreneurs.

For everyday purchases and consumer goods, middle-class Mexicans like to shop in glitzy modern malls, big supermarkets or hypermarkets and department stores. These are often in residential districts where travelers don't often go. In city centers you're more likely to find smaller, older shops and markets with a lot more character!

See p72 for an introduction to the many Mexican handicrafts: ceramics, masks, woodwork, jewelry, metalwork, lacquerware, indigenous textiles, bark paintings and *retablos* (also called *exvoto*). Below are many further fine products and good buys.

Bags

Bags come in all shapes and sizes, many incorporating indigenous designs; those made by the Huichol people are among the most authentic and original.

Baskets

Handmade baskets of multifarious shapes, sizes and patterns, made of materials from cane and bamboo to rush or palm-leaf strips, are common in Mexican markets. They can be useful for carrying other purchases home!

Clothes

Commercially produced clothing, whether based on traditional designs or with a Mexican take on international fashion trends, can be attractive and good value.

Hammocks

Usually made of cotton or nylon, hammocks come in a variety of widths and an infinite number of color patterns – easy to buy in Mérida, Palenque, Zipolite, Mitla and Juchitán.

Leather Goods

León is Mexico's shoe capital, and has dozens of stores; every other sizable city has plenty of good ones, too. Check quality and fit carefully before you buy. Mexicans use metric footwear sizes. Especially well-crafted belts, bags, *huaraches* (sandals), boots, clothes and saddles are available in northern and central ranching towns such as Zacatecas, Jerez, Hermosillo, Monterrey, Saltillo and Guadalajara.

Musical Instruments

Paracho, Michoacán, is the guitar capital of Mexico and also produces violins, cellos and other instruments. Elsewhere you'll come across maracas, tambourines, whistles, scrape boards and a variety of drums. Also keep an eye open for tongue drums – hollowed-out pieces of wood which are often cylindrical in shape and attractively carved or decorated, with two central tongues of wood, each giving a different note when struck.

Tablecloths

Particularly lovely tablecloths are made in Oaxaca and Michoacán states.

SOLO TRAVELERS

A single room normally costs well over half the price of a double room, but budget travelers can cut accommodation costs by staying in Mexico's increasing number of hostels, if they don't mind sharing a dorm. Hostels have the additional advantage of providing ready-made company, and often a lot of fun and helpful travel tips. Lone travelers need only remain on their own if they wish to when traveling in Mexico. It's very easy to pair up with others as there's a steady stream of people doing much the same sights around the country. In well-touristed places, notice boards advertise for traveling companions, flatmates, volunteer workers and so on. Half-day and full day tours are a good way to meet people and get more out of a place.

Solo travelers need to be especially watchful of their luggage when on the road and should stay in places with good security for their valuables so that they don't have to be burdened with them when out and about. One big drag of traveling alone is taking a quick dip in the ocean – you're stuck with your valuables and there's no one to watch out for them.

Traveling alone can be a very good way of getting into the local culture and it definitely improves your Spanish skills because it means that communication with Mexicans is essential. You can also get a kick out of doing what you want when you want. Eating by yourself night after night can get a bit tiresome, but you'll only be left alone if you want it that way, as Mexicans are very sociable.

TELEPHONE & FAX

Local calls are cheap. International calls can be expensive, but needn't be if you call from the right place at the right time.

Internet telephony (calls carried through an Internet server line instead of a phone line) has made an appearance at some Internet cafés in Mexico, and can be a lot cheaper than regular phone calls – at around US$0.20 per minute to the USA or US$0.30 a minute to Canada or Europe – though line quality can be very patchy. Internet telephony aside, there are two main types of public telephone service, with broadly similar costs: public card phones and call offices (*casetas de teléfono* or *casetas telefónicas*) where an on-the-spot operator connects the call for you. A third option is to call from your hotel, but hotels charge what they like for this service. It's nearly always cheaper to go elsewhere.

Calling Cards

Some calling cards from other countries can be used for calls from Mexico by dialing special access numbers:

AT&T (☎ 01-800-462-4240, 01-800-288-2872)
Bell Canada (☎ 01-800-123-0200, 01-800-021-1994)
BT Charge Card UK (☎ 01-800-123-02-44, 01-800-021-6644)
MCI (☎ 01-800-674-7000, 01-800-021-1000)
Sprint (☎ 01-800-877-8000)

Warning: if you get an operator who asks for your credit card instead of your calling card number, or says the service is unavailable, hang up. There have been scams in which calls are rerouted to super expensive credit card phone services.

Casetas de Teléfono

Costs in *casetas* are broadly similar to those in Telmex card phones (see p961), and their advantages are that they eliminate street noise and you don't need a phone card to use them. *Casetas* usually have a telephone symbol outside, or signs saying '*teléfono,*' 'Lada' or 'Larga Distancia.' In Baja California they are known as *cabinas*.

Collect Calls

A *llamada por cobrar* (collect call) can cost the receiving party much more than if they call you, so you may prefer to pay for a quick call to the other party to ask them to call you back. If you do need to make a collect call, you can do so from card phones without a card. Call an operator on ☎ 020 for domestic calls, or ☎ 090 for international calls, or use a 'home country direct' service through which you make an international collect call via an operator in the country you're calling. The Mexican term for 'home country direct' is *país directo*: Mexican international operators may know the access numbers for some countries, but it's best to get this information from your home country before you leave for Mexico.

Some telephone *casetas* and hotels will make collect calls for you, but they usually charge for the service.

Fax

Public fax service is offered in many Mexican towns by the public *telégrafos* (telegraph) office or the companies Telecomm and Computel. Also look for 'Fax' or 'Fax Público' signs on shops, businesses and telephone *casetas*, and in bus stations and airports. Typically you will pay around US$1 to US$2 a page to the US or Canada.

Mobile Phones

The most widespread mobile (cellular) phone system in Mexico is **Telcel** (www.telcel.com), with coverage virtually everywhere that has a significant population. Telcel has roaming partnerships with systems from many other countries, though using a phone from another country in Mexico can be expensive. For information, contact your service provider or visit www.gsmcoverage.co.uk, which has coverage maps, lists of roaming partners and links to phone companies' websites. Many top-end hotels have mobile phone rental booths in their lobbies. Telcel has a mobile phone rental and sales office at Mexico City airport. A typical new phone with some air time costs around US$200 to US$250 here. Telcel cards for additional air time are fairly widely available from newsstands and minimarts.

Prefixes & Codes

If you're calling a number in the town or city you're in, simply dial the local number (eight digits in Mexico City, Guadalajara and Monterrey; seven digits everywhere else).

To call another town or city in Mexico, you need to dial the long-distance prefix ☎ 01, followed by the area code (two digits for Mexico City, Guadalajara and Monterrey; three digits for everywhere else) and then the local number. For example, to call from Mexico City to Oaxaca, dial ☎ 01, then the Oaxaca area code ☎ 951, then the seven-digit local number. You'll find area codes listed under city and town headings through this book.

To make international calls, you need to dial the international prefix ☎ 00, followed by the country code, area code and local number. For example, to call New York City from Mexico, dial ☎ 00, then the US country code ☎ 1, then the New York City area code ☎ 212, then the local number.

To call a number in Mexico from another country, dial your international access code, then the Mexico country code ☎ 52, then the area code and number.

Public Card Phones

These are common in towns and cities: you'll usually find some at airports, bus stations and around the main plaza. Easily the most common, and most reliable on costs, are those marked with the name of the country's biggest phone company, Telmex. To use a Telmex card phone you need a phone card known as a *tarjeta Ladatel*. These are sold at kiosks and shops everywhere – look for the blue-and-yellow signs that read '*De venta aquí Ladatel*.' The cards come in denominations ranging from 10 pesos (about US$0.90) to 500 pesos (US$46).

Calls from Telmex card phones cost US$0.10 per minute for local calls; US$0.40 per minute long-distance within Mexico; US$0.50 per minute to the USA or Canada; US$1 per minute to Central America; US$2 per minute to Europe, Alaska or South America; and US$2.50 per minute to Hawaii, Australia, New Zealand or Asia.

In some parts of Mexico frequented by foreign tourists, you may notice a variety of phones that advertise that they accept credit cards or that you can make easy collect calls to the USA on them. While some of these phones may be a fair value, there are others on which very high rates are charged. Be very sure about what you'll pay before making a call on a non-Telmex phone.

Toll-Free & Operator Numbers

Mexican toll-free numbers (all ☎ 800 followed by seven digits) always require the ☎ 01 prefix. You can call these and the ☎ 060 emergency number from Telmex pay phones without inserting a telephone card.

Most US and Canadian toll-free numbers are ☎ 800 or ☎ 888 followed by seven digits. Some of these can be reached from Mexico (dial ☎ 00-1 before the 800), but you may have to pay a charge for the call.

For a Mexican domestic operator, dial ☎ 020; for an international operator, dial ☎ 090. For Mexican directory information, dial ☎ 040.

TIME

Most of Mexico is on Hora del Centro, the same as US Central Time (that's GMT minus six hours in winter, and GMT minus five hours during daylight saving). Five northern and western states, Chihuahua, Nayarit, Sinaloa, Sonora and Baja California Sur, are on Hora de las Montañas, the same as US Mountain Time (GMT minus seven hours in winter, GMT minus six hours during daylight saving). Baja California (Norte) observes Hora del Pacífico, the same as US Pacific Time (GMT minus eight hours in winter, GMT minus seven hours during daylight saving).

Daylight saving time (*horario de verano*, summer time) runs from the first Sunday in April to the last Sunday in October. Clocks go forward one hour in April and back one hour in October. The northwestern state of Sonora ignores daylight saving (like its US neighbor Arizona), so remains on GMT minus seven hours all year. Daylight saving is also ignored by a few remote rural zones such as the Sierra Norte of Oaxaca and the Marqués de Comillas area of eastern Chiapas (to the perdition of bus schedules from nearby towns such as Oaxaca and Palenque).

See the World Map at the back of this book if you need international time zone information.

TOILETS

Public toilets are rare, so take advantage of facilities in places such as hotels, restaurants, bus stations and museums. When out and about, carry some toilet paper with you if you think you're going to need it because it often won't be provided. If there's a bin beside the toilet, put paper in it because the drains can't cope otherwise.

TOURIST INFORMATION

Just about every town of touristic interest in Mexico has a state or municipal tourist office. They are generally helpful with maps, brochures and questions, and often some staff members speak English.

You can call the Mexico City office of the national tourism ministry **Sectur** (☎ 55-5250-0123, 800-903-92-00, 800-446-3942 in the USA & Canada; www.visitmexico.com) at any time – 24 hours a day, seven days a week – for information or help in English or Spanish.

Here are the contact details for the head tourism offices of each Mexican state:

Aguascalientes (☎ 449-915-95-04, 800-949-49-49; www.aguascalientes.gob.mx)

Baja California (☎ 078, 664-634-63-30; www.descubrebajacalifornia.com in Spanish)

Baja California Sur (☎ 612-124-01-00; www.gbcs.gob.mx in Spanish)

Campeche (☎ 981-816-67-67; www.campeche.gob.mx in Spanish)

Chiapas (☎ 961-612-55-11, 800-280-35-00; www.turismochiapas.gob.mx)

Chihuahua (☎ 614-410-10-77, 800-849-52-00; www.chihuahua.gob.mx/turismoweb in Spanish)

Coahuila (☎ 844-412-51-22, 800-718-42-20)

Colima (☎ 312-312-43-60; www.visitacolima.com.mx)

Durango (☎ 618-811-11-07; www.turismodurango.gob.mx)

Guanajuato (☎ 473-732-19-82, 800-714-10-86; www.guanajuato-travel.com)

Guerrero (☎ 747-472-95-66, 744-484-79-16; www.sectur.guerrero.gob.mx/spanish/homepage.html in Spanish)

Hidalgo (☎ 771-718-44-54, 800-718-26-00; www.hidalgo.gob.mx/turismo in Spanish)

Jalisco (☎ 33-3668-1600; 800-363-22-00; www.jalisco.gob.mx/srias/setur/espanol/inicio.html in Spanish)

Mexico City (☎ 55-5533-4700; www.mexicocity.gob.mx)

México (☎ 722-212-59-98, 800-849-13-33; www.edomexico.gob.mx/sedeco/turismo/home.html in Spanish)

Michoacán (☎ 443-312-80-81, 800-450-23-00; www.turismomichoacan.gob.mx in Spanish)

Morelos (☎ 777-314-38-72; www.morelostravel.com)

Nayarit (☎ 311-216-56-61, 311-212-08-36; www.turismonayarit.gob.mx in Spanish)

Nuevo León (☎ 81-8345-0870, 800-832-22-00, 800-235-24-38 in the US; www.nl.gob.mx in Spanish)

Oaxaca (☎ 951-576-48-28; www.oaxaca.gob.mx/sedetur in Spanish)

Puebla (☎ 222-246-20-44; www.turismopuebla.com.mx in Spanish)

Querétaro (☎ 442-238-50-00, 800-715-17-42; www.queretaro.gob.mx/turismo)

Quintana Roo (☎ 983-835-08-60; http://sedetur.qroo.gob.mx)

San Luis Potosí (☎ 444-812-99-39; www.descubresanluispotosi.com in Spanish)

Sinaloa (☎ 669-916-51-60; www.sinaloa-travel.com in Spanish)

Sonora (☎ 662-217-00-76, 800-716-25-55, 800-476-66-72 in the US; www.sonoraturismo.gob.mx)

Tabasco (☎ 993-316-36-33; www.visitetabasco.com)

Tamaulipas (☎ 834-315-61-36, 800-710-65-32, 888-580-59-68 in the US; http://turismo.tamaulipas.gob.mx in Spanish)

Tlaxcala (☎ 246-465-09-00/68, 800-509-65-57; www.tlaxcala.gob.mx/turismo)

Veracruz (☎ 228-812-73-45, 800-712-66-66; www.sedecover.gob.mx in Spanish)

Yucatán (☎ 999-924-92-90; www.mayayucatan.com)

Zacatecas (☎ 492-924-40-47, 800-712-40-78; www.turismozacatecas.gob.mx in Spanish)

TOURS

Taking an organized tour takes the strain out of travel planning and is especially worth considering if you have limited time. A knowledgeable and enthusiastic guide can add much to your understanding and enjoyment of a place, and group trips can also be a practical way of getting to remote attractions where public transportation isn't the greatest. Many companies both within Mexico and in other countries offer good activity-based or general tours.

Adventure Center USA (☎ 800-228-8747; www.adventurecenter.com; 1311 63rd St, Suite 200, Emeryville, CA 94608) Ecologically minded, community-focused, small-group camping and hotel trips in Mexico and Central and South America.

Adventures Selvazul Puebla (☎ 222-237-48-87; www.selvazul.com) Adventure eco-trips in Puebla, Veracruz and Chiapas include rafting, trekking, biking, rock climbing, mountaineering and sea kayaking. Team-building courses, too; one trip goes to the Lacandón jungle.

Adventure Specialists USA (☎ 719-630-7687 in winter, 719-783-2076 in the US; www.adventurespecialists.org; Bear Basin Ranch, Westcliffe, CO 81252) Barranca del Cobre (Copper Canyon) expeditions on foot, horseback or donkey.

Columbus Travel USA (☎ 800-843-1060; www.canyontravel.com; 900 Ridge Creek, Bulverde, TX 78163-2872) Barranca del Cobre explorations for individuals and small groups using local naturalist guides and private eco-lodges.

Ecocolors Cancún (☎ 998-884-36-67; www.ecotravelmexico.com) Small-group ecotours through the Mayan world; kayak, snorkel, dive, bird-watch or research the jaguar in the Sian Ka'an Biosphere Reserve.

Ecoturismo Yucatán Mérida (☎ 999-925-21-87; www.ecoyuc.com) Ecotours in the Maya world including biking, caving, kayaking, bird-watching and trekking, concentrating on culture and archaeology.

¡El Tour San Cristóbal de Las Casas (☎ 967-678-02-02; www.bikemexico.com) Bring-your-own bike tours of the Pacific coast, Yucatán Peninsula and Chiapas from one to 3½ weeks, with highly experienced English-speaking guides.

Explore Worldwide UK (☎ 01252-760000; www.explore.co.uk) Small-group land trips with interesting itineraries.

Field Guides USA (☎ 800-728-4953; www.fieldguides .com; 9433 Bee Cave Rd, Bldg 1, Ste 150, Austin, TX 78733) Bird-watching trips to southern Mexico.
GAP Adventures Canada (☎ 800-465-5600, www.gap .ca; 19 Duncan St, Ste 401, Toronto, Ontario M5H 3H1); USA (☎ 805-985-0922; 56/ W Channel Islands, Blvd 346, Port Hueneme, CA) Small-group tours in southern Mexico and neighboring Maya lands, mainly using local transportation and simple accommodations.
Global Exchange USA (☎ 415-255-7296, 800-497-1994; www.globalexchange.org; 2017 Mission St No 303, San Francisco, CA 94110) 'Reality tours' to Chiapas in which you get an in-depth look at the problems and conditions of people in particular regions; a one-week trip typically costs around US$750 plus airfares.
Journey Latin America UK (☎ 020-8747-3108; www.journeylatinamerica.co.uk; 12 & 13 Heathfield Tce, Chiswick, London W4 4JE) Organized outfit offering two- or three-week tours on a budget or more comfy basis. Also Baja sea-kayaking trips (combined with biking and bodyboarding if desired) and more up-market self-drive or escorted tours of Yucatán haciendas; three-week tours take in Guatemala and Belize as well as Mexico.
Marlene Ehrenberg Mexico City (☎ 55-5550-9080; www.marlene-ehrenberg.com.mx) Mexican-run ecological and cultural trips: stargaze in the desert, investigate the intriguing Huichol area near the abandoned mining village of Real de Catorce, or choose other beguiling options.
Mayatours USA (☎ 800-392-6292; www.mayatour .com) Tours and travel services to Mexico and Central America with emphasis on Mayan archaeology, ecology and diving; accommodations in four-star hotels or jungle lodges on request.
Tierraventura Oaxaca (☎ 951-501-13-63; www.tierra ventura.com) Small-group trips with multilingual guides to remote destinations in Oaxaca state, focusing on hiking, nature, crafts, traditional medicine, community tourism projects and meeting locals.
Tierra Dentro Oaxaca (☎ 951-514-92-84; welcome .to/tierradentro) Treks and ascents on Mexico's highest mountain, Pico de Orizaba.

You'll find information on tour companies of more local range throughout this book's regional chapters.

Websites with further information on tours in Mexico include the following:
AMTAVE (☎ 55-5375-7887; www.amtave.org; Felix Cuevas 224B, Colonia Del Valle) A group of over 80 'alternative tourism' operators around Mexico; its office is in Mexico City.
Earthfoot (www.earthfoot.org) Links to small-scale, low-impact, local ecotourism providers.
GORP (Great Outdoor Recreation Pages; www.gorp.com) Activity tours covering the whole gamut from butterflies to turtles to honeymoons to surfing.

Mexico Online (www.mexonline.com)
Planeta.com (www.planeta.com) Excellent site with many interesting contacts.

VISAS & DOCUMENTS
Every tourist must have an easily obtainable Mexican government tourist card. Some nationalities also need to obtain visas. Because the regulations sometimes change, it's wise to confirm them with a Mexican embassy or consulate before you go (see p951). The **Lonely Planet website** (www.lonelyplanet.com) has links to updated visa information.

Though it's not recommended, US and Canadian tourists can enter Mexico without a passport if they have official photo identification, such as a driver's license, plus some proof of their citizenship, such as an original birth certificate or voter's card (not a copy). Citizens of other countries who are permanent residents in the USA have to take their passports and permanent resident alien cards. Naturalized Canadian citizens require a valid passport.

In general it's much better to have a passport because officials of all countries are used to passports and may delay people who have other documents. In Mexico you will often need your passport when you change money.

All citizens of countries other than the US and Canada should have a passport that's valid for at least six months after they arrive in Mexico.

Travelers under 18 who are not accompanied by both their parents may need special documentation (see p947).

Mexicans with dual nationality must carry proof of both their citizenships and must identify themselves as Mexican when entering or leaving Mexico. They are considered Mexican by the Mexican authorities but are not subject to compulsory military service.

Citizens of the USA, Canada, the 15 EU countries (pre-EU expansion in 2004), Australia, New Zealand, the Czech Republic, Hungary, Iceland, Israel, Japan, Norway, Poland, South Africa and Switzerland are among those who do not require visas to enter Mexico as tourists. The list changes from time to time; check well ahead of travel with your local Mexican embassy or consulate. Visa procedures, for those who need them, can take several weeks.

Non-US citizens passing (even in transit) through the USA on the way to or from Mexico, or visiting Mexico from the USA, should check the passport and visa requirements for the USA.

Tourist Card & Tourist Fee

The Mexican tourist card – officially the *forma migratoria para turista* (FMT) – is a brief card document that you must fill out and get stamped by Mexican immigration when you enter Mexico and keep till you leave. It's available at official border crossings, international airports and ports, and often from airlines, travel agencies and Mexican consulates. At the US-Mexico border you won't usually be given one automatically – you have to ask for it.

At many US-Mexico border crossings you don't have to get the card stamped at the border itself, as the Instituto Nacional de Migración (INM, National Immigration Institute) has control points on the highways into the interior where it's also possible to do it. But it's preferable to get it done at the border itself, in case there are complications elsewhere.

One section of the card deals with the length of your stay in Mexico, and this section is filled out by the immigration officer. The maximum is 180 days but immigration officers will often put a much lower number (as little as 15 or 30 days in some cases) unless you tell them specifically that you need, say, 90 or 180 days. It's advisable to ask for more days than you think you'll need, in case you are delayed or change your plans.

Though the tourist card itself is free of charge, it brings with it the obligation to pay the tourist fee of about US$20, called the *derecho para no inmigrante* (DNI, non-immigrant fee). The exact amount of the fee may change from year to year. If you enter Mexico by air, the fee is included in your airfare. If you enter by land, you must pay the fee at a bank in Mexico at any time before you reenter the frontier zone on your way out of Mexico (or before you check in at an airport to fly out of Mexico). The frontier zone is the territory between the border itself and the INM's control points on the highways leading into the Mexican interior (usually 20km to 30km from the border). Most Mexican border posts have on-the-spot bank offices where you can pay the DNI fee immediately. When you pay at a bank, your tourist card will be stamped to prove that you have paid.

Look after your tourist card because it may be checked when you leave the country.

Tourist cards (and fees) are not necessary for visits shorter than 72 hours within the frontier zones along Mexico's northern and southern borders. A few extra zones are also exempt from the tourist card requirement for visits of less than 72 hours, including the Tijuana–Ensenada and Mexicali–San Felipe corridors in Baja California; and in Sonora, the Sonoita–Puerto Peñasco corridor.

A tourist card only permits you to engage in what are considered to be tourist activities (including sports, health, artistic and cultural activities). If the purpose of your visit is to work (even voluntarily), to report or to study, or to participate in humanitarian aid or human-rights observation, you may well need a visa. Check with a Mexican embassy or consulate (p951).

EXTENSIONS & LOST CARDS

If the number of days given on your tourist card is less than the 180-day maximum, its validity may be extended one or more times, at no cost, up to the maximum. To get a card extended you have to apply to the INM, which has offices in many towns and cities (you'll find its head office in each state listed on the INM website, www .inami.gob.mx, under 'Directorio'). The procedure costs around US$20 and should take between half an hour and three hours, depending on the cooperation of each particular immigration office. You'll need your passport, tourist card, photocopies of the important pages of these documents, and, at some offices, evidence of 'sufficient funds.' A major credit card is usually OK for the latter, or an amount in traveler's checks anywhere from US$100 to US$1000 depending on the office.

Most INM offices will not extend a card until a few days before it is due to expire; don't bother trying earlier.

If you lose your card or need further information, contact your nearest tourist office, or the **Sectur tourist office** (☎ 55-5250-0123, 800-903-92-00) in Mexico City, your embassy or consulate. Any of these should be able to give you an official note to take to your local INM office, which will issue a duplicate.

WOMEN

In this land that invented machismo, women have to make some concessions to local custom – but don't let that put you off. In general, Mexicans are great believers in the difference (rather than the equality) between the sexes.

Lone women must expect some catcalls and attempts to chat them up. Often these men only want to talk to you, but it can get tedious. You can discourage unwanted attention by avoiding eye contact (wear sunglasses), dressing modestly, moving confidently and speaking coolly but politely if you are addressed and feel that you must respond. Uninvited attention could result in a positive conversation if you make it clear that you are prepared to talk, but no more than that.

Don't put yourself in peril by doing things that Mexican women would not do, such as challenging a man's masculinity, drinking alone in a cantina, hitchhiking or going alone to isolated places. Unless you're flat-chested, wearing a bra will spare you a lot of comment and grief. A wedding ring might prove helpful too.

In beach resorts Mexican women dress in shorts, skimpy tops and dresses, and swimsuits of all sizes, though many do bow to modesty and swim in shorts and a T-shirt. On the streets of cities and towns you'll notice that women cover up and don't display too much leg or even their shoulders. The bare, pierced-belly look so popular in the West is not common.

When using local transportation it's best to don long or mid-calf-length trousers and a top that meets the top of your trousers, with sleeves of some sort. That way you'll feel most comfortable, and you can also stash your valuables out of sight with ease. Most of all, appear self-assured.

WORK

Mexicans themselves need jobs, and people who enter Mexico as tourists are not legally allowed to take employment. The many expats working in Mexico have usually been posted there by their companies or organizations with all the necessary papers.

English-speakers (and a few German or French speakers) may find teaching jobs in language schools, *preparatorias* (high schools) or universities, or can offer per-sonal tutoring. Mexico City is the best place to get English-teaching work; Guadalajara is also good. It's possible in other major cities. The pay is low, but you can live on it.

Press ads (especially in the various local English-language papers and magazines) and telephone yellow pages are sources of job opportunities. Pay rates for personal tutoring are rarely more than US$12 an hour. Positions in high schools or universities are more likely to become available at the beginning of each new term; contact institutions that offer bilingual programs or classes in English; for universities, ask for an appointment with the director of the language department. Language schools tend to offer short courses, so teaching opportunities with them come up more often and your commitment is for a shorter time, but they may pay less than high schools and universities.

A foreigner working in Mexico normally needs a permit or government license, but a school will often pay a foreign teacher in the form of a *beca* (scholarship), and thus circumvent the law, or the school's administration will procure the appropriate papers.

It's helpful to know at least a little Spanish, even though some institutes insist that only English be spoken in class.

Apart from teaching, you might find a little bar or restaurant work in tourist areas. It's likely to be part-time and short-term.

The **Learning Abroad Center** (www.istc.umn.edu) at the University of Minnesota is a good source of information on work, internships and volunteer opportunities internationally, with links to many other websites providing similar information.

Volunteer Work

Many opportunities exist for short- or longer-term unpaid work (or work that you pay to do) in Mexico. Projects range from sea turtle conservation to human-rights observation to work with abused children.

AmeriSpan (www.amerispan.com) Offers a range of volunteer opportunities in Mexico.

Amigos de las Américas (www.amigoslink.org) Sends paying volunteers from the US to work on summer health, community and youth projects in Latin America; volunteers receive prior training.

Casa de los Amigos (www.casadelosamigos.org in Spanish) This Quaker center in Mexico City places volunteers in some social and environmental projects in the city and also accepts volunteers to help run the Casa itself (see p145).

Ceduam (www.prodigyweb.net.mx/ceduamcal) Works on nutrition, gender issues, conservation and sustainable development; needs volunteers for various roles including work on its organic farm at Tlaxco, near Tlaxcala.

Earthwatch (www.earthwatch.org) With offices in the USA, Britain, Australia and Japan, Earthwatch runs environmental projects in Mexico (volunteers usually pay around US$1000 per week).

Global Exchange (www.globalexchange.org) Needs Spanish-speaking volunteer human-rights observers to live for six to eight weeks in peace camps in Chiapas villages threatened by violence. This program is run in collaboration with the Centro de Derechos Humanos Fray Bartolomé de Las Casas, a human-rights center in San Cristóbal de las Casas.

Sedepac (www.sedepac.org.mx) Mexico NGO that runs summer volunteer work camps in rural indigenous or peasant communities.

Sipaz (www.sipaz.org) An international peace group, Sipaz needs Spanish-speaking volunteers to work for a year or more in Chiapas.

Vive Mexico (www.vivemexico.org) Mexico-based NGO that coordinates international social, ecological and cultural work camps in Mexico.

The **Council on International Educational Exchange** (www.ciee.org), the **Alliance of European Voluntary Service Organisations** (www.alliance-network .org) and Unesco's **Coordinating Committee for International Voluntary Service** (www.unesco.org /ccivs) all have further information on volunteer programs in Mexico.

Transportation

CONTENTS

GETTING THERE & AWAY

ENTERING THE COUNTRY

Immigration officers won't usually keep you waiting any longer than it takes to flick through your passport and enter the length of your stay on your tourist card. Always remain patient and polite, even if procedures are slower than you would like. See p963 for further information on documents. Anyone traveling to Mexico via the USA should be sure to check US visa requirements.

AIR

Airports & Airlines

The following Mexican airports receive direct flights from the USA (some from several US cities, some from only one or two) and in some cases Canada. Only Mexico City and Cancún have flights from Europe or Latin America:

Acapulco (☎ 744-466-94-34)
Aguascalientes (☎ 449-915-81-32)
Bajío (León) (☎ 477-713-64-06)
Cancún (☎ 998-886-03-40)
Chihuahua (☎ 614-420-09-16)
Cozumel (☎ 987-872-49-16)
Durango (☎ 618-817-88-98)
Guadalajara (☎ 33-3688-5504)
Guaymas (☎ 622-221-05-11)

Hermosillo (☎ 662-261-01-42)
Ixtapa/Zihuatanejo (☎ 755-554-20-70)
La Paz (☎ 614-124-63-07)
Loreto (☎ 613-135-04-54)
Los Cabos (☎ 624-146 52 14)
Manzanillo (Playa de Oro; ☎ 314-333-25-25)
Mazatlán (☎ 669-928-04-38)
Mérida (☎ 999-946-25-00)
Mexico City (☎ 55-5571-3600; www.aicm.com.mx)
Monterrey (☎ 81-8369-0752)
Morelia (☎ 443-317-14-11)
Puerto Vallarta (☎ 322-221-28-48)
San Luis Potosí (☎ 444-822-23-96)
Tampico (☎ 833-224-48-00)
Tijuana (☎ 664-683-24-18)
Veracruz (☎ 229-934-70-00)
Villahermosa (☎ 993-356-01-57)
Zacatecas (☎ 492-985-02-23)

Mexico's two flag airlines are Mexicana and Aeroméxico. Their recent safety records are similar to major US and European airlines: Mexicana has had only one fatal crash in about two million flights since 1970, while Aeroméxico has suffered only one fatal event since 1986.

AIRLINES FLYING TO & FROM MEXICO

Aero California (code JR; ☎ 55-5207-1392; hub Tijuana)
Aerocaribe (code QA; ☎ 800-502-20-00; www.aerocaribe .com; hub Cancún)
Aerolitoral (code 5D; ☎ 800-800-23-76; www.aerolitoral .com; hub Monterrey)
Aeromar (code VW; ☎ 800-237-66-27; www.aeromar .com.mx; hub Mexico City)
Aeroméxico (code AM; ☎ 800-021-40-00; www.aero mexico.com; hub Mexico City)

THINGS CHANGE...

The information in this chapter is particularly vulnerable to change. Check directly with the airline or a travel agent to make sure you understand how a fare (and ticket you may buy) works and be aware of the security requirements for international travel. Shop carefully. The details given in this chapter should be regarded as pointers and are not a substitute for your own careful, up-to-date research.

TRANSPORTATION

Air Canada (code AC; ☎ 800-719-28-27; www.air canada.ca; hub Toronto)

Air Europa (code UX; www.aireuropa.com; hub Madrid)

Air France (code AF; ☎ 800-006-77-00; www.airfrance .com; hub Paris)

Alaska Airlines (code AS; ☎ 800-252-75-22; www.alaska-air.com; hub Seattle)

America West (code HP; ☎ 800-235-92-92; www.americawest.com; hub Phoenix)

American Airlines (code AA; ☎ 800-904-60-00; www.aa.com; hub Dallas)

ATA Airlines (code TZ; ☎ 33-3615-5755; www.ata.com; hub Chicago)

Aviacsa (code 6A; ☎ 800-006-22-00; www.aviacsa .com.mx; hub Mexico City)

Avianca (code AV; ☎ 800-705-79-00; www.avianca .com; hub Bogotá)

British Airways (code BA ; ☎ 55-5387-0300; www.britishairways.com; hub Heathrow Airport, London)

Continental Airlines (code CO; ☎ 800-900-50-00; www.continental.com; hub Houston)

Copa Airlines (code CM; ☎ 800-265-26-72; www.copaair.com; hub Panama City)

Cubana (code CU; ☎ 55-5250-3465; www.cubana.cu; hub Havana)

Delta Air Lines (code DL; ☎ 800-902-21-00; www.delta.com; hub Atlanta)

Iberia (code IB; ☎ 55-5130-3030; www.iberia.com; hub Madrid)

Japan Airlines (code JL; ☎ 800-024-01-50; www.jal.co.jp; hub Tokyo)

KLM (code KL; ☎ 55-5279-5390; www.klm.com; hub Amsterdam)

Lacsa (code LR; ☎ 55-5211-6640; www.taca.com; hub San José)

Lan-Chile (code LA; ☎ 800-700-67-00; www.lanchile .com; hub Santiago)

Líneas Aéreas Azteca (code ZE; ☎ 800-229-83-22; www.aazteca.com.mx; hub Mexico City)

Lufthansa (code LH; ☎ 55-5230-0000; www.lufthansa .com; hub Frankfurt)

Mexicana (code MX; ☎ 800-502-20-00; www.mexicana.com; hub Mexico City)

Northwest Airlines (code NW; ☎ 55-5279-5390; www.nwa.com; hubs Detroit, Minneapolis/St Paul, Memphis)

Singapore Airlines (code SQ; ☎ 55-5525-8787; www.singaporeair.com; hub Singapore)

Spirit Airlines (code NK; www.spiritair.com; hub Fort Lauderdale)

TACA (code TA; ☎ 55-5211-6640; www.taca.com; hub San Salvador)

United Airlines (code UA; ☎ 800-003-0777; www.ual.com; hub Los Angeles)

DEPARTURE TAX

A departure tax equivalent to about US$25 is levied on international flights from Mexico. It's usually included in your ticket cost, but if it isn't, you must pay in cash during airport check-in. Ask your travel agent in advance.

US Airways (code US; www.usairways.com; hub Philadelphia)

Varig (code RG; ☎ 55-5286-9027; www.varig.com.br; hub Sao Paulo)

Tickets

The cost of flying to Mexico is usually higher around Christmas and New Year, and during July and August. Weekends can be more costly than weekdays. In addition to ticket agents and websites such as those recommended in the following sections, it's often worth checking airline websites for special deals.

If Mexico is part of a bigger trip encompassing other countries in Latin America or elsewhere, the best ticket for you may be an open jaw (where you fly into one place and out of another, covering the intervening distance by land), or a round-the-world ticket (these can cost as little as UK£900 or A$2100), or a Circle Pacific ticket which uses a combination of airlines to circle the Pacific. Most of the recommended agents in the following sections can provide these types of ticket.

Australia & New Zealand

The cheapest route from Australia is usually via Japan on Japan Airlines or via the USA (normally Los Angeles). Going via South America tends to be more expensive. Typical round-trip fares from Sydney or Melbourne to Mexico City are between A$2400 and A$2800; you may have to add A$300 to A$400 in the high seasons. From Auckland, some of the cheapest fares are via Tahiti and the USA. You're normally looking at NZ$2200 to NZ$2800 round-trip.

The following are well-known agents for cheap fares, with branches throughout both countries:

Flight Centre Australia (☎ 133 133; www.flightcentre .com.au) New Zealand (☎ 0800 243 544; www.flightcentre .co.nz)

TRANSPORTATION

STA Travel Australia (☎ 1300 733 035; www.statravel.com
.au) New Zealand (☎ 0508 782 872; www.statravel.co.nz)

Try www.travel.com.au and www.travel.co
.nz for online fares.

Canada
Montreal, Toronto and Vancouver all have
direct flights to several Mexican airports.
Typical discounted round-trip fares from
Toronto are around C$800 to Mexico City,
C$900 to Cancún and C$1000 to Acapulco.
Discount ticket agents in Canada are known
as consolidators. **Travel Cuts** (☎ 800-667-2887;
www.travelcuts.com) is Canada's national student travel agency. For online bookings try
www.expedia.ca and www.travelocity.ca.

Central & South America & the Caribbean
You can fly direct to Mexico City from
nine cities in South America, five in Central America, and from Havana (Cuba)
and Santo Domingo (Dominican Republic), and to Cancún from many of the same
places plus Flores (Guatemala). Round-trip
fares to Mexico City start at around US$400
from Guatemala City, US$500 to US$600
from Caracas, Santiago or Buenos Aires or
US$800 from São Paulo. Fares to Cancún
are usually a little lower.

Recommended ticket agencies include the
following:
ASATEJ (☎ 54-011-4114-7595; www.asatej.com)
In Argentina.
IVI Tours (☎ 0212-993-6082; www.ividiomas.com)
In Venezuela.
Student Travel Bureau (☎ 3038-1555; www.stb.com
.br) In Brazil.
Viajo.com (www.viajo.com) Online and telephone book-
ings from several countries.

Europe
There are flights to Mexico City and Cancún.
Airlines flying nonstop are Aeroméxico,
Air France, British Airways, Iberia, KLM,
Lufthansa and Air Europa. An alternative is
to fly with a US airline or alliance partner,
changing planes in the USA.

You can normally get a discounted or
advance-purchase round-trip fare from cities in western Europe to Mexico City for
between UK£350 and UK£600 (€500 to
€875). Cancún flights are generally a little
more expensive.

TICKET AGENTS IN THE UK
Discount air travel is big business in London. Advertisements for many of the travel
agencies appear in the travel pages of the
weekend broadsheet newspapers, in *Time
Out*, the *Evening Standard* and the free
magazine *TNT*.

An excellent place to start your inquiries
is **Journey Latin America** (☎ 020-8747-3108; www
.journeylatinamerica.co.uk). Other recommended
agencies include the following:
Bridge the World (☎ 0870-444-7474; www.b-t-w.co.uk)
Flight Centre (☎ 0870-890-8099; www.flightcentre
.co.uk)
Flightbookers (☎ 0870-010-7000; www.ebookers.com)
STA Travel (☎ 0870-160-0599; www.statravel.co.uk)
For travelers under the age of 26.
Trailfinders (www.trailfinders.co.uk)

TICKET AGENTS ELSEWHERE IN EUROPE
Recommended ticket agencies include the
following:
France Nouvelles Frontières (☎ 0825-000-747; www
.nouvelles-frontieres.fr); Voyageurs du Monde (☎ 01
40 15 11 15; www.vdm.com); OTU Voyages (www.otu.fr)
A student and youth travel specialist.
Germany Expedia (www.expedia.de); Just Travel (☎ 089-
747-3330; www.justtravel.de); STA Travel (☎ 01805-456-
422; www.statravel.de) For travelers aged under 26.
Italy CTS Viaggi (☎ 06-462-0431; www.cts.it) A specialist
in student and youth travel.
Netherlands Airfair (☎ 020-620-5121; www.airfair.nl)
Scandinavia Kilroy Travels (www.kilroytravels.com)
Spain Barcelo Viajes (☎ 902-116-226; www.barceloviajes
.com); Viajes Zeppelin (☎ 902-384-253, www.v-zeppelin.es)

The USA
You can fly to Mexico without changing
planes from at least 22 US cities. There are
one-stop connecting flights from many
others.

Discount travel agents in the USA are
known as consolidators (although you
won't see a sign on the door saying 'Con-
solidator'). San Francisco is the ticket con-
solidator capital of the USA, but good deals
can also be found in other big cities. **STA
Travel** (☎ 800-781-4040; www.sta.com), the largest
student travel operator in the USA, has offices in many major cities.

The following sites are recommended for
online bookings:
■ www.cheaptickets.com
■ www.expedia.com
■ www.itn.net

TRANSPORTATION

- www.lowestfare.com
- www.onetravel.com
- www.orbitz.com
- www.smarterliving.com
- www.travelocity.com

Here are some typical discounted low-season round-trip fares:

From	To Mexico City	To Cancún	To Acapulco
Chicago	US$350	US$430	US$520
Dallas/Fort Worth	US$400	US$540	US$640
Los Angeles	US$390	US$500	US$520
Miami	US$420	US$450	US$500
New York	US$430	US$590	US$580

In high season you may have to pay US$100 more, though competitive fares are offered by some of the websites above for all times of year, if you book ahead.

LAND
Border Crossings
There are over 40 official crossing points on the US Mexico border, about 10 between Guatemala and Mexico, and two between Belize and Mexico. You'll find more practical information on the most important ones in this book's regional chapters.

Car & Motorcycle
The rules for taking a vehicle into Mexico change from time to time. You can check with the **American Automobile Association** (AAA; www.aaa.com), **Sanborn's** (☎ 800-222-0158; www.sanbornsinsurance.com), a Mexican consulate or the Mexican tourist information number in the USA and Canada (☎ 800-446-3942).

You won't usually find gasoline or mechanics available at Mexico's road borders: before crossing the border, make sure you'll be able to make it to the next sizable town inside Mexico. For information on practical aspects of driving and motorcycling once you're inside Mexico, see p977.

MOTOR INSURANCE
It is very foolish to drive in Mexico without Mexican liability insurance. If you are involved in an accident, you can be jailed and have your vehicle impounded while responsibility is assessed. If you are to blame for an accident causing injury or death, you may be detained until you guarantee restitution to the victims and payment of any fines. This could take weeks or months. Adequate Mexican insurance coverage is the only real protection: it is regarded as a guarantee that restitution will be paid, and will expedite release of the driver.

Mexican law recognizes only Mexican motor *seguro* (insurance), so a US or Canadian policy, even if it provides coverage, is not acceptable to Mexican officialdom. Mexican insurance is sold in US border towns; as you approach the border from the USA you will see billboards advertising offices selling Mexican policies. At the busiest border crossings (to Tijuana, Mexicali, Nogales, Agua Prieta, Ciudad Juárez, Nuevo Laredo, Reynosa and Matamoros), there are insurance offices open 24 hours a day. Some deals are better than others. Sanborn's and the **American Automobile Association** (AAA; www.aaa.com) are both well worth looking into for Mexico motor insurance. It's also worth checking the yellow pages in US border towns.

Short-term insurance is about US$15 a day for full coverage on a car worth under US$10,000; for periods of more than two weeks it's often cheaper to get an annual policy. Liability-only insurance costs around half the full coverage cost.

Insurance is considered invalid if the driver is under the influence of alcohol or drugs.

DRIVER'S LICENSE
To drive a motor vehicle in Mexico, you need a valid driver's license from your home country.

VEHICLE PERMIT
You will need a *permiso de importación temporal de vehículos* (temporary vehicle import permit) from Mexican customs if you want to take a vehicle beyond Baja California, beyond Puerto Peñasco in Sonora state, beyond the border zone that extends 20km to 30km into Mexico along the rest of the US frontier, and up to 70km from the Guatemalan and Belize frontiers. Officials at posts of the Instituto Nacional de Migración (INM; National Immigration Institute) in the border zones, and at the Baja California ports for ferries to mainland Mexico, will want to see the permit for your vehicle.

You must get the vehicle permit at the *aduana* (customs) office at a border crossing or, in Baja California, at the Pichilingue (La Paz) ferry terminal. (Permits are not available at Santa Rosalía, the other Baja ferry port.) Application forms for the vehicle permit are available online at www .banjercito.com.mx. The person importing the vehicle will need the original and two photocopies (people at the office may make photocopies for a small fee) of each of the following documents, which must as a rule all be in his/her own name (except that you can bring in your spouse's, parent's or child's vehicle if you can show documentation such as a marriage or birth certificate proving your relationship):

- tourist card (FMT): go to *migración* before you go to the *aduana*
- certificate of title or registration certificate for the vehicle (note: you will need both of these if you plan to drive through Mexico into Guatemala or Belize)
- a Visa, MasterCard or American Express credit card, issued by a non-Mexican institution; if you don't have one you must pay a returnable deposit of between US$200 and US$400 (depending on how old the car is) at the border. Your card details or deposit serve as a guarantee that you'll take the car out of Mexico before your tourist card (FMT) expires. If you're leaving Mexico at a different border crossing from the one you entered at, first make sure you will be able to recover your deposit there.
- proof of citizenship or residency such as a passport, birth certificate or voter's registration card accompanied by official photo ID such as a driver's license
- driver's license
- if the vehicle is not fully paid for, a letter of credit or partial invoice granted by the financing institution
- for a leased or rented vehicle, the original contract (plus a copy), which must be in the name of the person importing the car (few US rental firms allow their vehicles to be taken into Mexico)
- for a company car, proof of employment by the company and proof of the vehicle's ownership by the company

One person cannot bring in two vehicles. If you have a motorcycle attached to your car, you'll need another adult traveling with you to obtain a permit for the motorcycle, and he/she will need to have all the right papers for it. If the motorcycle is registered in your name, you'll need a notarized affidavit authorizing the other person to take it into Mexico.

At the border there will be a building with a parking area for vehicles awaiting permits. Go inside and find the right counter to present your papers. After some signing and stamping of papers, you sign a promise to take the car out of the country, the Banco del Ejército (also called Banjército; it's the army bank) charges a processing fee of about US$25 to your credit card, and you go and wait with your vehicle. Make sure you get back the originals of all documents. Eventually someone will come out and give you your vehicle permit and a sticker to be displayed on your windshield.

While in Mexico, other persons are allowed to drive the car only if the permit holder is in the car with them.

The vehicle permit entitles you to take the vehicle in and out of Mexico for the period shown on your tourist card. When you leave Mexico for the last time, you must have the permit canceled by the Mexican authorities. An official may do this as you enter the border zone, usually 20km to 30km before the border itself. If not, you'll have to find the right official at the border crossing. If you leave Mexico without having the permit canceled, once the permit expires the authorities may assume you've left the vehicle in the country illegally and decide to keep your deposit or charge a fine to your credit card.

Only the owner may take the vehicle out of Mexico. If the vehicle is wrecked completely, you must contact your embassy or consulate or a Mexican customs office to make arrangements to leave without it.

Belize

The Novelo's and Northern companies run some 20 buses a day between Belize City and Chetumal, Mexico (US$5.50 to US$7, four hours).

Guatemala

The road borders at La Mesilla/Ciudad Cuauhtémoc, Ciudad Tecún Umán/Ciudad Hidalgo and El Carmen/Talismán are all linked to Guatemala City, and nearby cities within Guatemala and Mexico, by plentiful buses and/or combis. **Transportes Galgos** (☎ 253-9131 in Guatemala City; www.transgalgosinter .com.gt) and **Tica Bus** (☎ 331-4279 in Guatemala City; www.ticabus.com) run a few buses daily all the way from Guatemala City to Tapachula, Chiapas (US$13 to US$17, six hours) via Escuintla and Mazatenango.

There are up to five direct daily buses from Flores, Guatemala, to Chetumal, Mexico (US$25 to US$35, seven to eight hours), run by **Línea Dorada/Mundo Maya** (☎ 926-1788 in Flores) and **San Juan Travel** (☎ 926-0041 in Flores). Buses go via Belize City.

For the Río Usumacinta route between Flores and Palenque, both **Fuente del Norte** (☎ 926-0517 in Flores) and Transportes Pinita run several daily 2nd-class buses to Bethel (US$3.50, four hours), on the Guatemalan

bank of the Usumacinta. The 40-minute boat trip from Bethel to Frontera Corozal, Mexico costs US$4 to US$6 per person; an alternative is to take a bus from Flores that continues through Bethel to La Técnica (US$4, five to six hours), from which it's only a US$0.70, five-minute river crossing to Frontera Corozal. Transportation between Frontera Corozal and Palenque (US$5, three to four hours) is provided by the combis of Autotransportes Río Chancalá and buses of Transportes Montebello. Travel agencies in Palenque and Flores offer bus-boat-bus packages between the two places for US$30 to US$35. If you're making this trip it's well worth the time and expense of detouring to the outstanding Mayan ruins at Yaxchilán, near Frontera Corozal: packages incorporating this are available.

BUS COMPANIES PROVIDING US–MEXICO INTERNATIONAL SERVICE

Company	☎ in US	Destinations
Autobuses Americanos/	☎ 213-688-0044 Los Angeles	US: California, Chicago, Denver, Phoenix,
Omnibus Americanos	☎ 303-292-0333 Denver	Albuquerque, Texas
	☎ 602-258-4331 Phoenix	Mexico: Ciudad Juárez, Chihuahua, Nuevo Laredo,
	☎ 713-928-8030 Houston	Monterrey, Saltillo, Matehuala, San Luis Potosí,
		San Miguel de Allende, Querétaro
Autobuses Amigos	☎ 956-550-8294 Brownsville	US: Houston, Brownsville
		Mexico: Matamoros, Tampico
Autobuses Crucero	☎ 602-528-0901 Phoenix	US: Los Angeles, Las Vegas, Phoenix, Tucson,
	☎ 520-287-5628 Nogales (AZ)	Nogales
		Mexico: Nogales, Hermosillo, Los Mochis,Mazatlán
El Expreso Bus Company	☎ 713-236-1926 Houston	US: Houston, Dallas, Atlanta, Florida,
		South Carolina
		Mexico: Matamoros
Los Paisanos	☎ 303-477-8888 Denver	US: Denver, El Paso
	☎ 915-532-2151 El Paso	Mexico: Ciudad Juárez, Chihuahua
Transportes Baldomero	☎ 602-258-2355 Phoenix	US: Phoenix, Tucson
Corral		Mexico: Nogales, Hermosillo, Guaymas, Álamos,
		Los Mochis, Culiacán
Transportes Golden State	☎ 303-675-0110 Denver	US: Yakima (WA), California, Las Vegas, Denver,
	☎ 213-627-2940 Los Angeles	Phoenix, Tucson
	☎ 602-269-0500 Phoenix	Mexico: Mexicali

Note: Americanos, Amigos and Crucero are affiliates of Greyhound.

The USA

BUS

Cross-border bus services link many US cities with northern Mexican cities. Mexican migrants are their main customers. While it can be marginally more convenient, and sometimes cheaper, to use one single service all the way from, say, Denver to Chihuahua, some cross-border buses can suffer delays at the border and you will usually lose little time by making your way to the border on one bus (or train), crossing it on foot or by local bus, and then catching an onward bus on the other side. **Greyhound** (in the USA ☎ 800-229-9424, in Mexico ☎ 800-710-88-19; www.greyhound.com) serves many US border cities; to reach others, transfer from Greyhound to a smaller bus line. Greyhound one-way fares to El Paso, for example, are US$45 from Los Angeles (16 hours), US$99 from Chicago (34 hours) and US$99 from New York (48 hours).

Listed below are some sample fares and journey times on cross-border buses.

Route	Fare	Duration
Los Angeles–Tijuana	US$20	4hr
Los Angeles–Hermosillo	US$74	15hr
Phoenix–Álamos	US$52	14hr
Phoenix–Mazatlán	US$96	20hr
Denver–Chihuahua	US$50-60	24hr
Dallas–Reynosa	US$40	13hr
Houston–Matamoros	US$25	9hr

CAR & MOTORCYCLE

If you are visiting the state of Sonora only, and are entering Mexico at Nogales and going to leave by the same route after not more than 180 days, you qualify for the Sonora Only permit and do not have to pay the US$25 fee or a guarantee. You just need to show – at the Km 21 checkpoint on highway 15 south of Nogales – your valid driver's license and proof of ownership or legal possession of the vehicle (such as registration, title, lease contract or notarized permission from leasing company or bank). Permits must be returned to this checkpoint within the allotted 180-day period.

If you are planning to buy a car specially for your Mexico trip, you can get an idea of used-car prices and trade-in values from the **Kelley Blue Book** (www.kbb.com). As little as US$2500 can buy you a car that will take you around Mexico and still be worth something at journey's end. The registration document can usually be obtained in one day, but the certificate of title can take a week, even if you ask for rush service.

TRAIN

Though there are no regular passenger trains on the Mexican side of the US–Mexico border, it's quite possible to reach the US side of the border by rail. Trains can be quicker and cheaper than buses, or slower and more expensive, depending on the route. **Amtrak** (☎ 800-872-7245; www.amtrak.com) serves four US cities from which access to Mexico is easy: San Diego, California (opposite Tijuana); El Paso, Texas (opposite Ciudad Juárez); Del Rio, Texas (opposite Ciudad Acuña) and San Antonio, Texas, which is linked by bus to Eagle Pass (opposite Piedras Negras) and Laredo (opposite Nuevo Laredo).

GETTING AROUND

AIR

All large and many smaller cities in Mexico have airports and passenger services. Depending on the fare you get, flying can be good value on longer journeys, especially considering the long bus trip that is probably the alternative. Domestic flights within Mexico are often cheaper if you book them before you go to Mexico, in conjunction with an international round-trip ticket.

Airlines in Mexico

Aeroméxico and Mexicana are the country's two major airlines. There are also numerous smaller ones, often flying routes between provincial cities ignored by the big two, most of whose flights begin or end at Mexico City.

The US Federal Aviation Administration (FAA) has assessed Mexico's civil aviation authority as in compliance with international aviation safety standards for overseeing Mexico's air carrier operations.

Fares

Fares can depend on whether you fly at a busy or quiet time of day, week or year, and how far ahead you book and pay. High season generally corresponds to the Mexican holiday seasons (see p954). You'll normally save money if you pay for the ticket a few

TRANSPORTATION

MEXICAN DOMESTIC AIRLINES

Airline	☎	Website	Areas served
Aero California	☎ 55-5207-1392	–	Mexico City, Baja California, north, west
Aero Cuahonte	☎ 452-524-00-32	www.aerocuahonte.com	Michoacán, Guadalajara
Aerocaribe	☎ 800-502-20-00	www.aerocaribe.com	Mexico City, Gulf coast, south, southeast
Aerocozumel	☎ 800-502-20-00	www.mexicana.com	Yucatán Peninsula
Aerolitoral	☎ 800-800-23-76	www.aerolitoral.com	Central Mexico, Baja California, north, west
Aeromar	☎ 800-237-66-27	www.aeromar.com.mx	Central Mexico, west, northeast, Gulf coast, southeast
Aeroméxico	☎ 800-021-40-00	www.aeromexico.com	over 50 cities nationwide
Aerotucán	☎ 800-640-41-48	www.aero-tucan.com	Oaxaca state
Aviacsa	☎ 800-006-22-00	www.aviacsa.com.mx	Mexico City, northwest, west, southeast, Monterrey, Acapulco
Líneas Aéreas Azteca	☎ 800-229-83-22	www.aazteca.com.mx	Mexico City, Cancún, north, west
Magnicharters	☎ 55-5566-8199	www.magnicharters.com	Mexico City, Guadalajara, Monterrey, Bajío, Torreón, San Luis Potosí, Morelia, Mérida, coastal resorts
Mexicana	☎ 800-502-20-00	www.mexicana.com	over 50 cities nationwide

Aerolitoral and Aeromar are affiliates of Aeroméxico and normally share its ticket offices and booking networks.
A similar arrangement exists between Aerocaribe, Aerocozumel and Mexicana.

days ahead or if you fly late in the evening. Independent airlines such as Aviacsa, Magnicharters and Aero California often offer fares significantly lower than Aeroméxico and Mexicana. Round-trip fares are usually simply twice the price of one-way tickets, though some advance-payment cheaper deals do exist.

Here are some examples of one-way, low-season, Mexicana fares from Mexico City, including taxes:

Destination	Fare
Acapulco	US$134
Cancún	US$167
Guadalajara	US$141
Mérida	US$162
Monterrey	US$149
Oaxaca	US$141
Puerto Vallarta	US$144
Tijuana	US$180

BICYCLE

Except for Baja California, cycling is not a common way to tour Mexico. The size of the country, reports of highway robbery, poor road surfaces, careless motorists and pedestrians and other road hazards (see p979) are deterrents. However, biking around is certainly possible if you're prepared for the challenges. You should be very fit, use the best equipment, and be fully able to handle your own repairs. Take the mountainous topography and hot climate into account when planning your route. Bike lanes are very rare.

Bicycling Mexico by Erica Weisbroth and Eric Ellman, published in 1990, is still a valuable help to anyone cycling in Mexico.

All cities have bicycle shops: a decent mountain bike suitable for a few weeks' touring costs around US$400 to US$500. You can't expect to get much of that back by selling it afterwards unless you have time on your side.

If you're interested in a long Mexican ride, consider the bring-your-own-bike tours of Pacific and southeast Mexico of up to a month offered by !El Tour, based in Chiapas (see p962 for more information).

BOAT

Vehicle and passenger ferries connecting Baja California with the Mexican mainland sail between Santa Rosalía and Guaymas, La Paz and Mazatlán, and La Paz and Topolobampo. One-way passenger fares range from US$46 to US$202; a car up to 5m in length costs between US$150 and US$200. There are also ferries from the Yucatán Peninsula to the offshore islands of Isla Mujeres (p909), Cozumel (p919) and Isla Holbox (p912).

BUS

Mexico has a good road and bus network, and comfortable, frequent, reasonably priced bus services connect all cities. Most cities and towns have one main bus terminal where all long-distance buses arrive and depart. It's usually called the Terminal de Autobuses, Central de Autobuses, Central Camionera or simply La Central (not to be confused with El Centro, the city center!) If there is no single main terminal, different bus companies will have separate terminals scattered around town.

Baggage is safe if stowed in the bus's baggage hold, but get a receipt for it when you hand it over. Keep your most valuable documents (passport, money, etc) in the cabin with you, and keep them closely protected.

Highway robbery happens very occasionally. The risk is higher at night, on isolated stretches of highway far from cities, and in 2nd-class buses.

Classes

DELUXE

De lujo services, sometimes termed ejecutivo (executive), run mainly on the busy routes. They are swift, modern and comfortable, with reclining seats, adequate legroom, air-conditioning, few or no stops, toilets on board (but not necessarily toilet paper), and sometimes drinks or snacks. Like 1st-class buses, deluxe buses often subject their passengers to violent third-rate movies: unless you close your eyes, you cannot avoid watching them as all seats face a video screen.

1ST CLASS

Primera (1a) clase buses have a comfortable numbered seat for each passenger. Their standards of comfort are perfectly adequate. They usually have air-conditioning and a toilet and they stop infrequently. Bring a sweater or jacket to combat over-zealous air-conditioning. All sizable towns have 1st-class bus service. As with deluxe buses, you buy your ticket in the bus station before boarding.

2ND CLASS

Segunda (2a) clase buses serve small towns and villages, and provide cheaper, slower travel on some intercity routes. A few are almost as quick, comfortable and direct as 1st-class buses. Others are old, slow and shabby.

Many 2nd-class services have no ticket office; you just pay your fare to the conductor. The small amount of money you save by traveling 2nd-class is not usually worth the discomfort or extra journey time entailed. These buses tend to take slow, nontoll roads in and out of big cities and will stop anywhere to pick up passengers: if you board mid-route you might make some of the trip standing.

Second-class buses can also be less safe than 1st-class or deluxe buses, for reasons of maintenance or driver standards or because they are more vulnerable to being boarded by bandits on some roads. Out in the remoter areas, however, you'll often find that 2nd-class buses are the only buses available.

Microbuses or 'micros' are small, usually fairly new, 2nd-class buses with around 25 seats, usually running short routes between nearby towns.

Costs

First-class buses typically cost around US$4 per hour of travel (70km to 80km). Deluxe buses may cost just 10% or 20% more than 1st-class, or about 60% more for superdeluxe services such as ETN, UNO and Turistar Ejecutivo. Second-class buses cost 10% or 20% less than 1st-class.

Reservations

For trips of up to four or five hours on busy routes, you can usually just go to the bus terminal, buy a ticket and head out

MEXICAN BUS COMPANIES

Company	☎	Website	Main regions/destinations
ABC	☎ 664-621-24-24	www.abc.com.mx	Baja California
ADO	☎ 800-702-80-00	www.ado.com.mx www.adogl.com.mx	Mexico City, Puebla, southeast, Veracruz state
Autotransportes Águila	☎ 612-122-42-70	–	Southern Baja California
Autovías	☎ 55-5277-7761	–	Mexico City, Michoacán, San Miguel de Allende, Zihuatanejo
Cristóbal Colón (OCC)	☎ 800-702-80-00	www.cristobalcolon.com.mx	Mexico City, Puebla, southeast
Elite	☎ 800-507-55-00	www.estrellablanca.com.mx	Mexico City, northwest, Pacific coast, Querétaro, San Luis Potosí
Estrella Blanca	☎ 800-507-55-00	www.estrellablanca.com.mx	Cuernavaca, Hermosillo, northern central highlands, Pacific coast
Estrella de Oro	☎ 55-5689-2006	www.estrelladeoro.com.mx	Acapulco, Cuernavaca, Mexico City, Taxco, Zihuatanejo
Estrella Roja	☎ 800-712-22-84	www.estrellaroja.com.mx	Cuernavaca, Mexico City, Puebla
ETN	☎ 55-5089-9200	www.etn.com.mx	Manzanillo, Mexico City, northern & western central highlands, Puerto Vallarta
Flecha Amarilla	☎ 800-375-75-87	www.flecha-amarilla.com	Manzanillo, Mexico City, Morelia, northern central highlands
Flecha Roja	☎ 800-507-55-00	www.estrellablanca.com.mx	Cuernavaca, Mexico City, Toluca
Futura	☎ 800-507-55-00	www.estrellablanca.com.mx	Guadalajara, Mexico City, Monterrey, Nuevo Laredo, northern central highlands, Pacific coast, Taxco
Maya de Oro	☎ 800-702-80-00	www.mayadeoro.com.mx	Mexico City, southeast
Ómnibus de México	☎ 800-849-02-08	www.omnibus.com.mx	Chihuahua, Ciudad Juárez, Guadalajara, Mexico City, Monterrey, northern central highlands, Saltillo
Primera Plus	☎ 55-5567-7176	www.primeraplus.com.mx	Manzanillo, Mexico City, northern & western central highlands, Puerto Vallarta
Pullman de Morelos	☎ 777-312-60-63	www.pullman.com.mx	Cuernavaca, Mexico City
TAP	☎ 668-812-57-49	–	Mexico City, northwest
Transportes Chihuahuenses	☎ 800-507-55-00	www.estrellablanca.com.mx	Chihuahua, Mexico City, Los Mochis, Zacatecas
Transportes del Norte	☎ 800-507-55-00	www.estrellablanca.com.mx	Mexico City, northeast, San Luis Potosí
Turistar	☎ 800-507-55-00	www.estrellablanca.com.mx	Mexico City, northeast, Pacific coast
UNO	☎ 800-702-80-00	www.uno.com.mx	Mexico City, Puebla, southeast, Veracruz state

Note: many bus lines are part of multi-line groups, which may share ticket desks at bus stations. ADO, Cristóbal Colón, Maya de Oro and UNO are all part of the ADO group. Elite, Estrella Blanca, Flecha Roja, Futura, Transportes Chihuahuenses, Transportes del Norte and Turistar are all part of Grupo Estrella Blanca.

HOW MANY STOPS?

It is important to know the type of bus service offered:

Sin escalas Nonstop.

Directo Very few stops.

Semi-directo A few more stops than *directo*.

Ordinario Stops wherever passengers want to get on or off the bus; deluxe and 1st-class buses are never *ordinario*.

Express Nonstop on short to medium-length trips; very few stops on long trips.

Local Bus that starts its journey at the bus station you're in and usually leaves on time; *local* service is preferable to *de paso*.

De paso Bus that started its journey somewhere else but is stopping to let off and take on passengers. A *de paso* bus may be late and may or may not have seats available; if the bus company does not have a computer booking system, you may have to wait until the bus arrives before any tickets are sold. If the bus is full, you may have to wait for the next one.

Viaje redondo Round-trip.

---

without much delay. For longer trips, or routes with infrequent service, book a ticket a day in advance, preferably two or three. Deluxe and most 1st-class bus companies have computerized ticket systems that allow you to select your seat from an on-screen diagram when you buy your ticket. Try to avoid the back of the bus, which is where the toilets are and also tends to give a bumpier ride.

Ticketbus (☎ 5133-2424, 800-702-80-00; www.ticket bus.com.mx) provides tickets and reservations by Internet or telephone or at any of its many offices in 24 cities for any service of the ADO group serving Mexico City, Puebla, the Gulf coast, Yucatán Peninsula, Oaxaca and Chiapas (including UNO, ADO-GL, Maya de Oro, ADO, Cristóbal Colón, Altos, Sur, Mayab, AU and Rápidos del Sur lines) and some other companies.

If you're paying for a bus ticket in cash, immediate cash refunds of 80% to 100% are available from many bus companies. To obtain this you have to cancel your ticket more than an hour or two before the listed departure time.

CAR & MOTORCYCLE

Driving in Mexico is not as easy as it is north of the border, but it is often easier and more convenient than the bus, and it's sometimes the only way to get to some of the most beautiful places or isolated towns and villages.

Bring Your Own Vehicle

Having a car in Mexico is most useful for travelers who:

- have plenty of time
- plan to go to remote places
- have surfboards, diving equipment or other cumbersome luggage
- will be traveling with at least one companion

Drivers should know some Spanish and have basic mechanical aptitude, reserves of patience and access to extra cash for emergencies. Good makes of car to take to Mexico are Volkswagen, Nissan, General Motors and Ford, which have manufacturing or assembly plants in Mexico and dealers in most big towns. Big cars are unwieldy on narrow roads and use a lot of gasoline. A sedan with a trunk (boot) provides safer storage than a station wagon or hatchback. Mexican mechanics are resourceful, and most repairs can be done quickly and inexpensively, but it still pays to take as many spare parts as you can manage (spare fuel filters are very useful). Tires (including spare), shock absorbers and suspension should be in good condition. For security, have something to immobilize the steering wheel, and consider getting a kill switch installed.

Motorcycling in Mexico is not for the fainthearted. Roads and traffic can be rough, and parts and mechanics hard to come by.

TRANSPORTATION

ROAD DISTANCES (KM)

	Acapulco	Cancún	Ciudad Juárez	Guadalajara	Guanajuato	Hermosillo	Matamoros	Mazatlán	Mérida	Mexico City	Monterrey	Morelia	Nogales	Oaxaca	Puebla	San Luis Potosí	Tapachula	Tijuana	Tuxtla Gutiérrez	Veracruz	Villahermosa
Cancún	2007																				
Ciudad Juárez	2258	3512																			
Guadalajara	889	2191	1578																		
Guanajuato	760	2014	1570	277																	
Hermosillo	2348	3608	769	1417	1694																
Matamoros	1370	2336	1530	774	1117	1848															
Mazatlán	1431	2891	1347	500	777	917	1250														
Mérida	1690	317	3195	1874	1697	3291	1959	2019													
Mexico City	395	1649	1863	542	365	1959	975	1042	1403												
Monterrey	1328	2363	1202	789	729	1520	328	928	1797	913											
Morelia	697	1951	1705	302	180	1719	954	802	1403	302	1056										
Nogales	2625	3885	620	1694	1971	277	2125	1194	3568	2359	2043	2043									
Oaxaca	828	1490	2333	1012	835	2429	1358	1512	470	545	687	820	2706								
Puebla	481	1526	1986	835	488	2082	1077	1165	1209	123	279	687	3318	347							
San Luis Potosí	810	2064	1448	340	215	1766	559	809	1512	415	609	609	3251	609	538						
Tapachula	1109	1376	3020	1699	1522	3116	1776	2199	564	1157	1459	1803	820	545	892	1034					
Tijuana	3237	4497	1312	2306	2583	889	2737	1806	4180	2348	2608	2638	3393	3251	2971	2615	1430				
Tuxtla Gutiérrez	967	1146	2878	1557	1380	2974	1634	2054	829	1015	1317	1661	3004	545	892	279	412	3250	671		
Veracruz	760	1373	2265	944	767	2361	963	1444	1056	402	704	990	3004	609	279	817	813	3616	284	492	
Villahermosa	1126	881	2631	1310	1133	2727	1455	1810	564	768	1070	1482	3004	609	645	1183	636	2425	284	492	1373
Zacatecas	1000	2254	1258	320	312	1576	979	619	1937	605	469	447	1853	1075	728	190	1762	1920	1576	1007	1373

The parts you'll most easily find will be for Kawasaki, Honda and Suzuki bikes.

Your home country license will suffice in Mexico. See p973 for the paperwork required for bringing a vehicle into Mexico and important information on insurance.

Gas (Petrol)

All *gasolina* (gasoline) and diesel fuel in Mexico is sold by the government's monopoly, Pemex (Petróleos Mexicanos). Most towns, even small ones, have a Pemex station, and the stations are pretty common on most major roads. Nevertheless, in remote areas you should fill up whenever you can. Only a few Pemex stations accept credit cards, and they'll often charge a 5% fee for doing so.

The gasoline on sale is all *sin plomo* (unleaded). There are two varieties: Magna Sin, roughly equivalent to US regular unleaded, and Premium, roughly equivalent to US super unleaded. At the time of research, Magna Sin cost about US$0.60 a liter (US$2.40 a US gallon), and Premium about US$0.70. Diesel fuel is widely available at around US$0.50 a liter. Regular Mexican diesel has a higher sulfur content than US diesel, but there is a 'Diesel Sin' with less sulfur. If diesel drivers change their oil and filter about every 3500km, they should have no problems.

Gas stations have pump attendants (who appreciate a small tip).

Maps

Mexican signposting can be poor. Mexican publisher Guía Roji's *Por Las Carreteras de México* road atlas (US$11) is an excellent investment. It's sold at good bookstores and some city newsstands in Mexico, and is available from Internet booksellers for a little more. It's updated annually and includes new highways.

Rental

Auto rental in Mexico is expensive by US or European standards, but is not hard to organize and can be a good way to visit a few places in a short time. It can also be useful for getting off the beaten track, where public transport is slow or scarce. You can rent cars at airports, at city center offices, at many big hotels and sometimes at bus terminals. You may need to book a

couple of days ahead. Booking by Internet or booking through a large international rental firm before you come to Mexico may save you a little money.

Renters must provide a valid driver's license (your home license is OK), passport and major credit card, and are usually required to be at least 21 (sometimes 25). Read the small print of the rental agreement. In addition to the basic daily or weekly rental rate, you pay tax and insurance costs to the rental company (fuel is not included in rates). Ask exactly what the insurance covers: it may only cover 90% of damage or theft costs and it may not cover 'partial theft,' such as wiper blades or tires, at all. Make sure you have plenty of liability coverage: Mexican law permits the jailing of drivers after an accident until they have met their obligations to third parties.

Most agencies offer a choice between a per-kilometer deal or unlimited kilometers. Work out which is best for you. Local firms are often cheaper than the big international ones. In most places the cheapest car available (often a Volkswagen Beetle) costs US$50 to US$60 a day including unlimited kilometers, insurance and tax. If you rent for a week, the seventh day is often free. The extra charge for drop-off in another city, when available, is usually about US$0.40 per kilometer.

Here's contact information (with Mexican phone numbers) for some major firms:

Alamo (☎ 55-1101-1100; www.alamo.com)
Avis (☎ 800-288-88-88; www.avis.com)
Budget (☎ 800-700-17-00; www.budget.com)
Dollar (☎ 33-3825-5080; www.dollar.com)
Europcar (☎ 800-201-20-84; www.europcar.com)
Hertz (☎ 800-709-50-00; www.hertz.com)
National (☎ 55-5661-5000; www.nationalcar.com)
Thrifty (☎ 55-5207-1100; www.thrifty.com)

Motorbikes or scooters are available to rent in a few tourist centers. You're usually required to have a driver's license and credit card. Note that a locally acquired motorcycle license is not valid under some travel insurance policies.

Road Conditions

Many Mexican highways, even some toll highways, are not up to the standards of US, Canadian or European ones. Still, the main roads are serviceable and fairly fast

TRANSPORTATION

LUCKY CHARMS

On some Mexican highways, especially those heading south from the US border, the army and police conduct fairly frequent drug and weapon searches. Old Mexico driving hands swear that any or all of the following items, visibly displayed, will indicate to officials that you are not a security risk and thus diminish your chances of being pulled over:

- a Virgin of Guadalupe charm or rosary beads hanging from the rear-view mirror
- a surfboard on the roof
- a bible or Lonely Planet guide on the dashboard!

---

when traffic is not heavy. Mexicans on the whole drive as cautiously and sensibly as people anywhere. Traffic density, poor surfaces and frequent hazards (potholes, speed bumps, animals, bicycles, children) all help to keep speeds down.

Driving on a dark night is best avoided since unlit vehicles, rocks, pedestrians and animals on the roads are common. Hijacks and robberies do occur.

In towns and cities, be especially wary of *Alto* (Stop) signs, *topes* (speed bumps) and holes in the road. They are often not where you'd expect, and missing one can cost you in traffic fines or car damage. Speed bumps are also used to slow traffic on highways that pass through built-up areas: they are not always signed, and some of them are severe!

BREAKDOWN ASSISTANCE

The Mexican tourism ministry, SECTUR, maintains a network of *Ángeles Verdes* (Green Angels) – bilingual mechanics in green uniforms and green trucks, who patrol major highways throughout the country daily during daylight hours looking for motorists in trouble. They make minor repairs, change tires, provide fuel and oil, and arrange towing and other assistance if necessary. Service is free; parts, gasoline and oil are provided at cost. If you are near a telephone when your car has problems, you can call their 24-hour hot line in Mexico City (☎ 55-5250-8221) or contact them through the national 24-hour tourist assistance numbers in Mexico City (☎ 55-5250-0123, 800-903-92-00).

CITY PARKING

It's not usually a good idea to park on the street overnight. If your hotel doesn't have parking, it's best to use a commercial *estacionamiento* (parking lot). These usually cost around US$5 overnight and US$1 per hour during the day.

TOLL ROADS

Mexico has more than 6000km of *autopistas* (toll roads), usually four-lane. They are generally in much better condition and a lot quicker than the alternative free roads. They also have a reputation for being safer from highway robbery. *Cuotas* (tolls) average about US$1 for every 10km to 20km. Toll information is available at www.capufe.gob.mx.

MOTORCYCLE HAZARDS

Certain aspects of Mexican roads make them particularly hazardous for bikers:

- poor signage of road and lane closures
- lots of dogs on the roads
- debris and deep potholes
- vehicles without taillights
- lack of highway lighting

Road Rules

Drive on the right-hand side of the road.

Speed limits are usually 100km per hour on highways and 40km per hour or 30km per hour in towns and cities. Traffic laws and speed limits rarely seem to be enforced on the highways. Obey the rules in the cities so you don't give the police an excuse to demand a 'fine' payable on the spot. (The standard bribe for minor traffic infringements is US$5.)

Antipollution rules in Mexico City ban most vehicles from the city's roads on one day each week (see p171).

One-way streets are the rule in cities. Priority at street intersections is indicated by thin black and red rectangles containing white arrows. A black rectangle means you have priority and a red one means you don't. Arrows indicate the direction of traffic on the cross street.

COLECTIVOS & OTHER VEHICLES

In some areas a variety of small vehicles provide alternatives to buses. *Colectivo* (collective) taxis, Volkswagen minibuses (combis) and more comfortable passenger-carrying vans, such as Chevrolet Suburbans, operate shuttle services between some towns, usually leaving whenever they have a full load of passengers. Fares are typically a little less than 1st-class buses. *Microbuses* or *'micros'* are small, usually fairly new, 2nd-class buses with around 25 seats, usually running short routes between nearby towns. More primitive are passenger-carrying *camionetas* (pickups) and *camiones* (trucks) with fares similar to 2nd-class bus fares. Standing in the back of a lurching truck with a couple of dozen *campesinos* (land workers) and their machetes and animals is always an experience to remember!

HITCHING

Hitchhiking is never entirely safe in any country in the world, and is not recommended. Travelers who decide to hitch should understand that they are taking a small but potentially serious risk. People who do choose to hitch will be safer if they travel in pairs and let someone know where they are planning to go. A woman traveling alone certainly should not hitchhike in Mexico, and even two women alone is not advisable.

However, hitching is not an uncommon way of getting to some of the off-the-beaten-track archaeological sites and other places poorly served by bus. Always be alert to possible dangers wherever you are. If the driver is another tourist or a private motorist, you may get the ride for free. If it is a work or commercial vehicle, you should offer to pay, something equivalent to the bus fare.

LOCAL TRANSPORTATION

Bicycle

Most Mexican towns and cities are flat enough to make cycling an option. Seek out the less traffic-infested routes and you should enjoy it. Even Mexico City has its biking enthusiasts. You can rent bikes in several towns and cities for US$10 to US$15 a day.

Boat

Here and there you may find yourself traveling by boat to an outlying beach, along a river or across a lake or lagoon. The craft are usually fast outboard *lanchas* (launches). Fares vary widely: an average is around US$1 a minute if you have to charter the whole boat (haggle!), or around US$1 for five to 10 minutes if it's a public service.

Bus

Generally known as *camiones*, local buses are the cheapest way to get around cities and out to nearby towns and villages. They run everywhere frequently and are cheap. Fares in cities are rarely more than US$0.50. Older buses are often noisy, dirty and crowded, but more and more cities have fleets of small, modern and much more pleasant microbuses.

In most cities, buses halt only at fixed *paradas* (bus stops), though in some you can hold your hand out to stop one at any street corner.

Colectivo, Combi, Microbus, Minibus & Pesero

These are all names for vehicles that function as something between a taxi and a bus, running along fixed urban routes usually displayed on the windshield. They're cheaper than taxis and quicker and less crowded than buses. They will pick you up or drop you off on any corner along their route: to stop one, go to the curb and wave your hand. Tell the driver where you want to go. Usually, you pay at the end of the trip and the fare (a little higher than a bus fare) depends on how far you go.

Metro

Mexico City, Guadalajara and Monterrey all have metro (subway, underground railway) systems. Mexico City's, in particular, is a quick, cheap and useful way of getting around. With 175 stations and being used by nearly 5 million people every weekday, it's the world's third-busiest subway.

Taxi

Taxis are common in towns and cities, and surprisingly economical. City rides cost around US$1 per km. (See p120 for a warning on taxi crime in Mexico City.) If a taxi has a meter, ask the driver if it's working ('*¿Funciona el taxímetro?*'). If it's not, or if the taxi doesn't have a meter, establish the price of the ride before getting in (this usually involves a bit of haggling.)

Some airports and big bus stations have a system of authorized ticket-taxis: you buy a fixed-price ticket to your destination from a special *taquilla* (ticket window) and then hand it to the driver instead of paying cash. This saves haggling and major rip-offs, but fares are usually higher than you could get on the street.

In some (usually rural) areas, some taxis operate on a colectivo basis, following set routes, often from one town or village to another, and picking up or dropping off passengers anywhere along that route. Fares per person are around one-fifth of the normal cab fare.

Renting a taxi for a day's out-of-town outing generally costs something similar

to a cheap rental car – around US$50 or US$60.

TRAIN

The spectacular Ferrocarril Chihuahua al Pacífico between Los Mochis and Chihuahua (p322), known in English as the Copper Canyon Railway, is one of the highlights of Mexico travel. But the rest of Mexico's regular passenger train system effectively ceased to exist after the railroads were privatized in the 1990s. The very few services remaining are either on routes of no interest to travelers or are special touristic excursion services. Most prominent among the latter are the **Tequila Express** (☎ 33-3880-9099) between Guadalajara and the tequila-distilling town of Amatitán (see p527), and the **Expreso Maya** (www.expresomaya.com) linking the Yucatán Peninsula, Palenque and Villahermosa.

Health Dr David Goldberg

CONTENTS

Travelers to Mexico need to be concerned chiefly about food-borne diseases, though mosquito-borne infections can also be a problem. Most of these illnesses are not life threatening, but they can certainly have an impact on your trip or even ruin it. Besides getting the proper vaccinations, it's important that you bring along a good insect repellent and exercise great care in what you eat and drink.

BEFORE YOU GO

Since most vaccines don't produce immunity until at least two weeks after they're given, visit a physician four to eight weeks before departure. Ask your doctor for an International Certificate of Vaccination (otherwise known as the yellow booklet), which will list all the vaccinations you've received. This is mandatory for countries that require proof of yellow fever vaccination upon entry, but it's a good idea to carry it wherever you travel.

Bring medications in their original containers, clearly labeled. A signed, dated letter from your physician describing all medical conditions and medications, including generic names, is also a good idea.

If carrying syringes or needles, be sure to have a physician's letter documenting their medical necessity.

INSURANCE

Mexican medical treatment is generally inexpensive for common diseases and minor treatment, but if you suffer some serious medical problem, you may want to find a private hospital or fly out for treatment. Travel insurance can typically cover the costs. Some US health insurance policies stay in effect (at least for a limited time) if you travel abroad, but it's worth checking exactly what you'll be covered for in Mexico. For people whose medical insurance or national health systems don't extend to Mexico – which includes most non-Americans – a travel policy is advisable. (Check the Subway section of the Lonely Planet website at www.lonelyplanet.com/subwwway for more information.)

You may prefer a policy that pays doctors or hospitals directly rather than requiring you to pay on the spot and claim later. If you have to claim later, keep all documentation. Some policies ask you to call collect to a center in your home country, where an immediate assessment of your problem is made. Check that the policy covers ambulances or an emergency flight home. Some policies offer lower and higher medical-expense options; the higher ones are chiefly for countries such as the USA, which have extremely high medical costs. There is a wide variety of policies available, so check the small print.

THE MAN SAYS...

It's usually a good idea to consult your government's travel health website before departure, if one is available:

- **Australia** www.dfat.gov.au/travel/
- **Canada** www.travelhealth.gc.ca
- **United Kingdom** www.doh.gov.uk /traveladvice/
- **United States** www.cdc.gov/travel/

HEALTH

IMMUNIZATIONS

The only required vaccine is yellow fever, and that's only if you're arriving in Mexico from a yellow fever–infected country in Africa or South America. However, a number of vaccines are recommended: see table below.

MEDICAL CHECKLIST

- Antibiotics
- Antidiarrheal drugs (eg loperamide)
- Acetaminophen/paracetamol (Tylenol) or aspirin
- Anti-inflammatory drugs (eg ibuprofen)
- Antihistamines (for hay fever and allergic reactions)
- Antibacterial ointment (eg Bactroban) for cuts and abrasions
- Steroid cream or cortisone (for poison ivy and other allergic rashes)
- Bandages, gauze, gauze rolls
- Adhesive or paper tape
- Scissors, safety pins, tweezers
- Thermometer
- Pocket knife
- DEET-containing insect repellent for the skin
- Permethrin-containing insect spray for clothing, tents and bed nets
- Sun block
- Oral rehydration salts
- Iodine tablets (for water purification)
- Syringes and sterile needles

INTERNET RESOURCES

There is a wealth of travel health advice on the Internet. For further information, the Lonely Planet website at www.lonelyplanet.com is a good place to start. The World Health Organization publishes a superb book called *International Travel and Health*, which is revised annually and is available online at no cost at www.who.int/ith. Another website of general interest is MD Travel Health at www.mdtravelhealth.com, which provides complete travel health rec-

RECOMMENDED VACCINATIONS

Vaccine	Recommended for	Dosage	Side effects
hepatitis A	all travelers	1 dose before trip; booster 6-12 months later	soreness at injection site; headaches; body aches
typhoid	all travelers	4 capsules by mouth, 1 taken every other day	abdominal pain; nausea; rash
yellow fever	required for travelers arriving from a yellow fever–infected area in Africa or the Americas	1 dose lasts 10 years	headaches; body aches; severe reactions are rare
hepatitis B	long-term travelers in close contact with the local population	3 doses over 6-month period	soreness at injection site; low-grade fever
rabies	travelers who may have contact with animals and may not have access to medical care	3 doses over 3-4 week period	soreness at injection site; headaches; body aches
tetanus-diphtheria	all travelers who haven't had booster within 10 years	1 dose lasts 10 years	soreness at injection site
measles	travelers born after 1956 who've had only 1 measles vaccination	1 dose	fever; rash; joint pains; allergic reactions
chickenpox	travelers who've never had chickenpox	2 doses 1 month apart	fever; mild case of chickenpox

HEALTH

ommendations for every country, updated daily, also at no cost.

FURTHER READING

For further information, see *Healthy Travel Central & South America,* also from Lonely Planet. If you're traveling with children, Lonely Planet's *Travel with Children* may be useful. The *ABC of Healthy Travel,* by E Walker et al, and *Medicine for the Outdoors,* by Paul S Auerbach, are other valuable resources.

IN TRANSIT

DEEP VEIN THROMBOSIS (DVT)

Blood clots may form in the legs (deep vein thrombosis) during plane flights, chiefly because of prolonged immobility. The longer the flight, the greater the risk. Though most blood clots are reabsorbed uneventfully, some may break off and travel through the blood vessels to the lungs, where they could cause life-threatening complications.

The chief symptom of DVT is swelling or pain of the foot, ankle, or calf, usually but not always on just one side. When a blood clot travels to the lungs, it may cause chest pain and difficulty breathing. Travelers with any of these symptoms should immediately seek medical attention.

To prevent the development of DVT on long flights you should walk about the cabin, perform isometric compressions of the leg muscles (ie contract the leg muscles while sitting), drink plenty of fluids, and avoid alcohol and tobacco.

JET LAG & MOTION SICKNESS

Jet lag is common when crossing more than five time zones, resulting in insomnia, fatigue, malaise or nausea. To avoid jet lag try drinking plenty of fluids (nonalcoholic) and eating light meals. Upon arrival, get exposure to natural sunlight and readjust your schedule (for meals, sleep etc) as soon as possible.

Antihistamines such as dimenhydrinate (Dramamine) and meclizine (Antivert, Bonine) are usually the first choice for treating motion sickness. Their main side effect is drowsiness. An herbal alternative is ginger, which works like a charm for some people.

IN MEXICO

AVAILABILITY & COST OF HEALTH CARE

There are a number of first-rate hospitals in Mexico City (p102). In general, private facilities offer better care, though at greater cost, than public hospitals.

Adequate medical care is available in other major cities, but facilities in rural areas may be limited. In many areas, the US consulate provides an online directory to local physicians and hospitals:

Ciudad Juarez http://ciudadjuarez.usconsulate.gov /wwwhacil.html
Guadalajara www.usembassy-mexico.gov/guadalajara /GeDoctors.htm
Hermosillo www.usembassy-mexico.gov/hermosillo /Hedoc.htm
Nogales www.usembassy-mexico.gov/nogales/NE_ACS _con1.htm

Many doctors and hospitals expect payment in cash, regardless of whether you have travel health insurance. If you develop a life-threatening medical problem, you'll probably want to be evacuated to a country with state-of-the-art medical care. Since this may cost tens of thousands of dollars, be sure you have insurance to cover this before you depart. You can find a list of medical evacuation and travel insurance companies on the US State Department website at www.travel .state.gov/medical.html.

Mexican pharmacies are identified by a green cross and a 'Farmacia' sign. Most are well supplied and the pharmacists well trained. Reliable pharmacy chains include Sanborns, Farmacia Guadalajara, Benavides and Farmacia Fenix. Some medications requiring a prescription in the US may be dispensed in Mexico without a prescription. To find an after-hours pharmacy, you can look in the local newspaper, ask your hotel concierge, or check the front door of a local pharmacy, which will often post the name of a nearby pharmacy that is open for the night.

INFECTIOUS DISEASES
Malaria

Malaria occurs in every country in Central America, including parts of Mexico. It's transmitted by mosquito bites, usually between dusk and dawn. The main symptom is high spiking fevers, which may be accompanied by chills, sweats, headache, body aches, weakness, vomiting, or diarrhea. Severe cases may involve the central nervous system and lead to seizures, confusion, coma and death.

Taking malaria pills is strongly recommended when visiting rural areas in the states of Oaxaca, Chiapas, Sinaloa, Michoacán, Nayarit, Guerrero, Tabasco, Quintana Roo and Campeche; for the mountainous northern areas in Jalisco; and for an area between 24° and 28° north latitude, and 106° and 110° west longitude, which includes parts of the states of Sonora, Chihuahua and Durango.

For Mexico, the first choice malaria pill is chloroquine, taken once weekly in a dosage of 500mg, starting one to two weeks before arrival and continuing through the trip and for four weeks after departure. Chloroquine is safe, inexpensive and highly effective. Side effects are typically mild and may include nausea, abdominal discomfort, headache, dizziness, blurred vision or itching. Severe reactions are uncommon.

Protecting yourself against mosquito bites is just as important as taking malaria pills (see p989), since no pills are 100% effective.

If you may not have access to medical care while traveling, bring along additional pills for emergency self-treatment, which you should take if you can't reach a doctor or develop symptoms that suggest malaria, such as high spiking fevers. One option is to take four tablets of Macaroni once daily for three days. If you start self-medication, you should try to see a doctor at the earliest possible opportunity.

If you develop a fever after returning home, see a physician, as malaria symptoms may not occur for months.

Malaria pills are not recommended for the major resorts along the Pacific and Gulf Coasts.

Dengue Fever

Dengue fever is a viral infection found throughout Central America. In Mexico, the risk is greatest along the Gulf Coast, especially from July to September. Dengue is transmitted by Aedes mosquitoes, which bite preferentially during the day and are usually found close to human habitations, often indoors. They breed primarily in artificial water containers, such as jars, barrels, cans, cisterns, metal drums, plastic containers and discarded tires. As a result, dengue is especially common in densely populated, urban environments.

Dengue usually causes flu-like symptoms including fever, muscle aches, joint pains, headaches, nausea and vomiting, often followed by a rash. The body aches may be quite uncomfortable, but most cases resolve uneventfully in a few days. Severe cases usually occur in children under age 15 who are experiencing their second dengue infection.

There is no specific treatment for dengue fever except to take analgesics such as acetaminophen/paracetamol (Tylenol) and drink plenty of fluids. Severe cases may require hospitalization for intravenous fluids and supportive care. There is no vaccine. The cornerstone of prevention is insect protection measures (see p989).

Hepatitis A

Hepatitis A occurs throughout Central America. It's a viral infection of the liver usually acquired by ingestion of contaminated water, food or ice, though it may also be acquired by direct contact with infected persons. The illness occurs worldwide, but the incidence is higher in developing nations. Symptoms may include fever, malaise, jaundice, nausea, vomiting and abdominal pain. Most cases resolve uneventfully, though hepatitis A occasionally causes severe liver damage. There is no treatment.

The vaccine for hepatitis A is extremely safe and highly effective. If you get a booster six to 12 months later, it lasts for at least 10 years. You really should get it before you go to Mexico or any other developing nation. Because the safety of hepatitis A vaccine has not been established for pregnant women or children under age two, they should instead be given a gammaglobulin injection.

Hepatitis B

Like hepatitis A, hepatitis B is a liver infection that occurs worldwide but is more common in developing nations. Unlike hepatitis A, the disease is usually acquired by sexual contact or by exposure to infected blood, generally through blood transfusions or contaminated needles. The vaccine is recommended only for long-term travelers (on the road more than six months) who expect to live in rural areas or have close physical contact with the local population. Additionally, the vaccine is recommended for anyone who anticipates sexual contact with the local inhabitants or a possible need for medical, dental or other treatments while abroad, especially if a need for transfusions or injections is expected.

Hepatitis B vaccine is safe and highly effective. However, a total of three injections are necessary to establish full immunity. Several countries added hepatitis B vaccine to the list of routine childhood immunizations in the 1980s, so many young adults are already protected.

Typhoid Fever

Typhoid fever is caused by ingestion of food or water contaminated by a species of *Salmonella* known as *Salmonella typhi*. Fever occurs in virtually all cases. Other symptoms may include headache, malaise, muscle aches, dizziness, loss of appetite, nausea and abdominal pain. Either diarrhea or constipation may occur. Possible complications include intestinal perforation, intestinal bleeding, confusion, delirium or (rarely) coma.

Unless you expect to take all your meals in major hotels and restaurants, typhoid vaccine is a good idea. It's usually given orally, but is also available as an injection. Neither vaccine is approved for use in children under age two.

The drug of choice for typhoid fever is usually a quinolone antibiotic such as ciprofloxacin (Cipro) or levofloxacin (Levaquin), which many travelers carry for treatment of travelers' diarrhea. However, if you self-treat for typhoid fever, you may also need to self-treat for malaria, since the symptoms of the two diseases can be indistinguishable.

Rabies

Rabies is a viral infection of the brain and spinal cord that is almost always fatal. The rabies virus is carried in the saliva of infected animals and is typically transmitted through an animal bite, though contamination of any break in the skin with infected saliva may result in rabies. Rabies occurs in all Central American countries. Most cases in Mexico are related to dog bites, but bats and other wild species remain important sources of infection.

Rabies vaccine is safe, but a full series requires three injections and is quite expensive. Those at high risk for rabies, such as animal handlers and spelunkers (cave explorers), should certainly get the vaccine. In addition, those at lower risk for animal bites should consider asking for the vaccine if they are traveling to remote areas and might not have access to appropriate medical care if needed. The treatment for a possibly rabid bite consists of rabies vaccine with rabies immune globulin. It's effective, but must be given promptly. Most travelers don't need rabies vaccine.

All animal bites and scratches must be promptly and thoroughly cleansed with large amounts of soap and water and local health authorities contacted to determine whether or not further treatment is necessary (see p990).

Yellow Fever

Yellow fever no longer occurs in Central America, but many Central American countries, including Mexico, require yellow fever vaccine before entry if you're arriving from a country in Africa or South America where yellow fever occurs. If you're not arriving from a country with yellow fever, the vaccine is neither required nor recommended. Yellow fever vaccine is given only in approved yellow fever vaccination centers, which provide validated International Certificates of Vaccination ('yellow booklets'). The vaccine should be given at least 10 days before departure and remains effective for approximately 10 years. Reactions to the vaccine are generally mild and may include headaches, muscle aches, low-grade fevers or discomfort at the injection site. Severe, life-threatening reactions have been described but are extremely rare.

Cholera

Cholera is an intestinal infection acquired through ingestion of contaminated food or water. The main symptom is profuse, watery diarrhea, which may be so severe that it causes life-threatening dehydration. The key treatment is drinking oral rehydration solution. Antibiotics are also given, usually tetracycline or doxycycline, though quinolone antibiotics such as ciprofloxacin and levofloxacin are also effective.

Only a handful of cases have been reported in Mexico over the last few years. Cholera vaccine is no longer recommended.

Other Infections

Gnathostomiasis is a parasite acquired by eating raw or undercooked freshwater fish, including ceviche, a popular lime-marinated fish salad. Cases have been reported from Acapulco and other parts of Mexico. The chief symptom is intermittent, migratory swellings under the skin, sometimes associated with joint pains, muscle pains or gastrointestinal problems. The symptoms may not begin until many months after exposure.

Leishmaniasis occurs in the mountains and jungles of all Central American countries. The infection is transmitted by sand flies, which are about one-third the size of mosquitoes. Leishmaniasis may be limited to the skin, causing slowly-growing ulcers over exposed parts of the body, or (less commonly) disseminate to the bone marrow, liver and spleen. The disease may be particularly severe in those with HIV. The disseminated form is rare in Mexico and is limited chiefly to the Balsas River basin in the southern states of Guerrero and Pueblas. There is no vaccine for leishmaniasis. To protect yourself from sand flies, follow the same precautions as for mosquitoes (p989), except that netting must be finer mesh (at least 18 holes to the linear inch).

Chagas' disease is a parasitic infection transmitted by triatomine insects (reduviid bugs), which inhabit crevices in the walls and roofs of substandard housing in South and Central America. In Mexico, most cases occur in southern and coastal areas. The triatomine insect lays its feces on human skin as it bites, usually at night. A person becomes infected when he or she unknowingly rubs the feces into the bite wound or any other open sore. Chagas' disease is extremely rare in travelers. However, if you sleep in a poorly constructed house, especially one made of mud, adobe or thatch, you should be sure to protect yourself with a bed net and good insecticide.

Histoplasmosis is caused by a soil-based fungus and acquired by inhalation, often when soil has been disrupted. Initial symptoms may include fever, chills, dry cough, chest pain and headache, sometimes leading to pneumonia. An outbreak was recently described among visitors to an Acapulco hotel.

Coccidioidomycosis, also known as 'valley fever,' is a fungal infection that is restricted to semiarid areas in the American southwest, nearby areas in northern Mexico, and limited foci in Central and South America. Valley fever is acquired by inhaling dust from contaminated soil. It begins as a lung infection, causing fever, chest pain and cough, and may spread to other organs, particularly the nervous system, skin and bone. Treatment requires high doses of antibiotics for prolonged periods and is not always curative.

Brucellosis is an infection occurring in domestic and wild animals that may be transmitted to humans through direct animal contact or by consumption of unpasteurized dairy products from infected animals. Symptoms may include fever, malaise, depression, loss of appetite, headache, muscle aches and back pain. Complications can include arthritis, hepatitis, meningitis and endocarditis (heart valve infection).

Tick-borne relapsing fever, which may be transmitted by either ticks or lice, has been reported from the plateau regions in central Mexico. Relapsing fever is caused by bacteria that are closely related to those which cause Lyme disease and syphilis. The illness is characterized by periods of fever, chills, headaches, body aches, muscle aches and cough, alternating with periods when the fever subsides and the person feels relatively well. To minimize the risk of relapsing fever, follow tick precautions as outlined below and practice good personal hygiene at all times.

Tularemia, also known as 'rabbit fever,' is a bacterial infection that primarily affects rodents, rabbits and hares. Humans generally become infected through tick or deerfly bites or by handling the carcass of an infected animal. Occasional cases are caused by inhalation of an infectious aerosol. In Mexico, most cases occur in rural areas in the northern part of the country. Tularemia may develop as a flu-like illness, pneumonia or skin ulcers with swollen glands, depending upon how the infection is acquired. It usually responds well to antibiotics.

Rocky Mountain spotted fever is a tick-borne infection characterized by fever, headache and muscle aches, followed by a rash. Complications may include pneumonia, meningitis, gangrene and kidney failure, and may be life threatening. Cases have been reported from the central part of the country, the Yucatán peninsula and Jalisco State.

Onchocerciasis (river blindness) is caused by a roundworm invading the eye, leading to blindness. The infection is transmitted by black flies, which breed along the banks of rapidly flowing rivers and streams. In Mexico, the disease is reported from highland areas in the states of Oaxaca, Chiapas and Guerrero.

Typhus may be transmitted by lice in scattered pockets of the country.

HIV/AIDS has been reported from all Central American countries. Be sure to use condoms for all sexual encounters.

TRAVELERS' DIARRHEA

To prevent diarrhea, avoid tap water unless it has been boiled, filtered or chemically disinfected (iodine tablets); only eat fresh fruits or vegetables if cooked or peeled; be wary of dairy products that might contain unpasteurized milk; and be highly selective when eating food from street vendors.

If you develop diarrhea, be sure to drink plenty of fluids, preferably an oral rehydration solution containing lots of salt and sugar. A few loose stools don't require treatment, but if you start having more than four or five stools a day you should start taking an antibiotic (usually a quinolone drug) and an antidiarrheal agent (such as loperamide). If diarrhea is bloody or persists for more than 72 hours or is accompanied by fever, shaking chills or severe abdominal pain you should seek medical attention.

ENVIRONMENTAL HAZARDS & TREATMENT
Altitude Sickness

Altitude sickness may develop in travelers who ascend rapidly to altitudes greater than 2500m. Being physically fit does not lessen your risk of altitude sickness. It seems to be chiefly a matter of genetic predisposition. Those who have experienced altitude sickness in the past are prone to future episodes. The risk increases with faster ascents, higher altitudes and greater exertion. Symptoms may include headaches, nausea, vomiting, dizziness, malaise, insomnia and loss of appetite. Severe cases may be complicated by fluid in the lungs (high-altitude pulmonary edema) or swelling of the brain (high-altitude cerebral edema). Most deaths are caused by high-altitude pulmonary edema.

The standard medication to prevent altitude sickness is a mild diuretic called acetazolamide (Diamox), which should be started 24 hours before ascent and continued for 48 hours after arrival at altitude. Possible side effects include increased urination, numbness, tingling, nausea, drowsiness, nearsightedness and temporary impotence. For those who cannot tolerate acetazolamide, most physicians prescribe dexamethasone, which is a type of steroid. A natural alternative is gingko, which some people find quite helpful. The usual dosage is 100mg twice daily.

To lessen the chance of altitude sickness, you should also be sure to ascend gradually to higher altitudes, avoid overexertion, eat light meals and avoid alcohol.

The symptoms of altitude sickness develop gradually so that, with proper care, serious complications can usually be prevented. If you or any of your companions show any symptoms of altitude sickness, you should not ascend to a higher altitude until the symptoms have cleared. If the symptoms become worse or if someone shows signs of cerebral or pulmonary edema, such as trouble breathing or mental confusion, you must immediately descend to a lower altitude. A descent of 500m to 1000m is generally adequate except in cases of cerebral edema, which may require a greater descent. Supplemental oxygen is helpful if available. Acetazolamide and dexamethasone may be used to treat altitude sickness as well as prevent it.

Travel to high altitudes is generally not recommended for those with a history of heart disease, lung disease, or sickle cell disease. It is also not recommended for pregnant women.

Mosquito Bites

To prevent mosquito bites, wear long sleeves, long pants, hats and shoes (rather than sandals). Bring along a good insect repellent, preferably one containing DEET, which should be applied to exposed skin and clothing, but not to eyes, mouth, cuts, wounds or irritated skin. Products containing lower concentrations of DEET are as effective, but for shorter periods of time. In

HEALTH

general, adults and children over 12 should use preparations containing 25% to 35% DEET, which usually lasts about six hours. Children between two and 12 years of age should use preparations containing no more than 10% DEET, applied sparingly, which will usually last about three hours. Neurological toxicity has been reported from DEET, especially in children, but appears to be extremely uncommon and generally related to overuse. Don't use DEET-containing compounds on children under age two.

Insect repellents containing certain botanical products, including oil of eucalyptus and soybean oil, are effective but last only 1½ to 2 hours. Where there is a high risk of malaria or yellow fever, use DEET-containing repellents. Products based on citronella are not effective.

For additional protection, apply permethrin to clothing, shoes, tents and bed nets. Permethrin treatments are safe and remain effective for at least two weeks, even when items are laundered. Permethrin should not be applied directly to skin.

Don't sleep with the window open unless there is a screen. If sleeping outdoors or in accommodation that allows entry of mosquitoes, use a bed net treated with permethrin, with edges tucked in under the mattress. The mesh size should be less than 1.5mm. Alternatively, use a mosquito coil, which will fill the room with insecticide through the night. Repellent-impregnated wristbands are not effective.

Tick Bites

To protect yourself from tick bites, follow the same precautions as for mosquitoes, except that boots are preferable to shoes, with pants tucked in. Be sure to perform a thorough tick check at the end of each day. You'll generally need the assistance of a friend or mirror for a full examination. Remove ticks with tweezers, grasping them firmly by the head. Insect repellents based on botanical products, described above, have not been adequately studied for insects other than mosquitoes and cannot be recommended to prevent tick bites.

Water

Tap water in Mexico is generally not safe to drink. Vigorous boiling for one minute is the most effective means of water purifica-

tion. At altitudes greater than 2000m, boil for three minutes.

Another option is to disinfect water with iodine pills. Instructions are usually enclosed and should be carefully followed. Or you can add 2% tincture of iodine to one quart or liter of water (five drops to clear water, 10 drops to cloudy water) and let stand for 30 minutes. If the water is cold, a longer time may be required. The taste of iodinated water can be improved by adding vitamin C (ascorbic acid). Don't consume iodinated water for more than a few weeks. Pregnant women, those with a history of thyroid disease and those allergic to iodine should not drink iodinated water.

A number of water filters are on the market. Those with smaller pores (reverse osmosis filters) provide the broadest protection, but they are relatively large and are readily plugged by debris. Those with somewhat larger pores (microstrainer filters) are ineffective against viruses, although they remove other organisms. Manufacturers' instructions must be carefully followed.

Sun

To protect yourself from excessive sun exposure, you should stay out of the midday sun, wear sunglasses and a wide-brimmed hat, and apply sunscreen with SPF 15 or higher, providing both UVA and UVB protection. Sunscreen should be generously applied to all exposed parts of the body approximately 30 minutes before sun exposure and be reapplied after swimming or vigorous activity. Drink plenty of fluids and avoid strenuous exercise when the temperature is high.

Air Pollution

Air pollution may be a significant problem, especially in Mexico City and Guadalajara. Pollution is typically most severe from December to May. Travelers with respiratory or cardiac conditions and those who are elderly or extremely young are at greatest risk for complications from air pollution, which may include cough, difficulty breathing, wheezing or chest pain. Minimize the risk by staying indoors, avoiding outdoor exercise and drinking plenty of fluids.

Animal Bites

Do not attempt to pet, handle or feed any animal, with the exception of domestic animals known to be free of any infectious disease. Most animal injuries are directly related to a person's attempt to touch or feed the animal.

Any bite or scratch by a mammal, including bats, should be promptly and thoroughly cleansed with large amounts of soap and water, followed by application of an antiseptic such as iodine or alcohol. Contact the local health authorities immediately for possible postexposure treatment, whether or not you've been immunized against rabies. It may also be advisable to start an antibiotic, since wounds caused by animal bites and scratches frequently become infected. One of the newer quinolones, such as levofloxacin (Levaquin), which many travelers carry in case of diarrhea, would be an appropriate choice.

Snake & Scorpion Bites

Venomous snakes in Central America include the bushmaster, fer-de-lance, coral snake and various species of rattlesnakes. The fer-de-lance is the most lethal. It generally does not attack without provocation, but may bite humans who accidentally come too close as its lies camouflaged on the forest floor. The bushmaster is the world's largest pit viper, measuring up to 4m in length. Like other pit vipers, the bushmaster has a heat-sensing pit between the eye and nostril on each side of its head, which it uses to detect the presence of warm-blooded prey.

Coral snakes are somewhat retiring and tend not to bite humans. North of Mexico City, all coral snakes have a red, yellow, black, yellow, red banding pattern, with red and yellow touching, in contrast to nonvenomous snakes, where the red and yellow bands are separated by black. South of Mexico City, the banding patterns become more complex and this distinction is not useful.

In the event of a venomous snake bite, place the victim at rest, keep the bitten area immobilized, and move them immediately to the nearest medical facility. Avoid tourniquets, which are no longer recommended.

TRADITIONAL MEDICINE

Problem	Treatment
jet lag	melatonin
motion sickness	ginger
mosquito bite prevention	oil of eucalyptus, soybean oil

Scorpions are a problem in many states. If stung, you should immediately apply ice or cold packs, immobilize the affected body part and go to the nearest emergency room. To prevent scorpion stings, be sure to inspect and shake out clothing, shoes and sleeping bags before use, and wear gloves and protective clothing when working around piles of wood or leaves.

CHILDREN & PREGNANT WOMEN

In general, it's safe for children and pregnant women to go to Mexico. However, because some of the vaccines listed previously are not approved for use in children and pregnancy, these travelers should be particularly careful not to drink tap water or consume any questionable food or beverage. Also, when traveling with children, make sure they're up to date on all routine immunizations. It's sometimes appropriate to give children some of their vaccines a little early before visiting a developing nation. You should discuss this with your pediatrician. If pregnant, bear in mind that should a complication such as premature labor develop while abroad, the quality of medical care may not be comparable to that in your home country.

Since yellow fever vaccine is not recommended for pregnant women or children less than nine months old, if you are arriving from a country with yellow fever, obtain a waiver letter, preferably written on letterhead stationery and bearing the stamp used by official immunization centers to validate the International Certificate of Vaccination.

HEALTH

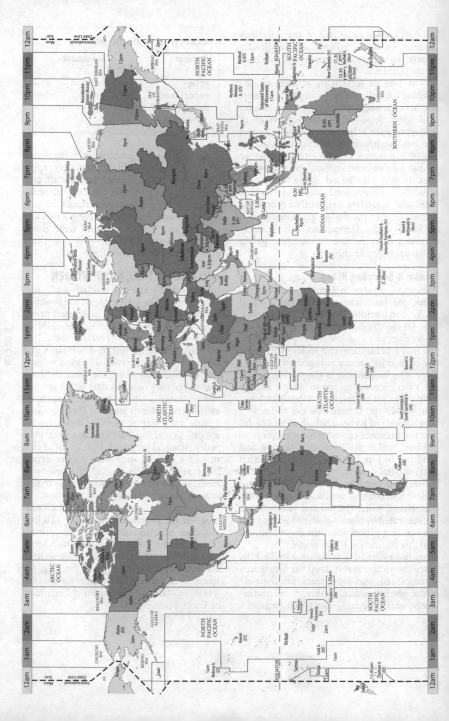

Language

CONTENTS

The predominant language of Mexico is Spanish. Mexican Spanish is unlike Castilian Spanish (the language of much of Spain) in two main respects: in Mexico the Castilian lisp has more or less disappeared and numerous indigenous words have been adopted. About 50 indigenous languages are spoken as a first language by more than seven million people, and about 15% of these don't speak Spanish.

Travelers in cities, towns and larger villages can almost always find someone who speaks at least some English. All the same, it is advantageous and courteous to know at least a few words and phrases in Spanish. Mexicans will generally respond much more positively if you attempt to speak to them in their own language.

It's easy enough to pick up some basic Spanish, and for those who want to learn the language in greater depth, courses are available in several cities in Mexico (see 'Courses' in the 'Directory' chapter on p949). You can also study books, records and tapes before you leave home. These resources are often available free at public libraries. Evening or college courses are also an excellent way to get started. For words and phrases for use when dining, see Eat Your Words on p90.

For a more comprehensive guide to the Spanish of Mexico, get a copy of Lonely Planet's *Mexican Spanish Phrasebook*.

PRONUNCIATION

Spanish spelling is phonetically consistent, meaning that there's a clear and consistent relationship between what you see in writing and how it's pronounced. In addition, most Spanish sounds have English equivalents, so English speakers shouldn't have too much trouble being understood.

Vowels

a	as in 'father'
e	as in 'met'
i	as in 'marine'
o	as in 'or' (without the 'r' sound)
u	as in 'rule'; the 'u' is not pronounced after **q** and in the letter combinations **gue** and **gui**, unless it's marked with a diaeresis (eg *argüir*), in which case it's pronounced as English 'w'
y	at the end of a word or when it stands alone, it's pronounced as the Spanish **i** (eg *ley*); between vowels within a word it's as the 'y' in 'yonder'

Consonants

As a rule, Spanish consonants resemble their English counterparts. The exceptions are listed below.

While the consonants **ch**, **ll** and **ñ** are generally considered distinct letters, **ch** and **ll** are now often listed alphabetically under **c** and **l** respectively. The letter **ñ** is still treated as a separate letter and comes after **n** in dictionaries.

b	similar to English 'b,' but softer; referred to as 'b larga'
c	as in 'celery' before **e** and **i**; otherwise as English 'k'
ch	as in 'church'
d	as in 'dog,' but between vowels and after **l** or **n**, the sound is closer to the 'th' in 'this'
g	as the 'ch' in the Scottish *loch* before **e** and **i** ('kh' in our guides to pronunciation); elsewhere, as in 'go'
h	invariably silent. If your name begins with this letter, listen carefully if you're waiting for public officials to call you.

LANGUAGE

j as the 'ch' in the Scottish *loch* (written as 'kh' in our guides to pronunciation)

ll as the 'y' in 'yellow'

ñ as the 'ni' in 'onion'

r a short **r** except at the beginning of a word, and after **l**, **n** or **s**, when it's often rolled

rr very strongly rolled

v similar to English 'b,' but softer; referred to as 'b corta'

x usually pronounced as **j** above; in some indigenous place names it's pronounced as an 's'; as in 'taxi' in other instances

z as the 's' in 'sun'

Word Stress

In general, words ending in vowels or the letters **n** or **s** have stress on the next-to-last syllable, while those with other endings have stress on the last syllable. Thus *vaca* (cow) and *caballos* (horses) both carry stress on the next-to-last syllable, while *ciudad* (city) and *infeliz* (unhappy) are both stressed on the last syllable.

Written accents will almost always appear in words that don't follow the rules above, eg *sótano* (basement), *América* and *porción* (portion).

GENDER & PLURALS

In Spanish, nouns are either masculine or feminine, and there are rules to help determine gender (there are of course some exceptions). Feminine nouns generally end with -**a** or with the groups -**ción**, -**sión** or -**dad**. Other endings typically signify a masculine noun. Endings for adjectives also change to agree with the gender of the noun they modify (masculine/feminine -**o**/-**a**). Where both masculine and feminine forms are included in this language guide, they are separated by a slash, with the masculine form first, eg *perdido/a*.

If a noun or adjective ends in a vowel, the plural is formed by adding **s** to the end. If it ends in a consonant, the plural is formed by adding **es** to the end.

ACCOMMODATIONS

I'm looking for ...	*Estoy buscando ...*	e·stoy boos·kan·do ...
Where is ...?	*¿Dónde hay ...?*	don·de ai ...
a cabin	*una cabaña*	oo·na ca·ba·nya
a camping ground	*un área para acampar*	oon a·re·a pa·ra a·kam·par
a guesthouse	*una pensión*	oo·na pen·syon
a hotel	*un hotel*	oon o·tel
a lodging house	*una casa de huespedes*	oo·na ka·sa de wes·pe·des
a posada	*una posada*	oo·na po·sa·da
a youth hostel	*un albergue juvenil*	oon al·ber·ge khoo·ve·neel

Are there any rooms available?

¿Hay habitaciones libres?	ay a·bee·ta·syon·es lee·bres	

I'd like a ... room.	*Quisiera una habitación ...*	kee·sye·ra·na a·bee·ta·syon ...
double	*doble*	do·ble
single	*individual*	een·dee·vee·dwal
twin	*con dos camas*	kon dos ka·mas

MAKING A RESERVATION

(for phone or written requests)

To ...	*A ...*
From ...	*De ...*
Date	*Fecha*
I'd like to book ...	*Quisiera reservar ...* (see the list under 'Accommodations' for bed and room options)
in the name of ...	*en nombre de ...*
for the nights of ...	*para las noches del ...*
credit card ...	*tarjeta de crédito ...*
number	*número*
expiry date	*fecha de vencimiento*
Please confirm ...	*Puede confirmar ...*
availability	*la disponibilidad*
price	*el precio*

How much is it per ...?	*¿Cuánto cuesta por ...?*	kwan·to kwes·ta por ...
night	*noche*	no·che
person	*persona*	per·so·na
week	*semana*	se·ma·na
full board	*pensión completa*	pen·syon kom·ple·ta
private/shared bathroom	*baño privado/ compartido*	ba·nyo pree·va·do/ kom·par·tee·do
too expensive	*demasiado caro*	de·ma·sya·do ka·ro
cheaper	*más económico*	mas e·ko·no·mee·ko
discount	*descuento*	des·kwen·to

Does it include breakfast?

¿Incluye el desayuno?   een-*kloo*-ye el de-sa-*yoo*-no

May I see the room?

¿Puedo ver la   *pwe*-do ver la
habitación?   a-bee-ta-*syon*

I don't like it.

No me gusta.   no me *goos*-ta

It's fine. I'll take it.

Está bien. La tomo.   es-*ta* byen la *to*-mo

I'm leaving now.

Me voy ahora.   me *voy* a-o-ra

CONVERSATION & ESSENTIALS

When approaching a stranger for information you should always extend a greeting, and use only the polite form of address, especially with the police and public officials. Young people may be less likely to expect this, but it's best to stick to the polite form unless you're quite sure you won't offend by using the informal mode. The polite form is used in all cases in this guide; where options are given, the form is indicated by the abbreviations 'pol' and 'inf.'

Saying *por favor* (please) and *gracias* (thank you) are second nature to most Mexicans and a recommended tool in your travel kit.

Hi.	*Hola.*	*o*-la (inf)
Hello.	*Buen día.*	*bwe*-n dee-a
Good morning.	*Buenos días.*	*bwe*-nos dee-as
Good afternoon.	*Buenas tardes.*	*bwe*-nas tar-des
Good evening/	*Buenas noches.*	*bwe*-nas no-ches
night.		
Goodbye.	*Adiós.*	a-*dyos*
Bye/See you soon.	*Hasta luego.*	as-ta *lwe*-go
Yes.	*Sí.*	see
No.	*No.*	no
Please.	*Por favor.*	por fa-*vor*
Thank you.	*Gracias.*	*gra*-syas
Many thanks.	*Muchas gracias.*	*moo*-chas *gra*-syas
You're welcome.	*De nada.*	de *na*-da
Apologies.	*Perdón.*	per-*don*
May I?	*Permiso.*	per-*mee*-so
(when asking permission)		
Excuse me.	*Disculpe.*	dees-*kool*-pe
(used before a request or when apologizing)		

How are things?

¿Qué tal?   ke tal

What's your name?

¿Cómo se llama usted?   *ko*-mo se *ya*-ma oo-*sted* (pol)
¿Cómo te llamas?   *ko*-mo te *ya*-mas (inf)

My name is ...

Me llamo ...   me *ya*-mo ...

It's a pleasure to meet you.

Mucho gusto.   *moo*-cho *goos*-to

The pleasure is mine.

El gusto es mío.   el *goos*-to es *mee*-o

Where are you from?

¿De dónde es/eres?   de *don*-de es/*er*-es (pol/inf)

I'm from ...

Soy de ...   soy de ...

Where are you staying?

¿Dónde está alojado?   *don*-de es-*ta* a-lo-*kha*-do (pol)
¿Dónde estás alojado?   *don*-de es-*tas* a-lo-*kha*-do (inf)

May I take a photo?

¿Puedo sacar una foto?   *pwe*-do sa-*kar* oo-na *fo*-to

SIGNS

Entrada	Entrance
Salida	Exit
Información	Information
Abierto	Open
Cerrado	Closed
Prohibido	Prohibited
Comisaria	Police Station
Servicios/Baños	Toilets
Hombres/Varones	Men
Mujeres/Damas	Women

DIRECTIONS

How do I get to ...?

¿Cómo llego a ...?   *ko*-mo ye-go a ...

Is it far?

¿Está lejos?   es-*ta* le-khos

Go straight ahead.

Siga/Vaya derecho.   *see*-ga/*va*-ya de-*re*-cho

Turn left.

Voltée a la izquierda.   vol-*te*-e a la ees-*kyer*-da

Turn right.

Voltée a la derecha.   vol-*te*-e a la de-*re*-cha

Can you show me (on the map)?

¿Me lo podría señalar   me lo po-*dree*-a se-nya-*lar*
(en el mapa)?   (en el *ma*-pa)

north	*norte*	*nor*-te
south	*sur*	soor
east	*este*	*es*-te
west	*oeste*	o-*es*-te
here	*aquí*	a-*kee*
there	*ahí*	a-*ee*
avenue	*avenida*	a-ve-*nee*-da
block	*cuadra*	*kwa*-dra
street	*calle/paseo*	*ka*-lye/pa-*se*-o

LANGUAGE

EMERGENCIES

Help!	¡Socorro!	so·ko·ro
Fire!	¡Fuego!	fwe·go
I've been robbed.	Me han robado.	me an ro·ba·do
Go away!	¡Déjeme!	de·khe·me
Get lost!	¡Váyase!	va·ya·se
Call ...!	¡Llame a ...!	ya·me a
the police	la policía	la po·lee·see·a
a doctor	un médico	oon me·dee·ko
an ambulance	una ambulancia	oo·na am·boo·lan·sya

It's an emergency.
Es una emergencia.   es oo·na e·mer·khen·sya
Could you help me, please?
¿Me puede ayudar, por favor?   me pwe·de a·yoo·dar por fa·vor
I'm lost.
Estoy perdido/a.   es·toy per·dee·do/a
Where are the toilets?
¿Dónde están los baños?   don·de es·tan los ba·nyos

HEALTH

I'm sick.
Estoy enfermo/a.   es·toy en·fer·mo/a
I need a doctor.
Necesito un doctor.   ne·se·see·to oon dok·tor
Where's the hospital?
¿Dónde está el hospital?   don·de es·ta el os·pee·tal
I'm pregnant.
Estoy embarazada.   es·toy em·ba·ra·sa·da
I've been vaccinated.
Estoy vacunado/a.   es·toy va·koo·na·do/a

I'm allergic to ...	Soy alérgico/a a ...	soy a·ler·khee·ko/a a ...
antibiotics	los antibióticos	los an·tee·byo·tee·kos
penicillin	la penicilina	la pe·nee·see·lee·na
nuts	las fruta secas	las froo·tas se·kas

I'm ...	Soy ...	soy ...
asthmatic	asmático/a	as·ma·tee·ko/a
diabetic	diabético/a	dya·be·tee·ko/a
epileptic	epiléptico/a	e·pee·lep·tee·ko/a

I have ...	Tengo ...	ten·go ...
diarrhea	diarrea	dya·re·a
nausea	náusea	now·se·a
a headache	un dolor de cabeza	oon do·lor de ka·be·sa
a cough	tos	tos

LANGUAGE DIFFICULTIES

Do you speak (English)?
¿Habla/Hablas (inglés)?   a·bla/a·blas (een·gles) (pol/inf)
Does anyone here speak English?
¿Hay alguien que hable inglés?   ai al·gyen ke a·ble een·gles
I (don't) understand.
(No) Entiendo.   (no) en·tyen·do
How do you say ...?
¿Cómo se dice ...?   ko·mo se dee·se ...
What does ...mean?
¿Qué significa ...?   ke seeg·nee·fee·ka ...

Could you please ...?	¿Puede ..., por favor?	pwe·de ... por fa·vor
repeat that	repetirlo	re·pe·teer·lo
speak more slowly	hablar más despacio	a·blar mas des·pa·syo
write it down	escribirlo	es·kree·beer·lo

NUMBERS

1	uno	oo·no
2	dos	dos
3	tres	tres
4	cuatro	kwa·tro
5	cinco	seen·ko
6	seis	says
7	siete	sye·te
8	ocho	o·cho
9	nueve	nwe·ve
10	diez	dyes
11	once	on·se
12	doce	do·se
13	trece	tre·se
14	catorce	ka·tor·se
15	quince	keen·se
16	dieciséis	dye·see·says
17	diecisiete	dye·see·sye·te
18	dieciocho	dye·see·o·cho
19	diecinueve	dye·see·nwe·ve
20	veinte	vayn·te
21	veintiuno	vayn·tee·oo·no
30	treinta	trayn·ta
31	treinta y uno	trayn·ta ee oo·no
40	cuarenta	kwa·ren·ta
50	cincuenta	seen·kwen·ta
60	sesenta	se·sen·ta
70	setenta	se·ten·ta
80	ochenta	o·chen·ta
90	noventa	no·ven·ta
100	cien	syen
101	ciento uno	syen·to oo·no
200	doscientos	do·syen·tos
1000	mil	meel
5000	cinco mil	seen·ko meel

PAPERWORK

birth certificate	certificado de nacimiento
border (frontier)	la frontera
car-owner's title	título de propiedad
car registration	registración
customs	aduana
driver's license	licencia de manejar
identification	identificación
immigration	migración
insurance	seguro
passport	pasaporte
temporary vehicle import permit	permiso de importación temporal de vehículo
tourist card	tarjeta de turista
visa	visado

SHOPPING & SERVICES

I'd like to buy ...
Quisiera comprar ...   kee·sye·ra kom·prar ...
I'm just looking.
Sólo estoy mirando.   so·lo es·toy mee·ran·do
May I look at it?
¿Puedo verlo/la?   pwe·do ver·lo/la
How much is it?
¿Cuánto cuesta?   kwan·to kwes·ta
That's too expensive for me.
Es demasiado caro   es de·ma·sya·do ka·ro
para mí.   pa·ra mee
Could you lower the price?
¿Podría bajar un poco   po·dree·a ba·khar oon po·ko
el precio?   el pre·syo
I don't like it.
No me gusta.   no me goos·ta
I'll take it.
Lo llevo.   lo ye·vo

Do you accept ...?	¿Aceptan ...?	a·sep·tan ...
American dollars	dólares americanos	do·la·res a·me·ree·ka·nos
credit cards	tarjetas de crédito	tar·khe·tas de kre·dee·to
traveler's checks	cheques de viajero	che·kes de vya·khe·ro

less	menos	me·nos
more	más	mas
large	grande	gran·de
small	pequeño/a	pe·ke·nyo/a

I'm looking for (the) ...	Estoy buscando ...	es·toy boos·kan·do
ATM	el cajero automático	el ka·khe·ro ow·to·ma·tee·ko

bank	el banco	el ban·ko
bookstore	la librería	la lee·bre·ree·a
exchange house	la casa de cambio	la ka·sa de kam·byo
general store	la tienda	la tyen·da
laundry	la lavandería	la la·van·de·ree·a
market	el mercado	el mer·ka·do
pharmacy/ chemist	la farmacia	la far·ma·sya
post office	la officina de correos	la o·fee·see·na de ko·re·os
supermarket	el supermercado	el soo·per·mer·ka·do
tourist office	la oficina de turismo	la o·fee·see·na de too·rees·mo

What time does it open/close?
¿A qué hora abre/cierra?
a ke o·ra a·bre/sye·ra
I want to change some money/traveler's checks.
Quisiera cambiar dinero/cheques de viajero.
kee·sye·ra kam·byar dee·ne·ro/che·kes de vya·khe·ro
What is the exchange rate?
¿Cuál es el tipo de cambio?
kwal es el tee·po de kam·byo
I want to call ...
Quisiera llamar a ...
kee·sye·ra lya·mar a ...

airmail	correo aéreo	ko·re·o a·e·re·o
letter	carta	kar·ta
registered (mail)	certificado	ser·tee·fee·ka·do
stamps	timbres	teem·bres

TIME & DATES

What time is it?	¿Qué hora es?	ke o·ra es
It's one o'clock.	Es la una.	es la oo·na
It's seven o'clock.	Son las siete.	son las sye·te
Half past two.	Dos y media.	dos ee me·dya
midnight	medianoche	me·dya·no·che
noon	mediodía	me·dyo·dee·a
half past two	dos y media	dos ee me·dya

now	ahora	a·o·ra
today	hoy	oy
tonight	esta noche	es·ta no·che
tomorrow	mañana	ma·nya·na
yesterday	ayer	a·yer

Monday	lunes	loo·nes
Tuesday	martes	mar·tes
Wednesday	miércoles	myer·ko·les
Thursday	jueves	khwe·ves
Friday	viernes	vyer·nes
Saturday	sábado	sa·ba·do
Sunday	domingo	do·meen·go

LANGUAGE

January	enero	e·*ne*·ro
February	febrero	fe·*bre*·ro
March	marzo	*mar*·so
April	abril	a·*breel*
May	mayo	*ma*·yo
June	junio	*khoo*·nyo
July	julio	*khoo*·lyo
August	agosto	a·*gos*·to
September	septiembre	sep·*tyem*·bre
October	octubre	ok·*too*·bre
November	noviembre	no·*vyem*·bre
December	diciembre	dee·*syem*·bre

TRANSPORT
Public Transport

What time does	¿A qué hora ...	a ke *o*·ra ...
... leave/arrive?	sale/llega?	sa·le/*ye*·ga
the boat	el barco	el *bar*·ko
the bus (city)	el camión	el ka·*myon*
the bus (intercity)	el autobus	el *ow*·to·*boos*
the minibus	el pesero	el pe·*se*·ro
the plane	el avión	el a·*vyon*
the train	el tren	el tren

the airport	el aeropuerto	el a·e·ro·*pwer*·to
the bus station	la estación de	la es·ta·*syon* de
	autobuses	ow·to·*boo*·ses
the bus stop	la parada de	la pa·*ra*·da de
	autobuses	ow·to·*boo*·ses
a luggage locker	un casillero	oon ka·see·*ye*·ro
the ticket office	la taquilla	la ta·*kee*·ya

A ticket to ..., please.
Un boleto a ..., por favor.   oon bo·*le*·to a ... por fa·*vor*
What's the fare to ...?
¿Cuánto cuesta hasta ...?   kwan·to *kwes*·ta a·sta ...

student's	de estudiante	de es·*too·dyan*·te
1st class	primera clase	pree·*me*·ra *kla*·se
2nd class	segunda clase	se·*goon*·da *kla*·se
single/one-way	viaje sencillo	vee·*a*·khe sen·*see*·yo
return/round trip	redondo	re·*don*·do
taxi	taxi	*tak*·see

Private Transport

I'd like to	Quisiera	kee·*sye*·ra
hire a/an ...	rentar ...	ren·*tar* ...
4WD	un cuator por	oon *kwa*·tro por
	cuatro	*kwa*·tro
car	un coche	oon *ko*·che
motorbike	una moto	*oo*·na *mo*·to

bicycle	bicicleta	bee·see·*kle*·ta
hitchhike	pedir aventón	pe·*deer* a·ven·*ton*
pickup (ute)	pickup	*pee*·kop
truck	camión	ka·*myon*

ROAD SIGNS

Though Mexico mostly uses the familiar international road signs, you should be prepared to encounter these other signs as well:

Acceso	Entrance
Aparcamiento	Parking
Camino en Reparación	Road Repairs
Ceda el Paso	Give way
Conserve Su Derecha	Keep to the Right
Curva Peligrosa	Dangerous Curve
Derrumbes	Landslides
Despacio	Slow
Desviación	Detour
Dirección Única	One-way
Escuela (Zona Escolar)	School (zone)
Hombres Trabajando	Men at Work
Mantenga Su Derecha	Keep to the Right
No Adelantar	No Passing
No Hay Paso	Road Closed
No Rebase	No Overtaking
Pare/Stop	Stop
Peaje	Toll
Peligro	Danger
Prepare Su Cuota	Have Toll Ready
Prohibido Aparcar/ No Estacionar	No Parking
Prohibido el Paso	No Entry
Puente Angosto	Narrow Bridge
Salida de Autopista	Exit Freeway
Topes/Vibradores	Speed Bumps
Tramo en Reparación	Road Under Repair
Vía Corta	Short Route (often a toll road)
Vía Cuota	Toll Highway

Where's a petrol station?
¿Dónde hay una   *don*·de ai oo·na
gasolinera?   ga·so·lee·*ne*·ra
How much is a liter of gasoline?
¿Cuánto cuesta el litro   kwan·to *kwes*·ta el *lee*·tro
de gasolina?   de ga·so·*lee*·na
Please fill it up.
Lleno, por favor.   *ye*·no por fa·*vor*
I'd like (20) pesos worth.
Quiero (veinte) litros.   *kye*·ro (*vayn*·te) *pe*·sos

diesel	diesel	*dee*·sel
leaded (regular)	gasolina con	ga·so·*lee*·na kon
	plomo	*plo*·mo
petrol (gas)	gasolina	ga·so·*lee*·na
unleaded	gasolina sin	ga·so·*lee*·na seen
	plomo	*plo*·mo

MEXICAN SLANG

Pepper your conversations with a few slang expressions! You'll hear many of these slang words and phrases all around Mexico, but others are particular to Mexico City.

¿Qué onda?
　　What's up?, What's happening?
¿Qué pasion? (Mexico City)
　　What's up?, What's going on?
¡Qué padre!
　　How cool!
fregón
　　really good at something, way cool, awesome
Este club está fregón.
　　This club is way cool.
El cantante es un fregón.
　　The singer is really awesome.
ser muy buena onda
　　to be really cool, nice
Mi novio es muy buena onda.
　　My boyfriend is really cool.
Eres muy buena onda.
　　You're really cool (nice).
pisto (in the north)
　　booze
alipús
　　booze
echarse un alipús, echarse un trago
　　to go get a drink
Echamos un alipús/trago.
　　Let's go have a drink.
tirar la onda
　　try to pick someone up, flirt
ligar
　　to flirt
irse de reventón
　　go partying
¡Vámonos de reventón!
　　Let's go party!
reven
　　a 'rave' (huge party with loud music and wild atmosphere)
un desmadre
　　a mess
Simón.
　　Yes.
Nel.
　　No.
No hay tos.
　　No problem. (literally 'there's no cough.')
¡Órale! (positive)
　　Sounds great! (responding to an invitation)

¡Órale! (negative)
　　What the *#&$!? (taunting exclamation)
¡Caray!
　　Shit!
¿Te cae?
　　Are you serious?
Me late.
　　Sounds really good to me.
Me vale.
　　I don't care, 'Whatever.'
Sale y vale.
　　I agree, Sounds good.
¡Paso sin ver!
　　I can't stand it!, No thank you!
¡Guácatelas! ¡Guácala!
　　How gross! That's disgusting!
¡Bájale!
　　Don't exaggerate!, Come on!
¡¿Chale?! (Mexico City)
　　No way!
¡Te pasas!
　　That's it! You've gone too far!
!No manches!
　　Get outta here!, You must be kidding!
un resto
　　a lot
lana
　　money, dough
carnal
　　brother
cuate, cuaderno
　　buddy
chavo
　　guy, dude
chava
　　girl, gal
jefe
　　father
jefa
　　mother
la tira, la julia
　　the police
la chota (Mexico City)
　　the police

LANGUAGE

oil	aceite	a-*say*-te
tire	llanta	yan-ta
puncture	agujero	a-goo-*khe*-ro

Is this the road to (...)?
¿Por acquí se va a (...)?
por a-*kee* se va a (...)

(How long) Can I park here?
¿(Por cuánto tiempo) Puedo estacionarme aquí?
(por *kwan*-to *tyem*-po) pwe-do ess-ta-syo-*nar*-me a-*kee*

Where do I pay?
¿Dónde se paga?
don-de se pa-ga

I need a mechanic/tow truck.
Necesito un mecánico/remolque.
ne-se-*see*-to oon me-*ka*-nee-ko/re-*mol*-ke

Is there a garage near here?
¿Hay un garaje cerca de aquí?
ai oon ga-*ra*-khe ser-ka de a-*kee*

The car has broken down (in ...).
El coche se descompuso (en ...)
el *ko*-che se des-kom-*poo*-so (en ...)

The motorbike won't start.
La moto no arranca.
la *mo*-to no a-*ran*-ka

I have a flat tire.
Tengo una llanta ponchada.
ten-go oo-na yan-ta pon-*cha*-da

I've run out of petrol.
Me quedé sin gasolina.
me ke-*de* seen ga-so-*lee*-na

I've had an accident.
Tuve un accidente.
too-ve oon ak-see-*den*-te

LANGUAGE

TRAVEL WITH CHILDREN

I need ...
Necesito ...
ne-se-*see*-to ...

Do you have ...?
¿Hay ...?
ai ...

a car baby seat
un asiento de seguridad para bebés
oon a-*syen*-to de se-goo-ree-*da* pa-ra be-*bes*

a child-minding service
oon club para niños
oon kloob pa-ra *nee*-nyos

a children's menu
un menú infantil
oon me-*noo* een-fan-*teel*

a creche
una guardería
oo-na gwar-de-*ree*-a

(disposable) diapers/nappies
pañales (de usar y tirar)
pa-*nya*-les de oo-*sar* ee tee-*rar*

an (English-speaking) babysitter
una niñera (que habla inglesa)
oo-na nee-*nye*-ra (ke *a*-bla een-*gle*-sa)

formula (milk)
leche en polvo
le-che en *pol*-vo

a highchair
una silla para bebé
oo-na *see*-ya pa-ra be-*be*

a potty
una bacinica
oo-na ba-see-*nee*-ka

a stroller
una carreola
oona ka-re-o-la

Do you mind if I breast-feed here?
¿Le molesta que dé el pecho aquí?
le mo-*les*-ta ke de el *pe*-cho a-*kee*

Are children allowed?
¿Se admiten niños?
se ad-*mee*-ten *nee*-nyos

Also available from Lonely Planet:
Mexican Spanish Phrasebook

Glossary

For more food and drink terms, also see the Food and Drink Glossary (p90); for transportation terms, see the Transportation chapter (p967); for general terms, see the Language chapter (p993).

AC – *antes de Cristo* (before Christ); equivalent to BC

adobe – sun-dried mud brick used for building

aduana – customs

agave – family of plants including the *maguey*

Alameda – name of formal parks in several Mexican cities

albergue de juventud – youth hostel

alfarería – potter's workshop

alfiz – rectangular frame around a curved arch; an Arabic influence on Spanish and Mexican buildings

Altiplano Central – dry plateau stretching across north central Mexico between the two Sierra Madre ranges

amate – paper made from tree bark

Ángeles Verdes – Green Angels; government-funded mechanics who patrol Mexico's major highways in green vehicles; they help stranded motorists with fuel and spare parts

antro – bar with (often loud) recorded music and usually some space to dance

Apdo – abbreviation for Apartado (Box) in addresses; hence Apdo Postal means Post Office Box

arroyo – brook, stream

artesanías – handicrafts, folk arts

atlas, atlantes (pl) – sculpted male figure(s) used instead of a pillar to support a roof or frieze; a *telamon*

atrium – churchyard, usually a big one

autopista – expressway, dual carriageway

azulejo – painted ceramic tile

bahía – bay

balneario – bathing place, often a natural hot spring

baluarte – bulwark, defensive wall

barrio – neighborhood of a town or city, often a poor neighborhood

billete – banknote

boleto – ticket

brujo/a – witch doctor, shaman; similar to *curandero/a*

burro – donkey

caballeros – literally 'horsemen,' but corresponds to 'gentlemen' in English; look for it on toilet doors

cabaña – cabin, simple shelter

cabina – Baja Californian term for a telephone *caseta*

cacique – regional warlord or political strongman

calle – street

callejón – alley

callejoneada – originally an Spanish tradition, still enjoyed in cities such as Guanajuato and Zacatecas, in which musicians lead a crowd of revelers through the streets, singing and telling stories as they go

calzada – grand boulevard or avenue

calzones – long baggy shorts worn by indigenous men

camarín – chapel beside the main altar in a church; contains ceremonial clothing for images of saints or the Virgin

camión – truck or bus

camioneta – pickup truck

campesino/a – country person, peasant

capilla abierta – open chapel; used in early Mexican monasteries for preaching to large crowds of indigenous people

casa de cambio – exchange house; place where currency is exchanged, faster to use than a bank

casa de huéspedes – cheap and congenial accommodations often to be found at a home converted into simple guest lodgings

caseta de larga distancia, caseta de teléfono, caseta telefónica – public telephone call station

cazuela – clay cooking pot; usually sold in a nested set

cenote – a limestone sinkhole filled with rainwater, used in Yucatán as a reservoir

central camionera – bus terminal

cerro – hill

Chac – Mayan rain god

chac-mool – pre-Hispanic stone sculpture of a hunched, belly-up figure; the stomach may have been used as a sacrificial altar

charreada – Mexican rodeo

charro – Mexican cowboy

chenes – well

chilango/a – citizen of Mexico City

chinampas – Aztec gardens built from lake mud and vegetation; versions still exist at Xochimilco, Mexico City

chingar – literally 'to fuck'; it has a wide range of colloquial usages in Mexican Spanish equivalent to those in English

chultún – cement-lined brick cistern found in the *chenes* (wells) region in the Puuc hills south of Mérida

Churrigueresque – Spanish late-baroque architectural style; found on many Mexican churches

cigarro – cigarette

clavadistas – the cliff divers of Acapulco and Mazatlán

Coatlicue – mother of the Aztec gods

colectivo – minibus or car that picks up and drops off passengers along a predetermined route; can also refer to other types of transport, such as boats, where passengers share the total fare

coleto/a – citizen of San Cristóbal de Las Casas

colonia – neighborhood of a city, often a wealthy residential area

combi – minibus

comida corrida – set lunch

completo – no vacancy, literally 'full up'; a sign you may see at hotel desks

conde – count (nobleman)

conquistador – early Spanish explorer-conqueror

cordillera – mountain range

correos – post office

coyote – person who smuggles Mexican immigrants into the USA

criollo – Mexican-born person of Spanish parentage; in colonial times considered inferior by peninsular Spaniards (see *gachupines, peninsulares*)

Cristeros – Roman Catholic rebels of the late 1920s

cuota – toll; a *vía cuota* is a toll road

curandero/a – literally 'curer'; a medicine man or woman who uses herbal and/or magical methods and often emphasizes spiritual aspects of disease

damas – ladies; the sign on toilet doors

danzantes – literally 'dancers'; stone carvings at Monte Albán

DC – *después de Cristo* (after Christ); equivalent to AD

de lujo – deluxe; often used with some license

de paso – a bus that began its route somewhere else, but stops to let passengers on or off at various points – often arriving late; a *local* bus is preferable

delegación – a large urban governmental subdivision in Mexico City comprising numerous *colonias*

descompuesto – broken, out of order

DF – Distrito Federal (Federal District); about half of Mexico City lies in the DF

edificio – building

ejido – communal landholding

embarcadero – jetty, boat landing

encomienda – a grant of indigenous labor or tribute to a *conquistador*; in return, the *conquistador* was supposed to protect the indigenous people in question and convert them to Catholicism, but in reality they were usually treated as little more than slaves

enramada – literally a bower or shelter, but it often refers to a thatch-covered, open-air restaurant

enredo – wraparound skirt

entremeses – hors d'oeuvres; also theatrical sketches, such as those performed during the Cervantino festival in Guanajuato

escuela – school

esq – abbreviation of *esquina* (corner) in addresses

estación de ferrocarril – train station

estípite – long, narrow, pyramid-shaped, upside-down pilaster; the hallmark of Churrigueresque architecture

ex-convento – former convent or monastery

excusado – toilet

faja – waist sash used in traditional indigenous costume

feria – fair or carnival, typically occurring during a religious holiday

ferrocarril – railway

ficha – a locker token available at bus terminals

fonda – inn

fraccionamiento – subdivision, housing development; similar to a *colonia*, often modern

frontera – a border between political entities

gachupines – derogatory term for the colonial *peninsulares*

giro – money order

gringo/a – US or Canadian (and sometimes European, Australasian etc) visitor to Latin America; can be used derogatorily

grito – literally 'shout'; the Grito de Dolores was the 1810 call to independence by parish priest Miguel Hidalgo, which sparked the struggle for independence from Spain

gruta – cave, grotto

guarache – also *huarache;* woven leather sandal, often with tire tread as the sole

guardería de equipaje – room for storing luggage (eg in a bus station)

guayabera – also *guayabarra;* man's shirt with pockets and appliquéd designs up the front, over the shoulders and down the back; worn in place of a jacket and tie in hot regions

güero/a – fair-haired, fair-complexioned person; a more polite alternative to *gringo/a*

hacendado – *hacienda* owner

hacha – flat carved-stone object from the Classic Veracruz civilization; connected with the ritual ball game

hacienda – estate; Hacienda (capitalized) is the Treasury Department

hay – there is, there are; you're equally likely to hear *no hay* (there isn't, there aren't)

henequén – agave fiber used to make sisal rope; grown particularly around Mérida

hombres – men; sign on toilet doors

huarache – see *guarache*

huevos – eggs; also slang for testicles

huipil, huipiles (pl) – indigenous woman's sleeveless tunic, usually highly decorated; can be thigh-length or reach the ankles

Huizilopochtli – Aztec tribal god

iglesia – church

INAH – Instituto Nacional de Antropología e Historia; the body in charge of most ancient sites and some museums

indígena – indigenous, pertaining to the original inhabitants of Latin America; can also refer to the people themselves

INI – Instituto Nacional Indigenista; set up in 1948 to improve the lot of indigenous Mexicans and to integrate them into society; sometimes accused of paternalism and trying to stifle protest

ISH – *impuesto sobre hospedaje*; lodging tax on the price of hotel rooms

isla – island

IVA – *impuesto de valor agregado*, or 'ee-bah'; a 15% sales tax added to the price of many items

ixtle – *maguey* fiber

jaguar – jaguar, a panther native to southern Mexico and Central America; principal symbol of the Olmec civilization

jai alai – the Basque game *pelota*, brought to Mexico by the Spanish; a bit like squash, played on a long court with curved baskets attached to the arm

jarocho/a – citizen of Veracruz

jefe – boss or leader, especially a political one

jipijapa – Yucatán name for a Panama hat

jorongo – small poncho worn by men

Kukulcán – Mayan name for the plumed serpent god Quetzalcóatl

lada – short for *larga distancia*

ladino – person of mixed (usually indigenous and Spanish) ancestry (ie most Mexicans)

lancha – fast, open, outboard boat

larga distancia – long-distance; usually refers to telephones

latifundio – large landholding; these sprang up after Mexico's independence from Spain

latifundista – powerful landowner who usurped communally owned land to form a *latifundio*

libramiento – road, highway

licenciado – university graduate, abbreviated as Lic and used as an honorific before a person's name; a status claimed by many who don't actually possess a degree

lista de correos – literally 'mail list,' a list displayed at a post office of people for whom letters are waiting; similar to General Delivery or Poste Restante

lleno – full, as with a car's fuel tank

local – can mean premises, such as a numbered shop or an office in a mall or block, or can mean local; a *local* bus is one whose route starts from the bus station you are in

machismo – Mexican masculine bravura

madre – literally 'mother,' but the term can also be used colloquially with an astonishing array of meanings

maguey – a type of agave, with thick pointed leaves growing straight out of the ground; *tequila* and *mezcal* are made from its sap

malecón – waterfront street, boulevard or promenade

mañana – literally 'tomorrow' or 'morning'; in some contexts it may just mean 'some time in the future'

maquiladora – assembly-plant operation, importing equipment, raw materials and parts for assembly or processing in Mexico, then exporting the products

mariachi – small ensemble of street musicians playing traditional ballads on guitars and trumpets

marimba – wooden xylophone-type instrument, popular in Veracruz and the south

Mayab – the lands of the Maya

mercado – market; often a building near the center of a town, with shops and open-air stalls in the surrounding streets

Mesoamerica – the region inhabited by the ancient Mexican and Mayan cultures

mestizaje – 'mixedness,' Mexico's mixed-blood heritage; officially an object of pride

mestizo – person of mixed (usually indigenous and Spanish) ancestry (ie most Mexicans)

metate – shallow stone bowl with legs, for grinding maize and other foods

Mexican Hat Dance – a courtship dance in which a girl and boy dance around the boy's hat

milpa – peasant's small cornfield, often cultivated by the slash-and-burn method

mirador, miradores (pl) – lookout point(s)

Montezuma's revenge – Mexican version of Delhi-belly or travelers' diarrhea

mordida – literally 'little bite,' a small bribe to keep the wheels of bureaucracy turning

mota – marijuana

Mudéjar – Moorish architectural style, imported to Mexico by the Spanish

mujeres – women; seen on toilet doors

municipio – small local-government area; Mexico is divided into 2394 of them

na – Mayan thatched hut

Nafta – North American Free Trade Agreement – see *TLC*

Náhuatl – language of the Nahua people, descendants of the Aztecs

naos – Spanish trading galleons

norteamericanos – North Americans, people from north of the US–Mexican border

Nte – abbreviation for *norte* (north), used in street names

Ote – abbreviation for *oriente* (east), used in street names

paceño/a – person from La Paz, Baja California Sur

palacio de gobierno – state capitol, state government headquarters

palacio municipal – town or city hall, headquarters of the municipal corporation

palapa – thatched-roof shelter, usually on a beach

palma – long, paddle-like, carved-stone object from the Classic Veracruz civilization; connected with the ritual ball game

panga – fiberglass skiff for fishing or whale-watching in Baja California

parada – bus stop, usually for city buses

parado – stationary, or standing up, as you often are on 2nd-class buses

parque nacional – national park; an environmentally protected area in which human exploitation is supposedly banned or restricted

parroquia – parish church

paseo – boulevard, walkway or pedestrian street; also the tradition of strolling in a circle around the plaza in the evening, men and women moving in opposite directions

Pemex – government-owned petroleum extraction, refining and retailing monopoly

peña – evening of Latin American folk songs, often with a political protest theme

peninsulares – those born in Spain and sent by the Spanish government to rule the colony in Mexico (see *criollo, gachupines*)

periférico – ring road

pesero – Mexico City's word for *colectivo*

petate – mat, usually made of palm or reed

peyote – a hallucinogenic cactus

pinacoteca – art gallery

piñata – clay pot or papier-mâché mold decorated to resemble an animal, pineapple, star etc; filled with sweets and gifts and smashed open at fiestas

playa – beach

plaza de toros – bullring

plazuela – small plaza

poblano/a – person from Puebla, or something in the style of Puebla

pollero – same as a *coyote*

Porfiriato – Porfirio Díaz's reign as president-dictator of Mexico for 30 years, until the 1910 revolution

portales – arcades

potosino – from the city or state of San Luis Potosí

presidio – fort or fort's garrison

PRI – Partido Revolucionario Institucional (Institutional Revolutionary Party); the political party that ruled Mexico for most of the 20th century

propina – tip; different from a *mordida*, which is closer to a bribe

Pte – abbreviation for *poniente* (west), used in street names

puerto – port

pulque – milky, low-alcohol brew made from the *maguey* plant

quechquémitl – indigenous woman's shoulder cape with an opening for the head; usually colorfully embroidered, often diamond-shaped

quetzal – crested bird with brilliant green, red and white plumage, native to southern Mexico, Central America and northern South America; quetzal feathers were highly prized in pre-Hispanic Mexico

Quetzalcóatl – plumed serpent god of pre-Hispanic Mexico

rebozo – long woolen or linen shawl covering the head or shoulders

refugio – a very basic cabin for shelter in the mountains

regiomontano/a – person from Monterrey

reja – wrought-iron window grille

reserva de la biósfera – biosphere reserve; an environmentally protected area where human exploitation is steered towards ecologically unharmful activities

retablo – altarpiece; or small painting on wood, tin, cardboard, glass etc, placed in a church to give thanks for miracles, answered prayers etc

río – river

s/n – *sin número* (without number); in street addresses

sacbé, sacbeob (pl) – ceremonial avenue(s) between great Mayan cities

sanatorio – hospital, particularly a small private one

sanitario – toilet, literally 'sanitary place'

sarape – blanket with opening for the head, worn as a cloak

Semana Santa – Holy Week, the week from Palm Sunday to Easter Sunday; Mexico's major holiday period, when accommodations and transport get very busy

servicios – toilets

sierra – mountain range

sitio – taxi stand

stele, steles or stelae (pl) – standing stone monument(s), usually carved

supermercado – supermarket; anything from a small corner store to a large, US-style supermarket

Sur – south; often seen in street names

taller – shop or workshop; a *taller mecánico* is a mechanic's shop, usually for cars; a *taller de llantas* is a tire-repair shop

talud-tablero – stepped building style typical of Teothuacán, with alternating vertical (*tablero*) and sloping (*talud*) sections

tapatío/a – person born in the state of Jalisco

taquilla – ticket window

telamon – statue of a male figure, used instead of a pillar to hold up the roof of a temple; see also *atlas*

telar de cintura – backstrap loom; the warp (lengthwise) threads are stretched between two horizontal bars, one of which is attached to a post or tree and the other to a strap around the weaver's lower back, and the weft (crosswise) threads are then woven in

teleférico – cable car

templo – church; anything from a chapel to a cathedral

teocalli – Aztec sacred precinct

Tezcatlipoca – multifaceted pre-Hispanic god, lord of life and death and protector of warriors; as a smoking mirror he could see into hearts, as the sun god he needed the blood of sacrificed warriors to ensure he would rise again

tezontle – light-red, porous volcanic rock used for buildings by the Aztecs and *conquistadores*

tianguis – Indigenous people's market

tienda – store

típico/a – characteristic of a region; particularly used to describe food

Tláloc – pre-Hispanic rain and water god

TLC – Tratado de Libre Comercio, the North American Free Trade Agreement (Nafta)

topes – speed bumps; found on the outskirts of many towns and villages, they are only sometimes marked by signs

trapiche – mill; in Baja California usually a sugar mill

tzompantli – rack for the skulls of Aztec sacrificial victims

UNAM – Universidad Nacional Autónoma de México (National Autonomous University of Mexico)

universidad – university

viajero/a – traveler

villa juvenil – youth sports center, often the location of an *albergue de juventud*

voladores – literally 'fliers,' the Totonac ritual in which men, suspended by their ankles, whirl around a tall pole

War of the Castes – bloody 19th-century Mayan uprising in the Yucatán Peninsula

were-jaguar – half-human, half-jaguar being, portrayed in Olmec art

yácata – ceremonial stone structure of the Tarascan civilization

yugo – U-shaped carved-stone object from the Classic Veracruz civilization; connected with the ritual ball game

zaguán – vestibule or foyer, sometimes a porch

zócalo – main plaza or square; a term used in some (but by no means all) Mexican towns

Zona Rosa – literally 'Pink Zone'; an area of expensive shops, hotels and restaurants in Mexico City frequented by the wealthy and tourists; by extension, a similar area in another city

Behind the Scenes

THIS BOOK

The 9th edition of *Mexico* was coordinated by John Noble, as were the last five editions. Past authors have included Doug Richmond, Dan Spitzer, Scott Wayne, Mark Balla, Wayne Bernhardson, Tom Brosnahan, Mark Honan, Nancy Keller and Scott Dogget as well as several authors of this edition. The Health chapter was written by Dr David Goldberg. Danny Palmerlee wrote the 'Hole Pozole!' boxed text (from *Mexico's Pacific Coast* guide). Author Sandra Bao's interesting asides also appear in this book. Neil Pyatt wrote the 'Oaxacan Art: the New Wave' box in the Oaxaca chapter, and Bruce Geddes wrote the 'Pulquerías: The Original Mexican Watering Hole' box in the Around Mexico City chapter.

THANKS from the Authors

John Noble Special thanks to Neil Pyatt, Danny Schechter and Myra Ingmanson for good company, hospitality, and for sharing their enormous knowledge of many things Mexican. And to all my 11 coauthors for info and tips and for sticking heroically to their task of not only updating the book but converting it to LP's new look, with rarely flagging enthusiasm despite an appalling barrage of style documents and amendments! And to the editors, cartographers and everyone else involved at LP Oakland and LP Melbourne for their skill, tact, good humour and patience in a very challenging task, above all Maria Donohoe for her dedication to getting the project moving at the start, and Commissioning Editor Suki Gear, who came cold to a

project already well under way and turned out to be a dream to work with.

Over in Melbourne, thank you Paul and Wendy for lending me your house, and thank you Peter and Kerry for lending me your laptop. Diverse thanks to Claudia and Yves, Ron Mader, Teresa Morales, Jonathan at Comala (Oaxaca), Dana Burton, Glenn and Ellen (Ocosingo) and Jorge Velasco. And thank you Harry Porter, Leo Meraz and Traviss Thomas for the fascinating facts I gleaned from you via Danny!

Sandra Bao Muchísimas gracias to every Mexican person I harassed for information at all those tourist offices, hotels, restaurants, bus terminals and street corners. Special thanks go to Stan Singleton and José Gutierrez, Walter and Bundy Illsley, Kevin Quigley and Arminda Flores, Charles Dews, and Steve and Maureen Rosenthal. And to my husband and soul mate, Ben Greensfelder, who accompanied me on this trip and enjoyed it as much as I did.

Susan Forsyth Special thanks to Gina Machorro from Puerto Escondido's tourist kiosk for her answers to multiple questions. Also in Puerto Escondido, Susan thanks Dan, Carmen and Isabel from El Cafecito for their help and patience with her constantly postponed arrival. In Puerto Ángel Gundi of Casa de Huéspedes Gundi y Tomas was, as usual, a mine of information, hospitable and good company. Fausto and Leila and Ana in San Agustinillo provided more good company and a

---

THE LONELY PLANET STORY

The story begins with a classic travel adventure: Tony and Maureen Wheeler's 1972 journey across Europe and Asia to Australia. There was no useful information about the overland trail then, so Tony and Maureen published the first Lonely Planet guidebook to meet a growing need.

From a kitchen table, Lonely Planet has grown to become the largest independent travel publisher in the world, with offices in Melbourne (Australia), Oakland (USA), London (UK) and Paris (France).

Today Lonely Planet guidebooks cover the globe. There is an ever-growing list of books and information in a variety of media. Some things haven't changed. The main aim is still to make it possible for adventurous travelers to get out there – to explore and better understand the world.

At Lonely Planet we believe travelers can make a positive contribution to the countries they visit – if they respect their host communities and spend their money wisely.

myriad of tips during Susan's mad dash around that beachside pueblo. In Huatulco, Gabriele Kratz of Buceo Sotavento was a terrific time saver with her invaluable titbits. Thanks too to children Isabella and Jack for putting up with Mum's hectic work schedule.

Beth Greenfield Thank you to the patient John Noble. Mil gracias to Rosario of Restaurant del Granero, who graciously led me out of confusing Torreón to the highway. And thank you Mom and Dad for inspiring me to travel, and to Kiki, for everything.

Michael Grosberg Thanks to all the strangers who helped me find my way and were always warm and kind. Special thanks to Pepe Quijano who became a fast friend in Monterrey, and for sharing his opinions and knowledge about the city, Mexico and the US. And to Jose Luis Enrique for his hospitality in Monterrey as well. Thanks also go out to Jerry and Susan Brite in Gómez Farías who took the time to teach me about birds and what makes birders tick and for an interesting drive into the mountains. And thanks also to Ricardo and Emilio Ebarra for the ride; otherwise I'd still be walking.

Morgan Konn Shouts out to Elaine, Wendy and Suki on the LP team. Muchisimo gracias Josephina en San Blas, Laura en Chacala, Paul, Rita y Victoria en Puerto Vallarta, Jim, Eva & Dewey en Troncones, Jeff, Nancy & George en Bucerias y los otres que yo no recuerdo. To Andres and my family, thanks for the support, encouragement and love.

Andrew Nystrom Mil gracias to Wendy, Suki, John, Danny and the LP crew; Barbra, John, Joe, Dolores and Morgan; Estela and Jon, Victoria Pratt, Leobardo Espinosa, the Virgin of Lujan and all the volunteer tope painters.

Michael Read Thanks to the many tourist offices, taxi drivers and random passersby who helped me find the hidden gems and cast out the stones. A meaningful nod goes to Ivan, Salvador and Yolanda of The 3 Amigos Canyon Expeditions in Creel for their friendship and tactical support, and to Luis F Trelles of Hermosillo, who revealed the subtle charms of that dusty desert metropolis. Michael gives muchas gracias to his stalwart travel companions Francesca 'Mulegé' Caprino, Lisa 'Tormenta' Colvin, and especially to his father, Kenneth 'Coot' Read, with whom he weathered the torrential rains of Bahuichivo.

Suzanne Plank Wendy Smith, thanks for inviting me on board. John Noble, thank you for your dedication and patience. Suki, it is a pleasure to work with you – thanks for everything. Ben, thank you so much for all your help; I'll never fill your sandals but it's been a joy to follow in your footsteps. Raúl y Geovanna, gracias por todo. Madeline (and Violene), thanks…for being. Nicole e Nelson, um abraço. Eduardo Rodriguez, muchísimas gracias por la hospitalidad; Lies, por la amistad. Shelley, thanks for the sunshine. Pirata, las estrellas.

Daniel Schechter Covering a city as vast as the DF is a formidable task, so I was fortunate to have the assistance of a number of people. Here's my chance to acknowledge their generous contributions of time and knowledge: Jeffrey A Wright kept me abreast of sports arcana and economic trends. The people at Bicitekas filled me in on the little-known practice of cycling in the Valle de México. Ricardo Castillo Mireles had much to say about bullfighting. Michael Schuessler and Brad Crownover enlightened me on gay culture in the capital. Paul Day, Nick Wilson, Miriam Martínez and Monica Campbell joined me on research forays, adding their invaluable ideas and opinions along the way. Special thanks are due to Carlos Mackinlay and Victor Heredia at Sectur GDF, and José Antonio Hernández and Olaf Carrera at American Chamber Mexico for answering my queries. Thank you, John Noble, for your usual thoughtful guidance throughout the research and writeup phases. Most of all, I want to thank my wife, Myra Ingmanson, for her huge contribution to the project. Myra's knowledge far exceeds my own in areas ranging from bus routes to Mac tools. Without her, I could not have done it.

Iain Stewart Above all thanks to Fiona (and Simone, Jan and Betty) for minding the fort – and the bairn – back home. In Mexico, my gratitude to Dana Burton for the gastro-tour of San Cristóbal and her many insights concerning her adopted city. I would also like to commend all the tourism personnel in Tabasco and Chiapas for putting up with my tedious questioning and quest for minutiae: Julio César Morales in Tuxtla, Gabriela Gudiño Gual in San Cristóbal and Karina Flores Hernádez in Tapachula were particularly patient. Thank you John Noble, the archaeologists Alfonso Morales and Julia Miller in Palenque for an illuminating morning, Chato and Enrique, Prem Cosio Villegas, the good people at Hospedaje Esmeralda, Nancy and David Orr and el gringo perdido in Puerto Arista. And Felix – let's hope the dating game with eMac works better next time!

Wendy Yanagihara For their expertise, help and kindness, thanks to Beatriz Jimenez and Antonio and Edgar in Tampico; José Bernabé, Karla Soria and Solomon Rodd in Xilitla; and Roy Dudley in Xalapa. Fuerte abrazos to Carmen & Henry in Xilitla, Gaudencio Simbrón González in Papantla, el chulo Fernando in Córdoba, and the table of 500 years in Veracruz. Thanks also to Elaine for getting me on the boat before jumping ship herself, and to Janey and Matt for letting me spread my papers and coffee mugs all over the dinner table.

CREDITS

Mexico 9 was commissioned and developed in Lonely Planet's Oakland office by Elaine Merrill, Maria Donohoe and Wendy Smith. Elaine and John Noble wrote the brief. Suki Gear came on board as Commissioning Editor when the authors were on the road. Cartography for this title was developed by Alison Lyall.

This sizable book had a tag team of coordinators: Rebecca Chau and Meg Worby (editorial) and Laurie Mikkelsen and Celia Wood (cartography). Susie Ashworth, Nina Rousseau, Kyla Gillzan, John Hinman, Jackey Coyle, Cherry Prior, Kate Evans, Katie Lynch, Carly Hall, Andrea Dobbin, Helen Yeates, Sally Steward, Holly Alexander and Sally O'Brien edited and proofed the book. Cartographic assistance was provided by Julie Sheridan, Owen Eszeki, Sarah Sloane, Anneka Imkamp, Andrew Smith, Barbara Benson, Tony Fankhauser and Wayne Murphy.

Vicki Beale and John Shippick laid the book out with assistance from Adam Bextream, Pablo Gastar, Katherine Marsh and Tamsin Wilson. The marvellous Gabbi Wilson shared editorial layout checking and layout, with help from Imogen Bannister and Brooke Lyons. Pepi Bluck designed the cover and Wendy Wright did the artwork. Quentin Frayne prepared the Language chapter. Victoria Harrison and Meg Worby prepared the index, assisted by Melanie Dankel. Overseeing production were Glenn van der Knijff (Project Manager) and Sally Darmody (Acting Project Manager), Darren O'Connell (Managing Editor) and Carolyn Boicos (Acting Managing Editor). Alison Lyall (Managing Cartographer) was assisted by Anthony Phelan.

THANKS from Lonely Planet

Many thanks to the hundreds of travelers who used the last edition and wrote to us with helpful hints, useful advice and interesting anecdotes:

A Tulio Aarun, Carmel Adelberg, Robert Adler, Anne-Grit Albrecht, Sanne L Albrectsen, Sid Anderson, Yeb Anema, Linda Anzalone, Sonia & George Archdale, Gillian Archibald, Cesar Arias, Lauren Armistead, Ruth Arnold, Kiersten Aschauer, Shara & Dev Atma, Monica Auger, David Authers, Carolina Avila, Francisco Luis Aviña-Cervantes **B** Eivor Back Salmonsson, Christine Baden, Roman Baedorf, Torsten Baeuerlen, Kevin Baitup, Klaus Bajohr-Mau, Lorraine Bajos, Ernest Baraniecki, Pashiera Barkhuysen, Ken Barnes, Jill Baron, Silke Baron, Anna Bassi, Greg Bauer, Vera Baumann, Ullvi Båve, Amanda Bayliss, Eva Bazant, Michael Beattie, Therese Beckman, Noreen Beg, Su-Li Beh, Ger Bekink, Margreet Bekker, Karolina Bengtsson, Esther Bergman, Stefanie Bernhard, Pierre Bernier, Danny Bernstein, Rory Bernstein, Alex Bertran, Adele Biagi, Lisa Bias, Patricia Bibb, Peter Bienstock, Albert Bihler, Liz Bissett, Mike Bissett, Aggie Black, Carol Blackburn, Vashti Blacker, Jan Blackman, Julia Blanc, Yves Blavet, Lee Blaylock, Susann Blum, Mary Boettcher, Lacy Boggs, Ondrea Boggs, Alberto Bollea, Richard Boltz, Trish Bondurant, Duane Bong, Laetitia Bonnet, Erica Boogers, Shirley Boudewijns, Tony Bourke, Ellen Bradbury-Reid, Richard Breakspear, A Bregman, Jo Brennan, Stephanie Brennan, Christine Brenner, Marko Brescak, Eleanor Bridger, Simon Briggs, Thomas Brooks, Steve Brough, Max Brouwers, Latoya Brown, Gerry Bryan, Michael Buckert, Nicole Buergin, Betty Buldan, Bette Jean Bullert, Lucy Burchmore, Dwight Burditt, Paul Burke, Mark Burton, Kressy Busch, Robert Wesley Butt, Brian Buuck **C** Catja Caemmerer, Stacey Cameron, Kate Camp, Jenny Campbell, Margaret Campbell, Paul Campbell, Douglas Campbell-Smith, Ellis Cane, Siobhan Canty, Anne Cariou, Marco Carlone, Ximena Carmona, Eleanor Carrington, James Carty, Rocio Castillo, Marianne Casto, Claire Catanach, Anthony Cawthorne, Mark Chamberlain, Iona Chamberlin, Silvia Chang,

Jane Charland, Peter Chartrand, Seth Chazin, Chan Hen Cheng, Wong Chi Lap, Elwin Chouinard, Chungwah Chow, Weihaw Chuang, Tina Clancy, Patrick Clarke, John Clayton, Andrew Clement, Ruth Clowes, E Coder, Dan Coffey, Rhonda Collis, George Comeau, James Condit, Gavan Connell, Eritrea Constantino, Kacey Cordes, Sergi Cormano Bel, Jerome Cosandey, Cathy Coulthard, Carol Courtney, Riff Coven, Stephaney Cox, Gareth Cross, Guy Crotty, Leonard Crowe, Emiliana Cruz, Dale Curtis **D** Liliana M D Valos, Jesper Dalgaard, Jan-Hendrik Damerau, Luisier Damien, Olle Danielsson, Jules Dares, M Davis, Kathy Davison, Justin Daza-Ritchie, Carla de Jonge, Willie de Kort, Henry De Marigny, Dan DeCoursey, Joyce Degens, Alexandra Delano, M Digel, Feng Ding, Pat Dobie, Anna Doddridge, Cara Dolan, Genevieve Dominguez, Gabi Dori, James du Bois, Keith Dumbleton, Huelo Dunn, Nathalie Dupraz, Jack Dwarswaard **E** Michael Eder, Joyce Edling, Carolann Edwards, David Eidell, Donald Eischen, John Eitzen, Lois Eley, Diane Elliott, R Ellis, Kilian Engel, Gundi Erhard, Rob Erickson, Tom & Karina Eriksen, Tandi Erlmann, Pamela Escobar, Mark Esposito, Nory Esteban, Robert Ettinger, Bob Evans, Michael Evoy **F** Alessandra Faleggi, Ray Farley, Max Farrar, Paul Fauset, Kim Felmingham, Elena Paula Fernandez, Araceli Fernandez, Macdara Ferris, Cecilia Fessler, Chris Field, Daniel Figueroa, Heather Finlay, Karin Fischenbeck, Jason R Fisher, Gary Fishman, Petra Fleck, Stephanie Fleming, Grant Fletcher, Melissa Floré, Annelies Florquin, Ben Flower, Andreas Foerster, Chris Ford, Robert Ford, Roy Forman, Barbara Fossati, David Foster, Brian Fowler, Claire Fraser, Helen Freimark, Kerstin Freudenthaler, Michael Friel, Val Friesen, Katia Fröhlich, Markus Fuchs, Andreas Funke **G** Linus Gabrielsson, Derek Gaither, Carlos R Galan Diaz, Sarah Gale, Daryl Galloway, Alejandro Gámez Handal, Jonathon Gandy, Alicia Juliana Garcia, Merav Gazit, Paul Gehrman, Sandra Gennai, Kris Genovese, Thomas Gentsch, Claudia Gerbino, Frank Gerritse, Roger Gerritzen, Valeria Ghisetti, Jill Gibbs, Kathleen Gibson, Gerald R Gilboe, Patrick Gill, Richard E Ginnold, Robert E Glass, Jeffrey Glazer, Jenny Glazer, Jean-Francois Gloux, Peter Godbeer, Grisha Golberg, Macario Gomes, Angela Gonzalez, Marco Gonzalez, Ernie Gorrie, LR & Silvia Gorski, Wessel Gossink, Hans-Herbert Gossmann, Stefan Graber, Sharon & Joe Graham, Jeff Granger, Francesco Greco, Brian Greene, Jeremy Greenwood, Bill Grimes, Dieter Groher, Hans-Herbert Grossmann, M Guenza, Paola Guido, Shaila Gupta, Steve Guthrie, Manuela Gutierrez Rebollo **H** Honza Haba, Marita Hagen, Enrico Halix, Camilla Hall, Lisa Hall, Peter Handel, Bob Haneveld, Mauricio Hanono, Julia Nicholson Harig, Jacob Harris, robbert Hart, Julie Hatfield, Juliette Hayes, Maria Healy, Lesley Hedges, Rickard Hedlund, Craig Heidig, Sharon Helgason, Tadeo Hernández, Joanne Heron, Carlos Herz, Jennifer Hess, Nancy Heuman, Vera Heybroek, Frank Hiatt, David Higgs, Kevin Hill, Michiel Hillenius, Matthias Hillenkamp, Pekka Hiltunen, Jill Himmelrick, Ana María Hintermann-Villamil, James Hodson, Tanya Hoeberechts, Sebastian Hoeft, Sebastian Hoffmann, Natalie Hohmann, Armin Holp, Daniel Houghton, Nicholas Houston, H Matthew Howarth, Rachel Howlett, Katy Howley, Celia Hoyles, Celina & Mirek Hrabanek, Margaret Huber, Michael Huerta, Fer Hurk, Maarten Hustinx, Jan Hutta, Brian Hyman, Natasha Hynes **I** Arnold Iniestra, Michael J Intintoli, Nadler Ishay, Patricia Ishimoto, Shamin Islam, Nikki & Goth Itoi J Nicki Jackson, Jennifer Jacobs, Lara Jacobson, Mary Lou Jacoby, Deborah James, Denys James, Justyna Janiszewska, Birgit Janke, Marjolaine Janvier-Houde, Meera Jayarajan, Anna Jephcote, Claus Jepsen, Bitten Jespersen, Mark Jitlal, Soames Job, Greg Johnson, Dan Johnston, Frank Jones, Sue Jones, Stine Ydegaard Jørgensen, Catherine Joyce, Karen Judge, Greg Juhl, Nadine Jung **K** Dennis Kaarsgaarn, Rebecca Kahn, Katrin Kalbfleisch, Claire Kalis, Jiri Kas, David Katzenstein, Tim Keeling, Liliane Keller, Stacey Kelly, Anne Kennedy, Michael Kennedy, Birgit Kern, Michael Kerr, Linda Kersey, Gareth Key, Tracey Kibble, Jenn Kipperman, Levente Kiss, Dave Knipe, Charlotte Knudtzen, Bart Konings, Bernard Koontz, Rebecka Koritz, Dragan Korkut, Daniel Kossick, Richard Kowalczyk, Angela Kowalick, Aarnoud Kraan, Peter Krebs, Silke Krob, Andrea Kunz, Phyllis Kynas **L** Simon La Greca, Shervin Lalezary, Stefan Landman, Christy Lanzl, Luke Larrassey, Daniel Lavoie, Andy Lawson, Khiem Lé, Alex Lea, Dan Leach, Martin Lessard, Stephan Leuenberger, Patricica Levitan, Avraham Lewin, John Lewis, Jeff Libman, Steve Lidgey, Dave Lieberman, Susan Lightfoot, Daniel & Roderick Limawan, Edwin Lipscomb, Karin Lock, Beatriz Lopez, Daniel Lott, Annie Lu, Sita Luca, Paolo Lucciarini, Matthew Luck, Bob Luckey, Abigail Lucking, Remko Lulof, Larry Lunsford, Brenda Lyon **M** Ian MacDonell, Christina Madrid, Silvana Magnaghi, Elaine Magree, Dee Mahan, Erika Malitzky, Terry Marcer, Yossi Margoninsky, Mary Markotic, Anna Marrant, Jeff Marshall, Christine Marshall-Smith, Gina Martin, Nicola Martin, Ulrike Martin, Rebecca Marvil, Giuliana Maselli, Hannah Mayell, Jessica Mayhew, Lloyd Mclean, Edward & Pamela McCamley, Sherry McCarnan, Jimmy McCarthy, Paul McCarthy, Melvin McClanahan, Kelli McCully, George McGolrick, Michael McKenna, Lachlan McKenzie, John McLaverty, Milagros McNeil, Janet McNicol, Amy McVay, Lynne Mellone, Clare Mendes, Erika Mendez, Mark Merkelbach, Colleen Meyer, Gary Meyer, Mateja Mikuz, Peter Milec, Ann Miller, David Miller, Duke Miller, Gretchen Miller, Hillary Miller, Russell Miller, Tim Miller, Michael Mina, Ute Minckert, Carolina Miranda, Natalia Misciattelli, Keren Moed, Mateo Monda, Heather Monell, Brigitte Monfils, Chariti Montez, Austin Moran, Rosa M Daunis, Steffi Morgner, Paola Morich, Jim Morris, Gail Morton, Lelde Muehlenbachs, Detlev Mueller, Eva Mueller-Holtz, Sabine Muff, Andrea Muller, Sonja Munnix, Abel Munoz, Fergus Murphy, Lorna Murphy, Susan Muscovitch, Jukka Mustonen **N** Ingrid Naden, Yohei Nagai, Talisa Navarro, Ken Nawrocki, Jocelyn & R Neal, Barb Neelley, Ulrich Netzel, Saskia Neuijen, Amotz Nevo, Gillian Newell, Eva Niepagenkemper, Jose Maria Nogales, Catherine Nolan-Ferrell, Lynda Noppe, Jeremy Norton, Katharina Nothelfer, Silvio Notz, Rachael Nugent **O** Michael O'Brien, Mary M O'Connor, Maureen O'Connor, Nick O'Kane, Feargal O'Suilleabhain, Bearnard & Verne O'Riain, Ketra Oberlander, Yuri Ogitani, Phillip Oppenheim, Sarah Orlowsky, Antonio Orozco, Yolanda Ortiz de Arri, Roy & Velia Ovenden, Sherman Owens, Pat Owsley **P** Otto & Inge Paar, Janis Packham, Linda Paisley, Claudia Paolicelli, Celine Paret, Leigh Paris, G Patrick, Ludovica & Pierpaolo Patroncini, Sheri Patterson, Dave Payne, Will Pearson, Jan M Pennington, Beth Perry, Roger & Michele Petitpas, Jerrald K Pfabe, Roberta Picconi, Mauro Pio, Flor

Podesta, Michelle Podmore, David Poland, Ellen Poler, Sandra Ponek, Rich Prager, Jim Premeaux, Gil Price, Angela Puddicombe **Q** Matt Quigley **R** Jurgen Rahmer, Krishna Rajendra, Marion Raming, Suma Ramzan, Rob Reid, Danielle Remmerswaal, Byron Rendar, Elaine Renegar, Charles Renn, Dave Rheault, David Richards, Anja Richartz, Brian Ridsdale, Patrick Rieger, Sally T Ringe, Rhiannon Roberts, Tyson Roberts, Peter Robinson, Elizabeth Rocco, Luis Fernando Rocha, Stacey Roe, Paul Roer, Jack Romanski, Benzi Ronen, Antoinette & Dey Rose, R Rose, Bob Rosen, Marvin Rosen, Klaus & Annette Rösmann, Gabriel Rubiera, Deborah Rubio, Victor Daniel Rubio Corona, Floren Rudy, Paul Ruiz, Liz Rusch, Marla Ryter **S** Dominic Sabatino, Bengt Sagnert, Rajasi Saha, Jeremy Salisbury, Allegra Salvadori, Solomon Sandberg, Ellen Sannen, Scott Savage, Laura Sawyer, Jonathan Scheffer, Henk Scherff, Matthias Schermaier, Roland Scheuerer, Ines Schihab, Christian Schild, Ed Schleicher, Henry Schlieman, Polly Schlodtmann, Christine Schmeisser, Theodore H Schmidkonz, Thomas Schmidt, Inga Schneider, Chris Schroers, Rich Schultz, Daniel Schulze, W Schuurman, John Schwartz, James Scott, Tom Scvown, Seth Seiderman, Rita Seith, Peter Seligman, Kristina Shapiro, Jade Shephard, Greg Shepherd, Mary Shirley, Barbara I Sholl, Constance Shore, Amit Irit Swartz, P Sibbles, Paul Siegler, Michael Siletti, Lincoln Siliakus, Mark Silverberg, Kati Sivula, Jo Skinner, Paul Sklar, Ajay Skolka, Mary Slade, Marijke Smalbraak, Mike Smet, Gary S Smith, Kate Smith, Samuel Smith, Sarah Smith, Chris Snell, Paul Sokal, Vicky Southgate, Drew Squires, Tommy Squires, Julie St Jean, Helen Stack, Howard & Val Staniforth, Daphne Stanley, Darin Stanley, Jeremy Stathan, Peg Steffensen, Rick Stephens, Terri Stern, Katie Sternberg, Greg Sterne, Luiza Stevenson, Andy Stock, Frank Stonehouse, Cecilia Stranneby, Leigh Streames, Ingrid Stulemeijer, Charles Sullivan, Hannah Sullivan, May Sutton, Irmgard Svenson **T** Celeste Tarricone, F Taylor, Graham Taylor, Emily Teplin, Mark Terry, Judith Teruel Sans, Paule Tetu, Kirstine Therkelsn, An Theunis, Norman Thibodeau, Gregg Thompson, Michelle Thompson, Craig Thomson, Mark Thorn, Giuseppe Tomassini, Ed Tompkins, Alexander Toniazzo, Daniel Torres, Laurent Toutain, Vu Tran, Tony Tschopp, Jude Tsouris, Aviad Tsuck **U** Zeev Unger **V** Karen Valls, Jeroen van Bijsterveld, Franklin van den Berg, Roel van den Berkmortel, Maurice van der Holst, Sytze van der Kooy, Thomas van der Lijke, Hester van der Linden, Ilse van der Veer, Wilna van Eyssen, Arie van Oosterwijk, Ron van Rooijen, Judy van Veen, Rob van Vroonhoven, Marja van Weeren, Cecilia Vargas, Fabian Vasconez, Charley & Mandy Vaughan, Angele Vautour, Rudy Velasquez, Brent Veltkamp, Fruzsina Veress, Federica Vettor, Marc Visser, Louis Visseren, Christian Voigt, Rolf Von Behrens, Tereza Vondrova **W** Thomas Wade, Ian Richard Walker, Mark Walker, Matt Walker, Todd & Susan Walker, Melanie Walsh, Katrin Wanner, Holger Warm, Dana Warren, Mike Warshauer, Evi Watt, Keith Webb, Julian Wedgwood, Jens Wehenkel, Monica Weinheimer, Ben Weiss, Joan Wells, Daniel Welsch, Monika Wescott, Kat West, Keith West, Reik Wetzig, Anne Wheelock, Brendan White, Chris White, John White, Michael White, Thomas Wicky, Anna-Karin Wikstrom, Michael Williams, Steve Wilson, Susanne Winter, Ben Wise, Emma Wise, Liz Wittmann-Todd, Courtenay Wolf, Lo & Eva Wolf, Erik Wolfers, Dr Kilian Wolters, Laura Wong-Pan, Velia Wortman, Walter R Wszolek, Marion Wu, Sacha Wunsch, Heather Wyant, Jon Wyler, Olivia Wyss **Y** Paul Yacht, Melek Yaprak, Ginger Yaunt, Susumu Yoda, Basil Yokarinis, Niki Young, Vincent Young, Tara Yudenfreund, J Yun **Z** Boris Zacharias, Gerhard Zanka, Dee Zduniak, Marion Zeindl, Hans R Zeller, Etay Zemach, Katherine Zibilich, Luca Daniel Zuppinger, Urs Zurbuchen

ACKNOWLEDGMENTS

Many thanks to the following for the use of their content:

Globe on back cover © Mountain High Maps 1993 Digital Wisdom, Inc.

Index

INDEX

INDEX

INDEX

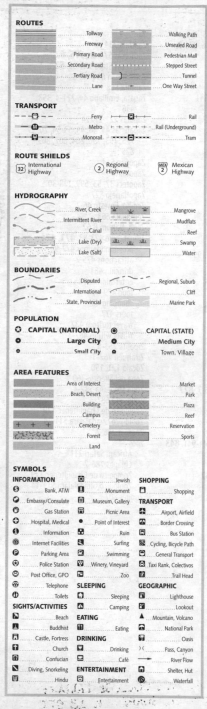

MAP LEGEND

ROUTES

Tollway	Walking Path
Freeway	Unsealed Road
Primary Road	Pedestrian Mall
Secondary Road	Stepped Street
Tertiary Road	Tunnel
Lane	One Way Street

TRANSPORT

Ferry	Rail
Metro	Rail (Underground)
Monorail	Tram

ROUTE SHIELDS

(32) International Highway	(2) Regional Highway	(MEX 2) Mexican Highway

HYDROGRAPHY

River, Creek	Mangrove
Intermittent River	Mudflats
Canal	Reef
Lake (Dry)	Swamp
Lake (Salt)	Water

BOUNDARIES

Disputed	Regional, Suburb
International	Cliff
State, Provincial	Marine Park

POPULATION

✪ CAPITAL (NATIONAL)	◉ CAPITAL (STATE)
● Large City	● Medium City
● Small City	● Town, Village

AREA FEATURES

Area of Interest	Market
Beach, Desert	Park
Building	Plaza
Campus	Reef
Cemetery	Reservation
Forest	Sports
Land	

SYMBOLS

INFORMATION

● Bank, ATM	✡ Jewish
❷ Embassy/Consulate	🏛 Monument
⛽ Gas Station	🏛 Museum, Gallery
➕ Hospital, Medical	Picnic Area
❶ Information	● Point of Interest
@ Internet Facilities	Ruin
❷ Parking Area	Surfing
✚ Police Station	Swimming
✉ Post Office, GPO	Winery, Vineyard
☎ Telephone	Zoo
🚻 Toilets	

SHOPPING

🛍 Shopping

TRANSPORT

✈ Airport, Airfield
Border Crossing
Bus Station
Cycling, Bicycle Path
General Transport
Taxi Rank, Colectivos
Trail Head

SLEEPING

☖ Sleeping
▲ Camping

SIGHTS/ACTIVITIES

Beach
Buddhist
Castle, Fortress
Church
Confucian
Diving, Snorkeling
Hindu

EATING

🍴 Eating

DRINKING

Drinking
Café

ENTERTAINMENT

Entertainment

GEOGRAPHIC

Lighthouse
Lookout
▲ Mountain, Volcano
National Park
Oasis
)(Pass, Canyon
→ River Flow
Shelter, Hut
Waterfall

LONELY PLANET OFFICES

Australia
Head Office
Locked Bag 1, Footscray, Victoria 3011
☎ 03 8379 8000, fax 03 8379 8111
talk2us@lonelyplanet.com.au

USA
150 Linden St, Oakland, CA 94607
☎ 510 893 8555, toll free 800 275 8555
fax 510 893 8572, info@lonelyplanet.com

UK
72–82 Rosebery Ave,
Clerkenwell, London EC1R 4RW
☎ 020 7841 9000, fax 020 7841 9001
go@lonelyplanet.co.uk

France
1 rue du Dahomey, 75011 Paris
☎ 01 55 25 33 00, fax 01 55 25 33 01
bip@lonelyplanet.fr, www.lonelyplanet.fr

Published by Lonely Planet Publications Pty Ltd
ABN 36 005 607 983